THE NEW PALGRAVE
DICTIONARY OF ECONOMICS
SECOND EDITION

THE NEW PALGRAVE

DICTIONARY OF ECONOMICS
SECOND EDITION

Edited by Steven N. Durlauf and Lawrence E. Blume

Volume 5   **Lardner – network goods (theory)**

palgrave
macmillan

This edition published 2008 by
PALGRAVE MACMILLAN
Houndmills, Basingstoke, Hampshire RG21 6XS and
175 Fifth Avenue, New York, N.Y. 10010
Companies and representatives throughout the world

PALGRAVE MACMILLAN is the global academic imprint of the Palgrave
Macmillan division of St. Martin's Press, LLC and of Palgrave Macmillan Ltd.
Macmillan® is a registered trademark in the United States, United Kingdom
and other countries. Palgrave is a registered trademark in the European
Union and other countries.

ISBN-10 0-230-22641-8   Volume 5
ISBN-13 978-0-230-22641-8   Volume 5

ISBN-10 0-333-78676-9   8-Volume set
ISBN-13 978-0-333-78676-5   8-Volume set

This book is printed on paper suitable for recycling and made from fully
managed and sustained forest sources. Logging, pulping and manufacturing processes
are expected to conform to the environmental regulations of the country of origin.

A catalogue record for this book is available from the British Library.

Library of Congress Cataloging-in-Publication Data

The new Palgrave dictionary of economics / edited by Steven N. Durlauf
and Lawrence E. Blume. – 2nd ed.
      v. cm.
   Rev. ed. of: The New Palgrave : a dictionary of economics. 1987.
   Includes bibliographical references.
   ISBN 978-0-333-78676-5 (alk. paper)

   1. Economics – Dictionaries.   I. Durlauf, Steven N.   II. Blume,
Lawrence.   III. New Palgrave.

HB61.N49 2008
330.03–dc22
                                                                 2007047205

10   9   8   7   6   5   4   3   2   1
17   16   15   14   13   12   11   10   09   08

Typesetting and XML coding by Macmillan Publishing Solutions, Bangalore, India
Printed in China

Contents

Publishing history

First edition of *Dictionary of Political Economy*,
edited by Robert Harry Inglis Palgrave, in three volumes:

Volume I, printed 1894.
Reprinted pages 1–256 with corrections, 1901, 1909.
Reprinted with corrections, 1915, 1919.

Volume II, printed 1896.
Reprinted 1900.
Reprinted with corrections, 1910, 1915.

Volume III, printed 1899.
Reprinted 1901.
Corrected with appendix, 1908.
Reprinted with corrections, 1910, 1913.
Reprinted, 1918.

New edition, retitled *Palgrave's Dictionary of Political Economy*,
edited by Henry Higgs, in three volumes:

Volume I, printed 1925.
Reprinted 1926.

Volume II, printed 1923.
Reprinted 1925, 1926.

Volume III, printed February 1926.
Reprinted May 1926.

The New Palgrave: A Dictionary of Economics,
edited by John Eatwell, Murray Milgate and Peter Newman.
Published in four volumes.

First published 1987.
Reprinted 1988 (twice).
Reprinted with corrections 1991.
Reprinted 1994, 1996.

First published in paperback 1998.
Reprinted 1999, 2003, 2004.

The New Palgrave Dictionary of Economics 2nd edition,
edited by Steven N. Durlauf and Lawrence E. Blume.
Published in eight volumes

List of entries A–Z

L
(CONTINUED)

Lardner, Dionysius (1793–1859)

Scientific popularizer and railway economist, Lardner was born in Dublin on 3 April 1793 and died on 29 April 1859. He was educated at Trinity College, Dublin, between 1817 and 1827 and is probably best known for his *Cabinet Cyclopaedia* of 133 volumes, published between 1829 and 1849. Although Lardner's series was graced by a number of distinguished contributors, he was satirized in the scientific community as 'Dionysius Diddler'. An astronomer as well as an essayist on numerous scientific topics, Lardner often took side trips into other fields. He studied railway engineering in Paris, and was probably well acquainted with the econo-engineering work at the Ecole des Ponts et Chaussées at a time when Jules Dupuit was actively pursuing economic topics. His sole work relating to economics, *Railway Economy* (1850), was filled with the kind of factual work and analysis being undertaken by the French engineers and by an American pupil of the Ecole, Charles Ellet. Lardner's work caught the eye of W.S. Jevons, who claimed that a reading of *Railway Economy* in 1857 led him to investigate economics in mathematical terms.

There is little doubt that Lardner's book contains important and creative insights into economic theory. An authority on Belgian railroads of the time, Lardner drew up a vast array of facts to develop a theory of the railway firm's costs and revenues. His theory of profit maximization derived from 'empirical' firm's costs and revenues may be set out graphically (see Figure 1).

The railway tariff, which Lardner identified as the independent variable, is displayed on the horizontal axis of the figure while total cost and receipts are measured on the horizontal. The total cost curve shows costs increasing as the tariff is lowered. At a prohibitive tariff Ox, that is, where no traffic would be transported, costs are some positive amount. Fixed costs, which exist whether traffic is carried or not, are an amount xL. As the tariff is lowered, increases in traffic carried cause total costs to increase until they reach maximum at a zero tariff. Both fixed and variable components of cost, then, are considered by Lardner.

Lardner formalized his conception of total receipts in the following terms. If, with Lardner, we let $r =$ the tariff imposed per mile on each ton of goods carried; $D =$ the average distance in miles to which each ton of goods is carried; $N =$ the number of tons booked, and; $R =$ the gross receipts from goods transport, then total receipts may be expressed as

$$R = NDr.$$

As the tariff is lowered from Ox, the average distance of each ton carried, D, and the number of tons booked, N, increase. With reference to Figure 1, lowering the tariff from Ox causes receipts, R in Lardner's equation, to increase to some maximum mp. Tariff reductions below Om, however, cause total receipts to fall, so that at a tariff

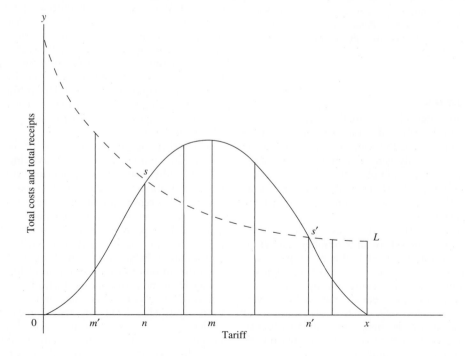

Figure 1

of zero, total receipts are zero (demand is inelastic for tariffs below Om).

Tariffs On' and On are 'break even' tariffs in Figure 1 and, significantly, Lardner argued that the profit-maximizing tariff would fall somewhere between the break-even tariff On' and the revenue-maximizing tariff Om. In modern terminology Lardner identified, if implicitly, the profit maximizing *quantity* as being where marginal cost equals marginal revenue. It is noteworthy that Lardner's analysis of profit maximization, which so impressed Jevons, is nowhere to be found in Jevons's writings.

In addition to a fine model of the profit-maximizing firm, Lardner presented a fairly complete theory of price discrimination related to location in his *Railway Economy*. Specifically, Lardner called for a reduction in long-haul rail rates and for the increase in short-haul rates in order to increase the aggregate profits of the railroad. The differing elasticities of demand for transport which made this discriminatory pricing structure possible were explained on the basis of spatially distributed demanders.

ROBERT B. EKELUND, JR.

Selected works

1850. *Railway Economy*. Reprinted, New York: A.M. Kelley, 1968.

Bibliography

Ekelund, R.B., Jr., Furubotn, E.G. and Gramm, W.P. 1972. *The Evolution of Modern Demand Theory*. Lexington, MA: Heath.
Hooks, D.L. 1971. Monopoly price discrimination in 1850: Dionysius Lardner. *History of Political Economy* 3, 208–23.
Robertson, R.M. 1951. Jevons and his precursors. *Econometrica* 19, 229–42.

large economies

Economists have often claimed that our theories were never intended to describe individual behaviour in all its idiosyncrasies. Instead, in this view, economic theory is supposed to explain only general patterns across large populations. The prime example is the theory of competitive markets, which is designed to deal with situations in which the influence of any individual agent on price formation is 'negligible'.

As in so many aspects of economics, Cournot (1838) was the first to make the role of large numbers explicit in his analysis. Cournot provided a theory of price and output which, as the number of competing suppliers increases without bound, asymptotically yields the competitive solution of price equals marginal and average cost. However, for any given finite number of competitors, an imperfectly competitive outcome results.

It took over a century for Cournot's insights on the role of large numbers to be fully appreciated. Edgeworth (1881) argued the convergence of his contract curve as the economy grew, and increasing numbers of authors assumed that the number of agents was 'sufficiently large' that each one's influence on quantity choices was negligible, but it was not until the contributions of Shubik (1959) and Debreu and Scarf (1963) to the study of the asymptotic properties of the core that the number of agents took a central role in economic analysis.

The crucial step in this line of analysis was taken by Aumann (1964). Arguing that, in terms of standard models of behaviour, an individual agent's actions could be considered to be negligible only if the individual were himself arbitrarily small relative to the collectivity, Aumann modelled the set of agents as being (indexed by) an atomless measure space. In this context, an individual agent corresponds to a set of measure zero, while aggregate quantities are represented as integrals (average, per capita amounts). Then changing the actions of a single individual (or any finite number) actually has no influence on aggregates.

The non-atomic measure space formulation brings three mathematical properties that have proven important. The first is that it provides a consistent modelling of the notion of individual negligibility: only in such a context is an individual truly able to exert no influence on prices. Thus, this model correctly represents the primary reason for appealing to 'large numbers': in it, competitive price-taking behaviour is rational. Moreover, this individual negligibility, when combined with an assumption that individual characteristics are sufficiently 'diffuse', means that discontinuities in individual demand disappear under aggregation (Sondermann, 1975).

The second property is that a (non-negligible) subset of agents drawn from an economy with a non-atomic continuum of agents is essentially sure to be a representative sample of the whole population. This property has proven crucial in the literature relating the core and competitive equilibrium. (See Hildenbrand, 1974, for a broad-ranging treatment of these issues.) It is also used in showing equivalence of core and value allocations (Aumann, 1975).

The other important property of the non-atomic continuum model is the convexifying effect. Even though individual entities (demand correspondences, upper-contour sets, production sets) may not be convex, Richter's theorem implies that the aggregates of these are convex sets when the set of agents is a non-atomic continuum. This property yields existence of competitive equilibrium in large economies even when the individual entities are ill behaved and no 'diffuseness' is assumed.

In the non-atomic continuum modelling, the individual agent formally disappears. Instead, one has coalitions (measurable sets of agents), and an individual is formally indistinguishable from any set of measure zero. The irrelevance of individuals is made very clear in the model of Vind (1964), where only coalitions are defined and individual agents play no part. Debreu (1967) showed the equivalence of Vind's and Aumann's approaches. A further extension of this line is to consider economies in terms only of the distributions of individual characteristics and allocations in terms of distributions of commodities. The strengths of this approach are shown in Hildenbrand (1974).

This disappearance of the individual is intuitively bothersome: economists are used to thinking about individual agents being negligible, but not about individuals having no existence whatsoever. Brown and Robinson (1972) provided an escape from this dilemma by their modelling of a large set of agents via non-standard analysis. This approach gives formal meaning to such notions as an infinitesimal that had been swept out of mathematics and replaced by 'epsilon-delta' arguments. In interpreting non-standard models, one distinguishes between how things appear from 'inside the model' and what they look like from 'outside'. From outside, these models may have an infinity of (individually negligible, infinitesimal) agents, yet from inside each agent is a well-defined, identifiable entity. Using this mathematical modelling eases the interpretation of large economies and also allows formalization of some very intuitive arguments that otherwise could not be made. Unfortunately, the difficulties of mastering the mathematics of non-standard analysis have limited the number of economists using this approach.

While these formal models capture the essential intuition about the nature of economic behaviour of large economies, results obtained in this context should be of interest only to the extent that these models provide a good approximation to large but finite economies. This point was first emphasized by Kannai (1970), and its elaboration was the central issue confronting mathematical general equilibrium theory through the 1960s and early 1970s. The issue is one of continuity: in what sense are infinite economy models the limits of finite economies as the economy grows, and do the various constructs of interest (competitive or Lindahl allocations, cores, value allocations, and so on) of the finite economies approach those of the limit, infinite economies? These questions are extremely subtle. A good introduction to them is Hildenbrand (1974).

The study of the limiting, asymptotic properties of various economic concepts represents an alternative, more direct (but often less tractable) approach to large economy questions than does working with infinite economies. This line begins with Cournot's (1838) treatment of the convergence of oligopoly to perfect competition, the general equilibrium development of which has been a major focus of recent activity (see Mas-Colell, 1982 and the references there). The work growing out of Edgeworth (1881) and Debreu and Scarf (1963) on the core-competitive equilibrium equivalence noted above also follows this line.

Once such convergence is established, the crucial question becomes that of the rate of convergence because asymptotic results are of limited interest if convergence is too slow. This question was first addressed for the core by Debreu (1975), who showed convergence at a rate of at least 1 over the number of agents.

A more direct approach to this issue of how large a market must be for its outcomes to be approximately competitive is to employ a model in which price formation is explicitly modelled. (Note that this is not a property of the Cournot or Arrow–Debreu analyses.) In a partial equilibrium context the Bertrand (1883) model of price-setting homogeneous oligopoly indicates that 'two is large', in that duopoly can yield price equal to marginal cost. Recent striking results in the same line for the double auction are due to Gresik and Satterthwaite (1985), who show that, even with individual reservation prices being private information, equilibrium under this institution can yield essentially competitive, welfare-maximizing volumes of trade with as few as six sellers and buyers.

This work is very heartening, for it tends to justify the profession's traditional reliance on competitive models which make formal sense only with an infinite set of agents. Another basis for optimism on this count comes from experimental work which shows strong tendencies for essentially competitive outcomes to be attained with quite small numbers. The further study of such institutions is clearly indicated.

JOHN ROBERTS

See also **non-standard analysis; perfect competition; Shapley–Folkman theorem.**

Bibliography

Aumann, R.J. 1964. Markets with a continuum of traders. *Econometrica* 32, 39–50.

Aumann, R.J. 1975. Values of markets with a continuum of traders. *Econometrica* 43, 611–46.

Bertrand, J. 1883. Theorie mathématique de la richesse sociale. *Journal des Savants* 48, 499–508.

Brown, D.J. and Robinson, A. 1972. A limit theorem on the cores of large standard exchange economies. *Proceedings of the National Academy of Sciences of the USA* 69, 1258–60.

Cournot, A. 1838. *Recherches sur les principes mathématiques de la théorie des richesses.* Paris: Hachette.

Debreu, G. 1967. Preference functions on measure spaces of economic agents. *Econometrica* 35, 111–22.

Debreu, G. 1975. The rate of convergence of the core of an economy. *Journal of Mathematical Economics* 2, 1–8.

Debreu, G. and Scarf, H. 1963. A limit theorem on the core of an economy. *International Economic Review* 4, 235–46.

Edgeworth, F.Y. 1881. *Mathematical Psychics.* London: Kegan Paul.

Gresik, T. and Satterthwaite, M. 1985. The rate at which a simple market becomes efficient as the number of traders increases: an asymptotic result for optimal trading mechanisms. Discussion Paper No. 641, Center for Mathematical Studies in Economics and Management Science, Northwestern University.

Hildenbrand, W. 1974. *Core and Equilibria of a Large Economy*. Princeton: Princeton University Press.

Kannai, Y. 1970. Continuity properties of the core of a market. *Econometrica* 38, 791–815.

Mas-Colell, A., ed. 1982. *Non-cooperative Approaches to the Theory of Perfect Competition*. New York: Academic Press.

Shubik, M. 1959. *Strategy and Market Structure: Competition, Oligopoly, and the Theory of Games*. New York: Wiley.

Sondermann, D. 1975. Smoothing demand by aggregation. *Journal of Mathematical Economics* 2, 201–24.

Vind, K. 1964. Edgeworth-allocations in an exchange economy with many traders. *International Economic Review* 5, 165–77.

large games (structural robustness)

Earlier literature on large (many players) cooperative games is surveyed in Aumann and Shapley (1974). For large strategic games, see Schmeidler (1973) and the follow-up literature on the purification of Nash equilibria. There is also substantial literature on large games with special structures, for example large auctions as reported in Rustichini, Satterthwaite, and Williams (1994).

Unlike the above, this survey concentrates on the structural robustness of (general) Bayesian games with many semi-anonymous players, as developed in Kalai (2004; 2005). (For additional notions of robustness in game theory, see Bergemann and Morris, 2005.)

Main message and examples

In simultaneous-move Bayesian games with many semi-anonymous players, all Nash equilibria are structurally robust. The equilibria survive under structural alterations that relax the simultaneous-play assumptions, and permit information transmission, revisions of choices, communication, commitments, delegation, and more.

Large economic and political systems and distributive systems such as the Web are examples of environments that give rise to such games. Immunity to alterations means that Nash equilibrium predictions are valid even in games whose structure is largely unknown to modellers or to players.

The next example illustrates immunity of equilibrium to revisions, or being *ex post* Nash, see Cremer and McLean (1985), Green and Laffont (1987) and Wilson (1987) for early examples.

Example 1 *Ex post stability illustrated in match pennies*
Simultaneously, each of k males and k females chooses one of two options, H or T. The payoff of every male is the proportion of females his choice matches and the payoff of every female is the proportion of males her choice *mis*matches. (When $k = 1$ this is the familiar match-pennies game.) Consider the mixed-strategy equilibrium where every player chooses H or T with equal probabilities.

Structural robustness implies that the equilibrium must be *ex post* Nash: it should survive in alterations that allow players to revise their choices after observing their opponents' choices. Clearly this is not the case when k is small. But as k becomes large, the equilibrium becomes arbitrarily close to being *ex post* Nash. More precisely, the Prob[some player can improve his payoff by more than ε *ex post*] decreases to zero at an exponential rate as k becomes large.

Example 2 *Invariance to sequential play illustrated in a computer choice game*
Simultaneously, each of n players chooses one of two computers, I or M. But before choosing, with $0.50 - 0.50$ i.i.d. probabilities, every player is privately informed that she is an I-type or an M-type. The payoff of every player is 0.1 if she chooses the computer of her type (zero otherwise) plus 0.9 times the proportion of opponents whose choices she matches. (Identical payoffs and prior probabilities are assumed only to ease the presentation. The robustness property holds without these assumptions.) Consider the favourite-computer equilibrium (FC) where every player chooses the computer of her type.

Structural robustness implies that the equilibrium must *be invariant to sequential play*: it should survive in alterations in which the (publicly observed) computer choices are made sequentially. Clearly this is not the case for small n, where any equilibrium must involve herding. But as n becomes large, the structural robustness theorem below implies that FC becomes an equilibrium in all sequential alterations. More precisely, the Prob[some player, by deviating to her non favorite computer, can achieve an ε-improvement at her turn] decreases to zero at an exponential rate.

The general definition of structural robustness, presented next, accommodates the above examples and much more.

Structural robustness

A mixed-strategy (Nash) equilibrium $\sigma = (\sigma_1, \ldots, \sigma_n)$ of a one-simultaneous-move n-person strategic game G is structurally robust if it *remains an equilibrium* in *every* structural *alteration* of G. Such an alteration is described by an extensive game, $\mathscr{A}$, and for σ to remain an equilibrium in $\mathscr{A}$ means that *every adaptation of σ to $\mathscr{A}$, $\sigma^{\mathscr{A}}$, must be an equilibrium in $\mathscr{A}$.*

Consider any n-person one-simultaneous-move Bayesian game G, like the Computer Choice game above.

Definition 1 *A (structural) alteration of G is any finite extensive game $\mathscr{A}$ with the following properties:*

1. *$\mathscr{A}$ includes the (original) G-players*: The players of $\mathscr{A}$ constitute a superset of the G-players (the players of G).
2. *Unaltered type structure*: At the first stage of $\mathscr{A}$, the G-players are assigned a profile of types by the same prior probability distribution as in G. Every player is informed of his own type.
3. *Playing $\mathscr{A}$ means playing G*: with every final node of $\mathscr{A}$, z, there is an associated unique profile of G pure-strategies, $a(z) = (a_1(z), \ldots, a_n(z))$.
4. *Unaltered payoffs*: the payoffs of the G-players at every final node z are the same as their payoffs in G (at the profile of realized types and final pure-strategies $a(z)$).
5. *Preservation of original strategies*: every pure-strategy a_i of a G-player i has at least one $\mathscr{A}$ adaptation. That is, an $\mathscr{A}$-strategy $a_i^{\mathscr{A}}$ that guarantees (w.p. 1) ending at a final node z with $a_i(z) = a_i$ (no matter what strategies are used by the opponents).

In the computer choice example, every play of an alteration $\mathscr{A}$ must produce a profile of computer allocations for the G-players. Their preferences in $\mathscr{A}$ are determined by their preferences over profiles of computer allocations in G. Moreover, every G-player i has at least one $\mathscr{A}$-strategy $I_i^{\mathscr{A}}$ (which guarantees ending at a final node where she is allocated I), and at least one $\mathscr{A}$-strategy $M_i^{\mathscr{A}}$ (which guarantees ending at a final node where she is allocated M).

Definition 2 *An $\mathscr{A}$ (mixed) strategy-profile, $\sigma^{\mathscr{A}}$, is an adaptation of a G (mixed) strategy-profile σ, if for every G-player i, every $\sigma_i^{\mathscr{A}}$ is an $\mathscr{A}$-adaptation of σ_i. That is, for every G pure-strategy a_i, $\sigma_i(a_i) = \sigma_i^{\mathscr{A}}(a_i^{\mathscr{A}})$ for some $\mathscr{A}$-adaptation $a_i^{\mathscr{A}}$ of a_i.*

In the computer choice example, for a G-strategy where player i randomizes 0.20 to 0.80 between I and M, an $\mathscr{A}$ adaptation must randomize 0.20–0.80 between a strategy of the type $I_i^{\mathscr{A}}$ and a strategy of the type $M_i^{\mathscr{A}}$.

Definition 3 *An equilibrium σ of G is structurally robust if in every alteration of G, $\mathscr{A}$, and in every adaptation of σ, $\sigma^{\mathscr{A}}$, the strategy of every G-player i, $\sigma_i^{\mathscr{A}}$, is best response to $\sigma_{-i}^{\mathscr{A}}$.*

Remark 1 The structural robustness theorem, discussed later, presents an asymptotic result: the equilibria are structurally robust up to two positive numbers (ε, ρ), which can be made arbitrarily small as n becomes large. The notion of approximate robustness is the following.

An equilibrium is (ε, ρ)-structurally robust if in every alteration and every adaptation as above, Prob[visiting an information set where a G-player can improve his payoff by more than ε] $\leq \rho$. (ε-improvement is computed conditional

on being at the information set. To gain such improvement the player may coordinate his deviation: he may make changes at the information set under consideration together with changes at forthcoming ones.)

For the sake of brevity, the next section discusses full structural robustness. But all the observations presented there also hold for the properly defined approximate counterparts. For example, the fact that structural robustness implies *ex post* Nash also implies that approximate structural robustness implies approximate *ex post* Nash. The implications of approximate (as opposed to full) structural robustness are important, due to the asymptotic nature of the structural robustness theorem.

Implications of structural robustness

Structural robustness of an equilibrium σ in a game G is a strong property, because the set of G-alterations that σ must survive is rich. The simple examples below are meant to suggest the richness of its implications, with the first two examples showing how it implies the notions already discussed (see Dubey and Kaneko, 1984 for related issues).

Remark 2 *Ex post Nash and being information-proof* G with revisions, $\mathscr{GR}$, is the following n-person extensive game. The n players are assigned types as in G (using the prior type distribution of G and informing every player of his own type). In a first round of simultaneous play, every player chooses one of his G pure strategies; the types realized and pure strategies chosen are all made public knowledge. Then, in a second round of simultaneous play, the players again choose pure strategies of G (to revise their first round choices). The payoffs are as in G, computed at the profile of realized types with the profile of pure strategies chosen in the *second* round.

Clearly $\mathscr{GR}$ satisfies the definition of an alteration (with no additional players), and every equilibrium σ of G has the following $\mathscr{GR}$ adaptation, σ^{NoRev}: in the first round the players choose their pure strategies according to σ, just as they do in G; in the second round nobody revises his first round choice.

Structural robustness of σ implies that σ^{NoRev} must be an equilibrium of $\mathscr{GR}$, that is, σ is *ex post* Nash.

Moreover, the above reasoning continues to hold even if the information revealed between the two rounds is partial and different for different players. The fact that σ^{NoRev} is an equilibrium in all such alterations shows that σ is *information-proof*: no revelation of information (even if strategically coordinated by G-players and outsiders) could give any player an incentive to revise. Thus, structural robustness is substantially stronger than all the variants of the *ex post* Nash condition. (In the non-approximate notions, being *ex post* Nash is equivalent to being information proof. But in the approximate notions information proofness is substantially stronger.)

Remark 3 *Invariance to order of play*
G played sequentially, $\mathcal{GS}$, is the following n-person extensive game. The n players are assigned types as in G. The play progresses sequentially, according to a fixed publicly known order. Every player, at his turn, knows all earlier choices.

Clearly, $\mathcal{GS}$ is an alteration of G, and every equilibrium σ of G has the following $\mathcal{GS}$ adaptation: At his turn, every player i chooses a pure-strategy with the same probability distribution σ_i as he does in the simultaneous-move game G. Structural robustness of σ implies that this adaptation of σ must be an equilibrium in every such $\mathcal{GS}$.

Moreover, the above reasoning continues to hold even if the order of play is determined dynamically, and even if it is strategically controlled by G-players and outsiders. Thus, a structurally robust equilibrium is invariant to the order of play in a strong sense.

Remark 4 *Invariance to revelation and delegation*
G with delegation, $\mathcal{GD}$, is the following $(n+1)$-players game. The original n G-players are assigned types as in G. In a first round of simultaneous play, every G-player chooses between (1) self-play and (2) delegate-the-play and report a type to an outsider, player $n+1$. In a second round of simultaneous play all the self-players choose their own G pure strategies, and the outsider chooses a profile of G pure strategies for all the delegators. The payoffs of the G players are as in G; the outsider may be assigned any payoffs.

Clearly, $\mathcal{GD}$ is an alteration of G, and every equilibrium σ of G has adaptations that involve no delegation.

In the computer choice game, for example, consider an outsider with incentives to coordinate: his payoff equals one when he chooses the same computer for all delegators, zero otherwise. This alteration has a new (more efficient) equilibrium, not available in G: everybody delegates and the outsider chooses the most-reported type.

Nevertheless, as structural robustness implies, FC remains an equilibrium in $\mathcal{GD}$ (nobody delegates in the first round and they choose their favorite computers in the second). Moreover, FC remains an equilibrium under any scheme that involves reporting and voluntary delegation of choices.

Remark 5 *Partially specified games*
Structurally robust equilibria survive under significantly more complex alterations than the ones above. For example, one could have multiple opportunities to revise, to delegate, to affect the order of play, to communicate, and more. Because of these strong invariance properties, such equilibria may be used in games which are only partially specified as illustrated by the following example.

Example 3 *A game played on the Web*
Suppose that instead of being played in one simultaneous move, the Computer Choice game has the following instruction: 'Go to Web site xyz before the end of the week, and click in your computer choice.' This instruction involves substantial structural uncertainty: In what order would the players choose? Who can observe whom? Who can talk to whom? Can players sign binding agreements? Can players revise their choices? Can players delegate their choices? And so forth.

Because it is unaffected by the answers to such questions, a structurally robust equilibrium σ of the one-simultaneous-move game can be played on the Web in a variety of ways without losing the equilibrium property. For example, players may make their choices according to their σ_i probabilities prior to the beginning of the click-in period, then go to the Web and click in their realized choices at individually selected times.

Remark 6 *Competitive prices in Shapley–Shubik market games*
For a simple illustration, consider the following n-trader market game (see Shapley and Shubik, 1977, and later references in Dubey and Geanakoplos, 2003, and McLean, Peck and Postlewaite, 2005). There are two fruits, apples and bananas, and a finite number of trader types. A type describes the fruit a player owns and the fruit he likes to consume. The players' types are determined according to individual independent prior probability distributions. Each trader knows his own type, and his payoff depends on his own type and the fruit he ends up with, as well as on the distribution of types and fruit ownership of his opponents (externalities are allowed, for example, a player may wish to own the fruit that most opponents like). In one simultaneous move, every player has to choose between (1) keeping his fruit and (2) trading it for the other kind.

The banana/apple price is determined proportionately (with one apple and banana added in to avoid division by zero). For example, if 199 bananas and 99 apples are traded, the price of bananas to apples would be $(199 + 1)/(99 + 1) = 2$, that is, every traded apple brings back two bananas and every traded banana brings back 0.5 apples.

With a small number of traders, the price is unlikely to be competitive. If players are allowed to re-trade after the realized price becomes known, they would, and a new price would emerge.

However, when n is large, approximate structural robustness implies being approximately information-proof. So even when the realized price becomes known, no player has significant incentive to re-trade, that is, the price is approximately competitive (Prob[some player can ε-improve his expected payoff by re-trading at the observed price] $\leq \rho$).

This is stronger than classical results relating Nash equilibrium to Walras equilibrium (for example, Dubey, Mas-Colell and Shubik, 1980). First, being conducted under incomplete information, the above relates Bayesian equilibria to rational expectations equilibria (rather than Walras). Also the competitive property described here is substantially stronger, due to the immunity of the equilibria to alterations represented by extensive games. If allowance is made for spot markets, coordinating institutions, trade on the Web, and so on, the Nash-equilibrium prices of the simple simultaneous-move game are sustained through the intermediary steps that may come up under such possibilities.

Remark 7 *Embedding a game in bigger worlds*
Alterations allow the inclusion of outside players who are not from G. Moreover, the restrictions imposed on the strategies and payoffs of the outsiders are quite limited. This means that alterations may describe bigger worlds in which G is embedded. Structural robustness of an equilibrium means that the small-world (G) equilibrium remains an equilibrium even when the game is embedded in such bigger worlds.

Remark 8 *Self-purification*
Schmeidler (1973) shows that in a normal-form game with a continuum of anonymous players, every strategy can be purified, that is, for every mixed-strategy equilibrium one can construct a pure-strategy equilibrium (Ali Khan and Sun, 2002 survey some of the large follow-up literature).

The *ex post* Nash property above constitutes a stronger (but asymptotic) result. Since the resulting play of a mixed strategy equilibrium yields pure-strategy profiles that are Nash equilibria (of the perfect information game), one does not need to construct pure-strategy equilibria: simply playing a mixed-strategy equilibrium yields pure-strategy profiles that are equilibria.

The approximate statement is: for every (ε, ρ) for sufficiently large n, Prob[ending at a pure strategy profile that is not an ε Nash equilibrium of the realized perfect information game] $\leq \rho$. Since both ε and ρ can be made arbitrarily small, this is asymptotic purification. Note that the model of Schmeidler, with a continuum of players, requires non-standard techniques to describe a continuum of independent random variables (the mixed strategies of the players). The asymptotic result stated here, dealing always with finitely many players, does not require any non-standard techniques.

Remark 9 *'As if' learning*
Kalai and Lehrer (1993) show that in playing an equilibrium of a Bayesian repeated game, after a sufficiently long time the players best-respond as if they know their opponents' realized types and, hence, their mixed strategies.

But being information-proof, at a structurally robust equilibrium (even of a one shot game) players' best respond (immediately) as if they know their opponents' realized types, their mixed strategies and even the pure-strategies they end up with.

Sufficient conditions for structural robustness

Theorem 1 *Structural Robustness* (rough statement): the equilibria of large one-simultaneous-move Bayesian games are (approximately) structurally robust if

(a) the players' types are drawn independently, and
(b) payoff functions are anonymous and continuous.

Payoff anonymity means that in addition to his own type and pure-strategy, every player's payoff may depend only on aggregate data of the opponents' types and pure-strategies. For example, in the computer choice game a player's payoff may depend on her own type and choice, and on the *proportions* of opponents in the four groups: I-types who chose I, I-types who chose M, M-types who chose I, and M-types who chose M.

The players in the games above are only semi-anonymous, because there are no additional symmetry or anonymity restrictions other than the restriction above. In particular, players may have different individual payoff functions and different prior probabilities (publicly known).

The continuity condition relates games of different sizes and rules out games of the type below.

Example 4 *Match the expert*
Each of n players has to choose one of two computers, I or M. Player 1 is equally likely to be one of two types: 'an expert who is informed that I is better' (I-better) or 'an expert who is informed that M is better' (M-better). Players 2, ... , n are of one possible 'non-expert' type. Every player's payoff is one if he chooses the better computer, zero otherwise. (Stated anonymously: choosing computer X pays one, if the proportion of the X-*better* type is positive, zero otherwise.)

Consider the equilibrium where player 1 chooses the computer he was told was better and every other player chooses I or M with equal probabilities. This equilibrium fails to be *ex post* Nash (and hence, fails structural robustness), especially as n becomes large, because after the play approximately one-half of the players would want to revise their choices to match the observed choice of player 1. (With a small n there may be 'accidental *ex post* Nash', but it becomes extremely unlikely as n becomes large.)

This failure is due to discontinuity of the payoff functions. The proportions of I-better types and M-better types in this game must be either $(1/n, 0)$ or $(0, 1/n)$, because only one of the n players is to be one of these types. Yet, whatever n is, every player's payoff is drastically affected (from 0 to 1 or from 1 to 0) when we switch from $(1/n, 0)$ to $(0, 1/n)$ (keeping everything else the same).

As n becomes large, this change in the type proportions becomes arbitrarily small, yet it continues to have a drastic effect on players' payoffs. This violates a condition of uniform equicontinuity imposed simultaneously on all the payoff functions in the games with $n = 1, 2, \ldots$ players.

EHUD KALAI

See also **Internet, economics of the; large economies; purification; rational expectations.**

Bibliography

Aumann, R.J. and Shapley, L.S. 1974. *Values of Nonatomic Games*. Princeton, NJ: Princeton University Press.

Bergemann, D. and Morris, S. 2005. Robust mechanism design. *Econometrica* 73, 1771–813.

Cremer, J. and McLean, R.P. 1985. Optimal selling strategies under uncertainty for a discriminating monopolist when demands are interdependent. *Econometrica* 53, 345–61.

Dubey, P., Mas-Colell, A. and Shubik, M. 1980. Efficiency properties of strategic market games: an axiomatic approach. *Journal of Economic Theory* 22, 339–62.

Dubey, P. and Kaneko, M. 1984. Information patterns and Nash equilibria in extensive games: 1. *Mathematical Social Sciences* 8, 111–39.

Dubey, P. and Geanakoplos, J. 2003. From Nash to Walras via Shapley–Shubik. *Journal of Mathematical Economics* 39, 391–400.

Green, J.R. and Laffont, J.J. 1987. Posterior implementability in a two-person decision problem. *Econometrica* 55, 69–94.

Kalai, E. 2004. Large robust games. *Econometrica* 72, 1631–66.

Kalai, E. 2005. Partially-specified large games. *Lecture Notes in Computer Science* 3828, 3–13.

Kalai, E. and Lehrer, E. 1993. Rational learning leads to Nash equilibrium. *Econometrica* 61, 1019–45.

Khan, A.M. and Sun, Y. 2002. Non-cooperative games with many players. In *Handbook of Game Theory with Economic Applications*, vol. 3, ed. R.J. Aumann and S. Hart. Amsterdam: North-Holland.

McLean, R., Peck, J. and Postlewaite, A. 2005. On price-taking behavior in asymmetric information economies. In *Essays in Dynamic General Equilibrium: Festschrift for David Cass*, ed. A. Citanna, J. Donaldson, H. Polemarchakis, P. Siconolfi and S. Spear. Berlin: Springer. Repr. in *Studies in Economic Theory* 20, 129–42.

Rustichini, A., Satterthwaite, M.A. and Williams, S.R. 1994. Convergence to efficiency in a simple market with incomplete information. *Econometrica* 62, 1041–64.

Schmeidler, D. 1973. Equilibrium points of nonatomic games. *Journal of Statistical Physics* 17, 295–300.

Shapley, L.S. and Shubik, M. 1977. Trade using one commodity as a means of payment. *Journal of Political Economy* 85, 937–68.

Wilson, R. 1987. Game-theoretic analyses of trading processes. In *Advances in Economic Theory: Fifth World Congress*, ed. T. Bewley. Cambridge: Cambridge University Press.

Laspeyres, Ernst Louis Etienne (1834–1913)

Laspeyres was born at Halle, Germany, on 28 November 1834 and died on 4 August 1913 at Giessen, Germany.

From 1853 to 1857, he studied at the universities of Tübingen, Berlin, Göttingen and Halle. He received a law degree from the University of Halle in 1857. He studied at the University of Heidelberg from 1857 to 1859, and in 1860 he obtained his Ph.D. from Heidelberg for the thesis, 'The Correlation between Population Growth and Wages'.

From 1860 until 1864 he worked as a lecturer at Heidelberg, where he wrote a history of the economic views of the Dutch (1863). In the following ten years, he taught at four different universities: 1864 – Basel; 1866 – the Polytechnic at Riga; 1869 – Dorpat; 1873 – Karlsruhe. Finally, from 1874 to 1900, he taught at the Justus-Liebig University at Giessen.

Laspeyres' main contribution to economics was his development of the index number formula that bears his name. Let the price and quantity of commodity n in period t be p_n^t and q_n^t respectively for $n = 1, \ldots, N$ and $t = 0, 1, \ldots, T$. Then the Laspeyres price index of the N commodities for period t (relative to the base period 0) is defined as

$$P_L \equiv \sum_{n=1}^{N} p_n^t q_n^0 \Big/ \sum_{n=1}^{N} p_n^0 q_n^0.$$

Laspeyres wrote his classic paper (1871), which suggested the above formula partly as an outgrowth of his empirical work on measuring price movements in Germany and partly to criticize the index number formula of Drobisch (1871). Using the notation defined above, the Drobisch price index for period t is defined as

$$P_D \equiv \left(\sum_{n=1}^{N} p_n^t q_n^t \Big/ \sum_{n=1}^{n} q_n^t \right) \Big/ \left(\sum_{n=1}^{N} p_n^0 q_n^0 \Big/ \sum_{n=1}^{N} q_n^0 \right).$$

Laspeyres criticized this formula by showing that the index generally changed even if all prices remained constant (that is, P_D does not satisfy an identity test, to use modern terminology). An even more effective criticism of P_D is that it is not invariant to changes in the units of measurement (whereas P_L is invariant).

Laspeyres did not write any further papers on index number theory. He wrote papers on economic history, the history of economic thought and on topical economic issues of his time; see Rinne (1981).

W.E. DIEWERT

Selected works

1863. *Geschichte der volkswirtschaftlichen Anschauungen der Niederländer und ihrer Literatur zur Zeit der Republik.* Leipzig.

1871. Die Berechnung einer mittleren Waarenpreissteigerung. *Jahrbücher für Nationalökonomie und Statistik* 16, 296–315.

Bibliography

Drobisch, M.W. 1871. Über die Berechnung der Veränderungen der Waarenpreise und des Geldswerths. *Jahrbücher für Nationalökonomie und Statistik* 16, 143–56.

Rinne, H. 1981. Ernst Louis Etienne Laspeyres 1834–1913. *Jahrböcher für Nationalökonomie und Statistik* 196, 194–216.

Lassalle, Ferdinand (1825–1864)

Born in Breslau, 13 April 1825; died in Geneva, 31 August 1864. The only son of a prosperous Jewish silk merchant, Lassalle studied philosophy and history at the University of Breslau and subsequently at the University of Berlin, where he encountered the radical ideas of the 'Young Hegelians' and of the French socialist thinkers. During the 1848 revolution he was associated with Marx and the *Neue Rheinische Zeitung*, and was arrested for his activities but acquitted by a jury in 1849. In the course of his short and turbulent life (which ended as a result of an absurd duel with the former fiancé of a woman he wished to marry), Lassalle became known primarily as a political and economic theorist, and as a leading figure in the radical and working-class movements, who organized in 1863 the first socialist party in Germany (the General Union of German Workers).

Lassalle's economic ideas were derived to a large extent from Marx, often without acknowledgement, but he diverged from the latter in important respects. As Bernstein (1891) observed: 'Lassalle was much more indebted to Marx than he admitted in his writings, but he was a disciple of Marx only in a restricted sense.' The main divergence can be summarized as the substitution of an evolutionary conception of the movement from capitalism to socialism for Marx's idea of a revolutionary transition. In his 'Workers' Programme' (1862) and his 'Open Letter' (1863), Lassalle advocated a course of political action for the working-class movement with two principal aims: first, the achievement of universal and equal suffrage; second, the development, with state aid, of workers' cooperatives that would lead to a gradual socialization of the economy. His reliance upon the action of the state (conceived in the manner of Hegel rather than Marx) was very great, and in the 'Open Letter' he adduced an 'iron law of wages', derived from classical political economy, to show that neither individually nor collectively could workers improve their conditions of life except by replacing the wage system with self-employment (cooperative production), for which the necessary capital must be provided by the state. It was in this context that Lassalle responded to Bismarck's invitation (11 May 1863) to express his views on 'working class conditions and problems' and subsequently had several meetings with him; a course of action which Engels (letter to Kautsky, 23 February 1891) later assessed harshly as a step towards allying the workers' movement with German nationalism and the monarchy.

Marx had a low opinion of Lassalle's abilities as an economist and political thinker, and in his *Critique of the Gotha Programme* (1875) on the occasion of the unification of the two existing German workers' parties (the Social Democratic Workers' Party and the General Union of German Workers) he strongly criticized the Lassallean ideas which were embodied in the draft programme; in particular, the erroneous restriction of ownership of the instruments of labour to the capitalist class, excluding landowners, and the confused notion of an 'iron law of wages', which is simply, Marx argued, 'the Malthusian theory of population'.

TOM BOTTOMORE

Selected works

1919–20. *Gesammelte Reden und Schriften*, 12 vols, edited with an Introduction by E. Bernstein. Berlin: Paul Cassirer.

Bibliography

Bernstein, E. 1891. *Ferdinand Lassalle as a Social Reformer*. London: Swan Sonnenschein, 1893. Reprinted, New York: Greenwood Press, 1969.

Footman, D. 1946. *The Primrose Path: A Life of Ferdinand Lassalle*. London: Cresset Press.

Lauderdale, Eighth Earl of [James Maitland] (1759–1839)

Born into a Scottish aristocratic family, Lauderdale entered the House of Commons at the age of 21 as a supporter of the Liberal Whig leader Charles Fox. Following the death of his father, he entered the House of Lords in 1790, where he became known for his defence of civil liberties. After a visit to France in 1792 he publicly expressed sympathy for the ideals of the French Revolution and supported a motion in Parliament (1795) to make peace with the new government of France. In his middle years he swung over to the Tory side and adamantly opposed most economic and political reform measures, especially bills to protect labour (even one which would restrict the use of young children in cleaning chimney flues). His views covered the political spectrum: in 1792 he flirted with Jacobinism, becoming a founding member of the Friends of the People; 40 years later he worked against the Reform Bill of 1832. He died in 1839 at 80, a ripe age indeed for a man known for his apoplectic temper.

Lauderdale had a sustained interest in trade policy, but here he also shifted ground. In 1804 he argued 'that all impediments thrown in the way of commercial communication, obstruct the increase of wealth' (1804, p. 365).

Yet in his pamphlet *A Letter on the Corn Laws* (1814) he claimed Adam Smith was in error, and advocated protection for agriculture, a position which he strongly held in the House of Lords for some 20 years.

Apart from some tracts on currency questions and debt policy, Lauderdale's contributions to economic thought are found in one major work, *An Inquiry into the Nature and Origin of Public Wealth* (1804). A second edition (1819) contained only minor revisions. This suggests that Lauderdale's involvement with economic theory was a one-time affair. The intellectual ferment generated by Ricardo's *Principles* (1st and 2nd editions), and the earlier tracts by Malthus, Edward West, and Ricardo on rent and profits seems to have passed him by: no mention of his contemporaries or the theoretical issues which they raised appeared in his new introduction or in the footnotes to the 1819 edition. The focus of both editions is the *Wealth of Nations*, and a large part of the *Inquiry* is given over to a negation of Smith's conclusions. Specifically, Lauderdale asserts that: (1) the maximization of private riches does not lead to maximum public wealth and welfare; (2) labour is not the cause of value or an adequate measure of value; (3) division of labour is not a major factor in economic growth; (4) parsimony and saving are frequently a public detriment as they may lead to over-investment and a capital glut; and (5) government tax revenues applied to rapid debt reduction ('a forced conversion of revenue into capital') will reduce aggregate consumption, deflate profits and capital values, and result in economic distress.

In developing these ideas Lauderdale exposes his deficiencies as a thinker. His analysis is sketchy, his style prolix and repetitious, and his conclusions based on weak or incomplete reasoning occasionally seem pretentious. Not surprisingly, his contemporaries focused on these flaws. Henry Brougham wrote a long very critical commentary on Lauderdale's *Inquiry* in the *Edinburgh Review* (July 1804), to which Lauderdale responded with an acerbic but not too effective pamphlet. Ricardo exposed several of his logical errors (Ricardo, 1823, pp. 267–77, 37ln., 384–5), and Malthus, who on a number of issues (capital glut, value theory and agricultural protectionism) was his intellectual heir, failed to acknowledge his intellectual debt; instead, he accused Lauderdale of 'going too far' in his condemnation of parsimony and savings (Malthus, 1836, p. 314), even though, as we shall see, their arguments were quite similar. Despite the negative opinions of his contemporaries, and his modest theoretical ability, Lauderdale now occupies a firm, albeit secondary, place in the history of economic doctrine. We may ask why.

The answer I believe lies in the fact that Lauderdale had a number of valuable insights into the workings of the economy which later economists thought important. Böhm-Bawerk considered Lauderdale's theory of profit a limited but significant step towards the true and complete explanation of interest and profit (that is, his own

theory). Following the appearance of Keynes's *General Theory* there was a re-examination of earlier writers who might have anticipated Keynesian ideas on saving, investment and employment. Malthus obviously was placed in the centre of this pantheon of economists, and Lauderdale as an earlier thinker espousing similar ideas was accorded lesser status. This is not a wholly satisfactory way of evaluating past intellectual contributions, but there is no doubt that each age searches for harmonious resonances in the historical literature. Here I shall try to broaden the perspective.

In the *Inquiry* Lauderdale challenged the natural harmony of interests propounded by Smith; namely, that individuals seeking private riches would lead a nation to maximize public wealth. To destroy this identity, Lauderdale tried to prove that the sum of private riches could increase while public wealth and welfare declined. Unfortunately, Lauderdale obfuscated the problem by treating the individual riches occasionally produced by monopoly or a sudden scarcity of supply as a *net* addition to aggregate riches when it was clear that Adam Smith meant aggregate riches in real terms, so the scarcity-induced gains of some are more than offset by real losses of others. Furthermore, Lauderdale overlooked Smith's postulate of free competition as a necessary condition for the coincidence of private and public interest. Ricardo came to Smith's defence and cleared up Lauderdale's ten pages of confusion in a couple of succinct paragraphs (Ricardo, 1823, p. 276).

But something positive came out of Lauderdale's discussion of value and riches. His examination of the effect of monopoly on total revenue led to an early and fairly sophisticated discussion of demand curves. Lauderdale reviews empirical estimates of the relationship between a percentage change in the price of a good and the percentage change in the quantity demanded, and notes that for various kinds of consumer goods elasticities may differ. In addition to the concept of price elasticity, Lauderdale gave us the beginnings of a theory of consumer choice, noting the utility sacrifices involved in giving up alternative bundles of goods when consumers make new choices in response to price changes (1804, pp. 59–86). Not surprisingly, Lauderdale rejected the labour theory of value, both as a cause of value and a measure of value (1804, p. 12). Although he related consumer preferences to demand, and was aware of demand in the schedule sense, he failed to relate costs to supply, and hence his theory of value suffered the inadequacies of all the early supply and demand theories, a weakness which Ricardo pointed out (1823, pp. 384–5).

We now come to the section of the *Inquiry* which has been of most interest in the post-Keynesian period: that dealing with saving, investment and fiscal policy. Lauderdale argues that the social benefits from savings have distinct limits: 'In every state of society, a certain quantity of capital, proportioned to the existing state of knowledge of mankind, may be usefully and profitably employed.' Invention may enlarge the scope for the application of capital, but outlets for profitable investment are still limited by the demand for consumer goods (Lauderdale, 1804, p. 227).

Individual parsimony may be misguided, but the harm it does tends to be offset by the prodigality of others. However, when a belief in parsimony leads to bad legislation such as a mandated sinking fund, which forces an increase in public parsimony through taxation and debt reduction, then the results may be 'fatal to the progress of wealth' (Lauderdale, 1804, pp. 228–30, 271). But there remains the question of what is the mechanism by which high savings rates or forced parsimony become 'fatal to the progress of wealth'. Superficially this discussion of the evils of parsimony has a Keynesian air to it, but actually Lauderdale (and Malthus) go on to describe a situation in which savings *are* invested, and it is over-investment relative to restricted consumption (made lower by taxation) which finally produces a collapse in profitability.

It is noteworthy that both writers developed a model in which productive applications of net additions to the capital stock are dependent on increases in consumption. They both also failed to recognize that for long periods a nation can use part of its investment for further investment – a deepening of the capital structure or, in Böhm-Bawerk's terms, a lengthening of the period of production, certainly an attribute of 19th-century capitalism. Whatever their limitations, it seems clear that the macroeconomic contributions of Lauderdale and Malthus are more closely related to the growth models of the Harrod–Domar type than to a short-run Keynesian analysis in which output drops because savings are *not* invested. Nevertheless, there is a tenuous connection with Keynes when we look at their descriptions of the late phase of the over-investment cycle. For Lauderdale over-investment reduces profits and the value of capital, and the resulting low prices 'discourage reproduction'. When we observe such deflation we 'must be cautious not to mistake for the effects of abundance that which in reality may be only the effect of failure of demand' (Lauderdale, 1804, pp. 263–4). Malthus wrote in a similar vein when he pointed to owners of floating capital vainly seeking investment outlets in the glutted capital markets of Europe (Malthus, 1836, p. 420).

We may conclude that the Lauderdale–Malthus theory of total output was not for the most part in the Keynesian mould, but surely that is no reason to downgrade it. Both men saw defects in the Smith–Say–Ricardo theory of total output and employment, and they recognized that restricted consumption and high rates of saving and investment could lead to a sectoral imbalance – a glut of capital, falling profits and, finally, a drop in the inducement to invest. In the policy arena, Lauderdale used these insights to oppose tax surpluses and debt reduction in a period of recession (Paglin, 1961, pp. 98–107; Lauderdale, 1829).

MORTON PAGLIN

See also **Malthus, Thomas Robert.**

Selected works

1797. *Thoughts on Finance*. 3rd edn. London: G.G. & J. Robinson.
1804. *An Inquiry into the Nature and Origin of Public Wealth*. Edinburgh. Reprinted, New York: Augustus M. Kelley, 1962.
1814. *A Letter on the Corn Laws*. Edinburgh: A. Constable.
1829. *Three Letters to the Duke of Wellington*. London: J. Murray.

Bibliography

Malthus, T.R. 1836. *Principles of Political Economy Considered with a View to Their Practical Application*. 2nd edn. London: William Pickering. Reprinted, New York: Augustus Kelley, 1964.
Paglin, M. 1961. *Malthus and Lauderdale: The Anti-Ricardian Tradition*. New York: Augustus Kelley.
Ricardo, D. 1823. *Principles of Political Economy and Taxation*. Ed. P. Sraffa, Cambridge: Cambridge University Press, 1951.

Laughlin, James Laurence (1850–1933)

Scholar, teacher, monetary reformer and university administrator, Laughlin was born in Deerfield, Ohio of middle-class parents of modest means. A scholarship plus outside work, largely tutoring, enabled him to attend Harvard. After completing his undergraduate study in history, he did graduate work under Henry Adams, receiving a Ph.D. for a thesis on 'The Anglo-Saxon Legal Procedure'. His subsequent academic career, however, was entirely in economics.

From 1878 to 1888 he taught at Harvard, from 1888 to 1890 he was successively Secretary and President of the Philadelphia Manufacturers' Mutual Fire Insurance Company, from 1890 to 1892 Professor of Political Economy and Finance at Cornell, and in 1892 was persuaded by President Harper to become Head Professor of Political Economy at the new University of Chicago, the position he held until he retired in 1916. From 1916 until his death in 1933 he continued his scientific writing and public activities.

Laughlin's scholarly work was almost entirely in the field of money and banking. Much of it, notably his *History of Bimetallism in the United States* (1885), consisted of a thorough and extremely careful presentation of historical evidence on the development of money and monetary institutions. But Laughlin also wrote extensively on monetary and banking theory, and on proposals for monetary reform. His work on these topics was marred by a dogmatic and rigid opposition to the quantity theory of money, an opposition that developed out of his public activities opposing the free silver movement. The proponents of free silver used a crude form of the quantity theory to support their position, which sufficed to render the theory anathema to Laughlin.

Laughlin's attack on the quantity theory had much in common with recent cost-push or structural or supply shock theories of inflation, in emphasizing the role of factors affecting specific goods and services rather than general monetary influences. Then, as now, such theories ran against the major stream of monetary analysis as exemplified in Laughlin's time by the work of Irving Fisher. As a result, his writings on theory have had no lasting influence on economic thought.

According to Wesley C. Mitchell, one of his students,

> Professor Laughlin's indubitable success as a teacher puzzled many who did not pass through his classroom. He was not an original thinker of great power. He did not enrich economics … . He did not even keep abreast of current developments in economic theory … . He had a prim and tidy mind, which he kept in perfect order by admitting nothing that did not harmonize with the furnishings installed in the 1880's … . Yet he held that a teacher's aim should be 'the acquisition of independent power and methods of work, rather than specific beliefs'.
>
> The very limitations I have listed helped Professor Laughlin to accomplish this aim. … [His] honesty of purpose impelled others to be honest, which meant that doubting students had to work out the reasons for their dissent … . Laughlin forced one to face intellectual conflicts in his own mind and find out where he stood in the world of ideas. That, I have long believed, was the secret of his success in helping so many students of such diverse capacities to make the most of their several gifts. (1941, pp. 879–80)

As monetary reformer, Laughlin was a leading opponent of the advocates of free silver. He wrote, lectured, and campaigned extensively in favour of 'hard money'. In his widely circulated free-silver pamphlet, *Coin's Financial School*, William Hope Harvey used Laughlin as a hard-money foil for the fictional Coin's free-silver argument. That episode terminated in a widely reported public debate in Chicago in 1885 between Laughlin and Harvey.

After the defeat of William Jennings Bryan and the free-silver forces in the presidential election of 1896, financial and commercial interests in the country organized the Indianapolis Monetary Commission to develop proposals for reform of the monetary and banking system. One of the 11 members of the commission, Laughlin was also the author of its extensive final report, which served as an important stepping-stone en route to the Aldrich–Vreeland Act of 1908 and the Federal Reserve Act of 1913. In addition, Laughlin served for nearly two years from 1911 to 1913, on leave from the University of

Chicago, as full-time chairman of the executive committee of the National Citizens League, an organization formed to mobilize public opinion in favour of banking reform.

Laughlin's close links with the Republican Party prevented him from playing any public role in the final preparation of the Federal Reserve Act under a Democratic administration. However, he exerted considerable influence behind the scenes through extensive private correspondence with his former student and assistant, H. Parker Willis, who, as banking expert for the House Banking and Currency Committee, has been regarded as primarily responsible for drafting the Act.

Laughlin's most important and lasting contribution was as head of the Department of Political Economy of the new University of Chicago. Though himself a hard-money man of rigidly conservative views, he demonstrated an extraordinary degree of tolerance for divergent views in staffing and guiding the department. At the very outset, he brought with him from Cornell Thorstein Veblen, who remained in the department for 14 years, the longest period Veblen spent at any single university during his stormy career. Veblen served as managing editor of the *Journal of Political Economy*, which Laughlin founded as one of his first acts at Chicago. Laughlin himself was the editor. As John U. Nef wrote in his obituary notice of Laughlin, 'his wide cultural interests combined with his other qualities to enable him to gather about him a more remarkable group of younger men than was to be found in any other economics department in the country and to help these men in making the most of their own gifts.' Nef notes that

> a very considerable portion of all the men who have made an important mark in economic thought between 1895 and 1930, beginning with Thorstein Veblen and coming down to Jacob Viner (Laughlin's last appointment) were connected at one time or another, as members or students, with the department of political economy. … Laughlin frequently chose the best men when they were of very different persuasions from his own. … And so it came about that one of the most conservative heads of an economics department in the country had politically the most liberal and economically the least orthodox department. (1934, p. 2)

Laughlin's emphasis on quality rather than ideology was combined with an emphasis on research by his faculty, as well as by graduate students as part of their training. A corollary was his belief in personal teaching as opposed to formal lecturing. These have remained key characteristics of the Chicago Department of Economics from that day to this. In more recent years, as in his day, the department has been widely regarded as a stronghold of proponents of a free-market economy. That reputation was justified in the sense that throughout the period the department had prominent members who held these views and presented them effectively. But they were always a minority. The department has been characterized by heterogeneity of policy views, not homogeneity. The economists at Chicago who held the generally fashionable views – who were 'liberal' in the 20th-century sense – could be matched at other institutions; the ones who were 'liberal' in the 19th-century sense could not be. That, plus the emphasis on economics as a serious scientific subject, capable of being tested by empirical and historical evidence, and of being used to illuminate important practical issues of conduct and policy, made Chicago economics unique. These were Laughlin's bequest to the department he built.

MILTON FRIEDMAN

Selected works

1885. *The History of Bimetallism in the United States*. New York: D. Appleton & Co.
1898. *Report of the Monetary Commission of the Indianapolis Convention of Boards of Trade, Chambers of Commerce, Commercial Clubs, and Other Similar Bodies of the United States*. Chicago: University of Chicago Press.
1903. *The Principles of Money*. New York: Charles Scribner's Sons.
1909. *Latter Day Problems*. New York: Charles Scribner's Sons.
1931. *A New Exposition of Money, Credit and Prices*, 2 vols. Chicago: University of Chicago Press.
1933. *The Federal Reserve Act: Its Origin and Problems*. New York: Macmillan.

Bibliography

Bornemann, A. 1940. *J. Laurence Laughlin*. Washington, DC: American Council on Public Affairs.
Mitchell, W.C. 1941. J. Laurence Laughlin. *Journal of Political Economy* 49, 875–81.
Nef, J.U. 1934. James Laurence Laughlin (1850–1933). *Journal of Political Economy* 42, 1–5.

Launhardt, Carl Friedrich Wilhelm (1832–1918)

Launhardt was born on 4 April 1832 in Hannover, where he died on 14 May 1918. His work is Germany's most important and in fact only significant contribution to the 'marginal revolution' in the last three decades of the 19th century. In the economic analysis of transportation and location, this contribution was not surpassed until the 1930s. Available only in German, some of it in publications that are hard to find, it still has not found the recognition it deserves, and Schumpeter's references in the *History of Economic Analysis* are inadequate.

Like Dupuit, Launhardt began his professional life as a civil engineer, working for the public road administration. In 1869 he joined the faculty of the Hannover Polytechnic Institute as a professor for roads, railways and bridges. This was the beginning of a distinguished academic career, in the course of which he served as the director of the institute and, when it became the Technische Hochschule Hannover, its first rector. He was made a member of the Königliche Akademie des Bauwesens and of the Preussische Herrenhaus. Dresden gave him an honorary degree for his contributions to the technology and economics of transportation.

Practical problems of highway planning led Launhardt to the gradually more general analysis of efficient transportation networks. This work was later systematized in *Theorie des Trassirens* (Theory of Network Planning). Part I, entitled 'Commercial Network Planning', contains the derivation of efficiency criteria without regard to topography. This part is the second edition, much revised and enlarged, of the 1872 publication, and also incorporates sections from the 1885 book. Part II, entitled 'Technical Network Planning for Railroads', applies economic efficiency criteria to curves and gradients imposed by topography; an earlier version was published in 1877.

The contributions to economics are found in Part I. This begins with a discussion of investment criteria. From a social point of view, networks should be planned in such a way that the sum of operating and capital costs is a minimum. Private capitalists, however, try to maximize the internal rate of return on their capital. Under perfect competition the two criteria would coincide, since the internal rate of return, if duly maximized, would equal the market rate of interest. In reality, however, since the railroad industry is inherently non-competitive, rates of return can be pushed above market rates of interest by keeping railroad investment below the social optimum. This was one of Launhardt's basic arguments for government ownership of railroads. For his own analysis he uses, of course, the social criterion.

Using geometry and calculus, Launhardt derives rules, depending on freight costs and volumes, for the optimal direction and density of highways connecting given market centres. He shows that highways of different quality (and thus with different freight costs) should meet at angles analogous to those of refracted light, a rule later popularized by Stackelberg as the 'law of refraction'. According to the 'law of nodes', transport costs on a star-shaped transportation network connecting three cities are minimized if the sines of the angles between its rays bear the same proportions as the total transportation costs per mile along the rays. The efficient combination of different modes, like highways, waterways and railways, is also considered.

Applying his analysis of network nodes to the location of plants, Launhardt produced the first substantial theory of industrial location (1882). In this basic contribution he determines the efficient location of a plant with given sources of supplies and given sales outlets by minimizing transportation costs. The optimum is found by an ingenious geometrical construction which became known as the 'pole principle', later amplified by Palander. It is given a mechanical interpretation as the centre of gravity of forces, representing freight rates, acting at the different input and output locations. After first assuming that the network of routes is being planned from scratch, Launhardt also derives rules for optimal additions to existing networks. The analysis is far superior to that in Alfred Weber's later book on the location of industries, in which Launhardt is not mentioned, and whose only claim to attention is the appendix by Georg Pick.

Launhardt's main contribution to the theory of railway rates is found in chapter 32 of (1885). It was elaborated in (1887) and further detail was added in (1890a) and (1890b), but these extensions add nothing for more general economic interest. The paper on 'Economic Problems of the Railway Industry' provides an extensive analysis, based on consumer surplus, of the social rate of return of railroads, both theoretical and numerical, including a cost–benefit analysis of future railway development.

For railway rates, Launhardt establishes the principle that the maximization of social welfare requires – in modern terminology – marginal cost pricing. But this, in turn, requires competition, while profit maximization by monopolistic railway firms implies that rates exceed marginal cost. In particular, if a railway transports homogeneous goods from a uniform plain to a market centre, the monopoly price is calculated to exceed marginal cost by 50 per cent (because, in modern terminology, freight volume reacts to the freight rate with an elasticity of – 2 and ton-miles thus with an elasticity of – 3). As a consequence, the freight volume is suboptimal. By perfect discrimination according to 'what the traffic will bear' over each distance, both railway profits and general welfare can be increased compared with simple monopoly. This, however, is only a second-best solution. For Launhardt, the efficiency of marginal cost pricing is another basic argument for government ownership.

Launhardt's main claim to a prominent place in the history of economic analysis is his slender treatise *Mathematische Begründung der Volkswirtschaftslehre* (Mathematical Foundations of Economics) of 1885. It was written in the light of Walras's *Mathematische Theorie der Preisbestimmung wirtschaftlicher Güter* (1881) and the second edition of Jevons's *Theory of Political Economy* (1879). At the same time, it is clearly pre-Marshall and pre-Edgeworth (though *Mathematical Psychics* had appeared in 1881). Two other books by Walras, sent by the author, arrived too late to be of use, nor was Launhardt acquainted with Cournot at that time. He reports that the copy he finally obtained from a library had apparently never been read, and Gossen could nowhere be found (because virtually no copies had been sold). Launhardt shows what a competent engineer with an economic turn of mind and a little calculus could do (and also what he could not do) in economics a hundred years ago. Launhardt's addiction to special functional forms, particularly quadratic utility functions, often results in spurious precision, limited generality and reduced lucidity, but the basic contributions are sound, important and original.

In his theory of exchange (Part I), Launhardt rightly criticizes Walras for believing (if taken literally) that there is no way for a trader to improve his position relative to free competition at uniform prices. His counter-examples relate to monopoly and price discrimination, leading him to the idea of an optimal tariff. While valid in principle, this analysis falls short of Edgeworth's. The discussion of the total gain from trade and its distribution, whose shortcomings were pointed out by Wicksell, was soon obsolete because of its dependence on the interpersonal additivity of utility.

In his discussion of distributive shares, Launhardt recognizes the backward-bending supply curve of labour and the effect of property incomes on labour supply and thus on wages. He also recognizes that the inter-occupational mobility of labour tends to equalize relative wage rates with both the ratios of the marginal products of labour and (to the extent an individual can choose between occupations) the ratio of its marginal disutilities. For profits, Launhardt's 'basic equation' expresses, substantially, the familiar optimality condition that the profit margin, as a percentage of price, is the inverse of the elasticity of demand (though this concept is not used, of course). It is clearly explained that the entrepreneur, in setting his price, considers only marginal costs, while prices are equalized to the average costs of the marginal firm by exit and entry. The profits of intra-marginal firms are correctly interpreted as rents, and the same principle is used to explain wage differentials.

Launhardt's theory of interest is Jevonian in spirit. Though brief and somewhat sketchy, it anticipates all the basic elements of Fisher's theory. In many respects Launhardt achieves more in 20 pages than Böhm-Bawerk in about 500. Using modern terminology, the rate of interest is explained by the interplay between a psychological preference for present consumption, modified by variations in expected income, and the marginal productivity of capital (ch. 24). Saving is interpreted as a sacrifice of current consumption for the sake of an infinite stream of additions to future consumption. It is shown mathematically that, with a rising rate of interest, given the rate of time preference, saving first rises to a maximum and then declines, because at high interest rates small savings are enough to buy a lot of future income. According to the 'basic principle of accumulation', the present value of the future marginal utility of income is made equal to the current marginal utility of income. In the course of time, optimal saving, if initially positive, will decline until a steady state is reached (ch. 15). Investments will be made up to the point where the marginal saving in operating costs is equal to the rate of interest.

The subject of Part III is the effect of transportation on production and consumption. Launhardt starts out by determining production and prices of a single seller supplying an unlimited market of uniform density. Delivered prices are seen to rise towards the periphery in the shape of a hollow cone, known as the 'Launhardt Funnel' (ch. 27). If sellers of differentiated products compete in a uniformly populated plain, their market areas are shown to be polygons, whose sides, depending on circumstances, are pieces of ellipses, hyperbolas or straight lines. In this context there emerges what Palander later called the Launhardt–Hotelling solution for heterogeneous duopoly. Forty-four years before Hotelling, Launhardt already used the paradigm of two competing suppliers, located at different points along a street, each maximizing his profits on the assumption that the price of his competitor is given. His solution, forgotten for half a century, is substantially identical to Hotelling's. An analogous analysis is provided for suppliers of differentiated products at the same location, showing how their ring-shaped market areas depend on transportation costs (ch. 29).

From the market areas of given suppliers, Launhardt shifts his attention to the supplying areas of given markets, which brings rent to the foreground. His description of the product 'rings' surrounding a single market city in an unlimited plain adds nothing to Von Thünen (ch. 30). The analysis is then extended to a number of markets, each with its limited supplying area. If identical cities are located in a pattern of regular triangles, the supplying areas are, of course, hexagonal. While this foreshadows Lösch's later work, Launhardt's triangular pattern is based on intuition and not on explicit optimality conditions. It is shown, however, how the mutual limitation of adjoining supplying areas raises rent and product prices (ch. 31). Much of this material was later incorporated in the second edition of *Commercial Network Planning* (1887).

Launhardt's monetary theory is far inferior to his microeconomics. Its centrepiece is the rejection of the quantity theory of money. In part, this is based, in the tradition of Senior and the Banking School, on the argument that under a gold standard an increase in the quantity of paper money just leads to an external (and/or internal) gold drain, while commodity prices remain tied to international prices or, in a closed economy, the gold price. To this extent, Launhardt is on firm ground. He went much further, however. In the theory of relative prices he had assumed that the marginal utility of money is constant. When first introduced, this was an innocuous simplification, but in the theory of money it became the source of fatal confusion, for it induced Launhardt to treat money incomes, which he chose as the proximate determinant of absolute prices, as if they were 'real' variables, independent of the money supply. After that, one is hardly surprised to read that higher interest rates result in higher prices and that gold discoveries have no influence on prices. The basic argument is found in *Mathematische Begründung* (1885); later

elaborations (1889; 1894) and historical illustrations and applications.

JÜRG NIEHANS

Selected works

1868. *Bestimmung der zweckmässigsten Steigungsverhältnisse der Chausseen*. Hannover.
1869. *Ueber Rentabilität and Richtungsfeststellung der Strassen*. Hannover.
1872. *Kommercielle Tracirung der Verkehrswege*. Hannover.
1877. *Die Betriebskosten der Eisenbahnen in ihrer Abhängigkeit von den Steigungs- und Krümmungsverhältnissen der Bahn*. *Handbuch für specielle Eisenbahn-Technik*, vol. 4, Supplement. Leipzig.
1882. *Die Bestimmung des zweckmässigsten Standortes einer gewerblichen Anlage*. *Zeitschrift des Vereines deutscher Ingenieure* 26, 106–15.
1883. *Wirtschaftliche Fragen des Eisenbahnwesens*. *Centralblatt der Bauverwaltung*, vol. 3.
1885. *Mathematische Begründung der Volkswirtschaftslehre*. Leipzig.
1887–8. *Theorie des Trassirens*. 2 parts. Hannover.
1889. *Die Quantitätshtheorie. Ein Beitrag zur Lehre vom Wesen des Geldes*. Hannover.
1890a. *Theorie der Tarifbildung der Eisenbahnen*. Berlin.
1890b. *Zur Frage einer besseren Feststellung des Personenfahrgeldes*. *Organ für die Fortschritte des Eisenbahnwesens*.
1894. *Mark, Rubel und Rupie Erläuterungen zur Währungsfrage und Erörterungen über das Wesen des Geldes*. Berlin.
1900. *Am sausenden Webstuhl der Zeit. Aus Natur und Geisteswelt*, vol. 23. Leipzig.

law of demand

The most familiar version of the law of demand says that as the price of a good increases the quantity demanded of the good falls. The principal use of the law of demand in economic theory is to provide sufficient and, in some contexts, necessary conditions for the uniqueness and stability of equilibrium, and for intuitive comparative statics. To guarantee such properties in equilibrium models with more than one good, the familiar one-good law of demand just stated is not sufficient – some multi-good version of the law is needed. In its multi-good form, the law of demand is said to hold for a particular change in prices if the prices and the quantities demanded move in opposite directions; in formal terms, the vector of price changes and the vector of resulting demand changes have a negative inner product.

In this article, we examine different formulations of the law of demand. They differ principally in the domain of price changes over which the law applies. It is not always the case that the law of demand is required to hold for *all* price changes: the version of the law which is required for stability analysis and comparative statics varies from one context to another. For each formulation of the law of demand, we discuss the conditions which are sufficient to guarantee that it is satisfied.

To point out the obvious, the law of demand, in whatever form, is not a universal law at all but a condition which may hold in some situations and not others. It is well known that, in transactions where asymmetric information is an important consideration, violations of the law can occur. For example, lowering the price of a set of used cars does not necessarily lead to higher demand if potential buyers think that the lower price reflects the quality of the cars being offered. (For a discussion of violations of the law of demand and other issues which arise when price has an impact on the perceived quality of the good being exchanged, see Stiglitz, 1987.) In this article we make the classical assumption that the features of the good being transacted are commonly known and independent of the price. As we shall see, even in this classical setting various forms of the law of demand will hold only under conditions which are often neither obviously onerous nor obviously innocuous; in these cases, one must necessarily turn to empirical work to ascertain whether or not the law holds.

We use the notation and terminology of Mas-Colell, Whinston and Green (1995, chs. 2, 3, 5) and assume that the reader is familiar with the basic consumer and producer theory described there. We assume that there are L commodities and that consumers are price-takers. The demand of a consumer of type α with income w at price vector $p = (p_\ell)_{\ell=1}^{L} \gg 0$ is the vector $x(p, w, \alpha) = (x_\ell(p, w, \alpha))_{\ell=1}^{L}$ in $\mathbb{R}_{+}^{L}$, satisfying the budget identity $p \cdot x(p, w, \alpha) = w$ for all p and w. Unless stated otherwise, we assume the demand function $x(\cdot, \cdot, \alpha)$ to be C^1. Then it has a Slutsky matrix of substitution effects $S(p,w,\alpha)$ with ℓj element $S_{\ell j}(p, w, \alpha) = \partial x_\ell(p, w, \alpha)/\partial p_j + [\partial x_\ell(p, w, \alpha)/\partial w]x_j(p, w, \alpha)$. The Slutsky matrix $S(p,w,\alpha)$ is the Jacobian matrix of the Slutsky-compensated demand function x^*, defined by $x^*(q) = x(q, q \cdot x(p, w, \alpha), \alpha)$, evaluated at $q = p$. The term $[\partial x_\ell(p, w, \alpha)/\partial w]x_j(p, w, \alpha)$ is called an income effect since it approximates the effect on the demand for good ℓ when income rises enough to compensate for a unit increase in the price of good j. If the consumer chooses demand bundles by maximizing a well-behaved utility function, then the Slutsky matrix is symmetric and negative semidefinite. The latter means that $v \cdot S(p, w, \alpha)v \leq 0$ for all $v \in \mathbb{R}^L$; in particular, the diagonal terms of the Slutsky matrix are non-positive.

One-good and multi-good laws of demand

The term 'law of demand' most often refers to the effect of price changes on consumers with fixed incomes. The law for a single good ℓ and a single consumer of type α is

$$(p_\ell - \bar{p}_\ell)(x_\ell(p, w, \alpha) - x_\ell(\bar{p}, w, \alpha)) \leq 0, \tag{1}$$

for p and $\bar{p}$, with $p_i = \bar{p}_i$ for all $i \neq \ell$ and income w fixed. (In the *strict* version of the law, the weak inequality in (1) is replaced by strict inequality when $p \neq \bar{p}$; all the laws of demand discussed in this article can be stated in their corresponding strict forms, though we generally do not do so.) The inequality (1) is equivalent to

$$0 \geq \frac{\partial x_\ell}{\partial p_\ell}(p, w, \alpha) = S_{\ell\ell}(p, w, \alpha)$$
$$- x_\ell(p, w, \alpha)\frac{\partial x_\ell}{\partial w}(p, w, \alpha),$$
$$\forall(p, w).$$

It holds if the substitution effect $S_{\ell\ell}$ is negative and larger in magnitude than the income effect $x_\ell(p, w, \alpha)\frac{\partial x_\ell}{\partial w}(p, w, \alpha)$. If the consumer is utility-maximizing, then $S_{\ell\ell} \leq 0$, so a sufficient condition for good ℓ to obey the law of demand is that the demand for this good is normal $(\partial x_\ell(p, w, \alpha)/\partial w \geq 0)$. If the demand for good ℓ is not normal, the price effect $\partial x_\ell/\partial p_\ell$ may be positive. This is called a Giffen effect and good ℓ is called a Giffen good. All goods are normal and Giffen effects are ruled out if the demand function is generated by homothetic preferences or by a concave additive utility function $(u(x) = \sum_{\ell=1}^{L} u_\ell(x_\ell))$, or, more generally, by a supermodular concave function u, that is, one in which all commodity pairs are Auspitz–Lieben–Edgeworth–Pareto complements: $\partial^2 u(x)/\partial x_j\partial x_\ell \geq 0$ for all $j \neq \ell$ (Chipman, 1977).

Giffen goods are rarely observed. Sometimes demand for a durable good like oil may increase with its current price if traders expect an even higher price in the future. However, if commodities are distinguished by date, this is not a Giffen effect since a future price changes along with the current price. A possible example of a Giffen good is proposed by Baruch and Kannai (2002). They give evidence suggesting that, in Japan of the 1970s, shochu, a cheap (and, by some accounts, nasty) alcoholic drink, fits the definition. One may explain the demand for shochu in the following way. A consumer chooses between sake (good 1) and shochu (good 2). He always prefers sake to shochu, but he also *must have* a minimum alcohol intake (which we fix at 1). Formally, his utility is $u(x_1, x_2) = x_1$, subject to the 'survival' constraint $x_1 + x_2 \geq 1$. If the consumer is sufficiently poor, both the budget and survival constraints bind, with the consumer consuming as much sake – and as little shochu – as possible. A fall in the price of shochu allows him to buy less shochu and more sake and still meet his alcohol requirement; this he chooses to do since he always prefers sake to shochu.

Turning now to multi-good laws of demand, let $P \subseteq \mathbb{R}_{++}^{L}$ be a set of prices and let $X : P \to \mathbb{R}^L$ be a function representing individual or aggregate demand of firms or of consumers. The natural multi-good generalization of the one-good law in (1) is

$$(p - p') \cdot (X(p) - X(p')) \leq 0 \tag{2}$$

for all (p, p') in some subset of $P \times P$. If P is convex and open and X is C^1, (2) holds on $P \times P$ if and only if the Jacobian matrix $\partial X(p)$ is negative semidefinite at each p (Hildenbrand and Kirman, 1988).

Suppose that the supply vector of the L goods changes from ω to ω'. Let p and p' be corresponding equilibrium prices so $X(p) = \omega$ and $X(p') = \omega'$. Then, if X obeys (2) for all prices, we obtain $(p - p') \cdot (\omega - \omega') \leq 0$. It is clear that this comparative statics property and the law of demand on X are essentially two sides of the same coin. Note also that, according to this property, an increase in the supply of good k, with the supply of all other goods held fixed, will lead to a fall in the price of k.

Suppose that P is open and X obeys the *strict* law of demand, that is, X satisfies (2) with strict inequality for all distinct p and p' in P. This implies in particular that X is 1–1 and that, for each $\bar{\omega}$ in $X(P)$, there is a unique equilibrium price vector $\bar{p} = X^{-1}(\bar{\omega})$. A tâtonnement path for the function $X - \bar{\omega}$ is the solution to $dp/dt = X(p(t)) - \bar{\omega}$ for some initial condition $p(0) = p'$ in P. We say that $X - \bar{\omega}$ is monotonically stable for $\bar{\omega}$ if each of its tâtonnement paths satisfies $d|p(t) - \bar{p}|^2/dt < 0$ whenever $p(t) \neq \bar{p}$. It is easy to check that $X - \bar{\omega}$ is monotonically stable for all $\bar{\omega}$ in $X(P)$ if and only if X obeys the strict law of demand. Furthermore, because P is open, a tâtonnement path for $X - \bar{\omega}$ which begins at a price sufficiently close to $\bar{p} = X^{-1}(\bar{\omega})$ stays in P for all $t > 0$. Lyapunov's second theorem then guarantees that the tâtonnement path converges to $\bar{p}$.

Laws of demand are thus useful as intuitive sufficient conditions for the uniqueness and stability of equilibrium and for comparative statics. We will examine, in different contexts, circumstances under which they hold.

Law of demand for competitive firms and consumers with quasilinear utility

For a firm with production set Y, profit maximizing net output vector y at price vector p and $\bar{y}$ at $\bar{p}$ satisfy $p \cdot y \geq p \cdot \bar{y}$ and $\bar{p} \cdot \bar{y} \geq \bar{p} \cdot y$. The net demand vectors $x = -y$ and $\bar{x} = -\bar{y}$ satisfy $p(x - \bar{x}) \leq 0$ and $\bar{p}(x - \bar{x}) \geq 0$, hence satisfy the law of demand: $(p - \bar{p}) \cdot (x - \bar{x}) \leq 0$. Similarly, a consumer with utility function $u(x_0, x) = x_0 + \phi(x_1, \ldots, x_L)$ (*quasilinear* with respect to good 0) and with sufficiently high income w satisfies the law of demand on a restricted domain, where the price of good 0 is fixed (say at 1). This is a special case of the law for firms. The consumer's optimal demand for goods 1 through L at p (the price vector for goods 1 to L) and income w maximizes $w - p \cdot x + \phi(x)$. This is equivalent to profit maximization with x an input vector and $\phi(x)$ the value of output.

Bewley (1977) shows that a long-lived consumer with a random income stream and a random but stationary time-separable utility function, who is constrained from borrowing, will accumulate savings so that the marginal utility of income is nearly constant. In the short run, this consumer acts (nearly) as if its utility is quasilinear with respect to money, and its short run demands for other goods satisfy the law of demand. Vives (1987) formalizes Marshall's idea (in his *Principles*) that consumer demands for goods with small expenditure shares are close to demands generated by quasilinear utility.

Multi-good laws of demand for a consumer

Suppose the demand of a consumer of type α is determined by maximizing a utility function u^α. The Hicksian compensated demand $h(p, \bar{u}, \alpha)$ is a bundle that minimizes $p \cdot x$ subject to $u^\alpha(x) \geq \bar{u}$. Keeping the utility level fixed at $\bar{u}$, this Hicksian demand function satisfies the multi-good law of demand: (2) holds for $X(p) = h(p, \bar{u}, \alpha)$. Utility maximization also guarantees that $x(\cdot, \cdot, \alpha)$ satisfies the *weak weak axiom of revealed preference*: $p \cdot x(p', w', \alpha) \leq w \Rightarrow p' \cdot x(p, w, \alpha) \geq w'$. Equivalently, for any fixed w, $X(p) = x(p, w, \alpha)$ satisfies (2) on the restricted domain with $p \cdot X(p') = w$. This is also called the compensated law of demand since the demand vector $X(p')$ remains barely affordable when the price vector changes from p' to p. The weak weak axiom is satisfied so long as the consumer maximizes a *complete* preference relation; the preferences need not be transitive. When $x(\cdot, \cdot, \alpha)$ is C^1, the following are equivalent: (i) $x(\cdot, \cdot, \alpha)$ obeys the weak weak axiom; (ii) its Slutsky matrix $S(p, w, \alpha)$ is negative semidefinite (but not necessarily symmetric); (iii) its Jacobian matrix $\partial_p x(p, w, \alpha)$ is negative semidefinite on the hyperplane orthogonal to $x(p, w, \alpha)$ (Kihlstrom, Mas-Colell and Sonnenschein, 1976; Brighi, 2004).

When we say that $x(\cdot, \cdot, \alpha)$ obeys the unrestricted law of demand (or law of demand, for short) we mean that for each w, $X(p) = x(p, w, \alpha)$ satisfies (2) for *all* price changes. Since this is equivalent to negative semidefiniteness of the Jacobian $\partial_p x(p, w, \alpha)$ for all p, it is stronger than simply saying that the diagonal terms of the matrix are non-positive. Thus it is not equivalent to the one-good law of demand for every good and does not follow from the assumption that the demand for every good is normal.

Let $M(p, w, \alpha)$ be the income effects matrix, with ℓj component $[\partial_w x_\ell(p, w, \alpha)] x_j(p, w, \alpha)$. From the Slutsky decomposition, $\partial_p x(p, w, \alpha) = S(p, w, \alpha) - M(p, w, \alpha)$, we see that type α satisfies the law of demand if it satisfies the weak weak axiom and $M(p, w, \alpha)$ is positive semidefinite at each p. However, the latter condition is strong; it occurs if and only if demand is linear in income for all goods, which excludes the possibility of luxuries or necessities.

A more promising approach is to find conditions under which the Slutsky matrix always 'dominates' the income effects matrix even when the latter 'misbehaves'. On the assumption that type α has a concave utility function u^α, a sufficient and (in a sense) necessary condition for the law of demand is $-[x^T \partial^2 u^\alpha(x) x]/(\partial u^\alpha(x) x) \leq 4, \forall x$.

This result was obtained independently by Milleron (1974) and Mitjuschin and Polterovich (1978) (see also Mas-Colell, Whinston and Green, 1995, p. 145, and an alternative formulation in Kannai, 1989).

An important application of this result is in the theory of portfolio choice. In that case, the demand bundle is the consumer's contingent consumption over L states of the world; it is standard to assume that the consumer has a von Neumann–Morgenstern utility function $u^\alpha(x) = \sum_{i=1}^{l} \pi_i v^\alpha(x_i)$, where π_i is the subjective probability of state i and $v^\alpha : R_{++} \to R$ is the Bernoulli utility function. Suppose the coefficient of relative risk aversion, $-yv^{\alpha\prime\prime}(y)/v^{\alpha\prime}(y)$, does not *vary* by more than four on the domain of v^α. Then the consumer's demand for contingent consumption at different state prices will obey the law of demand; this in turn implies that the law of demand holds for the consumer's demand for securities, whether or not the market is complete (Quah, 2003).

Laws of market demand when the income distribution is independent of price

Consider a large economy with consumers drawn at random from a probability space $A \times R_+$ of consumer types and their incomes, with distribution μ. The expected aggregate (market) demand vector at prices p is $X(p) = \int_{A \times R_+} x(p, w, \alpha) d\mu$. We are interested in conditions under which X obeys the unrestricted law of demand, that is, (2) holds for all price changes; equivalently, $\partial X(p)$ is negative semidefinite for all p. If $x(\cdot, \cdot, \alpha)$ obeys the law of demand for all α, then, clearly, so will X. One justification for studying the law of demand at the individual level is that it is preserved by aggregation.

Aggregating the Slutsky decomposition across all agents, the law of demand requires

$$
\begin{aligned}
v \cdot \partial X(p)v &= v \cdot \left[\int_{\alpha \in A} x(p, w, \alpha) d\mu \right] v \\
&= v \cdot \bar{S}(p)v - v \cdot \bar{M}(p)v \leq 0, \quad \forall v
\end{aligned}
$$
(3)

where $\bar{S}(p) = \int S(p, w, \alpha) d\mu$ is the mean Slutsky matrix, and $\bar{M}(p)$ is the mean income effects matrix, with ℓj element $\int [\partial x_\ell(p, w, \alpha)/\partial w] x_j(p, w, \alpha) \, d\mu$. (We assume here and below that these integrals exist.) If all consumers obey the weak weak axiom, which they do if they are utility maximizers, then $S(p,w,\alpha)$ and hence $\bar{S}(p)$ are negative semidefinite; so $\partial X(p)$ is negative semidefinite if $\bar{M}(p)$ is positive semidefinite.

The matrix $\bar{M}(p)$ is determined by the consumers' Engel curves $x(p\cdot, \cdot, \alpha)$ at p. Positive semidefiniteness of this matrix is known as *increasing spread* (Hildenbrand, 1994). To see why, note that

$$
2v \cdot \bar{M}(p)v = \partial_t \int [v \cdot x(p, w + t, \alpha)]^2 d\mu(\alpha, w)\big|_{t=0}.
$$
(4)

We can interpret $v \cdot x(p,w,\alpha)$ as α's demand for a commodity (call it T_v), which is consumed when the other goods are consumed; specifically, the consumption of one unit of good j requires v_j units of T_v. Then $\int [v \cdot x(p, w, \alpha)]^2 d\mu$ measures the spread of the consumers' demands for T_v around the origin. By (4), $\bar{M}(p)$ is positive semidefinite if and only if for every v the consumers' demands for T_v spread out from 0 as their incomes rise. This is the multi-good generalization of normality, where the consumers' demands for a single good increase (spread from 0) as their incomes rise.

We now consider various interpretable conditions on the distribution of consumer characteristics which guarantee increasing spread (and thus the law of demand). This property holds if consumers have the same demand function and income is distributed with a non-increasing density function ρ on $[0, \bar{w}]$ (Hildenbrand, 1983). In that case, integrating by parts, (4) becomes $2v \cdot \bar{M}(p)v = [v \cdot x(p, \bar{w}, \alpha)]^2 \rho(\bar{w}) - \int [v \cdot x(p, w, \alpha)]^2 \rho'(w) dw \geq 0$. While the non-increasing density condition is strong, imposing some weak restrictions on the Engel curves will guarantee increasing spread for a significantly larger class of income density functions (Chiappori, 1985). However, to guarantee increasing spread for *every* non-trivial income distribution requires stringent conditions on the consumers' Engel curves: $x(p, \cdot, \alpha)$ must lie in a single plane (depending on p) and the demand for each good is either a concave or convex function of income (Freixas and Mas-Colell, 1987; Jerison, 1999).

Increasing spread is also implied by certain kinds of behavioural heterogeneity across consumers. We consider consumers with the same income w and demands of the form $x_\ell(p, w, \alpha) = e^{\alpha_\ell} \hat{x}(e^{\alpha_1} p_1, \ldots, e^{\alpha_L} p_L, w)$, where $\hat{x}$ is an arbitrary demand function and $\alpha = (\alpha_1, \ldots, \alpha_L) \in R^L$. If $\hat{x}$ is generated by some utility function $\hat{u}$, then $x(\cdot, \cdot, \alpha)$ is generated by the utility function $u^\alpha(x) = \hat{u}(e^{-\alpha_1} x_1, \ldots, e^{-\alpha_L} x_L)$. Increasing spread is guaranteed if α has a sufficiently flat density over R^L. This condition also ensures that the mean Slutsky matrix $\bar{S}(p)$ is negative semidefinite even if $\hat{x}$, hence each $x(\cdot, \cdot, \alpha)$, violates the weak weak axiom (and so is *not* generated by a utility function). Thus when α has a sufficiently flat density, X satisfies the law of demand; in fact it can be shown that X is nearly generated by Cobb–Douglas preferences (Grandmont, 1992). Whether flatness of the α density implies heterogeneity (in some meaningful sense) of the consumers' demands depends on the behaviour of $\hat{x}$ (Giraud and Quah, 2003).

Even when $\bar{M}(p)$ is not positive semidefinite, that is, $v \cdot \bar{M}(p)v < 0$ for some v, it is clear from (3) that $v \cdot \partial X(p)v < 0$ can hold provided the substitution effects are large enough, that is, $v \cdot \bar{S}(p)v$ is sufficiently negative. This feature can be exploited; for example, one can substantially weaken the non-increasing density condition in Hildenbrand (1983; described above) and still obtain the law of demand if substitution effects are accounted for through restrictions on the utility function (Quah, 2000).

Similarly, a large enough positive income effect can compensate for consumers' violations of the weak weak axiom, that is, situations where, for some v, $v \cdot \bar{S}(p)v > 0$.

Whether the substitution effect $v \cdot \bar{S}(p)v$ dominates the income effect $v \cdot \bar{M}(p)v$ is an empirical question. The sizes of the effects must be estimated. Härdle, Hildenbrand and Jerison (1991) show how this can be done with cross-section data under standard econometric assumptions, without restrictions on the functional forms of the consumer demands. In most empirical demand analyses, consumers are grouped according to observable attributes other than income, and within a group, a, the consumers' budget share vectors are assumed to have the form $b^a(p, w) + \varepsilon$, where ε is a mean 0 random variable with distribution independent of income w. Under this assumption, a consumer's type is its attribute group and a realized value of ε. Within group a, the distribution of types with income w, denoted $\mu^a(\alpha|w)$, does not vary with w. Thus, if the income distribution in the group has a density ρ^a, then

$$\int \{\partial_w[v \cdot x(p, w, \alpha)]^2\}d\mu^a$$

$$= \int \{\partial_w \int [v \cdot x(p, w, \alpha)]^2 d\mu^a(\alpha|w)\}$$

$$\times \rho^a(w)dw, \forall v \in R^L. \quad (5)$$

The left side of (5) equals $2v \cdot M^a(p)v$, where $M^a(p)$ is the mean income effect matrix of the consumers in group a. The right side of (5) is the mean of the derivative of $\int [v \cdot x(p, w, \alpha)]^2 d\mu^a(\alpha|w)$ with respect to w. It can be efficiently estimated by the nonparametric method of average derivatives (Härdle and Stoker, 1989). The mean income effect matrix $\bar{M}(p)$ is a weighted average of the matrices $M^a(p)$, weighted by the shares of the population in the groups a. Condition (5), called metonymy, is weaker than the assumption that the budget shares have the form $b^a(p, w) + \varepsilon$, so weak, in fact, that it is not potentially refutable with infinite cross-section data (Evstigneev, Hildenbrand and Jerison, 1997; Jerison, 2001). Income effect matrices estimated in this way using cross-section expenditure data from several countries are all positive semidefinite (Härdle, Hildenbrand and Jerison, 1991; Hildenbrand and Kneip, 1993).

Laws of demand in private ownership economies

In the previous section, we assumed consumer incomes to be exogenously given independently of prices. This is plainly not true in general equilibrium. For example, consider a private ownership economy with consumers drawn randomly from a distribution μ over types, where type α has the demand function $x(\cdot, \cdot, \alpha)$ and an endowment vector ω^α. If the consumers receive no profits, the income of type α at price vector p is $p \cdot \omega^\alpha$. We are interested in laws of demand that can be satisfied by the consumer sector's aggregate demand

$\tilde{X}(p) = \int x(p, p \cdot \omega^\alpha, \alpha) \, d\mu$ or aggregate excess demand $\zeta(p) = \tilde{X}(p) - \bar{\omega}$, where $\bar{\omega} = \int \omega^\alpha d\mu$ is the aggregate endowment.

The first thing to note is that under standard assumptions, both $\tilde{X}$ and ζ are zero-homogeneous and, essentially for this reason, satisfy the unrestricted law of demand only in exceptional cases (Hildenbrand and Kirman, 1988). However, if the consumers' endowments are collinear (that is, if for each α there is some $k \geq 0$ with $\omega^\alpha = k\bar{\omega}$) then the sufficient conditions for the law of market demand given in the previous section are also sufficient for $\tilde{X}$ (and hence ζ) to satisfy (2) for p and p' in $P = \{p \in R^L_{++} : p \cdot \bar{\omega} = 1\}$; in other words, the law of demand holds for mean income preserving price changes. This is so because, when endowments are collinear, a price change which preserves mean income also preserves the income of *every* agent.

When we drop the strong assumption of collinear endowments, this restricted form of the law of demand is not guaranteed even if all consumers have homothetic preferences (Mas-Colell, Whinston and Green, 1995, p. 598). However, it *does* hold when the consumer sector has two properties: (*a*) all agents have homothetic preferences and (*b*) the preferences and endowments are independently distributed. Quah (1997) shows that this scenario can be understood as the idealization of a more general situation. The crucial feature of homothetic preferences here is that they generate demand functions which are linear in income. Retaining the independence assumption (*b*), one can show that, when substitution effects are non-trivial (in some specific sense), $\tilde{X}$ obeys the restricted law of demand provided the mean demand of agents with identical endowments is not 'too non-linear' in income. This last property can arise from an appropriate form of heterogeneity in demand behaviour, which can be modelled using the parametric framework employed by Grandmont (1987; 1992).

It is interesting to ask when aggregate consumer excess demand ζ satisfies the weak weak axiom: $p \cdot \zeta(p') \leq 0 \Rightarrow p' \cdot \zeta(p) \geq 0$. This condition ensures that the set of equilibrium prices is convex in all competitive production economies with convex technology and constant returns to scale; furthermore, it is the weakest restriction on ζ guaranteeing this conclusion (Mas-Colell, Whinston and Green, 1995, p. 609). The sufficiency of this condition hinges on the fact that the production side of the economy satisfies the law of demand. Since the equilibrium set is generically discrete, its convexity implies generic uniqueness of equilibrium (up to scalar multiple). When ζ satisfies the weak weak axiom it also satisfies the law of demand (2) on the restricted set with $p \cdot \zeta(p') = 0$. If (2) holds strictly on this set when p and p' are not collinear, then the unique equilibrium is globally stable under tâtonnement, and there are natural comparative statics.

With the use of a Slutsky decomposition, it can be shown that ζ satisfies the weak weak axiom if the mean

Slutsky matrix $S(p)$ is negative semidefinite (as it is if the consumers are utility maximizing) and the consumers' excess demand vectors spread apart on average when their incomes rise. The latter condition is called non-decreasing dispersion of excess demand (NDED). To formalize it, define $z(p, t, \alpha) \equiv x(p, t + p \cdot \omega^{\alpha}) - \omega^{\alpha}$, the excess demand of type α with income transfer t. The corresponding aggregate excess demand is $Z(p, t) \equiv \int z(p, t, \alpha) d\mu$. NDED holds if $\partial_t \int \{v \cdot [z(p, t, \alpha) - Z(p, t)]\}^2 d\mu|_{t=0} \geq 0$ for every $p \in R^L_{++}$ and every v with $v \cdot p = 0$ and $v \cdot \zeta(p) = 0$; in other words, the income transfers raise the variance of the composite excess demands $v \cdot z(p, t, \alpha)$ (Jerison, 1999). Quah's 1997 model (described above) is an example of an economy where NDED is satisfied approximately.

MICHAEL JERISON AND JOHN K.-H. QUAH

See also **comparative statics; Engel curve; general equilibrium; Giffen's paradox; revealed preference theory; risk aversion; tâtonnement and recontracting.**

Bibliography

Baruch, S. and Kannai, Y. 2002. Inferior goods, Giffen goods, and shochu. In *Economics Essays*, ed. G. Debreu, W. Neuefeind and W. Trockel. Berlin: Springer-Verlag.

Bewley, T. 1977. The permanent income hypothesis: a theoretical formulation. *Journal of Economic Theory* 16, 252–92.

Brighi, L. 2004. A stronger criterion for the weak weak axiom. *Journal of Mathematical Economics* 40, 93–103.

Chiappori, P.-A. 1985. Distribution of income and the 'law of demand'. *Econometrica* 53, 109–28.

Chipman, J. 1977. An empirical implication of Auspitz–Lieben–Edgeworth–Pareto complementarity. *Journal of Economic Theory* 14, 228–31.

Evstigneev, I.V., Hildenbrand, W. and Jerison, M. 1997. Metonymy and cross-section demand. *Journal of Mathematical Economics* 28, 397–414.

Freixas, X. and Mas-Colell, A. 1987. Engel curves leading to the weak axiom in the aggregate. *Econometrica* 55, 515–31.

Giraud, G. and Quah, J.K.-H. 2003. Homothetic or Cobb–Douglas behavior through aggregation. *Contributions to Theoretical Economics* 3(1), Article 8.

Grandmont, J.M. 1987. Distribution of preferences and the 'law of demand'. *Econometrica* 55, 155–61.

Grandmont, J.M. 1992. Transformations of the commodity space, behavioral heterogeneity, and the aggregation problem. *Journal of Economic Theory* 57, 1–35.

Härdle, W., Hildenbrand, W. and Jerison, M. 1991. Empirical evidence on the law of demand. *Econometrica* 59, 1525–49.

Härdle, W. and Stoker, T. 1989. Investigating smooth multiple regression by the method of average derivatives. *Journal of the American Statistical Association* 84, 986–95.

Hildenbrand, W. 1983. On the law of demand. *Econometrica* 51, 997–1019.

Hildenbrand, W. 1994. *Market Demand*. Princeton: Princeton University Press.

Hildenbrand, W. and Kirman, A. 1988. *Equilibrium Analysis*. Amsterdam: North-Holland.

Hildenbrand, W. and Kneip, A. 1993. Family expenditure data, heterscedasticity and the law of demand. *Ricerche Economiche* 47, 137–65.

Jerison, M. 1999. Dispersed excess demands, the weak axiom, and uniqueness of equilibrium. *Journal of Mathematical Economics* 31, 15–48.

Jerison, M. 2001. Demand dispersion, metonymy and ideal panel data. In *Economics Essays*, ed. G. Debreu, W. Neuefeind and W. Trockel. Berlin: Springer-Verlag.

Kannai, Y. 1989. A Characterization of monotone individual demand functions. *Journal of Mathematical Economics* 18, 87–94.

Kihlstrom, R., Mas-Colell, A. and Sonnenschein, H. 1976. The demand theory of the weak axiom of revealed preference. *Econometrica* 44, 971–78.

Mas-Colell, A. 1991. On the uniqueness of equilibrium once again. In *Equilibrium Theory and Applications*, ed. W. Barnett et al. Cambridge: Cambridge University Press.

Mas-Colell, A., Whinston, M.D. and Green, J.R. 1995. *Microeconomic Theory*. Oxford: Oxford University Press.

Milleron, J.C. 1974. Unicité et stabilité de l'équilibre en économie de distribution. Unpublished seminar paper, Séminaire d'Econométrie Roy-Malinvaud. Paris: CNRS.

Mitjuschin, L.G. and Polterovich, W.M. 1978. Criteria for monotonicity of demand functions. *Ekonomika i Matematicheskie Metody* 14, 122–8.

Quah, J.K.-H. 1997. The law of demand when income is price dependent. *Econometrica* 65, 1421–42.

Quah, J.K.-H. 2000. The monotonicity of individual and market demand. *Econometrica* 68, 911–30.

Quah, J.K.-H. 2003. The law of demand and risk aversion. *Econometrica* 71, 713–21.

Stiglitz, J.E. 1987. The Causes and consequences of the dependence of quality on price. *Journal of Economic Literature* 25(1), 1–48.

Vives, X. 1987. Small income effects: a Marshallian theory of consumer surplus and downward sloping demand. *Review of Economic Studies* 54, 87–103.

law, economic analysis of

Economic analysis of law seeks to identify the effects of legal rules on the behaviour of relevant actors and to determine whether these effects are socially desirable. The approach employed is that of economic analysis generally: the behaviour of individuals and firms is described on the assumption that they are forward looking and rational, and the framework of welfare economics is adopted to assess the social desirability of outcomes. The field may be said to have begun with Bentham (1789), who systematically examined how actors would behave in the face of legal incentives (especially criminal sanctions) and who evaluated outcomes with respect to a clearly stated measure of social welfare (utilitarianism). His work was left essentially undeveloped until four important contributions were made: Coase (1960) on externalities and liability, Becker (1968) on crime and law enforcement, Calabresi (1970) on accident law, and Posner (1972) on economic analysis of law in general. (Calabresi's book was the culmination of a series of articles, the first of which was published in 1961; see Calabresi, 1961.)

Our focus here is on the analytical foundations of five basic legal subjects: property, torts, contracts, civil litigation, and crime and law enforcement (on these, see generally Cooter and Ulen, 2003; Posner, 2003; Miceli, 1997; and Shavell, 2004). We do not treat more particular areas of law, such as antitrust, corporate and tax law, nor do we cite empirical work; for surveys of these and other areas of law and economics, including empirical studies, see Polinsky and Shavell (2007).

1. Property law
Justification and emergence of property rights
A beginning question is why there should be property rights in things. A number of arguments have been stressed, especially by early writers, including that property rights furnish incentives to work and to maintain durable things; that the rights make trade possible; and that, if such rights were absent, individuals would spend effort trying to take things from each other and protecting their things.

Property rights would be expected to emerge when their advantages become sufficiently great. For example, Demsetz (1967) explains the development of property rights in land among Indians as a way of preventing overly intensive hunting of valuable animals. Umbeck (1981) shows that when gold was discovered in California in 1848 property rights in gold-bearing land and river beds developed, as this encouraged individuals to pan for gold and to build sluices; it also curbed wasteful efforts to grab land from others. For a survey, see Libecap (1986).

Division of property rights
Property rights can be viewed as composed of *possessory* rights – rights of use – and rights to *transfer* possessory rights. Thus, what we commonly conceive of as ownership (say, of land) entails both a large swath of possessory rights (rights to build on land, plant on it, under most contingencies, and into the infinite future) and associated rights to transfer them. Property rights in things are generally held in substantially agglomerated bundles, but there is also significant partitioning of rights contemporaneously, over time and contingencies, and according to whether the rights are possessory or are for transfer. For example, an owner of land may not hold complete possessory rights, in that others may possess an easement giving them the right of passage upon his land, or the

right to take timber, or the right to extract oil if found (thus a contingent right). A rental agreement constitutes a division of property rights over time. Trust arrangements, such as those under which an adult manages property for a child, divide possessory rights and rights to transfer.

The division of property rights may be valuable when different parties derive different benefits from them, because gains can then be achieved if rights are allocated to those who obtain the most from them. There may, however, be disadvantages to the division of rights, including that externalities may arise (a person with a right of passage might trample crops).

Public property and its acquisition; takings and compensation
An important class of property is that owned by the public. As is well known, the main justification for public property concerns the difficulty that private providers would experience in charging for certain goods and services.

When it is desirable for the state to acquire property for public use, the state can either purchase it or take it through the exercise of the power of *eminent domain*. In the latter case, the law typically provides that the state must compensate property owners for the value of what has been taken from them.

A difference between purchase and compensated takings is that the amounts owners receive are determined by negotiation in the former case but unilaterally by the state in the latter. Because of errors in state determination of value, as well as concern about the behaviour of government officials, purchase would ordinarily be superior to compensated takings. When, however, the state needs to assemble many contiguous parcels, such as for a road, acquisition by purchase might be stymied by holdout problems, making the power to take socially advantageous.

On the assumption that there is a reason for the state to take property, a requirement to pay compensation may curb problems of overzealousness or abuse of authority by public officials, yet it may also exacerbate potential problems of insufficient public activity, because public authorities do not directly receive the benefits of takings (Kaplow, 1986). Payment of compensation also may lead property owners to invest excessively in property (see Blume, Rubinfeld and Shapiro, 1984).

Acquisition of property in unowned things
The law must determine the conditions under which a person will become a legal owner of previously unowned things, such as wild animals, fish, and mineral and oil deposits. Under the *finders-keepers rule*, incentives to invest in capture (such as to hunt for animals or explore for oil) are optimal if only one person is making the effort. However, if many individuals seek unowned things, they will invest a socially excessive amount of

resources in search: one person's investment usually will come, at least partly, at the expense of other person's likelihood of finding unowned things. Various aspects of the law ameliorate this problem of excessive search effort. For example, regulations may limit the quantities of fish and wild animals that can be taken; the right to search for minerals on the ocean floor may be auctioned; and oil extraction rights may be assigned to a single party.

Acquisition of good title when property is sold

A basic difficulty associated with sale of property that a legal system must solve is establishing validity of ownership or *title*. Good title is important for trade, since buyers want to be assured that they have property rights in what they purchase. But, if any sale gives a buyer good title, theft is encouraged, since thieves could then easily sell stolen goods. Under a *registration system*, good title means that one's name is listed in the registry as the owner, and title passes at the time of sale by an authorized change in the registry. Hence, buyers can clearly determine whether they are obtaining good title by checking the registry, and a thief could not easily sell stolen property by claiming that he has good title. Registries, however, are expensive to establish and maintain.

In the absence of registries, the law may employ the *original ownership rule*, under which the buyer does not obtain good title if the seller did not have good title. Alternatively, under the *bona fide purchase rule*, a buyer acquires good title as long as he had reason to think that the sale was legitimate, even if the item sold was in fact wrongfully obtained. This rule makes theft more attractive because thieves will often be able to sell their property to buyers who will be motivated to 'believe' that sales are bona fide.

Adverse possession

The legal doctrine of adverse possession allows involuntary transfer of land: a person is deemed to become the legal owner of land if he takes possession of it and uses it openly for at least a prescribed period, such as ten years. It may appear that this rule could be desirable because it encourages productive use of idle land. But this overlooks the possibility that a prospective adverse possessor could always bargain with the owner to rent or buy the land, and that there may be good reasons for allowing the land to remain idle. Additionally, the rule induces owners to expend resources policing incursions, and potential adverse possessors to attempt possession. A historical justification for the rule is that, before reliable land registries existed, it allowed a seller of land to establish good title to a buyer relatively easily: the seller need only show that he was on the land for the prescribed period.

Constraints on sale of property

Legal restrictions are often imposed on the sale of goods and services. One standard justification is externalities. For example, the sale of fireworks might be banned because of the externality that their ownership creates, namely, putting others at risk of injury. The other standard justification for legal restrictions on sale is lack of consumer information. For instance, a drug may not be sold without a prescription because of fear that otherwise buyers would not use it properly. Rather than restrict sales, however, the government could supply relevant information to consumers, such as by indicating that the drug has dangerous side effects, or that it should be taken only on the advice of a medical expert.

Externalities

When individuals use property, they may cause externalities, namely, harm or benefit to others. Generally, it is socially desirable for individuals to do more than is in their self-interest to reduce detrimental externalities and to act so as to increase beneficial externalities. The socially optimal resolution of harmful externalities often involves the behaviour of victims as well as that of injurers. If victims can do things to reduce the amount of harm more cheaply than injurers (say, install air filters to avoid pollution), it is optimal for victims to do so. Moreover, victims can sometimes alter their locations to reduce their exposure to harm.

Legal intervention can ameliorate problems of externalities. A major form of intervention that has been studied is *direct regulation*, under which the state restricts permissible behaviour, such as requiring factories to use smoke arrestors. Closely related is the *injunction*, whereby a potential victim can enlist the power of the state to force a potential injurer to take steps to prevent harm or to cease his activity. Society can also make use of financial incentives to induce injurers to reduce harmful externalities. Under the *corrective tax*, a party pays the state an amount equal to the expected harm he causes – for example, the expected harm due to a discharge of a pollutant into a lake. There is also *liability*, a privately initiated means of providing financial incentives, under which injurers pay for harm done if sued by victims. These methods differ in the information that the state needs to apply them, in whether they require or harness information that victims have about harm, and in other respects, such that each may be superior to the other in different circumstances (Shavell, 1993).

Parties affected by externalities will sometimes have the opportunity to make mutually beneficial agreements with those who generate the externalities, as Coase (1960) stressed. But bargaining may not occur, for many reasons: cost; collective action problems (such as when many victims each face small harms); and lack of knowledge of harm (such as from an invisible carcinogen). If bargaining does occur, it may not be successful, owing to asymmetric information. These difficulties often make bargaining a problematic solution to externality problems and imply that liability rules are needed, as discussed by Calabresi and Melamed (1972).

Property rights in information

The granting of property rights in information, notably the award of *patents* for inventions and *copyrights* for written works and certain other compositions, involves a major social benefit – the provision of incentives to create intellectual works – but also a social disadvantage – the creation of power to price above marginal cost. Patent and copyright law have been examined to ascertain how they reflect the trade-off between this benefit and disadvantage. A distinct form of legal protection is *trade secret law*, comprising various doctrines of contract and tort law that serve to protect a range of commercially valuable information that is not (or cannot be) protected by patent or copyright, such as customer lists. On property rights in information, see generally Landes and Posner (2003).

An alternative to property rights in information is for the state to offer *rewards* to creators of information, and for information that is developed to be made available to all who want it. Thus, an author of a book would receive a reward from the state for writing the book, possibly based on sales, but anyone who wanted to print it and sell it could do so. This system would create incentives for the creation of information without distorting prices, but requires the state to choose the magnitude of rewards.

Property rights in labels

Many goods and services are identified by labels, which have substantial social value because the quality of goods and services may be hard for consumers to determine directly. Labels enable consumers to purchase goods and services on the basis of product quality without requiring consumers to independently determine quality; a person who wants to stay at a high-quality hotel in another city can choose such a hotel merely by its label, such as 'Ritz Hotel'. In addition, sellers who label their output will have an incentive to produce goods and services of quality because consumers will recognize quality through sellers' labels. This basic reasoning is used to justify property rights in *trademarks*, as discussed by Landes and Posner (1987b).

2. Liability for accidents

Legal liability for accidents, which is governed by tort law, is a means by which society can reduce the risk of harm by threatening potential injurers with having to pay for the harms they cause. Liability is also frequently viewed as a device for compensating victims of harm, though we emphasize that insurance can provide compensation more cheaply than the liability system. There are two basic rules of liability. Under *strict liability*, an injurer must always pay for harm due to an accident that he causes. Under the *negligence rule*, an injurer must pay for harm caused only when he is found negligent, that is, only when his level of care was less than a standard of care chosen by the courts, often referred to as *due care*.

(There are various versions of these rules that depend on whether victims' care was insufficient.) In practice, the negligence rule is the dominant form of liability; strict liability is reserved mainly for certain especially dangerous activities. On economic analysis of liability for accidents, see generally Calabresi (1970), Landes and Posner (1987a), and Shavell (1987a).

Incentives to take care

In order to focus on how liability affects the incentive to prevent harm, assume first that parties are risk neutral and that accidents are *unilateral* – only injurers (not victims) influence risk by their choice of *care x*. Let $p(x)$ be the probability of an accident that causes harm h, where p is declining in x. Assume that the social objective is to minimize total expected costs, $x + p(x)h$, and let x^* denote the optimal x.

Under strict liability, injurers pay damages equal to h whenever an accident occurs, and they naturally bear the cost of care x. Thus, they minimize $x + p(x)h$; accordingly, they choose x^*.

Under the negligence rule, suppose that the due care level is set equal to x^*, meaning that an injurer who causes harm will have to pay h if $x < x^*$, but will not have to pay anything if $x \geq x^*$. Then it can be shown that the injurer will choose x^*: clearly, the injurer will not choose x greater than x^*; and he will not choose $x < x^*$, for then he will be liable (in which case the analysis of strict liability shows that he would not choose $x < x^*$). Thus, under both forms of liability, injurers are led to take optimal care. Note that to apply the negligence rule courts need sufficient information to calculate x^* and to observe x, whereas under strict liability they only have to observe x.

The analysis of incentives and liability has been undertaken as well for *bilateral* accidents, in which victims also take care, and when there is uncertainty in the determination of negligence (such as due to imperfect observation of x). On incentives and liability for unilateral and bilateral accidents, see originally Brown (1973) and also Diamond (1974).

Level of activity

An important extension allows for injurers to choose their *level of activity z*, which is interpreted as the (continuously variable) number of times they engage in their activity (or, if injurers are firms, their output). Let $b(z)$ be the benefit (or profit) from the activity, and assume the social objective is to maximize $b(z) - z(x + p(x)h)$; here $x + p(x)h$ is assumed to be the cost of care and expected harm each time an injurer engages in his activity. Let x^* and z^* be optimal values. Note that x^* minimizes $x + p(x)h$, so x^* is as described above, and that z^* is determined by $b'(z) = x^* + p(x^*)h$, which is to say, the marginal benefit from the activity equals the marginal social cost.

Under strict liability, an injurer will choose both the level of care and the level of activity optimally, as his objective will be the same as the social objective, to maximize $b(z) - z(x + p(x)h)$, because damage payments equal h whenever harm occurs. Under the negligence rule, an injurer will choose optimal care x^* as before, but his level of activity z will be socially excessive. In particular, because an injurer will escape liability by taking care x^*, he will choose z to maximize $b(z) - zx^*$, so that z will satisfy $b'(z) = x^*$. The injurer's cost of raising his level of activity is only his cost of care x^*, which is less than the social cost, which also includes $p(x^*)h$. On liability and the level of activity, see Shavell (1980b).

The failure of the negligence rule to control the level of activity arises because negligence is defined here (and also generally in practice) in terms of care alone. A justification for this restriction is the difficulty courts would face in determining the optimal activity level z^* and the actual z. The failure of the negligence rule to control the injurer's level of activity is applicable to any aspect of injurer behaviour that would be difficult to regulate directly (including, for example, research and development activity). If, however, courts were able to incorporate all aspects of injurer behaviour into the definition of due care, the negligence rule would result in optimal behaviour in all respects. (Note that the variable x in the original problem could be interpreted as a vector, with each element corresponding to a dimension of behaviour.)

Product liability
Another extension of the model of liability and incentives concerns product liability, the liability of firms for harms suffered by their customers. Here the degree to which liability creates incentives to reduce risk depends on customer knowledge of risk. If their knowledge is perfect, liability does not affect incentives since customers will recognize risky products and pay appropriately less for them. If their knowledge is imperfect, there is a role for liability, in many respects similar to what has been discussed above.

Risk-bearing and insurance
In addition to affecting incentives to reduce harm, the socially optimal resolution of the accident problem involves the spreading of risk to lessen risk-bearing by risk-averse parties. Risk-bearing is relevant not only because potential victims may face the risk of accident losses, but also because potential injurers may face the risk of liability. The former risk can be mitigated through so-called first-party insurance that covers losses suffered in accidents, and the latter through liability insurance.

Because risk-averse individuals tend to purchase insurance, the incentives associated with liability do not function in the direct way discussed above, but instead are mediated by the terms of insurance policies. To illustrate, consider strict liability in the unilateral accident model with care alone allowed to vary, and assume that insurance is sold at actuarially fair rates. If injurers are risk averse and liability insurers can observe their levels of care, injurers will purchase full liability insurance coverage and their premiums will depend on their level of care; their premiums will equal $p(x)h$. Thus, injurers will want to minimize their costs of care plus premiums, or $x + p(x)h$, so they will choose the optimal level of care x^*. In this instance, liability insurance eliminates risk for injurers, and the situation reduces to the previously analysed risk-neutral case. (Victims do not bear risk either because, in the present case, they are fully compensated for their losses.)

If, however, liability insurers cannot observe levels of care, insurance policies with full coverage could create severe moral hazard, and so might not be purchased. Instead, as we know from the theory of insurance, the typical amount of coverage purchased will be partial, for that leaves injurers with an incentive to reduce risk. In this case, therefore, the liability rule results in some direct incentive to take care because injurers are left bearing some risk after their purchase of liability insurance. But levels of care will still tend to be less than first-best.

This last observation raises the question of whether the sale of liability insurance is socially desirable. (We note that because of concern about diluted incentives, liability insurance was delayed for decades in many countries and is sometimes forbidden today, such as for punitive damages.) Notwithstanding the moral hazard problem, the sale of liability insurance is socially desirable, at least in basic models of accidents and some variations of them. This is because, if the liability insurer and the injurer together have to pay for the harm caused, the insurance policy will appropriately balance the social desire to reduce harm and the social desire to reduce risk-bearing.

Parallel observations apply under the negligence rule, where the focus of concern is on the bearing of risk by victims since injurers generally will take due care and not be liable. Risk-averse potential victims will tend to purchase first-party accident insurance.

The presence of insurance implies that the liability system cannot be justified primarily as a means of compensating risk-averse victims against loss. Rather, the justification for the liability system must lie in significant part in the incentives that it creates to reduce risk. To amplify, although both strict liability and the insurance system can compensate victims, the liability system is much more expensive than the insurance system (see below). Accordingly, if there were not a social need to create incentives to reduce risk, it would be best to dispense with the liability system and to rely on insurance to accomplish compensation. On liability and insurance, see Shavell (1982a).

Administrative costs
The administrative costs of the liability system – the legal costs and effort of litigants involved in suit, settlement

and trial – are substantial, generally exceeding the amounts received by victims. Consideration of administrative costs affects the comparison of liability rules, but it is not clear which rule involves greater expense: more cases are brought under strict liability than under the negligence rule (victims will not sue under the negligence rule if they believe the injurer was not negligent), but the cost of resolving a case should be greater under the negligence rule (because due care and the injurer's care level need to be ascertained). The presence of administrative costs raises the questions of whether the incentive benefits of the liability system justify incurring these costs, and whether the private incentive to sue is socially optimal. These questions are discussed in section 4.

3. Contracts

A contract is a specification of the actions that named parties are supposed to take at various times, as a function of the conditions that then obtain. A contract is said to be completely detailed, or simply *complete*, if the contract provides *explicitly* for all possible conditions. An incomplete contract may well cover all conditions by implication. A contract stating merely that a specified price will be paid for a bushel of wheat is incomplete because it does not mention many contingencies that might affect the parties. Note that such an incomplete contract has no *gaps*, as it stipulates what the parties are to do in all circumstances. Typically, incomplete contracts do not include conditions which, were they easy to include, would allow both parties to be made better off in an expected sense.

Contracts are here assumed to be enforced by a tribunal, which will usually be interpreted to be a state-authorized court, but it could also be another entity, such as an arbitrator or the decision-making body of a trade association or a religious group. (Reputation and other non-legal factors may also serve to enforce contracts, but we do not discuss these.) Enforcement refers to actions taken by the tribunal when one or more of the parties to the contract decide to come before it.

General reasons for contracts

Broadly speaking, parties make contracts when they have a need to make plans. They also want contracts enforced to prevent opportunistic behaviour that otherwise might occur during the course of the contractual relationship and stymie fulfilment of their plans.

There are two basic contexts in which parties make enforceable contracts. The first concerns virtually any kind of financial arrangement. The necessity of contract enforcement here is transparent. In financial arrangements, there is often a party who extends credit to another for some time period, and contract enforcement prevents his credit from being appropriated, which otherwise would render the arrangements impossible.

For example, if borrowers were not forced to repay loans, loans would be unworkable. In addition, financial contracts that allocate risk would generally be useless without enforcement because, once the risky outcome became known, one of the parties would not wish to honour the contract.

The second context in which parties make enforceable contracts involves the supply of customized or specialized goods and services which cannot be purchased on a spot market with a simultaneous exchange for money. The need for enforcement of agreements for supply of customized goods and services inheres in several advantages: averting problems of hold-up, which might distort incentives to invest in the contractual enterprise; allocation of risk; and prevention of inappropriate breach or performance, which can result from imperfect bargaining due to sheer cost or asymmetric information.

Contract formation

The formation of contracts is of interest, in several respects. One issue concerns search effort (Diamond and Maskin, 1979). Parties expend effort in finding contractual partners, and it is apparent that their search effort will not generally be socially optimal. On the one hand, they might not search enough: because the joint gain from contracting will generally be divided between the parties through the bargaining process, the private return to search may be less than the social return. On the other hand, parties might search more than is socially desirable because of a negative externality associated with discovery of a contract partner: when one party finds and contracts with a second, other parties are thereby prevented from contracting with that party.

A basic question that a tribunal must answer is: at what stage of interactions between parties does a contract become legally recognized? The general legal rule is that contracts are recognized if and only if both parties give a clear indication of assent, such as signing their names on a document. This rule allows parties to make enforceable contracts when they so desire, and it also protects parties from becoming legally obliged against their wishes, such as from one party's reliance on the other's statements (Bebchuk and Ben-Shahar, 2001; Wils, 1993). Mutual assent sometimes is not simultaneous; one party will make an offer and time will pass before the other agrees. An issue that this raises is how long, and under what circumstances, the offeror will want to be held to his offer, and whether he should be held to it. If an offeror is held to his terms, offerees will often be led to invest effort in investigating contractual opportunities. Otherwise, offerees might be taken advantage of by offerors if the offerees expressed serious interest after costly investigation (the offeror could change to less favourable terms). The anticipation of such offeror advantage-taking would reduce offerees' incentive to engage in investigation and thus diminish mutually beneficial contract formation (see, for example, Craswell, 1996; Katz, 1990; 1996).

Another issue of note is disclosure of information at the time of contract formation. Disclosure may be socially beneficial because the disclosed information may be desirably employed by one of the parties; for example, a buyer of a house may learn from the seller that the basement leaks and thus decide not to store valuables there. However, a disclosure obligation discourages parties from investing in acquisition of information (Kronman, 1978). For instance, an oil company contemplating buying land might decide against conducting a geological analysis of it to determine its oil-bearing potential if the company would be required to disclose its findings to the seller of the land, as the seller would then demand a price reflecting the value of the land. The social welfare consequences of the effect of a disclosure obligation on the motive to acquire information depend on whether the information is socially valuable or mere foreknowledge, on whether the party acquiring information is the buyer or the seller, and on inferences that would be drawn from silence (Shavell, 1994).

Even if both parties have given their assent, a contract will not be recognized if it was made when one of the parties was put under undue pressure – for example, if a party was physically or otherwise threatened by another. This legal rule has virtues similar to those of laws against theft; it reduces individuals' incentives to expend effort making threats and defending themselves against threats.

In addition, contracts may not be legally recognized if they are made in emergency situations, such as when the owner of a ship in distress promises to pay an exorbitant amount for rescue. Non-enforcement in such situations beneficially provides potential victims with implicit insurance against having to pay high prices, but it also reduces incentives for rescue.

Incomplete nature of contracts and their less-than-rigorous enforcement
Contracts are commonly observed to be significantly incomplete, leaving out all manner of variables and contingencies that are of potential relevance to contracting parties. Moreover, contracts are not enforced with high sanctions, and breach is not an uncommon event.

There are three reasons for the incompleteness of contracts. The first is the cost of writing more complete contracts. The second is that some variables (effort levels, technical production difficulties) cannot be verified by tribunals. The third is that the expected consequences of incompleteness may not be very harmful to contracting parties. Incompleteness may not be harmful because a tribunal might interpret an imperfect contract in a desirable manner. Also, as will be seen, the prospect of having to pay damages for breach of contract may serve as an implicit substitute for more detailed terms. Furthermore, the opportunity to renegotiate a contract often furnishes a way for parties to alter terms in the light of circumstances for which contractual provisions had not been made.

Interpretation of contracts
Contractual interpretation, which includes a tribunal's filling gaps, resolving ambiguities, and overriding literal language, can benefit parties by easing their drafting burdens or reducing their need to understand contractual detail. For example, if it is efficient to excuse a seller from having to perform if his factory burns down, the parties need not incur the cost of specifying this exception in their contract if they can trust the tribunal to interpret their contract as if the exception were specified. A method of interpretation can be viewed formally as a function that transforms the contract individuals write into the effective contract that the tribunal will enforce. Given a method of interpretation, parties will choose contracts in a constrained-efficient way. Notably, if the parties are concerned that an aspect of their contract would not be interpreted as they want, they could either bear the cost of writing a more explicit term that would be respected by the tribunal, or they could simply accept the expected loss from having a less-than-efficient term. The socially optimal method of interpretation will take this reaction of contracting parties into account and can be regarded as minimizing the sum of the costs the parties bear in writing contracts and the losses resulting from inefficient enforcement. (See Ayres and Gertner, 1989; Hadfield, 1994; Schwartz, 1992; Shavell, 2006.)

Damage measures for breach of contract
When parties breach a contract, they often have to pay damages in consequence. The damage measure, the formula governing what they should pay, can be determined by the tribunal or it can be stipulated in advance by the parties to the contract. One would expect parties to specify their own damage measure when it would better serve their purposes than the measure the tribunal would employ, and otherwise to allow the tribunal to select the damage measure. In either case, we now examine the utility of different damage measures to contracting parties, assuming initially that there is no renegotiation of contracts.

Clearly, the prospect of having to pay damages provides an incentive to perform contractual obligations, and thus generally promotes enforcement of contracts and the goals of the parties. Under the commonly employed *expectation measure*, damages equal the amount that compensates the victim of breach for his losses. Under this measure, a seller contemplating breach will be induced to perform if the cost of performance to the seller is less than the value of performance to the buyer, and to breach otherwise. Because the expectation measure leads to maximization of joint value, it would be chosen by the parties (ignoring consideration of investment incentives and risk bearing), as emphasized by Shavell (1980a). Another commonly employed measure of damages is the *reliance measure*: damages equal to the amount spent by the victim relying on contract performance, such as expenditures on advertising an entertainer who has contracted to appear at one's nightclub.

The point that the expectation measure of damages induces efficient performance of parties sheds light on the view of many legal commentators that breach is immoral. This view fails to account for the fact that contracts that are breached are generally incomplete, and that breach constitutes behaviour that the parties truly want and would have provided for in a complete contract.

Damage measures not only affect performance, they also influence the *ex ante* motive to make investments in reliance on contract performance. Under the expectation measure, reliance investments tend to exceed efficient levels: the buyer will treat an investment (like advertising an entertainer) as one with a sure payoff, since he will receive either performance or expectation damages, whereas the actual return to the investment is uncertain, due to the possibility of breach (advertising will be a waste if the entertainer does not appear); see Shavell (1980a). This tendency toward over-reliance stands in contrast to the problem of inadequate reliance investment associated with lack of contract enforcement.

Damage measures affect risk-bearing as well as incentives. Notably, because the expectation measure compensates the victim of a breach, the measure might be mutually desirable as a form of insurance if the victim is risk averse (Polinsky, 1983). However, the prospect of having to pay damages also constitutes a risk for a party who might commit breach (such as a seller whose costs suddenly rise), and he might be risk averse as well. The latter consideration may lead parties to want to lower damages or to employ damages less frequently by writing more detailed contracts (for instance, the parties could go to the expense of specifying in the contract that a seller can be excused from performance if his costs are unusually high).

Specific performance as a remedy for breach

An alternative to use of a damage measure for breach of contract is specific performance: requiring a party to satisfy his contractual obligation. Specific performance can be accomplished with a sufficiently high threat or by exercise of the state's police powers, such as by a sheriff removing a person from the land that he promised to convey. (Note that, if a monetary penalty can be employed to induce performance, then specific performance is equivalent to a damage measure with a high level of damages.)

It is apparent from what has been said about incomplete contracts and damage measures that parties should not want specific performance of many contracts that they write, for they do not wish their incomplete contracts always to be performed. It is therefore not surprising that, in fact, specific performance is not used as the remedy for breach for most contracts for production of goods or for provision of services. Additionally, specific performance might be peculiarly difficult to enforce in these contexts because of problems in monitoring and controlling parties' effort levels and the quality of production.

However, specific performance does have advantages for parties in certain contexts, such as in contracts for the transfer of things that already exist, like land, and specific performance is the usual legal remedy for sellers' breaches of contracts for the sale of land.

Renegotiation of contracts

Parties often have the opportunity to renegotiate their contracts when problems arise. Indeed, the assumption that they will do this has appeal because, having made an initial contract, the parties know of each other's existence and of many particulars of the contractual situation. For this reason, much of the economics literature (as opposed to law and economics literature) on contracts assumes that renegotiation always occurs and that, due to symmetric information between the parties, it always results in efficient performance. Hence, damage measures for breach of contract, or more generally, the mechanisms that the parties stipulate in their contracts, establish the threat points for renegotiation. If properly designed, the mechanisms can foster beneficial incentives to invest *ex ante* for both parties. On this extensive literature, see, for example, Rogerson (1984), Hart (1987), Hart and Moore (1988), and Bolton and Dewatripont (2005).

Legal overriding of contracts

A basic rationale for legislative or judicial overriding of contracts is the presence of externalities. Contracts that are likely to harm third parties are often not enforced, including, for example, agreements to commit crimes, price-fixing compacts, liability insurance policies against fines, and certain sales contracts (such as for machine guns).

Another general rationale for non-enforcement of contracts is to prevent a loss in welfare to one or both of the parties to a contract. This concern may justify non-enforcement when a party is incompetent, lacks relevant information, or is in an emergency situation. The rationale also applies in the context of contract interpretation by tribunals. As noted, contract interpretation may amount to the overriding of a written contractual term, and this practice may promote the welfare of contracting parties by allowing them to save writing costs, given that courts will step in and correct inefficient terms.

Additionally, contracts sometimes are not enforced because they involve the sale of things said to be inalienable, such as human organs, babies, and voting rights. In many of these cases, the inalienability justification for lack of enforcement can be recognized as involving externalities or the welfare of the contracting parties.

4. Litigation

We here consider the bringing and adjudication of lawsuits: the decision of a party who has suffered a loss whether to sue; the choice of the litigants whether to settle with each other or instead go to trial; and the choice of litigants, before or during trial, of how much to spend on litigation.

Suit

As a general rule, a party who has suffered loss, the plaintiff, will sue when the cost of suit c_P is less than the expected benefits from suit. The expected benefits from suit incorporate potential settlements or trial outcomes, but assume for simplicity that, if suit is brought, the plaintiff obtains for sure a judgment equal to harm suffered, h. Thus the plaintiff will sue when his litigation cost, c_P is less than h. (Obviously, if there is only a probability p of winning this amount, a risk-neutral plaintiff would sue when $c_P < ph$; and a risk-averse plaintiff would be less likely to sue.)

The private incentive to sue is fundamentally misaligned with the socially optimal incentive to sue, as emphasized by Shavell (1982b; 1997). The deviation could be in either direction. On the one hand, there is a divergence between private and social costs that can lead to socially excessive suit: when a plaintiff contemplates bringing suit, he bears only his own costs; he does not take into account the defendant's costs or the state's costs that his suit will engender. On the other hand, there is a difference between the private and social benefits of suit that can either lead to a socially inadequate level of suit or reinforce the cost-related tendency towards excessive suit. Specifically, the plaintiff considers his private benefit from suit (the gain he would obtain from prevailing) but not the social benefit (the deterrent effect on the behaviour of injurers generally). The private gain could be larger or smaller than the social benefit.

To illustrate, suppose that liability is strict. As stated, victims will sue if and only if $c_P < h$. Let x be the precaution expenditures that injurers will be induced to make if there is suit, q the probability of harm if suit is not brought, and q' the probability of harm if suit is brought. (Thus, q' will be less than q if x is spent on precautions.) Suit will be socially worthwhile if and only if $q'(c_P + c_D + c_S) < (q - q') h - x$, where c_D is the defendant's litigation cost and c_S is the state's cost. In other words, suit is socially worthwhile if the expected litigation costs are less than the deterrence benefits of suit net of the cost of precautions. The condition for victims to sue and the condition for suit to be socially optimal are very different. Whether victims will sue does not depend on the costs c_D and c_S. Moreover, the private benefit of suit is what the victim will receive as a damages award, h; in contrast, the social benefit is the harm weighted by the reduction in the accident probability, $q - q'$, net of the cost of precautions, x. It is evident, therefore, that victims might sue when suit is not socially desirable, or that victims might not sue even when suit would be socially beneficial.

The main implication of the private-social divergence is that state intervention may be desirable, either to correct a problem of excessive suit (notably by taxing suit or barring it in some domain) or a problem of inadequate suit (by subsidizing suit in some way). For the state to determine optimal policy, however, requires it to estimate the effects of suit on injurer behaviour and weigh them against the social costs of suit.

The importance of the private-social divergence in incentives to sue may be substantial. This is suggested by the high costs of using the legal system; indeed, legal costs may on average actually equal the amounts received by those who sue. Hence, the incentives created by the legal system must be significant to justify its use. Regardless of whether the legal system creates valuable incentives, however, the private motive to bring suit may be great, giving rise to a reason for social intervention. Conversely, in some domains the incentive to sue may be low (say, damages per plaintiff are not great) even though the value of deterrence is significant. This might justify the state's encouraging litigation.

Settlement versus trial

Assuming that a suit has been brought, we now consider whether parties will reach a settlement or go to trial. A settlement is a legally enforceable contract, usually involving a payment from the defendant to the plaintiff, in return for which the plaintiff agrees not to pursue his claim further. If the parties do not reach a settlement, we assume that they go to trial, that is, that some tribunal determines the outcome of their case. In fact, the vast majority of cases settle.

One model of the settlement-versus-trial decision presumes that the parties have somehow each come to a belief about the probability of the trial outcome (Posner, 2003, ch. 21; Shavell, 2004, ch. 17). Let p_P represent the plaintiff's opinion about his probability of prevailing, and let p_D be the defendant's opinion about that same probability. Let w be the amount that would be won (for simplicity assume that they agree about w). Assume also that the parties are risk neutral. The plaintiff's expected gain from trial, net of his litigation costs, is $p_P w - c_P$. The defendant's expected loss from trial, including his litigation costs, is $p_D w + c_D$. Hence, a settlement is possible if and only if $p_P w - c_P > p_D w + c_D$, in which case the settlement amount will be in the settlement range $[p_P w - c_P, p_D w + c_D]$. Note that, if the parties agree on the plaintiff's probability of prevailing, a settlement is feasible. A settlement range does not exist, and therefore trial will occur, if $p_P w - p_D w > c_P + c_D$. Risk aversion of the parties increases the size of the settlement range and thus, one presumes, makes settlement more likely: if the plaintiff is risk averse, he will be willing to settle for less than $p_P w - c_P$; and if the defendant is risk averse, she will be willing to pay more than $p_D w + c_D$.

The model just discussed does not explain the origin of the parties' beliefs and does not include a description of rational bargaining between them. Subsequently, standard asymmetric information models of settlement versus litigation were examined (Bebchuk, 1984; Reinganum and Wilde, 1986; Schweizer, 1989; Spier, 1992; Hay and Spier, 1998; Daughety, 2000). In a simple model of this type, there is one-sided asymmetry of information and the party without private information makes a take-it-or-leave-it settlement proposal. For example, the plaintiff makes a demand x to the defendant, who has private information about the probability p that he will lose at trial. If $pw + c_D < x$, the defendant will reject the demand and the plaintiff will therefore obtain only $pw - c_P$, but if $pw + c_D > x$, the defendant will accept and pay x. The plaintiff chooses x to maximize his expected payoff from settlement or trial. The higher his demand x, the more he will obtain if it is accepted, but the greater the likelihood of rejection and thus of his bearing trial costs. At the optimal demand for the plaintiff, there will generally be a positive probability of trial and also of settlement.

The virtues of such asymmetric information models are twofold. First, they include an explicit account of bargaining and thus of the probability of settlement and the magnitude of the settlement offer or demand. (The outcomes of these models depend, however, on essentially arbitrary modelling choices, such as whether the informed or the uninformed party makes the settlement proposal.) Second, the models explain differences of opinion that give rise to trial in terms of differences in possession of information. (However, the models do not account for why there should be differences in information, given that the parties have incentives to share information and may be forced to do so through legal discovery.)

The private and social incentives to settle generally diverge for several reasons. First, because the litigants do not bear all of the costs of a trial (such as the salaries of judges and the forgone value of juror time), they save less by settling than society does, which tends to make the private incentive to settle socially inadequate. Second, when there is asymmetric information, parties will fail to settle when the plaintiff's demand turns out to have been too high or the defendant's offer too low. But their desire to obtain from each other a greater share of the benefit from settling does not itself translate into any social benefit. Third, the prospect of settlement may reduce deterrence because defendants gain from settlement.

Litigation expenditures

A plaintiff will continue spending on litigation as long as this raises his expected return from settlement or trial (net of litigation costs), and a defendant will make such expenditures as long as this lowers his expected total outlays. The effects of each litigant's expenditures will generally depend on what the other does, and the two will often be spending to rebut one another.

There are several reasons why the private and social incentives to spend on litigation diverge. First, to the extent that their expenditures simply offset each other, without altering trial or settlement outcomes, the expenditures constitute a social waste. Second, the litigants' trial expenditures may mislead the tribunal rather than enhance the accuracy of the outcome, which has negative social value. Third, even if trial expenditures do improve the accuracy of outcomes, they may not be socially optimal in magnitude, for the parties consider only how their expenditures influence the litigation outcome, without regard to their influence (if any) on deterrence.

Because private and social incentives to spend on litigation may diverge, it may be beneficial for expenditures to be either curtailed or encouraged. In practice, courts often restrict the legal effort that parties can undertake, for example by limiting the extent of discovery and the number of testifying experts.

Other topics

A number of other topics that relate to litigation and the legal process have been studied, including the selection of suits for litigation (Priest and Klein, 1984); the accuracy of adjudication (Kaplow, 1994; Png, 1986); 'discovery', that is, mandated disclosure of information during litigation (Shavell, 1989); and the appeals process (Daughety and Reinganum, 2000; Shavell, 1995; Spitzer and Talley, 2000).

5. Public law enforcement and criminal law

Law enforcement often is the result of the efforts of public agents, such as inspectors, tax auditors, and police. We here discuss certain characteristics of optimal public law enforcement. As noted, this subject was first analysed by Bentham (1789) and Becker (1968) (for a survey, see Polinsky and Shavell, 2000).

Rationale of public enforcement

A basic question is why there is a need for public enforcement of law in the light of the availability of private suits brought by victims (Becker and Stigler, 1974; Landes and Posner, 1975; Polinsky, 1980). The answer depends importantly on the locus of information about the identity of injurers. When victims of harm naturally possess knowledge of the identity of injurers, allowing private suits for damages will motivate victims to sue and thus harness the information they have for purposes of law enforcement. This may help to explain why the enforcement of contractual obligations and of accident law is primarily private. When victims do not know who caused harm, however, or when finding injurers is difficult, society tends to rely instead on public investigation and prosecution; this is broadly true of crimes and of many violations of environmental and safety regulations.

Basic framework for analysing public enforcement

Suppose that, if an individual commits a harmful act, he obtains a gain and also faces the risk of being caught and sanctioned. The sanction could be a fine or a prison term. Fines will be treated as socially costless because they are mere transfers of money, whereas imprisonment is socially costly because of the expense of operating prisons and the disutility suffered by those imprisoned (which is not offset by gains to others). The higher the probability is of detecting and sanctioning violators, the more resources the state must devote to enforcement.

We assume that social welfare equals the sum of individuals' expected utilities. If individuals are risk neutral, social welfare can be expressed as the gains individuals obtain from committing their harmful acts, minus the harms caused and the costs of law enforcement. The enforcement authority's problem is to maximize social welfare by choosing enforcement expenditures, or, equivalently, a probability of detection, the form of sanctions, and their level.

Fines

Suppose that the sanction is a fine and that individuals are risk neutral. Then the optimal level of the fine is maximal, f_M, as emphasized in Becker (1968). If the fine were not maximal, society could save enforcement costs by simultaneously raising the fine and lowering the probability without affecting the level of deterrence. Formally, if $f < f_M$, then raise the fine to f_M and lower the probability from p to $(f/f_M)p$; the expected fine is still pf, so that deterrence is maintained, but expenditures on enforcement are reduced, implying that social welfare rises. Moreover, the optimal probability is such that there is some under-deterrence; in other words, at the optimal p the expected fine pf_M is less than the harm h. The reason for this result is that, if pf_M equals h, behaviour will be ideal, in which case decreasing p must be socially beneficial because the individuals thereby induced to commit the harmful act cause no net social losses (because their gains essentially equal the harm), but reducing p saves enforcement costs.

If individuals are risk averse, the optimal fine may well be below the maximal fine, as stressed in Polinsky and Shavell (1979). This is because the use of a very high fine would impose a substantial risk-bearing cost on individuals who commit harmful acts.

Imprisonment

Now suppose that the sanction is imprisonment and that individuals are risk neutral in imprisonment. Then the optimal imprisonment term is maximal. The reasoning is similar to that employed above with respect to fines: if the imprisonment term were not maximal, it could be raised and the probability of detection lowered so as to keep the expected prison term constant; neither individual behaviour nor the costs of imposing imprisonment are affected (because the expected prison term is the same), but enforcement expenditures fall.

If, instead, individuals are risk averse in imprisonment (the disutility of each additional year of imprisonment grows with the number of years in prison), there is a stronger argument for setting the imprisonment sanction maximally than when individuals are risk neutral. Now, when the imprisonment term is raised, the probability of detection can be lowered even more than in the risk-neutral case without reducing deterrence. Thus, not only are there greater savings in enforcement expenditures, but the social costs of imposing imprisonment sanctions decline because the expected prison term falls.

Last, suppose that individuals are risk preferring in imprisonment (the disutility of each additional year of imprisonment declines with the number of years in prison). This possibility seems particularly important: the first years of imprisonment may create unusually high disutility, due to brutalization of the prisoner or due to the stigma of having been imprisoned at all. In addition, individuals generally have positive time discount rates, which are thought to be especially significant for criminals. In the case of risk-preferring individuals, the optimal prison term may well be less than maximal: if the sentence were raised, the probability that maintains deterrence could not be lowered proportionally, implying that the expected prison term would rise. Thus, although there would be enforcement-cost savings, they might not be great enough to offset the increased sanctioning costs.

Fines versus imprisonment

Fines generally are preferable to prison terms as a means of deterrence, since fines are socially cheaper sanctions to impose (Becker, 1968). Hence, fines should be employed to the greatest extent possible – until a party's wealth is exhausted – before imprisonment is imposed. Further, imprisonment should be used as a sanction only if the harm prevented by the added deterrence is sufficiently great.

Fault-based liability

Our discussion so far has presumed that liability is strict, but liability may also be based on fault, an assessment of whether the act that caused harm was socially undesirable (analogous to the negligence rule and due-care standard discussed above in the accident context). Fault-based liability, like strict liability, can induce individuals to behave properly, but fault-based liability possesses an advantage when individuals are risk averse: if they act responsibly, they will not be found at fault, so will not bear the risk of being sanctioned. Similarly, fault-based liability is advantageous when the form of the sanction is imprisonment, for then, again, individuals may be led to behave optimally without the actual imposition of sanctions, and thus without social costs being incurred (Shavell, 1987b). To the extent that mistakes are made in determining fault, however, these two advantages are reduced because risk is imposed and sanctioning costs are incurred. Note, too, that fault-based liability is more difficult to implement, because it requires the state to determine optimal behaviour.

Incapacitation

Society may reduce harm not only through deterrence but also by imposing sanctions that remove parties from positions in which they are able to cause harm, that is, by incapacitating them. Imprisonment is the primary incapacitative sanction, although there are other examples: individuals can lose their drivers' licences, businesses can lose their right to operate in certain domains, and the like.

Suppose that the sole function of imprisonment is to incapacitate. Then it will be desirable to keep someone in jail as long as the reduction in crime from incapacitating him exceeds the costs of imprisonment (Shavell, 1987c). Although this condition could hold for a long period, it is unlikely to unless the harm prevented is very high, because the proclivity to commit crimes apparently declines sharply with age.

Note that, as a matter of economic logic, the incapacitation rationale might imply that a person should be imprisoned even if he has not committed a crime – because the danger he poses to society makes incapacitating him worthwhile. In practice, however, the fact that a person has committed a harmful act may be the best basis for predicting his future behaviour, in which case the incapacitation rationale would suggest imprisoning an individual only if he has committed such an act.

Two observations are worth noting about optimal enforcement when incapacitation is the goal as opposed to when deterrence is the goal. First, when enforcement is based on incapacitation, the optimal magnitude of the sanction is independent of the probability of apprehension, which contrasts with the case when enforcement is based on deterrence. Second, when enforcement is deterrence-oriented, the probability and magnitude of sanctions depend on the ability to deter, and, if this ability is limited (as, for instance, with the insane), a low expected sanction may be optimal, whereas a high sanction still might be called for to incapacitate.

Other issues

A number of other topics have been studied in the economic analysis of public law enforcement, including mistake, marginal deterrence (the effect of sanctions in reducing the severity of harm a party causes), self-reporting of violations (Kaplow and Shavell, 1994a; Innes, 1999), repeat offences, plea bargaining (Reinganum, 1988), general enforcement (when detection resources simultaneously influence the deterrence of a range of harmful acts) (Mookherjee and Png, 1992; and Shavell, 1991), and corruption of law-enforcement agents (Shleifer and Vishny, 1993; Rose-Ackerman, 1999; and Polinsky and Shavell, 2001).

Criminal law

The subject of criminal law may be viewed in the light of the theory of public law enforcement (Posner, 1985; Shavell, 1985). First, the fact that the acts in the core area of crime (robbery, murder, rape, and so forth) are punished by the sanction of imprisonment makes basic sense. Were society to rely on fines alone, deterrence of the acts in question would be grossly inadequate. Notably, the probability of detecting many of these acts is low, making the money sanction necessary for deterrence high, but the assets of individuals who commit these acts often are insubstantial. Hence, the threat of prison is needed for deterrence. Moreover, the incapacitative aspect of imprisonment is valuable because of the difficulty of deterring individuals who are prone to commit criminal acts.

Second, many of the doctrines of criminal law appear to enhance social welfare. This seems true of the basic feature of criminal law that punishment is not imposed on all harmful acts, but instead is usually confined to those that are undesirable. (For example, murder is subject to criminal sanctions, but not all accidental killing is.) As we have stressed, when the socially costly sanction of imprisonment is employed, the fault system is desirable because it results in less frequent imposition of punishment than strict liability. Also, the focus on intent in criminal law as a precondition for imposing sanctions may be sensible with regard to deterrence because those who intend to do harm are more likely to conceal their acts, and may be harder to discourage because of the benefits they anticipate. That unsuccessful attempts to do harm are punished in criminal law is an implicit way of raising the likelihood of sanctions for undesirable acts. Study of specific doctrines of criminal law seems to afford a rich opportunity for economic analysis.

6. Criticism of economic analysis of law

Many observers, and particularly non-economists, view economic analysis of law with scepticism. We consider several such criticisms here.

Description of behaviour

It is sometimes claimed that individuals and firms do not respond to legal rules as rational maximizers of their well-being. For example, it is often asserted that decisions to commit crimes are not governed by economists' usual assumptions. Some sceptics also suggest that, in predicting individuals' behaviour, certain standard assumptions are inapplicable. For example, in predicting compliance with a law, the assumption that preferences be taken as given would be inappropriate if a legal rule would change people's preferences, as some say was the case with civil rights laws and environmental laws. In addition, laws may frame individuals' understanding of problems, which could affect their probability assessments or willingness to pay. The emerging field of behavioural economics, as well as work in various disciplines that address social norms, is beginning to examine these sorts of issues (Jolls, Sunstein and Thaler, 1998).

Distribution of income
A frequent criticism of economic analysis of law concerns its focus on efficiency to the exclusion of the distribution of income. The claim of critics is that legal rules should be selected in a manner that takes into account their effects on the rich and the poor. But achieving sought-after redistribution through income tax and transfer programmes tends to be superior to redistribution through the choice of legal rules. This is because redistribution through legal rules and the tax-transfer system both will distort individuals' labour-leisure decisions in the same manner, but redistribution through legal rules often will require choosing an inefficient rule, which imposes an additional cost (Shavell, 1981; Kaplow and Shavell, 1994b).

Moreover, it is difficult to redistribute income systematically through the choice of legal rules. Many individuals are never involved in litigation; and for those who are there is substantial income heterogeneity among plaintiffs as well as among defendants. Additionally, in contractual contexts the choice of a legal rule often will not have any distributional effect because contract terms, notably the price, will adjust, so that any agreement into which parties enter will continue to reflect the initial distribution of bargaining power between them.

Concerns for fairness
An additional criticism is that the conventional economic approach slights important concerns about fairness, justice and rights. Some of these notions refer implicitly to the appropriateness of the distribution of income and, accordingly, are encompassed by our preceding remarks. Also, to some degree, the notions are motivated by instrumental concerns. For example, the attraction of paying fair compensation to victims must derive in part from the beneficial risk reduction effected by such payments, and the appeal of obeying contractual promises must rest in part on the desirable consequences contract performance has on production and exchange. To some extent, therefore, critics' concerns are already taken into account in standard economic analysis.

However, many who promote fairness, justice and rights do not regard these notions merely as some sort of proxy for attaining instrumental objectives. Instead, they believe that satisfying these notions is intrinsically valuable. This view also can be partially reconciled with the economic conception of social welfare: if individuals have a preference for a legal rule or institution because they regard it as fair, that should be credited in the determination of social welfare, just as any other preference should.

But many commentators take the position that conceptions of fairness are important as ethical principles in themselves, without regard to any possible relationship

the principles may have to individuals' welfare. This opinion is the subject of long-standing debate among moral philosophers. Some readers may be sceptical of normative views that are not grounded in individuals' well-being because embracing such views entails a willingness to sacrifice individuals' well-being. Indeed, consistently pursuing any non-welfarist principle must sometimes result in everyone being made worse off (see Kaplow and Shavell, 2001; 2002).

Efficiency of judge-made law
Also criticized is the contention of some economically oriented legal academics, notably Posner (1972), that judge-made law tends to be efficient (in contrast to legislation, which is said to reflect the influence of special interest groups). Some critics believe that judge-made law is guided by notions of fairness, or is influenced by legal culture or judges' biases, and thus will not necessarily be efficient. Whatever is the merit of the critics' claims, they are descriptive assertions about the law, and their validity does not bear on the power of economics to predict behaviour in response to legal rules or on the value of normative economic analysis of law.

A. MITCHELL POLINSKY AND STEVEN SHAVELL

See also **Coase theorem; law, public enforcement of; property law, economics and uncertainty; welfare economics.**

Bibliography
Ayres, I. and Gertner, R. 1989. Filling gaps in incomplete contracts: an economic theory of default rules. *Yale Law Journal* 99, 87–130.
Bebchuk, L. 1984. Litigation and settlement under imperfect information. *RAND Journal of Economics* 15, 404–15.
Bebchuk, L. and Ben-Shahar, O. 2001. Pre-contractual reliance. *Journal of Legal Studies* 30, 423–57.
Becker, G. 1968. Crime and punishment: an economic approach. *Journal of Political Economy* 76, 169–217.
Becker, G. and Stigler, G. 1974. Law enforcement, malfeasance, and compensation of enforcers. *Journal of Legal Studies* 3, 1–18.
Bentham, J. 1789. *An Introduction to the Principles of Morals and Legislation*, in *The Utilitarians*. Garden City, NY: Anchor Books, 1973.
Blume, L., Rubinfeld, D. and Shapiro, P. 1984. The taking of land: when should compensation be paid? *Quarterly Journal of Economics* 99, 71–92.
Bolton, P. and Dewatripont, M. 2005. *Contract Theory*. Cambridge, MA: MIT Press.
Brown, J. 1973. Toward an economic theory of liability. *Journal of Legal Studies* 2, 323–49.
Calabresi, G. 1961. Some thoughts on risk distribution and the law of torts. *Yale Law Journal* 70, 499–553.
Calabresi, G. 1970. *The Costs of Accidents: A Legal and Economic Analysis*. New Haven, CT: Yale University Press.

Calabresi, G. and Melamed, A. 1972. Property rules, liability rules, and inalienability: one view of the cathedral. *Harvard Law Review* 85, 1089–128.

Coase, R. 1960. The problem of social cost. *Journal of Law and Economics* 3, 1–44.

Cooter, R. and Ulen, T. 2003. *Law and Economics*, 4th edn. Reading, MA: Addison-Wesley.

Craswell, R. 1996. Offer, acceptance, and efficient reliance. *Stanford Law Review* 48, 481–553.

Daughety, A. 2000. Settlement. In *Encyclopedia of Law and Economics*, vol. 5, ed. B. Bouckaert and G. De Geest. Cheltenham: Edward Elgar.

Daughety, A. and Reinganum, J. 2000. Appealing judgments. *RAND Journal of Economics* 31, 502–25.

Demsetz, H. 1967. Toward a theory of property rights. *American Economic Review: Papers and Proceedings* 57, 347–59.

Diamond, P. 1974. Single activity accidents. *Journal of Legal Studies* 3, 107–64.

Diamond, P. and Maskin, E. 1979. An equilibrium analysis of search and breach of contract, I: steady states. *Bell Journal of Economics* 10, 282–316.

Hadfield, G. 1994. Judicial competence and the interpretation of incomplete contracts. *Journal of Legal Studies* 23, 159–84.

Hart, O. 1987. Incomplete contracts. In *The New Palgrave: A Dictionary of Economics*, vol. 2, ed. J. Eatwell, M. Milgate and P. Newman. New York: Macmillan.

Hart, O. and Moore, J. 1988. Incomplete contracts and renegotiation. *Econometrica* 56, 755–8.

Hay, B. and Spier, K. 1998. Settlement of litigation. In *The New Palgrave Dictionary of Economics and the Law*, vol. 3, ed. P. Newman. London: Macmillan.

Innes, R. 1999. Remediation and self-reporting in optimal law enforcement. *Journal of Public Economics* 72, 379–93.

Jolls, C., Sunstein, C. and Thaler, R. 1998. A behavioral approach to law and economics. *Stanford Law Review* 50, 1471–550.

Kaplow, L. 1986. An economic analysis of legal transitions. *Harvard Law Review* 99, 509–617.

Kaplow, L. 1994. The value of accuracy in adjudication: an economic analysis. *Journal of Legal Studies* 23, 307–401.

Kaplow, L. and Shavell, S. 1994a. Optimal law enforcement with self-reporting of behavior. *Journal of Political Economy* 102, 583–606.

Kaplow, L. and Shavell, S. 1994b. Why the legal system is less efficient than the income tax in redistributing income. *Journal of Legal Studies* 23, 667–681.

Kaplow, L. and Shavell, S. 2001. Any non-welfarist method of policy assessment violates the Pareto principle. *Journal of Political Economy* 109, 281–86.

Kaplow, L. and Shavell, S. 2002. *Fairness versus Welfare*. Cambridge, MA: Harvard University Press.

Katz, A. 1990. The strategic structure of offer and acceptance: game theory and the law of contract formation. *Michigan Law Review* 89, 215–95.

Katz, A. 1996. When should an offer stick? The economics of promissory estoppel in preliminary negotiations. *Yale Law Journal* 105, 1249–1309.

Kronman, A. 1978. Mistake, disclosure, information, and the law of contracts. *Journal of Legal Studies* 7, 1–34.

Landes, W. and Posner, R. 1975. The private enforcement of law. *Journal of Legal Studies* 4, 1–46.

Landes, W. and Posner, R. 1987a. *The Economic Structure of Tort Law*. Cambridge, MA: Harvard University Press.

Landes, W. and Posner, R. 1987b. Trademark law: an economic perspective. *Journal of Law and Economics* 30, 265–309.

Landes, W. and Posner, R. 2003. *The Economic Structure of Intellectual Property Law*. Cambridge, MA: Harvard University Press.

Libecap, G. 1986. Property rights in economic history: implications for research. *Explorations in Economic History* 23, 227–52.

Miceli, T. 1997. *Economics of the Law: Torts, Contracts, Property, Litigation*. New York: Oxford University Press.

Mookherjee, D. and Png, I. 1992. Monitoring vis-à-vis investigation in enforcement of law. *American Economic Review* 82, 556–65.

Png, I. 1986. Optimal subsidies and damages in the presence of judicial error. *International Review of Law and Economics* 6, 101–5.

Polinsky, A.M. 1980. Private versus public enforcement of fines. *Journal of Legal Studies* 9, 105–27.

Polinsky, A.M. 1983. Risk sharing through breach of contract remedies. *Journal of Legal Studies* 12, 427–44.

Polinsky, A.M. and Shavell, S. 1979. The optimal tradeoff between the probability and magnitude of fines. *American Economic Review* 69, 880–91.

Polinsky, A.M. and Shavell, S. 2000. The economic theory of public enforcement of law. *Journal of Economic Literature* 38, 45–76.

Polinsky, A.M. and Shavell, S. 2001. Corruption and optimal law enforcement. *Journal of Public Economics* 81, 1–24.

Polinsky, A.M. and Shavell, S., eds. 2007. *Handbook of Law and Economics*, vol. 1. Amsterdam: North-Holland.

Posner, R. 1972. *Economic Analysis of Law*. Boston: Little, Brown and Company.

Posner, R. 1985. An economic theory of the criminal law. *Columbia Law Review* 85, 1193–231.

Posner, R. 2003. *Economic Analysis of Law*, 6th edn. New York: Aspen Publishers.

Priest, G. and Klein, B. 1984. The selection of disputes for litigation. *Journal of Legal Studies* 13, 1–55.

Reinganum, J. 1988. Plea bargaining and prosecutorial discretion, *American Economic Review* 78, 713–28.

Reinganum, J. and Wilde, L. 1986. Settlement, litigation, and the allocation of litigation costs. *RAND Journal of Economics* 17, 557–66.

Rogerson, W. 1984. Efficient reliance and damage measures for breach of contract. *RAND Journal of Economics* 15, 39–53.

Rose-Ackerman, S. 1999. *Corruption and Government: Causes, Consequences and Reform*. New York: Cambridge University Press.

Schwartz, A. 1992. Relational contracts in the courts: an analysis of incomplete agreements and judicial strategies. *Journal of Legal Studies* 21, 271–318.

Schweizer, U. 1989. Litigation and settlement under two-sided incomplete information. *Review of Economic Studies* 56, 163–78.

Shavell, S. 1980a. Damage measures for breach of contract. *Bell Journal of Economics* 11, 466–90.

Shavell, S. 1980b. Strict liability versus negligence. *Journal of Legal Studies* 9, 1–25.

Shavell, S. 1981. A note on efficiency vs distributional equity in legal rulemaking: should distributional equity matter given optimal income taxation? *American Economic Review: Papers and Proceedings* 71, 414–18.

Shavell, S. 1982a. On liability and insurance. *Bell Journal of Economics* 13, 120–32.

Shavell, S. 1982b. The social versus the private incentive to bring suit in a costly legal system. *Journal of Legal Studies* 11, 333–9.

Shavell, S. 1985. Criminal law and the optimal use of nonmonetary sanctions as a deterrent. *Columbia Law Review* 85, 1232–62.

Shavell, S. 1987a. *Economic Analysis of Accident Law*. Cambridge, MA: Harvard University Press.

Shavell, S. 1987b. The optimal use of nonmonetary sanctions as a deterrent. *American Economic Review* 77, 584–92.

Shavell, S. 1987c. A model of optimal incapacitation. *American Economic Review: Papers and Proceedings* 77, 107–110.

Shavell, S. 1989. Sharing of information prior to settlement or litigation. *RAND Journal of Economics* 20, 183–95.

Shavell, S. 1991. Specific versus general enforcement of law. *Journal of Political Economy* 99, 1088–108.

Shavell, S. 1993. The optimal structure of law enforcement. *Journal of Law and Economics* 36, 255–87.

Shavell, S. 1994. Acquisition and disclosure of information prior to sale. *RAND Journal of Economics* 25, 20–36.

Shavell, S. 1995. The appeals process as a means of error correction. *Journal of Legal Studies* 24, 379–426.

Shavell, S. 1997. The fundamental divergence between the private and the social motive to use the legal system. *Journal of Legal Studies* 26, 575–612.

Shavell, S. 2004. *Foundations of Economic Analysis of Law*. Cambridge, MA: Harvard University Press.

Shavell, S. 2006. On the writing and interpretation of contracts. *Journal of Law, Economics, & Organization* 22, 289–314.

Shleifer, A. and Vishny, R. 1993. Corruption. *Quarterly Journal of Economics* 108, 599–617.

Spier, K. 1992. The dynamics of pretrial negotiation. *Review of Economic Studies* 59, 93–108.

Spitzer, M. and Talley, E. 2000. Judicial auditing. *Journal of Legal Studies* 29, 649–83.

Umbeck, J. 1981. *A Theory of Property Rights with Application to the California Gold Rush*. Ames: Iowa State University Press.

Wils, W. 1993. Who should bear the costs of failed negotiations? A functional inquiry into precontractual liability. *Journal des Economistes et des Etudes Humaines* 4, 93–134.

law of indifference

A designation applied by Jevons to the following fundamental proposition: 'In the same open market, at any one moment, there cannot be two prices for the same kind of article.'

This proposition, which is at the foundation of a large part of economic science, itself rests on certain ulterior grounds: namely, certain conditions of a perfect market. One is that monopolies should not exist, or at least should not exert that power in virtue of which a proprietor of a theatre, in Germany for instance, can make a different charge for the admission of soldiers and civilians, of men and women. The indivisibility of the articles dealt in appears to be another circumstance which may counteract the law of indifference in some kinds of market, where price is not regulated by cost of production.

[Jevons (1875), *Theory of Exchange*, 2nd edn, p. 99 (statement of the law). Walker (1886), *Political Economy*, art. 132 (a restatement). Mill (1848), *Political Economy*, bk. ii. ch. iv. § 3 (imperfections of actual markets). Edgeworth (1881), *Mathematical Psychics*, pp. 19, 46 (possible exceptions to the law of indifference).]

F.Y. EDGEWORTH

Reprinted from Palgrave's Dictionary of Political Economy.

Bibliography

Edgeworth, F.Y. 1881. *Mathematical Psychics*. London: Kegan Paul.

Jevons, W.S. 1875. *Money and the Mechanism of Exchange*. London: C. Kegan Paul & Co.

Mill, J.S. 1848. *Principles of Political Economy*. London: J.W. Parker.

Walker, F.A. 1886. *A Brief Textbook of Political Economy*. London.

Law, John (1671–1729)

John Law of Lauriston has been regarded by some observers as a monetary crank, by others as a precursor of modern schemes of managed money and Keynesian full-employment policies. He was the originator of the Mississippi Bubble, perhaps the greatest speculative bubble of all time.

Born in Edinburgh, the son of prosperous parents, Law was well educated in political economy. A fugitive from justice in 1694 for killing a man in a duel in

England, Law travelled extensively throughout Europe, observing and gaining experience in banking, insurance and finance. He proposed a number of unsuccessful schemes to set up a national bank of issue – in Paris in 1702, Edinburgh in 1705 and Savoy in 1712 – finally attaining success in France with the establishment in 1718 of the Banque Royale.

Law's theories on money and banking are contained in *Money and Trade Considered: With a Proposal for Supplying the Nation With Money* (1705) and other works (Hamilton, 1968; Harsin, 1934). Like other 18th-century writers Law adopted a disequilibrium theory of money, viewing it as a stimulant to trade. In a state of unemployment, Law maintained that an increase in the nation's money supply would stimulate employment and output without raising prices since the demand for money would rise with the increase in output. Moreover, once full employment was attained the monetary expansion would attract factors of production from abroad, so output would continue to increase.

According to Law, a paper-money standard was preferable to one based on precious metals. Suitable candidates for the money supply included government fiat, banknotes, stocks and bonds. Since the primary function of money was as a medium of exchange, it could best be served by a commodity (paper) not subject to considerable fluctuation in value and high resource costs. Thus Law advocated the establishment of note-issuing national banks that would extend productive loans (real bills), providing sufficient currency to guarantee prosperity. Two proposals for such banks, in Paris 1702 and Edinburgh 1705, would have had the note issues based on land initially valued in terms of silver.

From 1716 to 1720 John Law had the unique opportunity to apply his theories to the French economy. In 1715, the heritage of two exhausting wars was depression and deflation. Law succeeded in convincing the Regent (the Duke of Orleans) that a bank of issue would alleviate the problem of financing the national debt. Accordingly, he established in Paris on 2 May 1716 a private bank, the Banque Générale. In its 31 months of operation, the bank was remarkably successful; its notes (convertible into specie and payable as taxes) were issued in moderation and gained national circulation. On 4 December 1718, the Banque Générale was nationalized and renamed the Banque Royale, with Law in control, and in January 1719 it began to issue notes denominated in *livres tournois*, the unit of account, replacing the previously issued *écus de banque* representing fixed amounts of specie.

Alongside the bank, in August 1717, Law established the Compagnie d'Occident after obtaining the franchise on Louisiana and the monopoly of the Canadian fur trade. This company in the succeeding 22 months acquired the tobacco monopoly, the East India Company and the trading monopolies to Africa and China. Law changed its name in June 1719 to the Compagnie des Indes, and the following winter obtained the farm of the royal mints and of the indirect taxes. In October 1719 he refunded the national debt of 1.5 million *livres tournois*, and in January 1720 became Finance Minister.

The stock of the Compagnie des Indes, initially selling at a par value of £500, within half a year in an unprecedented speculative mania was bid up to many times its original price. The bubble burst in January 1720 after the price of the stock reached a peak of £18,000. To support the price Law made the mistake of pegging it at £9,000, thereby monetizing it and engendering a rapid expansion of notes (125 per cent in two months). In May 1720, in a desperate attempt to salvage his system Law issued a deflationary decree depreciating the stock and reducing the denomination of notes by stages. This decree led to a panic as the public, fearful of further capital losses, sold off both notes and stock. Law's dismissal by the Regent worsened the panic. He was quickly reinstated but his final attempt to restore confidence by reducing the outstanding note issue proved unsuccessful. By December 1720 the 'system' collapsed. Law fled to Belgium and payments quickly reverted to a specie basis. The collapse of the system ruined many in all walks of life and made the word 'bank' anathema in France for well over a century.

Though Law's system reduced unemployment and stimulated output, it was at the expense of doubling the price level. His system was undermined by his actions breaking the link between the note issue and specie convertibility; by retiring the national debt with bank notes convertible into stock; and by encouraging speculation in stock by declaring dividends unrelated to the company's true prospects. Monetizing the stock by pegging its price in the end destroyed the public's confidence in his system. Law was aware of many of the principles of sound money and banking, but by equating money with stock and relying on the real bills doctrine he sowed the seeds of disaster.

MICHAEL D. BORDO

Selected works

1705. *Money and Trade Considered: With a Proposal for Supplying the Nation With Money*. New York: Augustus Kelley, 1966.

Bibliography

Blaug, M. 1978. *Economic Theory in Retrospect*. 3rd edn. Cambridge: Cambridge University Press.

Hamilton, E.J. 1936. Prices and wages at Paris under John Law's system. *Quarterly Journal of Economics* 51, 42–70.

Hamilton, E.J. 1968. Law, John. In *International Encyclopedia of the Social Sciences*, vol. 9. New York: The Free Press.

Hamilton, E.J. 1969. The political economy of France at the time of John Law. *History of Political Economy* 1, 123–49.

Harsin, P., ed. 1934. *John Law: Oeuvres complètes*. 3 vols. Paris: Sirey.

Kindleberger, C.P. 1984. *A Financial History of Western Europe*. London: Allen & Unwin.

Neal, L. and Schubert, E. 1985. The first rational bubble: a new look at the Mississippi and South Sea schemes. Faculty Working Paper No. 1188, Bureau of Economic and Business Research, University of Illinois at Urbana-Champaign.

Rist, C.W. 1940. *A History of Monetary and Credit Theory from John Law to the Present Day*. London: Allen & Unwin.

Schumpeter, J.A. 1954. *History of Economic Analysis*. New York: Oxford University Press.

law(s) of large numbers

When we have a large number of independent replications of a random experiment, we observe that the frequency of the outcomes can be very well approximated by the probabilities of the corresponding events. The profits of many commercially successful enterprises – like casinos or insurance companies – are based on random events obeying some laws.

Mathematically, this idea was first formulated by Jacob Bernoulli, for experiments with only two outcomes ('Bernoulli experiments'). The terminology 'law of large numbers' was introduced by S.D. Poisson in 1835.

In the most basic version, LLN (the standard abbreviation for 'law(s) of large numbers') describes results of the following type. We assume that we have given a sequence of random variables $X_1, X_2, \ldots$ We say we have a LLN if

$$\frac{1}{N}(X_1 + \ldots X_N) \tag{1}$$

converges for $N \to \infty$, preferably to a constant.

For stating our results, we have to state the nature of the convergence in our LLN and impose some restrictions on the X_i. The more we restrict our X_i, the stronger our convergence results will be.

The weak law of large numbers

The 'weak law of large numbers' states that averages like (1) converge in a 'weak' sense (like for example convergence in probability) to a limit. In most cases, the requirements for the random variables involved are not very restrictive. A typical weak LLN is the following theorem.

Theorem 1 *Assume that the random variables X_i satisfy*

$$EX_i = 0, \tag{2}$$

$$\sup EX_i^2 < \infty \tag{3}$$

and

$$\lim_{M \to \infty} \sup_{|i-j| > M} |EX_i X_j| < \infty. \tag{4}$$

Then for $N \to \infty$

$$\frac{1}{N}(X_1 + \ldots X_N) \to^P 0,$$

where $\to^P$ denotes convergence in probability.

Our random variables have to be centred, of bounded variance, and condition (4) requires that the correlation of random variables 'far apart' converges to zero uniformly. This is a very general and important result. Another advantage is the simplicity of its proof: it is an elementary task to show that the variance of the average converges to zero. Then the theorem is an immediate consequence of Chebyshev's inequality. Moreover, the assumptions of the theorem can easily be checked, and only depend on the second moments of the X_i.

The strong law of large numbers

In some cases, we want to have more than convergence in probability of the averages. For this purpose, we have strong laws of large numbers. We do need, however, stricter requirements. The following theorem is a typical strong LLN. A more stringent discussion of this type of theorems

Theorem 2 *Assume that the random variables X_i satisfy (2),(3). Let $\mathfrak{F}_i$ be an increasing sequence of σ-algebras (for example. $\mathfrak{F}_{i-1} \subset \mathfrak{F}_i$) so that X_i is $\mathfrak{F}_i$ –measurable. Then let us assume that*

$$E(X_i / \mathfrak{F}_{i-1}) = 0. \tag{5}$$

Then

$$\frac{1}{N}(X_1 + \ldots X_N) \to 0 \ P - almost \ surely.$$

Heuristically, we can interpret $\mathfrak{F}_i$ as information available at time i. Then (5) postulates that we cannot predict X_i given the information at time $i - 1$. One important special case where (5) is fulfilled is the case of independent. In this case, we can choose $\mathfrak{F}_i$ to be the σ-algebra generated by $X_1, \ldots X_i$. Then, assuming the X_i to be independent, we have $E(X_i / \mathfrak{F}_{i-1}) = E(X_i)$.

Hence (5) is more general than the requirement of independence, but still far more restrictive than (4).

Ergodic theorems

We can easily see that (5) implies that our X_i are uncorrelated. In many applications, this requirement is unrealistic. Fortunately, there is a theory guaranteeing convergence of sums like (1) at least for stationary processes X_i. A process X_i, $i \in \mathbf{Z}$ is called (strictly) stationary if for all $n \in \mathbf{Z}$ the distributions of $(X_1, X_2, \ldots, X_m)$ and $(X_{n+1}, X_2, \ldots, X_{n+m})$ are the same. To describe the limits of our process, we need to introduce the transition operator T: This operator is a mapping defined on the space of random variables measurable with respect to the σ-algebra generated by the X_i, $i \in \mathbf{Z}$. For random variables

$$Y = f(X_{t_1}, X_{t_2}, \ldots X_{t_n}) \qquad (6)$$

we define the random variable TY by

$$TY = f(X_{t_1+1}, X_{t_2+1}, \ldots X_{t_n+1}). \qquad (7)$$

So the transition operator T shifts every random variable 'one step in the future'. (T can be considered as the inverse of the usual lag operator). One can show that the definition based on (6), (7) can be uniquely extended to the space of all X_i, $i \in Z$ measurable random variables. Then an event A is called *invariant* if

$$TI_A = I_A \text{ almost surely,}$$

where I_A is the indicator of the event A. It can be easily seen that the invariant events form a σ-algebra, which we denote by $\mathfrak{F}$. Then the ergodic theorem states that

$$\lim_{n \to \infty} \frac{1}{n} \sum_{i=1}^{n} X_i = E(X_i/\mathfrak{F}). \qquad (8)$$

(Since we are taking the conditional expectation with respect to $\mathfrak{F}$, it can easily be seen that $E(X_1/\mathfrak{F}) = E(X_2/\mathfrak{F}) = \ldots$).

The ergodic theorem is included in most of advanced textbooks on probability theory (see, for example, Billingsley, 1995). A more detailed exposition can be found in Gray (2007).

We now can take various conclusions from our theorem. First of all, we can regardless of the nature of the σ-algebra $\mathfrak{F}$ conclude that the limit of $\frac{1}{n} \sum_{i=1}^{n} X_i$ *exists*. In econometric theory, one often postulates the existence of limits of certain averages (that is, in regression theory we often assume that $\lim_{n \to \infty} \frac{1}{n} \sum_{i=1}^{n} x_i x_i'$ exists). In case of stationary processes, the theorem here makes assumptions of this type very plausible.

If the σ-algebra $\mathfrak{F}$ is trivial (that is, consists only of events of probability 0 and 1), then the right-hand side of (8) is constant. One sufficient criterion for this property is that the process is a causal function of i.i.d. random variables. So if

$$X_i = f(e_i, e_{i-1}, \ldots)$$

where e_i are i.i.d., $\mathfrak{F}$ is trivial.

Applications and uniform laws of large numbers

For many statistical applications, we need stronger results. As a first example, consider the asymptotic of the maximum likelihood estimator. As a simplest case, let us discuss the case of i.i.d. random variables X_i, distributed according to densities f_θ for parameters $\theta \in \Theta$, and let θ_0 be the true parameter. Then the LLN guarantees

that for every fixed θ

$$\frac{1}{n} \sum \ln(f_\theta(X_i)) \to \int \ln(f_\theta) f_{\theta_0}, \qquad (9)$$

and the function on the right-hand side is maximized if $\theta = \theta_0$. Since the maximum likelihood estimator maximizes the right-hand side, it seems reasonable to exploit this relation for a proof of consistency of the maximum likelihood estimator. The LLN guarantees only convergence for *fixed* θ, from our LLN we cannot say anything about the limiting behaviour of

$$\sup_{\theta \in \Theta} \ln\left(\frac{1}{n} \sum \ln(f_\theta(X_i))\right).$$

This problem would go away if one could establish that the convergence in (9) is *uniform* in θ. This strategy was first realized in a path breaking paper by A. Wald (Wald, 1949), where he first established the consistency of the maximum likelihood estimator. Today the techniques are a little more sophisticated. Nevertheless, consistency proofs for M-estimators still rely to good extend on Wald's idea.

Another application of uniform LLN is the consistency of 'plug-in' estimators. In many cases, the asymptotic variance of certain estimators can be expressed as a function of the expectations of certain random functions, possibly depending on the parameter to be estimated (for example, the well-known 'sandwich formula' derived by H. White; see for example Hayashi, 2000). A standard strategy is to estimate the parameter, then replace the expectation by an average (and hope that – due to the LLN – average and expectation are close together) and use the estimated parameter as an argument. One can easily see that only a uniform law of large numbers can justify procedures of this type.

Fortunately, there exist a lot of criteria to establish uniform laws of large numbers. For most cases of interest to econometricians, the papers by Andrews (1992) and Pötscher and Prucha (1989) will be sufficient.

A more general and abstract theory can be found in van der Vaart and Wellner (1996). These theories allow us also to estimate the cumulative distribution function of random variables directly. Suppose we have given random variables $X_i, \ldots, X_n$. Then the empirical distribution function F_n is defined as

$$F_n(x) = \frac{1}{n} \sum_{i=1}^{n} I(X_i \le x)$$

(that is F_n jumps $1/n$ in X_i and is constant in between the jumps). Then the theorem of Glivenko-Cantelli (see van der Vaart and Wellner, 1996) states that if the X_i are i.i.d. with cumulative distribution function F, then

$$\sup|F_n(x) - F(x)| \to 0.$$

It should be noted that there are generalizations to multivariate or even more general X_i. In these cases, however, one has to use slightly more sophisticated techniques. Instead of the 'empirical distribution function', one has to use the 'empirical measure' (a random measure, which puts mass $1/n$ in the points X_i, and instead of the maximum difference of the distribution functions one has to consider the maximal difference of the measures over certain classes ('VC-classes').

WERNER PLOBERGER

Bibliography

Andrews, D.W.K. 1992. Generic uniform convergence. *Econometric Theory* 8, 241–57.
Billingsley, P. 1995. *Probability and Measure*, 3rd edn. New York: Wiley.
Gray, R.M. 2007. *Probability, Random Processes, and Ergodic Properties*. Online. Available at http://ee.stanford.edu/~gray/arp.html, accessed 29 April 2007.
Hall, P. and Heyde, C.C. 1980. *Martingale Limit Theory and its Application*. San Diego: Academic Press.
Hayashi, F. 2000. *Econometrics*. Princeton: Princeton University Press.
Pötscher, B.M. and Prucha, I.R. 1989. A uniform law of large numbers for dependent and heterogeneous data processes. *Econometrica* 57, 675–83.
van der Vaart, A.W. and Wellner, J.A. 1996. *Weak Convergence and Empirical Processes*. New York: Springer.
Wald, A. 1949. Note on the consistency of the maximum likelihood estimate. *Annals of Mathematical Statistics* 20, 595–601.

law, public enforcement of

In this article we consider the theory of public enforcement of law – the use of public agents (inspectors, tax auditors, police, prosecutors) to detect and to sanction violators of legal rules. After briefly discussing the rationale for public (as opposed to private) enforcement, we present the basic elements of the theory: the probability of imposition of sanctions, the magnitude and form of sanctions (fines, imprisonment), and the rule of liability. We then examine a variety of extensions of the central theory, including the costs of imposing fines, mistakes, marginal deterrence, settlement, self-reporting, repeat offences, and incapacitation. (For a fuller treatment of the material in this entry, see Polinsky and Shavell, 2007.)

Before proceeding, we note that economically oriented analysis of public law enforcement dates primarily from the 18th century contribution of Jeremy Bentham (1789), whose analysis of deterrence was sophisticated and expansive. After Bentham, the subject of enforcement lay essentially dormant in economic scholarship until Gary Becker (1968) published a highly influential article, which has led to a voluminous literature.

Rationale of public enforcement

A basic question is why there is a need for public enforcement of law (see generally Becker and Stigler, 1974; Landes and Posner, 1975; Polinsky, 1980a). In particular, why not rely solely on private suits brought by victims? The answer depends importantly on the locus of information about the identity of injurers. When victims of harm naturally possess knowledge of the identity of injurers, allowing private suits for damages will motivate victims to sue and thus harness the information they have for purposes of law enforcement. This may explain why the enforcement of contractual obligations and of accident law is primarily private. When victims do not know who caused harm, however, or when finding injurers is difficult, society may need to rely instead on public investigation and prosecution; this is broadly true of crimes and of many violations of environmental and safety regulations.

Basic framework for analysing public enforcement

An individual who commits a harmful act obtains a gain and also faces the risk of being caught and sanctioned. The form of sanction could be a fine or a prison term. Fines generally will be treated as socially costless because they are mere transfers of money, whereas imprisonment will be considered as socially costly because of the expense of operating prisons and the disutility suffered by those imprisoned. The higher the probability of detecting violators, the more resources the state must devote to enforcement.

We assume that social welfare equals the sum of individuals' expected utilities. If individuals are risk neutral, social welfare can be expressed as the gains individuals obtain from committing their harmful acts, minus the harms caused and the costs of law enforcement. The enforcement authority's problem is to maximize social welfare by choosing enforcement expenditures (or, equivalently, a probability of detection), the form of sanctions, and their level.

Fines

Suppose that the sanction is a fine and that individuals are risk neutral. If the probability of detection p is taken as fixed, then the optimal fine is the harm h divided by the probability, that is, h/p; for then the expected fine $p(h/p)$ equals h. This fine is optimal because, facing it, an individual will commit a harmful act if, and only if, the gain he would derive exceeds the harm he would cause. Such behaviour is first-best. The fundamental formula h/p essentially was noted by Bentham (1789) and it has been observed by many others since.

If the probability of detection can be varied, the optimal fine is maximal, f_M, as emphasized by Becker (1968). If the fine were not maximal, society could save enforcement costs by simultaneously raising the fine and lowering the probability without affecting the level of deterrence. If $f < f_M$, then raise the fine to f_M and lower the probability from p to $(f/f_M)p$; the expected fine is still pf, so that deterrence is maintained but expenditures on enforcement are reduced, implying that social welfare rises.

The optimal probability p of imposing a fine is low in the sense that it results in some under-deterrence; that is, the optimal p is such that the expected fine pf_M is less than the harm h (Polinsky and Shavell, 1984). The reason is to economize on enforcement resources. In particular, if pf_M equals h, behaviour will be ideal, meaning that the individuals who are just deterred obtain gains essentially equal to the harm. These are the individuals who would be led to commit the harmful act if p were lowered slightly. That in turn must be socially beneficial because these individuals cause no net social losses (their gains essentially equal the harm), but reducing p saves enforcement costs. How much pf_M should be lowered below h depends on the saving in enforcement costs from reducing p compared with the net social costs of under-deterrence that will result if p is lowered non-trivially.

If individuals are risk averse, the optimal fine may be well less than the maximal fine, as first shown in Polinsky and Shavell (1979); see also Kaplow (1992). This is because a high fine would impose substantial risk-bearing costs on individuals who commit harmful acts. If $f < f_M$, it is still true that f can be raised and p lowered so as to maintain deterrence, but because of risk aversion this now implies that pf falls, meaning that fine revenue falls. The reduction in fine revenue reflects the disutility caused by imposing greater risk on risk-averse individuals. The decline in fine revenue could more than offset the savings in enforcement expenditures, causing social welfare to be lower.

Imprisonment
Now suppose that the sanction is imprisonment. If the probability of detection is fixed, there is no simple formula for the optimal imprisonment term (see Polinsky and Shavell, 1984). The optimal term could be such that there is either under-deterrence or over-deterrence. On the one hand, a relatively low imprisonment term, implying under-deterrence, might be socially desirable because imprisonment costs are reduced for those individuals who commit harmful acts. On the other hand, a relatively high term, implying over-deterrence, might be socially desirable because imprisonment costs are reduced due to fewer individuals committing harmful acts, even if some of these deterred individuals would have obtained gains exceeding the harm.

If the probability of detection can be varied and individuals are risk neutral in imprisonment, then the optimal imprisonment term is maximal. The reasoning is similar to that employed above: if the imprisonment term were not maximal, it could be raised and the probability of detection lowered so as to keep the expected prison term constant; neither individual behaviour nor

the costs of imprisonment are affected, but enforcement expenditures fall.

If, instead, individuals are risk averse in imprisonment (the disutility of each additional year of imprisonment grows with the number of years in prison), there is a stronger argument for setting the imprisonment sanction maximally (Polinsky and Shavell, 1999). Now when the imprisonment term is raised, the probability of detection can be lowered more than in the risk-neutral case without reducing deterrence. Thus, not only are there greater savings in enforcement expenditures, but also the costs of imposing imprisonment sanctions decline because the expected prison term falls.

Last, suppose that individuals are risk preferring in imprisonment (the disutility of each additional year of imprisonment declines with the number of years in prison). This possibility seems particularly important: the first years of imprisonment may create unusually high disutility, due to brutalization of the prisoner or to the stigma of having been imprisoned at all. Individuals' positive time discount rates, which are thought to be especially significant for criminals, also make the disutility of later years less significant. In the case of risk-preferring individuals, the optimal prison term may well be less than maximal: if the sentence were raised, the probability that maintains deterrence could not be lowered proportionally, implying that the expected prison term would rise. Thus, although there would be enforcement-cost savings, they might not be great enough to offset the increased sanctioning costs.

When the sanction is imprisonment, the optimal probability of detection may be such that there is either under-deterrence or over-deterrence. On the one hand, the motive to lower the probability is reinforced relative to the case of fines because imprisonment costs, as well as detection costs, decline if fewer offenders are caught. On the other hand, raising the probability of detection results in fewer offenders, which, everything else equal, decreases imprisonment costs because fewer are imprisoned. Either effect may dominate.

Fines versus imprisonment
Fines generally are preferable to prison terms as a means of deterrence, since fines are socially cheaper sanctions to impose (Becker, 1968; Polinsky and Shavell, 1984). Hence, fines should be employed to the greatest extent possible – until a party's wealth is exhausted – before imprisonment is imposed. Further, imprisonment should be used as a sanction only if the harm prevented by the added deterrence is sufficiently great.

Fault-based liability
Our discussion thus far has presumed that liability is strict (imposed whenever harm occurs), but liability may instead be based on fault (imposed only when behaviour was found to be socially undesirable). Fault-based liability, like strict liability, can induce individuals to behave

properly, but fault-based liability possesses an advantage when individuals are risk averse: if they act responsibly, they will not be found at fault, so will not bear the risk of being sanctioned. Similarly, fault-based liability is advantageous when the sanction is imprisonment, for then again individuals may be led to behave optimally without the actual imposition of sanctions, and thus without social costs being incurred (Shavell, 1987b). To the extent that mistakes are made in determining fault, however, these two advantages are reduced.

Fault-based liability is more difficult to implement because it requires more information than strict liability. To apply fault-based liability, the enforcement authority must be able to determine the proper fault standard – that is, socially desirable behaviour – and it must ascertain whether the defendant's conduct was in compliance with the fault standard. Under strict liability, the authority need only measure harm. (Moreover, for reasons we discuss below, strict liability encourages better decisions by injurers regarding their level of participation in harm-creating activities.)

This concludes the presentation of the basic theory of public enforcement of law. We now turn to various extensions and refinements of the analysis.

Accidental harms

We have been implicitly assuming that individuals decide whether or not to commit acts that cause harm with certainty, that is, they decide whether or not to cause intentional harms. In many circumstances, however, harms are accidental – they occur only with a probability. Essentially all that we have said above applies in a straightforward way when harms are accidental.

There is, however, an additional issue that arises when harm is uncertain: a sanction can be imposed either on the basis of the commission of an act that increases the chance of harm (such as storing chemicals in a substandard tank) or on the basis of the actual occurrence of harm (if the tank ruptures and results in a spill). In principle, either approach can achieve optimal deterrence – by setting the (expected) sanction equal to expected harm if liability is imposed whenever a dangerous act is committed, or equal to actual harm if liability is imposed only if harm occurs.

Several factors are relevant to the choice between act-based and harm-based sanctions (Shavell, 1993). First, act-based sanctions need not be as high as harm-based sanctions to accomplish a given level of deterrence (expected harm is less than actual harm), and thus offer an advantage because of parties' limited assets. Second, because act-based sanctions can accomplish a given level of deterrence with lower sanctions, they are preferable when parties are risk averse. Third, either act-based sanctions may be simpler to impose (it might be less difficult to determine whether an oil shipper properly maintains its vessels' holding tanks than to detect whether one of the vessels leaked oil), or harm-based sanctions may be easier to implement (a driver who causes harm might be caught without difficulty, but not one who speeds). Fourth, it may be hard to calculate the expected harm due to an act, but relatively easy to ascertain the actual harm if it eventuates, favoring harm-based sanctions.

Costs of imposing fines

The costs borne by enforcement authorities in imposing fines should be reflected in the fine. Recall that, if the probability of detection is taken as fixed and individuals are risk neutral, the optimal fine is h/p, the harm divided by the probability of detection. Now suppose there is a public cost k of imposing a fine. The optimal fine then becomes $h/p + k$; the cost k should be added to the fine that would otherwise be desirable (Becker, 1968; Polinsky and Shavell, 1992). The explanation is that, if an individual commits a harmful act, he causes society to bear not only the immediate harm h but also, with probability p, the cost k of imposing the fine – that is, his act results in an expected total social cost of $h + pk$. If the fine is $h/p + k$, the individual's expected fine is $p[h/p + k] = h + pk$, leading him to commit the harmful act if and only if his gain exceeds the expected total social cost of his act.

Not only does the state bear costs when fines are imposed, so do individuals who pay the fines (such as legal defence expenses). The costs borne by individuals, however, do not affect the formula for the optimal fine. Individuals properly take these costs into account because they bear them.

Level of activity

In many settings in which harm may occur, an individual chooses not only whether to commit a harmful act when engaging in an activity, but also the level at which to engage in the activity. Drivers decide how careful to be while driving, as well as how many miles to drive; similarly, firms choose safety precautions as well as their level of output. The socially optimal activity level is such that the actor's marginal utility from the activity just equals the marginal expected harm caused by the activity (we assume that optimal care is taken). Thus, the optimal number of miles driven is the level at which the marginal utility of driving an extra mile just equals the marginal expected harm per mile driven.

Under strict liability parties will choose the optimal level of activity because they will pay for all harm done. They will choose the optimal number of miles to drive because they will pay for all harm per mile driven. Under fault-based liability, however, parties generally do not pay for the harm they cause because they tend to behave so as not to be found at fault. As a consequence, they will choose an excessive level of activity (Shavell,

1980). Driving more miles increases expected harm, but this effect generally will be ignored under fault-based liability.

The interpretation of the preceding points in relation to firms is that under strict liability the product price will reflect the expected harm caused by production. Hence, the amount purchased, and thus the level of production, will tend to be socially optimal. However, under fault-based liability the product price will not reflect harm, but only the cost of precautions; thus, the level of output will be excessive (Polinsky, 1980b).

Relatedly, safety regulations and other regulatory requirements are often framed as standards of care that have to be met, but which, if met, free the regulated party from liability. Hence, regulations of this sort are subject to the criticism that they lead to excessive levels of the regulated activity. Making parties strictly liable for harm would be superior to safety regulation with respect to inducing socially correct activity levels.

Mistakes

An individual who should be found liable might mistakenly be acquitted. Conversely, an individual who should not be found liable might mistakenly be convicted. For an individual who has been detected, let the probabilities of these errors be ε_A and ε_C, respectively. Given the probability of detection p and the chances of these types of error, an individual will commit the wrongful act if and only if his gain g net of his expected fine if he does commit it exceeds his expected fine if he does not commit it, that is, when $g - p(1 - \varepsilon_A)f > - p\varepsilon_C f$, or, equivalently, when $g > (1 - \varepsilon_A - \varepsilon_C)pf$.

As emphasized by Png (1986), both types of error reduce deterrence: the term $(1 - \varepsilon_A - \varepsilon_C)pf$ is declining in both ε_A and ε_C. The first type of error diminishes deterrence because it lowers the expected fine if an individual violates the law. The second type of error lowers deterrence because it reduces the difference between the expected fine from violating the law and not violating it — the greater is ε_C, the smaller is the increase in the expected fine if one violates the law.

Because mistakes dilute deterrence, they reduce social welfare. Specifically, to achieve any level of deterrence, the probability p must be higher to offset the effect of errors. Mistaken convictions have the additional effect of discouraging socially desirable participation in the activity. Consequently, expenditures made to reduce errors may be socially beneficial (Kaplow and Shavell, 1994a).

Two other points regarding the implications of mistake are worth noting. First, if individuals are risk averse, the possibility of mistakes of either type generally lowers optimal sanctions (Block and Sidak, 1980). Second, as stressed by Craswell and Calfee (1986), individuals will often have a motive to take excessive precautions under fault-based liability in order to reduce the chance of being found erroneously at fault.

General enforcement

In many settings, enforcement may be said to be general in the sense that several different types of violations will be detected by an enforcement agent's activity. For example, a police officer waiting at the roadside may notice a driver who litters as well as one who goes through a red light or who speeds, and a tax auditor may detect a variety of infractions when he examines a tax return. (In contrast, if enforcement is specific, the probability is chosen independently for each type of harmful act.)

When enforcement is general, the optimal sanction rises with the level of harm, and is maximal only for relatively high harms (Shavell, 1991; Mookherjee and Png, 1992). To see why, assume that liability is strict, the sanction is a fine, and injurers are risk neutral. Let $f(h)$ be the fine given harm h. Then, for any general probability of detection p (that is, p applies regardless of h), the optimal fine schedule is h/p, provided that h/p is feasible; otherwise the optimal fine is maximal. This schedule is obviously optimal given p because it implies that the expected fine equals harm, thereby inducing ideal behaviour whenever that is possible. That sanctions should rise with the severity of harm up to a maximum when enforcement is general also holds if the sanction is imprisonment and if liability is fault-based.

Marginal deterrence

In many circumstances a person may consider which of several harmful acts to commit: for example, whether to release only a small amount of a pollutant into a river or a large amount, or whether to kidnap a person or also to kill the kidnap victim. In such contexts, sanctions influence which harmful acts individuals choose to commit (as well as whether to commit any harmful act). Marginal deterrence is said to occur when a more harmful act is deterred because its sanction exceeds that for a less harmful act (Stigler, 1970; Shavell, 1992; Wilde, 1992; Mookherjee and Png, 1994).

Other things being equal, it is socially desirable that enforcement policy creates marginal deterrence so that, when harmful acts do occur, less harm is done. One way to accomplish marginal deterrence is for sanctions to rise with the magnitude of harm, which means that sanctions generally will not be maximal. However, fostering marginal deterrence may conflict with achieving overall deterrence: in order for the schedule of sanctions to rise steeply enough to accomplish marginal deterrence, sanctions for less harmful acts may have to be so low that individuals are not deterred from committing some harmful act.

Note that marginal deterrence also can be promoted by increasing the probability of detection. Kidnappers can be better deterred from killing their victims if more police resources are devoted to apprehending kidnappers who murder their victims than to those who do not.

Principal–agent relationship

Although we have assumed that an injurer is a single actor, injurers often are more appropriately characterized as collective entities, and specifically as a principal and the principal's agent. For example, the principal could be a firm and the agent an employee, or the principal could be a contractor and the agent a subcontractor.

When harm is caused by the behaviour of principals and agents, many of our prior conclusions carry over to the sanctioning of principals. Notably, if a risk-neutral principal faces an expected fine equal to harm done, he will behave socially optimally in controlling his agents, and in particular will contract with them and monitor them in ways that will give the agents appropriate incentives to reduce harm (Newman and Wright, 1990; but see Arlen, 1994).

An issue that arises when there are principals and agents concerns the allocation of financial sanctions between the two parties. It is apparent that the particular allocation of sanctions does not matter when the parties can reallocate the sanctions through their own contract. For example, if the agent finds that he faces a large fine but is more risk averse than the principal, the principal can assume it; conversely, if the fine is imposed on the principal, he will retain it and not impose an internal sanction on the agent. Thus, the post-contract sanctions that the agent bears are not affected by the particular division of sanctions initially selected by the enforcement authority.

The allocation of monetary sanctions between principals and agents would matter, however, if some allocations allow the pair to reduce their total burden. An important example is when a fine is imposed only on the agent and he is unable to pay it (Sykes, 1981; Kornhauser, 1982). Then, he and the principal (who often would have higher assets) would jointly escape part of the fine, diluting deterrence. The fine therefore should be imposed on the principal rather than on the agent (or at least the part of the fine that the agent cannot pay).

A closely related point is that the imposition of imprisonment sanctions on agents may be desirable when their assets are less than the harm that they can cause, even if the principal's assets are sufficient to pay the optimal fine (Polinsky and Shavell, 1993). That an agent's assets are limited means that the principal may be unable to control him adequately through the use of contractually determined penalties, which can only be monetary. In such circumstances it may be socially valuable to use the threat of a jail sentence to better control agents' misconduct.

Settlements

It is common for lawbreakers to settle with public enforcement authorities prior to being found liable in a trial. (In the criminal context, the settlement usually takes the form of a plea bargain, an agreement in which the injurer pleads guilty to a reduced charge.) Both parties might prefer an out-of-court settlement to avoid the cost of a trial and to eliminate the risks inherent in the trial outcome (Cooter and Rubinfeld, 1989; on plea bargaining, see Reinganum, 1988, and Miceli, 1996).

These advantages suggest that settlement is socially valuable, but the effect of settlement on deterrence is a complicating factor. Specifically, settlements dilute deterrence: for if injurers desire to settle, it must be because the expected disutility of sanctions is lowered for them (Polinsky and Rubinfeld, 1988). The state may be able to offset this effect by increasing the level of sanctions.

Settlements may have other socially undesirable consequences. First, they may result in sanctions that are not as well tailored to harmful acts as would be true of court-determined sanctions. For example, if injurers have private information about the harm that they have caused, settlements will tend to reflect the average harm caused, resulting in high-harm (low-harm) injurers being under-deterred (over-deterred), whereas trial outcomes may better approximate the actual harm. Second, settlements hinder the amplification and development of the law through the setting of precedents. Third, if the sanction is imprisonment and defendants are risk averse, settlements necessitate longer terms than the expected sentence at trial in order to maintain deterrence, and thus increase public expenditures. On the social welfare evaluation of settlement, see, for example, Shavell (1997) and Spier (1997).

Self-reporting

We have assumed that individuals are subject to sanctions only if they are detected by an enforcement agent, but in fact parties sometimes disclose their own violations. For example, firms often report infractions of environmental and safety regulations, individuals usually notify police of their involvement in traffic accidents, and even criminals occasionally turn themselves in.

Self-reporting can be induced by lowering the sanction for individuals who disclose their own violations (Kaplow and Shavell, 1994b). Moreover, the reward for self-reporting can be made small, so that deterrence is only negligibly reduced. For example, if a risk-neutral individual commits a violation and does not self-report, his expected fine is pf. If he self-reports, the fine can be set just below pf, say at $pf - \varepsilon$, where $\varepsilon > 0$ is small. Then the individual will want to self-report but the deterrent effect of the sanction will be essentially the same as if he did not self-report.

There are several social advantages of self-reporting. First, self-reporting reduces enforcement costs because the enforcement authority does not have to identify and prove who the violator was. Second, self-reporting reduces risk (a relatively high sanction imposed with a relatively low probability is replaced by a certain punishment), and thus is advantageous if injurers are risk averse. Third, self-reporting may allow harm to be mitigated (early notice of an oil spill may facilitate its containment).

Repeat offenders

In practice, the law often sanctions repeat offenders more severely than first-time offenders. This policy cannot be socially advantageous if deterrence always induces first-best behaviour. For if the expected sanction for an offence equals its harm, then raising the sanction because an offender has a record of sanctions would over-deter him. Only if deterrence is inadequate is it possibly desirable to condition sanctions on offence history to increase deterrence. But, as we observed above, it usually will be worthwhile for the state to tolerate some under-deterrence in order to reduce enforcement expenses.

If there is under-deterrence, making sanctions depend on offence history may be beneficial. First, the use of offence history may create an additional incentive not to violate the law: if detection results not only in an immediate sanction but also in a higher sanction for any future violation, an individual will, everything else equal, be deterred to a greater extent (Polinsky and Shavell, 1998). Second, making sanctions depend on offence history allows society to take advantage of information about the dangerousness of individuals and the need to deter them: individuals with offence histories may be more likely than average to commit future violations, which might make it desirable to impose higher sanctions on them (Rubinstein, 1979; Polinsky and Rubinfeld, 1991). In addition, if repeat offenders have higher propensities to commit violations, they are more likely to be worth incapacitating by imprisonment (see below).

Imperfect knowledge about the probability and magnitude of sanctions

Individuals might not know the true probability of a sanction because the enforcement authority refrains from publishing information about the probability (perhaps hoping that individuals will believe it to be higher than it is in fact); or because the probability depends on factors that individuals do not fully understand; or because probabilities are difficult to assess. Also, individuals may have incomplete knowledge of the true magnitude of sanctions, particularly if the levels of sanctions are discretionary.

The implications of injurers' imperfect knowledge are straightforward. First, to predict how individuals behave, what is relevant, of course, is not the actual probability and magnitude of a sanction but the perceived levels or distributions of these variables. Second, to determine the optimal probability and magnitude of a sanction, account must be taken of the relationship between the actual and the perceived variables (Bebchuk and Kaplow, 1992; Kaplow, 1990). For example, if enforcement resources are increased in order to raise the probability of detection, there might be a delay before this increase is perceived by individuals, making such an investment less worthwhile.

Incapacitation

Society may reduce harm not only through deterrence, but also by imposing sanctions that remove parties from positions in which they are able to cause harm, that is, by incapacitating them. Imprisonment is the primary incapacitative sanction, although there are other examples: individuals can lose their driver's licences, businesses can lose their rights to operate in certain markets, and the like.

Suppose that the sole function of imprisonment is to incapacitate. Then it will be desirable to keep someone imprisoned as long as the reduction in criminal harm from incapacitating him exceeds the cost of imprisonment (Shavell, 1987c). Although this condition could hold for a long period, it often will not because the proclivity to commit crimes appears to decline sharply with age.

As a matter of economic logic, the incapacitation rationale might imply that a person should be imprisoned even if he has not committed a crime, because the danger he poses to society makes incapacitating him worthwhile. In practice, however, the commission of a harmful act may be a good basis for predicting a person's future behaviour, in which case the incapacitation rationale would suggest imprisoning an individual only if he has committed such an act.

Two observations are worth noting about the relationship between the incapacitation goal and the deterrence goal. First, when enforcement is based on incapacitation, the optimal magnitude of the sanction is independent of the probability of apprehension, which contrasts with the case when enforcement is based on deterrence. Second, when enforcement is deterrence-oriented, the probability and magnitude of sanctions depend on the ability to deter, and if this ability is limited (as, for instance, with the insane), a low expected sanction may be optimal, whereas a high sanction still might be called for to incapacitate.

Corruption

One form of corruption in the enforcement process is bribery, in which an enforcer accepts a payment in return for not reporting a violation (or for reducing the mandated sanction for the violation). A second form of corruption is framing and framing-related extortion, in which an enforcement agent may frame an innocent individual or threaten to frame him in order to extort money from him. On corruption of law enforcement, see Bowles and Garoupa (1997) and Polinsky and Shavell (2001) (and on corruption more generally, see, for example, Shleifer and Vishny, 1993, and Rose-Ackerman, 1999).

Bribery dilutes deterrence of violations of law because it results in a lower payment by an individual than the sanction for the offence. Framing and framing-related extortion also dilute deterrence. The reason is that framing and extortion imply that those who act innocently face an expected sanction, so that the difference between the expected sanction if an individual commits a violation and if he does not is lessened. (This point is essentially the same as the earlier observation that mistaken convictions dilute deterrence.)

One way to reduce corruption is to impose fines (or imprisonment sentences) on individuals caught engaging in bribery, extortion or framing. Corruption also can be reduced by paying enforcers rewards for reporting violations. Such payments will reduce their incentive to accept bribes because they will sacrifice their rewards if they fail to report violations. But high rewards give enforcers a greater incentive to frame innocent individuals. A third way to control corruption is to pay enforcers more than their reservation wage (that is, to pay them an efficiency wage). Then they would have more to lose if punished for corrupt behaviour and denied future employment.

A natural question is whether the deterrence-diluting effects of corruption can be offset by raising the fine on offenders. In the basic risk-neutral model of enforcement, it is not possible to raise the fine because the optimal fine is maximal. More realistically, however, the optimal fine is less than maximal for a variety of reasons, including those related to risk aversion, marginal deterrence, and general enforcement. While it would then be possible to raise the fine to offset the deterrence-diluting effects of corruption, doing so would lead to social costs (for example, by imposing greater risk).

Costly observation of wealth

Individuals and firms may be able to hide assets from government enforcers, including by hoarding cash, transferring assets to relatives or related legal entities, or moving money to offshore bank accounts. Consequently, an individual's level of wealth might not be able to be observed at all, or only after a costly audit.

Suppose first that the enforcement authority employs fines as sanctions and can audit an individual who claims that he cannot pay the fine (Polinsky, 2006). The optimal fine for misrepresenting one's wealth level equals the fine for the offence divided by the audit probability, and therefore generally exceeds the fine for the offence. This is a natural generalization of the formula for the optimal fine when the probability of detection is fixed, which is the harm divided by the probability. Auditing is valuable because it reduces misrepresentation of wealth and thereby increases deterrence.

Next, suppose that the enforcement authority cannot observe wealth because the cost of an audit is prohibitively high (Levitt, 1997; Polinsky, 2006). The authority would have used fines alone if it could have observed wealth at no cost, it would have imposed a higher fine on higher-wealth individuals. It obviously cannot do this when wealth is unobservable. Instead, it may be desirable to use the threat of an imprisonment sentence to induce individuals capable of paying a higher fine to do so. Alternatively, the enforcement authority might have used both fines and imprisonment if it could have observed wealth at no cost. Perhaps surprisingly, the inability to observe wealth might not be detrimental in this case. The reason is that the mix of fines and imprisonment that would be chosen when wealth is observable might impose a higher burden (though a lower fine) on low-wealth individuals. Then, high-wealth individuals will naturally want to identify themselves. Specifically, they will prefer to pay a higher fine and bear a shorter imprisonment sentence than to masquerade as low-wealth individuals, who will bear longer imprisonment sentences and a higher overall burden.

Social norms

To some extent, social norms and morality are substitutes for public law enforcement because they encourage in significant ways the attainment of desired behaviour (McAdams and Rasmusen, 2007; Posner, 1997; Shavell, 2002). Social norms influence behaviour partly through internal incentives: when a person obeys a moral rule, he will tend to feel virtuous, and if he disobeys the rule, he will tend to feel guilty. Social norms also affect behaviour through external incentives: when a person is observed by another party to have obeyed a moral rule, that party may bestow praise on the first party, who will enjoy the praise; and if the person is observed by the other party to have disobeyed the rule, the second party will tend to disapprove of the first party, who will dislike the disapproval. Because social norms channel behaviour in this way, some socially desirable conduct can be encouraged reasonably well without employing the legal system.

Notwithstanding these observations, there will, of course, often be a need for formal law enforcement. First, much conduct that society desires cannot be controlled through moral incentives alone. One reason is that the private gains from undesirable conduct are often large and dominate the moral incentives. Another reason is that external moral sanctions might be imposed only with a low probability (the robber, tax cheat or polluter might not be spotted by others). A second rationale of formal law enforcement is that the social harm from failing to control an act through moral incentives may be large. This makes the expense of law enforcement worth incurring (as in the case of controlling robbery, but not of breaking into a queue at a movie theatre).

Fairness

So far we have not considered the possibility that individuals have opinions about the fairness of sanctions or the arbitrariness of enforcement (Polinsky and Shavell, 2000b; Kaplow and Shavell, 2002). Suppose, first, that individuals believe that the magnitude of sanctions should reflect the gravity of the acts. As discussed previously, if individuals are risk neutral, the usual solution to the enforcement problem consists of the highest possible sanction and a relatively low probability of detection. When the issue of fairness is added to the analysis, however, the usual solution generally is not optimal because a very high sanction will be seen as unfair.

A consequence of the desire to keep sanctions at fair levels, meaning at quite constrained levels for acts that are not very harmful, is that the socially optimal probability of detection changes. The optimal probability could be higher than the conventionally optimal probability: to achieve a desired level of deterrence with a lower fairness-restricted sanction, the probability has to rise, perhaps significantly. Alternatively, the optimal probability could be lower than in the conventional case: the additional deterrence from raising the probability might be relatively low because the sanction is relatively low; and the lower the deterrent benefit from raising the probability, the lower would be the social incentive to devote resources to enforcement.

Another aspect of fairness concerns the probability of detection rather than the magnitude of sanctions. Suppose that individuals consider it unfair for some law-breakers to be sanctioned when others, who were lucky enough not to be caught, are not sanctioned. Then the optimal probability would be higher, and therefore the optimal sanction would be lower, than in the absence of this fairness concern.

A further notion of fairness involves the form of liability, whether liability is strict or based on fault. Individuals might prefer fault-based liability because sanctions are imposed on parties only if they behaved in a socially inappropriate way.

A final issue concerns the relevance of fairness considerations when firms, as opposed to individuals, are sanctioned. If what matters in terms of fairness is that the individuals responsible for harmful acts bear sanctions, as opposed to the artificial legal entity of a firm, one would want to identify the sanctions actually suffered by such persons within a firm if the firm bears a sanction. Note, too, that the imposition of sanctions on firms often penalizes individuals who are unlikely to be considered responsible for the harm, namely, shareholders and customers.

Criminal law

The subject of criminal law may be viewed in the light of the theory of public law enforcement (Posner, 1985; Shavell, 1985). First, the fact that the acts in the core area of crime (robbery, murder, rape, and so forth) are punished by the sanction of imprisonment makes basic sense. Were society to rely on fines alone, deterrence of the acts in question would be grossly inadequate. This is because the probability of detecting many of these acts is low, making the money sanction necessary for deterrence high, but the assets of individuals who commit these acts often are insubstantial. Hence, the threat of prison is needed for deterrence. Moreover, the incapacitative aspect of imprisonment is valuable because of the difficulty of deterring individuals who are prone to commit criminal acts.

Second, many of the doctrines of criminal law appear to enhance social welfare. This seems true of the basic feature of criminal law that punishment is not imposed on all harmful acts, but instead is usually confined to those that are especially undesirable. (For example, murder is subject to criminal sanctions, but some accidental killing is not.) As we have stressed, when the socially costly sanction of imprisonment is employed, the fault system is desirable because it results in less frequent imposition of punishment than strict liability. Also, the focus on intent in criminal law as a precondition for imposing sanctions may serve to foster deterrence because those who intend to do harm are more likely to conceal their acts, and may be harder to discourage because of the benefits they anticipate. An additional example of a welfare-enhancing doctrine in criminal law concerns attempts. That attempts to do harm are punished is an implicit way of raising the likelihood of sanctions for undesirable acts.

A. MITCHELL POLINSKY AND STEVEN SHAVELL

See also **deterrence (theory), economics of; externalities; law, economic analysis of; pecuniary versus non-pecuniary penalties.**

A. Mitchell Polinsky's research was supported by the John M. Olin Program in Law and Economics at Stanford Law School. Steven Shavell's research was supported by the John M. Olin Center for Law, Economics, and Business at Harvard Law School.

Bibliography

Arlen, J. 1994. The potentially perverse effects of corporate criminal liability. *Journal of Legal Studies* 23, 833–67.

Bebchuk, L. and Kaplow, L. 1992. Optimal sanctions when individuals are imperfectly informed about the probability of apprehension. *Journal of Legal Studies* 21, 365–70.

Becker, G. 1968. Crime and punishment: an economic approach. *Journal of Political Economy* 76, 169–217.

Becker, G. and Stigler, G. 1974. Law enforcement, malfeasance, and compensation of enforcers. *Journal of Legal Studies* 3, 1–18.

Bentham, J. 1789. An Introduction to the Principles of Morals and Legislation. In The Utilitarians, Garden City, NY: Anchor Books, 1973.

Block, M. and Sidak, J. 1980. The cost of antitrust deterrence: why not hang a price fixer now and then? *Georgetown Law Journal* 68, 1131–9.

Bowles, R. and Garoupa, N. 1997. Casual police corruption and the economics of crime. *International Review of Law and Economics* 17, 75–87.

Cooter, R. and Rubinfeld, D. 1989. Economic analysis of legal disputes and their resolution. *Journal of Economic Literature* 27, 1067–97.

Craswell, R. and Calfee, J.E. 1986. Deterrence and uncertain legal standards. *Journal of Law, Economics, & Organization* 2, 279–303.

Kaplow, L. 1990. Optimal deterrence, uninformed individuals, and acquiring information about whether acts are subject to sanctions. *Journal of Law, Economics, & Organization* 6, 93–128.

Kaplow, L. 1992. The optimal probability and magnitude of fines for acts that definitely are undesirable. *International Review of Law and Economics* 12, 3–11.

Kaplow, L. and Shavell, S. 1994a. Accuracy in the determination of liability. *Journal of Law and Economics* 37, 1–15.

Kaplow, L. and Shavell, S. 1994b. Optimal law enforcement with self–reporting of behavior. *Journal of Political Economy* 102, 583–606.

Kaplow, L. and Shavell, S. 2002. *Fairness versus Welfare*. Cambridge, MA: Harvard University Press.

Kornhauser, L. 1982. An economic analysis of the choice between enterprise and personal liability for accidents. *California Law Review* 70, 1345–92.

Landes, W. and Posner, R. 1975. The private enforcement of law. *Journal of Legal Studies* 4, 1–46.

Landes, W. and Posner, R. 1987. *The Economic Structure of Tort Law*. Cambridge, MA: Harvard University Press.

Levitt, S. 1997. Incentive compatibility constraints as an explanation for the use of prison sentences instead of fines. *International Review of Law and Economics* 17, 179–92.

McAdams, R. and Rasmusen, E. 2007. Norms in law and economics. In *Handbook of Law and Economics*, vol. 2, ed. A. Polinsky and S. Shavell. Amsterdam: North-Holland.

Miceli, T. 1996. Plea bargaining and deterrence: an institutional approach. *European Journal of Law and Economics* 3, 249–64.

Mookherjee, D. and Png, I. 1992. Monitoring vis-à-vis investigation in enforcement of law. *American Economic Review* 82, 556–65.

Mookherjee, D. and Png, I. 1994. Marginal deterrence in enforcement of law. *Journal of Political Economy* 102, 1039–66.

Newman, H. and Wright, D. 1990. Strict liability in a principal–agent model. *International Review of Law and Economics* 10, 219–31.

Png, I. 1986. Optimal subsidies and damages in the presence of judicial error. *International Review of Law and Economics* 6, 101–5.

Polinsky, A. 1980a. Private versus public enforcement of fines. *Journal of Legal Studies* 9, 105–27.

Polinsky, A. 1980b. Strict liability vs. negligence in a market setting. *American Economic Review* 70, 363–70.

Polinsky, A. 2006. The optimal use of fines and imprisment when wealth is unobservable. *Journal of Public Economics* 90, 823–35.

Polinsky, A. 2006. Optimal fines and auditing when wealth is costly to observe. *International Review of Law and Economics* 26, 232–35.

Polinsky, A. and Rubinfeld, D. 1988. The deterrent effects of settlements and trials. *International Review of Law and Economics* 8, 109–16.

Polinsky, A. and Rubinfeld, D. 1991. A model of optimal fines for repeat offenders. *Journal of Public Economics* 46, 291–306.

Polinsky, A. and Shavell, S. 1979. The optimal tradeoff between the probability and magnitude of fines. *American Economic Review* 69, 880–91.

Polinsky, A. and Shavell, S. 1984. The optimal use of fines and imprisonment. *Journal of Public Economics* 24, 89–99.

Polinsky, A. and Shavell, S. 1992. Enforcement costs and the optimal magnitude and probability of fines. *Journal of Law and Economics* 35, 133–48.

Polinsky, A. and Shavell, S. 1993. Should employees be subject to fines and imprisonment given the existence of corporate liability? *International Review of Law and Economics* 13, 239–57.

Polinsky, A. and Shavell, S. 1998. On offense history and the theory of deterrence. *International Review of Law and Economics* 18, 305–24.

Polinsky, A. and Shavell, S. 1999. On the disutility and discounting of imprisonment and the theory of deterrence. *Journal of Legal Studies* 28, 1–16.

Polinsky, A. and Shavell, S. 2000a. The economic theory of public enforcement of law. *Journal of Economic Literature* 38, 45–76.

Polinsky, A. and Shavell, S. 2000b. The fairness of sanctions: some implications for optimal enforcement policy. *American Law and Economics Review* 2, 223–37.

Polinsky, A. and Shavell, S. 2001. Corruption and optimal law enforcement. *Journal of Public Economics* 81, 1–24.

Polinsky, A. and Shavell, S. 2007. The theory of public enforcement of law. In *Handbook of Law and Economics*, vol. 1, ed. A. Polinsky and S. Shavell. Amsterdam: North-Holland.

Posner, R. 1985. An economic theory of the criminal law. *Columbia Law Review* 85, 1193–231.

Posner, R. 1997. Social norms and the law: an economic approach. *American Economic Review: Papers and Proceedings* 87, 365–9.

Reinganum, J. 1988. Plea bargaining and prosecutorial discretion. *American Economic Review* 78, 713–28.

Rose-Ackerman, S. 1999. *Corruption and Government: Causes, Consequences and Reform*. New York: Cambridge University Press.

Rubinstein, A. 1979. An optimal conviction policy for offenses that may have been committed by accident. In *Applied Game Theory*, ed. S. Brams, A. Schotter and G. Schwodiauer. Wurzburg: Physica-Verlag.

Shavell, S. 1980. Strict liability versus negligence. *Journal of Legal Studies* 9, 1–25.

Shavell, S. 1982. On liability and insurance. *Bell Journal of Economics* 13, 120–32.

Shavell, S. 1985. Criminal law and the optimal use of nonmonetary sanctions as a deterrent. *Columbia Law Review* 85, 1232–62.

Shavell, S. 1987a. The optimal use of nonmonetary sanctions as a deterrent. *American Economic Review* 77, 584–92.

Shavell, S. 1987b. A model of optimal incapacitation. *American Economic Review: Papers and Proceedings* 77, 107–10.

Shavell, S. 1987c. *Economic Analysis of Accident Law*. Cambridge, MA: Harvard University Press.

Shavell, S. 1991. Specific versus general enforcement of law. *Journal of Political Economy* 99, 1088–108.

Shavell, S. 1992. A note on marginal deterrence. *International Review of Law and Economics* 12, 345–55.

Shavell, S. 1993. The optimal structure of law enforcement. *Journal of Law and Economics* 36, 255–87.

Shavell, S. 1997. The fundamental divergence between the private and the social motive to use the legal system. *Journal of Legal Studies* 26, 575–612.

Shavell, S. 2002. Law versus morality as regulators of conduct. *American Law and Economics Review* 4, 227–57.

Shleifer, A. and Vishny, R. 1993. Corruption. *Quarterly Journal of Economics* 108, 599–617.

Spier, K. 1997. A note on the divergence between the private and the social motive to settle under a negligence rule. *Journal of Legal Studies* 26, 613–21.

Stigler, G. 1970. The optimum enforcement of laws. *Journal of Political Economy* 78, 526–36.

Sykes, A. 1981. An efficiency analysis of vicarious liability under the law of agency. *Yale Law Journal* 91, 168–206.

Wilde, L. 1992. Criminal choice, nonmonetary sanctions, and marginal deterrence: a normative analysis. *International Review of Law and Economics* 12, 333–44.

layoffs

The term 'layoff' is controversial in itself. For some the term connotes a temporary employer-initiated discharge, for others it represents any employer-initiated discharge that is without prejudice to the worker. The data on layoffs collected by the Bureau of Labor Statistics (BLS) in the United States (see, for example, various issues of the journal *Employment and Earnings*) takes the alternative types of layoffs into account across its firm and household surveys. Layoff data from the BLS survey of firms (the Job Openings and Labor Turnover Survey, JOLTS) provide data on employer-initiated discharges making no distinction as to whether the layoff is temporary or permanent. According to JOLTS, layoffs average about 1.1 per cent of US non-farm employment each month, which is about one-third of all worker separations. The BLS survey of households (the Current Population Survey, CPS) distinguishes between 'temporary layoffs' and 'permanent job losers' in tracking unemployment, where the former are layoffs for which recall is expected within six months and the latter are layoffs where employment ended involuntarily and the workers have begun looking for work. According to the CPS, about 50 per cent of all unemployed are classified as job losers and temporary layoffs account for one-third of the job losers.

The controversy over the terminology is dwarfed by the controversy over the occurrence of layoffs. When General Motors announces that it is laying off 20,000 of its workers indefinitely there is widespread press coverage. This attention is well deserved since substantial variation in layoffs (both temporary and permanent) is frequently observed, and layoffs play an important role in cyclical unemployment. Empirical studies of unemployment (for example, Davis, Haltiwanger and Schuh, 1996; Bleakley, Ferris and Fuhrer, 1999) indicate that the typical increase in unemployment during a business cycle slump is primarily due to an increase in employer-initiated discharges, that is, layoffs. For example, in the sharp 1982 recession in the USA, the fraction of the unemployed due to job loss peaked at 63 per cent while in the 2001 recession this fraction peaked at 56 per cent.

The increase in layoff unemployment during recessions is closely tied to the increase in gross job destruction in recessions. Davis, Haltiwanger and Schuh (1996) show that job destruction rises substantially during recessions and is increasingly driven by establishments contracting substantially (for example, with contractions greater than 25 per cent). In turn, Davis, Faberman and Haltiwanger (2006) show that establishments that are contracting intensively use layoffs as the primary means of contraction.

The structure of temporary and permanent layoffs over the cycle has varied over time. Groshen and Potter (2003) show that, in the four recessions in the USA between 1967 and 1990, both temporary layoff and permanent layoff unemployed surged in each of the recessions. However, starting with the 1990–1 recessions, temporary layoffs have played a much smaller role and the rise in job loss has been driven almost entirely by permanent layoffs.

The theory of layoff unemployment has evolved with the relative importance of temporary versus permanent layoffs. Given the important role for temporary layoffs in the 1970s, the so-called 'implicit contract models' (see, for example, Azariadis, 1975; Baily, 1974; and Burdett and Mortensen, 1980) were developed during that time to help account for the role of temporary layoffs. The temporary layoff models provide a basis for understanding how in a long-term employer–employee relationship it may be optimal for firms and workers to use temporary layoffs to respond to transitory shocks. However, the increased understanding and role of permanent job destruction and associated permanent job loss has pushed theoretical developments in new directions.

Recent theories that incorporate the evidence on permanent job destruction adopt the premise that the economy is subject to a continuous stream of allocative shocks – shocks that cause idiosyncratic variation in profitability among job sites and worker–job matches (see Davis and Haltiwanger, 1999; Mortensen and Pissarides, 1999; and Shimer, Rogerson and Wright, 2005 for an extensive survey of these theories). The continuous stream of allocative shocks generates the large-scale job and worker reallocation observed in the data. To explicitly model the job and worker reallocation process, these theories incorporate heterogeneity among workers and firms along one or more dimensions. Various theories also emphasize search costs, moving costs, sunk investments and other frictions that impede or otherwise distort the reallocation of factor inputs. The combination of frictions and heterogeneity gives rise to potentially important roles for allocative shocks and the reallocation process in aggregate economic fluctuations.

Theories of cyclical fluctuations in job and worker flows with such reallocation frictions can be classified into two broad types. One type treats fluctuations over time in the intensity of allocative shocks as an important driving force behind aggregate fluctuations and the pace of reallocation activity. A second type maintains that while allocative shocks and reallocation frictions are important, aggregate shocks drive business cycles and fluctuations in the pace of worker and job reallocation. Although different in emphasis, the two types of theories offer complementary views of labour market dynamics and business cycles, and both point toward a rich set of interactions between aggregate fluctuations and the reallocation process.

One can think of allocative shocks as events that alter the closeness of the match between the desired and actual characteristics of labour and capital inputs. Adverse aggregate consequences can result from such events because of the time and other costs of reallocation activity. In considering this view, it is important to emphasize that allocative shocks affect tangible inputs to the production process (labour and physical capital) and intangible inputs. These intangible inputs include the information capital embodied in an efficient sorting and matching of heterogeneous workers and jobs, knowledge about how to work productively with co-workers, knowledge about suitable locations for particular business activities and about idiosyncratic attributes of those locations, the information capital embodied in long-term customer–supplier and debtor–creditor relationships, and the organization capital embodied in sales, product distribution and job-finding networks. These remarks make clear why the economic adjustments to these

shocks are often costly and time consuming. It follows that sharp time variation in the intensity of allocative shocks can cause large fluctuations in gross job flows and in turn unemployment dynamics and layoffs in particular.

The connection between cyclical fluctuations in job destruction and layoffs may also stem from responses to adverse aggregate shocks. An adverse aggregate shock can push many declining and dying plants over an adjustment threshold. During boom times, a firm may choose to continue operating a plant that fails to recover its long-run average cost, because short-run revenues exceed short-run costs, or because of a sufficiently large option value to retaining the plant and its work force. A closely related mechanism emphasizes the changes in the incentives for reallocation over the cycle. The reallocation of specialized labour and capital inputs involves forgone production due to lost work time (for example, unemployment or additional schooling), worker retraining, the retooling of plant and equipment, the adoption of new technology, and the organization of new patterns of production and distribution. On average across firms and workers, the value of forgone production tends to fluctuate procyclically, rising during expansions and falling during recessions. This cyclical pattern generates incentives for both workers and firms to concentrate costly reallocation activity during recessions, when the opportunity cost of the resulting forgone production is relatively low. This mechanism is highlighted in the models of Davis and Haltiwanger (1999), Mortensen and Pissarides (1994) and Caballero and Hammour (1994).

A key question is whether the cyclical fluctuations in job destruction and layoffs reflect efficient or inefficient responses to shocks. Caballero and Hammour (1996) highlight the potential for labour markets to malfunction because of appropriability or hold-up problems. These problems arise whenever investment in a new production unit or the formation of a new employment relationship involves some degree of specificity for workers or employers, and there are difficulties in writing or enforcing complete contracts. In their model, Caballero and Hammour (1996) show that efficient restructuring involves synchronized job creation and destruction and relatively little unemployment. In contrast, the inefficient equilibrium restructuring process that emerges under incomplete contracts involves the decoupling of creation and destruction dynamics and relatively large unemployment responses to negative shocks. As discussed in Mortensen and Pissarides (1999), appropriability problems arise naturally in many search and matching models. Malcomson (1999) provides a broad discussion of hold-up problems in the labour market.

Overall, understanding layoffs requires understanding of the underlying dynamics of job and worker reallocation. New theories and new data sets have emerged that provide a rich new perspective on the dynamics of the labour market at the micro level and in turn the implications of these dynamics for aggregate fluctuations. Much work remains to be done on both theoretical and empirical questions, particularly on understanding the role of market imperfections in these dynamics. Along these lines, one continuing open question is not only to understand the driving forces of job loss but also the closely related forces of the job gains. After all, the loss of a job has much lower costs to the individual and the economy if the worker in question moves quickly to another job.

JOHN HALTIWANGER

See also **natural rate of unemployment; search models of unemployment.**

Bibliography

Ashenfelter, O. and Card, D., eds. 1999. *Handbook of Labor Economics*. Amsterdam: North-Holland.

Azariadis, C. 1975. Implicit contracts and underemployment equilibria. *Journal of Political Economy* 83, 1183–202.

Baily, M.N. 1974. Wages and employment under uncertain demand. *Review of Economic Studies* 41, 37–50.

Bleakley, H., Ferris, A. and Fuhrer, J. 1999. New data on worker flows during business cycles. *Federal Reserve Bank of Boston Review* July/August, 49–76.

Burdett, L. and Mortensen, D. 1980. Search, layoffs, and labor market equilibrium. *Journal of Political Economy* 88, 652–72.

Bureau of Labor Statistics. Current Population Survey. Online. Available at http://www.census.gov/cps, accessed 8 March 2007.

Bureau of Labour Statistics. Job Openings and Labor Turnover Survey. Online. Available at http://www.bls.gov/jlt, accessed 8 Match 2007.

Caballero, R. and Hammour, M. 1994. The cleansing effect of recessions. *American Economic Review* 84, 1350–68.

Caballero, R. and Hammour, M. 1996. On the timing and efficiency of creative destruction. *Quarterly Journal of Economics* 111, 805–52.

Davis, S.J., Haltiwanger, J. and Schuh, S. 1996. *Job Creation and Destruction*. Cambridge, MA: MIT Press.

Davis, S.J. and Haltiwanger, J. 1999. Gross job flows. In Ashenfelter and Card (1999).

Davis, S.J., Faberman, J. and Haltiwanger, J. 2006. The flow approach to labor markets: new data sources and micro-macro links. *Journal of Economic Perspectives* 20(3), 3–26.

Groshen, E. and Potter, S. 2003. Has structural change contributed to a jobless recovery? *Current Issues in Economics and Finance* 9(8), 1–7.

Malcomson, J.M. 1999. Individual employment contracts. In Ashenfelter and Card (1999).

Mortensen, D.T. and Pissarides, C. 1994. Job creation and job destruction in the theory of unemployment. *Review of Economic Studies* 61, 397–415.

Mortensen, D.T. and Pissarides, C. 1999. New developments in models of search in the labor market. In Ashenfelter and Card (1999).

Shimer, R., Rogerson, R. and Wright, R. 2005. Search theoretic models of the labor market. *Journal of Economic Literature* 43, 959–88.

U.S. Department of Labor. 2007. *Employment and Earnings*, various issues, Washington, DC: Government Printing Office.

Le Chatelier principle

Henri Louis Le Chatelier was a French chemist born in Paris in 1850. In 1884, he offered the following observation:

> Any system in stable chemical equilibrium, subjected to the influence of an external cause which tends to change either its temperature or its condensation (pressure, concentration, number of molecules in unit volume), either as a whole or in some of its parts, can only undergo such internal modifications as would, if produced alone, bring about a change of temperature or of condensation of opposite sign to that resulting from the external cause. (Oliver and Kurtz, 1992)

Later writers produced a more heuristic simplification: 'If the external conditions…are altered, the equilibrium … will tend to move in such a direction so as to oppose the change in external conditions' (Fermi, 1937, p. 111, cited in Samuelson, 1949, p. 639), or even more simply: if a stress is applied to a system at equilibrium, then the system readjusts, if possible, to reduce the stress. The Le Chatelier principle is a firmly established proposition in classical thermodynamics, though its verbal statement is somewhat vague in operational content. In the field of economics, the law of demand, which states that as a price increases, ceteris paribus, consumers will decrease their consumption of that good, is in fact a direct application of the Le Chatelier principle. Consumers (or firms) mitigate the adverse effects of the price increase by utilizing less of that good or input.

Following up a suggestion by his professor and mentor E.B. Wilson at Harvard, Paul Samuelson showed that this principle was a simple application of maximizing behaviour (see especially Samuelson, 1949; 1960a; 1974.) Moreover, physicists and economists – among economists, principally Samuelson – came to realize that the Le Chatelier principle was being used to describe two separate phenomena. The first referred to first-order changes in response to a change in a parameter value, such as a price. The second, which is what the Le Chatelier principle is now generally understood to mean, refers to *differences* in the changes as additional constraints are imposed on the system.

The general case
First-order effects
The most general comparative statics model with explicit maximizing behaviour is *maximize y = f(x, α)* subject to

$g(x, \alpha) = 0$, where $x(x_1, \ldots, x_n)$ is a vector of decision variables, $\alpha = (\alpha_1, \ldots, \alpha_m)$ is a vector of parameters (though for simplicity, we treat α as a scalar in the discussion below), and $g(\cdot)$ represents one or more constraints. Models at this level of generality, however, imply no refutable implications and are hence largely uninteresting. In particular, there are never refutable implications for parameters that enter the constraint (see, for example, Silberberg and Suen, 2000). Thus we restrict the analysis to models of the form

$$\text{maximize } y = f(x, \alpha) \qquad (1)$$

$$\text{subject to } g(x) = 0. \qquad (2)$$

Since it has no effect on the analysis to follow, we consider the case of only one external constraint. Also, parameters β, which enter the constraint but which do not enter the objective function, also do not affect the analysis, and hence we suppress them in the notation. The Lagrangian for this model is $L = f(x, \alpha) + \lambda g(x)$ producing the necessary first-order conditions (NFOC)

$$L_i = f_i(x, \alpha) + \lambda g_i(x) = 0 \quad i = 1, \ldots, n \qquad (3)$$

$$L_\lambda = g(x) = 0 \qquad (4)$$

Assuming the sufficient second-order conditions hold, we can in principle 'solve' for the $n + 1$ explicit choice functions $x = x^*(\alpha)$ and $\lambda^*(\alpha)$. Of course, since these choice functions are the result of solving the NFOC simultaneously, each individual x_i is a function of *all* the parameters, not just the ones which appear in L_i.

Substituting the x_i^*'s into the objective function yields the *indirect objective function* $\varphi(\alpha) = f(x^*(\alpha), \alpha)$, the maximum value of f for given α, subject to the constraint. Since $\varphi(\alpha)$ is by definition a maximum value, $\varphi(\alpha) \geq f(x, \alpha)$, but $\varphi(\alpha) = f(x, \alpha)$ when $x = x^*$. Thus the function $F(x, \alpha) = f(x, \alpha) - \varphi(\alpha)$ has a (constrained) maximum of zero, with respect to both x and α. Thus we consider the *primal-dual* model

$$\text{maximize } F(x, \alpha) = f(x, \alpha) - \varphi(\alpha) \qquad (5)$$

$$\text{subject to } g(x) = 0 \qquad (6)$$

where the maximization runs over x and also α. (In the latter instance, we ask, for given x_i's, what values of the parameters would make these x_i's the maximizing values?) The Lagrangian for this model is

$$L = f(x, \alpha) - \varphi(\alpha) + \lambda g(x) \qquad (7)$$

The first-order conditions with respect to x are the same as in the original model. With respect to α, the

NFOC yield the famous 'envelope theorem'

$$L_\alpha = f_\alpha - \varphi_\alpha = 0 \qquad (8)$$

When α enters the constraint also, we get the envelope theorem in its most general form,

$$\varphi_\alpha = L_\alpha = f_\alpha + \lambda g_\alpha \qquad (8a)$$

Importantly, however, since we have restricted the model so that the parameters α do not enter the constraint, the primal-dual model is *an unconstrained maximization in* α. Hence in the α dimensions, the second-order conditions are simply

$$F_{\alpha\alpha} = f_{\alpha\alpha} - \varphi_{\alpha\alpha} \leq 0. \qquad (9)$$

This inequality says that in the α dimensions, f is relatively more concave than φ. This is the fundamental geometrical property that underlies all comparative statics relationships and also the 'second-order' Le Chatelier relationships.

The NFOC (8) are identities when $x = x^*$. That is,

$$\varphi_\alpha(\alpha) \equiv f_\alpha(x^*(\alpha), \alpha) \qquad (10)$$

Differentiating with respect to α,

$$\varphi_{\alpha\alpha} \equiv \sum_1^n f_{\alpha i} \frac{\partial x_i^*}{\partial \alpha} + f_{\alpha\alpha} \qquad (11)$$

Rearranging terms, using (9) and invariance to the order of differentiation,

$$\varphi_{\alpha\alpha} - f_{\alpha\alpha} \equiv \sum_1^n f_{i\alpha} \frac{\partial x_i^*}{\partial \alpha} \geq 0 \qquad (12)$$

This is the fundamental relation of comparative statics. From it, we can derive Samuelson's famous 'conjugate pairs' theorem, namely, that refutable implications occur in maximization models when and only when a parameter enters one and only one first-order condition. For in that case, where say α enters only $L_i = 0$, $f_{j\alpha} \equiv 0$, $j \neq i$, and so (12) reduces to one term:

$$f_{i\alpha} \frac{\partial x_i^*}{\partial \alpha} \geq 0 \qquad (13)$$

In this case we can say that the response of x_i is in the same direction as the disturbance to the equilibrium (or, in the case of minimization models, in the opposite direction). These relationships constitute the 'first-order' Le Chatelier effects. Note that these results are identical to those in models with no constraints at all, or with multiple constraints, as long as those constraints do not contain the parameter that is changing.

Le Chatelier principle   51

Second-order effects

Suppose now the NFOC hold at the parameter value α^0 and consider now the imposition of an additional constraint, $h(x) = 0$, with the important restriction that this constraint does not change the original equilibrium, for example, a constraint holding some input fixed at the previous profit maximizing level. Then the new NFOC are solved for new explicit choice functions, $x_i = x_i^s(\alpha)$, where the superscript 's' stands for 'short run'. Substituting these short run choice functions into the objective function produces a new indirect objective function, $\psi(\alpha)$. Since the new constraint did not disturb the equilibrium, $\psi(\alpha^0) = \varphi(\alpha^0)$ at that point. However, since the objective function is now more constrained, for $\alpha \neq \alpha^0$, $\psi(\alpha) \leq \varphi(\alpha)$. Thus the function $G(\alpha) = \psi(\alpha) - \varphi(\alpha)$ has an unconstrained maximum (of zero) at $\alpha = \alpha^0$. The NFOC are

$$G_\alpha(\alpha) = \psi_\alpha(\alpha) - \varphi_\alpha(\alpha) = 0 \qquad (14)$$

We note that $\psi_\alpha(\alpha) = \varphi_\alpha(\alpha) = f_\alpha$ using the same analysis leading to eq. (8), since α appears in neither constraint. The second-order conditions are

$$G_{\alpha\alpha}(\alpha) = \psi_{\alpha\alpha}(\alpha) - \varphi_{\alpha\alpha}(\alpha) \leq 0 \qquad (15)$$

That is, the more constrained indirect objective function $\psi(\alpha)$ is tangent to $\varphi(\alpha)$ at $\alpha = \alpha^0$, but it is relatively more concave, or less convex. Using $\psi_\alpha(\alpha) \equiv \varphi_\alpha(\alpha) \equiv f_\alpha$ expressed as identities, and proceeding as in eqs. (10) through (12), inequality (15) yields the general second-order Le Chatelier effects:

$$\sum_1^n f_{i\alpha}\left(\frac{\partial x_i^*}{\partial \alpha} - \frac{\partial x_i^s}{\partial \alpha}\right) \geq 0 \qquad (16)$$

In the empirically important case where α enters only the ith first-order condition, this summation reduces to one term, producing

$$f_{i\alpha}\frac{\partial x_i^*}{\partial \alpha} \geq f_{i\alpha}\frac{\partial x_i^s}{\partial \alpha} \qquad (17)$$

Thus $\partial x_i^*/\partial \alpha \geq \partial x_i^s/\partial \alpha \geq 0$ when $f_{i\alpha} > 0$, and $\partial x_i^*/\partial \alpha \leq \partial x_i^s/\partial \alpha \leq 0$ when $f_{i\alpha} < 0$. In either case, $\left|\partial x_i^*/\partial \alpha\right| \geq \left|\partial x_i^s/\partial \alpha\right|$.

Examples

Profit maximization

Consider the profit-maximization model *maximize* $\pi = f(x, w, p) = p\theta(x_1 \ldots, x_n) - \sum w_i x_i$ Each parameter w_i enters only the ith NFOC, and $f_{x_i w_i} = -1$, so that (13) yields the negative slope property $\partial x_i/\partial w_i \leq 0$. Moreover, (17) yields, in addition, for any additional constraint (not involving w_i) imposed on the initial equilibrium,

$$\frac{\partial x_i^*}{\partial w_i} \leq \frac{\partial x_i^s}{\partial w_i} \leq 0 \qquad (18)$$

The 'long-run' factor demand functions are more elastic than any short-run factor demands defined as above.

In the case where the additional constraint is simply $x_n = x_n^0$, an analysis based on 'conditional demands' (Pollak, 1969) is available. If we substitute this constraint directly into the objective function, the 'short-run' demand functions are $x_i = x_i^s(w_1, \ldots w_{n-1}, p, x_n^0)$. These functions are related to the long-run demands by the identity

$$x_i^*(w_1, \ldots, w_n, p) \equiv x_i^s(w_1, \ldots w_{n-1},$$
$$p, x_n^*(w_1, \ldots, w_n, p)) \qquad (19)$$

Differentiating both sides of this identity with respect to w_i and w_n,

$$\frac{\partial x_i^*}{\partial w_i} \equiv \frac{\partial x_i^s}{\partial w_i} + \frac{\partial x_i^s}{\partial x_n^0}\frac{\partial x_n^*}{\partial w_i} \qquad (20)$$

$$\frac{\partial x_i^*}{\partial w_n} \equiv \frac{\partial x_i^s}{\partial x_n^0}\frac{\partial x_n^*}{\partial w_n} \qquad (21)$$

Substituting (21) into (20) and using a well-known reciprocity condition yields

$$\frac{\partial x_i^*}{\partial w_i} \equiv \frac{\partial x_i^s}{\partial w_i} + \frac{(\partial x_i^*/\partial w_n)^2}{\partial x_n^*/\partial w_n} \qquad (22)$$

Since the last term in (22) is negative, we get the Le Chatelier result (18).

Cost (expenditure) minimization

The cost functions in production theory are derived from the model, *minimize* $C = \sum w_i x_i$ subject to $f(x_1, \ldots, x_n) = y$, where y is now a parameter, that is, it is an arbitrary fixed level of output. This model is directly related to the profit maximization model. Write the profit maximization model as *maximize* $py - \sum w_i x_i$ subject to $f(x_1, \ldots, x_n) = y$. When output y is a variable, this model is the profit-maximization model. If y is parametric, it is the constrained cost minimization model. Thus we see that the cost minimization model is the profit maximization model with an added constraint. Denoting the factor demands derived from cost minimization as $x_i = x_i^y(w_1, w_n, y)$, we apply (13) and (17) to derive $\partial x_i^*/\partial w_i \leq \partial x_i^y/\partial w_i \leq 0$. The profit maximizing factor demand function, which incorporates an output effect, is always more elastic with respect to its own price than the constant output factor demand functions, regardless of whether the output effect is positive or negative. We can also show by this method that, if another constraint is imposed on the factors, these cost-minimizing demand functions become less elastic. When the additional constraint takes on the form of holding some factor fixed, as in the above profit-maximization model, a similar conditional demand process is available (see Silberberg and Suen, 2000).

Marginal cost functions

Many – perhaps most – important economic models incorporate a constraint of the form $g(x_1, \ldots, x_n) = k$. The cost minimization model is an example; so are the various two-factor two-good models in which endowment levels are fixed. The Lagrangian for the cost minimization model is $L = \sum w_i x_i + \lambda(y - f(x_1, \ldots, x_n))$. The indirect objective function is the cost function $C = C^*(w_1, \ldots, w_n, y)$. The envelope theorem (8a) identifies $\lambda^*(w_1, \ldots, w_n, y)$ as the marginal cost function: $C_y^* = \lambda^*$. We know from the above comparative statics discussion that cost minimization does not imply a sign for the slope of the marginal cost function, that is, $\partial \lambda^*/\partial y / 0 \rightarrow \partial \lambda^*/\partial y \gtreqless 0$. Nonetheless, we can still derive a Le Chatelier result for the marginal cost function.

Adding a new constraint $h(x) = 0$ to the cost minimization model consistent with the original equilibrium produces a new 'short run' cost function $C^s(w_1, \ldots w_n, y)$. Since this is more constrained than C^*, it must be the case that $C^* \leq C^s$, but the two are equal at the original equilibrium. Thus the function $F = C^* - C^s$ has an unconstrained maximum (of zero) with respect to all the parameters, and in particular, y. Thus $F_y = C_y^* - C_y^s = 0$ and $F_{yy} = C_{yy}^* - C_{yy}^s \leq 0$. But this latter inequality is $\partial \lambda^*/\partial y \leq \partial \lambda^s/\partial y$. That is, the long-run marginal cost function either falls faster or rises slower than the short-run marginal cost function. This is the mathematical foundation for the famous article by Viner (1932) and his draftsman Wong that started it all.

Extensions

The Le Chatelier principle is a local result. Even with the usual sufficient second-order conditions, if some price changes by a finite amount, it is not an implication of the model that the long-run effects are absolutely larger than the short-run effects. However, Milgrom and Roberts (1996) showed, using lattice theory, that, for example, for the profit-maximizing firm model, if all the cross-partials of the production function are everywhere non-negative, the Le Chatelier results hold in the large. A few years later, Suen, Silberberg and Tseng (2000) provided an easier proof of this result, showing also that the global Le Chatelier result held when the factors of production and the fixed factor do not switch from being substitutes to being complements (or vice versa) over the relevant price range.

Samuelson (1960a) analysed Le Chatelier phenomena for equilibrium systems not resulting from an explicit maximization hypothesis, using the 'well-known' theorem of reciprocal determinants of Jacobi. (I used to joke to my classes that the theorem was well-known to Jacobi and to Samuelson.) Lady and Quirk (2004) have analysed non-maximizing systems using a theory of cycles in determinants; they prove the Le Chatelier principle applies to systems identified by Morishima (1952), which allows substitutes and complements.

EUGENE SILBERBERG

See also **comparative statics; envelope theorem.**

Bibliography

Fermi, E. 1937. *Thermodynamics*. New York: Dover Publications, p. 111.

Lady, G. and Quirk, J. 2004. The scope of the Le Chatelier principle. Online. Available at http://optima-com.com/LeChat/The%20Scope%20of%20the%20LeChatelier%20Principle.doc, accessed 1 February 2006.

Milgrom, P. and Roberts, J. 1996. The Le Chatelier principle. *American Economic Review* 86, 173–9.

Morishima, M. 1952. On the laws of change in the price system in an economy which contains complementary commodities. *Osaka Economics Papers* 1, 101–13.

Oliver, J. and Kurtz, J. 1992. Henri Louis Le Chatelier, a man of principle. Woodrow Wilson Fellowship Foundation. Online. Available at http://www.woodrow.org/teachers/chemistry/institutes/1992/LeChatelier.html, accessed 31 December 2005.

Pollak, R. 1969. Conditional demand functions and consumption theory. *Quarterly Journal of Economics* 83, 60–78.

Samuelson, P. 1974. *Foundations of Economic Analysis*. Cambridge, MA: Harvard University Press.

Samuelson, P. 1949. *The Le Chatelier principle in linear programming*. RAND Corporation Monograph. Reprinted in *The Collected Scientific Papers of Paul Samuelson*, vol. 1, ed. J. Stiglitz. Cambridge, MA: MIT Press, 1966.

Samuelson, P. 1960a. Structure of a minimum equilibrium system. In *Essays in Economics and Econometrics: A Volume in Honor of Harold Hotelling*, ed. R. Pfouts. Chapel Hill: University of North Carolina Press.

Samuelson, P. 1960b. An extension of the le Chatelier principle. *Econometrica* 28, 368–79. Reprinted in *The Collected Scientific Papers of Paul Samuelson*, vol. 1, ed. J. Stiglitz. Cambridge, MA: MIT Press, 1966.

Silberberg, E. and Suen, W. 2000. *The Structure of Economics*, 3rd edn. New York: Irwin/McGraw-Hill.

Suen, W., Silberberg, E. and Tseng, P. 2000. The Le Chatelier principle: the long and the short of it. *Economic Theory* 16, 471–76.

Viner, J. 1932. Cost curves and supply curves. *Zeitschrift fur Nationalokonomie* 3, 23–46. Reprinted in American Economic Association, *Readings in Price Theory*. Chicago: Richard D. Irwin, 1952.

Le Trosne, Guillaume François (1728–1780)

French lawyer and economist. Born in Orléans, Le Trosne studied natural law philosophy with Pothier in preparation for work as a magistrate. In 1753 he was appointed Royal Councillor at the Orléans Presidial Court, whence he retired in 1773. Le Trosne joined the Physiocrats in 1764 by publishing a book defending the free trade in grain (1765) and articles in *Ephémérides* and other journals. His major economic work, *De l'ordre social*, appeared in 1777, its second volume, *De l'intérêt social*, having major economic content with its discussion of value, circulation, money, industry, and domestic, foreign and colonial trade, partly by way of criticism of Condillac's (1776) anti-physiocratic views on these subjects. Le Trosne died in Paris in 1780.

De l'ordre social sets out the laws required for good government designed to ensure and enhance the reproduction of subsistence and wealth. Two major laws are identified. The first demands freedom for economic activity and security of property (Le Trosne, 1777a, p. 38). The second seeks to secure sufficient government revenue to defray public expenses in providing not only security of property and defence but also public works in communication and transport most favourable to reproduction (1777a, p. 122). The second law entails an appropriate tax system ensured by gradual implementation of the single tax on net product (1777a, p. 147). The remaining discourses of the first volume develop the absolute necessity of these laws from historical examples and from their undesirable consequences when transgressed. Constitutional issues of good government defended in part by standard physiocratic arguments in lengthy footnotes (for example, on luxury, 1777a. pp. 214–19, and free trade, pp. 347–50) form the thrust of the argument in the first volume.

Le Trosne's second volume (1777b) is particularly noted for its theory of value (Meek, 1962, p. 389, n. 1), which distinguishes its various determinants such as usefulness, tastes, relative scarcity and competition but which identifies necessary expenses of production as the major influence on value, hence the name fundamental price (pp. 503–4). To analyse value effects on production and wealth Le Trosne distinguishes various value forms linking, for example, the excess of the price received for produce by the farmer over costs, to accumulation and the increase of wealth. Other roles for these complex value relationships are illustrated in Le Trosne's perceptive discussions of exchange, money, circulation, the sterility of industry and the benefits of trade for an agricultural nation. This analysis clearly confirms the value foundations of physiocratic theory, crystallized in his demonstration of the special productivity of agriculture by means of a simple example where all payments are assumed to be in kind ('*en nature*'), thereby demonstrating the inaccuracy of interpretations which neglect the sophisticated physiocratic value analysis (p. 590).

PETER GROENEWEGEN

Selected works

1765. *La liberté du commerce des grains, toujours utile et jamais nuisible*. Paris.

1777a. *De l'ordre social*. Paris. Reprinted, Munich: Kraus, 1980.

1777b. *De l'intérêt social, par rapport à la valeur, à la circulation, à l'industrie, & au commerce intérieur & extérieur*. Paris. Reprinted, Munich: Kraus, 1980.

Bibliography

Condillac, E.B. de. 1776. *Le commerce et le gouvernement considérés relativement l'un à l'autre*. Paris.

Meek, R.L. 1962. *The Economics of Physiocracy*. London: George Allen & Unwin.

learning and evolution in games: adaptive heuristics

'Adaptive heuristics' are simple behavioural rules that are directed towards payoff improvement but may be less than fully rational. The number and variety of such rules are virtually unlimited; here we survey several prominent examples drawn from psychology, computer science, statistics and game theory. Of particular interest are the informational inputs required by different learning rules and the forms of equilibrium to which they lead. We shall begin by considering very primitive heuristics, such as reinforcement learning, and work our way up to more complex forms, such as hypothesis testing, which still, however, fall well short of perfectly rational learning.

One of the simplest examples of a learning heuristic is *cumulative payoff matching*, in which the subject plays actions next period with probabilities proportional to their cumulative payoffs to date. Specifically, consider a finite stage game G that is played infinitely often, where all payoffs are assumed to be strictly positive. Let $a_{ij}(t)$ denote the cumulative payoff to player i over all those periods $0 \leq t' \leq t$ when he played action j, including some *initial propensity* $a_{ij}(0) > 0$. The cumulative payoff matching rule stipulates that in period $t + 1$, player i chooses action j with probability

$$p_{ij}(t + 1) = a_{ij}(t) \Big/ \sum_k a_{ik}(t). \qquad (1)$$

Notice that the distribution has full support given the assumption that the initial propensities are positive. This idea was first proposed by the psychologist Nathan Herrnstein (1970) to explain certain types of animal behaviour, and falls under the more general rubric of *reinforcement learning* (Bush and Mosteller, 1951; Suppes and Atkinson, 1960; Cross, 1983). The key feature of a reinforcement model is that the probability of choosing an action increases monotonically with the total payoff it has generated in the past (on the assumption that the payoffs are positive). In other words, taking an action and receiving a positive payoff *reinforces* the tendency to take that same action again. This means, in particular, that play can become concentrated on certain actions simply because they were played early and often, that is, play can be *habit-forming* (Roth and Erev, 1995; Erev and Roth, 1998).

Reinforcement models differ in various details that materially affect their theoretical behaviour as well as their empirical plausibility. Under cumulative payoff matching, for example, the payoffs are not discounted, which means that current payoffs have an impact on current behaviour that diminishes as $1/t$. Laboratory experiments suggest, however, that recent payoffs matter more than those long past (Erev and Roth, 1998); furthermore, the rate of discounting has implications for the asymptotic properties of such models (Arthur, 1991).

Another variation in this class of models relies on the concept of an *aspiration level*. This is a level of payoffs, sometimes endogenously determined by past play, that triggers a change in a player's behaviour when current payoffs fall below the level and inertial behaviour when payoffs are above the level. The theoretical properties of these models have been studied for 2×2 games, but relatively little is known about their behaviour in general games (Börgers and Sarin, 2000; Cho and Matsui, 2005).

Next we turn to a class of adaptive heuristics based on the notion of minimizing *regret*, about which more is known in a theoretical sense. Fix a particular player and let $\alpha(t)$ denote the average per period payoff that she received over all periods $t' \leq t$. Let $\alpha_j(t)$ denote the average payoff she *would have* received by playing action j in every period through t, on the assumption that the opponents played as they actually did. The difference $r_j(t) = \alpha_j(t) - \alpha(t)$ is the subject's *unconditional regret* from not having played j in every period through t. (In the computer science literature this is known as *external regret*; see Greenwald and Gondek, 2002.)

The following simple heuristic was proposed by Hart and Mas-Colell (2000; 2001) and is known as *unconditional regret matching*: play each action with a probability that is proportional to the positive part of its unconditional regret, that is,

$$p_j(t+1) = [r_j(t)]_+ \Big/ \sum_k [r_k(t)]_+. \qquad (2)$$

This learning rule has the following remarkable property: when used by any one player, his regrets become nonpositive almost surely as t goes to infinity *irrespective of the behaviour of the other players*. When all players use the rule, their time average behaviour converges almost surely to a generalization of correlated equilibrium known as the *Hannan set* or the *coarse correlated equilibrium set* (Hannan, 1957; Moulin and Vial, 1978; Hart and Mas-Colell, 2000; Young, 2004). In general, a *coarse correlated equilibrium* (CCE) is a probability distribution

over outcomes (joint actions) such that, given a choice between (*a*) committing *ex ante* to whatever joint action will be realized, and (*b*) committing *ex ante* to a fixed action, given that the others are committed to playing their part of whatever joint action will be realized, every player weakly prefers the former option. By contrast, a *correlated equilibrium* (CE) is a distribution such that, after a player's part of the realized joint action has been disclosed, he would just as soon play it as something else, given that the others are going to play their part of the realized joint action. It is straightforward to show that the coarse correlated equilibria form a convex set that contains the set of correlated equilibria (Young, 2004, ch. 3).

The heuristic specified in (2) belongs to a large family of rules whose time-average behaviour converges almost surely to the coarse correlated equilibrium set; equivalently, that assures no long-run regret for all players simultaneously. For example, this property holds if we let $p_j(t+1) = [r_j(t)]_+^\theta \big/ \sum_k [r_k(t)]_+^\theta$ for some exponent $\theta > 0$; one may even take different exponents for different players. Notice that these heuristics put positive probability only on actions that would have done strictly better (on average) than the player's realized average payoff. These are sometimes called *better reply rules*. Fictitious play, by contrast, puts positive probability only on action(s) that would have done *best* against the opponents' frequency distribution of play.

Fictitious play does not necessarily converge to the coarse correlated equilibrium set (CCES); indeed, in some 2×2 coordination games fictitious play causes perpetual miscoordination, in which case both players have unconditional long-run regret (Fudenberg and Kreps, 1993; Young, 1993). By choosing θ to be very large, however, we see that there exist better reply rules that are arbitrarily close to fictitious play and that do converge almost surely to the CCES. Fudenberg and Levine (1995; 1998; 1999) and Hart and Mas-Colell (2001) give general conditions under which stochastic forms of fictitious play converge in time average to the CCES.

Without complicating the adjustment process too much, one can construct rules whose time average behaviour converges almost surely to the *correlated equilibrium set* (CES). To define this class of heuristics we need to introduce the notion of conditional regret. Given a history of play through time t and a player i, consider the change in per period payoff if i had played action k in all those periods $t' \leq t$ when he actually played action j (and the opponents played what they did). If the difference is positive, player i has conditional regret – he wishes he had played k instead of j. Formally, i's *conditional regret* at playing j instead of k up through time t, $r_{jk}^i(t)$, is $1/t$ times the increase in payoff that would have resulted from playing k instead of j in all periods $t' \leq t$. Notice that the average is taken over all t periods to date; hence, if j was not played very often, $r_{jk}^i(t)$ will be small.

Consider the following *conditional regret matching* heuristic proposed by Hart and Mas-Colell (2000): if a given agent played action j in period t, then in period $t+1$ he plays according to the distribution

$$q_k(t+1) = \varepsilon r_{jk}(t)_+ \text{ for all } k \neq j, \text{ and}$$
$$q_j(t+1) = 1 - \varepsilon \sum_{k \neq j} r_{jk}(t)_+.$$

$$(3)$$

In effect $1-\varepsilon$ is the degree of inertia, which must be large enough that $q_k(t+1)$ is non-negative for all realizations of the conditional regrets $r_{jk}(t)$. If all players use conditional regret matching and ε is sufficiently small, then almost surely the joint frequency of play converges to the set of correlated equilibria (Hart and Mas-Colell, 2000). Notice that *pointwise* convergence is not guaranteed; the result says only that the empirical distribution converges to a convex *set*. In particular, the players' time-average behaviour may wander from one correlated equilibrium to another. It should also be remarked that, if a single player uses conditional regret matching, there is no assurance that his conditional regrets will become non-positive over time unless we assume that the other players use the same rule. This stands in contrast to unconditional regret matching, which assures non-positive unconditional regret for any player who uses it irrespective of the behaviour of the other players. One can, however, design more sophisticated updating procedures that unilaterally assure no conditional regret; see for example Foster and Vohra (1999), Fudenberg and Levine (1998, ch. 4), Hart and Mas-Colell (2000), and Young (2004, ch. 4).

A natural question now arises: do there exist simple heuristics that allow the players to learn *Nash* equilibrium instead of correlated or still coarser forms of equilibrium? The answer depends on how demanding we are about the long-run convergence properties of the learning dynamic. Notice that the preceding results on regret matching were concerned solely with time-average behaviour; no claim was made that period-by-period behaviour converges to any notion of equilibrium. Yet surely it is period-by-period behaviour that is most relevant if we want to assert that the players have 'learned' to play equilibrium. It turns out that it is very difficult to design adaptive learning rules under which period-by-period behaviour converges almost surely to Nash equilibrium in any finite game, unless one builds in some form of coordination among the players (Hart and Mas-Colell, 2003; 2006). The situation becomes even more problematic if one insists on fully rational, Bayesian learning. In this case it can be shown that there exist games of incomplete information in which no form of Bayesian rational learning causes period-by-period behaviours to come close to Nash equilibrium behaviour even in a probabilistic sense (Jordan, 1991, 1993;

Foster and Young, 2001; Young, 2004; see also LEARNING AND EVOLUTION IN GAMES: BELIEF LEARNING).

If one does not insist on full rationality, however, one can design stochastic adaptive heuristics that cause period-by-period behaviours to come close to Nash equilibrium – indeed close to subgame perfect equilibrium – most of the time (without necessarily *converging* to an equilibrium). Here is one approach due to Foster and Young (2003); for related work see Foster and Young (2006) and Germano and Lugosi (2007). Let G be a finite n-person game that is played infinitely often. At each point in time, each player thinks that the others are playing i.i.d. strategies. Specifically, at time t player i thinks that j is playing the i.i.d strategy $p_j(t)$ on j's action space, and that the opponents are playing independently; that is, their joint strategies are given by the product distribution $p_{-i}(t) = \prod_{j \neq i} p_j(t)$. Suppose that i's best response is to play a smoothed best response to $p_{-i}(t)$. Specifically, assume that i plays each action j with a probability proportional to $e^{\beta u_i(j, p_{-i})}$, where $u_i(j, p_{-i})$ is i's expected utility from playing j in every period when the opponents play p_{-i}, and $\beta > 0$ is a *response parameter*. This is known as a *quantal* or *log linear* response function. For brevity, denote i's response in period t by $q_i^\beta(t)$; this depends, of course, on $p_{-i}(t)$. Player i views $p_{-i}(t)$ as a hypothesis that he wishes to test against data. After first adopting this hypothesis he waits for a number of periods (say s) while he observes the opponents' behaviour, all the while playing $q_i^\beta(t)$. After s periods have elapsed, he compares the empirical frequency distribution of the opponents' play during these periods with his hypothesis. Notice that both the empirical frequency distribution and the hypothesized distribution lie in the same compact subset of Euclidean space. If the two differ by more than some tolerance level τ (in the Euclidean metric), he rejects his current hypothesis and chooses a new one.

In choosing a new hypothesis, he may wish to take account of information revealed during the course of play, but we shall also assume he engages in some *experimentation*. Specifically, let us suppose that he chooses a new hypothesis according to a probability density that is uniformly bounded away from zero on the space of hypotheses. One can show the following: given any $\varepsilon > 0$, if the response parameter β is sufficiently large, the test tolerance τ is sufficiently small (given β), and the amount of data collected s is sufficiently large (given β and τ), then the players' *period-by-period* behaviours constitute an ε-equilibrium of the stage game G at least $1 - \varepsilon$ of the time (Foster and Young, 2003). In other words, classical statistical hypothesis testing is a heuristic for learning Nash equilibria of the stage game. Moreover, if the players adopt hypotheses that condition on history, they can learn complex equilibria of the repeated game, including forms of subgame perfect equilibrium.

The theoretical literature on strategic learning has advanced rapidly in recent years. A much richer class of learning models has been identified since the mid-1990s, and more is known about their long-run convergence properties. There is also a greater understanding of the various kinds of equilibrium that different forms of learning deliver. An important open question is how these theoretical proposals relate to the empirical behaviour of laboratory subjects. While there is no reason to think that any of these rules can fully explain subjects' behaviour, they can nevertheless play a useful role by identifying phenomena that experimentalists should look for. In particular, the preceding discussion suggests that weaker forms of equilibrium may turn out to be more robust predictors of long-run behaviour than is Nash equilibrium.

H. PEYTON YOUNG

See also **behavioural game theory; learning and evolution in games: belief learning.**

Bibliography

Arthur, W.B. 1991. Designing agents that act like human agents: a behavioral approach to bounded rationality. *American Economic Association, Papers and Proceedings* 81, 353–9.

Börgers, T. and Sarin, R. 2000. Naïve reinforcement learning with endogenous aspirations. *International Economic Review* 31, 921–50.

Bush, R.R. and Mosteller, F. 1951. A mathematical model for simple learning. *Psychological Review* 58, 313–23.

Cho, I.-K. and Matsui, A. 2005. Learning aspiration in repeated games. *Journal of Economic Theory* 124, 171–201.

Cross, J. 1983. *A Theory of Adaptive Economic Behavior.* Cambridge: Cambridge University Press.

Erev, I. and Roth, A.E. 1998. Predicting how people play games: reinforcement learning in experimental games with unique, mixed strategy equilibria. *American Economic Review* 88, 848–81.

Foster, D.P. and Vohra, R. 1999. Regret in the on-line decision problem. *Games and Economic Behavior* 29, 7–35.

Foster, D.P. and Young, H.P. 2001. On the impossibility of predicting the behavior of rational agents. *Proceedings of the National Academy of Sciences of the USA* 98(222), 12848–53.

Foster, D.P. and Young, H.P. 2003. Learning, hypothesis testing, and Nash equilibrium. *Games and Economic Behavior* 45, 73–96.

Foster, D.P. and Young, H.P. 2006. Regret testing: learning Nash equilibrium without knowing you have an opponent. *Theoretical Economics* 1, 341–67.

Fudenberg, D. and Kreps, D. 1993. Learning mixed equilibria. *Games and Economic Behavior* 5, 320–67.

Fudenberg, D. and Levine, D. 1995. Universal consistency and cautious fictitious play. *Journal of Economic Dynamics and Control* 19, 1065–90.

Fudenberg, D. and Levine, D. 1998. *The Theory of Learning in Games.* Cambridge MA: MIT Press.

Fudenberg, D. and Levine, D. 1999. Conditional universal consistency. *Games and Economic Behavior* 29, 104–30.

Germano, F. and Lugosi, G. 2007. Global Nash convergence of Foster and Young's regret testing. *Games and Economic Behavior* 60, 135–54.

Greenwald, A. and Gondek, D. 2002. On no-regret learning and game-theoretic equilibria. *Journal of Machine Learning* 1, 1–20.

Hannan, J. 1957. Approximation to Bayes risk in repeated plays. In *Contributions to the Theory of Games*, vol. 3, ed. M. Dresher, A.W. Tucker and P. Wolfe. Princeton, NJ: Princeton University Press.

Hart, S. and Mas-Colell, A. 2000. A simple adaptive procedure leading to correlated equilibrium. *Econometrica* 68, 1127–50.

Hart, S. and Mas-Colell, A. 2001. A general class of adaptive strategies. *Journal of Economic Theory* 98, 26–54.

Hart, S. and Mas-Colell, A. 2003. Uncoupled dynamics do not lead to Nash equilibrium. *American Economic Review* 93, 1830–6.

Hart, S. and Mas-Colell, A. 2006. Stochastic uncoupled dynamics and Nash equilibrium. *Games and Economic Behavior* 57, 286–303.

Herrnstein, R.J. 1970. On the law of effect. *Journal of the Experimental Analysis of Behavior* 13, 243–66.

Jordan, J.S. 1991. Bayesian learning in normal form games. *Games and Economic Behavior* 3, 60–81.

Jordan, J.S. 1993. Three problems in learning mixed-strategy equilibria. *Games and Economic Behavior* 5, 368–86.

Moulin, H. and Vial, J.P. 1978. Strategically zero-sum games: the class of games whose completely mixed equilibria cannot be improved upon. *International Journal of Game Theory* 7, 201–21.

Roth, A.E. and Erev, I. 1995. Learning in extensive-form games: experimental data and simple dynamic models in the intermediate term. *Games and Economic Behavior* 8, 164–212.

Suppes, P. and Atkinson, R. 1960. *Markov Learning Models for Multiperson Interaction.* Stanford CA: Stanford University Press.

Young, H.P. 1993. The evolution of conventions. *Econometrica* 61, 57–84.

Young, H.P. 2004. *Strategic Learning and Its Limits.* Oxford: Oxford University Press.

learning and evolution in games: an overview

The theory of learning and evolution in games provides models of disequilibrium behaviour in strategic settings. Much of the theory focuses on whether and when disequilibrium behaviour will resolve in equilibrium play, and, if it does, on predicting which equilibrium will be played. But the theory also offers techniques for characterizing perpetual disequilibrium play.

1 A taxonomy

Models from *evolutionary game theory* consider the behaviour of large populations in strategic environments. In the biological strand of the theory, agents are genetically programmed to play fixed actions, and changes in the population's composition are the result of natural selection and random mutations. In economic approaches to the theory, agents actively choose which actions to play using simple myopic rules, so that changes in aggregate behaviour are the end result of many individual decisions. *Deterministic evolutionary dynamics*, usually taking the form of ordinary differential equations, are used to describe behaviour over moderate time spans, while *stochastic evolutionary dynamics*, modelled using Markov processes, are more commonly employed to study behaviour over very long time spans.

Models of *learning in games* focus on the behaviour of small groups of players, one of whom fills each role in a repeated game. These models too can be partitioned into two categories. Models of *heuristic learning* (or *adaptive learning*) resemble evolutionary models, in that their players base their decisions on simple myopic rules. One sometimes can distinguish the two sorts of models by the inputs to the agents' decision rules. In both the stochastic evolutionary model of c, Kandori, Mailath and Rob (1993) and the heuristic learning model of Young (1993), agents' decisions take the form of noisy best responses. But in the former model agents evaluate each action by its performance against the population's current behaviour, while in the latter they consider performance against the time averages of opponents' past play.

In models of *coordinated Bayesian learning* (or *rational learning*), each player forms explicit beliefs about the repeated game strategies employed by other players, and plays a best response to those beliefs in each period. The latter models assume a degree of coordination of players' prior beliefs that is sufficient to ensure that play converges to Nash equilibrium. By dropping this coordination assumption, one obtains the more general class of *Bayesian learning* (or *belief learning*) models. Since such models can entail quite naive beliefs, belief learning models overlap with heuristic learning models – see Section 3 below.

2 Evolutionary game theory

The roots of evolutionary game theory lie in mathematical biology. Maynard Smith and Price (1973) introduced the equilibrium notion of an *evolutionarily stable strategy* (or ESS) to capture the possible stable outcomes of a dynamic evolutionary process by way of a static definition. Later, Taylor and Jonker (1978) offered the *replicator dynamic* as an explicitly dynamic model of the natural selection process. The decade that followed saw an explosion of research on the replicator dynamic and related models of animal behaviour, population ecology,

and population genetics: see Hofbauer and Sigmund (1988).

In economics, evolutionary game theory studies the behaviour of populations of strategically interacting agents who actively choose among the actions available to them. Agents decide when to switch actions and which action to choose next using simple myopic rules known as *revision protocols* (see Sandholm, 2006). A population of agents, a game, and a revision protocol together define a stochastic process – in particular, a Markov process – on the set of population states.

2.1 Deterministic evolutionary dynamics

How the analysis proceeds depends on the time horizon of interest. Suppose that for the application in question, our interest is in moderate time spans. Then if the population size is large enough, the idiosyncratic noise in agent's choices is averaged away, so that the evolution of aggregate behaviour follows an almost deterministic path (Benaïm and Weibull, 2003). This path is described by a solution to an ordinary differential equation. For example, Björnerstedt and Weibull (1996) and Schlag (1998) show that if agents use certain revision protocols based on imitation of successful opponents, then the population's aggregate behaviour follows a solution to Taylor and Jonker's (1978) replicator dynamic. This argument provides an alternative, economic interpretation of this fundamental evolutionary model.

Much of the literature on deterministic evolutionary dynamics focuses on connections with traditional game theoretic solution concepts. For instance, under a wide range of deterministic dynamics, all Nash equilibria of the underlying game are rest points. While some dynamics (including the replicator dynamic) have additional non-Nash rest points, there are others under which rest points and Nash equilibria are identical (Brown and von Neumann, 1950; Smith, 1984; Sandholm, 2006).

A more important question, though, is whether Nash equilibrium will be approached from arbitrary disequilibrium states. For certain specific classes of games, general convergence results can be established (Hofbauer, 2000; Sandholm, 2007). But beyond these classes, convergence cannot be guaranteed. One can construct games under which no reasonable deterministic evolutionary dynamic will converge to equilibrium – instead, the population cycles through a range of disequilibrium states forever (Hofbauer and Swinkels, 1996; Hart and Mas-Colell, 2003). More surprisingly, one can construct games in which nearly all deterministic evolutionary dynamics not only cycle for ever, but also fail to eliminate strictly dominated strategies (Hofbauer and Sandholm, 2006). If we truly are interested in modelling the dynamics of behaviour, these results reveal that our predictions cannot always be confined to equilibria; rather, more complicated limit phenomena like cycles and chaotic attractors must also be permitted as predictions of play.

2.2 Stochastic evolutionary dynamics

If we are interested in behaviour over very long time horizons, deterministic approximations are no longer valid, and we must study our original Markov process directly. Under certain non-degeneracy assumptions, the long-run behaviour of this process is captured by its unique stationary distribution, which describes the proportion of time the process spends in each population state.

While stochastic evolutionary processes can be more difficult to analyse than their deterministic counterparts, they also permit us to make surprisingly tight predictions. By making the amount of noise in agents' choice rules vanishingly small, one can often ensure that all mass in the limiting stationary distribution is placed on a single population state. This *stochastically stable state* provides a unique prediction of play even in games with multiple strict equilibria (Foster and Young, 1990; Kandori, Mailath and Rob, 1993).

The most thoroughly studied model of stochastic evolution considers agents who usually play a best response to the current population state, but who occasionally choose a strategy at random. Kandori, Mailath and Rob (1993) show that if the agents are randomly matched to play a symmetric 2×2 coordination game, then taking the probability of 'mutations' to zero generates a unique stochastically stable state. In this state, called the *risk dominant equilibrium*, all agents play the action that is optimal against an opponent who is equally likely to choose each action.

Selection results of this sort have since been extended to cases in which the underlying game has an arbitrary number of strategies, as well as to settings in which agents are positioned on a fixed network, interacting only with neighbours (see Kandori and Rob, 1995; Blume, 2003; Ellison, 1993; 2000). Stochastic stability has also been employed in contexts where the underlying game has a nontrivial extensive form; these analyses have provided support for notions of backward induction (for example, subgame perfection) and forward induction (for example, signalling game equilibrium refinements): see Nöldeke and Samuelson (1993) and Hart (2002).

Still, these selection results must be interpreted with care. When the number of agents is large or the rate of 'mutation' is small, states that fail to be stochastically stable can be coordinated upon for great lengths of time (Binmore, Samuelson and Vaughan, 1995). Consequently, if the relevant time span for the application at hand is not long enough, the stochastically stable state may not be the only reasonable prediction of behaviour.

3 Learning in games

3.1 Heuristic learning

Learning models study disequilibrium adjustment processes in repeated games. Like evolutionary models, heuristic learning models assume that players employ simple myopic rules in deciding how to act. In the simplest of these models, each player decides how to act by considering the payoffs he has earned in the past. For instance, under reinforcement learning (Börgers and Sarin, 1997; Erev' and Roth, 1998), agents choose each strategy with probability proportional to the total payoff that the strategy has earned in past periods.

By considering rules that look not only at payoffs earned, but also at payoffs foregone, one can obtain surprisingly strong convergence results. Define a player's *regret* for (not having played) action a to be the difference between the average payoff he would have earned had he always played a in the past, and the average payoff he actually received. Under *regret matching†*, each action whose regret is positive is chosen with probability proportional to its regret. Hart and Mas-Colell (2000) show that regret matching is a *consistent* repeated game strategy: it forces a player's regret for each action to become nonpositive. If used by all players, regret matching ensures that their time-averaged behaviour converges to the set of *coarse correlated equilibria* of the underlying game. (*Coarse correlated equilibrium* is a generalization of correlated equilibrium under which players' incentive constraints must be satisfied at the *ex ante* stage rather than at the interim stage: see Young, 2004.)

Some of the most striking convergence results in the evolution and learning literature establish a stronger conclusion: namely, convergence of time-averaged behaviour to the set of *correlated equilibria*, regardless of the game at hand. The original result of this sort is due to Foster and Vohra (1997; 1998), who prove the result by constructing a calibrated procedure for forecasting opponents' play. A *forecasting procedure* produces probabilistic forecasts of how opponents will act. The procedure is *calibrated* if in those periods in which the forecast is given by the probability vector p, the empirical distribution of opponents' play is approximately p. It is not difficult to show that if players always choose myopic best responses to calibrated forecasts, then their time-averaged behaviour converges to the set of correlated equilibria.

Hart and Mas-Colell (2000) construct simpler procedures – in particular, procedures that define conditionally consistent repeated game strategies – also ensure convergence to correlated equilibrium. A repeated game strategy is *conditionally consistent* if for each frequently played action a, the agent would not have been better off had he always played an alternative action a' in place of a. As a matter of definition, the use of conditionally consistent strategies by all players leads time-averaged behavior to converge to the set of correlated equilibria.

Another variety of heuristic learning models, based on *random search and independent verification*, ensures a stochastic form of convergence to Nash equilibrium regardless of the game being played (Foster and Young, 2003). However, in these models the time required before equilibrium is first reached is quite long, making them most relevant to applications with especially long time horizons.

In some heuristic learning models, players use simple rules to predict how opponents will behave, and then respond optimally to those predictions. The leading examples of such models are *fictitious play* and its stochastic variants (Brown, 1951; Fudenberg and Kreps, 1993): in these models, the prediction about an opponents' next period play is given by the empirical frequencies of his past plays. Beginning with Robinson (1951), many authors have proved convergence results for standard and stochastic fictitious play in specific classes of games (see Hofbauer and Sandholm (2002) for an overview). But as Shapley (1964) and others have shown, these models do not lead to equilibrium play in all games.

3.2 Coordinated Bayesian learning

The prediction rule underlying two-player fictitious play can be described by a belief about the opponent's repeated game strategy that is updated using Bayes's rule in the face of observed play. This belief specifies that the opponent choose his stage game actions in an i.i.d. fashion, conditional on the value of an unknown parameter. (In fact, the player's beliefs about this parameter must come from the family of Dirichlet distributions, the conjugate family of distributions for multinomial trials.) Evidently, each player's beliefs about his opponent are wrong: player 1 believes that player 2 chooses actions in an i.i.d. fashion, whereas player 2 actually plays optimally in response to his own (i.i.d.) predictions about player 1's behaviour. It is therefore not surprising that fictitious play processes do not converge in all games.

In models of *coordinated Bayesian learning* (or *rational learning*), it is not only supposed that players form and respond optimally to beliefs about the opponent's repeated game strategy; it is also assumed that the players' initial beliefs are coordinated in some way. The most studied case is one in which prior beliefs satisfy an absolute continuity condition: if the distribution over play paths generated by the players' actual strategies assigns positive probability to some set of play paths, then so must the distribution generated by each player's prior. A strong sufficient condition for absolute continuity is that each player's prior assigns a positive probability to his opponent's actual strategy.

The fundamental result in this literature, due to Kalai and Lehrer (1993), shows that under absolute continuity, each player's forecast along the path of play is asymptotically correct, and the path of play is asymptotically consistent with Nash equilibrium play in the repeated game. Related convergence results have been proved for more complicated environments in which each player's stage game payoffs are private information (Jordan, 1995; Nyarko, 1998). If the distributions of players types are continuous, then the sense in which play converges to equilibrium can involve a form of purification: while actual play is pure, it appears random to an outside observer.

How much coordination of prior beliefs is needed to prove convergence to equilibrium play? Nachbar (2005) proves that for a large class of repeated games, for any belief learning model, there are no prior beliefs that satisfy three criteria: learnability, consistency with optimal play, and diversity. Thus, if players can learn to predict one another's behaviour, and are capable of responding optimally to their updated beliefs, then each player's beliefs about his opponents must rule out some seemingly natural strategies a priori. In this sense, the assumption of coordinated prior beliefs that ensures convergence to equilibrium in rational learning models does not seem dramatically weaker than a direct assumption of equilibrium play.

For additional details about the theory of learning and evolution in games, we refer the reader to the entries on specific topics listed in the cross-references below.

WILLIAM H. SANDHOLM

See also **deterministic evolutionary dynamics; learning and evolution in games: adaptive heuristics; learning and evolution in games: belief learning; learning and evolution in games: ESS; stochastic adaptive dynamics.**

The author thanks John Nachbar for a number of helpful conversations and for sharing his expertise on coordinated Bayesian learning. Financial support under NSF Grants SES-0092145 and SES-0617753 is gratefully acknowledged.

Bibliography

Benaïm, M. and Weibull, J.W. 2003. Deterministic approximation of stochastic evolution in games. *Econometrica* 71, 873–903.

Binmore, K., Samuelson, L. and Vaughan, R. 1995. Musical chairs: modeling noisy evolution. *Games and Economic Behavior* 11, 1–35.

Björnerstedt, J. and Weibull, J.W. 1996. Nash equilibrium and evolution by imitation. In *The Rational Foundations of Economic Behavior*, ed. K.J. Arrow, E. Colombatto, M. Perlman, and C. Schmidt. New York: St. Martin's Press.

Blume, L.E. 2003. How noise matters. *Games and Economic Behavior* 44, 251–71.

Börgers, T. and Sarin, R. 1997. Learning through reinforcement and the replicator dynamics. *Journal of Economic Theory* 77, 1–14.

Brown, G.W. 1951. Iterative solutions of games by fictitious play. In *Activity Analysis of Production and Allocation*, ed. T.C. Koopmans. New York: Wiley.

Brown, G.W. and von Neumann, J. 1950. Solutions of games by differential equations. In *Contributions to the Theory of Games I*, ed. H.W . Kuhn and A.W. Tucker, vol. 24 of *Annals of Mathematics Studies*. Princeton: Princeton University Press.

Ellison, G. 1993. Learning, local interaction, and coordination. *Econometrica* 61, 1047–71.

Ellison, G. 2000. Basins of attraction, long run equilibria, and the speed of step-by-step evolution. *Review of Economic Studies* 67, 17–45.

Erev, I. and Roth, A.E. 1998. Predicting how people play games: reinforcement learning in experimental games with unique, mixed strategy equilibria. *American Economic Review* 88, 848–81.

Foster, D.P. and Vohra, R. 1997. Calibrated learning and correlated equilibrium. *Games and Economic Behavior* 21, 40–55.

Foster, D.P. and Vohra, R. 1998. Asymptotic calibration. *Biometrika* 85, 379–90.

Foster, D.P. and Young, H.P. 1990. Stochastic evolutionary game dynamics. *Theoretical Population Biology* 38, 219–32.

Foster, D.P. and Young, H.P. 2003. Learning, hypothesis testing, and Nash equilibrium. *Games and Economic Behavior* 45, 73–96.

Fudenberg, D. and Kreps, D.M. 1993. Learning mixed equilibria. *Games and Economic Behavior* 5, 320–67.

Fudenberg, D. and Levine, D.K. 1998. *Theory of Learning in Games*. Cambridge: MIT Press.

Hart, S. 2002. Evolutionary dynamics and backward induction. *Games and Economic Behavior* 41, 227–64.

Hart, S. and Mas-Colell, A. 2000. A simple adaptive procedure leading to correlated equilibrium. *Econometrica* 68, 1127–50.

Hart, S. and Mas-Colell, A. 2003. Uncoupled dynamics do not lead to Nash equilibrium. *American Economic Review* 93, 1830–6.

Hofbauer, J. 2000. From Nash and Brown to Maynard Smith: equilibria, dynamics, and ESS. *Selection* 1, 81–8.

Hofbauer, J. and Sandholm, W.H. 2002. On the global convergence of stochastic fictitious play. *Econometrica* 70, 2265–94.

Hofbauer, J. and Sandholm, W.H. 2006. Survival of dominated strategies under evolutionary dynamics. Working paper. University of Vienna and University of Wisconsin.

Hofbauer, J. and Sigmund, K. 1988. *Theory of Evolution and Dynamical Systems*. Cambridge: Cambridge University Press.

Hofbauer, J. and Swinkels, J.M. 1996. A universal Shapley example. Working paper. University of Vienna and Northwestern University.

Jordan, J.S. 1995. Bayesian learning in repeated games. *Games and Economic Behavior* 9, 8–20.

Kalai, E. and Lehrer, E. 1993. Rational learning leads to Nash equilibrium. *Econometrica* 61, 1019–45.

Kandori, M., Mailath, G.J. and Rob, R. 1993. Learning, mutation, and long run equilibria in games. *Econometrica* 61, 29–56.

Kandori, M. and Rob, R. 1995. Evolution of equilibria in the long run: a general theory and applications. *Journal of Economic Theory* 65, 383–414.

Maynard Smith, J. and Price, G.R. 1973. The logic of animal conflict. *Nature* 246, 15–8.

Nachbar, J.H. 2005. Beliefs in repeated games. *Econometrica* 73, 459–80.

Nöldeke, G. and Samuelson, L. 1993. An evolutionary analysis of backward and forward induction. *Games and Economic Behavior* 5, 425–54.

Nyarko, Y. 1998. Bayesian learning and convergence to Nash equilibria without common priors. *Economic Theory* 11, 643–55.

Robinson, J. 1951. An iterative method of solving a game. *Annals of Mathematics* 54, 296–301.

Sandholm, W.H. 2006. Pairwise comparison dynamics and evolutionary foundations for Nash equilibrium. Working paper. University of Wisconsin.

Sandholm, W.H. 2007. Population games and evolutionary dynamics. Cambridge, MA: MIT Press.

Schlag, K.H. 1998. Why imitate, and if so, how? A boundedly rational approach to multi-armed bandits. *Journal of Economic Theory* 78, 130–56.

Shapley, L.S. 1964. Some topics in two person games. In *Advances in Game Theory*, ed. M. Dresher, L.S. Shapley and A.W. Tucker, vol. 52 of *Annals of Mathematics Studies*. Princeton: Princeton University Press.

Smith, M.J. 1984. The stability of a dynamic model of traffic assignment: an application of a method of Lyapunov. *Transportation Science* 18, 245–52.

Taylor, P.D. and Jonker, L. 1978. Evolutionarily stable strategies and game dynamics. *Mathematical Biosciences* 40, 145–56.

Young, H.P. 1993. The evolution of conventions. *Econometrica* 61, 57–84.

Young, H.P. 2004. *Strategic Learning and Its Limits*. Oxford: Oxford University Press.

learning and evolution in games: belief learning

In the context of learning in games, *belief learning* refers to models in which players are engaged in a dynamic game and each player optimizes, or ε optimizes, with respect to a *prediction rule* that gives a forecast of next period opponent behaviour as a function of the current history. This article focuses on the most studied class of dynamic games, two-player discounted repeated games with finite stage game action sets and perfect monitoring. An important example of a dynamic game that violates perfect monitoring and therefore falls outside this framework is Fudenberg and Levine (1993). For a more comprehensive survey of belief learning, see Fudenberg and Levine (1998).

The earliest example of belief learning is the *best-response dynamics* of Cournot (1838). In Cournot's model, each player predicts that her opponent will repeat next period whatever action her opponent chose in the previous period.

The most studied belief learning model is *fictitious play* (Brown, 1951), and its variants. In fictitious play, each player predicts that the probability that her opponent will play an action, say L, next period is a weighted sum of an initial probability on L and the frequency with which L has been chosen to date. The weight on the frequency is $t/(t+k)$, where t is the number of periods thus far and $k > 0$ is a parameter. The larger is k, the more periods for which the initial probability significantly affects forecasting.

The remainder of this article discusses four topics: (1) belief learning versus Bayesian learning, (2) convergence to equilibrium, (3) special issues in games with payoff uncertainty, and (4) sensible beliefs.

Belief learning versus Bayesian learning

Recall that, in a repeated game, a behaviour strategy gives, for every history, a probability over the player's stage game actions next period. In a Bayesian model, each player chooses a behaviour strategy that best responds to a *belief*, a probability distribution over the opponent's behaviour strategies.

Player 1's prediction rule about player 2 is mathematically identical to a behaviour strategy for player 2. Thus, any belief learning model is equivalent to a Bayesian model in which each player optimizes with respect to a belief that places probability 1 on her prediction rule, now reinterpreted as the opponent's behaviour strategy.

Conversely, any Bayesian model is equivalent to a belief learning model. Explicitly, for any belief over player 2's behaviour strategies there is a degenerate belief, assigning probability 1 to a particular behaviour strategy, that is equivalent in the sense that both beliefs induce the same distributions over play in the game, no matter what behaviour strategy player 1 herself adopts. This is a form of Kuhn's theorem (Kuhn, 1964). I refer to the behaviour strategy used in the degenerate belief as a *reduced form* of the original belief. Thus, any Bayesian model is equivalent to a Bayesian model in which each player's belief places probability 1 on the reduced form, and any such Bayesian model is equivalent to a belief learning model.

As an example, consider fictitious play. I focus on stage games with just two actions, L and R. By an i.i.d. strategy for player 2, I mean a behaviour strategy in which player 2 plays L with probability q, independent of history. Thus, if $q = 1/2$, then player 2 always randomizes 50:50 between L and R. Fictitious play is equivalent to a degenerate Bayesian model in which each player places probability 1 on the fictitious play prediction rule, and one can show that this is equivalent in turn to a non-degenerate Bayesian model in which the belief is represented as a beta distribution over q. The uniform distribution over q, for example, corresponds to taking the initial probability of L to be 1/2 and the parameter k to be 2.

There is a related but distinct literature in which players optimize with respect to *stochastic* prediction rules. In some cases (for example, Foster and Young, 2003), these models have a quasi-Bayesian interpretation: most of the time, players optimize with respect to fixed prediction rules, as in a Bayesian model, but occasionally players switch to new prediction rules, implicitly abandoning their priors.

Convergence to equilibrium

Within the belief learning literature, the investigation of convergence to equilibrium play splits into two branches. One branch investigates convergence within the context of specific classes of belief learning models. The best-response dynamics, for example, converge to equilibrium if the stage game is solvable by the iterated deletion of strictly dominated strategies. See Bernheim (1984) and, for a more general class of models, Milgrom and Roberts (1991). For an ε optimizing variant of fictitious play, convergence to approximate equilibrium play obtains for all zero-sum games, all games with an interior ESS, and all common interest games, in addition to all games that are strict dominance solvable, with the approximation closer the smaller is ε. Somewhat weaker convergence results are available for supermodular games. These claims follow from results in Hofbauer and Sandholm (2002).

In the results surveyed above, convergence is to repeated play of a single-stage game Nash equilibrium; in the case of ε fictitious play, this equilibrium may be mixed. There is a large body of work on convergence that is weaker than what I am considering here. In particular, there has been much work on convergence of the empirical marginal or joint distributions. For mixed strategy equilibrium, it is possible ;for empirical distributions to converge to equilibrium even though play does not resemble repeated equilibrium play; play may exhibit obvious cycles, for example. The study of convergence to equilibrium play is relatively recent and was catalysed by Fudenberg and Kreps (1993).

There are classes of games that cause convergence problems for many standard belief learning models, even when one considers only weak forms of convergence, such as convergence of the empirical marginal distributions (see Shapley, 1962; Jordan, 1993). Hart and Mas-Colell (2003; 2006) (hereafter HM) shed light on non-convergence by investigating learning models, including but not limited to belief learning models, that are *decoupled*, meaning that player 1's behaviour does not depend directly on player 2's stage game payoffs. A continuous time version of fictitious play fits into the framework of Hart and Mas-Colell (2003). The HM results imply that universal convergence is impossible for large classes of decoupled belief learning models: for any such model there exist stage games and initial conditions for which play fails to converge to equilibrium play.

The second branch of the literature, for which Kalai and Lehrer (1993a) (hereafter KL) is the central paper, takes a Bayesian perspective and asks what conditions on beliefs are sufficient to give convergence to equilibrium play. I find it helpful to characterize this literature in the following way. Say that a belief profile (giving a belief for each player) has the *learnable best-response property* (LBR) if there is a profile of best-response strategies (LBR strategies) such that, if the LBR strategies are played, then each player learns to predict the play path.

A player *learns to predict the play path* if her prediction of next period's play is asymptotically as good as if she knew her opponent's behaviour strategy. If the behaviour strategies call for randomization then players accurately predict the distribution over next period's play rather than the realization of next period's play. For example, consider a 2×2 game in which player 1 has stage game actions T and B and player 2 has stage game actions L and R. If player 2 is randomizing 50:50 every period and player 1 learns to predict the path of play, then for every ε there is a time, which depends on the realization of player 2's strategy, after which player 1's next period forecast puts the probability of L within ε of $1/2$. (This statement applies to a set of play paths that arises with probability 1 with respect to the underlying probability model; I gloss over this sort of complication both here and below.) For a more complicated example, suppose that in period t player 2 plays L with probability $1 - \alpha$, where α is the frequency that the players have played the profile (B, R). If player 1 learns to predict the play path, then for any ε there is a time, which now depends on the realization of both players' strategies, after which player 1's next period forecast puts the probability of L within ε of $1 - \alpha$.

Naively, if LBR holds, and players are using their LBR strategies, then, in the continuation game, players are optimizing with respect to posterior beliefs that are asymptotically correct and so continuation behaviour strategies should asymptotically be in equilibrium. This intuition is broadly correct, but there are three qualifications.

First, in general, convergence is to Nash equilibrium play in the *repeated* game, not necessarily to repeated play of a single stage game equilibrium. If players are myopic (meaning that players optimize each period as though their discount factors were zero), then the set of equilibrium play paths comprises all possible sequences of stage game Nash equilibria, which is a very large set if the stage game has more than one equilibrium. If players are patient, then the folk theorem applies and the set of possible equilibrium paths is typically even larger.

Second, convergence is to an equilibrium play path, not necessarily to an equilibrium of the repeated game. The issue is that LBR implies accurate forecasting only along the play path. A player's predictions about how her

opponent would respond to deviations may be grossly in error, for ever. Therefore, posterior beliefs need *not* be asymptotically correct and, unless players are myopic, continuation behaviour strategies need *not* be asymptotically in equilibrium. Kalai and Lehrer (1993b) shows that behaviour strategies can be doctored at information sets off the play path so that the modified behaviour strategies are asymptotically in equilibrium yet still generate the same play path. This implies that the play path of the original strategy profile was asymptotically an equilibrium play path.

Third, the exact sense in which play converges to equilibrium play depends on the strength of learning. See KL and also Sandroni (1998).

KL shows that a strong form of LBR holds if beliefs satisfy an absolute continuity condition: each player assigns positive probability to any (measurable) set of play paths that has positive probability given the players' actual strategies. A sufficient condition for this is that each player assigns positive, even if extremely low, probability to her opponent's actual strategy, a condition that KL call *grain of truth*. Nyarko (1998) provides the appropriate generalization of absolute continuity for games with type space structures, including the games with payoff uncertainty discussed below.

Games with payoff uncertainty

Suppose that, at the start of the repeated game, each player is privately informed of his or her stage game payoff function, which remains fixed throughout the course of the repeated game. Refer to player i's stage game payoff function as her *payoff type*. Assume that the joint distribution over payoff functions is independent (to avoid correlation issues that are not central to my discussion) and commonly known.

Each player can condition her behaviour strategy in the repeated game on her realized payoff type. A mathematically correct way of representing this conditioning is via distributional strategies (see Milgrom and Weber, 1985).

For any belief about player 2, now a probability distribution over player 2's distributional strategies, and given the probability distribution over player 2's payoff types, there is a behaviour strategy for player 2 in the repeated game that is equivalent in the sense that it generates the same distribution over play paths. Again, this is essentially Kuhn's theorem. And again, I refer to this behaviour strategy as a *reduced form*.

Say that a player *learns to predict the play path* if her forecast of next period's play is asymptotically as good as if she knew the reduced form of her opponent's distributional strategy. This definition specializes to the previous one if the distribution over types is degenerate. If distributional strategies are in equilibrium then, in effect, each player is optimizing with respect to a degenerate belief that puts probability one on her opponent's actual distributional strategy and in this case players trivially learn to predict the path of play.

One can define LBR for distributional strategies and, as in the payoff certainty case, one can show that LBR implies convergence to equilibrium play in the repeated game with payoff types. More interestingly, there is a sense in which play converges to equilibrium play of the *realized* repeated game – the repeated game determined by the realized type profile. The central paper is Jordan (1991). Other important papers include KL (cited above), Jordan (1995), Nyarko (1998), and Jackson and Kalai (1999) (which studies recurring rather than repeated games).

Suppose first that the realized type profile has positive probability. In this case, if a player learns to predict the play path, then, as shown by KL, her forecast is asymptotically as good as if she knew both her opponent's distributional strategy *and* her opponent's realized type. LBR then implies that actual play, meaning the distribution over play paths generated by the realized behaviour strategies, converges to equilibrium play of the realized repeated game. For example, suppose that the type profile for matching pennies gets positive probability. In the unique equilibrium of repeated matching pennies, players randomize 50:50 in every period. Therefore, LBR implies that, if the matching pennies type profile is realized, then each player's behaviour strategy in the realized repeated game involves 50:50 randomization asymptotically.

If the distribution over types admits a continuous density, so that no type profile receives positive probability, then the form of convergence is more subtle. Suppose that players are myopic and that the realized stage game is like matching pennies, with a unique and fully mixed equilibrium. Given myopia, the unique equilibrium of the realized repeated game calls for repeated play of the stage game equilibrium. In particular, it calls for players to randomize. It is not hard to show, however, that in a type space game with a continuous density, optimization calls for each player to play a pure strategy for almost every realized type. Thus, for almost every realized type profile in a neighbourhood of a game like matching pennies, actual play (again meaning the distribution over play paths generated by the realized behaviour strategies) cannot converge to equilibrium play, *even if the distributional strategies are in equilibrium.* Foster and Young (2001) provides a generalization for non-myopic players.

There is, however, a weaker sense in which play nevertheless does converge to equilibrium play in the realized repeated game. For simplicity, assume that each player knows the other's distributional strategy and that these strategies are in equilibrium. One can show that to an outsider observed play looks asymptotically like equilibrium play in the realized repeated game. In particular, if the realized game is like repeated matching pennies then observed play looks random. Moreover, to a player

in the game, opponent behaviour looks random because, even though she knows her opponent's distributional strategy, she does not know her opponent's type. As play proceeds, each player in effect learns more about her opponent's type, but never enough to zero in on her opponent's realized, pure, behaviour strategy. Thus, when the distribution over types admits a continuous density, convergence to equilibrium involves a form of purification in the sense of Harsanyi (1973), a point that has been emphasized by Nyarko (1998) and Jackson and Kalai (1999).

Sensible beliefs

A number of papers investigate classes of prediction rules that are sensible in that they exhibit desirable properties, such as the ability to detect certain kinds of patterns in opponent behaviour (see Aoyagi, 1996; Fudenberg and Levine, 1995; 1999; Sandroni, 2000).

Nachbar (2005) instead studies the issue of sensible beliefs from a Bayesian perspective. For simplicity, focus on learning models with known payoffs. Fix a belief profile, fix a subset of behaviour strategies for each player, and consider the following criteria for these subsets.

- *Learnability* – given beliefs, if players play a strategy profile drawn from these subsets then they learn to predict the play path.
- *Richness.* Informally (the formal statement is tedious), richness requires that if a behaviour strategy is included in one of the strategy subsets then certain variations on that strategy must be included as well. Richness, called CSP in Nachbar (2005), is satisfied automatically if the strategy subsets consist of all strategies satisfying a standard complexity bound, the same bound for both players. Thus richness holds if the subsets consist of all strategies with k-period memory, or all strategies that are automaton implementable, or all strategies that are Turing implementable, and so on.
- *Consistency* – each player's subset contains a best response to her belief.

The motivating idea is that, if beliefs are probability distributions over strategy subsets satisfying learnability, richness, and consistency, then beliefs are sensible, or at least are candidates for being considered sensible. Nachbar (2005) studies whether any such beliefs exist.

Consider, for example, the Bayesian interpretation of fictitious play in which beliefs are probability distributions over the i.i.d. strategies. The set of i.i.d. strategies satisfies learnability and richness. But for any stage game in which neither player has a weakly dominant action, the i.i.d. strategies violate consistency: any player who is optimizing will not be playing i.i.d.

Nachbar (2005) shows that this feature of Bayesian fictitious play extends to all Bayesian learning models. For large classes of repeated games, for *any* belief profile there are *no* strategy subsets that simultaneously satisfy learnability, richness, and consistency. Thus, for example, if each player believes the other is playing a strategy that has a *k*-period memory, then one can show that learnability and richness hold but consistency fails: best responding in this setting requires using a strategy with a memory of more than *k* periods. The impossibility result generalizes to ε optimization and ε consistency, for ε sufficiently small. The result also generalizes to games with payoff uncertainty (with learnability, richness, and consistency now defined in terms of distributional strategies) (see Nachbar, 2001).

I conclude with four remarks. First, since the set of all strategies satisfies richness and consistency, it follows that the set of all strategies is not learnable for *any* beliefs: for any belief profile there is a strategy profile that the players will not learn to predict. This can also be shown directly by a diagonalization argument along the lines of Oakes (1985) and Dawid (1985). The impossibility result of Nachbar (2005) can be viewed as a game theoretic version of Dawid (1985). For a description of what subsets *are* learnable, see Noguchi (2005).

Second, if one constructs a Bayesian learning model satisfying learnability and consistency then LBR holds and, if players play their LBR strategies, play converges to equilibrium play. This identifies a potentially attractive class of Bayesian models in which convergence obtains. The impossibility result says, however, that if learnability and consistency hold, then player beliefs must be partially equilibrated in the sense of, in effect, excluding some of the strategies required by richness.

Third, consistency is not *necessary* for LBR or convergence. For example, for many stage games, variants of fictitious play satisfy LBR and converge even though these learning models are inconsistent. The impossibility result is a statement about the ability to construct Bayesian models with certain properties; it is not a statement about convergence per se.

Last, learnability, richness, and consistency may be too strong to be taken as necessary conditions for beliefs to be considered sensible. It is an open question whether one can construct Bayesian models satisfying conditions that are weaker but still strong enough to be interesting.

JOHN NACHBAR

See also **deterministic evolutionary dynamics; learning and evolution in games: adaptive heuristics; learning and evolution in games: an overview; learning and evolution in games: ESS; purification; repeated games; stochastic adaptive dynamics.**

Bibliography

Aoyagi, M. 1996. Evolution of beliefs and the Nash equilibrium of normal form games. *Journal of Economic Theory* 70, 444–69.

Bernheim, B.D. 1984. Rationalizable strategic behavior. *Econometrica* 52, 1007–28.

Brown, G.W. 1951. Iterative solutions of games by fictitious play. In *Activity Analysis of Production and Allocation*, ed. T.J. Koopmans. New York: Wiley.

Cournot, A. 1838. Researches into the Mathematical Principles of the Theory of Wealth. Trans. N.T. Bacon, New York: Kelley, 1960.

Dawid, A.P. 1985. The impossibility of inductive inference. *Journal of the American Statistical Association* 80, 340–1.

Foster, D. and Young, P. 2001. On the impossibility of predicting the behavior of rational agents. *Proceedings of the National Academy of Sciences* 98, 12848–53.

Foster, D. and Young, P. 2003. Learning, hypothesis testing, and Nash equilibrium. *Games and Economic Behavior* 45, 73–96.

Fudenberg, D. and Kreps, D. 1993. Learning mixed equilibria. *Games and Economic Behavior* 5, 320–67.

Fudenberg, D. and Levine, D. 1993. Steady state learning and Nash equilibrium. *Econometrica* 61, 547–74.

Fudenberg, D. and Levine, D. 1995. Universal consistency and cautious fictitious play. *Journal of Economic Dynamics and Control* 19, 1065–89.

Fudenberg, D. and Levine, D. 1998. *Theory of Learning in Games*. Cambridge, MA: MIT Press.

Fudenberg, D. and Levine, D. 1999. Conditional universal consistency. *Games and Economic Behavior* 29, 104–30.

Harsanyi, J. 1973. Games with randomly disturbed payoffs: a new rationale for mixed-strategy equilibrium points. *International Journal of Game Theory* 2, 1–23.

Hart, S. and Mas-Colell, A. 2003. Uncoupled dynamics do not lead to Nash equilibrium. *American Economic Review* 93, 1830–6.

Hart, S. and Mas-Colell, A. 2006. Stochastic uncoupled dynamics and Nash equilibrium. *Games and Economic Behavior* 57, 286–303.

Hofbauer, J. and Sandholm, W. 2002. On the global convergence of stochastic fictitious play. *Econometrica* 70, 2265–94.

Jackson, M. and Kalai, E. 1999. False reputation in a society of players. *Journal of Economic Theory* 88, 40–59.

Jordan, J.S. 1991. Bayesian learning in normal form games. *Games and Economic Behavior* 3, 60–81.

Jordan, J.S. 1993. Three problems in learning mixed-strategy Nash equilibria. *Games and Economic Behavior* 5, 368–86.

Jordan, J.S. 1995. Bayesian learning in repeated games. *Games and Economic Behavior* 9, 8–20.

Kalai, E. and Lehrer, E. 1993a. Rational learning leads to Nash equilibrium. *Econometrica* 61, 1019–45.

Kalai, E. and Lehrer, E. 1993b. Subjective equilibrium in repeated games. *Econometrica* 61, 1231–40.

Kuhn, H.W. 1964. Extensive games and the problem of information. In *Contributions to the Theory of Games*, vol. 2, ed. M. Dresher, L.S. Shapley and A.W. Tucker. Princeton: Princeton University Press.

Milgrom, P. and Roberts, J. 1991. Adaptive and sophisticated learning in repeated normal form games. *Games and Economic Behavior* 3, 82–100.

Milgrom, P. and Weber, R. 1985. Distributional strategies for games with incomplete information. *Mathematics of Operations Research* 10, 619–32.

Nachbar, J.H. 2001. Bayesian learning in repeated games of incomplete information. *Social Choice and Welfare* 18, 303–26.

Nachbar, J.H. 2005. Beliefs in repeated games. *Econometrica* 73, 459–80.

Noguchi, Y. 2005. Merging with a set of probability measures: a characterization. Working paper, Kanto Gakuin University.

Nyarko, Y. 1998. Bayesian learning and convergence to Nash equilibria without common priors. *Economic Theory* 11, 643–55.

Oakes, D. 1985. Self-calibrating priors do not exist. *Journal of the American Statistical Association* 80, 339–42.

Sandroni, A. 1998. Necessary and sufficient conditions for convergence to Nash equilibrium: the almost absolute continuity hypothesis. *Games and Economic Behavior* 22, 121–47.

Sandroni, A. 2000. Reciprocity and cooperation in repeated coordination games: the principled-player approach. *Games and Economic Behavior* 32, 157–82.

Shapley, L. 1962. On the nonconvergence of fictitious play. Discussion Paper RM-3026, RAND.

learning and evolution in games: ESS

1. Introduction

According to John Maynard Smith in his influential book *Evolution and the Theory of Games* (1982, p.10), an ESS (that is, an *evolutionarily stable strategy*) is 'a strategy such that, if all members of the population adopt it, then no mutant strategy could invade the population under the influence of natural selection'. The ESS concept, based on static fitness comparisons, was originally introduced and developed in the biological literature (Maynard Smith and Price, 1973) as a means to predict the eventual outcome of evolution for individual behaviours in a single species. It avoids the complicated dynamics of the evolving population that may ultimately depend on spatial, genetic and population size effects.

To illustrate the Maynard Smith (1982) approach, suppose individual fitness is the expected payoff in a random pairwise contest. The ESS strategy p^* must then do at least as well as a mutant strategy p in their most common contests against p^* and, if these contests yield the same payoff, then p^* must do better than p in their rare contests against a mutant. That is, Maynard Smith's

definition applied to a symmetric two-player game says p^* is an ESS if and only if, for all $p \neq p^*$,

(i) $\pi(p, p^*) \leq \pi(p^*, p^*)$
(equilibrium condition)

(ii)   if $\pi(p, p^*) = \pi(p^*, p^*)$, $\pi(p, p) < \pi(p^*, p)$
(stability condition)

$$(1)$$

where $\pi(p, \hat{p})$ is the payoff of p against $\hat{p}$. One reason the ESS concept has proven so durable is that it has equivalent formulations that are equally intuitive (see especially the concepts of invasion barrier and local superiority in Section 2.1).

By (1) (i), an ESS is a Nash equilibrium (NE) with the extra refinement condition (ii) that seems heuristically related to dynamic stability. In fact, there is a complex relationship between the static ESS conditions and dynamic stability, as illustrated throughout this article with specific reference to the replicator equation. It is this relationship that formed the initial basis of what has come to be known as 'evolutionary game theory'.

ESS theory (and evolutionary game theory in general) has been extended to many classes of games besides those based on a symmetric two-player game. This article begins with ESS theory for symmetric normal form games before briefly describing the additional features that arise in each of several types of more general games. The unifying principle of local (or neighborhood) superiority will emerge in the process.

2. ESS for symmetric games

In a symmetric evolutionary game, there is a single set S of pure strategies available to the players, and the payoff to pure strategy e_i is a function π_i of the system's strategy distribution. In the following subsections we consider two-player symmetric games with S finite in normal and extensive forms (Sections 2.1 and 2.2 respectively) and with S a continuous set (Section 2.3).

2.1. Normal form games

Let $S \equiv \{e_1, \ldots, e_n\}$ be the set of pure strategies. A player may also use a mixed strategy $p \in \Delta^n \equiv \{p = (p_1, \ldots, p_n) | \sum p_i = 1, p_i \geq 0\}$ where p_i is the proportion of the time this individual uses pure strategy e_i. Pure strategy e_i is identified with the ith unit vector in Δ^n. The population state is $\hat{p} \in \Delta^n$ whose components are the current frequencies of strategy use in the population (that is, the strategy distribution). We assume the expected payoff to p is the bilinear function $\pi(p, \hat{p}) = \sum_{i,j=1}^n p_i \pi(e_i, e_j) \hat{p}_j$ resulting from random two-player contests.

Suppose the resident population is monomorphic at p^* (that is, all members adopt strategy p^*) and a monomorphic sub-population of mutants using p appears in the system. These mutants will not invade if there is a positive *invasion barrier* $\varepsilon_0(p)$ (Bomze and Pötscher, 1989). That is, if the proportion ε of mutants in the system is less than $\varepsilon_0(p)$, then the mutants will eventually die out due to their lower replication rate. In mathematical terms, $\varepsilon = 0$ is a (locally) asymptotically stable rest point of the corresponding resident-mutant invasion dynamics. For invasion dynamics based on replication, Bomze and Pötscher show p^* is an ESS (that is, satisfies (1)) if and only if every $p \neq p^*$ has a positive invasion barrier.

Important and somewhat surprising consequences of an ESS p^* are its asymptotic stability for many evolutionary dynamics beyond these monomorphic resident systems invaded by a single type of mutant. For instance, p^* is asymptotically stable when simultaneously invaded by several types of mutants and when a polymorphic resident system consisting of several (mixed) strategy types whose average strategy is p^* is invaded (see the 'strong stability' concept developed in Cressman, 1992). In particular, p^* is asymptotically stable for the replicator equation (Taylor and Jonker, 1978; Hofbauer, Schuster and Sigmund, 1979; Zeeman, 1980)

$$\dot{p}_i = p_i(\pi(e_i, p) - \pi(p, p)) \qquad (2)$$

when each individual player is a pure strategist.

Games that have a completely mixed ESS (that is, p^* is in the interior of Δ^n) enjoy further dynamic stability properties since these games are *strictly stable* (that is, $\pi(p - \hat{p}, p - \hat{p}) < 0$ for all $p \neq \hat{p}$) (Sandholm, 2006). The ESS of a strictly stable game is also globally asymptotically stable for the best response dynamics (the continuous-time version of fictitious play) (Hofbauer and Sigmund, 1998) and for the Brown–von Neumann–Nash dynamics (related to Nash's, 1951, proof of existence of NE) (Hofbauer and Sigmund, 2003).

The preceding two paragraphs provide a strong argument that an ESS will be the ultimate outcome of the evolutionary adjustment process. The proofs of these results use two other equivalent characterizations of an ESS p^* of a symmetric normal form game; namely,

(a) p^* has a *uniform* invasion barrier (i.e. $\varepsilon_0(p) > 0$ is independent of p)
(b) for all p sufficiently close (but not equal) to p^*

$$\pi(p, p) < \pi(p^*, p). \qquad (3)$$

It is this last characterization, called 'local superiority' (Weibull, 1995), that proves so useful for other classes of games (see below). Heuristically, (3) suggests p^* will be asymptotically stable since there is an incentive to shift towards p^* whenever the system is slightly perturbed from p^*.

Unfortunately, there are many normal form games that have no ESS. These include most three-strategy games classified by Zeeman (1980) and Bomze (1995).

Table 1   *The payoff matrix for the Rock–Scissors–Paper Game*

$$\begin{array}{c} \text{Rock} \\ \text{Scissors} \\ \text{Paper} \end{array} \begin{bmatrix} 0 & 1 & -1 \\ -1 & 0 & 1 \\ 1 & -1 & 0 \end{bmatrix}$$

Each entry is the payoff to the row player when column players are listed in the same order.

No mixed strategy p^* can be an ESS of a symmetric zero-sum game (that is, $\pi(\hat{p}, p) = -\pi(p, \hat{p})$ for all $p, \hat{p} \in \Delta^n$) since $\pi(p^*, p) = \pi(p^* - p, p) \leq 0 = \pi(p, p)$ for all $p \in \Delta^n$ in some direction from p^*. Thus, the classic zero-sum Rock–Scissors–Paper Game in Table 1 has no ESS since its only NE $\left(\frac{1}{3}, \frac{1}{3}, \frac{1}{3}\right)$ is interior. An early attempt to relax the ESS conditions to rectify this replaces the strict inequality in (1) (ii) by $\pi(p, p) \leq \pi(p^*, p)$. The NE p^* is then called a *neutrally stable strategy* (NSS) (Maynard Smith, 1982; Weibull, 1995). The only NE of the Rock–Scissors–Paper Game is a NSS.

Also, the normal forms of most interesting extensive form games have no ESS, especially when NE outcomes do not specify choices off the equilibrium path and so correspond to NE components. In general, when NE are not isolated, the *ESSet* introduced by Thomas (1985) is more important. This is a set E of NSS so that (1) (ii) holds for all $p^* \in E$ and $p \notin E$. An ESSet is a finite union of disjoint NE components, each of which must be an ESSet in its own right. Each ESSet has setwise dynamic stability consequences analogous to an ESS (Cressman, 2003). The ES structure of a game refers to its collection of ESSs and ESSets.

There are then several classes of symmetric games that always have an ESSet. Every two-strategy game has an ESSet (Cressman, 2003) which generically (that is, unless $\pi(\hat{p}, \hat{p}) = \pi(p, \hat{p})$ for all $p, \hat{p} \in \Delta^2$) is a finite set of ESSs. All games with symmetric payoff function (that is, $\pi(\hat{p}, p) = \pi(p, \hat{p})$ for all $p, \hat{p} \in \Delta^n$) have an ESSet corresponding to the set of local maxima of $\pi(p, p)$ which generically is a set of isolated ESSs). These are called partnership games (Hofbauer and Sigmund, 1998) or common interest games (Sandholm, 2006).

Symmetric games with payoff, $\pi_i(\hat{p})$, of pure strategy e_i nonlinear in the population state $\hat{p}$ are quite common in biology and in economics (Maynard Smith, 1982; Sandholm, 2006), where they are called playing-the-field models or population games. With $\pi(p, \hat{p}) = \sum_i p_i \pi_i(\hat{p})$, nonlinearity implies (1) is a weaker condition than (3), as examples in Bomze and Pötscher (1989) show. Local superiority (3) is then taken as the operative definition of an ESS p^* (Hofbauer and Sigmund, 1998) and it is equivalent to the existence of a uniform invasion barrier for p^*.

2.2. Extensive form games

The application of ESS theory to finite extensive form games has been less successful (see Figure 1). Every ESS

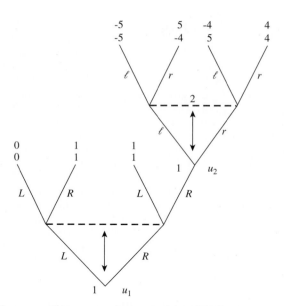

Figure 1 The extensive form tree of the van Damme example. For the construction of the tree of a symmetric extensive form game, see Selten (1983) or van Damme (1991)

can have no other realization equivalent strategies in its normal form (van Damme, 1991) and so, in particular, must be *pervasive strategy* (that is, it must reach every information set when played against itself). To ease these problems, Selten (1983) defined a *direct ESS* in terms of behaviour strategies (that is, strategies that specify the local behaviour at each player information set) as a b^* that satisfies (1) for any other behaviour strategy b. He showed each such b^* is subgame perfect and arises from the backward induction technique applied to the ES structure of the subgames and their corresponding truncations.

Consider backward induction applied to Figure 1. Its second-stage subgame $\begin{array}{c} \ell \\ r \end{array}\begin{bmatrix} -5 & 5 \\ -4 & 4 \end{bmatrix}$ has mixed ESS $b_2^* = \left(\frac{1}{2}, \frac{1}{2}\right)$ and, when the second decision point of player 1 is replaced by the payoff 0 from b_2^*, the truncated single-stage game $\begin{array}{c} L \\ R \end{array}\begin{bmatrix} 0 & 1 \\ 1 & 0 \end{bmatrix}$ also has a mixed ESS $b_1^* = \left(\frac{1}{2}, \frac{1}{2}\right)$. Since both stage games have a mixed ESS (and so a unique NE since they are strictly stable), (b_1^*, b_2^*) is the only NE of Figure 1 and it is pervasive. Surprisingly, this example has no direct ESS as Selten originally hoped since (b_1^*, b_2^*) can be invaded by the pure strategy that plays Rr (van Damme, 1991).

The same technique applied to Figure 1 with second-stage subgame replaced by $\begin{array}{c} \ell \\ r \end{array}\begin{bmatrix} -1 & 0 \\ 0 & -1 \end{bmatrix}$ yields $b_2^* = \left(\frac{1}{2}, \frac{1}{2}\right)$ and truncated single-stage game $\begin{array}{c} L \\ R \end{array}\begin{bmatrix} 0 & 1 \\ 1 & -1/2 \end{bmatrix}$

with $b_1^* = \left(\frac{3}{5}, \frac{2}{5}\right)$. This is an example of a two-stage War of Attrition with base game $\begin{bmatrix} 0 & 1 \\ 1 & 0 \end{bmatrix}$ where a player remains (R) at the first stage in the hope the opponent will leave (L) but incurs a waiting cost of one payoff unit if both players remain. This (b_1^*, b_2^*) is a direct ESS since all N-stage War of Attrition games are strictly stable (Cressman, 2003).

The examples in the preceding two paragraphs show that, although backward induction determines candidates for the ES structure, it is not useful for determining which candidates are actually direct ESSs. The situation is more discouraging for non-pervasive NE. For example, the only NE outcome of the two-stage repeated Prisoner's Dilemma game (Nachbar, 1992) with cumulative payoffs is mutual defection at each stage. This NE outcome cannot be an isolated behaviour strategy (that is, there is a corresponding NE component) and so there is no direct ESS. Worse, for typical single-stage payoffs such as $\begin{array}{c} \text{Defect} \\ \text{Cooperate} \end{array}\begin{bmatrix} -1 & 10 \\ -2 & 5 \end{bmatrix}$, this component does not satisfy setwise extensions of the ESS (for example, it is not an ESSet).

Characterization of NE found by backward induction with respect to dynamically stable rest points of the subgames and their truncations shows more promise. Each direct ESS b^* yields an ESSet in the game's normal form (Cressman, 2003) and so is dynamically stable. Furthermore, for the class of simultaneity games where both players know all player actions at earlier stages, Cressman shows that, if b^* is a pervasive NE, then it is asymptotically stable with respect to the replicator equation if and only if it comes from this backward induction process. In particular, the NE for Figure 1 and for the N-stage War of Attrition are (globally) asymptotically stable. Although the subgame perfect NE for the N-stage Prisoner's Dilemma game that defects at each decision point is not asymptotically stable, the eventual outcome of evolution is in the NE component (Nachbar, 1992; Cressman, 2003).

2.3. Continuous strategy space

Evolutionary game theory for symmetric games with a continuous set of pure strategies S has been slower to develop. Most recent work examines static payoff comparisons that predict an $x^* \in S$ is the evolutionary outcome. There are now fundamental differences between the ESS notion (1) and that of local superiority (3) as well as between invasion by monomorphic mutant subpopulations and the polymorphic model of the replicator equation. Here, we illustrate these differences when S is a subinterval of real numbers and $\pi(x, y)$ is a continuous payoff function of $x, y \in S$.

First, consider an $x^* \in S$ that satisfies (3). In particular,

$$\pi(x, x) < \pi(x^*, x) \qquad (4)$$

for all $x \in S$ sufficiently close (but not equal) to x^*. This is the *neighbourhood invader strategy* (NIS) condition of Apaloo (1997) that states x^* can invade any nearby monomorphism x. On the other hand, from (1), x^* cannot be invaded by these x if it is a *neighbourhood strict NE*, that is

$$\pi(x, x^*) < \pi(x^*, x^*) \tag{5}$$

for any other x sufficiently close to x^*. Inequalities (4) (5) are independent of each other and combine to assert that x^* strictly dominates x in all these two-strategy games $\{x^*, x\}$.

In the polymorphic model, populations are described by a P in the infinite dimensional set $\Delta(S)$ of probability distributions with support in S. When the expected payoff $\pi(x, P)$ is given through random pairwise contests, Cressman (2005) shows that strict domination implies x^* is *neighbourhood superior* (that is,

$$\pi(x^*, P) > \pi(P, P) \tag{6}$$

for all other $P \in \Delta(S)$ with support sufficiently close to x^*) and conversely, neighbourhood superiority implies weak domination. Furthermore, a neighborhood superior monomorphic population x^* (that is, the Dirac delta probability distribution δ_{x^*}) is asymptotically stable for all initial P with support sufficiently close to x^* (and containing x^*) under the replicator equation. This is now a dynamic on $\Delta(S)$ (Oechssler and Riedel, 2002) that models the evolution of the population distribution.

In the monomorphic model, the population is a monomorphism $x(t) \in S$ at all times. If a nearby mutant strategy $y \in S$ can invade x, the whole population is shifted in this direction. This intuition led Eshel (1983) to define a *continuously stable strategy* (CSS) as a neighbourhood strict NE x^* that satisfies, for all x sufficiently close to x^*,

$$\pi(y, x) > \pi(x, x) \tag{7}$$

for all y between x^* and x that are sufficiently close to x. Later, Dieckmann and Law (1996) developed the canonical equation of adaptive dynamics to model the evolution of this monomorphism and showed a neighbourhood strict NE x^* is a CSS if and only if it is an asymptotically stable rest point. Cressman (2005) shows x^* is a CSS if and only if it is *neighbourhood half-superior* (that is, there is a uniform invasion barrier of at least $\frac{1}{2}$ in the two-strategy games $\{x^*, x\}$) (see also the half-dominant concept of Morris, Rob and Shin, 1995).

For example, take $S = \mathbf{R}$ and payoff function

$$\pi(x, y) = -x^2 + bxy \tag{8}$$

that has strict NE $x^* = 0$ for all values of the fixed parameter b. x^* is a NIS (CSS) if and only if $b < 1$ $(b < 2)$ (Cressman and Hofbauer, 2005). Thus, there are strict NE when $b > 2$ that are not 'evolutionarily stable'.

3. Asymmetric games

Following Selten (1980) and van Damme (1991), in a two-player asymmetric game with two roles (or species), pairwise contests may involve players in the same or in opposite roles. First, consider ESS theory when there is a finite set of pure strategies $S = \{e_1, \ldots, e_n\}$ and $T = \{f_1, \ldots, f_m\}$ for players in role 1 and 2 respectively. Assume payoff to a mixed strategist is given by a bilinear payoff function and let $\pi_1(p; \hat{p}, \hat{q})$ be the payoff to a player in role one using $p \in \Delta^n$ when the current state of the population in roles 1 and 2 are $\hat{p}$ and $\hat{q}$ respectively. Similarly, $\pi_2(q; \hat{p}, \hat{q})$ is the payoff to a player in role 2 using $q \in \Delta^m$. For a discussion of resident-mutant invasion dynamics, see Cressman (1992), who shows the monomorphism (p^*, q^*) is uninvadable by any other mutant pair (p, q) if and only if it is a *two-species ESS*, that is, for all (p, q) sufficiently close (but not equal) to (p^*, q^*),

$$\text{either } \pi_1(p; p, q) < \pi_1(p^*; p, q) \text{ or}$$
$$\pi_2(q; p, q) < \pi_2(q^*; p, q). \tag{9}$$

The ESS condition (9) is the two-role version of local superiority (3) and has an equivalent formulation analogous to (1) (Cressman, 1992). This ESS also enjoys similar stability properties to the ESS of Subsection 2.1 such as its asymptotic stability under the (two-species) replicator equation (Cressman, 1992; 2003).

A particularly important class of asymmetric games consists of truly asymmetric games that have no contests between players in the same role (that is, there are no intraspecific contests). These are bimatrix games (that is, given by an $n \times m$ matrix whose ijth entry is the pair of payoffs $(\pi_1(e_i, f_j), \pi_2(e_i, f_j))$ for the interspecific contest between e_i and f_j). The ESS concept is now quite restrictive since Selten (1980) showed that (p^*, q^*) satisfies (9) if and only if it is a strict NE. This is also equivalent to asymptotic stability under the (two-species) replicator equation (Cressman, 2003). Standard examples (Cressman, 2003), with two strategies for each player include the Buyer–Seller Game that has no ESS since its only NE is in the interior. Another is the Owner–Intruder Game that has two strict NE Maynard Smith (1982) called the bourgeois ESS where the owners defend their territory and the paradoxical ESS where owners retreat.

Asymmetric games with continuous sets of strategies have recently received a great deal of attention (Leimar, 2006). For a discussion of neighbourhood (half) superiority conditions that generalize (6) and (7) to two-role truly asymmetric games with continuous payoff functions, see Cressman (2005). He also shows how these conditions are related to NIS and CSS concepts based on (9) and to equilibrium selection results for games with discontinuous payoff functions such as the Nash Demand Game (Binmore, Samuelson and Young, 2003).

ROSS CRESSMAN

See also **deterministic evolutionary dynamics; learning and evolution in games: an overview.**

Bibliography

Apaloo, J. 1997. Revisiting strategic models of evolution: the concept of neighborhood invader strategies. *Theoretical Population Biology* 52, 71–7.

Binmore, K., Samuelson, L. and Young, P. 2003. Equilibrium selection in bargaining models. *Games and Economic Behavior* 45, 296–328.

Bomze, I. 1995. Lotka–Volterra equation and replicator dynamics: new issues in classification. *Biological Cybernetics* 72, 447–53.

Bomze, I. and Pötscher, B. 1989. *Game Theoretical Foundations of Evolutionary Stability.* Lecture notes in economics and mathematical systems 324. Berlin: Springer-Verlag.

Cressman, R. 1992. *The Stability Concept of Evolutionary Games (A Dynamic Approach).* Lecture notes in biomathematics 94. Berlin: Springer-Verlag.

Cressman, R. 2003. *Evolutionary Dynamics and Extensive Form Games.* Cambridge, MA: MIT Press.

Cressman, R. 2005. Continuously stable strategies, neighborhood superiority and two-player games with continuous strategy space. Mimeo.

Cressman, R. and Hofbauer, J. 2005. Measure dynamics on a one-dimensional continuous trait space: theoretical foundations for adaptive dynamics. *Theoretical Population Biology* 67, 47–59.

Dieckmann, U. and Law, R. 1996. The dynamical theory of coevolution: a derivation from stochastic ecological processes. *Journal of Mathematical Biology* 34, 579–612.

Eshel, I. 1983. Evolutionary and continuous stability. *Journal of Theoretical Biology* 103, 99–111.

Hofbauer, J., Schuster, P. and Sigmund, K. 1979. A note on evolutionarily stable strategies and game dynamics. *Journal of Theoretical Biology* 81, 609–12.

Hofbauer, J. and Sigmund, K. 1998. *Evolutionary Games and Population Dynamics.* Cambridge: Cambridge University Press.

Hofbauer, J. and Sigmund, K. 2003. Evolutionary game dynamics. *Bulletin of the American Mathematical Society* 40, 479–519.

Leimar, O. 2006. Multidimensional convergence stability and the canonical adaptive dynamics. In *Elements of Adaptive Dynamics*, ed. U. Dieckmann and J. Metz. Cambridge University Press.

Maynard Smith, J. 1982. *Evolution and the Theory of Games.* Cambridge: Cambridge University Press.

Maynard Smith, J. and Price, G. 1973. The logic of animal conflicts. *Nature* 246, 15–18.

Morris, S., Rob, R. and Shin, H. 1995. Dominance and belief potential. *Econometrica* 63, 145–57.

Nachbar, J. 1992. Evolution in the finitely repeated Prisoner's Dilemma. *Journal of Economic Behavior and Organization* 19, 307–26.

Nash, J. 1951. Non-cooperative games. *Annals of Mathematics* 54, 286–95.

Oechssler, J. and Riedel, F. 2002. On the dynamic foundation of evolutionary stability in continuous models. *Journal of Economic Theory* 107, 223–52.

Sandholm, W. 2006. *Population Games and Evolutionary Dynamics.* Cambridge, MA: MIT Press.

Selten, R. 1980. A note on evolutionarily stable strategies in asymmetrical animal contests. *Journal of Theoretical Biology* 84, 93–101.

Selten, R. 1983. Evolutionary stability in extensive two-person games. *Mathematical Social Sciences* 5, 269–363.

Taylor, P. and Jonker, L. 1978. Evolutionarily stable strategies and game dynamics. *Mathematical Biosciences* 40, 145–156.

Thomas, B. 1985. On evolutionarily stable sets. *Journal of Mathematical Biology* 22, 105–15.

van Damme, E. 1991. *Stability and Perfection of Nash Equilibria*, 2nd edn. Berlin: Springer-Verlag.

Weibull, J. 1995. *Evolutionary Game Theory.* Cambridge, MA: MIT Press.

Zeeman, E. 1980. Population dynamics from game theory. In *Global Theory of Dynamical Systems*, ed. Z. Nitecki and C. Robinson. Lecture notes in mathematics 819. Berlin: Springer.

learning and information aggregation in networks

'Social learning' is a process whereby economic agents learn by observing the actions (but not the payoffs) of others; 'social learning in networks' applies this idea to situations in which individuals observe the other individuals to whom they are connected in a social network.

Griliches (1957) first studied the gradual adoption of corn planted with hybrid seed in the USA, a new agricultural technique, from the early 1930s to mid-1950s. He observed that at first farmers learned from salespersons; later they learned from their neighbours. The result was an S-shaped time profile of adoption. A number of recent papers, including Foster and Rosenzweig (1995), Conley and Udry (2001), Kremer and Miguel (2003) and Munshi (2004) examine how agents in developing countries learn from their social contacts when deciding whether to adopt new technologies.

The classical model of social learning, first studied by Banerjee (1992) and Bikhchandani, Hirshleifer and Welch (1992), and extended by Smith and Sørensen (2000), assumes a *pure information externality.* An agent's payoff $u(a, w)$ depends only on his own action a and an unknown state of nature w. Each agent i has private information about the state and his choice of action a will reflect that information. By observing an agent's action, it is possible to learn something about his information and make a better decision. The problem is that agents may rationally ignore their own information and 'follow the herd', that is, imitate the actions they see others choose. So-called *herd behaviour* and *informational cascades* can arise very rapidly, before much information has been revealed, and often result in inefficient choices. A number of experimental studies replicate herd behaviour in the laboratory.

The classical models assume that agents make decisions sequentially and observe the action chosen by each of their predecessors. In reality, individuals are bound together by a *social network*, the complex of relationships that brings them into contact with other agents, such as neighbours, co-workers, family, and so on. A specific framework, introduced by Gale and Kariv (2003), henceforth GK, assumes that individuals are bound together by a social network and can observe the agents to whom they are connected only through the network. The social network is represented by a *directed graph* in which nodes correspond to agents and agent i can observe agent j if there is an edge leading from node i to node j. In order to model the diffusion of information through the network, GK assume that agents choose actions simultaneously and revise their decisions as new information is received. More precisely, an agent whose current information is I chooses an action a to maximize his short-run payoff $E[u(a, w)|I]$. GK rationalize non-strategic behaviour by assuming there is a large number of agents of each type, so a single agent's decision has no impact on the future play of the game.

An agent's beliefs can be represented by a random sequence of probability distributions $P_t(\omega)$. At date t, an agent derives a posterior $P_{t+1}(w)$ from the prior $P_t(w)$ and the new information received. These beliefs satisfy the martingale property $E[P_{t+1}|I_t] = P_t$, and the martingale convergence theorem implies that these beliefs converge to a constant with probability one. The limiting beliefs are not necessarily uniform (different agents may have different beliefs) and need not be fully revealing. However, in *connected* networks, where every agent is connected directly or indirectly with every other agent, the initial diversity of actions is eventually replaced by uniformity. More precisely, except in cases of indifference, agents will choose the same action. This is the network-learning analogue of the herd behaviour found in the classical social learning model. The proof of uniformity makes use of the *imitation principle*. If agent i can observe the actions of agent j, agent i must be able to do as well as j on average (because one feasible strategy is to choose the same action j). In a connected network, all agents get the same payoff on average and this implies that they choose different actions only if they are indifferent.

Learning in a network is 'simply' a matter of Bayesian updating, but a rational agent must take account of the network architecture in order to update correctly. For example, suppose there are three (types of) agents, A, B, and C, arranged in a circle: A observes B, B observes C,

and C observes A. At the first decision, A has not yet had a chance to observe B, so he makes his decision based on his private information. Before the second decision, A observes B's first decision and uses it to update his beliefs about the true state of nature. Before the third decision, A observes B's second decision and realizes that any change from the first must be based on B's observation of C's first decision. So now A can make some inference about C's private information and update his beliefs accordingly. This learning can go on for some time. Eventually, A may observe changes in B's action that were prompted by changes in C's action that were prompted by C's observation of A. Even this is informative because it reveals how strong C's information is relative to A's. In any case, exploiting fully the information revealed in a network requires agents to consider not only what they observe, but also what their neighbours observe, what their neighbours' neighbors observe, and so on. The chains of inferences that rational individuals make naturally involve hierarchies of beliefs, that is, beliefs about a neighbour's beliefs about a neighbour's beliefs about ....

The complexity of Bayesian learning in networks has led some authors to suggest that models of *bounded rationality* are more appropriate for describing learning in networks. Bala and Goyal (1998) examine the decisions of boundedly rational agents, who try to extract information from the actions and payoffs of the agents they observe, but without taking account of the fact that those agents also observe other agents. Hence, there is private information in the Bala–Goyal model, but agents are assumed to ignore it. In the Bala–Goyal model, at each date, an agent chooses one of several available actions with unknown payoff distributions. Agents can observe the actions and payoffs of their neighbours (those to whom they are directly connected by the network) and use this information to update their beliefs about the payoff distribution. Thus, agents learn by observing the outcome (payoff) of an experiment (choice of action) rather than by inferring another agent's private information from his action. This is a model of *social experimentation*, in the sense that it generalizes the problem of a single agent experimenting with a multi-armed bandit to a social setting, rather than social learning. A model of social experimentation is quite different from a model of social learning because there is an informational externality but there is no informational asymmetry. As with Bayesian learning, boundedly rational learning implies convergence of beliefs and uniformity of actions in the limit.

Laboratory experiments provide the cleanest test for the theory since subjects' neighbourhoods and private information can be controlled. Choi, Gale and Kariv (2004; 2005) describe the results of an experimental investigation of learning in networks based on the model of GK. The experiments involve three-person, connected social networks. The experimental design uses three representative networks: the *complete network*, in which each agent can observe the actions chosen by the other agents; the *star network*, in which one agent, the centre, can observe the actions of the other two peripheral agents, and the peripheral agents can observe only the centre; and the *circle network*, in which each agent can observe only one other agent and each agent is observed by one other agent. Despite the small number of players in each game, it can be shown that myopic payoff maximization is rational: there is no gain to strategic behaviour. Nonetheless, larger-scale experiments might be informative.

The experimental data from these studies exhibit a strong tendency toward herd behaviour, but despite this tendency the efficiency of information aggregation is quite good. Although convergence to a uniform action is quite rapid, frequently occurring within two to three turns, there are significant differences between the behaviour of different networks. Most herds entail correct decisions, which is consistent with the predictions of the parametric model underlying the experimental design. Comparing the behaviour of different individuals indicates that there is indeed high variation in individual behaviour across subjects, but the error rates (the proportion of times a subject deviates from the best response) are uniformly fairly low.

These results suggest that the theory adequately accounts for large-scale features of the data, but in some situations the theory does less well in accounting for subjects' behaviour. It is likely that the theory fails in those situations because the complexity of the decision problem exceeds the bounded rationality of the subjects. Clearly, because of the lack of common knowledge in the networks, the decision problems faced by subjects require quite sophisticated reasoning. Subjects' success or failure in the experiment results from the appropriateness of the heuristics they use as much as the inherent difficulty of the decision-making. Thus, an important subject for future research is to identify 'black spots' where the theory does least well in interpreting the data and ask whether additional 'behavioural' explanations might be needed to account for the subjects' behaviour.

Many important questions about social learning in networks remain to be explored. While small networks can be very insightful, especially in experimental contexts, the development of the theory depends on properties of networks that can be generalized. The recent discovery of Barabási and Albert (1999) that many networks are *scale-free*, in the sense that a few nodes are *hubs*, which have a very large number of links to other nodes whereas most nodes have just a few, has significant implications for the efficiency of information aggregation. Once information reaches a hub it passes to numerous other nodes and spreads rapidly throughout the entire population, but if the hub's information is of poor quality its disproportionate influence becomes a disadvantage. Thus, the impact of hubs on the efficiency of information aggregation is not clear. Perhaps

the most important subject for future research is to identify the impact of network architecture on the efficiency and dynamics of social learning. Progress in this area requires both new theory and new experimental data.

DOUGLAS GALE AND SHACHAR KARIV

See also **behavioural game theory; experimental economics, history of; Griliches, Zvi; information cascades; learning and evolution in games: an overview; logit models of individual choice; network formation.**

Bibliography

Bala, V. and Goyal, S. 1998. Learning from neighbors. *Review of Economic Studies* 65, 595–621.

Banerjee, A. 1992. A simple model of herd behavior. *Quarterly Journal of Economics* 107, 797–817.

Barabási, A. and Albert, R. 1999. Emergence of scaling in random networks. *Science* 286, 509–12.

Bikhchandani, S., Hirshleifer, D. and Welch, I. 1992. A theory of fads, fashion, custom, and cultural change as informational cascade. *Journal of Political Economy* 100, 992–1026.

Choi, S., Gale, D. and Kariv, S. 2004. Learning in networks: an experimental study. Mimeo. New York: Center for Experimental Social Science (CESS), New York University.

Choi, S., Gale, D. and Kariv, S. 2005. Behavioral aspects of learning in social networks: an experimental study. *Experimental and Behavioral Economics Advances in Applied Microeconomics*, vol. 13, ed. J. Morgan. Oxford: JAI Press.

Conley, T. and Udry, C. 2001. Social learning through networks: the adoption of new agricultural technologies in Ghana. *American Journal of Agricultural Economics* 83, 668–73.

Foster, A. and Rosenzweig, M. 1995. Learning by doing and learning from others: human capital and technical change in agriculture. *Journal of Political Economy* 103, 1176–209.

Gale, D. and Kariv, S. 2003. Bayesian learning in social networks. *Games and Economic Behavior* 45, 329–46.

Griliches, Z. 1957. Hybrid corn: an exploration in the economics of technological change. *Econometrica* 25, 501–22.

Kremer, M. and Miguel, T. 2003. Networks, social learning, and technology adoption: the case of deworming drugs in Kenya. Mimeo. Berkeley: Department of Economics, University of California.

Munshi, K. 2004. Social learning in a heterogeneous population: technology diffusion in the Indian Green Revolution. *Journal of Development Economics* 73, 185–213.

Smith, L. and Sørensen, P. 2000. Pathological outcomes of observational learning. *Econometrica* 68, 371–98.

learning-by-doing

Empirical studies of the production process in various industries have demonstrated a positive association between current labour productivity and measures of past activity like past cumulative output or investment (see Wright, 1936; Hirsch, 1956; Alchian, 1963; Hollander, 1965; Sheshinski, 1967; Boston Consulting Group, 1972; 1974; 1978; and Lieberman 1984). A hypothesis advanced to explain this is that labour learns through experience and that experience is obtained during the production process. In other words, learning-by-doing is one of the reasons giving rise to dynamic economies of scale, because a firm knows that increasing current production reduces future average costs. If knowledge obtained within one firm cannot be communicated to other firms, we speak of learning without spillovers. There is some empirical evidence, though, that firms cannot totally exclude outsiders from their stock of knowledge, mainly because of labour turnover (see Boston Consulting Group, 1978, and Lieberman, 1984). Learning spillovers are a special case of positive externalities. The study of learning-by-doing, therefore, is a special case in the study of economies characterized by dynamic economies of scale and positive externalities.

Empirical studies of growth have demonstrated that increases in per capita output cannot be attributed solely, or even mainly, to increases in the capital–labour ratio (see Abramovitz, 1956; Solow, 1957; Kendrick, 1976). On the other hand, Verdoorn (1956) observed a positive relationship between past cumulative output and current labour productivity in the aggregate. This seems to suggest that the part of growth unexplained by increases in the capital–labour ratio could be accounted for by learning-by-doing. Once income per head increases for any reason, say because of an increase in the capital–labour ratio, it will keep on increasing for ever because the initial increase will improve labour productivity and income per head in the next period; after that, the chain of output increases resulting in productivity increases and vice versa is repeated for ever and for the right values of the coefficients it will generate unbounded growth even with stationary population.

Formal models of this process were constructed by Arrow (1962), Levhari (1966), Romer (1986), and Stokey (1986). None of these authors model the process of learning explicitly but consider a world of perfect information with features that are supposed to emerge from a process of learning going on behind the scenes. Here we analyse Romer's model, which is the more general and pays particular attention to existence.

Romer considers a continuous time model with infinitely lived agents who produce and consume a single final good out of a fixed, inexhaustible supply of primary factors. At any given moment in time, the final good can be either consumed or added to the indestructible stock of capital. There is an exogenously given number of firms; each firm's output at any moment in time depends on the amount of capital accumulated by the firm up to that moment, on the amount of natural resources it employs and on the total amount of capital accumulated by all firms up to that moment. In other words, knowledge can be communicated across firms and is incorporated in the capital stock. There are diminishing returns in private capital accumulation but increasing returns when the effect of a firm's accumulation on the total capital stock is taken into account. Notice that the assumption of diminishing returns in private capital accumulation implies that the technical process generated by new learning is capital-augmenting, not land-augmenting. Firms maximize profit and consumers maximize utility taking prices as given. Existence of Walrasian equilibria is demonstrated under the following assumptions: (a) firms do not recognize that their accumulation affects the total capital stock; (b) the growth rate of each firm's capital stock is uniformly bounded above and is a concave function of each firm's investment; (c) the production function is majorized by a constant plus a constant-elasticity function of the capital stock; (d) the discount factor is larger than the product of the above elasticity times the upper bound in the growth rate of the capital stock. Under some additional conditions, the equilibrium capital stock and consumption per head grow without bound. Equilibria are Pareto inefficient because firms do not take into account the fact that their private accumulation adds to the aggregate capital stock and therefore reduces everybody's future costs. Romer and Sasaki (1985) have generated unbounded growth with constant population and a fixed supply of exhaustible resources under more restrictive conditions on the coefficients.

Clearly, the main achievement of Romer's competitive model is to generate unbounded growth without assuming exogenous improvements in technology. The applicability and generality of the model, though, are restricted by the price-taking assumption and the related assumptions that all economies of scale are external to the firm and that the number of firms is fixed. Suppose for a moment that we accept the last two assumptions. Then, as Fudenberg and Tirole (1983) showed, if returns with respect to private capital accumulation are constant, no price-taking equilibrium exists; in other words, the assumption that technical progress is not land-augmenting is crucial. Also, there is no reason why firms should fail to recognize the effect of their actions on the capital stock. Spence (1981) and Fudenberg and Tirole (1983) constructed dynamic partial equilibrium models of learning without spillovers in which a fixed number of firms compete in quantities with Cournot expectations. Industry output may decline over time at a subgame perfect equilibrium, depending on how large is the discount factor relative to the number of firms. Stokey (1986) investigated the same model with spillovers and found that industry output increases over time. Given the importance of spillovers in generating growth, therefore, it seems worthwhile to study their determinants.

The next step is to remove the assumption that all dynamic economies of scale are external to the firm and that the number of firms is fixed. Even if one begins with a situation of purely external economies of scale, there are powerful economic incentives to internalize these economies by reductions in the number of firms, either by collusion or by competition that drives some firms out of business. The tendency to collude to internalize externalities is checked by the incentive of each firm to shirk (underinvest in learning) given that others have done their share of investment. The tendency of competition to reduce the number of firms is checked by entry when the number of firms is so small that a new entrant's gains by wiping out excess profits exceed losses due to lost economies of scale. The learning-by-doing model coupled with such a theory of firm size could generate more predictions about growth, concentration and distribution of income over time.

Finally, one has to address the issue of the evolution of the externalities themselves over time. The extent of learning spillovers is limited by concentration and by the creation of markets in order to transform the external effects into ordinary goods; both of these magnitudes are endogenous, and so the extent of learning spillovers should also be an endogenous variable. The current formulation of learning spillovers assumes a stable, exogenous relationship between measures of past activity and future productivity, but in a long-run model one would not expect such a relationship to hold, exactly because the number of firms and completeness of markets are variable in the long run.

SPYROS VASSILAKIS

Bibliography

Abramovitz, M. 1956. Resource and Output Trends in the U.S. since 1870. Occasional Paper No. 52, NBER.

Alchian, A. 1963. Reliability of progress curves in airframe production. *Econometrica* 31, 679–93.

Arrow, K.J. 1962. The economic implications of learning by doing. *Review of Economic Studies* 29, 155–73.

Boston Consulting Group. 1972. Perspectives in experience. Technical Report.

Boston Consulting Group. 1974. The experience curve reviewed: price stability. Technical Report.

Boston Consulting Group. 1978. Cross sectional experience curves. Technical Report.

Fudenberg, D. and Tirole, J. 1983. Learning-by-doing and market performance. *Bell Journal of Economics* 14, 522–30.

Hirsch, W.Z. 1956. Firm progress ratios. *Econometrica* 24(2), 136–44.

Hollander, S. 1965. *The Source of Increased Efficiency: A Study of DuPont Rayon Plants*. Cambridge, MA: MIT Press.

Kendrick, J.W. 1976. *The Formation and Stocks of Total Capital*. New York: NBER.

Levhari, D. 1966. Extensions of Arrow's learning by doing. *Review of Economic Studies* 33, 117–32.

Lieberman, D. 1984. The learning curve and pricing in the chemical processing industries. *RAND Journal of Economics* 15, 213–28.

Romer, P. 1986. Increasing returns and long-run growth. *Journal of Political Economy* 94, 1002–37.

Romer, P. and Sasaki, H. 1985. Monotonically decreasing natural resource prices under perfect foresight. Working Paper No. 19, Rochester Center for Economic Research, New York.

Sheshinski, E. 1967. Tests of the learning-by-doing hypothesis. *Review of Economics and Statistics* 49, 568–78.

Solow, R. 1957. Technical change and the aggregate production function. *Review of Economics and Statistics* 39, 312–20.

Spence, A.M. 1981. The learning curve and competition. *Bell Journal of Economics* 12, 49–70.

Stokey, N. 1986. The dynamics of industry-wide learning. In *Equilibrium Analysis: Essays in Honor of K.J. Arrow*, vol. 2, ed. W.P. Heller, R.M. Starr and D.A. Starrett. Cambridge: Cambridge University Press.

Verdoorn, P.J. 1956. Complementarity and long-range projections. *Econometrica* 24, 429–50.

Wright, T.P. 1936. Factors affecting the cost of airplanes. *Journal of Aeronautical Sciences* 3(4), 122–8.

learning in macroeconomics

Learning in macroeconomics refers to models of expectation formation in which agents revise their forecast rules over time, for example in response to new data. Expectations of future income, prices and sales play key roles in theories of saving and investment. Many other examples of the central role of expectations could be given.

1 Introduction

The current standard methodology for modelling expectations is to assume that the economy is in a rational expectations equilibrium (REE). REE is a model-consistent equilibrium in the two-way relationship between the influence of expectations on the economy and the dependence of expectations on the time path of the economy.

The standard formulation of REE makes strong assumptions on the information of economic agents. The true stochastic process of the economy is assumed known, with unforecastable random shocks constituting the remaining uncertainty. This assumption presupposes that the economic agents know much more than, say, the economists who in practice do not know the true stochastic structure and instead must estimate its parameters.

Recently, macroeconomic theory has been moving beyond the strict rational expectations (RE) hypothesis.

Explicit models of imperfect knowledge and associated learning processes have been developed. In models of learning economic agents try to improve their knowledge of the stochastic process of the economy over time as new information becomes available.

Different approaches to modelling learning behaviour have been employed. Perhaps the most common has been 'adaptive learning', which views economic agents as econometricians who estimate the parameters of their model and make forecasts using their estimates. In adaptive learning economic agents have limited common knowledge since they estimate their own perceived laws of motion.

A second approach, called 'eductive learning', assumes common knowledge of rationality: economic agents engage in a process of reasoning about the possible outcomes knowing that other agents engage in the same process. Eductive learning takes place in logical time. A third approach has been 'rational learning', which employs a Bayesian viewpoint. Full knowledge of economic parameters is then replaced by priors and Bayesian updating under a correctly specified model, including common knowledge that all agents share this knowledge. Rational learning thus retains a form of REE at each point of time.

Basic theories of learning were developed largely in the 1980s and 1990s. See Sargent (1993, 1999), Evans and Honkapohja (2001), Guesnerie (2005) and Beck and Wieland (2002) for references. Recently, models of learning have been applied to issues of macroeconomic, and especially monetary, policy. In this overview, we focus on adaptive learning as it has been the most widely used approach. (For references to the pre-2001 literature, see Evans and Honkapohja, 2001.)

2 Least squares learning

In adaptive learning it is commonly assumed that agents estimate their model of the dynamics of economic variables, called the *perceived law of motion* (PLM), by *recursive least squares* (RLS), arguably the most common estimation method in econometrics.

2.1 Overview

We illustrate the key concepts using the Cagan model of the price level $\hat{m} - p_t = -\psi(p_{t+1}^e - p_t) + \varphi' w_t + \varepsilon_t$, where p_t and $\hat{m}$ are logarithms of the price level and (constant) nominal money supply. Here $\psi > 0$ and p_{t+1}^e denotes the expectations of p_{t+1} formed at time t. w_t is a vector of observable exogenous variables, assumed to follow a stationary vector autoregression (VAR) process $w_t = F w_{t-1} + e_t$, in which F is taken as known for simplicity. ε_t is an unobservable i.i.d. shock.

The reduced form of the Cagan model is

$$p_t = \alpha_0 + \alpha_1 p_{t+1}^e + \beta' w_t + v_t, \qquad (1)$$

where $v_t = -(1 + \psi)^{-1} \varepsilon_t$ and α_0, α_1 and β depend on $\hat{m}$, ψ and φ. The model has a unique REE of the form $p_t = \bar{a} + \bar{b}' w_t + v_t$, where $\bar{a} = (1 - \alpha_1)^{-1} \alpha_0$, $\bar{b} = (I - \alpha_1 F')^{-1} \beta$.

Agents are assumed to use the PLM $p_t = a + b' w_t + \eta_t$, where η_t is a disturbance term. The PLM has the same functional form as the REE but possibly different coefficients since agents do not know the REE. To estimate the PLM, agents use data $\{p_i, w_i\}_{i=0}^{t-1}$ and forecast using the estimated model $E_t^* p_{t+1} = a_{t-1} + b_{t-1}' F w_t$.

These forecasts lead to a temporary equilibrium or *actual law of motion* (ALM) $p_t = T(\phi_{t-1})' z_t + v_t$, where $T(\phi)' = (\alpha_0 + \alpha_1 a, \alpha_1 b' F + \beta')$. The REE $(\bar{a}, \bar{b}')$ is a fixed point of the mapping $T(\phi)$ from the PLM to the ALM. If we let $\phi_t' = (a_t, b_t')$ and $z_t' = (1, w_t')$, RLS estimation is given by

$$\phi_t = \phi_{t-1} + t^{-1} R_t^{-1} z_t (p_t - \phi_{t-1}' z_t)$$
$$R_t = R_{t-1} + t^{-1} (z_t z_t' - R_{t-1}). \qquad (2)$$

where p_t is given by the ALM. We say that the REE is *stable under RLS learning* if $(a_{t-1}, b_{t-1}') \to (\bar{a}, \bar{b}')$ over time.

This model of learning involves bounded rationality. Each period agents maximize their objective, given their forecasts. However, agents treat the economy as having constant parameters, which is true only in the REE. Outside the REE the PLMs are misspecified, but misspecification vanishes as learning converges to the REE.

A key result, which holds in numerous models, is that RLS learning converges to RE under certain conditions on model parameters. Thus, the REE can be learned even though economic agents initially have limited knowledge and are boundedly rational.

Expectational stability (E-stability) is a convenient way for establishing the convergence conditions for RLS learning. Define the differential equation $d\phi/d\tau = T(\phi) - \phi$, which describes partial adjustment in virtual time τ. The REE is *E-stable* if it is locally stable under the differential equation. For models of the form (1), convergence is guaranteed if $0 < \alpha_1 < 1$, which is satisfied in the Cagan model since $\alpha_1 = \psi(1 + \psi)^{-1}$. Evans and Honkapohja (2001) contains a detailed discussion of convergence of RLS learning.

2.2 The roles of learning

Adaptive learning has several other important roles besides being a stability theory for REE. RE models can have multiple stationary equilibria, that is, *indeterminacy of equilibrium*. In such situations learning stability acts as a *selection criterion* to determine the plausibility of a particular REE.

As an example consider the non-stochastic Cagan model with government spending financed by seigniorage, with nonlinear reduced form $x_t = G(x_{t+1}^e)$, where x_t denotes inflation (see Evans and Honkapohja, 2001, chs. 11 and 12, for details). This model has two (interior) steady state solutions $\hat{x} = G(\hat{x})$. The low-inflation steady state x_L is stable under learning and the high-inflation steady state x_H is not. Learning selects a unique REE x_L in this model. In more general models, learning stability does not necessarily select a unique REE, but the set of 'plausible' REE is usually significantly smaller than the set of all REE.

The roles of RLS learning are not restricted to stability of REE and equilibrium selection. Learning can also provide new forms of dynamics as discussed below.

3 Monetary policy design

Indeterminacy of equilibria and instability of REE under RLS learning mean that the economy can be subject to persistent fluctuations. These instabilities can arise in the New Keynesian (NK) model (Woodford, 2003), which is widely used for studying monetary policy. Policy design has an important role in eliminating these instabilities and facilitating convergence to 'desirable' equilibria.

Consider the linearized NK model. The IS and PC curves $x_t = -\varphi(i_t - E_t^*\pi_{t+1}) + E_t^*x_{t+1} + g_t$ and $\pi_t = \lambda x_t + \beta E_t^*\pi_{t+1} + u_t$ summarize private sector behaviour. Here x_t, π_t and i_t denote the output gap, inflation and the nominal interest rate. φ and λ are positive parameters while $0 < \beta < 1$ is the discount factor. The shocks g_t and u_t are assumed to be observable and follow a known $VAR(1)$ process.

Central bank (CB) behaviour is described by an interest-rate rule. CB may use an instrument rule that is not based on explicit optimization. Examples are Taylor rules that depend on current data or forecasts, $i_t = \chi_\pi \pi_t + \chi_x x_t$ or $i_t = \chi_\pi E_t^*\pi_{t+1} + \chi_x E_t^*x_{t+1}$, where χ_π, $\chi_x > 0$.

The IS and PC equations, together with either Taylor rule, lead to a bivariate reduced form in (x_t, π_t), which can be examined for determinacy (uniqueness of equilibrium) and E-stability. Bullard and Mitra (2002) show that current-data Taylor rules yield both E-stability and determinacy iff $\lambda(\chi_\pi - 1) + (1 - \beta)\chi_x > 0$. Under forward-looking rules $\chi_\pi > 1$ and small χ_x yield E-stability and determinacy.

Optimal monetary policy under discretion and commitment has been examined by Evans and Honkapohja (2003a; 2003b; 2006). Various ways to implement optimal policy have been suggested. Some commonly suggested interest-rate rules, based on fundamental shocks and variables, can lead to E-instability and/or indeterminacy. Evans and Honkapohja advocate appropriate expectations-based rules that deliver both E-stability and determinacy.

Other aspects of learning are also important for monetary policy. One practical concern is the observability of private forecasts needed for forecast-based rules. Results by Honkapohja and Mitra (2005) show that using internal CB forecasts in place of private sector expectations normally delivers E-stability.

Another difficulty for optimal monetary policy is that it requires knowledge of structural parameters, which are in practice unknown. CB can learn the values of φ and λ by estimating IS and PC equations. Expectations-based optimal rules continue to deliver stability under simultaneous learning by private agents and the CB (see Evans and Honkapohja, 2003a; 2003b).

4 Fluctuations

A major issue in macroeconomics is economic fluctuations, for example, business cycles and asset price movements. Can learning help to explain these phenomena?

4.1 Stable sunspot fluctuations

One theory of macroeconomic fluctuations interprets them as rational 'sunspot' equilibria. Although many macroeconomic models – for example, the real business cycle (RBC) model or Taylor's overlapping contracts model – have a unique stationary solution under RE, other models can have indeterminacy. Examples include the overlapping generations (OLG) model and RBC models with increasing returns and monopolistic competition or tax distortions.

When multiple equilibria are present, some solutions may depend on variables, 'sunspots', that are completely extraneous to the economy. Such stationary sunspot equilibria (SSEs) exhibit self-fulfilling prophecies with the sunspot acting as a coordinating device: if expectations depend on a sunspot variable, then the actual economy, since it depends on expectations, can also depend rationally on the sunspot.

As already noted, learning stability is a selection device. Suppose agents' forecasts are a linear function of both the macroeconomic state and a sunspot variable. If the forecast functions have coefficients close to but not equal to SSE values, and if agents update the estimated coefficients using RLS, can the coefficients converge to SSE values? If not, this casts doubt on the plausibility of SSEs.

SSEs appear not to be stable under learning in indeterminate RBC models but are learnable in some other models. We first describe results for the NK model and then discuss the possibility of stable SSE in other models.

4.1.1 SSEs in the NK model

Consider again the linearized NK model augmented by either the current-data or forward-looking Taylor rule. As noted above, indeterminacy is likely when the 'Taylor principle' $\chi_\pi > 1$ is violated.

In practice CBs are said to use forward-looking rules, and Clarida, Gali and Gertler (2000) argue that empirical estimates of χ_π are less than 1 in the period before 1984, while they are greater than 1 for the subsequent period. Could SSEs explain the higher economic volatility in the earlier period?

Honkapohja and Mitra (2004) and Evans and McGough (2005) approach this question by asking when SSEs are stable under learning in the NK model. Surprisingly, SSEs appear never to be stable under learning for current-data Taylor rules. When the forward-looking Taylor rule is employed, stable SSEs occur not when $\chi_\pi < 1$, but rather when $\chi_\pi > 1$ and χ_π and χ_x are sufficiently large, that is, *overly* aggressive rules lead to learnable SSEs. However, this does not rule out the Clarida, Gali, Gertler explanation for pre-1984 instability because, if $\chi_\pi < 1$ leads to indeterminacy, *no* REE is stable under learning and aggregate instability would presumably result.

4.1.2 Stable SSEs in other models
Stability under learning is a demanding test for SSEs that is met in only some cases in the NK model. There are, however, other examples of stable SSEs, such as the basic OLG model.

Some nonlinear models can have multiple steady states that are locally stable under RLS learning. In this case there can also be SSEs that take the form of occasional random shifts between neighbourhoods of the distinct stable steady states. Examples of this are the 'animal spirits' model of Howitt and McAfee (1992), based on a positive search externality, and the 'growth cycles' model of Evans, Honkapohja and Romer (1998) based on monopolistic competition and complementarities between capital goods.

Two stable steady states also play a role in some important policy models. This can arise in a monetary inflation model with a fiscal constraint, developed by Evans, Honkapohja and Marimon (2001), and in the liquidity trap model of Evans and Honkapohja (2005). In these set-ups policy has an important role in eliminating undesirable steady states.

4.2 Dynamics with constant gain learning
An alternative route to explaining economic fluctuations is to modify RLS learning so that more recent observations are given a higher weight. A natural way to motivate this is to assume that agents are concerned about the possibility of structural change. In the RLS formula (2) this can be formally accomplished by replacing t^{-1} with a small 'constant gain' $0 < \gamma < 1$, yielding weights that geometrically decline with the age of observations.

This apparently small change leads to 'boundedly rational' fluctuations, with sometimes dramatic effects. Three main phenomena have emerged. First, as shown by Sargent (1999) and Cho, Williams and Sargent (2002), even when there is a unique equilibrium, occasional 'escape paths' can arise with learning dynamics temporarily driving the economy far from the equilibrium. Sargent shows how the reduction of inflation in the 1982–99 period might be due to such an escape path in which policymakers are led to stop attempting

to exploit a perceived (but misspecified) Phillips curve trade-off.

Second, in models with multiple steady states, learning dynamics can take the form of periodic shifts between regimes as a result of intrinsic random shocks interacting with learning dynamics. This is seen in the 'increasing social returns' example of Evans and Honkapohja (2001), the hyperinflation model of Marcet and Nicolini (2003), the exchange rate model of Kasa (2004) and the liquidity trap model of Evans and Honkapohja (2005).

Third, even when large escapes do not arise, there can be policy implications, because constant gain learning differs in small but persistent ways from full rationality. Orphanides and Williams (2005) show that policymakers attempting to implement optimal policy should be more hawkish against inflation than under RE.

5 Other developments
There continue to be many new applications of learning dynamics in macroeconomics, with closely related work in asset pricing and game theory.

One recent topic concerns the possibility that agents use a misspecified model. Under RLS learning agents may still converge, but to a restricted perceptions equilibrium, rather than to an REE (see Evans and Honkapohja, 2001). Another recent development is to allow agents to select from alternative predictors. In the Brock and Hommes (1997) model agents choose, based on recent past performance, between a costly sophisticated and a cheap naive predictor. This can lead to complex non-linear dynamics. Branch and Evans (2006) combine dynamic predictor selection with RLS learning and show the existence of 'misspecification equilibria' when all forecasting models are underparameterized.

Other topics and applications include empirical work on expectation formation, calibration and estimation of learning models to data, interaction of policymaker and private-sector learning, learning and robust policy, experimental studies of expectation formation, the role of calculation costs, expectations over long horizons, alternative learning algorithms, expectational and structural heterogeneity, transitional learning dynamics, consistent expectations and near-rationality.

Current interest in learning dynamics is evidenced by five recent Special Issues devoted to learning and bounded rationality, in *Macroeconomic Dynamics* (2003), *Journal of Economic Dynamics and Control* (two in 2005), *Review of Economic Dynamics* (2005), and *Journal of Economic Theory* (2005).

GEORGE W. EVANS AND SEPPO HONKAPOHJA

See also **animal spirits; determinacy and indeterminacy of equilibria; expectations; learning and evolution in games: an overview; multiple equilibria in macroeconomics; new Keynesian macroeconomics; rational expectations; rationality, bounded; sunspot equilibrium; two-stage least squares and the *k*-class estimator.**

Bibliography

Beck, G. and Wieland, V. 2002. Learning and control in a changing environment. *Journal of Economic Dynamics and Control* 26, 1359–77.

Branch, W. and Evans, G. 2006. Intrinsic heterogeneity in expectation formation. *Journal of Economic Theory* 127, 264–95.

Brock, W. and Hommes, C. 1997. A rational route to randomness. *Econometrica* 65, 1059–95.

Bullard, J. and Mitra, K. 2002. Learning monetary policy rules. *Journal of Monetary Economics* 49, 1105–29.

Cho, I.-K., Williams, N. and Sargent, T. 2002. Escaping Nash inflation. *Review of Economic Studies* 69, 1–40.

Clarida, R., Gali, J. and Gertler, M. 2000. Monetary policy rules and macroeconomic stability: evidence and some theory. *Quarterly Journal of Economics* 115, 147–80.

Evans, G. and Honkapohja, S. 2001. *Learning and Expectations in Macroeconomics*. Princeton, NJ: Princeton University Press.

Evans, G. and Honkapohja, S. 2003a. Expectations and the stability problem for optimal monetary policies. *Review of Economic Studies* 70, 807–24.

Evans, G. and Honkapohja, S. 2003b. Adaptive learning and monetary policy design. *Journal of Money Credit and Banking* 35, 1045–72.

Evans, G. and Honkapohja, S. 2005. Policy interaction, expectations and the liquidity trap. *Review of Economic Dynamics* 8, 303–23.

Evans, G. and Honkapohja, S. 2006. Monetary policy, expectations and commitment. *Scandinavian Journal of Economics* 108, 15–38.

Evans, G., Honkapohja, S. and Marimon, R. 2001. Convergence in monetary inflation models with heterogeneous learning rules. *Macroeconomic Dynamics* 5, 1–31.

Evans, G., Honkapohja, S. and Romer, P. 1998. Growth cycles. *American Economic Review* 88, 495–515.

Evans, G. and McGough, B. 2005. Monetary policy, indeterminacy and learning. *Journal of Economic Dynamics and Control* 29, 1809–40.

Guesnerie, R. 2005. *Assessing Rational Expectations 2: 'Eductive' Stability in Economics*. Cambridge, MA: MIT Press.

Honkapohja, S. and Mitra, K. 2004. Are non-fundamental equilibria learnable in models of monetary policy? *Journal of Monetary Economics* 51, 1743–70.

Honkapohja, S. and Mitra, K. 2005. Performance of monetary policy with internal central bank forecasting. *Journal of Economic Dynamics and Control* 29, 627–58.

Howitt, P. and McAfee, R. 1992. Animal spirits. *American Economic Review* 82, 493–507.

Kasa, K. 2004. Learning, large deviations and recurrent currency crises. *International Economic Review* 45, 141–73.

Marcet, A. and Nicolini, J. 2003. Recurrent hyperinflations and learning. *American Economic Review* 93, 1476–98.

Orphanides, A. and Williams, J. 2005. Imperfect knowledge, inflation expectations and monetary policy. In *The Inflation-Targeting Debate*, ed. B. Bernanke and M. Woodford. Chicago: University of Chicago Press.

Sargent, T. 1993. *Bounded Rationality in Macroeconomics*. Oxford: Oxford University Press.

Sargent, T. 1999. *The Conquest of American Inflation*. Princeton, NJ: Princeton University Press.

Woodford, M. 2003. *Interest and Prices*. Princeton, NJ: Princeton University Press.

Lederer, Emil (1882–1939)

Emil Lederer was a prominent economist and sociologist in the German Weimar Republic. He was born in the Bohemian town of Pilsen in 1882 and died in political exile in New York City in 1939. In Vienna and Berlin, where he studied both law and economics, Lederer participated in advanced seminars conducted by Menger, Böhm-Bawerk and Schmoller. From 1918 to 1931 he served as professor in Heidelberg and then succeeded Sombart in Berlin from 1931 to 1933. In collaboration with E. Jaffé, Schumpeter and Sombart as well as Max and Alfred Weber, he edited the *Archiv für Sozialwissenschaft und Sozialpolitik*, the renowned social science journal which ceased publication under the Nazi regime. After emigrating to New York in 1933 be became the first Dean of the New School for Social Research's Faculty of Political and Social Sciences, which was comprised of outstanding Continental scholars who had also sought asylum in the United States.

Lederer made pioneering contributions towards understanding the social, political and economic significance of large-scale, bureaucratic private enterprise. In a major theoretical and empirical study based on his *Habilitation*, Lederer undertook the first comprehensive analysis of the working conditions and political attitudes of salaried employees (Lederer, 1912). Subsequent work together with Jacob Marschak showed how rationalization of production along with bureaucratic division of labour in administration formed the basis for the rise of the new middle class (Lederer and Marschak, 1926). They concluded that the evolution of class structure in advanced capitalist societies undermines political stability and raises the spectre of fascism. Anxiety stemming from economic insecurity and abhorrence of collective action with organized labour weakens the growing middle class's support for democratic forms of government and strengthens its tolerance of authoritarian institutions to suppress the demands of the proletariat.

Lederer's advanced economics textbook contains an authoritative exposition and critique of objective and subjective value theories (Lederer, 1931a). The laws of the market economy, as depicted in the marginalist doctrine, are no longer in effect, since economies of large-scale production prevail. Adoption of modern technologies requires vertical integration, high proportion of fixed capital and substantial fixed costs for sales and general administrative overhead. Complementarities and decreasing marginal costs are the rule in basic industries (coal, steel, chemicals and utilities).

Increasing returns to scale is not only an anomaly which cannot be subsumed under the marginalist paradigm; it forms the starting point for business cycle theory (Lederer, 1924; 1927). Disproportionalities in growth of demand for investment and consumer goods are due to unavoidable price inflexibilities and absence of strong equilibrating tendencies. Cartels which administer prices and set production quotas are the natural outcome of the technically determined drive to realize economies of scale. The self-contained planning of separate industrial bureaucracies lacks inter-industry coordination and thus cannot prevent misallocation, underutilization and periodic decumulation of capital.

Rapid labour-saving technical change is regarded by Lederer as a key factor in explaining the severity of unemployment during the Great Depression (Lederer, 1931b; 1936a). In an upswing, dynamic enterprises exploit opportunities to realize above-normal returns on investment offered by introduction of highly mechanized techniques. Labour is displaced not only by rationalization of operations but also by diversion of capital from static enterprises which do not employ the new techniques. As productivity and productive capacity in dynamic enterprises increases, monopolistic market structures prevent prices from falling faster than wages. Redistribution of income from labour to capital decreases consumer goods demand, which in turn reduces the derived demand for capital goods and brings about excess capacity in capital goods production. Without incentives for accelerating the form of technical progress which creates new products, opens up new markets and stimulates labour-absorbing investment, technological unemployment persists.

Stressing the distinction between labour-saving and labour-absorbing forms of technical progress, Lederer criticized Keynes for his failure to analyse long-run dynamics (Lederer, 1936b). Investment in plant and equipment embodies new techniques. Not the lack of profitable investments, but rather an abundance of abnormally profitable rationalization investments creates structural unemployment in addition to the cyclical unemployment treated by Keynes. Government spending is necessary to stimulate the economy, but it is not sufficient to overcome mass unemployment. Democratic national planning is also necessary to attract capital to new industries offering additional employment opportunities.

Lederer's conviction that a mix of market and planned economies based on political consensus is practicable may be traced to his close association with the industrialist and statesman, Walther Rathenau, who was the architect of German economic mobilization in the First World War (Lederer, 1933; 1934).

Along with Schumpeter, Lederer cultivated an undogmatic Austrian style of theorizing. Both emphasized the significance of uncertainty, entrepreneurship (or its absence as a consequence of bureaucratization), disequilibrating forces, such as technical change, and underlying instability of capitalism. Schumpeter (1939; 1942) defended neoclassical equilibrium theory by asserting that the price system it represents moves automatically, but not without friction, towards a new equilibrium following the 'creative destruction' of an old equilibrium. Similarly, Lederer (1931b) wrote: 'The capitalist dynamic is not only "development" but also "destruction" '. However, Lederer combined neo-Ricardian (von Bortkiewicz, 1907) and Austro-Marxian (Hilferding, 1910) approaches to focus on the production system; accordingly, in his view there was no automatic mechanism to assure that investment brings about a rate and direction of technical change consistent with full employment equilibrium.

ROBERT A. DICKLER

Selected works

1912. *The Problem of the Modern Salaried Employee: Its Theoretical and Statistical Basis.* Trans. E.E. Warburg, New York: State Department of Social Welfare and the Department of Social Science, Columbia University, 1937.

1924. Konjunktur und Krise. *Grundriss der Sozialökonomik* 4(1). Tübingen: J.C.B. Möhr.

1926. (With J. Marschak.) *The New Middle Class.* Trans. S. Ellison, New York: State Department of Social Welfare and the Department of Social Science, Columbia University, 1937.

1927. Monopol und Konjunktur. *Vierteljahreshefte zur Konjunkturforschung*, vol. 2, Supplement 2. Berlin: Duncker & Humblot.

1931a. *Aufriss der ökonomischen Theorie.* 3rd edn. Tübingen: J.C.B. Möhr.

1931b. *Technischer Fortschritt und Arbeitslosigkeit.* Tübingen: J.C.B. Möhr.

1933. National economic planning. In *Encyclopaedia of the Social Sciences*, vol. 11. New York: Macmillan.

1934. Rathenau, Walther. In *Encyclopaedia of the Social Sciences*, vol. 13. New York: Macmillan.

1936a. *Technical Progress and Unemployment. An Enquiry into the Obstacles to Economic Expansion.* Studies and Reports, Series C, No. 22. Geneva: International Labor Office. Translation of revised edition of (1931a).

1936b. Commentary on Keynes. *Social Research* 3, 478–87.

1979. *Kapitalismus, Klassenstruktur und Probleme der Demokratie in Deutschland 1910–1940.* Göttingen: Vandenhoeck & Ruprecht. (Collection of essays, edited by J. Kocka with biographical essay by Hans Speier.)

Bibliography

Bortkiewicz, L. von. 1907. On the correction of Marx's fundamental theoretical construction in the third volume of *Capital*. In *Karl Marx and the Close of His System by E. von Böhm-Bawerk and Böhm-Bawerk's Criticism of Marx by R. Hilferding*, ed. P.M. Sweezy, New York: Kelley, 1949.

Hilferding, R. 1910. *Das Finanzkapital*. Vienna: I. Brand.

Schumpeter, J.A. 1939. *Business Cycles*. New York: McGraw-Hill.

Schumpeter, J.A. 1942. *Capitalism, Socialism and Democracy*, New York: Harper. 2nd edn, 1947.

leisure

What is 'leisure'? The Merriam-Webster Online Dictionary defines it as 'freedom provided by the cessation of activities; *especially*: time free from work or duties', while the Oxford English Dictionary suggests it is 'The state of having time at one's own disposal; time which one can spend as one pleases; free or unoccupied time'. (Both note that the adjective 'leisurely' describes an action that is done without haste, in a relaxed way.) In common parlance, attendance at a relative's funeral or time spent voting would therefore not generally be seen as 'leisure', because time spent on an activity due to a sense of civic or familial duty cannot qualify.

'Leisure' is therefore a problematic concept for economists, because the context and subjective interpretation of an activity is crucial to deciding whether it should be counted as work, duty or leisure – cooking or driving are, for example, activities that may be performed as parts of a paid occupational role, as a duty or for personal enjoyment. It is, in fact, not easy to think of an activity or time use that is not done sometimes for pay, sometimes for duty and sometimes for pleasure – perhaps by different people, but sometimes also by the same people. In many universities, the subtleties of such distinctions are explored in departments of 'Leisure Studies', which is now a recognized area of academic teaching and research. Peer-reviewed journals such as *Annals of Leisure Research* or *Leisure Sciences* report the latest research on leisure activities, and conferences are organized on such topics as 'Serious and Casual Leisure'.

Leisure as a residual category: the standard approach

However, for many economists, 'leisure' is simply the L in labour supply theory. This approach starts, in a one-period model, with each individual maximizing a utility function, where U is the individual's utility level, C represents consumption goods and L is leisure time, as in eq. (1):

$$Max\ U = u(C, L)\quad [u' > 0\quad u'' < 0]\qquad (1)$$

The wage rate available in the paid labour market (w) and total time (T) are seen as the fundamental constraints facing individuals. In this framework, the problem of utility maximization can be equivalently seen as one of 'labour supply' or 'leisure demand' since total time is divided between hours of paid work (H) and leisure time (L).

$$H + L = T \qquad (2)$$

$$C \leq wH. \qquad (3)$$

From this perspective, 'leisure' is whatever 'work' isn't – that is, leisure is a residual category, which is rarely examined directly or defined explicitly. Standard practice in economics journals is to focus on the hours of work decision – and 'work' is usually interpreted to mean 'paid employment'. In the JSTOR database of the top 26 economics journals, a keyword search, conducted in July 2005, for 'leisure' in archived articles published since 1995 yielded 823 'hits'. Of the top 100, sorted for 'relevance', only 25 had an explicit verbal definition of leisure – in most cases leisure was defined implicitly, as in eq. (2). If one discards the three articles discussing consumer demand for 'leisure goods' and focuses on time use, one finds the overwhelming majority of articles used leisure as a synonym for 'non-market time' – only three per cent recognized the possibility of 'on the job leisure' (but the definition was similarly residual – a lack of work effort – and implicit – for example, Dickinson, 1999, p. 639). Relatively few articles (about 15 per cent) considered the possibility that home production (such as shopping time) may be a form of 'work', while a similar number (about 13 per cent) argued that time spent in schooling or training preparatory to paid employment is not leisure. For a very few articles (three per cent), leisure was the residual time available after paid work and some other alternative, such as criminal activity.

When working time is defined as equal to hours of paid employment, commuting time is implicitly defined as part of leisure, although it is plausibly an intermediate input into paid employment. Commuting time is an important percentage of time use in modern societies – Putnam (2000, p. 212), for example, has ascribed much of the decline in civic engagement in the United States to increased commuting time and commented that 'American adults average seventy-two minutes every day behind the wheel....more than we spend cooking or eating and more than twice as much as the average parent spends with the kids.' However, commuting time is strangely absent from most labour–leisure models. As well, although 'retirement' is the particular form of non-work time consumed at the end of the life cycle, most economics articles implicitly exclude it from analysis, by concentrating on the working-age population.

All the same, although $L = T - H$ remains the dominant approach in economics, it has long been recognized that classifying time use as 'work' (painful) or 'leisure' (pleasurable) can be a bit oversimplified. A large body of research indicates, for example, that the unemployed are typically quite unhappy (Frey and Stutzer, 2002; Di Tella, McCulloch and Oswald, 2003) – time spent in unemployment seems to be qualitatively different from non-work time spent in other ways (that is, unpleasant). In general, people tend to rank their jobs fairly highly when asked to compare the satisfaction derived from specific activities (including jobs and types of housework and leisure). Juster and Stafford (1985) argued long ago that, in general, activities that involve social interaction – whether paid or unpaid – tend to be highly valued by individuals. Gary Becker (1965, p. 504) commented even earlier that 'Not only is it difficult to distinguish leisure from other non-work, but also even work from non-work.'

'Time-intensive commodities' and the disappearance of 'leisure': the Becker approach

Becker's solution to the time classification problem was to posit that 'commodities' (like dinner, or a sailing excursion) are what enters individuals' utility functions, and that the production of these commodities requires the input of both material goods and time. In this approach, 'leisure' therefore disappears as a distinct category, somewhat replaced by the concept of a 'time-intensive commodity'. The Becker perspective has important implications for the type of leisure activities that people are predicted to choose. Personal time is, essentially, the only input into commodities like contemplation or conversation or the pure enjoyment of peace and quiet – so their cost is just the opportunity cost of time (that is, the wage rate). The cost of goods-intensive non-work commodities (like speedboat racing) depends partly on the cost of those material goods. When (if) the wage rate rises, time-intensive leisure commodities increase in relative price compared with goods-intensive commodities. Hence, the Becker prediction is for greater materialism over time.

As well, consuming more 'commodities' in the same time period – for example, squeezing a tennis game and a sail and dinner and a night at the opera into the same day – is seen in the Becker model as representing an increase in the 'productivity of consumption time' (and more is always better), but some would also describe this as a more frenetic lifestyle. Winston (1987, p. 160) has commented that 'the most serious casualty [in Becker's approach] was loss of the sense of a leisurely and controlled pace that produces genuine satisfaction.'

However, Becker's approach has not, in fact, been much used. The straightforward work–leisure dichotomy continues to dominate economics journals. The pleasures of non-work time and the marginal disutility of labour were stressed by Marshall (1920, p. 117) many decades ago, and they continue to be the dominant framework today. Can one – should one – expect this constancy of perspective among economists to persist?

Social leisure and the coordination problem

One of the peculiarities of the traditional 'leisure demand–labour supply' perspective is its individualism. If utility really did depend only on the quantity of consumption goods and number of non-work hours experienced by individuals, a person's level of utility would be unaffected by solitary confinement, or by any other configuration of social interaction. However, time spent in isolation is, for most people, pleasurable only in small doses. Although one can choose to be alone, relatively few leisure activities are intrinsically asocial. Most leisure activities can be arranged on a continuum of 'teamness', and the vast majority of them are distinctly more pleasurable if done with others.

Playing softball or soccer are activities that make no sense if done alone. Singing to oneself may be something done in the shower, but singing with a choir is generally a different level of experience. Travelling to exotic foreign places or going for a walk are activities which are usually more pleasurable if done with a companion. Reading a novel is certainly solitary, but many people also like to talk about it afterwards, either formally in a book club or informally with friends over dinner.

To list these different possible leisure activities is to underscore the variety of leisure tastes that individuals have. This variety creates, for each individual, the problem of locating somebody congenial to play with, and scheduling the simultaneous free time to do so. The basic problem with wanting to have a social life is that individuals cannot do it unilaterally – arranging a social life involves a search process which is constrained by the social contacts available to each person, and by the availability of other people. This interdependence of leisure has generated a new literature, with a set of new insights.

Corneo (2005), for example, contrasts privately consumed leisure time (watching television) and socially enjoyed leisure (which requires investment in relationships). Across nations, average hours of television watching are *positively* correlated with average working time. Corneo explains this in terms of the strategic complementarities that arise in the organization of social leisure. If these complementarities are strong enough, equilibria with little social leisure but long hours of work and television viewing, and equilibria in which there is much social leisure along with short hours of work and television viewing, are both possible. Although workers will prefer the higher wages and lower hours of work of the latter, capitalists will prefer the former, since they realize a higher rate of return on their capital stock when total hours of work increase. And if desired working hours are conditional on what others do, individuals need coordination devices to ensure that social leisure is feasible – such as public holidays, a common weekend or working hours regulation – which implies a potentially crucial role for the state and for the relative power of workers and capitalists in influencing public policy.

Jenkins and Osberg (2005) argue that, although solo television watching is certainly feasible, companionship may nonetheless increase the utility derived from the activity. Their emphasis is on modelling more explicitly the constraints involved in locating leisure companions. They argue that the leisure time choices of household members depend on the opportunities for associational life that exist outside the household, and they show that the likelihood of associational activity for persons of a given age group depends on the percentage of persons in other age groups that also engage in that activity. They note that economic models of marriage have discussed the interdependence of spouses in income and material consumption, but it is also plausible that an important reason for marriage is that couples may like spending time together. Like Hamermesh (1998; 2002), they provide evidence on the synchronization and scheduling of spousal work and leisure time.

What are the implications of these new models of social leisure? From a theoretical perspective, the emphasis on the social nature of leisure opens up a whole new set of coordination issues – there is certainly no presumption that individualistic decision making will automatically produce a socially optimal equilibrium. However, the new models of social leisure nest the old labour–leisure choice perspective, since the option of 'solo leisure' is always there (albeit now one of several alternatives).

Kuhn (1970) argued that paradigms are replaced when they confront an important empirical anomaly that they are unable to resolve and when a more encompassing alternative theoretical perspective becomes available. The empirical fact which is now forcing a reconsideration of the analysis of leisure is the huge size of cross-national differences in the trend and level of non-work time. From 1980 to 2000, for example, average annual working hours per adult (ages 15–64) rose by 234 hours in the United States to 1,476 hours, but fell by 170 hours in Germany to 973, and by 210 hours in France to 957 (see Osberg, 2003a). By 2000, the cross-sectional difference was huge – non-work time per adult per week was some 9.7 hours greater in Germany, and 9.9 more hours greater in France, than in the United States.

In principle, an increase in hourly wages increases both potential income and the opportunity cost of leisure, so the demand for a normal good (like leisure) may rise or fall depending on the relative size of income and substitution effects. However, why should one be larger in Europe and the other larger in America? It is just not very satisfactory to say that 'tastes differ'.

Cross-country differences in average leisure time are due in part to inter-country differences in probability of employment, in part to differences in common entitlements to paid vacations and public holidays, and in part to differences in the usual hours of work of employees. Trends in these three components are driven by distinctly different processes – the number of paid public holidays

is, for example, determined by a set of political processes quite different from the determinants of individual decisions to enter the workforce and to work specific hours. A robust debate has emerged over the causes of these differences in total leisure time (for example, Bell and Freeman, 2001; Alesina, Glaeser and Sacerdote, 2005) – but it is clear that these differences are large enough to motivate both a concern over their implications and a discontent with the traditional labour–leisure choice model.

It has long been acknowledged that one reason why GDP per capita is a poor measure of economic well-being is that it does not recognize that leisure time has any value at all. If, as in the comparison of the United States with Germany or France, greater per capita GDP is obtained primarily from greater average working time, a comparison of economic well-being should measure both the cost of forgone individual leisure and the cost of the externality on the marginal utility of each individual's leisure as the decrease in the leisure time of everyone else impedes the feasibility of leisure time matches.

When (by increasing the availability of potential leisure matches) the choice of more leisure time by some individuals has a positive externality for other persons, there can be multiple equilibria in labour supply, in which the 'high work' equilibrium has unambiguously lower total utility. Societies which are better able to coordinate the level and timing of paid working hours may be better off in aggregate, because they enable their citizens to enjoy more satisfying social lives. To be specific, the leisure externality hypothesis suggests that Americans may work more hours than Europeans partly because they are more likely to have less satisfying social lives – because other Americans are also working more hours – and that they are worse off as a result.

Moreover, if authors such as Putnam (1993; 2000) and the OECD (2001) are correct in stressing the dependence of social capital on associational life and the importance of social capital for social and economic development, the costs of a high-work/low-social life equilibrium may be substantial, in terms of market income as well as utility. Knack and Keefer (1997) are representative of an empirical literature which argues that localities with an active civic society and associational life (and more generally a dense network of social ties among individuals, and a high level of trust) have higher growth rates of GDP per capita. This relationship has been argued to be due to a number of possible influences: for example lower transactions costs in capital, labour and product markets, more effective governance, lower costs of crime, labour conflict and political uncertainty, better health outcomes, and so on (see Osberg, 2003b). Whatever the channel of influence, it suggests that, although working longer hours may accelerate growth in GDP per capita in the short run, both income and social life may suffer in the longer run. There may be some wisdom in the old saying that: 'All work and no play makes Jack a dull boy.'

LARS OSBERG

See also **external economies; labour supply; social capital; time use.**

Bibliography

Alesina, A., Glaeser, E. and Sacerdote, B. 2005. Work and leisure in the U.S. and Europe: why so different? Working Paper No. 11278. Cambridge, MA: NBER.

Becker, G. 1965. A theory of the allocation of time. *Economic Journal* 75, 493–517.

Bell, L. and Freeman, R. 2001. The incentive for working hard: explaining hours worked differences in the US and Germany. *Labour Economics* 8, 181–202.

Corneo, G. 2005. Work and television. *European Journal of Political Economy* 21, 99–113.

Di Tella, R., MacCulloch, R. and Oswald, A. 2003. The macroeconomics of happiness. *Review of Economics and Statistics* 85, 809–27.

Dickinson, D. 1999. An experimental examination of labor supply and work intensities. *Journal of Labor Economics* 17, 638–70.

Frey, B. and Stutzer, A. 2002. *Happiness and Economics: How the Economy and Institutions Affect Well-Being*. Princeton: Princeton University Press.

Hamermesh, D. 1998. When we work. *American Economic Review* 88, 321–5.

Hamermesh, D. 2002. Timing, togetherness and time windfalls. *Journal of Population Economics* 15, 601–23.

Jenkins, S. and Osberg, L. 2005. Nobody to play with? The implications of leisure co-ordination. In *The Economics of Time Use*, ed. D. Hamermesh and G. Pfann. Amsterdam: Elsevier.

Juster, T. and Stafford, F., eds. 1985. *Time, Goods, and Well-Being*. Ann Arbor: Institute for Social Research, University of Michigan.

Knack, S. and Keefer, P. 1997. Does social capital have an economic payoff? A cross-country investigation. *Quarterly Journal of Economics* 112, 1251–88.

Kuhn, T. 1970. *The Structure of Scientific Revolutions*. Chicago: University of Chicago Press.

Marshall, A. 1920. *Principles of Economics*, 8th edn. London: Macmillan, 1961.

OECD (Organization for Economic Co-operation and Development). 2001. *The Well-being of Nations: The Role of Human and Social Capital*. Paris: OECD.

Osberg, L. 2003a. Understanding growth and inequality trends: the role of labour supply in the U.S.A. and Germany. *Canadian Public Policy* 29, Supplement 1, S163–S183.

Osberg, L., ed. 2003b. *The Economic Implications of Social Cohesion*. Toronto: University of Toronto Press.

Putnam, R. 1993. *Making Democracy Work: Civic Traditions in Modern Italy*. Princeton: Princeton University Press.

Putnam, R. 2000. *Bowling Alone: The Collapse and Revival of the American Community*. New York: Simon and Schuster.

Winston, G. 1987. Leisure. In *The New Palgrave: A Dictionary of Economics*, vol. 3, ed. J. Eatwell, M. Milgate and P. Newman. Basingstoke: Palgrave.

leisure class

This term became popular after Thorstein Veblen's book, *The Theory of the Leisure Class* (1899). In that book the author gives a historical and socio-economic explanation of the development of that wealthy class in the society of his time whose main characteristic was leisure. By 'leisure' Veblen means the non-productive spending of time which originates from a sense of the worthlessness of productive work and from the need to show pecuniary ability to afford a life of idleness. The basic social categories of Veblen's theory of the leisure class are pecuniary competition, conspicuous leisure and conspicuous consumption.

The leisure class is an old institution. The emergence of a leisure class coincides, according to Veblen, with the beginning of ownership. These two institutions (leisure class and ownership) are different aspects of the same general facts of social structure. The conditions for the appearance of the leisure class as a permanent form are: (1) the community has to be of a predatory type; and (2) the means of life must be affordable in a relatively easy way, so that part of the population can be liberated from routine work. It is necessary to make a proper distinction between the leisure and the labouring class. For the lower classes, as Veblen explains, since labour is their accepted and only mode of life, an emulative pride in a reputation for efficiency in their work becomes the only emulation that is open to them. For the 'superior pecuniary class' the most imperative secondary demand for emulation is the abstention from productive work. It is not sufficient to possess wealth or power. It becomes important to show that you have no need to do productive work. From the days of the Greek philosophers to the present a life of leisure is, as Veblen says, in a great part of secondary and derivative value (1936, p. 231).

Leisure does not usually bring about a material product; the result takes the form of non-material goods. Good examples of occupations that members of the leisure class choose to pursue are the knowledge of dead languages and the occult sciences, of correct spelling, of the various forms of music and other household arts, fashionable dress, furniture, games, sports, dogs and racehorses. Elegant speech shows the level of a speaker's emancipation from productive work. The leisure class is not interested in technological innovations and it is an obstruction to social and economic progress.

Veblen's critique of 'absentee ownership' is the next step in his analysis of modern civilization. The members of the leisure class do not want to have any connection with a production process and they leave the managing and guiding of this process to so-called 'captains of industry'. The last group is for Veblen the only positive power interested in technological development.

Veblen's critique of ownership and his opinion that the modern type of ownership is not compatible with industrial efficiency has been and still is unacceptable to many of his fellow economists. Like Marx, Max Weber and Karl Polanyi, Veblen had demonstrated the importance of studying primitive economies for general economic history and the interaction between economics and the society in general.

Veblen's leisure class seems very much like Marx's ruling capitalist class. Both of them see the bitter struggle between capital and labour. But they differ very much according to the methods of solving this contradiction. Marx's solution is, as is well known, a socialist revolution. In *The Theory of the Leisure Class* Veblen was not explicit about this issue. He was not sure about the end of this struggle, but he was very positive about the existence of the struggle. This goes very well with his Darwinian philosophy. A kind of trade unionism could be closer to Darwinism and is more acceptable for Veblen than neo-Hegelianism or Marxism.

Although his theory is based on Darwinian philosophy and although he argues for evolutionary socialism, in some of his later writings he was closer to the attitude that certain radical social movements could be the solution for breaking with old social institutions. In his search for emancipation of man, Veblen, together with other great humanists, had to become a socialist. His analysis of private ownership and the leisure class necessarily pushed him into this direction.

Nikolai Bukharin's *Economic Theory of the Leisure Class* (1919) is quite different from Veblen's book. This is not an economic account of the conditions which give rise to the existence of a leisure class in the manner of Veblen. The leisure class is not the central category in this work, as the title may suggest. Bukharin mentions the leisure class in the context of his critique from a Marxist point of view of the theory of marginal utility, especially that of the Austrian school. He gives no reference to Veblen. Bourgeois political economy, according to Bukharin, seeks to justify the capitalist system and therefore it loses its scientific role, contrary to the Marxist theory which claims its general validity precisely for the reason that it is the theoretical expression of the most advanced class – the working class.

In the critique of marginal utility theory Bukharin points out that this theory is the theoretical expression of the class of rentiers who have been eliminated from the process of production and are interested in disposing of their income from holdings of securities and bonds only. This marginal utility theory is, according to Bukharin, unhistorical: it starts with consumption not the production process. His critique of the logic and the method of subjective value theory is settled in direct confrontation with the labour theory of value.

J.K. Galbraith refers to Veblen's work, suggesting that the concepts 'conspicuous leisure' and 'conspicuous consumption' are still of significance (Galbraith, 1977). In the United States, as Galbraith explains, class as described by Veblen still exists: the members of the leisure class are still buying their social status.

It might have been expected that contemporary sociologists would have been more concerned with the concept of the leisure class. But this is not the case. They are very much occupied with leisure itself: it is common for sociologists to define leisure as the portion of time which remains when time for work and the basic requirements for existence have been satisfied, and this issue is related to the problem of how to spend leisure time. But this is a different problem and does not have a substantial relation to the problem of the leisure class.

F. STANKOVIĆ

See also **Bukharin, Nikolai Ivanovitch; conspicuous consumption; Veblen, Thorstein Bunde.**

Bibliography

Bukharin, N. 1919. *The Economic Theory of the Leisure Class*. New York: Monthly Review Press, 1972. (Originally published in Russian and first published in English in 1927.)

Galbraith, J.K. 1977. *The Age of Uncertainty*. Boston: Houghton Mifflin.

Veblen, T. 1899. *The Theory of the Leisure Class*. London: George Allen & Unwin.

Veblen, T. 1936. What Veblen taught. In *Selected Writings of Thorstein Veblen*, ed. W.C. Mitchell. New York: Viking Press.

Lenin, Vladimir Ilyich [Ulyanov] (1870–1924)

Vladimir Ilyich Ulyanov, who wrote and gained fame under the pseudonym Lenin, was born in April 1870, the second son of a Russian provincial official in Simbirsk (now Ulyanovsk). After the arrest and execution of his elder brother Alexander, in 1887 for alleged terrorist activity, Lenin became increasingly active in political study groups at Kazan, Samara and St Petersburg. He came to identify himself with the Marxist rather than the populist (Narodniki) stream in these study groups. He played an active part in the early theoretical debates between these two streams on the future course of Russia's economic and political development. At the time of the founding of the Russian Social Democratic Labour Party (RSDLP) in 1898, he was already known as its best young theorist. A split in the RSDLP took place in 1902 and Lenin became identified as the leader of the majority (Bolshevik) faction. He spent much of the early years of the 20th century in exile in London, Paris and Zurich. He returned to Russia in April 1917 after the February Revolution had initiated the post-tsarist phase of Russian politics. Lenin, unlike his fellow party members, correctly foresaw the instability of the political situation in which an unelected liberal democratic cabinet uneasily shared power with the federation of popularly elected factory committees (Soviets). He launched the Bolsheviks on a strategy of revolutionary rejection of the government and a platform of peace in the World War at any price. His analysis proved correct when in November 1917 the Bolsheviks won a majority in the All Russian Congress of Soviets and took power. Lenin led the communist government from that day until illness forced his withdrawal from active politics in March 1923. He died in January 1924.

Lenin's economic writing is extensive, comprising books, pamphlets, newspaper articles and occasional speeches (see Desai, 1986, for a full bibliography). His contributions can be placed under three headings: analysis of Russia's capitalist development in the period 1880–1900; the analysis of the developments in world capitalism in the period 1900–1916, where his concept of imperialism as a form of monopoly capitalism was an innovation; and lastly as a Marxist policy maker during the period 1917–23.

The development of capitalism in Russia

Lenin's book of this title published in 1898 is a substantial piece of work which traces the growth of commercial relations and specialization in agriculture leading to an erosion of the traditional communal forms. On the industrial side, Russia's late arrival entailed an active role for the tsarist state in fostering industrialization and an influx of foreign capital to finance the development. This meant that Russia, although a newly industrializing country in the 1890s, had a larger proportion of its industrial labour force in large factories than older industrialized countries like Britain. Lenin saw these as predictable consequences of rapid capitalist growth which made any going back to pre-capitalist communal forms of village organization impossible. The growth of large factories also meant concentration of workers in a few places, facilitating their combination in trade union activities. These economic circumstances – the growth of commercial relations in the countryside and of concentrations of the urban proletariat – dictated for Lenin the political strategy of a socialist party which hoped to win power by mass organization. Lenin's theory of the development of the democratic political movement follows the economic stages quite closely. In this sense he can be said to have developed an economic framework for a Marxist political theory. *The Development of Capitalism in Russia* is even to this day the only comprehensive economic history of a country from a Marxist perspective.

Imperialism, the highest stage of capitalism

In 1916, Lenin wrote his well-known economic pamphlet of this title. The background was provided by the First World War, which had broken out two years previously with enthusiastic participation by the working people of various combatant nations and the connivance of the socialist parties. The 'betrayal' by the workers and their political leaders was one factor in Lenin's urge to explain these events. The second urge was perhaps provided by a desire to integrate the facts of a war into a Marxist theory of the long-run development and eventual breakdown of capitalism.

Marx had predicted a tendency for the rate of profit to fall as capitalist development proceeded. Among the forces which may counteract this tendency was an increasing concentration in industry and the emergence of larger industrial units. In 1907, Hilferding in his *Finance Capital* had provided a theory and empirical evidence for the increasing integration of bank finance and industrial capital. The formation of trusts and cartels was helped by banks willing to finance mergers and controlling and interlocking equity holdings. Marxist economists saw the 20th century as entering a monopoly phase of capitalism in contrast to the competitive phase that Marx had written about.

Lenin's achievement is to add to the Marx–Hilferding account an international economic and political element. One part of his theory came from Hobson's *Imperialism*. As an underconsumptionist, Hobson linked the fight over African and Asian territory in the last decades of the 19th century among European nations to the search for outlets for surplus which could not be sold at home. Hobson took the view that this imperial search was irrational. Lenin, as a Marxist, saw the irrationality as a systematic functional element in a world of monopoly capital economies each of which was trying to stave off the falling rate of profit by exporting. The battle for markets could not however take place in a politically neutral context as envisaged by competitive economic theory. Large cartels and monopolies gave a few leading bankers and industrialists influence with the political governments of their country. The battle for markets thus became a struggle between developed capitalist nations for territory. It was the struggle for territory as a surrogate for markets which led to military confrontation between the major industrial nations and hence war. War was not however predicted to be a satisfactory solution to the problem of markets or of profitability. It was likely in Lenin's view to be the harbinger of proletarian uprising against the system in these countries which would end it.

Thus Lenin blends international political developments into a Marxian theory of capitalist development. Imperialism in Lenin's definition is the entire set of unequal economic relations between capitalist countries – between rival mature capitalist countries fighting for markets as well as between mature countries and developing economies which become their markets. Formal political control by one nation over another is not a necessary element in Lenin's view of imperialism. Although immensely influential in the interwar years due to Comintern orthodoxy, this theory has come under some attack recently (Warren, 1980). It lacks a coherent analytical theory of how monopoly capital differs from competitive capitalism and its empirical predictions proved only temporarily true when a series of political uprisings took place in Europe after the First World War. These uprisings did not mature into a full-scale collapse of capitalism, which continues many decades after Lenin foresaw its highest phase as having been achieved.

Socialist economic policy

As the first Marxist to lead a government, Lenin had to formulate practical economic policy. Given the notorious lack of discussion of socialist economic policy in Marx's writings, Lenin had to improvise. Two notions stand out as his distinctive contribution to this area. First, in his description of the post-revolutionary Russia as a transitional state from capitalism to socialism. During this transition, state capitalism was seen by Lenin as an advance upon private capitalism in as much as the political state was not a capitalist one but a workers' state. Lenin used the wartime German economic organization as the ideal of a fully integrated single economic unit which a planned socialist economy could beneficially emulate. Second, in the return to normality after the Civil War – in his pamphlet 'The Tax in Kind' – Lenin sketched a theory for the role of trade in reviving economic activity. The key was to move from a forced requisition of food surpluses to a policy of tax in kind and encouraging exchange. A revival of agriculture was required for an industrial revival but the terms of trade between the two sectors was a crucial policy variable in this respect. Trade is seen as an antidote to economic bureaucracy in this pamphlet. It was this pamphlet that inaugurated the New Economic Policy which could be said to have lasted from 1921 to 1929.

MEGHNAD DESAI

Selected works

1898. *The Development of Capitalism in Russia*. In *Collected Works*, vol. 3.

1916. *Imperialism; the Highest Stage of Capitalism*. In *Collected Works*, vol. 22.

1921. *The Tax in Kind*. In *Collected Works*, vol. 32.

1960–70. *Collected Works*, 45 vols. Trans. of the 4th enlarged Russian edn, Moscow: Progress Publishers.

Bibliography

Desai, M. 1986. *Lenin as an Economist*. London: Lawrence & Wishart.

Warren, B. 1980. *Imperialism: Pioneer of Capitalism*. London: New Left Books.

Bibliographic addendum

Studies of aspects of Lenin's life and thought continue to be produced because of his importance in world history.

Within this massive literature, valuable studies of his ideas include N. Harding, *Lenin's Political Thought*, 2 vols, New York: St. Martins Press, 1977 and 1981; and N. Harding, *Leninism*. Durham, NC: Duke University Press, 1996. An extensive general biography is R. Service, R. *Lenin: A Political Life*, 3 vols, Bloomington: Indiana University Press, 1985, 1991, and 1995. This massive study is synthesized and updated in R. Service, *Lenin*, Cambridge, MA: Harvard University Press, 2000.

Leontief paradox

The Heckscher–Ohlin–Samuelson (HOS) model of international trade with two factors of production and two commodities implies that a country will export the commodity that is produced intensively with the relatively abundant factor. Leontief (1953) discovered, to the surprise of the profession, that 1947 US exports were more labour-intensive than US imports in the sense that the capital per man required to produce a $1 million of exports was less than the capital per man required to produce a $1 million in import substitutes. This seemed to conflict sharply with the presupposition that the USA was abundant in capital compared with labour. Leontief's finding was so startling that it has been called a 'paradox', even though the result amounted to at most a single contradiction of the theory and even though no alternative model could be said to conform better with the facts.

Leontief's finding preceded and apparently stimulated a search of great breadth and intensity for a new theory of trade that could account for his result. It is in fact difficult to find another empirical result that has had as great an impact on the intellectual development of the discipline. Among the explanations of the finding are: (*a*) high productivity of US workers; (*b*) capital-biased consumption; (*c*) factor-intensity reversals; (*d*) tariffs; (*e*) abundance of natural resources; (*f*) abundance of human capital; (*g*) technological differences. These developments are surveyed in Chacholiades (1978, pp. 298–306).

It is surprising in retrospect that no one thought to examine the theoretical foundation for Leontief's inference that the factor content of US trade revealed the United States to be scarce in capital compared with labour, though a clear theory of the factor content of trade was not laid out until Vanek (1968). Vanek's model of the factor content of trade was first used in an overlooked article by Williams (1970) to criticize Leontief's inference. The very simple theoretical foundation for the Leontief calculation was clearly laid out in Leamer (1980), which shows that Leontief's data in fact reveal the United States to have been abundant in capital compared with labour.

Theoretical relationships that can serve as a foundation for studying the relative factor abundance revealed by international trade are the Heckscher–Ohlin–Vanek equations. These equations are derived from the simple identity that net exports of the services of a factor f are the difference between home supply and home demand: $T_f = X_f - M_f = S_f - D_f$, where T_f is the amount of factor f embodied in net exports, X_f is the amount of factor f required to produce the exported commodities, M_f is the amount required to produce the imported commodities, S_f is the domestic supply and D_f is the domestic demand. This identity is given empirical content by assuming identical homothetic tastes which implies that domestic demand for factor f is proportional to world supply, $D_f = sW_f$, where W_f is the world supply and s is the country's share of world consumption. With the use of this assumption, the net export equation can be written as

$$T_f/S_f = 1 - s(W_f/S_f).$$

In words, net exports as a share of domestic supply is positively related to factor abundance defined as the share of the world's total supply S_f/W_f. Accordingly, the relative scarcity of the factors is revealed by the ordering of the net export ratios T_f/S_f. Leamer (1980) shows that, although the net export of both capital and labour services were positive in 1947, the share of domestic supply of capital that was exported exceeded the share of labour exported, and consequently the United States was revealed by trade to be relatively abundant in capital compared with labour. In addition, Leamer (1980) shows that Leontief's finding that the exports were more capital intensive than imports is compatible with either ordering of factor abundance.

This fully resolves the apparent paradoxical ordering of capital and labour abundance, but a new problem arises. Brecher and Choudhri (1982) note that, if net exports are positive, the overall consumption share s must be less than the abundance ratio S_f/W_f. If trade is balanced, the consumption share is the ratio of home to world GNP, $s = \text{GNP}/\text{GNP}_w$. The inequality $S_f/W_f > s = \text{GNP}/\text{GNP}_w$ can be rewritten as $\text{GNP}_w/W_f > \text{GNP}/S_f$. Thus the United States is revealed by its positive net exports of labour services embodied in commodities to have had a per-capita GNP that is less than the rest of the world. Even after adjusting for the trade surplus, this is impossible to square with the facts. Another way of expressing this new paradox is that the positive export of labour services reveals that labour is abundant compared with other resources on the average since the consumption share s is an average of the abundance ratios.

It is ironic that this is one of the few empirical findings that can be said to have had a decided impact on the course of the profession and at the same time is based on a simple conceptual misunderstanding. The error that is implicit in Leontief's paradox is the use of an intuitive but false theorem which states that the ordering of capital per man in exports compared with imports reveals the relative abundance of capital and labour. This is true for the simple two-good model, but it is not the case for a multi-commodity reality. There is a lesson to be learned from this experience. Empirical work requires a fully articulated theoretical foundation. Intuition alone is not enough.

Although the precise form that Leontief's calculations took is inappropriate, the calculation of flows of factor services embodied in trade remains an interesting activity since these flows can be used to form a proper test of the Heckscher–Ohlin–Samuelson theorem and since the net effect of trade on the demand for factors of production can be an important input into trade policy that is intended to affect the distribution of income.

As it turns out, measurements of 1967 factor contents of trade reported in Bowen, Leamer and Sveikauskas (1987) rather badly violate the HOS model, thus reinvigorating the message of the Leontief paradox: there is something wrong with this model. One thing that is wrong is emphasized by Trefler's (1995) title: 'The Case of the Missing Trade'. Given the world's apparent unequal geographic distribution of capital, labour and land, the HOS model suggests that there should be much more trade than actually occurs. Trefler's solution to this puzzle is to allow in the model both home bias in consumption and also international productivity differences (for example, the United States is not so labour-scarce when allowance is made for the intensity of work). Also, Conway (2002) finds problems with the measurement of factor scarcity and calls for the model to include factor-specific differences in domestic factor mobility. It seems likely that we have not seen the end of the search for a model that most fully explains the nature of international trade.

EDWARD E. LEAMER

See also **Heckscher–Ohlin trade theory; input–output analysis.**

Bibliography

Bowen, H., Leamer, E. and Sveikauskas, L. 1987. Multicountry, multifactor tests of the factor abundance theory. *American Economic Review* 77, 791–809.

Brecher, R. and Choudhri, E. 1982. The Leontief Paradox, continued. *Journal of Political Economy* 90, 820–3.

Chacholiades, M. 1978. *International Trade Theory and Policy.* New York: McGraw-Hill.

Conway, P. 2002. The case of the missing trade and other mysteries: comment. *American Economic Review* 92, 394–404.

Leamer, E. 1980. The Leontief Paradox, reconsidered. *Journal of Political Economy* 88, 495–503.

Leontief, W. 1953. Domestic production and foreign trade: the American capital position re-examined. *Proceedings of the American Philosophical Society* 97, 332–49. Reprinted in *Readings in International Trade*, ed. H. Johnson and R. Caves. Homewood, IL: R.D. Irwin, 1968.

Trefler, D. 1995. The case of the missing trade and other mysteries. *American Economic Review* 85, 1029–46.

Vanek, J. 1968. The factor proportions theory: the N-factor case. *Kyklos* 21, 749–56.

Williams, J. 1970. The resource content in international trade. *Canadian Journal of Economics* 3, 111–22.

Leontief, Wassily (1906–1999)

Wassily Leontief was born on 5 August 1906 in St Petersburg, the only child of an academic family. He studied first at the University of Leningrad, earning the degree of 'Learned Economist' in 1925, and then at the University of Berlin (Ph.D., 1928). While working on his doctorate, he was appointed a research economist at the University of Kiel, where he remained for about three years, with a year out to serve as adviser to the Chinese Ministry of Railways in Nanking.

In 1931 he went to the United States to join the staff of the National Bureau of Economic Research, but after only a few months accepted an appointment at Harvard University, where he remained for the following 44 years. During those years he attained worldwide eminence, particularly for the invention and application of input–output analysis. Prominent among the honours he received during those years were election as President of the American Economic Association in 1970 and the Nobel Memorial Prize in Economics in 1973. In 1975 he accepted a chair at New York University, where he spent the remainder of his career.

Leontief had an exceptionally strong training in mathematics and a marked flair for mathematical and geometric reasoning. These qualities were displayed in his earliest papers, in the late 1920s and early 1930s, in which he applied his technical talents to a variety of topics including the estimation of elasticities of supply and demand, the measurement of industrial concentration, the use of indifference maps at a time when they were still novelties to explain patterns of international trade in a two-commodity, two-country model, analysis of the conditions under which cobweb cycles would converge or would expand explosively, and several others. These papers established his reputation as an economic theorist of first rank.

During this same period, he struck a theme that he was to emphasize repeatedly throughout his career: the thesis that economic concepts were meaningless and misleading unless they could be observed and measured. Thus, in 1936 he studied the significance of index numbers that purported to measure composite concepts such as the aggregate output of an economy or the general price level, and the following year published his famous diatribe against 'implicit theorizing', that is, explaining phenomena by introducing ill-defined concepts (the economist's version of Molière's doctor who attributed the effect of sleeping potions to their dormative propensities). Eleven years later, he returned to the measurement of aggregates much more profoundly and fruitfully in his 'Introduction to a Theory of the Internal Structure of Functional Relationships', which developed the mathematical conditions in which a single aggregate or index could replace a mass of detailed data without loss of information. And much later he devoted his presidential address to the American Economic Association to decrying 'Theoretical Assumptions and Nonobserved Facts' (1971).

These two characteristics – adroitness at mathematical expression and analysis and insistence that theoretical concepts be implementable – congealed in Leontief's major achievement, the invention, development, and application of input–output analysis. As a purely theoretical construct, input–output analysis had a long genealogy before Leontief began his work on it, around 1933. In the 18th century, François Quesnay used his *Tableau économique* to illustrate the relationships between agriculture and other sectors of the economy. A hundred years later, Marx demonstrated the relationships between the capital-goods and consumers' goods departments of an economy by a very similar two-sector table. The most important predecessor, however, was Walras's formulation of the general equilibrium of an economy, which employed a concept that is very similar to Leontief's input–output coefficients. In addition, as Leontief discovered after input–output analysis was well known, H.E. Bray had published essentially the same equations in 1922, and R. Remak had discovered them again in 1929.

The algebraic theory of input–output analysis had been explored by a number of late 19th-century algebraists, particularly by E. Frobenius and O. Perron, for whom the basic theorems have come to be named. All of these preceding theories expressed fundamental, abstract theoretical concepts; none could be used to specify the relationships among the sectors of an actual economy.

But throughout his career, Leontief has insisted that the task of a theorist only begins with the proposal of a well-formulated theory; the central task is to show that the theory can be applied to real economies, that it leads to interesting predictions about the behaviour of those economies, and that those predictions can be checked and found to be reasonably accurate. This radically operational point of view led Leontief to his critical contribution: the perception that the coefficients that express the relationships among the sectors of an economy can be estimated statistically, and that they are sufficiently stable so that they can be used in comparative static analyses to give quantitative estimates of the effects of different economic policies, taking into account their reverberations throughout the economy along with their effects on the industries affected in the first instance.

It is almost impossible now to appreciate the task of confirming these conjectures in the early 1930s. Input–output computations depend on inverting large matrices; the most powerful computing machines in existence then were punch-card machines that could multiply, after a fashion, but could not divide. Solving a half-dozen simultaneous linear equations was a formidable calculation; Leontief envisaged systems that numbered in the hundreds.

Input–output analysis also required data of an unfamiliar type – coefficients specifying the amounts of various raw materials and intermediate goods required per unit of product in each sector. The US Census of Manufactures included many of these coefficients, but by no means all. The remainder had to be compiled laboriously from trade journals and scattered sources.

Furthermore, the underlying assumption of the method, that the input–output coefficients remained essentially constant for substantial periods, was hard to reconcile with one of the main tenets of the theory of production – that factors of production were substituted for one another quite sensitively in response to price changes.

Beginning around 1933–4, Leontief concentrated on overcoming these difficulties by compiling coefficients for a 44-sector input–output table – about 2,000 coefficients – and making plans for their analysis. Since the solution of 44 simultaneous equations was far beyond the realm of the possible, the 44 sectors were consolidated into a scant ten for computational purposes. To check on the stability of the coefficients, tables were to be compiled for 1919 and 1929.

The first result of this study, 'Quantitative Input and Output Relations in the Economic System of the United States', appeared in 1936. Its centrepiece was a 41-sector input–output table for the United States in 1919, presenting the intersectoral flow coefficients along with sources and methods of estimation. The next year, Leontief published 'Interrelation of Prices, Output, Savings and Investment'. In the interim, he had made contact with Professor John B. Wilbur of the Massachusetts Institute of Technology, who had just invented an analog computer that could solve systems of up to nine linear equations. Accordingly, Leontief aggregated his 41-sector table into ten sectors and used Wilbur's computer to calculate the inverse. This was the first Leontief-inverse ever computed, and probably the first use of a large computer in economics or other social science.

By 1941, a parallel 41-sector table had been compiled for 1929 and the inverse of a ten-sector aggregation of it had been computed. The two tables were presented and compared in Leontief's first monograph, *The Structure of American Economy, 1919–1929*. The comparisons were intended to test whether the input coefficients were stable enough to yield useful empirical predictions. The comparisons were indecisive, in part for lack of a clear standard for judging the stability of the estimated coefficients.

The monograph did establish, however, that it was feasible to compile the raw data needed for an input–output table and to compute coefficients and an inverse table that appeared to make good economic sense. The importance of such tables for economic planning was recognized almost immediately. Within a few years, the US Bureau of Labour Statistics, with Leontief as a consultant, constructed a 400-sector table for projecting post-war employment by major industries, and the method was being applied all over the world for constructing economic development plans.

Leontief remained in the forefront of these developments. By 1944 he had calculated a table of input coefficients for 1939, comparable with the earlier two

tables, and found a satisfactory degree of stability for most of the coefficients extending over two decades. Using this up-to-date table, he published a sequence of three important papers in the *Quarterly Journal of Economics* for 1944 and 1946 exemplifying the use of input–output analysis for estimating the effects of exogenous disturbances on output, employment, wages, and prices in individual sectors.

In 1948, Leontief established the Harvard Economic Research Project as a centre for applying and extending input–output analysis. He became director of the Project, and headed it for the next 25 years. He was particularly active in developing interregional input–output analysis and in introducing capital–coefficient matrices to derive the investment implications of changes in final demand and, thereby, to use input–output analysis to generate growth paths as well as static equilibriums of economic systems.

This work led to two books, *The Structure of American Economy 1919–1939*, in 1951, and *Studies in the Structure of the American Economy*, in 1953, as well as several international conferences and a score of papers and articles. Probably the most striking discovery of this period of work has come to be called 'the Leontief paradox', the finding that, when indirect as well as direct input requirements are taken into account, American exports are more labour-intensive and less capital-intensive than American imports, although the United States is exceptionally well endowed with capital and has exceptionally high real wages.

Leontief and the staff of the Harvard Economic Research Project devised and implemented numerous other applications of input–output analysis. They included estimates of the inflationary impact of wage settlements, calculations of the direct and indirect effects of armament expenditures on the individual sectors of the economy, and methods for projecting the growth-paths of the sectors in a developing economy and for estimating capital requirements for economic development.

In the middle 1970s, Leontief became persuaded that, while competitive markets might guide an economy to a socially efficient equilibrium if given sufficient time, the process would be likely to be very protracted and unduly wasteful of mistakenly invested resources. Economic growth and efficient adjustments would be promoted better by establishing an economic planning board that would work out a number of detailed growth possibilities based on input–output analyses. The ultimate choice among these possibilities would be made by a political process. He advocated this type of indicative planning in a number of articles in *The New York Review of Books*, the *New York Times* 'op-ed page', and other general interest periodicals.

Leontief subsequently turned to the problems of worldwide economic growth, its environmental impact, its demands on the world's base of natural resources, and particularly on its implications for relations between the economies of the so-called First and Third Worlds. Under the sponsorship of the United Nations, he directed a study of the evolution of the world economy until the year 2000, based on a multiregional input–output model consisting of 15 regions, each comprised of 45 sectors, and linked by balanced trading relationships. This is, perhaps, the most ambitious input–output study yet undertaken. The results were published as *The Future of the World Economy* (1977). It found that, under a wide range of plausible assumptions, little progress would be made in closing the gap between the industrial and the developing regions unless current policies concerning international trade and finance were changed drastically in the directions of increased multinational aid and an increased flow of imports from the Third World to the First.

Leontief was a leader in improving the computational methods of economics, beginning with his use of Wilbur's analog equation solver in 1936. Subsequently he inverted input–output matrices on Howard Aiken's early Mark I and Mark II computers, the immediate predecessors of the electronic computer. In the 1980s the very large matrices required by his world economic models led him to be the first economist to use the so-called supercomputers and to apply parallel-processors and other highly efficient methods of computation.

Throughout his career, Leontief took an active interest in the education of the next generation of scholars. While at Harvard he served for 11 years as chairman of the Society of Fellows, the foundation that provides three-year, duty-free fellowships to promising young scholars, to enable them to reside at Harvard and pursue whatever interests they choose. He delighted in presiding over the weekly dinner meetings of the Society and leading conversations that range over all the fields of interest represented at the table.

R. DORFMAN

See also **input–output analysis.**

Selected works

Leontief's principal scientific contributions can be found in four volumes:.
1941. *The Structure of American Economy, 1919–1929.* Cambridge, MA: Harvard University Press and later editions.
1953. (With others.) *Studies in the Structure of the American Economy.* New York: Oxford University Press.
1966. *Essays in Economics: Theories and Theorizing.* New York: Oxford University Press, and later editions.
1977. *Essays in Economics*, Vol. 2. White Plains, NY: M.E. Sharpe.
Articles exemplifying Leontief's wide range of interests and activities can be found in:
Bulletin of the American Mathematical Society, April 1947.

New York Review of Books, 10 October 1968, 21 August 1969, 4 June 1970, 7 January 1971, 20 July 1972, 4 December 1980, 12 August 1982.
New York Times, op-ed page, 14 March 1974, 24 March 1977, 6 March 1979, 5 April 1981, 19 September 1983.
Scientific American, April 1961, September 1963, April 1965, September 1980.

Bibliographic addendum
A range of essays evaluating and extending Leontief's work may be found in
Dietzenbacher, E. and Lahr, M. 2004. *Wassily Leontief and Input–Output Economics.* Cambridge: Cambridge University Press.
Wood, J. 2001. *Wassily Leontief: Critical Assessments.* London and New York: Routledge.

Lerner, Abba Ptachya (1905–1982)

Lerner was one of the last of the great non-mathematical economists and certainly one of the most original, versatile and prolific members of the profession. Born in Rumania, raised from early childhood in the Jewish immigrant quarter of London's East End, he went to rabbinical school, started work at 16, working as tailor, capmaker, Hebrew School teacher, typesetter, and then founded his own printing shop. When that went bankrupt at the onset of the Great Depression, he enrolled as an evening student at the London School of Economics to find out the reason for his shop's failure. There, his outstanding logical faculties soon became evident and won him all the available prizes and fellowships, one of which took him to Cambridge to study with Keynes. He published many major articles already as an undergraduate, was appointed temporary assistant lecturer at the London School of Economics in 1935, assistant lecturer in 1936, and in 1937 a Rockefeller fellowship took him to the United States, where he remained, although his restlessness kept him from settling at any one university for more than a few years.

Lerner was a lifelong socialist, advocate of market pricing for its allocative efficiency, and believer in private enterprise, whose offer of private employment he considered an essential safeguard of individual freedom. That unusual combination of principles accounts for Lerner's loneliness and political isolation. In his economics, however, he knew how to reconcile those principles. His reconciliation of the first two made him into one of the founders (along with Oskar Lange) of the theory of market pricing in the decentralized socialist economy, and he sought to reconcile the first and third principles by advocating what he called socialist free enterprise: 'the freedom of both public and private enterprise to enter any industry on fair terms which, in each particular case, permit that form to prevail which serves the public best.'

Although Lerner's ambition was to improve the economy, not economics, he made many, often fundamental contributions to economic theory, mainly in the fields of welfare economics, international trade and macroeconomics but also in the theories of production, capital, monopoly, duopoly, spatial competition and index numbers. Furthermore, and hardly less important, he made generous use of his geometrical skill and genius for exposition in tidying up and clarifying other people's ideas. As a result, a number of important economic theorems and ideas, though first stated by others, became the profession's common property in Lerner's simpler and clearer formulations. An important example of that is the well-known rule that marginal cost pricing is a condition of welfare optimality. Another example is his definitive proof (Lerner, 1936a) that in the two-country, two-commodity model, export and import duties have identical consequences if their proceeds are spent in the same way.

In welfare economics, one of his first articles (Lerner, 1934a) not only introduced the notion that monopoly is a matter of degree, whose extent is best measured by the excess of price over marginal cost, but in the process also provided the first complete, comprehensive and clear statement and discussion of the nature and limitations of Pareto optimality, and of the equality between price and marginal cost and between price and marginal value product as necessary conditions of optimality. All that, along with Lerner's many papers on market pricing under socialism, was restated, elaborated and extended in his 1944 *The Economics of Control: Principles of Welfare Economics*.

That work, Lerner's best book, became and remains the most comprehensive non-mathematical text on welfare economics. Although written in the style of a handbook, with its propositions presented as rules for the planners and plant managers of a decentralized socialist economy to follow, the book is better described by the second than by the first half of its title. For most of those rules are nothing but the first-order conditions of optimality, presented with great care, clarity and completeness but without a hint at the practical obstacles in the way of putting them into actual practice. As a text on welfare economics, however, it is exceptionally meticulous and complete, it extends the scope of the welfare principle from resource allocation narrowly defined to taxation, macroeconomics and international trade and finance, and it contains the first logically based analysis of distributional optimality. Moreover, since a socialist economy, for Lerner, meant the use of private enterprise in some sectors, state-owned plants in others, depending on which was the more efficient in each, his guidebook for socialist planners also discusses why and when perfect competition leads to optimality and why and when real-life competition falls short of being perfect.

In the field of international trade theory, Lerner derived Samuelson's celebrated factor-price equalization theorem 15 years before Samuelson in a 1933 unpublished seminar paper printed only 19 years later (Lerner, 1952a). His elegant and ingenious resolution of a 19th-century controversy over the identity of import and export duties has already been mentioned; he devised (Lerner, 1932; 1934b) the standard geometry of the two-country, two-commodity model, which is well known from a whole generation of textbooks; and he was the first to raise and deal with the question of 'optimum currency areas' in his 1944 *Economics of Control*.

Most of Lerner's innovations in microeconomics and international trade theory were so basic and so useful that they promptly became integral parts of every economist's standard equipment. That is why it is hard to appreciate, at this late stage, the striking originality and elegant simplicity of his logic. One gets a glimpse of that by looking at his almost unknown proposal of how to counter OPEC's raising of the price of oil (Lerner, 1980a). He proposed the imposition of a variable import duty on oil (which he called extortion tax), whose level would always match the producer's profit margin, thereby rising and falling with the oil price and being higher on imports from high-priced and lower on those from low-priced producers. Since such a tariff would make consumers face much larger price changes than those decided upon by OPEC and much greater price differentials than those set by the different oil exporters, it would also make consumers' responses to those price changes and differentials correspondingly greater, thereby raising the price elasticity of demand for oil as it appears to producers. That would lower OPEC's monopoly power and so its profit maximizing monopoly price, and it would increase the rewards and the temptation for OPEC members to break up the coalition by defecting from it.

In macroeconomics, Lerner did as much as anyone to clarify, extend and popularize Keynes's *General Theory*; he was the first to recognize the inflationary implications of employment policies, the first to analyse in depth and in detail the causes and nature of inflation, and to propose a remedy for stagflation.

Lerner wrote the first article (1936b) to make Keynes's employment theory simple and generally intelligible, and in two short papers clarified Keynes's 'user cost' and 'marginal efficiency of capital' concepts (1943b; 1953). He wrote an interesting book (1951) to summarize and significantly extend Keynes's employment theory; he published an enlightening paper to explain the *General Theory*'s obscure Chapter 17 (1952b), thereby clearing up the complex role wage rigidity plays in rendering underemployment equilibrium possible; and he was the person best to elucidate the relation between macroeconomics and microeconomics by representing them as the two limiting cases of a more general type of economic analysis (1962).

Next to his work on welfare economics and international trade theory, Lerner's best known and most shockingly new contribution was his introduction of the idea of 'functional finance' (1943a; also restated in 1951, and in his 1944 *Economics of Control*), whose advocacy of Keynesian employment policies exposed the latter's logical implications and revolutionary nature. To careless readers, it also seemed like a wildly inflationary doctrine, although Lerner's concern over inflation and over the inflation effects of employment policies antedate everybody else's by many years.

Lerner's extensive work on inflation began with his distinguishing between low and high full employment (Lerner, 1951). High full employment is that beyond which further demand expansion presses against supply limitations and creates overspending (demand-pull) inflation; low full employment is the employment level below which the price level is stable. Levels of employment between the low and high full-employment levels create administered (cost-push) inflation, owing to labour's excessive bargaining strength. His 'low full employment' therefore is a forerunner (by 17 years) of Friedman's 'natural rate of unemployment'.

Lerner's theoretical papers on inflation contain many pioneering insights. One is his sharp analytic distinction between overspending or excess-demand inflation and administered or excess-claims inflation (1958; 1972), of which the former does, but the latter (according to him) does *not*, call for fiscal and/or monetary restraint. He later added a third category, expectational inflation (1972), which he also called defensive inflation to differentiate it from the aggressive nature of excess-claims inflation – arguing that incomes policy is effective against the former but ineffective against the latter. Another and well-known distinction which Lerner was the first to draw was that between expected and unexpected inflation (1949).

Since Lerner's heart was in reform, not in analytic niceties, his many discussions of inflation were just a preamble for working out a plan to control the main economic problem of his time, stagflation, that is, the combination of unemployment and inflation, which he considered characteristic of administered or excess-claims inflation. Restrictive policies were to him an inadmissible cure for that type of inflation, because he considered the creation of unemployment a prohibitive cost. Incomes policies he judged ineffective against all but expectational inflation, and he was too ardent a believer in the pricing mechanism to argue for wage and price controls. He wanted to stabilize the general price level without impeding the free movement of individual prices and wages. To accomplish that, he devised and, with David Colander's help, worked out in detail a scheme, called Market Anti-Inflation Plan, better known as MAP (1980b), for rationing the right of firms to raise the 'effective price' of their output, that is, the sum of profits and wages entering the price of their products (value added). The scheme would give every firm the right to increase its value added in the proportion of the estimated rise in the economy's overall productivity, but it would also allow them to sell their unused rights or the unused portion of their rights (in a market created for the purpose) to those other firms that want to increase their wages and/or profits (value added) in greater proportion.

Lerner developed his Market Anti-Inflation Plan gradually and published it at several stages and in several versions before it reached its final form in 1980. It was his last major contribution to economics and a fitting end to his career, because it well illustrates both the strengths and the weaknesses of his extraordinarily fertile and original mind. It is bold, elegant, ingenious and impeccably logical, with meticulous attention to every conceivable detail and exception, but combines those qualities with a slightly utopian flavour, all of which have characterized just about all of Lerner's many proposals for reform.

For the sheer novelty and stark logic of Lerner's arguments and policy proposals usually took people aback, but he was utterly unwilling and perhaps also unable to soften their impact in the interests of their easier acceptability. He was well aware of the reasons for the hostile reception of virtually all his recommendations but believed, with some justification, that, as time wore off their shocking novelty, they would become more acceptable and politically feasible. Lerner's MAP could well be the best remedy for stagflation but many less good remedies will first have to be tried and prove ineffective in order to render MAP politically acceptable.

T. SCITOVSKY

Selected works

1932. The diagrammatical representation of cost conditions in international trade. *Economica* 12, 346–56.
1934a. The concept of monopoly and the measurement of monopoly power. *Review of Economic Studies* 1(June). 157–75.
1934b. The diagrammatical representation of demand conditions in international trade. *Economica*, NS 1, 319–34.
1936a. The symmetry between import and export taxes. *Economica*, NS 3, 306–13.
1936b. Mr. Keynes' 'General Theory of Employment, Interest and Money'. *International Labour Review* 34, 435–54.
1943a. Functional finance and the federal debt. *Social Research* 10(February), 38–51.
1943b. User cost and prime user cost. *American Economic Review* 33(March), 131–2.
1944. *The Economics of Control: Principles of Welfare Economics*. New York: Macmillan.
1949. The inflationary process: some theoretical aspects. *Review of Economics and Statistics* 31(August), 193–200.
1951. *Economics of Employment*. New York: McGraw-Hill.
1952a. Factor prices and international trade. *Economica*, NS 19, 1–15.
1952b. The essential properties of interest and money. *Quarterly Journal of Economics* 66(May), 172–93.

1953. On the marginal product of capital and the marginal efficiency of investment. *Journal of Political Economy* 61(February), 1–14.

1958. Inflationary depression and the regulation of administered prices. *Joint Economic Committee Print*, Conference on Economic Stability and Growth, March.

1962. Macro-economics and micro-economics. In *Logic, Methodology and Philosophy of Science: Proceedings of the 1960 International Congress*, ed. E. Nagel, P. Suppes and A. Tarski. Stanford: Stanford University Press.

1972. *Flation: Not Inflation of Prices, Not Deflation of Jobs.* New York: Quadrangle Books.

1980a. OPEC – a plan – if you can't beat them, join them. *Atlantic Economic Journal* 8(3), 1–3.

1980b. (With D.C. Colander.) *MAP, A Market Anti-inflation Plan.* New York: Harcourt, Brace and Jovanovich.

For a representative collection of Lerner's best writings, see D.C. Colander, ed., *Selected Economic Writings of Abba P. Lerner*, New York: New York University Press, 1983. That volume contains most of the articles cited here and also has Lerner's complete bibliography.

For other, more detailed appraisals of Lerner's contribution to economics, see:

Samuelson, P.A. 1964. A.P. Lerner at sixty. *Review of Economic Studies* 31(June), 169–78.

Scitovsky, T. 1984. Lerner's contribution to economics. *Journal of Economic Literature* 22, 1547–71.

Sobel, I. 1979. Abba Lerner on employment and inflation: a post-Keynesian perspective. In *Essays in Post-Keynesian Inflation*, ed. J.H. Gapinski and C.E. Rockwood. Cambridge, Mass.: Ballinger.

Leroy-Beaulieu, Pierre-Paul (1843–1916)

French economist and journalist, Leroy-Beaulieu was born at Paris in 1843; he died there in 1916. His father was a Prefect and a Deputy under Louis-Philippe, his older brother a famous historian and a director of the Ecole des Sciences Politiques. His son Pierre, with whom he is sometimes confused, was also an economist. Initially trained in law, Paul Leroy-Beaulieu turned to economics in his early twenties, launching this new career with a prize-winning essay in 1867 on the effects of the moral and intellectual conditions of the working class on the rate of wages. Soon thereafter, he began collaborating on the *Revue des deux mondes*, and in 1871 he became editor of the *Journal des débats*. Two years later he founded the *Economiste française*, for which, as editor, he wrote weekly articles, missing only once in 43 years.

When Emile Boutmy established the Ecole Libre des Sciences Politiques in 1872, Leroy-Beaulieu accepted the chair of public finance. He later succeeded his father-in-law, Michel Chevalier, in the chair of political economy at the Collège de France. His ideas found wide exposure in countless journal articles and over a dozen books. A member of the French Institute and of the American Philosophical Society, he also received honorary degrees from the universities of Cambridge, Edinburgh, Dublin and Bologna.

Leroy-Beaulieu belonged to the French Liberal School of individualism and free trade. His major work, the *Traité théorique et pratique d'économie politique* (1896) is largely an exposition of classical theory. However, he rejected the pessimistic conclusions of Ricardo and Malthus, having argued in his *Essai sur la répartition des richesses* (1881) that there was no factual basis to either the Ricardian theory of rent or the 'iron law of wages'. Moreover, he sought to defuse the population bomb by arguing that the progress of civilization must always bring a declining birth rate because the altered demands and increased expenditures that accompany it are incompatible with the duties and responsibilities of parentage. In value theory, he followed the marginal analysis of the Austrians. Even as Walras was proselytizing on its behalf, however, Leroy-Beaulieu reviled the mathematical method as 'pure delusion and a hollow mockery ... [without] scientific foundation and ... practical use'. Showing equally poor judgement, he rejected the demand curve on frivolous grounds.

Leroy-Beaulieu's most enduring work was his treatise on public finance (1877), an effort that examines both public revenues and public credit. The second volume of this work rose somewhat above the first, remaining authoritative well into the 20th century.

R.F. HÉBERT

Selected works

1877. *Traité de la science des finances*, 2 vols. Paris: Guillaumin.

1881. *Essai sur la répartition des richesses et sur la tendance à une moindre inégalité des conditions.* Paris: Guillaumin.

1890. *L'état moderne et ses functions.* Paris: Guillaumin.

1896. *Traité théorique et pratique d'économie politique*, 4 vols. Paris: Guillaumin.

1913. *La question de la population.* Paris: F. Alcan.

Bibliography

Pirou, G. 1925. *Les doctrines économiques en France depuis 1870.* Paris: A. Colin.

Stourm, R. 1917. Paul Leroy-Beaulieu. *Revue des deux mondes*, Series VI 38, 532–53.

level accounting

Suppose that country A is observed to produce more output than country B: is this because it employs a larger amount of labour, a larger amount of capital or a larger amount of some other input? Or because it somehow succeeds (or endeavours) to make more effective use of given inputs? Level accounting refers to a particular approach to attacking these questions. In this approach, one computes indices of the quantities of each input participating in production in different countries, as well as the shares of each input in total income. The contribution of inputs (or of a subset of the inputs) to differences in output is then given by a geometric average of the inputs, with the shares acting as weights. The difference between the cross-country difference in output and the cross-country differences in inputs, a residual, is interpreted as a cross-country difference in the efficiency with which the inputs are employed, or in total factor productivity (TFP). Level accounting is therefore the cross-country analogue of GROWTH ACCOUNTING.

The earliest level-accounting exercises are a five-country study by Denison (1967) and a two-country comparison by Walters (1968). In the late 1970s Jorgenson and Nishimizu (1978) and Christensen, Cummings, and Jorgenson (1981) adapted the growth-accounting framework of Jorgenson's work with Griliches and Christensen to level comparisons between the United States and eight other advanced economies. They found substantial TFP differences.

More recently, level accounting has been a popular technique in addressing the sources of the enormous differences in income observed between the richest and poorest economies of the world (King and Levine, 1994; Klenow and Rodriguez-Clare, 1997; Hall and Jones, 1999). This trend has caused several authors to begin referring to it as 'development accounting'. While details vary, a consensus emerging from the development-accounting literature is that observed inputs of labour and capital account for at best 50 per cent of the observed variation in aggregate value added across a large sample (numbering about 100) of developed and developing countries. It is often argued that this evidence points to the need for developing countries to underemphasize saving and investment, and emphasize technical change and technology adoption.

Unfortunately, residual variation in development accounting poses at least as many problems of interpretation as residual variation in growth accounting. The problems are compounded by the appalling coarseness of the data. Instead of accounting for compositional differences amongst a large number of education, gender, race, and age categories, as mandated by the Jorgensonian framework, development accountants to date have mostly had to limit themselves to a rough correction for average years of schooling. Perhaps more importantly, instead of allowing for imperfect susbstitutability among different types of capital, again as prescribed by best accounting practice, measures of the capital stock are based on linear aggregation. Caselli and Wilson (2004) show that this could be a fatal flaw. Finally, most development-accounting exercises assume constant capital (and hence labour) shares across countries.

Creative improvements in the measurement of labour quality have recently been proposed by Weil (2007) and Jones and Schneider (2007). Weil proposes a way to account for differences in the productive capacity of the labour force caused by differences in health, while Jones and Schneider bring to bear cross-country differences in IQ. Both succeed in reducing residual variation considerably. These appear to be two (rare) instances where level accounting has introduced innovations that could potentially also be usefully incorporated into growth accounting, instead of the other way around.

Another recent extension of the development-accounting framework is due to Caselli and Coleman (2006), who show how to decompose the cross-country residual into differences in the efficiency with which different inputs are used. Caselli (2005) uses this technique to show that most differences in efficiency are differences in the efficiency with which labour is used. Caselli and Coleman (2006) further trace these differences to differences in the efficiency of skilled labour.

Cross-country level accounting can also be performed at the industry level, and indeed this seems a necessary step towards shedding light on the sources of large residual variation at the aggregate level. Conrad and Jorgenson (1985), and Jorgenson, Kuroda and Nishimizu (1987) presented industry-level productivity comparisons for the United States, Japan, and Germany. Despite the richness of their data they found surprisingly large TFP differences. The more recent development-accounting literature has only attempted an agriculture–nonagriculture decomposition. The most convincing effort to date is possibly due to Vollrath (2006), who appears to be able to eliminate a significant amount of residual variation in aggregate GDP by accounting for the allocation of factors across these two sectors.

FRANCESCO CASELLI

See also **growth accounting.**

Bibliography

Caselli, F. 2005. Accounting for cross-country income differences. In *Handbook of Economic Growth*, ed. P. Aghion and S. Durlauf. Amsterdam: North-Holland.

Caselli, F. and Coleman, J. 2006. The world technology frontier. *American Economic Review* 96, 499–522.

Caselli, F. and Wilson, D. 2004. Importing technology. *Journal of Monetary Economics* 51, 1–32.

Christensen, L., Cummings, D. and Jorgenson, D. 1981. Relative productivity levels, 1947–1973: an international comparison. In *New Developments in Productivity Measurement and Analysis, Studies in Income and Wealth*, vol. 41, ed. J. Kendrick and B. Vaccara. Chicago: University of Chicago Press.

Conrad, K. and Jorgenson, D. 1985. Sectoral productivity gaps between the United States, Japan, and Germany, 1960–1979. In *Probleme und Perspektiven der*

Wirtschaftlichen Entwicklung, ed. H. Giersch. Berlin: Duncker and Humblot.

Denison, E. 1967. *Why Growth Rates Differ?* Washington, DC: Brookings Institution.

Hall, R.E. and Jones, C.I. 1999. Why do some countries produce so much more output per worker than others? *Quarterly Journal of Economics* 114, 83–116.

Jones, G. and Schneider, J. 2007. IQ and productivity. Working paper, George Mason University.

Jorgenson, D., Kuroda, M. and Nishimizu, M. 1987. Japan–U.S. industry-level productivity comparisons, 1960–1979. *Journal of the Japanese and International Economies* 1, 1–30.

Jorgenson, D. and Nishimizu, M. 1978. U.S. and Japanese economic growth, 1952–1974. *Economic Journal* 88, 707–26.

King, R.G. and Levine, R. 1994. Capital fundamentalism, economic development, and economic growth. *Carnegie-Rochester Conference Series on Public Policy* 40, 259–92.

Klenow, P.J. and Rodriguez-Clare, A. 1997. The neoclassical revival in growth economics: has it gone too far? In *NBER Macroeconomics Annual 1997*, ed. B.S. Bernanke and J.J. Rotemberg. Cambridge, MA: MIT Press.

Vollrath, D. 2006. *How Important are Dual Economy Effects for Aggregate Productivity?* Houston: University of Houston Press.

Walters, D. 1968. *Canadian Income Levels and Growth: An International Perspective*. Ottawa: Economic Council of Canada.

Weil, D. 2007. Accounting for the effect of health on economic growth. *Quarterly Journal of Economics* 122 (forthcoming).

Lewis, W. Arthur (1915–1991)

W. Arthur Lewis was born on the island of St Lucia in the British West Indies on 23 January 1915. His early education was at St Mary's College on the island, where he completed a rigorous high school curriculum by the age of 14. This school is remarkable for having been attended not only by Lewis but also, 15 years later, by St Lucia's other Nobel Laureate, the poet Derek Walcott. A scholarship took Lewis to the London School of Economics in 1933, where he obtained a BA in Commerce with first class honours in 1937 and then went on to do a Ph.D. under the supervision of Arnold Plant, who incidentally was also the supervisor of Ronald Coase. In 1938 he was appointed as a junior member of the faculty, the first black man to receive such a position in the history of the institution. His very active teaching at the LSE on a very broad range of subjects undoubtedly prepared him well for his future work on economic development. He moved to Manchester University in 1947, where he held the Stanley Jevons Chair, previously occupied by J.R. Hicks, and where he was himself to be succeeded by

Harry Johnson. It was here that he did some of his most seminal work on development economics, the *Manchester School* article on 'Economic Development with Unlimited Supplies of Labor' (1954) and the treatise on *The Theory of Economic Growth* (1955). In the 1950s he was a senior official in agencies of the United Nations, and was for a time Vice Chancellor of the University of the West Indies. He went to Princeton in 1963, where he remained until his retirement in 1983: just as at the LSE, he was the first person of African descent ever to be appointed to the faculty. He held many part-time advisory positions with international organizations and governments in developing countries, particularly in West Africa and the Caribbean. He was awarded the Nobel Prize for Economics in 1979, together with T.W. Schultz, for their contributions to economic development. He died at his summer home in Barbados on 15 June 1991.

His earliest original research, including his Ph.D. thesis, was on the application of price theory to problems of industrial organization and public utilities. A number of studies published during the 1940s, such as 'The Two Part Tariff' (1941), 'Competition in Retailing' (1945), 'Fixed Costs' (1946), and other related topics, were brought together in a volume entitled *Overhead Costs*, published in 1949. Two other books published in the same year, based on his LSE lectures, were *Economic Survey 1919–1939* and *Principles of Economic Planning*. The first of these was an examination of the troubled economic history of the world economy in the interwar period, notable in particular for the way in which he linked together the experiences of the 'core' industrial countries with those of the primary producing 'periphery' of the world economy. The pessimism about the possibility of international trade to serve as a sustained 'engine of growth' for the developing countries, that has marked his subsequent writings on development economics down to his Nobel Prize Lecture in 1980 (entitled 'The Slowing Down of the Engine of Growth'), can perhaps be traced to his study of the inter-war period, an interesting parallel with the case of Ragnar Nurkse, who also came to the study of development problems after writing his *International Currency Experience* on the breakdown of the international monetary system in the 1930s. The book on planning, though written at an introductory level, was a penetrating early examination of the problems of coordinating government intervention and the market in a mixed economy.

Lewis's most famous and influential contribution to economics is undoubtedly the 1954 paper on development with 'unlimited supplies' of labour. He presents a stylized model in which the typical poor country is divided into a 'traditional' and a 'modern' sector. The former consists of peasant agriculture as well as self-employment of various sorts in urban areas, where the primary objective of economic activity is to maintain consumption. The 'modern' sector comprises commercial farming, plantations and mines and manufacturing, in all of which there is hired labour and profit is the motive for production organized by a class of capitalists and entrepreneurs. Lewis adopts a strictly classical viewpoint on two crucial features of his model. First, the real wage of unskilled labour in the modern sector is exogenously given, with employment and profits then being determined by the demand for labour corresponding to the fixed stock of capital in the short run. The second classical feature is that the accumulation of capital is governed by saving out of profits. The process of economic development is viewed as the expansion of the modern relative to the traditional sector until such time as the 'surplus labour' pool in the traditional sector is drained and an integrated labour market emerges with a neo-classically determined equilibrium real wage, rising steadily over time as growth proceeds. The model as a whole thus has two distinct phases, an initial 'classical' one with a fixed real wage, that is the main focus of the analysis, and a subsequent 'neoclassical' one with a rising real wage. The concept of a 'dual economy' in the first phase of the model has generated considerable controversy and an extensive polemical literature, to which references can be found in Findlay (1980), together with an appraisal, extensions and critique of the model itself. The most sophisticated and thorough theoretical defence of the dual economy and the associated notion of 'surplus labour' remains that provided by Sen (1966). The *Manchester School* in 2004 appropriately marked the 50th anniversary of the most celebrated article it ever published by a special issue, which contains a valuable survey of subsequent developments by Kirkpatrick and Barrientos (2004).

Another notable, but much less well-known, contribution of this seminal (1954) paper, in a neglected section on the open economy, is a model of the terms of trade between manufactures and primary products that is developed further, with empirical applications, in his (1969) Wicksell Lectures. The key idea is that the world price of manufactures, relative to the prices of tropical products such as coffee, tea, sugar, rubber and jute, is determined by the relative opportunity costs of labour in food production. Thus the Pittsburgh steel worker's wage is governed by the Kansas farmer's productivity, while the Brazilian coffee plantation wage is determined by the much lower productivity of peasant subsistence agriculture, which explains why a unit of steel in the world market commands so many more units of coffee. Since the transformation curves between steel and food and coffee and food are assumed to be linear, demand only determines quantities produced, consumed and traded, not relative prices, exactly as in the approach of the classical economists. Lewis applied this model in a very imaginative way to illuminate several key aspects of the history of the world economy in his last major work, *Growth and Fluctuations 1870–1913*, published in (1978). This volume extended his examination of the world economy in the inter-war period in *Economic Survey 1919–1939* back to the 'golden age' of globalization from 1870 to 1913, and is a deeply original piece of theoretical, statistical and historical research in the manner of Schumpeter and Kuznets. Both volumes are still essential reading for any serious student of the evolution of the world economy.

The reader can find an extensive collection of Lewis's articles and shorter monographs in the volume edited by Mark Gersovitz (1983). A measure of his influence on the field of development economics can be gathered from the volume of essays in his honour edited by Gersovitz and others (1982). Robert L. Tignor (2006) is a very valuable account of the life and inspiring achievements of this great pioneer of development economics, rightly drawing attention to the stoic courage and steely resolution with which he confronted and overcame the racial prejudice that was so virulent even in Western academic circles during his early career. The effect of these experiences may have made him appear to many as reserved, aloof and 'prickly' but to all who knew him well he was always kind, courteous and considerate, with a puckish sense of humour. The writer Pico Iyer (1997) described Derek Walcott, the other Nobel Laureate of St Lucia, as a 'Tropical Classical' because of the deep influence of Homer and other classical authors on his poetry. The designation fits Arthur Lewis admirably as well, and not only because of the influence of Ricardo and other classical authors on his economics.

RONALD FINDLAY

See also **dual economies.**

Selected works

1941. The two part tariff. *Economica*, NS 8, 240–70.
1945. Competition in retail trade. *Economica*, NS12, 202–34.
1946. Fixed costs. *Economica*, NS13, 231–58.
1949. *Economic Survey 1919–1939*. London: Allen & Unwin.
1949. *Overhead Costs*. London: Allen & Unwin.
1949. *The Principles of Economic Planning*. London: Allen & Unwin.
1954. Economic development with unlimited supplies of labor. *Manchester School* 22, 139–91.
1955. *The Theory of Economic Growth*. London: Allen & Unwin.
1969. *Aspects of Tropical Trade 1883–1965*. Wicksell Lectures, Stockholm: Almqvist & Wiksell.
1978. *Growth and Fluctuations 1870–1913*. London: Allen & Unwin.
1980. The slowing down of the engine of growth (Nobel Lecture). *American Economic Review*, 70, 555–64.

Bibliography

Findlay, R. 1980. On W. Arthur Lewis' contributions to economics. *Scandinavian Journal of Economics* 82(1), 62–76.
Gersovitz, M., Diaz-Alejandro, C.F., Ranis, G. and Rosenzweig, M.R. 1982. *The Theory and Experience of*

Economic Development: Essays in Honour of W. Arthur Lewis. London: George Allen & Unwin.

Gersovitz, M. 1983. *Selected Economic Writings of W. Arthur Lewis*. New York: New York University Press.

Iyer, P. 1997. *Tropical Classical: Essays from Several Directions*. New York: Vintage.

Kirkpatrick, C. and Barrientos, A. 2004. The Lewis model after 50 years. *Manchester School* 72, 679–90.

Nurkse, R. 1944. *International Currency Experience*. N.p.: League of Nations.

Sen, A.K. 1966. Peasants and dualism with or without surplus labor. *Journal of Political Economy* 74, 425–50.

Tignor, R.L. 2006. *W. Arthur Lewis and the Birth of Development Economics*. Princeton: Princeton University Press.

lexicographic orderings

Lexicographic orderings are orderings in which certain elements of the space being ordered have been selected for special treatment. I begin with an example. Suppose an agent has an ordering over commodities a and b. Although he or she likes both a and b, any bundle which has more of a is *preferred* to any bundle which has less of a. Of course among bundles which have the same amount of a, bundles with more b are preferred to those with less. Thus, there are no trade-offs between a and b and each indifference set is a single point. The name 'lexicographic' comes from the way words are ordered in a dictionary, alphabetically by the first letter and then the second and so on.

Lexicographic orderings were known chiefly as simple examples of orderings which *could not* be represented by a continuous real-valued function; see Debreu (1954) for the first discussion of this issue in economics. It is, however, in social choice theory and welfare economics where these orderings have come to prominence. To demonstrate their role a lexicographic maximin rule (leximin) follows. Let $u = (u_1, \ldots, u_N)$ be an element of a Euclidean N-space where u_n is the utility of person n. In each possible state of the world, say $\bar{u}_1 = (\bar{u}_1, \ldots, \bar{u}_n)$, let $r(\bar{u})$ be the person who is the rth best off. For example, if $N=3$ and $\bar{u} = (2, 7, 3)$ then $1(\bar{u}) = 2$ as person 2 has the highest utility, $2(\bar{u}) = 3$, and $3(\bar{u}) = 1$; ties are broken arbitrarily. An ordering R is a leximin rule if and only if for all $(u, \bar{u})$, $\bar{u}P\bar{u}$ if and only if there exists a k, $1 \leq k \leq N$, such that $\bar{u}_{k(u)} > \bar{u}_{k(u)}$ and for all $j > k$, $\bar{u}_{j(u)} = \bar{u}_{j(u)}$ where P is the strict preference relation, the asymmetric factor of R. That is, if the worst-off $N - k$ people have the same utility levels in $\bar{u}$ and $\bar{u}$ and the next worst-off person, k, is better off in $\bar{u}$ than in $\bar{u}$, then $\bar{u}$ is preferred to $\bar{u}$. Continuing the numerical example above let $\bar{u} = (2, 7, 2.5)$ so that $1(\bar{u}) = 2, 2(\bar{u}) = 3$, and $3(\bar{u}) = 1$. Then $k = 2, \bar{u}_{2(u)} = 3 > \bar{u}_{2(u)}$ and $\bar{u}_{3(u)} = 2 = \bar{u}_{3(u)}$ hence $\bar{u}P\bar{u}$.

It is important to notice that if each person's utility function were subjected to the same increasing transformation the above ordering would not change. This is a case where utility is ordinally measurable but fully comparable as levels of utility can be compared across individuals. That the leximin rule satisfies all of the original axioms of Arrow (1951; 1963) except for the comparability of levels of utility was first worked out by D'Aspremont and Gevers (1977).

Other types of lexicographic orderings appear frequently in social choice theory; see Sen (1986, section 6).

C. BLACKORBY

See also **orderings**.

Bibliography

Arrow, K.J. 1951. *Social Choice and Individual Values*. New York: Wiley. 2nd edn, 1963.

D'Aspremont, C. and Gevers, L. 1977. Equity and the informational basis of collective choice. *Review of Economic Studies* 44, 199–209.

Debreu, G. 1954. Representation of a preference ordering by a numerical function. In *Decision Processes*, ed. R. Thrall, C. Coombs and R. Davis. New York: Wiley.

Sen, A.K. 1986. Social choice theory. In *Handbook of Mathematical Economics*, vol. 3, ed. K. Arrow and M. Intriligator. Amsterdam and New York: North-Holland.

liability for accidents

Legal liability for accidents governs the circumstances under which parties who cause harm to others must compensate them. There are two basic rules of liability. Under *strict liability*, an injurer must always pay a victim for harm due to an accident that he causes. Under the *negligence rule*, an injurer must pay for harm caused only when he is found negligent, that is, only when his level of care was less than a standard of care chosen by the courts, often referred to as *due care*. (There are various versions of these rules that depend on victims' care, as will be discussed.) In fact, the negligence rule is the dominant form of liability; strict liability is reserved mainly for certain especially dangerous activities (such as the use of explosives). The amount that a liable injurer must pay a victim is known as *damages*.

Our discussion of liability begins by examining how liability rules create incentives to reduce risk. The allocation of risk and insurance is next addressed, and, following that, the factor of administrative costs. Then a number of topics are reviewed. Comprehensive economic treatments of accident liability are presented in Landes and Posner (1987) and Shavell (1987); an early, insightful informal, economically oriented treatment of liability is presented in Calabresi (1970). Empirical literature is surveyed in Kessler and Rubinfeld (2007) and is not considered here.

Incentives

In order to focus on liability and incentives to reduce risk, we assume in this section that parties are risk neutral. Further, we suppose that there are two classes of parties – injurers and victims – who do not have a contractual relationship. For example, injurers might be drivers and victims pedestrians, or injurers might be polluting firms and victims affected residents.

Unilateral accidents and the level of care

Here we suppose that injurers alone can reduce risk by choosing a level of *care*. Let x be expenditures on care (or the money value of effort) and $p(x)$ be the probability of an accident that causes harm h, where p is declining in x. Assume that the social objective is to minimize total expected costs, $x + p(x)h$, and let x^* denote the optimal x.

Under strict liability, injurers pay damages equal to h whenever an accident occurs, and they naturally bear the cost of care x. Thus, they minimize $x + p(x)h$; accordingly, they choose x^*.

Under the negligence rule, suppose that the due care level $\hat{x}$ is set equal to x^*, meaning that an injurer who causes harm will have to pay h if $x < x^*$ but will not have to pay anything if $x \geq x^*$. Then the injurer will choose x^*: he will not choose $x > x^*$, for that will cost him more and he escapes liability by choosing merely x^*; he will not choose $x < x^*$, for then he will be liable (in which case the analysis of strict liability shows that he would not choose $x < x^*$).

Thus, under both forms of liability, injurers are led to take optimal care, as first shown in Brown (1973). Note that under the negligence rule courts need to be able to calculate optimal care x^* and to observe actual care x, in addition to observing harm. Under strict liability courts need only to observe harm.

It should also be noticed that, under the negligence rule with due care $\hat{x}$ equal to x^*, negligence is never found, because injurers are induced to be non-negligent. Findings of negligence may occur, however, under a variety of modifications of our assumptions. Courts might make errors in observing injurers' care, so that an injurer whose true x is at least x^* might mistakenly be found negligent because his observed level of care is below x^*. Similarly, courts might err in calculating x^* and thus might set due care $\hat{x}$ above x^*. If so, an injurer who chooses x^* would be found negligent (even though care is accurately observed) because $\hat{x}$ exceeds x^*. As emphasized by Craswell and Calfee (1986), error in the negligence determination leads injurers to choose incorrect levels of care, and under some assumptions, to take excessive care in order to reduce the risk of being found negligent by mistake. Other explanations for findings of negligence are that individuals may not know x^* and thus take too little care, the judgment-proof problem (see below), which may lead individuals to choose to be negligent, and the inability of individuals to control their behaviour perfectly at every moment or of firms to control their employees.

Bilateral accidents and levels of care

We now assume that victims also choose a level of care y, that the probability of an accident is $p(x,y)$ and is declining in both variables, that the social goal is to minimize $x + y + p(x,y)h$, and that the optimal levels of care x^* and y^* are positive.

Under strict liability, injurers' incentives are optimal conditional on victims' level of care, but victims have no incentive to take care because they are fully compensated for their losses. However, the usual strict liability rule that applies in bilateral situations is strict liability with a defense of *contributory negligence*, meaning that an injurer is liable for harm only if the victim's level of care was not negligent, that is, his level of care was at least his due care level $\hat{y}$. If victims' due care level is y^*, then it is a unique equilibrium for both injurers and victims to act optimally: victims choose y^* in order to avoid having to bear their losses, and injurers choose x^* since they will be liable because victims are non-negligent.

Under the negligence rule, optimal behaviour is also the unique equilibrium. Injurers choose x^* to avoid being liable, and, since victims therefore bear their losses, they choose y^*. Two other variants of the negligence rule are negligence with the defence of contributory negligence (under which a negligent injurer is liable only if the victim is not negligent) and the comparative negligence rule (under which a negligent injurer is only partially liable if the victim is also negligent). These rules also induce optimal behaviour.

Thus, all of the negligence rules, and strict liability with the defence of contributory negligence, support optimal care, on the assumption due care levels are chosen optimally. Courts need to be able to calculate optimal care levels for at least one party under any of the rules, and in general this requires knowledge of the function $p(x,y)$. The main conclusions of this section were first proved by Brown (1973) (see also Diamond, 1974, for closely related results).

Unilateral accidents, level of care, and level of activity

Now let us reconsider unilateral accidents, allowing for injurers to choose their level of *activity* z, which is interpreted as the (continuously variable) number of times they engage in their activity (or, if injurers are firms, the scale of their output). Let $b(z)$ be the benefit from the activity, and assume the social object is to maximize $b(z) - z(x + p(x)h)$; here $x + p(x)h$ is assumed to be the cost of care and expected harm each time an injurer engages in his activity. Let x^* and z^* be optimal values. Note that, as before, x^* minimizes $x + p(x)h$, and that z^* satisfies $b'(z) = x^* + p(x^*)h$, the marginal benefit from the activity equals the marginal social cost, comprising the sum of the cost of optimal care and expected accident losses.

Under strict liability, injurers choose both the level of care and the level of activity optimally, as their objective is the social objective.

Under the negligence rule, injurers choose optimal care x^* as before, but their activity is socially excessive. Because an injurer escapes liability by taking care of x^*, he chooses z to maximize $b(z) - zx^*$, so that z satisfies $b'(z) = x^*$. The injurer's cost of raising his activity level is only his cost of care x^*, which is less than the social cost, as that also includes $p(x^*)h$. The excessive level of activity under the negligence rule is more important the larger is the expected harm $p(x^*)h$ from the activity.

The failure of the negligence rule to control the level of activity arises because negligence is defined here (and for the most part in reality) in terms of care alone. A justification for this assumption is that courts might face informational difficulties were they to include the activity level in the definition of negligence. The problem with the activity level under the negligence rule is applicable to any aspect of behaviour that would be difficult to incorporate into the negligence standard (including, for example, research and development activity). The distinction between levels of care and levels of activity was developed in Shavell (1980).

Bilateral accidents, levels of care, and levels of activity
If we consider levels of care and of activity for both injurers and victims, then none of the liability rules that we have considered leads to full optimality (on the assumption that activity levels are unobservable). The reason that full optimality cannot be achieved is in essence that injurers must bear full accident losses to induce them to choose the right level of their activity, but this means that victims will not choose the optimal level of their activity.

Risk-bearing and insurance
We next examine the implications of risk aversion and the role of insurance in the liability system (see Shavell, 1982a). A number of general points may be made.

First, the socially optimal resolution of the accident problem now involves not only the reduction of losses from accidents but also the protection of risk-averse parties against risk. Risk bearing is relevant for two reasons: not only because potential victims may face the risk of accident losses, but also because potential injurers may face the risk of liability. The former risk can be mitigated through accident insurance, and the latter through liability insurance.

Second, the incentives associated with liability do not function in the direct way discussed in the previous section, but instead are mediated by the terms of insurance policies. To illustrate, consider strict liability in the unilateral accident model with care alone variable, and assume that insurance is sold at actuarially fair rates. If injurers are risk averse and liability insurers can observe

their levels of care, injurers will purchase full liability insurance coverage and their premiums will depend on their level of care; their premiums will equal $p(x)h$. Thus, injurers will want to minimize their costs of care plus premiums, or $x + p(x)h$, so they will choose the optimal level of care x^*. In this instance, liability insurance eliminates risk for injurers, and the situation reduces to the previously analysed risk-neutral case.

If, however, liability insurers cannot observe levels of care, ownership of full coverage could create severe moral hazard, so would not be purchased. Instead, as is known from the theory of insurance, the typical amount of coverage purchased will be partial, for that leaves injurers with an incentive to reduce risk. In this case, therefore, the liability rule results in some direct incentive to take care because injurers are left bearing some risk after their purchase of liability insurance, but their level of care tends to be less than first best.

This last situation, in which liability insurance dilutes incentives, leads to a third point, concerning the question whether the sale of liability insurance is socially desirable. (We note that, because of fears about incentives, the sale of liability insurance was delayed for decades in many countries and that it was not allowed in the Soviet Union; further, in the United States liability insurance is sometimes forbidden against certain types of liability, such as against punitive damages.) The answer to the question is that, even though it may dilute incentives, sale of liability insurance is socially desirable, at least in basic models of accidents and some variations of them. In the case just considered, for example, injurers are made better off by the presence of liability insurance, as they choose to purchase it, and victims are indifferent to its purchase by injurers because victims are fully compensated for any harm suffered. This argument must be modified in other cases, such as when the damages injurers pay are less than harm because injurers are judgment-proof.

Fourth, consider how the comparison between strict liability and the negligence rule is affected by risk bearing. The immediate effect of strict liability is to shift the risk of loss from victims to injurers, whereas the immediate effect of the negligence rule is to leave the risk on victims (as injurers tend to act non-negligently). However, the presence of insurance means that victims and injurers can substantially shield themselves from risk, attenuating the relevance of risk bearing for the comparison of strict liability and negligence.

Finally, the presence of insurance implies that the liability system cannot be justified primarily as a means of compensating risk-averse victims against loss. Rather, the justification for the liability system must lie in significant part in the incentives that it creates to reduce risk. To amplify, although both the liability system and the insurance system can compensate victims, the liability system is much more expensive than the insurance system (see the next section). Accordingly, were there no social need to create incentives to reduce risk, it would be best to dispense with the liability system and to rely on insurance to accomplish compensation.

Administrative costs

The administrative costs of the liability system are the legal and other costs (notably the time of litigants) involved in bringing suit and resolving it through settlement or trial. These costs are substantial; a number of estimates suggest that, on average, administrative costs of a dollar or more are incurred for every dollar that a victim receives through the liability system (Shavell, 2004, p. 281).

Strict liability versus negligence

The factor of administrative costs affects the comparison of liability rules. On one hand, we would expect the volume of cases – and thus administrative costs – to be higher under strict liability than under the negligence rule. On the other hand, given that there is a case, we would anticipate administrative costs to be higher under the negligence rule because due care will be at issue. Hence, it is not clear which liability rule is administratively cheaper.

Social desirability of the liability system and private motives to sue

The existence and the surprisingly high magnitude of administrative costs raise rather sharply the question whether the liability system is socially worthwhile. Moreover, the private motive to sue is not in alignment with the social reasons for using the liability system. First, the private benefit of suit is the amount of money that would be obtained from it, whereas the social benefit is the deterrence that would be created. Second, the private cost of suit is the victim's cost, whereas the social cost includes also the injurer's and the state's cost. These differences give rise to the possibility of socially excessive or socially insufficient suit. To illustrate the former, suppose that care has no effect on the accident probability, so that it is socially undesirable for suit to be brought. Yet under strict liability a victim will bring suit as long as his cost is less than the harm suffered, so the volume of litigation activity could be high. To illustrate the possibility of socially inadequate suit, suppose that an expenditure on care of only one hundredth of harm will eliminate the possibility of otherwise certain harm, and suppose also that the magnitude of harm is less than the cost of suit. Then no suit will be brought. However, it would be desirable for victims to have an incentive to bring suit, for that would induce care to be taken, and, since no harm would then occur, no suit would ever occur. The private versus the social motive to make use of the legal system was first developed in Shavell (1982b, 1997); see also Polinsky and Rubinfeld (1988).

Topics

Damages

Under strict liability, damages must equal harm h for incentives to be optimal. Under the negligence rule, however, damages higher than h also would induce injurers to take optimal care of x^*. Higher damages will increase the incentive to be non-negligent; they will not lead injurers to take excessive care because injurers can escape liability merely by taking care of x^*. But when there is uncertainty in the negligence determination, damages higher than h may lead to problems of excessive care.

Damages exceeding h are desirable if injurers sometimes escape liability, as when injurers may be hard to identify (the origin of pollution may be difficult to trace). If the probability of liability for harm is q, then, if damages are raised to $(1/q)h$, expected liability will be h. Thus, the more likely an injurer is to escape liability, the higher should be damages. On these points and others about punitive damages, see Cooter (1989) and Polinsky and Shavell (1998).

Causation

A fundamental principle of liability law is that a party cannot be held liable unless he was the cause of losses. For example, if cancer occurs in an area where a firm has polluted, the firm will be liable only for the cancer that it caused, not for cancer due to other carcinogens. This principle is necessary to achieve social efficiency under strict liability, because otherwise incentives would be distorted. Socially desirable production might be rendered unprofitable if the firm were held responsible for all cases of cancer. Under the negligence rule, restricting liability to accidents caused by an actor may be less important than under strict liability: if negligent actors were held liable for harms they did not cause, they would only have greater reason to act non-negligently. On causation and incentives, see Calabresi (1975), Kahan (1989), and Shavell (1987).

Judgment-proof problem

The possibility that injurers may not be able to pay in full for the harm they cause is known as the judgment-proof problem and is of substantial importance, for individuals and firms often cause harms significantly exceeding their assets. When injurers are unable to pay fully for the harm they may cause, their incentives to reduce risk are inadequate, and their incentives to engage in risky activities excessive. Policy responses to the judgment-proof problem include vicarious liability (imposed on a party who has some control over the judgment-proof party), minimum asset requirements for participation in harmful activities, safety regulation, and criminal liability. On the judgment-proof problem and responses to it, see Kornhauser (1982), Pitchford (1995), Shavell (1986; 2005), and Sykes (1984).

Product liability

When victims are customers of firms, the role of liability in providing incentives may be attenuated or even non-existent. If customers have perfect knowledge of product risks, then they will pay less for risky products, and incentives to reduce risk will be optimal without liability. If, however, customer knowledge of risk is imperfect, liability is potentially useful in reducing risk. In the latter case, a question of interest is whether court-determined liability or market-determined liability, namely, warranties, is likely to be better, on which see Priest (1981), Rubin (1993), and Spence (1977).

Liability versus other means of controlling risk

Liability is only one method of controlling harm-causing behaviour; safety regulation and corrective taxes are among the alternatives. Liability harnesses the information that victims have about the occurrence of harm, and thus may be advantageous when victims, rather than the state, naturally observe how harm comes about; whereas when harm-causing behaviour and its occurrence requires state effort to be ascertained, regulation and taxation may be advantageous. In order for liability to function well as an incentive device, injurers must have assets approximating the harm they might cause, whereas regulation and taxation (based on expected harm rather than actual harm) do not require injurers to have substantial assets. Liability, however, may enjoy an administrative cost advantage over regulation and taxation, in that administrative costs are incurred under the liability system only when harm comes about, whereas such costs generally are incurred more often under regulation and taxation. On the comparison of the liability system and other means of controlling risk, see Calabresi and Melamed (1972), Kolstad, Ulen and Johnson (1990), and Shavell (1993).

STEVEN SHAVELL

See also **externalities; law, economic analysis of.**

Bibliography

Brown, J.P. 1973. Toward an economic theory of liability. *Journal of Legal Studies* 2, 323–49.

Calabresi, G. 1970. *The Costs of Accidents*. New Haven, CT: Yale University Press.

Calabresi, G. 1975. Concerning cause and the law of torts. *University of Chicago Law Review* 43, 69–108.

Calabresi, G. and Melamed, A.D. 1972. Property rules, liability rules, and inalienability: one view of the cathedral. *Harvard Law Review* 85, 1089–128.

Cooter, R.D. 1989. Punitive damages for deterrence: when and how much? *Alabama Law Review* 40, 1143–96.

Craswell, R. and Calfee, J.E. 1986. Deterrence and uncertain legal standards. *Journal of Law, Economics, & Organization* 2, 279–303.

Diamond, P.A. 1974. Single activity accidents. *Journal of Legal Studies* 3, 107–64.

Kahan, M. 1989. Causation and incentives to take care under the negligence rule. *Journal of Legal Studies* 18, 427–47.

Kessler, D. and Rubinfeld, D.R. 2007. Empirical study of the common law and legal process. In *Handbook of Law and Economics*, vol. 1, ed. A.M. Polinsky and S. Shavell. Amsterdam: North-Holland.

Kolstad, C.D., Ulen, T.S. and Johnson, G.V. 1990. Ex post liability vs. ex ante regulation: substitutes or complements? *American Economic Review* 80, 888–901.

Kornhauser, L. 1982. An economic analysis of the choice between enterprise and personal liability for accidents. *California Law Review* 70, 1345–92.

Landes, W.M. and Posner, R.A. 1987. *The Economic Structure of Tort Law*. Cambridge, MA: Harvard University Press.

Pitchford, R. 1995. How liable should a lender be? The case of judgment-proof firm and environmental risk. *American Economic Review* 85, 1171–86.

Polinsky, A.M. and Rubinfeld, D.R. 1988. The welfare implications of costly litigation for the level of liability. *Journal of Legal Studies* 17, 151–64.

Polinsky, A.M. and Shavell, S. 1998. Punitive damages: an economic analysis. *Harvard Law Review* 111, 869–962.

Priest, G.L. 1981. A theory of the consumer warranty. *Yale Law Journal* 90, 1297–352.

Rubin, P.H. 1993. *Tort Reform by Contract*. Washington, DC: AEI Press.

Shavell, S. 1980. Strict liability versus negligence. *Journal of Legal Studies* 9, 1–25.

Shavell, S. 1982a. On liability and insurance. *Bell Journal of Economics* 13, 120–32.

Shavell, S. 1982b. The social versus the private incentive to bring suit in a costly legal system. *Journal of Legal Studies* 11, 333–9.

Shavell, S. 1986. The judgment proof problem. *International Review of Law and Economics* 6, 45–58.

Shavell, S. 1987. *Economic Analysis of Accident Law*. Cambridge, MA: Harvard University Press.

Shavell, S. 1993. The optimal structure of law enforcement. *Journal of Law and Economics* 36, 255–87.

Shavell, S. 1997. The fundamental divergence between the private and the social motive to use the legal system. *Journal of Legal Studies* 26, 575–612.

Shavell, S. 2004. *Foundations of Economic Analysis of Law*. Cambridge, MA: Harvard University Press.

Shavell, S. 2005. Minimum asset requirements and compulsory liability insurance as solutions to the judgment-proof problem. *Rand Journal of Economics* 36, 63–77.

Spence, M. 1977. Consumer misperceptions, product failure, and producer liability. *Review of Economic Studies* 44, 561–72.

Sykes, A. 1984. The economics of vicarious liability. *Yale Law Journal* 93, 1231–80.

liberalism and economics

Liberalism is the theory and practice of reforms which has inspired two centuries of modern history. It grew out of the English Revolutions of the 17th century, spread to many countries in the wake of the American and French Revolutions of the 18th century, and dominated the better part of the 19th century. At that time, it also underwent changes. Some say it died, or gave way to socialism, or allowed itself to be perverted by socialist ideas; others regard the social reforms of the late 19th and 20th centuries as achievements of a new liberalism. More recently, interest in the original ideas of liberals has been revived. Thus, classical liberals, social liberals and neoliberals may be distinguished.

Classical liberalism is a simple, dramatic philosophy. Its central idea is liberty under the law. People must be allowed to follow their own interests and desires, constrained only by rules which prevent their encroachment on the liberty of others. Early liberals before and after John Locke (1690) liked to use the metaphor of a social contract to express this view. Society can be thought of as emerging from an agreement among its members to protect themselves against the selfish desires of others. Man's 'unsociable sociability' (Kant, 1784) makes rules necessary which bind all, but requires also the maximum feasible space for competition and conflict.

In fact, of course, early liberals were not concerned with building societies from scratch. They were concerned with forcing absolute rulers to yield to demands for liberty. The rule of law envisaged by liberals was a revolutionary force which heralded the enlightened phase of modernity.

The notion, rule of law, is not without ambiguity. It is, in the first instance, largely formal. One thinks of rules of the game applying to all and regulating the social, economic and political process. In theory, such rules are intended not to prejudge the outcome of the game itself. Still, even their formal conditions, equality before the law and due process, involved fundamental changes which justify speaking of a movement of reform. Throughout the history of liberalism, however, the question of certain substantive rights of man has been an issue. The inviolability of the person and the rights of free expression have been liberal causes along with constitutional rules. Liberals have rarely found it easy to reason for such substantive rights to their own satisfaction. A certain tension between liberal thought and the notion of natural rights is unmistakable.

The modern debate of these issues began in Scotland and England. John Locke, David Hume (1740) and Adam Smith (1776) are but three of many names to consider. From Britain, the ideas spread to the United States and to continental Europe. Montesqieu and Kant borrowed some of their ideas from British liberals. The American Declaration of Independence and the Constitution, the Declaration of the Rights of Man three years after the French Revolution are only two practical illustrations of the effect of the new ideas. If one wants to, one can distinguish, with Friedrich von Hayek, between a British 'evolutionary' and a continental 'constructivist' concept of liberalism. Either or both however became the dominant reform movements of the early 19th century and determined the dynamics of Europe and North America between the 1780s and the 1840s or 1850s.

Liberalism had consequences for economic, social and political thought. Its economic application was the most obvious and remains the most familiar. If rules of the game are all that can be justified whereas otherwise interests should be allowed a free reign, the scene is set for the operation of the market. It is the forum where equal rights of access and participation but divergent and competing interests lead, through the operation of an 'invisible hand' (Adam Smith), to the greatest welfare for all. Liberalism and market capitalism are inseparable, much as later European theorists (notably in Germany and Italy) have tried to dissociate the two.

The social application of liberalism analogously leads to the emergence of the public, if by 'public' we understand the meeting place of divergent views from which a 'public opinion' emerges. On the Continent, a more emphatic language is often preferred; here, one likes to speak of the emergence of society from under the state. Either way, the basic idea involves the same departure from an all-embracing system of domination by traditional authorities to one in which public authority is confined to certain tasks of regulation, and thus bound to grant and defend the freedom of individuals to express their views.

This is the point at which classical liberalism was not only instrumental for the promotion of market capitalism and social participation, but also for the development of what is called today, democracy. Again, the term is anything but clear. It can be understood to mean a system of government which is based on the competition of divergent views – individual views or group views – for power, constrained by rules which limit the instruments used in the process, and stipulate the possibility for change. In this sense, a variety of constitutional forms of democracy respond to liberal views, including versions of representative government as well as forms of plebiscite. Liberalism is not anarchism, but anarchism is in some ways an extreme form of liberalism. The law has a key role in liberal thinking, but for a long time the prevalent interest of liberals was that of liberating people from the fetters of control imposed by the tangible force of the state (and the church) or the abstract force of tradition. Not surprisingly, some authors took this intention of liberation to its extreme. If they believed in the essential goodness of man, they advocated the abolition of all social restraint; at times, Jean-Jacques Rousseau seems to argue this way. If on the other hand they believed in the ambivalence of human nature, they were not afraid to demand unlimited room for manoeuvre for 'the singular one and his property' (Max Stirner, 1845).

Perhaps this anarchist strain in early liberal thinking can be said to have been one of the reasons for the counter-reaction of the 19th century. Marx was the first to point out the historical advance brought about by 'bourgeois' equality before the law, including the contractual basis of economic action, but also the price paid by many for the 'anarchic' quality of the resulting market. The market – it was increasingly argued – was in fact not neutral, but favoured certain players to the systematic disadvantage of others. Mass poverty, conditions of labour, the state of industrial cities were cited as examples. Nor was this merely a view of anti-liberals. The great ambiguities in the thinking of John Stuart Mill tell the story.

There are two ways of describing the resulting history of thought and of social movements. One is to say that as the 19th century progressed, and certainly in the early decades of the 20th century, liberalism was replaced by socialism as a dominant force. People began to shrink back from the unconstrained market and sought new kinds of intervention. Today, authors would add that the 'structural change of the public' (J. Habermas, 1962) and the bureaucratization of democracy followed suit. Liberalism died a 'strange death'; it ceased to be a source of reform and became a defence of class interest.

Another view ascribes the new reforms to liberals also, albeit to a different kind of liberalism. In his Alfred Marshall Lectures of 1949, T.H. Marshall (1950) argued that the progress of citizenship rights had to involve, from a certain point onwards, their extension from the legal and the political to the social realm. Social citizenship rights turned out to be a necessary prerequisite for the exercise of equality before the law and universal suffrage. Thus, the social, or welfare state was no more than a logical extension of the process which began with the revolutions of the 18th century.

There is much to be said for this line of argument if one considers that the two men who above all determined the climate of political thought and action from the 1930s to the 1970s, John Maynard Keynes and William Beveridge, were both self-declared liberals. In effect if not in intention, they advanced ideas which led to restrictions on the operation of markets. One will be remembered as the author of economic policy as a deliberate effort by governments, the other has contributed much to the creation of transfer systems which are operated by governments in the light of an assumed common interest. In other words, these were liberals who pursued policies which led to strengthening rather than limiting the power of public authorities. Theirs was a substantive, a social liberalism.

Liberal parties have found it difficult to follow the twists of theoretical liberalism. Before the First World War, when socialist parties were still in their infancy and unable to determine policy in any major country, they were often the spokesmen of the deprived and underprivileged. At least one strand of the liberal tradition continued to be reformist. However, after the First World War, socialists or social democrats came to form governments in many countries. Their gain was the liberals' loss. Liberal parties declined to the point of insignificance, unless they merely kept the name and changed their policies out of recognition, either in the direction of social democracy (Canada) or in that of conservatism (Australia). Indeed, as a practical political movement, liberalism came to present such a confused picture that Hayek could argue that liberalism has become a mere intellectual, and not a political force.

The experience of totalitarianism interrupted this process without stopping it altogether. To the dismay but also to the surprise of many, basic human rights and the rules of the game of civil government became an issue again in the 1930s and 1940s. This gave rise to an important literature in which the underlying values of liberal thought were spelt out anew. Hayek's *Road to Serfdom* is one example, but the most important one is probably Karl Popper's *Open Society and Its Enemies* (1952). Popper developed above all what might be called the epistemology of liberalism. We are living in a world of uncertainty. Since no one can know all answers, let alone what the right answers are, it is of cardinal importance to make sure that different answers can be given at any one time, and especially over time. The path of politics, like that of knowledge, must be one of trial and error. The principle can be applied to economy and society as well.

The liberal revolt against totalitarianism waned with the memory of totalitarianism itself. While the term 'social market economy' was coined for Germany in the 1950s, the quarter-century of the economic miracle was in fact a social-democratic quarter-century. In it, economic growth was combined almost everywhere with a growing role of government and with the extension of the social state. Entitlements came to matter as much as achievements. Consensus counted for more than competition or conflict. Despite variations, this was a very successful period in the countries of the First World. But by the 1970s, the side effects of success had become major problems in their own right. These were not only obvious problems like environmental and social 'limits to growth', but systematic ones arising from the role of the state. Both Keynes and Beveridge gave rise to new questions. Neither stagflation in the 1970s nor boom unemployment in the 1980s seemed amenable to government intervention. The social state had got out of hand; it became harder and harder to finance, and its bureaucracies robbed it of much of its plausibility. There were demands for a reversal of trends.

Where such a reversal happened, it remained bitty, halting and inconsistent. However, the new climate gave rise also to elements of a new theory of liberalism. In one sense, this was, and is a return to the original project of asserting society against the state, the market against planning and regulation, the right of the individual against overpowering authorities and collectivities. American authors in particular restated the theory. Milton Friedman tried to show in a series of arguments that the role of government is usually contrary to the interests of people. Robert Nozick made a strong case for the 'minimal state' and against the arrogance of modern state power. James Buchanan (1975) and the 'constitutional economists' reconstructed the social contract and argued for severely limited rules and regulations, using the fiscal system as one of their main examples. This trend, more than the notion of supply-side economics (which in some ways is merely Keynes stood on his head) signifies the revival of liberalism.

There are other facets of the many-faceted term. For many, the extension of civil rights to hitherto disadvantaged groups is a liberal programme. Others still concentrate on the separation of church and state and the reduction of church influence. Again others regard liberalism as an advocacy of cultural values, including pluralism and creativity. It is not difficult to see the connection of such preferences with the mainstream of liberal thought.

This mainstream has three elements. Liberalism is a theory and a movement of *reform* to advance *individual liberties* in the horizon of *uncertainty*. This means by the same token that the prevailing theme of liberalism cannot be the same at all times. In the face of absolutism, it is liberty under the law; in the face of market capitalism, it is the full realization of citizenship rights; in the face of the 'cage of bondage' (Max Weber, 1922) of modern bureaucratic government, it is the optimal, if not the minimal state. The struggle for the social contract has become virulent in the advanced free societies. The crisis of the social state, the new unemployment, issues of law and order all raise basic questions of what is Caesar's and what are therefore the proper limits of individual desires. It is no accident that constitutional questions have come to the fore in several countries. At such a time, liberalism is gaining new momentum. It will not solve all issues, but it will remain a source of dynamism and progress towards more life chances for more people.

RALF DAHRENDORF

See also **invisible hand; libertarianism; property rights; utilitarianism and economic theory.**

Bibliography

Buchanan, J. 1975. *The Limits of Liberty*. Chicago: University of Chicago Press.
Habermas, J. 1962. *Strukturwandel der Öffentlichkeit*. Neuwied: Luchterhand.
Hume, D. 1740. *A Treatise of Human Nature*. Ed. L.A. Selby-Bigge, Oxford: Clarendon Press, 1888.
Kant, I. 1784. Idee zu einer allgemeinen Geschichte inweltbürgerlicher Absicht. In *Kants Populäre Schriften*, ed. P. Menzer, Berlin: Georg Reimer, 1911.
Locke, J. 1690. *Second Treatise of Government*. Ed. T.P. Peardon, New York: Liberal Arts Press, 1952.
Marshall, T.H. 1950. *Citizenship and Social Class*. Cambridge: Cambridge University Press.
Popper, K.R. 1952. *The Open Society and its Enemies*. 2nd edn. London: Routledge & Kegan Paul.
Smith, A. 1776. *An Inquiry into the Nature and Causes of the Wealth of Nations*. Oxford: Oxford University Press, 1976.
Stirner, M. 1845. *Der Einzige und sein Eigentum*. Leipzig: D. Wigand.
Weber, M. 1922. *Wirtschaft und Gesellschaft*. 4th edn, Töbingen: Mohr/Siebeck, 1956.

libertarianism

Libertarians, in current American usage and in this essay, are those who prefer to organize the world through the decentralized mechanisms of private property, trade, and voluntary cooperation rather than through government. Their position is thus a modern variant of the liberalism of the 19th century. Libertarians are likely to be critical of eminent domain, government regulation of business, paternalistic social policies, income redistribution, laws banning 'victimless crimes' such as drug use, gambling and prostitution, and much else. Since there are good arguments for government as well as good arguments against, only a minority of libertarians carry their position all the way to anarchism. Most accept some level of taxation to pay for the production of public goods such as national defence. Some accept government production or subsidy of things well short of pure public goods, such as schooling.

The term 'libertarian' is also sometimes applied to left anarchists, usually outside of the United States; its original meaning seems to have been believers in free will. The current American usage is largely a response to the shift in the meaning of 'liberal' over the first half of the 20th century. Since believers in what used to be called liberalism could no longer use that term without confusion, many adopted 'libertarian' as a substitute.

One reason for libertarians to support a less than perfectly libertarian society is the belief that, in terms of individual liberty, it is the best we can do. A second is the belief that, while liberty is important, it is not the only thing that is important. Support by many libertarians for government funding of some public goods – scientific research and public health are examples – is based on the idea not that their production makes us freer but that it makes us better off in other ways.

In this article I sketch the general arguments for a libertarian position, discuss libertarian views on particular issues, and finally consider different forms of libertarianism and the internal disagreements that define them.

Why liberty is right

Libertarian conclusions may be supported either by showing that restraints on individual liberty are wrong or by showing that they lead to undesirable consequences. The former approach is often put in terms of individual rights. Each person has a right to control his own body, a right violated by laws against using drugs, by a military draft, and by many other government acts. Each person has a right to control his legitimately acquired property, a right violated by taxation, regulation, price controls,....

Putting the argument in this form raises an obvious question: how to justify such claims. Libertarians offer a variety of answers, ranging from Objectivists, who believe that individual rights can be logically deduced from the nature of man, to intuitionists, who induce them by trying to generalize their moral intuitions (Rand, 1964; Den Uyl and Rasmussen, 1991; Rothbard, 1978; Lester, 2000; Nozick, 1974; Boaz, 1997; 1998).

It also raises questions about how rights are acquired and how far they extend. Almost nobody argues that my right to control my body includes the right to punch you in the nose. Whether it includes the right to make noise on my property that keeps you awake or burn coal in my fireplace whose smoke makes you cough is less clear.

Robert Bork, in the article (Bork, 1971) explaining why he was not a libertarian, argued that my disutility from knowing that you are doing something I disapprove of is just as real an externality as my disutility from breathing your smoke, hence that there is no rights-based case for individual freedom as libertarians understand it. If we treat everything I do that affects others without their consent as a trespass liable to be enjoined, we are left with no self-regarding actions and no liberty – the exception swallows the rule. A response from the standpoint of moral philosophy depends on some way of deriving rights that distinguishes between those sources of disutility to me that do and those that do not violate my rights – hitting me over the head versus living your life in a way I disapprove of.

The economic response starts by observing that the enforcement cost of a rule giving me control over my own body is low, since I already control my body. The enforcement cost of giving you control over my body is substantial. Hence the latter alternative is an inefficient definition of property rights, at least unless my use of my body clearly imposes substantial and measurable costs on you that cannot be dealt with by voluntary transactions along Coasean lines. Although your disutility from knowing that I am reading pornography may be just as real as your disutility from breathing my smoke, it is considerably harder to demonstrate to a court, so a liability rule awarding you damages for the disutility you suffer from my reading pornography is likely to result in inefficient outcomes and substantial litigation costs. Alternatively, a property rule giving you rather than me a property right in my behaviour – requiring me, before doing anything, to get permission from everyone who

objects – imposes transaction costs due to the hold-out problem sufficient to guarantee that nobody ever does anything, which is unlikely to be the efficient outcome. Following out this line of argument provides a defence of libertarian conclusions on consequentialist grounds.

'Liberty' and 'rights' are rhetorically powerful words, so it is not surprising that libertarians are not the only ones who claim them. Competing uses can be clarified by distinguishing between negative rights ('the area within which a man can act unobstructed by others', Berlin, 1969, p. 122) and positive rights. A negative right is a right to be left alone. A positive right is the right to some outcome. The right not to be killed is a negative right, the right to live – implying the right to be provided with what you need to live, such as food – a positive right. Other positive rights sometimes claimed include the right to decent housing, adequate food, medical care and equal treatment.

One problem with positive rights is that they contradict negative rights, including some that many find persuasive. If I have the right to decent housing and medical care, someone else must have the obligation to produce them, which is inconsistent with his right to control his own body. If I have the right to equal treatment, the right not to have an employer or homeowner decide whether to deal with me on the basis of my race or religion, someone else does not have the right of freedom of association, since he is required to deal with me even if he prefers not to. If I have the right not to be hated or despised for my sexual preferences, that means that I have a claim over the inside of your head, that being where your emotions are to be found. Thus the assertion of positive rights can be seen, and by libertarians often is seen, as the claim that some people are to some degree the slaves of others, required to serve them without having consented to do so – the violation of a deeply held negative right.

A second problem with positive rights is that they are more prone to internal inconsistency than negative rights. There is no conflict between my not killing or enslaving you and your not killing or enslaving me. But there is a conflict between my having adequate food, housing and medical care and your having them, if one or another of those goods happens to be in short supply.

Why liberty is useful

Large parts of the consequentialist argument for individual freedom go back to Adam Smith and should be familiar to every economist. Private property, exchange, prices provide a decentralized coordination mechanism that makes it possible for individuals with different objectives, knowledge and abilities to cooperate while pursuing their separate ends. In the limiting case of perfect competition, the result is provably efficient in the usual economic sense – cannot be improved by even a perfectly intelligent central planner with unlimited control over the actions of the planned. (For both the classical and modern versions of the First Efficiency Theorem, see Arrow, 1983, and references therein. For a non-technical sketch of the classical version, see D. Friedman, 1997, ch. 16.)

The fact that this argument is correct, non-obvious, and included in the professional training of any economist is part of the reason why libertarianism is more popular with economists than with most other academics and why even non-libertarian economists tend to be sympathetic to market approaches. To put it differently, one important reason for the rejection of libertarian conclusions by non-economists is the failure to understand price theory – how markets solve the coordination problem.

The case against

Yet not all economists, not even all good economists, are libertarians. The economic counter-argument starts with the facts that real markets are imperfectly competitive and real individuals are limited by, at least, imperfect information, transaction costs, and limited calculating ability. Once we drop the assumptions of the ideal model we are faced with the possibility of market failure, situations where individual rationality fails to lead to group rationality and hence where it is possible for restrictions on the actions of each to produce a better outcome for all. Familiar examples include the underproduction of public goods, the overproduction of negative externalities, and potentially beneficial transactions blocked by adverse selection.

These are real problems, but not always insoluble ones. A market failure results in an outcome inferior, for all concerned, to some alternative outcome. A sufficiently ingenious entrepreneur may be able to create that alternative and collect a share of the net benefit as his reward; a market failure is also a profit opportunity. Radio broadcasts are a pure public good produced privately. So are the services that Google provides to its users. Other forms of market failure may be dealt with by the development of systems of private norms (Ellickson, 1991; Posner, 2000). Where market failure exists we can expect private arrangements to produce imperfect outcomes, but less imperfect than casual consideration might suggest. (For an interesting example of a real world solution to a theoretically intractable market failure, see Cheung, 1973.)

A second objection to the argument for laissez-faire is that efficiency as defined in economics in the sense of Marshall or Hicks–Kaldor (D. Friedman, 1997, ch. 15) is inadequate as a normative criterion, so that a less efficient outcome may be preferable to a more efficient one. What is maximized by the market is value defined by willingness to pay, measured in dollars not utiles, so a transfer from rich to poor might decrease value measured in dollars but increase total utility.

This utilitarian argument for redistribution can be seen as a special case of the argument from market failure. Declining marginal utility is not merely a conjecture of philosophers; it is observed, in the form of risk aversion, in individual choices under uncertainty. In a perfect market, individuals would buy insurance against the risk of being born poor up to the point where the marginal utility costs of any resulting disincentives or transactions costs just balanced the marginal utility gain of transferring income from states of the world where they were rich to ones where they were poor. Thus the outcome of a perfect market would mirror the welfare programme that would be proposed by a utilitarian. It is merely our inconvenient inability to negotiate and sign insurance contracts prior to being born that prevents the market from solving the problem. The argument for utilitarianism in Harsanyi, 1955 – that it is what individuals would choose if they were designing a society behind a veil of ignorance with an equal probability of living any of its lives – makes it possible to view redistribution of income either as a way of increasing total utility or as a correction for market failure.

Other objections to market outcomes come from egalitarians who see equality as good in itself and from those who put substantial weight on values unrelated to individual humans achieving their objectives. If what really matters is the preservation of endangered species, whether or not of any value to human beings, there is no guarantee that the market to achieve it. The same is true if what really matters is behaving according to God's will, producing great art and literature, or doing justice whatever the consequences.

A libertarian response

It follows that one can imagine outcomes that improve, in one sense or another, on the outcome of pure laissez-faire. It does not follow that one can construct institutions that predictably produce such outcomes.

Consider the case of market failure. It exists because actions taken by A sometimes have effects on B. If A is free to ignore those effects he may make the pair on net worse off by taking actions that increase his welfare by less than they decrease B's or failing to take actions that would increase B's welfare by more than they decrease A's. A well-designed legal structure can sometimes make it in A's interest to take account of those effects, whether through property rules, liability rules, or bargaining between the parties. But sometimes, for reasons explored by Coase (1960) and others (D. Friedman, 2000, pp. 39–45), no legal structure can be constructed that makes it in the interest of all parties to make the efficient choices.

All this is true in private markets. But it is true far more often in the political markets that control the political institutions that are proposed as a solution to market failure in private markets.

Consider the naive model of democracy – politicians doing good because if they do not they will lose the next election. In order for it to work, individual voters have to acquire the information needed to know what politicians are doing and whether it is good. No politician campaigns on the slogan 'I'm the bad guy'. No farm bill is labelled 'An act to make farmers richer and city folk poorer'.

If I correctly identify the better candidate, vote for him, and – improbably – my vote proves decisive, the benefit is shared with everyone in the polity. The cost is borne by me alone. Time and energy spent acquiring the information necessary for informed voting produce something very close to a pure public good. Public goods are underproduced; one with a public of many millions is likely to be very badly underproduced. The implication is rational ignorance, voters failing to acquire the information they need to judge politicians because its value to them is less than its cost. That eliminates the simple argument for why politicians will find it in their political interest to act as we would wish them to.

A similar problem arises with a more sophisticated model in which political outcomes are driven by interest group pressure. The more an interest group stands to gain by passing or blocking a piece of legislation, the more it will offer politicians in order to support or oppose it. If that were the only relevant factor, the market for legislation would produce something close to an efficient outcome. If a bill produced net benefits, its supporters would spend more supporting it than its opponents spent to block it, and the bill would be likely to pass.

It is not the only relevant factor. An interest group lobbying for legislation is producing a public good for its members and faces an internal public good problem in doing so, since members that refuse to contribute will still benefit if the bill passes. Some interest groups are much better able than others to solve their internal public good problem. A concentrated interest group such as the auto industry – a handful of firms and one union – can raise a substantial fraction of the benefit it expects from an auto tariff in order to lobby for it. A dispersed interest group such as consumers of automobiles and producers of export goods, the people that bear most of the burden of such a tariff, can raise a negligible fraction of the cost to lobby against. Hence we would expect the political market to consistently redistribute from dispersed interest groups to concentrated ones, even when the benefit to the latter is much smaller than the cost to the former – as demonstrated by the continued existence of tariffs nearly two centuries after Ricardo demonstrated that they are, under most circumstances, injurious to the nation that imposes them.

In a private market, a producer receives a price that measures the value to consumers of what he produces, pays a cost that measures the cost to the suppliers of his inputs of producing them, and pockets the difference. It is only when special circumstances arise – externalities that cannot be dealt with by the market, information asymmetry, and the like – that his actions impose net costs or benefits on others. In the political market, in contrast, almost all decisions are made by people who bear few of the costs and receive few of the benefits those decisions produce. A legislator who passes an auto tariff imposes net costs of many billions of dollars on those affected, but all that comes out of his pocket is the extra cost of the car he buys. A judge whose precedent establishes a seriously inefficient legal rule might reduce national income by, say, a tenth of a percentage point – a staggering amount of damage for a single human being to do. But not only will he not pay any of the cost, he will never even know he made a mistake.

Consider, for example, *Davis v. Wyeth Laboratories, Inc.*, 399 F.2d 121 (9th Cir. (Idaho) Jan 22, 1968), where the court found Wyeth liable for the failure to adequately warn of the risk of polio vaccination. Their argument hinged on whether, if warned, Davis might reasonably have chosen not to be vaccinated. The court wrote: 'Thus appellant's risk of contracting the disease without immunization was about as great (or small) as his risk of contracting it from the vaccine. Under these circumstances we cannot agree with appellee that the choice to take the vaccine was clear.' They reached this conclusion by comparing the 0.9 in a million chance of getting polio from the vaccination with the 0.9 in a million *annual* rate of adult polio from natural causes. Since vaccination provided protection for many years, possibly a lifetime, the proper comparison was to the risk over many years, not one. The court made a mathematical error of more than an order of magnitude, set a precedent which substantially discouraged the development of new vaccines, caused many, perhaps thousands, of unnecessary deaths, and suffered no penalty for doing so.

Market failure is a real problem. It is a problem in ordinary private markets and a much more severe problem in political markets. That is an argument for shifting decisions, so far as possible, from political to private markets – an argument for, not against, the libertarian position.

A possible response is that decisions should be shifted to public markets only where private markets fail. But some degree of market failure can be alleged for almost any activity. Under legal rules permitting government intervention to correct any alleged market failure, intervention can be expected whenever it is politically profitable.

Libertarians vary in how far they are willing to push the arguments that I have just sketched. Consider the case of national defence, a public good with a very large public. The failure to produce it privately at an adequate level is likely to lead to a drastic reduction in liberty. That is an argument sufficiently strong to convince many, although not all, libertarians to include it in the proper functions of government.

So far I have been dealing with arguments based on market failure, but similar point cans be made with regard to other criticisms of market outcomes. It is true that the market takes account of values only to the extent that individuals do; if nobody cares about the survival of the oldest tree in the world or some threatened species of birds, there is no reason to expect the market to preserve it. But the same is true of the political system. It too is driven by the desires of individuals. It just does a much clumsier job of satisfying them.

Indeed, there are some reasons to expect the market to do a better job of serving 'non-economic' values than the political system. Many are things, not that nobody cares about, but only that most people don't, and the market is generally better at providing for small minorities than the political system. A religion followed by a per cent or two of the population has no difficulty getting the market to produce copies of its scriptures. If it is sufficiently unpopular with the majority, it may have problems getting the government to permit them to be printed. A minority in power might be able to do a better job of diverting resources to serve its values, whether religious or environmental, through the political system than through the market. But shifting decisions to the political system for that reason could be a risky gamble.

Another common criticism, but a mistaken one, is that the market ignores the interest of future generations. Future as well as present demand counts. It is worth planting hardwoods today for harvest a century hence as long as the return is at least as great as from alternative investments. Markets allocate resources over time, as Hotelling (1931) showed, in an economically efficient fashion. If it can be predicted that petroleum will be very valuable a century hence, it is profitable to leave it unpumped now so as to sell it then.

This argument depends on secure property rights. It breaks down if oil saved or a tree planted today is likely to be expropriated tomorrow, making holding it for future use a poor gamble. The alternative to decisions by the market is decisions by political mechanisms. Property rights in the political marketplace are much less secure than those in the private marketplace. A president who accepts costs today for benefits 10 or 20 years in the future can be reasonably confident that neither he nor his party will receive credit for those benefits. A dictator, unlike an entrepreneur, rarely has the opportunity to collect the benefit from investments expected to pay off in the future by transferring his long-term assets to a successor in exchange for immediate payment. Hence we would expect political institutions to be much more inclined to sacrifice the future to the present than market institutions, a conclusion supported by the evidence of environmental policy in the Soviet Union and Social Security in the United States.

What about income redistribution? Here again, the question is not whether there is an outcome that some would prefer to that produced by the market but whether there are institutions that predictably create such an outcome. The equal distribution of votes gives the poor some advantage on the political marketplace, but it may easily be outweighed by the very unequal distribution of other politically relevant resources. Modern governments are observed to redistribute from rich to poor via welfare, from poor to rich by subsidies for art, music, and – the big one – higher education, paid for mostly by state and local taxes and consumed mostly by people from the upper part of the income distribution. (The median family income of US college freshmen in 2001 was $67,200, compared with a median family income for all households of $42,228 – US Census Bureau, 2003, Tables 284 and 683. See Gwartney and Stroup, 1986, for a discussion of theory and evidence of the consequences of redistributional policies.) Similarly, farm policy provides a subsidy mostly to wealthy farmers and pays for it mainly by a regressive tax in the form of higher food prices.

A second problem with redistribution is rent seeking. In a polity that redistributes, it is in the interest of nearly everyone to spend resources trying to shift the redistribution in his favour, opposing redistribution from him and promoting redistribution to him (Tullock, 1967; D. Friedman, 1973, ch. 38; Krueger, 1974). The resulting deadweight cost might easily outweigh any utility gain from redistribution.

Issues

Libertarians differ in how far they are willing to carry their libertarianism. In the following discussion I present libertarian positions and the arguments for them while recognizing that in many cases the libertarian position is not supported by all who consider themselves libertarians.

The easy cases

Most of the arguments against price control, wage control, rent control, usury laws, and similar restrictions on the terms of market exchange are familiar to any economist. Many libertarians also argue that such restrictions violate individual rights. If I own my body, it is up to me to decide on what terms I will sell my labour to you. If I own my house, it is up to me to decide what terms I am willing to offer to potential tenants and up to them to decide what terms they are willing to accept. Thus many libertarians would reject not only rent and wage control but also legal restrictions on private discrimination in home sales, employment, and the like. (Nozick, 1974, ch. 7, provides an extended discussion and defence of a libertarian view of self-ownership.)

Libertarians taking that position may defend it either in terms of individual rights or by arguing that minorities are worse off in a world where such decisions are controlled by government than in one where they are controlled by private contract. State intervention in the

US South during the first half of the 20th century provides an obvious example. A prejudiced majority can do a great deal more harm to the minority it is prejudiced against where decisions are made by the government than where they are made privately.

Free trade is another easy case. If building cars in Detroit costs more than growing grain, putting it on ships, sending them out into the Pacific, and having them come back with Hondas on them, we are better off growing our cars instead of building them. A tariff forces us to use the more expensive technology instead of the less expensive; it protects American auto workers from the competition of American farmers, making Americans on the whole worse off. While economists can construct special circumstances in which a trade restriction might benefit the nation that imposed it, such as infant industries that require temporary protection, the restrictions we observe are not those suggested by such arguments: In the U.S., steel and auto are not infant industries. We observe instead the restrictions predicted by the public choice analysis offered earlier, policies that benefit concentrated interest groups at the expense of dispersed interest groups. (For an explanation of why tariff protection is particularly likely for declining industries such as steel, see D. Friedman, 1997, p. 294.)

Many libertarians find paternalism another easy case, since it contradicts the idea that each individual owns his own body and is free to make choices regarding it. As a practical matter, paternalistic regulations substitute for each individual's decisions about his own welfare the decisions of someone else. The regulator may have expert information the individual lacks, but he lacks both the individual's specialized knowledge about his own circumstances and the individual's incentive to act in that individual's interest. Thus professional licensing, justified as a paternalistic protection of the consumer, is in practice used by professions to reduce competition and so benefit themselves at the expense of their customers. (The classic discussion is M. Friedman, 1962, ch. 9). Similar arguments apply to laws against victimless crimes – the War on Drugs, laws against prostitution and gambling. Individuals might make the wrong decisions for themselves; others should be free to warn them against doing so. But the final decision ought to be made by each individual for himself.

A familiar example of the dangers of such regulation in the United States is the Food and Drug Administration (FDA). Letting a dangerous drug onto the market ends the regulator's career. Keeping a drug off the market for a few more years can do enormous damage – arguably an excess mortality on the order of a hundred thousand lives in the case of beta-blockers (Gieringer, 1985. For a webbed discussion, see FDAReview.org.) But damage that appears only in the mortality statistics is very nearly irrelevant, politically speaking. And the connection between over-regulation, higher prices and fewer new drugs is still less visible. (See Peltzman, 1973, for a classic examination of the effect of regulation on quality and rate of introduction of new drugs.)

Antitrust

There are legitimate arguments, widely supported by economists, in favour of government intervention against monopolies. Even libertarians are troubled by hypotheticals in which one firm owns the only well in the desert and insists on thirsty travellers giving all they own and indenturing their labour for decades into the future in exchange for a drink. Government regulation of monopoly, however, has its own problems. The regulator needs information he is unlikely to have – cost curves and demand curves – in order to force the firm to follow welfare-maximizing rather than profit-maximizing strategies (D. Friedman, 1997, pp. 238–43). And it is far from clear why a real-world regulator, driven by political rather than altruistic incentives, would attempt to regulate in the public interest rather than letting himself be captured by the regulated industry, a concentrated interest well positioned to reward politicians with money and regulators with future jobs (Stigler, 1971). An industry that is imperfectly competitive may be imperfectly efficient, but the situation is not improved by giving firms the opportunity to use government regulation, as the US railroad industry used the Interstate Commerce Commission (ICC), to exclude competitors and restrict competition (Kolko, 1977).

Such considerations persuade many libertarians that antitrust, both as a legal doctrine and as a basis for regulation, does more harm than good – that we would be better off putting up with any ills private monopoly may produce, since the cure is likely to be worse than the disease (M. Friedman, 1962, pp. 128–9). Others argue that the state need not prevent monopoly but ought not to support it, and can avoid doing so by refusing to enforce contracts in restraint of trade.

Immigration

The economic arguments for free movement of goods apply to capital and labour as well, implying that immigration produces net benefits for the country that permits it, just as free trade produces net benefits for the country that practises it. Freer immigration also produces what many would consider a desirable redistribution, since its major beneficiaries, the immigrants, are much poorer than those who might be made worse off by their move: workers in the country the immigrants go to, capitalists and landowners in the countries they come from.

This assumes a context of voluntary transactions. Some immigrants may come in order to profit by involuntary transactions, private or political – to commit robbery or collect welfare. And new immigrants, once they become citizens and voters, might use the political mechanism to advantage themselves at the cost of the rest of us. Such arguments help explain why not all libertarians support free immigration – despite empirical evidence that, at least under current circumstances, immigrants pay more in taxes than they collect in benefits (Simon, 1989; 1995).

The flip side to the 'immigrant as welfare recipient' argument is that, while the existence of a welfare state makes the desirability of free immigration less clear, free immigration makes it more difficult to maintain a welfare state. Free movement of people imposes limits on the ability of governments to exploit those they rule, similar to the limits that market competition imposes on the ability of firms to take advantage of their customers (Tiebout, 1956). For libertarians, that is an additional advantage to freer immigration.

Schooling

The usual argument for government provision or subsidy of schooling is that a democracy requires educated voters and an economy educated workers, hence that money spent educating my children benefits you and your children, hence that leaving education to the free market will result in too little.

The first part of that argument might be true, although it is hard to find evidence to support it. The second is simply bad economics. To the extent that education makes a worker more productive, the additional productivity is reflected in his wages; investing in human capital is no more a public good than investing in physical capital. In both cases the investor may receive less than the full value of his investment due to the distorting effect of taxation – some of my additional productivity goes, not to me, but to the Internal Revenue Service. But subsidizing the investment merely shifts the inefficiency to whoever pays the taxes that fund the subsidy.

There may be indirect externalities to subsidized education – a cure for cancer, say. But not all such externalities are positive. By educating my children I make them better able to use the political system to advantage themselves at the expense of your children. By sending my son to Harvard I give him an opportunity to feel superior to your son, who went to Podunk U. That is a benefit to me and my son, a cost to you and yours, and a negative externality produced by my expenditure on education. As Robert Frank (1986) has persuasively argued, one of the things humans care about and economists ought to take account of is relative status.

This example illustrates a common problem with arguments based on externalities. Those making them usually count only externalities that lead to the conclusion they want – positive if they want to subsidize something, negative if they want to ban it. If an activity produces both positive and negative externalities, as many do, and if we are unable to measure them accurately enough to determine the sign of their sum, we do not know whether we should be encouraging the activity or discouraging – in which case it might be wiser to do neither (D. Friedman, 1971).

Another argument for government involvement in schooling is that, since parents act in their own interest rather than that of their children, they may fail to pay the cost of schooling even when it produces a benefit larger than its cost. But shifting the decision to the political system means shifting it, not to children, but to other adults. Adults routinely make large sacrifices on behalf of their children, much more rarely on behalf of other people's children. So while a parent is not a perfect proxy for his children, he may be the best proxy available – a much better one than either the legislature or the teachers' unions.

Other government activities can be supported, and opposed, with similar arguments. Subsidies for basic research can be defended as producing a public good, rejected on the grounds that enough of the benefits can be privatized to make subsidy unnecessary (Kealey, 1997), that government involvement diverts too many smart people into whatever field is currently in fashion, and that it subverts the scientific enterprise by converting the search for truth into a search for grants.

The relevance of public good theory is less clear for police and courts, government activities traditionally accepted by believers in a minimal government. Law enforcers can choose to pursue criminals who commit crimes against those who have paid for their services and not those who have not; England survived with private thieftakers but without police in the modern sense until well into the 19th century. (Davies, 2002; D. Friedman, 1995. Both argue that there is no clear evidence that failure of the traditional system was the reason why it was eventually replaced.) Courts can refuse to settle disputes among those unwilling to pay for the service, and some – both private arbitrators and government courts – do. Many libertarians accept the conventional arguments for state provision of police and courts, paid for by taxation; others do not (D. Friedman 1973, part 3).

There are a few issues where libertarians disagree among themselves about which side is more libertarian. Intellectual property is one example. Some argue that a book or an invention, as the pure creation of a human mind, deserves strong protection. Others regard all intellectual property as coercive, a restriction on how individuals are permitted to use their own material property. Limited liability for corporations is another such. Many libertarians reject it on the grounds that individuals ought to be liable for their actions. Others see it as a legitimate consequence of freedom of association and contract and observe that, while it is possible for a corporation to impose costs it does not have the resources to compensate for, the same is true for an individual.

Foreign policy provides a particularly divisive example. Opponents of the United States in recent decades have been strikingly unfree societies – Hitler's Germany, Stalin's Russia, Mao's China, Ho Chi Minh's Vietnam – making a policy of overthrowing, or at least containing, them attractive to many libertarians. But such a policy is conducted by a government whose competence and motives libertarians find suspect – and badly done interventionism may well be worse than no interventionism (D. Friedman, 1989, ch. 45). Hence many libertarians favour the non-interventionist policy famously advocated by George Washington – peace and friendship with all, entangling alliances with none.

Libertarian: yes/no or more/less

Some libertarians propose a bright line definition of who is a libertarian, often along the lines of 'one who believes in never initiating force against another'. One problem with this is that libertarians do not have an entirely satisfactory account of what determines who owns what – in particular, of how unproduced resources, such as land, become property. Without a clear answer to that question, it is sometimes hard to distinguish the initiation of force from the use of force to defend what you justly own.

A second problem is that the bright line definition, taken literally, eliminates almost everyone, including almost all libertarians. Consider a scenario popularized by the late R.W. Bradford, editor of *Liberty Magazine*. You have carelessly fallen out of a 50th storey window. By good luck, you catch hold of the flagpole of the apartment immediately below you and start trying to climb in the window. The owner of the apartment objects that you are violating his property rights – not only by climbing in his window, but by using his flag pole without his permission. Do you let go and fall to your death? Such arguments suggest that 'libertarian' is more usefully defined as a continuum – more libertarian or less rather than libertarian or not.

An issue which has attracted a good deal of attention within the libertarian movement is whether there ought to be any government at all. One faction, sometimes labeled 'minarchist', supports a government that provides, at least, for courts, police, and national defence. The other – anarchists or anarcho-capitalists – argues that, with suitable institutions, voluntary cooperation in a free market can adequately provide all government services worth providing (D. Friedman, 1989, part 3; Rothbard, 1978). The latter position can be defended either on the (rights-based) grounds that all other alternatives involve violations of rights or on the (consequentialist) grounds that, just as the free market does a better job than government of building cars and growing food, it could also do a better job of producing laws and defending rights. While the latter claim seems obviously false to many when they first encounter it, it has proved sufficiently persuasive to be adopted by a significant minority of those seriously involved with libertarian ideas and libertarian argument. (Liberty Magazine Editors, 1999.)

Varieties of libertarianism

Does 'individuals have the right not to be coerced' mean that one should never initiate coercion or that one should act to minimize coercion? If rights are best protected by a tax-supported system of police and courts, should one support such taxes as a way of minimizing rights violations or oppose them as a violation of rights? (Nozick, 1974, pp. 28–35, discusses the distinction between rights as side constraints and a 'utilitarianism of rights' and offers arguments for the former.) One answer makes anarchism something close to a moral imperative, the other decides the anarchist/minarchist issue in terms of how well either alternative works.

It is useful for land to be treated as private property. But how does a claimant get ownership? Locke (1689, ch. 5, section 27) famously argued that he did it by mixing his labour with the land – clearing trees, plowing, removing boulders. But that argument included the proviso that there be as much land and as good available for other claimants, since otherwise the first claimants deprive others of the opportunity to claim land themselves. The value of the land is in part site value and in part value due to human effort; how does the owner get a just claim to the former?

Many libertarians avoid these questions by simply accepting existing titles to land. Others argue that such claims are legitimate only if based on a chain of voluntary transfer back to a legitimate appropriation, whether by Lockean mixing of labour with land or some other mechanism. A few, 'geolibertarians' or, more confusingly, 'left libertarians', reject unqualified private ownership of land entirely, arguing for the land tax of Henry George or something similar (Brody, 1983; D. Friedman, 1983; Valentyne and Steiner (2000a; 2000b); George, 1879.)

For a final variant on libertarianism, consider someone who accepts both the utilitarian argument for redistribution from rich to poor and libertarian arguments against government intervention in the market. He might favour a laissez-faire society combined with some very simple system of redistribution – say a flat tax used to finance a modest demogrant. (The best-known proposal along these lines is the negative income tax; M. Friedman, 1962, pp. 191–5. A more recent version is Murray, 2006.) Making the redistribution simple reduces the opportunity for individuals to spend resources trying to shift it in their favour. Putting all redistribution in one form eliminates arguments for other government interventions defended – often implausibly – as helping the poor. While many, perhaps most, libertarians would be reluctant to consider this a fully libertarian position, it provides a possible compromise for those who accept large parts of the consequentialist argument for libertarian policies while remaining unconvinced by libertarian arguments about rights.

DAVID FRIEDMAN

See also **antitrust enforcement; externalities; Friedman, Milton; international migration; laissez-faire, economists and; public choice; public goods; rent seeking; Rothbard, Murray N.**

Bibliography

Arrow, K. 1983. An extension of the basic theorems of classical welfare economics. In *Collected Papers of Kenneth J. Arrow, Volume 2: General Equilibrium.* Cambridge, MA: Belknap.

Berlin, I. 1969. *Four Essays on Liberty.* Oxford: Oxford University Press.

Boaz, D. 1997. *Libertarianism: A Primer.* New York: Free Press.

Boaz, D. 1998. *The Libertarian Reader: Classic and Contemporary Writings from Lao Tzu to Milton Friedman.* New York: Free Press.

Bork, R. 1971. Neutral principles and some First Amendment problems. *Indiana Law Journal* 47, 1–35.

Brody, B. 1983. Redistribution without egalitarianism. *Social Philosophy and Policy* 1, 71–87.

Cheung, S. 1973. The Fable of the Bees: an economic investigation. *Journal of Law and Economics* 16, 11–33.

Coase, R. 1960. The problem of social cost. *Journal of Law and Economics* 3, 1–44.

Davies, S. 2002. The private provision of police during the eighteenth and nineteenth centuries. In *The Voluntary City: Choice, Community, and Civil Society,* ed. D. Beito, P. Gordon and A. Tabarrok. Ann Arbor: University of Michigan Press.

Den Uyl, D. and Rasmussen, D. 1991. *Liberty and Nature.* Chicago: Open Court.

Ellickson, R. 1991. *Order Without Law: How Neighbors Settle Disputes.* Cambridge, MA: Harvard University Press.

FDAReview.org. Theory, evidence and examples of FDA harm. Online. Available at http://www.fdareview.org/harm.shtml, accessed 2 August 2006.

Frank, R. 1986. *Choosing the Right Pond: Human Behavior and the Quest for Status.* New York: Oxford University Press.

Friedman, D. 1971. Laissez-faire in population: the least bad solution. Occasional paper, Population Council. Online. Available at http://www.daviddfriedman.com/Academic/Laissez-Faire_In_Popn/L_F_in_Population.html, accessed 3 August 2006.

Friedman, D. 1973. *The Machinery of Freedom: Guide to a Radical Capitalism.* Chicago: Open Court, 1989.

Friedman, D. 1983. Comment on Brody 'Redistribution Without Egalitarianism'. *Social Philosophy and Policy* 1, 88–93.

Friedman, D. 1995. Making sense of English law enforcement in the eighteenth century. *University of Chicago Law School Roundtable* Spring/Summer, 475–505.

Friedman, D. 1989. *The Machinery of Freedom: Guide to a Radical Capitalism.* Chicago: Open Court.

Friedman, D. 1997. *Hidden Order: The Economics of Everyday Life.* New York: Collins.

Friedman, D. 2000. *Law's Order: What Economics Has to Do With Law and Why It Matters.* Princeton: Princeton University Press.

Friedman, M. 1962. *Capitalism and Freedom.* Chicago: University of Chicago Press.

George, H. 1879. *Progress and Poverty.* New York: Robert Schalkenbach Foundation, 2003.

Gieringer, D. 1985. The safety and efficacy of new drug approval. *Cato Journal* 5(1), 177–201.

Gwartney, J. and Stroup, R. 1986. Transfers, equality, and the limits of public policy. *Cato Journal* 6(1), 111–37.

Harsanyi, J. 1955. Cardinal welfare, individualistic ethics, and interpersonal comparisons of utility. *Journal of Political Economy* 64, 309–21.

Hotelling, H. 1931. The economics of exhaustible resources. *Journal of Political Economy* 39, 137–75.

Kealey, T. 1997. *The Economic Laws of Scientific Research.* New York: Palgrave Macmillan.

Kolko, G. 1977. *Railroads and Regulation, 1877–1916.* Westport, CT: Greenwood.

Krueger, A. 1974. The political economy of the rent seeking society. *American Economic Review* 64, 291–303.

Lester, J. 2000. *Escape From Leviathan: Liberty, Welfare, and Anarchy Reconciled.* New York: Palgrave Macmillan.

Liberty Magazine Editors. 1999. The liberty poll. *Liberty Magazine,* February, 11–22.

Locke, J. 1689. *Two Treatises of Government,* 2nd edn. Cambridge: Cambridge University Press, 1967.

Murray, C. 2006. *In Our Hands: A Plan To Replace The Welfare State.* Washington, DC: AEI Press.

Nozick, R. 1974. *Anarchy, State and Utopia.* Malden, MA: Blackwell.

Peltzman, S. 1973. An evaluation of consumer protection legislation: the 1962 drug amendments. *Journal of Political Economy* 81, 1049–91.

Posner, E. 2000. *Law and Social Norms.* Cambridge, MA: Harvard University Press.

Rand, A. 1964. Man's rights. In *The Virtue of Selfishness.* New York: Signet.

Rothbard, M. 1978. *For a New Liberty: The Libertarian Manifesto,* rev. edn. Lanham, MD: University Press of America.

Simon, J. 1989. *The Economic Consequences of Immigration.* Cambridge, MA: Blackwell.

Simon, J. 1995. *Immigration: The Demographic and Economic Facts.* Washington, DC: Cato Institute. Online. Available at http://www.cato.org/pubs/policy_report/pr-immig.html, accessed 3 August 2006.

Stigler, G. 1971. The theory of economic regulation. *Bell Journal of Economics and Management Science* 2, 3–21.

Tiebout, C. 1956. A pure theory of local public expenditures. *Journal of Political Economy* 64, 416–24.

Tullock, G. 1967. The welfare costs of tariffs, monopoly and theft. *Western Economic Journal* 5, 224–32.

US Census Bureau. 2003. *Statistical Abstract of the United States.* Online. Available at http://www.census.gov/prod/www/statistical-abstract-2001_2005.html, accessed 3 August 2006.

Valentyne, P. and Steiner, H., eds. 2000a. *The Origins of Left Libertarianism: An Anthology of Historical Writings.* New York: Palgrave.

Valentyne, P. and Steiner, H., eds. 2000b. *Left Libertarianism and Its Critics: The Contemporary Debate.* New York: Palgrave.

Lieben, Richard (1842–1919)

Lieben was born on 6 October 1842, in Vienna; he died there on 11 November 1919. After studying mathematics and engineering sciences, he became a partner in the Jewish family business bank and a respected member of the Viennese business community. In 1892 he advocated the adoption of a gold standard. He married late and had no children. He seems to have been of scholarly and artistic tastes, more contemplative than active.

Together with his cousin and brother-in-law Rudolf Auspitz, Lieben wrote the 'Researches on the Theory of Price' (1889), the only Austrian contribution to mathematical economics and one of the outstanding contributions in the last two decades of the 19th century. (This book is discussed in the dictionary entry on AUSPITZ, RUDOLF.)

As a correspondent to the *Economic Journal*, Lieben provided a lucid summary of their views on consumer's rent (1894). After his collaborator's death he concluded the controversy with Walras by a complex three-dimensional analysis of reciprocal demand curves (1908), gracefully acknowledging their original misunderstanding. Appropriate corrections were made in the French translation of the 'Researches' (1914). While it is impossible to separate Auspitz's and Lieben's contributions, these papers suggest that Lieben was more than a junior partner.

JÜRG NIEHANS

Selected works

1887. (With R. Auspitz.) *Zur Theorie des Preises*. Leipzig: Duncker & Humblot.
1889. (With R. Auspitz.) *Untersuchungen über die Theorie des Preises*. Leipzig: Duncker & Humblot. French translation by Louis Suret, Paris: M. Giard & E. Brière, 1914.
1890. (With R. Auspitz.) Reply. (To article by L. Walras in same publication.) *Revue d'économie politique* 4.
1894. On consumer's rent. *Economic Journal* 4, 716–19.
1897. Ueber die weitere Ausdehnung des Wasserstrassennetzes in Oesterreich in der Zukunft. *Verbands-Schriften des Deutsch-Oesterreichisch-Ungarischen Verbandes für Binnenschiffahrt*.
1898. Indian currency. *Economic Journal* 8, 151–2.
1908. Die mehrfachen Schnittpunkte zwischen der Angebots- und der Nachfragekurve. *Zeitschrift für Volkswirtschaft, Sozialpolitik und Verwaltung* 17, 607–16.

Bibliography

Weinberger, O. 1931. Rudolf Auspitz und Richard Lieben. *Zeitschrift für die gesamte Staatswissenschaft* 91.
Winter, J. 1927. *Fünfzig Jahre eines Wiener Hauses*. Vienna: F. Jasper.

life cycle hypothesis. See **bequests and the life cycle model; consumer expenditure; consumer expenditure (new developments and state of research); Modigliani, Franco.**

life tables

Life tables present the age incidence of mortality in a population. The population may be all those people in a country or other area, or some category within a country; it may be all persons counted at a particular moment or period of time, say 1980 (period table); or it may be those born at a particular time and followed through life (cohort table).

The abridged life table officially calculated for the United States deaths and population of 1983 (National Center for Health Statistics, 1983) is shown as Table 1. It is based on population estimated to mid-year ($_5P_x$ for age x to $x+4$ at last birthday) and extrapolated from the 1980 census, and corresponding deaths to residents occurring during the year 1980 ($_5D_x$). Unregistered deaths are few in developed countries, but population censuses tend to under count, and give a life table of too high mortality unless a correction is made. In most less developed countries registration of deaths is incomplete, and model (e.g. Coale and Demeny, 1983 or UN, 1982) tables fill the gap.

Having the age-specific death rates, $_5M_x=_5D_x/_5P_x$, the important step is calculating the probability that a person living at the beginning of the age interval will survive to the end. If the death rate within the interval can be assumed constant then the exact probability is $l_{x+5}/l_x = e^{-5_5M_x}$. In fact, for ages from about 10 onwards the death rate rises within as well as between intervals, and this is partly taken into account by the alternative more precise expression

$$\frac{l_{x+5}}{l_x} = \frac{1 - 5_5M_x/2}{1 + 5_5M_x/2}.$$

Greville (1943) gives a more general expression. More generally yet, if $p(x+t)$ is the continuous age distribution within the interval x to $x+5$, and $\mu(x+t)$ the continuous death rate, then we have the equation

$$_5M_x = \frac{\int_0^5 p(x+t)\mu(x+t)\,dt}{\int_0^5 p(x+t)\,dt}$$

from which it is required to extract the quantity

$$l_{x+5}/l_x = \exp\left[-\int_0^5 \mu(x+t)dt\right].$$

A solution (Keyfitz, 1985, p. 39) is obtained by expanding the p's and the μ's by Taylor's theorem.

Having obtained the probability of surviving from one point of age to the next, the life table is completed by cumulating these probabilities from age 0; with an arbitrary starting point ('radix') of 1 or 100000 the l_x column is obtained by successive multiplication

$$l_{x+5} = l_x\left(\frac{l_{x+5}}{l_x}\right), \quad \text{etc.}$$

Table 1 *Abridged life tables by race and sex: United States, 1980*

Age interval	Proportion dying	Of 100,000 born alive		Stationary population		Average remaining lifetime
Period of life between two exact ages stated in years (1)	Proportion of persons alive at beginning of age interval dying during interval (2)	Number living at beginning of age interval (3)	Number dying during age interval (4)	In the age interval (5)	In this subsequent age intervals (6)	Average number of years of life remaining of age interval (7)
X to $x+n$	$_nq_x$	L_x	$_nd_x$	$_nL_x$	T_x	$\mathring{e}_x$
All races						
0–1	0.0127	100,000	1,266	98,901	7,371,986	73.7
1–5	.0025	98,734	250	394,355	7,273,085	73.7
5–10	.0015	98,484	150	492,017	6,878,730	69.8
10–15	.0015	98,334	152	491,349	6,386,713	64.9
15–20	.0049	98,182	482	489,817	5,895,364	60.0
20–25	.0066	97,700	648	486,901	5,405,547	55.3
25–30	.0066	97,052	638	483,665	4,918,646	50.7
30–35	.0070	96,414	672	480,463	4,434,981	46.0
35–40	.0091	95,742	875	476,663	3,954,518	41.3
40–45	.0139	94,867	1,321	471,250	3,477,855	36.7
45–50	.0222	93,546	2,079	462,857	3,006,605	32.1
50–55	.0351	91,467	3,209	449,811	2,543,748	27.8
55–60	.0530	88,258	4,676	430,230	2,093,937	23.7
60–65	.0794	83,582	6,638	402,081	1,663,707	19.9
65–70	.1165	76,944	8,965	363,181	1,261,626	16.4
70–75	.1694	67,979	11,517	312,015	898,445	13.2
75–80	.2427	56,462	13,702	248,534	586,430	10.4
80–85	.3554	42,760	15,197	175,192	337,896	7.9
85 and over	1.0000	27,563	27,563	162,704	162,704	5.9

Source: National Center for Health Statistics (1983).

The l_x column has three interpretations: (1) The probability of a person just born surviving to age x. (2) The number of survivors in a hypothetic cohort (say starting with 100,000 births) by the time age x is reached. (3) The number of persons aged x in the stationary population.

For this last interpretation one integrates over one- or five-year age intervals, and so obtains $_5L_x = \int_0^5 l(x+t)\,dt$, the number of individuals in a stationary population (say one in which there are exactly 100,000 births per year) at age x to $x+4$ at last birthday.

What makes possible the simultaneous representation of these three quite different entities is a central assumption of the life table: that the actual number of deaths to occur will be the probability multiplied by the initial number exposed. In short, the life table is a deterministic model: if there are a million people, each with a probability of 0.01 of dying during the following year, there will be exactly 10,000 deaths. It also assumes that every individual of a given age and sex has the same probability of dying.

The estimators above do not make explicit allowance for withdrawals, nor for the individual times at death. With small populations, for instance those used in follow-up studies after a diagnosis of cancer, or after a particular treatment, more refined methods are needed. One such, called the product-limit method and using maximum likelihood, is due to Kaplan and Meier (1958). This and ways of dealing with withdrawals and censoring are taken up in Elandt-Johnson and Johnson (1980, ch. 6).

From the probability of surviving the life expectancy is calculated as $\mathring{e}_x = \int_0^{\omega-x} l(x+t)\,dt$. In the deterministic model this traces a (usually synthetic) cohort consisting of l_x individuals, who will live $_5L_x$ person-years over the next five years; $_5L_x+5$ over the five years after that, etc. These future years may be thought of as divided among the l_x persons, giving each of them an average of $\mathring{e}_x = \sum L_{x+h}/l_x$.

An original purpose of the life table was to calculate annuities and life insurance, and much of the modern notation has been developed by actuaries. If money carried no interest then the value of an annuity starting at age 65, say, would be $\int_{65}^{\omega} l(t)\,\mathrm{d}t$, and if this was to be paid for by yearly payments from age 20, the annual premium would be $\int_{65}^{\omega} l(t)\,\mathrm{d}t / \int_{20}^{65} l(t)\,\mathrm{d}t$. If money carries interest we need to discount this (say back to birth), and the premium will be less, being calculated as $\int_{65}^{\omega} e^{-it} l(t)\,\mathrm{d}t / \int_{20}^{65} e^{-it} l(t)\,\mathrm{d}t$, where i is the rate of interest compounded momently (Jordan, 1967).

The expectation of life at age 0 is a common measure of mortality, for comparing countries and other population aggregates: in the United States the life expectancy was 75 years in 1983, compared with 66 years for Mexico. Mexico's crude rate $(1000 \times D/P)$ is 6 per thousand against the US 9, a comparison that does not reflect true mortality because Mexico's population is much younger.

The third meaning of the life table can be generalized to represent the age distribution of a population that is increasing at a steady rate r; in this generalization the number of persons aged x to $x+4$ at last birthday is proportional to $\int_{0}^{5} e^{-(x+rt)} l(x+t)\,\mathrm{d}t$.

The life table idea is readily extended to more than two states of exit. One can work out the chance of dying from the several possible causes of death – cancer, heart disease, etc.; this is still a decrement table, but now with several causes of decrement.

While the notation and the concepts of the life tables were worked out for mortality, it is applied to many processes other than living and dying. A woman has a certain probability month by month of becoming pregnant; the probabilities can be cumulated to give the probability of still not being pregnant by the xth month, from which the expected months to pregnancy can be calculated for women who are fertile. An aircraft engine has a certain probability of breaking down in the first month, the second month, etc.; a life table shows the expected number of months of service, and by an extension the number of engines that will have to be kept in reserve for replacements up to a given level of security. Biological ecologists calculate life tables for many species of animals and insects. Probability of divorce in the first year, the second year, etc. after marriage can be worked out in the same two-state model, except that now first marriage and divorce rather than living and dead are the states in question. A table can be made for survival within the school system, in which the states are attending school and dropping out.

In increment–decrement tables persons can re-enter some of the states. For instance they can enter the labour force, then leave it, then enter again. The same applies to marriage, or to migration among regions of a country. For this a multi-dimensional analogue of the life table is available, and has been extensively used (Rogers, 1975, 1984; Schoen, 1975). The relevant formulas are matrix analogues of the ordinary life table formulas given above.

A main use of life tables is for population projection. If the population age x to $x+4$ at the jumping-off point is $_5P_x$, then 5 years later it will be $_5P_x {_5L_{x+5}}/{_5L_x}$ if the life table is appropriate and random variation and migration can be disregarded. (For the birth component and other aspects of projection, see Brass, 1974.)

In pursuing these and other purposes, one often deals with populations for which mortality data are deficient or altogether lacking. A common procedure in the past was to substitute a suitable member of a series (for example England and Wales at an appropriate date). Today it is more convenient to use one of the sets of model tables calculated for the purpose, based not on one country, but on all the countries for which reliable data are available (UN, 1982; Coale and Demeny, 1983).

Life tables are calculated on the (unrealistic) assumption that the population is homogeneous in respect of all unmeasured variables. Because the observed population is constantly being selected towards persons of greater robustness, the true expectation for a person initially of average robustness is less (by something of the order of one year) than that shown by published tables (Vaupel and Yashin, 1985).

NATHAN KEYFITZ

See also **economic demography; fertility in developing countries; Graunt, John; historical demography; mortality; stable population theory.**

Bibliography

Brass, W. 1971. On the scale of mortality. In *Biological Aspects of Demography*, ed. W. Brass. London: Taylor & Francis, 69–110.

Brass, W. 1974. Perspectives in population prediction, illustrated by the statistics of England and Wales. *Journal of the Royal Statistical Society*, Series A 137, 532–83.

Chiang, C.L. 1984. *The Life Table and Its Applications*. Malabar, Florida: Robert E. Krieger.

Coale, A.J. 1984. Life table construction on the basis of two enumerations of a closed population. *Population Index* 50(2), Summer, 193–213.

Coale, A.J. and Demeny, P. 1983. *Regional Model Life Tables and Stable Populations*. 2nd edn. New York: Academic Press.

Elandt-Johnson, R.C. and Johnson, N.L. 1980. *Survival Models and Data Analysis*. New York: John Wiley & Sons.

Greville, T.N.E. 1943. Short method of constructing abridged life tables. *Record American Institute Actuaries* 32, 29–43.

Jordan, C.W. 1967. *Life Contingencies*. Chicago: Society of Actuaries.

Kaplan, E.L. and Meier, P. 1958. Nonparametric estimation from incomplete observations. *Journal of the American Statistical Association* 53, 457–81.

Keyfitz, N. 1985. *Applied Mathematical Demography*. 2nd edn. New York: Springer-Verlag.

National Center for Health Statistics. 1983. *Advance Report of Final Mortality Statistics, 1980* 32(4), Supplement, US Department of Health and Human Services.

Rogers, A. 1975. *Introduction to Multiregional Mathematical Demography*. New York: John Wiley & Sons.

Rogers, A. 1984. *Migration, Urbanization, and Spatial Population Dynamics*. Boulder, Colorado: Westview Press.

Schoen, R. 1975. Constructing increment-decrement life tables. *Demography* 12, 313–24.

United Nations. 1982. *Model Life Tables for Developing Countries*. New York: United Nations.

Vaupel, J.W. and Yashin, A.I. 1985. The deviant dynamics of death in heterogeneous populations. In *Sociological Methodology 1985*, ed. N.B. Tuma. San Francisco: Jossey-Bass.

limit pricing

Modern economists generally trace models of limit pricing to Modigliani (1958). The idea of limit pricing is closely related to, and often not distinguished from, the much older idea that potential competition will induce a profit-maximizing incumbent monopolist or dominant group to set a price that would allow it (or, in some formulations, an entrant) only a normal rate of return (Giddings, 1887; Gunton, 1888; Liefmann, 1915; Marshall, 1890, p. 270; 1919, pp. 397–8, 524; Kaldor, 1935). With this second idea, it is the presence of potential entrants that constrains the options of incumbents, not the other way around.

Modigliani's (1958) more-than-a-book-review of Bain (1956) and Sylos-Labini (1957) offered a formal model based on what Modigliani called the Sylos postulate (1958, p. 217) 'that potential entrants behave as though they expected existing firms to adopt the policy … of maintaining output' in the face of entry. Given such beliefs, if incumbents produce a sufficiently large output that the best post-entry price a profit-maximizing entrant could expect would be below its average cost, entry would not occur.

Gaskins (1971) generalizes the static limit price model to a dynamic context, with a model in which incumbent pricing determines the rate of expansion of a fringe of price-taking suppliers. This might also be regarded as a dynamic generalization of the familiar Forchheimer–Auspitz–Lieben model of a dominant firm in a market with a price-taking fringe.

Friedman (1979) points out that, under conditions of complete and perfect information, profit-maximizing incumbents would not, in general, maintain post-entry output at pre-entry levels, and entrants would not expect them to do so. Much the same point had been made, less formally, by Bain (1949, p. 452). Without commitment, a low price fails as an entry-limiting device if entrants believe that in the post-entry market incumbents will act in their own self-interest.

One line of research that seeks to finesse the unsatisfactory nature of the Modigliani–Sylos postulate can be traced to Spence (1977) and Dixit (1979). They offer models in which an incumbent's pre-entry investment (in capacity) alters the incumbent's post-entry incentives, and by so doing gives credibility to post-entry conduct that renders entry unprofitable. See Allen et al. (2000) for careful discussion. The vast literature on strategic entry deterrence (Salop and Scheffman, 1983; Fudenberg and Tirole, 1984) springs from this root.

An alternative approach is taken by Kreps and Wilson (1982) and Milgrom and Roberts (1982). They give up the assumption of complete information and model entry-limiting behaviour based on an incumbent firm's reputation or entrants' uncertainty about an incumbent's costs. The modelling techniques employed here have been generalized to analyse predation and the conduct of regulation/competition policy under conditions of uncertainty.

The development of internally consistent theoretical models in which entry-limiting behaviour might occur as an equilibrium phenomenon was a major step in laying the game-theoretic foundation for modern industrial economics. The assembling of empirical evidence on the occurrence of limit pricing and other strategic reactions to entry has similarly followed the general trend of empirical research in industrial economics, studying particular markets for specific instances of entry-deterring behaviour.

There are case studies of limit-pricing behaviour (Blackstone, 1972). But empirical studies of entry suggest that theoretical models of entry and entry deterrence abstract from essential aspects of the phenomena (Simon, 2005, p. 1230).

Some real-world entry, no doubt, is like the entry of limit price and other entry-deterrence models – entry at large-scale into production of a standardized product hitherto offered by a small number of firms themselves aware of their oligopolistic interdependence. Archer Daniel Midland's well-known 1991 entry into lysine production is a case in point. Much more often, however, entry seems like the act of beginning small-scale production at a point on a Hotelling line, when location in characteristic space is largely fixed after entry and neither the entrant nor incumbents have a terribly good idea of the distribution of consumers in the region near the entrant's location.

Geroski (1995, p. 433) concludes in his careful survey that 'price is not frequently used by incumbents to deter entry, but that marketing activities are', and (1995, p. 434, fn. 7) 'work that has tried to test for the presence of limit pricing … in general … has produced somewhat ambiguous results.… Studies of the strategic use of excess capacity to block entry have also generally produced weak and fairly unpersuasive evidence on its importance.'

Empirical work suggests that the incumbent response to entry will vary with entrant and incumbent characteristics. The response to entry will sometimes be by lowering price, sometimes by other rival strategies, and sometimes by accommodating entry.

Scott Morton (1997) finds that longer-established entrants into turn-of-the-19th-century shipping cartels were less likely to evoke a hostile response, as were entrants with substantial financial resources. Podolny and Scott Morton (1999) suggest that a predatory response was less likely if social factors were present that would allow incumbents and entrants to judge each others' 'types'. Thomas (1999) finds that incumbent US breakfast cereal manufacturers are more likely to respond with advertising to entry into a product group by other incumbents, and more likely to lower price in response to entry by a new firm. Yamawaki (2002) finds a price response to Japanese entry by German manufacturers of luxury cars for the US market, but no such response by British manufacturers. In a study of entry into the US magazine industry, Simon (2005) finds that multi-market and single-market incumbents respond differently to entry. Multi-market incumbents are more likely to cut price in response to entry by a new firm, single-market incumbents more likely to cut price in response to entry by an established publisher. He also finds that a hostile response to entry is more likely the more concentrated the target market. Conlin and Kadiyali (2006) find some evidence of the use of excess capacity as an entry-deterring device in the Texas hotel market, and also that the maintenance of excess capacity is more likely by larger firms and by firms in more concentrated markets.

It thus appears that, while a strategic price response is one possible incumbent response to entry, it is only one. A full understanding of the determinants of equilibrium market structure in inherently oligopolistic industries must take the full range of possible responses into account.

STEPHEN MARTIN

See also **barriers to entry; market structure; monopoly; oligopoly; predatory pricing.**

Bibliography

Allen, B., Deneckere, R., Faith, T. and Kovenock, D. 2000. Capacity precommitment as a barrier to entry: a Bertrand–Edgeworth approach. *Economic Theory* 15, 501–30.

Auspitz, R. and Lieben, R. 1889. *Untersuchen über die Theorie des Preises*. Leipzig: Duncker & Humblot.

Bain, J.S. 1949. A note on pricing in monopoly and oligopoly. *American Economic Review* 39, 448–64.

Bain, J.S. 1954. Conditions of entry and the emergence of monopoly. In *Monopoly and Competition and their Regulation*, ed. E.H. Chamberlin. London: Macmillan.

Bain, J.S. 1956. *Barriers to New Competition*. Cambridge, MA: Harvard University Press.

Blackstone, E.A. 1972. Limit pricing and entry in the copying machine market. *Quarterly Review of Economics and Business* 12, 57–65.

Conlin, M. and Kadiyali, V. 2006. Entry-deterring capacity in the Texas lodging industry. *Journal of Economics and Management Strategy* 15, 167–85.

Dixit, A. 1979. A model of duopoly suggesting a theory of entry barriers. *Bell Journal of Economics* 10, 20–32.

Forchheimer, K. 1908. Theoretisches zum unvollstandigen Monopole. *Schmoller's Jahrbuch für Gesetzgebung, Verwaltung und Volkswirtschaft*, vol. 32. Munich, Leipzig: Duncker & Humblot.

Friedman, J.W. 1979. On entry preventing behavior and limit price models of entry. In *Applied Game Theory*, ed. S.J. Brams and G. Schwodiauer. Wurzburg and Vienna: Physica-Verlag.

Fudenberg, D. and Tirole, J. 1984. The fat-cat effect, the puppy-dog ploy, and the lean and hungry look. *American Economic Review* 74, 361–6.

Gaskins, Jr., D.W. 1971. Dynamic limit pricing: optimal limit pricing under threat of entry. *Journal of Economic Theory* 3, 306–22.

Geroski, P.A. 1995. What do we know about entry? *International Journal of Industrial Organization* 13, 421–40.

Giddings, F.H. 1887. The persistence of competition. *Political Science Quarterly* 2, 62–78.

Gunton, G. 1888. The economic and social aspect of trusts. *Political Science Quarterly* 3, 385–408.

Kaldor, N. 1935. Market imperfection and excess capacity. *Economica* NS 2, 33–50.

Kreps, D.M. and Wilson, R. 1982. Reputation and imperfect information. *Journal of Economic Theory* 27, 253–79.

Liefmann, R.L. 1915. Monopoly or competition as the basis of a government trust policy. *Quarterly Journal of Economics* 29, 308–25.

Marshall, A. 1890. Some aspects of competition. Presidential Address to the Economic Science and Statistics Section of the British Association, Leeds. In *Memorials of Alfred Marshall*, ed. A.C. Pigou. London: Macmillan, 1925.

Marshall, A. 1919. *Industry and Trade*, 4th edn. London: Macmillan, 1923.

Milgrom, P. and Roberts, J. 1982. Limit pricing and entry under incomplete information: an equilibrium analysis. *Econometrica* 50, 443–66.

Modigliani, F. 1958. New developments on the oligopoly front. *Journal of Political Economy* 66, 215–32.

Podolny, J.M. and Scott Morton, F.M. 1999. Social status, entry and predation: the case of British shipping cartels 1879–1929. *Journal of Industrial Economics* 47, 41–67.

Salop, S.C. and Scheffman, D.T. 1983. Raising rivals' costs. *American Economic Review* 73, 267–71.

Scott Morton, F. 1997. Entry and predation: British shipping cartels 1879–1929. *Journal of Economics and Management Strategy* 6, 679–724.

Simon, D. 2005. Incumbent pricing responses to entry. *Strategic Management Journal* 26, 1229–48.

Spence, A.M. 1977. Entry, capacity, investment oligopolistic pricing. *Bell Journal of Economics* 8, 534–44.

Sylos-Labini, P. 1957. *Oligopolio e Progresso Tecnico*. Milano: Giuffrè.

Sylos-Labini, P. 1962. *Oligopoly and Technical Progress*. Cambridge, MA: Harvard University Press.

Thomas, L.A. 1999. Incumbent firms' response to entry: price, advertising, and new product introduction. *International Journal of Industrial Organization* 17, 527–55.

Yamawaki, H. 2002. Price reactions to new competition: a study of US luxury car market, 1986–1997. *International Journal of Industrial Organization* 20, 19–39.

Lindahl equilibrium

Lindahl equilibrium attempts to solve the problem of determining the levels of public goods to be provided and their financing by adapting the price system in a way that maintains its central feature of an efficient allocation being the outcome of voluntary market activities within the context of private property rights. Instead of some political choice mechanism and coercive taxation, under the Lindahl approach each individual faces personalized prices at which he or she may buy total amounts of the public goods. In equilibrium, these prices are such that everyone demands the same levels of the public goods and thus agrees on the amounts of public goods that should be provided. Since each individual buys and consumes the total production of public goods, the price to producers is the sum of the prices paid by individuals, and equilibrium involves the supply at these prices equalling the common demand. Thus, Lindahl equilibrium brings unanimity about the level of public goods provision, with costs being shared in proportion to (marginal) benefits.

The basic idea of a market solution to the problem of providing public goods is due to Erik Lindahl (1919). In its modern formulation, Lindahl equilibrium has come to play a benchmark role in the study of economies with public goods, externalities, and government expenditure which parallels that played by Walrasian competitive equilibrium in the analysis of questions where these factors are absent. For example, tax incidence can be measured relative to the Lindahl equilibrium. On the other hand, the Lindahl concept does not share the competitive equilibrium's centrality of position as a predictor of the actual outcomes of economic activity.

This latter point involves some irony, because Lindahl's original exposition of the idea treats it as having both normative and descriptive/predictive value. Lindahl considered a legislature in which two parties represent the two homogeneous classes that constitute the electorate. (He also indicates how to extend the analysis to more classes and their representatives.) The issue is how much government activity should be carried out and how the costs of this activity should be shared between the two groups.

Lindahl identified two functions, say $f_A(s)$ and $f_B(s)$, which give, respectively, the expenditure on public activity that group A would want if it had to pay a fraction s of the corresponding costs and the level that B would want if it had to pay the complementary fraction $1 - s$. The value $x = f_A(s)$ is just the solution to the problem of maximizing the utility of after-tax income and public expenditure for group A, given that it will pay $100s\%$ of the costs, while f_B solves the corresponding problem for B. Ignoring income effects, Lindahl obtained $s = v'_A(f_A(s))$, where v_A is A's utility for public expenditure, and, correspondingly, $1 - s = v'_B(f_B(s))$. Note that f_A is decreasing and f_B is increasing. Thus, assuming $f_A(0) > f_B(0)$ or $f_A(1) < f_B(1)$, so that a group bearing all the costs wants less expenditure than does the group paying nothing, there is a unique value s^* strictly between zero and one at which the two groups agree on the desired level of expenditure, that is, $x^* = f_A(s^*) = f_B(s^*)$.

Much of Lindahl's analysis is in terms of bargaining between the two groups over x and s under the assumption that, at any partition of the costs, the smaller of the two proposed quantities will be implemented. (This reflects the connection to voluntary exchange, where no one is forced to transact.) He recognized that such bargaining would not automatically lead to s^*, x^*. However, he claimed that if both groups were equally adept at defending their interests, this outcome would result.

Foley (1970) provided the basic general equilibrium treatment of Lindahl's idea in the context of an Arrow–Debreu private ownership economy with both private and pure public goods (no rivalry in consumption and no possibility of exclusion) where there are zero endowments of public goods, these goods are never used as inputs, and production takes place under constant returns to scale. See Milleron (1972), Roberts (1973), and Kaneko (1977) for extensions and Roberts (1974) for a survey.

Foley's model focuses on prices for the public goods rather than cost shares. Individual demand functions for public goods, as depending on the prices of both private and public goods, are defined (exactly as for private goods) as the choices of quantities to consume that maximize utility subject to the budget constraint defined by the prices and the agent's endowment. Thus, the quantity demanded of any public good at a particular price vector differs with individual preferences and endowments. However, the nature of pure public goods requires that all agents' consumption of any of these goods be equal. Thus, if prices are to lead different individuals all to demand the same quantities of public goods, it is clear that the prices charged to consumers must be personalized, differing across individuals to reflect differences in preferences and incomes. The price received by a producer of public goods is then the sum of the price paid by individuals, because each unit of each public good is allocated to and paid for by every individual. Meanwhile, private goods markets involve standard competitive pricing. With this, Lindahl equilibrium is a vector p of private goods prices, a vector q_i of public goods prices for each consumer i, an allocation of private goods x_i to each i and a vector of public goods y such that: (x_i, y) is the most preferred consumption bundle for consumer i from those affordable at prices (p, q_i), given i's wealth as determined by p and i's initial endowment of private goods ω_i; and also such that the net input–output vector $(\sum_i x_i - \omega_i, y)$ is profit maximizing at the producer prices $(p, \sum_i q_i)$. Note that both consumers and producers are following standard, competitive, price-taking behaviour just as in the Walrasian equilibrium.

Further appreciation of the connection between Lindahl and Walrasian equilibria can be gained using Arrow's insight (1970) that externalities (and the public goods problem in particular) can be viewed as a phenomenon of missing markets. Given a public goods economy with I consumers, M private goods and N public goods such as studied by Foley, consider an associated economy with I consumers, $(M + K)$ private goods, and no public goods, where $K = IN$. In this economy, each public good n in the original economy is replaced by a collection of I private goods, each of which is of interest to and consumable by only one consumer and which together are joint products in production. A net input–output vector in this economy of the form

$$(z, \tilde{y}), \quad z \in R^M, \qquad \tilde{y} = (y^1, \ldots, y^{IN})$$
$$= (y_1, y_2, \ldots, \ldots, y_N, y_1, y_2, \ldots, y_N, \ldots, y_1,$$
$$y_2, \ldots, y_N) \in R_+^{IN}$$

is producible if and only if $(z, y_1, \ldots, y_N)$ is in the production set of the original public goods economy. A Walras equilibrium in this economy is a price vector $(p, q^1, \ldots, q^{IN}) \in R_+^{MK}$ and consumption vectors $(x_i, y_i^1, \ldots, y_i^{IN}) \in R^{M+K}, i = 1, \ldots, I$, where $(x_i, y_i^1, \ldots, y_i^{IN})$ is the most preferred bundle for i from among those costing no more than $p\omega_i$ and where $(\sum_i x_i - w_i, \sum_i y_i^1, \ldots, \sum_i y_i^{IN})$ is profit maximizing at prices $(p, q^1, \ldots, q^{IN})$. Clearly, these conditions imply $y_i^{jn} = 0$, for $i \neq j$ so that no consumer receives positive amounts of another's personalized goods, and $y_i^{in} = y_j^{in}$ for all i, j, and n, so that each individual consumes the same quantities of these personalized goods. Thus, Walras equilibria of the artificial economy exactly correspond to the Lindahl equilibria of the original economy, with a parallel correspondence between the feasible allocations in the two economies and between the Pareto optima.

This construction, which was used by Foley to prove existence of Lindahl equilibrium, illuminates the claim that the Lindahl equilibrium involves voluntary exchange in the context of maintaining private property rights. It also makes clear that Lindahl equilibria are Pareto optimal and that any optimum can be supported as an equilibrium with a reallocation of resources. (In fact, Silvestre, 1984, has characterized Lindahl allocations in terms of optimality plus a condition that no agent wants to reduce his or her contribution to paying for public goods if the level of provision would be proportionately reduced.) The Lindahl equilibrium's role as a benchmark is largely attributable to its having these properties, plus the fact that the Lindahl equilibrium allocations belong to the core if blocking is defined by a group being able to produce a more preferred consumption bundle for each of its members, even if non-members contribute nothing to public goods production (Foley, 1970). However, this construction also suggests some of the problems with the Lindahl equilibrium which prevent it from having great appeal as a positive prediction.

In particular, the usual complaint against a price-based solution to the public goods problem is that there would be no reason for an individual to take the Lindahl prices as given: misrepresentation of preferences should be profitable. Of course, as long as there are only a finite number of participants in a market, the behaviour of each typically has some influence on price formation, and so the assumption of price-taking in Walrasian, private goods equilibrium is questionable too.

Progress on this incentives question requires being more specific about the mechanism used to determine the allocation as a function of the initially dispersed information about the economic environment. In this context, Hurwicz (1972) formalized the idea that there must be incentive problems even with only private goods by showing that if a mechanism always yields Pareto optima and, if participation is voluntary, so that its outcomes must be unanimously preferred to the no-trade point, then it cannot be a dominant strategy always to report one's preferences (demand) correctly. The exactly parallel result for public goods was achieved by Ledyard and Roberts (see Roberts, 1976). Thus neither Walrasian nor Lindahl equilibria can be the outcome of a mechanism which is incentive compatible in this dominant-strategy sense.

Of course, the standard case in which the Walrasian equilibrium seems appealing is a 'large numbers' one where each individual's influence is small. This intuition has been formalized in a number of ways: revealing one's true demand for private goods generically is asymptotically a dominant strategy as the number of participants in the economy becomes large; only competitive allocations are in the core of large economies; Nash equilibria of various models in which individuals recognize their influence on prices converge to the competitive solution as the economy grows. However, with public goods the situation is much different: increasing the size of the economy makes price-taking less attractive. This too has been shown in various ways. Roberts (1976) showed that increasing numbers can worsen the incentives for correct revelation of preferences for public goods and that as the numbers grow, the departure of the outcome from efficiency can also increase. Muench (1972) showed that the core and Lindahl equilibria do not coincide in large economies, and Champsaur, Roberts and Rosenthal (1975) demonstrated that the core of a public goods economy may actually expand when the number of consumers increases. In terms of the artificial economy, the essential intuition is that the market for each of the personalized goods is monopsonized, and the joint-product interaction constrains the bargaining power of the producer which otherwise might permit an efficient outcome to the bilateral monopoly situation. Thus, it seems that in the large numbers situations that have been the traditional concern of economics, the price-taking assumption renders the Lindahl solution of little predictive or descriptive value.

These essentially negative results are in some contrast with the results on incentives for correct revelation in iterative planning procedures for determining public goods. This literature was begun by Malinvaud (1971a; 1971b) and Drèze and de la Vallée Poussin (1971) and is surveyed in Roberts (1986).

In this context, the notion of incentive-compatible behaviour is Nash equilibrium: each agent selects his/her responses to the central planning authority's proposals so as to maximize his/her payoff, given the strategies being used by the other agents to determine their responses. Such behaviour typically involves misrepresentation of preferences. However, various authors (Roberts, 1979, Champsaur and Laroque, 1982, and Truchon, 1984, for example), have shown that this misrepresentation need not prevent convergence to a Pareto optimum and, in particular, to the Lindahl allocation.

However, as argued in Roberts (1986), these results are of limited interest because they rely on the implausible assumption that each agent is perfectly informed about the other's preferences. (A similar criticism can be laid against the static mechanisms for obtaining Walrasian or Lindahl allocations as Nash equilibria; Hurwicz, 1979.) Moreover, once the (self-selection or truthful reporting) constraints associated with preferences being private information are recognized, it is not clear that any mechanism can achieve Lindahl allocations (see Laffont and Maskin, 1979; d'Aspremont and Gerard-Varet, 1979). This gives a further reason for doubting the empirical relevance of Lindahl equilibrium.

JOHN ROBERTS

See also **duality; incentive compatibility; public goods.**

Bibliography

Arrow, K.J. 1970. The organization of economic activity: issues pertinent to the choice of market versus non-market allocation. In *Public Expenditures and Policy Analysis*, ed. R.H. Haveman and J. Margolis. Chicago: Markham.

Champsaur, P. and Laroque, G. 1982. Strategic behavior in decentralized planning procedures. *Econometrica* 50, 325–44.

Champsaur, P., Roberts, J. and Rosenthal, R. 1975. Cores in economies with public goods. *International Economic Review* 16, 751–64.

d'Aspremont, C. and Gerard-Varet, L.A. 1979. On Bayesian incentive compatible mechanisms. In *Aggregation and Revelation of Preferences*, ed. J. Laffont. Amsterdam: North-Holland.

Drèze, J. and de la Vallée Poussin, D. 1971. A tâtonnement process for public goods. *Review of Economic Studies* 38, 133–50.

Foley, D. 1970. Lindahl's solution and the core of an economy with public goods. *Econometrica* 38, 66–72.

Hurwicz, L. 1972. On informationally decentralized systems. In *Decision and Organization: A Volume in Honor of Jacob Marschak*, ed. C.B. McGuire and R. Radner. Amsterdam: North-Holland.

Hurwicz, L. 1979. Outcome functions yielding Walrasian and Lindahl allocations at Nash equilibrium points. *Review of Economic Studies* 46, 217–27.

Kaneko, M. 1977. The ratio equilibrium and a voting game in a public goods economy. *Journal of Economic Theory* 16, 123–36.

Laffont, J. and Maskin, E. 1979. A differential approach to expected utility maximizing mechanisms. In *Aggregation and Revelation of Preferences*, ed. J. Laffont. Amsterdam: North-Holland.

Lindahl, E. 1919. *Die Gerechtigkeit der Besteuerung*. Lund: Gleerup. Part I, ch. 4, 'Positive Lösung', trans. E. Henderson and reprinted as 'Just taxation – a positive solution', in *Classics in the Theory of Public Finance*, ed. R.A. Musgrave and A.T. Peacock, London: Macmillan, 1958.

Malinvaud, E. 1971a. A planning approach to the public goods problem. *Swedish Journal of Economics* 11, 96–112.

Malinvaud, E. 1971b. Procedures for the determination of a program of collective consumption. *European Economic Review* 2, 187–217.

Milleron, J. 1972. Theory of value with public goods: a survey article. *Journal of Economic Theory* 5, 419–77.

Muench, T. 1972. The core and the Lindahl equilibrium of an economy with a public good: an example. *Journal of Economic Theory* 4, 241–55.

Roberts, J. 1973. Existence of Lindahl equilibrium with a measure space of consumers. *Journal of Economic Theory* 6, 355–81.

Roberts, J. 1974. The Lindahl solution for economies with public goods. *Journal of Public Economics* 3, 23–42.

Roberts, J. 1976. The incentives for correct revelation of preferences and the number of consumers. *Journal of Public Economics* 6, 359–74.

Roberts, J. 1979. Incentives in planning procedures for the provision of public goods. *Review of Economic Studies* 46, 283–92.

Roberts, J. 1986. Incentives, information and iterative planning. In *Information, Incentives, and Economic Mechanisms*, ed. T. Groves, R. Radner and S. Reiter. Minneapolis: University of Minnesota Press.

Silvestre, J. 1984. Voluntariness and efficiency in the provision of public goods. *Journal of Public Economics* 24, 249–56.

Truchon, M. 1984. Nonmyopic strategic behavior in the MDP planning procedure. *Econometrica* 52, 1179–89.

Lindahl, Erik Robert (1891–1960)

Lindahl was born on 21 November 1891 in Stockholm and died on 6 January 1960 in Uppsala, Sweden. He is now reckoned one of the great economists who were at work between the two world wars, and earned his reputation above all as a leading member within a group of Swedish economists during the 1930s consisting, besides himself, of Gunnar Myrdal, Bertil Ohlin, Dag Hammarskjöld, Alf Johansson, Erik Lundberg and Ingvar Svennilsson – a body which Ohlin (1937) had baptised the 'Stockholm School'.

The son of a prison governor, Lindahl grew up in Jönköping, the capital of a province in southern Sweden. After passing the *studentexamen* at a Stockholm Secondary School in spring 1910, he enrolled the following autumn as a student at the University of Lund, where economics soon became the favourite subject in his studies of humanities and law, which he passed with the degrees of the *filosofie kandidatexamen* (BA) in 1912 and the *juris kandidatexamen* (LLB) in 1914. Although Knut Wicksell was professor of economics and fiscal law in Lund at that time (1901–16), Lindahl did not have any personal contact with him during this period. However, Emil Sommarin, the successor to Wicksell's chair (1916–39) and at the time of Lindahl's student years *docent* (reader) in economics and a great admirer of Wicksell, succeeded in encouraging Lindahl to study the former's works to such an extent that the latter became in effect the first pupil of Wicksell. As Lindahl's dissertation of 1919, *Die Gerechtigkeit der Besteuerung*, was largely based on Wicksell's theory of public finance (1896), Sommarin let Wicksell read and comment on it, and, at the public defence of the thesis at Lund University on 13 December 1919, Wicksell officiated as the official 'challenger' appointed by the faculty of law (Lindahl, 1951, pp. 26–7).

With his doctoral thesis Lindahl had earned the title *docent* in public finance at Lund University (1920) and later also in economics and fiscal law at Uppsala University (1924), but not yet the position of a professor. In 1926 he became responsible for the planning of the voluminous investigations on *Wages, Cost of Living and National Income in Sweden 1860–1930* (see Lindahl, 1937a; and Benny Carlson, 1982, pp. 11–20) carried on in the following decade at the Institute for Social Sciences in

Stockholm University and financed by the Rockefeller Foundation. In his attempts to obtain a chair in economics Lindahl failed twice: in 1924 he lost the competition for a professorship at the University of Copenhagen to Bertil Ohlin, later his colleague in the Stockholm School, and in 1930 he was ranked as number two only for a chair in political economy and sociology at Gothenburg University, this time defeated by Gustaf Åkerman, like Lindahl an early pupil of Wicksell.

Only two years later, however, in 1932, Lindahl obtained the chair in political economy at the Gothenburg School of Business Economics without application, and from this time onwards Swedish universities competed to call him to their departments of economics. In 1939, the year of publication of his most famous work, *Studies in the Theory of Money and Capital*, he succeeded Sommarin at Lund University, and in 1942 he became professor at the University of Uppsala, where he retired in 1958. Internationally, Lindahl's outstanding position as economist was honoured by his election as President of the International Economic Association in 1956.

Lindahl's growing reputation from the early 1930s onwards also led to numerous calls for economic expertise by Sweden's governments and official institutions. When Sweden left the gold standard in 1931 he became an adviser to Riksbanken, the Swedish central bank. When as a result of the Great Depression the final report of the Swedish Unemployment Committee had to be given a theoretical foundation of its proposal for public works as remedy against unemployment (see Hammarskjöld, 1935, p. ix and ch. 1; Otto Steiger, 1971, p. 40; and Bent Hansen, 1981, pp. 266–7) and when, therefore, the character of Sweden's budget system had to be superseded in 1937 by a system deliberately designed to operate in a countercyclical manner (see Lindahl, 1935; cf. 1939a, app.), his expertise was sought by the Minister of Finance. Lindahl also became an economic adviser to the League of Nations (1936–9) and on two occasions to the United Nations (1949–50 and 1952–4).

Lindahl's work can be said to cover four major areas: (*a*) public finance; (*b*) methods of dynamic analysis; (*c*) monetary and macroeconomic theory; and (*d*) concepts of income and capital. Although Lindahl did not neglect empirical research, especially in public finance and national accounting, his contributions concentrated mainly on pure economic theory (see the detailed bibliography by Gertrud Lindahl and Olof Wallmén, 1960).

Public finance

Lindahl started his scientific career with a treatise on 'just taxation', his doctoral dissertation of 1919, which built on Wicksell (1896) and which, together with two re-examinations in 1928 and 1959, made it a pioneering contribution to the economic theory of the public household, today known as the 'Wicksell–Lindahl paradigm of just taxation' (Heinz Grossekettler, 2006, p. 557;

for more detail see Peter Bohm, 1987, and John Roberts, 1987). It can be characterized as a culmination of the neoclassical reformulation of the classical version of the benefit approach to the simultaneous determination of public revenue and expenditure – a reformulation which applied a new interpretation of the benefit rule as a condition of equilibrium instead of as a standard of justice as in the classical version.

Lindahl formulated this condition in a partial equilibrium framework, where 'financial equilibrium', that is, the equilibrium of *public* finance, is determined by equalization of the ratio of prices paid by each taxpayer for public and for private goods to his marginal benefits derived from public and from private goods, the equilibrating financial process brought about by the political mechanism in a parliamentary democracy (cf. Roberts, 1987). Lindahl was convinced that his model could explain voting behaviour and the influence of pressure groups on decisions of the government concerning public expenditures and taxes (Bohm, 1987, p. 201). However, this 'voluntary exchange approach' (Richard A. Musgrave, 1959, pp. 73–8) for a long time failed to meet with much understanding. The importance of Lindahl's path-breaking contribution was first acknowledged in the 1950s via the works on the pure theory of public expenditure of Paul A. Samuelson (1954) and Musgrave (1959) as well as by the English translation of important parts of his dissertation of 1919 in 1958 in the volume *Classics in Public Finance*, edited by Musgrave and Alan T. Peacock. In the 1970s and the 1980s, however, Lindahl's model came under attack. It was criticized for relying on the 'implausible assumption that each agent is perfectly informed about the other's preferences' (Roberts, 1987, p. 200), and also for lacking empirical relevance in face of today's, unlike in Lindahl's time, 'considerable amount of taxes raised for income distribution purposes' (Bohm, 1987, p. 201).

Methods of dynamic analysis

Lindahl's contributions to dynamic method were formulated as part of the theoretical core of his macroeconomic ideas, culminating in 1939 in his *Studies in the Theory of Money and Capital*. As has been shown by Björn Hansson (1982; cf. 1987; 1991, pp. 168–202; and Jan Petersson 1987), Lindahl's dynamic theory was developed by mutual influence within the Stockholm School, with himself and Myrdal as the key figures and mainly independent not only from influences from other contemporary economists but also – contrary to William P. Yohe (1959) – from Wicksell.

Already in his first macroeconomic treatise, the first edition of *Penningpolitikens mål* ([The aims of monetary policy], 1924, ch. 3), Lindahl stressed the *time* factor as a problem for economic analysis and used the notion of 'subjective calculations of the future' and also the term *ex post* (p. 33). A first coherent dynamic method was

formulated in his treatise on capital theory (1929a; cf. 1939a, pt. III), where Lindahl developed the famous notion of *intertemporal equilibrium*, that is, the analysis of the sequential character of an economy by a sequence of periods with equilibrium in each period as a consequence of the assumption of perfect foresight. This approach has been praised by Gérard Debreu (1959, p. 35) as being 'the first mathematical study of an economy whose activity extends over a finite number of elementary time-intervals'. However, as has been pointed out later (Murray Milgate, 1982, pp. 133–5), Friedrich A. Hayek had been moving on similar lines one year earlier. But this does not disturb the claim of Lindahl's originality, because a comparison of the 1929 and 1930 editions of his *Penningpolitikens medel* [The means of monetary policy] clearly shows that Lindahl became aware of Hayek's approach first after having worked out his own concept – Hayek's 1928 paper is referred to only in the second (1930, p. 11), not in the first edition (1929c, p. 10).

As has been shown by Hansson (1982, ch. 4, pp 59–67; 1987, pp. 504–5), Lindahl's formulation of intertemporal equilibrium, however, does not really represent a sequential process, since all prices and quantities are determined simultaneously at the beginning of the process for all periods. Lindahl became aware of this weakness when, under the influence of Myrdal's explicit introduction of expectations in equilibrium theory (1927, ch. 1), in the last section of his treatise on capital theory (1929a, pp. 80–1; cf. 1939a, pt. III, pp. 348–50) he substituted imperfect for perfect foresight. In *Penningpolitikens medel* (1930, pp. 18–24, 31–2; cf. 1939a, pt. II, pp. 158–9) Lindahl abandoned therefore, for the case of imperfect foresight, the method of intertemporal equilibrium for the notion of *temporary equilibrium*, that is, the analysis of the sequence of an economy as a series of very short periods of temporary equilibria with changes allowed only at the transition points of the periods. This notion looks closely akin to John R. Hicks's dynamic analysis in *Value and Capital* (1939, ch. 9) which in fact had been influenced decisively by Lindahl via personal contacts in 1934 and 1935, as later acknowledged by Hicks (cf. 1973, p. 8; 1985, pp. 66, 69; 1991, pp. 372–6; and Claes-Henric Siven, 2002, pp. 142–5). More important in a historical perspective, however, is the striking fact that general equilibrium theorists, from the late 1960s onwards, began to give up their mathematically more elaborated intertemporal equilibrium models of Arrow–Debreu type and to develop different notions of temporary equilibrium for very much the same reason as Lindahl in 1929 and 1930: recognition of the fact that intertemporal equilibrium does not reflect the sequential character of an economy in an essential way and the impossibility of handling imperfect foresight, that is, problems involving uncertainty and money.

However, under the influence of the criticism of his approach by Lundberg in 1930 and Myrdal in 1932 and

1933, Lindahl realized that even with the notion of temporary equilibrium there was no real causation between the periods when he applied this dynamic method to the analysis of the saving–investment mechanism during a Wicksellian cumulative process, since the equilibrium approach in the construction of temporary equilibrium cannot handle unforeseen events *during* a period. Therefore, he abandoned this notion and formulated instead the method of *sequence analysis*. This was done in the first part, Section 1, of his *Studies* (1939b, pp. 21–69), but a fully developed sequence analysis had already been presented in two unpublished papers of 1934a (published in Steiger, 1971, pp. 204–11) and 1935 (cf. Hansson, 1982, ch. 9). Furthermore, in Section 2 of the first part of his book Lindahl was the first economist who, in an extensive algebraic discussion of the relations between fundamental economic concepts (1939b, pp. 74–136), made the methodologically important distinction between 'micro-economic' and 'macro-economic terms' (p. 74) by which he tried to base the relations between macro values on some kind of microeconomic behaviour (pp. 111, 125; cf. Svennilsson, 1938, ch. 1; Siven, 1991, pp. 155–6; and Jens Christopher Andvig, 1991, p. 414). As shown by Hal R. Varian (1987, p. 461), this innovation has been wrongly attributed to Ragnar Frisch who, in an article of 1933 (pp. 172–3), had used the related terms 'micro-dynamic' and 'macro-dynamic analysis' in which he, however, 'was uninterested in the problems of microeconomic roots' of macroeconomics (Andvig, 1991, p. 415).

Incorporating the method of *ex ante* and *ex post* (cf. Steiger, 1987a) developed by Myrdal (1932; 1933) in his disequilbrium analysis and adopted by Ohlin (1934, ch. 1), where the former had criticized Lindahl's method of temporary equilibrium, and taking care of the sequence analysis of consecutive periods formulated by Hammarskjöld (1933a; 1933b, chs 1–5) and Svennilsson (1938, ch. 1), Lindahl's dynamic method in 1939b consisted of two parts: (*a*) a single-period analysis where *ex ante* plans determine *ex post* results; and (*b*) a continuation analysis where these *ex post* events lead to revised *ex ante* plans of a subsequent period. While Lindahl allowed for disequilibrium as long as he analysed a single period only, his analysis for several periods demanded equilibrium within each period. Because of this assumption Lindahl's sequence analysis – although it can be regarded as the first dynamic method with a meaningful sequential character, that is, not relying on the mutual interdependence of all events – did not imply the solution to the dynamic problem of establishing a convincing explanation of the causal connection between successive periods. In the end, while acknowledging Myrdal's plea for disequilibrium analysis, Lindahl hesitated to rely on the 'cumbersome *ex ante* and *ex post* terminology' (1939b, p. 68; cf. 1939c, pp. 264–5) because of its 'analytical complexity' (Siven, 2006b, p. 694; cf. 1985, p. 590; and Hansen, 1981, p. 274).

It was left to Lundberg's sequence analysis of 1937 (ch. 9) to overcome this limitation by allowing for disequilibrium within the different periods with the help of the assumption of constant expectation functions (cf. Hansson, 1982, ch. 10). Lindahl accepted Lundberg's method in his Studies (1939b, pp. 57–9), but was not keen on the time-related model sequences based on difference equations which were incorporated in the latter's construction. On the contrary, this dynamic method was rejected by Lindahl because of its mechanical character resulting from the assumption that expectations need not enter explicitly. However, it was exactly this approach which came to dominate dynamic theory until the late 1960s when general equilibrium theorists reintroduced the notion of temporary equilibrium and developed dynamic models which look very similar to Lindahl's sequence analysis (for example, Frank H. Hahn, 1980).

Monetary and macroeconomic theory

While Lindahl's contributions to dynamic analysis were formulated independently of Wicksell, his work on monetary and macroeconomic theory was clearly derived from the latter (1898; 1906). This influence can be traced back as far as Lindahl's first treatise on monetary matters, *Penningpolitikens mål* (1924; 1929b), where he systematized and extended the concepts used in the Swedish controversy between Wicksell and David Davidson before and after the First World War on the aim of monetary policy being to preserve the real value of contracts, that is, Wicksell's desideratum of a constant price level versus Davidson's proposal of price level variations in inverse proportion to changes in productivity (cf. Hammarskjöld, 1944; Carl G. Uhr, 1960, pp. 270–305; Klas Fregert, 1993; and Siven, 2002, 124–9). While Lindahl's analysis is worked out along Wicksellian lines, he ends up with Davidson's and not Wicksell's solution by showing that the latter's proposition of a '*normal*' rate of interest, that is, the particular level of the money rate which is equal to the 'natural' rate, determined by the marginal productivity of capital, does not hold for a constant price level in the face of productivity variations.

A more systematic treatment of Wicksell's concept of the normal rate was given in *Penningpolitikens medel* (1930, pp. 121–30; cf. 1939a, pt. II, pp. 245–57), where Lindahl was the first to show that this notion implies three different conditions for equilibrium: '(1) it corresponds to the *natural* or … the *real rate of interest*; (2) it establishes *equilibrium between the demand for and supply of saving* [that is, investment and savings]; and (3) it is *neutral in* relation to *the price level* – whereas a rate of interest above or below "normal" will influence the price level in a downward or upward direction' (1939a, pt. II, p. 246; cf. 1930, p. 122). It was this formulation which inspired Myrdal's famous reconstruction of Wicksell's normal rate (1932; 1933; 1939) in which the three conditions were characterized as *monet*ary equilibrium (cf. Steiger, 1987c, p. 507; Siven, 2006a, pp. 11–12; 2006b, pp. 672–4).

However, in the central part of *Penningpolitikens medel*, the analysis of the relation between the rate of interest and the price level, Lindahl (1930, pp. 131–4; cf. 1939a, pt. II, pp. 257–60; and 1939c, pp. 260–8) did not employ the notion of the normal rate, because his explicit consideration of expectations showed him the impossibility of a unique equilibrium rate irrespective of the rate of change of the level of prices – a reasoning very similar to John Maynard Keynes's emphasis in the *General Theory* (1936, pp. 242–4) that there are different normal rates for different levels of employment. Instead, Lindahl explained changes in the general price level with the help of another concept introduced by Wicksell (1906, p. 159): the approach of *aggregate demand and supply*. In Lindahl's formulation of this approach changes in the price level were determined by changes in the relation between the total demand for and the total supply of consumption goods, the total demand for consumption goods being defined as 'the portion of the total nominal income which is not saved', $E(1 - s)$ where E denotes total nominal income and s the ratio of saving to income, and the total supply defined as PQ, where P denotes the price level and Q the quantity of consumer goods of a certain period (1930, pp. 12–13; cf. 1939a, pt. I, pp. 142–3). In general, he never analysed imbalances in macroeconomic variables 'caused by "wrong" relative prices' (Siven, 2002, p. 141). Using Wicksell's suggestion of a perfect credit system, this approach left no room for the quantity of money either, and it was indeed, in Lindahl's analysis of the issue of money by the central bank, directed against the quantity theory of money, although he did not deprive it of all significance for the theory of money (cf. 1929d, p. 18; 1955, pp. 32–4). In fact, as has been first emphasized by Hansen (1979, p. 123) and later confirmed by Axel Leijonhufvud (1991, p. 464) and Lars Werin (1991, p. 178) as well as Mauro Boianovsky and Hans-Michael Trautwein (2006, pp. 881–2, 888–95), Lindahl in his later writings (cf. 1957, pp. 13–15, 19–21) was 'a true monetarist' and the first one to formulate the 'accelerationist' hypothesis in inflation theory offered a decade later by Edmund S. Phelps (1967) and Milton Friedman (1968). This hypothesis lies also at the heart of Lindahl's critical reformulation of *The General Theory*, in which he criticized Keynes's method of comparative statics in the equilibration of savings and investment by changes in income and employment, because it presupposes 'correct anticipations' (Lindahl, 1953, p. 27; cf. already 1934a, pp. 209–10; 1939c, pp. 264–5). Instead, Keynes should have relied on the dynamic analysis of changes of monetary and real variables where, like in his own analysis, expectations are allowed to adapt to the changes, but where expectational errors may nevertheless have effects that alter the equilibrium rates of interest and (un)employment

(cf. Boianovsky and Trautwein, 2006, p. 897). It is most interesting to note that Keynes (1934), in a correspondence with Lindahl (1934b) on the latter's paper of 1934a, rejected Lindahl's method because its 'dealing with time leads to undue complications and will be very difficult either to apply or to generalise about'.

Although Lindahl did not attempt to explicitly explain changes in output and employment, his aggregate analysis resulted in achievements which paved the way for Myrdal's (1932; 1933; 1939) and Ohlin's (1933; 1934, chs 1–3) monetary approaches, and which are still important for modern macroeconomics: (*a*) the use of the savings ratio s in the expression $E(1 - s)$ which related saving to expected income and which can be regarded as an alternative formulation of Keynes's (1936) propensity to consume, led to a definite distinction between saving and investment, with Lindahl (1929c, pp. 11–12, written in 1927–28; cf. Hansen, 1981, p. 261) being the first economist to see the independence of the latter from the former variable; (*b*) their distinction allowed him to divide aggregate income into saving and consumption demand and aggregate output into investment and consumer goods; (*c*) the 'paradox of savings' could be solved according to which a reduction in savings results in increased savings; (*d*) the assumption of unused resources was introduced (1930, pp. 42–51; cf. 1939a, 176–9 and 185–6), and unemployment was explained by deflation caused by a fall of aggregate demand where even the possibility of a stable unemployment equilibrium was visualized (1929c, pp. 43–4; 1930, p. 44); however, deleted in 1939a, pt. II; cf. Hansen, 1981, pp. 261–3. Compared with Keynes's principle of effective demand determining the equilibrium level of (un)employment there are, however, certain limitations in Lindahl's aggregate demand/supply approach: (*a*) unemployment equilibrium was considered only as an 'exceptional case', with – like in the other Stockholm School analyses on the relation between unemployment and wages (esp. Alf Johansson, 1934, ch. 5) – 'rigid money wages as a necessary condition for' and no 'complete macro model of unemployment' (Hansen, 1981, pp. 268–9; cf. Siven, 2002, p. 141); (*b*) the rate of interest was treated in its orthodox role as equilibrator of savings and investment in the long run; (*c*) saving and investment were not equilibrated by changes in aggregate income but by variations in its *distribution* (cf. the discussion initiated by Karl-Gustav Landgren, 1960, ch. 6:3; and followed up by Steiger, 1971, pp. 173–9; 1978, pp. 424–5; 1991, 129–30; Hansen, 1981, pp. 261–3; Don Patinkin, 1982, pp. 44–6; and Johan Myrman, 1991, pp. 272–6). In the analysis of this adjustment process, however, Lindahl was able to anticipate the whole neo-Keynesian or Kaldor–Pasinetti theory of distributive shares (cf. Guglielmo Chiodi and Kumaraswamy Velupillai, 1983; Velupillai, 1988).

On the other side, the equilibrating role of changes in total income with respect to saving and investment is implicit in Lindahl's sequence analysis of (1934a, pp. 208–11), where he showed how a difference between investment and saving *ex ante* leads to their *ex post* equality, and it was clearly visualized in his discussion of loan-financed public works as a means against unemployment (1932, pp. 136–7; 1935, pp. 1–5; cf. 1939a, app., pp. 356–67). As has been pointed out by Hansen (1955, p. 41), Lindahl in *Penningpolitikens medel* (1930, pp. 63–8; however, deleted in 1939a, pt. II) was the first economist to consider the possibility of a systematic use of variations in the relation between public expenditures and public incomes, that is, the budget balance, as a means to stabilize economic fluctuations because, as he recognized, a surplus in the balance can be defined as equivalent to state saving and a deficit as state investment (1930, p. 65). With this analysis he paved the way for Ohlin's (1934, ch. 5) and Myrdal's (1934, pts III–IV) more detailed analysis of loan-financed public works as remedies against unemployment. Unlike Keynesian economists, however, Lindahl in this discussion did not neglect the effects of such a fiscal policy for the national debt which he analysed in detail in 1944 (cf. 1946). There he formulated rules governing state borrowing which are very similar to those developed at the same time by Evsey D. Domar (1944), that is, that the problem of public debts is first and foremost a problem of the growth of national income.

Another innovation in Lindahl's monetary and macroeconomic theory was his discussion of how to organize the central banking system in a monetary union of independent nations (cf. 1930, pp. 170–9; however, deleted in 1939a, pt. II). As recently recognized by Gunnar Heinsohn and Steiger (2003, p. 13; cf. Steiger, 2007, pp. 43–5), Lindahl was the first economist to develop the model of a decentralized, two-stage central banking system for a common currency consisting of a main central bank and the national central banks, where the latter would receive the banknotes in the same way from the former like the domestic commercial banks of their national central bank. With this model he hoped to open the possibility for the main central bank to equilibrate differences in real rates of interest due to different rates of inflation between the union's members by allowing for differences in nominal rates of interest. With this proposal, Lindahl anticipated the central Achilles' heel of the Eurosystem, the central banking system of the European Monetary Union (EMU), where its Council can decide only on a unique nominal rate of interest (cf. Dieter Spethmann and Steiger, 2005, pp. 55–8). Furthermore, in spite of its name, the European Central Bank is not designed for issuing money and, therefore, not the central monetary authority of the EMU that could push through such a differentiation of credit. In his model, Lindahl (1930, p. 171) also demonstrated the necessity of a central fiscal authority in a monetary union to support the main central bank – another problem that has not been solved in the EMU (cf. Heinsohn and Steiger, 2003, pp. 13, 39).

Concepts of income and capital

While Lindahl's contributions to macroeconomic theory have been discussed extensively in the literature on the Stockholm School, his work on the macroeconomic concepts of income and capital have not received much attention (cf. Yohe, 1962).

The discussion of the notions of capital and income in Lindahl's theoretical framework stemmed from two different roots: (*a*) the approach to capital theory conceiving capital goods as stored services of land and labour, originally formulated by Eugen von Böhm-Bawerk (1889) and developed by Wicksell (1893; 1901) and Gustaf Åkerman (1923–4); and (*b*) the approach to the concept of income regarding income as a flow of benefits from the stock of capital and introduced into economic theory by Irving Fisher (1906). Both approaches had in common that *time* was included in a decisive manner and in concentrating on this element, Lindahl made the notions of income and capital essentially correlative.

In his piece on capital theory where he had introduced the method of intertemporal equilibrium (1929a; 1939a, pt. III), Lindahl avoided the theoretical difficulties of working with the concept of total capital in a world of heterogeneous capital goods by developing a completely disaggregated stationary equilibrium system – a 'Walrasian model with capital à la Wicksell' and with 'a striking similarity' to John von Neumann's model of equilibrium growth of 1937 (Hansen, 1970, pp. 199, 207–8). Although Lindahl did not make use of the concept of total capital in his equilibrium system, it can be shown that its total capital value can be determined on the basis of the term 'income' employed in his model – an insight which Lindahl formulated unequivocally in *Penningpolitikens medel* (1930, pp. 13–15; cf. 1939a, pt. II, pp. 143–6) and in more detail in his contributions on the concept of income (1933; 1937b, pp. 76–111).

Starting from Irving Fisher's basic premise that income consists of the services obtained from capital goods during a certain period, whereas capital is a stock existing at a given point of time, Lindahl (1933, pp. 400–1) looked upon *income as interest* accruing on the value of capital goods, and considered capital value as future income discounted. With this concept of income, implying that income is equal to the sum of consumption *and* saving, he solved the inconsistencies in Fisher's analysis of capital and income where saving, a flow term expressing the increase in capital value, had been excluded from income and incorporated into capital, a stock term. Consequently, Lindahl's discussion also made clear that changes in capital value, contrary to what had been the premises of Böhm-Bawerk, Wicksell and Åkerman, are not determined by changes in the use of capital but in the use of income, that is, the part which is not consumed: saving.

However, as Lindahl realized, this thesis holds true only under the assumption of perfect foresight. Following Myrdal's analysis of expectations of 1927, he showed that as soon as uncertainty about future events is introduced changes in anticipation of owners of capital assets lead to changes in capital value by *gains* and *losses* which cannot be regarded as positive or negative income, because like the stock of capital they refer not to a certain period but to a point of time (1929a, p. 75; 1939a, pt. III, p. 341; cf. Myrdal, 1927, p. 44, and the further discussion in Lindahl, 1939b, pp. 101–10). This insight led Lindahl to abandon the most practical concept of income – income as earnings – because it included gains and losses. Although Lindahl's concept of income – like his abstract classification of capital goods (Hansen, 1970, p. 200) – has been criticized for not being capable of empirical application and measurement, his contributions – together with Myrdal's approach of 1927 – have been acknowledged as 'the fundamental theoretical work concerning the notion of income' (Nicholas Kaldor, 1955, p. 162). This work should also become fundamental to Lindahl's research on national accounting (1937b; 1939b, pp. 74–136; 1954) which made him 'the father of Social Accounting *theory*' (Hicks, 1973, p. 8; cf. Carlson, 1982, 33–6).

During his lifetime – and until the late 1980s – Lindahl never earned a reputation comparable to that of his colleagues in the early Stockholm School, Gunnar Myrdal and Bertil Ohlin, and it has been argued by one of his younger colleagues (Lundberg, 1982, p. 275) that his contributions to economics were not distinguished by 'ingenious ideas' like those of Myrdal and Ohlin. As has been shown in this survey of Lindahl's work, however, the numerous original ideas in each of the four fields covered by his writings argue for quite different judgement. This holds especially true for Lindahl's monetary and macroeconomic theory, as has been demonstrated since the late 1980s by Boianovsky and Trautwein (2006), Leijonhufvud (1991), Siven (1991; 2002; 2006a; 2006b), Steiger (1987a; 1987b; 1987c; 2006a; 2006b; 2007), and Velupillai (1988).

The author wishes to thank Claes-Henric Siven (Stockholms Universitet) and Hans-Michael Trautwein (Universität Oldenburg) for valuable suggestions

OTTO STEIGER

See also **ex ante and ex post; Lindahl equilibrium; Myrdal, Gunnar; Ohlin, Bertil Gotthard; Stockholm School.**

Selected works

1919. *Die Gerechtigkeit der Besteuerung. Eine Analyse der Steuerprinzipien auf der Grundlage der Grenznutzentheorie.* Lund: Gleerupska Universitetsbokhandeln and H. Ohlsson. Ch. 4 trans. as 'Just taxation – a positive solution', in Musgrave and Peacock (1958).

1924. *Penningpolitikens mål och medel. Del I* [The aims and means of monetary policy. Part I]. Lund: C.W.K. Gleerup; Malmö: Försäkringsaktiebolaget. 1st edn of Lindahl (1929b).

1928. Einige strittige Fragen der Steuertheorie. In *Die Wirtschaftstheorie der Gegenwart*, vol. 4, ed. H. Mayer. Vienna: J. Springer; abridged trans. as 'Some controversial questions in the theory of taxation', in Musgrave and Peacock (1958).

1929a. Prisbildningsproblemets uppläggning från kapitalteoretisk synpunkt [The formulation of the theory of prices from the viewpoint of capital theory]. *Ekonomisk Tidskrift* 31, 31–81. Revised version trans. as Pt. III of Lindahl (1939a).

1929b. *Penningpolitikens mål* [The aims of monetary policy]. zund: C.W.K. Gleerup; Malmö: Försäkringsaktiebolaget. 2nd edn of Lindahl (1924).

1929c. *Penningpolitikens medel* [The means of monetary policy]. Lund: C.W.K. Gleerup; Malmö: Försäkringsaktiebolaget. 1st edn of Lindahl (1930).

1929d. *Om förhållandet mellan penningmängd och prisnivån* [On the relation between the quantity of money and the price level]. Uppsala: Lundequistska and Almqvist & Wiksell.

1930. *Penningpolitikens medel* [The means of monetary policy]. Lund: Gleerup; Malmö: Försökringsaktiebolaget. 2nd edn of Lindahl (1929c); revised version trans. as Pt. II of Lindahl (1939a).

1932. Offentliga arbeten i depressionstider [Public works in times of depression]. *Nationalekonomiska Föreningens Förhandlingar* [Proceedings of the Swedish Economic Association], Meeting of 25 November, pp. 127–37, 163–4.

1933. The concept of income. In *Economic Essays in Honour of Gustav Cassel*. October 20th, 1933. London: Allen & Unwin.

1934a. A note on the dynamic pricing problem. Mimeo, Gothenburg, 13 October. Quoted from the corrected version published in Steiger (1971).

1934b. Letter to John Maynard Keynes. Gothenburg, 7 November. In Steiger (1971).

1935. Arbetslöshet och finanspolitik [Unemployment and fiscal policy]. *Ekonomisk Tidskrift* 37, 1–36. Revised version trans. as App. to Lindahl (1939a).

1937a. (with E. Dahlgren and K. Kock.) *National Income of Sweden 1861–1930. In Two Parts*. Vol. III of *Wages, Cost of Living and National Income in Sweden 1860–1930*, ed. the Staff of the Institute for Social Sciences, University of Stockholm. London: P.S. King & Son; Stockholm: P.A. Norstedt & Söner.

1937b. 'National income', the concept and methods of estimation. In Lindahl (1937a), Pt. I.

1939a. *Studies in the Theory of Money and Capital*. London: Allen & Unwin.

1939b. The dynamic approach to economic theory. Pt. I of Lindahl (1939a).

1939c. Additional note (1939) (to Lindahl, 1939a, Pt. II). In Lindahl (1939a).

1944. Teorien för den offentliga skuldsättningen [The theory of the public debt]. In *Studier i ekonomi och historia tillägnade Eli F. Heckscher* [Studies in economics and history in honour of Eli F. Heckscher]. Uppsala: Almqvist & Wiksell. Abridged version trans. as Lindahl (1946).

1946. The problem of the growing national debt. *Skandinaviska Banken Quarterly Review* 27(2), 43–8. Abridged version of Lindahl (1944).

1951. Till hundraårsminnet av Knut Wicksells födelse [On the centenary of Knut Wicksell's birth]. *Ekonomisk Tidskrift* 53, 197–243. Quoted from the abridged version trans. as 'Wicksell's Life and Work', in K. Wicksell, *Selected Papers on Economic Theory*, ed. E. Lindahl. London: Allen & Unwin, 1958.

1953. Om Keynes' ekonomiska system. *Ekonomisk Tidskrift* 55, 186–243. Quoted from and trans. as 'On Keynes' economic system I–II', *Economic Record* 30 (1954), 19–32 and 159–71.

1954. Nationalbokföringens grundbegrepp. *Ekonomisk Tidskrift* 56, 87–138. Trans. as 'The basic concepts of national accounting', *International Economic Papers* 7 (1957), 71–100.

1955. Penningteoretiska utgångspunkter [Starting points in monetary theory]. In *Om Riksbankens sedelutgivningsrätt och därmed sammanhängande frågor* [On the Riksbanken's right to issue banknotes and related questions]. Stockholm: Statens offentligar utredningar 1955:43, 32–57.

1957. *Spelet om penningvärdet*. Stockholm: Kooperativa Förbundet. Quoted from and trans. as 'Das Spiel mit dem Geldwert', *Weltwirtschaftliches Archiv* 87 (1961), 7–53.

1959. Om skatteprinciper och skattepolitik. In *Ekonomi, politik, samhälle. En bok tillägnad Bertil Ohlin* [Economics, politics, society. A publication in honour of Bertil Ohlin], Stockholm: Folk & Samhälle and Esselte. Trans. as 'Tax principles and tax policy', *International Economic Papers* 10 (1960), 7–23.

Bibliography

Åkerman, J.G. 1923–4. *Realkapital und Kapitalzins*. 2 vols. Stockholm: Centraltryckeriet.

Andvig, J.C. 1991. Ragnar Frisch and the Stockholm School. In Jonung (1991).

Böhm-Bawerk, E. von 1889. *Kapital und Kapitalzins. Zweite Abteilung: Positive Theorie des Kapitales*. Jena: G. Fischer; 4th edn, 1921. Trans. as *Capital and Interest*, vols 2 and 3, South Holland, IL: Libertarian Press, 1959.

Bohm, P. 1987. Lindahl on public finance. In *The New Palgrave. A Dictionary of Economics*, vol. 3, ed. J. Eatwell, M. Milgate and P. Newman. London: Macmillan.

Boianovsky, M. and Trautwein, H.-M. 2006. Price expectations, capital accumulation and employment. Lindahl's macroeconomics from the 1920s to the 1950s. *Cambridge Journal of Economics* 30, 881–900.

Carlson, B. 1982. Bagge, Lindahl och nationalinkomsten. Om 'National Income of Sweden 1861–1930' [Bagge, Lindahl and the national income. On 'National Income of Sweden 1861–1930']. *Meddelande från*

Ekonomisk–historiska institutionen, Lunds Universitet, No. 27.

Chiodi, G. and Velupillai, K. 1983. A note on Lindahl's theory of distribution. *Kyklos* 36, 103–11.

Debreu, G. 1959. *Theory of Value. An Axiomatic Analysis of Economic Equilibrium*. New York: Wiley.

Domar, E.D. 1944. The 'burden of the debt' and the national income. *American Economic Review* 34, 798–827.

Fisher, I. 1906. *The Nature of Capital and Income*. New York: Macmillan. 2nd edn, 1912.

Frisch, R. 1933. Propagation problems and impulse problems in economic dynamics. In *Economic Essays in Honour of Gustav Cassel. October 20th, 1933*. London: Allen & Unwin.

Friedman, M. 1968. The role of monetary policy. *American Economic Review* 58, 1–17.

Fregert, K. 1993. Erik Lindahl's norm for monetary policy. In *Swedish Economic Thought. Explorations and Advances*, ed. L. Jonung. London: Routledge.

Grossekettler, H. 2006. Wicksell, Knut: Finanztheoretische Untersuchungen (1896). In *Lexikon der ökonomischen Werke. 650 wegweisende Schriften von der Antike bis ins 20. Jahrhundert*, ed. D. Herz and V. Weinberger. Düsseldorf: Verlag Wirtschaft und Finanzen.

Hahn, F.H. 1980. Unemployment from a theoretical viewpoint. *Economica* NS 47, 285–98.

Hammarskjöld, D. 1933a. Utkast till en algebraisk metod för dynamisk prisanalys [Outline of an algebraic method for the dynamic analysis of prices]. *Ekonomisk Tidskrift* 34(5–6) (1932, printed 1933), 157–76.

Hammarskjöld, D. 1933b. *Konjunkturspridningen. En teoretisk och historisk undersökning* [The propagation of business cycles. A theoretical and historical investigation]. Stockholm: Statens offentliga utredningar 1933:29.

Hammarskjöld, D. 1935. *Åtgärder mot arbetslöshet. Arbetslöshetsutredningens betänkande, del II* [Measures against unemployment. Report of the Swedish Unemployment Committee, Part II]. Stockholm: Statens offentliga utredningar 1935:6.

Hammarskjöld, D. 1944. Den svenska diskussionen om penningpolitikens mål. In *Studier i ekonomi och historia tillägnade Eli F. Heckscher* [Studies in economics and history in honour of Eli F. Heckscher]. Uppsala: Almqvist & Wiksell. Trans. as 'The Swedish discussion on the aims of monetary policy', *International Economic Papers* 5 (1955), 145–54.

Hansen, B. 1955. *Finanspolitikens ekonomiska teori*. Stockholm: Statens offentliga utredningar, 1955:25. Quoted from and trans. as *The Economic Theory of Fiscal Policy*, London: Allen & Unwin, 1958.

Hansen, B. 1970. *A Survey of General Equilibrium Systems*. New York: McGraw-Hill.

Hansen, B. 1979. Review of Erik Lundberg (ed.): Inflation Theory and Anti-Inflation Policy (1977). *Scandinavian Journal of Economics* 81, 119–25.

Hansen, B. 1981. Unemployment, Keynes, and the Stockholm School. *History of Political Economy* 13, 256–77.

Hansson, B. 1982. *The Stockholm School and the Development of Dynamic Method.* London: Croom Helm.

Hansson, B. 1987. Stockholm School. In *The New Palgrave. A Dictionary of Economics*, vol. 4, ed. J. Eatwell, M. Milgate and P. Newman. London: Macmillan.

Hansson, B. 1991. The Stockholm School and the development of dynamic method. In *The History of Swedish Economic Thought*, ed. B. Sandelin. London: Routledge.

Hayek, F.A. 1928. Das intertemporale Gleichgewichtssystem der Preise und die Bewegungen des 'Geldwertes'. *Weltwirtschaftliches Archiv* 28, 33–76. Trans. as 'Intertemporal price equilibrium and movements in the value of money', in F.A. von Hayek, *Money, Capital and Fluctuations. Early Essays*, ed. R. Cloughry. London: Routledge & Kegan Paul, 1984.

Heinsohn, G. and Steiger, O. 2003. The European Central Bank and the Eurosystem. An analysis of the missing central monetary institution in the European Monetary Union. ZEI Working Paper No. B03-09. Center for European Integration Studies (ZEI), Universität Bonn. Repr. in *The Euro, the Eurosystem, and the European Economic and Monetary Union*, ed. D. Ehrig and O. Steiger. Hamburg: LIT-Verlag, 2007.

Hicks, J.R. 1939. *Value and Capital. An Inquiry into Some Fundamental Principles of Economic Theory.* Oxford: Clarendon Press. 2nd edn, 1946.

Hicks, J.R. 1973. Recollections and documents. *Economica* NS 40, 2–11.

Hicks, Sir J. 1985. *Methods of Dynamic Economics.* Oxford: Oxford University Press.

Hicks, Sir J. 1991. The Swedish influence on *Value and Capital.* In Jonung (1991).

Johansson, A. 1934. *Löneutvecklingen och arbetslösheten* [The development of wages and unemployment]. Stockholm: Statens offentliga utredningar 1934:2.

Jonung, L., ed. 1991. *The Stockholm School of Economics Revisited.* Cambridge: Cambridge University Press.

Kaldor, N. 1955. *An Expenditure Tax.* London: Allen & Unwin. Quoted from the reprint of pp. 54–78, 'The concept of income in economic theory', in *Readings in the Concept and Measurement of Income*, ed. R.H. Parker and G.C. Harcourt. Cambridge: Cambridge University Press, 1969.

Keynes, J.M. 1934. Letter to Erik Lindahl. Bloomsbury, 8 December. Quoted from the reproduction in Steiger (1971).

Keynes, J.M. 1936. *The General Theory of Employment, Interest and Money.* London: Macmillan.

Landgren, K.-G. 1960. *Den 'nya ekonomien' i Sverige. J.M. Keynes, B. Ohlin och utvecklingen 1927–39* [The 'new economics' in Sweden. J.M. Keynes, B. Ohlin and the development 1927–39). Stockholm and Uppsala: Almqvist & Wiksell.

Leijonhufvud, A. 1991. Roundtable discussion. In Jonung (1991).

Lindahl, G. and Wallmén, O. 1960. Erik Lindahl. Bibliografi 1919–1960 [Erik Lindahl. Bibliography 1919–1960]. *Ekonomisk Tidskrift* 62, 59–74.

Lundberg, E. 1930. Om begreppet ekonomisk jämvikt [On the notion of economic equilibrium]. *Ekonomisk Tidskrift* 32, 133–60.

Lundberg, E. 1937. *Studies in the Theory of Economic Expansion.* Stockholm: Norstedt & Söner.

Lundberg, E. 1982. Lindahl, Erik. In *Svenskt biografiskt lexikon* [The Swedish Dictionary of Bibliography] 23. Stockholm: Norstedts Tryckeri.

Milgate, M. 1982. *Capital and Employment. A Study of Keynes's Economics.* London: Academic Press.

Musgrave, R.A. 1959. *The Theory of Public Finance.* New York: McGraw-Hill.

Musgrave, R.A. and Peacock, A.T., eds. 1958. *Classics in the Theory of Public Finance.* London: Macmillan. 2nd edn, 1967.

Myrdal, G. 1927. *Prisbildningsproblemet och föränderligheten* [The problem of price formation and changeability]. Uppsala and Stockholm: Almqvist & Wiksell.

Myrdal, G. 1932. Om penningteoretisk jämvikt. En studie över den 'normala räntan' i Wicksells penninglära [On monetary equilibrium. A study on the 'normal rate of interest' in Wicksell's monetary doctrine]. *Ekonomisk Tidskrift* 33 (1931, printed 1932), 191–302. Revised version trans. as Myrdal (1933).

Myrdal, G. 1933. Der Gleichgewichtsbegriff als Instrument der geldtheoretischen Analyse. In *Beiträge zur Geldtheorie*, ed. F.A. Hayek. Vienna: J. Springer. 1st rev. version of Myrdal (1932); 2nd rev. version trans. as Myrdal (1939).

Myrdal, G. 1934. *Finanspolitikens ekonomiska verkningar* [The economic effects of fiscal policy]. Stockholm: Statens offentliga utredningar 1934: 1.

Myrdal, G. 1939. *Monetary Equilibrium.* London: Hodge. Revised version of Myrdal (1933).

Myrman, J. 1991. The monetary economics of the Stockholm School. In Jonung (1991).

Neumann, J. von 1937. Über ein ökonomisches Gleichungssystem und eine Verallgemeinerung des Browerschen Fixpunktsatzes. In *Ergebnisse eines mathematischen Kolloquiums* 8, ed. K. Menger. Trans. as 'A model of general equilibrium', *Review of Economic Studies* 13 (1945–6), 1–9.

Ohlin, B. 1933. Till frågan om penningteoriens uppläggning [On the question of the method and structure in monetary theory]. *Ekonomisk Tidskrift* 35, 45–81. Quoted from and translated as 'On the formulation of monetary theory', *History of Political Economy* 10 (1978), 353–88.

Ohlin, B. 1934. *Penningpolitik, offentliga arbeten, subventioner och tullar som medel mot arbetslöshet. Bidrag till expansionens teori* [Monetary policy, public works, subsidies and tariffs as remedies for unemployment. A contribution to the theory of expansion]. Stockholm: Statens offentliga utredningar 1934:12.

Ohlin, B. 1937. Some notes on the Stockholm theory of savings and investment. I–II. *Economic Journal* 47, 53–69 and 221–240.

Patinkin, D. 1982. *Anticipations of the General Theory? And Other Essays on Keynes.* Chicago: University of Chicago Press.

Petersson, J. 1987. *Erik Lindahl och Stockholsskolans dynamiska metod* [Erik Lindahl and the dynamic method of the Stockholm School]. Lund: Universitetsförlaget Dialogus.

Phelps, E.S. 1967. Phillips Curves, expectations of inflation and optimal unemployment over time. *Economica* NS 34, 254–81.

Roberts, J. 1987. Lindahl equilibrium. In *The New Palgrave. A Dictionary of Economics*, vol. 3, ed. J. Eatwell, M. Milgate and P. Newman. London: Macmillan; New York: Stockton Press.

Samuelson, P.A. 1954. The pure theory of public expenditures. *Review of Economics and Statistics* 36, 387–9.

Siven, C.-H. 1985. The end of the Stockholm School. *Scandinavian Journal of Economics* 87, 577–93.

Siven, C.-H. 1991. Expectation and plan. The microeconomics of the Stockholm School. In Jonung (1991).

Siven, C.-H. 2002. Analytical foundations of Erik Lindahl's monetary analysis, 1924–1930. *History of Political Economy* 34, 111–53.

Siven, C.-H. 2006a. Stockholmsskolan och Keynes [The Stockholm School and Keynes]. *Økonomisk Forum* 60(6), 10–7.

Siven, C.-H. 2006b. Monetary equilibrium. *History of Political Economy* 38, 665–709.

Spethmann, D. and Steiger, O. 2005. The four Achilles' heels of the Eurosystem. Missing central monetary institution, different real rates of interest, nonmarketable securities, and missing lender of last resort. *International Journal of Political Economy* 34(2), (2004, printed Summer 2005) 46–68.

Steiger, O. 1971. *Studien zur Entstehung der Neuen Wirtschaftslehre in Schweden. Eine Anti-Kritik.* Berlin: Duncker & Humblot.

Steiger, O. 1978. Prelude to the theory of a monetary economy. Origins and significance of Ohlin's 1933 approach. *History of Political Economy* 10, 420–46.

Steiger, O. 1987a. *Ex ante* and *ex post*. In *The New Palgrave. A Dictionary of Economics*, vol. 2, ed. J. Eatwell, M. Milgate and P. Newman. London: Macmillan; New York: Stockton Press.

Steiger, O. 1987b. Lindahl, Erik Robert (1891–1960). In *The New Palgrave. A Dictionary of Economics*, vol. 3, ed. J. Eatwell, M. Milgate and P. Newman. London: Macmillan; New York: Stockton Press.

Steiger, O. 1987c. Monetary equilibrium. In *The New Palgrave. A Dictionary of Economics*, vol. 3, ed. J. Eatwell, M. Milgate and P. Newman. London: Macmillan; New York: Stockton Press.

Steiger, O. 1991. Comment on Eskil Wadensjö: 'The Committee of Unemployment and the Stockholm School'. In Jonung (1991).

Steiger, O. 2006a. Lindahl, Erik Robert: *Penningpolitikens medel* [The means of monetary policy] (1930). In *Lexikon der ökonomischen Werke. 650 wegweisende Schriften von der Antike bis ins 20. Jahrhundert*, ed. D. Herz and V. Weinberger. Düsseldorf: Verlag Wirtschaft und Finanzen.

Steiger, O. 2006b. Lindahl, Erik Robert: *Studies in the Theory of Money and Capital* (1939). In *Lexikon der ökonomischen Werke. 650 wegweisende Schriften von der Antike bis ins 20. Jahrhundert*, ed. D. Herz and V. Weinberger. Düsseldorf: Verlag Wirtschaft und Finanzen.

Steiger, O. 2007. Erik Lindahl och Eurosystemet [Erik Lindahl and the Eurosystem]. *Ekonomisk Debatt* 35(2), 42–5.

Svennilsson, I. 1938. *Ekonomisk planering. Teoretiska studier* [Economic planning. Theoretical studies]. Uppsala: Almqvist & Wiksell.

Uhr, C.G. 1960. *Economic Doctrines of Knut Wicksell.* Berkeley and Los Angeles: University of California Press.

Varian, H.R. 1987. Microeconomics. In *The New Palgrave. A Dictionary of Economics*, vol. 3, ed. J. Eatwell, M. Milgate and P. Newman. London: Macmillan.

Velupillai, K. 1988. Somer Swedish stepping stones to modern macroeconomics. *Eastern Economic Journal* 14, 87–98.

Werin, L. 1991. There were *two* Stockholm Schools. In Jonung (1991).

Wicksell, K. 1893. *Über Wert, Kapital und Rente.* Jena: G. Fischer. Trans. as *Value, Capital and Rent*, London: Allen & Unwin, 1954.

Wicksell, K. 1896. *Finanztheoretische Untersuchungen nebst Darstellung und Kritik des Steuerwesens Schwedens.* Jena: G. Fischer, iv–vi, 76–87, 101–59. Trans. as 'A new principle of just taxation', in Musgrave and Peacock (1958).

Wicksell, K. 1898. *Geldzins und Güterpreise. Eine Studie über die den Tauschwert des Geldes bestimmenden Ursachen.* Jena: G. Fischer. Trans. as *Interest and Prices. A Study of the Causes Regulating the Value of Money.* London: Macmillan, 1936.

Wicksell, K. 1901. *Föreläsningar i nationalekonomi.* Vol. 1, Stockholm: Fritzes; Lund: Berlingska. Trans. of the 3rd Swedish edn (1928) as *Lectures on Political Economy. Volume 1: General Theory*, London: Routledge & Sons, 1934.

Wicksell, K. 1906. *Föreläsningar i nationalekonomi.* Vol. 2: *Om penningar och kredit.* Stockholm: Fritzes; Lund:

Berlingska. Quoted from the trans. of the 3rd Swedish edn (1929), *Lectures on Political Economy. Volume 2: Money*, London: Routledge & Sons, 1935.

Yohe, W.P. 1959. *The Wicksellian Tradition in Swedish Macroeconomic Theory*. Ann Arbor, MI: University Microfilms.

Yohe, W.P. 1962. A note on some lesser known works of Erik Lindahl. *Canadian Journal of Economics and Political Science* 28, 274–80.

linear models

Von Neumann's linear economic model was first published in German in 1938 and translated into English in 1945. Since then there have been numerous economic and mathematical refinements, most of which are summarized in Burmeister and Dobell (1970) and/or Morishima (1969). The original von Neumann formulation did not admit either primary factors or final consumption. However, in the generalized von Neumann model described below, one primary factor, labour, is allowed, as well as a vector of final consumption goods. A further generalization allowing a vector of different primary factors is possible. Accordingly, linear models of Leontief–Sraffa (1960) type become a special case.

Assume there exist m alternative production activities for producing n different commodities, where $m \gtreqqless n$. Activity j operating at a unit intensity level requires a labour input a_{0j} and a vector of commodity inputs $(a_{1j}, a_{2j}, \ldots, a_{nj})$ to produce a vector of commodity outputs $(b_{1j}, b_{2j}, \ldots, b_{nj})$. Production takes one time period, so inputs at time t result in outputs at time $t+1$. Constant returns to scale is implied by linearity, and inputs $\lambda_{a_{0j}}$ and $(\lambda a_{1j}, \lambda a_{2j}, \ldots, \lambda a_{nj})$ yield outputs $(\lambda b_{1j}, \lambda b_{2j}, \ldots, \lambda b_{nj})$ for all $\lambda \geq 0$.

The vector of labour requirements for the m alternative production activities is written as $A_0 = (a_{01}, a_{02}, \ldots, a_{0m})$. The input matrix is

$$\left[\frac{A_0}{A}\right] = \begin{bmatrix} a_{01} & - & a_{0m} \\ a_{11} & & a_{1m} \\ \vdots & & \vdots \\ a_{n1}, & \cdots & , a_{nm} \end{bmatrix}$$

the output matrix is

$$B = \begin{bmatrix} b_{11} & \cdots & b_{1m} \\ \vdots & & \vdots \\ b_{11} & \cdots & b_{nm} \end{bmatrix}$$

and the intensity levels at which each of the m production activities is operated is given by the column vector

$$x = \begin{bmatrix} x_1 \\ \vdots \\ x_m \end{bmatrix}$$

Although in general some of the a_{0j}'s, a_{ij}'s and b_{ij}'s may be zero, here we assume that they are all positive; we thereby avoid some technical difficulties and gain expositional simplicity.

Assume that labour grows at the rate $g \geq 0$,

$$L(t + 1) = (1 + g)L(t), \tag{1}$$

and is fully employed with

$$L(t) = A_0(t)x(t). \tag{2}$$

For all t production must satisfy the resource constraint

$$Ax \leq Bx - C \tag{3}$$

where C denotes the column vector of commodities consumed

$$C = \begin{bmatrix} C_1 \\ \vdots \\ C_m \end{bmatrix}$$

The economy is capable of producing positive final consumption and balanced growth at the rate g provided the inequalities

$$(1 + g)Ax \leq Bx - C, \quad C \geq 0, \quad C \neq 0$$
$$x \geq 0, \quad x \neq 0 \tag{4}$$

are satisfied.

Prices for a unit of labour services and the n commodities are given by $p_0 \equiv w$ and the row vector $p = (p_1, p_2, \ldots, p_n)$, respectively, where

$$\sum_{i=0}^{n} p_i = 1$$

is one convenient normalization. The steady-state (or balanced growth) rate of interest (or profit rate) is denoted by r.

The economy can achieve a steady-state equilibrium at a given value of $r \geq 0$ if the von Neumann price system has a solution satisfying the inequalities

$$wA_0 + (1 + r)pA \geq pB, \quad w \geq 0, \quad w \neq 0$$
$$p \geq 0, \quad p \neq 0. \tag{5}$$

The quantity system (4) is dual to the price system (5) when $r=g$.

The von Neumann solution to (5) involves three economically essential inequalities:

(i) If the cost of operating an activity exceeds the revenue from that activity, then that activity is not used in a steady-state equilibrium solution, that is that activity is operated at a zero intensity level. Formally,

$$x_j = 0 \text{ if } wa_{0j} + (1+r)\sum_{i=1}^{n} p_i a_{ij} > \sum_{i=1}^{n} p_i b_{ij},$$

$$j = 1, \ldots, m.$$

$$(6)$$

(ii) If a commodity has a positive price, then its supply and demand are equal:

$$(1+g)\sum_{i=1}^{m} a_{ij}x_j = \sum_{j=1}^{m} b_{ij}x_j - C_i \text{ if } p_i > 0,$$

$$i = 1, \ldots, n.$$

$$(7)$$

(iii) The price of a commodity is zero if it is in excess supply:

$$p_i = 0 \text{ if } (1+g)\sum_{i=1}^{m} a_{ij}x_j < \sum_{j=1}^{m} b_{ij}x_j - C_i,$$

$$i = 1, \ldots, n.$$

$$(8)$$

The above generalized von Neumann model is not a general equilibrium model because there is one missing equation. Some behavioural equation involving the rate of interest and consumption is required to form a general equilibrium model. Nevertheless, this incomplete specification can be used to confirm and generalize many well known results.

For example, in steady-state equilibrium equations (5), (6), (7) and (8) imply that

$$(1+g)Ax + pC = pBx$$

$$= \text{value of output}$$

$$= wA_0 + p(1+r)Ax.$$

$$(9)$$

Using (2), the per capita value of commodity inputs or capital is given by

$$v = \frac{pAx}{A_0 x};$$

$$(10)$$

similarly the per capita value of consumption is

$$pc = \frac{pC}{A_0 x}.$$

$$(11)$$

Substituting (10) and (11) into (9) and rearranging yields

$$pc = w + (r - g)v.$$

$$(12)$$

The Golden Rule result that the value of per capita consumption is equal to the wage rate at the Golden Rule point where $r=g$ is an immediate consequence of (12). Other such results are easily derived; thus allowing for the possibility of joint production does not invalidate many economic results.

Two familiar classes of models are special cases of this generalized von Neumann model. First, Leontief–Sraffa models result simply by setting $m=n$ and $B=I$, which implies that the technology is free of joint production. Then if $p>0$ from (7)

$$C = [I - (1+g)A]x$$

$$(13)$$

where now the column vector x is interpreted as the output vector for commodities $1, \ldots, n$. Provided (4) has a solution, (13) may be solved for

$$x = [I - (1+g)A]^{-1}C,$$

$$(14)$$

and premultiplying (14) by the vector A_0 gives the consumption possibility frontier

$$A_0 x = L = [I - (1+g)A]^{-1}C.$$

$$(15)$$

Similarly, steady-state equilibrium prices for the Leontief–Sraffa model are given by

$$p = wA_0[I - (1+r)A]^{-1}.$$

$$(16)$$

Second, most neo-Austrian models of the type studied by Hicks (1973a) are a special case of this generalized von Neumann model. The latter fact is most easily demonstrated by considering the simple numerical example due to Burmeister (1974). A neo-Austrian process is a time sequence of input–output vectors

$$\{(a_t, b_t)\}_{t=0}^{T}$$

$$(17)$$

where a_t is the input of a commodity and b_t is the output (of the same commodity) in period t. Consider a process

$$\{(a_t, b_t)\}_{t=0}^{2} = \{(a_0, 0), (a_1, b_1), (a_2, 1)\}.$$

$$(18)$$

The neo-Austrian model (18) is *equivalent* to a von Neumann specification with

$$\left[\begin{array}{c} -\dfrac{A_0}{A} - \end{array}\right] = \begin{bmatrix} a_1 & a_1 & a_2 \\ - & - & - \\ 0 & 1 & 0 \\ 0 & 0 & 1 \\ 0 & 0 & 0 \end{bmatrix} \quad (19)$$

and

$$B = \begin{bmatrix} 1 & 0 & 0 \\ 0 & 1 & 0 \\ 0 & b_1 & 1 \end{bmatrix}; \qquad (20)$$

see Burmeister (1974, pp. 441–4).

We see, therefore, that the generalized von Neumann model is extraordinarily useful for unifying several apparently different ways of describing the production technology. However, when we do not restrict our attention to steady-state equilibria, the dynamic evolution of the model becomes extremely complex. The inequalities (4) and (5) must be satisfied for each t, as well as some additional equation to determine the interest rate r. Known results on the dynamics of models with heterogeneous capital goods – see, for examples the discussion and references cited in Chapters 5 and 6 of Burmeister (1980) – warn us that the task of completely characterizing the dynamic properties of von Neumann models will not be easy. The fact that the von Neumann formulation admits joint production makes the task even harder.

EDWIN BURMEISTER

See also **Hawkins–Simon conditions; input–output analysis; linear programming; Marxian value analysis; nonsubstitution theorems; Perron–Frobenius theorem; Sraffian economics.**

Bibliography

Burmeister, E. 1974. Synthesizing the neo-Austrian and alternative approaches to capital theory: a survey. *Journal of Economic Literature* 12(2), June, 413–56.
Burmeister, E. and Dobell, A.R. 1970. *Mathematical Theories of Economic Growth.* New York: Macmillan.
Burmeister, E. 1980. *Capital Theory and Dynamics.* New York: Cambridge University Press.
Burmeister, E. and Kuga, K. 1970. The factor-price frontier, duality and joint production. *Review of Economic Studies* 37(109), 11–19.
Hicks, J.R. 1973a. *Capital and Time. A Neo-Austrian Theory.* Oxford: Clarendon Press.
Hicks, J.R. 1973b. The Austrian theory of capital and its rebirth in modern economics. In *Carl Menger and the Austrian School of Economics,* ed. J.R. Hicks and W. Weber. New York and London: Oxford University Press.
Morishima, M. 1969. *Theory of Economic Growth.* Oxford: Clarendon Press.
Sraffa, P. 1960. *Production of Commodities by Means of Commodities: Prelude to a Critique of Economic Theory.* Cambridge: Cambridge University Press.
von Neumann, J. Über ein ökonomisches Gleichungssystem und eine Verallgemeinerung des Brouwerschen Fixpunktsatzes. *Ergebnisse eines mathematischen Kolloquiums,* Vol. 8, ed. K. Menger, Leipzig: Verlag. Trans. by G. Morgenstern as 'A model of general economic equilibrium', *Review of Economic Studies* 13, (1945–6), 1–9. Reprinted in *Readings in Mathematical Economics,* ed. P. Newman, Vol. II, Baltimore: Johns Hopkins University Press, 1968, 221–9.
von Weizsacker, C.C. 1971. *Steady State Capital Theory.* New York: Springer-Verlag.

linear programming

A list of applications of linear programming, since it was first proposed in 1947 by G. Dantzig, could fill a small volume. Both J. von Neumann and L. Kantorovich made important contributions prior to 1947. Its first use by G. Dantzig and M. Wood was for logistical planning and deployment of military forces. A. Charnes and W. Cooper in the early 1950s pioneered its use in the petroleum industry. S. Vajda and E.M.L. Beale were early pioneers in the field in Great Britain. In socialist countries, it is used to determine the plan for optimal growth of the economy. Thousands of linear programs are efficiently solved each day all over the world using the simplex method, an algorithm, also first proposed in 1947. Many problems which once could only be solved on high-speed mainframe computers can now be solved on personal computers.

The problem of minimizing or maximizing a function f_0 of several variables $X = (X_1, X_2, \ldots, X_n)$ subject to constraints $f_i(X) \leq 0$, $i = 1, \ldots, n$ is called a *mathematical program*. When all the functions f_i are linear, it is called a *linear program*; otherwise a *non-linear program*. If all f_i are convex functions, it is called a *convex program*. At first glance, linear inequality systems appear to be a very restricted class. However, as pointed out by T. C. Koopmans as early as 1948, linear programs can be used to approximate the broad class of convex functions commonly encountered in economic planning.

Linear programs may be viewed as a generalization of the Leontief Input–Output Model, one important difference being that alternative production processes (activities) are allowed to compete; another being the representation of capacity as an input that becomes available at a later point in time as an output (possibly depreciated). Solving a model with alternative activities requires not only software for efficiently solving on computers large systems of equations as in the Leontief case, but also software for selecting the best combination from an astronomical number of possible combinations of activities. (See the entry SIMPLEX METHOD FOR SOLVING LINEAR PROGRAMS.)

Formulating a linear program

Finding an optimal product mix (for example blend of gasoline, or metals, or mix of nuts, or animal feeds) is a typical application. For example, a manufacturer wishes

Table 1

Composition	Alloy A	B	C	D	Desired blend
% Lead	10	10	40	60	30%
% Zinc	10	30	50	30	30%
% Tin	80	60	10	10	40%
Cost/lb	4.1	4.3	5.8	6.0	Minimize cost per pound

to purchase at minimum total cost a number of solder alloys A, B, C, D which are available in the market-place in order to melt them down to make a blend of 30 per cent lead, 30 per cent zinc, and 40 per cent tin. Their respective costs per pound are shown in Table 1.

Suppose 100 pounds of blend is desired and X_A, X_B, X_C, X_D are the unknown number of pounds of A, B, C, D to be purchased. The problem to be solved is clearly: find Z and $(X_A, X_B, X_C, X_D) \geq 0$, such that:

$$0.1X_A + 0.1X_B + 0.4X_C + 0.6X_D = 30$$
$$0.1X_A + 0.3X_B + 0.5X_C + 0.3X_D = 30$$
$$0.8X_A + 0.6X_B + 0.1X_C + 0.1X_D = 40$$
$$\overline{4.1X_A + 4.3X_B + 5.8X_C + 6.0X_D = Z(\min)}$$

This example can be solved in a few seconds on a personal computer.

The standard form of a linear program is: find min z, $x = (x_1, \ldots, x_n) \geq 0$:

$$Ax = b, \quad cx = z(\min)$$

where A is a m by n matrix, b a column vector of m components and c a row vector of n components. The matrix A of coefficients is referred to as the *technology matrix*.

One way to formulate a linear program is to begin by (a) listing various constraints such as resources availability, demand for various goods by consumers, known bounds on productive capacity; (b) listing variables to be determined representing the levels of activities whose net inputs and outputs must satisfy the constraints, and finally (c) tabulating the coefficients of the various inequalities and equations.

Since linear programming models can be very large systems with thousands of inequalities and variables, it is necessary to use a special software, called *matrix generators*, to facilitate the model building process. Such systems have millions of coefficients, fortunately most of them are zero. Matrices with very few nonzero elements are called *sparse*. The World Bank uses software called GAMS to generate moderate-size sparse matrices A by rows. Another type of software called OMNI has been developed by Haverly Systems and has been used to generate very large sparse matrices by columns. When a model is formulated by columns, it is called *Activity Analysis*: the column of coefficients of a variable is the same as a recipe in a cook book – these are the input and output flows required to carry out one unit of an activity (or process). The variables, usually non-negative, are the unknown levels of activity to be determined. For example the activity of 'putting one unit (pound) of solder alloy A in the blend' has an input of $4.10 and outputs to the blend of 0.10 lb of lead, 0.10 lb of zinc, 0.80 lb of tin.

In economic applications, *output* coefficients are typically stated with + signs and *input* coefficients with − signs. Under this convention, the signs of the coefficients of the Z equation in the blending example should be reversed and, net revenues, $(-Z)$ maximized. In practice, instead of equations in non-negative variables, there can be a mix of equations and inequalities. Simple algebraic steps allow one to pass from one form of the system to another.

Primal and dual statements of the linear program

John von Neumann in 1947 was the first to point out that associated with a linear program is another called its *Dual*, formed by transposing the matrix A and interchanging the role of the RHS b and the 'cost' vector c. The original problem is called the *Primal*. Von Neumann expressed both of these LP in inequality form:

$$\text{Primal}: \quad \min \bar{z} = cX: \quad AX \geq b, \quad X \geq 0, \quad (P)$$
$$\text{Dual}: \quad \min \underline{z} = Y'b: \quad Y'A \leq c, \quad Y \geq 0, \quad (D)$$

where Y' is the transpose of column vector Y.

If we denote the jth column of A by $A(*, j)$, the n inequalities $Y'A \leq c$ may be rewritten as $Y'A(*, j) \leq c_j$ for $j = 1, \ldots, n$.

(P) expresses the physical constraints of the system under study. The variables Y of the dual (D) can be interpreted as *prices*. Mathematicians call them *Lagrange multipliers*. The dual conditions, $Y'A(*, j) - c_j \leq 0$ for $j = 1, \ldots, n$, may appear strange and just the opposite from what one would expect. They state that levels X_j of all activities j that show profit in the economy will rise to the point that all 'price out' nonprofitable. It turns out that when the value $\underline{z} = Y'b$ in (D) is maximized, all activities j that are operated at *positive* levels will just *break even*, i.e., just 'clear their books' and that all activities j operating at a strict loss will be operating at zero levels.

The famous duality theorem of von Neumann states that, when there exist 'feasible' solutions $AX \geq b$, $X \geq 0$ to (P) and $Y'A \leq c$, $Y \geq 0$ to (D),

$$\text{Max } \underline{z} = \text{Min } \bar{z}$$

It is easy to prove that *any* feasible solutions to (P) and (D) not necessarily optimum satisfy

$$\underline{z} = Y'b \leq cX = \bar{z},$$

so that if it happens that $Y^*b = cX^*$, for some feasible $X = X^*$, $Y = Y^*$ then by the duality theorem we know that such a pair (X^*, Y^*) are optimal solutions to (P) and (D).

This makes it possible to combine the primal and dual problems into the single problem of finding a feasible solution to the following: find $(X, \bar{X}, Y, \bar{Y}, \theta) \geq 0$:

$$\begin{bmatrix} 0 & A & -b \\ -A' & 0 & c' \\ b' & -c & 0 \end{bmatrix} \begin{bmatrix} Y \\ X \\ 1 \end{bmatrix} = \begin{bmatrix} \bar{Y} \\ \bar{X} \\ \theta \end{bmatrix} \quad \text{(P,D)}$$

where we have introduced two *slack* vectors $\bar{Y} \geq 0$ and $\bar{X} \geq 0$ which turn the inequality relations (P) and (D) into equality relations $AX - \bar{Y} = b$ and $Y'A + \bar{X}' = c$. The last relation is the single equation $Y'b - cX = \theta$ where $\theta \geq 0$ is a scalar.

It we multiply (P, D) by the vector $(Y', X', 1)$ on the left and perform all the matrix multiplications, everything on the left side cancels out because of the skew symmetry of the matrix and we are left with

$$0 = [Y'X'1][\bar{Y}\bar{X}\theta]' = \sum_i Y_i \bar{Y} + \sum_j X_j \bar{X}_j + \theta.$$

Because all terms are non-negative, it follows that

$$X_j \bar{X}_j = 0, \quad Y_i \bar{Y}_i = 0, \quad \theta = 0 \quad \text{for all } i \text{ and } j.$$

These are called *complementary slackness* or *Kuhn–Tucker* conditions for optimality.

Zero-sum matrix games

These games can be formulated as a special class of linear programs. The 'row' player chooses row i of a matrix while his opponent, the 'column' player, simultaneously chooses column j. Column player wins an amount a_{ij} if $a_{ij} \geq 0$ otherwise he pays the other player $-a_{ij}$. The *payoff* matrix is $A = [a_{ij}]$. It is called a *zero-sum* game because the sum of the payments each player receives adds up to zero. Von Neumann analysed this game in 1928 and introduced the notion of a *mixed strategy* $(Y_1, Y_2, \ldots, Y_m)$, $(X_1, X_2, \ldots, X_n)$ which are the probabilities of the players choosing any particular row and column. He showed that there exist optimal mixed strategies, $Y = Y^*$ for the row player and $X = X^*$ for the column player, such that if a player's mixed strategy is discovered by his opponent, it will have no effect on his expected payoff and hence no effect on the expected payoff of his opponent which is the negative of his.

The column player, if he plays conservatively and assumes his mixed strategy will become known to his opponent, will choose his probabilities $X_j \geq 0$ so as to maximize L where Max L and $X \geq 0$ are chosen so that

$$\sum_j a_{ij} X_j \geq L, \quad X_j \geq 0, \quad i = 1, \ldots, m$$

$$\sum_j X_j = 1. \quad \text{(C)}$$

Likewise the row player's-optimal mixed strategy, if he plays conservatively, will choose his probabilities $Y_i \geq 0$ so as to minimize K where Min K and $Y \geq 0$ are chosen so that

$$\sum_i Y_i a_{ij} \leq K, \quad Y_i \geq 0, \quad j = 1, \ldots, n$$

$$\sum_i Y_i = 1. \quad \text{(R)}$$

It is not difficult to prove that (C) and (R) are feasible linear programs and each is the dual of the other. Let $(Y_1^*, \ldots, Y_m^*)$ and $(X_1^*, \ldots, X_m^*)$ be optimal solutions to (R) and (C). Applying the duality theorem, we obtain von Neumann's famous *mini-max theorem* for zero-sum bimatrix games:

$$\max L = \min K = \sum_i \sum_j Y_i^* a_{ij} X_j^*,$$

the expected payoff to the column player.

Decomposition principle

Linear programming can be used in an iterative mode to aid a Central Authority to allocate scarce resources to factories in an optimal way without having to have detailed knowledge about each factory. Specifically the Central Authority proposes prices on the scarce commodities that induce the factories to submit a summary plan for approval of their requirement for scarce resources. The Central Authority blends these proposed plans with earlier ones submitted and uses them to generate new proposed prices. The entire cycle is then iterated. This method, first proposed by Dantzig and Wolfe in 1960, is known as the D–W or *Primal Decomposition Principle*.

The dual form of the Decomposition Principle is known as Benders Decomposition and was proposed by Benders in 1962. We illustrate it here in the context of a two-period planning problem.

$$\text{find } \min Z = c_1 X_1 + c_2 X_2 \text{ subject to :}$$
$$b_1 = A_1 X_1 \quad (X_1, X_2) \geq 0,$$
$$b_2 = -B_1 X_1 + A_2 X_2$$

where A_1, B_1, A_2 are matrices, b_1, b_2, c_1, c_2 vectors and $X_t \geq 0$ are the vectors of activity levels to be determined in periods $t = 1$ and 2.

The first period planners determine a feasible plan (p) that satisfies $b = AX_1^p, X_1^p \geq 0$ (augmented by certain necessary conditions, called 'cuts'), which they submit to the second period planners in the form of a vector $B_1 X_1^p$ which is used by them to solve the second period *sub* problem:

$$A_2 X_2 = b_2 + B_1 X_1^p, \quad X_2 \geq 0$$
$$c_2 X_2 = Z_2(\text{min}).$$

The second period planners respond with a vector of *optimality prices* π_2^k corresponding to the second period if the sub-problem is feasible, or with *infeasibility prices* σ_2^l (obtained at the end of phase 1 of the simplex method) if it is infeasible.

The first period planners then iteratively resolve, their problem augmented by $k' + l'$ additional necessary conditions (cuts) shown below:

Find $c_1 X_1 + \theta = Z(\text{min})$

$A_1 X_1 = b_1, \quad X_1 \geq 0,$

optimality cuts : $-(\pi_2^k B_1)X_1 + \theta \geq \pi_2^k b_2,$

$\quad k = 1, \ldots, k'$

infeasibility cuts : $-(\sigma_2^l B_1)X_1 \geq \sigma_2^l b \quad l = 1, \ldots, l'$

where $\theta = (c_2 X_2)$ is treated as an unknown variable. The interative process stops if $\theta = Z_2$, or $Z_2 - \theta = \Delta > 0$ is small enough.

Note that the additional conditions imposed on Period 1 are expressed in terms of Period-1 variables and θ only. These serve as surrogates for future periods (in this example for only one future period). The decomposition principle allows one to solve a multi-time-period problem one period at time and pass the ending conditions of one period on to initiate the next and to pass back price vectors to earlier periods that are translated into policy constraints called cuts. Applying this same approach to a multi-stage production line, one obtains an iterative process that can be viewed as an intelligent control system with learning.

GEORGE B. DANTZIG

See also **efficient allocation; nonlinear programming; simplex method for solving linear programs.**

Bibliography

Beale, E.M.L. 1954. Linear programming by the method of leading variables. Report of the Conference on Linear Programming, May, arranged by Ferranti Ltd, London.

Benders, J.F. 1962. Partitioning procedures for solving mixed-variable programming problems. *Numerische Mathematik* 4, 238–52.

Charnes, A., Cooper, W.W. and Mellon, B. 1952. Blending aviation gasolines – a study in programming interdependent activities in an integrated oil company. *Econometrica* 20(2), 135–59.

Dantzig, G.B. 1948. Programming in a linear structure. Comptroller, USAF, Washington, DC, February.

Dantzig, G. 1949, 1951. Programming of interdependent activities, II, mathematical model. In *Activity Analysis of Production and Allocation*, ed. T.C. Koopmans. New York: John Wiley, 330–35; also published in *Econometrica* 17 (3 and 4), 1949, 200–211.

Dantzig, G.B. 1963. *Linear Programming and Extensions*. Princeton: Princeton University Press.

Dantzig, G.B. and Wolfe, P. 1960. A decomposition principle for linear programs. *Operations Research* 8(1), 101–11.

Kantorovich, L.V. 1939. *Mathematical Methods in the Organization and Planning of Production*. Publication House of the Leningrad State University. Translated in *Management Science* 6 (1960), 366–422.

Koopmans, T.C., ed. 1951. *Activity Analysis of Production and Allocation*. New York: John Wiley.

Kuhn, H.W. and Tucker, A.W. 1951. [The symposium was held in 1950, but the proceedings volume was published in 1951.] Nonlinear programming. In *Proceedings of the Second Berkeley Symposium on Mathematical Statistics and Probability*, ed. Neyman. Berkeley: University of California Press, 481–92; also in *Econometrica* 19(1) (1951), 50–51 (abstract).

Leontief, W. 1951. *The Structure of the American Economy, 1919–1939*. New York: Oxford University Press.

Vajda, S. 1956. *The Theory of Games and Linear Programming*. New York: John Wiley.

von Neumann, J. 1928. Zur Theorie der Gesellschaftsspiele. *Mathematische Annalen* 100, 295–320. Translated by Sonya Bargmann in *Contributions to the Theory of Games*, vol. 4, ed. A.W. Tucker and R.D. Luce, Annals of Mathematics Study No 40, Princeton, NJ: Princeton University Press, 1959, pp. 13–42.

von Neumann, J. 1937. Über ein ökonomisches Gleichungsytem und eine Verallgemeinerung des Brouwerschen Fixpunktsatzes. *Ergebnisse eines Mathematischen Kolloquiums* No. 8. Translated in *Review of Economic Studies* 13(1) (1945–46), 1–9.

von Neumann, J. 1947. Discussion of a maximization problem. Manuscript, Institute for Advanced Study, Princeton, New Jersey, November.

von Neumann, J. *Collected Works*, Vol. VI, ed. A.H. Taub. Oxford: Pergamon Press. 1963, pp. 89–95.

Wood, M.K. and Dantzig, G.B. 1949, 1951. The programming of interdependent activities: general discussion. In *Activity Analysis of Production and Allocation*, ed. T.C. Koopmans. New York: John Wiley, 1951, 15–81; also in *Econometrica* 17(3 and 4) (1949), 193–9.

linkages

1 Introduction

Economic activities in different industries are linked to each other through aggregate income (horizontal linkages) and input–output relationships (vertical linkages). Could such linkages give rise to vicious circles of underdevelopment or virtuous circles of development when there are increasing returns to scale at the firm level? A standard account of a vicious circle goes as follows. Small-scale production methods in industry A lead to low output and income. This translates into low demand for industry B, which therefore also ends up using small-scale production methods and generating low output and income. The result is low demand for industry A, which justifies the small-scale production methods used in this industry. Low aggregate output and income are seen as the result of a vicious circle because the same economic environment is thought to be compatible with a high-income equilibrium where all industries use technologies that achieve high productivity at large scale. This high-income equilibrium is sustained by a virtuous circle. Large-scale production methods in industry A are profitable because of high income in industry B, and vice versa.

We will show that vicious or virtuous circles based on demand linkages are subject to a simple fallacy if increasing-returns-to-scale technologies differ from pre-industrial technologies only in that they are more productive at large scale. Still, vertical demand linkages will give rise to vicious or virtuous circles if increasing-returns-to-scale technologies use intermediate inputs more intensively than the technologies they replace. And horizontal demand linkages will do so if firms adopting increasing-returns-to-scale technologies must pay a compensating wage differential. Moreover, when there are both vertical demand and cost linkages, underdevelopment traps can be consistent with economic principles even if increasing-returns-to-scale technologies differ from pre-industrial technologies only in that they are more productive at large scale. We first discuss the role of horizontal demand linkages, then that of vertical demand linkages, and finally turn to vertical cost linkages.

Horizontal demand linkages. Imagine an economy populated by households and by firms in different industries. Suppose that each industry sells only to households. Assume also that the amount households spend on each industry is independent of prices (industry demand functions are unit elastic). In this case, demand linkages among industries are said to be *horizontal*. This simply means that economic activity in one industry affects spending on other industries only through the aggregate income of households.

Could horizontal demand linkages lead to economies being trapped into a situation of low income due to a vicious circle of low income and output? Rosenstein-Rodan (1943) and Nurkse (1953) thought so. They imagined a situation where low aggregate income was an obstacle to the adoption of technologies that achieve high productivity at large scale. But large-scale production methods would be profitable if all industries adopted them, because incomes generated in one industry would create demand for other industries.

The elements necessary for underdevelopment traps to be consistent with economic principles have always been subject to debate. Increasing returns to scale appeared to be crucial. But Fleming (1955) made clear that this was not enough. He imagined a situation where, because of low aggregate income, industry A cannot make a profit from adopting the increasing-returns-to-scale technology and that the same is true for industry B. Is it possible that the increasing-returns-to-scale technology becomes profitable if both A and B adopt it? Consider forcing A to adopt. In this case, the loss made in industry A will lower aggregate income. As a result, industry B will now face even lower demand and therefore make an even greater loss if it adopts the increasing-returns-to-scale technology. This means that aggregate income will fall further if we also force industry B to adopt the increasing-returns-to-scale technology. Hence, if the adoption of increasing-returns-to-scale technologies is unprofitable for any single industry, adoption in all industries will not be profitable either. Increasing returns alone can therefore not explain why industrialization does not take place although it would ultimately be profitable.

All accounts of underdevelopment traps did in fact feature (several) additional elements. In particular, Rosenstein-Rodan maintained that firms using large-scale production methods had to pay a compensating wage differential (partly because of the higher costs of living in urban areas, where industrial firms were located). Section 2 follows Murphy, Shleifer and Vishny (1989) in showing that underdevelopment traps may emerge when firms adopting the increasing-returns-to-scale technologies must pay a compensating wage premium.

Vertical demand linkages. Suppose now that industries sell goods to households and each other (to be used as intermediate inputs). Economic activity in one industry can then affect demand in another industry even if aggregate income remains unchanged. As a result, there are said to be *vertical* linkages. For example, consider the situation where industry B buys from A (industry A is *upstream* of B). In this case there is a *vertical demand* linkage as demand for the upstream industry A will depend on the economic activity in downstream industry B. There could also be a *vertical cost* linkage because the cost of production in downstream industry B is partly determined by the cost of goods produced in upstream industry A.

While the effects of horizontal demand linkages on economic development have always been subject to some controversy, there appears to be a consensus among early contributors that vertical demand linkages can lead to underdevelopment traps when technologies are subject to increasing returns to scale (Fleming, 1955; Scitovsky, 1954; Hirschman, 1958). It is simple to show however that this is not the case if increasing-returns-to-scale technologies differ from pre-industrial technologies only in that they are more productive at large scale. To see this, note that with vertical demand linkages the adoption of increasing-returns-to-scale technologies affects aggregate income directly and indirectly: directly through the profits made in the adopting industry, and indirectly through the profits made in supplying (upstream) industries. It would therefore seem that increasing-returns-to-scale technologies could be unprofitable in the adopting industry but still increase aggregate income. But this cannot happen when the increasing-returns-to-scale and the pre-industrial technologies use upstream inputs with the same intensity. In this case, the increase in the value of upstream goods demanded by a firm adopting increasing-returns-to-scale technologies is always a fraction of the (absolute value of the) loss that it makes. Moreover, as profits cannot exceed revenues, the increase in profits in supplying industries is necessarily smaller than the increase in the value of goods they sell. It therefore follows that the increase in profits in supplying industries (the positive indirect effect) can never compensate for the loss made in the industry adopting the increasing-returns-to-scale technology.

The empirical evidence indicates that the intermediate-input intensity of production increases with a country's level of industrialization. Increasing-returns-to-scale technologies may therefore be using intermediate inputs more intensively than the production methods they replace. Section 3 draws on Ciccone's (2002) model of input chains to show that vertical linkages can in this case explain why countries may be trapped into a vicious circle of underdevelopment, and why escaping this trap may be associated with large gains in aggregate income and productivity.

The interplay of vertical cost and demand linkages. The greater demand for intermediate inputs brought about by industrialization (vertical demand linkages) may partly be caused by falling intermediate input prices (vertical cost linkages). Falling intermediate input prices, on the other hand, are possible because of the higher productivity of large-scale production methods. Vertical cost and demand linkages therefore feed on each other (Young, 1928; Okuno-Fujiwara, 1988; Rodriguez-Clare, 1996). For example, Rodriguez-Clare considers a small open economy framework where the entry of new intermediate input varieties lowers the cost of intermediate inputs relative to labour, which leads final-good producers to substitute towards intermediate inputs. When this substitution effect is strong enough, it translates into greater revenues and profits for intermediate-input producers, which may validate intermediate-input producers' decision to start up new varieties in the first place.

Rodriguez-Clare shows that this interplay of vertical demand and cost linkages may lead to two equilibria: a low-income equilibrium where final-good producers use labour-intensive production methods because of the limited range of intermediate inputs available, and a high-income equilibrium where a large variety of intermediate inputs leads final-good producers to use intermediate-input intensive production methods. Okuno-Fujiwara (1988) considers a situation where vertical demand and cost linkages interact because greater demand for intermediate inputs leads to lower prices due to competition among a larger number of Cournot oligopolists. The final section of this entry uses the model with input chains to show that the interplay between vertical demand and cost linkages can result in underdevelopment traps even if increasing-returns-to-scale technologies differ from pre-industrial technologies only in that they are more productive at large scale.

2 A model of horizontal demand linkages

We will now examine the role of horizontal demand linkages for economic development using the model of Murphy, Shleifer, and Vishny (1989) (for a historical and methodological perspective on the horizontal-linkages literature, see Krugman, 1993; 1994). The first step is to describe the model set-up – the household sector, the production sector, and market structure. The second step is to characterize equilibrium prices and equilibrium allocations.

Households. There are L households, each of whom supplies one unit of labour inelastically (labour is the only production factor in this model and serves as the numeraire). Households spend an equal share of their incomes on each of the N goods produced in the economy.

Production. Each of the N goods demanded by households can be produced using two different production methods: a *pre-industrial* method requiring one unit of labour for each unit of output produced, and an *industrial* or increasing-returns-to-scale method, which is more efficient at the margin but subject to a fixed labour requirement (f). Formally, the increasing-returns-to-scale production method requires

$$l_i = f + cq_i \qquad (1)$$

units of labour to produce q_i units of good i, where $f > 0$ and $1 > c > 0$.

Industry wage premium. Working in the industrial sector generates a disutility $v \geq 0$ for households. Hence, relative to pre-industrial firms, industrial firms will have to pay a wage premium $v \geq 0$ as a compensating wage differential.

Market structure. Many firms are assumed to know the pre-industrial method to produce good i. As a result, the pre-industrial sector (also called competitive fringe) will be characterized by perfect competition. By contrast, only a single firm is taken to have the ability to produce each good in the industrial sector. These firms set prices optimally, taking the prices of all other firms as given. The labour market is taken to be perfectly competitive.

What keeps this model simple to analyse is that the equilibrium price of each good is unity whether the good is produced by the pre-industrial or the industrial sector. To see this, note that perfect competition and constant returns to scale in the pre-industrial sector imply that the price of goods produced in this sector must be equal to unity. A higher price would mean strictly positive profits and therefore further entry of pre-industrial producers, while a lower price would mean that no pre-industrial producer could break even. Now consider goods produced in the industrial sector. Clearly, the industrial producer will not set a price above unity, as she would lose the entire market to pre-industrial producers in this case. Moreover, industrial producers do not have an incentive to set a price below unity either, as households spend the same fraction of income on their good irrespectively of the price. Hence, industrial producers find it optimal to use a limit pricing strategy, setting prices exactly equal to the marginal cost of pre-industrial producers. As a result, the price of each of the N goods is equal to unity independently of the production method.

Pre-industrial equilibrium. Under what conditions will there be an equilibrium where all goods are produced with the pre-industrial method? In such an equilibrium, firms just break even, and aggregate income Y in the economy is therefore equal to aggregate labour income L. Because households spread income equally among all N goods, the quantity of good i demanded and supplied is $q_i = L/N$. The remaining question is whether firms in the industrial sector have an incentive to adopt the increasing-returns-to-scale method. The potential profit of such firms is $\pi_i = q_i^m - (f + cq_i^m)(1 + v)$, where q_i^m is the demand faced by the industrial producer of good i. As industrial and pre-industrial producers set the same price, the first industrial producer faces exactly the same demand as the pre-industrial producers she replaces, $q_i^m = L/N$. Her profits are therefore

$$\pi_i = L/N - (f + cL/N)(1 + v). \qquad (2)$$

If $\pi_i < 0$, an industrial producer has no incentive to adopt the increasing-returns-to-scale method, and it will be an equilibrium for all goods to be produced with the pre-industrial method. Hence, (2) implies that there is an equilibrium where all goods are produced with the pre-industrial method if

$$L(1 - c(1 + v)) < F(1 + v), \qquad (3)$$

where $F \equiv fN$.

Industrial equilibrium. What about equilibria where all goods are produced using the industrial method? We already know that prices of all goods will be equal to

unity in this equilibrium also. Moreover, households will keep spending the same share of income on all goods. Hence, all industries will employ the same amount of labour, L/N, in equilibrium. (1) therefore implies that the value of production in each industry is $(L/N - f)/c$. Summing across the N industries in the economy yields a value for gross domestic product, and hence aggregate household income, of $Y = (L - F)/c$ (recall that $F \equiv fN$).

Do firms make the profit necessary to sustain the industrial production method when all production takes place in the industrial sector? Profits of firms in the industrial sector are $\pi_i = q_i^m - (f + cq_i^m)(1 + v) \geq 0$, where q_i^m is the demand faced by the industrial producer of good i, $q_i^m = Y/N = (L - F)/cN$. Hence, there will be an equilibrium where firms using the increasing-returns-to-scale method make a profit if

$$L(1 - c(1 + v)) \geq F. \qquad (4)$$

Efficient allocation. When is the adoption of increasing-returns-to-scale technologies efficient? The aggregate value of production is $Y = (L - F)/c$ when industrial production methods are used and $Y = L$ with pre-industrial methods. The amount of goods necessary to pay the compensating wage differential when all workers are employed in the industrial sector is vL. Hence aggregate welfare will be higher with industrial production methods if and only if $(L - F)/c - vL \geq L$, or

$$L(1 - c(1 + v)) \geq F. \qquad (5)$$

Note that (4) and (5) coincide. Hence, an industrial equilibrium exists if and only if it is efficient.

Multiple equilibria and underdevelopment traps. Only one of the two inequalities in (3) and (4) can hold if there is no industry wage premium ($v = 0$). Hence, the equilibrium is unique in this case and, as a result, there cannot be development traps. Moreover, because an industrial equilibrium exists if and only if it is efficient, economies in a pre-industrial equilibrium actually do the best they can given the economic environment.

But when there is an industry wage premium ($v > 0$) there may be multiple equilibria as the inequalities in (3) and (4) can both be satisfied. When this is the case, economies may be stuck in a pre-industrial equilibrium, although the same economic environment would be compatible with an (efficient) industrial equilibrium. To understand why, suppose the economy is in a pre-industrial equilibrium when we force an industry to adopt the increasing-returns-to-scale technology. If (3) holds, then the adopting firm will make a loss. Still, its contribution to aggregate income is strictly positive. To see this, note that demand for this industry is L/N, and that this is also the amount of labour required to produce the amount of goods demanded using the pre-industrial production methods. Production with the increasing-returns-to-scale technology requires $cL/N + f$ units of labour, which is strictly smaller than L/N if (4) holds. Hence, the adoption of the increasing-returns-to-scale technology saves labour in the adopting industry, and therefore increases aggregate output and income. This increases demand faced by other industries and therefore raises the profitability of further adoption of the increasing-returns-to-scale technology. Eventually, industrialization raises aggregate income enough for increasing-returns-to-scale industries to break even. Hence, the industrial equilibrium can be seen as the result of a virtuous circle. The adoption of increasing-returns-to-scale technologies raises aggregate income and therefore the profitability of adopting increasing-returns-to-scale technologies. At the same time, the economic environment also allows for a development trap where low aggregate income is both the cause and the consequence of the failure to adopt increasing-returns-to-scale technologies.

3 Vertical demand linkages in an input chain model

The economic activity of different industries is linked to each other because the output of some industries is used as input in other industries. Can such vertical linkages give rise to vicious circles of underdevelopment or virtuous circles of development when there are increasing returns at the firm level? We will show that – just as for horizontal linkages – this cannot happen if increasing-returns-to-scale technologies differ from pre-industrial technologies only in that they are more productive at large scale.

Chenery, Robinson and Syrquin's (1986) comparative study of industrialization shows, however, that the industrialization of countries has typically been accompanied by an increase in the intermediate-input intensity of production. This suggests that industrial technologies may use intermediate inputs more intensively than the technologies they replace. We will therefore start by analysing a model of development where increasing-returns-to-scale technologies use intermediate inputs more intensively than pre-industrial technologies.

It will be useful to analyze the consequences of vertical linkages for industrialization in a framework that is as close as possible to the model of horizontal linkages of Murphy, Shleifer and Vishny. In particular, the aggregate amount of labour supplied by households continues to be L and households spend an equal share of their incomes on each of the N goods produced in the economy. On the production side, we continue to assume that each good can be produced using two different production methods, namely, a pre-industrial method and an industrial (increasing-returns-to-scale) method. The pre-industrial method requires one unit of labour for each unit of output. The increasing-returns-to-scale method will turn out to be cheaper at the margin but subject to a fixed labour requirement f. Many firms know the pre-industrial method, but for each good there is only a single firm with the ability to produce in the industrial sector.

Input chains and industrial production. The key difference with the horizontal linkages model is that now the increasing-returns-to-scale method is taken to be more intermediate-input intensive than the pre-industrial method. One way to model the intermediate-input structure of the economy is to think of goods being produced in S different locations along a river. Each location produces H different goods (the total number of goods is $N \equiv HS$). Goods at location 1 are produced using labour only. Goods at any location $s > 1$, on the other hand, are produced using all goods at location $s - 1$. This implies that all goods at locations $s < S$ may face intermediate-input demand from downstream industries in addition to consumption-goods demand from households (the exception are the H goods furthest downstream, at location S, which face consumption-goods demand only). In particular, we assume that, after having incurred the overhead labour cost, one unit of any good j located at $s > 1$ can be produced with c units of an intermediate-input composite $z_{j,s}$ that combines all H goods produced at location $s - 1$,

$$z_{j,s} = \prod_{i=1}^{H} \left(H q_{i,s-1} \right)^{1/H}, \tag{6}$$

where $q_{i,s-1}$ is the input of good i at location $s - 1$. This formulation implies that industrial firms spend the same amount on all upstream inputs. As a result, the marginal cost of the intermediate-input composite necessary for industrial production at location $s > 1$ is simply a geometrically weighted average of prices $p_{i,s-1}$ of the H upstream goods,

$$MC_s = \prod_{i=1}^{H} p_{i,s-1}^{\frac{1}{H}}. \tag{7}$$

Industrial production for goods at location $s = 1$ requires f units of overhead labour and c units of labour for each unit of output. (The assumption that the industrial overhead requires labour only while production at the margin requires intermediate inputs only simplifies the analysis considerably. Ciccone (2002) analyses the case where production of the overhead and at the margin use both labour and intermediate inputs.)

Just as in the horizontal linkages model, industrial firms find it optimal to use a limit pricing strategy for consumption goods vis-à-vis the competitive fringe. Their intermediate-input pricing strategy is potentially more complicated but also simplifies to a limit pricing strategy vis-à-vis the competitive fringe when H is sufficiently large.

Pre-industrial equilibrium. When will there be an equilibrium where all goods are produced with the pre-industrial method? It turns out that if H is sufficiently large the condition is

$$L(1 - c) < F, \tag{8}$$

which coincides with the condition for a pre-industrial equilibrium in the Murphy, Shleifer, and Vishny model of horizontal linkages. To see this, suppose that all goods are produced with the pre-industrial technology and their price is unity. When (8) holds, any single firm adopting the increasing-returns-to-scale method to produce consumption goods will make a loss. Moreover, when H is sufficiently large, (7) also implies that single industrial firms are unable to generate intermediate-input demand for their good even if they lower their price to the marginal cost of production. To see this, suppose that one industrial firm at location $S - 1$ is considering selling its good at marginal cost to firms at location S in order to generate intermediate-input demand. In this case, one of the H inputs of potential industrial firms at S would become available at price c and (7) implies that the marginal cost of production would therefore fall from c to $c^{(1+H)/H}$ (recall that the remaining $H - 1$ inputs are available at price of unity). Goods at S face demand L/N, which comes exclusively from households as there are no upstream industries. Hence, profits of the potential industrial firm at S producing at marginal cost $c^{(1+H)/H}$ would be $(1 - c^{(1+H)/H})L/N - f$, which is strictly negative if (8) holds and H is large enough. Potential industrial firms at location S would therefore find it unprofitable to start production even after the price cut, which implies that potential industrial firms at location $S - 1$ must break even on consumption-goods demand only. Applying the same argument sequentially to potential industrial firms in locations $S - 2$, $S - 3$, ..., 1 yields that pre-industrial production of all goods is an equilibrium when (7) holds and H is sufficiently large.

Industrial equilibrium. To determine the conditions for the existence of an industrial equilibrium, it is necessary to determine aggregate income when all goods at location σ and upstream of location σ are produced with the increasing-returns-to-scale technology. This turns out to be straightforward. If aggregate income is Y, the quantity of each good demanded by households is Y/N. The intermediate-input structure implies that industrial production of Y/N units of each of the H goods at location σ requires cY/N units of each of the H goods at location $\sigma - 1$. Hence, as Y/N units of good $\sigma - 1$ are demanded by households, production of each good at $\sigma - 1$ must be $Y/N + cY/N$. Production of this quantity of goods at $\sigma - 1$ requires $c(Y/N + cY/N)$ units of each good at $\sigma - 2$. Adding the Y/N units of goods at $\sigma - 2$ demanded by households, yields that production at $\sigma - 2$ must be $Y/N + cY/N + c^2 Y/N$. Continuing all the way upstream yields that the total production of each of the H goods at

location 1 must be

$$q_1 = Y/N + cY/N + c^2 Y/N + \dots$$
$$+ c^{\sigma - 1} Y/N = \frac{1 - c^\sigma}{1 - c} Y/N. \tag{9}$$

To turn to the labour market, f units of labour must be used as overhead in the production of each good produced with the industrial technology. Moreover, Y/N units of labour are required for the production of each good produced with the pre-industrial technology. Hence, the amount of labour available for production at the margin of the H goods at $s = 1$ is $L - \sigma H f - (N - \sigma H)Y/N$. Labour market clearing requires $cHq_1 = L - \sigma H f - (N - \sigma H)Y/N$. Substituting (9) yields aggregate income in an economy where the σ industries furthest upstream have industrialized:

$$Y(\sigma) = \frac{L - F(\sigma H/N)}{c\theta[\sigma](\sigma H/N) + (1 - (\sigma H/N))}$$
$$= \frac{L - F(\sigma H/N)}{1 - (\sigma H/N)(1 - c\theta[\sigma])}, \tag{10}$$

where

$$\theta[\sigma] \equiv \frac{1 - c^\sigma}{(1 - c)\sigma}.$$

$c\theta[\sigma]$ has a simple interpretation. It is the amount of labour required to produce one additional unit of goods located at σ if all industries upstream of (including) σ have adopted the industrial technology. Note that the amount of labour required to produce one additional unit of goods at location σ falls the longer the industrial input chain ($\theta[\sigma]$ is strictly decreasing in σ).

The intermediate-input structure implies that the demand for goods is greater the further upstream they are located. Hence, profits from adopting the increasing-returns-to-scale technology fall the further downstream industries are located. An equilibrium where all industrial firms make a profit will therefore exist if goods produced furthest downstream (at location S) can be produced using the increasing-returns-to-scale technology without a loss. Because firms furthest downstream sell to households only, their sales are equal to aggregate income divided by the number of goods, $Y[S]/N$ (recall that all firms set prices optimally at unity). As a result, their profits are positive if and only if $\pi_S = (1 - c)(Y[S]/N) - f \geq 0$ or, to make use of (10),

$$(1 - c)L \geq (c\theta[S] + (1 - c))F. \tag{11}$$

Multiple equilibria and underdevelopment traps. Comparison of (8) and (11) yields that, with input chains ($S > 1$), it is possible for the pre-industrial equilibrium and the industrial equilibrium to exist side by side.

(When $S = 1$ then $\theta = 1$ and the model is that of Murphy, Shleifer, and Vishny without an industry wage premium.) This is because the adoption of increasing-returns-to-scale technologies now has a direct and indirect effect on income. The direct effect is given by the profit or loss in the adopting industry. The indirect effect is equal to the profits generated upstream of the adopting industry. When the indirect profits generated by the increased intermediate-input demand more than offset direct losses of industrial technologies, then industrialization increases aggregate income. As a result, further industrialization becomes more profitable. When (7) and (10) hold simultaneously, this effect is strong enough to ensure that all industrial firms make a profit once all goods are produced with increasing-returns-to-scale technologies.

The pre-industrial and industrial equilibrium can exist side by side even if aggregate income is much greater in the industrial equilibrium. Note that aggregate income in the industrial equilibrium is $Y[S] = (L - F)/c\theta[S]$, see (10). As intermediate-input chains become longer, $\theta[S]$ in (10) tends to zero, and aggregate income in the industrial equilibrium increases. Aggregate income in the pre-industrial equilibrium, on the other hand, is independent of S as production does not rely on intermediate inputs. Moreover, the range of parameter values for which the industrial equilibrium exists increases. Hence, long input chains imply that equilibrium multiplicity is more likely and also that the aggregate income difference between industrial and pre-industrial equilibria may be very large.

Vertical linkages and equilibrium uniqueness. To see that the equilibrium is unique when increasing-returns-to-scale technologies use intermediate inputs as intensively as pre-industrial technologies, note that costs of production plus profit must add up to the value of firms' sales, $COST + \pi = q$. Suppose that intermediate inputs are a share α of costs of production for both the pre-industrial and the industrial production method. In this case, the demand for goods produced at $s - 1$ is equal to $\alpha COST_s = \alpha(q_s - \pi_s)$. Now suppose that all goods upstream of σ are produced with the increasing-returns-to-scale technology. Is it possible that aggregate income increases with the adoption of the increasing-returns-to-scale technology at σ even if the adopting firm makes a loss? A switch to industrial production at σ does not affect the value of goods produced at this location (q_σ is unchanged). Hence, the adoption of the increasing-returns-to-scale technology at σ increases demand for each good produced at $\sigma - 1$ by $-\alpha\pi_\sigma/H$. Loss-making industrialization at σ therefore leads to greater demand at $\sigma - 1$. But the profits generated by this input demand can never be greater than the initial loss π_σ. To see this, notice that total profits at location $\sigma - 1$ increase by $-(1 - c)\alpha\pi_\sigma$. Total profits at $\sigma - 2$ increase by $-(1 - c)\alpha^2 c\pi_\sigma$, where $-\alpha^2 c\pi_\sigma/H$ is the increase in demand for each good produced at $\sigma - 2$. The general formula is that total profits at location $\sigma - i$ increase

by $-(1 - c)\alpha^i c^{i-1}\pi_\sigma$. Summing profits across all locations yields $-(1 - c)\pi_\sigma\alpha[1 + \alpha c + (\alpha c)^2 + \ldots + (\alpha c)^{\sigma-1}]$, which is smaller than $-(1 - c)\pi_\sigma\alpha[1 + \alpha c + (\alpha c)^2 + \ldots] = -\pi_\sigma(\alpha - \alpha c)/(1 - \alpha c)$. Hence, $\alpha \leq 1$ implies that the sum of profits generated upstream of s by loss-making industrialization at s is always smaller than the initial loss (π_σ). Loss-making industrialization necessarily lowers aggregate income. The aggregate demand externality necessary for multiple equilibria is therefore absent when increasing-returns-to-scale technologies are no more intermediate-input intensive than pre-industrial technologies.

4 Vertical demand and cost linkages with input chains

So far firms adopting increasing returns to scale technologies did not have an incentive to cut prices. This eliminated virtuous circles of development where lower intermediate-input prices (vertical cost linkages) and greater intermediate-input demand (vertical demand linkages) feed on each other. A simple way to capture the interplay between vertical demand and cost linkages is to suppose that firms in the competitive fringe can produce one unit of goods at location $s > 1$ with $1 + \varepsilon > 1$ units of the intermediate-input composite in (6) or one unit of labour. That is, firms have access to two modes of production, a labour-intensive mode and an intermediate-input intensive mode. The exception continues to be goods at location 1, for which there is a labour-intensive mode of production only. Industrial firms at locations $s > 1$ also have access to a labour-intensive and an intermediate-input intensive mode of production, but are more efficient than pre-industrial firms at the margin. Once they have incurred the overhead labour requirement f, industrial firms can produce one unit of output with $c(1 + \varepsilon) < 1$ of the intermediate-input composite in (6) or $c < 1$ units of labour. Industrial firms producing goods at location 1 have access to the labour-intensive mode of production only. The assumption that the overhead is produced using labour only continues to simplify the analysis considerably. A new by-product of this assumption is that industrial firms now actually use intermediate inputs less intensively than pre-industrial firms at the same factor prices – the opposite of what we assumed in the previous section.

Pre-industrial equilibrium with labour-intensive production. Can there be an equilibrium where all goods are produced with the pre-industrial technology using labour only? The marginal cost of production with the pre-industrial technology in the labour-intensive mode is unity. Hence, the price of all goods would be equal to unity. To see that these prices make it optimal to use the labour-intensive mode of production, note that they imply that the marginal cost of intermediate-input composites in (7) is unity. The marginal cost of production using the intermediate-input intensive mode compared with the labour-intensive mode is therefore $1 + \varepsilon > 1$ (in the pre-industrial as well as the industrial sector). Hence, all firms will find it optimal to use the labour-intensive mode of production.

In a pre-industrial equilibrium, the adoption of the increasing-returns-to-scale technology by a single firm must lead to losses. If industrial firms can count on consumption-goods demand only, this will be the case if $L(1 - c) < F$. But an industrial firm may be able to generate additional demand by getting industries just downstream to switch to an intermediate-input intensive mode of production. While this can happen in principle, it will not happen if H is sufficiently large. To see this, consider the case where a single industrial firm supplies its good to downstream industries at marginal cost. In this case, (7) yields that the marginal cost of the intermediate input-intensive mode of production relative to the labour-intensive mode becomes $c^{1/H}(1 + \varepsilon)$, which will be greater than unity when H is sufficiently large (recall that $1 + \varepsilon > 1$). Hence, a single industrial firm cannot generate downstream intermediate-input demand even if it reduces its price to marginal cost. For H sufficiently large, a pre-industrial labour-intensive equilibrium will therefore exist if $L(1 - c) < F$.

Industrial equilibrium with intermediate-input intensive production. When is there an industrial equilibrium where all firms use the intermediate-input intensive mode of production? To simplify the analysis, suppose that industrial firms can price discriminate between households and industrial users of their goods. As before, industrial firms will find it optimal to follow a limit pricing strategy when it comes to sales to households. Industrial firms will therefore price consumption goods at unity. When it comes to intermediate-input sales to downstream industries, industrial firms must also take into account that users will switch to the labour-intensive mode of production if the cost of the intermediate-input composite is greater than $1/(1 + \varepsilon)$. Hence, each industrial firm will find it optimal to set a limit price of $1/(1 + \varepsilon)$ for intermediate inputs if other industrial intermediate-input suppliers do the same.

Aggregate income in the industrial equilibrium where all firms use the intermediate-input intensive mode of production can be determined following the argument that led to (10). The only difference is that an additional unit of all goods at location $s > 1$ now translates into a demand of $c(1 + \varepsilon)$ units of each good at location $s - 1$. Aggregate income when all goods are produced with the industrial technology in the intermediate-input intensive mode is therefore $Y[S] = (L - F)/c\hat{\theta}[S]$ where

$$\hat{\theta}[S] \equiv \frac{1 - (c(1 + \varepsilon))^S}{(1 - c(1 + \varepsilon))S}. \qquad (12)$$

An industrial equilibrium exists if the firm furthest downstream can break even given the demand for consumption goods, $\pi_S = (1 - c(1 + \varepsilon))(Y[S]/N) - f \geq 0$ or, to make

use of the expression for aggregate income just above,
$$(1 - c(1 + \varepsilon))L \geq \Big(c\hat{\theta}[S] + (1 - c(1 + \varepsilon)) \Big) F.$$

Multiple equilibria with vertical demand and cost linkages. There will be multiple equilibria if both $L(1 - c) < F$ and $(1 - c(1 + \varepsilon))L \geq \Big(c\hat{\theta}[S] + (1 - c(1 + \varepsilon)) \Big) F$. This implies that the pre-industrial equilibrium with labour-intensive production and the industrial equilibrium with intermediate-input intensive production may exist side by side if and only if there are input chains ($\hat{\theta}[S] < 1$). The virtuous circle sustaining industrial equilibria now consists of an interplay between vertical demand and cost linkages. The increase in the intermediate-input intensity of production necessary for increasing-returns-to-scale technologies to be profitable (vertical demand linkages) comes about because the adoption of increasing-returns-to-scale technologies translates into falling intermediate-input prices (vertical cost linkages). Note that, for this virtuous circle to be operative, the elasticity of substitution between intermediate inputs and labour in industrial production must be greater than unity (our model assumed that this elasticity is infinity for simplicity). In a pre-industrial equilibrium, on the other hand, pre-industrial technologies are both the cause and the consequence of labour-intensive modes of production.

5 Conclusion

Neither horizontal nor vertical demand linkages across industries lead to underdevelopment traps if increasing-returns-to-scale technologies differ from pre-industrial technologies only in that they are more productive at large scale. Nevertheless, theories of underdevelopment based on vicious circles of low demand and low productivity are consistent with economic principles. For example, in the case of vertical demand linkages, there can be development traps if increasing-returns-to-scale technologies use intermediate inputs more intensively than the technologies they replace. More generally, multiple equilibria in our models exist under assumptions that do not appear to be in contradiction by empirical evidence. The exception is that all our model economies were taken to be closed to international trade, but we could have assumed instead that only some goods are non-tradable or that all goods are tradable at some cost (for example, Okuno-Fujiwara, 1988; Rodriguez-Clare, 1996; Krugman and Venables, 1995). Still, it remains to be seen what part of international income differences can be attributed to development traps (for steps in this direction, see Fafchamps and Helms, 1996; Graham and Temple, 2006).

ANTONIO CICCONE

See also **balanced growth; development economics; external economies; externalities; multiple equilibria in macroeconomics; new economic geography; returns to scale; supermodularity and supermodular games.**

Bibliography

Chenery, H., Robinson, S. and Syrquin, M. 1986. *Industrialization and Growth: A Comparative Study.* New York: Oxford University Press.

Ciccone, A. 2002. Input chains and industrialization. *Review of Economic Studies* 69, 565–87.

Fafchamps, M. and Helms, B. 1996. Local demand, investment multipliers, and industrialization: theory and application to the Guatemalan highlands. *Journal of Development Economics* 49, 61–92.

Fleming, M. 1955. External economies and the doctrine of balanced growth. *Economic Journal* 65, 241–56.

Graham, B.S. and Temple, J.R.W. 2006. Rich nations, poor nations: how much can multiple equilibria explain? *Journal of Economic Growth* 11, 5–41.

Hirschman, A. 1958. *The Strategy of Economic Development.* New Haven, CT: Yale University Press.

Krugman, P. 1993. Toward a counter-counterrevolution in development theory. In *Proceedings of the World Bank Annual Conference on Development Economics*, ed. L.H. Summers and S. Shah. Washington, DC: World Bank.

Krugman, P. 1994. The fall and rise of development economics. In *Rethinking the Development Experience: Essays Provoked by the Work of Albert O. Hirschman*, ed. L. Rodwin and D.A. Schon. Washington, DC: Brookings Institution.

Krugman, P. and Venables, A.J. 1995. Globalization and the inequality of nations. *Quarterly Journal of Economics* 110, 857–80.

Murphy, K.M., Shleifer, A. and Vishny, R.W. 1989. Industrialization and the big push. *Journal of Political Economy* 97, 1003–26.

Nurkse, R. 1953. *Problems of Capital Formation in Underdeveloped Countries.* New York: Oxford University Press.

Okuno-Fujiwara, M. 1988. Interdependence of industries, coordination failure and strategic promotion of an industry. *Journal of International Economics* 25, 25–43.

Rodriguez-Clare, A. 1996. The division of labor and economic development. *Journal of Development Economics* 49, 3–32.

Rosenstein-Rodan, P. 1943. Problems of industrialization of Eastern and South-Eastern Europe. *Economic Journal* 53, 202–11.

Scitovsky, T. 1954. Two concepts of external economies. *Journal of Political Economy* 62, 143–51.

Young, A.A. 1928. Increasing returns and economic progress. *Economic Journal* 38, 527–42.

Lintner, John Virgil (1916–1983)

Lintner was born in Lone Elm, Kansas. He received the Ph.D. at Harvard University in 1946, becoming a member of the faculty a year earlier. He remained a member of the Harvard faculty throughout his career and was designated the George Gund Professor of Economics and Business Administration in 1964, with a joint appointment in the Business School and the Faculty of Arts and Sciences in Economics.

The contributions by John Lintner that are most frequently cited in the economic literature involve asset pricing, dividend policy, mergers, and capital formation under inflation. Along with others, Lintner was one of the independent creators of the modern theory of asset pricing. This model is usually referred to as the capital asset pricing model (CAPM) which holds that the equilibrium rates of return on all risky assets are a function of their covariance with the returns on the market portfolio.

In addition to his major contribution to the creation of the modern theory of financial markets, Lintner wrote the seminal articles on dividend policy which provided the foundations for further research and remain the basic references on the subject.

Mergers represented the third area of important contributions. An early study focused on the impact of taxes on mergers (Butters, Lintner and Cary, 1951). One important impact of taxes documented was the sale of companies to convert an earnings stream that would otherwise be subject to personal income tax rates to capital gains which would be taxed at lower rates. His later studies of mergers developed an analysis of the historical influences on mergers during the major merger movements of the United States. In addition, a theoretical rationale for pure conglomerate mergers was also developed (1971).

Many aspects of Lintner's interest in capital formation under inflation were brought together in his Presidential Address to the American Finance Association in December 1974 (1975). His subsequent work sought to develop further the major themes which he had set forth in his Presidential Address.

J. FRED WESTON

Selected works

1951. (With J.K. Butters and W.L. Cary.) *Effects of Taxation on Corporate Mergers.* Boston: Harvard Business School.

1956. Distribution of incomes of corporations among dividends, retained earnings and taxes. *American Economic Review* 46(May), 97–113.

1964. Optimal dividends and corporate growth under uncertainty. *Quarterly Journal of Economics* 78(February), 49–95.

1965. The valuation of risk assets and the selection of risky investments in stock portfolios and capital budgets. *Review of Economics and Statistics* 47(February), 13–37.

1965. Security prices, risk, and maximal gains from diversification. *Journal of Finance* 20, 587–615.

1969. The aggregation of investors' diverse judgments and preferences in purely competitive security markets. *Journal of Financial and Quantitative Analysis* 4, 347–400.

1971. Expectations, mergers, and equilibrium in purely competitive securities markets. *American Economic Review* 61(2), 101–11.

1975. Presidential address. American Finance Association Annual Meeting, San Francisco, California, 29 December 1974. *Journal of Finance* 30, 259–80.

liquidity constraints

A benchmark model

To explain what liquidity constraints are, and their implications for economic activity, it is useful to start with a simple benchmark model. Suppose a world with a continuum of households having unit mass. Time is indexed by $t = 0, 1, 2, \ldots$, and household i has preferences given by

$$E_0 \sum_{t=0}^{\infty} \beta^t u(c_{it}),$$

where E_0 is the expectation operator conditional on period 0 information, $0 < \beta < 1$, c_{it} is consumption, and $u(\cdot)$ is twice continuously differentiable, strictly concave, and has the property that $u'(0) = \infty$. Each household receives a random endowment of the perishable consumption good at the beginning of each period. That is, household i receives an endowment y_{it} in period t where y_{it} is assumed to be independent and identically distributed across households and over time. Assume that $\underline{y} \leq y_{it} \leq \bar{y}$, where $0 < \underline{y} < \bar{y}$. The law of large numbers then implies that the aggregate endowment is a constant, which we will denote by y. Therefore, this is an economy with no aggregate risk, but each household faces idiosyncratic risk associated with its endowment shocks.

Now, suppose that this economy has a complete set of markets. One market structure that gives completeness is contingent claims markets that open at $t = 0$ before households receive their period 0 endowments. All households trade on these markets, and a particular contingent claims market involves trade in claims to the consumption good deliverable at a particular date only under a particular realization for the path of endowment shocks for all households up to that date. Given this complete set of markets, what will be the equilibrium allocation of consumption across households at each date? All households are identical at the first date, and the result will be that, in equilibrium, $c_{it} = y$ for all i and t. The complete set of contingent claims markets provides perfect insurance for households. That is, they are able to share their risk efficiently, in that each household can shed the idiosyncratic risk associated with its endowment shocks. Indeed, the resulting equilibrium allocation of consumption is Pareto optimal.

Models with complete markets have proved to be very useful in economics, for example in the theory of asset pricing and in business cycle modelling. However, there are many applications where it is necessary that we depart from the complete markets paradigm, and the liquidity constraints literature is one such set of applications. To think about liquidity constraints we need to seriously address the frictions that will cause markets to work differently than in the complete markets case, and in some instances will cause some markets to shut down altogether. In the following sections we will explore some key departures from our benchmark model that illustrate the role of liquidity constraints.

Incomplete markets: a Bewley model

One approach to studying market incompleteness is to simply eliminate markets in the model under consideration, without asking questions about the underlying frictions which would cause incomplete markets. Bewley (1977) was a pioneer in this area, and Aiyagari (1994) provides a particularly clear treatment of the implications of incomplete markets.

As an example of the Bewley approach, suppose in our benchmark model that there is only one asset market, a market for non-contingent bonds on which trading occurs each period. Households can borrow and lend on this bond market. Assume that each bond is a one-period financial instrument. In period t, a bond sells for one unit of consumption goods, and is a promise to pay $1 + r_{t+1}$ units of consumption goods in period $t + 1$. Since there is no aggregate risk, there will exist a steady state competitive equilibrium where $r_{t+1} = r$, a constant, for all t.

We now need to write down the series of constraints that a household faces in the steady state equilibrium. The first of these is the sequence of budget constraints

$$c_{it} + b_{i,t+1} = y_{it} + (1 + r)b_{i,t},$$

for $t = 0, 1, 2, \ldots$, where b_{it} is the quantity of bonds acquired by household i in period t, and $b_{i0} = 0$ for all i. Typically in models of this type, there is also a borrowing constraint added, which could take the form

$$b_{it} \geq \underline{b}. \tag{1}$$

Constraint (1) serves a technical purpose, in that it prevents a household from borrowing an infinite amount so as to finance infinite consumption. Further, the constraint will affect the household's ability to smooth consumption over time in the face of fluctuating income. Constraint (1) is a kind of liquidity constraint, as it potentially prevents the household from borrowing against its lifetime wealth.

A competitive equilibrium will have the property that the bond market clears, that is the net stock of bonds in the population is zero in each period. This model is a special case of Aiyagari (1994), and so his results apply here. With Aiyagari's regularity conditions on $u(\cdot)$, a steady state competitive equilibrium will have the property that $r < \frac{1}{\beta} - 1$, that is, the equilibrium real interest rate is less than the rate of time preference. This reflects a precautionary savings motive, in that households wish to hold bonds to self-insure against having a string of bad luck, which in this case would be a string of low endowment shocks. Over time, a household will tend to increase its stock of bonds when its endowment is large, and to decrease the stock of bonds when its endowment is small. What we will observe in equilibrium is some distribution of bonds and consumption across the population of households. Households who have had good luck will tend to have a larger stock of bonds and higher consumption than those households who have had bad luck. The competitive equilibrium is therefore not in general Pareto optimal.

Another related application, from Bewley (1980), is to suppose that the single asset that is traded is money. For example, suppose that there is a fixed stock of money, M, for all t. Let P_t denote the price level in period t, and consider the steady state equilibrium where $P_t = P$, a constant, for all t. For the household, we can just reinterpret its constraints, in that $b_{i,t+1}$ is the real quantity of money carried over by the household into period $t + 1$, and $\underline{b} = 0$ as the household's money balances cannot fall below zero. An individual household in this set-up is even more severely liquidity-constrained than was the household in the Bewley model with borrowing and lending above. This is because the household cannot borrow at all, and cannot hold interest-bearing assets. Note that, in this monetary model, a household need only use money to buy consumption goods if it wishes to consume more than its endowment. Money is essentially held for insurance purposes, so as to smooth consumption over time.

Cash-in-advance

The idea for the basic cash-in-advance model seems to come from Clower (1967), but the important initial modelling work was done mainly by Robert Lucas, with a key contribution being Lucas (1980). Most cash-in-advance applications begin with the view that the basic frictions that might give rise to cash-in-advance constrained households need not be modelled, and that it is useful to proceed from the premise that money is necessary to purchase some goods and services.

Here, suppose in our basic model that there are no assets other than money, and that the only exchanges are trades of money for goods. Assume that a household's purchases of goods during the current period must be financed with money carried over from the previous period, and also suppose that the household cannot consume its own endowment. Let m_{it} denote the nominal money balances that household i has at the beginning of period t, and let P_t denote the price level. Then, the

household's budget constraint in period t is

$$P_t c_{it} + m_{i,t+1} = P_t y_{it} + m_{it}. \qquad (2)$$

The cash-in-advance constraint for the household is

$$P_t c_{it} \leq m_{it}. \qquad (3)$$

Thus, constraint (3) is another type of liquidity constraint. In this case, the interpretation is that some class of assets, which we refer to here as money, is necessary to carry out goods market spot exchanges.

Now, suppose that there is a fixed nominal stock of money M. Also, suppose that in equilibrium constraint (3) binds for each household i. Then, since in equilibrium the entire stock of money is held by households at the beginning of period and is spent to purchase the aggregate endowment, y, the equilibrium price level is

$$P_t = \frac{M}{y}$$

for all t. Then, given (2) and (3) with equality, we have

$$m_{i,t+1} = M \frac{y_{it}}{y},$$

which then implies, from (3) with equality, that

$$c_{it} = y_{i,t-1}.$$

Therefore, in this environment, households have essentially no ability to smooth consumption relative to income, as a result of this extreme type of liquidity constraint. The distribution of consumption across households in period t is determined by the distribution of income across households in the previous period.

Economists who are serious about monetary theory often treat cash-in-advance models with some disdain (see, for example, Wallace, 1996). As they see it, the problem is not that one cannot write down a model that is explicit about frictions and gives rise to cash-in-advance as an endogenous phenomenon. For example, suppose that we modify our benchmark model to permit an absence-of-double-coincidence friction of the type considered by early monetary theorists such as Jevons (1875). That is, assume that households are of N types, with measure $\frac{1}{N}$ households of each type, where type is indexed by $j = 1, 2, \ldots, N$. Type j households are endowed with good j, and consume the good which is endowed to type $j + 1$, modulo N. Further, suppose that a household has two members, a shopper that takes money from the household to buy goods in another market each period, and a seller who stays at home to sell the household's endowment. There are N distinct markets, and in a given period a shopper from a household of type j goes to market $j + 1$, modulo N, with money to buy goods, while a the seller stays behind and sells goods in market j. Note that this is still not enough to give us cash-in-advance, as we need to close off the possibility of credit arrangements among households which could take place through centralized communication, as is made clear in Kocherlakota (1998). Credit can be shut down by assuming that no communication is possible across markets, with buyers and sellers in a given market having no information about each other, beside the fact that sellers have identifiable goods and buyers have identifiable money balances. With competitive pricing in each of the N markets, we get exactly the set-up outlined above in this section, with a cash-in-advance constraint for each household. Given symmetry, there is an equilibrium where prices are the same in every market, and so the equilibrium allocation of consumption is identical to what was specified above.

The key problem that must be addressed in cash-in-advance environments involves what happens when there are other assets than money. For example, if we permit borrowing and lending by households, why is it that goods cannot be purchased with credit? How can money be dominated in rate of return by other assets? Why is it that government bonds, for example, are not used in transactions rather than money? Many cash-in-advance applications leave these questions unanswered.

Random matching

A useful way to extend our benchmark model at this point is to expand on the explicit cash-in-advance environment above to relate it more directly to the literature on monetary search and matching. The seminal work in this literature is by Jones (1976) and Kiyotaki and Wright (1989).

Suppose as above that there is a double coincidence problem, but here assume that there is one agent in a household, and that each household is randomly matched with one other household each period. Households produce different goods, and no household can consume its own endowment. Now, for a given household, assume that the probability is α that it is matched with another household whose goods it consumes, with the other household not wanting its goods (a single coincidence meeting). As well, assume that there is a probability γ that a household is matched with another household and there is a double coincidence of wants – each household consumes the other's goods. Suppose that $\alpha > 0$, $\gamma > 0$, and $2\alpha + \gamma < 1$. Suppose that a household in a bilateral match has no information about the other household, except that it can observe its quantity of money balances and its endowment. Thus, exchange can only involve bilateral exchanges of goods and money.

Now, suppose that household i and household k are matched. There is probability α that household i is a seller and k is a buyer. In this case, we have $c_{it} = 0$, $c_{kt} = y_{it}$, and

$$m_{i,t+1} = m_{it} + m(y_{it}, m_{it}, m_{kt}),$$
$$m_{k,t+1} = m_{k,t} - m(y_{it}, m_{it}, m_{kt}),$$

where $m(y_{it}, m_{it}, m_{kt})$ is the quantity of money exchanged for the y_{it} units of goods given up by the seller when the seller has m_{it} units of money and the buyer has m_{kt} units of money. As money balances must be non-negative, we have

$$-m_{it} \le m(y_{it}, m_{it}, m_{kt}) \le m_{kt} \qquad (4)$$

and these constraints are essentially liquidity constraints. Similarly, with probability α, household i is the buyer and k is the seller, in which case $c_{it} = y_{kt}$, $c_{kt} = 0$, and

$$m_{i,t+1} = m_{it} - m(y_{kt}, m_{kt}, m_{it}),$$
$$m_{k,t+1} = m_{k,t} + m(y_{kt}, m_{kt}, m_{it}),$$

with

$$-m_{kt} \le m(y_{kt}, m_{kt}, m_{it}) \le m_{it}. \qquad (5)$$

Finally, with probability γ there is a double coincidence, and household i and k exchange goods, so that $c_{it} = y_{kt}$, $c_{kt} = y_{it}$, and

$$m_{i,t+1} = m_{it} + b(y_{it}, y_{kt}, m_{it}, m_{kt}),$$
$$m_{k,t+1} = m_{k,t} - b(y_{it}, y_{kt}, m_{it}, m_{kt}),$$

where

$$-m_{it} \le b(y_{it}, y_{kt}, m_{it}, m_{kt}) \le m_{kt}. \qquad (6)$$

Here, $b(y_{it}, y_{kt}, m_{it}, m_{kt})$ is the quantity of money passed from household k to household i, which depends on the money balances and endowments of each household.

Note that this environment will give a clear sense in which money improves the equilibrium allocation. If money is not valued, then households can trade only when there is a double coincidence of wants, and this could severely limit exchange possibilities. In principle, the constraints (4), (5) and (6) will matter for the equilibrium allocation in important ways. However, the model as we have laid it out is quite intractable. It is possible to use a bargaining approach, as for example in Trejos and Wright (1995) or Shi (1995), to determine how much money is transferred in each type of match, but the key problem is in tracking the distribution of money balances in the population over time.

In some of the monetary search and matching literature, tractability is achieved through assuming that money and goods are indivisible (Kiyotaki and Wright, 1989) or that money is indivisible and goods are divisible (Trejos and Wright, 1995; Shi, 1995), and that there is an inventory constraint on money holdings. If a household can hold only one unit of money or nothing, and money is never disposed of, then the quantity of money outstanding tells us how many households have it and how much, and how many do not have it. Models with indivisible money yield some insights, but they are extremely awkward for dealing with some types of policy questions, such as those involving money growth and the effects of inflation. Some recent progress in the development of tractable search models of divisible money was achieved by Lagos and Wright (2005), who use a quasilinear utility setup with labour supply and alternating periods of centralized meeting and search. This type of model yields a result where, in the periods when centralized meeting takes place, economic agents optimally redistribute money among themselves in such a way that the distribution of money balances becomes degenerate. Recent research using this type of model (for example, Williamson, 2006; Berentsen, Camera and Waller, 2005) has been quite productive.

Private information and limited commitment

As an alternative to shutting down markets in an ad hoc fashion, imposing borrowing constraints, assuming cash-in-advance constraints, or making extreme informational assumptions that shut down all trade except monetary exchange, there are available approaches to facing frictions head-on that lead to incomplete insurance and imperfect credit. These approaches involve economies with private information and limited commitment.

A well-developed approach to dealing with private information frictions in large economies follows the pioneering work of Green (1987), Atkeson and Lucas (1993) and others. Extending our benchmark model, suppose now that endowments are private information. In our baseline environment, we know that if endowments are public information, then a Pareto optimal allocation that treats households identically has $c_{it} = y$ for all i,t. What is optimal from a social planner's point of view under private information?

It is clear that private information implies that the $c_{it} = y$ allocation cannot be implemented by the social planner. To see this, note that to achieve this allocation requires that household i make a transfer of $y_{it} - y$ to the planner in period t. But it would then be incentive compatible for every household in every period to report that its endowment was y, and so the planner could not achieve this allocation.

Following Green (1987) and Atkeson and Lucas (1995), one can solve for an optimal private information allocation by recursive methods. The state variable for any household is w_{it}, which is the level of expected utility promised to the household as of the beginning of period t. At the beginning of period t, the household reports its endowment y_{it} to the social planner, and it must be optimal for the household to report the truth (that is, the allocation must be incentive compatible). The planner delivers consumption $c(w_{it}, y_{it})$ to the household, which depends on its state and reported endowment, and promises expected utility $w(w_{it}, y_{it})$ for next period. There is a functional equation that solves for a cost function $V(w_{it})$, which is the cost to the social planner of delivering expected utility w_{it} to a particular

household. On the right-hand side of this functional equation is a cost minimization problem, and the minimization is subject, first, to a promise-keeping constraint, which is

$$w_{it} = \int \left\{ u\left[c(w_{it}, y_{it})\right] + \beta w(w_{it}, y_{it}) \right\} dF(y_{it}),$$

where $F(y_{it})$ is the distribution function for y_{it}. The remaining constraints are incentive compatibility constraints, written as

$$u\left[c(w_{it}, y_{it})\right] + \beta w(w_{it}, y_{it})$$
$$\geq u\left[c(w_{it}, \tilde{y}) + y_{it} - \tilde{y}\right] + \beta w(w_{it}, \tilde{y}),$$

for all $y_{it}, \tilde{y} \in y, \bar{y}$. The optimal allocation will typically have the property that some incentive compatibility constraints bind. For efficient risk sharing, we want households with high (low) endowments to be making positive (negative) transfers to the social planner. To accomplish this in an incentive compatible manner requires that households with high (low) endowments receive increases (decreases) in their future expected utility promises. Thus, the distribution of consumption will tend to fan out over time. Under some conditions, a vanishing fraction of households will ultimately consume the entire endowment. However, under other conditions there will be a limiting distribution of expected utility promises with mobility and a lower bound on expected utilities. If a household hits this lower bound (which is not absorbing), then this is much like having a borrowing constraint bind for this household. Thus, this type of set-up can yield what are essentially endogenous borrowing constraints or liquidity constraints.

An alternative approach to modeling frictions in a serious way is to assume some form of limited commitment. One approach to limited commitment is that of Kehoe and Levine (1993), which has elements of competitive equilibrium. Extending our benchmark model to illustrate the flavour of this modelling approach, suppose that there is only one type of intertemporal trade, involving one-period bonds, and that we wish to study a steady state where the real interest rate is a constant, r. Suppose that the key friction here is that a household may decide strategically to repudiate its debt, in which case it would be barred from the credit market for ever and would then consume its own endowment for ever. Thus, if a household does not repudiate its debt, then its budget constraint is given by

$$c_{it} + b_{i,t+1} = y_{it} + (1 + r)b_{it}, \tag{7}$$

where $b_{i,t+1}$ is the quantity of one-period bonds acquired in period t that each pay off $1 + r$ units of consumption in period $t + 1$. Let $v(b_{it}, y_{it})$ denote the expected utility of the household at the beginning of period t as a function of the household's asset position and endowment, determined by the functional equation

$$v(b_{it}, y_{it})$$
$$= \max_{c_{it}, b_{i,t+1}} \left[u(c_{it}) + \beta \int v(b_{i,t+1}, y_{i,t+1}) dF(y_{i,t+1}) \right]$$

subject to (7). To insure that the household does not repudiate its debt in equilibrium requires that the value of not repudiating is no smaller than the value of repudiating, or

$$v(b_{it}, y_{it}) \geq u(y_{it}) + \frac{\beta}{1 - \beta} \int u(\hat{y}) dF(\hat{y}). \tag{8}$$

Note that constraint (8) is another type of borrowing constraint or liquidity constraint. Typically, $v(b_{it}, y_{it})$ must be strictly increasing in b_{it} and so, given y_{it}, there will be some critical value of b_{it} for which the constraint binds. Thus, lenders cannot lend too much to a particular household, as doing so would imply debt repudiation.

Kocherlakota (1996) takes a somewhat different approach by examining a two-agent problem with limited commitment. In his set-up, two infinite-lived agents work out a risk-sharing arrangement subject to limited commitment. Kocherlakota's problem does not have some of the loose ends found in Kehoe and Levine (1993). In the Kehoe and Levine model, we are forced to accept an incomplete markets view of the world with no explanation for why the markets are missing, and it is not clear how credit market participants coordinate to discipline agents who repudiate their debts.

Aiyagari and Williamson (2000) integrate private information and limited commitment with a Bewley model of monetary exchange to study the relationship between money and credit. Credit arrangements are constrained by private information considerations, and if agents defect from credit arrangements their alternative is to be liquidity constrained in the manner of a Bewley-type consumer.

STEPHEN D. WILLIAMSON

See also **Aiyagari, S. Rao; incomplete markets; Lucas, Robert; money; money and general equilibrium.**

Bibliography

Aiyagari, R. 1994. Uninsured idiosyncratic risk and aggregate saving. *Quarterly Journal of Economics* 109, 659–84.

Aiyagari, R. and Williamson, S. 2000. Money and dynamic credit arrangements with private information. *Journal of Economic Theory* 91, 248–79.

Atkeson, A. and Lucas, R. 1993. On efficient distribution with private information. *Review of Economic Studies* 59, 427–53.

Atkeson, A. and Lucas, R. 1995. Efficiency and inequality in a simple model of unemployment insurance. *Journal of Economic Theory* 66, 64–88.

Berentsen, A., Camera, G. and Waller, C. 2005. The distribution of money balances and the nonneutrality of money. *International Economic Review* 46, 465–88.

Bewley, T. 1977. The permanent income hypothesis: a theoretical formulation. *Journal of Economic Theory* 16, 252–92.

Bewley, T. 1980. The optimum quantity of money. In *Models of Monetary Economies*, ed. J. Kareken and N. Wallace. Minneapolis, MN: Federal Reserve Bank of Minneapolis.

Clower, R. 1967. A reconsideration of the microfoundations of monetary theory. *Western Economic Journal* 6, 1–8.

Green, E. 1987. Lending and the smoothing of uninsurable income. In *Contractual Arrangements for Intertemporal Trade*, ed. E. Prescott and N. Wallace. Minneapolis: University of Minnesota Press.

Jevons, W.S. 1875. *Money and the Mechanism of Exchange.* London: Appleton.

Jones, R. 1976. The origin and development of media of exchange. *Journal of Political Economy* 84, 757–75.

Kehoe, T. and Levine, D. 1993. Debt-constrained asset markets. *Review of Economic Studies* 60, 865–88.

Kiyotaki, N. and Wright, R. 1989. On money as a medium of exchange. *Journal of Political Economy* 97, 927–54.

Kocherlakota, N. 1996. Implications of efficient risk-sharing without commitment. *Review of Economic Studies* 63, 595–610.

Kocherlakota, N. 1998. Money is memory. *Journal of Economic Theory* 81, 232–51.

Lagos, R. and Wright, R. 2005. A unified framework for monetary theory and policy analysis. *Journal of Political Economy* 113, 463–84.

Lucas, R. 1980. Equilibrium in a pure currency economy. In *Models of Monetary Economies*, ed. J. Kareken and N. Wallace. Minneapolis, MN: Federal Reserve Bank of Minneapolis.

Shi, S. 1995. Money and prices: a model of search and bargaining. *Journal of Economic Theory* 67, 467–96.

Trejos, A. and Wright, R. 1995. Search, bargaining, money, and prices. *Journal of Political Economy* 103, 118–41.

Wallace, N. 1996. A dictum for monetary theory. In *Foundations of Research in Economics: How do Economists do Economics?* ed. S.G. Medema and W.J. Samuels. Cheltenham: Edward Elgar.

Williamson, S. 2006. Search, limited participation, and monetary policy. *International Economic Review* 47, 107–28.

liquidity effects, models of

In macroeconomics, the term *liquidity effect* refers to a fall in nominal interest rates following an exogenous persistent increase in narrow measures of the money supply. According to the classical *Fisher effect*, however, an exogenous persistent increase in money is predicted to increase expected inflation and so increase nominal interest rates. Friedman (1968) argues that, in practice, both forces operate: a persistent increase in the money supply both reduces nominal interest rates and increases expected inflation so that the real rate – nominal minus expected inflation – also falls. Friedman (1968, pp. 5–7) speculates that nominal and real rates may fall below their typical levels for up to a year, but, over time, rates will then tend to increase before tending to the levels consistent with the inflation generated by the original monetary impulse.

Empirical macroeconomists have interpreted Friedman (1968) as follows. At long horizons real interest rates are determined by 'fundamentals' including the rate at which households discount the future and average productivity growth. Consequently, we should expect that long-horizon real interest rates are relatively stable and are unaffected by transitory monetary disturbances. Long-horizon nominal interest rates are this stable real rate plus expected inflation. At short horizons, however, Friedman's (1968) argument suggests that real and nominal interest rates are both volatile and positively correlated. His argument also suggests that short-horizon real rates and expected inflation are negatively correlated (Barr and Campbell, 1997, provide evidence consistent with this interpretation and Cochrane, 1989, provides specific evidence for liquidity effects at short horizons).

Perhaps the easiest way to interpret Friedman (1968) is in terms of the following market equilibrium scenario. Suppose that a monetary authority increases the money supply by conducting an unexpected outright purchase of bonds (an *open market operation*). At short horizons, nominal interest rates fall so that households are willing to hold a smaller quantity of bonds and a larger quantity of money. But this is only a partial equilibrium effect. As households spend their increased money holdings on goods, the price level increases and so real balances do not rise as fast as nominal balances. This general equilibrium effect mitigates the need for the nominal interest rate to fall. In many simple monetary models, households tend to spend money so 'fast' that the general equilibrium price level effect can completely overturn the partial equilibrium effect.

A textbook cash-in-advance (CIA) model with a constant aggregate endowment of goods ('output') and identically and independently distributed (IID) money growth shocks provides a stark example. In this model, households immediately spend an unexpected increase in money on a fixed quantity of goods. This increases the price level one-for-one with the increase in the money supply so that real balances are unchanged. In addition, because money growth is serially uncorrelated, expected inflation is constant. Taken together, constant real balances and constant expected inflation imply that the money market clears at a constant nominal interest rate. If instead monetary growth shocks are persistent then a

positive shock increases expected inflation and nominal interest rates increase. In short, there is a Fisher effect but no liquidity effect. CIA models that are carefully calibrated to empirical processes for money growth and output, such as Hodrick, Kocherlakota and Lucas (1991) and Giovannini and Labadie (1991), lead to similar conclusions, as do studies of conceptually similar production economies, such as Cooley and Hansen (1989).

We now turn to departures from the standard CIA model in which a liquidity effect dominates at short horizons while a Fisher effect dominates at long horizons. Although models with nominal rigidities are in principle capable of generating these liquidity effects, we instead focus on flexible price models in which a liquidity effect is generated by an *asset market friction* of one form or another. Each of the models we discuss – Lucas (1990), Grossman and Weiss (1983), and Alvarez, Atkeson and Kehoe (2002) – captures, albeit in different ways, some of the spirit of Friedman's (1968) intuition.

Lucas (1990) modifies the standard CIA endowment economy with a simple timing assumption: households have to allocate cash between a goods market and an asset market *before* observing the size of an open-market operation. Once that allocation has been made, there is a fixed quantity of cash sitting in the bond market. Now consider an unexpected purchase of bonds. Relative to the supply of bonds, there is now an unexpectedly large amount of cash available to purchase assets, so bond prices increase and the nominal interest rate falls.

Fuerst (1992) and Christiano and Eichenbaum (1995) integrate Lucas's (1990) timing assumption into otherwise standard real business cycle (RBC) models. The key innovation of these papers is that, in each period, firms have to borrow cash from financial intermediaries in order to pay their workers. After a positive monetary shock, the nominal interest rate decreases so that firms find it optimal to borrow the unexpected increase in money balances. This increases firms' labour demand and increases output. Thus, these models are consistent with the commonly held view that positive monetary shocks have a positive, albeit temporary, effect on output.

A limitation of models that use Lucas's (1990) timing assumption is that the liquidity effect is very transitory even when monetary shocks are persistent. Households can adjust their allocation of cash every period. Therefore, the liquidity effect is entirely driven by serially uncorrelated 'expectational errors' in cash allocation.

We now turn to Grossman and Weiss (1983) and Alvarez, Atkeson and Kehoe (2002). These are general equilibrium models inspired by Baumol (1952) and Tobin's (1956) 'inventory-theoretic' analyses of money demand. In this class of models, two key forces influence short-horizon liquidity effects. First, at any point in time, there are always some households that participate in asset markets and some households that do not. Second, because households do not acquire cash every period, they choose to spend their money holding slowly over time. The first force alone is sufficient to generate a liquidity effect; the second force provides an *amplification* mechanism.

In this setting, an open-market increase in the money supply must, in equilibrium, be held by the subset of households that are currently participating in asset markets. Therefore, even if the price level responds one-for-one with the increase in money supply, the *share* of aggregate real balances that must be held by these households increases. Hence, the nominal interest rate falls to clear the market. Also, because they hold a larger share of real balances, these households are able to increase their share of aggregate consumption and this drives down real interest rates. So, at short horizons, there is a liquidity effect.

Moreover, if households spend their money slowly over several subsequent periods then the price level does not respond one-for-one to an increase in the money supply. Instead, the price level responds slowly. This implies that aggregate real balances rise (equivalently, in a model with constant output, *velocity* falls) and this provides a second force driving down nominal interest rates. The liquidity effect is amplified.

The influential model of Grossman and Weiss (1983) is a deterministic CIA endowment economy that exhibits both effects. Households are imperfectly synchronized and only participate in asset markets every second period. They spend money on consumption goods over two periods (Rotemberg, 1984, studies a production version of essentially the same environment).

Alvarez, Atkeson and Kehoe (2002) endogenize the fraction of households that participate in asset markets. They assume that households can participate if they pay a fixed cost. If a household's individual real balances are neither too high nor too low, they do not pay the cost, do not participate in asset markets, and end up consuming their individual real balances. If their real balances are high, they pay the cost and invest money in the asset market. Similarly, if their real balances are low, they pay the cost in order to purchase goods with money invested in the asset market. The equilibrium amount of participation ends up depending on the curvature of the utility function, the expected growth rate of money and on the size of the fixed cost. For example, in a high-inflation economy almost all households pay the cost to participate in asset markets. Hence, increases in the money supply raise expected inflation and nominal interest rates as in a basic CIA model. By contrast, in a low inflation economy, more households choose not to participate and the effects of incomplete participation are larger and may be big enough to cause a liquidity effect (that is, to dominate the Fisher effect at short horizons).

To simplify their analysis, however, Alvarez, Atkeson and Kehoe (2002) set up the model so that both active and inactive households spend all their money each period. No households save money to spend on consumption over multiple periods. Therefore, velocity is

constant and the price level responds one-for-one with increases in the money supply. Alvarez, Atkeson and Kehoe (2002) can therefore generate a liquidity effect but without the amplification that is provided by a (transitory) fall in velocity. Alvarez, Atkeson and Edmond (2003) provide a stochastic counterpart to Grossman and Weiss (1983) where both forces are operative (but at the cost of reverting to an exogenous timing of transactions).

Limited participation models of the liquidity effect provide a number of important qualitative insights into the co-movements of money, interest, and prices (and, to a lesser extent, output). The *quantitative* insight provided by these models is, however, more debatable. To generate realistic co-movements of money, interest and prices, calibrated models of liquidity effects need 'large' asset market frictions. It is typically difficult to interpret the calibrated friction literally in terms of constraints faced by real-world firms and households (making it difficult, in the words of Manuelli and Sargent, 1988, p. 524, to 'find the people'). For example, the most successful parameterizations in Alvarez, Atkeson and Edmond (2003) require the representative household to make withdrawals of money (broadly defined) from an asset market account once every 24–36 months. Alvarez, Atkeson and Edmond (2003) defend this with an appeal to the low frequency of asset market participation observed in the *cross-section* by Vissing-Jorgensen (2002). Thus, the size of the friction is defended by appealing to the likely size of the friction facing a household representative of the US economy rather than by appealing to direct evidence of the heterogeneous frictions facing individual observations of US households.

Cole and Ohanian (2002) provide another demonstration of the difficulty of interpreting such models literally. They note that the distribution of money holdings between US firms and households has been quite unstable over the post-war period. When this observation is embedded in a model of liquidity effects, it implies a corresponding instability in the effects of money shocks on output – an instability that seems to be counterfactual.

In our opinion, these limitations should not be interpreted as reasons for rejecting models of asset market segmentation. If anything, these limitations are instead reasons for rejecting an implicit aggregation hypothesis. Traditional macro models work with relatively crude frictions that are intended to summarize a complicated array of micro frictions facing individual households and firms. For example, the literature on models of liquidity effects assumes only one level of market segmentation – either between households and asset markets, or between firms and asset markets. However, asset market segmentation seems to occur at numerous levels of financial intermediation. A large body of empirical evidence shows that phenomena consistent with market segmentation arise within the financial system – a system that might best be viewed as a collection of partially integrated and relatively specialized 'local' asset markets (see, among many others, Collin-Dufresne, Goldstein and Martin, 2001).

This evidence motivates us to ask how a collection of small segmentation frictions cumulates in the aggregate, and whether they add up to a quantitatively significant macro friction. If they do, then the models of liquidity effects that we have discussed here would indeed be natural laboratories for the analysis of the monetary transmission mechanism.

In short, we conjecture that addressing segmentation at a disaggregative level is likely to provide important empirical and theoretical insights into the relationship between patterns of intermediation in financial markets and traditional macro questions – including the size and stability of liquidity effects at short horizons and the monetary policy transmission mechanism more generally.

CHRIS EDMOND AND PIERRE-OLIVIER WEILL

See also **finance; Fisher, Irving; Friedman, Milton; inflation expectations; Lucas, Robert; money supply.**

Bibliography

Alvarez, F., Atkeson, A. and Edmond, C. 2003. On the sluggish response of prices to money in an inventory-theoretic model of money demand. Working Paper No. 10016. Cambridge, MA: NBER.

Alvarez, F., Atkeson, A. and Kehoe, P.J. 2002. Money, interest rates and exchange rates with endogenously segmented markets. *Journal of Political Economy* 110, 73–112.

Barr, D.G. and Campbell, J.Y. 1997. Inflation, real interest rates and the bond market: a study of UK nominal and index-linked government bond prices. *Journal of Monetary Economics* 39, 361–83.

Baumol, W.J. 1952. The transactions demand for cash: an inventory-theoretic approach. *Quarterly Journal of Economics* 66, 545–56.

Christiano, L.J. and Eichenbaum, M. 1995. Liquidity effects, monetary policy, and the business cycle. *Journal of Money, Credit and Banking* 27, 1113–36.

Cochrane, J.H. 1989. The return of the liquidity effect: a study of the short-run relation between money growth and interest rates. *Journal of Business and Economic Statistics* 7(1), 75–83.

Cole, H.L. and Ohanian, L.E. 2002. Shrinking money: the demand for money and the nonneutrality of money. *Journal of Monetary Economics* 49, 653–86.

Collin-Dufresne, P., Goldstein, R.S. and Martin, J.S. 2001. The determinants of credit spread changes. *Journal of Finance* 56, 653–86.

Cooley, T.F. and Hansen, G.D. 1989. The inflation tax in a real business cycle model. *American Economic Review* 79, 733–48.

Friedman, M. 1968. The role of monetary policy. *American Economic Review* 58, 1–17.

Fuerst, T.S. 1992. Liquidity, loanable funds, and real activity. *Journal of Monetary Economics* 29, 3–24.

Giovannini, A. and Labadie, P. 1991. Asset prices and interest rates in cash-in-advance models. *Journal of Political Economy* 99, 1215–51.

Grossman, S. and Weiss, L. 1983. A transactions-based model of the monetary transmission mechanism. *American Economic Review* 73, 871–80.

Hodrick, R.J., Kocherlakota, N. and Lucas, D. 1991. The variability of velocity in cash-in-advance models. *Journal of Political Economy* 99, 358–84.

Lucas, R.E., Jr. 1982. Interest rates and currency prices in a two-country world. *Journal of Monetary Economics* 10, 335–59.

Lucas, R.E., Jr. 1990. Liquidity and interest rates. *Journal of Economic Theory* 50, 237–64.

Manuelli, R. and Sargent, T.J. 1988. Models of business cycles: a review essay. *Journal of Monetary Economics* 22, 523–42.

Rotemberg, J.J. 1984. A monetary equilibrium model with transactions costs. *Journal of Political Economy* 92, 40–58.

Tobin, J. 1956. The interest-elasticity of the transactions demand for cash. *Review of Economics and Statistics* 38, 241–7.

Vissing-Jorgensen, A. 2002. Towards an explanation of household portfolio choice heterogeneity: nonfinancial income and participation cost structures. Working Paper No. 8884. Cambridge, MA: NBER.

liquidity preference

The notion of 'liquidity preference' has become generally used in the literature on monetary issues (particularly that concerned with the interest rate) following Keynes's contributions in the 1930s. It concerns the motives for demanding monetary instruments or other close substitutes. Earlier, the analysis of the demand for monetary instruments was based on other motives and concepts and led to different conclusions.

The analysis of the motives for demanding monetary instruments plays a specific role within monetary theory. The literature dealing with the interest rate, for instance, has always distinguished two different analytical steps. The first deals with the *variations* in the 'market interest rate', that is, that actually observed everyday: it *describes* how a change in this rate (or in the structure of the interest rates) comes about. To do that, it provides an analytical scheme which describes the behaviour of the money markets, by considering one after the other all different sources of demand for and supply of monetary instruments, pointing out the main causes of their variations. The second step deals with the *level* of the interest rate. It *explains* why this rate tends to remain, over a specific period of time, at a certain level, pointing out the factors determining it. The way in which these factors operate is then described by using the scheme provided in the first step of analysis. This clarifies the market mechanisms (that is, changes in the different components of demand and supply in the money markets) through which the prevailing level of the interest rate asserts itself.

The analysis of the motives for demanding monetary instruments thus properly belongs to the first step: it cooperates to describe the working of the money markets and the way in which variations in the interest rate (or in the structure of interest rates) occur.

This approach was followed by Smith, Ricardo, Tooke, J.S. Mill, Marx, Marshall, Wicksell, J.M. Keynes, Robertson, and so on, independently of the particular theory they proposed, that is whether the level of the 'average interest rate' (that prevailing over a specific period of time) was determined by the 'forces of productivity and thrift' or by other factors.

Prior to Keynes's contributions in the 1930s, it was assumed that monetary instruments (in most cases, central bank money) are demanded for two reasons. First, they are demanded by the household sector for the 'circulation of income'. Households, that is, hold in the form of currency a certain fraction of their income to carry out their daily consumption expenditure.

The second source of demand for central bank money, it was assumed, comes from the banking sector which requires liquid reserves to make payments to depositors and to meet the demand for bank loans of different maturity. Banks' decisions, it was argued, are concerned with protecting themselves against the risk of running out of liquid means while minimizing cost. In such analyses, which did not use modern portfolio choice tools, the amount of reserves banks demand depends upon the composition of their portfolio (particularly the maturity of their loans) and upon the degree of uncertainty they feel as to the smooth operation of the credit payment system. On the basis of these two elements, banks fix the desired ratio between their reserves in central bank money and the amount of loans they can supply.

As some authors noticed, the presence of uncertainty among the elements affecting the decisions of financial operators makes the credit payment system unstable. The desired ratio of reserves to loans changes continuously and sometimes sharply. Financial markets become tighter precisely when more liquid means are required. A higher degree of uncertainty as to the smooth operation of the system, for instance, leads the business and the banking sectors to desire to 'become more liquid'. The former tend to discount a larger amount of bills of exchange (that is, demand more short-term bank loans), while the latter set at a higher level the desired reserves–loans ratio, so supplying a smaller amount of bank loans.

The instability of the system and the variability of the interest rates were therefore recognized by some economists (a minority) and ascribed to the uncertainty felt by banks and business as to their ability to solve cash-flow problems.

This analysis of the demand for monetary instruments was dominant from Adam Smith onwards. Its basic points were still reflected in the famous 'Cambridge equation' presented by Pigou in his article 'The value of money' (1917) and in Keynes's *A Tract on Monetary Reform* (1923).

Keynes's analysis of liquidity preference

The analysis of the motives for demanding monetary instruments was considerably refined by J.M. Keynes in the 1930s. Developing the analysis inherited from Marshall and Pigou, Keynes distinguished three motives for demanding monetary instruments (by which was now meant member banks' money, that is, bank deposits).

First, monetary instruments are demanded for transaction purposes. The amount demanded due to this motive is a stable function of the level of income.

The second source of demand for monetary instruments is for precautionary purposes, defined as the demand coming from different sectors as a protection against the possibility that some unexpected payment has to be made, or that some expected receipts cannot be realized. This definition has been differently interpreted. Some authors (and the majority of textbooks) have interpreted it in a restrictive way, by identifying it with the households' holding of bank deposits as a precaution against extraordinary events (for example, payment of hospital bills). The precautionary demand for monetary instruments was typically lumped together with the transaction demand, both being an increasing function of the level of income. Other authors have instead given more extensive interpretation of this motive by including in it the demand coming from all financial operators feeling highly uncertain as to the future level of the interest rate. R. Kahn (1954) explained that people prefer holding part of their wealth in liquid means when their knowledge as to how the rate of interest is going to behave in the near future is so limited as to make it impossible to consider some future levels of this rate more probable than others.

This way of interpreting the precautionary motive makes it close to the third motive for demanding monetary instruments identified by Keynes: the speculative motive. Speculation in financial assets occurs because some agents expect with sufficient conviction that the rate of interest will move in a certain direction. The existence of uncertainty (that is, that lack of 'complete knowledge') is not denied. Yet the 'limited knowledge' available allows some agents to consider some future levels of the rate of interest more probable than others. Monetary instruments are so demanded (to avoid a loss in the capital value of financial assets) because a rise in the rate of interest is expected, and not because of the lack of any conviction as to the future of the rate of interest (as in the case of precautionary motive).

The novelty introduced by Keynes (some authors claim that it had been anticipated by Lavington, 1921) lies not in the fact that he recognized that money is also a 'store of value' (an element already present in previous literature), but in the fact that he made some specific sources of demand for monetary instruments depend upon the expected variations of the interest rate, and consequently on the expected variations in the capital value of financial assets.

On account of its magnitude, but principally on account of its high variability, which is due to the uncertain character of expectations about future events, this latter source of demand played a central role in Keynes's writing. It was considered to be *the* cause of variations in the rate of interest. Indeed, in subsequent years, some authors even identified the notion of liquidity preference with speculative motive, while many others put it at the centre of the intense debates on interest rate after the publication of the *General Theory of Employment, Interest and Money* (1936).

Keynes's innovations stimulated many controversies dealing with different aspects of the theory of interest and money. A central point in these debates was the evaluation of Keynes's own contribution: had he really presented a new theory of the rate of interest, alternative to the dominant marginalist one?

In the preparatory works and in the *General Theory* itself, Keynes had so characterized his contribution. He had tried to show the existence of logical inconsistency in the dominant real theory and, in opposition to it, had argued in favour of a *monetary* theory of the rate of interest based on historical and conventional factors.

The essential elements of the analysis of liquidity preference had already been introduced in *A Treatise of Money*, where the marginalist theory determining the 'natural' level of the interest rate on the basis of functions of demand for investment and supply of saving was still accepted. Here liquidity preference was integrated within the marginalist theory. In the *General Theory*, instead, the notion of a 'natural' interest rate was rejected. The 'average' level of the interest rate over a specific period of time was now determined by those factors able to affect the 'common opinion' as to the prevailing value of this rate in the future, and among these factors some importance was given to the policy of the monetary authority.

Thus, while in *A Treatise on Money* the novelty of liquidity preference referred to the first step of the analysis of the interest rate (that describing how variations in this rate come about), in the *General Theory*, the novelty regarded the second step of analysis, that is the theory determining the level of this rate.

Robertson's critique after the *General Theory*

The group of economists close to Keynes in those years, with whom he discussed the proofs of the *General Theory*, fully realized that only in this book had he turned the analysis of liquidity preference, already present in the *Treatise*, into a new theory of the interest rate. Not all of them, however, agreed with him. Robertson, brought up in the same Marshallian tradition as Keynes, defended the marginalist theory, claiming that Keynes was in the *General Theory* overstating the role played by monetary factors (see Keynes, 1973a, pp. 499, and Robertson, 1936; 1940). He invited Keynes to attribute to monetary and real forces their proper place, as he had done in *A Treatise on Money*. The abandonment of the 'forces of productivity and thrift', when dealing with the determination of the 'average' interest rate over long periods of time, left the 'expected normal value' of this rate unexplained. Robertson could not accept that 'the common opinion' as to the future value of the interest rate should be explained in terms of factors changing from one historical period to the others, rather than by referring to one specific set of factors able to affect the course of events in different historical contexts. If we ask, Robertson stated, 'what ultimately governs the judgement of wealthowners as to why the rate of interest should be different in the future from what it is today, we are surely led straight back to the fundamental phenomena of productivity and thrift' (Robertson, 1940, p. 25).

To clarify his view, Robertson translated Keynes's arguments into a different analytical framework based on 'flow' concepts. The determination of the 'market interest rate' (that actually observed daily) and of the 'average interest rate' (the one prevailing over long periods of time) was analysed in terms of 'loanable funds', to show that in both cases (but especially in the long-period case) the influence of the demand function for investment and the supply of saving could not be ignored. Within this discussion, Robertson also pointed out the need for extra funds to finance new investment.

The debate with Robertson was intense. Other economists also joined in to discuss the three issues raised: whether Keynes's theory left the determination of the average interest rate 'hanging in the air' (or 'hanging by its own bootstraps'); the role of speculative motive and saving and investment within a 'loanable-funds' approach; the 'finance' motive.

Hicks and the rise of the 'neoclassical synthesis'

While the debate with Robertson moved on the common ground of the Marshallian tradition, those with other economists were characterized, from the beginning, by greater problems of understanding and communication.

A major figure in these debates was J.R. Hicks, whose reviews of the *General Theory* (Hicks, 1936; 1937) were discussed with Keynes in an exchange of correspondence (see Keynes, 1973b, pp. 71–83). This correspondence reveals Keynes's insistence on his inability to understand the meaning and the aim of Hicks's claim that the validity of Keynes's theory of interest did not prove other theories to be wrong.

Hicks's aim was to integrate Keynes's ideas within an approach, different from the Marshallian one, based on a new version of the neoclassical theory of value which used the notion of *temporary* general equilibria. The rate of interest was determined, with the other distributive variables, relative prices and the level of activity, within an analysis characterized by interdependence between different markets and the simultaneous attainment of equilibrium between supply and demand in all of them. Equilibrium between saving and investment decisions was reached simultaneously with equilibrium between supply of and demand for monetary instruments. The application of 'Walras's Law' then made it possible to argue that the claim that the rate of interest is determined in the money market and the claim that it is determined in the market for saving and investment are equivalent.

Hicks's writings had a great impact on the literature. They opened the way to the interpretation of Keynes's work known as the 'neoclassical synthesis' and to the wide use of the famous IS–LM apparatus. Indeed, orthodox 'Keynesian economics' was derived from this line of development, rather than from Keynes's own writings, as the debate on interest rate shows.

The distinction between the two steps of an analysis of the interest rate was now obscured. In spite of Keynes's explicit claim to the contrary (Keynes, 1937, p. 215), the analysis of liquidity preference, which was intended as a means of describing the market mechanisms through which changes in the interest rate occur, became a theory determining the level of the interest rate. This theory was counter-posed to others – the 'loanable-funds theory' and the 'investment–saving theory' – in a long debate which in the end established what Hicks had hinted in his reviews of the *General Theory*, that is, that in a general equilibrium analysis to attribute the determination of a price or of a distributive variable to the attainment of equilibrium in one specific market makes no sense.

Now, none of the orthodox Keynesian literature mentioned any more what Keynes had emphasized: the instability of the speculative demand for money due to the uncertain character of the expectations about the future level of the interest rate. The integration of the market for monetary instruments within a general equilibrium analysis requires that the data determining the functions of demand for and supply of money have to be as stable as those determining the demand and supply functions in other markets.

The abandonment of Keynes's view of an unstable speculative demand for money was achieved by moving along two lines. First, the notion of an expected normal value of the interest rate was gradually abandoned. Second, the issue of stability was moved from a theoretical to an empirical level.

Already in *Value and Capital* (1939), Hicks had moved along the first line. After him, Modigliani (1944) derived a stable function of demand for money by referring to the risk of future increases in the interest rate, taking this risk

as independent of people's specific expectations. The risk is thus *in general* low when the interest rate is high and high when the interest rate is low. Reference to specific expectations of the future value of interest rate could, instead, make the risk high when the rate is high and low when the rate is low. Finally, Tobin (1958) with the explicit aim of making the theoretical treatment of uncertainty more precise in Keynesian analysis, proposed deriving the demand function for money by including, among the data, subjective probability distributions of the future level of the interest rate, not considering any particular variation in this rate more probable than others. (The similarity with Kahn's precautionary motive mentioned above is clear.) In this analysis, stability of the demand function for money can be achieved by adding one more assumption: any new piece of information acquired by agents does not change their subjective probability distribution. The meaning of this hypothesis is that agents have 'complete knowledge' of all relevant information, which amounts to assuming uncertainty away from the analysis. In his subsequent writings, Tobin did not return to this particular point, preferring to consider the issue of 'stability' an empirical, rather than a theoretical one. This line has been adopted by most followers of the orthodox Keynesian approach, thus avoiding complex theoretical problems. As a result, the possibility of reaching satisfactory conclusions on this issue appears more difficult.

Theories of the interest rate, which imply a departure from the dominant neoclassical tradition, whether Marshallian or modern general equilibrium versions, can also be found in the literature. They were held by authors close to Keynes during the preparation of the *General Theory*, like Joan Robinson and Kahn, and appear to reflect Keynes's original intentions more than other theories. Robinson and Kahn themselves, in subsequent years (see Robinson, 1937; 1951; Kahn, 1954) contributed to developing these analyses, which were also put forward by Kaldor (1939; 1970; 1982), and re-elaborated by a large group of economists, including Shackle (1967), Pasinetti (1974), Minsky (1975), Davidson (1978), Eatwell (1979), and Garegnani (1979).

Although there are some points of difference between these authors, they seem to agree on the instability of the speculative demand for money due to the uncertain character of the expectations about future level of the interest rate, and on the need to reject the neoclassical theory, for being either analytically inconsistent or for being based on the assumption of a simultaneous achievement of equilibrium in all markets, an assumption which neglects the different ways in which these markets are organized and operate.

The analyses of these authors have contributed to the development of a treatment of monetary issues which breaks with the traditional causal links between 'monetary' and 'real' variables, and where institutional elements, such as the way financial markets are organized over a certain period of time, play a central role. These analyses make it possible to argue in favour of a 'monetary' determination of the interest rate, based on historical and conventional factors, thus supporting Robinson's claim that *any* opinion 'that is widely believed tends to verify itself, so that there is a large element of "thinking makes it so" in the determination of the interest rates' (Robinson, 1951, p. 258).

The instability of the financial system and the variability of the interest rates are therefore recognized today, too, by some economists, who also allow for the influence of monetary factors on the level of activity and within the theory of value and distribution, in opposition to the dominant marginalist approach.

CARLO PANICO

See also **finance; Keynes, John Maynard.**

Bibliography

Davidson, P. 1978. *Money and the Real World*. London: Macmillan.

Eatwell, J.L. 1979. Theories of value, output and employment. In *Keynes's Economics and the Theory of Value and Distribution*, ed. J. Eatwell and M. Milgate. London: Duckworth, 1983.

Garegnani, P. 1979. Notes on consumption, investment and effective demand: II. *Cambridge Journal of Economics* 3(1), 63–82.

Hicks, J.R. 1936. Mr Keynes's theory of employment. *Economic Journal* 46, 238–53.

Hicks, J.R. 1937. Mr Keynes and the 'classics'; a suggested interpretation. *Econometrica* 5(April), 147–59.

Hicks, J.R. 1939. *Value and Capital*. Oxford: Clarendon Press.

Kahn, R.F. 1954. Some notes on liquidity preference. *Manchester School of Economics and Social Studies* 22, 229–57.

Kaldor, N. 1939. Speculation and economic stability. *Review of Economic Studies* 7(October), 1–27.

Kaldor, N. 1970. The new monetarism. *Lloyds Bank Review* No. 97, July, 1–18.

Kaldor, N. 1982. *The Scourge of Monetarism*. Oxford: Oxford University Press.

Keynes, J.M. 1923. A tract on monetary reform. In *Collected Writings of J.M. Keynes*, vol. 4, ed. D.E. Moggridge. London: Macmillan, 1971.

Keynes, J.M. 1930a. A treatise on money, vol. 1: The pure theory of money. In *Collected Writings of J.M. Keynes*, vol. 5, ed. D.E. Moggridge. London: Macmillan, 1971.

Keynes, J.M. 1930b. A treatise on money, Vol. 2: The applied theory of money. In *Collected Writings of J.M. Keynes*, vol. 6, ed. D.E. Moggridge. London: Macmillan, 1971.

Keynes, J.M. 1936. The general theory of employment, interest and money. In *Collected Writings of J.M. Keynes*, vol. 7, ed. D.E. Moggridge. London: Macmillan, 1973.

Keynes, J.M. 1937. Alternative theories of the rate of interest. *Economic Journal* 47, 241–52. In *The General Theory and After; Part II: Defence and Development, Collected Writings of J.M. Keynes*, vol. 14, ed. D.E. Moggridge, London: Macmillan, 1973.

Keynes, J.M. 1973a. The general theory and after; Part I: Preparation. In *Collected Writings of J.M. Keynes*, vol. 13, ed. D.E. Moggridge. London: Macmillan.

Keynes, J.M. 1973b. The general theory and after; Part II: Defence and development. In *Collected Writings of J.M. Keynes*, vol. 14, ed. D.E. Moggridge. London: Macmillan.

Keynes, J.M. 1979. The general theory and after: a supplement. In *Collected Writings of J.M. Keynes*, vol. 19, ed. D.E. Moggridge. London: Macmillan.

Lavington, F. 1921. *The English Capital Market*. London: Methuen.

Minsky, H.P. 1975. *John Maynard Keynes*. New York: Columbia University Press.

Modigliani, F. 1944. Liquidity preference and the theory of interest and money. *Econometrica* 12(January), 45–88.

Pasinetti, L.L. 1974. *Growth and Income Distribution*. Cambridge: Cambridge University Press.

Pigou, A.C. 1917. The value of money. *Quarterly Journal of Economics* 32(November), 38–65. Correction (February 1918), 209.

Robertson, D.H. 1936. Some notes on Mr Keynes' 'General Theory of Employment'. *Quarterly Journal of Economics* 51(November), 168–91.

Robertson, D.H. 1940. *Essays in Monetary Theory*. London: P.S. King.

Robinson, J.V. 1937. *Introduction to the Theory of Employment*. London: Macmillan.

Robinson, J.V. 1951. The rate of interest. *Econometrica* 19(April), 92–111. In *Collected Economic Papers of Joan Robinson*, vol. 2, Oxford: Blackwell, 1960.

Shackle, G.L.S. 1967. *The Years of High Theory*. Cambridge: Cambridge University Press.

Tobin, J. 1958. Liquidity preference as behavior risk. *Review of Economic Studies* 25(February), 65–86.

liquidity trap

A liquidity trap is defined as a situation in which the short-term nominal interest rate is zero. In this case, many argue, increasing money in circulation has no effect on either output or prices. The liquidity trap is originally a Keynesian idea and was contrasted with the quantity theory of money, which maintains that prices and output are, roughly speaking, proportional to the money supply.

According to the Keynesian theory, money supply has its effects on prices and output through the nominal interest rate. Increasing money supply reduces the interest rate through a money demand equation. Lower interest rates stimulate output and spending. The short-term nominal interest rate, however, cannot be less than zero, based on a basic arbitrage argument: no one will lend 100 dollars unless she gets at least 100 dollars back. This is often referred to as the 'zero bound' on the short-term nominal interest rate. Hence, the Keynesian argument goes, once the money supply has been increased to a level where the short-term interest rate is zero, there will be no further effect on either output or prices, no matter by how much money supply is increased.

The ideas that underlie the liquidity trap were conceived during the Great Depression. In that period the short-term nominal interest rate was close to zero. At the beginning of 1933, for example, the short-term nominal interest rate in the United States – as measured by three-month Treasuries – was only 0.05 per cent. As the memory of the Great Depression faded and several authors challenged the liquidity trap, many economists begun to regard it as a theoretical curiosity.

The liquidity trap received much more attention again in the late 1990s with the arrival of new data. The short-term nominal interest rate in Japan collapsed to zero in the second half of the 1990s. Furthermore, the Bank of Japan (BoJ) more than doubled the monetary base through traditional and non-traditional measures to increase prices and stimulate demand. The BoJ policy of 'quantitative easing' from 2001 to 2006, for example, increased the monetary base by over 70 per cent in that period. By most accounts, however, the effect on prices was sluggish at best. (As long as five years after the beginning of quantitative easing, the changes in the CPI and the GDP deflator were still only starting to approach positive territory.)

The modern view of the liquidity trap

The modern view of the liquidity trap is more subtle than the traditional Keynesian one. It relies on an intertemporal stochastic general equilibrium model whereby aggregate demand depends on current and expected future real interest rates rather than simply the current rate as in the old Keynesian models. In the modern framework, the liquidity trap arises when the zero bound on the short-term nominal interest rate prevents the central bank from fully accommodating sufficiently large deflationary shocks by interest rate cuts.

The aggregate demand relationship that underlies the model is usually expressed by a consumption Euler equation, derived from the maximization problem of a representative household. On the assumption that all output is consumed, that equation can be approximated as:

$$Y_t = E_t Y_{t+1} - \sigma(i_t - E_t \pi_{t+1} - r_t^e) \qquad (1)$$

where Y_t is the deviation of output from steady state, i_t is the short-term nominal interest rate, π_t is inflation, E_t is an expectation operator and r_t^e is an exogenous shock process (which can be due to host of factors). This equation says that current demand depends on expectations of future output (because spending depends on expected future income) and the real interest rate which is the difference between the nominal interest rate and expected future inflation (because lower real interest rates make spending today relatively cheaper than future spending). This equation can be forwarded to yield

$$Y_t = E_t Y_{T+1} - \sigma \sum_{s=t}^{T} E_t(i_s - \pi_{s+1} - r_s^e)$$

which illustrates that demand depends not only on the current short-term interest rate but on the entire expected path for future interest rates and expected inflation. Because long-term interest rates depend on expectations about current and future short-term rates, this equation can also be interpreted as saying that demand depends on long-term interest rates. Monetary policy works through the short-term nominal interest rate in the model, and is constrained by the fact that it cannot be set below zero,

$$i_t \geq 0. \qquad (2)$$

In contrast to the static Keynesian framework, monetary policy can still be effective in this model even when the current short-term nominal interest rate is zero. In order to be effective, however, expansionary monetary policy must change the public's expectations about future interest rates at the point in time when the zero bound will no longer be binding. For example, this may be the period in which the deflationary shocks are expected to subside. Thus, successful monetary easing in a liquidity trap involves committing to maintaining lower future nominal interest rates for any given price level in the future once deflationary pressures have subsided (see, for example, Reifschneider and Williams, 2000; Jung, Teranishi and Watanabe, 2005; Eggertsson and Woodford, 2003; Adam and Billi, 2006).

This was the rationale for the BoJ's announcement in the autumn of 2003 that it promised to keep the interest rate low until deflationary pressures had subsided and CPI inflation was projected to be in positive territory. It also underlay the logic of the Federal Reserve announcement in mid-2003 that it would keep interest rates low for a 'considerable period'. At that time, there was some fear of deflation in the United States (the short-term interest rates reached one per cent in the spring of 2003, its lowest level since the Great Depression, and some analysts voiced fears of deflation).

There is a direct correspondence between the nominal interest rate and the money supply in the model reviewed above. There is an underlying demand equation for real money balances derived from a representative household maximization problem (like the consumption Euler equation 1). This demand equation can be expressed as a relationship between the nominal interest rate and money supply

$$\frac{M_t}{P_t} \geq L(Y_t, i_t) \qquad (3)$$

where M_t is the nominal stock of money and P_t is a price level. On the assumption that both consumption and liquidity services are normal goods, this inequality says that the demand for money increases with lower interest rates and higher output. As the interest rate declines to zero, however, the demand for money is indeterminate because at that point households do not care whether they hold money or one-period riskless government bonds. The two are perfect substitutes: a government liability that has nominal value but pays no interest rate. Another way of stating the result discussed above is that a successful monetary easing (committing to lower *future* nominal interest rate for a given price level) involves committing to higher money supply *in the future* once interest rates have become positive again (see, for example, Eggertsson, 2006a).

Irrelevance results

According to the modern view outlined above, monetary policy will increase demand at zero interest rates only if it changes expectations about the future money supply or, equivalently, the path of future interest rates. The Keynesian liquidity trap is therefore only a true trap if the central bank cannot to stir expectations. There are several interesting conditions under which this is the case, so that monetary easing is ineffective. These 'irrelevance' results help explain why BoJ's increase in the monetary base in Japan through 'quantitative easing' in 2001–6 may have had a somewhat more limited effect on inflation and inflation expectations in that period than some proponents of the quantity theory of money expected.

Krugman (1998), for example, shows that at zero interest rates if the public expects the money supply in the future to revert to some constant value as soon as the interest rate is positive, quantitative easing will be ineffective. Any increase in the money supply in this case is expected to be reversed, and output and prices are unchanged.

Eggertsson and Woodford (2003) show that the same result applies if the public expects the central bank to follow a 'Taylor rule', which may indeed summarize behaviour of a number of central banks in industrial countries. A central bank following a Taylor rule raises interest rates in response to above-target inflation and above-trend output. Conversely, unless the zero bound is binding, the central bank reduces the interest rate if inflation is below target or output is below trend (an output gap). If the public expects the central bank to follow the Taylor rule, it anticipates an interest rate hike as soon as there are inflationary pressures in excess of the implicit inflation target. If the target is perceived to be price stability, this implies that quantitative easing has no effect, because a commitment to the Taylor rule implies that any increase in the monetary base is reversed as soon as deflationary pressures subside.

Eggertsson (2006a) demonstrates that, if a central bank is discretionary, that is, unable to commit to future policy, and minimizes a standard loss function that depends on inflation and the output gap, it will also be unable to increase inflationary expectations at the zero bound, because it will always have an incentive to renege on an inflation promise or extended 'quantitative easing' in order to achieve low *ex post* inflation. This deflation bias has the same implication as the previous two irrelevance propositions, namely, that the public will expect any increase in the monetary base to be reversed as soon as deflationary pressures subside. The deflation bias can be illustrated by the aid of a few additional equations, as illustrated in the next section.

The deflation bias and the optimal commitment

The deflation bias can be illustrated by completing the model that gave rise to (1), (2) and (3). In the model prices are not flexible because firms reset their price at random intervals. This gives rise to an aggregate supply equation which is often referred to as the 'New Keynesian' Phillips curve. It can be derived from the Euler equation of the firm's maximization problem (see, for example, Woodford, 2003)

$$\pi_t = \kappa(Y_t - Y_t^n) + \beta E_t \pi_{t+1} \qquad (4)$$

where Y_t^n is the natural rate of output (in deviation from steady state), which is the 'hypothetical' output produced if prices were perfectly flexible, β is the discount factor of the household in the model and the parameter $\kappa > 0$ is a function of preferences and technology parameters. This equation implies that inflation can increase output above its natural level because not all firms reset their prices instantaneously.

If the government's objective is to maximize the utility of the representative household, it can be approximated by

$$\sum_{t=0}^{\infty} \beta^t \{\pi_t^2 + \lambda_y (Y_t - Y_t^e)^2\} \qquad (5)$$

where the term Y_t^e is the target level of output. It is also referred to as the 'efficient level' or 'first-best level' of output. The standard 'inflation bias' first illustrated by Kydland and Prescott (1977) arises when the natural level of output is lower than the efficient level of output, that is, $Y_t^n < Y_t^e$.

Eggertsson (2006a) shows that there is also a deflation bias under certain circumstances. While the inflation bias is a steady state phenomenon, the deflation bias arises to temporary shocks. Consider the implied solution for the nominal interest rate when there is an inflation bias of $\bar{\pi}$. It is

$$i_t = \bar{\pi} + r_t^e.$$

This equation cannot be satisfied in the presence of sufficiently large deflationary shocks, that is, a negative r_t^e. In particular if $r_t^e < -\bar{\pi}$ this solution would imply a negative nominal interest rate. It can be shown (Eggertsson, 2006a) that a discretionary policymaker will in this case set the nominal interest rate to zero but set inflation equal to the 'inflation bias' solution $\bar{\pi}$ as soon as the deflationary pressures have subsided (that is, when the shock is $r_t^e \geq -\bar{\pi}_t$). If the disturbance r_t^e is low enough, the zero bound frustrates the central bank's ability to achieve its 'inflation target' $\bar{\pi}$ which can in turn lead to excessive deflation. (While deflation and zero interest rates are due to real shocks in the literature discussed above, an alternative way of modelling the liquidity trap is that it is the result of self-fulfilling deflationary expectations; see, for example, Benhabib, Schmitt-Grohe and Uribe, 2001.)

To illustrate this consider the following experiment. Suppose the term r_t^e is unexpectedly negative in period 0 $(r_t^e = r_L < 0)$ and then reverts back to its steady state value $\bar{r} > 0$ with a fixed probability α in every period. For simplicity assume that $\bar{\pi} = 0$. Then it is easy to verify

from eqs. (1), (4), the behaviour of the central bank described above and the assumed process for r_t^e that the solution for output and inflation is given by (see Eggertsson, 2006a, for details)

$$\pi_t = \frac{1}{\alpha(1 - \beta(1 - \alpha)) - \sigma\kappa(1 - \alpha)} \kappa\sigma r_L^e$$
$$\text{if } r_t^e = r_L^e \text{ and } \pi_t = 0 \text{ otherwise} \tag{6}$$

$$Y_t = \frac{1 - \beta(1 - \alpha)}{\alpha(1 - \beta(1 - \alpha)) - \sigma\kappa(1 - \alpha)} \sigma r_L^e$$
$$\text{if } r_t^e = r_L^e \text{ and } Y_t = 0 \text{ otherwise} \tag{7}$$

Figure 1 shows the solution in a calibrated example for numerical values of the model taken from Eggertsson and Woodford (2003). (Under this calibration $\alpha = 0.1$, $\kappa = 0.02$, $\beta = 0.99$ and $r_L = -\frac{0.02}{4}$ but the model is calibrated in quarterly frequencies.) The dashed line shows the solution under the contingency that the natural rate of interest reverts to positive level in 15 periods. The inability of the central bank to set negative nominal interest rate results in a 14 per cent output collapse and 10 per cent annual deflation. The fact that in each quarter there is a 90 per cent chance of the exogenous

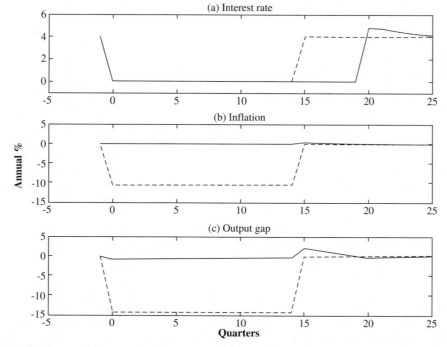

Figure 1   Response of the nominal interest rate, inflation and the output gap to a shocks that lasts for 15 quarters. *Note*: The dashed line shows the solution under policy discretion, the solid line the solution under the optimal policy commitment.

disturbance to remaining negative for the next quarter creates the expectation of future deflation and a continued output depression, which creates even further depression and deflation. Even if the central bank lowers the short-term nominal interest rate to zero, the real rate of interest is positive, because the private sector expects deflation. The same results applies when there is an inflation bias, that is, $\bar{\pi} > 0$, but in this case the disturbance r_t^e needs to be correspondingly more negative to lead to an output collapse.

The solution illustrated in Figure 1 is what Eggertsson (2006a) calls the deflation bias of monetary policy under discretion. The reason why this solution indicates a deflation bias is that the deflation and depression can largely be avoided by the correct *commitment* to optimal policy. The solid line shows the solution in the case that the central bank can commit to optimal future policy. In this case the deflation and the output contraction are largely avoided. In the optimal solution the central bank commits to keeping the nominal interest at zero for a considerable period beyond what is implied by the discretionary solution; that is, interest rates are kept at zero even if the deflationary shock r_t^e has subsided. Similarly, the central bank allows for an output boom once the deflationary shock subsides and accommodates mild inflation. Such commitment stimulates demand and reduces deflation through several channels. The expectation of future inflation lowers the real interest rate, even if the nominal interest rate cannot be reduced further, thus stimulating spending. Similarly, a commitment to lower future nominal interest rate (once the deflationary pressures have subsided) stimulates demand for the same reason. Finally, the expectation of higher future income, as manifested by the expected output boom, stimulates current spending, in accordance with the permanent income hypothesis (see Eggertsson and Woodford, 2003, for the derivation underlying this figures. The optimal commitment is also derived in Jung, Teranishi and Watanabe, 2005, and Adam and Billi, 2006, for alternative processes for the deflationary disturbance).

The discretionary solution indicates that this optimal commitment, however desirable, is not feasible if the central bank cannot commit to future policy. The discretionary policymaker is cursed by the deflation bias. To understand the logic of this curse, observe that the government's objective (5) involves minimizing deviations of inflation and output from their targets. Both these targets can be achieved at time $t = 15$ when the optimal commitment implies targeting positive inflation and generating an output boom. Hence the central bank has an incentive to renege on its previous commitment and achieve zero inflation and keep output at its optimal target. The private sector anticipates this, so that the solution under discretion is the one given in (6) and (7); this is the deflation bias of discretionary policy.

Shaping expectations

The lesson of the irrelevance results is that monetary policy is ineffective if it cannot stir expectations. The previous section illustrated, however, that shaping expectations in the correct way can be very important for minimizing the output contraction and deflation associated with deflationary shocks. This, however, may be difficult for a government that is expected to behave in a discretionary manner. How can the correct set of expectations be generated?

Perhaps the simplest solution is for the government to make clear *announcements* about its future policy through the appropriate 'policy rule'. This was the lesson of the 'rules vs. discretion' literature started by Kydland and Prescott (1977) to solve the inflation bias, and the same logic applies here even if the nature of the 'dynamic inconsistency' that gives rise to the deflation bias is different from the standard one. To the extent that announcements about future policy are believed, they can have a very big effect. There is a large literature on the different policy rules that minimize the distortions associated with deflationary shocks. One example is found in both Eggertsson and Woodford (2003) and Wolman (2005). They show that, if the government follows a form of price level targeting, the optimal commitment solution can be closely or even completely replicated, depending on the sophistication of the targeting regime. Under the proposed policy rule the central bank commits to keep the interest rate at zero until a particular price level is hit, which happens well after the deflationary shocks have subsided.

If the central bank, and the government as a whole, has a very low level of credibility, a mere announcement of future policy intentions through a new 'policy rule' may not be sufficient. This is especially true in a deflationary environment, for at least three reasons. First, the deflation bias implies that the government has an incentive to promise to deliver future expansion and higher inflation, and then to renege on this promise. Second, the deflationary shocks that give rise to this commitment problem are rare, and it is therefore harder for a central bank to build up a reputation for dealing with them well. Third, this problem is even further aggravated at zero interest rates because then the central bank cannot take any direct actions (that is, cutting interest rate) to show its new commitment to reflation. This has led many authors to consider other policy options for the government as a whole that make a reflation credible, that is, make the optimal commitment described in the previous section 'incentive compatible'.

Perhaps the most straightforward way to make a reflation credible is for the government to issue debt, for example by deficit spending. It is well known in the literature that government debt creates an inflationary incentive (see, for example, Calvo, 1978). Suppose the government promises future inflation and in addition prints one dollar of debt. If the government later reneges on its promised inflation, the real value of this one dollar of debt will increase by the same amount. Then the government will need to raise taxes to compensate for the increase in the real debt. To the extent that taxation is costly, it will no longer be in the interest of the government to renege on its promises to inflate the price level, even after deflationary pressures have subsided in the example above. This commitment device is explored in Eggertsson (2006a), which shows that this is an effective tool to battle deflation.

Jeanne and Svensson (2007) and Eggertsson (2006a) show that foreign exchange interventions also have this effect, for very similar reasons. The reason is that foreign exchange interventions change the balance sheet of the government so that a policy of reflation is incentive compatible. The reason is that, if the government prints nominal liabilities (such as government bonds or money) and purchases foreign exchange, it will incur balance-sheet losses if it reneges on an inflation promise because this would imply an exchange rate appreciation and thus a portfolio loss.

There are many other tools in the arsenal of the government to battle deflation. Real government spending, that is, government purchases of real goods and services, can also be effective to this end (Eggertsson, 2005). Perhaps the most surprising one is that policies that temporarily reduce the natural level of output, Y_t^n, can be shown to increase equilibrium output (Eggertsson, 2006b). The reason is that policies that suppress the natural level of output create actual and expected reflation in the price level and this effect is strong enough to generate recovery because of the impact on real interest rates.

Conclusion: the Great Depression and the liquidity trap

As mentioned in the introduction, the old literature on the liquidity trap was motivated by the Great Depression. The modern literature on the liquidity trap not only sheds light on recent events in Japan and the United States (as discussed above) but also provides new insights into the US recovery from the Great Depression. This article has reviewed theoretical results that indicate that a policy of reflation can induce a substantial increase in output when there are deflationary shocks (compare the solid line and the dashed line in Figure 1: moving from one equilibrium to the other implies a substantial increase in output). Interestingly, Franklin Delano Roosevelt (FDR) announced a policy of reflating the price level in 1933 to its pre-Depression level when he became President in 1933. To achieve reflation FDR not only announced an explicit objective of reflation but also implemented several policies which made this objective credible. These policies include all those reviewed in the previous section, such as massive deficit spending, higher real government spending, foreign exchange interventions, and even policies that reduced the natural level of output (the National Industrial Recovery Act and the Agricultural Adjustment Act: see Eggertsson, 2006b, for discussion). As discussed in Eggertsson (2005; 2006b) these policies may greatly have contributed to the end of the depression. Output increased by 39 per cent during 1933–7, with the turning point occurring immediately after FDR's inauguration, when he announced the policy objective of reflation. In 1937, however, the administration moved away from reflation and the stimulative policies that supported it – prematurely declaring victory over the depression – which helps explaining the downturn in 1937–8, when monthly industrial production fell by 30 per cent in less than a year. The recovery resumed once the administration recommitted to reflation (see Eggertsson and Puglsey, 2006). The modern analysis of the liquidity trap indicates that, while zero short-term interest rates made static changes in the money supply irrelevant during this period, expectations about the future evolution of the money supply and the interest rate were key factors determining aggregate demand. Thus, recent research indicates that monetary policy was far from being ineffective during the Great Depression, but it worked mainly through expectations.

GAUTI B. EGGERTSSON

See also **expectations; inflation expectations; optimal fiscal and monetary policy (with commitment); optimal fiscal and monetary policy (without commitment).**

Bibliography

Adam, K. and Billi, R. 2006. Optimal monetary policy under commitment with a zero bound on nominal interest rates. *Journal of Money, Credit and Banking* (forthcoming).

Benhabib, J., Schmitt-Grohe, S. and Uribe, M. 2001. Monetary policy and multiple equilibria. *American Economic Review* 91, 167–86.

Calvo, G. 1978. On the time consistency of optimal policy in a monetary economy. *Econometrica* 46, 1411–28.

Eggertsson, G. 2005. Great expectations and the end of the depression. Staff Report No. 234. Federal Reserve Bank of New York.

Eggertsson, G. 2006a. The deflation bias and committing to being irresponsible. *Journal of Money, Credit and Banking* 38, 283–322.

Eggertsson, G. 2006b. Was the New Deal contractionary? Working paper, Federal Reserve Bank of New York.

Eggertsson, G. and Pugsley, B. 2006. The mistake of 1937: a general equilibrium analysis. *Monetary and Economic Studies* 24(SI), 151–90.

Eggertsson, G. and Woodford, M. 2003. The zero bound on interest rates and optimal monetary policy. *Brookings Papers on Economic Activity* 2003(1), 212–19.

Jeanne, O. and Svensson, L. 2007. Credible commitment to optimal escape from a liquidity trap: the role of the balance sheet of an independent central bank. *American Economic Review* 97, 474–90.

Jung, T., Teranishi, Y. and Watanabe, T. 2005. Zero bound on nominal interest rates and optimal monetary policy. *Journal of Money, Credit and Banking* 37, 813–36.

Krugman, P. 1998. It's baaack! Japan's slump and the return of the liquidity trap. *Brookings Papers on Economic Activity* 1998(2), 137–87.

Kydland, F. and Prescott, E. 1977. Rules rather than discretion: the inconsistency of optimal plans. *Journal of Political Economy* 85, 473–91.

Reifschneider, D. and Williams, J. 2000. Three lessons for monetary policy in a low inflation era. *Journal of Money, Credit and Banking* 32, 936–66.

Wolman, A. 2005. Real implications of the zero bound on nominal interest rates. *Journal of Money, Credit and Banking* 37, 273–96.

Woodford, M. 2003. *Interest and Prices: Foundations of a Theory of Monetary Policy*. Princeton: Princeton University Press.

List, Friedrich (1789–1846)

Known chiefly as a proponent of economic nationalism and protection to 'infant industries', List's career followed a colourful, not to say disorderly course, from his engagement on behalf of a customs union in the early 1820s to exile and residence in the United States, agitation on behalf of railway construction, energetic economic journalism, and finally to his death by suicide in November 1846, depressed by his lack of success in promoting a commercial agreement between Prussia and Britain and also by chronic financial insecurity. Born into the family of a tanner on or about 6 August 1789 in Reutlingen, Württemberg, List's early life was unremarkable. After briefly working in his father's business, he entered service in the state administration as a clerk and in 1811 secured a position in Tübingen. There he began attending the occasional law lecture, giving up his appointment in 1813 to concentrate on his legal studies. He never sat for the final lawyers' examination, instead taking and passing the actuaries' examination in September 1814.

Re-entering the administration as an accountant, he was promoted in 1816 to the position of Chief Examiner of Accounts. At the same time he became involved in the publication of a reformist journal, contributing articles on the reform of local administration. Through his connections in Stuttgart he also became involved in proposals for the creation of a new faculty for state economy at the University of Tübingen; teaching began in January 1818 and List was appointed full professor of administrative practice. List seems to have made little effort to compensate for his lack of formal academic qualification for the post, and he was dismissed in mid-1819 for absenteeism.

It is at this point that List's 'life' begins; for it transpired that his absence during April 1819 was on account of his attendance at the founding meeting of the German Association for Trade and Commerce, a body dedicated to the abolition of internal barriers to trade and which appointed List consular secretary. During the following year List travelled on behalf of the Association, and was also elected to the Württemberg representative assembly as Deputy for Reutlingen. As a result of his activities in the latter role he was tried and sentenced for sedition in 1822; appealing from the sanctuary of Baden, he failed to get the verdict altered and began a life of exile, travelling in 1823 to Paris where he made the acquaintance of Lafayette. In May 1824, believing that he had been reprieved, List returned to Stuttgart, was promptly imprisoned and, in January 1825, exiled.

Acting on a suggestion of Lafayette, List set sail for America with his family in April 1825. Taking advantage of a tour that Lafayette was undertaking at the time, List travelled and studied, making the acquaintance of several leading political figures. Settling in Pennsylvania, where he briefly tried his hand at farming, he assumed in 1826 the editorship of a German-language newspaper, the *Readinger Adler*, and became closely associated with the Pennsylvania Society for the Encouragement of Manufactures and Mechanic Arts. Through this involvement he became a supporter of the 'American system' of protective tariffs, and published in late 1827 his first serious economic work, *Outlines of American Political Economy*, which was a critique of Thomas Cooper's free-trade *Elements of Political Economy*. Such was the success of this that the Pennsylvania Society asked List to write a school textbook on political economy, but only the first chapter of this work was ever written.

As a result of an interest in coal deposits List became involved in a railway construction company which eventually opened its railroad in 1831. By this time, List had supported the presidential campaign of Jackson in 1828 and had become an American citizen; he returned to Europe, settling there permanently in late 1832 and in 1834 was appointed American Consul in Leipzig. There he became involved with the construction of the Leipzig–Dresden railway and founded the *Eisenbahn-journal* (1835), but he parted with his fellow projectors in 1837 and moved to Paris, where he spent the next three years writing a prize essay and pursuing various journalistic projects.

After his period in Paris, he moved to Augsburg and then resumed his agitation on behalf of German economic unity and south German protectionism. As before, this was largely conducted through the medium of newspapers, one of these being the *Zollvereinsblatt*, founded in 1843. These last restless years brought literary success with the publication of his *National System of Political Economy*, but little effective influence on the formation of contemporary commercial policy.

List's contribution to the formation of the Zollverein was limited to the period between 1819 and 1820, when he travelled German courts representing the cause of tariff reform. His theoretical proposals concerning protection and 'infant industries' date from his American period and are indeed a direct result of his American experience of tariff debates in the later 1820s. Much of his writing is repetitive of simple themes, as one would expect of work produced in haste for newspapers, journals and pamphlets arguing for specific reforms. However, the general logic of his position can be summarized in the following terms.

The Smithian principle of 'natural liberty' and commercial freedom was a 'cosmopolitan doctrine' which erroneously generalized the situation of Britain to the rest of the world. Commercial freedom in this sense was a freedom for Britain to dominate the world economy, thanks to the degree of development of the British economy. Free trade and economic liberty were highly desirable for a true world economy, but were only appropriate to a world of economic equals. Such a world could be created only if those countries which were in the process of development could protect their key industries against premature competition. On the international front it was necessary to create a system of treaties and agreements which would regulate trade and competition in such a way that protective tariffs and other protectionist measures would one day be redundant. On the national level, it was important to abolish internal limitations to development, such as duties between German states which hindered trade and communication. A powerful device for the creation of strong national economies was the railway, perceived not so much for its freight capacity as for its role in promoting the freedom of movement of active populations. While the abolition of internal duties opened up the fiscal geography of an economy, this space was to be given shape by a railway network which would link major centres of population – and it is this emphasis on a communications *network* that distinguishes List's work in the 1830s.

List's writing on railway development is scattered in several articles and was never presented systematically, but his conception of economic liberty and world economic development is developed in the two books he published, and the prize essay which he wrote in Paris. His *Outlines of American Political Economy* clearly contrasts a 'Smithian' economy of individuals and of mankind with 'national economy'. The error of Smith was to believe that the promotion of 'individual economy' – the satisfaction of individual wants – would lead to 'the economy of mankind' or cosmo-political economy – securing the necessities and comforts of life to the whole human race. List argued that this would not happen; the true path to the economy of mankind lay through national economy, the consideration of measures and conditions appropriate to actually existing nations. The general laws of economics outlined by Smith and his followers could manifest themselves only through these nations, which necessarily modified the operation of these laws by force of their specific 'productive powers'.

The strength and independence of a national economy was secured through the control of the interior market, enabling the economy to flourish on the basis of its natural and human endowments.

The Natural System of Political Economy was written in 1837 as a response to questions concerning the ways of reconciling the interests of producers and consumers on the introduction of commercial liberty. This recapitulates the argument on individual and cosmopolitan economy already developed in the *Outlines*, but goes further in elaborating a general theory of economic development as a series of stages of agricultural, manufacturing and commercial activity. While the first stage involves a basic reliance on agriculture, by the fourth and final stage raw materials are imported for manufacture and re-export, while food is also imported.

The National System of Political Economy was published in 1841 and represents a rounding out of arguments already exposed in his earlier writing. Importantly, List now placed his arguments in a general conception of the civilizing process of international trade, underlining the fact that his opposition to free trade was by no means a narrowly nationalistic one. Also added to the original arguments is a conception of the international division of labour elaborated on the basis of the distinction of manufacture and agriculture. List divided the world into temperate zones naturally oriented towards manufacture, and hot zones with a natural advantage in the production of agricultural goods. A balanced development of the world economy, or in other words the civilizing process, requires that the nations in the temperate zone be in equilibrium with each other and that they neither singly nor jointly exploit the lands of the hot zone, which would otherwise become dependent on manufacturing powers.

Much of the *National System* is given over to a historical account of economic development which today is very dated, while List's critique of classical economics is likewise limited by the primarily non-academic readership to which he appealed. Nonetheless, his emphasis on productive powers rather than 'value and capital', and his insistence on the specificity of national endowments and conditions in considering world economic development remain of interest. While List's primary interest lay in political and economic reform, and his audience was emergent 'informed popular opinion', he nevertheless developed conceptions of economic space and economic development that have lasting intellectual merits.

K. TRIBE

Selected works

1827. *Outlines of American Political Economy*. Reprinted in *The Life of Friedrich List and Selection from his Writings*, ed. M.E. Hirst. London: Smith, Elder & Co., 1909.

1837. *The Natural System of Political Economy*. Trans. and ed. W.O. Henderson, London: Cass, 1983.

1841. *Das nationale System der politischen Oekonomie*. Stuttgart and Tübingen: J.G. Cotta. Trans. G.A. Matile as

National System of Political Economy, Philadelphia: J.B. Lippincott & Co., 1856. Trans. S.S. Lloyd as *The National System of Political Economy*, London: Longmans & Co., 1885.

1927–36. *Friedrich List. Schriften, Reden, Briefe*, 10 vols. Berlin.

litigation, economics of

Litigation refers to the process of taking an argument to a court of law where a decision will be made.

The discipline of economics has provided researchers – economists and legal scholars alike – with useful tools and frameworks for thinking about litigation. Is there too much litigation or too little? Why do some lawsuits go to trial while many others settle before trial? Should the losing party be required to reimburse the winning party's legal expenses? The first part of this article presents the main frameworks for studying the economics of litigation. The second part surveys just some of the active topics in the literature.

This article is largely a condensed version of Spier (2005). Previous surveys of this topic include Cooter and Rubinfeld (1989), Hay and Spier (1998), and Daughety (2000).

Basic framework

The decision to litigate

Suppose there are two *litigants*: one *plaintiff* and one *defendant*. The plaintiff is the injured party who seeks compensation; the defendant is the party who is potentially responsible for the plaintiff's injuries.

A plaintiff will rationally choose to bring suit when the expected gross return from litigation, x, exceeds the cost of pursuing the case, c_p. The gross return, x, represents the expected judgment at the end of a long and costly trial or a settlement that takes place at some time prior to the trial. It could also reflect other issues, such as the impact that a court decision will have on future cases or the plaintiff's concern for her business reputation. In general, the plaintiff's cost of pursuing the case, c_p, and the defendant's cost of fighting back, c_d, would influence the gross return, x, and could be modelled in a similar way to other economic contests (Dixit, 1987). For the moment, however, we will treat them as exogenous.

The plaintiff's incentive to bring suit typically diverges from what is best for society as a whole (see Shavell, 1982b; 1997). Consider a situation where accidents are totally avoided if the defendant makes a small investment in precautions. If the plaintiff were expected to sue following an accident, the defendant would rationally take the precautions. No accidents would occur and no litigation costs would be incurred. If $c_p > x$, however, then the plaintiff lacks a credible threat to sue. Knowing this, the defendant has no incentive to take the precautions

(however inexpensive). In this example, the plaintiff's private incentive to sue is *socially insufficient*. This is not always the case, however. Suppose that the defendant's investment is totally ineffective: accidents occur whether or not the defendant takes precautions. Following an accident, the plaintiff will sue the defendant when $c_p < x$. The plaintiff's incentive to bring suit is *socially excessive* in this example. Litigation is a socially wasteful activity here because there is nothing the defendant could have done to avoid the accident.

Settlement

Not surprisingly, the overwhelming majority of lawsuits settle before trial. (Fewer than four per cent of civil cases that are filed in the US State Courts go to trial; see Ostrom, Kauder and La Fountain, 2001, p. 29). To use our earlier notation, the plaintiff will receive a net payoff of $x - c_p$ if the case goes to court and the defendant will receive $-x - c_d$. Although x represents a simple transfer from the defendant to the plaintiff, the litigation costs, $c_p + c_d$, represent a deadweight loss. Any out-of-court transfer $S \in (x - c_p, x + c_d)$ from the defendant to the plaintiff would be a Pareto improvement. The precise outcome of settlement negotiations will hinge on a variety of factors, including the timing of offers and counteroffers, the information and beliefs of the two litigants, and the nature of the broader legal and strategic environment.

Settlement with symmetric information

Suppose that the litigants are symmetrically informed and play an alternating-offer game with $T-1$ rounds of bargaining before trial in round T. At trial, the defendant pays x to the plaintiff and the litigation costs, c_p and c_d, are incurred. The litigants share a common discount factor, δ.

This game is easily solved by backwards induction. Suppose that the plaintiff is designated to make the last settlement offer in period $T-1$. The defendant will accept any offer that is better than going to trial, so the plaintiff will offer $S_{T-1} = \delta(x + c_d)$, minus a penny perhaps. If the case hasn't settled earlier, it will certainly settle on the courthouse steps. If we work backwards, the litigants are willing to settle for $S_{T-2} = \delta^2(x + c_d)$ in period $T-2$, and (by an extension of this logic) are willing to settle for $S_1 = \delta^{T-1}(x + c_d)$ in period 1.

Two observations about this example are in order. First, the allocation of the bargaining surplus is sensitive to the timing of the settlement offers. If the defendant were the one to make the last offer instead, then the case would settle for $S_{T-1} = \delta(x - c_p)$ in the last round and, working backwards, we would have $S_1 = \delta^{T-1}(x - c_p)$. In other words, the party who makes the last offer succeeds in extracting all of the bargaining surplus. The bargaining surplus would, of course, be more evenly allocated in a random-offer or framework where the two litigants flip a coin to determine who makes an offer.

Second, this simple example does not predict exactly *when* settlement will take place. The litigants are, in fact, indifferent between settling for $S_1 = \delta^{T-1}(x + c_d)$ in period 1 and for $S_{T-1} = \delta(x + c_d)$ on the courthouse steps. The reason for this is straightforward: there is no inefficiency associated with delay when the litigation costs are entirely borne at trial. (Settlement models differ from the related models of bilateral trade. There, discounting causes the pie to shrink. Here, discounting by itself does not affect the size of the pie.) If the costs of litigation were incurred gradually over time instead, so the first $T-1$ rounds of bargaining were costly as well, then there would be a unique subgame-perfect equilibrium with settlement in period 1 (Bebchuk, 1996).

Settlement with asymmetric information

Asymmetric information is common in litigation settings. Plaintiffs often have first-hand knowledge about the damages they have suffered; defendants often have first-hand knowledge about their degree of involvement in the accident. Litigants also receive private signals concerning the credibility of their witnesses and the quality and work ethic of their lawyers. Some of this information will become commonly known over time – the parties surely learn a great deal through pretrial proceedings and discovery. Other information may never come to light at all, but can nevertheless affect trial outcomes.

Suppose that the defendant has private information about x, the expected judgment at trial. A similar analysis would follow if the plaintiff were privately informed instead. Formally, suppose x drawn from a nicely behaved probability density function $f(x)$ on $[\underline{x}, \bar{x}]$ with cumulative density $F(x)$. Starting with P'ng (1983) and Bebchuk (1984), many papers assume that the uninformed player – the plaintiff in our example – makes a single take-it-or-leave-it settlement offer, S, before trial. The defendant accepts S if it is lower than what he would expect to pay at trial, $S < \delta(x + c_d)$. The offer generates a 'cut-off,' $\hat{x} = \delta^{-1}S - c_d$, where defendant types above the cut-off accept the offer and those below the cut-off reject the offer and go to court.

The plaintiff's optimization problem may be written as a function of the cutoff, $\hat{x}$: $Max \int_{\underline{x}}^{\hat{x}} \delta(x - c_p)f(x)\,dx + [1 - F(\hat{x})]\delta(\hat{x} + c_d)$. The first term represents the plaintiff's net payoff associated with those types who reject the settlement offer, and the second term reflects the settlement payments from the defendant types above the cut-off, $\hat{x}$, who accept the offer. Any interior solution is characterized by the following first-order condition:

$$1 - F(\hat{x}) - (c_p + c_d)f(\hat{x}) = 0.$$

At least some cases will settle – the plaintiff will certainly make a settlement offer that is accepted by the most liable defendants – and an interior solution exists when $(c_p + c_d)$ is not too high.

Bebchuk's basic model has been extended in a variety of ways. Nalebuff (1987) argues that the plaintiff may no longer have a credible commitment to take the case to trial following the rejection of the settlement offer, and explicitly incorporates a credibility constraint. Spier (1992) allows the plaintiff to make a sequence of settlement offers before trial. When litigation costs are all borne at trial (so there is no efficiency loss from delay), the plaintiff waits until the very last moment to offer $S_{T-1} = \delta(\hat{x} + c_d)$, where $\hat{x}$ is defined above. (The deadline effect is less pronounced when there are pretrial costs as well.) Reinganum and Wilde (1986) let the informed litigant made a single take-it-or-leave-it offer before trial and characterize a perfect Bayesian equilibrium – unique under the D1 refinement of Cho and Kreps (1987). The defendant's equilibrium offer $S(x) = \delta(x - c_p)$ perfectly reveals his type. Making the correct inference, the plaintiff is indifferent and accepts the settlement offer with probability

$$\pi(x) = e^{-(\bar{x}-x)/(c_p+c_d)}.$$

Note that this probability is increasing in the defendant's expected liability, x. This is implied by incentive compatibility; the defendant must be rewarded in equilibrium for making higher settlement offers with a higher rate of acceptance by the plaintiff.

Some scholars have used mechanism-design techniques to study settlement and have shown, among other things, that some cases will *necessarily* go to trial when the litigation costs are not too large (Spier, 1994a). In contrast to Myerson and Satterthwaite's (1983) analysis of bilateral trade, settlement bargaining breaks down with one-sided incomplete information and despite common knowledge that gains from trade exist. (Schweizer, 1989, and Daughety and Reinganum, 1994, explore extensive form games with two-sided asymmetric information.) Finally, it is important to mention an older literature where litigants have different priors about the outcome at trial. Landes (1971), Posner (1973), and Gould (1973) show that settlement negotiations may fail when the two sides are sufficiently optimistic. (See Loewenstein et al., 1993, for empirical evidence on self-serving biases.)

Normative implications

There are strong normative arguments in favour of settlement. Through a private settlement, the parties can avoid their litigation costs and (if they are risk averse) the risk premium associated with trials. *All else equal*, private settlement serves society's interest. What makes this topic more interesting – and sometimes exceptionally challenging – is that *all else is not equal*. First, settlement dilutes a defendant's incentives to avoid accidents. Following an accident, the defendant is better off if he has the option to settle his claim. Anticipating settlement on relatively advantageous terms, the defendant has less incentive to take precautions to avoid the lawsuit to begin with (Polinsky and Rubinfeld, 1988). (This not necessarily a bad thing: when cases settle out of court the litigations costs are avoided so the social cost of an accident is lower. Therefore, the defendant *should* be taking less care than if all cases went to trial.) Spier (1997) shows that the defendant's incentives are diluted even further if the defendant has private information. Second, the plaintiff is made better off through settlement than she would be going to trial and is therefore more likely to bring the suit. Therefore, the anticipation of settlement raises the *overall volume of cases* that are pursued.

Topics

Accuracy

Several papers present formal analyses of the social value of accuracy in legal settings. Kaplow and Shavell (1996) argue that the *ex post* accurate verification of the victim's damages is socially valuable if the injurer knew the victim's damages at the time when he chose his precaution level. Accuracy is not valuable, however, if the victim's damages could not have been known by the injurer *ex ante*. The 'scheduling' of damages, or standardizing awards for injuries that fall into particular categories (as in workers' compensation), may be desirable in these cases. Scheduling also makes the future outcome of the case more transparent – there is less to argue about – and can help to promote settlement (Spier, 1994b). Kaplow and Shavell (1992) argue that accuracy gives injurers an incentive to learn about the injuries that their activities might cause and will subsequently fine-tune their precautions. (Accurate information created by earlier trials may also help future actors fine-tune their actions; Hua and Spier, 2005.)

Alternative dispute resolution

Alternative dispute resolution (ADR) refers to the formal and informal proceedings that help parties resolve their disputes *outside* of formal litigation. Unlike settlement, which is typically achieved by the litigants themselves (and their lawyers), ADR proceedings often involve third parties who offer opinions and/or advice. Many of these systems are part of the court system, but many others are designed by the parties themselves (for example, ADR clauses in commercial contracts). In either case, ADR reflects the need to reduce the transaction costs of litigation and to make accurate decisions (Shavell, 1994; Mnookin, 1998). Farber and White's (1991) empirical study of medical malpractice claims suggests that non-binding arbitration provides an informative signal and encourages subsequent settlement. Yoon (2004) confirms this result, but finds that ADR neither reduces litigation costs nor significantly shortens the delay. The importance of this topic and the relative dearth of research – both theoretical and empirical – makes ADR a ripe topic for further investigation.

Appeals

In most legal systems, a litigant who is dissatisfied with a lower court's decision can appeal to a higher court. In Shavell (1995), appeals can be an efficient means of correcting the errors made at the lower-court level. Appeals harness the private information of the litigants themselves: an incorrectly convicted defendant is more likely to appeal an earlier ruling since the probability of reversal is higher. In this way, resources are saved relative to random auditing. (See also Spitzer and Talley, 2000.) Daughety and Reinganum (2000a) consider a Bayesian model of appeals where the upper court perceives the private decision to appeal as informative and tries to rule 'correctly' given its posterior beliefs.

Bifurcation

Landes (1993) was the first to formally analyse 'bifurcated' trials where the court establishes the defendant's negligence before determining the plaintiff's damages. One benefit of bifurcation is that, once the defendant is absolved of liability, no further costs are incurred. The effect on the settlement rate is ambiguous, however. Chen, Chien and Chu (1997) consider these issues in a model with asymmetric information. Daughety and Reinganum (2000b) endogenize the level of litigation spending. White (2002), in her empirical analysis of asbestos trials, shows bifurcation raises the plaintiffs' expected returns and increases the number of cases that are filed.

Case selection

The cases that go to trial are the tip of the iceberg – the vast majority of cases are settled before trial. These tried cases are likely to differ – perhaps systematically – from the cases that never reach the courtroom. Suppose the defendant is privately informed about the expected judgment at trial. Both the screening (Bebchuk, 1984) and signalling (Reinganum and Wilde, 1986) approaches discussed earlier predict that defendants with weak cases are more likely to settle out of court than defendants with strong cases. Intuitively, a defendant who expects an adverse judgment is more likely to accept a settlement offer. This result would be reversed if the plaintiff has private information instead. Many authors have explored case selection using models with non-common priors instead of asymmetric information. Most notably, Priest and Klein (1984) predicted that, for tried cases, the plaintiff win rate will tend towards 50 per cent. This stark result depends on the symmetry of the litigants, among other things. (With asymmetric information, Shavell, 1996, shows that any plaintiff win rate is possible.) More generally, however, the Priest–Klein framework suggests ways that trial rates may be systematically related to plaintiff win rates. Waldfogel (1995) estimates a structural model and finds results roughly consistent with the Priest–Klein theory.

Class actions

When an injurer has harmed a group of victims, these victims may (under some circumstances) join their claims for the purpose of litigation and/or settlement. One advantage of consolidation is the scale economies associated with common proceedings and legal representation. Che (1996) assumes that plaintiffs who join a class forgo a fine-tuned award and receive instead the average damage of the group. Absent settlement, it is clear that plaintiffs with weak cases are more likely to join a class. This adverse selection problem is mitigated when plaintiffs are privately informed. Weak plaintiffs have an incentive to remain independent, too, in an attempt to 'signal' that they have strong cases and, in equilibrium, fewer weak plaintiffs join the class. Che (2002) argues that classes may form to increase the members' bargaining power via information aggregation. The defendant is more generous when bargaining with the class as a whole than when bargaining with individuals.

Contingent fees

In the United States, plaintiffs' attorneys are often paid on a contingent basis, receiving a third (say) of any settlement or judgment but nothing if the case is lost. The use of contingent fees is regulated in the US. In particular, lawyers are prohibited from purchasing cases from their clients (Santore and Viard, 2001). Many European countries prohibit contingent fees altogether. There are many economic rationales for contingent fees. First, they give liquidity-constrained plaintiffs a way to finance their cases and shift some of the risk to the attorney. They also mitigate moral hazard (Danzon, 1983) and adverse selection problems. In Rubinfeld and Scotchmer (1993), attorneys have private information about their abilities and signal high quality through a willingness to accept contingent payment. Menus of contingent fees also arise when the clients have private information. (See also the mechanism-design model of Klement and Neeman, 2004.) In Dana and Spier (1993), the attorney has private information about the merits of the plaintiff's case. With contingent fees, the plaintiff can rest assured that the attorney will decline cases that are sure to lose. Finally, contingent fees can also be used strategically to make plaintiffs into 'tougher' negotiators (Hay, 1997; Bebchuk and Guzman, 1996). In empirical studies, Danzon and Lillard (1983) show a higher drop rate with contingent fees, and Helland and Tabarrok (2003) find that contingent fees are associated with higher-quality cases and faster case resolution.

Decoupling

It may be socially desirable to tax or subsidize the plaintiff's damage award. In Polinsky and Che (1991), a defendant chooses his level of precautions and, if injured, the plaintiff decides whether to bring suit. The optimal decoupled scheme taxes the plaintiff's award so that only a handful of cases are brought, but, at the same time, it makes the award very large so that the defendant's incentives are maintained. Since the defendant's stakes are large relative to the plaintiff's, the defendant will tend to spend more at trial (Kahan and Tuckman, 1995; Choi and Sanchirico, 2004). Daughety and Reinganum (2003) consider these issues in a model with asymmetric information.

Disclosure and discovery

Litigants may voluntarily share information before trial. Indeed, the 'unravelling' logic of Grossman (1981) implies that all private information would come to light because an adverse inference would be drawn from silence. Full unravelling cannot occur, however, when hard evidence is simply unavailable. Guilty defendants have an incentive to pool with the innocent defendants who are unable to prove their innocence, for example. This suggests an important role for laws that require litigants to share information before trial. 'Discovery' can improve the accuracy of later court decisions (Hay, 1994; Cooter and Rubinfeld, 1994) and facilitate settlement negotiations before trial by narrowing the scope of asymmetric information (Shavell, 1989). (In contrast, Schrag, 1999, argues that discovery can lead to higher litigation costs and longer delays.) In Farber and White's (1991) sample of medical malpractice cases, many lawsuits are settled or dropped following discovery. Using a survey of attorneys in federal civil cases, Shepherd (1999) finds defendants increase their discovery efforts, 'tit-for-tat', in response to heightened discovery requests by the plaintiff.

The English Rule

In the United States, litigants bear their own costs of litigation – the 'American Rule'. In contrast, the 'English Rule' shifts the winner's costs to the loser. Shavell (1982a) and Katz (1990) show that the English Rule discourages the filing of low-probability-of-prevailing cases but encourages high-probability-of-prevailing cases. (Kaplow, 1993, and Polinsky and Rubinfeld, 1998, discuss the normative implications.) The English Rule also tends to raise the litigation rate when parties disagree about the probability of winning (Bebchuk, 1984; Shavell, 1982a). Intuitively, the scope for disagreement is even higher because the parties have different beliefs about who will bear the litigation costs. Finally, the English Rule tends to raise the level of litigation spending (Braeutigam, Owen and Panzar, 1984; Hause, 1989; Katz, 1987). Intuitively, the marginal cost associated with spending is lower since the costs are partially externalized.

Inquisitorial versus adversarial systems

In adversarial systems, each side gathers and processes information separately. In inquisitorial systems – such as those found in continental Europe – these activities are more centralized and often presided over by a judge (see the discussion in Parisi, 2002). Adversarial systems are often criticized for giving litigants an incentive to hide relevant information from each other and from the court. They also can lead to the wasteful duplication of effort. On the other hand, adversarial systems may provide better incentives for information gathering (Dewatripont and Tirole, 1999). Milgrom and Roberts (1986) present a persuasion game where the parties have equal access to all of the relevant evidence and show that accuracy is not compromised in equilibrium. This stark result may no longer hold when parties have asymmetric access to evidence or when evidence is costly to gather and disclose; see also Shin (1998), Daughety and Reinganum (2000b) and Froeb and Kobayashi (1996).

Insurance contracts

It is common for insurance contracts to place an upper bound on the level of coverage. This creates a potential conflict between the defendant and his insurer when deciding to settle a case (Meurer, 1992; Sykes, 1994). The insurance company is averse to settling because the defendant will bear the downside of a very large judgment at trial. Nevertheless, the defendant may delegate settlement authority to his insurer as a strategic commitment to be 'tough' in settlement negotiations. By reducing the most that the insurer is willing to pay in settlement, the insurance contract serves to extract value from the plaintiff. These contracts may be undesirable from a social welfare perspective, however, since the toughness of the insurer can increase the litigation rate (and the associated litigation costs). Formally, these ideas are related to Aghion and Bolton's (1987) analysis of contracts as a barrier to entry. (Spier and Sykes, 1998, show that corporate debt has a similar strategic value.)

Joint and several liability

There are many situations where a single victim is harmed by the actions of many injurers (for example, toxic-tort and price-fixing cases). Common rules for allocating responsibility include non-joint liability, where each losing defendant is responsible for his own share of damages, and joint and several liability, where a single losing defendant can be held responsible for the entirety of the plaintiff's damages. Kornhauser and Revesz (1994) analyse settlement incentives when the liability of a non-settling defendant is reduced, dollar for dollar, by the value of the previous settlements. (If the plaintiff's damages are $80 and one defendant settles for S, the remaining defendant may be responsible for $80 - S$.) This rule encourages settlement when the cases are positively correlated but discourages settlement when the cases are independent. Some empirical support has been found in disputes between the Environmental Protection Agency (EPA) and Superfund defendants (Chang and Sigman, 2000).

Most-favoured-nation clauses

Settlement contracts in environments with multiple plaintiffs sometimes include 'most-favoured-nation' (MFN) clauses. They work in the following way: if an early settlement agreement includes an MFN clause and the defendant settles later with another plaintiff for more money, the early settlers receive the better terms, too. Spier (2003a) argues that MFN clauses economize on delay costs when a single defendant makes repeated offers to privately informed plaintiffs. MFNs may also be used to extract value from future plaintiffs (Spier, 2003b; Daughety and Reinganum, 2004). Intuitively, an MFN commits the defendant to be tough in future negotiations, allowing the defendant and the early plaintiffs to capture a greater share of the future bargaining surplus. The welfare effects of most-favoured-nation clauses are ambiguous. They can make early settlement negotiations more efficient but may lead later negotiations to fail.

Negative expected value claims

Suppose that a plaintiff has a negative expected value (NEV) claim – he stands to lose money if the case proceeds all the way to trial. Could this plaintiff succeed in extracting a settlement from the defendant? Interestingly, the *divisibility* of litigation costs over time can make the plaintiff's threat to litigate the NEV claim credible (Bebchuk, 1996). Here is the intuition. With divisibility, the bulk of the costs are sunk once the case reaches the courthouse steps. At that point, the plaintiff's threat to litigate is credible, so the defendant will settle. If we work backwards, the plaintiff's threat to continue may be credible at all stages of the game. Furthermore, a privately informed plaintiff with a NEV claim may mimic a plaintiff with a positive expected value claim and the defendant (not knowing for sure) may capitulate (Bebchuk, 1988; Katz, 1990). Finally, Rosenberg and Shavell (1985) present a model where the defendant must sink some defence costs or risk a summary judgment before trial.

Offer-of-judgment rules

Under Rule 68 of the United States Rules of Civil Procedure, if a plaintiff rejects a settlement offer and later receives a judgment that is less favourable, then the plaintiff is forced to bear the defendant's post-offer costs. Other rules allow for two-sided cost shifting. Spier (1994a) shows that these rules raise the settlement rate when liability is acknowledged but there is private information about damages. Intuitively, the rule serves to discipline aggressive settlement tactics (but see Farmer and Pecorino, 2000, and Miller, 1986). Bebchuk and Chang (1999) show that offer-of-judgment rules level the playing field in bargaining and lead to settlements that more accurately reflect the expected judgment at trial.

Patent litigation

Suppose that a patentee and an imitator are trying to settle a dispute. At trial, the patent may be invalidated, in which case the imitator will compete on equal footing with the patentee. Settlement provides an opportunity for collusion. Shapiro (2003) discusses these mechanisms and proposed criteria for judicial approval of patent settlements; see also Meurer (1989). Marshall, Meurer and Richard (1994) argue that the mere threat of patent litigation may be enough to soften competition in a patent race; see also Choi (1998). Lanjouw and Schankerman (2001) document interesting correlations between litigation decisions and the characteristics of the patents. In particular, a patent is more likely to be litigated if it serves as the 'base of a cumulative chain' or, in other words, there are more rents to be captured from future innovators.

Plea bargaining

In criminal cases in the United States, the prosecutor and the defendant often negotiate a guilty plea in exchange for a lighter sentence – a process known as plea bargaining. Landes (1971), in the first formal analysis of plea bargaining, assumes that the prosecutor maximizes the sum of expected sentences subject to a resource constraint. Grossman and Katz (1983) assume that the defendant privately observes his guilt and the uninformed prosecutor makes a single take-it-or-leave-it offer of a reduced sentence in exchange for a guilty plea. In the screening equilibrium, the guilty defendants accept the offer and the innocent defendants reject the offer and go to trial. This is, of course, similar to Bebchuk's (1984) analysis of civil settlement. In Reinganum (1988), the prosecutor's offer signals the prosecutor's private information and, as in Reingaum and Wilde's (1986) analysis of civil settlement, the offers with high sentences are rejected more. In contrast to Grossman and Katz (1983), trials are more likely when the defendant is guilty. (In Reinganum, 2000, an informed defendant makes an offer to an uninformed prosecutor.)

Precedent

In Anglo-American legal systems, laws can be created and changed by judges over time. Cooter, Kornhauser and Lane (1979) present an early formal model where the courts learn about – and subsequently adjust – standards of care for injurers and victims. Landes and Posner (1976) consider the possibility of judicial bias, but argue that the threat of being overruled mitigates a judge's incentive to pursue his own agenda. Gennaioli and Shleifer (2005) present a formal model with a different conclusion. Rasmusen (1994) formalizes strategic interactions among a sequence of judges in a dynamic framework and shows that judges may cooperate in equilibrium and follow past precedents because violations would lead to future breakdowns where their own precedents would be violated by others; see also Schwartz (1992), Daughety and Reinganum (1999b) and Kornhauser (1992). Levy (2005) presents a model where judges have career concerns and go against precedent to signal their abilities. (A set of related rules and doctrines, 'collateral estoppel', applies when at least one litigant is

involved in multiple suits; see Spurr, 1991, and Che and Yi, 1993.)

Secret settlement

It is not uncommon lawsuits to settle secretly, where neither the existence of the suit nor the terms of the settlement are observed by the public. Secrecy may be facilitated through 'gag orders' or through private contracts. In Daughety and Reinganum (1999a; 2002), open settlements publicize the defendant's involvement in a case and increase the likelihood that other plaintiffs will file suit in the future. They also provide future plaintiffs with information about the expected value of their claims. Daughety and Reinganum (1999a) show that, because of the publicity effect, early plaintiffs can extract 'hush money' from defendants, enriching themselves at the expense of later plaintiffs. Importantly, secrecy can compromise firms' behaviour and product safety choices in a market setting (Daughety and Reinganum, 2005).

Standards of proof

How confident should a judge or jury be before convicting a defendant or finding in favour of a plaintiff? Rubinfeld and Sappington (1987) present a framework where the defendant can manipulate the signal received by the court, and shows how the optimal standard of proof balances litigation costs and *ex ante* deterrence concerns. Sanchirico (1997) presents a model where plaintiffs, as well as defendants, make investments in their cases. Demougin and Fluet (2006) explores the trade-offs when the defendant's wealth is limited. See Bernardo, Talley and Welch (2000) and Hay and Spier (1997) for discussions of the burden of proof.

KATHRYN E. SPIER

See also **dispute resolution; law, economic analysis of.**

The author thanks the Searle Fund for financial support.

Bibliography

Aghion, P. and Bolton, P. 1987. Contracts as a barrier to entry. *American Economic Review* 77, 388–401.

Bebchuk, L. 1984. Litigation and settlement under imperfect information. *RAND Journal of Economics* 15, 404–15.

Bebchuk, L. 1988. Suing solely to extract a settlement offer. *Journal of Legal Studies* 17, 437–50.

Bebchuk, L. 1996. A new theory concerning the credibility and success of threats to sue. *Journal of Legal Studies* 25, 1–25.

Bebchuk, L. and Chang, H. 1999. The effect of offer-of-settlement rules on the terms of settlement. *Journal of Legal Studies* 28, 489–513.

Bebchuk, L. and Guzman, A. 1996. How would you like to pay for that? The strategic effects of fee arrangements on settlement terms. *Harvard Negotiation Law Review* 1, 3–63.

Bernardo, A., Talley, E. and Welch, I. 2000. A theory of legal presumptions. *Journal of Law, Economics, and Organization* 16, 1–49.

Braeutigam, R., Owen, B. and Panzar, J. 1984. An economic analysis of alternative fee shifting systems. *Law and Contemporary Problems* 47, 173–204.

Chang, H.F. and Sigman, H. 2000. Incentives to settle under joint and several liability: an empirical analysis of superfund litigation. *Journal of Legal Studies* 24, 205–36.

Che, Y.-K. 1996. Equilibrium formation of class action suits. *Journal of Public Economics* 62, 339–61.

Che, Y.-K. 2002. The economics of collective negotiations in pretrial bargaining. *International Economic Review* 43, 549–76.

Che, Y.-K. and Yi, J.G. 1993. The role of precedents in repeated litigation. *Journal of Law, Economics, and Organization* 9, 399–424.

Chen, K.-P., Chien, H.-K. and Chu, C.Y.C. 1997. Sequential versus unitary trials with asymmetric information. *Journal of Legal Studies* 26, 239–58.

Cho, I.-K. and Kreps, D. 1987. Signalling games and stable equilibria. *Quarterly Journal of Economics* 102, 179–221.

Choi, A.H. and Sanchirico, C.W. 2004. Should plaintiffs win what defendants lose? Litigation stakes, litigation effort, and the benefits of decoupling. *Journal of Legal Studies* 33, 323–54.

Choi, J.P. 1998. Patent litigation as an information-transmission mechanism. *American Economic Review* 88, 1249–63.

Cooter, R., Kornhauser, L. and Lane, D. 1979. Liability rules, limited information, and the role of precedent. *Bell Journal of Economics* 10, 366–73.

Cooter, R. and Rubinfeld, D. 1989. Economic analysis of legal disputes and their resolution. *Journal of Economic Literature* 27, 1067–97.

Cooter, R. and Rubinfeld, D. 1994. An economic model of legal discovery. *Journal of Legal Studies* 23, 435–64.

Dana, J. and Spier, K. 1993. Expertise and contingent fees: the role of asymmetric information in attorney compensation. *Journal of Law, Economics, and Organization* 9, 349–67.

Danzon, P. 1983. Contingent fees for personal injury litigation. *Bell Journal of Economics* 14, 213–23.

Danzon, P. and Lillard, L. 1983. Settlement out of court: the disposition of medical malpractice claims. *Journal of Legal Studies* 12, 345–78.

Daughety, A. 2000. Settlement. In *Encyclopedia of Law and Economics*, vol. 5, ed. B. Bouckaert and G. De Geest. Cheltenham: Edward Elgar.

Daughety, A. and Reinganum, J. 1994. Settlement negotiations with two-sided asymmetric information: model duality, information distribution, and efficiency. *International Review of Law and Economics* 14, 283–98.

Daughety, A. and Reinganum, J. 1999a. Hush money. *RAND Journal of Economics* 30, 661–78.

Daughety, A. and Reinganum, J. 1999b. Stampede to judgment: persuasive influence and herding behavior by courts. *American Law and Economics Review* 1, 158–89.

Daughety, A. and Reinganum, J. 2000a. Appealing judgments. *RAND Journal of Economics* 31, 502–25.

Daughety, A. and Reinganum, J. 2000b. On the economics of trials: adversarial process, evidence, and equilibrium bias. *Journal of Law, Economics, and Organization* 16, 365–94.

Daughety, A. and Reinganum, J. 2002. Information externalities in settlement bargaining: confidentiality and correlated culpability. *RAND Journal of Economics* 334, 587–604.

Daughety, A. and Reinganum, J. 2003. Found money? Split-award statutes and settlement of punitive damages cases. *American Law and Economics Review* 5, 134–64.

Daughety, A. and Reinganum, J. 2004. Exploiting future settlements: a signaling model of most-favored-nation clauses in settlement bargaining. *RAND Journal of Economics* 35, 467–85.

Daughety, A. and Reinganum, J. 2005. Secrecy and safety. *American Economic Review* 95, 1074–91.

Demougin, D. and Fluet, C. 2006. Preponderance of evidence. *European Economic Review* 50, 963–76.

Dewatripont, M. and Tirole, J. 1999. Advocates. *Journal of Political Economy* 107, 1–39.

Dixit, A. 1987. Strategic behavior in contests. *American Economic Review* 77, 891–98.

Farber, H. and White, M. 1991. Medical malpractice: an empirical examination of the litigation process. *RAND Journal of Economics* 22, 199–217.

Farmer, A. and Pecorino, P. 2000. Conditional cost shifting and the incidence of trial: pretrial bargaining in the face of a Rule 68 offer. *American Law and Economics Review* 2, 318–40.

Froeb, L. and Kobayashi, B. 1996. Naive, biased, yet Bayesian: can juries interpret selectively produced evidence? *Journal of Law, Economics, and Organization* 12, 257–76.

Gennaioli, N. and Shleifer, A. 2005. The evolution of precedent. Working Paper No. 11265. Cambridge, MA: NBER.

Gould, J. 1973. The economics of legal conflicts. *Journal of Legal Studies* 2, 279–300.

Grossman, S. 1981. The informational role of warranties and private disclosure about product quality. *Journal of Law and Economics* 24, 461–83.

Grossman, G. and Katz, M. 1983. Plea bargaining and social welfare. *American Economic Review* 73, 749–57.

Hause, J. 1989. Indemnity, settlement, and litigation, or 'I'll be suing you'. *Journal of Legal Studies* 18, 157–80.

Hay, B. 1994. Civil discovery: its effects and optimal scope. *Journal of Legal Studies* 23, 481–517.

Hay, B. 1997. Optimal contingent fees in a world of settlement. *Journal of Legal Studies* 26, 259–78.

Hay, B. and Spier, K. 1997. Burdens of proof in civil litigation. *Journal of Legal Studies* 26, 413–33.

Hay, B. and Spier, K. 1998. Settlement of litigation. In *The New Palgrave Dictionary of Economics and the Law*, ed. P. Newman. London: Macmillan.

Helland, E. and Tabarrok, A. 2003. Contingency fees, settlement delay, and low-quality litigation: empirical evidence from two datasets. *Journal of Law, Economics, and Organization* 19, 517–42.

Hua, X. and Spier, K. 2005. Information and externalities in sequential litigation. *Journal of Institutional and Theoretical Economics* 161, 215–32.

Kahan, M. and Tuckman, B. 1995. Special levies for punitive damages. *International Review of Law and Economics* 15, 175–85.

Kaplow, L. 1993. Shifting plaintiffs' fees versus increasing damage awards. *RAND Journal of Economics* 24, 625–30.

Kaplow, L. and Shavell, S. 1992. Private versus socially optimal provision of ex-ante legal advice. *Journal of Law, Economics, and Organization* 8, 306–20.

Kaplow, L. and Shavell, S. 1996. Accuracy in the assessment of damages. *Journal of Law and Economics* 39, 191–209.

Katz, A. 1987. Measuring the demand for litigation: is the English Rule really cheaper? *Journal of Law, Economics, and Organization* 3, 143–76.

Katz, A. 1990. The effect of frivolous lawsuits on the settlement of litigation. *International Review of Law and Economics* 10, 3–27.

Klement, A. and Neeman, Z. 2004. Incentive structures for class action lawyers. *Journal of Law, Economics, and Organization* 20, 102–24.

Kornhauser, L. 1992. Modeling collegial courts, 2: Legal doctrine. *Journal of Law, Economics, and Organization* 8, 441–70.

Kornhauser, L. and Revesz, R. 1994. Multidefendant settlements: the impact of joint and several liability. *Journal of Legal Studies* 23, 41–76.

Landes, W. 1971. An economic analysis of the courts. *Journal of Law and Economics* 14, 61–107.

Landes, W. 1993. Sequential versus unitary trials: an economic analysis. *Journal of Legal Studies* 22, 99–134.

Landes, W. and Posner, R. 1976. Legal precedents: a theoretical and empirical analysis. *Journal of Law and Economics* 19, 249–307.

Lanjouw, J. and Schankerman, M. 2001. Characteristics of patent litigation: a window on competition. *RAND Journal of Economics* 32, 129–51.

Levy, G. 2005. Careerist judges. *RAND Journal of Economics* 36, 275–97.

Loewenstein, G., Issacharoff, S., Camerer, C. and Babcock, L. 1993. Self-serving assessments of fairness and pretrial bargaining. *Journal of Legal Studies* 22, 135–58.

Marshall, R., Meurer, M. and Richard, J. 1994. Litigation settlement and collusion. *Quarterly Journal of Economics* 109, 211–39.

Meurer, M. 1989. The settlement of patent litigation. *RAND Journal of Economics* 20, 77–91.

Meurer, M. 1992. The gains from faith in an unfaithful agent: settlement conflict between defendants and liability insurer. *Journal of Law, Economics and Organization* 8, 502–22.

Milgrom, P. and Roberts, J. 1986. Relying on the information of interested parties. *RAND Journal of Economics* 17, 18–32.

Miller, G. 1986. An economic analysis of Rule 68. *Journal of Legal Studies* 15, 93–125.

Miller, G. 1987. Some agency problems in settlement. *Journal of Legal Studies* 161, 189–215.

Mnookin, R. 1998. Alternative dispute resolution. In *The New Palgrave Dictionary of Economics and the Law*, ed. P. Newman. London: Macmillan.

Myerson, R. and Satterthwaite, M. 1983. Efficient mechanisms for bilateral trading. *Journal of Economic Theory* 29, 265–81.

Nalebuff, B. 1987. Credible pretrial negotiation. *RAND Journal of Economics* 18, 198–210.

Ostrom, B., Kauder, N. and LaFountain, R. 2001. *Examining the Work of the State Courts, 1999–2000*. Williamsburg, VA: National Center for State Courts.

Parisi, F. 2002. Rent seeking through litigation: adversarial and inquisitorial systems compared. *International Review of Law and Economics* 22, 193–216.

P'ng, I.P.L. 1983. Strategic behavior in suit, settlement, and trial. *RAND Journal of Economics* 14, 539–50.

Polinsky, A. and Che, Y.-K. 1991. Decoupling liability: optimal incentives for care and litigation. *RAND Journal of Economics* 22, 562–70.

Polinsky, A. and Rubinfeld, D. 1988. The deterrent effects of settlements and trials. *International Review of Law and Economics* 8, 109–16.

Polinsky, A. and Rubinfeld, D. 1998. Does the English Rule discourage low-probability-of-prevailing plaintiffs? *Journal of Legal-Studies* 27, 519–35.

Posner, R. 1973. An economic approach to legal procedure and judicial administration. *Journal of Legal Studies* 2, 399–458.

Priest, G. and Klein, B. 1984. The selection of disputes for litigation. *Journal of Legal Studies* 13, 1–55.

Rasmusen, E. 1994. Judicial legitimacy as a repeated game. *Journal of Law, Economics, and Organization* 10, 63–83.

Reinganum, J. 1988. Plea bargaining and prosecutorial discretion. *American Economic Review* 78, 713–28.

Reinganum, J. 2000. Sentencing guidelines, judicial discretion, and plea bargaining. *RAND Journal of Economics* 31, 62–81.

Reinganum, J. and Wilde, L. 1986. Settlement, litigation, and the allocation of litigation costs. *RAND Journal of Economics* 17, 557–68.

Rosenberg, D. and Shavell, S. 1985. A model in which lawsuits are brought for their nuisance value. *International Review of Law and Economics* 5, 3–13.

Rubinfeld, D. and Sappington, D. 1987. Efficient awards and standards of proof in judicial proceedings. *RAND Journal of Economics* 18, 308–15.

Rubinfeld, D. and Scotchmer, S. 1993. Contingent fees for attorneys: an economic analysis. *RAND Journal of Economics* 24, 343–56.

Sanchirico, C. 1997. The burden of proof in civil litigation: a simple model of mechanism design. *International Review of Law and Economics* 17, 431–47.

Santore, R. and Viard, A.D. 2001. Legal fee restrictions, moral hazard, and attorney rights. *Journal of Law and Economics* 44, 549–72.

Schrag, J. 1999. Managerial judges: an economic analysis of the judicial management of legal discovery. *RAND Journal of Economics* 30, 305–23.

Schwartz, E. 1992. Policy, precedent, and power: a positive theory of supreme-court decision making. *Journal of Law, Economics, and Organization* 8, 219–52.

Schweizer, U. 1989. Litigation and settlement under two sided incomplete information. *Review of Economic Studies* 56, 163–77.

Shapiro, C. 2003. Antitrust limits to patent settlements. *RAND Journal of Economics* 34, 391–411.

Shavell, S. 1982a. Suit, settlement and trial: a theoretical analysis under alternative methods for the allocation of legal costs. *Journal of Legal Studies* 11, 55–82.

Shavell, S. 1982b. The social versus the private incentive to bring suit in a costly legal system. *Journal of Legal Studies* 11, 333–9.

Shavell, S. 1989. The sharing of information prior to settlement or litigation. *RAND Journal of Economics* 20, 183–95.

Shavell, S. 1993. Suit versus settlement when parties seek nonmonetary judgments. *Journal of Legal Studies* 22, 1–14.

Shavell, S. 1994. Alternative dispute resolution: an economic analysis. *Journal of Legal Studies* 24, 1–28.

Shavell, S. 1995. The appeals process as a means of error correction. *Journal of Legal Studies* 24, 379–426.

Shavell, S. 1996. Any probability of plaintiff victory at trial is possible. *Journal of Legal Studies* 25, 493–501.

Shavell, S. 1997. The fundamental divergence between the private and the social motive to use the legal system. *Journal of Legal Studies* 26, 575–613.

Shepherd, G. 1999. An empirical study of the effects of pretrial discovery. *International Review of Law and Economics* 19, 245–63.

Shin, H. 1998. Adversarial and inquisitorial procedures in arbitration. *RAND Journal of Economics* 29, 378–405.

Spier, K. 1992. The dynamics of pretrial negotiation. *Review of Economic Studies* 59, 93–108.

Spier, K. 1994a. Pretrial bargaining and the design of fee-shifting rules. *RAND Journal of Economics* 25, 197–214.

Spier, K. 1994b. Settlement bargaining and the design of damage awards. *Journal of Law, Economics, and Organization* 10, 84–95.

Spier, K. 1997. A note on the divergence between the private and social motive to settle under a negligence rule. *Journal of Legal Studies* 26, 613–23.

Spier, K. 2003a. The use of most-favored-nation clauses in settlement of litigation. *RAND Journal of Economics* 34, 78–95.

Spier, K. 2003b. Tied to the mast: most-favored-nation clauses in settlement contracts. *Journal of Legal Studies* 32, 91–120.

Spier, K. 2005. Litigation. In *The Handbook of Law and Economics*, ed. A. Mitchell Polinsky and S. Shavell. Amsterdam: North-Holland.

Spier, K. and Sykes, A. 1998. Capital structure, priority rules, and the settlement of civil claims. *International Review of Law and Economics* 18, 187–200.

Spitzer, M. and Talley, E. 2000. Judicial auditing. *Journal of Legal Studies* 24, 649–83.

Spurr, S. 1991. An economic analysis of collateral estoppel. *International Review of Law and Economics* 11, 47–61.

Sykes, A. 1994. 'Bad faith' refusal to settle by liability insurers: some implications of the judgment-proof problem. *Journal of Legal Studies* 23, 77–110.

Waldfogel, J. 1995. The selection hypothesis and the relationship between trial and plaintiff victory. *Journal of Political Economy* 103, 229–60.

White, M. 2002. Explaining the flood of asbestos litigation: consolidation, bifurcation, and bouquet trials. Working Paper No. 9362. Cambridge, MA: NBER.

Yoon, A. 2004. Mandatory arbitration and civil litigation: an empirical study of medical malpractice litigation in the west. *American Law and Economics Review* 6, 95–134.

Lloyd, William Forster (1794–1852)

Lloyd was Drummond Professor of Political Economy at the University of Oxford from 1832 to 1837. During those years he delivered a series of lectures which display marked originality and willingness to differ from the current canons of received wisdom among political economists. Twelve of the lectures were published. The manuscripts of the remaining lectures, approximately 24 in number, have not been found (Romano, 1977).

Among the published lectures, that of 1833 and the second set of 1836 are quite outstanding. His lecture on Value (1833) has moved some leading historians of economic thought to hail Lloyd as one of the first writers to articulate the marginal utility theory of value. Less celebrated, but equally notable, is his analysis of the manner in which the operations of the contemporary British economy condemn unskilled labourers to poverty. Against the popular Malthusianism of his day, he argues in favour of the principle of poor laws and of the proposition that relief of the poor is a matter of social justice (rather than individual charity).

In the course of his 1836 lectures Lloyd constructs a model of the British economy which, he believes, demonstrates that the present situation of unskilled labourers is akin to that of slaves. Further, he observes, contemporary British society is dividing progressively into two mutually exclusive classes, and the degree of concentration of ownership and control of capital in the nation is increasing. Under existing circumstances, the unskilled worker is obliged to give ever greater quantities of his 'power of labouring' in order to obtain in return a subsistence wage.

As a person, Lloyd remains an elusive, even enigmatic, figure. He followed an older brother Charles (later, Regius Professor of Divinity and Bishop of Oxford) to Christ Church in 1812. There he studied mathematics and classics, took an MA in 1818 and was ordained in 1822. Before Lloyd succeeded Richard Whately in the Drummond Chair, he was Reader in Greek (1823) and lecturer in mathematics (1824). In 1834 he was elected a Fellow of the Royal Society. At the end of his period as Professor of Political Economy, Lloyd left Oxford to live at Prestwood, Great Missenden, Buckinghamshire, where he died in 1852. During his last 15 years Lloyd appears to have lived very quietly and published nothing. There is as yet no satisfactory explanation as to why this able and well-connected scholar chose to remain silent.

BARRY GORDON

Selected works

Twelve of Lloyd's lectures, 1834–36, were published collectively as *Lectures on Population, Value, Poor Laws and Rent*, London, 1837; reprinted, New York: A.M. Kelley, 1968. The collection includes: Two Lectures on the Checks to Population, delivered in 1834; A Lecture on the Notion of Value as Distinguishable not only from Utility, but also from Value in Exchange, delivered in 1833; Four Lectures on Poor Laws, delivered in Hilary term, 1836; Two Lectures on the Justice of Poor-Laws, and One Lecture on Rent, delivered in Michaelmas term, 1836. Earlier, Lloyd had published *Prices of Corn in Oxford in the Beginning of the Fourteenth Century: Also from the Year 1583 to the Present Time*, Oxford, 1830.

Bibliography

Bowley, M. 1972. The predecessors of Jevons – the revolution that wasn't. *Manchester School of Economic and Social Studies* 40(1), 9–29.

Gordon, B.J. 1966. W.F. Lloyd: a neglected contribution. *Oxford Economic Papers*, NS 18(1), 64–70.

Harrod, R.F. 1927. An early exposition of final utility: W.F. Lloyd's lecture on the notion of value (1833) reprinted. *Economic History* (supplement to the *Economic Journal*), May, 168–83.

Romano, R.M. 1971. W.F. Lloyd – a comment. *Oxford Economic Papers* 23, 285–90.

Romano, R.M. 1977. William Forster Lloyd – a non-Ricardian? *History of Political Economy* 9, 412–41.

loanable funds

The term 'loanable funds' was used by the late D.H. Robertson, the chief advocate of the loanable funds theory of the interest rate, in the sense of what Marshall used to call 'capital disposal' or 'command over capital', (Robertson, 1940, p. 2). In a money-using economy where money is the only accepted means of payment, however, loanable funds are simply sums of money offered and demanded during a given period of time for immediate use at a certain price.

The loanable funds theory of interest is the theory which maintains that the interest rate, i.e. the price for the use of such funds per unit of time, must be determined by the supply and demand for such funds.

The insistence on the *flow* nature of loanable funds is based upon the crucial conception that in a money-using world the major bulk of money normally exists in a continuous circular flow. It is constantly passing out of the hands of one person as the means of payment for his expenditures into the hands of others as the embodiment of their incomes and sales proceeds, which will in turn be expended, and so on *ad infinitum*. A part of the money in this endless circular flow, however, is observed to be constantly being diverted into a side stream leading to the money market, where it constitutes the supply of loanable funds. From there borrowers of loanable funds would then take them off and in general would put them back into the main circular flow of expenditures and incomes (receipts).

This emphasis on the flow nature of loanable funds does not imply that the loanable funds theory would be unaware that there are sometimes money balances held inactive, like stagnant puddles lying off the main stream of the money flow. The loanable funds theory, however, would maintain that the stocks of money off the circular flow, as well as the stock of money inside the circular flow, have no direct influence on the money market. It is only when people attempt to divert money from the circular flow into the money market (saving), or into the stagnant puddles (hoarding), or conversely try to withdraw the inactive money from the stagnant puddles for re-injection into the circular flow or into the money market (dishoarding), that the interest rate will be directly affected. In other words, only *adjustments* in the idle balances (hoarding or dishoarding) together with the flows of savings and investment exert direct influences on the interest rate.

Since flows must be measured over time, we must choose a convenient unit to measure time. To take account of the fact that money does not circulate with infinite velocity, Robertson defined the unit period as one 'during which, at the outset of our inquiry, the stock of money changes hands once in final exchange for the constituents of the community's real income or output' (Robertson, 1940, p. 65). In my opinion, however, it would be more consistent and convenient to define the unit period as one during which, at the outset, the stock of money changes hands once in exchange for all commodities and services instead of restricting the objects of exchange to final products only (Tsiang, 1956, esp. pp. 545–7). The reason for this will be clear later. Based on our new definition of the unit period, all gross incomes and sales proceeds from goods and services received during the current period cannot be spent on anything until the next period when they are then said to be 'disposable'.

The definition of the unit period, however, does not preclude the funds borrowed or realized from sales of financial assets from being expendable during the same period. This differential treatment of the proceeds of sales of financial assets as distinguished from the proceeds of sales from goods and services is also an attempt to simulate the real situation in our present world; for the velocity of circulation of money against financial assets is in fact observed to be many times faster than that against goods and services. Assuming that there is a fixed unit period in our short period analysis does not necessarily imply that we are *ipso facto* assuming the invariability of the velocity of circulation of money; for short period variations in the velocity of money can be taken care of in terms of increases or decreases in the idle balances held.

Under this definition of the unit period and the implicit assumptions behind it, each individual, therefore, faces a financial constraint in that during a given unit period he can spend only his disposable income and his idle balances (the sum of the two constitutes the entire stock of money he possesses at the beginning of the period) plus the money he can currently borrow on the money market. Buying on credit is to be treated as first borrowing the money and then spending it. Thus when he plans to spend more than his disposable income and the amount he is willing to dishoard from his idle balances, he must borrow the excess from the money market to satisfy his total demand for finance. Since additions to the demand side are equivalent to deductions from the supply side, and vice versa, we need not dispute with Robertson when he classifies the demand for, and the supply of, loanable funds on the money market as follows (Robertson, 1940, p. 3).

On the demand side, he lists, with terminology slightly changed:

D1 funds required to finance current expenditures on investment of fixed or working capital;

D2 funds required to finance current expenditures on maintenance or replacement of existing fixed or working capital (note here that if our unit period were defined in the way Robertson defined it, i.e., as the period during which the total stock of money changes hands only once in the final exchange for the constituents of the community's real income, then the current expenditure on maintenance and replacement, i.e., on intermediate products, cannot be said to require a dollar for dollar provision of finance as would expenditures on final products);

D3 funds to be added to inactive balances held as liquid reserves;

D4 funds required to finance current expenditures on consumption in excess of disposable income.

Correspondingly, on the supply side, he gives:

S1 current savings defined as disposable income minus planned current consumption expenditure;

S2 current depreciation or depletion allowances for fixed and working capital taken out of the gross sales proceeds of the preceding period;

S3 dishoarding withdrawn from previously held inactive balances of money;

S4 net creation of additional money by banks.

The function of the money market is to match the flow demands for loanable funds to the flow supplies, and the instrument with which it operates to achieve equilibrium between the two sides is the vector of interest rates. It is to be noted that in the flow equilibrium condition the total stock of money does not figure at all.

Nevertheless, it must be pointed out that the flow equilibrium condition of the money market as conceived by the loanable funds theorists can imply the stock equilibrium condition as conceived by the liquidity preference theorists, provided two necessary conditions are satisfied. Of the four demands for loanable funds listed above, D1, D2 and D4 are the additional demands for transactions balances (or what Keynes in 1937 called the finance demand for liquidity) needed by some firms and consumers to finance their current planned expenditures. And of the four sources of supply of loanable funds, S1 and S2 are but the reductions in demand for finance which other consumers of firms can spare during the current period. Therefore, D1, D2 and D4 minus S1 and S2 must be equal to the net aggregate increase which the community as a whole would want to add to their transaction balances.

Similarly, D3 minus S3 is the net increase which the community would want to add to their inactive balances (including precautionary, speculative, and investment balances).

Thus the equilibrium condition of the demand for and supply of loanable funds, i.e.,

$$D1 + D2 + D3 + D4 = S1 + S2 + S3 + S4,$$

which can be rearranged as:

$$[D1 + D2 + D4 - (S1 + S2)] + (D3 - S3) = S4,$$

implies that the total increases in aggregate demand for transaction balances (finance) and for inactive balances equal the net current increases in money supply created by banks. Provided it may be presumed (*a*) that the previous stock supply of and demand for money were originally equal to each other, and (*b*) that the current increases (or decreases) in supply and demand for money (treated above as flow supply and demand for loanable funds) represent the full unlagged adjustments of the previous stock supply and demand to their new equilibrium values, the flow equilibrium of the loanable funds should necessarily imply a new stock equilibrium (Tsiang, 1982).

The two necessary provisos used to be taken for granted by the liquidity preference theorists, who generally think that full stock equilibrium can be achieved instantaneously at any point in time. However, Professor James Tobin, in his Nobel lecture given in 1981 (Tobin, 1982), has come to recognize that the money market cannot operate within a dimensionless point of time, but must operate in finite time periods, which he called slices of time. Furthermore, he recognized that the equilibrium which can be expected in such a short slice of time can only be that between the adjustments in the stock demanded and in the stock supplied during the period. Since adjustments in stocks per time period are flows, Tobin's new approach is thus really a sort of flow equilibrium analysis.

Moreover, Tobin, at the same time, also admitted that in such a short period as a slice of time, portfolios of individual agents cannot adjust fully to new market information. Lags in response are inevitable and rational in view of the costs of transactions and decisions. Thus neither of the two necessary conditions is satisfied in the real world. Consequently, even when the money market has brought the flow demand for and supply of loanable funds to equality, the stock demand for money and the total money stock need not have reached mutual equilibrium, which the Keynesians and the stock-approach economists used to assume as being attainable at every point of time.

Finally, it should be realized that the demand for finance for planned investment expenditure, which Keynes (1937, p. 667) admitted he should not have overlooked in his *General Theory*, is of the nature of a flow generated by a flow decision to invest. It is not just a partial adjustment of the stock demand for money towards its new equilibrium value as treated in Tobin's new theory (Tobin, 1982). As Keynes put it in his reply to Ohlin (1937), '"Finance" is a revolving fund …. As soon as it is used in the sense of being expended, the lack of liquidity is automatically made good and the readiness to become temporarily unliquid is available to be used over again' (Keynes, 1937, p. 666). This is essentially a reaffirmation of the traditional conception of the circular flow of money, which loanable funds theorists had emphasized from the outset, but which Keynes himself had pushed into the dark background with his emphasis that the entire stock of money is being held voluntarily in portfolio allocation.

The rediscovery of the demand for finance by Keynes and the more recent unheralded switch on the part of Tobin towards the flow approach from his usual stock approach indicate that the loanable funds theory is perhaps the more appropriate approach at least for short period dynamic analysis.

S.C. TSIANG

See also **liquidity preference.**

Bibliography
Keynes, J.M. 1937. The ex-ante theory of the rate of interest. *Economic Journal* 47(December), 663–9.

Ohlin, B. 1937. Some notes on the Stockholm theory of savings and investment, I. *Economic Journal* 47(March), 53–69.

Ohlin, B. 1937. Some notes on the Stockholm theory of savings and investment, II. *Economic Journal* 47(June), 221–40.

Robertson, D.H. 1940. *Essays in Monetary Theory*. London: P.S. King.

Tobin, J. 1982. Money and finance in the macroeconomic process. *Journal of Money, Credit and Banking* 14(May), 171–204.

Tsiang, S.C. 1956. Liquidity preference and loanable funds theories, multiplier and velocity analysis: a synthesis. *American Economic Review* 46(September), 539–64.

Tsiang, S.C. 1982. Stock or portfolio approach to monetary theory and the neo-Keynesian school of James Tobin. *IHS-Journal* 6, 149–71.

local public finance

Economic analysis of the taxation and expenditure policies of local public authorities has become far more sophisticated as theoretical enquiry has directed attention towards the uniquely local aspects of public finance and as national policies have increased the importance of the local public sector.

Many of the issues that arise in the analysis of the local public sector are familiar reflections of the important questions in public finance that have been addressed at the national level; for example, the incidence of taxation and the welfare losses from revenue instruments; the effect of government expenditures on consumer welfare and the distribution of well-being; the effect of public sector distortions on resource allocation and relative prices.

However, the principal difference between the economic analysis of public finance at the national and at the local levels is the potential for mobility among jurisdictions by the transport of final products and inputs, and especially by residents who finance local government and consume public output. Critically, this mobility may be endogenous to the revenue or expenditure actions taken by the local public authority, and this must be considered in any economic analysis of local finance.

This insight, as it affects efficiency in the allocation of local public output and the incidence of local taxes, goes back at least to the fifth edition of Marshall's *Principles*

(1907, Appendix G). Marshall presented a lucid discussion of the effect of local public expenditures on residential mobility ('A high rate spent on providing good primary and secondary schools may attract artisan residents while repelling the well-to-do' – Marshall, 1920, p. 794). He also noted the effects of mobility upon the incidence of local taxes.

Given the increased complexity of decentralized taxation and expenditure patterns when compared to national government policies, one may begin by asking which economic functions of government ought to be undertaken by the central (national) government rather than by local authorities. Consider the original Musgrave (1959) taxonomy of public sector functions: distribution, stabilization and allocation. It seems clear that a system of local taxes and expenditures is inappropriate for achieving distributional or stabilization goals. After the adoption of any system of taxation and redistribution by a locality, even one which reflects a unanimous view of the citizens, it will be in the interests of those bearing the burden of the tax to relocate in other jurisdictions and in the interests of potential beneficiaries of the redistribution to move into the jurisdiction. Similarly, locally adopted monetary and fiscal policies are unlikely to further stabilization objectives, even if such objectives are uniformly held by local citizens. Import leakages are so large that the local benefits of stabilization policies (for example, local public employment programmes) are almost certain to be less than their costs.

It is precisely the mobility of households, goods and factors across jurisdictions that defeats local stabilization and redistribution policies. Conversely, however, the same 'openness' of the local economy means that the decentralized local provision of public goods will in many cases improve the allocative efficiency of the economy. In particular, the smaller and more homogeneous a community in a system of local government, the more likely is it that the provision of public goods by any community will be consistent with the demands of its citizens. In the limit, of course, if public goods are financed by a head tax, and if there are neither economies of scale in production nor externalities in consumption, then provision by a system of small jurisdictions, each with citizens of homogeneous tastes and incomes, will result in an efficient allocation.

If, however, there are economies of scale in production, it makes sense to have larger jurisdictions. But when the public good is produced by a larger entity, 'congestion' may result; that is, the quality of the good may decline as it is shared with more people. In larger jurisdictions, moreover, citizen demands may be more heterogeneous. The problem of balancing the benefits of cost-sharing in production, on the one hand, with the sacrifice in well-being by compromising individual consumers' demands or by introducing 'congestion' in public goods consumption, on the other, has been central

to the normative analysis of the local provision of public goods.

Consider, for example, a 'club' providing some collective benefit to identical individuals (Buchanan, 1965). Suppose an organization supplies some public output Q subject to congestion, or equivalently, suppose it supplies a good whose standardized cost $C(N)$ increases with population N. Individuals of income Y are assessed the average cost of service provision and allocate their remaining income to some numeraire good X. A community of N identical individuals will choose public output to maximize utility, $U(Q,X)$, subject to the individual budget constraint, $Y = X + [C(N)/N] Q$. This implies the familiar Samuelson (1954) condition:

$$N[(\partial U/\partial Q)/(\partial U/\partial X)] = C(N). \qquad (1)$$

The level of public good provision is chosen by the club of fixed size N so that the *sum* of the individual marginal rates of substitution (MRS) between private and public goods equals the marginal rate of transformation (MRT) in production. Given this level of public output, from the budget constraint it also follows that choice of club size to maximize utility is:

$$C'(N) = C(N)/N. \qquad (2)$$

The optimum size of the club is the membership at which the average cost of public output is equal to the marginal cost of adding another member. From equations (1) and (2) it follows that for a pure public good, that is, $C'(N) = 0$, the optimal size of the club is unbounded, while for a private good, where $C(N) = PN$, the *individual* MRS is equal to the MRT and the size of the club is indeterminate.

Applied to local public finance, the model indicates that a system of communities, each with identical individuals and of that size which minimizes average cost, would be a stable and efficient mechanism for public service provision. Homogeneity of demands is necessary for efficiency even if the tax structure (or club dues) is of the Lindahl variety. Each group in a heterogeneous community would be better off by moving to a jurisdiction with identical tax shares.

Theoretical analyses of local public economies are much more complicated when the partitioning of individuals into political jurisdictions is 'non-anonymous', that is, when the characteristics of the other members (in addition to their incomes) matter to those in the club. In many cases, an equilibrium allocation of residents to jurisdictions may not exist at all (Scotchmer, 1997). As noted below, non-anonymous crowding may also affect the costs of public goods provision and the interpretation of demands for local public goods.

The 'club' model of the provision of local public goods is a special case of the so-called Tiebout (1956) model, probably the most influential idea in the modern analysis of local public finance. Tiebout's stylized and informal analysis assumes that residential mobility is costless, that local jurisdictions provide public goods at minimum average cost and that local government is financed by non-distortionary lump-sum taxes. Under these circumstances, Tiebout argues that the provision of public goods by a system of competitive local governments may be no less efficient than the allocation of private goods by the market economy. The conclusion of this argument also depends crucially upon the availability to citizens of a sufficiently large number of jurisdictions offering differing packages of local public goods and upon the absence of inter-jurisdictional externalities, as well as more conventional assumptions about full information. In reality, in most metropolitan areas, local public output is supplied by a small number of communities (small, at least, relative to the number of types of demanders); local mobility is quite costly and is motivated by many non-fiscal concerns. Individuals often live in one jurisdiction and work in another, and there are externalities among jurisdictions. Finally, revenues are raised, not by head taxes but by a variety of local levies, especially *ad valorem* taxes on real property. Each of these factors limits the economic efficiency of the local public sector in important ways.

The externalities or 'spillouts' of the benefits of public service provision mean that such goods will be under-provided without coordination by local communities – since each community will only consider the benefits accruing to its own citizens in choosing the level of service provision. For public goods and services with substantial spillouts of benefits, efficient levels of production can be stimulated by a system of open-ended matching grants to localities by the central government. As Pigou (1932) originally demonstrated, if the matching rate (the fraction of local spending reimbursed by higher government) corresponds to the fraction of local public output, which spills out to non-residents, then the externality will be internalized. It is, of course, rather difficult to implement this maxim of local public finance (Oates, 1972).

The heavy reliance upon local property taxes for financing the local public sector, especially in Britain, Canada and the United States, is another source of allocative inefficiency in local finance. Clearly, a property tax alters the housing consumption decision and leads to underconsumption of housing as well as to inefficiency in public goods consumption. Until rather recently the system of local property taxes was viewed as a system of excises (Netzer, 1966), regressive levies on property and housing consumption, in contrast to the original Henry George (1879) position on land taxes. Modern theoretical analyses (following Mieszkowski, 1972), which assume that capital is mobile across jurisdictions and that the supply of capital is insensitive to its rate of return, have led to a reconsideration of the regressive nature of the tax. The inelastic supply of aggregate capital means that a national system of local property taxes will reduce

returns to capitalists by the average level of the tax. The geographical mobility of capital implies that capital will flee from high-tax jurisdictions, raising marginal productivity and pre-tax returns, to low-tax jurisdictions, depressing pre-tax returns. Thus the incidence of the system of property taxes depends upon the magnitude of the average level of the tax, relative to the deviations from that average, as well as distribution of households among high-tax and low-tax jurisdictions. Despite the ambiguities in resolving these detailed empirical issues, this theoretical argument suggests that the burden of property taxation is heavily skewed towards the owners of capital. Empirically, this conclusion is probably modified by regressive appraisal and administrative procedures. It should be noted, moreover, that from local governments' perspective an increase in the level of the property tax to finance service provision is an excise on property users (since a change in any one community's property tax rate can have only a negligible effect on the average level of rates for the nation).

The distortion inherent in property tax financing may lead to local policies of exclusionary zoning. If, for example, the benefits of the local public sector were roughly equal per household, then it would be in the interests of current residents to force incoming households to consume more housing than the average household. Current residents may attempt to enforce this by imposing minimum lot-size restrictions or by other exclusionary practices to increase the housing consumption of newcomers. Of course, as noted before, unless there are sufficient communities so that the households residing within a jurisdiction are literally identical, those who chose to consume less housing will typically enjoy a fiscal residual.

Despite these clear examples of allocative inefficiency in the system of local public finance and service provision, there is a substantial body of evidence that variations in property tax rates are reflected in property values and that variations in public services (for example, school quality) are capitalized into the sale prices of residential property. These findings are certainly consistent with the process of 'voting with one's feet' implied by the Tiebout model, but the capitalization of taxes and services is not necessary to efficiency in local government, nor does efficient service provision necessarily imply capitalization.

The observation that individuals register their demands for publicly financed services in their choices of community has other important implications, however. Specifically, information about the public goods provided by different jurisdictions, together with information about the characteristics of the residents of those jurisdictions, may be sufficient to identify consumer demands for public services. Extensive analyses of these issues have been undertaken, combining economic theories of the local political process with aggregate data on local public finance and choice of output. Under rather restrictive assumptions, the political process which determines the level of service provision can be modelled as the choice of the median voter of the community. Given the characteristics of that individual (or rather, estimates obtained from aggregate information), the 'tax price' that individual confronts, and the level of public output chosen, the parameters of the demand curve are estimated econometrically. The 'tax price' is the marginal cost to the individual of purchasing an additional dollar of public output. With property tax financing, this is typically approximated by the median voter's house value as a fraction of the community's taxable real property per household.

As noted above, the residents of localities may 'care' about the characteristics of other residents simply because their characteristics affect the cost of producing public services. One example may involve local schools, which absorb the largest share of local government spending on public services. To the extent that peers 'matter' in the production of educational outputs in primary school, policies of matching grants to local governments based on disadvantaged residents are called for (see Nechyba, 2003). The specification of empirical models of the demand for local public services is much more problematic when the demographic characteristics reflect either tastes for public goods or the costs of supplying them, or both.

Nevertheless, the results of these empirical investigations have proven useful in the positive analysis of citizen demands for public services and in the analysis of local finance. Nevertheless, the underlying economic model of local government behaviour is open to questions, both technical (for example, the requirement that preferences exhibit single peakedness) and substantive (for example, the neglect of the role of bureaucracy in government decisions). For example, if the median voter determines the demand for local public output, then the propensity for a community to spend out of lump-sum aid from higher government ought to be no different from the propensity to spend out of income generated by local taxation. Yet empirical evidence suggests that the propensity of communities to spend out of untied grant income greatly exceeds the propensity to spend out of ordinary income. A variety of alternative models of local finance have been espoused to help explain this 'flypaper' effect ('money sticks where it lands') in the context of bureaucratic decision-making. Chief among them are the so-called Leviathan models of a government that exploits its citizens by maximizing revenues extracted by taxation (Brennan and Buchanan, 1980). Clearly, however, more theoretical work needs to be done to resolve the contradictions between mobile consumers of local public output and sluggish suppliers.

Finally, it has been suggested that the inherent nature of local output and the traditional financing mechanisms of local government combine to exacerbate the economic and administrative problems of the local public sector

(Baumol, 1967). Local output consists largely of labour-intensive services, where technical change is inherently slow, and is typically financed by income-inelastic tax instruments. Under reasonable demand conditions, these may produce a more or less continuous 'crisis' in local public finance, as service costs escalate more rapidly than revenue increments. Given these characteristics of the local financing mechanism, as well as the redistributive nature of many local services, there may thus be a strong case for revenue or tax-base sharing at the national level.

JOHN M. QUIGLEY

See also **fiscal federalism; public finance; public goods; Tiebout hypothesis; urban economics.**

Bibliography

Baumol, W.J. 1967. Macroeconomics of unbalanced growth: the anatomy of urban crisis. *American Economic Review* 62, 415–26.

Brennan, G. and Buchanan, J.M. 1980. *The Power to Tax: Analytical Foundations of a Fiscal Constitution.* Cambridge: Cambridge University Press.

Buchanan, J.M. 1965. An economic theory of clubs. *Economica* 32, 1–14.

George, H. 1879. *Progress and Poverty.* New York: Appleton.

Inman, R.P. 1979. The fiscal performance of local governments: an interpretive review. In *Current Issues in Urban Economics*, ed. P. Mieszkowszki and M. Straszheim. Baltimore, MD: Johns Hopkins University Press.

Marshall, A. 1907. *Principles of Economics*, 5th edn. 8th edn, London: Macmillan, 1920.

Mieszkowski, P. 1972. The property tax: an excise tax or a property tax? *Journal of Public Economics* 1, 73–96.

Musgrave, R.A. 1959. *The Theory of Public Finance.* New York: McGraw-Hill.

Nechyba, T. 2003. School finance, spatial income segregation, and the nature of communities. *Journal of Urban Economics* 54, 61–88.

Netzer, D. 1966. *Economics of the Property Tax.* Washington, DC: Brookings Institution.

Oates, W.E. 1972. *Fiscal Federalism.* New York: Harcourt Brace Jovanovich.

Pigou, A.C. 1932. *The Economics of Welfare*, 4th edn. London: Macmillan.

Rubinfeld, D.L. 1985. The economics of the local public sector. In *Handbook of Public Economics*, vol. 2, ed. J. Auerbach and M. Feldstein. Amsterdam: North-Holland.

Samuelson, P.A. 1954. The pure theory of public expenditure. *Review of Economics and Statistics* 36, 387–9.

Scotchmer, S. 1997. On price-taking equilibria in club economies with nonanonymous crowding. *Journal of Public Economics* 65, 75–87.

Tiebout, C.M. 1956. A pure theory of local expenditures. *Journal of Political Economy* 64, 416–24.

local regression models

Local regression models are regression models where the parameters are 'localized', that is, they are allowed to vary with some or all of the covariates in a general way. Suppose that (Y, X) are random variables and let

$$E(Y|X = x) = m(x) \qquad (1)$$

when it exists. The regression function $m(x)$ is of primary interest because it describes how X affects Y. One may also be interested in derivatives of m or averages thereof or in derived quantities like conditional variance $var(Y|X = x) = E(Y^2|X = x) - E^2(Y|X = x)$. In cases of heavy-tailed distributions, the conditional expectation may not exist, in which case one may instead work with other location functionals like trimmed mean or median. The conditional expectation is particularly easy to deal with but a lot of what is done for the mean can also be done for the median or other quantities.

A parametric regression model for $m(x)$ is a family of functions $M(x;\theta)$, $\theta \in \Theta \subset \mathbb{R}^p$, where for each θ, $M(,;\theta)$ is a known function. The true parameter θ_0 for which $M(x;\theta_0) = m(x)$ for all $x \in \mathcal{X}$ is unknown and has to be estimated from data. For example, $M(x;\theta) = x^\top\theta$ would correspond to the linear regression case, which is the central model of econometrics. A key concept is that of identifiability: M is identifiable when distinct parameter values lead to different values of M for at least some x values. See Rothenberg (1971) for discussion. Parametric models arise frequently in economics and are of central importance. However, such models arise only when one has imposed specific functional forms on utility or production functions. Without these ad hoc assumptions one only gets much milder restrictions on functional form like concavity, symmetry, homogeneity and so on. The nonparametric approach is based on the belief that parametric models are usually mis-specified and may result in incorrect inferences. In this approach one treats the regression function $m(x)$ as being of unknown functional form. One usually assumes that m is a continuous function or even differentiable, although there are cases of interest where $m(x)$ is, say, continuous only from the right (left) with limits on the left (right), that is, there may be jumps at certain known or unknown locations in the support $\mathcal{X}$ of X (see Delgado and Hidalgo, 2000). By not restricting the functional form one obtains valid inferences for a much larger range of circumstances. In practice, the applicability depends on the sample size and the quality of data available. The theory and methods for carrying out such estimation are well understood, and are reviewed elsewhere (Härdle and Linton, 1994). Local regression models are one way of interpreting the nonparametric approach.

A local regression model is a family of functions

$$M(x;\theta(x)), \qquad \theta \in \Theta = \{\theta : \mathcal{X} \to \mathbb{R}^p\}, \qquad (2)$$

where $M(x;\theta)$ is a known function of both arguments. The true (functional) parameter $\theta_0(\cdot)$ for which $M(x;\theta_0(x)) = m(x)$ for all $x \in \mathcal{X}$ is unknown. It is usually assumed to be smooth. In other words this is a standard parametric regression model except that the parameters vary with the covariate value. There are a number of special cases. At one extreme lies the parametric model in which $\theta(x) = \theta$ for all $x \in \mathcal{X} \subset \mathbb{R}^d$, but the true θ_0 is unknown. At the other extreme lies the fully nonparametric case where $\theta(\cdot)$ is not subject to any exclusion restrictions.

Many different M functions will generally do. For example, the local constant case corresponds to $M(x;\theta) = \theta$ and the local linear case corresponds to $M(x;\theta) = \theta_0 + \theta_1 x$. These cases along with higher-order polynomials have been widely studied (see, for example, Fan and Gijbels, 1996). There are also other possibilities. Consider the Cobb–Douglas parametric model

$$M(x;\theta) = \theta_0 x_1^{\theta_1} \cdots x_d^{\theta_d}, \qquad (3)$$

which is widely used in studies of production. By making $\theta = (\theta_0, \theta_1, \ldots, \theta_d)$ vary freely with x one can match with any function $m(x)$ so long as the supports coincide (see, for example, Charnes, Cooper and Schinnar, 1976). For binary data where it is known that $m(x) \in [0, 1]$ it is appropriate to take $M(x;\theta) = F(\theta_0 + \theta_1 x)$ for some given c.d.f. F like the normal or logit. In that case, for a given x, there exists $\theta_0(x), \theta_1(x)$ such that $m(x) = F(\theta_0(x) + \theta_1(x)x)$. This example illustrates some pitfalls; for example, when $m(x) > 1$ for some x of interest. In that case, taking $M(x;\theta) = F(\theta_0 + \theta_1 x)$ will not be satisfactory.

The statistical justification for using local constant, local linear, and more generally local polynomial models is that any smooth function $m(x)$ can be approximated near the point x_0 by Taylor series expansions, so for p-times continuously differentiable scalar functions we have

$$m(x) = \sum_{j=0}^{p} \frac{1}{j!} \frac{d^j m}{dx^j}(x_0)(x - x_0)^j + R(x, x_0),$$

$$(4)$$

where the remainder term satisfies $R(x, x_0)/|x - x_0|^p \to 0$ as $x \to x_0$. Thus the function m is locally well approximated by a polynomial of order p, $\sum_{j=0}^{p}\alpha_j(x - x_0)^j$, where α_j can be identified with $j!^{-1}d^j m(x_0)/dx^j$. This justifies using local polynomial regression. But why should one ever work with local regression models outside the local polynomial class? First, any other local parametric model $M(x, \theta)$ that is p-times continuously differentiable in x at x_0, satisfies a similar expansion to (4), $\sum_{j=0}^{p}\beta_j(x - x_0)^j$, where β_j are functions of θ. By equating coefficients one obtains the same leading terms as long as there are 'enough' parameters in θ. Therefore, the same approximating objectives are reached by any such model. In some cases other equivalent classes may provide better approximations. Polynomials can sometimes violate some known features, like for example $m(x) \in [0, 1]$. In that case, taking $M(x;\theta)$ to be a c.d.f. of a polynomial provides the same approximation (so long as the c.d.f. chosen is also smooth enough) but imposes the boundedness restriction. Second, the local parameters may also be of interest in themselves. In the Cobb–Douglas case, the $\theta_j(x)$ can be interpreted as local elasticities. A third benefit is that the local model nests the parametric model. This leads to better statistical properties for estimators and test statistics when the model is true or approximately true, the 'home turf' case (see Hjort and Glad, 1995). When the default parametric model in the area of interest is nonlinear, as is true in many fields, there are some advantages to taking a localization of this in the nonparametric approach.

The issue of identification in local regression models is not well explored but some results are known (see Gozalo and Linton, 2000). The expansion (4) is clearly crucial for identification. If the function m is continuous but not differentiable, then only a single parameter is identifiable, which corresponds to the first term in (4); additional parameters remain unidentified. It is also necessary that there is a neighbourhood of the estimation point that contains enough observations (this is guaranteed when the marginal density exists and is positive).

Estimation of local regression models can be carried out by localization of the usual estimation criteria adopted for estimation of the corresponding parametric model like maximum likelihood or the method of moments where the localization is carried out by multiplying the contribution of observation i to the sample average objective function by the weight $w_{ni} = K((x - Xi)/h)$, where K is called the kernel and usually satisfies at least $\int K(u)du = 1$, while $h = h(n)$ is the bandwidth, a sequence designed to go to zero with sample size. The effect of the weighting factor w_{ni} is to emphasize observations close to the point of interest x and to de-emphasize observations far from x, whence the appellation 'localization'.

In the multivariate case, the expansion (4) becomes much more complicated: there are d first order partial derivatives, $d(d - 1)/2$ second order partial derivatives, and so on. With $p = 5$ and $d = 10$ the local parametric model would have over 1,000 parameters, which is too many for practical use. There are many interesting and important cases lying between the two extremes of parametric and fully nonparametric models, where some of the θ_j vary with only a subset of x. In this case, the local parametric model is imposing exclusion restrictions on the function m and the expansion is reduced. We next give some examples.

A function $m(x)$ is additively separable if

$$m(x) = \sum_{j=1}^{d} m_j(x_j)$$

for some functions m_j. In terms of the framework of the previous section $p = d$ and

$$M(x; \theta) = \sum_{j=1}^{d} M_j(x_j, \theta_j) \quad ; \quad \theta_j(x) = \theta_j(x_j).$$

The functions $\theta_j(x_j)$ are one-dimensional but of unknown form. This implies that $m(x) = \sum_{j=1}^{d} m_j(x_j)$, where $m_j(x_j) = \theta_j(x_j)$. In this case, each function $\theta_j(x)$ has $d - 1$ exclusion restrictions. This is consistent with strong separability as defined in Goldman and Uzawa (1964). A generalization of this is to the so-called generalized additive models where $M(x; \theta) = G\left(\sum_{j=1}^{d} M_j(x_j, \theta_j)\right)$, where $\theta_j(x) = \theta_j(x_j)$, in which G is a known 'link' function, while θ_j are univariate functions as before. For example, G could be the c.d.f. of a random variable like the normal or logit. Linton and Nielsen (1995) discuss estimation of additive models.

In time series one is often interested in the relationship

$$E[y_t | I_{t-1}] = m(I_{t-1}),$$

where the information set $I_{t-1} = \{y_{t-1}, \dots\}$ includes all past variables, either for estimation or forecasting purposes. This situation is complicated because I_{t-1} contains infinitely many variables and apart from the important class of Markov models m generally depends on all of them. A common assumption here is some kind of mixing condition that guarantees that the effect of y_{t-k} on y_t dies out as $k \to \infty$. For example, an invertible $MA(1)$ process has $m(I_{t-1}) = \sum_{j=1}^{\infty} \theta^{j-1} y_{t-j}$ for some $|\theta| < 1$. A natural generalization of this is the model $m(I_{t-1}) = \sum_{j=1}^{\infty} m_j(y_{t-j})$, where m_j is a sequence of functions such that the sum is well defined, that is, $m_j(\cdot)$ must decline in importance as $j \to \infty$. This model is hard to analyse and to estimate. Instead, consider the more restrictive version

$$m(I_{t-1}) = \sum_{j=1}^{\infty} \theta^{j-1} m(y_{t-j}) \qquad (5)$$

for some unknown function $m(\cdot)$ and parameter θ. When $m(y) = y$ this includes the MA(1) process as a special case, but includes many other nonlinear models. By taking a local parametric model $M(y) = a_0(y) + a_1(y)y + a_2(y)y^2$ for m one can nest the GARCH$(1, 1)$ model of Bollerslev (1986). Linton and Mammen (2005) have recently developed a theory of estimation for this class of models.

Another popular approach is the locally stationary models pioneered by Dahlhaus (1997). A locally stationary AR(1) process is $y_t = \rho(t/T)y_{t-1} + \varepsilon_t$, where ε_t is i.i.d. and $\rho(\cdot)$ is a smooth but unknown form. By taking the local parametric model $M(y) = a_0$ one can nest the conventional autoregression, although there are other possibilities. Dahlhaus actually deals with a more general class of linear processes with $y_t = \sum_{j=0}^{\infty} c_j(t/T)\varepsilon_{t-j}$, where $c_j(\cdot)$ are unknown but smooth functions.

OLIVER B. LINTON

See also **kernel estimators in econometrics; nonparametric structural models; semiparametric estimation.**

Bibliography

Bollerslev, T. 1986. Generalized autoregressive conditional heteroskedasticity. *Journal of Econometrics* 31, 307–27.

Charnes, A., Cooper, W. and Schinnar, A. 1976. A theorem on homogeneous functions and extended Cobb–Douglas forms. *Proceedings of the National Academy of Science, USA* 73, 3747–4748.

Dahlhaus, R. 1997. Fitting time series models to nonstationary processes. *Annals of Statistics* 25, 1–37.

Delgado, M. and Hidalgo, F. 2000. Nonparametric inference on structural breaks. *Journal of Econometrics* 96, 113–44.

Fan, J. and Gijbels, I. 1996. *Local Polynomial Modelling and its Applications.* London: Chapman and Hall.

Goldman, S. and Uzawa, H. 1964. A note on separability and demand analysis. *Econometrica* 32, 387–98.

Gozalo, P. and Linton, O. 2000. Local nonlinear least squares estimation: using parametric information nonparametrically. *Journal of Econometrics* 99, 63–106.

Härdle, W. and Linton, O. 1994. Applied nonparametric methods. In *The Handbook of Econometrics*, vol. 4, ed. D. McFadden and R. Engle. Amsterdam: North- Holland.

Hjort, N. and Glad, I. 1995. Nonparametric density estimation with a parametric start. *Annals of Statistics* 23, 882–904.

Linton, O. and Mammen, E. 2005. Estimating semiparametric ARCH models by kernel smoothing methods. *Econometrica* 73, 771–836.

Linton, O. and Nielsen, J. 1995. A kernel method of estimating structured nonparametric regression based on marginal integration. *Biometrika* 82, 93–100.

Rothenberg, T. 1971. Identification in parametric models. *Econometrica* 39, 577–91.

location theory

From a historical perspective, location theory has been at both the centre and the periphery of economic theory. It has been at the centre to the extent that it has followed the tradition taking its roots in Hotelling's classical paper 'Stability in Competition' (1929) and has used the spatial framework as a metaphor to explain issues involving heterogeneity and diversity across agents (Rosen, 2002). Examples include the supply of differentiated products, electoral competition between political parties, the matching process on the labour market, competition between communities to attract residents or firms, and the number and size of jurisdictions. Location theory has been at the periphery to the extent that space

has not been a major concern for most economists. Indeed, it is rare to find a principles textbook in which location issues are covered, let alone mentioned. This is despite their obvious importance for the way actual markets function, as shown, for instance, by the debate raging in many industrialized countries about the consequences of globalization for the location of jobs.

The theory of optimal location for a firm has long been dominated by the minisum model in which the firm aims at minimizing its total transportation costs (Weber, 1909). Formally, this is achieved by minimizing the weighted sum of distances to a finite number of points, which represent input and output markets. When the length of the shortest path connecting any two points of a transportation network measures the distance between these points, the firm's optimal location is an input/output market, or a node of the network, or both (Hurter and Martinich, 1988). Hence, *the locational choice of a firm is either sluggish or catastrophic.* Another interesting feature of that model is that the firm's optimal location is the outcome of the interplay of a system of forces pulling the firm in different directions. When several competing firms are to be located, the system of forces becomes richer in that it involves what are called 'agglomeration' and 'dispersion' forces.

Spatial competition between firms

To see how such a system of forces works, we consider the framework developed by Hotelling (1929). The market of a homogeneous good is made up of consumers who request one unit of the good. Because any single consumer is negligible to firms, Hotelling assumes that consumers are continuously distributed along a linear and bounded segment: think of Main Street. For simplicity, consumers are also supposed to be uniformly distributed along the linear segment. Two stores, aiming to maximize their respective profits, seek a location along the same segment. Because they are dispersed across locations, consumers differ in their access to the same store. In such a context, firms anticipate correctly that each consumer will buy from the store posting the lower full price, namely, the price at the firm's gate, called 'mill price', augmented by the travel costs that consumers must bear to go to the store they patronize. Accordingly, once they are located firms have some monopoly power over the consumers located in their vicinity, which enables them to choose their price. Of course, this choice is restricted by the possibility that consumers have to supply themselves from the competing firm. Note that any firm is supposed to have a single location – that is, an *address* – because increasing returns and indivisibilities do not allow it to run a large number of outlets dispersed along Main Street without incurring major losses (Koopmans, 1957).

Since each firm is aware that its price choice affects the consumer segment supplied by its rival, *spatial competition is inherently strategic.* This is one of the main innovations introduced by Hotelling, who uses a two-stage game to model the process of spatial competition. In the first stage, stores choose their location non-cooperatively; in the second, these locations being publicly observed, firms select their selling price. The use of a sequential procedure means that firms anticipate the consequences of their locational choices on their subsequent choices of prices, thus imparting to the model an implicit dynamic structure. The game is solved by backward induction. For an arbitrary pair of locations, Hotelling starts by solving the price subgame corresponding to the second stage. The resulting equilibrium prices are introduced into the profit functions, which then depend only upon the locations chosen by the firms. These functions stand for the payoffs that firms will maximize during the first stage of the game. Such an approach anticipates by several decades the concept of subgame perfect Nash equilibrium introduced by Selten (1965).

Whereas the individual purchase decision is discontinuous – a consumer buying only from one firm – Hotelling finds it reasonable to suppose that firms' aggregated demands are continuous with respect to prices. Supposing that each consumer is negligible solves the apparent contradiction between discontinuity at the individual level and continuity at the aggregated level. In other words, when consumers are continuously distributed across locations aggregated demands are 'often' continuous. The hypothesis of the continuum that had been popularized much later by Aumann (1964) is found here to represent the idea that competitive agents have a negligible impact on the market outcome. However, Hotelling considers a richer setting involving both 'dwarfs' – consumers – whose behaviour is competitive and 'giants' – firms – whose behaviour is strategic because they can manipulate the market outcome.

Hotelling's claim was that the process of spatial competition leads firms to agglomerate at the market centre. If true, this provides us with a rationale for the observed spatial concentration of firms selling similar goods (such as restaurants, movie theatres, or fashion clothes shops). But Hotelling's analysis is undermined by a mistake that invalidates his main conclusion: when firms are sufficiently close, the corresponding subgame does not have a Nash equilibrium in pure strategies, so that the payoffs used by Hotelling in the first stage are wrong (d'Aspremont, Gabszewicz and Thisse, 1979). This negative conclusion has led d'Aspremont et al. to slightly modify the Hotelling setting by assuming that the travel costs borne by consumers are quadratic in the distance covered, instead of being linear as in Hotelling. This new assumption captures the idea that the marginal cost of time increases with the length of the trip to the store. In this modified version, d'Aspremont et al. show that any price subgame has one and only one Nash equilibrium in pure strategies. Plugging these prices into the profit functions, they show that firms choose to set up at

the two extremities of the linear segment. Firms do so because this allows them to relax price competition and to restore their profit margins. Indeed, when prices are fixed and equal the quest for customer proximity – or, equivalently, for a larger market area – leads the two firms to agglomerate at the market centre. The tendency for firms to choose distinct locations or products has been confirmed by many works, and has led Tirole (1988) to call it the 'Principle of Differentiation'.

Consequently, *price competition is a dispersion force*, whereas *the market area effect is an agglomeration force*. What the Principle of Differentiation tells us is that the dispersion force always dominates the agglomeration force, at least when firms sell a homogeneous product and compete in price. Hence, the Hotelling setting is to be enriched if we want to be able to understand why firms selling similar products often form spatial clusters. This has been accomplished by following two different research strategies. In the first, the purpose is to identify market mechanisms allowing firms to relax price competition without being spatially separated. From this perspective, the most natural approach is to assume that firms sell products that are differentiated in the space of characteristics. It combines both spatial and product differentiation per se. An alternative approach, however, is to appeal to some form of collusion between firms that permits them to avoid the devastating effects of price competition. This is especially relevant when products can hardly be differentiated. The second research strategy is based on Stigler (1961) and develops the idea that consumers are imperfectly informed about the places where the existing varieties are made available. In such a context, consumers must undertake some search before finding a good match.

Product differentiation and collusion
Several papers have shown that firms selling differentiated varieties choose to agglomerate at the market centre when products are sufficiently differentiated, transportation costs borne by the consumers are low enough, or both (de Palma et al., 1985). This can be understood as follows. When consumers have different tastes and when residential locations and tastes are not correlated (or, alternatively, when individuals exhibit a love of variety), each firm supplies what is the best match for consumers who are otherwise dispersed across all locations. Price competition is relaxed by product differentiation, so that firms may afford to set up at the place offering the best accessibility to their potential customers. Such a place is obviously the market centre when the consumer distribution along Main Street is uniform. In addition, it is never profitable for a firm to leave the cluster when transportation costs are low because the benefit of a good match dominates the additional transportation costs that the consumer must bear to buy her best match. All of this seems to fit modern economies characterized by more and more variety and decreasing travel costs.

In a nutshell, we may then safely conclude that one of the main reasons for agglomeration is that *firms substitute product differentiation for spatial separation*, very much as *Newsweek* and *Time* are supplied in the same stores but differentiated by their cover stories (Irmen and Thisse, 1998).

The welfare analysis of such an outcome is somewhat unexpected. At the optimum, prices are set equal to the common marginal cost so that consumers' well-being depends only upon firms' locations. In the case of a homogeneous good, maximizing total welfare boils down to minimizing aggregate transportation costs. However, once we introduce differentiation across varieties, consumers no longer patronize the nearest firm on each trip because they now benefit from intrinsic differentiation between stores. In this context, one needs a more general approach accounting for both distance and product diversity effects, the appropriate measure being the consumers' indirect utility. As a result, the formation of a cluster need not be socially sub-optimal. Quite the opposite: when products are sufficiently differentiated, transportation costs are low, or both, it is socially desirable to have all firms agglomerated within a cluster. Hence, unlike what Hotelling thought, such an extreme concentration may be socially optimal.

Under what became known as 'semi-collusion', it has been shown that firms that anticipate some form of collusion in the price stage, which is typically repeated, will choose to locate together at the market centre (Jehiel, 1992; Friedman and Thisse, 1993). In this case, selling a homogenous product makes it easier to sustain price collusion because the punishment for a defecting firm is more severe. Of course, collusion is not easy to maintain in the long run, so that firms face a positive probability that price collusion will break down. In this case, firms select separated locations but do not seek to maximize their spatial differentiation. Specifically, Jehiel, Friedman and Thisse (1995) have established that the higher the probability that the price agreement will break down, the larger is the distance between firms.

Search

When firms sell differentiated products, it is reasonable to assume that consumers are incompletely informed about the varieties that are supplied. Even though the typical consumer knows which varieties are available in the market, she is unsure about which variety is offered where (and at which price). If consumers have to compare alternatives before buying, they must undertake *search* among firms. Stated differently, when the only way for consumers to find out which variety is on offer in a particular store is to visit this store, they must bear the corresponding travel cost. Gathering information being costly, each consumer must compare the cost of an additional bit of information with the expected gain in terms of surplus. In a spatial setting, both the cost and the gain vary with consumers' and firms' locations.

When several stores are located together, it is reasonable to assume that the typical consumer knows the location and size of the cluster but not its composition. Once she arrives at the cluster, the travel costs are sunk and she can visit any store at a very low cost. But she must pay the transportation cost to each isolated store she visits. Spatial clustering of stores is, therefore, a particular means by which firms can facilitate consumer search. Indeed, a consumer is more likely to visit a cluster of stores than an isolated one because of the higher probability she faces of finding there a good match and a good price. When firms realize this fact, each of them understands that it might be in its own interest to form a marketplace with others. When a firm considers the possibility of joining competitors within the same marketplace, it thus faces a trade-off between a negative competition effect and a positive market area effect, both being generated by the pooling of firms selling similar products.

In the case of a market with a fixed size, Wolinsky (1983) has shown that the market outcome involves all firms forming a single marketplace once transportation costs are sufficiently low and when there are enough stores to make the cluster attractive. It is worth noting that the agglomeration may arise away from the market centre. Any point such that no single firm is able to find an alternative location far enough to induce some consumers to visit it before the cluster is a spatial equilibrium. Of course, the cluster cannot be too far from the market centre because stores need to offer a good accessibility to *all* consumers. Accordingly, once the urban area extends far away into the same direction, this implies that some firms will want to create a new cluster away from the original one.

Schulz and Stahl (1996) show that it is possible to uncover additional and surprising results by considering a market of variable size. To this end, they consider an unbounded space that allows them to capture the idea that more competition within the cluster may attract new customers coming from more distant locations, thus allowing the demand for each variety to increase. More concretely, the entry of a new variety may lead to an increase in the cluster's demand that outweighs the decrease in market area inflicted on existing varieties. Although price competition becomes fiercer, it appears here that firms may take advantage of the extensive margin effect to increase their prices in equilibrium. Clearly, when the number of varieties is not too large, such positive effects associated with the gathering of firms strengthen the agglomeration force that lies behind the cluster. Though collectively several firms might want to form a new market, it may not pay an individual firm to open a new market in the absence of a coordinating device. Consequently, a new firm entering the market will choose instead to join the incumbents, thus leading to a larger agglomeration. In this case, *the entry of a new firm creates a positive externality for the existing firms by making total demand larger.* This in turn explains the common fact that department stores encourage the location of competing firms within the shopping centre.

The relationship with new economic geography

It appears that location theory and new economic geography have a lot in common, a fact that has been overlooked in the literature. Such a relationship between the two domains is worth noting because economic geography models are developed in general equilibrium frameworks involving monopolistic competition on the product market, whereas location theory uses partial equilibrium models under oligopolistic competition. Indeed, one of the main conditions identified in spatial competition for a cluster of firms to emerge corresponds with the main finding established in 'new economic geography', that is, firms agglomerate when trade costs are sufficiently low (Krugman, 1991; Fujita, Krugman and Venables, 1999). Likewise, product differentiation fosters agglomeration whereas, by its mere existence, a cluster generates a lock-in effect similar to those encountered in economic geography. In both settings, the absence of increasing returns would lead to the emergence of 'backyard capitalism' in which each household produces its own consumption bundle. Finally, the market size effect uncovered in search models is similar to the agglomeration effect identified by Krugman and others.

Spatial competition and urban economics

So far, consumers have been able to seek where to buy but not where to live. Yet it is reasonable to assume that consumers adjust their residential choices to the locations selected by large firms and/or by public facilities. For the resulting distribution to be non-degenerate, a land market must be introduced in which consumers compete for land use. In such a context, the demand of a consumer for the firm's output becomes in turn endogenous in that it depends on the income left after the land rent is paid. This brings into the picture some general equilibrium ingredients in that firms and households locations are interdependent. Fujita and Thisse (1986) consider a setting in which firms choose their locations, anticipating consumers' residential choices, this sequence reflecting the fact that firms have market power whereas consumers adjust their locational choices to those made by firms. Because they compete for land, consumers are spread around firms in a way such that no consumer can find a better place to live. In the case of two firms selling a homogeneous good at a common given price, the agglomeration of the two firms is always a Nash equilibrium. However, dispersed equilibria may also coexist when travel costs are sufficiently high. This is because the decrease in individual consumption resulting from a move toward the rival dominates the market area effect. In other words, firms may not find it advantageous to

agglomerate, thus showing that *competition for land acts a major dispersion force.*

Public facilities

Cities provide a large variety of local public goods. Because its location interacts with the locational choices of firms and households, a large public facility which consumers wish to access influences the nature of the urban structure. In particular, one expects the presence of a major equipment to act as an agglomeration force on the private sector (Thisse and Wildasin, 1992). When topographical boundaries have no impact on the location of the public facility, this one is always established at the centre of the urban area and there is a tendency for this facility to draw the private firms together as income rises with respect to transportation costs. When the facility is set up near the edge of the area available for urban use – think of an urban area on the coast of a body of water – the resulting asymmetry has a significant impact on the locational interactions between firms: the two private firms are located together at the centre of the urban area. Hence, *the public facility may serve as the center of a dispersed spatial configuration, or it may induce the agglomeration of firms in a location different from that of the public facility itself*. In both cases, it vastly contributes to the shaping of the city structure.

Local labour markets

Due to the evolution of technological progress and the concomitant expansion of metropolitan areas, the urban labour force has become more heterogeneous whereas the labour market has been segmented in thinner sub-markets. The force inducing the formation of local labour markets finds its origin, at least partially, in the skill and geographical heterogeneity of workers (Brueckner, Thisse and Zenou, 2002). When workers have heterogeneous skills, firms have different job requirements because they have incentives to differentiate their job offers in order to gain market power in the labour market. This in turn implies that the labour market works as an *oligopsony* in which firms with different skill needs and different urban locations compete for mobile and skill-heterogeneous workers. In terms of urban economics, each firm may be considered as a company town attracting workers who also choose to reside near this firm. As in the case of firms selling consumption goods, firms are separated in the geographical space because this allows them to enjoy market power over the workers situated in their vicinity. Consequently, the economy may be viewed as a system of cities in which each firm/city competes to attract workers who are also residents. *The fact that each firm is anchored in a distinct location is a fundamental reason for the emergence of local labour markets.*

When workers bear the training cost that allows them to erase any mismatch between their innate skills and the skill needs of their employer, the net wage is lower for workers whose 'skill distance' from their employer is larger. Firms understand that, in the residential equilibrium, commuting distance is positively related to a worker's skill distance from the firm. In such a context, the equilibrium residential location of workers is governed by the quality of their match in the labour market. Knowledge of the connection between skill and commute distances affects the firm's interaction with its rivals as it competes for labour. The critical issue is that the equilibrium wage depends on the commuting cost parameters, yielding a link between the urban structure and the labour market. More precisely, low-skill workers incur high commuting costs, which may in turn lead low-skill workers not to take a job. Unemployment may arise, therefore, because some workers turn out to be too 'distant' from firms in *both* the skill and urban spaces. As in the foregoing, two different spatial components interact to shape the social structure of cities.

JACQUES-FRANÇOIS THISSE

See also **new economic geography; product differentiation; spatial economics; systems of cities; urban agglomeration; urban economics.**

Bibliography

Aumann, R. 1964. Markets with a continuum of traders. *Econometrica* 32, 39–50.

Brueckner, J., Thisse J.-F. and Zenou, Y. 2002. Local labor markets, job matching and urban location. *International Economic Review* 43, 155–71.

d'Aspremont, C., Gabszewicz, J. and Thisse, J.-F. 1979. ·On Hotelling's 'Stability in Competition'. *Econometrica* 47, 1045–50.

de Palma, A., Ginsburgh, V., Papageorgiou, Y.Y. and Thisse, J.-F. 1985. The principle of minimum differentiation holds under sufficient heterogeneity. *Econometrica* 53, 767–81.

Friedman, J. and Thisse, J.-F. 1993. Partial collusion fosters minimum product differentiation. *RAND Journal of Economics* 24, 631–45.

Fujita, M., Krugman, P. and Venables, A. 1999. *The Spatial Economy: Cities, Regions and International Trade.* Cambridge, MA: MIT Press.

Fujita, M. and Thisse, J.-F. 1986. Spatial competition with a land market: Hotelling and von Thünen unified. *Review of Economic Studies* 53, 819–41.

Hotelling, H. 1929. Stability in competition. *Economic Journal* 39, 41–57.

Hurter, A. and Martinich, J. 1988. *Facility Location and the Theory of Production.* Dordrecht: Kluwer.

Irmen, A. and Thisse, J.-F. 1998. Competition in multi-characteristics spaces: Hotelling was almost right. *Journal of Economic Theory* 78, 76–102.

Jehiel, P. 1992. Product differentiation and price collusion. *International Journal of Industrial Organization* 10, 633–41.

Jehiel, P., Friedman, J. and Thisse, J.-F. 1995. Collusion and antitrust detection. *Japanese Economic Review* 46, 226–46.

Koopmans, T. 1957. *Three Essays on the State of Economic Science.* New York: McGraw-Hill.

Krugman, P. 1991. Increasing returns and economic geography. *Journal of Political Economy* 99, 483–99.

Rosen, S. 2002. Markets and diversity. *American Economic Review* 92, 1–15.

Schulz, N. and Stahl, K. 1996. Do consumers search for the highest price? Equilibrium and monopolistic optimum in differentiated products markets. *RAND Journal of Economics* 27, 542–62.

Selten, R. 1965. Spieltheoretische Behandlung eines Oligopolmodells mit Nachfrageträgheit. *Zeitschrift für die gesamte Staatswissenschaft* 121, 301–24.

Stigler, G. 1961. The economics of information. *Journal of Political Economy* 69, 213–25.

Thisse, J.-F. and Wildasin, D. 1992. Public facility location and urban spatial structure. *Journal of Public Economics* 48, 83–118.

Tirole, J. 1988. *The Theory of Industrial Organization.* Cambridge, MA: MIT Press.

Weber, A. 1909. *Ueber den Standort der Industrien*, Tübingen, J.C.B. Mohr. English translation: *The Theory of the Location of Industries.* Chicago: Chicago University Press, 1929.

Wolinsky, A. 1983. Retail trade concentration due to consumers' imperfect information. *Bell Journal of Economics* 14, 275–82.

logit models of individual choice

The logit function is the reciprocal function to the sigmoid *logistic* function. It maps the interval [0,1] into the real line and is written as:

$$logit(p) = \ln(p/(1-p)).$$

Two traditions are involved in the modern theory of logit models of individual choices. The first one concerns *curve fitting* as exposed by Berkson (1944), who coined the term 'logit' after its close competitor 'probit' which is derived from the normal distribution. Both models are by far the most popular econometric methods used in applied work to estimate models for binary variables, even though the development of semiparametric and nonparametric alternatives since the mid-1970s has been intensive (Horowitz and Savin, 2001).

In the second strand of literature, models of discrete variables and discrete choices as originally set up by Thurstone (1927) in psychometrics have been known as 'random utility models' (RUM) since Marschak (1960) introduced them to economists. As the availability of individual databases and the need for tools to forecast aggregate demands derived from discrete choices were increasing from the 1960s onwards, different waves of innovations, fostered by McFadden (see his Nobel lecture, 2001) elaborated more and more sophisticated and flexible logit models. The use of these models and of simulation methods has triggered burgeoning applied research in demand analysis in recent years.

Those who wish to study the subject in greater detail are referred to Gouriéroux (2000), McFadden (2001) or Train (2003), where references to applications in economics and marketing can also be found.

Measurement models

As Berkson (1951, p. 327) put it, logit (or probit) models may be seen as 'merely a convenient way of graphically representing and fitting a function'. They are used for any empirical phenomenon delivering a binary random variable Y_i, taking values 0 and 1, to be analysed. In a logit model, it is postulated that its probability distribution conditional on a vector of covariates X_i is given by:

$$\Pr(Y_i = 1|X_i) = \frac{\exp(X_i\beta)}{1 + \exp(X_i\beta)}$$

where β is a vector of parameters. This model can also be derived from more general frameworks in statistical mechanics or spatial statistics (Strauss, 1992).

With the use of cross-sectional samples, the parameter of interest is estimated using maximum likelihood or by generalized linear models (GLM) methods where the link function is logit (McCullagh and Nelder, 1989). Under the maintained assumption that it is the true model and other standard assumptions, the maximum likelihood estimator (MLE) is consistent, asymptotically normal and efficient (Amemiya, 1985). Nevertheless, the MLE may fail to exist, or more exactly be at the bounds of the parameter space, when the samples are uniformly composed of 0 s or 1 s, for instance (Berkson, 1955).

When repeated observations are available, the method of Berkson delivers an estimator close to MLE since they are asymptotically equivalent. Observe first that the logit function of the true probability obeys the linear equation:

$$logit(\Pr(Y_c = 1|X_c)) = X_c\beta$$

where the covariates X_c now take a discrete number of values defining each cell, c. Second, use the observed frequency in each cell, $\hat{p}_c$, and contrast it with the theoretical probability, p_c, as:

$$logit(\hat{p}_c) = X_c\beta + (logit(\hat{p}_c) - logit(p_c))$$
$$= X_c\beta + \varepsilon_c.$$

The random term ε_c properly scaled by the square root of the number of observations in cell c is asymptotically normally distributed with variance equal to $1/(p_c(1 - p_c))$. The method of Berkson then consists in

using minimum chi-square, that is, a method of moments, to estimate β, an instance of what is know as minimum distance or asymptotic least squares (Gouriéroux, Monfort and Trognon, 1985).

When measurements for a single individual are repeated, Rasch (1960) suspected that individual effects might be important and proposed to write:

$$logit(\Pr(Y_{it} = 1|X_{it})) = X_{it}\beta + \delta_i$$

where t indexes the different items that are measured and δ_i is an individual specific intercept or fixed effect. Items can be different questions in performance tests or different periods. In the original Rasch formulation, parameters were allowed to be different across items, β_t, and there were no covariates.

Given that the number of items is small, it is well known that the estimation of such a model runs into the problem of incidental parameters (see Lancaster, 2000). As the number of parameters δ_i increases with the cross-section dimension, the MLE is inconsistent (Chamberlain, 1984). Nevertheless, the nuisance parameters δ_i can be differenced out using conditional likelihood methods (Andersen, 1973) because:

$$logit(\Pr(Y_{it} = 1|X_{it}, Y_{it} + Y_{it'} = 1)) = (X_{it} - X_{it'})\beta.$$

The conditional likelihood estimator of β is consistent and root n asymptotically normal but it is not efficient, although no efficient estimator is known. Furthermore, when binary variables Y_{it} are independent, conditionally on X_i, the only model where a root n consistent estimator exists is a logit model (Chamberlain, 1992). Extensions of Rasch rely on the fact that root n consistent estimators exist if and only if $Y_{it} + Y_{it'}$ is a sufficient statistic for the nuisance parameters δ_i (Magnac, 2004). When the number of items or periods becomes large, profile likelihood methods where individual effects are treated as parameters seem to be accurate in Monte Carlo experiments as soon as the number of periods is four or five (Arellano, 2003).

Multinomial logit (or in disuse 'conditional logit') is to binary logit what a multinomial is to a binomial distribution (Theil, 1969). Given a vector Y_i consisting of K elements which are binary random variables and lie in the $\mathbb{R}^K$– simplex (their sum is equal to 1), it is postulated that:

$$\Pr(Y_i^{(k)} = 1|X_i) = \frac{\exp(X_i\beta^{(k)})}{1 + \sum_{k=2}^{K}\exp(X_i\beta^{(k)})}$$

where by normalization, $\beta^{(1)} = 0$. Ordered logit has a different flavour since it applies to rank-ordered data such as education levels (Gouriéroux, 2000).

As probits, logit models are very tightly specified parametric models and can be substantially generalized. Much effort has been exerted to relax parametric and conditional independence assumptions, starting with Manski (1975). Manski (1988) analyses the identifying restrictions in binary models, and Horowitz (1998) reviews estimation methods. In some cases, Lewbel (2000) and Matzkin (1992) offer alternatives.

Random utility models

The theory of discrete choice is directly set up in a multiple alternative framework. A choice of an alternative k belonging to a set C is assumed to be probabilistic either because preferences are stochastic or heterogenous, or because choices are perturbed in a random way. By definition, choice probability functions map each alternative and choice sets into the simplex of $\mathbb{R}^K$.

A strong restriction on choices is the axiom of Independence of Irrelevant Alternatives (IIA, Luce, 1959). The axiom states that the choice between two alternatives is independent of any other alternative in the choice set. The version that allows for zero probabilities (McFadden, 2001) states that for any pair of choice set C,C' such that $\{k,k'\} \in C$ and $C \subset C'$:

$$\Pr(k \text{ is chosen in } C') = \Pr(k \text{ is chosen in } C).$$
$$\Pr(\text{An element of } C \text{ is chosen in } C').$$

Under this axiom, choice probabilities take a multinomial generalized logit form.

Moreover, assume that choices are associated with utility functions, $\{u^{(k)}\}_k$ that depend on determinants X_i and random shocks:

$$u^{(k)} = X\beta^{(k)} + \varepsilon^{(k)},$$

and that the actual choice of the decision maker yields maximum utility to her. Then, the IIA axiom is verified if and only if $\varepsilon^{(k)}$ are independent and extreme value distributed (McFadden, 1974). Extensions of decision theory under IIA were proposed in the continuous case (Resnick and Roy, 1991) or in an intertemporal context (Dagsvik, 2002).

The IIA axiom is a strong restriction as in the famous red and blue bus example where, if IIA is assumed, the existence of different colours affects choices of transport between bus and other modes while introspection suggests that colours should indeed be irrelevant. Several generalizations which proceed from logit were proposed to bypass IIA. Hierarchical or tree structures were the first to be used. At the upper level, the choice set consists of broad groups of alternatives. In each of these groups, there are various alternatives which can consist themselves of subsets of alternatives, and so on. The best-known model is the two-level nested logit, where alternatives are grouped by similarities. For instance, the first level is the choice of the type of the car, the second level is the make of the car. The formula

of choice probabilities for nested logit,

$$p^{(k)} = \frac{\exp(X\beta^{(k)}/\lambda_{B_s})\left(\sum_{j\in B_s}\exp(X\beta^{(j)}/\lambda_{B_s})\right)^{\lambda_{B_s}-1}}{\sum_{t=1}^{T}\left(\sum_{j\in B_t}\exp(X\beta^{(j)}/\lambda_{B_s})\right)^{\lambda_{B_t}}},$$

where alternative k belongs to B_s, is not illuminating but the logic of construction is clear. Choices at each level are modelled as multinomial logit (Train, 2003).

General extreme value distributions (McFadden, 1984) provide more extensions, although they do not generate all configurations of choice probabilities. In contrast, mixed logit does, as shown by McFadden and Train (2000). Instead of considering that parameters are deterministic, make them random or heterogeneous across agents. The result is a mixture model where individual probabilities of choice are obtained by integrating out the random elements as in

$$p^{(k)} = \int p^{(k)}(\beta)f(\beta)d\beta.$$

Integrals are computed using simulation methods (MacFadden, 2001). The same principle is used by Berry, Levinsohn and Pakes (1995) with a view to generalizing the aggregate logit choice models using market data. Logit models are still very much in use in applied settings in demand analysis and marketing, and are equivalent to a representative consumer model (Anderson, de Palma and Thisse, 1992). Mixed logits permit much more general patterns of substitution between alternatives and should probably become the standard tool in the near future.

THIERRY MAGNAC

See also **categorical data; econometrics; hierarchical Bayes models; maximum likelihood; McFadden, Daniel; mixture models; nonlinear panel data models; product differentiation; rational behaviour; utility.**

Bibliography

Amemiya, T. 1985. *Advanced Econometrics.* Cambridge, MA: Harvard University Press.
Andersen, E.B. 1973. *Conditional Inference and Models for Measuring.* Copenhagen: Mentalhygiejnisk Forlag.
Anderson, S.P., de Palma, A. and Thisse, J.F. 1992. *Discrete Choice Theory of Product Differentiation.* Cambridge, MA: MIT Press.
Arellano, M. 2003. Discrete choices with panel data. *Investigaciones Economicas* 27, 423–58.
Berkson, J. 1944. Application of the logistic function to bioassay. *Journal of the American Statistical Association* 39, 357–65.
Berkson, J. 1951. Why I prefer logits to probits. *Biometrics* 7, 327–39.
Berkson, J. 1955. Maximum likelihood and minimum chi-square estimates of the logistic function. *Journal of the American Statistical Association* 50, 130–62.

Berry, S.T., Levinsohn, J.A. and Pakes, A. 1995. Automobile prices in market equilibrium. *Econometrica* 63, 841–90.

Chamberlain, G. 1984. Panel data. In *Handbook of Econometrics*, vol. 2, ed. Z. Griliches and M. Intriligator. Amsterdam: North-Holland.

Chamberlain, G. 1992. Binary response models for panel data: identification and information. Unpublished manuscript, Harvard University.

Dagsvik, J. 2002. Discrete choice in continuous time: implications of an intertemporal version of IAA. *Econometrica* 70, 817–31.

Gouriéroux, C. 2000. *Econometrics of Qualitative Dependent Variables*. Cambridge: Cambridge University Press.

Gouriéroux, C., Monfort, A. and Trognon, A. 1985. Moindres carrés asymptotiques. *Annales de l'INSEE* 58, 91–121.

Horowitz, J. 1998. *Semiparametric Methods in Econometrics*. Berlin: Springer.

Horowitz, J.L. and Savin, N.E. 2001. Binary response models: logits, probits and semiparametrics. *Journal of Economic Perspectives* 15(4), 43–56.

Lancaster, T. 2000. The incidental parameter problem since 1948. *Journal of Econometrics* 95, 391–413.

Lewbel, A. 2000. Semiparametric qualitative response model estimation with unknown heteroskedasticity or instrumental variables. *Journal of Econometrics* 97, 145–77.

Luce, R. 1959. *Individual Choice Behavior: A Theoretical Analysis*. New York: Wiley.

Magnac, T. 2004. Panel binary variables and sufficiency: generalizing conditional logit. *Econometrica* 72, 1859–77.

Manski, C.F. 1975. The maximum score estimation of the stochastic utility model of choice. *Journal of Econometrics* 3, 205–28.

Manski, C.F. 1988. Identification of binary response models. *Journal of the American Statistical Association* 83, 729–38.

Marschak, J. 1960. Binary choice constraints and random utility indicators. In *Mathematical Methods in the Social Sciences*, ed. K. Arrow. Stanford: Stanford University Press.

Matzkin, R. 1992. Nonparametric and distribution-free estimation of the binary threshold crossing and the binary choice models. *Econometrica* 60, 239–70.

McCullagh, P. and Nelder, J.A. 1989. *Generalized Linear Models*. London: Chapman and Hall.

McFadden, D. 1974. Conditional logit analysis of qualitative choice behavior. In *Frontiers in Econometrics*, ed. P. Zarembka. New York: Academic Press.

McFadden, D. 1984. Econometric analysis of qualitative response models. In *Handbook of Econometrics*, vol. 2, ed. Z. Griliches and M.D. Intriligator. Amsterdam: North-Holland.

McFadden, D. 2001. Economic choices. *American Economic Review* 91, 351–78.

McFadden, D. and Train, K. 2000. Mixed MNL models for discrete responses. *Journal of Applied Econometrics* 15, 447–70.

Rasch, G. 1960. *Probabilistic Models for Some Intelligence and Attainment Tests*. Copenhagen: Denmark Paedagogiske Institut.

Resnick, S.I. and Roy, R. 1991. Random USC functions, max stable process and continuous choice. *Annals of Applied Probability* 1, 267–92.

Strauss, D. 1992. The many faces of logistic regression. *American Statistician* 46, 321–27.

Theil, H. 1969. A multinomial extension of the linear logit model. *International Economic Review* 10, 251–9.

Thurstone, L. 1927. A law of comparative judgement. *Psychological Review* 34, 273–86.

Train, K. 2003. *Discrete Choice Methods with Simulation*. Cambridge: Cambridge University Press.

lognormal distribution

If there is a number, θ, such that $Y = \log_e(X - \theta)$ is normally distributed, the distribution of X is *lognormal*. The important special case of $\theta = 0$ gives the two parameter lognormal distribution, $X \sim \Lambda(\mu, \sigma^2)$ with $Y \sim N(\mu, \sigma^2)$, where μ and σ^2 denote the mean and variance of $\log_e X$. The classic work on the subject is by Aitchison and Brown (1957). A useful survey is provided by Johnson, Kotz and Balakrishnan (1994, ch. 14). They also summarize the history of this distribution: the pioneer contributions by Galton (1879) on its genesis, and by McAlister (1879) on its measures of location and dispersion, were followed by Kapteyn (1903), who studied its genesis in more detail and also devised an analogue machine to generate it. Gibrat's (1931) study of economic size distributions was a most important development because of his law of proportionate effect. Since then there has been an immense number of applications of the lognormal distribution in the natural, behavioural and social sciences.

Why does the lognormal distribution appear to occur so frequently? One plausible answer is based on the central limit theorems used to explain the genesis of a normal curve. If a large number of random shocks, some positive, some negative, change the size of a particular variable, X, in an additive fashion, the distribution of that variable will tend to become normal as the number of shocks increases. But if these shocks act multiplicatively, changing the value of X by randomly distributed proportions instead of absolute amounts, the central limit theorems apply to $Y = \log_e X$ which tends to be normally distributed. Hence X has a lognormal distribution.

The substitution of multiplicative for additive random shocks generates a positively skew, leptokurtic, lognormal distribution instead of the symmetric, mesokurtic normal curve. But the degree of skewness and kurtosis of the two-parameter lognormal curve depends solely on σ^2, so if this is low enough, the lognormal approximates the normal curve. The important difference is that X cannot take zero or negative values which may make the lognormal distribution a more appropriate representation of variables, such as height and weight, which must take positive values. Clearly, the widespread occurrence of positive variables in practice, coupled with the great flexibility of the shape of the lognormal, provide further reasons for its frequent application.

P.E. HART

See also **Gini ratio; inequality (measurement); Lorenz curve; Pareto distribution.**

Bibliography

Aitchison, J. and Brown, J.A.C. 1957. *The Lognormal Distribution.* Cambridge: Cambridge University Press.

Galton, F. 1879. The geometric mean in vital and social statistics. *Proceedings of the Royal Society of London* 29, 365–7.

Galton, F. 1889. *Natural Inheritance.* London: Macmillan.

Galton, F. 1892. *Hereditary Genius.* London: Macmillan.

Gibrat, R. 1931. *Les inégalites économiques.* Paris: Librairie du Recueil Sirey.

Johnson, N., Kotz, S. and Balakrishnan, L. 1994. *Continuous Univariate Distributions*, vol. 1. New York: John Wiley.

Kapteyn, J.C. 1903. *Skew Frequency Curves in Biology and Statistics.* Astronomical Laboratory, Groningen: Noordhoff.

McAlister, D. 1879. The law of the geometric mean. *Proceedings of the Royal Society of London* 29, 367–75.

long memory models

Much analysis of economic and financial time series focuses on stochastic modelling. Deterministic sequences, based on polynomials and dummy variables, can explain some trending or cyclic behaviour, but residuals typically exhibit serial dependence. Stochastic components have often been modelled by stationary, weakly dependent processes: parametric models include stationary and invertible autoregressive moving average (ARMA) processes, while a non-parametric approach usually focuses on a smooth spectral density. In many cases, however, we need to allow for a greater degree of persistence or 'memory'. This is characterized by stationary time series whose autocorrelations are not summable or whose spectral densities are unbounded, or by non-stationary series evolving over time. The latter are partly covered by unit root processes, but considerably greater flexibility is possible.

Basic models

Early empirical evidence of slowly decaying autocorrelations emerged long ago, in analyses of astronomical, chemical, agricultural and hydrological data, and then in economics and finance. A stationary parametric model which attracted early interest is 'fractional noise'. Let x_t, $t = 0, \pm 1, \ldots$, be a covariance stationary discrete time process, so its autocovariance $cov(x_t, x_{t+u})$ depends only on u, and thus may be denoted by γ_u. Then fractional noise x_t has autocovariance

$$\gamma_u = \gamma_0 \left\{ |u+1|^{2d+1} - 2|u|^{2d+1} + |u-1|^{2d+1} \right\},$$
$$u = 0, \pm 1, \ldots, \tag{1}$$

where the parameter d is called the 'memory parameter', and satisfies $-\frac{1}{2} < d < \frac{1}{2}$. When $d = 0$ (1) implies that $\gamma_u = 0$ for $u \neq 0$, so x_t is white noise. But if $0 < d < \frac{1}{2}$, we have

$$\gamma_u \sim 2d \left(d + \frac{1}{2} \right) \gamma_0 |u|^{2d-1}, \quad \text{as } |u| \to \infty, \tag{2}$$

where '$\sim$' means that the ratio of left- and right-hand sides tends to one. It follows from (2) that γ_u does decrease with lag u, but so slowly that

$$\sum_{u=-\infty}^{\infty} \gamma_u = \infty. \tag{3}$$

In the frequency domain, when x_t has a spectral density $f(\lambda)$, $\lambda \in (-\pi, \pi)$ given by

$$f(\lambda) = (2\pi)^{-1} \sum_{u=-\infty}^{\infty} \gamma_u \cos(u\lambda), \quad \lambda \in (-\pi, \pi),$$

the property (3) is equivalent to

$$f(0) = \infty, \tag{4}$$

and more precisely a fractional noise process x_t has spectral density satisfying

$$f(\lambda) \sim C\lambda^{-2d}, \quad \text{as } \lambda = 0 +. \tag{5}$$

In general we can regard (3) and (4) as basic indicators of a 'long memory' process x_t, and (2) and (5) as providing more detailed description of autocorrelation structure at long lags, or spectral behaviour at low frequencies. By contrast, if x_t were a stationary ARMA, γ_u would decay exponentially and $f(\lambda)$ would be analytic at all frequencies. The structure (5) is similar to Granger's (1966) 'typical spectral shape of an economic variable'.

The model (1) is connected with the physical property of 'self-similarity', and, so far as economic and financial data are concerned, found early application in work of Mandelbrot (1972) and others. However, (1) imposes a very rigid structure, with autocorrelations decaying monotonically and depending on a single parameter. In addition, though a formula for $f(\lambda)$ corresponding to (1) can be written down, it is complicated, and (1) does not connect well mathematically with other important time series models, and does not lend itself readily to forecasting.

An alternative class of 'fractionally integrated' processes leads to a satisfactory resolution of these concerns. This is conveniently expressed in terms of the lag operator L, where $Lx_t = x_{t-1}$. Given the formal expansion

$$(1-s)^d = \sum_{j=0}^{\infty} \frac{\Gamma(j+d)}{\Gamma(d)\Gamma(j+1)} s^j,$$

we consider generating x_t from a zero-mean stationary sequence u_t, $t = 0, \pm 1, \ldots$, by

$$(1-L)^d(x_t - \mu) = v_t, \tag{6}$$

where $\mu = Ex_t$ and

$$|d| < \frac{1}{2}.$$

If v_t has absolutely summable autocorrelations, that satisfy some mild additional conditions, both the properties (2) and (5) hold. In the simplest case of (6), v_t is a white noise sequence. Then γ_u decays monotonically when $d \in (0, \frac{1}{2})$ and indeed behaves very much like (1). This model may have originated in Adenstedt (1974), though he stressed the case $d \in (-\frac{1}{2}, 0)$, where x_t is said to have 'negative dependence' or 'antipersistence'. Taking v_t to be a stationary and invertible ARMA process, with autoregressive order p and moving average order q, gives the FARIMA (p, d, q) process of Granger and Joyeux (1980). In principle, the short memory process v_t in (6) can be specified in any number of ways so as to yield (2) and/or (5); a process satisfying this condition is sometimes called $I(d)$.

Statistical inference

Given observations x_t, $t = 1, \ldots, n$ there is interest in estimating d. If v_t has parametric autocorrelation, as when x_t is a FARIMA (p, d, q), one can form a Gaussian maximum likelihood estimate of d and any other parameters. This estimate has the classical properties of being $n^{1/2}$-consistent and asymptotically normal and efficient. Computationally somewhat more convenient estimates, called Whittle estimates, have the same asymptotic properties. Indeed, for standard FARIMA (p, d, q) parameterizations, say, the estimates of d and of ARMA coefficients have asymptotic variance matrix that is unaffected by many departures from Gaussianity. Though these asymptotic properties are of the same type as one obtains for estimates of short memory processes, such as ARMAs, their proof is considerably more difficult (see Fox and Taqqu, 1986), due to the spectral singularity (4). In econometrics, generalized method of moments (GMM) estimation has become very popular, and GMM estimates have been proposed for long memory models. However, unless a suitable weighting is

used, they are not efficient under Gaussianity, are not more robust asymptotically to non-Gaussianity, and are not even asymptotically normal when $d > \frac{1}{4}$.

If the parametric autocorrelation is mis-specified, for example if in the FARIMA (p, d, q) p or q are chosen too small or both are chosen too large, then the procedures described in the previous paragraph will generally produce inconsistent estimates of d, as well as of other parameters. Essentially, the attempt to model the short memory component of x_t damages estimation of the long memory component. This difficulty can be tackled by a 'semiparametric' approach, if one regards the local or asymptotic specifications (2) or (5) as the model, and estimates d using only information in low frequencies or in long lags. Frequency domain versions are by far the more popular here, having the nicest asymptotic statistical properties. In the log periodogram estimate of d, logged periodograms are regressed on a logged local approximation to $f(\lambda)$, over the m Fourier frequencies closest to the origin (Geweke and Porter-Hudak, 1983), m having the character of a bandwidth number similar to those used in smoothed nonparametric functional estimation. An alternative approach optimizes a local Whittle function, again based on the lowest m Fourier frequencies (Künsch, 1987). In the asymptotics for both types of estimate (see Robinson, 1995a; 1995b) m must increase with n, but more slowly (to avoid bias); both the log periodogram and local Whittle estimates are $m^{1/2}$-consistent and asymptotically normal, with the latter the more efficient (though it is computationally more onerous, being only implicitly defined). Because both converge more slowly than estimates of correctly specified parametric models, a larger amount of data may be necessary for estimates to be reasonably precise. Moreover, estimates are sensitive to the choice of m. However, automatic and other rules are available for determining m; and semiparametric methods of estimating memory parameters have become very popular not only because of the robust character of the asymptotic results, but because of their relative simplicity.

The long memory processes we have been discussing exhibit an excess of low frequency power (5). But one can also consider parametric or semiparametric models for a spectral density with one or more poles at non-zero frequencies. These models can be used to describe seasonal or cyclic behaviour (see Arteche and Robinson, 2000). It is also possible to estimate the unknown location of a pole, that is, cycle (see Giraitis, Hidalgo and Robinson, 2001).

Nonlinear models

In non-Gaussian series, not all information is contained in first and second moments. In particular, in many financial series observations x_t may appear to have little or no autocorrelation, but instantaneous nonlinear functions, such as squares x_t^2, exhibit long memory behaviour.

We can develop models to describe such phenomena. For example, let

$$x_t = \varepsilon_t h_t, \qquad (7)$$

where x_t is a sequence of independent and identically distributed random variables with unit variance, whereas h_t is a stationary autocorrelated sequence, such that ε_s and h_t are independent for all s, t. Then for all $u \neq 0$, $cov = (x, x_{t+u}) = 0$ but $cov(x_t^2, x_{t+u}^2) = cov(h_t^2, h_{t+u}^2)$, which in general can be non-zero. In particular, if h_t^2 has long memory, so has x_t^2. In a more fundamental modelling we can take h_t to be a nonlinear function of an underlying long memory Gaussian processes, with the functional form of h determining the extent of any long memory in h_t^2; these issues were discussed in some generality by Robinson (2001). The models form a class of long memory stochastic volatility models, whose estimation has been discussed by Hurvich, Moulines and Soulier (2005), for example.

The fractional class (6) can be modified or extended to describe a wide class of nonstationary behaviour. For $d \geq \frac{1}{2}$ the variance of x_t (6) explodes, but we can consider truncated versions such as

$$x_t = (1 - L)^{-d}\{v_t 1(t \geq 1)\}$$

where $1(\cdot)$ is the indicator function, or

$$x_t = (1 - L)^{-k}\{w_t 1(t \geq 1)\}$$

for integer $k \geq 1$, where w_t is a stationary $I(c)$ process, $|c| < \frac{1}{2}$, and $d = k + c$. In either case we might call x_t a (nonstationary) $I(d)$ process, for $d \geq \frac{1}{2}$. Both models include the unit root case $d = 1$ that has proved so popular in econometrics. However, the fractional class $I(d)$, for real-valued d, bridges the gap between short memory and unit root processes, allowing also for the possibility of arbitrarily long memory d. The 'smoothness' of the $I(d)$ family is associated with classical asymptotic theory, which is not found in autoregressive based models around a unit root. Robinson (1994) showed that Lagrange multiplier tests for the value of d, and any other parameters, have asymptotic null χ^2 distributions for all real d. Also, under nonstationary suitably modified parametric and semiparametric methods of estimating d, extending those for the stationary case, tend still to be respectively $n^{1/2}$- and $m^{1/2}$-consistent, and asymptotically normal, unlike, say, the lag-one sample autocorrelation of a unit root series.

Multivariate models

Often in economics and finance we are concerned with a vector of jointly dependent series, so x_t is vector-valued. Such series can be modelled, either parametrically or semiparametrically, to have long memory, with different elements of x_t possibly having different memory parameters, and being stationary or nonstationary. Methods of statistical inference developed for the univariate case can be extended to such settings. However, multivariate data introduces the possibility of (fractional) cointegration, where a linear combination of x_t (the cointegrating error) can have smaller memory parameter than the elements of x_t. Cointegration has been extensively developed for the case x_t is $I(1)$ and cointegrating errors are $I(0)$, and methods developed for this case can fail to detect fractional cointegration. Moreover, it is possible for stationary series, not only nonstationary ones, to be fractionally cointegrated, as seems relevant in financial series. In either case, methods of analysing cointegration that allow memory parameters of observables and cointegrating errors to be unknown (see, for example, Hualde and Robinson, 2004) afford considerable flexibility.

P. M. ROBINSON

See also **central limit theorems; econometrics; nonparametric structural models; semiparametric estimation; time series analysis.**

Research supported by ESRC Grant R000239936.

Bibliography

Adenstedt, R. 1974. On large-sample estimation for the mean of a stationary random sequence. *Annals of Statistics* 2, 1095–107.

Arteche, J. and Robinson, P. 2000. Semiparametric inference in seasonal and cyclic long memory processes. *Journal of Time Series Analysis* 21, 1–25.

Fox, R. and Taqqu, M.S. 1986. Large sample properties of parameter estimates of strongly dependent stationary Gaussian time series. *Annals of Statistics* 14, 517–32.

Geweke, J. and Porter-Hudak, S. 1983. The estimation and application of long memory time series models. *Journal of Time Series Analysis* 4, 221–38.

Giraitis, L., Hidalgo, J. and Robinson, P. 2001. Gaussian estimation of parametric spectral density with unknown pole. *Annals of Statistics* 29, 987–1023.

Granger, C. 1966. The typical spectral shape of an economic variable. *Econometrica* 34, 150–67.

Granger, C. and Joyeux, R. 1980. An introduction to long memory time series models and fractional differencing. *Journal of Time Series Analysis* 1, 15–39.

Hualde, J. and Robinson, P. 2004. Semiparametric estimation of fractional cointegration. Mimeo, London School of Economics.

Hurvich, C., Moulines, E. and Soulier, P. 2005. Estimating long memory in volatility. *Econometrica* 73, 1283–328.

Künsch, H. 1987. Statistical aspects of self-similar processes. In *Proceedings of the First World Congress of the Bernoulli Society*, vol. 1, ed. Y. Prohorov and V. Sazonov. Utrecht: VNU Science Press.

Mandelbrot, D. 1972. Statistical methodology for non-periodic cycles: from the covariance to R/S analysis. *Annals of Economic and Social Measurement* 1, 259–90.

Robinson, P. 1994. Efficient tests of nonstationary hypotheses. *Journal of the American Statistical Association* 89, 1420–37.

Robinson, P. 1995a. Log-periodogram regression of time series with long range dependence. *Annals of Statistics* 23, 1048–72.

Robinson, P. 1995b. Gaussian semiparametric estimation of long range dependence. *Annals of Statistics* 5, 1630–61.

Robinson, P. 2001. The memory of stochastic volatility models. *Journal of Econometrics* 101, 192–218.

long run and short run

The distinction between long-run and short-run (or long-period and short-period) equilibrium, introduced by Marshall (see Marshall, 1890, pp. 363–80; hints at this distinction are also to be found in some of Marshall's early works, dated 1870–71, recently re-presented in Whitaker, 1975, pp. 119–64), reflected a method which was the generally accepted one at the time, and essentially the same as the method of the classical political economists and of Marx. The use of the method was not affected by the deep change undergone by the theory of value and distribution around the 1870s with the advent of what is nowadays called the 'neoclassical' school. This method, called 'method of long-period positions' (Garegnani, 1976), however, has been abandoned in much of the modern mainstream work on value. Further, there is no uniform meaning attributed to the terms 'short-period' and 'long-period', but rather a variety of usages depending on the theoretical framework of the writer, a situation responsible for many misunderstandings and debates at cross purposes.

The classical political economists

Since its origin in the writings of 18th-century authors, economic theory has used what has been subsequently named the 'long-period method' of analysis to investigate how production, distribution and accumulation take place within a market economy. According to Quesnay and A. Smith, the system 'market economy' produces results which are 'independent of men's will' (Quesnay, 1758). Competition, Smith thought, tends to establish uniformity in the 'average' or 'natural' rates of wages, profits and rent. 'Market' prices, that is, observed prices, thus tend to gravitate towards their 'natural' levels (also called 'average prices' or 'prices of production'), defined as those which allowed the payment of wages, profits and rents at their average or natural rates (Smith, 1776, pp. 57–61).

According to the classical political economists, a divergence between the 'market' and the 'natural' price of a commodity is caused by a divergence between the amount supplied by producers and the 'effectual demand' for it, that is, 'the demand of those who are willing to pay the natural price of the commodity, or the whole value of rent, labour and profit, which must be paid in order to bring it thither' (Smith, 1776, p. 58). This divergence implies windfall profits or losses for that commodity. If supply coincides with 'effectual demand', 'market' price corresponds to 'natural' price. The rate of profit earned in that sector is equal to the one which is uniformly earned in the whole economy. Equilibrium conditions are said to prevail. Within this approach, therefore, fluctuations of supply and demand explain nothing but the deviations of 'market' prices from 'natural' prices.

The idea that the interaction of competitive market forces pushes the actual level of economic variables towards their 'natural' or 'average' level was applied to different fields of economic theory. Marx, for instance, applied it to the analysis of the 'market' and the 'average' interest rate (see Marx, 1972, pp. 355–66). The latter rate, according to Marx, was determined by 'the average conditions of competition, the balance between lender and borrower' (Marx, 1972, p. 363) in the money market over a certain historical period (Marx, 1972, p. 363). He rejected previous views determining this rate in terms of 'natural' laws, like the rate of growth of timber in central Europe forests (Marx, 1972, p. 363 n.) or in terms of the rate of return on capital invested in the productive sectors depending upon the material or technological conditions of production of commodities (Marx, 1972, p. 363). In his historically relative determination, the 'average' interest rate, being constrained by no 'natural' or 'material' law, can be at any level. At the same time, the interaction of demand and supply determines the daily variations of the 'market' interest rate and makes it converge towards its 'average' level.

The application of the 'long-period method' to the analysis of the interest rate makes it clear that the essential element of the method is the reference to an 'average' or 'normal' position around which the actual values of the variable considered gravitate. Reference to the attainment of a uniform rate of profit in all sectors is not strictly necessary if the theory does not determine the variable considered on the basis of the technological conditions of production. In Marx's analysis, since the 'average' interest rate is independent of the rate of profits, it is possible to separate the study of the factors determining the former rate from the study of the technological links between distributive variables and commodity prices, where competitive forces set in motion a gravitation process when windfall profits or losses appear in particular industries. The notion of 'average' interest rate, which may be used to identify a position of long-period equilibrium for this variable, can thus be introduced and analysed by referring to a normal position of this variable, which has actually prevailed over a certain period, without making reference to a uniform rate of profits. In a theory determining the 'natural' interest rate on the basis of technological conditions of production, instead, no separation can be made between the analysis of the average interest rate and that of the links between commodity prices and distributive variables. In this case, the condition of a uniform rate for return on capital defines the 'long-period equilibrium' position for both commodity prices and interest rate.

The rise of neoclassical economics

The long-period method was also used by those economists (like Walras, Menger, Jevons, Böhm-Bawerk, J.B. Clark, Wicksell, et al.) who some years later introduced and developed the 'neoclassical' theory of value and distribution. *No question was raised by these authors as to the use of this method.*

The new theory, unlike the previous one, determined prices, output and distribution simultaneously. The 'natural' or 'equilibrium' values of all these variables (including the interest rate and the level of activity in the economy, which turns out to be a full employment level) depended, among other things, upon the technological conditions of production and were thus associated with the attainment of a uniform rate of profits in the economy.

Among the earlier neoclassical economists, Marshall deserves special consideration, since he introduced the notion of short- and long-period equilibrium (see Marshall, 1890, pp. 80). In his writings, Marshall tried to show how the neoclassical principles of price determination in terms of supply and demand functions could be applied to analytical levels which were closer to actual events. He thus analysed price determination for each single market (partial equilibrium) and within this analysis he referred to three different notions of equilibrium (temporary, short-period and long-period), which differed as to the conditions determining the supply functions. In a temporary equilibrium, it was supposed, there is no time to change the supply of the commodity. The amount supplied is fixed and the equilibrium price is that which allows that quantity to be demanded.

Analyses of short-period equilibrium assume that there is time to change supply through production, but there is no time to change the structure of *fixed capital* goods existing in *that* industry. This assumption constrains the technological possibilities of production. As in the case of temporary equilibrium, short-period equilibrium is compatible with windfall profits or losses.

In long-period analyses, it is assumed instead that there is time to adapt the structure of fixed capital goods of the industry so that quasi-rents (that is, entrepreneurial net profits) disappear. The price then guarantees just the 'normal rate of profits' (that is, the 'equilibrium' real rate of return on capital which is uniform in the whole economy).

Marshall's partial equilibrium analysis appears to rely on general equilibrium analysis for the determination of the 'equilibrium' rate of return on capital and of 'ceteris paribus' prices. The view that the 'general equilibrium' analysis was logically prior appears accepted in some major contributions of the debate on Marshall's theory of value of the 1920s and the early 1930s (see Sraffa, 1925 and 1926, and Pigou's reply, 1927). Marshall's starting point thus was the same as that of Walras, Wicksell, and of the other neoclassical economists mentioned above.

Long-period general equilibrium must not be confused with 'secular' equilibrium, which results from allowing enough time for factor endowments to change under the influences of demographic factors and propensity to save, so as to cause the economy to reach 'stationary' or 'steady growth' conditions (see Robbins, 1930).

Short- and long-period in Keynes

By the end of the 1920s, dissatisfaction with the neoclassical conclusions as to the level of activity of the economy and with the analysis of capital led some economists to new analytical developments, which affected for the first time the method used too.

J.M. Keynes criticized the neoclassical conclusion that the market economy has an inherent tendency towards full employment. In the preparatory works and in the introduction to the *General Theory* he insisted that his concern was not the analysis of the temporary and cyclical fluctuations of the level of activity, but the theory dealing with the more fundamental forces which tend to prevail in the economic system (see Keynes, 1936, pp. 4–5; 1973; pp. 405–7; and 1979, pp. 54–7). He wanted thus to replace the neoclassical long-period theory of the level of output with a new one. Yet the way he presented his new theory has raised many problems of interpretation also related to the method used.

First of all, Keynes stated in his book that he assumed as given the structure of *fixed capital* goods existing in the economy. This can lead to consider his theory as a short-period one, arguing that it would determine the level of capacity utilization in the economy. It is difficult, however, to support this interpretation also with the argument that in the *General Theory* Keynes was following Marshall's definition of short-period, which was confined to partial equilibrium analysis. Marshall knew that the time required for adjustment of the structure of fixed capital goods differed from one industry to the other, so that it would have been unreasonable to extend the hypothesis of a fixed structure from one industry to the whole economy, as Keynes did. This element of ambiguity as to the use of the concepts has raised many puzzling questions among the interpreters of Keynes.

At the same time, Keynes explicitly stated that his theory was meant to explain why the level of employment, over a specific historical period, oscillates round an intermediate or average position (often not a full-employment one), whereas in other periods it oscillates round a different one (Keynes, 1936, p. 254). This reference to 'specific historical periods' and to 'average or normal positions' can lead to consider Keynes's theory as a long-period one, in the same way as Marx's theory of the 'average' interest rate. The assumption of a fixed structure of capital goods would thus play a secondary role in Keynes's theory.

Besides, Keynes hinted towards an analysis of accumulation which emphasizes the role played by effective demand (Keynes, 1936, p. 372–80). The trend followed by a growing economy in which adjustment in the structure of fixed capital goods has occurred, is affected by the level of effective demand. The possibility of assuming in this analysis an adjusted structure of fixed capital goods (to which a uniform rate of profits corresponds) can lead to consider this as the *long-period theory* present in the *General Theory*.

Finally, the maintenance in the *General Theory* of elements belonging to the neoclassical tradition, like the acceptance of the principle of diminishing marginal returns for capital from which the existence of a full-employment level of the rate of interest is derived (see Keynes, 1936, pp. 147–8, 178, 203, 235 and 243; Keynes, 1973, pp. 456, 615, 630) has allowed some interpreters to consider Keynes's 'underemployment equilibrium' as a situation in which market forces have not yet worked out their effects fully, consequently defining it as a position of 'short-period equilibrium' (see Patinkin, 1976, pp. 116–19; Winch, 1969, p. 167).

The presence of several lines of development of its basic principle (that of effective demand) and the lack of precision and coherence as to the concepts and the analytical elements used appear to be an endless source of discussion as to the interpretation of Keynes's work. The existing evidence does not seem to support, however, the view that the *General Theory* wanted to move along the same lines as Hayek, Hicks and others, who in those years were proposing the neoclassical theory of value, distribution and the level of output on the basis of a method of analysis different from the long-period one.

Post-Walrasian developments

In the same years, dissatisfaction with the neoclassical analysis of capital was leading to a shift in method, owing to the adoption of what may be called 'post-Walrasian' notions of general equilibrium, elaborated by Hayek and Lindahl around the 1930s, but first proposed to a wider audience in 1939 by Hicks's *Value and Capital* (see Garegnani, 1976; Milgate 1979). The change in method derives from the change in the treatment of the capital endowment.

In the traditional neoclassical treatment, dominant up to the 1950s, the conception of equilibrium as a centre

of gravitation of time-consuming adjustments (a conception incompatible with taking as given the equilibrium endowments of the several capital goods) had been reconciled with the supply-and-demand approach to factor pricing by conceiving capital as a *single* factor of production, capable of changing 'form' (that is, of embodying itself into different vectors of heterogeneous capital goods) without changing in 'quantity', so that its 'form' (that is, composition) could be left to be determined by the equilibrium condition of a uniform rate of return on the supply price of capital goods – the distinguishing element of long-period positions. Capital so conceived had ultimately to be measured as an amount of value, because in equilibrium different capital goods earn rewards proportional to their values. Within the neoclassical framework, therefore, the reference to a homogeneous factor 'capital', a value magnitude, was a logical necessity, entailed by the attempt to explain distribution through the equilibrium between demand for and supply of 'factors of production', without abandoning the traditional method of long-period positions (Petri, 2004). With one exception, this conception of capital was in fact more or less explicitly adopted by all founders of neoclassical theory and it was the target of the Cambridge critique of the 1960s (Harcourt, 1969; Garegnani, 1970). The only exception had been Walras, who intended as well to determine a long-period equilibrium and accordingly maintained the uniform-profit-rate condition, but took as data the endowment of each kind of capital goods, with the result that his model was generally devoid of solutions.

Walras's treatment of the capital endowment as a given vector is maintained in post-Walrasian general equilibrium analyses, but the condition of uniform profit rate on supply price is dropped. Existing capital goods are treated like natural resources; commodities are dated, so prices of future commodities are distinguished from prices of currently available commodities; and the current composition of the production of new capital goods is determined in either of two ways: by assuming the existence of complete futures markets (intertemporal equilibria, see for example Debreu, 1959), or through the introduction of expectations among the data (temporary equilibria, see for example Hicks, 1939 and Grandmont, 1977).

The difference between the notion of equilibrium entailed by such a treatment of capital and that entailed by the long-period method of analysis warrants emphasis (Garegnani, 1990). The latter attempts to represent states of the economy which have the role of centres of gravitation of observed day-to-day magnitudes: chance movements away from such a state set off forces tending to bring the economy back to it. Changes in the economy can then be studied by comparing the long-period positions corresponding to the situation before and after the change. Post-Walrasian equilibria cannot have such a role, because they rely on data some of which (the endowments of capital goods and, where futures markets are not complete, expectations) would be altered by any chance deviation from the equilibrium: thus the forces set off by this deviation would not tend to bring the economy back to the same equilibrium. For the same reason, stability questions relative to post-Walrasian equilibria can only be asked for imaginary atemporal adjustment processes which exclude the implementation of disequilibrium production decisions before the equilibrium is reached.

A variety of usages

The introduction of new equilibrium concepts, together with the tendency to overlook the existence of differences with previous ones and to use the same terminology for the former and for the latter, has been a source of confusion and misunderstandings in recent debates on theoretical and applied work.

The term 'short-period equilibria' has been sometimes applied to post-Walrasian equilibria (including 'fix price' equilibria with quantity adjustments, which share the same impermanence of data). On other occasions, Keynes's notion of equilibrium has been identified with temporary equilibrium. In both cases, the very great difference between Marshall's and Keynes's analyses on one side and post-Walrasian analyses on the other side has been neglected: in post-Walrasian models, *all* capital goods, including circulating capital goods, are given, while in Marshall's short-period analyses only the fixed plant of a single industry is a datum, and in Keynes's work only the fixed capital goods of the whole economy are given.

At the same time, the term 'long-period equilibrium' has been used in recent years to refer (*a*) to post-Walrasian intertemporal equilibria with futures markets extending far into the future; (*b*) to sequences of temporary equilibria; (*c*) to stationary or steady-growth equilibria. In all these cases, an incomplete grasp of the changes introduced in the notion of equilibrium appears to emerge.

Finally, modern neoclassical economists sometimes develop applied analyses using the traditional method of long-period positions, although rejecting, as their theoretical foundations, the traditional versions of neoclassical theory in favour of the post-Walrasian ones, which are not compatible with that method.

CARLO PANICO AND FABIO PETRI

See also **Marshall, Alfred.**

Bibliography

Debreu, G. 1959. *Theory of Value.* New York: Wiley.
Garegnani, P. 1970. Heterogeneous capital, the production function and the theory of distribution. *Review of Economic Studies* 37, 407–36.
Garegnani, P. 1976. On a change in the notion of equilibrium in recent work on value and distribution.

In *Essays in Modern Capital Theory*, ed. M. Brown, K. Sato and P. Zarembka. Amsterdam: North-Holland.
Garegnani, P. 1990. Quantity of capital. In *Capital Theory*, ed. J. Eatwell, M. Milgate and P. Newman. London: Macmillan.
Grandmont, J.M. 1977. Temporary general equilibrium theory. *Econometrica* 45, 535–72.
Harcourt, G.C. 1969. Some Cambridge controversies in the theory of capital. *Journal of Economic Literature* 7, 369–405.
Hicks, J.R. 1939. *Value and Capital.* Oxford: Clarendon Press.
Keynes, J.M. 1936. The General Theory of Employment, Interest and Money. In *The Collected Writings of J.M. Keynes*, vol. VII, ed. D. Moggridge. London: Macmillan.
Keynes, J.M. 1973. The General Theory and After. Part I: Preparation. In *The Collected Writings of J.M. Keynes*, vol. XIII, ed. D. Moggridge. London: Macmillan.
Keynes, J.M. 1979. The General Theory and After: A Supplement. In *The Collected Writings of J.M. Keynes*, vol. XXIX, ed. D. Moggridge. London: Macmillan.
Marshall, A. 1890. *Principles of Economics.* 8th edn, London: Macmillan, 1920.
Marx, K. 1972. *Capital*, vol. 3. London: Lawrence & Wishart.
Milgate, M. 1979. On the origin of the notion of 'intertemporal equilibrium'. *Economica* 46, 1–10.
Patinkin, D. 1976. *Keynes' Monetary Thought.* Durham, NC: Duke University Press.
Petri, F. 2004. *General Equilibrium, Capital and Macroeconomics. A Key to Recent Controversies in Equilibrium Theory.* Cheltenham: Edward Elgar.
Pigou, A.C. 1927. The laws of diminishing and increasing cost. *Economic Journal* 37(June), 188–97.
Quesnay, F. 1758. *Tableau économique.* Reproduced and trans. as *Quesnay's Tableau économique*, ed. M. Kuczynski and R.L. Meek, London: Macmillan, 1972.
Robbins, L. 1930. On a certain ambiguity in the conception of stationary equilibrium. *Economic Journal* 40(June), 194–214.
Smith, A. 1776. *An Inquiry into the Nature and Causes of the Wealth of Nations.* Ed. E. Cannan, London: Methuen, 1904.
Sraffa, P. 1925. Sulle relazioni fra costo e quantità prodotta. *Annali di Economia* 2, 277–328.
Sraffa, P. 1926. The laws of returns under competitive conditions. *Economic Journal* 36(December), 535–50.
Whitaker, J.K., ed. 1975. *The Early Economic Writings of Alfred Marshall, 1867– 1890.* London: Macmillan.
Winch, D. 1969. *Economics and Policy: A Historical Study.* London: Hodder & Stoughton.

Longfield, Mountifort (1802–1884)

Longfield was born at Desertserges, Country Cork, Ireland, in 1802. Although he graduated from Trinity College, Dublin, in 1823 with first class honours in natural sciences, he was elected a Fellow of his college in

1825 as 'jurist'. His subsequent career was primarily in real property law, but when Archbishop Whately founded the professorship of political economy at Trinity College, Dublin, in 1832, Longfield was the successful candidate and became the first holder of the chair, from 1832 until 1836. In 1834 he was appointed Regius Professor of Feudal and English Law and in 1849 became one of the first Commissioners of the newly established Irish Incubered Estates Commission. When this was transmuted into the Landed Estates Court in 1858, Longfield was appointed a Judge of that court, retiring in 1867. He died in Dublin in 1884.

In 1847 he was one of the founder members of the Dublin Statistical Society (later re-named the Statistical and Social Inquiry Society of Ireland) and followed Whately as its President in 1863, but his many other public services derived primarily from his positions as advocate and judge. In his later years Longfield never returned to political economy but continued to write on questions of Irish land tenure and social reform.

The three volumes of lectures which Longfield published during his tenure of the Whately chair attracted little attention at the time, but have since been recognized as containing contributions to economic theory of outstanding originality. In his *Lectures on Political Economy* (1834a) Longfield dealt with the central issues of classical theory, those of value and distribution, in a manner which displayed a very clear grasp of the structure of Ricardian theory, but which in content diverged fundamentally from Ricardo's approach. He laid stress on the determination of market rather than natural values and presented remarkably complete demand-and-supply theory supplemented by elements of utility analysis. Perhaps his most original contribution was made in the area of distribution, where he formulated a theory of profits as determined by the marginal productivity of physical capital and a theory of wages as determined by the specific productivity of the labourer.

Longfield rejected the idea that the 'natural price' of labour was determined by subsistence, arguing that the 'wages of the labourer depend upon the value of his labour and not upon his wants' (1834a, p. 206). Although, like Ricardo, Longfield predicted a rise in rents, a fall in profits and a rise in wages in the progress of society, his view of the long-term prospects for economic growth was optimistic. He expected the effects of increased population to be offset by technical progress in agriculture, and foresaw many benefits from the increased accumulations of capital which would lower profits, not least among them the increased productivity of labour, which would raise wages.

Longfield's two other published courses of lectures are more concerned with current economic problems, but his *Lectures on Commerce* (1835) contained several anticipations of later developments in international trade theory. His analysis of the causes of international specialization extended to all variations in factor endowments and he specifically treated the case of trade in more than two commodities, showing that each country would tend to export those commodities in which the productivity of its labour was above average and import those in which it was below average.

In his *Lectures on Poor Laws* (1834b) Longfield endorsed Senior's stern principle that assistance to the able-bodied should be confined to the barest subsistence – perhaps, ironically, because of the very optimism of his views about the likely trends of profits and wages. On the other hand, he favoured generous public assistance to those unable, through age or disability, to fend for themselves – even to the extent of advocating non-contributory old-age pensions. Longfield repeated this proposal in 1872, when he specifically considered state interference with the distribution of wealth; unlike most of his contemporaries he was then prepared also to advocate public dispensaries and hospitals to which access would not be means-tested, improved sanitary regulation of housing standards, free public education and improved public recreation facilities.

Longfield's economic writings appear to have had little influence on his contemporaries, but since his rediscovery by Seligman (1903) the originality of his contributions has come to be generally recognized.

R.D. COLLISON BLACK

Selected works

1834a. *Lectures on Political Economy, delivered in Trinity and Michaelmas Terms, 1833*. Dublin: R. Milliken & Son. Reprinted, 1971.

1834b. *Four Lectures on Poor Laws Delivered in Trinity Term, 1834*. Dublin: R. Milliken & Son. Reprinted, 1971.

1835. *Three Lectures on Commerce, and one on Absenteeism, delivered in Michaelmas Term, 1834*. Dublin: William Curry, Junior & Co. Reprinted, 1971.

1840. Banking and currency. *Dublin University Magazine* 15, 3–15, 218–33, 369–89, 609–20. Reprinted, 1971.

1870. Tenure of land in Ireland. *Systems of Land Tenure*. Cobden Club, London.

1872a. The limits of state interference with the distribution of wealth in applying taxation to the assistance of the public. *Journal of the Statistical and Social Inquiry Society of Ireland* 6, 105–14.

1872b. *Elementary Treatise on Series*. Dublin.

1971. *The Economic Writings of Mountifort Longfield*. Ed. R.D. Collison Black, New York: A.M. Kelley.

Bibliography

Black, R.D.C. 1945. Trinity College, Dublin, and the theory of value 1832–1863. *Economica*, NS 12, 140–48.

Black, R.D.C. 1984. The Irish dissenters and nineteenth-century political economy. In *Economists and the Irish Economy*, ed. A.E. Murphy. Dublin: Irish Academic Press, 120–37.

Moss, L.S. 1976. *Mountifort Longfield, Ireland's First Professor of Political Economy*. Ottowa, III.: Green Hill Publishers.

Murphy, A.E. 1984. Mountifort Longfield's appointment to the chair of political economy in trinity College, Dublin, 1832. In *Economists and the Irish Economy*, ed. A.E. Murphy. Dublin: Irish Academic Press, 13–24.

Seligman, E.R.A. 1903. On some neglected British economists. *Economic Journal* 13, 335–63, 511–35. Revised version published in E.R.A. Seligman, *Essays in Economics*, New York: Macmillan, 1925.

longitudinal data analysis

1 Why panel data?

'Longitudinal data' (or 'panel data') refers to data-sets that contain time series observations of a number of individuals. In other words, it provides multiple observations for each individual in the sample. Compared with cross-sectional data, in which observations for a number of individuals are available only for a given time, or time-series data, in which a single entity is observed over time, panel data have the obvious advantages of more degrees of freedom and less collinearity among explanatory variables, and so provide the possibility of obtaining more accurate parameter estimates. More importantly, by blending inter-individual differences with intra-individual dynamics, panel data allow the investigation of more complicated behavioural hypotheses than those that can be addressed using cross-sectional or time-series data.

For instance, suppose a cross-sectional sample yields an average labour-participation rate of 50 per cent for married women. Given that the standard assumption for the analysis of cross-sectional data is that, conditional on certain variables, each woman is a random draw from a homogeneous population, this would imply that each woman has a 50 per cent chance of being in the labour force at any given time. Hence, a married woman would be expected to spend half of her married life in the labour force and half out of it. The job turnover would be frequent, and the expected average job duration would be just two years (Ben-Porath, 1973). However, the cross-sectional data could be drawn from a heterogeneous population in which 50 per cent of the sample was drawn from the population that always works and 50 per cent from the population that never works. In this situation, there is no turnover and a woman's current work status is a perfect predictor of her future work status. To discriminate between these two possibilities, we need information on individual labour-force histories in different sub-intervals of the life cycle, which can be provided only if information is available on the intertemporal dynamics of individual entities. On the other hand, although time series data provide information on dynamic adjustment, variables over time tend to move collinearly, hence making it difficult to identify micro-dynamic or macro-dynamic effects. Often, estimation of distributed lag models has to rely on strong prior restrictions like the Koyck or Almon lag, with very little empirical justification (for example, Griliches, 1967). With panel data, the inter-individual differences can often lessen the problem of multicollinearity and provide the possibility of estimating unrestricted time adjustment patterns (for example, Pakes and Griliches, 1984).

By utilizing information on both the intertemporal dynamics and the individuality of the entities, panel data may also allow an investigator to control the effects of missing or unobserved variables. For instance, MaCurdy's (1981) life-cycle labour supply of prime-age males with perfect foresight model assumes that the logarithm of hours worked is a linear function of the real wage rate and the logarithm of the worker's marginal utility of initial wealth, which is unobserved. Since the wage rate and the marginal utility of initial wealth are correlated, any instrument that is correlated with the wage rate will be correlated with the marginal utility of initial wealth. There is no way one can obtain a consistent estimate of the coefficient of the wage rate with cross-sectional data. But, if panel data are available and since marginal utility of initial wealth stays constant over time, one can take the difference of the labour supply model over time to get rid of the marginal utility of initial wealth as an explanatory variable. Regressing change in hour on change in wage rate and other socio-demographic variables can yield consistent estimates of the coefficient of the wage rate and other explanatory variables.

Panel data may also provide microfoundations for aggregate data analysis. Aggregate data analysis often invokes the 'representative agent' assumption. If micro units are heterogeneous, the time series properties of aggregate data may be very different from those of disaggregate data (for example, Granger, 1990; Lewbel, 1994) and policy evaluation based on aggregate data could also be grossly misleading (for example, Hsiao, Shen and Fujiki, 2005). By providing time series observations for a number of individuals, panel data are ideal for the investigation of the homogeneity issue.

Panel data involve observations of two or more dimensions. In normal circumstances, one would expect the computation and inference of panel data models to be more complicated than those of cross-section or time series data. However, in certain situations the availability of panel data actually simplifies inference. For instance, statistical inference for non-stationary panel data can be complicated (for example, Phillips, 1986). But, if observations are independently distributed across cross-sectional units, central limit theorems applied across cross-sectional units lead to asymptotically normally distributed statistics (for example, Levin, Lin and Chu, 2002; Im, Pesaran and Shin, 2003).

2 Issues of panel data analysis

Standard statistical methodology is based on the assumption that the outcomes, say y, conditional on certain variables, say x, are random outcomes from a probability distribution that is characterized by a fixed dimensional parameter vector, $\theta, f(y \mid x; \theta)$. For instance, the standard linear regression model assumes that $f(y \mid x; \theta)$ takes the form that $E(y \mid x) = \alpha + \beta' x$, and $\mathrm{Var}(y \mid x) = \sigma^2$, where $\theta' = (\alpha, \beta', \sigma^2)$. Panel data, by their nature, focus on individual outcomes. Factors affecting individual outcomes are numerous. It is rare to be able to assume a common conditional probability density function of y conditional on x for all cross-sectional units, i, at all time, t. If the conditional density of y given x varies across i and over t, the fundamental theorems for statistical inference, the laws of large numbers and central limit theorems, will be difficult to implement. Ignoring the heterogeneity across i and over t that are not captured by x can lead to severely biased inference. For instance, suppose that the data is generated by

$$y_{it} = \alpha_i + \beta' x_{it} + v_{it}, \quad \begin{matrix} i = 1, \ldots, N, \\ t = 1, \ldots, T. \end{matrix} \quad (2.1)$$

as depicted by Figure 1 in which the broken-time ellipses represent the point scatter of individual observation around the mean, represented by the broken straight lines. If an investigator ignores the presence of unobserved individual-specific effects, α_i, and mistakenly estimates a model of the form

$$y_{it} = \alpha + \beta' x_{it} + v_{it}^* \quad (2.2)$$

the following equation solid line in Figure 1 would depict the pooled least squares regression result which could completely contradict the individual relation between y and x.

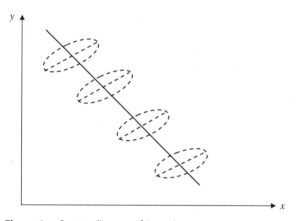

Figure 1   Scatter diagram of (y_{it}, x_{it})

One way to restore homogeneity across i and/or over t is to add more conditional variables, say z,

$$f(y_{it} \mid x_{it}, z_{it}; \theta). \quad (2.3)$$

However, the dimension of z can be large. A model is a simplification of reality, not an exact representation of reality. The inclusion of z may confuse the fundamental relationship between y and x, in particular when there is a shortage of degrees of freedom or multicollinearity, and so on. Moreover, z may not be observable. If an investigator is interested only in the relationship between y and x, one approach to characterize the heterogeneity not captured by x is to assume that the parameter vector varies across i and over t, θ_{it}, so that the conditional density of y given x takes the form $f(y_{it} \mid x_{it}; \theta_{it})$. However, without a structure being imposed on θ_{it}, such a model has only descriptive value; it is not possible to draw any inference on θ_{it} from observed data.

One primary focus of methodological panel data literature is to suggest possible structures for θ_{it}. One way to impose some structure on θ_{it} is to decompose θ_{it} into (β, γ_{it}), where β is the same across i and over t, referred to as *structural parameters*, and γ_{it} as *incidental parameters* because when observations in cross-sectional units and/or time series units increase, there are rising numbers of γ_{it} to be estimated. The focus then will be on how to make valid inference on β after controlling the impact of γ_{it}.

Without imposing structure for γ_{it}, again it is not possible to make any inference on β because the unknown γ_{it} will exhaust all available sample information. On the assumption that the impacts of observable variables, x, are the same across i and over t, represented by the structure parameters, β, the incidental parameters γ_{it} represent the heterogeneity across i and over t that are not captured by x_{it}. They can be considered as composed of the effects of omitted individual time-invariant, α_i, period individual-invariant, λ_t, and individual time-varying variables, δ_{it}. The individual time-invariant variables are variables that are the same for a given cross-sectional unit through time but that vary across cross-sectional units, such as individual-firm management, ability, gender, and socio-economic background. The period individual-invariant variables are variables that are the same for all cross-sectional units at a given time but that vary though time, such as prices, interest rates, and widespread optimism or pessimism. The individual time-varying variables are variables that vary across cross-sectional units at a given point in time and also exhibit variations through time, such as firm profits, sales and capital stock. The unobserved heterogeneity as represented by the individual-specific effects, α_i and time specific effects, λ_t, or individual time-varying effects, δ_{it} can be assumed to be either random variables (referred to as the *random effects* model) or fixed parameters (referred to as the *fixed effects* model).

3 Linear static models

A widely used panel data model assumes that the effects of observed explanatory variables, x, are identical across cross-sectional units, i, and over time, t, while the effects of omitted variables can be decomposed into the individual-specific effects, α_i, time-specific effects, λ_t, and individual time-varying effects, $\delta_{it} = u_{it}$, as follows:

$$y_{it} = \beta' x_{it} + \alpha_i + \lambda_t + u_{it}, \quad \begin{aligned} i &= 1, \ldots, N, \\ t &= 1, \ldots, T. \end{aligned}$$

$$(3.1)$$

In a single equation framework, individual time effects, u, are assumed random and uncorrelated with x, while α_i and λ_t may or may not be correlated with x. When α_i and λ_t are treated as fixed constants, they are parameters to be estimated, so whether they are correlated with x is not an issue. On the other hand, when α_i and λ_t are treated as random, they are typically assumed to be uncorrelated with x_{it}.

For ease of exposition, we assume that there are no time-specific effects, that is, $\lambda_t = 0$ for all t and u_{it} are independently, identically distributed (i.i.d) across i and over t. Stack an individual's T time series observations of (y_{it}, x'_{it}) into a vector and a matrix, (3.1) may alternatively be written as

$$y_i = X_i \beta + e \alpha_i + u_i, i = 1, \ldots, N, \quad (3.2)$$

where $y_i = (y_{i1}, \ldots, y_{iT})', X_i = (x_{i1}, \ldots, x_{iT})', u_i = (u_{i1}, \ldots, u_{iT})'$, and e is a $T \times 1$ vector of 1's.

Let Q be a $T \times T$ matrix satisfying the condition that $Q e = 0$. Pre-multiplying (3.2) by Q yields

$$Q y_i = Q X_i \beta + Q u_i, \quad i = 1, \ldots, N. \quad (3.3)$$

Equation (3.3) no longer involves α_i. The issue of whether α_i is correlated with x_{it} or whether α_i should be treated as fixed or random is no longer relevant for (3.3). Moreover, since X_i is exogenous, $E(QX_i u_i' Q') = QE(X_i u_i')Q' = 0$ and $EQu_i u_i' Q' = \sigma_u^2 QQ'$. An efficient estimator of β is the generalized least squares estimator (GLS),

$$\hat{\beta} = \left[\sum_{i=1}^{N} X_i' Q'(QQ')^- QX_i \right]^{-1} \left[\sum_{i=1}^{N} X_i' Q'(QQ')^- QY_i \right],$$

$$(3.4)$$

where $(Q'Q)^-$ denotes the Moore–Penrose generalized inverse (for example, Rao, 1973).

When $Q = I_T - \frac{1}{T} e e'$, Q is idempotent. The Moore–Penrose generalized inverse of $(Q'Q)^-$ is just $Q = I_T - \frac{1}{T} e e'$ itself. Pre-multiplying (3.3) by Q is equivalent to transforming (3.1) into a model

$$(y_{it} - \bar{y}_i) = \beta'(x_{it} - \bar{x}_i) + (u_{it} - \bar{u}_i), \quad \begin{aligned} 1 &= 1, \ldots, N, \\ t &= 1, \ldots, T. \end{aligned}$$

$$(3.5)$$

where $\bar{y}_i = \frac{1}{T}\sum_{t=1}^{T} y_{it}, \bar{x}_i = \frac{1}{T}\sum_{t=1}^{T} x_{it}$ and $\bar{u}_i = \frac{1}{T}\sum_{t=1}^{T} u_{it}$. The transformation is called *covariance transformation*. The least squares estimator (LS) (or a generalized least squares estimator, GLS) of (3.5),

$$\hat{\beta}_{cv} = \left[\sum_{i=1}^{N} \sum_{t=1}^{T} (x_{it} - \bar{x}_i)(x_{it} - \bar{x}_i)' \right]^{-1}$$

$$\times \left[\sum_{t=1}^{N} \sum_{t=1}^{T} (x_{it} - \bar{x}_i)(y_{it} - \bar{y}_i) \right],$$

$$(3.6)$$

is called *covariance estimator* or *within* estimator because the estimation of β only makes use of within (group) variation of y_{it} and x_{it} only. The covariance estimator of β turns out to be also the least squares estimator of (3.1) when $\lambda_t = 0$. It is the best linear unbiased estimator of β if α_i is treated as fixed and u_{it} is i.i.d.

If α_i is random, transforming (3.2) into (3.3) transforms T independent equations (or observations) into $(T - 1)$ independent equations, hence the covariance estimator is not as efficient as the efficient generalized least squares estimator if $E\alpha_i x_{it}' = 0$. When α_i is independent of x_{it} and is independently, identically distributed across i with mean 0 and variance σ_α^2, the best linear unbiased estimator (BLUE) of β is GLS,

$$\hat{\beta} = \left[\sum_{i=1}^{N} X_i' V^{-1} X_i \right]^{-1} \left[\sum_{i=1}^{N} X_i' V^{-1} Y_i \right],$$

$$(3.7)$$

where $V = \sigma_u^2 I_T + \sigma_\alpha^2 e e', V^{-1} = \frac{1}{\sigma_u^2}\left[I_T - \frac{\sigma_\alpha^2}{\sigma_u^2 + T\sigma_\alpha^2} e e' \right]$. Let $\psi = \frac{\sigma_u^2}{\sigma_u^2 + T\sigma_\alpha^2}$, the GLS is equivalent to first transforming the data by subtracting a fraction $(1 - \psi^{1/2})$ of individual means $\bar{y}_i$ and $\bar{x}_i$ from their corresponding y_{it} and x_{it}, then regressing $[y_{it} - (1 - \psi^{1/2})\bar{y}_i]$ on $[x_{it} - (1 - \psi^{1/2})\bar{x}_i]$. (for detail, see Baltagi, 2001; Hsiao, 2003).

When α_i is treated as fixed, the covariance estimator is equivalent to applying LS to the transformed model (3.5). If a variable is time-invariant, like a gender dummy, $x_{kit} = x_{kis} = \bar{x}_{ki}$, the transformation eliminates the corresponding variable from the specification. Hence, the coefficients of time-invariant variables cannot be estimated. On the other hand, if α_i is random and uncorrelated with $\underset{\sim}{x}_i$, $\psi \neq 1$, the GLS can still estimate the coefficients of those time-invariant variables.

4 Dynamic models

When the regressors of a linear model contains lagged dependent variables, say, of the form (for example, Balestra and Nerlove, 1966)

$$
\begin{aligned}
\underset{\sim}{y}_i &= \underset{\sim}{y}_{i,-1}\gamma + X_i\underset{\sim}{\beta} + \underset{\sim}{e}\,\alpha_i + \underset{\sim}{u}_i \\
&= Z_i\underset{\sim}{\theta} + \underset{\sim}{e}\,\alpha_i + \underset{\sim}{u}_i, \quad i = 1, \ldots, N.
\end{aligned}
\tag{4.1}
$$

where $\underset{\sim}{y}_{i,-1} = (y_{i0}, \ldots, y_{i,T-1})'$, $Z_i = (\underset{\sim}{y}_{i,-1}, X_i)$ and $\underset{\sim}{\theta} = (\gamma, \beta')'$. For ease of notation, we assume that y_{i0} are observable. Technically, we can still eliminate the individual-specific effects by pre-multiplying (4.1) by the transformation matrix $Q(Q\underset{\sim}{e} = \underset{\sim}{0})$,

$$
Q\underset{\sim}{y}_i = QZ_i\underset{\sim}{\theta} + Q\underset{\sim}{u}_i.
\tag{4.2}
$$

However, because of the presence of lagged dependent variables, $EQZ_i\underset{\sim}{u}_i'Q' \neq 0$ even with the assumption that u_{it} is independently, identically distributed across i and over t. For instance, the covariance transformation matrix $Q = I_T - \frac{1}{T}\underset{\sim}{e}\,\underset{\sim}{e}'$ transforms (4.1) into the form

$$
\begin{aligned}
(y_{it} - \bar{y}_i) &= (y_{i,t-1} - \bar{y}_{i,-1})\gamma + (\underset{\sim}{x}_{it} - \bar{\underset{\sim}{x}}_i)'\underset{\sim}{\beta} \\
&\quad + (u_{it} - \bar{u}_i), \quad \begin{aligned} i &= 1, \ldots, N, \\ t &= 1, \ldots, T. \end{aligned}
\end{aligned}
\tag{4.3}
$$

where $\bar{y}_i = \frac{1}{T}\sum_{t=1}^{T}y_{it}, \bar{y}_{i,-1} = \frac{1}{T}\sum_{t=1}^{T}y_{i,t-1}$ and $\bar{u}_i = \frac{1}{T}\sum_{t=1}^{T}u_{it}$. Although, $y_{i,t-1}$ and u_{it} are uncorrelated under the assumption of serial independence of u_{it}, the covariance between $\bar{y}_{i,-1}$ and u_{it} or $y_{i,t-1}$ and $\bar{u}_i$ is of order $(1/T)$ if $|\gamma| < 1$. Therefore, the covariance estimator of $\underset{\sim}{\theta}$ creates a bias of order $(1/T)$ when $N \to \infty$ (Anderson and Hsiao, 1981; 1982; Nickell, 1981). Since most panel data contain large N but small T, the magnitude of the bias can not be ignored (for example, with $T = 10$ and $\gamma = 0.5$, the asymptotic bias is -0.167).

When $EQZ_i\underset{\sim}{u}_i'Q' \neq \underset{\sim}{0}$, one way to obtain a consistent estimator for $\underset{\sim}{\theta}$ is to find instruments W_i that satisfy

$$
EW_i\underset{\sim}{u}_i'Q' = \underset{\sim}{0},
\tag{4.4}
$$

and

$$
\text{rank}(W_iQZ_i) = k,
\tag{4.5}
$$

where k denotes the dimension of $(\gamma, \beta')'$, then apply the generalized instrumental variable or generalized method of moments (GMM) estimator by minimizing the objective function

$$
\begin{aligned}
&\left[\sum_{i=1}^{N}W_i(Q\underset{\sim}{y}_i - QZ_i\underset{\sim}{\theta})\right]'\left[\sum_{i=1}^{N}(W_iQ\underset{\sim}{u}_i\underset{\sim}{u}_i'Q'W_i')\right]^{-1} \\
&\quad \times \left[\sum_{i=1}^{N}W_i(Q\underset{\sim}{y}_i - QZ_i'\underset{\sim}{\theta})\right],
\end{aligned}
\tag{4.6}
$$

with respect to $\underset{\sim}{\theta}$ (for example, Arellano, 2003; Ahn and Schmidt, 1995; Arellano and Bond, 1991; Arellano and Bover, 1995). For instance, one may let Q be a $(T-1) \times T$ matrix of the form

$$
D = \begin{bmatrix} -1 & 1 & 0 & . & . \\ 0 & -1 & 1 & . & . \\ 0 & . & . & . & . \\ . & . & . & -1 & 1 \end{bmatrix},
\tag{4.7}
$$

then the transformation (4.2) is equivalent to taking the first difference of (4.1) over time to eliminate α_i for $t = 2, \ldots, T$,

$$
\Delta y_{it} = \Delta y_{i,t-1}\gamma + \Delta\underset{\sim}{x}_{it}'\underset{\sim}{\beta} + \Delta u_{it}, \quad \begin{aligned} i &= 1, \ldots, N, \\ t &= 2, \ldots, T, \end{aligned}
\tag{4.8}
$$

where $\Delta = (1 - L)$ and L denotes the lag operator, $Ly_t = y_{t-1}$. Since $\Delta u_{it} = (u_{it} - u_{i,t-1})$ is uncorrelated with $y_{i,t-j}$ for $j \geq 2$ and $\underset{\sim}{x}_{is}$, for all s, when u_{it} is independently distributed over time and $\underset{\sim}{x}_{it}$ is exogenous, one can let W_i be a $T(T-1)[K + \frac{1}{2}] \times (T-1)$ matrix of the form

$$
W_i = \begin{bmatrix} \underset{\sim}{q}_{i2} & 0 & . & . \\ 0 & \underset{\sim}{q}_{i3} & . & . \\ . & . & . & . \\ . & . & . & . \\ . & . & . & \underset{\sim}{q}_{iT} \end{bmatrix},
\tag{4.9}
$$

where $\underset{\sim}{q}_{it} = (y_{i0}, y_{i1}, \ldots, y_{i,t-2}, \underset{\sim}{x}_i')$, $\underset{\sim}{x}_i = (\underset{\sim}{x}_{i1}', \ldots, \underset{\sim}{x}_{iT}')'$, and $K = k - 1$. Under the assumption that $(\underset{\sim}{y}_i', \underset{\sim}{x}_i')$ are independently, identically distributed across i, the

Arellano–Bover (1995) GMM estimator takes the form

$$\underset{\sim AB,GMM}{\hat{\theta}}$$

$$= \left\{ \left[\sum_{i=1}^{N} Z_i' D' W_i' \right] \left[\sum_{i=1}^{N} W_i A W_i' \right]^{-1} \left[\sum_{i=1}^{N} W_i D Z_i \right] \right\}^{-1}$$

$$\times \left\{ \left[\sum_{i=1}^{N} Z_i' D' W_i' \right] \left[\sum_{i=1}^{N} W_i A W_i' \right]^{-1} \left[\sum_{i=1}^{N} W_i D \underset{\sim i}{y} \right] \right\},$$

(4.10)

where A is a $(T-1) \times (T-1)$ matrix with 2 on the diagonal elements, -1 on the elements above and below the diagonal elements, and 0 elsewhere.

The GMM estimator has the advantage that it is consistent and asymptotically normally distributed whether α_i is treated as fixed or random because it eliminates α_i from the specification. However, the number of moment conditions increases at the order of T^2, which can create severe downward bias in finite sample (Zilak, 1997). An alternative is to use a (quasi-) likelihood approach which has the advantage of having a fixed number of orthogonality conditions independent of the sample size. It also has the advantage of making use of all the available samples, hence can yield a more efficient estimator than (4.10) (for example, Hsiao, Pesaran and Tahmiscioglu, 2002; Binder, Hsiao and Pesaran, 2005). Since there is no reason to assume the data-generating process of initial observations, y_{i0}, to be different from the rest of y_{it}, the likelihood approach has to formulate the joint likelihood function of $(y_{i0}, y_{i1}, \ldots, y_{iT})$ (or the conditional likelihood function $(y_{i1}, \ldots, y_{iT} | y_{i0})$). However, y_{i0} depends on previous values of $\underset{\sim i,-j}{x}$ and α_i, which are unavailable. Bhargava and Sargan (1983) suggest circumscribing this missing data problem by conditioning y_{i0} on $\underset{\sim i}{x}$ and α_i if α_i is treated as random, while Hsiao, Pesaran and Tahmiscioglu (2002) propose conditioning $(y_{i1} - y_{i0})$ on the first difference of $\underset{\sim i}{x}$ if α_i is treated as a fixed constant.

5 Random vs. fixed effects specification

The advantages of random effects (RE) specifications are as follows:

1. The number of parameters stays constant when sample size increases.
2. It allows the derivation of efficient estimators that make use of both within- and between-(group) variation.
3. It allows the estimation of the impact of time-invariant variables.

The disadvantages of RE specification are that it typically assumes that the individual- and/or time-specific effects are randomly distributed with a common mean and are independent of $\underset{\sim it}{x}$. If the effects are correlated with $\underset{\sim it}{x}$ or if there is a fundamental difference

among individual units, that is, conditional on $\underset{\sim it}{x}, y_{it}$ cannot be viewed as a random draw from a common distribution, the common RE model is mis-specified and the resulting estimator is biased.

The advantages of fixed effects (FE) specification are that it allows the individual-and/or time-specific effects to be correlated with explanatory variables $\underset{\sim}{x}$. Neither does it require an investigator to model their correlation patterns.

The disadvantages of the FE specification are as follows:

1. The number of unknown parameters increases with the number of sample observations. In the case when T (or N for λ_t) is finite, it introduces the classical incidental parameter problem (for example, Neyman and Scott, 1948).
2. The FE estimator does not allow the estimation of the coefficients that are time-invariant.

In other words, the advantages of RE specification are the disadvantages of FE specification, and the disadvantages of RE specification are the advantages of FE specification. To choose between the two specifications, Hausman (1978) notes that the FE estimator (or GMM), $\underset{\sim FE}{\hat{\theta}}$, is consistent whether α_i is fixed or random. On the other hand, the commonly used RE estimator (or GLS), $\underset{\sim RE}{\hat{\theta}}$, is consistent and efficient only when α_i is indeed uncorrelated with $\underset{\sim it}{x}$. If α_i is correlated with $\underset{\sim it}{x}$, the RE estimator is inconsistent. Therefore, Hausman (1978) suggests using the statistic

$$\left(\underset{\sim FE}{\hat{\theta}} - \underset{\sim RE}{\hat{\theta}} \right)' \left[\text{cov}\left(\underset{\sim FE}{\hat{\theta}} \right) - \text{cov}\left(\underset{\sim RE}{\hat{\theta}} \right) \right]^{-} \left(\underset{\sim FE}{\hat{\theta}} - \underset{\sim RE}{\hat{\theta}} \right)$$

(5.1)

to test RE vs FE specification. The statistic (5.1) is asymptotically chi-square distributed with degrees of freedom equal to the rank of $[\text{cov}(\underset{\sim FE}{\hat{\theta}}) - \text{cov}(\underset{\sim RE}{\hat{\theta}})]$.

6 Nonlinear models

The introduction of individual-specific effects, α_i, and/or time-specific effects, λ_t, provides a simple way to capture the unobserved heterogeneity across i and over t. However, the likelihood functions are in terms of observables, $(y_i, x_i), i = 1, \ldots, N$. Therefore, we will have either to treat α_i as unknown parameters (fixed effects) and consider the conditional likelihood,

$$f(\underset{\sim i}{y} | \underset{\sim i}{x}, \underset{\sim}{\beta}, \alpha_i), \quad i = 1, \ldots, N,$$

(6.1)

or to treat α_i as random and consider the marginal likelihood

$$f\left(\underset{\sim i}{y} | \underset{\sim i}{x}, \underset{\sim}{\beta} \right) = \int f(y_i | \underset{\sim i}{x}, \underset{\sim}{\beta}, \alpha_i) f(\alpha_i | \underset{\sim i}{x}) d\alpha_i,$$

$$i = 1, \ldots, N,$$

(6.2)

where $f(\alpha_i|\underset{\sim}{x}_i)$ denotes the conditional density of α_i given $\underset{\sim}{x}_i$.

When the unobserved individual specific effects, α_i, (and or time-specific effects, λ_t) affect the outcome, y_{it}, linearly, one can avoid the consideration of random versus fixed effects specification by eliminating them from the specification through some linear transformation such as the covariance transformation (3.3) or first difference transformation (4.8). However, if α_i affects y_{it} nonlinearly, it is not easy to find a transformation that can eliminate α_i. For instance, consider the following binary choice model where the observed y_{it} takes the value of either 1 or 0 depending on the latent response function

$$y_{it}^* = \beta' \underset{\sim}{x}_{it} + \alpha_i + u_{it}, \qquad (6.3)$$

and

$$y_{it} = \begin{cases} 1, & \text{if } y_{it}^* > 0, \\ 0, & \text{if } y_{it}^* \le 0, \end{cases} \qquad (6.4)$$

where u_{it} is independently, identically distributed with density function $f(u_{it})$. Let

$$y_{it} = E(y_{it}|\underset{\sim}{x}_{it}, \alpha_i) + \varepsilon_{it}, \qquad (6.5)$$

then

$$E(y_{it}|\underset{\sim}{x}_{it}, \alpha_i) = \int_{-(\beta' \underset{\sim}{x}_{it} + \alpha_i)}^{\infty} f(u)\,du$$

$$= [1 - F(-\beta' \underset{\sim}{x}_{it} - \alpha_i)]. \qquad (6.6)$$

Since α_i affects $E(y_{it}|\underset{\sim}{x}_{it}, \alpha_i)$ nonlinearly, α_i remains after taking successive difference of y_{it},

$$y_{it} - y_{i,t-1} = [1 - F(-\beta' \underset{\sim}{x}_{it} - \alpha_i)]$$
$$- [1 - F(-\beta' \underset{\sim}{x}_{i,t-1} - \alpha_i)]$$
$$+ (\varepsilon_{it} - \varepsilon_{i,t-1}). \qquad (6.7)$$

The likelihood function conditional on $\underset{\sim}{x}_i$ and α_i takes the form,

$$\prod_{i=1}^{N} \prod_{t=1}^{T} [F(-\beta' \underset{\sim}{x}_{it} - \alpha_i)]^{1-y_{it}} \\ \times [1 - F(-\beta' \underset{\sim}{x}_{it} - \alpha_i)]^{y_{it}}. \qquad (6.8)$$

If T is large, a consistent estimator of β and α_i can be obtained by maximizing (6.8). If T is finite, there is only limited information about α_i no matter how large N is. The presence of incidental parameters, α_i, violates the regularity conditions for the consistency of the maximum likelihood estimator of $\underset{\sim}{\beta}$.

If $f(\alpha_i|\underset{\sim}{x}_i)$ is known, and is characterized by a fixed dimensional parameter vector, a consistent estimator of β can be obtained by maximizing the marginal likelihood function,

$$\prod_{i=1}^{N} \int \prod_{t=1}^{T} [F(-\beta' \underset{\sim}{x}_{it} - \alpha_i)]^{1-y_{it}} \\ \times [1 - F(-\beta' \underset{\sim}{x}_{it} - \alpha_i)]^{y_{it}} f(\alpha_i|\underset{\sim}{x}_i)\,d\alpha_i. \qquad (6.9)$$

However, maximizing (6.9) involves T-dimensional integration. Butler and Moffitt (1982), Chamberlain (1984), Heckman (1981), and others have suggested methods to simplify the computation.

The advantage of RE specification is that there is no incidental parameter problem. The problem is that $f(\alpha_i|\underset{\sim}{x}_i)$ is in general unknown. If a wrong $f(\alpha_i|\underset{\sim}{x}_i)$ is postulated, maximizing the wrong likelihood function will not yield a consistent estimator of β. Moreover, the derivation of marginal likelihood through multiple integration may be computationally infeasible. The advantage of FE specification is that there is no need to specify $f(\alpha_i|\underset{\sim}{x}_i)$. The likelihood function will be the product of individual likelihood (for example, (6.8)) if the errors are assumed i.i.d. The disadvantage is that it introduces incidental parameters.

A general approach to estimating a model involving incidental parameters is to find transformations to transform the original model into a model that does not involve incidental parameters. Unfortunately, there is no general rule available for nonlinear models. One has to explore the specific structure of a nonlinear model to find such a transformation. For instance, if $f(u)$ in (6.3) is logistic, then

$$\text{Prob}(y_{it} = 1|\underset{\sim}{x}_{it}, \alpha_i) = \frac{e^{\beta' \underset{\sim}{x}_{it} + \alpha_i}}{1 + e^{\beta' \underset{\sim}{x}_{it} + \alpha_i}}. \qquad (6.10)$$

Since, in a logit model, the denominators of Prob $(y_{it} = 1|\underset{\sim}{x}_{it}, \alpha_i)$ and Prob $(y_{it} = 0|\underset{\sim}{x}_{it}, \alpha_i)$ are identical and the numerator of any sequence $\{y_{i1}, \ldots, y_{iT}\}$ with $\sum_{t=1}^{T} y_{it} = s$ always equal to $\exp(\alpha_i s) \cdot \exp\{\sum_{t=1}^{T} (\beta' \underset{\sim}{x}_{it}) y_{it}\}$, the conditional likelihood function conditional on $\sum_{t=1}^{T} y_{it} = s$ will not involve the incidental parameters α_i. For instance, consider the simple case that $T = 2$, then

$$\text{Prob}(y_{i1} = 1, y_{i2} = 0|y_{i1} + y_{i2} = 1)$$

$$= \frac{e^{\beta' \underset{\sim}{x}_{i1}}}{e^{\beta' \underset{\sim}{x}_{i1}} + e^{\beta' \underset{\sim}{x}_{i2}}} = \frac{1}{1 + e^{\beta' \Delta \underset{\sim}{x}_{i2}}} \qquad (6.11)$$

and

$$\text{Prob}(y_{i1} = 0, y_{i2} = 1 | y_{i1} + y_{i2} = 1) = \frac{e^{\beta' \Delta x_{i2}}}{1 + e^{\beta' \Delta x_{i2}}},$$

$$(6.12)$$

(Chamberlain, 1980; Hsiao, 2003).

This approach works because of the logit structure. In the case when $f(u)$ is unknown, Manski (1987) exploits the latent linear structure of (6.3) by noting that, for given i,

$$\beta' x_{it} > \beta' x_{i,t-1} \Leftrightarrow E(y_{it} | x_{it}, \alpha_i) > E(y_{i,t-1} | x_{i,t-1}, \alpha_i),$$
$$\beta' x_{it} = \beta' x_{i,t-1} \Leftrightarrow E(y_{it} | x_{it}, \alpha_i) = E(y_{i,t-1} | x_{i,t-1}, \alpha_i),$$
$$\beta' x_{it} < \beta' x_{i,t-1} \Leftrightarrow E(y_{it} | x_{it}, \alpha_i) < E(y_{i,t-1} | x_{i,t-1}, \alpha_i),$$

$$(6.13)$$

and suggests maximizing the objective function

$$H_N(b) = \frac{1}{N} \sum_{i=1}^{N} \sum_{t=2}^{T} sgn(b' \Delta x_{it}) \Delta y_{it},$$

$$(6.14)$$

where $sgn(w) = 1$ if $w > 0$, $= 0$ if $w = 0$, and -1 if $w < 0$. The advantage of the Manski (1987) maximum score estimator is that it is consistent without the knowledge of $f(u)$. The disadvantage is that (6.13) holds for any $c\beta$ where $c > 0$. Only the relative magnitude of the coefficients can be estimated with some normalization rule, say $\| \beta \| = 1$. Moreover, the speed of convergence is considerably slower ($N^{1/3}$) and the limiting distribution is quite complicated. Horowitz (1992) and Lee (1999) have proposed modified estimators that improve the speed of convergence and are asymptotically normally distributed.

Other examples of exploiting specific structure of nonlinear models to eliminate the effects of incidental parameters α_i include dynamic discrete choice models (Chamberlain, 1993; Honoré and Kyriazidou, 2000; Hsiao et al., 2005), symmetrically trimmed least squares estimator for truncated and censored data (tobit models) (Honoré, 1992), sample selection models (or type II tobit models) (Kyriazidou, 1997), and so on. However, often they impose very severe restrictions on the data such that not much of it can be utilized to obtain parameter estimates. Moreover, there are models that do not appear to yield consistent estimator when T is finite.

An alternative to consistent estimators is to consider bias-reduced estimators. The advantage of such an approach is that the bias-reduced estimators may still allow the use of all the sample information so that, from a mean square error point of view, the bias-reduced estimator may still dominate consistent estimators because

the latter often have to throw away a lot of the sample, and thus tend to have large variances.

Following the ideas of Cox and Reid (1987), Arellano (2001) and Carro (2006) propose to derive the modified MLE by maximizing the modified log-likelihood function

$$L^*(\beta) = \sum_{i=1}^{N} \left[\ell_i^*(\beta, \hat{\alpha}_i(\beta)) - \frac{1}{2} \log \ell_{i,\alpha_i\alpha_i}^*(\beta, \hat{\alpha}_i(\beta)) \right]$$

$$(6.15)$$

where $\ell_i^*(\beta, \hat{\alpha}_i(\beta))$ denotes the concentrated log-likelihood function of y_i after substituting the MLE of α_i in terms of β, $\hat{\alpha}_i(\beta)$ (that is, the solution of $\frac{\partial \log L}{\partial \alpha_i} = 0$ in terms of β, $i = 1, \ldots, N$) into the log-likelihood function and $\ell_{i,\alpha_i,\alpha_i}^*(\beta, \hat{\alpha}_i(\beta))$ denotes the second derivative of ℓ_i^* with respect to α_i. The bias correction term is derived by noting that to the order of $(1/T)$ the first derivative of ℓ_i^* with respect to β converges to $\frac{1}{2} \frac{E[\ell_{i,\beta\alpha_i\alpha_i}^*(\beta,\alpha_i)]}{E[\ell_{i,\alpha_i\alpha_i}^*(\beta,\alpha_i)]}$. By subtracting the order $(1/T)$ bias from the likelihood function, the modified MLE is biased only to the order of $(1/T^2)$, without increasing the asymptotic variance.

Monte Carlo experiments conducted by Carro (2006) have shown that, when $T = 8$, the bias of modified MLE for dynamic probit and logit models is negligible. Another advantage of the Arellano–Carro approach is its generality. For instance, a dynamic logit model with time dummy explanatory variable does not meet the Honoré and Kyriazidou (2000) conditions for generating consistent estimators, but will not affect the asymptotic properties of the modified MLE.

7 Modelling cross-sectional dependence

Most panel studies assume that, apart from the possible presence of individual invariant but period-varying time-specific effects, λ_t, the effects of omitted variables are independently distributed across cross-sectional units. However, often economic theory predicts that agents take actions that lead to interdependence among themselves. For example, the prediction that risk-averse agents will make insurance contracts allowing them to smooth idiosyncratic shocks implies dependence in consumption across individuals. Ignoring cross-sectional dependence can lead to inconsistent estimators, in particular when T is finite (for example, Hsiao and Tahmiscioglu, 2005). Unfortunately, contrary to the time series data in which the time label gives a natural ordering and structure, general forms of dependence for cross-sectional dimension are difficult to formulate. Therefore, econometricians have relied on strong parametric assumptions to model cross-sectional dependence. Two approaches have been proposed to model cross-sectional dependence: economic distance (or a spatial approach) and a factor approach.

In regional science, correlation across cross-section units is assumed to follow a certain spatial ordering, that is, dependence among cross-sectional units is related to location and distance, in a geographic or more general economic or social network space (for example, Anselin, 1988; Anselin and Griffith, 1988; Anselin, Le Gallo and Jayet, 2006). A known spatial weights matrix, $W = (w_{ij})$, an $N \times N$ positive matrix in which the rows and columns correspond to the cross-sectional units, is specified to express the prior strength of the interaction between individual (location) i (in the row of the matrix) and individual (location) j (column), w_{ij}. By convention, the diagonal elements, $w_{ii} = 0$. The weights are often standardized so that the sum of each row, $\sum_{j=1}^{N} w_{ij} = 1$.

The spatial weight matrix, W, is often included into a model specification to the dependent variable, to the explanatory variables, or to the error term. For instance, a *spatial lag* model for the $NT \times 1$ variable $\underset{\sim}{y} = (\underset{\sim 1}{y}', \ldots, \underset{\sim N}{y}')', \underset{\sim i}{y} = (y_{i1}, \ldots, y_{iT})'$, may take the form

$$\underset{\sim}{y} = \rho(W \otimes I_T)\underset{\sim}{y} + X\underset{\sim}{\beta} + \underset{\sim}{u} \tag{7.1}$$

where X and $\underset{\sim}{u}$ denote the $NT \times 1$ explanatory variables and $NT \times 1$ vector of error terms, respectively, and $\otimes$ denotes the Kronecker product. A *spatial error* model may take the form

$$\underset{\sim}{y} = X\underset{\sim}{\beta} + \underset{\sim}{v} \tag{7.2}$$

where $\underset{\sim}{v}$ may be specified as in a *spatial autoregressive* form,

$$\underset{\sim}{v} = \theta(W \otimes I_T)\underset{\sim}{v} + \underset{\sim}{u}, \tag{7.3}$$

or a spatial moving average form,

$$\underset{\sim}{v} = \gamma(W \otimes I_T)\underset{\sim}{u} + \underset{\sim}{u}. \tag{7.4}$$

The spatial model can be estimated by the instrumental variables (GMM estimator) or the maximum likelihood method. However, the approach of defining cross-sectional dependence in terms of 'economic distance' measure requires that the econometricians have information regarding this 'economic distance'. Another approach to model cross-sectional dependence is to assume that the error of a model, say model (7.3), follows a linear factor model,

$$v_{it} = \sum_{j=1}^{r} b_{ij} f_{jt} + u_{it}, \tag{7.5}$$

where $\underset{\sim t}{f} = (f_{1t}, \ldots, f_{rt})'$ is a $r \times 1$ vector of random factors, $\underset{\sim i}{b}' = (b_{i1}, \ldots, b_{ir})$, is $r \times 1$ non-random factor

loading coefficients, u_{it}, represents the effects of idiosyncratic shocks which is independent of $\underset{\sim t}{f}$ and is independently distributed across i. (for example, Bai and Ng, 2002; Moon and Perron, 2004; Pesaran, 2006). The conventional time-specific effects model is a special case of (7.5) when $r = 1$ and $b_i = b_\ell$ for all i and ℓ.

The factor approach requires considerably less prior information than the economic distance approach. Moreover, the number of time-varying factors, r, and factor load matrix $B = (b_{ij})$ can be empirically identified if both N and T are large. However, when T is large, one can estimate the covariance between i and j, σ_{ij}, by $\frac{1}{T}\sum_{t=1}^{T} \hat{v}_{it}\hat{v}_{jt}$ directly, then apply the generalized least squares method, where $\hat{v}_{it}$ is some preliminary estimate of v_{it}.

8 Large-N and large-T panels

Our discussion has been mostly focusing on panels with large N and finite T. There are panel data sets, like the Penn-World tables, covering different individuals, industries and countries over long periods. In general, if an estimator is consistent in the fixed-T, large-N case, it will remain consistent if both N and T tend to infinity. Moreover, even in the case that an estimator is inconsistent for fixed T and large N (say, the MLE of dynamic model (4.1) or fixed effects probit or logit models (6.6)), it can become consistent if T also tends to infinity. The probability limit of an estimator, in general, is identical irrespective of how N and T tend to infinity. However, the properly scaled limiting distribution may depend on how the two indexes, N and T, tend to infinity.

There are several approaches for deriving the limits of large-N, large-T panels:

1. *Sequential limits.* First, fix one index, say N, and allow the other, say T, to go to infinity, giving an intermediate limit, then let N go to infinity.
2. *Diagonal-path limits.* Let the two indexes, N and T, pass to infinity along a specific diagonal path, say $T = T(N)$ as $N \to \infty$.
3. *Joint limits.* Let N and T pass to infinity simultaneously without placing specific diagonal path restrictions on the divergence.

In many applications, sequential limits are easy to derive. However, sometimes sequential limits can give misleading asymptotic results. A joint limit will give a more robust result than either a sequential limit or a diagonal-path limit, but will also be substantially more difficult to derive and will apply only under stronger conditions, such as the existence of higher moments. Phillips and Moon (1999) have given a set of sufficient conditions that ensures that sequential limits are equivalent to joint limits.

When T is large, there is a need to consider serial correlations more generally, including both short-memory and persistent components. For instance, if unit roots are present in y and x (that is, both are integrated of order 1) but are not cointegrated, Phillips and Moon (1999) show that, if N is fixed but $T \to \infty$, the least squares regression of y on x is a non-degenerate random variable that is a functional of Brownian motion that does not converge to the long-run average relation between y and x, but it does if N also tends to infinity. In other words, the issue of spurious regression will not arise in a panel with large N (for example, Kao, 1999).

Both theoretical and applied researchers have paid a great deal of attention to the unit root and spurious regression properties of variables. When N is finite and T is large, standard time-series techniques can be used to derive the statistical properties of panel data estimators. When N is large and cross-sectional units are independently distributed across i, central limit theorems can be invoked along the cross-sectional dimension. Asymptotically normal estimators and test statistics (with suitably adjustment for finite T bias) for unit roots and cointegration have been proposed (for example, Baltagi and Kao, 2000; Im, Pesaran and Shin, 2003; Levin, Lin and Chu, 2002). They, in general, gain statistical power over their standard time series counterpart (for example, Choi, 2001).

When both N and T are large and cross-sectional units are not independent, a factor analytic framework of the form (7.5) has been proposed to model cross-sectional dependency and variants of unit root tests are proposed (for example, Moon and Perron, 2004). However, the implementation of those panel unit root tests is quite complicated. When $N \to \infty, \frac{1}{N}\sum_{i=1}^{N} u_{it} \to 0,$ (7.5) implies that $\bar{v}_t = \underset{\sim}{\bar{b}}' \underset{\sim}{f}_t$, where $\underset{\sim}{\bar{b}}'$ is the cross-sectional average of $\underset{\sim}{b}_i' = (b_{i1}, \ldots, b_{ir})$. Approximating $\underset{\sim}{b}_i' \underset{\sim}{f}_t$ by its cross-sectional mean function, Pesaran (2005; 2006) suggests a simple approach to filter out the cross-sectional dependency by augmenting the cross-sectional means, $\bar{y}_t$ and $\underset{\sim}{\bar{x}}_t$ to the regression model (7.2),

$$y_{it} = \underset{\sim}{x}_{it}' \underset{\sim}{\beta} + \alpha_i + \bar{y}_t c_i + \underset{\sim}{\bar{x}}_t' \underset{\sim}{d}_i + e_{it}, \quad (8.1)$$

or $\bar{y}_t, \Delta\bar{y}_{t-j}$ to the Dickey–Fuller (1979) type regression model,

$$\Delta y_{it} = \alpha_i + \delta_i t + \gamma_i y_{i,t-1} + \sum_{\ell=1}^{p_i} \phi_{i\ell} \Delta y_{i,t-\ell}$$

$$+ c_i \bar{y}_{t-1} + \sum_{\ell=1}^{p_i} d_{i\ell} \Delta\bar{y}_{t-\ell} + e_{it},$$

$$(8.2)$$

for testing of unit root, where $\bar{y}_t = \frac{1}{N}\sum_{i=1}^{N} y_{it}, \underset{\sim}{\bar{x}}_t = \frac{1}{N}\sum_{i=1}^{N}\underset{\sim}{x}_{it}, \Delta\bar{y}_{t-j} = \frac{1}{N}\sum_{i=1}^{N}\Delta y_{i,t-j}$ and $\Delta = (1-L), L$ denotes the lag operator. The resulting pooled estimator will again be asymptotically normally distributed.

When cross-sectional dependency is of unknown form, Chang (2002) suggests using nonlinear transformations of the lagged level variable, $y_{i,t-1}, F(y_{i,t-1})$, as instrumental variables (IV) for the usual augmented Dickey–Fuller (1979) type regression. The test static for the unit root hypothesis is simply defined as a standardized sum of individual IV t-ratios. As long as $F(\cdot)$ is regularly integrable, say $F(y_{i,t-1}) = y_{i,t-1}e^{-c_i|y_{i,t-1}|}$, where c_i is a positive constant, the product of the nonlinear instruments $F(y_{i,t-1})$ and $F(y_{j,t-1})$ from different cross-sectional units i and j are asymptotically uncorrelated, even the variables $y_{i,t-1}$ and $y_{j,t-1}$ generating the instruments are correlated. Hence, the usual central limit theorems can be invoked and the standardized sum of individual IV t-ratios is asymptotically normally distributed.

For further review of the literature on unit roots and cointegration in panels, see Breitung and Pesaran (2006) and Choi (2006).

9 Concluding remarks

In this paper we have tried to provide a summary of the advantages of using panel data and the fundamental issues of panel data analysis. Assuming that the heterogeneity across cross-sectional units and over time that is not captured by the observed variables can be captured by period-invariant individual specific and/or individual-invariant time-specific effects, we surveyed the fundamental methods for the analysis of linear static and dynamic models. We have also discussed difficulties in analysing nonlinear models and modelling cross-sectional dependence. There are many important issues, such as the modelling of joint dependence or simultaneous equations models, time-varying parameter models (for example, Hsiao, 1996; 2003; Hsiao and Pesaran, 2006), unbalanced panel, measurement errors (Griliches and Hausman, 1986; Wansbeek and Koning, 1989), and so on, that were not discussed, but can be found in Arellano (2003), Baltagi (2001) or Hsiao (2003).

Although panel data offer many advantages, they are no panacea. The power of panel data to isolate the effects of specific actions, treatments or more general policies depends critically on the compatibility of the assumptions of statistical tools with the data-generating process. In choosing the proper method for exploiting the richness and unique properties of the panel, it might be helpful to keep the following questions in mind. First, in investigating economic issues what advantages do panel data offer us over data-sets consisting of a single cross section or time series? Second, what are the limitations of panel data and the econometric methods that have been proposed for analysing such data? Third, when using panel data, how can we increase the efficiency of parameter estimates? Fourth, are the assumptions underlying the statistical inference procedures and the data-generating process compatible?

I would like to thank Steven Durlauf for helpful comments.

CHENG HSIAO

Bibliography

Ahn, S.C. and Schmidt, P. 1995. Efficient estimation of models for dynamic panel data. *Journal of Econometrics* 68, 5–27.

Anderson, T.W. and Hsiao, C. 1981. Estimation of dynamic models with error components. *Journal of the American Statistical Association* 76, 598–606.

Anderson, T.W. and Hsiao, C. 1982. Formulation and estimation of dynamic models using panel data. *Journal of Econometrics* 18, 47–82.

Anselin, L. 1988. *Spatial Econometrics: Methods and Models.* Boston: Kluwer.

Anselin, L. and Griffith, D.A. 1988. Do spatial effects really matter in regression analysis? *Papers of the Regional Science Association* 65, 11–34.

Anselin, L., Le Gallo, J. and Jayet, H. 2006. Spatial panel econometrics. In *The Econometrics of Panel Data: Fundamentals and Recent Developments in Theory and Practice.* 3rd edn, ed. L. Matyas and P. Sevestre. Dordrecht: Kluwer.

Arellano, M. 2001. Discrete choice with panel data. Working Paper No. 0101. Madrid: CEMFI.

Arellano, M. 2003. *Panel Data Econometrics.* Oxford: Oxford University Press.

Arellano, M. and Bond, S.R. 1991. Some tests of specification for panel data: Monte Carlo evidence and an application to employment equations. *Review of Economic Studies* 58, 277–97.

Arellano, M. and Bover, O. 1995. Another look at the instrumental variable estimation of error-components models. *Journal of Econometrics* 68, 29–51.

Bai, J. and Ng, S. 2002. Determining the number of factors in approximate factor models. *Econometrica* 70, 91–121.

Balestra, P. and Nerlove, M. 1966. Pooling cross-section and time series data in the estimation of a dynamic model: the demand for natural gas. *Econometrica* 34, 585–612.

Baltagi, B.H. 2001. *Econometric Analysis of Panel Data.* 2nd edn. New York: Wiley.

Baltagi, B.H. and Kao, C. 2000. Nonstationary panels, cointegration in panels and dynamic panel: a survey. In *Nonstationary Panels Panel Cointegration, and Dynamic Panels,* ed. B. Baltagi. Amsterdam: JAI Press.

Ben-Porath, Y. 1973. Labor force participation rates and the supply of labor. *Journal of Political Economy* 81, 697–704.

Bhargava, A. and Sargan, J.D. 1983. Estimating dynamic random effects models from panel data covering short time periods. *Econometrica* 51, 1635–59.

Binder, M., Hsiao, C. and Pesaran, M.H. 2005. Estimation and inference in short panel vector autoregressions with unit roots and cointegration. *Econometric Theory* 21, 795–837.

Breitung, J. and Pesaran, M.H. 2006. Unit roots and cointegration in panels. In *The Econometrics of Panel Data: Fundamentals and Recent Developments in Theory and Practice.* 3rd edn, ed. L. Matyas and P. Sevestre. Dordrecht: Kluwer.

Butler, J.S. and Moffitt, R. 1982. A computationally efficient quadrature procedure for the one factor multinomial probit model. *Econometrica* 50, 761–4.

Carro, J.M. 2006. Estimating dynamic panel data discrete choice models with fixed effects. *Journal of Econometrics* (forthcoming).

Chamberlain, G. 1980. Analysis of covariance with qualitative data. *Review of Economic Studies* 47, 225–38.

Chamberlain, G. 1984. Panel data. In *Handbook of Econometrics,* vol. 2, ed. Z. Griliches and M. Intriligato. Amsterdam: North-Holland.

Chamberlain, G. 1993. Feedback in panel data models. Mimeo, Department of Economics, Harvard University.

Chang, Y. 2002. Nonlinear IV unit root tests in panels with cross-sectional dependency. *Journal of Econometrics* 110, 261–92.

Choi, I. 2001. Unit root tests for panel data. *Journal of International Money and Finance* 20, 249–72.

Choi, I. 2006. Nonstationary panels. In *Palgrave Handbooks of Econometrics,* vol. 1, ed. T.C. Mills and K.D. Patterson. Basingstoke: Palgrave Macmillan.

Cox, D.R. and Reid, N. 1987. Parameter orthogonality and approximate conditional inference. *Journal of the Royal Statistical Society, B* 49, 1–39.

Dickey, D.A. and Fuller, W.A. 1979. Distribution of the estimators for autoregressive time series with a unit root. *Journal of the American Statistical Association* 74, 427–31.

Granger, C.W.J. 1990. Aggregation of time-series variables: a survey. In *Disaggregation in Econometric Modeling,* ed. T. Barker and M.H. Pesaran. London: Routledge.

Griliches, Z. 1967. Distributed lags: a survey. *Econometrica* 35, 16–49.

Griliches, Z. and Hausman, J.A. 1986. Errors-in-variables in panel data. *Journal of Econometrics* 31, 93–118.

Hausman, J.A. 1978. Specification tests in econometrics. *Econometrica* 46, 1251–71.

Heckman, J.J. 1981. Statistical models for discrete panel data. In *Structural Analysis of Discrete Data with Econometric Applications,* ed. C.F. Manski and D. McFadden. Cambridge, MA: MIT Press.

Honoré, B. 1992. Trimmed LAD and least squares estimation of truncated and censored regression models with fixed effects. *Econometrica* 60, 533–67.

Honoré, B. and Kyriazidou, E. 2000. Panel data discrete choice models with lagged dependent variables. *Econometrica* 68, 839–74.

Horowitz, J.L. 1992. A smoothed maximum score estimator for the binary response model. *Econometrica* 60, 505–31.

Hsiao, C. 1996. Random coefficient models. In *The Econometrics of Panel Data*. 2nd edn, ed. L. Matyas and P. Sevestre. Dordrecht: Kluwer.

Hsiao, C. 2003. *Analysis of Panel Data*, 2nd edn. Cambridge: Cambridge University Press.

Hsiao, C. and Pesaran, M.H. 2006. Random coefficients models. In *The Econometrics of Panel Data: Fundamentals and Recent Developments in Theory and Practice*. 3rd edn, ed. L. Matyas and P. Sevestre. Dordrecht: Kluwer.

Hsiao, C., Pesaran, M.H. and Tahmiscioglu, A.K. 2002. Maximum likelihood estimation of fixed effects dynamic panel data models covering short time periods. *Journal of Econometrics* 109, 107–50.

Hsiao, C., Shen, Y. and Fujiki, H. 2005. Aggregate vs disaggregate data analysis – a paradox in the estimation of money demand function of Japan under the low interest rate policy. *Journal of Applied Econometrics* 20, 579–601.

Hsiao, C., Shen, Y., Wang, B. and Weeks, G. 2005. Evaluating the effectiveness of Washington State repeated job search services on the employment rate of prime-age female welfare recipients. Mimeo, University of Southern California.

Hsiao, C. and Tahmiscioglu, A.K. 2005. Estimation of dynamic panel data models with both individual and time specific effects. Mimeo.

Im, K., Pesaran, M.H. and Shin, Y. 2003. Testing for unit roots in heterogeneous panels. *Journal of Econometrics* 115, 53–74.

Kao, C. 1999. Spurious regression and residual-based tests for cointegration in panel data. *Journal of Econometrics* 90, 1–44.

Kyriazidou, E. 1997. Estimation of a panel data sample selection model. *Econometrica* 65, 1335–64.

Lee, M.J. 1999. A root-N-consistent semiparametric estimator for related effects binary response panel data. *Econometrica* 67, 427–33.

Levin, A., Lin, C. and Chu, J. 2002. Unit root tests in panel data: asymptotic and finite sample properties. *Journal of Econometrics* 108, 21–24.

Lewbel, A. 1994. Aggregation and simple dynamics. *American Economic Review* 84, 905–18.

MaCurdy, T.E. 1981. An empirical model of labor supply in a life cycle setting. *Journal of Political Economy* 89, 1059–85.

Manski, C.F. 1987. Semiparametric analysis of random effects linear models from binary panel data. *Econometrica* 55, 357–62.

Moon, H.R. and Perron, B. 2004. Testing for a unit root in panels with dynamic factors. *Journal of Econometrics* 122, 81–126.

Neyman, J. and Scott, E.L. 1948. Consistent estimates based on partially consistent observations. *Econometrica* 16, 1–32.

Nickell, S. 1981. Biases in dynamic models with fixed effects. *Econometrica* 49, 1399–416.

Pakes, A. and Griliches, Z. 1984. Estimating distributed lags in short panels with an application to the specification of depreciation patterns and capital stock constructs. *Review of Economic Studies* 51, 243–62.

Pesaran, M.H. 2005. A simple panel unit root test in the presence of cross-section dependence. DAE Working Paper No. 0346, Cambridge University.

Pesaran, M.H. 2006. Estimation and inference in large heterogeneous panels with a multifactor error structure. *Econometrica* 74, 967–1012.

Phillips, P.C. 1986. Understanding spurious regressions in econometrics. *Journal of Econometrics* 33, 311–40.

Phillips, P.C. and Moon, H.R 1999. Linear regression limit theory for nonstationary panel data. *Econometrica* 67, 1057–111.

Rao, C.R. 1973. *Linear Statistical Inference and Its Applications*, 2nd edn. New York: Wiley.

Wansbeek, T.J. and Koning, R.H. 1989. Measurement error and panel data. *Statistica Neerlandica* 45, 85–92.

Zilak, J.P. 1997. Efficient estimation with panel data when instruments are predetermined: an empirical comparison of moment-condition estimators. *Journal of Business and Economic Statistics* 15, 419–31.

Lorenz curve

The Lorenz curve is the most widely used technique to represent and analyse the size distribution of income and wealth. The curve plots cumulative proportion of income units and the cumulative proportion of income received when income units are arranged in ascending order of their income. Max Otto Lorenz, a statistician (born 19 September 1876 in Burlington, USA; retired 1944), proposed this curve in 1905 in order to compare and analyse inequalities of wealth in a country during different epochs, or in different countries during the same epoch – and since then, the curve has been widely used as a convenient graphical device to summarize the information collected about the distributions of income and wealth.

The Lorenz curve may be represented by a function $L(p)$, which is interpreted as the fraction of total income received by the lowest pth fraction of income units. It satisfies the following conditions (Kakwani, 1980):

(a) if $p = 0$, $L(p) = 0$
(b) if $p = 1$, $L(p) = 1$
(c) $L'(p) = (x/\mu) \geq 0$ and $L''(p) = (1/\mu\, f(x)) > 0$
(d) $L(p) \geq p$

where income x of a unit (which can be negative for some units but is assumed to be non-negative here for notational convenience) is a random variable with the probability density function $f(x)$ with mean μ and $L'(p)$ and $L''(p)$ are the first and second derivatives of $L(p)$ with respect to p, respectively.

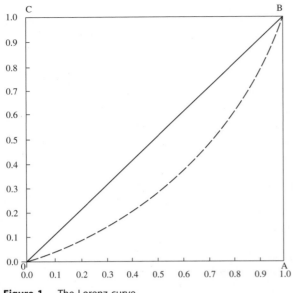

Figure 1   The Lorenz curve

A hypothetical Lorenz curve is illustrated in Figure 1. The ordinate and abscissa of the curve are $L(p)$ and p, respectively. The slope of the Lorenz curve is positive and increases monotonically, in other words, the curve is convex to the p-axis. From this it follows that $L(p) < p$. The straight line represented by the equation $L(p)=p$, is called the egalitarian line. The curve lies below this line. If, however, the curve coincides with the egalitarian line, it means that each unit receives the same income, which is the case of perfect equality of incomes. In the case of perfect inequality of incomes, the Lorenz curve coincides with OA and AB, which implies that all income is received by only one unit.

Since the Lorenz curve displays the deviation of each individual income from perfect equality, it captures, in a sense, the essence of inequality. The nearer the Lorenz curve is to the egalitarian line, the more equal the distribution of income will be. Consequently, the Lorenz curve could be used as a criterion for ranking income distributions: for if the Lorenz curve for one distribution, X, lies everywhere above that for another distribution, Y, then the distribution X may be said to be more equal than the distribution Y. However, the ranking provided by the curve is only partial – when two Lorenz curves intersect, neither distribution can be said to be more equal than the other. This partial ranking (or quasi-ordering as Sen (1973) calls it) need not, however, be considered a weakness of the Lorenz curve. In fact Sen (1973) criticizes the inequality measures that provide complete orderings on the grounds that 'the concept of inequality has different facets which may point in different directions and sometimes a total ranking can not be expected to emerge'. According to him, the concept of inequality is essentially a question of partial ranking

and the Lorenz curve is consistent with such a notion of inequality.

Is there any relation between the Lorenz curve ranking of distributions and social welfare? The answer has been provided by Atkinson (1970) who proved a theorem which shows that if social welfare is the sum of the individual utilities and every individual has an identical utility function which is concave, the ranking of distributions according to the Lorenz curve criterion is identical to the ranking implied by the social welfare function, provided the distributions have the same mean income and their Lorenz curves do not intersect. This theorem implies that one can judge between the distributions without knowing the form of the utility function except that it is increasing and concave. If the Lorenz curves do intersect, however, two utility functions that will rank the distributions differently can always be found.

Atkinson's theorem is based on the assumption that the social welfare function is equal to the sum of individual utilities and that every individual has the same utility function. These assumptions are somewhat limited and have been criticized by DasGupta, Sen and Starrett (1973) as well as by Rothschild and Stiglitz (1973), who have demonstrated that the result is, in fact, more general and would hold for any symmetric welfare function that is quasi-concave.

The Lorenz curve makes distributional judgements independently of the size of income, which as Sen (1973) points out, 'will make sense only if the relative ordering of welfare levels of distributions were strictly neutral to the operation of multiplying everybody's income by a given number'. This is rather an extreme requirement because social welfare depends on both size and the distribution of income.

Working independently on extensions of the Lorenz partial ordering, Shorrocks (1983) and Kakwani (1984) arrived at a criterion which would rank any two distributions with different mean incomes. The new criterion is given by $L(\mu, p)$, which is the product of the mean income μ and the Lorenz curve $L(p)$, whereas the Lorenz curve ranking is based only on $L(p)$. Ranking the distributions according to $L(\mu, p)$ will be identical to the Lorenz ranking if the distributions have the same mean income. This criterion of ranking has been justified from the welfare point of view in terms of several alternative classes of social welfare functions. Kakwani (1984) has used this criterion for international comparison of welfare using data from 72 countries.

As pointed out in the beginning, the Lorenz curve technique was devised as a convenient graphical method to represent and analyse the size distributions of income and wealth. The technique has proved to be extremely powerful and its applications in many areas of applied economics have recently been explored. In analysing data on consumer expenditures Mahalanobis (1960) developed a new technique 'Fractile Graphical Analyses' for comparison of socioeconomic groups at different places or points of time. In this paper, he proposed to extend and generalize the concept of the Lorenz curve to deal with problems of consumer behaviour patterns with respect to different commodities. He suggested that generalized Lorenz curves be called concentration curves, and in fact, used them as a convenient graphical device to describe consumption patterns for different commodities based on data from the National Sample Survey of India.

Kakwani (1977, 1980) provided, however, a more general and rigorous treatment of concentration curves in order to study the relationships among the distributions of different economic variables. He proved theorems which have many applications, particularly in the field of public finance where the effect of taxation and public spending of income distribution is analysed. Other areas in which concentration curves can be applied are inflation as it affects income distribution, estimation of Engel elasticities, disaggregation of total inequality by factor components, and economic growth and income distribution. In a later contribution he used concentration curves to explore how the sense of envy felt by individuals affects the optimal tax structure (Kakwani, 1985).

NANAK KAKWANI

See also **Gini ratio; Pareto distribution; poverty.**

Bibliography

Atkinson, A.B. 1970. On the measurement of inequality. *Journal of Economic Theory* 2, 244–63.

Dasgupta, P., Sen, A.K. and Starrett, D. 1973. Notes on the measurement of inequality. *Journal of Economic Theory* 6, 180–87.

Kakwani, N. 1977. Applications of Lorenz curves in economic analysis. *Econometrica* 45, 719–27.

Kakwani, N. 1980. *Inequality and Poverty: Methods of Estimation and Policy Applications.* New York: Oxford University Press.

Kakwani, N. 1984. Welfare ranking of income distributions. *Advances in Econometrics*, 191–213.

Kakwani, N. 1985. Applications of concentration curves to optimal negative income taxation. *Journal of Quantitative Economics* 1(1).

Lorenz, M.O. 1905. Methods for measuring concentration of wealth. *Journal of the American Statistical Association* 9, 209–19.

Mahalanobis, P.C. 1960. A method of fractile graphical analysis. *Econometrica* 28, 325–51.

Rothschild, M. and Stiglitz, J.E. 1973. Some further results on the measurement of inequality. *Journal of Economic Theory* 6(2), April,188–204.

Sen, A. 1973. *On Economic Inequality.* Oxford: Clarendon Press.

Shorrocks, A.F. 1983. Ranking income distributions. *Economica* 50, 3–18.

Lösch, August (1906–1945)

Lösch was born on 15 October 1906 in Oehringen (Württ), though he considered Heidenheim (Brenz) his home. He went to school there, studied in Freiburg with Eucken and in Bonn with Schumpeter and Spiethoff. He was twice a Rockefeller Fellow in the United States, where he did most of the theoretical and empirical work on *Die räumliche Ordnung der Wirtschaft* (1939a), published in the United States as the *Economics of Location* in 1954. His Habilitation (that is, his qualification to teach at a university) on population waves and business cycles was accepted but its unpopular conclusions and his known anti-Nazi views prevented him from getting the *venia legendi*, the actual permission to teach. He found refuge with the Kiel Institut für Weltwirtschaft, where he became chief of his own research group while at the same time suffering from political interference. He wrote a number of reports for the institute, one of which was published with his conclusions reversed. He kept his personal integrity at great personal cost. He died on 30 May 1945 in Ratzeburg (Holstein) of scarlet fever, which his weakened condition could not tolerate. In 1971, the City of Heidenheim honoured his memory by sponsoring biennial international conferences on location problems, establishing a prize for the best theses in the field and, a few years later, a special honour for older scholars in the field.

Although Lösch's first published paper dealt with the transfer problem, and he continued to be interested in international monetary problems, his only other publications in that field are two discussions of the transfer problem and an extensive fragment in the posthumously published 'Theory of Foreign Exchanges'. The two major subjects of his published work were the relation of population and business cycles and, of course, his highly original *Räumliche Ordnung der Wirtschaft*.

The discussions of population problems anticipate many later developments. Waves of population increase were neither sufficient nor necessary for the explanation of business cycles. With detailed statistics, some going back to the 17th century, Lösch showed that any relation went from business cycles to population waves, much as recent theory suggests. Though Lösch can claim priority there is no evidence that he actually influenced later developments.

The investigations about a declining and ageing population resulted, however, in quite different conclusions from what was then either politically or academically acceptable. The ageing of the population (the German 'Vergreisung' has sinister overtones absent from the English equivalent) had its economic compensations. It allowed the better training of the younger generation and increased capital accumulation and productivity. Even in military terms, fewer but better trained and better equipped people were preferable to more but less skilled individuals. In short, fewer young people allowed greater savings and investments leading to increased productivity and growth. This differed substantially from the then prevalent secular stagnation thesis and is much more in keeping with the warnings of present-day development economists of the dangers of rapid population growth. Lösch's earlier *Was ist vom Geburtenrückgang zu halten?* (1932) was later put on the index by the Nazis and his doctoral thesis on the same topic was effectively suppressed.

Lösch's greatest contribution dealt, in most general terms, with general equilibrium theory applied to space. Distance itself becomes the central phenomenon. Lösch's intellectual predecessors dealt with this problem essentially in two ways. They either solved a partial equilibrium system (Alfred Weber) or they substituted a series of smaller regions for one large one (Ohlin).

Going from partial to general equilibrium, and investigating the structure of the region instead of taking it as given, involved the substitution of a very general set of assumptions for the usual *ceteris paribus* assumptions made. In Weber (and practically everyone else) the locations of markets, raw materials and populations are assumed. In Lösch the basic assumption is a perfectly even distribution of population and of all raw materials. With these extraordinarily general and brilliantly unrealistic assumptions Lösch succeeds in showing that competitive forces alone will establish a system of locations which, in turn, can be understood either as agglomerations of productions or the intersection of fewer or more crossroads, all being simultaneously determined.

Lösch presents a Walrasian model with distance built in as a system of coordinates of location. His most famous contribution, however, is the analysis of the *structure* of an economic landscape on the basis of the simple generalized assumptions mentioned. The empirical work related mostly to the American Mid-West, where the assumptions are approximately realistic. One test of the genius of the model is that, unlike with most theoretical models, the introduction of more realistic assumptions simplifies rather than complicates the model.

In the 'ideal' Lösch landscape the basic unit is a hexagon. This follows from the condition that consumers are initially equidistant from each other, that each producer and consumer must lie within the market area of each good and that there must be no empty corners. Modifications introduced are rectangular areas on the model of, say, the layout of American counties; or the effect of different resource endowments of different areas; or of a border separating what might otherwise be one market area.

The work does not exhaust itself with equilibrium analysis or the structure of economic landscapes. There is a dynamic analytical and empirical study of how business cycles spread over the economic landscape or how transfers are made over and between areas through intraregional adjustments in connected areas and from one sub-market to another. Thus the initial impact of a change in demand in one landscape capital might first be felt in the capital in the centre of another landscape and spread from there in declining ripples to the border. There is a study of how the Great Depression spread in time and geographically through an area. The usual multiplier is supplemented by a spatial one.

The Lösch analyses the *Gestalt* of a region rather than defining it by such criteria as the immobility of factors of production between but not within regions: all factors are mobile at a cost which varies with distance, even land whose physical immobility is substituted for by changes in its utilization. The case of completely specific resources is investigated, though considered rare.

Lösch left a number of unfinished studies, and plans for many more. His is probably the most original book published on economics in the German language between the two world wars. Most scholars would consider themselves lucky if they had added a layer of bricks to an existing wall. Only few scholars can claim to have started a new wall, and even fewer to have started a new building. Lösch is one of those few scholars.

WOLFGANG F. STOLPER

See also **location theory.**

Selected works

1930. Eine Auseinandersetzung über das Transfer Problem. *Schmollers Jahrbuch* 54, 1193–206.

1932. *Was ist vom Geburtenrückgang zu halten?* 2 vols, Heidenheim: privately published.

1936a. *Bevölkerungswellen und Wechsellagen.* Jena: Gustav Fischer.

1936b. Die Vergreisung wirtschaftlich gesehen. *Schmollers Jahrbuch* 60, 577–685.

1936–7. Population cycles as a cause of business cycles. *Quarterly Journal of Economics* 51, 649–62.

1938. The nature of economic regions. *Southern Economic Journal* 5(1), 71–8.

1939a. *Die räumliche Ordnung der Wirtschaft. Eine Untersuchung über Standort, Wirtschaftsgebiete und Internationalen Handel.* 2nd revised edn, 1944. 3rd edn (reprint of the 2nd edn), Jena: Gustav Fischer, 1962. 2nd edn trans. as *The Economics of Location*, New Haven: Yale University Press, 1954.

1939b. Eine neue Theorie des Internationalen Handel. *Weltwirtschaftliches Archiv* 50, 308–28. Trans. as 'A new theory of international trade', *International Economic Papers* No. 6, London: Macmillan, 1956.

1949. Theorie der Währung. Ein Fragment. *Weltwirtschaftliches Archiv* 62, 35–88.

Bibliography

Riegger, R., ed. 1971. *August Lösch in Memoriam.* Heidenheim: Verlag der Buchhandlung Meuer. Contains eight contributions and a bibliography of 78 items, including literature about Lösch.

Valavanis, S. 1955. Lösch on location. *American Economic Review* 45, 637–44.

Zottmann, A. 1949. Dr. Habil. August Lösch, gestorben am 30. Mai 1945. *Weltwirtschaftliches Archiv* 62(1), 28–31. Appended bibliography, 32–4.

Lowe, Adolph (1893–1995)

Born on 4 March 1893 in Stuttgart, Adolph Lowe was educated at Berlin and Tübingen and received the Dr. Juris. from Tübingen in 1918. From 1919 to 1924 he was Section Head in the Ministries of Labour and Economics of the Weimar Republic, and was largely responsible for the practical planning and management of the currency reforms that brought the great hyperinflation to an end. From 1924 to 1926 he was Head of the International Division of the Federal Statistical Bureau, a politically sensitive post in the light of disputes over reparations payments. In 1926 he became Director of Research at the Institute of World Economics at the University of Kiel, where he established an important centre for research into business cycles and their control and regulation through planning. In 1931 he was appointed Professor of Political Economy at the University of Frankfurt, where he joined the leaders of a major renaissance in social and socialist thinking. But in March 1933 he became the first professor in the social sciences to be fired by Hitler. He moved immediately to England, where he held a post at Manchester until 1940, when he moved to the New School for Social Research in New York, where he was Professor of Economics, Director of Research at the Institute of World Affairs, and then Professor Emeritus, remaining active in the Department until his return to Germany, in March 1983, 50 years after his forced departure. In 1984 he was awarded the Dr. *honoris causa* by the University of Bremen.

His publications include 'Wie Ist Konjunkturtheorie Überhaupt Moglich?' (1926), *Economics and Sociology* (1935), *The Price of Liberty* (1937), 'The Classical Theory of Economic Growth' (1954), *On Economic Knowledge* (1965; 1977) and *The Path of Economic Growth* (1976). *Economic Means and Social Ends*, edited by Robert L. Heilbroner, was published in 1969 in honour of Professor Lowe's 75th birthday.

Unlike many economists, Lowe considered economics inseparable from social inquiry in general. In his view, the central question of economics is the determination of the path of economic growth and its relation to technical progress and social change. Lowe developed a strikingly simple three-sector model in which structural changes during expansion could be displayed. Growth will normally not take place in a balanced manner; more commonly the actual path will be a 'traverse' from one desired path to another, which is likely to shift again before it is reached. But the problem has to be understood in the light of what Lowe calls 'instrumental analysis'. Conventional economic theory begins with knowledge of the prevailing situation and a set of well-defined behavioural laws, based on maximizing. From these two givens one can deduce/predict the future configuration of the economy. This approach worked well in the early stages of capitalism, when the pressure of poverty on labour and competition on capital ensured stable patterns of behaviour. But mass production and economies of scale undermine competition, while affluence and unionization, together with the growth of the middle class, lead both to unpredictable wage bargaining and to unstable consumer spending. Tastes become volatile, while consumption can be postponed or redirected, and businesses plan strategically, often in cooperation with their rivals, instead of maximizing on a short horizon – so the traditional approach is no longer appropriate. The historical conditions do not constrain behaviour sufficiently for maximizing models, even complex ones, to picture it accurately, so that the conventional method must be set aside. (Which means, as well, that the forces of the market cannot be relied upon; they are no longer determinate.) Instead, the givens should be the existing conditions and the *desired terminal position*, and the job of economic analysis then becomes to find the 'goal-adequate' sequences of change, together with the stimuli and/or constraints that will create the necessary behaviour patterns. Such stimuli and constraints must be imposed by government. Economic analysis becomes a form of planning, and Lowe's work in his last years analysed the relation of planning to freedom.

EDWARD J. NELL

Selected works

1926. Wie ist Konjunkturtheorie überhaupt möglich? *Weltwirtschaftliches Archiv* 24(2), 165–97.

1935. *Economies and Sociology: A Plea for Co-operation in the Social Sciences*. London: G. Allen & Unwin.

1937. *The Price of Liberty: A German on Contemporary Britain*. London: L. and Virginia Woolf at the Hogarth Press.

1954. The classical theory of economic growth. *Social Research* 21(July), 127–58.

1965. *On Economic Knowledge*. New York: Harpers; London: Longmans. Enlarged edn, New York and London: M.E. Sharpe, 1977.

1969. *Economic Means and Social Ends: Essays in Politics Economics*, ed. R. L. Heilbroner. Englewood Cliffs, NJ: Prentice-Hall.

1976. *The Path of Economic Growth*. Cambridge: Cambridge University Press.

1988. *Has Freedom a Future?* New York: Praeger.

low-income housing policy

Low-income housing assistance is an important part of the welfare system in many countries.

Rationales

The most compelling rationale for this government activity is that some taxpayers care about low-income households and think that the decision makers in some of these households spend too little of their income on housing for their own good. Another important argument is that some taxpayers are particularly concerned about the well-being of the children in low-income households and prefer housing subsidies to unrestricted cash grants in order to better target assistance to the objects of their concern. These rationales imply that a successful housing programme induces its recipients to occupy better housing and consume less of other goods than they would choose in response to an unrestricted cash grant in an amount equal to the housing subsidy.

Programme types

Governments have tried many methods of providing housing assistance. The most important distinction between rental housing programmes is whether the subsidy is attached to the dwelling unit or to the assisted household. If the subsidy is attached to a rental dwelling unit, each family must accept the particular unit offered in order to receive assistance and loses its subsidy when it moves. Each family offered recipient-based rental assistance has a choice among many units in the private market that meet the programme's standards, and the family can retain its subsidy when it moves. The analogous distinction for homeownership programmes is between programmes that require eligible families to buy from selected sellers in order to receive a subsidy and programmes that provide subsidies to eligible families that are free to buy from any seller that provides housing meeting the programme's standards.

There are two broad types of unit-based rental assistance, namely, public housing and privately owned subsidized projects. Public housing projects are owned and operated by government entities. In public housing programmes, civil servants make all of the decisions made by private owners of unsubsidized housing. Governments also contract with private parties to provide unit-based assistance in subsidized housing projects. In the United States, the majority of these private parties are for-profit firms, but non-profit organizations have a significant presence. Under most programmes, these private parties agree to provide rental housing meeting certain standards at restricted rents to households with particular characteristics for a specified number of years. The overwhelming majority of the projects were newly built under a subsidized construction programme. Almost all of the rest were substantially rehabilitated as a condition for participation in the programme. None of the programmes that subsidize privately owned projects provide subsidies to all suppliers who would like to participate.

In 2004, the United States government spent about $15 billion on its housing voucher programme, more than $15 billion to subsidize private projects for low-income households, and about $7.5 billion to subsidize public housing projects. The US Department of Housing and Urban Development's Section 8 New Construction and Substantial Rehabilitation Program and the Internal Revenue Service's Low-Income Housing Tax Credit Program are the two largest programmes that subsidize private rental projects, accounting for about 75 per cent of public expenditure on programmes of this type. In total, these rental programmes served about seven million households. During the same year, the US government spent only $4 billion to subsidize low-income homeowners. These programmes tend to provide shallower subsidies to households with substantially higher incomes than the rental programmes.

Theory

Economic theory that accounts for the most rudimentary features of real housing programmes does not have strong implications about their effects. For example, these programmes may induce households to occupy worse housing even if housing is a normal good. Such counterintuitive outcomes result from the nonlinear budget frontiers facing households offered housing assistance. For instance, a household offered a unit in a subsidized housing project is offered an all-or-nothing choice of a particular dwelling unit at a below-market rent. This unit might be worse than the household's current unit, but the household may accept the offer because the reduction in its rent enables it to consume more of other goods.

Evidence

The remainder of this article summarizes the evidence on the effects of the major rental housing programmes in the United States. The United States has rental programmes of each broad type, and a disproportionate share of the evidence on the performance of low-income housing programmes throughout the world pertains to these programmes. Homeownership programmes are a small part of the current system, and little is known about their effects.

Different rental housing programmes have different effects. Indeed, the same programme has different effects in different circumstances. Olsen (2003) provides a more detailed account of the evidence on the performance of individual programmes, and the bibliography to this article contains references to some of the more important recent studies. This article endeavours to characterize what is typical of these programmes and the differences in the average effect of programmes of different types.

The most important finding of the empirical literature on the effects of different housing programmes from the viewpoint of housing policy is that recipient-based housing assistance has provided equally good housing at a much lower total cost than any type of unit-based assistance. The reasons for this result suggest that it would apply generally. These reasons include the absence of a financial incentive for good decisions on the part of civil servants who operate public housing, the excessive profits that inevitably result from allocating subsidies to selected developers of private subsidized projects, and the distortions in usage of inputs resulting from the subsidy formulas. Another reason for the excess cost of unit-based assistance is that this assistance is usually tied to the construction of new units. The least expensive approach to improving the housing conditions of low-income households involves heavy reliance on upgrading the existing housing stock.

Since housing programmes are intended to produce particular changes in consumption of housing services compared with consumption of other goods, knowledge of these changes is important for evaluating these programmes. The overwhelming majority of recipients of housing assistance occupy better housing than they would occupy in the absence of assistance. More importantly, they typically occupy better housing than they would occupy if they were given cash grants in amounts equal to their housing subsidies. Most recipients of rental housing assistance pay significantly less for their housing and hence have more to spend on other goods.

One aspect of the housing bundle broadly conceived that has attracted considerable attention is its neighbourhood. Recipients of tenant-based vouchers and occupants of privately owned subsidized projects typically live in somewhat better and less racially segregated neighbourhoods than in the absence of housing assistance. Occupants of public housing typically live in noticeably worse and more racially segregated neighbourhoods.

A careful theoretical analysis that accounts for a key feature of low-income housing programmes has shown that, even if the subsidy under the programme declines with increases in earnings and leisure is a normal good, the programme will not necessarily induce the recipient to work less (Schone, 1992). Nevertheless, evidence based on a controlled experiment indicates that voucher recipients reduce their earnings about 13 per cent on average (Patterson et al., 2004). Other evidence indicates that programmes of unit-based assistance have somewhat larger work disincentive effects (Olsen et al., 2005).

Low-income housing programmes differ substantially from unrestricted cash grants in their effects. The mean value of project-based housing assistance as judged by recipients is much less than 75 per cent of the mean housing subsidy (that is, the difference between the market rent of the subsidized unit and the tenant's contribution). The mean value of tenant-based housing assistance as judged by recipients is about 80 per cent of the mean housing subsidy.

Consistent with their intentions, the mean benefit to recipients in these programmes is greater for poorer and larger households among households that are the same in other respects. Mean benefit varies little with the age, race and sex of the head of the household after other household characteristics are accounted for. The variance in benefit among recipients with the same characteristics is large under construction programmes that have produced new units for many years. In these mature construction programmes, there is an enormous difference between the best and the worst units, and a tenant with specified characteristics would pay the same rent for these units.

Unit-based or recipient-based housing programmes can make the neighbourhoods into which subsidized households move better or worse places to live. Neighbourhood property values capture these effects. On average across all units in a programme, the evidence indicates that no programme has had a significant effect on neighbourhood property values.

Housing programmes affect the rents of unsubsidized units with unchanging characteristics. Evidence from the Housing Assistance Supply Experiment indicates that an entitlement housing voucher programme for which the poorest 20 per cent of the population is eligible will have small effects on market rents (Lowry, 1983). No evidence is available for construction programmes. However, economic theory suggests that, if a construction programme leads to a larger housing stock, it will result in higher market rents because it will drive up the prices of inputs used heavily in the housing industry. This effect might be small, however, because the evidence indicates that subsidized construction crowds out unsubsidized construction to a considerable extent (Malpezzi and Vandell, 2002; Sinai and Waldfogel, 2005; and references in Olsen, 2003).

An important recent literature estimates a wide range of impacts of offering portable vouchers to families living in the worst public housing projects or in public housing projects in the poorest neighbourhoods. The larger strand of this research is based on data from a controlled experiment called Moving to Opportunity, in which one experimental group was offered a housing voucher without any restriction on the neighbourhood where it could be used and another experimental group had to move for at least a year to a neighbourhood where the poverty rate was less than ten per cent prior to the experiment (Orr et al., 2003). These treatments led their recipients to live in better housing and neighbourhoods without a reduction in expenditure on other goods. However, they did not lead to some expected outcomes. After four to seven years in the experiment, the treatment groups did not increase their earnings and their children's educational performance did not improve. With a few notable exceptions such as the mental health of girls and their mothers, the treatments had minimal effects on health outcomes. The treatments generally had effects in opposite directions on the delinquency and risky behaviour of boys and girls. The effects on boys were negative, though these effects were not usually statistically significant. A smaller strand of this literature is based on data on natural experiments such as when public housing tenants must move because their project is torn down (Jacob, 2004).

EDGAR O. OLSEN

See also **crowding out; housing policy in the United States; housing supply; welfare state.**

Bibliography

Jacob, B. 2004. Public housing, housing vouchers, and student achievement: evidence from public housing demolitions in Chicago. *American Economic Review* 94, 233–58.

Lowry, I.S., ed. 1983. *Experimenting with Housing Allowances: The Final Report of the Housing Assistance Supply Experiment.* Cambridge, MA: Oelgeschlager, Gunn & Hain.

Malpezzi, S. and Vandell, K. 2002. Does the low-income housing tax credit increase the supply of housing? *Journal of Housing Economics* 11, 360–80.

Olsen, E.O. 2003. Housing programs for low-income households. In *Means-Tested Transfer Programs in the United States*, ed. R. Moffitt. Chicago: University of Chicago Press.

Olsen, E.O., Tyler, C.A., King, J.W. and Carrillo, P.E. 2005. The effects of different types of housing assistance on earnings and employment. *Cityscape* 8, 163–87.

Orr, L. et al. 2003. *Moving to Opportunity for Fair Housing Demonstration Program: Interim Impacts Evaluation.* Washington, DC: US Department of Housing and Urban Development.

Patterson, R. et al. 2004. *Evaluation of the Welfare to Work Voucher Program: Report to Congress.* Washington, DC: US Department of Housing and Urban Development.

Schone, B.S. 1992. Do means tested transfers reduce labor supply? *Economics Letters* 40, 353–8.

Sinai, T. and Waldfogel, J. 2005. Do low-income housing subsidies increase the occupied housing stock? *Journal of Public Economics* 11–12, 2137–64.

Lucas, Robert (born 1937)

In 1995, Robert E. Lucas, Jr received the Nobel Prize in Economic Sciences 'for having developed and applied the hypothesis of rational expectations, and thereby having transformed macroeconomic analysis and deepened our understanding of economic policy' (Press Release announcing the Nobel Prize, 1995; repr. in Svensson, 1996, p. 1).

Robert Lucas was born in Yakima, Washington on 15 September 1937. He received his BA in History in 1959, and his Ph.D. in Economics in 1964, both from the University of Chicago. He began his career as an assistant professor at Carnegie Mellon University, where he became an associate professor in 1967 and a full professor in 1970. He joined the Department of Economics at the University of Chicago as a full professor in 1975, and since 1980 has served as John Dewey Distinguished Service Professor of Economics there. He is a fellow of the Econometric Society, the American Academy of Arts and Sciences, and the American Finance Association; a member of the National Academy of Sciences and the American Philosophical Society and a titular member of the European Academy of Arts, Sciences and Humanities. Lucas served as the President of the Econometric Society in 1997 and as the President of the American Economic Association in 2002.

Robert Lucas's seminal contributions in the early 1970s led to a paradigm shift in macroeconomics: the rational expectations revolution. By the late 1970s–early 1980s, due to the efforts of Robert Lucas and others (including Robert Barro, William Brock, Edward Prescott, Thomas Sargent and Neil Wallace) the frontier of macroeconomic research had moved away from models with static or adaptive expectations towards models in which agents act in their best interest, utilizing all available information about past, present and future. As a result, dynamic stochastic general equilibrium models with rigorous microfoundations have been developed to understand economic fluctuations and growth and to analyse the effects of monetary and fiscal policies. While these models have become increasingly complex in an effort to better understand the economy, almost all of them are built on the principles set forth by Robert Lucas.

The beginning of the rational expectations revolution: expectations and the neutrality of money

Robert Lucas's 'Expectations and Neutrality of Money', published in 1972 in the *Journal of Economic Theory*, was the first paper to incorporate the idea of rational expectations into a dynamic general equilibrium model. (RATIONAL EXPECTATIONS were introduced by Muth, 1961. In their ground-breaking study of investment under uncertainty, Lucas and Prescott, 1971 applied the notion of rational expectations in a dynamic partial equilibrium model of a competitive industry facing stochastic demand.)

The agents in Lucas's (1972b) model are fully rational: based on the available information, they form expectations about future prices and quantities, and based on these expectations they act to maximize their expected lifetime utility. This paper also was the first to provide sound theoretical underpinnings to Milton Friedman's (1968) and Edmund Phelps's (1968) view of the long-run neutrality of money, and at the same time to provide an explanation of the observed positive correlation between output and inflation, famously depicted by the Phillips curve.

Lucas's model is built on Paul Samuelson's (1958) overlapping generations model. Agents live for two periods. In each period the young generation works, consumes and saves. The old generation consumes its savings. Goods are perishable and there is only one savings instrument in the economy, money.

The population in the economy is allocated into two distinct markets (islands) across which no communication is possible. The old generation is equally divided between the islands. The allocation of the young generation across the islands is a random variable. The amount of money holdings by the old generation is also a random variable, because it depends on the realization of a random shock in the money growth rate: each dollar carried from one period to another is multiplied by the realized money growth rate between these two periods. Agents do not observe the current allocation of young across islands and the money growth rate, but know their underlying probability distributions. To solve for the optimal amount of labour supply and savings, the young must form expectations about the future value of money, that is, the future price level. How does one form such expectations? Lucas's answer is, rationally. He defined and explicitly solved for the rational expectations equilibrium, in which agents correctly predict how the price level depends on the state of the economy. Of course, to do so each agent also must correctly understand the actions of all other agents in the current and future generations and how these actions affect prices (and quantities).

In the model, the positive correlation between the money growth rate and output arises because the young, when faced with a high demand for their goods, are unable to distinguish its source: the demand could be high because of a higher money growth rate, or because of a lower fraction of the young workers on the island. Due to their inability to infer exactly the source of the high demand, the young find it optimal to produce whenever they face a high demand. Consequently, a positive money growth shock leads to an economic expansion on both islands. Without uncertainty about the money growth rate, the neutrality of money is immediately attained. Any pre-announced proportional money growth rule – for example, the $k\%$ rule advocated by Milton Friedman – results in the same real outcomes.

Lucas showed that invariance of real outcomes to the pre-announced part of the money growth rule holds also when there are shocks to money growth. This finding is often characterized as a 'policy ineffectiveness' result, because it implies that, although there is a positive correlation between output and money growth, this correlation cannot be exploited by the monetary authority to influence real economic activity.

Prior to Lucas's (1972b) work, economists often emphasized that a distinction should be drawn between the long-run and the short-run effects of monetary shocks. An important corollary of Lucas's work is that this distinction often is misleading. The true distinction must be made between anticipated and unanticipated monetary disturbances, because their effects on real economic activity are likely to be very different. Most of the subsequent monetary business cycle literature embraces this distinction.

Econometric policy evaluation: the Lucas critique

Lucas (1976), known as the LUCAS CRITIQUE, marked the turning point in how economists approached econometric policy evaluation. Thomas Sargent's (1996) account of the events following the Lucas critique gives a sense of its tremendous impact:

> [W]e didn't understand what was going on until, upon reading Lucas's 'Econometric Policy Evaluation' in Spring of 1973, we were stunned into terminating our long standing Minneapolis Fed research project to design, estimate and optimally control a Keynesian macroeconometric model. We realized that Kareken, Muench, and Wallace's (1973) defense of the 'look-at-everything' feedback rule for policy – which was thoroughly based on 'best responses' for the monetary authority exploiting a 'no response' private sector – could not be the foundation of a sensible research program, but was better viewed as a memorial plaque to the Keynesian tradition in which we had been trained to work. (Sargent, 1996, p. 539)

The essence of the Lucas critique stems naturally from the concept of rational expectations. Indeed, rationality of the private sector implies that it cannot be modelled as a 'no response' entity. Rather, any observed or anticipated change in monetary policy, including the 'best response' of the monetary authority, will induce the 'best responses' from the agents in the private sector. This, in turn, implies that the effects of a new policy cannot be assessed according to econometric estimation of the private sector's behaviour under the old policy.

Other major contributions

Robert Lucas has made several other major contributions in different areas of economics. A small subset of them is presented below, in chronological order.

Lucas (1978a) elegantly introduced the first general equilibrium model of asset pricing. In the model economy, physical assets are represented by what nowadays typically is referred to as 'Lucas trees': infinitely lived objects that generate stochastic dividends (fruits). Lucas explicitly derived asset prices as functions of the economy's state variables. The logic of Lucas's asset pricing equation forms the foundation of many models in macro and financial economics.

Lucas (1980b) and Lucas and Stokey (1987) helped to lay the foundations of monetary economics. The ideas and the methodology developed in these papers continue to guide monetary economists, particularly in applied research. Lucas (1980b) is the first general equilibrium study of the determination of prices in an economy in which the use of money arises from a cash-in-advance constraint. The model in Lucas and Stokey (1987), which is the prototype for a number of widely used dynamic stochastic general equilibrium monetary models, features both real and nominal shocks. Methods developed by Lucas and Stokey for establishing the existence of, characterizing and solving for the equilibrium of such models have proven to be powerful tools in applied and theoretical research.

Lucas (1982) extended the logic of his earlier contributions, Lucas (1978a) and Lucas (1980b), to a two-country stochastic general equilibrium model with infinitely lived agents, in which he explicitly derived formulas for pricing real assets and nominal bonds as well as for determining exchange rates. The framework developed in this paper serves as a point of departure for many models in international economics.

Lucas and Stokey (1983) is a major contribution to modern public finance. Lucas and Stokey studied the Ramsey (1927) problem – the problem of optimal taxation when non-distortionary tax instruments are unavailable – in dynamic stochastic economies without physical capital. Their paper provided a number of important insights about the structure and time consistency of optimal fiscal and monetary policies. Lucas and Stokey showed that a sufficiently rich debt maturity structure could allow for time consistency of the optimal fiscal policy.

Lucas (1988) is a seminal contribution in the economic development and growth literature (see also the 1991 Fisher and Shultz Lecture at the European Meetings of Econometric Society, published as Lucas, 1993). Lucas (1988) and an earlier paper by Paul Romer (1986) heralded the birth of endogenous growth theory and the resurgence of research on economic growth in the late 1980s and the 1990s. These papers offered an escape from 'the straightjacket of the neoclassical growth model, in which the long term per capita (output) growth is pegged by the rate of exogenous technological progress' (Barro and Sala-i-Martin, 2004, p. 19), by showing that factor accumulation does not need to run into diminishing returns to scale and, therefore, could lead to perpetual growth. In particular, Lucas emphasized the role of human capital, and externalities generated by it, as important sources of long-run economic growth.

Robert Lucas has written a number of seminal books. Among them are *Models of Business Cycles* (1987) and, with N. Stokey and E. Prescott, *Recursive Methods in Economic Dynamics* (1989). The former presents a critical assessment of the business cycle literature of the 1970s and the early 1980s and offers novel insights about economic fluctuations. This monograph contains Lucas's famous calculation of the cost of business cycles, which he argued to be insignificant. (In a similar spirit, Lucas, 2000a provided a quantitative assessment of the welfare cost of inflation. In this paper, he found that the gains from reducing inflation could be non-negligible. Subsequent research often has taken his calculations of the cost of business cycles and of the cost of inflation as benchmarks.) Another indispensable volume, *Recursive Methods in Economic Dynamics* (1989), deals with stochastic dynamic programming. It has been widely used as a textbook in graduate macroeconomics courses and as a guide for formulating and solving dynamic stochastic general equilibrium models.

LEVON BARSEGHYAN

See also **Lucas critique; monetary business cycles (imperfect information); neutrality of money; Phillips curve; rational expectations.**

In writing this article I have drawn from Fisher (1996), Hall (1996), Svensson (1996), Sargent (1996), Lucas (1996) and Chari (1998).

Selected works

1962. (With Z. Griliches, G.S. Maddala, and N. Wallace). Notes on estimated aggregate quarterly consumption functions. *Econometrica* 30, 491–500.

1967a. Optimal investment policy and the flexible accelerator. *International Economic Review* 8, 78–85.

1967b. Tests of a capital-theoretic model of technological change. *Review of Economic Studies* 34, 175–89.

1967c. Adjustment costs and the theory of supply. *Journal of Political Economy* 75, 321–34.

1968. (With T. McGuire, J. Farley and W. Ring.) Estimation and inference for linear models in which subsets of the dependent variable are constrained. *Journal of the American Statistical Association* 63, 1201–13.

1969a. (With L. Rapping.) Real wages, employment, and inflation. *Journal of Political Economy* 77, 721–54.

1969b. (With L. Rapping.) Price expectations and the Phillips curve. *American Economic Review* 59, 342–50.

1970a. Capacity, overtime and empirical production functions. *American Economic Review* 60, 23–7.

1970b. (With L.A. Rapping et al.) Real wages, employment and inflation. In *The New Microeconomics in Employment and Inflation Theory*, ed. E.S. Phelps et al. New York: W.W. Norton.

1971. (With E.C. Prescott.) Investment under uncertainty. *Econometrica* 39, 659–81.

1972a. (With E.C. Prescott.) A note on price systems in infinite dimensional space. *International Economic Review* 13, 416–22.

1972b. Expectations and the neutrality of money. *Journal of Economic Theory* 4, 103–24.

1972c. (With L. Rapping.) Unemployment in the great depression: is there a full explanation? *Journal of Political Economy* 80, 186–91.

1972d. Econometric testing of the natural rate hypothesis. In *The Econometrics of Price Determination Conference*, ed. O. Eckstein. Washington, DC: Board of Governors of the Federal Reserve System.

1973. Some international evidence on output-inflation trade-offs. *American Economic Review* 63, 326–34.

1974. (With E.C. Prescott.) Equilibrium search and unemployment. *Journal of Economic Theory* 7, 188–209.

1975. An equilibrium model of the business cycle. *Journal of Political Economy* 83, 1113–44.

1976. Econometric policy evaluation: a critique. *Carnegie-Rochester Conference Series on Public Policy*, vol. 1. First publ. in *The Phillips Curve and Labor Markets*, ed. K. Brunner and A. Meltzer. Amsterdam: North-Holland, 1975.

1977. Understanding business cycles. In *Stabilization of the Domestic and International Economy*, ed. K. Brunner and A. Meltzer. Amsterdam: North-Holland.

1978a. Asset prices in an exchange economy. *Econometrica* 46, 1429–45.

1978b. On the size distribution of business firms. *Bell Journal of Economics* 508–23.

1978c. Unemployment policy. *American Economic Review* 68, 353–57.

1979. (With T.J. Sargent.) After Keynesian macroeconometrics. In *After the Phillips Curve*, Federal Reserve Bank of Boston, Conference Series No. 19: 49–72. Repr. in *Federal Reserve Bank of Minneapolis Quarterly Review* 3, 1–6.

1980a. Rules, discretion and the role of the economic advisor. In *Rational Expectations and Economic Policy*, ed. S. Fischer. Chicago: University of Chicago Press for the NBER.

1980b. Equilibrium in a pure currency economy. In *Models of Monetary Economics*, ed. J.H. Karaken and N. Wallace. Minneapolis: Federal Reserve Bank of Minneapolis.

1980c. Two illustrations of the quantity theory of money. *American Economic Review* 1970, 1005–14.

1980d. Methods and problems in business cycle theory. *Journal of Money, Credit and Banking* 12, 696–717.

1981a. (With T.J. Sargent.) *Rational Expectations and Econometric Practice*. Minneapolis: University of Minnesota Press.

1981b. *Studies in Business-Cycle Theory*. Cambridge, MA: MIT Press.

1981c. Distributed lags and optimal investment policy. In Lucas and Sargent (1981a).

1981d. Optimal investment with rational expectations. In Lucas and Sargent (1981a).

1982. Interest rates and currency prices in a two-country world. *Journal of Monetary Economics* 10, 335–60.

1983. (With N.L. Stokey.) Optimal fiscal and monetary policy in an economy without capital. *Journal of Monetary Economics* 12, 55–94.

1984a. (With N.L. Stokey.) Optimal growth with many consumers. *Journal of Economic Theory* 32, 139–71.

1984b. Money in a theory of finance. In *Essays on Macroeconomic Implications of Financial and Labor Markets and Political Processes*, eds. K. Brunner and A. Meltzer. Amsterdam: North-Holland.

1986a. Principles of fiscal and monetary policy. *Journal of Monetary Economics* 17, 117–34.

1986b. Adaptive behavior and economic theory. *Journal of Business* 59, S401–S426.

1987. (With N.L. Stokey.) Money and interest in a cash-in-advance economy. *Econometrica* 55, 491–514.

1987. *Models of Business Cycles*. Y. Jahnsson Lectures.Oxford: Basil Blackwell.

1988. On the mechanics of economic development. *Journal of Monetary Economics* 22, 3–42.

1989. (With N.L. Stokey and E.C. Prescott.) *Recursive Methods in Economic Dynamics*. Cambridge, MA: Harvard University Press.

1990a. Liquidity and interest rates. *Journal of Economic Theory* 50, 237–64.

1990b. Why doesn't capital flow from rich to poor countries? *American Economic Review* 80, 92–6.

1990c. Supply side economics: an analytical review. *Oxford Economic Papers* 42, 293–316.

1992a. (With A.G. Atkeson.) On efficient distribution with private information. *Review of Economic Studies* 59, 427–53.

1992b. On efficiency and distribution. *Economic Journal* 102, 233–47.

1993. Making a miracle. *Econometrica* 61, 251–72.

1995. (With A.G. Atkeson.) Efficiency and equality in a simple model of efficient unemployment insurance. *Journal of Economic Theory* 66, 64–88.

1996. Nobel lecture: monetary neutrality. *Journal of Political Economy* 104, 661–82.

2000a. Inflation and welfare. *Econometrica* 68, 247–74.

2000b. Some macroeconomics for the 21st century. *Journal of Economic Perspectives* 14(1), 159–68.

2001a. *Lectures on Economic Growth*. Cambridge, MA: Harvard University Press.

2001b. Externalities and cities. *Review of Economic Dynamics* 4, 245–74.

2002. (With E. Rossi-Hansberg.) On the internal structure of cities. *Econometrica* 70, 1445–76.

2003. Macroeconomic priorities. *American Economic Review* 93, 1–14.

2004. Life earnings and rural-urban migration. *Journal of Political Economy* 112(S1), S29–S59.

2007. (With M. Golosov.) Menu costs and Phillips curves. *Journal of Political Economy* 115, 171–99.

2007. (With F. Alvarez.) General equilibrium analysis of the Eaton–Kortum model of international trade. *Journal of Monetary Economics*.

Bibliography

Barro, R. and Sala-i-Martin, X. 2004. *Economic Growth*, 2nd edn. Cambridge, MA: MIT Press.

Chari, V.V. 1998. Nobel Laureate Robert E. Lucas, Jr.: architect of modern macroeconomics. *Journal of Economic Perspectives* 12(1), 171–86 Repr. in *Federal Reserve Bank of Minneapolis Quarterly Review* 23, 2–12, 1999.

Fisher, S. 1996. Robert Lucas's Nobel memorial prize. *Scandinavian Journal of Economics* 98, 11–31.

Friedman, M. 1968. The role of monetary policy. *American Economic Review* 58, 1–15.

Hall, R.E. 1996. Robert Lucas, recipient of the 1995 Nobel memorial prize in economics. *Scandinavian Journal of Economics* 98, 33–48.

Kareken, J.A., Muench, T. and Wallace, N. 1973. Optimal open market strategy: the use of information variables. *American Economic Review* 63, 156–72.

Muth, J.F. 1961. Rational expectations and the theory of price movements. *Econometrica* 29, 315–35.

Phelps, E. 1968. Money-wage dynamics and labor market equilibrium. *Journal of Political Economy* 76, 687–711.

Ramsey, F.P. 1927. A contribution to the theory of taxation. *Economic Journal* 37, 47–61.

Romer, P. 1986. Increasing returns and long run growth. *Journal of Political Economy* 94, 1002–37.

Samuelson, P.A. 1958. An exact consumption-loan model of interest with or without the contrivance of money. *Journal of Political Economy* 66, 467–82.

Sargent, T.J. 1996. Expectations and nonneutrality of Lucas. *Journal of Monetary Economics* 37, 535–48.

Svensson, L.E.O. 1996. The scientific contributions of Robert E. Lucas, Jr. *Scandinavian Journal of Economics* 98, 1–10.

Lucas critique

The 'Lucas critique' is a criticism of econometric policy evaluation procedures that fail to recognize the following economic logic:

> [G]iven that the structure of an econometric model consists of optimal decision rules of economic agents, and that optimal decision rules vary systematically with changes in the structure of series relevant to the decision maker, it follows that any changes in policy will systematically alter the structure of econometric models. (Lucas, 1976, p. 41)

At the time of his writing, Robert E. Lucas, Jr. (1976) was criticizing the prevailing approach to quantitative macroeconomic policy evaluation for ignoring this logic and, hence, as being fundamentally inconsistent with economic theory. To fully appreciate Lucas's critique, we first consider a general theoretical argument and then turn to a particular example.

At each date t there is a vector s_t of state variables summarizing all aspects of the history that are relevant to the economy's future evolution; for example, the vector might include the economy's capital stock. The economy is also described by a vector x_t of government policy variables and a vector ε_t of random shocks – for example, shocks to technology or to government policy. For given specifications of the processes governing x_t and ε_t, it is common in macroeconomic theory to analyse models that yield an equilibrium law of motion in form of a difference equation,

$$s_{t+1} = f(s_t, x_t, \varepsilon_t). \tag{1}$$

(For many textbook examples of stochastic rational expectations models that yield such a recursive equilibrium representation; see Ljungqvist and Sargent, 2004.) Equation (1) is also the point of departure for the econometric policy evaluation procedures criticized by Lucas, who argued that their approach failed to recognize the optimization behaviour of economic agents that is implicit in eq. (1). Specifically, the criticized approach proceeds as follows. First, historical data are used to estimate the equation

$$s_{t+1} = F(\theta, s_t, x_t, \mu_t), \tag{2}$$

where F is specified in advance, θ is a fixed parameter vector to be estimated, and μ_t is a vector of random disturbances. Second, with the use of the estimated eq. (2), policy evaluations are performed by comparing economic outcomes for different paths of government policy variables $\{x_t\}$. The policy choice that produces the most desirable economic outcome is deemed to be the best policy. But, as argued by Lucas, this approach violates the premises for economic theory because the parameter vector θ depends partly on agents' decision rules that are not invariant to the conduct of government policy. That is, if the government changes its policy, the parameter θ will also change, so that the consequences of a new policy cannot be evaluated on the basis of the historical relationship in eq. (2).

Lucas's argument is best illustrated with an example. Consider the classic example of the so-called 'Phillips curve'. Phillips (1958) had estimated a negative relationship between wage inflation and unemployment using British data for the period 1861–1957. Samuelson and Solow (1960) and others interpreted this and related empirical findings as evidence of a structural trade-off between an economy's inflation rate and its unemployment rate. That is, the parameter θ in eq. (2), estimated with historical data, was considered to be fixed and to describe how unemployment would respond to inflation outcomes associated with different monetary policies. Friedman (1968) and Phelps (1968) argued against the existence of such an exploitable trade-off because it was inconsistent with economic theory based on rational agents. To understand the fallacy of the Phillips curve and its extension – the fallacy of the econometric policy evaluation procedures criticized by Lucas – consider the monetary model of Lucas (1972). Exchange in the economy takes place in physically separated markets.

Producers in a market base their output decisions on the local market-clearing price level without knowing the current economy-wide price level. The price in a market varies stochastically because there are exogenous random shocks both to the distribution of producers across markets and to the aggregate quantity of nominal money, none of which is directly observable to the agents. Hence, information on the current state of these real and monetary shocks is transmitted to agents only through the price in the market where each agent happens to be. In an equilibrium, producers in a market would like to increase their output in response to a high price driven by real but not nominal shocks. A high price due to a real shock means that the ratio of producers to consumers is low in that market and, therefore, profits on sales are high in real terms (when evaluated in terms of the economy-wide price level). But a high price in a market due to an expansion of the aggregate quantity of nominal money means that prices tend to be high in all markets and, therefore, profits on sales are high in nominal but not real terms. The inference and decision problems solved by the agents in this model are shown to give rise to a Phillips curve, as had been estimated with real-world data, but where the model's apparent trade-off between inflation and output cannot be systematically exploited by the government in its choice of monetary policy.

To further convey the insights from this general equilibrium model of the Phillips curve, we adopt a version of Lucas's (1976) simplified model that does not spell out all the details of the economic environment but instead postulates three equations that capture the forces at work in the fully articulated model. The economy-wide price level (in logs), p_t, is given by

$$p_t = \bar{p}_t + m_t, \qquad (3)$$

where $\bar{p}_t$ reflects a systematic component of monetary policy that is known to all agents, and m_t reflects an i.i.d. shock to monetary policy. It is assumed that the random variable m_t is normally distributed with mean zero and variance σ_m^2. The price (in logs) in market i at time t, p_{it}, is given by

$$p_{it} = p_t + z_{it}, \qquad (4)$$

where z_{it} is a deviation from the economy-wide price level because of shocks to the distribution of producers across markets. The real shock z_{it} is assumed to be a normal, i.i.d. random variable with mean zero and variance σ_z^2. Finally, let y_{it} denote the log-deviation of output from its 'natural rate' in market i at time t which varies with the perceived, relative price:

$$y_{it} = \alpha[p_{it} - E(p_t|I_{it})], \qquad (5)$$

where $\alpha > 0$ reflects intertemporal substitution possibilities in supply (determined by technological factors and tastes for substituting labour over time), and $E(\cdot|I_{it})$ denotes the mathematical expectation conditioned upon

information I_{it} available in market i at time t. The agents' prediction problem in eq. (5) is straightforward to solve (see, for example, Ljungqvist and Sargent, 2004, ch. 5):

$$E(p_t|I_{it}) = E(p_t|p_{it}, \bar{p}_t) = (1 - \Omega)p_{it} + \Omega\bar{p}_t, \qquad (6)$$

where $\Omega = \sigma_z^2/(\sigma_m^2 + \sigma_z^2)$. The substitution of eqs. (3), (4) and (6) into eq. (5) yields

$$y_{it} = \alpha\Omega(m_t + z_{it}). \qquad (7)$$

Thus, output in market i varies with the sum of nominal and real shocks, $(m_t + z_{it})$, because producers cannot perfectly disentangle these shocks but must make inferences based on the observed price p_{it}. Producers' willingness to vary output from its natural rate depends on how likely observed price variations are due to real rather than nominal shocks, as captured by the magnitude of $\Omega \in [0, 1]$. Under the assumption of a large number N of markets, the real shocks, $\{z_{it}\}$, cancel each other out when averaged over markets, and the economy's deviation from its natural rate of output, y_t, becomes

$$y_t = \frac{1}{N}\sum_{i=1}^{N} y_{it} = \alpha\Omega m_t = \alpha\Omega(p_t - \bar{p}_t), \qquad (8)$$

where the last equality invokes eq. (3) and, hence, the economy exhibits a positive relationship between unanticipated inflation and output.

If estimations were performed using data on output and inflation from the described economy, we would find a Phillips curve along which increases in inflation are associated with higher output realizations. However, any attempts by the government to exploit that relationship would fail. For example, a government that permanently increases the growth rate of the money supply to generate higher inflation in order to stimulate output will ultimately see no real effects from that change in policy. The reason for this is that, after agents have become aware of the higher underlying inflation rate in the economy, they will change their expectations when making predictions about relative price movements due to real disturbances. Formally, the change in monetary policy represents an increase in the component $\bar{p}_t$ and, when that systematic change becomes known to the agents, it will not affect unanticipated inflation, $(p_t - \bar{p}_t) = m_t$, so output is left unaffected in eq. (8).

This example illustrates Lucas's general criticism of econometric policy evaluation procedures that fail to recognize that the estimated eq. (2) depends partly on agents' decision rules and is therefore not invariant to changes in government policy. For a proper policy evaluation procedure, we need to revise the econometric formulation in eq. (2) so that it becomes consistent with equilibrium outcomes as represented by eq. (1).

Recall that the latter equation is derived for given specifications of the processes governing x_t and ε_t. In particular, to analyse agents' optimization behaviour, we need to specify the environment in which they live, including their perceptions about future government policy. As Lucas (1976, p. 40) remarked, 'one cannot meaningfully discuss optimal decisions of agents under arbitrary sequences $\{x_t\}$ of future shocks'. Instead, Lucas suggested that one proceeds by viewing government policy as a function of the state of the economy,

$$x_t = G(\lambda, s_t, \eta_t), \qquad (9)$$

where λ is a parameter vector that characterizes government policy, and η_t is a vector of random disturbances. Then the new version of eq. (2) becomes

$$s_{t+1} = F(\theta(\lambda), s_t, x_t, \mu_t), \qquad (10)$$

and the econometric problem is that of estimating the function $\theta(\lambda)$. A change in government policy is viewed as a change in the parameter λ affecting the behaviour of the system in two ways: first, by altering the time series behaviour of $\{x_t\}$, and second, by leading to modification of the parameter θ governing the rest of the system, which reflects changes in agents' decision rules in response to the new policy.

A constructive response to the Lucas critique has been the development of rational expectations econometrics. A goal of that approach has been to estimate the 'primitives' of dynamic rational expectations models, in the form of parameters describing tastes and technologies. If historical data can be used to obtain such estimates, the economic model can in principle be used to evaluate alternative government policies that could be without precedent, as explained by Lucas and Sargent (1981). That is, knowledge about the primitives of a model enables us to derive agents' decision rules and equilibrium outcomes for any specified policy process. In terms of eq. (10), this explains how the function $\theta(\lambda)$ could conceivably be estimated even if the historical data have been generated under a single government policy λ.

Though one of the key contributors to the methodology of rational expectations econometrics, Sargent (1984) has raised a philosophical conundrum with this approach to policy evaluation (as earlier discussed by Sargent and Wallace, 1976). Suppose that the primitives of an economic model have been estimated during an estimation period in which government policy was specified to be λ, and then the estimated model is used to compare alternative policies in order to find the best future policy λ^*. But such a procedure leads to an internal contradiction under the assumption of rational expectations, because, if the procedure were in fact likely to be persuasive in having the policy recommendation actually adopted soon, it would mean that the original

econometric model with it specified policy λ had been mis-specified. As pointed out by Sargent (1984, p. 413): 'A rational expectations model during the estimation period ought to reflect the procedure by which policy is thought later to be influenced, for agents are posited to be speculating about government decisions into the indefinite future.'

Given its fundamental impact on questions of economic policy both in practice and in theory, the Lucas critique figured prominently in the list of contributions when the Royal Swedish Academy of Sciences (1995) awarded Robert E. Lucas, Jr. the Nobel Prize in economics 'for having developed and applied the hypothesis of rational expectations, and thereby having transformed macroeconomic analysis and deepened our understanding of economic policy.'

LARS LJUNGQVIST

See also **Phillips curve; rational expectations.**

Bibliography

Friedman, M. 1968. The role of monetary policy. *American Economic Review* 58, 1–17.

Ljungqvist, L. and Sargent, T.J. 2004. *Recursive Macroeconomic Theory*, 2nd edn. Cambridge, MA: MIT Press.

Lucas, R.E., Jr. 1972. Expectations and the neutrality of money. *Journal of Economic Theory* 4, 103–24.

Lucas, R.E., Jr. 1976. Econometric policy evaluation: a critique. In *The Phillips Curve and the Labor Market*, ed. K. Brunner and A. Meltzer, Vol. 1 of Carnegie-Rochester Conference on Public Policy. Amsterdam, North-Holland.

Lucas, R.E., Jr. and Sargent, T.J. 1981. *Rational Expectations and Econometric Practice*. Minneapolis: University of Minnesota Press.

Phelps, E.S. 1968. Money wage dynamics and labor market equilibrium. *Journal of Political Economy* 76, 687–711.

Phillips, A.W. 1958. The relation between unemployment and the rate of change of money wage rates in the United Kingdom, 1861–1957. *Econometrica* 25, 283–99.

Royal Swedish Academy of Sciences 1995. The Sveriges Riksbank Prize in Economic Sciences in Memory of Alfred Nobel for 1995. Press release, 10 October. Online. Available at http://nobelprize.org/economics/laureates/1995/press.html, accessed 4 October 2006.

Samuelson, P.A. and Solow, R.M. 1960. Analytical aspects of anti-inflation policy. *American Economic Review* 50, 177–94.

Sargent, T.J. 1984. Autoregressions, expectations, and advice. *American Economic Review* 74, 408–15.

Sargent, T.J. and Wallace, N. 1976. Rational expectations and the theory of economic policy. *Journal of Monetary Economics* 2, 169–83.

lump sum taxes

A lump sum tax is fixed in amount and of such a nature that no action by the victim (short of emigration or suicide) can alter his or her liability. An example would be a poll tax, perhaps differentiated on the basis of sex and age.

It is difficult to find other examples. Differentiation on the basis of ability, wealth, income or expenditure would clearly lead to taxes that were not lump sum. Ability can be disguised. Wealth can be consumed. Leisure can be substituted for income, and saving for spending. All such actions would reduce tax. This implies that the principal criteria one might like to use as a basis for redistributive taxation are ruled out if one is confined to lump sum taxes. It also implies that it may be difficult to relate lump sum taxes to ability to pay. A feature of lump sum taxation is that what taxpayers bear is exactly balanced (in monetary terms) by what the fisc gains. That is because there is no tax at the margin. (If there were tax at the margin, taxpayers could vary their liabilities by varying their activities, and the tax would not be lump sum.) The absence of tax at the margin means that no transaction is killed off by the driving of a wedge between what one party pays and the other receives. When there is such a wedge (caused by a tax that is not lump sum) transactions are not entered into which, but for the tax, would have been mutually advantageous to the parties; and the loss to the parties is not balanced by any gain to the fisc. This is the 'excess burden' of taxation. It can never occur when taxes are lump sum.

In general equilibrium analysis the imposition of a set of lump sum taxes and bounties is equivalent to an adjustment of initial endowments. The attainment of equilibrium is not impaired, but its position will usually be altered. In welfare economics the conditions are investigated under which such an equilibrium may also represent a general optimum of production and exchange (in the sense of Pareto). If these conditions are met, it will not be possible to make one person better off without making someone else worse off. But the distribution of wealth may be very unequal: in an extreme case one person could end up with everything, the others with nothing. Lump sum taxes can, in theory, correct this situation without impairing the general optimum. In this sense, they are an ideal form of taxation.

Lump sum taxes are thus of some importance in theoretical work. But in the real world, poll taxes being their only viable form, they are rarely encountered precisely because they cannot in practice be matched to ability to pay or used to achieve a redistribution of income of wealth without ceasing to be lump sum. At most they are a benchmark against which the less than perfect taxes we normally encounter can be measured.

J. DE V. GRAAFF

See also **compensation principle; neutral taxation; optimal taxation.**

Lundberg, Erik Filip (1907–1987)

Lundberg was born in Stockholm and obtained a Ph.D. in economics in 1937 at the Stockholms Högskola. From 1937 to 1955 he was director of the Government Economic Research Institute (Konjunkturinstitutet), and from 1946 to 1965 he was professor of economics at the University of Stockholm; he held the same post at the Stockholm School of Economics from 1965 to 1970. He was president of the Royal Swedish Academy of Science from 1973 to 1976, and chairman of the Nobel Prize Committee for Economics from 1975 to 1980. He held numerous visiting professorships throughout the world.

Lundberg's main contributions to economic theory are his models of macroeconomic fluctuations and his analysis of the problems of economic policy, in particular the conflicts between stabilization policy and policies for the allocation of resources and the distribution of income.

His *Studies in The Theory of Economic Expansion* (1937) is an early work of high originality about the instability of growth, the main analytical technique being systems of difference equations of multiplier and accelerator mechanisms (with some consideration to the possibilities of flexible coefficients), embedded in a simple macroeconomic framework. Lags between inputs, output, income formation and spending play strategic roles (the lag between output and income-formation is often referred to as 'the Lundberg lag'). Rather than providing reduced-form solutions to the system, Lundberg presented numerical sequences of various macroeconomic variables and their relations, so-called 'sequence analysis'.

The part of the book which had the strongest immediate influence on other theorists is perhaps the inventory model. Non-anticipated increases in sales, while first resulting in a fall in inventories, later on, due to attempts by firms to restore the initial relation of inventory stocks to production levels, result in various kinds of inventory cycles. Lundberg's inventory analysis inspired, for instance, Lloyd Metzler's inventory model, as well as the inventory analysis, with more elaborate microeconomic underpinnings, by Holt and Modigliani.

Among Lundberg's contributions to the analysis of economic policy, *Business Cycles and Economic Policy* (1953 in Swedish; 1957 in English), stands out as a particularly important piece of work. The analysis is characterized by rather informal theorizing, though using concepts of traditional economic theory, both for the 'international' and the Swedish economy. Calculations of *ex ante* inflation and deflation gaps, by way of excess demand (supply) in the goods market and/or the labour market, are important instruments of analysis.

Lundberg was also a pioneer in analysing the role of taxation for 'cost inflation', a point formalized by an equation expressing how much nominal wage rates would have to rise to guarantee a one per cent increase in after-tax real wage rates, after considering both the marginal tax rates and the price effects of wage increases (the Lundberg wage-multiplier).

When analysing long-term growth problems, Lundberg also discovered the so-called 'Horndal effect', expressing how labour productivity can go on rising over long periods of time without new investment, hence providing an indication of disembodied productivity growth (1961). Lundberg also made interesting comparative studies of growth, fluctuations and economic policy in various countries, for instance in *Instability and Economic Growth* (1968).

He also participated frequently in Swedish economic policy discussion, emphasizing the importance of avoiding overvalued exchange rates. His own policy recommendations, in addition, built on combining *general*, market-orientated stabilization policies with rather selective social policies to achieve economic security and desired income redistributions.

ASSAR LINDBECK

Selected works

1930. Om ekonomisk jämvikt. *Ekonomisk Tidskrift* 32(4), 133–60.

1937. *Studies in the Theory of Economic Expansion*. London: P.S. King & Sons. Oxford: Blackwell, 1955.

1953. *Konjunkturer och Ekonomisk Politik*. Stockholm: SNS. English edn, *Business Cycles and Economic Policy*, London: Allen & Unwin, 1957.

1959. The profitability of investment. *Economic Journal* 69, 653–77.

1961. *Produktivitet och räntabilitet*. Stockholm: SNS.

1968. *Instability and Economic Growth*. New Haven: Yale University Press.

1972. Productivity and structural change – a policy issue in Sweden. *Economic Journal* 82, March, Supplement, 465–85.

1985. The rise and fall of the Swedish model. *Journal of Economic Literature* 23, 1–36.

Lyapunov functions

Within twelve years, from Poincaré's *Mémoire sur les courbes définies par une équation différentielle* (1881–6) to Lyapunov's thesis *Obshčaya zadača ob unstoičivosti dviženiya* (1892), the qualitative theory of differential equations emerged almot from scratch as the core of a new field in mathematics; both Poincaré and Lyapunov were motivated by problems in mechanics, celestial mechanics above all. Even if he did not match Poincaré's prodigious creativity between 1880 and 1883, Lyapunov developed from 1888 to 1892 a theory of dynamical stability which makes his 1892 thesis both a pioneering piece of work and a classic; in particular he developed a general stability criterion which now bears his name: the Lyapunov function.

Consider a system of ordinary differential equations

$$\dot{x} = f(x, t)$$

where x is a vector in R^n and depends on t (t is in general interpreted as time), where $\dot{x} = dx/dt$ is the derivative of x with respect to t and where f is a function from R^{n+1} to R^n. A trajectory of the system is a function x from an interval T in R to R^n

$$x : T \to R^n : t \to x(t)$$
$$\dot{x}(t) \equiv f(x(t), t)$$

which is a solution of the system, i.e. such that $\dot{x}(t)$ and $f[x(t), t]$ are identical on T; T is often of the form $[t_0, +\infty]$.

In what follows we shall limit ourselves to autonomous systems, i.e. systems of the form $\dot{x} = f(x)$, where f is dependent on t only through x. However, our whole presentation is easily generalized to non-autonomous systems, as is done in Rouche et al. (1977) and Rouche and Mawhin (1980).

It would appear at first sight that the system $\dot{x} = f(x)$ suffers from another restriction: it is a first-order system, in the sense that its equations include first-order derivatives only. This might be seen a serious restriction indeed; think for example of the system formalizing the dynamics of the simple frictionless pendulum

$$\ddot{x}_1 + \sin x_1 = 0$$

where x_1 is the angular distance from the vertical line. However, it is always possible to transform a system including derivatives of order higher than one into a first-order system with a higher number of equations. For example, the former system consisting of one second-order equation is equivalent to the following system of two first-order equations:

$$\dot{x}_1 = x_2$$
$$\dot{x}_2 = -\sin x_1$$

To investigate the stability properties of the pendulum, it is thus immediately possible to make use of the general concepts and methods available for first-order systems.

In order to introduce these concepts and methods in the spirit of Lyapunov, and then to see how they operate in economic models, we first have to be slightly more precise in defining an autonomous differential system as a system of first-order differential equations

$$(DS) \qquad \dot{x} = f(x)$$

where f is a continuous Lipschitzian function from an open subset Ω of R^n to R^n, i.e.

$$f : \Omega \to R^n : x \to f(x).$$

'Lipschitzian' means that there exists a constant α such that

$$\forall x^1, \quad x^2 \in \Omega, \quad \|f(x^1) - f(x^2)\| \leq \alpha \|x^1 - x^2\|;$$

this assumption is very convenient because it ensures (see Coddington and Levinson, 1955) that through any point in Ω there passes one and only one trajectory of (DS); hence trajectories do not cross. However this assumption is not strictly necessary for what follows (see Aubin and Cellina, 1984 and Rouche et al. 1977).

We may now introduce the basic concepts of stability and attractivity for equilibria of dynamic systems. A point x^e in Ω is an equilibrium of (DS) if $f(x^e)=0$; in other words, x^e is an equilibrium if for any t_0 in R the function

$$x : [t_0, +\infty| \to R^n : t \to x^e$$

is a trajectory.

Stability: an equilibrium x^e is stable if a trajectory which comes sufficiently close to x^e never after recedes too far from x^e.

More precisely an equilibrium x^e is stable if, for any neighbourhood B_δ of x^e included in Ω, there exists a neighbourhood $B_\eta \subset B_\varepsilon$ such that any trajectory passing through B_η remains in B_ε ever after (see Figure 1).

Local attractivity: an equilibrium x^e is a local attractor if a trajectory which comes sufficiently close to x^e later on tends to x^e.

More precisely an equilibrium x^e is a local attractor if there exists a neighbourhood B_δ of x^e included in Ω such that any trajectory which passes through B_δ tends to x^e as $t \to +\infty$; this does not mean that the trajectory always remains in B_δ (see Figure 2).

An equilibrium may be stable without being a local attractor, as in the case of the frictionless pendulum. It is also true that an equilibrium may be a local attractor, without being stable, but this is much more difficult to illustrate (see section 40 in Hahn, 1967). An equilibrium which is both stable and a local attractor is often called asymptotically stable.

Global attractivity: given a subset Ω_s of Ω, an equilibrium x^e in Ω_s is a global attractor with respect to Ω_s if any trajectory which passes through Ω_s tends to x^e as $t \to +\infty$.

An equilibrium which is both stable and a global attractor with respect to some Ω_s is often called globally asymptotically stable (globally with respect to Ω_s).

The convenient way, often the sole way, to deal with stability and attractivity as defined above, is in general to find a suitable Lyapunov function.

Lyapunov function: consider a subset Δ of Ω and a function of class C^1 (i.e. continuous and having continuous first-order partial derivatives)

$$W : \Delta \to R : x \to W(x).$$

W is a Lyapunov function if it satisfies the following requirements:

(i)   it is bounded below on Δ, i.e.

$$\exists a \in R \text{ such that,} \quad \forall x \in \Delta, \quad W(x) \geq a.$$

(ii)   it tends to infinity as x does, i.e.

$$\text{if } \|x\| \to +\infty, \quad \text{then} \quad W(x) \to +\infty.$$

(iii)   its time derivative $\dot{W}(x)$ is nonpositive on Δ, i.e.

$$\forall x \in \Delta, \quad \dot{W}(x) \leq 0$$

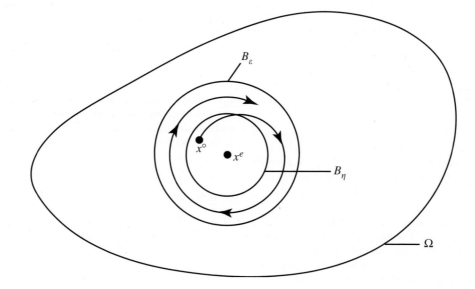

Figure 1

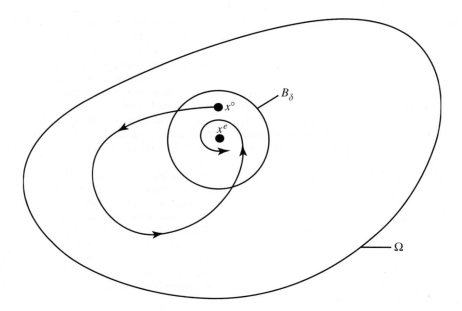

Figure 2

where the time derivative is defined as

$$\dot{W} : \Delta \to R : x \to \dot{W}(x) = \sum_{k-1}^{x} \frac{\partial W(x)}{\partial x_k} f_h(x).$$

The name 'time derivative' is warranted as

$$\dot{W}[x(t)] = \sum_{k-1}^{x} \frac{\partial W[x(t)]}{\partial x_k} \dot{x}_k(t) = \frac{\mathrm{d}W[x(t)]}{\mathrm{d}t}$$

along any trajectory in Δ.

It is possible for $n=2$ to draw level curves of W in the subset Δ of the plane (x_1, x_2). On Figure 3 two level curves are drawn, with $k' < k''$, as well as a trajectory. W is non-increasing along any trajectory in Δ; hence, as soon as a trajectory reaches a level curve, say k', it never again comes back to points on level curves k with $k > k'$, for example $k=k''$. This suggests deriving properties of stability and attractivity from the existence of a Lyapunov function; we indeed have:

Proposition 1: if there exists on some neighbourhood B of the equilibrium x^e a Lyapunov function W and if x^e is an isolated minimum of W on B, then x^e is a stable equilibrium. If moreover x^e is the only point in B where $\dot{W} = 0$, then x^e is also a local attractor.

These are sufficient conditions for stability and local attractivity. It turns out that the existence of a Lyapunov function is also a necessary condition (for a general exposition and complete proofs which are valid even for nonautonomous systems, see Rouche et al. (1977) and Rouche and Mawhin (1980)).

The first part of Proposition 1, but not the second part, applies to the frictionless pendulum, the Lyapunov function being here the total energy $\frac{1}{2}x_2^2 - \cos x_1 + 1$. Both parts of Proposition 1 apply to the tâtonnement process in a competitive economy where all goods are gross substitutes for all prices. Let n be the number of goods; let p be the price vector normalized in such a way that it is in the $n - 1$ dimensional unit simplex $\bar{\Sigma}$ defined by $\Sigma_{j=1}^{n} p_j = 1$; and let $z_j(p)$ be the aggregate excess demand function for good j. Let Σ be the interior of $\bar{\Sigma}$. Gross substitutability implies that there exists one and only one general competitive equilibrium price vector p^e and that p^e is in Σ, i.e. p_j^e is strictly positive for all goods j (for more details see Arrow and Hahn, 1971).

Consider then the well-known tâtonnement process

(TP) $\dot{p} = z(p).$

It is a (DS) system, with $\Omega=\Sigma$; being the unique general competitive equilibrium price vector, p^e is also the unique equilibrium of the differential system (TP). Consider on Σ the function

$$W(p) = \|p - p^e\|^2.$$

Its time derivative is

$$\dot{W}(p) = \sum_{j-1}^{x} \frac{\partial W(p)}{\partial p_j} z_j(p)$$

$$= 2 \sum_{j-1}^{x} (p_j - p_j^e) z_j(p) = -2p^e \cdot z(p),$$

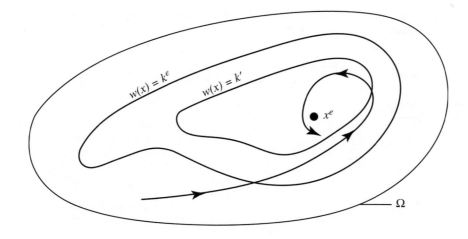

Figure 3

because of Walras's law. On the other hand, it is a consequence of gross substitutability that

$$\forall p \neq p^e, \quad p^e \cdot z(p) > 0.$$

It is thus clear that W is a Lyapunov function, that p^e is its unique minimum on Σ and that $\dot{W}$ is zero only at p^e; hence p^e is stable and is a local attractor for the tâtonnement process. Is it a global attractor with respect to Σ? The answer is not within the range of proposition 1. Something more is needed.

Proposition 2: consider a system (DS) and a bounded subset Δ of Ω which is such that there exists a Lyapunov function W

$$W : \Delta \to R : x \to W(x)$$

satisfying the additional requirement that $\dot{W}$ is zero only at equilibria of the system, i.e.

$$\dot{W}(x) = 0 \Rightarrow f(x) = 0.$$

Then, if all the limit points of a trajectory are in Δ, they are equilibria of the system; if moreover all the equilibria of the system are isolated, this trajectory tends to one of them as $t \to +\infty$.

Corollary: if the system has a unique equilibrium, if Δ is open and if any trajectory which passes through Δ has all its limit points in Δ, then the equilibrium is a global attractor with respect to Δ and it is stable.

This corollary has no general counterpart when there are several isolated equilibria, because a trajectory starting in the neighbourhood of one equilibrium may tend to another one. However, if an equilibrium is an isolated minimum of W, proposition 1 ensures that it is stable and is a local attractor.

Proposition 2 and its corollary allow us to answer the question, left unanswered above, about the tâtonnement process: as Σ is bounded and as gross substitutability prevents any trajectory from having a limit point on the boundary of Σ, all conditions in proposition 2 and in the corollary are met; so p^e is a global attractor with respect to Σ.

Another well-known application of Lyapunov functions is in the theory of public goods. Consider an economy with N consumers ($i=1,\ldots, N$), m public goods ($k=1,\ldots, m$) and one private good used as numeraire. Let $x \in R_+^m$ denote the bundle of public goods made available to the consumers, and let y^i denote the amount of numeraire consumed by $i=1,\ldots, N$; this means that $(x, y^i) \in R_+^{m+1}$ describe the total consumption of i. His preferences are formalized by a utility function

$$u^i : R_+^{m+1} \to R : (x, y^i) \to u^i(x, y^i);$$

this function is of class C^1, quasi-concave, nondecreasing with respect to each of its arguments, and is strictly increasing with respect to the consumption of the numeraire, i.e.

$$\frac{\partial u^i}{\partial y^i} > 0 \text{ on } R_+^{m+1}.$$

Let Z be the set of feasible allocations, i.e. the set of all $z = (x, y^1, \ldots, y^N)$ in R_+^{m+N} which can be made available for consumption, given the technical possibilities and the initial resources of the economy. Z is of course bounded; it is reasonable to consider that it is closed and convex; hence it is a compact convex subset of R_+^{m+N}.

How to reach a Pareto-optimal feasible allocation? The MDP (for Malinvaud–Drèze–Poussin, see Champsaur et al., 1977) planning procedure gives the following answer: starting from any feasible allocation, revise z

continuously according to the following differential system, which is a (DS) system:

$$(\text{MDP}) \quad \frac{dx_k}{dt} = \sum_{i=1}^{N} \pi_k^i(z) - \gamma_k(z), k = 1, \ldots, m$$

$$\frac{dy^i}{dt} = -\sum_{k=1}^{m} \pi_k^i(z) \frac{dx_k}{dt}$$

$$+ \delta^i \sum_{k=1}^{m} \frac{dx_k}{dt} \left[\sum_{j=1}^{N} \pi_k^j(z) - \gamma_k(z) \right],$$

$$i = 1, \ldots, N$$

where $\pi_k^i(z)$ is the marginal willingness to pay of consumer i for public good k, and $\gamma_k(z)$ is the marginal cost of public good k. The $\delta_i, i = 1, \ldots, N$, are non-negative weights summing up to 1: $\sum_{i=1}^{N} \delta^i = 1$. These differential equations mean that the quantity made available of each public good is revised according to the difference between the total marginal willingness to pay for that public good and its marginal cost; simultaneously every consumer pays an amount of numéraire equal to his willingness to pay for this set of revisions, and receives a fraction of the total surplus that the revisions generate.

Consider the function

$$W : Z \to R : z \to W(z) = -u^i(x, y^i)$$

where i is chosen among those i for which $\delta^i > 0$. Straightforward calculations lead to

$$\dot{W}(z) = -\delta^i \sum_{k-1}^{m} [\pi_k^i(z) - \gamma_k(z)]^2 \frac{\partial u^i}{\partial y^i},$$

which is nonpositive everywhere on Z and is zero if and only if z is an equilibrium of (MDP). W is a Lyapunov function and Proposition 2 applies with $\Delta = Z$. As Z is compact it is even possible to conclude that any limit point of any trajectory which is included in Z is an equilibrium of (MDP). If all the utility functions u^i, $i = 1, \ldots, N$, are strictly quasi-concave, the result is sharpened in the sense that any trajectory which is included in Z tends to an equilibrium as $t \to +\infty$. The economic significance of these results proceeds from the fact that all the equilibria of (MDP) are Pareto optima.

However, it is not guaranteed that all trajectories of (MDP) starting in Z are included in Z, as the revisions generated by the equations

$$\frac{dx_k}{dt} = \sum_{i=1}^{N} \pi_k^i(z) - \gamma_k(z), k = 1, \ldots, m$$

may lead to negative values of the public goods. We would then have a meaningless procedure. In order to avoid this possibility the above equations must be replaced in (MDP) by:

$$\frac{dx_k}{dt} = \begin{cases} \sum_{i=1}^{N} \pi_k^i(z) - \gamma_k(z) & \text{for } x_k > 0 \\ \max \left[\sum_{i=1}^{N} \pi_k^i(z) - \gamma_k(z), 0 \right] & \text{for } x_k = 0. \end{cases}$$

It is then immediate that any trajectory of (MDP) starting in Z is included in Z. But do trajectories still exist? and if they exist, do they actually tend to equilibria of (MDP)? The answers are not trivial, as there are significant discontinuities in the right-hand sides of the new equations. These answers nevertheless turn out to be positive; this is a by-product of the extension of existence and stability theorems to multivalued dynamical systems

$$\frac{dz}{dt} \in F(z)$$

where F is an upper hemicontinuous correspondence such that the image $F(z)$, of any point z in an open subset Ω of R^n, is a compact convex subset of R^n. For such systems, Lyapunov functions have been defined with the same purposes as for ordinary systems (see Champsaur et al., 1977; Aubin and Cellina, 1984).

Lyapunov functions are used in many other economic models, to prove the convergence of non-tâtonnement processes for example (see Arrow and Hahn, 1971) or to investigate the stability properties of a process of free entry and exit of firms, facing random demand and guided by expected profits (see Drèze and Sheshinski, 1984). Of particular interest is the use of a Lyapunov function of the form $(Q - Q^e) \cdot (k - k^e)$, where k is the vector of capital stocks in the economy and Q is the vector of current prices for investment goods, to show that any optimal growth path tends to the (suitably modified) golden rule capital stock k^* when the discount rate is not too large (see Brock and Scheinkman, 1976; Cass and Shell, 1976).

Till now we have dealt only with dynamical stability, i.e. with questions typically like the following one: two trajectories happen to pass through two neighbouring points; does it imply that they will ever after remain close to each other? Around 1970, G. Debreu and S. Smale introduced structural stability into economic theory, i.e. stability with respect to parameters of the system; a typical question is here: is the configuration of competitive equilibria of an economy (for example the fact that they are isolated) stable when the initial endowments of the agents in the economy change? Almost a century before, Poincaré introduced and systematically explored the concept of bifurcation in mathematics (see Poincaré, 1881); the word came to him as a natural comparison with daily experience:

On voit que les deux catégories d'ellipsoïdes forment deux séries continues de figures d'équilibre. Mais il y a une figure qui est commune aux deux séries et qui est, si l'on veut me permettre cette comparaison, un point de bifurcation. (Poincaré, 1892, p. 810)

Bifurcation is a basic concept for the study of structural stability; even if the latter expression was to come much later, the essence of the approach is in Poincaré's works.

In the introduction (Poincaré, 1882), Poincaré refers to 'les recherches ultérieures parmi lesquelles les plus importantes sont, sans contredit, celles de M. Liapounoff'. It seems indeed that no other mathematician of the time saw better than Lyapunov did the significance of Poincaré's new concepts and methods. In the three volumes (Lyapunov, 1906–1912), Lyapunov explored in great detail the bifurcation of the equilibrium configurations of a rotating homogeneous mass of liquid. The ultimate goal was to explain the evolution of stars. As long as the angular velocity Ω of the rotating mass is less than or equal to a critical value ω^c, there is one and only one equilibrium configuration for each velocity ω, and it is an ellipsoid. But at ω^c a bifurcation appears: at ω^c the equilibrium configuration is still unique and is an ellipsoid but, in Lyapunov's own words, 'C'est l'ellipsoïde, par lequel on entre dans la série des figures d'équilibre que M. Poincaré a appelé pyriformes' (Lyapunov, 1906–1912, vol. 3, p. 6). It is indeed shown (Lyapunov, 1906–1912, vol. 1, pp. 216–17 and vol. 3, p. 106) that there exists an interval $[\omega^c, \bar{\omega}]$ such that, for every ω in this interval there are two equilibrium configurations: the usual ellipsoid and a pear-shaped configuration, whose symmetry and stability properties were systematically investigated by Lyapunov. This is a study in structural stability, the last one to appear before 1937, at which time Andronov and Pontrjagin (1937) picked up the subject, which has been exploding since then.

It has recently been shown that in (strictly deterministic) economic growth models, bifurcation phenomena can take place which are strikingly similar to those explored by Lyapunov: ω is replaced by the discount rate r, the ellipsoids by steady states and the pear-shaped configurations by closed cycles that bifurcate from the steady state for some value r_0 of r (see Benhabib and Nishimura, 1979). Bifurcations even appear in stationary competitive monetary economies: at critical values of some parameters of the economy – for example the degree of concavity of utility functions – a stationary equilibrium bifurcates towards a line (a 'série', in Poincaré's words) of stationary equilibria on one hand, and a simultaneous line of closed cycles; the latter are the business cycles of the model, and their stability under suitable assumptions has been shown using Poincaré–Lyapunov methods (see Grandmont, 1985).

Economists tend to know Lyapunov for his celebrated functions, it appears that there is even more to interest them in the various approaches to stability that Lyapunov has developed during his lifelong study of dynamical systems.

C. HENRY

See also **correspondence principle; gross substitutes.**

Bibliography

Andronov, A.A. and Pontrjagin, L.S. 1937. Systèmes grossiers. *Doklady Akademii Nauk* 14, 247–51.

Arrow, K. and Hahn, F. 1971. *General Competitive Analysis*. San Francisco: Holden-Day.

Aubin, J.P. and Cellina, A. 1984. *Differential Inclusions*. Berlin: Springer.

Benhabib, J. and Nishimura, K. 1979. The Hopf bifurcation and the existence and stability of closed orbits in multisector models of optimal economic growth. *Journal of Economic Theory* 21, 421–44.

Brock, W.A. and Scheinkman, J.A. 1976. Global asymptotic stability of optimal control systems with applications to the theory of economic growth. *Journal of Economic Theory* 12, 164–90.

Cass, D. and Shell, K. 1976. The structure and stability of competitive dynamical systems. *Journal of Economic Theory* 12, 31–70.

Champsaur, P., Drèze, J. and Henry, C. 1977. Stability theorems with economic applications. *Econometrica* 45, 273–94.

Coddington, E.A. and Levinson, N. 1955. *Theory of Ordinary Differential Equations*. New York: McGraw-Hill.

Drèze, J.H. and Sheshinski, E. 1984. On industry equilibrium under uncertainty. *Journal of Economic Theory* 33, 88–97.

Grandmont, J.M. 1985. On endogenous competitive business cycles. *Econometrica* 53, 995–1045.

Hahn, W. 1967. *Stability of Motion*. Berlin: Springer.

Lyapunov, A. 1892. Obshčaya zadača ob ustoičivosti dviženiya (The general problem of the stability of motion). *Soc. Math. Kharkov*. The 1907 French translation has been reproduced in *Annals of Mathematics Studies* 17, Princeton: Princeton University Press, 1949.

Lyapunov, A. 1906–12. *Sur les figures d'équilibre peu différentes des ellipsoïdes d'une masse liquide homogène douée d'un mouvement de rotation*. 3 vols, Académie impériale des Sciences, St. Petersburg.

Poincaré, H. 1881. Mémoire sur les courbes définies par une équation différentielle. *Journal de Mathématiques Pures et Appliquées* 7(3), 1881, 375–422; 8(3), 1882, 251–96; 1(4), 1885, 167–244; 2(4), 1886, 151–217.

Poincaré, H. 1882. Les formes d'équilibre d'une masse fluide en rotation. *Revue Générale des Sciences* 3, 809–15.

Rouche, N., Habets, P. and Laloy, M. 1977. *Stability Theory by Lyapunov's Direct Method*. Applied Mathematical Sciences No. 22, Berlin: Springer.

Rouche, N. and Mawhin, J. 1980. *Ordinary Differential, Equations: Stability and Periodic Solutions*. Surveys and Reference Works in Mathematics, London: Pitman.

M

machinery question

That machinery is of benefit to the manufacturer who introduces it has never been a point of discussion in the history of economics and the machinery question is solely a dispute over whether society benefits from the introduction of machinery, the most pressing social issue being the displacement of labour by machinery and the consequent threat of widespread unemployment. In general terms, the social benefits of machinery were well appreciated by the middle of the 18th century. However, the greatly increased use of machinery at the end of the 18th century gave a new intensity to the debate at the beginning of the 19th century. The analytical tools used by classical economists to tackle this general equilibrium problem were however quite inadequate and it is doubtful whether a deeper understanding of the issue was achieved by the heroic abstractions of the 19th century.

The earliest explicit discussions of machinery appear to be in the pamphlets of John Cary (1695), *A Discourse on Trade*. It was a time when the competitiveness of English industry was being much discussed and John Cary pointed out that England retained her business advantage because of the ability of English manufacturers to invent.

> Tobacco is cut by Engines: Books are printed; Deal Boards are sawn with Mills; Lead is smelted by Wind-Furnaces; all which save the Labour of many Hands, so the Wages of those employed need not be fallen. ...
>
> New Projections are every Day set on Foot to render the making our Woollen Manufactures easy, which should be rendered cheaper by the Contrivance of the Manufacturers, not by falling the Price of Labour: Cheapness creates Expence, and gives fresh Employments, whereby the Poor will be still kept at Work. (Cary, 1695, pp. 99–100)

A few years later, in his *Considerations of the East-India Trade* (1701), Henry Martin advocated the import of cheaper cloth from the East Indies by comparing it with the effects of machinery:

> Arts, and Mills, and Engines, which save the labour of Hands, are ways of doing things with less labour, and consequently with labour of less price, tho' the Wages of Men imploy'd to do them shou'd not be abated. The *East-India* Trade procures things with less and cheaper labour than would be necessary to make the like in *England*; it is therefore very likely to be the cause of the invention of Arts, and Mills, and Engines, to save the labour of Hands in other Manufactures. Such things are successively invented to do a great deal of work with little labour of Hands; they are the effects of Necessity and Emulation; every Man must be still inventing himself, or be still advancing to farther perfection upon

the invention of other Men ... (Martin, 1701, pp. 589–90)

At this stage the effect of machinery in preserving competitiveness receives primary emphasis. There is as yet no link drawn between high wages and the incentive to create machinery. In the years that followed only the prolific Daniel Defoe paid serious attention to the role of machinery without making any substantive analytical contribution. Indeed, Defoe even wondered whether machinery were not sometimes an evil because it displaced labour. In parliamentary debates in 1738 on the making of buttons by loom instead of by hand, Henry Archer implicitly subscribed to the full employment and sustainability thesis in a speech of considerable eloquence:

> As to the honourable gentleman's other arguments, drawn from the number of hands employed in the needle-work manufacture ... it is, in my humble opinion, a very good argument for dismissing this Bill; because, as the manufacture may be carried on by a much fewer number of hands, with equal advantage to our trade in general, those who are employed in the needle-work way, are so many hands taken from other arts and other manufactures, in which they might be employed to much better purpose.

Archer goes on to use an example that was repeated often by classical economists:

> There was a time, Sir, when all the learning of this kingdom, and the rest of Europe, was contained in manuscripts, the writing of which employed great numbers of hands, and took up a vast deal of time in re-copying. But, Sir, how ridiculous would it have been, if on the discovery of the art of printing, the transcribers and copers of those manuscripts had joined in a petition to the legislature, that it would be pleased to prohibit the art of printing, for the same reason which the honourable gentleman now uses, because great numbers would thereby be deprived of bread! (Archer, 1742)

The next advance was stimulated by Montesquieu's claim in *The Spirit of the Laws* that the introduction of machinery was not necessarily beneficial. This provoked Josiah Tucker to provide one of the best statements on the effects of machinery:

> What is the Consequence of this Abridgment of Labour, both regarding the Price of the Goods, and the Number of Persons employed? The Answer is very short and full, *viz.* That the Price of Goods is thereby prodigiously lowered from what otherwise it must have been; and that a much greater Number of Hands are employed....
>
> And the first Step is, that Cheapness, *ceteris paribus* is an Inducement to buy, – and that many Buyers cause a great Demand, – and that a great Demand brings on a great Consumption; – which great Consumption must necessarily employ a vast Variety of Hands, whether the

original Material is considered, or the Number and Repair of Machines, or the Materials out of which those Machines are made, or the Persons necessarily employed in tending upon and conducting them: Not to mention those Branches of the Manufacture, Package, Porterage, Stationary Articles, and Book-keeping, &c. &c. which must inevitably be performed by human Labour....

That System of Machines, which so greatly reduces the Price of Labour, as to enable the Generality of a People to become Purchasers of the Goods, will in the End, though not immediately, employ more Hands in the Manufacture, than could possibly have found Employment, had no such machines been invented. And every manufacturing Place, when duly considered, is an Evidence in this Point. (Tucker, 1757, pp. 241–2)

The subject received little further impetus in the half-century that followed. The tangential discussion of machinery by Adam Smith in the *Wealth of Nations* perhaps contributed to this state of affairs. The only notable treatment is in the lectures of Dugald Stewart at Edinburgh (1858–78), which were very influential as part of an oral tradition, but which were not available in print till the 1860s. Stewart's contribution lay in seeing the machinery question as part of a much larger and more fundamental policy issue – the trade-off between individual losses and social gains. He therefore links together three issues that had hitherto been separately discussed – the creation of large farms, the benefits of enclosures and the use of machinery. In each case Stewart grants that the hardships imposed on individuals were undeniable. He then continues;

In judging of the policy of such innovations … it is absolutely necessary to abstract from the individual hardships that may fall under our notice, and to fix our attention on those general principles which influence the national prosperity. (Stewart, 1856, vol. 8, p. 131)

In deciding upon the benefits of introducing machinery, Stewart observes that the material improvement of mankind and the use of machinery are practically inseparable. The policy recommendation was thus unequivocal.

It is hardly possible to introduce suddenly the smallest innovation into the Political Economy of a State, let it be ever so reasonable, nay, ever so profitable, without incurring some inconveniences. But temporary inconveniences furnish no objection to solid improvements. Those which may arise from the sudden introduction of a machine cannot possibly be of long continuance. The workmen will, in all probability, be soon able to turn their industry into some other channel; and they are certainly entitled to every assistance the public can give them, when they are thus forced to change their professional habits. (1856, vol. 8, p. 193)

The severe post-Napoleonic depression contributed greatly to a reconsideration of the effects of machinery and John Barton should perhaps be given most credit for

the new interest with his pamphlet, *Observations on the Circumstances which Influence the Condition of the Labouring Classes of Society* (1817). Commenting on the distinction, inherited from Adam Smith, between circulating and fixed capital, Barton pointed out that only the former serves to employ labour – the latter is embodied in machinery. Since it appeared empirically undeniable that progress involved a greater proportionate use of fixed capital Barton argued that the funds for employing labour, or circulating capital, must be subject to proportionate decrease and lead to greater unemployment. Barton was very clear about the role of high wages in inducing the adoption of machinery.

It is the proportion which the wages of labour at any particular time bear to the whole produce of that labour, which appears to me to determine the appropriation of capital in one way or the other. For if at any time the rate of wages should decline, while the price of goods remained the same, or if goods should rise, while wages remained the same, the profit of the employer would increase, and he would be induced to hire more hands. If, on the other hand, wages should rise, in proportion to commodities, the labour's share in the produce of his own industry would be increased at the expense of his master, who would of course keep as few hands as possible. – He would aim at performing every thing by machinery, rather than by manual labour. (Barton, 1817, pp. 17–18)

How far David Ricardo was directly influenced by Barton in reversing his initial optimistic position on the benefits of machinery is unclear, but in the third edition of his *Principles of Political Economy and Taxation* (1821, pp. 388–95) Ricardo tried to justify some of the pessimistic attitudes to machinery by means of a numerical example. To begin with, we have a farmer whose yearly activities can be summarized as follows:

Fixed Capital	7,000
Wages (Circulating)	13,000

	20,000
Profits (10 per cent)	2,000 (used for consumption)

Total	22,000

The circulating capital is said to 'replace the value of 15,000', that is, to provide the required profit of 2,000. In year 1, the capitalist sets half his workers to construct machines. As surplus value arises from circulating capital, the profits of 2,000 arises in equal parts from the workers in farming and the workers in machines:

Fixed Capital (Old)	7,000
Wages (Farming)	6,500
Profits (Farming)	1,000

Wages (Machines)	6,500 (Embodied in machines)
Profits (Machines)	1,000
	- - - - - -
Total	22,000
	- - - - - -

If the farmer still spends 2,000 for his own consumption, he is left with 5,500 to spend on wages the next year. In other words, the wage bill falls from 13,000 to 5,500 because of the construction of machines. The gross produce consists of profits, rent and wages, while the net produce consists of profits and rent only. In our case, there is no rent, so the gross produce falls from 15,000 to 7,500 while the net produce stays at 2,000. Ricardo concludes as follows:

> In this case, then, although the net produce will not be diminished in value, although its power of purchasing commodities may be greatly increased, the gross produce will have fallen from a value of 15,000 *l* to a value of 7,500 *l*, and as the power of supporting a population, and employing labour, depends always on the gross produce of a nation, and not on its net produce, there will necessarily be a diminution in the demand for labour, population will become redundant, and the situation of the labouring classes will be that of distress and poverty.

Subsequently, Ricardo concedes that more workers can be employed in producing goods that the capitalist may wish to consume with his increased real power of consumption, but this may not be strong enough to compensate for the initial loss of employment.

> All I wish to prove, is, that the discovery and use of machinery may be attended with a diminution of gross produce; and whenever that is the case, it will be injurious to the labouring class, as some of their number will be thrown out of employment, and population will become redundant, compared with the funds which are to employ it.

There are a number of curious features about Ricardo's analysis which, though based on a simple numerical example, is claimed to have some relevance. First, it is not at all clear whether Say's Law, which Ricardo adhered to so vehemently on other occasions, also operates when labour is displaced by machinery. Secondly, Ricardo simply presents the initial disruption of new machinery without saying anything about the nature of the new equilibrium or the adjustment process leading to it. This contrasts sharply with his usual emphasis upon permanent effects – indeed, in assuming that the new machines made will be able to realize 1,000 units of profit Ricardo is implicitly assuming some sort of pervasive equilibrium. Thirdly, Ricardo appears to deny the practical importance of his example at the end of the chapter when he emphasizes that his argument holds only when the new machinery is introduced suddenly.

The statements which I have made will not, I hope, lead to the inference that machinery should not be encouraged. To elucidate the principle, I have been supposing, that improved machinery is *suddenly* discovered, and extensively used; but the truth is, that these discoveries are gradual, and rather operate in determining the employment of the capital which is saved and accumulated, than in diverting capital from its actual employment.

This point gains additional force from Ricardo's insistence that the state take no action to discourage technological progress. Most subsequent economists, from Malthus onwards, took exception to the collection of assumptions necessary to produce Ricardo's result.

Of the classical economists who followed, only Nassau Senior and John Stuart Mill tried to justify Ricardo's reasoning, sometimes with the same surprising pattern of argument that characterized Ricardo. For example, John Stuart Mill (1848) begins by asserting that workers suffer temporarily when circulating capital is converted to fixed capital; almost immediately however he adds that this is a case which scarcely ever occurs in practice. An attempt by J.E. Tozer to provide a mathematical formulation of the question does not go beyond the framework set of by Ricardo. Tozer (1838) grants that there is an initial deduction from the wages fund but points out that the fund is replenished over time as the additional output from the machinery is produced. There does not appear to be a serious effort at going beyond Ricardo's analytical schema until the writings of Knut Wicksell.

With his usual clarity, Wicksell begins his section on production and distribution by setting forth the technical conditions necessary for the validity of the marginal productivity theory of distribution. He recognizes that the distributive impact of machinery depends upon the manner in which machinery alters the marginal productivities of labour and capital and that simple answers to such a question are unlikely. One issue which he analyses with considerable acumen is the position of Ricardo that machinery may actually diminish the gross product. Wicksell takes issue with Ricardo's conclusion and claims that Ricardo did not follow his premises to their logical conclusion – under free competition, changes in technique cannot lead to a diminution of gross product. This is proved as follows:

> Let x and y denote the number of labourers per acre using the old and new methods of cultivation, and let $f(x)$ and $\phi(y)$ denote the production functions of these lands. If m acres are cultivated by the old method and n acres by the new method, then the problem of maximizing total product is

> Maximize

> $$mf(x) + n\phi(y)$$

subject to

$$m + n = B$$
$$mx + ny = A$$

where B is the total number of acres and A is the total amount of labour available. The first order conditions for a maximum are,

$$f'(x) = \phi'(y) \text{ and } f(x) - xf'(x) = \phi(y) - y\phi'(y)$$

where the prime denotes differentiation. The first condition states that total product is maximized when the marginal product of labour is equal, under both methods and the second condition states the equality of rents per acre. Wicksell now observes that these are precisely the conditions achieved by pure competition and hence that Ricardo was wrong to claim that a diminution of gross product was possible. Modern readers will note that Wicksell assumes throughout the validity of interior maxima. Subject to this qualification, Wicksell's analysis is a considerable improvement on anything produced before him.

The problem just discussed considered labour and land as the only explicit factors of production. Even here, Wicksell feels that 'It is scarcely possible to discover a simple and intelligible criterion which will indicate whether a change in the technique of production is in itself likely to raise or lower wages'. When Wicksell goes on to add capital as a factor of production, he has to concede that inventions may reduce the marginal product and share of labour. This leads him to say that 'The capitalist saver is ... fundamentally, the friend of labour, though the technical inventor is not infrequently its enemy' (Wicksell, 1911, pp. 140, 143, 164).

A satisfactory treatment of the machinery question depends upon modelling the general equilibrium of an economy and of following its transition from an initial equilibrium to the new equilibrium after the introduction of machinery. Even today, such a treatment is by no means easily achieved. Perhaps the classical economists would have done best to accept the general benefits of machinery, subject to transitional difficulties, as expounded by economists such as Tucker and Stewart, and wait until the proper analytical tools to discuss the issue satisfactorily had been developed.

S. RASHID

See also **Ricardo, David; Tozer, John Edward.**

Bibliography

Archer, H. 1742. Second Parliament of George II: Fourth session (8 of 9, begins 7/4/1738). *The History and Proceedings of the House of Commons: Volume 10: 1737–1739* (1742), pp. 258–92. Online. Available at http://www.british-history.ac.uk/report.asp?compid= 37804, accessed 19 July 2007.

Barton, J. 1817. *Observations on the Circumstances which Influence the Conditions of the Labouring Classes of Society.* London.

Cary, J. 1695. *A Discourse on Trade.* 3rd edn, London, 1745.

Defoe, D. 1704. *Giving Alms no Charity.* London.

Martin, H. 1701. *Considerations on the East-India Trade.* Reprinted in *A Select Collection of Scarce and Valuable Economic Tracts*, ed. J.R. McCulloch. London, 1856.

Mill, J.S. 1848. Principles of Political Economy with Some of Their Applications to Social Philosophy. In *Collected Works of John Stuart Mill*, ed. J.M. Robson. Toronto: University of Toronto Press, 1970.

Ricardo, D. 1821. Principles of Political Economy and Taxation. 3rd edn. In *The Works and Correspondence of David Ricardo*, ed. P. Sraffa. Cambridge: Cambridge University Press, 1951.

Stewart, D. 1856. Lectures on Political Economy. In *Collected Works of Dugald Stewart*, vols 8 and 9, ed. Sir W. Hamilton. Edinburgh: Thomas Constable & Co., 1854–60.

Tozer, J.E. 1838. *A Mathematical Investigation of the Effect of Machinery.* ed. D. Collard. New York: A.M. Kelley, 1968.

Tucker, J. 1757. *Instructions for Travellers.* Repr. in R.L. Schuyler, *Josiah Tucker.* New York: Columbia University Press, 1931.

Wicksell, K. 1911. *Lectures on Political Economy.* 2nd edn. trans. E. Classen. London: G. Routledge & Sons, 2 vols, 1934–5.

Machlup, Fritz (1902–1983)

Fritz Machlup was born in Wiener Neustadt, south of Vienna, on 15 December 1902, and died in New York on 30 January 1983. He studied economics at the University of Vienna in the 1920s under Friedrich von Wieser and Ludwig von Mises, and wrote his doctoral dissertation on the gold-exchange standard (Machlup, 1925) under the latter. In the years 1922–32 he pursued a business career in the family cardboard-manufacturing partnership while continuing his intellectual interests in economics and philosophy of science in association with von Mises, Hayek, Haberler, Morgenstern, Felix Kaufmann and Alfred Schütz. During this period he wrote two more books including one (Machlup, 1931) dealing with the role of stock-market speculation in capital formation. As business conditions deteriorated in the 1930s he took leave from his partners to accept a Rockefeller fellowship, and spent 1933–35 in the United States. Upon receiving an appointment at the University of Buffalo in 1935 he liquidated his Austrian business interests, and following a brief stay in England began an academic career in the United States. He moved to Johns Hopkins in 1947, and to Princeton in 1960 to succeed Jacob Viner. At Hopkins he had a profound influence as a graduate teacher and in building up a first-rate graduate programme that achieved national prominence; a list of his students is contained in Machlup (1963), and tributes and testimonials from many of them will be found in Dreyer (1978). At Princeton he was extremely active in his direction of the International Finance Section. Upon his retirement in 1971 he resumed his active career at New York University until his death shortly after his 80th birthday. He was president of the Southern Economic Association (1959), the American Association of University Professors (1962–64), the American Economic Association (1966), and the International Economic Association (1971–4).

Machlup's two great areas of research were international monetary economics and industrial organization, the latter with special emphasis on the 'knowledge industry', an activity which began with a study of the patent system (Machlup and Penrose, 1950; Machlup, 1958), continued with the development of a formal theory of invention, innovation, and the optimal lag of imitation behind innovation (see Bitros, 1976, pp. 439–502), and culminated in a monograph on the subject (1962), the multi-volumed second edition of which remained unfinished at the time of his death (Machlup, 1980b; 1982b; 1983). What was especially original in his contributions was his peculiar talent, resulting from his business background and study of philosophy of science, of being able to formulate a theory that took into account – in addition to the usual economic facts – the theories or rationalizations put forward by economic agents to justify their own actions. This was used to support his contention that economic agents engage in maximizing behaviour even though they may deny this. Such perceptions permeate his works on industrial organization (Machlup, 1949; 1952a; 1952b) and were developed in numerous articles collected in Machlup (1963).

Machlup's contributions to international economics were likewise characterized by a combination of clear logical thinking and intimate knowledge of the workings of economic institutions. His two-country extension of the theory of the multiplier (1943) was especially illuminating in bringing out the implicit financial assumptions of Keynesian theory. His work on the theory and policy of foreign-exchange markets and international economic adjustment (collected in Machlup, 1964) was very influential. His classic (1939–40) article developing Haberler's concepts of demand and supply of foreign exchange was required reading for a generation of graduate students. In his famous controversy with Sidney Alexander, while stressing the importance of relative prices he proved himself to be always the eclectic, never espousing one narrow 'approach' to the exclusion of all others. At first countering 'elasticity pessimism' and championing flexible exchange rates in his academic writings, he later became the prime architect of plans to reform the international monetary system in his organization of the 'Bellagio group' (Machlup and Malkiel, 1964). These activities have been recounted by Robert

Triffin and John Williamson in Dreyer (1978). Machlup's last contributions to international economics included a series of penetrating analyses of the Eurodollar market (starting with Machlup, 1970) and his one foray into 'real' international trade, a work on the theory of economic integration (Machlup, 1977).

Machlup had a remarkable and unforgettable personality. He was brilliant and as sharp as a whistle in his keen analysis and grasp of economic issues; he was lucid and patient as a teacher, yet tough; he was charming and witty; he was a great music-lover and an avid sportsman to the end of his days. Above all he was a man of extraordinary energy and passion.

Most of Machlup's important articles have been reprinted in Machlup (1963; 1964) and Bitros (1976); the first and third of these contain bibliographies of his work. Further information concerning his life and work will be found in Dreyer (1978), Chipman (1979), Machlup (1980a; 1982a), and Haberler (1983). The latter concludes with an apt poetic tribute by Kenneth Boulding.

JOHN S. CHIPMAN

Selected works

1925. *Die Goldkernwährung*. Halberstadt: Meyer.
1931. *Börsenkredit, Industriekredit und Kapitalbildung*. Vienna: Julius Springer. Revised English edn, *The Stock Market, Credit and Capital Formation*, London: Hodge; New York: Macmillan, 1940.
1943. *International Trade and the National Income Multiplier*. Philadelphia: Blakiston.
1949. *The Basing-point System*. Philadelphia: Blakiston.
1950. (With E. Penrose.) The patent controversy in the nineteenth century. *Journal of Economic History* 10, 1–29.
1952a. *The Economics of Sellers' Competition*. Baltimore: Johns Hopkins Press.
1952b. *The Political Economy of Monopoly*. Baltimore: Johns Hopkins Press.
1958. *An Economic Review of the Patent System*. Study of the Subcommittee on Patents, Trademarks, and Copyrights of the Committee on the Judiciary, US Senate, Study No. 15. Washington, DC: Government Printing Office.
1962. *The Production and Distribution of Knowledge in the United States*. Princeton: Princeton University Press.
1963. *Essays on Economic Semantics*. Englewood Cliffs, NJ: Prentice-Hall.
1964. *International Payments, Debts, and Gold*. New York: Scribner's. 2nd edn, New York: New York University Press, 1976.
1964. (With G. Malkiel, eds.) *International Monetary Arrangements: The Problem of Choice*. Princeton: International Finance Section, Department of Economics, Princeton University.
1970. Euro-dollar creation: a mystery story. *Banca Nazionale del Lavoro Quarterly Review* 23, 219–60. Reprinted in Bitros (1976).
1977. *A History of Thought on Economic Integration*. New York: Columbia University Press.

1980a. My early work on international monetary problems. *Banca Nazionale del Lavoro Quarterly Review* 35, 115–46.

1980b, 1982b, 1983. *Knowledge: Its Creation, Distribution, and Economic Significance.* Vol. 1: *Knowledge and Knowledge Production.* Vol. 2: *The Branches of Learning.* Vol. 3: *The Economics of Information and Human Capital.* Princeton: Princeton University Press.

1982a. My work on international monetary problems, 1940–1964. *Banca Nazionale del Lavoro Quarterly Review* 35, 3–36.

Bibliography

Bitros, G., ed. 1976. *Selected Economic Writings of Fritz Machlup.* New York: New York University Press.

Chipman, J.S. 1979. Machlup, Fritz. In *International Encyclopedia of the Social Sciences*, vol. 18. New York: Free Press.

Dreyer, J.S., ed. 1978. *Breadth and Depth in Economics: Fritz Machlup – The Man and His Ideas.* Lexington, MA: D.C. Heath.

Haberler, G. 1983. Fritz Machlup zum Gedenken. *Neue Zürcher Zeitung*, 16 February, 19. Fritz Machlup: in memoriam. *Cato Journal* 3, Spring, 11–14.

Macleod, Henry Dunning (1821–1902)

Macleod warrants special mention in this *Dictionary* if only because in the late 1850s and early 1860s he undertook to produce single-handedly a dictionary of economics on a grand scale – and, what is more, one to which he was to be the sole contributor. In the event the task proved to be beyond him, as it would for any mortal, and all that appeared was the first volume covering the letters A–C. Macleod never held an academic appointment, though he applied unsuccessfully for chairs at Cambridge (1863), Edinburgh (1871), and Oxford (1888).

Macleod, the son of a Scottish landholder, was born in Edinburgh. After graduation from Cambridge (BA, Trinity, 1843) and admission to the Bar (1849), he wrote a report on the administration of poor relief in the nine local parishes of the district of Easter Ross in Scotland (1851). This report led directly to the establishment of a poorhouse under Scotland's first Poor Law Union. In 1854, he joined the Royal British Bank and wrote a memorandum and opinion on that bank's legal position under the Joint Stock Banking Act of 1845. This first excursion into financial matters stimulated him to study the literature of economics on the subject, but he found that

> for the purpose of describing the actual principles and mechanisms of commerce they [Smith, Ricardo and Mill] were absolutely worthless. ... I saw that the

greatest opportunity that had come to any man since Galileo had come to me, and I then determined to devote myself to the construction of a real science of Economics on the model of the already established physical sciences. (1896b, pp. 142–3)

To his credit he stuck fast to his task. His detractors, however, have passed harsh judgement on its results (see, for example, the assessment of him in Higgs's edition of *Palgrave's Dictionary*); his sympathetic readers have been more generous (see, for example, Hayek, 1933). Given the sheer magnitude of his project, there would seem to be more to be said for the position of the critics.

Macleod's employment in the banking system led to what is perhaps his most important book on that subject: *The Theory and Practice of Banking* (1855–6). Its two most interesting features for the modern reader are, perhaps, the discussion of discount policy and the insistence on the proposition that 'the distinction between capital and currency ... is of the most profound delusions that ever existed' (1855, vol. 2, p. lxxii; see also the entry on 'Credit' in his *Dictionary*). Not surprisingly, for one who kept fast to the basic position of the Bullion Report, this latter notion introduced a number of ambiguities into the argument. However, not withstanding these peculiarities, the book was apparently quite successful, going through five editions by the 1890s and being reprinted soon after his death. Charles Rist referred to it as Macleod's 'great book' (1940, p. 261).

There followed many publications on monetary matters of which two may be singled out. In *Bimetallism* (1894), he criticized the proponents of a dual standard for advocating 'an impossibility'; a position which put him at odds with many of his contemporaries. This polemic was continued in two short tracts issued by the Gold Standard Defence Association in 1895 under the titles 'Gresham's Law' and 'Bimetallism in France'. Secondly, in 1898, he published two contributions to the debate surrounding the Fowler Commission on Indian currency arrangements: *Indian Currency* and *A Tentative Scheme for Restoring a Gold Currency to India*.

Macleod's project of reconstructing economic science continued on more general matters with *Elements of Political Economy* (1858). The book is interesting as an example of Macleod's advocacy of a definition of economics as the 'science of exchanges', or catallactics, which Marshall claimed 'anticipated much both of the form and substance of recent criticisms on the classical doctrine of value in relation to cost, by Profs. Walras and Carl Menger' (1920, p. 821), and for the fact that in it he introduces into the vocabulary of economics the phrase 'Gresham's Law'.

One of Macleod's interesting habits was that of publishing the same material in different forms and under different titles. In this he reminds one of McCulloch. Thus, *Bimetallism* was itself an expanded version of the seventh chapter of his *Theory of Credit* (1889–91), his

Elements of Political Economy (1858) appeared in successive editions under the titles *The Principles of Economic Philosophy* (1872–5) and *The Elements of Economics* (1881–6), and his *History of Economics* (1896b) seems to be made up of material from his unfinished dictionary.

Macleod died at Norwood on 16 July 1902.

MURRAY MILGATE AND ALASTAIR LEVY

See also **catallactics.**

Selected works

1851. *The Results of the Operation of the Poorhouse System in Ross.* Inverness: Courier Office, repr. from the *Inverness Courier.*

1855–6. *The Theory and Practice of Banking; with the Elementary Principles of Currency, Prices, Credit and Exchanges.* 2 vols. London: Longman, Brown, Green and Longmans.

1858. *The Elements of Political Economy.* London: Longman, Brown, Green, Longmans and Roberts.

1863. *A Dictionary of Political Economy: Biographical, Bibliographical, Historical and Practical: A–C.* London: Longmans, Green, Longman, Roberts, and Green.

1889–91. *The Theory of Credit.* 2 vols. London: Longmans, Green & Co.

1894. *Bimetallism.* London: Longmans, Green & Co.

1896a. *A History of Banking in all the Leading Nations.* 2 vols. London: Bliss, Sands & Co.

1896b. *The History of Economics.* London: Bliss, Sands & Co.

1898. *Indian Currency.* Longmans: Green & Co.

Bibliography

Hayek, F.A. 1933. Henry Dunning Macleod. In *Encyclopedia of the Social Sciences*, vol. 10, ed. E.R.A. Seligman. New York: Macmillan.

Marshall, A. 1920. *Principles of Economics.* 8th edn. London: Macmillan.

Rist, C. 1940. *History of Monetary and Credit Theory from John Law to the Present Day.* Trans. J. Degras from the French edn of 1938, New York: Macmillan; London: G. Allen & Unwin. Reprinted, New York: A.M. Kelley, 1966.

macroeconomic effects of international trade

The field of open economy macroeconomics deals with the macroeconomic behaviour of economies that trade with each other. International trade can have macroeconomic effects by helping the transmission of disturbances from one economy to another as well as by affecting the impact of macroeconomic policies on economic activity. This article discusses several representative open economy macro models, highlighting the role different theoretical features play in influencing the channels through which trade flows can have macro effects.

Keynesian framework

At its simplest level, international trade is linked to macroeconomic activity through the national income relation. Consider the Keynesian income–expenditure model of a small open economy, in which prices and the interest rate are given, foreign demand for exports is exogenous, and domestic output is determined by demand. With these assumptions, an exogenous increase in domestic expenditures raises domestic income and worsens the current account balance; however, income rises less than in a closed economy because of leakages from the income stream through imports and through saving. In contrast, an exogenous increase in foreign demand for domestic goods leads to an increase in both exports and domestic income. Because the increased direct demand for exports is only partially offset by the expansion of imports induced by higher income, the current account improves overall. The resulting rise in domestic output implies positive cross-country transmission of the foreign disturbance.

Income multiplier effects through changes in trade also characterize open economy extensions of the Keynesian framework, such as the classic Mundell–Fleming model. This model also takes prices as given, but allows the income effects of monetary stimulus and exogenous expenditure changes to take account of interest rate changes depending on the degree of international capital mobility and of exchange rate changes, which in turn depend on the exchange rate regime. With a flexible exchange rate regime, exchange rate changes affect the relative demand for domestic and foreign goods. Thus, for example, domestic monetary stimulus that reduces the interest rate, raises income, and creates an excess demand for foreign exchange also depreciates the domestic currency. If the Marshall–Lerner–Robinson condition is satisfied, that is, the sum of price elasticities of domestic and foreign demands for imports exceeds unity, then the lower relative price of domestic goods switches demand from foreign to domestic goods and raises the current account balance, causing domestic income to increase and foreign income to decrease. Accordingly, the domestic income multiplier effect of the monetary stimulus is augmented by the expenditure-switching effect of the exchange rate; in addition, the trade transmission effect of domestic monetary shocks to foreign income is negative.

In these models crucial parameters affecting transmission effects include the marginal propensity to import and the elasticity of trade with respect to the exchange rate. Thus, for example, an increase in the marginal propensity to import out of income lessens the multiplier effects of domestic policy stimulus.

New open economy macro models

New open-economy macroeconomic models (NOEM) integrate older fixed-price Keynesian models of macroeconomic fluctuations with dynamic intertemporal analysis based on microeconomic foundations and optimizing agents. These models embed imperfect competition and short-run nominal rigidities in a general equilibrium framework and provide clear welfare criteria in the form of the utility of the representative consumer. They also assume that bond (but not equity) markets are integrated, providing a consumption-smoothing role for net trade flows via the current account. Thus, for example, a temporary productivity shock that raises domestic output induces higher saving and a temporary current account surplus (though with investment dynamics a current account deficit may result if the increase in investment exceeds the increase in saving).

In a seminal paper, Obstfeld and Rogoff (1995) use a two-country framework in which each country specializes in producing a subset of tradable goods, and domestic and foreign consumers have identical preferences over a basket of both domestic and foreign goods. They show that monetary shocks have a positive effect on domestic output and a negative transmission effect on foreign output, as in the Mundell–Fleming model. Because monetary stimulus depreciates the domestic currency, it lowers the domestic country's terms of trade, reduces the purchasing power of domestic residents and raises the purchasing power of foreign residents. This terms-of-trade effect makes foreign residents better off and domestic residents worse off, but not by enough to offset the domestic gains from greater output. A temporary current account surplus is generated as well via the intertemporal consumption-smoothing channel.

A key parameter in NOEM models is the elasticity of substitution between goods embedded in consumer preferences. Obstfeld and Rogoff assume that the elasticity of substitution between goods produced in the same country is the same as the elasticity of substitution between goods produced in different countries. Several papers show how the international transmission of shocks is affected by relaxing this assumption. Tille (2001) shows that, if the elasticity of substitution of domestic and foreign goods exceeds unity, the Marshall–Lerner–Robinson condition holds. In this case, a currency depreciation and decline in the terms of trade results in a large demand switch towards domestic goods and a rise in export revenue. Tille also shows that, if there is less substitutability between domestic and foreign goods across countries than within countries (the empirically more relevant case), the terms-of-trade effect of domestic monetary expansion may be large enough to lower domestic welfare (termed a 'beggar-thyself' effect), while raising foreign welfare. In contrast, greater fiscal expenditures on domestic output raise the domestic terms of trade and domestic welfare, while reducing relative demand for foreign goods and foreign welfare (a 'beggar-thy-neighbour' effect), particularly when domestic and foreign goods are poor substitutes.

Corsetti and Pesenti (2001) deal with the special case in which the elasticity of substitution between domestic

and foreign goods is unity, implying constant expenditure shares on domestic and foreign goods. This specification implies that the current account is always in balance. The reason is that, with unit elasticity between domestic and foreign goods, an increase in the foreign price of foreign goods results in a proportionate decrease in the quantity of foreign demand for domestic goods, leaving expenditures on exports constant and the current account unaffected.

Other extensions to NOEM models that affect the transmission of policy include consumption bias for domestic over foreign goods (Warnock, 2003), pricing-to-market behaviour (Betts and Devereux, 1998), and non-traded distribution services (Burstein, Eichenbaum and Rebelo, 2006).

International real business cycle models

The tendency of macro aggregates, such as output, to move together in different countries is well documented (Backus, Kehoe and Kydland, 1992; Baxter, 1995). Cross-country business cycle correlations depend on the interaction of common international shocks, country-specific shocks, and the transmission of these shocks between countries. An important question in international macroeconomics is how much these comovements reflect the transmission of shocks across borders through international trade linkages. International real business cycle (IRBC) models analyse this issue within a dynamic general equilibrium framework based on microfoundations. Unlike NOEM models, these models typically assume flexible prices and complete markets, though more recent work has introduced price rigidity and incomplete asset markets.

On theoretical grounds, the effect of international trade links on the comovement of national business cycles is ambiguous. On the one hand, greater integration can increase intra-industry specialization and production-sharing because of low elasticity of substitution between intermediate inputs produced in different countries; in addition, it may allow demand shocks to propagate more easily across national borders, which may lead to a higher correlation of business cycles when countries trade more. On the other hand, greater trade integration can increase inter-industry specialization if countries specialize more in the goods in which they have a comparative advantage in order to achieve gains from trade; this case, if industry-specific shocks are a dominant source of business cycle movements, may lead to a lower correlation of business cycles when countries trade more.

On balance, the empirical evidence suggests that the former effect dominates, and that countries with a lot of bilateral trade tend to have more synchronized business cycles (for example, Frankel and Rose, 1998; Baxter and Kouparitsas, 2005). However, since the early 1980s business cycle synchronization has not in fact increased among industrial countries despite increasing trade integration. Stock and Watson (2005) provide a partial explanation by showing that common international shocks experienced by G-7 countries have been smaller in the 1980s and 1990s than they were in the 1960s and 1970s. But they also show that cyclical comovements have increased for subgroups of countries, notably within Europe and North America. Burstein, Kurz and Tesar (2005) construct a model that is consistent with this development in which trade between core countries and their periphery (for example, the United States and Canada) involves more production sharing than does trade between core regions (for example, the United States and Europe). Consequently, one should observe higher output correlations between core and peripheral countries than between core regions. IRBC models have been less successful in explaining the quantitative magnitude of the relation between trade intensity and the cross-country correlation of business cycles; that is, a given change in bilateral trade intensity generates a much smaller change in output correlations than is apparent in the data; this is referred to as the 'trade comovement gap puzzle' (Kose and Yi, 2006).

The finding that greater trade intensity is associated with greater cross-country comovements in business cycles suggests that these comovements depend on policies that enhance international trade, such as lowering of trade barriers or reductions in exchange rate costs due to membership in currency unions. Frankel and Rose (2002) find that the positive effect of currency unions on trade in turn has a large effect on output in member countries. Since the main cost of joining a currency area is the cost of giving up monetary independence, this has the implication that a pair of countries with business cycles that are dissimilar *ex ante* (making the act of joining a currency union appear costly) might have more correlated business cycles *ex post* because the increase in trade stimulated by the currency union tends to synchronize business cycles.

Trade frictions and macro models

The international tradability of goods depends not just on the degree of substitutability in consumption, but also on transport costs and other trade frictions. In fact, Obstfeld and Rogoff (2000) argue that introducing real trade costs helps explain a variety of puzzles in international economics, including the low cross-country correlation of consumption (consumption correlations puzzle), the limited magnitude of current account imbalances (Feldstein–Horioka puzzle), international price discrepancies (purchasing power parity puzzle), and home bias in trade and asset holdings.

Taken to the extreme, trade frictions play a role in explaining why some goods may not be traded at all. While open economy macroeconomics by definition analyses trade across national borders, the field has long found it useful to assume that a given exogenous set of goods is non-traded. This traded/non-traded distinction is essential to many well-known results in the field, such as the Balassa–Samuelson effect, which says that, as the productivity of traded goods rises relative to that of non-traded goods, there will be tendency for the real exchange rate to appreciate.

The international trade literature has explained non-tradedness as an outcome of trade frictions. For example, Dornbusch, Fischer and Samuelson (1977) show how a range of non-traded goods can arise in the presence of cross-country trade costs within a model in which differences in labour productivity across a continuum of goods determine the range of goods a country produces as well as the pattern of trade.

A growing field of international economics research tries to integrate models of trade and macroeconomics and treats the set of tradable goods not as exogenously given but rather as an endogenously determined characteristic of the analysis. Several authors (Ghironi and Melitz, 2005; Bergin, Glick, and Taylor, 2006) formulate open economy macro models with monopolistic competition and heterogeneously productive firms, in which firms face fixed costs of selling in domestic and export markets, to explain phenomena such as the Balassa–Samuelson effect. Since only relatively more productive firms are profitable enough to engage in trade, they endogenously satisfy the precondition of the Balassa–Samuelson story that productivity gains are concentrated in the traded goods sector.

Loose ends

International trade can influence macroeconomic activity through other channels. For example, as highlighted in endogenous growth models, technological progress may depend on incentives to undertake R&D and innovate, which, in turn, may depend on externalities or spillover effects from greater markets provided by international trade (Grossman and Helpman, 1991). Greater openness to trade can also complicate the optimal conduct of monetary policy because of the impact of the exchange rate on real activity and inflation. Clarida, Gali and Gertler (2001) show how more openness to international trade can influence a central bank following an optimal policy feedback rule to raise the domestic interest rate more aggressively in response to inflation pressures. Lastly, trade may serve as a transmission channel through which financial crises may spread contagiously across countries (Glick and Rose, 1999).

REUVEN GLICK

See also **growth and international trade; international real business cycles; international trade and heterogeneous firms; international trade theory; Marshall–Lerner condition; new open economy macroeconomics; trade costs; tradable and non-tradable commodities.**

Bibliography

Backus, D., Kehoe, P. and Kydland, F. 1992. International real business cycles. *Journal of Political Economy* 100, 745–75.

Baxter, M. 1995. International trade and business cycles. In *Handbook of International Economics*, vol. 3, ed. G. Grossman and K. Rogoff. Amsterdam: North-Holland.

Baxter, M. and Kouparitsas, M. 2005. Determinants of business cycle comovement: a robust analysis. *Journal of Monetary Economics* 52, 113–57.

Bergin, P., Glick, R. and Taylor, A. 2006. Productivity, tradability, and the long-run price puzzle. *Journal of Monetary Economics* 53, 2041–66.

Betts, C. and Devereux, M. 1998. Exchange rate dynamics in a model of pricing to market. *Journal of International Economics* 50, 215–44.

Burstein, A., Eichenbaum, M. and Rebelo, S. 2006. The importance of nontradable goods' prices in cyclical real exchange rate fluctuations. *Japan and the World Economy* 18, 247–53.

Burstein, A., Kurz, C. and Tesar, L. 2005. International trade, production sharing and the transmission of business cycles. Working paper, University of California at Los Angeles.

Clarida, R., Gali, J. and Gertler, M. 2001. Optimal monetary policy in open versus closed economies: an integrated approach. *American Economic Review* 91, 248–52.

Corsetti, G. and Pesenti, P. 2001. Welfare and macroeconomic interdependence. *Quarterly Journal of Economics* 116, 421–45.

Dornbusch, R., Fischer, S. and Samuelson, P. 1977. Comparative advantage, trade, and payments in a Ricardian model with a continuum of goods. *American Economic Review* 67, 823–39.

Frankel, J. and Rose, A. 1998. The endogeneity of the optimum currency area criteria. *Economic Journal* 108, 1009–25.

Frankel, J.A. and Rose, A. 2002. An estimate of the effect of common currencies on trade and income. *Quarterly Journal of Economics* 117, 437–66.

Ghironi, F. and Melitz, M. 2005. International trade and macroeconomic dynamics with heterogenous firms. *Quarterly Journal of Economics* 120, 865–915.

Glick, R. and Rose, A. 1999. Contagion and trade: why are currency crises regional? *Journal of International Money and Finance* 18, 603–17.

Grossman, G. and Helpman, E. 1991. *Innovation and Growth in the Global Economy*. Cambridge, MA: MIT Press.

Kose, M. and Yi, K.-M. 2006. Can the standard international business cycle model explain the relation between trade and comovement? *Journal of International Economics* 68, 267–95.

Obstfeld, M. and Rogoff, K. 1995. Exchange rate dynamics redux. *Journal of Political Economy* 103, 624–60.

Obstfeld, M. and Rogoff, K. 2000. The six major puzzles in international macroeconomics: is there a common cause? In *NBER Macroeconomics Annual*, ed. B. Bernanke and K. Rogoff. Cambridge, MA: MIT Press.

Stock, J. and Watson, M. 2005. Understanding changes in international business cycle dynamics. *Journal of the European Economic Association* 3, 968–1006.

Tille, C. 2001. The role of consumption substitutability in the international transmission of monetary shocks. *Journal of International Economics* 53, 421–44.

Warnock, F. 2003. Exchange rate dynamics and the welfare effects of monetary policy in a two-country model with home-product bias. *Journal of International Money and Finance* 22, 343–63.

macroeconomic forecasting

Macroeconomic forecasts are 'guesses' of the future values of important macroeconomic aggregates such as GDP, inflation, or the unemployment rate. These forecasts inform the decisions of business, policymakers, investors, and consumers. Macroeconomic forecasts are regularly constructed by government agencies and private companies. For example, every quarter the Bank of England publishes its *Inflation Report*, which contains forecasts of inflation over the next three years. Federal Reserve policymakers also rely on forecasts from the Green Book; however, unlike the Bank of England, the Fed does not release its forecasts to the public. The Federal Reserve Bank of Philadelphia summarizes private sector macroeconomic forecasts for the United States in its quarterly *Survey of Professional Forecasters*.

Macroeconomic forecasts are constructed using a variety of methods. These methods can be grouped into four categories: (1) leading indicator indexes; (2) structural econometric models; (3) time series models; and (4) judgement.

The origin of leading indicator indexes can be traced to the 1930s when, at the request of the US Secretary of the Treasury, Wesley Mitchell proposed a set of variables that historically had moved in anticipation of the business cycle. Averages of these leading indicators are an index of leading indicators. Such an index was constructed in the United States for several years by the Department of Commerce and is now maintained and published monthly by the Conference Board, which also publishes leading indicator indexes for several other countries.

Structural econometric models construct forecasts using dynamic relationships suggested by economic theory and estimated by statistical methods. Work on these models by Tinbergen, Klein and Haavelmo resulted in Nobel prizes for these researchers in 1969, 1980 and 1989 respectively. Large-scale structural models with hundreds of equations were developed in the 1960s and early 1970s, but forecast failures in the 1970s led researchers to question both the economic theory used in the models and the statistical procedures used to fit the models' equations. Refinements in theory (notably the importance of expectations and dynamic adjustment) and statistical methods (notably time series methods) are incorporated in the current generation of large-scale structural models. Currently, there is a significant research effort aimed at constructing small-scale structural models ('dynamic stochastic general equilibrium' models) for policy evaluation and forecasting.

Time series models use serial correlation (or persistence) in variables to construct forecasts. For example, a simple autoregressive model (AR) has the form $y_t = \alpha + \phi y_{t-1} + \varepsilon_t$, where y_t is an economic variable of interest and ε_t is a zero-mean serially uncorrelated random shock. When ϕ is positive (negative), larger than average values of y_{t-1} tend to be associated with larger (smaller) than average values of y_t. Thus, an autoregressive forecast of y_{T+1} using data through time T is $y_{T+1/T} = \alpha + \phi y_T$. Many macroeconomic variables display short-run dependence, and time series models typically produce more accurate short-run forecasts than other forecasting methods. Time series models have been developed to construct forecasts based on linear and nonlinear dependence properties in macroeconomic variables, and multivariate time series models, such as vector autoregressions (VARs), are widely used for short-horizon macroeconomic forecasting.

Professional forecasters also rely on judgement when constructing their forecasts. That is, while the macroeconomic forecasts published by the Bank of England or the Fed's Green Book forecasts rely on econometric models, the forecasts are not identical to model-based forecasts. Professional forecasters typically use judgement to adjust model-based forecasts. These adjustments – sometimes called 'add-factors' – allow forecasters (so they argue) to incorporate information that is not captured in the economic model. As an empirical matter, good judgement appears to improve the accuracy of model-based forecasts.

Much of the theory of forecasting can be derived from elementary concepts in probability theory. Let y_{T+1} denote the variable to be forecast and X_T denote a set of variables to be used for constructing the forecast. In general, X_T will include y_T, y_{T-1}, and longer lags, as well as current and lagged values of other series. Let $g(X_T)$ denote the forecast or 'guess' of y_{T+1} constructed from X_T, where good choices of $g(\, . \,)$ lead to more accurate forecasts. The forecast error is $e_{T+1} = y_{T+1} - g(X_T)$, and accuracy can be measured by mean squared forecast error (MSFE), where the conditional MSFE $= E(e_{T+1}^2 | X_T)$. A fundamental result from probability theory is that $E(e_{T+1}^2 | X_T)$ is minimized using $g(X_T) = E(y_{T+1} | X_T)$; that is, the regression (conditional expectation) produces the minimum mean squared forecast error.

A key implication of this theoretical result is that more information is always better – that is, it never hurts to include more variables in X_T, and the information in these additional variables will often reduce the MSFE. But, this result assumes that the regression function

$E(y_{T+1} | X_T)$ is known, and in practice this function must be estimated using sample data. Including many variables in X_T means that many parameters must be estimated to characterize the regression function, and estimating a large number of parameters leads to statistical estimation error that increases the MSFE. This trade-off between including more variables in X_T to capture more information about y_{T+1} and the increased statistical error associated with estimating additional parameters for the forecasting model is one of the major practical problems in forecasting.

Another major problem is the temporal stability of the forecasting model. That is, the regression $E(y_{T+1} | X_T)$ might change over time, so that a regression estimated using past data might provide poor forecasts for future values of y_T. These two problems – developing methods for forecasting using many past variables and problems associated with instability – are active areas of current research. The relevant chapters in Elliott, Granger and Timmerman (2006) summarize current research on these and other important topics in economic forecasting.

MARK W. WATSON

See also **time series analysis; vector autoregressions.**

Bibliography

Bank of England. 2007. *Inflation Report*. Online. Available at http://www.bankofengland.co.uk/publications/inflationreport/index.htm, accessed 19 February 2007.

Elliott, G., Granger, C.W.J. and Timmerman, A.C., eds. 2006. *Handbook of Economic Forecasting*, vol. 1. Amsterdam: North-Holland.

Federal Reserve Bank of Philadelphia. 2007. *Survey of Professional Forecasters*. Online. Available at http://www.phil.frb.org/econ/spf, accessed 19 February 2007.

macroeconomics, origins and history of

Macroeconomics analyses a whole economy or economies, dealing with aggregate output and employment, the price level and interest rate, rather than with the prices or quantities of particular commodities. It became a recognized field as textbooks and course offerings responded to John Maynard Keynes's *General Theory of Employment, Interest and Money* (1936; 1971–89, vol. 7), to the mathematical and diagrammatic reformulations of Keynes by David Champernowne, Brian Reddaway, Roy Harrod, J.R. Hicks, James Meade, Oskar Lange, Mabel Timlin and Franco Modigliani (Hicks, 1937; Young, 1987), and to the first aggregate econometric models such as Tinbergen (1939). Ragnar Frisch (1933) introduced the terms 'macrodynamics' and 'macroanalysis', and his distinction between macroanalysis and microanalysis is the same as the subsequent distinction between macroeconomics and microeconomics. Michal Kalecki (1935) first used 'macrodynamic' in a title, and by the time that Lawrence Klein (1946) used 'macroeconomics' in the title of a journal article, he presumed that its meaning would be clear to his readers. But just as Molière's *bourgeois gentilhomme* spoke prose long before he knew he was doing so, economists wrote macroeconomics long before they called it by that name. Macroeconomics grew out of two long-standing traditions within economics: business cycle analysis and the theory of money.

Macroeconomic themes in pre-classical and classical political economy

The quantity theory of money is the oldest surviving theory in economics, yet remained, in David Laidler's (1991a) phrase, 'always and everywhere controversial' (primarily over whether changes in the quantity of money are exogenous or endogenous). Holding that a change in the money supply will ultimately change prices in the same proportion, the quantity theory was first used in the 16th century by Martin Navarro de Azpilcueta (writing in Latin as Navarrus) and other scholastics at the University of Salamanca (Grice-Hutchinson, 1952), and then by Jean Bodin in France, to explain the 'Price Revolution', the inflation following the inflow of silver from the Spanish colonies in the New World. John Locke, Richard Cantillon and Isaac Gervaise contributed to understanding the velocity of circulation and the adjustment of international payments (Vickers, 1959). The economic essays in David Hume's *Political Discourses* (see Hume, 1752) mark a high-point of pre-classical monetary economics (see Humphrey, 1993). Hume's analysis of the specie-flow mechanism of adjustment under the gold standard showed that an increase in the quantity of gold in one country would increase prices and spending in that country, causing a trade deficit and gold inflow until balance of payments of equilibrium was restored with the world's gold distributed among countries in proportion to their demand for real money balances. Hume's specie-flow mechanism provided a crushing rejoinder to mercantilist schemes for increasing the amount of gold in a country by promoting exports and restricting imports. Such tariffs, quotas and subsidies would distort resource allocation without producing a lasting trade surplus, and would raise prices rather than the real wealth of a nation. Hume recognized that an increased money supply would provide a temporary stimulus to real output, which would fade as prices and wages adjusted. While Hume linked each country's price level to that country's money stock and emphasized relative price effects on trade balances, his younger contemporary and friend Adam Smith anticipated the monetary approach to the balance of payments by assuming purchasing power parity (with the world price level set by the world gold stock and world demand for real money balances) with adjustment taking place, not through relative price changes, but through the direct

effect of a nation's excess demand for or supply of money on spending, hence on the balance of payments and on the country's stock of gold.

Keynes's *General Theory* revived interest in the debate in the years after the Napoleonic Wars about the possibility of a general glut of commodities. Keynes deplored the victory of David Ricardo's sharper analysis and endorsement of Say's (or James Mill's) Law of Markets over what Keynes regarded as Thomas Robert Malthus's deeper (but fuzzier) insight that insufficient effective demand could result in an excess supply of labour without an excess demand for any good (other than money). Malthus's insight was obscured by his failure to distinguish between a decision to save and a decision to invest, and hence to see the significance of hoarding. Statements of the Law of Markets by classical economists were more varied and complex, often subtler, and sometimes more confused and contradictory than Keynes suggested in short quotations from the classics, which sometimes misled when taken out of context (see Link, 1959, and Corry, 1962, on the macroeconomics of English classical economists and their critics, and Sowell, 1972, on Say's Law). John Stuart Mill and others searched for a statement of the Law of Markets that would be the stronger truism that Oskar Lange later labelled as Say's Equality (if each and every commodity market is in equilibrium, then the sum of excess demand over all commodity markets much add to zero) but weaker than what Lange called Say's Identity, that excess demand for all commodity markets (that is, all markets except money) always sums to zero for any set of prices, regardless of whether any individual market is in equilibrium. Say's Identity, taken together with the adding up of budget constraints that Lange termed Walras's Law, implies that the money market always clears for any prices, leaving the absolute level of prices indeterminate. The policy implications that classical economists drew from their analysis are also more varied and pragmatic than the later textbook caricature: Jean-Baptiste Say recommended public works as a temporary response to unemployment during periods of adjustment, and criticized Ricardo for ignoring the possibility that savings might be hoarded if investment opportunities were inadequate. Ricardo, whose economic writings had begun with a pamphlet arguing that the premium on bullion demonstrated the wartime overissue and depreciation of inconvertible banknotes, was willing after the end of the war to support restoration of gold convertibility at the depreciated parity, rather than deflation to restore the pre-war parity. Henry Thornton (1802) introduced the concept of the central bank as the lender of last resort to support solvent but illiquid banks against bank runs. The proper role, if any, of the Bank of England generated prolonged controversy among the Banking, Currency, and Free Banking Schools in the first three quarters of the 19th century, producing analyses of lasting significance for monetary economics (V. Smith, 1936; Fetter, 1965).

François Quesnay's *Tableau Economique*, the crowning achievement of Physiocratic economics in France at the time of Hume and Smith, represented the circular flow of income and spending. It was not taken up by the mainstream of British and French classical political economy, but, a century after Quesnay, the *Tableau Economique* inspired Karl Marx's schemes of simple and expanded reproduction in the second volume of *Capital* (published posthumously in 1885), relating output and reinvestment rates in Department I (capital goods) and Department II (wage goods). For decades, this pioneering two-sector growth model was used only by Marxist economists such as Rosa Luxemburg and Otto Bauer constructing models of the supposed inevitable breakdown of capitalism, and then in 1928 by G.A. Fel'dman, proposing a growth theory for a planned economy. Fel'dman's articles were part of a false dawn of modern growth theory, appearing in the same year as the December 1928 issue of the *Economic Journal* that contained Allyn Young on increasing returns and economic progress (inspired by Adam Smith) and Frank Ramsey's application of calculus of variations to optimal capital accumulation by a representative agent, but by 1930 Young and Ramsey were dead and Fel'dman had vanished in Stalin's purges (see Fel'dman, Ramsey and Young in Dimand, 2002, vol. 3, and Bauer in vol. 5). Neoclassical hostility to Marx's theory of value and exploitation led to neglect of his contribution to growth theory, just as classical rejection of the Physiocratic doctrine of the exclusive net productivity of agriculture diverted attention from the circular flow. Marx also analysed the cyclical fluctuation of the profit rate around a downward trend, with cyclical troughs in the profit rate causing layoffs that force down wages by swelling the reserve army of the unemployed and cyclical peaks in the profit rate leading to realization crises as redistribution away from wages reduces demand for output (since Marx rejected Say's Law). However, his analysis of the increasing severity of crisis (as of the downward trend of the profit rate) was conducted within the special terminology and assumptions of his labour theory of value, which limited its influence on the mainstream of economics.

Business cycles

Recognition of the more or less periodic recurrence of crises and prosperity goes back at least to Thomas Tooke's discussion in 1823 of 'waves' in prices (Arnon, 1991), the beginning of the vast literature on cyclical fluctuations most conveniently sampled in the multivolume anthologies of O'Brien (1997), Hagemann (2001) and Boianovsky (2005), and in the encyclopedia of Glasner (1997). Clément Juglar (1862) and W. Stanley Jevons (1884, collecting essays written from 1862 to 1882) advanced the analysis of economic fluctuations as periodic oscillations to a higher level, surpassing earlier descriptive and classificatory works (such as Max Wirth's *Geschichte der Handelskrisen* in 1858) and displacing the

perception of crises as the result of occasional events. Jevons built upon Hyde Clarke's 1847 suggestion of a meteorological cause for the recurrence of crises every ten years or so (Hyde Clarke also perceived multiple, overlapping cycles, including a longer period of 54 years, anticipating Kondratiev). Jevons's sunspot theory of the trade cycle has so fallen out of favour that the term 'sunspots' in now used in the field of business cycles to refer to any intrinsically irrelevant variables (and even the term 'business cycles' is no longer taken to imply that fluctuations are in fact periodic cycles). This is unfair to Jevons, who was following the accepted meteorology of his era, which held that the cycle in solar activity affected weather. Cycles in weather would affect harvests, which, in a still largely agricultural world economy, would affect all economic sectors. Jevons's sunspot theory, together with his warnings about the impending exhaustion of coal, did much more than his marginal utility analysis of relative prices to persuaded the British Association for the Advancement of Science that economics was sufficiently scientific for Section F to remain in the Association. Nonetheless, as Wesley Mitchell (1927, p. 384) remarked,

> Jevons had an admirably candid mind; yet in 1875, when the sun-spot cycle was supposed to last 11.1 years, he was able to get from Thorold Rogers' *History of Agriculture and Prices in England* a period of 11 years in price fluctuations, and when the sun-spot cycle was revised to 10.45 years he was able to make the average interval between English crises 10.466 years.

Jevons was misled by the belief that an economic cycle must have a cause that is itself cyclical, but, as Knut Wicksell put it, the motion of a rocking horse does not resemble the motion of the stick that started it rocking (cited by Frisch, 1933). Jevons's sunspot theory has distracted attention from such lasting contributions as the seasonal cycle (in his essay on the annual autumnal pressure on the Bank of England) and his use of index numbers to trace the effects of the Australian and California gold discoveries.

Wesley Mitchell (1913; 1927) was the leading figure in the statistical approach to business cycle analysis. In 1920, Mitchell founded the National Bureau of Economic Research (NBER), which was the model for institutes of business cycle or conjuncture research in Berlin, Vienna (directed first by Friedrich Hayek and then by Oskar Morgenstern), Belgium, Sofia, Moscow (directed by Nikolai D. Kondratiev, the theorist of long waves), and Warsaw (where Kalecki worked), Britain's National Institute of Economic and Social Research, and the Institute of World Economics in Kiel. Although his Columbia lectures on types of economic theory were famous, Mitchell was sceptical about taking any single explicit economic theory, such as the quantity theory of money or utility maximization, as a starting point, as he felt that many of the theories surveyed in Mitchell (1927) captured something of the truth, but none the whole truth. Mitchell was influenced by his teacher at the University of Chicago, the institutionalist Thorstein Veblen (1904), who coined the term 'neoclassical' to describe the sort of Marshallian economics of which he disapproved. Mitchell and Arthur F. Burns (his successor directing the NBER) concentrated on investigating the statistical properties of time series, looking for patterns of leads and lags and for superimposed cycles of different periods and amplitudes. The widely reported index of leading indicators continues the original NBER approach.

Sir William Beveridge, director of the London School of Economics, used the periodogram, an early version of spectral analysis, to decompose wheat prices into 19 cycles with periods varying from 2.735 years to 68 years (Beveridge, 1921; 1922). Finding so many cycles led sceptics, such as Harvard statistician E.B. Wilson, to wonder whether there were any truly periodic oscillations in economic time series (apart from seasonality), since with enough cycles any series could be represented as a summation of cycles. Eugen Slutsky (1937, originally published in Russian in 1927), used a moving average of the last three digits of the winning Moscow lottery numbers to show that summation of random series could produce apparent cycles. Slutsky (1937) and Frisch (1933) influenced economists to consider fluctuations as oscillatory responses to random shocks (real or monetary), turning away from the emphasis of Jevons, Juglar, Mitchell, Beveridge and Kondratiev on underlying cycles. Cowles Commission director Tjalling Koopmans (1947) denounced Burns and Mitchell's *Measuring Business Cycles* (1946) as 'Measurement without Theory', and argued instead for simultaneous equation macroeconometric models, with the equations identified by exclusionary restrictions derived from a priori economic theory. Koopmans's Chicago colleague Milton Friedman (whose Columbia dissertation had been supervised by Burns) responded by writing down a formal model representing Mitchell's business cycle analysis (Friedman, 1952, Section III and Appendix, pp. 257–82). The vector autoregressions (VAR) of Christopher Sims (1980) marks a return (with more modern statistical techniques) to the NBER approach of investigating the statistical properties of macroeconomic time series with only limited reliance on a priori restrictions drawn from theory.

1886 and all that: the dawn of modern monetary macroeconomics, 1886–1914

Around 1886, during a period of depression, analysis of cycles and crises acquired a new emphasis on fluctuation of employment as the problem and variations in the general price level as a preventable cause. Carroll Wright (1886) devoted his first annual report as US Commissioner of Labor to a statistical study, *Industrial Depressions*, finding such depressions to be largely contemporaneous across manufacturing nations and advocating profit-sharing to mitigate the severity of

fluctuations (a proposal independently rediscovered nearly a century later by Martin Weitzman). In the same year, Britain had a Royal Commission on the Depression of Trade and Industry, chaired by Lord Iddesleigh (Stafford Northcote) and including Professor Bonamy Price of Oxford but most notable for the evidence of Professor Alfred Marshall of Cambridge. In his evidence to that inquiry and to the Gold and Silver Commission of 1887–8 (both reprinted in Marshall, 1926, edited by Keynes), and in a paper to the Industrial Remuneration Conference of 1885, Marshall considered how far remediable causes adversely affect continuity of employment. This led him to suggest 'Remedies for Fluctuations of General Prices' in the *Contemporary Review* in March 1887 (reprinted in Pigou, 1925), revising Ricardo's ingot plan to make the monetary unit a claim on a fixed weight of gold plus a fixed weight of silver, a step toward pegging the monetary unit to a basket of commodities (Irving Fisher's compensated dollar). This symmetallism proved incomprehensible to bimetallists, who persisted in plans that would require pegging the relative price of gold and silver. Also in 1886 (two years after writing the introduction to the posthumous collections of Jevons's *Investigations in Currency and Finance*), Herbert Foxwell published a lecture on *Irregularity of Employment and Fluctuations of Prices* (in Dimand, 2002, vol. 1). Like his colleague Marshall (both were fellows of St John's College, Cambridge), Foxwell emphasized fluctuations in employment as the crucial challenge posed by economic instability, and argued that the problem 'How to secure greater industrial stability' could be reformulated as 'How to diminish price fluctuations'. A young Swedish student named Knut Wicksell attended Foxwell's lectures at University College London in 1886. As Wesley Mitchell (1927, p. 7) observed, 'Before the end of the nineteenth century there had accumulated a body of observations and speculations sufficient to justify the writing of histories of the theories of crises': Eugen von Bergmann's *Die Wirtschaftskrisen: Geschichte der nationalökonomischen Krisentheorien*, published in Stuttgart in 1895, and E.D. Jones's *Economic Crises*, published in New York in 1900 (see also Barnett, 1941). In 1909, the year of Beatrice and Sidney Webb's Minority Report of the Poor Law Commission and of the first edition of Beveridge's *Unemployment*, the London School of Economics published a 71-page bibliography of unemployment and the unemployed by F. Isabel Taylor.

The cover of David Laidler's *The Golden Age of the Quantity Theory* (1991b) shows the three economists who dominated monetary economics before the First World War, making the case for monetary shocks and imbalances as the avoidable source of fluctuations: Alfred Marshall, Knut Wicksell and Irving Fisher.

In *Interest and Prices* in 1898 and then in his *Lectures on Political Economy* (1915), Wicksell distinguished the market rate of interest, set by the banking system, from the natural rate, the interest rate at which desired saving and investment would balance and the price level would not change. If a technical innovation raises the natural rate, or the banking system lowers the market rate, it will be profitable for entrepreneurs to borrow for new investment projects as long as the natural rate exceeds the market rate, causing (in a pure credit economy with no cash drain) a cumulative inflation. If the market rate exceeded the natural rate, a cumulative deflation would ensue. Although he considered himself a quantity theorist following in the footsteps of Ricardo, Wicksell was a pioneer in analysing a pure credit economy, not anchored by gold or other base money, which is why Michael Woodford deliberately chose Wicksell's title *Interest and Prices* for his 2003 treatise analysing a world in which financial innovation has greatly reduced the role of cash and bank reserves. Wicksell's economic contributions (which included using what came to be called the Cobb–Douglas production function four years before Cobb and Douglas) were continued by a Stockholm School including Dag Hammarskjold, Karin Kock (1929), Erik Lindahl (1939), Erik Lundberg (1937), Gunnar Myrdal (1939) and Bertil Ohlin – a list including three Nobel laureates (two in economics, one in peace) and four Swedish cabinet ministers. The Stockholm economists later expressed confidence that, even if Keynes had never written *The General Theory*, they would have discovered it themselves, but Don Patinkin (1982) expressed doubt, because the focus of Wicksell's heirs was on price dynamics, not the equilibrium level of employment and national income. Keynes's earlier *Treatise on Money* in 1930 (1971–89, vols 5 and 6) was much more Wicksellian than *The General Theory* in its emphasis on cumulative inflation or deflation when the interest rate does not equate planned investment to planned saving.

J. Bradford De Long (2000) writes:

> The story of 20th century macroeconomics begins with Irving Fisher. In his books *Appreciations and Interest* (1896), *The Rate of Interest* (1907), and *The Purchasing Power of Money* (1911) [Fisher, 1997, vols. 1, 3, and 4], Fisher fueled the intellectual fire that much later became monetarism. To understand the determination of prices and interest rates and the course of the business cycle, monetarism holds, look first (and often last) at the stock of money – at the quantities in the economy of those assets that constitute readily spendable purchasing power. ... It is true that the ideas that we see as necessarily producing the quantity theory of money go back to David Hume, if not before. But the equation-of-exchange and the transformation of the quantity theory of money into a tool for making quantitative analyses and predictions of the price level, inflation, and interest rates was the creation of Irving Fisher.

In *Appreciation and Interest*, Fisher argued that the difference between interest rates expressed in two standards (money and commodities, gold and silver, dollars and francs) is the expected rate of appreciation of one standard in terms of the other, deriving from this uncovered interest parity between two countries, the expectations theory of the term structure of interest rates, and the Fisher relation that nominal interest is the sum of real interest and expected inflation (plus a cross-product term). In *The Rate of Interest*, Fisher introduced the Fisher diagram, showing the optimal smoothing of consumption over two periods (assuming perfect credit markets) and an individual's saving or dissaving in each period. In *The Purchasing Power of Money*, Fisher (with his former student Harry G. Brown) upheld the quantity theory both against bimetallists who predicted permanent real benefits from expanding the money supply and against hard-money opponents of bimetallism (notably J. Laurence Laughlin of the University of Chicago), who denied the path of US prices could be explained by changes in the money supply. Fisher and Brown explained economic fluctuations by the slow adjustment of nominal interest to monetary shocks during 'transition periods' (lasting perhaps ten years), so that fluctuations could be avoided either by educating the public against what Fisher later termed 'the money illusion' (so that expected inflation and hence nominal interest would adjust to monetary shocks, leaving real interest unaltered) or by a monetary policy rule of varying the exchange rate (the dollar price of gold) to hold constant a price index (for which Fisher later proposed the Fisher ideal index, the geometric mean of the Paasche and Laspeyres indexes). Fisher's 1926 article, 'A statistical relation between unemployment and price changes' (in Fisher, 1997, vol. 8), correlated unemployment with a distributed lag of past price level changes (as a proxy for expected inflation), and was reprinted in the *Journal of Political Economy* in 1973 under the heading 'Lost and Found: I Discovered the Phillips Curve – Irving Fisher'. Unlike Marshall in Cambridge and Wicksell in Stockholm, Fisher did not attract a school of disciples at Yale. Through his role in establishing the Econometric Society and the Cowles Commission, Fisher advanced his preferred economic methodology of formal theorizing using mathematical and statistical techniques, but his contributions to monetary economics and economic fluctuations (like those of Hayek, Hawtrey, and many others) were long overshadowed by Keynes's *General Theory*, notwithstanding Keynes's acknowledgement of Fisher as his intellectual great-grandparent in appreciating the real effects of monetary changes.

Although Alfred Marshall's *Money, Credit and Commerce* was not published until 1923, the year before his death, parts of it were drafted as early as the 1870s, and his ideas had long circulated through his lectures, his evidence to official inquiries (gathered by Keynes in Marshall 1926), and the 'Cambridge oral tradition' of monetary theory (Eshag, 1963; Bridel, 1987; Laidler; 1999). Marshall, his professorial successor A.C. Pigou, Pigou's successor D.H. Robertson (1926), the young J.M. Keynes, and Cambridge economics lecturers

Frederick Lavington and J.R. Bellerby used a cash balance version of the quantity theory, relating the number of units of purchasing power the public wished to hold as cash to the level of income (in contrast to Fisher's logically equivalent version, which expressed the quantity theory in terms of the velocity of circulation of money).

Departure from the gold standard during the First World War and the post-war central European hyperinflations provided the occasion for the highest achievement of Marshallian monetary economics, Keynes's *Tract on Monetary Reform* in 1923 (Keynes 1971–89, vol. 4), an innovative work but one that innovated within the tradition established by Marshall. Keynes analysed inflation as a form of taxation of real money balances, identified as a social cost the consequent reduction in desired holdings of real money balances (M/P), and introduced covered interest parity (the spread between forward and spot exchange rates equals the difference between interest rates in the two currencies). Keynes calculated that real money balances had fallen by 92 per cent during the German hyperinflation, as a result of the soaring opportunity cost of holding money. Others had mistakenly argued that since the price level (P) was rising faster than the money supply (M), monetary expansion could not be the cause of the price inflation, and the Reichsbank president Rudolf Havenstein promised that, with 38 new high-speed printing presses, the Reichsbank would be able to print enough money to catch up with the prices. Robertson (1926), then collaborating closely with Keynes, examined forced saving ('induced lacking' in Robertson's terminology) caused by inflation. Turning from inflation to deflation, Keynes wrote *The Economic Consequences of Mr. Churchill* (in Keynes 1971–89, vol. 9) to oppose Britain's return to the gold standard at the pre-war parity in 1925, arguing that restoration of the pre-war parity would require a reduction of prices and money wages that could be achieved only through prolonged unemployment (see June Flanders, 1989, on the development of international monetary economics).

Keynesian Revolution and monetarist counter-revolution

The Great Depression of the 1930s helped provide a receptive audience for John Maynard Keynes's *General Theory of Employment, Interest and Money* (1936; 1971–89, vol. 7), which argued that involuntary unemployment could persist unless the government intervened with appropriate management of aggregate demand (Clarke, 1988; Dimand, 1988; Backhouse, 1995). *The General Theory* challenged Lionel Robbins and Friedrich Hayek of the London School of Economics, who argued against expansionary fiscal and monetary policy and for letting the depression take its course, and William Beveridge, who held (until his conversion to Keynesianism) that the existing level of British unemployment could be fully accounted for by structural, frictional and seasonal unemployment without invoking any deficiency of aggregate demand. To the rising generation of new economists,

from Harvard students Paul Samuelson and James Tobin to LSE economists Abba Lerner and Nicholas Kaldor, Keynes offered a message of hope that depressions were curable and preventable without adopting a Soviet-style centrally planned economy. Attempts to dismiss or ignore Keynes (Burns and Mitchell, 1946, mentioned Keynes in one sentence, in a footnote) were futile. Keynes provided an agenda for economists providing public policy advice and a framework for empirical, policy-oriented modelling, at a time when depression and war greatly expanded the role of governments.

Keynes's success in winning over the next generation of economists obscured the extent to which his contemporaries in economics shared his policy views rather than those of Robbins and Hayek: although Keynes used Pigou (1933) as the target of his attack on classical theory, he recognized how close they stood on practical policy. Even Ralph Hawtrey, the Treasury economist associated with the 'Treasury view' about crowding out and the ineffectiveness of fiscal policy, was convinced of the effectiveness of (and need for) stabilizing monetary policy (and contributed intriguing numerical examples to the development of the Kahn–Keynes spending multiplier; see Hawtrey, 1932). Keynes's caricature in *The General Theory* of 'classical economists' from Ricardo to Pigou as upholders of a rigid version of Say's Law, denying any role to aggregate demand in explaining unemployment (in contrast to the superior insight but fuzzier analytics of mercantilists, Malthus, and the underconsumptionists Hobson and Mummery), was more widely noted than his subsequent clarification that he did not consider Fisher or Hawtrey or Robertson or Wicksell as classical. However, support for expansionary fiscal or monetary policy during the Depression did not necessarily imply anticipation of Keynesian economics: proposals circulated for emergency public works financed by cutting other government spending and for domestic monetary expansion while keeping the exchange rate fixed, and in the United States the New Deal's National Recovery Administration was an attempt to raise price toward pre-Depression levels by restricting supply, rather than by stimulating demand. Keynes provided a framework within which the implications of such policies could be analysed. Independently of Keynes, starting from Marx and Rosa Luxemburg, Michal Kalecki in Poland developed a theory very close to Keynes's income–expenditure analysis, and in 1934 published in Polish a three-equation model of goods market equilibrium, money market equilibrium and aggregate supply. Patinkin (1982) argued that Kalecki was concerned with the dynamics of cyclical fluctuations, Keynes with determining the equilibrium level of income that equates saving to desired investment, and that Kalecki's 1934 essay (which Kalecki did not choose to be translated among his selected articles in 1966 and 1971, or refer to in other works) was not part of his central message.

The analytical framework that dominated macroeconomics for at least a quarter century after the Second

World War was based on Keynes's aggregate supply and aggregate demand functions (generally with more attention to aggregate demand than to aggregate supply) and the small system of simultaneous equations behind the Hicks–Hansen IS/LM diagram, which included Keynes's money demand function (liquidity preference) and later substitutes for his consumption function (De Vroey and Hoover 2004). The system of equations representing Keynes's message in a form equivalent to IS/LM was a four-equation model in Keynes's Cambridge lectures in December 1933, attended by David Champernowne and Brian Reddaway, the first economists to use such a model in print, but Keynes did not include it in *The General Theory*, perhaps following Marshall's advice to use mathematics as a tool of inquiry but to then translate the analysis into English and burn the mathematics (Rymes, 1989; Dimand, 1988). The resulting framework (extended to open economies by Robert Mundell and J. Marcus Fleming in the 1960s) did not capture all of Keynes's message (or messages), notably his distinction between fundamental uncertainty and insurable risk. Econometric estimation of macroeconomic models was pioneered, independently of Keynes, by Ragnar Frisch, Jan Tinbergen and Trygve Haavelmo (and Keynes's review of the first volume of Tinbergen, 1939, expressed severe scepticism), but it was taken up with enthusiasm by such Keynesians as Lawrence Klein. The claim in Chapter 2 of *The General Theory* that real and money wages move in opposite directions over the course of the cycle (and by implication, that real wages vary counter-cyclically) was challenged empirically by John Dunlop and Lorie Tarshis and on theoretical grounds by Michal Kalecki, leading Keynes in 1939 to acknowledge the cyclical pattern of real wages as an open question, which it remains to this day.

Milton Friedman and his students (Friedman, 1956) offered a renewed quantity theory of money as a challenge to Keynesianism, claiming to follow a Chicago oral tradition of monetary theory. Certainly it drew on such Chicago landmarks as Henry Simons's 1936 argument for rules rather than authorities in monetary policy (reprinted in Simons, 1948), but the intellectual inheritance from non-Chicago quantity theorists such as Irving Fisher and Clark Warburton (and even the young Keynes of *A Tract on Monetary Reform*) gradually came to be recognized. As Patinkin (1981) noted, a key element of Friedman's approach, the demand for money as a function of a small number of variables, originated in Keynes's *General Theory*. Although others had come close (in 1930, Fisher stated the marginal opportunity cost of holding cash balances), Keynes was the first to write the demand for money as a function of income and the interest rate. A further irony was that, though the spread of Keynesianism stemmed largely from its apparent ability to explain the Great Depression, the monetary interpretation of the Great Depression by Friedman and Schwartz (1963), as the consequence of mistaken Federal Reserve policy that permitted the US money supply to

contract by a third, was crucial in persuading many economists of the explanatory power of monetarism, the revived form of the quantity theory. For an overview of the development of macroeconomics from Keynes through Friedman to the New Classical and New Keynesian research programs (and the non-mainstream Post Keynesian and Austrian schools, from Keynesian fundamental uncertainty and Mises–Hayek trade cycle theory, respectively), enlivened with interviews with leading participants (see Snowdon and Vane, 2005).

Recurring themes

Certain issues reappear throughout the history of economics. Do fluctuations result from monetary disturbances, as Hawtrey (1913; 1932) and Fisher argued, or from real productivity shocks such as Schumpeterian innovations? Is unemployment best analysed as the functioning or malfunctioning of the labour market (as in Beveridge, 1930, and Hutt, 1939) or in terms of the demand for and supply of output as a whole (Keynes)? Is there a role for demand management to offset instability caused by volatile private investment reflecting the fundamental uncertainty of future profitability (Keynes) or is government itself the source of instability (von Mises, Hayek)? Should a central bank follow a rule rather than having discretion (as Henry Simons asked in 1936), or need there even be a central bank (as Hayek's student Vera Smith asked the same year)? Are recessions undesirable and preventable disequilibrium phenomena, or, as Arthur Ellis (1879) and Friedrich Hayek (1931) held, are they a normal and necessary part of the equilibrium path of the economy? Should analysis of economic fluctuations should be primarily a study of the statistical properties of the fluctuations, as in Burns and Mitchell (1946) and decades later Sims's vector autoregressions, or should the analysis be explicitly grounded in formal economic theory? As macroeconomists continue to theorize, measure, test and argue about these issues, they stand, knowingly or not, on the 'shoulders of giants' who discussed these questions before. De Long (2000, p. 83) notes that 'The New Classical research program walks in the footprints of Joseph Schumpeter's *Business Cycles* (1939) [and of Schumpeter, 1912, and Robertson, 1915], holding that the key to the business cycle is the stochastic nature of economic growth [so that] the "cycle" should be analyzed with the same models used to understand the "trend"', while the name of the New Keynesian research program (which emphasizes frictions that prevent instantaneous adjustment to nominal shocks) indicates its historical antecedents (although, as De Long points out, it also incorporates important features of Milton Friedman's contributions, such as emphasis on policy rules and on monetary rather than fiscal policy). Insights have sometimes long preceded the ability to formalize them; even Adam Smith's famous increasing returns through the division of labour, revived in Allyn Young's 1928 essay on economic progress, did not make its mark on the theories of international trade and endogenous growth until the last decades of the 20th century, when ways were devised to incorporate increasing returns to scale in formal models. The field has experienced major changes, as when Keynes made determining the equilibrium level of national income the central issue, or when monetarism posed inflation as the central problem instead of unemployment, or when attention shifted from fluctuations to long-term growth, but in each case the change was a transformation of a rich heritage.

ROBERT W. DIMAND

Bibliography

Arnon, A. 1991. *Thomas Tooke, Pioneer of Monetary Theory*. Aldershot, UK: Edward Elgar.

Backhouse, R.E. 1995. *Interpreting Macroeconomics: Explorations in the History of Macroeconomic Thought*. London and New York: Routledge.

Barnett, P. 1941. *Business-Cycle Theory in the United States, 1860–1900*. Chicago: University of Chicago Press.

Beveridge, W.H. 1921. Weather and harvest cycles. *Economic Journal* 21, 429–52.

Beveridge, W.H. 1922. Wheat prices and rainfall in Western Europe. *Journal of the Royal Statistical Society* 85, 412–59.

Beveridge, W.H. 1930. *Unemployment, a Problem of Industry (1909 and 1930)*. London: Longmans, Green.

Boianovsky, M., ed. 2005. *Business Cycle Theories: Selected Texts 1860–1939*, vols. 5–8, London: Pickering & Chatto.

Bridel, P. 1987. *Cambridge Monetary Thought: The Development of Saving–Investment Analysis from Marshall to Keynes*. Basingstoke: Macmillan.

Burns, A.F. and Mitchell, W.C. 1946. *Measuring Business Cycles*. New York: NBER.

Clarke, H. 1847. *Physical Economy: A Preliminary Inquiry into the Physical Laws Governing the Periods of Famines and Panics*. London (Cat. No. 34987.8, Kress Library, Harvard University).

Clarke, P. 1988. *The Keynesian Revolution in the Making 1924–1936*. Oxford: Oxford University Press.

Corry, B. 1962. *Money, Saving and Investment in English Economics 1800–1850*. London: Macmillan.

De Long, J.B. 2000. The triumph of monetarism? *Journal of Economic Perspectives* 14(1), 83–94.

De Vroey, M. and Hoover, K.D., eds. 2004. *The IS–LM Model: Its Rise, Fall, and Strange Persistence*. Durham, NC: Duke University Press. *Annual Supplement to History of Political Economy* 36.

Dimand, R.W. 1988. *The Origins of the Keynesian Revolution*. Aldershot, UK: Edward Elgar, and Stanford, CA: Stanford University Press.

Dimand, R.W., ed. 2002. *The Origins of Macroeconomics*, 10 vols. London and New York: Routledge.

Ellis, A. 1879. *The Rationale of Market Fluctuations*, 4th edn. London: Effingham Wilson.

Eshag, E. 1963. *From Marshall to Keynes: An Essay on the Monetary Theory of the Cambridge School*. Oxford: Basil Blackwell.

Fetter, F.W. 1965. *The Development of British Monetary Orthodoxy 1797–1875*. Cambridge, MA: Harvard University Press.

Fisher, I. 1997. *The Works of Irving Fisher*, 14 vols, ed. W.J. Barber assisted by R. Dimand and K. Foster, consulting ed. J. Tobin. London: Pickering & Chatto.

Flanders, M.J. 1989. *International Monetary Economics 1870–1960*. Cambridge: Cambridge University Press.

Friedman, M. 1952. The economist theorist. In *Wesley Clair Mitchell: The Economic Scientist*, ed. A.F. Burns. New York: NBER.

Friedman, M., ed. 1956. *Studies in the Quantity Theory of Money*. Chicago: University of Chicago Press.

Friedman, M. and Schwartz, A.J. 1963. *A Monetary History of the United States, 1867–1960*. Princeton, NJ: Princeton University Press for NBER.

Frisch, R. 1933. Propagation problems and impulse problems in dynamic economics. In *Economic Essays in Honour of Gustav Cassell*, London: George Allen & Unwin.

Glasner, D., ed. 1997. *Business Cycles and Depressions: An Encyclopedia*. New York: Garland.

Grice-Hutchinson, M. 1952. *The School of Salamanca: Readings in Spanish Monetary Theory 1544–1605*. Oxford: Clarendon Press.

Hagemann, H., ed. 2001. *Business Cycle Theories: Selected Texts 1860–1939*, 4 vols. London: Pickering & Chatto.

Hawtrey, R.G. 1913. *Good and Bad Trade*. London: Constable. Reprinted New York: A.M. Kelley, 1970 (with 1962 preface by author).

Hawtrey, R.G. 1932. *The Art of Central Banking*. London: Longmans, Green.

Hayek, F.A. 1931. *Prices and Production*. London: Routledge.

Hicks, J.R. 1937. Mr. Keynes and the classics: a suggested interpretation. *Econometrica* 5, 147–59.

Hume, D. 1752. *Writings on Economics*, ed. E. Rotwein. Madison: University of Wisconsin Press, 1955.

Humphrey, T.M. 1993. *Money, Banking, and Inflation: Essays in the History of Monetary Thought*. Aldershot, UK, and Brookfield, VT: Edward Elgar.

Hutt, W.H. 1939. *The Theory of Idle Resources*. London: Cape.

Jevons, W.S. 1884. *Investigations in Currency and Finance*, ed. H.S. Foxwell. London: Macmillan.

Juglar, C. 1862. *Des crises commerciales et de leur retour périodique en France, en Angleterre et aux Etats-Unis*. Paris: Guillaumin.

Kalecki, M. 1934. Trzy uktady [Three economic models]. *Ekonomista* 34, 54–70. Trans. C.A. Kisel. In M. Kalecki, *Collected Works of Michal Kalecki, Volume 1: Capitalism, Business Cycles and Full Employment*, ed. J. Ostiatynski. Oxford: Clarendon Press, 1990.

Kalecki, M. 1935. A macrodynamic theory of the business cycle. *Econometrica* 3, 327–44.

Keynes, J.M. 1971–89. *Collected Writings of John Maynard Keynes*, 30 vols., ed. D.E. Moggridge and E.A.G. Robinson. London: Macmillan, and New York: Cambridge University Press, for the Royal Economic Society.

Klein, L.R. 1946. Macroeconomics and the theory of rational behavior. *Econometrica* 14(2), 93–108.

Kock, K. 1929. *A Study of Interest Rates*. Stockholm Economic Studies No. 1. London: P.S. King.

Koopmans, T.C. 1947. Measurement without theory. *Review of Economic Statistics* 29, 161–72.

Laidler, D. 1991a. *The Golden Age of the Quantity Theory*. Princeton, NJ: Princeton University Press.

Laidler, D. 1991b. The quantity theory is always and everywhere controversial – why? *Economic Record* 67, 289–306.

Laidler, D. 1999. *Fabricating the Keynesian Revolution: Studies of the Inter-war Literature on Money, the Cycle, and Unemployment*. Cambridge: Cambridge University Press.

Laidler, D. 2003. *Macroeconomics in Retrospect: Selected Essays*. Cheltenham, UK, and Northampton, MA: Edward Elgar.

Lindahl, E. 1939. *Studies in the Theory of Money and Capital*. London: George Allen & Unwin.

Link, R. 1959. *English Theories of Economic Fluctuations 1815–1848*. New York: Columbia University Press.

Lundberg, E. 1937. *Studies in the Theory of Economic Expansion*. London: P.S. King.

Marshall, A. 1923. *Money, Credit and Commerce*. London: Macmillan.

Marshall, A. 1926. *Official Papers*, ed. J.M. Keynes. London: Macmillan.

Mises, L. von. 1935. *The Theory of Money and Credit*, trans. H. Batson. London: Cape.

Mitchell, W.C. 1913. *Business Cycles*. Berkeley: University of California Press.

Mitchell, W.C. 1927. *Business Cycles: The Problem and Its Setting*. New York: NBER.

Myrdal, G. 1939. *Monetary Equilibrium*, trans. R. Bryce and N. Stolper. London: W. Hodge.

O'Brien, D.P., ed. 1997. *Foundations of Business Cycle Theory*, 3 vols. Cheltenham, UK, and Brookfield, VT: Edward Elgar.

Patinkin, D. 1981. *Essays on and in the Chicago Tradition*. Durham, NC: Duke University Press.

Patinkin, D. 1982. *Anticipations of the General Theory? And Other Essays on Keynes*. Chicago: University of Chicago Press.

Pigou, A.C., ed. 1925. *Memorials of Alfred Marshall*. London: Macmillan.

Pigou, A.C. 1933. *Theory of Unemployment*. London: Macmillan.

Robertson, D.H. 1915. *A Study of Industrial Fluctuation*. London: P.S. King.

Robertson, D.H. 1926. *Banking Policy and the Price Level*. London: P.S. King.

Rymes, T.K. 1989. *Keynes's Lectures, 1932–35: Notes of a Representative Student*. Basingstoke: Macmillan, and Ann Arbor: University of Michigan Press.

Schumpeter, J.A. 1912. *The Theory of Economic Development*, trans. R. Opie. Cambridge, MA: Harvard University Press, 1934.

Schumpeter, J.A. 1939. *Business Cycles*, 2 vols. New York: McGraw-Hill.

Simons, H. 1948. *Economic Policy for a Free Society*. Chicago: University of Chicago Press.

Sims, C. 1980. Macroeconomics and reality. *Econometrica* 48, 1–48.

Slutsky, E. 1937. The summation of random causes as the source of cyclic processes. *Econometrica* 5, 105–46.

Smith, V.C. 1936. *The Rationale of Central Banking*. London: P.S. King.

Snowdon, B. and Vane, H.R. 2005. *Modern Macroeconomics: Its Origins, Development and Current State*. Cheltenham: Edward Elgar.

Sowell, T. 1972. *Say's Law: A Historical Analysis*. Princeton, NJ: Princeton University Press.

Thornton, H. 1802. *An Enquiry into the Nature and Effects of the Paper Credit of Great Britain*, ed. F.A. Hayek. New York: A.M. Kelley, 1965.

Tinbergen, J. 1939. *Statistical Testing of Business Cycle Theories*, 2 vols. Geneva: League of Nations. Reprinted New York: Agathon Press, 1968.

Veblen, T. 1904. *The Theory of Business Enterprise*. New York: Charles Scribner's Sons.

Vickers, D. 1959. *Studies in the Theory of Money 1690–1776*. New York: Chilton.

Wicksell, K. 1898. *Interest and Prices*, trans. R. Kahn. London: Macmillan, 1936.

Wicksell, K. 1915. *Lectures on Political Economy*, vol. 2, trans. E. Claasen. London: Routledge, 1935.

Wirth, M. 1858. *Geschichte der Handelskrisen*. 4th edn, Frankfurt am Main, 1890.

Woodford, M. 2003. *Interest and Prices: Foundations of a Theory of Monetary Policy*. Princeton, NJ: Princeton University Press.

Wright, C.D. 1886. *Industrial Depressions: The First Annual Report of the Commissioner of Labor, March, 1886*. Washington, DC: Government Printing Office. Reprinted New York: Augustus M. Kelley, 1968.

Young, A.A. 1928. Increasing returns and economic progress. *Economic Journal* 38, 527–42.

Young, W. 1987. *Interpreting Mr. Keynes: The IS–LM Enigma*. Oxford: Polity Press and Boulder, CO: Westview.

Maddala, G.S. (1933–1999)

G.S. Maddala (universally known as 'G.S.') was born on 21 May 1933 in the south Indian state of Andhra Pradesh, where he had his high-school education. G.S. held the University Eminent Chair at the Ohio State University when he died on 4 June 1999 due to congestive heart failure.

G.S.'s father was a schoolteacher of modest means, and his mother, though having only an elementary education, was well versed in Sanskrit and the works of the great Indian philosopher Sankara. After graduating from high school in 1947, G.S. had to drop out of college for a few years due to health and other reasons. In 1955 he graduated first in his class from Andhra University with a BA in mathematics, and went on to graduate in First Class from Bombay University with an MA in statistics in 1957. With a Fulbright Fellowship, G.S. travelled to the University of Chicago in 1960 and completed his Ph.D. in 1963 under the supervision of the late Zvi Griliches. In that year, he was offered the job of Assistant Professor of Economics at Stanford University. Before joining Ohio State in 1993, G.S. taught at the University of Rochester (1967–75) and at the University of Florida (1975–93). He also held visiting appointments at Cornell, Yale, CORE, Monash, Columbia, Caltech (as the Fairchild Distinguished Scholar), Emory and Oakridge Labs. The fascinating narration of his journey from an early college dropout in a remote Indian village in 1947 to a faculty position at Stanford in 1963 can be found in the Introduction ('How I Became an Econometrician') to the two-volume selected works of Maddala (1994). More detailed biographical information, his life story and philosophy can be found in Lahiri and Phillips (1999), Lahiri (1999), Griliches (1999), Rosen (2000) and Hsiao (2003).

Beginning with his first published paper (with Zvi Griliches, Robert Lucas, and Neil Wallace) in 1962, through the next four decades, G.S. published 12 books and more than 110 articles covering almost every emerging area of econometrics – distributed lags, generalized least squares, panel data, simultaneous equations, measurement errors, tests of significance, switching and disequilibrium models, qualitative and limited dependent variable models, selection and self-selection models, exact small sample distributions of estimators, outliers and bootstrap methods, robust estimators and more. The list is practically endless. Throughout his career G.S. used sample theory and Bayesian techniques freely in his research, a rarity in the econometrics profession, and was one of the early proponents of Bayesian approach in econometrics. Through his many books and the breadth of his own research, G.S. became a veritable textbook himself – a pre-eminent teacher in econometrics and an authority on almost every econometrics topic. Not surprisingly, according to the *Social Science Citation Index*, G.S. was one of the top five most-cited econometricians during each of the years 1988–93, and he was cited more times in 1994 and 1996 than each of the six econometricians who won the Clark Medal during 1970–2000.

During the 1960s, G.S. contributed heavily towards the formulation and estimation of production functions and technical change. His doctoral dissertation was on productivity and technical change in the US bituminous coal industry. His two papers with Jay Kadane in 1966 and 1967 considered, respectively, the importance of alternative exogeneity assumptions in the estimation of the constant elasticity of substitution production functions parameters inclusive of the share equations; and the bias in the estimation of the returns to scale parameter when the production function is incorrectly specified as a Cobb Douglas. The rigour and depth in these papers were undoubtedly ahead of their time.

The early 1970s saw a flurry of activity on efficient estimation methods of alternative distributed lag models. One of G.S.'s widely cited papers (1971a) showed why certain commonly used two-step procedures are asymptotically less efficient than the maximum likelihood estimator in the presence of lagged dependent variables as regressors. This sort of problem is encountered also in dynamic panel data models with individual heterogeneity. The key result in this paper is that in these models the information matrix of the slope parameters and the parameters embedded in the covariance matrix of residuals are not diagonal. Using this as a starting point, Pagan (1986) developed a more thorough and modern characterization of numerous two-step procedures with estimated covariance matrix in the context of various econometric models.

With Dave Grether in 1973, G.S. studied the effects of errors in variables in distributed lag models with serial correlation. They showed analytically that the estimated speed of adjustment can be severely biased, and can give the spurious appearance of a long lag in adjustment. In two influential papers with A.S. Rao in 1971 and 1973, G.S. developed maximum likelihood procedures for Solow's Pascal lag and Jorgenson's rational distributed lag models, and compared the power of tests for serial correlation in regression models with lagged dependent variables. One important conclusion that emerged from the latter study was that the nature of the autocorrelation and trend in the exogenous variable is crucial in determining the small sample behaviour of the test statistics and the estimators – hinting at much of the work on integrated variables that would come in the 1980s.

During the early 1970s G.S. also produced a number of important papers on the use and estimation of panel data models, and rightfully became one of the three 'fathers' (together with Yair Mundlak and Marc Nerlove) of modern panel data analysis in econometrics. In his influential *Econometrica* (1971b) paper, G.S. demonstrated – with his characteristic clarity – that the error component estimator is a weighted combination of within and between estimators, and thus the use of dummies entails substantial loss of information by ignoring the 'between' variation in the data. In another *Econometrica* (1971c) paper, G.S. discussed the problem of pooling cross-section and time series data, and emphasized tests for consistency between time series and cross-section information. The paper contains a very deep analysis of an alternative Bayesian approach with diffuse priors and concludes that the two approaches should be complementary. (Publishing three full-length articles in *Econometrica* in a year has to be some kind of a record for an economist!) The profession quickly saw the enduring value of these publications and elected G.S. a fellow of the Econometric Society in 1975.

During the 1970s, like many other econometrics stalwarts of the period, G.S. was also involved in the development of econometric methodology in simultaneous equations models. He worked on appropriate estimation strategies in large and medium-size econometric models (1971d), and studied the power characteristics of alternative tests of significance associated with simultaneous equation estimation (1974a). His *Econometrica* (1974b) paper showed that 'diffuse' and 'non-informative' priors might lead to sharp posterior distributions even in under-identified models. Only recently have Chao and Phillips (2002) fully solved the so-called 'Maddala paradox' using Jeffreys prior. They interpret the pathological result in terms of a naive use of the diffuse prior that fails to downweight sufficiently that part of the parameter space where the rank condition either fails or nearly fails. In another potent contribution to an important recent work on weak instruments, Maddala and Jeong (1992) correctly showed that the bimodal distribution of the instrumental variable estimator obtained in the literature is merely due to the illustrative model used, where the correlation between the structural and the first-stage errors is perfect. Phillips (2006) gives a complete characterization of the bimodality problem when instruments are weak.

From the mid-1970s, G.S. was primarily focused on developing estimation and test procedures for qualitative and limited dependent variable models, and produced nearly 40 articles. This line of research also dealt with models with selection, self-selection, disequilibrium and controlled prices. His work at Rochester with Forrest Nelson (1974) on disequilibrium models and with Lung-Fei Lee (1976) on recursive models with qualitative endogenous variables and generalized selection models represents a long and very fruitful period of research on this topic. His 1983 Econometric Society monograph, *Limited Dependent and Qualitative Variables in Econometrics*, was an immediate best-seller and was declared a citation classic in *Current Contents* (vol. 30, 16 July 1993). It has fuelled much of the innovative applied and theoretical research using these tools since the mid-1980s, and has served as a bible to empirical researchers in applied microeconomics. The strength of the book lies in its comprehensiveness, expositional simplicity, and depth. As of June 2006, the Google Scholar reports a record 3,721 citations of this advanced monograph. G.S. also wrote a number of theoretical and empirical papers analysing limited dependent and qualitative variable models with panel data, and wrote widely cited expository articles for use in other disciplines such as accounting, finance, transportation, and health.

It is notable that G.S. can jointly claim a statistical distribution – the Singh–Maddala (1976) distribution – a much better name than the Burr type 12 to which it is related. Maddala and Singh's proposed statistical distribution has triggered much research in describing the actual size distribution of incomes, and is a generalization of the Pareto distribution and the Weibull distribution used in analysis of equipment failures. As aptly noted by Sherwin Rosen (2000) while delivering the

first Maddala lecture at Ohio State University on 26 April 2000, 'Coase may have his Theorem, Stigler his Laws, Black and Scholes their Formula, and Lucas his critique, but what economist aside from Pareto (who was just as much a sociologist and political scientist and only one third economist) has half ownership of a distribution? And what an elegant economic derivation it has.'

G.S. had a deep interest in rational expectations models, in the validity of the hypothesis that can be gleaned from recorded survey data, and in how econometric disequilibrium models play out in this framework. Maddala, Fishe and Lahiri (1983) developed methods to estimate aggregate expectations when available survey data are partly qualitative and partly quantitative. He had done pioneering work (Maddala, 1983a) on the estimation for models with bounded price variation, and with Scott Shonkwiler (1985) applied the methodology to the corn market. With Steve Donald (1992), G.S. studied the disequilibrium model with upper and lower bounds on prices under rational expectations. The latter paper foreshadowed much work on exchange rate determination in a target zone in the 1990s. Undoubtedly, the full potential of this line of research initiated by G.S. is yet to be realized.

With failing health, G.S. spent much of the 1990s working primarily on bootstrap techniques and time series models with cointegration and structural breaks. During this period, he also wrote important papers on tests of unit roots in panel data models, robust inference, errors in variables problems in finance, Bayesian shrinkage estimation, outliers and influential observations, neural nets, and many others. Thus, ill health neither slowed down his research nor dampened his passion for mentoring and supervising Ph.D. students. In total G.S. supervised close to 60 doctoral students, co-authoring more than 65 published articles with them.

While testing the rationality of survey data on interest rate expectations in the context of a multiple-indicator single index model with heteroskedasticity, Maddala and Jeong in the mid-1990s used the weighted double bootstrap method to implement the Wald test in finite samples. His work with Hongyi Li in 1996 explored the use of different bootstrap techniques in cointegration regressions, financial and non-linear models. With Wu (1999) on panel data unit root test, G.S. suggested the use of a novel Fisher test that combines N individual tests with bootstrap-based critical values. Since much remains to be done to extend the Fisher approach to combining individual tests that are correlated, further generalizations of the Maddala–Wu test are certainly to come.

Much of his work on modern time series analysis has been summarized in his seminal book with In-Moo Kim (1998). This book also presents a comprehensive and lucid review of unit root and cointegration tests, and estimation with integrated variables. It discusses problems of unit root tests and cointegration under structural change, outliers, robust methods, the Markov switching model, and Harvey's structural time series model. The book contains a welcome chapter on the Bayesian approach to many of these problems and bootstrap methods for small-sample inference.

G.S. contributed to a number of purely policy-oriented and applied areas. Some of these topics include consumption, production and cost functions, money demand, regulation, pseudo-data, returns to college education, housing markets, energy demand, stock prices, international macro, and cross-country growth analysis. In all these papers, G.S. made serious attempts to grapple with substantive and important issues of the day. However, one common characteristic that flows through all these papers is that they unfailingly reflect the discriminating judgement of a consummate econometrician.

G.S. had the gift of a brilliant expositor – the ability to cut through the technical superstructure to reveal only essential details, while retaining the nerve centre of the subject matter he sought to explain. He loved to write econometrics in plain English. There was magic in how he could cut to the core, strip away all the irrelevant details and illuminate the essence of the issue in a quiet and unassuming way. This exceptional expository capability made him revered by applied and theoretical econometricians alike. This skill was apparent in all his writing and was a central element in his textbook expositions. His 1977 econometrics text redefined the boundaries of econometrics that could be integrated into graduate teaching, and became a new standard for subsequent econometrics textbooks. His advanced undergraduate textbook *An Introduction to Econometrics* has gone into its third edition (2000), and all his textbooks have been translated into a number of foreign languages.

G.S.'s style was to take a critical but constructive look at evolving econometric techniques – in particular those that have little practical significance. In this, G.S. had something that was close to perfect pitch in econometrics. He was one of the few econometricians who constantly asked whether the questions being answered were worth asking – always maintaining a clear perspective on a wide range of issues in econometrics and their relationship to economic problems. In doing so, he never hesitated to go against the tide of the profession. While much of his work was undoubtedly constructive, much was also critical of many current fads in econometrics. That is also a very important contribution.

KAJAL LAHIRI

See also **Bayesian econometrics; bootstrap; categorical data; distributed lags; econometrics; elasticity of substitution; expectations; fixed effects and random effects; inequality (measurement); rational expectations; Roy model; selection bias and self-selection; shrinkage-biased estimation in econometrics; time series analysis.**

I am grateful to Anthony Davies, Cheng Hsiao, Kay, Tara and Vivek Maddala, Thad Mirer, Peter Phillips and others who have contributed to this biography.

Selected works

1962. (With Z. Griliches, R.E. Lucas and N. Wallace.) Notes on estimated aggregate consumption functions. *Econometrica* 30, 491–500.

1965. Productivity change in the bituminous coal industry. *Journal of Political Economy* 73, 352–65.

1966. (With J.R. Kadane.) Notes on the estimation of elasticity of substitution. *Review of Economics and Statistics* 48, 340–4.

1967. (With J.R. Kadane.) Estimation of returns to scale and elasticity of substitution. *Econometrica* 35, 419–23.

1971a. Generalized least squares with an estimated covariance matrix. *Econometrica* 39, 23–33.

1971b. On the use of variance component models in pooling cross-section and time series data. *Econometrica* 39, 341–58.

1971c. The likelihood approach to pooling cross-section and time series data. *Econometrica* 39, 939–53.

1971d. Simultaneous equations methods for large and medium-sized econometric models. *Review of Economic Studies* 38, 435–45.

1971. (With A.S. Rao.) Maximum likelihood estimation of Solow's and Jorgenson's distributed lag models. *Review of Economics and Statistics* 53, 80–8.

1972. (With D.M. Grether.) On the asymptotic properties of two-step procedures used in the estimation of distributed lag models. *International Economic Review* 13, 737–44.

1973. (With D.M. Grether.) Errors in variables and serially correlated residuals in distributed lag models. *Econometrica* 41, 255–62.

1973. (With A.S. Rao.) Tests for serial correlation in regression models with lagged dependent variables and serially correlated errors. *Econometrica* 41, 255–62.

1974a. Some small sample evidence on tests of significance in simultaneous models. *Econometrica* 42, 841–51.

1974b. Weak priors and sharp posteriors in simultaneous equation models. *Econometrica* 44, 345–51.

1974. (With F.D. Nelson.) Maximum likelihood methods for models of markets in disequilibrium. *Econometrica* 42, 1013–30.

1976. (With L.-F. Lee.) Recursive models with qualitative endogenous variables. *Annals of Social and Economic Measurement* 5, 525–45.

1976. (With S.K. Singh.) A function for size distribution of incomes. *Econometrica* 44, 963–70.

1977. *Econometrics.* New York: McGraw Hill.

1983a. Methods for models of markets with bounded price variation. *International Economic Review* 24, 361–78.

1983b. *Limited Dependent and Qualitative Variables in Econometrics.* Cambridge: Cambridge University Press.

1983. (With R.P. Fishe and K. Lahiri.) A time series analysis of popular expectations data. In *Economic Applications of Time-Series Analysis*, ed. A. Zellner. Washington, DC: U.S. Census Bureau.

1985. (With J.S. Shonkwiler.) Modeling expectations of bounded prices: an application to the market for corn. *Review of Economics and Statistics* 67, 697–702.

1992. (With J. Jeong.) On the exact small sample distribution of the instrumental variable estimator. *Econometrica* 60, 181–3.

1992. (With S. Donald.) A note on the estimation of limited dependent variable models under rational expectations. *Economics Letters* 38, 17–23.

1994. *Econometric Methods and Applications: Selected Papers of G.S. Maddala*, 2 vols. Aldershot: Edward Elgar.

1996. (With H. Li.) Bootstrapping time series models (with discussion). *Econometric Reviews* 15, 115–95.

1998. (With I.-M. Kim.) *Unit Roots, Cointegration and Structural Change*. Cambridge: Cambridge University Press.

1999. (With S. Wu.) A comparative study of unit root tests with panel data and a new simple test. *Oxford Bulletin of Economics and Statistics* 61, 631–52.

2000. *An Introduction to Econometrics*, 3rd edn. Chichester: Wiley.

Bibliography

Chao, J.C. and Phillips, P.C. 2002. Jeffreys prior analysis with simultaneous equations models in the case with n+1 endogenous variables. *Journal of Econometrics* 111, 251–82.

Griliches, Z. 1999. Forward. In *Analysis of Panels and Limited Dependent Variable Models* (essays in honor of G.S. Maddala), ed. C. Hsiao et al. Cambridge: Cambridge University Press.

Hsiao, C. 2003. In Memoriam: G.S. Maddala. *Econometric Reviews* 22, vii–viii.

Hsiao, C., Lahiri, K., Lee, L.-F. and Pesaran, M.H. 1999. *Analysis of Panels and Limited Dependent Variable Models* (essays in honor of G.S. Maddala). Cambridge University Press.

Lahiri, K. 1999. ET Interview: Professor G.S. Maddala. *Econometric Theory* 15, 753–76.

Lahiri, K. and Phillips, P.C. 1999. Obituary: G.S. Maddala, 1933–1999. *Econometric Theory* 15, 639–41.

Pagan, A.R. 1986. Two stage and related estimators and their applications. *Review of Economic Studies* 53, 517–38.

Phillips, P.C. 2006. A remark on bimodality and weak instrumentation in structural equation estimation. *Econometric Theory* 22, 947–60.

Rosen, S. 2000. G.S. Maddala Memoir. First G.S. Maddala Lecture. Department of Economics, Ohio State University, Columbus, 26 April.

Mahalanobis, Prasanta Chandra (1893–1972)

Mahalanobis was born in Calcutta of a well-to-do Bengali middle-class family with a reformed outlook on Hindu religion. He was educated first at Presidency College, Calcutta, and then at Cambridge, where he graduated with a First in Natural Sciences from King's College in 1915. He became a Fellow of the Royal Society in 1946 and received many other scientific honours. While Mahalanobis served as Professor of Physics at Presidency College for nearly three decades, his scientific work consisted chiefly of developing statistical theory and techniques that had application to a wide range of subjects, beginning with meteorology and anthropology and ending in economics.

Mahalanobis established a firm international reputation on the basis of his work on the design of large-scale sample surveys (for example, 1944) and thus laid the basis for systematic collection of a large variety of data relating to socio-economic conditions. Mahalanobis's sense of realism was combined with a deep understanding of the problems of statistical inference. This led him to place stress on 'non-sampling errors' in addition to the standard preoccupation with sampling errors. He devised his system of 'interpenetrating network of sub-samples' to derive among other things, an idea of 'non-sampling errors' which are inherently associated with large-scale collection of data.

Mahalanobis's work on experimental designs developed with a view to estimating crop yields (1946) was highly influential in laying down the basis for collection of agricultural statistics in India. In multivariate statistics, Mahalanobis's measure of distance between two populations (1936), usually known as Mahalanobis's D^2 statistic, is a major contribution that is much used in anthropometry and elsewhere.

Mahalanobis maintained a keen interest in problems of national planning even before India had gained Independence. He recognized very early that such planning had to have a firm statistical base, and from the beginning of the 1950s, when the Indian Five Year Plan was launched, began to devote a very large part of his time and attention to questions of estimating national income and the factors determining its rate of growth. His approach to planning issues, with its strong emphasis on quantification, was significantly different from the qualitative approach favoured by the Indian economists of his generation. However, Mahalanobis was no exclusive believer in narrowly conceived quantitative techniques. He developed an important blend between qualitative and quantitative considerations, which is reflected in his 'Approach of Operational Research to Planning in India' (1955).

The second Five Year Plan, whose analytical structure was largely the handiwork of Mahalanobis, stands out as a very distinguished document in the development of planning theory. Mahalanobis is generally regarded as one of the prominent advocates of the inward-looking strategy of industrialization, along with Raul Prebisch. But the analytical foundation of the Mahalanobis approach was derived from somewhat different premises. While Prebisch began his theoretical study from what he thought was a historical fact, that is, the secular decline in terms of the trade of primary producing countries, Mahalanobis developed a two-sector model of growth to deduce a strategy of industrial development which he thought was best suited to India. The classification of the economy into sectors resembled in some respects Marx's famous Departmental Schema, although they were not identical.

Mahalanobis's sector-schema (1953) distinguished between 'capital goods' and 'consumer goods', but the assumption of vertical integration made in the interest of simplicity made statistical implementation difficult. The essential point of the model is that the capacity of the capital goods sector determines the potential rate of expansion of the consumer goods sector, and not the other way round. Further, at any given instant, capacities are not directly transferable from one sector to the other. Labour is not considered to be a constraint on expanding production. The model was developed initially for a closed economy but has been subsequently extended to open economies, with an exogenously given profile of export earnings. Mahalanobis used the model to illustrate the nature of the trade-off between present and future consumption, given the objective characteristics of the two sectors.

For the dynamic closure of the model he used the ratio of the output of the capital goods sector that is ploughed back into itself ('λ_k' in his notation), to deduce a 'gradualist growth' path of consumption. For any given value λ_k maintained over time, the rate of growth of aggregate output tends, over a sufficiently long period, to a magnitude $\lambda_k\beta_k$, where β_k is the output–capital ratio of the capital goods sector. The Mahalanobis model was subsequently freed from the assumption of an exogenously stipulated λ_k Exercises carried out by Stoleru (1965), Chakravarty (1969), Dasgupta (1969) and others introduced explicit intertemporal social utility functions along with a production technology of the Mahalanobis type. They deduced the characteristics of optimal growth paths with the help of variational calculus. $\lambda_k(t)$ was deduced as a solution of the optimizing exercise. It was shown that while the assumption of 'non-shiftability' critical to Mahalanobis's model could in several cases give rise to a preference for capital goods sector in early stages of growth (a strategy preferred by Mahalanobis himself), one could not obtain a universal rule of priority for capital goods irrespective of initial conditions, or the nature of social utility functions over time.

In all these exercises, the coefficients pertaining to the 'capital goods sector', sometimes identified as the 'machine tool sector', turned out to be an important determinant of the growth process. Earlier literature on business cycle theory originating with Marx, Tugan Baranovsky and Adolph Lowe had placed emphasis on the 'machine tools sector', without linking it up with an explicit growth model. In the growth-theoretic area Fel'dman alone appears to be the true predecessor of Mahalanobis, as is evident from Domar's discussion (1957).

Mahalanobis extended the two-sector model to a four-sector model, to focus on issues of reduction in unemployment along with increases in income. Mahalanobis came to the 'dual development thesis', which consisted in assigning high weights to the capital goods sector in the interests of long-term growth, and emphasis on the highly labour-intensive consumer goods sector in the short run. In the literature on planning, this has on occasion been referred to as the strategy of 'walking on two legs', with authorship occasionally ascribed to Mao Tse Tung.

Towards the end of his life, Mahalanobis returned to issues of statistical methodology and concentrated on developing what he called 'fractile graphical analysis' (1960), which is based on a geometrical concept of error and can also provide a generalized measure of separation between two 'different universes' of study.

Mahalanobis's work remains important for economists who are working on quantitative approaches to problems of plan formulation, especially in the context of large-sized economies. His work on sample surveys has generated a very valuable literature to which economic statisticians from India and elsewhere have made notable contributions.

SUKHAMOY CHAKRAVARTY

See also **development economics; Fel'dman, Grigorii Alexandrovich.**

Selected works

1936. On generalized distance in statistics. National Institute of Science, India, *Proceedings* 2, 49–55.
1944. On large scale sample surveys. *Philosophical Transactions*, Series B 231, 392–451. London: The Royal Society.
1946. Sample surveys of crop yields. *Sankhya* 7, 269–80.
1953. Some observations on the process of growth of national income. *Sankhya* 12, 307–12.
1955. The approach of operational research to planning in India. *Sankhya* 16(1–2), 3–130.
1958. Science and national planning. *Sankhya* 20, 69–106.
1960. A method of fractile graphical analysis. *Econometrica* 28, 325–51.
1961. *Talks on Planning*. Bombay and London: Asia Publishing House.

Bibliography

Bhagwati, J.N. and Chakravarty, S. 1969. Contributions to Indian economic analysis – a survey. *American Economic Review* (Supplement) 59(4), 1–73.
Chakravarty, S. 1969. *Capital and Development Planning*. Cambridge, MA: MIT Press.
Dasgupta, P.S. 1969. Optimum growth when capital is non-transferable. *Review of Economic Studies* 36(1), 77–88.
Domar, E.D. 1957. *Essays in the Theory of Economic Growth*. New York and Oxford: Oxford University Press.

Rao, C.R. 1973. Prasanta Chandra Mahalanobis. In *Biographical Memoirs of the Fellows of Royal Society* 19. London: The Royal Society.

Stoleru, L.G. 1965. An optimal policy for economic growth. *Econometrica* 33, 321–48.

Makower, Helen (1910–1998)

Helen Makower was educated at Cambridge and obtained her doctorate from London University. From 1938 until her retirement in 1973 she taught at the London School of Economics and Political Science. In collaboration with Jacob Marschak she made a pioneering contribution to modern asset portfolio theory and to the study of labour mobility. After the Second World War her analytical insights and interest in work then being performed at the Cowles Commission in Chicago led to her being one of the important links through which such techniques as activity analysis entered the academic scene in Britain. Her 1957 book and other papers made original contributions to the application of linear methods in economic analysis. One of her important insights was into the analogy between production and consumption, a precursor of later work on the household production and characteristics approaches to consumer theory.

K.J. LANCASTER

Selected works

1938. (With J. Marschak.) Assets, prices and monetary theory. *Economica* N.S. 5(August), 261–88.

1939–40. (With J. Marschak and H.W. Robinson.) Studies in the mobility of labour: analysis for Great Britain. Pt. I–II. *Oxford Economic Papers* 2(May 1939), 70–97; 4 (September 1940), 39–62.

1950. The analogy between producer and consumer equilibrium analysis. *Economica* N.S. 17(February), 63–8.

1957. *Activity Analysis and the Theory of Economic Equilibrium*. London: Macmillan.

Malthus, Thomas Robert (1766–1834)

Malthus has the unusual distinction not only of being a founder of classical economics – mainly because of his principle of population – but also of being instrumental in attempts to overthrow classical economics, mainly because of his principle of effective demand and its influence on John Maynard Keynes.

The most comprehensive and authoritative source of biographical information on Malthus is James (1979), from which the following brief details have been largely derived. Additional information can be found in the first edition of *The New Palgrave: A Dictionary of Economics* (Pullen, 1987), Malthus (1989b, pp. xv–lxix), and the *Oxford Dictionary of National Biography* (Pullen, 2004). Malthus was born on 13 February 1766, near Wotton, in the county of Surrey, England, and died on 29 December 1834, at Bath. He was buried in Bath Abbey where there is a commemorative plaque. Although he was baptized Thomas Robert, he used his full name only in formal situations; in less formal correspondence he signed himself T. Robert Malthus or Robert Malthus, and was known to family and close friends as Robert or Bob.

He was the son of Henrietta (née Graham) (1733–1800) and Daniel Malthus (1730–1800). The latter, having inherited independent means, cultivated literary, artistic, scientific and theatrical interests. He was an admirer and correspondent of Rousseau, who once visited the family home soon after Malthus's birth. The extensive library of Daniel Malthus was eventually passed on to Malthus and, supplemented by acquisitions of his own and other family members, is now held in Jesus College, Cambridge.

Malthus graduated in 1788, and in 1789 was ordained deacon with title to a stipendiary curacy at the small chapel at Okewood in the parish of Wotton. He was ordained priest in 1791, was appointed non-resident Rector of Walesby in Lincolnshire in 1803, and succeeded to the perpetual curacy of Okewood in 1824. He married in 1804 and had three children, but no grandchildren. In 1805 he was appointed to the East India College as 'Professor of General History, Politics, Commerce and Finance', a title later altered to 'Professor of History and Political Economy'. He held the post for the rest of his life, residing in the College at Haileybury, near Hertford. As well as performing his teaching duties, he preached regularly in the college chapel. The important collection of Malthus manuscripts held at Kanto Gakuen University in Japan (Malthus, 1997; 2004) contains four of his sermons. They corroborate the statement of his colleague William Empson: 'Mr. Malthus was a clergyman – a most conscientious one, pure and pious. We never knew one of this description so entirely free of the vices of his caste' (Empson, 1837, p. 481). His main publications were *An Essay on the Principle of Population*, first published in 1798, with five further editions in 1803, 1806, 1807, 1817 and 1826, and *Principles of Political Economy*, first published in 1820 with a posthumous second edition in 1836. He also published at least 20 smaller works – his authorship of a 21st is disputed – and evidence he gave at two public enquiries can be found in the published reports. There is a full list of his publications in *The New Palgrave* (Pullen, 1987) or in Malthus (1986, vol. 1, pp. 41–4). He engaged in extensive correspondence throughout his career, with Ricardo and many others. More than 230 letters to and from over 50 correspondents are known to have survived.

Malthus's methodology: 'the doctrine of proportions'

Before considering particular aspects of Malthus's political economy, it is important to understand some of the peculiar features of his methodology. Failure to do so has resulted in many misunderstandings and unnecessary disagreements among commentators.

One of the most important, but one of the most unrecognized, aspects of Malthus's methodology was the principle that he called the 'doctrine of proportions'. This was the traditional ethical notion of the just mean or middle way. As Leslie Stephen (1893) said, in the first *Dictionary of National Biography*, Malthus was always 'a lover of the golden mean'. The distinctive innovation of Malthus lay in applying the concept to political economy, and in giving it such a prominent and consistent role.

He stated that his aim was to show 'how frequently the doctrine of proportions meets us at every turn, and how much the wealth of nations depends upon the relation of parts'. It was his view that 'all the great results in political economy, respecting wealth, depend upon *proportions*', and warned that the 'tendency to extremes is one of the great sources of error in political economy, where so much depends upon proportions'. He added that 'It is not, however, in political economy alone that so much depends upon proportions, but throughout the whole range of nature and art' (1989b, vol. 1, pp. 352, 432; vol. 2, pp. 252, 269, 278).

Malthus's doctrine of proportions is thus essentially the same as the concept of the optimum. Although he did not use the term 'optimum', he must be recognized as having been one of the first to introduce the concept of the optimum into economics. In giving this central role to the doctrine of proportions, he has in effect said that *the* economic problem is the problem of balance, not the problem of choice.

But, despite his widespread use of the doctrine of proportions, Malthus recognized that precise determination of optimum points would be difficult. In discussing the optimum level of saving, he acknowledged that 'the resources of political economy may not be able to ascertain it' (1989b, vol. 1, p. 9), and, in discussing the just means for saving and the division of landed property, he said 'the extremes are obvious and striking, but the most advantageous mean cannot be marked' (1989b, vol. 1, p. 10).

The moderation and balance implied by the doctrine of proportions was evident in Malthus's personal temperament. Bishop Otter, who knew Malthus for nearly 50 years, said that he 'scarcely ever saw him ruffled, never angry, never above measure, elated or depressed', and that Malthus possessed 'a degree of temperance and prudence, very rare at that period, and carried by him even into his academical pursuits' (in Otter, 1836, pp. xxxii, xlix); and William Empson said in reference to the doctrine of proportions: 'The lesson which he sought to impress on others, he faithfully applied to himself; and so successfully, that few characters have ever existed of more perfect symmetry and order' (Empson, 1837, pp. 476–7).

Malthus has been given credit for introducing or propagating, either alone or with others, a number of key ideas in the history of economics; notably, the principle of population, the law of diminishing returns, and the role of effective demand. The doctrine of proportions could be added to the list.

Limitations and exceptions

Another facet of Malthus's methodology was his insistence on limitations and exceptions to the general principles in political economy. This could be seen either as a corollary of his doctrine of proportions or as another way of expressing the same doctrine. He believed that there are some general principles in political economy to which exceptions are 'most rare', but added 'yet there is no truth of which I feel a stronger conviction than that there are many important propositions in political economy which absolutely require limitations and exceptions' (1989b, vol. 1, p. 8). In this respect, he departed from the absolutist and universalist aspirations of some of his contemporaries, who, anxious to promote the scientific credentials of political economy, pretentiously declared them to be 'laws'. He was critical of the 'precipitate attempt to simplify and generalize', which he regarded as the 'principal cause of error, and of the differences which prevail at present among the scientific writers on political economy' (1989b, vol. 1, pp. 5–6).

Malthus has been accused, in his own day and now, of lacking in logic, especially by comparison with Ricardo. The accusation that his views did not constitute a logical and coherent system appears to have emanated from a failure to appreciate that his views were formulated in the context of his doctrine of proportions, and that he believed exceptions and limitations frequently have to be admitted when principles are used to formulate policies for application to particular real-world circumstances.

Laissez-faire and government intervention

Malthus strongly supported the principle of laissez-faire or freedom of trade: 'the wealth of nations is best secured by allowing every person, as long as he adheres to the rules of justice, to pursue his own interest in his own way', and 'governments should not interfere in the direction of capital and industry, but leave every person, so long as he obeys the laws of justice, to pursue his own interest in his own way'. He described this as a 'great principle' and as 'one of the most general rules of political economy' (1989b, vol. 1, pp. 3, 13, 518).

But he also argued that some exceptions to the principle of laissez-faire have to be recognized, and that the principle of non-interference is 'necessarily limited in practice' (1989b, vol. 1, 18–19, 525). He believed that there are certain duties that belong to the government – for example, in areas such as education; support of the poor; construction and maintenance of roads, canals, and public docks; colonization and emigration; and the support of forts and establishments in foreign countries – although he recognized that there may be differences of opinion about the extent to which government should share in such matters. In particular, the 'necessity of taxation … impels the government to action, and puts an end to the possibility of letting things alone' (1989b, vol. 1, pp. 18–19).

Thus, although Malthus strongly supported the principle of laissez-faire, his support, like that of Adam Smith, was pragmatic and conditional rather than dogmatic and absolute. There was, however, a major difference in their conception of the laissez-faire principle. In what Donald Winch has described as 'an attack on a central feature of the *Wealth of Nations*' and as 'a major qualification to Smith's system of natural liberty', Malthus doubted whether economic growth has always been, or will always be, advantageous to the mass of society. Malthus criticized Smith's view that the economic growth of Britain during the 18th century had improved the living standards of the labouring classes; he recognized that investments in trade and manufacturing had benefited individual capitalists, but argued that they were of less benefit to society as a whole. Thus Malthus raised the possibility of conflict between economic growth and human happiness, and implied that interventionist welfare policies by government might be justified. In this respect, as Winch has argued, 'if general allegiance to the system of natural liberty, as interpreted by Smith and upheld under the different circumstances by some of his followers, is the hallmark of an orthodox political economist during the first half of the nineteenth century, Malthus occupies a decidedly ambivalent position' (Winch, 1987, pp. 32, 59–61, 76–7).

Population

Malthus's first published work – *An Essay on the Principle of Population* (1798) – was written primarily to controvert the perfectibilist notions of Godwin and Condorcet. He believed that the growth of population presented a major obstacle to unlimited human progress. He argued that population will constantly tend to exceed the food supply, with the result that human progress will be neither rapid nor unlimited, and will be accompanied by sufferings and evils arising from the operation of unavoidable checks to population growth.

To support his views on the threat of overpopulation to human progress, Malthus introduced the notion of the two ratios. He argued that population will tend to increase in a geometrical ratio (1, 2, 4, 8 …) doubling every 25 years; but the food supply will increase only in an arithmetical ratio (1, 2, 3, 4 …). He believed that the population of 'this Island' was then about seven million, and that after the first 25 years it would reach 14 million, after 50 years 28 million, after 75 years 56 million, and so on. But the utmost that could be expected for the supply of food is that there would be sufficient to feed 14 million after 25 years, 21 million after 50 years, 28 million after 75 years, and so on. Thus, after the first 25 years, the food supply would become insufficient, and any further progress in the size of the population and the standard of living would be impossible. He concluded that this argument is conclusive against the perfectibility of the mass of mankind.

Opinions differ on whether Malthus's principle of population depends essentially on the empirical accuracy of these ratios or whether they were intended merely as approximate tendencies, or as a mathematical metaphor. Whatever his intention, there is no doubt that the ratios have exerted a powerful rhetorical influence in promoting his message and his fame.

Malthus was not the first writer to issue a warning about the dangers of overpopulation, as he himself acknowledged, but for a variety of reasons his arguments have become the best-known, and have exerted a great influence on human thought and human affairs. He alerted the world to the problem of overpopulation, and his views continue to affect the population policies of governments through the world today.

Having presented his basic arguments in the first two chapters of the *Essay*, Malthus then proceeded to discuss the 'checks' to population. As he said in his first postulate, people cannot live without food, and therefore it would be impossible to have a situation where 28 million people were in existence but the food supply was adequate for only 21 million. There must therefore be some mechanisms or checks whereby populations are prevented from exceeding the food supply. The bulk of the *Essay*, especially in the much enlarged later editions, was devoted to a detailed description of the checks that have operated in different countries and at different times.

He classified the checks as either positive checks that reduce normal life expectancy and increase the death rate, or preventive checks that reduce the birth rate. Among his list of positive checks he included common diseases, epidemics, wars, plagues, pestilence, famines, infanticide, unwholesome occupations and habitations, severe labour, exposure to the seasons, extreme poverty, bad nursing of children, great cities, and excesses of all kinds.

The preventive checks, described in circumspect language ('vicious customs with respect to women'), included prostitution and birth control, but the only preventive check that he approved of and advocated was prudential restraint, by which he meant delaying marriage until sufficient resources of food, accommodation and other necessaries are available to provide the parents and the expected number of children with an acceptable standard of living. He noted that prudential restraint is practised, and should be practised, by those who want to maintain after marriage the social and economic status they enjoyed before marriage. The case for prudential restraint was even more vigorously argued in the later editions, where those who marry and raise children without ensuring that they have sufficient resources are accused of irresponsible and immoral behaviour.

He also classified the population checks as either vice or misery, but did not clearly show how the vice-and-misery classification is related to the positive-and-preventive. Presumably he meant that, among the positive checks, some, such as war and infanticide, are vices, and all lead to misery; and among the preventive checks all except prudential restraint are vices, and all are likely to lead to misery; and although prudential restraint is a virtue, not a vice, it often leads to vice.

> Restraints upon marriage are but too conspicuous in the consequent vices that are produced in almost every part of the world; vices, that are continually involving both sexes in 'inextricable unhappiness'. (1986, vol. 1, p. 28)

In admitting that prudential restraint might also be a cause of misery, he might have been speaking from personal experience, being in 1798 a 32-year-old bachelor with an income as a curate insufficient to support a wife and family in a socially acceptable manner.

In the second and later editions, he introduced the expression 'moral restraint', by which he meant prudential restraint conducted in accordance with Christian moral precepts regarding premarital sex, but the *concept* of moral restraint is *implicit* in the first edition. It is unlikely that, in advocating prudential restraint, Malthus as a Protestant clergyman would have intended to condone prudential restraint that was accompanied by immoral sexual behaviour.

In the second (and later) editions of the *Essay*, he softened some of the harshest conclusions of the first by arguing that, if people could be made aware of the harm done by improvident procreation, then moral restraint, though still a difficult challenge, could be practised without causing misery and without leading to vicious practices. He objected to contraception on moral grounds and also because, by facilitating control of the birth rate and reducing the pressure of population, it would remove one of the incentives needed to overcome our natural indolence, to promote economic growth, and to encourage the 'growth of mind'. It is ironical that the expression 'Malthusian practices' became synonymous with contraception, and that contraception has become the method most commonly adopted throughout the world to control population. The world has responded to Malthus's warnings of the danger of overpopulation by adopting a remedy he strongly rejected.

Arguments in favour of population growth

The popular and superficial view of Malthus is that he was opposed to population growth. But there are numerous instances in his writings which show that he regarded an increase of population, under certain conditions, as desirable in itself, and as a necessary cause of economic growth. For example, he spoke of the 'pursuit of the desirable object of population' (1986, vol. 3, p. 455); and, referring to the possibility of a great increase of

population in Ireland in the 19th century, he said 'so great an increase of human beings, if they could be well supported, would be highly desirable' (1986, vol. 4, p. 32). In a similar vein he said: 'That an increase of population, when it follows in its natural order, is … a great positive good in itself, … I should be the last to deny' (1989a, vol. 1, p. 439). And those who use Malthus to support a policy of population reduction forget that on one occasion he argued that a diminution of population would be harmful: 'It is evidently therefore regulation and direction which are required with regard to the principle of population, not diminution or alteration' (1989a, vol. 2, p. 94).

Some of his most forceful statements in favour of population growth occurred in the appendices added to the third (1806) and fifth (1817) editions of the *Essay*, in response to critics who had accused him of being anti-population. The fact that these appendices have been omitted from some modern reprints of the *Essay* might explain the limited awareness of his pro-population ideas.

Malthus's pro-population views can even be seen when he was advocating prudential restraint: 'Prudential habits with regard to marriage carried to a considerable extent, among the labouring classes of a country mainly depending upon manufactures and commerce, might injure it' (1989b, vol. 1, p. 236; vol. 2, p. 215). This is a surprising argument, given that he had said that the preventive check of prudential restraint should be a principal remedy for overpopulation. It shows that he wished the doctrine of proportions to be applied as a check to the preventive check!

Malthus's pro-population views can also be seen in his statements on population as a *necessary* cause of economic growth. He admitted that population growth alone will not promote economic growth; for example, he argued that 'the increase of population alone … does not furnish an effective stimulus to the continued increase of wealth' (1989b, vol. 1, pp. 347–8), 'population alone cannot create an effective demand for wealth' (1989b, vol. 1, p. 350) and 'encouragements to population … will not alone furnish an adequate stimulus to the increase of wealth' (1989b, vol. 1, p. 351). But he also stated:

> That a permanent increase of population is a powerful and necessary element of increasing demand, will be most readily allowed. (1989b, vol. 1, p. 347; in the second edition, 'permanent' was changed to 'continued')

and

> That an increase of population, when it follows in its natural order, is … absolutely necessary to a further increase in the annual produce of the land and labour of any country, I should be the last to deny. (1989a, vol. 1, p. 439)

In other words, although Malthus recognized that population growth is not a *sufficient* cause of economic growth, he nevertheless regarded it as a *necessary* cause.

In some circumstances, according to Malthus, an increase in population will bring about a decrease in living standards; but in other circumstances it will bring about an increase in living standards, and a decrease in population will bring about a decrease in living standards. Living standards can be both a direct and an inverse function of population. Some critics would regard this as self-contradictory, as proof of his lack of logic, and as a justification for William Cobbett's epithet 'muddle-headed Malthus'. Others would see it as a reasonable, parabolic application of the doctrine of proportions.

Theological aspects of the principle of population

The early chapters of the first edition of the *Essay* have a rather pessimistic tone. They appear to be saying that the pressure of population against the food supply will keep the mass of the population at or near subsistence level, and that this struggle between food and population will be accompanied by miseries and vices. However, in the last two chapters of the first edition of the *Essay* Malthus explored the theological implications of his principle of population. His published contributions in theology are too limited for him to be considered as a theologian in a professional sense, but his theological views are interesting in their own right, because of their heterodox nature, and because they seem to have been presented, not as a mere afterthought or pious homily, but in an attempt to integrate his principle of population into a comprehensive world view, in opposition to that of Godwin and Condorcet. As a Christian minister he would have been concerned to show that his view of population did not conflict with Christian ideas about the nature of God. He had due cause for concern. In saying that misery and vice can come from obeying the biblical injunction to go forth and multiply, he was accused by some critics of blasphemously denying the Creator's omnipotence, omniscience and benevolence.

However, in the last two chapters of the first edition of the *Essay* he argued, on the contrary, that population pressure is providentially ordained by God as a means whereby human development ('the growth of mind') is stimulated. He argued that the constant pressure of population against food supply, although it might produce some moral and physical evils, would also produce an overbalance of good. The first edition of the *Essay* thus finished on a note of moral and theological optimism.

The last two chapters were omitted from subsequent editions of the *Essay*. Comments contained in his correspondence (1997, pp. 73–7) and remarks from other contemporaries indicate that the omission occurred at the instigation of friends. Some commentators interpret the omission as a recantation. Others find traces of his theology in the later editions, and argue that his growth-of-mind theology remained an essential, if only implicit, framework throughout all editions of the *Essay*. They argue that to ignore its theological aspect is to ignore an essential element of his total population theory and, contrary to his intentions, to reduce the *Essay* to a mere economic or political tract.

Poor Laws

Although Malthus believed that population pressure was a phenomenon common to most societies, he argued that the problem had been exacerbated in England by the Poor Laws. They were intended to alleviate poverty, but only succeeded in creating the poor they sought to maintain. They encouraged people to marry too early and have large families, in the expectation that food and accommodation would be provided for them; and they discouraged hard work and the development of productive skills.

In his earlier writings Malthus had argued for abolition of the Poor Laws, both as a principle and as a practical policy; but in later writings and in correspondence (see James, 1979, p. 450; Winch, 1996, pp. 320–1) his position moved from complete abolition to gradual abolition, and then to administrative reform, arguing that a fundamental change involving complete abolition would present practical and political difficulties, and that the most that could be achieved in the current circumstances would be an amelioration of the present system through improved administration.

This is an example of his insistence on the need for limitations and exceptions in the practical application of general principles. He did not see any contradiction in subscribing to the idea in principle while at the same time rejecting it as a practical policy for a particular place and time. Another example of this feature of his methodology occurred in his views on the Corn Laws.

Corn Laws

Although Malthus strongly supported the principle of laissez-faire, he published a pamphlet in 1815 supporting the retention of the Corn Laws, which prohibited, for example, the import of wheat when the home price fell below 80 shillings a quarter. This radical departure from laissez-faire caused dismay among other political economists and among his Whig friends who opposed the protectionist policy of the Tory government. In admitting this exception to the principle of laissez-faire, he was in effect reaffirming his view that, unlike the laws of mathematics, the principles of political economy should not be applied in an absolutist and universalist manner.

It has been argued that in his later years Malthus changed his mind and recanted his earlier support for the Corn Laws. The arguments for and against this change-of-mind hypothesis have been elaborated elsewhere (Hollander, 1992; 1995; Pullen, 1995), and are too detailed to be repeated here. It would probably be fair to say that, on the basis of the textual and contextual evidence so far presented, there is no clear, unambiguous statement of a recantation by Malthus. But it should also be said that Malthus was strongly in favour of the principle of free trade, and that he strongly regretted the need for an exception in the case of the Corn Laws. It is obvious from his writings and correspondence that, if the circumstances that necessitated the exception were removed, he would have gladly removed his support for agricultural protection.

Economic growth, effective demand and Say's Law

Malthus's views on economic growth are to be found scattered throughout his many publications, with his most systematic (but not comprehensive) treatment of this topic in the final chapter of the *Principles*, namely chapter 7, 'On the Immediate Causes of the Progress of Wealth'. He divided the immediate causes of progress into two categories: 'the powers of production' and 'the means of distribution'. On the production side he discussed four causes: population, accumulation, soil fertility and inventions (which, by combining the second and the fourth, could be reclassified as labour, capital and land). On the distribution side he discussed three causes: the division of landed property, commerce (internal and external), and unproductive consumers. His views on the production side were unremarkable at the time, and would be quite acceptable in standard texts today, but his views on the distribution side have proved to be controversial because of their emphasis on the role of effective demand.

By effective or effectual demand Malthus meant the *power* to purchase at a price sufficient to cover the vendor's costs and required profit, combined with the *willingness* to purchase. His distinction between power and will, or means and motives, was a recurring theme in his political economy. He stressed that production requires more than the power to produce; it requires also the motive to produce, which comes from effective demand.

> … the powers of production, to whatever extent they may exist, are not alone sufficient to secure the creation of a proportionate degree of wealth. Something else seems to be necessary in order to call these powers fully into action. This is an effectual and unchecked demand for all that is produced. (1989b, vol. 1, p. 413; vol. 2, pp. 263, 447)

The powers of production will be 'called into action, in proportion to the effective demand for them' and 'General wealth, like particular portions of it will always follow effective demand (1989b, vol. 1, pp. 414, 417). In effect he was saying that demand-side forces are as powerful and as necessary as the supply-side forces of natural resources, capital accumulation, division of labour, and so on.

He believed that an important cause of an adequate level of effective demand was the existence of a body of 'unproductive consumers', who purchase material products but do not produce material products. They would include menial servants, military personnel, actors, clergymen and other service providers. The concept was completely misunderstood by Ricardo who said that unproductive consumption is as useful as a fire in a warehouse or the destruction of war. Malthus later recognized that the term 'unproductive' had pejorative implications, and altered it to 'the provision of services'. However, the concept could also include those who live on their investments in the national debt and those whose wealth enables them to consume without either producing material goods or providing services, thus inviting Marx's description of Malthus as a protector of the ruling classes and the idle rich.

Malthus's views on effective demand were largely rejected during his lifetime, and largely ignored for the next hundred years. It was generally believed with James Mill, Jean-Baptiste Say and others that the purchasing power generated during the production process would be sufficient for all the products to be sold, that aggregate demand deficiency would never be a cause of economic decline, and that a general glut of products would be impossible. This view, known as Say's Law or Mill's Principle, and popularly expressed as 'supply creates its own demand', became a standard theme of classical economics, and still finds its supporters, even though Malthus showed, and Say virtually admitted, that its validity relies on a tautological definition of 'supply' and 'product'. The experience of the depression of the 1930s and the publication of J.M. Keynes's *General Theory* (1936) cast doubt on this conventional wisdom of Say's Law, and rescued Malthus's views on effective demand from oblivion.

Effective demand and the division of landed property

Malthus's views on effective demand as a stimulus to economic progress led him to advocate a wider distribution of wealth, because 'Practically it has always been found that the excessive wealth of the few is in no respect equivalent, with regard to effective demand, to the mere moderate wealth of the many' (1989b, vol. 1, p. 431). But this redistribution of property has often been neglected, and sometimes even denied, in the secondary literature. Karl Marx, in particular, misinterpreted Malthus in this regard, and some other commentators appear to have taken their views of Malthus from Marx; and, like Marx, have not bothered to test them against Malthus's text.

Admittedly, there are passages in some parts of Malthus's writings that support a pro-landlordism interpretation. But in other passages he was critical of the distribution of land and other property, and described the existing maldistribution as unjust and as an impediment to economic growth; for example

> A very large proprietor, surrounded by very poor peasants, presents a distribution of property most unfavourable to effective demand … Thirty or forty proprietors, with incomes answering to between one

thousand and five thousand a year, would create a much more effective demand for wheaten bread, good meat, and manufactured products, than a single proprietor possessing a hundred thousand a year. (1989b, vol. 2, 373–4)

In his view, 'the division of landed property is one of the great means of the distribution of wealth', and without 'an easy subdivision of landed property ... a country with great natural resources might slumber for ages with an uncultivated soil, and a scanty yet starving population' (1989b, vol. 1, pp. 439–40).

He did not propose that either private property in land or the class of landed proprietors should be abolished. He regarded both as necessary. But he did not regard 'the present great inequality of property' as 'either necessary or useful to society'; and added that 'On the contrary, it must certainly be considered as an evil, and every institution that promotes it is essentially bad and impolitic' (Malthus, 1986, vol. 1, p. 102). Less inequality in land ownership would mean that rents would be enjoyed by a larger number of proprietors.

However, he did not wish the division of property to be pushed too far:

> The division and distribution of property, which is so beneficial when carried only to a certain extent, is fatal to production when pushed to extremity. (1989a, I, 372)

This argument is an excellent illustration of his characteristic middle-way methodology. He himself regarded the question of the division of property as the most important application of the doctrine of proportions.

> It will be found, I believe, true that all the great results in political economy, respecting wealth, depend upon *proportions* ... But there is no part of the whole subject, where the efficacy of proportions in the production of wealth is so strikingly exemplified, as in the division of landed and other property; and where it is so very obvious that a division to a certain extent must be beneficial, and beyond a certain extent prejudicial to the increase of wealth. (1989b, vol. 1, pp. 432–3)

Distribution as a factor of production

Other writers, before and after Malthus, have discussed production and distribution, but generally their approach has been to regard distribution as the process whereby the proceeds of production are shared out after they have been produced by the factors of production. Their theory of distribution is worked out independently of their theory of production.

Malthus also looked at the problem of distribution in this way, with separate chapters analysing the way in which wages, profits and rents are determined. But in addition he looked at distribution from another direction. For Malthus, distribution is not merely concerned with sharing out the spoils of production. It has a further

function. It is an essential determinant of production, and an integral part of the production process considered in its totality. Without a proper distribution, there would be no production – except at a self-subsistence level. He saw distribution as a problem to be resolved *before* (as well as after) production takes place. Whereas others were concerned mainly with how the distribution of the product between wages, profits and rent is affected by economic development, Malthus made a major contribution by stressing that the distribution of the product in turn affects economic development. He was in effect saying, if not in these precise words, that distribution must be regarded as a factor of production, along with the conventional listing of the other factors of production – land, labour and capital. They represent only the supply side of the production process; but, if production is to occur, there must be a motive to produce as well as the means. In an exchange system, there will be no motive for producers to produce unless there are prospects of profits, and there will be no profit prospects unless there is an adequate effective demand for the products. This effective demand from potential consumers will not be forthcoming unless there has been a proper distribution of spending power. As Malthus said, 'there is certainly no indirect cause of production as powerful as consumption' (1989b, vol. 2, p. 34). The effective demand generated by a proper distribution provides demanders with the power or means to demand, and this provides suppliers with the will or motive to supply. It is obvious that, unless there has been production, there can be no distribution. But Malthus insisted that maximum production will not be achieved unless an optimum spread of distribution is established.

The separation and dichotomy between production and distribution that is presented in typical textbooks would therefore have been unacceptable to Malthus, for whom any listing of the factors of production would have to include distribution. It is this relationship of reciprocal causation between distribution and production that makes Malthus's theory of distribution innovative and distinctive.

Saving, investment and hoarding

Some commentators have interpreted Malthus as holding that savings are always invested; and have concluded that in Malthus's theory saving is not a leakage from the circular flow, does not constitute a reduction in effective demand, is not an impediment to economic growth, and must always be beneficial. In this respect, they see a major difference between Malthus and Keynes. They deny the claim that Malthus was a precursor of Keynes, and argue that Keynes was mistaken in regarding Malthus as a precursor. This interpretation appears to have been based in part on statements such as:

> it is stated by Adam Smith, and it must be allowed to be stated justly, that the produce which is annually saved is

as regularly consumed as that which is annually spent, but that it is consumed by a different set of people. (Malthus, 1989b, vol. 1, p. 31)

Malthus appears here to agree with Adam Smith that savings will always find an outlet in investment, and that there will never be a surplus of savings over investment. However, that interpretation is doubtful, given that 'and it must be allowed to be stated justly' was omitted from the second edition of the *Principles* (see Malthus 1989b, vol. 2, pp. 28, 300–1). Ricardo in his *Notes on Malthus* had said that a saving-equals-investment interpretation is inconsistent with the views expressed elsewhere by Malthus on saving. It would be reasonable to conclude that the omission was made by Malthus in response to Ricardo's note (Ricardo, 1951–73, vol. 2, p. 15, n. 4).

Another possible source for attributing a saving-equals-investment view to Malthus might be Malthus's statement 'No political economist of the present day can by saving mean mere hoarding' (1989b, vol. 1, p. 32). Some commentators have interpreted this to mean that, in Malthus's view, savings are always invested, never hoarded, and never intended to be hoarded. If correct, such an interpretation would also constitute a major difference between Malthus and Keynes.

But there is another, more plausible, interpretation. Malthus here was not saying that savings are never held as idle cash balances. He was not precluding the possibility that savings might remain uninvested and idle, not on purpose but because a satisfactory investment outlet cannot be found. This alternative interpretation negates a saving-equals-investment interpretation.

There are numerous instances in Malthus's writings that support this alternative interpretation. They clearly show that, in his view, savings will not always be invested, and that excessive savings are harmful. For example, Adam Smith had said that 'every frugal man [appears to be] a publick benefactor' and that the increase of wealth depends on a favourable balance of production over consumption (Smith, 1776, book II, ch. 3, para. 25; book IV, ch. 3, iii, para. c.15), but Malthus disagreed:

> That these propositions are true to a great extent is perfectly unquestionable ... but it is quite obvious that they are not true to an indefinite extent. (1989b, vol. 1, 8)

To say that Malthus identified or equated saving and investment is to ignore his frequent use of expressions such as redundant capital, excessive capital, idle capital, spare capital, premature supply of capital, unemployed capital, vacant capital, capitalists at a loss where they can safely employ their capitals, capitals at a loss for employment, and so on. These expressions refer to funds that arise through savings and are intended for investment but for which an actual investment, at an acceptable degree of profit and risk, cannot be found. Malthus was thus recognizing the possible existence of an inequality between *ex ante* or intended investment and *ex post* or

actual investment, because of the exhaustion of profitable investment outlets. This gap between savings intended for investment and savings actually invested could be described as unintended or residual hoarding – although Malthus did not use those terms – as distinct from the intended hoarding of a miser, or 'mere hoarding'.

Malthus and Ricardo

The correspondence between Malthus and Ricardo provides a revealing insight into the minds and characters of two of the most important contributors to the development of political economy in England during its formative years in the early 19th century (see Ricardo, 1951–73, vols 6–9). They expressed their arguments forcefully but politely, although at times hints of frustration and exasperation began to appear, as they struggled to comprehend and to counter the other's point of view, especially when in an era without carbon copies and photocopies they seemed to forget what they had previously written. And despite their doctrinal and methodological differences, they remained close friends, with frequent visits to one another's homes. Ricardo's last letter to Malthus concluded with the statement: 'I should not like you more than I do if you agreed in opinion with me' (Ricardo, 1951–73, vol. 9, p. 382); and Malthus, after the death of Ricardo, was reported to have said: 'I never loved any body out of my own family so much' (Empson, 1837, p. 489). Ricardo had offered to assist Malthus financially by investing money for him in a stockbroking venture; and at one stage Malthus might have been seriously considering a personal involvement in international trading in commodities and bullion, using statistics and advice provided by Ricardo (see Malthus, 2004, ch. 3). After Ricardo's death, Malthus defended him against critics who Malthus considered had gone too far in their criticisms; and, in lectures read to the Royal Society of Literature in 1825 and 1827, Malthus developed a theory of value which, while maintaining his previous emphasis on demand and supply as determinants of value, gave greater recognition to Ricardo's emphasis on the cost of production (Malthus, 1986, vol. 7, pp. 301–23).

Opinions differ on who was the greater economist – Malthus or Ricardo. Who made the more significant contributions to the development of economics? On the one hand there are those who see Malthus as muddle-headed, and Ricardo as the better logician. On the other hand, there are those who reject the claim that Ricardo was a better logician, and who argue that Malthus's understanding of the multi-causal complexity of the real world was of far greater value to the progress of economics than Ricardo's abstract theorizing. The most famous member of the latter group, J.M. Keynes, said that the world would be 'a much wiser and richer place' if 'Malthus, instead of Ricardo, had been the parent stem from which nineteenth-century economics proceeded'; and that 'the almost total obliteration of Malthus's line of approach and the complete domination of Ricardo's for a period of a hundred years has been a disaster to the progress of economics' (Keynes, 1933, pp. 120, 117).

J.M. PULLEN

See also **Corn Laws, free trade and protectionism; history of economic thought; Keynes, John Maynard; laissez-faire, economists and; Malthusian economy; Smith, Adam.**

Selected works

1986. *The Works of Thomas Robert Malthus*, 8 vols, ed. E. Wrigley and D. Souden. London: William Pickering.

1989a. *An Essay on the Principle of Population*, variorum edn, 2 vols, ed. P. James. Cambridge: Cambridge University Press for the Royal Economic Society.

1989b. *Principles of Political Economy*, variorum edn, 2 vols, ed. J. Pullen. Cambridge: Cambridge University Press for the Royal Economic Society.

1997. *T.R. Malthus: The Unpublished Papers in the Collection of Kanto Gakuen University*, vol. 1, ed. J. Pullen and T. Hughes Parry. Cambridge: Cambridge University Press for the Royal Economic Society.

2004. *T.R. Malthus: The Unpublished Papers in the Collection of Kanto Gakuen University*, vol. 2, ed. J. Pullen and T. Hughes Parry. Cambridge: Cambridge University Press for the Royal Economic Society.

Bibliography

Bonar, J. 1924. *Malthus and His Work*, 2nd edn. London: George Allen and Unwin.

Bonar, J. 1925–6. Thomas Robert Malthus. In *Palgrave's Dictionary of Political Economy*, 2nd edn, ed. H. Higgs. London: Macmillan.

Dupâquier, J., Fauve-Chamoux, A. and Grebenik, E. 1903. *Malthus Past and Present*. London: Academic Press.

Empson, W. 1837. Life, writings and character of Mr Malthus. *Edinburgh Review* 64(January), 496–506.

Ghosh, R. 1963. 'Malthus on emigration and colonization. Letters to Wilmot-Horton'. *Economica* 30, 45–62.

Hollander, S. 1992. Malthus's abandonment of agricultural protectionism: a discovery in the history of economic thought. *American Economic Review* 82, 650–9.

Hollander, S. 1995. More on Malthus and agricultural protection. *History of Political Economy* 27, 531–7.

Hollander, S. 1997. *The Economics of Thomas Robert Malthus*. Toronto: University of Toronto Press.

James, P. 1966. *The Travel Diaries of Thomas Robert Malthus*. Cambridge: Cambridge University Press.

James, P. 1979. *Population Malthus: His Life and Times*. London: Routledge and Kegan Paul.

Keynes, J.M. 1933. Robert Malthus. In *Essays in Biography*. London: Macmillan, 1961.

Keynes, J.M. 1936. *The General Theory of Employment, Interest and Money*. London: Macmillan.

McCleary, G. 1953. *The Malthusian Population Theory*. London: Faber and Faber.

Meek, R., ed. 1953. *Marx and Engels on Malthus*. London: Lawrence and Wishart.

Otter, W. 1836. Memoir of Robert Malthus. In T.R. Malthus, *Principles of Political Economy*, 2nd edn. New York: Augustus M. Kelley, 1951.

Pullen, J. 1987. Malthus, Thomas Robert. In *The New Palgrave: A Dictionary of Economics*, vol. 3, ed. J. Eatwell, M. Milgate and P. Newman. London: Macmillan.

Pullen, J. 1995. Malthus on agricultural protection: an alternative view. *History of Political Economy* 27, 517–29.

Pullen, J. 2004. Malthus, Thomas Robert. In *Oxford Dictionary of National Biography*. Oxford: Oxford University Press.

Ricardo, D. 1951–73. *The Works and Correspondence of David Ricardo*, 11 vols, ed. P. Sraffa with the collaboration of M. Dobb. Cambridge: Cambridge University Press for the Royal Economic Society.

Smith, A. 1776. *An Inquiry into the Nature and Causes of the Wealth of Nations*, ed. R. Campbell and A. Skinner; textual editor W. Todd. Oxford: Clarendon Press, 1976.

Stephen, L. 1893. Malthus, Thomas Robert. In *Dictionary of National Biography*, vol. 12. London: Oxford University Press.

Waterman, A. 1991. *Revolution, Economics and Religion: Christian Political Economy, 1798–1833*. Cambridge: Cambridge University Press.

Winch, D. 1983. Higher maxims: happiness versus wealth in Malthus and Ricardo. In *That Noble Science of Politics*, ed. S. Collini, D. Winch and J. Burrow. Cambridge: Cambridge University Press.

Winch, D. 1987. *Malthus*. Oxford: Oxford University Press.

Winch, D. 1996. *Riches and Poverty: An Intellectual History of Political Economy in Britain, 1750–1834*. Part 3, 'Robert Malthus as Political Moralist'. Cambridge: Cambridge University Press.

Malthusian economy

The Malthusian economy is the economic system which prevails whenever a society's production technology advances so slowly that population growth forces incomes down to the subsistence level. In such an economy material welfare is independent of natural resources, technology and capital accumulation, but instead depends solely on the factors governing fertility and mortality. The resulting subsistence income can, however, vary widely across societies. Some Malthusian economies were rich by the standards of most countries in modern Africa, for example.

Almost all societies until 1800 were Malthusian, from the original foragers of the African savannah 50,000 years ago down through settled agrarian societies of considerable sophistication such as England, France, China and Japan in 1800. The operation of all human societies through history up until the Industrial Revolution can thus seemingly be described by this one simple economic system. An implication of this is that there was most likely no gain in material welfare between the evolution of anatomically modern humans and the onset of the Industrial Revolution.

Government actions, in so far as they change fertility or mortality, can influence material welfare in the Malthusian economy, but in a contradictory fashion. Good governments that reduced mortality through order and security made people poorer. Bad governments that increased mortality through warfare and banditry made them wealthier.

The economic logic of these societies was first, though only partially, appreciated by Thomas Malthus in his famous *Essay on a Principle of Population* of 1798. Malthus's insights were elaborated by writers such as David Ricardo and James Stuart Mill into the system called classical political economy in the early 19th century. Ironically, this intellectual development happened just as for the first time the rate of technological advance was becoming sufficiently rapid to bring the Malthusian era to a close.

Insight into the Malthusian economy starts from the insight that the biological capacity of women to produce offspring is much greater than the number of births required to reproduce the population. If fertility is unrestricted women can have 12 or more children. Social institutions regulating marriage and contraceptive practices will determine the actual numbers of births per women. In modern societies these institutions and practices vary greatly, so the number of births per women varies greatly. Completed fertility now ranges across the world from a low of 1.15 in Spain to a high of 8.0 in Niger. Only where women happen on average to have two children who survive to adulthood will population be stable. Even small deviations from this number will cause rapid increases or decreases in population. Thus modern populations are not stable.

Despite this potential for explosive population growth, pre-industrial populations were remarkably stable over the long run. The average annual growth rate of world population from 10,000 years BC to AD 1800 was 0.05 per cent. The typical woman before 1800 thus had 2.02 children who survived to reproductive age. As an extreme case the population of Egypt, for example, is estimated at between four million and five million at 1000 years BC. The population in Greek and Roman Egypt a millennium later is estimated at this same four million to five million. The first modern census in 1848 suggests a population of 4.5 million. Thus over nearly 3,000 years the Egyptian population growth rate was to a close approximation zero, and women on average had two surviving children. Yet it is estimated that in Roman Egypt the average woman gave birth to six children. Some mechanism kept fertility and mortality in balance in these pre-industrial economies.

The Malthusian equilibrium

The simple Malthusian model of how pre-industrial society functioned supplies an economic mechanism to explain its population stability. In its simplest version there are just three assumptions:

1. The *birth rate*, the number of births per year per thousand people, is a socially determined constant, independent of material living standards. Birth rates will vary across societies, but in this simplest model they are assumed to be independent in any given society of material living conditions.
2. The *death rate*, the number of deaths per year per thousand persons, declines as material living standards increase. Again, the death rate will differ across societies depending on climate and lifestyles, but it assumed that in all societies it will decline as material living conditions improve.
3. *Material living standards* decline as population increases.

Figure 1 shows the first two assumptions of the simple Malthusian model in graphical form in the upper panel. The birth and death rates are plotted on the vertical axis, material income per capita on the horizontal axis. The first two assumptions of the simple Malthusian model imply that there is only one level of real incomes at which the birth rate equals the death rate, denoted as y^*. And this constitutes a stable equilibrium. Thus y^* is called the 'subsistence income' of the society: it is the income at which the population barely subsists, in the sense of just reproducing itself. This subsistence income is determined without any reference to the production technology. It depends only on the factors which determine birth and death rates. Once we know these factors we can determine the subsistence income.

Another aspect of human welfare is life expectancy at birth, that is, the average number of years a person will live. In the Malthusian era life expectancy at birth also depended only on the factors determining birth and death rates. This is because with a *stable* population, where annual births have equalled deaths for a long time, life expectancy at birth is the inverse of the crude birth rate. With fertility not restricted in any way crude birth rates would be 50–60 per thousand in pre-industrial populations (based on modern experience). This would imply a life expectancy at birth of 20 years or less.

The term 'subsistence income' can lead to the confused notion that in the Malthusian economy people were always living on the edge of starvation. In fact, in almost all Malthusian economies the subsistence income was considerably above the income required for the physiological minimum daily diet. All pre-industrial societies for which we have good demographic records limited fertility below the biological maximum. Differences in the location of the mortality and fertility schedules generated subsistence incomes at very different levels. Thus,

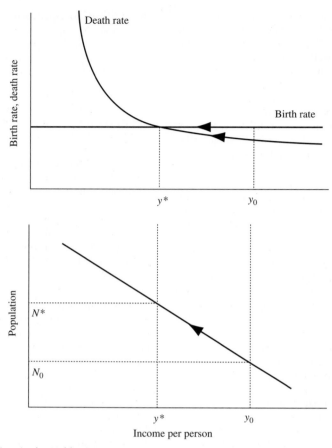

Figure 1 Long-run equilibrium in the Malthusian economy

both 1450 and 1650 were periods of population stability in England, and hence periods where by definition income was at subsistence. But the wage of unskilled agricultural labourers was equivalent to about 6 lb of wheat flour per day in 1650, compared with 18 lb in 1450. Even the 1650 unskilled wage was well above the physiological minimum. A diet of about 1.33 lb of wheat flour per day would keep a labourer alive and fit for work (it would supply about 2,400 calories per day). Thus, pre-industrial societies, while they were subsistence societies, were not starvation regimes. England in 1450, indeed, was wealthy even by the standards of many modern societies such as those in sub-Saharan Africa.

The bottom panel of Figure 1 illustrates the third assumption. The panel has on the vertical axis the population, N, and on the horizontal axis the material income. As population increased material income per person by assumption declined. The justification for this assumption is the law of diminishing returns. Since one important factor of production, land, is always in fixed supply in pre-industrial economies, the law of diminishing returns implies that average output per worker fell as the labour supply increased as long as the technology

remained static. Thus the average amount of material consumption available per person fell with population.

Figure 1 also shows how an equilibrium birth rate, death rate, population level and real income were arrived at in the long run in a pre-industrial economy. Suppose we start at an arbitrary initial population N_0 in the diagram, greater than N^*. This generates an income y_0, above the subsistence income. At this income the birth rate exceeds the death rate, so population grows until income falls to y^* and population equals N^*.

Changes in the birth rate, death rate and 'technology' schedules

Suppose that the birth rate schedule in Figure 1 was higher. Then at the equilibrium, real income would be lower, and the population greater. Thus any increase in birth rates in the Malthusian world drove down real incomes and reduced life expectancy. Conversely, anything which limited birth rates drove up real incomes and increased life expectancy. Thus in the pre-industrial era birth rates were a crucial determinant of material living conditions.

If the death rate schedule was higher, so that at each income there was a higher death rate, then the equilibrium real income would be higher. But if the birth rate was not responsive to income then a greater death rate increased real incomes but in the long run had no effect on the annual death rate or on life expectancy at birth. Thus in this simplest Malthusian model higher mortality risks at a given income were unambiguously a good thing, at least in the long run.

The simple Malthusian world thus exhibits an almost counter-intuitive logic. Anything that raised the death rate schedule, the death rate at a given income, such as war, disorder, disease or poor sanitary practices, increased material living standards without changing life expectancy at birth. Anything that reduced the death rate schedule, such as advances in medical technology, or better public sanitation, or public provision for harvest failures, or peace, reduced material living standards without any gain in life expectancy at birth.

While the real income was determined from the birth and death schedules, the population size depended on the schedule linking population and real incomes. Above I labelled this the 'technology' schedule, because in general the major cause of changes in this schedule has been technological advances. But other things could shift this schedule – a larger capital stock, improvements in the terms of trade, climate improvements, and a more productive organization of the economy. A shift upwards in this schedule, in the short run, since population can change only slowly, would have increased real incomes. But the increased real incomes reduced the death rate, so that births exceeded deaths and population began growing. The growth of population ended only when the income returned to the subsistence level, y^*. At this new equilibrium the only effect of the technological change

was to increase the population supported. There was no lasting change in the living standards of the average person.

More complicated Malthusian models

An issue that has exercised historical demographers is whether the birth rate in pre-industrial societies was 'self-regulating'. What they mean by this is shown in Figure 2, which shows the birth and death schedules of a simplified Malthusian model, as well as a modified birth schedule, which slopes upwards with material incomes. In the modified Malthusian model it is assumed that in good times people married earlier and more people married, so that fertility increased, whereas in bad times fewer married, and they married later, so that fertility declined.

It should be clear that a positive association of fertility and income does not change the basic equilibrium of the model. The only difference is that increases in the death rate at any given material income are now not so unambiguously good, since they will be associated with higher fertility and mortality rates and hence lower incomes. The evidence for societies such as pre-industrial England, however, shows no response of fertility to income (Wrigley et al., 1997). Thus the simple model may well describe pre-industrial societies well.

What causes many more potential complications is a birth schedule that declines with material incomes. Suppose that as real incomes go up one of the responses of people is to desire fewer children. With a birth rate that declines with real incomes the model could have multiple crossings between the birth rate and death rate schedules. At those places where the birth rate schedule was declining more steeply than the death rate schedule the

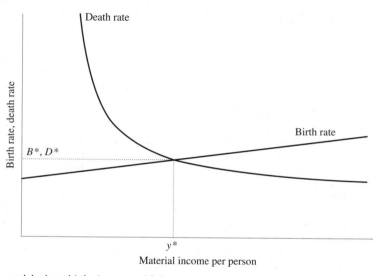

Figure 2   A Malthusian model where births increase with income

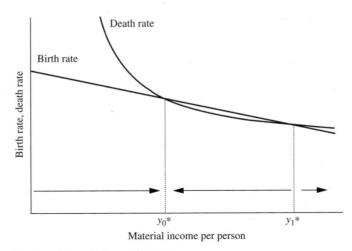

Figure 3   A Malthusian model where births decline with income

equilibrium would be unstable. Figure 3 gives a declining birth rate schedule that twice intersects the death rate schedule. The intersection at the lower real income, y_0, is a stable equilibrium. But the second higher income equilibrium at y_1 is unstable. If real incomes drop below this level by any amount then population starts to grow, leading real incomes all the way down to the stable equilibrium at y_0. Conversely if they increase at all above y_1 then deaths will exceed births and real incomes continue to grow indefinitely. The population will fall eventually to zero.

In this case there is a 'Malthusian trap' in the pre-industrial economy. A society can be stuck in the subsistence income equilibrium unless some jolt such as acquiring extra land, experiencing a much higher death rate, or experiencing faster technological progress pushes up wages enough so that fertility falls permanently. The shock of the Black Death, however, which tripled real incomes for the poorest workers in England by 1450, did not lead to any permanent movement towards lower fertility and the escape from the Malthusian trap. Again, the evidence for pre-industrial demography suggests no declines in fertility with higher incomes.

The empirical implications of the Malthusian model

The most interesting empirical implication of the Malthusian model is that material living conditions for people, including life expectancy at birth, may well have been unchanged between the dawn of humanity and AD 1800. Were the people in sophisticated societies such as England, France, the Netherlands, Japan and China in 1800 really no better off than the original hunter-gatherers? This seems particularly counter-intuitive for England, reckoned to be the richest country the world by 1800.

By then England was a society that would not seem that different from our own. The middle and upper classes in London breakfasted at coffee shops as they read

the daily newspapers. They dwelled in homes of brick and glass with water supplied by lead pipes, lighted at night by oil harvested from sperm whales taken thousands of miles away in the oceans. There was extensive trade for luxury products from the tropics – cottons, silks, spices. How could the material condition of humanity not be better then than in the savage past when our ancestors faced the elements naked, and sought shelter at night in depressions in the ground or in crude lean-tos?

But even in England in 1800 the living conditions of the mass of the population were still primitive. The largest employment was still agriculture, where the average day wage in 1800–9 was the equivalent of 5.7 lb of wheat flour. This was enough to keep a family fed only if most of the income was spent on the cheapest forms of food such as bread. Farm labourers lived in simple structures little better than those of the medieval period. They slept when it was dark because they could not afford lighting. They could afford one new set of clothing per year. English farm labourers six hundred years before, in 1200–9, received a wage which was the equivalent of 12 lb of flour, significantly more than in 1800. And at the best time for pre-industrial workers in England, circa 1450, when the population losses of the plagues which ravaged Europe from 1348 on were their greatest, the real wage was much higher, equivalent to 18 lb of flour. In the years 1200–1800 in England there is no sign of long-run gains in real wages for the mass of workers. We know also the real day wage of farm workers in Roman Egypt circa AD 250 was the equivalent of 5 lb of flour, not much less than England in 1800.

How did English material living conditions around 1800 compare with hunter-gatherer societies such as those that constituted society through the great bulk of human history? We can obtain insight on this in two ways. The first is by comparing living conditions in England in 1800 with those of the few surviving hunter-gatherer groups. Since the diets were very different here we have to use measures such as the number of calories consumed per person per day. In 1787–96 for the families of English farm workers this was a meagre 1,508 calories. For a group of eight hunter-gatherer societies studied in the 1960s to 1980s the average consumption was 2,272 calories, much better than for England. On this measure the English on the eve of the Industrial Revolution seem to have lived less well than the average hunter-gatherer. Another aspect of the quality of life is life expectancy at birth. One measure of this is the fraction of infants that survived the first year of life. In England as a whole this is estimated at 83 per cent in the second half of the 18th century. For modern hunter-gatherer societies survival rates were a little lower at 79 per cent. But this is still not that much lower than for the richest society in the world in 1800. And survival rates for infants in London, the richest part of England, were only 70 per cent because of the health hazards of city life.

A second measure is the average stature of people. Height is a good index of material living conditions, since it depends on both food consumption and the amount of sickness people experience as they grow. Average heights for adult males in England circa 1800 were 67 inches or less. This was very good by the standards of societies just before industrialization. Average male heights in Japan in the late 19th century were 61 inches and in India in the early 19th century 64 inches. Yet these heights in England are little if any better than those recorded from skeletons of hunter-gatherers in the Mesolithic (10,000–5000 BC) and Neolithic (5000–1000 BC) in Europe. Average male height from these skeletons is estimated at 66 inches. So overall, if we look at agrarian societies across the world in 1800 AD, the stature evidence suggests a decline in living conditions from hunter-gatherer society.

Thus, the evidence is that for the mass of humanity on the eve of the Industrial Revolution living conditions were no better and probably worse than in the hunter-gatherer past.

GREGORY CLARK

See also **anthropometric history; historical demography; industrial revolution; Malthus, Thomas Robert.**

Bibliography

Bennike, P. 1985. *Paleopathology of Danish Skeletons.* Copenhagen: Akademisk Forlag.
Clark, G. 2007. *A Farewell to Alms: A Brief Economic History of the World.* Princeton, NJ: Princeton University Press.
Koepke, N. and Baten, J. 2005. The biological standard of living in Europe during the last two millennia. *European Review of Economic History* 9, 61–95.
Malthus, T. 1798. *An Essay on a Principle of Population.* 6th edn. London: John Murray, 1826.
Miller, M. and Upton, C. 1986. *Macroeconomics: A Neoclassical Introduction.* Chicago: University of Chicago Press.
Steckel, R. and Rose, J., eds. 2001. *The Backbone of History: Health and Nutrition in the Western Hemisphere.* Cambridge: Cambridge University Press.
Wrigley, E., Davies, R., Oeppen, J. and Schofield, R. 1997. *English Population History from Family Reconstruction: 1580–1837.* Cambridge and New York: Cambridge University Press.

Malynes, Gerard de (*fl.* 1586–1623)

A merchant of English parentage, born in Antwerp at an unknown date, Malynes was a commissioner of trade in the Low Countries about 1586. He came to London and was frequently consulted on commercial questions by the Privy Council in the reigns of Elizabeth I and James I. He became an assay master at the mint and obtained a patent to supply farthings; he was imprisoned for a time, complaining later that he had been ruined by being paid in his own coins. He also served as a spy for England. Called on by the standing commission on trade for evidence on the state of the coinage, he published a series of pamphlets on money and prices. A mercantilist and a bullionist, he was heavily influenced by Scholastic literature.

Malynes viewed individual commodity prices as determined by demand and supply. However, he was more interested in the price level, governed by the quantity of money (Malynes, 1601b; 1603). An expanding money supply, associated with a rising price level, decreased interest rates and stimulated the economy (1601b; 1622a). Therefore Malynes viewed usury as at best a necessary evil (see Muchmore, 1969, p. 346) and, above all, opposed any export of specie whatsoever.

Rejecting the balance of trade theory, Malynes charged that 'bankers' (exchange dealers) controlled the exchange rate (1601b; 1622a; 1622b; 1623). By their incorporation of usury in the price of a bill of exchange and through speculation, they conspired to undervalue sterling, leading to a deterioration in England's terms of trade ('overbalancing') and a specie outflow (1601b; 1622a; 1623). But overvalued sterling would not lead to a specie inflow, because the export proceeds would be spent on luxury imports (1601b). Yet Malynes (1601b) has a theory of price level changes in response to exchange rates differing from mint parity and money flowing between countries – a price specie-flow mechanism, marred only by the assumption of inelastic demand. His solution to the twin problems of specie outflow and terms of trade deterioration is comprehensive exchange control with enforced exchange dealings at rates fixed at mint parities (Malynes, 1601b; 1622a; 1622b; Muchmore, 1969, pp. 347–8).

LAWRENCE H. OFFICER

Selected works

1601a. *Saint George for England, allegorically described.* London: Richard Field for William Tymme.

1601b. *A Treatise of the Canker of England's Commonwealth.* London: Richard Field for William Iohnes. Reprinted in part in *Tudor Economic Documents*, vol. 3, ed. R.H. Tawney and E. Power. London: Longmans, Green, 1924.

1603. *England's View, in the Unmasking of Two Paradoxes.* London: Richard Field.

1622a. *Consuetudo, vel lex mercatoria, or the Ancient Law-merchant.* London: Adam Islip.

1622b. *The Maintenance of Free Trade.* London: I. Legatt for W. Sheffard.

1623. *The Centre of the Circle of Commerce.* London: William Iones.

Bibliography

Johnson, E. 1933. Gerard de Malynes and the theory of the foreign exchanges. *American Economic Review* 22, 441–55.

Muchmore, L. 1969. Gerrard de Malynes and mercantile economics. *History of Political Economy* 1, 336–58.

Officer, L.H. 1982. The purchasing-power-parity theory of Gerrard de Malynes. *History of Political Economy* 14, 251–5.

Roover, R. de 1974. *Business, Banking and Economic Thought.* Chicago: University of Chicago Press.

Schumpeter, J. 1954. *History of Economic Analysis.* Oxford: Oxford University Press.

Spiegel, H. 1971. *The Growth of Economic Thought.* Englewood Cliffs, NJ: Prentice-Hall.

Wu, C.-Y. 1939. *An Outline of International Price Theories.* London: George Routledge & Sons.

Manchester School

The Manchester School was the name given by Disraeli after the event to the leaders of the successful agitation conducted between 1838 and 1846 to abolish the Corn Laws. It is wrongly associated with the arch-advocacy of laissez-faire. The people of the School were not in fact united by any single idea, other than believing in the complete and immediate repeal of the tariff on grain.

Within the School there were five discernible groups in the sense of there being five different reasons why people wanted repeal or purposes that directed them. Some were compatible with others, and one group could agree with another over what was important but differ over how important it was. The arguments that each group made do not, when taken together, constitute a cogent or even coherent whole but taken separately could be both, and are always interesting. Moreover, the campaign for repeal is itself an instructive event in the history of economic policy.

(1) One group was the mill-owners of Lancashire who provided most of the money for the campaign and formed the National Anti-Corn Law League to conduct it. Some believed that repeal, by reducing the price of bread, would reduce money wages, hence the cost of production in their mills. The belief comes from the Ricardian principle that real wages are constant in the long run. It could have made the businessmen believe the export of grain should be protected, since that too could reduce its price, hence have placed them in the interesting but not unusual position of half-believing in the free market.

They in fact did not support protection because a greater reason for their wanting repeal was to increase the export of manufactured goods. The economic argument most often made was that importing more grain would provide foreigners with more income to spend on British exports, with the result that income and employment would increase at home. The mill-owners were repeatedly accused of simply wanting to cut wages. Cobden privately warned them to stay out of the repeal campaign if they could not come in with clean hands. Publicly he offered to support a Factory Bill of Lord Ashley – the 'universal syllabub of philanthropic twaddle', in Carlyle's description – if Ashley would pay his farm hands what the workers in Cobden's factory were paid. The offer was declined.

Another economic augument for repeal was that it would retard the growth of manufacturing abroad and so keep Britain in its leading industrial position. Why the owner of a small mill would profit by his country's having more mills than any other was not made clear (although he might by way of an externality of some sort). The argument is nevertheless noteworthy. It was revived after 1945, when the undeveloped countries hastened to industrialize in the belief that doing so was a necessary condition of their progress. The argument is also part of the curious notion, entertained by historians, that Britain's free trade was an instrument of its imperialism. They reason that Britain, by keeping others in a non-industrial condition, could dominate them, exploit them, and/or make them dependent on it. Why one country would choose to be mistreated by another when it could choose a trading partner that did not mistreat it, as in a system of free trade it could do, is not explained. Or is there an explanation of why a dollar's worth of manufactured goods adds more to total welfare than a dollar's worth of goods that are not manufactured?

(2) Among the businessmen working for repeal were those who believed it would make life better for the lower classes. They have been called the humanitarian employers. They did more for their workers than the market or the law required, providing schools for the children, reading rooms and meeting places for the men and women, helping them to form friendly societies, cooperatives and cultural groups. Some employed a 'salaried visitor' (social worker) to call at the homes. These business people also undertook to improve the communities where they were established. One such effort was the Manchester Statistical Society which collected information on living conditions and used it to improve them. The Greg family stood out in this group.

(3) The radical businessmen, working on a larger scale than the humanitarians, aspired to improve the nation and the world. In economic affairs their great end was free trade and after the repeal of the Corn Laws they had a part in the abolition of the Navigation Laws. In politics they looked toward democratic government and worked to extend the franchise until all adult males had the right to vote. The radicals believed free trade would first increase the influence of the business classes, increase their members in Parliament, then (in a way not fully explained) increase the power of the working classes.

John Bright was the leader of this group, which itself was the Manchester version of the middle-class radicalism of the time. It had a finger or a hand or more in most reform movements, great and small, from the abolition of slavery and removal of religious disabilities to the penny post and repeal of the taxes on knowledge. The radicals were disrespectful of authority, indifferent to custom, unmindful of the ridiculous figure they often cut, and they were meddlesome, tiresome, persistent and effective. Like Pancks, what they did, they did, they did indeed, and when they finished there were noble institutions in ruins.

(4) The Philosophic or London Radicals had a different place from that of the radical businessmen, grounding their reform on a considered application of Bentham's utilitarianism and conducting themselves in the mannerly, measured way that made them heard and respected but unheeded and ineffectual. They did not care for the rough and ready way of Manchester and had to be reminded of where they were before it took on the repeal of the Corn Laws. Before them, Charles Villiers, a leading Benthamite, had each year moved in the House that it constitute itself a committee of the whole to consider the repeal of the Corn Laws, and each year the motion was defeated. The leadership of the free trade bloc passed to Cobden when he became a Member of Parliament, an instance, his friends said, of talent giving way to genius. Francis Place, who was on the edge of the London Radicals, put things plainly and said that when the Manchester people wanted something done they did it.

(5) Cobden represented the pacifists of the School. They believed that trading nations had a material interest in peace, an idea Ricardo had stated in his *Essay on Profits* in 1815, and that they were natural friends by virtue of meeting on the market, an idea Ricardo was too realistic to entertain. Oddly, the pacifists seem not to have noticed they could have drawn an argument from the *Wealth of Nations*. No pacifist himself, Smith said Britain should not engage in trade that would diminish its military power. The implication is that free trade makes nations unable to go to war as well as unwilling.

The pacifists, although not the largest group within the School, were even more influential than the radicals.

Cobden wanted to graft the peace movement onto the repeal campaign although he would not permit the franchise to be so joined, as Bright wanted to do. After repeal, the franchise had more public support than the peace movement and grew until all adults had the vote. Nevertheless those who believe free trade is conducive to peace can and do point out that the 19th century was a time when trade was freer than ever and was the only century in recent history when there has not been a world war.

Cobden wanted free trade because it would bring peace, Bright because it would bring the franchise. Others in the School had each of them his own purpose. They made common cause for seven years until the Corn Laws were brought down, then returned to their separate ways.

The Manchester School was a coalition around a single issue. It was not a group of ideologues committed to laissez-faire, as historians have carelessly said, nor did it express the pure spirit of the middle class, as some contemporaries believed. It was not a rent-seeking force, as Public Choice economists are tempted to say, nor did it preach the principles of huckstering (Disraeli), nor were its leaders 'bartering Jews' (Engels), nor were they 'the official representatives of the bourgeoisie' (Marx). If the Manchester School is to be described simply, it was a remarkably successful effort to remove a major obstacle in the way of the market.

WILLIAM D. GRAMPP

See also **Bright, John; Cobden, Richard.**

Bibliography

Grampp, W.D. 1960. *The Manchester School of Economics*. Stanford: Stanford University Press; London: Oxford University Press.

Hirst, F.W., ed. 1903. *Free Trade and other Fundamental Doctrines of the Manchester School*. London, New York: Harper & Bros.

McCord, N. 1958. *The Anti-Corn Law League 1838–1846*. London: Allen & Unwin.

Morley, J. 1881. *The Life of Richard Cobden*. London: Chapman & Hall.

Prentice, A. 1853. *History of the Anti-Corn Law League*. London: W. & F.G. Cash.

Proceedings of the Chamber of Commerce and Manufactures at Manchester. 1821–1865. Mss. at the Manchester Central Library.

Students in the Honours School of History in the University of Manchester and Arthur Redford. 1934. *Manchester Merchants and Foreign Trade 1794–1858*. Manchester: Publications of the University of Manchester, Economic History Series.

Trevelyan, G.M. 1913. *The Life of John Bright*. London: Constable.

mandated employer provision of employee benefits

The provision of social benefits can be financed in a number of different ways: through broad income taxation, through taxation of payroll only, or through mandates on employers to provide those benefits for their employees. The last channel is one of sizable and growing importance in the United States, although less so in other nations that tend to rely more on tax-financed government provision. Yet, until the late 1980s, the impacts of mandates were not much studied. The implicit assumption in economic analysis was that such mandates could be analysed using the standard tools of tax incidence and efficiency.

A very influential article by Summers (1989) changed all that. Summers pointed out that mandating employer provision of benefits to their employees had two effects on labour market equilibrium. On the one hand, a reduction in labour demand naturally accompanies the imposition of extra costs on employers. On the other hand, however, mandates should also cause an outward shift in labour supply, since individuals are now being effectively compensated more highly for their labour; they are receiving their previous compensation plus the mandated benefit. This shifts more of the costs of benefits to workers and reduces the deadweight loss from their provision. Indeed, as Summers pointed out, if employees valued the mandated benefit at its cost to the employer, then these supply and demand shifts would be equal. The end result would be 'full shifting to wages': a decline in wages by exactly the cost of the benefit with no impact on total labour supplied to the market and no efficiency consequences. Employees would simply be buying a benefit they value with their wages.

This article inspired a large follow-up literature, mostly empirical, investigating the equity and efficiency properties of mandates. I review that literature here, in three steps. First, I comment on the theoretical points made by Summers. Second, I discuss the empirical evidence available on the impacts of mandates. Finally, I discuss the key unanswered questions that must be addressed by future research.

Theoretical background

Summers' analysis was as straightforward as it was insightful, highlighting the impacts of mandates in a simple demand and supply framework. The mathematics behind this analysis is explored in Gruber (1992), Gruber and Krueger (1991) and Anderson and Meyer (1997). These analyses show that the incidence of mandated benefits depends on the elasticities of supply and demand, as with any tax, along with a new parameter: the valuation of the benefit by employees. If valuation is equal to the cost paid by the employer for the benefit, then there is full shifting to wages.

But this analysis misses an important point: Summers' analysis is in no way restricted to mandates. Indeed, the

analysis is exactly the same for Unemployment Insurance, a US programme which provides tax-financed benefit to unemployed workers. The key to Summers' analysis is not the form of provision (mandate or tax); rather, the key is that the benefits are *restricted to workers*, generating the labour supply increase that offsets some of the efficiency consequences of the intervention. For example, a payroll tax-financed expansion of health insurance to workers fits into this framework, but a payroll tax-financed expansion of health insurance to all individuals in society does not. In the latter case, there would not be the corresponding increase in labour supply, since individuals would not have to work to receive the benefit.

Another question raised by Summers' analysis is this: if there were full incidence on wages, why wouldn't employers simply provide the benefit voluntarily? Why is government coercion necessary to promote employer provision of a benefit fully valued by employees? The best answer here, as pointed out by Summers, is that there may be market failures that lead employers to not reflect workers' valuation of this programme without a government mandate. Most obviously, adverse selection in the market for benefits could cause employer reluctance to be, for example, the one employer in town that offered health insurance or paid maternity leave. This standard adverse selection problem may keep employers from offering benefits that are fully valued by employees. (Indeed, if there is such a market failure, it is feasible that a programme such as workers' compensation could *raise* the quantity of labour in the market. If workers value workers' compensation at more than its cost to employers – as might be the case if workers are risk averse – the labour supply curve would shift out by more than the demand curve shifted in; workers would be willing to accept a wage cut of *more* than the cost of workers' compensation in order to have this benefit. This would actually raise employment.)

Empirical evidence

During the 1990s a large number of articles explored the empirical impact of mandates, in particular the extent to which mandated costs were shifted to wages. This literature is reviewed in detail in Gruber (2001); I provide an overview here. The consensus of this literature is that, over the medium to long term, the cost of mandates is fully reflected in wages.

Gruber and Krueger (1991) provide the first such analysis, dealing with increases in the employer costs of Workers' Compensation (WC) insurance across US industries and states over time. WC provides cash benefits and health coverage to workers injured on the job, and much of the variation in costs in the authors' data comes from increases in the health care component of this programme. They focus on workers in five industries for which WC costs are high and rapidly growing; in some industries and states, these costs amounted to over 25 per cent of payroll by 1987, the end of their sample period. They use both micro-data on wages and aggregate data on employment and wages by state/industry. They include state and industry fixed effects in their models, so that they are controlling for general differences in pay across industries and places, and estimating only how that pay changed when the costs of WC rose. In both data-sets, they find that for these sets of industries 85 per cent of increases in workers compensation costs were shifted to wages.

Anderson and Meyer (1997) undertake a similar analysis for Unemployment Insurance (UI), which provides cash benefits to unemployed workers. This programme is not a mandate, but it should operate in the same fashion as it levies payroll taxes on firms to provide benefits to their workers. Anderson and Meyer's conclusion is similar to Gruber and Krueger: general differences in UI payroll taxes appear to be fully reflected in wages with little effect on labour supply.

There is also a long literature on the impact of payroll taxation on wages that is reviewed by Hamermesh (1987). This literature is much more mixed in its conclusions, although the variation in payroll taxes mostly comes over time, and it is difficult to estimate its incidence separately from other time series factors in the United States where there is little variation across workers in payroll tax rates. More recent evidence is consistent, however, with the notion of full shifting to wages in other countries (for example, Gruber, 1997).

Labour supply is not simply a discrete choice, however, but rather a combination of participation and hours of work decisions. Increases in costs will effect both the supply of and the demand for work hours conditional on participation. From the employer perspective, increases in health insurance costs are an increase in the fixed cost of employment and are as a result more costly (as a fraction of labour payments) for low-hours employees. Employers will therefore desire increased hours by fewer workers, lowering the cost per hour of the health insurance for a given total labour supply. Of course, if the wage offset is lower for low-hours workers, workers will demand the opposite outcome: there will be increasing demand for part-time work, with hours falling and employment increasing. Moreover, since part-time workers may be more readily excluded from health insurance coverage, there may also be a countervailing effect on the employer side, as full-time employees are replaced with their (uninsured) part-time counterparts. In this case as well, hours would fall and employment would rise. Thus, the effect on hours of work is uncertain. Several studies have addressed this issue, and the general consensus is that mandating fixed costs of employment leads to rises in hours and falls in employment (Gruber, 1994; Cutler and Madrian, 1998).

Remaining questions

While there have been significant gains in our understanding of the impacts of mandates, important questions remain unanswered. The most important is the question of heterogeneity across workers: how do mandates affect workers differentially within the workplace? Consider the example of mandated health insurance. The cost of health insurance will not be uniform throughout the workplace; costs are higher for family insurance than for individual coverage, or for older workers than for younger workers. In the limit, with extensive experience rating, costs vary worker by worker, depending on their underlying health status. Gruber (1992) extends the model of Gruber and Krueger (1991) to the case of two groups of workers, where costs increase for one but not the other. If there is group-specific shifting, then the solution collapses to the one group model. If not, however, the substitutability of these groups will also determine the resulting labour market equilibrium; in general, there will be effects on both the group for which costs increase and the group for which they do not.

In practice, there may be a number of barriers to group-specific, and in particular individual-specific, shifting. Most obviously, there are anti-discrimination regulations which prohibit differential pay for the same job across particular demographic groups, or which prevent differential promotion decisions by demographic characteristic. Workplace norms which prohibit different pay across groups or union rules about equality of pay may have similar effects. Thus, a central question for incidence analysis is *how finely* firms can shift increased costs to workers' wages. If there is imperfect group- or worker-specific shifting, there may be pressure on employers to discriminate against costly workers in their hiring decisions.

Two studies suggest that there is within-workplace shifting to wages. Gruber (1994) studied the effect of state laws (and a follow-up federal law) that mandated in the mid-1970s that the costs of pregnancy and childbirth be covered comprehensively. Before this time, health insurance plans provided very little coverage for the costs associated with normal pregnancy and childbirth, while providing generous coverage for other medical conditions. This distinction was viewed as discriminatory by some state governments, leading to the state laws mandating that pregnancy costs be covered as completely as other medical costs. These laws significantly increased the insurance costs for women of childbearing age in those states, thereby raising the costs of employing a specific group of workers (or their husbands, who may provide them with insurance). I estimated full shifting to wages for these groups. Further corroborating evidence on this point is provided by Sheiner (1999), who found that, when health-care costs rise in a city, the wages of workers who have the highest costs (older and married workers) fall the most.

This research suggests that within-workplace shifting to wages is possible. The news here is good for efficiency: mandates which have differential effects across broad groups of workers will not necessarily lead to displacement of the high-cost group. The news is potentially bad for equity, however: other groups will not cross-subsidize the high costs imposed on one group in the workplace. In any case, neither of these studies addresses the extent to which within-firm shifting is possible; in the limit, it is hard to conceive that employers could shift costs to wages on a worker-by-worker basis.

Other questions have not been addressed at all by the literature. First, how rapidly does shifting to wages occur? Despite the evidence that mandates are fully reflected in wages, employers vociferously oppose mandated benefits as costing jobs. The reason for their opposition could be that wages cannot adjust quickly enough in the short run to offset displacement effects; the studies cited earlier show full shifting only over several-year periods.

Second, what are the effects of existing constraints on compensation design in the labour market? For example, for workers already at the minimum wage, firms will be unable to shift to wages increases in the cost of health insurance. Similarly, union contract or other workplace pay norms may interfere with the adjustment of wages to reflect higher costs. These institutional features could increase the disemployment effects of rising health costs.

Third, what is the underlying structural mechanism behind a finding of full shifting to wages? In the simple labour market framework above, there are two reasons why increased costs might be shifted to wages: because individuals value the benefits that they are getting fully; or because labour supply is perfectly inelastic. Disentangling these alternatives is very important for future policy analysis. Consider the example of national health insurance, which is financed by a mandate, with an additional payroll tax to cover non-workers. If the full shifting documented earlier is due to full employee valuation with somewhat elastic labour supply, then national health insurance will have important disemployment effects, since labour supply will not increase in response to a benefit that is not restricted to workers. If full shifting is due to inelastic supply, however, then the population which is receiving benefits is irrelevant; in any case the costs will be passed on to workers' wages, so national health insurance will not cause disemployment. Existing evidence, as reviewed in Gruber (2001), is mixed on which of these channels is at work.

Conclusion

Since the early 1990s there has been a substantial growth in research on mandated benefits. The conclusions from the work to date are clear: the costs of mandated benefits are fully shifted onto wages, with little impact on total labour supply. But important questions about the mechanisms behind such shifting remain unanswered.

JONATHAN GRUBER

Bibliography

Anderson, P. and Meyer, B. 1997. The effect of firm specific taxes and government mandates with an application to the U.S. Unemployment Insurance program. *Journal of Public Economics* 65, 119–44.

Cutler, D. and Madrian, B. 1998. Labor market responses to rising health insurance costs: evidence on hours worked. *RAND Journal of Economics* 29, 509–30.

Gruber, J. 1992. The efficiency of a group-specific mandated benefit: evidence from health insurance benefits for maternity. Working Paper No. 4157. Cambridge, MA: NBER.

Gruber, J. 1994. The incidence of mandated maternity benefits. *American Economic Review* 84, 622–41.

Gruber, J. 1997. The incidence of payroll taxation: evidence from Chile. *Journal of Labor Economics* 15(3, Part 2), S72–S101.

Gruber, J. 2001. Health insurance and the labor market. In *The Handbook of Health Economics*, ed. J. Newhouse and A. Culyer. Amsterdam: North-Holland.

Gruber, J. and Krueger, A. 1991. The incidence of mandated employer-provided insurance: lessons from Workers' Compensation insurance. In *Tax Policy and the Economy* 5, ed. D. Bradford. Cambridge, MA: MIT Press.

Hamermesh, D.S. 1987. Payroll taxes. In *The New Palgrave: A Dictionary of Economics*, vol. 3, ed. J. Eatwell, M. Milgate and P. Newman. London: Macmillan.

Sheiner, L. 1999. Health care costs, wages, and aging. Finance and Economics Discussion Series 1999–19, Board of Governors of the Federal Reserve System.

Summers, L. 1989. Some simple economics of mandated benefits. *American Economic Review* 79, 177–83.

Mandel, Ernest (1923–1995)

Ernest Mandel was born of Jewish parents in Frankfurt-am-Main on 5 April 1923. The family emigrated to Antwerp. By 1939 he was actively involved in socialist and trade union politics. When the Nazis invaded Belgium in 1940, he became a member of the resistance. On three occasions he was arrested and imprisoned, but each time he escaped. He was arrested for a final time in October 1944 and liberated by the Allies in March 1945. He obtained a higher education in Brussels and Paris. His name was prominent in academia in the 1960s and 1970s when Marxism and Trotskyism enjoyed significant popularity, particularly among university students. He died on 20 July 1995.

His *Marxist Economic Theory* was first published in French in 1962 and in English in 1968. When student revolts and labour unrest broke out in the late 1960s, Mandel's text and the much shorter *Introduction to Marxist Economic Theory* (1967) were available for the growing numbers interested in Marxist economics. His *Marxist Economic Theory* was widely praised and his

Introduction sold over half a million copies and was translated into 30 languages.

His *Formation of the Economic Thought of Karl Marx* was published in French in 1967 and in English in 1971. It was one of the first works in English to analyse Marx's *Grundrisse*, which did not appear in complete form in English until 1973.

In his *Europe vs. America* – published in German in 1968 and in English in 1970 – he predicted relative economic decline and increasing 'public squalor' in the United States, sustained rapid economic growth in Japan, and the achievement of productivity levels in the western European 'core' regions to rival those in America.

In his *Late Capitalism* – published in German in 1972 and in English in 1975 – he revisited the idea that capitalism was subject to repeated waves of boom and stagnation in 45–60 year cycles. Not only did Mandel predict the downturn of the 1970s on the basis of this analysis, but also this work help to revive academic interest in the study of long waves, which has continued to the present day. However, his analysis has been criticized for misunderstanding Trotsky's criticisms of Kondratiev (Day, 1976) and lacking a plausible mechanism to explain the complete long-wave cycle (Tylecote, 1992).

Mandel wrote introductions to the new English translations of the three volumes of Marx's *Capital*, published by Penguin (Marx, 1976; 1978; 1981). He was obliged to consider the stormy technical debates in the 1970s over the labour theory of value and Marx's theory of the tendency of the rate of profit to fall (Steedman, 1977). However, instead of addressing the detailed critical arguments, he simply brushed them aside.

In 1978 Mandel was invited by the University of Cambridge to give the prestigious Alfred Marshall Memorial lectures. These were published as *Long Waves of Capitalist Development* (1980): a restatement and development of ideas in *Late Capitalism*. Further weaknesses in his position emerged when it became clear that mass unemployment in the West was not leading to political advances for socialism. Instead the period saw a resurgent political individualism and neoliberalism.

Like Trotsky, Mandel opposed the view that the Soviet-type economies were another type of 'capitalism', envisaged a collapse of the Soviet regimes, and expected that the working class would rise up in defence of state planning and nationalized property. Even after their collapse in 1989–91, in his *Power and Money* (1992) he hoped for a new workers' movement in eastern Europe and predicted that capitalism would not be easily re-established. Overall, the theoretical weakness of his outlook became increasingly clear in the last 15 years of his life.

GEOFFREY M. HODGSON

See also **capitalism; Kondratieff cycles; Marx's analysis of capitalist production; socialism; socialism (new perspectives); Soviet economic reform; Trotsky, Lev Davidovitch.**

Selected works

1967. *An Introduction to Marxist Economic Theory.* New York: USA.

1968. *Marxist Economic Theory*, 2 vols, trans. B. Pearce from the French edition of 1962. London: Merlin.

1970. *Europe vs. America: Contradictions of Imperialism*, trans. from the German edition of 1968. New York: Modern Reader.

1971. *The Formation of the Economic Thought of Karl Marx: 1843 to Capital*, trans. B. Pearce from the French edition of 1967. London: NLB.

1975. *Late Capitalism*, trans. from the German edition of 1972. London: NLB.

1980. *Long Waves of Capitalist Development: The Marxist Interpretation.* Cambridge: Cambridge University Press.

1992. *Power and Money: A Marxist Theory of Bureaucracy.* London: Verso.

Bibliography

Day, R. 1976. The theory of long waves: Kondratiev, Trotsky, Mandel. *New Left Review* 99, 67–82.

Marx, K. 1976. *Capital*, vol. 1, trans. B. Fowkes from the fourth German edition of 1890. Harmondsworth: Pelican.

Marx, K. 1978. *Capital*, vol. 2, trans. D. Fernbach from the German edition of 1893. Harmondsworth: Pelican.

Marx, K. 1981. *Capital*, vol. 3, trans. D. Fernbach from the German edition of 1894. Harmondsworth: Pelican.

Steedman, I. 1977. *Marx After Sraffa.* London: NLB.

Tylecote, A. 1992. *Long Waves in the World Economy: The Present Crisis in Historical Perspective.* London: Routledge.

Mandeville, Bernard (1670–1733)

Mandeville was born in or near Rotterdam in 1670 and died in Hackney, London, in 1733. He was awarded the degree of Doctor of Medicine from the University of Leyden in 1961. He took up the practice of medicine, specializing in the 'Hypochondriack and Hysterick Diseases', a subject on which he later published a treatise. Mandeville travelled to England, married there in 1699, and lived in England for the rest of his life. He was very widely read in the 18th century. His writings have often led to his being referred to as a satirist, but that is an inadequate and misleading classification.

Although Mandeville was not an economist, his writings were influential in shaping the direction of economic thinking in the 18th century. In 1705 he published a pamphlet, in doggerel verse, under the title *The Grumbling Hive: Or Knaves turn'd Honest.* In 1714 it was republished under its better-known title, *The Fable of the Bees: or, Private Vices, Publick Benefits.* This and subsequent editions included extensive expansions, clarifications and 'vindications' of his earlier themes. The grumbling hive was originally a thriving and powerful community. When, however, its inhabitants were suddenly and miraculously converted from a vicious to a virtuous moral condition, the community was swiftly reduced to an impoverished and depopulated state.

Mandeville's central theme is that public benefits are the product of private vices and not of private virtues. His paradox, which was widely regarded as scandalous, was achieved by employing a highly ascetic and self-denying definition of virtue. Since behaviour that could be shown to be actuated by even the slightest degree of self-regarding motive – pride, vanity, avarice or lust – was classified as vice, Mandeville had little difficulty in concluding that a successful social order must inevitably be one where public benefits are built upon a foundation of private vices.

> ... I flatter myself to have demonstrated that, neither the Friendly Qualities and kind Affections that are natural to Man, nor the real Virtues he is capable of acquiring by Reason and Self-Denial, are the Foundation of Society; but that what we call Evil in this World, Moral as well as Natural, is the grand Principle that makes us sociable Creatures, the solid Basis, the Life and Support of all Trades and Employments without Exception: That there we must look for the true Origin of all Arts and Sciences, and that the Moment Evil ceases, the Society must be spoiled, if not totally dissolved. (Mandeville, 1732, vol. 1, p. 369)

What was of more enduring significance in Mandeville's views was his forceful and unapologetic popularization of the belief that socially desirable consequences would flow from the individual pursuit of self-interest. It is an essential part of Mandeville's argument that a viable social order can emerge out of the spontaneous actions of purely egoistic impulses, requiring neither the regulation of government officials, on the one hand, nor altruistic individual behaviour, on the other.

> As it is Folly to set up Trades that are not wanted, so what is next to it is to increase in any one Trade the Numbers beyond what are required. As things are managed with us, it would be preposterous to have as many Brewers as there are Bakers, or as many Woolen-drapers as there are Shoe-makers. This Proportion as to Numbers in every Trade finds it self, and is never better kept than when nobody meddles or interferes with it. (Mandeville, 1732, vol. 1, pp. 299–300)

Thus, Mandeville enunciates a vision of an economy that organizes itself and that allocates resources through the market place. Although there is no serious analysis of the workings of the market mechanism, there is the clear assertion that the unregulated market provides a system of signals and inducements such that the interactions of purely egoistic motives will somehow produce results that will advance the public good.

In developing his views, Mandeville offered many acute observations on the causes as well as the consequences

of the division of labour in society. He regarded the division of labour as the great engine of economic improvement over the ages. It is the most reliable way for 'savage People' to go about 'meliorating their Condition'. For

> ... if one will wholly apply himself to the making of Bows and Arrows, whilst another provides Food, a third builds Huts, a fourth makes Garments, and a fifth Utensils, they not only become useful to one another, but the Callings and Employments themselves will in the same Number of Years receive much greater Improvements, than if all had been promiscuously follow'd by every one of the Five. (Mandeville, 1729, vol. 2, p. 284)

Although one can identify a number of possible precursors to Adam Smith's celebrated views on the division of labour, it is well established that Smith had in fact read and digested Mandeville carefully. Smith's marvellous description of the extensive division of labour involved in the production of a day-labourer's coat, with which he closes the first chapter of the *Wealth of Nations*, may be traced to Mandeville's earlier treatment of the same subject – a treatment which, indeed, Smith extensively paraphrases. Moreover, the passage in the *Wealth of Nations* containing the often quoted statement that 'It is not from the benevolence of the butcher, the brewer, or the baker, that we expect our dinner, but from their regard to their own interest' (Smith, 1776, p. 14) is in a direct lineage from Mandeville's earlier observation:

> ... The whole Superstructure [of Civil Society] is made up of the reciprocal Services, which Men do to each other. How to get these Services perform'd by others, when we have Occasion for them, is the grand and almost constant Sollicitude in Life of every individual Person. To expect, that others should serve us for nothing, is unreasonable; therefore all Commerce, that Men can have together, must be a continual bartering of one thing for another. (Mandeville, 1729, vol. 2, p. 349)

Thus Mandeville was, in some important respects, an early advocate of laissez-faire (although this advocacy did not extend to foreign trade, where Mandeville's views were still distinctly Mercantilist). He articulated a vision of the role of the division of labour in society, and of the forces making for social change and evolution, as well as for social cohesion, that were in many respects distinctly precocious, and that exercised a powerful influence in shaping the intellectual agenda of economists and other social scientists later in the 18th century.

N. ROSENBERG

Selected works

1714; 1729; 1732. *The Fable of the Bees*, 2 vols, ed. F.B. Kaye. London: Oxford University Press, 1924. (This is the definitive edition.)

Bibliography

Hayek, F.A. 1978. Dr. Bernard Mandeville. In *New Studies in Philosophy, Politics, Economics and the History of Ideas*, ed. F.A. Hayek. Chicago: University of Chicago Press.

Primer, I., ed. 1975. *Mandeville Studies*. The Hague: Martinus Nijhoff.

Rosenberg, N. 1963. Mandeville and laissez-faire. *Journal of the History of Ideas* 24(2), 183–96.

Smith, A. 1776. *An Inquiry into the Nature and Causes of the Wealth of Nations*. New York: Modern Library, 1937.

Stephen, L. 1876. *History of English Thought in the Eighteenth Century*, 2 vols. London: Smith, Elder.

Viner, J. 1953. *Introduction to Bernard Mandeville, A Letter to Dion*. Los Angeles: Augustan Reprint Society, Publication No. 41.

Mangoldt, Hans Karl Emil von (1824–1868)

Mangoldt was born in Dresden in 1824 and died in 1868 of a heart attack after a short life. He was an eminent theorist in economics, yet greatly underrated by his German contemporaries. He received his doctorate in Tübingen (1847) and was afterwards a civil servant in the Ministry of Foreign Affairs – a post he resigned for political reasons – and became editor of the official *Weimarer Zeitung* (1852). His academic career began in 1855 as Privatdozent in Göttingen and ended as Professor of Political Science and Political Economic after only six years (1862–8) at the University of Freiburg (Breisgau).

Mangoldt ranks among those pioneers in Germany, like von Thünen, von Buquoy, von Hermann, Gossen and Launhardt, who applied formal analysis to explain economic phenomena. Yet the predominant influence of the Historical School diminished the impact of his methods and ideas on German university economists. He shared this fate with Cournot and Walras. A second reason for this underrating of his pioneering achievements at home was his strong interest in classical economics. Thus it is not surprising that his reputation was much higher in England (via Edgeworth and Marshall) than in 19th-century Germany.

In his most important books, *Unternehmergewinn* (1855) and *Grundriss* (1863), he argues in the classic tradition, examines its hypotheses in the light of economic and political reality and modifies them considerably. Like Cournot (earlier) and Marshall (later) Mangoldt uses a novel apparatus of partial analysis – Frisch's microanalysis – to expound originally a mathematical theory of prices that goes far beyond Cournot. He describes in a very modern way the process from one equilibrium to another, analyses multiple equilibria and explains joint supplies and demands, a concept which Marshall would take up later on. Further, he has deeply influenced our theories of profit and rent by interpreting the entrepreneurial gain as rents of differential ability.

Indeed, Mangoldt definitely anticipates Schumpeter's theory of the entrepreneur. He clearly distinguishes profit as an independent category of income from interest (of the capitalist), by stressing different elements of gain such as the compensation for risk-bearing or for new goods or techniques of production and sale. The pioneer function of the entrepreneur, motivated also by intangibles, as in Smith's concept, is clearly expressed in the statement

> … die Auffindung und Verwirklichung der besten Produktionsmethoden … die Ausbeutung der von der Natur gegebenen Hilfsmittel, die Herstellung der Güter in der für das Bedürfnis dienlichsten Weise [the discovery and realization of the best methods of production, … the exploitation of natural resources, the manufacturing of goods in a way that is most appropriate for the need]. (1855, p. 68)

This means, of course, novel improvements as well.

Unfortunately, Mangoldt did not attempt to make these realistic and dynamic elements an essential part of his price theory via a notion of *evolutionary* competition as did Smith and Schumpeter. Thus he neglected the different properties and intensities of competition in different stages in the life cycle of a product.

Furthermore, his contribution to allocation theory was as pioneering as his analysis of coalitions on the labour market. Here he objected to profit participation by workers without risk-sharing. Finally, it is notable that Mangoldt originally extended Ricardo's theory of comparative costs by applying, although in rather vague terms, the notion of elasticity of demand and supply in the theory of international trade.

Mangoldt was, no doubt, one of the eminent theorists and rare pioneers in the 19th century whose achievements are still underrated and whose use of mathematics seems to be rather overrated. Though an abstract thinker, he seldom lost the binding ties to reality.

H.C. RECKTENWALD

Selected works

1847. Über die Aufgabe, Stellung und Einrichtung der Sparkassen. Dissertation, Tübingen University.

1855. *Die Lehre vom Unternehmergewinn: ein Beitrag zur Volkswirtschaftslehre*. Leipzig: Teuber.

1863. *Grundriss der Volkswirtschaftslehre*, 2nd edn. Stuttgart: Maier. A chapter was translated as 'The Exchange Ratio of Goods', *International Economic Papers* 11. (1962), 32–59.

Bibliography

Recktenwald, H.C. 1951. Zur Lehre von den Marktformen. *Weltwirtschaftliches Archiv* 67(2), 298–326.

Recktenwald, H.C. 1985. Über das Selbstverständnis der ökonomischen Wissenschaft. *Jahrbuch der Leibniz-Akademie der Wissenschaften und der Literatur*. Wiesbaden: Steiner.

Recktenwald, H.C. and Samuelson, P.A. 1986. *Über Thünens 'Der isolierte Staat'*. Darmstadt and Dusseldorf: Wirtschaft und Finanzen.

Maoist economics

Ten thousand years is too long; seize the day, seize the hour.

> (Mao Zedong, *Mengjianghong – A Reply to Comrade Guo Moruo*, 1963)

Had Mao died in 1956, there would be no doubt that he was a great leader of the Chinese people, a respected, loved and outstanding great man in the proletarian revolutionary movement of the world. Had he died in 1966, his meritorious achievements would have been somewhat tarnished but still very good. Since he actually died in 1976, there is nothing we can do about it.

> (Chen Yun at the Central Party Work Conference, November–December 1978. Quoted from Lardy and Lieberthal, 1983. *Ming-Pao* (Hong Kong) 15 January 1979)

'Maoist economics' refers to the collection of economic policies implemented by the Communist Party of China (CPC) during the Maoist era, which began with the founding of the People's Republic in 1949 and ended shortly after the demise of Chairman Mao Zedong in 1976. Thanks to the CPC's meticulous cultivation of Mao's personality cult, Mao was able to exploit his 'mass line' political strategy by exhorting the masses to follow his vision when the CPC hierarchy was unwilling. As a result, Mao could set major policy initiatives with few checks and balances. But to attribute all major decisions to Mao would be an oversimplification, especially before 1958. The leadership of the CPC in Beijing and local cadres, often split into factions with different policy agendas and preferences (for a detailed historical account of the policy debates within the leadership circle in China in the 1950s and 1960s, see for example, Lardy and Lieberthal, 1983; Riskin, 1987; and Bachman, 1997), contributed not only to policy implementation but also to policy formulation. Maoist economics is therefore not synonymous with 'Mao Zedong Thought' on economic matters. ('Mao Zedong Thought' is considered an extension of Marxism–Leninism derived from the teachings of Mao Zedong and the distillation of the experience of the Communist revolution in China. It has been enshrined in the Constitution of the CPC as part of the party's official ideology since 1945. As China has embarked on market-oriented reforms since 1978, 'Deng Xiaoping Theory', which advocated the pragmatic concept of 'socialism with Chinese characteristics', has served as the party's working doctrine.)

The aim of this article is to outline a consistent framework for organizing and understanding the economic policies that were formulated and implemented during the Maoist era.

Agricultural taxation and the Chinese-style central planning

When on 1 October 1949 Chairman Mao proclaimed that the Chinese people had finally stood up at the ceremony for the founding of the People's Republic, China was a desperately poor agrarian economy ravaged by more than a century of internal turmoil, foreign invasions and civil wars. With most of her industrial assets either destroyed or looted by the Soviet forces that occupied Manchuria at the end of the Second World War, or removed to Taiwan and Hong Kong ahead of advancing Communist troops, China was 'poor and blank', as Mao (1958) put it. With 90 per cent of her population of 550 million living in abject poverty in the countryside and toiling on small plots of land using traditional labour-intensive farming technology, China was barely able to feed and clothe her population.

Since poor peasants made up the vast majority of the population, the CPC under Mao had focused on building its support base among peasants by, among other things, promising to deliver what every peasant wanted: a private plot of land. Between 1946 and 1953, the CPC launched land reform, first in the territories under its control and then in all ethnically Chinese areas on the mainland after 1949. The process generally involved assigning each rural family a class status; motivating the poor, lower-middle, middle and initially the 'rich' peasants to engage in 'class struggle' against landlords and expropriating land, draft animals, farm implements and property from landlords and redistributing them to landless peasants (Fairbank, 1992). The 'class struggle', which included public trials, denunciations and mass executions of landlords and counter-revolutionaries, created an atmosphere of terror. But the land reform solidified support for the CPC among the poor and middle peasantry. (For an on-the-ground observation of the land reform in a Chinese village, see Hinton, 1967.)

As the CPC secured military and political control of the mainland, its priority shifted to managing and rebuilding the war-torn economy. With the economy rebounding quickly, Chinese leaders turned their attention to long-run economic development, aimed at building a socialist, industrial nation. Having secured material and technical support from the Soviet Union, they adopted a Soviet-style, heavy-industry-oriented development strategy in the first Five Year Plan (FYP 1953–7). The plan called for massive industrial investment, including the construction of 156 industrial plants outfitted with imported Soviet equipment. The Soviet contributions to this big push included loans amounting to about four per cent of the total investment, technology transfers and

10,000 Soviet specialists (Fairbank, 1992). The success of this ambitious plan therefore hinged on the ability of the government to mobilize investable surplus internally. Without a significant industrial and commercial sector, the government had to extract the needed surplus from the vast agricultural sector.

Throughout Chinese history, agricultural taxes, collected in kind, have been the primary source of government revenue. (Indeed the Chinese character for tax, *shui*, as a portmanteau of grain and convert, refers to a levy on the use of land payable in grain.) In the 1950s, China had a three-tiered agricultural tax structure. At the first tier was an in-kind levy on grain production, known as the 'government grain'. Peasants received no compensation for turning over the government grain to the State Grain Bureau. At a statutory rate of 15 per cent in 1950, this tax accounted for 39 per cent of government revenue. (This figure is calculated using data posted on the official website of China's Ministry of Finance.) In later years, as the price scissors – the differences between the prices on industrial and agricultural goods – widened, and as the industrial sector grew rapidly because of the massive capital expenditure funded largely by agricultural taxes, the share of explicit agricultural taxes dropped to six per cent by 1976.)

At the second tier was an implicit tax, a grain procurement quota, which dictated how much each peasant household had to sell to the State Grain Bureau out of their after-tax grain at below-market procurement prices. After meeting these two obligations, peasants would usually be left with just enough grain to sustain a subsistent living. Markets still existed in the early 1950s, where peasants could exchange some of their surplus produce for other goods. At the third tier was an in-kind levy on rural labour. Under the traditional subsistence farming practice in China, peasants would take a break or work less intensively during agricultural off-seasons in order to conserve food energy. To the government, this idling was unacceptable. Dams, irrigation systems, roads and other large-scale infrastructure projects could be worked on more intensively during off-seasons by drafting peasants to carry out backbreaking manual labour. Utilizing a mixture of exhortation and coercion, the government mobilized tens of millions of peasants for large construction projects in the 1950s.

Collecting the three-tiered taxes from hundreds of millions of independent peasant households was a daunting task. Tax enforcement became even harder when market prices of grain rose substantially in 1952 as a result of increased demand caused by rapid industrialization and urbanization and by the need to export agricultural products in exchange for Soviet equipment. In response, the government in 1953 closed the grain market and monopolized grain trade by fiat, making it illegal for anyone other than the government to engage in large-scale grain trade. In 1954, it expanded the control to include oil seeds, cotton, pork, and other key agricultural commodities.

Extracting agricultural surplus was further hampered by the lower level of agricultural productivity in China than in more developed countries. With nearly 90 per cent of the population living in the countryside, China was producing barely enough food and wearable fibres to meet basic domestic needs. Estimates by Ashton et al. (1984) suggest that the daily average food energy intake in China in the 1950s was around 2,000 calories per capita, below the 2,350 calories recommended by the United Nations.

To further improve its extractive capability and to raise agricultural productivity, the government turned to collectivization. By organizing peasant households into collectives, the CPC could extend its political control down to the village level. The grass-roots party organizations could effectively monitor production to further improve tax compliance. Rooted in the prevailing ideology, Chinese leaders also believed that collectivization would enable peasants to take advantage of economies of scale, to learn best practices in scientific farming, to accelerate the adoption of high-yield seeds and modern inputs, and therefore to realize a great leap in agricultural productivity. (Apparently influenced by Soviet propaganda, Chinese leaders were taken in by the miraculous claims of productivity-boosting farming techniques made by a group of pseudo-scientists who dominated the Soviet agricultural science establishment. Because these pseudoscientific techniques contradicted the farming experience of Chinese peasants, the only way to propagate them was to make it a political task for rural collectives and grass-roots party organizations. For an account of Lysenkoism in the Soviet Union and its influence in China during the Maoist era, see Becker, 1996.)

Collectivization, however, represented a radical reorganization of rural life in China. Given the importance of agriculture in the Chinese economy and the traumatic experience of forced collectivization in the Soviet Union (Becker, 1996), China's first FYP emphasized voluntary participation and set out a relatively conservative and flexible timetable, calling for socialist transformation in agriculture to be accomplished in 10–15 years. Between 1952 and 1954, collectivization proceeded gradually. By 1954, only 11 per cent of peasant households were enrolled in elementary Agricultural Producers' Cooperatives (APCs), where members pooled their privately owned land, draft animals and large tools and used them jointly. APC members were paid wages for their labour as well as rents for their contributions in land and capital. While wage rates and rents were supposedly set at market levels, actual practice left many richer peasants complaining that the rents were insufficient. Reports of richer peasants exiting the cooperatives, selling and killing their draft animals, and downing trees on their plots in 1954 started to alarm leaders in Beijing. In January 1955, the CPC issued an urgent order for the protection of draft animals. The combination of state monopolization of grain trade and collectivization had, by the authorities' own admission, dampened the 'enthusiasm' of the peasants for production. Emergency measures that the government implemented included fixing procurement quotas and putting on hold any further push for collectivization in the spring of 1955. But any reprieve that peasants got was short-lived.

By the summer of 1955, imbalances in the economy from implementing the aggressive first FYP had reached record levels. The supply of agricultural products, raw materials and consumer goods could not keep up with the growing demand. With tax revenues insufficient to meet the funding needs in the first FYP, the government was running a large fiscal deficit. (In 1955, debt issuance by the government reached a record high of 2.5 per cent of GDP.) Factors that contributed to the imbalances included the agricultural bottleneck exacerbated by the collectivization movement, the ambitious first FYP that allocated massive investment to heavy industry, and the inherent difficulties of managing a centrally planned economy.

Mao's own analysis, however, identified over-centralization as a serious problem of the Soviet-style central planning whereby the planners tried to do what could be done better by local cadres. The solution that Mao put forth was not to stop the expansion of the role of the state in the economy, but to limit the role of the nascent central planning bureaucracy and expand the role of local governments. He faulted the planners in Beijing for not doing enough to harness the enthusiasm of local cadres, workers and peasants for socialist transformation both in industry and in agriculture. In a policy speech delivered on 31 July 1955, Mao made the argument for accelerating socialist transformation in general and collectivization in particular.

> [Some] comrades fail to understand that socialist industrialization cannot be carried out in isolation from the cooperative transformation of agriculture. In the first place, as everyone knows, China's current level of production of commodity grain and raw materials for industry is low, whereas the state's need for them is growing year by year, and this presents a sharp contradiction. If we cannot basically solve the problem of agricultural cooperation within roughly three five-year plans, that is to say, if our agriculture cannot make a leap from small-scale farming with animal-drawn implements to large-scale mechanized farming, ... then we shall fail to resolve the contradiction between the ever-increasing need for commodity grain and industrial raw materials and the present generally low output of staple crops, and we shall run into formidable difficulties in our socialist industrialization and be unable to complete it. (Mao, 1977, pp. 196–7)

To ensure that Mao's vision was turned quickly into action, the CPC passed in October 1955 a resolution that reiterated the policy directive for accelerating collectivization and authorized the party hierarchy to criticize any

party member who disagreed with the policy as a 'right-leaning opportunist'. ('The Resolution Regarding Agricultural Collectivization' was passed in the 6th Plenary Meeting of the 7th CPC Congress held in Beijing from 4–11 October 1955.)

As local cadres who moved decisively and quickly to implement this policy directive were publicly praised, and laggards were publicly criticized, local cadres found themselves locked into a rat race on who could coerce peasants to form bigger collectives at a faster pace. By the end of 1956, 96.3 per cent of all peasant households had joined collectives, more than ten years ahead of the schedule set in the first FYP.

Mao's administrative decentralization was not a repudiation of the concept of central planning. It was an attempt to redefine central planning in the Chinese context with perhaps an implicit intent to enlarge the sphere of Mao's influence. By weakening the nascent central planning bureaucracy, Mao effectively strengthened his own influence in enunciating broad policy directives in the form of slogans that could be easily passed down to local cadres. To align the interests of local cadres with the centre, Mao offered high-powered incentives: those who found innovative ways to implement the centre's directives irrespective of economic consequences were rewarded with public praise and promotion, while those who ignored the centre's policy directives were punished with the humiliation of public criticism and denunciation. In more serious cases, those who resisted the centre's policy directives could be purged as 'rightists' or 'counter-revolutionaries'. Mao also made frequent use of brutal political campaigns against nonconformists and instilled an atmosphere of terror. (One of the most notorious political campaigns was the 1957 'anti-rightist' campaign; Fairbank, 1992.) The resulting political system was one in which Mao could exploit his personality cult in enunciating broad policy directives without the inconveniences of checks and balances. Mao's administrative decentralization thus marked the beginning of the politicization of economic policy formulation and implementation in China. When Mao launched the Great Leap Forward (GLF) movement in 1958, the inaugural year of the second FYP, there was hardly any dissenting voice.

The Great Leap Forward

By setting production targets even more aggressively in the second FYP, the CPC hoped that China would grow out of the imbalances created during the first FYP by exhorting local cadres and the masses to make selfless sacrifices in order to transform China into an industrial, socialist nation. In March 1958, the CPC issued a new directive, calling local cadres to amalgamate smaller cooperatives into larger ones. Zealous local cadres in Henan province created township-sized collectives, dubbed 'People's Communes'. Each of the communes was an all-encompassing institution that functioned as a local government, an agricultural collective, local government-owned industrial and commercial enterprises (one of the enduring legacies of Mao's administrative decentralization was the policy directive that encouraged the creation of local government-owned enterprises), local schools, and a militia integrated into the national defence system. In these collectives, communalization went beyond all means of production and invaded the private lives of peasants. For example, family kitchens were banned and were replaced by communal kitchens that offered members free meals (Li and Yang, 2005). 'People's Communes are good because they are big and communal', declared Mao. By early autumn, communes had spread across China.

Believing that collectivization significantly boosted agricultural productivity, the CPC created a new rat race for local cadres by exhorting them to 'overcome reactionary conservatism' (*People's Daily*, 10 September 1958). Unable to deliver the expected increase in grain output, local cadres started to outdo each other in statistical gamesmanship by making wild claims about grain output. An initial tally of the 1958 grain output after the autumn harvest pegged it at 525 million metric tons (MMTs), up by nearly 170 per cent from 1957. The figure was subsequently revised down to a more modest 375 MMTs. (The downward revisions did not stop here. Two more were made: first to 250 on 22 August 1959 and then to 200 in 1979; Li and Yang, 2005.)

With the numbers indicating that collectivization had permanently resolved China's agricultural bottleneck, the government raised agricultural taxes: grain procurement (including government grain) was increased from 46 million metric tons in 1957 to 64 in 1959; 16.4 million peasants, about twice the size of the industrial labour force in 1957, were relocated to cities in 1958 to support the expansion of industry and construction; and more than 100 million peasants were mobilized in the winter of 1957–8 to undertake large irrigation and land reclamation projects, and to operate millions of small 'backyard iron furnaces'. (Built using mud and bricks, these furnaces melted scrap metal – for example, iron woks made obsolete by communal kitchens – to produce iron, which even the government admitted was of useless quality; Becker, 1996.) The increase in agricultural taxes allowed the government to raise national savings from 24.9 per cent of national income (measured by net material product) in 1957 to 43.8 per cent in 1959. These savings were almost exclusively invested in heavy industries (Riskin, 1987, p. 142). Grain export was raised from an average of 2.11 million tons between 1953 and 1957 to 3.95 million tons in 1959 to meet payment obligations for importing capital goods.

The collectivization miracle was, however, a mirage. Lin (1990) finds that incentive problems within large collectives had deleterious effects on agricultural productivity. With actual grain output significantly lower than the falsified statistics, the agricultural taxes were excessive. Grain retained in rural areas fell sharply from 273 kg per capita in 1957 to 193 kg in 1959, and further down to 182 kg in 1960. Since grain was the primary source of food energy in China at the time, the drop in per capita food availability coincided with the onset of worst famine in human history. (Demographers who extrapolated mortality trends in China estimated the total number of premature deaths during the GLF famine at between 16.5 and 30 million; see Li and Yang, 2005.)

As the disastrous consequences of the GLF policies became known in 1959, Mao temporarily stepped aside to let his pragmatic colleagues, Liu Shaoqi and Deng Xiaoping, take responsibility in managing both government and party affairs. The pragmatic leaders started to reverse course: they reduced grain procurement by ten million tons, increased agricultural labour force by more than 50 million between 1958 and 1962 by sending back new industrial recruits back to the countryside, dismantled communal kitchens, downsized the collectives and started to import grain. More importantly, they allowed spontaneous, bottom-up experimentation with market-oriented reforms in 1961. Grain output began to recover in 1961, but did not surpass its pre-GLF level of 195 million metric tons (recorded in 1957) until 1966, the first year of yet another political upheaval – the Cultural Revolution.

The model

To better understand the trade-offs faced by Chinese policymakers and the key factors that contributed to the GLF disaster, I turn next to Mao's policy directive for accelerating collectivization with the aid of a simple two-sector dynamic model developed in Li and Yang (2005).

A key feature of the Li–Yang model is the explicit dependence of agricultural labour productivity on nutrition. For simplicity, assume that in the agricultural sector labour is the only factor and the technology exhibits constant returns to scale. If L_t is labour allocated to agriculture, the aggregate grain output in year t can be written as

$$Q_t = af(c_t)L_t \qquad (1)$$

where $af(c_t)$ measures the contribution of nutrition to the labour productivity of an average worker who consumes c_t amount of grain in year t, and a is a productivity parameter. Experimental and empirical studies have found that $f(\cdot)$ tends to be an increasing, S-shaped function with $f''(c) \geq 0$ at a very low level of food intake, and $f''(c) < 0$ as food intake reaches a sufficiently high level. (For a survey on health, nutrition and economic development, see Strauss and Thomas, 1998.) If the government taxes away p_t amount of grain output from each agricultural worker after the harvest in year t, the amount of grain saved for consumption in year $t+1$ is then

$$c_{t+1} = af(c_t) - p_t. \qquad (2)$$

The industrial sector uses a Leontief technology that produces one unit of industrial output by employing one unit of labour, d units of capital service and m units of grain as an intermediate input in fixed proportions. Assume that all capital goods must be imported and paid for by exporting grain, and the exchange rate is one unit of grain to one unit of capital service. With abundant grain supply and the economy's labour supply normalized to 1, the industrial output is simply $1 - L_t$. The government is assumed to maximize a discounted flow of industrial output, $\sum_{t=0}^{\infty} \beta^t (1 - L_t)$, subject to the following budget constraint:

$$p_t L_t \geq (d + m + n)(1 - L_t), \qquad (3)$$

where $\beta < 1$ is the government's discount factor and n is the food entitlement of each industrial worker. (For more discussion on food entitlement, see Li and Yang, 2005. In 1956, the national average of monthly ration of grain for labourers assigned to the most physically demanding jobs was 25 kg. Retail prices of food items in stores were set by the government and played little role in resource allocation.) This constraint, which captures China's key bottleneck during the Maoist era, states that the amount of grain procured must be sufficient to meet export demand for the importation of capital goods, industrial demand for intermediate inputs, and food demand from industrial workers.

Given the government objective, the optimal solution calls for allocating just enough labour to grain production, so the constraint (3) is binding in each year. This implies that the optimal allocation of labour to grain production should be $L_t = (d + m + n)/(p_t + d + m + n)$. Substituting this binding constraint into eq. (2), one can show that the government's optimal policy is a solution to the following Euler equation for a given initial level of food consumption c_0:

$$a\beta f'(c_{t+1}) = \left(\frac{af(c_{t+1}) - c_{t+2} + d + m + n}{af(c_t) - c_{t+1} + d + m + n} \right)^2. \qquad (4)$$

The optimal steady state policy is to set the food consumption per agricultural work $\bar{c}$ such that $f'(\bar{c}) = (a\beta)^{-1}$. The steady state is asymptotically stable if $f''(\bar{c}) < 0$. This stability condition is satisfied if the productivity effect of nutrition exhibits diminishing returns around the steady state per capita food consumption, which is consistent with previous experimental findings.

Under the stability condition, the steady state grain procurement $\bar{p}$ and industrial output $1 - \bar{L}$ are both increasing functions of agricultural productivity a and the discount factor β. The model therefore validates Mao's claim in his quoted policy speech that raising agricultural productivity would contribute to the relaxation of the agricultural bottleneck and hence permit a

faster pace of industrialization. It also proves that patience is a virtue: a more patient government, one that uses a larger discount factor β (or a lower discount rate) in setting intertemporal policies, can sustain a higher level of steady state agricultural and industrial production. The intuition is as follows. A more patient government, one that discounts future industrial production at a lower rate and is content with a lower growth rate, would set a lower tax rate on peasants, allowing them to improve nutrition and labour productivity. The improved productivity would in turn increase the tax base sufficiently high to more than compensate for any revenue loss from lowering the tax rate. As a result, both the grain procurement and industrial production are higher in the steady state for a more patient government.

Like Stalin, Mao was impatient. (In a speech delivered in 1931, Stalin, 1952, used nationalistic rhetoric to demonstrate the imperative to press on with rapid industrialization regardless of the obstacles during the first Five Year Plan of 1928–32 in the USSR.) And, like Stalin, Mao saw collectivization as a means to achieve rapid industrialization. Expecting collectivization to raise a, the increasingly impatient planners exhorted local cadres to increase grain procurement and to divert more agricultural labour to industrial production and large infrastructure projects. Since collectivization actually caused a to fall, the GLF policies left many peasants with insufficient amount of grain for consumption. Malnutrition (and famine in several grain-producing provinces) significantly reduced labour productivity, leading to a collapse in grain production. The further reduction in grain output caused malnutrition and famine to spread from the countryside into cities. The linkage between nutrition and productivity thus offers a dynamic explanation of why the negative incentive effect of collectivization could cascade into a major catastrophe. Empirical investigation by Li and Yang (2005) finds that the GLF policies were principally responsible for this disaster. As the GLF policies were reversed by Liu Shaoqi and Deng Xiaoping, the Chinese economy began to stabilize in 1962. In 1966, when the economy appeared to have fully recovered by 1966, Mao launched another political campaign – the Great Proletarian Cultural Revolution.

The Cultural Revolution

The post-GLF policies had some noteworthy features. First, the centre–province distribution of power was rebalanced in favour of the centre. The task of collecting reliable information on the prevalence and severity of famine was simply too important to be delegated to local cadres. Second, collectives were downsized by making village-level 'production brigades' responsible for their own finances, and communal kitchens were closed. More important, the policies permitted spontaneous experimentation with household responsibility schemes within collectives, allowed peasant families to keep small private plots, and reopened markets in which peasants could sell their surplus produce. These policies arrested the downward momentum and brought about a gradual recovery.

But they represented a humiliating retreat in the campaign towards socialism. As long as the retreat was tactical, Mao was content standing on the sideline. However, Khrushchev's denunciation of Stalin's rule in 1956 and the subsequent de-Stalinization in the Soviet Union gave Mao reasons to be concerned about his own legacy. As soon as the economy recovered, Mao moved to reclaim power so that he could purge those who had the potential to become China's Khrushchev. In 1966, Mao turned against Liu and Deng. Exploiting his personality cult, Mao kicked off the 'Great Proletarian Cultural Revolution' in 1966 by exhorting the Red Guards, made up primarily of students and other urban youths, to rebel against the power base of Liu and Deng – the government and party hierarchy. Liu and Deng, along with many of their colleagues, were labelled 'capitalist roaders' and were purged in 1968.

Mindful of the fragile conditions in the Chinese countryside, moderate leaders did their best to keep the revolution from spreading into the countryside, preventing a rerun of the famine during the GLF. But the market-oriented reforms permitted under Liu and Deng were nullified. Agricultural productivity continued to stagnate until market-oriented reforms were restarted in 1978. The demand for food, however, continued to grow as a result of the post-war baby boom. Unable to raise grain procurement quotas to meet the growing demand for food rations in the cities, the government resorted to sending millions of urban youths to the countryside to grow their own food and to receive 're-education'.

The Cultural Revolution brought politicization to every facet of life in China. It was better to be revolutionary (that is, loyal to Mao) than productive. Intellectuals and experts, considered less loyal to Mao, were sent to re-education camps in the countryside. Colleges were closed at first and were reopened later to admit only students from 'revolutionary families' – families of workers, peasants and soldiers – based on recommendations from grass-roots party organizations. Seasoned bureaucrats and factory managers were purged by the Red Guards, and 'Revolutionary Committees', comprised of workers, peasants and students, took over government offices and state-owned enterprises.

The revolution paralysed the government and the nascent economic planning apparatus. With neither the plan nor the market to guide the allocation of resources, the economy fell into a state of anarchy. As coordination across regions fell by the wayside, regional self-sufficiency, a policy stance endorsed by Mao, became a necessity. Specialization based on regional comparative advantage gave way to the duplication of industrial structure across provinces. The economy stagnated until

1978, when a rehabilitated Deng Xiaoping restarted market-oriented reforms.

Discussion

One of the classic tenets of Marxian economics is that, with planning eliminating the 'anarchy of production', a planned economy can avoid or at least better manage large aggregate economic fluctuations (Ellman, 1989). The experience of the Chinese-style central planning offers little support for this claim. The analysis of the GLF disaster by Li and Yang (2005) suggests that, on the contrary, central planning as practised in China exposed the economy to a new systemic risk. Because policy directives formulated at the centre had to be carried out in all localities, policy failures had generated large economic imbalances, severe economic and political crises, and prolonged stagnation. The source of the risk is the concentration of economic and political power in the hands of the planners. In the case of China, Chairman Mao, a charismatic leader, maintained a near monopoly on economic and political policies. With no effective checks and balances during the Maoist era, the economic and political system in China was incapable of arresting the momentum of apparently deleterious policy directives.

The Maoist era was tumultuous. It saw spectacular post-war reconstruction, the build-up of a rudimentary industrial economy aided by Soviet assistance and the formation of a decentralized government administration that emphasized regional self-sufficiency on the one hand and economic collapse, stagnation, a personality cult and brutal 'class struggle' on the other. It conditioned a generation of pragmatic leaders who, after the demise of Mao, would restart market-oriented reforms through decentralized regional experimentation, disown the personality cult, ban mass movements and depoliticize economic policymaking, while resolutely maintaining the CPC's hold on power. The historical significance of Maoist economics may lie not in what it is but in what it is not.

WEI LI

See also **agriculture and economic development; China, economics in; Chinese economic reforms; command economy; famines; planning.**

Bibliography

Ashton, B., Hill, K., Piazza, A. and Zeitz, R. 1984. Famine in China: 1958–61. *Population and Development Review* 10, 613–45.

Bachman, D.M. 1997. *Bureaucracy, Economy, and Leadership in China: The Institutional Origins of the Great Leap Forward.* Cambridge: Cambridge University Press.

Becker, J. 1996. *Hungry Ghosts: Mao's Secret Famine.* New York: Henry Holt and Company.

Communist Party of China. Constitution. Online. Available at http://news.xinhuanet.com/ziliao/2004-11/24/content_2255749.htm, accessed 13 June 2007.

Ellman, M. 1989. *Socialist Planning*. Cambridge: Cambridge University Press.

Fairbank, J.K. 1992. *China: A New History*. Cambridge, MA: Harvard University Press.

Hinton, W. 1967. *Fanshen: A Documentary of Revolution in a Chinese Village*. New York: Monthly Review Press.

Lardy, N.R. and Lieberthal, K. 1983. Introduction. In *Chen Yun's Strategy for China's Development: A Non-Maoist Alternative*, ed. N.R. Lardy and K. Lieberthal. The China Book Project. Armonk, NY: M.E. Sharpe.

Li, W. and Yang, D.T. 2005. The Great Leap Forward: anatomy of a central planning disaster. *Journal of Political Economy* 113, 840–77.

Lin, J.Y. 1990. Collectivization and China's agricultural crisis in 1959–61. *Journal of Political Economy* 98, 1228–52.

Mao, Z. 1958. Introducing a cooperative. In Mao (1977).

Mao, Z. 1977. *Selected Work of Mao Zedong*, vol. 5. Beijing: Foreign Language Press.

Ministry of Finance, People's Republic of China. Online. Available at http://www.mof.gov.cn, accessed 20 February 2007.

Riskin, C. 1987. *China's Political Economy*. Oxford: Oxford University Press.

Stalin, J.V. 1952. *Economic Problems of Socialism in the USSR*. Moscow: Foreign Language Publishing House.

Strauss, J. and Thomas, D. 1998. Health, nutrition, and economic development. *Journal of Economic Literature* 36, 866–17.

Marcet, Jane Haldimand (1769–1858)

The classical political economist Jane Haldimand Marcet was born in London, the eldest of ten children of Anthony (Antoine) Haldimand, a Swiss citizen who was a successful London banker and property developer, and his English wife, Jane Pickersgill. She was tutored at home, studying the same subjects as her brothers, and took charge of the household at the age of 15, when her mother died. In December 1799 she married Alexander Marcet, a London physician from Geneva. Since her father bequeathed all his children an equal share of the family fortune, regardless of gender, she was independently wealthy, with no need to write for money. Nonetheless, she wrote 30 educational books on chemistry, political economy, botany, mineralogy, grammar and history, many written in the form of conversations. Her first book, an introduction to experimental chemistry, was published in 1806 after attending Humphrey Davy's lectures at the Royal Institution and after repeating Davy's experiments at home in Alexander Marcet's laboratory. The book was adapted in the United States as a college text, and its tremendous commercial success is shown by the many plagiarized editions that emerged in a period with no effective international copyright law. It introduced the young Michael Faraday to science.

Jane Marcet encountered the ideas of Adam Smith through Sydney Smith's lectures on moral philosophy at the Royal Institution in 1804 and 1806. Alexander Marcet and David Ricardo were both elected to the Geological Society in 1808. Jane Marcet's younger brother, William Haldimand (who lived with the Marcets), was elected a director of the Bank of England in 1809 at the age of 25, and, like his sister, shared Ricardo's attribution of the rising price of bullion to the excessive issue of bank notes, which was very much a minority view among the directors of the Bank of England. James Mill and Thomas Robert Malthus were also friends of the Marcets. Jane Marcet's *Conversations on Political Economy*, published anonymously in 1816, attempted to make the economic ideas of Smith, Malthus, Ricardo and Jean-Baptiste Say accessible to a wider public. Robert Torrens declared her 'one female, at least, fully competent to instruct the members of the present cabinet in Political Economy', while J.R. McCulloch considered her book 'on the whole, the best introduction to the science that has yet appeared'. Ricardo's daughter read the book at her father's recommendation, and Say wrote for permission to 'translate sizeable passages from her excellent book' for his political economy class (Polkinghorn, 1993, p. 55).

Jane Marcet (1816; 1833; 1851) was a successful popularizer of classical political economy, but she was also fully capable of independent judgement, sharing Ricardo's opposition to the Corn Laws rather than Malthus's support for them, and supporting the proposed Factory Act in 1833, contrary to the beliefs of her younger friend, Harriet Martineau. Marcet was more optimistic than Ricardo or Malthus about the prospects for economic growth, being less concerned that the working class would erode gains in the standard of living by heedlessly multiplying. Like Say, she placed more emphasis on utility than labour cost as a source of value: when Malthus, after high praise of her discussion of rent, protested that 'I think you have given too much sanction to Mr. Say's opinion reflecting utility', she cut out and discarded the rest of his letter (Polkinghorn, 1986). A talented educational writer and the first woman to expound the principles of economics, Jane Marcet succeeded in bringing classical political economy (and other disciplines such as chemistry, botany and mineralogy) to a wider public.

ROBERT W. DIMAND AND EVELYN L. FORGET

See also **British classical economics; Corn Laws, free trade and protectionism; Malthus, Thomas Robert; Martineau, Harriet; Ricardo, David; Say, Jean-Baptiste.**

Selected works

1816. *Conversations on Political Economy*. 3rd edn. London: Longman, 1818.

1833. *John Hopkins's Notions on Political Economy.* London: Longman.

1851. *Rich and Poor.* London: Longman.

Bibliography

Bodkin, R.G. 1999. The issue of female agency in classical economic thought: Jane Marcet, Harriet Martineau, and the men. *Gender Issues* 17, 62–73.

Polkinghorn, B. 1986. An unpublished letter from Malthus to Jane Marcet. *American Economic Review* 76, 845–7.

Polkinghorn, B. 1993. *Jane Marcet: An Uncommon Woman.* Aldermaston, UK: Forestwood Publications.

Shackleton, J.R. 1990. Jane Marcet and Harriet Martineau: pioneers of economic education. *History of Education* 19, 283–97.

Marget, Arthur William (1899–1962)

A leading monetary theorist during the first half of his career, Marget went on to make an even greater contribution by formulating and implementing government policies regarding international banking and finance. Born in Chelsea, Massachusetts, on 17 October 1899, he graduated from Harvard with AB (1920) and MA (1921) degrees in Semitics, and a Ph.D. in economics (1927). He taught economics at Harvard (1920–7) and the University of Minnesota (1927–43; resigned 1948). He died in Guatemala City on 5 September 1962.

As an academician, Marget's principal concern was with the central problems of monetary theory, and since these had been so strikingly shaped by John Maynard Keynes, much of Marget's work became a critique of his views. Marget regarded himself as building upon an enduring neoclassical tradition, and saw the Keynesian Revolution as a largely misdirected episode that had the merit, however, of making some genuine contributions, and especially of stimulating the sort of re-examinations and refinements of doctrine exemplified by his own writings. His most significant critical contributions were his evaluations of Keynes's *Treatise on Money*, of liquidity preference, of Keynes's treatment of expectations, and of the implications of Keynes's *General Theory of Employment, Interest and Money* for the theory of prices (Marget, 1938; 1942). Marget's principal positive contributions were an extension and refinement of the concepts of the velocity of circulation of money and of goods; his reformulation of the quantity equation relating prices, output and money; his argument that the cash-balance approach is useful only in connection with the analysis of changes in the velocity of the circulation of money; and his analysis of the relevance of particular demand curves and their elasticity to the structure of money prices (Marget, 1938; 1942). The valuable elements of his critique of 20th-century theory and of his constructive writings have been assimilated into the discipline and are no longer a focus of discussion. Marget also undertook some studies in the history of thought which are among the best work on the subjects with which he dealt. Particularly worthy of note are his examinations of the monetary theory of 19th-century neoclassical economists (Marget, 1931; 1935; 1938; 1942).

As an applied economist, Marget was concerned with international financial policies. While a major (1943–5) and a lieutenant colonel (1945) in the US Army, he devoted himself to preparations to bring about the economic and financial rehabilitation of Austria. He then became chief of the finance division of the US Allied Command for Austria (1946–9); a member of the US delegation in London that prepared for the treaty with Austria (1947); and a member of the US delegation to the Council of Foreign Ministers, which was charged with negotiating that treaty in London and Moscow (1947). His subsequent career included the positions of Chief of the Finance Division at the headquarters of the Marshall Plan in Paris (July 1948–December 1949), consultant to the US Treasury (1948), and Director of the Division of International Finance of the Federal Reserve Board of Governors (January 1950–April 1961). Among other activities, he represented the Board at meetings of the central banks of the western hemisphere in Bogotá (1956) and Guatemala City (1958). He then became the US representative to the Central American Common Market in Guatemala City and an adviser to the Common Market Bank in Honduras (April 1961–September 1962). In the latter roles he was instrumental in promoting the effectiveness of the Common Market policies.

Marget's scholarly work was distinguished by an insistence on logical clarity and an amassing of scholarly detail in the presentation of his expositions. His bureaucratic work was distinguished by an outstanding ability to suggest workable new financial institutions and procedures.

DONALD A. WALKER

Selected works

1931. Léon Walras and the 'cash-balance approach' to the problem of the value of money. *Journal of Political Economy* 39, 569–600.

1932. The relation between the velocity of circulation of money and the velocity of circulation of goods. Parts I and II. *Journal of Political Economy* 40, 289–313; 477–512.

1935. The monetary aspects of the Walrasian system. *Journal of Political Economy* 43, 145–86.

1938, 1942. *The Theory of Prices: A Re-Examination of the Central Problems of Monetary Theory.* 2 vols. New York: Prentice-Hall.

marginal and average cost pricing

In a pure and simple static world of perfect competition, where production units purchase or rent all their inputs in competitive markets and each sells a single homogeneous product competitively, production takes place at a point of constant returns to scale where the marginal cost and average cost of the product are equal to each other and to its price. If in addition there are no neighbourhood effects or externalities operating outside the market, the result will be Pareto efficient, meaning that there is no feasible alternative arrangement that would be better for someone and no worse for anyone.

Difficulties with the concept of average cost

As soon as production takes place with durable capital facilities that must be adapted to the needs of an individual firm there may no longer be an effective market for these facilities and a cost of their use during any particular period must be determined by other means. In the rather extreme case of the 'one-horse-shay' asset that in a static environment yields a stream of identical services over a known lifetime, a constant periodic rental cost can be derived by the use of a 'sinking fund' method of depreciation in which the rent is the sum of an increasing depreciation charge and a decreasing interest charge on the net value. But where the value of the service varies over time, whether because of physical deterioration, an increasing cost of maintenance needed to keep the item in 'as new' condition, or shifts in demand, this would in principle cause depreciation charges to vary; in practice this is done in one of a number of arbitrary ways by using 'straight-line' or various forms of 'accelerated' depreciation. If these charges are used as a basis for pricing, where competition is imperfect enough to give some leeway, the results can be correspondingly arbitrary.

More serious problems arise in the increasingly widespread cases of joint production of several distinguishable products or services. Where competitive markets exist, the market conditions dictate the allocation of joint costs among the various products, as when a meat-packing establishment produces steaks, hides, glue and offals. There is no way in which one can determine a meaningful average cost of hides by considering only the production process. Where the products, though economically widely different, are physically similar, it is tempting to cut the Gordian knot and average over the entire output, often at the cost of serious impairment of economic efficiency. Even when elaborate rationales are concocted by cost accountants, unless demand conditions as well as production conditions are taken into account the results are essentially arbitrary.

One can do a little better with marginal cost, at least if one is seeking a short-run marginal social cost (hereafter SRMSC), which is the concept that would be relevant for efficiency-promoting pricing decisions. Unless a consumer is presented with a price that correctly represents the marginal social cost associated with the various alternatives open to him, he is likely to make inefficient decisions.

The importance of emphasizing the short run

One often finds in the literature proposals to use a 'long-run marginal cost' as a basis for setting rates. The trouble is that in an operation producing a multitude of products with interrelated costs it is not possible even to define in any precise way what could be meant by a 'long-run marginal cost', any more than one could define a relevant long-run marginal cost for the hides and steak that are derived from the same carcass in the face of fluctuations over time in relative demand.

The attempt to use a long-run concept seems to be motivated in part by the notion that in some sense the long-run concept is more inclusive in that it allows for variation in capital investment and would include a return on such investment, whereas short-run marginal costs would fail to cover the costs of capital investment. In the single-product steady-state case, however, which is the only case for which the long-run marginal cost can be clearly defined, if the investment in plant is at the optimal level, i.e. the level which will result in the given output being produced at the lowest total cost, short- and long-run average cost curves will be tangent to each other at the given output, and short- and long-term marginal costs will be equal. Short run marginal-cost prices will therefore cover just as much of the total cost as will prices based on 'long-run marginal cost'. If short-run marginal cost is below the long-run marginal cost, this would indicate that the installed plant is larger than optimum, and conversely if plant is below optimum size, short-run marginal cost will be above long-run marginal cost.

Flexible versus stable prices

A long-run approach is sometimes advocated on the ground that it results in more stable prices. Price rigidity, however, exacts a high toll in terms of reduced efficiency. It is sometimes argued that stable prices are required for intelligent planning for installations that commit the investor to the use of a given volume of service. There is nothing in a SRMSC pricing policy, however, that precludes providing the consumer with estimates of the probable course of prices in the longer term, or even entering into long-term contracts to purchase specified quantities of service. If they are not to interfere with efficiency, however, such contracts should allow for the possibility of purchasing additional amounts at the eventual going rates, or of selling back some of the contracted-for output if this should prove profitable for the consumer.

Lack of flexibility in pricing has, indeed, been a major source of inefficiency in the use of utility services, whether arising as a result of the cumbersomeness of the regulatory procedures in privately owned utilities, or of bureaucratic inertia in publicly owned ones. At times it has even appeared that it takes longer to carry out the bureaucratic procedures involved in altering a price than to install additional capacity, whereas in terms of the underlying capabilities prices can and should be altered on shorter notice than the time taken to adjust fixed capital installations.

Optimal decision-making sequence

The efficient pattern of decision-making consists of first establishing a pricing policy to be followed in the future (as distinct from the application of that policy to produce a specific set of prices), then planning adjustments to fixed capital installations according to a cost-benefit analysis based on predicted demand patterns and predicted application of the pricing policy, subject to whatever financial constraints may be applicable, and then eventually determining prices on a day-to-day or month-to-month basis in terms of conditions as they actually develop.

Too often a rigid adherence to inappropriate financial constraints results in a pattern of pricing over time that leads to gross inefficiency in the utilization of facilities that are added in large increments. In the setting of tolls on bridges, for example, a high fixed toll is often imposed from the start in an attempt to minimize early shortfalls of revenues below interest and amortization charges. When the indebtedness incurred to finance the facility is finally paid off, tolls are often eliminated, sometimes just at the time that they should be increased in order to check the growth of traffic and congestion and defer the necessity for the construction of additional facilities.

The forward-looking character of marginal cost

Since changes in present usage cannot affect costs incurred or irrevocably committed to in the past, it is only present and future costs that are of concern in the determination of marginal cost. Past recorded costs are relevant only as predictors of what current and future costs will turn out to be. The marginal cost of ten gallons of gasoline pumped into a car is not determined by what the service station paid for that gasoline, but by the cost expected to be incurred to replace that gasoline at the next delivery. The substantial time-lag that often exists between a change in price at the raw material level and its reflection at the retail level is one of the pervasive failings that contributes to the inefficiency of the economic system.

Another more important case in which future impacts are of vital importance in the calculation of marginal cost is where congestion accumulates a backlog of demand that has to be worked off over a period of time. A particularly striking case of this occurs when traffic regularly accumulates in a queue during rush hours at a bottleneck such as a toll bridge. The consequence of adding a car to the traffic stream is that there will be one more car waiting in the queue from the time the car joins the queue until the queue is eventually worked off, assuming that the flow through the bottleneck will be unaffected by the lengthening of the queue.

The marginal cost of a vehicle trip will be measured in terms of a number of vehicle hours of delay equal to the interval from the time the car would have arrived at the choke point if there had been no delay, to the time the queue is finally worked off. This is not measured by the length of the queue at the moment, but will be determined by the subsequent arrival of traffic over an extended period. A car arriving at the queue after it began to accumulate at 7:30 may get through the bottleneck at 8:00, after being delayed by only 15 minutes, but if the bottleneck will not be worked off until 10:00 the marginal cost will be $2\frac{1}{4}$ vehicle hours of which only $\frac{1}{4}$ hour is borne by the added car itself. The remaining two hours, if evaluated at $5 per vehicle hour, would indicate that under these conditions the toll that would represent this externality would be $10. Marginal cost cannot be determined exclusively from conditions at the moment, but may well depend, often to an important extent, on predictions as to what the impact of current consumption will be on conditions some distance into the future.

Marginal cost of heterogeneous sets of uses

It will often happen, for various reasons, that the same price will have to be applied to a non-homogeneous set of uses. To set such a price properly, the marginal costs of the various uses within the set covered must be combined in some way to get a marginal cost relevant to this decision. It would be wrong, however, merely to average the marginal costs of all the uses for which this price is to be charged. Rather, the decision as to whether a decrease in a given price is desirable must consider the cost of the increments or decrements in the various outputs that will be bought as a result of the price change. In averaging the marginal costs of the various usage categories, the weighting will have to be in proportion to the responsiveness of each usage category to the change in price.

For example, if a price is to be set for electricity consumption on summer weekday afternoons, in a system where air-conditioning is an important load, consumption and marginal cost may be higher on hot days than on warm days, but it may be considered too difficult to differentiate in price between the two categories of days. An increase in the price for this entire set of periods may induce some customers to adjust the thermostat setting. But during hot days the equipment may work full tilt without reducing the temperature to the thermostat setting, whereas on warm days there will be a reduction in power consumption. The marginal cost relevant to the setting of the common price would then be determined predominantly by the lower marginal cost of the warm-day consumption, and relatively little, if at all, by the higher marginal cost hot-day consumption.

Anticipatory marginal cost

In many cases a customer will make his effective decision to consume an item some time in advance, and it will be the expected price as perceived by him at that time that determines his decision. If, as in services subject to reservation, a firm price must be quoted the time the reservation is made, it is the expected marginal cost as of that moment that should govern the price charged. In the case of a service where the demand is highly variable and to a considerable extent unpredictable, such an expected marginal cost would be an average of marginal costs that might arise under alternative possible developments, possibly ranging from a very low value, if there turns out to be unused capacity, to the possibly quite high value if another latecomer must be turned away. The respective probabilities of these outcomes, as estimated at a given time, will vary with the proportion of the total supply already sold, the time remaining to the delivery of the service, and the pricing policy to be followed in the interim.

At one extreme, for long-haul airline reservations where the unit of sale is large, one might find it worth while to have a fairly elaborate pricing scheme in which the price quoted would vary according to the proportion of seats on a given flight already sold and the time remaining to departure, in simulation of what an ideal speculators' market might produce, the price at any time being an estimate of the price which, if maintained thereafter, would result in all the remaining seats being just sold out at departure time. This would correspond to marginal cost in that the sale of a seat at any given time would slightly raise the price during the remaining period to decrease demand by one unit, at a price that would be expected to be on the average equal to the price at which the seat was sold, indicating that the price was equal to the value of the seat to the alternative passenger.

Quality-volume interrelationships

In principle, in the absence of barriers to entry, competition would induce the supply of just sufficient seats on the various routes to cause revenues produced by such pricing to just cover costs. Even this, however, would be optimal only on those routes where traffic is so heavy that even with planes of a size producing the lowest cost per seat, further increases in service frequency would be of negligible value. On most routes there will remain economies of scale in that either providing more seats at the same frequency of service with larger planes would reduce costs per seat, or providing more seats with the same size of planes would provide an increased frequency of service that would be of value to others than the additional riders. In the latter case the marginal cost of providing for the additional passengers would be calculated by deducting the increase in the value of the service by reason of increased frequency from the cost of providing the added seats.

If it were possible to adjust plane size and frequency in a continuous fashion, then if the situation is optimal the two marginal costs would be equal. In practice both plane size and service frequency can be varied only in discrete jumps, so that this relation would be only approximate. Optimal price would be above a downward marginal cost calculated on the basis of a reduction in service, and below an upward marginal cost calculated on the basis of an increase in service. The decreases and increases might involve a combination of frequency and plane size changes. To preserve the formulation that price should equal marginal cost it may be useful to define marginal cost in such cases as consisting of the range between these upward and downward values rather than as a single point.

In practice, between the existence of economies of scale and the imperfect cross-elasticity of demand between flights at various times and with different amenities, removal of regulation tends to result in an emphasis on non-price competition, attempts to subdivide the market by various devices and restrictions to permit discriminatory pricing, and a bunching of service schedules at salient times and places that provides a lower overall level of convenience than would be possible were the given number of seat miles distributed more efficiently.

Where the unit of sale is small it may not be worth while to incur the transaction costs of varying price in strict conformity with SRMSC. One could, in theory, apply the same principle to the sale of newspapers at a given outlet. The price of a newspaper would vary according to the number of unsold papers remaining and the time of day. This would result in less disappointment of customers having an urgent desire for a paper late in the day and encountering a sold-out condition, and fewer unsold papers returned. But unless some ingenious device can be found for executing such a programme at low transaction costs, it probably would not be considered worth while, even by the most sanguine advocate of marginal cost pricing.

Wear and tear, depreciation and marginal cost

Even in the absence of lumpiness or technological change, existing methods of charging for capital use often fail to give a proper evaluation of marginal cost. This is especially true where the useful life of a unit of equipment is determined more by amount of use than by lapse of time. In the extreme case of equipment that must be retired at the end of a given number of miles or hours of active service, or after the production of so many kwh of energy, and which, in one-horse-shay fashion, gives a uniform quality of service over its lifetime without requiring increasing levels of maintenance, the marginal cost of use at a given time will be the consequent advancing of the time of retirement of the equipment. The marginal cost of using the newest units will be the lowest, and will advance over time at a rate equal to the rate of interest as the equipment ages and the advancement of replacement consequent upon use becomes less and less remote.

In a service subject to daily and weekly peaks, the newest equipment will be allocated to the heaviest service, operating during both peak and off-peak hours. Equipment will be relegated to less and less intense service as it ages. The marginal cost of service at a particular moment will be that for the oldest unit that has to be pressed into service at that instant. The rental charge for the use of the unit will vary gradually over the entire range of demands, rather than dropping off to zero whenever the full complement of equipment is not required. At the other end, in this extreme case, the service provided would not necessarily be held constant by price variation over an extended peak period: under the conditions postulated it would be possible to provide for needle peaks by planning for the stretching out over time of the final service units of the oldest equipment. In this way the required peak capacity can be provided at a cost much lower than that which would be calculated by loading all the capital charges for the added equipment on this brief period of use.

Another way of looking at the matter is to appeal to the proposition that perfect competition under conditions of perfect foresight will produce optimal results. To this end one can suppose a situation in which vehicles are rented by the hour from a large number of lessors operating in a competitive market. For simplicity, initially, one can assume all vehicles to be of the one-horse-shay variety, being equivalent to bundles of hours of active service, with the quality of service being independent of age up to a final 'bubble-burst' collapse. Also, for simplicity, assume a steady state in which vehicles are scrapped and replaced at a constant rate over time, so that at any given moment vehicles are evenly distributed by age.

A common market rental price for all vehicles at any given time of the week will emerge, being higher as the number of vehicles in service at the time is greater. During any given week, each renter will have a reservation price for his vehicle, such that he will rent his vehicle during those hours for which the market rental is above this reservation price and never when the market rate is lower. This reservation price will increase over time for any given vehicle at the market rate of interest, since a renter will rent his vehicle if and only if the net present value of the rental discounted back to the time of purchase exceeds some fixed amount. The owner would not want to rent his vehicle for a net present value less than he could have got by selling one of this stock of service units at some other time at or just below his reservation price. New buses will have the lowest reservation price and will be assigned to the schedules calling for the most hours of service per week, while old buses will be held idle during slack hours and used only for peak service. As each bus ages it will be assigned to less and less heavy service along the load-duration curve.

This pattern of usage can be regarded as resulting from a desire to recover the capital tied up in the usage units of each bus as rapidly as possible. It is related to the practice in electric utilities of using the newest units for peak service, in that case motivated in part by the tendency for the newer units to be more efficient in thermal terms. To be sure, occasionally new units are designed specifically for peaking service, with a correspondingly low capital cost, though this is a relatively recent phenomenon related to a slowing-down of secular increases in potential thermal efficiency.

In any case, where wear-and-tear is a factor, one cannot properly allocate depreciation charges primarily to peak service, however defined, nor should they be spread evenly over all service, much less spread evenly over hours of the week so that vehicle hours in off-peak periods would get higher charges than during the peak. Rather the depreciation charge per vehicle hour will vary gradually and in a positive direction with the intensity of use of the equipment at any given hour.

The analysis becomes a little complicated when equipment life is dependent on mileage or loading or intensity of use as well as hours of active service, so that different rentals would properly be chargeable according to the nature of the service for which the unit is being rented. Also further analysis is required if equipment is laid up between runs at isolated terminals rather than at a central depot where a market could be postulated, or if the fleet contains vehicles varying in size or other characteristics. It would even be theoretically appropriate to charge different fares for the same trip at the same time if made on vehicles with different origins or destinations. (In Hong Kong, indeed, the practice is to charge a flat fare on each route, but to differentiate the fare fairly elaborately as among routes. On segments where routes converge, this has the unfortunate result of unduly concentrating riding on buses with the lower fares, even where the higher fare buses have empty seats and are making stops in any case for other passengers.)

Costs of major overhauls that are performed at relatively long intervals would also complicate the picture. There are also problems associated with gradual or sudden changes in overall demand levels, or special events that can be anticipated sufficiently to present an opportunity for reacting in terms of a change in price. The picture can be further complicated if, as was discussed above, there are changes in available technologies or other changes in quality or cost. But the same method of analysis in terms of a hypothetical competitive market can be used to obtain appropriate results.

For the sake of simplicity the above analysis has been couched mainly in terms of a bus service, but the analysis is applicable wherever the useful life of equipment is in part a function of the intensity with which it is used.

Responsive pricing

In some cases, notably in telephone and electric power services, the technical possibility exists for conveying information as to the current price to customers at the instant of consumption, and for customers to respond to such information in a worthwhile manner at modest cost. In the case of telephone service the information as to the level of charges for local calls can be substituted for the dial tone, with information on rates for long distance calls provided to users who wait for it before dialling the final digits. If the charge exceeds what the customer is willing to pay the call can be aborted with little occupancy of equipment or inconvenience to the user. Prices can be varied from moment to moment in accordance with marginal cost, as estimated from the degree of busyness of the relevant sets of equipment.

In the case of electric power, the costs of providing for a variation of the price according to the conditions of the moment would be somewhat greater. But if the facilities take the form of remote meter reading, either by carrier current over the power lines or by a separate communications channel, much of the cost would be covered by the avoidance of costs involved in manual meter reading. A signal of rate changes can then be provided to the customer as a by-product of the signal required to initiate a new rate period. The customer can then respond either manually or by installing automatic equipment which will adjust the operation of such items as air-conditioning and refrigeration compressors, water heaters and the like, according to the level of rates in a manner determined by the customer himself. Retrofitting of existing meters by attaching a pulse-generating device such as a mirror and photo-electric cell to the rotor shaft of the existing meter and feeding the pulses to electronic counters and registers should be possible at relatively low cost.

Such responsive pricing would be especially valuable in dealing with emergencies, providing greater assurance of the maintenance of essential services than is possible with existing techniques, and making it possible to reduce substantially the cost of providing reserve capacity. In the case of floods, conflagrations, breakdowns in transit, or other emergencies that under present conditions tend to result in the overloading of telephone facilities and difficulties in completing calls of a vital nature, rates can be charged that are high enough to inhibit a sufficient number of less important calls so that the ability of the system to handle vital calls promptly is preserved. This is difficult to do with present techniques, for while it is relatively easy to give priority to calls originating at such points as police stations, hospitals, and the like, most emergency calls are calls to rather than from these points and it is much more difficult to distinguish such calls close to the point of origin. And there are always a certain number of vital calls not distinguishable in terms of either origin or destination.

Again, in the case of unscheduled power cuts, it would be possible to cause an almost instantaneous shedding of substantial water-heating and refrigeration loads, followed, in the case of an extended cut, by partial shedding of elevator, transit and batch process loads for which it is more inconvenient to respond quite so promptly, after which a sufficient refrigeration load can be picked up as needed to avoid food spoilage. Many of the serious consequences of major power blackouts could have been avoided had such a system been in place at the time. Reserve capacity might well be cut back to provision for scheduled maintenance, leaving the load-shedding capability of responsive pricing to function as a reserve. In many cases the speed of response possible with responsive pricing would be faster than the reaction time within which reserve capacity can pick up load, leading to better voltage regulation and a higher quality of service to customers remaining on the line. And if, in spite of everything, areas must be cut off completely, responsive pricing would also be of considerable help in facilitating a smooth recovery from an outage: instead of having a whole army of motors trying to start up at once upon the restoration of power, with consequent load surges, voltage fluctuations, and malfunction of equipment, load could be picked up smoothly and gradually as the price is lowered from the inhibiting level.

Preserving incentives with escrow funds

With privately owned utilities the regulatory process is too slow to permit prices established directly by regulation to be constantly adjusted to changing current conditions, unless indeed the regulators were to assume a large part of what are normally the responsibilities of management. The problem thus arises of how to allow the prices to be paid by customers to be varied by the utility management without giving rise to incentives for behaviour contrary to the public interest. Even if a formula could be devised that would require the utility to adjust prices to track short-run marginal cost, if the utility were allowed to keep the revenues thus generated without restriction, this would set up undesirable incentives for the utility to skimp on the provision of capacity in order to drive up the marginal cost, price, revenues, and profits.

A resolution of this dilemma can be achieved by separating the revenue to be retained by the utility from the amounts to be paid by customers. We can have the 'responsive' prices paid by customers vary according to short-run marginal social cost, while the revenues to be retained by the utility are determined by a 'standard' price schedule fixed by regulation in the normal manner, the difference being paid into or out of an escrow fund. Failure of the utility to expand capacity adequately would drive marginal cost up, and with it the responsive price, causing revenues to flow into the escrow fund, but the only way the utility could draw on these funds would be to expand capacity sufficiently to drive marginal cost down, causing the responsive rate to fall below the standard rate on the average, entitling the utility to make up the difference from the escrow fund as long as it lasts. Excessive expansion would result in the escrow fund being exhausted, with a corresponding constraint on the revenues obtainable by the utility from the unaugmented low responsive rates.

The setting of the responsive rates would have to be to a large extent at the discretion of the operating utility, though the regulatory commission could monitor the process and even attempt to establish guidelines according to which the responsive price should be set. The utility would normally have no incentive to set the responsive rate below marginal cost, since this would merely increase sales and hence costs by more than any possible long-run increase in revenues to the utility. To be sure, in the short run it might be able to draw on the escrow fund to the extent of the excess, if any, of the standard rate over the responsive rate, but since from a long-run perspective there will normally be other more advantageous ways of drawing on this fund this will not be attractive.

When marginal cost is below the standard price, which would tend to be the usual situation, the utility would in general have an incentive to set the price between the marginal cost and the standard price, since each additional sale produced by the lower price will yield an immediate net revenue equal to the difference between marginal cost and the standard price, offset only by the drawing down of the escrow fund by the difference between the responsive and the standard price. When marginal cost is above the standard price, which with a properly designed standard rate schedule with time-of-day variation should happen relatively rarely, the utility would have an incentive to set the price at least at the marginal cost level, since to set it lower would tend to increase output at a cost in excess of anything the utility could ever recover. How much higher than marginal cost the price might be set would in theory be limited by the condition that the price could not be high enough to curtail demand sufficiently to drive marginal cost below the standard price. If the standard price has an adequate time-of-day variation, this constraint, loose as it may seem, may be sufficient. Additional guidelines could of course be imposed by the regulatory commission for those rare occasions where this constraint might seem insufficient to keep prices within bounds.

Actual steps towards responsive pricing

Some actual practices of utility companies are steps in the direction of responsive pricing. Contracts for 'interruptible' power provide for load shedding at the discretion of the utility subject to some overall limits. As these are fairly long-term contracts that usually require ad hoc communication between the utility and the customer, their applicability is limited and there is no assurance that the necessary shedding will be done in the most economical manner. Many customers are reluctant to submit to load shedding that is not under their control at least to some extent, and that might be imposed under awkward circumstances. Where reserves are ample and interruption is highly unlikely, such contracts have been challenged as being a form of concealed discriminatory concession. On the other hand customers entering into such contracts in the expectation of not being interrupted may feel aggrieved if interruption actually takes place.

Another experimental provision applied by a company with a heavy summer air-conditioning load is for a special surcharge to be applied to the usage of larger customers on days when the temperature at some standard location exceeds a critical level. And another company bases its demand charge on the individual customer's demand recorded at the time that turns out to have been the monthly system peak load, supplying the customers with information as to moment-to-moment variations in the system load. This leads to interesting game-playing on the part of customers as they attempt to keep their own consumption down at times that look as though they might become the monthly peak, with the result that this action may itself shift the peak to another time.

Economies of scale, subsidy and second best pricing

Where there are economies of scale, prices set at marginal cost will fail to cover total costs, thus requiring a subsidy. One reason for wanting to avoid such a subsidy is that if an agency is considered eligible for a subsidy much of the pressure on management to operate efficiently will be lost and management effort will be diverted from controlling costs to pleading for an enhancement of the subsidy. This effect can be minimized by establishing the base for the subsidy in a manner as little susceptible as possible to untoward pressure from management. But it is unlikely that this can be as effective in preserving incentives for cost containment as a requirement that the operation be financially self-sustaining. To achieve this, prices must be raised above marginal cost, and in a multi-product operation the question arises as to how these margins should vary from one price to another within the agency.

Another objection to subsidy is that it raises hard questions of who should bear the burden of the subsidy. More fundamentally the taxes imposed to provide the subsidy will often have distorting effects of their own, and minimizing the overall distortion would again require prices to be raised above marginal cost. One can, indeed, regard these excesses of price over marginal cost as excise taxes comparable to other excise taxes that might be levied to raise a specified amount of revenue.

The answer given to the problem of how to allocate excise taxes and other margins of price above marginal cost so as to minimize the overall loss of economic efficiency given by Frank Ramsey in 1927 can be expressed for the case of independent demands as the inverse elasticity rule, which says that the margin of price over marginal cost as a percentage of the price shall be inversely proportional to the elasticity of demand. A more general formulation is one that states that prices shall be such that consumption of the various services would be decreased by a uniform percentage from that which would have been consumed if price had been set at marginal cost and demand had been a linear extrapolation from the neighbourhood of the 'second-best' point.

A more transparent formulation, devised by Bernard Sobin in work for the US Postal Service, is the requirement of a uniform 'leakage ratio', leakage being the difference between the net revenue actually derivable from a small increment in a particular price and the hypothetical revenue that would have been obtained had there been no change in consumption as a result of this increment. Leakage is the algebraic sum of the products of the changes in consumption of the various related products induced by the small change in a given price, and the respective margins between their prices and marginal costs. Leakage is a measure of the loss of efficiency resulting from the change in the particular price, and the leakage ratio is the ratio of this loss of efficiency to the hypothetical gain in gross revenue if there had been no change in consumption. If one leakage ratio should be greater than another, the same net revenue could be obtained at greater economic efficiency by getting more revenue from the price with the smaller leakage ratio and less from the other. The second-best solution accordingly requires that all leakage ratios be equal.

This analysis can be extended to the case where the agency is being subsidized by taxes which involve an adverse impact on the economy, in terms of marginal distorting effects, compliance costs, and collection costs, which can be expressed as the 'marginal cost of public funds' (MCPF). For a net decrease in the subsidy derived by increasing a price, which can be considered to be equivalent to imposing a tax equal to the difference between the marginal cost and the price, $MCPF = LR/(1 - LR)$, where LR is the leakage ratio. A second-best optimum is then one where the MCPF's are equalized over both external and internal taxes.

Special sources of subsidy: land rents and congestion charges

In the case of goods and services with economies of scale that are provided primarily to consumers within a particular urbanized area, methods of financing may be available that involve no marginal cost of public funds or even result in an enhancement of efficiency. The existence of large cities, indeed, is to a predominant extent due to the availability in the city of goods and services produced under conditions of economies of scale: if there were no economies of scale, activity could be scattered about the landscape in hamlets, with great reduction in the high transportation costs involved in movement about a large city. If prices of these services are reduced to marginal cost, the increased attractiveness of the city as a consequence would tend to drive up land rents within the city, and it appears quite appropriate that a levy on such rents should be used to finance the required subsidies. And while there are practical and conceptual difficulties in defining exactly how land rents or land values should be specified for purposes of levying a tax, it is generally considered that a tax on land values, properly defined, has negligible adverse impacts on the efficient allocation of resources.

Indeed, there is a theorem of spatial economics which states that in a system of perfect competition among cities, the availability in the city of services and products subject to economies of scale, priced at their respective marginal social costs, will generate land rents just sufficient to supply the subsidies required to permit prices to be lowered to marginal cost. Among the more important of these services are utility services such as electric power, telephone, cable communications, water supply, mail collection and delivery, sewers and waste disposal, and local transit. It is not clear just how broad the conditions are under which this theorem would hold, and there are difficulties in capturing all land rents for subsidy purposes, but steps in this direction are clearly desirable.

On a more intuitive level, one can note that a person who occupies or uses land that is provided with services such as the availability of transit, electricity, telephone, mail delivery and the like will be requiring that these services be carried past his property to serve others whether or not he himself uses them. The user of tennis courts located conveniently in a built-up area should no more be excused from contributing to the costs of carrying these services past the courts, even though no direct use is made of electric power, telephone, mail, or other services, than he should expect his auto dealer to cut the price of an automobile by the cost of the headlights and windshield wipers merely because he asserts that he will never drive at night or in bad weather. Tennis players will indeed pay a rent enhanced by the presence of these services and the consequent greater demand for the land for other purposes, but the rent will go to the landlord, not to the purveyor of the services, and the price of the services to those who do use them will be too high for efficiency, unless indeed they are subsidized by other taxes that have their own distorting effects.

It is a corollary of this theorem that it would be to the advantage of the landlords in the area, *faute de mieux*, to agree collectively to pay a tax based on their land values, in order to subsidize the various utility services to enable the prices to be set closer to marginal social cost. They could expect in the long run that this action would increase their rents by as much or more than the taxes. To be sure, they might do better by getting someone else to pull their chestnuts out of the fire, but they can do this only at considerable damage to the overall efficiency of the economy of the city, to say nothing of the inequity of such a parasitic relationship.

In addition to land rents in the conventional sense, there is the land used for city streets for the use of which no adequate rental is generally charged. Charging on the basis of SRMSC for the use of congested city streets would in most cases yield a revenue far in excess of the cost of maintaining such facilities, which could appropriately be used for the subsidy of other urban facilities. Properly adjusted, such charges would increase efficiency by bringing home to the users the costs that their use directly imposes on others.

Formerly it would have been considered impractical to attempt to charge for the use of city streets according to the amount of congestion caused: the collection of tolls by manual methods at a multitude of points within the city might well create more congestion than it averted. Advances in technology have, however, made it possible to do this at minimal interference with traffic flow and at modest cost. One method, proposed as long ago as 1959 and recently carried to the point, is to require all vehicles using the congested facilities to be equipped with electronic response units which will permit individual vehicles to be identified as they pass scanning stations suitably distributed within and around the congested area so that the records thus generated can be processed by computer and appropriate bills sent to the registered owners at convenient intervals. If properly done, this would greatly improve traffic conditions so that the net cost of the revenue to the road users would be far less than the amount collected as revenue. A pilot installation has recently been tested in Hong Kong with satisfactory results, but full implementation appears to have been deferred, because of the political situation associated with the impending transfer of sovereignty.

Indeed, one can define 'hypercongestion' as a condition where so many cars are attempting to move in a given area that fewer vehicle miles of travel are being accomplished than could be if fewer vehicles were in the area but could move more rapidly; for example if 1000 vehicles in an area move at 8 mph and produce 8000 vehicle miles of travel per hour, reducing the number of cars in the area at a given time to 800 might raise speed to 11 mph producing 8800 vehicle miles of travel per hour. By restricting the flow of traffic in the period leading up to the hypercongestion period, road pricing could prevent hypercongestion from occurring, except possibly sporadically, and in any case so improve conditions that more movement would be accomplished during the peak period at faster speeds. The improvement during peak periods might even be such that total movement throughout the day would be increased, and where conditions are now severe users could find that they are better off than before, even inclusive of the payment of the congestion charge.

If there are bridges, tunnels, or other special facilities for which a toll is already being charged, and which

regularly back up a queue during the morning rush-hour, substantial revenues can be obtained at no overall net cost to the users by adding a surcharge to the toll during the period where queueing regularly threatens, rising gradually from zero to a maximum and down again in such a way that by gradual adjustment regular queueing is substantially eliminated. The toll surcharge will then be taking the place of the queue in influencing decisions as to when to travel, and in general those who plan their trips in terms of time of arrival at their destination will be able to leave as many minutes later as they formerly wasted in the queue, pass the bottleneck at the same time as before, and arrive at their destinations at the same time as before. The extra toll will be roughly the equivalent of the value of the extra time enjoyed at the origin point, and the revenue will in effect be obtained at no net burden on the users. In practice the results may be even better than this as a result of the added encouragement to car-pooling, the reduction of obstruction to cross-traffic, and the expediting of emergency or other trips where the delay had been a particularly serious matter.

Gains in the evening may be not quite so dramatic. The situation is not symmetrical, as typically the timing of the trip will be determined in terms of time of departure, which is separated by the queue from the time at the bottleneck. On the other hand the risk of conditions approaching gridlock is greater, since the accumulation of queues inside circumferential bottlenecks is more likely to create congestion, and there is less of a physical barrier to the simultaneous emergence of large quantities of traffic from parking lots into the downtown streets than there is in the morning to the convergence on the congested area of traffic arriving from the outside.

Congestion charges should be imposed, at least notionally, without exception on all forms of traffic. Such charges would be a necessary element in the cost-benefit analysis by which decisions are made as to the level and pattern of bus service to be provided, even though they would not be directly relevant to the determination of the price structure to be applied to that service.

Paradoxes in the behaviour of marginal social cost

A strict calculation of marginal social cost in particular circumstances may produce what may appear to be quite paradoxical results. For example, in many circumstances it will be optimal, and even essential, to maintain at least a minimum frequency of service in off-peak hours with buses of a standard size, resulting in there being practically always a large number of empty seats in each bus. Under these circumstances the cost of carrying additional passengers is predominantly the cost of boarding and alighting, including the time of the driver and the other passengers on the bus who are delayed in the process. This cost will be relatively higher if the bus is half full than if it is nearly empty. The result is likely to be that the cost of a trip from a point near one end of the run to a point near the other end, at both of which points the bus is likely to be lightly loaded, may be smaller than for a shorter trip between points near the middle of the run where the bus is likely to be more heavily loaded. This is not a trivial matter: if it were there would be no sense to the refusal of express buses with empty seats to pick up local passengers. It is highly unlikely, however, that fares based on such a seemingly perverse behaviour of cost would meet with popular approval. Indeed, the original US interstate commerce legislation contained prohibitions against higher rates being charged shorter hauls than for any longer hauls within which they might be included.

Another paradoxical example can occur in mixed hydrothermal electric power systems: an increase in fuel prices could result in the marginal cost of power at particular times being reduced rather than increased. If hydro dams are spilling water at certain seasons of the year, increased fuel costs may make it economical to increase the installed generating capacity to make use of the spilling water, even for a briefer period of time over the year than was previously worth while. If during the wet season installed hydro generating capacity is more than sufficient to meet trough demand, marginal cost during such periods will be substantially zero, or at most limited to a small element of wear and tear on equipment pressed into service. Installing more turbo-generators would expand the period during which this low marginal cost is effective, so that while increased fuel costs cause marginal cost to rise during the peak, the result could also be to lower marginal cost in these intervals into which the period of exclusive hydro supply expands.

In the case of long distance telephone service, the drastic reductions in the cost of bulk line-haul transmission have created a situation where distance, especially beyond the range where separate wire transmission is economical, is relatively unimportant as a cost factor, and where satellite transmission is involved, ground distance is indeed irrelevant. What remains important is the number of successive circuits, with their associated termination and switching equipment, involved in the making of a call. Thus a call between two small communities over a moderate distance, for which the volume of calling is insufficient to warrant the provision of a separate circuit, will generally cost substantially more than a call between important centres over a much longer distance, since the latter will involve only a single long-haul circuit, while the former will require patching through two or more long-haul circuits.

Another anomaly occurs when an innovation promising substantial reductions in costs appears on the horizon, such as has happened repeatedly in telecommunications. Any further installation of the old technology in the interim before the new technology is actually available will involve an investment which will have its capital value diminished over a brief period to that determined by its competition with the new technology. High depreciation or obsolescence charges are in order, and the prospect of the new lower costs results in higher current prices which would serve to hold back current demand and lessen the amount of old technology required to be installed.

Marginal cost pricing is thus not a matter of merely lowering the general level of prices with the aid of a subsidy; with or without subsidy it calls for drastic restructuring of pricing practices, with opportunities for very substantial improvements in efficiency at critical points.

WILLIAM VICKREY

See also **congestion; ideal output.**

Bibliography

Beckwith, B.P. 1955. *Marginal Cost Price-Output Control*. New York: Columbia University Press.

Mitchell, M., Manning, G. and Acton, J.P. 1978. *Peak-Load Pricing*. Cambridge, MA: Ballinger.

Nelson, J.R., ed. 1964. *Marginal Cost Pricing in Practice*. Englewood Cliffs, NJ: Prentice-Hall.

Ramsey, F. 1927. A contribution to the theory of taxation. *Economic Journal* 37, 47–61.

Vickrey, W. 1967. Optimization of traffic and facilities. *Journal of Transport Economics and Policy* 1(2), 1–14.

Vickrey, W. 1969. Congestion theory and transport investment. *American Economic Review* 59, 251–60.

Vickrey, W. 1970. The city as a firm. In *The Economics of Public Services*, ed. M.S. Feldstein and R.F. Inman, Proceedings of a conference held by the International Economic Association, Turin, Italy. London: Macmillan; New York: Wiley, 334–43.

Vickrey, W. 1971. Responsive pricing of public utility services. *Bell Journal of Economics and Management Science* 2(1), 337–46.

marginal productivity theory

Marginal productivity theory is an approach to explaining the rewards received by the various factors or resources that cooperate in production. Broadly stated, it holds that the wage or other payment for the services of a unit of a factor is equal to the decrease in the value of commodities produced that would result if any unit of that factor were withdrawn from the productive process, the amounts of all other factors remaining the same.

The basic justification of this assertion is highly intuitive. It rests on three assumptions: that the product is sold and the factor services are purchased in competitive markets; that the firms in those markets operate so as to maximize their profits; and that the products sold are produced by technologies that satisfy the 'law of variable proportions', which holds that successive equal increments of one factor of production, the amounts of all other factors remaining unchanged, will yield successively smaller increments of physical output. It follows immediately from these assumptions that if the wage of any factor exceeds the value of the output that would be lost if a unit less of that factor were employed, then a unit less of that factor will be employed, and successive units will be released until the inequality is annihilated. Similarly, if the wage of any factor is less than the value of the output that an additional unit could produce, successive units of that factor will be employed until the inequality vanishes.

The motivating concept in the foregoing argument was the effect on the value of output of small changes in the quantities used of different factors of production. This idea is so important that a special vocabulary has developed in order to discuss it with precision. The marginal product of a factor of production is the ratio of the greatest change in the output of some product that can be obtained by a small change in the use of the factor to the change in the use of the factor. The marginal product multiplied by the price of the product is the value of the marginal product. Marginal productivity theory holds that the payment for any factor of production tends to be about equal to the value of its marginal product, where, in a multiproduct firm, the product used in the calculation is the one for which the value of marginal product is greatest.

Clearly, the marginal product and its value may depend on the size of the 'small' change in the amount of the factor that is used in the calculation. To avoid being ambiguous when the amount of the factor is a continuous variable, the concept of marginal productivity is used: the marginal productivity of a factor is the limit that its marginal product approaches as the change in the quantity of the factor approaches zero. The result of multiplying the marginal productivity by the price of the product is called, somewhat inaccurately, the value of the marginal product; confusion rarely results.

Two of the assumptions made above to justify the marginal productivity doctrine can be relaxed. First, if the assumption that the firm produces for a competitive market is dropped, the conclusions of the theorem has to be weakened slightly. If a firm produces for a market that is not perfectly competitive, it will recognize that it cannot change the quantity of any of the commodities it sells without simultaneously changing the price. Consequently, it will take account of the fact that if it changes the amount used of any factor, the resulting change in sales revenue will not equal the value of the factor's marginal product, but that value adjusted for the induced change in price. The ratio of the change in sales revenue to the change in the employment of a factor, for 'small' changes, is called the factor's marginal revenue product. Then the reasoning used to deduce the marginal productivity doctrine leads to the conclusion that the firm will employ each factor at the level where its marginal revenue product equals its rate of pay, whether or not the firm sells in a competitive market. In competitive markets, the marginal revenue product of a factor equals the value of its marginal product, but not necessarily in other market types.

The assumption that firms operate so as to maximize their profits can also be weakened for some purposes. If the firm operates only so as to produce its outputs at the lowest possible total cost, the same line of argument shows that the rates of pay for any two factors used by the firm will be proportional to the marginal revenue products of the factors. This is a weaker conclusion than was found for profit-maximizing firms, and does not imply any particular relationship between a factor's rate of pay and its marginal revenue product or the value of its marginal product.

Development of the concept

Simple as it may appear, the marginal productivity principle was seen clearly only after a long, slow evolution. It was first presented in essentially its modern form around 1890, by J.B. Clark and Alfred Marshall, who apparently arrived at it independently. Their formulation built on the work of numerous predecessors, each of whom saw an important aspect of the principle but did not perceive its full generality.

The problem that gave rise to the marginal productivity principle – to explain the distribution of the national income among the great social classes and, especially to explain the shares claimed by the owners of capital and land – was at the top of the agenda of 19th-century economics. Thus, originally, only three very broad factors of production were considered: land, labour and capital, corresponding to the three social classes.

The first application of the principle occurred in the Malthus–Ricardo theory of rent, in particular in the concept of the intensive margin, which held that doses of labour and capital (in unspecified proportions) would be applied to each parcel of land until the value of the increase in product equalled the cost of the dose. The separate rewards to labour and capital were explained on other grounds.

In 1833, Longfield argued that the rate of interest was governed by the earnings of the least productive unit of capital, using a marginal argument. But he did not extend the reasoning to wages. At around the same time, von Thünen applied the principle to both wages and interest but did not publish his findings until much later, and then so obscurely that they had no influence. Jevons, in 1871, accounted for the rate of interest by a marginal argument, but explained wages as a residual after rent and interest were paid. Indeed, Jevons's theory is remarkably similar to Longfield's.

The ingredient that all these applications of the marginal principle missed was that the equality of marginal product and factor reward applied to all factors. Walras in 1874 (and, indeed, J.-B. Say three-quarters of a century before) insisted on treating the various factors of production symmetrically, but he did not derive any of the factor shares by a marginal argument until the later editions of the *Elements*, and then only awkwardly. Thus the marginal insight was not applied symmetrically to all factors until Clark published the papers that led to his *The Distribution of Wealth* (1899), and Marshall published his *Principles of Economics* (1890), thereby introducing a unified theory of income distribution.

The achievement of the unified theory raised a puzzling question: if each unit of every factor was paid the value of that factor's marginal product, would the total value produced be neither more nor less than just sufficient to make all the factor payments? In 1894 Philip Wicksteed showed that the answer is affirmative for production processes with constant returns to scale, thus establishing the internal consistency of the marginal productivity principle. (Clark had believed it all along, but on inadequate grounds.) Wicksteed's proof amounted to an independent rediscovery of part of Euler's Theorem for Homogeneous Functions.

Beginning with the late 1880s, when the various partial glimpses of the doctrine congealed, marginal productivity theory became an essential part of the accepted explanation of the general level of wages and of the rate of interest, with important implications for practical economic issues. For example, it is often held that unions are powerless to raise the average level of wages because wages are governed by the marginal productivity of the labour force, which union activity cannot affect.

Although the marginal productivity concept was originally applied to explain the rewards of the broad social classes – the workers, landowners and entrepreneur–capitalists – beginning with Walras it became absorbed into the general theory of production and value. In that context it is used to explain the payments for the services of all the classes of factors that enter into production, and the definitions of these classes can be chosen freely to fit the problem under study. The tripartite classification continues to be used frequently, however.

Qualifications

The marginal productivity doctrine does not purport to be a complete explanation, even in principle, of the payments received by factors of production. As the simple, basic argument indicated, it explains only the amount of each factor that an enterprise will employ at different rates of payment for its services and in the presence of given quantities of the other factors used; that is, the demand curves for the factors. Supply curves also are needed to complete the explanation of the equilibrium level of use and rate of payment for the factors.

Furthermore, especially in the version that deals with numerous factors, rather than just two, a high degree of simultaneity arises. The demand curve for each factor depends on the amounts used of the other factors, but those amounts, depend on the amount used of the first factor, so, in the end, the rates of payment and the quantities used of all the factors are determined simultaneously. Consequently, the rates of payment for the various factors cannot be explained except in the context of a full-fledged general equilibrium model. Still, in such a model it often turns out that the payment received by each factor corresponds to its marginal productivity in each productive process in which it is used and in which marginal productivity is a well-defined concept. These complications will be clarified by considering a more formal and rigorous derivation and statement of the principle.

Formal derivation of the marginal productivity thesis

The theory is based on the behaviour of a profit-maximizing firm in a competitive industry. To describe that behaviour, imagine a firm that produces m products by the use of n factors or inputs. Suppose that the price of the ith product is p_i and that the quantity produced (per year) is y_i. Then the gross revenues per year will be $R = \Sigma p_i y_i$. Similarly, let w_j be the price per unit of the jth factor used. If the jth factor is a kind of labour or a purchased input w_j is simply its price or wage, but if it is a kind of fixed capital, then w_j should be regarded as its rental cost, normally interest on its purchase or construction cost plus a depreciation allowance. The amount of the jth factor used will be denoted by x_j. Then the total cost incurred per year will be $C = \Sigma w_j x_j$. The profit that the firm seeks to maximize is $R - C$.

The quantities (per year) of output, y_i and input x_j, cannot be chosen freely. This basic presentation will be limited to the simplest situation, in which the choices are constrained only by an explicit, differentiable production function, which will be written $g(y_1, \ldots, y_m, x_1, \ldots, x_n) = c$. The implicit constraint that none of the arguments of $g(., ., \ldots)$ can be negative has important consequences that will be noted below.

In this set-up, invoking the assumptions mentioned in the second paragraph of this entry, the necessary conditions for a choice of y and x to maximize the firm's profits are the familiar marginal equalities. Specifically:

(1) Marginal rates of substitution. The marginal rate of substitution between two factors, say the jth and the kth is the rate at which small amounts of the jth factor can be substituted for the kth with no effect on the rates of output in accordance with the production function constraint. Denote it by $\delta x_j / \delta x_k$. Mathematically, it is the ratio of the partial derivatives of the production function, or $\delta x_j / \delta x_k = -(\partial g / \partial x_k)/(\partial g / \partial x_k)$. Economically, when the firm's

profits are being maximized $\delta x_j/\delta x_k = w_k/w_j$. The intuitive content is clearest when the maximizing condition is written as $w_j\delta x_j = w_k\delta x_k$, which requires that when profits are being maximized the amounts of factors that can be substituted for each other in accordance with the production function must have equal monetary value.

(2) Marginal rates of transformation. There is a similar relationship among the rates at which the outputs can be 'transformed' into one another in accordance with the production function constraint. Let $\delta y_i/\delta y_k$ denote the ratio at which production of the ith output can replace production of the kth. Mathematically, $\delta y_i/\delta y_k = -(\partial g/\partial y_k)/(\partial g/\partial y_i)$. Economically, when profits are being maximized $\delta y_i/\delta y_k = p_k/p_i$. Again, this result asserts that when profits are being maximized a small quantity of one of the outputs can be replaced by a quantity of equal value of any of the other outputs.

(3) Marginal productivity of a factor. The final necessary marginal equality relates small changes in the quantity of an input, say x_j, to the resulting changes in the quantity of any of the outputs, say y_i, in accordance with the production function. Mathematically, $\delta y_i/\delta x_j = -(\partial g/\partial x_j)/(\partial g/\partial y_i)$. When profits are being maximized $\delta y_i/\delta x_j = w_j/p_i$. Economically, this is seen to require that if any output is increased by a small amount, the use of some factor must be increased by an amount of equal value.

This third differential equality, of course, is the marginal productivity doctrine, which is seen to be one of the consequences of the theory of profit maximization under competitive conditions. It is often written in the form $\text{VMP}_j = p_i(\delta y_i/\delta x_j) = w_j$, for all values of i. This formula defines the value of the marginal product of the jth factor to be the increase in the value produced of any product for which that factor is used, per unit increase in the use of the factor, and holds that the price per unit of that factor's services will be equal to the VMP when profits are being maximized.

Evaluation

At present the marginal productivity principle is used to explain the demand for factors of production in both a two-factor version using aggregate capital and aggregate labour as the factors, and an n-factor version, where n is the number of distinguishable factors used in the production process.

To use the two-factor version it is necessary to establish quantitative measures of the aggregates of dissimilar objects that are given the names 'capital' and 'labour', a task that has never been performed to anyone's satisfaction. For a long time, until the publication of J. Robinson's disturbing paper, 'The production function and the theory of capital' (1953), the lack of satisfactory measures of the aggregates was regarded as a technicality that did not affect the essential insight. But that paper drove home the realization that in the absence of those measures the marginal productivities, i.e. $\partial g/\partial K$ and $\partial g/\partial L$, were essentially undefined. From that time forth, analyses that use the two-factor version have been regarded as simplified 'parables', useful for making an intuitive point, but not to be taken literally. Clarifying the meaning of 'capital' and 'labour' regarded as homogeneous factors of production continues to be one of the main problems of capital theory.

The n-factor version avoids the impossible task of aggregating apples and bulldozers, but has problems of its own. The formulation considered in this article is too simple to fit most industrial or commercial situations. It presumes that the constraints on choices can be described reasonably well by a single well-behaved, differentiable production function. This is generally not the case. Extreme examples are production functions in which factors are used or outputs are produced in fixed proportions. Any cooking recipe provides an example. More usual are cases in which the choices of input and output quantities are constrained by several functional relationships. The typical example is a firm or industry in which several different machines are each used in the production of several different products. Then there will be a functional relationship for each type of machine, to express the capacity of that type required for each combination of quantities of the different products. This is the sort of problem that has given rise to the use of linear programming in production planning and economic planning generally.

Where there are several constraints, the formulation used above does not apply because, essentially, the amounts of the inputs and outputs cannot be varied two at a time if they are connected by more than a single constraint. Marginal productivity is still a well-defined concept, but it no longer satisfies simple formulas like $\text{MP}_j = p_j(\delta y_i/\delta x_j)$ for any value of i. Instead, the marginal productivities, as defined above, are identified with the shadow prices in the solution to a mathematical programming problem, which is a considerably less intuitive concept.

Very frequently, if the problem of finding the combination of factor inputs that maximizes profits is solved straightforwardly, some of the input levels in the solution turn out to be negative – which is nonsense. Then, again, resort must be had to mathematical programming types of formulation and interpretation. The essential perceptions of marginal productivity theory still apply, but they can no longer be expressed by equalities between price ratios and ratios of marginal changes.

ROBERT DORFMAN

See also **capital theory (paradoxes); Clark, John Bates; classical distribution theories.**

Bibliography

Expositions of marginal productivity theory can be found in any standard text on microeconomics, for example Mansfield (1985). A famous and thoughtful presentation is contained in Hicks (1932). More advanced, and more mathematical, treatments, can be found in Baumol (1977) and Malinvaud (1972). For the relation between marginal productivity and mathematical programming, see Dorfman et al. (1958). The standard, and excellent, reference on the history of the doctrine is Stigler (1941).

Baumol, W.J. 1977. *Economic Theory and Operations Analysis*. Englewood Cliffs, NJ: Prentice-Hall.

Dorfman, R., Samuelson, P.A. and Solow, R.M. 1958. *Linear Programming and Economic Analysis*. New York: McGraw-Hill.

Hicks, J.R. 1932. *The Theory of Wages*. New York: Macmillan.

Malinvaud, E. 1972. *Lectures on Microeconomic Theory*. Amsterdam and London: North-Holland.

Mansfield, E. 1985. *Microeconomics: Theory and Applications*. New York: Norton.

Stigler, G.J. 1941. *Production and Distribution Theories: The Formative Period*. New York: Macmillan.

marginal revolution

The marginal revolution (sometimes called the marginal utility revolution) refers to the introduction into economics, in 1870–1, of the concept of marginal utility by William Stanley Jevons, Léon Walras and Carl Menger and which has widely been seen as involving a revolutionary break with the 'classical' economics of David Ricardo, John Stuart Mill and many of their contemporaries (see Blaug, 1996, ch. 8). The value of a commodity was no longer explained in terms of its cost of production (possibly reducible to the labour required to produce it) but in terms of its value to the consumer. The concept of utility was used to explain consumer choices, marginal utility being seen by some (though not all) authors as replacing cost of production as the foundation on which the theory of value rested. In the 1890s marginal techniques were then applied systematically to the problem of income distribution. This change, it is argued, revolutionized economics, laying the foundations on which modern economic theory is built. Its many dimensions – viewing behaviour as optimization, using utility to describe individual behaviour, focusing on individual agents, the use of mathematics – attest to its importance (Hutchison, 1978, provides a longer list; Maas, 2005, ch. 1, sketches more recent attempts to choose between them). There is disagreement over the extent to which the change should be described as a revolutionary or as an evolutionary change going back many decades, and over its exact significance; but the marginal revolution is firmly established in histories of economic thought. However, while it describes certain developments in economic theory, to understand the changes that took place in economics around this time one should place it in a broader historical context.

Varieties of marginalism

The most important qualification to the idea of a marginal revolution is the heterogeneity of economics during this period. Classical ideas were dominant in Britain, but even within classical economics there was great variety, and it has even been argued that marginalist ideas can be traced back as far as Steuart (see ENGLISH SCHOOL OF POLITICAL ECONOMY). At some time, virtually every element in the classical system outlined above had been challenged, many of these challenges leaving their mark. Much of this variety was captured within Mill's *Principles of Political Economy*, which went through seven editions between 1848 and 1873, and was undoubtedly the leading treatment of the subject: he worked with a very broad supply and demand theory of value and had accommodated many modifications to the Ricardian theory of income distribution. From Mill, the jump to marginalist theories was much easier than from Ricardo. Indeed, Alfred Marshall, though unfairly praising Ricardo at the expense of Mill (see O'Brien, 1990), derived his theory of value by translating Mill into mathematics during the 1860s; when he encountered Jevons's work, it was a simple matter to graft marginal utility on to a mathematical treatment of supply and demand (Whitaker, 1975).

There was also great variety across countries. In Ireland, it has been argued that an independent tradition of subjective value theory had been established at Trinity College Dublin, by successive holders of the Whately Chair (Black, 1945). Ireland also produced two leading exponents of a historical approach to economics, T.E. Cliffe Leslie and John Kells Ingram. Leslie's assault on deductive theorizing was a significant factor in the shaking of confidence in classical economics in Britain in the 1870s (see Hutchison, 1953). In Germany, supply and demand theories had a long history, a supply and demand diagram having been used in a textbook as early as 1843 by Heinrich Rau (see Streissler, 1990). In France, Smithian political economy had been mediated not through Ricardo but through Jean-Baptiste Say. The work of Augustin Cournot and the engineers of the École des ponts et chaussées, whose analysis rested on the concept of a demand curve, created an intellectual background very different from that prevailing in Britain.

These differences, together with profound differences in their personal backgrounds, meant that the work of Jevons, Walras and Menger, though often bracketed together, was far from homogeneous (see Jaffe, 1975). Though Jevons and Walras both advocated the importance of mathematical argument, their emphases differed. Walras, closer to French rationalism, saw his general equilibrium equations as an abstract system that could solve the same problem that was solved in the real world by other means. Jevons focused on mechanical analogies and the notion that the same methods could be applied to physical and social sciences (Maas, 2005). The contrast was even more marked in their applied work, where Jevons was a pioneer in the use of statistics but Walras was not. Menger, in contrast with both of them, rejected the use of mathematics, seeing the use of simultaneous equations as incompatible with identifying the causal relations between human needs and the value of commodities.

The varieties of marginalism increase further when later marginalists are brought into the account. Jevons, Walras and Menger did have disciples, most of them took their analysis in new directions and many are in many ways originals, the best examples being Marshall, Joseph Alois Schumpeter (Austrian, geographically and intellectually, yet an admirer of Walras), Knut Wicksell (whose Swedish synthesis of Austrian and Walrasian ideas bore little resemblance to Schumpeter's) and John Bates Clark (who constructed a non-mathematical American version of marginalism). Given this variety, it is not surprising that the marginal revolution can also be portrayed as a very slow process. Even in the 1880s and 1890s, some economists were still writing textbooks organized on classical lines, marginalist ways of thinking co-existing with other lines of enquiry.

The wider context

While scholars might, at one time, have been content to explain the advent of marginalist ideas in terms of economists coming to see the truth about consumers and value, historians are no longer satisfied with such explanations, arguing that economic ideas have to be explained in terms of the context out of which they arose. One context is that of 19th-century science. The most widely discussed explanation has been Mirowski's (1984; 1989) argument that marginalist economics reflects developments in physics (see De Marchi, 1993). The 1860s saw the rise of energetics – the attempt to reduce all physical phenomena to energy. If physical phenomena could be reduced to energy, then so should social phenomena. More than that, adopting the methods of physical scientists and the mathematics of maximization and energy conservation offered economists the possibility of acquiring the status of physicists, adopting similar standards of rigour. Mirowski directed historians' attention to the many passages where Jevons, Walras and others stated explicitly that this was what they were doing. Though Mirowski drew normative conclusions about which many historians have been sceptical, and though his interpretation clearly does not fit some of the most important marginalists (notably Menger and Marshall), historians have taken up the idea that a major dimension to the marginal revolution was seeing economics as amenable to the methods of the physical sciences rather than as something radically different (see Maas, 2005; Schabas, 2005).

Moreover, at this period, physics was not the only prestigious natural science: controversies over evolution were at their height, following the publication of Charles Darwin's *Origin of Species* and the application of evolutionary arguments to human society by Herbert Spencer. This cannot explain the advent of marginalism, but it represents an important additional connection between economics and contemporary science and helps explain why economics looked very different at the end of the 19th century from the way it looked in the 1860s. Raffaelli (2003) has pointed out that Marshall, perhaps the most significant figure in late-19th century marginalist economics, based his economics, not on the Benthamite utilitarianism used by Jevons, but on evolutionary psychology. Human nature was moulded by experience. Evolutionary ideas thus reinforced the notion that human beings had to be seen as different from one another and that they could be changed. This way of thinking could lead into eugenics, a widely entertained body of ideas that developed towards the end of the century (see Peart and Levy, 2005). But such ideas also served to undermine the Malthusian bogey that had provided an argument against much social reform throughout the century (Stedman Jones, 1984). Marshall, for example, though he used the static, mechanical apparatus of supply and demand, used it to discuss dynamic processes. He saw industries evolving as biological species, and human character changing in response to human activities, a process that was too complicated to be represented mathematically, and as a result never worked with formal dynamic models: they would have been too mechanical. Against such arguments that evolution became influential at that time, Schabas (2005), though stressing that neoclassical economists were very interested in psychology, has recently questioned whether Darwin has as much influence as has been claimed.

The significance of evolutionary ideas points to another aspect of the context against which the advent of marginalist ideas needs to be set: the political climate. The late 19th century has been called the liberal age, when Europe moved towards freer trade and the franchise became more democratic. The progress of liberal ideas and policies varied greatly from country to country, but everywhere there was debate over the merits of liberalism and collectivism, with the latter taking many forms, ranging from Fabian 'municipal socialism' to Marxian socialism. In Britain, the mid-century radicals, amongst whom Mill was pre-eminent, were liberals who wanted to reform the institutions of society in ways consistent with their liberalism. But, by the end of the century, following the extension of the franchise to much of the working class in 1867 and 1884, radicalism became increasingly collectivist. Against Social Darwinist arguments for individualism were ranged ethical arguments for reform, from the American Social Gospel movement to the variety of movements for social reform inspired in Britain by the Oxford philosopher T.H. Green (see Richter, 1964). In the same way that the Great Depression motivated many who came into economics in the 1930s and 1940s, the problem of poverty affected this earlier generation. Economists' attitudes towards policy changed (see Hutchison, 1978), as did the way they developed their theories, the most noticeable example being the development of welfare economics by the Cambridge School, J.A. Hobson, and others.

Though it was again a process the speed of which varied greatly from country to country, a further element of the context in which the marginal revolution took place was the professionalization of economics. By the middle of the 19th century, economics was being developed by a mixture of academics and members of a broader educated elite; those recognized as economists might be politicians or businessmen. Specialist journals existed in some countries, but original work in the subject was also published in journals read by non-specialists. By the end of the century economics, like many other disciplines, had changed, becoming an academic discipline in which the main communication was between specialists. This made possible a different type of discourse, more technical and addressing issues that might seem more tenuously related to issues of concern to lay people.

Conclusions

The marginal revolution, like other revolutions in economics, is associated with changes in economic theory that undoubtedly altered the way economics was conceived. However, picking out a single theoretical or methodological innovation that explains why the marginal revolution was apparently so important has proved difficult. The reason may be that, as in the case of the Keynesian Revolution, though economics changed profoundly in the closing decades of the 19th century, these changes owed as much, if not more, to deeper changes in the social, political and intellectual context in which economists were working as to any specific innovation in economic theory.

ROGER E. BACKHOUSE

See also **English School of political economy; Jevons, William Stanley; Marshall, Alfred; Menger, Carl; Walras, Léon.**

Bibliography

Black, R.D.C. 1945. Trinity College Dublin and the theory of value. *Economica* 47, 140–8.
Blaug, M. 1996. *Economic Theory in Retrospect*, 5th edn. Cambridge: Cambridge University Press.
De Marchi, N., ed. 1993. *Non-natural Social Science: Reflecting on the Enterprise of More Heat than Light*.
Durham, NC: Duke University Press. Also in *History of Political Economy* 25 (supplement), 271–82.
Hutchison, T.W. 1953. *A Review of Economic Doctrines, 1870–1929*. Oxford: Oxford University Press.
Hutchison, T.W. 1978. *On Revolutions and Progress in Economic Knowledge*. Cambridge: Cambridge University Press.
Jaffe, W. 1975. Menger, Jevons and Walras dehomogenized. *Economic Inquiry* 14, 511–24.
Maas, H.B.J.B. 2005. *William Stanley Jevons and the Making of Modern Economics*. Cambridge: Cambridge University Press.
Mirowski, P. 1984. Physics and the marginalist revolution. *Cambridge Journal of Economics* 8, 361–79.
Mirowski, P. 1989. *More Heat Than Light: Economics as Social Physics, Physics as Nature's Economics*. Cambridge: Cambridge University Press.
O'Brien, D.P. 1990. Marshall's work in relation to classical economics. In *Centenary Essays on Alfred Marshall*, ed. J. Whitaker. Cambridge: Cambridge University Press.
Peart, S. and Levy, D. 2005. *The Vanity of the Philosopher: From Equality to Hierarchy in Post-Classical Economics*. Ann Arbor: University of Michigan Press.
Raffaelli, T. 2003. *Marshall's Evolutionary Economics*. London: Routledge.
Richter, M. 1964. *The Politics of Conscience: T.H. Green and His Age*. London: Weidenfeld & Nicolson.
Schabas, M. 2005. *The Natural Origins of Economics*. Chicago: University of Chicago Press.
Stedman Jones, G. 1984. *Outcast London: A Study in the Relationship between Classes in Victorian Society*, 2nd edn. New York: Pantheon Books.
Streissler, E.W. 1990. The influence of German economics on the work of Menger and Marshall. *History of Political Economy* 22 (annual supplement), 31–68.
Whitaker, J.K., ed. 1975. *The Early Economic Writings of Alfred Marshall, 1867–1890*. London: Macmillan.

marginal utility of money

Interest in the marginal utility of money probably dates from Alfred Marshall's identification of consumer surplus as the area under the demand curve. Marshall went on to add a qualification to his analysis:

> In the same way if we were to neglect for the moment the fact that the same sum of money represents a different amount of pleasure to different people, we might measure the surplus satisfaction which the sale of tea affords, say, in the London market, by the aggregate of the sums by which the prices shown in a complete list of demand prices of tea exceeds its selling price. (Marshall, 1920, p. 106)

In the mathematical appendix (Note VI), Marshall identifies the 'total utility of the commodity' with the area under the demand curve, defined by an integral, but then qualifies that analysis by saying 'we assume that the marginal utility of money to the individual purchaser is the same throughout'. The meaning of these phrases is anything but clear. The text phrase seems to indicate that interpersonal comparisons of utility are a necessary prerequisite for the use of consumer's surplus; in the appendix, Marshall's concern is that, as more of a commodity is purchased, money will yield less satisfaction to the consumer, destroying any linear relationship between money and utility.

Later interpretation of 'constant marginal utility of money' was further complicated by the use of the word 'money' in two different contexts. To Marshall, money provided no direct utility to the consumer; it was a device solely for lowering the transactions cost of exchange. The concurrently developed general equilibrium theory of Walras, however, treated money as that one good which happened to have the additional property of serving as the medium of exchange, a numéraire commodity whose price was unity.

We now analyse the connection between the marginal utility of money and consumer's surplus. The consumer is assumed to maximize $U = U(x_1, \ldots, x_n)$ subject to $\sum p_i x_i = M$. We derive the Marshallian (money income held constant) demand functions $x_i = x_i^M(p_1, \ldots, p_n, M)$ along with $\lambda^M(p_1, \ldots, p_n, M)$ using the Lagrangian $L = U + \lambda(M - \sum p_i x_i)$.

The indirect utility function $U^*(p_1, \ldots, p_n, M) = U(x_1^M, \ldots, x_n^M)$ indicates the maximum utility for given prices and money income. Using the envelope theorem, $\partial U^*/\partial M = \lambda^M$, the marginal utility of money income. Also, $\partial U^*/\partial p_i = -\lambda^M x_i^M$ (Roy's identity). The Hicksian (utility held constant) or 'compensated' demand functions $x_i^U(p_1, \ldots, p_n, U)$ are derived from minimizing $M = \sum p_i x_i$ subject to $U(x_1, \ldots, x_n) = U^0$. The expenditure function $M^*(p_1, \ldots, p_n, U^0) = \sum p_i x_i^u$ indicates the minimum cost of maintaining utility level U^0 for arbitrary prices $p_1, \ldots, p_n$. By the envelope theorem, the Hicksian demands are the first partials of the expenditure function: $x_i^U = \partial M^*/\partial p_i$. (See HICKSIAN AND MARSHALLIAN DEMANDS.)

The area to the left of a consumer's demand curve between two prices (where the initial price is higher than the final price), is $-\int x_i \partial p_i$. The units of this integral are that of money income, being price times quantity. Suppose this area equals some value A. The issue is: what question does A answer, and what is the relation between that answer and the marginal utility of money? Since a Hicksian demand function is the first partial of the expenditure function, the area to the left of this demand curve is simply a change in the expenditure function:

$$-\int x_i^U \mathrm{d}p_i = -\int (\partial M^*/\partial p_i)\, \mathrm{d}p_i$$
$$= M^*(p^0, U^0) - M^*(p^1, U^0)$$

where p^0 and p^1 are the initial and final price vectors over which the integral is taken. The area to the left of Hicksian demand function therefore represents a change in expenditure with utility held constant; this area indicates the amount a consumer would be willing to pay (or have to be paid) to willingly accept some change in the purchase price of some good. Moreover, there is no need to invoke any assumption at all about the marginal utility of money.

The area to the left of the Marshallian demand function, however, has no such easy interpretation, because unlike the Hicksian demands, the Marshallian demand functions are *not* in general the partial derivatives of some integral function; therefore the integrals of the Marshallian demands are not expressible in terms of changes in some well-defined function of the initial and final prices and income levels. From Roy's equality, the Marshallian demands are the first partials of the indirect utility function *divided by the marginal utility of income*. Thus

$$-\int x_i^M \mathrm{d}p_i = -\int (1/\lambda^M)(\lambda^M x_i^M)\, \mathrm{d}p_i$$
$$= \int (1/\lambda^M)(\partial U^*/\partial p_i)\, \mathrm{d}p_i.$$

However, if the marginal utility of money term is 'constant', that is, independent of prices, it can be moved in front of the integral sign; only then can this expression be integrated to yield a function of the endpoint prices (and money income):

$$-\int x_i^M \mathrm{d}p_i = (1/\lambda^M)\int (\partial U^*/\partial p_i)\, \mathrm{d}p_i$$
$$= (1/\lambda^M)[U(p^1) - U(p^0)].$$

Thus, in this case, the area to the left of the Marshallian demand function would equal a change in utility divided by the marginal utility of money, thus converting that change in utility into units of money. Marshall's claim that the area to the left of a demand curve may be interpreted as a change in utility under the assumption of constant marginal utility of money would thus be technically correct for the demand functions derived from utility maximization, though how much of the above discussion he had in mind can easily be debated.

The problem with this analysis is that λ^M cannot literally be a 'constant,' as shown by Samuelson (1942). Since $\lambda^M = U_i/p_i$ a proportionate change (for example, doubling) of prices and income leaves the amount of the goods consumed unchanged (since the Marshallian demand functions are homogeneous of degree zero in prices and income), and thus the numerator of this expression unchanged. However, the denominator has doubled, meaning λ^M has halved. Thus $\lambda^M = (p_1, \ldots, p_n, M)$ must be homogeneous of degree −1; it can be independent of at most n of its arguments. It can, for example, be independent of all prices, but not income also, or it can be independent of $n - 1$ prices and income.

Since $\partial U^*/\partial p_i = -\lambda^M x_i^M$ and $\partial U^*/\partial M = \lambda^M$, Young's theorem on invariance of partial derivatives to the order of differentiation yields (omitting superscripts)

$$M^*_{p_i M} = -[\lambda \partial x_i/\partial M + x_i \partial \lambda/\partial M]$$
$$= \partial \lambda/\partial p_i = M^*_{Mp_i}.$$

Suppose

$$\partial \lambda^M/\partial p_i = 0, \quad i = 1, \ldots, n.$$

Then

$$(M/x_i)(\partial x_i/\partial M) = -(M/\lambda)(\partial \lambda/\partial M)$$
$$\text{for} \quad i = 1, \ldots, n.$$

That is, the income elasticities are all equal (necessarily to unity, from the budget constraint); thus the utility function must be homothetic. Denoting the Marshallian area CS, we have

$$CS = (1/\lambda^M)[U^*(p^1, M) - U^*(p^0, M)].$$

Thus for homothetic utility functions, where the indifference curves are all radial blow-ups of each other, the Marshallian area represents the unique monetary equivalent of a change in utility; the coefficient which converts 'utiles' to money income is invariant over the price change.

Suppose now that λ^M is a function of one price only, say p_n. Then from the above equation, $\partial x_i^M/\partial M = 0, i = 1, \ldots, n - 1$. Since there is no income effect for goods 1 to $n - 1$, the Marshallian demand functions for those goods coincide with the Hicksian demands. This is the famous case of 'vertically parallel' indifference curves. Therefore the interpretation of the area to the left of any of these Marshallian demand curves is identical to the case of the Hicksian demands, that is, the willingness to pay to face the lower price.

EUGENE SILBERBERG

See also **consumer surplus; Giffen's paradox; Hicksian and Marshallian demands; indirect utility function; Marshall, Alfred.**

Bibliography

Marshall, A. 1920. *Principles of Economics*, 8th edn. London: Macmillan.

Samuelson, P.A. 1942. Constancy of the marginal utility of money. In *Studies in Mathematical Economics and Econometrics: In Memory of Henry Schultz*, ed. O. Lange, F. McIntyre and T.O. Yntema. Chicago: University of Chicago Press.

Silberberg, E. and Suen, W. 2000. *The Structure of Economics*, 3rd edn. New York: McGraw-Hill.

market competition and selection

Realized positive profits, not *maximum* profits, are the mark of success and viability. It does not matter through what process of reasoning or motivation such success was achieved. The fact of its accomplishment is sufficient. This is the criterion by which the economic system selects survivors: those who realize *positive profits* are the survivors; those who suffer losses disappear. (Alchian, 1950, p. 213)

Most economic models make use of extreme rationality hypotheses: firms maximize profits with full knowledge of their technology and prices, and investors are subjective expected utility maximizers whose beliefs are correct. Surely some firms and some investors do not always behave as these models hypothesize, but does this matter for predictions of market outcomes? It could be that the aggregation that takes place in supply and demand results in prices and market quantities that agree with the predictions of models using extreme versions of rationality. It could be that, over time, firms and investors learn to behave as these models predict and so market outcomes converge to those predicted by the models. Finally, it could be that markets select for firms and investors who behave 'as if' they are rational. This last defence of the use of rationality is the essence of the quote from Alchian (1950).

There is a long history in economics of using market selection arguments in defence of rationality hypotheses. The early literature focused on selection for profit maximizing firms. Among its best-known proponents is Friedman (1953, p. 22): 'The process of natural selection thus helps to validate the hypothesis (of profit maximization) or, rather, given natural selection, acceptance of the hypothesis can be based largely on the judgment that it summarizes appropriately the conditions for survival.' Of course, even if the selection reasoning is correct, selection can only work over those types of behaviours that are present in the economy. If no firm maximizes profits, then no profit-maximizing firm can be selected. Alchian was acutely aware of this:

The pertinent requirement – positive profits through relative efficiency – is weaker than 'maximized profits,' with which, unfortunately, it has been confused. Positive profits accrue to those who are better than their actual competitors, even if the participants are ignorant, intelligent, skilful, etc. The crucial element is one's aggregate position relative to actual competitors, not some hypothetically perfect competitors. As in a race, the award goes to the relatively fastest, even if all the competitors loaf. (Alchain, 1950, p. 213)

Enke (1951) argued that, at least in competitive industries, the relatively fastest will in fact be profit maximizers, and so in this case selection will lead to the survival only of profit maximizing firms:

> In the long run, however, if firms are in active competition with one another rather than constituting a number of isolated monopolies, natural selection will tend to permit the survival of only those firms that either through good luck or great skill have managed, almost or completely, to optimize their position and earn the normal profits necessary for survival. In these instances the economist can make aggregate predictions *as if* each and every firm knew how to secure maximum long-run profits. (Enke, 1951, p. 567)

Similar market selection arguments have been proposed to justify strong rationality hypotheses on the part of investors. Fama argues that:

> dependency in the noise generating process would tend to produce 'bubbles' in the price series ... If there are many sophisticated traders in the market, however, they may cause these 'bubbles' to burst before they have a chance to really get underway. (Fama, 1965, p. 38)

According to Fama, 'A superior analyst is one whose gains over many periods of time are *consistently* greater than those of the market'. This is at least indirectly an argument for market selection and its affect on the efficiency of prices. Cootner was an early, clear proponent of this argument:

> Given the uncertainty of the real world, the many actual and virtual traders will have many, perhaps equally many, forecasts ... If any group of traders was consistently better than average in forecasting stock prices, they would accumulate wealth and give their forecasts greater and greater weight. In this process, they would bring the present price closer to the true value. (Cootner, 1967, p. 80)

In this article we examine the more recent analyses of whether these arguments for market selection, and its impact on efficiency, are correct. We consider in turn, selection over firms and selection over investors.

Selection over firms

Alchain, Friedman and Enke argue that a profit dynamic will select for firms that, for whatever reason, maximize profits. Correspondingly, according to this argument, those that do not act as profit maximizers will be driven out of the market. But how is it that non-maximizers are driven out? The implicit idea is that, in the presence of maximizers, the non-maximizers experience losses that deplete their financial capital, which forces them out of the market. The literature has explored two avenues by which losses of financial capital could have this effect. One is that if the firm's operations are financed from retained earnings, then firms that consistently experience losses would eventually exhaust their retained earnings, causing

them to vanish. A second argument is that unsuccessful firms will not be able to raise capital in the financial markets, and may not even be able to retain their initial capital. Thus, so this argument goes, the markets will punish unsuccessful firms, which will eventually vanish.

Winter (1964; 1971) and Nelson and Winter (1982) analyse a retained earnings dynamic. They argue that the retained earnings of profit maximizers will grow fastest, and thus these firms will eventually dominate the market. These authors construct a partial equilibrium model in which the 'as if' hypothesis of profit maximization describes the long-run steady state behaviour of firms. In their analysis, prices are fixed and all firms have access to the same technology. This structure leads to the existence of a uniformly most-fit firm, which is selected for by a retained earnings-based investment dynamic.

The early work on market selection was greatly concerned with the meaning of profit maximization when profits are random. Dutta and Radner (1999) directly take up the question of whether markets select for firms that maximize expected profits. Their answer is 'no': the decision rules that maximize the long probability of survival are not those that maximize expected profits. Dutta and Radner's firms are owned by investors who choose how much of the firm's earnings to reinvest in the firms and how much to withdraw as dividends. An expected profit maximizing firm is one that maximizes the expectation of present discounted value of dividends paid to its owners. This policy results in an upper bound on the retained earnings left in the firm, and from this level of retained earnings any firm can experience a string of losses that results in bankruptcy.

There are two parts to the argument for market selection of profit maximizers. First, there is the issue of whether the market selects for profit maximizers. Second, there is the issue of whether in the long run the economy behaves as if only profit mazimizing firms exist. The Dutta and Radner analysis casts doubt about a positive answer to the first question in stochastic settings. Koopmans (1957) cast doubts about a positive answer to the second question even in a deterministic setting. According to his analysis, appealing to an external dynamic process to defend the profit maximization assumption is not a satisfactory way to proceed. Instead, he believed that the dynamic process itself should be modelled. Nelson and Winter (1982, p. 58) were also aware that the co-evolution of firm behaviour and the economic environment resulting from a complete model of the dynamic process could pose problems for the evolutionary defence of profit maximization. They observed that among the 'less obvious snags for evolutionary arguments that aim to provide a prop for orthodoxy' is 'that the relative profitability ranking of decision rules may not be invariant with respect to market conditions'. They do not, however, go on to provide a general equilibrium analysis of the consequences of replacing static profit maximization with a selection dynamic.

Blume and Easley (2002) showed that Koopman's concern about the market selection dynamic in a general equilibrium setting is correct. They show that although only profit maximizers persist in any steady state of the retained earnings dynamic, the long run of the economy need not be well described by assuming that only profit maximizing firms exist. The difficulty arises because of the endogeneity of prices, which causes the relative profitability of firms to depend on the allocation of capital across the firms. As a result, the retained earnings dynamic need not settle down, and efficient firms can be driven out of the market by inefficient firms.

In addition to raising working capital through retained earnings, firms also enter the capital markets. Whether these markets reinforce the market selection hypothesis, as Friedman argues, or undermine it, depends on how well these markets function. If markets are complete (without the securities created by non-maximizing firms) and investors are expected utility maximizers with rational expectations, then investors would not allocate capital to non-maximizing firms. Such firms would never produce, and the selection hypothesis would be trivially, and instantly, correct. Alternatively, if some investors have incorrect expectations, then they could invest in non-maximizing firms. The fate of these firms depends on the fate of their investors. So, in this case, the question of selection for profit maximizing firms reduces to the question of selection for investors who act as expected utility maximizers with rational expectations.

Selection over investors

Friedman, Fama and Cootner argue that asset markets will select for rational investors, and that because of this selection, assets will eventually be priced efficiently. Two interesting approaches have been taken to the selection for rational investors question. First, suppose traders use a variety of portfolio rules. Is it the case that traders whose rules are not rational will lose their money to those who do act as if they are rational? Second, suppose that all traders are subjective expected utility maximizers. Is it the case that markets select for those whose expectations are correct, or most nearly correct?

In order to pose these questions precisely rationality has to be defined (see RATIONALITY). The selection literature has asked about selection for a very strong form of rationality – expected utility maximization with correct expectations about the payoffs to assets. This is the interesting question because in economies populated by subjective expected utility maximizers whose beliefs are not tied down by a rational expectations hypothesis we have little to say about asset prices. The mere assumption that investors are subjective expected utility maximizers (in the sense of Savage, 1951) places no restrictions on the stochastic process of Arrow security prices (Blume and Easley, 2005).

Selection over rules

Consider an intertemporal general equilibrium economy with a collection of Arrow securities and one physical good available at each date. Suppose traders are characterized by their stochastic processes of endowments of the good and by portfolio and savings rules. A savings rule describes the fraction of wealth the trader saves and invests at each date given any partial history of states. Similarly, a portfolio rule describes the fraction of savings the trader allocates to each Arrow security. The savings and portfolio rules that rational traders could choose form one such class of rules; but other, non-rationally motivated rules are also possible.

Three questions arise about the dynamics of wealth selection in this economy. First, is there any kind of selection at all? Second, is it possible to characterize the rules which win? Third, if selection does take place, does every trader using a rational rule survive, and in the presence of such a trader do all non-rational traders vanish?

In repeated betting, with exogenous odds, the betting rule that maximizes the expected growth rate of wealth is known as the Kelly rule (Kelly, 1956). The use of this formula in betting with fixed, but favourable odds was further explored by Breiman (1961). In asset markets the 'odds' are not fixed; instead they are determined by equilibrium asset prices, which in turn depend on traders' portfolio and savings rules. Nonetheless, the market selects over rules according to the expected growth rate of wealth share they induce. Blume and Easley (1992) show that if there is a unique trader using a rule that is globally maximal with respect to this criterion, then this trader eventually controls all the wealth in the economy, and prices are set as if he is the only trader in the economy. A trader whose savings rate is maximal and whose portfolio rule is, in each partial history, the conditional probability of states for tomorrow has a maximal expected growth rate of wealth share. This rule is consistent with the trader having logarithmic utility for consumption, rational expectations and a discount factor that is as large as any trader's savings rate. Thus, if this trader exists, he is selected for. However, rationality alone does not guarantee a maximal expected growth rate of wealth share. There are rational portfolio rules that do not maximize fitness (even controlling for savings rates), and traders who use these rules can be driven out of the market by traders who use rules that are inconsistent with rationality.

Amir et al. (2005) and Evstigneev, Hens and Schenk-Hoppe (2006) take an alternative approach to selection over rules in asset markets. They consider general one-period assets and ask if there are simple portfolio rules that are selected for, or are evolutionarily stable, when the market is populated by other simple (not explicitly price dependent) portfolio rules. In this research, either all winnings are invested, or equivalently, all investors are assumed to invest an equal fraction of their winnings. So selection operates only over portfolio rules. Amir et al. (2005) find that an investor who apportions his wealth across assets according to their conditional expected relative payoffs drives out all other investors as long as none of the other investors end up holding the market. This result is consistent with Blume and Easley (1992) as the log optimal portfolio rule agrees with the conditional expected relative payoff rule when only these two rules exist in the market. Hence, both these rules hold the market in the limit. Evstigneev, Hens and Schenk-Hoppe (2006) use notions of stability from evolutionary game theory to show that the expected relative payoffs rule is evolutionarily stable.

Selection among subjective expected utility maximizers

DeLong et al. (1990; 1991) analyse selection over traders who are subjective expected utility maximizers with differing beliefs. In an overlapping generations model they show (1990) that traders with incorrect beliefs can earn higher expected returns, because they take on extra risk. But as survival is not determined by expected returns, this result does not answer the selection question. DeLong et al. (1991) argue that traders whose beliefs reflect irrational overconfidence can eventually dominate an asset market in which prices are set exogenously. This result appears to contradict Alchian's and Friedman's intuitions. But, as prices are exogenous, these traders are not really trading with each other; if they were, then were traders with incorrect beliefs to dominate the market, prices would reflect their beliefs and rational traders might be able to take advantage of them.

In an economy with complete markets and traders who have a common discount factor, Alchian and Friedman's intuition is correct. Sandroni (2000) shows, in a Lucas trees economy with some rational-expectations traders, that if traders have a common discount factor, then all traders who survive have rational expectations. Blume and Easley (2006) show that this result holds in any Pareto optimal allocation in any bounded classical economy and thus for any complete markets equilibrium. To see why the market selection hypothesis is true for these economies suppose that states are iid and that traders have differing, fixed iid beliefs. Then each trader assigns zero probability to almost all the infinite sample paths that any other trader believes to be possible. Each trader would be willing to give up all his endowment on the sample paths he believes to be impossible in order to obtain more consumption on those he believes to be possible. Since markets are complete, these trades are effectively possible. But, if only one trader has correct beliefs, then only one trader puts positive probability on the infinite sample paths that actually occur. So only this trader will have positive consumption, and thus positive wealth, in the limit.

For bounded complete market economies there is a survival index that determines which traders survive and which vanish. This index depends only on discount factors, the actual stochastic process of states, and, traders' beliefs about this stochastic process. Most importantly, for these economies, attitudes towards risk do not matter for survival. The literature also provides various results demonstrating how the market selects among learning rules. The market selects for traders who learn the true process over those who do not learn the truth, for Bayesians with the truth in the support of their prior over comparable non-Bayesians, and among Bayesians according to the dimension of the support of their prior (assuming that the truth is in the support).

In economies with incomplete markets, the market selection hypothesis can fail to be true. Blume and Easley (2006) show that if markets are incomplete, then rational traders may choose either savings rates or portfolio rules that are dominated by those selected by traders with incorrect beliefs. If some traders are irrationally optimistic about the payoff to assets, then the price of those assets may be high enough for rational traders to choose to consume more now, and less in the future. Their low savings rates are optimal, but as a result of their low savings rates the rational traders do not survive.

An alternative version of the market selection hypothesis is that asset markets select for traders with superior information. The research discussed above asks about selection over traders with different, but exogenously given, beliefs. Alternatively, if traders begin with a common prior and receive differential information they will have differing beliefs, but now they will care about each others' beliefs. In this case, the selection question is difficult because the information that traders have will be reflected in prices. If the economy is in a fully revealing rational expectations equilibrium, then there is no advantage to having superior information; see Grossman and Stiglitz (1980). So the question only makes sense in the more natural, but far more complex, case in which information is not fully revealed by market statistics. Figlewski (1978) shows that traders with information which is not correctly reflected in prices have an advantage in terms of expected wealth gain over those whose information is fully impounded in prices. But as expected wealth gain does not determine fitness this result does not fully answer the question. Mailath and Sandroni (2003) consider a Lucas trees economy with log utility traders and noise traders. They show that the quality of information affects survival, but so does the level of noise in the economy. Scuibba (2005) considers a Grossman and Stiglitz (1980) economy in which informed traders pay for information and shows that in this case uninformed traders do not vanish.

Conclusion

The modern literature has shown that the market selection hypothesis needs to be qualified. For some economies it acts much as the earlier writers conjectured; in others it does not select for profit maximizers or rational traders. Much work remains to be done, however. Blume and Easley (2006) and Sandroni (2000) mostly discuss selection in complete markets. Sandroni, though, points out that even when markets are incomplete, traders with log utility and rational expectations are favoured, while Blume and Easley construct some examples to show that the outcome of market selection can depend on market completeness. The connection between market structure and market selection is not well understood. The implications of market selection for asset pricing are known only for complete markets in the long run and some examples. Most economists' intuition about market behaviour and asset pricing comes from the study of market models that allow little or no agent heterogeneity. Taking heterogeneity seriously and chasing down its implications for market performance promises to be a rich area for future research.

LAWRENCE BLUME AND DAVID EASLEY

See also **general equilibrium; rational expectations; rationality.**

Bibliography

Alchian, A. 1950. Uncertainty, evolution and economic theory. *Journal of Political Economy* 58, 211–21.

Amir, R., Evstigneev, I., Hens, T. and Schenk-Hoppe, K.R. 2005. Market selection and survival of investment strategies. *Journal of Mathematical Economics* 41, 105–22.

Blume, L. and Easley, D. 1992. Evolution and market behavior. *Journal of Economic Theory* 58, 9–40.

Blume, L. and Easley, D. 2002. Optimality and natural selection in markets. *Journal of Economic Theory* 107, 95–130.

Blume, L. and Easley, D. 2005. Rationality and selection in asset markets. In *The Economy as an Evolving Complex System*, ed. L. Blume and S. Durlauf. Oxford: Oxford University Press.

Blume, L. and Easley, D. 2006. If you're so smart, why aren't you rich? Belief selection in complete and incomplete markets. *Econometrica* 74, 929–66.

Breiman, L. 1961. Optimal gambling systems for favorable games. In *Proceedings of the Fourth Berkeley Symposium on Mathematical Statistics and Probability*, ed. J. Neyman. Berkeley: University of California Press.

Cootner, P. 1967. *The Random Character of Stock Market Prices*. Cambridge, MA: MIT Press.

DeLong, J.B., Shleifer, A., Summers, L. and Waldmann, R. 1990. Noise trader risk in financial markets. *Journal of Political Economy* 98, 703–38.

DeLong, J.B., Shleifer, A., Summers, L. and Waldmann, R. 1991. The survival of noise traders in financial markets. *Journal of Business* 64, 1–19.

Dutta, P. and Radner, R. 1999. Profit maximization and the market selection hypothesis. *Review of Economic Studies* 66, 769–98.

Enke, S. 1951. On maximizing profits: a distinction between Chamberlin and Robinson. *American Economic Review* 41, 566–78.

Evstigneev, I., Hens, T. and Schenk-Hoppe, K.R. 2006. Evolutionary stable stock markets. *Economic Theory* 27, 449–68.

Fama, E. 1965. The behavior of stock market prices. *Journal of Business* 38, 34–105.

Figlewski, S. 1978. Market 'efficiency' in a market with heterogeneous information. *Journal of Political Economy* 86, 581–97.

Friedman, M. 1953. *Essays in Positive Economics*. Chicago: University of Chicago Press.

Grossman, S.J. and Stiglitz, J.E. 1980. On the impossibility of informationally efficient markets. *American Economic Review* 70, 393–408.

Kelly, J.L. 1956. A new interpretation of information rate. *Bell System Technical Journal* 35, 917–26.

Koopmans, T. 1957. *Three Essays on the State of Economic Science*. New York: McGraw-Hill.

Mailath, G. and Sandroni, A. 2003. Market selection and asymmetric information. *Review of Economic Studies* 70, 343–68.

Nelson, R. and Winter, S. 1982. *An Evolutionary Theory of Economic Change*. Cambridge, MA: Harvard University Press.

Sandroni, A. 2000. Do markets favor agents able to make accurate predictions? *Econometrica* 68, 1303–42.

Savage, L.J. 1951. The theory of statistical decision. *Journal of the American Statistical Association* 46, 55–67.

Scuibba, E. 2005. Asymmetric information and survival in financial markets. *Economic Theory* 25, 353–79.

Winter, S. 1964. Economic natural selection and the theory of the firm. *Yale Economic Essays* 4, 225–72.

Winter, S. 1971. Satisficing, selection and the innovating remnant. *Quarterly Journal of Economics* 85, 237–61.

market failure

The best way to understand market failure is first to understand market success, the ability of a collection of idealized competitive markets to achieve an equilibrium allocation of resources that is Pareto optimal. This characteristic of markets, which was loosely conjectured by Adam Smith, has received its clearest expression in the theorems of modern welfare economics. For our purposes, the first of these, named the first fundamental theorem of welfare economics, is of most interest. Simply stated it reads: (1) if there are enough markets, (2) if all consumers and producers behave competitively, and (3) if an equilibrium exists, then the allocation of resources in that equilibrium will be Pareto optimal (see Arrow, 1951; Debreu, 1959). Market failure is said to occur when the conclusion of this theorem is false; that is, when the allocations achieved with markets are not efficient.

Market failure is often the justification for political intervention in the marketplace (for one view, see Bator, 1958, section V). The standard argument is that if market allocations are inefficient, everyone can and should be made better off. To understand the feasibility and desirability of such Pareto-improving interventions, we must achieve a deeper understanding of the sources of market failure. Since each must be due to the failure of at least one of the three conditions of the first theorem, we will consider those conditions one at a time.

The first condition requires there to be enough markets. Although there are no definitive guidelines as to what constitutes 'enough', the general principle is that if any actor in the economy cares about something that also involves an interaction with at least one other actor, then there should be a market for that something; it should have a price (Arrow, 1969). This is true whether the something is consumption of bread, consumption of the smoke from a factory, or the amount of national defence. The first of these examples is a standard private good, the second is an externality, and the third is a public good. All need to be priced if we are to achieve a Pareto-optimal allocation of resources; without these markets, actors may be unable to inform others about mutually beneficial trades which can leave both better off.

The informational role of markets is clearly highlighted by a classic example of market failure analysed by Scitovsky (1954). In this example, a steel industry, which must decide now whether to operate, will be profitable if and only if a railway industry begins operations within five years. The railway industry will be profitable if and only if the steel industry is operating when the railway industry begins its own operations. Clearly each cares about the other and it is efficient for each to operate; the steel industry begins today and the railway industry begins later. Nevertheless, if there are only spot markets for steel, the railway industry cannot easily inform the steel industry of its interests through the marketplace. This inability to communicate desirable interactions and to coordinate timing is an example of market failure and has been used as a justification for public involvement in development efforts; a justification for national planning. However, if we correctly recognize that there are simply too few markets, we can easily find another solution by creating a futures market for steel. If the railway industry is able to pay today for delivery of steel at some specified date in the future then both steel and railway industries are able to make the other aware of their interests through the marketplace. It is easy to show that as long as agents behave competitively and equilibrium exists, the addition of futures markets will solve this type of market failure.

A completely different example of the informational role of markets arises when actors in the marketplace are asymmetrically informed about the true state of an uncertain world. The classic example involves securities markets where insiders may know something that outsiders do not. Even if it is important and potentially profitable for the uninformed actor to know the information held by the informed actor, there may not be enough markets to generate an efficient allocation of resources. To see this most clearly, suppose there are only two possible states of the world. Further, suppose there are two consumers, one of whom knows the true state and one of whom thinks each state is equally likely. If the only markets that exist are markets for physical commodities, then the equilibrium allocation will not in general be Pareto optimal. One solution is to create a contingent claims market. An 'insurance' contract can be created in which delivery and acceptance of a specified amount of the commodity is contingent on the true state of the world. Assuming both parties can, *ex post*, mutually verify which is indeed the true state of the world, if both behave competitively and an equilibrium allocation exists, it will be Pareto optimal, given the information structure. A more general and precise version of this theorem can be found in Radner (1968).

Analysing this example further we note that in equilibrium the prices of commodities in the state that is not true will be close to or equal to zero, since at positive prices the informed actor will always be willing to supply an infinite amount contingent on the false state, knowing delivery will be unnecessary. If the uninformed actor is clever and realizes that prices will behave this way in equilibrium then he can become informed simply by observing which contingency prices are zero. If he then uses this information, which has been freely provided by the market, the equilibrium will be Pareto optimal under full information. In a very simple form, this is the idea behind rational expectations (see Muth, 1961). With clever competitive actors, it may not be necessary to create all markets in order to achieve a Pareto-efficient equilibrium allocation.

Completing markets seems to be an easy technique to correct market failure. The suggestions that taxes and subsidies (Pigou, 1932) or property rights reassignments (Coase, 1960) can cure market failure follow directly from this observation. However, an unintended consequence can sometimes occur after the creation of these markets. In some cases, adding more markets may cause conditions (2) and (3) of the first theorem to be false. Curing one form of market failure can lead to another. To understand how this happens and how the second condition requiring competitive behaviour can be affected, consider the informed consumer in our previous example. If he realizes that the uninformed consumer is going to make inferences based indirectly on his actions then he should not behave competitively because he could do better by pretending to be uninformed. He can, by strategically limiting the supply of information of which he is the monopoly holder, do better than if he behaved competitively. It is only his willingness to supply infinite amounts of the commodity in the false state that gives away his knowledge. Supplying only a little commodity contingent on that (false) state in return for a small payment today would not allow the uninformed agent to infer anything and would allow the informed agent to make a profit from his monopoly position. This is not very different from the standard example of a violation of condition (2), monopoly supply of a commodity.

A different example of this phenomenon of unintended outcomes arises when markets are created to allocate public goods. It is now well known that the introduction of personal, Lindahl prices to price individual demands for a public good does indeed lead to Pareto-optimal allocations if consumers behave competitively (see Foley, 1970). However, under this scheme, each agent becomes a monopsonist in one of the created markets and, therefore, has an incentive to understate demand and not to take prices as given. This is the phenomenon of 'free riding', often alluded to as the reason why the creation of markets may not be a viable solution to market failure. To understand why, let us now examine the second condition of the first theorem in more detail.

The second condition of the first theorem about market success is that all actors in the marketplace behave competitively. This means that each must act as if they cannot affect prices and, given prices, as if they follow optimizing behaviour. Consumers maximize preferences subject to budget constraints and producers maximize profits, each taking prices as fixed parameters. This condition will be violated when actors can affect the values that equilibrium prices take and in so doing be better off. The standard example of market failure due to a violation of this condition is monopoly, in which one actor is the sole supplier of an output. By artificially restricting supply, this actor can cause higher prices and make himself or herself better off even though the resulting equilibrium allocation will be inefficient.

Can we correct market failure due to non-competitive behaviour? To find an answer let us first isolate those conditions under which agents find it in their interests to follow competitive behaviour. The work of Roberts and Postlewaite (1976) has established that if each agent holds only a small amount of resources relative to the aggregate available, then they will usually be unable to manipulate prices in any significant way and will act as price takers. It is the depth of the market that is important. This is also true when the commodity is information. If each agent is informationally small, in the sense that he either knows very little or what he does know is of little importance to others, then he loses little by behaving competitively (see Postlewaite and Schmeidler, 1986). On the other hand, if he is informationally important, as in the earlier example, he may have an incentive to behave non-competitively. The key is the size of the agent's resources, both real and informational, relative to the market.

The solution to market failure from non-competitive behaviour then seems to be to ensure that all agents are both resource and informationally small. Of course this must be accomplished through direct intervention as in the antitrust laws and the securities market regulations of the United States and may not be feasible. For example, it may not be possible to correct this type of market failure by simply telling agents to behave competitively. In such an attempt, one would try to enforce a public policy that all firms must charge prices equal to the marginal cost of output. But, unless the costs and production technology of the firm can be directly monitored, a monopolist can easily act as if he were setting price equal to marginal cost while using a false cost curve. It would be impossible for an outside observer to distinguish this non-competitive behaviour from competitive behaviour without directly monitoring the cost curve. If the monopolist were a consumer whose preferences were unobservable, then even monitoring would not help. In general, market failure from non-competitive behaviour is difficult to correct while still retaining markets. We will hint at some alternatives below.

Expansion of the number of markets can also lead to violations of the third condition of the first theorem. For illustration we consider three examples. The first and simplest of these is the case of increasing returns to scale in production. The classic case is a product that requires a fixed set-up cost and a constant marginal cost to produce. (More generally we could consider non-convex production possibilities sets.) If the firm acts competitively in this industry and if the price is above marginal cost the firm will supply an infinite amount. If the price is at or below marginal cost the firm will produce nothing. If the consumers' quantity demand is positive and finite at a price equal to marginal cost, then there is no price such that supply equals demand. Equilibrium does not exist. The real implication of this situation is not that markets do not equilibrate or that trade does not take place, it is that a natural monopoly exists. There is room for at most one efficient firm in this industry. Again it is the assumption of competitive behaviour that is ultimately violated.

The next example, due to Starrett (1972), involves an external diseconomy. Suppose there is an upstream firm that pollutes the water and a downstream firm that requires clean water as an input into its production process. It is easy to show that if such a diseconomy exists and if the downstream firm always has the option of inaction (that is, it can use no inputs to produce no outputs at zero cost), then the aggregate production possibilities set of the economy when expanded to allow enough markets cannot be convex (see Ledyard, 1976 for a formal proof). If the production possibilities set of the economy is non-convex, then, as in the last example, it is possible that a competitive equilibrium will not exist. Expansion of the number of markets to solve the inefficiencies due to external diseconomies can lead to a situation in which there is no competitive equilibrium.

The last example, first observed by Green (1977) and Kreps (1977), arises in situations of asymmetric information. Recall the earlier example in which one agent was fully informed about the state of the world while the other thought each state was equally likely. Suppose preferences and endowments in each state are such that if both know the state then the equilibrium prices in each state are the same. Further, suppose that if the uninformed agent makes no inferences about the state from the other's behaviour then there will be different prices in each state. Then no (rational expectations) equilibrium will exist. If the informed agent tries to make inferences the prices will not inform him, and if the uninformed agent does not try to make inferences the prices will inform him. Further, it is fairly easy to show that if a market for information could be created (ignoring incentives to hide information) the resulting possibilities set is in general non-convex. In either case there is no equilibrium.

Most examples of non-existence of equilibrium seem to lead inevitably to non-competitive behaviour. In our example of non-existence due to informational asymmetries, it is natural for the informed agent to behave as a monopolist with respect to that information. In the example of the diseconomy, if a market is created between the upstream and the downstream firm, each becomes a monopoly. If there is a single polluter and many pollutees, the polluter holds a position similar to a monopsony. The non-existence problem due to the fundamental non-convexity caused by the use of markets to eliminate external diseconomies is simply finessed by one or more of the participants assuming non-competitive behaviour. An outcome occurs but it is not competitive and, therefore, not efficient.

Market failure, the inefficient allocation of resources with markets, can occur if there are too few markets, non-competitive behaviour, or non-existence problems. Many suggested solutions for market failure, such as tax-subsidy schemes, property rights assignments, and special pricing arrangements, are simply devices for the creation of more markets. If this can be done in a way that avoids non-convexities and ensures depth of participation, then the remedy can be beneficial and the new allocation should be efficient. On the other hand, if the addition of markets creates either non-convexities or shallow participation, then attempts to cure market failure from too few markets will simply lead to market failure from monopolistic behaviour. Market failure in this latter situation is fundamental. Examples are natural monopolies, external diseconomies, public goods and informational monopolies. If one wants to achieve efficient allocations of resources in the presence of such fundamental failures one must accept self-interested behaviour and explore non-market alternatives. A literature using this approach, sometimes called implementation theory and sometimes called mechanism design theory, was initiated by Hurwicz (1972) and is surveyed in Groves and Ledyard (1986). More recent results can be found at MECHANISM DESIGN and MECHANISM DESIGN (RECENT DEVELOPMENTS).

JOHN O. LEDYARD

See also **incentive compatibility; incomplete contracts; incomplete markets; mechanism design; mechanism design (new developments); Pareto efficiency; welfare economics.**

Bibliography

Arrow, K. 1951. An extension of the basic theorems of classical welfare economics. In *Proceedings of the Second Berkeley Symposium on Mathematical Statistics and Probability*, ed. J. Neyman. Berkeley: University of California Press.

Arrow, K. 1969. The organization of economic activity: issues pertinent to the choice of market versus non-market allocation. In Joint Economic Committee, *The Analysis and Evaluation of Public Expenditures: The PPB System*, Washington, DC: Government Printing Office.

Bator, F. 1958. The anatomy of market failure. *Quarterly Journal of Economics*, 351–79.

Coase, R. 1960. The problem of social cost. *Journal of Law and Economics* 3, 1–44.

Debreu, G. 1959. *Theory of Value: An Axiomatic Analysis of Economic Equilibrium*. Cowles Foundation Monograph No. 17. New York: Wiley.

Foley, D. 1970. Lindahl's solution and the core of an economy with public goods. *Econometrica* 38, 66–72.

Green, J. 1977. The nonexistence of informational equilibria. *Review of Economic Studies* 44, 451–63.

Groves, T. and Ledyard, J. 1986. Incentive compatibility ten years later. In *Information, Incentives, and Economic Mechanisms*, ed. T. Groves, R. Radner and S. Reiter. Minneapolis: University of Minnesota Press.

Hurwicz, L. 1972. On informationally decentralized systems. In *Decision and Organization*, ed. C.B. McGuire and R. Radner. Amsterdam: North-Holland.

Kreps, D. 1977. A note on 'fullfilled expectations' equilibria. *Journal of Economic Theory* 14, 32–43.

Ledyard, J. 1976. Discussion of 'on the nature of externalities'. In *Theory and Measurement of Economic Externalities*, ed. S. Lin. New York: Academic Press.

Muth, J. 1961. Rational expectations and the theory of price movements. *Econometrica* 29, 315–35.

Pigou, A. 1932. *The Economics of Welfare*, 4th edn. New York: Macmillan.

Postlewaite, A. and Schmeidler, D. 1986. Differential information and strategic behavior in economic environments: a general equilibrium approach. In *Information, Incentives, and Economic Mechanisms*, ed. T. Groves, R. Radner and S. Reiter. Minneapolis: University of Minnesota Press.

Radner, R. 1968. Competitive equilibrium under uncertainty. *Econometrica* 36, 31–58.

Roberts, J. and Postlewaite, A. 1976. The incentives for price-taking behavior in large exchange economies. *Econometrica* 44, 115–27.

Scitovsky, T. 1954. Two concepts of external economies. *Journal of Political Economy* 62, 70–82.

Starrett, D. 1972. Fundamental non-convexities in the theory of externalities. *Journal of Economic Theory* 4, 180–99.

market institutions

In order to work as they should, markets need institutions. Defining the rules of the game, institutions consist of the constraints, formal and informal, on economic and political actors (North, 1991). Market institutions serve to limit transaction costs: the time and money spent locating trading partners, comparing their prices, evaluating the quality of the goods for sale, negotiating agreements, monitoring performance and settling disputes (McMillan, 2002).

The notion that institutions matter is as old as the study of economics. For markets to create gains from trade, as Adam Smith recognized, the state must define property rights and enforce contracts.

That institutions matter is also one of the chief insights from modern economics. In the presence of informational asymmetries, markets can falter. If buyer and seller have different information about the item to be exchanged, a 'lemons market' may arise. Unable to distinguish high-quality goods, buyers may be unwilling to pay a price that elicits supply of anything other than low-quality items. Potential gains from trade go unrealized (Akerlof, 1970). When information is distributed unevenly – as is ubiquitous in the real world of economics, even if most of the textbooks have yet to bring it on board – prices do not incorporate all relevant information, and so non-price information is needed (Spence, 1973; Rothschild and Stiglitz, 1976). Limiting the inefficiencies from informational asymmetries requires mechanisms for signalling and screening: devices like reputation, warranties and credentials, as well as in some cases government-set rules and regulations. A more nuanced view of market processes is called for than the institution-free textbook account of price equilibration via supply and demand.

Evidence on the role of market-supporting institutions is accumulating. Much of the evidence comes from developing countries and countries in transition from communist central planning. Where markets work smoothly, in affluent countries, the market-supporting institutions are almost invisible. It is hard to find evidence of lemons markets in a country like the United States, because institutional solutions have evolved. By contrast, where markets work badly, in poor countries, the absence of institutions is conspicuous (Klitgaard, 1991). A few examples are given in what follows.

Property rights and contracting

Institutional innovation sometimes occurs even in affluent countries. An experiment in property rights has arisen in fisheries. Worldwide, fisheries are in crisis. Overfishing results from an externality: the costs of any one fisher's taking too many fish are mostly borne by others. Applying the idea of Ronald Coase (1960) of defining property rights to solve an externality, the New Zealand government has created, essentially, property rights in the fish. Fishers are assigned quotas that define, by species, their allowable fish catch. The quotas are tradable, so they end up with those fishers with the highest willingness to pay, which probably leads to an efficient allocation. Property rights in fish do not come for free, however, but require extensive costly government monitoring (Grafton, Squires and Fox, 2000). Military aircraft patrol the oceans. Each step of every single fish's journey from landing to final sale is documented, with catch reports, buyers' receipts, cold-storage records and export invoices being collated. Fishery inspectors police breaches. The costs of overseeing the quotas have yielded a return, as fish stocks have been successfully conserved.

Another property-rights experiment has occurred in residential land. In cities in every developing country there are squatters, poor people living on land to which they hold no legal rights. Ad hoc property rights exist even in the absence of formal legal protections, as neighbourhood associations and the squatters themselves guard the land. However, the inability to appeal to the law brings some inefficiencies. Hernando de Soto (2000) argued that, if the impoverished squatters held land titles, they would acquire access to capital markets, because they would then have collateral to offer. In Peru, following de Soto's advocacy, over a million squatter households were granted title to the land they occupied. The effects of this huge inauguration of property rights showed up, unexpectedly, not in the capital market but in the labour market. Householders' borrowing increased little, but hours worked outside the home by adult household members increased and hours worked by their children decreased (Field, 2003; Field and Torero, 2004). Without land titles, householders stayed at home to watch over their property, sending their children out to work. Holding land titles, they felt secure enough to enter the workforce. Establishing the market institution brought instant welfare gains. However, the gains came in an unforeseen form, illustrating the difficulty in general of anticipating the effects of institutional reform (McMillan, 2004).

With contracting, as with property rights, informal substitutes operate in the absence of formal institutions. Small firms make deals with each other and get finance, using personal networks and ongoing relationships to substitute for missing laws of contract and using retained earnings and trade credit to make up for a lack of access to financial markets (Fafchamps, 2004; McMillan and

Woodruff, 2002). Large firms also can prosper without institutions, coping instead by cultivating favours from politicians. Where the lack of institutions shows up is for small firms wishing to grow. Needing to make large, discrete investments, they can no longer rely on retained earnings and trade credit, so they may be unable to grow if the financial market is underdeveloped. Needing to deal with increasing numbers of trading partners, they cannot continue to rely on personal connections but must start to use the law of contract. The firm-size distribution in a typical developing country shows a missing middle, with a lot of employment in tiny firms and quite a lot in large firms, but not much in mid-sized firms (Snodgrass and Biggs, 1996). The missing middle is a symptom of weak legal and regulatory institutions.

Information transmission

An archetypical lemons market existed in India in the 1970s (Klitgaard, 1991). Quality fresh milk was hard to find because vendors routinely watered it down. Buyers could not assess the milk's butterfat content, and so the low-quality milk drove out the high-quality milk. Launching a campaign against adulterated milk, the National Dairy Development Board provided inexpensive machines to measure butterfat content as the milk moved from farmer to wholesaler to vendor. It also set up payment schemes making the price of milk reflect its measured quality and created brand names to give buyers trust in what they were getting. As a result of this coordinated initiative, quality improved and consumption rose.

The loan market is impeded by information asymmetries: both adverse selection (a lender may find it hard to distinguish whether any given loan applicant is a good credit risk) and moral hazard (a borrower, having received a loan, may have an incentive to default). Since these transaction costs are proportionately larger for small than for large loans, small lenders often pay exorbitant interest rates or are frozen out of the loan market. In Bangladesh's Grameen Bank and other microcredit banks, tiny loans are made to poor people via groups of borrowers. Each group member is held responsible for any other member's loan. Being neighbours, the group members know each other's business better than any banker, can monitor each other's use of the loans and can invoke social sanctions to discipline defaulters. Group lending is an elegant solution to the loan market's informational asymmetries.

The equity market relies heavily on institutions. For shareholders, who lack information about the firm's affairs, evaluating managers is difficult, and so a lemons market may arise. In many countries, lax oversights allow controlling shareholders to expropriate minority shareholders (Johnson et al., 2000). If the rules governing the financial markets are inadequate, investors are reluctant to buy stocks because they are unwilling to trust managers, and so firms do not get the finance they need.

A well-functioning equity market relies on a complex set of interrelated institutions, formal and informal, to foster information flow (Black, 2001). First, reputations for honest dealings must be built up by auditors, law firms, investment banks and the business press. Second, there are self-regulating private-sector bodies such as industry associations as well as the stock exchange, with its rules on listing firms' financial reporting and its sanction of delisting. Third, the equity market rests on state-provided mechanisms: not only laws requiring that investors receive accurate data, but also an activist regulator. The law's transaction costs (Glaeser and Shleifer, 2003) mean that a regulator supplements the courts in setting and enforcing the rules of the game.

Conclusion

Market-supporting institutions ensure that property rights are respected, that people can be trusted to live up to their promises, that externalities are held in check, that competition is fostered and that information flows smoothly (McMillan, 2002). Without institutions, the promise of efficient markets goes unrealized.

JOHN MCMILLAN

See also **Akerlof, George Arthur; Arrow, Kenneth Joseph; development economics; growth and institutions; institutionalism, old; micro-credit; property law, economics and search theory (new perspectives); Spence, A. Michael; Stiglitz, Joseph E.**

Bibliography

Akerlof, G. 1970. The market for 'lemons'. *Quarterly Journal of Economics* 84, 488–500.
Black, B. 2001. The legal and institutional preconditions for strong stock markets. *UCLA Law Review* 48, 781–855.
Coase, R. 1960. The problem of social cost. *Journal of Law and Economics* 3, 1–44.
de Soto, Hernando. 2000. *The Mystery of Capital.* New York: Basic Books.
Fafchamps, M. 2004. *Market Institutions in Sub-Saharan Africa.* Cambridge, MA: MIT Press.
Field, E. 2003. Entitled to work. Unpublished manuscript. Cambridge, MA: Harvard University.
Field, E. and Torero, M. 2004. Do property titles increase credit access among the urban poor? Unpublished manuscript. Cambridge, MA: Harvard University.
Glaeser, E. and Shleifer, A. 2003. The rise of the regulatory state. *Journal of Economic Literature* 41, 401–25.
Grafton, R., Squires, D. and Fox, K.J. 2000. Private property and economic efficiency. *Journal of Law and Economics* 43, 679–714.
Johnson, S., La Porta, R., Lopez-de-Silanes, F. and Shleifer, A. 2000. Tunneling. *American Economic Review Papers and Proceedings* 90, 22–7.

Klitgaard, R. 1991. *Adjusting to Reality*. San Francisco: ICS Press.

McMillan, J. 2002. *Reinventing the Bazaar*. New York: Norton.

McMillan, J. 2004. Avoid hubris. *Finance and Development* 41, 34–7.

McMillan, J. and Woodruff, C. 2002. The central role of entrepreneurs in transition economies. *Journal of Economic Perspectives* 16, 153–70.

North, D. 1991. Institutions. *Journal of Economic Perspectives* 5, 97–112.

Rothschild, M. and Stiglitz, J.E. 1976. Equilibrium in competitive insurance markets. *Quarterly Journal of Economics* 90, 629–50.

Snodgrass, D. and Biggs, T. 1996. *Industrialization and the Small Firm*. San Francisco: ICS Press.

Spence, A. 1973. Job market signaling. *Quarterly Journal of Economics* 87, 355–74.

market microstructure

Market microstructure studies the behaviour and formation of prices in asset markets. Whereas economic analyses of price formation generally abstract from any particular price-setting mechanisms, market microstructure relies on the specific rules and protocols of markets to analyse how prices are determined. This focus on the microstructure of the market provides insights into how the design of markets affects the price process, detailing both how individual prices are determined and how those prices evolve over time. Such insights are useful for a wide range of issues in asset pricing, as well as for guiding econometric investigations of high frequency data. In addition, microstructure research analyses structural issues in securities trading, such as the role and function of exchanges, the optimal design of trading systems, and the optimal regulation of securities markets.

Fundamental to microstructure research is the realization that asset prices are set in actual markets, and not by fictional auctioneers. Thus, while the forces of supply and demand ultimately underlie all asset prices, the specific formation and evolution of prices is much more complex. Buyers and sellers, for example, need not arrive synchronously, making the determination of a market-clearing price at a point in time problematic. When traders do arrive at markets, they may also face a range of market frictions such as transactions costs, search costs and the like (see Stoll, 2001). Furthermore, the value of assets may change over time, with some traders potentially knowing more about future values than other traders. Markets facilitate the trading of assets by providing liquidity and price discovery, and how they do so depends on the rules and structure of the market (see O'Hara, 2003).

Canonical models in microstructure

Early microstructure models focused on the specific market structure found in organized stock markets. In such markets, a designated market-maker or specialist quotes prices to buy or sell units of the asset. By serving as counter-party to buyers and sellers, the market-maker solves the asynchronicity problem noted above by standing ready to provide liquidity on either side of the market. The market-maker earns the 'spread', or the difference between the price at which he buys shares (the bid) and the price at which he will sell shares (the ask). In return, however, the market-maker has to bear inventory risk, essentially going long when traders wish to sell, and short when traders wish to buy.

There is an extensive literature analysing the market-maker's pricing problem in the presence of inventory risk (for a review of models, see O'Hara, 1995). In general, such models assume risk-averse market-makers facing exogenous holding costs in a setting in which all agents are symmetrically informed and 'true' asset prices are assumed fixed or, at least, stationary processes. An important feature of the equilibrium is that there is no single price: the price the market-maker sets depends upon whether the trader wishes to buy or sell, and on how much he wishes to trade. Prices change over time in response to the specialist's inventory position, his market power and parameters relating to the supply and demand for the asset. Such inventory models have been extended to a wide variety of market settings such as foreign exchange, bond markets, and options and futures markets. Empirical analyses find substantial support for the predictions of inventory models.

An alternative class of microstructure models considers price-setting when some agents have better information about the asset's true value than do other agents. The impetus for such models was an early paper by Treynor (1971), who noted that traders arriving at the market included those who needed to trade for liquidity reasons, those with better information about the asset's true value, and those who thought they had better information but were in fact incorrect. Treynor conjectured that the market-maker's prices were a balancing act offsetting his losses to the informed traders with his gains from the liquidity and noise traders. Viewed from this perspective, a spread arises naturally in security markets, independent of any inventory or transactions costs explanations. Fisher Black (1986) expanded on this notion to highlight the important role played by noise or liquidity traders in allowing markets to become efficient.

An intriguing implication of this research is that, if some traders do have better information about the asset's true value, then the nature of the order flow can be informative as to future asset values. Consequently, the market-maker's price-setting problem evolves from being a simple balancing of expected gains and losses to that of learning how to extract information from the order flow. With the market-maker drawing inferences from the order flow, this sets the stage for traders to consider the impact of their trades as well, particularly if they are attempting to profit on private information.

There are two general approaches to modelling price-setting in the presence of asymmetric information, sequential trade models and Kyle (1985) models. Glosten and Milgrom (1985) consider a risk-neutral market-maker facing known populations of informed and uninformed traders, where traders arrive sequentially to the market. The market-maker knows these population parameters, but does not know the identity of any individual trader. The market-maker does know, however, that traders informed of good news will all want to buy, while those informed of bad news will all want to sell. Consequently, the market-maker's conditional expectation of the asset's value also differs with trade direction, and it is these conditional expectations that become his bid and ask prices. Based on the trade that actually occurs, the market-maker updates his beliefs regarding the asset's value using Bayes' rule. The continued one-sided trading of the informed traders eventually forces prices to the true equilibrium level.

Sequential trade models provide an elegant means to characterize the relation between trades and prices on a tick-by-tick basis. Because the market-maker learns from trades, the evolution of prices depends on the order flow, as does the size and movement of the spread. More complex analyses demonstrate a role for other market information in affecting price behaviour. Trade size, for example, may be informative as informed traders prefer to trade larger rather than smaller amounts (Easley and O'Hara, 1987). The time between trades may also have information content as a signal of the existence of new information, and this, in turn, can impart information content to volume (Easley and O'Hara, 1992). Trade location, trade in correlated assets, and alternative order types can also have information content. Because of their tick-by-tick focus, sequential models are particularly useful for guiding empirical analysis of microstructure data, an issue we will return to shortly.

An alternative modelling approach is a Kyle (1985) model. Kyle models focus on the dual problems facing the market-maker, who must figure out what the informed traders know, and the informed trader, who wishes to exploit his private information for profit. The Kyle model uses a batch-auction framework in which the market-maker sees the aggregated trades of both the informed traders and the noise or liquidity traders, and based on this order flow he sets a single price. The market-maker conjectures a trading strategy for the informed trader that is linear in the asset's true value, while the informed trader conjectures a pricing strategy for the market-maker that is linear in the total order flow. In equilibrium, both conjectures must be correct, a feature typical of rational expectations equilibrium models. As in sequential trade models, the market-maker's price reflects his conditional expected value for the asset, this conditional expectation changes as he learns from the order flow, and prices eventually adjust to true values. Back and Baruch (2004) demonstrate conditions under which the Kyle and Glosten–Milgrom models essentially converge.

An important feature of Kyle models is their ability to characterize the trading strategy of the informed trader. The optimal strategy for the informed trader is essentially to hide his trades in the noise trade, and he varies his trades over time in response to the market-maker's growing precision of his beliefs about the asset's true value. Holden and Subrahmanyam (1992) show that, if there are many informed traders, then their combined trading actions force prices almost instantaneously to true values, a result again reminiscent of rational expectations models. A wide range of research has considered variants of the Kyle model allowing for different types of information structures, for uninformed traders to also act strategically, and for the market-maker to have differential information.

These two asymmetric information-based modelling approaches allow researchers to address a broad range of issues in the trading of financial assets, and are particularly useful in demonstrating how markets perform their price discovery function. Because market-makers are risk neutral and unconstrained as to their inventory holdings, liquidity issues in these models reflect more difficulties induced by the potential information content of trades, rather than the risk-bearing considerations that arise in inventory models. As both effects are likely to be present in actual markets, a wide range of research has investigated empirically how spreads and price changes are influenced by information, inventory, and the fixed costs of making markets.

Research directions in microstructure research

The growth of financial asset markets worldwide, as well as the increasing availability of high frequency microstructure data from a wide array of markets, has allowed microstructure researchers to investigate a broad range of issues, both empirical and theoretical. I highlight here a few areas that are of particular importance.

Econometrics of high-frequency data

Microstructure data allows researchers to analyse the evolution of prices and market data on a second-by-second basis. Indeed, most microstructure data sets include millions of observations, raising a range of econometric issues. Of particular importance are the periodicity of the data, biases introduced by market structure protocols, optimal statistical models for evaluating the behaviour of prices and spreads, and data sampling issues. Hasbrouck (2006) discusses each of these topics.

Because prices arise only when there are trades, price data is not spaced uniformly throughout the trading day. This introduces a censored sampling problem as prices can be thought of as draws from the true asset value distribution, but where the timing of the draws may not be independent of evolution of the value process itself. Engle and Russell (1998) exploit this insight to develop the auto-conditional duration (ACD) model to analyse the evolution of intra-day volatility. A related problem is sampling across assets, as non-synchronicity of trading may result in price observations that lag true value innovations across stocks. A number of authors have considered the implications of non-synchronous trading for cross-sectional econometric analyses.

A variety of authors also consider the time-series properties of microstructure data, with a particular focus on decomposing price movements into those associated with the value process and those reflecting noise arising from the microstructure such as tick size constraints, bid/ask bounce, price continuity rules, and so on. These econometric issues are particularly important for asset pricing research.

Asset pricing – liquidity and information risk
Microstructure models analyse the liquidity and price discovery roles markets play in asset pricing. Recent research has focused on whether these two market roles also affect asset returns. Amihud and Mendelson (1986) first suggested that liquidity could influence asset returns by affecting an investor's overall cost of trading. Numerous empirical researchers have investigated whether spreads, a proxy for these liquidity costs, are related to asset returns, but the empirical evidence has been mixed. More recent research by Pastor and Stambaugh (2004) using lagged volume measures of liquidity provides stronger evidence, and the authors propose a liquidity factor to explain asset returns. One reason why this effect may arise is commonality in liquidity. Chordia, Roll and Subrahmanyam (2000) find that liquidity measures appear to vary systematically across stocks, and these effects may be time-varying. Other researchers have found similar commonality effects in bond market liquidity measures.

A second research stream considers the price discovery process, and whether investors require higher returns to hold stocks for which a greater fraction of the available information is private rather than public. Easley, Hvidkjaer and O'Hara (2002) derive measures of information-based trading using a structural microstructure model, and demonstrate that asset returns are explained by these information measures. What generates this effect is the inability to diversify optimally, as uninformed traders always lose to informed traders, who are better able to shift their portfolio weights to reflect true values. Empirical research supports a distinct role for both liquidity and information risk in affecting asset returns.

Electronic markets and trading systems
Microstructure models have typically analysed price-setting on a centralized market with a designated market-maker (or makers). While such a setting corresponds well to an exchange or dealer market, it is less applicable to the wide variety of electronic markets now used to trade many financial assets. Of particular importance are electronic trading systems which rely on the aggregation of limit orders to effectuate trades. Orders to buy and sell at a specific price and quantity are collected in the 'book', with price and time priority rules dictating how such orders are handled. At any point in time, a spread exists between the highest (lowest) price at which someone is willing to buy (sell) the asset. In such systems, trades arise when orders cross, imparting an importance to the order decisions of individual traders.

Traders face complex decision problems in placing orders due to the uncertainty of execution of any order. Of particular concern is that uninformed traders may face an adverse selection problem in that their trades are more likely to execute when there is new information, causing them to buy when there is bad news and sell when there is good news. This difficulty is further compounded by trading protocols that allow limit orders to 'sweep the book' and thereby trigger the execution of many individual orders as the opposite side of a large order. There is a substantial literature looking at the behaviour of such electronic markets, but the complexity of these markets leaves many important issues yet to be resolved.

Market structure
Microstructure research is traditionally concerned with issues related to the design and structure of markets. The rise of new markets and trading technologies has raised a plethora of market structure issues. Of particular interest to many researchers are questions relating to transparency, or what information is available to traders and when can they see it. Bond markets, for example, were traditionally opaque, but new reporting rules have increased their transparency. Numerous authors have investigated how this has changed the liquidity and efficiency of the bond market. Option markets traditionally faced little competition, but the development of a national options market in the United States, along with the rise of electronic competitors, has changed this market structure. Regulatory changes in the United States and Europe have also dramatically affected market structure in equities, raising questions as to the efficacy of these new rules. Finally, the markets themselves are evolving from member-owned cooperatives to publicly traded firms, raising a host of issues relating to corporate governance and self-regulation. Microstructure research provides a means to evaluate the economic impact of these changes and to suggest alternative structures for the trading of financial assets.

MAUREEN O'HARA

See also **adverse selection; noise traders.**

Bibliography

Amihud, Y. and Mendelson, H. 1986. Asset pricing and the bid-ask spread. *Journal of Financial Economics* 17, 223–49.

Back, K. and Baruch, S. 2004. Information in securities markets: Kyle meets Glosten and Milgrom. *Econometrica* 72, 433–65.

Black, F. 1986. Noise. *Journal of Finance* 41, 529–43.

Chordia, T., Roll, R. and Subrahmanyam, A. 2000. Commonality in liquidity. *Journal of Financial Economics* 56, 3–28.

Easley, D. and O'Hara, M. 1987. Price, trade size, and information in securities markets. *Journal of Financial Economics* 19, 69–90.

Easley, D. and O'Hara, M. 1992. Time and the process of security price adjustment. *Journal of Finance* 47, 577–605.

Easley, D., Hvidkjaer, S. and O'Hara, M. 2002. Is information risk a determinant of asset prices? *Journal of Finance* 56, 2185–221.

Engle, R. and Russell, J.R. 1998. Autoregressive conditional duration: a new model for irregularly spaced data. *Econometrica* 66, 1127–62.

Glosten, L. and Milgrom, P. 1985. Bid, ask, and transaction prices in a specialist market with heterogeneously informed traders. *Journal of Financial Economics* 14, 71–100.

Hasbrouck, J. 2006. *Empirical Market Microstructure: The Institutions, Economics, and Econometrics of Securities Trading.* New York: Oxford Economic Press.

Holden, C.W. and Subrahmanyam, A. 1992. Long-lived private information and imperfect competition. *Journal of Finance* 47, 247–70.

Kyle, A. 1985. Continuous auctions and insider trading. *Econometrica* 53, 1315–35.

O'Hara, M. 1995. *Market Microstructure Theory.* Boston: Blackwell.

O'Hara, M. 2003. Presidential address: liquidity and price discovery. *Journal of Finance* 58, 1335–54.

Pastor, L. and Stambaugh, R. 2004. Liquidity risk and expected stock returns. *Journal of Political Economy*, 111, 642–85.

Stoll, H. 2001. Market frictions. *Journal of Finance* 55, 1479–514.

Treynor, J. 1971. The only game in town. *Financial Analysts Journal* 27, 12–14, 22.

market period

The concept of market period was introduced by Marshall to define markets according to the time period over which they extended. It was thus an additional classification of markets to that of location or space (*Principles*, V.i.6). This distinction became the modern textbook one between the short period and the long, reducing Marshall's more complex three-period classification. As he put it,

we shall find that if the period is short, the supply is limited to the stores which happen to be at hand; if the period is long, the supply will be influenced, more or less, by the cost of producing the commodity in question; and if the period is very long, this cost will in its turn be influenced, more or less, by the cost of producing the labour and material things required for producing the commodity.

Hence the short run is that period for which stocks are constant, the long run that period where price is determined by the costs of production (but factors are constant) and the very long run that period where all factors vary.

The Marshallian market period was, as Hicks pointed out (1965, ch. 5) one of the ways in which Marshall used his 'static method'. For in the short period, Hicks goes on to say, Marshall could treat the industry as if it were in static equilibrium. Capital, fixed in the short period, is like land in Ricardo, and it earns a rent. In the longer run, the static method breaks down, as capital becomes variable, like labour.

The concept of Marshallian short period has been used extensively in the theory of the firm, in terms of short- and long-run equilibria, and the defining of cost curves according to this classification. Harrod, in 1934, linked this Marshallian concept with the new theory of imperfect competition developed by Joan Robinson (and Chamberlin), to look at the process of imperfect competition and the impact of entry on short- and long-run profit maximization.

The Marshallian short run concept was taken over into macroeconomics by Keynes as one of three components of Marshall's theory which he used to construct the *General Theory* (the others were partial equilibrium and thus exogenous expectations, and the representative firm aggregate which Keynes took over as the economy). However the Keynesian use of market period was not universally adopted in macroeconomics and it is Hicks's much more restrictive concept used in the IS–LM framework which is now much more familiar. The Hicksian 'week' is a market period in which fundamentally it is stocks that are constant, while the Keynesian 'year' allows for an element of 'user cost' whereby the utilization of capital affects the future demand for capital.

The Hicksian week and the concept of temporary equilibrium associated with it were first set out by Hicks in the middle chapters of *Value and Capital* in 1939, and were subsequently revised in an important, somewhat neglected essay entitled 'Methods of Dynamic Analysis' in 1956, reprinted in *Money, Interest and Wages* (1982). These concepts formed part of an attempt to construct a theory of dynamics, going beyond Marshall's static analysis. The alternative extreme hypothesis of allowing all factors to vary is a longer-run theory, and forms the basis of general equilibrium and growth theory. Both the Hicksian and Keynesian theories attempt to construct an intermediary period, and for each the corresponding problems were to decide which factors are to be allowed to vary, which to stay constant and what process of adjustment to vary, which to be employed by firms. But once these theoretical assumptions have been made, the individual periods become discrete rather than continuous (as in the longer-run case). Thus a theory of dynamics based on the Hicksian week requires an additional theory by which to link the discrete periods together to form a continuous model. We need to know how to get from one period to another. Both Keynes and Hicks resorted in one way or another to a link via expectations, though both provided what now appear to be inadequate explanations of their formation.

The modern new classical theory of macroeconomic equilibrium avoids the short and the long run distinction by appealing both to the perfectibility of markets per se, and to a theory of expectations which is itself based on perfect markets. Thus although the rational expectations approach 'solves' the problem of linking market periods, it does so in a way which avoids rather than solves the problems of market period analysis. Perfect markets do not have dynamics with limited time horizons and rigidities and thus, in the rational expectations perfect foresight model, there is really no need for market period analysis. It is clear however that market imperfections in real variables and expectations do exist, and hence that short-run temporary equilibria cannot easily be linked together.

D.R. HELM

See also **long run and short run; Marshall, Alfred; reservation price and reservation demand; temporary equilibrium.**

Bibliography

Harrod, R. 1934. Doctrines of imperfect competition. *Quarterly Journal of Economics* 48, 442–70.
Hicks, J.R. 1956. Methods of dynamic analysis. In *25 Essays in Honour of Erik Lindahl*, Stockholm. Repr. in J.R. Hicks, *Money, Interest and Wages*. Oxford: Basil Blackwell, 1982.
Hicks, J.R. 1965. The method of Marshall. In *Capital and Growth*, ed. J.R. Hicks. Oxford: Clarendon Press.
Marshall, A. 1920. *Principles of Economics*. 8th edn, London: Macmillan.

marketplaces

Marketplaces in the long-run

The history of marketplaces is traced here as a sequence of pivotal events that began at least 60,000 years ago

when, archaeologists suggest, the earliest appearance of trade in Europe can be inferred from the discovery of made objects – amber mollusc shells and worked stone – that had been moved to sites hundreds of kilometers from their sources. But the origins of trade may extend back even further in time, for 'the archaeological record does not reveal *any* time in the history of man in Europe in which there was no movement of "manufactured" objects' (Grantham, 1997, p. 18).

A giant leap takes us to Mesopotamia 10,000 years ago. Having by now collected abundant evidence of the deleterious effect of settled agriculture on human health in the Neolithic, it has been suggested by some paleopathologists that the Agricultural Revolution – the sedentary cultivation of grain, sugar, flax, wool, sisal, jute and hemp – may have been driven less by the quest for food security than by the high value these staple crops could earn in trade.

Study of the 4,000 year-old Heqanakht Papyri reveals Heqanakht himself to have been 'obsessed' with running his farm to make a profit and augment his wealth, and the economy of Pharaonic Egypt to have been one *not* of priestly redistribution, as had been thought, but of private property, money prices, cash crops, rental land, wage labour and marketplaces (Allen, 2002).

Ten centuries before the Christian era, the marketplaces rimming the Aegean Basin were specializing in the export of high-value wines, olives and oil to trade for imports of grains, raw materials and slaves from the 'barbarians' north of the Mediterranean.

In the eighth and seventh centuries BC, Phoenicia's legendary traders integrated the markets of the eastern and western Mediterranean; the Etruscans made contact with the Celts; and the merchants of India reached the northwest coast of England.

In the Bible, The Book of Ezekiel, written, it is thought, in the sixth century BC, describes in chapters 26–27 the prosperous city of Tyre whose marketplaces overflowed with an abundance of fir trees from Senir, cedars from Lebanon, ivory benches from the isle of Chittim, fine linen from Egypt, silver, iron tin and lead from Tarshish, emeralds, purple, coral, agate and fine linen from Syria, wheat from Minnith, honey, oil and balm from Pannag wine and white wool from Helbon, lambs, rams and goats from Arabia, spices from Sheba and Ra-amah, and skilled artisans, labourers, seafaring men, and merchants from all over the eastern Mediterranean.

Most exotic of all were the marketplaces that grew up along the Silk Road, established by the Han Dynasty in the second century BC as China's only link to the West. Along much of its length, the Silk Road was less a 'road' than a hazardous path around the world's most unlivable desert, through the world's most inaccessible mountain passes, over the world's highest peaks, and among the world's most isolated and hostile peoples. The Road started in what is now Xian on China's northwest border, and made its way west through Kazakstan, Kyrgyzstan,

Uzbekistan, Tajikistan and Afghanistan, encircling the Hindu Kush, until, crossing the Black Sea, it ended in Roman Syria – which is as much as to say, in Venice! The marketplaces of this commerce were the oases of central Asia and the fabled 'Arabian Nights' cities they became: Xian, Islamabad, Tehran, Kashi, Samarkand, Bukhara, Kabul, Kandahar, Tashkent, Aleppo, Lahore, Baghdad, Ankara, Istanbul. For 15 centuries, caravans of up to 1,000 camels each made the journey from oasis to oasis for months on end, under armed guard, bearing gold, metals, ivory, precious stones, myrrh, frankincense, ostrich eggs, horses, glass, silks, porcelain, guns, powder, jade, bronzes, lacquer – and the great religious civilizations of Buddhism and Islam.

On the European end of the Silk Road great 'diaspora networks' were founded by Greek, Armenian and Jewish merchant families of the eastern Mediterranean, who traded a world away with the diaspora networks of India, China, Japan and Indonesia (McCabe, Harlaftis and Minoglou, 2005).

In time, the Romans would discover the secret of making silk, Europeans would find a sea route to China, the Silk Road with its storied past would disappear beneath the sand, the Mongol hordes would burst out of the East, and Europe would reap the whirlwind. In the Black Death that ravaged the continent between 1348 and 1351, Europe lost as much as 40 per cent of its population.

To a demographic event so catastrophic no system, no institution, no mode of production could remain impervious. Especially transformed were Europe's labour markets. In England, those who survived the Black Death lived to enjoy 'the sole golden age of the English peasantry' (Hatcher 1987, p. 281). The Statute of Artificers notwithstanding, the general response of the manorial economy to the desperate scarcity of labour, the abundance of abandoned land, and rising prices in grain markets was to relax feudal constraints on the mobility of labour, to raise nominal wages, lower rents, and make concessions on customary dues and obligations. In a word, peasants under villein tenure were able to secure copyhold and leasehold tenancies. By the 17th century, England had become 'a peasant-free zone' (R.M. Smith in Scott, 1998, p. 346).

In Russia, in stunning contrast, the response to depopulation was the establishment of serfdom. In the face of acute labour scarcity and expanding grain markets, the Boyars demanded tighter and tighter legal restrictions on the mobility of peasants until, by an Act of the Duma in 1649, serfs and their households were made the personal property of the lord – effectively slaves (Domar, 1970, pp. 13–32).

Thus, 'peasant' in the European context came to be a status that defies definition: some were well on the way to yeomanry by 1600, others were only a technicality away from a heritable condition of slavery.

Marketplaces and peasants

From the 14th century to the 18th, the history of marketplaces is linked to the history of peasants, as that of peasants is to marketplaces. In Brueghel's exuberant paintings of peasants tumbling about in overflowing marketplaces the link has become an icon of Flemish art. 'Historically, peasants only exist when markets exist, even if they do not fully participate in them' (Scott, 1998, p. 2).

Having for well over a century minutely observed a vast number of peasant societies, the characteristics of peasant markets, and the behaviour of peasants with respect to them, it has been anthropology, rather than economics, that has become, to use Grantham's phrase (1997, p. 19), 'the referent social science' of the peasant economy. Peasant villages, whether in Indo-China, West Africa, the Stone Age, or – improbably – colonial New England, are said to have this in common: that the village marketplace is 'embedded in' the social fabric of the community; the rules governing it, and the motivations of buyers and sellers and borrowers and lenders transacting in it are subordinate to and constrained by the non-market values of the ambient culture, and stand as epicentres of resistance to the encroachment of the 'disembedded', protocapitalist, dynamic, hegemonic Market, with a capital M.

Influential as this model has been, there is a counternarrative, accepted even by some anthropologists. Thus, for example, among the Panajachelenos of the Guatemalan highlands, 'Commerce is the breath of life' (Tax, 1963, p. 132). According to Sol Tax, both men and women spend more time buying and selling and talking about buying and selling than doing anything else. When they have nothing to sell, they buy something in a cheap market and carry it to a dear one to sell. The Maoris of New Zealand, the Ifugao of the Philippines, the Senegambian, Afikpo, Esusu, Yoruba, Hausa, Tiv and Dahomean peoples of West Africa, the northeastern Malays, the Javanese and the Trobriand Islanders have all been found to engage in price- and quantity-bargaining, to 'seek maximal advantage' in marketplace transactions (Firth and Yamey, 1964), and to exhibit in their market-dependence the same U-shaped relationship to their disposable assets as is associated with risk-averse behaviour in developed economies.

A case in point is a new study of African markets by Marcel Fafchamps (2004) who argues that sub-Saharan Africa today is decisively 'market-oriented'. The development of Africa, Fafchamps insists, has been impeded not by the cultural incongruity of markets, or the absence of markets, or the lack of a market *mentalité*, but by the accommodation that traders in sub-Saharan markets have had to make to the ubiquity of market imperfections. In the absence of well-defined property rights, intermediary institutions, notaries public and contract enforcement, the sole bar against asymmetric information, adverse selection and moral hazard has been what might be called 'insider trading': repeated transactions among networks of friends and relations bound to one another by webs of trust. In the context of sub-Saharan Africa these webs, although intimate, are not cooperative, says Fafchamps, but strategic; the object is not to avoid the discipline of the market but more nearly to satisfy its assumptions.

Few peasant economies fit the 'moral economy' model (Rothenberg, 1992, chap. 2). And those that do may, like 15th-century French villages, have been torn by strife, the collective experience 'rubbed raw' (Hoffman, 1996, p. 77) by the face-to-face pursuit of what Avner Offer (1997) has called 'regard'. But the principal critique of a non-market model is that it is a steady-state model, and that has tended to impart a Durkheimian steady-state bias to peasant studies. It is a bias very much 'at home' with a methodology in anthropology itself in which scrutiny ever closer is leveled at subjects ever narrower – from tribe, to village, clan, household, extended family, nuclear family, gender – thereby surrendering to economists the trade *among* groups and the articulation *between* market-places that generates growth. It is in regulating that process that the community asserts its dominion over what Braudel (1982, p. 58) has called 'the insidious tentacles of the economy'.

Regulating the marketplace

Such interventions have a very long history, coming down to us, Blackstone thought, from Saxon times when no title to goods valued above 20 pence could change hands without witnesses. But such impediments to trade could not have persisted were it not for law. It is the province of any law worthy of the name to recognize in 'You have got what belongs to me' its sphere of action (Pollock and Maitland, 1895, p. 33), and nowhere more urgently than at the point of transferring the ownership of chattels by sale. For what but law can distinguish sale from theft, right from use, ownership from possession, *dominium* from *seisin*?

As the frequency of trade increased in the 13th century, exchange in an open market established by royal grant – a 'market ouvert' – sufficed, in lieu of witnesses, to divest a seller. With outdoor marketplaces came rules, regula-tions and ordinances establishing, locating, restricting and supervising open markets, covered markets, fairs, merchant courts and piepoudre courts for itinerant mer-chants; appointing ringers of opening and closing bells, monitors of weights and measures, collectors of fees and fines, inspectors of quality, enforcers of Just Prices and wardens to patrol the perimeters of the marketplace. This regulatory 'apparatus' was brought to the American colonies and given the force of law in the municipal marketplaces of all large towns in Massachusetts and throughout the colonies.

'The Laws and Liberties of Massachusetts', codified between 1641 and 1691, declared the taking of excessive wages by mechanics and day labourers and the charging of unreasonable prices by shopkeepers and merchants punishable by double restitution or imprisonment. They set the weight of the pennyloaf of white bread, and authorized the selection of two able persons annually to enter into the houses of all bakers 'as oft as they see cause' to inspect and weigh all bread found there on pain of forfeiture. Two persons were appointed annually to ascertain the range of prevailing wheat prices each month and set the price at which bakers shall bake their bread. 'The Laws and Liberties' also set the days of the week when a marketplace shall be kept in Boston, Salem, Lynn and Charlestown, set the times of the ringing of the opening and closing bells, forbade all trade outside the perimeter of the marketplace, and set the two days a year when Boston, Salem, Watertown and Dorchester shall have fairs (Cushing, 1976).

In 1737, Faneuil Hall, Boston's beleaguered market-place, was besieged by farmers from the surrounding hinterland who 'donned the livery of heaven' (disguised themselves as clergy) and burned it to the ground (Brown, 1900, chap. 8). By the early 1820s, the regulated 'market ouvert' and the legal doctrine of implied contract expressed by it were abandoned in favour of the rule of *caveat emptor*. Contract, not Community, would come increasingly to regulate markets.

Marshallian markets: the marketplace after 1900

With the publication of Alfred Marshall's *Principles of Economics* in 1900, economics became the referent social science of markets. It may therefore come as something of a surprise to discover that in this, the urtext of economics, marketplaces have vanished! Marshall's definition of a market is of an abstraction, outside of spatial coordinates, oblivious of cultural context, and functioning homeo-statically in accordance with laws of its own making. 'The distinction of locality is not necessary,' he wrote. 'Economists understand by the term "Market" not any particular marketplace in which things are bought and sold, but the whole of any region in which buyers and sellers are in such free intercourse with one another that the prices of the same good tend to equality easily and quickly' (Marshall, 1890, p. 324).

Thus, the market is not a place but a *process* that expands in space and unfolds in time, driven by the pace at which different prices for the same good converge toward a single price. Called the Law of One Price, that convergence is the unintended consequence of arbitrage between buyers seeking cheap markets and sellers seeking dear markets.

But as long as a wedge between 'cheap' and 'dear' markets persists, that is, as long as the convergence pro-cess is incomplete, marketplaces remain significant, not as 'spots of ground' but as transitional nodes of price-formation that become 'folded in' as the market process advances along its dendritic expansion-path. The story we have followed for 60,000 years has not, even in a Marshallian sense, become irrelevant.

At the same time, economics itself, as the referent social science of markets, is expanding its narrow field of vision beyond its Marshallian boundaries in an attempt to comprehend the wider social and psychological foundations of economic behaviour. I am reminded of the earthquake of 8 October 2005, which that struck high up in the Kashmiri Himalayas. Within a week of the catastrophe, survivors set up a village marketplace (BBC News). Seventy-three thousand had been killed, three million were made homeless, none had necessities, none had surpluses, but within days they made a marketplace.

WINIFRED B. ROTHENBERG

See also **Braudel, Fernand; Domar, Evsey David; market institutions; peasant economy; peasants; Polanyi, Karl.**

Bibliography

Allen, J.P. 2002. *The Heqanakht Papyri.* New York: Metropolitan Museum of Art and Yale University Press.
Braudel, F. 1982. *The Wheels of Commerce: Civilization & Capitalism, 15th–18th Century*, vol. 2. New York: Harper and Row.
Brown, A.E. 1900. *Faneuil Hall and the Faneuil Hall Market, Or Peter Faneuil's Gift.* Boston: Lee and Shepard.
Curtin, P.D. 1975. *Economic Change in Precolonial Africa: Senegambia in the Era of the Slave Trade.* Madison: University of Wisconsin Press.
Cushing, D. 1976. *The Laws and Liberties of Massachusetts, 1641–1691*, 3 vols. Wilmington: Scholarly Resources.
Domar, E.D. 1970. The causes of slavery and serfdom: a hypothesis. *Journal of Economic History* 30, 18–32.
Ellis, F. 1988. *Peasant Economics: Farm Households and Agrarian Development.* Cambridge: Cambridge University Press.
Fafchamps, M. 2004. *Market Institutions in Sub-Saharan Africa.* Cambridge, MA: MIT Press.
Firth, R. and Yamey, B.S., eds. 1964. *Capital, Saving and Credit in Peasant Societies: Studies from Asia, Oceania, the Caribbean, and Middle America.* Chicago: Aldine.
Gonzales, R. 2005. The Geography of the Silk Road. http://www.humboldt.edu/~geog3091/ideas/raysilk.html. Accessed 21 July 2005.
Grantham, G. 1997. The shards of trade: archaeology and the economic history of the super-long-run. Paper delivered at the Economic History Association Conference, August 1997, p. 18.
Hatcher, J. 1987. English serfdom and villeinage: towards a reassessment. In *Landlords, Peasants and Politics in Medieval England*, ed. T. Aston. Cambridge: Cambridge University Press.
Hoffman, P.T. 1996. *Growth in a Traditional Society: The French Countryside, 1450–1815.* Princeton: Princeton University Press.
Hughes, J.R.T. 1976. *Social Control in the Colonial Economy.* Charlottesville: University Press of Virginia.

Kohn, M. 2003. Organized Markets in Pre-Industrial Europe. Working paper. Dartmouth College, July 2003.
Marshall, A. 1890. *Principles of Economics.* 8th edn, London: Macmillan, 1946.
Mazower, M. 2004. *Salonica, City of Ghosts: Christians, Muslims, and Jews, 1430–1950.* New York: Alfred Knopf.
McCabe, I.B., Harlaftis, G. and Minoglou, I., eds. 2005. *Diaspora Entrepreneurial Networks: Four Centuries of History.* New York: Berg.
McNeill, W.H. 1976. *Plagues and Peoples.* Garden City: Anchor/Doubleday.
Offer, A. 1997. Between the gift and the market: the economy of regard. *Economic History Review* 50, 450–76.
Polanyi, K. 1944. *The Great Transformation: The Political and Economic Origins of Our Time.* Boston: Beacon Press.
Pollock, F. and Maitland, F. 1895. *The History of English Law before the Time of Edward*, vol. 2. Cambridge: Cambridge University Press, 1968.
Rothenberg, W.B. 1992. *From Market-Places to a Market Economy: The Transformation of Rural Massachusetts, 1750–1850.* Chicago: University of Chicago Press.
Scott, T., ed. 1998. *The Peasantries of Europe: From the Fourteenth to the Eighteenth Centuries.* New York: Addison Wesley Longman.
Tax, S. 1963. *Penny Capitalism: A Guatemalan Indian Economy.* Chicago: University of Chicago Press.

market power and collusion in laboratory markets

The robustness of competitive market predictions stands as one of the most impressive results in experimental economics. Laboratory markets regularly generate competitive outcomes in environments populated by just two or three sellers. However, as in natural contexts, competitive outcomes do not always emerge. This article reviews results of laboratory markets in which price increases are driven by factors such as the exercise of unilateral market power or by collusion.

Before reviewing the main concepts and contributions in this area, I offer two observations. First, laboratory methods represent an important but limited complement to existing empirical tools for investigating market performance. Given the stark simplicity and limited duration of laboratory markets, experimentalists can aspire to say little about specific naturally occurring markets. Experiments can, however, provide important insights into the behavioural relevance of theories upon which antitrust policies are based.

Second, the trading rules defining negotiations and contracting can exert first-order effects on market competitiveness. For example, markets organized under the double auction trading rules used in many financial exchanges, are much more robustly competitive than markets organized under the posted-offer trading rules used in most retail exchanges: duopoly or even monopoly sellers are less able to increase market prices in double-auction than in posted-offer markets (Davis and Holt, 1993, chs 3, 4; Holt, 1995). Indeed, one of the motivating factors in the emerging field of institutional design was an interest in developing institutional rules that promoted efficient market outcomes.

For specificity I focus here on results from posted-offer markets, primarily because posted-offer markets allow a particularly intuitive illustration of the factors affecting market competitiveness. However, a host of other trading institutions exist, ranging from single and multi-unit auctions, to multi-sided computerized 'smart' markets, and again to institutions that exist primarily as theoretical constructs, such as quantity-setting Cournot mechanisms. The competitive implications of each of these institutions must be evaluated independently.

Posted-offer markets and unilateral market power

Unilateral market power is perhaps the most frequently observed reason why prices in laboratory markets deviate from competitive predictions. This market power exists when one or more sellers, acting on their own, find it profitable to raise prices above the competitive level. The supply and demand structures shown in the two panels of Figure 1 illustrate how capacity restrictions can create market power. In each panel, the market consists of three sellers, S1, S2 and S3, each of whom offers four units for sale, under the conditions that two units cost $2.00 and two units cost $3.00. A buyer will purchase a fixed number of units (seven in the left panel or ten in the right panel) at prices less than or equal to $6.00.

Exchange in these markets proceeds in a number of trading periods. At the outset of each period, sellers simultaneously make price decisions. Production is 'to order' in the sense that sellers incur costs only for the units that actually sell. Once all sellers post prices, a simulated fully revealing buyer makes all possible purchases, starting with the least expensive units first. In the case of a tie, the buyer rotates purchases among the tied sellers.

In the market shown in the left panel of Figure 1 the buyer will purchase at most seven units. Given an aggregate supply of 12 units, sellers in this market have no market power: at any common price above $3.00, each seller can increase sales from an expected 2.33 units to four units by posting a price just slightly below the common price. For any vector of heterogeneous prices above $3.00 only the seller posting the lowest price will sell all four units. The seller posting the second highest price will sell three units, while the high-pricing seller will sell nothing. The unique Nash equilibrium for the stage game has each seller posting the competitive price of $3.00, selling 2.33 units in expectation and earning $2.00.

Expanding demand to ten units, as shown in the right panel of Figure 1, limits excess supply, and thus creates market power. Given that the highest price seller is now certain to sell at least two units, the competitive price of $3.00 is no longer a Nash equilibrium for the stage game. At a common price of $3.00 each seller sells 3.33 units (in expectation) and earns $2.00. By posting a price of $6.00, any seller can sell two units and increase earnings to $8.00. A common price of $6.00 is not an equilibrium for the stage game, since any seller would find that deviating from $6.00 increases sales to four units. Sellers have similar incentives to undercut any common price down to a minimum $p_{min}=\$4.50$, where the profits from selling four units as the lowest pricing seller equals earnings at the limit price. The equilibrium for this game involves mixing over the range from $4.50 to $6.00. As shown in the figure, the unique symmetric equilibrium is $4.71.

An extensive series of experiments show that sellers respond to unilateral market power by raising prices. Further, power drives pricing outcomes more powerfully than do changes in the number of sellers. For example, when they reallocated units among five sellers to create market power, Davis and Holt (1994) observed substantial price increases. However, reducing the number of sellers from five to three in a way that held market power conditions fixed, Davis and Holt observed only modest additional price increases. Market power of the sort illustrated in the right panel of Figure 1 has wide applications, ranging from distortions in markets for emissions trading (Godby, 2000) and for electricity transmission (Rassenti, Smith and Wilson, 2003), to price stickiness in the face of aggregate demand shocks (Wilson, 1998).

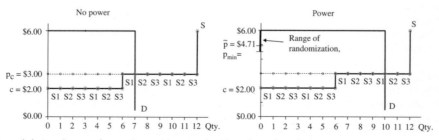

Figure 1   Supply and demand arrays for markets without and with unilateral market power

Tacit collusion

Experimentalists have also observed supra-competitive prices in repeated market games where sellers have no market power. This *tacit collusion* has been observed most frequently in duopolies (for example, Alger, 1987; Fouraker and Seigel, 1963). However, tacit collusion has also been observed in thicker markets where sellers possess no market power. For example, Cason and Williams (1990) observe persistently high prices in a four-seller design similar to that shown as the left panel of Figure 1. Experimentalists often measure tacit collusion as the difference between observed prices and prices consistent with the Nash equilibrium for the market analysed as a stage game. Importantly, other than exceeding equilibrium price predictions, tacitly collusive laboratory outcomes typically exhibit no obvious signs of coordinated activity.

Tacit collusion may coexist with market power. For example, prices in the market power sessions reported by Davis and Holt (1994) were significantly above prices consistent with the equilibrium mixing distribution. In this context, the difference between mean observed prices and the mean of the equilibrium mixing distribution may be reasonably taken as a measure of tacit collusion.

Tacit collusion is not yet well understood, and isolating the causes of tacit collusion represents an important project for future experimental work. Price signalling activity at least partially explains tacit collusion (for example, Durham et al., 2004). However, evidence suggests that more than price signals and responses may be at play. Dufwenberg and Gneezy (2000) report an experiment where duopolists deviate from the static Nash (competitive) prediction for a game, even when sellers are rematched into different markets after each decision. In such a context price signalling is not possible.

Explicit collusion

Given opportunities to explicitly discuss pricing, laboratory sellers quite persistently organize profit-increasing cartels (Isaac, Ramey and Williams, 1984). However, a capacity to monitor agreements and prevent secret discounts appears critical to the success of these arrangements (Davis and Holt, 1998). Given the illegality of explicit agreements, the more interesting questions regarding explicit collusion concern the capacity of authorities to detect such arrangements through the actions of sellers in the market (Davis and Wilson, 2002).

Other factors affecting pricing

A host of experimental studies indicate that standard 'facilitating practices' can contribute to price increases. Experimental studies where supra-competitive prices have been attributed to facilitating practices include 'most favoured nation' and 'meet-or-release' clauses (Grether and Plott, 1984), non-binding price signals (Holt and Davis, 1990) and multi-market competition (Phillips and Mason, 1991).

Buyer behaviour can also affect market outcomes. When buyer decisions are simulated, details of the purchasing rules can have a large effect on prices (Kruse, 1993). Powerful human buyers can substantially undermine both market power and tacit collusion (Ruffle, 2000). However, the use of real rather than simulated buyers appears to generate more competitive prices even when the human buyers engage in no strategic behaviour (Coursey et al., 1984).

Finally, information conditions and even sellers' expectations can significantly affect pricing outcomes. For example, Huck, Norman and Oechssler (2000) report that information regarding underlying supply and demand conditions facilitates the exercise of predicted market power (markets are drawn to static Nash predictions). However, information on rival sellers' profits made markets more competitive in a market where the high-profit seller has the highest market share, so imitation by others will tend to expand quantity and reduce price. Also, in a Cournot context, Huck et al. (2007) report that seller aspirations for increased profits helped consolidated sellers maintain prices substantially above static Nash levels.

DOUGLAS D. DAVIS

See also **antitrust enforcement; Bertrand competition; experimental economics; market institutions.**

Bibliography

Alger, D. 1987. Laboratory tests of equilibrium predictions with disequilibrium price data. *Review of Economic Studies* 54, 105–45.

Cason, T.N. and Williams, A.W. 1990. Competitive equilibrium convergence in posted-offer markets with extreme earnings inequities. *Journal of Economic Behavior and Organization* 14, 331–52.

Coursey, D., Isaac, R.M., Luke, M. and Smith, V.L. 1984. Market contestability in the presence of sunk (entry) costs. *RAND Journal of Economics* 15, 69–84.

Davis, D.D. and Holt, C.A. 1993. *Experimental Economics.* Princeton: Princeton University Press.

Davis, D.D. and Holt, C.A. 1994. Market power and mergers in laboratory markets with posted prices. *RAND Journal of Economics* 25, 467–87.

Davis, D.D. and Holt, C.A. 1998. Conspiracies and secret discounts in laboratory markets. *Economic Journal* 108, 736–56.

Davis, D.D. and Wilson, B. 2002. An experimental investigation of methods for detecting collusion. *Economic Inquiry* 40, 213–30.

Dufwenberg, M. and Gneezy, U. 2000. Price competition and market concentration: an experimental study. *International Journal of Industrial Organization* 18, 7–22.

Durham, Y., McCabe, K., Olson, M.A., Rassenti, S. and Smith, V. 2004. Oligopoly competition in fixed cost environments. *International Journal of Industrial Organization* 22, 147–62.

Fouraker, L.E. and Siegel, S. 1963. *Bargaining Behavior.* New York: McGraw-Hill.

Godby, R. 2000. Market power and emission trading: theory and laboratory results. *Pacific Economic Review* 5, 349–64.

Grether, D.M. and Plott, C.R. 1984. The effects of market practices in oligopolistic markets: an experimental examination of the ethyl case. *Economic Inquiry* 24, 479–507.

Holt, C.A. 1995. Industrial organization: a survey of laboratory research. In *The Handbook of Industrial Organization*, ed. J.H. Kagel and A.E. Roth. Princeton: Princeton University Press.

Holt, C.A. and Davis, D.D. 1990. The effects of non-binding price announcements on posted-offer markets. *Economics Letters* 34, 307–10.

Huck, S., Normann, H. and Oechssler, J. 2000. Does information about competitors' actions increase or decrease competition in experimental oligopoly markets? *International Journal of Industrial Organization* 18, 39–57.

Huck, S., Konrad, K.A., Müller, W. and Normann, H.T. 2007. The merger paradox and why aspiration levels let it fail in the laboratory. *Economic Journal* 117, 1073–95.

Isaac, R.M., Ramey, V. and Williams, A. 1984. The effects of market organization on conspiracies in restraint of trade. *Journal of Economic Behavior and Organization* 5, 191–222.

Kruse, J.B. 1993. Nash equilibrium and buyer rationing rules: experimental evidence. *Economic Inquiry* 31, 631–66.

Phillips, O.R. and Mason, C.F. 1991. Mutual forbearance in experimental congolomerate markets. *RAND Journal of Economics* 23, 395–414.

Rassenti, S.J., Smith, V.L. and Wilson, B.J. 2003. Controlling market power and price spikes in electricity networks: demand-side bidding. *Proceedings of the National Academy of Sciences* 100, 2998–3003.

Ruffle, B.J. 2000. Some factors affecting demand withholding in posted-offer markets. *Economic Theory* 16, 529–44.

Wilson, B.J. 1998. What collusion? Unilateral market power as a catalyst for countercyclical markups. *Experimental Economics* 1, 133–45.

market price

The market price, or market value, is defined as the actual price paid for a commodity during a certain period of time, and may be contrasted with the natural or normal price, which is determined by the long-term forces and the permanent causes of the value of commodities (*see* NATURAL PRICE).

The distinction between market price and the intrinsic value of a good can be traced back to the origins of economic science. Before Adam Smith, Richard Cantillon had already analysed the causes which influence the temporary value of a commodity (Hollander, 1973, p. 41).

Many different causes can affect the market price of a commodity and it is difficult to explain the day-to-day changes in its value. However, economic theory has generally singled out the relationship between the demand for a product and its supply on the market as the main force determining the market value. For Smith, the existence of a positive difference between the effectual demand for a commodity and the quantity of it which has been produced and brought to the market leads to a high market price vis-à-vis the natural value, and vice versa. But if there is free competition between producers, market prices cannot be too different from natural prices for a long period of time. Market competition forces lead to the gravitation of market prices around the natural prices. Therefore in classical political economy the two concepts are carefully listed. In particular, the market price is continuously brought towards the natural price.

The concept of market price is an important feature of Adam Smith's description of the competitive mechanism and the way in which it leads to a uniform rate of profit in all sectors of the economy. For instance, when the supply of a commodity falls short of its effectual demand the market price is higher than the natural one, because of the competition between the buyers who are eager to purchase that good (Smith, 1776, pp. 73–4). Either one or more of the three component elements of value – wages, profits and rent – is paid at a rate higher than the natural rate. In a freely competitive economy producers compare their rate of profit with profit rates earned in other activities. Thus entrepreneurs invest their capital in the sectors which yield the highest rates or profit. This leads to an increase in the output of the commodities whose market prices are higher than natural ones, and vice versa a decrease when market prices are lower than natural values. Therefore the concept of market price is part of Smith's explanation of the changes in output which occur from one production period to another in each sector.

Given the natural price, and the corresponding level of effectual demand, the increase in output leads to a market situation in which more consumers (willing to pay for the good at its natural price) can be satisfied. There is less competition than before between the consumers, and the market price tends to move towards the natural price. Again, the entrepreneurs compare market prices and profit rates in all sectors of the economy and capital will move if the rate of profit is not uniform. Only when all the demand is matched by an equal supply at a market price level which equals the natural one will competition stop; in this situation the market price is exactly the right amount to pay all the components of price at their natural values. The market price depends on excess demand (or supply) on the market at any moment in time, but cannot be too far away from the natural price for a long period of time, because competition tends to bring it towards this level.

Alfred Marshall's distinction between the market and normal value of commodities is similar to Adam Smith's. Normal value is related to the cost production of commodities, while market prices are mainly influenced by utility and demand (Marshall, 1920, pp. 289–90). Marshall also believes that it is difficult to work out a precise theory to determine the market values of commodities; they are affected by too many factors. Marshall argues that there are long and short period forces acting on prices. But he is much more sceptical than Smith about the existence of a precise mechanism, namely competition, which should prevent short-term market prices from moving too far away from the normal price of commodities.

G. VAGGI

See also **natural price**.

Bibliography

Hollander, S. 1973. *The Economics of Adam Smith*. London: Heinemann.

Marshall, A. 1920. *Principles of Economics*. 8th edn. Reprinted, London: Macmillan, 1972.

Smith, A. 1776. *An Inquiry into the Nature and Causes of the Wealth of Nations*. Oxford: Oxford University Press, 1976.

market structure

Why is the world market for large commercial jet aircraft dominated by just two firms, while oil tankers are produced by a large number of firms spread over many countries? This is the kind of question addressed in the literature on 'market structure', a field once seen as a rather arcane area, in which explanatory theories were weak and in which discussion tended to focus on rival interpretations of 'statistical regularities' reported in empirical studies. The most famous of these 'regularities' related to a supposed link, across different industries, between the degree to which the industry was dominated by a few large firms ('concentration'), and some average measure of the rate of return (profit) on fixed assets enjoyed by firms in the industry. (Popular summary measures of concentration include the 'k-firm concentration ratio', that is, the share of industry sales revenue accounted for by the top k firms, and the Herfindahl index, defined as the sum of squares of all firms' market shares). Now the presence of a (positive) relation of this

kind would raise the question, 'why do industries with high rates of profit not attract entry, to the point where such differences are eroded?' This question was countered in the older literature, following Bain (1956), by appealing to the supposed existence of 'barriers to entry' in various industries. These barriers fell into three categories. The first related to factors intrinsic to the industry's methods of production ('scale economies'). If the average cost of production falls sharply as output rises to a certain level, then we might regard that level as a 'minimum efficient scale', and postulate that the industry is large enough to accommodate only a small number of firms of this size. This point was, and remains, uncontroversial. The second category related to institutional barriers associated with legal or regulatory impediments, or poor access to financial markets, and so on, but, while barriers of this category may be important in some industries and for some countries, they are probably of secondary relevance to the general run of industries in market economies. The third type of barrier related to the role played by advertising and R&D, and it is here that some serious difficulties arise, a point to which we turn in what follows.

The series of ideas just set out came to be known as the Bain paradigm, or the Structure–Conduct–Performance paradigm. Expressed briefly, this view held that a more concentrated structure, however sustained, allowed firms to operate less intensive forms of price competition ('conduct'), and this in turn led to high profits ('performance'). This view was seriously undermined in the 1980s as a result of two developments in the literature. The first of these developments was empirical: it became clear, in the light of new empirical studies, that the claim for a positive relationship between concentration and profitability was not well-founded. (For a review of the evidence, see Schmalensee, 1989.) The second development was theoretical: it was clear that any successful explanation of differences in concentration across industries could not rely solely on 'scale economies' and 'institutional barriers'; the role played by advertising and R&D in raising the stakes required of entrants to an industry seemed crucial. But here a problem arises: the levels of advertising and R&D, unlike the degree of scale economies, are matters that are under the control of the firms themselves. The levels of expenditure firms undertake in these areas are ground out as part of the competitive process – and so we cannot treat their levels as a given, and claim that, when we observe a high ratio of advertising and/or R&D to industry sales revenue, this constitutes a 'barrier to entry' that explains the industry's high level of concentration. Rather, an explanation of market structure must explain *both* the level of concentration *and* the levels of advertising and R&D intensity. The 'given' that distinguishes one industry from another must not be the observed (or 'equilibrium') *level* of advertising or R&D, but rather the underlying (industry-specific) relationship between any firm's level of spending on these fixed outlays and the resulting benefit ('perceived product quality', say, or, more generally, any effect leading to an outward shift in the firm's demand schedule or a fall in its unit cost of production).

These problems with the older literature led from the late 1980s onwards to the development of a new literature on market structure. (See, for example, Dasgupta and Stiglitz, 1980; Shaked and Sutton, 1986; Sutton, 1991; 1998. A full technical review of the literature will be found in Sutton, 2007.) The point of departure of this literature lies in modelling the evolution of structure by reference to a 'free entry' model, in which any one of a number of potential entrants is free to enter the industry, and to choose its level of outlays on advertising, R&D, and so on, in the light of the choices made by its rivals.

The modern game-theoretic literature

The models used in the modern literature take the form of 'multi-stage games'. In the simplest example, a firm decides, at stage 1, to enter (and pay some positive, minimal, entry fee whose size is a given, and which can, for example, be interpreted as the cost of building a production plant of 'minimum efficient scale'). At stage 2, each firm, knowing the number of firms that have entered, chooses its level(s) of advertising and/or R&D. Its choices will depend inter alia on the (industry-specific) degree of effectiveness of these expenditures in influencing consumer demand for its product(s). In 'commodity' type industries, where this effectiveness is very low, these outlays will be close to zero. Finally, in stage 3, firms compete in price, taking as given the attributes of their respective products, and they realize corresponding levels of (gross) profits. (It is always assumed that firms have constant marginal costs of production, and that they face downward-sloping demand schedules.)

The central idea that emerges from these ('endogenous sunk costs') models is as follows: as the size of the market increases (in the sense of having a larger number of consumers, so that each firm's demand schedule shifts outwards) the industry may adjust to this in two ways: the number of firms may rise ('entry'), and/or the spending level per firm on advertising, R&D, and so on, may rise – because, in the absence of a proportional rise in the number of firms, each firm now enjoys a higher level of demand, and so the marginal return it gains from being able to charge a given price premium for a higher-quality product rises ('escalation'). Now the degree to which one or other of these effects operates depends inter alia on the effectiveness of advertising and/or R&D. It also depends on the degree to which high-quality products can draw customers away from rival products of a lower quality. Suppose, for example, that products differ not only in quality, but in other attributes also, and that customers differ in their preferences over these latter attributes. Then it will be correspondingly harder for a firm that raises its 'perceived quality' level to attract sales from rivals. An example may be helpful here: consider, for instance, the market for flowmeters. These devices are used to measure the rate of flow of liquids, and they come in a large number of types. An increase in R&D spending by a producer of 'electromagnetic' flowmeters will have only a limited impact in drawing consumers away from 'ultrasonic' flowmeters, since the latter type of meter has attributes that makes it better suited than the electromagnetic type in certain applications. By way of contrast, consider the case of the (civil) aircraft industry, as it developed since the late 1920s. At that period, there were many types of plane in operation (monoplanes/biplanes, metal/wood construction, land/seaplanes, and so on). Yet all makers faced a market where all buyers (airlines) sought to achieve the same objective: to minimize the carrying cost per passenger mile. As soon as it became clear which type of design best achieved this single aim, plane-makers converged on the solution (an all metal monoplane with a cantilever wing design, following the Douglas DC3). Thereafter, technical developments were focused on pushing forward the performance of this type of plane, and, as plane-makers escalated their efforts in this direction, the stakes required to keep up with rival firms' innovations rose, and there was a 'shake-out' of all but a handful of firms. This story was repeated at the dawn of the jet age in the 1950s. Here a growing world market led, not to the entry of new plane-makers, but to an increasing flow of development outlays by the surviving firms, so that only Boeing and Airbus remain in the wide-body commercial jet business today. (For the details of this story, and the rise of Airbus, see Sutton, 1998, ch. 15.)

Where does this leave us? The kind of market profiles that emerge are these: (*a*) those with high R&D outlays and high global concentration (for example, wide-body commercial jets); (*b*) those with high R&D outlays, low concentration and a fragmented set of distinct product categories (for example, flowmeters); and (*c*) those with low R&D spending, where, once the size of the market is large, the level of concentration may become arbitrarily low.

Within advertising-intensive industries, a simpler picture emerges. Here, the fact that a firm can use a single brand to span a range of product types in a market means that we can, with few exceptions, define markets in a way that avoids the complication posed by the presence of sub-markets for distinct product types, of the kind we encountered in the flowmeter example above. Here, the theory leads to a very simple prediction: if we take a cross-section of markets of different sizes (by looking, say, at a single industry across a number of countries of different sizes), then we will find a sharp difference in the market size–concentration relationship as between the 'advertising-intensive' industries and a control group of industries in which advertising plays an insignificant role. In the latter group, very low levels of concentration may be reached as market size increases. In the former group, concentration levels will necessarily remain above some critical level in all countries, no matter how large the size of the country (the 'non-convergence' property). This prediction, and related predictions of the theory, have been widely tested over the past decade and appears to be closely in line with what is found in the data (for a review, see Sutton, 2007).

One further comment is called for in relation to this prediction: what is predicted is not an actual or equilibrium level of concentration, but rather a *lower bound* to the level of concentration that can emerge under given circumstances. It is intrinsic to models of this kind that a range of different outcomes is possible, depending on such factors as the form of the entry process (simultaneous, sequential, and so on). The most graphic illustration of this point comes from thinking about the pattern of ownership of plants spread over some geographic region large enough to support many plants. There will be a 'fragmented' equilibrium in which every plant is owned by a different firm, and there will be other equilibria in which the number of plants will remain (roughly) the same, but several of these plants will be owned by the same firm. In other words, a range of outcomes can arise as equilibria, depending on the form of the entry process and the nature of price competition, and the theoretical focus of interest lies in asking, not about the actual outcome, but about the range of possible outcomes, or, more specifically, about the lower bound to the level of concentration that can emerge.

Extensions: learning effects and network externalities

Two further ('dynamic') mechanisms play a role in explaining high levels of concentration. First, if each firm's unit cost level falls over time as a function of its cumulated volume of output to date, then an early entrant may build a dominant market position by setting an initial low price – possibly below its current unit variable cost of production – with a view to achieving a high output volume, and so a relatively low level of unit cost in the future. In a small number of industries – aircraft, semiconductors and chemical fibres – this effect is quite large.

Second, if the attractiveness of a firm's product to new consumers increases with the number of consumers it has supplied in the past, then again a firm may use an initial low price to build up its early client base and so stimulate future demand (Katz and Shapiro, 1985). Examples of such effects abound in the information technology sector: as an item of hardware becomes more widely owned, more firms in the software industry will find it attractive to develop dedicated software for it, thus reinforcing its initial popularity.

What both these examples have in common with the endogenous sunk cost models described earlier becomes clear once we interpret the 'planned losses' incurred in the initial phase as a fixed outlay – analogous to an outlay on R&D or advertising – which yields a payoff in the later phase, either through lower unit costs or increased demand. The novel element which arises in these 'learning' or 'network effects' models is that these effects can be cumulative over time, and so a small initial disparity in the costs or sales of two firms may in principle become amplified over time.

Structure, conduct and performance revisited

What does this imply for the Structure–Conduct–Performance paradigm? If high concentration is merely the natural outcome of the competitive process, should we still see high concentration in an industry as an indication that policy intervention might be warranted?

At a conceptual level, what remains is this: it is still true within the modern 'free entry' models discussed above that structure affects conduct. It is also true that conduct affects performance; but now there is a feedback loop through which high levels of profit may attract new entry, that is, structure is not a given, but is now determined as part of the market process. One consequence that emerges from this is that there is no simple and general link, of the kind central to the old literature, between high concentration and high profitability: it is possible, for example, to have industries with widely different levels of concentration that exhibit no difference in their rates of return on investment. High ('supernormal') profits can, however, arise in these 'free entry' models, through a number of channels. Most notably, they may arise because of asymmetries in the entry process ('first mover advantages'): an early entrant to the market may build up a level of investment in R&D, for example, and so enjoy both a high market share and a high rate of return on its investments, so that the industry-wide levels of concentration and profitability are relatively high. A second channel relates to the important but neglected role of 'integer effects', that is, if there is room in market at equilibrium for only a small number of entrants, then it may be, for example, that two firms can both make supernormal profits, but the entry of a third firm would drive the profit rate below a normal rate of return, so further entry does not occur. Finally, and most importantly, variations in productivity (unit costs) across firms associated with non-imitable advantages can lead to positive (supernormal) profits for (all) intra-marginal firms – a free entry condition implies 'zero profits' only for the marginal entrant (Demsetz, 1973).

One key issue remains: what of comparisons between alternative forms of market structure within any one industry? This is the question that lies at the heart of competition policy regarding mergers. As we have seen, the normal workings of the competitive process fix a lower bound to the level of concentration that must come about under free competition. This bound can, in the case of some industries, be very high in absolute terms, even in a large market; but in other industries it will be very low. Above this bound, varying levels of concentration can emerge since various patterns of market structure can be sustained as equilibria (as in the example of geographically dispersed plants mentioned above). What remains true of the Structure–Conduct–Performance story is that these different market structures may have different welfare properties; a proposed merger that moves us towards a more concentrated structure which will lead to reduced consumer welfare will be subject to the traditional objections. On the other hand, it may be that a merger arises merely as a response to changes in external conditions, and represents a shift away from a form of market structure that constituted an equilibrium outcome under the previous setting, but is no longer sustainable as an equilibrium in this changed environment. Distinguishing between these two possibilities in any specific instance is one of the (many) challenges in dealing with merger cases.

Why does it matter?

The traditional rationale for studying market structure was based on its link to profitability and to social welfare. There is, however, another line of argument that has gained considerable force as a result of the empirical success of the modern free entry models in explaining cross-industry differences in concentration. This line of argument rests on the claim that the success of these models provides convincing, though indirect, evidence for the workings of some key competitive mechanisms that appear to operate in a more or less uniform way across a wide range of industries.

To place this in perspective, it is worth noting that the conventional wisdom in economics from the 1950s to the late 1980s was deeply pessimistic in respect of models that lay between the two polar cases of perfect competition or (Chamberlinian) monopolistic competition, on the one hand, and monopoly on the other. This pessimism was typically expressed in the observation, 'with oligopoly, anything can happen'. The new game-theoretic literature of the 1980s formalized oligopoly theory using the Nash equilibrium concept, and offered it as a general framework within which perfect competition and monopoly appeared as special (limiting) cases. While this new literature appeared to some critics to simply reinforce the negative view of oligopoly theory, the successful application of these game-theoretic models to the task of 'explaining market structure' suggests that the early pessimism is unwarranted: it seems that these models capture at least some 'robust' competitive mechanisms that operate in a more or less uniform way across the general run of industries.

JOHN SUTTON

See also **airline industry; antitrust enforcement.**

Bibliography
Bain, J. 1956. *Barriers to New Competition.* Cambridge, MA: Harvard University Press.
Dasgupta, P. and Stiglitz, J.E. 1980. Industrial structure and the nature of innovative activity. *Economic Journal* 90, 266–93.
Demsetz, H. 1973. Industry structure, market rivalry, and public policy. *Journal of Law and Economics* 20, 113–24.
Katz, M.L. and Shapiro, C. 1985. Network externalities, competition and compatibility. *American Economic Review* 75, 424–40.
Schmalensee, R. 1989. Inter-industry studies of structure and performance. In *Handbook of Industrial Organization*, vol. 2, ed. R. Schmalensee and R. Willig. Amsterdam: North-Holland.
Shaked, A. and Sutton, J. 1986. Product differentiation and market structure. *Journal of Industrial Economics* 36, 131–46.
Sutton, J. 1991. *Sunk Costs and Market Structure.* Cambridge, MA: MIT Press.
Sutton, J. 1998. *Technology and Market Structure.* Cambridge, MA: MIT Press.
Sutton, J. 2007. Market structure: theory and evidence. In *Handbook of Industrial Organization*, vol. 3, ed. M. Armstrong and R. Porter. Amsterdam: North-Holland.

marketing boards

Marketing boards are state-controlled or state-sanctioned entities legally granted control over the purchase or sale of agricultural commodities. They can be divided into two broad categories. Monopolistic marketing boards that create a single-commodity seller are found mainly in developed countries. Monopsonistic marketing boards concentrating buyer-side market power in one institution were commonplace for many years in developing countries. Monopolistic marketing boards were typically established with the main objective of maintaining or raising and stabilizing farm prices and incomes in an administratively practical and politically acceptable manner. By contrast, monopsonistic marketing boards were typically established to give the state control over commodity prices – normally for the benefit of foreign and urban buyers – and capacity to tax agriculture so as to subsidize industrialization.

Marketing boards in developed countries

Marketing boards are state-sponsored trading enterprises legally invested with monopoly powers to organize the marketing of agricultural commodities. These statutory entities typically operate under direct or indirect producer control. Among the earliest boards were the New Zealand Meat Producers Board and the New Zealand Dairy Board, each established in 1922, the Australia Queensland Sugar Board of 1923, and the Australia

Wheat Board, formed in 1939. In Australia, marketing boards used import protection and home consumption price schemes to stabilize producer prices. They initially received financial support from the state, although such support later declined as the focus of the boards changed. A number of state and commonwealth-level marketing boards were later established, with varying degrees of authority and responsibilities in the marketing of agricultural products such as wool, dairy, meat, wine and brandy, honey and horticultural products. The marketing boards in New Zealand evolved in a similar manner, with regulatory authority in export marketing and licensing but no direct financial support from the state. These boards, involved in the marketing of dairy, apple and pear, kiwi fruit, horticulture, meat and wool products, all used activities such as single-desk selling, price pooling, revenue pooling and preferential financing to seek higher producer prices.

The earliest major marketing schemes in Britain were the milk, potatoes and bacon marketing boards formed under the British Marketing Acts of 1931 and 1933. These acts enabled producers to set up marketing schemes that had the legislative power to ensure conformity by all producers. The core purpose of the marketing boards was to maintain or raise producer prices of basic agricultural commodities through acreage restrictions, direct or indirect limits on saleable quantities, and price discrimination, with higher prices in sheltered markets and lower prices in exposed ones. In addition, monopolies of processed products were legalized, leading to the organization of processor and distributor schemes. The marketing boards thus held the monopoly power to control supply, the terms of sale and the channels and conditions of sale (Bauer, 1948). By 1948 marketing boards had spread to include all major agricultural commodities. In Canada, marketing boards were also formed in response to the price fluctuations of the Great Depression. The Dominion Marketing Board, a federal agency established under the National Farm Products Act of 1934, exercised extensive market power over the sale of regulated products, transferable to provincial-level producer-organized boards. The Agricultural Marketing Acts of 1940 and 1956 delineated the powers of regulation and market control activities for the established and new federal and provincial marketing boards. The result was marketing boards with diverse market powers and scope of operations across provinces, and across boards within the same province. Some marketing boards act only in a supervisory capacity, whereas others wield more extensive powers in market regulation and control. Activities generally range from negotiating minimum prices, regulating quantity and quality of marketed products, collecting and distributing payments, as well as grading and quality control.

Several common features distinguish marketing boards in developed countries from those found in developing nations. First, marketing boards in developed countries tend to be specialized in both scale and scope of operations. For example, New Zealand currently runs strictly export monopolies, such as the Dairy Board, that have control over the country's agricultural exports but negligible influence over domestic production, sales, imports or tariff rates.

Second, marketing boards in developed countries tend to subsidize farmers at the expense of consumers, as evidenced by their mandate to maintain high producer prices for farmers through limited supply. One result is that marketing boards in developed countries have tended to generate windfall profits for the owners of farm land and other sector-specific assets in agriculture.

Third, and following directly from their role in subsidizing farmers, state trading enterprises tend to encourage and support cartels at producer, processor and distributor levels. Developed country agricultural marketing boards have been a major issue in international trade because historically they dominated certain markets. For example, McCalla and Schmitz (1982) estimated that 95 per cent of world wheat trade in 1973–7 involved a state marketing board on at least one side of the transaction. Because marketing boards enjoy greater flexibility than private traders in pricing – for example, they can commonly delay payments to producers, pool payments so as to reduce producer price risk, and can practise discriminatory pricing among export or import markets – their operations are closely scrutinized by the World Trade Organization for prospectively anti-competitive practices.

Marketing boards in developing countries

Marketing boards in developing countries were typically begun during colonial times for purposes distinct from those of their counterpart marketing boards in developed economies. And they have followed a somewhat different trajectory from those of marketing boards in developed countries.

European colonial powers formed marketing boards in large measure to facilitate the export of agricultural commodities to Europe and to stabilize prices faced by colonial elites (for food crops) and metropolitan buyers (for export crops). Post-independence governments generally maintained marketing boards because these were considered simpler to manage and more efficient in conducting organized trade than the traditional, decentralized private sector. More compellingly, marketing boards provided a convenient way for the governments to maintain control over the marketing of strategic commodities, such as the food staples and important export crops (Lele and Christiansen, 1989). The marketing boards system was most prevalent in the anglophone African and South Asian countries, but widespread as well in francophone and lusophone African countries and in Asia and Latin America.

Marketing boards were both state-owned and state-funded, based on centralized decision making systems.

They possessed the sole legal authority to purchase commodities from farmers and to engage in trade. Through the boards, governments typically fixed official producer prices for all controlled commodities, often in a pan-seasonal and pan-territorial manner whereby a single price was set for the whole marketing season and for all regions of the country. Marketing boards provided a guaranteed market for the farmers, absorbing all marketed surplus at the official producer prices, and maintaining extensive buying networks and storage facilities throughout the production regions. Pan-seasonal and pan-territorial pricing practices eliminated any opportunities for arbitrage, discouraging private investment in commodity storage or transport capacity, and reinforcing the government's control over the marketing channel. Unlike marketing boards in developed countries, producer sales into the network were rarely rationed, because the marketing boards' objective was normally to increase supply and lower prices for consumers, as opposed to controlling supply for the benefit of producers.

Two features of the export crop marketing boards – as distinct from those handling staple food commodities – are worth noting. First, the marketing boards held the sole legal rights in commodity export, and had a mandate to generate income for the state. Therefore, storage costs were maintained at low levels through selling policies such as rapid evacuation and forward selling. In addition, local producer prices were typically set at levels lower than the international free-on-board prices, through price fixing or overvalued exchange rates. Essentially, export crop marketing boards were used as a means to tax agriculture in order to develop the industrial sector in these agrarian economies. The taxes were often quite severe. In Tanzania, for example, local producer prices for coffee and tobacco fell to 23 per cent and 15 per cent of international prices, respectively, by the mid-1980s.

Second, because export crop marketing boards served foreign demand, no price controls existed on the selling end. Marketing boards could trade on an open market for the highest possible selling prices. However, because most of the former European colonies enjoyed preferential access to European markets under the Lomé Convention, most commodities were sold to Europe. In addition, some export crops enjoyed commodity price stabilization through international commodity agreements such as the International Coffee Agreement or the International Rubber Agreement. In those cases where a country enjoys world market power, a state marketing board can, at least in theory, increase prices and thereby extract consumer surplus from foreign buyers to benefit the exporting country, including its producers. This is one of the concerns surrounding state trading enterprises within global trade policy fora.

Even though the export crop marketing boards were generally established first, in most developing countries staple food commodity marketing boards became at least as significant a part of the parastatal system. For food commodities, government control extended to every stage of the market chain, to include farm gate, wholesale and retail price controls. In-country commodity movement was restricted, especially the movement of strategic food commodities, and private trade was either illegal or legal only by licence. To achieve food security objectives, food subsidies were generally offered, mostly implicitly, in the form of fixed consumer prices set at levels lower than the market price. Although farm prices were generally set at a below-market level as well, the government often offered implicit subsidies to farmers, through price stabilization operations, and input and credit subsidies administered through the marketing boards (Lele and Christiansen, 1989). Moreover, pan-territorial pricing typically implied subsidies for farmers in more remote smallholder regions. In some countries and for some crops, these arrangements likely stimulated greater crop production than would have occurred under open market arrangements.

Grain marketing boards commonly also handled the strategic food reserves for emergency situations, and had the responsibility to import food in shortage seasons. These parastatals therefore held most of their nations' inter-seasonal and inter-annual grain storage capacity, a legacy that would affect inter-seasonal commodity price movements after the liberalization of commodity marketing systems in the 1980s and 1990s. Although processing was not their core business, marketing boards, in some cases, were also involved in preliminary processing, such as milling rice or maize, or in licensing and monitoring the processing industry activities. This underscores an important difference from developed country marketing boards: the breadth of commodity marketing boards' mandate in most developing countries.

Over time, the fiscal sustainability of marketing boards in developing countries became questionable. The broad range of marketing operations handled by marketing boards and the politically charged manner in which these operations were typically handled led to massive inefficiencies and deficits that cash-strapped central governments had an increasingly difficult time covering. The subsidies embedded in grains pricing systems, coupled with heavy overhead costs associated with high administrative, transportation and storage costs, soon created huge tax burdens. In an attempt to ensure food security, the state would generally increase producer prices with less than proportional increases in consumer prices, taking on responsibility for a significant share of the marketing costs associated with moving food from farm to table. The pan-territorial pricing system meant higher transportation and handling costs in moving commodities from some remote areas, and the management of large volumes of commodities in storage was costly. In addition, the monitoring of private trade was not only costly but generally ineffective, especially for food commodities in shortage seasons, when parallel markets flourished to meet local demand. In Mali, for example, even though private cereals trade was illegal before 1981, only 30–40 per cent of total grain trade was actually handled by the state trading agency, OPAM (Staatz, Dioné and Dembélé, 1989). On the international market, marketing boards faced decreasing real commodity prices for export crops, further undermining their sustainability.

By the end of the 1970s budget deficits resulting from the management and mismanagement of parastatals had reached astronomical levels in most countries. In Mali, OPAM's annual deficit reached US$80 million by 1980, three times the board's annual grain sales. In Tanzania, the National Marketing Corporation's overdrafts were about $250 million in 1993, against total state expenditures on agriculture of $12million. The National Cereals and Produce Board (NCPB) of Kenya accumulated an estimated loss of about $300 million by 1993, in contrast with central government expenditure on agriculture of $33 million (Dembélé and Staatz, 2002; Lele and Christiansen, 1989). These patterns were by no means exclusive to Africa. Indonesia's price stabilization scheme for rice, managed by the National Logistics Supply Organization (BULOG), also proved a high price to pay for self-sufficiency, as did the Food Corporation of India.

In addition to budgetary complications, marketing boards also faced organizational challenges. Their susceptibility to bureaucracy and corruption increased both the inefficiency in their operations and the transactions costs for farmers and consumers. For example, Arhin, Hesp and van der Laan (1985) argue that by the mid-1970s the Ghana Cocoa Marketing Board had become little more than an instrument of the government for the purpose of mobilizing political support for the incumbent government.

Mounting deficits, poor management and the perverse incentives created by anti-competitive behaviour brought marketing boards and price stabilization systems under attack, based in part on seminal research into the welfare effects of government interventions to stabilize commodity prices (Newbery and Stiglitz, 1981). These deficit problems, coupled with the new economic insights, triggered widespread agricultural market reforms in the 1980s and 1990s throughout the developing world, implemented mainly but not exclusively, in the context of structural adjustment programmes (SAPs) of the World Bank and the International Monetary Fund.

Agricultural marketing reforms generally aimed to reduce the role of the public sector in marketing and to encourage private sector participation so as to let markets allocate scarce goods more efficiently. Marketing boards experienced major reforms under these programmes, comprising the elimination of price controls, termination of farm input and consumer food subsidies, removal of marketing boards' monopsony power and deregulation of private trade. In many cases, marketing boards were privatized or at least commercialized, the latter referring to cases where marketing boards remained government owned, but with autonomous decision-making power

and an explicit objective to maximize profits. The logic was that, by removing political interference in the marketing process, market forces would lead to efficient resource allocation and price discovery. Market deregulation was thus expected to improve marketing efficiency by reducing transactions costs, increasing producer prices, thus inducing increased production and potentially also lowering consumer prices.

The response of the market was immediate and quite dramatic in many cases. Entry into formerly controlled agricultural markets was massive in most countries, although with continued bottlenecks in functions requiring significant capital outlays, such as bulk inter-seasonal storage and long-haul motorized transport, entry was typically restricted to niches with low entry barriers (Barrett, 1997). Nonetheless, formal and informal private traders became a significant part of the marketing channel, performing most of the trade activities that the marketing boards previously performed.

In spite of widespread liberalization, marketing operations for most 'strategic' food and export crops changed little. Newly privatized or commercialized marketing boards were often replaced with 'new' marketing boards that were initially intended to provide public goods, but eventually and predictably became involved in crop marketing. In Zambia, for example, the government-owned Food Reserve Agency (FRA) that replaced the National Agricultural Marketing Board (NAMBOARD) in 1995, charged with maintaining the strategic grain reserve and acting as a buyer of last resort for smallholder farmers, in time took up prior NAMBOARD responsibilities such as fertilizer distribution. Moreover, some of the commercialized marketing boards did not significantly change their pricing systems and continued to use the power of the state to remain dominant players in the current market system. In Indonesia for example, even though the market was opened to private traders, BULOG remained a price leader by operating a major buffer stock, purchasing rice when rice prices fell below a stated floor price and releasing stocks when prices rose above a price ceiling. Similarly, in the Kenyan maize sector the NCPB continued to intervene directly in markets to support maize prices; and in Malawi ADMARC remains the dominant maize buyer and distributor of inputs. Zimbabwe went so far as to reinstate the monopsony power of the Grain Marketing Board and its pre-reform operations. Not surprisingly, the budget deficit of these marketing boards actually increased after reforms.

These trends reflect governments' reluctance to relinquish control over marketing board operations, particularly the setting of prices for key food and export crops, given political sensitivity to these issues. As it turned out, such concerns were not completely unwarranted. In many developing countries the legacy of private underinvestment in storage and transport capacity, inadequate commercial trading skills in the nascent private sector, combined with limited access to finance, restricted entry into key niches of the marketing channel. These market conditions facilitated the emergence of new monopolies, often substituting private for public market power. Problems of weak contract enforcement, unreliable physical security and underdeveloped communications and transport infrastructure often impeded business expansion, market integration and price transmission. Despite increased private investment in transportation and storage infrastructure after reforms, the weaknesses of the existing systems implied considerable business risk. Consequently, private traders did not fully or quickly fill the voids left by the withdrawal of the marketing boards from core commodity market intermediation functions. Price volatility increased sharply in many countries. Moreover, farmers' access to seasonal credit dropped significantly as market liberalization ended formerly monopsonistic marketing boards' willingness to extend seasonal credit to growers that were collateralized by future sales. Reduced credit often led to fewer purchased inputs and lower crop output. In an attempt to restore market stability and production volumes, states often suspended or reversed reforms, reinstating price controls and trade restrictions, thereby further exacerbating instability and undermining investor confidence. The result has been incomplete reforms in most developing countries, where private sector involvement remains pervasive but small-scale and weak, while unprofitable commercialized marketing boards remain prominent and prone to government interference.

The current state of play

Far fewer marketing boards exist than previously. Because they reduce or eliminate competition, marketing boards are widely believed to induce inefficiency in marketing and sluggishness in price discovery. Therefore, government involvement in agricultural marketing has been weakening in both developed and developing countries since the mid-1980s, a result of the adoption of more liberal domestic economic policies, coupled with global pressure to conform to international trade rules steadily expanding their coverage of agriculture. The monopoly or monopsony powers of all but a few marketing boards have been lifted, and the marketing and processing activities of the boards have been streamlined. Where reforms have been widespread and successful, marketing boards have vanished or retreated to providing public goods, such as strategic grain reserves or insurance against extraordinary price fluctuations. Where reforms have been halting or unsuccessful, the weaknesses of private agricultural marketing channels have been laid bare by the rollback of marketing boards.

CHRISTOPHER B. BARRETT AND EMELLY MUTAMBATSERE

See also **agricultural markets in developing countries; agriculture and economic development; international trade theory.**

Bibliography

Arhin, K., Hesp, P. and van der Laan, L. 1985. *Marketing Boards in Tropical Africa*. Nairobi: KIP Limited.

Barrett, C. 1997. Food marketing liberalization and trader entry: evidence from Madagascar. *World Development* 25, 763–77.

Bauer, P. 1948. A review of the agricultural marketing schemes. *Economica* 15, 132–50.

Dembélé, N. and Staatz, J. 2002. The impact of market reform on agricultural transformation in Mali. In *Perspectives on Agricultural Transformation: A View from Africa*, ed. T. Jayne, I. Minde and G. Argwings-Kodhek. Hauppauge, NY: Nova Science Publishers Inc.

Lele, U. and Christiansen, R. 1989. *Markets, Marketing Boards and Cooperatives in Africa, Issues in Adjustment Policy*. MADIA Discussion Paper 11. Washington, DC: World Bank.

McCalla, A. and Schmitz, A. 1982. State trading in grain. In *State Trading in International Markets*, ed. M. Kostecki. New York: St Martin's Press.

Newbery, D. and Stiglitz, J. 1981. *The Theory of Commodity Price Stabilization*. Oxford: Clarendon Press.

Staatz, J., Dioné, J. and Dembélé, N. 1989. Cereals market liberalization in Mali. *World Development* 17, 703–18.

markets

Markets dominate modern life, and economists have for long been concerned about market prices, but, despite this ongoing preoccupation, until recently there has been little discussion of the nature and operation of markets themselves.

No fewer than three Nobel Laureates in economics have noted this paradox. George Stigler (1967, p. 291) wrote: 'The efficacy of markets should be of great interest to the economist: Economic theory is concerned with markets much more than with factories or kitchens. It is, therefore, a source of embarrassment that so little attention has been paid to the theory of markets and that little chiefly to speculation.' Stigler made a plea for the theoretical study of markets, which for a long time went unheard.

Ten years later Douglass North (1977, p. 710) similarly remarked: 'It is a peculiar fact that the literature on economics and economic history contains so little discussion of the central institution that underlies neoclassical economics – the market'. Another 11 years had passed when Ronald Coase (1988, p. 7) observed that 'in modern economic theory the market itself has an even more shadowy role than the firm'. Economists are interested only in 'the determination of market prices' whereas 'discussion of the market place itself has entirely disappeared'.

Economists have had little to say about the nature of markets, other than classifying them by their degrees of competition and their numbers of buyers and sellers. Beyond this, the institutional aspects of markets have been widely neglected. For much of the 20th century there has been little discussion of how specific markets are structured to select and authenticate information, and of how specific prices are actually formed. Furthermore, 'the market' was treated as a relatively homogeneous and undifferentiated entity, with little consideration of different market mechanisms and structures. When market mechanisms were addressed this was typically confined within the framework of general equilibrium theory, with relatively little attention to the institutional details and alternative market structures.

Inspection of standard economics textbooks confirms these observations. While market outcomes such as prices are always central to the discussion, there is generally little consideration of the detailed rules and mechanisms through which prices are formed, and the concept of the market itself often goes undefined. Indeed, there is an entry on markets in neither the massive 1968 edition of the *Encyclopaedia of the Social Sciences* nor the otherwise comprehensive 1987 edition of *The New Palgrave: A Dictionary of Economics*.

Three questions arise. First, what briefly is the nature of markets and how can the market be defined? Second, why has the specific anatomy of markets been neglected by economists? Third, what recent developments in economics and elsewhere help to remedy the deficiency? After a brief historical discussion this article addresses these questions.

Historical background

Goods have changed hands within human societies for hundreds of thousands of years. However, much of this internal circulation was powered by custom and tradition. Transfers of goods often involved ceremony and personal, reciprocal actions. These personal and kin-based exchanges contrast with the organized and competitive pecuniary ambiance of modern markets. Ceremonial transfers involved 'the continuous definition, maintenance and fulfilment of mutual roles within an elaborate machinery of status and privilege' (Clarke, 1987, p. 4). Most of this internal circulation of goods was devoid of any conception of the voluntary, contractual transfer of ownership or property rights. These reciprocal transfers of goods were more to do with the validation of custom and social rank.

Something more akin to trade existed at least as far back as the last ice age. However, this trade was largely peripheral and occurred at the meeting of different tribal groups. As Max Weber (1927, p. 195) attested, it did not take place 'between members of the same tribe or of the same community' but was 'in the oldest social communities an external phenomenon, being directed only towards foreign tribes'. This contention that trade began externally and between communities rather than within them has withstood subsequent scholarly examination. Trade was typically a collective and *inter*-social enterprise between one tribe and another.

With the rise of the ancient civilizations, both external and internal trade increased substantially. The development of money and coinage facilitated its expansion. A definable internal commodity market (or *agora*), with multiple buyers and sellers, first appeared in a designated open space in Athens in the sixth century BC (Polanyi, 1971; North, 1977). The *agora* opened frequently and had strict trading rules. At around the same time there existed an annual auction market on Babylonia: young women were put on display and male bidders competed for marriage rights (Cassady, 1967). Nevertheless, some scholars have warned against the view that these ancient civilizations were generally and predominantly market economies (Finley, 1962; Polanyi, Arensberg and Pearson, 1957). By contrast, researchers such as Peter Temin (2006) have argued that the Roman Empire in particular contained developed and interlocking markets with variable prices, albeit without a highly developed banking system and with a relatively limited market for capital.

European and Mediterranean trade contracted after the fall of the Roman Empire. When commerce began to develop again in medieval times, internal markets then had a limited role in the medieval economy. 'Strange though it may seem', wrote the historian Henri Pirenne (1937, p. 140), 'medieval commerce developed from the beginning not of local but of export trade.' Although there are likely to have been other earlier organized markets in England, systematic evidence of the king enforcing his right to license all markets and fairs does not appear until the 13th century.

Markets for slaves existed in classical antiquity and persisted in some regions until the modern era. By contrast, feudal serfs were not owned as chattels, but they did not enjoy the right to choose their masters. Feudal institutions, driven by traditional obligations rather than voluntary contract, meant that the hiring of labourers was marginalized and markets for wage labourers were rare. With the decline of bonded labour, which began as early as the 14th century in England, employment contracts were limited largely to casual labourers, alongside a large number of self-employed producers and others in peasant family units. In England it was not until about the 18th century that a class of potentially mobile wage labourers emerged who constituted the most important source of labour power. Organized markets for employees, involving labour exchanges or employment agents, did not become prominent until the 19th century.

To turn to capital markets, an early market for debts was the French *courratier de change* in the 12th century. In the 13th century, after the development of a banking system in Venice, trade began in government securities in several Italian cities. In 1309 a 'Beurse' was organised in Bruges in Flanders, named after the Van der Beurse family, who had previously hosted regular commodity exchanges in their residence. Soon after, similar 'Beurzen' opened in Ghent and Amsterdam. In 1602 the Dutch East India Company issued the first shares on the Amsterdam

Bourse or Stock Exchange. The London Stock Exchange, founded in 1801, traces its origins to 1697 when commodity and stock prices began to be published in a London coffee house. The origins of the New York Stock Exchange go back to 1792, when 24 stockbrokers organized a regular market for stocks in Wall Street. Accordingly, developed capital markets first appeared in the Netherlands in the 17th century and later spread to other countries.

Overall, in the last 400 years markets have expanded enormously in scope, volume and economic importance. Markets have come to pervade internal as well as external trade and to dominate the global economic system. The modern era of globalization is often identified with the growth of global commodity and financial markets since the middle of the 19th century.

This brief historical sketch is background for the task of defining markets. At least three options emerge, involving different degrees of historical specificity. The broadest definition would be to use the term 'market' to refer to all forms of transfer of goods or services between persons, including the age-old customary or ceremonial transfers within tribes and households, exchanges of property between tribes, and modern organized markets with multiple buyers and sellers. We consider this option and some more restrictive alternatives next.

The nature of markets

The Austrian school economist Ludwig von Mises (1949) is exceptional among economists in devoting a lengthy chapter to 'the market'. He sees the market economy as 'the social system of the division of labour under private ownership of the means of production' (1949, p. 257). He explicitly excludes economies under social or state ownership of the means of production from this category, but nevertheless regards such systems as strictly 'not realizable'. Consequently, the historical and territorial boundaries of his concept of the market depend very much on what is regarded as 'private ownership'. He associates private ownership with the rise of civilization, and defines ownership in terms of full control of the services that derive from a good, rather than in legal terms. Together these specifications amount to a definition of the market that embraces all forms of trade or exchange that involve private property, defined loosely as assets under private control.

Although von Mises associates secure private property and exchange with the rise of civilization, these terms are defined in a manner that does not exclude their application to earlier periods of human history. It then becomes problematic whether or not ceremonial transfers and ritualistic gift-giving are regarded as 'exchanges' of 'property' and whether or not these activities come within the sphere of 'the market'. Essentially, the historical compass of the latter term depends very much on what we mean by notions such as exchange and property.

In downplaying the legal aspects of property and exchange, von Mises also fails to probe the nature of the rights that form part of the exchange. Instead he sustains the notion that uncoerced and informed consent by the parties to the transaction is a sufficient basis to constitute the contractual and property rights involved. A problem with this idea is that mutual individual consent itself requires a legislative and institutional framework to legitimize, scrutinize and protect those individual rights. The importance of this legal and constitutional framework is widely recognized, including by other Austrian theorists such as Friedrich Hayek (1960). Several historical cases of the spontaneous evolution of systems of enforced property rights do exist, but they generally rely on reputational and other monitoring mechanisms that are more difficult to sustain in large-scale, complex societies (Sened, 1997).

An alternative intellectual tradition places more emphasis on the legal and statutory basis of individual rights. This approach pervaded the 19th-century German Historical School and their predecessors such as Karl Heinrich Rau, and continued into the 20th century in the original American Institutionalist School, particularly in the writings of John Rogers Commons. Both Rau and Commons (1924) argued that exchange is more than a voluntary and reciprocal transfer of resources: it also involves the contractual interchange of statutory property rights. For them, exchange had to be understood and analysed in terms of the key institutions that are required to sustain it.

This narrower and more legalistic understanding of private property and contractual exchange confine them both in longevity and scale. Statutorily endorsed property rights, applied to moveable goods and services, were not codified until the ancient civilizations. In feudal times, much of the transfer of goods and services was achieved by custom or coercion rather than by contract and consent. Indeed, economic historians such as North (1981), who attempt to explore the origins of modern markets and commodity exchange, generally focus on the late medieval or early modern period as the era in which well-defined individual property rights began to spread widely from specific parts of the world.

A second important dilemma emerges. This is whether the market is regarded as coextensive with the exchange of private property per se or whether it is given an even narrower meaning and used to refer to forms of *organized* exchange activity. Two major factors lead us to consider an even narrower meaning for the term.

The first consideration is the commonplace use of the term 'market' itself and its equivalent in other languages. The word 'market' originally appeared as a noun to describe a specific place where people gathered and exchanges of a particular kind took place. The first market in Athens in the sixth century BC had rules concerning who could buy or sell, what could be bought or sold, and how trading should take place. In medieval England markets were permitted by royal charters and located in specific towns. In Europe and elsewhere in the last 300 years organized town and village markets have become commonplace. There are also permanent buildings that function as 'exchanges', for agricultural products, minerals, financial stocks, and so on. Although it has acquired additional meanings, the noun 'market' still refers to a place or gathering where trade is organized.

The second issue is the existence of a well-researched form of exchange that takes place in different contexts and involves different considerations. In three seminal and influential works, George B. Richardson (1972), Victor P. Goldberg (1980) and Ronald Dore (1983) point out that many real-world commercial transactions do not take place in the competitive arena of a market. Instead they involve firms in ongoing contact, which exchange relevant information before, during and after the contract itself. The relationship is durable and the contract is often renewed. This is most often described as 'relational exchange'. A question in the derivative literature is to examine the reason for the mutual choice of an ongoing exchange relationship rather than the more competitive institution of the market. Among the explanations is the importance of establishing ongoing trust in circumstances of uncertainty where product characteristics are complex, relatively unique or involve continuous potential improvements. Whatever the reason for its existence, such relational contracting is very different from the more anonymous exchanges in organized markets. Relational exchanges are nevertheless still contractual exchanges of property rights, in their fullest and most meaningful sense. If they are distinguished by definition from market exchanges, then not all exchanges take place in markets. Furthermore, the exchange of goods or services that are strictly unique may be regarded as a non-market phenomenon, even if the exchange is not relational. The term 'market' is thus reserved for forms of exchange activity with many similar exchanges involving multiple buyers or sellers.

In part, it is the degree of organization of exchange activity that makes markets different from relational exchange. In financial markets, for example, there are typically strict rules concerning who can trade and how trading should be conducted. In such relatively volatile markets, specific institutions sift information and present it to traders to help the formation of price expectations and norms. Market institutions in other contexts monitor the quality of goods and the instruments of weight and measure. Within these structures, trading networks emerge on the basis of business connections and reputations.

Modern telecommunications mean that a market does not have to be organized in a specific location. Either bidders can communicate with the market centre over long distances, as with many financial markets, or the market *place* can itself disappear, as in the case of Internet-based markets, such as eBay. The latter case

nevertheless remains a market, because it is an organized (virtual) forum, subject to specific procedures and rules.

We thus arrive at a definition of a market in the following terms. Markets involve multiple exchanges, multiple buyers or multiple sellers, and thereby a degree of competition. A market is defined as an institution through which multiple buyers or multiple sellers recurrently exchange a substantial number of similar commodities of a particular type. Exchanges themselves take place in a framework of law and contract enforceability. Markets involve legal and other rules that help to structure, organize and legitimize exchange transactions. They involve pricing and trading routines that help to establish a consensus over prices, and often help by communicating information regarding products, prices, quantities, potential buyers or possible sellers. Markets, in short, are organized and institutionalized recurrent exchange.

Of course, it is often difficult to draw the line between organized and relational exchange. There are many possible intermediate cases. However, such difficulties are typical when dealing with highly varied phenomena and are commonplace in some other sciences, notably biology. Similar difficulties exist in distinguishing other economic forms, such as making the important distinction between employment contracts and contracts for services. Nevertheless, such distinctions are important. The difficulty of defining a species does not mean that species should not be defined.

The operation of the law of one price is often taken as an indication of the existence of a market. Of course, imperfect information and quality variations can explain variations within a market from a single price. Nevertheless, the organized competition of the market and its associated information facilities are necessary institutional conditions for any gravitation by similar commodities to a single price level.

Taking stock, we may contrast the narrower definition of the market given above – as an institution with multiple buyers or multiple sellers, and recurrent exchanges of a specific type of commodity – with the much broader definitions raised earlier. These differences in definition do not simply affect the degree of historical specificity of 'market' phenomena, they also sustain different theoretical frameworks and promote different questions for research. Some explanations for this divergence arise in the next section.

Why have economists neglected the institutional character of markets?

For much of the 20th century, the institutional character of markets has been neglected by economists because institutions generally have been neglected. The exceptions consist of economists who placed a special emphasis on institutions. The institutional character of markets was emphasised by German historical economists such as

Gustav Schmoller and Werner Sombart in the 19th century (Hodgson, 2001). The British dissident economist John A. Hobson (1902, p. 144) wrote: 'A market, however crudely formed, is a social institution'. Likewise, for the American institutionalist John Maurice Clark (1957, p. 53): 'the mechanism of the market, which dominates the values that purport to be economic, is not a mere mechanism for neutral recording of people's preferences, but a social institution with biases of its own'. Coase, North and others have effectively revived an interest in the institutional structure of markets that was eclipsed by developments in mainstream economics during much of the 20th century.

A further clue to help explain why generations of economists have neglected the institutional character of markets lies in the preceding section, where the problem of defining the boundaries of key concepts such as property, exchange and market was raised. Many economists have maintained that the principles of the subject should be as universal as possible – like physics – to the extent that substantial consideration of historically or nationally specific institutional structures is lost. The idea that economics should be defined as a general 'science of choice' (Robbins, 1932) is part of this tradition. Consequently, terms such as property, exchange and market are given a wide meaning. Accordingly, many forms of human interaction have been regarded as 'exchange' and the summation of such 'exchanges' as 'markets'. In these terms, there is little difficulty in applying these concepts to many different types of system, from tribal societies through classical antiquity to the modern capitalist world.

Consequently, the idea of the market assumes a de-institutionalized form, as if it was the primeval and universal ether of all human interactions. Whenever people gather together in the name of self-interest, then a market somehow emerges in their midst. The market springs up simply as a result of these spontaneous interactions: it results neither from a protracted process of multiple institution-building nor from the full development of a historically specific commercial culture.

Incidentally, many sociologists have also assumed a de-institutionalized concept of the market. This is partly the result of the influence of a notion, promoted by Talcott Parsons and others, that sociology should also aspire to a high degree of historical generality. It is also a result of the influence of Marxism within sociology. Despite its emphasis on historical specificity, Marxism also treats markets as uniform entities, ultimately permeated by just one specific set of pecuniary imperatives and cultural norms.

From the 1940s to the 1970s, general equilibrium theory provided the framework in which economists attempted to understand the functioning of markets in wide-ranging terms. Even here, however, some significant attention had to be paid to institutional mechanisms and structures. Something special like the 'Walrasian auctioneer' had to be assumed in order to make the model work (Arrow and Hahn, 1971). Some elemental institutional structures had to be brought in to make the model function in its own terms. The limits to this project of theoretical generalization became more apparent in the 1970s, when it was shown that few general conclusions could be derived. In particular, Hugo Sonnenschein (1972) and others demonstrated that within general equilibrium theory the aggregated excess demand functions can take almost any form (Rizvi, 1994).

The existence of 'missing markets' always poses a problem for the general equilibrium approach: a complete set of markets for all present and future commodities in all possible states of the world is typically assumed as a basis for general clearance in all markets. However, if market institutions are themselves scarce and costly to establish, then some may be missing for that reason. Furthermore, while capitalism has historically promoted market institutions, modern developed capitalism prohibits several types of market, such as markets for slaves, votes, drugs, or futures markets for labour. In so far as capitalism makes such prohibitions, 'missing markets' are inevitable within capitalism.

The technical problems exposed by Sonnenschein and others led economists to shift their attention away from general equilibrium theory. Instead, game theory became the cutting edge of theoretical analysis. By its nature, game theory tends to lead to less general propositions and points instead to more specific rules and institutions. As game theory became fashionable in the 1980s, it became a theoretical tool in the 'new institutionalist' revival in economic theory.

The revival of the notion of markets as institutions

At least three further developments helped to promote the study of markets as social institutions. First, the basic theory of auctions emerged in the 1970s and 1980s (McAfee and McMillan, 1987; Wolfstetter, 1996). It was assumed from the outset that participants in an exchange did not have complete information, and on this basis it was shown that choices concerning auction forms and rules could significantly affect market outcomes. These ideas assumed centre stage in the 1990s with the use by governments of auction mechanisms in electricity and telecommunications deregulation, most notably in the selling of the electromagnetic spectrum for telecommunications services, and subsequently with the growth of auctions on the Internet (McAfee and McMillan, 1996).

A second and closely related development was the rise of experimental economics, which began to be recognized as an important subdiscipline in the 1980s. Modern experimental economists, in simulating markets in the laboratory, have found that they have had also to face the unavoidable problem of setting up its specific institutional structure. Simply calling it a market is not enough to provide the experimenter with the institutionally specific structures and procedural rules. As leading experimental economist Vernon Smith (1982, p. 923) wrote: 'it is not possible to design a laboratory resource allocation experiment without designing an institution in all its detail'. Work within experimental economics has underlined the importance of these specific rules, by showing that market outcomes are sometimes relatively insensitive to the information processing capacities of the agents involved, because particular constraints govern the results (Gode and Sunder, 1993).

In reality, each particular market is entwined with other institutions and a particular social culture. Accordingly, there is not just one type of market but many different markets, each depending on its inherent routines, cultural norms and institutional make-up. Differentiating markets by market structure according to textbook typology – from perfect competition through oligopoly to monopoly – is not enough. Institutions, routines and culture have to be brought into the picture. Experimental economists have discovered an equivalent truth in laboratory settings, and have learned that experimental outcomes often depend on the tacit assumptions and cultural settings of participants. Different types of market institution are possible, involving different routines, pricing procedures, and so on. This has been acknowledged by a growing number of economists, as the notion of a single universal type of market has lost credibility (McMillan, 2002).

Third, these theoretical developments were dramatized by events. Following the collapse of the Eastern bloc in 1989–91, a number of economists presumed that many markets would emerge spontaneously in the vacuum created by the breakdown of central planning. This view turned out to be mistaken, as capital and other markets were slow to develop and their growth was thwarted by the lack of an appropriate institutional infrastructrure. Several formerly planned economics slipped back into recession. Critics such as Coase (1992, p. 718) drew attention to the necessary institutional foundations of the market system: 'The ex-communist countries are advised to move to a market economy … but without the appropriate institutions, no market of any significance is possible'.

While sociologists, like economists, had previously paid relatively little attention to market institutions, the revitalization of the sub-discipline of economic sociology led to a series of studies by sociologists of financial and other markets (Abolafia, 1996; Baker, 1984; Burt, 1992; Fligstein, 2001; Lie, 1997; Swedberg, 1994; White, 1981; 1988). These works show how specific networks and social relationships between actors structure exchanges, and how cultural norms govern market operations and outcomes. Similar considerations have emerged in empirical and simulation work by economists that stresses the importance of learning and previous experience in trading partner selection and in the decision to accept a transaction (Kirman and Vignes, 1991; Härdle and Kirman, 1995).

Taken as a whole, these literatures testify to a much more nuanced conception of market phenomena. As a result of all these developments, the treatment by economists and others of markets began to change. Both economists and sociologists are now paying detailed attention to the nature of specific market rules and mechanisms. A milestone paper by Alvin Roth (2002) challenges the view of a single universal theory of market behaviour. While those economists who had paid attention to different market mechanisms had typically been preoccupied with a search for 'optimal' rules and institutional forms, gradually this has become a will-o'-the-wisp with the realization that typical assumptions in the emerging literature concerning cognitive and information impairments have made this search difficult or impossible (Lee, 1998; Mirowski, 2007).

Nevertheless, while the search for optimal institutional blueprints is intractable, these theoretical developments have begun to provide an analytical framework within which the limits and potentialities of different types of market mechanism can be appraised. An outcome is to abandon the former widespread notion – shared by all kinds of theorists from Marxists to the Austrian School – that 'the market' is a singular type of entity entirely understandable in terms of the same principles or laws. While Hayek and his followers should be given inspirational credit for their emphasis on the informational limitations inherent in all complex economic systems, they stressed that markets are the most effective processors of information while downplaying or ignoring the differences between various types of market.

In this context, markets reappear as varied and historically specific phenomena. The general equilibrium approach has been overshadowed by an array of theoretical and empirical methodologies, including game theory, agent-based modelling, laboratory experimentation and real-world observation.

Conclusions

A number of options for defining a market have been outlined here. The broadest option is to regard the market as the universal ether of human interaction, depending on little more than the division of labour. A second option is to regard the market as synonymous with commodity exchange, in which case it dates at least as far back to the dawn of civilization.

By contrast, several considerations militate in favour of a narrower definition, and recent developments in economic theory point in this direction. In the narrower sense, markets are organized exchange. Where they exist, markets help to structure, organize and legitimize numerous exchange transactions. Pricing and trading procedures within markets help to establish a consensus over prices, and communicate information regarding products, prices, quantities, potential buyers or possible sellers.

Variation in market rules and procedures means that markets differ substantially, especially when we consider markets in different cultures. The markets of 2,000 years ago were very different from (say) the electronic financial markets of today. In the real world, and even in a single country, we may come across many different examples of the market. The market itself is neither a natural datum nor an ubiquitous ether, but is itself a social institution, governed by sets of rules restricting some and legitimizing other behaviours. Furthermore, the market is necessarily entwined with other social institutions, such as in many cases the local or national state. It can emerge spontaneously, but it can also be promoted or guided by conscious design.

A clear implication of this argument is that the unnuanced but familiar pro- and anti-market policy stances are both insensitive to the possibility of different types of market institution. Instead of recognizing the important role of different possible cultures and trading customs, both the opponents and the advocates of the market have focused exclusively on its general features. Thus, for instance, Marxists have deduced that the mere existence of private property and markets will themselves encourage acquisitive, greedy behaviour, with no further reference in their analysis to the role of ideas and culture in helping to form the aspirations of social actors. This is the source of their 'agoraphobia', or fear of markets. Obversely, overenthusiastic advocates of the market claim that its benefits stem simply and unambiguously from the existence of private property and exchange, without regard to possible variations in detailed market mechanism or cultural context. As strange bedfellows, both Marxists and some market advocates have underestimated the degree to which all market economies are unavoidably made up of densely layered social institutions.

GEOFFREY M. HODGSON

See also **arbitrage; auctioneer; auctions (applications); Austrian economics; capitalism; competition; competition and selection; competition, Austrian; competition, classical; computing in mechanism design; contemporary capitalism; economic sociology; econophysics; efficient markets hypothesis; electricity markets; existence of general equilibrium; experimental economics; general equilibrium; general equilibrium (new developments); institutionalism, old; labour market institutions; land markets; market institutions; market microstructure; marketplaces; marketing boards; marriage markets; Marx's analysis of capitalist production; property rights; tâtonnement and recontracting; two-sided markets.**

Bibliography

Abolafia, M. 1996. *Making Markets: Opportunism and Restraint on Wall Street.* Cambridge, MA: Harvard University Press.

Arrow, K. and Hahn, F. 1971. *General Competitive Analysis.* Edinburgh: Oliver and Boyd.

Baker, W. 1984. The social structure of a national securities market. *American Journal of Sociology* 89, 775–811.

Burt, R. 1992. *Structural Holes: The Social Structure of Competition.* Cambridge, MA: Harvard University Press.

Cassady, R. 1967. *Auctions and Auctioneering.* Berkeley and Los Angeles: University of California Press.

Clark, J. 1957. *Economic Institutions and Human Welfare.* New York: Alfred Knopf.

Clarke, D. 1987. Trade and industry in barbarian Europe till Roman times. In *The Cambridge Economic History of Europe, Volume II: Trade and Industry in the Middle Ages*, 2nd edn, ed. M. Postan and E. Miller. Cambridge: Cambridge University Press.

Coase, R. 1988. *The Firm, the Market, and the Law.* Chicago: University of Chicago Press.

Coase, R. 1992. The institutional structure of production. *American Economic Review* 82, 713–19.

Commons, J. 1924. *Legal Foundations of Capitalism.* New York: Macmillan.

Dore, R. 1983. Goodwill and the spirit of market capitalism. *British Journal of Sociology* 34, 459–82.

Finley, M., ed. 1962. *Second International Conference of Economic History, Volume. I: Trade and Politics in the Ancient World.* New York: Arno.

Fligstein, N. 2001. *The Architecture of Markets: An Economic Sociology of Twenty-First Century Capitalist Societies.* Princeton, NJ: Princeton University Press.

Gode, D. and Sunder, S. 1993. Allocative efficiency of markets with zero-intelligence traders: market as a partial substitute for individual rationality. *Journal of Political Economy* 101, 119–37.

Goldberg, V. 1980. Relational exchange: economics and complex contracts. *American Behavioral Scientist* 23, 337–52.

Härdle, W. and Kirman, A. 1995. Nonclassical demand: a model-free examination of price quantity relations in the Marseille fish market. *Journal of Econometrics* 67, 227–7.

Hayek, F. 1960. *The Constitution of Liberty.* London and Chicago: Routledge and Kegan Paul, and University of Chicago Press.

Hobson, J. 1902. *The Social Problem: Life and Work.* London: James Nisbet.

Hodgson, G. 2001. *How Economics Forgot History: The Problem of Historical Specificity in Social Science.* London and New York: Routledge.

Kirman, Alan P. and Vignes, A. 1991. Price dispersion: theoretical considerations and empirical evidence from the Marseilles fish market. In *Issues in Contemporary Economics: Proceedings of the Ninth World Congress of the International Economic Association*, ed. K. Arrow. New York: New York University Press.

Lee, R. 1998. *What Is an Exchange? The Automation, Management, and Regulation of Financial Markets.* Oxford: Oxford University Press.

Lie, J. 1997. Sociology of markets. *Annual Review of Sociology* 23, 341–60.

McAfee, R.P. and McMillan, J. 1987. Auctions and Bidding. *Journal of Economic Literature* 25, 699–738.

McAfee, R. and McMillan, J. 1996. Analyzing the airwaves auction. *Journal of Economic Perspectives* 10(1), 199–76.

McMillan, J. 2002. *Reinventing the Bazaar: A Natural History of Markets*. New York and London: Norton.

McMillan, J. 2003. Market design: the policy uses of theory. *American Economic Review (Papers and Proceedings)* 93, 139–44.

Mirowski, P. 2007. Markets come to bits: evolution, computation and markomata in economic science. *Journal of Economic Behavior and Organization*. 63, 209–42

Mises, L. von. 1949. *Human Action: A Treatise on Economics*. London and New Haven: William Hodge and Yale University Press.

North, D. 1977. Markets and other allocation systems in history: the challenge of Karl Polanyi. *Journal of European Economic History* 6, 703–16.

North, D. 1981. *Structure and Change in Economic History*. New York: Norton.

Pirenne, H. 1937. *Economic and Social History of Medieval Europe*. New York: Harcourt Brace.

Polanyi, K. 1971. *Primitive and Modern Economics: Essays of Karl Polanyi*. Boston: Beacon Press.

Polanyi, K., Arensberg, C. and Pearson, H., eds. 1957. *Trade and Market in the Early Empires*. Chicago: Henry Regnery.

Richardson, G. 1972. The organisation of industry. *Economic Journal* 82, 883–96.

Rizvi, S. 1994. The microfoundations project in general equilibrium theory. *Cambridge Journal of Economics* 18, 357–77.

Robbins, L. 1932. *An Essay on the Nature and Significance of Economic Science*. London: Macmillan.

Roth, A. 2002. The economist as engineer: game theory, experimentation, and computation as tools for design economics. *Econometrica* 70, 1341–78.

Sened, I. 1997. *The Political Institution of Private Property*. Cambridge: Cambridge University Press.

Smith, V. 1982. Microeconomic systems as an experimental science. *American Economic Review* 72, 923–55.

Sonnenschein, H. 1972. Market excess demand functions. *Econometrica* 40, 549–63.

Stigler, G. 1967. Imperfections in the capital market. *Journal of Political Economy* 75, 287–92.

Swedberg, R. 1994. Markets as social structures. In *Handbook of Economic Sociology*, ed. N. Smelser and R. Swedberg. Princeton: Princeton University Press.

Temin, P. 2006. The economy of the early Roman Empire. *Journal of Economic Perspectives* 20(1), 133–51.

Weber, M. 1927. *General Economic History*. London: Allen and Unwin.

White, H. 1981. Where do markets come from? *American Journal of Sociology* 87, 517–47.

White, H. 1988. Varieties of markets. In *Social Structure: A Network Approach*, ed. B. Wellman and S. Berkowitz. Cambridge, MA: Harvard University Press.

Wolfstetter, E. 1996. Auctions: an introduction. *Journal of Economic Surveys* 10, 367–420.

Markov chain Monte Carlo methods

1 Introduction

Markov chain Monte Carlo methods, popularly called MCMC methods, are a class of Monte Carlo methods for sampling a given univariate or multivariate probability distribution (the target distribution). These methods play a central role in the theory and practice of modern Bayesian methods where they are used for the numerical calculation of quantities (such as the moments and quantiles of posterior and predictive densities) that arise in the Bayesian prior–posterior analysis. They have transformed the fields of Bayesian statistics and econometrics.

Suppose that in a given Bayesian model the prior density is $\pi(\boldsymbol{\theta})$ and the sampling density or likelihood function is $f(\mathbf{y}|\boldsymbol{\theta})$, where $\mathbf{y}$ is a vector of observations and $\boldsymbol{\theta} \in \Re^d$ is an unknown parameter. In the Bayesian context, inferences about $\boldsymbol{\theta}$ are based on the posterior density $\pi(\boldsymbol{\theta}|\mathbf{y}) \propto \pi(\boldsymbol{\theta})f(\mathbf{y}|\boldsymbol{\theta})$. Now suppose that one is interested in finding the mean of the posterior density

$$E(\boldsymbol{\theta}|\mathbf{y}) = \int \boldsymbol{\theta}\pi(\boldsymbol{\theta}|\mathbf{y})d\boldsymbol{\theta}$$

but that the integral cannot be computed analytically. In that case one can compute the integral by Monte Carlo sampling methods. The general idea is to calculate the integral from a sample

$$\boldsymbol{\theta}^{(1)}, \ldots, \boldsymbol{\theta}^{(M)} \sim \pi(\boldsymbol{\theta}|\mathbf{y}),$$

that is drawn from the posterior density. This sample can be used to estimate the posterior mean and other features of the posterior density. For instance, the posterior mean can be estimated by the average of the sampled draws, and the quantiles of the posterior density by the quantiles of the sampled output.

The requisite sampling of the target density is made possible by MCMC methods. In a MCMC simulation, one samples the target density in an indirect way: by simulating a suitably constructed Markov chain whose invariant distribution is the target density. Then the draws beyond some chosen burn-in period are taken as a (correlated) sample from the target density. The defining feature of Markov chains is the property that the conditional density of $\boldsymbol{\theta}^{(j)}$ (the jth element of the sequence) conditioned on the entire preceding history of the chain depends only on the previous value $\boldsymbol{\theta}^{(j-1)}$. Denote this conditional density, the transition density of the Markov chain, by $p(\boldsymbol{\theta}^{(j-1)}, \cdot|\mathbf{y})$. Then, in the MCMC framework, a sample is produced by simulating the transition density as

$$\boldsymbol{\theta}^{(1)} \sim p(\boldsymbol{\theta}^{(0)}, \cdot|\mathbf{y})$$
$$\vdots$$
$$\boldsymbol{\theta}^{(j)} \sim p(\boldsymbol{\theta}^{(j-1)}, \cdot|\mathbf{y})$$
$$\vdots$$

If we let the first n_0 cycles represent the burn-in phase, for some choice of n_0, the draws

$$\boldsymbol{\theta}^{(n_0+1)}, \boldsymbol{\theta}^{(n_0+2)}, \ldots, \boldsymbol{\theta}^{(n_0+M)}$$

are treated as those from $\pi(\boldsymbol{\theta}|\mathbf{y})$. Even though the sampled variates are correlated, laws of large numbers for Markov sequences can be used to show that, under regularity conditions, the sample average of any integrable function $g(\boldsymbol{\theta})$ converges to its posterior expectation:

$$M^{-1} \sum_{j=1}^{M} g(\boldsymbol{\theta}^{(j)}) \rightarrow \int g(\boldsymbol{\theta})\pi(\boldsymbol{\theta}|\mathbf{y})d\boldsymbol{\theta}, \qquad (1)$$

as M becomes large.

There are two common ways of constructing a transition density $p(\boldsymbol{\theta}^{(j-1)}, \cdot|\mathbf{y})$ whose limiting distribution is the required target density. One way is by a method called the Metropolis–Hastings (M–H) algorithm, which was introduced by Metropolis et al. (1953) and Hastings (1970). Key references about this method are Tierney (1994), and Chib and Greenberg (1995). A second approach is by the so-called Gibbs sampling algorithm. This method was introduced by Geman and Geman (1984), Tanner and Wong (1987) and Gelfand and Smith (1990), and was the impetus for the current interest in Markov chain sampling methods. A summary of many aspects of MCMC methods is contained in Chib (2001) while textbook accounts include Gilks, Richardson and Spiegelhalter (1996), Chen, Shao and Ibrahim (2000), Liu (2001) and Robert and Casella (2004).

2 Metropolis–Hastings algorithm

Suppose that we are interested in sampling the target density $\pi(\boldsymbol{\theta}|\mathbf{y})$, where $\boldsymbol{\theta}$ is a vector-valued parameter and $\pi(\boldsymbol{\theta}|\mathbf{y})$ is a continuous density. The idea behind the M–H algorithm is to simulate a proposal value $\boldsymbol{\theta}'$ from a transition density $q(\boldsymbol{\theta}, \boldsymbol{\theta}'|\mathbf{y})$ that is convenient to stimulate but does not necessarily have the correct limiting distribution and then to subject the proposal value to a specific randomization to ensure that the resulting Markov chain has the correct limiting distribution.

To define the M–H algorithm, let $\boldsymbol{\theta}^{(j-1)}$ be the current value. Then the next value $\boldsymbol{\theta}^{(j)}$ is produced by a two-step process consisting of a 'proposal step' and a 'move step'.

- *Proposal step*: Sample a proposal value $\boldsymbol{\theta}'$ from $q(\boldsymbol{\theta}^{(j-1)}, \boldsymbol{\theta}|\mathbf{y})$ and calculate the quantity

$$\alpha(\boldsymbol{\theta}^{(j-1)}, \boldsymbol{\theta}'|\mathbf{y})$$
$$= \min\left\{1, \frac{\pi(\boldsymbol{\theta}'|\mathbf{y})}{\pi(\boldsymbol{\theta}^{(j-1)}|\mathbf{y})} \frac{q(\boldsymbol{\theta}', \boldsymbol{\theta}^{(j-1)}|\mathbf{y})}{q(\boldsymbol{\theta}^{(j-1)}, \boldsymbol{\theta}'|\mathbf{y})}\right\}. \qquad (2)$$

- *Move step*: Let $\boldsymbol{\theta}^{(j)} = \boldsymbol{\theta}'$ with probability $\alpha(\boldsymbol{\theta}^{(j-1)}, \boldsymbol{\theta}'|\mathbf{y})$; remain at the current value $\boldsymbol{\theta}^{(j-1)}$ with probability $1 - \alpha(\boldsymbol{\theta}^{(j-1)}, \boldsymbol{\theta}'|\mathbf{y})$.

In terms of nomenclature, the source density $q(\boldsymbol{\theta}, \boldsymbol{\theta}'|\mathbf{y})$ is called the candidate generating density or proposal density, and $\alpha(\boldsymbol{\theta}^{(j-1)}, \boldsymbol{\theta}'|\mathbf{y})$ the *acceptance probability* or, more descriptively, the *probability of move*. Note also that the function $\alpha(\boldsymbol{\theta}^{(j-1)}, \boldsymbol{\theta}'|\mathbf{y})$ in this algorithm can be computed without knowledge of the norming constant of the posterior density $\pi(\boldsymbol{\theta}|\mathbf{y})$. In addition, if the proposal density is symmetric, satisfying the condition $q(\boldsymbol{\theta}, \boldsymbol{\theta}'|\mathbf{y}) = q(\boldsymbol{\theta}', \boldsymbol{\theta}|\mathbf{y})$, then the acceptance probability reduces to $\pi(\boldsymbol{\theta}'|\mathbf{y})/\pi(\boldsymbol{\theta}^{(j-1)}|\mathbf{y})$; hence, if $\pi(\boldsymbol{\theta}') \geq \pi(\boldsymbol{\theta}^{(j-1)}|\mathbf{y})$, the chain moves to $\boldsymbol{\theta}'$, otherwise it moves to $\boldsymbol{\theta}'$ with probability given by $\pi(\boldsymbol{\theta}'|\mathbf{y})/\pi(\boldsymbol{\theta}^{(j-1)}|\mathbf{y})$. The latter is the algorithm of Metropolis et al. (1953).

Remark 1 *Derivation of the M–H algorithm*: A question of some interest is the justification of this two-step approach. This question was tackled by Chib and Greenberg (1995), who derived the method from the logic of reversibility. A Markov transition density $p(\boldsymbol{\theta}, \boldsymbol{\theta}'|\mathbf{y})$ is said to be reversible for $\pi(\boldsymbol{\theta}|\mathbf{y})$ if the following condition holds for every $(\boldsymbol{\theta}, \boldsymbol{\theta}')$ in the support of the target distribution:

$$\pi(\boldsymbol{\theta}|\mathbf{y})p(\boldsymbol{\theta}, \boldsymbol{\theta}'|\mathbf{y}) = \pi(\boldsymbol{\theta}'|\mathbf{y})p(\boldsymbol{\theta}', \boldsymbol{\theta}|\mathbf{y}). \qquad (3)$$

The reversibility condition is important because reversible chains are invariant. Invariance refers to the property that

$$\pi(\boldsymbol{\theta}'|\mathbf{y}) = \int p(\boldsymbol{\theta}, \boldsymbol{\theta}'|\mathbf{y})\pi(\boldsymbol{\theta}|\mathbf{y}) \, d\boldsymbol{\theta} \qquad (4)$$

which means that, if the transition density is invariant for the target density, then, once convergence is achieved, a subsequent value $\boldsymbol{\theta}'$ drawn from the transition density is also from the target density. To see that reversibility implies invariance one simply integrates both sides of (3) over $\boldsymbol{\theta}$. This leads to the invariance condition since $\int p(\boldsymbol{\theta}, \boldsymbol{\theta}'|\mathbf{y}) \, d\boldsymbol{\theta}' = 1$ by virtue of being a transition density. Now consider the Markov chain induced by the proposal density $q(\boldsymbol{\theta}, \boldsymbol{\theta}'|\mathbf{y})$. Because this was formulated without the reversibility condition in mind it is unlikely to satisfy reversibility. Suppose that for a pair of points $(\boldsymbol{\theta}, \boldsymbol{\theta}')$ it is true that

$$\pi(\boldsymbol{\theta}|\mathbf{y})q(\boldsymbol{\theta}, \boldsymbol{\theta}'|\mathbf{y}) > \pi(\boldsymbol{\theta}'|\mathbf{y})q(\boldsymbol{\theta}', \boldsymbol{\theta}|\mathbf{y}), \qquad (5)$$

which means informally that the process moves from θ to θ' too frequently and too rarely in the reverse direction. This situation can be corrected by reducing the flow from θ to θ' by introducing probabilities $\alpha(\theta, \theta'|\mathbf{y})$ and $\alpha(\theta', \theta|\mathbf{y})$ of making the moves in either direction so that

$$\pi(\theta|\mathbf{y})q(\theta, \theta'|\mathbf{y})\alpha(\theta, \theta'|\mathbf{y})$$
$$= \pi(\theta'|\mathbf{y})q(\theta', \theta|\mathbf{y})\alpha(\theta', \theta|\mathbf{y}).$$

One now sets $\alpha(\theta', \theta|\mathbf{y})$ to be as high as possible, namely, equal to 1. Solving for $\alpha(\theta, \theta'|\mathbf{y})$ one then gets

$$\alpha(\theta, \theta'|\mathbf{y}) = \frac{\pi(\theta'|\mathbf{y})}{\pi(\theta|\mathbf{y})}\frac{q(\theta', \theta|\mathbf{y})}{q(\theta, \theta'|\mathbf{y})}.$$

Because one started from (5) this is clearly less than 1. On the other hand, if the inequality in (5) were reversed, the same argumentation leads to the conclusion that $\alpha(\theta, \theta'|\mathbf{y}) = 1$. Thus, on combining these two cases we reproduce the expression of $\alpha(\theta, \theta'|\mathbf{y})$ given in (2).

Remark 2 *Transition density of the M–H chain*: The transition density of the M–H chain has two components – one for the move away from θ and given by $\alpha(\theta, \theta'|\mathbf{y})q(\theta, \theta'|\mathbf{y})$ and one for the probability of staying at θ given by $r(\theta|\mathbf{y}) = 1 - \int \alpha(\theta, \theta'|\mathbf{y})q(\theta, \theta'|\mathbf{y})\, d\theta'$. In particular,

$$p_{MH}(\theta, \theta'|\mathbf{y}) = \alpha(\theta, \theta'|\mathbf{y})q(\theta, \theta'|\mathbf{y}) + \delta_\theta(\theta')r(\theta|\mathbf{y})$$

where $\delta_\theta(\theta')$ is the Dirac-function at θ defined as $\delta_\theta(\theta') = 0$ for $\theta' \neq \theta$ and $\int \delta_\theta(\theta')\, d\theta' = 1$. It is easy to check that the integral of the transition density over all possible values of θ is 1, as required.

Remark 3 *Convergence properties*: The theoretical properties of the M–H algorithm (in particular the ergodic behaviour of the chain from an arbitrarily specified initial value) depend crucially on the nature of the proposal density. One requirement is that the proposal density be everywhere positive in the support of the posterior density, which means that the M–H chain can make a transition to any point in its support in one step. Further discussion of the conditions is given in Tierney (1994) and Robert and Casella (2004).

Remark 4 *Mixing*: The sampled values from the M–H algorithm (as from any Markov chain) are correlated. The goal in any particular application is to ensure that the serial correlation is not excessive. One diagnostic to check for the degree of serial correlation in the sampled draws is the *autocorrelation time* or *inefficiency factor* of each component θ_k of θ defined as

$$a_k = \left\{1 + 2\sum_{s=1}^{M}(1 - \frac{s}{M})\rho_{ks}\right\},$$

where ρ_{ks} is the sample autocorrelation at lag s from the M sampled draws $\theta_k^{(n_0+1)}, \ldots, \theta_k^{(n_0+M)}$. One can interpret this quantity in terms of the *effective sample size*, or ESS, defined for the kth component of θ as $ESS_k = \frac{M}{a_k}$. With independent sampling the autocorrelation times are theoretically equal to 1, and the effective sample size is M. When the inefficiency factors are high, the effective sample size is much smaller than M.

2.1 Choice of proposal density

One family of candidate-generating densities is given by $q(\theta, \theta'|\mathbf{y}) = q(\theta' - \theta)$. The candidate θ' is thus drawn according to the process $\theta' = \theta + \mathbf{z}$, where $\mathbf{z}$ follows the distribution q, and is called the *random walk M–H chain*. The random walk M–H chain is quite popular in applications. One has to be careful in setting the variance of $\mathbf{z}$ because if it is too large the chain may remain stuck at a particular value for many iterations, while if it is too small the chain will tend to make small moves and move inefficiently through the support of the target distribution.

Another possibility is to let $q(\theta, \theta'|\mathbf{y}) = q(\theta'|\mathbf{y})$, an *independence M–H chain* in the terminology of Tierney (1994). One way to implement such chains is by tailoring the proposal density to the target at the mode by a multivariate normal or multivariate-t distribution with location given by the mode of the target and the dispersion given by inverse of the Hessian evaluated at the mode (Chib and Greenberg, 1994; 1995).

Yet another way to generate proposal values is through a Markov chain version of the accept–reject method (Tierney, 1994; Chib and Greenberg, 1995). To explain this method, suppose $c > 0$ is a known constant and $h(\theta)$ a source density. Let $C = \{\theta : \pi(\theta|\mathbf{y}) \leq ch(\theta)\}$ denote the set of value for which $ch(\theta)$ dominates the target density. Given $\theta^{(j-1)} = \theta$ the next value $\theta^{(j)}$ is obtained as follows. First, a candidate value θ' is obtained, independent of the current value θ, by applying the accept–reject algorithm with $ch(\cdot)$ as the 'pseudo-dominating' density. The candidates θ' that are produced under this scheme have density $q(\theta'|\mathbf{y}) \propto \min\{\pi(\theta'|\mathbf{y}), ch(\theta')\}$. Then, the M–H probability of move is given by

$$\alpha(\theta, \theta'|\mathbf{y})$$
$$= \begin{cases} 1 & \text{if } \theta \in C \\ 1/w(\theta) & \text{if } \theta \notin C, \ \theta' \in C \\ \min\{w(\theta')/w(\theta), 1\} & \text{if } \theta \notin C, \ \theta' \notin C \end{cases}$$
$$(6)$$

where $w(\theta) = c^{-1}\pi(\theta|\mathbf{y})/h(\theta)$.

2.2 Example

To illustrate the M–H algorithm, consider the binary response data in Table 1, on the occurrence or non-occurrence

Table 1 *Caesarean infection data*

y(1/0)	x_1	x_2	x_3
11/87	1	1	1
1/17	0	1	1
0/2	0	0	1
23/3	1	1	0
28/30	0	1	0
0/9	1	0	0
8/32	0	0	0

Source: Fahrmeir and Tutz (1994).

Table 2 *Caesarean data: prior–posterior summary based on 5,000 draws (beyond a burn-in of 100 cycles) from the tailored M–H algorithm*

	Prior		Posterior			
	Mean	Std dev	Mean	Std dev	Lower	Upper
β_0	0.000	2.236	−1.080	0.220	−1.526	−0.670
β_1	0.000	2.236	0.593	0.249	0.116	1.095
β_2	0.000	2.236	1.181	0.254	0.680	1.694
β_3	0.000	2.236	−1.889	0.266	−2.421	−1.385

of infection following birth by Caesarean section. The response variable y is 1 if the Caesarean birth resulted in an infection, and zero if not. There are three covariates: x_1, an indicator of whether the caesarean was non-planned; x_2, an indicator of whether risk factors were present at the time of birth; and x_3, an indicator of whether antibiotics were given as a prophylaxis. The data in the table contains information from 251 births. Under the column of the response, an entry such as 11/87 means that there were 98 deliveries with covariates $(1,1,1)$ of whom 11 developed an infection and 87 did not. Suppose that the probability of infection for the ith birth $(i \leq 251)$ is

$$\Pr(y_i = 1|\mathbf{x}_i, \boldsymbol{\beta}) = \Phi(\mathbf{x}_i'\boldsymbol{\beta}), \qquad (7)$$

$$\boldsymbol{\beta} \sim N_4(\mathbf{0}, 5\mathbf{I}_4) \qquad (8)$$

where $\mathbf{x}_i = (1, x_{i1}, x_{i2}, x_{i3})^\top$ is the covariate vector, $\boldsymbol{\beta} = (\beta_0, \beta_1, \beta_2, \beta_3)$ is the vector of unknown coefficients, Φ is the cdf of the standard normal random variable and $\mathbf{I}_4$ is the four-dimensional identity matrix. The target posterior density, under the assumption that the outcomes $\mathbf{y} = (y_1, y_2, ..., y_{251})$ are conditionally independent, is

$$\pi(\boldsymbol{\beta}|\mathbf{y}) \propto \pi(\boldsymbol{\beta}) \prod_{i=1}^{251} \Phi(\mathbf{x}_i'\boldsymbol{\beta})^{y_i} \left\{ 1 - \Phi(\mathbf{x}_i'\boldsymbol{\beta}) \right\}^{(1-y_i)}$$

where $\pi(\boldsymbol{\beta})$ is the density of the $N(0, 10\mathbf{I}_4)$ distribution.

To define the Chib and Greenberg (1994) tailored proposal density, let

$$\hat{\boldsymbol{\beta}} = (-1.093022 \quad 0.607643 \quad 1.197543 \quad -1.904739)'$$

be the maximum likelihood estimate and let

$$\mathbf{V} = \begin{pmatrix} 0.040745 & -0.007038 & -0.039399 & 0.004829 \\ & 0.073101 & -0.006940 & -0.050162 \\ & & 0.062292 & -0.016803 \\ & & & 0.080788 \end{pmatrix}$$

be the symmetric matrix obtained by inverting the negative of the Hessian matrix (the matrix of second derivatives)

of the log-likelihood function evaluated at $\hat{\boldsymbol{\beta}}$. To generate proposal values, we use a multivariate-t density with 15 degrees of freedom, location given by $\hat{\boldsymbol{\beta}}$ and dispersion given by $\mathbf{V}$. The M–H algorithm is run for 5,000 iterations beyond a burn-in of 100 iterations. The prior–posterior summary is reported in Table 2. It contains the first two moments (the mean and the standard deviation) of the prior and posterior and the 2.5th (lower) and 97.5th (upper) percentiles of the marginal densities of $\boldsymbol{\beta}$.

In addition, we plot in Figure 1 the four marginal posterior densities. These are derived by smoothing the histogram of the simulated values with a Gaussian kernel. In the same plot we also report the autocorrelation functions (correlation against lag) for each of the sampled parameter values. The serial correlations decline quickly to zero indicating that the algorithm is mixing well.

2.3 Multiple-block M–H algorithm

When the dimension of $\boldsymbol{\theta}$ is large it is often necessary to divide the parameters into smaller groups or blocks and then to sample the blocks in turn. For simplicity suppose that two blocks are adequate and that $\boldsymbol{\theta}$ is written as $(\boldsymbol{\theta}_1, \boldsymbol{\theta}_2)$, with $\boldsymbol{\theta}_k \in \Omega_k \subseteq \Re^{d_k}$. To sample these blocks let

$$q_1(\boldsymbol{\theta}_1, \boldsymbol{\theta}_1'|\mathbf{y}, \boldsymbol{\theta}_2); q_2(\boldsymbol{\theta}_2, \boldsymbol{\theta}_2'|\mathbf{y}, \boldsymbol{\theta}_1),$$

denote the two proposal densities, one for each block $\boldsymbol{\theta}_k$, where the proposal density q_k may depend on the current value of the remaining block. Also, define

$$\alpha(\boldsymbol{\theta}_1, \boldsymbol{\theta}_1'|\mathbf{y}, \boldsymbol{\theta}_2) = \min\left\{ \frac{\pi(\boldsymbol{\theta}_1', \boldsymbol{\theta}_2|\mathbf{y}) q_1(\boldsymbol{\theta}_1', \boldsymbol{\theta}_1|\mathbf{y}, \boldsymbol{\theta}_2)}{\pi(\boldsymbol{\theta}_1, \boldsymbol{\theta}_2|\mathbf{y}) q_1(\boldsymbol{\theta}_1, \boldsymbol{\theta}_1'|\mathbf{y}, \boldsymbol{\theta}_2)}, 1 \right\}$$

and

$$\alpha(\boldsymbol{\theta}_2, \boldsymbol{\theta}_2'|\mathbf{y}, \boldsymbol{\theta}_1) = \min\left\{ \frac{\pi(\boldsymbol{\theta}_1, \boldsymbol{\theta}_2'|\mathbf{y}) q_2(\boldsymbol{\theta}_2', \boldsymbol{\theta}_2|\mathbf{y}, \boldsymbol{\theta}_1)}{\pi(\boldsymbol{\theta}_1, \boldsymbol{\theta}_2|\mathbf{y}) q_2(\boldsymbol{\theta}_2, \boldsymbol{\theta}_2'|\mathbf{y}, \boldsymbol{\theta}_1)}, 1 \right\},$$

as the probability of move for block $\boldsymbol{\theta}_k$ conditioned on the other block. Then, in what may be called the multiple-block M–H algorithm, one updates each block using an M–H step with the above probability of move, given the most current value of the other block. The method can be extended to several blocks in the same way.

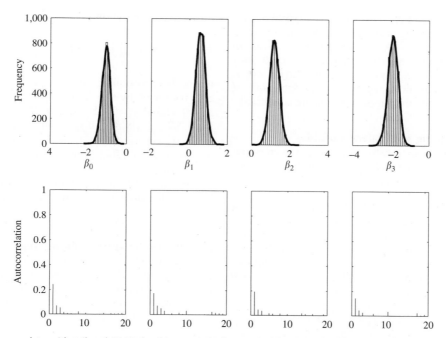

Figure 1 Caesarean data with tailored M–H algorithm: marginal posterior densities (top panel) and autocorrelation plot (bottom panel)

Remark 5 An important special case arises if each proposal density is the full conditional density of that block. Specifically, if we set

$$q_1(\boldsymbol{\theta}_1, \boldsymbol{\theta}_1' | \mathbf{y}, \boldsymbol{\theta}_2) \propto \pi(\boldsymbol{\theta}_1', \boldsymbol{\theta}_2 | \mathbf{y}),$$
$$q_1(\boldsymbol{\theta}_1', \boldsymbol{\theta}_1 | \mathbf{y}, \boldsymbol{\theta}_2) \propto \pi(\boldsymbol{\theta}_1, \boldsymbol{\theta}_2 | \mathbf{y})$$

and

$$q_2(\boldsymbol{\theta}_2, \boldsymbol{\theta}_2' | \mathbf{y}, \boldsymbol{\theta}_1) \propto \pi(\boldsymbol{\theta}_1, \boldsymbol{\theta}_2' | \mathbf{y}),$$
$$q_2(\boldsymbol{\theta}_2', \boldsymbol{\theta}_2 | \mathbf{y}, \boldsymbol{\theta}_1) \propto \pi(\boldsymbol{\theta}_1, \boldsymbol{\theta}_2 | \mathbf{y})$$

then an interesting simplification occurs. The probability of move (for the first block) becomes

$$\alpha_1(\boldsymbol{\theta}_1, \boldsymbol{\theta}_1' | \mathbf{y}, \boldsymbol{\theta}_2) = \min\left\{1, \frac{\pi(\boldsymbol{\theta}_1', \boldsymbol{\theta}_2 | \mathbf{y})\pi(\boldsymbol{\theta}_1, \boldsymbol{\theta}_2 | \mathbf{y})}{\pi(\boldsymbol{\theta}_1, \boldsymbol{\theta}_2 | \mathbf{y})\pi(\boldsymbol{\theta}_1', \boldsymbol{\theta}_2 | \mathbf{y})}\right\}$$
$$= 1,$$

and similarly for the second block, implying that, if proposal values are drawn from their full conditional densities, then the proposal values are accepted with probability one. This special case is called the Gibbs sampling algorithm.

3 The Gibbs sampling algorithm

The Gibbs sampling was introduced by Geman and Geman (1984) in the context of image processing and then discussed in the context of missing data problems by Tanner and Wong (1987). It was brought into prominence by Gelfand and Smith (1990) who demonstrated its use in a range of Bayesian problems.

3.1 The algorithm

Suppose that the parameters are grouped into two p blocks $(\boldsymbol{\theta}_1, \boldsymbol{\theta}_2, \dots, \boldsymbol{\theta}_p)$ with the associated set of full conditional distributions

$$\{\pi(\boldsymbol{\theta}_1 | \mathbf{y}, \boldsymbol{\theta}_2, \dots, \boldsymbol{\theta}_p); \pi(\boldsymbol{\theta}_2 | \mathbf{y}, \boldsymbol{\theta}_1, \boldsymbol{\theta}_3, \dots, \boldsymbol{\theta}_p); \dots,$$
$$\pi(\boldsymbol{\theta}_p | \mathbf{y}, \boldsymbol{\theta}_1, \dots, \boldsymbol{\theta}_{d-1})\},$$

where each full conditional distribution is proportional to $\pi(\boldsymbol{\theta}_1, \boldsymbol{\theta}_2, \dots, \boldsymbol{\theta}_p) | \mathbf{y})$. Then, one cycle of the Gibbs sampling algorithm is completed by simulating $\{\boldsymbol{\theta}_k\}_{k=1}^{p}$ from these distributions, recursively refreshing the conditioning variables.

3.2 Sufficient conditions for convergence

Under rather general conditions, the Markov chain generated by the Gibbs sampling algorithm converges to the target density as the number of iterations become large. Formally, if we let $p_G(\boldsymbol{\theta}, \boldsymbol{\theta}' | \mathbf{y})$ represent the transition density of the Gibbs algorithm and let $p_G^{(M)}(\boldsymbol{\theta}_0, \boldsymbol{\theta} | \mathbf{y})$ be the density of the draw $\boldsymbol{\theta}'$ after M iterations given the starting value $\boldsymbol{\theta}_0$, then

$$\|p_G^{(M)}(\boldsymbol{\theta}^{(0)}, \boldsymbol{\theta}' | \mathbf{y}) - \pi(\boldsymbol{\theta}' | \mathbf{y})\| \to 0, \tag{9}$$
$$\text{as} \quad M \to \infty.$$

Roberts and Smith (1994) (see also Chan, 1993) have shown that this convergence occurs under the following weak conditions: (i) $\pi(\theta|\mathbf{y}) > 0$ implies there exists an open neighbourhood N_θ containing θ and $\varepsilon > 0$ such that, for all $\theta' \in N_\theta$, $\pi(\theta'|\mathbf{y}) \geq \varepsilon > 0$; (ii) $\int \pi(\theta|\mathbf{y})d\theta_k$ is locally bounded for all k, where θ_k is the kth block of parameters; and (iii) the support of θ is arc connected.

4 MCMC sampling with latent variables

MCMC sampling can involve not just parameters but also latent variables. This idea was called data augmentation by Tanner and Wong (1987) in the context of missing data problems.

To fix notations, suppose that $\mathbf{z}$ denotes a vector of latent variables and let the modified target distribution be $\pi(\theta, \mathbf{z}|\mathbf{y})$. If the latent variables are tactically introduced, the conditional distribution of θ (or sub-components of θ) given $\mathbf{z}$ may be easy to derive. Then, a multiple-block M–H simulation is conducted with the blocks θ and $\mathbf{z}$ leading to the sample

$$\left(\theta^{(n_0+1)}, \mathbf{z}^{(n_0+1)}\right), \ldots, \left(\theta^{(n_0+M)}, \mathbf{z}^{(n_0+M)}\right)$$
$$\sim \pi(\theta, \mathbf{z}|\mathbf{y}),$$

where the draws on θ, ignoring those on the latent data, are from $\pi(\theta|\mathbf{y})$, as required.

To demonstrate this technique in action, consider the probit regression example discussed in Section 2.2. Albert and Chib (1993) introduced a technique for this and related models that capitalizes on the simplifications afforded by introducing latent data into the sampling. The Albert–Chib method has found wide use and has made possible the routine analysis of models for categorical responses. To begin, let

$$z_i|\boldsymbol{\beta} \sim N(\mathbf{x}_i'\boldsymbol{\beta}, 1),$$

$$y_i = I[z_i > 0], \quad i \leq n,$$

$$\boldsymbol{\beta} \sim N_k(\boldsymbol{\beta}_0, \mathbf{B}_0). \tag{10}$$

This specification is equivalent to the probit model since $\Pr(y_i = 1|\mathbf{x}_i, \boldsymbol{\beta}) = \Pr(z_i > 0|\mathbf{x}_i, \boldsymbol{\beta}) = \Phi(\mathbf{x}_i'\boldsymbol{\beta})$. Now the MCMC sampling is based on the full conditional distributions

$$\boldsymbol{\beta}|\mathbf{y}, \{z_i\}; \quad \{z_i\}|\mathbf{y}, \boldsymbol{\beta},$$

which are both tractable. In particular, the distribution of $\boldsymbol{\beta}$ conditioned on the latent data becomes independent of the observed data and has the same form as in the Gaussian linear regression model with the response data given by $\{z_i\}$ and is multivariate normal with mean $\hat{\boldsymbol{\beta}} = \mathbf{B}(\mathbf{B}_0^{-1}\boldsymbol{\beta}_0 + \sum_{i=1}^n \mathbf{x}_i z_i)$ and variance matrix $\mathbf{B} = (\mathbf{B}_0^{-1} + \sum_{i=1}^n \mathbf{x}_i \mathbf{x}_i')^{-1}$. Next, the distribution of the latent data conditioned on the data and the parameters factor into a set of n independent distributions with each depending

on the data through y_i:

$$\{z_i\}|\mathbf{y}, \boldsymbol{\beta} \stackrel{d}{=} \prod_{i=1}^n z_i|y_i, \boldsymbol{\beta},$$

where the distribution $z_i|y_i, \beta$ is the normal distribution $z_i|\beta$ truncated by the knowledge of y_i; if $y_i = 0$, then $z_i \leq 0$ and if $y_i = 1$, then $z_i > 0$. Thus, one samples z_i from $TN_{(-\infty,0)}(\mathbf{x}_i'\beta, 1)$ if $y_i = 0$ and from $TN_{(0,\infty)}(\mathbf{x}_i'\beta, 1)$ if $y_i = 1$, where $TN_{(a,b)}(\mu, \sigma^2)$ denotes the $N(\mu, \sigma^2)$ distribution truncated to the region (a,b).

We apply this method to the example considered in Section 2.2 above and report the results in Figure 2. We see the close agreement between the two sets of results.

5 Strategies for improving mixing

In practice, while implementing MCMC methods it is important to construct samplers that mix well, where mixing is measured by the autocorrelation time, because such samplers can be expected to converge more quickly to the invariant distribution.

5.1 Choice of blocking

As a general rule, sets of parameters that are highly correlated should be treated as one block when applying the multiple-block M–H algorithm. Otherwise, it would be difficult to develop proposal densities that lead to large moves through the support of the target distribution.

Blocks can be combined by the method of composition. For example, suppose that θ_1, θ_2 and θ_3 denote three blocks and that the distribution $\theta_1|\mathbf{y}, \theta_3$ is tractable (that is, can be sampled directly). Then, the blocks (θ_1, θ_2) can be collapsed by first sampling, θ_1 from $\theta_1|\mathbf{y}, \theta_3$ followed by θ_2 from $\theta_2|\mathbf{y}, \theta_1, \theta_3$. This amounts to a two-block MCMC algorithm. In addition, if it is possible to sample (θ_1, θ_2) marginalized over θ_3 then the number of blocks is reduced to one. Liu (1994) discusses the value of these strategies in the context of a three-block Gibbs MCMC chain. Roberts and Sahu (1997) provide further discussion of the role of blocking in the context of Gibbs Markov chains used to sample multivariate normal target distributions.

5.2 Tuning the proposal density

The proposal density in an M–H algorithm has an important bearing on the mixing of the MCMC chain. Chib and Greenberg (1994; 1995), Tierney (1994), Tierney and Mira (1999) and Liu (2001) discuss various possibilities for formulating proposal density that can be helpful in a variety of problems.

6 Prediction and model choice

In some settings, for example in models for time series data, an important goal is prediction. In the Bayesian context, a future observation y_f is predicted through the

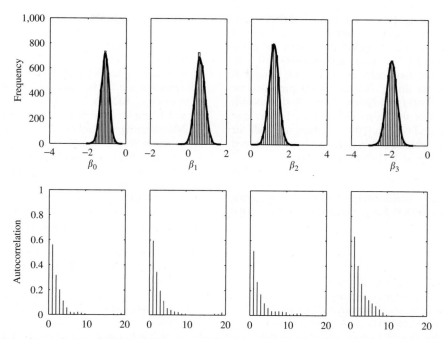

Figure 2 Caesarean data with Albert–Chib algorithm: marginal posterior densities (top panel) and autocorrelation plot (bottom panel)

(predictive) density defined as

$$f(y_f|\mathbf{y}) = \int f(y_f|\mathbf{y}, \boldsymbol{\theta})\pi(\boldsymbol{\theta}|\mathbf{y}) \, d\boldsymbol{\theta},$$

where $f(y_f|\mathbf{y}, \mathcal{M}, \boldsymbol{\theta})$ is the conditional density of y_f given $(\mathbf{y}, \boldsymbol{\theta})$. In general, the predictive density is not available in closed form. It can be shown, however, that, if one simulates $y_f^{(j)} \sim f(y_f|\mathbf{y}, \boldsymbol{\theta}^{(j)})$ for each sampled draw $\boldsymbol{\theta}^{(j)}$ from the MCMC simulation, then the collection of simulated values $\{y_f^{(1)}, \ldots, y_f^{(M)}\}$ is a sample from $f(y_f|\mathbf{y})$. This simulated sample can be summarized in the usual way.

MCMC methods have also been widely applied to the problem of the model choice. Suppose that there are K possible models $\mathcal{M}_1, \ldots, \mathcal{M}_K$ for the observed data defined by the sampling densities $\{f(\mathbf{y}|\boldsymbol{\theta}_k, \mathcal{M}_k)\}$ and proper prior densities $\{p(\boldsymbol{\theta}_k|\mathcal{M}_k)\}$ and the objective is to find the evidence in the data for the different models. In the Bayesian approach this question is answered by placing prior probabilities $\text{Pr}(\mathcal{M}_k)$ on each of the K models and using the Bayes calculus to find the posterior probabilities $\{\text{Pr}(\mathcal{M}_1|\mathbf{y}), \ldots, \text{Pr}(\mathcal{M}_K|\mathbf{y})\}$ conditioned on the data but marginalized over the unknowns $\boldsymbol{\theta}_k$ (Jeffreys, 1961). Specifically, the posterior probability of $\mathcal{M}_k$ is given by the expression

$$\text{Pr}(\mathcal{M}_k|\mathbf{y}) = \frac{\text{Pr}(\mathcal{M}_k)m(\mathbf{y}|\mathcal{M}_k)}{\sum_{l=1}^{K}\text{Pr}(\mathcal{M}_l)m(\mathbf{y}|\mathcal{M}_l)}$$
$$\propto \text{Pr}(\mathcal{M}_k)m(\mathbf{y}|\mathcal{M}_k), \quad (k \leq K)$$

where $m(\mathbf{y}|\mathcal{M}_k)$ is the marginal likelihood of $\mathcal{M}_k$.

A problem in estimating the marginal likelihood is that it is an integral of the sampling density over the prior distribution of $\boldsymbol{\theta}_k$. Thus, MCMC methods, which deliver sample values from the posterior density, cannot be used to directly average the sampling density. One method for dealing with this difficulty is due to Chib (1995). The starting point is the expression

$$m(\mathbf{y}|\mathcal{M}_k) = \frac{f(\mathbf{y}|\boldsymbol{\theta}_k, \mathcal{M}_k)p(\boldsymbol{\theta}_k|\mathcal{M}_k)}{\pi(\boldsymbol{\theta}_k|\mathbf{y}, \mathcal{M}_k)}$$

which is an identity in $\boldsymbol{\theta}_k$. From here an estimate of the marginal likelihood on the log-scale is given by

$$\begin{aligned}\log\hat{m}(\mathbf{y}|\mathcal{M}_k) &= \log f(\mathbf{y}|\boldsymbol{\theta}_k^*, \mathcal{M}_k) \\ &\quad + \log p(\boldsymbol{\theta}_k^*|\mathcal{M}_k) - \log\hat{\pi}(\boldsymbol{\theta}_k^*|\mathbf{y}, \mathcal{M}_k)\end{aligned}$$

where $\boldsymbol{\theta}_k^*$ denotes an arbitrarily chosen point and $\hat{\pi}(\boldsymbol{\theta}_k^*|\mathbf{y}, \mathcal{M}_k)$ is the estimate of the posterior density at that single point. To estimate the posterior ordinate one utilizes the Gibbs output in conjunction with a decomposition of the ordinate into marginal and conditional components. Chib and Jeliazkov (2001) extend this approach for output produced by the M–H algorithm while Basu and Chib (2003) show how the method can be applied in semiparametric models.

In some cases one is interested in a large number of candidate models, each with parameters $\boldsymbol{\theta}_k \in B_k \subseteq R^{d_k}$. In such cases one can get information about the relative support for the contending models from a model space-parameter space MCMC algorithm. In these algorithms, the models are represented by a categorical variable $\mathscr{M}$ which is then sampled along with the parameters of each model. The posterior distribution of $\mathscr{M}$ is computed as the frequency of times each model is visited. Methods for doing this have been proposed by Carlin and Chib (1995) and Green (1995). Both methods are closely related as shown by Dellaportas, Forster and Ntzoufras (2002) and Godsill (2001). Related methods for the problem of variable selection have also been developed starting with George and McCulloch (1993).

SIDDHARTHA CHIB

See also **Bayesian econometrics; Bayesian statistics; econometrics; hierarchical Bayes models; simulation-based estimation.**

Bibliography

Albert, J.H. and Chib, S. 1993. Bayesian analysis of binary and polychotomous response data. *Journal of the American Statistical Association* 88, 669–79.

Basu, S. and Chib, S. 2003. Marginal likelihood and Bayes factors for Dirichlet process mixture models. *Journal of the American Statistical Association* 98, 224–35.

Carlin, B.P. and Chib, S. 1995. Bayesian model choice via Markov chain Monte Carlo. *Journal of Royal Statistical Society, Series B* 57, 473–84.

Chan, K.S. 1993. Asymptotic behavior of the Gibbs sampler. *Journal of the American Statistical Association* 88, 320–6.

Chen, M.H., Shao, Q.M. and Ibrahim, J.G. 2000. *Monte Carlo Methods in Bayesian Computation.* New York: Springer.

Chib, S. 1995. Marginal likelihood from the Gibbs output. *Journal of the American Statistical Association* 90, 1313–21.

Chib, S. 2001. Markov chain Monte Carlo methods: computation and inference. In *Handbook of Econometrics,* vol. 5, ed. J.J. Heckman and E. Leamer. Amsterdam: North-Holland.

Chib, S. and Greenberg, E. 1994. Bayes inference in regression models with ARMA (p,q) errors. *Journal of Econometrics* 64, 183–206.

Chib, S. and Greenberg, E. 1995. Understanding the Metropolis–Hastings algorithm. *American Statistician* 49, 327–35.

Chib, S. and Jeliazkov, I. 2001. Marginal likelihood from the Metropolis–Hastings output. *Journal of the American Statistical Association* 96, 270–81.

Dellaportas, P., Forster, J.J. and Ntzoufras, I. 2002. On Bayesian model and variable selection using MCMC. *Statistics and Computing* 12, 27–36.

Fahrmeir, L. and Tutz, G. 1994. *Multivariate Statistical Modelling Based on Generalized Linear Models.* Berlin: Springer.

Gelfand, A.E. and Smith, A.F. 1990. Sampling-based approaches to calculating marginal densities. *Journal of the American Statistical Association* 85, 398–409.

Geman, S. and Geman, D. 1984. Stochastic relaxation, Gibbs distribution and the Bayesian restoration of images. *IEEE Transactions, PAMI* 6, 721–41.

George, E.I. and McCulloch, R.E. 1993. Variable selection via Gibbs sampling. *Journal Of The American Statistical Association* 88, 881–9.

Gilks, W.K., Richardson, S. and Spiegelhalter, D.J. 1996. *Markov Chain Monte Carlo in Practice.* London: Chapman & Hall.

Godsill, S.J. 2001. On the relationship between Markov chain Monte Carlo methods for model uncertainty. *Journal of Computational And Graphical Statistics* 10, 230–48.

Green, P.J. 1995. Reversible jump Markov chain Monte Carlo computation and Bayesian model determination. *Biometrika* 82, 711–32.

Hastings, W.K. 1970. Monte-Carlo sampling methods using Markov chains and their applications. *Biometrika* 57, 97–109.

Jeffreys, H. 1961. *Theory of Probability,* 3rd edn. Oxford: Oxford University Press.

Liu, J.S. 1994. The collapsed Gibbs sampler in Bayesian computations with applications to a gene-regulation problem. *Journal of the American Statistical Association* 89, 958–66.

Liu, J.S. 2001. *Monte Carlo Strategies in Scientific Computing.* New York: Springer.

Metropolis, N., Rosenbluth, A.W., Rosenbluth, M.N., Teller, A.H. et al. 1953. Equations of state calculations by fast computing machines. *Journal of Chemical Physics* 21, 1087–92.

Robert, C.P. and Casella, G. 2004. *Monte Carlo Statistical Methods,* 2nd edn. New York: Springer.

Roberts, G.O. and Sahu, S.K. 1997. Updating schemes, correlation structure, blocking and parameterization for the Gibbs sampler. *Journal of the Royal Statistical Society, Series B* 59, 291–317.

Roberts, G.O. and Smith, A.F.M. 1994. Simple conditions for the convergence of the Gibbs sampler and Metropolis-Hastings algorithms. *Stochastic Processes and Their Applications* 49, 207–16.

Tanner, M.A. and Wong, W.H. 1987. The calculation of posterior distributions by data augmentation (with discussion). *Journal of the American Statistical Association* 82, 528–50.

Tierney, L. 1994. Markov chains for exploring posterior distributions (with discussion). *Annals of Statistics* 21, 1701–62.

Tierney, L. and Mira, A. 1999. Some adaptive Monte Carlo methods for Bayesian inference. *Statistics in Medicine* 18, 2507–15.

Markov equilibria in macroeconomics

We say that a dynamic economy has a Markovian structure (or is Markovian, for short) if the stochastic processes that specify the fundamentals of the economy (such as endowments, preferences and technologies) are Markov processes. Note that deterministic economies are special cases in which the stochastic processes for the fundamentals have degenerate distributions. In many applications attention is restricted to first-order Markov processes in which the probability distributions over fundamentals today are functions exclusively of their values yesterday.

In dynamic economies sequential equilibria are sequences of functions mapping histories of realizations of the stochastic process of the fundamentals into allocations and prices such that all agents in the economy maximize their objectives, given prices, and all markets clear. Under fairly mild conditions (that is, convexity and continuity assumptions on the primitives) such equilibria exist. However, in order to characterize and compute equilibria it is often useful to look for equilibria of a different form.

Recursive Markov equilibria can be characterized by a state space, a policy function and a transition function. The policy function maps the state today into current endogenous choices and prices, and the transition function maps the state today into a probability distribution over states tomorrow (see, for example, the definition in Ljungqvist and Sargent's 2000 textbook). In most of this survey we will use the terms 'Markov equilibria' and 'recursive Markov equilibria' interchangeably; however, below we also consider Markov equilibria which are not recursive and refer to these as 'generalized Markov equilibria'. This characterization leaves open, of course, what the appropriate state variables are that constitute the state space.

Most simply, the state space would consist of the set of possible exogenous shocks governing endowments, preferences and technologies. But, other than in exceptional cases (see, for example, Lucas's 1978 asset pricing application where asset prices are solely functions of the underlying shocks to technology), such a strongly stationary Markov equilibrium does not exist.

In addition to the exogenous shocks, endogenous variables have to be included in the state space to assure existence of a Markov equilibrium. We define as the minimal state space the space of all exogenous shocks and endogenous variables that are payoff-relevant today, in that they affect current production or consumption sets or preferences (see Maskin and Tirole, 2001). We call Markov equilibria with this minimal state space 'simple Markov equilibria'. In the remainder of this article we want to discuss what we know about the existence and uniqueness of such Markov equilibria, both in general and for important specific examples. As it turns out, when equilibria are Pareto efficient, and thus equilibrium allocation can be determined by solving a suitable social planner problem, simple Markov equilibria can be shown to exist under fairly mild conditions. We therefore discuss this case first. On the other hand, when equilibria are not Pareto efficient – for example, when markets are incomplete or economic agents behave strategically – forward-looking variables often have to be included for a Markov equilibrium to exist; therefore, simple Markov equilibria in the sense defined above do not exist in general. We discuss this case in Section 2.

1 Markov equilibria in economies where equilibria are Pareto optimal

In this section we discuss the existence and uniqueness of simple Markov equilibria in economies whose sequential market equilibrium allocations can be determined as solutions to a suitable social planner problem. In these economies the problem of proving the existence of a Markov equilibrium reduces to showing that the solution of the social planner can be written as a time-invariant optimal policy function of the minimal set of state variables, as defined above.

This is commonly done by reformulating the optimization problem of the social planner as a functional equation and showing that the optimal Markov policy function generates a sequential allocation which solves the original social planner problem; this is what Bellman (1957) called the principle of optimality. This principle can be established under weak conditions (see Stokey, Lucas and Prescott, 1989). Equipped with this result, the existence of a Markov equilibrium then follows from the existence of a solution to the functional equation associated with the social planner problem.

If the functional equation can be shown to be a contraction mapping (sufficient conditions for this were provided by Blackwell, 1965), then it follows that there exists a unique value function solving the functional equation and an optimal policy correspondence. In addition, the contraction mapping theorem also gives an iterative procedure to find the solution to the functional equation from any starting guess, which is helpful for numerical work.

Under weaker conditions other fixed-point theorems may be employed to argue at least for the existence (if not uniqueness) of a solution to the functional equation, with associated optimal Markov policy correspondence. In order to establish that the policy correspondence is actually a function (and thus the Markov equilibrium is unique), in general strict concavity of the return function needs to be assumed. Stokey, Lucas and Prescott (1989) provide a summary of the main results in the general theory of dynamic programming.

This technique of analysing and computing dynamic equilibria in Pareto optimal economies is now widely used in macroeconomics. Its first application can be found in Lucas and Prescott (1971) in their study of optimal investment behaviour under uncertainty.

Lucas (1978) used recursive techniques to study asset prices in an endowment economy and showed that the Markov equilibrium has a particularly simple form. Kydland and Prescott (1982) showed how powerful these techniques are for a quantitative study of the business cycle implications of the neoclassical growth model with technology shocks to production. The volume by Cooley (1995) provides a comprehensive overview over this line of research.

2 Generalized Markov equilibria

In models where the first welfare theorem is not applicable (for example, models with incomplete financial markets or with distorting taxes), in models where there are infinitely many agents (such as overlapping generations models) or in models with strategic interaction the existence of simple Markov equilibria (that is, Markov equilibria with minimal state space) cannot be guaranteed. See Santos, 2002; Krebs, 2004; Kubler and Schmedders, 2002; and Kubler and Polemarchakis, 2004; for simple counter-examples. An important exception is Bewley-style models with incomplete markets where simple recursive Markov equilibria exist; see, for example, Krebs, 2006. The functional equations characterizing equilibrium have no contraction properties, and more general fixed-point theorems than the contraction mapping theorem, such as Schauder's fixed-point theorem, cannot be applied because it is difficult to guarantee compactness of the space of admissible functions. Coleman (1991) is an important example where existence can be shown. However, his results rely on monotonicity conditions on the equilibrium dynamics which are not satisfied in general models.

In the applied literature a solution to this problem was suggested early on. For example Kydland and Prescott (1980) analyse a Ramsey dynamic optimal taxation problem. To make the problem recursive they add as a state variable last period's marginal utility.

On the theoretical side Duffie et al. (1994) were the first to rigorously analyse situations where recursive equilibria may fail to exist in general equilibrium models. Kubler and Schmedders (2003) and Miao and Santos (2005) refine their approach and make it applicable for computations. Miao and Santos, (2005), also give a clear explanation of how this approach relates to the work by Abreu, Pearce and Stacchetti (1990). We now present their basic idea.

Consider a Markovian economy where a date-event (or node) can be associated with a finite history of shocks, $S^t = (s_0, \ldots, s_t)$. The shocks follow a Markov chain with support $\mathscr{S} = \{1, \ldots, S\}$. Denote by $z(s^t)$ the vector of all endogenous variables at node s^t. Typically this would include the vector of household asset holdings across individuals and the capital stock at the beginning of the period, but also prices and endogenous choices at note s^t, as well as shadow variables

such as Lagrange multipliers. A competitive equilibrium is a process of endogenous variables $\{z(s^t)\}$ with $z(s^t) \in \mathscr{Z} \subset \mathbb{R}^M$, which solve the optimization problems of all agents in the economy, and clear markets. The set $\mathscr{Z}$ denotes the set of all possible values of the endogenous variables.

We focus on dynamic economic models where an equilibrium can be characterized by a set of equations relating current-period exogenous and endogenous variables to endogenous and exogenous variables next period. It is straightforward to incorporate inequality constraints into this framework. For expositional purposes we focus on equations. Examples of such equations are the Euler equations of individual households, first order conditions of firms, as well as market-clearing conditions for all markets. We assume that such a set of equations characterizing equilibrium is given and denote it by

$$h(\hat{s}, \hat{z}, z_1, \ldots, z_S) = 0.$$

The arguments $(\hat{s}, \hat{z})$ denote the exogenous state variables and endogenous variables for the current period. Note that the endogenous variables might contain variables which were determined in the previous period, such as the capital stock and individuals' assets. The variables $(z_s)_{s=1}^{S}$ denote endogenous variables in the subsequent period, in states $s = 1, \ldots, S$, respectively. We refer to $h(\cdot) = 0$ as the set of 'equilibrium equations'.

As explained above, to analyse Markov equilibria one needs to specify an appropriate state space. We assume that the equilibrium set $\mathscr{Z}$ can be written as the product $\mathscr{Y} \times \hat{\mathscr{Z}}$, where $\mathscr{Y}$ denotes the set into which the endogenous state variables fall. In the neoclassical growth model, $\mathscr{Y}$ would consist of the set of possible values of the capital stock; in models with heterogeneous agents one would need to add the set of possible wealth distributions across agents. Unfortunately, as the references cited above show, a recursive Markov equilibrium with this state space may not exist. We therefore require a more general notion of Markov equilibrium for these types of economies.

A *generalized Markov equilibrium* consists of a (nonempty valued) 'policy correspondence', P, that maps the state today into possible endogenous variables today, and a 'transition function', F, that maps the state and endogenous variables today into endogenous variables next period. Formally, the maps

$$P : \mathscr{S} \times \mathscr{Y} \rightrightarrows \hat{\mathscr{Z}} \quad \text{and} \quad F : \text{graph}(P) \to \mathscr{Z}^S$$

should satisfy that for all shocks and endogenous variables in the current period, $(\hat{s}, \hat{z}) \in \text{graph}(P)$, the transition function prescribes values next period that are consistent with the equilibrium equations, that is,

$$h(\hat{s}, \hat{z}, F(\hat{s}, \hat{z})) = 0,$$

and lie in the policy correspondence, that is,

$$(s, F_s(\hat{s}, \hat{z})) \in \text{graph}(P) \quad \text{for all} \quad s \in \mathscr{S}.$$

It follows that a generalized Markov equilibrium is recursive, according to our earlier definition, if the associated policy correspondence is single valued. It is simple if the state space is the natural minimal state space.

It is easy to see that Markov equilibria are in fact competitive equilibria in the usual sense. Duffie et al. (1994) show that, under mild assumptions on the primitives of the model, generalized Markov equilibria exist whenever competitive equilibria exist. The basic idea of their approach is very similar to backward induction, using critically a natural monotonicity property of the inverse of the equilibrium equations. (See their original paper, Kubler and Schmedders (2003) or Miao and Santos (2005) for details.)

For practical purposes it is of course crucial that the chosen state space is relatively small and that the Markov equilibrium is recursive. In an asset pricing model with heterogeneous agents, Kubler and Schmedders choose the state space to consist of the beginning-of-period wealth distribution, but can show the existence only of a generalized Markov equilibrium. One cannot rule out the possibility that the equilibrium is not recursive; the same value of the state variables might occur with different values of the endogenous variables. The counter-examples to existence mentioned above show that this is precisely the problem. If for given initial conditions there exist multiple competitive equilibria, the one that realizes is pinned down by lagged variables. Without ruling out multiplicity of equilibria, it does not seem possible to prove the existence of recursive equilibria with the natural state space.

Miao and Santos (2005) enlarge the state space with the shadow values of investment of all agents and prove that with this larger state space a recursive Markov equilibrium exists. The basic insight of their approach is that one needs to add variables to the natural state space that uniquely select one out of several possible endogenous variables.

The main practical problem with the approach originated by Duffie et al. (1994) and refined by Miao and Santos (2005) is that it provides a method to construct all Markov equilibria. There might exist some recursive equilibria for the natural (minimal) state space, but this approach naturally solves for all other recursive Markov equilibria as well. Datta et al., 2005, provide ideas for solving for the one Markov equilibrium with minimal state space.

In many recent applications of recursive methods to macroeconomics the focus of researchers studying non-optimal economies is to find a recursive equilibrium with minimal state space. Notable examples in which even this natural state space is large are Rios-Rull (1996), Heaton and Lucas (1996) and Krusell and Smith (1998).

They mark the boundary of economies that currently can be analysed with recursive techniques.

In dynamic endowment economies with either informational frictions or limited enforceability of contracts, constrained-efficient (efficient, subject to the informational or enforcement constraints) consumption allocations usually display a high degree of dependence on past endowment shocks, even though the natural state space contains only the current endowment shock. Therefore, Markov equilibria with minimal state space do not exist. However, using ideas by Spear and Srivastava (1987) and Abreu, Pearce, and Stacchetti (1990), the papers by Atkeson and Lucas (1992) and Thomas and Worrall (1988) demonstrate that nevertheless the constrained social planner problem has a convenient recursive structure if one includes promised lifetime utility as a state variable into the recursive problem. This approach or its close alternative, namely, to introduce as an additional state variable Lagrange multipliers on the incentive or enforcement constraints (as in Marcet and Marimon, 1998), has seen many applications in macroeconomics, since it facilitates making a large class of dynamic models with informational or enforcement frictions recursive and hence tractable. Miao and Santos (2005) show how such problems with strategic interactions can be incorporated into the framework above.

In optimal policy problems in which the government has no access to a commitment technology, a discussion has emerged about the desirability of a restriction to Markov policies with minimal state space. Such restrictions rule out reputation if one confines attention to smooth policies. See Phelan and Stacchetti (2001) and Klein and Rios-Rull (2003) for examples of the two opposing views on this issue. However, as Krusell and Smith (2003) argue, if one allows discontinuous policy functions reputation effects can be generated even with Markov policies. (While Krusell and Smith discuss optimal decision rules in a consumption–savings problem with quasi-geometric discounting, their results carry over to optimal policy problems without commitment on the part of the policymaker.)

DIRK KRUEGER AND FELIX KUBLER

See also **computation of general equilibria; decentralization; Euler equations; existence of general equilibrium; functional analysis; general equilibrium; general equilibrium (new developments); income taxation and optimal policies; incomplete markets; Markov processes; optimal fiscal and monetary policy (without commitment); Pareto efficiency; recursive competitive equilibrium; recursive contracts.**

Bibliography

Abreu, D., Pearce, D. and Stacchetti, E. 1990. Toward a theory of repeated games with discounting. *Econometrica* 58, 1041–63.

Atkeson, A. and Lucas, R. 1992. On efficient distribution with private information, *Review of Economic Studies* 59, 427–53.

Bellman, R. 1957. *Dynamic Programming*. Princeton, NJ: Princeton University Press.

Blackwell, D. 1965. Discounted dynamic programming. *Annals of Mathematical Statistics* 36, 226–35.

Coleman, J. 1991. Equilibrium in a production economy with an income tax. *Econometrica* 59, 1091–104.

Cooley, T. 1995. *Frontiers of Business Cycle Research*. Princeton, NJ: Princeton University Press.

Datta, M., Mirman, L., Morand, O. and Reffett, K. 2005. Markovian equilibrium in infinite horizon economies with incomplete markets and public policy. *Journal of Mathematical Economics* 41, 505–44.

Duffie, D., Geanakoplos, J., Mas-Colell, A. and McLennan, A. 1994. Stationary Markov equilibria. *Econometrica* 62, 745–81.

Heaton, H. and Lucas, D. 1996. Evaluating the effects of incomplete markets on risk sharing and asset pricing. *Journal of Political Economy* 104, 443–87.

Klein, P. and Rios-Rull, V. 2003. Time consistent optimal fiscal policy. *International Economic Review* 44, 1217–46.

Krebs, T. 2004. Non-existence of recursive equilibria on compact state spaces when markets are incomplete. *Journal of Economic Theory* 115, 134–50.

Krebs, T. 2006. Recursive equilibrium in endogenous growth models with incomplete markets, *Economic Theory*, 29, 505–23.

Krusell, P. and Smith, A. 1998. Income and wealth heterogeneity in the macroeconomy. *Journal of Political Economy* 106, 867–96.

Krusell, P. and Smith, A. 2003. Consumption–savings decisions with quasi–geometric discounting. *Econometrica* 71, 365–76.

Kubler, F. and Polemarchakis, H. 2004. Stationary Markov equilibria for overlapping generations. *Economic Theory* 24, 623–43.

Kubler, F. and Schmedders, K. 2002. Recursive equilibria in economies with incomplete markets. *Macroeconomic Dynamics* 6, 284–306.

Kubler, F. and Schmedders, K. 2003. Stationary equilibria in asset-pricing models with incomplete markets and collateral. *Econometrica* 71, 1767–95.

Kydland, F. and Prescott, E. 1980. Dynamic optimal taxation, rational expectations and optimal control. *Journal of Economic Dynamics and Control* 2, 79–91.

Kydland, F. and Prescott, E. 1982. Time to build and aggregate fluctuations, *Econometrica* 50, 1345–71.

Ljungqvist, L. and Sargent, T. 2000. *Recursive Macroeconomic Theory*. Cambridge, MA: MIT Press.

Lucas, R. 1978. Asset prices in an exchange economy. *Econometrica* 46, 1426–45.

Lucas, R. and Prescott, E. 1971. Investment under uncertainty. *Econometrica* 39, 659–81.

Marcet, A. and Marimon, R. 1998. Recursive contracts. Working paper, University Pompeu Fabra, Barcelona.

Maskin, E. and Tirole, J. 2001. Markov perfect equilibrium. *Journal of Economic Theory* 100, 191–219.

Miao, J. and Santos, M. 2005. Existence and computation of Markov equilibria for dynamic non–optimal economies. Working paper, Department of Economics, Boston University.

Phelan, C. and Stacchetti, E. 2001. Sequential equilibria in a Ramsey tax model. *Econometrica* 69, 1491–518.

Rios-Rull, V. 1996. Life cycle economies with aggregate fluctuations. *Review of Economic Studies* 63, 465–90.

Santos, M. 2002. On non-existence of Markov equilibria for competitive-market economies. *Journal of Economic Theory* 105, 73–98.

Spear, S. and Srivastava, S. 1987. On repeated moral hazard with discounting, *Review of Economic Studies* 54, 599–617.

Stokey, N., Lucas, R. and Prescott, E. 1989. *Recursive Methods in Economic Dynamics*. Cambridge, MA: Harvard University Press.

Thomas, J. and Worrall, T. 1988. Self-enforcing wage contracts. *Review of Economic Studies* 55, 541–54.

Markov processes

Unless one is clairvoyant, the only temporally evolving processes which are tractable are those whose future behaviour can be predicted on the basis of data which is available at the time when the prediction is being made. Of course, in general, the behaviour of even such an evolution will be impossible to predict. For example, if, in order to make a prediction, one has to know the detailed history of everything that has happened during the entire history of the entire universe, one's chance of making a prediction may be a practical, if not a theoretical, impossibility. For this reason, one tries to study evolutions mathematically with models in which most of the distant past can be ignored when one makes predictions about the future. In fact, many mathematical models of evolutions have the property that, for the purpose of predicting the future, the past becomes irrelevant as soon as one knows the present, in which case the evolution is said to be a 'Markov process', the topic at hand, after Andrei Andreyevich Markov (1856–1922).

The components of a Markov process are its *state space* $\mathbb{S}$ and its *transition rule T*. Mathematically, $\mathbb{S}$ is just some non-empty set, which in applications will encode all the possible states in which the evolving system can find itself, and $T : \mathbb{S} \to \mathbb{S}$ is a function from $\mathbb{S}$ into itself which gives the *transition rule*. More precisely, if now the system is in state x, it will be next in state $T(x)$, from which it will go to $T^2(x) = T(T(x))$, and so on. (Here we are thinking of time being discrete. Thus, 'next' means after one unit of time has passed.)

To give a sense of the sort of reasoning required to construct a Markov process, consider a (classical) physical particle whose motion is governed by Newton's equation $\vec{F} = m\vec{a}$ ('force equals mass times acceleration'). At least in theory, Newton's equation says that, on the assumption that one knows the mass of the particle and the force field $\vec{F}$ which acts on it, one can predict where the particle will be in the future as soon as one knows what its position and velocity are now. On the other hand, knowing only its present position is not sufficient by itself. Thus, even though one may care about nothing but its position, in order to produce a Markov process for a particle evolving according to Newton's equation it is necessary to adopt the attitude that the *state* of the particle consists of its position *and* velocity, not just its position alone. Of course, in that velocity is the derivative of position, the two are so inextricably intertwined that one might be tempted to concentrate on position on the grounds that one will be able to compute the velocity whenever necessary. However, this tack destroys the Markov property, namely, there is no way of computing the velocity of a particle 'now' if all one knows is its position 'now'. For this reason, physicists consider the state of a particle to be a composite of its position and velocity, and the resulting state space $\mathbb{R}^6 = \mathbb{R}^3 \times \mathbb{R}^3$ (three coordinates for position and three for velocity) they call the *phase space* of the particle.

The same point may be clearer in the following example. Suppose that one has an evolution on a state space $\mathbb{S}$ which proceeds according to the rule that, if the present state is x_n and the preceding state was x_{n-1}, then the next state will be $x_{n+1} = T(x_{n-1}, x_n)$. This is *not* a Markov process. Nonetheless, it can be 'Markovized'. Indeed, replace the original state space by $\hat{\mathbb{S}} = \mathbb{S} \times \mathbb{S}$, the set of ordered pairs (x, y) with x and y from $\mathbb{S}$, and define $\hat{T}((x, y)) = (y, T(x, y))$. It is then an easy matter to check that, if the original system was in state x_{-1} at time -1 and state x_0 at time 0, then its state at time $n \geq 1$ will be x_n, the second component of the pair $(x_{n-1}, x_n) = \hat{T}^n((x_{-1}, x_0))$.

The moral to be drawn from these examples is that *the presence or absence of the Markov property is in the eye of the beholder.* That is, a change of venue (the state space) can make the Markov property appear in circumstances where it was not originally apparent. In fact, by making the state space sufficiently large, any evolution can be forced to be Markov. On the other hand, the more complicated the state space, the less useful is the Markov property. Thus, in practice, what one seeks is the 'simplest' state space on which one's evolution possesses the Markov property.

Stochastic Markov processes

Roughly speaking, Markov processes fall into one of two categories. Those in the first category are 'deterministic' in the sense that their state space is sufficiently detailed that the individual states give complete and unambiguous information. Both the examples given above are deterministic. The mathematical analysis of deterministic

Markov processes has a proud history going back to Newton which includes major contributions by such luminaries as P. Chebyshev, A. Markov, A. Lyapounov, H. Poincaré, and J. Moser. The second category of Markov processes, and the one on which the rest of this article will concentrate, are 'probabilistic' or 'stochastic' Markov processes. To understand where and why these processes arise, consider the problem of describing the state of all the gas molecules in a room. Each litre of gas contains approximately Avogrado's number, $6.02214199 \times 10^{23}$, of molecules. Thus, even a small room will contain something on the order of 10^{26} molecules. Moreover, because, by Newton's laws of motion, the state of each individual molecule will lie in its individual phase space, the state of the entire system of molecules will have to specify the positions and velocities of all 10^{26} molecules. Stated mathematically, the state space of the system will be $\mathbb{R}^{6 \times 10^{26}}$, on which any sort serious analysis is too daunting to contemplate.

When one is confronted with a problem which is intractable as presented, the time-honoured procedure of choice is to reformulate the problem in a way which makes it more tractable. In the case just described, the reformulation was made by G.W. Gibbs (1902) and L. Boltzmann (1896; 1898), the fathers of statistical mechanics. They abandoned any hope of saying exactly where all the molecules will be and reconciled themselves to settling for a description of the statistics of the molecules. That is, instead of asking exactly where all the molecules would be, they asked what would be the probability of finding a molecule in various regions of phase space. From this point of view, the state of the system will not be an element of $\mathbb{R}^{6 \times 10^{26}}$ but of $\mathbf{M}_1(\mathbb{R}^6)$, the space probability distributions on the individual phase space $\mathbb{R}^6$. Of course, Gibbs and Boltzmann's reformulation only changes the problem, it does not solve it. Indeed, although Newton's equation determines how the system of molecules evolves and therefore how their distribution will evolve, the use of Newton's equation would remove the advantage which Boltzmann and Gibbs hoped to gain from their reformulation. Thus, they had to come up with an alternative way of describing the transition rule which governs the evolution of the distribution of the system as a Markov process on $\mathbf{M}_1(\mathbb{R}^6)$. The description proposed by Boltzmann is given by the famous Boltzmann equation. Unfortunately, Boltzmann's equation is itself so complicated that it is only recently that substantial progress has been made toward understanding it in any generality. On the other hand, Gibbs and Boltzmann's idea of studying Markov processes on the space of probability distributions is seminal and has proved to be both ubiquitous and powerful.

The abstract setting for a stochastic Markov process starts with a non-empty set $\mathbb{S}$, the deterministic state space, and the associated space $\mathbf{M}_1(\mathbb{S})$ of probability distributions on $\mathbb{S}$. The easiest and most commonly studied stochastic Markov processes are those for which the transition rule $T : \mathbf{M}_1(\mathbb{S}) \to \mathbf{M}_1(\mathbb{S})$ is a linear (more correctly, an affine) function. To be definite, suppose $\mathbb{S}$ is a finite set. Then $\mathbf{M}_1(\mathbb{S})$ is the set of all functions μ on $\mathbb{S}$ which assign each $x \in \mathbb{S}$ a number $\mu(\{x\}) \in [0, 1]$ (the probability of $\{x\}$ under μ) in such a way that $\sum_{x \in \mathbb{S}} \mu(\{x\}) = 1$. (The use of $\mu(\{x\})$ instead of $\mu(x)$ here is a little pedantic. However, one must remember that probabilities are assigned to *events* – that is, subsets of the sample space – and that $\{x\}$ is the event that 'x occurred'.) Clearly, if μ and v are in $\mathbf{M}_1(\mathbb{S})$ and $\theta \in [0, 1]$, then the convex combination $\theta\mu + (1 - \theta)v$ is again an element of $\mathbf{M}_1(\mathbb{S})$. Sets with this property are said to be 'affine' (as distinguished from 'linear', which refers to sets which are closed under all linear, not just convex, combinations), and a function on an affine set is said to be affine if it commutes with convex combinations. Thus, for $\mathbf{M}_1(\mathbb{S})$, the transition rule T is affine if $T(\theta\mu + (1 - \theta)v) = \theta T(\mu) + (1 - \theta)T(v)$. Because $\mathbb{S}$ is finite, one can dissect such transition rules in the following way. First, for each $x \in \mathbb{S}$, let δ_x denote the element of $\mathbf{M}_1(\mathbb{S})$ which assigns 1 to $\{x\}$ (and therefore 0 to $\mathbb{S} \setminus \{x\}$). Next, set $\mathbf{P}(x, \cdot) = T(\delta_x)$. That is, $\mathbf{P}(x, \cdot)$ is the element of $\mathbf{M}_1(\mathbb{S})$ to which T takes $T(\delta_x)$, and so $\mathbf{P}(x, \{y\}) = [T(\delta_x)](\{y\})$. Because, for any $\mu \in \mathbf{M}_1(\mathbb{S})$ which is not equal to δ_x, $\mu = \mu(\{x\})\delta_x + (1 - \mu(\{x\}))\mu^x$, where $\mu^x \in \mathbf{M}_1(\mathbb{S})$ is determined so that $\mu^x(\{y\})$ equals $(1 - \mu(\{x\}))^{-1}\mu(\{y\})$ or 0 depending on whether $y \neq x$ or $y = x$, the affine property of T means that $T(\mu) = \mu(\{x\})\mathbf{P}(x, \cdot) + (1 - \mu(\{x\}))T(\mu^x)$. Hence, after peeling off one x at a time, one concludes that

$$T(\mu) = \sum_{x \in \mathbb{S}} \mu(\{x\})\mathbf{P}(x, \cdot) \qquad (1)$$

when T is affine.

Probabilistic interpretation

The representation of T given by (1) admits an intuitively pleasing probabilistic interpretation: namely, $\mathbf{P}(x, \{y\})$ can be thought of as the probability that the system will next be in the state y given that is now in state x. With this interpretation in mind, probabilists call $x \in \mathbb{S} \mapsto \mathbf{P}(x, \cdot) \in \mathbf{M}_1(\mathbb{S})$ a *transition probability* on the state space $\mathbb{S}$. The terminology here is confusing. From the point of view adopted earlier, one might, and should, have thought that $\mathbf{M}_1(\mathbb{S})$ is the state space. However, the probabilistic interpretation is most easily appreciated if one thinks of $\mathbb{S}$ as the state space and $x \in \mathbb{S} \to (x, \cdot) \in \mathbf{M}_1(\mathbb{S})$ as a random transition rule. To complete this picture, probabilists introduce random variables to represent the random points in $\mathbb{S}$ visited. More precisely, again assume that $\mathbb{S}$ is finite, and suppose that $\mu \in \mathbf{M}_1(\mathbb{S})$ describes the initial distribution of the process under consideration. Then probabilists construct a sequence $\{X_n : n \geq 0\}$ of random variables, called a *Markov chain*, in such a way that,

for any $n \geq 0$,

$$\begin{aligned}
\mathbf{P}(X_0 &= x_0, \ldots, X_n = x_n) \\
&= \mu(\{x_0\})\mathbf{P}(x_0, \{x_1\}) \cdots \mathbf{P}(x_{n-1}, \{x_n\}).
\end{aligned}$$

In words, this says that the right-hand side above is the probability that the chain with initial distribution μ starts at x_0 and then goes on to visit, successively, the points x_1 through x_n.

To see that the probabilistic interpretation is completely consistent in the deterministic case, observe that a deterministic Markov process can be formulated as a stochastic Markov process. That is, if T is the transition rule for the deterministic process, take $\mathbf{P}(x, \cdot) = \delta_{T(x)}$, and check that, with probability 1, the Markov chain with transition probability $\mathbf{P}(x, \cdot)$ follows the same path as the deterministic one with transition rule T. Equivalently, with probability 1, $X_n = T^n(X_0)$ for all $n \geq 1$.

Ergodic theory of Markov chains

Continue in the setting of the preceding section. One of the phenomena predicted by Gibbs in connection with his and Boltzmann's study of gases was that, no matter what the initial distribution of the gas, after a long time the gas should equilibrate in the sense that it will achieve a *stationary distribution* (that is, a distribution that does not change with time) which does not depend on how it was distributed initially. One's experience with the behaviour of gases makes this prediction entirely plausible: place an opened bottle of perfume in the corner of a room; wait an hour, and confirm that the perfume will have become more or less equi-distributed throughout the room. Be that as it may, the prediction, which goes by the name of Gibbs's 'ergodic hypothesis', has been mathematically verified in only one physically realistic model. Nonetheless, as will be explained next, ergodicity is relatively easy to verify for most stochastic Markov processes on a finite state space.

To develop some intuition for what ergodicity means and why it might hold for a stochastic Markov process on a finite state space $\mathbb{S}$, it is best to first know how to recognize when a $\mu \in \mathbf{M}_1(\mathbb{S})$ is stationary. But, if μ is stationary, then it is left unchanged as the system evolves, and, in terms of the transition probability, this means that

$$\mu(\{y\}) = \sum_{x \in \mathbb{S}} \mu(\{x\})\mathbf{P}(x, \{y\}) \quad \text{for all } y \in \mathbb{S}.$$

$$(2)$$

Now suppose that $\mathbb{S} = \{1, 2\}$, and consider the problem of finding a solution to (2). That is, we want to find $\mu \in \mathbf{M}_1(\{1, 2\})$ so that

$$\begin{aligned}
\mu(\{1\}) &= \mu(\{1\})\mathbf{P}(1, \{1\}) + \mu(\{2\})\mathbf{P}(2, \{1\})\mu(\{2\}) \\
&= \mu(\{1\})\mathbf{P}(1, \{2\}) + \mu(\{2\})\mathbf{P}(2, \{2\}).
\end{aligned}$$

$$(3)$$

At first sight, there appear to be too many conditions on μ: not only must it satisfy the two equations in (3), it also has to satisfy $\mu(\{1\}) + \mu(\{2\}) = 1$ as well as being non-negative. Even if one ignores the non-negativity, one suspects that three linear equations are just too many for a pair of numbers to satisfy. On the other hand, after a little manipulation, one sees (remember that $\mathbf{P}(1, \cdot)$ and $\mathbf{P}(2, \cdot)$ are probability distributions) that both the equations in (3) are equivalent to $\mu(\{1\})\mathbf{P}(1, \{2\}) = \mu(\{2\})\mathbf{P}(2, \{1\})$. Hence the two equations in (3) are equivalent, and so there are really only two equations to be satisfied: $\mu(\{1\})\mathbf{P}(1, \{2\}) = \mu(\{2\})\mathbf{P}(2, \{1\})$ and $\mu(\{1\}) + \mu(\{2\}) = 1$. There are two cases to be considered. The first case is when the chain never moves, or, equivalently, $\mathbf{P}(1, \{2\}) = 0 = \mathbf{P}(2, \{1\})$. In this case there are two solutions, namely, δ_1 and δ_2, which is exactly what one should expect for a chain which never moves. In the second case, the one corresponding to a chain which can move, either $\mathbf{P}(1, \{2\}) > 0$ or $\mathbf{P}(2, \{1\}) > 0$. In both these cases, one can easily check that the one and only solution to (3) is given by

$$\mu(\{1\}) = \frac{\mathbf{P}(2, \{1\})}{\mathbf{P}(1, \{2\}) + \mathbf{P}(2, \{1\})} \quad and$$

$$\mu(\{2\}) = \frac{\mathbf{P}(1, \{2\})}{\mathbf{P}(1, \{2\}) + \mathbf{P}(2, \{1\})}.$$

Continuing in the setting of the preceding, we want to examine when Gibbs's ergodic hypothesis holds. Obviously, at the very least, ergodicity requires that there be only one stationary μ, otherwise we could start the chain with one of them as initial distribution, in which case it would never get to the other. Thus, we need to assume that $\mathbf{P}(1, \{2\}) + \mathbf{P}(2, \{1\}) > 0$, and, to simplify matters, we will assume more, namely, that $m \equiv m_1 + m_2 > 0$, where $m_1 = \min\{P(1, \{1\}), P(2, \{1\})\}$ and $m_2 = \min\{P(1, \{2\}), P(2, \{2\})\}$, and, under this assumption we (following Doeblin) will show that, for any $v \in \mathbf{M}_1(\{1, 2\})$

$$\|v\mathbf{P} - \mu\| \le (1 - m)\|v - \mu\|, \tag{4}$$

where $v\mathbf{P} \in \mathbf{M}_1(\{1, 2\})$ is determined by

$$v\mathbf{P}(\{y\}) \equiv \sum_{x=1}^{2} v(\{x\})\mathbf{P}(x, \{y\})$$

and, for any pair $v_1, v_2 \in \mathbf{M}_1(\{1, 2\})$, $\|v_2 - v_1\| \equiv \sum_{x=1}^{2} |v_2(\{x\}) - v_1(\{x\})|$. To prove (4), first observe that, because μ is stationary, $\mu = \mu\mathbf{P}$, and therefore, since $\sum_{x=1}^{2}(v(\{x\}) - \mu(\{x\})) = 1 - 1 = 0$,

$$v\mathbf{P}(\{y\}) - \mu(\{y\}) = \sum_{x=1}^{2}(v(\{x\}) - \mu(\{x\}))\mathbf{P}(x, \{y\})$$

$$= \sum_{x=1}^{2}(v(\{x\}) - \mu(\{x\})) \times (\mathbf{P}(x, \{y\}) - m_y).$$

Next, take the absolute value of both sides, remember that the absolute value of a sum of numbers is dominated by the sum of their absolute values, and arrive at

$$\|v\mathbf{P} - \mu\| \le \sum_{y=1}^{2}\left(\sum_{x=1}^{2}|v(\{x\}) - \mu(\{x\})|(\mathbf{P}(x, \{y\}) - m_y)\right)$$

$$= \sum_{x=1}^{2}\left(\sum_{y=1}^{2}|v(\{x\}) - \mu(\{x\})|(\mathbf{P}(x, \{y\}) - m_y)\right)$$

$$= (1 - m)\|v - \mu\|.$$

Given (4), it becomes an easy matter to check ergodicity. Indeed, $v\mathbf{P}$ is the distribution of the chain at time 1 when it is started with initial distribution v. Similarly, its distribution at time 2 will be $v\mathbf{P}^2 = (v\mathbf{P})\mathbf{P}$, and so $\|v\mathbf{P}^2 - \mu\| \le (1 - m)\|v\mathbf{P} - \mu\| \le (1 - m)^2\|v - \mu\|$. Proceeding by induction, one sees that distribution $v\mathbf{P}^n = (v\mathbf{P}^{n-1})\mathbf{P}$ at time n will satisfy $\|v\mathbf{P}^n - \mu\| \le (1 - m)^n\|v - \mu\|$. Hence, because $m > 0$, this implies that $\|v\mathbf{P}^n - \mu\|$ tends to 0 exponentially fast, which means that the chain possesses an extremely strong form of ergodicity.

Other directions

In this article we have discussed only the most elementary examples of Markov processes. In particular, in order to avoid technical difficulties, all our considerations have been about processes for which the time parameter is discrete. As soon as one moves into the realm of processes with a continuous time parameter, the theory becomes much more technically involved. However, the price which one has to pay in technicalities is amply rewarded by the richness of the continuous time theory. To wit, Brownian motion (also known as the Wiener process) is a continuous parameter Markov process which makes an appearance in a surprising, and ever growing, number of places: harmonic analysis in pure mathematics, filtering and separation of signal from noise in electrical engineering, the kinetic theory of gases in physics, price fluctuations on the stock market in economics, and so on. Thus, for the sake of the curious, the bibliography below gives a very brief and enormously inadequate list of places where one can learn more about Markov processes.

DANIEL W. STROOCK

Bibliography
Elementary texts

Karlin, S. and Taylor, H. 1975. *A First Course in Stochastic Processes*, 2nd edn. New York: Academic Press.
Norris, J. 1997. *Markov Chains*. Cambridge Series in Statistical and Probabilistic Mathematics. Cambridge: Cambridge University Press.
Stroock, D. 2005. *An Introduction to Markov Processes*. Graduate Text Series No. 230. Heidelberg: Springer-Verlag.

Advanced texts

Dynkin, E. 1965. *Markov Processes*, vols. 1 and 2. Grundlehren Nos. 121 and 122. Heidelberg: Springer-Verlag.

Ethier, S. and Kurtz, T. 1986. *Markov Processes: Characterization and Convergence*. New York: Wiley.

Revuz, D. 1984. *Markov Chains*. North-Holland Mathematical Library, vol. 11. Amsterdam and New York: North-Holland.

Stroock, D. 2003. *Markov Processes from K. Itô's Perspective*. Annals of Mathematical Studies No. 155. Princeton, NJ: Princeton University Press.

Physics texts

Boltzmann, L. 1896, 1898. *Lectures on Gas Theory*, 2 vols, trans. S. Brush. New York: Dover Publications, 1995.

Gibbs, J. 1902. *Elementary Principles in Statistical Mechanics*. New York: Scribner.

Markowitz, Harry Max (born 1927)

Harry M. Markowitz is a Nobel laureate who shared a 1990 prize with Merton Miller and William Sharpe for their contributions to financial economics. A native of Chicago, he received undergraduate and graduate degrees from the University of Chicago, culminating in a Ph.D. in 1954. His article on portfolio selection (1952a), drawn from his dissertation, was a path-breaking contribution that would be fully developed in his 1959 Cowles Foundation monograph, *Portfolio Selection: Efficient Diversification of Investments*. The monograph provided a strong case for receiving the Nobel Memorial Prize.

Markowitz is a gifted applied mathematical economist who responds creatively to observed behaviour and has a strong interest in providing tools that facilitate applications of economics. As a graduate student he published a second influential article (1952b), which extended and qualified an important contribution by Friedman and Savage (1948) that proposed an explanation for why individuals both insure and gamble. Specifically, he transformed their argument to describe bets that involved deviations from an individual's 'customary wealth', which is wealth exclusive of recent windfall gains or losses, and imposed a third inflection point, which was needed to satisfy the expected utility hypothesis requirement that a utility function be bounded from below. By describing how the Friedman and Savage model could not account for some commonly observed behaviour, this article afforded a clear insight into the way Markowitz analysed decisions about risk. It takes only one simple division to transform deviations from an individual's customary wealth to rates of return on customary wealth.

Markowitz's article on portfolio selection lucidly explained why focusing on the expected rate of return (hereafter, 'return' means 'rate of return') was inadequate to account for widely observed portfolio diversification. By simultaneously considering expected return and the variance of return (E and V), he developed a set of efficient EV portfolios that would have a maximum return for an arbitrary variance of return. Further, almost all of these efficient portfolios would have more than one asset and thus be diversified. Using elegant geometric arguments, the article explained how in a problem involving N securities the set of efficient portfolios could be represented by a set of connected line segments. This insight underlies the algorithm for computing efficient portfolios that is presented in his monograph.

In that article and in his monograph, Markowitz was careful to emphasize that he was developing a method for using an investor's beliefs (or perhaps those of security analysts) about expected return and variance so that he or she could use them in an optimal way. In neither did he explain how expectations should be formed. Similarly, he was agnostic about whether the probabilities investors used in forming expectations were objective or subjective. Finally, he did not assume that returns were normally distributed or that an investor had a quadratic utility function, although one of these conditions is formally necessary to describe portfolio choice in terms of expected return and variance of return. The complications raised in the preceding three sentences are briefly considered in the final section of the monograph and would absorb many journal pages in the coming years. Levy and Markowitz (1979) addressed the limitations of restricting attention to expected return and variance and argued that by focusing on these two measures investors were not likely often to be misled.

The monograph was an expositional tour de force and consequently had an enormous impact on the theory and practice of finance. Its first chapters were quite intuitive and made no technical demands on the reader. The third and fourth chapters contain elementary discussions of the concepts of expected return and variance, the fifth and sixth generalize the discussion to cover large numbers of securities and aggregation over time, and the seventh provides a clear geometric interpretation of efficient portfolios. The eighth chapter presents the critical line method for isolating efficient portfolios and solving the underlying quadratic programming problem. The ninth chapter restates the argument using a semi-variance. The remaining four chapters describe rational portfolio behaviour and discuss how the expected utility hypothesis can be applied to the portfolio selection problem. They include the topics of portfolio choice over time and when objective and subjective probabilities differ.

Technical derivation of the critical line method is reported in Appendix A in the monograph, which generalizes its original exposition in Markowitz (1956). The method works because the set of efficient portfolios is convex, in part because there are assumed to be upper and lower bounds on the holdings of any asset. In the monograph no short sales are allowed, although this restriction can be relaxed. If we ignore some minor technical issues involving singularities that cannot be dealt with here, the method can be described intuitively. It is initiated by finding the security with the highest expected return. A portfolio fully invested in this security is an element in the set of efficient portfolios. Then, find the security or linear combination of securities that can be substituted for that highest-yielding security in a manner which respects the balance sheet identity that the sum of asset shares equals unity and provides the minimum reduction in return per unit decrease in variance. This substitution is continued until one or more of the securities reach zero (or a lower bound) or until a security not in this combination can be beneficially introduced, at which point another linear combination is chosen. The algorithm stops when no substitution is possible that further lowers the variance of a portfolio.

The monograph and a contemporaneous paper by Tobin (1958) underlay the development of the capital asset pricing model (CAPM) by Sharpe (1964), which argued that an asset's return was determined by its correlation with the return of the market portfolio. This model greatly increased interest in EV models among practitioners and the academic community. In his presidential address to the American Finance Association, however, Markowitz (1983) expressed some reservations about the CAPM because it failed to take into account limits on borrowing.

Apart from his work on modelling portfolio decisions, Markowitz made significant contributions to management science. In Markowitz (1957), he developed sparse matrix techniques for simplifying the solution of linear programming problems, which continue to be used in present-day algorithms that employ Cholesky factorizations. In Markowitz and Manne (1957) an important set of applications, discrete programming problems, were analysed. In Manne and Markowitz (1963), applications of 'process analysis' are reported in which Markowitz was a co-author on several papers that studied metal-working industries. Process analysis examines production capabilities in an industry. Also, he made many contributions that led to improvements in simulations, including the construction of a programming language, SIMSCRIPT (see Markowitz, Hausner and Karr, 1963, and Dimsdale and Markowitz, 1999).

Markowitz spent much of his career outside academia. From 1952 through 1963 he was on the staff of the RAND Corporation and from 1974 through 1983 he was at IBM's T. J. Watson Research Center. His monograph was largely written when he was a visitor at Yale University in 1955–6, on leave from RAND. He joined the faculty of Baruch College of the City University of New York as a distinguished professor of finance and economics in 1982, and in 2004 was a research professor at the University of California at San Diego. In 1989 he was awarded the prestigious Von Neumann Prize in Operations Research

by the Operations Research Society of America and The Institute of Management Science for his work on 'portfolio selection, mathematical programming, and simulation'.

DONALD D. HESTER

See also **computational methods in econometrics; efficiency bounds; expected utility hypothesis; foreign direct investment; risk; risk-coping strategies; Sharpe, William F.; Tobin, James; uncertainty.**

Selected works

1952a. Portfolio selection. *Journal of Finance* 7, 77–91.
1952b. The utility of wealth. *Journal of Political Economy* 60(2), 151–58.
1956. The optimization of a quadratic function subject to linear constraints. *Naval Research Logistics Quarterly* 3, 111–33.
1957. The elimination form of the inverse and its application to linear programming. *Management Science* 3, 255–69.
1957. (With A. Manne.) On the solution of discrete programming problems. *Econometrica* 25, 84–110.
1959. *Portfolio Selection: Efficient Diversification of Investments.* Cowles Foundation Monograph 16. New York: John Wiley and Sons.
1963. (With B. Hausner and H. Karr.) *SIMSCRIPT: A Simulation Programming Language.* Englewood Cliffs, NJ: Prentice Hall.
1963. (Co-edited with A. Manne.) *Studies in Process Analysis: Economy-Wide Production Capabilities.* Cowles Foundation Monograph 18. New York: John Wiley and Sons.
1979. (With H. Levy.) Approximating expected utility by a function of mean and variance. *American Economic Review* 69, 308–17.
1983. Negative or not nonnegative: a question about CAPMs. *Journal of Finance* 38, 283–95.
1999. (With B. Dimsdale.) A description of the SIMSCRIPT language. IBM Systems Journal 38 (2/3), 151–61.

Bibliography

Friedman, M. and Savage, L. 1948. The utility analysis of choices involving risk. *Journal of Political Economy* 56, 279–304.
Sharpe, W. 1964. Capital asset prices: a theory of market equilibrium under conditions of risk. *Journal of Finance* 19, 425–42.
Tobin, J. 1958. Liquidity preference as behavior towards risk. *Review of Economic Studies* 25, 65–86.

marriage and divorce

This article summarizes the economic analysis of marriage markets. The first section provides a description of stylized facts that motivate the interest of economists in this problem. It is shown that marital status is closely tied with 'economic' variables such as work and wages.

We illustrate these facts using mainly US data but the patterns are similar in all developed countries. The second section demonstrates how the tools of economists bear on 'non-economic' subjects such as marriage, fertility and divorce, often analysed by researchers from other fields. The final section highlights some connections between the theory and empirical evidence.

Basic facts
Marriage and divorce
The 20th century was characterized by substantial changes in family structure (Figure 1). More men and women are now divorced and unmarried or have alternative arrangements, such as cohabitation. Interestingly, the rise in divorce rates is associated with an increase in remarriage rates (relative to first marriage rates), reflecting higher turnover. Most people had a first marriage, and most divorces end in remarriage. Moreover, the remarriage rate is greater than the first marriage rate and far exceeds the divorce rate, suggesting that, despite the larger turnover, marriage is still a 'natural' state (Table 1). Women enter the first marriage faster than men. However, following divorce, men remarry at higher rates than women, especially at old ages. This pattern reflects the

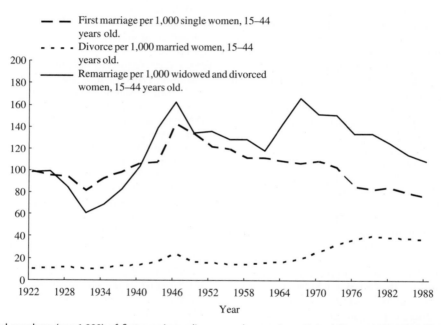

Figure 1   Annual numbers (per 1,000) of first marriage, divorce, and remarriage: United States, 1921–1989 (three-year averages). *Source*: National Center of Health Statistics.

Table 1   *Marital histories of men and women, United States, 1996*

Age in 1966	Ever married by 1966 (%)		Divorced from first marriage by 1966 (%)		Remarried after first divorce by 1966 (%)	
	Men	Women	Men	Women	Men	Women
25	31.8	50.0	4.6	12.2	55.5	44.0
30	65.4	71.1	16.7	17.2	35.6	49.7
35	77.4	84.1	26.9	26.4	60.7	65.1
40	80.9	85.2	34.0	36.5	66.4	67.6
45	87.3	89.8	41.1	41.6	71.6	68.1
50	93.2	91.3	39.8	42.4	78.3	68.9
55	94.5	95.3	38.2	38.0	79.0	64.1
60	96.6	94.9	34.3	30.7	86.9	64.7

Source: US Census Bureau, Survey of Income and Program Participation (SIPP), 1996 Panel, Wave 2 Topical Module.

earlier marriage of women and their longer lives, which causes the ratio of men to women to decline with age.

One consequence of higher marital turnover is the large number of children who live in single-parent and step-parent households. In 2002, 23 per cent of US children younger than 18 years lived only with their mother, and five per cent lived only with their father. Children of broken families are more likely to live in poverty and to underperform in school. Lower attainments of such children are observed also prior to the occurrence of divorce, suggesting that bad marriage rather than divorce may be the cause (Piketty, 2003).

Marriage and work

Time use data (Table 2) show that men work more than women in the market; women do more housework than men. Per day, single women work at home three hours while single men work less than two hours. These figures roughly double for married couples with young children, showing clearly that children require a substantial investment of time and that most of this load is carried by the mother. The total time worked and the corresponding amount of leisure is about the same for married men and women.

Figure 2 displays the work patterns within couples. The most common situation is that the husband works full-time and the wife works part-time or does not work at all. However, the proportion of such couples has declined and the proportion of couples where *both* partners work full-time has risen sharply, reflecting the increased entry of married women into the labour force.

Marriage and wages

Male–female wage differences of full-time workers are larger among married than among single persons. Married men have consistently the highest wage among men, while never-married women have the highest wage among women. The wage gap between married men and women rises as the cohort ages, reflecting the cumulative effects of gender differences in the acquisition of labour market experience (Figures 3 and 4). The increased participation of married women, associated with the increase in their wages, has increased their wage relative to those of never-married women and their husbands (Table 3).

Economic theory of marriage and divorce

From an economic point of view, marriage is a voluntary partnership for the purpose of joint production and joint consumption. As such, it is comparable to other economic organizations that aim to maximize some private gains but are subject to market discipline.

Gains from marriage

Consumption and production in the family are broadly defined to include non-marketable goods and services, such as companionship and children. Indeed, the production and rearing of children is the most commonly recognized role of the family. We mention here five broad

Table 2 *Daily hours of work of men and women (age 20–59) in the market and at home, by marital status, selected countries and years*

	US 1985	Can. 1982	UK 1985	Ger. 1992	Italy 1989	Norw. 1990
Paid work						
Single men	5.5	5.6	4.2	6.4	4.9	4.7
Single women	4.6	4.3	3.3	5.0	3.3	4.0
Married men, no child	6.2	6.2	5.5	6.3	5.5	5.7
Married women, no child	3.3	4.0	3.8	3.3	2.0	4.2
Married men, child 5–17	6.1	5.9	5.7	6.7	6.1	6.0
Married women, child 5–17	3.5	3.7	2.6	3.2	2.2	3.6
Married men, child < 5	6.9	6.2	6.1	6.8	6.2	5.7
Married women, child < 5	1.9	2.4	2.0	2.2	1.9	2.1
Housework (including child care)						
Single men	1.6	1.7	2.2	1.6	0.7	1.7
Single women	2.8	3.3	3.9	3.4	3.1	2.9
Married men, no child	1.8	2.0	3.3	2.2	1.3	2.1
Married women, no child	4.1	3.9	3.8	4.8	6.4	3.5
Married men, child 5–17	2.3	2.5	2.1	2.3	1.2	2.4
Married women, child 5–17	4.4	4.7	5.5	5.5	7.0	4.5
Married men, child < 5	2.3	3.2	2.3	2.8	1.5	3.2
Married women, child < 5	6.4	6.8	3.8	6.9	7.6	6.1

Source: Multinational Time Use Study.

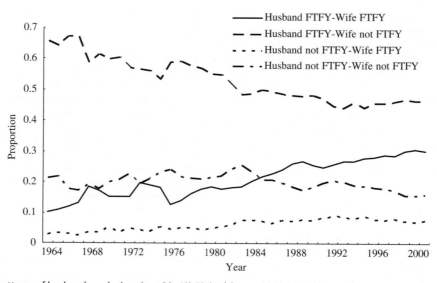

Figure 2   Work patterns of husbands and wives (age 30–40), United States, 1964–2001. Note: A Spouse is employed full-time-full-year (FTFY) if he/she works 50 weeks or more and hours exceed 34 per week. *Source*: Current Population Surveys.

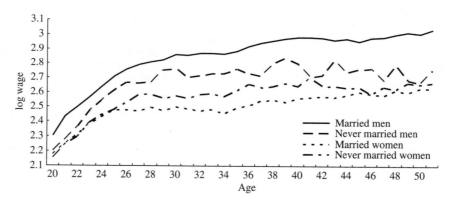

Figure 3   Hourly wages (in logs) of fully employed married and never-married US men and women born in 1946–1950, by age. *Source*: Current Population Surveys.

sources of *economic* gain from marriage, that is, why 'two are better than one':

1. Sharing of collective (non-rival) goods; both partners can equally enjoy their children, share the same information and use the same home.
2. Division of labour to exploit comparative advantage or increasing returns; one partner works at home and the other works in the market.
3. Extending credit and coordination of investment activities; one partner works when the other is in school.
4. Risk-pooling; one partner works when the other is sick or unemployed.

5. Coordination of child care, which is a collective good for the parents. Although children can be produced and raised outside the family, the family has a substantial advantage in carrying out these activities. Two interrelated factors cause this advantage: by nature, parents care about their own children and, because of this mutual interest, it is more efficient that the parents themselves determine the expenditure on their children. If the parents live separately, whether single or remarried, the non-custodian parent loses control of child expenditures. Lack of contact further reduces the incentive or ability to contribute time and money to the children. Together, these factors reduce the

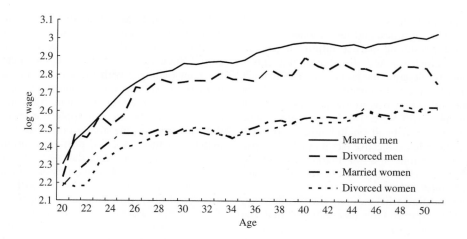

Figure 4 Hourly wages (in logs) of fully employed married and divorced US men and women born in 1946–1950, by age. *Source*: Current Population Surveys.

Table 3 *Relative wage gaps associated with marital status for fully employed men and women, by year and age, United States, 1965–2001*

Years/age	Married–never married		Married–divorced		Mar. men–mar. women between groups	Husband–wife within couples
	Men	Women	Men	Women		
1965–74						
25–34	13.8	−8.8	9.6	4.5	37.2	32.5
35–44	21.5	−17.6	17.1	−1.6	52.1	42.7
1975–84						
25–34	15.6	−6.5	8.5	−.5	35.4	29.6
35–44	21.0	−17.5	12.4	−2.8	52.1	43.8
1985–94						
25–34	15.6	−2.0	15.4	7.7	23.6	21.1
35–44	21.3	−9.9	15.4	2.4	38.7	32.1
1995–2001						
25–34	13.6	2.3	13.6	2.3	17.0	18.1
35–44	23.7	−1.8	21.4	7.8	31.7	27.5

Source: Current Population Surveys.

welfare of both parents and children when they live apart (Weiss and Willis, 1985).

Family decision making

The existence of potential gains from marriage is not sufficient to motivate marriage and to sustain it. Prospective mates are concerned whether the potential gains will be realized and how they are divided. Family members have potentially conflicting interests and a basic question is how families reach decisions. The old notion that families maximize a common objective appears to be

too narrow. Instead of this *unitary* model, it is now more common to consider *collective* models in which partners with different preferences reach some binding agreement that specifies an *efficient* allocation of resources and a *stable sharing rule*. (Browning, Chiappori and Weiss, 2005, ch. 3).

In a special case, referred to as *transferable utility*, it is possible to separate the issues of efficiency and distribution. This situation arises if there is a commodity (say, money) that, upon changing hands, shifts utilities between the partners at a fixed rate of exchange. In this case, the family decision process can be broken into two steps: actions are first chosen to maximize a weighted *sum* of the individual utilities, and then money is transferred to divide the resulting marital output. In general, the problems of efficiency and distribution are intertwined. We may still describe the family as maximizing a weighted sum of the individual utilities, but the weights depend on the individual bargaining powers, and any shift in the weights will affect the family choice. The bargaining power may depend on individual attributes such as earning capacity, subjective factors such as impatience and risk aversion, and on market conditions, such as the sex ratio and availability of alternative mates (Lundberg and Pollak, 1993).

The question remains: what enforces the coordination between family members? One possibility is that the partners sign a formal 'marriage contract' that is enforced by law. However, such contracts are quite rare in modern societies, which can be probably ascribed to a larger reliance than in the past on emotional commitments and the presumption that too much contracting can 'kill love'. In the absence of legal enforcement, efficient contracts may be supported by repeated interactions and the possibility to trade favours and punishments. This possibility arises because marriage is a durable relationship, forged by the long-term investment in children and the accumulation of marital specific capital, which is lost or diminished in value if separation occurs. However, repeated game arguments cannot explain unconditional giving, such as taking care of a spouse stricken by Alzheimers who would never be able to return the favour. Emotional commitments and altruism play a central role in enforcing family contracts (Becker, 1991, ch. 8).

The marriage market
Individuals in society have many potential partners. An undesired marriage can be avoided or replaced by a better one. This situation creates competition over the potential gains from marriage. In modern societies, explicit price mechanisms are not observed. Nevertheless, the assignment of partners and the sharing of the gains from marriage can be analysed within a market framework.

Matching models provide a starting point for such analysis. These models investigate the mapping from preferences over prospective matches into a stable assignment (Roth and Sotomayor, 1990). An assignment is said to be *stable* if no married person would rather be single and no two (married or unmarried) persons prefer to form a new union. To illustrate, assume that each male is endowed with a single trait, m, and each female is endowed with a single trait, f. Let

$$z = h(m, f). \qquad (1)$$

be the *household production function* that summarizes the impact of traits of the matched partners on marital output, z, and assume that $h(m, f)$ is increasing in m and f.

Suppose, first, that z is a public good that the partners must consume jointly. Then, the only stable assignment is such that males with high m marry females with high f, and, if there are more (fewer) eligible men than women, the men (women) with the fewest endowments remain unmarried. All men want to marry the best woman, and she will accept only the best man. After this pair is taken 'out of the game', we can apply the same argument to the next-best couple and proceed sequentially. Such a matching pattern is called positive *assortative matching*.

If one assumes, instead, that z can be divided between the two partners and that utility is transferable, then a man with low m may obtain women with high f by giving up part of his private share in the gains from marriage. The type of interaction in the gains from marriage determines the willingness to pay for the different attributes. Complementarity (substitution) means that the two traits interact in such a way that the benefits from a woman with high f are higher (lower) for a male with high m than for a male with low m. Thus, a positive (negative) assortative matching occurs if the two traits are complements (substitutes). An important lesson is that in a marriage market with sufficient scope for compensation within marriage, the best man is not necessarily the one married to the best women, because, with negative interaction, either one of them can be bid away by the second-best of the opposite sex (Becker, 1991, ch. 4).

What determines the division of marital gains? If each couple is considered in isolation then, in principle, any efficient outcome is possible, and one has to use bargaining arguments to determine the allocation. However, in an 'ideal' frictionless case, where partners are free to break marriages and swap partners at will, the outcome depends on the joint distribution of male and female characteristics in the market at large. Traits of the partners in a particular marriage have no direct impact on the shares of the two partners, because these traits are endogenously determined by the requirement of stable matching.

These features show up more clearly if one assumes a continuum of agents and continuous marital attributes. Let $F(m)$ and $G(f)$ be the cumulative distributions of the male and female traits, respectively, and let the measure of women in the total population be r, where the measure of men is normalized to 1. Assume that the female and male traits are complements and transferable utility. Then, if man m' is married to woman f', the set of men with m exceeding m' must have the same measure as the set of women with f above f'. Thus, for all m and f in the set of married couples,

$$1 - F(m) = r(1 - G(f)). \qquad (2)$$

This simple relationship determines a positively sloped matching function, $m = \phi(f)$.

A *sharing rule* specifies the shares of the wife and husband in every marriage that forms. Let $v(m)$ be the *reservation utility* that man *m* requires in *any* marriage and let *u*(*f*) be the reservation utility of woman *f*. Then the sharing rule that supports a stable assignment must satisfy

$$v(m) = \max_{f} (h(f, m) - u(f)),$$

$$\text{and} \qquad (3)$$

$$u(f) = \max_{y} (h(z, y) - v(y)).$$

That is, each married partner gets the spouse that maximizes his or her 'profit' from the partnership over all possible alternatives. As we move across matched couples, the welfare of each partner changes according to the *marginal* contribution of his/her *own* trait to the *marital* output, irrespective of the potential impact on the partner whom one marries. With a continuum of agents, there are no rents in the marriage market because everyone receives roughly what can be obtained in the next-best alternative. Another condition for a stable assignment is that, if there are unmarried men, the least attractive married man cannot get any surplus from marriage. Otherwise, slightly less attractive men could bid away his match. A similar condition applies for unmarried women.

From these considerations, one can obtain a unique sharing rule, provided that $r \neq 1$. Basically, one first finds the sharing in the least attractive match, using the no-rent condition. Then the division in better marriages is determined sequentially, by using the condition that along the stable matching profile each partner receives his or her marginal contribution to the marital output. The sharing rule is fully determined by the sex ratio and the respective trait distributions of the two sexes. It can be shown that a marginal increase in the ratio of women to men in the marriage market improves (or leaves unchanged) the welfare of all men, and reduces (or leaves unchanged) the welfare of all women. From (2), it is seen that an upward (downward) first-order shift in the distributions of traits is equivalent (in terms of the effects on the sharing rule) to a marginal increase (decrease) in the female–male ratio. In this regard, there is close correspondence between the impact of changes in quality (that is, the average trait) and size of the two groups that are matched in the marriage market (Browning, Chiappori and Weiss 2005, ch. 9).

Search

The process of matching in real life is characterized by scarcity of information about potential matches. Models of search add realism to the assignment model because they provide an explicit description of the sorting process that happens in real time.

Following Mortensen (1988), consider infinitely lived agents and assume that meetings are governed by a Poisson random process (these two assumptions are made to ensure a stationary environment). The total marital output is observed upon meeting and, on the assumption of transferable utility, marriage will occur whenever this marital output exceeds the *sum* of the values of continued search of the matched partners. This rule holds because it implies the existence of a division within marriage that makes both partners better off. Because meetings are random and sparse in time, those who actually meet and choose to marry enjoy a positive rent. The division of these rents between the partners is an important issue. Two considerations determine the division of the gains from marriage: outside options, reflected in the value of continued search, and the self-enforcing allocation that would emerge if the marriage continued without agreement (Wolinsky, 1987). If these two considerations are combined, the sharing rule is influenced by both the value of search as single and the value of continued search during the bargaining process, including the option of leaving when an outside offer arrives. In this way, a link is created between the division of marital output gains and market conditions.

Search models explain why, despite the gains from marriage, part of the population is not married and individuals move between married and single states. The steady state proportions of the population in each state are such that the flows into and out of each state are equalized. These two flows are determined by the search strategies that individuals adopt.

Search models may have significant externalities. For instance, it may be easier to find a mate if there are many singles searching for mates. There are several possible reasons for such *increasing returns* in the matching process. One reason is that the two sexes meet in a variety of situations (work, sport, social life and so on) but many of these meetings are 'wasted' in the sense that one of the individuals is already attached and not willing to divorce. A second reason is that the establishment of more focused channels, where singles meet only singles, is costly. These will be created only if the 'size of the market' is large enough. Third, the intensity of search by unattached decreases with the proportion of attached people in the population who are less likely to respond to an offer (Mortensen, 1988). In such a case, the marriage (divorce) rates will be above (below) their efficient levels, as each person fails to consider the effect of marriage or separation on the prospects of other participants in the marriage market.

Search and assortative matching

The presence of frictions modifies somewhat the results on assortative matching. Following Burdett and Coles (1999), consider a case of non-transferable utility with frictions. Assume that if man *m* marries women *f*, he gets *f* and she gets *m*. There is a continuum of types with continuous distributions and meetings are generated by a Poisson process with parameter λ. Upon meeting, each partner decides whether to accept the match or to continue the search. Marriage occurs only if both partners accept each other and, by assumption, a match cannot be broken.

Each man (woman) chooses a reservation policy that determines which women (men) to accept. The reservation values for men and women, R_m and R_f, respectively, depend on the individual's own trait. Agents at the top of the distribution of each gender can be choosier because they know that they will be accepted by most people on the other side of the market. Hence, continued search is more valuable for them. Formally, let

$$R_m = b_m + \frac{\lambda \mu_m}{r} \int_{R_m}^{\bar{f}} (f - R_m) dG_m(f),$$

$$(4)$$

$$R_f = b_f + \frac{\lambda \mu_f}{r} \int_{R_f}^{\bar{m}} (m - R_f) dF_f(m)$$

where the flow of benefits as single, b, the proportion of meetings that end in marriage, μ, and the distribution of 'offers' if marriage occurs, all depend on traits, as indicated by the m and f subscripts. The common discount factor, r, represents the cost of waiting.

In equilibrium, the reservation values of all agents must be a best response against each other, yielding a (stationary) Nash equilibrium. In particular, the 'best' woman and the 'best' man will adopt the policies

$$R_{\tilde{m}} = b_{\tilde{m}} + \frac{\lambda}{r} \int_{R_{\tilde{m}}}^{\bar{f}} (f - R_{\tilde{m}}) dG(f), \qquad (5)$$

$$R_{\tilde{f}} = b_{\tilde{f}} + \frac{\lambda}{r} \int_{R_{\tilde{f}}}^{\tilde{m}} (m - R_{\tilde{f}}) dF(m).$$

Thus, the best man accepts some women who are inferior to the best woman and the best woman accepts some men who are inferior to the best man, because a bird in the hand is worth two in the bush.

The assumption that the ranking of men and women is based on a single trait introduces a strong commonality in preferences whereby all men agree on the ranking of all women and vice versa. Because all individuals of the opposite sex accept the best woman and all women accept the best man, μ is set to 1 in eq. (5) and the distribution of offers equals the distribution of types in the population. Moreover, if the best man accepts all women with f in the range $[R_{\tilde{m}}, \bar{f}]$, then all men who are inferior in quality will also accept such women. But this means that all women in the range $[R_{\tilde{m}}, \bar{f}]$ are sure that all men accept them and therefore will have the *same* reservation value, $R_{\tilde{f}}$, which in turn implies that all men in the range $[R_{\tilde{f}}, \tilde{m}]$ will have the same reservation value, $R_{\tilde{m}}$.

These considerations lead to a *class structure* with a finite number of distinct classes in which individuals

marry each other. Having identified the upper class, we can then examine the considerations of the top man and woman in the rest of the population. Lower-class individuals face $\mu < 1$ and a *truncated* distribution of offers because not all meetings end in marriage but, in principle, these can be calculated and then one can find the reservation values for the highest two types and all other individuals in the group forming the second class. Proceeding in this manner to the bottom, it is possible to determine all classes. This pattern is similar to the case without frictions and non-transferable utility except that, because of the need to compromise, low- and high-quality types mix within each class.

With frictions and transferable utility, there is still a tendency towards positive (negative) assortative matching based on the interaction in traits. If the traits are complements, individuals of either sex with a higher endowment will adopt a more selective reservation policy and will be matched, on the average, with a highly endowed person of the opposite sex. However, with sufficient friction it is possible to have negative assortative matching even under complementarity. This, again, is driven by the need to compromise. With low frequency of meetings and costs of waiting, males with low m expect some women with high f to accept them. If the gain from such a match is large enough, they will reject all women with low f and wait until a high f woman arrives.

Divorce and remarriage

Divorce is motivated by uncertainty and changing circumstances. Thus, individuals may enter a relationship and then break it if a better match is met. Or changing economic and emotional circumstances may dissipate the gains from marriage. As time passes, new information on match quality and outside options is accumulated, and each partner decides whether to dissolve the partnership. In making this choice, partners consider the expected value of each alternative, where the value of remaining married includes the option of later divorce and the value of divorcing includes the option of later remarriage. Under divorce at will, divorce occurs endogenously whenever one partner has an alternative option that the current spouse cannot, or is unwilling to, match by a redistribution of the gains from marriage.

Following divorce, the options for sharing and coordination of activities diminish. The divorced partners may have different economic prospects, especially if children are present. Asymmetries arise because the mother usually loses earning capacity as a result of having a child. To mitigate these risks, the partners have a mutual interest in signing binding contracts that stipulate post-divorce transfers. Such contracts are negotiated 'in the shadow of the law' and are legally binding. Child support payments are mandatory but the non-custodial father may augment the transfer to influence child expenditures by the custodial mother. Payments made to the custodial mother are usually fungible and, therefore, the amount that actually reaches the children depends on the mother's marital status. If she remarries, child expenditures depend on the new husband's net income, including his child-support commitments to his ex-wife. Hence, the willingness of each parent to provide child support depends on commitments of others. These interdependencies can yield *multiple equilibria*, with and without children and correspondingly low and high divorce rates (Browning, Chiappori and Weiss, 2005, ch. 11).

Theory and evidence

There is a growing body of empirical research that addresses the testable implications of the models outlined above.

1. The unitary model of the household implies that the consumption levels of husband and wife depend only on *total* family income. This, however, is rejected by the data (Lundberg, Pollak and Wales, 1997). Nevertheless, consumption and work patterns of married couples indicate that they act efficiently (Browning and Chiappori, 1994), implying that a collective model fits the data.
2. Matching models with transferable utility imply positive assortative matching based on the spouses' schooling but negative matching based on their wages (Becker, 1991, ch. 10). In fact, the correlation between the education levels of married partners (about .6) is substantially higher than the correlation between their wages (about .3).
3. Because partners are matched based on their traits as observed at the time of marriage, both positive or negative *surprises* trigger divorce (Becker, 1991, ch. 10). Weiss and Willis (1997) find an impact of unexpected changes in husband's and wife's incomes on the probability of divorce.
4. Unanticipated shocks are less destabilizing if partners are well matched. Anticipating that, couples would sort into marriage according to characteristics that enhance the stability of marriage. In fact, individuals with similar schooling are less likely to divorce and are more likely to marry. This pattern holds for religion and ethnicity, too (Weiss and Willis, 1997).
5. Individual types congregate into locations that facilitate matching; gays in San Francisco (Black et al., 2000) or Jews in New York (Bisin, Topa and Verdier, 2004). Such patterns suggest increasing returns in search. Higher wage variability among men induces women to search longer for their first or second husband, consistently with an optimal search strategy (Gould and Paserman, 2003).
6. Marital choices and family decisions respond to aggregate marriage market conditions. Black women in the United States delay their marriage and have children out of wedlock because of a shortage of eligible black men (Willis, 1999); a higher male–female ratio reduces the hours worked by wives and raises the hours worked by husbands (Chiappori, Fortin and Lacroix, 2002).
7. The sharp increase in divorce in the United States and other countries during 1965–75 seems to constitute a switch across two different equilibria. A marriage market is capable of such abrupt change because of inherent positive feedbacks in matching and contracting. Explanations for the timing of the change include the appearance of the contraceptive pill, the break-up of norms and legal reforms (Michael, 1988; Goldin and Katz, 2002).

YORAM WEISS

See also **assortative matching; collective models of the household; marriage markets.**

Bibliography

Becker, G. 1991. *Treatise on the Family*. Cambridge, MA: Harvard University Press.

Bisin, A., Topa, G. and Verdier, T. 2004. Religious intermarriage and socialization in the US. *Journal of Political Economy* 112, 612–65.

Black, D., Gates, G., Sanders, S. and Taylor, L. 2000. Demographics of the gay and lesbian population in the United States: evidence from available systematic data sources. *Demography* 37, 139–54.

Browning, M. and Chiappori, P. 1994. Efficient intra-household allocations: characterization and empirical tests. *Econometrica* 66, 1241–78.

Browning, M., Chiappori, P. and Weiss, Y. 2005. *Family Economics*. Cambridge: Cambridge University Press.

Burdett, K. and Coles, M. 1999. Long-term partnership formation: marriage and employment. *Economic Journal* 109, F307–F334.

Chiappori, P., Fortin, B. and Lacroix, G. 2002. Marriage market, divorce legislation, and household labor supply. *Journal of Political Economy* 110, 37–72.

Goldin, C. and Katz, L. 2002. The power of the pill: oral contraceptives and women's career and marriage decisions. *Journal of Political Economy* 110, 730–70.

Gould, E. and Paserman, D. 2003. Waiting for Mr Right: rising inequality and declining marriage rates. *Journal of Urban Economics* 53, 257–81.

Lundberg, S. and Pollak, R. 1993. Separate spheres bargaining and the marriage market. *Journal of Political Economy* 101, 988–1010.

Lundberg, S., Pollak, R. and Wales, T. 1997. Do husbands and wives pool resources? Evidence from UK Child Benefit. *Journal of Human Resources* 32, 463–80.

Michael, R. 1988. Why did the divorce rate double within a decade? *Research in Population Economics* 6, 367–99.

Mortensen, D. 1988. Matching: finding a partner for life or otherwise. *American Journal of Sociology* 94(supplement), s215–s240.

Piketty, T. 2003. The impact of divorce on school performance: evidence from France, 1968–2002. Discussion Paper No. 4146. London: CEPR.

Roth, A. and Sotomayor, M. 1990. *Two Sided Matching: A Study in Game-theoretic Modeling and Analysis.* Cambridge: Cambridge University Press.

Weiss, Y. and Willis, R. 1985. Children as collective goods. *Journal of Labor Economics* 3, 268–92.

Weiss, Y. and Willis, R. 1997. Match quality, new information, and marital dissolution. *Journal of Labor Economics* 15, S293–S329.

Willis, R. 1999. A theory of out-of-wedlock childbearing. *Journal of Political Economy* 107(6), S33–S64.

Wolinsky, A. 1987. Matching, search, and bargaining. *Journal of Economic Theory* 42, 311–33.

marriage markets

The marriage market is a term used by economists to characterize the process that determines how men and women are matched to each other through marriage. Formally the marriage market may be thought of as an allocative process that, given the preferences and endowments of two sets of individuals (men and women), yields a set of couples and unmatched individuals and a distribution of resources within each match. Marriage markets are generally distinguished from other sorting processes such as worker–firm matching by the assumption that each member of each set of individuals is matched to at most one member of the other set. However, the basic concept of the marriage market may also be applied to other cases such as polygamy or same-sex partnerships. It is also generally assumed that one's well-being within marriage is determined by the characteristics of one's partner and the distribution of resources within the marriage, but not the matches of other individuals in the marriage market conditional on these factors. The economics literature on the marriage market has built importantly on a two-part foundational article on the economics of marriage published in 1973 and 1974 (Becker, 1973; 1974). However, the phrase 'marriage market' is considerably older, with a first citation in the *Oxford English Dictionary* of 1842.

Stable assignment

Central to the notion of a marriage market is the notion of stable assignment. A stable assignment may be characterized as a set of partner allocations and distributions of resources within marriage so that no individual of one sex would be willing to make an offer (in terms of partnership and a distribution of resources within that partnership) to an individual of the other sex which that individual strictly prefers to his or her equilibrium allocation.

An early and important divide in terms of economic models of marriage arises with respect to the question of transferable utility. Transferable utility arises when well-being within the household may be freely transferred between members of the household through a reallocation of household resources. Under these conditions the question of who marries whom can be importantly separated from the question of how resources are distributed within marriage and any stable marriage assignment can be characterized as the outcome of the maximization of a linear programme (Bergstrom, 1997).

At the other extreme from a transferable utility model is one in which there is no possibility of transferring resources within or across marriage. A key feature of such models is that there is generally a wide variety of possible stable equilibria. Gale and Shapley (1962) illustrate two such stable equilibria, by the construction of two matching algorithms based on who makes offers and who makes the decision to accept, tentatively accept, or reject those offers. Each man is at least as well off in the equilibrium in which men make offers relative to the equilibrium in which women makes offers and vice versa.

Distributive effects

Becker's (1973) pioneering analysis of the marriage market considered, among other things, the effects of the marriage market on household distribution. Consider, for example, a simplified version of this model in which there is heterogeneity in tastes for being single, transferable utility within marriage, and no heterogeneity across couples in total utility within marriage. The outcome of the model is a distribution parameter that characterizes the share of total marital utility going to each partner within marriage and a number of marriages, with those individuals of both sexes with the highest taste for being single remaining unmarried. Among other things the model illustrates how a rise in the female wage raises the utility of married females within marriage even when married women are not active in the labour market. The increased opportunities for women outside marriage implies that women must, at the margin, receive a higher share of marital utility in order to be willing to marry.

There is substantial debate about the importance of marriage market structure in influencing transfers between partners and their respective households of origin at the time of marriage. Of particular relevance is the evidence of a historical transition from bride-price to dowry in parts of South Asia and the very large levels of dowry relative to annual income that are sometimes observed in that region. A number of factors have been argued to play an important role in this regard, including changes in the relative sizes of female and male populations of marriageable age associated with population growth and the gap in typical ages at marriage, changes in inequality and economic opportunity, and changes in the relative merits of different forms of parental transfers in their children.

Assortative mating

A second issue that has received significant theoretical and empirical scrutiny is the question of the extent to which the marriage market matches men and women with similar characteristics. This issue is thought to be important because of its implications for interhousehold inequality and for intergenerational transmission of inequality. If high-earning men match with high-earning women, and these high-earning couples transfer these resources to their children in the form of financial assistance and/or human capital, then inequality is likely to be more persistent across generations than would be the case otherwise. Assortative mating by religion and/or immigrant status is also thought to be both an indicator of and contributor to the process of assimilation. Finally, assortative mating on unobservable (to analysts) attributes can affect inferences about household behaviour that condition on household composition. For example, if men with a high unobservable taste for child human capital match with more educated women, then highly educated women will appear to have more educated children even if there is no direct effect.

A simple transferable utility model in which marital output is increasing in the product of male and female quality yields the prediction that there should be positive assortative mating on such attributes as intelligence, wealth and beauty. A possible exception arises with respect to market earnings capacity to the extent that, as postulated by Becker (1973), one member of the couple specializes in the production of non-market goods. Interestingly, the theoretical prediction of positive assortative mating across classes of individuals can arise within the marriage market with imperfect information (Burdett and Coles, 1997).

The evidence supports the prediction of positive assertive mating on partner attributes, although there have been changes over time in the degree to which this is observed. In particular, the degree of educational assortative mating fell between 1940 and 1960 in the United States but has increased subsequently, largely due to a decline in the share of low-education individuals marrying (Schwartz and Mare, 2005). There has also been a shift in the sign of the correlation in partner earnings from negative to positive since the 1960s (Schwartz, 2005), a pattern that has contributed to the overall increase in interhousehold inequality in income.

Marriage timing

A third set of marriage-market issues relates to the timing of marriage, particularly for women. It is argued that early marriage can result in higher fertility, lower rates of human capital investment, and an adverse bargaining position from the perspective of women. Boulier and Rosenzweig (1984), in an early contribution on this subject, showed how unobserved attractiveness could lead to incorrect inference about the role of education in delaying marriage and increasing spousal quality. Bergstrom and Bagnoli (1993) show how the process of uncertainty resolution with regard to the marital prospects may differentially affect the timing of marriage for men and women of different qualities. It also is the case that timing of marriage can play an important role in the equilibration of marriage markets given substantial differences in the relative numbers of eligible men and women arising from sex differences in mortality or a gap in the age at marriage for men and women for a growing population. In particular, because of how changes in the timing of marriage for sequential cohorts of eligible men and women affect the number of marriages taking place at a particular point in time, a persistent ten per cent excess in the number of eligible females relative to males can be accommodated with an increase in the female relative to male age at marriage by just one year over a decade (Foster, Khan and Protik, 2004).

ANDREW FOSTER

See also **assortative matching; Becker, Gary S.; family economics; household production and public goods; marriage and divorce; matching and market design.**

Bibliography

Becker, G.S. 1973. A theory of marriage: part I. *Journal of Political Economy* 81, 813–46.

Becker, G.S. 1974. A theory of marriage: part II. *Journal of Political Economy* 82, S11–26.

Bergstrom, T. 1997. A survey of theories of the family. In *Handbook of Population and Family Economics*, vol. 1A, ed. M.R. Rosenzweig and O. Stark. New York: North-Holland.

Bergstrom, T.C. and Bagnoli, M. 1993. Courtship as a waiting game. *Journal of Political Economy* 101, 185–202.

Boulier, B. and Rosenzweig, M. 1984. Schooling, search and spouse selection: testing economic theories of marriage and household behavior. *Journal of Political Economy* 92, 712–32.

Burdett, K. and Coles, M. 1997. Marriage and class. *Quarterly Journal of Economics* 112, 141–68.

Foster, A., Khan, N. and Protik, A. 2004. Equilibrating the marriage market in a rapidly growing population: evidence from rural Bangladesh. Working paper, Department of Economics, Brown University.

Gale, D. and Shapley, L. 1962. College admissions and the stability of marriage. *American Mathematical Monthly* 69, 9–15.

Schwartz, C.R. 2005. Earnings inequality among married couples and the increasing association between spouses' earnings. Working paper, Department of Economics, UCLA.

Schwartz, C.R. and Mare, R.D. 2005. Trends in educational assortative marriage from 1940 to 2003. *Demography* 42, 621–46.

Marschak, Jacob (1898–1977)

The diversity of Jacob Marschak's education and early experience made it likely that he would approach the study of economic behaviour with more than the average breadth of interest and vision. He was born in Kiev on 23 July 1898, and studied mechanical engineering at the Kiev Institute of Technology. At the beginning of the Russian Revolution he served briefly as Minister of Labour in the Menshevik government of Georgia but was forced to escape to Germany. There he went first to the University of Berlin, where he studied economics and statistics with L.V. Bortkiewicz, and then to the University of Heidelberg, where he received his Ph.D. in economics in 1922. His professors at Heidelberg included E. Lederer in economics, A. Weber in sociology, K. Jaspers in philosophy and G. Anschuetz in public law.

Following his doctoral studies at Heidelberg, he earned his living for the next eight years as an economic journalist and applied economist. He was economic editor for the *Frankfurter Zeitung* (1924–5), a research associate at the Research Centre for Economic Policy in Berlin (1926–8), and supervisor and editor of research for a Parliamentary Commission of Exporting Industries, at the Institute of World Economics of the University of Kiel (1928–30). Also, in 1926 he spent time in London on a travelling fellowship from the University of Heidelberg.

In 1930 he was appointed as a Privatdozent in economics at the University of Heidelberg, but three years later, once again the victim of political events, he left Germany and went to Oxford as a university lecturer. In 1935 he became Reader in Statistics and Director of the Oxford Institute of Statistics, where he remained until 1939. During this period he wrote extensively on theoretical and statistical aspects of demand analysis, a field in which he was a pioneer (Marschak, 1931).

In 1939 Marschak moved to the United States, where he lived the rest of his life, teaching at the New School for Social Research (1940–42), the University of Chicago (1943–55), Yale University (1955–60), and the University of California at Los Angeles (1960–77).

During the first dozen years Marschak was an active participant in the econometric revolution that is commonly associated with the Cowles Commission for Research in Economics. This revolution was nurtured at an early and crucial stage by the seminar on econometric methods and results that Marschak organized at the National Bureau of Economic Research, while he was on the faculty of the New School for Social Research. The intensive contacts fostered in this seminar led, in particular, to three fundamental papers on the statistical estimation of systems of simultaneous equations, by Haavelmo (1943), Mann and Wald (1943), and Marschak and Andrews (1944). Two further publication landmarks in this movement were the Cowles Commission Monographs No. 10 and No. 14, to which Marschak contributed the opening chapters (Marschak, 1950a; 1953).

Two other topics on which Marschak worked presaged his later work on decision and organization. First, he was, for a number of years, interested in the demand for money, and through his work and that of others the idea evolved that this demand could be better understood in the context of a more general theory of the joint demand for various assets (Marschak, 1938; 1949; 1950b). Furthermore, since the ultimate values of assets are rarely known with certainty at the time they are acquired, such a general theory needed to be based on a more systematic theory of decision in the face of uncertainty than was then available.

A second topic was the subject of his first scientific publication, a contribution to the debate on the efficiency, or even viability, of socialism. A central issue in that debate was whether the centralization of economic authority in a socialist state was compatible with the decentralization of information necessary in a complex economy.

From 1950 on, Marschak's research and writing was concerned with the general area of decision, information and organization. More specifically, one can identify at least three topics to which he made substantial contributions: (1) stochastic decision, (2) the economic value of information, and (3) the theory of teams.

Stochastic decision

In a series of articles (Marschak, 1959a; 1964a; Marschak and Block, 1960; Marschak and Davidson, 1959b; Marschak, Becker and DeGroot, 1963a; 1963b; 1963c; 1964b), Marschak proposed and elaborated the theory of stochastic decision and reported on a number of experiments. This work had its roots in the theory of rational economic choice or utility theory and in certain theories of psychological measurement.

Marschak developed a framework for describing the behaviour of economic decision makers who are approximately rational or consistent, or whose consistency of behaviour cannot be exactly verified through observation because of the observer's inability to control or identify all of the relevant factors in the decision-making situation.

It had long been recognized that economic decision makers did not exhibit exact consistency in their detailed choices. Economists were and remain loath to abandon the general framework of rational decision making that has appeared to be so fruitful in the analysis of the economic system as a whole, Marschak's theory provided a theoretical model that could be used for econometric studies of individual choice behaviour and that was connected in a coherent way with the general hypothesis of economic rationality. The work of Marschak and his co-authors was at first more appreciated by psychologists than by economists. His papers on this subject are still standard references in the theory of psychological scaling (Luce, Bush and Galanter, 1963, vol. 3, ch. 19).

More recently, this theory has provided the basis of statistical studies of individual choice behaviour (McFadden, 1982), as well as of a new approach to the theory of economic equilibrium that takes account of the uncertainty of individual behaviour (Hildenbrand, 1971; Bhattacharya and Majumdar, 1973).

Economic value of information

Marschak was probably the first to develop a systematic theory of the economic value of information. In this development he recognized that the measurement of quantity of information used by communication engineers, and associated with the work of Wiener and Shannon, was not adequate to measure the value of information. Indeed, it was not possible to identify a single measure of information such that more is always better.

Instead, Marschak turned to the newly developed theory of statistical decision for the source of his framework. For him, the value of a particular information system – or more generally, a system of information gathering, communication and decision – was related to the particular class of economic decision problems under consideration. His theoretical analysis of the value and cost of information pointed to the importance of more empirical knowledge concerning the technology of observation, information processing, communication and decision making, although he, himself, did not do any empirical work in this field. These ideas are elaborated in a long series of papers beginning with his contribution to *Decision Processes* (Marschak, 1954) and summarized in his paper 'Economics of Information Systems' (1971).

Economic theory of teams and organization

In an economic or other organization, the members of the organization typically differ in (1) the actions or strategies available to them, (2) the information on which their actions can be based, and (3) their preferences among alternative outcomes and their beliefs concerning the likelihoods of alternative outcomes given any particular organization action. Marschak recognized that the difficulty of determining a solution concept in the theory of games was related to differences of type 3. However, a model of an organization in which only differences of types 1 and 2 existed, which he called a team, presented no such difficulty of solution concept, and promised to provide a useful tool for the analysis of problems of efficient use of information in organizations. Such a model provided a framework for analysing the problems of decentralization of information so central to both the theory of competition and the operation of a socialist economy. The idea of a team was introduced in Marschak (1954; 1955), and a systematic development of the theory of teams is provided in Marschak and Radner (1972).

Towards the end of his career, Marschak returned to the theoretical issues concerning conflict of interest among the members of a decentralized organization. He approached this primarily in terms of the normative problem of devising incentives for the members of a 'team' to behave in accord with the goals of the organization. Of course, to the extent that such incentives are needed, the organization is no longer a team, in the technical sense of the term and the problem is back in the domain of the more general theory of games. It was left to others to make substantial progress on this set of problems. An important early effort in this direction was by T. Groves, who in his doctoral dissertation (1969) and his subsequent article, 'Incentives in Teams' (1973) presented – in a particular case – a solution to the problem of providing incentives to decentralized decision makers to both send truthful messages and make optimal decisions. These ideas were further developed in the contexts of the theory of public goods, the allocation of resources in a divisionalized firm and the principal–agent relationship. (For references to the literature on these developments see Groves and Ledyard, 1987; Hurwicz, 1979; Radner, 1986.)

Besides the significance of Marschak's individual contributions to economic analysis, I would like to emphasize the cumulative significance of his life's work. Through his work ran the important message that economists must come to grips with problems of uncertainty. He led the way, not only through his own research, but through his indefatigable and successful efforts at explaining these problems to his colleagues in economics and related disciplines. His work drew from psychology, statistics and engineering, and in turn influenced research in those disciplines. Indeed, more than any other economist I know, Marschak typified the best in behavioural science.

ROY RADNER

Selected works

A bibliography of Marschak's publications (excluding most book reviews and all newspaper articles) can be found in McGuire and Radner (1986). A large number of his papers have been reprinted in Marschak (1974).

1923. Wirtschaftsrechnung und Gemeinwirtschaft. *Archiv für Sozialwissenschaft* 51, 501–20.

1931. *Elastizität der Nachfrage*. Tübingen: J.C.B. Mohr.

1938. Money and the theory of assets. *Econometrica* 6, 311–25.

1944. (With W.H. Andrews.) Random simultaneous equations and the theory of production. *Econometrica* 12, 143–205.

1949. Role of liquidity under complete and incomplete information. *American Economic Review* 39, 182–95.

1950a. Statistical inference in economics: an introduction. In *Statistical Inference in Dynamic Economic Models*, ed. T.C. Koopmans. New York: Wiley.

1950b. The rationale of the demand for money and 'money illusion'. *Metroeconomica* 2, 71–100.

1953. Economic measurements for policy and prediction. In *Studies in Econometric Method*, ed. W.C. Hood and T.C. Koopmans. New York: Wiley.

1954. Towards an economic theory of organization and information. In *Decision Processes*, ed. R.M. Thrall, C.H. Coombs and R.L. Davis. New York: Wiley.

1955. Elements for a theory of teams. *Management Science* 1, 127–37.

1959a. Binary-choice constraints and random utility indicators. In *Mathematical Methods in Social Sciences*, ed. K.J. Arrow, S. Karlin and P. Suppes. Stanford: Stanford University Press.

1959b. (With D. Davidson.) Experimental tests of stochastic decision theory. In *Measurement: Definitions and Theory*, ed. C.W. Churchman and P. Ratoosh. New York: Wiley.

1960. (With H.D. Block.) Random orderings and stochastic theories of responses. In *Contributions to Probability and Statistics: Essays in Honor of Harold Hotelling*, ed. I. Olkin et al. Stanford: Stanford University Press.

1963a. (With G. Becker and M. DeGroot.) Stochastic models of choice behavior. *Behavioral Science* 8, 41–55.

1963b. (With G. Becker and M. DeGroot.) An experimental study of some stochastic models for wagers. *Behavioral Science* 8, 199–202.

1963c. (With G. Becker and M. DeGroot.) Probability of choices among very similar objects: an experiment to decide between two models. *Behavioral Science* 8, 306–11.

1964a. Actual versus consistent decision behavior. *Behavioral Science* 9, 103–10.

1964b. (With G. Becker and M. DeGroot.) Measuring utility by a single-response sequential method. *Behavioral Science* 9, 226–32.

1971. Economics of information systems. In *Frontiers of Quantitative Economics*, ed. M. Intriligator. Amsterdam: North-Holland.

1972. (With R. Radner.) *Economic Theory of Teams*. New Haven: Yale University Press.

1974. *Economic Information, Decision, and Prediction*. 3 vols. Dordrecht: Reidl.

Bibliography

Bhattacharya, R.N. and Majumdar, M.K. 1973. Random exchange economies. *Journal of Economic Theory* 6, 37–67.

Groves, T. 1973. Incentives in teams. *Econometrica* 41, 617–31.

Groves, T. and Ledyard, J. 1987. Incentive compatibility ten years later. In *Information, Incentives, and Economic Mechanisms: Essays in Honor of Leonid Hurwicz*, ed. T. Groves, R. Radner and S. Reiter. Minneapolis: University of Minnesota Press.

Haavelmo, T. 1943. The statistical implications of a system of simultaneous equations. *Econometrica* 11, 1–12.

Hildenbrand, W. 1971. Random preferences and equilibrium. *Journal of Economic Theory* 3, 414–29.

Hurwicz, L. 1979. On the interaction between information and incentives in organizations. In *Communication and Control in Society*, ed. K. Drittendorf. New York: Gordon Breach.

Luce, R.D., Bush, R. and Galanter, E., eds. 1963–5. *Handbook of Mathematical Psychology*. 3 vols. New York: Wiley.

Mann, H.B. and Wald, A. 1943. On the statistical treatment of linear stochastic difference equations. *Econometrica* 11, 173–220.

McFadden, D. 1982. Qualitative choice models. In *Advances in Economic Theory*, ed. W. Hildenbrand. Cambridge: Cambridge University Press.

McGuire, C.B. and Radner, R., eds. 1986. *Decision and Organization*. 2nd edn. Minneapolis: University of Minnesota Press. Originally published Amsterdam: North-Holland, 1972.

Radner, R. 1986. The internal economy of large firms. *Economic Journal* 96, Supplement, 1–22.

Marshall, Alfred (1842–1924)

Alfred Marshall, Professor of Political Economy at the University of Cambridge from 1885 to 1908 and founder of the Cambridge School of Economics, was born in Bermondsey, a London suburb, on 26 July 1842. He died at Balliol Croft, his Cambridge home of many years, on 13 July 1924 at the age of 81. His magnum opus, *Principles of Economics* (1890a) evolved through eight editions in his lifetime, the final edition (1920) being most commonly cited today. It was one of the most influential treatises of its era and was for many years the Bible of British economics, introducing many still familiar concepts. The Cambridge School rose to great eminence in the 1920s and 1930s. A.C. Pigou and J.M. Keynes, the most important figures in this development, were among Marshall's pupils.

Marshall's biography and career are outlined initially, after which descriptions are given of his views on the social setting, aims and methods of economics, and his intellectual debts to others. An analysis of his fundamental ideas on theories of value and distribution, which were mainly set out in *Principles*, follows, after which his contributions to monetary and international-trade theory are considered briefly. A final section provides additional documentation and general suggestions for further reading. Also, some of the more technical sections have attached to them brief 'bibliographic notes' offering suggestions for further exploration. All bibliographic references lacking an author's name are to works by Marshall, and the bibliographic details of all his cited publications can be found in the list of 'Selected works' below. The bibliographic details for all cited works written or edited by others are listed in the concluding 'Bibliography'.

Biography and career

Marshall grew up in the London suburb of Clapham, being educated at the Merchant Taylors' School where he showed academic promise and a particular aptitude for mathematics. Eschewing the more obvious path of a closed scholarship to Oxford and a classical education, he entered St John's College, Cambridge, in 1862 on an open exhibition. There he read for the Mathematical Tripos, Cambridge University's most prestigious degree competition, emerging in 1865 in the exalted position of Second Wrangler, bettered only by the future Lord Rayleigh. This success ensured Marshall's election to a Fellowship at St John's. Supplementing his stipend by some mathematical coaching, and abandoning – doubtless because of a loss of religious conviction – half-formed earlier intentions of a clerical career, he became engrossed in the study of the philosophical foundations and moral bases for human behaviour and social organization. In 1868 he became a College Lecturer in Moral Sciences at St John's, coming to specialize in teaching political economy. By about 1870 he seems to have committed his career to developing this subject, seemingly ripe for reform, and helping to transform it into a new science of economics.

For several years he laboured persistently to develop and refine his economic ideas, and to deepen his understanding and grasp of both the existing economic literature and the economic reality that was its subject matter. In 1875 he visited the United States to probe economic conditions, and throughout his life he was tireless in his efforts to master the practicalities of the economic world. Prior to 1879 his publications were meagre. He had embarked on a book on international trade and problems of protectionism in the mid-1870s, and before that he had worked out many of his distinctive theoretical ideas in the form of short essays, many now reproduced in Whitaker (1975). But the only part of this material to be made public was four chapters from the theoretical appendices for the proposed international-trade volume. In 1879 Henry Sidgwick had these printed for private circulation under the title *The Pure Theory of Foreign Trade: The Pure Theory of Domestic Values* (1879a). (An amplified version together with surviving portions of the text of the abandoned trade volume is also reproduced in Whitaker, 1975.) The year 1879 also saw the publication of Marshall's first book, *The Economics of Industry* (1879b), written jointly with his wife Mary Paley Marshall.

Mary Paley had been one of the first group of students at Newnham Hall (later Newnham College) where Marshall, an early supporter of the informal scheme of Cambridge lectures for women, taught her political economy. Their marriage in 1877 required Marshall to give up his Cambridge position under the celibacy rules then in force. He found a new livelihood as principal of the recently established University College, Bristol, where he also became Professor of Political Economy. There *The Economics of Industry* was brought to completion and published by the house of Macmillan, which continued as Marshall's publisher thereafter. Ostensibly an elementary primer, this book contained the first general statement of Marshall's emerging theories, and a considerable

sophistication lay beneath its deceptively simple surface. Together with the powerful *Pure Theory* chapters published by Sidgwick, a few copies of which circulated outside Cambridge, *The Economics of Industry* marked Marshall as a rising star in the economics firmament. With the death of W.S. Jevons in 1881, he moved into the public eye as the leader in Britain of the new scientific school of economics.

The duties of the Bristol principalship proved irksome to Marshall, especially as the college was struggling financially. He was anxious to proceed with his writing, having by 1877 conceived the plan for the book that was to become the *Principles*. His frustrations were increased by the onset in 1879 of a debilitating illness, diagnosed as kidney stones, which restricted his activities. He was persuaded to continue as principal until 1881, when he resigned both posts at the college. The next year was spent travelling, with an extended sojourn in Palermo, and it was in this year that composition of the new book began in earnest.

At Bristol, Marshall had got to know well Benjamin Jowett, the famed Master of Balliol, who was one of the governors of the struggling college. It was probably by Jowett's generosity that Marshall was able to return to Bristol in 1882 as Professor of Political Economy. And it was doubtless at Jowett's instigation that the Marshalls moved to Oxford in 1883, when a Balliol lectureship became vacant on the unexpected death of Arnold Toynbee. Marshall had considerable success as a teacher in Oxford and appeared settled in for an indefinite stay. But an 'Oxford School of Economics' was not to be. The sudden death of Henry Fawcett, who had been Professor of Political Economy at Cambridge since 1863, opened up the irresistible prospect of a return to Cambridge and a position with great potential for academic leadership. Marshall, the dominant candidate, was duly elected in December 1884, holding the chair until 1908, when he resigned to devote himself entirely to writing.

In many ways Cambridge's inviting prospects were to prove illusory. Economics was taught as part of the Historical and Moral Sciences Triposes, but neither avenue provided a supply of able interested students, nor was there much scope for advanced work. Marshall struggled for many years, with limited success, to increase the scope for economic teaching. But it was not until 1903, with the establishment of a new Tripos in Economics and Politics, that his goal was achieved. Even then, few resources were made available by the university and colleges for the teaching of economics, and the staffing of the new Tripos relied heavily on Marshall's willingness to support two young lecturers from his own pocket. The flowering of the new school came about mainly after his retirement, but the seeds were certainly planted by his efforts.

Absorbed in the struggle for his own subject, Marshall took relatively little part in general university affairs.

Indeed, his rather obsessive personality and proneness to magnify details would have made him ineffectual as a university statesman even if he had aspired in that direction. But he did play a prominent part in the successful campaign of 1896–7 against the granting of Cambridge degrees to students of the women's colleges – this despite his wife being at the time a lecturer at Newnham. He was not opposed to women's education, indeed had been a warm supporter in his early days, but was vehemently opposed to the assimilation of women into an educational system designed for men.

But the dominant fact in Marshall's life after his return to Cambridge, and certainly the aspect of greatest interest to posterity, is his long struggle to give adequate written expression to the stores of economic knowledge and understanding he had accumulated. The demands of teaching and administration left him little time or energy for sustained composition during term time and it was in the jealously guarded long vacations, usually spent away from Cambridge on the south coast of England or in the Tyrol of Austria, that the only real progress could be made. By 1887 the book commenced in 1881 had grown into a projected two-volume treatise. He hoped to complete the first volume in time for it to appear in the autumn of that year with the second volume appearing by 1889. In fact, the first volume (1890a) appeared as the *Principles of Economics, Volume One*, only in July 1890, when it was received with great and immediate acclaim and established Marshall firmly as one of the world's leading economists. The second volume never appeared. It was to have covered foreign trade, money, trade fluctuations, taxation, collectivism and aims for the future – a tall order!

Marshall struggled for the next 13 years with his intractable second volume, meanwhile spending much time on substantial, but not very substantive, recastings of the first volume in new editions of 1891, 1895 and 1898, and in preparing a digest of it to replace the earlier *Economics of Industry* which he had come to dislike intensely. (The digest, 1892, appeared under the title *Elements of the Economics of Industry, Volume One*. Like the earlier work it included material on trades unions that was never incorporated into *Principles*.) By 1903 much material had been accumulated for the second volume, but the scope was becoming unmanageable as Marshall became increasingly preoccupied with problems of trusts, trades unions, international trade, and comparative economic development, and decreasingly concerned with matters of pure theory. In that year, partly from the impetus of writing a private memorandum on trade policy for the use of the then Chancellor of the Exchequer, and partly because the tariff controversy was at full heat, Marshall was tempted into writing a short topical book on foreign trade questions, intending to publish it speedily. But this project too grew unmanageably in his hands. In 1907, the preface to the fifth edition of *Principles* (the last major rewriting) announced the abandonment of the proposed continuation and promised instead a volume, already partly in print, on 'National Industry and Trade', to be followed soon by a companion volume on 'Money, Credit and Employment' (Guillebaud, 1961, vol. 2, p. 46). To reflect this change, the title of the sixth and subsequent editions of *Principles* was changed to *Principles of Economics: An Introductory Volume*. Retirement in 1908, at the age of 66, freed Marshall to concentrate on these projects, but progress continued to be slow. He appears to have suffered from recurrent dyspepsia and high blood pressure, necessitating a strict regimen and limiting his ability to work. But the more fundamental problem was that the world kept changing and the increasingly realistic and factual tone of his enquiry called for incessant recasting and revision. Nothing had been completed by the time war broke out in 1914, and then much rewriting was required to take into account the radical changes that were transforming the world economy and its post-war prospects. At last, when Marshall was 77 years old, *Industry and Trade* (1919), his second masterpiece, finally appeared. It was a magisterial, largely factual, consideration of trends in the British and international economy and of future economic prospects. But, lacking an obvious theoretical skeleton, it has not received from economists the kind of attention lavished on *Principles*, although interest in it is now beginning to stir among historians of economics.

In its final form, *Industry and Trade* was narrower in scope than had been intended earlier, while the proposed book on 'Money, Credit and Employment' still remained to be written. Over the next four years, by a remarkable effort, and despite rapidly waning powers, some of the mass of accumulated raw material remaining was pulled together in *Money, Credit and Commerce* (1923). This contains Marshall's fullest treatment of the theories of money and international trade, but it is an imperfect pastiche of earlier material, some dating back almost 50 years.

In the last months of his life, Marshall toyed with the occasional writings and the memoranda and evidence for governmental enquiries that he had prepared at various stages during his career, with the hope of editing them for publication in book form. This was not to be, but his plan was largely fulfilled after his death in two books sponsored by the Royal Economic Society (Pigou, 1925; Keynes, 1926).

Judged by what might have been, Marshall's authorial performance after 1890 was a sorry one, marked by repeated procrastination and inconstancy and by chronically over-optimistic expectations. The mantle of leadership that he had assumed on Jevons's death had proved a heavy one. Both temperamentally and by virtue of his acknowledged position as the doyen of British economists, Marshall was compelled to attempt the magisterial and to denigrate the kind of forceful direct essay of which he was eminently capable.

As Cambridge professor and unquestioned leader of British orthodox economists, Marshall could hardly avoid becoming a public figure whose pronouncements carried more than a personal weight. His consciousness of this, and of the precarious public standing of economics, as well as his own temperament, made him peculiarly reluctant to enter into public controversy, although he would on occasion fire off a letter to *The Times* on some issue of the day. He served as an expert witness for several government enquiries and was an influential member of the Royal Commission on Labour of 1890–94. As President of Section F of the British Association in 1890 he took the formal lead in the movement to found the British (later Royal) Economic Association, but he was not a prime mover. Indeed, he was not a clubbable or organizational man and relied on others to further whatever goals he desired for economics and the economics profession at large. But neither was he a recluse. Balliol Croft received a continuing stream of visitors, ranging from working class leaders to distinguished foreign economists, while students or young colleagues were always welcomed and offered generous advice mixed with exhortation.

Although able students interested in economics were in short supply, Marshall did over the years teach and influence several students who were to make contributions to the subject. From the early Cambridge period H.S. Foxwell, H.H. Cunynghame, J.N. Keynes and J.S. Nicholson might be mentioned. The Oxford period brought L.L.F.R. Price and E.C.K. Gonner, while the period as Professor in Cambridge produced, among others, A. Berry, A.W. Flux, C.P. Sanger, A.L. Bowley, S.J. Chapman, A.C. Pigou, J.H. Clapham, D.H. Macgregor, C.R. Fay, and, last but not least, J.M. Keynes.

The undoubted fact of Marshall's professional leadership of British economics calls for some explanation. He was far from suited to such a role by temperament, and his fussiness and inflexibility could be irritating. For example, Sidgwick, J.N. Keynes, and Foxwell, the most important of his early allies in Cambridge, were all eventually alienated. Marshall's success can be attributed partly to sheer persistence. As in the case of the new Tripos, he had a clear idea of what he wanted to accomplish and worried away at it until he exhausted the opposition and was allowed to have his way. But it must also have been due to the lack of any alternative. The relevant question is not 'Why Marshall?' but 'Who else?' Economics was rapidly evolving as a profession around the turn of the 20th twentieth century, creating a leadership vacuum. Leadership was unlikely to emanate from outside Oxford, Cambridge or London, but F.Y. Edgeworth at Oxford was perhaps the last man capable of meeting the need, while E. Cannan at the new London School of Economics, although more suited than Marshall to the hurly-burly of professional politics, was too much the perennial critic and iconoclast to fill the bill. Moreover, whatever Marshall's foibles, the sheer power of his intellectual vision, his international standing as Britain's leading economic thinker, and his ability to inspire an impressive flow of budding scholars, all conspired to make him the only feasible contender.

Marshall's views on the social setting, aims and methods of economics

Marshall saw economics as concerned with those aspects of human behaviour open to pecuniary influences and sufficiently regular and ubiquitous to permit statements of broad scope and some persistence. While maintaining, especially in earlier work, that some heeded moral imperatives might be impervious to pecuniary considerations, he conceded that most behaviour lay within the ambit of the measuring rod of money. On the other hand, he emphasized that motivation was not merely a matter of pursuing pecuniary self-interest, even if broadly conceived to include interests of family and friends. He was anxious to lay the ghost of *homo economicus* and emphasized the human desires to obtain social approbation or distinction and to enjoy the pleasures of skilful activity. He saw actors as diverse as captains of industry and sculptors driven more by the joys of creative activity and the striving for the regard of peers than by the desire for material acquisition.

As well as not being pecuniary maximizers in any narrow sense, individuals were for the most part seen as imperfect optimizers. The working classes, especially, often lacked the knowledge and foresight to judge their long-term interests. Marshall's actors were not imbued with complete knowledge of their environment but had to acquire knowledge slowly, and often painfully, through experience. Nor were they endowed with fixed desires and an intrinsic, unchanging character. Indeed, character and preferences evolved as individuals were exposed to new possibilities and chose to enter into new activities. The workplace, in particular, was an important moulder of character. Self-improvement and character development induced by environmental changes, planned or unplanned, both figured largely in Marshall's world view. He believed that social institutions, such as land tenancy practices, were pliable and ultimately moulded themselves into conformity with the individual interests involved, rather than presenting a permanent constraint on mutually desired accommodations. (For this he was taken to task by his most vehement critic, W. Cunningham, who denied the applicability of modern economic theory to medieval practices – see Cunningham, 1892.) But institutional change must be slow, slower even than changes in individual character and wants, because informal customs and tacit agreements are hard to change. Thus, while the institutions and informal understandings and prohibitions that constrain and mould economic behaviour might ultimately be endogenous they will often be ill adapted to current circumstances and thereby act as an independent constraint on the pursuit of mutually desired accommodations. Institutions, in the broad sense, are important and not always socially rational constraints on individual action.

Marshall was impelled to economics because 'the study of the causes of poverty is the study of the causes of the degradation of a large part of mankind' (1920, p. 3). For the bulk of the population, mired in poor living and working conditions, little progress in habits, aspirations and self-esteem could be expected without prior improvement in economic conditions. Such improvement was socially important not so much for its own sake, at least once the pangs of immediate want were assuaged, but because of its instrumental role in permitting and stimulating improvement in the quality and character of the population. What Marshall really valued was not improvement in the standard of living but the enhancement of the standard of life that this improvement made possible. And he entertained little doubt about what constituted a qualitative improvement here, even though – or perhaps because – his values may seem quite parochial and culture-bound.

Economic improvement required appropriate institutions, incentives and attitudes, and would be threatened by wide-scale government intrusions into economic affairs, although some forced income redistribution could be tolerated. But even if economic conditions were improved, the full yield of social betterment would be garnered only if enlarged consumption were turned to ennobling and horizon-expanding channels (rather than, say, to strong drink), involved a due consumption of beneficial leisure, and was accompanied by healthier and less stultifying conditions of working and town life. The government had a guiding role to play here. But even more important would be the assistance and example of employers and the upper and middle classes, who must first rid themselves of a frequent propensity to showy and ostentatious consumption and excessive materialism. The working-class leaders and skilled artisans who had already raised their own standard of life had an important leadership role too. Voluntary individual efforts to assist the rise of the underprivileged must rest on an adequate understanding of economic consequences. For this, as well as to secure an informed electorate, the diffusion of sound economic knowledge was an essential and integral element in the process of socio-economic transformation. Economics thus was itself a noble activity of high importance for the future of mankind.

The broad view of the economy suggested by the foregoing is of a complex evolutionary process of combined economic, social and individual change in which each individual's abilities, character, preferences and knowledge develop jointly, along with social institutions, markets and the technologies of production and communication. The pursuit of self-interest, broadly conceived, is ubiquitous in directing this evolutionary process, but is subject to inertia, ignorance and limited foresight, not to mention individual mutability.

Unfortunately, Marshall was able to bring little formal analysis to bear on this general 'biological' vision of the economy and could only evoke it descriptively. It might be true that 'the Mecca of the economist lies in economic biology rather than in economic dynamics' (1920, p. xiv). Nevertheless, the only available analytical tools were those of classical mechanics, tools that Marshall's early mathematical training had equipped him to employ skillfully. In fact, chief reliance had to be put on that branch of classical mechanics dealing with statics. Dynamics, beyond a few qualitative applications, required more precise information than was likely to be available. Perforce then, much of Marshall's formal analysis, like that of W.S. Jevons or Léon Walras, was based on simple assumptions of individual optimization and market equilibrium, taking preferences, technology and market institutions for granted. Such provisional or tentative 'statical' treatments could often be valuable. Indeed Marshall viewed them as indispensable for the correct analysis of many questions. But he was always anxious to stress that the analysis was preliminary, and perhaps of only transitory validity. This awareness made him impatient of over-elaboration, so that, for example, he showed no interest at all in pushing the statical approach to its logical conclusion in the general equilibrium analysis of the stationary state. For him, equilibrium analysis was an indispensable but rough and ready instrument that needed to be employed with due caution and a continuing awareness of its limitations in the face of a complex ever-evolving reality. It was only a tool and did not itself constitute concrete knowledge.

Marshall had no great profundity as a philosopher of science and had little patience with metaphysics: 'in a sense … he held no views on method' (Coase, 1975, p. 27). Marshall's discussions of methodology largely reflect the philosophical presuppositions of his day. His method was in the general deductive tradition of John Stuart Mill, but he sought to emphasize the relativity of particular theories, as contrasted with the universality of the general theoretical 'organon' or economists' toolbox. Anxious to present a public image of the unity of economics in the face of the Methodenstreit among economists in the late 19th century, he attempted to maintain an uneasy balance on method, decrying extended chains of deductive reasoning but denying the possibility of purely inductive inference unguided by a coherent conceptual framework. Economics had room for specialists in both deductive and inductive methods, but both must ultimately be co-workers. Assumptions must be selected with close regard to the facts of the case and potential disturbing causes must be kept prominently in mind and due allowance made for them. J.N. Keynes described Marshall's analytical method as 'deductive political economy guided by observation' (1891, p. 217n) and Keynes's chapter 'On the Deductive Method in Political Economy' (1891, pp. 204–35) is perhaps as good a rationalization of Marshall's method as one can find.

Intellectual debts

The intellectual background to Marshall's work in economics was established in the 1860s, partly in his stringent mathematical training, but perhaps more importantly in the heady mixture of utilitarianism, evolutionism and German idealism which he eagerly imbibed in the years immediately following his graduation. He seems to have started on economics from J.S. Mill's *Principles of Political Economy* (1848), moving on to the classic works of Smith and Ricardo. At a fairly early stage, probably around 1868, he discovered Cournot's *Récherches* (1838), which provided examples of the application of mathematics to economic questions. Acquaintance with J.H. von Thünen's work, which influenced Marshall's distribution theory, must have come somewhat later, in the early to mid-1870s. During the 1870s and early 1880s Marshall also read widely on economic development and socialism, including much literature in German, the only foreign language he mastered thoroughly. After that, his reading seems to have been concentrated mainly on factual and practical matters. Once his own theoretical views had crystallized, he appears to have been reluctant to do more than attempt to explain and clarify them to others, and to have taken remarkably little interest in new theoretical issues or in the theoretical ideas of others.

In many ways, the list of Marshall's denials of theoretical indebtedness is more remarkable than that of his acknowledgments. He claimed to have developed his ideas on consumer surplus before learning of anticipations by J. Dupuit and H. Fleeming Jenkin. The grudging attitude to W.S. Jevons's marginal utility theory shown in his review (1872) of Jevons (1871), although subsequently relaxed, was never replaced by any acknowledgement of indebtedness. He showed little or no interest in the work of Walras, gave meagre credit to Carl Menger, whose work must have become known to him by the early 1880s, patronized Pantaleoni and Böhm-Bawerk, largely ignored Pareto, and so on. Even in the case of Edgeworth, one of his few intimates, Marshall felt that undoubted theoretical powers were guided by an unreliable judgement and refused to follow Edgeworth's subtle elaborations far. In fact, the only major theorist of the day to command Marshall's entire admiration and respect was J.B. Clark, and even here there was no acknowledgement of serious indebtedness. This tendency to denigrate the work of his contemporaries was matched by an equally strong tendency to overvalue the achievements of the British Classical School led by A. Smith, D. Ricardo and J.S. Mill. For one reason or another – perhaps a personality quirk, perhaps an effort to boost the public esteem of economics – Marshall was prone to exaggerate the intellectual continuity and maturity of his subject – see O'Brien (1990) on this.

A growing interest in wider intellectual influences on Marshall in his formative years 1865–70 has been sparked by the publication and analysis of his early philosophical manuscripts (Raffaelli, 1994, 2003), especially a paper entitled 'Ye Machine' that outlines a mechanism capable of learning new routines from experience, thus freeing its limited learning ability to gradually establish new and higher level routines, and so on. It appears that Marshall's ambitions in these early years lay in the area of 'psychology' or perhaps better in the 'philosophy of mind'. Whether the world lost more than economics gained from his switch to economics remains an open and perhaps insoluble question. But it does appear that the pattern of a sequential routinizing of new methods, continually leading to new levels of individual or organizational complexity, continued to play a significant part in Marshall's economic thought. More generally it is clear that he read philosophical literature widely in his formative years: Kant, Hegel, H. Spencer, and others. But whether and how these sources influenced his economic thought remains uncertain, partly because evidence is slight or absent.

Demand theory

So far the discussion has remained on a very general level, dealing with broad aspects of Marshall's life and work. At this point there begins a much more detailed and technical consideration of various aspects of his theoretical contributions, commencing with his demand theory. Marshall's treatment of the theory of demand is sketchy and incomplete, concentrating on the demand for a single commodity, or commodity group, against a loosely defined background. A utility-maximizing individual's utility is defined by $u(x) + w(y)$ where x is the individual's consumption of the particular good X, while y is the individual's expenditure on all other goods. This expenditure is measured in money of constant purchasing power: that is, deflated by a general price index. How this index is defined and whether, as seems appropriate, the price of X is excluded from it, is left unclear. Such money can be treated as a composite good, Y, and y can be regarded as the amount of this composite good consumed. If m is the individual's initial endowment of Y, then $y = m$ whenever $x = 0$, while if X can be freely purchased at a fixed price of p units of Y per unit of X then x and y must satisfy the constraint $px + y = m$. Marshall assumes that the utility functions $u(x)$ and $w(y)$ have positive but diminishing marginal utility so that $u'(x) > 0 > u''(x)$ and $w'(y) > 0 > w''(y)$, where single and double primes are used to denote first and second derivatives. The maximum expenditure, e, that the individual is willing to make to secure x units of X is implicitly defined as a function $e(x, m)$ by $u(x) + w(m - e) - w(m) = 0$. Providing that x and y are both positive, the rate at which e increases with x is $u'(x)/w'(m - e)$ by the implicit function theorem. This ratio would be the demand price for the xth unit of X if all previous units had been acquired at their corresponding demand prices: that is, if the individual had faced perfect price discrimination in exchanging Y for X. Alternatively, if the individual had been able to obtain any amount of X at fixed per unit price, p, the resulting demand function $x(p, m)$ for X would be implicitly defined (given x and y are both positive) by the first-order condition $u'(x) - pw'(m - px) = 0$. Partial differentiation of $x(p, m)$ shows that x falls as p increases, while an increase in m increases both x and y: thus, the Giffen possibility of an increase in p increasing the quantity of X demanded is excluded. But an increase in p may lower or raise the value of px, so that demand for X may be price elastic or price inelastic at a given p.

The possibility of buying at a fixed price rather than facing perfect price discrimination creates a consumer surplus of $e(x(p, m), m) - px(p, m)$. This is the additional amount that could have been extracted by perfect price discrimination for all units up to the price-taking optimal one. That this surplus is positive follows from the fact that every infra-marginal unit of X acquired creates a surplus utility when the individual faces a fixed price (since $u'(x) > pw'(m - px)$ for each such x) but no surplus when the individual is faced with perfect price discrimination.

Marshall's mathematical notes (1920, pp. 838–42) on his general case are obscure and puzzling. Doubtless he felt this case was too dependent on unobservables to be of much practical value. He therefore emphasized the special case in which the marginal utility of money is treated as a constant. The rationale offered is that an individual's 'expenditure on any one thing … is only a small part of his whole expenditure' (1920, p. 842). This simplifies $e = e(x, m)$ above to $e = u(x)/w'(m)$ while $x(p, m)$ is now defined implicitly by $u'(x)/w'(m) = p$. At the x value defined by the latter equation, consumer surplus arising from the ability to buy any amount of X at the per-unit price p can be expressed in utility terms as $u(x) - xu'(x)$ or in money terms as $u(x)/w'(m) - xu'(x)/w'(m)$. These formulae are exactly analogous to the standard formula for Ricardian land rent, with the first term the output obtained on a piece of land from the application of x doses of variable input, each dose remunerated at the common marginal product. Partly because of this analogy, Marshall used the term 'consumer rent' rather than 'consumer surplus' prior to 1898.

Although priority must go to Dupuit, Marshall's simple concept of consumer surplus based on the assumption of a constant marginal utility of money has been influential. But he was well aware of the complications arising from variation in the marginal utility of money: 'Strictly speaking we ought to take account of the fact that if he spent less on tea the marginal utility of money to him would be less than it is, and he would get an element of consumers' surplus from buying other things at prices which now yield him no such rent' (1920, p. 842). Although such influences may be 'of the second order of smallness' they raise the more disquieting issue of assessing the overall welfare effects of changes that affect many markets simultaneously. On this Marshall had little to say: 'the task of adding together the total utilities of all commodities, so as to obtain the aggregate of the total utility of all wealth, is beyond the range of any but the most elaborate mathematical formulae' (1920, p. 131n.). It was a task he chose not to pursue. Apart from generalizing for the possibility that a certain quantity of good X might be indispensable, Marshall elected not to develop his demand theory further, or even to generalize it to incorporate utility functions that were not additively separable (1920, p. 845). It is clear that each commodity in turn might take the spotlighted role of good X and that in certain circumstances simultaneous consumer surpluses for several goods might be added (1920, p. 842). An unpublished early manuscript note from the 1870s on the theory of taxation (Whitaker, 1975, vol. 2, pp. 285–305) had advanced matters considerably further by working formally with the maximization of utility under a budget constraint, but this lead was not followed up in print and some of its lessons for welfare economics were apparently forgotten. *Principles* gave a clear intuitive account of the consumer's overall optimization problem (1920, pp. 117–23), but failed to connect it to the resulting interrelated set of demand functions for the various goods consumed. Indeed, it is clear that for positive purposes Marshall was willing to treat market demand functions in a quite pragmatic way, admitting, for example, close substitutes or complements and the Giffen exception, all inconsistent with the simple formal theory set out above. In judging this, it must be borne in mind that consistency and generality of 'statical' analysis were not Marshall's real goal. Rather, 'fragmentary statical hypotheses are used as temporary auxiliaries to dynamical – or rather biological – conceptions' (1920, p. xv).

The market demand for a good that is offered to all actual or potential buyers at the same given price is of course obtained as a function of that price by summing the amounts demanded at that price by all the consumers. A sufficient but not necessary condition for market demand to fall as price increases is that each individual's demand decreases. The now familiar concept of market demand elasticity – proportional quantity change divided by proportional price change – was first introduced by Marshall, although several authors had come close to the idea previously. It appeared without flourish in (1885c), and appeared more prominently in *Principles*. But Marshall himself made relatively little use of it.

Bibliographic note: Marshall's treatment of demand is essentially contained in (1920, pp. 92–137, 838–43). An influential, although controversial, interpretation of Marshall's demand theory is given by Friedman (1949). Biswas (1977) gives another alternative to the orthodox reading provided by Stigler (1950) that is largely adopted here. An excellent overview is Aldrich (1996). On consumer surplus see Chipman (1990).

Production and long-period competitive supply

In deriving the long-period supply curve of a commodity in *Principles*, Marshall envisages production as organized by firms, typically family businesses. Each firm strives to minimize its production costs, substituting one productive factor or production method for another according to the 'Principle of Substitution'. In its simpler forms this involves marginalist adjustment to bring relative marginal value products into line with relative marginal costs. But more generally, the Principle of Substitution is akin to a natural selection process, being 'a special and limited application of the law of survival of the fittest' (1920, p. 597). Marshall's firms do not have costless access to a common production function, but must grope and experiment their way to cost-reducing modifications. The long-period supply curve is defined for a given state of general scientific and technical knowledge. But each firm must explore this to some extent anew.

Although the distinction is not entirely clear – distinctions seldom are for Marshall – two polar cases may be distinguished within his theory of long-period competitive supply. These will be referred to as the 'agricultural' and the 'industrial' cases. The former is much the more straightforward and involves an industry in which production is relatively simple, internal economies of scale are minimal, and the product is homogeneous and easily marketed. The optimal firm size is small, and management is sufficiently routine to need no exceptional ability to keep a firm operating efficiently. As the overall market expands, new firms may be added, but changing composition of the population of firms is not an essential feature of this case.

The long-period supply price per unit of output at which such an industry can supply any quantity of output must just cover the cost of maintaining that level of output indefinitely. That is, it must just suffice to pay all the inputs (including management) needed to produce that level of output in a cost-minimizing way at rates that just ensure that the requisite input quantities will continue to be forthcoming indefinitely. In the case of skilled workers, in particular, the rate must just suffice to induce parents to apprentice new workers to the industry at a rate exactly offsetting the attrition through retirement and other causes. Similarly, the return to fixed capital must just suffice to induce replacement of the existing stock of fixed assets, while the return to management must keep up the necessary replacement flow of managers. On the other hand, the return to land services must just suffice to prevent these services from migrating elsewhere, replacement not being necessary. As the level of industry output being considered is increased, the supply price will probably rise, mainly because of the need to pay a higher return to land so as to attract a greater supply from other uses, but perhaps also because of the need to pay more for rare natural talents that, like land, must be attracted in greater quantity from other uses, not being capable of replication through education and

training. Such a tendency for long-period supply price to rise with output may be mitigated though seldom eliminated by substitution against inputs whose supply price is rising, and by possible external economies that increase each firm's efficiency by influences that depend, not on its own output, but on the entire industry's output. A tendency for supply price to rise with output will imply that infra-marginal units of those inputs whose supply prices are rising receive rents, since all units will be remunerated at the rate necessary to induce continuing supply of the marginal unit. In the absence of external economies (or diseconomies) the total rent or producer surplus generated will be the 'triangular' area above the supply curve. That is, it will be

$$R = xg(x) - \int_0^x g(v)\mathrm{d}v$$

where $g(x)$ is the supply price of output quantity x, an increasing function of x. This result does not apply in the presence of external economies. In later editions of the *Principles*, Marshall introduced the device of the 'particular expenses curve' (1920, pp. 810–12) to display rent in such a case, but this *ex post* construction does not give an independent basis for determining rent.

It is clear that the long-period supply curve of an industry depends on the general economic background against which the industry is assumed to operate. As is the case with demand, Marshall does not consider this background in detail. He assumes prices to be expressed in money of constant purchasing power and recognizes on occasion that there may be close interrelations between two industries (for example, they may compete for the same specialized land). He also recognizes that 'a theoretically perfect long period must give time enough to enable not only the factors of production of the commodity to be adjusted to the demand, but also for the factors of production of those factors of production to be adjusted and so on' (1920, p. 379n.), and that this leads ultimately to the assumption of a stationary state. But he is not willing to follow this route far and is content in general to take the supply conditions of the factors of production for granted when analyzing long-period price determination.

In the 'manufacturing' case, to which we now turn, the product is differentiated, marketing is difficult, and each firm must build up and retain goodwill and a customer connection for its own specialized product. There are substantial internal economies of scale in production and successful management calls for business ability of a high and rare character. In this environment, a family business may be built up by an exceptional founder, but this build-up must be slow because of the difficulty of establishing a market and perhaps also because of constraints on financing. And when the founder passes on, his successors are unlikely to have equal talents or even the lesser talents required to prevent the firm's business from languishing. By the third generation of succession, the firm is likely to expire. Even a joint stock company (a case added rather as an afterthought) is likely to ossify into bureaucratic stagnation, and presumably the same is true of family businesses that rely on paid managers. Thus, the typical firm in the manufacturing case passes through a finite life cycle, and the industry is comprised of a population of such firms at various phases of the life cycle, some in the early expanding phase, others in decline.

The long-period supply price at which such an industry can supply a specified level of output must now be regarded as an index of the prices of all the different firms' products. It must meet all the conditions required in the agricultural case. Thus, the price must allow for a continuing replacement flow of the various types of workers (including managers) and fixed assets, as well as the retention of the necessary 'land' services. But now there must also be a surplus sufficient to induce a replacement flow of new firms – a supply of 'business organization' that will just suffice to replace the expiring firms and keep the age distribution of firms constant.

Industry equilibrium does not require each firm to be in an unchanging equilibrium any more than the trees in the proverbial forest. A new firm will be established if the prospective earnings over the expected life cycle appear to justify the cost and trouble involved. The firm's initial earnings are likely to be negative as it slowly builds up its technical expertise and market connections, but these early losses can be regarded as investments to be recouped in the later stages of the firm's prospective life cycle.

It is here that Marshall's 'representative firm' enters the picture. It is best regarded as a parable that avoids the need to consider the entire distribution of firms. By definition, the long-period supply price of any level of industry output is the average cost of the representative firm at that level of output. Industry-level magnitudes may then be regarded as if they were generated by a fixed number of unchanging representative firms rather than by the actual heterogeneous body of ever-changing firms. In other words, the manufacturing case may be treated as if it were an agricultural case populated by representative firms only. Such arguments add nothing conceptually and are prone to confuse, although it might be noted that Marshall believed an acute well-informed observer could select an actual firm that was close to being representative in this sense.

The average cost and size of the representative firm will change as industry output changes. There are two main reasons for this. A larger industry output is likely to generate more external economies, lowering the costs of every firm. But more importantly, the larger industry demand is, the easier it will be for a new firm to build up a market, and so the larger the size to which firms will grow before they begin to decline. This will bring about greater access on average to unexhausted internal

economies of scale, again leading to lower costs on average. For both these reasons, long-period supply price is likely to decline as a larger industry output is considered, even though the opportunity cost of obtaining greater supplies of land services and rare natural talents may rise. Again, the particular expenses curve may be used to display the producer surpluses or rents accruing to such scarce factors at any given level of industry output, but the relationship of this family of curves to the long-period supply curve is tenuous and complex. Rent obviously cannot be represented by a 'welfare triangle' above the supply curve when the latter is falling.

The conception of competition in Marshall's manufacturing case is much closer to later ideas of imperfect or monopolistic competition than to modern notions of perfect competition. Products are differentiated and firms are not price takers, but face at any time downward-sloping demand curves in their special markets. Even if the difficulties of rapidly building up a firm's internal organization can be overcome, the resulting enlarged output cannot be sold at a price covering cost – even granted substantial scale economies in production – without going through the slow process of building up a clientele and shifting the firm's particular demand curve. The time this takes is assumed to be considerable relative to the duration of the firm's initial vitality. But in some cases the difficulties of rapid expansion may be overcome. They may not have been very severe, as when different firms' products are highly substitutable, or the firm's founder may have unusual genius. In such cases the industry will pass into a monopoly or be dominated by a few, strategically interacting firms, or 'conditional monopolies' as Marshall termed them.

Marshall's reconciliation of persisting competition with increasing returns and falling supply price is complex and problematic, but it does not depend in any essential way on scale economies being external to the firm. The concept of external economies is one of his significant contributions, although his treatment of it can hardly be called pellucid. But it was added more for verisimilitude than because it was theoretically essential to the structure of his theory.

The issues surrounding Marshall's representative firm, and the problem of reconciling the persistence of competition with the presence of unexhausted internal economies of scale, continue to receive attention among historians of economic thought but no definitive reading has yet been attained, or perhaps ever will be. The account given above is well supported by Marshall's text, but as is often the case with Marshall, elements of ambiguity and vagueness remain.

Bibliographic note: Marshall's treatment of long-period competitive supply is to be found in (1920, pp. 314–22, 337–80, 455–61, 805–12) and (1919, pp. 178–96). The earliest version, dating from the early 1870s is reproduced in Whitaker (1975, vol. 1, pp. 119–59) and see also

(1879a). Key early commentaries and criticisms of Marshall's theory of supply are Sraffa (1926), Robbins (1928), D.H. Robertson, Sraffa and Shove (1930), Viner (1931), Frisch (1950), Hague (1958) and Newman (1960).

Price determination and period analysis

The long-period supply curve for any good indicates for each market quantity the least price at which that quantity will continue to be supplied indefinitely. The long-period equilibrium price and quantity are determined by the intersection of this supply curve with the market demand curve, assumed to be negatively sloped, that indicates the highest uniform price at which any total quantity can be sold. In the agricultural case, equilibrium will be unique as the supply curve slopes positively. But in the manufacturing case, the supply curve, as well as the demand curve, may have negative slope, so that multiple equilibria can occur. Equilibrium is adjudged locally stable if demand price is above (below) supply price at a quantity just below (above) the equilibrium quantity. The intuitive justification for this is that the actual price of any available quantity is determined by the demand price, while quantity produced tends to increase (through both expansion of existing firms and entry of new firms) whenever an excess of market price over supply price promises high profits, while it tends to decrease in the opposite case.

This stability argument is sketchy and, in any case, there still remains the question of exactly how a new long-period equilibrium is attained following some change, such as a permanent shift in the demand curve. One possibility would be to consider explicitly the adjustment process through time, but Marshall preferred to approach the problem by another route – his period analysis, one of his most memorable and lasting contributions. (His passing claim (1920, p. 808) that the long-period supply curve may not be reversible, supply price depending upon past-peak output as well as current output, is something of an exception to this generalization. It appears to rest on some restriction of the degree of downward supply adjustment, and so not to involve a true long-period analysis, or else to invoke a kind of learning by doing that once attained is not readily lost.)

Period analysis is Marshall's most explicit and self-conscious application of the comparative-static, partial-equilibrium method with which his name will always be associated. As he observed,

> the most important among the many uses of this method is to classify forces with reference to the time which they require for their work; and to impound in *Caeteris Paribus* those forces which are of minor importance relatively to the particular time we have in view. (Guillebaud, 1961, vol. 2, p. 67)

Which forces or variables are to be hypothetically frozen or impounded, and which are to be determined by the requirements of equilibrium (an equilibrium contingent upon the contents of the *ceteris paribus* pound, of course), should be determined pragmatically in each case with the aim of focusing on the features deemed dominant in that case. As a general rule, those forces should be impounded which move very slowly, or else bounce around very rapidly, relative to the length of 'the particular time we have in view'. This is well illustrated by Marshall's example of a fish market, where the focus may be on the determinants of price over a few days, a few months, or several years, or even decades (1920, pp. 369–71). As an expositional matter, however, and also to embody distinctions of wide (but not universal) applicability, Marshall emphasized three broad cases. Temporary or market equilibrium analysis proceeded on the assumption of a fixed stock of output already available or in the pipeline. Short-period normal equilibrium analysis permitted output to be varied, but not the stock of productive 'appliances' available to produce that output. 'Appliances' must be taken here to cover skilled labour and business organization as well as fixed capital assets, so that the existing set of firms is to be taken as given. Finally, long-period normal equilibrium, which has already been considered, allows the stock of appliances, as well as the level of output, to be freely varied. In this case equilibrium incorporates the conditions necessary for inducing an exact replacement flow of each kind of appliance, including a replacement flow of new firms in the manufacturing case.

Temporary equilibrium for a perishable commodity is simply a matter of selling off the existing stock. Marshall recognizes the possibility of 'false trading' – sales at a non-equilibrium price – but argues that (*a*) this will not affect the eventual price if the marginal utility of money is constant, and (*b*) price will quickly settle close to the uniform price that would just clear the market if used in all transactions. With a storable good there is the further speculative possibility of holding back supply for future sale, and this gives expected future cost of production an indirect role in influencing current market price. Cost of production already incurred is an irrelevant bygone, however.

In short-period normal equilibrium, output is adapted to demand within the constraints set by the fixed supply of available 'appliances'. High demand will raise equilibrium output, but only within the limits possible by working existing appliances more intensively or pulling in versatile unspecialized labour and land from elsewhere. Low demand will lead to low utilization of appliances, perhaps idleness of some, and migration of unspecialized inputs to elsewhere. In the agricultural case a firm will change output until marginal prime or variable cost equals market price. In the manufacturing case, a fear of spoiling the future market or invoking retaliation from competitors tends to make a firm's output more responsive to variation in market price, and hence to make market price less responsive to demand shifts.

Otherwise, the two cases are similar, both involving a fixed population of firms and a rising supply curve.

The return received by an appliance will often exceed the minimum necessary to induce its operation at the chosen intensity (its prime cost) and this excess is a 'quasi rent'. To the extent that land and rare natural talents are immobile in the short period, or less mobile in the short period than the long, their returns too will often have a quasi-rent element. Otherwise, they will receive only differential rents, though often at rates differing from their long-period values. It should be stressed that the concepts of quasi-rent and differential rent are relative to a specific use. The prime cost necessary to retain an input in this use may itself include rent or quasi-rent when viewed in the context of a more inclusive set of alternative uses. Thus, from the viewpoint of all possible uses in the economy, the return to any factor in fixed supply is entirely a rent or quasi-rent (the latter if fixity is only short-period).

Marshall paid little attention to the possibility that forces similar to those constraining the adjustment of supply when time is limited might also operate on the side of demand. Thus the same considerations underlie the market demand curve whether it is coupled with a temporary, short-period or long-period supply curve. In each case, market equilibrium price and quantity are determined by the intersection of the appropriate demand and supply curve. The stability of temporary equilibrium is directly asserted. The stability of short-period equilibrium depends on the same quantity-adjustment argument invoked for long-period equilibrium, but since the short-period supply curve is always positively sloped, uniqueness and stability are assured.

The theory of short-period normal equilibrium was designed as a tool for analysing unemployment and economic fluctuations in the never-completed second volume of *Principles*. But it also has use in explaining adjustment to a permanent disturbance. Suppose, for instance, that an industry is in long-period equilibrium when a permanent shift in demand occurs. The immediate or short-period effects can be analysed by freezing output and stocks of appliances at their initial levels. Insight into the actual adjustment through time can then be obtained by appropriately changing the output level assumed in the temporary equilibrium, so that movement of temporary equilibrium towards short-period equilibrium can be traced out as output , but not stocks of appliances, adjusts. Similarly, the levels assumed for the stocks of appliances in this short-period equilibrium can be allowed to change and the movement of short-period equilibrium towards long-period equilibrium traced out. Such arguments are now a staple of elementary pedagogy. They clearly require additional assumptions about the adjustment of output and the way in which investment or disinvestment in appliances proceeds, and are only a poor and ambiguous substitute for an explicit dynamic analysis. But such 'statical'

procedures, although imperfect, may, in Marshall's words, be 'the first step towards a provisional and partial solution in problems so complex that a complete dynamical solution is beyond our attainment' (Pigou, 1925, p. 312).

Marshall's period analysis, and more generally his partial-equilibrium approach to price determination, was designed in large part as a usable tool for the analysis of concrete issues. Its longevity amply testifies to its usefulness in this respect. But it was also meant to serve the more doctrinal purpose of clarifying the respective roles utility and cost of production play in determining value. The aim was to show that the greater the scope for supply adjustment permitted in the definition of equilibrium, the more dominant the supply side influence on price becomes. This doctrinal goal helps to account for the rather heavy weight given to long-period analysis in *Principles*. For, as Marshall recognized, its value as a tool of applied analysis is seriously qualified by the fact that 'violence is required for keeping broad forces in the pound of Caeteris Paribus during, say, a whole generation, on the ground that they have only an indirect bearing on the question in hand' (1920, p. 379n). That is, there is no good ground for assuming that background forces such as technology and tastes will remain constant for the length of time required for long-period equilibrium to be practically relevant. For concrete analysis of problems of such long duration it will often be necessary to transcend the period analysis, with its reliance on statical equilibrium, and undertake directly an analysis of secular change, of which Book 6, Ch. 12 of *Principles* on the 'General Influence of Economic Progress' (1920, pp. 668–88) offers the main example, but not a very impressive one.

In emphasizing the role that cost of production plays in the determination of long-period value, Marshall was not content to rest on money costs of production but sought to go behind these costs to the real costs – the efforts and abstinences – for which in a non-coercive economy the money costs are recompense. In doing so he purported to follow Ricardian tradition, but is more plausibly viewed as attempting to place the newer subjective value theories in broader (but still subjective) focus. Just as the price paid by a consumer serves as a measure of marginal utility, with a consumer surplus gained on infra-marginal units, so the unit price received by a worker or saver measures the real cost or disutility at the margin, with a producer surplus on the inframarginal units of effort or abstinence. But, as Marshall recognized, the parallel holds imperfectly in the long period when workers must be regarded as produced means of production as well as final consumers and cost bearers. In particular, parental sacrifice for raising and training offspring obtains little or no direct pecuniary reward.

Bibliographic note: Marshall's treatment of period analysis is concentrated in (1920, pp. 363–80) but see Whitaker (1975, vol. I, pp. 119–59) for the earliest version. For commentary and exposition see especially Viner (1931), Opie (1931), Frisch (1950), Whitaker (1982). On temporary equilibrium see (1920, pp. 331–6, 791–3, 844–5) and Walker (1969). On short-period normal value see Gee (1983).

Normal value and normal profit

Implicit in the preceding discussion are Marshall's conceptions of normal value and normal profit. Normal value is defined as the value that would result 'if the economic conditions under view had time to work out undisturbed their full effect' (1920, p. vii). It is contrasted with market value, which is 'the actual value at any time' (1920, p. 349). Normal value is hypothetical, resting on a *ceteris paribus* condition, its role being to indicate underlying tendencies. The normal value of a commodity may approximate its average value over periods sufficiently long for the 'fitful and irregular causes' (1920, pp. 349–50) that dominate market value to cancel out, but this should not be presupposed automatically outside a hypothetical stationary state.

The distinction between normal and market value is closely related to the distinction between natural and market value found in the work of Smith and the classical economists. In 1879 Marshall had identified normal value with 'the results which competition would bring about in the long run' (1879b, p. vii), but in *Principles* he switched to the view that 'Normal does not mean Competitive' (1920, p. 347) and admitted any kind of regular influence so long as it was sufficiently persistent. The economic forces hypothetically permitted to achieve full mutual accommodation could now be chosen appropriately for each case. In particular, the distinction between short-period and long-period normal (or 'sub-normal' and 'true-normal' in earlier editions) was emphasized.

Profit was viewed by Marshall as the residual income accruing to a firm's owner, a return on the investment of the owner's own capital and recompense for the pains of exercising 'business power' in planning, supervision and control. Normal profit is essentially an opportunity cost, the minimum return necessary to secure the owner's inputs to their current use, or rather to accomplish this for an owner of normal ability. Marshall presumes that there is a large and elastic supply of versatile actual or potential owner managers of normal ability. In long-period equilibrium each of these must just receive the same normal rates of return on investment and exercise of business power whatever the line of business. However, those who are exceptional may do better, essentially by exerting greater business power.

These common rates of normal return are simultaneously determined, along with the normal returns to other kinds of effort and abstinence, by Marshall's macroeconomic theory of the long-period determination of factor incomes (see below). Although it is the case that profits are a residual, rather than a contractually agreed amount like other incomes, this difference is immaterial in long-period equilibrium. In particular, a long-period equilibrium analogy between ordinary wages and the normal earnings of business power is stressed. Normal profit is a necessary element in the costs that underlie the long-period normal supply curve, but actual profit is a quasi-rent or producer surplus for shorter periods.

Normal profits are a return to 'business power in command of capital' and compensate for three distinct elements: 'the supply of capital, the supply of the business power to manage it, and the supply of the organization by which the two are brought together and made effective for production' (1920, p. 596). The combined compensation of the latter two components comprises 'gross earnings of management', the return to the second component being 'net earnings of management'. In long-period equilibrium, the normal return to the first element is imputed at the market interest rate on default-free loans, and that to the second component at the rate paid to hired managers performing comparable tasks. The residual third element, the return to 'organization', is most straightforwardly interpreted as an extra return on owned capital equivalent to the premium for default risk, or 'personal risk', that would have to be paid on borrowed capital. In the manufacturing case, the annual level of normal profit for each firm in an industry must be interpreted as the annualized equivalent of the expected stream of returns that is just sufficient to induce an individual of normal ability to found a firm in the industry rather than divert energies and capital elsewhere. Normal ability here is defined relative to other potential founders of firms, a group already exceptional relative to the population as a whole. By construction, such normal profits must be earned by the representative firm.

Bibliographic note: The most pertinent commentary is Frisch (1950). For Marshall's views on normal value see (1879b, pp. v–vii, 65–71, 146–9; 1920, pp. vii, 33–6, 337–50, 363–80). For his views on normal profit see (1879b, pp. 135–45; 1920, pp. 73–4, 291–313, 596–628). For the role of 'personal risk' see Guillebaud (1961, vol. 2, p. 672).

Welfare economics

To serve as a tool of welfare economics, monetary measures of consumer surplus, producer surplus and rent must be aggregated over individuals. But how are the resulting sums to be interpreted? Marshall's very limited and proximate attempts at formal welfare arguments are carried out within a utilitarian framework, for which the goal is maximizing aggregate utility. He implies that interpersonal utility comparisons are possible in principle and that utility functions will be similar for all members of any group that is homogeneous in terms of mental, physical and social attributes. Within such a group, the marginal utility of money will be the same for two individuals having the same income, and lower for the richer of two individuals with differing incomes, on the assumption in each case that both individuals face the same trading opportunities. A postulated government action may impose gains and losses on various individuals that can be measured and aggregated in money-equivalent terms. But how can these measures be translated into statements about aggregate gains and losses of utility? Marshall emphasizes two special cases. First, if the gains and losses are both proportionately distributed over income classes in exactly the same way, then net aggregate gain (positive or negative) in money will serve as an ordinal index for the net aggregate gain in utility. A corollary of this is that if two alternative actions affecting the same group have the same relative distributions of gains and losses over income classes then the alternative yielding the greater net aggregate gain in money must have the greater net aggregate gain in utility. Second, if some change makes for a zero net aggregate change in money terms, but the gains accrue to individuals of lower income than those bearing the costs, then the aggregate net utility gain must be positive – a warrant for certain redistributive policies. In other cases he sees that careful assessments of the marginal utility of money to the various injured and benefited groups would be needed, assessments that could be used to transform monetary gains and losses into utility measures. He toys (1920, pp. 135, 842–3) with using the Bernoulli hypothesis on the relation between wealth and utility as a basis for such calculations, but gives little indication as to how assessments might be made in practice.

Marshall's best known and most successful foray into formal welfare analysis was his proof that total welfare might be increased by using the proceeds of a tax on an 'agricultural' industry to subsidize a 'manufacturing' industry. All comparisons involved long-period equilibria and relied on the validity of aggregated money-equivalent measures of gains and losses. He demonstrated that the gain in consumer surplus in the expanded decreasing-cost manufacturing industry might exceed the combined loss in consumer and producer surplus in the contracted increasing-cost agricultural industry. No formal account was taken of a possible gain in producer surplus in the manufacturing industry as this merely makes the argument hold *a fortiori*. The crucial point in this argument, as Marshall recognized, is that producers are not harmed by 'a fall in price which results from improvements in industrial organization' (1920, p. 472). It is immaterial whether the improved organization of the enlarged manufacturing industry is due to external economies or to internal economies resulting from an increase in the size of the representative firm. Contrary to much subsequent opinion, Marshall's tax-subsidy argument is not necessarily dependent upon external economies.

Another significant, but overlooked, welfare analysis provided by Marshall was that of a monopolistic public enterprise in a situation where taxation involves an excess burden (1920, pp. 487–93, 857–8). In the absence of this excess burden Marshall proposes that the enterprise seek to maximize 'total benefit', the sum of net profit and consumer surplus. This implies marginal cost pricing, since the area below the demand curve and above the marginal cost curve is maximized when the two curves intersect. But, given that taxation involves an excess burden, it may be desirable to augment tax receipts from monopoly revenue if the sacrifice of consumer surplus is small. Marshall proposes the alternative goal of maximizing 'compromise benefit', the sum of consumer surplus and monopoly revenue when the latter is in effect multiplied by the marginal cost of raising a unit of government revenue from other sources. Maximization of compromise benefit leads to the setting of what has come to be termed a 'Ramsey price'.

The two examples of welfare analysis just described proceed within a partial equilibrium framework, treating each industry as negligible compared to the entire economy and regarding the marginal utility of money as approximately constant to each individual. Marshall's rather fragmentary remarks on optimal tax systems, income redistribution and the 'doctrine of maximum satisfaction' cannot be restricted in this way, and so raise serious unresolved analytical difficulties. On the other hand, his tax-subsidy argument was a valid counter-example to arguments that competition must lead to a social optimum, or that optimal indirect tax systems must involve uniform tax rates. It must also be borne in mind that utilitarian welfare economics was for Marshall only a first step towards a more evolutionary analysis of possible modes of improving the physical quality and the values and activities of mankind.

Bibliographic note: Marshall's treatment of welfare economics is to be found in (1920, pp. 18–19, 124–37, 462–76, 487–93). Ellis and Fellner (1943) is a good statement of the standard interpretation of the Marshall–Pigou tax-subsidy argument, emphasizing external effects. See also Bharadwaj (1972). On Marshall's treatment of compromise benefit see Whitaker (1986, pp.186–8). Myint (1948) gives a useful general perspective on Marshall's welfare theory. Albon (1989) offers an intriguing insight into Marshall's attempt to apply welfare analysis to issues surrounding the British Post Office monopoly.

Interrelated markets and distribution theory

Marshall was anxious to emphasize the interdependence of markets and introduced his treatment of joint and composite demand and supply largely for this purpose. A group of goods is jointly supplied if all are outputs of a single productive activity and jointly demanded if all are inputs. On the other hand, a particular good is compositely supplied or demanded if it is provided or acquired by several distinct productive activities. Marshall's formal treatment of joint demand and supply proceeded on the general assumption that the products involved were consumed or produced in fixed proportions, as did his related analysis of the 'derived demand' for any one of several jointly demanded inputs – 'derived' since the demand for such inputs is derived from the demand for their joint product. The derived demand curve for a specific input can be constructed conceptually by supposing that its supply is perfectly elastic at an arbitrary price and that the markets for the output and all the inputs (including the specific input) adjust to equate quantity demanded to quantity supplied in each market. This gives a price quantity combination on the derived demand curve for the specific input. Other such combinations can be obtained by varying the arbitrarily chosen price and repeating the exercise, and so on. Marshall laid down four rules for inelasticity of derived demand. These were that the input should have no good substitutes, that the product it helps make should be inelastically demanded, that the input should account for only a small part of production costs, and that cooperating inputs should be inelastically supplied. Fixity of input ratios guaranteed the first condition, but the more general case was asserted rather than proven. The advantage of working with the derived demand curve for an input is that it permits a more transparent analysis of the effects of changes in the supply conditions of the singled-out input.

The prime example of joint demand is the demand for productive inputs, and Marshall's analysis of market interdependence was carried through more fully in this specific connection, the role of substitution among inputs receiving full acknowledgement. The principle of substitution ensured that input usage tended to be adjusted by firms so as to minimize the total production cost of any level of output. Thus, the value of the marginal product of an input (or the 'net product' as Marshall termed it) tended under competition to equal the unit price of the input. There has been some confusion about the relation between 'net product' and marginal product because the former allows usage of other inputs to adjust consequentially when the chosen input is increased while the latter does not. But, provided that the initial situation is cost-minimizing, the adjustment of other inputs (if small) has no effect on the change in output – an application of the envelope theorem. Marshall recognizes this explicitly (1920, p. 409n) and there is no good reason for refusing to classify him as a marginal productivity theorist.

Interdependence among input markets was further highlighted in the analysis of the competition of several industries for an input that is in temporarily or permanently fixed overall supply. A peculiarity of this last analysis was the insistence on excluding from the marginal cost of any industry the cost of bidding such fixed resources away from other uses. This is a perfectly legitimate application of the general envelope theorem: provided resource use is optimally adjusted, the marginal

cost of increasing output will be the same whatever input or sub-group of inputs is increased. But Marshall's insistence on asymmetry where there is really symmetry can be accounted for only by his desire to legitimize, and extend to quasi-rent, the classical doctrine that rent is price determined rather than a price-determining element of cost.

Marshall's vision of market interdependence culminates in his treatment of income distribution, where he seeks to bring out the extents to which the interests of different factors of production are harmonious or conflicting. Distribution is determined by the interaction of the demands and supplies for the various inputs, the demands being essentially joint demands. Marginal productivity is a theory of input demand, not a complete theory of distribution, because the supplies of the various inputs cannot be viewed as fixed, at least in the long period. Indeed, in the long period the dominant influences on the prices of factors other than land are exerted by their supply conditions. The costs that then have to be met must ensure that various kinds of labour and capital continue to be replaced in their existing uses and quantities.

From an overall view 'The net aggregate of all the commodities produced is itself the true source from which flow the demand prices for all these commodities, and therefore for the agents of production used in making them' (1920, p. 536). This aggregate, 'the national dividend', is distributed among the factors of production. It is at once the

> aggregate net product of, and the sole source of payment for, all the agents of production within the country: it is divided up into earnings of labour; interest of capital; and lastly the producer's surplus, or rent, of land and of other differential advantages for production. It constitutes the whole of them, and the whole of it is distributed among them; and the larger it is, the larger, other things being equal, will be the share of each of them. (1920, p. 536)

The share going to any class of inputs will depend upon the need people have for its services: 'not the *total* need, but the *marginal* need' (p. 536, italics original). But a complicating influence for distribution theory, although one 'more full of hope for the future of the human race than any that is known to us' lies in the fact that 'highly paid labour is generally efficient and therefore not dear labour' (p. 510). Influenced by F.A. Walker, Marshall was a strong proponent of the 'economy of high wages' argument that high wages increase labour efficiency, not perhaps immediately, but cumulatively over time and perhaps over generations: effects that transcend simple theorizing in terms of static equilibrium.

All the different productive factors cooperating in production have a common interest in increasing the size of the pie to be shared, the national dividend or income, but each factor has a selfish interest in restrictive practices that increase its own share, even if they reduce the size of the pie slightly. A prime question of social policy for Marshall is how these divergent incentives can be reconciled: how combined action by various groups, such as unions, can be prevented from assuming forms that, while perhaps individually beneficial to any one group in isolation, are certainly mutually harmful if undertaken by all.

Marshall here enters into macroeconomic forms of argument, and it is indeed true that he did toy with the formal specification of macroeconomic models of growth and distribution (see Whitaker, 1975, vol. 2, pp. 305–16). But, with this exception, it should be emphasized that his treatment of market interdependence fell far short of a full theory of general equilibrium on Walrasian lines. Even when formalizing market interdependence in the mathematical appendix to *Principles* (1920, pp. 846–56), he simply treated the demand or supply of each commodity as a function of nothing but the price of the commodity itself. The links between the generation of income in factor markets and the expenditure of that income in product markets were left quite vague. Again, it must be recalled that the development of comprehensive fully articulated equilibrium theories was not Marshall's aim.

Bibliographic note: The key sections for Marshall's treatment of interrelated markets and distribution theory are (1920, pp. 381–54, 504–45, 660–67, 846–56). For general commentaries on Marshall's distribution theory see Stigler (1941), H.M. Robertson (1970), Whitaker (1974; 1988). On Marshall's treatment of labour supply see Walker (1974; 1975), Matthews (1990). On the economy of high wages see Petridis (1996).

Monopoly and combination

Marshall's analysis of price and output determination by a profit-maximizing monopolist, and of the effects of taxing such a monopolist, followed the lead of Cournot. The concept of marginal revenue was implicit in the mathematical statement, but Marshall's chosen vehicle was geometrical. Curves of average revenue and cost, and of their difference, average net revenue, y, (all functions of the quantity sold, x) were superimposed on a grid of iso-profit hyperbolae of form $xy = constant$. Profit was maximized when the average net revenue curve touched the highest such iso-profit curve. Weighting consumer surplus into the maximand, as well as net revenue, gave rise to the welfare analysis of 'compromise benefit' already mentioned.

Monopoly analysis was applied to trades unions, with the use of the concept of the derived demand for an input. A union controlling a labour input for which derived demand is inelastic can certainly raise wages – not only the wage rate but the total wages received – although at the price of unemployment of some members. Whether such a monopolistic restriction

can be sustained for long is more doubtful, as there will be pressures both to enter the union and to evade its grasp by the relocation or reorganization of production.

A more problematic question was whether 'labour's disadvantage in bargaining' meant that combined action by workers could raise wages, even without any restriction of labour supply. Marshall believed that it did, but emphasized that the result might be less capital accumulation by non-workers, an outcome that could harm workers eventually.

The extremes of monopoly and competition were both covered by the theory of normal value, even though the competition might be more akin to later concepts of imperfect or monopolistic competition than to any ideal form of perfect competition. But 'normal action falls into the background, when Trusts are striving for the mastery of a large market' (1920, p. xiv). The incidents, tactics and alliances of oligopolistic conflict defied reduction to a simple general theory. They were to have been considered in the uncompleted second volume of *Principles* and were to some extent covered by *Industry and Trade*. The latter's treatment of entry-limiting behaviour by a 'conditional monopolist', who dominates the market but does not control entry, is of considerable interest in the light of much recent work on this class of problems.

Bibliographic note: Marshall's treatment of monopoly theory is to be found in (1879b, pp. 180–86; 1920, pp. 477–95, 856–8). For his views on trusts and conditional monopolies see (1890b; 1919, pp. 395–635, especially 395–422). For his views on trades unions see (1879b, pp. 187–213; 1892, pp. 362–402; 1920, pp. 689–722) and Petridis (1973). On 'labour's disadvantage in bargaining' see Hicks (1930). Liebhafsky (1955) summarizes the relevant arguments of *Industry and Trade*.

Monetary theory

Marshall was in full command of previous British discussions of monetary issues, but not himself a major contributor to the development of monetary theory. His evidence before royal commissions in 1887 and 1899 showed an impressive mastery of monetary analysis, both domestic and international, and was minutely examined by successive generations of Cambridge students, serving for many years virtually as a textbook. But it was not until 1923, with the appearance of *Money Credit and Commerce*, that Marshall put forward his monetary views in a systematic way. By then these had not the novelty, nor he the vigour, to advance contemporary discussion.

Marshall's most important contribution to monetary theory was to place the overall demand for money in the context of individual choices as to the fraction of one's wealth to keep on hand as ready cash. This approach, set out clearly in a manuscript of the early 1870s (Whitaker, 1975, Vol. I, pp. 164–77), was developed by Marshall's Cambridge successors, especially A.C. Pigou and F. Lavington, into what is termed the 'Cambridge k' approach. It laid the background for the treatment of the demand for money in J.M. Keynes (1936). On international monetary theory, Marshall espoused a form of purchasing power parity.

Marshall's name is particularly associated with his proposals for 'symmetalism', the use of a fixed-weight combination of gold and silver as the monetary base, and for indexed contracts based on a 'tabular standard of value', or price index, to be maintained by the government. The former was offered as an improvement on fixed-ratio bimetallism, of which he was never more than a lukewarm adherent.

Marshall had interesting, if fragmentary, insights into business fluctuations and general unemployment, which he viewed as temporary disequilibrium consequences of credit market dislocations. These spilled over into general coordination failures, with unemployment in one market spreading to others by reducing demand in cumulative fashion – the germ at least of the multiplier concept. On the other hand, Say's Law was maintained as an equilibrium truth of great importance. He saw the remedies for cyclical unemployment in the 'continuous adjustment of means to ends, in such a way that credit can be based on the solid foundation of fairly accurate forecasts', and in curbs on reckless inflations of credit that are 'the chief cause of all economic malaise' (1920, p. 710).

Bibliographic note: Marshall's monetary evidence is reproduced in J.M. Keynes (1926, pp. 3–195, 265–326). Other sources for his monetary views are Whitaker (1975, vol. 1, pp. 164–77), and Marshall (1887; 1923, pp. 12–97, 140–54, 225–33, 264–320). The standard treatment of Marshall's monetary views is Eshag (1963). For Marshall's views on business fluctuations see his (1879b, pp. 150–57; 1885a; 1892, pp. 400–3; 1920, pp. 710–11; 1923, pp. 234–63). Also see Wolfe (1956), Laidler (1990).

International trade

Marshall's major contribution to international trade theory was his well-known geometrical analysis of the equilibrium and stability of two-country trade by means of intersecting offer curves. Each country's offer curve indicated the number of 'bales' of home goods it was prepared to exchange for a specified number of bales of foreign goods, demand being elastic or inelastic as an increase in the latter caused the former to increase or decrease. Possibilities of multiple and unstable offer-curve intersections were noted. The offer curves themselves were taken as data, although complex readjustments of production and consumption underlay them. The need for a separate theory of international trade was justified, in classical vein, by the supposed international immobility of factors of production that remain mobile domestically.

The main purpose of this theoretical apparatus was to examine the effects of tariffs. A country might gain by selfishly exploiting its monopoly power through restricting trade, and would certainly gain if trading equilibrium occurred on an inelastic portion of the foreign offer curve. But Marshall came to doubt increasingly the transferability of this result to a multi-country case, although admitting that it might apply to an export tax on an exceptional commodity (like British steam coal) lacking close substitutes and incapable of being produced elsewhere.

A related attempt to construct a theoretical measure of the 'net benefit' a country gains from foreign trade, analogous to the measures of consumer and producer surplus, was not entirely satisfactory as the partial equilibrium context had clearly been transcended.

On matters of concrete trade policy for Britain, Marshall was a firm but cautious adherent of free trade, even unilateral free trade, but became increasingly concerned with the prospects for Britain's position in the world economy. The discussion in *Industry and Trade* of the links between foreign competition and domestic industrial organization and structure reflected this concern.

Bibliographic note: For Marshall's treatment of the theory of international trade by offer curves see Whitaker (1975, vol. 1, pp. 260–79; vol. 2, pp. 111–81), Marshall (1923, pp. 155–224, 330–60). For the net benefit measure see Whitaker (1975, vol. 1, pp. 379–81) and Marshall (1923, pp. 338–40). Commentaries on Marshall's theory are to be found in Viner (1937, pp. 527–92), Chipman (1965), Johnson and Bhagwati (1960) and Creedy (1990). For Marshall's views on trade policy and trends see Marshall (1919, pp. 1–177, 681–784; 1923, pp. 98–139, 201–24) and J.M. Keynes (1926, pp. 367–420).

A brief survey of Marshall's writings with suggestions for further reading

The first editions of Marshall's five books were (1879b), (1890a), (1892), (1919), (1923). *Economics of Industry* (1879b) had a new edition in 1881 and was reprinted with minor changes several times up to 1892. It is an important source for Marshall's views on distribution theory, trades unions and business fluctuations. His magnum opus, *Principles* (1890a), had new editions in 1891, 1895, 1898, 1907, 1910, 1916 and 1920. The title was changed to its final form (as in (1920)) in the fifth edition. *Principles* is the basic source for Marshall's views on the theories of value and distribution as well as his broader views on economics and social welfare. Since the rewritings between editions were substantial, the ninth variorum edition, edited by C.W. Guillebaud, Marshall's nephew (Guillebaud, 1961), is essential for serious study. The first of its two volumes is a facsimile of the eighth edition of 1920. The second volume contains deleted passages from earlier editions, editorial notes, and various supporting documents. Users of the differently paginated Macmillan paperback edition of the eighth edition should note that all page references to the eighth edition given above must be located by using the table of correspondences appended to the paperback version.

Elements of the Economics of Industry (1892) had new editions in 1896 and 1899 and frequent reprintings. The last preface is dated 1907. It is essentially an abridgement of *Principles*, designed to replace *Economics of Industry*, a book that Marshall had come to despise, quite unjustifiably. *Elements* contains Marshall's fullest treatment of trades unions. *Industry and Trade* (1919) had new editions in 1919, 1920 and 1923 but only the first of these involved significant changes. Its three books deal with 'Some origins of present problems of industry and trade', 'Dominant tendencies of business organization', and 'Monopolistic tendencies: their relations to public well-being'. It adopts a largely historical and comparative approach and focuses on contemporary issues. Nevertheless, it contains many passages and insights of permanent interest and warrants closer attention by economists than it has received until recently. *Money Credit and Commerce* (1923) had only one edition and conveys Marshall's views on money, international trade and business fluctuations. Although blemished, it should not be dismissed.

An almost comprehensive annotated list of Marshall's occasional writings is found in Pigou (1925, pp. 500–8), which also reprints many of the texts of these writings. Guillebaud (1961) reproduces further occasional pieces. The 'Pure Theory' chapters (1879a), privately printed by Sidgwick, were first published in reprint form in 1930. A corrected and amplified version is included in Whitaker (1975). The two volumes of the latter also reproduce Marshall's unpublished early manuscripts, mainly from the 1870s, including several manuscript chapters from the abandoned volume on foreign trade. Marshall's important contributions to official enquiries are collected in J.M. Keynes (1926), a book that is supplemented by Groenewegen (1996).

The literature on Marshall's life and thought is too extensive to allow for more than a highlighting of some significant contributions. The splendid memorial essay by J.M. Keynes (1924) is not to be missed, although outdated on some points, nor is the charming memoir by Marshall's wife (M.P. Marshall 1944). Pigou (1925) includes fascinating vignettes by several of Marshall's colleagues and friends and Guillebaud (1971) gives a nephew's reminiscences. A major scholarly biography (Groenewegen 1995) covers Marshall's life and thought exhaustively, while a comprehensive three-volume edition of Marshall's correspondence (Whitaker 1996) provides much new information. Additional primary material on Marshall is provided in Raffaelli, Biagini and McWilliams-Tullberg (1995), where notes on Marshall's 1873 lectures to women students are reproduced, and

Raffaelli (1994), where Marshall's essays on philosophical and psychological manuscripts from the late 1860s are reproduced and analyzed. See also Harrison (1963). Newspaper reports on public lectures Marshall gave during his years in Bristol are reproduced in Coase and Stigler (1969), Whitaker (1972) and Butler (1995).

Valuable overall assessments of Marshall are provided by Cannan (1924), Schumpeter (1941), Viner (1941), Shove (1942) and O'Brien (1981). Maloney (1985) studies Marshall's involvement in the professionalization of British economics. An extensive body of detailed analysis and criticism of Marshall's thought, mainly conducted in academic journals, continues to expand, with growing tributaries from Italy and Japan in particular. Wood (1982; 1996) assembles in eight volumes a somewhat miscellaneous collection of 239 pieces on Marshall, but standard bibliographic aids such as EconLit are recommended for a comprehensive search. The 1990 centenary of the publication of *Principles* produced two books of essays on Marshall (Whitaker 1990, McWilliams-Tullberg 1990) and several symposia on Marshall in economics journals. Samples of recent research can be found in Arena and Quéré (2003). On Marshall's social and behavioural views see Parsons (1931; 1932), Whitaker (1977) and Chasse (1984). For Marshall's views on socialism and trades unions see, respectively, McWilliams-Tullberg (1975) and Petridis (1973).

JOHN K. WHITAKER

See also **ceteris paribus; consumer surplus; demand price; external economies; Marshall, Mary Paley.**

Selected works

1872. Review of Jevons (1871). *Academy*, April. Reprinted in Pigou (1925).

1874. The future of the working classes. *The Eagle*. Reprinted in Pigou (1925).

1876. On Mr. Mill's theory of value. *Fortnightly Review*, April. Reprinted in Pigou (1925).

1879a. *The Pure Theory of Foreign Trade. The Pure Theory of Domestic Values*. Privately printed. Reprinted in 1930, London: London School of Economics, Scarce Works in Political Economy No. 1; and in amplified form in Whitaker (1975).

1879b. (With M.P. Marshall.) *The Economics of Industry*, 2nd edn. London: Macmillan, 1881.

1884. Where to house the London poor. *Contemporary Review*, March. Reprinted in Pigou (1925).

1885a. How far do remediable causes influence prejudicially (a) the continuity of employment (b) the rate of wages? with four appendices. In *Report of Proceedings and Papers of the Industrial Remuneration Conference*, ed. C. Dilke. London: Cassel. The important appendix on 'Theories and facts about wages' is also reproduced in Guillebaud (1961).

1885b. *The Present Position of Political Economy: An Inaugural Lecture delivered at the Senate House*

Cambridge in February 1885. London: Macmillan. Reprinted in Pigou (1925).

1885c. On the graphic method of statistics. *Jubilee Volume*, a supplement to *Journal of the [London] Statistical Society*. Reprinted in Pigou (1925).

1887. Remedies for fluctuations of general prices. *Contemporary Review*, March. Reprinted in Pigou (1925).

1889. Cooperation. Presidential address to the 21st annual Cooperative Congress, Ipswich. Reprinted in Pigou (1925).

1890a. *Principles of Economics, Volume One.* London: Macmillan.

1890b. Some aspects of competition. Presidential address to Section F of the British Association for the Advancement of Science. Reprinted in Pigou (1925).

1892. *Elements of Economics of Industry*, 3rd edn. London: Macmillan, 1899.

1893. On rent. *Economic Journal* 3, 74–90. Reprinted in Guillebaud (1961).

1897. The old generation of economists and the new. *Quarterly Journal of Economics* 11, 115–35. Reprinted in Pigou (1925).

1898. Distribution and exchange. *Economic Journal* 8, 37–59. Portions are reprinted in Pigou (1925) and Guillebaud (1961).

1902. *A Plea for the Creation of a Curriculum in Economics and Associated Branches of Political Science.* London: Macmillan. Reprinted in Guillebaud (1961).

1907. The social possibilities of economic chivalry. *Economic Journal* 17, 7–29. Reprinted in Pigou (1925).

1917. National taxation after the war. In *After-War Problems*, ed. W. Dawson. London: George Allen and Unwin. Partly reproduced in Pigou (1925).

1919. *Industry and Trade*, 4th edn. London: Macmillan, 1923.

1920. *Principles of Economics: An Introductory Volume.* London: Macmillan. The eighth edition of Marshall (1890a).

1923. *Money, Credit and Commerce.* London: Macmillan.

Bibliography

Albon, R. 1989. Alfred Marshall and the consumers' loss from the British Post Office monopoly. *History of Political Economy* 21, 679–88.

Aldrich, J. 1996. The course of Marshall's theorizing about demand. *History of Political Economy* 28, 171–218.

American Economic Association. 1953. *Readings in Price Theory.* Homewood, IL: Irwin.

Arena, R. and Quéré, M., eds. 2003. *The Economics of Alfred Marshall: Revisiting Marshall's Legacy.* Basingstoke and New York: Palgrave Macmillan.

Bharadwaj, K. 1972. Marshall on Pigou's Wealth and Welfare. *Economica* 39, 32–46.

Biswas, T. 1977. The Marshallian consumer. *Economica* 44, 47–56.

Butler, R.W. 1995. 'The economic condition of America': Marshall's missing speech at University College, Bristol. *History of Political Economy* 27, 405–16.

Cannan, E. 1924. Alfred Marshall, 1842–1924. *Economica* 4, 257–61.

Chasse, J. 1984. Marshall, the human agent and economic growth: wants and activities revisited. *History of Political Economy* 16, 381–404.

Chipman, J. 1965. A survey of international trade: Part 2, the neoclassical theory. *Econometrica* 33, 685–760.

Chipman, J. 1990. Marshall's consumer's surplus in modern perspective. In Whitaker (1990).

Coase, R. 1975. Marshall on method. *Journal of Law and Economics* 18, 25–31.

Coase, R. and Stigler, G. 1969. Alfred Marshall's lectures on progress and poverty. *Journal of Law and Economics* 12, 181–226.

Cournot, A. 1838. *Mathematical Principles of the Theory of Wealth.* Trans. N. Bacon, New York: Macmillan, 1897.

Creedy, J. 1990. Marshall and international trade. In Whitaker (1990).

Cunningham, W. 1892. The perversion of economic history. *Economic Journal* 2, 491–506.

Ellis, H. and Fellner, W. 1943. External economies and diseconomies. *American Economic Review* 33, 493–511.

Eshag, E. 1963. *From Marshall to Keynes: An Essay on the Monetary Theory of the Cambridge School.* Oxford: Blackwell.

Friedman, M. 1949. The Marshallian demand curve. *Journal of Political Economy* 57, 463–95. Reprinted in M. Friedman, *Essays in Positive Economics*, Chicago: University of Chicago Press, 1953.

Frisch, R. 1950. Alfred Marshall's theory of value. *Quarterly Journal of Economics* 64, 495–524.

Gee, J. 1983. Marshall's views on 'short period' value formation. *History of Political Economy* 15, 181–205.

Groenewegen, P. 1995. *A Soaring Eagle: Alfred Marshall 1842– 1924.* Aldershot and Brookfield, VT: Edward Elgar.

Groenewegen, P., ed. 1996. *Official Papers of Alfred Marshall: A Supplement.* Cambridge: Cambridge University Press.

Guillebaud, C., ed. 1961. *Alfred Marshall: Principles of Economics: Ninth (Variorum) Edition*, 2 vols. London: Macmillan.

Guillebaud, C. 1971. Some personal reminiscences of Alfred Marshall. *History of Political Economy* 3, 1–8.

Hague, D. 1958. Alfred Marshall and the competitive firm. *Economic Journal* 68, 673–90.

Harrison, R. 1963. Two early articles by Alfred Marshall. *Economic Journal* 73, 2–30.

Hicks, J. 1930. Edgeworth, Marshall and the indeterminateness of wages. *Economic Journal* 40, 215–31.

Jevons, W. 1871. *The Theory of Political Economy.* London: Macmillan.

Johnson, H. and Bhagwati, J. 1960. Notes on some controversies in the theory of international trade. *Economic Journal* 70, 74–93.

Keynes, J. 1924. Alfred Marshall, 1842–1924. *Economic Journal* 34, 311–72. Reprinted with slight changes in Pigou (1925).

Keynes, J.M., ed. 1926. *Official Papers of Alfred Marshall*. London: Macmillan.

Keynes, J.M. 1936. *The General Theory of Employment, Interest and Money*. London: Macmillan.

Keynes, J.N. 1891. *The Scope and Method of Political Economy*. London: Macmillan.

Laidler, D. 1990. Alfred Marshall and the development of monetary economics. In Whitaker (1990).

Liebhafsky, H. 1955. A curious case of neglect: Marshall's *Industry and Trade*. *Canadian Journal of Economics* 21, 339–53.

McWilliams-Tullberg, R. 1975. Marshall's 'tendency to socialism'. *History of Political Economy* 7, 75–111.

McWilliams-Tullberg, R., ed. 1990. *Alfred Marshall in Retrospect*. Aldershot and Brookfield VT: Edward Elgar.

Maloney, J. 1985. *Marshall, Orthodoxy and the Professionalisation of Economics*. Cambridge: Cambridge University Press.

Marshall, M. 1944. *What I Remember*. Cambridge: Cambridge University Press.

Matthews, R. 1990. Marshall and the labour market. In Whitaker (1990).

Mill, J.S. 1848. *Principles of Political Economy*. London: Parker. Many subsequent editions.

Myint, H. 1948. *Theories of Welfare Economics*. London: London School of Economics.

Newman, P. 1960. The erosion of Marshall's theory of value. *Quarterly Journal of Economics* 74, 587–600.

O'Brien, D.P. 1981. Alfred Marshall, 1842–1924. In *Pioneers of Modern Economics in Britain*, ed. D. O'Brien and J. Presley. London: Macmillan.

O'Brien, D. 1990. Marshall's work in relation to Classical economics. In Whitaker (1990).

Opie, R. 1931. Marshall's time analysis. *Economic Journal* 41, 199–215.

Parsons, T. 1931. Wants and activities in Marshall. *Quarterly Journal of Economics* 46, 101–40.

Parsons, T. 1932. Economics and sociology: Marshall in relation to the thought of his time. *Quarterly Journal of Economics* 46, 316–47.

Petridis, A. 1973. Alfred Marshall's attitudes to and economic analysis of trade unions: a case of anomalies in a competitive system. *History of Political Economy* 5, 165–98.

Petridis, A. 1996. Brassey's law and the economy of high wages in nineteenth century economics. *History of Political Economy* 28, 583–606.

Pigou, A., ed. 1925. *Memorials of Alfred Marshall*. London: Macmillan.

Raffaelli, T. 1994. Alfred Marshall's early philosophical writings. *Research in the History of Economic Thought and Methodology: Archival Supplement* 4, 51–158.

Raffaelli, T. 2003. *Marshall's Evolutionary Economics*. London and New York: Routledge.

Raffaelli, T., Biagini, E. and McWilliams-Tullberg, R., eds. 1995. *Alfred Marshall's Lectures to Women: Some Economic Questions Directly Connected to the Welfare of the Laborer*. Aldershot and Brookfield, VT: Edward Elgar.

Robbins, L. 1928. The representative firm. *Economic Journal* 38, 387–404.

Robertson, D., Sraffa, P. and Shove, G. 1930. Increasing returns and the representative firm. *Economic Journal* 40, 76–116.

Robertson, H. 1970. Alfred Marshall's aims and methods illustrated from his treatment of distribution. *History of Political Economy* 2, 1–65.

Schumpeter, J. 1941. Alfred Marshall's *Principles*: a semi-centennial appraisal. *American Economic Review* 31, 236–48.

Shove, G. 1942. The place of Marshall's *Principles* in the development of economic theory. *Economic Journal* 52, 294–329.

Sraffa, P. 1926. The laws of returns under competitive conditions. *Economic Journal* 36, 535–50.

Stigler, G. 1941. *Production and Distribution Theories: The Formative Period*. New York: Macmillan.

Stigler, G. 1950. The development of utility theory. *Journal of Political Economy* 58, 307–27; 373–96.

Viner, J. 1931. Cost curves and supply curves. *Zeitschrift für Nationalökonomie* 3, 23–46. Reprinted in American Economic Association (1953).

Viner, J. 1937. *Studies in the Theory of International Trade*. New York: Harper.

Viner, J. 1941. Marshall's economics in relation to the man and his times. *American Economic Review* 31, 223–35.

Walker, D. 1969. Marshall's theory of competitive exchange. *Canadian Journal of Economics* 2, 590–98.

Walker, D. 1974. Marshall on the long-run supply of labor. *Zeitschrift für die Gesamte Staatswissenschaft* 130, 691–705.

Walker, D. 1975. Marshall on the short-run supply of labor. *Southern Economic Journal* 41, 429–41.

Whitaker, J. 1972. Alfred Marshall: the years 1877 to 1885. *History of Political Economy* 4, 1–61.

Whitaker, J. 1974. The Marshallian system in 1881: distribution and growth. *Economic Journal* 84, 1–17.

Whitaker, J., ed. 1975. *The Early Economic Writings of Alfred Marshall, 1867–1890*, 2 vols. London: Macmillan.

Whitaker, J. 1977. Some neglected aspects of Alfred Marshall's economic and social thought. *History of Political Economy* 9, 161–97.

Whitaker, J. 1982. The emergence of Marshall's period analysis. *Eastern Economic Journal* 8, 15–29.

Whitaker, J. 1986. The continuing relevance of Alfred Marshall. In *Ideas in Economics*, ed. R. Black. London: Macmillan.

Whitaker, J. 1988. The distribution theory of Marshall's Principles. In *Theories of Income Distribution*, ed. A. Asimakopulos. Boston, Dordrecht and Lancaster: Kluwer Academic.

Whitaker, J., ed. 1990. *Centenary Essays on Alfred Marshall*. Cambridge: Cambridge University Press.

Whitaker, J., ed. 1996. *The Correspondence of Alfred Marshall, Economist*, 3 vols. Cambridge: Cambridge University Press.

Wolfe, J. 1956. Marshall and the trade cycle. *Oxford Economic Papers* 8, 90–101.

Wood, J. 1982. *Alfred Marshall: Critical Assessments*, 4 vols. London: Croom Helm.

Wood, J. 1996. *Alfred Marshall: Critical Assessments, Second Series*, 4 vols. London: Routledge.

Marshall, Mary Paley (1850–1944)

British economist, born in Ufford (Nottinghamshire) on 24 October 1850; died in Cambridge 7 March 1944. Great-granddaughter of the great theologian William Paley, she was brought up in a strictly evangelical faith in Ufford, her father's vicarage. Thomas Paley, had taken a good degree in mathematics (33rd wrangler) in 1833 at Cambridge, and had been, for a period, a fellow of St John's College. Mary had one elder sister and two younger brothers.

In 1871, with a scholarship, she went up to Cambridge to complete her education with studies at university level. Under the whimsical chaperon Anne J. Clough (sister of the poet), and the teaching of a handful of young voluntary dons committed to the cause of higher education of women (among them Henry Sidgwick and Alfred Marshall), she took the Moral Sciences Tripos. She graduated, albeit informally, in 1874 (the first woman to achieve such a distinction in Cambridge) but the board of examiners (W.S. Jevons was among them) was so bitterly divided that in the certificate they recorded, very unusually, that she had received two votes for a first class and two for a second.

Shortly after her degree Mary Paley began to teach and to tutor female students in the newly opened Newnham Hall. In 1876, on request, she began to write a small economic textbook for Extension Lectures, that eventually became *The Economics of Industry* (1879). In the same year she became engaged to Alfred Marshall. They married in Ufford in July 1877. From that date onwards, till the death of Alfred Marshall in 1924, her life was essentially devoted, first in Bristol, where they settled after marriage, then in Oxford (1883–4) and finally in Cambridge, to helping him in his scientific work and to saving him from all the normal nuisances of life.

For several decades Mary Paley Marshall taught and tutored female students of economics in Newnham college. A member of many associations (Charity Organization Society, Ethical Society, and so on) she participated in the founding group of the British Economic Association. After 1924 she became the first librarian of the newly founded Marshall Library, which she visited regularly until her 90th year. In 1928 the University of

Bristol awarded her an honorary degree. She was a gifted amateur water colour painter and her posthumous Memoir, *What I Remember* (1947), shows glimpses of literary talent. Mary was not buried beside Alfred, but her ashes were scattered in the garden of her house.

Mary Paley Marshall's claims to be considered as an economist by herself are, strictly speaking, unassessable. Personally she signed only a few short notes in the early issues of the *Economic Journal*, which show a clear mind, a good style and a balanced judgement, but no more. Her only title to fame resides in the green-covered *Economics of Industry*, co-authored with Alfred Marshall. This small textbook, reprinted many times and translated into several foreign languages, was rated very highly by contemporaries. J.M. Keynes went so far as to say: 'It was, in fact, an extremely good book; nothing more serviceable for its purpose was produced for many years, if ever.' From the viewpoint of the development of economic analysis the book is relevant as a sort of half-way house between the *Principles* of J.S. Mill and the *Principles* of A. Marshall. Despite some hints to the contrary by J.M. Keynes, the respective positions (teacher and pupil) and ages (Alfred was older by eight years) suggest that Mary Paley's contribution was only secondary and subordinate.

Worthy of mention is the help she afforded Alfred Marshall in preparing and amending all his works. In a letter to John Neville Keynes, there is a hint of a substantial collaboration: 'My wife and I', writes Alfred Marshall, alluding to an article by J.L. Laughlin (*Quarterly Journal of Economics*, 1887), 'find it very hard to see Laughlin's points & perhaps we underrate the strength of his attack.'

Had it not been for the suffocating influence of Alfred, Mary Paley, with her clear mind, earnestness and strong will, would have become herself, we can confidently guess, an economist of repute and not, as is the case, a minor figure in the shadow of Alfred Marshall.

G. BECATTINI

Selected works

1879. (With Alfred Marshall.) *The Economics of Industry*. London: Macmillan.2nd edn, 1881.

1896. Conference of women workers. *Economic Journal* 6(21), 107–9.

1947. *What I Remember*. Cambridge: Cambridge University Press.

Bibliography

Clough, B.A. and Strachey, J.P. 1944. Mrs Alfred Marshall (Mary Paley) 1850–1944. *Cambridge Review* 65(1597), 300.

Constable, W.G. 1960. Art and economics in Cambridge. *The Eagle*, April.

Keynes, J.M. 1944. Mary Paley Marshall 1850–1944. *Economic Journal* 54, June–September, 268–84. Reprinted in J.M. Keynes, *Essays in Biography*, ed. G. Keynes. London: Rupert Hart-Davis. 2nd edn, 1951.

Keynes, J.N. Letter 1(58), kept in the Marshall Library, Cambridge.

Marshall–Lerner condition

In the comparative-statical calculations of the simplest two-commodity barter theory of international trade, the outcomes invariably depend on the magnitude of the sum of the two import-demand elasticities, one relating to the country under study (the 'home' country) and the other to the rest of the world (collectively, the 'foreign' country); in particular, the response of a variable to a disturbance will be in one direction if the sum of elasticities is less than minus 1 and in the opposite direction if the sum is greater than minus 1. On the other hand, for some dynamic or 'disequilibrium' models of international trade it is a necessary and sufficient condition of local stability that the same sum of elasticities be less than minus 1. Let us define Δ as one plus the sum of the two elasticities of import demand. Then the so-called Marshall–Lerner condition requires that Δ be negative. Evidently the condition provides a link between the comparative-statics of international trade and some forms of trade dynamics. That such a link exists is, of course, the essence of Samuelson's correspondence principle.

Proceeding to a more detailed account of the Marshall–Lerner condition, let us suppose that the home country imports the first commodity, the foreign country the second; and let us denote by p the world price of the second commodity in terms of the first and by α and α^* parameters of the home and foreign economies, respectively. Then, in the absence of trade impediments and autonomous international transfers, we may write the general-equilibrium or *mutatis mutandis* home import-demand function as $\phi(1/p, \alpha)$, the foreign import-demand function as $\phi^*(p, \alpha^*)$ and the condition of world equilibrium as

$$\phi(1/p, \alpha) - p\phi^*(p, \alpha^*) = 0. \tag{1}$$

Suppose now that an initial equilibrium is disturbed by small changes in α and α^*. Differentiating (1) totally we obtain

$$\left(p^{-2}\phi_{1/p} + \phi^* + p\phi_p^*\right)\mathrm{d}p = \phi_\alpha \mathrm{d}\alpha - p\phi_{\alpha^*}^*\mathrm{d}\alpha^*$$

or, equivalently,

$$\Delta \mathrm{d}p \equiv \left(1 + \xi + \xi^*\right)\mathrm{d}p = \left(\phi_\alpha \mathrm{d}\alpha - p\phi_{\alpha^*}^*\mathrm{d}\alpha^*\right)/\phi^* \tag{2}$$

where the subscripts indicate partial derivatives and where $\xi \equiv \phi_{1/p}/(p\phi)$ and $\xi^* \equiv p\phi_p^*/\phi^*$ are the price

elasticities of home and foreign import demand, respectively.

On the other hand, we may consider the dynamic tâtonnement defined by the differential equation

$$\dot{p} \equiv \mathrm{d}p/\mathrm{d}t = f\left[\phi^*(p, \alpha^*) - \phi(1/p, \alpha)/p\right] \tag{3}$$

where f is a differentiable sign-preserving function of the world excess demand for the second commodity and t denotes time. Evidently (3) is a dynamic extension of (1). For the local stability of p at an equilibrium value it is necessary and sufficient that $\mathrm{d}f/\mathrm{d}p$ be negative in a sufficiently small neighbourhood of the equilibrium value. Now a little calculation shows that $\mathrm{d}f/\mathrm{d}p = f'\Delta\phi^*/p$, where the prime indicates differentiation; moreover, since f is differentiable and sign-preserving, f' is necessarily positive sufficiently near the equilibrium value of p. For local stability, therefore, it is necessary and sufficient that Δ be negative.

By way of illustration we may consider the traditional 'transfer problem'. Identifying $\alpha = \alpha^*$ with the amount transferred from the foreign to the home country, in terms of the numeraire, eq. (1) reduces to

$$\phi(1/p, \alpha) - p\phi^*(p, \alpha) - \alpha = 0$$

and, if α is initially zero, eq. (2) reduces to

$$\Delta \mathrm{d}p = \left(\phi_\alpha - 1 + p\phi_\alpha^*\right)\mathrm{d}\alpha/\phi^*.$$

Evidently ϕ_α and $1 - p\phi_\alpha^*$ are home and foreign marginal propensities to consume the first commodity. Thus, in stable systems, the terms of trade move in favour of the recipient of a small payment if and only if that country's marginal propensity to consume the imported commodity is less than the foreign country's marginal propensity to consume the same commodity.

The home and foreign economies have been specified in terms of the functions ϕ and ϕ^* only. Whether in any particular context the Marshall–Lerner condition is satisfied depends on the structure imposed on ϕ and ϕ^* by the context. Evidently the appropriate structure will be quite different for economies with and without chronic unemployment and, more generally, for economies with and without internal market-clearing. It will also be quite different for rural and industrial economies, for growing and declining economies and for rich and poor economies.

While the inequality $\Delta < 0$ is now widely known as the Marshall–Lerner condition, the label is inappropriate in a context of dynamic analysis. For Alfred Marshall developed a quite different stability condition (see Marshall, 1879, II; 1923, Appendix J; Samuelson, 1947, pp. 266–7); Amano, 1968; Kemp, 1964, pp. 89–90); and Abba Lerner was not at all concerned with disequilibrium dynamics (see Lerner, 1944).

MURRAY C. KEMP

Bibliography

Amano, A. 1968. Stability conditions in the pure theory of international trade: a rehabilitation of the Marshallian approach. *Quarterly Journal of Economics* 82(2), 326–39.

Kemp, M.C. 1964. *The Pure Theory of International Trade and Investment*. Englewood Cliffs, NJ: Prentice-Hall.

Lerner, A.P. 1944. *The Economics of Control*. New York: Macmillan.

Marshall, A. 1879. *The Pure Theory of Foreign Trade*. Published privately. Reprinted with *The Pure Theory of Domestic Values*. London: London School of Economics and Political Science, 1949.

Marshall, A. 1923. *Money, Credit and Commerce*. London: Macmillan.

Samuelson, P.A. 1947. *Foundations of Economic Analysis*. Cambridge, MA: Harvard University Press.

Martineau, Harriet (1802–1876)

Harriet Martineau, the best-selling popularizer of classical political economy, was born in Norwich, England, on 12 June 1802, the sixth of eight children of Thomas Martineau, a Unitarian textile manufacturer, and Elizabeth Rankin Martineau. She was educated at home, except that from 1813 to 1815 she studied French, Latin, and English composition at a school run by the Reverend Isaac Perry. Her early writings were religious, beginning with an article on 'Female Writers on Practical Divinity' for the *Monthly Repository*. After her father's death in 1826, she became engaged, but her fiancé died before they could be married. She remained single for the rest of her life. Investment losses in 1829 forced her to support herself by writing: William Johnson Fox's *Monthly Review* hired her as a book reviewer for 15 pounds a year, and when the Central Unitarian Association offered prizes for essays to convert Catholics, Jews, and Muslims, Martineau won all three prizes, for 15 guineas each. These prizes enabled her to visit her brother in Dublin in 1831. While there, she planned the series *Illustrations of Political Economy*, stories that would expound (especially to the working classes) the principles of classical political economy, to which she had been introduced by Jane Marcet's *Conversations on Political Economy* (1816) and James Mill's *Elements of Political Economy* (1821). The first of the 34 tales of political economy, of the Poor Laws, and of taxation was published in February 1832 by Charles Fox (brother of William Fox), and distributed by the Society for the Diffusion of Useful Knowledge. By 10 February, the first printing of 1,500 copies had all been sold, and a second printing of 5,000 copies ordered.

The success of *Illustrations of Political Economy* (1832–4; 2004a) made Martineau a celebrity: Henry Brougham, the Lord Chancellor, provided her with private papers on the impending reform of the Poor Law, while Robert Owen attempted, without success, to convert her to socialism. Although poor health interrupted her work several times, Harriet Martineau refused offers of government pensions from Lord Grey in 1835, Lord Melbourne in 1841, and W.E. Gladstone in 1873, lest her independence be compromised. Instead, her friends raised funds for an annuity for her in 1843, and, when her health permitted she worked with great diligence, writing more than 1,600 articles for the *Daily News* from 1852 to 1866. Although her income was modest, she was a philanthropist, founding a building society among other charitable projects.

Harriet Martineau disclaimed originality for *Illustrations of Political Economy*, insisting that its purpose was didactic, making established principles better known. Her presentation of the principles was original, and her work stood out for its recognition of women as rational economic agents (1985). In her *Illustrations*, Martineau upheld laissez-faire and property rights. In later life, Martineau endorsed married women's property rights, condemned slavery as an illegitimate form of property, gave qualified support to workers' cooperatives, and accepted the need for state intervention in certain very limited circumstances. Her lectures at working men's institutions stressed education rather than state intervention as the remedy for most social ills. Her subsequent writings on America and slavery (1837; 2002) demonstrated that she was an adept economic analyst, not just a popularizer. For example, Martineau recognized the limited demand for the services of prostitutes in the South as evidence of the sexual exploitation of slaves, and identified the inability of slaveholders to make credible long-term commitments to their slaves as a source of inefficiency in slave agriculture (Levy, 2003). Martineau's *Society in America* (1837) emphasized the incompatibility of slavery and of the legal, political, and economic position of American women (lacking votes and, if married, property rights) with America's founding rhetoric of liberty. Her study of the United States was accompanied by her *How to Observe Morals and Manners* (1838), a methodological manual on comparative sociology and ethnography. In 1853, Martineau published a translation and abridgement of the pioneer sociologist Auguste Comte's *Philosophie positive*, an adaptation that pleased Comte so much that he had it translated back into French.

In 1855, anticipating death from heart disease, Martineau wrote her autobiography for posthumous publication (1877), but she lived until 27 June 1876.

ROBERT W. DIMAND AND EVELYN L. FORGET

See also **British classical economics; Marcet, Jane Haldimand; slavery.**

Selected Works

1832–4. *Illustrations of Political Economy, Taxation, Poor Law and Paupers*, 13 vols. London: C. Fox; repr. with new introduction by C. Franklin. Bristol: Thoemmes, 2001.

1837. *Society in America*. London: Saunders and Otley. Abridged edn, ed. S.M. Lipset, New Brunswick, NJ: Transaction, 1981.

1838. *How to Observe Morals and Manners*. London: C. Knight. Repr. 1989, ed. M.R. Hill. New Brunswick, NJ: Transaction.

1877. *Harriet Martineau's Autobiography*, 2 vols. London: Smith, Elder; repr. London: Virago, 1983.

1985. *Harriet Martineau on Women*, ed. G.G. Yates. New Brunswick, NJ: Rutgers University Press.

2002. *Writings on Slavery and the American Civil War by Harriet Martineau*, ed. D.A. Logan. DeKalb, IL: Northern Illinois University Press.

2004a. *Illustrations of Political Economy: Selected Tales*, ed. D.A. Logan. Peterborough, ON: Broadview Press.

2004b. *Harriet Martineau's Writings on the British Empire*, 5 vols, ed. D.A. Logan. London: Pickering & Chatto.

2005. *Harriet Martineau: Writings on British History and Military Reform*, 6 vols, ed. D.A. Logan. London: Pickering & Chatto.

2006. *The Collected Letters of Harriet Martineau*, 5 vols, ed. D.A. Logan. London: Pickering & Chatto.

Bibliography

Henderson, W. 1992. Harriet Martineau or when political economy was popular. *History of Education* 21, 383–403.

Levy, D. 2003. Taking Harriet Martineau's economics seriously. In *The Status of Women in Classical Economic Thought*, ed. R. Dimand and C. Nyland. Cheltenham, and Northampton, MA: Edward Elgar.

Logan, D.A. 2002. *The Hour and the Woman: Harriet Martineau's 'Somewhat Remarkable' Life*. DeKalb: Northern Illinois University Press.

Marcet, J. 1816. *Conversations on Political Economy*. 3rd edn, London: Longman, 1818.

Mill, J. 1821. *The Elements of Political Economy*. London: Baldwin, Cradock & Joy.

Orazem, C. 1999. *Political Economy and Fiction in the Early Writings of Harriet Martineau*. Frankfurt: Peter Lang.

Webb, R.K. 1960. *Harriet Martineau, a Radical Victorian*. London: Heinemann, and New York: Columbia University Press.

martingales

A martingale is a mathematical model of a fair game, or of some other process that is incrementally random noise. The term, which also denotes part of a horse's harness or a ship's rigging, refers in addition to a gambling system in which every losing bet is doubled; it was introduced into probability theory by J.L. Doob. Among stochastic processes, martingales have particular constancy properties with respect to conditioning. The time parameter may be either discrete or continuous, but since the latter is more important in economic applications, we concentrate on it.

Suppose that on a basic probability space there is defined a *history* $\mathscr{H} = (\mathscr{H}_t)_{t \geq 0}$ representing observable events as a function of time. For each t, $(\mathscr{H}_t)$ is the σ-algebra comprising events determined by observations over the interval $[0,t]$, so that $(\mathscr{H}_s) \subseteq (\mathscr{H}_t)$ when $s \leq t$. Then a stochastic process $M = (M_t)_{t \geq 0}$ is a *martingale* with respect to this history if

(a) For each t, M_t is $\mathscr{H}_t$ measurable (i.e., the state of the process at t is observable over $[0,t]$);
(b) $E[|M_t|] < \infty$ for each t;
(c) The 'martingale property' holds: whenever $s \leqslant t$,

$$E[M_t | \mathscr{H}_s] = M_s. \qquad (1)$$

When no history is specified, it is usually understood that $\mathscr{H}_t = \sigma(M_s; s \leq t)$. One specific consequence is that $E[M_t] = E[M_0]$ for each t, so that a martingale is constant in the mean.

Written as

$$E[M_t - M_s | \mathscr{H}_s] = 0, \quad s \leq t,$$

the martingale property implies that the optimal (in the sense of minimum mean squared error, or MMSE) predictor of a future increment of a martingale is zero. Thus, a martingale is indeed a mathematical idealization of a fair game. In some ways this property is clearest in differential form: assuming that the differential dM_t, which always extends *forward* in time from t, can be defined, then M is a martingale provided that

$$E[dM_t | \mathscr{H}_t] = 0 \qquad (2)$$

for each t. Thus, a martingale can be interpreted as a 'noise' process, in which the MMSE prediction of the differential dM_t is simply zero; in many applications this interpretation becomes quite literal. Martingales are also analogous to the residuals in a regression problem, where what remains unexplained by the model should reduce, ideally, to chance variation.

One can also define *supermartingales*, for which (1) becomes

$$E[M_t | \mathscr{H}_t] \leq M_s, \qquad (3)$$

and *submartingales*, in which the sense of the inequality in (3) is reversed. A supermartingale represents a less-than-fair game.

All martingales are in some sense convex combinations of (generalizations of) two key examples, namely the Wiener and Poisson processes. If (W_t) is a Wiener process (Brownian motion), then the processes W_t and $W_t^2 - t$ are both martingales; in fact, these properties characterize the Wiener process. In discrete time, martingales generalize sums of independent, mean zero random variables; the Wiener process, which has independent and stationary increments, is a continuous time counterpart of these partial sum processes.

If (N_t) is a point process (or counting process), with N_t the number of events occurring in $[0, t]$, then under quite general assumptions there exists a nonnegative, predictable (a technical term, which in practice means left-continuous) random process (λ_t), the stochastic intensity of N, such that the process $M_t = N_t - \int_0^t \lambda_s ds$ is a martingale. Since $\lambda_t dt = E[dN_t|\mathcal{H}_t]$, M represents the new information realized as a function of time and, because of this and applications in statistics and state estimation, is known as the innovation martingale. For a Poisson process, which like the Wiener process has independent and stationary increments, the stochastic intensity is deterministic and equal to the rate of the process.

Square integrable martingales are especially important. A martingale M is *square integrable* if $\sup_t E[M_t^2] < \infty$, and in this case there exists a predictable process $\langle M \rangle$, the *predictable variation* of M, such that $M_t^2 - \langle M \rangle_t$ is a martingale. That the predictable variation is incrementally a conditional variance is confirmed by the differential relationship

$$d\langle M \rangle_t = E[(dM_t - E[dM_t|\mathcal{H}_t])^2|\mathcal{H}_t]$$
$$= E[(dM_t)^2|\mathcal{H}_t].$$

Here the second equality holds because M is a martingale.

For the Wiener process $\langle W \rangle_t \equiv t$ in particular, the predictable variation is deterministic, a property characteristic of processes with independent increments. For a point process N with stochastic intensity λ, the predictable variation of the innovation martingale $dM_t = dN_t - \lambda_t dt$ is given by $d\langle M \rangle_t = \lambda_t dt$, which implies that a point process is locally and conditionally Poisson, in the sense that the incremental conditional mean and variance coincide.

Existence of the predictable variation is proved via the Doob-Meyer decomposition theorem, a cornerstone of the theory. The principal theoretical results pertaining to martingales fall into three classes: inequalities, convergence theorems and optimal sampling theorems.

So-called maximal inequalities, which provide upper bounds for probabilities of the form $P\{\sup_{s \leq t}|M_s| > c\}$, are not only of inherent interest, but also the key tools for proving convergence theorems. Moreover, these inequalities form the basis of a profound connection between martingales and classical mathematical analysis.

Under various assumptions, given a martingale M there exists a random variable M_∞ such that $M_t \to M_\infty$ almost surely as $t \to \infty$. Convergence obtains both almost surely and in L^1 if M is uniformly integrable, and in this case $M_t = E[M_\infty|\mathcal{H}_t]$ for each t. Not all martingles converge, however; those that fail to converge include, for example, the Wiener process and most innovation martingales.

Optimal sampling theorems require the further concept of a stopping time. A random time T (a random variable with values in $[0, \infty]$, interpreted as the time at which some event occurs – with $T=\infty$ corresponding to its not occurring) is a *stopping time* of the history $\mathcal{H}$ if $\{T \leq t\} \in \mathcal{H}_t$ for each t. Intuitively, whether a stopping time has occurred by t can be determined from observations over $[0, t]$, and does not require prescient knowledge of the future. The rule by which a gambler quits a game must be a stopping time. Associated with a stopping time T is a σ-algebra $\mathcal{H}_t$ representing events determined by observations over the random time interval $[0, T]$ in the same way that for deterministic t, $\mathcal{H}_t$ corresponds to the interval $[0, t]$.

Martingale property extends from deterministic times to stopping times, and imply in particular that an unfair game cannot be made fair by means of a stopping time. More precisely, if M is a martingale and S and T are stopping times with $S \leq T$, then under broad–albeit not universal – conditions,

$$E[M_T|\mathcal{H}_s] \leq M_s. \qquad (4)$$

With $S=0$ in (4), taking expectations yields $E[M_T] = E[M_0]$. The corresponding result for supermartingales,

$$E[M_T|\mathcal{H}_s] \leq M_s, \qquad (5)$$

demonstrates that an unfair game cannot be made fair via a stopping time, and dooms gambling systems without infinite resources to eventual failure.

Significant applications of martingales include mathematical statistics (likelihood ratio processes are martingales), queueing theory, filtering and prediction (for example, in signal processing) and economics.

A common feature of these applications is that they involve a random system 'driven' by a martingale in precisely the same manner that a dynamical system is driven by a forcing function. Given a (square integrable) martingale M and a predictable process C fulfilling integrability restrictions, the stochastic integral process

$$(C*M)_t = \int_0^t C_s dM_s$$

is itself a martingale, for which M acts as driving term. (Since M may change state discontinuously, whether endpoints are included in the interval of integration must be specified; in this case, the integral is over the closed interval $[0, t]$.) Construction of stochastic integrals is a difficult, subtle problem: none of the conventional definitions can be applied pathwise (typically the sample paths of M are not of bounded variation), and instead one must employ sophisticated probability theory. The predictable variations satisfy

$$d\langle C*M \rangle_t = C_t^2 d\langle M \rangle_t.$$

Economic applications include, e.g., models of securities prices.

In applications, the inclusion of a 'dt'-integral is often desirable or necessary, leading to *semimartingales*, which are random processes Z of the form

$$Z_t = \int_0^t A_s ds + \int_0^t C_s dM_s, \qquad (6)$$

where M is a martingale, C is a predictable process and A fulfills a technical property known as progressive measurability. (Integrability conditions must be satisfied as well.) The differential version of (6) is

$$dZ_t = A_t dt + C_t dM_t. \qquad (7)$$

If the processes A and C, rather than specified exogenously, are functionals of Z, then (7) becomes a stochastic differential equation

$$dZ_t = \mu(Z_t)dt + \sigma(Z_t)dM_t, \qquad (8)$$

or, more generally,

$$dZ_t = \mu(Z_s; s \le t)dt + \sigma(Z_s; s \le t)dM_t. \qquad (9)$$

These equations can be solved – however, not using pathwise methods – under a variety of assumptions, but essentially only when the driving term is a martingale. For example, if the martingale is the Wiener process, solutions to (8) and (9) are known as diffusions and Itō processes, respectively, and the resultant theory as the Itō calculus, after its principal inventor, K. Itō. Alternatively, if M is the innovation martingale associated with a point process N then, inter alia, solutions to (8) can be used to construct recursive methods for filtering to extract signals from noise.

ALAN F. KARR

Bibliography

Brémaud, P. 1981. *Point Processes and Queues: Martingale Dynamics.* Berlin: Springer-Verlag.

Hall, P. and Heyde, C.C. 1980. *Martingale Limit Theory and its Applications.* New York: Academic Press.

Kallianpur, G. 1980. *Stochastic Filtering Theory.* New York: Springer-Verlag.

Karr, A.F. 1986. *Point Processes and their Statistical Inference.* New York: Marcel Dekker.

Lipster, R.S. and Shiryayev, A.N. 1978. *Statistics of Random Processes,* I and II. Berlin: Springer-Verlag.

Metivier, M. and Pellaumail, J. 1980. *Stochastic Integration.* New York: Academic Press.

Shiryayev, A.N. 1981. Martingales: recent developments, results and applications. *International Statistical Review* 49, 199–233.

Marx, Karl Heinrich (1818–1883)

Karl Marx was born on 5 May 1818, the son of the lawyer Heinrich Marx and Henriette Pressburg. His father was descended from an old family of Jewish rabbis, but was himself a liberal admirer of the Enlightenment and not religious. He converted to Protestantism a few years before Karl was born to escape restrictions still imposed upon Jews in Prussia. His mother was of Dutch-Jewish origin.

Life and work

Karl Marx studied at the *Friedrich-Wilhelm Gymnasium* in Trier, and at the universities of Bonn and Berlin. His doctoral thesis, *Differenz der demokritischen und epikurischen Naturphilosophie*, was accepted at the University of Jena on 15 April 1841. In 1843 he married Jenny von Westphalen, daughter of Baron von Westphalen, a high Prussian government official.

Marx's university studies covered many fields, but centred around philosophy and religion. He frequented the circle of the more radical followers of the great philosopher Hegel, befriended one of their main representatives, Bruno Bauer, and was especially influenced by the publication in 1841 of Ludwig Feuerbach's *Das Wesen des Christentums* (The Nature of Christianity). He had intended to teach philosophy at the university, but that quickly proved to be unrealistic. He then turned towards journalism, both to propagandize his ideas and to gain a livelihood. He became editor of the *Rheinische Zeitung*, a liberal newspaper of Cologne, in May 1942. His interest turned more and more to political and social questions, which he treated in an increasingly radical way. The paper was banned by the Prussian authorities a year later.

Karl Marx then planned to publish a magazine called *Deutsch-Französische Jahrbücher* in Paris, in order to escape Prussian censorship and to be more closely linked and identified with the real struggles for political and social emancipation which, at that time, were centred around France. He emigrated to Paris with his wife and met there his lifelong friend Friedrich Engels.

Marx had become critical of Hegel's philosophical political system, a criticism which would lead to his first major work, Zur Kritik des *Hegelschen Rechtsphilosophie* (A Critique of Hegel's Philosophy of Right). Intensively studying history and political economy during his stay in Paris, he became strongly influenced by socialist and working-class circles in the French capital. With his 'Paris Manuscripts' (*Oekonomisch-philosophische Manuskripte*, 1844), he definitely became a communist, i.e. a proponent of collective ownership of the means of production.

He was expelled from France at the beginning of 1845 through pressure from the Prussian embassy and migrated to Brussels. His definite turn towards historical materialism (see below) would occur with his manuscript *Die Deutsche Ideologie* (1845–6) culminating in the eleven *Theses on Feuerbach*, written together with Engels but never published during his lifetime.

This led also to a polemical break with the most influential French socialist of that period, Proudhon, expressed in the only book Marx would write in French, *Misère de la Philosophie* (1846).

Simultaneously he became more and more involved in practical socialist politics, and started to work with the Communist League, which asked Engels and himself to draft their declaration of principle. This is the origin of the *Communist Manifesto* (1848, *Manifest der Kommunistischen Partei*).

As soon as the revolution of 1848 broke out, he was in turn expelled from Belgium and went first to France, then, from April 1848 on, to Cologne. His political activity during the German revolution of 1848 centred around the publication of the daily paper *Neue Rheinische Zeitung*, which enjoyed wide popular support. After the victory of the Prussian counter-revolution, the paper was banned in May 1849 and Marx was expelled from Prussia. He never succeeded in recovering his citizenship. Marx emigrated to London, where he would stay, with short interruptions, till the end of his life. For fifteen years, his time would be mainly taken up with economic studies, which would lead to the publication first of *Zur Kritik der Politischen Oekonomie* (1859) and later of *Das Kapital*, Vol. I (1867). He spent long hours at the British Museum, studying the writings of all the major economists, as well as the government Blue Books, Hansard and many other contemporary sources on social and economic conditions in Britain and the world. His reading also covered technology, ethnology and anthropology, besides political economy and economic history; many notebooks were filled with excerpts from the books he read.

But while the activity was mainly studious, he never completely abandoned practical politics. He first hoped that the Communist League would be kept alive, thanks to a revival of revolution. When this did not occur, he progressively dropped out of emigré politics, but not without writing a scathing indictment of French counter-revolution in *Der 18. Brumaire des Louis Bonaparte* (1852), which was in a certain sense the balance sheet of his political activity and an analysis of the 1848–52 cycle of revolution and counter-revolution. He would befriend British trade-union leaders and gradually attempt to draw them towards international working class interests and politics. These efforts culminated in the creation of the International Working Men's Association (1864) – the so-called First International – in which Marx and Engels would play a leading role, politically as well as organizationally.

It was not only his political interest and revolutionary passion that prevented Marx from becoming an economist pure and simple. It was also the pressure of material necessity. Contrary to his hope, he never succeeded in earning enough money from his scientific writings to sustain himself and his growing family. He had to turn to journalism to make a living. He had initial, be it modest, success in this field, when he became European correspondent of the *New York Daily Tribune* in the summer of 1851. But he never had a regular income from that collaboration, and it ended after ten years.

So the years of his London exile were mainly years of great material deprivation and moral suffering. Marx suffered greatly from the fact that he could not provide a minimum of normal living conditions for his wife and children, whom he loved deeply. Bad lodgings in cholera-stricken Soho, insufficient food and medical care, led to a chronic deterioration of his wife's and his own health and to the death of several of their children; that of his oldest son Edgar in 1855 struck him an especially heavy blow. Of his seven children, only three daughters survived, Jenny, Laura and Eleanor (Tussy). All three were very gifted and would play a significant role in the international labour movement, Eleanor in Britain, Jenny and Laura in France (where they married the socialist leaders Longuet and Lafargue).

During this long period of material misery, Marx survived thanks to the financial and moral support of his friend Friedrich Engels, whose devotion to him stands as an exceptional example of friendship in the history of science and politics. Things started to improve when Marx came into his mother's inheritance; when the first independent working-class parties (followers of Lassalle on the one hand, of Marx and Engels on the other) developed in Germany, creating a broader market for his writings; when the IWMA became influential in several European countries, and when Engels' financial conditions improved to the point where he would sustain the Marx family on a more regular basis.

The period 1865–71 was one in which Marx's concentration on economic studies and on the drafting of *Das Kapital* was interrupted more and more by current political commitments to the IWMA, culminating in his impassioned defence of the Paris Commune (*Der Bürgerkrieg in Frankreich* [*The Civil War in France*] 1871). But the satisfaction of being able to participate a second time in a real revolution – be it only vicariously – was troubled by the deep divisions inside the IMWA, which led to the split with the anarchists grouped around Michael Bakunin.

Marx did not succeed in finishing a final version of *Das Kapital* vols II and III, which were published posthumously, after extensive editing, by Engels. It remains controversial whether he intended to add two more volumes to these, according to an initial plan. More than 25 years after the death of Marx, Karl Kautsky edited what is often called vol. IV of *Das Kapital*, his extensive critique of other economists: *Theorien über den Mehrwert* (*Theories of Surplus Value*).

Marx's final years were increasingly marked by bad health, in spite of slightly improved living conditions. Bad health was probably the main reason why the final version of vols II and III of *Capital* could not be finished. Although he wrote a strong critique of the Programme which was adopted by the unification congress (1878) of German social democracy (*Kritik Des Gothaer Program*), he was heartened by the creation of that united working-class party in his native land, by the spread of socialist organizations throughout Europe, and by the growing influence of his ideas in the socialist movement. His wife fell ill in 1880 and died the next year. This came as a deadly blow to Karl Marx, who did not survive her for long. He himself died in London on 14 March 1883.

Historical materialism

Outside his specific economic theories, Marx's main contribution to the social sciences has been his theory of historical materialism. Its starting point is anthropological. Human beings cannot survive without social organization. Social organization is based upon social labour and social communication. Social labour always occurs within a given framework of specific, historically determined, social relations of production. These social relations of production determine in the last analysis all other social relations, including those of social communication. It is social existence which determines social consciousness and not the other way around.

Historical materialism posits that relations of production which become stabilized and reproduce themselves are structures which can no longer be changed gradually, piecemeal. They are modes of production. To use Hegel's dialectical language, which was largely adopted (and adapted) by Marx: they can only change qualitatively through a complete social upheaval, a social revolution or counter-revolution. Quantitative changes can occur within modes of production, but they do not modify the basic structure. In each mode of production, a given set of relations of production constitutes the basis (infrastructure) on which is erected a complex superstructure, encompassing the state and the law (except in classless society), ideology, religion, philosophy, the arts, morality etc.

Relations of production are the sum total of social relations which human beings establish among themselves in the production of their material lives. They are therefore not limited to what actually happens at the point of production. Humankind could not survive, i.e. produce, if there did not exist specific forms of circulation of goods, e.g. between producing units (circulation of tools and raw materials) and between producing units and consumers. A priori allocation of goods determines other relations of production than does allocation of goods through the market. Partial commodity production (what Marx calls 'simple commodity production' or 'petty commodity production' – 'einfache Warenproduktion') also implies other relations of production than does generalized commodity production.

Except in the case of classless societies, modes of production, centred around prevailing relations of production, are embodied in specific class relations which, in the last analysis, overdetermine relations between individuals.

Historical materialism does not deny the individual's free will, his attempts to make choices concerning his existence according to his individual passions, his interests as he understands them, his convictions, his moral options etc. What historical materialism does state is: (1) that these choices are strongly predetermined by the social framework (education, prevailing ideology and moral 'values', variants of behaviour limited by material conditions etc); (2) that the outcome of the collision of millions of different passions, interests and options is essentially a phenomenon of social logic and not of individual psychology. Here, class interests are predominant.

There is no example in history of a ruling class not trying to defend its class rule, or of an exploited class not trying to limit (and occasionally eliminate) the exploitation it suffers. So outside classless society, the class struggle is a permanent feature of human society. In fact, one of the key theses of historical materialism is that 'the history of humankind is the history of class struggles' (Marx, *Communist Manifesto*, 1848).

The immediate object of class struggle is economic and material. It is a struggle for the division of the social product between the direct producers (the productive, exploited class) and those who appropriate what Marx calls the social surplus product, the residuum of the social product once the producers and their offspring are fed (in the large sense of the word; i.e. the sum total of the consumer goods consumed by that class) and the initial stock of tools and raw materials is reproduced (including the restoration of initial fertility of the soil). The ruling class functions as ruling class essentially through the appropriation of the social surplus product. By getting possession of the social surplus product, it acquires the means to foster and maintain most of the superstructural activities mentioned above; and by doing so, it can largely determine their function – to maintain and reproduce the given social structure, the given mode of production – and their contents.

We say 'largely determine' and not 'completely determine'. First, there is an 'immanent dialectical', i.e. an autonomous movement, of each specific superstructural sphere of activity. Each generation of scientists, artists, philosophers, theologists, lawyers and politicians finds a given *corpus* of ideas, forms, rules, techniques, ways of thinking, to which it is initiated through education and current practice, etc. It is not forced to simply continue and reproduce these elements. It can transform them, modify them, change their interconnections, even negate them. Again: historical materialism does not deny that there is a specific history of science, a history of art, a history of philosophy, a history of political and moral ideas, a history of religion etc., which all follow their own logic. It tries to *explain* why a certain number of scientific, artistic, philosophical, ideological, juridical changes or even revolutions occur at a given time and in given countries, quite different from other ones which occurred some centuries earlier elsewhere. The nexus of these 'revolutions' with given historical periods is a nexus of class interests.

Second, each social formation (i.e. a given country in a given epoch) while being characterized by predominant relations of production (i.e. a given mode or production at a certain phase of its development) includes different relations of production which are largely remnants of the past, but also sometimes nuclei of future modes of production. Thus there exists not only the ruling class and the exploited class characteristic of that prevailing mode of production (capitalists and wage earners under capitalism). There also exist remnants of social classes which were predominant when other relations of production prevailed and which, while having lost their hegemony, still manage to survive in the interstices of the new society. This is for example the case with petty commodity producers (peasants, handicraftsmen, small merchants), semifeudal landowners, and even slave-owners, in many already predominantly capitalist social formations throughout the 19th and part of the 20th centuries. Each of these social classes has its own ideology, its own religious and moral values, which are intertwined with the ideology of the hegemonic ruling class, without becoming completely absorbed by that.

Third, even after a given ruling class (e.g. the feudal or semi-feudal nobility) has disappeared as a ruling class, its ideology can survive through sheer force of social inertia and routine (custom). The survival of traditional *ancien régime* catholic ideology in France during a large part of the 19th century, in spite of the sweeping social, political and ideological changes ushered in by the French revolution, is an illustration of that rule.

Finally, Marx's statement that the ruling ideology of each epoch is the ideology of the ruling class – another basic tenet of historical materialism – does not express more than it actually says. It implies that other ideologies can exist side by side with that ruling ideology without being hegemonic. To cite the most important of these occurrences: exploited and (or) oppressed social classes can develop their own ideology, which will start to challenge the prevailing hegemonic one. In fact, an ideological class struggle accompanies and sometimes even precedes the political class struggle properly speaking. Religious and philosophical struggles preceding the classical bourgeois revolutions; the first socialist critiques of bourgeois society preceding the constitution of the first working-class parties and revolutions, are examples of that type.

The class struggle has been up to now the great motor of history. Human beings make their own history. No mode of production can be replaced by another one without deliberate actions by large social forces, i.e., without social revolutions (or counter-revolutions). Whether these revolutions or counter-revolutions actually lead to the long-term implementation of deliberate projects of social reorganization is another matter altogether. Very often, their outcome is to a large extent different from the intention of the main actors.

Human beings act consciously, but they can act with false consciousness. They do not necessarily understand why they want to realize certain social and (or) political plans, why they want to maintain or to change economic or juridical institutions; and especially, they rarely understand in a scientific sense the laws of social change, the material and social preconditions for successfully conserving or changing such institutions. Indeed, Marx claims that only with the discovery of the main tenets of historical materialism have we made a significant step forward towards understanding these laws, without being able to predict 'all' future developments of society.

Social change, social revolutions and counter-revolutions are furthermore occurring within determined material constraints. The level of development of the productive forces – essentially tools and human skills, including their effects upon the fertility of the soil – limits the possibilities of institutional change. Slave labour has shown itself to be largely incompatible with the factory system based upon contemporary machines. Socialism would not be durably built upon the basis of the wooden plough and the potter's wheel. A social revolution generally widens the scope for the development of the productive forces and leads to social progress in most fields of human activity in a momentous way. Likewise, an epoch of deep social crisis is ushered in when there is a growing conflict between the prevailing mode of production (i.e. the existing social order) on the one hand, and the further development of the productive forces on the other. Such a social crisis will then manifest itself on all major fields and social activity: politics, ideology, morals and law, as well as in the realm of the economic life properly speaking.

Historical materialism thereby provides a measuring stick for human progress: the growth of the productive forces, measurable through the growth of the average productivity of labour, and the number, longevity and skill of the human species. This measuring stick in no way abstracts from the natural preconditions for human survival and human growth (in the broadest sense of the concept). Nor does it abstract from the conditional and partial character of such progress, in terms of social organization and individual alienation.

In the last analysis, the division of society into antagonistic social classes reflects, from the point of view of historical materialism, an inevitable limitation of human freedom. For Marx and Engels, the real measuring rod of human freedom, i.e. of human wealth, is not 'productive labour'; this only creates the material pre-condition for that freedom. The real measuring rod is leisure time, not in the sense of 'time for doing nothing' but in the sense of time freed from the iron necessity to produce and reproduce material livelihood, and therefore disposable for all-round and free development of the individual talents, wishes, capacities, potentialities, of each human being.

As long as society is too poor, as long as goods and services satisfying basic needs are too scarce, only part of society can be freed from the necessity to devote most of its life to 'work for a livelihood' (i.e. of forced labour, in the anthropological/sociological sense of the word, that is in relation to desires, aspirations and talents, not to a juridical status of bonded labour). That is essentially what represents the freedom of the ruling classes and their hangers-on, who are 'being paid to think', to create, to invent, to administer, because they have become free from the obligation to bake their own bread, weave their own clothes and build their own houses.

Once the productive forces are developed far enough to guarantee all human beings satisfaction of their basic needs by 'productive labour' limited to a minor fraction of lifetime (the half work-day or less), then the material need of the division of society in classes disappears. Then, there remains no objective basis for part of society to monopolize administration, access to information, knowledge, intellectual labour. For that reason, historical materialism explains both the reasons why class societies and class struggles arose in history, and why they will disappear in the future in a classless society of democratically self-administering associated producers.

Historical materialism therefore contains an attempt at explaining the origin, the functions, and the future withering away of the state as a specific institution, as well as an attempt to explain politics and political activity in general, as an expression of social conflicts centred around different social interest (mainly, but not only, those of different social classes; important fractions of classes, as well as non-class social groupings, also come into play).

For Marx and Engels, the state is not existent with human society as such, or with 'organized society' or even with 'civilized society' in the abstract; neither is it the result of any voluntarily concluded 'social contract' between individuals. That state is the sum total of apparatuses, i.e. special groups of people separate and apart from the rest (majority) of society, that appropriate to themselves functions of a repressive or integrative nature which were initially exercised by all citizens. This process of alienation occurs in conjunction with the emergence of social classes. The state is an instrument for fostering, conserving and reproducing a given class structure, and not a neutral arbiter between antagonistic class interests.

The emergence of a classless society is therefore closely intertwined, for adherents to historical materialism, with the process of withering away of the state, i.e. of gradual devolution to the whole of society (self-management, self-administration) of all specific functions today exercised by special apparatuses, i.e. of the dissolution of these apparatuses. Marx and Engels visualized the dictatorship of the proletariat, the last form of the state and of political class rule, as an instrument for assuring the transition from class society to classless society. It should itself be a state of a special kind, organizing its own gradual disappearance.

We said above that, from the point of view of historical materialism, the immediate object of class struggle is the division of the social product between different social classes. Even the political class struggle in the final analysis serves that main purpose; but it also covers a much broader field of social conflicts. As all state activities have some bearing upon the relative stability or instability of a given social formation, and the class rule to which it is submitted, the class struggle can extend to all fields of politics, from foreign policy to educational problems and religious conflicts. This has of course to be proven through painstaking analysis, and not proclaimed as an axiom or a revealed truth. When conducted successfully, such exercises in class analysis and class definition of political, social and even literary struggles become impressive works of historical explanation, as for example Marx's *Class Struggles in France 1848–50*, Engels' *The German Peasant War*, Franz Mehring's *Die Lessing-Legende*, Trotsky's *History of the Russian Revolution*, etc.

Marx's economic theory – general approach and influence

A general appraisal of Marx's method of economic analysis is called for prior to an outline of his main economic theories (theses and hypotheses).

Marx is distinct from most important economists of the 19th and 20th centuries in that he does not consider himself at all an 'economist' pure and simple.

The idea that 'economic science' as a special science completely separate from sociology, history, anthropology etc. cannot exist, underlies most of his economic analysis. Indeed, historical materialism is an attempt at unifying all social sciences, if not all sciences about humankind, into a single 'science of society'.

For sure, within the framework of this general 'science of society', economic phenomena could and should be submitted to analysis as specific phenomena. So economic theory, economical science, have a definite autonomy after all; but is only a partial and relative one.

Probably the best formula for characterizing Marx's economic theory would be to call it an endeavour to explain the social economy. This would be true in a double sense. For Marx, there are no eternal economic laws, valid in every epoch of human prehistory and history. Each mode of production has its own specific economic laws, which lose their relevance once the general social framework has fundamentally changed. For Marx likewise, there are no economic laws separate and apart from specific relations between human beings, in the primary (but not only, as already summarized) social relations of production. All attempts to reduce economic problems to purely material, objective ones, to relations between things, or between things and human beings, would be considered by Marx as manifestations of mystification, of false consciousness, expressing itself through the attempted reification of human relations. Behind relations between things, economic science should try to discover the specific relations between human beings which they hide. Real economic science has therefore also a demystifying function compared to vulgar 'economics', which takes a certain number of 'things' for granted without asking the question: Are they really only what they appear to be? From where do they originate? What explains these appearances? What lies behind them? Where do they lead? How could they (will they) disappear? *Problemblindheit*, the refusal to see that facts are generally more problematic than they appear at first sight, is certainly not a reproach one could address to Marx's economic thought.

Marx's economic analysis is therefore characterized by a strong ground current of *historical relativism*, with a strong recourse to the genetical and evolutionary method of thinking (that is why the parallel with Darwin has often been made, sometimes in an excessive way). The formula 'genetic structuralism' has also been used in relation to Marx's general approach to economic analysis. Be that as it may, one could state that Marx's economic theory is essentially geared to the discovery of specific 'laws of motion' for successive modes of production. While his theoretical effort has been mainly centred around the discovery of these laws of motion for capitalist society, his work contains indications of such laws – different ones, to be sure – for precapitalist and postcapitalist social formations too.

The main link between Marx's sociology and anthropology on the one hand, and his economic analysis on the other, lies in the key role of social labour as the basic anthropological feature underlying all forms of social organization. Social labour can be organized in quite different forms, thereby giving rise to quite different economic phenomena ('facts'). Basically different forms of social labour organization lead to basically different sets of economic institutions and dynamics, following basically different logics (obeying basically different 'laws of motion').

All human societies must assure the satisfaction of a certain number of basic needs, in order to survive and reproduce themselves. This leads to the necessity of establishing some sort of equilibrium between socially recognized needs, i.e. current consumption and current production. But this abstract banality does not tell us anything about the concrete way in which social labour is organized in order to achieve that goal.

Society can recognize all individual labour as *immediately social labour*. Indeed, it does so in innumerable primitive tribal and village communities, as it does in the contemporary *kibbutz*. Directly social labour can be organized in a despotic or in a democratic way, through custom and superstition as well as through an attempt at applying advanced science to economic organization; but it will always be immediately recognized social labour, in as much as it is based upon *a prior* assignment of the producers to their specific work (again: irrespective of the form this assignation takes, whether it is voluntary or compulsory, despotic or simply through custom etc.).

But when social decision-taking about work assignation (and resource allocation closely tied to it) is fragmented into different units operating independently from each other – as a result of private control (property) of the means of production, in the economic and not necessarily the juridical sense of the word – then social labour in turn is fragmented into private labours which are not automatically recognized as socially necessary ones (whose expenditure is not automatically compensated by society). Then the private producers have to exchange parts or all of their products in order to satisfy some or all of their basic needs. Then these products become commodities. The economy becomes a (partial or generalized) market economy. Only by measuring the results of the sale of his products can the producer (or owner) ascertain what part of his private labour expenditure has been recognized (compensated) as social labour, and what part has not.

Even if we operate with such simple analytical tools as 'directly social labour', 'private labour', 'socially recognized social labour', we have to make quite an effort at abstracting from immediately apparent phenomena in order to understand their relevance for economic analysis. This is true for all scientific analysis, in natural as well as in social sciences. Marx's economic analysis, as presented in his main books, has not been extremely popular reading; but then, there are not yet so many scientists in these circumstances. This has nothing to do with any innate obscurity of the author, but rather with the nature of scientific analysis as such.

The relatively limited number of readers of Marx's economic writings (the first English paperback edition of *Das Kapital* appeared only in 1974!) is clearly tied to Marx's scientific rigour, his effort at a systematic and all-sided analysis of the phenomena of the capitalist economy.

But while his economic analysis lacked popularity, his political and historical projections became more and more influential. With the rise of independent working-class mass parties, an increasing number of these proclaimed themselves as being guided or influenced by Marx, at least in the epoch of the Second and the Third Internationals, roughly the half century from 1890 till 1940. Beginning with the Russian revolution of 1917, a growing number of governments and of states claimed to base their policies and constitutions on concepts developed by Marx. (Whether this was legitimate or not is another question.) But the fact itself testifies to Marx's great influence on contemporary social and political developments, evolutionary and revolutionary alike.

Likewise, his diffused influence on social science, including academic economic theory, goes far beyond general acceptance or even substantial knowledge of his main writings. Some key ideas of historical materialism and of economic analysis which permeate his work – e.g. that economic interests to a large extent influence, if not determine, political struggles; that historic evolution is linked to important changes in material conditions; that economic crises ('the business cycle') are unavoidable under conditions of capitalist market economy – have become near-platitudes. It is sufficient to notice how major economists and historians strongly denied their validity throughout the 19th century and at least until the 1920s, to understand how deep has been Marx's influence on contemporary social science in general.

Marx's labour theory of value

As an economist, Marx is generally situated in the continuity of the great classical school of Adam Smith and Ricardo. He obviously owes a lot to Ricardo, and conducts a current dialogue with that master in most of his mature economic writings.

Marx inherited the labour theory of value from the classical school. Here the continuity is even more pronounced; but there is also a radical break. For Ricardo, labour is essentially a numeraire, which enables a common computation of labour and capital as basic elements of production costs. For Marx, labour is value. Value is nothing but that fragment of the total labour potential existing in a given society in a certain period (e.g. a year or a month) which is used for the output of a given commodity, at the average social productivity of labour existing then and there, divided by the total number of these commodities produced, and expressed in hours (or minutes), days, weeks, months of labour.

Value is therefore essentially a social, objective and historically relative category. It is social because it is determined by the overall result of the fluctuating efforts of each individual producer (under capitalism: of each individual firm or factory). It is objective because it is given, once the production of a given commodity is finished and is thus independent from personal (or collective) valuations of customers on the market place; and it is historically relative because it changes with each important change (progress or regression) of the average productivity of labour in a given branch of output, including in agriculture and transportation.

This does not imply that Marx's concept of value is in any way completely detached from consumption. It only means that the feedback of consumers' behaviour and wishes upon value is always mediated through changes in allocation of labour inputs in production, labour seen as subdivided into living labour and dead (dated) labour, i.e. tools and raw materials. The market emits signals to which the producing units react. Value changes after these reactions, not before them. Market price changes can of course occur prior to changes in value. In fact, changes in market prices are among the key signals which

can lead to changes in labour allocation between different branches of production, i.e. to changes in labour quantities necessary to produce given commodities. But then, for Marx, values determine prices only basically and in the medium-term sense of the word. This determination only appears clearly as an explication of *medium and long-term price movements*. In the shorter run, prices fluctuate around values as axes. Marx never intended to negate the operation of market laws, of the law of supply and demand, in determining these short-term fluctuations.

The 'law of value' is but Marx's version of Adam Smith's 'invisible hand'. In a society dominated by private labour, private producers and private ownership of productive inputs, it is this 'law of value', an objective economic law operating behind the backs of all people, all 'agents' involved in production and consumption, which, in the final analysis, regulates the economy, determines what is produced and how it is produced (and therefore also what can be consumed). The 'law of value' regulates the exchange between commodities, according to the quantities of socially necessary abstract labour they embody (the quantity of such labour spent in their production). Through regulating the exchange between commodities, the 'law of value' also regulates, after some interval, the distribution of society's labour potential and of society's non-living productive resources between different branches of production. Again, the analogy with Smith's 'invisible hand' is striking.

Marx's critique of the 'invisible hand' concept does not dwell essentially on the analysis of how a market economy actually operates. It would above all insist that this operation is not eternal, not immanent in 'human nature', but created by specific historical circumstances, a product of a special way of social organization, and due to disappear at some stage of historical evolution as it appeared during a previous stage. And it would also stress that this 'invisible hand' leads neither to the maximum of economic growth nor to the optimum of human wellbeing for the greatest number of individuals, i.e. it would stress the heavy economic and social price humankind had to pay, and is still currently paying, for the undeniable progress the market economy produced at a given stage of historical evolution.

The formula 'quantities of abstract human labour' refers to labour seen strictly as a fraction of the total labour potential of a given society at a given time, say a labour potential of 2 billion hours a year (1 million potential producers supposedly capable of working each 2000 hours a year). It therefore implies making abstraction of the specific trade or occupation of a given male or female producer, the product of a day's work of a weaver not being worth less or more than that of a peasant, a miner, a housebuilder, a milliner or a seamstress. At the basis of that concept of 'abstract human labour' lies a social condition, a specific set of social relations of production, in which small independent producers are essentially equal. Without that equality, social division of labour, and therefore satisfaction of basic consumers' needs, would be seriously endangered under that specific organizational set-up of the economy. Such an equality between small commodity owners and producers is later transformed into an equality between owners of capital under the capitalist mode of production.

But the concept of homogeneity of productive human labour, underlying that of 'abstract human labour' as the essence of value, does not imply a negation of the difference between skilled and unskilled labour. Again: a negation of that difference would lead to breakdown of the necessary division of labour, as would any basic heterogeneity of labour inputs in different branches of output. It would then not pay to acquire skills: most of them would disappear. So Marx's labour theory of value, in an internally coherent way, leads to the conclusion that one hour of skilled labour represents more value than one hour of unskilled labour, say represents the equivalent of 1.5 hours of unskilled labour. The difference would result from the imputation of the labour it costs to acquire the given skill. While an unskilled labourer would have a labour potential of 120,000 hours during his adult life, a skilled labourer would only have a labour potential of 80,000 hours, 40,000 hours being used for acquiring, maintaining and developing his skill. Only if one hour of skilled labour embodies the same value of 1.5 hours of unskilled labour, will the equality of all 'economic agents' be maintained under these circumstances, i.e. will it 'pay' economically to acquire a skill.

Marx himself never extensively dwelled on this solution of the so-called *reduction problem*. This remains indeed one of the most obscure parts of his general economic theory. It has led to some, generally rather mild, controversy. Much more heat has been generated by another facet of Marx's labour theory of value, the so-called *transformation problem*. Indeed, from Böhm-Bawerk writing a century ago till the recent contributions of Sraffa (1960) and Steedman (1977), the way Marx dealt with the transformation of values into 'prices of production' in *Capital* Vol. III has been considered by many of his critics as the main problem of his 'system', including being a reason to reject the labour theory of value out of hand.

The problem arises out of the obvious modification in the functioning of a market economy when *capitalist* commodity production substitutes itself for *simple* commodity production. In simple commodity production, with generally stable technology and stable (or easily reproduceable) tools, living labour is the only variable of the quantity and subdivision of social production. The mobility of labour is the only dynamic factor in the economy. As Engels pointed out in his Addendum to *Capital* Vol. III (Marx, g, pp. 1034–7) in such an economy, commodities would be exchanged at prices which would be immediately proportional to values, to the labour inputs they embody.

But under the capitalist mode of production, this is no longer the case. Economic decision-taking is not in the hands of the direct producers. It is in the hands of the capitalist entrepreneurs in the wider sense of the word (bankers – distributors of credit – playing a key role in that decision-taking, besides entrepreneurs in the productive sector properly speaking). Investment decisions, i.e. decisions for creating, expanding, reducing or closing enterprises, determine economic life. It is the *mobility of capital* and not the mobility of labour which becomes the motive force of the economy. Mobility of labour becomes essentially an epiphenomenon of the mobility of capital.

Capitalist production is production for profit. Mobility of capital is determined by existing or expected profit differentials. Capital leaves branches (countries, regions) with lower profits (or profit expectations) and flows towards branches (countries, regions) with higher ones. These movements lead to an equalization of the rate of profit between different branches of production. But approximately equal returns on all invested capital (at least under conditions of prevailing 'free competition') coexist with unequal proportions of inputs of labour in these different branches. So there is a disparity between the direct value of a commodity and its 'price of production', that 'price of production' being defined by Marx as the sum of production costs (costs of fixed capital and raw materials plus wages) and the average rate of profit multiplied with the capital spent in the given production.

The so-called 'transformation problem' relates to the question of whether a relation can nevertheless be established between value and these 'prices of production', what is the degree of coherence (or incoherence) of the relation with the 'law of value' (the labour theory of value in general), and what is the correct quantitative way to express that relation, if it exists.

We shall leave aside here the last aspect of the problem, to which extensive analysis has recently been devoted (Mandel and Freeman, 1984). From Marx's point of view, there is no incoherence between the formation of 'prices of production' and the labour theory of value. Nor is it true that he came upon that alleged difficulty when he started to prepare *Capital* III, i.e. to deal with capitalist competition, as several critics have argued (see e.g. Joan Robinson, 1942). In fact, his solution of the transformation problem is already present in the *Grundrisse* (Marx, d), before he even started to draft *Capital* Vol. I.

The sum total of value produced in a given country during a given span of time (e.g. one year) is determined by the sum total of labour-inputs. Competition and movements of capital cannot change that quantity. The sum total of values equals the sum total of 'prices of production'. The only effect of capital competition and capital mobility is to *redistribute* that given sum – and this through a redistribution of surplus value (see below) – between different capitals, to the benefit of some and at the expense of others.

Now this redistribution does not occur in a haphazard or arbitrary way. Essentially value (surplus-value) is transferred from technically less advanced branches to technologically more advanced branches. And here the concept of 'quantities of socially necessary labour' comes into its own, under the conditions of constant revolutions of productive technology that characterize the capitalist mode of production. Branches with lower than average technology (organic composition of capital, see below) can be considered as wasting socially necessary labour. Part of the labour spent in production in their realm is therefore not compensated by society. Branches with higher than average technology (organic composition of capital) can be considered to be economizing social labour; their labour inputs can therefore be considered as more intensive than average, embodying more value. In this way, the transfer of value (surplus-value) between different branches, far from being in contradiction with the law of value, is precisely the way it operates and should operate under conditions of 'capitalist equality', given the pressure of rapid technological change.

As to the logical inconsistency often supposedly to be found in Marx's method of solving the 'transformation problem' – first advanced by von Bortkiewicz (1907) – it is based upon a misunderstanding in our opinion. It is alleged that in his 'transformation schemas' (or tables) (Marx, g, pp. 255–6) Marx calculates inputs in 'values' and outputs in 'prices of production', thereby omitting the feedback effect of the latter on the former. But that feedback effect is unrealistic and unnecessary, once one recognizes that inputs are essentially data. Movements of capital posterior to the purchase of machinery or raw materials, including ups and downs of prices of finished products produced with these raw materials, cannot lead to a change in prices and therefore of profits of the said machinery and raw materials, on sales which have already occurred. What critics present as an inconsistency between 'values' and 'prices of production' is simply a recognition of *two different time-frameworks* (cycles) in which the equalization of the rate of profit has been achieved, a first one for inputs, and a second, later one for outputs.

Marx's theory of rent

The labour theory of value defines value as the socially necessary quantity of labour determined by the average productivity of labour of each given sector of production. But these values are not mathematically fixed data. They are simply the expression of a *process* going on in real life, under capitalist commodity production. So this average is only ascertained in the course of a certain time-span. There is a lot of logical argument and empirical evidence to advance the hypothesis that the normal time-span for essentially modifying the value of commodities is the business cycle, from one crisis of over-production (recession) to the next one.

Before technological progress and (or) better (more 'rational') labour organization etc. determines a more than marginal change (in general: decline) in the value of a commodity, and the crisis eliminates less efficient firms, there will be a coexistence of firms with various 'individual values' of a given commodity in a given branch of output, even assuming a single market price. So, in his step-for-step approach towards explaining the immediate phenomena (facts of economic life) like prices and profits, by their essence, Marx introduces at this point of his analysis a new mediating concept, that of *market value* (Marx, g, ch. 10). The market value of a commodity is the 'individual value' of the firm, or a group of firms, in a given branch of production, around which the market price will fluctuate. That 'market value' is not necessarily the mathematical (weighted) average of labour expenditure of all firms of that branch. It can be below, equal or above that average, for a certain period (generally less than the duration of the business cycle, at least under 'free competition'), according to whether social demand is saturated, just covered or to an important extent not covered by current output plus existing stocks. In these three cases respectively, the more (most) efficient firms, the firms of average efficiency, or even firms with labour productivity below average, will determine the market value of that given commodity.

This implies that the more efficient firms enjoy *surplus profits* (profits over and above the average profit) in case 2 and 3 and that a certain number of firms work at less than average profit in all three cases, but especially in case 1.

The mobility of capital, i.e. normal capitalist competition, generally eliminates such situations after a certain lapse of time. But when that mobility of capital is impeded for long periods by either unavoidable scarcity (natural conditions not renewable or non-substitutable, like land and mineral deposits) or through the operation of institutional obstacles (private property of land and mineral resources forbidding access to available capital, except in exchange for payments over and above average profit), these surplus profits can be frozen and maintained for decades. They thus become *rents*, of which *ground rent* and *mineral rent* are the most obvious examples in Marx's time, extensively analysed in *Capital* vol. III (Marx, g, part 6).

Marx's theory of rent is the most difficult part of his economic theory, the one which has witnessed fewer comments and developments, by followers and critics alike, than other major parts of his 'system'. But it is not obscure. And in contrast to Ricardo's or Rodbertus's theories of rent, it represents a straightforward application of the labour theory of value. It does not imply any emergence of 'supplementary' value (surplus value, profits) in the market, in the process of circulation of commodities, which is anathema to Marx and to all consistent upholders of the labour theory of value.

Nor does it in any way suggest that land or mineral deposits 'create' value.

It simply means that in agriculture and mining less productive labour (as in the general case analysed above) determines the market value of food or minerals, and that therefore more efficient farms and mines enjoy surplus profits which Marx calls differential (land and mining) rent. It also means that as long as productivity of labour in agriculture is generally below the average of the economy as a whole (or more correctly: that the organic composition of capital, the expenditure in machinery and raw materials as against wages, is inferior in agriculture to that of industry and transportation), the sum-total of surplus-value produced in agriculture will accrue to landowners + capitalist farmers taken together, and will not enter the general process of (re)distribution of profit throughout the economy as a whole.

This creates the basis for a supplementary form of rent, over and above differential rent, rent which Marx calls absolute land rent. This is, incidentally, the basis for a long-term separation of capitalist landowners from entrepreneurs in farming or animal husbandry, distinct from feudal or semi-feudal landowners or great landowners under conditions of predominantly petty commodity production, or in the Asiatic mode of production, with free peasants.

The validity of Marx's theory of land and mining rents has been confirmed by historical evidence, especially in the 20th century. Not only has history substantiated Marx's prediction that, in spite of the obstacle of land and mining rent, mechanization would end up by penetrating food and raw materials production too, as it has for a long time dominated industry and transportation, thereby causing a growing decline of differential rent (this has occurred increasingly in agriculture in the last 25–50 years, first in North America, and then in Western Europe and even elsewhere). It has also demonstrated that once the structural scarcity of food disappears, the institutional obstacle (private property) loses most of its efficiency as a brake upon the mobility of capital. Therefore the participation of surplus-value produced in agriculture in the general process of profit equalization throughout the economy cannot be prevented any more. Thereby absolute rent tends to wither away and, with it, the separation of land ownership from entrepreneurial farming and animal husbandry. It is true that farmers can then fall under the sway of the banks, but they do so as private owners of their land which becomes mortgaged, not as share-croppers or entrepreneurs renting land from separate owners.

On the other hand, the reappearance of structural scarcity in the realm of energy enabled the OPEC countries to multiply the price of oil by ten in the 1970s, i.e. to have it determined by the oilfields where production costs are the highest, thereby assuring the owners of the cheapest oil wells in Arabia, Iran, Libya, etc. of huge differential mineral rents.

Marx's theory of land and mineral rent can be easily extended into a general theory of rent, applicable to all fields of production where formidable difficulties of entry limit mobility of capital for extended periods of time. It thereby becomes the basis of a Marxist theory of monopoly and monopoly surplus profits, i.e. in the form of cartel rents (Hilferding, 1910) or of technological rent (Mandel, 1972). Lenin's and Bukharin's theories of surplus profit are based upon analogous but not identical reasoning (Bukharin, 1914, 1926; Lenin, 1917).

But in all these cases of general application of the Marxist theory of rent, the same caution should apply as Marx applied to his theory of land rent. By its very nature, capitalism, based upon private property, i.e. 'many capitals' – that is, competition – cannot tolerate any 'eternal' monopoly, a 'permanent' surplus profit deducted from the sum total of profits which is divided among the capitalist class as a whole. Technological innovations, substitution of new products for old ones including the field of raw materials and of food, will in the long run reduce or eliminate all monopoly situations, especially if the profit differential is large enough to justify huge research and investment outlays.

Marx's theory of money

In the same way as his theory of rent, Marx's theory of money is a straightforward application of the labour theory of value. As value is but the embodiment of socially necessary labour, commodities exchange with each other in proportion of the labour quanta they contain. This is true for the exchange of iron against wheat as it is true for the exchange of iron against gold or silver. Marx's theory of money is therefore in the first place a commodity theory of money. A given commodity can play the role of universal medium of exchange, as well as fulfil all the other functions of money, precisely because it is a commodity, i.e. because it is itself the product of socially necessary labour. This applies to the precious metals in the same way it applies to all the various commodities which, throughout history, have played the role of money.

It follows that strong upheavals in the 'intrinsic' value of the money-commodity will cause strong upheavals in the general price level. In Marx's theory of money, (market) prices are nothing but the expression of the value of commodities in the value of the money commodity chosen as a monetary standard. If £1 sterling = $\frac{1}{10}$ ounce of gold, the formula 'the price of 10 quarters of wheat is £1' means that 10 quarters of wheat have been produced in the same socially necessary labour time as $\frac{1}{10}$ ounce of gold. A strong decrease in the average productivity of labour in gold mining (as a result for example of a depletion of the richer gold veins) will lead to a general depression of the average price level, all other things remaining equal. Likewise, a sudden and radical increase in the average productivity of labour in gold mining, through the discovery of new rich gold fields (California after 1848; the Rand in South Africa in the 1890s) or through the application of new revolutionary technology, will lead to a general increase in the price level of all other commodities.

Leaving aside short-term oscillations, the general price level will move in medium and long-term periods according to the relation between the fluctuations of the productivity of labour in agriculture and industry on the one hand, and the fluctuations of the productivity of labour in gold mining (if gold is the money-commodity), on the other.

Basing himself on that commodity theory of money. Marx therefore criticized as inconsistent Ricardo's quantity theory (Marx, h, part 2). But for exactly the same reason of a consistent application of the labour theory of value, the quantity of money in circulation enters Marx's economic analysis when he deals with the phenomenon of paper money (Marx, c).

As gold has an intrinsic value, like all other commodities, there can be no 'gold inflation', as little as there can be a 'steel inflation'. Abstraction made of short-term price fluctuations caused by fluctuations between supply and demand, a persistent decline of the value of gold (exactly as for all other commodities) can only be the result of a persistent increase in the average productivity of labour in gold mining, and not of an 'excess' of circulation in gold. If the demand for gold falls consistently, this can only indirectly trigger off a decline in the value of gold through causing the closure of the least productive gold mines. But in the case of the money-commodity, such overproduction can hardly occur, given the special function of gold of serving as a universal reserve fund, nationally and internationally. It will always therefore find a buyer, be it not, of course, always at the same 'prices' (in Marx's economic theory, the concept of 'price of gold' is meaningless. As the price of a commodity is precisely its expression in the value of gold, the 'price of gold' would be the expression of the value of gold in the value of gold).

Paper money, bank notes, are a *money sign* representing a given quantity of the money-commodity. Starting from the above-mentioned example, a banknote of £1 represents $\frac{1}{10}$ ounce of gold. This is an objective 'fact of life', which no government or monetary authority can arbitrarily alter. It follows that any emission of paper money in excess of that given proportion will automatically lead to an increase in the general price level, always other things remaining equal. If £1 suddenly represents only $\frac{1}{20}$ ounce of gold, because paper money circulation has doubled without a significant increase in the total labour time spent in the economy, then the price level will tend to double too. The value of $\frac{1}{10}$ ounce of gold remains equal to the value of 10 quarters of wheat. But as $\frac{1}{10}$ ounce of gold is now represented by £2 in paper banknotes instead of being represented by £1, the price of wheat will move from £1 to £2 for 10 quarters (from two shillings

to four shillings a quarter before the introduction of the decimal system).

This does not mean that in the case of paper money, Marx himself has become an advocate of a quantity theory of money. While there are obvious analogies between his theory of paper money and the quantity theory, the main difference is the rejection by Marx of any mechanical automatism between the quantity of paper money emitted on the one hand, and the general dynamic of the economy (including on the price level) on the other.

In Marx's explanation of the movement of the capitalist economy in its totality, the formula *ceteris paribus* is meaningless. Excessive (or insufficient) emission of paper money never occurs in a vacuum. It always occurs at a given stage of the business cycle, and in a given phase of the longer-term historical evolution of capitalism. It is thereby always combined with given ups and downs of the rate of profit, of productivity of labour, of output, of market conditions (overproduction or insufficient production). Only in connection with these other fluctuations can the effect of paper money 'inflation' or 'deflation' be judged, including the effect on the general price level. The key variables are in the field of production. The key synthetic resultant is in the field of profit. Price movements are generally epiphenomena as much as they are signals. To untwine the tangle, more is necessary than a simple analysis of the fluctuations of the quantity of money. Only in the case of extreme runaway inflation of paper money would this be otherwise; and even in that border case, *relative* price movements (different degrees of price increases for different commodities) would still confirm that, in the last analysis, the law of value rules, and not the arbitrary decisions of the Central Bank, or any other authority controlling or emitting paper money.

Marx's theory of surplus-value

Marx himself considered his theory of surplus-value his most important contribution to the progress of economic analysis (Marx, l; letter to Engels of 24 August 1867). It is through this theory that the wide scope of his sociological and historical thought enables him simultaneously to place the capitalist mode of production in its historical context, and to find the roots of its inner economic contradictions and its laws of motion in the specific relations of production on which it is based.

As said before, Marx's theory of classes is based on the recognition that in each class society, part of society (the ruling class) appropriates the social surplus product. But that surplus product can take three essentially different forms (or a combination of them). It can take the form of straightforward unpaid surplus labour, as in the slave mode of production, early feudalism or some sectors of the Asian mode of production (unpaid corvée labour for the Empire). It can take the form of goods appropriated by the ruling class in the form of use-values pure and simple (the products of surplus labour), as under feudalism when feudal rent is paid in a certain amount of produce (produce rent) or in its more modern remnants, such as sharecropping. And it can take a money form, like money-rent in the final phases of feudalism, and capitalist profits. Surplus-value is essentially just that: the money form of the social surplus produce or, what amounts to the same, the money product of surplus labour. It has therefore a common root with all other forms of surplus product: unpaid labour.

This means that Marx's theory of surplus-value is basically a deduction (or residual) theory of the ruling classes' income. The whole social product (the net national income) is produced in the course of the process of production, exactly as the whole crop is harvested by the peasants. What happens on the market (or through appropriation of the produce) is a distribution (or redistribution) of what already has been created. The surplus product, and therefore also its money form, surplus-value, is the residual of that new (net) social product (income) which remains after the producing classes have received their compensation (under capitalism: their wages). This 'deduction' theory of the ruling classes' income is thus *ipso facto* an exploitation theory. Not in the ethical sense of the word – although Marx and Engels obviously manifested a lot of understandable moral indignation at the fate of all the exploited throughout history, and especially at the fate of the modern proletariat – but in the economical one. The income of the ruling classes can always be reduced in the final analysis to the product of unpaid labour: that is the heart of Marx's theory of exploitation.

That is also the reason why Marx attached so much importance to treating *surplus-value as a general category*, over and above profits (themselves subdivided into industrial profits, bank profits, commercial profits etc.), interest and rent, which are all part of the total surplus product produced by wage labour. It is this general category which explains both the existence (the common interest) of the ruling class (all those who live off surplus value), and the origins of the class struggle under capitalism.

Marx likewise laid bare the economic mechanism through which surplus-value originates. As the basis of that economic mechanism is a huge social upheaval which started in Western Europe in the 15th century and slowly spread over the rest of the continent and all other continents (in many so-called underdeveloped countries, it is still going on to this day).

Through many concomitant economic (including technical), social, political and cultural transformations, the mass of the direct producers, essentially peasants and handicraftsmen, are separated from their means of production and cut off from free access to the land. They are therefore unable to produce their livelihood on their own account. In order to keep themselves and their families alive, they have to hire out their arms, their muscles and their brains, to the owners of the means of production

(including land). If and when these owners have enough money capital at their disposal to buy raw materials and pay wages, they can start to organize production on a capitalist basis, using wage labour to transform the raw materials which they buy, with the tools they own, into finished products which they then automatically own too.

The capitalist mode of production thus presupposes that the producers' *labour power has become a commodity*. Like all other commodities, the commodity labour power has an exchange value and a use value. The exchange value of labour power, like the exchange value of all other commodities, is the amount of socially necessary labour embodied in it, i.e. its reproduction costs. This means concretely the value of all the consumer goods and services necessary for a labourer to work day after day, week after week, month after month, at approximately the same level of intensity, and for the members of the labouring classes to remain approximately stable in number and skill (i.e. for a certain number of working-class children to be fed, kept and schooled, so as to replace their parents when they are unable to work any more, or die). But the use value of the commodity labour power is precisely its capacity to create new value, including its potential to create more value than its own reproduction costs. Surplus-value is but that difference between the total new value created by the commodity labour power, and its own value, its own reproduction costs.

The whole Marxian theory of surplus-value is therefore based upon that subtle distinction between 'labour power' and 'labour' (or value). But there is nothing 'metaphysical' about this distinction. It is simply an explanation (demystification) of a process which occurs daily in millions of cases.

The capitalist does not buy the worker's 'labour'. If he did that there would be obvious theft, for the worker's wage is obviously smaller than the total value he adds to that of the raw materials in the course of the process of production. No: the capitalist buys 'labour power', and often (not always of course) he buys it at its *justum pretium*, at its real value. So he feels unjustly accused when he is said to have caused a 'dishonest' operation. The worker is victim not of vulgar theft but of a social set-up which condemns him first to transform his productive capacity into a commodity, then to sell that labour power on a specific market (the labour market) characterized by institutional inequality, and finally to content himself with the market price he can get for that commodity, irrespective of whether the new value he creates during the process of production exceeds that market price (his wage) by a small amount, a large amount, or an enormous amount.

The labour power the capitalist has bought 'adds value' to that of the used-up raw materials and tools (machinery, buildings etc.). If, and until that point of time, this added value is inferior or equal to the workers' wages, surplus-value cannot originate. But in that case, the capitalist has obviously no interest in hiring wage labour. He only hires it because that wage labour has the quality (the use value) to add to the raw materials' value more than its own value (i.e. its own wages). This 'additional added value' (the difference between total 'value added' and wages) is precisely surplus-value. Its emergence from the process of production is the precondition for the capitalists' hiring workers, for the existence of the capitalist mode of production.

The institutional inequality existing on the labour market (masked for liberal economists, sociologists and moral philosophers alike by juridical equality) arises from the very fact that the capitalist mode of production is based upon generalized commodity production, generalized market economy. This implies that a propertyless labourer, who owns no capital, who has no reserves of larger sums of money but who has to buy his food and clothes, pay his rent and even elementary public transportation for journeying between home and workplace, *in a continuous way* in exchange of money, is under the *economic compulsion* to sell the only commodity he possesses, to wit his labour power, also on a continuous basis. He cannot withdraw from the labour market until the wages go up. He cannot wait.

But the capitalist, who has money reserves, can temporarily withdraw from the labour market. He can lay his workers off, can even close or sell his enterprise and wait a couple of years before starting again in business. This institutional difference makes price determination of the labour market a game with loaded dice, heavily biased against the working class. One just has to imagine a social set-up in which each citizen would be guaranteed an annual minimum income by the community, irrespective or whether he is employed or not, to understand that 'wage determination' under these circumstances would be quite different from what it is under capitalism. In such a set-up the individual would really have the economic choice whether to sell his labour power to another person (or a firm) or not. Under capitalism, he has no choice. His is forced by economic compulsion to go through with that sale, practically at any price.

The economic function and importance of trade unions for the wage-earners also clearly arises from that elementary analysis. For it is precisely the workers' 'combination' and their assembling a collective resistance fund (what was called by the first French unions *caisses de résistance*, 'reserve deposits') which enables them, for example though a strike, to withdraw the supply of labour power temporarily from the market so as to stop a downward trend of wages or induce a wage increase. There is nothing 'unjust' in such a temporary withdrawal of the supply of labour power, as there are constant withdrawals of demand for labour power by the capitalists, sometimes on a huge scale never equalled by strikes. Through the functioning of strong labour unions, the working class tries to correct, albeit partially and

modestly, the institutional inequality on the labour market of which it is a victim, without ever being able to neutralize it durably or completely.

It cannot neutralize it durably because in the very way in which capitalism functions there is a powerful built-in corrective in favour of capital: the inevitable emergence of an industrial reserve army of labour. There are three key sources for that reserve army: the mass of precapitalist producers and self-employed (independent peasants, handicraftsmen, trades-people, professional people, small and medium-sized capitalists); the mass of housewives (and to a lesser extent, children); the mass of the wage-earners themselves, who potentially can be thrown out of employment.

The first two sources have to be visualized not only in each capitalist country seen separately but on a world scale, through the operations of international migration. They are still unlimited to a great extent, although the number of wage-earners the world over (including agricultural wage labourers) has already passed the one billion mark. At the third source, while it is obviously not unlimited (if wage labour would disappear altogether, if all wage labourers would be fired, surplus-value production would disappear too; that is why 'total robotism' is impossible under capitalism), its reserves are enormous, precisely in tandem with the enormous growth of the absolute number of wage earners.

The fluctuations of the industrial reserve army are determined both by the business cycle and by long-term trends of capital accumulation. Rapidly increasing capital accumulation attracts wage labour on a massive scale, including through international migration. Likewise, deceleration, stagnation or even decline of capital accumulation inflates the reserve army of labour. There is thus an upper limit to wage increases, when profits (realized profits and expected profits) are 'excessively' reduced in the eyes of the capitalists, which triggers off such decelerated, stagnating or declining capital accumulation, thereby decreasing employment and wages, till a 'reasonable' level of profits is restored.

This process does not correspond to any 'natural economic law' (or necessity), nor does it correspond to any 'immanent justice'. It just expresses the inner logic of the *capitalist* mode of production, which is geared to profit. Other forms of economic organization could function, have functioned and are functioning on the basis of other logics, which do not lead to periodic massive unemployment. On the contrary, a socialist would say – and Marx certainly thought so – that the capitalist system is an 'unjust', or better stated 'alienating', 'inhuman' social system, precisely because it cannot function without periodically reducing employment and the satisfaction of elementary needs for tens of millions of human beings.

Marx's theory of surplus-value is therefore closely intertwined with a *theory of wages* which is far away from Malthus's, Ricardo's or the early socialists' (like

Ferdinand Lassalle's) 'iron law of wages', in which wages tend to fluctuate around the physiological minimum. That crude theory of 'absolute pauperization' of the working class under capitalism, attributed to Marx by many authors (Popper, 1945, et al.), is not Marx's at all, as many contemporary authors have convincingly demonstrated (see among others Rosdolsky, 1968). Such an 'iron law of wages' is essentially a demographic one, in which birth rates and the frequency of marriages determine the fluctuation of employment and unemployment and thereby the level of wages.

The logical and empirical inconsistencies of such a theory are obvious. Let it be sufficient to point out that while fluctuations in the supply of wage-labourers are considered essential, fluctuations in the demand for labour power are left out of the analysis. It is certainly a paradox that the staunch opponent of capitalism, Karl Marx, pointed out already in the middle of the 19th century the potential for wage increases under capitalism, even though not unlimited in time and space. Marx also stressed the fact that for each capitalist wage increases of other capitalists' workers are considered increases of potential purchasing power, not increases in costs (Marx, d).

Marx distinguishes two parts in the workers' wage, two elements of reproduction costs of the commodity labour power. One is purely physiological, and can be expressed in calories and energy quanta; this is the bottom below which the wage cannot fall without destroying slowly or rapidly the workers' labour capacity. The second one is historical-moral, as Marx calls it (Marx, i), and consists of those additional goods and services which a shift in the class relationship of forces, such as a victorious class struggle, enables the working class to incorporate into the average wage, the socially necessary (recognized) reproduction costs of the commodity labour power (e.g. paid holidays after the French general strike of June 1936). This part of the wage is essentially flexible. It will differ from country to country, continent to continent, and from epoch to epoch, according to many variables. But it has the upper limit indicated above: the ceiling from which profits threaten to disappear, or to become insufficient in the eyes of the capitalists, who then go on an 'investment strike'.

So Marx's theory of wages is essentially an *accumulation-of-capital theory of wages* which sends us back to what Marx considered the first 'law of motion' of the capitalist mode of production: the compulsion for the capitalists to step up constantly the rate of capital accumulation.

The laws of motion of the capitalist mode of production

Marx's theory of surplus-value is his most revolutionary contribution to economic science, his discovery of the basic long-term 'laws of motion' (development trends) of the capitalist mode of production constitutes undoubtedly his most impressive scientific achievement. No other 19th-century author has been able to foresee in such a coherent way how capitalism would function, would develop and would transform the world, as did Karl Marx. Many of the most distinguished contemporary economists, starting with Wassily Leontief (1938), and Joseph Schumpeter (1942), have recognized this.

While some of these 'laws of motion' have obviously created much controversy, we shall nevertheless list them in logical order, rather than according to the degree of consensus they command.

(a) *The capitalist's compulsion to accumulate.* Capital appears in the form of accumulated money, thrown into circulation in order to increase in value. No owner of money capital will engage in business in order to recoup exactly the sum initially invested, and nothing more than that. By definition, the search for profit is at the basis of all economic operations by owners of capital.

Profit (surplus-value, accretion of value) can originate outside the sphere of production in a precapitalist society. It represents then essentially a *transfer of value* (so-called primitive accumulation of capital); but under the capitalist mode of production, in which capital has penetrated the sphere of production and dominates it, surplus-value is currently produced by wage labour. It represents a constant increase in value.

Capital can only appear in the form of many capitals, given its very historical-social origin in private property (appropriation) of the means of production. 'Many capitals' imply unavoidable competition. Competition in a capitalist mode of production is competition for selling commodities in an anonymous market. While surplus-value is produced in the process of production, it is *realized* in the process of circulation, i.e. through the sale of the commodities. The capitalist wants to sell at maximum profit. In practice, he will be satisfied if he gets the average profit, which is a percentage really existing in his consciousness (e.g. Mr. Charles Wilson, the then head of the US automobile firm General Motors, stated before a Congressional enquiry: we used to fix the expected sales price of our cars by adding 15% to production costs). But he can never be sure of this. He cannot even be sure that all the commodities produced will find a buyer.

Given these uncertainties, he has to strive constantly to get the better of his competitors. This can only occur through operating with more capital. This means that at least part of the surplus-value produced will not be unproductively consumed by the capitalists and their hangers-on through luxury consumption, but will be accumulated, added to the previously existing capital.

The inner logic of capitalism is therefore not only to 'work for profit', but also to 'work for capital accumulation'. 'Accumulate, accumulate; that is Moses and the Prophets', states Marx in *Capital*, Vol. I (Marx, e, p. 742). Capitalists are *compelled* to act in that way as a result of competition. It is competition which basically fuels this

terrifying snowball logic: initial value of capital →
accretion of value (surplus-value) → accretion of capital
→ more accretion of surplus-value → more accretion of
capital etc. 'Without competition, the fire of growth
would burn out' (Marx, *g*, p. 368).

(b) *The tendency towards constant technological
revolutions.* In the capitalist mode of production, accumulation of capital is in the first place accumulation of
productive capital, or capital invested to produce more
and more commodities. Competition is therefore above
all competition between productive capitals, i.e. 'many
capitals' engaged in mining, manufacturing, transportation, agriculture, telecommunications. The main weapon
in competition between capitalist firms is cutting production costs. More advanced production techniques and
more 'rational' labour organization are the main means
to achieve that purpose. The basic tend of capital accumulation in the capitalist mode of production is therefore a trend towards more and more sophisticated
machinery. Capitalist growth takes the dual form of
higher and higher value of capital and of constant revolutions in the techniques of production, of constant
technological progress.

(c) *The capitalists' unquenchable thirst for surplus-value
extraction.* The compulsion for capital to grow, the irresistible urge for capital accumulation, realizes itself above
all through a constant drive for the increase of the production of surplus-value. Capital accumulation is nothing but surplus-value capitalization, the transformation
of part of the new surplus-value into additional capital. There is no other source of additional capital than
additional surplus-value produced in the process of
production.

Marx distinguishes two different forms of additional
surplus-value production. *Absolute surplus-value* accretion occurs essentially through the extension of the work
day. If the worker reproduces the equivalent of his wages
in 4 hours a day, an extension of the work day from 10 to
12 hours will increase surplus-value from 6 to 8 hours.
Relative surplus-value accretion occurs through an
increase of the productivity of labour in the wage-goods
sector of the economy. Such an increase in productivity
implies that the equivalent of the value of an identical
basket of goods and services consumed by the worker
could be produced in 2 hours instead of 4 hours of
labour. If the work day remains stable at 10 hours and
real wages remain stable too, surplus-value will then
increase from 6 to 8 hours.

While both processes occur throughout the history of
the capitalist mode of production (viz. the contemporary
pressure of employers in favour of overtime!), the first
one was prevalent first, the second one became prevalent
since the second half of the 19th century, first in Britain,
France and Belgium, then in the USA and Germany, later
in the other industrialized capitalist countries, and later
still in the semi-industrialized ones. Marx calls this process the *real subsumption* (subordination) of *labour under*
capital (Marx, *k*), for it represents not only an economic
but also a physical subordination of the wage-earner
under the machine. This physical subordination can only
be realized through social control. The history of the
capitalist mode of production is therefore also the history
of successive forms of – tighter and tighter – control of
capital over the workers inside the factories (Braverman,
1974); and of attempts at realizing that tightening of
control in society as a whole.

The increase in the production of relative surplus-value
is the goal for which capitalism tends to periodically
substitute machinery for labour, i.e. to expand the industrial reserve army of labour. Likewise, it is the main tool
for maintaining a modicum of social equilibrium, for
when productivity of labour strongly increases, above all
in the wage-good producing sectors of the economy, real
wages and profits (surplus-value) can both expand simultaneously. What were previously luxury goods can even
become mass-produced wage goods.

(d) *The tendency towards growing concentration and
centralization of capital.* The growth of the value of capital means that each successful capitalist firm will be
operating with more and more capital. Marx calls this
the tendency towards growing concentration of capital.
But in the competitive process, there are victors and
vanquished. The victors grow. The vanquished go bankrupt or are absorbed by the victors. This process Marx
calls the centralization of capital. It results in a declining
number of firms which survive in each of the key fields of
production. Many small and medium-sized capitalists
disappear as independent business men and women.
They become in turn salary earners, employed by
successful capitalist firms. Capitalism itself is the big
'expropriating' force, suppressing private property of the
means of production for many, in favour of private
property for few.

(e) *The tendency for the 'organic composition of capital'
to increase.* Productive capital has a double form. It
appears in the form of *constant* capital: buildings,
machinery, raw materials, energy. It appears in the form
of *variable* capital: capital spent on wages of productive
workers. Marx calls the part of capital used in buying
labour power variable, because only that part produces
additional value. In the process of production, the value
of constant capital is simply maintained (transferred
in toto or in part into the value of the finished product).
Variable capital on the contrary is the unique source of
'added value'.

Marx postulates that the basic historic trend of capital
accumulation is to increase investment in constant capital at a quicker pace than investment in variable capital;
the relation between the two he calls the 'organic composition of capital'. This is both a technical/physical relation (a given production technique implies the use of a
given number of productive wage earners, even if not in
an absolutely mechanical way) and a value relation. The
trend towards an increase in the 'organic composition of

capital' is therefore a historical trend towards *basically labour-saving technological progress*.

This tendency has often been challenged by critics of Marx. Living in the age of semi-automation and 'robotism', it is hard to understand that challenge. The conceptual confusion on which this challenge is mostly based is an operation with the 'national wage bill', i.e. a confusion between wages in general and variable capital, which is only the wage bill of productive labour. A more correct index would be the part of the labour costs in total production costs in the manufacturing (and mining) sector. It is hard to deny that this proportion shows a downward secular trend.

(f) *The tendency of the rate of profit to decline.* For the workers, the basic relation they are concerned with is the rate of surplus-value, i.e. the division of 'value added' by them between wages and surplus-value. When this goes up, their exploitation (the unpaid labour they produce) obviously goes up. For the capitalists however, this relationship is not meaningful. They are concerned with the relation between surplus-value and the *totality* of capital invested, never mind whether in the form of machinery and raw materials or in the form of wages. This relation is the *rate of profit*. It is a function of two variables, the organic composition of capital and the rate of surplus-value. If the value of constant capital is represented by c, the value of variable capital (wages of productive workers) by v and surplus-value by s, the rate of profit will be $s/(c + v)$. This can be rewritten as

$$\frac{s/v}{(c+v)/(v)} + 1$$

with the two variables emerging $((c + v)/(v)$ obviously reflects c).

Marx postulates that the increase in the rate of surplus value has definite limits, while the increase in the organic composition of capital has practically none (automation, robotism). There will therefore be a basic tendency for the rate of profit to decline.

This is however absolutely true only on a very long-term, i.e. essentially 'secular', basis. In other time-frameworks, the rate of profit can fluctuate under the influence of countervailing forces. Constant capital can be devalorized, through 'capital saving' technical process, and through economic crises (see below). The rate of surplus-value can be strongly increased in the short or medium term, although each strongly increase makes a further increase more difficult (Marx, *d*, pp. 335–6); and capital can flow to countries (e.g. 'Third World' ones) or branches (e.g. service sectors) where the organic composition of capital is significantly lower than in the previously industrialized ones, thereby raising the average rate of profit.

Finally, the increase in the mass of *surplus-value* – especially through the extension of wage labour in general, i.e. the total number of workers – offsets to a large extent the depressing effects of moderate declines of the average rate of profit. Capitalism will not go out of business if the mass of surplus-value produced increases 'only' from £10 to £17 billion, while the total mass of capital has moved from 100 to 200 billion; and capital accumulation will not stop under these circumstances, nor necessarily slow down significantly. It would be sufficient to have the unproductively consumed part of surplus-value pass e.g. from £3 to £2 billion, to obtain a rate of capital accumulation of 15/200, i.e. 7.5%, even higher than the previous one of 7/100, in spite of a decline of the rate of profit from 10 to 8.5%.

(g) *The inevitability of class struggle under capitalism.* One of the most impressive projections by Marx was that of the inevitability of elementary class struggle under capitalism. Irrespective of the social global framework or of their own historical background, wage-earners will fight everywhere for higher real wages and a shorter work day. They will form elementary organizations for the collective instead of the individual sale of the commodity labour power, i.e. trade unions. While at the moment Marx made that projection there were less than half a million organized workers in at the most half a dozen countries in the world, today trade unions encompass hundreds of millions of wage-earners spread around the globe. There is no country, however remote it might be, where the introduction of wage labour has not led to the appearance of workers' coalitions.

While elementary class struggle and elementary unionization of the working class are inevitable under capitalism, higher, especially political forms of class struggle, depend on a multitude of variables as to the rapidity with which they extend beyond smaller minorities of each 'national' working class and internationally. But there too the basic secular trend is clear. There were in 1900 innumerably more conscious socialists than in 1850, fighting not only for better wages but, to use Marx's words, for the abolition of wage labour (Marx, *i*) and organizing working class parties for that purpose. There are today many more than in 1900.

(h) *The tendency towards growing social polarization.* From two previously enumerated trends, the trend towards growing centralization of capital and the trend towards the growth of the mass of surplus-value, flows the trend towards growing social polarization under capitalism. The proportion of the active population represented by wage-labour in general, i.e. by the modern proletariat (which extends far beyond productive workers in and by themselves) increases. The proportion represented by self-employed (small, medium-sized and big capitalists, as well as independent peasants, handicraftsmen, tradespeople and 'free professions' working without wage-labour) decreases. In fact, in several capitalist countries, the first category has already passed the 90 per cent mark, while in Marx's time it was below 50 per cent everywhere but in Britain. In most industrialized (imperialist) countries, it has reached 80–85 per cent.

This does not mean that the petty entrepreneurs have tended to disappear. Ten or 15–20 per cent out of 30 million people, not to say out of 120 million, still represent a significant social layer. While many small businesses disappear, especially in times of economic depression, as a result of severe competition, they also are constantly created, especially in the interstices between big firms, and in new sectors where they play an exploratory role. Also, the overall social results of growing proletarization are not simultaneous with the economic process in and by itself. From the point of view of class consciousness, culture, political attitude, there can exist significant time-lags between the transformation of an independent farmer, grocer or doctor into a wage-earner, and his acceptance of socialism as an overall social solution for his own and society's ills. But again, the secular trend is towards *growing homogeneity*, less and less heterogeneity, of the mass of the wage-earning class, and not the other way around. It is sufficient to compare the differences in consumer patterns, attitudes towards unionization or voting habits between manual workers, bank employees and government functionaries in say 1900 and today, to note that they have decreased and not increased.

(i) *The tendency towards growing objective socialization of labour.* Capitalism starts in the form of private production on a medium-sized scale for a limited number of largely unknown customers, on an uncontrollably wide market, i.e. under conditions of near complete fragmentation of social labour and anarchy of the economic process. But as a result of growing technological progress, tremendously increased concentration of capital, the conquest of wider and wider markets throughout the world, and the very nature of the labour organization inside large and even medium-sized capitalist factories, a powerful process of objective socialization of labour is simultaneously set in motion. This process constantly extends the sphere of economy in which not blind market laws by conscious decisions and even large-scale cooperation prevail.

This is true especially inside mammoth firms (inside multinational corporations, such 'planning' prevails far beyond the boundaries of nation-states, even the most powerful ones!) and inside large-scale factories; but it is also increasingly true for buyer/seller relations, in the first place on an inter-firm basis, between public authorities and firms, and more often than one thinks between traders and consumers too. In all these instances, the rule of the law of value becomes more and more remote, indirect and discontinuous. Planning prevails on a short and even medium-term basis.

Certainly, the economy still remains capitalist. The rule of the law of value imposes itself brutally through the outburst of economic crises. Wars and social crises are increasingly added to these economic crises to remind society that, under capitalism, this growing objective socialization of labour and production is indissolubly linked to private appropriation, i.e. to the profit motive as motor of economic growth. That linkage makes the system more and more crisis-ridden; but at the same time the growing socialization of labour and production creates the objective basis for a general socialization of the economy, i.e. represents the basis of the coming socialist order created by capitalism itself, within the framework of its own system.

(j) *The inevitability of economic crises under capitalism.* This is another of Marx's projections which has been strikingly confirmed by history. Marx ascertained that periodic crises of overproduction were unavoidable under capitalism. In fact, since the crisis of 1825, the first one occurring on the world market for industrial goods to use Marx's own formula, there have been twenty-one business cycles ending (or beginning, according to the method of analysis and measurement used) with twenty-one crises of overproduction. A twenty-second is appearing on the horizon as we are writing.

Capitalist economic crises are always crises of *overproduction of commodities* (*exchange values*), as opposed to pre- and post-capitalist economic crises, which are essentially crises of *underproduction of use-values*. Under capitalist crises, *expanded reproduction* – economic growth – is brutally interrupted, not because too few commodities have been produced but, on the contrary, because a mountain of produced commodities finds no buyers. This unleashes a spiral movement of collapse of firms, firing of workers, contraction of sales (or orders) for raw materials and machinery, new redundancies, new contraction of sales of consumer goods etc. Through this *contracted reproduction*, prices (gold prices) collapse, production and income is reduced, capital loses value. At the end of the declining spiral, output (and stocks) have been reduced more than purchasing power. Then production can pick up again; and as the crisis has both increased the rate of surplus-value (through a decline of wages and a more 'rational' labour organization) and decreased the value of capital, the average rate of profit increases. This stimulates investment. Employment increases, value production and national income expand, and we enter a new cycle of economic revival, prosperity, overheating and the next crisis.

No amount of capitalists' (essentially large combines' and monopolies') 'self-regulation', no amount of government intervention, has been able to suppress this cyclical movement of capitalist production. Nor can they succeed in achieving that result. This cyclical movement is inextricably linked to production for profit and private property (competition), which imply periodic over-shooting (too little or too much investment and output), precisely because each firm's attempt at maximizing profit unavoidably leads to a lower rate of profit for the system as a whole. It is likewise linked to the separation of value production and value realization.

The only way to avoid crises of overproduction is to eliminate all basic sources of disequilibrium in the economy, including the disequilibrium between productive capacity and purchasing power of the 'final consumers'. This calls for elimination of generalized commodity production, of private property and of class exploitation, i.e. for the elimination of capitalism.

Marx's theory of crises

Marx did not write a systematic treatise on capitalist crises. His major comments on the subject are spread around his major economic writings, as well as his articles for the *New York Daily Tribune*. The longest treatment of the subject is in his *Theorien über den Mehrwert*, subpart on Ricardo (Marx, *h*, Part 2). Starting from these profound but unsystematic remarks, many interpretation of the 'Marxist theory or crisis' have been offered by economists who consider themselves Marxists. 'Monocausal' ones generally centre around 'disproportionality' (Bukharin, Hilferding, Otto Bauer) – anarchy of production as the key cause of crises – or 'underconsumption' – lack of purchasing power of the 'final consumers' as the cause of crises (Rosa Luxemburg, Sweezy). 'Non-monocausal' ones try to elaborate Marx's own *dictum* according to which *all* basic contradictions of the capitalist mode of production come into play in the process leading to a capitalist crisis (Grossman, Mandel).

The question of determining whether according to Marx, a crisis of overproduction is first of all a crisis of overproduction of commodities or a crisis of overproduction of capital is really meaningless in the framework of Marx's economic analysis. The mass of commodities is but one specific form of capital, commodity capital. Under capitalism, which is generalized commodity production, no overproduction is possible which is not simultaneously overproduction of commodities and overproduction of capital (over-accumulation).

Likewise, the question to know whether the crisis 'centres' on the sphere of production or the sphere of circulation is largely meaningless. The crisis is a disturbance (interruption) of the process of enlarged reproduction; and according to Marx, the process of reproduction is precisely a (contradictory) unity of production and circulation. For capitalists, both individually (as separate firms) and as the sum total of firms, it is irrelevant whether more surplus-value has actually been produced in the process of production, if that surplus-value cannot be totally realized in the process of circulation. Contrary to many economists, academic and Marxist alike, Marx explicitly rejected any Say-like illusion that production more or less automatically finds its own market.

It is correct that in the last analysis, capitalist crises of overproduction result from a downslide of the average rate of profit. But this does not represent a variant of the 'monocausal' explanation of crisis. It means that, under capitalism, the fluctuations of the average rate of profit are in a sense the seismograph of what happens in the system as a whole. So that formula just refers back to the sum-total of partially independent variables, whose interplay causes the fluctuations of the average rate of profit.

Capitalist growth is always disproportionate growth, i.e. growth with increasing disequilibrium, both between different departments of output (Marx basically distinguishes department I, producing means of production, and department II, producing means of consumption; other authors add a department III producing non-reproductive goods – luxury goods and arms – to that list), between different branches and between production and final consumption. In fact, 'equilibrium' under capitalism is but a conceptual hypothesis practically never attained in real life, except as a border case. The above mentioned tendency of 'overshooting' is only an illustration of that more general phenomenon. So 'average' capital accumulation leads to overaccumulation which leads to the crisis and to a prolonged phenomenon of 'underinvestment' during the depression. Output is then consistently inferior to current demand, which spurs on capital accumulation, first to a 'normal' level and then to renewed overaccumulation, all the more so as each successive phase of economic revival starts with new machinery of a higher technological level (leading to a higher average productivity of labour, and to a bigger and bigger mountain of a produced commodities. Indeed, the very duration of the business cycle (in average 7.5 years for the last 160 years) seemed for Marx determined by the 'moral' life-time of fixed capital, i.e. the duration of the reproduction cycle (in value terms, not in possible physical survival) of machinery.

The ups and downs of the rate of the profit during the business cycle do not reflect only the gyrations of the output/disposable income relation; or of the 'organic composition of capital'. They also express the varying correlation of forces between the major contending classes of bourgeois society, in the first place the short-term fluctuations of the rate of surplus-value reflecting major victories or defeats of the working class in trying to uplift or defend its standard of living and its working conditions. Technological progress and labour organization 'rationalizations' are capital's weapons for neutralizing the effects of these fluctuations on the average rate of profit and on the rate of capital accumulation.

In general, Marx rejected any idea that the working class (or the unions) 'cause' the crisis by 'excessive wage demands'. He would recognize that under conditions of overheating and 'full employment', real wages generally increase, but the rate of surplus-value can simultaneously increase too. It can, however, not increase in the same proportion as the organic composition of capital. Hence the decline of the average rate of profit. Hence the crisis.

But if real wages do not increase in time of boom, and as they unavoidably decrease in times of depression, the average level of wages during the cycle in its totality would be such as to cause even larger overproduction of wage goods, which would induce an even stronger collapse of investment at the height of the cycle, and in no way help to avoid the crisis.

Marx energetically rejected any idea that capitalist production, while it appears as 'production for production's sake', can really emancipate itself from dependence on 'final consumption' (as alleged e.g. by Tugan-Baranowsky). While capitalist technology implies indeed a more and more 'roundabout-way-of-production', and a relative shift of resources from department II to department I (that is what the 'growing organic composition of capital' really means, after all), it can never develop the productive capacity of department I without developing in the medium and long-term the productivity capacity of department II too, admittedly at a slower pace and in a lesser proportion. So any medium or long-term contraction of final consumption, or final consumers' purchasing power, increases instead of eliminates the causes of the crisis.

Marx visualized the business cycle as intimately intertwined with a *credit cycle*, which can acquire a *relative* autonomy in relation to what occurs in production properly speaking (Marx, g, pp. 570–73). An (over)expansion of credit can enable the capitalist system to sell temporarily more goods that the sum of real incomes created in current production plus past savings could buy. Likewise, credit (over)expansion can enable them to invest temporarily more capital than really accumulated surplus-value (plus depreciation allowances and recovered value of raw materials) would have enabled them to invest (the first part of the formula refers to net investments; the second to gross investment).

But all this is only true temporarily. In the longer run, debts must be paid; and they are not automatically paid through the results of expanded output and income made possible by credit expansion. Hence the risk of a *krach*, of a credit or banking crisis, adding fuel to the mass of explosives which cause the crisis of overproduction.

Does Marx's theory of crisis imply a theory of an inevitable final collapse of capitalism through purely economic mechanisms? A controversy has raged around this issue, called the 'collapse' or 'breakdown' controversy. Marx's own remarks on the matter are supposed to be enigmatic. They are essentially contained in the famous chapter 32 of volume I of *Capital* entitled 'The historical tendency of capitalist accumulation', a section culminating in the battle cry: 'The expropriators are expropriated' (Marx, e, p. 929). But the relevant paragraphs of that chapter describe in a clearly non-enigmatic way, an interplay of 'objective' and 'subjective' transformations to bring about a downfall of capitalism, and not a purely economic process. They list among the causes of the overthrow of capitalism not only economic crisis and growing centralization of capital, but also the growth of exploitation of the workers and of their indignation and revolt in the face of that exploitation, as well as the growing level of skill, organization and unity of

the working class. Beyond these general remarks, Marx, however, does not go.

Marx and Engels on the economy of post-capitalist societies

Marx was disinclined to comment at length about how a socialist or communist economy would operate. He thought such comments to be essentially speculative. Nevertheless, in his major works, especially the *Grundrisse* and *Das Kapital*, there are some sparse comments on the subject. Marx returns to them at greater length in two works he was to write in the final part of his life, his comments on the *Gotha Programme* of united German social-democracy (Marx, j), and the chapters on economics and socialism he wrote or collaborated with for Engels' *Anti-Dühring* (1878). Generally his comments, limited and sketchy as they are, can be summarized in the following points.

Socialism is an economic system based upon conscious planning of production by associated producers (nowhere does Marx say: by the state), made possible by the abolition of private property of the means of production. As soon as that private property is completely abolished, goods produced cease to be commodities. Value and exchange value disappear. Production becomes production for use, for the satisfaction of needs, determined by conscious choice (*ex ante* decisions) of the mass of the associated producers themselves. But overall economic organization in a postcapitalist society will pass through two stages.

In the first stage, generally called 'socialism', there will be relative scarcity of a number of consumer goods (and services), making it necessary to measure exactly distribution based on the actual labour inputs of each individual (Marx nowhere refers to different quantities and *qualities* of labour; Engels explicitly *rejects* the idea that an architect, because he has more skill, should consume more than a manual labourer). Likewise, there will still be the need to use incentives for getting people to work in general. This will be based upon strict equality of access for all trades and professions to consumption. But as human needs are unequal, that formal equality masks the survival of real inequality.

In a second phase, generally called 'communism', there will be plenty, i.e. output will reach a saturation point of needs covered by material goods. Under these circumstances, any form of precise measurement of consumption (distribution) will wither away. The principle of full needs satisfaction covering all different needs of *different* individuals will prevail. No incentive will be needed any more to induce people to work. 'Labour' will have transformed itself into meaningful many-fold activity, making possible all-round development of each individual's human personality. The division of labour between manual and intellectual labour, the separation of town and countryside, will wither away. Humankind will be organized into a free federation of producers' and consumers' communes.

Selected works

There is still no complete edition of all of Marx's and Engels's writings. The standard German and Russian editions by the Moscow and East Berlin Institutes for Marxism-Leninism, generally referred to as *Marx-Engels-Werke* (MEW), do not include hundreds of pages printed elsewhere (e.g. Marx's *Enthüllungen zur Geschichte der Diplomatie im 18. Jahrhundert* [Revelations on the History of 18th-century Diplomacy]), and several thousand pages of manuscripts not yet printed at the time these editions were published. At present, a monumental edition called *Marx-Engels-Gesamtausgabe* (MEGA) has been started, again both in German and in Russian, by the same Institutes. It already encompasses many of the unpublished manuscripts referred to above, in the first place a previously unknown economic work which makes a bridge between the *Grundrisse* and vol. 1 of *Capital*, and which was written in the years 1861–3 (published under the title *Zur Kritik der Politischen Oekonomie – Contribution to a Critique of Political Economy 1861–1863* in MEGA II/3/1–6, Berlin Dietz Verlag, 1976–1982). Whether it will include all of Marx's and Engels's writings remains to be seen.

In English, key works by Marx and Engels have been systematically published by Progress Publishers, Moscow, and Lawrence & Wishart, London; but this undertaking is by no means an approximation of the *Marx-Engels-Werke* mentioned above. The quality of the translation is often poor. The translations of Marx's and Engels's writings published by Penguin Books in the *Marx Pelican Library* are quite superior to it. We therefore systematically refer to the latter edition whenever there is a choice. Marx's and Engels's books and pamphlets referred to in the present text are mostly in chronological order:

(Marx *a*) *Die Deutsche Ideologie* (1846), together with Friedrich Engels.
(Marx *b*) *Manifest der Kommunistischen Partei* (1848), written in collaboration with Friedrich Engels. In English: *Manifesto of the Communist Party*, in *Marx: The Revolutions of 1848*, Harmondsworth: Penguin Books, 1973.
(Marx *c*) *Zur Kritik der Politischen Oekonomie* (1858). In English: *Contribution to the Critique of Political Economy*, London: Lawrence & Wishart, 1970.
(Marx *d*) *Grundrisse der Kritik der Politischen Oekonomie* (written in 1858–1859, first published in 1939). English edition: *Foundations of a Critique of Political Economy*, Harmondsworth: Penguin Books, 1972.
(Marx *e*): *Das Kapital, Band I* (1867). In English: *Capital*, Vol. I, Harmondsworth: Penguin Books, 1976.
(Marx *f*) *Das Kapital, Band II*, published by Engels in 1885. In English: *Capital*, Vol. II, Harmondsworth: Penguin Books, 1978.

(Marx *g*) *Das Kapital, Band III*, published by Engels in 1894. In English: *Capital*, Vol. III, Harmondsworth: Penguin Books, 1981.
(Marx *h*) *Theorien über den Mehrwert*, published by Karl Kautsky 1905–10. In English: *Theories of Surplus Value*, Moscow: Progress Publishers, 1963.
(Marx *i*) *Lohn, Preis und Profit*, written in 1865. In English: *Wages, Price and Profits*, in *Marx-Engels Selected Works*, Vol. II, Moscow: Progress Publishers, 1969.
(Marx *j*) *Kritik des Gothaer Programms*, written in 1878 in collaboration with Engels. In English: *Critique of the Gotha Programme*, in *Marx-Engels: The First International and After*, Harmondsworth: Penguin Books, 1974.
(Marx *k*) *Resultate des unmittelbaren Produktionsprozesses* (unpublished section VII of Vol. I of *Capital*), first published in 1933. In English: *Results of the Immediate Process of Production, Appendix to Capital*, Vol. I, Harmondsworth: Penguin Books, 1976.
(Marx *l*) *Marx-Engels: Briefwechsel (Letters)*. There is no complete English edition of the letters. Some are included in the *Selected Works* in 3 vols, published by Progress Publishers, Moscow.
(Engels): *Anti-Dühring* (1878). The chapter on economy was written by Marx, who also read all the other parts and collaborated in their final draft. In English: *Anti-Dühring*, London: Lawrence & Wishart, 1955.

ERNEST MANDEL

Bibliography

There are innumerable books and articles devoted to comments or elaborations on Marx's economic thought, or which criticize them. We list here those works we refer to in the above text, as well as those we consider the most important ones (based, needless to say, upon subjective judgement).

Baran, P.A. 1957. *The Political Economy of Growth*. London: John Calder.
Baran, P.A. and Sweezy, P.M. 1966. *Monopoly Capital*. New York and London: Monthly Review Press.
Böhm-Bawerk, E. von. 1896. *Zum Abschluss des Marxschen Systems*. English edn, *Karl Marx and the Close of this System*, including a reply by Rudolf Hilferding, *Böhm-Bawerk's Criticism of Karl Marx*, ed. P.M. Sweezy, New York: Augustus M. Kelley, 1949.
Bortkiewicz, L. von. 1907. *Zur Berichtigung der grundlegenden theoretischen Konstruktion von Marx im Dritten Band des 'Kapital'*. Trans. by P.M. Sweezy as 'On the Correction of Marx's Fundamental Theoretical Construction in the third volume of *Capital*'. In Böhm-Bawerk (1949), 197–221.
Braverman, H. 1974. *Labor and Monopoly Capital: the degradation of work in the twentieth century*. New York and London: Monthly Review Press.
Bronfenbrenner, M. 1970. *The Vicissitudes of Marxian Economics*. London.

Bukharin, N. 1914. *Imperialism and World Economy.* English trans., London: M. Lawrence, 1915.

Bukharin, N. 1926. *Imperialism and the Accumulation of Capital.* Trans. by R. Wichmann, ed. K.J. Tarbuck, London: Allen Lane, 1972.

Dobb, M. 1937. *Political Economy and Capitalism: some essays in economic tradition.* London: G. Routledge & Sons. Reprinted Westport, Conn.: Greenwood Press, 1972.

Emmanuel, A. 1969. *L'échange inégal. Essai sur les antagonismes dans les rapports économiques internationaux.* Paris: François Maspero. Trans. by B. Pearce as *Unequal Exchange: a study of the imperialism of trade,* London: New Left Books, 1972.

Grossman, H. 1929. *Das Akkumulations- und Zusammenbruchsgesetz des kapitalistischen Systems.* Leipzig: C.L. Hirschfeld.

Hayek, F.A. von. 1944. *The Road to Serfdom.* Chicago: University of Chicago Press: London: G. Routledge & Sons.

Hilferding, R. 1910. *Das Finanzkapital.* Vienna: Wiener Volksbuchhandlung. Trans. by M. Watnick and S. Gordon, ed. T. Bottomore as *Finance Capital,* London: Routledge & Kegan Paul, 1981.

Itoh, M. 1980. *Value and Crisis: Essays on Marxian Economics in Japan.* London: Pluto.

Kolakowski, L. 1976–8. *Main Currents of Marxism: its rise, growth and dissolution,* 3 vols. Trans. P.S. Falla, Oxford: Clarendon Press, 1978.

Lange, O. 1963. *Political Economy,* 2 vols. Trans., ed. P.F. Knightsfield, Oxford: Pergamon Press; Warsaw: PWN – Polish Scientific Publishers.

Lange, O. and Taylor, F.M. 1938. *On the Economic Theory of Socialism.* 2 vols, Minneapolis: University of Minnesota Press.

Lenin, V.I. 1917. *Imperialism, Last Stage of Capitalism.* Petrograd. English trans., *Imperialism, the Highest Stage of Capitalism,* Moscow: Foreign Languages Publishing House, 1947.

Leontief, W. 1938. The significance of Marxian economics for present-day economic theory. *American Economic Review,* Supplement, March. Reprinted in *Marx and Modern Economists,* ed. D. Horowitz, London: MacGibbon & Kee, 1968.

Luxemburg, R. 1913. *Akkumulation des Kapitals.* Trans. A. Schwarzschild, with an introduction by J. Robinson, as *The Accumulation of Capital,* London: Routledge & Kegan Paul, 1951.

Mandel, E. 1962. *Traité d'économie marxiste.* Paris: R. Juillard. Trans. B. Pearce as *Marxist Economic Theory,* 2 vols, London: Merlin Press, 1968.

Mandel, E. 1972. *Der Spätkapitalismus.* Frankfurt am Main: Suhrkampf. Trans. J. De Bres as *Late Capitalism,* London: New Left Books. Revised edn, 1975.

Mandel, E. 1980. *Long Waves of Capitalist Development: the Marxist interpretation.* Cambridge: Cambridge University Press.

Mandel, E. and Freeman, A., eds. 1984. *Ricardo, Marx, Sraffa.* London: Verso.

Mattick, P. 1969. *Marx and Keynes: the limits of the Mixed Economy.* Boston: P. Sargent.

Mises, L. von. 1920. Die Wirtschaftsrechnung im sozialistischen Gemeinwesen. Trans. S. Adler as 'Economic calculations in the socialist commonwealth', in *Collectivist Economic Planning,* ed. F.A. von Hayek, London: G. Routledge & Sons, 1935.

Morishima, M. 1973. *Marx's Economics: A Dual Theory of Value and Growth.* Cambridge: Cambridge University Press.

Nutzinger, H.G. and Wolfstetter, E., eds. 1974. *Die Marx'sche Theorie und ihre Kritik.* 2 vols, Frankfurt am Main: Campus.

Pareto, V. 1966. *Marxisme et économie pure.* Geneva: Droz.

Popper, K. 1945. *The Open Society and its Enemies.* 2 vols, London: G. Routledge & Sons.

Robinson, J. 1942. *An Essay on Marxian Economics.* London: Macmillan. 2nd edn, 1966.

Rosdolsky, R. 1968. *Entstehungsgeschichte des Marxschen 'Kapital'.* Frankfurt am Main: Europäische Verlagsanstalt. Trans. P. Burgess as *The Making of Marx's Capital,* London: Pluto Press, 1977.

Rubin, I.I. 1928. *Essays on Marx's Theory of Value.* Moscow. English trans., Detroit: Black and Red, 1972.

Schumpeter, J. 1942. *Capitalism, Socialism and Democracy.* New York and London: Harper & Brothers.

Sraffa, D. 1960. *Production of Commodities by Means of Commodities.* Cambridge: Cambridge University Press.

Steedman, I. 1977. *Marx after Sraffa.* London: New Left Books.

Sternberg, F. 1926. *Der Imperialismus.* Berlin: Malik-Verlag.

Sweezy, P.M. 1942. *The Theory of Capitalist Development.* New York: Monthly Review Press.

Tugan-Baranowsky, M. von. 1905. *Theoretische Grundlagen der Marxismus* Leipzig: Duncker & Humblot.

Wygodsky, S. *Der gegenwärtige Kapitalismus.* Trans. by C.S.V. Salt as *The Story of a Great Discovery: How Karl Marx wrote 'Capital',* Tunbridge Wells: Abacus Press, 1972.

Bibliographic addendum

While diminished since the 1980s, Karl Marx's influence throughout the social sciences is still significant. Even the relatively recent literature on his life and thought is overwhelming. Valuable explications of Marxian economics include:

Foley, D. 1986. *Understanding Capital: Marx's Economic Theory.* Cambridge, MA: Harvard University Press.

Roemer, J. 1981. *Analytical Foundations of Marxian Economic Theory.* Cambridge: Cambridge University Press.

Roemer, J. 1988. *Free to Lose: An Introduction to Marxist Economic Philosophy.* London: Radius.

Outside of economics, important studies include:

Buchanan, A. 1982. *Marx and Justice.* Totowa, NJ: Rowan and Allanhead.

Carver, T. 1998. *The Post-Modern Marx.* Manchester: Manchester University Press.

Cohen, G.A. 1988. *History, Labour, and Freedom: Themes from Marx*. Oxford: Oxford University Press.

Cohen, G.A. 2000. *Karl Marx's Theory of History: A Defence*. 2nd edn. Oxford: Clarendon Press.

Elster, J. 1985. *Making Sense of Marx*. Cambridge: Cambridge University Press.

Kain, P. 1989. *Marx and Ethics*. Oxford: Oxford University Press.

Roemer, J., ed. 1986. *Analytical Marxism*. Cambridge: Cambridge University Press.

Rockmore, T. 2002. *Marx After Marxism*. Oxford: Basil Blackwell.

Van den Berg, A. 1989. *The Immanent Utopia: From Marxism on the State to the State of Marxism*. Princeton: Princeton University Press.

Wolff, J. 2002. *Why Read Marx Today?* Oxford: Oxford University Press.

Wood, A. 2004. *Karl Marx*. 2nd edn. London: Routledge.

All of these are complemented by what remains a classic short introduction to Marx's ideas:

Berlin, I. 1985. *Karl Marx*. 4th edn. Oxford: Oxford University Press.

as well as the standard biography of Marx:

McLellan, D. 1996. *Karl Marx: A Biography*. 3rd revised edn. London: Palgrave Macmillan.

Finally,

Bottomore, T., ed. 1983. *A Dictionary of Marxist Thought*. Cambridge, MA: Harvard University Press.

is helpful both as a survey and as a mechanism for overcoming language differences between Marxist approaches and others.

Marxian transformation problem

Marx's framework: value, surplus-value, prices and competition

Marx consistently distinguishes the notions of *value* and *price*, in contrast to contemporary economic language, which uses the term 'value' to refer to prices in a situation of general equilibrium, though the use of the term is rather flexible; for example 'value added' is actually the value of net product measured in price terms. For Marx, value is a 'social substance' manifested in economic relations in the 'form' of prices, though prices are not necessarily proportional to values, as we will see.

Value and surplus-value

We first recall Marx's basic concepts (see also MARX'S ANALYSIS OF CAPITALIST PRODUCTION). Central to Marx's framework of analysis in *Capital* is the *labour theory of value* (LTV), which defines the value of a commodity as the 'socially necessary' labour time required by its production, that is, the labour time required by average available techniques of production for workers of average skill.

The LTV is central to Marx's theory of exploitation, a term he uses to describe a situation in which one individual or group lives on the product of the labour of others. According to the LTV, when commodities are exchanged through sale and purchase, no value is created. But this principle does not apply to capitalists' purchase of the *labour power* of workers. Workers sell their labour power, that is, their capability to work, to a firm, owned by a capitalist. The buyer uses this labour power in production to add value to the commodity produced. The *value of labour power* is the labour time required by the production of the commodities the worker buys. But the worker can typically work more hours than are on average required to produce this bundle of commodities. For example, the goods the worker can buy may require eight hours of labour per day, when the labour-day lasts 12 hours. The difference, four hours, is unpaid labour time. If an hour of social labour on average produces a value whose price form is $10, four hours of unpaid labour time results in a surplus-value whose price form is $40, which is appropriated by the capitalist. The *rate of surplus-value* is the ratio of unpaid to paid labour time, in this case 4/8, that is, 50 per cent.

Two laws of exchange

Marx situates his discussion in the context of the distinction made by Adam Smith and David Ricardo between 'market prices' and 'natural prices'. Market prices are the prices at which commodities actually exchange from day to day in the market. Smith and Ricardo, however, regarded market prices as fluctuating (or 'gravitating') around centres of attraction they called 'natural prices'. ('Gravitation' means that the economy is in a permanent situation of disequilibrium, though in a vicinity of equilibrium where natural prices would prevail.)

In the above analysis, Marx assumes that commodities tend to exchange at their values (at *prices proportional to values*), that is, in proportion to the labour time embodied in them. 'Tend' means here that deviations are obviously possible, but that such prices will 'regulate' the market, in the sense that if the prevailing set of prices systematically under-compensates the labour used in the production of a commodity, labour will move to the production of better-paid commodities. As a result, the supply of the under-compensated commodity will decline, and its price will rise. In reality prices would gravitate around values, which would play the role of natural prices in such an economy. This is the *commodity law of exchange*.

In a capitalist economy, however, capitalists buy not only the labour power of workers (which Marx denotes as *variable capital*), but also non-labour inputs, such as raw materials, and fixed capital, such as machinery (which Marx denotes as *constant capital*). If natural prices were proportional to labour inputs, as the commodity law of exchange posits, capitalists using more constant capital per worker than the average would realize smaller profit in comparison to their total capital advanced, that is, lower profit rates. Marx accepts the idea that competition tends to equalize profit rates in various industries, despite differences in capital advanced per worker, which is the *capitalist law of exchange*. Marx uses the term 'prices of production' to describe a system of prices which guarantee to the capitalists of various industries a uniform profit rate. Capitalists will invest more where profit rates are larger, and conversely in the symmetrical case. They move their capital from one industry to another seeking maximum profit rates, and this movement results in a gravitation of market prices around prices of production. Marx regards prices of production as the centres of gravitation of market prices, and thus the natural prices relevant to a competitive capitalist economy.

Is the theory of surplus-value compatible with the theory of competition?

The problem is posed of the compatibility of the capitalist law of exchange at prices of production with the theory of exploitation as extraction of surplus-value. Marx's line of argument is that surplus-value is *created* in production through the exploitation of labour, that is, in proportion to labour expended, but *realized* proportionally to total capital invested. According to Marx, this separation between the locus of extraction and the locus of realization does not contradict the theory of exploitation so that capitalist competition is compatible with his theory of exploitation through the appropriation of surplus-value from unpaid labour time.

To support this argument, Marx presents a pair of tables (1981, ch. 9) showing the redistribution of surplus-value through deviations of price from values proportional to embodied labour times. All variables are measured in hours of labour time, and as a result prices of production are expressed in the same unit. Because Marx's own calculations involve some extraneous

complexity (differential turnover rates among sectors), it is more useful to consider the simplified case shown in Table 1. Two industries exist, each of which advances the same capital of 100, but divided in different proportions between the purchase of non-labour inputs (C) and labour inputs (V). All capital is used up during the period, so that the rate of profit is the ratio of surplus-value to total capital advanced, $r = s/(c+v)$. The rate of surplus-value is uniform and equal to 100 per cent. Consequently, surplus-values are equal to variable capitals. Surplus-values and values are computed in each industry. When prices are proportional to values, profit rates differ between the two sectors. Prices of production are determined in Marx's procedure by summing up all surplus-value, a total of 40, and redistributing it in proportion to total capital, that is 20 in each industry, to equalize profit rates on the capitals advanced.

The procedure illustrates a straightforward 'redistribution' of surplus-value. Clearly, the sum of prices, 240, is equal to the sum of values, and total surplus-value is, by construction, conserved in the form of profit. These observations are expressed in two *Marxian equations* concerning the entire economy:

Sum of values = sum of prices of production

Sum of surplus − value = sum of profits

Note that these compact formulations are not rigorous, since values and surplus-value are measured in labour time and prices and profits in money. Thus, 'Sum of values' should read 'Sum of prices proportional to values'. A simple way out of the problem of units is to use one of these equations to define the general level of prices. For example, the sum of prices of production could be set equal to the number of hours corresponding to the sum of values. Then, Marx's line of argument implies that the surpluses in both sets of prices are equal, as in the second equation. This simple calculation illustrates the idea that profits are 'forms' of surplus-value, that is, unpaid labour.

Approximations

Marx is, however, aware that the type of computation illustrated in Table 1 is not satisfactory, since the evaluations of constant and variable capital have not been modified despite the fact that prices have changed.

Table 1   *Marx's calculation of prices of production from values*

Industry	Constant capitals, C	Variable capitals, V	Total capitals, K=C+V	Surplus-values, S=V	Values of commodities produced, $\Lambda = K+S$	Profits, Π	'Prices of production' of commodities produced, $P = K+1\Pi$
1	70	30	100	30	130	20	120
2	90	10	100	10	110	20	120
Total economy	160	40	200	40	240	40	240

First, when natural prices are prices of production, non-labour inputs are purchased on the market at prices of production, not at prices proportional to values. It is, therefore, not correct to conserve the evaluation of constant capital:

> We had originally assumed that the cost-price of a commodity equalled the value of the commodities consumed in its production. But for the buyer the price of production of a specific commodity is its cost-price, and may thus pass as cost-price into the prices of other commodities. Since the price of production may differ from the value of a commodity, it follows that the cost-price of a commodity containing this price of production of another commodity may also stand above or below that portion of its total value derived from the value of the means of production consumed by it. It is necessary to remember this modified significance of the cost-price, and to bear in mind that there is always the possibility of an error if the cost-price of a commodity in any particular sphere is identified with the value of the means of production consumed by it. Our present analysis does not necessitate a closer examination of this point. (Marx, 1981, ch. 9)

Second, there is a similar problem concerning variable capital. When commodities exchange at prices of production, workers will not be able to buy the same bundle of commodities with a wage corresponding to a purchasing power expressed, as in Marx's calculation, as a certain number of hours of labour time, as when prices are proportional to values. Marx is also aware of this problem:

> [...] the average daily wage is indeed always equal to the value produced in the number of hours the labourer must work to produce the necessities of life. But this number of hours is in its turn obscured by the deviation of the prices of production of the necessities of life from their values. However, this always resolves itself to one commodity receiving too little of the surplus-value while another receives too much, so that the deviations from the values which are embodied in the prices of production compensate one another. Under capitalist production, the general law acts as the prevailing tendency only in a very complicated and approximate manner, as a never ascertainable average of ceaseless fluctuations. (Marx, 1981, ch. 9)

It is not easy to understand Marx's position from these notes (which he never revised for publication). It does seem that the analysis requires a 'closer analysis', since the revaluation of constant capital at prices of production will in general make the sum of prices of production deviate from the sum of values, or make the sum of profits deviate from the sum of surplus-values. While it is true that a redistribution of surplus-value through a system of prices of production does not alter the living labour expended in production, so that over the whole economy the deviations from value 'compensate one another', the value of labour power will remain constant only if workers consume commodities in the same proportion as they are produced in the whole economy, which is implausible. The phrase 'average of ceaseless fluctuations' suggests the averaging out of market prices to prices of production rather than the averaging of surplus-value across sectors.

If Marx's use of the term 'approximately' is taken literally, it would appear that the LTV and the theory of exploitation he introduced in Volume 1 of *Capital* are only 'approximately' true! Although Marx is conscious of the problem, it is impossible to consider his solution as rigorous. In the formulation of the two equations above, it appears that, when the calculation is done rigorously as in the formal setting below, the second equation *does not hold*! Later critics have judged this a devastating refutation of Marx's theories of value and exploitation, which in turn has led to ongoing controversy.

Earlier approaches

The foundations of the transformation problem can be found in the first analyses of competition and prices in capitalism, beginning with Adam Smith and David Ricardo, on which Marx elaborated. The distinction between values and prices remains somewhat fuzzy in these authors. Smith fails to establish a clear relationship between value and profit rate equalization as the principle determining 'natural prices'. Thus, one characteristic feature of these approaches, from which Marx was unable to depart completely, is that two sets of prices (the two laws of exchange above) are considered, one proportional to values (embodied labour times), and the other equalizing profit rates (a *dual system*), when only one price system prevails in real-world capitalism (a *single system*):

1. A system of prices proportional to values (embodied labour times) plays a role in the analyses of Smith, Ricardo and Marx. Only Marx, however, clearly distinguishes the two systems from the start.
2. The determination of the 'surplus', when such a concept exists (as in Ricardo and Marx), is posed in the first system and imported into the second, instead of being analysed directly within the second system.

This dual system approach lies at the basis of the phrase 'transformation problem', which refers to the transformation from one system into the other.

Adam Smith

Smith's point of departure is an 'early, rude' state of society, before the establishment of private property in land and means of production. There, Smith contends, products of human labour will exchange in proportion to the labour time required to produce them. Smith offers as an example that, if it requires two days on average to kill a beaver, but one day to kill a deer, a beaver will tend to exchange for two deer. Smith's argument supporting this conclusion rests on the assumption that any hunter can choose to allocate time to hunting deer or beaver, so that, if the exchange ratio were higher or lower than the labour time ratio, hunters would shift from the under- to the over-remunerated productive activity, and force the exchange ratio back toward the labour time ratio. The viewpoint is clearly that of the commodity law of exchange.

Smith applies the same type of reasoning to argue that, once means of production have become private property (which he calls 'stock', and later economists called 'capital'), the ability of owners to shift their capital from one line of production to another will tend to equalize the profit rate across different sectors of production. The viewpoint is now that of the capitalist law of exchange.

David Ricardo

Ricardo critiques and corrects Smith's analysis. Ricardo originally based his theories of prices and distribution on Smith's first principle that the labour expended in producing a commodity determines its price in exchange. But Ricardo, elaborating on the dual system approach, examines the necessary quantitative difference between the two principles that might determine natural prices more carefully than Smith. Ricardo understood that the proportion between capitals invested in non-labour inputs and labour is not uniform across industries, and that this fact implies a discrepancy between the two sets of prices, but he regarded these deviations as quantitatively limited. Prefiguring Marx's investigation, Ricardo was concerned to work out the properties of the first system (values) to derive conclusions concerning distribution, which he supposed were also valid in the second system (prices of production).

First, when natural prices are proportional to values (embodied labour times), it is obvious that there is a trade-off between the shares of output which respectively go to workers and capitalists: workers create all the value added to inputs, and buy a share of output whose production requires less labour time than they expend. In contrast to Smith, Ricardo had a clear view of this mechanism. This division of total output between workers and capitalists was crucial to his analysis, because of its implications in terms of economic policy. (For example, Ricardo was in favour of a low price of corn, which, in his opinion, would increase the profits of capitalists by lowering wages – and encourage capital accumulation.)

Second, Ricardo would have liked to conserve the straightforward distributional properties he derived from the assumption of prices proportional to values, even while acknowledging the quantitative difference between such natural prices proportional to values and natural prices that would equalize profit rates across industries. But Ricardo understood that, in the profit rate-equalizing system, the natural prices of commodities may change with a change in the real wage (due to the distinct compositions of capital) even if the labour required in production remains unaltered, contrary to what happens in the first system, where values remain unchanged with a change in the wage. Thus, with Ricardo's analysis, we are getting closer to Marx's framework and problems.

The rebellious classical legacy in Marx

Marx adopted key elements from Smith and Ricardo's works: (a) a dual system approach to natural prices in capitalism (beginning, with Smith, as if labour was the unique input); (b) Ricardo's analysis of distribution as a 'trade-off' between wages and profit; and (c) Smith's analysis of competition that Ricardo had also adopted.

The two classical economists were the mainstream when Marx started his study of economics. Marx seized this opportunity to establish his theory of exploitation, in which surplus-value arises from unpaid labour time, on 'mainstream' grounds. Then he devoted hundreds of pages (in the manuscripts known as *The Theories of Surplus-value*) to the inability of these 'bourgeois' economists to establish a theory of exploitation, although Ricardo came close. This very smart political move on Marx's part eventually forced mainstream economic theory to abandon these 'dangerous' implications of the LTV.

The transformation controversy

A large literature is devoted to the transformation problem, starting with the critical contributions of Eugen Böhm-Bawerk (1890) and Ladislaus von Bortkiewicz (1952) in the late 19th and early 20th centuries. This literature has led to considerable formal advance, though it has failed to resolve the basic controversy over which of Marx's conclusions, if any, are logically valid.

There are fundamentally two points raised by these critiques. First, the critics claim that the value system is useless as a preliminary to the calculation of prices of production. Paul Samuelson puts this point in the following manner: 'Contemplate two alternative and discordant systems. Write down one. Now transform by taking an eraser and rubbing it out. Then fill in the other one. *Voilá!* You have completed your transformation algorithm' (1971, p. 400). This point is, however, not really relevant, since Marx's objective was not to show that it is impossible to compute prices of production if values have not been previously determined, but rather to show that the theory of exploitation is consistent with the principle of capitalist competition.

Second, the main focus of this critique is the incompatibility of the two Marxian equations. This literature calculates surplus-value by deducting the value of a given bundle of worker's consumption from the worker's labour time. Profits, on the other hand, are calculated by deducting the price of this same bundle at prices of production from the value added (in prices).

When prices of production are not proportional to values, these two quantities are not equal, violating the second Marxian equation. This treatment of the wage of workers, which allocates their purchasing power to particular commodities, departs from Marx's apparent stipulation in his discussion of the transformation problem of the rate of surplus-value.

In face of this quantitative inequality between surplus-value and profit, the Fundamental Marxian Theorem (see Morishima, 1973) argues that the LTV does provide a qualitative foundation for Marx's theory of exploitation, since the rate of profit will be positive if and only if the rate of surplus-value is positive. This interesting observation, however, falls short of fulfilling Marx's ambition to found his theory of exploitation on the LTV through the two Marxian equations.

A crucial moment in the criticism of Marx's transformation was the publication of Piero Sraffa (1960). This book is simultaneously a critique of Marx and of neo-classical economics, but it is, above all, a bold attempt to elaborate Ricardo's analysis. It is the origin of the neo-Ricardian school, represented by, in particular, Ian Steedman (1977) and Pierangelo Garegnani (1984). The central point, in the neo-Ricardian School, is that the LTV is useless, with respect to both the determination of prices of production and exploitation. The dual-system approach of Ricardo is abandoned in favour of the price of production system, as the reference to value is deemed irrelevant. Sraffa calculates prices of production directly from a description of technology and distribution. In this framework, he shows that Ricardo's trade-off between wages and the profit rate can be derived formally as a downward sloping relation (see the mathematical section below).

The price of net product-unallocated purchasing power labour theory of value (PNP-UPP LTV) approach to exploitation

In the late 1970s, Gérard Duménil (1980; 1983; 1984) and Duncan Foley (1982) (independently) proposed new lines of interpretation of Marx's theory of value. In doing so, they followed distinct routes, but the basic principles underlying these reformulations converge to the same basic framework. This interpretation is inappropriately referred to, in the literature, as the 'New Interpretation'. It is more precise to describe it as the 'price of net product-unallocated purchasing power labour theory of value' (PNP-UPP LTV). It was rapidly adopted by Alain Lipietz (1982).

Value and exploitation in the PNP-UPP LTV approach
Beginning with Marx's two equations, as is traditional, there are two basic principles to this interpretation. First, Marx's equation concerning the 'sum of values' and 'sum of prices' holds for the net product of the period. 'Net product' means here, as in Marx's reproduction schemes and national accounting frameworks, output minus non-labour inputs inherited from the previous period.

The important idea here is that it is the expenditure of living labour that creates value. Marx regards the value of a commodity as equal to the value transferred by the inputs consumed and the new value created by labour during the period. But the two perspectives are equivalent:

Value transferred from inputs
  + value created by new labour
    = value of output
Value created by new labour
  = value of output
    − value transferred from inputs

The price form of the value created by the total productive labour expended during a period of time is the price of the net product of the period. (As is well known, the price of this net product is equal to total income, wages plus profits.) The PNP-UPP LTV interpretation argues that, when Marx (in the first quotation above) points to the fact that the cost-prices of commodities used as inputs to production must be adjusted to reflect the change to prices of production, the correct formulation would have been to exclude them from the first Marxian equation, which would then read 'Sum of values of net product = sum of price of net product'. Since values are expressed in labour time, while prices of production are expressed in terms of money, this equation implicitly defines an equivalence between value-creating labour time and money, the *monetary expression of value or labour time* (MELT), which is the ratio of the price of net product (value added measured in money) to the productive labour time expended. If, for example, 250 billion hours of productive labour were expended in an economy to produce a net product worth $10 trillion, the monetary expression of labour time would be $40 per hour. The MELT expresses quantitatively (as a ratio of the price of the net product to the living labour expended) what Marx calls the 'price form' of the total value created during the period.

Second, the PNP-UPP LTV views the term 'surplus-value' in the second Marxian equation as referring to the monetary equivalent of unpaid labour time. The wage, as in Marx's calculation, is regarded as unallocated purchasing power giving workers the potential to buy a fraction of the net product. (This is the way capitalists look at wage payments, since the individual capitalist has no interest in how workers actually spend their wages.) Individual workers can allocate this purchasing power among the commodities they jointly produced (or even save some of it), in whatever proportions they choose. This can be described as the unallocated purchasing power (UPP) approach to exploitation. With this definition of surplus-value, the Marxian second equation immediately holds as an identity. The PNP-UPP LTV holds the rate of surplus-value rather than the consumption bundle of workers constant.

There is a sharp contrast between the PNP-UPP LTV and the traditional interpretation in the way they conceptualize distribution. Following Marx's procedure in his calculation, represented in the simplified example introduced earlier, it is impossible to assume that workers can buy the same bundle of commodities before and after the redistribution of surplus-value, since the purchasing power they receive will be spent at different prices. Consequently, the wage must be changed to keep the bundle of workers' consumption unchanged (and the rate of surplus-value must be altered – hence the controversy). The UPP approach to exploitation conserves the rate of exploitation, or, more rigorously, measures the value of labour power as the value whose price form is the price of the commodities workers can buy: an unallocated purchasing power on any commodities. The rate of surplus-value, as in Marx's calculation, is unchanged.

A single-system approach and exploitation in any set of prices

A key aspect of the PNP-UPP LTV interpretation is that value is present in the theory of exploitation, as a social substance extracted in one place in the economy (firm, industry), and realized in another. But there is no logical anteriority in the value system, compared to the price system. This interpretation is a single-system approach to the LTV.

This property has important analytical consequences. There is only one economy, one system, not two. There is no 'underlying', hidden economy, which operates in 'values' where the distributional realities that structure the functioning of capitalism could be determined. The theory of exploitation is not dependent on the prevalence of any particular set of prices. The consideration of prices of production is not central to Marx's argument concerning exploitation, only an example that illustrates a much more general conclusion. Prices of production are just *one case* in which such a demonstration must be made, which Marx focused on because of the importance of this particular set of prices in competitive capitalism, as centres of gravitation of market prices.

The specific property expressed in the equality of the profit rate among industries cannot play any role in the theory of exploitation. Prices may deviate from prices of production because of gravitation; the amounts of surplus-value realized in each industry may also differ from what is implied by the prevalence of uniform profit rates because of the existence of non-reproducible resources and their rents; counteracting factors, such as monopoly, may also prevent equalization of profit rates. These deviations, inherent to capitalism, and also mentioned in Marx's analysis, do not invalidate his theory of value and exploitation.

An ongoing debate

The shift of perspective to single-system interpretations of Marx's labour theory of value has led to further debate in this vein. Fred Moseley (2003) proposes to apply the reasoning of the SS-LTV approach not just to variable capital, but to constant capital as well. Moseley argues for retaining the original form of the Marxian equations by defining the total value of a commodity as the labour-time equivalent of the price of constant capital plus the living labour expended in adding value. Moseley argues that Marx's comments in the quotations above are unnecessary because Marx's tables themselves express his underlying understanding of the labour theory of value.

Alan Freeman, Giugelmo Carchedi, Alan Kliman, and their co-authors (Freeman and Carchedi, 1996) have put forward a 'temporal single-system' (TSS) interpretation of the labour theory of value. This interpretation sets the transformation problem in a temporal context, defining the value of commodities as the sum of the labour time equivalent of constant capital (calculated using a monetary expression of labour time) and the living labour expended in the current period in production. By construction, this interpretation makes the first Marxian equation hold for the total product, while the second Marxian equation holds when the monetary expression of labour time is appropriately defined (as in the SS-LTV). It is, however, clear in Marx's analysis that the value of a commodity is not determined by the actual amount of labour its production required in the past, but by the labour time it requires under present prevailing conditions:

> ... the value of commodities is not determined by the labour-time originally expended in their production, but by the labour-time expended in their reproduction, and this decreases continually owing to the development of the social productivity of labour. On a higher level of social productivity, all available capital appears, for this reason, to be the result of a relatively short period of reproduction, instead of a long process of accumulation of capital. (Marx, 1981, ch. 24)

This evaluation at 'replacement costs', however, does not imply that the economy is necessarily in a stationary state as the TSS critique has claimed.

A mathematical setting

The use of numerical examples to work out the quantitative implications of theoretical ideas is now outdated. The most common framework in the contemporary literature on the transformation problem is a pure circulating-capital model with a single technique in each sector, in which basic properties of solutions and interpretations can be elegantly and compactly expressed. A single homogeneous labour input works with stocks of an arbitrary but finite number of produced commodities available at the beginning of a production period.

One unit of each commodity is produced by a single technique of production. This framework is consistent with the example in the first table above but not with Marx's tables since the circulating capital model does not include fixed capital, while Marx's examples do.

1. *Techniques of production.* The number of goods is n, also the number of techniques. A technique of production, indexed by j, is characterized by a column vector, $a_j = (a_{j1,\dots}, a_{ji,\dots}, a_{jn})$, and a scalar l_j, where a_{ji} is interpreted as the quantity of the commodity i required as inputs, and l_j as the quantity of labour required for the production of one unit of commodity j. A technology consisting of the set of all available techniques is described by collecting corresponding inputs into a matrix $\mathbf{A}$, and the labour input scalars into a row vector l'. A pattern of economic production is described by a vector of levels of operation of the techniques, $x = (x_1, \dots, x_j, \dots, x_n)$. The inputs required with this pattern of production can compactly be written in matrix notation as $\mathbf{A}x$, while the total labour required is $l'x$.

2. *The determination of values.* The value, λ_j, of commodity j is the sum of the direct labour, l_j, expended in its production, and the indirect labour contained in produced inputs required for its production, $\lambda_1 a_{j1} + \cdots + \lambda_n a_{jn} = \lambda' a_j$, that is $\lambda_j = \lambda' a_j + l_j$. The vector of values of commodities, λ', satisfies the equation: $\lambda' = \lambda'\mathbf{A} + l'$. It can be written as:

$$\lambda' = l'(\mathbf{I} - \mathbf{A})^{-1}$$

The value of the net product $y = (\mathbf{I} - \mathbf{A})x$, is equal to the total labour time expended: $\lambda'y = l'x$. It is the sum of variable capital (wages paid), and total surplus-value. We denote τ as the rate of surplus-value, and v, the value of one unit of labour power, or the share of wages in the net product. These two variables are linked by the relationship $v = 1/(1+\tau)$.

3. *The example of the table.* Each element in the table (upper-case notation) refers to industries, that is the product of unit variables (lower-case notation) by levels of operation (industries are marked by the subscript j, while vectors have no subscript). Below we will use the notation, P_j, for the price of the output of industry j, p_j for the price of one unit of commodity j, and p' for the vector of unit prices.

Constant capitals: $C_j = \lambda' a_j x_j$ and $C = \lambda'\mathbf{A}\,x$.
Variable capitals: $V_j = v\,l_j x_j$ and $V = v\,l'x$, with $v = 1/(1+\tau)$ or $\tau = (1-v)/v$.
Total capitals: $K_j = C_j + V_j$ and $K = C + V$.
Surplus-values: $S_j = \tau\,V_j = (1-v)\,l_j x_j$ and $S = \tau\,V = (1-v)\,l'x$.
Values of commodities: $\Lambda_j = K_j + S_j = (\lambda' a_j + l_j)\,x_j = \lambda_j x_j$ and $\Lambda = K + S = (\lambda'\mathbf{A} + l')\,x = \lambda'x$.

Marx determines the total surplus-value, S, and allocates it proportionally to total capital in each industry, so that the profit rates, r_j, in each industry is uniform: $r = S/K$

(or, equivalently, $1+r = \Lambda/K$). Profits in each industry are: $\Pi_j = r\,K_j$. By construction, total profits are equal to total surplus-value. The price of production of the total output of industry j is: $P_j = K_j + \Pi_j = (1+r)K_j$. For the price of one unit of commodity j, one has:

$$p_j = (1+r)(\lambda' a_j + vl_j) \text{ and } p' = (1+r)(\lambda'\mathbf{A} + vl').$$

As is obvious, the two equations Sum of values $(\Lambda = \lambda'x) = $ Sum of 'prices of production' $(P = p'x)$ and Sum of surplus-value $(S) = $ Sum of profits $(\Pi = r\,K)$ are satisfied.

4. *The determination of prices of production.* In the above calculation, Marx simply transfers the values of inputs to the price of production system instead of estimating them at their prices of production. Prices of production are a stationary price system (in which inputs have the same prices as outputs, as would be the case in a long-period equilibrium) at which profit rates in all sectors are equal to a given r, when the wage is paid at the beginning of the production period:

$$p' = (1+r)(p'\mathbf{A} + wl'), \quad \text{which implies}$$
$$p'[r, w] = w(1+r)l'(\mathbf{I} - (1+r)\mathbf{A})^{-1}.$$

The profit rate equalization conditions are n equations (one for each produced commodity) in $n+2$ variables, the n prices p', r, and w. Since the accounting units in which prices and the wage are expressed are arbitrary, it is possible without loss of generality to add one further equation normalizing prices, such as $p'N = 1$, where N is a nonnegative bundle of commodities chosen as numéraire for the price system, or, alternatively $w = 1$, which specifies the unit wage as the numéraire.

In the treatment of the transformation problem the most intuitive normalization is to express prices in labour time units. These prices are often called 'direct prices', and the general price level in this metric is determined by: $p'y = l'\,x$. The price of the net product $p'y$, evaluated at direct prices, is equal to the total labour time expended: $l'x$. This is equivalent to saying that the numéraire is the net product divided by the total number of hours expended: $N = y/l'x$. Using this numéraire one has:

$$p'[r] = \frac{l'x}{l'(\mathbf{I} - (1+r)\mathbf{A})^{-1}y}l'(\mathbf{I} - (1+r)\mathbf{A})^{-1}$$

Using this relationship and the expression of $p'[r,w]$ above, one can determine the negative relation between wages and the profit rate, à la Ricardo and Sraffa:

$$w = \frac{1}{1+r}\frac{l'x}{l'(\mathbf{I} - (1+r)\mathbf{A})^{-1}y}$$

When the profit rate is 0, we have $w = 1$, and $p' = l'(\mathbf{I} - \mathbf{A})^{-1} = \lambda'$: direct prices are equal to values.

5. *The historical transformation controversy.* The dual-system critique is based on comparing the aggregates (sum of values to sum of prices, and sum of surplus-values with sum of prices) under the assumption of a given real wage as a bundle, d, of commodities. Thus, the value of labour power and surplus-value are respectively: $v = \lambda' d$, and $S = (1-v)\,l'x$. Workers are assumed to buy the same commodities when prices of production prevail, so that $w = p'd$. Substituting $p'[r,w]$, as above, for p' in this expression, the profit rate is the solution of the following implicit equation:

$$(1+r)l(I - (1+r)A)^{-1}d = 1.$$

One can then calculate Π, which has no reason to be equal to S: in the general case, the second Marxian equation does not hold.

6. *The PNP-UPP LTV.* In the PNP-UPP LTV interpretation, in contrast, the same situation of distribution means the same rate of surplus-value. In general this means that workers will not be able to buy the same bundle of commodities at prices of production. The rate of surplus-values is: $\tau^P = \Pi / W$. If, in the two systems, the price of production of the net product is set equal to its value, of which it is the price form (or, equivalently, if the monetary expression of value is set to 1), that is $p'y = \lambda'y = l'x$, then the total price of profits is equal to the sum of surplus-value, of which it is the price form. Thus the two Marxian equations (the first interpreted in terms of the net product) hold.

DUNCAN FOLEY AND GÉRARD DUMÉNIL

See also **absolute and exchangeable value; classical production theories; competition, classical; labour theory of value; linear models; market price; Marxian value analysis; Marx's analysis of capitalist production; natural price; neo-Ricardian economics.**

Bibliography

Böhm-Bawerk, E. von. 1890. *Capital and Interest.* New York: Kelley and Millman, 1957.

Bortkiewicz, L. von. 1952. Value and price in the Marxian system. *International Economic Papers* 1952(2), 5–60.

Duménil, G. 1980. *De la valeur aux prix de production.* Paris: Economica.

Duménil, G. 1983. Beyond the transformation riddle: a labor theory of value. *Science and Society* 47, 427–50.

Duménil, G. 1984. The so-called 'transformation problem' revisited: a brief comment. *Journal of Economic Theory* 33, 340–8.

Duménil, G. and Lévy, D. 1984. The unifying formalism of domination: value, price, distribution and growth in joint production. *Zeitschrift für Nationalökonomie* 44, 349–71.

Foley, D.K. 1982. The value of money, the value of labor power, and the Marxian transformation problem. *Review of Radical Political Economics* 14(2), 37–47.

Foley, D.K. 2000. Recent developments in the labor theory of value. *Review of Radical Political Economy* 32(1), 1–39.

Freeman, A. and Carchedi, G., eds. 1996. *Marx and Non-equilibrium Economics.* Brookfield, Vermont: Edward Elgar.

Garegnani, P. 1984. Value and distribution in the classical economists and Marx. *Oxford Economic Papers* 26, 291–325.

Lipietz, A. 1982. The 'so-called transformation problem' revisited. *Journal of Economic Theory* 26, 59–88.

Marx, K. 1976; 1978; 1981. *Capital*, vols. 1, 2, and 3. New York: Random House.

Morishima, M. 1973. *Marx's Economics.* Cambridge: Cambridge University Press.

Moseley, F. 2003. Money and totality: Marx's logic in volume 1 of capital. In *The Constitution of Capital: Essays on Volume 1 of Capital*, eds. R. Bellofiore and N. Taylor. Basingstoke: Palgrave Macmillan.

Samuelson, P.A. 1971. Understanding the Marxian notion of exploitation: a summary of the so-called transformation problem between Marxian values and competitive prices. *Journal of Economic Literature* 9, 399–431.

Sraffa, P. 1960. *Production of Commodities by Means of Commodities: Prelude to a Critique of Economic Theory.* Cambridge: Cambridge University Press.

Steedman, I. 1977. *Marx after Sraffa.* London: New Left Books.

Marxian value analysis

For Marx, the labour theory of value was not a theory of price, but a method for measuring the exploitation of labour. The exploitation of labour, in turn, was important for explaining the production of a surplus in a capitalist economy. In a feudal economy, the emergence of a net product, surplus to the consumption of producers and to the inputs consumed in production, was palpable. For the serf reproduced himself on his family plot of land during part of the week, and then worked for the lord, doing demesne or corvée labour during the other part. There was a temporal and physical division between production for subsistence or reproduction, and production which generated an economic surplus and was appropriated by the lord. Under capitalism, with the division of labour, such a demarcation no longer existed. If capitalism is characterized by competitive markets, where each factor is paid its true 'value', and no one makes a windfall profit by cheating his partner in exchange, how could a surplus emerge? In what manner could a sequence of equal exchanges transform an initial set of inputs into a larger quantity of outputs, with the surplus being appropriated systematically by one class, the capitalists? Marx's project was to explain the origin of profits in a perfectly competitive model, where each factor, including labour, received its competitive price in exchange.

Marx thought he had discovered the answer to this apparent economic sleight of hand by tracing what happened to labour as it passed from the workers who expended it, to the products in which it became embodied, and eventually to the profits of capitalists who sold these commodities. In some of his writings, notably in *Capital*, Volume I, he simplified the argument by assuming that the prices of goods were equal to the amounts of labour they embodied. The embodied labour in a good is the amount of labour necessary to produce that good, and to reproduce all inputs used up in its production. (Assume the only non-produced input is labour.) In particular, this is true also for the good 'labour power'; the embodied labour in a week's labour supplied by a worker is the amount of labour necessary to produce the goods which that worker consumes to reproduce himself for work the following week. If all goods exchange at their embodied labour values (the simplifying assumption) then, in particular, the worker receives a wage in consumption commodities (say, corn) which is just necessary to reproduce himself (which includes the reproduction of the working-class family). The secret of accumulation, for Marx, lay in the discovery that the embodied labour value of one week's labour was, let us say, four days of labour. In four days of socially expended labour, given the existing technology and stock of capital, the consumption commodities necessary to reproduce the worker could be produced. Thus the worker was paid an amount of corn which required four days to produce, his wage for seven days' labour. The surplus labour of three days became embodied in commodities which were the rightful property of the capitalist who hired the worker. Why would the worker agree to such a deal? Because he had no access to the means of production necessary for producing his consumption goods on any better terms. Those means of production were owned by the capitalist class. (Although the simplifying assumption, that equilibrium prices are equal to or proportional to embodied labour values, is rarely true, Marx conjectured that the deviation of prices from labour values was not crucial to understanding the origin of profits. On this point he was correct. Much ink has been spent on the 'transformation problem', which tries to relate embodied labour values to equilibrium prices in general. As will be shown below, prices need not be proportional to embodied labour values for the theory of class and exploitation to be sensible. Hence the study of the transformation problem is a pointless detour.)

Imagine a corn economy, where there are two technologies for producing corn, a Farm and a Factory: – Farm: 3 days' labour produces 1 corn output – Factory: 1 days' labour + 1 corn (seed) produces 2 corn output. On the Farm, corn is produced from labour alone, perhaps by cultivating wild corn on marginal land. In the capital-intensive Factory technology, seed corn is used as capital. One unit of seed capital reproduces itself and produces one additional corn output with one day of labour. Suppose both techniques require one week for the corn to grow to maturity. Let there be 1000 agents, ten of whom each own 50 units of seed corn. The other 990 peasants own only their labour power. Suppose a person requires one corn per week to survive; his preferences are to consume that amount, and then to take leisure. Assume that if he owns a stock of seed corn, he is not willing to run it down: he must replenish the inputs which he uses up before consuming. What is an equilibrium for this economy, which is guaranteed to reproduce the stocks with which it begins?

Since there are only 500 bushels of seed corn, the required consumption of 1000 corn cannot be reproduced using only the Factory technology, since the seed capital of 500 must be replaced. Capital is scarce relative to the labour which is available for it to employ. The wage which the 'capitalists', who own the seed corn, will offer at equilibrium to those whom they employ will therefore be bid down to the wage which peasants can earn in the marginal Farm technology: 1/3 corn per day labour. At any higher wage, all peasants will wish to sell their labour to the capitalists, and there is insufficient capital to employ them all. (It is assumed peasants have no preference for life on the Farm over life in the Factory. All they care about is rate at which they can exchange labour for corn.) At the wage of 1/3 corn per day, 500/3 peasants become workers in the Factory, each working for three days, planting three units of seed corn, and earning a wage of one corn. This exhausts the capital stock. The remaining peasants stay on the Farm, and also earn one corn with three days' labour. The ten capitalists each work zero days; altogether, they make a profit of $(500 - 500/3) = 333.3$ corn, after paying wages and replenishing their seed stock.

In the Factory technology, the embodied labour value of one corn is one day's labour; that amount of labour produces one corn output and reproduces the seed capital used. But the worker, at equilibrium, must work three days to earn one corn. This is so because he does not own the capital stock required for operating the efficient Factory method. His alternative is to eke out a subsistence of one corn by doing three days' labour on the Farm. The worker is said to be *exploited* if the labour embodied in the wage goods he is paid is less than the labour he expends in production. This is the case here, and it is evidently what makes possible the production of a surplus, in an economy where all agents wish only to work long enough to reproduce themselves (and their capital stock). Note this last statement characterizes, as well, the capitalists: in this story, they get 333 corn profits and expend no labour, a result consistent with their having subsistence preferences, where each desires to work only so long as he must to consume his one corn per week.

Contrast this capitalist economy, where three classes have emerged – capitalists, workers, and peasants – to the following subsistence, peasant economy. Everything is the same as above, except the initial distribution of corn: let each of the 1000 persons own initially 0.5 corn. At equilibrium, each agent will work two days and consume one corn. First, he uses the Factory to turn his 0.5 seed corn into 0.5 corn net output, which costs him 0.5 days of labour; then he must produce another 0.5 corn for consumption, for which he turns to the Farm, where he works for 1.5 days. Each agent consumes one corn with two days' labour, an egalitarian society, which is classless. (There are other ways of arranging the equilibrium in this economy, in which one group of agents hires another group to work up its capital stock, while they, in turn, work on the Farm. But the final allocation of corn and labour is the same as in the equilibrium just described.) There is a fine point here: perhaps one should say, in both economies, that the amount of labour socially embodied in one corn is two days (not one, as written above), for that is what is required to produce society's necessary corn consumption given the capital stock and available techniques. This will not change the verdict that the workers in the capitalist economy are exploited, while no one is exploited in the egalitarian society.

Contrast these two economies, which differ only in the initial distribution of the capital stock. Inequality in the distribution of the means of production gives rise to: (1) the production of a surplus above subsistence needs, or accumulation; (2) exploitation, in the sense that some agents expend more labour than is embodied in the goods they consume and others expend less labour than is embodied in what the consume; and (3) classes of agents, some of whom hire labour, some of whom sell labour, and some of whom work for themselves. The exploitation of labour emerges with the unequal ownership of capital, or the 'separation' of workers from the means of production. The existence of an industrial reserve army (here, the peasantry) who have access to an inferior technology to reproduce themselves explains the equilibration of the wage at a level below that which exhausts the product of labour in the capitalist sector. Moreover, exploitation may be an indicator of an injustice of capitalism. If it does not seem fair that a serf must work three days a week for the lord perhaps it is not fair either that a wage labourer must expend more labour than is embodied in the wage goods he receives. That verdict, however, is not obvious and requires further analysis. Although the story can be made complicated, these simple models demonstrate the main features of the Marxian theory of labour exploitation.

Class, exploitation and wealth

Consider an economy of N agents, with n produced commodities and labour. The input–output matrix which specifies the linear technology is A, and the row vector of direct labour inputs needed to operate the technology is L. Agent i has an initial endowment vector

of goods w^i and one unit of labour power. For simplicity, assume as above subsistence preferences: each agent wishes to earn enough income to purchase some fixed consumption vector b, and not run down the value of his initial endowment, valued at equilibrium prices. After working enough to earn that amount, he takes leisure. It is clear that each agent will only operate activities, at a given price vector, which generate the maximum rate of profit. Normalize prices by setting the wage at unity. For all activities to operate at equilibrium, the commodity price vector p must satisfy:

$$p = (1 + \pi)(pA + L) \qquad (1)$$

Prices p obeying (1) generate a uniform and hence maximal rate of profit π for all activities. (The only activities we observe are the ones reported in A and hence without loss of generality, we may assume the profit rate must be equalized for all sectors of production, since agents only operate maximal profit rate activities.)

The vector of embodied labour values in commodities is Λ:

$$\Lambda = \Lambda(1 - A)^{-1} \qquad (2)$$

A worker, whose initial endowments are none except his labour power, must earn wages sufficient to purchase the subsistence vector b, which requries:

$$pb = 1 \qquad (3)$$

From these three equations, it can be demonstrated (see Morishima, 1973; Roemer, 1981) that:

$$\pi > 0 \text{ if and only if } \Lambda b < 1 \qquad (4)$$

Equivalence (4) was coined by Morishima the 'fundamental Marxian theorem', as it shows that profits are positive precisely when labour is exploited (for the second inequality says that the labour embodied in the wage bundle is less than one unit of labour).

An agent in this model minimizes the labour he expends subject to earning revenues sufficient to buying his consumption b, and to replace the finance capital he uses. Suppose, for simplicity, there is no borrowing and all production must be financed from initial wealth. In general, an agent will optimize by hiring some labour, selling some of his own labour, and/or working on his own capital stock. Let x^i be the vector of activity levels which agent i operates himself, financed with his wealth; let y^i be the vector of activity levels he hires others to operate, which he finances; let z^i be the amount of labour he sells to other operators. His problem is to choose vectors x^i, y^i, and z^i to:

$$\min Lx^i + z^i$$

subject to

(i) $pAx^i + pAy^i \leq pw^i$

(ii) $p(q - A)x^i + p(q - A)y^i - Ly^i + z^i \geq pb$

The first constraint requires him to finance the activities operated out of his endowment, and the second requires that his revenues, net of wages paid and replacement costs, suffice to purchase the consumption bundle b. As well as the price vector satisfying (1), equilibrium requires that the markets for production inputs, consumption goods, and labour must clear. It can be proved that at such a 'reproducible solution', society is divided into five classes of agents, characterized by their relation to the hiring or selling of labour, as follows. There is a class of *pure capitalists*, who only hire labour (y^i is non-zero, but x^i and z^i are zero vectors); there is a class of *mixed capitalists*, who hire labour and work for themselves as well ($y^i \neq 0 \neq x^i, z^i = 0$); there is a class of *petty bourgeoisie*, who only work for themselves, and neither hire nor sell labour ($x^i \neq 0; y^i = 0 = z^i$); there is a class of *mixed proletarians*, who work for themselves part-time, and also sell their labour power on the market ($x^i \neq 0 \neq z^i, y^i = 0$); and there are *proletarians*, who only sell their labour power ($z^i \neq 0, x^i = 0 = y^i$). It is clear, from consulting the agent's programme, that this last class comprises those agents who own nothing but their labour power. More generally, the *Class-Wealth Correspondence Theorem* states that the five classes named, in that order, list agents in descending order of wealth. This verifies an intuition of classical Marxism.

There is, as well, a relation of class to exploitation. The *Class–Exploitation Correspondence Principle* states that the agents who hire labour are exploiters and the agents who sell labour are exploited. The exploitation status of agents in the petty bourgeoisie is ambiguous. Exploitation is defined as before: an agent is exploited if he expends more labour than is embodied in the vector b, and he is an exploiter if he expends less labour than that. It is important to note that this relationship of class to exploitation is a theorem of the model, not a postulate. Both the class and exploitation status of an agent emerge in the model as a consequence of optimizing behaviour, determined by the initial distribution of endowments, technology and preferences. These aspects of agents which in classical Marxism were taken as given (their class and exploitation status) are here proved to emerge as part of the description of agents in equilibrium, from initial given data of a more fundamental sort (endowments, etc.). For this reason, the model described provides microfoundations for classical Marxian descriptions. Generalizations and discussion of the model are pursued in Roemer (1982, 1985a). See Wright (1985) and Bardhan (1984, ch. 13) for empirical applications. For a general evaluation of the Marxian theory of exploitation and class, see Elster (1985, ch. 2, 4 and 5).

From the viewpoint of modern capitalism, many criticisms can be levelled against these stories. Foremost among them, perhaps, is the assumption of subsistence preferences. What happens if agents have more general preferences for income and leisure? The Class–Exploitation Correspondence Principle continues to hold, but the correspondence between class and wealth may fail. It fails, however, only for preference orderings which are unusual: the Class–Wealth Correspondence is true if the elasticity of labour supplied by the population viewed cross-sectionally with respect to its wealth is less than or equal to unity. There can, therefore, be no general claim that exploitation corresponds to wealth, in the classical way – that the poor are exploited by the rich. Whether the exploitation–wealth correspondence holds depends on the labour supply behaviour of agents as their wealth changes.

Exploitation as a statistic

Note that the fundamental conclusions of classical Marxian value analysis – the association of exploitation with class, in a certain way, and the association of exploitation with profits and accumulation – hold even when equilibrium prices are not proportional to labour values. For the prices of equation (1) are not, except in a singular case, proportional to the labour values of equation (2). Therefore, the usefulness of exploitation theory need not rest upon the false labour theory of value. It is for this reason that the transformation problem, for so long a central concern in Marxian economics, is unimportant.

That usefulness, instead, depends on how good a statistic exploitation is for the phenomena it purports to represent. Does the exploitation of labour explain accumulation? The 'fundamental Marxian theorem' would seem to say so. But, in fact, it can be shown that in an economy capable of producing a surplus, every commodity can be viewed as exploited, not just labour power. If corn is chosen as the value numeraire, then the amount of corn value embodied in a unit of corn is less than one unit of corn, so long as profits are positive. Thus labour power is not unique, as Marx thought, in regard to its potential for being exploited, and it is a false inference that the exploitation of labour 'explains' profits any more than the exploitation of corn or steel or land does. (For versions of this 'generalized commodity exploitation theorem', see Vegara (1979), Bowles and Gintis (1981), Samuelson (1982), and Roemer (1982).)

Is exploitation a good statistic for the injustice of capitalist appropriation of the surplus? Only if the initial distribution of endowments, which gives rise to such appropriation, is unjust. Marx claimed this was so, by arguing that initial capitalist property was established by plunder and enclosure (*Capital*, Volume 1, Part 8). But suppose there were a clean capitalism, in which initial inequalities in the ownership of capital were generated by differential hard work, skills, risk-taking postures, and perhaps luck of the agents. Would the ensuing class structure, exploitation and differential wealth indicate an injustice, or would it reflect the consequences of persons exercising traits which are rightfully theirs, and from which they deserve differentially to benefit? These topics are pursued in Cohen (1979) and Roemer (1985b).

In sum, the Marxian theory of exploitation is liberated from the labour theory of value. The link between class and exploitation is robust; but Marx's claim that the exploitation of labour is the unique explanans of accumulation is false. If one's class, defined above as one's relation to hiring or selling of labour, is important sociologically in determining behaviour (such as collective action against another class) and preferences, then the positive theory of class determination described is of use. Exploitation remains a statistic, of some value, for the inequality in the distribution of productive assets. But in this role, exploitation may not correspond to wealth as in the classical story: if the labour supplied by agents responds with excessive enthusiasm to increases in their wealth, then the rich can be 'exploited' by the poor. The ethical conclusion from an observation of exploitation is in this case unclear.

Even aside from this peculiar case, exploitation is a circuitous proxy for differential wealth in productive assets, and one's normative evaluation of exploitation depends on one's view of the process that generates that inequality. If agents are the rightful owners of their alienable means of production, because they accumulated them based on the exercise of their rightfully owned talents and preferences then exploitation does not represent unjust expropriation. If agents are not entitled to own alienable productive assets, either because they have no right to their talents and preferences (whose distribution is morally arbitrary), or because they came to possess those assets in some other unjustifiable way, then exploitation represents an expropriation. Inheritance, for example, might be an unjust way of acquiring assets which were originally acquired in an untainted manner. The essential question which lies behind the theory of exploitation concerns the fairness of a system of property allowing private ownership of alienable productive assets. The concept of exploitation based on the calculation of surplus labour accounts is, in this writer's view, a circuitous route towards the discussion of that central issue.

Ethical views concerning what kinds of asset may justifiably be privately appropriated change through history. Property in other persons, as in slavery, or more limited rights over the powers of other persons, as in feudalism, are no longer viewed as legitimate. The Marxian theory of exploitation is associated with a call for the abolition of private property in the productive assets external to persons. (Marx himself did not explicitly base his call for the abolition of such property on grounds of fairness, but on grounds of efficiency, despite the clear ethical tone of his attacks on capitalism. For an evaluation of the debate surrounding this question, see Geras (1985).) The cogency of that call must be established independently of the theory of exploitation.

J.E. ROEMER

See also **exploitation; labour theory of value; market price; Marx, Karl Heinrich.**

Bibliography

Bardhan, P. 1984. *Land, Labor and Rural Poverty: Essays in Development Economics.* New York: Columbia University Press.

Bowles, S. and Gintis, H. 1981. Structure and practice in the labor theory of value. *Review of Radical Political Economics* 12(4), 1–26.

Cohen, G.A. 1979. The labor theory of value and the concept of exploitation. *Philosophy and Public Affairs* 8(4), Summer, 338–60.

Elster, J. 1985. *Making Sense of Marx.* Cambridge: Cambridge University Press.

Geras, N. 1985. The controversy about Marx and justice. *New Left Review* No. 150, March–April, 47–85.

Morishima, M. 1973. *Marx's Economics.* Cambridge: Cambridge University Press.

Roemer, J.E. 1981. *Analytical Foundations of Marxian Economic Theory.* Cambridge: Cambridge University Press.

Roemer, J.E. 1982. *A General Theory of Exploitation and Class.* Cambridge, Mass.: Harvard University Press.

Roemer, J.E. 1985a. *Value, Exploitation, and Class.* London: Harwood Academic Publishers.

Roemer, J.E. 1985b. Should Marxists be interested in exploitation? *Philosophy and Public Affairs* 14(1), Winter, 30–65.

Samuelson, P. 1982. The normative and positivistic inferiority of Marx's values paradigm. *Southern Economic Journal* 49(1), July,11–18.

Vegara, J.M. 1979. *Economia politica y modelos multisectoriales.* Madrid: Editorial Tecnos.

Wright, E.O. 1985. *Classes.* London: New Left Books.

Marx's analysis of capitalist production

Karl Marx's analysis of capitalist production is best understood in the context of his broad theory of human societies and their history, namely, *historical materialism.* This theory argues that, after passing through various stages in which societies are divided into classes and the exploitation of a majority of producers by a privileged minority prevails, humanity will finally eliminate classes and class domination by a revolutionary process conducted by the organized *proletariat* in capitalism. This revolutionary stand was based on a 'scientific' investigation of history in general and capitalism in particular, with a special emphasis on economics, always with a political perspective. Whether historical materialism has a scientific or ideological character obviously remains controversial between Marxists and non-Marxists: Marxist theory is considered a discredited doctrine of the past by non-Marxists, while Marxists consider mainstream social and economic thinking as a continuing apologetics of capitalism.

After an introductory section devoted to locating the capitalist mode of production as a particular epoch in human history, the main focus below is on Marx's analysis of capitalist production. There are two facets to the theory of capital in the strict sense: *surplus value* (exploitation), and *the circuit of capital* (its 'circulation'). These are introduced separately, and then gradually combined in the analysis of more complex phenomena. Finally, we consider three broad sets of basic mechanisms directly related to the hold of capital on the functioning of the economy: (1) competition, (2) accumulation, technological and distributional changes, and (3) crises and the business cycle. We do not consider other important aspects of Marx's thinking such as his analysis of class struggle, and his theory of the state. The interpretation of even very fundamental aspects of Marx's thought remains contested among Marxist scholars. The bibliography contains a selective list of works that represent some of these different perspectives.

The capitalist mode of production

The historical materialist point of view starts from the observation that all human societies must produce in order to reproduce both individuals and society itself. Production in this general sense always involves the combination of human labour with previously produced means of production and the natural resources of the earth. With the emergence of settled agriculture a *surplus product* over and above what is necessary for reproduction becomes possible. In societies with a surplus product, class exploitation, an institutionalized form of inequality, arises. Societies divide into a small *exploiting class* which appropriates, controls, and distributes the surplus product created by the labour of a much larger *exploited class* of producers who receive on average only what is necessary for their reproduction. Marx and Engels distinguish two aspects of these *class societies*. The *forces of production* comprise the population, natural resources, and technology which make a surplus product possible; the *social* relations *of production* comprise the institutional framework (such as property relations) through which the exploiting class appropriates the surplus product. The forces and social relations of production together constitute a *mode of production*. For example, in the slave mode of production characteristic of ancient Greek and Roman civilizations, the institution of slavery sustained by military force and political power was the means through which slave-owners appropriated a surplus product created by

the labour of slaves, who received a minimum subsistence. In the feudal mode of production, the institutions of serfdom sustained by military force and religious and political power were the means through which the lords of the manor appropriated a fraction of the labour time of serfs, who also laboured in their own fields to feed and reproduce themselves (or the serf had to pay a rent in kind or, later, in money, in addition to various taxes). This is what *exploitation* means in Marx's thought: to live on the product of the labour of other people.

From the historical materialist point of view, capitalism is a class society in which the institutions of private property in the means of production and free wage labour are the means through which capitalists appropriate the *surplus value* created by workers producing commodities (or services), who receive wages. In feudalism, the exploitation of the serfs was transparent: the serfs worked a certain part of the week on their own plots for their own subsistence, and a certain part of the week on the lord's land to supply his consumption and armies. Marx's theory of capitalism demonstrates that, though the mechanism of capitalist exploitation through the social relation of wage labour based on the formal legal equality of workers and employers is less transparent, capitalists also appropriate the surplus labour time of the workers. Capitalism, therefore, defines a specific stage of the history of class societies. Capitalism's decentralized, highly competitive organization creates powerful incentives for the rapid development of the forces of production through population growth, technical innovation, and a widening division of labour, but it is unable to control the forces it has itself stimulated.

Marx and Engels expected that the capitalist working class (the *proletariat*), once it had a clear understanding of capitalist exploitation and reached a high degree of organization, would overthrow the social relations of capitalism in a revolution to establish a classless society based on social control of the large surplus product made possible by the forces of production developed by capitalism. A violent transition was required, the *dictatorship of the proletariat,* to attain socialism and finally communism, marking the end of the 'prehistory' of humanity. Marx developed this analysis in collaboration with Friedrich Engels in *The Communist Manifesto* (1848).

Marx's main work, *Capital*, is devoted to the analysis of capitalist production. The first volume was published, in 1867, while Marx (1818–83) was still alive. Volumes II and III were published later by Friedrich Engels, from extensive notebooks still in draft form at the time of Marx's death. In what follows, we refer to *Capital* by volumes and chapters; for example, 'III, 25' means Chapter 25 of Volume III. References and quotations can be found on Internet, for example in the *Marx/Engels Library*, http://www.marxists.org/archive/marx/works, or in Marx (1976; 1978; 1981). We have put square brackets around our own interpolations in quotes; everything else comes from the source.

The definition of capital (I, 4)

Marx defines capital as *value* (to be defined below) participating in a dynamic process of self-expansion. A capitalist spends money to hire workers and buy means of production, and then sells the resulting output for enough money to cover his initial outlay and secure a profit (the form taken by 'surplus value'). In this process value appears in various forms: first under the form of money; then as the value of productive inputs (labour power, raw materials, machinery, and buildings); then as the value of the commodities produced; and finally as money value again after the produced commodities have been sold. This process of capital is pointless unless, as is normally the case when capitalists make a profit, the money realized in the sale of commodities is greater than the money initially spent to start the process. Capital is not value as such, but value in movement:

> If we pin down the specific forms of appearance assumed in turn by self-valorising value, in the course of its life, we reach the following elucidation: capital is money, capital is commodities. In truth, however, value is here the subject of a process in which, while constantly assuming the form in turn of money and commodities, it changes its own magnitude, throwing off surplus-value from itself considered as original value. (I, 4)

Two aspects of capital are present in this definition: (1) capital is expanding value; and (2) capital value changes its form. These two aspects of capital are also called the *process of self-expansion* (sometimes called *valorization*), and the *process of circulation of capital* (or circuit of capital). Marx means here that: (1) the capitalist invests a certain capital with the intent of making profits (expansion); (2) capital is invested in commodities and money, and constantly passes from one form to the other (for example, when an output is sold, value changes form from commodity to money).

The first two volumes of *Capital* treat the processes of *self-expansion* and *circulation* of capital separately (with a few exceptions); the third volume considers the combination of these two elements. Before entering into the analysis of capital, it is necessary, however, to introduce two other preliminary concepts, *commodity* and *money*, and the related concepts of *value* (at the centre of the definition of capital) and *price*, to which Marx devotes the first three chapters of Volume I, prior to the analysis of capital. In Volumes I and II, the three concepts are considered successively: commodity (including value), money (including price), and capital (valorization and circulation). (This outline is logical, not historical: historically commodities and money reach their full development only with the capitalist mode of production.) We will follow this outline in our exposition here.

Commodities, value, money, and prices

Commodities and value (I, 1)

A *product* is the result of human labour, working with produced means of production and the natural resources of the earth. Useful products become *commodities* when they are regularly exchanged rather than being consumed directly by their producers. 'Useful' must be taken in a very broad sense as something desired by someone, for whatever reason. A producer who exchanges his product receives social recognition for his own labour in the form of the other commodities he acquires. Marx denotes the labour time required for the production of a commodity under average conditions, as *socially necessary labour time*. As the outcome of a parcel of social labour time, the commodity has an *exchange value*, or more briefly a *value*. Thus, according to Marx (who here follows Adam Smith), a commodity has a dual character as: (1) *object of utility*, or equivalently a *use value*, and (2) an *exchange value*, or *value*. The value of the commodity is the sum of labour embodied in previously produced inputs, *dead labour*, and newly incorporated labour, *living labour*. Marx sometimes calls this definition the *law of value*, although he rarely uses the expression. Later economists often refer to this framework as the *labour theory of value*.

The dual character of the commodity is reflected on labour itself. The concrete quality of labour (weaving, computer-programming) corresponds to the use-value aspect of the commodity it produces. But all categories of social labour materialized in the production of commodities have in common the ability to produce exchange values and, as such, are defined as *abstract labour*. There is no a priori rule accounting for this process of abstraction. Exchange dissolves the specific character of concrete labours, and the repetition of exchange establishes their quantitative equivalence. If one category of concrete labour is not adequately compensated, its supply will decline, and its wage will rise. In a similar manner, it is exchange which establishes the normal degree of intensity, skill, and technical efficiency in production.

Abstracting from the capitalist character of production, commodities would 'normally' exchange in proportion to their values. For example, if the value of commodity A is twice that of commodity B, one unit of A will exchange for two of B. If the exchange ratio were only one B for one A, producers of A would switch to producing B; a shortage of A would ensue and the exchange value of A would rise. This is the *commodity law of exchange*, sometimes confused with the law of value. The distinction is important because the law of value is a fundamental characteristic of commodity production, whether commodities exchange in proportion to their values or not. (In competitive capitalist economies they typically do not, as we will see.)

Money and prices (I, 3)

We begin with the definition of money, and its first function as *measure of value*, and introduce the other functions of money, and the concept of the *price form* of value.

The value of commodities cannot be expressed on the market directly in abstract labour time (which nobody can observe or measure). In the exchange of two commodities, such as linen for a coat, the value of one commodity is expressed in the body of the other (measured in units such as a length or weight) as its direct *equivalent*. With the repetition of exchange, some specific commodity, such as gold, will emerge as a *socially accepted general equivalent*, that is, as *money*. Thus for Marx the original function of money is as *measure of value*. In addition to its function as measure of value, money comes to serve as *medium of circulation* if purchases and sales are paid for directly, and as *means of payment* if payment is deferred. Value can be accumulated temporarily in money hoards. Another function of money is, therefore, as a *store of value* (though any durable, valuable commodity can serve as a store of value).

Prices are values as expressed in monetary units. They are *forms of value*. When commodities exchange at prices proportional to their values, the price of a commodity expresses the socially necessary (abstract) labour time required for its production of this commodity, qualitatively and quantitatively in a straightforward manner. This is the framework of Volumes I and II. But the prices of commodities may deviate from their values, and we will later return to this issue. The State can establish a *standard of price* by defining a local currency unit such as the franc or dollar as a certain amount of gold or other money commodity. Valueless tokens, 'symbols or tokens of value' in Marx's words, such as paper currency, may also be circulated in place of commodity money:

> In the same way as the exchange-value of commodities is crystallised into gold money as a result of exchange, so gold money in circulation is sublimated into its own symbol, first in the shape of worn gold coin, then in the shape of subsidiary metal coin, and finally in the shape of worthless counters, scraps of paper, mere *tokens of value*. (Marx, 1859, 2.B.2.c)

Money also takes the form of a stock of purchasing power in an account in a financial institution. In contemporary capitalism, there is no commodity money.

The monetary expression of value and the quantity of money

Inherent in Marx's theory is the relation between abstract labour time and its price form in money terms. There is a quantitative aspect to this relation. The ratio – for example, dollars per hour of abstract socially necessary labour time – can be called the monetary expression of labour time, or the monetary expression of value.

The determination of this ratio, which is a way of looking at the general price level in an economy, is discussed by Marx in his critique of Ricardo's quantity of money theory of prices, under the assumption of the existence of a commodity money. Marx explains that the quantity of money required to circulate the mass of commodities produced in any period depends on the quantity of the commodities exchanged, their money prices, determined by their costs of production, and the velocity of money, the average number of transactions in which each unit of money participates in the period (an institutional characteristic). Money flows in and out of hoards (reserves) to accommodate the requirements of circulation. He interprets this principle as governing the quantity of money required for purchases and sales, in contrast to Ricardo's quantity of money theory of prices, which sees the prices of commodities adjusting to a given quantity of money. In Marx's theory the general level of prices is determined by the relative costs of production of the money commodity and other commodities when a commodity like gold is used as money. (The critique of Ricardo's theory is developed in Marx, 1859, 2.C.)

The theory of surplus value

The labour theory of value is the foundation of Marx's theory of exploitation, or surplus value. When a produced commodity is purchased or sold no new value is created. If a commodity sells at a price proportional to its value, given the monetary expression of value, the buyer and seller exchange money and commodity representing equal values. If the commodity sells above or below its value, the value gained by one party is just offset by the value lost by the other.

Productive labour-power and surplus-value (I, 7–9)

Marx explains surplus value in relation to the purchase of the labour power of waged workers. The capability to work, denoted as *labour power*, is a commodity, with a use-value and a value. The *use value* of labour power is labour itself, because a capitalist buys labour power to obtain the right to use the labour of the worker. The *value* of labour power is the value equivalent of the purchasing power of the wage on the commodities the worker can buy. (We will discuss later Marx's view of the actual purchasing power of workers.)

Only 'productive workers', that is, workers involved directly in production within capitalist enterprises, produce new value in Marx's analysis, in contrast to 'unproductive workers', whose labour power is employed by capitalists to maximize their profit rate. If the value of the labour power of productive workers is less than the value they produce, capitalist production on average adds more value in the production of commodities than it expends in hiring workers. (One can, equivalently, say that the money wage must be smaller than the monetary expression of the labour time expended by the average worker.) Because capitalist production can produce a surplus over the subsistence of productive workers, typically the value of labour power is smaller than the value labour produces, and surplus value results.

Thus, labour power has a property not shared by other commodities. While the purchase and sale of a produced commodity can only redistribute a given value between buyer and seller, the capitalist's purchase and use of labour-power, in contrast, results in the creation of surplus-value. The capitalist buys labour-power at a wage reflecting the necessary labour time required by the production of the consumption basket of the worker, say, four hours a day, but on average the worker can work longer, say, eight hours. Thus, the capitalist can appropriate *surplus labour*, here four hours, in the form of surplus value. (If the monetary expression of labour time is ten dollars per hour, the surplus value created by an average worker in a day under these assumptions would be 40 dollars.) Under the wage system, once a capitalist has paid a worker the agreed wage, the product of the worker's labour and its value belong to the capitalist. The production of surplus value is thus compatible with transactions at prices proportional to values, including the purchase of labour power at a wage proportional to the value of productive labour power. Marx argues that capitalist exploitation does not violate the commodity law of exchange, that is, it would take place even if all commodities exchanged at prices proportional to their values.

The actual appearance of labour power available for hire historically depends on two preconditions. First, workers must be legally free to sell their labour power. This explains the historic hostility of capitalism to bound forms of labour such as serfdom and slavery. Second, workers cannot have access to their own means of production, such as the feudal commons, so that they have no choice but to sell their labour power to the owner of means of production to live. This explains the historic support of capitalism for the enclosure of common lands and their conversion into private property. Marx devotes the last part of Volume I to *primitive accumulation*, the actual historical process through which the capitalist mode of production came into being. There he shows how, in the first steps of accumulation in England, the availability of labour power was achieved by way of straightforward social violence. The *enclosure* of common lands deprived the rural population of its old conditions of reproduction, and subjected it to the dependency on capital. It is important to keep such mechanisms in mind in the investigation of the historical dynamics of capitalism. Marx emphasizes the crucial historical importance of the transformation of produced means of production and labour, which are universal aspects of human production,

into the specific commodity forms of capital, including labour power.

The value of the produced inputs the capitalist purchases to undertake production is recovered in the sales price unchanged, so that Marx calls it *constant capital*, denoted by the symbol c. The value of the labour power the capitalist buys as an input to production, on the other hand, is recovered in the sales price expanded by the addition of the surplus value, so that Marx calls it *variable capital*, denoted by the symbol v. The sum of constant capital, c, variable capital, v, and surplus value, s, is the total value of the product. The sum $c + v$ is the total cost of the commodity. The sum $v + s$ is the *living labour*, as opposed to *dead labour, c*, and measures the *value added* by the production process. The *rate of surplus value*, s/v, is the ratio of *unpaid* to *paid* labour time, so that Marx also calls it the *rate of exploitation*. The ratio c/v, which measures the ratio of dead to living labour in the cost of the commodity, is the *value composition* of capital.

This decomposition of the value of a commodity is parallel to the income statement of a capitalist firm, which exhibits *profit* (Marx's surplus-value, s) as the difference between sales price (Marx's value of the commodity, $c + v + s$), and the cost of the means of production and wages required to produce the commodity (Marx's $c + v$).

Absolute and relative surplus value, manufacture and industry (I, 12–16)

Identifying surplus value as surplus labour time does not tell what determines its magnitude and variation. Many natural, social and political conditions are involved, and vary historically. Labour performed by members of the family at home, women in particular, crucially affects the level of exploitation compatible with the reproduction of the workers and their families. In his analysis of surplus value in Volume I, Marx introduces important developments concerning the historical transformation of technology and organization.

Surplus value can be increased in two analytically distinct ways (which can be combined in real production): first, by lengthening the duration of labour time without increasing the value of labour power, *absolute surplus value*; second, by diminishing the value of labour power by cheapening worker's consumption through productivity gains holding the duration of labour time constant, *relative surplus value*. In Marx's view relative surplus value is the origin of the most important developments in the historical transformation of the organization of labour and technology by capitalism.

Marx sees distinct periods in which this transformation of production took different forms. In 'manufacture', a large number of individual workers, each processing his or her own means of production, are brought together in one location primarily for the purpose of increasing the capitalist's surveillance and control of production (which

Marx describes as the 'formal subsumption' of labour to capital). In 'large-scale industry', the capitalist takes the further step of imposing a detailed division of labour on the production process, transforming the workers' relation to the production process (which Marx describes as the 'real subsumption of labour to capital'). Both technology and organization enter into these transformations. In manufacture, workers originally worked with the same tools they previously used in production at home; in large-scale industry, by contrast, capital has completely transformed technology and the organization of labour.

We will return to Marx's theory of technical change in capitalism in the discussion of the falling rate of profit.

The circulation of capital

As defined earlier, capital is self-expanding value moving through various forms (money, commodity...). We now turn to the analysis of the circulation of capital. The emphasis is on the motion from one form to the other, and the coexistence of the various fractions of capital under the three forms at a given point in time.

The circuit of capital (II, 1–4)

A capitalist spends money to buy inputs (means of production and labour power); organizes production; stockpiles and sells the resulting product; and realizes a certain amount of money in sales revenue, normally larger than the original capital outlay. Each atom of capital goes through the various *forms*: money-capital, M, commodity capital in the form of inputs to production, C, productive capital, P, the value of partially finished commodities and plant and equipment in the workshop, and again commodity capital in the form of inventories of commodities awaiting sale, C', and finally returning to money through the sale of the produced commodities, M'. Marx represents this sequence in a diagram of the *circuit of capital*:

$$M—C\ldots P\ldots C'—M'$$

Here M is the money the capitalist uses to buy inputs to production C, P represents the actual production process, and C' are the produced commodities which are sold for money M'. The dashes represent purchase and sale of commodities on the market. The circuit is a chain, which can be viewed as beginning in M, C, or P, the *circuits of money, commodity*, and *productive capital*, three distinct formula of the same circuit.

The speeds at which the values of the various components of capital go through the productive form of capital, P, can be quite different. The value of some components, like raw materials, returns quickly to the money form in the sale of the commodity, while others like the value of buildings and machinery (whose value is only transferred to the product along their service life) returns only after a long period of time. From these differences in turnover time follows the distinction between *circulating* and *fixed capital*.

Capital is also a stock of value at any point in time. All the circuits overlap simultaneously: at the same moment new means of production and labour-power are being purchased while production is going on and finished output is being sold. The capital of a capitalist is the total value, tied up at any moment in these circuits. The total capital, K, is divided into three component stocks: *money capital, M, commodity capital, C*, and *productive capital, P*. The sum $K = M+C+P$ parallels the total of the assets on the capitalist's balance sheet.

Industrial, commercial and money-dealing capital (III, 16; III, 19)

Industrial capital undergoes the complete circuit of capital as above, taking on the forms M, C, and P in turn. Some capitals, however, are specialized to limited segments of the circuit. The first is *commercial capital*, which buys finished commodities from industrial capitalists to sell them to final purchasers, in the reduced circuit $M—C—M'$: commercial capitalists buy in order to sell the same commodity. The second category, *money-dealing capital*, refers to the technical activity of banks in handling money payments into and out of accounts (and the exchange of currencies). Since no productive labour is expanded in these circuits, no surplus value is created. How industries engaged in such activities can make profits is part of the theory of competition considered below.

Marx's schemes of reproduction (II, 18–21)

Although Volume II of *Capital* is devoted to the circulation of capital, the analysis of the *schemes of reproduction* combines valorization (c, v, s) and circulation (M, C and P).

Three departments are distinguished which produce the physical commodities to satisfy the demand emanating from c, v, and s: Department I produces means of production, Department II commodities consumed by workers, and Department III commodities consumed by capitalists. If all of the surplus value is consumed, no accumulation takes place, and the size of the capitalist economy remains unchanged, the case of *simple reproduction*. If a fraction of the surplus value is accumulated, the corresponding purchasing power is spent on additional means of production, and the capitalist economy expands, the case of *expanded reproduction*.

Marx assumes that all capital in the three industries accomplishes exactly one circuit: at the beginning and at the end of the period, all capital is assumed to be under the form C (the stocks of means of production and worker and capitalist consumption goods waiting to be sold). In this setting reproduction requires certain proportionalities to hold: for example, in simple reproduction the value added of Department I must equal the constant capital of Departments II and III.

In this framework, Marx considers two types of issues. The first issue is the definition of output and its relation to income. The *net product* is the value of the final product, C', minus the value of what is now denoted as intermediate inputs, either produced in the previous period, in C, or during the present period but purchased as inputs by firms. Marx shows that the value of this net product is equal to total income or *value added*, as in contemporary national accounting, the sum of wages and surplus value (including rent, interest and profit as we will see): $v+s$. Second, Marx investigates the circulation of money. He attempts to demonstrate how the money thrown into circulation by capitalists returns as sales revenue, taking into account the activities of a sector producing the money commodity if such a money commodity exists.

The functions of the capitalist and their delegation to employees (II, 6)

Being a capitalist is not a sinecure: both the appropriation of surplus value and the circuit of capital require active attention. In contemporary language: enterprises must be managed. Marx refers to these tasks as 'capitalist functions', in particular commercial transactions:

> The transformations of the forms of capital from commodities into money and from money into commodities are at the same time transactions of the capitalist, acts of purchase and sale. The time in which these transformations of forms take place constitutes subjectively, from the standpoint of the capitalist, the time of purchase and sale; … the time in which the capitalist buys and sells and scours the market is a necessary part of the time in which he functions as a capitalist, i.e., as personified capital. It is a part of his business hours. (II, 6)

The tasks considered are variegated, from the overseeing of labour in the workshop to the acceleration of the circuit of capital (as in the market activities mentioned above). All these tasks are unproductive, though they are useful. Their purpose is the *maximizing of the profit rate* of the capitalist. (The profit rate is defined below in the treatment of competition.)

The capitalist delegates some of these unproductive tasks to employees. They require means of production as well as labour power, like industrial capitalist production, though they produce no value. The wage and capital costs of these unproductive activities are a deduction from the surplus value. Marx denotes them as 'costs', in particular *costs of circulation* (the control and acceleration of the circuit of capital). As a consequence Marx categorizes some wage labour employed in capitalist production as unproductive, as in, for example, the case of overseers and employees in trade.

The distribution of surplus value as income

In Volume III, surplus value in its relation to both self-expansion and circulation is renamed *profit*. Profit is a form of surplus value. Once extracted, surplus value is at the origin of various categories of incomes, which appear as deductions from profit. The payment of such incomes to agents who employ no labour is thus consistent with the labour theories of value and surplus value. These channels of distribution of surplus value correspond to specific fractions of ruling classes in capitalism, such as active capitalists (entrepreneurs), money capitalists and landowners.

Interest and profit of enterprise: interest-bearing capital (III, 21–3)

Some capitalists do not engage directly in capitalist production, but put their capital at the disposal of another functioning industrial capitalist, the *active capitalist* (or *entrepreneur*). This transaction may take the form of a loan in exchange for a share of the surplus value as *interest*, or the purchase of shares of stock in the firm which pays *dividends*. Marx treats both cases as *interest-bearing capital*, and this category of capitalists as *money capitalists* (sometimes referred to as 'financial capitalists'). Marx explains interest as a portion of the surplus-value realized by active capitalists. The profit remaining after the active capitalist has paid dividends and interest is *profit of enterprise*. The existence of a developed loan market with a uniform rate of interest (for each maturity and risk of the loan) leads active capitalists to regard their own capital as loan capital, and to impute interest on it as an opportunity cost. Thus profit of enterprise appears as a kind of wage to the entrepreneurial activities of the active capitalist.

Rent (III, 38, 45)

Owners of scarce natural resources ('land' in the terminology of the classical political economists) also receive incomes in deduction from profits, in the form of rents. Due to their monopoly ownership of specific pieces of land, landowners can bargain with individual capitalists for a share of the surplus-value as rent (or royalties in other instances). How rents are quantitatively determined can only be examined in relation of the theory of competition.

Finance
Banking capital and money capitalists (II, 19; III, 29)

The tasks of money-dealing capital are performed by banks. This represents their first source of income.

Banks also concentrate and use available masses of capital. One source of funds for banks is the idle balances of money in the economy, which are deposited in bank accounts. Thus, the money capital of enterprises is pooled within banks together with the balances of money held by other agents, such as households. While individual balances fluctuate, the aggregate pools are much more stable. A second source of funds is the capital of money capitalists (interest-bearing capital, including stock shares), who, instead of dealing directly with entrepreneurs, use banks as intermediaries. (Marx is aware of the capability of banks to 'create' money, but his view of banking mechanisms remains dominated by intermediation.) The theory of banking capital unites these two facets of the theory of capital: money-dealing capital and the handling of the capital of money capitalists.

Besides the management of accounts, the main function of banks is to make these funds available to agents seeking financing. Banks actually become the 'administrators' of the capital of money capitalists, and 'confront' capital as used by enterprises:

> Borrowing and lending money becomes their [banks'] particular business. They act as middlemen between the actual lender and the borrower of money capital. Generally speaking, this aspect of the banking business consists of concentrating large amounts of the loanable money capital in the bankers' hands, so that, in place of the individual money-lender, the bankers confront the industrial capitalists and commercial capitalists as representatives of all money-lenders. They become the general managers of money capital. On the other hand by borrowing for the entire world of commerce, they concentrate all the borrowers vis-à-vis all the lenders. A bank represents a centralisation of money capital of the lenders, on the one hand, and, on the other, a centralisation of the borrowers. (III, 25)

It is in these pages of Volume III of *Capital* that Marx analyses the issuance of paper currency by private banks and the Bank of England.

Fictitious capital and financial instability (III, 25)

Marx's original definition of capital, as value in a movement of self-expansion, does not apply to securities like Treasury bills, or even to the stock shares of corporations. To refer to these securities, Marx uses the phrase *fictitious capital*. A public bond is in no way 'fictitious' for its holder, but it has no counterpart in the M, C and P of the circuit of capital. Once bonds or equities have been sold by a capitalist firm and are being traded on a secondary market, their values are also fictitious. The emergence of a market interest rate leads to the phenomenon of the *capitalization* of income flows such as the interest on government debt and dividends on equity: the market, where expectations concerning the future of these flows are taken into account, assigns a principal value to any flow of income. Thus, the accumulation of capital is paralleled in capitalism by that of such fictitious capital. Marx sees this capitalization of revenue flows as a source of instability.

The institutional framework of modern capitalism (III, 21–3)

As noted earlier, with the development of capitalism, the functions of the active capitalist are gradually delegated to managers and employees. This configuration, in which funding is provided by money capitalists with banks acting as intermediary, and the bulk of capitalist functions is delegated to a salaried personnel is that of modern capitalism:

> But since, on the one hand, the mere owner of capital, the money capitalist, has to face the functioning capitalist, while money capital itself assumes a social character with the advance of credit, being concentrated in banks and loaned out by them instead of its original owners, and since, on the other hand, the mere manager who has no title whatever to the capital, whether through borrowing it or otherwise, performs all the real functions pertaining to the functioning capitalist as such, only the functionary remains and the capitalist disappears as superfluous from the production process. (III, 23)

The trinity formula of capital and classes in capitalism (III, 48; III, 52)

A major objective of *Capital* is to establish surplus value as the source of all incomes in capitalist society except wages. But capitalist practice hides this origin of capitalist incomes in what Marx calls the 'trinity formula':

> *Capital—profit (profit of enterprise plus interest), land—ground-rent, labour—wages*, this is the trinity formula which comprises all the secrets of the social production process. (III, 48)

Actually, this configuration is again altered in what we called above the institutions of modern capitalism:

> Furthermore, since as previously demonstrated interest appears as the specific characteristic product of capital and profit of enterprise on the contrary appears as wages independent of capital, the above trinity formula reduces itself more specifically to the following: *Capital—interest, land—ground-rent, labour—wages*, where profit, the specific characteristic form of surplus-value belonging to the capitalist mode of production, is fortunately eliminated. (III, 48)

To Marx, this trinity formula is 'irrational', because it confuses the source of incomes in the distribution of surplus-value with the role of necessary inputs in the production of use-values.

Volume III of *Capital* stops on a single-page chapter (obviously incomplete), entitled 'Classes'. There Marx establishes a straightforward relationship between his analysis of incomes and the fundamental class pattern of capitalism:

> The owners merely of labour-power, owners of capital, and land-owners, whose respective sources of income

are wages, profit and ground-rent, in other words, wage-labourers, capitalists and land-owners, constitute the three big classes of modern society based upon the capitalist mode of production. (III, 52)

To this one could add fractions of capitalist classes corresponding to the various circuits of capital and the division of surplus value as above: (1) industrial capitalists, commercial capitalists, bankers, and (2) entrepreneurs (active capitalists) and money capitalists.

The distribution of surplus value through competition

The analysis of capitalist production we have summarized so far, based on the idea that surplus value (and hence capitalist profit) arises from the exploitation of productive labour, runs counter to the apparent linkage of profit to the value of capital invested, regardless of the amount of labour it employs, or indeed whether or not that labour produces commodities at all. Marx offers a systematic account of the way in which competition among capitals gives rise to this linkage of profit with total capital invested by redistributing the surplus value created by productive labour.

Prices and the collective character of exploitation (III, 9)
Because prices are not necessarily proportional to values, surplus value is not necessarily realized by the capitalists who hired the labour-power that created it. Exploitation is thus a 'collective' mechanism for the capitalist class. It is as if surplus labour was collected in a single pool, and then distributed among capitalists in proportion to their invested capital (though the division of the surplus value among the individual capitals is actually the result of a fierce competitive struggle):

> Thus, although in selling their commodities the capitalists of the various spheres of production recover the value of the capital consumed in their production, they do not secure the surplus-value, and consequently the profit, created in their own sphere by the production of these commodities. What they secure is only as much surplus-value, and hence profit, as falls, when uniformly distributed, to the share of every aliquot part of the total social capital from the total social surplus-value, or profit, produced in a given time by the social capital in all spheres of production. ... So far as profits are concerned, the various capitalists are just so many [100] stockholders in a stock company in which the shares of profit are uniformly divided per 100, so that profits differ in the case of the individual capitalists only in accordance with the amount of capital invested by each in the aggregate enterprise, i.e., according to his investment in social production as a whole, according to the number of his shares. (III, 9)

It is, consequently, necessary to distinguish between the mechanisms which govern the overall *appropriation* of surplus-value and its *realization* by particular capitalists:

1. The total surplus value depends on the value of labour power and the total number of workers capitalists employ.
2. Any system of commodity prices 'distributes' this total surplus value to individual producers (and landowners).

Marx describes this process of redistribution of surplus value as a 'metabolism' of value. Note that prices remain 'forms of value', as stated in the analysis of money and prices, but the hours of social abstract labour are reshuffled. At issue is no longer the labour actually expended to produce each commodity individually, but value as socially 'distributed' by prices (purchasing power as a fraction of social value 'conveyed' by the price of each commodity).

The transformation problem (III, 9)
At the beginning of Volume III, Marx pursues two objectives simultaneously. On the one hand, he analyses the basic mechanisms of competition in capitalism, in which the determination of a particular set of prices is implied, with equalized profit rates among industries, and, on the other hand, he uses this particular case to discuss the metabolism of value introduced above. This exposition obscures the fact that the underlying mechanism of exploitation operates whatever the prevailing system of prices; the theory of exploitation does not depend on the particular properties of commodity prices and, in particular, not on the attainment of a market equilibrium at which profit rates are equalized. The failure to separate the two projects, and to appreciate the restricted context of the discussion of the metabolism of value in this particular case, has created much confusion in the history of Marxist economic theory.

In the later literature the two problems, those of the metabolism of value and the prevalence of a particular set of prices in capitalist competition, are usually treated jointly as the *transformation problem*. Because of its importance in the history of Marxism, a specific entry is devoted to this controversial issue (see MARXIAN TRANSFORMATION PROBLEM).

The classical Marxian long-period equilibrium: prices of production (III, 10)
The analysis of this process of redistribution of surplus value through competition marks an important break in the present account of Marx's analysis in *Capital*. Beginning with the definition of capital (and the corresponding requirement of the analysis of commodity and money, actually a preliminary to the exposition of capital), we first followed Marx in his investigation of the two components of the theory of capital: the extraction of surplus value and the circuit of capital. These two

aspects were then combined in analyses such as the reproduction schemes or capitalist functions. Finally, attention turned to the division of surplus value: (1) its distribution as interest and dividends to money capitalists, and as rents to landowners; (2) its realization by various categories of capitals, such as commercial capital and banking capital, in which no surplus value is produced; and (3), in the present section, its reallocation to capitalists of various industries independently of the extraction by individual capitalists, as in competition. We now enter a new category of developments, in which dynamic processes are involved: the mechanisms of competition, accumulation and employment, technical and distributional changes, and crises and the business cycle.

The basic idea in the analysis of capitalist competition is straightforward. If capital is free to move from one line of production to another in search of profit, the competitive movement of capitals will tend to move prices of specific commodities up or down until the rate of profit is equalized in all sectors. The *equalization of the rate of profit*, clearly stated by Adam Smith and David Ricardo, represents competition at the most fundamental level of analysis. The appropriation and realization of surplus value, as stated above, is thus specified quantitatively: one industry where little labour is used proportionally to total capital, in comparison to another industry, realizes more surplus value as profit than its workers actually contribute to the total surplus value (and conversely).

The *profit rate* is central in this analysis of competition. The profit rate is defined as the ratio of profit, s, to total capital, $K = M + C + P$, that is $r = s/K$. The ratio of the value of the average total capital invested during one unit of time (for example, a year) to the flow of value corresponding to the cost of production engaged during this unit of time, $T = K/(c + v)$, is the *turnover time* of capital measured in units of time such as months or years. In the Marxist literature, the turnover time is often implicitly or explicitly assumed to be unity, in which case the profit rate $r = s/K$ is equal to the *profit margin*, the ratio of profit to costs of production, $s/(c + v)$.

The movement of capital in the pursuit of profit results in a tendency toward the equalization of profit rates among industries. Marx calls commodity prices which are consistent with an equalized profit rate *prices of production*:

> But capital withdraws from a sphere with a low rate of profit and invades others, which yield a higher profit. Through this incessant outflow and influx, or, briefly, through its distribution among the various spheres, which depends on how the rate of profit falls here and rises there, it creates such a ratio of supply to demand that the average profit in the various spheres of production becomes the same, and values are, therefore, converted into prices of production. (III, 10)

Actual *market prices* tend to gravitate around prices of production, and this property defines the *capitalist law of exchange* (which supersedes the commodity law of exchange when production is organized by capital). As stated earlier, Marx calls the substitution of one law of exchange for the other a 'transformation', the *transformation of values* (actually prices proportional to individual values) *into prices of production*.

The profit of commercial and money-dealing capital (III, 16; III, 19)

Although commercial and money-dealing capitals do not contribute to the extraction of surplus value, they do participate in its realization, along the lines indicated above, like any other capital. Commercial capital, for example, must secure a profit by buying commodities from industrial capitalists at prices below the prices at which those commodities will be sold to final purchasers. In this way commercial capital appropriates part of the surplus value actually created in the circuit of industrial capital. Similarly, the fees charged by money-dealing capital transfer surplus value created in the circuit of other capitals (abstracting from interest paid by other agents such as households or the state). Thus, the profit of commercial and money-dealing capital is part of the surplus value produced by labour employed by industrial capital.

Differential and absolute rent (III, 38; III, 45)

The level at which rents can be established is directly related to the level of the average and tendentially uniform profit rate in the overall economy. The condition for the cultivation of a land of lesser fertility or for a more intensive investment is that the marginal investment must yield the average profit rate. All capitalists (including capitalist farmers) expect to realize the average profit rate prevailing throughout the economy. This condition is assured if landowners bargain for rents just high enough to assure capitalists the average rate of profit on their land. This defines *differential rent*. Marx also assumes that landowners as a class may withhold their lands until a minimum rent is paid, which defines *absolute rent*.

The centralization and concentration of capital, monopoly (I, 25)

The Classical–Marxian analysis, which assumes equalized profit rates among industries (not firms, because of differences in their productive efficiency), does not seem to match the features of competition in modern capitalism. Followers of Marx, from Hilferding and Lenin in the early 20th century to contemporary Marxist economics, point to the historical transformation of competition through the emergence of monopolies and oligopolies. The notion of the interplay of large firms is already part of Marx's analysis. In the process of accumulation the size of individual capitalist firms is altered by the *concentration* and *centralization* of capital. In Marx's account, concentration refers to the rise of the size of firms which parallels accumulation, while centralization denotes the outcome of merger or acquisition (and the process of competitive elimination of smaller and less efficient firms in an industry). Monopoly capital is not, however, part of Marx's analysis of capitalism, and Marx does not question the classical analysis of competition on such grounds. Rather than the view that the size of firms could hamper the process of equalization of profit rates among industries, Marx repeatedly asserts that credit mechanisms, including banks, are a crucial factor in the ability of capital to migrate among industries and, therefore, in the formation of prices of production.

Accumulation, and technological and distributional change

The *accumulation of capital* refers to the situation where a fraction of surplus value is saved and devoted to increasing the value of capital. While the analysis of expanded reproduction considers a steady growth path of the economy (on which the key ratios, the rate of surplus value, the organic composition of capital, the value of labour power, and the composition of demand, are assumed to remain constant), Marx's theory of accumulation incorporates the qualitative change in capitalist production that actually accompanies its expansion.

Capital accumulation and employment (I, 25)

For accumulation to succeed, a number of conditions must be met. In particular, an expanded supply of labour power must be made available to permit the expansion of production, an issue which Marx addresses at the end of Volume I. Marx rejects the conclusions of classical economists such as Thomas Malthus, who proposed universal laws governing population growth and a 'natural' path of accumulation of capital, and blamed low wages on the fecundity of workers and the limits of natural resources. Marx argues that each mode of production evolves its own characteristic laws of population, and that capitalism in particular gives rise to a number of mechanisms that ensure a rough proportionality between population growth and the accumulation of capital.

How much labour is necessary to meet the demands of capital accumulation? How is the supply of labour roughly adapted to accumulation? Marx explains, in his *law of capitalist accumulation*, that the amount of labour required depends on (1) the pace of accumulation and (2) technical change as manifested in the variation of the composition of capital – that is, the ratio of capital outlays on means of production (*constant capital*) to capital outlays on wages (*variable capital*). If accumulation is rapid, and the composition of capital unaltered, the demand for labour power grows in proportion to accumulation and real wages tend to increase. This is the most favourable situation for workers. Technical change may moderate this tendency through an increase in

the composition of capital, as the same accumulation requires less additional labour, and the demand for labour power grows more slowly than capital as a whole. A priori, any relation between the pace of accumulation and the change in the composition of capital may occur. Marx points, however, to the fact that the composition of capital tends historically to rise and, thus, the pressure on employment is regularly relaxed.

Two mechanisms contribute to remedy any potential lack of available labour power. First, technical change leading to increases in the composition of capital makes some employed labour redundant. Second, recurrent crises periodically restore what Marx calls the *floating reserve army of labour*, with the decline of output. Thus, the process of accumulation is uneven. Accumulation first proceeds during phases of more or less balanced growth; gradually the reserve army of unemployed workers is reabsorbed and wages rises. This is an inducement towards technical change increasing the composition of capital. If, however, the demand for labour grows too rapidly, a crisis occurs, the demand for labour is relaxed. Finally, a new wave of accumulation resumes after the crisis, during which a fraction of capital is devalued or destroyed. We will return below to these episodes in which a rise of wages provokes crises, which Marx calls situations of 'over-accumulation'.

In addition to this recurring fluctuation of unemployment, capitalism historically has drawn workers from the *latent reserve army*, through the destruction of traditional agricultural modes of production, and the consequent migration of displaced workers to the capitalist labour market. The potential competition of the latent reserve army puts a long-term downward pressure on wages as well.

The overall interaction of these factors is complex, because technical change and the income distribution cannot be treated as independent mechanisms. Marx considers that rising wages, and a correspondingly diminished rate of surplus value, increase the incentives for capitalists to seek labour-saving technical changes. This leads to a rise in the composition of capital, as more machinery is employed, precisely in order to avoid increased wage costs. This analysis must be supplemented by the consideration of fundamental political conditions, in particular, the strength of workers' class struggle, since Marx believed that, over and above the mechanisms involved in the law of capitalist accumulation, organized labour struggles could influence both wages and the length of the working day.

One of Marx's main goals in presenting his theory of accumulation, at the end of Volume I of *Capital*, is to show that the scarcity of labour power is not an absolute barrier to capital accumulation. The main thesis there is that, in the race between capital accumulation and the supply of labour power that governs the evolution of real wages, employment, and the rate of surplus value, capital has the edge over labour as a result of the capability of capital to substitute fixed capital (machinery) for labour:

> The same causes which develop the expansive power of capital, develop also the labour-power at its disposal. The relative mass of the industrial reserve army increases therefore with the potential energy of wealth. But the greater this reserve army in proportion to the active labour-army, the greater is the mass of a consolidated surplus-population, whose misery is in inverse ratio to its torment of labour. The more extensive, finally, the Lazarus-layers of the working-class, and the industrial reserve army, the greater is official pauperism. *This is the absolute general law of capitalist accumulation.* Like all other laws it is modified in its working by many circumstances, the analysis of which does not concern us here. (I, 25-4)

Besides the resistance of organized workers, this capability of capitalism to perpetuate an available reserve army by technical change is limited by the cost of the addition of capital which is required to displace labour, as Marx will contend in his analysis of technical change and the tendency for the profit rate to fall.

Technical change (III, 13–15)

The social and technical conditions of production and their historical transformation are central to Marx's analysis of capitalist production. The term 'technology' is convenient but somewhat misleading. Marx always describes conditions of production in a perspective which combines technology in the strict sense and organization, that is, the institutional framework in which production is performed; the notion of social relations cannot be neglected in this context. This is the case, for example, in the analysis of relative surplus value, as discussed earlier in reference to manufacture and large-scale industry.

Although Marx often discussed specific historical determinants of technical innovations, his main theory of technical change in capitalism sees it as an endogenous response to pressures from competitors and workers. Each capitalist has a strong motivation to find cost-reducing technical innovations (or profit-increasing product innovations) because the firm which first successfully exploits such innovations is in a position to capture higher-than-average profit rates ('super-profits') as a result of its temporary monopoly on the innovation. Innovating capitalists may also use their cost advantage aggressively to increase their market share. (In this respect Marx develops the theory of technical change Ricardo, 1817, presents in his chapter on machinery.) Over time, competitors will find equivalent innovations and the advantage of the innovating capitalist will erode.

Capitalist technical innovation in Marx's framework begins with the discovery of a range of potential new productive techniques and forms of labour organization. The accumulated store of technical knowledge available

to capitalist society at any moment is the result of this historical process of innovation: there is no set of pre-determined techniques as is assumed in the neoclassical production function. Marx's theory of induced technical change is basically evolutionary. The capitalist evaluates the cost of these alternatives at prevailing prices and wages, and forms expectations concerning profit rates. Only those technologies that promise to reduce costs or increase profits at prevailing prices and wages are *viable* candidates for adoption. The criterion is an increased profit rate.

Marx emphasizes that, because capitalism places both strong incentives for technical change and the power to implement in the hands of competing capitalist firms, it is a *technically progressive* mode of production, in contrast to slavery and feudalism. In this respect Marx resembles Smith, who emphasizes increasing returns inherent in the division of labour, rather than Ricardo, who emphasizes diminishing returns due to limited natural resources (land).

The tendency for the profit rate to fall (III, 13–15)

In Volume III of *Capital*, Marx describes trajectories of technical and distributional changes that he denotes as *historical tendencies*. They are unbalanced (nonhomothetic) growth trajectories, which Marx considered typical of the dynamics of capitalism, which we will describe as *trajectories à la Marx*. Along such very long-term paths, the growth rates of capital, output, and employment gradually fall, labour productivity and the composition of capital rise, the share of wages in total income is constant or diminishing, and the profit rate declines. In the speaking of historical tendencies, 'historical' refers to a very long-term time frame; 'tendency' means that though accumulation in capitalism tends to follow such trajectories, the trajectory does not necessarily prevail due to the action of what Marx labels *counteracting factors*. It is in this framework that Marx defines the *tendential fall in the rate of profit*. This 'law' expresses sophisticated insights into the historical dynamics of capitalist economic growth. It is one of the major disputed issues in contemporary Marxist economics (along with the transformation problem).

In Volume III, the profit rate is written as a ratio of two flows or, equivalently, the turnover time of capital is assumed to be unity: $r = s/K = s/(c + v)$. Dividing by v, Marx obtains: $r = (s/v)/(c/v + 1)$. The numerator is the rate of surplus value, and the denominator is the *value composition of capital, the ratio of constant to variable capital*, plus 1. Marx calls this value composition the *organic composition* of capital. In this simple presentation, the conflicting impacts of the rate of exploitation and the organic composition of capital are clearly evident.

Although *labour productivity* does not appear in this formal setting, it is explicitly a key variable in Marx's analysis. Without altering the basic framework, it is possible to write: $r = (s/(v + s))/((c + v)/(v + s))$. Here, $s/(v + s)$

is the share of profit in total income, and $(c+v)/(v+s)$ is total capital per hour worked, which is another measure of the organic composition of capital. (This ratio can also be read as the ratio of capital to output, since output is equal to total income, or equivalently the inverse of what is frequently loosely called 'capital productivity'.) The numerator, the share of profit, can be written $1 - (v/(v+s))$, that is, 1 minus the share of wages. The share of wages is equal to real wages divided by labour productivity. Thus, the profit rate can be expressed as the ratio of the profit share to the total capital per hour worked, which we call simply the *composition of capital*:

$$\text{profit rate} = \frac{1 - \frac{\text{real wage}}{\text{labor productivity}}}{\text{composition of capital}}$$

Marx's fundamental insight can be sketched as follows. To maintain or increase profits (which appear in the numerator of the profit rate), when there is no fall in the real wage, capitalists must increase the productivity of labour, which is the mechanism of relative surplus value. Marx contends, however, that this increase has a considerable cost for capitalists because increases in labour productivity typically require the investment of more capital per hour worked: productivity gains are realized by way of an increased mechanization of production. Thus, the composition of capital rises, and the rate of profit may fall. The actual evolution of the rate of profit also depends on what happens to the real wage and, consequently, to the rate of surplus value as labour productivity increases, which depends on labour market factors and class struggle, which are beyond the control of any individual capitalist.

Marx considers the case where the rate of surplus value remains constant to refute the argument that the falling profit rate is the result of an excessive growth in the cost of labour to the capitalists. When the productivity of labour rises, a constant rate of surplus value implies a rising real wage. Thus in making this argument, Marx does not assume a constant real wage. His thesis is rather that it is difficult for capitalists to counteract rising wages by technical change, since a more efficient technique in terms of labour productivity typically requires a rising composition of capital. The linchpin of Marx's thesis is, therefore, a hypothesis on the features of available techniques, that is, the profile of innovation: it is comparatively easy to find labour-saving devices if the cost of mechanization is not considered, but opportunities to reduce labour costs without inflating capital costs are rare.

Thus, on trajectories à la Marx the productivity of labour rises, while the productivity of capital (the inverse of the composition of capital) falls, a pattern of technical change sometimes called *Marx-biased*:

> The law of the falling rate of profit, which expresses the same, or even a higher, rate of surplus-value, states,

in other words, that any quantity of the average social capital, say, a capital of 100, comprises an ever larger portion of means of production, and an ever smaller portion of living labour. Therefore, since the aggregate mass of living labour operating the means of production decreases in relation to the value of these means of production, it follows that the unpaid labour and the portion of value in which it is expressed must decline as compared to the value of the advanced total capital. ... The relative decrease of the variable and increase of the constant capital, however much both parts may grow in absolute magnitude, is, as we have said, but another expression for greater productivity of labour. (III, 13)

Though Marx never articulated the entire framework, this analysis of the biased pattern of technical change supplements the mechanisms at work in the law of capitalist accumulation. Accumulation recurrently pushes employment to the limits of the supply of labour power available and drives real wages upward. Technical change and recurrent crises allow for the partial relaxation of this pressure (as we have seen), but, in typical periods, the new techniques available are such that technical change can only partially offset the rise in real wages, and the profit rate falls. Accumulation is pursued in spite of the diminished profit rate, which will only be apparent after the fact, when a major crisis occurs.

The analysis Engels published from Marx's notes in Volume III of *Capital* is incomplete, and was not intended for publication in the form in which we read it. Consequently, it is not too surprising that Marx's analysis of the tendency for the profit rate to fall remains controversial among Marxists. A central issue is the assumption made concerning real wages, and its relationship to the profitability criterion in the adoption of new techniques. Marx is clear that the innovating capitalist initially makes a surplus profit, while his competitors gradually adopt the new technique and prices fall through competition towards the prices of production corresponding to the new technology. Marx contends that the new uniform average profit rate tends to be lower than the original one. Nobuo Okishio (1972) has demonstrated that if the real wage remains unchanged during this process the new average profit rate can never fall. But along a trajectory à la Marx real wages do increase, as we have explained, although the possibility of a tendency for the rate of profit to fall is consistent with Marx's assumption that the rate of surplus value is constant or even rising.

The problem of the evolution of real wages, the value of labour power, and the rate of surplus value over time as labour productivity rises is controversial among Marxists, due to a change of Marx's view on this subject during his lifetime. Engels explained that Marx originally accepted the so-called *iron law of wages*, which assumes that real wages are constantly driven downward to a minimum compatible with the reproduction of the labour force, but later abandoned it. Marx sometimes refers to a 'socially and historically determined' cost of reproduction of labour power, as an external constraint on the evolution of the real wage. But this 'exogenous' variable is explicitly subject to a number of economic and social determinations: (i) class struggle impacts on wages and the duration of labour; and (ii) the outcome of struggles crucially depends on the conditions of accumulation and the population available to work (as in the law of accumulation). Marx's understanding of the determination of wages is similar to his view of technical change: the path of real wages is the result of the interaction of extra-economic factors with economic mechanisms such as accumulation and crises.

Crises and the business cycle (III, 15)

There is no systematic treatment of crises and of the business cycle in Marx's work, although the issue plays a prominent role in his analysis of capitalism. In early works, like the *Communist Manifesto*, even prior to Marx's serious study of political economy, the idea that crises will prove more violent with the evolution of capitalism is central. Recurrent crises became a feature of capitalism during the first half of the 19th century. This link between economic mechanisms and class struggle had a considerable impact on Marx's view of the historical dynamics of capitalism. Then, Marx became gradually better aware of the complexity of the phenomenon of crises, in particular the relationship between real and financial mechanisms and crises.

Partial crises and crises of general overproduction

Before capitalism, poor crops and the devastation of war and disease were the major causes of disruptions of production. David Ricardo (1817) observed the existence of recurring crises more directly related to the nature of capitalism, which he called *states of distress*. These crises struck specific industries, like textiles. Consequently, Ricardo interpreted these situations as the effect of *disproportions*, that is, the outcome of the excessive accumulation of capital in one industry. Ricardo did not believe in the possibility of a general glut of the market. Marx devoted much energy to the refutation of Ricardo's interpretation. He contended that the existence of a delay between the sale of a commodity and the spending of its money price on another commodity invalidates 'Say's Law', the principle that the sale of a commodity constitutes a direct demand for another commodity. Monetary exchange thus implies the *possibility* of crises, because, by functioning as intermediary in exchanges, money allows for the interruption of the chain of exchanges. Only the 'possibility' of crises is, however, implied, not their actual mechanisms in capitalism.

Marx identified a new category of crises, *crises of general overproduction,* where all industries were simultaneously affected. Marx did not deny the existence of crises specific to particular industries, that he called *partial crises,* but contrasted the two types of situations, partial and general, and was specifically concerned with the latter.

The ultimate ground of crisis: profitability and social needs

Marx described general crises of overproduction as typical of capitalism. In capitalism, the purpose of production is not the satisfaction of the needs of the population, but the appropriation of profits. The 'ultimate ground' of crisis in capitalism is this disconnection between production and social needs:

> The ultimate reason [*ground*] for all real crises always remains the poverty and restricted consumption of the masses as opposed to the drive of capitalist production to develop the productive forces as though only the absolute consuming power of society constituted their limit. (III, 30)

This quotation is often misunderstood. Marx did not believe that higher wages would solve the problem of crises in capitalism. The cause of crises, proper to capitalism, is the recurrent inability to pursue production *at a certain rate of profit*. Therefore, profitability is always the crucial variable in Marx's explanation of crises:

> Over-production of capital is never anything more than overproduction of means of production – of means of labour and necessities of life – which may serve as capital, *i.e.*, may serve to exploit labour at a given degree of exploitation; ... too many means of labour and necessities of life are produced at times to permit of their serving as means for the exploitation of labourers at a certain rate of profit. (III, 15-3)

The business cycle and its determinants

Marx described the fluctuating pattern of production in capitalism as 'the cycles in which modern industry moves – state of inactivity, mounting revival, prosperity, over-production, crisis, stagnation, state of inactivity, etc.' (III, 22).

Production is recurrently destabilized by mechanisms which affect the profitability of capital in the short run (a sudden decline rather than a steady downward trend). The first mechanism is *over-accumulation*. Periodically, employment gets closer to the limits of the population available to work (the reserve army is reabsorbed, as in the law of capitalist accumulation). Wages tend to rise, and profitability is diminished. A second mechanism is the rise of interest rates. During the phase of rapid accumulation, the mass of credits increases and, at a certain point, interest rates rise. Again, profitability is affected and the economy destabilized. Marx is well aware of the relationship between real and financial mechanism, and he interprets the direction of causation as reciprocal.

As stated above, Marx did not explain crises by the deficient level of wages (except in his very early work), and refuted this explanation in the manuscripts of Volume II:

> It is sheer tautology to say that crises are caused by the scarcity of effective consumption, or of effective consumers. The capitalist system does not know any other modes of consumption than effective ones, except that of *sub forma pauperis* or of the swindler. That commodities are unsalable means only that no effective purchasers have been found for them, i.e., consumers (since commodities are bought in the final analysis for productive or individual consumption). But if one were to attempt to give this tautology the semblance of a profounder justification by saying that the working-class receives too small a portion of its own product and the evil would be remedied as soon as it receives a larger share of it and its wages increase in consequence, one could only remark that crises are always prepared by precisely a period in which wages rise generally [over-accumulation] and the working-class actually gets a larger share of that part of the annual product which is intended for consumption. From the point of view of these advocates of sound and 'simple' (!) common sense, such a period should rather remove the crisis. (II, 20)

Structural crises and the falling profit rate

Since the profitability of capital is central in Marx analysis of crises, there is a link between the tendency for the profit rate to fall and crises. Marx's view is that actual phases of decline of the profit rate make crises more likely, more frequent and deeper. He points to the existence of periods of sustained instability, which, although Marx does not use the term, can be called *structural crises*. A declining and depressed profit rate (both the tendency and levels are at issue) disturbs capitalist accumulation:

> …in view of the fact that the rate at which the total capital is valorised, i.e. the rate of profit, is the spur to capitalist production …, a fall in this rate slows down the formation of new, independent capitals and thus appears as a threat to the development of the capitalist production process; it promotes overproduction, speculation and crises, and leads to the existence of excess capital alongside a surplus population. (III, 15)

This insight concerning the link between the profit rate and the occurrence of periods of historical perturbation in the course of accumulation provides a powerful framework for understanding the real history of capitalist economies.

DUNCAN FOLEY AND GÉRARD DUMÉNIL

See also **British classical economics; capitalism; class; classical distribution theories; classical growth model;** **commodity fetishism; commodity money; exploitation; labour theory of value; labour's share of income; Marx, Karl Heinrich; Marxian transformation problem; Marxian value analysis; 'political economy'; profit and profit theory.**

Bibliography

Arthur, C.J. 2004. *New Dialectic and Marx's Capital*. Leiden, Boston: Brill.

Brewer, A. 1984. *Guide to Marx's Capital*. Cambridge: Cambridge University Press.

Cleaver, H. 2000. *Reading Capital Politically*. Edinburgh: AK Press.

Duménil, G. and Lévy, D. 1993. *Economics of the Profit Rate: Competition, Crises, and Historical Tendencies in Capitalism*. Aldershot: Edward Elgar.

Duménil, G. and Lévy, D. 2003. *Économie Marxiste du Capitalisme*. Paris: La Découverte.

Fine, B. 1975. *Marx's Capital*. Leiden, Boston: Brill.

Fine, B. and Saad-Filho, A. 2004. *Marx's Capital*. New York: Pluto.

Foley, D. 1986. *Understanding Capital: Marx's Economic Theory*. Cambridge, MA: Harvard University Press.

Itoh, M. and Bullock, P. 1987. *The Basic Theory of Capitalism: The Forms and Substance of the Capitalist Economy*. Lanham, MD: Rowman and Littlefield.

Marx, K. 1859. *A Contribution to the Critique of Political Economy*, ed. M. Dobb. New York: International Publishers, 1970.

Marx, K. 1976, 1978, 1981. *Capital, Volumes I, II, III*. New York: Random House.

Marx, K. and Engels, F. 1848. *The Communist Manifesto*. New York: Signet Classics, 1998.

Moseley, F. 1993. *Marx's Method in Capital: A Reexamination*. Leiden, Boston: Brill.

Okishio, N. 1972. On Marx's production prices. *Keizaigaku Kenkyu* 19, 38–63.

Pilling, G. 1980. *Marx's Capital*. London, New York: Routledge.

Ricardo, D. 1817. *On the Principles of Political Economy and Taxation*. Cambridge: Cambridge University Press, 1951.

Rosdolsky, R. 2005. *The Making of Marx's Capital*. London: Pluto Press.

Rubin, I. 1972. *Essays on Marx's Economic Theory*. Detroit: Black and Red.

Sekine, T. 1997. *Outline of the Dialectic of Capital*. London: Palgrave Macmillan.

Shaikh, A. and Tonak, E. 1996. *Measuring the Wealth of Nations: The Political Economy of National Accounts*. Cambridge: Cambridge University Press.

Sweezy, P. 1970. *Theory of Capitalist Development*. New York: Monthly Review Press.

Weeks, J. 1994. *Capital and Exploitation*. Princeton: Princeton University Press.

Wolff, R. and Cohen, M. 1985. *Understanding Marx: A Reconstructive and Critique of Capital*. Princeton: Princeton University Press.

Mason, Edward Sagendorph (1899–1992)

Edward Mason had a significant impact on the economics profession in four disparate areas: through his influence on the Harvard Economics Department; through his role in two separate sub-fields of the discipline – industrial and development economics; and by exemplifying the dual role of academic and practitioner.

When he came to Harvard in 1919 as a graduate student, he was not in the Harvard mould: he was from the public schools of Kansas and its University. Later, another newcomer and 'provincial', J. Kenneth Galbraith, characterized young Mason's presence by saying 'even when he was an Instructor, where Ed Mason sat there was the head of the table'. He remained a central figure in Harvard Economics for well over 50 years, his only absence a stint in Washington during the Second World War (1941–44). He was one of a handful of senior faculty who dominated the department during its glory days, when it produced about half of all economics Ph.D. degree holders in the United States and was responsible for a substantial fraction of the research produced in the country.

Mason's role at Harvard extended beyond economics. He served for 11 years (1947–58) as Dean of the School of Public Administration and for a short period was second-in-command of the university. While he was its Dean the School of Public Administration became the leading exponent of an emphasis on policy analysis, especially economic analysis, rather than administrative tools and institutions.

Mason taught many of the economists who expanded industrial economics from a preoccupation with regulation and monopoly to an analysis of markets and firms. The 'Masonic Lodge' of ex-students, together with its Grand Master, came to dominate the newly developed applied discipline of industrial organization. Mason stimulated the work by his proposition that the performance of a firm was largely explained by the structure of the market in which it operated. The controversy stimulated by this idea and by the concept of monopolistic competition to which he contributed, helped the subfield of industrial economics to flourish intellectually.

It was typical of Mason to come to research from policy concerns; he exemplified the practitioner–academician. Mason's advice was sought by governments and he was privy to their problems and the facts at their disposal. During the Second World War, he headed the economic staff of the OSS, probably the first US intelligence agency to gather economic intelligence systematically and to analyse possibilities for economic warfare. Later he was Deputy Assistant Secretary of State in charge of Economic Affairs and chief economic adviser to the US delegation at the 1947 Moscow Conference.

In the early 1950s, development economists began to apply many of the standard tools of economics to the special problems and institutions of the poor countries. Mason developed an interest in this subject in typical fashion by setting out to deal with a specific set of policy problems. After returning to Harvard at the end of the war, as Dean of Public Administration, he was asked to organize technical assistance to help Pakistan carry out the economic analysis crucial to rational government decision making. Out of that effort emerged another institution that rightfully could be seen as created by Mason; the Development Advisory Service, later the Harvard Institute of International Development. A surprising proportion of those who consider themselves development economists had their initial field experience as an adviser, or as their local counter part, in one of the teams fielded by an organization that existed only because Mason managed to persuade Harvard to undertake the non-traditional university function of advising foreign governments.

GUSTAV F. PAPANEK

Selected works

1926. The doctrine of comparative cost. *Quarterly Journal of Economics* 41, November 63–93.

1932. *The Street Railway in Massachusetts.* Cambridge, MA: Harvard University Press.

1937. Monopoly in law and economics. *Yale Law Journal* 47(1), 34–49. Repr. in *Public Policy and the Modern Corporation: Selected Readings*, ed. D. Grunewald and H.L. Bass. New York: Meredith, 1966.

1938. Price inflexibility. *Review of Economics and Statistics* 20, May, 53–64.

1939. Price and production policies of larger-scale enterprise. *American Economic Review* 29, 61–74. Repr. in American Economic Association, *Readings in Industrial Organization and Public Policy*, ed. R.B. Hefelbower and G.W. Stocking. Homewood, IL: Richard D. Irwin, 1958.

1946. *Controlling World Trade Cartels and Commodity Agreements.* New York: McGraw-Hill.

1949a. The effectiveness of the federal anti-trust laws: a symposium. *American Economic Review* 39, 712–13. Repr. in *Monopoly Power and Economic Performance: The Problems of Industrial Concentration*, ed. E. Mansfield. New York: W.W. Norton, 1964. Also reprinted in *Problems of the Modern Economy*, ed. E.S. Phelps. New York: W.W. Norton, 1966.

1949b. The current status of the monopoly problem in the United States. *Harvard Law Review* 62, 1265–85.

1956. Market power and business conduct: some comments on the Report of the Attorney General's Committee on Antitrust Policy. *American Economic Review, Papers and Proceedings* 46, 471–81.

1957. *Economic Concentration and the Monopoly Problem.* Cambridge, MA: Harvard University Press.

1958. The apologetics of 'Managerialism'. *Journal of Business* 31, January, 1–11. Repr. in *The Business System: Readings in Ideas and Concepts* (vols 1–3). *In Commemoration of the Fiftieth Anniversary, Graduate School of Business, Columbia University, 1966*, ed. C.C. Walton and R.S. Eells. New York: Arkville Press, 1967.

1959, ed. *The Corporation in Modern Society*. Cambridge. MA: Harvard University Press.

1952. Raw materials, rearmament, and economic development. *Quarterly Journal of Economics* 66, 327–41.

1960. The role of government in economic development. *American Economic Review, Papers and Proceedings* 50, 636–40. Repr. in *Studies in Economic Development*, ed. A.M. Okun and R.W. Richardson. New York: Holt, Rinehart & Winston, 1961.

1962. Some aspects of the strategy of development planning: centralization vs. decentralization. In *Organizations, Planning and Programming for Economic Development*, vol. 8 of Science, Technology and Development; US papers prepared for the U.N. Conference on the Application of Science and Technology for the Benefit of the Less Developed Area, Washington, DC: Government Printing Office.

1963. Interests, ideologies and the problem of stability and growth. *American Economic Review* 53, 1–18.

1964. *Foreign Aid and Foreign Policy*. New York: Harper and Row for the Council on Foreign Relations.

1966. *Economic Development in India and Pakistan*. Cambridge, MA: Center for International Affairs, Harvard University.

1967. Monopolistic competition and the growth process in less developed countries: Chamberlin and the Schumpeterian dimension. In *Monopolistic Competition Theory: Studies in Impact. Essays in Honor of Edward H. Chamberlin*, ed. R.E. Kuenne. New York: John Wiley.

1971. Controlling industry. In D.V. Brown et al., *The Economics of the Recovery Program*. New York: Da Capo.

1973. (With R.E. Asher.) *The World Bank since Bretton Woods*. Washington, DC: Brookings Institution.

1980. (With others.) *The Economic and Social Modernization of the Republic of Korea*. Cambridge, MA: Harvard University Press.

Massé, Pierre (1898–1987)

Massé was born on 13 January 1898, the same day that Emile Zola in his 'J'accuse' revealed the truth about the Dreyfus Affair, which arouses so much passion in French political circles to this day. His family was quick to take sides – in defence of the innocent – and from them Massé quite probably inherited his deep humanism, in which realistic thought was allied with optimism in action.

In 1916, he passed the competitive entrance examinations to both the Ecole Normale Supérieure, in science, and the Ecole Polytechnique. He was a Second Lieutenant in the Artillery from 1917 to 1918, and then opted for the Polytechnique and a career as an engineer. This choice of career foreshadowed a life in which, in a happy marriage, thought and action were to mingle unceasingly. A further spell of training at the Ecole des Ponts et Chaussées, and the start of his career as a government servant, channelled him towards major civil engineering works, and then, quite soon, towards the business world and hydroelectrical improvement works.

This was a decisive turning-point for both the man of action, the builder, and for the thinking economist. Obliged to deal with the management problems raised by the water stocks accumulated in reservoirs, and also with the need to turn them to account, Massé identified the key role of reserves as the means of regulating systems in order to cope with random factors. In his first work, *Les réserves et la régulation de l'avenir*, published in 1946, whose findings had been published two years previously in a paper submitted to the Société Statistique de Paris, Pierre Massé can be seen to be a forerunner of dynamic programming and of the theory of optimum control. In particular, he set forth in this paper two rules for the optimal management of random processes: (*a*) reservoirs should be managed so as to equalize the marginal utility of the water releases and the marginal expected value of the water held in stock; and (*b*) in order to calculate that expected value a strategy for the future should be defined, that is, a sequence of conditional decisions combining at any time the impact of past decisions, the actual outcome of the random processes, and the perception of what future natural conditions will probably be. Kenneth Arrow was later to note, in 1956, that this was the earliest formulation of Richard Bellman's Optimum Principle.

Massé's work was deeply marked by the recognition that in a random world – and the more so with an uncertain future – one could not confine oneself to just a single forecast, and by the need to adopt strategies and regulate stocks. This was to be borne out 20 years later, when he was in charge of the French Commissariat au Plan (Planning Commission). The consistency of the forecasts carried out as part of the National Accounts exercise certainly went some way towards making the plan a 'reducer of uncertainties'. Moreover, under his guidance this achievement was crowned by a forecasting approach in which the seeking of a consensus on the type of development that was desirable was combined with the concern to identify 'factors with potential for the future', and by the devising of 'warning lights', as instruments for marking the future course that were capable of setting corrective actions in motion.

He was Directeur de l'Equipement at Electricité de France in 1946 for the start of the Plan Monnet and became its Directeur Général Adjoint two-and-a-half years later, a post he held until 1959. In those 12 years he developed, and then applied, linear programming techniques for determining the overall volume of electricity generating plant, and furnished justification for using a national discount rate for setting off present and future income and expenditure against each other. He tirelessly argued with the government in favour of using these clear and rigorous tools, already finding support on the Commissariat Général du Plan. In 1957, he published

Le choix des investissements, a work which was to become authoritative both in France and abroad.

In February 1959, General de Gaulle appointed Massé to head the Commissariat Général du Plan. He took up his duties backed by the sound experience of a microeconomist who was thoroughly at ease with the idea of maximizing the benefit to the community in managing a public service, and who was attached to the pricing system and to its role in providing guidance and regulation. He sought to make the Plan – which had been largely governed by the concern for consistency and accordingly gave pride of place to analysing interlocking strengths and weaknesses – a structure better directed towards achieving competitiveness, both domestically and on foreign markets. His aim was not only to produce more, but also to produce better quality, with consciousness of costs.

With these goals, he strove to lighten the Plan's structure and make it interlocking with, and not a substitute for, the market. Without losing the valuable contribution of a generalized market survey, backed up with the use of an input–output matrix, he endeavoured to better pinpoint future price and income trends: in this way, programming by volume was to be backed up by an early attempt at programming by value. While the market could show what present prices were, it said practically nothing about future prices, since forward markets covered only narrow sectors and near time-horizons. By the light it shed on the future, the Plan was seen to be an indispensable adjunct to a smoothly working market economy. The 'Centre' had the task of successfully conveying to the 'Periphery' the right price system, and on the basis of this information, the Periphery was able to return to the Centre information on what the intentions were of the decentralized economic agents concerning volumes of goods to be consumed or invested in, and the volumes of factors to be mobilized. In this way, consultation was established between the Centre and the Periphery, converging, after a few successive iterations, towards a dynamic equilibrium. Pierre Massé had already analysed this converging dialogue between the Centre and the Periphery as early as 1952, in 'Pratique et philosophie de l'investissement'. The Commissariat au Plan in fact organized consultations among the major socio-occupational categories; experts could intervene to put figures to the impacts from selecting the options adopted, while the representatives of the state were there to ensure observance of the major policy guidelines defined by the government in agreement with Parliament. Such at least was the theory. Certain departures from it were unavoidable in practice.

However, 'at the same time as it was an act of faith', the Plan continued to be 'an affirmation of the will'. Concerned as he was for a 'less incomplete view of man' to be taken into consideration, Massé succeeded in convincing the most influential circles in his country that a better balance should be struck between private and collective consumption. Thus, a feature of the early 1960s was a new concern for developing communal infrastructures. At the same time, while investigating various development scenarios, he concluded that it was necessary to raise the discount rate (of profitability) – an indicator of the scarcity of capital for government investors – so that it actually corresponded to the marginal efficiency of capital. He also concerned himself with disseminating the practice of constant-price calculations, so that, while changes in relative prices were not ignored, the profitability of infrastructure projects was not made attributable to inflated profits.

Having stressed future values, Massé necessarily broadened the scope of studies to cover price and income trends, and unavoidably brought discussion round to the knotty point of social tensions. To clarify and persuade, he worked on surplus accounts, establishing a rigorous relationship between the overall productivity gains made from one year to the next, and the sum of benefits available for distribution to customers, suppliers, workers and investors. From this attempt there at least remains a learning approach which the Centre d'Etude des Revenus et des Coûts, set up in 1966 at his instigation, has been engaged in disseminating and extending.

After helping start the Fifth Plan, Massé returned to Electricité de France, of which he was chairman for three years, and secured from the political authorities a sounder channelling of the necessary efforts for investment in the generation of electricity by nuclear power. He thereupon resumed acquaintanceship with business economics, though he did not forsake reflections upon the problems of the national economy, which he was never to abandon thereafter.

In 1977, Massé was elected a member of the Institut de France, which for almost 200 years has gathered together the most eminent French personalities in the humanities, science, history, philosophy and art. He pursued research for the remainder of his life. His body of work attests to a lifelong endeavour to reconcile macro and microeconomists and to ensure the cross-fertilization of their ideas for the social good.

MARCEL P. BOITEUX

Selected works

1946. *Les résberves et la régulation de l'avenir dans la vie économique*. Paris:Hermann.

1952. Pratique et philosophie de l'investissement. *Economie appliquée* 5, 625–58.

1953. Les investissements électriques. *Revue de statistique appliquée* 1(3–4), 119–29.

1957. (With R. Gibrat.) Application of linear programming to investments in the electric power industry. *Management Science* 3(2), 149–66.

1959. Prévision et prospective. *Cahiers de prospective*. Paris.

1964. *Le choix des investissements*. 2nd edn. Paris: Dunod.

1965. *Le plan ou l'anti-hasard*. Paris: Gallimard.

1969. (With P. Bernard.) *Les dividendes du progrès*. Paris: Le Seuil.

1973. *La crise du développement*. Paris: Gallimard.

1976. *Prédation et création. Etudes*. Paris.

1982. *Le chiffré et le vécu, 1960–1980. Revue des sciences morales et politiques*. Paris.

1984. *Aléas et Progrès, entre Candide et Cassandre*. Paris: Economica.

matching

Matching (or job-matching) is the process whereby a firm and a worker meet, learn whether their characteristics combine productively and, in light of this information, sequentially contract a wage and decide whether to separate or to continue production.

In many respects, a job is like a marriage. Two parties (a firm and a worker) engage in a long-run relationship, whose success depends on a myriad of factors, all quite difficult to describe. Only the actual outcome of the match can reveal the underlying 'fit'. If the match works, it continues; otherwise it is scrapped and the partners try their luck elsewhere.

Jovanovic (1979a) formalizes the job-matching hypothesis in a dynamic, rational-expectations context. This hypothesis hinges on two pivotal ideas: learning and selection. The emphasis on selection follows the tradition of equilibrium sorting in labour markets going back to the static Roy model (Roy, 1951). Now, dynamics and imperfect information take centre stage. A job is viewed as an 'inspection' as well as an 'experience' good. The worker and the firm have to 'taste' the match to decide its value, just like two people first date (to 'inspect' the match) then possibly get married (to 'experience' the match), with varying degrees of success. Unlike in marriage markets, utility is typically transferable through the wage. The fit between firm and worker characteristics is modelled as a match-specific productivity component, a parameter of the output process, summarizing how well the innumerable relevant characteristics of the worker and of the task actually dovetail. Random noise in production creates a signal extraction problem. The firm and/or the worker continuously observe the output performance of the match, incorporate this information in wages, and reassess it against alternative opportunities offered by the market.

A job-matching model

Output y_t is produced at time $t = 1, 2...$ by a firm and a worker with a 1:1 Leontief technology:

$$y_t = \theta + \varepsilon_t.$$

There is no hours or effort choice. θ is average productivity or 'match quality', drawn by nature, unobserved by firm and worker, at the beginning of the match from

$\theta : N(m_{-1}, 1/h_{-1})$, which are also parties' prior beliefs. $\varepsilon_t : N(0, 1/p_\varepsilon)$ is white noise, i.i.d. and independent of θ. Therefore, risk-neutral firm and worker are interested in the permanent component θ. Following the bulk of the literature, assume that firm and worker are symmetrically informed. This is not a crucial assumption: all that matters is that *some* learning drives match selection.

Upon matching at time 0, parties inspect the match and observe a signal

$$x = \theta + \eta$$

where $\eta : N(0, 1/p_\eta)$ independent of θ. By Bayes' rule, $\theta|x : N(m_0, 1/h_0)$, where $h_0 = h_{-1} + p_\eta$ and $h_0 m_0 = m_{-1}h_{-1} + xp_\eta$. If the match begins and output is produced at $t = 1, 2...$, posterior beliefs about match quality conditional on the worker's track record are recursively updated as follows:

$$\theta|x, y_1, y_2, \ldots y_t : N(m_t, 1/h_t)$$
where
$$h_t = h_{-1} + p_\eta + tp_\varepsilon$$
$$h_t m_t = h_{t-1}m_{t-1} + p_\varepsilon y_t.$$

That is, m_t and h_t are the mean and precision of the normal posterior distribution of θ, conditional on all information available to date t. After solving backward, m_t is an average of the prior expectation m_{-1}, the initial signal x and the history of output $\Sigma_{s=1}^t y_s$, weighted by their respective precisions. Given the model's parameters, history and beliefs are summarized by expected productivity m_t and by tenure t, which jointly measure the specific human capital accumulated in the relationship.

With no uncertainty and perfect information ($h_{-1} = \infty$ and/or $p_\eta = \infty$), workers and firms would immediately discard unpromising matches and keep drawing better and better outcomes. With imperfect information, equilibrium behaviour is 'sequential' and non-trivial. Equilibrium cannot be perfectly competitive, due to the specificity of match quality and consequently of human capital. Nonetheless, with free entry, no mobility and no capital costs, there is a contracting equilibrium where the wage offered by the firm to the worker equals the worker's expected (marginal) productivity m_t, and firms break even. The worker captures the entire option value of learning. By Bayes's rule, the distribution of the future wage m_{t+1}, unconditional on unknown match quality θ but conditional on current beliefs $\{m_t, t\}$, is normal with

$$E[m_{t+1}|m_t, t] = m_t \text{ and } Var[m_{t+1}|m_t, t]$$
$$= \frac{p_\varepsilon}{[h_{-1} + p_\eta + (t+1)p_\varepsilon](h_{-1} + p_\eta + tp_\varepsilon)}$$

$$(1)$$

The worker's value of employment solves the Bellman equation

$$V(m_t, t) = \max\langle \beta E[V(\tilde{m}_0, 0)], m_t$$
$$+ \beta E[V(m_{t+1}, t+1)|m_t, t\rangle$$
(2)

for some discount factor $\beta \in [0, 1]$. At each point in time, including $t = 0$ right after observing the initial signal x and before starting production, the worker decides whether to quit this match at once and to inspect another one next period (expected value $E[V(\tilde{m}_0, 0)]$, independent of $\{m_t, t\}$ because θ is match-specific) or to accept the wage m_t, produce, observe the output realization y_t, update beliefs to $\{m_{t+1}, t+1\}$, and decide again.

The worker's employment value $V(m, t)$ is increasing in expected match quality m and decreasing in tenure t. The first effect is obvious. Formally, an increase in m_t raises the right-hand side of (2) directly and, by (1), the normal distribution of future wages in a first-order stochastic dominance sense. Standard dynamic programming arguments establish monotonicity of V. To see why the value V is also decreasing in tenure t, consider the following thought experiment. Before deciding whether to quit or to produce y_{t+1}, the worker is provided with a free signal v which has the same distribution as y_{t+1}, and is then informative about match quality. After observing this signal, the worker cannot do worse, because he or she can always ignore it. So, before observing v, she must value this additional information:

$$E_v[E[V(m_{t+1}, t+1)|v, m_t, t]] \geq V(m_t, t)$$
$$= V(E_v[E[m_{t+1}|m_t, t, v]], t)$$

where the equality follows from $v : y_{t+1}$ and then $E_v[E[m_{t+1}|m_t, t, v]] = E[m_{t+1}|m_t, t] = m_t$. The inequality implies that V is convex in m. Since tenure t reduces the variance of m from (1), it follows from Jensen's inequality that $V(m,t)$ declines in t for given m. Intuitively, a match of equally expected but more uncertain productivity is more valuable: there is some chance it will turn out to be great, otherwise it can always be scrapped.

Testable implications and empirical evidence

The key implications of the model derive from selection and learning, and those implications that are testable have indeed found strong empirical support.

Selection

Given the properties of V, the worker quits as soon as the wage falls short of a reservation wage, which is increasing in tenure. As the option value of learning is consumed, a given expected match quality is no longer sufficient to support the match. Reservation wages are not directly observable, but the resulting selection does have indirect, testable implications. Only promising matches survive, so

the average m_t (wage) in continuing jobs increases (cross-sectionally) with tenure t. Indeed, seniority has modest but consistently positive wage returns (Altonji and Williams, 2005). As better matches are less likely to end, the hazard rate of separation, after an initial 'discovery' phase, declines with tenure, a very robust stylized fact (Farber, 1994). Finally, censoring bad matches skews the distribution of wage residuals, conditional on observable worker and firm exogenous characteristics: a symmetric and thin-tailed Gaussian distribution of output turns into a distribution of 'unexplained' wages with a thick Pareto upper tail (Moscarini, 2005), as in a typical empirical wage distribution.

Learning

From (1), unconditional on the unobserved quality of the match, the wage m_t is a martingale, with variance of innovations declining with tenure t. Beliefs updated in a Bayesian fashion cannot be expected to drift in any direction, for the same reason that asset prices are a random walk in efficient financial markets. Thus, unconditionally on tenure, within-job wage changes are uncorrelated and, as uncertainty about match quality is resolved, have declining variance (Mortensen, 1988). Wage growth slows down over the course of a career. Indeed, the search for serial correlation in wage changes has been inconclusive, but the slowdown of wage growth is prevalent (Topel and Ward, 1992). The wages of a cohort of workers 'fan out', as some workers are luckier than others and find earlier a good match that pays a high wage, and as commonly observed empirically. When a match separates due to an exogenous layoff (not modelled here, but easy to accommodate), the worker loses the entire match-specific human capital, so she suffers a persistent wage loss. This fully agrees with the available evidence (Jacobson, Lalonde and Sullivan, 1993). More problematic is the prediction (Mortensen, 1988) that, as $V(m, t)$ falls with t, separation rises with tenure given the wage: empirical evidence (Topel and Ward, 1992) suggests the opposite.

Alternative hypotheses about worker turnover

In light of its intuitive appeal and empirical success, job-matching has become the benchmark model of worker turnover. It has in part inspired the canonical search-and-matching model of the labour market (Mortensen and Pissarides, 1994), where *ex post* idiosyncratic uncertainty drives job flows while search frictions account for involuntary unemployment. But, despite its vast influence, the job-matching approach still faces alternative and competing views of worker turnover, which provide conceptually quite different explanations for the same set of stylized facts. The starker contrast is with pure search models, which may dispose of heterogeneity altogether. In the search literature, wage dispersion and dynamics originate from firms' power of monopsony and commitment to contracts, due to purely strategic considerations. Retention concerns and counter-offers (Burdett and Mortensen, 1998; Burdett and Coles, 2003) explain returns to seniority, declining separations rate and so forth. Closer to the job-matching approach is a class of models that retain heterogeneity and selection, but allow for the quality of the job to change physically over time, while in the job-matching model everything is predetermined, and parties only have to learn their fate. Notable examples are firm-specific training (Jovanovic, 1979b) and learning-by-doing, as well as stochastic match-specific productivity shocks (Mortensen and Pissarides, 1994). In these models, general properties of Bayesian learning, like the declining variance of inno-vations, must be assumed as ad hoc properties of the productivity process. Nonetheless, this lack of iden-tification poses a formidable challenge, and motivates an ongoing research effort.

GIUSEPPE MOSCARINI

See also **assortative matching; bandit problems; learning in macroeconomics; matching and market design; Roy model; search theory; selection bias and self-selection; sequential analysis.**

Bibliography

Altonji, J. and Williams, N. 2005. Do wages rise with job seniority? A reassessment. *Industrial and Labor Relations Review* 58, 370–97.

Burdett, K. and Coles, M. 2003. Equilibrium wage-tenure contracts. *Econometrica* 71, 1377–404.

Burdett, K. and Mortensen, D. 1998. Wage differentials, employer size, and unemployment. *International Economic Review* 39, 257–73.

Farber, H. 1994. The analysis of interfirm worker mobility. *Journal of Labor Economics* 12, 554–93.

Jacobson, L., Lalonde, R. and Sullivan, D. 1993, Earnings losses of displaced workers. *American Economic Review* 83, 685–709.

Jovanovic, B. 1979a. Job matching and the theory of turnover. *Journal of Political Economy* 87, 972–90.

Jovanovic, B. 1979b. Firm-specific capital and turnover. *Journal of Political Economy* 87, 1246–60.

Mortensen, D. 1988. Wages, separations, and job tenure: on-the-job specific training or matching? *Journal of Labor Economics* 6, 445–71.

Mortensen, D. and Pissarides, C. 1994. Job creation and job destruction in the theory of unemployment. *Review of Economic Studies* 61, 397–415.

Moscarini, G. 2005. Job matching and the wage distribution. *Econometrica* 73, 481–516.

Roy, A. 1951. Some thoughts on the distribution of earnings. *Oxford Economic Papers* 3, 135–46.

Topel, R. and Ward, M. 1992. Job mobility and the careers of young men. *Quarterly Journal of Economics* 107, 439–79.

matching and market design

'Matching' is the part of economics that focuses on the question of who gets what, particularly when the scarce goods to be allocated are heterogeneous and indivisible; for example, who works at which job, which students go to which school, who receives which transplantable organ, and so on. Studying how particular matching markets succeed at creating efficient matches, or fail to do so, has yielded insights into how markets in general work well or badly.

Because market failures have sometimes been success-fully fixed by devising new rules for both centralized and decentralized market organization, matching has been a major focus of the emerging field of market design. Some designs by economists have included labour market clearing houses for doctors and other health-care workers in the United States, both for their first jobs and as they enter specialties. Clearing houses have also been imple-mented in less traditional markets, which cannot adjust prices or wages to help clear the market, such as the matching of students to schools in New York City and in Boston. And new clearing houses are being implemented for the organization of live-donor kidney exchanges among patients in need of a kidney transplant who have willing donors with whom they are incompatible.

In the next section we review some studies of matching, including some market failures that have been addressed either by introducing appropriate rules to a decentralized market (as in admissions to graduate programmes in American universities), or by introducing a centralized clearing house (as in the markets for new doctors in the United States, Canada, and Britain). The subsequent two sections consider the simple theory behind some clearinghouse designs. Then we return to some of the successful market design applications, which build on the theoretical models, but handle practical problems that are sometimes not yet fully understood in theory.

We focus on three kinds of market failure that sometimes impede efficient matching.

1. Failure to provide *thickness*; that is, to bring together enough buyers and sellers (or firms and workers, schools and students, and so forth) to transact with each other.
2. Failure to overcome the *congestion* that thickness can bring, that is, that can result when lots of buyers and sellers are trying to transact. That is, failure to provide enough time, or failure to make transactions fast enough so that market participants can consider enough alter-native possible transactions to arrive at satisfactory ones.
3. Failure to make it *safe* for market participants to reliably reveal or otherwise act on their information.

Some market failures and their consequences

Unravelling, congestion and centralized clearing houses A variety of professional labour markets have suffered from the *unravelling* of appointment dates: from year to year, appointments were made earlier and earlier in advance of actual employment. Markets that had once been thick, with many employers and applicants on the market at the same time, became thin, as potential employees faced early offers, dispersed in time, to which they had to respond before they could learn what other offers might be forthcoming. That is, applicants often received 'exploding' offers that had to be accepted or rejected without waiting to see whether a more desirable offer might be forthcoming. An applicant who accepts such an offer, in the case that acceptances are binding, will never learn of the more desirable offers that might have become available, but if the offer is reasonably desirable rejecting it might be very risky. And, when applicants are quickly accepting offers in this way, employers, when they make offers, have to start taking into account whether the offer is likely to be accepted, since by the time an offer is rejected other desirable applicants may have already accepted offers elsewhere. This often makes unravelling a dynamic process, with offers being made earlier and shorter in duration from year to year. This kind of unravelling has been described in detail in markets for lawyers (Avery et al., 2001), gastroenterologists (Niederle, Proctor and Roth, 2006) and many others (see Roth and Xing, 1994). A clear example is the market for new doctors (Roth, 1984).

The first job for almost all new doctors in the United States and Canada is as an intern or resident at a hospital. In the early 1900s, medical graduates were hired for such jobs near the end of their fourth year of medical school, just before graduation. By the 1930s, hiring was largely completed half a year before graduation, and by the 1940s it had moved to sometimes as much as two years before graduation. That is, in the early 1940s, students were being hired long before they would begin work, at dispersed times, and without much opportunity to consider alternatives, and long before they had sufficient experience to reveal either to employers or to themselves what kinds of medicine they would most prefer and be best able to practise. There was widespread recognition among the participants that the market was often failing to create the most productive matches of doctors to hospitals, both because there was too little opportunity to consider alternatives and because the matching was being done before important information about students became available.

One way in which many markets tried to address this failure was by attempting to establish rules concerning when offers could be made. In the market for new American doctors, the most concerted attempt at this kind of solution began in 1945 with the help of the medical schools, which agreed not to release any information to hospitals about students until a specified date.

However, the market experienced *congestion* in that hospitals found that they did not always have enough time to make all the offers they would like if their first offer was declined. Over the next few years students were

called upon to make increasingly prompt decisions whether to accept offers. In 1945 offers were supposed to remain open for 10 days. By 1949 a deadline of 12 hours had been rejected as too long. Hospitals were finding that, if an offer was rejected after even a brief period of consideration, it was often too late for them to reach their next most preferred candidates before they had accepted other offers. Even when there was a long deadline much of this action was compressed into the last moments, because a student who had been offered a position that wasn't his first choice would be inclined to wait as long as possible before accepting, in the hope of eventually being offered a preferable position. So hospitals felt compelled to pressure students to reply immediately, and offers conveyed by telegram were frequently followed by phone calls requesting an immediate reply.

Congestion can be a problem in any market in which transactions take some time, but it is especially visible in entry-level professional labour markets in which many workers and jobs become available at the same time (for example, after graduation from university, medical school, law school, and so on).

In the face of congestion, many markets unravel, as employers try to gain more time to make offers by starting to do so earlier (Roth and Xing, 1994). But the market for new doctors found a solution in the form of a centralized clearing house. Starting in the early 1950s, the various medical groups organized a centralized clearing house, which remains in use today, having undergone some changes over the years. Nowadays, a medical student applies to hospitals and goes on interviews in the winter of the final year of medical school, and then in February submits an ordered preference list of positions to the centralized clearing house, the National Resident Matching Program (NRMP). At the same time, the residency programmes (the employers) submit an ordered preference list of candidates. Once all the preference lists are collected, the clearing house uses an algorithm to produce a match, and residency programmes and applicants are informed to whom they have been matched. Although this clearing house began as an entirely voluntary one, it has been so successful that today it is virtually the only way that most residencies are filled. As we will see below, that success depends critically on the matching algorithm.

The NRMP, and clearing houses like it, also make very clear the kinds of issues involved for a marketplace to make it safe for participants to reveal their information. In a clearing house in which you are asked to state your preferences, the question is simply: is it a good idea to state your true preferences, or would you do better otherwise? For the NRMP we'll see that stating true preferences is indeed both safe and sensible. We'll also discuss clearing houses that failed this test, like the one for placing students into schools in Boston that consequently failed to accomplish their objectives in other ways also, and were redesigned.

Before presenting some formal models that will allow us to start to explain which matching algorithms and clearing houses have been successful and which have failed, it will be helpful to think about several different kinds of matching markets.

Two-sided and one-sided matching markets

Labour markets, like the market for new doctors, are usually modelled as two-sided markets, in which agents on one side of the market (workers) need to be matched with agents on the other side (employers), and each agent has preferences over possible matches. We'll see below that this two-sided structure allows strong conclusions to be drawn about the properties of matchings and matching mechanisms.

In many markets this two-sided structure is absent. One way this occurs is when any participant in the market can be matched with any other. For example, if a group of people want to form pairs to be roommates or bridge partners, any one of them can in principle be matched with any other, although not all matchings would be efficient. We encounter markets of this kind when we speak of kidney exchange.

Another way in which markets can be one-sided is if the agents in the market need to be matched to objects, for example when people need to be assigned rooms in a dormitory, or places in a public school that doesn't itself have preferences or take strategic actions (unlike in a two-sided matching market). That is, such a market matches people to places, but only one side, the people, are active participants in the market. Some markets can also be hybrids, with both two and one-sided properties (as when schools aren't strategic players, but still have priorities over students).

Below we consider some static models of two and one-sided matching that have proved useful in the design of clearing houses, and in understanding what they do. In the section on design, we'll also speak about some decentralized design solutions to various market failures, such as unravelling. While there has been some good initial progress on formal models of decentralized markets, and dynamic models in which phenomena like unravelling can play out over time (see for example, Li and Rosen, 1998), these areas are still in need of development, and have not yet received the theoretical attention commensurate with their importance in the study of markets generally (though see Niederle and Yariv, 2007).

Formal models of matching

Two-sided matching models

The workhorse models of two-sided matching come in several varieties. The simplest, presented in detail below, is the 'marriage model' in which each firm seeks to hire only a single worker, and wages and other kinds of price adjustment are represented simply in the preferences that workers and firms have for each other (for

example, in these models, wages are part of the job description that determines preferences). However the kinds of results we present here generalize to models in which wage and price formation is explicitly included, some pointers to such models are included in the references.

The marriage model consists of two disjoint sets of agents, men $= \{m_1, \ldots, m_n\}$ and women $= \{w_1, \ldots, w_p\}$, each of whom has complete and transitive preferences over the agents on the other side (and the possibility of being unmatched, which we model as being 'matched to yourself'). Preferences can be represented as rank order lists, for example, if man m_i's first choice is w_3, his second choice w_2 $[w_3 > m_i w_2]$ and so on, until at some point he prefers to remain unmatched, that is $P(m_i) = w_3, w_2, \ldots m_i \ldots$. If agent k (on either side of the market) prefers to remain single rather than be matched to agent j, that is, if $k > k$ j, then j is said to be *unacceptable* to k. If an agent is not indifferent between any two acceptable mates, or between being matched and unmatched, we'll say he/she has *strict* preferences.

An *outcome* of the game is a *matching*: μ: $M \cup W \rightarrow M \cup W$ such that $w = \mu(m)$ iff $\mu(w) = m$, and for all m and w either $\mu(w)$ is in M or $\mu(w) = w$, and either $\mu(m)$ is in W or $\mu(m) = m$. That is, a matching matches agents on one side to agents on the other side, or to themselves, and if w is matched to m, then m is matched to w.

A matching μ is *blocked by an individual* k if k prefers being single to being matched with $\mu(k)$, that is, $k > k$ $\mu(k)$. A matching μ is *blocked by a pair of agents* (m,w) if they each prefer each other to the partner they receive at μ, that is, $w > m$ $\mu(m)$ and $m > w$ $\mu(w)$.

A matching μ is *stable* if it isn't blocked by any individual or pair of agents.

A stable matching is Pareto efficient, and in the core, and in this simple model the set of (pairwise) stable matchings equals the core.

Theorem 1 (Gale and Shapley, 1962). A stable matching exists for every marriage market.

Gale and Shapley approached this problem from a purely theoretical perspective, but proved this theorem via a constructive algorithm of the kind that has subsequently turned up at the heart of a variety of clearing houses.

Deferred acceptance algorithm, with men proposing (roughly the Gale and Shapley, 1962 version)

Step 0. If some preferences are not strict, arbitrarily break ties (for example, if some m is indifferent between wi and wj, order them consecutively in alphabetical order. Different agents may break ties differently: that is, tie-breaking can be decentralized by having each agent fill out a strict preference list...).

Step 1(a). Each man m proposes to his 1st choice (if he has any acceptable choices).

Step1(b). Each woman rejects any unacceptable proposals and, if more than one acceptable proposal is received, 'holds' the most preferred and rejects all others... .

Step k(a). Any man who was rejected at step k-1 makes a new proposal to its most preferred acceptable mate who hasn't yet rejected him. (If no acceptable choices remain, he makes no proposal.)

Step k(b). Each woman holds her most preferred acceptable offer to date, and rejects the rest. STOP: when no further proposals are made, and match each woman to the man (if any) whose proposal she is holding.

Note that the proof of the theorem now follows from the observation that the matching produced in this way is itself stable. If some man would prefer to be matched to a woman other than his assigned mate, he must, according to the algorithm, have already proposed to her, and she has rejected him, meaning she has a man she strictly prefers, hence they cannot form a blocking pair.

Roth (1984) showed that the algorithm adopted by the medical clearing house in the 1950s was equivalent to the hospital proposing deferred acceptance algorithm. Gale and Shapley observed that which side of the market proposes in a deferred acceptance algorithm has consequences.

Theorem 2 (Gale and Shapley, 1962). When all men and women have strict preferences, there always exists an M-optimal stable matching (that every man likes at least as well as any other stable matching), and a W-optimal stable matching. Furthermore, the matching μM produced by the deferred acceptance algorithm with men proposing is the M-optimal stable matching. The W-optimal stable matching is the matching μW produced by the algorithm when the women propose.

Note that the algorithm has been stated as if people take actions in the course of the algorithm, and we can ask whether those actions would best serve their interests. To put it another way, is it possible to design a clearing house in which a matching is produced from participants' stated rank order lists in such a way that it will never be in someone's interest to submit a rank order list different from their true preferences? The following theorem answers that question in the negative.

Theorem 3 Impossibility Theorem (Roth – see Roth and Sotomayor, 1990). No stable matching mechanism exists for which stating the true preferences is a dominant strategy for every agent.

However it is possible to design the mechanism so that one side of the market can never do any better than to state their true preferences.

Theorem 4 (Dubins and Freedman, Roth – see Roth and Sotomayor, 1990).

The mechanism that yields the M-optimal stable matching (in terms of the stated preferences) makes it a dominant strategy for each man to state his true preferences.

The conclusions of Theorems 1–3 also hold for a variety of related models (in which firms employ multiple workers, and wages are explicitly allowed to vary; see, for example, Shapley and Shubik, 1971; Kelso and Crawford, 1982, for notable early models of matching with money, and see Roth and Sotomayor, 1990; Hatfield and Milgrom, 2005). However, when we look at many-to-one matching models (in which firms employ multiple workers but workers seek just one job), we have to be careful. It turns out that no procedures exist that give firms a dominant strategy, but that a worker proposing deferred acceptance algorithm still makes it a dominant strategy for workers to state their true preferences (see Roth and Sotomayor, 1990 for more details and further references). (These results are closely connected to related results in auction theory; see in particular Hatfield and Milgrom, 2005; Milgrom, 2004.)

When the market for medical residents was redesigned (Roth and Peranson, 1999), a number of practical complications had to be dealt with, such as the fact that about 1,000 graduates a year go through the match as couples who wish to be matched to nearby jobs, and hence have joint preferences over pairs of residency programmes. While this can cause the set of stable matchings to be empty, in practice this has not proved to be a significant problem (see also Roth, 2002, on engineering aspects of economic design).

One-sided matching models

Shapley and Scarf's 'house' markets

Another basic model of matching markets was introduced by Shapley and Scarf (1974). They model a simple barter economy in which each one of n agents owns an indivisible good (which they call a house) and has preferences over all houses in the economy. Each agent has use for only one house and trade is only feasible in houses (that is, there is no money in their model). An allocation μ in this context is a matching of houses and agents so that each agent receives one and only one house. An exchange in this market does not need to be bilateral. An allocation μ is in the core if no coalition (including single agent coalitions) of agents can improve upon it (in the sense that all are weakly better off and at least one is strictly better off) by swapping their own houses. Shapley and Scarf attribute to David Gale the following *top trading cycles* algorithm (TTC) which can be used to find a core allocation for any housing market:

Step 1: Each agent points to the owner of her most preferred house (which could possibly be herself). Since there are finite number of agents there is at least one *cycle* (where a cycle is an ordered list $(i_1, i_2, \ldots, i_k)$ of agents with each agent pointing to the next agent in the list and agent *ik* pointing to agent i_1). In each cycle the implied exchange is carried out and the procedure is repeated with the remaining agents.

In general, at

Step k: Each remaining agent points to the owner of her most preferred house among the remaining houses. There is at least one cycle. In each cycle the implied exchange is carried out and the procedure is repeated with the remaining agents.

The algorithm terminates when each agent receives a house.

Theorem 5 (Shapley and Scarf, 1974). The TTC algorithm yields an allocation in the core for each housing market.

The core has some remarkable properties in the context of housing markets. The following propositions summarize the most notable of these results.

While exchange is feasible only in houses, a *competitive allocation* of a housing market can be defined via 'token money'. There is an important relation between the core and the competitive allocation for this very basic barter economy.

Theorem 6 (Roth and Postlewaite, 1977). There is a unique allocation in the core (which can be obtained with the TTC algorithm) when agents have strict preferences over houses. Moreover the unique core allocation coincides with the unique competitive allocation.

Another remarkable feature of this model is that the top trading cycles mechanism makes it safe for agents to reveal their true preferences.

Theorem 7 (Roth, 1982). The core as a mechanism is *strategy-proof* when agents have strict preferences over houses. That is, truth-telling is a dominant strategy for all agents in the preference revelation game in which TTC is applied to the stated preferences to produce an allocation.

Moreover, it is essentially the only mechanism that is strategy-proof among those that are Pareto efficient and *individually rational* (in the sense that an agent never receives a house inferior to her own).

Theorem 8 (Ma, 1994). The core is the only mechanism that is Pareto efficient, individually rational and strategy-proof.

House allocation problems

Hylland and Zeckhauser (1979) introduced the *house allocation problem* which only differs from housing markets in *property rights*: There are *n* houses to be allocated for *n* agents where each agent has use for only one house and has strict preferences over all houses. Unlike in housing markets, no agent owns a specific house. The mechanism known as *random serial dictatorship* (RSD) is widely used in real-life allocation problems of this sort, such as assigning students to dormitory rooms. Under RSD agents are randomly ordered (from a uniform distribution) in a list and the first agent in the list is assigned her top choice house, the next agent is assigned her top choice among the remaining houses, and so on. In addition to its popularity in practice, RSD has good incentive and efficiency properties.

Theorem 9 RSD is *ex post* Pareto efficient and strategy-proof.

Recall that the only difference between house allocation problems and housing markets is the initial property rights, and the core is very well-behaved in the context of the latter. This observation motivates the mechanism *core from random endowments* (CRE): randomly assign houses to agents with uniform distribution, interpret the resulting matching as the initial allocation of houses, and pick the core of the resulting housing market. It turns out, CRE is equivalent to RSD.

Theorem 10 (Abdulkadiroglu and Sönmez, 1998). For any house allocation problem CRE and RSD yield the same lottery and hence they are equivalent mechanisms.

House allocation with existing tenants

Housing markets and house allocation problems have very different property rights. The former is a pure private ownership economy where each house 'belongs' to a specific agent, whereas in the latter no strict subset of the grand coalition has claims on any house. Abdulkadiroglu and Sönmez (1999) introduced the following hybrid *house allocation with existing tenants* model. There are two kinds of agents: *existing tenants* each of whom owns a house, and *newcomers* none of whom has claims on a specific house. In addition to the *occupied houses* owned by existing tenants, there are also *vacant houses*. As in house allocation problems no specific person or group has claims on any vacant house. Suppose that the number of newcomers is equal to the number of vacant houses and hence the number of agents is equal to the number of houses. Agents have strict preferences over all houses and each existing tenant is allowed to keep her current house.

Abdulkadiroglu and Sönmez introduced the following *you request my house – I get your turn* algorithm

(YRMH–IGYT) which generalizes TTC as well as RSD. Under YRMH–IGYT, agents are randomly ordered in a line and initially only the vacant houses are *available*. The first agent in the line is assigned her top choice provided that it is either her own house or an available house (in which case her own house becomes available) and the process continues with the next agent in the line. If, however, her top choice is an occupied house, the line is adjusted and the owner of the requested house is moved right in front of the requester. The process continues in a similar way with either the owner of the requested house getting assigned his own house or an available house (making his own house available), or otherwise his requesting an occupied house and upgrading its owner to the top of the line. When the process continues in a similar way there will either be a *cycle* of existing tenants (as in TTC) who can swap their own houses or a *chain* $(i_1, i_2, \ldots, i_k)$ of agents where agent i_1 is assigned an available house and each of the following agents is assigned the preceding agent's house.

The resulting mechanism inherits the attractive properties of its 'parents'.

Theorem 11 (Abdulkadiroglu and Sönmez, 1999). The YRMH–IGYT mechanism is strategy-proof, *ex post* Pareto efficient, and individually rational (in the sense that no existing tenant receives a house inferior to her own).

Kidney exchange

Living donors are an important source of kidneys for transplantation. But a patient with a willing living donor may not be able to receive a transplant because of a blood-type or immunologic incompatibility between her and her donor. Recently transplant centres around the world developed the possibility of *pairwise kidney exchange* in which two such pairs can exchange donors in case the donor in each pair is compatible with the patient in the other. Another interesting option is *indirect kidney exchange* in which the patient of an incompatible pair receives priority in the deceased donor waiting list if her incompatible donor donates a kidney to that waiting list. However, prior to 2004 only a very few exchanges had been accomplished, in large part because the market wasn't thick, and no databases were being maintained of incompatible patient–donor pairs. In an effort to organize kidney exchange on a larger scale, Roth, Sönmez and Ünver (2004) introduced the following *kidney exchange* model. There are a number of patients each with a (possibly) incompatible donor. For each patient a subset of donors can feasibly donate a kidney and the patient has strict preferences over these donors and his own donor (who may or may not be compatible with him). In addition to ranking all compatible donors, each patient also ranks a 'waiting list option' which represents trading his donor's kidney with a priority in the waitlist. An *allocation* in this context is a matching of patients and donors such that:

- each patient is matched with either a donor or the waiting list option, and
- each donor can be matched with at most one patient while the waiting list option may be matched with multiple patients.

(The donors who remain unmatched are offered to the waitlist in exchange for the equal number of priorities awarded by the allocation). We are only interested in *individually rational* allocations where patients receive neither a donor nor the waiting list option unless it is indicated to be at least as good as his donor's kidney. If the waiting list option is ranked inferior to his donor for a patient, that means the patient is not interested in such an exchange. As in the case of house allocation with existing tenants model, an allocation consists of cycles and chains where

- each patient in a cycle receives a kidney from the donor of the next patient in the cycle, and
- all but the last patient in a chain receive a kidney from the donor of the next patient in the chain whereas the last patient in the chain receives a priority in the waiting list.

If the waiting list option is infeasible, then the resulting problem is formally equivalent to a housing market and therefore has a unique allocation in the core which can be obtained via the TTC algorithm. In this simpler model an allocation (including the one in the core) consists of only cycles. When the waiting list option is feasible an allocation can also have chains (which are indirect exchanges and their more elaborate versions). In this more general model Roth, Sönmez and Ünver (2004) introduce a class of *top trading cycles and chains* (TTCC) algorithms each of which extend the TTC. Among these algorithms Roth, Sönmez and Ünver (2004) identify one that is Pareto efficient and strategy-proof:

Theorem 12 (Roth, Sönmez and Ünver, 2004). There exists a TTCC mechanism that is Pareto efficient and strategy-proof.

In practice, as kidney exchanges have become organized on a larger scale in New England and elsewhere (see Roth, Sönmez and Ünver, 2005a; 2005b; 2007), there has been a focus, for logistical reasons, on cycles and chains that are relatively short, typically only involving exchanges among two or three patient–donor pairs.

The deferred acceptance algorithm (for two-sided markets) also has some uses in one-sided allocation problems in which children are to be allocated to schools, if the schools, although not active strategic players, have priorities over students that need to be treated like preferences (Abdulkadiroglu and Sönmez, 2003).

Design and engineering

Introducing a centralized stable match

Of the several dozen markets and submarkets we know of that established clearing houses in response to unravelling in a (two-sided) labour market, those that produce stable matchings have been most successful. Of particular note in this regard are the markets used in the various regions of the British National Health Service. In the 1960s, these markets suffered from the same kind of unravelling that had afflicted the American medical market in the 1940s. A Royal Commission recommended that each region organize a centralized clearing house (see Roth, 1991), and the various regions each invented their own matching algorithms, some of which were stable and some of which were not (an example of such unstable algorithms will be given later). Those clearing houses that produced stable matches succeeded, while those that did not most often failed and were abandoned. But over a broad range of markets, the correlation between stability and success in halting unravelling isn't perfect; some unstable mechanisms remain in use, and some stable mechanism have occasionally failed, as we will discuss later. And there are other differences between markets than the way their clearing houses are designed. This is why, in order to establish that producing a stable outcome is an important feature for the success of a match, controlled experiments in the laboratory can be informative.

The laboratory experiments reported by Kagel and Roth (2002) help to verify the influence of a stable or unstable matching mechanism. After unravelling had begun in a small laboratory market, a clearing house was introduced using either the stable deferred acceptance algorithm or the unstable algorithms that failed in various regions of the British National Health service (Roth, 1991). In the lab, as in the field, participants learned to wait for and use the stable algorithm, but learned to arrange their matches early and thus avoid using the unstable algorithm. Note that a laboratory market is quite different from a naturally occurring labour market, but it has the advantage that it allows the effect of the different algorithms to be observed in an environment in which everything else is the same.

Centralized clearing houses that yield stable outcomes have sometimes been introduced to organize markets suffering from failures other than unravelling (and the resulting lack of thickness), but related to congestion or the safety of revealing private information.

Examples of algorithms that produce unstable outcomes, but have been used in a number of market clearing houses, are so called priority algorithms, used for example by some British clearing houses, and also in several school choice problems in the United States. A priority algorithm classifies different matches in terms of priorities, based on the rank orders submitted, and then makes feasible matches in order of priority. In Boston, for example, the centralized system attempted to give as many students as possible their first choice school. The difficulty with the system was that students who did not get assigned to their first choice were much less likely to be assigned to the school they had listed as their second choice than they would have been if they had listed it as their first choice, since those schools often get filled by students who list them as their first choice. This means participants have strong incentives to not report their preferences truthfully, if there is a good chance that they would not be admitted to their true first choice school; it might be wiser to list their second-choice school as their first choice. The newly adopted Boston clearing house fixes this problem using a deferred acceptance algorithm (Abdulkadiroglu et al., 2005; 2006).

Some markets manage to halt unravelling, but still suffer from congestion. The market for clinical psychologists (before it reorganized through a modified deferred acceptance algorithm, see Roth and Xing, 1997) and the match of students to New York City high schools before it was redesigned (Abdulkadiroglu et al., 2005; 2006) are good examples. Clinical psychologists tried to run a deferred acceptance algorithm over the phone in the course of a day, 'match day,' from 9:00 a.m. to 4:00 p.m.. All offers had to remain open until 4 p.m., and students were supposed to hold only one offer at a time. Even though turnaround time in this market was very fast (offers took about five minutes, rejections about one minute), simulating a deferred acceptance algorithm in real time, for a market with about 2,000 positions in 500 programmes, takes much longer than the seven hours of match day. (And making the market longer may increase the effects of congestion, if it means that participants can no longer stay by the phone for the whole market, so that the time for an offer to be made and rejected becomes disproportionately longer.) Congestion is an issue whenever a large number of offers have to be made. The system used to assign students to New York City high schools used to be carried out through the mails, and over 30,000 students a year were 'stranded' on waiting lists and had to be assigned to a school for which they had expressed no preference. The new New York City clearing house is able to process preferences quickly, and in the four years following its adoption in 2003 fewer than 3,000 students had to be assigned each year to a school for which they had expressed no preference.

What are the effects of a centralized match?

Centralized clearing houses can help make markets thick and uncongested, and avoid unravelling. Studying their effect on various markets can also help us understand how clearing houses and the timing of the market (for example, how far a labour market operates in advance of employment) influence the outcome of the market in other respects. For example, the market for gastroenterology fellows provides us with a natural case study of the effects of a clearing house not only on hiring practices (namely the timing of the market, and the kinds of offers that are made), but also employment opportunities, job placement and the potential impact on wages.

Gastroenterology fellows are doctors who have completed three years of residency in internal medicine, and are now employed in a fellowship that will result in their becoming board certified sub-specialists in gastroenterology. The market in which gastroenterology fellows are hired operated in a decentralized way for many years, and experienced the problems of congestion, unravelling and exploding offers, as described above in connection with the market for medical residents. In 1986, various internal medicine sub-specialties organized a clearing house called the Medical Specialties Matching Program (MSMP), sponsored by and organized along the same lines as the NRMP (which operates the resident match). But in the mid-1990s, gastroenterology fellowship programmes, and applicants, started to defect from the match, and the gastroenterology market again unravelled. A match was successfully re-established only in 2006 (Niederle, Proctor and Roth, 2006). In those intervening years, as the market unravelled, the national market broke up into more local markets (Niederle and Roth, 2003b). Fellowship programmes, particularly smaller ones, had a larger tendency to hire their own residents than under a centralized match.

A second aspect of the outcome that received prominence in 2002 is the question of whether a match affects wages. An antitrust lawsuit against the NRMP and numerous other defendants was brought in 2002 by 16 law firms on behalf of three former residents seeking to represent the class of all former residents (and naming as defendants a class including all hospitals that employ residents).

Niederle and Roth (2003a) showed empirically that in fact there is no difference in wages between medicine sub-specialties that use a match and those that don't. The suit was dismissed in 2004 following legislation intended to clarify that the medical match is a marketplace and does not violate antitrust laws.

The theory of the complaint was that a match holds down wages for residents and fellows. Bulow and Levin (2006) present a very stylized theoretical model providing some logical support for this possibility, by comparing a market with impersonal prices (to represent the NRMP) with perfectly competitive prices at which each worker is paid his or her marginal product. Subsequent theoretical papers have shown that the conclusion about wage suppression doesn't necessarily follow if the model is expanded to include the possibility of firms hiring more than one worker (Kojima, 2007), or when the model incorporates the actual procedures by which the medical match is conducted (Niederle, 2007). Furthermore, decentralized markets may often fail to achieve stable outcomes (Niederle and Yariv, 2007).

Beyond centralized matching: why do some markets work well, while others do not?

We have seen that stability is an important feature for a centralized match to remain in use. However, the history of the gastroenterology market shows that producing a stable outcome is not sufficient to guarantee a successful clearing house. For a centralized match to work well, participants need to have incentives to participate in the match. McKinney, Niederle and Roth (2005) observed that the collapse of the gastroenterology fellowship match seems to have been caused by an unusual shock to the supply of highly qualified gastroenterology fellows, a kind of shock that was not observed in other internal medicine sub-specialties that continued to use a match. Furthermore, market conditions seemed to have stabilized, so that a centralized match would work well once again, if it could be successfully reinstated.

However, many gastroenterology fellowship programmes, when they considered reinstituting a match, were concerned that, while they were willing to refrain from making the early offers that had become customary, and wait for the match, their main competitors would continue to make early exploding offers to promising applicants. Such concerns could effectively prevent a successful restart of a centralized clearing house.

This raises the more general question as to why some markets unravel and experience congestion problems in the first place, while others do not. Empirically, most markets that experience congestion also experience that employers (hospitals, federal judges, colleges...) make short-term offers, with a binding deadline, and in which the acceptance of an offer is often effectively binding (Niederle and Roth, 2007, for descriptions in the markets for law graduates, and for college admissions, see for example, Avery et al., 2001; 2007; Avery, Fairbanks and Zeckhauser, 2003).

On the other hand there are markets that do not unravel, such as the market for graduate school admission. In this market, a policy (adopted by the large majority of universities) states that offers of admission and financial support to graduate students should remain open until 15 April. Furthermore, a student faced with an earlier deadline is explicitly encouraged to accept this offer, and, in case a better one is received before 15 April, to renege on that former acceptance. This of course makes early exploding offers much less attractive to make. Niederle and Roth (2007) explore environments in which either eliminating the possibility of making exploding offers or making early acceptances non-binding helps prevents markets from operating inefficiently early.

These insights were used to help reorganizing the gastroenterology fellowship match. To reduce the concerns of programmes that their competitors would start making exploding offers before the match, a resolution was adopted by the four main professional gastroenterology organizations that stated that acceptances made before the match were not to be considered binding, and such applicants could still change their minds and participate in the match. For an account of the effects of a centralized clearinghouse on the outcomes of a market, and the experience of the gastroenterology fellowship market, see Niederle and Roth (2008).

Directions for future research

As economists' understanding of the matching function of markets increases, and as economists are more often called upon to help design markets, one challenge will be to understand better how decentralized markets work well or badly, and not only in the final transactions.

For example, a common problem in many entry-level labour markets (and in dating and marriage markets) is that participants do not have well formed preferences over potential matching partners, and forming those preferences is often very costly. For example, in the American market for assistant professors, economics departments receive hundreds of applications for any position, but in general interview only about 30 candidates at the annual winter meetings. From among those they interview, they must decide whom to fly out for extended campus visits and seminars, and it is from among this latter set of candidates that they eventually choose to whom to make an offer. Because this is a time-consuming and costly process many departments have to take care to interview applicants who not only have a good chance of being desirable colleagues, but who also have a good chance of accepting an offer if one is made. This often amounts to a coordination problem: not all departments should interview the same applicants. Allowing applicants to credibly submit information about their interest in particular schools can help alleviate this coordination problem, and in 2007 the American Economic Association implemented a signalling mechanism of this sort in the market for economists.

In general, the study of the matching function of markets has directed attention at the design of rules and procedures of both centralized and decentralized markets. The goal of the growing interest among economists in matching and market design is to understand the operation of markets, both centralized and decentralized, well enough so we can fix them when they're broken.

MURIEL NIEDERLE, ALVIN E. ROTH AND TAYFUN SÖNMEZ

See also **experimental economics; experimental labour economics; game theory; labour market institutions; matching; mechanism design experiments; mechanism design (new developments).**

Bibliography

Abdulkadiroglu, A., Pathak, P.A. and Roth, A.E. 2005. The New York City high school match. *American Economic Review* 95, 364–67.

Abdulkadiroglu, A., Pathak, P.A. and Roth, A.E. 2006. Strategy-proofness versus efficiency in matching with indifferences: redesigning the NYC high school match, Working paper, Harvard University.

Abdulkadiroglu, A. and Sönmez, T. 1998. Random serial dictatorship and the core from random endowments in house allocation problems. *Econometrica* 66, 689–701.

Abdulkadiroglu, A. and Sönmez, T. 1999. House allocation with existing tenants. *Journal of Economic Theory* 88, 233–60.

Abdulkadiroglu, A. and Sönmez, T. 2003. School choice: a mechanism design approach. *American Economic Review* 93, 729–47.

Abdulkadiroglu, A., Pathak, P.A., Roth, A.E. and Sönmez, T. 2005. The Boston public school match. *American Economic Review* 95, 368–71.

Abdulkadiroglu, A., Pathak, P.A., Roth, A.E. and Sönmez, T. 2006. Changing the Boston school choice mechanism, Working Paper No. 11965. Cambridge, MA: NBER.

Avery, C., Fairbanks, A. and Zeckhauser, R. 2003. *The Early Admissions Game: Joining the Elite*. Cambridge, MA: Harvard University Press.

Avery, C., Jolls, C., Posner, R.A. and Roth, A.E. 2001. The market for federal judicial law clerks. *University of Chicago Law Review* 68, 793–902.

Avery, C., Jolls, C., Posner, R.A. and Roth, A.E. 2007. The new market for federal judicial law clerks. *University of Chicago Law Review* 74, 447–86.

Bulow, J. and Levin, J. 2006. Matching and price competition. *American Economic Review* 96, 652–68.

Gale, D. and Shapley, L.S. 1962. College admissions and the stability of marriage. *American Mathematical Monthly* 69, 9–15.

Hatfield, J. and Milgrom, P. 2005. Matching with contracts. *American Economic Review* 95, 913–35.

Hylland, A. and Zeckhauser, R. 1979. The efficient allocation of individuals to positions. *Journal of Political Economy* 87, 293–314.

Kagel, J.H. and Roth, A.E. 2000. The dynamics of reorganization in matching markets: a laboratory experiment motivated by a natural experiment. *Quarterly Journal of Economics* 115, 201–35.

Kelso, A.S. and Crawford, V.P. 1982. Job matching, coalition formation, and gross substitutes. *Econometrica* 50, 1483–504.

Kojima, F. 2007. Matching and price competition: comment. *American Economic Review* 97, 1027–31.

Li, H. and Rosen, S. 1998. Unraveling in matching markets. *American Economic Review* 88, 371–87.

Ma, J. 1994. Strategy-proofness and the strict core in a market with indivisibilities. *International Journal of Game Theory* 23, 75–83.

Milgrom, P. 2004. *Putting Auction Theory to Work*. Cambridge: Cambridge University Press.

McKinney, C.N., Niederle, M. and Roth, A.E. 2005. The collapse of a medical labor clearinghouse (and why such failures are rare). *American Economic Review* 95, 878–89.

Niederle, M. 2007. Competitive wages in a match with ordered contracts, *American Economic Review*.

Niederle, M., Proctor, D.D. and Roth, A.E. 2006. What will be needed for the new GI fellowship match to succeed? *Gastroenterology* 130, 218–24.

Niederle, M. and Roth, A.E. 2003a. Relationship between wages and presence of a match in medical fellowships. *Journal of the American Medical Association* 290, 1153–4.

Niederle, M. and Roth, A.E. 2003b. Unraveling reduces mobility in a labor market: gastroenterology with and without a centralized match. *Journal of Political Economy* 111, 1342–52.

Niederle, M. and Roth, A.E. 2007. Making markets thick: how norms governing exploding offers affect market performance. Working paper.

Niederle, M. and Roth, A.E. 2008. The effects of a central clearinghouse on job placement, wages, and hiring practices. In *Labor Market Intermediation*, ed. D. Autor. Chicago: University of Chicago Press.

Niederle, M. and Yariv, L. 2007. Matching through decentralized markets. Working paper.

Roth, A.E. 1982. Incentive compatibility in a market with indivisible goods. *Economics Letters* 9, 127–32.

Roth, A.E. 1984. The evolution of the labor market for medical interns and residents: a case study in game theory. *Journal of Political Economy* 92, 991–1016.

Roth, A.E. 1991. A natural experiment in the organization of entry level labor markets: regional markets for new physicians and surgeons in the U.K. *American Economic Review* 81, 415–40.

Roth, A.E. 2002. The economist as engineer: game theory, experimental economics and computation as tools of design economics. *Econometrica* 70, 1341–78.

Roth, A.E. and Peranson, E. 1999. The redesign of the matching market for American physicians: some engineering aspects of economic design. *American Economic Review* 89, 748–79.

Roth, A.E. and Postlewaite, A. 1977. Weak versus strong domination in a market with indivisible goods. *Journal of Mathematical Economics* 4, 131–7.

Roth, A.E., Sönmez, T. and Ünver, M.U. 2004. Kidney exchange. *Quarterly Journal of Economics* 119, 457–88.

Roth, A.E., Sönmez, T. and Ünver, M.U. 2005a. A kidney exchange clearinghouse in New England. *American Economic Review* 95, 376–80.

Roth, A.E., Sönmez, T. and Ünver, M.U. 2005b. Pairwise kidney exchange. *Journal of Economic Theory* 125, 151–88.

Roth, A.E., Sönmez, T. and Ünver, M.U. 2007. Efficient kidney exchange: coincidence of wants in markets with compatibility-based preferences. *American Economic Review* 97, 828–51.

Roth, A.E. and Sotomayor, M. 1990. *Two-Sided Matching: A Study in Game-Theoretic Modeling and Analysis*. New York: Cambridge University Press.

Roth, A.E. and Xing, X. 1994. Jumping the gun: imperfections and institutions related to the timing of market transactions. *American Economic Review* 84, 992–1044.

Roth, A.E. and Xing, X. 1997. Turnaround time and bottlenecks in market clearing: decentralized matching in the market for clinical psychologists. *Journal of Political Economy* 105, 284–329.

Roth, A.E., Sönmez, T., Ünver, M.U., Delmonico, F.L. and Saidman, S.L. 2006. Utilizing list exchange and undirected Good Samaritan donation through 'chain' paired kidney donations. *American Journal of Transplantation* 6, 2694–705.

Shapley, L. and Scarf, H. 1974. On cores and indivisibility. *Journal of Mathematical Economics* 1, 23–37.

Shapley, L. and Shubik, M. 1971. The assignment game I: the core. *International Journal of Game Theory* 1, 111–30.

matching estimators

1 Introduction

Matching is a widely used non-experimental method of evaluation that can be used to estimate the average effect of a treatment or programme intervention. The method compares the outcomes of programme participants with those of matched non-participants, where matches are chosen on the basis of similarity in observed characteristics. One of the main advantages of matching estimators is that they typically do not require specifying the functional form of the outcome equation and are therefore not susceptible to misspecification bias along that dimension. Traditional matching estimators pair each programme participant with a single matched non-participant (see, for example, Rosenbaum and Rubin, 1983), whereas more recently developed estimators pair programme participants with multiple non-participants and use weighted averaging to construct the matched outcomes.

We next define some notation and discuss how matching estimators solve the evaluation problem. Much of the treatment effect literature is built on the potential outcomes framework of Fisher (1935), exposited more recently in Rubin (1974) and Holland (1986). The framework assumes that there are two potential outcomes, denoted (Y_0, Y_1) that represent the states of being without and with treatment. An individual can be in only one state at a time, so only one of the outcomes is observed. The outcome that is not observed is termed a *counterfactual outcome*. The treatment impact for an individual is

$$\Delta = Y_1 - Y_0,$$

which is not directly observable. Assessing the impact of a programme intervention requires making an inference about what outcomes would have been observed in the no-programme state. Let $D = 1$ for persons who participate in the programme and $D = 0$ for persons who do not. The $D = 1$ sample often represents a select group of persons who were deemed eligible for a programme, applied to it, got accepted into it and decided to participate in it. The outcome that is observed is $Y = DY_1 + (1 - D)Y_0$.

Before considering different parameters of interest and their estimation, we first consider what is available directly from the data. The conditional distributions $F(Y_1|X, D = 1)$ and $F(Y_0|X, D = 0)$ can be recovered from the observations on Y_1 and Y_0, but not the joint distributions $F(Y_0, Y_1|X, D = 1)$, $F(Y_0, Y_1|X)$ or the impact distribution, $F(\Delta|X, D = 1)$. Because of this missing data problem, researchers often aim instead on recovering some features of the impact distribution, such as its mean. The parameter that is most commonly the focus of evaluation studies is the *mean impact of treatment on the treated*, $TT = E(Y_1 - Y_0|D = 1)$, which gives the benefit of the programme to programme participants. (If the outcome were earnings and the TT parameter exceeded the average cost of the programme, then the programme might be considered to at least cover its costs.)

Matching estimators typically assume that there exist a set of observed characteristics Z such that outcomes are independent of programme participation conditional on Z. That is, it is assumed that the outcomes (Y_0, Y_1) are independent of participation status D conditional on Z,

$$(Y_0, Y_1) \perp\!\!\!\perp D | Z. \tag{1}$$

The independence condition can be equivalently represented as $\Pr(D = 1|Y_0, Y_1, Z) = \Pr(D = 1|Z)$, or $E(D|Y_0, Y_1, Z) = E(D|Z)$. In the terminology of Rosenbaum and Rubin, 1983, treatment assignment is 'strictly ignorable' given Z. It is also assumed that for all Z there is a positive probability of either participating ($D = 1$) or not participating ($D = 0$) in the programme: that is,

$$0 < \Pr(D = 1|Z) < 1. \tag{2}$$

This assumption is required so that matches for $D = 0$ and $D = 1$ observations can be found. If assumptions (1) and (2) are satisfied, then the problem of determining mean programme impacts can be solved by substituting the Y_0 distribution observed for matched on Z non-participants for the missing participant Y_0 distribution.

The above assumptions are overly strong if the parameter of interest is the mean impact of treatment on the treated (TT), in which case a weaker conditional mean independence assumption on Y_0 suffices (see Heckman,

Ichimura and Todd, 1998):

$$E(Y_0|Z, D = 1) = E(Y_0|Z, D = 0) = E(Y_0|Z). \tag{3}$$

Furthermore, when TT is the parameter of interest, the condition $0 < \Pr(D = 1|Z)$ is also not required, because that condition is only needed to guarantee a participant analogue for each non-participant. The TT parameter requires only

$$\Pr(D = 1|Z) < 1. \tag{4}$$

Under these assumptions, the mean impact of the programme on programme participants can be written as

$$\begin{aligned} \Delta_{TT} &= E(Y_1 - Y_0|D = 1) \\ &= E(Y_1|D = 1) - E_{Z|D=1}\{E_Y(Y|D = 1, Z)\} \\ &= E(Y_1|D = 1) - E_{Z|D=1}\{E_Y(Y|D = 0, Z)\}, \end{aligned}$$

where the second term can be estimated from the mean outcomes of the matched on Z comparison group. (The notation $E_{Z|D=1}$ denotes that the expectation is taken with respect to the $f(Z|D = 1)$ density.)

Assumption (3) implies that D does not help predict values of Y_0 conditional on Z which rules out selection into the programme directly on values of Y_0. However, there is no similar restriction imposed on Y_1, so the method does allow individuals who expect to experience higher levels of Y_1 to select into the programme on the basis of that information. For estimating the TT parameter, matching methods allow selection into treatment to be based on possibly unobserved components of the anticipated programme impact, but only in so far as the programme participation decisions are based on the unobservable determinants of Y_1 and not those of Y_0.

Second, the matching method also requires that the distribution of the matching variables, Z, not be affected by whether the treatment is received. For example, age, gender, and race would generally be valid matching variables, but marital status may not be if it were potentially affected by receipt of the programme. To see why this assumption is necessary, consider the term

$$E_{Z|D=1}\{E_Y(Y|D = 0, Z)\} = \int_{z \in Z} \int_{y \in Y} y \, f(y|D = 0, z) f(z|D = 1) \mathrm{d}z.$$

It uses the $f(z|D = 1)$ conditional density to represent the density that would also have been observed in the no treatment ($D = 0$) state, which rules out the possibility that receipt of treatment changes the density of Z. Variables that are likely to be affected by the treatment or programme intervention cannot be used in the set of matching variables.

With non-experimental data, there may or may not exist a set of observed conditioning variables for which

(1) and (2), or (3) and (4), hold. A finding of Heckman, Ichimura and Todd (1997) and Heckman et al. (1996; 1998) in their application of matching methods to data from the Job Training and Partnership Act (JTPA) programme is that (2) and (4) were not satisfied, because no match could be found for a fraction of the participants. If there are regions where the support of Z does not overlap for the $D=1$ and $D=0$ groups, then matching is justified only when performed over the *region of common support*. The estimated treatment effect must then be defined conditionally on the region of overlap. Some methods for empirically determining the overlap region are described below.

Matching estimators can be difficult to implement when the set of conditioning variables Z is large. If Z are discrete, small-cell problems may arise. If Z are continuous and the conditional mean $E(Y_0|D=0,Z)$ is estimated nonparametrically, then convergence rates will be slow due to the so-called *curse of dimensionality* problem. Rosenbaum and Rubin (1983) provide a theorem that can be used to address this dimensionality problem. They show that for random variables Y and Z and a discrete random variable D

$$E(D|Y, P(D=1|Z))$$
$$= E(E(D|Y,Z)|Y, \Pr(D=1|Z)),$$

so that

$$E(D|Y,Z) = E(D|Z) \Rightarrow E(D|Y, \Pr(D=1|Z))$$
$$= E(D|\Pr(D=1|Z)).$$

This result implies that, when Y_0 outcomes are independent of programme participation conditional on Z, they are also independent of participation conditional on the probability of participation, $P(Z) = \Pr(D=1|Z)$. That is, when matching on Z is valid, matching on the summary statistic $\Pr(D=1|Z)$ (the *propensity score*) is also valid. Provided that $P(Z)$ can be estimated parametrically (or semiparametrically at a rate faster than the nonparametric rate), matching on the propensity score reduces the dimensionality of the matching problem to that of a univariate problem. For this reason, much of the literature on matching focuses on propensity score matching methods. (Heckman, Ichumura and Todd, 1998, and Hahn, 1998, consider whether it is better in terms of efficiency to match on $P(X)$ or on X directly.) With the use of the Rosenbaum and Rubin (1983) theorem, the matching procedure can be broken down into two stages. In the first stage, the propensity score $\Pr(D=1|Z)$ is estimated, using a binary discrete choice model. (Options for first the stage estimation include, for example, a parametric logit or probit model or a semiparametric estimator, such as semiparametric least squares – Ichimura, 1993 – maximum score – Manski, 1973 – smoothed maximum score – Horowitz, 1992 – or semiparametric maximum likelihood – Klein and Spady, 1993. If $P(Z)$ were estimated using a fully nonparametric method, then the curse of dimensionality problem would

reappear.) In the second stage, individuals are matched on the basis of their predicted probabilities of participation.

We next describe a simple model of the programme participation decision to illustrate the kinds of assumptions needed to justify matching. (This model is similar to an example given in Heckman, Lalonde and Smith, 1999.) Assume that an individual chooses whether to apply to a training programme on the basis of the expected benefits. He or she compares the expected earnings streams with and without participating, taking into account opportunity costs and net of some random training cost ε, which may include a psychic component expressed in monetary terms. The participation decision is made at time $t=0$ and the training programme lasts for periods 1 through τ, during which time earnings are zero. The information set used to determine expected earnings is denoted by W, which might include, for example, earnings and employment history. The participation model is

$$D=1 \text{ if } E\left(\sum_{j=\tau}^{T} \frac{Y_{1j}}{(1+r)^j} - \sum_{k=1}^{T} \frac{Y_{0k}}{(1+r)^k} |W \right)$$
$$> \varepsilon + Y_{00}, \text{ else } D=0.$$

The terms in the right-hand side of the inequality are assumed to be known to the individual but not to the econometrician.

If $f(Y_{0k}|\varepsilon + Y_{00}, X) = f(Y_{0k}|X)$, then

$$E(Y_{0k}|X, D=1) = E(Y_{0k}|X, \varepsilon + Y_{00} < \eta(W))$$
$$= E(Y_{0k}|X),$$

which would justify application of a matching estimator. This assumption places restrictions on the correlation structure of the earnings residuals. For example, the assumption would not be plausible if $X=W$ and $Y_{00} = Y_{0k}$, because knowing that a person selected into the programme ($D=1$) would likely be informative about subsequent earnings. We could assume, however, a model for earnings such as

$$Y_{0k} = \phi(X) + v_{0k},$$

where v_{0k} follows an MA(q) process with $q<k$, which would imply that Y_{0k} and Y_{00} are uncorrelated conditional on X. The matching method does not require that everything in the information set be known, but it does assume sufficient information to make the selection on observables assumption plausible.

2 Cross-sectional matching methods
For notational simplicity, let $P=P(Z)$. A prototypical propensity score matching estimator takes the form

$$\hat{\alpha}_M = \frac{1}{n_1} \sum_{i \in I_1 \cap S_P} [Y_{1i} - \hat{E}(Y_{0i}|D=1, P_i)]$$

$$(5)$$

$$\hat{E}(Y_{0i}|D = 1, P_i) = \sum_{j \in I_0} W(i,j) Y_{0j},$$

where I_1 denotes the set of programme participants, I_0 the set of non-participants, S_P the region of common support (see below for ways of constructing this set). n_1 is the number of persons in the set $I_1 \cap S_P$. The match for each participant $I \in I_1 \cap S_P$ is constructed as a weighted average over the outcomes of non-participants, where the weights $W(i,j)$ depend on the distance between P_i and P_j. Define a neighbourhood $C(P_i)$ for each i in the participant sample. Neighbours for i are non-participants $j \in I_0$ for whom $P_j \in C(P_i)$. The persons matched to i are those people in set A_i where $A_i = \{j \in I_0 | P_j \in C(P_i)\}$. We describe a number of alternative matching estimators below, that differ in how the neighbourhood is defined and in how the weights $W(i,j)$ are constructed.

2.1 Alternative ways of constructing matched outcomes

2.1.1 Nearest-neighbour matching
Traditional, pairwise matching, also called *nearest-neighbour matching*, sets:

$$C(P_i) = \min_j ||P_i - P_j||, \ j \in I_0.$$

That is, the non-participant with the value of P_j that is closest to P_i is selected as the match and A_i is a singleton set. The estimator can be implemented either matching with or without replacement. When matching is performed with replacement, the same comparison group observation can be used repeatedly as a match. A drawback of matching without replacement is that the final estimate will usually depend on the initial ordering of the treated observations for which the matches were selected.

Caliper matching (Cochran and Rubin, 1973) is a variation of nearest neighbour matching that attempts to avoid 'bad' matches (those for which P_j is far from P_i) by imposing a tolerance on the maximum distance $||P_i - P_j||$ allowed. That is, a match for person i is selected only if $||P_i - P_j|| < \varepsilon, \ j \in I_0$, where ε is a pre-specified tolerance. Treated persons for whom no matches can be found within the caliper are excluded from the analysis, which is one way of imposing a common support condition. A drawback of caliper matching is that it is difficult to know a priori what choice for the tolerance level is reasonable.

2.1.2 Stratification or interval matching
In this variant of matching, the common support of P is partitioned into a set of intervals, and average treatment impacts are calculating through simple averaging within each interval. A weighted average of the interval impact estimates, using the fraction of the $D = 1$ population in each interval for the weights, provides an overall average impact estimate. Implementing this method requires a decision on how wide the intervals should be. Dehejia and Wahba (1999) implement interval matching using intervals that are selected such that the mean values of the estimated P_i and P_j are not statistically different from each other within intervals.

2.1.3 Kernel and local linear matching
More recently developed matching estimators construct a match for each programme participant using a weighted average over multiple persons in the comparison group. Consider, for example, the nonparametric *kernel matching estimator*, given by

$$\hat{\alpha}_{KM} = \frac{1}{n_1} \sum_{i \in I_1} \left\{ Y_{1i} - \frac{\sum_{j \in I_0} Y_{0j} G\left(\frac{P_j - P_i}{a_n}\right)}{\sum_{k \in I_0} G\left(\frac{P_k - P_i}{a_n}\right)} \right\}$$

where $G(\cdot)$ is a kernel function and a_n is a bandwidth parameter. (See Heckman, Ichimura and Todd, 1997; 1998; and Heckman et al., 1998.) In terms of eq. (5), the weighting function, $W(i,j)$, is equal to

$$\frac{G\left(\frac{P_j - P_i}{a_n}\right)}{\sum_{k \in I_0} G\left(\frac{P_k - P_i}{a_n}\right)}.$$

For a kernel function bounded between -1 and 1, the neighbourhood is

$$C(P_i) = \left\{ \left| \frac{P_i - P_j}{a_n} \right| \leq 1 \right\}, \ j \in I_0.$$

Under standard conditions on the bandwidth and kernel,

$$\frac{\sum_{j \in I_0} Y_{0j} G\left(\frac{P_j - P_i}{a_n}\right)}{\sum_{k \in I_0} G\left(\frac{P_k - P_i}{a_n}\right)}$$

is a consistent estimator of $E(Y_0|D = 1, P_i)$. (Specifically, we require that $G(\cdot)$ integrates to one, has mean zero and that $a_n \to 0$ as $n \to \infty$ and $na_n \to \infty$. One example of a kernel function is the quartic kernel, given by $G(s) = \frac{15}{16}(s^2 - 1)^2$ if $|s| < 1$, $G(s) = 0$ otherwise.)

Heckman, Ichimura and Todd (1997) also propose a generalized version of kernel matching, called local linear matching. Recent research by Fan, 1992a; 1992b, demonstrated advantages of local linear estimation over more standard kernel estimation methods. These advantages include a faster rate of convergence near boundary points and greater robustness to different data design densities; see Fan, 1992a; 1992b.) The local linear weighting function is given by

$$W(i,j) = \frac{G_{ij}\sum_{k\in I_0}G_{ik}(P_k - P_i)^2 - [G_{ij}(P_j - P_i)]\left[\sum_{k\in I_0}G_{ik}(P_k - P_i)\right]}{\sum_{j\in I_0}G_{ij}\sum_{k\in I_0}G_{ij}(P_k - P_i)^2 - \left(\sum_{k\in I_0}G_{ik}(P_k - P_i)\right)^2}.$$

$$(6)$$

As demonstrated in research by Fan (1992a; 1992b), local linear estimation has some advantages over standard kernel estimation. These advantages include a faster rate of convergence near boundary points and greater robustness to different data design densities (see Fan, 1992a; 1992b). Thus, local linear regression would be expected to perform better than kernel estimation in cases where the non-participant observations on P fall on one side of the participant observations.

To implement the matching estimator given by eq. (5), the region of common support S_P needs to be determined. The common support region can be estimated by

$$\hat{S}_P = \{P : \hat{f}(P|D=1) > 0 \text{ and } \hat{f}(P|D=0) > c_q\},$$

where $\hat{f}(P|D=d)$, $d \in \{0,1\}$ are standard nonparametric density estimators. To ensure that the densities are strictly greater than zero, it is required that the densities be strictly positive (that is, exceed zero by a certain amount), determined using a 'trimming level' q. That is, after excluding any P points for which the estimated density is zero, an additional small percentage of the remaining P points is excluded for which the estimated density is positive but very low. The set of eligible matches is thus given by

$$\hat{S}_q = \{P \in \hat{S}_P : \hat{f}(P|D=1) > c_q \text{ and } \hat{f}(P|D=0) > c_q\},$$

where c_q is the density cut-off level that satisfies

$$\sup_{c_q} \frac{1}{2J} \sum_{\{i\in I_1 \cap \hat{S}_P\}} \{1(\hat{f}(P|D=1))$$
$$< c_q + 1(1(\hat{f}(P|D=0)) < c_q)\} \leq q.$$

Here, J is the cardinality of the set of observed values of P that lie in $I_1 \cap \hat{S}_P$. That is, matches are constructed only for the programme participants for which the propensity scores lie in $\hat{S}_q$.

The above estimators are representations of matching estimators and are commonly used. They can be easily adapted to estimate other parameters of interest, such as the average effect of treatment on the untreated (UT $= E(Y_1 - Y_0 | D = 0, X)$), or the average treatment effect (ATE $= E(Y_1 - Y_0 | X)$), which is just a weighted average of treatment on the treated (TT) and treatment on the untreated (UT).

The recent literature has also developed alternative matching estimators that employ different weighting schemes to increase efficiency. See, for example, Hahn (1998) and Hirano, Imbens and Ridder (2003) for estimators that attain the semiparametric efficiency bound. The methods are not described in detail here, because those studies focus on the ATE and not on the average effect of treatment on the treated (TT) parameter. Heckman, Ichimura and Todd (1998) develop a regression-adjusted version of the matching estimator, which replaces Y_{0j} as the dependent variable with the residual from a regression of Y_{0j} on a vector of exogenous covariates. The estimator uses a Robinson (1988) type estimation approach to incorporate exclusion restrictions: that is, that some of the conditioning variables in an equation for the outcomes do not enter into the participation equation or vice versa. In principle, imposing exclusion restrictions can increase efficiency. In practice, though, researchers have not observed much gain from using the regression-adjusted matching estimator. Some alternatives to propensity score matching are discussed in Diamond and Sekhon (2005).

2.2 When does bias arise in matching?
The success of a matching estimator depends on the availability of observable data to construct the conditioning set Z, such that (1) and (2) are satisfied. Suppose only a subset $Z_0 \subset Z$ of the required variables is observed. The propensity score matching estimator based on Z_0 then converges to

$$\alpha'_M = E_{P(Z_0)|D=1}(E(Y_1|P(Z_0), D=1)$$
$$- E(Y_0|P(Z_0), D=0)). \qquad (7)$$

The bias for the parameter of interest, $E(Y_1 - Y_0 | D=1)$, is

$$\text{bias}_M = E(Y_0|D=1) - E_{P(Z_0)|D=1}\{E(Y_0|P(Z_0), D=0)\}.$$

There is no way of a priori choosing the set of Z variables to satisfy the matching condition or of testing whether a particular set meets the requirements. In rare cases, where data are available on a randomized social experiment, it is sometimes possible to ascertain the bias (see, for example, Heckman, Ichimura, and Todd, 1997; Dehejia and Wahba, 1999; 2002; Smith and Todd, 2005).

3 Difference-in-difference matching estimators
The estimators described above assume that, after conditioning on a set of observable characteristics, outcomes are conditionally mean independent of programme participation. However, for a variety of reasons there may be systematic differences between participant and non-participant outcomes, even after conditioning on observables, which could lead to a violation of the identification conditions required for matching. Such differences may arise, for example, because of programme selectivity on unmeasured characteristics or because of levels differences in outcomes that might arise when participants and non-participants reside in different local

labour markets or if the survey questionnaires used to gather the data differ in some ways across groups.

A difference-in-differences (DID) matching strategy, as defined in Heckman, Ichimura and Todd (1997) and Heckman et al. (1998), allows for temporally invariant differences in outcomes between participants and non-participants. This type of estimator matches on the basis of differences in outcomes using the same weighting functions described above. The propensity score DID matching estimator requires that

$$E(Y_{0t} - Y_{0t'}|P, D = 1) = E(Y_{0t} - Y_{0t'}|P, D = 0),$$

where t and t' are time periods after and before the programme enrolment date. This estimator also requires the support condition given above, which must now hold in both periods t and t'. The local linear difference-in-difference estimator is given by

$$\hat{\alpha}_{DM} = \frac{1}{n_1} \sum_{i \in I_1 \cap S_P} \{(Y_{1ti} - Y_{0t'i})\} \\ - \sum_{j \in I_0 \cap S_P} W(i,j)(Y_{0tj} - Y_{0t'j})\},$$

where the weights correspond to the local linear weights defined above. If repeated cross-section data are available, instead of longitudinal data, the estimator can be implemented as

$$\hat{\alpha}_{DM} = \frac{1}{n_{1t}} \sum_{i \in I_{1t} \cap S_P} \left\{(Y_{1ti} - \sum_{j \in I_{0t} \cap S_P} W(i,j) Y_{0tj}\right\} \\ - \frac{1}{n_{1t'}} \sum_{i \in I_{1t'} \cap S_P} \left\{(Y_{1t'i} - \sum_{j \in I_{0t'}} W(i,j) Y_{0t'j}\right\},$$

where $I_{1t}, I_{1t'}, I_{0t}, I_{0t'}$ denote the treatment and comparison group data-sets in each time period.

Finally, the DID matching estimator allows selection into the programme to be based on anticipated gains from the programme in the sense that D can help predict the value of Y_1 given P. However, the method assumes that D does not help predict changes $Y_{0t} - Y_{0t'}$ conditional on a set of observables (Z) used in estimating the propensity score. In their analysis of the effectiveness of matching estimators, Smith and Todd (2005) found difference-in-difference matching estimators to perform much better than cross-sectional methods in cases where participants and non-participants were drawn from different regional labour markets and/or were given different survey questionnaires.

4 Matching when the data are choice-based sampled

The samples used in evaluating the impacts of programmes are often choice-based, with programme participants oversampled relative to their frequency in the population of persons eligible for the programme.

Under choice-based sampling, weights are generally required to consistently estimate the probabilities of programme participation. (See, for example, Manski and Lerman, 1977, for discussion of weighting for logistic regressions.) When the weights are unknown, Heckman and Todd (1995) show that with a slight modification matching methods can still be applied, because the odds ratio ($P/(1-P)$) estimated using a logistic model with incorrect weights (that is, ignoring the fact that samples are choice-based) is a scalar multiple of the true odds ratio, which is itself a monotonic transformation of the propensity scores. Therefore, matching can proceed on the (misweighted) estimate of the odds ratio (or on the log odds ratio).

5 Using balancing tests to check the specification of the propensity score model

As described earlier, the propensity score matching estimator requires the outcome variable to be mean independent of the treatment indicator conditional on the propensity score, $P(Z)$. An important consideration in implementation is how to choose Z. Unfortunately, there is no theoretical basis for choosing a particular set Z to satisfy the identifying assumptions, and the set is not necessarily the most inclusive one.

To guide in the selection of Z, there is some accumulated empirical evidence on how bias estimates depended on the choice of Z in particular applications. For example, Heckman et al. (1998), Heckman, Ichimura and Todd (1997) and Lechner (2001) show that the choice of variables included in Z can make a substantial difference to the estimator's performance. These papers found that biases tended to be higher when the participation equation was estimated using a cruder set of conditioning variables. One approach adopted is to select the set Z to maximize the percentage of people correctly classified under the model. Another finding in these papers is that the matching estimators performed best when the treatment and control groups were located in the same geographic area and when the same survey instrument was administered to both treatments and controls to ensure comparable measurement of outcomes.

Rosenbaum and Rubin (1983) suggest a method to aid in the specification of the propensity score model. The method does not provide guidance in choosing which variables to include in Z, but can help to determine which interactions and higher-order terms to include in the model for a given Z set. They note that for the true propensity score, the following holds:

$$Z \perp\!\!\!\perp D|\Pr(D = 1|Z),$$

or equivalently $E(D|Z, \Pr(D = 1|Z)) = E(D|\Pr(D = 1|Z))$. The basic intuition is that, after conditioning on $\Pr(D = 1|Z)$, additional conditioning on Z should not provide new information about D. If after conditioning on the estimated values of $P(D=1|Z)$ there is still dependence on Z, this suggests misspecification in the model used to estimate $\Pr(D=1|Z)$. The theorem holds for any Z, including sets Z that do not satisfy the conditional independence condition required to justify matching. As such, the theorem is not informative about what set of variables to include in Z.

This result motivates a specification test for $\Pr(D=1|Z)$, that is a test whether or not there are differences in Z between the $D=1$ and $D=0$ groups after conditioning on $P(Z)$. The test has been implemented in the literature a number of ways (see, for example Eichler and Lechner, 2002; Dehijia and Wahba, 1999; 2002; Smith and Todd, 2002; Diamond and Sekohn, 2005).

6 Assessing the variability of matching estimators

The distribution theory for the cross-sectional and difference-in-difference kernel and local linear matching estimators described above is derived in Heckman, Ichimura and Todd (1998). However, implementing the asymptotic standard error formulae can be cumbersome, so standard errors for matching estimators are often instead generating using bootstrap resampling methods. (See Efron and Tibshirani, 1993, for an introduction to bootstrap methods, and Horowitz, 2003, for a recent survey of bootstrapping in econometrics.) A recent paper by Abadie and Imbens (2006a) shows that standard bootstrap resampling methods are not valid for assessing the variability of nearest neighbour estimators, but can be applied to assess the variability of kernel or local linear matching estimators for a suitably chosen bandwidth. Abadie and Imbens (2006b) present alternative standard error formulae for assessing the variability of nearest neighbour matching estimators.

7 Applications

There have been numerous evaluations of matching estimators in recent decades. For a survey of many applications in the context of evaluating the effects of labour market programmes (see Heckman, Lalonde and Smith, 1999). More recently, propensity score matching estimators have been used in evaluating the impacts of a variety of programme interventions in developing countries. Jalan and Ravallion (1999) assess the impact of a workfare programme in Argentina (the *Trabajar* programme), and Jalan and Ravallion (2003) study the effects of public investments in piped water on child health outcomes in rural India. Galiani, Gertler and Schargrodsky (2005) use difference-in-difference matching methods to analyse the effects of privatization of water services on child mortality in Argentina. Other applications include Gertler, Levine and Ames (2004) in a study of the effects of parental death on child outcomes, Lavy (2004) in a study of the effects of a teacher incentive programme in Israel on student performance, Angrist and Lavy (2001) in a study of the effects of teacher training on children's test scores in Israel, and Chen and Ravallion (2003) in a study of a poverty reduction project in China.

Behrman, Cheng and Todd (2004) use a modified version of a propensity score matching estimator to evaluate the effects of a preschool programme in Bolivia on child health and cognitive outcomes. They identify programme effects by comparing children with different lengths of duration in the programme, using matching to control for selectivity into alternative durations. Also, see Imbens (2000) and Hirano and Imbens (2004) for an analysis of the role of the propensity score with continuous treatments. Lechner (2001) extends propensity score analysis for the case of multiple treatments.

PETRA E. TODD

See also **propensity score; selection bias and self-selection; semiparametric estimation; treatment effect.**

Bibliography

Abadie, A. and Imbens, G. 2006a. On the failure of the bootstrap for matching estimators. Technical Working Paper No. 325. Cambridge, MA: NBER.

Abadie, A. and Imbens, G. 2006b. Large sample properties of matching estimators for average treatment effects. *Econometrica* 74, 235–67.

Angrist, J. and Lavy, V. 2001. Does teacher training affect pupil learning? Evidence from matched comparisons in Jerusalem public schools. *Journal of Labor Economics* 19, 343–69.

Behrman, J., Cheng, Y. and Todd, P. 2004. Evaluating preschool programs when length of exposure to the program varies: a nonparametric approach. *Review of Economics and Statistics* 86, 108–32.

Chen, S. and Ravallion, M. 2003. Hidden impact? Ex-post evaluation of an anti-poverty program. Policy Research Working Paper No. 3049. Washington, DC: World Bank.

Cochran, W. and Rubin, D. 1973. Controlling bias in observational studies. *Sankyha* 35, 417–46.

Dehejia, R. and Wahba, S. 1999. Causal effects in non-experimental studies: reevaluating the evaluation of training programs. *Journal of the American Statistical Association* 94, 1053–62.

Dehejia, R. and Wahba, S. 2002. Propensity score matching methods for nonexperimental causal studies. *Review of Economics and Statistics* 84, 151–61.

Diamond, A. and Sekhon, J.S. 2005. Genetic matching for estimating causal effects: a general multivariate matching method for achieving balance in observational studies. Working paper, Department of Political Science, Berkeley.

Efron, B. and Tibshirani, R. 1993. *An Introduction to the Bootstrap*. New York: Chapman and Hall.

Eichler, M. and Lechner, M. 2002. An evaluation of public employment programmes in the East German state of Sachsen-Anhalt. *Labour Economics* 9, 143–86.

Fan, J. 1992a. Design adaptive nonparametric regression. *Journal of the American Statistical Association* 87, 998–1004.

Fan, J. 1992b. Local linear regression smoothers and their minimax efficiencies. *Annals of Statistics* 21, 196–216.

Fisher, R.A. 1935. *Design of Experiments.* New York: Hafner.

Friedlander, D. and Robins, P. 1995. Evaluating program evaluations: new evidence on commonly used nonexperimental methods. *American Economic Review* 85, 923–37.

Galiani, S., Gertler, P. and Schargrodsky, E. 2005. Water for life: the impact of the privatization of water services on child mortality in Argentina. *Journal of Political Economy* 113, 83–120.

Gertler, P., Levine, D. and Ames, M. 2004. Schooling and parental death. *Review of Economics and Statistics* 86, 211–25.

Hahn, J. 1998. On the role of the propensity score in efficient estimation of average treatment effects. *Econometrica* 66, 315–31.

Heckman, J., Ichimura, H. and Todd, P. 1997. Matching as an econometric evaluation estimator: evidence from evaluating a job training program. *Review of Economic Studies* 64, 605–54.

Heckman, J., Ichimura, H. and Todd, P. 1998. Matching as an econometric evaluation estimator. *Review of Economic Studies* 65, 261–94.

Heckman, J., Lalonde, R. and Smith, J. 1999. The economics and econometrics of active labor market programs. In *Handbook of Labor Economics*, vol. 3A, ed. O. Ashenfelter and D. Card. Amsterdam: North-Holland.

Heckman, J., Smith, J. and Clements, N. 1997. Making the most out of social experiments: accounting for heterogeneity in programme impacts. *Review of Economic Studies* 64, 487–536.

Heckman, J. and Todd, P. 1995. Adapting propensity score matching and selection models to choice-based samples. Manuscript, Department of Economics, University of Chicago.

Heckman, J., Ichimura, H., Smith, J. and Todd, P. 1996. Sources of selection bias in evaluating social programs: an interpretation of conventional measures and evidence on the effectiveness of matching as a program evaluation method. *Proceedings of the National Academy of Sciences* 93, 13416–20.

Heckman, J., Ichimura, H., Smith, J. and Todd, P. 1998. Characterizing selection bias using experimental data. *Econometrica* 66, 1017–98.

Hirano, K., Imbens, G. and Ridder, G. 2003. Efficient estimation of average treatment effects using the estimated propensity score. *Econometrica* 71, 1161–89.

Hirano, K. and Imbens, G. 2004. The propensity score with continuous treatments. In *Applied Bayesian Modeling and Causal Inference from Incomplete Data Perspectives*, ed. A. Gelman and X.L. Meng. New York: Wiley.

Holland, P.W. 1986. Statistics and causal inference (with discussion). *Journal of the American Statistical Association* 81, 945–70.

Horowitz, J.L. 1992. A smoothed maximum score estimator for the binary response model. *Econometrica* 60, 505–32.

Horowitz, J.L. 2003. The bootstrap. *Handbook of Econometrics*, vol. 5, ed. J.J. Heckman and E.E. Leamer. Amsterdam: North-Holland.

Ichimura, H. 1993. Semiparametric least squares and weighted SLS estimation of single index models. *Journal of Econometrics* 58, 71–120.

Imbens, G. 2000. The role of the propensity score in estimating dose-response functions. *Biometrika* 87, 706–10.

Jalan, J. and Ravallion, M. 1999. Efficient estimation of average treatment effects: evidence for Argentina's Trabajar program. Policy Research Working Paper. Washington, DC: World Bank.

Jalan, J. and Ravallion, M. 2003. Does piped water reduce diarrhea for children in rural India. *Journal of Econometrics* 112, 153–73.

Klein, R.W. and Spady, R.H. 1993. An efficient semiparametric estimator for binary response models. *Econometrica* 61, 387–422.

LaLonde, R. 1986. Evaluating the econometric evaluations of training programs with experimental data. *American Economic Review* 76, 604–20.

Lavy, V. 2002. Evaluating the effects of teachers' group performance incentives on pupil achievement. *Journal of Political Economics* 110, 1286–387.

Lavy, V. 2004. Performance pay and teachers' effort, productivity and grading ethics. Working Paper No. 10622. Cambridge, MA: NBER.

Lechner, M. 2001. Identification and estimation of causal effects of multiple treatments under the conditional independence assumption. In *Econometric Evaluations of Active Labor Market Policies in Europe*, ed. M. Lechner and F. Pfeiffer. Heidelberg: Physica.

Manski, C. 1973. Maximum score estimation of the stochastic utility model of choice. *Journal of Econometrics* 3, 205–28.

Manski, C. and Lerman, S. 1977. The estimation of choice probabilities from choice-based samples. *Econometrica* 45, 1977–88.

Robinson, P. 1988. Root-N consistent nonparametric regression. *Econometrica* 56, 931–54.

Rosenbaum, P. and Rubin, D. 1983. The central role of the propensity score in observational studies for causal effects. *Biometrika* 70, 41–55.

Rosenbaum, P. and Rubin, D. 1985. Constructing a control group using multivariate matched sampling methods that incorporate the propensity score. *American Statistician* 39, 33–8.

Rubin, D.B. 1974. Estimating causal effects of treatments in randomized and nonrandomized studies. *Journal of Educational Psychology* 66, 688–701.

Silverman, B.W. 1986. *Density Estimation for Statistics and Data Analysis.* London: Chapman and Hall.

Smith, J. and Todd, P. 2005. Does matching overcome Lalonde's critique of nonexperimental estimators? *Journal of Econometrics* 125, 305–53.

material balances

A material balance is a simple planning device developed (if not originated) early in Soviet planning for the purpose of equating prospective availabilities of a given good and its prospective requirements over the plan period (or at some target date in case of a stock). It occupies a central role in Soviet-type planning. The phrase, a literal rendering of the Russian *material'nyi balans*, is somewhat inexact and possibly confusing inasmuch as each of the two words has a variety of meanings in English. A more exact term would be 'sources-and-uses account' for a flow or 'balance sheet' for a stock. As such, material balances have counterparts in planning and management the world over.

In Soviet-type planning, a material balance is typically constructed *ex ante*. It can pertain to any good or resource requiring planners' attention or administrative disposition; thus, 'balance' is drawn up not only for material products, but also for labour, capacity, foreign exchange, and so on. While it can be drawn up at any level of the hierarchy of a command economy and by any relevant organizational entity, these alternatives carry important economic, bureaucratic and even political implications in a Soviet-type economy. 'In the course of preparing the annual plan … the USSR State Planning Commission draws up [some] 2,000 single-product balances, the State Commission for Supply – up to 15,000, and the ministries – up to 50,000' (*EKO*, August, 1983, p. 26). Though there may be some duplication in terms of goods between these figures, they nonetheless do suggest the magnitude of the annual task, especially if one bears in mind the interconnections.

In Soviet-type practice a material balance not only has the passive purpose of checking requirements against availabilities, but forms the operational basis for specific production or import directives to designated organizations and firms, and for specific acquisition permits to designated users of the good. Note that nearly all producer goods are administratively allocated (rationed) to users.

A material balance may take the following form (adapted from Levine, 1959):

Table 1

Material balance for good X for (year)	
Sources	*Uses (distribution)*
1. Current production – by major producing organizations, firms	1. For production – by organizations, firms
2. Imports	2. For construction – by organizations, firms
3. Other sources	3. For household sector ('market fund')
4. Beginning-year stocks – by organizations	4. For export

Table 1. (*Continued*)

Material balance for good X for (year)	
Sources	*Uses (distribution)*
5. Total sources	5. To central reserve stocks
	6. End-year stocks at suppliers – by organizations, firms
	7. Total uses (distribution)

Two kinds of questions arise: (*a*) operational – how is the balance initially compiled and 'balanced', and later adjusted for outside effects (from other balances) and the extent to which successive iterations are required to converge? and (*b*) policy – the bounds and degree of aggregation of a 'good', the organizational locus and level of compilation, and so on?

Little is known about the initial compilation. There must be serious problems of the requisite detailed information in the case of many goods, given that the preparation of the annual plan extends over most of the pre-plan year (and often into the plan year). Thus, the database may anticipate the plan year by one-and-a-half to two years whose projection is obviously subject to uncertainty. A common problem is the uncertainty of going-on-stream of capacity under construction. Also, the data may not be very accurate to start with, given the cat-and-mouse game that firms and other subordinates play with their superiors. What is more, thousands of balances are being drawn up simultaneously, often by different organizations or subdivisions, with the obvious difficulty of mutual coordination.

The 'balancer' must take into account – in addition to technical parameters – political and other high-level decisions, existing economic programmes, bureaucratic politics, and the usual pressure to squeeze more out of the economy's resources. Corruption is not unknown. The work is largely done manually and inevitably to some extent subjectively. While computers are beginning to be used, the input–output technique – which in principle is eminently suitable for the purpose – seems to be applied for the grosser computations and checks, not for the drawing up of operational, short-term material balances. The main reasons are that the sectors in even the largest matrices are too aggregative for the material balances, and the data underlying the technical coefficients are not current enough.

Among the balancer's technical parameters, pride of place is occupied by the 'norm' – a disaggregated input–output ratio, which assists the compiler in filling in parts of both sides of the account. Much effort goes into computation of the norms, given their crucial role in the preparation of plans and the issuing of specific assignments. They are supposed to be 'scientific', that is, representing the best applicable engineering practice (note: for technical rather than economic efficiency), but given their enormous number and informational problems, this remains an ideal. In the event, the balancer must employ short-cuts and resort to optimistic assumptions in order to achieve equality of requirements and availabilities while under pressure to deliver high ('taut') production targets. A common and much criticized short-cut is simply to raise output targets of all producers by a uniform percentage, with corresponding adjustments of the norms.

The weakest link in the material balance method is coordination among the many balances to achieve a reasonably internally consistent plan for the whole economy or a sector thereof. (Montias, 1959, discusses this at length.) Even if the implicit inter-industry matrix is close to triangular, every iteration is a major undertaking under the actual conditions. Aggregating the goods would simplify the iteration process, but would not suit well the demands posed by detailed production assignments and allocation orders. So would the holding of ample reserve stocks, which are not always there or accessible. In fact, adjustments and corrections tend ordinarily to be carried to only a few adjoining balances.

The overall annual plan that emerges is typically of low internal consistency (not to say, economic efficiency), causing considerable difficulties to those charged with its implementation and necessitating continual further correction and adjustment during the plan year, with the same effect.

GREGORY GROSSMAN

See also **command economy; economic calculation in socialist countries; planning.**

Bibliography

Levine, H.S. 1959. The centralized planning of supply in Soviet industry. In U.S. Congress, Joint Economic Committee, *Comparison of the United States and Soviet Economies* I. Washington, DC.

Montias, J.M. 1959. Planning with material balances in Soviet-type economies. *American Economic Review* 49, 963–85.

mathematical economics

I. The steady course on which mathematical economics has held for the past four decades sharply contrasts with its progress during the preceding century, which was marked by several major scientific accidents. One of them occurred in 1838, at the beginning of that period, with the publication of Augustin Cournot's *Recherches sur les principes mathématiques de la théorie des richesses*. By its mathematical form and by its economic content, his book stands in splendid isolation in time; and in explaining its data historians of economic analysis in the first

half of the 19th century must use a wide confidence interval.

The University of Lausanne was responsible for two other of those accidents. When Léon Walras delivered his first professorial lecture there on 16 December 1870, he had held no previous academic appointment; he had published a novel and a short story but he had not contributed to economic theory before 1870; and he was exactly 36. The risk that his university took was vindicated by the appearance of the *Eléments d'économie politique pure* in 1874–7. For Vilfredo Pareto, who succeeded Walras in his chair in 1893, it was also a first academic appointment; he had not contributed to economic theory before 1892; and he was 45. This second gamble of the University of Lausanne paid off when Pareto's *Cours d'économie politique* appeared in 1896–97, followed by his *Manuel d'économie politique* in 1909, and by the article 'Economie mathématique' in 1911.

In the contemporary period of development of mathematical economics, profoundly influenced by John von Neumann, his article of 1928 on games and his paper of 1937 on economic growth also stand out as major accidents, even in a career with so many facets.

The preceding local views would yield a distorted historical perception, however, if they were not complemented by a global view which sees in the development of mathematical economics a powerful, irresistible current of thought. Deductive reasoning about social phenomena invited the use of mathematics from the first. Among the social sciences, economics was in a privileged position to respond to that invitation, for two of its central concepts, commodity and price, are quantified in a unique manner, as soon as units of measurement are chosen. Thus for an economy with a finite number of commodities, the action of an economic agent is described by listing his input, or his output, of each commodity. Once a sign convention distinguishing inputs from outputs is made, the action of an agent is represented by a point in the commodity space, a finite-dimensional real vector space. Similarly the prices in the economy are represented by a point in the price space, the real vector space dual of the commodity space. The rich mathematical structure of those two spaces provides an ideal basis for the development of a large part of economic theory.

Finite dimensional commodity and price spaces can be, and usually are, identified and treated as a Euclidean space. The stage is thus set for geometric intuition to take a lead role in economic analysis. That role is manifest in the figures that abound in the economics literature, and some of the great theorists have substituted virtuosity in reasoning on diagrams for the use of mathematical form. As for mathematical economists, geometric insight into the commodity-price space has often provided the key to the solution of problems in economic theory.

The differential calculus and linear algebra were applied to that space at first as a matter of course. By the time John Hicks's *Value and Capital* appeared in 1939, Maurice Allais' *A la recherche d'une discipline économique* in 1943, and Paul Samuelson's *Foundations of Economic Analysis* in 1947, they had both served economic theory well. They would serve it well again, but the publication of the *Theory of Games and Economic Behavior* in 1944 signalled that action was also going to take new directions. In mathematical form, the book of von Neumann and Oskar Morgenstern set a new level of logical rigour for economic reasoning, and it introduced convex analysis in economic theory by its elementary proof of the MiniMax theorem. In the next few years convexity became one of the central mathematical concepts, first in activity analysis and in linear programming, as the *Activity Analysis of Production and Allocation* edited by Tjalling Koopmans attested in 1951, and then in the mainstream of economic theory. In consumption theory as in production theory, in welfare economics as in efficiency analysis, in theory of general economic equilibrium and in the theory of the core, the picture of a convex set supported by a hyperplane kept reappearing, and the supporting hyperplane theorem supplied a standard technique for obtaining implicit prices. The applications of that theorem to economics were a ready consequence of the real vector space structure of the commodity space; yet they were made more than thirty years after Minkowski proved it in 1911.

Algebraic topology entered economic theory in 1937, when von Neumann generalized Brouwer's fixed point theorem in a lemma devised to prove the existence of an optimal growth path in his model. The lag from Brouwer's result of 1911 to its first economic application was shorter than for Minkowski's result. It should, however, have been significantly longer, for von Neumann's lemma was far too powerful a tool for his proof of existence. Several authors later obtained more elementary demonstrations, and David Gale in particular based his in 1956 on the supporting hyperplane theorem. Thus von Neumann's lemma, reformulated in 1941 as Kakutani's fixed point theorem, was an accident within an accidental paper. But in a global historical view, the perfect fit between the mathematical concept of a fixed point and the social science concept of an equilibrium stands out. A state of a social system is described by listing an action for each one of its agents. Considering such a state, each agent reacts by selecting the action that is optimal for him given the actions of all the others. Listing those reactions yields a new state, and thereby a transformation of the set of states of the social system into itself is defined. A state of the system is an equilibrium if, and only if, it is a fixed point of that transformation. More generally, if the optimal reactions of the agents to a given state are not uniquely determined, one is led to associate a set of new states, instead of a single state, with every state of the system. A point-to-set transformation of the set of states of the social system into itself is thereby defined; and a state of the system is an equilibrium if, and

only if, it is a fixed point of that transformation. In this view, fixed point theorems were slated for the prominent part they played in game theory and in the theory of general economic equilibrium after John Nash's one-page note of 1950.

A perfect fit of mathematical form to economic content was also found when the traditional concept of a set of negligible agents was formulated exactly. In 1881, in *Mathematical Psychics*, Francis Edgeworth had studied in his box the asymptotic equality of the 'contract curve' of an economy and of its set of competitive allocations. Basic to his proof of convergence is the fact that in his limiting process every agent tends to become negligible. A long period of neglect of his contribution ended in 1959, when Martin Shubik brought out the connection between the contract curve and the game theoretic concept of the core. After the second impulse given in 1962 by Herbert Scarf's first extension of Edgeworth's result, a new phase of development of the economic theory of the core was under way; and in 1964 Robert Aumann formalized the concept of a set of negligible agents as the unit interval of the real line with its Lebesgue measure. The power of that formulation was demonstrated as Aumann proved that in an exchange economy with that set of agents, the core and the set of competitive allocations coincide. Karl Vind then gave, also in 1964, a different formulation of this remarkable result in the context of a measure space of agents without atoms, and showed that it is a direct consequence of Lyapunov's theorem of 1940 on the range of an atomless vector measure. The convexity of that range explains the convexing effect of large economies. In the important case of a set of negligible agents, it justifies the convexity assumption on aggregate sets to which economic theory frequently appeals. A privileged place was clearly marked for measure theory in mathematical economics.

An alternative formulation of the concept of a set of negligible agents was proposed by Donald Brown and Abraham Robinson in 1972 in terms of Non-standard Analysis, created by Robinson in the early 1960s. Innovations in the mathematical tools of economic theory had not always been immediately and universally adopted in the past. In this case the lag from mathematical discovery to economic application was exceptionally short, and Non-standard Analysis had not been widely accepted by mathematicians themselves. Predictably the intrusion of this strange, sophisticated new tool in economic theory was greeted mostly with indifference or with scepticism. Yet it led to the form given by Robert Anderson to inequalities on the deviation of core allocations from competitive allocations, which are central to the theory of the core. In the article published by Anderson in 1978 those inequalities are stated and proved in an elementary manner, but their expression was found by means of Non-standard Analysis.

The differential calculus, which had been used earlier on too broad a spectrum of economic problems, turned out in the 1970s to supply the proper mathematical machinery for the study of the set of competitive equilibria of an economy. A partial explanation of the observed state of an economic system had been provided by proofs of existence of equilibrium based on fixed point theorems. A more complete explanation would have followed from persuasive assumptions on a mathematical model of the economy ensuring uniqueness of equilibrium. Unfortunately the assumptions proposed to that end were excessively stringent, and the requirement of global uniqueness had to be relaxed to that of local uniqueness. Even then an economy composed of agents on their best mathematical behaviour (for instance each having a concave utility function and a demand function both indefinitely differentiable) may be ill-behaved and fail to have locally unique equilibria. If one considers the question from the generic viewpoint, however, one sees that the set of those ill-behaved economies is negligible. This time the ideal mathematical tool for the proof of that assertion is Sard's theorem of 1942 on the set of critical values of a differentiable function. By providing appropriate techniques for the study of the set of equilibria, differential topology and global analysis came to occupy in mathematical economics a place that seemed to have been long reserved for them.

As new fields of mathematics were introduced into economic theory and solved some of its fundamental problems, a growth-generating cycle operated. The mathematical interest of the questions raised by economic theory attracted mathematicians who in turn made the subject mathematically more interesting. The resulting expansion of mathematical economics was unexpectedly rapid. Attempting to quantify it, one can use as an index the total number of pages published yearly by the five main periodicals in the field: *Econometrica* and the *Review of Economic Studies* (which both started publishing in 1933), the *International Economic Review* (1960), the *Journal of Economic Theory* (1969), and the *Journal of Mathematical Economics* (1974). The graph of that index is eloquent. It shows a first phase of decline to 1943, followed by a 33-year period of exuberant, nearly exponential growth. The annual rate of increase that would carry the index exponentially from its 1944 level to its 1977 level is 8.2 per cent, a rate that implies doubling in slightly less than nine years and that cannot easily be sustained. The years 1977–84 have indeed marked a pause that will soon resemble a stagnation phase if it persists. Among its imperfections the index gives equal weights to *Econometrica*, the *Review of Economic Studies*, and the *International Economic Review*, all of which publish articles on econometrics as well as on mathematical economics, and to the *Journal of Economic Theory* and the *Journal of Mathematical Economics*, which do not. But given lower relative weights to the first three yields even higher annual rates of exponential growth of the index for the period 1944–77.

The sweeping movement that took place from 1944 to 1977 suggests an inevitable phase in the evolution of mathematical economics. The graph illustrating that phase hints at the deep transformation of departments of economics during those 33 years. It also hints at the proliferation of discussion papers and at the metamorphosis of professional journals like the *American Economic Review*, which was almost pure of mathematical symbols in 1933 but had lost its innocence by the late 1950s. Figure 1.

II. As a formal model of an economy acquires a mathematical life of its own, it becomes the object of an inexorable process in which rigour, generality and simplicity are relentlessly pursued.

Before 1944, articles on economic theory only exceptionally met the standards of rigour common in mathematical periodicals. But several of the exceptions were outstanding, among them the two papers of von Neumann of 1928 and of 1937, and the three papers of Abraham Wald of 1935–6 on the existence of a general economic equilibrium. In 1944 the *Theory of Games and Economic Behavior* gained full rights for uncompromising rigour in

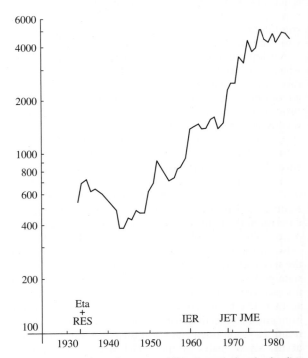

Figure 1   Number of pages published yearly by the leading journals in mathematical economics (Econometrica (abbr. Eta), *Review of Economic Studies*, (For the first 29 years the *Review of Economic Studies* was published on an academic rather than on a calendar year basis. As a result, only one issue appeared in 1933, compared with three in 1934; hence the spurious initial increase in the graph.) *International Economic Review, Journal of Economic Theory, Journal of Mathematical Economics*).

economic theory and prepared the way for its axiomatization. An axiomatized theory first selects its primitive concepts and represents each one of them by a mathematical object. For instance the consumption of a consumer, his set of possible consumptions and his preferences are represented respectively by a point in the commodity space, a subset of the commodity space and a binary relation in that subset. Next, assumptions on the objects representing the primitive concepts are specified, and consequences are mathematically derived from them. The economic interpretation of the theorems so obtained is the last step of the analysis. According to this schema, an axiomatized theory has a mathematical form that is completely separated from its economic content. If one removes the economic interpretation of the primitive concepts, of the assumptions and of the conclusions of the model, its bare mathematical structure must still stand. This severe test is passed only by a small minority of the papers on economic theory published by *Econometrica* and by the *Review of Economic Studies* during their first decade.

The divorce of form and content immediately yields a new theory whenever a novel interpretation of a primitive concept is discovered. A textbook illustration of this application of the axiomatic method occurred in the economic theory of uncertainty. The traditional characteristics of a commodity were its physical description, its date, and its location when in 1953 Kenneth Arrow proposed adding the state of the world in which it will be available. This reinterpretation of the concept of a commodity led, without any formal change in the model developed for the case of certainty, to a theory of uncertainty which eventually gained broad acceptance, notably among finance theorists.

The pursuit of logical rigour also contributed powerfully to the rapid expansion of mathematical economics after World War II. It made it possible for research workers to use the precisely stated and flawlessly proved results that appeared in the literature without scrutinizing their statements and their proofs in every detail. Another cumulative process could thus gather great momentum.

The exact formulation of assumptions and of conclusions turned out, moreover, to be an effective safeguard against the ever-present temptation to apply an economic theory beyond its domain of validity. And by the exactness of that formulation, economic analysis was sometimes brought closer to its ideology-free ideal. The case of the two main theorems of welfare economics is symptomatic. They respectively give conditions under which an equilibrium relative to a price system is a Pareto optimum, and under which the converse holds. Foes of state intervention read in those two theorems a mathematical demonstration of the unqualified superiority of market economies, while advocates of state intervention welcome the same theorems because the explicitness of their assumptions emphasizes discrepancies between the theoretic model and the economies that they observe.

Still another consequence of the axiomatization of economic theory has been a greater clarity of expression, one of the most significant gains that it has achieved. To that effect, axiomatization does more than making assumptions and conclusions explicit and exposing the deductions linking them. The very definition of an economic concept is usually marred by a substantial margin of ambiguity. An axiomatized theory substitutes for that ambiguous concept a mathematical object that is subjected to definite rules of reasoning. Thus an axiomatic theorist succeeds in communicating the meaning he intends to give to a primitive concept because of the completely specified formal context in which he operates. The more developed this context is, the richer it is in theorems, and in other primitive concepts, the smaller will be the margin of ambiguity in the intended interpretation.

Although an axiomatic theory may flaunt the separation of its mathematical form and its economic content in print, their interaction is sometimes close in the discovery and elaboration phases. As an instance, consider the characterization of aggregate excess demand functions in an *l*-commodity exchange economy. Such a function maps a positive price vector into an aggregate excess demand vector, and Walras' Law says that those two vectors are orthogonal in the Euclidean commodity-price space. That function is also homogeneous of degree zero. For a mathematician, these are compelling reasons for normalizing the price vector so that it belongs to the unit sphere. Then aggregate excess demand can be represented by a vector tangent to the sphere at the price vector with which it is associated. In other words, the aggregate excess demand function is a vector field on the positive unit sphere. Hugo Sonnenschein conjectured in 1973 that any continuous function satisfying Walras' Law is the aggregate excess demand function of a finite exchange economy. A proof of that conjecture (Debreu, 1974) was suggested by the preceding geometric interpretation since any vector field on the positive unit sphere can be written as a sum of *l* elementary vector fields, each one obtained by projecting a positive vector on one of the *l* coordinate axes into the tangent hyperplane. There only remains to note that every continuous elementary vector field is the excess demand function of a mathematically well-behaved consumer. Mathematical form and economic content alternately took the lead in the development of this proof.

The pursuit of generality in a formalized theory is no less imperative than the pursuit of rigour, and the mathematician's compulsive search for ever weaker assumptions is reinforced by the economist's awareness of the limitations of his postulates. It has, for example, expurgated superfluous differentiability assumptions from economic theory, and prompted its extension to general commodity spaces.

Akin in motivation, execution and consequences is the pursuit of simplicity. One of its expressions is the quest for the most direct link between the assumptions and the conclusions of a theorem. Strongly motivated by aesthetic appeal, this quest is responsible for more transparent proofs in which logical flaws cannot remain hidden, and which are more easily communicated. In extreme cases the proof of an economic proposition becomes so simple that it can dispense with mathematical symbols. The first main theorem of welfare economics, according to which an equilibrium relative to a price system is a Pareto optimum, is such a case.

In the demonstration, we study an economy consisting of a set of agents who have collectively at their disposal positive amounts of a certain number of commodities and who want to allocate these total resources among themselves. By the consumption of an agent, we mean a list of the amounts of each commodity that he consumes. And by an allocation, we mean a specification of the consumption of each agent such that the sum of all those individual consumptions equals the total resources. Following Pareto, we compare two allocations according to a unanimity principle. We say that the second allocation is collectively preferred to the first allocation if every agent prefers the consumption that he receives in the second to the consumption that he receives in the first. According to this definition, an allocation is optimal if no other allocation is collectively preferred to it. Now imagine that the agents use a price system, and consider a certain allocation. We say that each agent is in equilibrium relative to the given price system if he cannot satisfy his preferences better than he does with his allotted consumption unless he spends more than he does for that consumption. We claim that an allocation in which every agent is in equilibrium relative to a price system is optimal. Suppose, by contradiction, that there is a second allocation collectively preferred to the first. Then every agent prefers his consumption in the second allocation to his consumption in the first. Therefore the consumption of every agent in the second allocation is more expensive than his consumption in the first. Consequently the total consumption of all the agents in the second allocation is more expensive than their total consumption in the first. For both allocations, however, the total consumption equals the total resources at the disposal of the economy. Thus we asserted that the value of the total resources relative to the price system is greater than itself. A contradiction has been obtained, and the claim that the first allocation is optimal has been established.

This result, which provides an essential insight into the role of prices in an economy and which requires no assumption within the model, is remarkable in another way. The two concepts that it relates might have been isolated, and its symbol-free proof might have been given early in the history of economic theory and without any help from mathematics. In fact that demonstration is a late by-product of the development of the mathematical theory of welfare economics. But to economists who have even a casual acquaintance with mathematical symbols,

the previous exercise is not more than an artificial *tour de force* that has lost the incisive conciseness of a proof imposing no bar against the use of mathematics. That conciseness is one of the most highly prized aspects of the simplicity of expression of a mathematized theory.

In close relationship with its axiomatization, economic theory became concerned with more fundamental questions and also more abstract. The problem of existence of a general economic equilibrium is representative of those trends. The model proposed by Walras in 1874–7 sought to explain the observed state of an economy as an equilibrium resulting from the interaction of a large number of small agents through markets for commodities. Over the century that followed its publication, that model came to be a common intellectual framework for many economists, theorists as well as practitioners. This eventually made it compelling for mathematical economists to specify assumptions that guarantee the existence of the central concept of Walrasian theory. Only through such a specification, in particular, could the explanatory power of the model be fully appraised. The early proofs of existence of Wald in 1935–6 were followed by a pause of nearly two decades, and then by the contemporary phase of development beginning in 1954 with the articles of Arrow and Debreu, and of Lionel McKenzie.

In the reformulation that the theory of general economic equilibrium underwent, it reached a higher level of abstraction. From that new viewpoint a deeper understanding both of the mathematical form and of the economic content of the model was gained. Its role as a benchmark was also perceived more clearly, a role which prompted extensions to incomplete markets for contingent commodities, externalities, indivisibilities, increasing returns, public goods, temporary equilibrium, … .

In an unanticipated, yet not unprecedented, way greater abstraction brought Walrasian theory closer to concrete applications. When different areas of the field of computable general equilibrium were opened to research at the University of Oslo, at the Cowles Foundation, and at the World Bank, the algorithms of Scarf included in their lineage proofs of existence of a general economic equilibrium by means of fixed point theorems. This article has credited the mathematical form of theoretic models with many assets. Their sum is so large as to turn occasionally into a liability, as the seductiveness of that form becomes almost irresistible. In its pursuit, research may be tempted to forget economic content and to shun economic problems that are not readily amenable to mathematization. No attempt will be made here, however, to draw a balance sheet, to the debit side of which justice would not be done. Economic theory is fated for a long mathematical future, and in other editions of Palgrave authors will have the opportunity, and possibly the inclination, to choose as a theme 'Mathematical Form vs. Economic Content'.

GERARD DEBREU

First published in Econometrica, November 1986, with revisions.

See also **computation of general equilibria; cores; existence of general equilibrium; game theory; regular economies; uncertainty and general equilibrium.**

Bibliography

Allais, M. 1943. *A la recherche d'une discipline économique.* Paris: Imprimerie Nationale.

Anderson, R.M. 1978. An elementary core equivalence theorem. *Econometrica* 46, 1483–7.

Arrow, K.J. 1951. An extension of the basic theorems of classical welfare economics. In *Proceedings of the Second Berkeley Symposium on Mathematical Statistics and Probability*, ed. J. Neyman, Berkeley: University of California Press, 507–32.

Arrow, K.J. 1953. Le rôle des valeurs boursières pour la répartition la meilleure des risques. *Econométrie*, Paris: Centre National de la Recherche Scientifique, 41–8.

Arrow, K.J. and Debreu, G. 1954. Existence of an equilibrium for a competitive economy. *Econometrica* 22, 265–90.

Arrow, K.J. and Hahn, F.H. 1971. *General Competitive Analysis.* San Francisco: Holden-Day.

Arrow, K.J. and Intriligator, M.D., (eds.) 1981–5. *Handbook of Mathematical Economics*, vols 1,2 and 3. Amsterdam: North-Holland Publishing Company.

Aumann, R.J. 1964. Markets with a continuum of traders. *Econometrica* 32, 39–50.

Balasko, Y. 1986. *Foundations of the Theory of General Equilibrium.* New York: Academic Press.

Brouwer, L.E.J. 1912. Über Abbildungen von Mannigfaltigkeiten. *Mathematische Annalen* 71, 97–115.

Brown, D.J. and Robinson, A. 1972. A limit theorem on the cores of large standard exchange economies. *Proceedings of the National Academy of Sciences of the USA* 69, 1258–60.

Cournot, A. 1838. *Recherches sur les principes mathématiques de la théorie des richesses.* Paris: L. Hachette.

Debreu, G. 1951. The coefficient of resource utilization. *Econometrica* 19, 273–92.

Debreu, G. 1952. A social equilibrium existence theorem. *Proceedings of the National Academy of Sciences of the USA* 38, 886–93.

Debreu, G. 1959. *Theory of Value: an Axiomatic Analysis of Economic Equilibrium.* New York: Wiley.

Debreu, G. 1970. Economies with a finite set of equilibria. *Econometrica* 38, 387–92.

Debreu, G. 1974. Excess demand functions. *Journal of Mathematical Economics* 1, 15–21.

Debreu, G. 1977. The axiomatization of economic theory. Unpublished lecture given at the University of Bonn, 22 April.

Debreu, G. 1982. Existence of competitive equilibrium. Chapter 15 in Arrow and Intriligator (1981–5).

Dierker, E. 1974. *Topological Methods in Walrasian Economics.* Berlin: Springer.

Dierker, E. 1975. Gains and losses at core allocations. *Journal of Mathematical Economics* 2, 119–28.

Dierker, E. 1982. Regular economies. Chapter 17 in Arrow and Intriligator (1981–5).

Edgeworth, F.Y. 1881. *Mathematical Psychics.* London: Kegan Paul.

Gale, D. 1956. The closed linear model of production. In *Linear Inequalities and Related Systems*, ed. H.W. Kuhn and A.W. Tucker, Princeton: Princeton University Press.

Hildenbrand, W. 1974. *Core and Equilibria of a Large Economy.* Princeton: Princeton University Press.

Hildenbrand, W. 1982. Core of an economy. Chapter 18 in Arrow and Intriligator (1981–5).

Hicks, J.R. 1939. *Value and Capital.* Oxford: Clarendon Press.

Kakutani, S. 1941. A generalization of Brouwer's fixed point theorem. *Duke Mathematical Journal* 8, 457–9.

Koopmans, T.C., (ed.) 1951. *Activity Analysis of Production and Allocation.* New York: Wiley.

Lyapunov, A.A. 1940. Sur les fonctions-vecteurs complètement additives. *Izvestiia Akademii Nauk SSSR* 4, 465–78.

Mantel, R. 1974. On the characterization of aggregate excess demand. *Journal of Economic Theory* 7, 348–53.

Mas-Colell, A. 1985. *The Theory of General Economic Equilibrium: a Differentiable Approach.* Cambridge: Cambridge University Press.

McKenzie, L.W. 1954. On equilibrium in Graham's model of world trade and other competitive systems. *Econometrica* 22, 147–61.

Minkowski, H. 1911. Theorie der konvexen Körper. *Gesammelte Abhandlungen*, Leipzig and Berlin: Teubner, vol. 3, 131–229.

Nash, J.F. 1950. Equilibrium points in n-person games. *Proceedings of the National Academy of Sciences of the USA* 36, 48–9.

Neumann, J.von. 1928. Zur Theorie der Gesellschaftsspiele. *Mathematische Annalen* 100, 295–320.

Neumann, J.von. 1937. Über ein ökonomisches Gleichungssystem und eine Verallgemeinerung des Brouwerschen Fixpunktsatzes. In *Ergebnisse eines mathematischen Kolloquiums*, vol. 8, 73–83.

Neumann, J.von. and Morgenstern, O. 1944. *Theory of Games and Economic Behavior.* Princeton: Princeton University Press.

Pareto, V. 1896–7. *Cours d'économie politique.* Lausanne: Rouge.

Pareto, V. 1909. *Manuel d'économie politique.* Paris: Giard.

Pareto, V. 1911. Economie mathématique. In *Encyclopédie des sciences mathématiques*, Paris: Gauthier-Villars, vol. I(4), 591–640.

Robinson, A. 1966. *Non-standard Analysis.* Amsterdam: North-Holland.

Samuelson, P.A. 1947. *Foundations of Economic Analysis.* Cambridge, Mass.: Harvard University Press.

Sard, A. 1942. The measure of the critical points of differentiable maps. *Bulletin of the American Mathematical Society* 48, 883–90.

Scarf, H. 1962. An analysis of markets with a large number of participants. In H. Scarf, *Recent Advances in Game Theory*, Princeton: Princeton University Press.

Scarf, H. 1973. (With the collaboration of T. Hansen) *The Computation of Economic Equilibria*. New Haven: Yale University Press.

Scarf, H. 1982. The computation of equilibrium prices: an exposition. Chapter 21 in Arrow and Intriligator (1981–5).

Scarf, H.E. and Shoven, J.B. 1984. *Applied General Equilibrium Analysis*. Cambridge: Cambridge University Press.

Shubik, M. 1959. Edgeworth market games. In *Contributions to the Theory of Games*, vol. 4, Annals of Mathematical Studies 40, Princeton: Princeton University Press.

Smale, S. 1981. Global analysis and economics. Chapter 8 in Arrow and Intriligator (1981–5).

Sonnenschein, H. 1973. Do Walras' identity and continuity characterize the class of community excess demand functions? *Journal of Economic Theory* 6, 345–54.

Vind, K. 1964. Edgeworth-allocations in an exchange economy with many traders. *International Economic Review* 5, 165–77.

Wald, A. 1935. Über die eindeutige positive Lösbarkeit der neuen Produktionsgleichungen. *Ergebnisse eines mathematischen Kolloquiums* 6, 12–20.

Wald, A. 1936a. Über die Produktionsgleichungen der ökonomischen Wertlehre. In *Ergebnisse eines mathematischen Kolloquiums*. 7, 1–6.

Wald, A. 1936b. Über einige Gleichungssysteme der mathematischen Ökonomie. *Zeitschrift für Nationalökonomie* 7, 637–70.

Walras, L. 1874–7. *Eléments d'économie politique pure*. Lausanne: L. Corbaz.

mathematical methods in political economy

The idea of applying mathematics to human affairs may appear at first sight an absurdity worthy of Swift's Laputa. Yet there is one department of social science which by general consent has proved amenable to mathematical reasoning – statistics. The operations not only of arithmetic, but also of the higher calculus, are applicable to statistics. What has long been admitted with respect to the average results of human action has within the last half-century been claimed for the general laws of political economy. The latter, indeed, unlike the former, do not usually present numerical constants; but they possess the essential condition for the application of mathematics: constancy of *quantitative* – though not necessarily numerical – relations. Such, for example, is the character of the law of Diminishing Returns: that an increase in the capital and labour applied to land is (tends to be) attended with a less than proportionate increase in produce. The language of Functions is well adapted to express such relations. When, as in the example given, and frequently in economics (see Marshall, *Principles*, 5th edn, Preface, p. xix), the relation is between *increments* of quantities, the differential calculus is appropriate. In the simpler cases the geometrical representations of functions and their differentials may with advantage be employed.

Among the branches of the economic calculus *simultaneous equations* are conspicuous. Given several quantitative – though not in general numerical – relations between several variable quantities, the economist needs to know whether the quantities are to be regarded as *determinate*, or not. A beautiful example of numerous prices determined by numerous conditions of supply and demand is presented by Professor Marshall in his 'bird's-eye view of the problems of joint demand, composite demand, joint supply, and composite supply' (*Principles*, Mathematical Appendix, note xxi). 'However complex the problem may become, we can see that it is theoretically determinate' (ibid., cf. Preface, p. xx). When we have to do with only *two* conditions, two *curves* may be advantageously employed instead of two *equations*.

The mathematical operations which have been mentioned, and others – in particular the integral calculus, are all contained in the calculus of *maxima* and *minima*, or, as it is called, of *variations;* which seems to comprehend all the higher problems of abstract economics. For instance, Prof. Marshall, after writing out a number of equations 'representing the causes that govern the investment of capital and effort in any undertaking', adds, 'they may all be regarded as mathematically contained in the statement that H–V [the net advantages] is to be made a maximum' (*Principles*, Mathematical Appendix, 2nd and later editions, note xiv). It was profoundly said by Malthus, 'Many of the questions both in morals and politics seem to be of the nature of the problems *de maximis et minimis* in fluxions.' The analogy between economics and mechanics in this respect is well indicated by Dr Irving Fisher in his masterly *Mathematical Investigations*.

The property of dealing with quantities not expressible in numbers, which is characteristic of mathematical economics, is not to be regarded as a degrading peculiarity. It is quite familiar and allowed in ordinary mathematics. For instance, if one side of a plane triangle is greater than another, the angle opposite the greater side is greater than the angle opposite the less side (*Euclid*, Book I). Quantitative statements almost as loose as those employed in abstract economics occur in the less perfectly conquered portions of mathematical physics, with respect to the distances of the fixed stars, for instance (see Sir Robert Ball, *Story of the Heavens*, ch. xxi); e.g. before 1853 it was only known that 'the distance of 61 Cygni could not be *more* than sixty billions of miles'. It is really less than forty billions.

The instance of astronomy suggests a secondary or indirect use of mathematical method in economics, which physical science has outgrown. As the dawn of the Newtonian, or even of the Copernican, theory put to flight the vain shadows of astrology, so the mere statement of an economic problem in a mathematical form may correct fallacies. Attention is directed to the data which would be required for a scientific solution of the problem. Variable quantities expressed in symbols are less liable to be treated as constant. This sort of advantage is obtained by formulating the relation between quantity of precious metal in circulation and the general level of prices, as Sir John Lubbock (senior) has done in his pamphlet *On currency* (anonymous, 1840). Thus the mathematical method contributes to that negative or dialectic use of theory which consists in meeting fallacious arguments on their own ground of abstract reasoning (see some remarks on this use of theory by Prof. Simon Newcomb in the June number of the *Quarterly Journal of Economics*, 1893; and compare Prof. Edgeworth, *Economic Journal*, vol. i, p. 627). The mathematical method is useful in clearing away the rubbish which obstructs the foundation of economic science, as well as in affording a plan for the more regular part of the structure.

The modest claims here made for the mathematical method of political economy may be illustrated by comparing it with the literary or classical method in the treatment of some of the higher problems of the science. The fundamental principle of supply and demand has been stated by J.S. Mill with much precision in ordinary language (*Political Economy*, book iii, ch. 2, §§ 4, 5, and, better, review of Thornton, *Dissertations*, vol. iv). But he is not very happy in indicating the distinction between a rise of price which is due to a diminution of supply – the dispositions of the buyers, the Demand Curves remaining constant – and the rise of price which is due to a displacement of the demand curve. He appears not to perceive that the position of equilibrium between supply and demand is *determinate*, even where it is not *unique* – a conception supplied by equations with multiple roots or curves intersecting in several points. The want of this conception seems to involve even Mill's treatment of the subject in obscurity (*Political Economy*, book iii, ch. 18, § 6).

The use of simultaneous equations or intersecting curves facilitates the comprehension of the 'fundamental symmetry' (Marshall) between the forces of demand and supply; the littérateurs lose themselves in wordy disputes as to which of the two factors 'regulates' or 'determines' value.

The disturbance of the conditions of supply by a tax or bounty, or other impediment or aid, gives rise to problems too complicated for the unaided intellect to deal with. Prof. Marshall, employing the mathematical theory of Consumers' rent, reaches the conclusion that it might *theoretically* be advantageous to tax commodities obeying

the law of decreasing returns in order with the proceeds to give bounty to commodities following the opposite law (*Principles*, book v, ch. xiii, § 7). The want of the theory of consumer's rent renders obscure Mill's treatment of the 'gain' which a country may draw to itself by taxing exports or imports (*Political Economy*, book v, ch. 4, § 6; cf. book iii, ch. 18, § 5). This matter is much more clearly expressed by the curves of Messrs. Auspitz and Lieben (*Untersuchungen*, Article 81).

The preceding examples presuppose free competition; the following relate to monopoly. The relation between the rates and the traffic of a railway is shown with remarkable clearness by the aid of a diagram in the appendix to Prof. Hadley's *Railroad Transportation*. By means of elaborate curves Prof. Marshall shows that a government having regard to the interest of the consuming public, as well as to its revenue, may fix a much lower price than a monopolist actuated by mere self-interest. The taxation of monopolies presents problems which require the mathematical method initiated by Cournot. His reasoning convinces of error the following statement made by Mill (book v, chs 4, 6) and others: 'A tax on rare and high-priced wines will fall only on the owners of the vineyard,' for 'when the article is a strict monopoly ... the price cannot be further raised to compensate for the tax'. Cournot obtains by mathematical reasoning the remarkable theorem that in cases where there is a joint demand for articles monopolized by different individuals, the purchaser may come off worse than if he had dealt with a single monopolist. This case is more important than at first appears (Marshall, *Principles*, 2nd edn, book v, ch. x, § 4; 5th edn, book v, ch. xi, § 7).

Under the head of monopoly may be placed the case of two individuals or corporate units dealing with each other. The indeterminateness of the bargain in this case is perhaps best contemplated by the aid of diagrams.

These examples, which might be multiplied, seem to prove the usefulness of the mathematical method. But the estimate would be imperfect without taking into account the abuses and defects to which the method is liable. One of these is common to every *organon* – especially new ones – liability to be overrated. As Prof. Marshall says, 'When the actual conditions of particular problems have not been studied, such [mathematical] knowledge is little better than a derrick for sinking oil-wells where there are no oil-bearing strata.' Again, the mathematical method is a machinery, the use of which is very liable to be overbalanced by the cost to others than the maker of acquiring it. Not only is mathematics a foreign language 'to the general'; but even to mathematicians a new notation is an unknown dialect which it may not repay to learn. As Prof. Marshall says, 'It seems doubtful whether any one spends his time well in reading lengthy translations of economic doctrines into mathematics that have not been made by himself.'

This estimate of the uses and dangers of mathematical method may be confirmed by reference to the works in the subjoined list; which does not pretend to be exhaustive.

F.Y. EDGEWORTH

Reprinted from Palgrave's Dictionary of Political Economy.

Bibliography

Auspitz, R. and Lieben, R. 1889. *Untersuchungen über die Theorie des Preises.* Leipzig: Duncker & Humblot.

Cournot, A. 1838. *Recherches sur les principes mathématiques de la théorie des richesses.* Paris: Hachette.

Dupuit, E.T. 1844. De la mesure de l'utilité des travaux publics. *Annales des Ponts et Chaussées*, 2nd series 8, 332–75.

Dupuit, E.T. 1849. *De l'influence des Péages.* Paris: Guillaumin.

Edgeworth, F.Y. 1881. *Mathematical Psychics.* London: Kegan Paul.

Gossen, H.H. 1854. *Entwicklung der Gesetze des menschlichen Verkehrs.* 2nd edn, Berlin: Praeger, 1889.

Jevons, W.S. 1871. *Theory of Political Economy.* 3rd edn, London: Macmillan, 1888.

Keynes, J.N. 1891. *The Scope and Method of Political Economy.* 3rd edn, revised, London: Macmillan, 1904.

Launhardt, W. 1885. *Mathematische Begründung der Volkswirthschaftslehre.* Leipzig.

Marshall, A. 1890. *Principles of Economics.* London: Macmillan 2nd edn, 1891; 5th edn, 1907.

Pantaleoni, M. 1889. *Principii di economia pura.* Florence: G. Barbčra.

Pareto, V. 1896. *Cours d'économie politique.* Lausanne: Rouge.

Walras, L. 1874. *Eléments d'économie politique pure.* 2nd edn, Lausanne: F. Rouge, 1889.

Wicksteed, P.H. 1888. *Alphabet of Economic Science.* London: Macmillan.

mathematics and economics

Understanding the connection between mathematics and economics is not the same as understanding the nature and role of mathematical economics. 'Mathematical economics' is the employment of mathematics in economics itself. Explaining or justifying mathematical economics often involves essentialist arguments concerning the true nature of economic objects and the true nature of the economy, as well as arguments suggesting that employing mathematics is appropriate since the underlying 'economy' is quantitative in nature. Consequently, an historical discussion of mathematical economics will be a narrative of increased sophistication over time in economics, as mathematical tools, techniques and methods move into economic discourse and enrich economic analysis.

Alternatively, one can discuss the relation between mathematics and economics in terms of separate intellectual activities performed in separate intellectual communities, and in that case one will wish to look over time at the interpenetration of the ideas and practices of the two communities across their highly permeable boundaries. The history of mathematics concerns the changing body of mathematical knowledge such as new theorems proved, new research areas opened, and new techniques developed. But the history also involves changing images of mathematical knowledge: changing perspectives and understandings, for example, about the nature of mathematical objects, what constitutes a proof, what constitutes rigour, what constitutes useful versus not useful mathematics, and so forth (see Corry, 1996, p. 3). Similarly the history of economics involves a history of not only the development of economic knowledge, but the development and changes in images of economic knowledge: what constitutes the economy, what constitutes a good explanation in economics, what constitutes serious empirical work in economics, what a good model is, and so on. Consequently a discussion of the interconnection of mathematics and economics requires not just attention to the interconnection of the bodies of knowledge, as is reflected in the historical discussion of mathematical economics, but a historical discussion of the interconnection of their respective images of knowledge. Put another way, a discussion of the connection of mathematics and economics must reflect economists' changing conceptions of the image of mathematical knowledge and not just their changing understandings of the body of mathematical knowledge.

This distinction between the body of knowledge and the images of knowledge provides a different perspective on the relation between mathematics and economics. The central point for economists to understand is that there were three distinct shifts in the image of mathematics from the beginning of the 19th century to the end the 20th century.

From geometry to mechanics

As a starting point, consider the conditions and perspectives under which mathematics was produced early in the 19th century. Looking closely, we see, particularly in England, the importance of both Euclid's *Elements* and Newton's *Principia.* That is, from relatively early in the 19th century, through the modifications of the Cambridge Tripos in 1849, and on through the middle third of the 19th century at Cambridge, mathematics was understood as flowing, in its purpose and nature, from both Euclid and Newton. From Euclid one understood that geometry was the paradigm of mathematics, and that it was a path to truth. Theorems were derived from assumptions called axioms, where the truth of those assumptions was self-evident from our understanding of the physical world. To learn geometry was to understand how rigorous arguments could lead to truth. One studied mathematics, specifically geometry, as an exemplar of how one deduced truths about the world, and thus mathematics was the paradigm of deductive thought and logical ratiocination. Parallel to this view of how deductive reasoning from true premises could lead to true conclusions, Newton's *Principia* (his mathematical proofs of course were all based on Euclidian geometry – even the calculus derivations were geometrical), suggested how this kind of mathematics could also open up an understanding of the physical world. Students were required to study mathematics because it provided a way of achieving truth.

This image of mathematics is at the root of Ricardo's arithmetical models, and is present in Whewell's papers (1829; 1831; 1850) on economics using mathematics, for Whewell himself was central in reconstructing the Cambridge Tripos around Euclidean geometry and Newton's *Principia* at mid-19th century. Economics was to employ a particular kind of mathematics, Euclidean geometry, to demonstrate its propositions. Just as Newton employed geometrical proofs of his propositions, so too did Marshall. It is an interesting exercise to open Alfred Marshall's *Principles* next to the Newton's *Principia* and see the physical similarity of the proofs or demonstrations of the propositions in each book. Marshall, as Second Wrangler in the Mathematical Tripos of January 1865, had had to master both Euclid and Newton.

The first change in the image of mathematics was developed from a new conception of what mathematical truth might mean. It occurred over the second third of the 19th century and was then well incorporated in the Continental tradition in mathematics. That is, outside Britain there was a change in the image of mathematics between the time of Whewell's defence of mathematics in the educational process, a defence based in the notion that mathematics (*vide* Euclid, Newton) was the paradigm of certain and secure knowledge (the time of Marshall's student days), and Marshall's later time as Professor of Political Economy. The emergence of non-Euclidean geometries had made Whewell's argument about axiomatics, and inevitable truth, ring hollow long before the turn of the 20th century. In the time of the new geometries, the difficulty of linking mathematical truth to a particular (Euclidean) geometry produced a real crisis of confidence for Victorian educational practice (Richards, 1988). This first crisis prepared the late Victorian mind for the new idea that mathematical rigour had to be associated with physical argumentation. And it was this new image of mathematics in science that helps us to understand the concerns of individuals like Edgeworth and Pareto.

An emergent set of themes in mathematics developed from the increased awareness of alternatives to Euclidean geometry, and the recognition that no one set of axioms could be selected for demonstrating the truth of all mathematical propositions. Thus the success of the new rational mechanics (Lagrange's programme of applying techniques of advanced calculus to the study of motions of solids and liquids) in making sense of the world of physical systems encouraged a refinement of the truth-producing view of mathematics. That is, in the last third of the 19th century, in Britain as well as Italy, France and Germany, a rigorous mathematical argument began to be seen as one based on a substrate of physical reasoning. For an argument to be rigorous, and thus believable, the mathematical structure had to be founded generally on the most successful of applied mathematical practices, namely, rational mechanics. *A valid and good and useful mathematical model was a model that had physical interpretations.* The 'marginal revolution' in economics was precisely this new understanding. One sees this very clearly in Marshall, who was at the cusp of this changed image of mathematics, for his derivations were offered using Euclidian geometry, but whose mathematical arguments about equilibrium and stability are instantiations of mechanical devices like an egg in a bowl, or a pair of scissors. Put another way, through much of the 19th century in British mathematics, and thus to a degree among insular British economists for whom British mathematics *was* mathematics, rigour in argument was associated with geometric proofs based on assumptions, called axioms, that could be linked to constrained optimization processes associated with particular physical systems. Rational mechanics was taken as a paradigm for what economists came to call the marginal revolution, which, however, was hardly revolutionary but rather the migration of rational mechanical ideas into economic discourse (Mirowski, 1989). Thus, by the last decades of the 19th century one finds economists employing specific mechanical models of economic behaviour. Walras, Pareto, Marshall, Edgeworth and Fisher were producing rigorous mathematical models of economic processes, where rigour was associated with a mathematics tied to physical processes.

From mechanics to axiomatics

But by 1900 the images of, and styles of doing, mathematics were beginning to change again in response to new challenges in mathematics and physics. In mathematics, there were problems associated with the foundations of mathematics. There were apparent inconsistencies in set theory associated with Georg Cantor's new ideas on 'infinity' (that is, transfinite cardinals, and the continuum of real numbers), and apparent inconsistencies in the foundations of arithmetic and logic, associated with work by Frege and Peano. Similarly troubling was the failure of physics, particularly rational mechanics, to solve the new problems associated with black-body radiation, quanta and relativity. If the deterministic mechanical mode of physical argumentation was to be replaced by an alternative physical theory, what constituted a rigorous mathematical argument had to be re-described. In any event, some established areas of mathematics were no longer connected to a canonical physical model (Weintraub, 2002).

Consequently, around the end of the 19th century, just as economists had begun to understand that constructing a mathematical science required basing argumentation of the physical reasoning of rational mechanics, and the measurement of quantities to further ground those reasoning chains, the image of mathematical knowledge was again changing. Modelling the concerns of the new physics appeared to require a new mathematics, based less on deterministic dynamical systems and more on statistical argumentation, algebra, and new beliefs about appropriate axioms for logic and arithmetic.

Just as the objects of the physical world appeared changed – gone were billiard balls, newly present were quanta – the recognition that the paradoxes of set theory and logic were intertwined led mathematicians to seek new foundations for their subject. Analysis of those foundations of set theory, logic and arithmetic, and thus the foundations of sciences based on mathematics, were now to be based on axiomatic thinking. A rigorous argument was to be one built on strong foundations, and axiomatizing the structure of theories, in both physics and mathematics, was a path to the development of those theories (Hilbert, 1918). Thus, following a late 19th century period in which mathematical rigour was to be established by basing the mathematics on physical reasoning, around 1900 – as understanding of the physical world became less secure – *mathematical truth was to be established not relative to physical reasoning but relative to other mathematical theories and objects*. From a physical reductionism mathematics moved to a mathematical reductionism, in the guise of one or another set of ideas about formalism: problems and paradoxes and confusions in turn-of-the-century mathematics were to be resolved by a re-conceptualization of the nature of the fundamental objects of mathematics. The images of mathematical knowledge and ideas of rigour, truth, formalization and proof all changed over this period.

It took a number of decades for this new image of mathematics to become securely established in the mathematical community. From Hilbert's 1918 call for axiomatization as the road to knowledge in mathematics and science, through the interwar years, mathematicians were slow to reframe their working concerns. So too did economists' use of mathematics in the interwar period reflect the earlier perspectives of modelling economic problems as constrained optimization demonstrations imitating 19th century mechanics. Beginning in the 1930s, however, a group of French mathematicians, collectively called 'Nicholas Bourbaki', began rewriting mathematics from the foundationalist perspective (Weintraub and Mirowski, 1994). Mathematics was conceived of, in their project, as growing organically from very basic ideas about sets, which led inexorably to the identification of a small number of 'mother structures' (algebraic, order, and topological) from which other structures, other branches of mathematics, could be derived. Rigorous mathematics was not grounded in

physical models but rather in mathematics itself. Mathematics was to concern itself with analyses of mathematical structures. Over the next few decades pure mathematics, or mathematics uncontaminated by applications and disengaged from the world of applications, gained sway in the mathematics community. It was in this period that the eminent mathematician Paul Halmos (1981) famously titled an article 'Applied mathematics is bad mathematics'. In economics, this concatenation of ideas moved into mainstream theory with the work of Gerard Debreu, Kenneth Arrow and Tjalling Koopmans. The Cowles Commission, in the 1940s at the University of Chicago, became the site for production of this kind of work in mathematical economic theory, particularly general equilibrium theory.

Yet, even as a pure mathematics was taking hold in economics, the exigencies of the Second World War, and economists' involvement with scientists, engineers and other social scientists, moved mathematical economists' concerns back from axiomatization and into what would become operations research. This, of course, was not 'pure' at all, but based on concrete problems of real systems. As Amy Dahan Dalmedico, the historian of mathematics, noted:

> The second World War initiated what I shall call 'image war' or 'representation war' concerning what mathematics was about, what it dealt with, and how. Over the course of the 1950s and 1960s, this 'war' was progressively developed until the balance of power began to shift perceptibly at the end of the 1970s and during the 1980s. This 'war' was focused mainly on the cleavage between pure and applied mathematics, and on the tacit hierarchy – of concepts as much as of values – informing these categories of 'pure' and 'applied'. (Dalmedico, 2001, p. 224)

Thus, Bourbakist images of mathematics were becoming dominant in economics at the same time as the major challenge to those ideas was forming outside 'pure' theory. The image of mathematics as a discipline concerned with understanding the structures of mathematical objects was indeed dominant in the 1950s and 60 s, not only in the United States but in a number of other countries. Yet, from the Second World War on through the cold war, applied mathematics was taking root in disparately profound ways, and was attracting more and more support in the form of grants and contracts and students. New fields of statistics, computer science and operations research flourished. Consequently, economists' ideas about mathematics began to undergo changes, as usual with some time lag, mirroring the changing images of mathematics that were reshaping interests and methods in the mathematics community itself. 'While *structure* was the emblematic term of the 1960s, *model* has now taken its place. In the physical sciences, climatology, engineering science, economics, and the social sciences, the practice of model-building has gradually dominated the terrain. It is today absolutely massive and intrinsically bound up with numerical experimentation and simulation' (Dalmedico, 2001, 249).

If the important lesson from mathematics in the first third of the 19th century was that economics needed to become a deductive science (as geometry was), in the late 19th century the lesson from mathematics was that economics needed to model itself on rational mechanics. Over the first two thirds of the 20th century the lesson was that economics was to become scientific by grounding its models and theories on a modest set of axioms concerning pure economic agents' preferences and choices. But, beginning nearly at mid-century, mathematics was re-imagining itself as a discipline that historically had developed by solving real problems presented to it from other sciences. And in a similar fashion, and partially in response to that changing image of mathematical knowledge, the notion of a serious economic science, connected to data-based reasoning, was reshaping the idea of rigorous argumentation in economics. Econometrics and applied microeconomics were to form the reconstructed core of economic science much as work in algorithmics and applied mathematics were re-commanding attention in the mathematics community. 'At the Berlin International Congress of Mathematicians in August 1998, the old opposition between the pure and the applied – still widely shared in the community – has been formulated in quite different terms: "mathematicians who build models versus those who prove theorems". [Mumford, 1998]. But the respect enjoyed by the former is now definitely as high as that of the latter' (Dalmedico, 2001, p. 249). So too in economics, as the prestige accorded 'good work' in applied economics now rivals that accorded to work in pure theory.

E. ROY WEINTRAUB

See also **Debreu, Gerard; existence of general equilibrium; Fisher, Irving; Marshall, Alfred; mathematical economics; mathematical methods in political economy; Whewell, William.**

Bibliography

Corry, L. 1996. *Modern Algebra and the Rise of Mathematical Structures.* Boston: Birkhäuser.

Dalmedico, A. 2001. An image conflict in mathematics after 1945. In *Changing Images in Mathematics: From the French Revolution to the New Millennium*, ed. U. Bottazzini and A. Dalmedico. London and New York: Routledge.

Halmos, P. 1981. Applied mathematics is bad mathematics. In *Mathematics Tomorrow*, ed. L. Steen. New York and Heidelberg: Springer-Verlag.

Hilbert, D. 1918. Axiomatisches Denken. *Mathematische Annalen* 78, 405–15.

Mirowski, P. 1989. *More Heat Than Light*. New York and Cambridge: Cambridge University Press.

Mumford, D. 1998. Trends in the profession of mathematics: choosing our directions. *Berlin Intelligencer*, ICM August 1998, 2–5.

Richards, J. 1988. *Mathematical Visions: the Pursuit of Geometry in Victorian England.* San Diego: Academic Press.

Weintraub, E. 2002. *How Economics Became a Mathematical Science.* Durham, NC: Duke University Press.

Weintraub, E. and Mirowski, P. 1994. The pure and the applied: Bourbakism comes to mathematical economics. *Science in Context* 72, 245–72.

Whewell, W. 1829; 1831; 1850. *Mathematical Exposition of Some Doctrines of Political Economy.* Reprints of Economic Classics. New York: Augustus M. Kelley, 1971.

mathematics of networks

In much of economic theory it is assumed that economic agents interact, directly or indirectly, with all others, or at least that they have the opportunity to do so in order to achieve a desired outcome for themselves. In reality, as common sense tells us, things are quite different. Traders in a market have preferred trading partners, perhaps because of an established history of trust, or simply for convenience. Buyers and sellers have preferred suppliers and customers. Consumers have preferred brands and outlets. And most individuals limit their interactions, economic or otherwise, to a select circle of partners or acquaintances. In many cases partners are chosen not on economic grounds but for social reasons: individuals tend overwhelmingly to deal with others who revolve in the same circles as they do, socially, intellectually or culturally.

The patterns of connections between agents form a social network (Figure 1), and it is intuitively clear that the structure of such networks must affect the pattern of economic transactions, not to mention essentially every other type of social interaction among human beings. Any theory of interaction that ignores these networks is necessarily incomplete. In the last few decades, therefore, researchers have conducted extensive investigations of networks in economics, mathematics, sociology and a number of other fields, in an effort to understand and explain network effects.

The study of social (and other) networks has three primary components. First, empirical studies of networks probe network structure using a variety of techniques such as interviews, questionnaires, direct observation of individuals, use of archival records, and specialist tools like 'snowball sampling' and 'ego-centred' studies. The goal of such studies is to create a picture of the connections between individuals, of the type shown in Figure 1. Since there are many different kinds of possible connections between people – business relationships, personal relationships, and so forth – studies must be designed appropriately to measure the particular connections of interest to the experimenter.

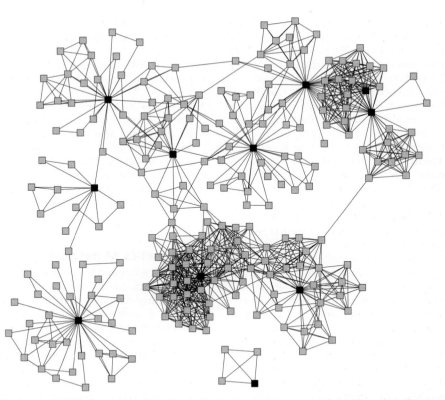

Figure 1   A social network of collaborative links. *Note*: The nodes (squares) represent people and the edges (lines) social ties between them.

Second, once one has empirical data on a network, one can answer questions about the community the network represents using mathematical or statistical analyses. This is the domain of classical social network analysis, which focuses on issues such as: who are the most central members of a network and who are the most peripheral? Which people have most influence over others? Does the community break down into smaller groups, and if so what are they? Which connections are most crucial to the functioning of a group?

And third, building on the insights obtained from observational data and its quantitative analysis, one can create models, such as mathematical models or computer models, of processes taking place in networked systems – the interactions of traders, for example, or the diffusion of information or innovations through a community. Modelling work of this type allows us to make predictions about the behaviour of a community as a function of the parameters affecting the system.

After a brief historical review, the primary purpose of this article is to describe the mathematical techniques involved in the second and third of these three components: the quantitative analysis of network data and the mathematical modelling of networked systems. Necessarily, this review is short. Much more substantial coverage can be found in the many books and review articles in the field (Wasserman and Faust, 1994; Scott, 2000; West, 1996; Harary, 1995; Ahuja, Magnanti and Orlin, 1993; Dorogovtsev and Mendes, 2003; Albert and Barabási, 2002; Newman, 2003).

History of social network analysis
The study of social networks has roots in the 19th-century beginnings of sociology, especially the 'gestalt' tradition of Koehler and others, but is widely regarded as having begun in earnest in the 1930s with the work of psychologist Jacob Moreno, a Romanian immigrant to the United States who had spent a number of years in Vienna and was influenced there by the work of Freud. Moreno advocated an approach to psychoanalysis that involved participants discussing or physically enacting issues that concerned them in front of the analyst. Another approach, which Moreno employed with schoolchildren among others, involved the analyst passively watching participants' interactions with one another and recording their nature and pattern. In the process of his studies he developed a new tool, the sociogram, which was a map of interactions between individuals drawn on paper as a set of points and lines (Moreno, 1934, p. 38).

In 1933 Moreno presented some of his sociograms during a lecture at a medical conference in New York City, and the work attracted sufficient interest to be featured in the *New York Times*. In everything but name, Moreno's sociograms were what we would now call social networks, and his methods, although strange by today's standards, were the intellectual precursor of social network analysis, which is now a flourishing branch of the social sciences (Wasserman and Faust, 1994). (The term 'social network' was not invented until some years later; it is usually credited to John Barnes,1954.)

Apart from a gap during the war years, social network analysis was pursued vigorously following its early popularization. Particularly well-known studies include the 'southern women' study of Davis, Davis, and Gardner (1941), Anatol Rapoport's investigations of friendship networks among school children in the 1950s (Rapoport and Horvath, 1961), Pool and Kochen's (1978) mathematical models of social networks that circulated widely in the 1950s and 1960s (although they were not published until much later), and Stanley Milgram's (1967) famous 'small world' experiments. Today, social network analysis is one of the standard quantitative tools in the social science toolbox, finding use both in academia and in the business world as a microscope with which to view the details of social interactions.

Mathematics of networks

Turning to the mathematical methods of network analysis, which are the principal focus of this article, let us begin with some simple definitions. A network – also called a *graph* in the mathematics literature – is made up of points, usually called *nodes* or *vertices*, and lines connecting them, usually called *edges*. Mathematically, a network can be represented by a matrix called the *adjacency matrix* **A**, which in the simplest case is an $n \times n$ symmetric matrix, where n is the number of vertices in the network. The adjacency matrix has elements

$$A_{ij} = \begin{cases} 1 & \text{if there is an edge between vertices } i \text{ and } j, \\ 0 & \text{otherwise.} \end{cases}$$

(1)

The matrix is symmetric since if there is an edge between i and j then clearly there is also an edge between j and i. Thus $A_{ij} = A_{ji}$.

In some networks the edges are *weighted*, meaning that some edges represent stronger connections than others, in which case the nonzero elements of the adjacency matrix can be generalized to values other than unity to represent stronger and weaker connections. Another variant is the *directed network*, in which edges point in a particular direction between two vertices. For instance, in a network of cash sales between buyers and sellers the directions of edges might represent the direction of the flow of goods (or conversely of money) between

individuals. Directed networks can be represented by an asymmetric adjacency matrix in which $A_{ij} = 1$ implies the existence (conventionally) of an edge pointing from j to i (note the direction), which will in general be independent of the existence of an edge from i to j.

Networks may also have *multiedges* (repeated edges between the same pair of vertices), *self-edges* (edges connecting a vertex to itself), *hyperedges* (edges that connect more than two vertices together) and many other features. We here concentrate primarily on the simplest networks, having undirected, unweighted single edges between pairs of vertices.

Centrality measures

Now let us consider the analysis of network data. We start by looking at *centrality measures*, which are some of the most fundamental and frequently used measures of network structure. Centrality measures address the question, 'Who is the most important or central person in this network?' There are many answers to this question, depending on what we mean by 'important'. Perhaps the simplest of centrality measures is *degree centrality*, also called simply *degree*. The degree of a vertex in a network is the number of edges attached to it. In mathematical terms, the degree k_i of a vertex i is

$$k_i = \sum_{j=1}^{n} A_{ij}.$$

(2)

Though simple, degree is often a highly effective measure of the influence or importance of a node: in many social settings people with more connections have more power.

A more sophisticated version of the same idea is the so-called *eigenvector centrality*. Where degree centrality gives a simple count of the number of connections a vertex has, eigenvector centrality acknowledges that not all connections are equal. In general, connections to people who are themselves influential will lend a person more influence than connections to less influential people. If we denote the centrality of vertex i by x_i, then we can allow for this effect by making x_i proportional to the average of the centralities of i's network neighbours:

$$x_i = \frac{1}{\lambda} \sum_{j=1}^{n} A_{ij} x_j,$$

(3)

where λ is a constant. Defining the vector of centralities $\mathbf{x} = (x_1, x_2, \ldots)$, we can rewrite this equation in matrix form as

$$\lambda \mathbf{x} = \mathbf{A} \cdot \mathbf{x},$$

(4)

and hence we see that **x** is an eigenvector of the adjacency matrix with eigenvalue λ. On the assumption that we wish the centralities to be non-negative, it can be shown (using the Perron–Frobenius theorem) that λ must be the largest eigenvalue of the adjacency matrix and $\mathbf{x}$ the corresponding eigenvector.

The eigenvector centrality defined in this way accords each vertex a centrality that depends on both the number and the quality of its connections: having a large number of connections still counts for something, but a vertex with a smaller number of high-quality contacts may outrank one with a larger number of mediocre contacts. Eigenvector centrality turns out to be a revealing measure in many situations. For example, a variant of eigenvector centrality is employed by the well-known Web search engine Google to rank Web pages, and works well in that context.

Two other useful centrality measures are *closeness centrality* and *betweenness centrality*. Both are based upon on the concept of network paths. A path in a network is a sequence of vertices traversed by following edges from one vertex to another across the network. A *geodesic path* is the shortest path, in terms of number of edges traversed, between a specified pair of vertices. (Geodesic paths need not be unique; two or more paths can tie for the title of shortest.) The closeness centrality of vertex i is the mean geodesic distance (that is, the mean length of a geodesic path) from vertex i to every other vertex. Closeness centrality is *lower* for vertices that are more central in the sense of having a shorter network distance on average to other vertices. (Some writers define closeness centrality to be the reciprocal of the average so that higher numbers indicate greater centrality. Also, some vertices may not be reachable from vertex i – two vertices can lie in separate 'components' of a network, with no connection between the components at all. In this case closeness as above is not well defined. The usual solution to this problem is simply to define closeness to be the average geodesic distance to all *reachable* vertices, excluding those to which no path exists.)

The betweenness centrality of vertex i is the fraction of geodesic paths between other vertices that i lies on. That is, we find the shortest path (or paths) between every pair of vertices, and ask on what fraction of those paths vertex i lies. Betweenness is a crude measure of the control i exerts over the flow of information (or any other commodity) between others. If we imagine information flowing between all pairs of individuals in the network and always taking the shortest possible path, then betweenness centrality measures the fraction of that information that will flow through i on its way to wherever it is going. In many social contexts a vertex with high betweenness will exert substantial influence by virtue not of being in the middle of the network (although it may be) but of lying 'between' other vertices in this way. It is in most cases only an approximation to assume that information flows along geodesic paths; normally it will not, and variations of betweenness centrality such as 'flow betweenness' and 'random walk betweenness' have been proposed to allow for this. In many practical cases, however, the simple (geodesic path) betweenness centrality gives quite informative answers.

Other network properties

The study of shortest paths on networks also leads to another interesting network concept, the *small-world effect*. It is found that in most networks the mean geodesic distance between vertex pairs is small compared with the size of the network as a whole. In a famous experiment conducted in the 1960s, the psychologist Stanley Milgram (1967) asked participants (located in the United States) to get a message to a specified target person elsewhere in the country by passing it from one acquaintance to another, stepwise through the population. Milgram's remarkable finding that the typical message passed though just six people on its journey between (roughly) randomly chosen initial and final individuals has been immortalized in popular culture in the phrase 'six degrees of separation', which was the title of a 1990 Broadway play by John Guare in which one of the characters discusses the small-world effect. Since Milgram's experiment, the small-world effect has been confirmed experimentally in many other networks, both social and nonsocial.

Other network properties that have attracted the attention of researchers in recent years include network *transitivity* or *clustering* (the tendency for triangles of connections to appear frequently in networks – in common parlance, 'the friend of my friend is also my friend'), vertex similarity (the extent to which two given vertices do or do not occupy similar positions in the network), communities or groups within networks and methods for their detection, and, crucially, the distribution of vertex degrees, a topic discussed in more detail below.

Models of networks

Turning to models of networks and of the behaviour of networked systems, we find that perhaps the simplest useful model of a network (and one of the oldest) is the *Bernoulli random graph*, often called just the *random graph* for short (Solomonoff and Rapoport, 1951; Erdős and Rényi, 1960; Bollobás, 2001). In this model one takes a certain number of vertices n and creates edges between them with independent probability p for each vertex pair. When p is small there are only a few edges in the network, and most vertices exist in isolation or in small groups of connected vertices. Conversely, for large p almost every possible edge is present between the $\binom{n}{2}$ possible vertex pairs, and all or almost all of the vertices join together in a single large connected group. One might imagine that for intermediate values of p the sizes of groups would just grow smoothly from small to large, but this is not the case. It is found instead that there is a *phase transition* at a special value $p = 1/n$ above which a *giant component* forms, a group of connected vertices occupying a fixed fraction of the whole network, i.e., with size varying as n. For values of p less than this, only small groups of vertices exist of a typical size that is independent of n. Many real-world networks show behaviour reminiscent of this model, with a large component of connected vertices filling a sizable fraction of the entire network, the remaining vertices falling in much smaller components that are unconnected to the rest of the network.

The random graph has a major shortcoming, however: the distribution of the degrees of the vertices is quite unlike that seen in most real-world networks. The fraction p_k of vertices in a random graph having degree k is given by the binomial distribution, which becomes Poisson in the limit of large n:

$$p_k = \binom{n-1}{k} p^k (1-p)^{n-1-k} ; \frac{z^k e^{-z}}{k!}, \quad (5)$$

where $z = (n-1)p$ is the mean degree. Empirical observations of real networks, social and otherwise, show that most have highly non-Poisson distributions of degree, often heavily right-skewed with a fat tail of vertices having unusually high degree (Albert and Barabási, 2002; Dorogovtsev and Mendes, 2003). These high-degree nodes or 'hubs' in the tail can, it turns out, have a substantial effect on the behaviour of a networked system.

To allow for non-Poisson degree distributions, one can generalize the random graph, specifying a particular, arbitrary degree distribution p_k and then forming a graph that has that distribution but is otherwise random. A simple algorithm for doing this is to choose the degrees of the n vertices from the specified distribution, draw each vertex with the appropriate number of 'stubs' of edges emerging from it, and then pick stubs in pairs uniformly at random and connect them to create complete edges. The resulting model network (or more properly the ensemble of such networks) is called the *configuration model*.

The configuration model also shows a phase transition, similar to that of the Bernoulli random graph, at which a giant component forms. To see this, consider a set of connected vertices and consider the 'boundary vertices' that are immediate neighbours of that set. Let us grow our set by adding the boundary vertices to it one by one. When we add one boundary vertex to our set the number of boundary vertices goes down by 1. However, the number of boundary vertices also increases by the number of new neighbours of the vertex added, which is one less than the degree k of that vertex. Thus the total change in the number of boundary vertices is $-1 + (k-1) = k - 2$. However, the probability of a particular vertex being a boundary vertex is proportional to k, since there are k times as many edges by which a vertex of degree k could be connected to our set than there are for a vertex of degree 1. Thus the average change in the number of boundary vertices when we add one vertex to our set is a weighted average

$\Sigma_i k_i (k_i - 2)/\Sigma_j k_j = \Sigma_i k_i (k_i - 2)/(nz)$, where z is again the mean degree. If this quantity is less than zero, then the number of boundary vertices dwindles as our set grows bigger and will in the end reach zero, so that the set will stop growing. Thus in this regime all connected sets of vertices are of finite size. If on the other hand this number is greater than zero, then the number of boundary vertices will grow without limit, and hence the size of our set of connected vertices is limited only by the size of the network.

Thus, a giant component exists in the network if and only if

$$\langle k^2 \rangle - 2\langle k \rangle > 0, \quad (6)$$

where $\langle k \rangle = z = n^{-1}\Sigma_i k_i$ is the mean degree and $\langle k^2 \rangle = n^{-1}\Sigma_i k_i^2$ is the mean-square degree.

The mean-square degree appears over and over in the mathematics of networks. Another context in which it appears is in the spread of information (or anything else) over a network. Taking a simple model of the spread of an idea (or a rumour or a disease), imagine that each person who has heard an idea communicates it with independent probability q to each of his or her friends. If the person's degree is k, then there are $k - 1$ friends to communicate the idea to, not counting the one from whom he or she heard it in the first place, so the expected number who hear it is $q(k - 1)$. Performing the weighted average over vertices again, we find that the average number of people a person passes the idea onto, also called the *basic reproductive number* R_0, is

$$R_0 = q \frac{\sum_i k_i (k_i - 1)}{\sum_i k_i} = q \frac{\langle k^2 \rangle - \langle k \rangle}{\langle k \rangle}. \quad (7)$$

If R_0 is greater than 1, then the number of people hearing the idea grows as it gets passed around and it will take off exponentially. If R_0 is less than 1 then the idea will die. Again, we have a phase transition, or *tipping point*, for the spread of the idea: it spreads if and only if

$$q > \frac{\langle k \rangle}{\langle k^2 \rangle - \langle k \rangle}. \quad (8)$$

The simple understanding behind the appearance of the mean-square degree in this expression is the following. If a person with high degree hears this idea he or she can spread it to many others, by virtue of having many friends. However, such a person is also more likely to hear the idea in the first place because of having many friends to hear it from. Thus, the degree enters twice into the process: a person with degree 10 is $10 \times 10 = 100$ times more effective at spreading the idea than a person with degree 1.

The appearance of the mean-square degree in expressions like (6) and (8) can have substantial effects. Of particular interest are networks whose degree distributions have fat tails. It is possible for such networks to have very large values of $\langle k^2 \rangle$ – in the hundreds or thousands – so that, for example, the right-hand side of eq. (8) is very small. This means that the probability of each individual person spreading an idea (or rumour or disease) need not be large for it still to spread through the whole community.

Another important class of network models is the class of generative models, models that posit a quantitative mechanism or mechanisms by which a network forms, usually as a way of explaining how the observed structure of the network arises. The best-known example of such a model is the 'cumulative advantage' or 'preferential attachment' model (Price, 1976; Barabási and Albert, 1999), which aims to explain the fat-tailed degree distributions observed in some networks. In its simplest form this model envisages a network that grows by the steady addition of vertices, one at a time. Many networks, such as the World Wide Web and citation networks, grow this way; it is a matter of current debate whether the model applies to social networks as well. Each vertex is added with a certain number m of edges emerging from it, whose other ends connect to pre-existing vertices with probability proportional to those vertices' current degree. That is, the higher the current degree of a vertex, the more likely that vertex is to acquire new edges when the graph grows. This kind of rich-get-richer phenomenon is plausible in many network contexts and is known to generate Pareto degree distributions. Using a rate-equation method (Price, 1976; Simon, 1955; Krapivsky, Redner and Leyvraz, 2000), we find that in the limit of large network size the degree distribution obeys:

$$p_k = \frac{2m(m+1)}{k(k+1)(k+2)}. \tag{9}$$

This distribution has a tail going as $p_k : k^{-3}$ in the large-k limit, which is strongly reminiscent of the degree distributions seen particularly in citation networks and also in the World Wide Web. Generative models of this type have been a source of considerable interest in recent years and have been much extended by a number of authors (Dorogovtsev and Mendes, 2003; Albert and Barabási, 2002) beyond the simple ideas described here.

Concepts such as those appearing in this article can be developed a great deal further and lead to a variety of useful, and in some cases surprising, results about the function of networked systems. More details can be found in the references.

M.E.J. NEWMAN

See also **artificial neural networks; business networks; graph theory; interacting agents in finance; network formation; Pareto distribution; Perron–Frobenius theorem; power laws; psychology of social networks; small-world networks; social networks in labour markets.**

Bibliography

Ahuja, R., Magnanti, T. and Orlin, J. 1993. *Network Flows: Theory, Algorithms, and Applications.* Upper Saddle River, NJ: Prentice Hall.

Albert, R. and Barabási, A.-L. 2002. Statistical mechanics of complex networks. *Reviews of Modern Physics* 74, 47–97.

Barabási, A.-L. and Albert, R. 1999. Emergence of scaling in random networks. *Science* 286, 509–12.

Barnes, J. 1954. Class and committees in a Norwegian island parish. *Human Relations* 7, 39–58.

Bollobás, B. 2001. *Random Graphs,* 2nd edn. New York: Academic Press.

Davis, A., Gardner, B. and Gardner, M. 1941. *Deep South.* Chicago: University of Chicago Press.

Dorogovtsev, S. and Mendes, J. 2003. *Evolution of Networks: From Biological Nets to the Internet and WWW.* Oxford: Oxford University Press.

Erdős, P. and Rényi, A. 1960. On the evolution of random graphs. *Publications of the Mathematical Institute of the Hungarian Academy of Sciences* 5, 17–61.

Harary, F. 1995. *Graph Theory.* Cambridge, MA: Perseus.

Krapivsky, P., Redner, S. and Leyvraz, F. 2000. Connectivity of growing random networks. *Physical Review Letters* 85, 4629–32.

Milgram, S. 1967. The small world problem. *Psychology Today* 2, 60–7.

Moreno, J. 1934. *Who Shall Survive?* Beacon, NY: Beacon House.

Newman, M. 2003. The structure and function of complex networks. *SIAM Review* 45, 167–256.

Pool, I. and Kochen, M. 1978. Contacts and influence. *Social Networks* 1, 1–48.

Price, D. 1976. A general theory of bibliometric and other cumulative advantage processes. *Journal of American Society for Information Science* 27, 292–306.

Rapoport, A. and Horvath, W. 1961. A study of a large sociogram. *Behavioral Science* 6, 279–91.

Scott, J. 2000. *Social Network Analysis:* A Handbook, 2nd edn. London: Sage.

Simon, H. 1955. On a class of skew distribution functions. *Biometrika* 42, 425–40.

Solomonoff, R. and Rapoport, A. 1951. Connectivity of random nets. *Bulletin of Mathematical Biophysics* 13, 107–17.

Wasserman, S. and Faust, K. 1994. *Social Network Analysis.* Cambridge: Cambridge University Press.

West, D. 1996. *Introduction to Graph Theory.* Upper Saddle River, NJ: Prentice Hall.

maximum likelihood

Given data from some member of a parametric family of distributions, maximum likelihood provides a general purpose method of estimation frequently accompanied by useful statistical properties.

In a series of papers, R.A. Fisher (1922; 1925; 1934) proposed and argued for a method of estimation he dubbed 'maximum likelihood'. The intuitive appeal and broad applicability continue to drive its use as a primary tool of statisticians. Suppose data $z = (z_1, \ldots, z_n)$ is drawn from a distribution with density $f_n(z; \theta_0)$, and further suppose that this distribution is a member of a family of parametric distributions with densities $\{f_n(z; \theta) : \theta \in \Theta \subset \mathbb{R}^k\}$ (for k finite and $\theta_0 \in \Theta$). The likelihood function is simply defined by the joint density as the function $l_n(\theta, z) = f_n(z; \theta)$ with argument θ and data z held fixed. The maximum likelihood estimator (MLE) is then defined as

$$\hat{\theta}_{ML} = \arg \min_{\theta \in \Theta} l_n(\theta, z).$$

One motivation for the MLE comes from the likelihood principle, which implies that statistical inference on θ given data z should be based solely on the likelihood function, $l_n(\theta, z)$ (Berger and Wolpert, 1988). According to this principle the relative evidence on two different values of θ given by the data is fully summarized by their likelihood ratio. In this sense, the MLE is the value of θ most supported by the data. Of course, most econometric work involving maximum likelihood does not take a strict likelihood principle viewpoint, but is typically more concerned with sampling properties from a frequentist viewpoint. It is this perspective that will be our main emphasis in what follows.

It is often convenient to (equivalently) think of the MLE as maximizing the log likelihood ratio, $\mathscr{L}_n(\theta) = \ln \frac{f_n(z; \theta)}{f_n(z; \theta_0)}$. When the data is independent and identically distributed (i.i.d.) with marginal density f, the log likelihood ratio can be written $\mathscr{L}_n(\theta) = \sum_{i=1}^n \ln \frac{f(z_i; \theta)}{f(z_i; \theta_0)}$. By the law of large numbers, the normalized log likelihood ratio $(\frac{1}{n} \mathscr{L}_n(\theta))$ approaches $\mathscr{L}(\theta) = E_{\theta_0}[\ln \frac{f(z_i; \theta)}{f(z_i; \theta_0)}]$ (where the expectation is taken with respect to the 'population' density $f(z_i; \theta_0)$) asymptotically. Though $-\mathscr{L}(\theta)$ does not satisfy the formal definition of metric, it is often taken as distance measure between the densities $f(z; \theta)$ and $f(z; \theta_0)$. Not surprisingly, this distance is minimized at $\theta = \theta_0$ (when the identification condition that $f(z; \theta) \neq f(z; \theta_0)$ for $\theta \neq \theta_0$ is satisfied). The log likelihood ratio $\mathscr{L}_n(\theta)$ can be interpreted as a sample approximation to this discrepancy measure, which is minimized at the MLE. The likelihood ratio test statistic, for testing the null hypothesis that $\theta = \theta_0$, is also based on this value.

Fisher emphasized the usefulness of the maximized likelihood itself. The density $f_n(z; \hat{\theta}_{ML})$ provides an approximation to the population density. If, for instance, there is interest in some feature of $f_n(z; \theta_0)$, then an approximation can often be obtained from the corresponding feature of $f_n(z; \hat{\theta}_{ML})$ (as in the parametric bootstrap). More generally, Efron (1982) notes that $f_n(z; \hat{\theta}_{ML})$ acts as a data summary.

Properties

For most commonly used parametric distributional families, the MLE is consistent. Note, for instance, that when $\mathscr{L}(\theta)$ is maximized at θ_0, and the convergence of the log likelihood ratio $\frac{1}{n} \mathscr{L}(\theta)$ mentioned above is uniform on Θ, then $\hat{\theta}_{ML}$ will correspondingly converge to θ_0. More general sufficient conditions for consistency are also available; see Ibragimov and Has'minskii (1981).

Under appropriate regularity conditions (which essentially amount to smoothness of the parametric model), the MLE is asymptotically normal.

$$\sqrt{n}(\hat{\theta}_{ML} - \theta_0) \xrightarrow{d} N(0, J(\theta_0)^{-1})$$

where $J(\theta)$ is the Fisher information matrix, with value $E_{\theta}[\nabla_{\theta} \ln f(z; \theta)(\nabla_{\theta} \ln f(z; \theta))']$ when the data is i.i.d. and $\nabla_{\theta} \ln f(z; \theta)$ is called the 'score function'. Define the Hessian as $H(\theta) = E_{\theta}[\nabla_{\theta\theta} \ln f(z_i; \theta)]$. By the information matrix equality, $J(\theta) = -H(\theta)$, which adds to the variety of estimators for the information matrix. Frequentist confidence intervals are then immediately available based on the asymptotic normality property and an estimator for $J(\theta_0)$.

Other approximations for the distribution of the MLE are also available for certain statistical models. Barndorff-Nielsen (1983) provides an accurate approximation to the conditional distribution of the MLE given a maximal ancillary statistic. (An ancillary statistic is a statistic whose distribution does not depend on θ, and if every ancillary statistic is a function of a given ancillary statistic then that statistic is called maximal.) When the MLE is sufficient, Barndorff-Nielsen's formula is exact. For non-regular models, asymptotic normality may no longer hold and a general limiting distribution result is then unavailable. Ibragimov and Has'minskii (1981), for instance, characterize the asymptotic behavior of the MLE for certain non-regular classes of models.

The Fisher information matrix is additionally useful as an efficiency bound. Accordingly, the MLE itself enjoys certain optimality properties. For regular models, the MLE is asymptotically efficient under classical criteria. Hirano and Porter (2005) show that a shifted version of the MLE is asymptotically efficient for an even broader class of statistical models (and allow for asymmetric loss). Higher-order efficiency of the MLE has been established in Pfanzagl and Wefelmeyer (1978).

Intuition for the asymptotic normality and efficiency of the MLE can be gained through a consideration of the behaviour of the log likelihood ratio in the i.i.d. case. If we re-parametrize the likelihood in terms of the 'local' parameter $h = \sqrt{n}(\theta - \theta_0)$, then with enough smoothness the log likelihood ratio can be expanded as follows

$$\sum_{i=1}^n \ln \frac{f(z_i; \theta_0 + h/\sqrt{n})}{f(z_i; \theta_0)} \approx \frac{h'}{\sqrt{n}} \sum_{i=1}^n \nabla_{\theta} \ln f(z; \theta_0)$$
$$+ \frac{1}{2} \cdot \frac{1}{n} \sum_{i=1}^n h' \nabla_{\theta\theta} \ln f(z; \theta_0) h.$$

Under regularity conditions, the log likelihood ratio converges in distribution (for each h) to $N(-\frac{1}{2}h'J(\theta_0)h, h'J(\theta_0)h)$. (This kind of 'Taylor' expansion actually holds under a mild condition of differentiability in quadratic mean which is weaker than the twice continuous differentiability of the likelihood that appears necessary.) Models with log likelihood ratios obeying this kind of convergence are called 'locally asymptotically normal'. Now, consider the statistical model consisting of a single observation on a random variable $X \sim N(h, J(\theta_0)^{-1})$. Notably, the log likelihood ratio for this simple statistical model $\{N(h, J(\theta_0)^{-1}) : h \in \mathbb{R}^k\}$ has the same distribution as the asymptotic distribution for the log likelihood ratio of the general model above. Since the log likelihood ratio captures all the statistical information in a given statistical model, there is an equivalence between the asymptotic behaviour of the original model with densities $\prod_{i=1}^{n} f(z_i; \theta)$ and the much simpler model given by a single observation from a normal with unknown mean h (and known variance-covariance, $J(\theta_0)^{-1}$). This equivalence is formalized in the limits of experiments theory (Le Cam, 1986). Intuitively, one might expect that the MLE for the local parameter $\hat{h}_{ML} = \sqrt{n}(\hat{\theta}_{ML} - \theta_0)$ in the original model will behave (asymptotically) like the MLE of the 'limit' normal model, which is simply given by X. The normality of X and the efficiency (minimax) of the mean in a normal model then corresponds to the asymptotic normality and asymptotic efficiency of the MLE in the original model.

Other important properties of the MLE are invariance and sufficiency. The MLE is necessarily a function of all sufficient statistics. The MLE is also invariant to parametrization of the family of distributions. So, if the distributions are re-parametrized in terms of $\lambda = T(\theta)$, then $\hat{\lambda}_{ML} = T(\hat{\theta}_{ML})$. Additionally, the MLE satisfies a group equivariance property (Eaton, 1989). Suppose the family of distributions is invariant under the group of transformations $\mathscr{G}$ defined on both the sample and parameter spaces. If $g \in \mathscr{G}$, then $\hat{\theta}_{ML}(gz) = g\hat{\theta}_{ML}(z)$, where the MLE is written as a function of the observations.

Limitations

Since densities are not uniquely defined, the likelihood criterion on which the MLE is based is not uniquely defined. For a given likelihood, a solution to the maximization problem that defines the MLE need not necessarily exist (or multiple solutions are also possible).

The consistency, asymptotic normality and efficiency properties (discussed above) are all asymptotic, leaving the possibility that the small sample behaviour of the MLE may be quite poor in given applications. Even the asymptotic properties themselves are assured under regularity conditions. Neyman and Scott (1948) describe a famous example where maximum likelihood can be poorly behaved in small samples. The random variables

x_{ij} are distributed $N(\mu_i, \sigma^2)$ for $i = 1, \ldots, n$, $j = 1, \ldots, J$, and all random variables are independent. Consider the case with fixed n and $J = 2$. Since $x_{i2} - x_{i1}$ is distributed $N(0, 2\sigma^2)$, $s_n^2 = \frac{1}{2}\frac{1}{n}\sum_{i=1}^{n}(x_{i2} - x_{i1})^2$ is a natural and reasonable estimator for σ^2. But $\hat{\sigma}_{ML}^2 = \frac{1}{2}s_n^2$, which could be a quite poor estimator with significant bias. This poor small sample performance is particularly notable, since this model consists only of independent normally distributed random variables. Asymptotically, if n remains fixed and J grows, then the MLE has all the usual favourable large sample properties. If J is fixed and n grows, then the assumption of a finite dimensional parameter space is violated, and the MLE is not even consistent.

Stein's well-known shrinkage estimator shows that, even in a simple normal model with known variance-covariance and unknown mean, the MLE need not be (mean-squared error) optimal. It is also notable that, outside of regular models, asymptotic efficiency of the MLE can frequently fail. A simple example of such a non-regular model is data drawn from a uniform distribution on $[0, \theta]$. More general, parameter-dependent support models can be found in the auction literature, and the MLE is generally suboptimal by traditional asymptotic efficiency criteria (Hirano and Porter, 2003). Le Cam (1990) lists a number of additional examples where the deficiencies of maximum likelihood are highlighted.

Extensions

Suppose the parameter is partitioned $\theta' = (\theta_1', \theta_2')$, and we define $\theta_2^*(\theta_1) = \arg\max_{\theta_2} l_n(\theta_1, \theta_2)$. Then, the profiled likelihood, $l_n(\theta_1, \theta_2^*(\theta_1))$ can be maximized to give the MLE for θ_1. Sometimes this is useful for computational purposes. This formulation has also been useful for conceptual purposes, such as developing semiparametric efficiency bounds, where θ_2 contains nuisance parameters. Maximum likelihood theory also extends immediately to conditional likelihood formulations. Other methods have been developed to ease the computational burden of maximum likelihood in certain problems. The EM algorithm can be especially helpful in missing data cases (MacLachlan and Krishnan, 1997). Simulated maximum likelihood is useful when the likelihood can be expressed as high-dimensional integral without a closed form solution (Hajivassiliou and Ruud, 1994).

A natural concern with maximum likelihood is its reliance on correct specification of the family of distributions. Quasi-likelihood methods suggest parametric families that have robustness properties beyond the family specified. Exponential linear families often play a prominent role in this approach (Gourieroux, Monfort and Trognon, 1984). Typically, efficiency is sacrificed, but consistency and asymptotic normality still hold where the asymptotic variance of the limiting normal distribution is given by the 'sandwich' formula, $H(\theta_0)^{-1}J(\theta_0)H(\theta_0)^{-1}$.

Extensions of maximum likelihood have also been usefully applied in semiparametric and nonparametric contexts. Ai (1997) considers semiparametric estimation in a model with unknown conditional density that is assumed only to satisfy an index restriction. The conditional density is estimated nonparametrically, and the corresponding score function is constructed to produce a semiparametric maximum likelihood estimate of a finite-dimensional parameter of the model. Tibshirani and Hastie (1987) introduced the notion of local likelihood estimation where regression functions are fit locally according to a maximum likelihood criterion. This idea has been extended to density estimation and other regression-type settings (Fan, Farmen and Gijbels 1998). Linton and Xiao (2007) develop an adaptive nonparametric regression approach that estimates the unknown density of the disturbance (or its score function) and then uses this estimate for local likelihood estimation of the unknown regression function. Empirical likelihood methods are another offshoot of nonparametric maximum likelihood. The basic insight that the empirical distribution function is the nonparametric MLE for a general cumulative distribution function has led to new approaches to confidence region formation, estimation in regression models, generalized method of moments inference, and bootstrapping (Owen, 2001; Brown and Newey, 2002).

JACK R. PORTER

See also **classical distribution theories; econometrics; efficiency bounds; empirical likelihood; Fisher, Ronald Aylmer; nonparametric structural models; optimality and efficiency; semiparametric estimation; statistical inference.**

Bibliography

Ai, C. 1997. A semiparametric maximum likelihood estimator. *Econometrica* 65, 933–63.
Barndorff-Nielsen, O.E. 1983. On a formula for the distribution of the maximum likelihood estimator. *Biometrika* 70, 343–65.
Berger, J. and Wolpert, R. 1988. *The Likelihood Principle*. Hayward, CA: Institute of Mathematical Statistics.
Brown, B. and Newey, W. 2002. Generalized method of moments, efficient bootstrapping, and improved inference. *Journal of Business and Economic Statistics* 20, 507–17.
Eaton, M. 1989. *Group Invariance Applications in Statistics*. Hayward, CA: Institute of Mathematical Statistics.
Efron, B. 1982. Maximum likelihood and decision theory. *Annals of Statistics* 10, 340–56.
Fan, J., Farmen, M. and Gijbels, I. 1998. Local maximum likelihood estimation and inference. *Journal of the Royal Statistical Society* (Series B) 60, 591–608.
Fisher, R.A. 1922. On the mathematical foundations of theoretical statistics. *Philosophical Transactions of the Royal Society of London* A 222, 309–60.
Fisher, R.A. 1925. Theory of statistical estimation. *Proceedings of the Cambridge Philosophical Society* 22, 700–25.
Fisher, R.A. 1934. Two new properties of mathematical likelihood. *Proceedings of the Royal Society of London* A 144, 285–307.
Gourieroux, C., Monfort, A. and Trognon, A. 1984. Pseudo maximum likelihood methods: theory. *Econometrica* 52, 681–700.
Hajivassiliou, V. and Ruud, P. 1994. Classical estimation methods for LDV models using simulation. *Handbook of Econometrics*, vol. 4, ed. D. McFadden and R. Engle. Amsterdam: North-Holland.
Hirano, K. and Porter, J. 2003. Asymptotic efficiency in parametric structural models with parameter dependent support. *Econometrica* 71, 1307–38.
Hirano, K. and Porter, J. 2005. Efficiency in asymptotic shift models. Working paper, University of Wisconsin.
Ibragimov, I.A. and Has'minskii, R.Z. 1981. *Statistical Estimation: Asymptotic Theory*. New York: Springer-Verlag.
Le Cam, L. 1986. *Asymptotic Methods in Statistical Decision Theory*. New York: Springer-Verlag.
Le Cam, L. 1990. Maximum likelihood: an introduction. *International Statistical Review* 58, 153–71.
Linton, O. and Xiao, Z. 2007. A nonparametric regression estimator that adapts to error distribution of unknown form. *Econometric Theory* 23(3) (forthcoming).
MacLachlan, G. and Krishnan, T. 1997. *The EM Algorithm and Extensions*. New York: Wiley.
Neyman, J. and Scott, E.L. 1948. Consistent estimates based on partially consistent observations. *Econometrica* 16, 1–32.
Owen, A.B. 2001. *Empirical Likelihood*. New York: Chapman-Hall.
Pfanzagl, J. and Wefelmeyer, W. 1978. A Third-order optimum property of the maximum likelihood estimator. *Journal of Multivariate Analysis* 8, 1–29.
Tibshirani, R. and Hastie, T. 1987. Local likelihood estimation. *Journal of the American Statistical Association* 82, 559–67.

maximum score methods

In a seminal paper, Manski (1975) introduces the maximum score estimator (MSE) of the structural parameters of a multinomial choice model and proves consistency without assuming knowledge of the distribution of the error terms in the model. As such, the MSE is the first instance of a semiparametric estimator of a limited dependent variable model in the econometrics literature.

Maximum score estimation of the parameters of a binary choice model has received the most attention in the literature. Manski (1975) covers this model, but Manski (1985) focuses on it. The key assumption that Manski (1985) makes is that the latent variable underlying the observed binary data satisfies a linear α-quantile regression specification. (He focuses on the linear median regression case, where $\alpha = 0.5$.) This is perhaps an under-appreciated fact about maximum score estimation in the binary choice setting. If the latent variable were observed, then classical quantile regression estimation (Koenker and Bassett, 1978), using the latent data, would estimate, albeit more efficiently, the same regression parameters that would be estimated by maximum score estimation using the binary data. In short, the estimands would be the same for these two estimation procedures.

Assuming that the underlying latent variable satisfies a linear α-quantile regression specification is equivalent to assuming that the regression parameters in the linear model do not depend on the regressors and that the error term in the model has zero α-quantile conditional on the regressors. Under these assumptions, Manski (1985) proves strong consistency of the MSE. The zero conditional α-quantile assumption does not require the existence of any error moments and allows heteroskedastic errors of an unknown form. This flexibility is in contrast to many semiparametric estimators of comparable structural parameters for the binary choice model. As discussed in Powell (1994), many of these latter estimators require the existence of error moments and most require more restrictive assumptions governing the relation of errors to regressors.

The weak zero conditional α-quantile assumption comes at a price, however. Extrapolation power is limited: off the observed support of the regressors it is not possible to identify the conditional probability of the choice of interest, but only whether this probability is above or below $1 - \alpha$. See Manski (1995, pp. 149–50). There are also disadvantages associated with the estimation procedure. The maximum score criterion function is a sum of indicator functions of sets involving parameters. This lack of smoothness precludes using standard optimization routines to compute the MSE. Moreover, Kim and Pollard (1990) show that this type of discontinuity leads to a convergence rate of $n^{-1/3}$ rather than the $n^{-1/2}$ convergence rate attained by most semiparametric estimators of parameters in this model. In addition, Kim and Pollard (1990) show that the MSE has a nonstandard limiting distribution. The properties of this distribution are largely unknown, making asymptotic inference problematic. Also, Abrevaya and Huang (2005) prove that the bootstrapped MSE is an inconsistent estimator of the parameters of interest, precluding bootstrap inference.

To repair some of these shortcomings, Horowitz (1992) develops a smoothed MSE (SMSE) for the linear median regression case. This estimator retains the attractive flexibility properties of the MSE, but can be computed using standard optimization routines. In addition, the SMSE converges at a faster rate than the MSE and has a normal limit law allowing first order asymptotic inference. Horowitz (2002) proves that bootstrapped SMSE provides asymptotic refinements and in various simulations demonstrates the superiority of bootstrap tests over first-order asymptotic tests. Kordas (2006) generalizes Horowitz's (1992) SMSE to cover all α-quantiles.

In the next section, we present the multinomial choice model under random utility maximization as well as some intuition behind maximum score estimation in this context. We then discuss the relation between maximum score estimation in the binary response model and quantile regression. Next, we present Kim and Pollard's (1990) heuristic argument for the nonstandard rate of convergence of the MSE in the binary model. Finally, we discuss the method of Horowitz (1992) for smoothing the MSE.

The random utility maximization model of choice and the MSE

Manski (1975) developed the MSE for the multinomial choice model in the context of random utility maximization. Suppose the ith individual in a sample of size n from a population of interest must make exactly one of J choices, where $J \geq 2$.

For $i \in \{1, 2, \ldots, n\}$ and $j \in \{1, 2, \ldots, J\}$, let U_{ij} denote the utility to individual i of making choice j. Assume the structural form $U_{ij} = X'_{ij}\beta + \varepsilon_{ij}$ where X_{ij} is an observable $m \times 1$ vector of explanatory variables, β is an unknown $m \times 1$ parameter vector, and ε_{ij} is an unobservable random disturbance. (A more general set-up can be accommodated. For example, there can be a different parameter vector associated with each choice.)

The utilities associated with the choices an individual faces are latent, or unobservable. However, an individual's choice is observable. Suppose we adopt the maximum utility model of choice: if individual i makes choice j then $U_{ij} > U_{ik}$ for all $k \neq j$. For any event E, define the indicator function $\{E\} = 1$ if E occurs and 0 otherwise. Define

$$Y_{ij} = \{U_{ij} > U_{ik}, \text{ for all } k \neq j\}$$
$$= \{X'_{ij}\beta + \varepsilon_{ij} > X'_{ij}\beta + \varepsilon_{ik}, \text{ for all } k \neq j\}. \tag{1}$$

If choice j has maximum utility, then $Y_{ij} = 1$. Otherwise, $Y_{ij} = 0$. Thus, for each individual i, we observe X_{ij}, $j = 1, 2, \ldots, J$ and Y_{ij}, $j = 1, 2, \ldots, J$.

The traditional approach to estimating β in the multinomial choice model under the assumption of random utility maximization is the method of maximum likelihood in which the errors are iid with a distribution known up to scale. The likelihood function to be maximized has the form

$$\sum_{i=1}^{n} \sum_{j=1}^{J} Y_{ij} \, \log P\{Y_{ij} = 1 | X_{i1}, X_{i2}, \ldots, X_{iJ}, b\}.$$

For example, when ε_{ij} has the Type 1 extreme-value cdf $F(t) = \exp(-\exp(-t))$, $t \in R$, McFadden (1974) shows that the likelihood probabilities have the multinomial logit specification $\exp(X'_{ij}b)\left[\sum_{k=1}^{J}\exp(X'_{ij}b)\right]^{-1}$. The corresponding likelihood function is analytic and globally concave. Despite the consequent computational advantages, this specification makes very strong assumptions about the distribution of the errors. The MSE is consistent under much weaker assumptions about the errors. Manski (1975) only assumes that the disturbances ε_{ij} are independent and identically distributed (iid) across choices and independent but not necessarily identically distributed across individuals.

Write b for a generic element of the parameter space. It follows trivially from (1) that the infeasible criterion function

$$\sum_{i=1}^{n}\sum_{j=1}^{J} Y_{ij}\{X'_{ij}b + \varepsilon_{ij} > X'_{ik}b + \varepsilon_{ik}, k \neq j\}$$

attains its maximum value of n at $b = \beta$. Since, for each i, the disturbances ε_{ij} are iid variates, this suggests estimating β with the maximizer of the so-called score function

$$\sum_{i=1}^{n}\sum_{j=1}^{J} Y_{ij}\{X'_{ij}b > X'_{ij}b, k \neq j\} .$$

A score for a parameter b is the number of correct predictions made by predicting Y_{ij} to be 1 whenever $X'_{ij}b$ exceeds $X'_{ij}b$ for all $k \neq j$. A maximizer of the score function is an MSE of β. The maximizer need not be unique.

The MSE in the binary choice model and quantile regression

Now consider the binary model where $J = 2$. Define $Y_i = Y_{i1}$ (implying $Y_{i2} = 1 - Y_i$) and $X_i = X_{i1} - X_{i2}$. Then the score function in (2) reduces to

$$\sum_{i=1}^{n}[Y_i\{X'_i b > 0\} + (1 - Y_i)\{X'_i b < 0\}].$$

$$(3)$$

Substitute $1 - \{X'_i b > 0\}$ for $\{X'_i b < 0\}$ in (3) and expand each summand to see that maximizing (3) is equivalent to maximizing

$$S_n(b) = n^{-1}\sum_{i=1}^{n}(2Y_i - 1)\{X'_i b > 0\}. \quad (4)$$

Note that $Y_i = \{Y_i^* > 0\}$ where $Y_i^* = X'_i\beta + \varepsilon_i$ with $\varepsilon_i = \varepsilon_{i1} - \varepsilon_{i2}$. For ease of exposition, write (Y^*, Y, X, ε) for $(Y_1^*, Y_1, X_1, \varepsilon_1)$ and x for an arbitrary point in the support of X. Thus, $Y = \{Y^* > 0\}$ where $Y^* = X'\beta + \varepsilon$.

Before proceeding further, we must consider what interpretation to give to the parameter β in the last paragraph. The interpretation depends on our assumptions. For example, if we assume that β does not depend on x and that for every x, $E[Y^*|x] = x'\beta$, then β is such that the conditional mean of Y^* given $X = x$ is equal to $x'\beta$. However, if we assume that MED $(Y^*|x) = x'\beta$, then β is such that the conditional median of Y^* given $X = x$ is equal to $x'\beta$. In general, the β satisfying the conditional mean assumption will be different from the β satisfying the conditional median assumption. Similarly, if we assume that for $a \neq 0.5$, the conditional α-quantile of Y^* given x is equal to $x'\beta$, then this β will, in general, be different from the β satisfying the conditional median assumption.

With this in mind, for $\alpha \in (0,1)$, write $Q_\alpha(Y^*|x)$ for the α-quantile of Y^* given $X = x$. Fix an $\alpha \in (0,1)$ and assume the linear α-quantile regression specification. That is, assume that for each x in the support of X, there exists a unique parameter β_α, depending on α but not on x, such that $Q_\alpha(Y^*|x) = x'\beta_\alpha$. This implies a zero conditional α-quantile restriction on ε: $Q_\alpha(\varepsilon|x) = 0$ for all x.

For $\alpha \in (0, 1)$, define

$$S_n^\alpha(b) = n^{-1}\sum_{i=1}^{n}[(2Y_i - 1) - (1 - 2\alpha)]\{X'_i b > 0\} .$$

$$(5)$$

Clearly, $S_n^{0.5}(b) = S_n(b)$ in (4). Assume that the linear α-quantile regression specification holds for some $\alpha \in (0,1)$. To see that it makes sense, under this assumption, to estimate β_α with the maximizer of $S_n^\alpha(b)$, consider $S^\alpha(b) = ES_n^\alpha(b)$. We see that

$$S^\alpha(b) = E^X[E[(2Y - 1) - (1 - 2\alpha)]\{X'b > 0\}|X]$$
$$= E^X[[(2P\{-\varepsilon < X'\beta_\alpha|X\} - 1)$$
$$- (1 - 2\alpha)]\{X'b > 0\}].$$

The linear α-quantile regression specification implies a zero conditional α-quantile restriction on ε: for all x, $P\{\varepsilon \leq 0|x\} \leq \alpha$ and $P\{\varepsilon \geq 0|x\} \geq 1 - \alpha$. Thus, $x'\beta_\alpha > 0$ if and only if $P\{-\varepsilon \leq x'\beta_\alpha|x\} \geq P\{-\varepsilon \leq 0|x\} \geq 1 - \alpha$. Deduce that for each possible value of X, the term in outer brackets in the last expression is maximized at $b = \beta_\alpha$. It follows that $S^\alpha(b)$ is maximized at $b = \beta_\alpha$. The analogy principle (Manski, 1988) prescribes using a maximizer of $S_n^\alpha(b)$ to estimate β_α.

The nonstandard convergence rate

The summands of the criterion function in (5) depend on b only through indicator functions of sets. As such, each summand has a 'sharp edge', to use the terminology of Kim and Pollard (1990). These authors provide a beautiful heuristic for why estimators that optimize empirical processes with sharp-edge summands converge at rate $n^{-1/3}$, rather than the usual $n^{-1/2}$ rate. They decompose the sample criterion function into a deterministic trend plus noise. Then, for each possible parameter value, they consider how the trend and the noise compete for dominance. Only a parameter value for which the trend does not overwhelm the standard deviation of the noise has a fighting chance of being an optimizer. Sharp edges produce standard errors with nonstandard sizes leading to the nonstandard $n^{-1/3}$ rate. We now examine how their argument works for the MSE for a very simple model.

Assume the median regression specification for the model $Y = \{\beta - X - \varepsilon > 0\}$. Thus, $\beta_{0.5} = (\beta, -1)$ where the slope coefficient is known to equal -1 and the intercept β is the unknown parameter of interest. Assume that ε has median zero and is independent of X, so that the conditional median zero restriction is trivially satisfied. Also, assume that the distributions of X and ε have everywhere positive Lebesgue densities.

Refer to (4). Define $S(b) = ES_n(b) = E(2Y - 1)\{X'b > 0\}$. In the intercept example, $S(b) = E(2\{\varepsilon < \beta - X\} - 1)\{X < b\}$. Simple calculations show that

$$S(b) = 2 \int_{-\infty}^{b} F_\varepsilon(\beta - t) f_x(t) dt - F_x(b)$$

where $F_\varepsilon(\cdot)$ is the cdf of ε, $f_x(\cdot)$ is the pdf of X, and $F_x(\cdot)$ is the cdf of X. Write $f_\varepsilon(\cdot)$ for the pdf of ε. Again, simple calculations show that

$$S'(b) = 2F_\varepsilon(\beta - b) f_x(b) - f_x(b)$$
$$S''(b) = 2F_\varepsilon(\beta - b) f'_x(b) - f_x(b) 2 f_\varepsilon(\beta - b) - f'_x(b) .$$

By the median restriction, we see that $S'(\beta) = 0$ and $S''(\beta) = -2f_x(\beta) f_\varepsilon(0) < 0$. Thus, $S(b)$ is locally maximized at $b = \beta$. In fact, the given assumptions imply that $S(b)$ is globally and uniquely maximized at $b = \beta$. The MSE maximizes $S_n(b) - S_n(\beta)$. For each b, decompose $S_n(b) - S_n(\beta)$ into a sum of a deterministic trend and a random perturbation:

$$S_n(b) - S_n(\beta) = S(b) - S(\beta) + [S_n(b) - S_n(\beta) - [S(b) - S(\beta)]] .$$

A Taylor expansion about β shows that for b near β, the trend $S(b) - S(\beta)$ is approximately quadratic with maximum value zero at $b = \beta$:

$$S(b) - S(\beta) \approx S''(\beta)(b - \beta)^2 .$$

By a central limit theorem, for large n, the random contribution $S_n(b) - S_n(\beta) - [S(b) - S(\beta)]$ is approximately normally distributed with mean zero and variance σ_b^2/n where

$$\sigma_b^2 = E[(2Y - 1)[\{X < b\} - \{X < \beta\}]]^2$$
$$- [E(2Y - 1)[\{X < b\} - \{X < \beta\}]]^2 .$$

For b near β, the second term is much smaller than the first. It is the first term that accounts for the sharp-edge effect. It equals

$$F_x(\beta) + F_x(b) - 2[F_x(\beta)\{b > \beta\} + F_x(b)\{b < \beta\}] .$$

A Taylor expansion of both $F_x(b)$ terms about β shows that this term is approximately equal to $|b - \beta| f_x(\beta)$ for b near β. Thus, near β, the criterion function $S_n(b) - S_n(\beta)$ is approximately equal to a quadratic maximized at β, namely, $-c_1(b - \beta)^2$ for $c_1 > 0$, plus a zero-mean random variable with standard deviation equal to $c_2 n^{-1/2} |b - \beta|^{1/2}$ for $c_2 > 0$. Values of b for which $-c_1(b - \beta)^2$ is much bigger in absolute value than $c_2 n^{-1/2} |b - \beta|^{-1/2}$ have little chance of maximizing $S_n(b) - S_n(\beta)$. Rather, the maximizer is likely to be among those b values for which, for some $c > 0$,

$$(b - \beta)^2 \leq cn^{-1/2} |b - \beta|^{1/2} .$$

Rearranging, we see that the maximizer is likely to be among the b values for which

$$|b - \beta| \leq cn^{-1/3} .$$

This is the essence of the heuristic presented by Kim and Pollard (1990) for $n^{-1/3}$ convergence rates. These authors also note that, when criterion functions are smooth, the variance of the random perturbation usually has order $|b - \beta|^2$ (instead of $|b - \beta|$) which, by the same heuristic, leads to the faster $n^{-1/2}$ convergence rate.

Smoothing the MSE

In order to remedy some of the shortcomings of the MSE, Horowitz (1992) develops a smoothed maximum score estimator (SMSE) under a linear median regression specification for the latent variable in the binary model. He replaces the indicator function in (4) with a smooth approximation. His SMSE maximizes a criterion function of the form

$$n^{-1} \sum_{i=1}^{n} (2Y_i - 1) K(X'_i b / \sigma_n)$$

where K is essentially a smooth cdf and σ_n approaches zero as the sample size increases. Thus, $K(X'_i b / \sigma_n)$ approaches the indicator function $\{X'_i b > 0\}$ as $n \to \infty$. By smoothing out the sharp-edge of the indicator function in (4), Horowitz is able to use Taylor expansion arguments to show that the SMSE, under slightly stronger conditions than those required for consistency of the MSE, converges at rate n^δ for $2/5 \leq \delta < 1/2$ and has a normal limit. The exact rate of convergence depends on certain smoothness assumptions and satisfies an optimality property (see Horowitz, 1993). The normality result makes it possible to do standard asymptotic inference with the SMSE. Horowitz (2002) shows that the bootstrapped SMSE provides asymptotic refinements.

Kordas (2006) applies the smoothing technique of Horowitz (1992) to the criterion function in (5) and obtains asymptotic results similar to those of Horowitz (1992) for any $\alpha \in (0, 1)$.

ROBERT P. SHERMAN

See also **quantile regression.**

Bibliography

Abrevaya, J. and Huang, J. 2005. On the bootstrap of the maximum score estimator. *Econometrica* 73, 1175–204.

Horowitz, J.L. 1992. A smoothed maximum score estimator for the binary response model. *Econometrica* 60, 505–31.

Horowitz, J.L. 1993. Optimal rates of convergence of parameter estimators in the binary response model with weak distributional assumptions. *Econometric Theory* 9, 1–18.

Horowitz, J.L. 2002. Bootstrap critical values for tests based on the smoothed maximum score estimator. *Econometrica* 111, 141–67.

Kim, J. and Pollard, D. 1990. Cube root asymptotics. *Annals of Statistics* 18, 191–219.

Koenker, R. and Bassett, G., Jr. 1978. Regression quantiles. *Econometrica* 46, 33–50.

Kordas, G. 2006. Smoothed binary regression quantiles. *Journal of Applied Econometrics* 21, 387–407.

Manski, C.F. 1975. Maximum score estimation of the stochastic utility model of choice. *Journal of Econometrics* 3, 205–28.

Manski, C.F. 1985. Semiparametric analysis of discrete response: asymptotic properties of the maximum score estimator. *Journal of Econometrics* 27, 313–33.

Manski, C.F. 1988. *Analog Estimation Methods in Econometrics*. New York: Chapman and Hall.

Manski, C.F. 1995. *Identification Problems in the Social Sciences*. Cambridge, MA: Harvard University Press.

McFadden, D. 1974. Conditional logit analysis of qualitative choice behavior. In *Frontiers in Econometrics*, ed. P. Zarembka. New York: Academic Press.

Powell, J.L. 1994. Estimation of semiparametric models. In *Handbook of Econometrics*, vol. 4, ed. R. Engle and D. McFadden. Amsterdam: North-Holland.

Mazzola, Ugo (1863–1899)

Italian economist, born in Naples on 16 September 1863; died in Courmayeur on 14 August 1899. When he was just 20 years old, he graduated from the University of Naples, where his economic course had been largely based on the ideas of Francesco Ferrara. He did post-graduate research in Berlin, where he came in touch with Adolf Wagner and carried out research on behalf of the Italian Ministry of Agriculture into the problems associated with providing insurance for the working classes. At the age of 24 Mazzola was appointed to the Chair of Public Finance at the University of Pavia, where in 1896 he, with other economists, bought up the *Giornale degli Economisti* and transformed it into a centre of liberal thought. It was in this journal that the most eminent economists of the time, Maffeo Pantaleoni, Antonio De Viti De Marco, and Vilfredo Pareto, had their work published.

Mazzola believed fervently in the concept of free trade and he fought the protectionist trends which were threatening the country as it moved towards industrialization. In economic doctrine he was attracted to marginalist theory, as advocated by Jevons and Menger, and to its more comprehensive version in general equilibrium theory. Using these tools of analysis he wrote *I dati scientifici della finanza pubblica*, published in 1890, and thus made 'a lasting contribution' (to quote Pantaleoni) to the foundation of the theory of public finance. Mazzola was an expert on German fiscal theories, but he disagreed with the rather ambiguous way in which they differentiated between individual and collective aims. Mazzola stressed that, in his view, individual objectives are conditioned by public aims (defence, security, and so on) which can only be achieved by means of political cooperation. He believed that the provision of public welfare was necessary for the attainment of collective aims. So he analysed the characteristics of public welfare and then examined the process of price determination by means of the principles of maximization of utility – characteristics of the marginalist theory. In this way the phenomenon of fiscal theory was brought within the sphere of general economic analysis.

F. CAFFÈ

Selected works

1886. *L'assicurazione degli operai nella scienza e nella legislazione germanica*. Rome: Botta.

1890. *I dati scientifici della finanza pubblica*. Rome: Loescher.

1895. *L'imposta progressiva in economia pura e sociale*. Pavia.

1967. The formation of the prices of public goods. In *Classics in the Theory of Public Finance*, ed. R.A. Musgrave and A.T. Peacock. London: Macmillan.

Bibliography

Pantaleoni, M. 1899. Ugo Mazzola. *Giornale degli Economisti*. 2nd Series, 19(September), 189–98.

McCulloch, John Ramsay (1789–1864)

McCulloch was born in Galloway, Scotland on 1 March 1789. After attending Edinburgh University he secured employment as a lawyer's clerk. In 1816 he began his contributions to economics with two essays on the national debt. He was editor of *The Scotsman*, 1817–21, and a contributor to that paper until 1827. In 1818 he began writing for the *Edinburgh Review* and continued doing so until 1837, contributing nearly 80 articles. He also contributed to *Encyclopaedia Britannica* and was a prolific author, his works including editions of the *Wealth of Nations*, a *Commercial Dictionary*, a *Geographical Dictionary*, *Principles of Political Economy*, a *Statistical Account of the British Empire* and a *Treatise on Taxation*. He was a noted bibliophile, and after his death his library was purchased by his friend Lord Overstone and ultimately presented to Reading University.

It was not only as an author that McCulloch was influential; he was also called as an expert witness before the Select Committee on machinery of 1824 and that on Ireland of 1825. He was also one of the first public teachers of economics. He began lecturing in Edinburgh in 1820, and although attempts to establish a chair at Edinburgh University on his behalf in 1825 failed, he had been selected in 1824 to give the Ricardo Memorial lectures in London. In 1828, largely through the agency of James Mill, he was appointed the first professor of political economy at London University. He remained professor until 1837, though largely supporting himself by his pen; but in 1838 he was appointed Comptroller of the Stationery Office, a post he occupied until his death in 1864. This did not prevent him from continuing his literary activities and he remained active as an author, producing new editions of his earlier works and some completely new ones, notably the *Treatise on Taxation* (1845, 1852, 1863) and the *Geographical Dictionary* (1841–2, 1845–6, 1849, 1852, 1854).

As an economist, McCulloch was at one stage very much under the influence of Ricardo, but the influence was transient. He put forward a simple labour theory of value under the influence of Ricardo, while aware that this was a simplified version (assuming away the problem of capital), for popular exposition. But though the emphasis is on labour quantity, and undoubtedly derived from Ricardo, it was a theory of relative (exchangeable) value, and McCulloch's analysis never borrowed from Ricardo the fundamental (to Ricardo) concept of the invariable measure. Indeed, McCulloch rejected the concept emphatically.

The vicissitudes of McCulloch's exposition over the years included, without doubt, a number of erroneous positions and a strange solution to the origin of profits as being in stored labour continuing to work. He also attempted to make labour cost a real (disutility) cost. But in the second edition (1830) of his *Principles* he advanced an almost complete cost of production theory, where cost was, as in an earlier *Scotsman* article, marginal cost. Labour cost, amortization and profit were now recognized as costs as they had been with Smith; the influences of Ricardo was now largely apparent in treating rent not as a cost but as a price-determined surplus, thus ignoring transfer earnings. Finally, in the 1838 edition of his notes to the *Wealth of Nations*, McCulloch clarified the nature of the profit reward with both waiting (as stressed by Ricardo) and productivity (as stressed by McCulloch) combining to produce a positive return.

McCulloch's treatment of money and banking derived from Smith, Hume and Thornton, though he long followed Ricardo in advancing the idea that the value of commodity money was determined by its cost of production, an idea he finally abandoned in his contributions to the eighth edition of *Encyclopaedia Britannica*. He accepted Hume's theory of the distribution of the precious metals, drawing also on Smith and especially Thornton, though he did accept, at least in relation to external losses of metal, the Ricardian definition of excess. In considering the internal level of activity in relation to money, he accepted Say's identify as an equilibrium proposition; but he also recognized the possibility that excess demand for money in disequilibrium might cause economic dislocation, thus magnifying fluctuations originating in the real side of the economy, such as over-investment. He also recognized, and approved, in contrast to Ricardo, the effects of mild inflation in producing forced saving and economic growth. On the issue of banking control he at first accepted Ricardo's view that convertibility was its own safeguard, but he came to recognize the problems of over-issue of notes much earlier than many writers – he was firmly opposed to laissez-faire in banking – and was one of the earliest writers to put forward the principle that a note issue should fluctuate in amount in response to the balance of payments exactly as an identically circumstanced metallic money would do, though he saw this as providing only a partial solution to monetary control.

McCulloch's analysis of international trade followed Smith rather than Ricardo, in basing trade on absolute advantage assuming international factor mobility. McCulloch may have done this because he saw that the possibility of trade advantage, as explained in comparative cost theory, was incomplete until this was translated into relative costs and prices. At all events he considered Ricardo's treatment of international trade to be faulty. In his view there was a complete parallel between international and inter-regional trade. McCulloch's treatment went well beyond that of Smith in some respects; and in particular, his analysis of the transfer problem, based on the work of Parnell, was an important precursor of modern developments. He discussed not only the effects of a transfer in the form of specie, or of commodities, but also a demand transfer of the kind made famous by Ohlin in his controversy with Keynes after the First World War. On matters of trade policy McCulloch has had the image of a crude free trader: but in fact, though he recognized the harm that protection could do, freedom of trade could, in his view, involve the imposition of substantial import duties – even as high as 25 per cent – as long as these were balanced by home excise duties so as to avoid distortion of choice.

McCulloch's treatment of public finance used the Smithian framework: the analysis inevitably acquired a number of Ricardian accretions, but many of these were ultimately discarded. Moreover, McCulloch drew on a wide range of earlier writers on taxation and was particularly indebted to Hume and to Robert Hamilton. He presented a broad synthetic treatment which did much to give tax theory practicality after the Ricardian detour into the corn model. His main focus of attention was the use of fiscal policy in such a way as to ensure the maintenance of growth. Heavy taxation could interfere with growth; but if taxation was sensibly used it could be a stimulus to growth, increasing the supply of both effort and savings. A widely based regime of moderate indirect taxes, extending even to postage, was what McCulloch favoured, on ability-to-pay grounds, despite the distortions of the price system and the regressive elements. He opposed Gladstone's taxation policy, not only reliance upon income tax which McCulloch believed to interfere with growth, failing to stimulate effort and, where not proportional, subverting economic motivation.

The basic process of economic development was seen largely in terms of Smith's apparatus involving the accumulation of capital (but including human capital) and division of labour. It also involved the institutional requirements of security of property, internal freedom of trade, and a substantial role for government including education, control of public utilities, and employer liability for accidents. On to this Smithian basis McCulloch grafted specific Ricardian features, notably the Ricardian explanation for the declining rate of profit. However, he finally rejected the idea of inevitably diminishing returns in agriculture, as well as the inverse movement of wages and profits, and the Ricardian stagnation thesis. Writing later than Smith, McCulloch's treatment of development shows a much heavier emphasis on technology. Indeed, this was the basis of a fundamental disagreement with Ricardo over the role of machinery, and led him also to reject the primacy which Smith had afforded to agriculture – he attached key importance to the manufacturing sector though he was worried about the distributional consequences.

On agriculture itself however he wrote a good deal. He believed in large-scale capitalist farming (and supported primogeniture though not entails), and came, after a long period of believing in the (at least ultimate) inevitability of diminishing returns, to the view that under such a system improvements might continuously offset the diminution of returns. Thus his attack on the Corn Laws did not emphasize the Ricardian concept of stagnation but other matters, notably the idea that they encouraged price fluctuation. In this context he employed not only arguments about elasticity of demand and supply but also an agricultural cobweb. On this basis he argued, in contrast to Ricardo, that all classes, including the landlords, lost by the Corn Laws (though he followed Ricardo's argument for a measure of agricultural protection) and he also came to reject Ricardo's argument that improvements were against the interest of the landlords.

Classical economics, unlike modern economics, contained, as an integral part, a theory of population, which served in turn as the basis for various theorems about wages and welfare. McCulloch's population theory initially followed the first two editions of Malthus's celebrated Essay. But, probably under the influence of Nassau Senior, he become opposed to the Malthusian argument, believing prudential restraints to predominate. Indeed, amongst mainstream classical economists he was probably the most extreme anti-Malthusian, a development which harmonized with his move away from Ricardo's influence. Having sided with Malthus and Ricardo in opposing the Poor Law, he changed his mind quite openly after 1826 and became a supporter of the old Poor Law, believing that it did not undermine prudential restraint and that it preserved social stability. He opposed the 1834 Poor Law as harsh and over-centralized. As a measure to raise wages generally he supported emigration and colonization, though he did not favour retention of control of colonies, and objected, in particular, to Wakefield's schemes for 'scientific' colonization.

All this raises directly McCulloch's concept of the operation of the labour market. McCulloch is particularly associated with the idea of the wage fund, because of his Essay on Wages (1826); and with a given wage fund, reducing supply will raise wages, as implied in McCulloch's treatment of emigration. His analysis of demand for labour thus equated capital with demand for labour, though in his more careful treatments he distinguished total and wage capital (and total population and labour supply). But this only provided half the analysis: on the supply side McCulloch employed four different labour supply functions, including a rising supply schedule as normal; two negatively inclined short-run schedules (the first when wages rose after excessive hours had been required to survive at the previous level of wages, the second where women and children entered the labour force as wages fell, to maintain family income). Fourthly, there was a secular population function. McCulloch favoured high wages, and his writings in defence of trades unions were important in the successful struggle to secure repeal of the Combination Laws.

As an economist, McCulloch was a fairly representative classical writer in that his work involved a synthesis of elements deriving from Smith and Ricardo. Yet McCulloch's case is particularly interesting because his own evolution over they very long period (48 years) of his writings, mirrors the development of classical economics itself. Starting from a basis of Smith and Malthus, he fell under the influence of Ricardo's magnetic personality and remarkable powers of abstraction; but he gradually passed through this phase, the Smithian elements in his work resuming their predominance and leading in turn to an emphasis on empirical work and a methodological position foreign to the tenor of Ricardo's work.

D.P. O'BRIEN

Selected works

1825. *The Principles of Political Economy: with some inquiries respecting their application, and a sketch of the rise and progress of the science*, 3rd edn. Edinburgh: W. Tait, 1843.

1832. *A Dictionary Practical, Theoretical, and Historical, of Commerce and Commercial Navigation*, 10th edn. London: Longmans, 1859.

1845. *A Treatise on the Principles and Practical Influence of Taxation and the Funding System*, ed. D.P. O'Brien. Edinburgh: Scottish Academic Press for The Scottish Economics Society, 1975.

Bibliography

O'Brien, D.P. 1970. *J.R. McCulloch: A Study in Classical Economics*. London: Allen & Unwin.

McFadden, Daniel (born 1937)

1 Introduction

Daniel L. McFadden, the E. Morris Cox Professor of Economics at the University of California at Berkeley, was the 2000 co-recipient of the Nobel Prize in Economics, awarded 'for his development of theory and methods of analyzing discrete choice'. (The prize was split with James J. Heckman, awarded 'for his development of theory and methods for analyzing selective samples'). McFadden was born in North Carolina, USA, in 1937 and received a BS in physics from the University of Minnesota (with highest honors) in 1956, and a Ph.D. in economics from Minnesota in 1962. His academic career began as a postdoctoral fellow at the University of Pittsburgh. In 1963 he was appointed as assistant professor of economics at the University of California at Berkeley, and tenured in 1966. He has also held tenured appointments at Yale University (as Irving Fisher Research Professor in 1977), and at the Massachusetts Institute of Technology (from 1978 to 1991). In 1990 he was awarded the E. Morris Cox Chair at the University of California at Berkeley, where he has also served as Department Chair and as Director of the Econometrics Laboratory.

2 Research contributions

McFadden is best known for his fundamental contributions to the theory and econometric methods for analysing *discrete choice*. Building on a highly abstract, axiomatic literature on *probabilistic choice theory* due to Thurstone (1927), Block and Marschak (1960), and Luce (1959), McFadden developed the econometric methodology for estimating the utility functions underlying probabilistic choice theory. McFadden's primary contribution was to provide the econometric tools that permitted widespread *practical empirical application* of discrete choice models, in economics and other

disciplines. According to his autobiography (McFadden, 2001),

> In 1964, I was working with a graduate student, Phoebe Cottingham, who had data on freeway routing decisions of the California Department of Transportation, and was looking for a way to analyze these data to study institutional decision-making behavior. I worked out for her an econometric model based on an axiomatic theory of choice behavior developed by the psychologist Duncan Luce. Drawing upon the work of Thurstone and Marshak, I was able to show how this model linked to the economic theory of choice behavior. These developments, now called the multinomial logit model and the random utility model for choice behavior, have turned out to be widely useful in economics and other social sciences. They are used, for example, to study travel modes, choice of occupation, brand of automobile purchase, and decisions on marriage and number of children.

Thousands of papers applying his technique have been published since his path-breaking papers, 'Conditional Logit Analysis of Qualitative Choice Behavior' (1973) and 'The Revealed Preferences of a Government Bureaucracy: Empirical Evidence' (1976). In December 2005, a search of the term 'discrete choice' using the Google search engine yielded 10,200,000 entries, and a search on the Google Scholar search engine (which limits search to academic articles) returned 759,000 items.

Besides the discrete choice literature itself, McFadden's work has spawned a number of related literatures in econometrics, theory, and industrial organization that are among the most active and productive parts of the economic literature in the present day. This includes work in game theory and industrial organization (for example, the work on discrete choice and product differentiation of Anderson, De Palma and Thisse (1992), estimation of discrete games of incomplete information (Bajari et al., 2005), and discrete choice modelling in the empirical industrial organization literature (Berry, Levinsohn and Pakes, 1995, and Goldberg, 1995), the econometric literature on semiparametric estimation of discrete choice models (Manski, 1985; McFadden and Train, 2000), the literature on discrete/continuous choice models and its connection to durable goods and energy demand modelling (Dagsvik, 1994; Dubin and McFadden, 1984; Hannemann, 1984), the econometric literature on choice based and stratified sampling (Cosslett, 1981; Manski and McFadden, 1981), the econometric literature on 'simulation estimation' (McFadden, 1994; Hajivassiliou and Ruud, 1994; Pakes and Pollard, 1989), and the work on structural estimation of dynamic discrete choice models and extensions thereof (Dagsvik, 1983; Eckstein and Wolpin, 1989; Heckman, 1981; Rust, 1994).

McFadden has also made significant contributions to other fields, particularly to economic theory and production economics. Due to space limitations, I can only briefly mention several of his best known contributions here. McFadden's earliest published work was in pure theory, including seminal work on duality theory of production functions that was subsequently published in his book on Production Economics edited with Melvyn Fuss in 1978. McFadden made important contributions to growth theory including his 1967 Review of Economic Studies paper that showed how the overtaking criterion could be used to evaluate infinite horizon development programmes, resolving an outstanding paradox raised by Diamond and Koopmans. In a series of papers with Mitra and Majumdar (1976; 1980), McFadden extended the classical competitive equilibrium welfare theorems established by Debreu and others in finite economies, (that is, competitive equilibria are Pareto efficient, and any Pareto efficient allocation can be sustained as a competitive equilibrium after a suitable reallocation of resources), to infinite horizon economies. This work was not a simple technical extension or previous work by Debreu: it resolved serious conceptual problems created by the fact that in an infinite horizon economy (which includes standard overlapping generations models) the commodity space is infinite-dimensional and the number of consumers is infinite. These papers provided sufficient conditions for the existence of these fundamental welfare theorems, resolving paradoxes raised by Paul Samuelson, who showed special cases of infinite horizon overlapping generation economies where competitive equilibria can be strikingly inefficient. Another landmark paper is McFadden's (1974) paper on excess demand functions with Mantel, Mas-Colell and Richter. This paper provided one of the most general proofs of a classic conjecture by Hugo Sonnenschein that the necessary and sufficient properties of any system of aggregate excess demand functions are that it satisfy the following three properties: (1) homogeneity, (2) continuity, and (3) Walras's Law. McFadden has made numerous other contributions to economic theory that I do not have space to cover here. Instead, I now return to a more in depth review of McFadden's contributions to the discrete choice literature, the primary contributions that were cited in his Nobel Prize award.

3 Contributions to discrete choice

McFadden's contributions built on prior work in the literature on *mathematical psychology* (see LOGIT MODELS OF INDIVIDUAL CHOICE for further details). McFadden's contribution to this literature was to recognize how to operationalize the random utility interpretation in an empirically tractable way. In particular, he provided the first a random utility interpretation of the multinomial logit (MNL) model. His other fundamental contribution was to solve an analogue of the *revealed preference problem*: that is, using data on the actual choices and states of a sample of agents $\{(d_i, x_i)\}_{i=1}^{N}$, he showed how it was

possible to 'reconstruct' their underlying random utility functions via the method of maximum likelihood, where the likelihood is a product of individuals' *conditional choice probabilities*. Given the simplicity of the MNL choice probabilities, this worked helped to spawn a huge empirical literature that applied discrete choice models to a wide variety of phenomena. Further, McFadden introduced a new class of multivariate distributions, the *generalized extreme value family* (GEV), and derived tractable formulas for the implied choice probabilities including the *nested multinomial logit model*, and showed that these models relax some of the empirically implausible restrictions implied by the multinomial logit model, particularly the *independence from irrelevant alternatives* (IIA) property.

3.1 Multivariate extreme value distributions and the multinomial logit model

McFadden assumed that an individual's utility function has the following *additive separable* representation

$$U(x, z, d, \theta) = u(x, d, \theta) + v(z, d). \quad (3.1)$$

Define $\varepsilon(d) \equiv v(z, d)$. It follows that an assumption on the distribution of the random vector z implies a distribution for the random vector $\varepsilon \equiv \{\varepsilon(d)|d \in D(x)\}$. McFadden's approach was to make assumptions directly about the distribution of ε, rather than making assumptions about the distribution of z and deriving the implied distribution of ε. Standard assumptions for the distribution of ε that have been considered include the *multivariate normal* which yields the *multivariate probit* variant of the discrete choice model. Unfortunately, in problems where there are more than only two alternatives (the case that Thurstone studied), the multinomial probit model becomes intractable in higher dimensional problems. The reason is that, in order to derive the conditional choice probabilities, one must do numerical integrations that have a dimension equal to $|D(x)|$, the number of elements in the choice set. In general this multivariate integration is computationally infeasible when $|D(x)|$ is larger than 5 or 6, using standard quadrature methods on modern computers.

McFadden introduced an alternative assumption for the distribution of ε, namely the *multivariate extreme value distribution* given by

$$F(z|x) = Pr\{\varepsilon_d \leq z_d | d \in D(x)\}$$
$$= \prod_{d \in D(x)} \exp\{-\exp\{-(z_d - \mu_d)/\sigma)\}\},$$

$$(3.2)$$

and showed that (when the location parameters μ_d are normalized to) the corresponding random utility model produces choice probabilities given by the multinomial logit formula

$$P(d|x,\theta) = \frac{\exp\{u(x,d,\theta)/\sigma\}}{\sum_{d'\in D(x)}\exp\{u(x,d',\theta)/\sigma\}}.$$

This is McFadden's key result, that is, the *MNL choice probability is implied by a random utility model when the random utilities have extreme value distributions*. It leads to the insight that the *independence from irrelevant alternatives* (IIA) property of the MNL model is a consequence of the statistical independence in the random utilities. In particular, even if the *observed attributes* of two alternatives d and d' are identical (which implies $u(x, d, \theta) = u(x, d', \theta)$), the statistical independence of unobservable components $\varepsilon(d)$ and $\varepsilon(d')$ implies alternatives d and d' are not perfect substitutes even when their observed characteristics are identical. In many cases this is not problematic: individuals may have different idiosyncratic perceptions and preferences for two different items that have the same observed attributes. However in the case of the 'red bus/blue bus' example or the concert ticket example discussed by Debreu (1960), there are cases where it is plausible to believe that the observed attributes provide a sufficiently good description of an agent's perception of the desirability of two alternatives. In such cases, the hypothesis that choices are also affected by additive, *independent* unobservables $\varepsilon(d)$ provides a poor representation of an agent's decisions. What is required in such cases is a random utility model that has the property that the degree of correlation in the unobserved components of utility $\varepsilon(d)$ and $\varepsilon(d')$ for two alternatives d, $d' \in D(x)$ is a function of the degree of closeness in the observed attributes. This type of dependence can be captured by a *random coefficient probit model*. This is a random utility model of the form $U(x, z, d, \theta) = x_d(\theta + z)$ where x_d is a $k \times 1$ vector of observed attributes of alternative d, and θ is a $k \times 1$ vector of utility weights representing the mean weights individuals assign to the various attributes in x_d in the population and $z \sim N(0, \Omega)$ is a $k \times 1$ normally distributed random vector representing agent specific deviations in their weighting of the attributes relative the population average values, θ. Under the random coefficients probit specification of the random utility model, when $x_d = x_{d'}$, alternatives d and d' are in fact perfect substitutes for each other and this model is able to provide the intuitively plausible prediction of the effect of introducing an irrelevant alternative – the red bus – in the red bus/blue bus problem (see, for example, Hausman and Wise, 1978).

3.2 Generalized extreme value distributions and nested logit models

McFadden (1981) introduced the generalized extreme value (GEV) family of distributions. This family relaxes the independence assumption of the extreme value specification while still yielding tractable expressions for choice probabilities. The GEV distribution is given by

$$F(z|x) = Pr\{\varepsilon_d \le z_d | d \in D(x)\}$$
$$= \exp\{-H(\exp\{-z_1\}, \ldots,$$
$$\exp\{-z_{|D(x)|}\}, x, D(x))\},$$

for any function $H(z, x, D(x))$ satisfying certain consistency properties. McFadden showed that choice probabilities for the GEV distribution are given by

$$P(d|x,\theta) =$$
$$\frac{\exp\{u(x,d,\theta)\}H_d(\exp\{u(x,1,\theta)\},\ldots,\exp\{u(x,|D(x)|,\theta)\},x,D(x))}{H(\exp\{u(x,1,\theta)\},\ldots,\exp\{u(x,|D(x)|,\theta)\},x,D(x)),}$$

where $H_d(z, x, D(x)) = \partial/\partial_{Zd} H(z, x, D(x))$. A prominent subclass of GEV distributions is given by H functions of the form

$$H(z,y,D(x)) = \sum_{i=1}^{n}\left[\sum_{d\in D_i(x)} z_d^{1/\sigma_i}\right]^{\sigma_i},$$

where $\{D_1(x), \ldots, D_n(x)\}$ is a partition of the full choice set $D(x)$. This subclass of GEV distributions yields the *nested multinomial logit* (NMNL) choice probabilities (see LOGIT MODELS OF INDIVIDUAL CHOICE for further details).

The NMNL model has been applied in numerous empirical studies especially to study demand where there are an extremely large number of alternatives, such as modelling consumer choice of automobiles (for example, Berkovec, 1985; Goldberg, 1995). In many of these consumer choice problems there is a natural partitioning of the choice set in terms of *product classes* (for example, luxury, compact, intermediate, sport-utility, and so on, classes in the case of autos). The nesting avoids the problems with the IIA property and results in more reasonable implied estimates of demand elasticities than those obtained using the MNL model. In fact, Dagsvik (1995) has shown that the class of random utility models with GEV distributed utilities is 'dense' in the class of all random utility models, in the sense that choice probabilities implied from any random utility model can be approximated arbitrarily closely by a random utility model in the GEV class. However a limitation of nested logit models is that they imply a highly structured pattern of correlation in the unobservables induced by the econometrician's specification of how the overall choice set $D(x)$ is to be partitioned, and the number of levels in the nested logit 'tree'. Even though the NMNL model can be nested to arbitrarily many levels to achieve additional flexibility, it is desirable to have a method where patterns of correlation in unobservables can be estimated from the data rather than being imposed by the analyst. Further, even though McFadden and Train (2000) recognize Dagsvik's (1995) finding as a 'powerful theoretical result', they conclude that 'its practical econometric application is limited by the difficulty of specifying estimating and testing the consistency of relatively abstract generalized Extreme Value RUM' (McFadden and Train, 2000, p. 452).

3.3 Method of simulated moments and simulation based inference for discrete choice

As noted above, the random coefficients probit model has many attractive features: it allows a flexibly specified covariance matrix representing correlation between unobservable components of utilities that avoid many of the undesirable features implied by the IIA property of the MNL model, in a somewhat more direct and intuitive fashion than is possible via the GEV family. However as noted above, the multinomial probit model is intractable for applications with more than four or five alternatives due to the 'curse of dimensionality' of the numerical integrations required, at least using deterministic numerical integration methods such as Gaussian quadrature. One of McFadden's most important contributions was his (1989) *Econometrica* paper that introduced the *method of simulated moments* (MSM). This was a major breakthrough that introduced a new econometric method that made it feasible to estimate the parameters of multinomial probit models with arbitrarily large numbers of alternatives.

The basic idea underlying McFadden's contribution is to use *Monte Carlo integration* to approximate the probit choice probabilities. While this idea had been previously proposed by others, it was never developed into a practical, widespread estimation method because 'it requires an impractical number of Monte Carlo draws to estimate small choice probabilities and their derivatives with acceptable precision' (McFadden, 1989, p. 997). However McFadden's insight was that it is not necessary to have extremely accurate (and thus very computationally time-intensive) Monte Carlo estimates of choice probabilities in order to obtain an estimator for the parameters of a multinomial probit model that is consistent and asymptotically normal and performs well in finite samples. McFadden's insight is that the *noise from Monte Carlo simulations can be treated in the same way as random sampling error and will thus 'average out' in large samples*. In particular, his MSM estimator has good asymptotic properties even when *only a single Monte Carlo draw is used to estimate each agent's choice probability*. See SIMULATION-BASED ESTIMATION for further details on the MSM estimator.

The idea behind the MSM estimator is quite general and can be applied in many other settings besides the multinomial probit model. McFadden's work helped to spawn a large literature on 'simulation estimation' that developed rapidly during the 1990s and resulted in computationally feasible estimators for a large new class of econometric models that were previously considered to be computationally infeasible. However, there are even better simulation estimators for the multinomial probit model, which generally outperform the MSM estimator in terms of having lower asymptotic variance and better finite sample performance, and which are easier to compute. One problem with the simple Monte Carlo estimator $\hat{P}(x_i, \theta)$ underlying the MSM estimator is that it is a discontinuous and 'locally flat' function of the parameters θ, and thus the MSM criterion function is difficult to optimize. Hajivassiliou and McFadden (1998) introduced the *method of simulated scores* (MSS) that is based on Monte Carlo methods for simulating the *scores* of the likelihood function for a multinomial probit model and a wide class of other *limited dependent variable models* such as Tobit and other types of censored regression models. (In the case of a discrete choice model, the score for the ith observation is $\partial/\partial\theta \log(P(d_i|x_i, \theta))$.) Because it simulates the score of the likelihood rather than using a method of moments criterion, the MSS estimator is more efficient than the MSM estimator. Also, the MSS is based on a *smooth simulator* (that is, a method of simulation that results in an estimation criterion that is a continuously differentiable function of the parameters θ), so the MSS estimator is much easier to compute than the MSM estimator. Based on numerous Monte Carlo studies and empirical applications, MSS (and a closely related simulated maximum likelihood estimator based on the Geweke–Hajivassiliou–Keane', GHK, smoother simulator) are now regarded as the estimation methods of choice for a wide class of econometric models with limited dependent variable that are commonly encountered in empirical applications (see SIMULATION-BASED ESTIMATION for further details).

3.4 Mixed logit models

A mixed MNL model has choice probabilities of the form

$$P(d|x, \theta) = \int \left[\frac{\exp\{u(x, d, \alpha)}{\sum_{d' \in D(x)} \exp\{u(x, d', \alpha)\}} \right] G(d\alpha|\theta).$$

$$(3.3)$$

There are several possible random utility interpretations of the mixed logit model. One interpretation is that the α vector represents 'unobserved heterogeneity' in the preference parameters in the population, so the relevant choice probability is marginalized using the population distribution for the α parameters in the population, $G(\alpha|\theta)$. The other interpretation is that α is similar to vector ε, that is, it represents information that agents observe and which affects their choices (similar to ε) but which is unobserved by the econometrician, except that the components of ε, $\varepsilon(d)$ enter the utility function additively separably, whereas the variables α are allowed to enter in a non-additively separable fashion and the random vectors α and ε are statistically independent. It is easy to see that, under either interpretation, the mixed logit model will not satisfy the IIA property, and thus is not subject to its undesirable implications. McFadden and Train proposed several alternative ways to estimate mixed logit models, including maximum simulated likelihood and MSM. In each case, Monte Carlo integration is used to approximate the integral in equation (3.3) with respect to $G(\alpha|\theta)$. Both of these estimators are smooth functions of the parameters θ, and both benefit from the computational tractability of the MNL while at the same time having the flexibility to approximate virtually any type of random utility model. The intuition behind McFadden and Train's approximation theorem is that a mixed logit model can be regarded as a certain type of *neural network* using the MNL model as the underlying 'squashing function'. Neural networks are known to have the ability to approximate arbitrary types of functions and enjoy certain optimality properties, that is, the number of parameters (that is, the dimension of the α vector) needed to approximate arbitrary choice probabilities grows only linearly in the number of included covariates x. (Other approximation methods, such as *series estimators* formed as tensor products of bases that are univariate functions of each of the components of x, require a much larger number of coefficients to provide an comparable approximation, and the number of such coefficients grows exponentially fast with the dimension of the x vector.)

4 Conclusion

This brief survey of McFadden's contributions to the discrete choice literature has revealed the immense practical benefits of his ability to link theory and econometrics, innovations that lead to a vast empirical literature and widespread applications of discrete choice models. Beginning with his initial discovery, that is, his demonstration that multinomial logit choice probabilities result from a random utility model with multivariate extreme value distributed unobservables, McFadden has made a series of fundamental contributions that have enabled researchers to circumvent the problematic implications of the IIA property of the MNL model, providing computationally tractable methods for estimating ever wider and more flexible classes of random utility and limited dependent-variable models in econometrics.

JOHN RUST

See also **logit models of individual choice; simulation-based estimation.**

Selected works

1967. The evaluation of development programmes. *Review of Economic Studies* 34, 25–50.
1973. Conditional logit analysis of qualitative choice behavior. In *Frontiers of Econometrics*, ed. P. Zarembka. New York: Academic Press.
1974. The measurement of urban travel demand. *Journal of Public Economics* 3, 303–28.

1974. (With R. Mantel, A. Mas-Colell and M.K. Richter.) A characterization of community excess demand functions. *Journal of Economic Theory* 9, 361–74.
1976. The revealed preferences of a government bureaucracy: empirical evidence. *Bell Journal of Economics and Management Science* 7, 55–72.
1976. (With M. Majumdar and T. Mitra.) On efficiency and Pareto optimality of competitive programs in closed multisector models. *Journal of Economic Theory* 13, 26–46.
1978. Cost, revenue, and profit functions. In *Production Economics: A Dual Approach to Theory and Applications*, vol. 1, ed. M. Fuss and D. McFadden. Amsterdam: North-Holland.
1980. (With T. Mitra and M. Majumdar, M.) Pareto optimality and competitive equilibrium in infinite horizon economies. *Journal of Mathematical Economics* 7, 1–26.
1981. Econometric models of probabilistic choice. In *Structural Analysis of Discrete Data with Econometric Applications*, ed. C.F. Manski and D. McFadden. Cambridge, MA: MIT Press.
1981. (With C.F. Manski, ed.) *Structural Analysis of Discrete Data with Econometric Applications*. Cambridge, MA: MIT Press.
1984. Econometric models of qualitative response models. In *Handbook of Econometrics*, vol. 2, ed. Z. Griliches and M. Intriligator. Amsterdam: North-Holland.
1989. A method of simulated moments for estimation of discrete response models without numerical integration. *Econometrica* 57, 995–1026.
1994. (With P. Ruud.) Estimation by simulation. *Review of Economics and Statistics* 76, 591–608.
2000. (With K. Train.) Mixed MNL models of discrete response. *Journal of Applied Econometrics* 15, 447–70.
2001. Autobiography. In *Les Prix Nobel. The Nobel Prizes 2000*, ed. T. Frängsmyr. Stockholm: Nobel Foundation.

Bibliography

Anderson, S.P., De Palma, A. and Thisse, J.F. 1992. *Discrete Choice Theory of Product Differentiation*. Cambridge: MIT Press.
Bajari, P., Hong, H., Krainer, J. and Nekipelov, D. 2005. Estimating static models of strategic interactions. Manuscript, University of Michigan.
Berkovec, J. 1985. New car sales and used car stocks: a model of the automobile market. *RAND Journal of Economics* 16, 195–214.
Berry, S., Levinsohn, J. and Pakes, A. 1995. Automobile prices in market equilibrium. *Econometrica* 63, 841–90.
Block, H. and Marschak, J. 1960. Random orderings and stochastic theories of response. In *Contributions to Probability and Statistics*, ed. I. Olkin. Stanford: Stanford University Press.
Cosslett, S.R. 1981. Efficient estimation of discrete-choice models. In *Structural Analysis of Discrete Data with*

Econometric Applications, ed. C.F. Manski and D. McFadden. Cambridge, MA: MIT Press.

Dagsvik, J.K. 1983. Discrete dynamic choice: an extension of the choice models of Luce and Thurstone. *Journal of Mathematical Psychology* 27, 1–43.

Dagsvik, J.K. 1994. Discrete and continuous choice, max-stable processes and independence from irrelevant attributes. *Econometrica* 62, 1179–205.

Dagsvik, J.K. 1995. How large is the class of generalized extreme value models? *Journal of Mathematical Psychology* 39, 90–8.

Debreu, G. 1960. Review of R.D. Luce '*Individual Choice Behavior*'. *American Economic Review* 50, 186–8.

Dubin, J. and McFadden, D. 1984. An econometric analysis of residential electric appliance holdings and consumption. *Econometrica* 52, 345–62.

Eckstein, Z. and Wolpin, K. 1989. The specification and estimation of dynamic stochastic discrete choice models. *Journal of Human Resources* 24, 562–98.

Goldberg, P. 1995. Product differentiation and oligopoly in international markets: i the case of the U.S. automobile industry. *Econometrica* 63, 891–951.

Hajivassiliou, V. and McFadden, D.L. 1998. The method of simulated scores for the estimation of LDV models. *Econometrica* 66, 863–96.

Hajivassiliou, V.A. and Ruud, P.A. 1994. Classical estimation methods for LDV models using simulation. In *Handbook of Econometrics*, vol. IV, ed. R.F. Engle and D.L. McFadden. Amsterdam: Elsevier.

Hannemann, M. 1984. Discrete/continuous models of consumer demand. *Econometrica* 52, 541–62.

Hausman, J. and Wise, D. 1978. A conditional probit model of qualitative choice: discrete decisions recognizing interdependence and heterogeneous preferences. *Econometrica* 46, 403–26.

Heckman, J.J. 1981. Statistical models for discrete panel data. In *Structural Analysis of Discrete Data with Econometric Applications*, ed. C.F. Manski and D. McFadden. Cambridge, MA: MIT Press.

Luce, R.D. 1959. *Individual Choice Behavior: A Theoretical Analysis*. New York: Wiley.

Manski, C.F. 1985. Semiparametric estimation of discrete response: asymptotics of the maximum score estimator. *Journal of Econometrics* 27, 303–33.

Manski, C.F. 2001. Dan McFadden and the econometric analysis of discrete choice. *Scandinavian Journal of Economics* 103, 217–29.

Pakes, A. and Pollard, D. 1989. Simulation and the asymptotics of optimization estimators. *Econometrica* 57, 1027–57.

Rust, J. 1994. Structural estimation of Markov decision processes. In *Handbook of Econometrics*, vol. 4, ed. R.F. Engle and D.L. McFadden. Amsterdam: Elsevier.

Thurstone, L.L. 1927. Psychophysical analysis. *American Journal of Psychology* 38, 368–89.

Meade, James Edward (1907–1995)

James Meade was one of the truly great economists of the 20th century. He was profoundly internationalist in his outlook, and was awarded the Nobel Memorial Prize in Economics in 1977, jointly with Bertil Ohlin, for *The Theory of International Economic Policy* (1951–5). But his contributions spanned the whole of the discipline. He made fundamental, and widely influential, contributions to economic theory, in both macroeconomics and microeconomics. More than this, his main concern was always with the part that economic analysis has to play in the solution of practical economic policy problems. As a result, he contributed to the theory of economic policy in a very wide range of subjects, including macroeconomic management, trade policy reform, public finance, economic growth, income distribution, wage determination, and population growth. He served actively in policy-making as an economist for the League of Nations, and in the Economic Section of the UK Cabinet Office during, and immediately after, the Second World War. In all that he did, Meade saw the role of an economist as helping to design a better society – both by the creation of good institutions of economic management and by the provision of appropriate incentives for private individuals.

In this article I concentrate on four main issues. I first explain the large part that Meade played in the creation of Keynes's *General Theory* in the 1930s. After this, I describe his work with Keynes during the Second World War in the creation of the International Monetary Fund and the GATT (which has since become the World Trade Organization, or WTO). I then turn to Meade's work on international economics at the London School of Economics (LSE), immediately after the war, for which he was awarded the Nobel Prize; I spend some time showing how this theoretical work was related to his earlier work on policy with Keynes. Finally, I set out the role that Meade played, along with a group of young economists to which I belonged, in the construction of the inflation-targeting regime that became the centrepiece of British macroeconomic policymaking in the 1990s.

1 Activities before the Second World War: Keynesian macroeconomics

Meade was born on 23 June 1907 in Swanage, Dorset, and brought up in Bath. He went to school at Malvern College, and then won a scholarship in classics to Oriel College in Oxford. But like many others of his generation he was appalled by the problem of mass unemployment, which, as he said, caused 'poverty in the midst of plenty'. As a result he turned to the study of economics for the last two years of his university education. Meade gained greatly from studying classics, but, as a result of doing so, he had to teach himself the mathematics that he later used extensively.

Immediately upon graduating in 1930, Meade was elected to a fellowship at Hertford College, and appointed to a lectureship in economics at Oxford University. But in October 1930 his college first sent him to Cambridge for the academic year 1930/31, 'to learn my subject before I started to teach it. I had the greatest good fortune of being taken into Trinity College … by Dennis Robertson, to whose teaching that year I owe a deep debt of gratitude. At an early stage he told me that there was a young man in Kings called Richard Kahn whom I should get to know' (Meade, 1983b, p. 263).

And so Meade spent a formative and creative year as a member of the 'Circus' which was gathered around Keynes. This group of people were debating Keynes' *Treatise on Money* (Keynes, 1930) which had just been published, and included Joan and Austin Robinson, and Piero Sraffa, as well as Kahn. Meade enjoyed describing the 'workshop style' of the Circus meetings. Keynes took no part in the proceedings, but after each meeting Richard Kahn orally recounted to Keynes the subject matter of the discussions and the lines of argument.

> From the point of view of a humble mortal like myself Keynes seemed to play the role of God in a morality play; he dominated the play but rarely appeared on the stage. Kahn was the Messenger Angel who brought messages and problems from Keynes to the 'Circus' and went back to Heaven with the result of our deliberations. (Keynes, 1971–88, vol. 13, p. 339; see also p. 338)

The casting of Keynes in this role was first suggested by Meade's wife Margaret in 1934 when they were staying for the weekend with Austin and Joan Robinson in Cambridge. That weekend, too, was dominated by messages from people who had just spoken with Keynes, though Keynes himself never appeared in person.

The Circus was discussing the failure of Keynes's *Treatise*. Keynes had expected that book to become his magnum opus. In it he set out the theoretical work which he had done since the end of the First World War, about the causes of the economic cycle, and about how this cycle should be managed on a national basis and internationally. There is much modern macroeconomics in the *Treatise*, and the international macroeconomics is particularly good: it is possible to find elements of the Swan diagram, of the Fleming–Mundell model, and even of the Dornbusch model (see Vines, 2003). But the *Treatise* contains a fatal flaw. It aims to analyse the problem of the economic cycle, but the discussion rests upon a formal model in which the level of economic activity is exogenous. This mistaken model is nevertheless of interest because it contains the necessary clues about what Keynes needed to do next. In the *Treatise*, an increase in aggregate demand, caused – say – by an exogenous increase in investment, and not prevented by the central bank from having an overall effect on aggregate demand, would cause demand to increase relative to supply, which was assumed to be fixed, and so would cause a rise in the level of prices. This would redistribute income to profits, away from wages, because the level of the money wage is

'somewhat sticky' in the model. That would raise the overall level of savings, because the propensity to save is assumed to be higher for capitalists than for workers. A new equilibrium would be regained after the working out of a 'multiplier' process: one in which the price level rises by the amount necessary to re-equilibrate leakages (the extra savings) with injections (the increased investment). This all makes sense, except if the model is meant to help in a discussion of booms and slumps in *output*, which it cannot do because output is exogenous. Sorting out this mess required Keynes to write the *General Theory of Employment, Interest and Money*, which took him until 1936.

By the time Meade arrived in Cambridge in October, Kahn had already drafted his famous article on the 'multiplier' (Kahn, 1931). In this piece Kahn showed that, if output is endogenous, one can sum an infinite geometric series to show that the overall effect on output of an increase in investment is 'multiplied' because of the increases in consumption which happen as output increases. It appears that it was Meade, the young graduate student from Oxford, who showed how Kahn's multiplier analysis could be connected with Keynes's argument in the *Treatise*. There were two steps in this demonstration.

First, Meade showed, by summing the series of the effects of output on savings instead of the series of the effects of output on consumption, that movements in output would cause an increase in savings which would be equal to the original increase in investment. This idea, called 'Mr Meade's Relation' in Kahn's article, was written down in a note which was subsequently lost. It has become fundamental to our understanding of the multiplier process, and is explained in all basic macroeconomics textbooks. Meade (1993) explains the way in which his approach was complementary to that of Kahn. This approach was useful to the Circus, in that it showed how Kahn's multiplier process was a flex-output version of the fixed-output argument of the *Treatise* explained above.

Meade once described the second step of his demonstration to me as follows. 'I said the following to the other members of the Circus. "Haven't any of you read Marshall's *Principles of Economics*? In that book, in the short run, the economy lies on a short-run, upward-sloping, supply curve. But that curve adds an extra equation to the model. This means that – in comparison with the model in the *Treatise* – we can make *both* prices *and* output endogenous at the same time."' This second idea of Meade's is explained, with much less clarity, in Kahn's article. Once it was properly understood, it led the Circus to the view that it is primarily variations in the level of *output* which bring savings into line with investment, and so re-establish the conditions of macroeconomic equilibrium, rather than variations only in the level of *prices*, as had been supposed, unsatisfactorily, by Keynes in the *Treatise*. Kahn himself warmly acknowledged his debt to

Meade, both in his article of 1931 and in his fascinating account of the period published in 1984 and called *The Making of Keynes' General Theory* (Kahn, 1984).

Meade stated (Keynes, 1971–88, vol. 13, p. 342) that when he returned to Oxford in 1931 he took back with him in his head 'most of the essential ingredients of the subsequent system of the *General Theory*'. In his 'Simplified model of Mr. Keynes' system' (Meade, 1937) Meade set out these 'essential ingredients' in a system of eight equations, which included those of the IS–LM model. It is known that Hicks saw a draft of this paper before he prepared his own celebrated article explaining the IS–LM system (Hicks, 1937); indeed Hicks uses Meade's notation in his presentation (see Young, 1987). Meade's 'simplified model' is more general than that of Hicks, because it includes the upward-sloping supply curve discussed above. It therefore enables one to see *much* more of what is going on in the *General Theory*. But Meade's article is very difficult to understand, because it takes so much for granted. One can read it carefully without ever seeing the point that Hicks was concerned to make about the relationship between Keynes and the 'classics', and it was Hicks who invented the famous diagram to explain this point. This appears to be the first of a number of occasions during Meade's career on which he would set out a fully specified piece of economic theory, only to find that someone else would extract a simple, essential, idea from what Meade had written, publish it, and become famous as a consequence.

Meade taught in Oxford until 1937. During this period he synthesized with great clarity the ideas of the Keynesian Revolution in *An Introduction to Economic Analysis and Policy* (1936), published almost simultaneously with the *General Theory*. This was the first-ever economics textbook: until then books had been written as a means of expounding new ideas in economics. Many undergraduates in Cambridge at that time were confused by the turbulent debate concerning the Keynesian Revolution which swirled around them, and bemused by the associated misunderstandings, a number of which seemed to be deliberate. Subsequent oral tradition in Cambridge maintained that many of these people found Meade's book exceptionally helpful, since it cut straight through all of these difficulties.

Interestingly, the Keynesian model is expounded in Meade's book using an exogenous rate of interest. That is, Meade set out the 'Keynesian-cross' version of Keynes's model, rather than setting out the full IS–LM system. My own view of the reason for this is that Meade never really believed in the LM curve and so thought, like many of us now do, that the IS–LM system was a distraction. The reason that I say this is that in Meade (1937) he discusses the (realistic) possibility that banks might adjust the quantity of money, in the face of shocks to the economy, so as to keep the interest rate unchanged, unlike what happens in the IS–LM system (except in an extreme case). This view of his was in turn based on the analysis

in his first published article (Meade, 1934), in which he invented the money-multiplier – quite independently of the work in the United States begun by Phillips (1920) – and in which he carefully showed what banks would need to do in order to behave in this way. That Meade should have presented the Keynesian system in this way right back at the beginning, even although he fully understood the IS–LM system, has implications for understanding why – as discussed below – he proceeded the same way when he wrote *The Balance of Payments* in the late 1940s.

Economic Analysis and Policy also contains a discussion of longer-run growth, and presents an exposition of the Ramsey model of optimal growth. This was nearly ten years before Harrod and Domar invented what now looks like a very primitive version of growth theory, and long before the famous papers of Solow (1956) and Swan (1956), who invented a simplified version of the Ramsey model, in which the savings rate is *exogenous*. In two key pages, published 20 years before the papers by Swan and Solow, Meade explains how the optimal savings rate could be chosen *endogenously* in order to produce a welfare-maximizing growth process. These pages provide an astonishingly clear verbal exposition of the first order-conditions which must be satisfied if growth is to be optimal.

A second edition of *Economic Analysis and Policy* was published in 1937. This gave an exposition of the new ideas in imperfect competition, invented by Edwin Chamberlin and Joan Robinson, which were challenging Marshallian microeconomics in the 1930s (see Shackle, 1967). These ideas only really bore fruit in mainstream microeconomics, and in macroeconomics, in the 1970s and 1980s, after the rise of game theory. But they had a more or less immediate effect on Meade's work in macroeconomics, as I will show below.

Economic Analysis and Policy also includes a section on problems of international order and disorder, which shows that, already as a young man, Meade (unlike many in Britain and America at this time) was thinking about the macroeconomic problems of the world, as distinct from those of an individual nation. In this part of the book, Meade expands on the ideas on international macroeconomics, which were already to be found in Keynes's *Treatise*, as I have described above. (Notably, Joan Robinson, 1937, and Roy Harrod, 1933, were also busy doing the same thing.) Meade's volume ends with a prescient chapter on the economic causes of war. It is chilling to re-read this chapter, written three or four years before the outbreak of the Second World War. One also realizes that many of the problems connected with internationally ill-coordinated macroeconomic policies, which emerged in the world economy in the 1980s, and which have re-emerged at the beginning of the new millennium, are very like those which Meade wrote about nearly 75 years ago.

Throughout his time at Oxford, Meade was actively involved with the group of Fabian socialist intellectuals who were helping the British Labour Party to recover its sense of purpose, after the disastrous collapse of the Labour Government in 1931. Meade contributed to discussions across the same wide range of macroeconomic, microeconomic and international issues that he had treated in *Economic Analysis and Policy*, and he was most influential in his advocacy of expansionary Keynesian policies (Durbin, 1985, see especially pp. 136–44, 194–8, 211–12 and 220).

Meade elaborated on this last theme in *Consumers' Credits and Unemployment* (1938). In this work, he proposes Keynesian demand management in the form of *automatic*, countercyclical variations in taxation to stabilize macroeconomic fluctuations. This book foreshadows both the Full Employment White Paper of 1944, and the nominal-income targeting project on which he worked for ten years from 1978, both of which are discussed in more detail below. *Consumers' Credits and Unemployment* is perhaps the earliest official published advocacy of fine-tuned Keynesian policies.

In 1937 Meade went with his wife and young family to Geneva, where he was to stay for three years, as an economist for the League of Nations. Meade often spoke with admiration of the remarkable band that were assembled there, which included Tinbergen, Koopmans, Haberler, Nurkse, and Marcus Fleming. His job was to prepare, more or less single-handed, the *World Economic Survey* (the forerunner of the present IMF *World Economic Outlook*) and he transformed this publication. Keynes was much influenced by Meade's work in Geneva. In the *General Theory*, Keynes had made use of an upward-sloping short-run supply curve, as described above in my account of the discussions of the Circus, which relies on goods being produced in a manner subject to diminishing returns, and being supplied under competitive conditions. Keynes's important article of 1939 makes extensive reference to Meade's work, and then goes on to argue that the quantity produced in an economy is determined by demand, even if there are constant marginal costs. But this was inconsistent with the competitive analysis that Keynes had utilized in the *General Theory*, which requires the assumption of increasing marginal costs. This article by Keynes was exceptionally difficult to understand. It was extensively discussed in Cambridge in the 1970s, when people were comparing Keynes's macroeconomics with that of Kalecki, who had carefully evaded this difficulty by assuming 'markup' pricing. The confusion was resolved only by the arrival of the classic Dixit and Stiglitz (1977) paper. That paper brought Chamberlin's ideas about imperfect competition into macroeconomics, suggesting a setup in which each individual profit-maximizing producer faces a downward-sloping demand curve and sets prices above marginal costs, but in which the existence of free entry prevents the emergence of monopoly profits. I know, from working with Meade from the late 1970s onwards, that the standard macroeconomic model which he used

daily, as part of his mental equipment, had this feature, and I believe that, unlike many others, this had been true for him since the mid-1930s, when he wrote the material on imperfect competition in *Economic Analysis and Policy*, which I described above. It is probable that this framework influenced his empirical work in Geneva, and thus influenced Keynes's article of 1939.

The war finally caused the Meades to leave Geneva for London in 1940, with three young children, the smallest a three-week old infant. They set out in a small car for one of the Channel ports, not knowing that at this very time the Germans had broken through at Sedan. After an increasingly desperate journey the family ended up in Nantes as refugees, and finally crossed the Channel in an RAF 'transport ship' – a converted tramp steamer – at the very time of the Dunkirk evacuation.

2 The war years, 1940–45: building the post-war world order

On his return to Britain, Meade was brought into the Economic Section of the Cabinet Office. There was a grim feeling of impotence amongst the economists, who wished to do something for the war effort. Keynes's *How to Pay for the War* (Keynes, 1940) had just been published. Meade therefore set to work on a set of national accounts, so that, at the very least, those making war policy might be able to attach some numbers to Keynes's ideas. Richard Stone who had only recently graduated in economics from Gonville and Caius College, Cambridge, was brought in to help with this work. Together they produced what is probably the first full logical structure of 'double-entry' national accounts (Meade and Stone, 1941; 1944). Meade recalled how in the statistical work he quickly became Stone's research assistant – and so began Stone's work on national income accounting that eventually led to another Nobel Prize.

During his subsequent time at the Economic Section, Meade worked in three crucial areas. He was to become Director of the Economic Section from 1945 to 1947.

First, Meade was involved in the planning for post-war international monetary arrangements. He participated in the initial excited responses in Whitehall to Keynes's 'Clearing Union' plan for a new post-war international monetary system (Keynes, 1971–88, vol. 25, pp. 41–67; see also van Dormael, 1978). He became a member of the British delegation to Washington in September 1943 which discussed these issues with Harry Dexter White and others (Keynes, 1971–88, vol. 25, pp. 338 ff.). And he took part in the subsequent British deliberations, leading up to the Bretton Woods conference in 1944 at which the International Monetary Fund was established.

I have described the analytical content of these negotiations in some detail in Vines (2003), drawing on the wonderful historical account by Skidelsky (2000), and on the papers of Keynes and Meade. Keynes's policy objectives were to create a post-war global system in which full-employment policies could be adopted by the Allied nations, and in which such full-employment policies could be reconciled with the requirement that their trade balances not get too far out of line. Keynes's initial response to this problem was a highly illiberal one: balance-of-payments restrictions should be the mechanism which re-equilibrated exports with imports after any negative external shock to a country (through tariffs, quotas, and 'managed' trade). He was persuaded away from this view by an 'outstandingly able group of economists' (Williamson, 1983a, p. 91) which included Meade and also Marcus Fleming, Roy Harrod, Lionel Robbins, and Dennis Robertson. This group managed to convince Keynes that exchange rate devaluation should be the adjustment device. Keynes vacillated literally for years on the issue, deliberately suspending judgement, drawing forth from this talented group an extraordinary collection of papers, particularly on the tariffs-versus-devaluation issue (Keynes, 1971–88, vol. 26, ch. 2 and pp. 239–327). James Meade once told me that, one day in a particularly tedious meeting at the Board of Trade in 1944, Keynes scribbled a note to him to the effect that he (Keynes) was, at last, intellectually converted to a regime in which external adjustment would be achieved by exchange-rate change.

Second, when Keynes produced his Clearing Union plan, Meade quickly produced a project for a 'Commercial Union' as a companion piece. It was on the basis of this document that the debate in Whitehall on post-war commercial policy (concerning such sensitive issues as imperial preference and the use of import restrictions on balance-of-payments grounds) took place. Meade devoted much time to drafting and redrafting these ideas and, as he said, 'helping to get them through Whitehall'. And it was to promote these ideas that he was a member of the September 1943 delegation to Washington (mentioned above), and he was subsequently a member of the British delegation to the international conferences in London in 1946 and in Geneva in 1947 which worked on a charter for a proposed International Trade Organization (ITO). Although in the end the ITO proved to be unacceptable to the United States, the Geneva conference resulted in a General Agreement on Tariffs and Trade (GATT) which took on many of the projected functions of the ITO (see Keynes, 1971–88, vol. 26, ch. 2). And the GATT was eventually turned into the World Trade Organization (WTO) in 1994.

These international discussions laid down, amongst other things, the conditions under which nations should be permitted to form regional free-trade-areas, in which discriminatory regional preference is allowed to overrule the most-favoured-nation rule for international trade which lies at the centre of the WTO, and which lay at the centre of the GATT. Those discussions duly led to Article 24 of the GATT (and to a similar provisions in the international agreements which underpin the WTO). The technical discussions on this Article were particularly

difficult, since the relevant theory by Viner and Meade, on 'trade creation' and 'trade diversion', had not yet been invented. (This theory is discussed in Section 3 below.) The discussions also contained much which was non-technical, which dealt more fundamentally with the nature of the international trading system. On one occasion, Meade told me, he could not understand why a senior US official – I believe that it was Dean Acheson – was speaking up so strongly against imperial preference, and yet so much in favour of Britain joining up with European nations, a joining-up which has, in due course, led to the European Common Market, and ultimately to the creation of the European Union. 'I have relatives who are farmers in New Zealand', said Meade, 'who sell their lamb to Britain. They a natural part of the British economic system. Why should we not have an Imperial Free Trade Area which includes them? This would be just like your setup in the US, in which you have a free trade area which includes all 50 of your states?'. 'But there is a lot of water between Britain and New Zealand', replied Acheson. 'There is also quite a lot of water between Britain and France', replied Meade.

If we take these two activities together, it is clear that Meade was one of the architects, on both the monetary side and the trade side, of the liberal world economic regime which sustained the long post-war boom in the Western world from 1945 to 1973. Meade always believed that *both* pieces of this regime stand or fall together. Free trade would – he thought – be resisted if there were severe global macroeconomic imbalances. (This point became clear once again in the mid-1980s, and it is becoming even more clear in the mid-2000s. But conversely, if there is not free trade then macroeconomic order will be difficult to maintain, since devaluation will tend to be much less effective at adjusting trade imbalances. Meade summarized this point clearly, in a diary entry which he made on 31 December 1944 (Meade, 1988–90, vol. 4, p. 22.) He emphasized 'the need for flexible exchange rates to adjust balance of payments [to avoid pushing the burden of adjustment onto] rigid trade controls … in a world in which internal wage levels were not easily reduced. [But such adjustment might be] more easily acceptable if it was preceded by an international agreement to lower trade barriers, since in that case smaller movements in exchange rates would be required'. This belief – that macro management and micro liberalism should go together – had already informed his work in the 1930s. It would form the central organizing principle for the work that Meade did at the LSE on international economics, which I discuss immediately below. As noted in the introduction and conclusion to this article, it recurs again and again throughout his work.

At the meeting at the Board of Trade in 1944, to which I referred above, Keynes followed up his scribble with a sketch, on the back of an envelope, of the desired features of the whole international system that he and his colleagues were trying to build (see Vines, 2003). This sketch went something like the following.

Objective	Instrument (s)	Responsible authority
Full employment	Demand management (mainly fiscal)	National governments
Balance of payments adjustment	Pegged but adjustable exchange rates	International Monetary Fund
Promotion of international trade	Tariff reductions etc.	International Trade Organisation
Economic development	Official international lending	World Bank

Keynes was aware that this plan would need to work, not just for individual countries, but for the global system as a whole. (It would have been surprising if someone who had invented macroeconomics did not take such an overall, systemic view.) I discuss in some detail in Vines (2003) how Keynes feared that difficulties in the balance-of-payments adjustment process might impose, on deficit countries, an obligation to deflate demand below full employment, something which might not be matched by symmetrical over-expansion by surplus countries, and might thereby create pressures towards global deflation. I also describe how Keynes differed in this view from Harry Dexter White, his US counterpart in the Washington negotiations, who feared an outcome in which the International Monetary Fund would be so expansive with liquidity that there would be a great post-war inflation, worldwide. In that article I claim that, during these discussions, Keynes' negotiating strategy in pursuit of a balanced global outcome was underpinned by a significant theoretical understanding of what was going on. In particular I maintain that (*a*) Keynes took from his *Treatise* something akin to an IS–LM–BP model (without the flaw in the analysis of the *Treatise*, which had been fixed up by the invention of the multiplier and the publication of the *General Theory*), and (*b*) Keynes, as he negotiated, was using something akin to a two-country version of that model to understand what was being discussed. These two claims of mine are vital for a proper understanding of the work that Meade did at the LSE on international economics, which I discuss below.

I will be brief about Meade's third activity while he was in the Economic Section during the war, although it was important. Meade's paper 'Internal Measures for the Prevention of General Unemployment', dated 8 July 1941, reached the Intern-Departmental Committee

on Post-War Internal Economic Problems in November, and as Skidelsky (2000, p. 270) says 'never quite lost its place as front-runner in the development of post-war employment policy'. This was, in effect, the first draft of what finally became the Full Employment White Paper, published as an official paper with the title of *Employment Policy* (Minister of Reconstruction, 1944), which laid the basis for a transformed macroeconomic management within the United Kingdom after the war. In the drafting of this document, there were long discussions between Meade and Keynes on the possibility and desirability of automatic fiscal fine-tuning (see Keynes, 1971–88, vol. 27, pp. 207–19 and 308–79; Wilson, 1982). Meade advocated countercyclical variations in social security contributions; this proposal featured in the final White Paper and was endorsed by Keynes. That idea would remain more or less an article of faith for Meade, and underpinned his work in inflation targeting which I describe in Section 5.

3 The LSE, 1947–58: international economics

Meade became Professor of Commerce (with special reference to international trade) at the LSE in 1947, where he was to stay for ten years, and where his great work on international economics was done.

It had been Meade's intention to begin his time back at a university by rewriting his textbook *Economic Analysis and Policy*. But this was not to happen. Someone once observed to me how different the teaching of our subject might have been if Meade had actually rewritten his book, rather than leaving the field open for Samuelson's great *Principles* book (Samuelson, 1948), which was not published until 12 years after Meade's book had first appeared. In his Nobel Prize autobiography Meade (1977a) explained why this did not happen.

> I realised that it might be necessary to [rewrite the book] in more than one volume. So, as I was appointed at the LSE to teach international economics, I started on *The Theory of International Economic Policy*. It grew into my two books, *The Balance of Payments*, and *Trade and Welfare*, with their two mathematical appendices....These books took up practically the whole of my ten years at the LSE; but even so they did not cover the whole of the international problem.... My original project was over-ambitious; but the part which I did manage to cover was sufficient, eventually, to gain for me the Nobel award. (Meade, 1977a.)

It is characteristic of Meade's modesty that he should describe the work for which he received the Nobel Prize as an attempt to rewrite a textbook.

The balance of payments

In his introduction the *The Balance of Payments* (Meade, 1951–5), he had, equally modestly, described it as a book which 'does not claim to make any significant contribution of original work in the fundamentals of pure economic analysis' (p. vii). This is something which turns out not to be true.

Meade also said of his book that it is one which has an 'indebtedness to the ideas of Lord Keynes [which] is too obvious to need any emphasis' (p. ix). Many people have said to me that they think that this remark is there because the book contains lots of 'multiplier Keynesianism', of a kind derived from the *General Theory*, which was still new and exciting in the 1950s. If that reading is correct, the generous acknowledgement of Keynes's contributions would not be particularly significant. But I believe the remark meant something rather different and rather more interesting. On more than one occasion Meade said to me that all he had done in this book was to write down what he learned from his work with Keynes during the war, about how to understand the international position of the British economy, and about how the world economy should be managed. That is a much more thought-provoking connection to acknowledge. (He did also admit that he had added quite a lot of algebra in the appendix.)

Volume I of the *Theory of International Economic Policy* (Meade, 1951–5) was entitled *The Balance of Payments*. There were three new features of this book. First, at the level of technical analysis, it integrated income effects and price effects so as to study the balance of payments in a general-equilibrium framework. In doing so, it extended the theory of the balance of payments beyond its traditional identification with the current account to so as to consider the overall balance by including international capital movements. Second, it had a policy orientation, focusing on two instruments (exchange rate adjustment and domestic demand management) and two targets (internal balance – that is, full employment – and external balance – that is, a satisfactory overall balance of payments position). Third, Meade carried out his tasks in this book using a two-country model rather than merely developing the analysis for a single open economy.

At the level of technical analysis, investigations of the effects of exchange rate change had previously been separated from investigations of Keynesian income–expenditure theory. The former was normally based on the assumption of constant incomes, and carried out in terms of Marshallian partial equilibrium concepts, using the elasticities approach. (For a few key exceptions, see Robinson, 1937; Harrod, 1933; Laursen and Metzler, 1950; and Harberger 1950.) The latter was normally carried out using fixprice models, which led to the 'absorption' approach to the balance of payments, published by Alexander in the same year as Meade's book (Alexander, 1952). The formal integration of the elasticities approach and the absorption approach to balance-of-payments theory, which Meade achieved, was very important.

At the level of the theory of economic policy, Meade's basic idea – that, if internal and external balance are to be attained simultaneously, then two policy instruments are needed (exchange rate adjustment and the management of domestic demand) – was not a new one to him. He would have been familiar with this idea from his work with Keynes at the beginning of the war on Keynes' book *How to Pay for the War*, and also from his work with Keynes on Britain's financial crisis at the end of the war. (See Vines, 2003, for a detailed discussion of this claim.) Furthermore, as noted at the beginning of this article, many of the necessary components of this idea are already to be found in the *Treatise*, published more than 20 years earlier; and many of them are also to be found in *Economic Analysis and Policy*, published 15 years earlier, and in the work of Robinson and Harrod referred to above.

Indeed, this idea now seems deeply obvious to all of us. But that is only because we know the Swan diagram, which collapses all of the complex analysis by Meade into just one diagram (Swan, 1963), just like Hicks had done with the IS–LM system. At the time, Meade's idea was absolutely revolutionary. In reminding ourselves of this fact, we should not forget that Tinbergen was awarded the Nobel Prize in 1969 for stating a more general, but equally obvious, idea – that to achieve *n* targets simultaneously one (normally) needs *n* instruments. (Tinbergen's analysis was developed simultaneously to, and independently of, Meade's book.) And it took a *very* long time for Meade's idea to be learned. For many years after the Second World War in the UK, full employment policies appear to have been carried out without sufficient regard for their effects on the balance of payments, and they often needed to be reversed at times of balance-of-payments crisis. Also, to take another example, many policymakers still continue to forget that if a devaluation is to improve a current-account deficit then it must be accompanied by a reduction in domestic absorption relative to domestic output, so as to release the resources needed to improve the trade account.

All of what I have said so far is about open-economy macroeconomics. We should also notice the third important feature of Meade's book which I have mentioned above – that it develops everything for a two-country world, and discusses *global* macroeconomics, not just *open-economy* macroeconomics. You might think that this would be the obvious way to proceed. After all, any treatment of *trade* theory is normally done this way, by analysing trade in a two-country world, and this is what Meade himself would do in Volume II of the *Theory of International Economic Policy*, published a few years later. Furthermore, all of us have now lived through the 1980s, in which we studied the effects of Reaganomics on Europe, something which clearly required a *two*-country model. (We are all at present trying to understand the interrelationships between the United States, East Asia and Europe, which seems to need a *three*-country model.) But nobody had ever done global macroeconomics before Meade wrote his book. As I note in

Vines (2003), even Keynes, when writing down of the key components of the necessary theory in the *Treatise* in 1930, wrote about nearly everything for a single open economy rather than for a global system. But in Vines (2003) I also develop the argument, described at the end of Section 2 above, that Keynes worked out, informally, aspects of the needed two-country model when he was negotiating with Harry Dexter White about the establishment of the IMF. It is my belief that Meade had seen, when working on these negotiations with Keynes, that such a model was necessary for a systemic discussion of global, policy-related, questions. This is my view of why he set out his analysis in this way, even although doing this made his book *much* harder to read.

Harry Johnson made two important criticisms of Meade's book at the level of technical analysis. The first, developed in Johnson's long review of the book (Johnson, 1951), concerned the treatment of saving in the model. Meade assumes that the amount of real saving coming from a given real income is independent of the terms of trade. Laursen and Metzler (1950) and Harberger (1950) had already shown how to avoid this mistake; many practitioners of open economy macroeconomics still forget how hard it is to defend what Meade assumes.

Johnson's second criticism, made in the paper which Johnson published at the time the Meade received the Nobel Prize (Johnson, 1978), leads in a valuable direction. What Johnson said was that Meade did not succeed in fully integrating real and monetary theory in his book. What he meant by this is that Meade assumed a flexible money supply policy designed to maintain a given exogenous rate of interest, with monetary policy changes being expressed in terms of (exogenous) interest rate changes. In the IS–LM–BP model subsequently developed by Fleming (1962) and Mundell (1962), the interest rate instead becomes endogenous, so as to ensure that the economy lies on a given LM curve. Under fixed exchange rates, the LM curve moves around because of the endogeneity of the money supply, unless monetary sterilization is possible, in a way which was analysed in the monetary theory of the balance of payments (which led to fame for Harry Johnson). Under floating exchange rates the money supply is held constant, and the interest rate and the exchange rate together become jointly endogenous, along with output. It seems odd that Meade did not think to make the interest rate endogenous by introducing an LM curve into his model, since this is exactly what he had done, more than 15 years earlier, when he had explained Keynes's *General Theory* to the world. Had Meade done this, surely he would have instantly invented the Fleming–Mundell model. My suggestion of the reason why that didn't happen is related to my view, stated earlier, that Meade never really believed in the LM curve. In his subsequent work, which I discuss below, work that was contemporaneous with that of John Taylor, Meade allowed for the endogeneity of the interest rate without having to make the ridiculous assumption

of a fixed money supply – essentially by supposing that the interest rate would follow something like a Taylor rule. One can easily build a Fleming–Mundell-like model with a Taylor rule in it, instead of an LM curve. I believe that, although Meade did not like the way that the interest rate was made endogenous in the LM curve, at the time he was writing *The Balance of Payments* he could not yet see how to replace the LM curve by a policy–behaviour relationship like the Taylor rule. This is why, I think, it was not possible for him to take the next step and construct something akin to the Fleming–Mundell model.

Trade and welfare

The second volume of the *Theory of International Economic Policy* was titled *Trade and Welfare*. In this, Meade presented a systematic analysis of neoclassical trade theory, essentially the theory of Heckscher and Ohlin, with the latter of whom he shared the Nobel Prize. But he combined this with an analysis of trade in factors – both capital and labour. He discusses policy in this book – the issue of protection versus free trade – but in relation to the movement of *both* goods and factors of production. Meade's inclusion of international factor movements, in the main corpus of his theory of international trade, was innovative, and chimed with growing concerns, at the time, and since, about the 'brain drain', foreign direct investment, and the multinational corporation. Surprisingly, very few expositors of trade theory have followed Meade in explaining trade theory in this way, so that these subjects are more normally studied in isolation. Perhaps, again, it is because Meade's integrated analysis makes for such difficult reading.

The book made a number of important innovations at the level of technical analysis, whose influence in economic theory went far beyond the study of international phenomena.

First, Meade introduced a new method for measuring small changes in welfare, which was a generalization of Marshallian consumer surplus, with its attendant limitations. And he then went on to present a whole new approach to welfare economics, defining overall welfare as an appropriately weighted sum of individual welfares. Johnson (1978) describes it as a brilliant feat of imagination for Meade to see that he could take over this approach from Fleming (1951) and then rework it into a powerful general technique for welfare analysis of practical policy problems. Doing this enabled Meade to escape from the nihilism of the new welfare economics, which worked in terms of 'potential welfare' and the 'compensation principles', but which made it difficult to say anything practical at all about the welfare effects of economic policy changes. Nearly all of us now do welfare economics in the manner pioneered by Meade.

Second, Meade invented the theory of domestic distortions in order to show that a move towards free trade may not be welfare-improving if there are already distortions elsewhere in the economy. This idea was later carried forward by Bhagwati and Ramaswami (1963) and Johnson (1965). Meade invented the theory of the second best in his discussion of these ideas (inventing the technical term 'second best' as he did so), and explored many of its implications. As Corden (1996a) says, it is hard to see how something which now seems so obvious needed to be invented. Jacob Viner, in a book on customs unions (Viner, 1950), had already established the distinction between trade creation and trade diversion in the creation of free trade areas. This also seems totally obvious to us now, but it really only became obvious after Meade published the *Theory of Customs Unions* (1955b), which clarified and extended Viner's distinction, and located it within his general theory of the second best.

Finally, it is important to add that the *Trade and Economic Welfare* includes a discussion of the meaning of optimum population and of optimum savings and of the relationship between these two concepts. This discussion, too, broke new ground.

Phillips

While at the LSE, Meade also did something else which was stunningly important: he brought Bill Phillips into economics. Meade once said to me that Phillips was the closest to genius of anyone that he had ever known. Phillips's really important work in economics was on the use of control theory for macroeconomic stabilization purposes, rather than in estimating the 'Phillips curve' (for which he is so famous, but which he did in a rush in a few weeks, just before leaving London go on sabbatical leave).

Phillips had trained before the war as an electrical engineer (having previously left school without any formal qualifications), and immediately after the war he had graduated from the LSE with a third-class honours degree in sociology. One day, soon after receiving this unremarkable qualification, Phillips explained to Meade that he wished to build a strange 'water-machine' model of a macroeconomic system. Meade listened patiently because 'the pipes seemed to have the right labels', and so encouraged Phillips to build the machine, offering Phillips the inducement that he could demonstrate it at Lionel Robbins's prestigious seminar for graduate students. The machine was duly built, and it is described in Phillips (1950). A brilliant performance followed at the Robbins seminar, in front of most of the London economics professoriat, who had got word of what was coming. In the course of that seminar, said Meade, Phillips gave the best exposition that anyone present had ever heard of the Keynes-versus-Robertson debate, about whether the rate of interest was determined by liquidity preference or by the supply of, and demand for, loanable funds. This, said Phillips, was an argument about stocks versus flows; he then illustrated his claim by displaying the effects of water sitting in tanks, on the one hand, and water flowing through pipes, on the other. Phillips was

duly instructed to write up his machine in a Ph.D. thesis, and John Hicks, who was by then Drummond Professor of Political Economy in Oxford, was asked to examine the thesis so as to ensure that somebody with a third-class degree in sociology could be given a Ph.D. in economics with a clear conscience. Phillips was then promptly brought on to the staff, and became one of the professors in the department within a few years. In Vines (1996) I give a detailed account of how the Phillips machine works. In particular I describe the stock–flow intuition which it provides, which is almost impossible to obtain any other way than by looking at this machine in action, and which certainly cannot be obtained from modern computer simulation models. As I describe below, Meade was closely involved with the use of the machine.

Work on his machine led Phillips to write his classic article on the use of control theory to help stabilize an economy (Phillips, 1954). This paper argued that a feedback policy can have destabilizing effects if the instrument of policy responds too strongly to a disturbance to the target of policy, and there is a lag in the effect of the instrument on the target. In a subsequent paper, Phillips concluded on a cautious note: 'the problem of economic stabilisation is, even in principle, a very intricate one, and … a much more thorough investigation of both theoretical principles and empirical relationships would be needed before detailed policy recommendations could be justified' (Phillips, 1957, p. 275). Meade was involved with the preparation of both of these papers, and he agreed with their conclusions.

Milton Friedman came to hold similar views on the potentially destabilizing effects of macroeconomic policy, at a very similar time (Friedman, 1953). He went on to declare that active macroeconomic policymaking is too difficult to do properly and, worse still, too dangerous. Friedman's response to this problem was to set off in pursuit of his holy grail: a non-interventionist macroeconomic policy.

Meade's and Phillips's response to this problem was rather different. Phillips thought that it would be possible to do good macroeconomic policy, but only if the policy was carefully designed. Indeed he ended his 1957 paper on an optimistic note. He called for the use of multivariable control methods, to regulate multiple objectives in an economy in the face of multiple disturbances, and he noted that methods for doing this were just, in the late 1950s, becoming available. He also called for the econometric estimation of the parameters of the econometric model which would be necessary for the study of such regulation. Meade said to me on more than one occasion that he regarded his own last big project, carried out more than 20 years later, and described in Section 5 below, as a response to Phillips's call to action.

Other activities

At the LSE Meade acquired a further generation of very able young disciples, drawn from many countries, who included Max Corden, Richard Lipsey, Robert Mundell and Harry Johnson, the last of these 'at one remove' (Johnson, 1978, p. 66). Meade had persuaded Phillips to build two of his water machines, joined together by an ingenious model of a foreign-exchange market. Peter Kenen (now retired from Princeton) vividly remembers a graduate student seminar in which he was asked to run fiscal and monetary policy for the United States on one of these machines. At the same time on the other machine Richard Cooper (now retired from Harvard) was required to run fiscal and monetary policy for Europe. They made the world develop unstable cycles – and spilt a lot of water (Vines, 1996). By such means did that generation of students learn about the need for an international coordination of macroeconomic policies, 25 years before the subject became fashionable.

During this time Meade also went on sabbatical leave to Australia. With Eric Russell of Adelaide he wrote a short theoretical analysis of the effects of the Korean War boom on the Australian economy, via its effects in raising the world price of wool, which was – at that time – a major export commodity for Australia (Meade and Russell, 1957). This article is one of the most profound pieces ever written about that economy. (Harcourt, 1982, ch. 21, describes how it came to be written: Meade became the expositor of Russell's perceptions, which then existed only in note form.) The authors first explain the 'Stolper–Samuelson' theorem concerning the effects of protection on income distribution. Their exposition is different from the one given by Stolper and Samuelson, and much more like that to be found in the original source of that theorem – the Brigden Report of 1929 on the Australia tariff (Brigden et al., 1929). This is because it discusses the effects of protection on income distribution in an Australian 'dependent-economy' model, in which there are non-traded goods as well as traded goods. (See Vines, 1994.) Meade and Russell then use this model to examine what has subsequently become called the 'Dutch Disease'. They show how an export boom can, by raising wages, give rise to cost pressures for the protected sector, which can cause it to contract, even at a time of general boom. Their paper directly influenced the subsequent discussion of this problem, first in Australia in the 1970s (see Gregory, 1976), and then worldwide in the 1980s (see Corden, 1984). This 'problem' has returned in a big way in the early 21st century, with the high prices of primary commodities, worldwide.

4 Cambridge, 1957–69: growth theory

Meade became Professor of Political Economy at Cambridge in 1957, when he succeeded his teacher, Dennis Robertson. When Meade moved to Cambridge, growth theory was in the air. His useful book, *A Neo-Classical Theory of Economic Growth* (1961b), 'brings the subject within the range of the undergraduate student, covers a number of aspects (such as the presence of the fixed factor land) usually omitted in more high powered mathematical treatments, and presents in detail the mathematics of a two-sector growth model' (Johnson, 1978, p. 79). He also made advanced contributions to growth theory (1965, with Frank Hahn, and 1966). But his lasting contribution in this area is his essay *Efficiency, Equality, and the Ownership of Property* (1964). This 'provides a very suggestive account of the forces underlying the accumulation of capital and the relationship between earned and unearned income' and 'stimulated much of the revival of interest in this subject, at least in the United Kingdom' (Corden and Atkinson, 1979, p. 530). Meade regarded this as, in many ways, his best book, because it puts together into a single synoptic framework his views on economic growth, on the microeconomic role of the price mechanism, on the size and the genetic composition of the population, and on the distributional implications of property ownership. He analysed further the interplay of these last factors in his Keynes Lecture on 'The Inheritance of Inequalities: Some Biological, Demographic, Social, and Economic Factors' (Meade, 1973c).

In 1960 Meade visited Mauritius and contributed to a report to the Governor, applying for the first time his ideas on growth theory and on population policy to the problems of a less developed country (Meade 1961a). His prediction for Mauritius of Malthusian stagnation turned out to be spectacularly wrong, in interesting ways.

In 1973 Meade also began in Cambridge a grand scheme of work entitled *The Principles of Political Economy*. The purpose of this series of books was 'to bring the best of modern theory within the range of an intelligent and educated adult, the volumes being intended to tackle successively departures from the assumptions of a model of perfect static general equilibrium' (Johnson, 1978, p. 79).

5 Retirement, 1969–95

In 1969 Meade took early retirement, five years before the statutory retiring age. As Atkinson and Weale (2000) say, '[a]lways the most gentle and courteous of men, he had found extremely depressing the quarrels between those labelled "post Keynesian" and those in the Faculty who researched the mainstream of Economics'. But he did not stop working; indeed the next quarter century was to be one of his most productive.

Meade initially worked on the *Principles of Political Economy* but subsequently, perhaps sensing that this enterprise did not provide the best outlet for his unflagging energy, he turned to other schemes. The *Intelligent Radical's Guide to Economic Policy* (1975a) had 'wide influence in Britain, particularly on debates about economic planning' (Corden, and Atkinson, 1979, p. 530). In it Meade returned to a theme set forth in his *Planning and the Price Mechanism* (1948a) which I summarize in my concluding section below.

An expenditure tax

Meade's first big activity in retirement was to chair a committee which was established by the Institute of Fiscal Studies, to look into the structure of the UK tax system and to advise on how it might be simplified. The report, entitled *The Structure and Reform of Direct Taxation* (1978a), is a monumental study of British personal taxation. As Atkinson and Weale (2000) say,

> The Committee observed that the tax system at the time was a mixture of taxes on income and taxes on expenditure, and concluded that it should be more desirable that tax should be levied on one or the other, all but one of the Committee favouring a shift towards an expenditure tax. In the 20 years since the report was written, exemptions for saving have appeared in the form of TESSAs, PEPs and ISAs, and the shift to indirect taxation has been a move towards a tax on expenditure. In this respect, the Report was influential, but its lasting value lies in the outstandingly high quality of the analysis.

Meade was fortunate in having as assistants for that committee three additional able young scholars, John Flemming, John Kay and Mervyn King, who all subsequently achieved distinction in various aspects of public life.

A return to the theory of macroeconomic policy

In 1977 Meade returned to the great questions of national macroeconomic management, at the age of 70, when most people might have felt ready for a holiday. His work began with his Nobel Prize lecture entitled 'The Meaning of Internal Balance' (Meade, 1978b). It has been explained above how, in the *Balance of Payments* (1951) – one of the volumes for which Meade received the prize – he talked about the problems of reconciling internal balance (full employment) with external balance (a satisfactory overall balance of payments position). In his Nobel Prize lecture, Meade returned to question this framework, arguing that the concept of 'internal balance can now no longer be taken merely to refer to the achievement of full employment, but must also make reference to the achievement of low and stable inflation' (Meade, 1978b). He argued that it is not sufficient to rely on incomes policy, of the conventional kind which was still fashionable in Britain. The fundamental problem is that a commitment to 'full employment' removes the threat of unemployment as a response to over-rapid wage increases, and it is on this threat which wage and price stability in part depends. As a result, Meade argued that Keynesian policies should be 'stood on their head'. Demand management policy should be responsible for the maintenance of a slow and restrained rate of growth of money incomes, so as to put a 'lid' upon inflationary pressures. Incomes policy, or, more generally, the 'reform of wage-fixing', should

be used – he argued – not to hold down prices but to promote employment.

This lecture contained three striking claims.

First, Meade's assertion that demand management would, inevitably, be excessively expansionary and would thereby promote inflation was essentially the same claim as that made the following year by Kydland and Prescott (1978) – a claim which went on to help them, too, to win the Nobel Prize. Meade's claim was made five years before the macroeconomic implications of the Kydland and Prescott idea were properly worked out by Barro and Gordon (1983).

Second, Meade's claim that macroeconomic policy should be confined to 'putting a lid on inflation' implied that employment would no longer be determined by a macroeconomic policy which was promoting full employment. As a result the levels of employment and of unemployment would be determined in some other way. At any point in time, said Meade, the 'reform of wage fixing' could be taken as given, and that would determine what we would now call the non-accelerating inflation rate of unemployment, or NAIRU. Meade then said that unemployment would gravitate towards the NAIRU, using the following argument. If unemployment was lower than the NAIRU, then inflation would be rising. But if the rate of growth of money incomes was effectively controlled by policy, then this would mean that policy would need to ensure that output fell, so as to prevent the growth of money incomes from rising above target. That would cause unemployment to rise towards the NAIRU, which would – in turn – stop inflation from rising. Meade used a similar argument to describe what would happen if unemployment was above the NAIRU. This line of reasoning effectively made Meade a follower of Friedman, who had claimed, in his fundamental paper published ten years earlier, that macroeconomic policy could not itself control the level of unemployment (Friedman, 1968). Friedman's idea had been publicly broadcast in Great Britain, by Prime Minister Callaghan, in a famous speech given two years before Meade's lecture. But at the time this idea was too revolutionary for most macroeconomists in Britain. It was still widely thought that only monetarists believed something like this; Bob Rowthorn had caused uproar amongst the Cambridge Keynesians by claiming something of this kind just a year before Meade gave his lecture (Rowthorn, 1977). Meade's lecture had the effect of detaching such a claim from its monetarist proponents, and began the process of making this claim mainstream in Britain, something which was eventually achieved by Layard, Nickell and Jackman (1991).

Third, Meade discussed how, exactly, demand management policy (that is, fiscal and monetary policy) should be used to achieve the required slow and restrained growth of money incomes. His answer was that this should be done mainly by fine-tuned changes in tax rates, which, as mentioned above, he had discussed in

Consumers' Credit and Employment (1938) and as he had suggested in his draft of the Full Employment White Paper in 1944. This answer made him very *unlike* Milton Friedman. In a subsequent mischievous talk to the Royal Economic Society, Meade (1981) created a taxonomy, so as to compare his new proposals with orthodox Keynesianism on the one hand and monetarism on the other. His mischief was to make the monetarists end up on the far left of his taxonomy, and to make the 'old-fashioned' Keynesians end up on the far right.

Meade presented a draft of this Nobel Prize lecture to the Marshall Society – Cambridge's student economics society. I was a research student in Cambridge at the time. As I recall, we did not know that Meade had just been awarded the Nobel Prize, or that what we were hearing was a dry run for his lecture in Stockholm. His lecture was a bit too un-Keynesian for me, and I stood up and said so. Meade defended his claims to the (large) audience, using the argument that policy works well when each policymaker is given an objective which he is likely to be able to achieve – and that macroeconomic policymakers would be able to achieve a nominal income target, but would not be able to achieve an excessively optimistic employment target. (This was, again, a very Barro–Gordon-like answer.) But I had, by that time, read the papers by Phillips referred to above. So I stood up again and – rather bravely – said that, although this might be true, I thought that if his system was set up as a set of differential equations it would probably be unstable.

This question was to set in train a large research programme in the Department of Applied Economics in Cambridge. I had never met Meade before this lecture, but within a week he had asked me to work with him, and he then gradually gathered a large team to work with us, which included Andy Blake, Nicos Christodoulakis, Martin Weale and Peter Westaway, and also brought the control engineer Jan Maciejowski into the group. The resulting activity led to four substantial books (Meade, 1982; Meade et al., 1983a; Meade, 1986a; and Meade et al., 1989) and also to a number of tracts and articles in both technical and popular journals. Two main strands emerged in this work; we can describe these as being about inflation targeting and about supply side reforms.

Inflation targeting

The second and fourth of the books just described set out Meade's proposed policy regime, in which there would be a target for nominal GDP, to be controlled primarily by means of changes in taxes. In Meade et al. (1983a) it was shown, using an estimated econometric model of the economy, that fine-tuned feedback rules for taxes really could be found which would keep nominal income close to a target path. The work used the multivariable control methods which Phillips (1957) had predicted would become available, which were supplied to the group by Jan Maciejowski.

This work culminated in Meade et al. (1989), called *Macroeconomic Policy: Inflation, Wealth and the Exchange Rate*. As a central part of the work for this book, Martin Weale oversaw the construction of an original empirical macroeconomic model, which developed the model being used at the National Institute of Economics Research in London at the time. It contained a number of rational-expectations features, which, at that time, were highly innovative. In particular, the model investment was driven by Tobin's q (that is, by the value of the stock market), which, following earlier work by Blanchard, was forward-looking, and which jumped in response to the expected future level of the interest rate (in exactly the same way as the exchange rate jumps in the Dornbusch model). And the model contained a forward-looking consumption function, with consumption partly depending on expected future income and thus on the expected future level of taxes. This is by now all rather familiar, but was ground-breaking at the time, although some of the underlying ideas had already been explained by Meade himself, nearly 20 years earlier, in *The Growing Economy* (Meade, 1968).

Meade's policies were tried out on this model, using taxes as the policy instrument (and also the interest rate, for reasons explained below). This required the application of feedback control to a forward-looking model. That was necessary, given the rational-expectations features in the model, which made consumption and investment at any point in time depend on the expected level of taxes and the interest rate in the future, as has been explained above. The new ideas necessary for this work were developed jointly by the group in Cambridge, by a group in London led by David Currie and Paul Levine, and by Marcus Miller and Willem Buiter in Warwick and Bristol. The central idea driving that work on control methods was that rule-bound policies are necessary to guide an economy, if the world is forward-looking, since what economic agents do now depends on what they expect policy to do in the future. Such ideas were largely put on one side in the early to mid-1990s, when inflation-target regimes were first analysed theoretically, using simple backward-looking models (see, for example, Bean, 1998.) But many of them have re-emerged in more recent technical work on targeting inflation in forward-looking, dynamic economies. For example, the idea of 'stabilization bias', which was understood very clearly by this group of people in England in the mid-1980s, was rediscovered and made popular by Michael Woodford nearly 15 years later, in the late 1990s.

Meade's young colleagues came to experience his skill at running a group of researchers – which I have begun to think he partly inherited from his experience in the Cambridge Circus so many years previously. As he passed 80 years of age, Meade presided over a weekly programme of meetings, at which his research group discussed the rational-expectations developments which I have described above. The day after each meeting, Meade would sit at home, in his village outside Cambridge, and write down an algebraic formulation of what we had all discussed. He would then walk to his local post office and send us a letter containing a photocopy of these hand-written notes. We would all then analyse his algebra and diagrams, in preparation for the next week's meeting.

It is fair to say that the policy proposals, which Meade's group developed, have not withstood the test of time. There are two explanations for this.

First, we now target the rate of inflation, not nominal incomes; Meade's nominal-income target regime was, effectively, only a precursor to the inflation-target regime which is now in place in the UK. Meade proposed a nominal income target, in part, because it was inherently more flexible than a *rigid* inflation target. It did not require that the inflation rate be exactly pinned down to an exactly pre-announced rate, but instead allowed, as explained above, for a (temporary) increase in inflation to be met by a (temporary) reduction in output, so as to ensure – on balance – that there would be no change in the rate of growth of nominal incomes. We now know that a *flexible* inflation-target regime is better than such a nominal-income target regime. But it took some years of research for us to understand just why this is so, work which is described, for example, in Hall and Mankiw (1993), Leiderman and Svensson (1995), and Woodford, (2003). We have realized that the chief disadvantage of a nominal income target is that it does not 'let bygones be bygones': it requires that any overshoot which has occurred in the *level* of prices be clawed back, by means of a recession and lower subsequent inflation. But – at the same time – we have also realized that significant institutional development is required if one is to move from a purely rule-based system, like a nominal-income-target regime, to something like a rule-based but flexible inflation-target regime. To do this requires that the macroeconomic policy-making authorities be shielded from political influences which might force them to use their flexibility in an over-inflationary manner.

Second, we now use changes in interest rates, not changes in tax rates, in order to control inflation. We do this for three well-known reasons. First, it is easier to shield monetary policy from political influence than it is to do this for fiscal policy. Second the interest rate can be changed more regularly than taxes can be changed, and more quickly in response to new information – although fiscal procedures are less inflexible in some countries (such as the UK and New Zealand) than in others (such as the United States). Third, in an open economy monetary policy can have effects beyond those which can be caused by changes in taxes, because it can cause changes in a country's exchange rate which can, in turn, cause movements in exports and imports. This allows a country to externalize some of the costs of controlling shocks. That is a good idea if shocks in the world happen at different times in different countries.

Thus, as to both target and instrument, it appears that the world has moved on from Meade's proposals.

Nevertheless Meade's proposals had more general features, which *do* seem to have survived the test of time. Meade came to describe them as 'New Keynesian'. They were 'Keynesian' since, unlike Friedman, Meade continued to see the need for interventionist macroeconomic policies. (On this see Gordon, 1990.) They were 'new' because Meade proposed a target for a nominal variable (nominal income) instead of having a target for real output. And, in addition, they were proposals for rule-bound policies. It is hard to remember how unusual, and how original, it was to combine these three features, in the early 1990s.

These three features of Meade's proposals seem to have had a significant influence on the development of macroeconomic policymaking in the UK in the early 1990s. It is also hard to remember just what a mess macroeconomic policymaking was in Britain at that time. Following the country's brief flirtation with monetarism, it had joined the ill-fated 'exchange-rate mechanism' of the European Monetary System, which, in retrospect, appears to have been a pretty stupid policy framework. Following the UK's ejection from that system in September 1992, the Bank of England needed to quickly design a new policy regime. There was very little good theoretical guidance on what to do – other than Meade's. I say this, in particular, because the proposals of John Taylor, that monetary policy could follow a 'Taylor rule', really emerged only two years later (Taylor, 1994). When the new regime was announced by the Bank, *within days*, it had Meade's three features – it was one in which interest rates would be actively used, in pursuit of a nominal variable (the inflation target), in a rule-bound (if flexible) manner. The outcome was one of the world's earliest inflation-targeting regimes (the British regime was second only to that established in New Zealand), a set-up which has developed into the world's best inflation-targeting system. I believe that *Macroeconomic Policy* (Meade et al., 1989) exerted some influence in the construction of this valuable new regime in Britain.

Furthermore, there are aspects of Meade's proposals which may yield further benefits in the future. *Macroeconomic Policy* suggests that policy should not just pursue a nominal anchor (taken to be a nominal income target in that book but it could just as well be an inflation target). The book also suggests that policy should pursue a target for the allocation of GDP between consumption and investment, so as to avoid 'selling off the family silver' (a phrase much discussed at the time), that is, so as to ensure that the supply side of the economy grows sufficiently rapidly. To do this, the book suggests that there should be rule-bound procedures for *two* policy instruments (both monetary policy – that is, interest-rate policy – and fiscal policy) in the joint pursuit of *two* targets (both the nominal anchor and the consumption–investment split). This was a very Meade-like suggestion in two ways: it synthesized a number of different ideas being discussed at the time, and it was characteristically complex and difficult to investigate (making this aspect of *Macroeconomic Policy* quite hard to understand).

One might argue that, in most circumstances, interest-rate policy can adequately control inflation, in the short to medium run, leaving fiscal policy to be more gradually adjusted so as to being about any desired changes in the consumption–investment mix, in the longer term. This is, for example, how the current British macroeconomic policymaking framework operates. In such cases monetary policy and fiscal policy can be considered separately, and a complex analysis of two instruments in pursuit of two targets is positively unhelpful.

Nevertheless, practical experience – in the United States, Japan, Europe and Australia – has shown that there are circumstances in which fiscal policy may need to assist in the pursuit of the inflation target, particularly when there are large falls, or increases, in demand. (See Garnaut, 2005.) And recent theoretical work has shown that there may be more general advantages if fiscal and monetary policymakers can rely on each other to act in appropriate ways. (See Allsopp and Vines, 2005.) The problems which might arise if the monetary and fiscal authorities cannot do this, and act independently of each other, were examined in Meade's very last published journal article (Meade and Weale, 1995b). These problems have arisen very seriously in the Eurozone, where the European Central Bank and European governments do not cooperate, but not much, if at all, in the United Kingdom, for reasons examined theoretically in Kirsanova, Stehn and Vines (2005).

The reform of wage fixing
The second part of Meade's project considered measures to promote employment through the reform of wage fixing. These were described in Meade (1982; 1984a; 1986a; 1986b). Looking back, one can credit Meade with having helped to create a sea change in the 1980s in British discussion of how wages ought to be fixed. Gone entirely are the ideas of rigid, centralized policies to hold down wages and prices by centralized administration. In their stead are proposals for policies which reinforce market mechanisms and which have their major impact as employment-creating rather than price-controlling devices (Layard, 1986). Meade's own suggestions included proposals for arbitration, a wage inflation tax and profit sharing.

On profit sharing and related topics Meade had already written a number of papers, starting in 1972 with 'The Theory of Labour Managed Firms and of Profit Sharing'; and his views on this subject also become influential in Britain. He was sympathetic to the ideas about workers' remuneration espoused in Weitzman's book *The Share Economy* (1984). But his criticisms of Weitzman were also important. Profit sharing *might* have

beneficial effects for macroeconomic stability, through encouraging greater flexibility of workers' remuneration. But it *might also* do the opposite, if workers who concede profit sharing also come to exert an influence on the employment decisions of their firms, and use this influence to restrict employment opportunities and raise their own wages.

Meade went on working in this second area, long after the group of those working on demand management broke up after the publication of *Macroeconomic Policy* in the late 1980s. An important driving force in this work, and something which I have not discussed adequately in this article, was Meade's interest in the reform of the social security system. Such reform might make it possible to reconcile an efficient labour market – which might necessitate a pay-bargaining system that delivered low wages to some people – with a distribution of income which was equitable and just.

The year 1995 saw the production of Meade's last book *Full Employment Regained* (Meade, 1995a), in which he attempted a synthesis of his ideas on demand management and on supply side reforms, arguing that full employment was possible providing that the appropriate reforms were undertaken. This, as Atkinson and Weale (2000) say, brought his career full circle. That career began, and ended, with Meade being concerned about the waste of resources and misery generated by high levels of unemployment. The Institute of Fiscal Studies hosted a seminar at which the ideas in his book were discussed. This was his last public appearance. And it was a gathering of many of the people whom he had influenced throughout his long career.

6 Influence

There can be no doubt that the *Theory of International Economic Policy* had an enormous influence upon our discipline. Corden and Atkinson (1979) and Johnson (1978) pay eloquent tribute to this. What I have said above suggests that there are many other ways in which he has exerted considerable influence. However, it is true that Meade is not as visible as some others of his generation.

This is probably due to his difficult manner of writing. This meant that his books were not as widely read as they might have been. Immediately one must exempt from this blanket statement Meade's popular articles and semi-popular tracts, which were beautifully written, and which displayed Meade's classical training to great effect, at the same time as being very persuasive. However his form of exposition, when he was doing fundamental economic theory, was very different. His 'style of work and presentation consists in the development of a *general* mathematical model of a problem, followed by translation of analysis of the various possible cases into literary English illustrated at most by arithmetical examples or simple diagrams' (Johnson, 1978, p. 65; emphasis added).

Johnson went on (p. 66) to complain about his 'taxonomic approach and dependence on rather inelegant personal mathematics'. This means, said Johnson, that 'students find it incredibly tedious to read his books and [find it] difficult to convince themselves that the effort is worthwhile in terms of the knowledge gained' (p. 65).

Corden and Atkinson made similar complaints, specifically about Meade's *Theory of International Economic Policy*, but by implication about his other work as well:

> ... the ... model of *The Balance of Payments* was very influential and ... had a rapid impact on key writers and policy makers in the field.... By contrast, the influence of Trade and Welfare was more delayed, and to a great extent many of its original ideas were rediscovered later ... Both books ... are written in a taxonomic and rather heavy style, with no footnote references to the literature and a failure to highlight the author's original contributions. Although the books are immensely rewarding to serious students, their messages often reach a wider audience only through the intermediation of more succinct, if less original, writers. (Corden and Atkinson, 1979, p. 530)

Elsewhere Corden and Atkinson talk of Meade's 'distinctive literary–arithmetical style', which now seems somewhat old fashioned compared with modern concise, simple algebraic expositions. Johnson (1978, p. 74) sums up the complaints, talking about the 'reader-repellent character of Meade's literary-arithmetical-cum-idiosyncratic-mathematical-appendix style of presentation'.

All this enables one to see why the spread of Meade's ideas had to rely, more than is usual, on his personal influence over his colleagues. It is easy to see how, in such circumstances, his influence could be underrated.

Yet one can easily see, too, why Meade deliberately chose to work in the way just described. It was his prodigious power to generalize – to see competing theories about any subject as part of a yet larger encompassing scheme of things – which caused him to create his vast architectural structures of taxonomy. These put off many readers. But, the structures having been created, a dedicated band of followers managed to climb up onto them, and then – when they came down again – to explain what they had seen to the rest of the profession. It was obviously easier to do this for those disciples and colleagues who had the good fortune to work directly with Meade, for they were able to discuss the insights of his work with him, as they worked through it. As will be clear, there were many such disciples and colleagues throughout Meade's long career. It is mainly through them, and thus mainly indirectly, that his influence spread so far.

Those who worked with Meade shared in his zest for life and in his acute sense of fun, some of which may be apparent to the reader of this account. They saw, too, his respect for careful argument, and his pleasure in a slow and measured conversation, through which such argument can be developed. But, especially, Meade conveyed to them his sense of the underlying moral purpose of our discipline. It is appropriate to end this assessment of Meade's work by discussing his views on that subject.

7 Underlying philosophy

I mentioned in the introduction that Meade took up the study of economics because he wanted to help make the world a better place for ordinary men and women. In this he stood in the great Cambridge tradition of secular moralists, who might in the early Victorian age have become priests, but under the later influences of Darwinism and religious doubt turned instead to social improvement. The first volume of Skidelsky's biography of Keynes (Skidelsky, 1983) links Keynes back to Marshall and Sidgwick in that enterprise. Meade, in turn, emphasized this shared objective as 'the decisive factor in binding me so closely to [Keynes] ... he had ... a passionate desire to devise a better domestic and international society' (Meade, 1983b, p 268).

What is the conception of this better society that Meade strove for? And what is the role of the economist in helping to create it? The following few paragraphs, taken from a review article which he wrote in the late 1940s (Meade, 1948b, p. 34), summarize some of his key ideas with a deceptive simplicity.

Meade writes that one's overall purpose is that 'of combining freedom, efficiency and equity in social affairs ...'

> Two points should, however, be emphasised. First, this does not beg the question of planning. There may well be occasions ... on which the State should rightly prepare general programmes for far-reaching structural changes in the use of the community's resources; and there may be sections of the economy (such as public investment) where the State should on all occasions plan ahead. But where planning takes place, it is still possible to use money and prices as a main, if not the main, instrument for getting the plan carried out.

> Secondly, there is no suggestion that on those occasions in which money and prices have been extensively used in the past the arrangements have been satisfactory. Far from it. In order that money and prices may fulfil their purpose three main conditions must be fulfilled. First, the total supply of monetary counters must be neither too great nor too small in relation to the total supply of goods and services to be purchased. Secondly, the total supply of monetary counters must be equitably distributed so that no one obtains more than a fair share of command over resources. Thirdly, no private person or body of persons must be allowed to remain in a sufficiently powerful position to rig the market for his own advantage.

> These conditions have not been fulfilled in the past. On the contrary, considerable state planning and much state intervention is required to ensure that

these conditions are fulfilled. If, however, we wish to combine freedom, efficiency and equity in our economic life, we should proceed to make arrangements to see that these fundamental conditions are satisfied; and as they are more and more nearly fulfilled we should make a progressively greater use of the monetary and pricing systems....

These 'fundamental conditions' have indeed been more nearly satisfied, in OECD countries, in the several decades since Meade wrote these words. But there is still much work to do. We still need to design intelligent monetary and pricing systems to deal with pressing global microeconomic problems (such as the threat of global warming, or the miserable health of the world poorest people), and with pressing global macroeconomic problems (such as large international imbalances, and the risks of financial crises in emerging market economies). It remains Meade's challenge to economists that we should develop policymaking institutions, and pricing systems, to deal with these problems, in ways which combine all of freedom, efficiency and equity, as much as possible.

DAVID VINES

See also **absorption approach to the balance of payments; elasticities approach to the balance of payments; Heckscher–Ohlin trade theory; inflation targeting; International Monetary Fund; World Trade Organization.**

Selected works

This article is a development of my entry about Meade in the first edition of *The New Palgrave: A Dictionary of Economics* (Vines, 1987). That piece made use of two full-scale assessments of his work by Harry Johnson (1978) and by Corden and Atkinson (1979), and also used the short account by Harcourt (1985). In writing this piece I have been helped by a number of full-scale assessments of Meade's work which have appeared since 1987, by Atkinson (1996), Atkinson and Weale (2000), and Howson (2000). I have also referred to shorter accounts in Solow (1987), Greenaway (1990), and Corden (1996a; 1996b). There is a bibliography of Meade's work attached to Johnson (1978), which was complete when it was assembled, except for 'a number of ephemeral newspaper articles and reviews'. From 1978 until his death in 1995, Meade continued to publish a remarkable amount, and a full bibliography is attached to Howson (2000). Accordingly, in the list below I include only those pieces of Meade's work to which I have referred explicitly, plus a few other particularly important pieces to which I do not refer. The bibliography, of course, includes all the pieces by other authors to which I make reference.

1933. *The Rate of Interest in a Progressive State.* London: Macmillan.
1934. The amount of money and the banking system. *Economic Journal* 4, 98–107.

1936. *An Introduction to Economic Analysis and Policy.* London: Oxford University Press. 2nd edn, 1937. American edition, ed. C.J. Hitch with an Introduction by A.J. Hanson, New York: Oxford University Press, 1938.
1937. A simplified model of Mr Keynes' system. *Review of Economic Studies* 4, 98–107.
1938. *Consumers' Credits and Unemployment.* London: Oxford University Press.
1940. *The Economic Basis of a Durable Peace.* London: Oxford University Press.
1941. (With J.R.N. Stone.) The construction of Tables of National Income, Expenditure, Savings and Investment. *Economic Journal* 51, 216–33.
1944. (With J.R.N. Stone.) *National Income and Expenditure.* London: Oxford University Press.
1948a. *Planning and the Price Mechanism: The Liberal Socialist Solution.* London: Allen & Unwin; New York: Macmillan, 1949.
1948b. Planning without prices. *Economica NS* 15, 28–35.
1951–5. *The Theory of International Economic Policy.* Vol. 1: *The Balance of Payments* (1951); Vol. 2: *Trade and Welfare* (1955a); with mathematical supplements. London and New York: Oxford University Press.
1952. *A Geometry of International Trade.* New York: A. Kelley, 1969. London: Allen & Unwin.
1953a. *The Atlantic Community and the Dollar Gap.* London: Friends of the Atlantic Union.
1953b. *Problems of Economic Union.* The Charles R. Walgreen Foundation Lectures. Chicago: University of Chicago Press.
1955b. *The Theory of Customs Unions.* The De Vries Lectures, Vol. 1. Amsterdam: North-Holland.
1955c. The case for variable exchange rates. *Three Banks Review* 27(September), 3–27. Reprinted in *Readings in Money, National Income and Stabilization Policy*, ed. W. Smith and R. Teigen. Chicago: Richard D. Irwin, 1965.
1956a. *The Belgium–Luxembourg Economic Union, 1921–39: Lessons from an Early Experiment.* Essays in International Finance No. 25. Princeton: International Finance Section.
1956b. *Japan and the General Agreement on Tariffs and Trade.* The Joseph Fisher Lectures in Commerce, Adelaide University. Adelaide: Adelaide University Press.
1957. (With E.A. Russell.) Wage rates, the cost of living and the balance of payments. *Economic Record* 33(April), 23–8.
1958. *The Control of Inflation.* Inaugural Lecture, Cambridge University. London: Cambridge University Press.
1961a. (With others.) *The Economic and Social Structure of Mauritius.* Report to the Governor of Mauritius. London: Methuen.
1961b. *A Neo-Classical Theory of Economic Growth.* London: Allen & Unwin. 2nd edn, 1964.
1964. *Efficiency, Equality and the Ownership of Property.* London: Allen & Unwin.
1965. *Principles of Political Economy: I. The Stationary Economy.* London: Allen & Unwin; Chicago: Aldine Press.

1965. (With F.H. Hahn.) The rate of profit in a growing economy. *Economic Journal* 75, 445–8.

1966. The outcome of the Pasinetti process: a note. *Economic Journal* 76, 161–5.

1968. *Principles of Political Economy: 1I. The Growing Economy*. London: Allen & Unwin; Chicago: University of Chicago Press.

1971a. *Principles of Political Economy: III. The Controlled Economy*. London: Allen & Unwin.

1971b. *Wages and Prices in a Mixed Economy*. Occasional Paper No. 35. London: Institute of Economic Affairs.

1972. The theory of labour managed firms and of profit sharing. *Economic Journal* 82, 402–28.

1973a. *The Theory of Economic Externalities*. Geneva: Institut Universitaire des Hautes Etudes Internationales.

1973b. Economic policy and the threat of doom. In *Resources and Population*, ed. B. Benjamin, P. Cox and J. Peel. London: Academic Press.

1973c. The inheritance of inequalities: some biological, demographic, social and economic factors. *Proceedings of the British Academy* 59, Oxford: Oxford University Press.

1975a. *The Intelligent Radical's Guide to Economic Policy*. London: Allen & Unwin.

1975b. The Keynesian revolution. In *Essays on John Maynard Keynes*, ed. M. Keynes. London: Macmillan.

1976. *Principles of Political Economy: IV. The Just Economy*. London: Allen & Unwin.

1977a. Contrib Title: Autobiography.In *Nobel Lectures: Economics 1969–80*, ed. A. Lindbeck. Singapore: World Scientific Publishing Co, 1992. Online. Available at http://nobelprize.org/nobel_prizes/economics/laureates/1977/meade-autobio.html, accessed 27 March 2007.

1977b. Banquet Speech on award of the Nobel Prize. In *Les Prix Nobel. The Nobel prizes 1977*, ed. W. Odelberg. Stockholm: Nobel Foundation. Online. Available at http://nobelprize.org/nobel_prizes/economics/laureates/1977/meade-speech.html, accessed 27 March 2007.

1978a. (With others.) *The Structure and Reform of Direct Taxation*. London: Allen & Unwin.

1978b. The meaning of internal balance. *Economic Journal* 88, 423–35.

1981. Comment on the papers by Professors Laidler and Tobin. *Economic Journal* 91, 49–55.

1982. *Stagflation, Vol. I: Wage Fixing*. London: Allen & Unwin.

1983a. (with D. Vines and J. Maciejowski.) *Stagflation, Vol. II: Demand Management*. London: Allen & Unwin.

1983b. Impressions of Maynard Keynes. In Worswick and Trevithic (1983).

1984b. A new Keynesian Bretton Woods. *Three Banks Review* (June), 8–25.

1984c. A new Keynesian approach to full employment. *Lloyds Bank Review* (150), 1–18.

1984a. *Wage Fixing Revisited*. Occasional Paper No. 72.London: Institute of Economic Affairs.

1986a. *Alternative Systems of Business Organization and Workers' Remuneration*. London: Allen & Unwin.

1986b. *Different Forms of Share Economy*. London: Public Policy Centre, London.

1988–90. *The Collected Papers of James Meade Volumes I–IV*, (Volume IV jointly edited with D. Moggridge). London:Unwin Hyman.

1989. (With M. Weale, A. Blake, N. Christodoulakis and D. Vines.) *Macroeconomic Policy: Inflation, Wealth and the Exchange Rate*. London: Unwin and Hyman.

1993. The relation of Mr Meade's relation to Kahn's multiplier. *Economic Journal* 103, 464–5.

1995a. *Full Employment Regained*. Occasional Paper No. 61, Department of Applied Economics, Cambridge University.

1995b. (With M. Weale.) Monetary union and the assignment problem. *Scandinavian Journal of Economics* 97, 201–22.

Bibliography

Alexander, S. 1952. The effects of a devaluation on a trade balance. *IMF Staff Papers* 2, 263–78.

Allsopp, C. and Vines, D. 2005. The macroeconomic role of fiscal policy. *Oxford Review of Economic Policy* 21, 485–508.

Atkinson, A. 1996. James Meade's vision: full employment and social justice. *National Institute Economic Review* (July), 90–7.

Atkinson, A. and Weale, M. 2000. James Meade: a memoir. In *1999 Lectures and Memoirs*. London: published for the British Academy by Oxford University Press.

Barro, R. and Gordon, D. 1983. A positive theory of monetary policy in a natural rate model. *Journal of Political Economy* 91, 589–610.

Bean, C. 1998. The new UK monetary arrangements: a view from the literature. *Economic Journal* 108, 1795–809.

Bhagwati, J. and Ramaswami, V.K. 1963. Domestic distortions, tariffs, and the theory of optimum subsidy. *Journal of Political Economy* 71, 44–50.

Brigden, J., Copeland, D., Dyason, E., Giblin, L. and Wickens, C. 1929. *The Australian Tariff: An Economic Enquiry*. Melbourne: Melbourne University Press.

Corden, W.M. 1984. Booming sector and Dutch Disease economics: Survey and consolidation. *Oxford Economic Papers* 36, 359–80.

Corden, W.M. 1996a. Special profile: James Meade, 1907–1995. *Review of International Economics* 4, 382–6.

Corden, W.M. 1996b. James Meade 1907–1995. *Economic Record* 72, 172–4.

Corden, W.M. and Atkinson, A. 1979. Meade James E. In *International Enyclopaedia of the Social Sciences Bibliographical Supplement*, vol. 18, ed. D.L. Sills. New York: Free Press; London: Macmillan.

Durbin, E. 1985. *New Jerusalems*. London: Routledge & Kegan Paul.

Dixit, A. and Stiglitz, J. 1977. Monopolistic competition and optimum product diversity. *American Economic Review* 57, 297–308.

Fleming, J.M. 1951. On making the best of balance of payments restrictions on imports. *Economic Journal* 61, 48–71.

Fleming, J.M. 1962. Domestic financial policies under fixed and under floating exchange rates. *IMF Staff Papers* 9, 369–79.

Friedman, M. 1953. The effects of a full employment policy on economic stability: a formal analysis. In *Essays in Positive Economics*. Chicago: Chicago University Press.

Friedman, M. 1968. The role of monetary policy. *American Economic Review* 58, 1–17.

Garnaut, R. 2005. Is macroeconomics dead? Monetary and fiscal policy in historical context. *Oxford Review of Economic Policy* 21, 524–31.

Gordon, R. 1990. What is New Keynesian Economics? *Journal of Economic Literature* 28, 1115–71.

Greenaway, D. 1990. The intelligent radical on economic policy: an essay on the work of James Meade. *Scottish Journal of Political Economy* 37, 288–98.

Gregory, R. 1976. Some implications of the growth of the mineral sector. *Australian Journal of Agricultural Economics* 20(2), 71–91.

Harberger, A.C. 1950. Currency depreciation, income and the balance of trade. *Journal of Political Economy* 58, 47–60.

Hall, R. and Mankiw, G. 1993. Nominal income targeting, NBER Working Paper no 4439. Published in *Monetary Policy*, ed. G. Mankiw. Chicago: University of Chicago Press, 1994.

Harcourt, G.C. 1982. The Social Science Imperialists: Selected Essays, ed. P. Kerr. London: Routledge & Kegan Paul.

Harcourt, G.C. 1985. Meade, James (1907–). In *The Social Science Encyclopaedia*, ed. A. Kuper and J. Kuper. London: Routledge & Kegan Paul.

Harrod, R.F. 1933. *International Economics*. London: Nisbet.

Hicks, J. 1937. Mr Keynes and the classics: a suggested simplification. *Econometrica* 5, 147–59.

Howson, S. 2000. James Meade. *Economic Journal* 110, 122–45.

Johnson, H.G. 1951. The taxonomic approach to economic policy. *Economic Journal* 61, 812–32.

Johnson, H.G. 1965. Optimal trade intervention in the presence of domestic distortions. In *Trade Growth and the Balance of Payments*, ed. R. Baldwin. Amsterdam: North-Holland.

Johnson, H.G. 1978. James Meade's contribution to economics. *Scandinavian Journal of Economics* 80, 64–85.

Kahn, R. 1931. The relation of home investment to unemployment. *Economic Journal* 41, 173–98.

Kahn, R. 1984. *The Making of Keynes' General Theory*. Cambridge: Cambridge University Press.

Keynes, J.M. 1930. *A Treatise on Money*. London: Macmillan.

Keynes, J.M. 1936. *The General Theory of Employment, Interest and Money*. London: Macmillan.

Keynes, J.M. 1939. Relative movements of real wages and output. *Economic Journal* 49, 34–51.

Keynes, J.M. 1940. *How to Pay for the War*. Repr. in Keynes (1971–88, vol. 9). London: Macmillan.

Keynes, J.M. 1971–88. *The Collected Writings of John Maynard Keynes*. London: Macmillan.

Kirsanova, T., Stehn, J. and Vines, D. 2005. The interactions between fiscal policy and monetary policy. *Oxford Review of Economic Policy* 21, 532–64.

Kydland, F.E. and Prescott, E.C. 1978. Rules rather than discretion. *Journal of Political Economy* 84, 473–91.

Laursen, S. and Metzler, L. 1950. Flexible exchange rates and the theory of employment. *Review of Economics and Statistics* 32, 281–99.

Layard, R. 1986. *How to Beat Unemployment*. Oxford: Oxford University Press.

Layard, R., Nickell, S. and Jackman, R. 1991. *Unemployment: Macroeconomic Performance and the Labour Market*. Oxford: Oxford University Press.

Leiderman, L. and Svensson, L., eds. 1995. *Inflation Targets*. London: CEPR.

Minister of Reconstruction. 1944. *Employment Policy*. Cmd. 6527. London: HMSO.

Mundell, R.A. 1962. The appropriate use of fiscal and monetary policy for internal and external stability. *IMF Staff Papers* 9, 70–7.

Phillips, A.W. 1950. Mechanical models in economic dynamics. *Economica* 17, 283–305.

Phillips, A.W. 1954. Stabilization policy in a closed economy. *Economic Journal* 64, 290–323.

Phillips, A.W. 1957. Stabilization policy and the time form of lagged responses. *Economic Journal* 67, 265–77.

Phillips, C. 1920. *Bank Credit*. New York: Macmillan.

Robinson, J. 1937. The foreign exchanges. In *Essays in the Theory of Employment*. London: Macmillan. 2nd edn, 1947.

Rowthorn, R. 1977. Conflict, inflation and money. *Cambridge Journal of Economics* 1, 215–39.

Samuelson, P. 1948. *Economics*. New York: McGraw Hill.

Shackle, G.L.S. 1967. *The Years of High Theory*. Cambridge: Cambridge University Press.

Skidelsky, R. 1983. *John Maynard Keynes: Hopes Betrayed 1883–1920*. London: Macmillan.

Skidelsky, R. 2000. *John Maynard Keynes: Fighting for Britain 1937–1946*. London: Macmillan.

Solow, R.M. 1956. A contribution to the theory of economic growth. *Quarterly Journal of Economics* 70, 65–94.

Solow, R.M. 1987. James Meade at eighty. *Economic Journal* 97, 986–8.

Swan, T.W. 1956. Economic growth and capital accumulation. *Economic Record* 32, 334–61.

Swan, T. 1963. Longer run problems of the balance of payments. In *The Australian Economy*, ed. H.W. Arndt and W.M. Corden. Melbourne: Cheshire. Repr. in *Readings in International Economics*, ed. R. Caves and H. Johnson. Homewood, IL: Irwin, 1968.

Taylor, J. 1994. *Macroeconomic Policy in a World Economy: From Econometric Design to Practical Operation*. New York: Norton.

Van Dormael, A. 1978. *Bretton Woods: Birth of a Monetary System*. London: Macmillan.

Viner, J. 1950. *The Customs Union Issue*. New York: Carnegie Institute for International Peace.

Vines, D. 1987. Meade James Edward. In *The New Palgrave: A Dictionary of Economics*, vol. 3, ed. J. Eatwell, M. Milgate and P. Newman. London: Macmillan.

Vines, D. 1994. Unfinished business: Australian protectionism, Australian trade liberalisation and APEC. Shann Memorial Lecture, University of Western Australia. In *Australian Macroeconomic Policy Debates: Contributions from the Shann Memorial Lectures, 1991–2000*, ed. P.L. Crompton. Perth: University of Western Australia Press, 2005.

Vines, D. 1996. The Phillips machine. In *A.W. Phillips: Collected Writings in Contemporary Perspective*, ed. R. Leeson. Cambridge: Cambridge University Press.

Vines, D. 2003. John Maynard Keynes, 1937–1946: The creation of international macroeconomics. *Economic Journal* 113, F338–361.

Weitzman, M. 1984. *The Share Economy*. Cambridge, MA: Harvard University Press.

Williamson, J. 1983a. Keynes and the international economic order. In Worswick and Trevithick (1983).

Williamson, J. 1983b. *The Exchange Rate System*. Washington, DC: Institute for International Economics.

Wilson, T. 1982. Planning for the war and for the peace. In *Keynes as a Policy Adviser*, ed. A.P. Thirlwall. London: Macmillan.

Woodford, M. 2003. *Interest and Prices*. Princeton: Princeton University Press.

Worswick, D. and Trevithick, D., eds. 1983. *Keynes and the Modern World*. Cambridge: Cambridge University Press.

Young, W. 1987. *Interpreting Mr Keynes: The IS/LM Enigma*. Cambridge: Polity Press.

meaningfulness and invariance

Few disavow the principle that scientific propositions should be meaningful in the sense of asserting something that is verifiable or falsifiable about the qualitative or empirical situation under discussion. What makes this principle tricky to apply in practice is that much of what is said is formulated not as simple assertions about qualitative or empirical events – such as a certain object sinks when placed in water – but as laws formulated in rather abstract, often mathematical, terms. It is not always apparent exactly what class of qualitative observations corresponds to such (often numerical) laws. Theories of meaningfulness are methods for investigating such matters, and invariance concepts are their primary tools.

The problem of meaningfulness, which has been around since the inception of mathematical science in ancient times, has proved to be difficult and subtle; even today it has not been fully resolved. This article surveys some of the current ideas about it, and illustrates, through examples, some of its uses. The presentation requires some elementary technical concepts of measurement theory (such as representation, scale type, and so on), which are explained in MEASUREMENT, THEORY OF.

1 Concepts of meaningfulness

1.1 Some notation and definitions

The operation of functional composition is denoted $*$. The Cartesian product of $T_1, \ldots, T_n$ is denoted $\prod_i^n T_i$.

A *scale* $\mathscr{S}$ is a set of functions from a qualitative domain, a set X endowed with one or more relations, into the real numbers. Elements of $\mathscr{S}$ are called *representations*. An example is the usual physical scale to measure length. Two of its representations are the *foot representation* and the *centimeter representation*. $\mathscr{S}$ is said to be

- a *ratio scale* if and only if for each ϕ in $\mathscr{S}$,

$$\mathscr{S} = \{r\phi \,|\, r > 0\},$$

- an *interval scale* if and only if for each ϕ in $\mathscr{S}$,

$$\mathscr{S} = \{r\phi + s \,|\, r > 0, s \text{ a real}\},$$

- an *ordinal scale* if and only if for each ϕ in $\mathscr{S}$, the range of ϕ is a (possibly infinite) interval of reals and

$$\mathscr{S} = \{f * \phi \,|\, f \text{ is a strictly monotonic function}$$
$$\text{from the range of } \phi \text{ onto itself}\}.$$

1.2 Intuitive formulation of meaningfulness and some examples

The following example, taken from Suppes and Zinnes (1963), nicely illustrates part of the problem in a very elementary way. Which of the following four sentences are meaningful?

(i) Stendhal weighed 150 on 2 September 1839.
(ii) The ratio of Stendhal's weight to Jane Austen's on 3 July 1814 was 1.42.
(iii) The ratio of the maximum temperature today to the maximum temperature yesterday is 1.10.
(iv) The ratio of the difference between today's and yesterday's maximum temperature to the difference between today's and tomorrow's maximum temperature will be 0.95.

Suppose that weight is measured in terms of the ratio scale $\mathscr{W}$ (which includes among its representations the pound and kilogram representations and all those obtained by just a change of unit), and that temperature is measured by the interval scale $\mathscr{T}$, which for this example includes the Fahrenheit and Celsius representations. (The Kelvin representation for temperature, which assumes an absolute zero temperature, is not in $\mathscr{T}$.)

Then Statement (*ii*) is meaningful, because with respect to each representation in $\mathscr{W}$ it says the same thing, that is, its truth value is the same no matter which representation in $\mathscr{W}$ is used to measure weight. That is not true for Statement (*i*), because (*i*) is true for exactly one representation in $\mathscr{W}$ and false for all of the rest. Thus we say that (*i*) is 'meaningless'. Similarly, (*iv*) is meaningful with respect to $\mathscr{T}$ but (*iii*) is not.

The somewhat intuitive concept of meaningfulness suggested by these examples is usually stated as follows. Suppose a qualitative or empirical attribute is measured by a representation from a scale of representations $\mathscr{S}$. Then a numerical statement involving values of the representation is said to be *quantitatively meaningful* if and only if its truth (or falsity) is constant no matter which representation in $\mathscr{S}$ is used to assign numbers to the attribute. There are obvious formal difficulties with this definition, for example the concept of 'numerical statement' is not a precise one. More seriously, it is unclear under what conditions this is the 'right' definition of meaningfulness, for it does not always lead to correct results in some well-understood and non-controversial situations. (See the discussion involving situations where the measurement scale consists of a single representation for an example.) Nevertheless, it is the concept most frequently employed in the literature, and invoking it often provides insight into the correct way of handling a quantitative situation – as the following still elementary but somewhat less obvious example shows.

Consider a situation where M persons rate N objects (for example, M judges judging N contestants in a sporting event). For simplicity, assume that person i rates objects according to the ratio scale of representations $\mathscr{R}_i$. The problem is to find an ordering on the N objects that aggregates the judgements of the judges in a reasonable way. It can be shown that their judgements cannot be coordinated in such a way that, for all R_i in $\mathscr{R}_i$ and R_j in $\mathscr{R}_j$ that for some object a, the assertion $R_i(a) = R_j(a)$ is justified philosophically. The difficulties underlying such a coordination are essentially those that arise in attempting to compare individual utility functions. The latter problem – the 'interpersonal comparison of utilities' – has been much discussed in the literature, as for example in Narens and Luce (1983). It is generally agreed that there are great, if not insurmountable, difficulties in carrying out such comparisons. Any rule that does not involve coordination among the raters can be formulated as follows. First, let F be a function that assigns to an object the value $F(r_1, \ldots, r_M)$ whenever person i assigns the number r_i to the object. Second, assume that object a is ranked just as high as b if and only if the value assigned by F to a is at least as great as that assigned by F to b. In practice F is often taken to be the arithmetic mean of the ratings $r_1, \ldots, r_M$ (for example, Pickering, Harrison and Cohen, 1973). Observe, however, that arithmetic means for this kind of rating situation, in general, produce a non-quantitatively meaningful ranking of objects,

as illustrated by the following special case. Suppose $M = 2$ and, for $i = 1, 2$, R_i is person's i representation that is being used for generating ratings, and

$$R_1(a) = 2, \quad R_1(b) = 3, \quad R_2(a) = 3, \quad and \quad R_2(b) = 1.$$

Then the arithmetical mean of the ratings for a, 2.5, is greater than that for b, 2, and thus a is ranked above b. However, meaningfulness requires the same order if any other representations of persons 1 and 2 rating scales are used, for example, $10R_1$ and $2R_2$. But for this choice of representations, the arithmetic mean of a, 13, is less than that of b, 16, and thus b is ranked higher than a.

It is easy to check that the geometrical mean of rankings for an object,

$$F(r_1, \ldots, r_M) = [r_1 \cdots r_M]^{\frac{1}{M}},$$

gives rise to a quantitatively meaningful, non-coordinated rule for ranking objects. It can be shown under plausible conditions that all other meaningful, non-coordinated rules give rise to the same ranking as that given by the geometric mean (Aczél and Roberts, 1989).

Many other applications of quantitative meaningfulness have been given by various researchers. In particular, Roberts (1985) provides a wide range of social science examples. In some contexts, quantitative meaningfulness presents certain technical difficulties that require some modification in its definition (see, for example, Roberts and Franke, 1976; Falmagne and Narens, 1983).

1.3 Meaningfulness and statistics

Another area of importance to social scientists in which invariance notions are thought to be relevant is applying statistics to numerical data. The role of measurement considerations in statistics and of invariance under admissible scale transformations was first emphasized by Stevens (1946; 1951); this view quickly became popularized in numerous textbooks, and it produced extensive debates in the literature. Continued disagreement exists, mainly created by confusion arising from the following two simple facts:

- Measurement scales are characterized by groups of admissible transformations of the real numbers.
- Statistical distributions exhibit certain invariances under appropriate transformation groups, often the same groups (especially the affine transformations), as those that arise from measurement considerations.

Because of these facts, some scientists have concluded that the suitability of a statistical test is determined, in part, by whether or not the measurement and distribution groups are the same. Thus, it is said that one may be able to apply a test, such as a *t*-test, that rests on the Gaussian distribution to ratio or interval scale data, but surely not to ordinal data, because the Gaussian distribution is invariant under the group of positive affine transformations, $x \to rx + s$, r, s real, $r > 0$ – which arises in both the ratio and the interval case but not in the ordinal one. Neither half of the assertion is correct. First, a significance test should be applied only when its distributional assumptions are met, and they may very well hold for some particular representation of ordinal data. And second, a specific distributional assumption may well not be met by data arising from a particular scale of measurement. For example, reaction times, being times, are measured on a physical ratio scale, but they are rarely well approximated by a Gaussian distribution.

What is true, however, is that any proposition (hypothesis) that one plans to put to statistical test or to use in estimation had better, itself, be quantitatively meaningful with respect to the scale used for the measurements. In general, it is not quantitatively meaningful to assert that two means are equal when the quantities are measured by an ordinal scale, because equality of means is not invariant under strictly increasing transformations. Thus, no matter what distribution holds and no matter what test is performed, the result may not be quantitatively meaningful, because the hypothesis is not. In particular, if an hypothesis is about the measurement structure itself, for example that the representation is additive over a concatenation operation, then it is essential that the following propositions (*a*) and (*b*) hold, where a *symmetry* of a structure is by definition an isomorphism of the structure onto itself: (*a*) the hypothesis be invariant under the symmetries of the structure and therefore invariant under the scale used to measure the structure. (Because it is assumed that scales of measurement are structure preserving functions from a qualitative structure onto a quantitative one, (*a*) immediately follows). And (*b*) the hypotheses of the statistical test be met without going outside the transformations of the measurement representation. See Luce et al. (1990) for a more detailed discussion of this issue.

2 Concepts of invariance

Measurement laws are quantitative laws based primarily on interrelationships of scales of measurement. They have in common with quantitative meaningfulness that they are derived through considerations of admissible transformations of the measurements of relevant variables. In the view of Falmagne and Narens (1983, p. 298) they arise in an empirical situation 'that is governed by an empirical law of which we know little of its mathematical form and a little of its invariance properties, but a lot about the structure of the admissible transformations of its variables, and use this information to greatly delimit the possible equations that express the law'. They are generalizations of the kind of laws that have a long-standing tradition in physics, where they are known as laws derived according principles of 'dimensional analysis'. These principles involve the assertion that laws

of nature are in a deep sense invariant under changes of unit, which correspond to invariance under symmetries. Thus, knowledge of the scale type of the relevant variables – a strong presupposition – greatly limits the forms of laws.

2.1 Measurement laws: simplest case
These principles were introduced into the behavioural sciences by Luce (1959), which was concerned with special cases of 'possible psychophysical laws'. He generalized dimensional analysis, which only assumed ratio scale transformations of the several variables, to the more general situation of the measurement scale types described by S.S. Stevens. Luce (1964) extended the 1959 formulation to include a few important cases of a single function of many variables.

Luce (1959) considered the case where the independent variable x and the dependent variable y were related by a law, $y = f(x)$, where f was some continuous function. He assumed that this law was invariant under admissible transformations of measurements, that is, for each admissible transformation ϕ of the independent variable, there was an admissible transformation ψ of the dependent variable such that for all x and y,

$$y = f(x) \text{ iff } \psi(y) = f(\phi(x)). \quad (1)$$

The following is an example of a use of Luce's theory. Suppose x is an objective variable measured by a ratio scale, for example, a physical variable such as the intensity of light or the weight of gold, and y is the subjective evaluation of x, for example, the subjective brightness of light, the subjective value of gold, and f is the law linking x and y. Suppose x and y are both measured on ratio scales and f is continuous. Suppose further that f satisfies eq. (1). Under these conditions, Luce shows that there are real numbers r and a, a depending on ψ, such that

$$f(x) = ax^r. \quad (2)$$

His method of proof was to show that eq. (1) implied that f satisfied the functional equation $h(s)f(t) = f(st)$ for some continuous function h and all positive s and t, and that this functional equation had eq. (2) as its only solution.

For most applications, such as the above brightness and subjective value examples, the scale for the independent variable is known and continuity is a reasonable idealized approximation. Sometimes theory will specify the measurement scale for the dependent variable. However, often the scale for the dependent variable is unknown, and in many cases, unobservable, as, for example, when it is subjective. In such situations, the measurement scale for the dependent variable has to be hypothesized or derived from theory. It can be hypothesized to be one of several theoretically reasonable types of measurement scales, and then methods similar to the one used to derive Equation (2) can be used to arrive at a measurement law for each type of hypothesized scale. The set of resultant measurement laws provides a clear set of quantitative hypotheses for empirical testing. Quite often such hypotheses turn out to be a good place to begin a scientific investigation.

2.2 Measurement laws: more complex cases

In a number of ways, Falmagne and Narens (1983) greatly generalized Luce's 1959 approach for deriving laws from measurement considerations. In particular:

- Instead of one independent variable and one dependent variable, they assumed n independent variables and one dependent variable. (They formulated matters for two independent variables to simplify notation, but their approach easily extends to n independent variables.)
- They allowed for a general relationship R among the admissible transformations of the independent variables to hold; that is, for the sets T_i of admissible transformations of the independent variables $x_1, \ldots, x_n$, R can be any nonempty subset of $\prod_i^n T_i$.
- They allowed for more general kinds of laws by allowing for a family $\mathscr{F}$ of functions to relate the dependent variable with n independent variables. They interpret $\mathscr{F}$ as follows. Initially, representations $\varphi_1, \ldots, \varphi_n$ are used to measure the n independent variables, $x_1, \ldots, x_n$. These measurements determine a function $f(\varphi_1(x_1), \ldots, \varphi_n(x_n))$ that is the value of the dependent variable measured on an unknown scale when $x_1, \ldots, x_n$ are measured by $\varphi_1, \ldots, \varphi_n$. There are other equally valid ways of measuring *each* independent variable x_i. These are obtained by transforming φ_i by the elements of T_i. However, valid measurements for the *set* of independent variables may be additionally constrained by the empirical law relating the dependent variable to the independent variables. The additional constraint is captured by the relation R. Thus each other valid measurement of the independent variables is given by $\tau_1*\varphi_1, \ldots, \tau_n*\varphi_n$ for some $\tau_1, \ldots, \tau_n$ such that $R(\tau_1, \ldots, \tau_n)$. The law giving the numerical value of the dependent variable, when the set of independent variables $x_1, \ldots, x_n$ are measured respectively by $\tau_1*\varphi_1, \ldots, \tau_n*\varphi_n$, is given by

$$f_{\tau_1, \ldots, \tau_n}(\tau_1*\varphi_1(x_1), \ldots, \tau_n*\varphi_n(x_n)).$$

In this way, it is the family of functions,

$$\mathscr{F} = \{f_{\tau_1, \ldots, \tau_n}(\tau_1*\varphi_1(x_1), \ldots,$$
$$\tau_n*\varphi_n(x_n))|R(\tau_1, \ldots, \tau_n)\},$$

that expresses the empirical law relating the dependent variable to the independent variables $x_1, \ldots, x_n$. Only in very restrictive cases will $\mathscr{F}$ consist of a single function.

2.3 Order meaningfulness

In place of assuming the scale type of the dependent variable, they assume 'order meaningfulness', that is, they assume the following. Using the just presented notation, suppose $\mathscr{F}$ is a family of functions that is a law relating the dependent variable with n independent variables and $f_{\sigma_1, \ldots, \sigma_n}$ and $f_{\tau_1, \ldots, \tau_n}$ are in $\mathscr{F}$. Then for all $x_1, \ldots, x_n$ and $u_1, \ldots, u_n$, $f_{\sigma_1, \ldots, \sigma_n}(\sigma_1*\varphi_1(x_1), \ldots, \sigma_n*\varphi_n(x_n)) \leq f_{\sigma_1, \ldots, \sigma_n}(\sigma_1*\varphi_1(u_1), \ldots, \sigma_n*\varphi_n(u_n))$ if and only if $f_{\tau_1, \ldots, \tau_n}(\tau_1*\varphi_1(x_1), \ldots, \tau_n*\varphi_n(x_n)) \leq f_{\tau_1, \ldots, \tau_n}(\tau_1*\varphi_1(u_1), \ldots, \tau_n*\varphi_n(u_n))$.

By considering families of functions rather than a single function for laws, Falmagne and Narens generalized the notion of 'dimensional constants' that appear in many laws. Their generalization allows for the formulation of behavioural laws (Falmagne and Narens, 1983; Falmagne, 1985) and physical laws (Falmagne, 2004) that cannot be obtained by considering only a single function. Of course, Falmagne and Narens' theory also allows for the case of a single function, by allowing the family of functions to degenerate to a set consisting of a single function.

In many situations order meaningfulness is a testable condition, making it a preferable assumption to assuming a scale type for a dependent variable unless, of course, one already has a well-developed theory for the dependent variable. In the Falmagne–Narens theory, the scale type of the dependent variable is not needed to obtain the law linking the independent and dependent variables.

For the case where the family $\mathscr{F}$ consists of a single function f of n-independent variables, Aczél, Roberts and Rosenbaum (1986) provided more general results. Through an insightful mathematical argument, they were able to characterize measurement laws using only measurability assumptions from real analysis about f instead of monotonicity or continuity assumptions. Aczél and Roberts (1989) use the general approach of Aczél, Roberts and Rosenbaum (1986) to derive measurement laws of economic interest.

3 Relation between meaningfulness and invariance

Quantitative meaningfulness lacks a serious account as to why it is a good concept of meaningfulness; that is, it lacks a sound theory as to why it should yield correct results. Formulating a serious account for it is difficult. One tack (Krantz et al., 1971; Luce, 1978; Narens, 1981) is to observe that, if meaningfulness expresses valid qualitative relationships, then it must correspond to something purely qualitative, and therefore it should have a purely qualitative description. A long tradition in mathematics for formulating qualitative relationships that belong naturally to some structure or concept goes back to at least 19th-century geometry and was the centrepiece of the famous Erlanger Programme for geometry of Felix Klein. It was based on the idea that associated with each geometry was a set of transformations $\mathscr{T}$, and the relations and concepts belonging to the geometry were exactly those that were left invariant by all the transformations in $\mathscr{T}$. There are strong connections between (a) geometric techniques of establishing coordinate systems and measurement techniques for establishing scales, and (b) the Erlanger Programme's concept of 'geometric' and the measurement-theoretic concept 'meaningfulness'. To examine these connections, some definitions and conventions are needed.

3.1 Convention
Throughout the remainder of this article, it is assumed that $\mathscr{X}$ is a qualitative structure, which consists of a qualitative set X as its domain and relations based on X (called the *primitives of* $\mathscr{X}$); $\mathscr{N}$ is a numerically based structure, that is, $\mathscr{N}$ is a structure that has a subset of the real numbers as its domain; and $\mathscr{S}$ is the measurement scale consisting of all isomorphisms from $\mathscr{X}$ onto $\mathscr{N}$. (See MEASUREMENT, THEORY OF for a more detailed description of this kind of measurement scale.)

3.2 Qualitative meaningfulness
An isomorphism of $\mathscr{X}$ onto itself is called a *symmetry* (or *automorphism*) of $\mathscr{X}$. It easily follows that if α is a symmetry of $\mathscr{X}$ and ϕ and ψ are elements of $\mathscr{S}$, then

- $\phi*\alpha$ is in $\mathscr{S}$,
- $\phi^{-1}*\psi$ is a symmetry of χ,
- $\theta=\phi*\psi^{-1}$ is an admissible transformation of $\mathscr{S}$, that is, $\phi*\eta$ is in $\mathscr{S}$ for each η in $\mathscr{S}$, and all admissible transformations can be obtained in the just mentioned manner by appropriate selections of ϕ and ψ.

An n-ary relation R on X is said to be *qualitatively meaningful* if and only if it is invariant under the symmetries of $\mathscr{X}$, that is, if and only if for each symmetry α of $\mathscr{X}$ and each $x_1,\ldots,x_n$ in X,

$$R(x_1,\ldots,x_n) \text{ iff } R(\alpha(x_1),\ldots,\alpha(x_n)).$$

3.3 Quantitative meaningfulness
Although a relation T being 'quantitatively meaningful' was previously defined, it is defined again here to make explicit the role the scale $\mathscr{S}$ plays in qualitative meaningfulness: an n-ary relation T on N is said to be *quantitatively $\mathscr{S}$-meaningful* if and only if for each admissible transformation τ of $\mathscr{S}$ and each $r_1,\ldots,r_n$ in N,

$$T(r_1,\ldots,r_n) \text{ iff } T(\tau(r_1),\ldots,\tau(r_n)).$$

$\mathscr{S}$ can be used to interpret T as a relation U on X as follows. The n-ary relation U on X is said to be the $\mathscr{S}$-interpretation of T if and only if for all ϕ in $\mathscr{S}$ and all $r_1,\ldots,r_n$

$$T(r_1,\ldots,r_n) \text{ iff } U(\phi^{-1}(r_1),\ldots,\phi^{-1}(r_n)).$$

3.4 Basic result
The above definitions and relationships between symmetries and admissible transformations immediately yield the following theorem relating qualitatively and quantitatively meaningful relations:

Theorem *A relation T is quantitatively $\mathscr{S}$-meaningful if and only if its $\mathscr{S}$-interpretation is qualitatively meaningful.*

The above theorem shows that each quantitatively meaningful relation has, through measurement, a corresponding qualitatively meaningful relation. Luce (1978) used this idea to provide a qualitative theory for practice of dimensional analysis in physics: Luce produced a qualitative structure $\mathscr{X}$ for measuring physical attributes. He showed that, under measurement, the quantitatively meaningful relationships among the attributes were the 'dimensionally invariant functions' of dimensional analysis. It is a principle of dimensional analysis that physical laws are such dimensionally invariant functions. Thus, by the just mentioned theorem, it then follows from the principles of dimensional analysis that each physical law corresponds to a qualitatively meaningful relation of $\mathscr{X}$. (Measurement-theoretic foundations for dimensional analysis can be found in Krantz et al., 1971; Luce et al., 1990; Narens, 2002.)

Qualitative meaningfulness is just the Erlanger concept of 'geometric' applied to science. Mathematically, the two concepts are identical. The Erlanger Programme, as formulated by Klein (1872) and as used in mathematics, lacks a serious justification for assuming that the invariance of a relation under the symmetries of a geometry implies that the relation belongs to the geometry.

3.5 Scientific definability
Narens (2002; 2007) sought to find a justification for Klein's assumption. He thought that a reasonable concept of a relation R belonging to a structure $\mathscr{X}$ was that R should somehow be definable in terms of the primitives of $\mathscr{X}$. But the usual concepts of 'definable' used in logic failed to provide a match with the Erlanger's concept of 'geometric'. Narens developed a new definability concept to capture the Erlanger Programme's concept of 'geometric'. He called the new concept *scientific definability*.

Scientific definability assumes that the quantitative world is constructed from relationships based on real numbers and is completely separated from the qualitative situation under investigation, $\mathscr{X}$, which is conceptualized as a qualitative structure. Unlike definability concepts from logic, scientific definability allows the free use of concepts from the quantitative world for defining relationships based on the domain X of a qualitative structure $\mathscr{X}$. Narens shows that a relation on X is qualitatively meaningful if and only if it is scientifically defined in terms of $\mathscr{X}$.

There is one obvious case where the Erlanger Programme appears to produce a remarkably poor concept of 'geometric'. This is where the geometry $\mathcal{X}$ has the identity function as its only symmetry, yielding that every relation on X is 'geometric', and for measurement situations where the scale consists of a single representation, making each relation on the domain of the numerical representing structure quantitatively meaningful, and thus, by the above theorem, each relation on X qualitatively meaningful. There are many important examples of this case, for example the geometry of physical universe under Einstein's general theory of relativity.

Narens (2002) provides generalizations of 'scientific definability' that appear to yield reasonable and productive concepts of 'geometric' ('qualitatively meaningful') for situations where the geometry (qualitative structure) has the identity as its only symmetry. The main idea for the generalizations is the following. Instead of formulating meaningfulness in terms of a single qualitative structure, a family $\mathcal{F}$ of isomorphic qualitative structures is used. It is assumed that all the structures in $\mathcal{F}$ have the same domain called the *common domain* (of $\mathcal{F}$). A relation R on the common domain is said to be $\mathcal{F}$-*meaningful* if and only if there exist a structure $\mathcal{X}$ in $\mathcal{F}$, primitives $R_{j_1}, \ldots, R_{j_n}$ of $\mathcal{X}$, and a formula φ used for scientific definitions such that

(i) R has a scientific definition in terms $R_{j_1}, \ldots, R_{j_n}$ and φ, and

(ii) R has the same scientific definition for all $\mathcal{X}' = \langle X, R'_j \rangle_{j \in J}$ in $\mathcal{F}$; that is, R has the same scientific definition as in (i) but with $R_{j_1}, \ldots, R_{j_n}$ replaced by $R'_{j_1}, \ldots, R'_{j_n}$.

For the case where $\mathcal{F}$ consists of a single structure, $\mathcal{F}$-meaningfulness coincides with qualitative meaningfulness.

LOUIS NARENS AND R. DUNCAN LUCE

See also **measurement, theory of.**

Bibliography

Aczél, J. and Roberts, F.S. 1989. On the possible merging functions. *Mathematical Social Sciences* 17, 205–43.

Aczél, J., Roberts, F.S. and Rosenbaum, Z. 1986. On scientific laws without dimensional constants. *Journal of Mathematical Analysis and Applications* 119, 389–416.

Falmagne, J.-C. 1985. *Elements of Psychophysical Theory.* New York: Cambridge University Press.

Falmagne, J.-C. 2004. Meaningfulness and order-invariance: two fundamental principles for scientific laws. *Foundations of Physics* 34, 1341–8.

Falmagne, J.-C. and Narens, L. 1983. Scales and meaningfulness of quantitative laws. *Synthese* 55, 287–325.

Klein, F. 1872. *Vergleichende Betrachtungen über neuere geometrische Vorschungen: Programm zu Eintritt in die philosophische Facultät und den Senat der Universität zu Erlangen.* Erlangen: Deichert.

Krantz, D.H., Luce, R.D., Suppes, P. and Tversky, A. 1971. *Foundations of Measurement*, vol. 1, New York: Academic Press.

Luce, R.D. 1959. On the possible psychophysical laws. *Psychological Review* 66(2), 81–95.

Luce, R.D. 1964. A generalization of a theorem of dimensional analysis. *Journal of Mathematical Psychology* 1, 278–84.

Luce, R.D. 1978. Dimensionally invariant numerical laws correspond to meaningful qualitative relations. *Philosophy of Science* 45, 1–16.

Luce, R.D., Krantz, D.H., Suppes, P. and Tversky, A. 1990. *Foundations of Measurement*, vol. 3, New York: Academic Press.

Narens, L. 1981. A general theory of ratio scalability with remarks about the measurement-theoretic concept of meaningfulness. *Theory and Decision* 13, 1–70.

Narens, L. 1985. *Abstract Measurement Theory.* Cambridge, MA: MIT Press.

Narens, L. 2002. *Theories of Meaningfulness.* Mahwah: Lawrence Erlbaum and Associates.

Narens, L. 2007. *Introduction to the Theories of Measurement and Meaningfulness and the Role of Invariance in Science.* Mahwah: Lawrence Erlbaum and Associates.

Narens, L. and Luce, R.D. 1983. How we may have been misled into believing in the interpersonal comparability of utility. *Theory and Decision* 15, 247–60.

Pfanzagl, J. 1968. *Theory of Measurement.* New York: Wiley. 2nd edn., Vienna: Physica, 1971.

Pickering, J.F., Harrison, J.A. and Cohen, C.D. 1973. Identification and measurement of consumer confidence: methodology and some preliminary results. *Journal of the Royal Statistical Society* Series A 136, 43–63.

Roberts, F.S. 1980. On Luce's theory of meaningfulness. *Philosophy of Science* 47, 424–33.

Roberts, F.S. 1985. Applications of the theory of meaningfulness to psychology. *Journal of Mathematical Psychology* 229, 311–32.

Roberts, F.S. and Franke, C.H. 1976. On the theory of uniqueness in measurement. *Journal of Mathematical Psychology* 14, 211–18.

Stevens, S.S. 1946. On the theory of scales of measurement. *Science* 103, 677–80.

Stevens, S.S. 1951. Mathematics, measurement and psychophysics. In *Handbook of Experimental Psychology*, ed. S.S. Stevens. New York: Wiley.

Suppes, P. and Zinnes, J.L. 1963. Basic measurement theory. In *Handbook of Mathematical Psychology*, vol. 1, eds. R.D. Luce, R.R. Bush and E. Galanter. New York: Wiley.

Means, Gardiner Coit (1896–1988)

The Modern Corporation and Private Property appeared in 1932, co-authored by Means and Adolph Berle. This book fused the abilities of a great economist and a great lawyer, and became deservedly famous.

The prevalent economic and legal thinking at that time did not recognize adequately the emergence of corporate giantism. It envisaged a system characterized in the main by small private enterprises. And it assumed that this worked well because the law of supply and demand would determine price levels and thus automatically produce adjustments assuring the greatest good of the greatest number. This laissez-faire approach made private property almost sacrosanct and almost free from public intervention.

Berle and Means *proved* that this was not how the economy actually worked. As they revealed, the monster size of existing corporations and their dominating power negated the attributes of private property as then conceived; their ability and determination to fix or 'administer' prices prevented the benign operation of supply and demand. These findings suggested that increased government intervention in the private sector was essential in the public interest; and this was fortified by the book's additional findings *in re* economic concentration and the separation between ownership and control. Thus the book indicated among other things the need for legal change, including judicial reinterpretations of governmental powers under the Constitution.

Substantial parts of the book were used to support New Deal and judicial action between 1933 and 1939, which viewed corporations and private property in a new light. And the New Deal brought Means to Washington. He alone among three economic advisers to the Secretary of Agriculture dealt with the effect of farm conditions upon the overall economy. Next, he was Director of the industrial division of the National Resources Planning Board (NRPB), where he developed techniques for depicting what composition of business activity would maintain full employment. This type of work, continued by him on the staff of the Committee for Economic Development (after a spell as fiscal analyst in the Bureau of the Budget) was intrinsic to the Committee's portrayal of the post-war markets requisite to full employment.

During subsequent decades, Means poured forth a Niagara of writing and speeches. Insistently, he built upon his original thesis of corporate power, especially through its pricing practices. Refuting the prevalent view among economists that there is a 'trade-off' between unemployment and inflation, he showed that the great increases in inflation during recent decades have come mainly, not during a highly used economy near full employment, but rather during periods when the economy moved into stagnation and recession. This squared with his early finding that the modern corporation can and does lift prices to compensate for low volume. It also revealed that his humanistic concern about full employment and economic justice must reject the frequent and unsuccessful efforts to achieve price stability by spawning the misery of vast unemployment. Always, unlike so many economists, Means eschewed outmoded or untested theories, and spent himself in exhaustive empirical studies in aid of his own analysis and policy recommendations.

LEON H. KEYSERLING

See also **Berle, Adolf Augustus, Jr.**

Selected work

1932. (With A.A. Berle.) *The Modern Corporation and Private Property*. New York: Commerce Clearing House.

mean-variance analysis

In a mean–variance portfolio analysis (Markowitz, 1959) an n-component vector (portfolio) X is called feasible if it satisfies

$$AX = b \qquad X \geq O$$

where A is an $m \times n$ matrix of constraint coefficients, and b an m-component constant vector. An EV combination is called feasible if

$$E = \mu^T X$$
$$V = X^T C X$$

for some feasible portfolio. Here E is the expected return of the portfolio, V the variance of the portfolio, μ the vector of expected returns of securities, and C a positive semidefinite covariance matrix of returns among securities.

A feasible EV combination is called inefficient if some other feasible combination has either less V and no less E, or else greater E and no greater V. A feasible EV combination is called efficient if it is not inefficient. A feasible portfolio X is efficient or inefficient according to whether its EV combination meets the one definition or the other. As in linear programming, the constraints $(AX = b, X \geq O)$ can represent inequalities by introducing slack variables, and can incorporate variables which are allowed to be negative, by separating the positive and negative parts of such variables.

Markowitz (1956) shows that if V is strictly convex over the set of feasible portfolios – for example when C is positive definite – the set of efficient portfolios is piecewise linear, and the set of efficient EV combinations is piecewise parabolic. There may or may not be a kink in the efficient EV set at a 'corner portfolio', where two pieces of the efficient portfolio set meet. Markowitz (1959, Appendix A), shows for arbitrary semidefinite C that, while there may be more than one efficient portfolio for given efficient EV combination, there is a piecewise linear set of efficient portfolios which contains one and only one efficient portfolio for each efficient EV combination. The piecewise linear nature of the efficient set is illustrated graphically, for small n, in Markowitz (1952) and (1959).

The fact that the mean–variance analysis selects a portfolio for only one period does not imply that the investor plans to retire at the end of the period. Rather, it assumes that in the dynamic programming (Bellman, 1957) solution to the many period investment problem, current wealth is the only state variable to enter the implied single period utility function (see Markowitz, 1959, Ch. 13; Samuelson, 1969; Ziemba and Vickson, 1975). Mossin (1968) shows conditions under which the optimum solution to the many period problem is 'myopic' in that the single period utility function is the same as an end-of-game utility function. This is an example of – but not the only example of – a class of games in which wealth is the only state variable.

The Markowitz (1959) justification for the use of mean-variance analysis further assumes that if one knows the E and V of a portfolio one can estimate with acceptable accuracy the expected value of the one-period utility function. Samuelson (1970) and Ohlson (1975) present conditions under which mean and variance are asymptotically sufficient as the length of holding periods – that is, the intervals between portfolio revisions – approaches zero. For 'long' holding periods, for example for time between revisions as long as a year, Markowitz (1959), Young and Trent (1969), Levy and Markowitz (1979), Pulley (1981) and Kroll, Levy and Markowitz (1984) have each found mean-variance approximations to be quite accurate for a variety of utility functions and historical distributions of portfolio return.

This leads to an apparent anomaly: if you know mean and variance you practically know expected utility; the mean-variance approximation to expected utility is based on a quadratic approximation to the single-period utility function; yet Arrow (1965) and Pratt (1964) show that any quadratic utility function has the objectionable property that an investor with such a utility function becomes increasingly averse to risks of a given dollar amount as his wealth increases. Levy and Markowitz (1979) show that the anomaly disappears if you distinguish three types of quadratic approximation:

(1) Assuming that the investor has a utility-of-wealth function that remains constant through time – so that as the investor's wealth changes he moves along the curve to a new position – fit a quadratic to this curve at some instant of time, and continue to use this same approximation subsequently. (Note that the assumption here, that the investor has a constant utility-of-wealth function is sufficient, but not necessary, for the investor to have a single period utility function at each period.)

(2) Fit the quadratic to the investor's current single period utility function. For example, if the investor has an unchanging utility-of-wealth function, choose a quadratic to fit well near current wealth (i.e. near portfolio return equal zero).

(3) Allow the quadratic approximation to vary from one portfolio to another, that is, let the approximation depend on the mean, and perhaps the standard deviation, of the probability distribution whose expected value is to be estimated.

The Pratt–Arrow objections apply to an approximation of type (1). The approximations proposed in Markowitz (1959) are of types (2) and (3). Levy and Markowitz (1979) show that, under quite general assumptions, the type 3 mean-variance maximizer has the same risk aversion in the small (in the sense of Pratt) as does the original expected utility maximizer.

Uses of mean-variance analysis

Two areas of use deal with: (a) actual portfolio management using mean–variance analysis, and (b) implications for the economy as a whole of the assumption that all investors act according to the mean–variance criteria. We refer to these, respectively, as 'normative' and 'positive' uses of mean–variance analysis.

The positive application of mean-variance analysis is dealt with elsewhere in this Dictionary. Seminal works in the field include the Tobin (1958) analysis of liquidity preference; and the Sharpe (1964), Lintner (1965) and Mossin (1966) Capital Asset Pricing Models (CAPMs). As in the Tobin model, these CAPMs assume that the investor can either lend all he has or borrow all he wants at the same 'risk-free' rate of interest. From this assumption (plus assumptions that all investors have the same beliefs and seek mean–variance efficiency subject to the same constraint set) they conclude that the excess return on each security (its expected return minus the risk-free rate) is proportional to its 'beta', where the latter is the regression of the security's return against the return of the market as a whole. Black (1972) drops the assumption that the investor can borrow at a risk-free rate; assumes instead that the investor can sell short and use the proceeds to buy long; and derives a formula for excess return just like that of Sharpe–Lintner–Mossin except that the expected return on a zero-beta portfolio is substituted for the risk-free rate in the formula for excess return. Merton (1969) has developed mean–variance theory in continuous time. This has been used, for example, in the analysis of option prices by Black and Scholes (1973) from which a vast literature of further implications followed.

As compared with the models used in normative analysis, the models of positive analysis tend to use quite simple constraint sets and other special assumptions (e.g. all investors have the same beliefs). The justification for such assumptions is that they give concrete, therefore testable, implications; and indeed have been the subject of extensive empirical testing.

In the use of mean-variance analysis for actual money management, the question immediately arises as to how to estimate the large number of required covariances.

Sharpe (1963) concluded, and Cohen and Pogue (1967) confirmed, that a simple one-factor model of covariance was sufficient. King (1966) showed that, in addition to one pervasive factor, there were ample industry sources of covariance. By the mid-1970s it was clear to many practitioners that the one-factor model was not adequate, since, for example, sometimes 'the market', as measured by some broad index, went up while high beta stocks went down, to an extent that could not be explained by chance. Many-factor models such as that of Rosenberg (1974) are now widely used.

Other models of covariance used in practice include scenario and combined scenario and factor models (Markowitz and Perold, 1981), and a model which assumes that all correlation coefficients are the same (Elton and Gruber, 1973). The use of factor, scenario or constant correlation models, in addition to simplifying the parameter estimation problem, can considerably accelerate the computation of efficient sets for analyses containing hundreds of securities. For example, the Perold (1984) code will solve large portfolio selection problems for arbitrary A and C, but is especially efficient in handling upper bounds on variables and sparse (mostly zero) A and C matrices. (The introduction of 'dummy' securities into the analysis allows one to 'sparsify' the C matrix for factor, scenario or constant correlation models.) Even faster solutions are obtained by Elton, Gruber and Padberg (1976 and 1978) for the one-factor and constant correlation models for certain common constraint sets.

HARRY M. MARKOWITZ

See also **capital asset pricing model; finance.**

Bibliography

Arrow, K. 1965. *Aspects of the Theory of Risk Bearing.* Helsinki: Yrjö Jahnsson Foundation.

Bellman, R.E. 1957. *Dynamic Programming.* Princeton: Princeton University Press.

Black, F. 1972. Capital market equilibrium with restricted borrowing. *Journal of Business* 45, 444–55.

Black, F. and Scholes, M. 1973. The pricing of options and corporate liabilities. *Journal of Political Economy* 81, 637–54.

Cohen, J.K. and Pogue, J.A. 1967. An empirical evaluation of alternative portfolio-selection models. *Journal of Business* 40, April, 166–93.

Elton, E.J. and Gruber, M.J. 1973. Estimating the dependence structure of share prices. *Journal of Finance* 28, 1203–32.

Elton, E.J., Gruber, M.J. and Padberg, M.W. 1976. Simple criteria for optimal portfolio selection. *Journal of Finance* 31, 1341–57.

Elton, E.J., Gruber, M.J. and Padberg, M.W. 1978. Simple criteria for optimal portfolio selection: tracing out the efficient frontier. *Journal of Finance* 33, 296–302.

King, B.F. 1966. Market and industry factors in stock price behavior. *Journal of Business* 39, Supplement, January, 139–90.

Kroll, Y., Levy, H. and Markowitz, H.M. 1984. Mean variance versus direct utility maximization. *Journal of Finance* 39, 47–61.

Levy, H. and Markowitz, H.M. 1979. Approximating expected utility by a function of mean and variance. *American Economic Review* 69, 308–17.

Lintner, J. 1965. The valuation of risk assets and the selection of risky investments in stock portfolios and capital budgets. *Review of Economics and Statistics* 47, February, 13–37.

Markowitz, H.M. 1952. Portfolio selection. *Journal of Finance* 7, 77–91.

Markowitz, H.M. 1956. The optimization of a quadratic function subject to linear constraints. *Naval Research Logistics Quarterly* 3, 111–33.

Markowitz, H.M. 1959. *Portfolio Selection: Efficient Diversification of Investments.* New Haven: Yale University Press. Reprinted, New York: John Wiley and Sons, 1970.

Markowitz, H.M. and Perold, A. 1981. Portfolio analysis with factors and scenarios. *Journal of Finance* 36, 871–7.

Merton, R.C. 1969. Lifetime portfolio selection under uncertainty: the continuous-time case. *Review of Economics and Statistics* 51(3), 247–57.

Mossin, J. 1966. Equilibrium in a capital asset market. *Econometrica* 34, 768–83.

Mossin, J. 1968. Optimal multiperiod portfolio policies. *Journal of Business* 41, 215–29.

Ohlson, J.A. 1975. The asymptotic validity of quadratic utility as the trading interval approaches zero. In *Stochastic Optimization Models in Finance*, ed. W.T. Ziemba and R.G. Vickson. New York: Academic Press.

Perold, A.F. 1984. Large-scale portfolio optimization. *Management Science* 30, 1143–60.

Pratt, J.W. 1964. Risk aversion in the small and in the large. *Econometrica* 32, 122–36.

Pulley, L.B. 1981. A general mean-variance approximation to expected utility for short holding periods. *Journal of Financial and Quantitative Analysis* 16, 361–73.

Rosenberg, B. 1974. Extra-market components of covariance in security returns. *Journal of Financial and Quantitative Analysis* 9(2), 263–74.

Samuelson, P.A. 1969. Lifetime portfolio selection by dynamic stochastic programming. *Review of Economics and Statistics* 51(3), 239–46.

Samuelson, P.A. 1970. The fundamental approximation theorem of portfolio analysis in terms of means, variances and higher moments. *Review of Economic Studies* 37, 537–42.

Sharpe, W.F. 1963. A simplified model for portfolio analysis. *Management Science* 9(2), 277–93.

Sharpe, W.F. 1964. Capital asset prices: a theory of market equilibrium under conditions of risk. *Journal of Finance* 19, 425–42.

Tobin, J. 1958. Liquidity preference as behavior toward risk. *Review of Economic Studies* 25, 65–86.

Young, W.E. and Trent, R.H. 1969. Geometric mean approximations of individual security and portfolio performance. *Journal of Financial and Quantitative Analysis* 4(2), 179–99.

Ziemba, W.T. and Vickson, R.G., eds. 1975. *Stochastic Optimization Models in Finance*. New York: Academic Press.

measure theory

Measure theory is that part of mathematics which is concerned with the attribution of weights of 'measure' to the subsets of some given set. Such a measure is required to satisfy a natural condition of additivity, that is that the measure of the union of disjoint sets should be equal to the sum of the measure of those sets. The fundamental problems of measure arise when one has to treat infinite sets or infinite unions of sets. It is perhaps not clear why such a tool should be of use in economics.

Apart from the rather trivial observation that, since measure theory provides the basis for probability theory it underlies all of the economics of uncertainty, there have been direct applications of this theory to several basic problems in economic theory (for a more detailed account, see Kirman, 1982). A first example of such an application is given by the idea of 'pure' or 'perfect' competition. The fundamental characteristic of a perfectly competitive economic situation is one in which no individual can influence the outcome. Thus, in a competitive market economy, although prices are the result of the collective activity of all the agents, no individual by acting alone can modify them and hence takes them as given. Now strictly speaking in a finite economy this cannot be true and in the work of Torrens, Cournot and Edgeworth can be found lengthy discussions as to whether it is rational for individuals to behave in a perfectly competitive way. Indeed, as Viner once observed, the fact that it is profitable for them to do otherwise is a 'skeleton in the cupboard of free trade'.

Economists have typically avoided the contradiction involved in analysing economies in which individuals do have positive influence but behave as if they do not, by saying that individuals behave 'as if' or 'believe that' they have no effect on the outcome. To a mathematician there is no contradiction involved in the idea of individual elements having no weight but sets of such elements having positive weight. If we think of the unit interval, each point has no length but sub-intervals made up of such points do have positive weight. This is, of course, due to the fact that there are infinitely many, indeed a continuum, of such points. Aumann (1964) in his path-breaking article made use of these ideas to define an 'ideal' or 'continuum' economy which corresponded logically to the idea of perfect competition. If instead of

the set of agents A in an economy being finite, we substitute the unit interval [0, 1] a continuum exchange economy can be defined by $e[0, 1] \rightarrow \mathscr{P}_{mo} \times R^l_+$ where l is the number of goods and $\mathscr{P}_{mo}$ is the set of monotonic continuous preferences on R^l_+ positive orthant of Euclidian l space. Thus with each agent or point is associated a preference relation and an initial bundle of goods. Now we have defined an economy which has the right framework for perfect competition. To be able to use this model requires a little more. If we think of an allocation f which assigns to each agent a bundle of goods how do we say that what is allocated is equal to the sum of the initial resources $e(a)$ of the agents. To write

$$\sum_{\alpha \in A} e(a) = \sum_{\alpha \in A} f(a)$$

no longer makes sense. However, in a finite economy with n agents, we could also write.

$$\underset{\text{averages resources}}{1/n \sum e(a)} = \underset{\text{average allocation}}{1/n \sum f(a)}$$

without changing anything. In the continuum economy, just such a statement can be made by writing

$$\int e(a) = \int f(a).$$

When taking an average in this way by integrating we are assigning weights to the various subsets of agents. In other words, we integrate 'with respect to some measure μ'. In the case where $A=[0, 1]$ there is a natural measure (Lebesgue measure) which corresonds to the length of the intervals which make up a set. This allows us to carry through all the standard analysis in such an economy and indeed allows one to obtain two interesting results which do not hold in finite economies. The first is that in such an economy a competitive equilibrium exists even if preferences are not convex. The second is that the set of Walrasian allocations $W(\varepsilon)$ is equal to the set of allocations which no coalition can improve upon, called the core $C(\varepsilon)$ of the economy (see CORES). This last result is the 'perfect' or 'ideal' version of an old result of Edgeworth. In fact, Aumann's results can be shown to be approximately true for large but finite economies and thus, as one might hope, the ideal case gives us a good idea of what happens in large economies.

Two observations are in order. In fact, the choice of the unit interval and Lebesgue measure is arbitrary. All that one needs is a *measure space* $(A, \mathscr{A}, \mu)$ where A is the set of agents $\mathscr{A}$ is the collection of subsets or coalitions of agents and μ is the measure of these subsets. $\mathscr{A}$ can be thought of as the set of all subsets of A although strictly speaking this is not correct. What is required to model perfect competition is that no individual has weight. Thus one must add the condition that the measure space be 'atomless' that is for any set C with $\mu(C) > 0$ there must be a subset B contained in C with $\mu(C) > \mu(B) > 0$. This is in contradiction with the standard term 'atomistic competition' which is supposed to describe perfect competition. Another aspect of economies which implicitly makes use of the notion of a continuum economy is the discussion of the *distribution of agents' characteristics*. It is common practice in economics to use a continuous function such as the Pareto distribution to describe the income distribution. For this to be fully appropriate a continuum economy is needed. How may we formally describe distributions? Suppose that we start with a measure space of agents as explained above. Now consider an economy ε i.e. an attribution of preferences and initial resources to each agent. Take a set B in the characteristics space and consider the set C of those agents who have characteristics in B i.e. $C = \varepsilon^{-1}(B)$ Now let the measure $\psi(B) = \mu(C)$ Thus the measure μ on the set of agents induces another measure ψ on the set of characteristics. This defines the distribution of characteristics in that economy. Now, one could maintain that a good argument for the distribution approach would be that two economies with the same distribution of characteristics should have the same equilibria, for example. Hildenbrand (1975) gives a detailed discussion of this problem. The general merit of the distribution approach is of course that individualistic descriptions of the characteristics of agents make little economic sense in very large economies. Furthermore, in such economies, putting conditions on the distribution of characteristics may help in restricting the class of outcomes that may be observed. An illustration of the necessity for this is given by the results of Sonnenschein (1973) and Debreu (1974) which show that all the standard individualistic assumptions on individuals put no restrictions on the aggregate excess demand of an economy other than continuity and Walras's Law. This means that there is essentially no *a priori* restriction on the form of aggregate excess demand functions and hence on observable outcomes. Indeed, in finite economies, even specifying the income distribution does not help (see Kirman and Koch, 1986). However, Hildenbrand (1983) has shown that, in a continuum economy, if one puts a condition on the income distribution, then the 'law of demand' is satisfied. This 'normality' of goods with respect to prices is a fairly strong restriction on excess demand functions and indicates that other results in the same direction might be obtained.

Rather than make assumptions about the specific form of the distribution it is sometimes useful to be able to say something about how 'dispersed' agents characteristics are. This involves requiring that the 'support' of the measure ψ representing the distribution of characteristics, that is the smallest set which has full measure, should not be 'too small'. For example, a bothersome feature of the standard assumption of convex rather than strictly convex preferences is that demand is a

'correspondence' rather than a function. This involves considerable technical difficulties. However, it has been shown by various authors (an account may be found in Mas-Colell (1985) for example) that if the support of the distribution of agents characteristics is sufficiently large then aggregate demand will be a function and not a correspondence.

Another use of measure theory is to give precision to the idea that phenomena are 'unlikely'. Thus one cannot exclude, for example, the possibility that an economy will have an infinite set, even a continuum, of equilibrium allocations. However, as Debreu (1970) has shown, 'almost no' economies have this property. To see the idea consider an Edgeworth box representing a two man, two good exchange economy. Each point in the box can be considered as a possible location of the individual endowments. Naturally, the equilibria vary with initial endowments. What is true is that if we consider the set of endowments which give rise to infinite equilibria, its 'area' or 'measure' is zero. Thus the probability that an economy drawn at random, in some sense, will have infinite equilibria is zero.

A classic problem which has received considerable attention is that of how to divide some object fairly among n individuals. Suppose that the object is not homogeneous, a cake with different layers for example, then if an individual assigns value 1 to the whole cake he can give a value to any piece of the cake. In other words, each individual i has a measure μ_i on the cake. It has been shown that it is possible to find partitions of U ($U_1 \dots U_n$) so that each individual i considers that his share U_i is worth more than $1/n$ of the cake. This does not exclude some individuals being jealous of each other. However, Dubins and Spanier (1961) have shown that it is possible to find partitions where each individual considers that all the pieces U_i of the cake are worth $1/n$. Thus:

$$\mu(U_j) = 1/n \quad i, j = 1 \dots n$$

and everybody believes that the division is perfectly equitable.

Another illustration of the measure theoretic approach is the following. Arrow (1963) discussed the problem of establishing a rule which aggregates individual preferences on a set of social allocations into social preferences. He showed that if all individual preferences are allowed then no rule satisfying certain basic axioms exists. In particular, he showed that his first axioms implied that there must be a 'dictator', who has the property that if he prefers state x to state y, then society prefers x to y. Fishburn (1970) showed that this was not true in a society with an infinite number of individuals, thus raising hopes that in large economies Arrow's result loses its importance. In fact, this is not the case, Arrow's axioms impose a very special structure on those sets of individuals who 'dictate' society's preferences in the above sense. This structure implies that no matter how large the finite economy there will always be a dictator. Thus the infinite case is exceptional. However, in the infinite society individuals make little sense and one can give a measure theoretic equivalent of Arrow's result. For a society in which the set of individuals is represented by the unit interval then any dictatorial set C contains a dictatorial set B with positive but smaller measure that is

$$\mu(C) > \mu(B) > 0 \quad \text{with } B \subset C.$$

Thus there are dictatorial sets of arbitrarily small measure.

As a last example consider the problem of 'temporary equilibrium'. In an economy in which one can only transfer wealth to the future by keeping money and in which individuals anticipate future prices, one wishes to find an equilibrium for the goods and money markets today. Each individual forms a distribution over tomorrow's prices p_2 as a function ψ of today's prices p_1. Now if for example, individuals always expect prices tomorrow to be higher than today there may be no incentive at any prices to hold money. In this case, there can be no equilibrium. However, if we require that prices tomorrow should not be 'too dependent' on today's then equilibrium exists. Formally, we require that the family of the price distributions ψ over all prices should be 'tight'. An explanation of this with results is given by Grandmont (1977). However, intuitively, it is clear that one excludes the ever increasing expectations that lead to hyperinflation.

These examples illustrate the ways in which a formal mathematical tool, measure theory, has been incorporated into economic theory. In particular, its use in characterizing ideal economies, those corresponding to the notion of perfect competition, has been invaluable.

A.P. KIRMAN

See also **cores; functional analysis; Lyapunov functions; non-standard analysis.**

Bibliography

Any standard text in measure theory such as Halmos (1971) will give the essential mathematical notions, and more specialized references are given in the bibliographies of the articles cited here.

Arrow, K.J. 1963. *Social Choice and Individual Values*. 2nd edn, New York: Wiley.
Aumann, R.J. 1964. Markets with a continuum of traders. *Econometrica* 32, 39–50.
Debreu, G. 1970. Economies with a finite set of equilibria. *Econometrica* 38, 387–92.
Debreu, G. 1974. Excess demand functions. *Journal of Mathematical Economics* 1(1), 15–21.
Dubins, I.E. and Spanier, E.H. 1961. How to cut a cake fairly. *American Mathematical Monthly* 1, 1–17.
Fishburn, P.C. 1970. Arrow's impossibility theorem, concise proof and infinite voters. *Journal of Economic Theory* 2, 103–6.
Grandmont, J.M. 1977. Temporary general equilibrium theory. *Econometrica* 45(3), 535–72.
Halmos, P.R. 1961. *Measure Theory*. 7th edn, Princeton: Van Nostrand.
Hildenbrand, W. 1975. Distributions of agents characteristics. *Journal of Mathematical Economics* 2, 129–38.
Hildenbrand, W. 1983. On the law of demand. *Econometrica* 51(4), 997–1020.
Kirman, A.P. 1982. Measure theory with applications to economics. Chapter 5 in *Handbook of Mathematical Economics*, ed. K.J. Arrow and M. Intriligator, Vol. 1, 159–209.
Kirman, A.P. and Koch, K.J. 1986. Market excess demand in economies with identical preferences and co-linear endowments. *Review of Economic Studies* 53(3), 457–64.
Mas-Colell, A. 1985. *The Theory of General Economic Equilibrium*. Cambridge; Cambridge University Press.
Sonnenschein, H. 1973. Do Walras's identity and continuity characterise the class of community excess demand functions. *Journal of Economic Theory* 6(4), 345–54.

measurement

The dominant measurement theory is the representational theory of measurement (RTM), which takes measurement as a process of assigning numbers to attributes of the empirical world in such a way that the relevant qualitative empirical relations among these attributes are reflected in the numbers themselves as well as in important properties of the number system.

The RTM defines measurement set-theoretically. Given a set of empirical relations $\mathbf{R} = \{R_1, \ldots, R_m\}$ on a set of extra-mathematical entities $\mathbf{X}$ and a set of numerical relations $\mathbf{P} = \{P_1, \ldots, P_m\}$ on the set of numbers $\mathbf{N}$ (in general a subset of the set of real numbers), a function ϕ from $\mathbf{X}$ into $\mathbf{N}$ takes each R_i into P_i, $i = 1, \ldots, m$, provided that the elements $x, y, \ldots$, in $\mathbf{X}$ stand in relation R_i if and only if the corresponding numbers $\phi(x), \phi(y), \ldots$, stand in relation P_i. In other words, measurement is conceived of as establishing homomorphisms (also called scales) from empirical relational structures $\langle \mathbf{X}, \mathbf{R} \rangle$ into numerical relational structures $\langle \mathbf{N}, \mathbf{P} \rangle$. A numerical relational structure representing an empirical relational structure is also called a model, therefore the RTM is sometimes called the model theory of measurement.

The problem is that when the requirements for choosing a representation or model are not further qualified, it can easily lead to an operationalist position, which is most explicitly expressed by Stevens (1959, p. 19): 'Measurement is the assignment of numerals to objects or events according to rule – any rule.' A model should meet certain criteria to be considered homomorphic to an empirical relational structure. In economics, there are two different foundational approaches, an axiomatic and an empirical approach (Boumans, 2007).

Axiomatic theory

The axiomatic theory is most comprehensively presented in Krantz et al. (1971–90). According to this literature the foundations of measurement are established by axiomatization. The analysis into the foundations of measurement involves, for any particular empirical relation structure, the formulation of a set of axioms that is sufficient to establish two types of theorems, a representation theorem and a uniqueness theorem.

A representation theorem asserts that if a given relational structure satisfies certain axioms, then a homomorphism into a certain numerical relational structure can be constructed. A uniqueness theorem sets forth the permissible transformations $\phi \rightarrow \phi'$. A transformation $\phi \rightarrow \phi'$ is permissible if and only if ϕ and ϕ' are both homomorphisms of $\langle \mathbf{X}, \mathbf{R} \rangle$ into the same numerical structure $\langle \mathbf{N}, \mathbf{P} \rangle$.

Probably the first example of the axiomatic approach in economics is Frisch (1926), in which three axioms define utility as a quantity. The work more often referred to as the one that introduced the axiomatic approach to economics, however, is Von Neumann and Morgenstern (1944). They required the transformation $\phi : \mathbf{X} \rightarrow \mathbf{N}$ to be order-preserving: $x > y$ implies $\phi(x) > \phi(y)$, and linear:

$$\phi(\alpha x + (1 - \alpha)y) = \alpha\phi(x) + (1 - \alpha)\phi(y),$$

$$\text{where } \alpha \in (0, 1).$$

Another field in economics in which the axiomatic approach has been influential is the axiomatic index theory. This theory originates from Fisher's work on index numbers (1911; 1922). Fisher evaluated in a systematic manner a very large number of indices with respect to a number of criteria. These criteria were called 'tests'. Fisher himself did not expect that it would be possible to devise an index number that would satisfy all these tests. Moreover, Frisch (1930) proved the impossibility of maintaining a certain set of Fisher's tests simultaneously. It is, however, Eichhorn and Voeller (1976) who provide a definite evaluation of Fisher's tests by their axiomatic approach.

Eichhorn and Voeller (1976) look systematically at the inconsistencies between various tests (and how to prove such inconsistencies) by means of the functional equation theory. Functional equation theory is transferred into index theory if the price index is defined as a positive function $P(\mathbf{p}_s, \mathbf{x}_s, \mathbf{p}_t, \mathbf{x}_t)$ that satisfies a number of axioms, where $\mathbf{p}$ is a price vector and $\mathbf{x}$ a commodity vector, and the subscripts are time indices. These axioms do not, however, determine a unique form of the price index function. Several additional tests are needed for assessing the quality of a potential price index. Both axioms and tests are formalized as functional equations. When the axioms are formalized as functional equations, inconsistency theorems can then be proven by showing that for the relevant combinations of functional equations, the solution space is empty.

In current axiomatic index theory, axioms specify mathematical properties that are essential or desirable for an index formula. One of the problems of axiomatic index theory is the impossibility of simultaneously satisfying all axioms. In practice, however, a universally applicable solution to this problem is not necessary. The specifics of the problem at hand, including the purpose of the index and the characteristics of the data, determine the relative merits of the possible attributes of the index formula.

Empirical approach

Relation-rich structures, in contrast to object-rich structures, do not lend themselves to axiomatization. This does not mean, however, that measurement is impossible, but that a representation should, beside theoretical requirements, also satisfy empirical criteria. Moreover, economic measurements are often developed for purposes of economic policy; so, representations should also satisfy criteria of applicability. For example, a national account system should be a consistent structure of interdependent definitions, enabling uniform analysis and comparison of various economic phenomena.

To understand empirical measurement approaches, let us consider the problem of measuring a property x of an economic phenomenon. $y_i \ (i = 1, \ldots, n)$ are repeated observations to be used to determine value x. Each observation involves an observational error, ε_i. This error term, representing noise, reflects the operation of many different, sometimes unknown, background conditions, indicated by B:

$$y_i = f(x, B_i) = f(x, 0) + \varepsilon_i \quad (i = 1, \ldots n)$$

$$(1)$$

Now, accuracy is obtained by reducing noise as much as possible. One way of obtaining accuracy is by taking care that the background conditions B are held constant, in other words, that *ceteris paribus* conditions are imposed. To show this, eq. (1) is rewritten to expresses how x and possible other conditions (B) influence the observations:

$$\Delta y = f_x \Delta x + f_B \Delta B = f_x \Delta x + \Delta \varepsilon \qquad (2)$$

Then, imposing *ceteris paribus* conditions: $\Delta B \approx 0$ reduces noise.

However, *ceteris paribus* conditions imply full control of the circumstances and complete knowledge of all potential influence quantities. However, in economics we have often to deal with open systems, in which full control is not feasible. As a result, accuracy has to be obtained by modelling in a specific way. To measure x a model M has to be specified of which the values of the observations y_i functions as input and the output estimate $\hat{x}$ as measurement result: $\hat{x} = M[y_i; \alpha]$, where α denotes the parameter set of the model. If one substitute eq. (1) into model M, one can derive that, assuming that M is a linear operator (usually the case):

$$\hat{x} = M[f(x) + \varepsilon; \alpha] = M_x[x; \alpha] + M_\varepsilon[\varepsilon; \alpha]. \tag{3}$$

A necessary condition for the measurement of x is that a model M must entail a representation of the measurand, M_x, and a representation of the environment of the measurand, M_ε.

The performance of a model built for measuring purposes is described by the terms accuracy and precision. In metrology, accuracy is defined as the statement about the closeness of the model's outcome to a value declared as the standard. Precision is a statement about the spread of the estimated measurement errors. The usual procedure to attain precision is by minimizing the variance of errors. The procedure to obtain accuracy is calibration, which is the establishment of the relationship between values indicated by a model and the corresponding values realized by standards. So, we can split the measurement error in three parts:

$$\hat{\varepsilon} = \hat{x} - x = M_\varepsilon + (M_x - S) + (S - x) \tag{4}$$

where S represents a standard value. The error term M_ε is reduced as much as possible by aiming at precision. $(M_x - S)$ is the part of the error term that is reduced by calibration. The reduction of the last term $(S - x)$ is called standardization and is dealt with by finding an invariant structure representing the measurement system.

Attempting to find these invariant structures, we have to deal with the so-called problem of passive observation: it is not possible to identify the reason for a disturbing influence, say z, being negligible, $f_z \Delta z \approx 0$. We cannot distinguish whether its potential influence is very small, $f_z \approx 0$, or whether the factual variation of this quantity over the period under consideration is too small, $\Delta z \approx 0$. The variation of z is determined by other relationships within the economic system. In some cases, a virtually dormant quantity may become active because of changes in the economic system elsewhere. Each found empirical relationship is a representation of a specific data-set. So, for each data-set it is not clear whether potential influences are negligible or only dormant. This is what Haavelmo (1944) called the problem of autonomy. Some of the empirical found relations have very little 'autonomy' because their existence depends upon the simultaneous fulfilment of a great many other relations. Autonomous relations are those relations that could be expected to have a great degree of invariance with respect to various changes in the economic system.

This problem of autonomy is dealt with by the following modelling strategy: when a relationship appears to be inaccurate, this is an indication that a potential factor is omitted. As long as the resulting relationship is inaccurate, potential relevant factors should be added. The expectation is that this strategy will result in the fulfilment of two requirements: (a) the resulting model captures a complete list of factors that exert large and systematic influences and (b) all remaining influences can be treated as a small noise component. The problem of passive observations is solved by accumulation of data-sets: the expectation is that we converge bit by bit to a closer approximation to the complete model, as all the most important factors reveal their influence. This strategy, however, is not applicable in cases when there are influences that we cannot measure, proxy or control for, but which exert a large and systematic influence on the outcomes.

A very influential paper in macroeconometrics (Lucas, 1976) showed that the estimated so-called structural parameters (α) achieved by the above strategy are not invariant under changes of policy rules. Policy-invariant parameters should be obtained in an alternative way. Either they could be supplied from independent microeconometric studies, accounting identities or institutional facts, or they are chosen to secure a good match between a selected set of characteristics of the actual observed time series and those of the simulated model output. These alternative ways of obtaining parameter values are all covered by the label calibration. It is important that, whatever the source, the facts being used for calibration should be as stable as possible. An important result of this calibration strategy is that for accurate measurement it is no longer required for representations to be homomorphic to an empirical relational structure.

MARCEL BOUMANS

See also **calibration; ceteris paribus; econometrics; meaningfulness and invariance; measurement error models; measurement, theory of.**

Bibliography

Boumans, M. 2007. *Measurement in Economics: A Handbook.* Elsevier.

Eichhorn, W. and Voeller, J. 1976. *Theory of the Price Index.* Berlin: Springer.

Fisher, I. 1911. *The Purchasing Power of Money.* New York: Kelley, 1963.

Fisher, I. 1922. *The Making of Index Number.* New York: Kelley, 1967.

Frisch, R. 1930. Necessary and sufficient conditions regarding the form of an index number which shall meet certain of Fisher's tests. *Journal of the American Statistical Association* 25, 397–406.

Frisch, R. 1926. On a problem in pure economics. In *Preferences, Utility, and Demand*, eds. J. S. Chipman,

L. Hurwicz, M.K. Richter and H.F. Sonnenschein. New York: Harcourt Brace Jovanovich, 1971.

Haavelmo, T. 1944. The probability approach in econometrics. *Econometrica* 12, 1–118.

Krantz, D.H., Luce, R.D., Suppes, P. and Tversky, A. 1971–90. *Foundations of Measurement*, 3, vols. New York: Academic Press.

Lucas, R. 1976. Econometric policy evaluation: a critique. In *The Phillips Curve and Labor Markets*, eds. K. Brunner and A.H. Meltzer. Amsterdam: North-Holland.

Stevens, S.S. 1959. Measurement, psychophysics, and utility. In *Measurement. Definitions and Theories*, eds. C.W. Churchman and P. Ratoosh. New York: Wiley.

Von Neumann, J. and Morgenstern, O. 1944. *Theory of Games and Economic Behavior*. Princeton: Princeton University Press, 1956.

measurement error models

1. Introduction

Many economic data-sets are contaminated by the mismeasured variables. Measurement error is one of the fundamental problems in empirical economics. The presence of measurement errors causes biased and inconsistent parameter estimates, and leads to erroneous conclusions to various degrees in both linear and non-linear econometric models. Techniques for addressing measurement error problems can be classified along two dimensions. Different techniques are used in linear models and in nonlinear models. Measurement error models that are valid under the classical measurement error assumption often are not applicable when the classical measurement error assumption does not hold.

2. Linear models with classical measurement errors

The classical measurement error assumption maintains that the measurement errors in any of the variables in a data-set are independent of all the true variables that are the objects of interest. The implication of this assumption in the linear least square regression model $y_i^* = x_i^{*'}\beta + \varepsilon_i$ is well understood and is usually described in standard econometrics textbooks. Under this assumption, measurement errors in the dependent variable $y_i = y_i^* + v_i$ do not lead to inconsistent estimates of the regression coefficients. Its only consequence is to inflate the standard errors of those regression coefficient estimates. On the other hand, independent errors that are present in the observations of the regressors $x_i = x_i^* + \eta_i$ lead to attenuation bias in simple univariate regression models and to inconsistent regression coefficient estimates in general. The importance of measurement errors in analysing the empirical implications of economic

theories is highlighted in Milton Friedman's seminal book on the consumption theory of the permanent income hypothesis (Friedman, 1957). In Friedman's model, both consumption and income consist of a permanent component and a transitory component that can arise from measurement errors or genuine fluctuations. The marginal propensity to consume relates the permanent component of consumption to the permanent income component. Friedman showed that, because of the attenuation bias, the slope coefficient of a regression of observed consumption on observed income would lead to an underestimate of the marginal propensity to consume.

Econometric work on linear models with classical independent additive measurement error dates back to Frish (1934), who derived bounds on the slope and the constant term. Instrumental variables (IV) is a popular method for obtaining consistent point estimators of the parameters of interest in this classical independent additive measurement error model. A valid instrument often comes from the second measurement of the error-prone true variable: $w_i = x_i^* + v_i$ which is subject to another independent measurement error v_i. The second measurement w_i is a valid instrument for the first measurement x_i because it is independent of both ε_i and η_i, but is correlated with the regressor x_i based on the first measurement.

The double-measurement instrumental variable method for linear regression models has been generalized by Hausman et al. (1991) to certain nonlinear regression models in which the regressors are polynomial functions of the error-prone variables. The following is a simplified version of the polynomial regression model that they considered:

$$y = \sum_{j=0}^{K} \beta_j z^j + r'\phi + \varepsilon.$$

Among the two sets of regressors z and r, r is precisely observed but z is observed only with errors. In particular, two measurements of z, x and w, are observed which satisfy

$$x = z + \eta \quad \text{and} \quad w = z + v.$$

An i.i.d. sample of observations is assumed to be available. Therefore we focus on identification of population moments. For convenience, assume that ε, η and v are mutually independent and they are independent of all the true regressors in the model.

First assume that $\phi = 0$, then identification of β depends on population moments $\xi_j \equiv E(yz^j), j = 0, \ldots,$ K and $\zeta_m \equiv Ez^m, m = 0, \ldots, 2K$, which are the elements of the population normal equations for solving for β. Except for ξ_0 and ζ_0, these moments depend on z which is not observed, but they can be solved from the moments of observable variables Exw^{j-1}, Ew^j for

$j = 0, \ldots, 2K$ and Eyw^j, $j = 0, \ldots, K$. Define $v_k = Ev^k$. Then the observable moments satisfy the following relations:

$$Exw^j = E(z+\eta)(z+v)^j = E \sum_{l=0}^{j} \binom{j}{l}(z+\eta)z^l v^{j-l}$$

$$= \sum_{l=0}^{j} \binom{j}{l} \zeta_{l+1} v_{j-l}, \quad j = 1, 2K - 1,$$

$$(1)$$

and

$$Ew^j = E(z+v)^j = E \sum_{l=0}^{j} \binom{j}{l} z^l v^{j-l}$$

$$= \sum_{l=0}^{j} \binom{j}{l} \zeta_l v_{j-l},$$

$$j = 1, \ldots, 2K, \quad (2)$$

and

$$Eyw^j = Ey(z+v)^j = E \sum_{l=0}^{j} \binom{j}{l} yz^l v^{j-l}$$

$$= \sum_{l=0}^{j} \binom{j}{l} \xi_l v_{j-l},$$

$$j = 1, \ldots, K. \quad (3)$$

Since $v_1 = 0$, we have a total of $(5K - 1)$ unknowns in $\zeta_1, \ldots, \zeta_{2K}, \xi_1, \ldots, \xi_K$ and $v_2, \ldots, v_{2K}$. Equations (1), (3) and (4) give a total of $5K - 1$ equations that can be used to solve for these $5K - 1$ unknowns. In particular, the $4K - 1$ eqs. in (1) and (3) jointly solve for $\zeta_1, \ldots, \zeta_{2K}, v_2, \ldots, v_{2K}$. Subsequently, given knowledge of these ζ's and v's, ξ's can then be recovered from eq. (4). Finally, we can use these identified quantities of $\xi_j, j = 0, \ldots, K$ and $\zeta_m, m = 0, \ldots, 2K$ to recover the parameters β from the normal equations

$$\xi_l = \sum_{j=0}^{K} \beta_j \zeta_{j+l}, \quad l = 0, \ldots, K.$$

When $\phi \neq 0$, Hausman et al. (1991) noted that the normal equations for the identification of β and ϕ depends on a second set of moments Eyr, Err' and $Erz^j, j = 0, \ldots, K$, in addition to the first set of moments ξ's and ζ's. Since Eyr and Err' can be directly observed from the data, it only remains to identify $Erz^j, j = 0, \ldots, K$. But these can be solved from the following system of

equations, for $j = 0, \ldots, K$:

$$Erw^j = Er(z+v)^j = E \sum_{l=0}^{j} \binom{j}{l} rz^l v^{j-l}$$

$$= \sum_{l=0}^{j} \binom{j}{l} (Erz^l) v_{j-l}, j = 0, \ldots, K.$$

In particular, using the previously determined v coefficients, the jth row of the previous equation can be solved recursively to obtain

$$Erz^j = Erw^j - \sum_{l=0}^{j-1} \binom{j}{l} (Ez^l r) v_{j-l}.$$

Once all these elements of the normal equations are identified, the coefficients β and ϕ can then be solved from the normal equations $[EyZ', Eyr]' = D[\beta', \phi']$, where $Z = (1, z, \ldots, z^K)$ and $D = E[(Z'r'), (Z'r')]$.

3. Nonlinear model with classical measurement errors

The deconvolution method is a useful technique to analyse general nonlinear model

$$Em(y^*; \beta) = 0$$

under the classical measurement error assumption with double measurements. These techniques are developed by Schennach (2004), Li (2002) and Taupin (2001). Suppose one knows the characteristic function $\psi_\eta(t) = Ee^{it\eta_i}$ of the errors η_i where only $y_i = y_i^* + \eta_i$ is observed and $y^i \in R^k$. Then the characteristic function of y_i^* can be recovered from the ratio of the characteristic functions $\hat{\phi}_y(t)$ and $\phi_n(t)$ of y_i and η_i:

$$\hat{\phi}_{y^*}(t) = \hat{\phi}_y(t) / \phi_\eta(t).$$

where $\hat{\phi}_y(t)$ can be estimated using a smooth version of $\frac{1}{n}\sum_{i=1}^{n} e^{ity_i}$. Once the characteristic function of y^* is known, its density can be recovered from the inverse Fourier transformations

$$\hat{f}(y^*) = \left(\frac{1}{2\pi}\right)^k \int \hat{\phi}_{\mathbf{y}^*}(\mathbf{t}) e^{-iy^{*'}\mathbf{t}} d\mathbf{t}.$$

For each β, a sample analog of the moment condition can then be estimated by

$$\int m(y^*; \beta) \hat{f}(y^*) dy^*.$$

A semiparametric generalized method of moment (GMM) estimator can be formed by minimizing over β a quadratic distance of the above estimated moment condition from zeros. Often, the characteristic function of the measurement errors $\phi_n(t)$ might not be known. However, if two independent measurements of the latent true variable y^* with additive errors are observed and the errors are i.i.d, an estimate of $\hat{\phi}_y(t)$ can be obtained using the two independent measurements.

For certain parametric families of the measurement error distribution, $\phi_n(t)$ can be parameterized and its parameters can be estimated jointly with β. Hong and Tamer (2003) assume that the marginal distributions of the measurement errors are Laplace (double exponential) with zero means and unknown variances, and the measurement errors are independent of the latent variables and are independent of each other. Under these assumptions, they derive simple revised moment conditions in terms of the observed variables that lead to a simple estimator for nonlinear method of moment models with measurement error of the classical type when no additional data are available.

When the distributions of η are independent double Laplace, its characteristic function takes the form of

$$\phi_\eta(t) = \Pi_{j=1}^k \left(1 + \frac{1}{2}\sigma_j^2 t_j^2\right)^{-1}.$$

Using this characteristic function, Hong and Tamer (2003) (Theorem 1) show that the moment condition $Em(y^*; \beta)$ can be translated into observable variable y as

$$Em(\mathbf{y}^*; \beta)$$

$$= Em(\mathbf{y}; \beta) + \sum_{l=1}^k \left(-\frac{1}{2}\right)^l \sum_{j_1 < \cdots < j_l} \cdots \sum \sigma_{j_1}^2 \cdots$$

$$\sigma_{j_l}^2 \times E \frac{\partial^{2l}}{\partial y_{j_1}^2 \cdots \partial x_{j_l}^2} m(\mathbf{y}; \beta).$$

For each candidate parameter value β, the right-hand side of the above can be estimated from the sample analog by replacing the expectation with the empirical sum. It can then be used to form a quadratic GMM objective function which can be used to estimate jointly β and the variance parameters $\sigma_j's$ of the double exponential distributions.

4. Non-classical measurement errors

The recent applied economics literature has raised concerns about the validity of the classical measurement error assumption. For example, in economic data it is often the case that data-sets rely on individual respondents to provide information. It may be hard to tell whether or not respondents are making up their answers and, more crucially, whether the measurement error is correlated with some of the variables. Studies by Bound and Krueger (1991), Bound et al. (1994) and Bollinger (1998) have all documented evidences of non-classical measurement errors. In order to obtain consistent estimates of the parameters β in the moment conditions

$m(y^*; \beta)$, Chen, Hong and Tamer (2005) and Chen, Hong and Tarozzi (2004) make use of an auxiliary data-set to recover the correlation between the measurement errors and the underlying true variables by estimating the conditional distribution of the measurement errors given the observed reported variables or proxy variables. In their model, the auxiliary data-set is a subset of the primary data, indicated by a dummy variable $D = 0$, which contains both the reported variable Y and the validated true variable Y^*. Y^* is not observed in the rest of the primary data-set ($D = 1$) which is not validated. The authors assume that the conditional distribution of the true variables given the reported variables can be recovered from the auxiliary data-set:

Assumption 4.1 $Y^* \perp D|Y$.

Under this assumption, an application of the law of iterated expectations gives

$$E[m(Y^*; \beta)] = \int g(Y; \beta)f(Y)dY \quad \text{where} \quad g(Y; \beta)$$

$$= E[m(Y^*; \beta)|Y, D = 0].$$

This suggests a semiparametric GMM estimator for the parameter β. For each value of β in the parameter space, the conditional expectation function $g(Y; \beta)$ can be nonparametrically estimated using the auxiliary data-set where $D = 0$.

Chen, Hong, and Tamer (2005) suggest using sieve methods to implement this nonparametric regression. Let n denote the size of the entire primary data-set and let n_a denote the size of the auxiliary data-set where $D = 0$. Let $\{q_l(Y), l = 1, 2, \ldots\}$ denote a sequence of known basis functions that can approximate any square-measurable function of X arbitrarily well. Also let

$$q^{k(n_a)}(Y) = \left(q_1(Y), \ldots, q_{k(n_a)}(Y)\right)' \quad \text{and}$$

$$Q_a = \left(q^{k(n_a)}(Y_{a1}), \ldots, q^{k(n_a)}(Y_{an_a})\right)'$$

for some integer $k(n_a)$, with $k(n_a) \to \infty$ and $k(n_a)/n \to 0$ when $n \to \infty$. In the above Y_{aj} denotes the jth observation in the auxiliary sample. Then for each given β, the first step nonparametric estimation can be defined as,

$$\hat{g}(Y; \beta) = \sum_{j=1}^{n_a} m\left(Y_{aj}^*; \beta\right) q^{k(n_a)}(Y_{aj})$$

$$\times (Q_a'Q_a)^{-1} q^{k(n_a)}(Y).$$

A GMM estimator for β_0 can then be defined using a positive definite weighting matrix $\hat{W}$ as

$$\hat{\beta} = \arg\min_{\beta \in B} \left(\frac{1}{n}\sum_{i=1}^n \hat{g}(Y_i; \beta)\right)' \hat{W} \left(\frac{1}{n}\sum_{i=1}^n \hat{g}(Y_i; \beta)\right).$$

Chen, Hong, and Tarozzi (2004) show that a proper choice of $\hat{W}$ achieves the semiparametric efficiency bound for the estimation of β. They called this estimator the 'conditional expectation projection estimator'.

Assumption (4.1) allows the auxiliary data-set to be collected using a *stratified sampling* design where a *non-random response-based subsample* of the primary data is validated. In a typical example of this stratified sampling design, we first oversample a certain subpopulation of the mismeasured variables Y, and then validate the true variables Y^* corresponding to this nonrandom stratified subsample of Y. It is very natural and sensible to oversample a sub-population of the primary data-set where more severe measurement error is suspected to be present. Assumption 3.1 is valid as long as, in this sampling procedure of the auxiliary data-set, the sampling scheme of Y in the auxiliary data is based only on the information available in the distribution of the primary data-set $\{Y\}$. For example, one can choose a subset of the primary data-set $\{Y\}$ and validate the corresponding $\{Y^*\}$, in which case the Y's in the auxiliary data set are a subset of the primary data Y. The stratified sampling procedure can be illustrated as follows. Let U_{pi} be i.i.d $U(0,1)$ random variables independent of both Y_{pi} and Y_{pi}^*, and let $T(Y_{pi}) \in (0,1)$ be a measurable function of the primary data. The stratified sample is obtained by validating every observation for which $U_{pi} < T(Y_{pi})$. In other words, $T(Y_{pi})$ specifies the probability of validating an observation after Y_{pi} is observed.

A special case of assumption 3.1 is when the auxiliary data is generated from the same population as the primary data, where a full independence assumption is satisfied:

Assumption 4.2 $Y, Y^* \perp D$.

This case is often referred to as a validation sample. Semiparametric estimators that make use of a validation sample include Carroll and Wand (1991), Sepanski and Carroll (1993), Lee and Sepanski (1995), and the recent work of Devereux and Tripathi (2005). Interestingly, in the case of a validation sample, Lee and Sepanski (1995) suggest that the nonparametric estimation of the conditional expectation function $g(Y;\beta)$ can be replaced by a finite dimensional linear projection $h(Y;\beta)$ into a fixed set of functions of Y. In other words, instead of requiring that $k(n_a) \to \infty$ and $k(n_a)/n \to 0$, we can hold $k(n_a)$ to be a fixed constant in the above least square regression for $\hat{g}(Y;\beta)$. Lee and Sepenski (1995) show that this will still produce a consistent and asymptotically normal estimator for β as long as the auxiliary sample is also a validation sample that satisfies assumption 4.2. However, if the auxiliary sample satisfies assumption 4.1 but not assumption 4.2, then it is necessary to require $k(n_a) \to \infty$ to obtain consistency. Furthermore, even in the case of a validation sample, requiring $k(n_a) \to \infty$ typically results in a more efficient estimator for β than a constant $k(n_a)$.

An alternative consistent estimator that is valid under assumption 4.1 is based on the *inverse probability weighting* principle which provides an equivalent representation of the moment condition $Em(y^*;\beta)$. Define $p(Y) = p(D = 1|Y)$,

$$Em(y^*; \beta) = E\left[m(Y^*; \beta_0)\frac{1-p}{1-p(Y)}|D=0\right].$$

To see this, note that

$$E\left[m(Y^*; \beta_0)\frac{1-p}{1-p(Y)}|D=0\right]$$
$$= \int m(Y^*; \beta_0)\frac{1-p}{1-p(Y)}\frac{f(Y)(1-p(Y))f(Y^*|Y,D=0)}{1-p}dY^*dY$$
$$= \int m(Y^*; \beta_0)f(Y^*|Y)f(Y)dY^*dY = Em(y^*; \beta),$$

where the third equality follows from assumption 3.1 that $f(Y^*|Y, D = 0) = f(Y^*|Y)$.

This equivalent reformulation of the moment condition $Em(Y^*;\beta)$ suggests a two-step inverse probability weighting estimation procedure. In the first step, one typically obtains a parametric or nonparametric estimate of the so-called propensity score $\hat{p}(Y)$ using, for example, a logistic binary choice model with a flexible functional form. In the second step, a sample analog of the re-weighted moment conditions is computed using the auxiliary data-set:

$$\hat{g}(\beta) = \frac{1}{n_a}\sum_{j=1}^{n_a} m\left(Y_j^*; \beta\right)\frac{1}{1-\hat{p}(Y_j)}.$$

This is then used to form a quadratic norm to provide a GMM estimator:

$$\hat{\beta} = \arg\ \min_{\beta} \hat{g}(\beta)\ W_n\hat{g}(\beta).$$

Interestingly, an analog of the conditional independence assumption 4.1 is also rooted in the program evaluation literature and is typically referred to as the assumption of un-confoundedness, or selection based on observables. Semiparametric efficiency results for the mean treatment effect parameters to nonlinear GMM models have been developed by, among other, Robins, Mark, and Newey (1992), Hahn (1998), Hirano, Imbens, and Ridder (2003) and Imbens, Newey, and Ridder (2005). Many of the results presented here generalize these results for the mean treatment effect parameters to nonlinear GMM models.

5. Misclassification of binary of discrete variables
Measurement problems on binary or discrete variables usually take the form of *mis-classification*: for example, a unionized worker might be mis-classified as one who is not unionized. When the variable of interest and its

measurement are both binary, the measurement error can not be independent of the true binary variable. Typically, mis-classification introduces a negative correlation, or mean reversion, between the errors and the true values. Estimation methods that address the mis-classification problem have been developed by, among others, Abrevaya, Hausman, and Scott-Morton (1998), Manski and Horowitz (1995), Molinari (2005) and Mahajan (2006).

In particular, the recent work by Mahajan (2006) studies a nonparametric regression model where one of the true regressors is a binary variable:

$$y = g(x^*, z) + \varepsilon, \quad \text{where} \quad E(\varepsilon|x^*, z) = 0.$$

Instead of observing x^*, the researchers are able only to observe a potentially misreported binary value x of x^*. In the rest of this section we present the identification and estimation results developed in Mahajan (2006).

Mahajan (2006) assumes that, in addition, another random variable v is observed such that the following four assumptions hold.

Assumption 5.1 $E(y|x^*, z, x, v) = g(x^*, z)$.

Assumption (5.1) requires that conditional on the true variable x^*, the measurement error $x - x^*$ does not provide additional information about the outcome variable y. It also requires that v satisfies the following additional assumptions.

Assumption 5.2 $x \perp v|x^*, z$,

and for $\eta_2^*(z, v) = P(x^* = 1|z, v)$,

Assumption 5.3 $\eta_2^*(z, v)$ is a non-trivial function of v.

Mahajan (2006) calls the variable v an *instrument like variable* that is conditionally independence of the outcome y (assumption 5.1) and of the misreported value x (assumption 5.2), but is correlated with x^* given z (assumption 5.3). Assumption 5.1 is similar to the exclusion restriction for instrument variables in standard linear models. Assumption 5.3 is analogous to the requirement that an instrument should be correlated with regressors. Because of assumption 5.2, assumption 5.3 implies that $\eta_2(z, v) = P(x = 1|z, v)$ is also a non-trivial function of v given z.

In addition, Mahajan (2006) also imposes the following monotonicity assumption to restrict the extent of misclassification:

Assumption 5.4 Define $\eta_0(z) = P(x = 1|x^* = 0, z)$, and $\eta_1(z) = P(x = 0|x^* = 1, z)$. $\eta_0(z) + \eta_1(z) < 1$.

This assumption is innocuous since it can almost certainly be satisfied by relabelling the binary variables.

Under these assumptions, Mahajan (2006) demonstrates that the regression function $g(x^*, z)$ can be nonparametrically identified. To see this, note that $\eta^2(z, v)$ is observable and note the following relations:

$$E(x|z, v) \equiv \eta_2(z, v) = (1 - \eta_1(z))\eta_2^*(z, v) + \eta_0(z)(1 - \eta_2^*(z, v))$$

$$E(y|z, v) = g(1, z)\,\eta_2^*(z, v) + g(0, z)(1 - \eta_2^*(z, v))$$

$$E(yx|z, v) = g(1, z)(1 - \eta_1(z))\,\eta_2^*(z, v) + g(0, z)\,\eta_0(z)(1 - \eta_2^*(z, v)).$$

Suppose v takes n_v values. For each z, $\eta_0(z)$, $\eta_1(z)$, $g(0, z)$, $g(1, z)$ and $\eta_2^*(z, v)$ are unknown. There are $4 + n_v$ parameters. There are $3n_v$ equations. Therefore, as long as $n_v \geq 2$, all the parameters can possibly be identified. Intuitively, if $\eta_2^*(z, v)$ is known, the second moment condition $E(y|z, v)$ identifies $g(1, z)$ and $g(0, z)$. Information from the other moment conditions also allows one to identify both $\eta_1(z)$ and $\eta_0(z)$.

A constructive proof is given in Mahajan (2006) using the above three moment conditions. First of all, using the first moment condition

$$\eta_2^*(z, v) = \frac{\eta_2(z, v) - \eta_0(z)}{1 - \eta_0(z) - \eta_1(z)}.$$

If this is substituted into the next two moment conditions, then one can write

$$E(y|z, v) = g(0, z) + (g(1, z)$$
$$- g(0, z))\frac{\eta_2(z, v) - \eta_0(z)}{1 - \eta_0(z) - \eta_1(z)}$$
$$= g(0, z) - \frac{(g(1, z) - g(0, z))\eta_0(z)}{1 - \eta_0(z) - \eta_1(z)}$$
$$+ \frac{g(1, z) - g(0, z)}{1 - \eta_0(z) - \eta_1(z)}\eta_2(z, v)$$

$$E(yx|z, v) = g(0, z)\eta_0(z) - [g(1, z)\,(1 - \eta_1(z))$$
$$- g(0, z)\eta_0(z)]\frac{\eta_0(z)}{1 - \eta_0(z) - \eta_1(z)}$$
$$+ \frac{[g(1, z)(1 - \eta_1(z)) - g(0, z)\eta_0(z)]}{1 - \eta_0(z) - \eta_1(z)}\eta_2(z, v)$$
$$= -\frac{(g(1, z) - g(1, z))\eta_0(z)\,(1 - \eta_1(z))}{1 - \eta_0(z) - \eta_1(z)}$$
$$+ \frac{[g(1, z)\,(1 - \eta_1(z)) - g(0, z)\eta_0(z)]}{1 - \eta_0(z) - \eta_1(z)}\eta_2(z, v).$$

Mahajan (2006) suggests that, if one runs a regression of $E(y|z, v)$ on $\eta_2(z, v)$ and runs a regression of $E(yx|z, v)$ on $\eta_2(z, v)$, then one can recover the intercepts and the slope coefficients:

$$a = g(0,z) - \frac{(g(1,z) - g(0,z))\eta_0(z)}{1 - \eta_0(z) - \eta_1(z)}$$

$$b = \frac{g(1,z) - g(0,z)}{1 - \eta_0(z) - \eta_1(z)}$$

$$c = g(0,z)\eta_0(z) - [g(1,z)(1 - \eta_1(z))$$
$$\quad - m(0,z)\eta_0(z)] \frac{\eta_0(z)}{1 - \eta_0(z) - \eta_1(z)}$$
$$\quad = -\frac{(g(1,z) - g(1,z))\eta_0(z)\,(1 - \eta_1(z))}{1 - \eta_0(z) - \eta_1(z)}$$

$$d = \frac{[g(1,z)\,(1 - \eta_1(z)) - g(0,z)\eta_0(z)]}{1 - \eta_0(z) - \eta_1(z)}.$$

Therefore, one can write

$$a = m(0,z) - \eta_0(z)b \qquad (4)$$

$$c = m(0,z)\eta_0(z) - d\eta_0(z) \qquad (5)$$

and

$$c = -b(1 - \eta_1(z))\,\eta_0(z). \qquad (6)$$

Equation (4) can be used to concentrate out $m(0,z)$. One can then substitute it into (5) and make use of (6) to write

$$(a + \eta_0(z)b)\,\eta_0(z) - d\eta_0(z)$$
$$= -b(1 - \eta_1(z))\,\eta_0(z).$$

Then we can factor out $\eta_0(z)$ and rearrange:

$$1 - \eta_1(z) + \eta_0(z) = \frac{d - a}{b}. \qquad (7)$$

Now we have two eqs. (6) and (7) in two unknowns $1 - \eta_1(z)$ and $\eta_0(z)$. Obviously the solutions to this quadratic system of equation is unique only up to an exchange between $1 - \eta_1(z)$ and $\eta_0(z)$. However, assumption 5.4 rules out one of these two possibilities and allows for point identification. Hence Mahajan (2006) demonstrates that the model is identified.

Mahajan (2006) further develops his identification strategy into a nonparametric estimator, and also develops a semiparametric estimator for a single index model.

6. Conclusion

Despite numerous articles that have been written on the topic of measurement errors in econometrics and statistics over the years, there are still many unresolved important questions that are related to models of measurement errors. For example, the implications of measurement errors and data contaminations on complex structural models in labour economics and industrial

organization are yet to be understood and studied. Recent empirical studies of precautionary saving and the permanent income hypothesis make use of panel data to address the issue of measurement errors (see, for example, Parker and Preston, 2005). Also, it is often the case that not all variables are validated in auxiliary data-sets. How to make use of partial information in validation studies is also an open question.

HAN HONG

See also **econometrics; efficiency bounds; linear models; semiparametric estimation.**

The author acknowledges generous research support from the NSF (SES-0452143) and the Sloan Foundation.

Bibliography

Abrevaya, J., Hausman, J. and Scott-Morton, F. 1998. Identification and estimation of polynomial errors-in-variables models. *Journal of Econometrics* 87, 239–69.

Bollinger, C. 1998. Measurement error in the current population survey: a nonparametric look. *Journal of Labor Economics* 16, 576–94.

Bound, J., Brown, C., Duncan, G. and Rodgers, W. 1994. Evidence on the validity of cross-sectional and longitudinal labor market data. *Journal of Labor Economics* 12, 345–68.

Bound, J. and Krueger, A. 1991. The extent of measurement error in longitudinal earnings data: do two wrongs make a right. *Journal of Labor Economics* 12, 1–24.

Carroll, R. and Wand, M. 1991. Semiparametric estimation in logistic measurement error models. *Journal of the Royal Statistical Society* 53, 573–85.

Chen, X., Hong, H. and Tamer, E. 2005. Measurement error models with auxiliary data. *Review of Economic Studies* 72, 343–66.

Chen, X., Hong, H. and Tarozzi, A. 2004. Semiparametric efficiency in GMM models nonclassical measurement errors. Working paper, Duke University and New York University.

Devereux, P. and Tripathi, G. 2005. Combining datasets to overcome selection caused by censoring and truncation in moment bases models. Working paper, University of Connecticut and UCLA.

Friedman, M. 1957. *A Theory of the Consumption Function*. Princeton: Princeton University Press.

Frish, R. 1934. *Statistical Confluence Study*. Oslo: University Institute of Economics.

Hahn, J. 1998. On the role of propensity score in efficient semiparametric estimation of average treatment effects. *Econometrica* 66, 315–32.

Hausman, J., Ichimura, H., Newey, W. and Powell, J. 1991. Measurement errors in polynomial regression models. *Journal of Econometrics* 50, 271–95.

Hirano, K., Imbens, G. and Ridder, G. 2003. Efficient estimation of average treatment effects using the estimated propensity score. *Econometrica* 71, 1161–89.

Hong, H. and Tamer, E. 2003. A simple estimator for nonlinear error in variable models. *Journal of Econometrics* 117, 1–19.

Imbens, G., Newey, W. and Ridder, G. 2005. Mean-squared-error calculations for average treatment effects. Working paper, Harvard University, MIT and USC.

Lee, L. and Sepanski, J. 1995. Estimation of linear and nonlinear errors-in-variables models using validation data. *Journal of the American Statistical Association* 90(429), 130–40.

Li, T. 2002. Robust and consistent estimation of nonlinear errors-in-variables models. *Journal of Econometrics* 110, 1–26.

Mahajan, A. 2006. Identification and estimation of regression models with misclassification. *Econometrica* 74, 631–65.

Manski, C. and Horowitz, J. 1995. Identification and robustness with contaminated and corrupted data. *Econometrica* 63, 281–302.

Molinari, F. 2005. Partial identification of probability distributions with misclassified data. Working paper, Cornell University.

Parker, J. and Preston, B. 2005. Precautionary savings and consumption fluctuations. *American Economic Review* 95, 1119–44.

Robins, J., Mark, S. and Newey, W. 1992. Estimating exposure effects by modelling the expectation of exposure conditional on confounders. *Biometrics* 48, 479–95.

Schennach, S. 2004. Estimation of nonlinear models with measurement error. *Econometrica* 72, 33–75.

Sepanski, J. and Carroll, R. 1993. Semiparametric quasi-likelihood and variance estimation in measurement error models. *Journal of Econometrics* 58, 223–56.

Taupin, M. 2001. Semiparametric estimation in the nonlinear structural errors-in-variables model. *Annals of Statistics* 29, 66–93.

measurement, theory of

Most mathematical sciences rest upon quantitative models, and the theory of measurement is devoted to making explicit the qualitative assumptions that underlie them. This is accomplished by first stating the qualitative assumptions – empirical laws of the most elementary sort – in axiomatic form and then showing that there are structure preserving mappings, often but not always isomorphisms, from the qualitative structure into a quantitative one. The set of such mappings forms what is called a 'scale of measurement'.

A theory of the possible numerical scales plays an important role throughout measurement – and therefore throughout science. Just as the qualitative assumptions of a class of structures narrowly determine the nature of the possible scales, so also the nature of the underlying scales greatly limits the possible qualitative structures that give rise to such scales. Two major themes of this entry reflect research results of the 1970s and 1980s: (*a*) the possible scales that are useful in science are necessarily very limited; (*b*) once a type of scale is selected (or assumed to exist) for a qualitative structure, then a great deal is known about that structure and its quantitative models. A third theme concerns applications of these ideas to the behavioural sciences, especially to utility theory and psychophysics from 1980 onward.

There are several general references to the axiomatic theory. Perhaps the most elementary and the one with the most examples is Roberts (1979). Pfanzagl (1968) and Krantz et al. (1971) are on a par, with the latter more comprehensive. Narens (1985), which is the mathematically most sophisticated, covers much of the basic material mentioned here. Later additions are: Luce et al. (1990), which has much in common with Narens (1985); Suppes et al. (1989), which is focused on geometric representations and probability generalizations; Narens (2007), which is a more narrowly focused introductory book with examples mainly from psychophysics; and Suppes (2002). Mostly, we cite only references not included in wither Krantz et al. (1971) or Narens (1985).

1 Axiomatizability

The qualitative situation is usually conceptualized as a relational structure $\mathscr{X} = \langle X, S_0, S_1, \ldots \rangle$, where the S_0, $S_1, \ldots$ are finitary relations on X. The number of relations can be either finite or infinite, but in applications almost always finite. X is called the domain of the structure and the S_i its primitive relations. In most applications, S_0 will be some type of ordering relation that is usually written as $\succsim$. The following are some examples of qualitative structures used in measurement situations.

The first goes back to Helmholtz (see Section 4). It has for its domain a set X of objects with the properties like those of mass. There are two primitive relations. The first, $\succsim$, is a binary ordering according to mass (which may be determined, for example, by using an equal-arm pan balance so that $x \succsim y$ means that the pans either remain level or the one containing x drops). The second is a binary operation o, which formally is a ternary relation. For mass it is empirically defined as follows: if x and y are placed in the same pan and are exactly balanced by z, then we write $xoy \sim z$, where $\sim$ means equivalence in the attribute. Other interpretations of the primitives of $\langle X, \succsim, o \rangle$ can be found in the above references. Axiomatic treatments of the structure $\langle X, \succsim, o \rangle$ are discussed in Section 4.

A second example is from economics. Suppose that $C_1, \ldots, C_n$ are sets each consisting of different amounts of a commodity, and $\succsim$ is a preference ordering exhibited by a person or an institution over the set of possible commodity bundles $C = \prod_i C_i$. $\langle C, \succsim \rangle$ is called a *conjoint structure*, and axioms about it are given that among other things induce an ordering, $\succsim_i$, of an individual's preferences for the commodities associated with each component i.

A third example, due to B. de Finetti, has as its domain an algebra of subsets, called 'events', of some non-empty set Ω. The primitives of the structure consist of an ordering relation $\succsim$ of 'at least as likely as', the events Ω and $\emptyset$ and the set theoretical operations of union $\cup$, intersection $\cap$, and complementation $\neg$.

The relational structure

$$\mathscr{P} = \langle \mathscr{E}, \succsim, \Omega, \emptyset, \cup, \cap, \neg \rangle \qquad (1)$$

is intended to characterize qualitatively probability-like situations. The primitive $\succsim$ can arise from many different processes, depending upon the situation. In one, which is of considerable importance to Bayesian probability theorists and statisticians, $\succsim$ represents a person's ordering of events according to how likely they seem, using whatever basis he or she wishes in making the judgements.

In such a case, $\mathscr{P}$ is thought of as a *subjective or personal probability structure*. In another, $\succsim$ is an ordering of events based on some probability model for the situation (possibly one coupled with estimated relative frequencies), as in much of classical probability theory.

2 Ordered structure

2.1 Weak order, Dedekind completeness, and unboundedness

Two types of 'quantitative' representations have played a major role in science: systems of coordinate geometry and the real number system (the latter being the one-dimensional specialization of the former). Results about the former are in Suppes et al. (1989), but our focus here is the latter. The absolutely simplest case, included in all of the above examples, is the order-preserving representation ϕ of $\langle X, \succsim \rangle$ into $\langle \mathbb{R}, \geq \rangle$, where $\mathbb{R}$ denotes the real numbers. An immediate implication is that $\succsim$ must be transitive, reflexive, and connected (for all x and y, either $x \succsim y$ or $y \succsim x$). Such relations are given many different names including *weak order*. An antisymmetric weak order is called a total or *simple order*. There has been much empirical controversy about the transitivity of $\succsim$, with the most recent Bayesian analyses favouring transitivity of $\succ$ but not of $\sim$ (Myung, Karabatsos and Iverson, 2005). Some doubt has been expressed about completeness. Nevertheless, most of the well-developed measurement-theoretic techniques assume both the completeness and transitivity of $\succsim$ as idealizations.

G. Cantor showed that for $\langle X, \succsim \rangle$ to be so represented, necessary and sufficient conditions are that $\succsim$ be a weak order and that there be a finite or countable subset Y of X that is order dense in X (that is, for each $x \succ z$ there exists a y in Y such that $x \succsim y \succsim z$). For many purposes, this subset plays the same role as do the rational numbers within the system of real numbers.

In order for the representation to be onto either $\langle \mathbb{R}, \geq \rangle \langle \mathbb{R}^+, \geq \rangle$, where $\mathbb{R}^+$ denotes the positive real numbers, which often happens in physical measurement, two additional conditions are necessary and sufficient: *Dedekind completeness* (each non-empty bounded subset of X has a least upper bound in X) and *unboundedness* (there is neither a least nor a greatest element).

In measurement axiomatizations, one usually does not postulate a countable, order-dense subset, but derives it from axioms that are intuitively more natural. For example, with a binary operation of combining objects, order density follows from a number of properties including an *Archimedean axiom* which states in some fashion that no object is either infinitely larger than or infinitesimally close to another object. When the structure is Dedekind complete and the operation is monotonic, it is also Archimedean. Dedekind completeness and Archimedeaness are what logicians call 'second-order axioms', and in principle they are incapable of direct empirical verification.

The most fruitful and intensively examined measurement structures are those with a weak ordering $\succsim$ and an associative, positive binary operation o that is strictly monotonic ($x \succsim y$ iff $xoz \succsim yoz$). They have been the basis of much physical measurement. However, for much of the 20th century they played little role in the behavioural and social sciences but, as seen in Sections 6 and 7, since the 1997s such operations have come to be useful. The development of a general non-associative and non-positive ($x \succsim xoy$ for some x and y) theory began in 1976, and it is moderately well understood in certain situations having many symmetries. (Technically, symmetries or automorphisms of the structure are isomorphic transformations of the structure onto itself.) This, and its specialization to associative structures, is the focus of Section 3.

2.2 Representations and scales

A key concept in the theory of measurement is that of a *representation*, which is defined to be a structure preserving map ϕ of the qualitative, weakly ordered relational structure $\mathscr{X}$ into a quantitative one, $\mathscr{R}$, in which the domain is a subset of the real numbers. Representations are either isomorphisms or homomorphisms. The latter are used in cases where equivalences play an important role (for example, conjoint structures where trade-offs between components are the essence of the matter), in which case equivalence classes of equivalent elements are assigned the same number. We say ϕ is a $\mathscr{R}$-representation for $\mathscr{X}$.

From 1960 to 1990, measurement theorists were largely focused on certain types of qualitative structures for which numerical representations exist. The questions faced are two. The first, the 'existence' problem, is to establish that the set of $\mathscr{R}$-representations is non-empty for $\mathscr{X}$. Cantor's conditions above establish existence of a numerical representation of any weak order. The second, the 'uniqueness', problem is to describe compactly the set of all $\mathscr{R}$-representations. Several examples are cited. Since 1990, the focus has been increasingly on applying these insights to behaviour. We cite aspects of utility theory, global psychophysics, and probability.

For the qualitative mass structure $\mathscr{X} = \langle X, \gtrsim o \rangle$ described previously, the qualitative representing structure is taken to be $\mathscr{R} = \langle \mathbb{R}^+, \geq, + \rangle$ where $\geq$ and $+$ have their usual meanings in $\mathbb{R}^+$. The set of $\mathscr{R}$-representations of $\mathscr{X}$ consist of all functions ϕ from X into $\mathbb{R}^+$ such that for each x and y in X,

(i) $x \gtrsim y$ iff $\phi(x) \geq \phi(y)$, and
(ii) $\phi(xoy) = \phi(x) + \phi(y)$.

Such a function is called a *homomorphism for $\mathscr{X}$*, and the set of all of them is called a *scale (for $\mathscr{X}$)*. In addition to Helmholtz, others – including Hölder, Suppes, Luce and Marley, and Falmagne – have stated axioms about the primitives that are sufficient to show the existence of such homomorphisms and to show the following uniqueness theorem: any two homomorphisms ϕ and ψ are related by positive multiplication, that is, there is some real $r > 0$ such that $\psi = r\phi$. In the language introduced by Stevens (1946), such a form of measurement is said to form a 'ratio scale'. For cases where is an operation (defined for all pairs), Alimov (1950) and Roberts and Luce (1968) gave necessary and sufficient conditions for such a representation. Such a complete characterization as this one is rather unusual in measurement; sufficient conditions are far more the norm. Often they entail structural assumptions, such as a solvability condition, as well as necessary ones.

Representations of the structure $\mathscr{C} = \langle \prod_i C_i, \gtrsim \rangle$ of commodity bundles are usually taken in economics to be n-tuples $\langle \phi_1, \ldots, \phi_n \rangle$ of functions, where ϕ_i maps C_i into $\mathbb{R}^+$, such that for each x_i and y_i in C_i, $i = 1, \ldots, n$,

$$(x_1, \ldots, x_n) \gtrsim (y_1, \ldots, y_n) \quad \text{iff}$$
$$\sum_i \phi_i(x_i) \geq \sum_i \phi_i(y_i). \quad (2)$$

In the measurement literature such a conjoint representation is called 'additive'.

Debreu, Luce and Tukey, Scott, Tversky, and others gave axioms about $\mathscr{C}$ for which existence of an additive representation can be shown, and such that any two representations $\langle \phi_1, \ldots, \phi_n \rangle$ and $\langle \psi_1, \ldots, \psi_n \rangle$ are related by affine transformations of the form $\psi_I = r\phi_I + s_i$, $i = 1, \ldots, n$, $r > 0$. Note that r is common to all components. In Stevens' nomenclature, the set of such representations ψ_i for each fixed i are said to form an 'interval scale'.

In the example of the subjective probability structure, eq. (1), the usual sort of representation is a probability function P from $\mathscr{E}$ into $[0, 1]$, such that, for all A, B in $\mathscr{E}$,

(i) $P(\Omega) = 1$ and $P(\emptyset) = 0$,
(ii) $A \gtrsim B$ iff $P(A) \geq P(B)$, and
(iii) if $A \cap B = \emptyset$, then $P(A \cup B) = P(A) + P(B)$.

Unlike the previous two examples, here any two representations are identical, which scales Stevens called 'absolute'. Such a scale might be appropriate for representing a qualitative structure describing a relative frequency approach to probability. However, for subjective probability, it is better to view P as being a representation of the bounded ratio scale $\{rP | r > 0\}$ that is normalized by setting the bound, Ω, to be $1 = rP(\Omega)$.

A number of authors have given sufficient conditions in terms of the primitives for P to exist. Fine (1973) gave the first good, early summary of a variety of approaches to probability. Additional approaches to qualitative and subjective probability can be found in Narens (2008).

2.3 Interlocked measurement structures

A very common, and fundamentally important, feature of measurement is the existence of two or more ways to manipulate the same attribute. Again, mass measurement is illustrative. The mass order $\langle X, \gtrsim \rangle$ is determined as above. Mass can be manipulated in at least two ways by varying volumes and/or substances. Let $\langle V, \gtrsim', o_V \rangle$ be a structure for combining volumes, where o_V is a set of volumes and V is a strictly monotonic, positive, and associative operation over V, and let $X = V \times S$ be a structure of masses, where S is a set of homogeneous substances of various densities. (v, s) is interpreted as an object of volume v filled with substance s and that, therefore, has mass. By definition, o_V is the operation on $V \times \{s\}$ such that $(v,s)o_V(v',s) = (vo_Vv',s)$. The first manipulation is to vary $\gtrsim$ via volume concatenation of a single homogeneous material $s, \langle V \times \{s\}, \gtrsim, o_V \rangle$. The second is to manipulate the conjoint trade-off between volumes and substances, $\langle V \times S, \gtrsim \rangle$. Let m and m^* be the resulting representations of mass which, because they both preserve $\gtrsim$, must be strictly monotonically related. The ordering interlock alone is insufficient to develop measurement as was done in classical physics and as reflected in the familiar structure of physical units. Comparable developments are now beginning to appear in the behavioural and social sciences. The two structures must be interlocked beyond $\gtrsim$. Such interlocks are often types of distribution laws. In the mass case, the *distributive interlock* is: For u, $v \in V$ and r, $s \in S$,

$$(u, r) \sim (v, s) \text{ and } (u', r) \sim (v', s)$$
$$\text{imply } (u, o_V u', r) \sim (u, o_V v', s).$$

For much more detail, see Luce et al. (1990). Such laws are the source of the structure reflected in the units of physical measurement that are used and underlie dimensional analysis (Krantz et al., 1971; Luce et al., 1990; Narens, 2002).

Typically, one is able to use the two separate numerical representations to reduce the interlock to solving a functional equation. (A functional equation resembles a differential one in that its solutions are the unknown functions satisfying the equation. It is unlike a differential equation in that no derivatives are involved; rather, the equation relates the value of the function at several values of the independent variable. See Aczél (1966; 1987) for a general introduction and classical examples of functional equations. Some arising in the behavioural and social sciences were novel and have required the aid of specialists to solve.)

Behavioural examples of interlocked structures are cited in Sections 6 and 7.

2.4 Empirical usefulness of axiomatic treatments

One, seemingly under-appreciated, advantage of a measurement approach to some scientific questions is that it offers an alternative way of testing quantitative models other than attempting to fit the representation to data and to evaluate it by a measure of goodness of fit. Because representations, such as utility and subjective probability, in general have free parameters and often free functions, estimation is necessary. In contrast, the axioms underlying such representations are (usually) parameter free. Testing the axioms often makes clear the source of a problem, thereby giving insight into what must be altered. Not everyone values the overall axiomatic (as compared with an analytic mathematical) approach to scientific questions; in particular, Anderson (1981, pp. 347–56) has sharply attacked it.

A familiar economic example arose in the theory of subjective expected utility (Fishburn, 1970; Savage, 1954). In its simplest form the domain is gambles of the form $xo_A y$, meaning that x is the consequence attached to the occurrence of the chance event A, whereas y is the consequence when the chance outcome is $\neg A$. The x and y may be pure consequences or may be themselves gambles, and the theory postulates a preference ordering $\succsim$ over the pure consequences and gambles constructed from pure consequences and gambles. Classical axiomatizations establish conditions on preferences over gambles so that there exists a probability measure P on the algebra of events, as in a probability structure, and a 'utility function' U over the gambles such that U preserves $\succsim$ and

$$U(xo_A y) = P(A)U(x) + [1 - P(A)]U(y). \tag{3}$$

A series of early empirical studies (for summaries see Allais and Hagen, 1979; Kahneman and Tversky, 1979) made clear that this representation, which can be readily defended on grounds of rationality, fails to describe human behaviour. Among its axioms, the one that appears to be the major source of difficulty is the 'extended sure-thing principle'. It may be stated as

follows: For events A, B and C, with C disjoint from A and B,

$$xo_A y \succsim xo_B y \text{ iff } xo_{A \cup C} y \succsim xo_{B \cup C} y. \tag{4}$$

It is easy to verify that eq. (3) implies equation eq. (4), but people seem unwilling to abide by eq. (4). Any attempt at a descriptive theory must abandon it (see below).

2.5 Non-uniqueness of axiom systems

The isolation of properties in the axiomatic approach has an apparently happenstance quality because the choice of qualitative axioms is by no means uniquely determined by the representation. Any infinite structure has an infinity of equivalent axiom systems, and it is by no means clear why we select the ones that we do. It is entirely possible for a descriptive failure to be easily described in one axiomatization and to be totally obscure in another. Thus, some effort is spent on finding alternative but equivalent axiomatizations.

A related use of axiomatic methods, including the notion of scale (see Sections 2.2 and 3) is to study scientific meaningfulness, which is treated under MEANINGFULNESS AND INVARIANCE.

3 Scale types

3.1 Classification

As was noted in the examples, scale type has to do with the nature of the set of maps from one numerical representation of a structure into all other equally good representations, in a particular numerical structure such as the multiplicative real numbers. For some fixed numerical structure $\mathscr{R}$, a scale of the structure $\mathscr{X}$ is the collection of all $\mathscr{R}$-representations of $\mathscr{X}$. Much the simplest case, the one to which we confine most of our attention, occurs when $\mathscr{X}$ is totally ordered, the domain of $\mathscr{R}$ is either $\mathbb{R}$ or $\mathbb{R}^+$, and the $\mathscr{R}$-representations are all onto the domain and so are isomorphisms. Such scales are then usually described in terms of the (mathematical) group of real transformations that take one representation into another. As Stevens (1946) noted, four distinct groups of transformations have appeared in physical measurement: any strictly monotonic function, any linear function $rx + s$, $r > 0$, any similarity transformation rx, $r > 0$, and the identity map. The corresponding scales are called *ordinal*, *interval*, *ratio*, and *absolute*. (Throughout this article, although not in all of the literature, ratio scales are assumed to be onto $\mathbb{R}^+$ thereby ruling out cases where an object maps to zero.)

A property of the first three scale types, called *homogeneity*, is that for each element x in the qualitative structure and each real number r in the domain of $\mathscr{R}$, some representation maps x into r. Homogeneity, which is typical of physical measurement, plays an important role in formulating many physical laws. Two general questions are: what are the possible groups associated with homogeneous scales, and what are the general classes of structures that can are represented by homogeneous scales?

It is easiest to formulate answers to these questions in terms of automorphisms (= symmetries), that is, isomorphisms of the qualitative structure onto itself. The representations and the automorphisms of the structure are in one-to-one correspondence, because, if ϕ and ψ are two representations and juxtaposition denotes function composition, then $\psi^{-1}\phi$ is an automorphism of the structure, and if ϕ is a representation and α is an automorphism, then $\psi = \phi\alpha$ is a representation.

It is not difficult to see that homogeneity of a scale simply corresponds to there being an automorphism that takes any element of the domain of the structure into any other element. To make this more specific, for M a positive integer, $\mathscr{X}$ is said to be *M-point homogeneous* if and only if each strictly ordered set of M points can be mapped by an automorphism onto any other strictly ordered set of M points. A structure that fails to be homogeneous for $M = 1$ is said to be *0-point homogeneous*; one that is homogeneous for every positive integer M is said to be ∞ *-point homogeneous*.

A second important feature of a scale is its degree of redundancy, formulated as follows: a scale is said to be *N-point unique*, where N is a non-negative integer if and only if for every two representations ϕ and ψ in the scale that agree at N distinct points, $\phi = \psi$. By this definition, ratio scales are 1-point unique, interval scales are 2-point unique, and absolute scales 0-point unique. Scales, such as ordinal ones, that take infinitely many points to determine a representation are said to be ∞ *-point unique*. Equally, we speak of the structure being *N-point unique* if and only if every two automorphisms that agree at N distinct points are identical.

The abstract concept of scale type can be given in terms of these concepts. The *scale type* of $\mathscr{X}$ is the pair (M, N) such that M is the maximum degree of homogeneity and N is the minimum degree of uniqueness of $\mathscr{X}$. For the types of cases under consideration, it can be shown that $M \leq N$. Ratio scales are of type $(1, 1)$ and interval scales of type $(2, 2)$. Narens (1981a; 1981b) showed that the converses of both statements are true. And Alper (1987) showed that, if $M > 0$ and $N < \infty$, then $N = 1$ or 2. The group in the $(1, 2)$ case consists of transformations of the form $rx + s$, where s is any real number and r is in some non-trivial, proper subgroup of the multiplicative group $\langle \mathbb{R}^+, \cdot \rangle$, One example is $r = k^n$, where $k > 0$ is fixed and n ranges over the integers. So a structure is homogeneous if and only if it is of type $(1, 1)$, $(1, 2)$, $(2, 2)$, or (M, ∞). The (M, ∞) case is not fully understood. Ordinal scalable (∞, ∞) structures appear frequently in science, and a $(1, \infty)$ structure for threshold measurement appears in psychophysics. We focus here on the $(1, 1)$, $(1, 2)$, $(2, 2)$ cases. For detailed references, see Luce et al. (1990), Narens (1985), or Narens (2007).

3.2 Unit representations of homogeneous concatenation structures

The next question is: which structures have scales of these types? Although the full answer is unknown, it is completely understood for ordered structures with binary operations. This is useful because, as was noted, the associative form of these operations plays a central role in much physical measurement and, as we shall see below, both associative and non-associative forms arise naturally in two distinct ways of interest to behavioural and social scientists.

Consider real concatenation structures of the form $\mathscr{R} = \langle \mathbb{R}^+, \geq, *' \rangle$ where $\geq$ has its usual meaning and we have replaced $+$ by a general binary, numerical operation $*'$ that is strictly monotonic in each variable. The major result is that if $\mathscr{X}$ satisfies $M > 0$ and $N < \infty$ (a sufficient condition for finite N is that $*'$ be continuous – Luce and Narens, 1985) then the structure can be mapped canonically into an isomorphic one of the form $\langle \mathbb{R}^+, \geq, * \rangle$, with a function f from $\mathbb{R}^+$ onto $\mathbb{R}^+$ such that

(i) f is strictly increasing,
(ii) $f(x)/x$ is strictly decreasing, and
(iii) for all x, y in $\mathbb{R}^+$, $x * y = yf(x/y)$ (Cohen and Narens, 1979)

This type of canonical representation, which is called a *unit representation*, is invariant under the similarities of a ratio scale, that is, for each positive real r,

$$rx * ry = ryf(rx/ry) = ryf(x/y) = r(x * y).$$

The two most familiar examples of unit representations are ordinary additivity, for which $f(z) = 1 + z$ and so $x * y = x + y$, and bisymmetry, for which $f(z) = z^c$, $c \in (0, 1)$, and so $x * y = x^c y^{1-c}$. Situations where such representations arise are discussed later.

A simple invariance property of the function f corresponds to the three finite scale types (Luce and Narens, 1985). Consider the values of $\rho > 0$ for which $f(x^\rho) = f(x)^\rho$ for all $x > 0$. The structure is of scale type $(1, 1)$ if and only if $\rho = 1$; of type $(1, 2)$ if and only if for some fixed $k > 0$ and all integers n, $\rho = k^n$; and of type $(2, 2)$ if and only if there are constants c and d in $(0, 1)$ such that

$$f(z) = \begin{cases} z^c, & z \geq 1 \\ z^d, & z < 1. \end{cases}$$

If, as is the usual practice in the social sciences (see subjective expected utility, Section 6), but not in physics, the above representation is transformed by taking logarithms, it becomes a weighted additive form on $\mathbb{R}$:

$$x * y = \begin{cases} cx + (1 - c)y, & x \geq y \\ dx + (1 - d)y, & x < y. \end{cases}$$

That representation is called *dual bilinear* and the underlying structures are called dual bisymmetric (when $c = d$, the 'dual' is dropped). For references see Luce et al. (1990).

4 Axiomatization of concatenation structures

Given this understanding of the possible representations of homogeneous, finitely unique concatenation structures, it is natural to return to the classical question of axiomatizing the qualitative properties that lead to them. Until the 1970s, the only two cases that were understood axiomatically were those leading to additivity and averaging (see below). We now know more, but our knowledge remains incomplete.

4.1 Additive representations

The key mathematical result underlying extensive measurement, due to O. Hölder, states that when a group operation and a total ordering interlock so that the operation is strictly monotonic and is Archimedean in the sense that sufficient copies of any positive element (that is, any element greater than the identity element) will exceed any fixed element, then the group is isomorphic to an ordered subgroup of the additive real numbers. Basically, the theory of extensive measurement restricts itself to the positive subsemigroup of such a structure. Extensive structures can be shown to be of scale type (1, 1).

Various generalizations involving partial operations (defined for only some pairs of objects) have been developed. (For a summary, see Krantz et al., 1971, chs 2, 3, and 5; Luce et al., 1990, ch. 19). Not only are these structures with partial operations more realistic, they are essential to an understanding of the partial additivity that arises in such cases as probability structures. They can be shown to be of scale type (0, 1). Michell (1999) gives an alternative perspective on measurement in the behavioural sciences and a critique of axiomatic measurement approaches.

The representation theory for extensive structures not only asserts the existence of a numerical representation, but provides a systematic algorithm (involving the Archimedean property) for constructing one to any pre-assigned degree of accuracy. This construction, directly or indirectly, underlies the extensive scales used in practice.

The second classical case, due to J. Pfanzagl, leads to weighted average representations. The conditions are monotonicity of the operation, a form of solvability, an Archimedean condition, and bisymmetry, $(xou)o(yov) \sim (xoy)o(uov)$ which replaces associativity. One method of developing these representations involves two steps: first, the bisymmetric operation is recoded as a conjoint one (see Section 5) as follows: $(u, v) \gtrsim (x, y)$ iff $uov \gtrsim xoy$; and second, the conjoint structure is recoded as an extensive operation on one of its components. This reduces the proof of the representation theorem to that of extensive measurement, that is to Hölder's theorem, and so it too is constructive.

4.2 Non-additive representations

The most completely understood generalization of extensive structures, called positive concatenation structures or PCSs for short, simply drops the assumption of associativity. Narens and Luce (see Narens, 1985; Luce et al., 1990, ch. 19) showed that this was sufficient to get a numerical representation and that, under a slight restriction which has since been removed, the structure is 1-point unique, but not necessarily 1-point homogeneous. Indeed, Cohen and Narens (1979) showed that the automorphism group is an Archimedean ordered group and so is isomorphic to a subgroup of the additive real numbers; it is homogeneous only when the isomorphism is to the full group. As in the extensive case, one can use the Archimedean axiom to construct representations, but the general case is a good deal more complex than the extensive one and almost certainly requires computer assistance to be practical.

For Dedekind complete PCSs that map onto $\mathbb{R}^+$, a nice criterion for 1-point homogeneity is that, for each positive integer n and every x and y, then $n(xoy) = nxony$, where by definition $1x = x$ and $nx = (n-1)xox$. The form of the representations of all such homogeneous representations was described earlier.

The remaining broad type of concatenation structures consists of those that are idempotent: that is, for all x, $xox = x$. The following conditions have been shown to be sufficient for idempotent structures to have a numerical representation (Luce and Narens, 1985): o is an operation that is strictly monotonic and satisfies an Archimedean condition (for differences) and a solvability condition that says for each x and y, there exist u and v such that $uox = y = xov$. If, in addition, such a structure is Dedekind complete, it can be shown that it is N-point unique with $N \leq 2$.

5 Axiomatization of conjoint structures

5.1 Binary structures

A second major class of measurement structures, widely familiar from both physics and the social sciences, comprises those involving two or more independent variables exhibiting a trade-off in the to-be-measured dependent variable. Their commonness and importance in physics is illustrated by familiar physical relations among three basic attributes, such as kinetic energy $= mv^2/2$, where m is the mass and v the velocity of a moving body. Such conjoint trade-off structures are equally common in the behavioural and social sciences: preference between commodity bundles or between gambles; loudness of pure tones as a function of signal intensity and frequency; trade-off between delay and amount of a reward, and so on. Although there is some theory for more than two independent variables in the additive case, with the general representation given by eq. (2), for present purposes we confine attention to the two-variable case $\langle X \times S, \succsim \rangle$. Michell (1990) gives detailed analyses of a number of behavioural examples.

As with concatenation structures, the simplest case to understand is the additive one in which the major non-structural properties are:

(i)   *independence (monotonicity)*: if $(x, s) \succsim (x', s)$ holds for some s, then it holds for all s in S, and the parallel statement for the other component. Note that this property allows us to induce natural orderings, $\succsim_X$ on X and $\succsim_S$ on S;

(ii) *Thomsen condition*: if $(x, r) \sim (y, t)$ and $(y, s) \sim (z, r)$, then $(x, s) \sim (z, t)$; and

(iii) an *Archimedean condition* which says that if $\{x_i\}$ is a bounded sequence and if for some $r \sim s$ it satisfies $(x_i, r) \sim (x_{i+1}, s)$, then the sequence is finite. A similar statement holds for the other component.

These properties, together with some solvability in the structure, are sufficient to prove the existence of an interval scale, additive representation (for a summary of various results, see Krantz et al., 1971, chs 6, 7, and 9). The result has been generalized to non-additive representations by dropping the Thomsen condition, which leads to the existence of a non-additive numerical representation (Luce et al., 1990, chs 19 and 20). The basic strategy is to define an operation, say o_X on component X, that captures the information embodied in the trade-off between components. The induced structure can be shown to consist of two PCSs pieced together at an element that acts like a natural zero of the concatenation structure. The results for PCSs are then used to construct the representation. As might be anticipated, o_X is associative if and only if the conjoint structure satisfies the Thomsen condition.

6 Interlocked structures and applications to utility theory

6.1 Interlocked conjoint/extensive structures

The next more complex structure has the form $\mathscr{D} = \langle X \times S, \succsim, o \rangle$, where o is an operation on S. Such structures appear in the construction of the dimensional structure of physical units. The key qualitative axioms for physical measurement are that $\langle X \times S, \succsim \rangle$ is a conjoint structure satisfying independence, $\langle S, \succsim_s, o \rangle$ is an extensive structure, where $\succsim_s$ is the induced ordering on S, and $\mathscr{D}$ is distributive, that is,

$$\text{if } (x, p) \sim (y, q) \text{ and } (x, s) \sim (y, t),$$
$$\text{then } (x, pos) \sim (y, qot).$$

These axioms yield the following representation for $\mathscr{D}$: There exists a ratio scale S for the extensive structure $\langle S, \succsim_s, o \rangle$ such that for each $\phi \in S$ there exists ψ from X into the positive reals such that for all x, y in X and all s, t,

p, q in S, there exists a representation ϕ on S that is part of a multiplicative representation of the conjoint structure and additive over the concatenation operation: that is,

(i) $(x, s) \succsim (y, t)$ iff $\psi(x)\phi(s) \geq \psi(y)\phi(t)$, and
(ii) $\phi(poq) = \phi(p) + \phi(q)$.

Discussions of how to construct the full algebra of physical dimensions using distributive structures and how to generalize these algebras to situations where there are no primitive associative operations are discussed in Luce et al. (1990) and Narens (2002).

6.2 Rationality assumptions in traditional utility theory

As was noted earlier, an extensive literature exists on preferences among uncertain alternatives, often called 'gambles'. The first major theoretical development was the axiomatization of subjective expected utility (SEU), which is a representation satisfying, in the binary case, eq. (3). Although such axiomatizations are defensible theories in terms of principles of rationality, they fail as descriptions of human behaviour. The rationality axioms invoked are of three quite distinct types.

First, preference is assumed to be transitive. This assumption has been shown to fail in various empirical contexts (especially multifactor ones), with perhaps the most pervasive and still ill-understood example being the 'preference reversal phenomenon', discovered by Slovic and Lichtenstein and investigated extensively by others, most famously by Grether and Plott (1979), and several later references given in Luce (2000, pp. 39–45). Nevertheless, transitivity is the axiom that is least easy to give up. Even subjects who violate it are not inclined to defend their 'errors'. A few attempts have been made to develop theories without it, but so far they are complex and have not received much empirical scrutiny (Bell, 1982; Fishburn, 1982; 1985; Suppes et al., 1989, chs 16 and 17).

The second type of rationality postulates so-called 'accounting' principles in which two gambles are asserted to be equivalent in preference because when analysed into their component outcomes they are seen to be identical. For example, if $xo_A y$ is a gamble and $(xo_A y)o_B y$ means that if the event B occurs first and then, independent of it, A occurs, then on accounting grounds $(xo_A y)o_B y \sim (xo_B y)o_A y$ is rational because, on both sides, x is the outcome when A and B both occur (although in opposite orders) and y otherwise. One of the first 'paradoxes' of utility theory, that of Allais, is a violation of an accounting equation which assumes that certain probability calculations also take place.

The third type of rationality condition is the extended sure-thing principle, eq. (4). Its failure, which occurs regularly in experiments, is substantially the 'paradox' pointed out earlier by Ellsberg. Subjects have insisted on the reasonableness of their violations of this principle (MacCrimmon, 1967).

6.3 Some generalizations of SEU

Kahneman and Tversky (1979) proposed a binary modi-fication of the expected utility representation designed to accommodate the last two types of violations, and Tversky and Kahneman (1992) generalized it to general finite gambles. During the 1980s and 1990s a great deal of attention was devoted to this general class of so-called rank- (and sometimes sign-) dependent representations (RDU or RSDU) (also called cumulative and Choquet, 1953, representations). Summaries of this work, much of it of an axiomatic character for both risky cases, where probabilities are assumed known, and uncertain cases, where a subjective probability function is constructed, can be found in Quiggin (1993) and Luce (2000). These developments rests very heavily on modifying the distri-bution laws that are assumed. A far more general survey of utility theory, covering many aspects of it from an economic but not primarily an axiomatic measurement-theoretic perspective, is Barberà, Hammond and Seidl (1998; 2004).

To return to an axiomatic approach, suppose in what follows that $x_1 \gtrsim x_2 \gtrsim \cdots \gtrsim x_n$ and their associated event partition is $(E_1, E_2, \ldots, E_n)$. Define $E(i) = \cup_{j=1}^{i} E_j$. The class of RDU representations involve proving from the axioms the existence of an order-preserving, utility func-tion U over pure consequences and gambles and, in general, non-additive weighting function S over the chance events such that

$$U(x_1, E_1; x_2, E_2; \ldots; x_n, E_n)$$
$$= \sum_{i=1}^{n} U(x_i)[S(E_i \cup E(i-1)) - S(E(i-1))].$$
$$(5)$$

Note that the weighting function is essentially the incre-mental impact of adding E_i to $E(i-1)$. When S is finitely additive, that is, for disjoint A and B, $S(A \cup B) = S(A) + S(B)$, then eq. (5) reduces to subjective expected utility (SEU).

If there is a unique consequence e, sometimes called a reference level and sometimes taken to be no change from the status quo, then the consequences and gambles can be partitioned into gains, where $x_i \gtrsim e$, and the remainder, losses. In such cases, usually it follows from the assumptions made that $U(e)=0$ and, usually, the weighting functions are sign dependent (that is, their form depends on whether their consequences are positive with respect to e or negative). Also, the RSDU represen-tation includes cumulative prospect theory (Tversky and Kahneman, 1992) as a special case having added restrictions on both U and S.

Other interesting developments involving different patterns of weighting are cited in Luce (2000).

A great deal of attention has been paid to issues of accounting for empirical phenomena discovered over the years that have discredited SEU and EU as descriptive models of human behaviour. For some summaries see Luce (2000) and Marley and Luce (2005). M.H. Birnbaum (numerous citations of his articles appear in the last reference) has discovered experimental designs that discredit a major feature of eq. (5) called *coalescing* or, equally, *event splitting*: Suppose $x_k = x_k = y$, then

$$(x_1, E_1; \ldots; y, E_k; y, E_{k+1}; \ldots; x_n, E_n)$$
$$\sim (x_1, E_1; \ldots; y, E_k \cup E_{k+1}; \ldots; x_n, E_n).$$
$$(6)$$

The left-hand side of eq. (6) is called 'split' because y is attached to each of two events, E_k and E_{k+1}. The right-hand side is called 'coalesced' because y is attached to the single coalesced event $E_k \cup E_{k+1}$. Birnbaum has vividly demonstrated that experimental subjects often fail to split gambles in ways that help facilitate rational decisions. The other direction, coalescing, is effortless because no choice is involved. Indeed, Birnbaum (2007) has shown that splitting the branch (x_1, E_1), which has the best consequence, x_1, enhances the apparent worth of a gamble, whereas splitting (x_n, E_n), the branch with the poorest consequence, diminishes it. Long ago, he pro-posed a modified representation, called TAX, because it 'taxes' the poorest consequence in favour of the best one, which accommodates many empirical phenomena, including this one, but neither he nor anyone else has offered a measurement axiomatization of TAX. This remains an open problem.

6.4 Joint receipt

Beginning in 1990, Luce and collaborators have investi-gated an operation $\oplus$ of joint receipt in gambling structures and ways that it may interlock with gambling structures. Its interpretation is suggested by its name, having two goods at once which, because $\oplus$ is assumed to be associative and commutative, can be extended to any finite number of goods. Several possible interlocking laws have been studied, and improved axiomatizations involving them have been given for a number of classical representations (for a summary, see Luce, 2000). The representation that has arisen naturally is called p-additive (so named, at the suggestion of A.J. Marley, because it is the only polynomial form that can be transformed into an additive one), namely, for some real δ,

$$U(x \oplus y) = U(x) + U(y) + \delta U(x)U(y).$$

(By rescaling U there is no loss of generality in assuming that δ is either -1, 0, or 1.)

6.5 Lack of idempotence and the utility of gambling

A feature of very many utility models, in particular, of all RDU or RSDU ones, is *idempotence*:

$$(x, E_1; \ldots; x, E_i; \ldots; x, E_n) \sim x.$$

Among other things, this has been thought to be a way to connect gambles to pure consequences, but that feature is redundant with the certainty principle $(x, E(n)) \sim x$. Further, if there is an inherent utility or disutility to risk or gambling, as widespread behaviour suggests there is – witness Las Vegas and mountain climbing – violations of idempotence assess it. Luce and Marley (2000) proposed partitioning a gamble g into a pure consequence, called a *kernel equivalent of g*, $KE(g)$, with the joint receipt, $\oplus$, of its unrewarded event structure $(e, E_1; \dots; e, E_i; \dots; e, E_n)$, which is called an *element of chance*. Although they found properties of such a decomposition based on the assumption that utility is additive over joint receipt, $\oplus$, they did not discover much about the form of the utility of an element of chance. In the case of risk, further work has led to a detailed axiomatic formulation of that leads either to EU plus a Shannon entropy term, or to a linear weighted form plus entropy of some degree different from 1. In the case of uncertainty, the form for elements of risk is much less restrictive (Luce et al., 2008a; 2008b). This risky form was first arrived at by Meginniss (1976) using a non-axiomatic approach. Because of the symmetry of entropy, this representation is unable to account for Birnbaum's differential event splitting data. This approach needs much more work.

7 Other applications of behavioural interest

7.1 A psychophysical one

A modified version of one of the RDU axiomatizations has been reinterpreted as a theory of global psychophysics, meaning that the focus is on the full dynamic range of intensity dimensions (for example, in audition the range 5–130 dB SPL; contemporary IRBs restrict the top of the range to 85 dB), not just local ranges as in discrimination studies. An example of the primitives are sound intensities x and y to the left and right ears, respectively, denoted (x, u), about which the respondent makes loudness judgments. Given two such stimuli, (x, x) and (y, y), $x > y$, and a positive number p, the respondent also can be requested to judge which stimulus (z, z) makes the subjective 'interval' from (y, y) to (z, z) seem to be p times the 'interval' from (y, y) to (x, x). The data are z, which we may denote in operator notation as $(x, x) o_p (y, y) := (z, z)$. Luce (2002; 2004) (for a summary of theory, tests, and references, see Luce and Steingrimsson, 2006) provided testable axioms, it is shown that there is a real valued mapping ψ, called a psychophysical function, and a numerical distortion function W such that

$$\Psi(x, u) = \Psi(x, 0) + \Psi(0, u)$$
$$+ \delta\Psi(x, 0)\Psi(0, u) \quad (\delta \geq 0),$$

$$(7)$$

$$W(p) = \frac{\Psi[(x, x) o_p (y, y)] - \Psi(y, y)}{\Psi(x, x) - \Psi(y, y)} \quad (x > y \geq 0).$$

$$(8)$$

The axioms have been empirically tested by Steingrimsson and Luce in four papers. The 2005a focused on each structure, the conjoint one and the operator; the 2005b focused on the interlocks between them for audition. The results are supportive of the theory. Possible mathematical forms for Ψ and W have been reduced to testable conditions that, with one exception (the cases where $\delta \neq 0$, $\Psi(x, 0)$ and $\Psi(0, x)$ are both power functions but with different exponents), were evaluated with considerable, but not perfect, support, for power functions (2006; 2007). Narens (1996) earlier proposed a closely related theory that included an axiom that forced $W(1) = 1$. Empirical data of Ellermeier and Faulhammer (2000) and Zimmer (2005) soundly rejected the joint hypothesis that W is a power function with $W(1) = 1$. Subsequent theory and experiments found considerable support for power functions with $W(1) \neq 1$.

7.2 Foundations of probability

Today, the usual approach to probability theory is the classical one due to Kolmogorov (1933). It assumes that probability is a σ-additive (the countable extension of finite additivity) measure function P with a sure event having probability 1. It defines the important concepts of independence and conditional probability in terms of P.

There are many objections to this approach as a foundation for probability. A summary of most of them can be found in Fine (1973) and Narens (2008). In particular, independence and conditional probability appear to be more basic concepts than unconditional probability: for example, one often needs to know the independence of events in order to estimate probabilities. Also, in most empirical situations one cannot exactly pin down the probabilities: that is, there are many probability functions consistent with the data. This suggests that in such situations the underlying probabilistic concept should be a family of probability functions instead of a single probability function. Obviously, with many consistent probability functions explaining the data, the Kolmogorov method of defining independence by $P(A \cap B) = P(A)P(B)$ really does not work. These and other difficulties disappear with measurement-theoretic approaches to probability (for example, see Krantz et al., 1971; Fine, 1973; Narens, 1985; 2008). The qualitative approach provides richer and more flexible methods than Kolmogorov's for formulating and investigating the foundations of probability.

Both the Kolmogorov and the measurement-theoretic approaches assume an event space that is a Boolean algebra of subsets. This assumption works for most applications in science and is routinely assumed in theoretical and empirical studies of subjective probability.

A major exception to it is quantum mechanics, where a different event space is needed (von Neumann, 1995).

It is well-known that Boolean algebras of events correspond to the classical propositional calculus of logic. The classical propositional calculus captures deductions for propositions that are either true or false. It is not adequate for capturing various concepts of 'vagueness', 'ambiguity', or 'incompleteness based on lack of knowledge'. For these, logicians use nonclassical propositional calculi. In general, these nonclassical calculi cannot be interpreted as the classical propositional calculus with 'true' and 'false' replaced with probabilities. It is plausible that some of the just-mentioned concepts are relevant to how individuals make judgements and decisions. Their incorporation into formal descriptions of behaviour requires the event space to be changed from the usual algebra of events used in the Kolmogorov approach to probability to a different kind of event space. This issue and proposals for alternative event spaces are discussed in detail in Narens (2008).

In summary, the Kolmogorov approach to probability is flawed at a foundational level and is too narrow to account for many important scientific phenomena. The measurement-theoretic approach is one alternative for providing a better foundation and generalizations for the kind of probability theory described by Kolmogorov. One should also consider the possibility of developing probabilistic theories for event spaces different from algebras of events, especially for phenomena that fall outside of usual forms of observation, including various phenomena arising from mentation.

R. DUNCAN LUCE AND LOUIS NARENS

See also **expected utility hypothesis; meaningfulness and invariance; measurement; non-expected utility theory; prospect theory; Savage's subjective expected utility model; utility.**

Bibliography

Aczél, J. 1966. *Lectures on Functional Equations and their Applications.* New York/London: Academic Press.

Aczél, J. 1987. *A Short Course on Functional Equations: Based upon Recent Applications to the Social and Behavioral Sciences.* Dordrecht: Reidel.

Alimov, N.G. 1950. On ordered semigroups. *Izvestia Akademii Nauk SSSR, Serija Mat.* 14, 569–76.

Allais, M. and Hagen, O. 1979. *Expected Utility Hypotheses and the Allais Paradox.* Dordrecht: Reidel.

Alper, T.M. 1987. A classification of all order-preserving homeomorphism groups that satisfy uniqueness. *Journal of Mathematical Psychology* 31, 135–54.

Anderson, N.H. 1981. *Foundations of Information Integration Theory.* New York: Academic.

Barberà, S., Hammond, P. and Seidl, C. 1998, 2004. *Handbook of Utility Theory. Vol. I: Principles; Vol. II: Extensions.* Boston: Kluwer.

Bell, D. 1982. Regret in decision making under uncertainty. *Operations Research* 30, 961–81.

Birnbaum, M.H. 2007. Tests of branch splitting and branch-splitting independence in Allais paradoxes with positive and mixed consequences. *Organizational Behavior and Human Decision Processes* 102, 154–73.

Choquet, G. 1953. Theory of capacities. *Annals Institut Fourier* 5, 131–295.

Cohen, M. and Narens, L. 1979. Fundamental unit structures: a theory of ratio scalability. *Journal of Mathematical Psychology* 20, 193–232.

Ellermeier, W. and Faulhammer, G. 2000. Empirical evaluation of axioms fundamental to Stevens's ratio-scaling approach: I. Loudness production. *Perception and Psychophysics* 62, 1505–11.

Fine, T. 1973. *Theories of Probability.* New York: Academic.

Fishburn, P.C. 1970. *Utility Theory for Decision Making.* New York: Wiley.

Fishburn, P.C. 1982. Nontransitive measurable utility. *Journal of Mathematical Psychology* 26, 31–67.

Fishburn, P.C. 1985. Nontransitive preference theory and the preference reversal phenomenon. *International Review of Economics and Business* 32, 39–50.

Grether, D.M. and Plott, C.R. 1979. Economic theory of choice and the preference reversal phenomenon. *American Economic Review* 69, 623–38.

Kahneman, D. and Tversky, A. 1979. Prospect theory: an analysis of decision under risk. *Econometrica* 47, 263–91.

Kolmogorov, A. 1933. *Grundbegriffe der Wahrscheinlichkeitsrechnung.* New York: Chelsea, 1946.

Krantz, D.H., Luce, R.D., Suppes, P. and Tversky, A. 1971. *Foundations of Measurement,* vol. 1. New York: Academic. Repr. New York: Dover, 2007.

Luce, R.D. 2000. *Utility of Gains and Losses: Measurement-Theoretical and Experimental Approaches.* Mahwah, NJ: Erlbaum. Errata: see Luce's web page at http://www.socsci.uci.edu.

Luce, R.D. 2002. A psychophysical theory of intensity proportions, joint presentations, and matches. *Psychological Review* 109, 520–32.

Luce, R.D. 2004. Symmetric and asymmetric matching of joint presentations. *Psychological Review* 111, 446–54.

Luce, R.D., Krantz, D.H., Suppes, P. and Tversky, A. 1990. *Foundations of Measurement,* vol. 3. New York: Academic. Repr. New York: Dover, 2007.

Luce, R.D. and Marley, A.A.J. 2000. On elements of chance. *Theory and Decision* 49, 97–126.

Luce, R.D. and Narens, L. 1985. Classification of concatenation measurement structures according to scale type. *Journal of Mathematical Psychology* 29, 1–72.

Luce, R.D., Ng, C.T., Aczél, J. and Marley, A.A.J. 2008a. Utility of gambling I: entropy-modified linear weighted utility. *Economic Theory.*

Luce, R.D., Ng, C.T., Aczél, J. and Marley, A.A.J. 2008b. Utility of gambling II:. risk, paradoxes, data. *Economic Theory.*

Luce, R.D. and Steingrimsson, R. 2006. Global psychophysical judgments of intensity: summary of a theory and experiments. In *Measurement and Representations of Sensations*, ed. H. Colonious and E. Dzharfov. Mahwah, NJ: Lawrence Erlbaum Associates.

MacCrimmon, K.R. 1967. Descriptive and normative implications of the decision theory postulates. In *Risk and Uncertainty*, ed. K. Borch and J. Mossin. New York: Macmillan.

Marley, A.A.J. and Luce, R.D. 2005. Independence properties vis-à-vis several utility representations. *Theory and Decision* 58, 77–143.

Meginniss, J.R. 1976. A new class of symmetric utility rules for gambles, subjective marginal probability functions, and a generalized Bayes' rule. *Proceedings of the American Statistical Association, Business and Economic Statistics Section* , 471–6.

Michell, J. 1990. *An Introduction to the Logic of Psychological Measurement*. Hillsdale, NJ: Lawrence Erlbaum Associates.

Michell, J. 1999. *Measurement in Psychology: Critical History of a Methodological Concept*. Cambridge: Cambridge University Press.

Myung, J.I., Karabatsos, G. and Iverson, G.J. 2005. A Bayesian approach to testing decision making axioms. *Journal of Mathematical Psychology* 49, 205–25.

Narens, L. 1981a. A general theory of ratio scalability with remarks about the measurement-theoretic concept of meaningfulness. *Theory and Decision* 13, 1–70.

Narens, L. 1981b. On the scales of measurement. *Journal of Mathematical Psychology* 24, 249–75.

Narens, L. 1985. *Abstract Measurement Theory*. Cambridge, MA: MIT Press.

Narens, L. 1996. A theory of ratio magnitude estimation. *Journal of Mathematical Psychology* 40, 109–29.

Narens, L. 2002. *Theories of Meaningfulness*. Mahwah, NJ: Lawrence Erlbaum Associates.

Narens, L. 2007. *Introduction to the Theories of Measurement and Meaningfulness and the Use of Invariance in Science*. Mahwah, NJ: Lawrence Erlbaum Associates.

Narens, L. 2008. *Theories of Probability: An Examination of Logical and Qualitative Foundations*. London: World Scientific.

Pfanzagl, J. 1968. *Theory of Measurement*. New York: Wiley. 2nd edn, Vienna: Physica, 1971.

Quiggin, J. 1993. *Generalized Expected Utility Theory: The Rank-Dependent Model*. Boston: Kluwer.

Roberts, F.S. 1979. *Measurement Theory*. Reading, MA: Addison-Wesley.

Roberts, F.S. and Luce, R.D. 1968. Axiomatic thermodynamics and extensive measurement. *Synthese* 18, 311–26.

Savage, L.J. 1954. *The Foundations of Probability*. New York: Wiley.

Steingrimsson, R. and Luce, R.D. 2005a. Evaluating a model of global psychophysical judgments I: behavioral properties of summations and productions. *Journal of Mathematical Psychology* 49, 290–306.

Steingrimsson, R. and Luce, R.D. 2005b. Evaluating a model of global psychophysical judgments II: behavioral properties linking summations and productions. *Journal of Mathematical Psychology* 49, 308–19.

Steingrimsson, R. and Luce, R.D. 2006. Empirical Evaluation of a model of global psychophysical judgments III: a form for the psychophysical and perceptual filtering. *Journal of Mathematical Psychology* 50, 15–29.

Steingrimsson, R. and Luce, R.D. 2007. Empirical Evaluation of a model of global psychophysical judgments IV: Forms for the weighting function. *Journal of Mathematical Psychology* 51, 29–44.

Stevens, S.S. 1946. On the theory of scales of measurement. *Science* 103, 677–80.

Suppes, P. 2002. *Representation and Invariance of Scientific Structures*. Stanford, CA: CSLI publications.

Suppes, P., Krantz, D.H., Luce, R.D. and Tversky, A. 1989. *Foundations of Measurement*, vol. 2. New York: Academic. Repr. New York: Dover, 2007.

Tversky, A. and Kahneman, D. 1992. Advances in prospect theory: cumulative representation of uncertainty. *Journal of Risk and Uncertainty* 5, 297–323.

von Neumann, J. 1995. *Mathematical Foundations of Quantum Mechanics*. Princeton, NJ: Princeton University Press.

Zimmer, K. 2005. Examining the validity of numerical ratios in loudness fractionation. *Perception & Psychophysics* 67, 569–79.

mechanism design

Overview

A mechanism is a specification of how economic decisions are determined as a function of the information that is known by the individuals in the economy. In this sense, almost any kind of market institution or economic organization can be viewed, in principle, as a mechanism. Thus mechanism theory can offer a unifying conceptual structure in which a wide range of institutions can be compared, and optimal institutions can be identified.

The basic insight of mechanism theory is that *incentive constraints* should be considered coequally with *resource constraints* in the formulation of the economic problem. In situations where individuals' private information and actions are difficult to monitor, the need to give people an incentive to share information and exert efforts may impose constraints on economic systems just as much as the limited availability of raw materials. The theory of mechanism design is the fundamental mathematical methodology for analysing these constraints.

The study of mechanisms begins with a special class of mechanisms called *direct-revelation* mechanisms, which operate as follows. There is assumed to be a mediator who can communicate separately and confidentially with every individual in the economy. This mediator may be thought of as a trustworthy person, or as a computer tied into a telephone network. At each stage of the economic process, each individual is asked to report all of his private information (that is, everything that he knows that other individuals in the economy might not know) to the mediator. After receiving these reports confidentially from every individual, the mediator may then confidentially recommend some action or move to each individual. A direct-revelation mechanism is any rule for specifying how the mediator's recommendations are determined, as a function of the reports received.

A direct-revelation mechanism is said to be *incentive compatible* if, when each individual expects that the others will be honest and obedient to the mediator, then no individual could ever expect to do better (given the information available to him) by reporting dishonestly to the mediator or by disobeying the mediator's recommendations. That is, if honesty and obedience is an equilibrium (in the game-theoretic sense), then the mechanism is incentive compatible.

The analysis of such incentive-compatible direct-revelation mechanisms might at first seem to be of rather narrow interest, because such fully centralized mediation of economic systems is rare, and incentives for dishonesty and disobedience are commonly observed in real economic institutions. The importance of studying such mechanisms is derived from two key insights: (i) for any equilibrium of any general mechanism, there is an incentive-compatible direct-revelation mechanism that is essentially equivalent; and (ii) the set of incentive-compatible direct-revelation mechanisms has simple mathematical properties that often make it easy to characterize, because it can be defined by a set of linear inequalities. Thus, by analysing incentive-compatible direct-revelation mechanisms, we can characterize what can be accomplished in all possible equilibria of all possible mechanisms, for a given economic situation.

Insight (i) above is known as the *revelation principle*. It was first recognized by Gibbard (1973), but for a somewhat narrower solution concept (dominant strategies, instead of Bayesian equilibrium) and for the case where only informational honesty is problematic (no moral hazard). The formulation of the revelation principle for the broader solution concept of Bayesian equilibrium, but still in the case of purely informational problems, was recognized independently by many authors around 1978 (see Dasgupta, Hammond and Maskin, 1979; Harris and Townsend, 1981; Holmstrom, 1977; Myerson, 1979; Rosenthal, 1978). Aumann's (1974; 1987) concept of *correlated equilibrium* gave the first expression to the revelation principle in the case where only obedient choice of actions is problematic (pure moral hazard, no adverse selection). The synthesis of the revelation principle for general Bayesian games with incomplete information,

where both honesty and obedience are problematic, was given by Myerson (1982). A generalization of the revelation principle to multistage games was stated by Myerson (1986).

The intuition behind the revelation principle is as follows. First, a central mediator who has collected all relevant information known by all individuals in the economy could issue recommendations to the individuals so as to simulate the outcome of any organizational or market system, centralized or decentralized. After the individuals have revealed all of their information to the mediator, he can simply tell them to do whatever they would have done in the other system. Second, the more information that an individual has, the harder it may be to prevent him from finding ways to gain by disobeying the mediator. So the incentive constraints will be least binding when the mediator reveals to each individual only the minimal information needed to identify his own recommended action, and nothing else about the reports or recommendations of other individuals. So, if we assume that the mediator is a discrete and trustworthy information-processing device, with no costs of processing information, then there is no loss of generality in assuming that each individual will confidentially reveal all of his information to the mediator (maximal revelation to the trustworthy mediator), and the mediator in return will reveal to each individual only his own recommended action (minimal revelation to the individuals whose behaviour is subject to incentive constraints).

The formal proof of the revelation principle is difficult only because it is cumbersome to develop the notation for defining, in full generality, the set of all general mechanisms, and for defining equilibrium behaviour by the individuals in any given mechanism. Once all of this notation is in place, the construction of the equivalent incentive-compatible direct-revelation mechanism is straightforward. Given any mechanism and any equilibrium of the mechanism, we simply specify that the mediator's recommended actions are those that would result in the given mechanism if everyone behaved as specified in the given equilibrium when his actual private information was as reported to the mediator. To check that this constructed direct-revelation mechanism is incentive compatible, notice that any player who could gain by disobeying the mediator could also gain by similarly disobeying his own strategy in the given equilibrium of the given mechanism, which is impossible (by definition of equilibrium).

Mathematical formulations

Let us offer a precise general formulation of the proof of the revelation principle in the case where individuals have private information about which they could lie, but there is no question of disobedience of recommended actions or choices. For a general model, suppose that there are n individuals, numbered 1 to n. Let C denote the set of all possible combinations of actions or resource allocations that the individuals may choose in the economy. Each individual in the economy may have some private information about his preferences and endowments, and about his beliefs about other individuals' private information. Following Harsanyi (1967), we may refer to the state of an individual's private information as his *type*. Let T_i denote the set of possible types for any individual i, and let $T = T_i \times \ldots \times T_n$ denote the set of all possible combinations of types for all individuals.

The preferences of each individual i may be generally described by some *payoff function* $u_i : C \times T \to \mathbb{R}$, where $u_i(c,(t_i,\ldots,t_n))$ denotes the payoff, measured in some von Neumann–Morgenstern utility scale, that individual i would get if c was the realized resource allocation in C when $(t_i,\ldots,t_n)$ denotes the actual types of the individuals $1,\ldots,n$ respectively. For short, we may write $t = (t_i,\ldots,t_n)$ to describe a combination of types for all individuals.

The beliefs of each individual i, as a function of his type, may be generally described by some function $p_i(\cdot \,|\, \cdot)$, where $p_i(t_1,\ldots,t_{i-1}, t_{i+1},\ldots,t_n | t_i)$ denotes the probability that individual i would assign to the event that the other individuals have types as in $(t_1,\ldots,t_{i-1}, t_{i+1},\ldots,t_n)$, when i knows that his own type is t_i. For short, we may write $t_{-i} = (t_1,\ldots,t_{i-1}, t_{i+1},\ldots,t_n)$, to describe a combination of types for all individuals other than i. We may let $T_{-i} = T_1 \times \ldots \times T_{i-1} \times T_{i+1} \times \ldots \times T_n$ denote the set of all possible combinations of types for the individuals other than i.

The general model of an economy defined by these structures $(C, T_1,\ldots,T_n, u_1,\ldots,u_n, p_1,\ldots,p_n)$ is called a Bayesian collective-choice problem.

Given a Bayesian collective-choice problem, a general mechanism would be any function of the form γ: $S_1 \times \ldots \times S_n \to C$, where, for each i, S_i is a nonempty set that denotes the set of strategies that are available for individual i in this mechanism. That is, a general mechanism specifies the strategic options that each individual may choose among, and the social choice or allocation of resources that would result from any combination of strategies that the individuals might choose. Given a mechanism, an equilibrium is any specification of how each individual may choose his strategy in the mechanism as a function of his type, so that no individual, given only his own information, could expect to do better by unilaterally deviating from the equilibrium. That is, $\sigma = (\sigma_1,\ldots,\sigma_n)$ is an equilibrium of the mechanism γ if, for each individual i, σ_i is a function from T_i to S_i, and, for every t_i in T_i and every s_i in S_i,

$$\Sigma_{t_{-i} \in T_{-i}} \; p_i(t_{-i}|t_i)u_i(\gamma(\sigma(t)), t)$$
$$\geq \Sigma_{t_{-i} \in T_{-i}} \; p_i(t_{-i}|t_i)u_i(\gamma(\sigma_{-i}(t_{-i}), s_i), t).$$

(Here $\sigma(t) = (\sigma_1(t_1),\ldots,\sigma_n(t_n))$ and $(\sigma_{-i}(t_{-i}), s_i) = (\sigma_1(t_1),\ldots,\sigma_{i-1}(t_{i-1}), s_i, \sigma_{i+1}(t_{i+1}),\ldots,\sigma_n(t_n))$.) Thus, in an equilibrium σ, no individual i, knowing only his own type t_i, could increase his expected payoff by changing his

strategy from $\sigma_i(t_i)$ to some other strategy s_i, when he expects all other individuals to behave as specified by the equilibrium σ. (This concept of equilibrium is sometimes often called *Bayesian equilibrium* because it respects the assumption that each player knows only his own type when he chooses his strategy in S_i. For a comparison with other concepts of equilibrium, see Dasgupta, Hammond and Maskin, 1979, and Palfrey and Srivastava, 1987.)

In this context, a direct-revelation mechanism is any mechanism such that the set S_i of possible strategies for each player i is the same as his set of possible types T_i. A direct-revelation mechanism is (Bayesian) incentive-compatible iff it is an equilibrium (in the Bayesian sense defined above) for every individual always to report his true type. Thus, $\mu : T_1 \times \ldots \times T_n \to C$ is an incentive-compatible direct-revelation mechanism if, for each individual i and every pair of types t_i and r_i in T_i,

$$\Sigma_{t_{-i} \in T_{-i}} \; p_i(t_{-i}|t_i)u_i(\mu(t), t)$$
$$\geq \Sigma_{t_{-i} \in T_{-i}} \; p_i(t_{-i}|t_i)u_i(\mu(t_{-i}, r_i), t).$$

(Here $(t_{-i}, r_i) = (t_1,\ldots,t_{i-1}, r_i, t_{i+1},\ldots,t_n)$.) We may refer to these constraints as the *informational incentive constraints* on the direct-revelation mechanism μ. These informational incentive constraints are the formal representation of the economic problem of *adverse selection*, so they may also be called adverse-selection constraints (or self-selection constraints).

Now, to prove the revelation principle, given any general mechanism γ and any Bayesian equilibrium σ of the mechanism γ, let μ be the direct-revelation mechanism μ defined so that, for every t in T,

$$\mu(t) = \gamma(\sigma(t)).$$

Then this mechanism μ always leads to the same social choice as γ does, when the individuals behave as in the equilibrium σ. Furthermore, μ is incentive compatible because, for any individual i and any two types t_i and r_i in T_i,

$$\Sigma_{t_{-i} \in T_{-i}} \; p_i(t_{-i}|t_i)u_i(\mu(t), t)$$
$$= \Sigma_{t_{-i} \in T_{-i}} \; p_i(t_{-i}|t_i)u_i(\gamma(\sigma(t)), t)$$
$$\geq \Sigma_{t_{-i} \in T_{-i}} \; p_i(t_{-i}|t_i)u_i(\gamma(\sigma_{-i}(t_{-i}), \sigma_i(r_i)), t)$$
$$= \Sigma_{t_{-i} \in T_{-i}} \; p_i(t_{-i}|t_i)u_i(\mu(t_{-i}, r_i), t).$$

Thus, μ is an incentive-compatible direct-revelation mechanism that is equivalent to the given mechanism γ with its equilibrium σ.

Notice that the revelation principle asserts that any pair consisting of a mechanism *and* an equilibrium is equivalent to an incentive-compatible direct-revelation mechanism. Thus, a general mechanism that has several equilibria may correspond to several different incentive-compatible mechanisms, depending on which equilibrium is considered.

Furthermore, the same general mechanism will generally have different equilibria in the context of different Bayesian collective-choice problems, where the structure of individuals' beliefs and payoffs are different. For example, consider a first-price sealed-bid auction where there are five potential bidders who are risk-neutral with independent private values drawn from the same distribution over \$0 to \$10. If the bidders' values are drawn from a uniform distribution over this interval, then there is an equilibrium in which each bidder bids 4/5 of his value. On the other hand, if the bidders' values are drawn instead from a distribution with a probability density that is proportional to the square of the value, then there is an equilibrium in which each bidder bids 8/9 of his value. So in one situation the first-price sealed-bid auction (a general mechanism) corresponds to an incentive-compatible mechanism in which the bidder who reports the highest value gets the object for 4/5 of his reported value; but in the other situation it corresponds to an incentive-compatible mechanism in which the bidder who reports the highest value gets the object for 8/9 of his reported value. There is no incentive-compatible direct-revelation mechanism that is equivalent to the first-price sealed-bid auction in all situations, independently of the bidders' beliefs about each others' values. Thus, if we want to design a mechanism that has good properties in the context of many different Bayesian collective-choice problems, we cannot necessarily restrict our attention to incentive-compatible direct-revelation mechanisms, and so our task is correspondingly more difficult. (See Wilson, 1985, for a remarkable effort at this kind of difficult question.)

Even an incentive-compatible mechanism itself may have other dishonest equilibria that correspond to different incentive-compatible mechanisms. Thus, when we talk about selecting an incentive-compatible mechanism and assume that it will then be played according to its honest equilibrium, we are implicitly making an assumption about the selection of an equilibrium as well as of a mechanism or communication structure. Thus, for example, when we say that a particular incentive-compatible mechanism maximizes a given individual's expected utility, we mean that, if you could choose any general mechanism for coordinating the individuals in the economy and if you could also (by some public statement, as a focal arbitrator, using Schelling's, 1960, *focal-point effect*) designate the equilibrium that the individuals would play in your mechanism, then you could not give this given individual a higher expected utility than by choosing this incentive-compatible mechanism and its honest equilibrium.

In many situations, an individual may have a right to refuse to participate in an economic system or organization. For example, a consumer generally has the right to refuse to participate in any trading scheme and instead just consume his initial endowment. If we let $w_i(t_i)$ denote the utility payoff that individual i would get if he refused to participate when his type is t_i, and if we assume that an individual can make the choice not to participate after learning his type, then an incentive-compatible mechanism μ must also satisfy the following constraint, for every individual i and every possible type t_i:

$$\Sigma_{t_{-i} \in T_{-i}} \; p_i(t_{-i}|t_i)u_i(\mu(t), t) \geq w_i(t_i).$$

These constraints are called *participational incentive constraints*, or *individual-rationality* constraints.

In the analysis of Bayesian collective-choice problems, we have supposed that the only incentive problem was to get people to share their information, and to agree to participate in the mechanism in the first place. More generally, a social choice may be privately controlled by one or more individuals who cannot be trusted to follow some pre-specified plan when it is not in their best interests. For example, suppose now that the choice in C is privately controlled by some individual (call him 'individual 0') whose choice of an action in C cannot be regulated. To simplify matters here, let us suppose that this individual 0 has no private information. Let $p_0(t)$ denote the probability that this individual would assign to the event that $t=(t_1,\ldots,t_n)$ is the profile of types for the other n individuals, and let $u_0(c, t)$ denote the utility payoff that this individual receives if he chooses action c when t is the actual profile of types. Then, to give this active individual an incentive to obey the recommendations of a mediator who is implementing the direct-revelation mechanism μ, μ must satisfy

$$\Sigma_{t \in T} \; p_0(t)u_0(\mu(t), t) \geq \Sigma_{t \in T} \; p_0(t)u_0(\delta(\mu(t)), t)$$

for every function $\delta: C \rightarrow C$. These constraints assert that obeying the actions recommended by the mediator is better for this individual than any disobedient strategy δ under which he would choose $\delta(c)$ if the mediator recommended c. Such constraints are called *strategic incentive constraints* or *moral-hazard constraints*, because they are the formal representation of the economic problem of moral hazard.

For a formulation of general incentive constraints that apply when individuals both have private information and control private actions, see Myerson (1982) or (1985).

Applications

In general, the mechanism-theoretic approach to economic problems is to list the constraints that an incentive-compatible mechanism must satisfy, and to try to characterize the incentive-compatible mechanisms that have properties of interest.

For example, one early contribution of mechanism theory was the derivation of general *revenue equivalence* theorems in auction theory. Ortega-Reichert (1968) found that, when bidders are risk-neutral and have private values for the object being sold that are independent and drawn from the same distribution, then a remarkably diverse collection of different auction mechanisms all generate the same expected revenue to the seller, when bidders use equilibrium strategies. In all of these different mechanisms and equilibria, it turned out that the bidder whose value for the object was highest would always end up getting the object, while a bidder whose value for the object was zero would never pay anything. By analysing the incentive constraints, Harris and Raviv (1981), Myerson (1981) and Riley and Samuelson (1981) showed that all incentive-compatible mechanisms with these properties would necessarily generate the same expected revenue, in such economic situations.

Using methods of constrained optimization, the problem of finding the incentive-compatible mechanism that maximizes some given objective (one individual's expected utility, or some social welfare function) can be solved for many examples. The resulting optimal mechanisms often have remarkable qualitative properties.

For example, suppose a seller, with a single indivisible object to sell, faces five potential buyers or bidders, whose private values for the object are independently drawn from a uniform distribution over the interval from $0 to $10. If the objective is to maximize the sellers' expected revenue, optimal auction mechanisms exist and all have the property that the object is sold to the bidder with the highest value for it, except that the seller keeps the object in the event that the bidders' values are all less than $5. Such a result may seem surprising, because this event could occur with positive probability (1/32) and in this event the seller is getting no revenue in an 'optimal' auction, even though any bidder would almost surely be willing to pay him a positive price for the object. Nevertheless, no incentive-compatible mechanism (satisfying the participational and informational incentive constraints) can offer the seller higher expected utility than these optimal auctions, and thus no equilibrium of any general auction mechanism can offer higher expected revenue either. Maximizing expected revenue requires a positive probability of seemingly wasteful allocation.

The threat of keeping the object, when all bidders report values below $5, increases the seller's expected revenue because it gives the bidders an incentive to bid higher and pay more when their values are above $5. In many other economic environments, we can similarly prove the optimality of mechanisms in which seemingly wasteful threats are carried out with positive probability. People have intuitively understood that costly threats are often made to give some individual an incentive to reveal some information or choose some action, and the analysis of incentive constraints allows us to formalize this understanding rigorously.

In some situations, incentive constraints imply that such seemingly wasteful allocations may have to occur with positive probability in all incentive-compatible mechanisms, and so also in all equilibria of all general mechanisms. For example, Myerson and Satterthwaite (1983) considered bilateral bargaining problems between a seller of some object and a potential buyer, both of whom are risk-neutral and have independent private values for the object that are drawn out of distributions that have continuous positive probability densities over some pair of intervals that have an intersection of positive length. Under these technical (but apparently quite weak) assumptions, it is impossible to satisfy the participational and informational incentive constraints with any mechanism in which the buyer gets the object whenever it is worth more to him than to the seller. Thus, we cannot hope to guarantee the attainment of full *ex post* efficiency of resource allocations in bilateral bargaining problems where the buyer and seller are uncertain about each other's reservation prices. If we are concerned with welfare and efficiency questions, it may be more productive to try to characterize the incentive-compatible mechanisms that maximize the expected total gains from trade, or that maximize the probability that a mutually beneficial trade will occur. For example, in the bilateral bargaining problem where the seller's and buyer's private values for the object are independent random variables drawn from a uniform distribution over the interval from $0 to $10, both of these objectives are maximized subject to incentive constraints by mechanisms in which the buyer gets the object if and only if his value is greater than the seller's value by $2.50 or more. Under such a mechanism, the event that the seller will keep the object when it is actually worth more to the buyer has probability 7/32, but no equilibrium of any general mechanism can generate a lower probability of this event.

The theory of mechanism design has fundamental implications about the domain of applicability of Coase's (1960) theorem, which asserts the irrelevance of initial property rights to efficiency of final, allocations. The unavoidable possibility of failure to realize mutually beneficial trades, in such bilateral trading problems with two-sided uncertainty, can be interpreted as one of the 'transaction costs' that limits the validity of Coase's theorem. Indeed, as Samuelson (1985) has emphasized, reassignment of property rights generally changes the payoffs that individuals can guarantee themselves without selling anything, which changes the right-hand sides of the participational incentive constraints, which in turn can change the maximal social welfare achievable by an optimal incentive-compatible mechanism.

For example, consider again the case where there is one object and two individuals who have private values for the object that are independent random variables drawn from a uniform distribution over the interval from $0 to $10. When we assumed above that one was the 'seller', we meant that he had the right to keep the object and pay nothing to anyone, until he agreed to some other arrangement. Now, let us suppose instead that the rights to the object are distributed equally between the two individuals. Suppose that the object is a divisible good and each individual has a right to take half of the good and pay nothing, unless he agrees to some other arrangement. (Assume that, if an individual's value for the whole good is t_i, then his value for half would be $t_i/2$.) With this symmetric assignment of property rights, we can design incentive-compatible mechanisms in which the object always ends up being owned entirely by the individual who has the higher value for it, as Cramton, Gibbons and Klemperer (1987) have shown.

For example, consider the game in which each individual independently puts money in an envelope, and then the individual who put more money in his envelope gets the object, while the other individual takes the money in both envelopes. This game has an equilibrium in which each individual puts into his envelope an amount equal to one-third of his value for the whole good. This equilibrium of this game is equivalent to an incentive-compatible direct-revelation mechanism in which the individual who reports the higher value pays one-third of his value to buy out the other individual's half-share. This mechanism would violate the participational incentive constraints if one individual had a right to the whole good (in which case, for example, if his value were $10 then he would be paying $3.33 under this mechanism for a good that he already owned). But with rights to only half of the good, no type of either individual could expect to do better (at the beginning of the game, when he knows his own value but not the other's) by keeping his half and refusing to participate in this mechanism.

More generally, redistribution of property rights tends to reduce the welfare losses caused by incentive constraints when it creates what Lewis and Sappington (1989) have called *countervailing incentives*. In games where one individual is the seller and the other is the buyer, if either individual has an incentive to lie, it is usually because the seller wants to overstate his value or the buyer wants to understate his value. In the case where either individual may buy the other's half-share, neither individual can be sure at first whether he will be the buyer or the seller (unless he has the highest or lowest possible value). Thus, a buyer-like incentive to understate values, in the event where the other's value is lower, may help to cancel out a seller-like incentive to overstate values, in the event where the other's value is higher.

The theory of mechanism design can also help us to appreciate the importance of mediation in economic relationships and transactions. There are situations in which, if the individuals were required to communicate with each other only through perfect noiseless communication channels (for example, in face-to-face dialogue), then the set of all possible equilibria would be much smaller than the set of incentive-compatible mechanisms that are achievable with a mediator. (Of course, the revelation principle asserts that the former set cannot be larger than the latter.)

For example, consider the following 'sender–receiver game' due to J. Farrell. Player 1 has a privately known type that may be α or β, but he has no payoff-relevant action to choose. Player 2 has no private information, but he must choose an action from the set $\{x, y, z\}$. The payoffs to players 1 and 2 respectively depend on 1's type and 2's action as follows.

	x	y	z
α	2, 3	1, 2	0, 0
β	4, -3	8, -1	0, 0

At the beginning of the game, player 2 believes that each of 1's two possible types has probability 1/2.

Suppose that, knowing his type, player 1 is allowed to choose a message in some arbitrarily rich language, and player 2 will hear player 1's message (with no noise or distortion) before choosing his action. In every equilibrium of this game, including the randomized equilibria, player 2 must choose y with probability 1, after every message that player 1 may choose in equilibrium (see Farrell, 1993; Myerson, 1988). If there were some message that player 1 could use to increase the probability of player 2 choosing x (for example, 'I am α, so choosing x would be best for us both!'), then he would always send such a message when his type was α. (It can be shown that no message could ever induce player 2 to randomize between x and z.) So not receiving such a message would lead 2 to infer that 1's type was β, which implies that 2 would rationally choose z whenever such a message was not sent, so that both types of 1 should always send the message (any randomization between x and y is better than z for both types of 1). But a message that is always sent by player 1, no matter what his type is, would convey no information to player 2, so that 2 would rationally choose his *ex ante* optimal action y.

If we now allow the players to communicate through a mediator who uses a randomized mechanism, then we can apply the revelation principle to characterize the surprisingly large set of possible incentive-compatible mechanisms. Among all direct-revelation mechanisms that satisfy the relevant informational incentive constraints for player 1 and strategic incentive constraints for player 2, the best for player 2 is as follows: if player 1 reports to the mediator that his type is α then with probability 2/3 the mediator recommends x to player 2, and with probability 1/3 the mediator recommends y to player 2; if player 1 reports to the mediator that his type is β then with probability 2/3 the mediator recommends y to player 2, and with probability 1/3 the mediator recommends z to player 2. Notice that this mechanism is also better for player 1 than the unmediated equilibria when 1's type is α, although it is worse for 1 when his type is β.

Other mechanisms that player 2 might prefer would violate the strategic incentive constraint that player 2 should not expect to gain by choosing z instead of y when y is recommended. If player 2 could pre-commit himself always to obey the mediator's recommendations, then better mechanisms could be designed.

Efficiency

The concept of efficiency becomes more difficult to define in economic situations where individuals have different private information at the time when the basic decisions about production and allocation are made. A welfare economist or social planner who analyses the Pareto efficiency of an economic system must use the perspective of an outsider, so he cannot base his analysis on the individuals' private information. Otherwise, public testimony as to whether an economic mechanism or its outcome would be 'efficient' could implicitly reveal some individuals' private information to other individuals, which could in turn alter their rational behaviour and change the outcome of the mechanism! Thus, Holmstrom and Myerson (1983) argued that efficiency should be considered as a property of mechanisms, rather than of the outcome or allocation ultimately realized by the mechanism (which will depend on the individuals' private information).

Thus, a definition of Pareto efficiency in a Bayesian collective-choice problem must look something like this: 'a mechanism is efficient if there is no other feasible mechanism that may make some other individuals better off and will certainly not make other individuals worse off.' However, this definition is ambiguous in at least two ways.

First, we must specify whether the concept of feasibility takes incentive constraints into account or not. The concept of feasibility that ignores incentive constraints may be called *classical feasibility*. In these terms, the fundamental insight of mechanism theory is that incentive constraints are just as real as resource constraints, so that incentive compatibility may be a more fruitful concept than classical feasibility for welfare economics.

Second, we must specify what information is to be considered in determining whether an individual is 'better off' or 'worse off'. One possibility is to say that an individual is made worse off by a change that decreases his expected utility payoff as would be computed before his own type or any other individuals' types are specified. This is called the *ex ante* welfare criterion. A second possibility is to say that an individual is made worse off by a change that decreases his conditionally expected utility, given his own type (but not given the types of any other individuals). An outside observer, who does not know any individual's type, would then say that an individual may be made worse off, in this sense, if this conditionally expected utility were decreased for at least one possible type of the individual. This is called the *interim* welfare criterion. A third possibility is to say that an individual is made worse off by a change that decreases his conditionally expected utility given the types of all individuals. An outside observer would then say that an individual may be worse off in this sense if his conditionally expected utility were decreased for at least one possible combination of types for all the individuals. This is called the *ex post* welfare criterion.

If each individual knows his own type at the time when economic plans and decisions are made, then the interim welfare criterion should be most relevant to a social planner. Thus, Holmstrom and Myerson (1983) argue that, for welfare analysis in a Bayesian collective-choice problem, the most appropriate concept of efficiency is that which combines the interim welfare criterion and the incentive-compatible definition of feasibility. This concept is called *incentive efficiency*, or *interim incentive efficiency*. That is, a mechanism $\mu: T \to C$ is incentive efficient if it is an incentive-compatible mechanism and there does not exist any other incentive-compatible mechanism $\gamma: T \to C$ such that for every individual i and every type t_i in T_i,

$$\Sigma_{t_{-i} \in T_{-i}} \ p_i(t_{-i}|t_i)u_i(\gamma(t), t)$$
$$\geq \Sigma_{t_{-i} \in T_{-i}} \ p_i(t_{-i}|t_i)u_i(\mu(t), t),$$

and there is at least one type of at least one individual for which this inequality is strict. If a mechanism is incentive efficient, then it cannot be common knowledge among the individuals, at the stage when each knows only his own type, that there is some other incentive-compatible mechanism that no one would consider worse (given his own information) and some might consider strictly better.

For comparison, another important concept is classical *ex post* efficiency, defined using the *ex post* welfare criterion and the classical feasibility concept. That is, a mechanism $\mu: T \to C$ is (*classically*) *ex post efficient* iff there does not exist any other mechanism $\gamma: T \to C$ (not necessarily incentive compatible) such that, for every individual i and every combination of individuals' types t in $T = T_1 \times \ldots \times T_n$,

$$u_i(\gamma(t), t) \geq u_i(\mu(t), t),$$

with strict inequality for at least one individual and at least one combination of individuals' types.

The appeal of *ex post* efficiency is that there may seem to be something unstable about a mechanism that sometimes leads to outcomes such that, if everyone could share their information, they could identify another outcome that would make them all better off. However, we have seen that bargaining situations exist where no incentive-compatible mechanisms are *ex post* efficient. In such situations, the incentive constraints imply that rational individuals would be unable to share their information to achieve these gains, because if everyone were expected to do so then at least one type of one individual would have an incentive to lie.

Thus, a benevolent outside social planner who is persuaded by the usual Paretian arguments should choose some incentive-efficient mechanism. To determine more specifically an 'optimal' mechanism within this set, a social welfare function is needed that defines tradeoffs, not only between the expected payoffs of different individuals but also between the expected payoffs of different types of each individual. That is, given any positive utility-weights $\lambda_i(t_i)$ for each type t_i of each individual i, one can generate an incentive-efficient mechanism by maximizing

$$\Sigma_{i=1}^n \ \Sigma_{t_i \in T_i} \ \lambda_i(t_i) \ \Sigma_{t_{-i} \in T_{-i}} \ p_i(t_{-i}|t_i)u_i(\mu(t),t)$$

over all $\mu: T \to C$ that satisfy the incentive constraints; but different vectors of utility weights may generate different incentive-efficient mechanisms.

Bargaining over mechanisms

A positive economic theory must go beyond welfare economics and try to predict the economic institutions that may actually be chosen by the individuals in an economy. Having established that a social planner can restrict his attention to incentive-compatible direct-revelation mechanisms, which is a mathematically simple set, it is natural to assume that rational economic agents who are themselves negotiating the structure of their economic institutions should be able to bargain over the set of incentive-compatible direct-revelation mechanisms. But if we assume that individuals know their types already at the time when fundamental economic plans and decisions are made, then we need a theory of mechanism selection by individuals who have private information.

When we consider bargaining games in which individuals can bargain over mechanisms, there should be no loss of generality in restricting our attention to equilibria in which there is one incentive-compatible mechanism that is selected with probability 1 independently of anyone's type. This proposition, called the *inscrutability principle*, can be justified by viewing the mechanism-selection process as itself part of a more broadly defined general mechanism and applying the revelation principle. For example, suppose that there is an equilibrium of the mechanism-selection game in which some mechanism μ would be chosen if individual 1's type were α and some other mechanism ν would be chosen if 1's type were β. Then there should exist an equivalent equilibrium of the mechanism-selection game in which the individuals always select a direct-revelation mechanism that coincides with mechanism μ when individual 1 confidentially reports type α to the mediator (in the implementation of the mechanism, after it has been selected), and that coincides with mechanism ν when 1 reports type β to the mediator.

However, the inscrutability principle does not imply that the possibility of revealing information during a mechanism-selection process is irrelevant. There may be some mechanisms that we should expect not to be selected by the individuals in such a process, precisely because some individuals would choose to reveal information about their types rather than let these mechanisms be selected. For example, consider the following Bayesian collective-choice problem, due to Holmstrom and Myerson (1983). There are two individuals, 1 and 2, each of whom has two possible types, α and β, which are independent and equally likely. There are three social choice options, called x, y and z. Each individual's utility for these options depends on his type according to the following table.

Option	$1, \alpha$	$1, \beta$	$2, \alpha$	$2, \beta$
x	2	0	2	2
y	1	4	1	1
z	0	9	0	-8

The incentive-efficient mechanism that maximizes the *ex ante* expected sum of the two individuals' utilities is as follows: if 1 reports type α and 2 reports α then choose x, if 1 reports type β and 2 reports α then choose z, and if 2 reports β then choose y (regardless of 1's report). However, Holmstrom and Myerson argue that such a mechanism would not be chosen in a mechanism-selection game that is played when 1 already knows his type, because, when 1 knows that his type is α, he could do better by proposing to select the mechanism that always chooses x, and 2 would always want to accept this proposal. That is, because 1 would have no incentive to conceal his type from 2 in a mechanism-selection game if his type were α (when his interests would then have no conflict with 2's), we should not expect the individuals in a mechanism-selection game to agree inscrutably to an incentive-efficient mechanism that implicitly puts as much weight on 1's type-β payoff as the mechanism described above.

For another example, consider again the sender–receiver game due to Farrell. Recall that y would be the only possible equilibrium outcome if the individuals could communicate only face-to-face, with no mediation or other noise in their communication channel. Suppose that the mechanism-selection process is as follows: first 2 proposes a mediator who is committed to implement some incentive-compatible mechanism; then 1 can either accept this mediator and communicate with 2 thereafter only through him, or 1 can reject this mediator and thereafter communicate with 2 only face-to-face. Suppose now that 2 proposes that they should use a mediator who will implement the incentive-compatible mediation plan that is best for 2 (recommending x with probability 2/3 and y with probability 1/3 if 1 reports α, recommending y with probability 2/3 and z with probability 1/3 if 1 reports β). We have seen that this mechanism is worse than y for 1 if his type is β. Furthermore, this mechanism would be worse than y for player 1 under the *ex ante* welfare criterion, when his expected payoffs for type α and type β are averaged, each with weight 1/2. However, it is an equilibrium of this mechanism-selection game for player 1 always to accept this proposal, no matter what his type is. If 1 rejected 2's proposed mediator, then 2 might reasonably infer that 1's type was β, in which case 2's rational choice would be z instead of y, and z is the worse possible outcome for both of 1's types.

Now consider a different mechanism-selection process for this example, in which the informed player 1 can select any incentive-compatible mechanism himself, with only the restriction that 2 must know what mechanism has been selected by 1. For any incentive-compatible mechanism μ, there is an equilibrium in which 1 chooses μ for sure, no matter what his type is, and they thereafter play the honest and obedient equilibrium of this mechanism. To support such an equilibrium, it suffices to suppose that, if any mechanism other than μ were selected, then 2 would infer that 1's type was β and therefore choose z. Thus, concepts like sequential equilibrium from non-cooperative game theory cannot determine the outcome of this mechanism-selection game, beyond what we already know from the revelation principle; we cannot even say that 1's selected mechanism will be incentive-efficient. To get incentive efficiency as a result of mechanism-selection games, we need some further assumptions, like those of cooperative game theory.

An attempt to extend traditional solution concepts from cooperative game theory to the problem of bargaining over mechanisms has been proposed by Myerson (1983; 1984a; 1984b). In making such an extension, one must consider not only the traditional problem of how to define reasonable compromises between the conflicting interests of different individuals, but also the problem of how to define reasonable compromises between the conflicting interests of different types of the same individual. That is, to conceal his type in the mechanism-selection process, an individual should bargain for some inscrutable compromise between what he really wants and what he would have wanted if his type had been different; and we need some formal theory to predict what a reasonable inscrutable compromise might be. In the above sender–receiver game, where only type β of player 1 should feel any incentive to conceal his type, we might expect an inscrutable compromise to be resolved in favor of type α. That is, in the mechanism-selection game where 1 selects the mechanism, we might expect both types of 1 to select the incentive-compatible mechanism that is best for type α. (In this mechanism, the mediator recommends x with probability 0.8 and y with probability 0.2 if 1 reports α; and the mediator recommends x with probability 0.4, y with probability 0.4, and z with probability 0.2 if 1 reports β.) This mechanism is the

neutral optimum for player 1, in the sense of Myerson (1983).

ROGER B. MYERSON

See also **incentive compatibility; mechanism design experiments; mechanism design (new developments); revelation principle.**

Bibliography

Aumann, R.J. 1974. Subjectivity and correlation in randomized strategies. *Journal of Mathematical Economics* 1, 67–96.

Aumann, R.J. 1987. Correlated equilibrium as an expression of Bayesian rationality. *Econometrica* 55, 1–18.

Coase, R. 1960. The problem of social cost. *Journal of Law and Economics* 3, 1–44.

Cramton, P., Gibbons, R. and Klemperer, P. 1987. Dissolving a partnership efficiently. *Econometrica* 55, 615–32.

Dasgupta, P., Hammond, P. and Maskin, E. 1979. The implementation of social choice rules: some general results on incentive compatibility. *Review of Economic Studies* 46, 185–216.

Farrell, J. 1993. Meaning and credibility in cheap-talk games. *Games and Economic Behavior* 5, 514–31. Repr. in *Mathematical Models in Economics*, ed. M. Bacharach and M. Dempster. Oxford: Oxford University Press, 1997.

Gibbard, A. 1973. Manipulation of voting schemes: a general result. *Econometrica* 41, 587–602.

Harris, M. and Raviv, A. 1981. Allocation mechanisms and the design of auctions. *Econometrica* 49, 1477–99.

Harris, M. and Townsend, R.M. 1981. Resource allocation under asymmetric information. *Econometrica* 49, 33–64.

Harsanyi, J.C. 1967. Games with incomplete information played by Bayesian players. *Management Science* 14, 159–82, 320–34, 481–502.

Holmstrom, B. 1977. On incentives and control in organizations. Ph.D. thesis, Graduate School of Business, Stanford University.

Holmstrom, B. and Myerson, R.B. 1983. Efficient and durable decision rules with incomplete information. *Econometrica* 51, 1799–19.

Lewis, T.R. and Sappington, D.E.M. 1989. Countervailing incentives in agency problems. *Journal of Economic Theory* 49, 294–313.

Myerson, R.B. 1979. Incentive compatibility and the bargaining problem. *Econometrica* 47, 61–74.

Myerson, R.B. 1981. Optimal auction design. *Mathematics of Operation Research* 6, 58–73.

Myerson, R.B. 1982. Optimal coordination mechanisms in generalized principal–agent problems. *Journal of Mathematical Economics* 10, 67–81.

Myerson, R.B. 1983. Mechanism design by an informed principal. *Econometrica* 51, 1767–97.

Myerson, R.B. 1984a. Two-person bargaining problems with incomplete information. *Econometrica* 52, 461–87.

Myerson, R.B. 1984b. Cooperative games with incomplete information. *International Journal of Game Theory* 13, 69–86.

Myerson, R.B. 1985. Bayesian equilibrium and incentive compatibility. In *Social Goals and Social Organization*, ed. L. Hurwicz, D. Schmeidler and H. Sonnenschein. Cambridge: Cambridge University Press.

Myerson, R.B. 1986. Multistage games with communication. *Econometrica* 54, 323–58.

Myerson, R.B. 1988. Incentive constraints and optimal communication systems. In *Proceedings of the Second Conference on Theoretical Aspects of Reasoning about Knowledge*, ed. M.Y. Vardi. Los Altos: Morgan Kaufmann.

Myerson, R.B. and Satterthwaite, M. 1983. Efficient mechanisms for bilateral trading. *Journal of Economic Theory* 29, 265–81.

Ortega-Reichert, A. 1968. Models for competitive bidding under uncertainty. Ph.D. thesis, Department of Operations Research, Stanford University.

Palfrey, T. and Srivastava, S. 1987. On Bayesian implementable allocations. *Review of Economic Studies* 54, 193–208.

Riley, J.G. and Samuelson, W.F. 1981. Optimal auctions. *American Economic Review* 71, 381–92.

Rosenthal, R.W. 1978. Arbitration of two-party disputes under uncertainty. *Review of Economic Studies* 45, 595–604.

Samuelson, W. 1985. A comment on the Coase Theorem. In *Game-Theoretic Models of Bargaining*, ed. A.E. Roth. Cambridge: Cambridge University Press.

Schelling, T.C. 1960. *The Strategy of Conflict*. Cambridge, MA: Harvard University Press.

Wilson, R. 1985. Incentive efficiency of double auctions. *Econometrica* 53, 1101–15.

mechanism design (new developments)

1 Possibility results and robustness

Game theory provides methods to predict the outcome of a given game. Mechanism design concerns the *reverse* question: given some desirable outcome, can we design a game which produces it? Formally, the *environment* is $\langle A, N, \Theta \rangle$, where A is a set of feasible and verifiable alternatives or outcomes, $N = \{1, \ldots, n\}$ is a set of agents, and Θ is a set of possible *states of the world*. Except where indicated, we consider *private values* environments, where a state is $\theta = (\theta_1, \ldots, \theta_n) \in \times_i \Theta_i = \Theta$, each agent i knows his own 'type' $\theta_i \in \Theta_i$, and his payoff $u_i(a, \theta_i)$ depends only on the chosen alternative and his own type. (This does not rule out the possibility that the agents know something about each others' types.) If values are not private, then they are said to be *interdependent*. A *mechanism* or *contract* $\Gamma = (S, h)$ specifies a set of feasible actions S_i for each agent i, and an outcome function $h : S \equiv \times_{i=1}^{n} S_i \to A$. An outside party

(a principal or social planner), or the agents themselves, want to design a mechanism which produces optimal outcomes. These are often represented by a *social choice rule* (SCR) $F : \Theta \to A$. A *social choice function* (SCF) is a single-valued SCR. Implicitly, it is assumed that the mechanism designer does not know the true θ, and this lack of information makes it impossible for her to directly choose an outcome in $F(\theta)$. Instead, she uses the more roundabout method of designing a mechanism which produces an outcome in $F(\theta)$, *whatever the true θ may be*.

In a *revelation mechanism*, each agent simply reports what he knows (so if agent i only knows θ_i then $S_i = \Theta_i$). By definition, an *incentive compatible* revelation mechanism has a *truthful* Bayesian–Nash equilibrium, that is, it achieves *truthful implementation*. Truthful implementation plays an important role in the theory because of the revelation principle (see the dictionary entry on MECHANISM DESIGN, which surveys the early literature on truthful implementation). The early literature produced powerful results on optimal mechanisms for auction design, bargaining problems, and other applications. However, it generally made quite strong assumptions, for example, that the agents and the principal share a common prior over Θ, that the principal can *commit* to a mechanism, that the agents cannot side-contract and always use equilibrium strategies, and so on. We survey the recent literature which deals with these issues. In addition, we note that the notion of truthful implementation has a drawback: it does not rule out the possibility that non-truthful equilibria also exist, and these may produce suboptimal outcomes. (A non-truthful equilibrium may even Pareto dominate the truthful equilibrium for the agents, and hence provide a natural focal point for coordinating their actions.) To rule out the possibility of suboptimal equilibria, we may require *full implementation*: for all $\theta \in \Theta$, the set of equilibrium outcomes should precisely equal $F(\theta)$.

Maskin (1999) assumed *complete information*: each agent knows the true θ. If $n \geq 3$ agents know θ, then any SCF can be truthfully implemented: let the agents report θ, and if at least $n - 1$ agents announce the same θ then implement the outcome $F(\theta)$. Unilateral deviations from a consensus are disregarded, so truth-telling is a Nash equilibrium. Of course, this revelation mechanism will also have non-truthful equilibria. For full implementation, more complex mechanisms are required. (Even if $n = 2$, any SCF can be truthfully implemented if the principal can credibly threaten to 'punish' both agents if they report different states; in an economic environment, this might be achieved by making each agent pay a fine.)

A necessary condition for full Nash implementation is *(Maskin) monotonicity* (Maskin, 1999). Intuitively, monotonicity requires that moving an alternative *up* in the agents' preference rankings should not make it *less* likely to be optimal. This condition can be surprisingly difficult to satisfy. For example, if the agents can have any complete and transitive preference relation on A, then any Maskin monotonic SCF must be a constant function (Saijo, 1987). The situation is quite different if we consider *refinements* of Nash equilibrium. For example, there is a sense in which almost any (ordinal) SCR can be fully implemented in *undominated Nash equilibrium* when the agents have complete information (Palfrey and Srivastava, 1991; Jackson, Palfrey and Srivastava, 1994; Sjöström, 1994). Chung and Ely (2003) showed that this possibility result is not robust to small perturbations of the information structure that violate private values (there is a small chance that agent i knows more about agent j's preferences than agent j does). The violation of private values is key. For example, in Sjöström's (1994) mechanism, an agent who knows his own preferences can eliminate his dominated strategies, and a second round of elimination of *strictly* dominated strategies generates the optimal outcome. This construction is robust to small perturbations that respect private values.

A different kind of robustness was studied by McLean and Postlewaite (2002). Consider an economic environment where each agent i observes an independently drawn signal t_i which is correlated with the state θ. The complete information structure is approximated by letting each agent's signal be very accurate. With complete information, any SCF can be truthfully implemented. McLean and Postlewaite (2002) show robustness to perturbations of the information structure: any outcome can be approximated by an incentive-compatible allocation, if the agents' signals are accurate enough. There is no need to assume private values.

The literature on *Bayesian mechanism design* typically assumes each agent i knows only his own type $\theta_i \in \Theta_i$, the agents share a common prior p over $\Theta \equiv \times_{i=1}^{n} \Theta_i$, and the principal knows p. In fact, for truthful implementation with $n \geq 3$, the assumption that the principal knows p is redundant. Suppose for any common prior p on Θ, there is an incentive-compatible revelation mechanism $\Gamma_p = (\times_{i=1}^{n} \Theta_i, h_p)$. By definition, Γ_p truthfully implements the SCF $F_p \equiv h_p$. The mechanism Γ_p is 'parametric', that is, it depends on p. To be specific, consider a quasi-linear public goods environment with independent types, and suppose Γ_p is the well-known mechanism of d'Aspremont and Gérard-Varet (1979). Now consider a nonparametric mechanism Γ, where each agent i announces p and θ_i. If at least $n-1$ agents report the same p, the outcome is $h_p(\theta_1, \ldots, \theta_n)$. Now, if agent i thinks everyone will announce p truthfully, he may as well do so. If in addition he thinks the other agents report θ_{-i} truthfully, then he should announce θ_i truthfully by incentive compatibility of Γ_p. Therefore, for any common prior p, the nonparametric mechanism Γ truthfully implements F_p. In this sense, the principal can use Γ to extract the agents' shared information about p. Of course, this particular mechanism also has non-truthful equilibria. Choi and Kim (1999) *fully* implemented the d'Aspremont and Gérard-Varet (1979) outcome in

undominated Bayesian–Nash equilibrium, using a nonparametric mechanism. Naturally, their mechanism is quite complex. Suppose we restrict attention to mechanisms where each agent i only reports θ_i, truthfully in equilibrium. Then the necessary and sufficient condition for full nonparametric Bayesian–Nash implementation for any common prior p is (dominant strategy) incentive compatibility plus the *rectangular property* (Cason et al., 2006).

The d'Aspremont and Gérard-Varet (1979) mechanism is budget balanced and surplus maximizing. The above argument shows that such outcomes can be truthfully implemented by a nonparametric mechanism in quasi-linear environments with independent types. As is well known, this cannot be achieved by any dominant strategy mechanism. Thus, in general, nonparametric truthful implementation is easier than dominant strategy implementation. However, there are circumstances where the two concepts coincide. Bergemann and Morris (2005a) consider a model where each agent i has a *payoff type* $\theta_i \in \Theta_i$ and a *belief type* π_i. The payoff type determines the payoff function $u_i(a, \theta_i)$, while the belief type determines beliefs over other agents' types. The set of socially optimal outcomes $F(\theta)$ depends on payoff types, but not on beliefs. Bergemann and Morris (2005a) show that in quasi-linear environments with no restrictions on side payments (hence no budget-balance requirement), truthful implementation for all possible type spaces with a common prior implies dominant strategy implementation. (For related results, see Section 4.)

Bergemann and Morris (2005b) consider *full* implementation of SCFs in a similar framework. The SCF $F : \Theta \to A$ is *fully robustly implemented* if there exists a mechanism which fully implements F on all possible type spaces. They make no common prior assumption. Full robust implementation turns out to be equivalent to implementation using iterated elimination of strictly dominated strategies. Although a demanding concept, there are situations where full robust implementation is possible. For example, a Vickrey-Clarke-Groves (VCG) mechanism in a public goods economy with private values and strictly concave valuation functions achieves implementation in strictly dominant strategies. However, Bergemann and Morris (2005b) show the impossibility of full robust implementation when values are sufficiently interdependent.

A generalization of Maskin monotonicity called *Bayesian monotonicity* is necessary for ('parametric') full Bayesian-Nash implementation (Postlewaite and Schmeidler, 1986; Palfrey and Srivastava, 1989a; Jackson, 1991). Again, refinements lead to possibility results (Palfrey and Srivastava, 1989b). Another way to expand the set of implementable SCRs is *virtual* implementation (Abreu and Sen, 1991; Duggan, 1997). Serrano and Vohra (2001) argue that the sufficient conditions for virtual implementation are in fact quite strong.

The work discussed so far is *consequentialist*: only the final outcome matters. The mechanisms are clearly not meant to be descriptive of real-world institutions. For example, they typically require the agents to report 'all they know' before any decision is reached, an extreme form of centralized decision making hardly ever encountered in the real world. (The question of how much information must be transmitted in order to implement a given SCR is addressed by Hurwicz and Reiter, 2006, and Segal, 2004.) Delegating the power to make (verifiable) decisions to the agents would only create additional 'moral hazard' constraints, as discussed in the entry on MECHANISM DESIGN. Since centralization eliminates these moral hazard constraints, it typically strictly dominates decentralization in the basic model. However, as discussed below, by introducing additional aspects such as renegotiation and collusion, we can frequently prove the optimality of more realistic decentralized mechanisms. The implicit assumption is that decentralized decision making is in itself a good thing, which is a mild form of non-consequentialism. (Other non-consequentialist arguments are discussed in Section 4.) We might add that there is, of course, no way to eliminate the moral hazard constraints if the agents take *unverifiable* decisions that cannot be contracted upon. In this case, the issue of centralization versus decentralization of decisions is moot.

2 Renegotiation and credibility

Suppose $n = 2$ and both agents know the true θ. If a revelation mechanism is used and the agents announce different states, then we cannot identify a deviator from a 'consensus', so it may be necessary to punish *both* agents in order to support a truth-telling equilibrium. But this threat is not credible if the agents can avoid punishment by renegotiating the outcome. Maskin and Moore (1999) capture the renegotiation process by an exogenously given function $r : A \times \Theta \to A$ which maps outcome a in state θ into an efficient outcome $r(a, \theta)$. They derive an incentive-compatibility condition which is necessary for truth-telling when $n = 2$, and show that *renegotiation monotonicity* is necessary for full Nash implementation (see also Segal and Whinston, 2002).

The idea that renegotiation may preclude the implementation of the first-best outcome, even when information is complete, has received attention in models of bilateral trade with relationship-specific investments (the hold-up problem). It is possible to implement the first-best outcome if trade is one-dimensional and investments are 'selfish', in the sense that each agent's investment does not directly influence the other agent's payoff (Nöldeke and Schmidt, 1995; Edlin and Reichelstein, 1996). If investments are not selfish, then the first-best cannot always be achieved, while the second-best can often be implemented without any explicit contract (Che and Hausch, 1999). Segal (1999) found a similar result in a model with k goods and selfish investments, for k

large (see also Maskin and Tirole, 1999; Hart and Moore, 1999). It should be noted that the case $n = 2$ is quite special, and adding a third party often alleviates the problem of renegotiation (Baliga and Sjöström, 2006).

Credibility and renegotiation also impact trading with asymmetric information. Suppose the seller can produce goods of different quality, but the buyer's valuation is his private information. It is typically second-best optimal for the seller to offer a contract such that low-valuation buyers consume less than first-best quality ('under-production'), while high-valuation buyers enjoy 'information rents'. Incentive compatibility guarantees that the buyer reveals his true valuation. Now suppose trading takes place twice, and the buyer's valuation does not change. Suppose the seller cannot credibly commit to a long-run (two-period) contract. If the buyer reveals his true valuation in the first period, then in the second period the seller will leave him no rent. This is typically not the second-best outcome. The seller may prefer a 'pooling' contract which does not fully reveal valuations in the first period, a commitment device which limits his ability to extract second period rents. This idea has important applications. When a regulator cannot commit to a long-run contract, a regulated firm may hide information or exert less effort to cut costs, the *ratchet effect* (Freixas, Guesnerie and Tirole, 1985). A borrower may not exert effort to improve a project knowing that a lender with deep pockets will bail him out, the *soft budget constraint* (Dewatripont and Maskin, 1995a). These problems are exacerbated if the principal is well informed and cannot commit not to use his information. Institutional or organizational design can alleviate the problems. By committing to acquire less information via 'incomplete contracts', or by maintaining an 'arm's-length relationship', the principal can improve efficiency (Dewatripont and Maskin, 1995b; Crémer, 1995). Less frequent regulatory reviews offset the ratchet effect, and a decentralized credit market helps to cut off borrowers from future funding. Long-run contracts can help, but they may be vulnerable to renegotiation (Dewatripont, 1989). In particular, the second-period outcome may be renegotiated if quality levels are known to be different from the first-best. Again, some degree of pooling may be optimal.

If the principal cannot commit even to short-run contracts, then, after receiving the agents' messages, she always chooses an outcome that is optimal given her beliefs. She cannot credibly threaten punishments that she would not want to carry out. Refinements proposed in the cheap-talk literature suggest that a putative pooling equilibrium may be destroyed if an agent can reveal information by 'objecting' in a credible way. This leads to a necessary condition for full implementation with complete information which is reminiscent of Maskin monotonicity, but which involves the principal's preferences (Baliga, Corchón and Sjöström, 1997).

3 Collusion

A large literature on collusion was inspired by Tirole (1986). A key contribution was made by Laffont and Martimort (1997), who assumed an uninformed third party proposes side contracts. This circumvents the signalling problems that might arise if a privately informed agent makes collusive proposals. A side contract for a group of colluding agents is a *collusive mechanism* which must respect incentive compatibility, individual rationality and feasibility constraints. The original mechanism Γ, designed by the principal, is called the *grand mechanism*. The objective is to design an optimal grand mechanism when collusion is possible. Typically, collusion imposes severe limits on what can be achieved.

Baliga and Sjöström (1998) study a model with moral hazard and limited liability. Two agents share information not known to the principal: agent 1's effort is observed by both agents. Agent 2's effort is known only to himself. In the absence of collusion, the optimal grand mechanism specifies a 'message game': agent 2 reports agent 1's effort to the principal. Now suppose the agents can side contract on agent 1's effort, but not on agent 2's effort (which is unobserved). Side contracts can specify side transfers as a function of realized output, but must respect limited liability. This collusion may destroy centralized 'message games', and we obtain a theory of optimal delegation of decision making. For some parameters, it is optimal for the principal to contract only with agent 2, and let agent 2 subcontract with agent 1. This is intuitive, since agent 2 observes agent 1's effort and can contract directly on it. More surprisingly, there are parameter values where it is better for the principal to contract only with agent 1.

Mookherjee and Tsumagari (2004) study a similar model, but with adverse selection: the agents privately observe their own production costs. In this model, delegating to a 'prime supplier' creates 'double marginalization of rents': the prime supplier uses underproduction to minimize the other agent's information rent. A centralized contract avoids this problem. Hence, in this model delegation is always strictly dominated by centralization, even though the agents can collude.

Mookherjee and Tsumagari (2004) assume the agents can side contract before deciding to participate in the grand contract. Che and Kim (2006) assume side contracting occurs only after the decision to participate in the grand mechanism has been made. In this case, collusion does not limit what the principal can achieve. Hence, the timing of side contracting is important. In a complete information environment with $n \geq 3$, Sjöström (1999) showed that neither renegotiation nor collusion limit the possibility of undominated Nash implementation.

4 Other theoretical issues

In quasi-linear environments with uncorrelated types, there exist incentive-compatible mechanisms which maximize the social surplus (for example, d'Aspremont and Gérard-Varet, 1979). But the principal cannot extract all the surplus: the agents must get informational rents. However, Crémer and McLean (1988) showed that the principal can extract all the surplus in auctions with *correlated types*. McAfee and Reny (1992) extended this result to general quasi-linear environments.

Jehiel and Moldovanu (2001) considered a quasi-linear environment with multidimensional (uncorrelated) types and interdependent values. Generically, a standard revelation mechanism cannot be designed to extract information about multidimensional types, and no incentive-compatible and surplus-maximizing mechanism exists. Mezzetti (2004) presents an ingenious *two-stage* mechanism which maximizes the surplus in interdependent values environments, even when types are independent and multidimensional. In the first stage, the mechanism specifies an outcome decision but not transfers. Transfers are determined in the second stage by reports on payoffs realized by the outcome decision. Mezzetti (2007) shows that the principal can sometimes extract all the surplus by this method, even if types are independent. For optimal mechanisms for a profit-maximizing monopolist when consumers have multidimensional types and private values, see Armstrong (1996).

Incentive compatibility does not require that each agent has a dominant strategy. Nevertheless, incentive-compatible outcomes can often be replicated by dominant strategy mechanisms (Mookherjee and Reichelstein, 1992). In quasi-linear environments, all incentive-compatible mechanisms that maximize the social surplus are *payoff-equivalent* to dominant strategy (VCG) mechanisms (Krishna and Perry, 1997; Williams, 1999). However, as pointed out above, dominant strategies (but not incentive compatibility) rules out budget balance.

Bergemann and Välimäki (2002) assume agents can update a common prior by costly information acquisition. Suppose a single-unit auction has two bidders i and j who observe statistically independent private signals θ_i and θ_j. Bidder i's valuation of the good is $u_i(\theta_i, \theta_j) = \alpha\theta_i + \beta\theta_j$, where $\alpha > \beta > 0$. Thus, values are interdependent. Efficiency requires that bidder i gets the good if and only if $\theta_i \geq \theta_j$. Suppose bidders report their signals, the good is allocated efficiently given their reports, and the winning bidder i pays the price $(\alpha + \beta)\theta_j$. This VCG mechanism is incentive compatible (Maskin, 1992). If bidder i acquires negative information which causes him to lose the auction, then he imposes a negative externality on the other bidder (as $\beta > 0$). This implies the bidders have an incentive to collect too much information. Conversely, there is an incentive to collect too little information when $\beta < 0$. Bergemann and Välimäki (2002) provide a general analysis of these externalities. Similar externalities occur when members of a committee must collect information before voting. If the committee is large, each vote is unlikely to be pivotal, and free riding occurs. Persico (2004) shows how the optimal committee is designed to encourage the members to collect information.

Some authors reject consequentialism and instead emphasize agents' *rights*. For example, suppose a mechanism implements *envy-free outcomes*. An agent might still feel unfairly treated if his own bundle is worse than a bundle which another agent *had the right to choose* (but did not). Such agents may demand 'equal rights' (Gaspart, 1995). Unfortunately, once we leave the classical exchange economy, Sen's 'Paretian liberal' paradox (Sen, 1970) suggests that rights are incompatible with efficiency (Deb, Pattanaik and Razzolini, 1997). Sen originally considered rights embodied in SCRs rather than mechanisms. Peleg and Winter (2002) study *constitutional implementation* where the mechanism embodies the same rights as the SCR it implements.

5 Learning from experiments

Cabrales, Charness and Corchón (2003) tested the so-called canonical mechanism for Nash implementation. A Nash equilibrium was played only 13 per cent of the time (20 per cent when monetary fines were used). Remarkably, the optimal outcome was implemented 68 per cent of the time (80 per cent with 'fines'), because deviations from equilibrium strategies frequently did not affect the outcome. This suggests that a desirable property of a mechanism is *fault-tolerance*: it should produce optimal outcomes even if some 'faulty' players deviate from the theoretical predictions. Eliaz (2002) showed that, if at most $k < \frac{1}{2} n - 1$ players are 'faulty' (that is, unpredictable), then full Nash implementation is possible if *no-veto-power* and $(k + 1)$-*monotonicity hold*.

Equilibrium play can be justified by epistemic or dynamic theories. According to epistemic theories, common knowledge about various aspects of the game implies equilibrium play even in one-shot games. Experiments provide little support for this. However, there is evidence that players can reach equilibrium through a dynamic adjustment process. If a game is played repeatedly, with no player knowing any other player's payoff function, the outcome frequently converges to a Nash equilibrium of the one-shot complete information game (Smith, 1979). Dynamic theories have been applied to the mechanism design problem (for example, Cabrales and Ponti, 2000). Chen and Tang (1998) and Chen and Gazzale (2004) argue that mechanisms which induce supermodular games produce good long-run outcomes. Unfortunately, these convergence results are irrelevant for decisions that are taken infrequently, or if the principal is too impatient to care only about the long-run outcome.

The idea of dominant strategies is less controversial than Nash equilibrium, and should be more relevant for decisions that are taken infrequently. Unfortunately, experiments on dominant-strategy mechanisms have yielded negative results. Attiyeh, Franciosi and Isaac (2000, p. 112) conclude pessimistically, 'we do not believe that the pivot mechanism warrants further practical consideration … . This is due to the fundamental failure of the mechanism, in our laboratory experiments, to induce truthful value revelation.' However, VCG mechanisms (such as the pivotal mechanism) frequently have a multiplicity of Nash equilibria, some of which produce suboptimal outcomes. Cason et al. (2006) did experiments with *secure* mechanisms, which fully implement an SCR both in dominant strategies and in Nash equilibria. The players were much more likely to use their dominant strategies in secure than in non-secure mechanisms. In the non-secure mechanisms, deviations from dominant strategies tended to correspond to Nash equilibria. However, these deviations typically did not lead to suboptimal outcomes. In this sense, the non-secure mechanisms were fault-tolerant. Kawagoe and Mori (2001) report experiments where deviations from dominant strategies typically corresponded to suboptimal Nash equilibria.

In experiments, subjects often violate standard axioms of rational decision making. Alternative theories, such as prospect theory, fit the experimental evidence better. But, if we modify the axioms of individual behaviour, the optimal mechanisms will change. Esteban and Miyagawa (2005) assume the agents have Gul–Pesendorfer preferences (Gul and Pesendorfer, 2001). They suffer from 'temptation', and may prefer a smaller menu (choice set) to a larger one. Suppose each agent first chooses a menu, and then chooses an alternative from this menu. Optimal menus may contain 'tempting' alternatives which are never chosen in equilibrium, because this relaxes the incentive-compatibility constraints pertaining to the choice of menu. Eliaz and Spiegler (2006) assume some agents are 'sophisticated' and some are 'naive'. Sophisticated agents know that they are dynamically inconsistent, and would like to commit to a future decision. Naive agents are unaware that they are dynamically inconsistent. The optimal mechanism screens the agents by providing commitment devices that are chosen only by sophisticated agents.

Experiments reveal the importance of human emotions such as spite or kindness (Andreoni, 1995; Saijo, 2003). In many mechanisms in the theoretical literature, by changing his strategy an agent can have a big impact on another agent's payoff without materially changing his own. Such mechanisms may have little hope of practical success if agents are inclined to manipulate each others' payoffs due to feelings of spite or kindness.

SANDEEP BALIGA AND TOMAS SJÖSTRÖM

See also **auctions (experiments); auctions (theory); contract theory; hold-up problem; incentive compatibility; mechanism design; revelation principle.**

Bibliography

Abreu, D. and Sen, A. 1991. Virtual implementation in Nash equilibria. *Econometrica* 59, 997–1022.

Andreoni, J. 1995. Cooperation in public goods experiments: kindness or confusion? *American Economic Review* 85, 891–904.

Armstrong, M. 1996. Multiproduct nonlinear pricing. *Econometrica* 64, 51–75.

Attiyeh, G., Franciosi, R. and Isaac, R.M. 2000. Experiments with the pivotal process for providing public goods. *Public Choice* 102, 95–114.

Baliga, S., Corchón, L. and Sjöström, T. 1997. The theory of implementation when the planner is a player. *Journal of Economic Theory* 77, 15–33.

Baliga, S. and Sjöström, T. 1998. Decentralization and collusion. *Journal of Economic Theory* 83, 196–232.

Baliga, S. and Sjöström, T. 2006. Contracting with third parties. Working paper No. 75, CSIO, Northwestern University.

Bergemann, D. and Morris, S. 2005a. Robust mechanism design. *Econometrica* 73, 1771–813.

Bergemann, D. and Morris, S. 2005b. Robust implementation: the role of large type spaces. Discussion Paper No. 1519, Cowles Foundation, Yale University.

Bergemann, D. and Välimäki, J. 2002. Information acquisition and efficient mechanism design. *Econometrica* 70, 1007–34.

Cabrales, A., Charness, G. and Corchón, L. 2003. An experiment on Nash implementation. *Journal of Economic Behavior and Organization* 51, 161–93.

Cabrales, A. and Ponti, G. 2000. Implementation, elimination of weakly dominated strategies and evolutionary dynamics. *Review of Economic Dynamics* 3, 247–82.

Cason, T., Saijo, T., Sjöström, T. and Yamato, T. 2006. Secure implementation experiments: do strategy-proof mechanisms really work? *Games and Economic Behavior* 57, 206–35.

Che, Y.K. and Hausch, D. 1999. Cooperative investments and the value of contracting. *American Economic Review* 89, 125–47.

Che, Y.K. and Kim, J. 2006. Robustly collusion-proof implementation. *Econometrica* 74, 1063–107.

Chen, Y. and Gazzale, R. 2004. When does learning in games generate convergence to Nash equilibria? *American Economic Review* 94, 1505–35.

Chen, Y. and Tang, F.F. 1998. Learning and incentive compatible mechanisms for public goods provision: an experimental study. *Journal of Political Economy* 106, 633–62.

Choi, J. and Kim, T. 1999. A nonparametric, efficient public decision mechanism: undominated Bayesian Nash implementation. *Games and Economic Behavior* 27, 64–85.

Chung, K. and Ely, J. 2003. Implementation with near-complete information. *Econometrica* 71, 857–71.

Crémer, J. 1995. Arm's length relationships. *Quarterly Journal of Economics* 110, 275–95.

Crémer, J. and McLean, R. 1988. Full extraction of the surplus in Bayesian and dominant strategy auctions. *Econometrica* 56, 1247–57.

d'Aspremont, C. and Gérard-Varet, L.A. 1979. Incentives and incomplete information. *Journal of Public Economics* 11, 25–45.

Deb, R., Pattanaik, P. and Razzolini, L. 1997. Game forms, rights and the efficiency of social outcomes. *Journal of Economic Theory* 72, 74–95.

Dewatripont, M. 1989. Renegotiation and information revelation over time: the case of optimal labor contracts, *Quarterly Journal of Economics* 104, 589–619.

Dewatripont, M. and Maskin, E. 1995a. Credit and efficiency in centralized and decentralized economies. *Review of Economic Studies* 62, 541–55.

Dewatripont, M. and Maskin, E. 1995b. Contractual contingencies and renegotiation. *RAND Journal of Economics* 26, 704–19.

Duggan, J. 1997. Virtual Bayesian implementation. *Econometrica* 67, 1175–99.

Edlin, A. and Reichelstein, S. 1996. Hold-ups, standard breach remedies and optimal investment. *American Economic Review* 86, 478–501.

Eliaz, K. 2002. Fault tolerant implementation. *Review of Economic Studies* 69, 589–610.

Eliaz, K. and Spiegler, R. 2006. Contracting with diversely naive agents. *Review of Economic Studies* 73, 689–714.

Esteban, S. and Miyagawa, E. 2005. Optimal menu of menus with self-control preferences. Unpublished paper, Penn State University.

Freixas, X., Guesnerie, R. and Tirole, J. 1985. Planning under incomplete information and the ratchet effect. *Review of Economic Studies* 52, 173–92.

Gaspart, F. 1995. Fair implementation in the cooperative production problem: two properties of normal form mechanisms. Unpublished manuscript, FUNDP Namur.

Gul, F. and Pesendorfer, W. 2001. Temptation and self-control. *Econometrica* 69, 1403–35.

Hart, O. and Moore, J. 1999. Foundations of incomplete contracts. *Review of Economic Studies* 66, 115–38.

Hurwicz, L. and Reiter, S. 2006. *Designing Economic Mechanisms*. New York: Cambridge University Press.

Jackson, M. 1991. Bayesian implementation. *Econometrica* 59, 461–77.

Jackson, M., Palfrey, T. and Srivastava, S. 1994. Undominated Nash implementation in bounded mechanisms. *Games and Economic Behavior* 6, 474–501.

Jehiel, P. and Moldovanu, B. 2001. Efficient design with interdependent valuations. *Econometrica* 69, 1237–59.

Kawagoe, T. and Mori, T. 2001. Can the pivotal mechanism induce truthtelling? *Public Choice* 108, 331–54.

Krishna, V. and Perry, M. 1997. Efficient mechanism design. Unpublished manuscript, Penn State University.

Laffont, J.J. and Martimort, D. 1997. Collusion under asymmetric information. *Econometrica* 65, 875–911.

McAfee, P. and Reny, P. 1992. Correlated information and mechanism design. *Econometrica* 60, 395–421.

McLean, R. and Postlewaite, A. 2002. Informational size and incentive compatibility. *Econometrica* 70, 2421–53.

Maskin, E. 1992. Auctions and privatization. In *Privatization*, ed. H. Siebert. Tübingen: J.C.B. Mohr.

Maskin, E. 1999. Nash equilibrium and welfare optimality. *Review of Economic Studies* 66, 23–38.

Maskin, E. and Moore, J. 1999. Implementation and renegotiation. *Review of Economic Studies* 66, 39–56.

Maskin, E. and Tirole, J. 1999. Two remarks on the property rights literature. *Review of Economic Studies* 66, 139–50.

Mezzetti, C. 2004. Mechanism design with interdependent valuations: efficiency. *Econometrica* 72, 1617–26.

Mezzetti, C. 2007. Mechanism design with interdependent valuations: surplus extraction. *Economic Theory* 3, 473–99.

Mookherjee, D. and Reichelstein, S. 1992. Dominant strategy implementation of Bayesian incentive compatible allocation rules. *Journal of Economic Theory* 56, 378–99.

Mookherjee, D. and Tsumagari, M. 2004. The organization of supplier networks: effects of delegation and intermediation. *Econometrica* 72, 1179–219.

Nöldeke, G. and Schmidt, K. 1995. Option contracts and renegotiation: a solution to the hold–up problem. *RAND Journal of Economics* 26, 163–79.

Palfrey, T. and Srivastava, S. 1989a. Implementation with incomplete information in exchange economies. *Econometrica* 57, 115–34.

Palfrey, T. and Srivastava, S. 1989b. Mechanism design with incomplete information: a solution to the implementation problem. *Journal of Political Economy* 97, 668–91.

Palfrey, T. and Srivastava, S. 1991. Nash implementation using undominated strategies. *Econometrica* 59, 479–501.

Peleg, B. and Winter, E. 2002. Constitutional implementation. *Review of Economic Design* 7, 187–204.

Persico, N. 2004. Committee design with endogenous information. *Review of Economic Studies* 71, 165–91.

Postlewaite, A. and Schmeidler, D. 1986. Implementation in differential information economies. *Journal of Economic Theory* 39, 14–33.

Saijo, T. 1987. On constant Maskin monotonic social choice functions. *Journal of Economic Theory* 42, 382–86.

Saijo, T. 2003. Spiteful behavior in voluntary contribution mechanism experiments. In *Handbook of Experimental Economics Results*, ed. C. Plott and V. Smith, Elsevier Science.

Segal, I. 1999. Complexity and renegotiation: a foundation for incomplete contracts. *Review of Economic Studies* 66, 57–82.

Segal, I. 2004. The communication requirements of social choice rules and supporting budget sets. Working Paper No. 39, School of Social Science, Institute for Advanced Study, Princeton.

Segal, I. and Whinston, M. 2002. The Mirrlees approach to mechanism design with renegotiation. *Econometrica* 70, 1–46.

Sen, A. 1970. The impossibility of a Paretian liberal. *Journal of Political Economy* 78, 152–7.

Serrano, R. and Vohra, R. 2001. Some limitations of virtual Bayesian implementation. *Econometrica* 69, 785–92.

Sjöström, T. 1994. Implementation in undominated Nash equilibria without using integer games. *Games and Economic Behavior* 6, 502–11.

Sjöström, T. 1999. Undominated Nash implementation with collusion and renegotiation. *Games and Economic Behavior* 26, 337–52.

Smith, V. 1979. Incentive compatible experimental processes for the provision of public goods. In *Research in Experimental Economics*, vol. 1, ed. V. Smith. Greenwich, CT: JAI Press.

Tirole, J. 1986. Hierarchies and bureaucracies. *Journal of Law, Economics and Organization* 2, 181–214.

Williams, S. 1999. A characterization of efficient, Bayesian incentive compatible mechanisms. *Economic Theory* 14, 155–80.

mechanism design experiments

Mechanism design is the art of designing institutions that align individual incentives with overall social goals. Mechanism design theory was initiated by Hurwicz (1972) and is surveyed in Groves and Ledyard (1987). To bridge the gap between a theoretical mechanism and an actual economic process that solves fundamental social problems, it is important to observe and evaluate the performance of the mechanism in the context of actual decision problems faced by real people with real incentives. These situations can be created and carefully controlled in a laboratory. A mechanism design experiment takes a theoretical mechanism, recreates it in a simple environment in a laboratory with human subjects as economic agents, observes the behaviour of human subjects under the mechanism, and assesses its performance in relation to what it was created to do and to the theory upon which its creation rests. The laboratory serves as a wind tunnel for new mechanisms, providing evidence which one can use to eliminate fragile ones, and to identify the characteristics of successful ones.

When a mechanism is put to test in a laboratory, behavioural assumptions made in theory are seriously challenged. Theory assumes perfectly rational agents who can compute the equilibrium strategies via introspection. When a mechanism is implemented among boundedly rational agents, however, characteristics peripheral to theoretical implementations, such as transparency, complexity and dynamic stability, become important, or even central, to the success of a mechanism in a laboratory, and we suspect, ultimately in the real world. Mechanism design experiments cover several major domains, including public goods and externalities, matching, contract theory, auctions, market design and information markets. In what follows, we will review the experimental results of some of these topics.

Public goods and externalities

With the presence of public goods and externalities, competitive equilibria are not Pareto optimal. This is often referred to as market failure, since competitive markets on their own either result in underprovision of public goods (that is, the free-rider problem) or over-provision of negative externalities, such as pollution. To solve the free-rider problem in public goods economies, incentive-compatible mechanisms use innovative tax-subsidy schemes that utilize agents' own messages to achieve the Pareto optimal levels of public goods provision. A series of experiments test these mechanisms in the laboratory (see Chen, 2008, for a comprehensive survey).

When preferences are quasi-linear, the Vickrey–Clarke–Groves (VCG) mechanism (Vickrey, 1961; Clarke, 1971; Groves, 1973) is strategy-proof, in the sense that reporting one's preferences truthfully is always a dominant strategy. It has also been shown that any strategy-proof mechanism selecting an efficient public decision at every profile must be of this type (Green and Laffont, 1977). Two forms of the VCG mechanism have been tested in the field and laboratory by various groups of researchers. The pivot mechanism refers to the VCG mechanism when the public project choice is binary, while the cVCG mechanism refers to the VCG mechanism when the level of the public good is selected from a continuum. Under the pivot mechanism, misrevelation can be prevalent. Attiyeh, Franciosi and Isaac (2000) show that about ten per cent of the bids were truthfully revealing their values. Furthermore, there was no convergence tendency towards value revelation. In a follow-up study, Kawagoe and Mori (2001) show that more information about the payoff structure helps reduce the degree of misrevelation. More recently, Cason et al. (2006) provide a novel explanation for the problem of misrevelation in strategy-proof mechanisms. As Saijo et al. (2005) point out, the standard strategy-proofness concept in implementation theory has serious drawbacks, that is, almost all strategy-proof mechanisms have a continuum of Nash equilibria. They propose a new implementation concept, secure implementation, which requires the set of dominant strategy equilibria and the set of Nash equilibria to coincide. Cason et al. (2006) compare the performance of two strategy-proof mechanisms in the laboratory: the Pivot mechanism where implementation is not secure and truthful preference revelation is a weakly dominant strategy, and the cVCG mechanism with single-peaked preferences where implementation is secure. Results indicate that subjects play dominant strategies significantly more often in the secure cVCG mechanism (81 per cent) than in the non-secure Pivot mechanism (50 per cent). The importance of secure implementation in dominant strategy implementation is replicated in Healy (2006), where he compares five public goods mechanisms, voluntary contributions, proportional taxation, Groves–Ledyard, Walker

and cVCG. The cVCG is found to be the most efficient of all mechanisms.

Although the VCG mechanism admits dominant strategies, the allocation is not fully Pareto-efficient. In fact, it is impossible to design a mechanism for making collective allocation decisions, which is informationally decentralized, non-manipulable and Pareto optimal. This impossibility has been demonstrated in the work of Hurwicz (1975), Green and Laffont (1977), Roberts (1979), Walker (1980) and Mailath and Postlewaite (1990) in the context of resource allocation with public goods.

Many 'next-best' mechanisms preserve Pareto optimality at the cost of non-manipulability, some of which preserve 'some degree' of non-manipulability. Some mechanisms have been discovered which have the property that Nash equilibria are Pareto optimal. These can be found in the work of Groves and Ledyard (1977), Hurwicz (1979), Walker (1981), Tian (1989), Kim (1993), Peleg (1996), Falkinger (1996) and Chen (2002). Other implementation concepts include perfect Nash equilibrium (Bagnoli and Lipman, 1989), undominated Nash equilibrium (Jackson and Moulin, 1992), subgame perfect equilibrium (Varian, 1994), strong equilibrium (Corchon and Wilkie, 1996), and the core (Kaneko, 1977), and so forth. Apart from the above non-Bayesian mechanisms, Ledyard and Palfrey (1994) propose a class of Bayesian Nash mechanisms for public goods provision.

Experiments on Nash-efficient public goods mechanisms underscore the importance of dynamic stability, that is, whether a mechanism converges under various learning dynamics. Most of the experimental studies of Nash-efficient mechanisms focus on the Groves–Ledyard mechanism (Smith, 1979a; 1979b; Harstad and Marrese, 1981; 1982; Mori, 1989; Chen and Plott, 1996; Arifovic and Ledyard, 2006). Chen and Tang (1998) also compare the Walker mechanism with the Groves–Ledyard mechanism. Falkinger et al. (2000) study the Falkinger mechanism. Healy (2006) compares Nash-efficient mechanisms to cVCG and other benchmarks.

Among the series of experiments exploring dynamic stability, Chen and Plott (1996) first assessed the performance of the Groves–Ledyard mechanism under different punishment parameters. They found that by varying the punishment parameter the dynamics and stability changed dramatically. For a large enough parameter, the system converged very quickly to its stage game Nash equilibrium and remained stable; while under a small parameter, the system did not converge to its stage game Nash equilibrium. This finding was replicated by Chen and Tang (1998) with more independent sessions and a longer time series in an experiment designed to study the learning dynamics.

Figure 1 presents the time series data from Chen and Tang (1998) for two out of five types of players. Each graph presents the mean (the black dots) and standard

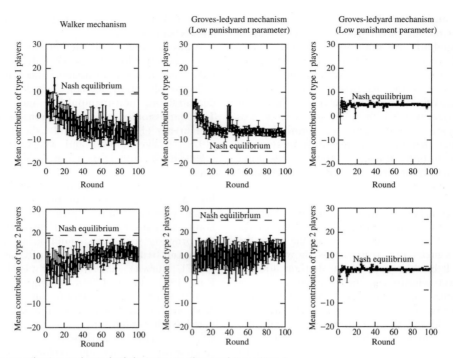

Figure 1   Mean contribution and standard deviation in Chen and Tang (1998)

deviation (the error bars) for each of the two different types averaged over seven independent sessions for each mechanism – the Walker mechanism, the Groves–Ledyard mechanism under a low punishment parameter (GL1), and the Groves–Ledyard mechanism under a high punishment parameter (GL100). From these graphs, it is apparent that GL100 converged very quickly to its stage game Nash equilibrium and remained stable, while the same mechanism did not converge under a low punishment parameter; the Walker mechanism did not converge to its stage game Nash equilibrium either.

Because of its good dynamic properties, GL100 had significantly better performance than GL1 and Walker, evaluated in terms of system efficiency, close to Pareto optimal level of public goods provision, fewer violations of individual rationality constraints and convergence to its stage game equilibrium.

These past experiments serendipitously studied supermodular mechanisms. Two recent studies systematically vary the parameters from below, close to, at and above the supermodularity threshold to assess the effects of supermodularity on learning dynamics.

Arifovic and Ledyard (2006) conduct computer simulations of an individual learning model in the context of a class of the Groves–Ledyard mechanisms. They vary the punishment parameter systematically, from extremely small to extremely high. They find that their model converges to Nash equilibrium for all values of the punishment parameter. However, the speed of convergence

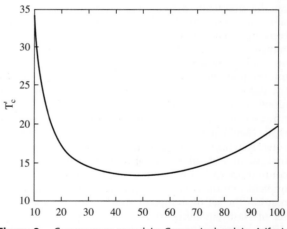

Figure 2   Convergence speed in Groves–Ledyard in Arifovic and Ledyard (2006)

depends on the value of the parameter. As shown in Figure 2, the speed of convergence is U-shaped: very low and very high values of the punishment parameter require long periods for convergence, while a range of intermediate values requires the minimum time. In fact, the optimal punishment parameter identified in the simulation is much lower than the supermudularity threshold. Predictions of the computation model are validated by experimental data with human subjects.

In a parallel research project on the role of supermodularity on convergence, Chen and Gazzale (2004) experimentally study the generalized version of the compensation mechanism (Varian, 1994), which implements efficient allocations as subgame-perfect equilibria for economic environments involving externalities and public goods. The basic idea is that each player offers to compensate the other for the 'costs' incurred by making the efficient choice. They systematically vary the free parameter from below, close to, at and beyond the threshold of supermodularity to assess the effects of supermodularity on the performance of the mechanism. They have three main findings. First, in terms of proportion of equilibrium play and efficiency, they find that supermodular and 'near supermodular' mechanisms perform significantly better than those far below the threshold. This finding is consistent with previous experimental findings. Second, they find that from a little below the threshold to the threshold, the improvement in performance is statistically insignificant. This implies that the performance of 'near supermodular' mechanisms, such as the Falkinger mechanism, ought to be comparable to supermodular mechanisms. Therefore, the mechanism designer need not be overly concerned with setting parameters that are firmly above the supermodular threshold – close is just as good. This enlarges the set of robustly stable mechanisms. The third finding concerns the selection of mechanisms within the class of supermodular mechanisms. Again, theory is silent on this issue. Chen and Gazzale find that within the class of supermodular mechanisms, increasing the parameter far beyond the threshold does not significantly improve the performance of the mechanism. Furthermore, increasing another free parameter, which is not related to whether or not the mechanism is supermodular, does improve convergence.

In contrast to the previous stream of work which identifies supermodularity as a robust sufficient condition for convergence, Healy (2006) develops a k-period average best response learning model and calibrates this new learning model on the data-set to study the learning dynamics. He shows that subject behaviour is well approximated by a model in which agents best respond to the average strategy choices over the last five periods under all mechanisms. Healy's work bridges the behavioural hypotheses that have existed separately in dominant strategy and Nash-efficient mechanism experiments.

In summary, experiments testing public goods mechanisms show that dominant strategy mechanisms should also be secure, while Nash implementation mechanisms should satisfy dynamic stability, if any mechanism is to be considered for application in the real world in a repeated interaction setting.

While experimental research demonstrates that incentive-compatible public goods mechanisms can be effective in inducing efficient levels of public goods provision, almost all the mechanisms rely on monetary transfers, which limit the scope of implementation of these mechanisms in the real world. In many interesting real world settings, such as open source software development and online communities, sizable contributions to public goods are made without the use of monetary incentives. We next review a related social psychology literature, which studies contribution to public goods without the use of monetary incentives.

Social loafing

Analogous to free riding, social loafing refers to the phenomenon whereby individuals exert less effort on a collective task than they do on a comparable individual task. To determine conditions under which individuals do or do not engage in social loafing, social psychologists have developed and tested various theoretical accounts. Karau and Williams (1993) present a review of this literature and develop a collective effort model, which integrates elements of expectancy value, social identity and self-validation theories, to explain social loafing. A meta-analysis of 78 studies shows that social loafing is robust across studies. Consistent with the prediction of the model, several variables are found to moderate social loafing. The following factors are of particular interests to a mechanism designer.

1. *Evaluation potential*: Harkins (1987) and others show that social loafing can be reduced or sometimes eliminated when a participant's contribution is identifiable and evaluable. In a related public goods experiment, Andreoni and Petrie (2004) find a substantial increase (59 per cent) in contribution to public goods compared to the baseline of a typical VCM experiment, when both the amount of individual contribution and the (photo) identification of donors are revealed.
2. *Task valence*: the collective effort model predicts that the individual tendency to engage in social loafing decreases as task valence (or perceived meaningfulness) increases.
3. *Group valence and group-level comparison standards*: Social identity theory (Tajfel and Turner, 1986) suggests that 'individuals gain positive self-identity through the accomplishments of the groups to which they belong' (Karau and Williams, 1993, p. 686). Therefore, enhancing group cohesiveness or group identity might reduce or eliminate social loafing. In a closely related economics experiment, Eckel and Grossman (2005) use induced group identity to study the effects of varying strength of identity on cooperative behaviour in a repeated public goods game. They find that while cooperation is unaffected by simple and artificial group identity, actions designed to enhance group identity contribute to higher levels of cooperation. This stream of research suggests that high degrees of group identification may limit individual shirking and free riding in environments with a public good.

4. *Expectation of co-worker performance influences individual effort.* This set of theories might be sensitive to individual valuations for the public good as well as the public goods production functions. The meta-analysis indicates that individuals loafed when they expected their co-workers to perform well, but did not loaf otherwise.

5. *Uniqueness of individual inputs*: individuals loafed when they believed that their inputs were redundant, but did not loaf when they believe that their individual inputs to the collective product were unique. In an interesting application, Beenen et al. (2004) conducted a field experiment in an online community called MovieLens. They found that users who were reminded of the uniqueness of their contributions rated significantly more movies than the control group.

6. *Task complexity*: individuals were more likely to loaf on simple tasks, but less likely on complex tasks. This finding might be related to increased interests when solving complex tasks.

Exploring non-monetary incentives to increase contribution to public goods is an important and promising direction for future research. Mathematical models of social psychology theories are likely to shed insights on the necessary and sufficient conditions for a reduction or even elimination of social loafing.

Matching

Matching theory has been credited as 'one of the outstanding successful stories of the theory of games' (Auman, 1992). It has been used to understand existing markets and to guide the design of new markets or allocation mechanisms in a variety of real world contexts. Matching experiments serve two purposes: to test new matching algorithms in the laboratory before implementing them in the real world, and to understanding how existing institutions evolved. We focus on one-sided matching experiments, and refer the reader to MATCHING AND MARKET DESIGN for a summary of the two-sided matching experiments.

One-sided matching is the assignment of indivisible items to agents without a medium of exchange, such as money. Examples include the assignment of college students to dormitory rooms and public housing units, the assignment of offices and tasks to individuals, the assignment of students to public schools, the allocation of course seats to students (mostly in business schools and law schools), and timeshare exchange. The key mechanisms in this class of problems are the top trading cycles (TTC) mechanism (Shapley and Scarf, 1974), the Gale–Shapley deferred acceptance mechanism (Gale and Shapley, 1962), and variants of the serial dictatorship mechanism (Abdulkadiroglu and Sonmez, 1998). Matching experiments explore several issues. For strategy-proof mechanisms, they explore the extent to which subjects

recognize and use their dominant strategies without prompting. For mechanisms which are not strategy-proof, they explore the extent of preference manipulation and the resulting efficiency loss. As a result, they examine the robustness of theoretical efficiency comparisons when the mechanisms are implemented among boundedly rational subjects and across different environments.

For the class of house allocation problems, two mechanisms have been compared and tested in the laboratory. The random serial dictatorship with squatting rights (RSD) is used by many US universities for on-campus housing allocation, while the TTC mechanism is theoretically superior. Chen and Sonmez (2002) report the first experimental study of these two mechanisms. They find that TTC is significantly more efficient than RSD because it induces significantly higher participation rate of existing tenants.

Another application of one-sided matching is the time-share problem. Wang and Krishna (2006) study the top trading cycles chains and spacebank mechanism (TTCCS), and two status quo mechanisms in the time-share industry, that is, the deposit first mechanism and the request first mechanism, neither of which is efficient. In the experiment, the observed efficiency of TTCCS is significantly higher than that of the deposit first mechanism, which in turn, is more efficient than the request first mechanism. In fact, efficiency under TTCCS converged to 100 per cent quickly, while the other two mechanisms do not show any increase in efficiency over time.

More recently, the school choice problem has received much attention. We review two experimental studies. Chen and Sonmez (2006) present an experimental study of three school choice mechanisms. The Boston mechanism is influential in practice, while the Gale–Shapley and TTC mechanisms have superior theoretical properties. Consistent with theory, this study indicates a high preference manipulation rate under Boston. As a result, efficiency under Boston is significantly lower than that of the two competing mechanisms in the designed environment. However, contrary to theory, Gale–Shapley outperforms TTC and generates the highest efficiency. The main reason is that a much higher proportion of subjects did not realize that truth-telling was a dominant strategy under TTC, and thus manipulated their preferences and ended up worse off. While Chen and Sonmez (2006) examine these mechanisms under partial information, where an agent only knows his own preference ranking, and not those of other agents, a follow-up study by Pais and Pinter (2006), investigates the same three mechanisms under different information conditions, ranging from complete ignorance about the other participants' preferences and school priorities to complete information on all elements of the game. They show that information condition has a significant effect on the rate of truthful preference revelation. In particular, having no information results in a significantly higher proportion of truth-telling than under any treatment with additional information. Interestingly, there is no significant difference in the efficiency between partial and full information treatments. Unlike Chen and Sonmez (2006), in this experiment, TTC outperforms in terms of efficiency. Furthermore, TTC is also less sensitive to the amount of information in the environment.

Owing to their important applications in the real world, one-sided matching experiments provide insights on the actual manipulability of the matching mechanisms which are valuable in their real world implementations. Some issues, such as the role of information on the performance of the mechanisms, remain open questions.

Combinatorial auctions

In many applications of mechanism design, theory is not yet up to the task of identifying the optimal design or even comparing alternative designs. One case in which this has been true is in the design of auctions to sell collections of heterogeneous items with value complementarities, which occur when the value of a combination of items can be higher than the sum of the values for separate items. Value complementarities arise naturally in many contexts, such as broadcast spectrum rights auctioned by the Federal Communications Commission, pollution emissions allowances for consecutive years bought and sold under the RECLAIM programme of the South Coast Air Quality Management District in Los Angeles, aircraft take-off and landing slots, logistics services, and advertising time slots. Because individuals may want to express bids for combinations of the items for sale, requiring up to 2^N bids per person when there are N items, these auctions have come to be known as combinatorial auctions.

As was discussed earlier under public goods mechanisms, theory has identified the VCG mechanism as the unique auction design that would implement an efficient allocation assuming bidders use dominant strategies. Theory has not yet identified the revenue-maximizing combinatorial auction, although Ledyard (2007) shows that it is not the VCG mechanism. Theory has also been of little use in comparing the expected revenue collection between different auction designs. This has opened the way for many significantly different auction designs to be proposed, and sometimes even deployed, with little evidence to back up various claims of superiority.

To give some idea of the complexity of the problem we describe just some of the various design choices one can make. Should the auctions be run as a sealed bid or should some kind of iterative procedure be used? And, if the latter, should iteration be synchronous or asynchronous? What kinds of bids should be allowed? Proposals for allowable bids include only bids for a single item, bids for any package, and some which allow only a limited list of packages to be bid on. What stopping rule should be used? Proposals have included fixed stopping times, stop after an iteration in which revenue does not increase by more than x per cent, stop if demand is less than or equal to supply, and an imaginative but complex system of eligibility and activity rules created for the Federal Communications Commission (FCC) auctions. Should winners pay what they bid or something else? Alternatives to pay what you bid include VCG prices and second-best prices based on the dual variables to the programme that picks the provisional winners. What should bidders be told during the auction? Some designs provide information on all bids and provisional winners and the full identity of the bidders involved in them. Some designs provide minimal information such as only the winning bids without even the information as to who made them. The permutations and combinations are many. Because theory has not developed enough to sort out what is best, experiments have been used to provide some evidence.

The very first experimental analysis of a combinatoric auction can be found in Rassenti, Smith and Bulfin (1982), where they compared a sealed bid auction (RSB) allowing package bids to a uniform price sealed bid auction (GIP), proposed by Grether, Isaac and Plott (1981), that did not allow package bids. Both designs included a double auction market for re-trading after the auction results were known. The RSB design yielded higher efficiencies than the GIP design. Banks, Ledyard and Porter (1989) compared a continuous, asynchronous design (AUSM), a generalization of the English auction with package bidding, to a synchronous iterative design with myopic VCG pricing and found AUSM to yield higher efficiencies and revenues on average. Ledyard, Porter and Rangel (1997) compare the continuous AUSM to a synchronous iterative design (SMR) developed by Millgrom (2000) for the FCC auctions, which only allowed simultaneous single item bids. The testing found that ASUM yielded significantly higher efficiencies and revenues. Kwasnica et al. (2005) compare an iterative design (RAD) with package bidding and price feedback to both AUSM and SMR. RAD and SMR use the same stopping rule. Efficiencies observed with RAD and AUSM are similar and higher than those for SMR, but revenue is higher in SMR since many bidders lose money due to a phenomenon known as the exposure problem, which is identified in Bykowsky, Cull and Ledyard (2000). If it is assumed that bidders default on bids on which they make losses and thus set the prices of such bids to zero, revenues are in fact higher under AUSM and RAD than under SMR. At the behest of the FCC, Banks et al. (2003) ran an experiment to compare an iterative, package bidding design (CRA) from Charles River Associates and Market Design (1998) with the FCC SMR auction format. They also found that the package bidding design provides more efficient allocations but less revenue, due to bidder losses in the SMR.

Parkes and Unger (2000) proposed an ascending price, generalized VCG auction (iBEA) that maintains nonlinear and non-anonymous prices on packages, and charges VCG prices to the winners. The design would theoretically produce efficient allocations as long as bidders bid in a straightforward manner. Straightforward bidding is myopic and non-strategic and involves bidding on packages that yield the locally highest payoff in utility. There is no evidence that actual bidders will behave this way. Chen and Takeuchi (2005) have experimentally tested iBEA against the VCG sealed bid auction and found that VCG was superior in both revenue generation and efficiency attained. Takeuchi et al. (2006) tested RAD against VCG and found that RAD generated higher efficiencies, especially in the earlier auctions. They were using experiments to test combinatoric auctions as a potential alternative to scheduling processes in situations with valuation complementarities. In many cases current procedures request orderings from users and then employ a knapsack algorithm of some kind to choose good allocations without any concern for incentive compatibility. Takeuchi et al. (2006) find that both RAD and VCG yield higher efficiencies than the knapsack approach. Ledyard, Porter and Noussair (1996) found similar results when comparing a more vanilla combinatoric auction to an administrative approach. These findings suggest there are significant improvements in organization performance being overlooked by management.

Porter et al. (2003) proposed and tested a combinatorial clock (CC) auction. After bids are submitted, a simple algorithm determines the demand for each item by each bidder and for those items that have more than one bidder demanding more units than are available the clock price is raised. They test their design against the SMR and CRA. They do not report revenue but in their tests the CC design attained an almost perfect average efficiency of 99.9 per cent. CRA attained an average of 93 per cent, while SMR attained only 88 per cent. Brunner et al. (2006) have carried out a systematic comparison of SMR and three alternatives, CC, RAD and a new FCC design called SMRPB, which takes the basic RAD design and changes two things. SMRPB allows bidders to win at most one package and the pricing feedback rule includes some inertia that RAD does not. They find that in terms of efficiency RAD is better than CC which is equivalent to SMRPB which is better than SMR. In terms of revenue, they find CC is better than RAD which is better than SMRPB which is better than SMR.

Most of these papers compare only two or three auction designs at a time and the environments used as the basis for comparison is often different in different papers. Further, environments can often be chosen that favour one auction over another. To deal with this, many research teams stress test their results by looking at boundary environments' collections of payoff parameters that give each auction under examination its best or worst chance of yielding high revenue or efficiency. But it is still unusual for a research team to report on a comparative test of several auctions in which their own design

ends up being out-performed by another. Nevertheless, there are some tentative conclusions one can draw from this research.

The easiest and most obvious conclusion is that allowing package bidding improves both efficiency and revenue. In all the studies listed, anything that limits bidders' ability to express the full extent of their willingness to pay for all packages does interfere with efficiency and revenue. Less obvious but also easy to see is that simultaneity and iteration are also good design features. Bidding in situations in which value complementarities exist can be difficult since bidders need to discover where their willingness to pay is more than others but also where they fit with others interests. Getting this right improves both efficiency and revenue. Iteration and relevant price feedback both help here. Stopping rules also matter. Although this is an area that could benefit from more research, it is clear that in many cases complicated stopping rules that allow auctions to proceed for very long periods of time provide little gain in revenue or efficiency.

Summary

Mechanism design experiments identify features of mechanisms that lead to good performance when they are implemented among real people. Experiments testing public goods mechanisms show that dominant strategy mechanisms should also be secure, while Nash-efficient mechanisms should satisfy dynamic stability if it is to be considered for application in the real world in a repeated interaction setting. For matching mechanisms, transparency of the dominant strategy leads to better performance in the laboratory. Lastly, in combinatorial auctions, package bidding, simultaneity and iteration are shown to be good design features. In addition to the three domains covered in this article, there has been a growing experimental literature on market design, information markets and contract theory. We do not cover them in this article, due to lack of robust empirical regularities. However, they are excellent areas in which to make a new contribution.

YAN CHEN AND JOHN O. LEDYARD

See also **computing in mechanism design; matching and market design; mechanism design; public goods.**

Bibliography

Abdulkadiroglu, A. and Sönmez, T. 1998. Random serial dictatorship and the core from random endowments in house allocation problems. *Econometrica* 66, 689–701.

Andreoni, J. and Petrie, R. 2004. Public goods experiments without confidentiality: a glimpse into fund-raising. *Journal of Public Economics* 88, 1605–23.

Arifovic, J. and Ledyard, J. 2006. Computer testbeds and mechanism design: application to the class of Groves-Ledyard mechanisms for provision of public goods. Caltech working paper. Pasadena, CA.

Attiyeh, G., Franciosi, R. and Isaac, M. 2000. Experiments with the pivot process for providing public goods. *Public Choice* 102, 95–114.

Aumann, R. 1992. Foreword. In *Two-Sided Matching: A Study in Game-Theoretic Modeling and Analysis*, ed. E. Alvin, M.A. Roth, O. Sotomayor. Cambridge: Cambridge University Press.

Bagnoli, M. and Lipman, B. 1989. Provision of public goods: fully implementing the core through private contributions. *Review of Economic Studies* 56, 583–602.

Banks, J.S., Ledyard, J.O. and Porter, D.P. 1989. Allocating uncertain and unresponsive resources: an experimental approach. *Rand Journal of Economics* 20, 1–25.

Banks, J., Olson, M., Porter, D., Rassenti, S. and Smith, V. 2003. Theory, experiment and the federal communications commission spectrum auctions. *Journal of Economic Behavior and Organization* 51, 303–50.

Beenen, G., Ling, K., Wang, X., Chang, K., Frankowski, D., Resnick, P. and Kraut, R. 2004. In *Proceedings of ACM Computer Supported Cooperative Work 2004*, Conference on Computer Supported Cooperative Work. Chicago, IL: ACM.

Brunner, C., Goeree, J., Holt, C. and Ledyard, J. 2006. Combinatorial auctioneering, Caltech working paper. Pasadena, CA.

Bykowsky, M., Cull, R. and Ledyard, J. 2000. Mutually destructive bidding: the FCC auction design problem. *Journal of Regulatory Economics* 17, 205–28.

Cason, T., Saijo, T., Sjöström, T. and Yamato, T. 2006. Secure implementation experiments: do strategy-proof mechanisms really work? *Games and Economic Behavior* 57, 206–35.

Charles River Associates Inc. and Market Design Inc. 1998. Report No. 1351–00.

Chen, Y. 2002. A family of supermodular Nash mechanisms implementing Lindahl allocations. *Economic Theory* 19, 773–90.

Chen, Y. 2008. Incentive-compatible mechanisms for pure public goods: a survey of experimental literature. In *The Handbook of Experimental Economics Results*, ed. C. Plott and V. Smith. Amsterdam: Elsevier.

Chen, Y. and Gazzale, R. 2004. Supermodularity and convergence: an experimental study of the compensation mechanism. *American Economic Review* 94, 1505–35.

Chen, Y. and Plott, C.R. 1996. The Groves–Ledyard mechanism: an experimental study of institutional design. *Journal of Public Economics* 59, 335–64.

Chen, Y. and Sonmez, T. 2002. Improving efficiency of on-campus housing: an experimental study. *American Economic Review* 92, 1669–86.

Chen, Y. and Sonmez, T. 2006. School choice: an experimental study. *Journal of Economic Theory* 127, 202–31.

Chen, Y. and Tang, F.-F. 1998. Learning and incentive compatible mechanisms for public goods provision: an experimental study. *Journal of Political Economy* 106, 633–62.

Chen, Y. and Takeuchi, K. 2005. Multi-object auctions with package bidding: an experimental comparison of Vickrey and iBEA. Working paper.

Clarke, E.H. 1971. Multipart pricing of public goods. *Public Choice* 11, 17–33.

Corchon, L. and Wilkie, S. 1996. Double implementation of the ratio correspondence by a market mechanism. *Review of Economic Design* 2, 325–37.

Eckel, C. and Grossman, P. 2005. Managing diversity by creating team identity. *Journal of Economic Behavior & Organization* 58, 371–92.

Falkinger, J. 1996. Efficient private provision of public goods by rewarding deviations from average. *Journal of Public Economics* 62, 413–22.

Falkinger, J., Fehr, E., Gächter, S. and Winter-Ebmer, R. 2000. A simple mechanism for the efficient provision of public goods: experimental evidence. *American Economic Review* 90, 247–64.

Gale, D. and Shapley, L. 1962. College admissions and the stability of marriage. *American Mathematical Monthly* 69, 9–15.

Green, J. and Laffont, J.-J. 1977. Characterization of satisfactory mechanisms for the revelation of the preferences for public goods. *Econometrica* 45, 427–38.

Grether, D., Isaac, M. and Plott, C. 1981. The allocation of landing rights by unanimity among competitiors. *American Economic Review* 71, 166–71.

Groves, T. 1973. Incentives in Teams. *Econometrica* 41, 617–31.

Groves, T. and Ledyard, J. 1977. Optimal allocation of public goods: a solution to the 'free rider' problem. *Econometrica* 45, 783–809.

Groves, T. and Ledyard, J. 1987. Incentive compatibility since 1972. In *Essays in Honor of Leonid Hurwicz*, ed. T. Groves, R. Radner and S. Reiter. Minneapolis: University of Minnesota Press.

Harkins, S.G. 1987. Social loafing and social facilitation. *Journal of Experimental Social Psychology* 23, 1–18.

Harstad, R.M. and Marrese, M. 1981. Implementation of mechanism by processes: public good allocation experiments. *Journal of Economic Behavior & Organization* 2, 129–51.

Harstad, R.M. and Marrese, M. 1982. Behavioral explanations of efficient public good allocations. *Journal of Public Economics* 19, 367–83.

Healy, P.J. 2006. Learning dynamics for mechanism design: an experimental comparison of public goods mechanisms. *Journal of Economic Theory* 129, 114–49.

Hurwicz, L. 1972. On informationally decentralized systems. In *Decision and Organization*, ed. C. McGuire and R. Radner. Amsterdam: North-Holland.

Hurwicz, L. 1975. On the existence of allocation systems whose manipulative Nash equilibria are Pareto-optimal. Paper presented at Third World Congress of the Econometric Society, Toronto.

Hurwicz, L. 1979. Outcome functions yielding Walrasian and Lindahl allocations at Nash equilibrium points. *Review of Economic Studies* 46, 217–25.

Isaac, R. and James, D. 2000. Robustness of the incentive compatible combinatorial auction. *Experimental Economics* 3, 31–53.

Jackson, M. and Moulin, H. 1992. Implementing a public project and distributing its cost. *Journal of Economic Theory* 57, 125–40.

Kaneko, M. 1977. The ratio equilibria and the core of the voting game in a public goods economy. *Econometrica* 45, 1589–94.

Kauru, S.J. and Williams, K.D. 1993. Social loafing: a meta-analytic review and theoretical integration. *Journal of Personality and Social Psychology* 65, 681–706.

Kawagoe, T. and Mori, T. 2001. Can pivotal mechanism induce truth-telling? An experimental study. *Public Choice* 108, 331–54.

Kim, T. 1986. On the nonexistence of a stable Nash mechanism implementing Lindahl allocations. Mimeo. University of Minnesota.

Kim, T. 1993. A stable Nash mechanism implementing Lindahl allocations for quasi-linear environments. *Journal of Mathematical Economics* 22, 359–71.

Kwasnica, A.M., Ledyard, J.O., Porter, D. and DeMartini, C. 2005. A new and improved design for multi-object iterative auctions. *Management Science* 51, 419–34.

Ledyard, J. 2007. Optimal combinatoric auctions with single-minded bidders. *Proceedings of the 8th ACM Conference on Electronic Commerce.* San Diego, CA: ACM.

Ledyard, J., Olson, M., Porter, D., Swanson, J. and Torma, D. 2002. The first use of a combined value auction for transportation services. *Interfaces* 32, 4–12.

Ledyard, J. and Palfrey, T. 1994. Voting and lottery drafts as efficient public goods mechanisms. *Review of Economic Studies* 61, 327–55.

Ledyard, J., Porter, D. and Noussair, C. 1996. The allocation of a shared resource within an organization. *Economic Design* 2, 163–92.

Ledyard, J., Porter, D. and Rangel, A. 1997. Experiments testing multiobject allocation mechanisms. *Journal of Economics and Management Strategy* 6, 639–75.

Mailath, G. and Postlewaite, A. 1990. Asymmetric information bargaining problems with many agents. *Review of Economic Studies* 57, 351–67.

McAfee, P.R. and McMillan, J. 1996. Analyzing the airwaves auction. *Journal of Economic Perspectives* 10(1), 159–75.

McCabe, K., Rassenti, S. and Smith, V. 1989. Designing 'Smart' computer assisted markets. *European Journal of Political Economy* 5, 259–83.

Millgrom, P. 2000. Putting auction theory to work: the simultaneous ascending auction. *Journal of Political Economy* 108, 245–272a.

Milgrom, P. and Roberts, J. 1990. Rationalizability, learning and equilibrium in games with strategic complementarities. *Econometrica* 58, 1255–77.

Milgrom, P. and Shannon, C. 1994. Monotone comparative statics. *Econometrica* 62, 157–80.

Mori, T. 1989. Effectiveness of mechanisms for public goods provision: an experimental study. *Economic Studies* 40, 234–46.

Pais, J. and Pintér, A. 2006. School choice and information: an experimental study on matching mechanisms. Working Paper, Institute for Economics and Business Administration (ISEG). Lisbon: Technical University.

Parkes, D. and Unger, L. 2000. Iterative combinatorial auctions: theory and practice. In *Proceedings of the 17th National Conference on Artificial Intelligence* (AAAI-00).

Peleg, B. 1996. Double implementation of the Lindahl equilibrium by a continuous mechanism. *Economic Design* 2, 311–24.

Porter, D.P. 1999. The effect of bid withdrawal in a multi-object auction. *Review of Economic Design* 4, 73–97.

Porter, D., Rassenti, S., Roopnarine, A. and Smith, V. 2003. Combinatorial auction design. *Proceedings of the National Academy of Sciences* 100, 11153–7.

Rassenti, S., Smith, V. and Bulfin, R. 1982. A combinatorial auction mechanism for airport time slot allocation. *Bell Journal of Economics* 13, 402–17.

Roberts, J. 1979. Incentives and planning procedures for the provision of public goods. *Review of Economic Studies* 46, 283–92.

Saijo, T., Sjöström, T. and Yamato, T. 2005. Secure Implementation. Working Paper, No. 567-0047. Osaka: Institute of Social and Economic Research, Osaka University.

Shapley, L.S. and Scarf, H. 1974. On cores and indivisibilities. *Journal of Mathematical Economics* 1, 23–37.

Smith, V. 1979a. Incentive compatible experimental processes for the provision of public goods. In *Experimental Economics*, vol. 1, ed. R. Smith. Greenwich, CT: JAI Press.

Smith, V. 1979b. An experimental comparison of three public goods decision mechanisms. *Scandinavian Journal of Economics* 81, 198–251.

Tajfel, H. and Turner, J.C. 1986. The social identity theory of intergroup behaviour. In *Psychology of Intergroup Relations*, ed. S. Worchel and W. Austin. Chicago: Nelson-Hall.

Takeuchi, K., Lin, J., Chen, Y. and Finholt, T. 2006. Shake it up baby: scheduling with package auctions. Working paper. School of Information, University of Michigan.

Tian, G. 1989. Implementation of the Lindahl correspondence by a single-valued, feasible, and continuous mechanism. *Review of Economic Studies* 56, 613–21.

Varian, H. 1994. A solution to the problems of externalities when agents are well-informed. *American Economic Review* 84, 1278–93.

Vickrey, W. 1961. Counterspeculation, auctions and competitive sealed tenders. *Journal of Finance* 16, 8–37.

Walker, M. 1980. On the impossibility of a dominant strategy mechanism to optimally decide public questions. *Econometrica* 48, 1521–40.

Walker, M. 1981. A simple incentive compatible scheme for attaining Lindahl allocations. *Econometrica* 49, 65–71.

Wang, Y. and Krishna, A. 2006. Timeshare exchange mechanisms. *Management Science* 52, 1123–37.

medieval guilds

Guilds operated throughout Europe during the Middle Ages, and in many places, lasted into the early modern era. Guilds were groups of individuals with common goals whose activities, characteristics, and composition varied greatly across centuries, regions, and industries.

Guilds filled many niches in medieval economy and society. Typical taxonomies divide urban occupational guilds into two types: merchant and craft.

Merchant guilds were organizations of merchants who were involved in long-distance commerce and local wholesale trade, and may also have been retail sellers of commodities in their home cities and distant venues where they possessed rights to set up shop. The largest and most influential merchant guilds participated in international commerce and politics and established colonies in foreign cities. In many cases, they evolved into or became inextricably intertwined with the governments of their home towns.

Merchant guilds enforced contracts among members and between members and outsiders. Guilds policed members' behaviour because medieval commerce operated according to the community responsibility system. If a merchant from a particular town failed to fulfil his part of a bargain or pay his debts, all members of his guild could be held liable. When they were in a foreign port, their goods could be seized and sold to alleviate the bad debt. They would then return to their hometown, where they would seek compensation from the original defaulter.

Merchant guilds also protected members against predation by rulers. Rulers seeking revenue had an incentive to seize money and merchandise from foreign merchants. Guilds threatened to boycott the realms of rulers who did this, a practice known as *withernam* in medieval England. Since boycotts impoverished both kingdoms which depended on commerce and governments for whom tariffs were the principal source of revenue, the threat of retaliation deterred medieval potentates from excessive expropriations.

Craft guilds were organized along lines of particular trades. Members of these guilds typically owned and operated small businesses or family workshops. Craft guilds operated in many sectors of the economy. Guilds of victuallers bought agricultural commodities, converted them to consumables, and sold finished foodstuffs. Examples included bakers, brewers, and butchers. Guilds of manufacturers made durable goods and, when profitable, exported them from their towns to consumers in distant markets. Examples include makers of textiles, military equipment, and metalware. Guilds of a third type sold skills and services. Examples include clerks, teamsters, and entertainers.

These occupational organizations engaged in a wide array of economic activities. Some manipulated input and output markets to their own advantage. Others established reputations for quality, fostering the expansion of anonymous exchange and making everyone better off. Because of the underlying economic realities, victualling guilds tended towards the former. Manufacturing guilds tended towards the latter. Guilds of service providers fell somewhere in between. All three types of guilds managed labour markets, lowered wages, and advanced their own interests at their subordinates' expense. These undertakings had a common theme. Merchant and craft guilds acted to increase and stabilize members' incomes.

Non-occupational guilds also operated in medieval towns and cities. These organizations had both secular and religious functions. Historians refer to these organizations as social, religious, or parish guilds as well as fraternities and confraternities. The secular activities of these organizations included providing members with mutual insurance, extending credit to members in times of need, aiding members in courts of law, and helping the children of members afford apprenticeships and dowries.

The principal pious objective was the salvation of the soul and escape from Purgatory. Guilds served as mechanisms for organizing, managing, and financing members' collective quest for eternal salvation. Efforts centered on three types of tasks. The first were routine and participatory religious services such as prayers, processions, the singing of psalms, the illumination of holy symbols, and the distribution of alms to the poor. The second category consisted of actions performed on members' behalf after their deaths and for the benefit of their souls. Post-mortem services began with funerals and continued perpetually as guilds prayed (or hired priests to pray) for the salvation of the souls of all deceased members. The third category involved indoctrination and monitoring to maintain the piety of members.

Righteous living was important because members' fates were linked together. The more pious one's brethren, the more helpful their prayers, and the more quickly one escaped from purgatory. So, in hopes of minimizing purgatorial pain and maximizing eternal happiness, guilds beseeched members to restrain physical desires and forgo worldly pleasures.

Guilds also operated in villages and the countryside. Rural guilds performed the same tasks as social and religious guilds in towns and cities. Recent research on medieval England indicates that guilds operated in most, if not all, villages. Villages often possessed multiple guilds. Most rural residents belonged to a guild. Some may have joined more than one organization.

Guilds often spanned multiple dimensions of this taxonomy. Members of craft guilds participated in wholesale commerce. Members of merchant guilds opened retail shops. Social and religious guilds evolved into occupational associations. All merchant and craft guilds possessed religious and fraternal features.

In sum, guild members sought prosperity in this life and providence in the next. Members wanted high and stable incomes, quick passage through Purgatory, and eternity in heaven. Guilds helped them coordinate their collective efforts to attain these goals.

To attain their collective goals, guilds had to persuade members to contribute to the common good and deter free riding. Guilds that wished to develop respected reputations had to get all members to sell superior merchandise. Guilds that wished to lower the costs of labour had to get all masters to reduce wages. Guilds that wished to raise the prices of products had to get all masters to restrict output. Guilds whose members wished to enter heaven had to get all members to live piously, abstaining both from the pleasures of the flesh and the material temptations of secular society.

To persuade members to cooperate and advance their common interests, guilds formed stable, self-enforcing associations that possessed structures for making and implementing collective decisions. A guild's members met periodically to elect officers, audit accounts, induct new members, debate policies, and amend ordinances. Officers administered a nexus of agreements among a guild's members. Details of these agreements varied greatly from guild to guild, but the issues addressed were similar in all cases. Members agreed to contribute certain resources or take certain actions that furthered the guild's occupational and spiritual endeavors.

Members who failed to fulfil their obligations faced punishments. Punishments varied across transgressions, guilds, time and place, but a pattern existed. First-time offenders were punished lightly, perhaps suffering public scolding and paying small monetary fines, and repeat offenders punished harshly. The ultimate threat was expulsion.

Within large guilds, a hierarchy existed. Masters were full members who usually owned their own workshops, retail outlets, or trading vessels. Masters employed journeymen, who were labourers who worked for wages on short-term contracts or a daily basis (hence the term journeyman, from *jour*, the French word for 'day'). Journeymen hoped to one day advance to the level of master. To do this, journeymen usually had to save enough money to open a workshop and pay for admittance, or, if they were lucky, receive a workshop through marriage or inheritance.

Masters also supervised apprentices, who were usually boys in their teens who worked for room, board and perhaps a small stipend in exchange for a vocational education. Both guilds and government regulated apprenticeships, usually to ensure that masters fulfilled their part of the apprenticeship agreement. Terms of apprenticeships varied, usually lasting from five to nine years.

Relationships between guilds and governments varied over centuries and around Europe. Guilds typically began as voluntary associations with little legal standing. Most guilds operated without formal recognition or authorization from the government. Successful occupational guilds aspired to attain recognition as a self-governing association

with the right to possess property and other legal privileges. Merchant and craft guilds often purchased these rights from municipal and royal authorities.

The history of guilds stretches back to times with few written records. In the late Roman Empire, organizations resembling guilds existed in most towns and cities. These voluntary associations of artisans, known as *collegia*, were organized along trade lines. Members shared religious observances and fraternal dinners. Most of these organizations disappeared during the Dark Ages, when the Western Roman Empire disintegrated and urban life collapsed. In the Eastern Roman Empire, some *collegia* may have survived from late antiquity and evolved into medieval guilds, but it is unlikely that even the most resilient *collegia* survived in Western Europe.

In the centuries following the collapse of the Roman Empire, evidence indicates that guild-like associations operated in most towns and many rural areas. These organizations functioned as modern burial and benefit societies, whose objectives included prayers for the souls of deceased members, payments of *weregilds* in cases of justifiable homicide, and supporting members involved in legal disputes. These rural guilds were descendents of Germanic social organizations known as *gilda* which the Roman historian Tacitus referred to as *convivium*.

During the 11th through 13th centuries, considerable economic development occurred. The revival of long-distance trade coincided with the expansion of urban areas. Merchant guilds formed an institutional foundation for this commercial revolution. Merchant guilds sprung up in towns throughout Europe, and in many places rose to prominence in urban political structures. Merchant guilds' principal accomplishment was establishing the institutional foundations for long-distance commerce.

Merchant guilds first flourished in Italian cities in the 12th century. Craft guilds became ubiquitous in Italy during the succeeding century. In northern Europe, merchant guilds rose to prominence a century later, when local merchant guilds in trading cities such as Lubeck and Bremen formed alliances with merchants throughout the Baltic region. The alliance system grew into the Hanseatic League which dominated trade around the Baltic and North Seas and in northern Germany.

As economic expansion continued in the 13th and 14 centuries, the influence of the Catholic Church grew, and the doctrine of Purgatory developed. The doctrine inspired the creation of countless religious guilds, since the doctrine provided members with strong incentives to want to belong to a group whose prayers would help one enter heaven and it provided guilds with mechanisms to induce members to exert effort on behalf of the organization.

The number of guilds grew rapidly after the Black Death, for several reasons. The decline in population raised per capita incomes, which encouraged the expansion of consumption and commerce, which in turn necessitated the formation of institutions to satisfy this demand.

Repeated epidemics decreased family sizes, particularly in cities, where the typical adult had on average perhaps 1.5 surviving children, few surviving siblings, and only a small extended family, if any. Guilds replaced extended families in a form of fictive kinship. The decline in family size and impoverishment of the Church also forced individuals to rely on their guild more in times of trouble, since they no longer could rely on relatives and priests to sustain them through periods of crisis. All of these changes bound individuals more closely to guilds, discouraged free riding, and encouraged the expansion of collective institutions.

For nearly two centuries after the Black Death, guilds dominated life in medieval towns. Any town resident of consequence belonged to a guild. Most urban residents thought guild membership to be indispensable. Guilds dominated manufacturing, marketing, and commerce. Guilds dominated local politics and influenced national and international affairs. Guilds were the centre of social and spiritual life.

The heyday of guilds lasted into the 16th century. The Reformation weakened guilds. Afterwards, in Protestant nations the influence of guilds waned. Guilds often asked governments for assistance. Guilds requested monopolies on manufacturing and commerce and asked courts to force members to live up to their obligations. Guilds lingered where governments provided such assistance. Guilds faded where governments did not. Guilds retained strength in nations which remained Catholic until they were swept away by the reforms following the French Revolution and the Napoleonic Wars.

GARY RICHARDSON

Bibliography

Basing, P. 1990. *Trades and Crafts in Medieval Manuscripts*. London: British Library.
Cooper, R.C.H. 1985. *The Archives of the City of London Livery Companies and Related Organizations*. London: Guildhall Library.
Davidson, C. 1996. *Technology, Guilds, and Early English Drama*. Early Drama, Art, and Music Monograph Series 23. Kalamazoo, MI: Medieval Institute Publications, Western Michigan University.
Epstein, S.R. 1998. Craft guilds, apprenticeships, and technological change in pre-industrial Europe. *Journal of Economic History* 58, 684–713.
Epstein, S. 1991. *Wage and Labor Guilds in Medieval Europe*. Chapel Hill, NC: University of North Carolina Press.
Gross, C. 1890. *The Guild Merchant: A Contribution to British Municipal History*. Oxford: Clarendon Press.
Gustafsson, B. 1987. The rise and economic behavior of medieval craft guilds: an economic-theoretical interpretation. *Scandinavian Journal of Economics* 35, 1–40.
Hanawalt, B. 1984. Keepers of the lights: late medieval English parish guilds. *Journal of Medieval and Renaissance Studies* 14, 21–37.
Hatcher, J. and Miller, E. 1995. *Medieval England: Towns, Commerce and Crafts, 1086–1348*. London: Longman.
Hickson, C.R. and Thompson, E.A. 1991. A new theory of guilds and European economic development. *Explorations in Economic History* 28, 127–68.
Lopez, R. 1971. *The Commercial Revolution of the Middle Ages, 950–1350*. Englewood Cliffs, NJ: Prentice-Hall.
Mokyr, J. 1990. *The Lever of Riches: Technological Creativity and Economic Progress*. Oxford: Oxford University Press.
Pirenne, H. 1952. *Medieval Cities: Their Origins and the Revival of Trade*, trans. F. Halsey. Princeton: Princeton University Press.
Richardson, G. 2001. A tale of two theories: monopolies and craft guilds in medieval England and modern imagination. *Journal of the History of Economic Thought* 23, 217–42.
Richardson, G. 2000. Brand Names Before the Industrial Revolution. Working paper, UC Irvine.
Richardson, G. 2004. Guilds, laws, and markets for manufactured merchandise in late-medieval England. *Explorations in Economic History* 41, 1–25.
Richardson, G. 2005. Christianity and craft guilds in late medieval England: a rational choice analysis. *Rationality and Society* 17, 139–89.
Richardson, G. 2005. The prudent village: risk pooling institutions in medieval English agriculture. *Journal of Economic History* 65, 386–413.
Smith, T. 1870. *English Guilds*. London: N. Trübner & Co.
Swanson, H. 1983. *Building Craftsmen in Late Medieval York*. York: University of York Press.
Thrupp, S. 1989. *The Merchant Class of Medieval London 1300–1500*. Chicago: University of Chicago Press.
Unwin, G. 1904. *The Guilds and Companies of London*. London: Methuen & Company.
Ward, J. 1997. *Metropolitan Communities: Trade Guilds, Identity, and Change in Early Modern London*. Palo Alto: Stanford University Press.
Westlake, H.F. 1919. *The Parish Guilds of Mediaeval England*. London: Society for Promotion of Christian Knowledge.

Menger, Carl (1840–1921)

Carl Menger is known as one of the co-founders, along with W.S. Jevons and Leon Walras, of marginal utility analysis. As such, he can be counted as one of the originators of modern neoclassical economics. He is also recognized as the founder of the Austrian School of economics which developed a distinct tradition of economic thought over the century following his writing.

Menger was born in Neu-Sandez, Galizieu, a part of Austria that later became Poland. His family were mostly civil servants and army officers. Menger's father was a lawyer, and Carl studied law and political science first at the University of Vienna (1859–60) and then at Prague (1860–63). He took a doctorate at the University of Cracow and soon after, began a career in journalism. He worked in Lemberg and later Vienna where his main interests were in economic and fiscal problems of Austria. In 1871, Menger entered the Austrian civil service. However, 1871 was also the year in which his first book, *Grundsätze der Volkswirtschaftslehre*, later translated as *Principles of Economics*, was published. He presented this work for his habilitation for the faculty of law and political science at the University of Vienna. As a consequence, he became a 'privatdozent' and quit his position in the civil service. In 1873, he was appointed extraordinary professor and began his very long and very successful academic career. In 1876, Menger was appointed tutor to Crown Prince Rudolf of Austria and for two years accompanied him on travels through Germany, France, Switzerland and the British Isles. Upon his return, he resumed his teaching responsibilities, and he received a chair in political economy in 1879. He continued to teach until 1903 when, at the comparatively early age of 63, he retired to devote himself exclusively to completing the treatise he had begun with the *Principles*. He died within three days of his 81st birthday in 1921, his project still incomplete. He was survived by his one son, Karl.

The *Principles of Economics*

When Menger published the *Principles*, he was 31 years old and a journalist who had recently been appointed to the prestigious 'Ministerratsprasidium' in the Austrian civil service. Several biographers report that during his years as a journalist Menger became interested in economics because he observed that current economic theories did not seem to explain current economic events. He therefore wanted to work out the laws of economics for himself. It is apparent from the internal textual evidence of the *Principles*, however, that Menger must have had a more than cursory interest in the subject of economics during his years as a student. He must have read deeply and widely in the history of economics, since his first major work cites a wide range of earlier thinkers on economic problems including Aristotle, the medieval scholastics, Turgot, Smith, Ricardo, the German historicists and the contemporary socialists. Menger's knowledge of the history of economic thought is also evidenced by the outstanding library he accumulated during his lifetime, and by the fact that most of the major works in economic thought bear the marks of his close study.

Menger's clear purpose was to show how his theory of value could solve satisfactorily and in a unified manner all the problems of economic theory posed by earlier thinkers. The major target of his work was the labour theory of value which he believed was not only incorrect as an explanation of value and prices, but also failed to provide a unified explanation for factor prices on its own terms. However, Menger also took as his task to explain away the paradox of value, the erroneous view of Aristotle that exchange was an exchange of equivalent values, the mistaken view that capital as such was productive and the notion that money had to be explained according to different principles from other goods. In fact, every chapter of the *Principles* contains a refutation of some earlier doctrine or other that required a correct theory of value to elucidate.

Menger was writing partly against the background of classical economics. He was also, however, writing to an audience of German scholars who, in their rejection of classical economics were also rejecting the whole notion that one could develop a scientific theory of economic phenomena. Nothing, however, could be further from Menger's approach. Part of his aim, then, was to explain to the German historical economists that scientific economic theory was possible and compatible with empirical reality. To that end, Menger dedicated the book 'with respectful esteem to D. Wilhelm Roscher', a major figure in the older German Historical School.

To Menger, the central unifying principle of economics was the phenomenon of value. One had to explain the source of value before any of its particular manifestations could be understood. However, to develop adequately a theory of value, Menger had to prepare the ground upon which the theory rests. For Menger, that meant spending the first two chapters of his book (62 pages and over one-fourth the main text) on an exhaustive discussion of the meaning of a good and of an economic good in particular. While to the modern reader this might seem excessively thorough, Menger, the innovator, wished to take nothing for granted in establishing the firm basis of his theory. One had to move from the notion of useful things to the notion of a good to the concept of an economic good before one could understand the real meaning of economic value. Since all of economic theory hangs on this concept, he must have believed it imperative to be sure the reader understands each step of the argument.

Right from the beginning we see Menger's distinctive approach to economic theory. 'All things are subject to the law of cause and effect' (*Principles*, p. 51). Economic theory is an exercise in discovering and explaining the causal relationship between things and human values. He thus begins by pointing out that there are many useful things in the world, but for a useful thing to have 'goods-character', men must (*a*) recognize a causal connection between the good and its ability to satisfy a need and (*b*) have the power to make use of the thing for need satisfaction. (Goods, Menger points out, can be concrete things or they can be intangible relationships such as firms, copyrights or good will, an observation that is distinctly modern.) This is a pattern repeated again and again in Menger's writing: men must have knowledge and power. Economic life is built around gaining knowledge and power; knowledge of causal relationship between things and satisfaction, knowledge of technical production relationships, knowledge of trading opportunities, knowledge of 'economic' prices, knowledge of the qualities of goods, and the power to make the best use of man's knowledge.

Knowledge of causal connections among goods permits men to rank goods in accordance with their relationship to want satisfaction. Goods that have the ability to satisfy needs directly (consumer goods), Menger called 'first order goods'. Goods that can only indirectly satisfy needs by being transformed with complementary goods into first order goods, Menger called 'goods of a higher order' (inputs). Furthermore, higher order goods are not valued in themselves, but derive their 'goods character' from first order goods, an observation that will later allow Menger to develop his refutation of the labour theory of value.

Having established the concept of a good in general in Chapter 1, Menger goes on in Chapter 2 to explain the concept of an economic good. Menger's definition of an economic good is completely familiar to modern readers; the way in which Menger develops his argument is not. Menger sees men's strictly economizing activities as taking place within the context of an overall plan through time. He argues that men must estimate both their needs for various goods and the quantities of goods that will be available for fulfilling their consumption plans for specific periods of time. Their estimated needs, he calls their 'requirements' (bedarfs) a concept for which we have no modern equivalent although Stigler (1941, p. 140) has argued that requirements are the quantities of goods sufficient to make marginal utility go to zero (all the economic goods men could rationally consume). An economic good, then, is one where available quantities fall short of men's requirements.

The notion of requirements is important to Menger's argument because it allows him to discuss how men get information about requirements and quantities of goods and how they plan for their consumption in the face of uncertainty. It is obvious in this discussion that Menger does not hypothesize given utility functions which are maximized subject to fixed constraints. While he eventually gets to a verbal explanation of economizing behaviour that is consistent with the standard model, to him the interesting questions involve how men go about estimating their requirements over time and how they plan to satisfy them. Their planning activities require not only that they estimate future needs based on present tastes and preferences, but that they take into account the fact that their needs may change in unexpected ways. Further, their planning activity also encompasses plans to change the quantities of goods available. Hence, the plan is one of production as well as consumption. Only after Menger establishes the importance of human planning through time does he go on to discuss economizing behaviour in the modern sense of maximizing satisfaction within the known resource constraints.

Economizing to Menger, then, is a two-step process that involves first formulating a general plan for meeting one's requirements by assessing probable needs given an uncertain future and gathering information about the probable availability of goods, and then actually economizing based on the actual needs and quantities available at a moment in time.

Menger's discussion of an economic good is rich with associated insights. In this chapter, he gives an account of how non-economic goods become economic (through growth of population, growth of human needs and advances in knowledge as civilization progresses), a description of public goods (goods that are economic goods in general but are provided in such a way that people treat them as non-economic goods), an account of the origin and function of private property (to protect economic goods owned by the haves from the predation of the have-nots). Property is the 'only practically possible solution of the problem that is, in the nature of things, imposed upon us by the disparity between requirements for, and available quantities of, all economic goods' (*Principles*, p. 97), and a discussion of the economic implications of differing qualities of goods. He devotes part of his discussion of economic goods to discussing the nature of individual wealth – the entire sum of economic goods at an individual's command – and of national wealth – a slippery concept that can only be accurately described as 'a complex of wealths linked together by intercourse and trade' (*Principles*, p. 112).

Finally, after this detailed groundwork, Menger gets to his theory of value in Chapter 3. Menger has been called a member of the 'psychological school' because of his thoroughly subjective notion of value. However, it is not a Jevons-like utilitarian subjectivism. Goods are valued not because they provide various quantities of utils to individuals, but because they serve various uses that have different levels of importance to individuals. The difference may seem small to the reader, but it makes for subtle but important differences in understanding the valuation process. 'Value is ... the importance that individual goods or quantities of goods attain for us because we are conscious of being dependent on command of them for the satisfaction of our needs' (*Principles*, p. 115). Value is a judgement men make about the importance of goods; it adheres in concrete units of goods and not in abstract utility. The problem of a theory of value is to explain the differences in value among different goods.

Menger develops his theory of value in two stages. First he shows, with the use of a numerical table, how the importance men attach to the acquisition of additional units of a good that satisfies a particular need declines as more of the good is acquired, and by comparing the declining satisfactions associated with the acquisition of increasing amounts of various goods, he explains why a man might satisfy some of his desire for tobacco, for example, before he has completely satisfied his desire for food. In fact, Menger's tables are vivid examples of Gossen's first and second laws. Menger's use of numbers may give the impression that he is explaining utility as a cardinally measurable quantity. However, the impression is immediately dispelled when he points out that his chart is merely illustrative of a general psychological principle and is not meant to be taken literally. Furthermore, his chart, he explains, describes only a special case of valuation – the case where a single good serves for a single satisfaction. The more important case – where a single good has multiple uses – is more complex and requires more discussion. Interestingly, it is only in the context of the following more complex case that he states clearly his principle of diminishing marginal valuation.

When a single good, such as sacks of grain or pails of water, can serve many different uses, the first units will be used to serve the most important uses for the good while successive units of the good will be put to less and less important uses. Menger concludes, then, that the value of any one sack of grain is equal to the satisfaction associated with the least important use that would go unsatisfied if one sack of grain is removed, a statement of diminishing marginal utility that is completely free of mathematical metaphor.

Menger drew two immediate implications from his value theory: (1) the diamonds–water paradox was easily solved because given their respective quantities, the marginal unit of water in most cases served no use while the marginal unit of scarce diamonds had very important desires to satisfy, and (2) the labour theory of value was obviously incorrect.

> The determining factor in the value of a good, then, is neither the quantity of labor or other goods necessary for its production not the quantity necessary for its reproduction, but rather the magnitude of importance of those satisfactions with respect to which we are conscious of being dependent on command of the good. This principle of value determination is universally valid, and no exception to it can be found in human economy. (*Principles*, p. 145)

This leads Menger to one of the most important theoretical implications of his theory – that the value of goods of a higher order depends on the prospective value of corresponding goods of lower order. In fact, the value of an input is equal to the satisfaction that would be forgone if the input were not available for use. Note that this is not so much a marginal productivity theory of factor value as it is a 'marginal utility product' theory completely consistent with his subjective theory of value.

Despite his comments on the value of goods of a higher order, Menger did not develop a theory of production in the modern sense. He did observe, however, that all production takes place in time, and that the higher the order of goods employed, the more distant in time will be the final satisfaction obtained. The only way men can increase output is 'to lengthen the period of time over which their provident activity is to extend in the same degree that they progress to goods of higher order' (*Principles*, p. 153). This suggestion was the basis upon which Böhm-Bawerk constructed his theory of the

period of production that led to so much controversy by the end of the 19th century. Menger also points out that the limit to economic progress is the degree to which men value the same satisfaction more highly in the present rather than the future. Later called 'time-preference' by Austrian economists, Menger believed it was a consequence of men's continuous and finite life span. Without time preference, one would have to expect infinite capital accumulation. Notice that time preference is an explanation for why there is a limit to capital accumulation rather than an explanation for why capital is accumulated at all.

Menger is best known for his theory of value and its implication for goods of a higher order. His theory of exchange and price is neither so well-known nor so highly regarded. This is a pity since the chapters following the theory of value are equally rich with economic insights and deserve close attention by modern readers. Predictably, Menger's theory of exchange is derived from his theory of value. His starting point is Adam Smith's statement that men are possessed of a 'propensity to truck, barter and exchange one good for another', a statement Menger finds objectionable since it provides no explanation for the particular kinds of trade men make or for the limits of their trading activity. Men do not trade because of a propensity to do so, but because of a rational desire to improve their well-being. Men seek out trade opportunities in order to exchange something less valuable for something more valuable and hence trade is productive of value for both trading partners. The problem for the economist, then, is to determine the limit of trade, limits that will be reached when neither party any longer stands to gain.

While Menger's theory of trade is fairly standard, less standard is his very modern discussion of the importance of transactions costs in limiting trade. These 'economic sacrifices of exchange' (*Principles*, p. 189) arise because men and their possessions are separate in space and time and must be brought together for trade to take place. Sometimes these economic sacrifices are so great that a potentially productive trade does not take place at all. It is the role of market intermediaries (including entrepreneurs) to reduce the economic sacrifices of trade through improved knowledge and improved market organizations. Entrepreneurs bring together potential traders, and the source of the intermediary's income is the gain in satisfaction permitted by his activities. The idea of transactions costs and the role of market 'intermediaries' in reducing transactions costs was rediscovered in the 1950s.

Menger's theory of exchange leads him to develop his theory of price. This chapter eventually arrives at propositions that are now standard in price theory, but it does so in a peculiar way. Menger states in the very beginning of the chapter that contrary to the beliefs of some earlier thinkers, price is not the fundamental feature of exchange. While price is directly observable, it is derivative of the real fundamental feature of exchange: the utility gain from trade. Price is merely a 'symptom of an economic equilibrium between the economies of individuals' (*Principles*, p. 191). There should be no misunderstanding then about exchange involving an exchange of equivalent values. If such were the case, men would be willing to reverse their trades since there would be no gain or loss involved. But we do not observe such 'reversible' trades in the real world because trades are not of equivalent values but of subjective values that differ for each party to the trade. Price theory, then, is not a theory of establishing equivalents for exchange but rather a theory that seeks to explain why men give specific quantities of goods for specific quantities of other goods.

Menger approaches this problem in a way that was to become common in neoclassical economics – according to the number of traders in the market. However, instead of taking the case of many buyers and sellers as the norm and examining various monopolies as deviations, he begins with the simplest case of two party exchange ('isolated exchange') and progresses through various monopoly models finally to reach the case of 'bilateral competition'. The reason for this progression is not simply analytic simplicity; he believed that this was the way trade actually developed in history with monopolies giving way to more and more competitive conditions, and he gives several historical examples to support his case.

Under isolated exchange, price will fall within a range set by the marginal utilities of the two traders. The actual price is indeterminate from the point of view of theory, but in most cases, Menger argued, neither party will have any special bargaining power and they will agree to a price that gives them a more or less equal utility gain.

From there Menger progresses to the case where a monopolist provides a single good to several competing buyers. In this case, the limits within which price will fall are narrowed by the intensity of demand of the most eager buyer and the one next most eager to acquire the good.

The case of monopoly provision of several units of a good to competing buyers is even more interesting. There, assuming a uniform price is established:

> price formation takes place between the limits that are set by the equivalent of one unit of the monopolized good to the individual least eager and least able to compete who still participates in the exchange and the equivalent of one unit of the monopolized good to the individual most eager and best able to compete of the competitors who are economically excluded from the exchange. (*Principles*, p. 207)

One important implication is that the larger the quantity offered for sale by the monopolist, the 'lower in terms of purchasing power and eagerness to trade will he have to descend among the classes of competitors for the monopolized good in order to sell the whole quantity, and hence the lower also will be the price of one unit of the monopolized good' (*Principles*, p. 207). In this way, Menger established the inverse price–quantity relationship that had been assumed by economists prior to the introduction of marginalism into economic thought.

What is interesting in Menger's approach is that he emphasizes that the process of price formation is the same regardless of the market conditions. Monopolists are subject to the limits placed on their actions by the utilities of the buyers just as competitors are so limited. What does vary according to market conditions are the policies of sellers. Monopolists may well follow a policy of restricting supply in order to sell few units at higher prices, or they may follow a policy of selling different units at different prices depending on the buyers. Competitors in supply of a product, however, will never find those policies to their advantage and hence under bilateral competition, one would expect prices to be lower and quantities supplied to be greater.

There is some debate as to whether Menger was offering an equilibrium theory of price determination in the *Principles* (Streissler, 1972; Jaffé, 1976). Certainly, his method of reasoning implies some underlying equilibrium price within any given market, and he even states that from time to time equilibrium prices will be observed. Equilibrium prices are 'economic' prices in that transactions at these prices are the result of economizing behaviour where no one could have been better off at another price. Further, he describes prices that reflect the full 'economic situation', a phrase that seems to indicate a more widespread economic equilibrium. However, it is also true that Menger did not describe economies settling down to a strict general equilibrium in the manner of Walras. Indeed, given the barriers to strict economic behaviour, especially barriers of incomplete knowledge, that are inherent in real life, Menger would find a Walrasian general equilibrium in principle unattainable. Men did the best they could, and with economic progress their best got better, but the very conception of a Walrasian general equilibrium is foreign to Menger's method of reasoning. This will become clearer below when Menger's methodology is discussed.

The next two chapters, 'Use Value and Exchange Value' and 'The Theory of the Commodity', while containing several interesting discussions about market organization, are really prelude to the very important last chapter on 'The Theory of Money'. In the 'Commodity' chapter, Menger defines a commodity as a good intended for sale and then discusses the varying degrees of saleability of commodities based on their characteristics and market organization. The point he is leading to is to define money as the most marketable of all commodities, his starting point for the last chapter.

Menger does not develop a theory of the value of money in the *Principles*. While he does stress the importance of holding precautionary balances, to Menger the most important questions are how does money come to exist and what functions does it serve. These are questions he addresses both in his *Principles*, in the later work on methodology and in his two articles on money written in 1892. From a modern perspective, there are two particularly interesting features of Menger's discussion that should be noted. First, Menger's account of the origin of money is developed in a way reminiscent of the reasoning of the Scottish Enlightenment and Adam Smith's 'invisible hand' in particular (although it is doubtful that the writers of the Scottish Enlightenment were the direct sources for his reasoning. In fact, at one point, he criticizes Adam Smith for a too mechanistic and rationalistic view of economic and social institutions! [*Investigations*, p. 177]). Money, according to Menger, arises out of the self-interested actions of individuals aimed at attaining their own ends through trade, but not specifically aimed at developing a money commodity as such. Second, because money arises as an unintended by-product of human action, it is not a creation of government.

The process Menger describes for the origin of money is a straightforward extension of his theory of economizing behaviour through trade. Following Aristotle, Menger points out the difficulties men face under barter in finding trading partners, (the problem of the 'double coincidence of wants'). Rational men soon come to realize that goods have different degrees of marketability. A cow, for instance, is far more marketable than custom made shoes. Hence, men learn that if they exchange their less marketable goods for goods that may not directly satisfy their needs but that are more marketable, they will be more successful at bartering for what they really need. Eventually, Menger reasons, some one commodity will emerge as the most marketable commodity and men will be willing always to accept it in exchange for other goods because they know they will have no trouble trading it for what they really want. This most marketable commodity then becomes money. While specific money commodities have differed from one society to another, in the most developed countries, precious metals become the money commodity because of their suitable characteristics: their portability, divisibility, scarcity, and so on.

Obviously, in such a theory money cannot be a creation of government because it is a naturally evolved social institution. Government can enhance the acceptability of a money commodity by declaring it legal tender, but government cannot create money. In this way, Menger's theory is meant to solve several long-standing controversies in the theory of money. The nominalist–realist debate is resolved by acknowledging that the value of money commodity is equal to the value of the money (except for small coins where it would be uneconomic to spend the resources to make full-weight coins) but by also pointing out that the actual commodity can be anything consistent with the accepted standards and level of development of the community. The commodity–fiat debate is resolved by showing a role for government in enhancing the acceptability of money even though it

originates first through a natural process of human choices.

The last chapter is not the only place in which Menger discusses the origin of an economic phenomenon. All through the *Principles*, Menger is interested in establishing the origin and meaning of phenomena where the meaning is often elucidated through a description of their evolution through time. Erich Streissler (1972, p. 430) has gone so far as to credit Menger with presenting foremost a theory of economic development in the *Principles*. There is much to recommend that position. One of Menger's main themes is that economic development is a process of increasing knowledge and the consequent improvement in the variety and quality of goods available. Economic development is characterized by better communication among traders, more complex trading institutions, more and better commodities, and a greater ability of men to establish 'economic' prices.

We can perhaps understand Menger's vision better if we remember how he thought of the human predicament. Man in his original state is ignorant of his environment and uncertain about his (finite) future. He must plan for the satisfaction of his wants in this difficult world, and his primary aid is his ability to learn. The progress of civilization is nothing so much as a process of reducing ignorance and developing institutions that make dealing with the uncertain future more manageable. Smith emphasized the division of labour and capital accumulation as the causes of the wealth of nations. Menger emphasized the priority of improved knowledge to the improvement of wealth. Indeed, progress is evidenced by 'the increasing understanding of the causal connections between things and human welfare' (*Principles*, p. 74).

Methodology

While Menger's *Principles* was well received and eventually became very influential in his native Austria, his theories came in for criticism – or, more to the point, apathy and neglect – in the one audience Menger had most hoped to convince, the German Historical School. While the older members of the historical school, Knies, Roscher and Hildebrand, understood classical economic theory and wanted to overcome its shortcomings with detailed historical investigations which would have the purpose of allowing them to infer them empirical regularities in economic events, the younger Germans, led by Gustav Schmoller, rejected the theory entirely. They believed there could be no such thing as scientific economic theory, and they insisted on viewing an economy as an organic whole at one with politics, law and custom. Menger's new theory, then, was considered not only incorrect, but useless. To Menger, who was convinced that he had discovered the key to unlocking the mysteries of all economic phenomena, such cavalier dismissal must have been particularly galling.

Having failed to make headway with his new theory in Germany on what appeared to be methodological grounds, Menger began work in 1875 on his second book, *Untersuchungen über die Methode der Social-wissenschaften und der politischen Oekonomie insbeson-dere* (*Investigations into the Method of the Social Sciences with special reference to Economics*). This book, essentially a defence of economic theory and an account of its relationship to historical methods, was published in 1883. Menger's ambition was this time to attract the attention of German academics. This time he succeeded, but unfortunately, the attention he attracted was negative. Gustav Schmoller's review of the *Investigations* was particularly unsympathetic and incited Menger to respond with an impassioned pamphlet entitled *The Errors of Historicism* in 1884. In this pamphlet, Menger dropped all attempts at cordial conciliation and, in Hayek's words, 'ruthlessly demolished Schmoller's position' (Hayek, 1981, p. 24). If so, Schmoller never discovered the demolition since he returned the book to Menger unread and wrote a final scathing attack on Menger in his journal.

This exchange has been referred to as the 'Method-enstreit' or war of methods, a war that at the time seemed to have no clear winners and certainly led to no resolution of the opposing views. Ultimately, of course, Menger's position was far closer to the methodological turn economics took in the subsequent century, although in Germany, Menger's approach and the school that formed around it remained excluded from the university curriculum well into the 20th century.

The vehemence and hostility with which the Germans greeted Menger's *Investigations* is to some degree surprising. Far from an attempt to displace the approach of the Historical School, Menger's *Investigations* is a conscious plan for incorporating many of the features of the historical–empirical approach into a more comprehensive general methodology. (Although it must be admitted that Menger's tone is not always cordial when discussing the mistaken views of the Historical School.) Menger divides economics into three parts: the historical–statistical which investigates the individual nature and individual connection of economic phenomena, the theoretical which investigates the general nature and general connections of phenomena, and the 'practical sciences of national economy', the basic principles for suitable action in the field of national economy, or in modern terminology, economic policy (*Investigations*, pp. 38–9). Menger defends the idea that science requires knowledge *both* of individual (or concrete) aspects of phenomena and of the general (formal) aspects. Presumably, the methods of the Historical School are appropriate to the investigation of concrete aspects of economic phenomena while economic theory is necessary to understand the general aspects. The general form of things, Menger calls *types* and the general form of relationships, Menger calls *typical*.

Menger defends the scientific quality of economic theory despite the fact that its laws are not as strict as some other sciences may be. All sciences, Menger argues, show varying degrees of strictness, and 'the number of natural sciences which absolutely comprise strict laws of nature is also small, and the value of those which only show empirical laws is nevertheless beyond question' (*Investigations*, p. 52). Economic science develops exact laws, but the observation of these laws in reality is hindered by the complexity of the events in which they are manifested and by the impingement of non-economic goals on the actions of observable human beings. Hence, one can never refute the exact laws of economics by pointing to contrary empirical cases. Such a procedure would be analogous to testing the laws of geometry by measuring triangular shapes. In any case, the fact that economic laws are not as strict as some other sciences is irrelevant to its scientific character.

The problem of economic science is to find the causal laws of typical events even though they are manifested in complex reality. Hence it is necessary to 'ascertain the simplest elements of everything real, elements which must be thought of as strictly typical just because they are the simplest' (*Investigations*, p. 60). The appropriate procedure, then, is to start with the simplest elements of economic phenomena and from there investigate the laws by which more complicated human phenomena are formed from simplest elements. Menger called this the 'causal–genetic' approach. Obviously, the simplest elements of economic theory are human valuations and from this can be derived the more complicated economic relationships that are observable in the real world. While Menger does not call this approach 'methodological individualism', it is clear from his discussion of the exact approach and his later criticisms of the excesses of the organic approach that he is a methodological individualist where that means explaining economic phenomena in terms of the choices and consequences of individual human valuation.

Menger's example that he uses to contrast the exact approach with the 'realistic–empirical' is particularly interesting since it clarifies a point of debate about his use of equilibrium constructs. He claims that the exact method can be used to predict 'economic prices' even though one rarely observes true economic prices in the real world. The four criteria for prices to be 'economic' are that (*a*) individuals protect their economic interests completely; (*b*) people have complete knowledge about their goals and their means to achieving them; (*c*) they know the full economic situation (complete knowledge about quantities offered for sale and what prices are being charged) and (*d*) they have the freedom to act in their own interests according to their knowledge. It does not take much imagination to see in these requirements a form of perfect competition where complete knowledge and freedom of entry and exit allow economic man full scope to arrive at equilibrium prices. However, while the laws which predict economic prices are true and exact, the empirical manifestation of them will vary due to circumstances. Indeed, Menger argues that it would be surprising indeed if any of the circumstances required for the establishment of 'economic' prices were ever met completely in the real world. Real prices will deviate from economic prices, and the role of the realistic–empirical approach, then, is to discover to what degree real prices deviate from economic prices. The realistic–empirical approach, however, must take the exact theory of economic prices as the point of departure.

While Menger insists on the necessity of an exact theory of economics to understand economic phenomena, it is clear that he does not believe economics is an all-purpose science. Economics provides exact laws, but only of a subset of human action. In answer to the charge that his vision of human experience is too limited, he emphasizes that a full understanding of social phenomena requires the aid of the totality of exact sciences of man as well as the historical context of the actions. He is also careful to point out that his assumption of economic man – man guided exclusively by self-interest – is a fiction that does not capture real action. The theory of political economy 'teaches us to follow and understand in an exact way the manifestations of human self-interest in the efforts of economic humans aimed at the provision of their material needs' (*Investigations*, p. 87) but this provides understanding of a special side, by no means the only side, of human life.

One of the criticisms of economic theory that Menger attempted to answer was the charge that pure theory ignored the reality of development and change in economic life and failed to take account of the organic nature of real economic phenomena. While Menger in principle acknowledged the importance of change brought about in time both to empirical forms and to strict types, he believed that the way to explain such change was always with reference to exact theory. In fact, those who discussed organic development missed one of the most important sources of institutional change in social organization. In the *Principles*, Menger had developed a theory of the origin of money as an unintended social order. In the *Investigations*, Menger generalized his theory to encompass many different social forms. The Historical School's emphasis on historical development required a theory of development, a theory that explained how institutions arise from the unintended consequences of human attempts to improve their own well-being.

Menger saw the problem of exact research to be to discover 'how institutions which serve the common welfare and are extremely significant for its development come into being without a *common will* directed toward establishing them?' (*Investigations*, p. 146). His answer, developed using examples of such social institutions as money, law, language, markets, the origin of communities and of the state itself, was that individuals following

their own economic interests provide spillovers to others in the form of increased knowledge of potential advantages or increased ability to pursue their interests. Money, as we have already learned, arises as individuals attempt to overcome the difficulties of barter by acquiring more saleable commodities for the purposes of trade. New localities develop as individuals of different abilities and different professions settle in new areas because they believe they have a better market for their skills. States mostly came into being as families living in close proximity to each other decided it was to their advantage to unite. Most such social organization, Menger argued were not the consequences of conscious planning, but the unconscious result of human will directed toward other, more personal ends. This is the nature of organic development in social science.

What makes Menger's discussion of 'organic' orders (or 'spontaneous orders' as Hayek was later to call them) particularly interesting, is the fact that he not only describes them, but he also provides a brief theoretical analysis of how they can develop. He mentions in his theory of the origin of money that some individuals will be quicker than others to recognize the advantages of acquiring more marketable commodities because it helps them to come closer to their own ends. Not everyone will discover the advantages of indirect exchange at once, but they will soon learn because 'there is no better means to enlighten people about their economic interests than their perceiving the economic successes of those who put the right means to work for attaining them' (*Investigations*, p. 155). It does not take much of a leap to interpret Menger's theory as describing the development of an organic order as a process of discovery and transmission of new information through imitation, motivated by the interests of economic persons. Menger's theory of unintended organic institutions is thus an attempt to reconcile the organic and developmental approach to economics with the exact laws of economic science.

Compared to the frenetic publishing activity of a 20th-century economist, Menger published relatively little during his long career. Nevertheless, he had a major influence on the history of economic thought primarily because he attracted a number of bright and ambitious students. Although his two major disciples, Friedrich Wieser and Eugen Böhm-Bawerk, were never technically his students (both had studied at the University of Vienna before Menger began teaching there), they were clearly his students in the most important sense: they absorbed and finally extended major aspects of the work of the master. Wieser worked specifically on the problem of imputation which led him to be the first to use the term 'opportunity cost', the utility of the forgone alternative. Wieser also extended Menger's notion of national economy in ways that brought him closer to the to the general equilibrium school. Böhm-Bawerk is best known for his development of Menger's suggestions about the importance of time in production and the implication of goods of higher order for a theory of the structure of production.

While Wieser and Böhm-Bawerk were the best known of Menger's students, there were many others who gathered around him and formed a school. Those who published works in the Austrian tradition included Emil Sax, Johann von Komorzynski, Robert Zuckerkandl, and H. von Schullern-Schrattenhofen. Although not directly his student, Ludwig von Mises (who actually studied under Böhm-Bawerk) made his first major contribution to economics by extending Menger's notion of marginal utility combined with Menger's process analysis to develop a theory of the value of money. Friedrich Hayek, a student of von Mises, later developed Menger's ideas of spontaneous orders and the problem of knowledge into a comprehensive social theory. Both Mises and Hayek, in turn, have inspired a number of contemporary economists to work in the tradition of Menger to reformulate modern economics in a more 'Austrian' form.

KAREN I. VAUGHN

See also **Austrian economics.**

Selected works

1871. *Grundsätze der Volkswirtschaftslehre.* Trans. J. Dingwall and B.F. Hoselitz as *Principles of Economics* with an Introduction by F.A. Hayek. New York and London: New York University Press, 1981.
1883. *Untersuchungen über die Methode der Sozialwissenschaften und der politischen Ökonomie insbesondere.* Trans. F.J. Nock as *Problems of Economics and Sociology,* edited and with an Introduction by L. Schneider. Urbana: University of Illinois Press, 1963. Reprinted as *Investigations into the Method of the Social Sciences with Special Reference to Economics* with a new Introduction by L.H. White, New York and London: New York University Press, 1985.
1884. *Irrthümer des Historismus in der deutschen Nationalökonomie.* Vienna: Hölder.
1887. *Zur Kritik der politischen Ökonomie.* Vienna.
1888. Zur Theorie des Kapitals. *Conrad's Jahrbücher für Nationalökonomie und Statistik* 17, 1–49.
1889. Grundzüge einer Klassifikation der Wirtschaftswissenschaften. *Conrad's Jahrbücher für Nationalökonomie und Statistik* 14.
1892. Geld. In *Handwörterbuch der Staatswissenschaften,* vol. 3. Vienna.
1892a. Die Valutaregulierung in Österreich-Ungarn. *Conrad's Jahrbücher fur Nationalökonomie und Statistik* 3.
1892b. *Der Übergang zur Goldwahrung. In Untersuchungen über die Wertprobleme der österreichisch-ungarischen Valutareform.* Vienna.
1892c. La monnaie mesure de la valeur. *Revue d'économie politique* 6.
1892d. On the origin of money. *Economic Journal* 2(6), 239–55.

Bibliography

Alter, M., 1982. Carl Menger and Homo Oeconomicus: some thoughts on Austrian theory and methodology. *Journal of Economic Issues* 16(1), 149–60.
Bloch, H.-S., 1940. Carl Menger: the founder of the Austrian school. *Journal of Political Economy* 48, 428–33.
Hayek, F.A. 1981. Carl Menger. Introduction to Carl Menger, *Principles of Economics.* New York and London: New York University Press.
Hicks, J.R. and Weber, W., eds. 1973. *Carl Menger and the Austrian School of Economics.* Oxford: Clarendon Press.
Jaffé, W. 1976. Menger, Jevons and Walras de-homogenized. *Economic Inquiry* 14, 511–24.
Kauder, E. 1957. Intellectual and political roots of the older Austrian school. *Zeitschrift für Nationalökonomie* 17, 411–25.
Kauder, E. 1959. Menger and his library. *Economic Review* 10 (Hitotsubashi University).
Kauder, E. 1965. *A History of Marginal Utility Theory.* Princeton: Princeton University Press.
Kirzner, I.M. 1979. The entrepreneurial role in Menger's system. In *Perception, Opportunity and Profit: Studies in the Theory of Entrepreneurship,* ed. I.M. Kirzner. Chicago: University of Chicago Press.
Martin, D.T. 1979. Alternative views of Mengerian entrepreneurship. *History of Political Economy* 11, 271–85.
Mises, L. von. 1978. Carl Menger and the Austrian school of economics. In *The Clash of Group Interests and Other Essays.* ed. L. von. Mises. New York: Center for Libertarian Studies.
Schumpeter, J.A. 1951. Carl Menger, 1840–1921. In *Ten Great Economists, From Marx to Keynes.* ed. J.A. Schumpeter. New York: Oxford University Press.
Stigler, G.J. 1941. Carl Menger. In *Production and Distribution Theories,* ed. G.J. Stigler. New York: Macmillan.
Streissler, E. 1972. To what extent was the Austrian School marginalist? *History of Political Economy* 4, 426–41.
Wagner, R.E. et al. 1978. Carl Menger and Austrian economics. *Atlantic Economic Journal* 6(3), Special Issue. Contributions by R.E. Wagner, S. Bostaph, L.S. Moss, I.Kirzner, H. Nelson Gram and V.C. Walsh, L.M. Lachmann and K.I. Vaughn.

Bibliographic addendum

See also M. Alter, *Carl Menger and the Origins of Austrian Economics,* Boulder, CO: Westview Press, 1990. Different facets of Menger's work are discussed in B. Caldwell, ed., *Carl Menger and His Legacy in Economics,* Durham, NC: Duke University Press, 1991. M. Latzer and S. Schmitz, eds, *Carl Menger and the Evolution of Payments Systems,* Cheltenham: Edward Elgar, 2002, provides the first English translation of Menger's 'Geld' as well as essays both evaluating Menger's views on monetary systems and applying them to contemporaneous issues.

mercantilism

Mercantilism is economic nationalism that seeks to limit the competition faced by domestic producers. The tools of mercantilist policies include the granting of monopoly privileges, regulation of prices and business practices and especially prohibitions, tariffs, subsidies and other regulations regarding the conduct of international trade. The goals of mercantilism are supposedly to contribute to the development of a rich and powerful state; however, the principal beneficiaries are the merchants and producers who are protected or encouraged under a mercantile system. Although mercantilism was frequently promoted as means of obtaining long-term development objectives, it is significant that such promotion typically increased in fervour following periods of trade crisis, such as that in England in the 1620s.

Mercantilism refers to the economic thought and policies that were characteristic of the dominant western European trading nations during the transition from medieval feudalism to modern capitalism from the 16th to the late 18th century. Adam Smith (1776, p. 399) characterized the 'principle of the commercial or mercantile system' – that a 'favourable' balance of trade would bring gold or silver into the country – which could be used to 'carry on foreign wars, and to maintain fleets and armies in distant countries'. Import restraints and encouragement to exportation were the mercantile policies that would enrich and empower the newly emerging nation-states. At the end of the 19th century authors of the German Historical School popularized the term 'mercantilism' while rationalizing the mercantile policies as necessary for the unification of feudal power centres by large competitive states.

The mercantile era emerged following the discovery of the New World and the East Indies by European explorers at the close of the 15th century. Shipping and trading grew in importance during this period as did the frequency of military battles at sea and in the colonies. Anglo-French rivalry remained intense, and Henry VIII invested heavily in shipping while fortifying the coastline against possible attack. Meanwhile, the Spanish Habsburgs were at war all over Europe. Mercantile economic warfare complemented the military objectives of the antagonistic nations and served to unify each nation against an external threat.

As a concept of society, mercantilism reflects the medieval view that wise government intervention is necessary to delicately balance the tendencies of unbridled competition to produce unjust wages or income below a subsistence level, when too many workers or businesses operate in a particular activity, or to result in an unregulated monopoly that would reap unjust profits charging prices that are too high. The market could certainly not be left to itself to find a 'just price' or wage. The 1563 Statute of Artificers marked one of the first efforts by Queen Elizabeth of England to extend the restrictive and regulatory policies of medieval towns to the nation as a whole. A century later, Louis XIV of France, with the assistance of his powerful mercantilist finance minister Jean-Baptiste Colbert, undertook similar national regulation of industry and simplification of the internal tolls of France which Heckscher (1935, vol. 1, p. 103) 'ranks with Elizabeth's Statute of Artificers as one of the two unquestionable triumphs of mercantilism in the sphere of economic unification'.

The granting of monopoly privileges was a relatively more important form of state protection during the earlier part of the mercantile era. The British East India Company was granted a monopoly charter by Queen Elizabeth in 1600 which encouraged the United Provinces to consolidate the independent Dutch traders into the Dutch East India Company in 1604. A number of short-lived East Indies trading monopolies were chartered by the French Crown throughout the first half of the 17th century, culminating in the 1664 charter of, and royal participation in, the French East Indies Company. These privileges were intended to benefit the developing shipping and long-distance trading industries themselves as well as to provide revenues to the state either directly, in the case of state monopolies, or indirectly through modest duties on imports of the private monopolies.

When, however, the successful conclusion of the Dutch Revolt in 1648 exposed the English to an increased level of competition in intra-European shipping and trading, Cromwell eventually responded with the first Navigation Act of 1651. This Act stipulated that all goods imported into England or her territories had to be carried in English ships, unless they were carried directly from a European country of origin on ships owned and crewed by citizens of that country of origin, and that no foreign vessels could engage in the coastal trade among English ports. Furthermore, no type of salted fish or fishing by-product of the type usually caught and processed by English people could be imported unless it was caught and processed by an English ship. Additional navigation laws further protected English fishing, shipping and trading industries from competition, especially from the Dutch, who largely dominated maritime activity at the time.

More general industrial protection followed the navigation laws, although several early examples of discriminatory protective policies were already in existence. The 1667 anti-Dutch tariff imposed by Colbert in France, and the subsequent quadrupling of import duties in England during the 15 years following the 1688 accession to the throne of William III and Mary marked the major shift from moderate revenue-generating customs duties on imports and exports to the more protective import tariffs as well as bounties and drawbacks on exports that constituted the mercantile system in Smith's view. English export duties on woollens were abolished in 1700 and export duties were abolished in general by the Walpole customs reform of 1722. Protection was further extended throughout the 18th century until 'the building up of the protective system showed signs of becoming a general and recognized policy ... in the decade in which Adam Smith was collecting material and writing his great blast against commercial regulation, *The Wealth of Nations*' (Davis, 1966, p. 314).

Following Smith's (1776, p. 418) lengthy examination of the 'popular notion that wealth consists in money', mercantilism has often been depicted as the school of thought that confused money with wealth. Although this interpretation has been thoroughly debated, there is certainly much evidence to suggest that mercantile pamphleteers did believe an inflow of precious metals would increase the wealth of the nation and that foreign but not domestic or internal trade was the only way to increase the wealth of a nation that did not possess gold or silver mines. Exportation of bullion or coin had generally been regulated or prohibited since medieval times, and it was in an effort to get those restrictions relaxed that mercantilist authors such as Mun (1664, p. 5), a director of the British East Indies Trading Company, argued that the 'means therefore to increase our wealth and treasure is by *Foreign Trade*, wherein we must ever observe this rule; to sell more to strangers yearly than we consume of theirs in value'. That the wealth of the nation was not perceived to be primarily related to its ability to provide goods and services to its consumers is revealed when reading Mun's (1664, p. 7) recommendations for reducing imports such as using waste grounds 'to supply our selves and prevent the importations of Hemp, Flax, Cordage, Tobacco and divers other things which we now fetch from strangers to our great impoverishing'.

In all fairness, the proponents of an export surplus did not generally advocate the accumulation of specie for the simple purpose of hoarding it, although they did like to make the analogy between the kingdom and an individual that would grow poor if its purchases exceeded its income. Of course, neither the individual nor the kingdom will grow poor if the purchases include investment expenditures that yield a rate of return in excess of the borrowing cost. As a store of value, money is only a component of wealth to the extent that one intends to spend it one day, and there is a limit to this precautionary motive for accumulating specie. It is sensible to accumulate specie following a period of declining reserves (excessive expenditure) or in response to increased uncertainty, which requires a larger precautionary balance, or in response to increased hostility, which requires a larger defence balance, but not ad infinitum, except perhaps to maintain a desired ratio of specie to growing royal expenditures over time. For the merchant adventurers engaged in long-distance trading, specie was a valuable factor of production as a medium of exchange, and they recognized the relationship between the quantity of money in circulation and the amount of trading activity that could be financed. Mun (1664, p. 68) was careful to recommend that the royal treasure should not be augmented by more than the favourable balance of

trade, 'for if he should mass up more money than is gained by the over-balance of his foreign trade, he shall not *Fleece*, but *Flea* his Subjects, ... whereby the life of lands and arts must fail and fall to the ruin both of the public and private wealth'. This indicates that he perceived a relationship between the quantity of money and the level of national economic activity, although his immediate concern was probably the economic activity of his own British East India Company, which imported exotic goods that could not be produced at home.

More important, perhaps, than enabling the royal treasure to be augmented, an export surplus is generally perceived to stimulate domestic employment directly or indirectly by reducing interest rates. According to Heckscher (1935, vol. 2, p. 121), the '"fear of goods" was nourished ... by the idea of creating work at home and of taking measures against unemployment'. References to the unemployment argument date back to the early 15th century, and in English legislation in 1455, 'foreign competition was blamed for having caused the unemployment in the silk industry' (Heckscher, 1935, vol. 2, p. 122). The preference for encouraging exportation of manufactured consumer goods, as opposed to raw materials or productive equipment, and allowing the importation of raw materials are consistent with this employment concern. An export surplus – an excess of domestic saving over investment – naturally arises when productivity growth outpaces the growth of profitable domestic investment opportunities, and this may include an accumulation of international reserves to finance the growth of monetized transactions; but to try to engineer such a surplus with protective trade policies would be futile at best. In addition to competitively induced innovation and increased specialization, limited by the extent of the market, productive investment is the true source of a sustainable increase in the wealth of a nation, and there is no reason to suppose, a priori, that domestic investment is inferior to foreign investment.

Most of the vestiges of the mercantile era were removed during the laissez-faire era of the 19th and early 20th centuries, especially in England, where monarchical power was weaker and property rights were clearer than in France and Spain. Yet mercantilism has remained a topic of considerable debate, especially since Heckscher's broad treatment of the subject and the emergence of global depression in the 1930s (Heckscher, 1935; Viner, 1937; Minchinton, 1969; Coleman, 1969; Magnusson, 1993). Whether mercantilist policies re-emerge in the 21st century will depend on the institutional framework within which the special interests seeking protection must function (Ekelund and Tollison, 1997), as there exists no coherent economic doctrine to support such policies.

LAURA LAHAYE

See also **cameralism; Colbert, Jean-Baptiste; Hume, David; Misselden, Edward; Mun, Thomas; Schmoller, Gustav von.**

Bibliography

Coleman, D. 1969. *Revisions in Mercantilism*. London: Methuen.

Davis, R. 1966. The rise of protection in England, 1689–1786. *Economic History Review* 19, 306–17.

Ekelund, R. and Tollison, R. 1997. *Politicized Economies: Monarch, Monopoly and Mercantilism*. College Station: Texas A & M University Press.

Heckscher, E. 1935. *Mercantilism*, 2 vols. London: Allen & Unwin.

LaHaye, L. 2007. Mercantilism. In *The Concise Encyclopedia of Economics*, ed. D. Henderson. Indianapolis: Liberty Fund.

Magnusson, L. 1993. *Mercantilist Economics*. Boston: Kluwer.

Magnusson, L. 1994. *Mercantilism, the Shaping of an Economic Language*. London: Routledge.

Minchinton, W. 1969. *Mercantilism, System or Expediency?* Lexington: Raytheon.

Mun, T. 1664. *England's Treasure by Foreign Trade or The Balance of our Foreign Trade is the Rule of our Treasure*. London. Reprints of Economic Classics, New York: Kelley, 1968.

Smith, A. 1776. *The Wealth of Nations*. Edwin Cannan edn. New York: Random House, 1937.

Viner, J. 1937. *Studies in the Theory of International Trade*. New York: Harper.

Mercier De La Rivière, Pierre-Paul (Mercier or Lemercier) (1720–1793/4)

Lawyer, administrator and economist, born into a financier's family in 1720. From 1749 to 1759, he was Councillor of the Paris Parlement; from 1759 to 1764, Governor of Martinique. Although Garnier (1854, p. 188) claims that Mercier became acquainted with Quesnay and Mirabeau while Governor of Martinique, this is doubtful. However, after 1765 he became a prominent Physiocrat and published what many (for example, Smith, 1776, p. 679; Mill, 1824, p. 712) considered to be the most comprehensive exposition of Physiocratic doctrine in his *L'ordre naturel et essentiel des sociétés politiques* (1767). This gained him both Catherine the Great's invitation to advise her on a new legal code and the enmity of Voltaire (1768), who devastatingly satirized his cumbrous prose. Du Pont (1768) wrote a summary of Mercier's work for *Ephémérides*, confirming thereby its enormous importance for the Physiocrats. Subsequently, Mercier published a reply to Galiani's dialogues attacking the Physiocratic position on the grain trade (1770) and an essay on the importance of public education dedicated to the King of Sweden (1775). He died in Paris in either 1793 or 1794.

Mercier's *L'ordre naturel* (1767) is therefore the major general treatise of Physiocratic doctrine both political and economic. The work divides into three parts with a concluding summary chapter. Part I develops the theory and necessity of the social order based on the duties and rights inherent in private property, without which a society cannot be sustained. 'The greatest possible happiness comes from the greatest possible abundance of means of enjoyment and the greatest possible freedom to profit from [the ownership of property]' (1767, I, pp. 42–3). Hence the sanctity of private property and complete freedom for its owners to use it are the first principles of the theory of natural order (pp. 45, 50–51). These principles need to be inculcated in society through a system of public instruction (pp. 91–2). Part II discusses the manner in which social order is achieved in practice through the establishment of three fundamental institutions: law and magistrature, the sovereign as bearer of authority, and institutions of public instruction for spreading knowledge of the social order among all members of society. In his lengthy elaboration on these institutions (chs 11–24) Mercier presents his famous defence of legal despotism.

Part III (the greater part of Volume 2 in the original edition) further discusses the practical promotion of the social order by examining the political economy of wealth creation. After reviewing the essential association between the king and his subjects (ch. 25) the theory of taxation is presented as the way in which kings share the net product of their common property with the landlords (chs 28–34). The dogmatic presentation of Physiocratic tax theory was the special target of Voltaire (1768). These chapters also contain interesting economic contributions. In them Mercier emphasizes the role of consumption and effective demand in stimulating reproduction (vol. 2, pp. 138–9); presents an argument showing the possibility of a downward spiral in economic activity 'in geometrical progression' if taxation reduces the advances of agriculture (pp. 150–1), an analysis having both real and value aspects (pp. 160–4). The second half of Part III examines commerce and industry and their function in the Physiocratic social order (chs 35–43), the last chapter being a particularly dogmatic demonstration of these activities' unproductive nature. However, they likewise contain interesting analytical contributions on the role of money and its circulation (vol. 2, pp. 262–3, 297–9, 334), the impact of trade on wealth via the profits of agriculture and hence accumulation when it provides a wider market for agricultural produce (p. 273) and a critique of the balance of trade doctrine based on the logical impossibility for all nations to enjoy a favourable balance (p. 349) and a type of specie mechanism argument (pp. 360–7) from which Mercier concludes that nations can have too much as well as too little money (pp. 368–9). His discussion of commerce and industry highlights, in particular, the richness of Physiocratic value theory and its importance for their theory of distribution and economic development. As Vaggi (1987) has demonstrated, recognition of this importance is indispensable for a proper understanding of Physiocracy, as is the full social and political framework in which their policy recommendations are framed and for which Mercier was particularly noted by his contemporaries.

PETER GROENEWEGEN

Selected works

1767. *L'ordre naturel et essentiel des sociétés politiques.* London and Paris.

1770. *L'intérêt général de l'état, ou la liberté du commerce des blés, avec une réfutation d'un nouveau système publié par l'abbé Galiani en forme de dialogues sur le commerce des blés.* Amsterdam and Paris.

1775. *De l'instruction publique, ou considérations morales et politiques sur la nécessité, la nature et la source de cette institution.* Stockholm and Paris.

Bibliography

Du Pont de Nemours, P.S. 1768. De l'origine et des progrès d'une science nouvelle. Reprinted in *Physiocrates*, vol. 1, ed. E. Daire, Paris, 1846, .

Garnier, J. 1854. Mirabeau. In *Dictionnaire de l'économie politique*, vol. 2, ed. Ch. Coquelin and Guillaumin. Paris.

Mill, J. 1824. Economists. Supplement to *Encyclopaedia Britannica*, vol. 3. Edinburgh.

Smith, A. 1776. *An Inquiry into the Nature and Causes of the Wealth of Nations.* Ed. R.H. Campbell, A.S. Skinner and W.B. Todd. Oxford: Clarendon Press, 1976.

Vaggi, G. 1987. *The Economics of François Quesnay.* London: Macmillan.

Voltaire, F.M.A. de. 1768. *The Man of Forty Crowns.* London, trans. from the French.

Mercosur

Mercado Común del Sur (Mercosur, Southern Common Market) is an ambitious economic integration project which includes Argentina, Brazil, Paraguay and Uruguay. It represents 70 per cent of the gross domestic product (GDP) of South America and 60 per cent of its population. In terms of geographic size, Mercosur is four times larger than the European Union, which would rank Mercosur as the largest customs union in the world. Its economic size, however, is similar to that of the Netherlands.

Mercosur was launched in March 1991 with the signing of the Asunción Treaty. Aiming at creating a common market, Article I calls for full internal mobility of goods, services and factors of production, the implementation of common external policies in these areas, as well as the coordination of macroeconomic policies and cooperation in education, health and transport policies.

It is an agreement that is open to accession by all members of the Latin American Integration Association (which regulates partial bilateral trade agreements among members). By 1996 Bolivia and Chile were associate members of Mercosur; later, a free-trade agreement

(FTA) was signed with the Andean Community. At the time of writing other Latin American countries are in different stages of association with Mercosur. Negotiations for trade agreements are ongoing with China, the European Union, Mexico, India, South Africa, Egypt, and Morocco.

Mercosur members had agreed in the Asunción Treaty to create the common market within four years. However, this proved politically impossible and little progress was made a part from very rapid reductions in internal tariffs (with some negotiated exceptions). Very quickly it became clear that the ambitious objectives of the Asunción Treaty had to be scaled back. An imperfect customs union became a more realistic objective, and the Protocol of Ouro Preto signed in December 1994 called for the implementation of a common external tariff (CET) by early 1995. It was an imperfect 'common' external tariff as each member was allowed some deviations from the negotiated CET; and more than ten years later the CET is still to be defined in some politically entrenched sectors (such as sugar). Nevertheless, by 1996 internal tariffs were applied on less than three per cent of tariff lines, and the CET was implemented in 80 per cent of tariff lines.

In all other areas progress has been slow or non-existent. For example, non-tariff barriers (NTBs) are not only not subject to common external policies but are routinely used as an impediment to intra-regional trade, contrary to what is explicitly required in Article V of the Asunción Treaty. For example, non-automatic import licensing, sanitary measures and other technical regulations (such as labelling) on Brazilian imports of powdered milk impose an equivalent tax of 54 per cent on Argentina's exporters (Berlinski, 2004). Internal trade in the automobile sector is managed with bilateral trade quotas at the firm level (for those firms with a presence in several Mercosur members) and a trade balance constraint on global automobile trade, which if removed could double bilateral trade (Brambilla, 2005). Negotiations on services trade and factor mobility were still at a very early stage 15 years after the treaty was signed. The Services Trade Protocol signed in 1997 merely states the multilateral commitments of Mercosur members at the World Trade Organization (WTO). The dispute settlement mechanism (DSM) remained unused until 1997; an appeal court was created only in 2002. Steps have been taken for the mutual recognition of standards, but enforcement has been largely absent (for example, in the area of education, mutual recognition stops at the high-school level). Macroeconomic coordination is limited to routine exchange of (public) information.

Internal tariffs and the FTA

In spite of the slow progress in the 'non-tariff' areas (NTBs, services, factor mobility, macroeconomic coordination), by the late 1990s Mercosur was considered one of the most successful attempts at regional integration between developing countries. This was partly due to the unprecedented rapid elimination of internal tariffs, a sixfold increase in intra-regional trade, a twentyfold increase in flows of foreign direct investment (FDI) (mainly from the United States and Spain), and the longevity that the agreement was achieving in spite of several financial, economic and institutional crises.

A more careful analysis, however, reveals a more subtle picture. Let me start with the rapid increase in trade. Yeats (1998) argued that intra-regional trade appeared to be concentrated in products in which Mercosur did not have a clear comparative advantage (capital goods), and that these were the goods with the most rapid growth after the creation of Mercosur. He concluded that this provided evidence of trade diversion and should raise questions regarding the (static) welfare impacts of such rapid growth in intra-regional trade. Olarreaga and Soloaga (1998) showed that fast-growing intra-regional trade was concentrated on products with trade-diverting potential partly because deviations from zero internal tariffs occurred in products with substantial trade-creation potential, as predicted by the theoretical political economy literature on regional agreements.

External tariffs and the CET

It has also been argued that a significant part of the increase in intra-regional trade need not be attributed to the creation of Mercosur, but rather to the tremendous trade liberalization vis-à-vis the rest of the world that Mercosur members were independently undertaking after the mid-1980s. For example, Brazil's external tariff declined from an average of 80 per cent in the mid-1980s to an average of 15 per cent by the mid-1990s. This can explain a large share of the rapid growth in imports, including those from other Mercosur members. On the other hand, it has been suggested that the important external liberalization undertaken by Mercosur members needs to be partly attributed to the creation of Mercosur. Without the significant competitive pressure imposed by the increase in intra-regional flows, the move towards lower external tariffs would have been more difficult. Bohara, Gawande and Sanguinetti (2004) showed that the lobbying for high external tariffs was eroded by the increase in intra-regional trade due to internal tariff preferences. Also, it has been shown that a significant force for lower CET was the prospect of the elimination of duty drawbacks for intra-regional exports (a by-product of the creation of Mercosur) as agreed in Ouro Preto. Indeed, the elimination of duty drawbacks on intra-regional exports increased counter-lobbying by regional exporters for lower tariffs on their imports of intermediate inputs from the rest of the world. This led to a 25 per cent reduction in the negotiated CET (Cadot, de Melo and Olarreaga, 2003).

An additional trade-related benefit for Mercosur members is that rest-of-the-world exporters to the regional market started pricing their products more competitively due to the more intense competition in the internal market brought by tariff preferences granted to other Mercosur members. This led to significant welfare gains for Mercosur consumers of imported products at the expense of foreign firms exporting to the region (Chang and Winters, 2002). Schiff and Chang (2003) further showed that the pro-competitive forces that led rest-of-the-world exporters to price more competitively after the creation of Mercosur were also present even when Mercosur partners did not export to each other, as long as they had the potential to do so (that is, markets were contestable). Thus, Mercosur created trade-related gains to its members even in the absence of any intra-regional trade flow or external tariff reduction.

Beyond tariffs

Moreover, regardless of whether Mercosur led to trade diversion, it has been shown that most households and in particular poor households within the region benefited from the agreement. Porto (2006) provided evidence of a pro-poor bias of Mercosur in Argentina: on average, poor households gain more from the reform than middle-income households, whereas the effects on rich families are positive but not statistically significant. Prior to Mercosur, Argentine trade policy protected the rich over the poor. As relative pre-Mercosur tariffs are higher on relatively skill-intensive goods, the tariff removals tend to benefit the poor over the rich. Thus, Mercosur not only helps reduce poverty in Argentina, but it improves the distribution of income.

Regarding the rapid increase in FDI flows, it seems that the creation of Mercosur was not the main cause. Most statistical analysis shows no direct causality between the creation of Mercosur and the rapid growth in FDI (Castilho and Zignago, 2002). The main forces were the simultaneous privatization processes in Argentina and Brazil, the macroeconomic stabilization and the external tariff reduction independently undertaken by Mercosur members, which provided foreign firms investing in the region access to imported inputs (Chudnovski, 2001). The creation of a larger regional market only marginally contributed to foreign firms' decisions to invest in Mercosur.

The longevity of Mercosur has come at the cost of achievements in the area of internal free trade, the implementation of the CET, and an (implicit) consensus to move slowly in other areas. For example, at the end of 1992 Argentina increased its statistical import tax surcharge (applied to intra-Mercosur imports) from three to ten per cent as its trade deficit with Brazil widened. An optional increase in external tariffs of up to three percentage points was authorized in 1997. In June 2001, on the eve of a major financial and fiscal crisis, the Argentine government unilaterally altered its tariff rates on capital goods and consumer goods. A waiver was granted by the Common Market Council. In 2006, duty drawbacks and temporary admission regimes which were to be eliminated by 2000 were still in place; the customs code drafted in 1994 had not been adopted by any of the members' parliaments; and no common safeguard mechanism had been put in place to deal with unforeseen changes in competitive pressures, leading to the adoption of unilateral ad hoc measures and private sector marketing agreements (for example, dairy, paper and steel) after the devaluation of the real in January 1999. In sum, flexibility rather than consistency has been the norm, and time-inconsistent policies have often been reversed with the associated cost for the credibility of Mercosur institutions (Bouzas, 2002).

Regional institutions

From the very beginning Mercosur decisions were driven by national private-sector interests, and weak and relatively politicized regional institutions emerged, partly because Brazil (the largest member) wanted to preserve its hegemony. Mercosur is ruled by a Consejo del Mercado Común (CMC, Common Market Council), which is responsible for the political decisions of the integration process. Sitting members are the four national presidents and their cabinets, who regularly meet twice a year. The Grupo Mercado Común (GMC, Common Market Group) is directly answerable to the CMC and is the executive organ, which includes the ministers of foreign affairs and economics, the chairmen of the central banks, and the permanent coordinators from each member country. The GMC enforces resolutions. The GMC branches out into the Trade Commission of Mercosur, which is responsible for counselling and enforcing trade policy instruments as well as setting directives; the Joint Parliamentary Commission in representation of the four parliaments; the Economic and Social Consultation Forum, which has representatives from the different economic and social groups; and finally a weak Administrative and Technical Secretariat, which supports the whole operation from Montevideo. With such a structure, any decision is likely to be highly politicized (Vaillant, 2005).

The absence of strong regional institutions has been particularly felt in the area of macroeconomic coordination. Throughout the 1990s the variability of nominal exchange rates within the region was twice as great as in other comparable countries, leading to the strong backlashes against regional integration discussed above. This led some regional leaders, including the former Argentine President Carlos Menem, to call for the creation of a monetary union. As argued by Eichengreen (1998), this is the optimal instrument to avoid wide fluctuations in intra-regional exchange rates while keeping some flexibility with respect to bilateral exchange rates with the rest of the world. However, a monetary union will not be an option as long as the other institutions of Mercosur remained politicized and weak. As the experience of the European Union shows, a monetary union not only requires a strong and politically independent central bank but should also be part of an interlocking web of strong economic and political agreements, all of which could be jeopardized if a country abandoned the single currency. The latter acts as a significant barrier to exit for members, reinforcing credibility and stabilizing markets. Mercosur members have all taken significant steps towards central-bank independence. But in terms of barriers to exit there is not much apart from a relatively well-functioning customs union. Very little has been achieved in terms of common trade, economic, social or security policies. If Mercosur does not engage in a deeper integration project, a monetary union cannot be successful.

To conclude, Mercosur is an unprecedented example of successful and enduring regional integration among developing countries. It has proven its resilience by emerging relatively unscathed from acute financial and fiscal crises in the region. However, the most difficult and challenging steps towards the economic integration envisaged in the Treaty of Asunción remain to be taken.

MARCELO OLARREAGA

See also **currency unions; foreign direct investment; regional and preferential trade agreements.**

Bibliography

Berlinski, J. 2004. *Los impactos de la política comercial: Argentina y Brazil (1988–1997)*. Buenos Aires: Siglo XXI.

Bohara, A., Gawande, K. and Sanguinetti, P. 2004. Trade diversion and declining tariffs: evidence from Mercosur. *Journal of International Economics* 64, 65–88.

Bouzas, R. 2002. MERCOSUR after ten years: learning process or déjà-vu? In *Paths to Regional Integration: The Case of Mercosur*, ed. J. Tulchin and R. Espach. Washington, DC: Woodrow Wilson International Center.

Brambilla, I. 2005. A customs union with multinational firms: the automobile market in Argentina and Brazil. Working Paper No. 11745. Cambridge, MA: NBER.

Cadot, O., de Melo, J. and Olarreaga, M. 2003. The protectionist bias of duty drawbacks: evidence from Mercosur. *Journal of International Economics* 59, 161–82.

Castilho, M. and Zignago, S. 2002. Trade effects of FDI in Mercosur: a disaggregated Analysis. In *An Integrated Approach to the EU-Mercosur Association*, ed. P. Giordano. Paris: Sciences Po.

Chang, W. and Winters, L. 2002. How regional blocs affect excluded countries: the price effects of Mercosur. *American Economic Review* 92, 889–904.

Chudnovski, D. 2001. *El boom de la inversión extranjera directa en el MERCOSUR*. Buenos Aires: Siglo XXI.

Eichengreen, B. 1998. Does Mercosur need a single currency? Working Paper No. 1018, Center for International and Development Economic Research, UC Berkeley.

Olarreaga, M. and Soloaga, I. 1998. Endogenous tariff formation: the case of Mercosur. *World Bank Economic Review* 12(1), 297–320.

Porto, G. 2006. Using survey data to assess the distributional effects of trade policy. *Journal of International Economics* 70(1), 140–60'.

Schiff, M. and Chang, W. 2003. Market presence, contestability and the terms-of-trade effects of regional integration. *Journal of International Economics* 60, 161–75.

Vaillant, M. 2005. Mercosur: southern integration under construction. *Internationale Politik und Gesellschaft* 2, 52–71.

Yeats, A. 1998. Does Mercosur's trade performance raise concerns about the effects of regional trade arrangements? *World Bank Economic Review* 12(3), 1–28.

merger analysis (United States)

In the economics literature, a merger is the combination of the assets of two or more firms. Economists usually distinguish three different types of merger: horizontal, vertical, and conglomerate. Horizontal mergers are between rivals; vertical mergers involve firms one of which supplies inputs to the other(s); conglomerate mergers are between firms in unrelated businesses. Mergers represent one way for a firm to acquire assets as an already assembled package.

We first discuss why a merger is sometimes a desirable way to expand a firm. Then we turn to the evidence on the amount of merger activity. Finally, we address one of the important questions surrounding mergers: whether they are motivated by the desire to improve efficiency or by the desire to acquire market power. Although the evidence is sometimes ambiguous, the overwhelming consensus is that most merger activity in the United States is motivated by efficiency considerations.

Reasons for mergers

The most important obvious reason for mergers is to increase efficiency. There is a variety of ways in which mergers can enhance efficiency. By increasing its size, a firm may be able to achieve economies of scale in production, distribution, management, or other aspects of the firm's operation, such as research and development. By eliminating duplication of certain management functions, firms may be able to cut their total costs. Certain scale efficiencies may arise naturally when firms are regulated or have reporting requirements. For example, a merged firm may have to submit tax and other government forms only once as a result of the merger.

By increasing the number of its activities, the merged firm may achieve economies of scope, efficiencies that result from engaging in related activities done together in one firm. For example, the ability of one firm to provide a wide range of products may make distribution easier. Alternatively, the ability to use in one activity knowledge gained in another can make it more efficient to have one firm perform both activities rather than having each activity performed by a different firm.

A common reason for vertical mergers is to eliminate transaction costs associated with using the marketplace to obtain supplies. (Of course, there is the offsetting cost of running a larger firm.) An example of a transaction cost is opportunism. In marketplace transactions, a buyer may (unexpectedly) be able to exploit the seller (or vice versa). For example, the seller may have no other possible buyer in the short run, and the buyer could demand a lower price than the once originally agreed upon. A vertical merger is an alternative to other mechanisms such as reputations or contract litigation to deal with this problem.

A vertical merger may eliminate the distortion of an upstream (input) monopoly. Prior to merger, the downstream (output) firm decides how to produce and how to price its output based on this distorted input price. If the output is produced with variable input proportions, there is a loss of efficiency to the economy that a vertical merger can fix. There is a private incentive to vertically integrate, but the effect on social welfare is ambiguous.

If both the upstream and the downstream firms are non-competitive, a vertical merger eliminates 'double marginalization'. An upstream firm with market power raises its price above its marginal cost. Then the downstream firm adds an additional markup so that the final consumers pay a double markup. If the firms merge, they set only a single markup, causing output price to fall, output to expand and social welfare to rise.

So far, these explanations do not answer the question why one firm merges with another rather than buying the underlying assets and assembling them itself. Aside from competitive effects, one answer is that another firm is a package of already assembled assets and it may be cheaper to buy an existing firm than to create one.

Mergers can also be used to transfer assets from the control of bad managers (or investors) to good ones. Suppose that Firm X has very smart managers, while Firm Y has either incompetent managers or managers who are not performing well because no one is monitoring their actions. Here, a transfer of assets to X should allow Y's assets to be more productive. X should be able to pay more for Y's assets than they are worth based on the market's valuation of Y's cash flows under its current incompetent management. This disparity in value creates an incentive for X to purchase Y. To avoid being taken over, Y's managers can improve their performance (that is, the takeover threat disciplines them) or engage in defensive tactics designed to thwart such a takeover in order to save their jobs. If these defensive tactics induce the acquiring firm to raise its price for Y, the tactics can benefit Y's shareholders. There is a large literature on defensive tactics as well as their sometimes ambiguous efficiency consequences. In a hostile takeover, X buys Y despite the desire of Y (or its managers) to remain independent. The use of hostile takeovers in the 1980s coincided with the ability of acquiring firms to obtain financing through junk bonds (bonds below investment grade).

Aside from efficiency motivations, another rationale for a merger is to eliminate competition between the merging firms. The antitrust laws of the United States forbid mergers that result in a lessening of competition with a consequent increase in price. Although antitrust concerns about mergers mainly arise in the context of horizontal mergers, such concerns can also arise with vertical mergers. One concern is that a vertical merger could eliminate a key supplier for a rival firm. Typically, theories of vertical harm are much less certain in their predictions than theories of competitive harm arising from horizontal mergers.

In addition to efficiency and market power explanations, there is a variety of other reasons for mergers. Tax considerations can sometimes make it advantageous for one firm to merge with another. For example, if one firm has a loss and another a profit, a merger can lower their total tax liability. The merged firm may be able to report no profit and therefore owe no corporate tax. Separately, one of the firms (the profitable one) would have to pay a tax. Mergers can also allow managers to engage in empire building, or allow a firm to have an 'excuse' ('I'm no longer in charge') to renege on certain informal promises made to workers or other firms.

Evidence: merger activity

Mergers come in waves, being common in certain industries at certain times. Because no single data series on merger activity goes back to 1900, we must splice together sometimes inconsistent data sources to study mergers over the 20th century. Figure 1 presents data on the amount of US merger activity relative to the size of the economy back to 1900. By controlling for the economy's size (a larger economy is likely to generate more merger activity), we can compare the intensity of merger activity at different times.

Figure 1 indicates that there have been several waves of merger activity. The first, around 1900, was (relatively) the largest and represents the creation of some of the best-known firms in the United States, such as General Electric and U.S. Steel. This was a time of great change with significant developments in transportation and communications. The second wave was in the 1920s and helped to create several oligopolies. The third, in the 1960s, involved conglomerate mergers. In the 1980s, the fourth wave (which would be more evident in the figure if we had dollar value of merger activity instead of the number of mergers) arose as hostile takeovers became popular in the United States. The fifth was in the late 1990s and disproportionately involved airlines, telecommunications, banking and other industries that had previously been heavily regulated.

The timing of merger waves seems to coincide with stock market booms for reasons no one has completely explained. One recent explanation by Shleifer and Vishny (2003) maintains that during stock booms stocks are overvalued (a fact known by managers but not outside investors) and managers use the (overvalued) stock to purchase other firms. In stock market booms, the use of

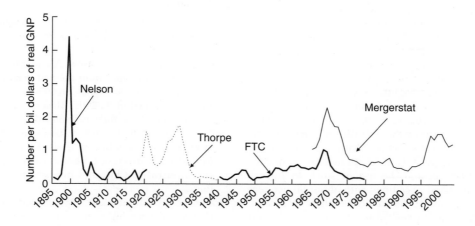

Figure 1   Annual number of mergers and acquisitions per billion US dollars of real GNP (United States, 1895–2003). 1982 dollars. *Sources:* Nelson Series, Federal Trade Commission (FTC) 'Board' series and Mergerstat. In 2003 the Bureau of Economic Analysis made comprehensive revisions to its National Income and Product Accounts. These revised figures were used to calculate deflators for the FTC series and Mergerstat. The Mergerstat series has broader converage (for example, more industries, lower thresholds for reporting) than the FTC series. Adapted from Golbe and White (1998, Figure 9.7).

stock rather than cash to buy other firms' assets does increase, consistent with the hypothesis.

Empirical evidence: rationales for mergers

A central question is whether mergers improve efficiency or, especially in the case of horizontal mergers, reduce competition and harm consumers. Despite an enormous number of studies of this question, the answer is still somewhat controversial. Our conclusion is that, although there is no doubt that some mergers are poorly motivated and turn out badly for the firms, and that some horizontal mergers reduce competition and harm consumers, most are expected to be profitable, to enhance efficiency and not to reduce competition.

Researchers have used three types of data: stock market data, accounting data, and price or output data. Because of their availability, stock market data have been used most often. Stock market studies rely on the premise that stock market prices are a good indication of a firm's expected future profitability (and make subtle assumptions about when information gets reflected in prices). These stock market studies can capture the effect of a merger on the acquiring firm, the acquired (target) firm, and rivals. Accounting data may have certain biases that can be hard to correct, and can be difficult to obtain. The same is true of data on price and output. In contrast to stock market studies, studies using either accounting or performance data are *ex post* studies of mergers (what happened after the mergers), while studies using stock market data are *ex ante* studies (what is expected to happen). We present a brief summary of the major findings (see Carlton and Perloff, 2005, and the references cited there, especially Andrade and Stafford, 2001, and Pautler, 2003).

Shareholders of an acquired firm earn a premium of between 16 and 25 per cent above the price prevailing prior to the merger. This premium is now higher than it used to be before the Williams Act of 1968 was passed. The Williams Act requires a firm to reveal publicly its intentions to acquire another firm.

Shareholders of the acquiring firm do not do very well. Although they earned slightly positive returns in the 1960s (plus four per cent), their returns became slightly negative (minus three per cent) in the 1980s and 1990s. Interestingly, the form of the acquisition (whether cash or stock) influences the return, with acquirers doing better when more cash is used, though it is unclear why this should occur. (The use of stock to finance mergers has increased over time, with about 60 per cent of transactions in the 1990s financed entirely by stock.)

Overall, the total return (which is what matters for efficiency) to the combined acquiring and acquired firms is positive. That is, the total value of the merged firm is about 2–7.5 per cent higher after a merger than the sum of each firm's value pre-merger.

Researchers using accounting or other performance data have had more difficulty documenting gains from mergers. Using data from the 1960s and 1970s, Scherer (1988) and Ravenscreft and Scherer (1987) do not find increased profits post-merger. Andrade and Stafford (2001) use Scherer's data and show that the data support the efficiency hypothesis if one controls for industry benchmarks. Lichtenberg and Siegal (1987) find significant positive effects of mergers on productivity.

Studies of stock markets and of individual industries have been used to investigate whether horizontal mergers generally create market power. The stock market studies exploit the idea that a merger that creates efficiency will cause the stock price of the (to-be-merged) firm to rise and that of its rivals to fall. In contrast, a horizontal merger that eliminates a rival should be expected to also benefit other rivals (since industry price will rise if competition is eliminated). Banerjee and Eckard (1998) show that, even for the massive merger wave around 1900 (prior to strict enforcement of antitrust laws forbidding mergers that eliminated competition), rival firms suffered as a result of a horizontal merger, supporting the efficiency hypothesis. There are of course exceptions, and some studies of recent mergers (for example, some airline mergers) show that horizontal mergers can harm competition and raise price. However, most of the literature (though certainly not all) supports the view that mergers generally should be expected to help consumers.

DENNIS W. CARLTON AND JEFFREY M. PERLOFF

See also **firm boundaries (empirical studies); mergers, endogenous; merger simulations.**

This article draws heavily on Carlton and Perloff (2005, ch. 2). The reader interested in more detailed discussion should consult that work together with the references cited therein.

Bibliography

Andrade, G. and Stafford, E. 2001. New evidence and perspectives on mergers. *Journal of Economic Perspectives* 15(2), 103–20.

Banerjee, A. and Eckard, E. 1998. Are mega-mergers anti-competitive? Evidence from the first great merger wave. *RAND Journal of Economics* 29, 803–27.

Carlton, D. and Perloff, J., 2005. *Modern Industrial Organization*. New York: Pearson Addison Wesley.

Golbe, D. and White, L. 1988. A time series analysis of mergers and acquisitions in the US Economy. In *Corporate Takeovers: Causes and Consequences*, ed. A. Auerbach. Chicago: University of Chicago Press.

Lichtenberg, F. and Siegal, D. 1987. Productivity and changes in ownership of manufacturing plants. *Brookings Papers on Economic Activity* 1987(3), 63–83.

Pautler, P. 2003. Evidence on mergers and acquisitions. *Antitrust Bulletin* 48, 119–221.

Ravenscraft, D. and Scherer, F. 1987. *Mergers, Sell-offs and Economic Efficiency*. Washington, DC: Brookings Institution.

Scherer, F. 1988. Corporate takeovers: the efficiency arguments. *Journal of Economic Perspectives* 2(1), 69–82.

Shleifer, A. and Vishny, R. 2003. Stock market driven acquisitions. *Journal of Financial Economics* 70, 295–311.

merger simulations

The key in an evaluation of a proposed merger is to determine whether the reduction of competition it would cause is outweighed by potential cost reductions. Traditional analysis of mergers is primarily based on industry-concentration measures. A market is defined and market shares of the relevant firms are used to compute a pre-merger concentration measure as well as a change in this measure due to the merger. Both the pre-merger level and the change in concentration are then compared with preset levels. The intuition is that, if the industry is concentrated, or if the change in concentration is large, then the anti-competitive effect will dominate. Using this approach to evaluate mergers in some industries is problematic for at least two reasons. In many cases the product offerings make the definition of the relevant product (or geographic) market difficult. Even if the relevant market can be defined, the computed concentration index provides a reasonable standard by which to judge the competitive effects of the merger only under strong assumptions.

Merger simulation attempts to deal with these challenges. The basic idea consists of 'front-end' estimation, in which the structural primitives of the model are estimated, and a 'back-end' analysis, in which the estimates are used to simulate the post-merger equilibrium. The approach proceeds as follows.

First, demand parameters are recovered by econometric estimation, if the data are rich enough, or, if data (with enough variation) are not available, then marketing and other anecdotal evidence can be used to approximate the effects of prices on demand (Werden and Froeb, 1994). Estimation has to deal with two main challenges: a flexible functional form, especially with a large number of products, and reasonable identifying assumptions. The most commonly used approaches, to deal with the large number of products, are multi-level budgeting (Hausman, Leonard and Zona, 1994) and the discrete-choice, characteristics, approach (Berry, Levinsohn and Pakes, 1995; Nevo, 2000). Prices are set endogenously and typically respond to demand shocks that are unobserved by the researcher, and therefore instrumental variables are needed. Two common instrumental variables are observed characteristics of other products (Bresnahan, 1987; Berry, Levinsohn and Pakes, 1995) and out-of-market prices (Hausman, Leonard and Zona, 1994; Nevo 2000).

Second, pre-merger cost parameters are recovered. One approach is to assume a model of pricing (Bertrand, say) and to use it jointly with the estimated demand parameters to recover implied marginal costs. If needed, the implied marginal costs can be regressed on characteristics in order to recover cost functions. Alternatively, the pricing equation, and the cost functions, can be estimated jointly with demand. Either way, the model of pricing can, and should, be tested (Porter, 1983; Bresnahan, 1987; Nevo, 2001). Finally, marginal cost can be approximated from accounting data, but these tend to be unreliable.

Third, the recovered marginal costs and estimated demand parameters are used jointly to simulate the new equilibria that would result from a merger. Usually, the analysis focuses on 'unilateral effects', with the likelihood of (tacit) collusion fixed. In principle, however, the simulation can use a different model of competition post-merger from the one used to recover the parameters. In order to address potential cost reductions, the simulation can be performed with marginal cost fixed, by changing marginal costs or by asking what cost saving is required to keep consumer welfare, or any other measure, at a certain level (Nevo, 2000). Finally, the model can be used to assess the likelihood of entry and/or the change in incentive to collude.

The end result is a prediction of post-merger prices and quantities under several scenarios. With the use of the estimated demand and supply functions, these equilibrium quantities can be converted into consumer welfare and (variable) profits. The change in welfare and profits can be used as the basis for evaluating the merger instead of the change in concentration. This has the advantage of being linked to economic theory and the underlying trade-off between reduction in competition and improved efficiency. It also allows the parties to assess the accuracy of the prediction due to the assumptions by simulating under different assumptions, or due to the data by computing standard errors.

There are several potential pitfalls in using merger simulation. The simulation is only as good as the model it is based on and the parameter estimates that go into the simulation. Therefore, one should take extra care in choosing a model suitable for the industry. Furthermore, in some cases data and time constraints might limit the ability to consistently estimate the parameters required for the simulation.

Despite the fact that merger simulation has been used extensively in practice, there is little work testing its accuracy with the use of post-merger data. One exception is a study of mergers in the airline industry (Peters, 2003) that finds that simulation methods do a reasonable job at predicting the price effects of mergers. Peters also finds that a large fraction of the unexplained change in prices comes from changes in marginal costs or firm conduct (his analysis cannot separate the two). Retrospective analysis of this sort is useful not just in evaluating the quality of predictions but also in pointing to directions in which the modelling and analysis can be improved.

For further readings and details see Whinston (2005, ch. 3).

AVIV NEVO

Bibliography

Berry, S., Levinsohn, J. and Pakes, A. 1995. Automobile prices in market equilibrium. *Econometrica* 63, 841–90.

Bresnahan, T. 1987. Competition and collusion in the American automobile oligopoly: the 1955 price war. *Journal of Industrial Economics* 35, 457–82.

Hausman, J., Leonard, G. and Zona, J. 1994. Competitive analysis with differentiated products. *Annales d'Economie et de Statistique* 34, 159–80.

Nevo, A. 2000. Mergers with differentiated products: the case of the ready-to-eat cereal industry. *RAND Journal of Economics* 31, 395–421. Reprinted in *Empirical Industrial Organization*, ed. P. Joskow and M. Waterson. Cheltenham: Edward Elgar, 2004.

Nevo, A. 2001. Measuring market power in the ready-to-eat cereal industry. *Econometrica* 69, 307–42.

Peters, C. 2003. Evaluating the performance of merger simulation: evidence from the US airline industry. Working Paper No. 32. Center for the Study of Industrial Organization, Northwestern University.

Porter, R. 1983. A study of cartel stability: The Joint Executive Committee, 1880–1886. *Bell Journal of Economics* 14, 301–14.

Werden, G. and Froeb, L. 1994. The effects of mergers in differentiated products industries: logit demand and merger policy. *Journal of Law, Economics and Organization* 10, 407–26.

Whinston, M. 2005. *Lectures on Antitrust Economics*. Cambridge, MA: MIT Press.

mergers, endogenous

The term 'endogenous mergers' reflects the view in economic theory that mergers are equilibrium outcomes. The literature on endogenous mergers explicitly analyses firms' incentives to merge and makes predictions on the volume and type of mergers that are likely to occur. In this literature, merger formation is modelled as a bidding game or non-cooperative coalition formation game (Kamien and Zang, 1990; Gowrisankaran, 1999; Nocke, 2000; Pesendorfer, 2005), or as an anonymous merger market where firms can buy or sell corporate assets (Jovanovic and Rousseau, 2002; Nocke and Yeaple, 2006). The literature on endogenous mergers is conceptually distinct from the literature on *exogenous* mergers, which considers the positive and normative effects of a merger between a given ('exogenous') set of firms.

To analyse the endogenous merger process, one first needs to understand why firms may want to merge. Several motives for mergers have been identified in the literature.

First, firms may want to merge to realize efficiency gains or 'synergies'. Mergers may allow firms to exploit complementarities in their capabilities (Nocke and Yeaple, 2007), or they may be an efficient way to reallocate used capital from less productive firms to more productive firms (Jovanovic and Rousseau, 2002).

Second, firms may want to merge to increase their market power. However, as Salant, Switzer and Reynolds (1983) have shown for the Cournot model, a merger solely aimed at increasing market power may not be profitable: to the extent that merging firms want to reduce joint output to raise price, non-participating outsiders will increase their output in response, imposing a negative externality on the merging firms. (This point relies heavily on the Cournot assumption; see Deneckere and Davidson, 1985.) While it has generally been acknowledged that horizontal mergers (between firms competing in the same market) may lead to higher prices and lower welfare, the Chicago School of antitrust has long held the view that vertical mergers (between upstream suppliers and their downstream customers) are efficiency-enhancing. By showing that vertical mergers may allow foreclosure of upstream suppliers or downstream buyers, this view has recently been refuted in a series of articles (see Rey and Tirole, 2005, for a survey).

Third, firms may want to merge to facilitate collusion. A horizontal merger may facilitate collusion by reducing the number of players in the industry, or by reallocating industry capacity in a way that equalizes firms' incentives to cheat (Compte, Jenny and Rey, 2002). A vertical merger may facilitate upstream collusion by reducing the number of downstream outlets through which an upstream firm can profitably deviate. Furthermore, to the extent that collusion is sustainable only if the vertically integrated firm receives a larger market share than an unintegrated firm, firms may have an incentive to merge so as to demand and obtain a larger share of the collusive pie (Nocke and White, 2003).

Finally, a variety of other motives for merger have been proposed, some of which are based on the view that firms do not necessarily maximize profits. For example, it has been argued that managers may have an incentive to engage in empire building.

Focusing on the market power motive, much of the recent literature on endogenous mergers has been concerned with studying the limits to monopolization through mergers and acquisitions, and making predictions on the relationship between concentration levels and industry characteristics (Kamien and Zang, 1990; Nocke, 2000; Gowrisankaran and Holmes, 2004). The starting point of this literature is the observation by Stigler (1950, pp. 25–6) that 'the promoter of a merger is likely to receive much encouragement from each firm – almost every encouragement, in fact, except participation'.

To understand Stigler's point that a merger to monopoly may not obtain even when feasible, consider an industry with N firms, each running a single plant to produce a homogeneous or differentiated good. If a subset of these firms merge, they will internalize any externality in the price/output decisions they impose on each other. Unless efficiency gains from merging are large, a merged entity would thus produce a smaller output per plant than a single-plant firm: a firm participating in the merger ('insider') would be better off than a firm not participating ('outsider'). Let $\Pi(N; 0)$ denote monopoly profits, and $\Pi(1; N - 1)$ the profit of a single-plant firm competing with a larger firm owning $N - 1$ plants. Assume the merger would take place even when only $N - 1$ firms agreed to merge. Then, firm i will agree to merge with its $N - 1$ rivals only if $\Pi(1; N - 1) \leq s_i \Pi(N; 0)$, where s_i is firm i's equity share in the merged entity. Since this must hold for any firm i, merger to monopoly will occur only if $\Pi(1; N - 1) \leq \Pi(N; 0)/N$. In standard oligopoly models, this inequality is often violated if efficiency gains from merging are small, the number of firms is large, and competition is not too 'tough'. Merger to monopoly may thus fail to occur, even though it would maximize joint profits, as some firm(s) may be better off staying outside and taking a free ride on the merged entity's effort to restrict output.

There may also be limits to monopolization through mergers and acquisitions because of entry. To the extent that a merger makes the industry *less* competitive, a merger between incumbents may induce more entry in the future, reducing the incumbents' profits. By not merging with their rivals, incumbent firms may thus credibly commit to compete vigorously and deter further entry.

VOLKER NOCKE

See also **cartels; merger analysis (United States); merger simulations.**

Bibliography

Compte, O., Jenny, F. and Rey, P. 2002. Capacity constraints, mergers and collusion. *European Economic Review* 46, 1–29.
Deneckere, R. and Davidson, C. 1985. Incentives to form coalitions with Bertrand competition. *RAND Journal of Economics* 16, 473–86.
Gowrisankaran, G. 1999. A dynamic model of endogenous horizontal mergers. *RAND Journal of Economics* 30, 56–83.
Gowrisankaran, G. and Holmes, T.J. 2004. Mergers and the evolution of industry concentration: results from the dominant firm model. *RAND Journal of Economics* 35, 561–82.
Jovanovic, B. and Rousseau, P.L. 2002. The Q-theory of mergers. *American Economic, Review Papers and Proceedings* 92, 198–204.
Kamien, M.I. and Zang, I. 1990. The limits of monopolization through acquisition. *Quarterly Journal of Economics* 105, 465–99.
Nocke, V. 2000. Monopolisation and industry structure. Economics Working Paper No. 2000-W27, Nuffield College, Oxford.
Nocke, V. and White, L. 2003. Do vertical mergers facilitate upstream collusion? Working Paper No. 03-033, PIER, University of Pennsylvania.
Nocke, V. and Yeaple, S. 2007. Cross-border mergers and acquisitions versus greenfield foreign direct investment: the role of firm heterogeneity. *Journal of International Economics* 72(2), 336–65.
Pesendorfer, M. 2005. Mergers under entry. *RAND Journal of Economics* 36, 661–79.
Rey, P. and Tirole, J. 2005. A primer on foreclosure. In *Handbook of Industrial Organization*, vol. 3, ed. M. Armstrong and R. Porter. Amsterdam: North-Holland.
Salant, S.W., Switzer, S. and Reynolds, R.J. 1983. Losses from horizontal merger: the effects of an exogenous change in industry structure on Cournot–Nash equilibrium. *Quarterly Journal of Economics* 98, 185–99.
Stigler, G.J. 1950. Monopoly and oligopoly by merger. *American Economic Review, Papers and Proceedings* 40, 23–34.

merit goods

The concept of merit goods, since its introduction thirty years ago (Musgrave, 1957, 1959), has been widely discussed and given divergent interpretations (for surveys, see Head, 1966; Andel, 1984). Since no patent attaches to the term, it is thus difficult to provide a unique definition. However, most interpretations relate to situations where evaluation of a good (its merit or demerit) derives not simply from the norm of consumer sovereignty but involves an alternative norm. In the following, various situations and their bearing on the concept will be considered.

1. Merit goods, private goods and public goods

While the concept of merit goods was raised in the context of fiscal theory, the term has broader application and should not be confused with that of public (Musgrave, 1957, 1959) goods. The distinction between private and public or social goods arises from the mode in which benefits become available, i.e., rival in the one and non-rival in the other case (see Public Goods). As a result, conditions of Pareto optimality differ, as do the appropriate mechanisms of choice. But whether met through a market or political process, both choices and the normative evaluation of outcomes squarely rest on the premise of individual preference. Consumer sovereignty is taken to apply to both cases. The concept of merit (or, for that matter, of demerit) goods questions that premise. It thus cuts across the traditional distinction between private and public goods. A more fundamental set of issues is raised, issues which do not readily fit into the conventional framework of micro theory as based on a clearly designed concept of free consumer choice.

2. Pathological cases

Next, we consider various settings where the norm of consumer sovereignty remains the preferred solution, but where difficulties in implementation have to be met. The most extreme case arises with regard to the mentally deficient or children. In both cases, some guidance is needed and custodial choices have to be made. These, however, may be viewed as exceptional circumstances and not part of the essential merit good problem. It is also evident that rational choice requires correct information, and that the quality of choice is impeded where information is imperfect or misleading. Situations may arise, as in the design of educational programmes, where the quality of choice as eventually valued by the beneficiary's own preference is improved by initial delegation of choice to others whose prior information is superior. Once more, the implementation of individual preferences is affected, but without questioning their dominance at the normative level.

Other instances arise where rational choice is impeded by oversight or myopia. Individuals, though informed and generally competent to choose, may be inclined to depart from rational choice on certain issues. Thus future consumption tends to be undervalued relative to present consumption (Pigou, 1928), while public services may be overvalued because they seem free or undervalued due to dislike of taxation. Rational choice may be impeded in the context of risk-taking, and so forth. Certain goods may thus come to be under or oversupplied for such reasons of misjudgment and their promotion or restriction may be called for. Such situations again pose some departure from the premise of rational choice, but they deal with defects in the implementation of consumer sovereignty, rather than its rejection as a norm.

3. Rule of fashion

By assuming individuals to have a well-defined preference structure which may then be interfered with, it is tempting to bypass the fact that individual preferences are not fixed in isolation but are affected by the societal setting in which individuals operate. Taking an extreme view of this dependence (Galbraith, 1958), the existence of independent preferences may be denied. Individual preferences become mirror images of fashions in what society approves or holds desirable. But this is too extreme a position. While societal influences enter, they are nevertheless met by individual responses, leaving effective preferences to differ across individuals. Though the preferences of individuals are conditioned by their social environment, own-preferences enter in shaping the individual's responses thereto. It thus seems inappropriate to equate the concept of merit goods with that of fashion.

4. Community preferences

As distinct from the rule of fashion, consider a setting where individuals, as members of the community, accept certain community values or preferences, even though their personal preferences might differ. Concern for maintenance of historical sites, respect for national holidays, regard for environment or for learning and the arts are cases in point. Such acceptance in turn may affect one's choice of private goods or lead to budgetary support of public goods even though own preferences speak otherwise. By the same token, society may come to reject or penalize certain activities or products which are regarded as demerit goods. Restriction of drug use or of prostitution as offences to human dignity (quite apart from potentially costly externalities) may be seen to fit this pattern. Community values are thus taken to give rise to merit or demerit goods. The hard-bitten reader regards this as merely another instance of fashion which may be disposed of accordingly. But such is not the case. Without resorting to the notion of an 'organic community', common values may be taken to reflect the outcome of a historical process of interaction among individuals, leading to the formation of common values or preferences which are transmitted thereafter (Colm, 1965). As this author sees it, this is the setting in which the concept of merit or demerit goods is most clearly appropriate, and where consumer sovereignty is replaced by an alternative norm.

5. Paternalism in distribution

In viewing the problem of individual choice and preferences, we so far have assumed that the individual's endowment from which to choose is given. It remains to consider a set of problems which arise in the context of distribution.

We begin with the case of voluntary giving (Hochman and Rogers, 1969). Donor D may derive utility from giving to recipient R, but more so if the grant is specified in kind (e.g., milk) than given in cash (and used for beer). Such paternalistic giving interferes with R's preferences. While R cannot be damaged (the grant can be refused) his or her gain is less than it would be from a cash grant. Charity by way of paternalistic giving thus involves imposition of D's preferences, of what goods *he* considers of merit for R. At the same time, giving in kind is in line with consumer sovereignty at the donor level, as D's satisfaction depends on what R consumes. Moreover, R cannot suffer a loss, since the grant may be rejected.

A similar problem arises in the context of redistribution through the political process of majority rule. Here, taking as well as giving is involved. While the Rs would prefer to take cash, they may do better by setting for in-kind programmes which appeal to the Ds. Redistribution by majority vote may thus take in-kind form. Once more the Ds may impose their preferences on the Rs, but subject to the terms of the social contract which now permits such intervention via majority rule. Many budget programmes rendering services to the poor (such as health, welfare, and low-cost housing) are of this type, and have indeed come to be classified as merit goods (OECD, 1985).

Having considered merit goods in relation to redistribution, it remains to note their bearing on the more basic issue of *primary* distribution. Models of distributive justice have taken a variety of forms, including entitlement to earnings in the Lockean tradition, utilitarian criteria, and entitlement to 'fair shares' (Vickrey, 1960; Harsanyi, 1955; Rawls, 1971). The latter may be viewed in terms of fair shares in income and wealth, while leaving its use to individual choice; or, it may be viewed in terms of a fair share in particular goods or bundles thereof. The role of merit goods arises in the latter context, and indeed bears some relation to the philosopher's concept of 'primary goods'. Moreover, both approaches may be combined in various ways. Thus, society may view it as fair to modify the distribution of income via a tax-transfer scheme, while also arranging the distribution of certain goods (e.g., scarce medical treatment) outside the market rule (Tobin, 1970), or society may wish to assure an adequate minimum provision, but do so by providing for a bundle of necessities rather than an equivalent minimum income to be spent at the recipient's choice. Goods separated out for non-market distribution might then be viewed as merit goods.

6. Multiple preferences or 'higher values'

The reader will note that up to this point we have dealt with settings which, in one way or another, involve some form of departure from the rule of consumer sovereignty. It remains to consider a further perspective, which views the problem within the sovereignty context. This approach postulates that preferences may derive from conflicting sets. This has been noted over the ages, from Artstotle's concept of 'atrasia,' over the Kantian imperative and Faust's 'two souls' to Adam Smith's impartial observer (Smith, 1759). Later the same thought appears in Harsanyi's distinction between subjective and ethical preferences (Harsanyi, 1955). A recent illustration follows in Rawls's concept of disinterested choice (Rawls, 1971) and Sen's usage of commitment (Sen, 1977). The term merit goods has then been applied to goods chosen under the latter ('ethically superior') set of preferences. Such choice may involve private as well as public goods, although they may be more likely to enter in the latter context where they may prove less costly due to the sharing of tax burdens (Brennan, and Lomasky 1983).

Conclusion

As the preceding discussion shows, the term merit goods has been applied to a variety of situations. In (1) we have noted that the merit good concept should not be confused with that of public goods. In section (2) we noted that a variety of situations may arise where interference with individual choice is needed but without questioning its validity as the basic norm. In (3) we have granted that individual preferences are influenced by social environment, but not to the point of excluding individual-preference based responses. None of these cases offered an appropriate setting in which to apply the merit or demerit concept. The case considered in section (4), offering community values as a restraint on individual choice, did, however, fit the pattern and, as I see it, goes to the heart of the merit concept. Section (5) posed related issues in the context of distribution. Voluntary giving was shown to permit the donor to impose his or her preferences on the donee, and this remains the case, if with lesser force, for political redistribution. Redistribution will tend to be in goods which the donor consider meritorious for the donee. Turning to primary distribution, we noted that society may define fair shares in cash or kind, the latter chosen with regard to what are considered meritorious items for the recipient. Only in section (6) did use of the merit goods concept remain within the context of the sovereignty norm, dealing now with preferences (merit or demerit wants) of a higher or lower kind. In all, it seems difficult to assign a unique meaning to the term. This writer's preference, as noted before, would reserve its use for the setting dealt with under (4), but that of (5) and (6) may also have a claim.

RICHARD A. MUSGRAVE

See also **public finance; public goods.**

Bibliography

Andel, N. 1984. Zum Konzept der meritorischen Güter. *Finanz Archiv*, New Series 42(3), where extensive literature references are given.

Brennan, G. and Lomasky, L. 1983. Institutional aspects of merit goods analysis. *Finanz Archiv*, New Series 41, 183–206.

Colm, G. 1965. National goals analysis and marginal utility economics. *Finanz Archiv*, New Series 24, 209–24.

Galbraith, K. 1958. *The Affluent Society*. Boston: Houghton Mifflin.

Harsanyi, J. 1955. Cardinal welfare, individualistic ethics, and interpersonal comparisons of utility. *Journal of Political Economy* 63, 309–21.

Head, J.C. 1966. On merit goods. *Finanz Archiv*, New Series 25(1), 1–29.

Hochman, H.H. and Rogers, J.D. 1969. Pareto-optimal redistribution. *American Economic Review* 59, 542–57.

Musgrave, R.A. 1957. A multiple theory of budget determination. *Finanz Archiv*, New Series 17, 333–43.

Musgrave, R.A. 1959. *The Theory of Public Finance.* New York: McGraw-Hill.

OECD. 1985. *The Role of the Public Sector.* Paris: OECD.

Pigou, A.C. 1928. *A Study in Public Finance.* London: Macmillan.

Rawls, J. 1971. *A Theory of Justice.* Cambridge, Mass.: Harvard University Press.

Sen, A. 1977. Rational fools: a critique of the behavioral foundations of economic theory. *Philosophy and Public Affairs* 6, 317–44.

Smith, A. 1749. *The Theory of Moral Sentiments.* Reprinted, New York: Liberty, 1969.

Tobin, J. 1970. On limiting the domain of inequality. *Journal of Law and Economics* 13, 263–77.

Veblen, T. 1899. *The Theory of the Leisure Class.* New York: New American Library.

Vickrey, W. 1960. Utility, strategy, and social decision rules. *Quarterly Journal of Economics* 74, 507–35.

Merton, Robert C. (born 1944)

Robert C. Merton, awarded the 1997 Nobel Memorial Prize in Economics, was born in New York City on 31 July 1944. His father, Robert K. Merton, was a noted sociologist, to say the least. This biographical sketch of Robert C. Merton and his contributions to financial economics may seem brief, given the gigantic impact that he had on economics and financial-market practice.

Merton's university education veered from applied mathematics at Columbia University (BS, 1966) and the California Institute of Technology (MS, 1967) to economics at MIT (Ph.D., 1970), where he quickly joined Paul Samuelson as student, then research assistant, faculty colleague, and collaborator. Their paper on warrant pricing (1969a) hinted at Merton's later massive contributions to 'the option-pricing formula' and to dynamic investment theory, which followed almost immediately. Within a few years of his arrival at MIT in 1967, it is no exaggeration to say that Merton had transformed his newly chosen field of financial economics and, more broadly, dynamic modelling in economics.

Only a decade before Merton framed his revolutionary new approach to financial modelling, Modigliani and Miller (1958) had used arbitrage reasoning to discover the irrelevance of corporate capital structure and dividend policy in perfect capital markets. About five years before Merton came on to the scene, William Sharpe (1964) had adapted Markowitz's mean-variance investment theory to establish the relationship between risk and expected return in market equilibrium. These pre-Merton breakthroughs were based on static reasoning. Merton exploited stochastic calculus – a completely new approach to dynamic modelling under uncertainty – in order to extend these insights and to open entirely new paths of discovery. The crucial tool of stochastic calculus that Merton brought into financial modelling is the

formula of Kiyoshi Itô (1951), whereby, under suitable technical regularity, the rate of change of the conditional expectation of $f(X(t), t)$, for an Itô process X and a smooth function $f(\cdot\cdot)$, is

$$f_t(X(t), t) + f_x(X(t), t)m(t) + \tfrac{1}{2}f_{xx}(X(t), t)v(t), \qquad (1)$$

where $m(t)$ is the rate of change of the conditional expectation of $X(t)$, and $v(t)$ is the rate of change of the conditional variance of $X(t)$. (Subscripts indicate partial derivatives.)

Consider, for example, Merton's approach (1969b; 1971) to investment, in which $X(t)$ is the wealth of a risk-averse investor whose current optimal conditional expected utility for final wealth is $f(X(t), t)$. (The conjectured dependence of indirect utility on wealth and time only is tantamount to the independence over time of asset returns, which Merton relaxed in 1973b.) The current portfolio p of investments determines the 'local mean' $m(t, p)$ and 'local variance' $v(t, p)$ of changes in wealth. At anything other than an optimal portfolio strategy, Bellman's principle of optimality implies that the conditional expected change of $f(X(t), t)$ is negative, so (1) suggests that

$$\text{Max}_p \quad f_t(X(t), t) + f_x(X(t), t)m(t, p) + \tfrac{1}{2}f_{xx}(X(t), t)v(t, p) = 0. \qquad (2)$$

Because the mean $m(t, p)$ and variance $v(t, p)$ of the 'local return' on wealth are linear and quadratic, respectively, with respect to the portfolio choice p, the first-order optimality conditions for (2) provide an explicit solution for p in terms of the derivatives of $f(\cdot\cdot)$. Substitution of this solution for p into the same equation (2) leaves a partial differential equation to solve for $f(x, t)$. Merton was able to give explicit solutions in certain cases. For example, with expected power utility for final wealth, the indirect utility must inherit the same degree of homogeneity with respect to wealth. Merton's problem is still the classic textbook example of stochastic control to which graduate students in finance and other fields, even beyond economics, are first exposed. The associated insights into lifetime investment planning are striking, and have led to an immense literature of extensions.

Although this is no place to derive it, the Black–Scholes formula $f(x, t)$ for the price at time t of an option on an asset whose current market value is x is similarly obtained by the 'risk-neutral' valuation equation

$$f_t(x, t) + f_x(x, t)rx + \tfrac{1}{2}f_{xx}(x, t)\sigma^2 x^2 = rf(x, t), \qquad (3)$$

where r is the continuously compounding risk-free borrowing rate and σ is the volatility (the standard deviation of annualized continuously compounding returns) of the underlying asset. The boundary condition for (3), in the case of a call option with an exercise date T and exercise price K, is $f(x, T) = max(x - K, 0)$, because this is the market value of the right, but not the obligation, to buy the stock for K when it trades in the market for x. Black and Scholes (1973) solved this equation with the famous formula named for them. For the market value of a general contingent claim paying $g(X(T))$ at T, the same differential equation (3) applies under technical conditions, with the boundary condition $f(x, T) = g(x)$.

By virtue of Itô's formula (1), one can view (3) as a statement that the option's expected rate of return may be treated as the risk-free rate of return, provided that we replace the actual mean rate of return on the underlying asset with the risk-free rate. Indeed, this is roughly how Black and Scholes (1973) interpreted their original derivation of (3), which was based on a particular general-equilibrium model. Merton, however, noted that changes in the market value of the option over time could actually be replicated by trading the underlying asset, financing any cash needs with risk-free borrowing. This 'arbitrage' strategy leads to (3) without reference to a particular general-equilibrium model, since arbitrage is ruled out in any equilibrium. Black and Scholes acknowledged Merton for this alternative approach, which was the genesis of both an enormous academic literature on contingent claims pricing and the professional practice of 'financial engineering', a field that includes a vast array of financial pricing and risk-management methods.

Among the most influential applications that Merton developed on the basis of his approach to derivative asset pricing was his insight (1974) that the equity and debt of a corporation may be viewed as derivative securities written on the assets of the firm, and priced accordingly. This idea was developed independently in Black and Scholes (1973). In any case, this widely known 'Merton model of corporate debt' is the basis of much modern fundamental market analysis of corporate debt and credit derivatives, in practice and academic research, including both pricing and default prediction.

Rounding out the series of major results that Merton produced within a stunningly short period of time were his intertemporal capital asset pricing model (ICAPM) (1973b) and his theory of rational option pricing (1973a). Merton's ICAPM extended Sharpe's CAPM to a dynamic framework, relieving it of its dependence on mean-variance utility because, from (2), we see that only the ('instantaneous') mean and variance of returns matter for conditional mean rates of change of utility, under technical conditions. More importantly, the ICAPM showed how the expected returns of assets in a multi-period setting compensate not only for exposure to the risk associated with the return of the market portfolio but also for exposure to the risks associated with changes in state variables determining future conditional distributions of asset returns. These latter risks introduce hedging motives not present in a static model. Merton's Theory of Rational Option Pricing (1973a) shored up the foundations of the Black–Scholes option

pricing model and treated a variety of related issues, in particular a rational approach to exercising and pricing American options. A few years later Merton (1977) provided deeper foundations for the basic arbitrage reasoning underlying the pricing of derivatives by replacing his earlier 'instantaneous return' arbitrage argument, the original basis of the Black–Scholes formula, with the construction of dynamic portfolio trading strategies that specified, at each state and date, the actual quantities of each type of security that an investor would hold in order to replicate the final payoff of the target contingent claim.

After 1978 Merton shifted his attention from foundational theories of investment and asset pricing to applications of those theories, paying special attention to the institutional features of financial markets and to related issues of public policy. For example, a series of papers addressed pension planning, social security, and bank deposit insurance. He also worked on corporate capital budgeting, labour contracts, financial intermediation, and the risk management of financial institutions, among many other applications. Merton even turned his hand to some empirical research on investments. His 1987 presidential address to the American Finance Association raised some influential new ideas regarding the impact of market imperfections and incomplete information on equilibrium asset prices.

In 1988 Merton moved from MIT, of whose faculty he had been a member since 1970, to Harvard University. While he has maintained direct involvement in financial markets in various capacities throughout his professional career, for example as a consultant, in 1993 Merton took a more significant step in this direction by becoming one of the first principals of the now notorious hedge fund, Long-Term Capital Management (LTCM). In its first years, the great financial successes of LTCM were attributed in large measure to the unusually deep team of talented financial minds, notably including both Merton and Myron Scholes, which had been assembled by John Merriwether, LTCM's founder. When LTCM failed spectacularly in 1998, some pundits ironically blamed undue reliance on sophisticated financial modelling, in some cases singling out Merton and Scholes. The record, however, seems to point to initial successes based on high leverage, attractive financing, and good trading, and then failure caused by high leverage coupled with the results of some unwise or unlucky trading, exacerbated by a 'rush to the exits' by other investors who held large positions similar to those of LTCM. In 2002, Merton co-founded Integrated Finance, a financial advisory firm.

As of this writing, Merton continues to publish and speak influentially, and remains on Harvard's faculty. In addition to the Nobel Prize, Merton is the recipient of numerous awards and honorary degrees, and is widely viewed as one of the all-time most respected leaders and researchers of his profession.

DARRELL DUFFIE

See also **contingent valuation; Miller, Merton; Modigliani, Franco; Scholes, Myron; Sharpe, William F.; social insurance; Social Security in the United States.**

Selected works

1969a. (With P. Samuelson.) A complete model of warrant pricing that maximizes utility. *Industrial Management Review* 10 (Winter), 17–46. Chapter 7 in *Continuous-Time Finance*.

1969b. Lifetime portfolio selection under uncertainty: the continuous-time case. *Review of Economics and Statistics* 51, 247–57. Chapter 4 in *Continuous-Time Finance*. 1992.

1971. Optimum consumption and portfolio rules in a continuous-time model. *Journal of Economic Theory* 3, 373–413. Chapter 5 in *Continuous-Time Finance*, 1992.

1973a. Theory of rational option pricing. Bell Journal of Economics and Management Science 4, 141–83. Chapter 8 in *Continuous-Time Finance*, 1992.

1973b. An intertemporal capital asset pricing model. *Econometrica* 41, 867–87. Chapter 15 in *Continuous-Time Finance*, 1992.

1974. On the pricing of corporate debt: the risk structure of interest rates. *Journal of Finance* 29, 449–70. Chapter 12 in *Continuous-Time Finance*, 1992.

1976. Option pricing when underlying stock returns are discontinuous. *Journal of Financial Economics* 3, 125–44. Chapter 9 in *Continuous Time Finance*, 1992.

1977. On the pricing of contingent claims and the Modigliani–Miller theorem. *Journal of Financial Economics* 5, 241–9. Chapter 13 in *Continuous Time Finance*, 1992.

1978. On the cost of deposit insurance when there are surveillance costs. *Journal of Business* 51, 439–52. Chapter 20 in *Continuous-Time Finance*, 1992.

1980. On estimating the expected return on the market: an exploratory investigation. *Journal of Financial Economics* 8, 323–61.

1983a. On the role of social security as a means for efficient risk-bearing in an economy where human capital is not tradeable. In *Financial Aspects of the US Pension System*, ed. Z. Bodie and J. Shoven. Chicago: University of Chicago Press.

1983b. On consumption-indexed public pension plans. In *Financial Aspects of the US Pension System*, ed. Z. Bodie and J. Shoven. Chicago: University of Chicago Press 1983. Chapter 18 in *Continuous-Time Finance*, 1992.

1985. Implicit labor contracts viewed as options: a discussion of 'Insurance Aspects of Pensions'. In *Pensions, Labor, and Individual Choice*, ed. D. Wise. Chicago: University of Chicago Press.

1987a. (With Z. Bodie and A. Marcus.) Pension plan integration as insurance against social security risk. In *Issues in Pension Economics*, ed. Z. Bodie, J. Shoven and D. Wise. Chicago: University of Chicago Press.

1987b. A simple model of capital market equilibrium with incomplete information. *Journal of Finance* 42, 483–510.

1987c. (With Z. Bodie and A. Marcus.) Defined benefit versus defined contribution pension plans: what are the real tradeoffs? In *Pensions in the U.S. Economy*, ed. J. Shoven and D. Wise. Chicago: University of Chicago Press.

1990. The financial system and economic performance. *Journal of Financial Services Research* 4, 263–300.

1992. *Continuous-Time Finance*. Rev. edn. Cambridge, MA: Basil Blackwell.

1993a. (With Z. Bodie.) Deposit insurance reform: a functional approach. *Carnegie–Rochester Conference Series on Public Policy* 38, 1–34.

1993b. (With A. Perold.) Theory of risk capital in financial firms. *Journal of Applied Corporate Finance* (Fall), 16–32.

1993c. (With Z. Bodie.) Pension benefit guarantees in the United States: a functional analysis. In *The Future of Pensions in the United States*, ed. R. Schmitt. Philadelphia: University of Pennsylvania Press.

1995. Financial innovation and the management and regulation of financial institutions. *Journal of Banking and Finance* 19, 461–81.

1997. A model of contract guarantees for credit-sensitive, opaque financial intermediaries. *European Finance Review* 1, 1–13.

2000. (With Z. Bodie.) *Finance*. New Jersey: Prentice-Hall.

2005. (With Z. Bodie.) The design of financial systems: towards a synthesis of function and structure. *Journal of Investment Management* 3, 1–23.

Bibliography

Bernstein, P. 1992. *Capital Ideas*. New York: Free Press.

Black, F. 1989. How we came up with the option formula. *Journal of Portfolio Management* 15, 4–8.

Black, F. and Scholes, M. 1973. The pricing of options and corporate liabilities. *Journal of Political Economy* 81, 637–54.

Duffie, D. 1998. Black, Merton and Scholes – their central contributions to economics. *Scandinavian Journal of Economics* 100, 411–24.

Greenspan, A. 1998. private-sector refinancing of the large hedge fund, Long-Term Capital Management. Testimony before the Committee on Banking and Financial Services, US House of Representatives, 1 October. Online. Available at http://www.federalreserve.gov/boarddocs/testimony/19981001.htm, accessed 26 July 2005.

Itô, K. 1951. On a formula concerning stochastic differentials. *Nagoya Mathematics Journal* 3, 55–65.

Jarrow, R. and Protter, P. 2004. A short history of stochastic integration and mathematical finance: the early years, 1880–1970. In *The Herman Rubin Festschrift, IMS Lecture Notes* 45, 75–91. Institute of Mathematical Statistics: Bethesda, MD.

Markowitz, H. 1959. *Portfolio Selection: Efficient Diversification of Investment*. New York: Wiley.

Modigliani, F. and Miller, M. 1958. The cost of capital, corporation finance, and the theory of investment. *American Economic Review* 48, 261–97.

Royal Swedish Academy of Sciences. 1998. The Nobel
  Memorial Prize in Economics 1997. *Scandinavian Journal
  of Economics* 100, 405–9.
Schaefer, S. 1998. Robert Merton, Myron Scholes and the
  development of derivative pricing. *Scandinavian Journal
  of Economics* 100, 425–45.
Sharpe, W. 1964. Capital asset prices: a theory of market
  equilibrium under conditions of risk. *Journal of Finance*
  19, 425–42.

Methodenstreit

The 'battle of methods' between Carl Menger (1840–1921) and Gustav Schmoller (1838–1917) is one of the most important methodological debates in the history of economics. It began with the publication of Menger's book on method (1883), which made the case for pure theory based on assumptions about behaviour and antecedent conditions. Schmoller responded with a strongly worded review (1883) that argued for principles of economics based on empirical historical data and the inductive method. Menger answered with an equally vehement statement of *The Errors of Historicism* (1884). The infuriated Schmoller refused even to read it (Schmoller, 1884). A torrent of books and papers by others followed over the next several decades. The best summary of the entire controversy is Ritzel (1951).

Like most disputes over method in economics, the opposing views were related to more complex disagreements over the nature and scope of economics and its policy implications. Menger's assumptions about behaviour implied a social system composed of selfishly motivated individuals; Schmoller assumed the existence of individuals grouped into nations, with group as well as individual goals. More important, Menger's conclusions emphasized the primacy of laissez-faire policies designed to allow as large a scope as possible to market adjustment processes. Schmoller's conclusions supported the interventionist and state-building policies of the newly unified German nation. In addition, the Ministry of Education in Berlin gave almost exclusive preference to the Schmoller school in appointing university professors. Menger was attacking the 'official' economics prevailing in Germany and its almost monopolistic control over university appointments. In addition to economic method, academic freedom and the role of the state were at issue.

On the basic issue of the place of theory and empirical studies in economics, Menger and Schmoller agreed that both were necessary. They disagreed, however, on the emphasis to be placed on each and their role in the development of conclusions. Menger argued that 'pure' economics based on assumptions of wide and perhaps universal generality, could be developed through correct logical analysis to arrive at conclusions of equally broad applicability and usefulness. Propositions based on empirical data, however, would be correct only for the limited data on which they were based. Since empirical data were always partial, as well as bounded by time and space, the conclusions drawn from them must be both problematic and of limited generality. Correct and general propositions could be derived through rigorous logic from assumptions not bounded by time, space or special circumstance, however.

Empirical studies entered Menger's method in two ways. First, they could be used to verify or illustrate the results of theoretic inquiry. Second, they were necessary when theoretic principles were applied to specific instances or policy problems. Empirical studies were required to define the situation to which theoretic principles were applied, and to delimit the applicability of the conclusions. Data acted as a bridge between the principles of pure economics and the policy problems of applied economics. Indeed, Menger warned against application of pure theory to applied problems without thorough empirical studies.

Schmoller also advocated use of both empirical studies and theory, but in a different combination. He rejected Menger's logical deductive method for three chief reasons: its assumptions were unrealistic, its high degree of abstraction made it largely irrelevant to the real-world economy, and it was devoid of empirical content. The theory was therefore useless in studying the chief questions of importance to economists: how have the economic institutions of the modern world developed to their present state, and what are the laws and regularities that govern them? The proper method was induction of general principles from historical–empirical studies (Schmoller, 1883). In the Hegelian tradition of 19th-century German scholarship, Schmoller conceived of the economy as a dynamic and evolving set of interrelated institutions whose laws of development could not be understood in terms of an abstract theory of constrained choice. One reason for the polarized arguments of the Methodenstreit was that the disputants were talking about different things.

How were the historical laws of economic development and change to be determined? Schmoller was not clear on that point, although he devoted five chapters of the introductory section of his *Grundriss* to a survey of the history and method of economics (Schmoller, 1900–4). The starting point of his method was empirical research rather than assumptions. The second step was to organize the data in a logical fashion, to bring out the essential nature of economic phenomena. The third step was to identify the relationship between phenomena in the context of their continually changing interaction and development. At all stages of the inquiry, empirical research was to be used to obtain the propositions of steps two and three. The connecting link between data and generalizations was not spelled out, although in retrospect we can interpret the procedure as an early version of the gestalt method and the use of pattern models.

The Methodenstreit had a significant impact on the development of economics. Schmoller's attack on the logical deductive method as inherently devoid of empirical content coincided with similar critiques by the British economic historians, John A. Hobson and the American institutionalists led by Thorstein Veblen. These critics forced the adherents of neoclassical economics to bring empirical studies more fully into the mainstream of economic thought and practice. After the Methodenstreit a combination of theory and empirical studies was almost universally accepted by economists as necessary.

Menger's method of combining them was adopted, however. In the 20th century economics became increasingly a theoretic discipline based on 'as if' assumptions, which are developed by rigorous logical methods to derive general propositions. Hypotheses about reality, derived from the general propositions, are then tested against empirical studies. Schmoller's vision of an empirical discipline based on factual studies, in which generalizations are both derived from and tested against data as they are developed, remains only among critics of the mainstream in a new battle of methods that has erupted a hundred years later.

DANIEL R. FUSFELD

See also **Historical School, German; institutional economics; Menger, Carl; methodology of economics; Schmoller, Gustav von.**

Bibliography

Menger, K. 1883. *Untersuchungen über die Methode der Sozialwissenschaften, und der politischen Oekonomie insbesondere.* Berlin: Duncker & Humblot. Ed. L. Schneider and trans. F.J. Nock as *Problems of Economics and Sociology*, Urbana: University of Illinois Press, 1963.
Menger, K. 1884. *Die Irrthümer des Historismus in der deutschen Nationalökonomie.* Vienna: Alfred Hölder.
Ritzel, G. 1951. *Schmoller Versus Menger.* Offenbach: Bollwerk-Verlag.
Schmoller, G. von. 1883. Zur Methodologie der Staats- und Sozialwissenschaften. *Jahrbuch für Gesetzgebung, Verwaltung und Volkswirtschaft im deutschen Reich* 8, 974–94.
Schmoller, G. von. 1884. *Jahrbuch für Gesetzgebung, Verwaltung und Volkwirtschaft in deutschen Reich*, 677.
Schmoller, G. von. 1900–4. *Grundriss der allgemeinen Volkswirtschaftslehre.* Leipzig: Duncker & Humblot.

methodological individualism

Methodological individualism is a doctrine in the social sciences according to which a proper explanation of a social regularity or phenomenon is one that is grounded in individual motivations and behaviour. In other words, according to this methodology, individual human beings are the basic units from which we must build *up* in order to understand the functioning of society, economy and polity. We may not in all our research succeed in doing so but to committed methodological individualists such research must be viewed as provisional and ideally be accompanied by a slight feeling of inadequacy on the part of the researcher.

The social scientists who have been the focus of much of the debate on methodological individualism and, paradoxically, also the ones least touched by the debate are economists. Economists are typically held up as examples of the most unbending methodological individualists; and, on the rare occasions when economists have joined this debate, they have tended to agree with this. The difference is that most non-economists mean this as criticism, whereas most economists take it as praise.

At first sight this characterization of economics seems right. Textbooks of microeconomics almost invariably begin by specifying individual utility functions or preference relations and asserting that human beings are rational in the sense that they behave so as to maximize their own utilities. They then build up from this to explain market phenomena, make claims about social welfare and discuss prospects of national economic growth. In some macroeconomic models economists are unable to build all the way up from individual behaviour and use aggregate behaviour descriptions as the starting point. But these models are almost always accompanied by an effort to 'complete' them with proper micro-foundations; and the profession regards these models as somewhat incomplete and awaiting the definitive work.

That economics may not actually be quite as methodologically individualistic as often presumed by both the discipline's admirers and its critics is a matter to which I return below. What is interesting to note here is that the debate on methodological individualism has been a surprisingly cantankerous one that has spawned enemies and intrigues. Some social scientists have sworn by it: no other method is worth its salt. Others have castigated it as an instrument of exploitation and maintenance of the status quo. Concepts and categorizations have multiplied over the years. We have come across methodological holism, methodological solipsism, atomism, 'MIs' (that is, methodological individualisms) of different types – 1, 2, 3 ... – creating the impression that the British intelligence had somehow got involved in the quest to understand this elusive concept.

One cause of the controversy is the confounding of positive and normative social science. To some commentators, methodological individualism implies that it is fine to leave it all to individuals, and by implication it amounts to an argument against government intervention. Friedrich von Hayek (1942) and James Buchanan (1989), for instance, have taken this line, as have some sociologists, who felt that the conservatism of traditional economics is founded in its adherence to methodological individualism. But this happens because of a possibly logical error, a failure to appreciate Hume's law, namely, that a normative proposition cannot be derived from a purely positive analysis. Kenneth Arrow (1994) has rightly criticized the tendency of some writers to treat methodological individualism and 'normative individualism' as inextricably linked. Similarly, Marxists often link methodological individualism automatically to certain ethical implications. Roemer (1981) and Elster (1982) argue that this is not a valid link. In what follows I treat the two as separate and assume that methodological individualism has no automatic normative implications.

Origins

The term 'methodological individualism' was probably used for the first time in the English language in 1909 by Joseph Schumpeter. Even if that is not so, Schumpeter certainly thought so, and he pointed out in his paper in the *Quarterly Journal of Economics* that year that he had actually coined the term in German the previous year. But methodological individualism had been *practised* from much earlier, at least as early as Adam Smith (1776), and was described as a deliberate methodology, though without the term itself being used, by Carl Menger in 1883 (Menger, 1883). Max Weber's later exposition of it was published posthumously in 1922 (Weber, 1922).

From the perspective of economics it seems reasonable to treat Menger as the first proponent of methodological individualism. He did so vociferously, dismissing the German historical school of economists and their methods as outdated and flawed. He advanced the idea of 'spontaneous order' in society, which sprang from atomistic individual behaviour, reminiscent of Adam Smith's 'invisible hand' and the efficiency of markets that was an outcome of rational, self-interested behaviour on the part of individuals. Menger not only failed to acknowledge that some of his ideas on spontaneous social order were already there in Adam Smith but wrote in a tone almost suggesting that Smith had taken those ideas from him.

A distinction is often drawn in philosophy between methodological individualism and 'atomism'. The latter is treated as a more extreme version of individualism, in which it is possible to characterize each individual fully without reference to society and then explain social behaviour by simply imagining such individuals being brought together in one society. Since the proponents of these ideas did not really define terms with that much care – and when they did, they went on to write in a way that disregarded their own definitions – I shall refrain from drawing fine distinctions and treat these neighbouring terms as all representing the broad *idea* of methodological individualism. Moreover, concepts like these are probably innately indefinable. They are understood through a combination of approximate definitions and repeated use.

It is useful in an exposition like this to think of the polar opposite of the term under consideration. This is captured in the concept of 'methodological holism', developed (without endorsement) by the philosopher John Watkins. Methodological holism is the belief that there are 'macroscopic laws that are *sui generis* and apply to the system as an organic whole' (Watkins, 1952, p. 187), and the behaviour of its components had to be deduced from it. In economics, this would imply beginning our analysis by stating the laws of an aggregate economy and, perhaps, the behaviour of prices and industries and, from that, deducing how individuals behaved and what motivated them. Stated in these terms, it immediately becomes clear from a perusal of almost any microeconomics textbook that economics belongs essentially to the methodological individualist end of the spectrum defined by methodological holism at one end and individualism at the other.

After these writings, interest in the subject flagged. Social scientists, especially economists, continued to do research without trying to explicitly articulate the method that they were in fact using. The feeling developed among economists that the issue of methodological individualism was either trivial or had been resolved in their favour.

In the early 1990s the economists' gathering insouciance was challenged by Rajeev Bhargava (1993) and Kenneth Arrow (1994). Bhargava summarizes various points of view on the subject and then challenges the orthodoxy, especially within economics. But he also expresses well the philosopher's inevitable anxiety in a debate like this, which stems from not knowing whether what one is grappling with is something profound or trivial. As he writes, 'On reading the literature one is swung between exuberance and despair, from feeling that all problems have been resolved to one that none has … Gradually an intense frustration overwhelms the reader: perhaps there was nothing worth discussing in the first place. What on earth was all the fuss about?' (1993, p. 5).

What he settles for as the best face of methodological individualism is 'intentionalism'. The intentional man is somewhere between the imaginary *homo economicus* and equally rare *homo sociologicus*. He can choose and decide individually but he is not a relentless, maximizing agent. He has psychology and a sense of social norms, which get in the way of selfish maximization. Bhargava then develops the idea of 'contextualism' as a challenge to methodological individualism, including intentionalism. The challenge consists of arguing that a variety of beliefs and practices in everyday life make sense only in the *context* of the society where they occur. Hence, in describing a society or an economy we are compelled to use concepts which are *irreducibly social*.

The reason why the assertion that certain beliefs and concepts are inextricably social is unlikely to stir a hornet's nest is that, although many economists claim to be rigid adherents of methodological individualism, they do use and have always used social concepts and categories. This is convincingly argued by Arrow. He points out how a variable such as price in a competitive model is an irreducibly social concept. Each individual takes the price to be given but the price that comes to prevail is an outcome of the choices made by all the individuals. So economists constructing equilibrium models, who claim to be hardened methodological individualists, are actually not so, at least in the sense that they use some concepts that are irreducibly social. Knowingly or unknowingly they follow a method which uses social categories. In fact, this was explicitly recognized by Schumpeter in his classic essay on methodological individualism, where he noted 'prices are obviously social phenomena' (1909, p. 217).

Preferences and groups

There are more contentious claims that one can make about the role of social concepts in economics. One of these relates to the *permissibility* of a certain class of propositions in social science, such as: 'The landlord will undertake action A, *because* it is in the landlord's class interest to do so.' (Action A could, for instance, be: 'refuse to hire a servant who has fled another landlord's employment and offers to work for this landlord for a low wage'). Let me call this proposition P.

The bone of contention between neoclassical and traditional Marxist economists is frequently whether such propositions are permissible. Many neoclassical economists and some political scientists (especially those belonging to the positive political economy school) believe that P is not permissible – a person's class interest must be not be treated as an innate characteristic in the same way that his self-interest may be. A small group of writers maintain that even Marxism is compatible with methodological individualism and that class and other aggregate behaviour should, ideally, be built from individual motivations and preferences (Roemer, 1981; Elster, 1982).

In any case, whether or not proposition P is wrong, mainstream economics certainly considers it so. If an economist were to use an axiom like proposition P, she would usually want to first satisfy herself why it may be in the landlord's *self*-interest to behave in a way which is in his *class* interest. However, this does not negate the use of beliefs and other concepts and variables which are irreducibly social. It is not clear whether a researcher who does both (that is, resists explaining individual behaviour solely in terms of its ability to serve group or class interests but uses concepts and beliefs which are inherently social) is a methodological individualist. But this is a purely definitional matter and of no great consequence. The important and contestable question is whether assumptions like proposition P should or should not be used. I take the view that it is best to avoid such assumptions as far as possible, without making that into a dogma.

There are some fundamental ways in which modern economics has moved further away from methodological individualism than merely by using irreducibly social concepts, like prices, and even without using propositions, like P. I here mention two. First, most models of economics make use of the idea of 'rules of the game'. In Cournot oligopoly, firms choose quantities and then wait for prices to form. In Bertrand oligopoly, firms set prices and then wait to sell what the market demands from them. In most real-life situations, these rules evolve over time through intrinsically social processes. We may not fully understand what these social processes are, but few individuals will deny their existence. Arrow (1994) has emphasized this and also the importance of 'social knowledge.'

Second, there is increasing recognition in economics that individual preferences are endogenous. They evolve over time and may be responsive to what happens in society at large. As Thorstein Veblen (1899) recognized, around the time when neoclassical economics was taking shape, human preferences for certain objects often depend on who else is consuming those objects. If a film star wears a brand-name shirt, you may be willing to pay more for that same shirt. If the elite likes a particular wine, then some people will acquire a taste for that wine; moreover, such people will be viewed by others as belonging to the elite because of their taste in wine. In other words, people often use goods to associate themselves with other people who use those goods (Basu, 1989). These are obvious matters (though they were sidelined during the time of Veblen) and any economist whose ability to think is not damaged by excessive textbook education will recognize that these kinds of preference endogeneity exist. What is remarkable about Schumpeter's (1909) essay is that he understood (admittedly in a somewhat inchoate way) that this recognition may cut into the methodological individualism of economics. He observed how, given the human tendency to conform to society, 'there will be a tendency to give [each individual's] utility curves shapes similar to those of other members of the community' (1909, p. 219).

To see how this can ruffle methodological individualism, suppose that each person likes to wear jeans if more than 60 per cent of society wears jeans; more precisely, suppose that, if over 60 per cent of society wears jeans, each person is willing to pay for jeans more than the marginal cost of producing them; otherwise they are willing to pay less. This society will have two possible equilibria: one in which no one wears jeans and another (however revolting it may be to visualize this) in which everyone wears jeans. In models of this kind there is an interdependence between society's behaviour and each individual's preference. Once we recognize this, there is no reason to start our analysis by characterizing the individual. We may still do so through force of habit. But we could equally begin by considering a social behaviour postulate – for instance, that 50 per cent of people wear jeans. Then we work out how much each individual prefers to wear jeans (and so how much each is willing to pay for his or her jeans) and check whether the initial social postulate is sustainable. If it is, then we have found an equilibrium. If not (as in the above example), then the behaviour is not one that will prevail in equilibrium. This method is one of neither methodological individualism nor methodological holism. It is therefore evident that, as economics becomes more sophisticated, it is moving away from pure individualism towards this kind of a hybrid methodology.

Normative statements

An interesting and unexpected area where methodological individualism is violated is in some of our normative statements. We often pass moral judgement on groups of people which cannot be reduced to the individuals in the group. Normative propositions of the following kind are common: 'It is a shame that no one in your university does research on poverty.' If you asked the person making this observation whether he was blaming you for not doing research on poverty, he would typically claim that he was not; in fact, he would deny that he was casting aspersions on *any* individual but criticizing the collectivity of individuals in the university. This amounts to an implicit rejection of individualism.

Methodological individualism in the context of normative statements like the above one has not been much analysed, but Ronald Dworkin has provided an interesting analysis. He argues that in situations of group responsibility it may be reasonable to *personify* the group. Thus, when a corporation produces a dangerously defective good but it is not possible to pin down the responsibility on any particular individual, we may need to treat the corporation as a moral agent and apply 'facsimiles of our principles about individual fault and responsibility to it' (Dworkin, 1986, p. 170). And *then*, by virtue of the *corporation's* responsibility, we may proceed to hold some or all of the individual *members* of the corporation responsible. This is interesting because it comes as close to Watkins's 'methodological holism' as we are likely to encounter anywhere. Individuals are still essential units in Dworkin's analysis but, unlike in standard methodological individualism, judgement of the group *precedes* judgement of the individual.

Dworkin argues that we unwittingly often use this method. This happens when we talk of the state's responsibility for certain kinds of individual rights. Thus we talk of the state's obligation to ensure that no one is assaulted by others. Moreover, we do this even before agreeing on how this responsibility is to be apportioned across various units and agents of the state, such as the police and the bureaucracy. Dworkin (1986, p. 171) points out how we discuss the community's responsibility and 'leave for

separate consideration the different issue of which arrangement of official duties would best acquit the communal responsibility' (emphasis added).

It is possible to criticize Dworkin's line (see Basu, 2000) by arguing that the personification of the corporation or the community has to be an interim construct. It will be sustained if we *can* then apportion the blame among the members of the corporation. If, however, we find that we are not able to spread the blame among the individuals in some reasonable way, then we may have to forgo our initial stand, which held the corporation responsible, or at least maintain that there is no way to take the next step of tracing the fault to individuals.

Interestingly, this brings us back to the kind of analysis defended in the case of endogenous preferences. And this suggests, once again, that what is needed for modern social science is neither holism not individualism but a hybrid methodology that, at least for now, lacks a name.

KAUSHIK BASU

See also **collective rationality; economic man; individualism versus holism; social norms.**

Bibliography

Arrow, K. 1994. Methodological individualism and social knowledge. *American Economic Review* 84, 1–10.

Basu, K. 1989. A theory of association: social status, prices and markets. *Oxford Economic Papers* 41, 653–71.

Basu, K. 2000. *Prelude to Political Economy: A Study of the Social and Political Foundations of Economics*. Oxford: Oxford University Press.

Bhargava, R. 1993. *Individualism in Social Science: Forms and Limits of Methodology*. Oxford: Oxford University Press.

Buchanan, J. 1989. The State of Economic Science. In *The State of Economic Science*, ed. W. Sichel. Kalamazoo, MI: Upjohn Institute for Employment Research.

Dworkin, R. 1986. *Law's Empire*. Cambridge, MA: Harvard University Press.

Elster, J. 1982. Marxism, functionalism and game theory. *Theory and Society* 11, 453–82.

Hayek, F. von. 1942. Scientism and the study of science. *Economica* 9, 267–91.

Menger, C. 1883. *Investigations into the Method of the Social Sciences with Special Reference to Economics*. English translation. New York: New York University Press, 1986.

Roemer, J. 1981. *Analytical Foundations of Marxian Economic Theory*. Cambridge: Cambridge University Press.

Schumpeter, J. 1909. On the concept of social value. *Quarterly Journal of Economics* 23, 213–32.

Smith, A. 1776. *Inquiry into the Nature and Causes of the Wealth of Nations*. Indianapolis: Liberty Classics, 1981.

Veblen, T. 1899. *The Theory of the Leisure Class*. London: Macmillan.

Watkins, J. 1952. The principle of methodological individualism. *British Journal for the Philosophy of Science* 3, 186–89.

Weber, M. 1922. *Economy and Society*, vol. 1. New York: Bedminster Press, 1968.

methodology of economics

Since the 1970s, the methodology of economics has developed from a series of reflections by practising economists on the methods employed in their field, to a field at the boundaries of economics and philosophy (and to a lesser extent sociology). After an initial focus on falsificationism, the range of issues pursued has considerably broadened.

In the social sciences, which include economics, the term 'methodology' is used with two different meanings. When an article or thesis contains a section called 'methodology' in which the author explains how a piece of research was conducted the word is used as a synonym for 'method'. In the literature on 'the methodology of economics', on the other hand, it is used as a label for enquiries into the principles underlying economic reasoning. This article is concerned only with the second of these two meanings.

The methodology of economics is inevitably an interdisciplinary activity. Economists may analyse their own reasoning using ideas drawn from philosophy, sociology, linguistics or discourse analysis, or they can draw simply on their own experience as practising economists. For philosophers, enquiries into economic methodology are part of philosophy – a branch of the philosophy of science or, if the word science is thought inappropriate, of knowledge. Economic methodology is thus largely covered by the article on PHILOSOPHY AND ECONOMICS. The two are, however not synonymous, for the latter covers decision theory, rational choice and ethics, fields not traditionally thought of as economic methodology. That article traces the interrelations between these disciplines from the 19th century to the present. However, though this overlaps with the story of economic methodology, the two are not synonymous.

The explicit study of methodology has always had a mixed reputation within economics. Most of the time, economists simply get on with their work, reflecting on specific methodological problems as and when they arise, refraining from more general speculation. They are suspicious of general theories about how to practise economics (or any other subject for that matter), especially when such theories are written by those who do not themselves engage in the research they are analysing. Against this there are those who believe that methodological reflection by those who are more distant from practice, whether they are trained as economists or philosophers, even if it does not tell economists how to do their work better, can provide a valuable perspective on what economists do that would be otherwise be missed. When it comes to publication, some, even if they find methodological argument valuable, hold that it should not have a place within economics journals as it is not economics, but writing about economics. A further reason for scepticism is that methodological arguments are frequently used by non-economists and heterodox economists to show that certain economic theories cannot possibly be right: it is held that, rather than speculate on methodology, those who believe this would do better if they showed by example, how things could be done better. This attitude has a parallel in divisions within the field of economic methodology between those who believe that the task of methodology is primarily to understand what economists do (a stance that does not imply an absence of criticism, even if the methodologist deliberately refrains from telling economists what to do) and those who use methodological arguments to argue for heterodox positions within economics. These two categories overlap significantly, but this divide nevertheless reflects important tensions within the field.

Historical background

The 19th century was an age when disciplinary boundaries began to be established. Given the extremely high regard in which John Stuart Mill was held by contemporaries, both as a philosopher and as an economist, it would be rash to classify him according to modern disciplinary categories. His *Logic* (1843) was a standard textbook in the philosophy of science and his *Essays on Some Unsettled Questions of Political Economy* (1844) were an influential statement of economic methodology. Methodological arguments among economists were frequent (see, for example, the work collected in Smyth, 1962; Backhouse, 1997) and were primarily by economists using methodological arguments to criticize positions with which they disagreed. Cliffe Leslie and John Elliott Cairnes are good examples. Both established reputations for their work in economics itself, but wrote extensively on methodology, Leslie in a series of essays (1879) and Cairnes in *The Character and Logical Method of Political Economy* (1857). William Stanley Jevons made a methodological case for a particular way of practising economics in his *Theory of Political Economy* (1871) but in addition to being a leading economist was also the author of *The Principles of Science* (1873), a major textbook in the philosophy of science. If anyone should be classified as a professional methodologist in this period, it is John Neville Keynes, author of a textbook in formal logic, but whose *The Scope and Method of Political Economy* (1890) was his major work. Even if some considered it a worthy book, but one that students did not in practice need to bother with, it played a role in establishing the Marshallian consensus within British economics and preventing the methodological dispute between the Carl Menger (1883) and the German Historical School from dividing the British profession in the same way as it divided German-speaking economists. There were methodological disputes over historicism in British economics, but they were nowhere nearly as divisive as the German.

The tradition of economists writing article and occasionally book-length reflections on methodology continued through the 20th century, and was linked to disputes over the direction in which economics should be moving. In the first half of that century, the most influential such work was undoubtedly Lionel Robbins's *An Essay on the Nature and Significance of Economic science* (1932), which helped define modern welfare economics and, more broadly to redefine the subject, though this took much longer than is commonly believed (Backhouse and Medema, 2007). The 1930s saw a profusion of articles and books on methodology, many of which discussed Robbins's *Essay*. However, what we find is a literature that, though containing much that was perceptive, can be seen as a series of comparatively isolated works in which trends are hard to identify.

After the Second World War, this pattern continued, though the literature became more focused, due to the way economic theory was developing. There was also, in the background, the emergence of what came to be known as the 'received view' in the philosophy of science and the work of Karl Popper, though lags in translation meant that this permeated the economic literature only gradually. Several of the leading economists wrote on methodology, their work being given focus, despite their varied perspectives, by their concern with models and the role of assumptions. The most influential work was Milton Friedman's 'The Methodology of Positive Economics' (1953) with its provocative thesis that it was actually desirable for the assumptions of a theory to be unrealistic. Good theories are ones that pick out the relevant features of reality, using a sparse set of assumptions to explain a wide range of phenomena, which means that they must be descriptively unrealistic. Tjalling Koopmans included an essay defending unrealistic models on quite different grounds in his *Three Essays on the State of Economic Science* (1957): unrealistic models should be seen not in isolation but as part of a series of models – they are prototypes of subsequent models that will be more realistic. These, and above all Friedman's essay, provoked a significant literature. The question of testability linked this with issues being discussed in the philosophy of science in a way that was not generally true of the period before the Second World War (an exception was Hutchison, 1938).

Methodology of economics as a field

The emergence of the methodology of economics as a recognizable field within economics, into which this earlier literature could (retrospectively) be incorporated, is best dated to the appearance of Mark Blaug's *The Methodology of Economics* (1980). This was not the first textbook on economic methodology but it served to define a field in a way that previous textbooks (for example, Stewart, 1979) had not. It offered a survey of what economists needed to know about the philosophy of science and a series of case studies in economics. The theme of the book was the importance of falsificationism, as found in the work of Karl Popper and Imre Lakatos. He offered a typically robust conclusion:

> [T]he ultimate question we can and must pose about any research program is the one made familiar by Popper: what events, if they materialized, would lead us to reject that program? A program that cannot meet that question has fallen short of the highest standards that scientific knowledge can attain. (Blaug, 1980, p. 264)

The common practice among economists was what he called 'innocuous falsificationism': to preach falsificationism but not to practise it. The theme of his case studies was that the subject had made progress when economists had sought to test theories, even when such testing had, as in the examples of human capital theory or monetarism, been inconclusive.

Blaug's book was important. His thesis offered a challenge, both to those who felt that there must be reasons why economists approached their subject in ways that, according to Blaug, were fundamentally flawed, and to those who were concerned about the philosophical coherence of falsificationism. This defined a research agenda. His approach to methodology also pointed to ways in which it could be combined with the history of economic thought. Popperian methodology, especially in its Lakatosian variant, with its focus on progress, provided a criterion that could be used to assess the history of economics, an approach already explored in Latsis (1976). For the first time, economic methodology came to be linked with the history of economic thought.

A further stimulus to economic methodology came from heterodox economics. Movements such as radical economics, Post Keynesian economics and Austrian economics, though their proponents might construct longer histories, originated in the late 1960s and early 1970s, and were characterized by methodological critiques of the way they saw economic enquires being undertaken. Their interest in both methodology and the history of economics brought tensions: their interest in the subject was welcomed but this was associated with concerns that their ideological commitments might cause a problem for the field (in his article on HISTORY OF ECONOMIC THOUGHT, Goodwin hints at similar concerns).

The result of this activity was the emergence of an identifiable field of economic methodology, defined not simply by textbooks but by a community of specialists engaging with each other as well as economists and philosophers who chose to explore the subject. This blend of economics and philosophy was reflected in the specialist journals, those publishing articles in English including

Economics and Philosophy (established 1985), *Journal of Economic Methodology* (1994), *Research in the History of Economic Thought and Methodology* (1983), and in anthologies such as Caldwell (1993) or Hausman (1994) (the former contains a useful list of previously anthologized articles). There are also foreign-language journals, of which *Revue de philosophie économique* has begun publication in English. The difference between the *Journal of Economic Methodology* and *Economics and Philosophy* illustrates the point made earlier that, though there is substantial overlap, economic methodology is not synonymous with philosophy and economics.

The emergence of the field of economic methodology was centred on the philosophy of Popper and Lakatos. By 1990, these approaches had ceased to be dominant. Though some (for example, Blaug, Lawrence Boland and Terence Hutchison) continued to defend it, falsificationism was generally seen as too restrictive a criterion against which to appraise economic theories: the methodologies of Popper and Lakatos had technical problems and there were good reasons why economists behaved differently. The most significant problem arises from the fact that theories are almost never testable on their own, creating problems with what it means for a theory to be falsifiable (see FALSIFICATIONISM). Lakatosian methodology raised questions concerning the definition of a research programme and the meaning of novelty (see PARADIGMS). Corroboration seemed more important than either Popper or Lakatos admitted.

The most influential alternative was articulated by Daniel Hausman's *The Inexact and Separate Science of Economics* (1992). Dismissive of Popper and Lakatos, this book opened up other themes, such as ways of thinking about economic models, but its significance was engaging in what Hausman elsewhere summarized as 'empirical philosophy of science'. This involved exploring in detail economists' practices, his main example being the way economists had responded to the phenomenon of preference reversals. Hausman defended the view that economics was, as Mill had expressed it in the mid-19th century, an inexact science, but he was more critical of the motivation, implicit in economists' responses to experimental evidence, to keep their science separate from any dependence on philosophy. This conclusion may, at least in part, have been rendered out of date by the rise of behavioural economics, but its significance lay in the method of starting from economics, drawing out methodological conclusions (as opposed to the method) characteristic of the Popperian era, and of applying the methodology developed in the context of natural science to economics.

The problems involved in defining Lakatosian research programmes were widely considered to render the concept a rather blunt tool for analysing economics. Instead, the trend was towards analysing problems that arose in particular fields of economics. The rise of experimental economics raised new methodological questions about experimental procedures and the transferability of experimental results to behaviour out of the laboratory. Econometric practices raised issues not covered in traditional methodology such as the significance of data mining, the meaning of causality and how measurement of economic quantities should be understood. Disagreements over the relation between macro and microeconomics raised questions about individualism and the meaning of aggregate analysis, many of which were familiar to the philosophy of social science. Economists had come, almost universally, to argue in terms of models, raising the question of what was going on in the process of economic modelling. Postmodernism failed to have anything like the effect that it had in some other social sciences, but some postmodern ideas were explored. Older questions, such as conventionalism, instrumentalism, positivism and falsification, all concerned with questions of theory appraisal, remained, but they received proportionately much less attention.

The methodology of economics today

The methodology of economics has remained a field with very elastic boundaries. There is a substantial literature in which specialists in the field engage with each other, but perhaps more than most fields in economics, it is one where outsiders, who engage in varying degrees with this literature, have much to say. These outsiders include philosophers, economists specializing in other fields and other social scientists. This results in a variety of perspectives, one of the main divides concerning the extent to which writers see methodology as aimed at understanding economists' practices and the extent to which they seek to criticize those practices. Sometimes these aims overlap, but sometimes they do not, those concerned with explication considering that others do not take economics sufficiently seriously, and those concerned with criticism considering that the others are too defensive about what they find within the discipline.

The result is that it has become increasingly difficult to find a framework within which to offer a coherent survey of the field. The most comprehensive recent attempt is Wade Hands's *Reflection without Rules* (2001), which he describes as an 'interpretive survey' of the economic methodology. Part of the difficulty with such a task is, as Hands (2001, p. ix) recognized, that any such survey is aiming at a moving target. That would be true in any field; however, a further difficulty is that much work on methodology cuts across the philosophical categories he employs to structure his survey and hence provide the basis for his interpretation. His starting point (as for Blaug, 1980; Caldwell, 1982), was the breakdown of the received view within the philosophy of science, after which he identified a series of turns – the naturalistic, the sociological, the pragmatic and the economic – as well as attempts to develop the Popperian, Millian and other traditions. From the point of view of elucidating the philosophical foundations of economic methodology, this is a successful strategy. However, this framework does not shed much light on some practice-based methodological work. For example Hoover's (2001a; 2001b) work on macroeconomics and causality could be fitted into its framework but, despite its deep philosophical engagement, it is not clear that it is helpful to do so. The problems with work by reflective practitioners, such as Reder (1999) or Goldfarb (1997), simply does not fit at all.

Economic methodology has become a very active field that tackles a range of questions that is much broader than was the case in, say, 1950. In part this reflects the broadening that has taken place within economics, which has meant that methodologists have faced the challenge of broadening their focus to encompass developments as varied as experimental economics and time-series econometric methods. There has also been a shift away from abstract questions of theory appraisal towards understanding the variety of practices found in economics, the aim being to work out a philosophical framework that is appropriate to economics rather than simply applying one derived from consideration of natural science. Finally, economic methodology has turned not only to philosophy of science, as that term has traditionally been understood, but also to disciplines such as sociology, linguistics and science studies. This plethora of new developments suggests that it may change as much in the next quarter century as it has done in the past.

ROGER E. BACKHOUSE

See also **assumptions controversy; causality in economics and econometrics; conventionalism; data mining; economics, definition of; experimental methods in economics; explanation; falsificationism; Historical School, German; history of economic thought; individualism versus holism; instrumentalism and operationalism; measurement; models; paradigms; philosophy and economics; pluralism in economics; positive economics; positivism; postmodernism; stylized facts; theory appraisal.**

Bibliography

Backhouse, R.E. 1997. *The Methodology of Economics: Nineteenth-Century British Contributions*, 6 vols. London and Bristol: Routledge & Thoemmes Press.

Backhouse, R.E. and Medema, S.G. 2007. Defining economics: Robbins's essay in theory and practice. Working paper. Abstract online. Available at http://ssrn.com/abstract=969994, accessed 19 May 2007.

Blaug, M. 1980. *The Methodology of Economics: How Economists Explain*, 2nd edn. Cambridge: Cambridge University Press, 1992.

Cairnes, J.E. 1857. *The Character and Logical Method of Political Economy*. London: Macmillan, 1888.

Caldwell, B.J. 1982. *Beyond Positivism: Economic Methodology in the Twentieth Century*. London: Allen & Unwin.

Caldwell, B.J. 1993. *The Philosophy and Methodology of Economics*, 3 vols. Cheltenham: Edward Elgar.

Friedman, M. 1953. The methodology of positive economics. In *Essays in Positive Economics*, ed. M. Friedman. Chicago: University of Chicago Press.

Goldfarb, R. 1997. Now you see it, now you don't: emerging contrary results in economics. *Journal of Economic Methodology* 4, 221–44.

Hands, D.W. 2001. *Reflection without Rules: Economic Methodology and Contemporary Science Theory*. Cambridge: Cambridge University Press.

Hausman, D.M. 1992. *The Inexact and Separate Science of Economics*. Cambridge: Cambridge University Press.

Hausman, D.M. 1994. *The Philosophy of Economics: An Anthology*. Cambridge: Cambridge University Press.

Hoover, K.D. 2001a. *The Methodology of Empirical Macroeconomics*. Cambridge: Cambridge University Press.

Hoover, K.D. 2001b. *Causality in Economics*. Cambridge: Cambridge University Press.

Hutchison, T.W. 1938. *The Significance and Basic Postulates of Economic Theory*. London: Macmillan.

Jevons, W.S. 1873. *The Principles of Science: A Treatise on Logic and Scientific Method*, 2nd edn. London: Macmillan, 1877.

Jevons, W.S. 1871. *The Theory of Political Economy*, 2nd edn. London: Macmillan, 1879.

Keynes, J.N. 1890. *The Scope and Method of Political Economy*. London: Macmillan, 1917.

Koopmans, T.C. 1957. *Three Essays on the State of Economic Science*. New York: McGraw Hill.

Latsis, S.J. 1976. *Method and Appraisal in Economics*. Cambridge: Cambridge University Press.

Leslie, T.E.C. 1879. *Essays on Political and Moral Philosophy*. Dublin: Hodges, Foster & Figgis.

Menger, C. 1883. *Investigations into the Method of the Social Sciences with Special Reference to Economics*, tr. F.J Nock. New York: New York University Press, 1985.

Mill, J.S. 1843. *A System of Logic. The Collected Works of John Stuart Mill*, vols 7–8, ed. J.M. Robson. Toronto: University of Toronto Press, 1974.

Mill, J.S. 1844. Essays on Some Unsettled Questions of Political Economy. in *The Collected Works of John Stuart Mill*, vol. 4, ed. J.M. Robson. Toronto: University of Toronto Press, 1967.

Reder, M.W. 1999. *Economics: The Culture of a Controversial Science*. Chicago: University of Chicago Press.

Robbins, L.C. 1932. *An Essay on the Nature and Significance of Economic Science*. London: Macmillan, 1935.

Smyth, R.L. 1962. *Essays in Economic Method: Selected Papers read to Section F of the British Association for the Advancement of Science, 1860– 1913*. London: Duckworth.

Stewart, I. 1979. *Reasoning and Method in Economics*. New York: McGraw Hill.

Metzler, Lloyd Appleton (1913–1980)

Metzler was born in Lost Springs, Kansas and took AB and MBA degrees at the University of Kansas. He was one of a long line of brilliant students that John Ise sent to Harvard, where Metzler arrived in 1937. He served as an instructor and tutor, receiving his Ph.D. in 1942. From 1943 to 1946 he held a number of positions with government agencies in wartime Washington, including the Office of Strategic Services, several economic policy and planning commissions, and, from 1944 to 1946, with the research staff of the Board of Governors of the Federal Reserve System. From 1946 to 1947 he was a member of the economics department of Yale University. In 1947 he joined the department at the University of Chicago, where he remained until his death. His health declined in the early 1950s; removal of a brain tumour in 1952 left him with a markedly reduced energy level. He continued to teach and produced an occasional paper for the next 20 years.

Metzler's *Collected Papers*, most of them written between 1941 and 1951, were published by Harvard University Press in 1973. A Festschrift, *Trade, Stability, and Macroeconomics*, co-edited by his fellow student Paul Samuelson and one of his own students, George Horwich, was published by Academic Press in 1974.

I. Metzler's contribution to the business cycle literature centred on his integration of inventories into a dynamic model of income determination. Employing the income/expenditure multiplier/accelerator framework pioneered by Robertson, Keynes, Hicks, Lundberg, Samuelson and others, Metzler added a rigorous formulation of inventory behaviour against a backdrop of production lags and endogenously determined anticipation of sales.

His initial assumption, supported by his later empirical investigation (1948), was that the response of output to sales receipts was the longest of the three basic lags in the circular flow of income, of which the other two were the lag between the receipt of income and consumption spending and the lag between output and the distribution of earnings to factors of production. Featuring the output/sales lag, his classic study, 'The Nature and Stability of Inventory Cycles' (1941), demonstrated that any disturbance, such as an autonomous increase in investment, tended to produce cycles about the new level of income provided that the marginal propensity to consume is less than unity. The cycles are damped if businesses demand a constant level of inventories and expect sales in the current period to be unchanged at the level of the preceding period. Explosive cycles may occur if anticipated sales change when actual sales change and if firms try to maintain a constant ratio of inventories to anticipated sales.

If inventory demand varies with anticipated sales, a reduction in inventories below desired levels during an expansionary phase of the business cycle raises the demand for inventories and hence reinforces the rise in income and expenditures. The increases gradually taper off, causing a fall in planned inventory investment. Income and sales therefore fall and inventories rise about desired levels. The demand for inventories drops further and reinforces the decline in income. The model thus gives rise to predictions about the relative timing of movements in income, sales, and inventories, and of response coefficients for which the cyclical process will converge to a new equilibrium.

Investigations in the 30 years following the 1941 paper, including several of his own (1946; 1947b; 1973e), tended to support Metzler's initial formulation. The basic model was also enriched by the addition of monetary factors and the rate of interest, the price level, and a disaggregation of inventories into finished goods and goods in process (Zarnowitz, 1985, pp. 541–2).

II. Metzler's contribution to macro-monetary theory came from a single influential paper, 'Wealth, Saving, and the Rate of Interest' (1951b). Metzler wrote in the wake of the great debates between Keynes and his critics (Haberler, 1941; Pigou, 1943; 1947; Scitovszky, 1941), who had invoked a positive relation between real cash balances and expenditures on goods and services as the basis of achieving a stable macro equilibrium. Metzler, taking a broader view of wealth as including both real balances and financial claims to the capital stock, argued that the implied inverse wealth/saving relation introduced a monetary element in the determination of the interest rate. Whereas money was traditionally without any lasting influence on the real side of the 'classical' model, the presence of the wealth/saving relation meant that the exchange of money and securities (the prototype of which is an interest-bearing equity claim) between the central bank and the private sector altered the latter's perceived wealth total and hence its rate of saving and the equilibrium rate of interest.

In Metzler's analysis, an open-market purchase, for example, raises cash balances and removes securities from private portfolios. In the resulting adjustment process, real balances are reduced by the rise of the general price level, but securities are not restored. The consequent net wealth loss stimulates a greater rate of saving and a lower rate of interest in the post-purchase equilibrium.

Most commentators disputed Metzler's claim that in the classical tradition, monetary changes tended not to affect the equilibrium rate of interest (Haberler, 1952, p. 245; Patinkin, 1956, pp. 260–1). On the other hand, the early critics would probably have agreed that Metzler was the first to articulate a specific influence on the interest rate that sprang from open-market operations in a model containing the wealth/saving relation.

Later critics, notably Robert Mundell (1960), questioned the *direction* of that influence on the interest rate. Metzler had been careful to account for the disposition of the earnings on the securities acquired by the central bank in the open-market purchase. In order to prevent private disposable income from falling continuously as these earnings are received by the bank in the future, the fiscal authority is assumed to reduce taxes by an equal amount (Metzler, 1951b, p. 109n). Mundell pointed out that if the taxes reduced are those on capitalizable income, the securities sold to the central bank are exactly replaced by an upward revaluation of remaining privately held securities. The wealth effect of the operations, taking account of the inflation-induced loss of real balances, is a 'wash'. A reduction in taxes on capital, however, also raises the net return to capital and hence the investment demand schedule. In the new equilibrium, the rate of interest is higher.

Metzler (1973d, pp. 354–62) replied that capitalizable federal taxes are at most 30 per cent of total federal taxes. Proportionately, 70 per cent of a tax cut falls on non-capitalizable personal income. Only a small part of the value of securities sold to the bank is thus recovered by any likely tax cut, and the operation's wealth effects remain predominantly as Metzler described them.

David McCord Wright (1952) pointed out that the lower equilibrium interest rate generated by Metzler's open-market purchase will itself promote a more rapid investment rate, offsetting thereby the community's loss of securities and real wealth due to the purchase. Metzler (1952) objected that such an offset fell outside the limited time frame that his analysis and macrotheory generally were properly concerned with.

George Horwich (1962; 1964) argued that offsetting wealth changes due to forced saving tend to characterize the very process by which the new equilibrium interest rate is reached. While Wright saw a long-run wealth offset spurred by the wealth/saving-induced lower rate of interest, Horwich questioned whether the short-run adjustment creating a reduced equilibrium interest rate was viable. His characterization of the adjustment process (influenced by Metzler's account of the securities markets underlying the model) emphasized the equilibrating role of new or flow security supply and demand originating in new investment and saving, respectively. The excess of investment over saving created by the operation is thus, in its financial counterpart, an excess supply of new securities that directly moves the interest rate towards its new equilibrium and funds additional investment spending. If, through forced saving, the excess investment is realized in additional real capital, the excess new securities tend to replace those sold to the bank. The process of reaching any post-operation equilibrium is thus one in which additional security issues and increments of capital stock are necessarily involved and tend, more or less, to maintain the pre-operation level of wealth.

Niehans (1978) questioned Metzler's specification of the capital stock as a determinant of saving, while real balances, which are at desired levels in equilibrium, are not so specified. Both wealth components, Niehans argued (1978, pp. 91–2), should be at desired (optimum)

levels in equilibrium and should not appear in individual demand functions. He saw the main contribution of the 'wealth' article in its elegant formulation of the neo-classical synthesis (see also Haberler, 1952, p. 246 for this viewpoint), in the distinction it made in the differing impacts of the various types of monetary change, and in its broad influence on the methodology employed by the major monetary writers of the next quarter century.

III. At least half of Metzler's papers are related to the field of international trade. He is probably best known for papers on tariff theory, international macro-economics, and the transfer problem, but other work includes a lucid survey (1949a), a discussion of difficulties of applying purchasing power parity in post-Second World War exchange rate realignments (1947a), and a discussion of the views of Frank Graham (1950a).

In tariff theory, Metzler's contribution has largely been summarized in the statement that, in a two-country, two-good world, a tariff can fail to be protective in the sense that it can lead to a reduction in the domestic relative price of the import-competing good. This is the so-called 'Metzler paradox'. It is ironic that Metzler himself described this result as well known, and viewed his own contribution as analyzing the implications for income distribution of such a non-protective tariff (1949b, p. 10). Metzler's papers on this topic were apparently motivated by pronouncements of Australian economists, and the two papers (1949b; 1949c) include discussion of alternative assumptions about expenditure of tariff revenue – by government (non-dutiable) or the private sector (dutiable), with various marginal propensities to consume, and from a zero or non-zero initial tariff. However the cleanest and best-known result comes with zero initial tariff and with tariff revenue implicitly going to the private sector as an increase in disposable income. Metzler shows that the domestic relative price will not change if the elasticity of import demand in the foreign country is equal to 1 minus the marginal propensity to import in the home (tariff-levying) country.

This foregoing result is easily understood by considering the world market for the home importable. The imposition of a trade tax, at constant domestic relative price, will imply a vertical shift of the foreign export supply curve (as in an elementary tax-incidence problem), since foreign export supply is a function of world relative price. If the foreign offer curve is elastic, this implies decreased export supply by the foreign country at the fixed domestic price, but if the foreign offer curve is inelastic (implying that the export supply curve is backward-bending), then the result is increased export supply at a given domestic price. On the demand side, a fixed domestic price implies a lower world relative price of the home importable. Thus the home country is better off, via the improvement in its terms of trade. If the importable is a normal good, the improved real income in the home country implies a rightward shift of the home import demand curve. In a Walrasian-stable market, the domestic price falls if and only if the shifts in home import demand and foreign export supply combine to yield excess supply at the initial domestic price. Metzler's condition is a requirement that the shifts in the two curves exactly offset each other. Thus, if the importable good is normal at home, an inelastic foreign offer curve is necessary, but not sufficient, for the Metzler paradox.

The subsequent literature has enshrined this simplest version of the non-protective tariff (despite at least one attempt to refute the result). It is now understood that, given the normality assumption, the Metzler paradox is inconsistent with the home country levying the so-called optimal tariff; thus the 'paradox' is just one of many possible consequences of a second-best situation (from a myopic national viewpoint).

Another result to bear Metzler's name is the Laursen–Metzler effect, in honour of the joint authors (1950). Laursen and Metzler were concerned with integrating models of flexible exchange rates which focused either on income–expenditure effects or on terms of trade effects, but not on both simultaneously. They posited a channel from devaluation through the terms of trade and onto expenditure; specifically, a deterioration in the terms of trade was assumed to lead to increased expenditure with given nominal income. This was then applied to discussion of the extent of insulation via flexible exchange rates, and of the 'acceptability' of exchange rate changes in certain policy scenarios. The Laursen–Metzler effect has been integrated into the literature, although it was eclipsed in periods where there was extreme emphasis on flexible product prices (thus weakening the link from exchange rate changes to changes in the terms of trade) and although there is some question as to the sign of the effect. In a period of current-account and government-budget imbalances, there has been some emphasis on real intertemporal models of trade. With more sophisticated models of simultaneous intertemporal and intratemporal optimization than were available to Laursen and Metzler, a deeper understanding of the link between intratemporal terms of trade and current expenditure is now possible.

Many of Metzler's international papers involved the transfer problem; see Metzler (1942; 1951a; 1951c; 1973b; 1973c). Metzler's focus was on endogenous income and expenditure effects, holding prices and interest rates fixed. In later papers, the analysis is tied to Metzler's contributions to the applications of matrix theory to economics. In the transfer problem, since the initial transfer is a pure redistribution, the analytic question concerns what changes in endogenous variables are required to re-establish equilibrium. The pure trade literature has emphasized the endogenous adjustment of the terms of trade in real, flexible-price models – including a somewhat incestuous literature, mainly involving Samuelson and Jones, on the likelihood of orthodox or anti-orthodox bias. More recently, the

possibility of 'paradox' in a multi-country setting has been the central topic. Metzler's assumption of constant prices led to analysis of the impact on trade balances and income at home and abroad, with discussion of the role of stability conditions nationally and globally and of the relevant roles for alternative income concepts in the presence of imported inputs for production. Chapter 4 of the *Collected Papers* (1973c) comes closest to linking up to the orthodox theory. While Metzler was one of many contributors to the transfer literature, his strong Keynesian perspective may have limited the long-term importance of his contribution more on this topic than on those mentioned earlier.

IV. In the field of mathematical economics, Metzler has been honoured by having a matrix named after him. The central paper is perhaps Metzler (1945), but see also Metzler (1950b; 1951a; 1951c). The Metzler matrix is a square matrix with positive diagonal elements, negative off-diagonal elements, positive principal minors and determinant, and a positive inverse matrix. Metzler investigated this class of matrices in the context of market stability (1945) and comparative statics (1950b). The stability analysis linked the Hicksian concept of market stability, which can be interpreted as essentially static, and Samuelson's explicitly dynamic approach to stability.

Metzler showed that if multiple markets are stable for any (relative) speeds of adjustment, then they must satisfy Hicks's concept of perfect stability. Perfect stability says that a fall in price in any single market creates excess demand in that market – after any subset of other prices is adjusted to clear the 'own' markets – and all other prices are held fixed. Metzler's proof revolved about the alternating sign of principal minors of a matrix of partial derivatives of excess demands with respect to prices, the negative of this matrix leading to a Metzler matrix. Metzler also showed, by counterexample, that Hicksian perfect stability does not imply Samuelsonian dynamic stability. Another Metzler result showed that in the presence of gross substitutability, dynamic stability and perfect stability are equivalent. Gross substitutability guarantees that the matrix of partial derivatives has negative diagonal terms and positive off-diagonal terms, so that its negative has the sign pattern of a Metzler matrix. The intuition of the gross substitute case is that the impact of a change in 'own price' on excess demand for a good exceeds the aggregate impact of all 'other price' changes; thus, in a sense, the system generalizes the intuition of single-market stability analysis. While cross-effects can exist, the own effects dominate in each market. Metzler applied this theory to the comparative statics of fixed-coefficient regional models, multi-country income transfers, and taxes and subsidies in fixed-coefficient models. As is better understood after integrative work on matrices with dominant diagonals (McKenzie, 1960) and on P-matrices (Gale and Nikaido, 1965), strong results in 'square' – that is, $n \times n$ systems –

usually require strong assumptions closely related to the existence of appropriate Metzler matrices. While there were many other contributors in this area, for example Hawkins and Simon, and while the majority of key results were already known to mathematicians, Metzler's work provided a crucial synthesis of stability literature and an important step in the evolution of matrix theory as applied in economics.

GEORGE HORWICH, JOHN POMERY

Selected works

1941. The nature and stability of inventory cycles. *Review of Economics and Statistics* 23(3), 113–29.

1942. The transfer problem reconsidered. *Journal of Political Economy* 50, 397–414.

1945. Stability of multiple markets: the Hicks conditions. *Econometrica* 13(4), 277–92.

1946. Business cycles and the theory of employment. *American Economic Review* 36, 278–91.

1947a. Exchange rates and the International Monetary Fund. In *International Monetary Policies*, Postwar Economic Studies No. 7., ed. L.A. Metzler, R. Triffin and G. Haberler. Washington, DC: Board of Governors of the Federal Reserve System.

1947b. Factors governing the length of inventory cycles. *Review of Economics and Statistics* 29(1), 1–15.

1948. Three lags in the circular flow of income. In *Income, Employment, and Public Policy: Essays in Honor of Alvin H. Hansen*, ed. L.A. Metzler. New York: W.W. Norton.

1949a. The theory of international trade. In *A Survey of Contemporary Economics*, ed. H.S. Ellis. Philadelphia: Blakiston.

1949b. Tariffs, the terms of trade, and the distribution of national income, *Journal of Political Economy* 57, 1–29.

1949c. Tariffs, international demand, and domestic prices. *Journal of Political Economy* 57, 345–51.

1950a. Graham's theory of international values. *American Economic Review* 40, 301–22.

1950b. A multiple-region theory of income and trade. *Econometrica*18(4), 329–54.

1950. (With S. Laursen.) Flexible exchange rates and the theory of employment. *Review of Economics and Statistics* 32(4), 281–99.

1951a. A multiple-country theory of income transfers. *Journal of Political Economy* 59, 14–29.

1951b. Wealth, saving, and the rate of interest. *Journal of Political Economy* 59, 93–116.

1951c. Taxes and subsidies in Leontief's input–output model. *Quarterly Journal of Economics* 65, 433–38.

1952. A reply. *Journal of Political Economy* 60, 249–52.

1973a. *Collected Papers*. Cambridge, MA: Harvard University Press.

1973b. Imported raw materials, the transfer problem, and the concepts of income. In Metzler (1973a).

1973c. Flexible exchange rates, the transfer problem, and the balance-budget theorem. In Metzler (1973a).

1973d. The structure of taxes, open-market operations, and the rate of interest. In Metzler (1973a).

1973e. Partial adjustment and the stability of inventory cycles. In Metzler (1973a).

Bibliography

Gale, D. and Nikaido, H. 1965. The Jacobian matrix and the global univalence of mappings. *Mathematische Annalen* 159(2), 81–93.

Haberler, G. 1941. *Prosperity and Depression*. 3rd edn. Geneva: League of Nations.

Haberler, G. 1952. The Pigou effect once more. *Journal of Political Economy* 60, 240–6.

Horwich, G. 1962. Real assets and the theory of interest. *Journal of Political Economy* 70, 157–69.

Horwich, G. 1964. *Money, Capital, and Prices*. Homewood, IL: R.D. Irwin.

Horwich, G. and Samuelson, P.A., eds. 1974. *Trade, Stability, and Macroeconomics: Essays in Honor of Lloyd A. Metzler*. New York: Academic Press.

McKenzie, L. 1960. Matrices with dominant diagonals and economic theory. In *Mathematical Methods in the Social Sciences 1959*, ed. K.J. Arrow, S. Karlin and P. Suppes. Stanford: Stanford University Press.

Mundell, R.A. 1960. The public debt, corporate income taxes, and the rate of interest. *Journal of Political Economy* 68, 622–26.

Niehans, J. 1978. Metzler, wealth, and macroeconomics: a review. *Journal of Economic Literature* 16, 84–95.

Patinkin, D. 1956. *Money, Interest and Prices: An Integration of Monetary and Value Theory*. Evanston: Row, Peterson.

Pigou, A.C. 1943. The classical stationary state. *Economic Journal* 53, 343–51.

Pigou, A.C. 1947. Economic progress in a stable environment. *Economica*, NS 14(55), 180–8.

Scitovszky, T. 1941. Capital accumulation, employment, and price rigidity. *Review of Economic Studies* 8(2), 69–88.

Wright, D.M. 1952. Professor Metzler and the rate of interest. *Journal of Political Economy* 60, 247–9.

Zarnowitz, V. 1985. Recent work on business cycles in historical perspective: a review of theories and evidence. *Journal of Economic Literature* 23, 523–80.

micro-credit

Micro-credit encompasses a broad movement to supply professional banking services to poor households; micro-credit innovations offer new insights into the economics of information and new mechanisms for reducing poverty.

Karl Marx (1867) famously tied inequality in access to capital to broader social and economic inequalities driven by markets; micro-credit presents the promise that market mechanisms may instead help to broaden capital access.

The economics of information shows why poor customers are usually shunned by commercial lenders.

Customers typically lack the assets and ownership documents that banks require as collateral, and banks lack cost-effective ways to monitor and enforce contracts. Theorists demonstrate how credit rationing can emerge in these contexts, with adverse selection and moral hazard as culprits. The challenge for banks is exacerbated by the small size of transactions. The *MicroBanking Bulletin*'s (2006) survey of 302 leading micro-credit institutions, for example, found that the average loan balance was 436 dollars for the median 'micro-bank'. For the median micro-bank focusing on poorer customers, the average loan balance was just 109 dollars. These amounts tend to fall below the threshold of interest for large commercial banks, even in low-income economies. Hence the poor lose twice: they begin with less income and fewer assets than others, and, as a result, they have worse access to the financial institutions that might offer a route away from poverty. To this extent, poverty reinforces poverty.

Micro-credit is part of an approach that aims to undo this equation. Despite the challenges, providers of micro-credit aim to deliver reliable and reasonably priced financial services to the under-served, and most institutions aim to do so without ongoing subsidies. While loans are relatively small, advocates argue that the funds are sufficient to finance small businesses and cover emergency consumption needs – and thus to contribute meaningfully to poverty reduction.

Early micro-credit successes were realized in Bangladesh, Indonesia and Bolivia, gaining global attention in the 1980s. By the end of 2005, one annual survey counted over 3,000 institutions, collectively serving 113 million customers worldwide (Daley-Harris, 2006). Of these, 82 million customers were classified as being among the 'poorest', and 84 per cent of those were women. Rough estimates place unmet demand at over one billion people. The 2006 Nobel Peace Prize to Muhammad Yunus and the Grameen Bank of Bangladesh recognized the potential of micro-credit to reduce global poverty, though Yunus's boldest claims about the potential scale and impact of micro-credit remain untested with reliable data.

The *MicroBanking Bulletin* (2006) survey shows both the promise and the challenges of micro-credit. The survey, which is skewed towards institutions with strong commitments to financial self-sufficiency, finds that 69 per cent of the 302 institutions were earning profits in 2004, and just two per cent of loan portfolios were deemed 'at risk' as a result of loan payments left unpaid beyond 30 days. Real interest rates on loans average about 25–35 per cent per year in the survey, though some top 90 per cent per year.

The encouragement of profit and the tolerance of relatively high interest rates are central to the logic of micro-credit policy. Escaping reliance on subsidy, it has been argued, allows institutions to expand beyond the constraints imposed by donors' purses, creating the prospect of a truly global market-based industry. Despite innovations, though, institutions focused on the poorest customers face stiff challenges in generating profits. The *MicroBanking Bulletin* (2006) survey shows that the median micro-bank serving the poorest customers faces almost twice the cost of lending (per unit of assets) compared with the median micro-bank serving better-off (but still low-income) customers. The extent of trade-offs between meeting profit targets and achieving social objectives remains largely unexplored, as does the nature of productivity-enhancing roles for subsidy (Armendáriz de Aghion and Morduch, 2005, ch. 9).

Group lending

The high rates of loan repayment are attributed to innovative loan contracts, most notably the 'group lending' contract. The group approach is associated with the Grameen Bank, although it has been employed more faithfully by others. The Grameen approach begins with the bank entering a village and inviting villagers to form themselves into five-person groups. A cluster of groups is then formed into a centre that meets once a week in the village, where all business is transacted by a loan officer from the bank. Loans are given to individuals, but the group is deployed to improve incentives and provide a support network. As long as all loans are repaid on time, loans continue to be made to group members, but if any group member cannot repay his or her loan (and the four others cannot fix the problem themselves), the entire group is excluded from future borrowing. This element of the contract is often referred to as creating 'joint liability' – even though, in the Grameen model at least, individuals are not explicitly liable for the repayment of fellow group members.

The contract addresses moral hazard by giving borrowers incentives to monitor each other and to sanction members whose lack of effort jeopardizes loan repayments. The customers often have advantages in these activities, which stem from living and working alongside each other and from being able to employ 'social' sanctions that the bank cannot use. The contracts may also foster mutual support mechanisms that provide insurance and other assistance, a point stressed by Muhammad Yunus, Grameen's founder. Early theoretical analyses on moral hazard in group lending include Stiglitz (1990), while Besley and Coate (1995) raise the possibility of collusive behaviour by borrowers.

The contracts, in principle, can also address adverse selection (and the inefficiencies created by the withdrawal of safer borrowers in markets with asymmetric information; Stiglitz and Weiss, 1981). Adverse selection in credit markets arises because banks cannot distinguish between potential customers who are likely to reliably repay loans and those that will not. Without such information, the bank must charge all customers the same interest rate, and the safer borrowers implicitly subsidize the riskier ones.

In principle, the process of group formation can improve outcomes by screening risky borrowers and matching safer individuals with other relatively safe individuals. Because the effective cost of the loan depends in part on the probability that one's fellow group members will default, safer individuals will then face lower effective borrowing costs than riskier individuals – even when all individuals face identical nominal contracts; the contract combined with the sorting process reduces the extent of cross-subsidization and thus adverse selection (Ghatak, 1999; see also references in Armendáriz de Aghion and Morduch, 2005, ch. 3). This mechanism has received little empirical verification, though, and in practice lenders devote substantial resources to information acquisition.

Beyond group lending

The use of groups has clear attractions but has proved cumbersome when customers have diverse needs and growth prospects. It also relies on the willingness and ability of customers to carry out monitoring and enforcement tasks that are usually the responsibility of bankers. Rai and Sjöström (2004) point to inefficiencies in group lending that can be mitigated through simple information revelation mechanisms, and, as noted above, collusion remains a theoretical possibility. A push to move beyond group lending with joint liability reached an important milestone in practice when two early pioneers, BancoSol of Bolivia and the Grameen Bank, independently abandoned group lending with joint liability as the basis of their operations.

The move beyond group lending highlights other contract innovations that have been overshadowed. Among the most important is the repayment schedule. In Grameen Bank loan contracts, for example, loans are repaid in small increments weekly over the course of several months to a year. It is an odd structure for loans that are ostensibly for business investments that may take time to bear fruit. The schedule, though, allows households to repay loans from other income sources in small, manageable increments. In this way, loans can often be repaid even if businesses fail. Perhaps more important, the structure allows households to easily use loans to finance consumption, strengthening the ability to cope with health crises, pay school fees and keep food on the table. The extent to which such 'diversion' occurs, and its costs and benefits, has yet to receive much research attention, but it may hold a key to new directions for micro-credit.

A second important mechanism is the use of long-term lending relationships. Lenders gain information and instill incentives for loan repayment by repeatedly interacting with customers, allowing borrowers to start with small loans and become eligible for steadily larger loans with each successful cycle.

From micro-credit to 'micro-finance'

Most of the evidence in favour of micro-credit is anecdotal, though rigorous empirical studies are accumulating

(Armendáriz de Aghion and Morduch, 2005, ch. 8). In data from Mexico, for example, McKenzie and Woodruff (2006) find returns to capital of above 20 per cent per month for small-scale businesses with capital stocks below 200 dollars. As capital stocks rise above 400 dollars, estimated returns to capital fall to around five per cent per month. These returns are still substantial and help to explain the ability to pay relatively high interest rates.

The returns pose a puzzle, though. There are no signs of poverty traps, and if returns are so high, why have households been unable to save more on their own, overcoming credit gaps through self-finance? With the realization that customers indeed seek better ways to save and insure (and seek credit for a wide range of uses), micro-banks have started expanding their services. The next wave of innovations focuses there, and draws in part on insights from behavioural economics (for example, Ashraf, Karlan, and Yin, 2006). The focus will thus continue to shift from 'micro-credit' to 'micro-finance' more broadly.

JONATHAN MORDUCH

See also **adverse selection; credit rationing; development economics; moral hazard; poverty alleviation programmes; poverty traps.**

Bibliography

Armendáriz de Aghion, B. and Morduch, J. 2005. *The Economics of Microfinance*. Cambridge, MA: MIT Press.

Ashraf, N., Karlan, D. and Yin, W. 2006. Tying Odysseus to the mast: evidence from a commitment savings product in the Philippines. *Quarterly Journal of Economics* 121, 635–72.

Beck, T., Demirguc-Kunt, A. and Martinez Peria, M.S. 2006. Banking services for everyone? Barriers to bank access and use around the world. World Bank Policy Research Working Paper 4079. Washington, DC: World Bank.

Besley, T. and Coate, S. 1995. Group lending, repayment incentives, and social collateral. *Journal of Development Economics* 46, 1–18.

Daley-Harris, S. 2006. *State of the Microcredit Summit Campaign Report 2006*. Washington, DC: Microcredit Summit.

Ghatak, M. 1999. Group lending, local information and peer selection. *Journal of Development Economics* 60, 27–50.

Marx, K. 1867. *Capital*, vol. 1, tr. Ben Fowkes. Harmondsworth: Penguin, 1990.

McKenzie, D. and Woodruff, C. 2006. Do entry costs provide an empirical basis for poverty traps? Evidence from Mexican microenterprises. *Economic Development and Cultural Change* 55, 3–42.

Microbanking Bulletin 12. 2006. Washington, DC: Microfinance Information Exchange.

Rai, A. and Sjöström, T. 2004. Is Grameen lending effcient? Repayment incentives and insurance in village economies. *Review of Economic Studies* 71, 217–34.

Stiglitz, J. 1990. Peer monitoring and credit markets. *World Bank Economic Review* 4, 351–66.

Stiglitz, J. and Weiss, A. 1981. Credit markets with imperfect information. *American Economic Review* 71, 393–410.

microfoundations

The quest to understand microfoundations is an effort to understand aggregate economic phenomena in terms of the behaviour of individual economic entities and their interactions. These interactions can involve both market and non-market interactions. The quest for microfoundations grew out of the widely felt, but rarely explicitly stated, desire to stick to the position of methodological individualism (see Agassi, 1960; 1975; Brodbeck, 1958), and also out of the growing uneasiness among economists in the late 1950s and 1960s with the coexistence of two sub-disciplines – namely, microeconomics and macroeconomics – both aiming to explain features of the economy as a whole. Methodological individualism is the view that proper explanations in the social sciences are those that are grounded in individual motivations and their behaviour. The urge to make microeconomics and macro-economics compatible can be understood from the perspective of the unity-of-science discussion initiated by the Vienna Circle in the philosophy of science in the beginning of the 20th century (see Nelson, 1984).

Efforts to understand microfoundations go far beyond the questions that lie at the heart of formal aggregation theory, that is, the analysis of how to map aggregate economic variables and relationships back to similar individual variables and relationships that underlie them. One crucial issue in the microfoundations literature is the extent to which aggregate economic variables and/or relationships exhibit features that are similar to the features of individual variables and/or relationships, and in particular whether certain features are emergent properties at the macro level that do not have a natural counterpart at the individual level. An important early example of emergence is Schelling's analysis (1978) of segregation. He shows that segregation in neighbourhoods may be an emergent property at the micro level that can be viewed as an unintended consequence of the individual decisions concerning where to live.

The discussion on emergence shows that there is no reason to assume or expect macro behaviour to be in any way similar or analogous to the behaviour of individual units. In order to have 'proper' microfoundations in line with methodological individualism, it is thus by no means required that aggregate outcomes are represented as if they were the outcome of a single agent's decision problem. On the contrary, the restriction to single individual decision problems found in modern macroeconomics is self-imposed and not implied by the methodological position of methodological individualism (see Kirman, 1989). In fact, one may argue that the interaction between different, and possibly heterogeneous, individual units should be at the core of macroeconomic analysis.

As the quest for 'proper' microfoundations has arisen in the debate concerning the microfoundations for macroeconomics, this article's main focus is on this debate. The article starts with a historical perspective on this debate and continues to discuss New Classical and New Keynesian approaches to macroeconomics that emerged out of the microfoundations debate. The role of equilibrium notions and expectations is discussed in a separate section. The article argues that the microfoundations for macroeconomics literature is best understood from the perspective of attempting to make microeconomics and macroeconomics compatible with each other. The article closes with a discussion of non-mainstream approaches to microfoundations and more recent approaches to microfoundations using the perspective of evolutionary forces and boundedly rational behaviour.

Historical background to the microfoundations for macroeconomics debate

Around the mid-1950s two more or less separate approaches existed to studying economy-wide phenomena: general equilibrium theory and (Keynesian) macroeconomics. Some of the more important theoretical issues within each of these approaches were settled. Existence of a general equilibrium point was proved by Arrow and Debreu (1954) and the macroeconomic IS–LM framework was well established (following the seminal paper by Hicks, 1937). Of course, some other issues were still to be tackled, such as questions related to how to deal with imperfect competition, incomplete markets and/or overlapping generations.

Both approaches explained economy-wide phenomena, but there were important differences between the perspectives from which they started. Flexible prices and market-clearing were at the core of general equilibrium theory; involuntary unemployment and effective demand were important concepts in macroeconomics. The neoclassical synthesis reconciled general equilibrium theory and (Keynesian) macroeconomics by giving each of them its own domain of applicability: macroeconomics (with its assumption of sticky money wages) gives an accurate description of the economy in the short run, while long-run developments of the economy were considered to be adequately described by the general equilibrium approach.

From a theoretical point of view this state of affairs was unsatisfactory. One cannot simply attribute unemployment to sticky money wages while leaving the theoretical structure of general equilibrium theory intact: the imposition of a fixed money wage (or, more generally, fixed prices) deeply affects the theory of supply and demand. It was natural, then, to inquire into the relationship between the two approaches, especially given that they study the same phenomena. In addition, the generally accepted view was that it is the market interaction between many individual agents from which economy-wide phenomena result, implying that general equilibrium theory is the more fundamental theory of the two. The quest for microfoundations was born.

The rise of interest in microfoundations can also be at least party conceived as being driven by the perceived failings of important elements of empirical macroeconomics and in particular the fact that the Phillips curve turned out to be not a stable relationship that can be used for economic policy purposes (see, for example, Friedman, 1968). Several essays in Phelps (1970) are written to reconcile microeconomic theory with the apparent temporary trade-off between wages and unemployment embodied in the new interpretation of the Phillips curve.

New Classical and New Keynesian economics

One key controversy in the quest for microfoundations is how to explain the widely observed phenomenon of unemployment. From a market-clearing perspective, unemployment simply means that at the current (real) wage rate people do not want to supply more labour to the market. If there is registered unemployment, it is thus either of a 'voluntary' nature or a short-run phenomenon that quickly disappears. In this vein, Lucas (1978, p. 354) argued that involuntary unemployment is not a fact that needs to be explained, but rather a theoretical construct Keynes introduced in the hope it would be helpful in explaining fluctuations in measured unemployment.

In line with these ideas, New Classical economists have attempted to reconcile macroeconomic phenomena such as inflation and unemployment, and the empirical observed trade-off between the two measured by the Phillips curve, with a Walrasian notion of market clearing. Early models, such as Lucas and Rapping (1969) and Lucas (1972), stressed the idea that incomplete information about the money supply may cause business fluctuations. Later real business cycle models (such as that of Kydland and Prescott, 1982) looked at technology shocks to explain cyclical behaviour. Thus, an important difference between the Lucas–Rapping approach and early real business cycle models is that the former, but not the latter, introduces frictions to explain business cycles. With these New Classical models, the concept of the representative agent (consumer, firm or producer/consumer agent) became widely used in modern macroeconomics. In its most extreme form, the economy as a whole is represented as if it were the outcome of a single individual's decision problem. The possible differences between individual and aggregate economic behaviour are thereby assumed away.

Economists who were oriented towards Keynesian ideas thought that there is an involuntary, non-transient component in observed unemployment figures. Many New Keynesian contributions therefore try to reconcile

the notion of involuntary unemployment with a notion of market equilibrium.

A first approach considers the question how to incorporate the notion of price stickiness, especially concerning money wages into the traditional theory of demand and supply. This issue was first studied by Clower (1965). He emphasized that, because of the interdependence of markets, demand and supply curves on all markets are affected if money wages are fixed. If prices are restrained from bringing about market clearing allocations, then other variables have to bring about some kind of fixed-price equilibrium. Clower (1965) and Leijonhufvud (1968) set out a research programme studying the existence of fixed-price equilibria and their properties. The resulting equilibrium notion and the properties of such fixprice equilibria were formulated by Barro and Grossman (1971), Drèze (1975) and Benassy (1975), among others. The idea of this literature is that agents express their demands on the basis of market prices and perceived quantity constraints. These models have microfoundations in the sense that they are based on decision-making individuals and a notion of equilibrium. Moreover, it turned out that the fixprice models capture quite a number of ideas associated with Keynesian economics. By means of these alternative equilibrium notions, involuntary unemployment could be regarded as an equilibrium phenomenon in which optimizing households face a quantity constraint on the amount of labour they can supply. Also, the Keynesian notions of effective demand and the multiplier were reformulated within the new models. Finally, the models provided arguments for demand policies by the government. Of course, from a market-clearing perspective, these fixprice models are unsatisfactory as they do not explain why (rational) individuals do not propose changes to the terms of trade at which they exchange. Clearly, if prices are fixed at no market clearing levels, some agents in the economy can mutually benefit by exchanging at different prices, and therefore have an incentive to propose changes in prices. A literature on small menu cost appeared arguing that introducing a very small cost for economic agents to change prices may result in large fluctuations in aggregate output (see Mankiw, 1985).

Another approach New Keynesian economists followed is to incorporate the literature on imperfect competition into macroeconomic models. Hart (1982), Blanchard and Kiyotaki (1987), Kiyotaki (1988) and d'Aspremont, Dos Santos Ferreira and Gérard-Varet (1990) are among the pioneering articles in this area. These models can explain why aggregate output is below the optimal full employment output level. Unemployment can be involuntary when there is imperfect competition in the labour market.

A third approach to explaining non-competitive wages is to introduce some type of informational problem, as in the literature on efficiency wages. The basic idea of this literature is that the average labour productivity is positively related to the wage a firm offers. Firms may set wages above the competitive level in order to induce employees to work harder, and therefore may be unwilling to lower their wage offers (see Yellen, 1984; Lindbeck and Snower, 1987).

Yet another approach relies on coordination failures formally analysed in terms of multiple equilibria (see Bryant, 1983; Roberts, 1987). Cooper and John (1988) point out that many New Keynesian models are based on strategic complementarities between agents' actions, that is, these models do not rely on an assumption that prices cannot adjust to their market equilibrium values. When strategic complementarity exists, there may be multiple equilibria that can be Pareto-ranked. Agents may then find themselves in a 'bad' equilibrium, but individually they cannot benefit by deviating to another choice. The authors call this a 'coordination failure'.

There is a parallel between the coordination failures literature and the overlapping generations general equilibrium literature (see, for example, Geanakoplos and Polemarchakis, 1986). The latter literature views the economy as a process without definite end, such that what happens today is underdetermined as it depends on what people expect to happen tomorrow, which in turn depends on what people expect to happen the day after tomorrow, and so on. In such a world there is a continuum of equilibria. Geanakoplos and Polemarchakis (1986) show that, depending on how this indeterminacy is solved, that is, which variables are chosen to be exogenously determined, classical or Keynesian-oriented conclusions may be derived.

Work on all these different models has resulted in a shared methodology of how to go about building macroeconomic models. The traditional distinction in macroeconomics between Keynesian and classical economists is disappearing and a common methodology is surfacing. Economists share the understanding that the ultimate question that matters is how well markets function. The differences in importance attached to various market frictions are more a matter of degree than of fundamental divergence between different methodologies. The nature of what used to be macroeconomic theory has undergone dramatic changes alongside these developments. Traditional macroeconomic issues such as how to explain the business cycle or how to account for inflation are now studied with the same tools and techniques as those that are used in microeconomics. Along these lines, and by using the assumption of the representative agent, modern macroeconomics has assumed away the heterogeneity that may exist at the individual level. Lucas's prediction that we may soon simply speak of economic theory instead of separate microeconomic and macroeconomic theories has turned out to be fairly accurate (see Lucas, 1987, pp. 107–8). Somewhat paradoxically, one may say that the modern economist who still is a 'hard line microeconomist' is now called a macroeconomist.

Rationality, equilibrium and expectations

The efforts to create microfoundations for macroeconomics have resulted in a more unified approach to doing economic theory. The approaches discussed so far (also Keynesian-oriented models) all postulate rational behaviour on the part of economic agents and some notion of equilibrium. If expectations are important, it is postulated that agents' expectations concerning important variables coincide with the model's predicted values concerning these same variables. This assumption concerning agents' expectations have been termed 'rational expectations' (see Muth, 1961).

Parallel to the microfoundations literature, a literature questioning the eductive justifications for the notions of equilibrium and rational expectations emerged. This literature on the foundations of game theory basically argued that, if we assume that agents (players) are rational and that their rationality and the model (game) in which they operate are common knowledge, then it is not implied that these agents will play according to an equilibrium of the game. Fundamental papers in this respect are Bernheim (1984) and Pearce (1984), among others. These and other papers show that a much weaker notion, named (correlated) rationalizability, can be derived from assumptions regarding common knowledge of the rationality of players.

On the basis of this literature, Guesnerie (1992) argues that rational expectations should be regarded as an equilibrium notion that is also not solely based on postulates regarding the rational behaviour of individual players. It is rational for individual players to have 'rational expectations' if other players have these very same 'rational expectations', but not necessarily otherwise. As the notion of rational expectations is essentially an equilibrium or consistency notion, it suffers from the same drawbacks in that it is not implied by the individual rationality assumptions that players will form rational expectations.

Another literature (see, for example, Bray and Savin, 1986, and several essays in Frydman and Phelps, 1983) studies the question whether in a decentralized economy economic agents may learn over time to have expectations that are consistent with those that are assumed by the rational expectations hypothesis. The general conclusion of this literature is that, due to the feedback from expectations to economic behaviour, the outcomes of an economic model with learning agents do not converge to the rational expectations solution.

It then follows that the microfoundations literature mentioned so far has not really succeeded in deriving all macroeconomic propositions from fundamental hypotheses on the behaviour of individual agents. The requirements of methodological individualism have thus not been satisfied by the microfoundations literature, which has predominantly presumed that individuals behave rationally (see Janssen, 1993).

Non-mainstream approaches to the microfoundations of macroeconomics

Apart from a long-lasting debate in the mainstream literature, the term 'microfoundations' has also stimulated work by other economists, and they have publicized their views on the relation between microeconomics and macroeconomics. Horwitz (2000) provides an overview of the Austrian perspective where individual knowledge, prices as conveyers of information, and subjective evaluations play important roles. The essays in Hayek (1948) and his views on spontaneous order are especially important in this respect. It may seem, then, that macroeconomics is not an important term in the Austrian vocabulary. However, this is only partly true. From an Austrian perspective an important question is what kind of monetary system will most likely preserve the communicative function of prices. Austrian economists have, as Horwitz shows, addressed such issues in a way that is compatible with methodological individualism.

A post-Keynesian view of the economy holds that long-term expectations are largely determined by non-economic processes such as those determined by mass psychology. These expectations therefore should be regarded as exogenous to the economic model, rather than as endogenously determined as in the case of rational expectations. Interestingly, this post-Keynesian view comes close to the result that is established by Geanakoplos and Polemarchakis (1986) in their overlapping generations general equilibrium model, where they show that indeterminacy of equilibria implies that expectations concerning future market outcomes may be chosen exogenously. Important investment decisions are, according to post-Keynesian economists, by their nature long-term decisions, and these decisions are thus largely determined by the state of these long-term expectations. This fundamental uncertainty requires a different decision-theoretic approach from what is typically used by mainstream economics. Informally, some post-Keynesians have argued for the irreducibility of macroeconomic issues to purely microeconomic considerations where individuals' actions are based on expected utility calculations (see Weintraub, 1979).

Alternative types of microfoundations

Most of the literature up to the 1990s discussing the microfoundations of macroeconomics has focused on rationally behaving self-interested economic agents. More recently, attention has shifted to other forms of behaviour. Using evolutionary mechanisms or learning, economists have studied the evolutionary foundations of equilibrium notions (see Kandori, Mailath and Rob, 1993; Young, 1993). Allowing agents to imitate best practices they observe around them, or choosing best replies to some adaptively formed expectations of what others will do, the literature shows that under some conditions concerning the dynamic process the economy will converge to equilibrium play. Early work in this direction by Schelling (1978) shows, as noted in the introduction to this article, that macro phenomena such as racial segregation may be regarded as the unintended long-run outcome of the interactive effects of decisions of individual households to move into other neighbourhoods.

Alternatively, economists such as Fehr and Falk (1999) have looked at the consequences of non-selfish preferences for macroeconomic outcomes. They consider preferences for fairness and reciprocity to be important in explaining why managers do not consider cutting employees' wages. Wage cuts may be perceived as unfair and hostile, and managers fear that they will be followed by hostile actions on the part of employees. This literature provides an alternative foundation for the downward rigidity of monetary wages, and may start a literature on behavioural macroeconomics.

Conclusions

The microfoundations literature has brought about many changes in economic theory. Macroeconomic theory in the form of studies of the interplay of a few aggregate relationships is almost non-existent nowadays. Instead, an extreme form of 'microfoundations' is sometimes used in which the economy as a whole is represented in terms of a single agent decision problem. In this way, emergent properties appearing at the macro level that do not exist at the individual level are precluded from the analysis as the micro and macro level simply coincide!

Along with the many other models in the microfoundations literature reviewed in this article, we now see a wide spectrum of partly overlapping models dealing with different types of market frictions and market imperfections. Most of the literature before the 1990s adopts fairly traditional assumptions concerning individual behaviour. More recent contributions in the area of behavioural economics and evolutionary models with (adaptively) learning individuals are starting to explore the implications of different behavioural assumptions at the individual level and to consider the macro implications. These models have the potential to analyse how macro phenomena may emerge from the interactions among a heterogeneous set of individuals. Thereby, they may provide economic theory with a more plausible empirical underpinning, while sticking to the requirements of methodological individualism.

MAARTEN C.W. JANSSEN

See also **involuntary unemployment; methodological individualism; social interactions (theory).**

Bibliography

Agassi, J. 1960. Methodological individualism. *British Journal of Sociology* 11, 144–70.

Agassi, J. 1975. Institutional individualism, *British Journal of Sociology* 26, 144–55.

Arrow, K. and Debreu, G. 1954. Existence of an equilibrium for a competitive economy. *Econometrica* 22, 265–90.

d'Aspremont, C., Dos Santos Ferreira, R. and Gérard-Varet, L. 1990. On monopolistic competition and involuntary unemployment. *Quarterly Journal of Economics* 105, 895–919.

Barro, R. and Grossman, H. 1971. A general disequilibrium model of income and employment. *American Economic Review* 61, 82–93.

Benassy, J.-P. 1975. Neo-Keynesian disequilibrium theory in a monetary economy. *Review of Economic Studies* 42, 502–23.

Bernheim, D. 1984. Rationalizable strategic behavior. *Econometrica* 52, 1007–28.

Blanchard, O. and Kiyotaki, N. 1987. Monopolistic competition and the effects on aggregate demand. *American Economic Review* 77, 647–66.

Bray, M. and Savin, N. 1986. Rational expectations equilibria, learning and model specification. *Econometrica* 54, 1129–60.

Brodbeck, M. 1958. Methodological individualisms: definition and reduction. *Philosophy of Science* 25, 1–22.

Bryant, J. 1983. A rational expectations Keynes type model. *Quarterly Journal of Economics* 98, 525–9.

Clower, R. 1965. The Keynesian counterrevolution: a theoretical appraisal. In *The Theory of Interest Rates*, ed. F. Hahn and F. Brechling. London: Macmillan.

Cooper, R. and John, A. 1988. Coordinating coordination failures in Keynesian models. *Quarterly Journal of Economics* 103, 441–63.

Drèze, J. 1975. Existence of an equilibrium with price rigidity and quantity rationing. *International Economic Review* 16, 301–20.

Fehr, E. and Falk, A. 1999. Wage rigidity in a competitive incomplete contract labour market. *Journal of Political Economy* 107, 106–34.

Friedman, M. 1968. The role of monetary policy. *American Economic Review* 58, 1–17.

Frydman, R. and Phelps, E., eds. 1983. *Individual Forecasting and Aggregate Outcomes*. Cambridge: Cambridge University Press.

Geanakoplos, J. and Polemarchakis, H. 1986. Walrasian indeterminacy and Keynesian macroeconomics. *Review of Economic Studies* 53, 755–79.

Guesnerie, R. 1992. An exploration of the eductive justifications of the rational expectations hypothesis. *American Economic Review* 82, 1254–78.

Hart, O. 1982. A model of imperfect competition with Keynesian features. *Quarterly Journal of Economics* 97, 109–38.

Hayek, F. 1948. *Individualism and Economic Order*. Chicago: Chicago University Press.

Hicks, J. 1937. Mr. Keynes and the classics: a suggested interpretation. *Econometrica* 5, 147–59.

Horwitz, S. 2000. *Microfoundations and Macroeconomics: An Austrian Perspective*. London: Routledge.

Janssen, M. 1993. *Microfoundations: A Critical Inquiry*. London: Routledge.

Kandori, M., Mailath, G. and Rob, R. 1993. Learning, mutation and long-run equilibria in games. *Econometrica* 61, 29–56.

Kirman, A. 1989. The intrinsic limits of modern economic theory: the emperor has no clothes. *Economic Journal* 99(supplement), 126–39.

Kirman, A. 1992. Whom or what does the representative individual represent? *Journal of Economic Perspectives* 6(2), 117–36.

Kiyotaki, N. 1988. Multiple expectational equilibria under monopolistic competition. *Quarterly Journal of Economics* 103, 695–713.

Kydland, F. and Prescott, E. 1982. Time to build and aggregate fluctuations. *Econometrica* 50, 1345–70.

Leijonhufvud, A. 1968. *On Keynesian Economics and the Economics of Keynes*. New York: Oxford University Press.

Lindbeck, A. and Snower, D. 1987. Efficiency wages versus insiders and outsiders. *European Economic Review* 31, 407–16.

Lucas, R. 1972. Expectations and the neutrality of money. *Journal of Economic Theory* 4, 103–24.

Lucas, R. 1978. Unemployment policy. *American Economic Review* 68, 353–7.

Lucas, R. 1987. *Models of Business Cycles*. Oxford: Basil Blackwell.

Lucas, R. and Rapping, L. 1969. Real wages, employment and inflation. *Journal of Political Economy* 77, 721–54.

Mankiw, N. 1985. Small menu cost and large business cycles: a macroeconomic model of monopoly. *Quarterly Journal of Economics* 100, 529–37.

Muth, J. 1961. Rational expectations and the theory of price movements. *Econometrica* 29, 315–35.

Nelson, A. 1984. Some issues surrounding the reduction from macroeconomics to microeconomics. *Philosophy of Science* 51, 573–94.

Pearce, D. 1984. Rationalizable strategic behavior and the problem of perfection. *Econometrica* 52, 1029–50.

Phelps, E., ed. 1970. *Microeconomic Foundations of Unemployment and Inflation Theory*. London: Macmillan.

Roberts, J. 1987. An equilibrium model with involuntary unemployment at flexible competitive prices and wages. *American Economic Review* 57, 856–74.

Schelling, T. 1978. *Micromotives and Macrobehavior*. New York: Norton.

Weintraub, E. 1979. *Microfoundations*. Cambridge: Cambridge University Press.

Yellen, J. 1984. Efficiency-wage models of unemployment. *American Economic Review* 74, 200–5.

Young, H. 1993. The evolution of conventions. *Econometrica* 61, 57–84.

Mill, James (1773–1836)

Mill was born in a village near Montrose in Scotland, the son of a cobbler-cum-smallholder. With the support of a local laird, Sir John Stuart, he was able to attend Montrose Academy and then, in 1790, Edinburgh University, where his original goal was to become a minister in the Scottish Kirk. During the seven years he spent in Edinburgh, he appears to have virtually become a member of the Stuart family, acting as tutor to the daughter of the house. Mill attended Dugald Stewart's lectures on moral philosophy and may have attended his class on political economy as well. Mill obtained his MA in 1794 and acquired a licence to preach in 1798. After an unsuccessful spell as an itinerant preacher and tutor, he moved to London in 1802, where he became part of an expatriate community of young Scots attempting to make their way in the world through journalism. In addition to various freelance jobs, Mill edited the *Literary Journal* from 1803 to 1806, writing most of the articles dealing with political and economic topics. This enabled him to marry in 1805 and begin a family of nine children that was to prove a strain on his finances and temperament. He also began work on what was to be an 11-year enterprise, the research for and writing of his *History of British India* (1817). In addition to his income from journalism, Mill obtained assistance from Jeremy Bentham, whose disciple and intermediary with the world of affairs he became after 1808. In this way, and especially through his articles for the Supplement to the 4th, 5th and 6th editions of the Encyclopaedia *Britannica* (1815–24), Mill became the leading light of the movement known as philosophic radicalism, an intellectual grouping dedicated to the reform of parliament and other legal and political institutions according to Benthamite criteria for 'good government'. In contradistinction to Bentham, however, Mill was a mature devotee of associationist psychology, as can be judged from his *Analysis of the Phenomena of the Human Mind* (1829). Mill also provided his eldest son, John Stuart, with an education which became part of the father's claim, both positive and negative, to have formed his son's mind and character. In 1819, partly as a result of the reception given to his *History*, Mill was appointed to the post of Assistant Examiner with the East India Company, rising to the post of Chief Examiner in 1830, a position he held until his death in 1836.

Mill's early economic writings consist of a large body of articles and two pamphlets, the first of which was *An Essay on the Impolicy of a Bounty on the Exportation of Grain* (1804), constructed along Smithian lines, the second entitled *Commerce Defended: An Argument by which Mr. Spence, Mr. Cobbett, and others have attempted to prove that Commerce is not a source of National Wealth* (1808). The latter is of interest to the history of economics, for two main reasons. The work contains the first enunciation in English of what was originally known as the Say–Mill law of markets; and it

was through this work that Mill made the acquaintance of David Ricardo. The pamphlet was an attack on the views of those neo-physiocratic authors who argued during the period of Napoleon's economic blockade that agriculture rather than manufacturing and commerce was the true source of Britain's wealth. Mill agreed that claims on behalf of commerce had frequently been pitched too high, but he defended the Smithian view that manufacturing and other profits were a legitimate form of net surplus. He also upheld a pre-comparative cost interpretation of the gains from trade judged by the difference between the real costs incurred in producing goods for export and the putative domestic cost of producing imported goods. In countering Spence's underconsumptionist arguments on the relationship between capital accumulation, consumption and public expenditure, Mill defended Smith's distinction between productive and unproductive labour, translating it into the goods consumed by each category in order to show the importance of accumulation and productive consumption to economic growth. In refuting the idea of excessive accumulation, or general overproduction, Mill invoked Say's principle: 'The production of commodities creates, and is the one and universal cause which creates a market for the commodities produced' (1808, p. 135). Since the argument was conducted in barter terms, however, it amounts to little more than a statement of Say's identity, though the implication was that the conclusions applied equally to a money economy. Hence Mill's conclusion: the claims of commerce could be exaggerated whenever it was suggested that the extension of foreign markets was necessary to guarantee full employment. Here then was the English origin of the idea, expressed in characteristically unqualified terms, that was to lie at the heart of the controversy between Ricardo and Malthus over general gluts, and was later to be taken up by Keynes as the distinguishing mark of orthodox classical (and neo-classical) macroeconomics – an intellectual obstacle that had to be removed by a new theory of effective demand in order to open the way for an explanation of involuntary unemployment in the *General Theory*.

It was largely as a result of Mill's encouragement that Ricardo overcame his doubts as to his capacity to move from being an economic pamphleteer to writing his *Principles of Political Economy*, which embodied those new doctrines that were necessary in order to replace those of Smith and other predecessors. Mill became Ricardo's impresario, coach and disciple; he was responsible for completing Ricardo's education and inducing him to enter parliament as spokesman for the 'true' principles of political economy and the reform programme of philosophic radicalism. Mill wrote one of the first 'schoolbook' accounts of Ricardo's doctrines in his *Elements of Political Economy* (1821), a record of what his son was taught at the tender age of 13. Ricardian doctrines appear in their most simplified and abstract form, but arranged according to the model provided by Jean

Baptiste Say's *Traité d'économie politique* (1814), and with some embellishments that were not always acceptable to Ricardo himself. Thus in attempting to defend Ricardo's labour theory of value from attack by Robert Torrens, Mill bowdlerized the theory.

On policy matters, however, Mill struck out more boldly than Ricardo on two main issues: the advocacy of birth control as a solution to the problem of low wages, and a proposal for taxing the increment in rents accruing to landowners as a result of any legislative action which increased the demand for land. (Mill chiefly had the Corn Laws in mind.) He was sympathetic to land nationalization (if only as a way of frightening the landed aristocracy) and to the view that taxes on rent were one of the best means of raising government revenue; but he recognized that such proposals could not be introduced into a country where property had already exchanged hands at prices reflecting rental expectations. Nevertheless, since this only gave a legitimate expectation to present rents, plus an allowance for improvements undertaken by the landowner, Mill was in favour of levying what would later be called a 'betterment' charge on increments in rent beyond this. In adopting this position he believed he was merely carrying Ricardo's conclusions on the special nature of rent, as compared with wages and profits, to their logical policy conclusion.

Mill then, rather than Ricardo, is the source of that strand of radical thinking on the 'law of rent' that was to be passed on via his son to the Fabians. More significantly, when judged by results, the official positions occupied by Mill and his son in India House ensured that their views on taxation and land revenue were influential in practice. It was primarily through his efforts that a determined attempt was made in the Bengal provinces to replace a landowner-based (*zemindari*) system of land tenure with one based on the view that the government should retain the ultimate rights in land and deal directly with the peasant cultivator or *ryot*, basing the tax assessment on Ricardian or pure rent.

Mill is also of some importance for his views on the methodology of political economy and other moral sciences, as can be best illustrated – negatively at least – by the attack mounted by Macaulay on Mill's essay on 'Government' for the *Encyclopaedia Britannica*. Mill was an extreme upholder of the virtues of the deductive method, and a critic of practical men who professed to be 'all for fact and nothing for theory'. In this respect Mill is sometimes credited with an influence on, certainly as encouraging, Ricardo's adoption of the a priori method of working from unqualified assumptions to 'strong cases', and from there to policy conclusions. Since there is little firm evidence to establish this proposition, those who are either critical or defensive of the Ricardian method should probably dispense with Mill rather than attempt to draw attention to similarities or differences between the practice of both men. We do know, however, that Mill produced a son who believed that his education

had peculiarly fitted him to engage in 'the science of science itself, the science of investigation – of method'. We also know that in the aftermath of the Macaulay attack the son wrote an essay 'On the Definition of Political Economy; and on the Method of Investigation Proper to it', later to be the basis for Book VI of his *System of Logic* (1843), in which he criticized both his father and Macaulay in the course of expounding an interpretation of the role of deductive methods in political economy which remained canonical for much of the 19th century.

DONALD WINCH

See also **classical distribution theories; Enlightenment, Scottish; land tax; Mill, John Stuart; Ricardo, David; Say, Jean-Baptiste.**

Selected works

1804. *An Essay on the Impolicy of a Bounty on the Exportation of Grain*. London. Repr. in Winch (1966).

1808. *Commerce Defended: An Argument by which Mr. Spence, Mr. Cobbett, and others have attempted to prove that Commerce is not a source of National Wealth*. Repr. in Winch (1966).

1817. *History of British India*. London: Baldwin & Cradock.

1821. *Elements of Political Economy*. London: Baldwin Cradock & Joy; 2nd edn, 1824; 3rd edn, 1826. Repr. in Winch (1966).

1829. *Analysis of the Phenomena of the Human Mind*. London: Baldwin & Cradock.

Bibliography

Bain, A. 1882. *James Mill: A Biography*. London: Longmans.

Ball, T. 1992. *James Mill: Political Writings*. Cambridge: Cambridge University Press.

De Marchi, N.B. 1983. The case for James Mill. In *Methodological Controversy in Economics: Historical Essays in Honor of T.W. Hutchison*, ed. A.W. Coats. Greenwich, CT: JAI Press.

Keynes, J.M. 1936. *General Theory of Employment Interest and Money*. London: Macmillan.

Macaulay, T.B. 1829. Mill's essay on government: utilitarian logic and politics. *Edinburgh Review* 97 (March).

Mill, J.S. 1844. On the definition of political economy; and on the method of investigation proper to it. In *Essays on Some Unsettled Questions in Political Economy*. London: Parker. [Written 1829; first published in the *London and Westminster Review*, 1836.]

Mill, J.S., 1843. *A System of Logic*. London: Parker.

Ricardo, D. 1817. *Principles of Political Economy and Taxation*. London: John Murray.

Say, J.-B. 1814. *Traité d'économie politique*, 2nd edn. Paris: A.-A. Renouard.

Winch, D. 1966. *James Mill: Selected Economic Writings*. Edinburgh: Oliver & Boyd. Reissue, New Brunswick: Transaction, 2006.

Mill, John Stuart (1806–1873)

John Stuart Mill was the pre-eminent British economist of the mid-19th century. But he was much more besides, commanding a hearing in public debates on subjects from logic to liberty, the position of women to the problem of Ireland. Yet, though his *Principles of Economics, with Some of Their Applications to Social Philosophy* (1848) dominated economic discourse for 40 years, there is little in it of technical, or even conceptual, advance that would justify placing him in a pantheon of great economists, if one judges by what is understood as economics today. Mill should be known and honoured more for his vision of an improved condition for humankind and for the novel economic views that formed part of that vision than for his economic analysis as such.

Approaching Mill's economic ideas from this perspective necessitates attending to his passage from early Benthamite propagandist and defender of Ricardian doctrine to more pragmatic reform strategist, with a greatly expanded notion of happiness. The transformation was traumatic in that it involved a lapse, and relapses, into depression, and it meant modifying some old convictions. Positively, however, Mill also discovered the possibility of cultivating feelings – 'of inward joy, of sympathetic and imaginative pleasure' – and began to see for others the prospect of 'perennial sources of happiness, when all the greater evils of life shall have been removed' (1873, pp. 147, 151). Certain elements in this prospect seemed to him to require, ultimately, the replacement of competition with cooperation, and there were various other novel economic aspects to this notion. But the inspiration was quite different from the motivations reflected in the economics Mill had learned from James Mill (his father) and Ricardo. This makes it hard to find the strong logical link between economic doctrine and social philosophy implied by the word 'Applications' in the subtitle of his *Principles*. In fact there is a switch in mode between the doctrines and the applications, from the demonstrative to the conditional – from result to possibility – which seriously weakens that link. There is also a difference of tone: Mill wrote with great immediacy and verve about possibilities for the improvement of humankind, but defensively on the economic doctrines he had inherited. He embraced new social thinkers, borrowing freely from them even if, as he often allowed, their views were incomplete, not always coherent and even downright misleading in certain respects. But he chose not to keep up with new developments in economics, more especially those that employed mathematics. Instead he stuck to the method that was his forte, clearing up terminological and logical confusion and thus 'perplexities'.

1 The constraints of a Benthamite education

Mill was the eldest of eight children born to James Mill and Harriet (née Barrow). He was home-schooled by his demanding father, whom he eventually succeeded as Examiner in the East India Company. The elder Mill was a Scots literary émigré in London, disciple of Bentham, and a leading protagonist of utilitarian reform. His writing took precedence, and, besides giving John basic instruction, he largely turned over to him the education of the younger children. John's mother, worn down, developed no intellectual interests, and became for him a model of what women should not be, in sharp contrast to Harriet Taylor, with whom he fell in love in the 1830s and married in 1851. Harriet Taylor shared Mill's reformist ideas and emboldened him in expressing his notions concerning autonomy, not least for women.

John's spectacular childhood achievements are well known: beginning to learn Greek words at the age of three, and starting Latin at eight, acquiring the language by dint of having to instruct his siblings. Studies in Logic began at 12, and Political Economy at 13. Instruction in the latter took the form of lectures from his father, which he was to summarize and repeat the following day, on their daily walk. James Mill's *Elements of Political Economy* (1821), which the daily lectures became, was essentially a set of logical propositions. John always regarded logical analysis as the most valuable of all mental trainings.

At the age of 20, however, Mill discovered that something was lacking. In describing what he would later call a crisis in his mental history, he recalls imagining the accomplishment of all the Benthamite reforms for which he was agitating, but finding himself without satisfaction at the prospect. Recovery was effected, he tells us, through reading new authors and modifying his circle of friends; central to the process, however, was the realization that the Benthamite views he had imbibed were entirely too narrow.

During Mill's childhood the family spent their summers close to Bentham, and in 1821 he began reading him – in fact Dumont's edited version of notes, published as the *Traité de Législation*. This work gave him 'a vista of improvement' for human life based on coherent laws and opinions founded on the principle of utility (1873, pp. 69, 71). Somewhat later Mill was given the task of editing Bentham's manuscript of *The Rationale of Judicial Evidence* (1827); so, by the time of his depression, Mill must have been as well equipped as anyone in Britain to convey accurately Bentham's thinking on government and to comment on matters of English law, which he did, frequently, in the daily and periodical press.

Mill's post-depression reappraisals were cautious, even after Bentham and his own father had died. In 1838, however, he was able to present a lengthy and balanced account. He praised Bentham for having accomplished the first scientific investigation of the large and messy body of precepts that comprised English law, using as his tool what Mill called 'the method of detail'– separating wholes into their parts, resolving abstractions into concrete things – in short, 'breaking every question into pieces before attempting to solve it' (1838, pp. 83, 100). The method was Baconian; Bentham's originality lay not in having invented it, but in having applied it to the law. He had not yet had the impact that he deserved, partly because of his obsessive verbal partitioning of every topic. This resulted in tedious intricacies for which few readers cared. But the method had the great merit of bringing into question even commonly accepted truths and constituted a tool for identifying the rationale, or lack of it, in every existing or proposed law.

Take murder, for example. According to common sense and religion it is a crime. But why? A rational examination would ask whether the benefits to the perpetrator were outweighed by costs, in terms of the suffering inflicted on the victim; the feelings of insecurity aroused in others; and the discouragement to certain sorts of industry and useful pursuits through fear, as well as any diversion of resources to warding off the perceived danger. If the costs dominate, then murder must count as a crime and the infliction of punishment is warranted (1838, p. 83). Mill judged it useful to challenge even basic truths in this way, both because they support many subsidiary truths, and for the mental discipline involved, which we need in order to guard us against too readily following moralists who invoke, unexamined, phrases such as 'law of nature' or 'right reason', and politicians who call for 'liberty' and 'social order' (1838, p. 84; 1873, p. 67).

On the negative side, Mill found Bentham's approach cripplingly narrow. By focusing on pain and pleasure exclusively Bentham implied that human beings are governed solely by their own immediate interest and their sympathy or antipathy towards others.

Among things ignored are a feeling of moral approbation or disapprobation (conscience); standards of excellence or the desire of perfection as an end in itself; a sense of honour or personal dignity; a love of beauty; the passion of the artist; love of the congruency or consistency of things, or of their conforming to their intended ends (1838, pp. 95–6). This philosophy, devoid of morality and spiritual interests, did not sit well with the new Mill, who had now 'learnt by experience that the passive susceptibilities needed to be cultivated as well as the active capacities' (1873, p. 147). But neither was Bentham's philosophy able to cope well with even the purely business aspects of life, since in practice every action influences our own and others' affections and desires (1838, p. 98).

Mill's own revised aspiration was to give due place to the *moral*, *aesthetic*, and *sympathetic* aspect of every human action. We must ask of each, is it right or wrong? Is it beautiful – inspiring, estimable? And is it 'loveable?' (1838, p. 112). These additions could have come from Smith's *Theory of Moral Sentiments* (1759), though it is not clear that Mill knew that work.

Returning to Bentham's philosophy, Mill concluded that, since it ignored feelings and the moral, the inspiring

and the lovable, it simply offered a crude guide to desirable outward circumstances and regulations to effect them. But circumstances and punishments cannot instil the sympathy that binds us. Mill drew from the aftermath of the French Revolution the lesson that social feelings are only shallow-rooted in human nature, that, once a society has torn down old institutions that have grown corrupt, conflicting interests are likely to produce anarchy (1838, p. 99). For sympathy to prevail, then, there must be education directed towards making it second nature to care for others as we care for ourselves.

On the political level, Bentham, it was true, had urged that government be delegated to those whose interests are identical with the interests of the population at large. But Mill feared giving even such a group control over the whole; without a serious opposition its members are apt to become tyrannical (1838, pp. 106–8). Mill's fears in this regard presage those expressed by Hayek in his *Road to Serfdom* (1944).

What did it mean to be a Benthamite propagandist, as Mill was before 1826? Two examples will illustrate. He distributed pamphlets on methods of birth control, convinced that the average condition of the working classes could be permanently improved only by voluntary reduction in their numbers relative to the means available for their support. And he opposed the Corn Laws because, in restricting imports, they kept the price of grain higher than it need be, making the most basic means of sustenance less accessible, which was a clear net loss of aggregate happiness. By contrast with these cut-and-dried policy choices, Mill's views in the decade or so after 1826 were largely an outworking of the enlarged basis for personal and social happiness that he had adopted.

He also became more practical; he saw that radicals must co-opt conservatives to command a parliamentary majority. The new Mill judged that there is no simple and direct connection between first principles, such as the principle of utility, and actions that will increase happiness. For individuals differ in their primary beliefs, making happiness 'too complex and indefinite an end' to pursue in the Benthamite manner (1838, p. 110). Fortunately, division on ultimate standards does not preclude agreement on intermediate ends. During the 1830s, therefore, Mill strove to engage erstwhile opponents on such intermediate goals, arguing, for example, that the landed interest's support for the Corn Laws would be weakened if it could be shown that those laws actually increased wage costs, harming landowners both as employers and consumers.

2 Early political economy

Philosophically and in terms of political practice Mill's new views had far-reaching implications for his life and writing. Much of his political economy, however, underwent relatively little change. Not only prior to 1826, but even in his *Principles* he retained and defended the core doctrines of his father's *Elements* and Ricardo's *Principles of Political Economy and Taxation* (1817). At times, especially early on, his defence was conducted with a fierceness that blinded him to any merit in alternative views. In the 1840s, by which time he wanted to make place, alongside the old core doctrines, for many additional topics in economic analysis as well as for his favourite ideas for improving society, the combination lent to his *Principles* the appearance of a patchwork. An illustration of his early treatment of critics can be given here; the patchwork aspect of the *Principles* will be touched upon in Section 5.

The illustration concerns the central subject of value. Ricardo and James Mill chose to discuss value strictly in terms of exchange value, for both wanted to show that, as population grows, the value of food *relative* to manufactures rises because land of lesser productivity has to be brought under cultivation. On the assumption that returns in manufacturing are constant but unit labour costs in agriculture are rising, it is obvious what causes an observed rising trend in the relative price of food.

Smith, however, in addition to allowing value to be relative, stressed the pain cost of labour and insisted that the true cost of goods is how much labour they command. Behind this emphasis was a concern that the sacrifice of ease involves a loss of happiness, since ease for Smith was linked with tranquillity of mind, and the latter with happiness. Mill understood this (see 1848, pp. 580–1). Nevertheless, as a young defender of his father and Ricardo, he dismissed Smith's alternative measure of value lest readers be deflected from focusing on relative labour input, so central to the case against the Corn Laws. Hence, when Malthus, in his *Measure of Value* (1823), opted for Smith's sacrifice measure, Mill, aged 17, portrayed him as logically incompetent: to make labour command a measure of value, Malthus had in fact to assume what he needed to show, that the value of wages is always the same (1823, p. 57). Mill was correct but also quite one-eyed. Malthus showed in his *Definitions in Political Economy* (1827) that he too grasped the difference between an invariable measure of value and exchange value, yet preferred to measure even exchange value by how much labour commodities can command because that is appropriate if one's purpose is to ascertain 'the sacrifice which people are willing to make in order to obtain [commodities]' (1827, p. 211).

Against this crabbed performance, it is refreshing to find Mill, a very few years later, writing comparatively wide-ranging and subtle analyses of current events. The best of these was an essay, 'Paper Currency and Commercial Distress', in the short-lived radical *Parliamentary Review* of 1826, on the recent 'commercial revulsion'.

Mill insisted that the proximate cause of recession in this case was a prior speculation, not in new ventures, but in existing activities. The dominant group of parliamentarians instead blamed an over-issue of small notes by country bankers – an attribution of causation, Mill suggested, that betrayed a deeper scepticism about paper currency. Drawing on Tooke's recently revised *Considerations on the State of the Currency* (1826), Mill showed that the speculation had begun after trade papers reported below normal stocks in a few key goods, including grains. In the usual way this had induced dealers to increase their purchases, causing an immediate price increase, a pattern that then extended itself, though for purely speculative reasons, to a wider range of goods. Mill agreed that there had been an increase in credit associated with speculative buying, but observed that this did not require small notes: trade credit and bills of exchange would have sufficed. He also showed that the observed movements in the currency were not what one would expect from an expansion of the circulation. What had happened was merely a redistribution of, rather than an overall expansion in, the circulation. When grain prices first began to rise, means of circulation shifted from London to the country, sustaining the rise in agricultural prices but lowering the prices of manufactures in the city. Manufactured exports therefore rose, and, because grain imports were restricted under the Corn Laws, the exports occasioned an influx of gold. This would have happened whether the medium of circulation was metallic or paper, and no net expansion of their notes by country bankers need have been involved. It followed that the ultimate culprit was the Corn Laws, which prevented imports from offsetting the speculative purchases occasioned by the initial shortfalls in stocks of grain.

This was a tour de force in applied economic analysis. Mill contrasted his analysis with an account of why the parliamentarians had got it wrong. At root they lacked general principles. Inevitably, then, the views of 'practical men' – men who observed a few facts near at hand and generalized on that inadequate basis – prevailed with them.

Practical men as nemesis was a theme in Mill's famous essay 'On the Definition of Political Economy; and on the Method of Investigation Proper to It', which was published in 1836 and again, along with other youthful exercises in clarification of the principles of the new political economy, in *Essays on Some Unsettled Questions of Political Economy* (1844). From an economist's point of view perhaps the most useful portion of Mill's *System of Logic, Ratiocinative and Inductive* (1843) was his extended analysis of the social scientist's equivalent of experimentation: the various methods of ascertaining causes (Book III). The earlier methodological essay started him down that road.

The methodological essay is by far the most sophisticated of the set published in 1844, the others, with two other exceptions, suffering from being of the crabbed, defensive sort. In an essay on 'The Influence of Consumption on Production' Mill allowed that a general glut could occur, temporarily, if there were a sudden general preference for liquidity. The other exception was an essay on 'The Laws of Interchange between Nations', in which Mill elaborated on his father's suggestion that the division of the gains from trade would depend on the relative strengths of demand of the participating countries. This was one of Mill's few lasting contributions to economic analysis. Marshall utilized it in his essay *The Pure Theory of Foreign Trade* (1879), and his demonstration, in the context of the 1903 tariff debate that whether the foreigner bears the cost of a tariff will depend on the shape of his offer curve.

3 Espousing selective conservatism, and incorporating social evolution

By the late 1830s, as we have seen, Mill had begun to make explicit what was required to make good on Bentham's omissions. But how exactly were these to be supplied? Here Mill had recourse to German views, conveyed in language more palatable to English minds by the poet and essayist Samuel Taylor Coleridge. He also drew on the writings of the Saint Simonians, particularly the early work of Auguste Comte.

Mill took from Coleridge the idea that education should assist in forming national character. The young need to be imbued with an 'active principle of cohesion', of sympathy, not hostility; union, not separation. This might require heroes, or at least common beliefs; either way the goal must be to make caring for others second nature. By implication, there was a very active role here for government, a role more positive than either the pre-revolutionary French philosophers had allowed, or than their English counterparts had felt to be necessary. The French had wanted to tear down corrupt and spent institutions, after which government should basically leave people be (laissez-faire). On the English side, the national discomfort with conflict and a preference for compromise had asserted itself in the 18th century; after the strife of the 17th century the English had settled for living with whatever institutions there were, provided they were reduced to practical nullities (1840, pp. 142–4, 146). There was no sense in England that education should be reformed to build national character and supply an active force for social cohesion.

Mill picked up on three intriguing ways in which government might contribute to or reflect cohesion; and each had an economic aspect. First, the state 'ought to be considered as a great benefit society, or mutual insurance company, for helping (under the necessary regulations for preventing abuse) that large proportion of its members who cannot help themselves' (1840, p. 156). The details of this idea were not filled in, and it does not reappear in Mill's later work, but it sounds not unlike the Social Security system of the United States or the mandatory contributions towards retirement now applied in many countries.

Second, the land must be considered a trust. Mill distinguished this notion from calls for the state to reclaim private property, though he noted that the law of real property originally applied only to movables. It was his view that, if an owner possesses more land than is necessary for him to sustain himself and his family by his own labour, the excess confers on him power over others and the state may require that this power not be abused. This meant that even the system of cultivation is a proper concern of society (1840, pp. 157–8). The notion reappears in the *Principles*, though as one among several possibilities for limiting bequest and tenure (1848, p. 227).

Third, Mill insisted that education, being of almost boundless power, should be used by the state to foster public opinion in favour of the attracting forces within society. These forces derive from our love of praise, favour, admiration and respect, and our dread of shame and ill repute – again, ideas central to Smith's *Moral Sentiments*, though Smith was not acknowledged by Mill. Mill held that, once the basic means of living has been obtained, almost the whole of our remaining effort is directed to acquiring the favourable regard of others. In fact this is the driving force behind the industrial and commercial activity that advances civilization. Love of praise, however, is also the source of the selfish thirst for aggrandizement; hence the state must tip the balance in favour of social sympathy (1840, pp. 410–1).

A possible explanation of Mill's slighting of Smith is available in this instance. Mill might easily have seen Smith as insufficiently positive about the role of government. Smith, for example, advocated basic education for the poor in the hope that, for those condemned by excessive specialization to repetitive, trivial tasks, it might mitigate the risk of moral deformity (1776, p. 788). But for Mill that was too feeble a response, too restrained an expectation. For him education was the key to all future social and personal improvement.

The expectation of improvement also impelled Mill farther in a related direction. There is an implication for distribution in the notion that mutuality of interests makes it easier to cultivate and fix social feelings (1861, p. 231). Mill took from Comte the conviction that there had been considerable social progress towards cooperation, a trend likely to continue. The cooperative spirit, in turn, ought to make it possible for individuals to regard working for the benefit of others as a good it itself, requiring no compensation. Ideally, what we get for ourselves should not be viewed as a quid pro quo for our cooperation but in terms of 'how much the circumstances of society permit to be assigned' to us, 'consistent with the just claims of others'. The market method of settling a worker's share of the produce may be a temporary practical necessity, but morally is not ideal. Society, Mill understood, was not yet ready to relinquish the market, so he judged it better to let competition decide rather than to impose any artificial mode of distribution as yet untried – save in the army, where it was the de facto norm (1865, pp. 340–1). The idea reappears in the discussion, in the *Principles*, of cooperative arrangements in industry, though Mill's emphasis there was strongly on shared ownership for harnessing 'productive energies', and cooperation as still for the future, while competition is not only dominant but also has its positive side emphasized (1848, pp. 216, 337, 356).

4 Happiness: an enlarged view

Feelings aside, morals, aesthetics and sympathy – the other three missing elements in Bentham's philosophy – put happiness firmly in the social sphere. Mill continued to hold, with Bentham, that the general end should be the multiplication of happiness, but increasingly happiness had to involve the desire to care for others. Even if by nature we have only a small germ of this feeling it is one which can and should be 'laid hold of and nourished by the contagion of sympathy and the influences of education' and supported by external sanctions (1861, p. 233). Social ends would thus be rendered part of our inmost motivation.

On the one hand, then, Mill naturally came to think of happiness as linked to the growth of the cooperative spirit. On the other, he also saw it, crucially, as involving the development of the inward man, which is where the three added dimensions really have their purchase on our emotions and motives. He would eventually redefine individual happiness as a satisfied life, one with a balance between tranquillity and excitement. A person who finds this balance can be content with little pleasure, and can even be reconciled to much pain (1861, p. 215). Mill saw no reason why the mass of humankind could not unite tranquillity with excitement, since, even without great improvement in outward circumstances, the inward balance could be struck.

Notice, however, that inward happiness, since it does not depend essentially on a person's material resources or situation, removes the end – happiness – from the status of positional good. It may be that this realization predisposed Mill to accept Comte's ideas on cooperation – that cooperation itself is made easier if the overall end in view does not involve rivalry – though there is no collaborating evidence for this.

5 Mill's mature political economy

Mill's *Principles* was an uneasy amalgam of Smith, Ricardo, Mill's own refined insights on various discrete topics, and new social ideas.

The treatise can be dissected for its insights on a wide range of topics, as Hollander has done in his full-length study of Mill (1985). Hollander shows Mill to have had an unusually clear grasp of mechanisms: the determination of (long-run or cost) prices by variation of supply; of the rate of return by the proportion of the work day required to produce wage goods; of the alternative to wage reduction that exists in population control, as a way of equating the growth rates of population and capital accumulation; of the feedback between speculation engendered by a declining rate of profit and the loss of capital due to business failures, which in itself will raise the rate of profit; of a general desire to hold money as a cause of depressions; and so on.

These mechanisms summarize clearly and appropriately Mill's analytical contribution, which he even recorded on occasion as a list of propositions established (for example 1848, pp. 497–9). Since, however, there are various possibilities implicit in the application of such propositions, circumstances matter, as Mill himself stressed in his essay on method. This distinction between demonstrated truth and institutional possibilities inevitably loosened the logical connection between Mill's economic analysis and his social views. Thus he could analyse in a Malthusian-cum-Ricardian way the growth tendencies that issue in stationariness: given diminishing returns in agriculture, constant population growth and a fixed state of the productive arts, growth will eventually cease. Yet he could also freely explore possibilities for human nature, society and the 'Art of Living' in the stationary state, unconstrained by those economic tendency laws.

This is partly responsible for the patchwork appearance of the *Principles* noted earlier; yet it probably owes as much or more to Mill's having retained key doctrines from Ricardo and his father while accepting that they had not always elaborated the general case. In acknowledging this, on rent for example, Mill ended up incorporating qualifications that the reader must locate here and there – in the case of rent, in four separate chapters, spread across three books.

Marshall chose an alternative way of addressing rent. He noted that rent of land is 'no isolated economic doctrine' but 'simply the chief species of a large genus of economic phenomena' (1890, I, p. 629). Mill, sticking to the Ricardian view that rent of land is 'differential and peculiar' (1848, p. 495), concluded that rent only enters into the cost of production if there is a scarcity element involved – cases 'rather conceivable than actually existing' (1848, p. 498). Marshall, however, constructed a continuum of cases in which, at one extreme, a productive resource is in strictly fixed supply and its return therefore a surplus or 'rent in the strictest sense of the term', while at the other end the resource is quickly reproducible and its return no more than the interest on the money cost of obtaining more of it. There are multiple combinations in between where revenue might temporarily diverge from interest, for reasons originating either on the supply or the demand side. Specifying the exact circumstances may have consequences, as when a choice must be made whether to impose a tax on producers rather than consumers. Marshall's point was that interest and quasi-rent 'shade into one another gradually', making such choices very difficult (1890, I, pp. 412–21). Hence, as to 'rent not entering into cost', he concluded that the phrase cannot be rescued by verbal analysis but 'only by experience'. At the same time, it is a 'denial of subtle truths' to generalize either in the direction chosen by Mill or its opposite (1890, II, p. 439). Mill's fierce defence of Ricardian doctrine in this instance, as in some others, did not advance the cause of clarity nor did it allow experience the crucial role his own method suggested it should have.

As noted, Mill incorporated analytical developments in economics selectively; he left aside those that involved mathematics – not the strongest component in his early education (1873, p. 15, though see also p. 59) and a mode of reasoning he later came to suspect of strengthening the false claim that moral, political and 'supersensual' truth may be had without self-observation and common experience (1832, p. 331; 1873, p. 233). Not to speak of French works, he failed to mention even contemporary English analyses of profit-maximizing equilibrium, and the gains and losses from the supposition of various changes (in technique – hence machinery – or in taxes), such as those due to Tozer (1838) and Lardner (1850). Much later he responded to Jevons, though probably not from having studied the *Theory of Political Economy* (1871) at first hand. And from reviews of the *Theory* Mill *mis*judged that Jevons just offered 'a notation implying the existence of greater precision in the data than the questions admit of' (Mill to Cairnes, 5 December 1871, in Mill, 1963–91, vol. 17, p. 1862).

There remain, as the freshest contributions of the *Principles*, those of Mill's notions on future social possibilities that have some economic content.

1. In the context of reflecting on possible distributions of property (Book II, Ch. 1), Mill posited that a society might be in the position of having to choose between communal ownership and private. He supplied arguments why the communal arrangement ought not to be rejected out of hand. Shirking, he allowed, would be a serious problem; moreover, the experiment should not be tried without universal education first being implemented and numbers (population) controlled, so that none would lack for subsistence. Under such circumstances one might assume more public spirit than we are used to seeing. Nevertheless, and difficulties with the alternative notwithstanding, he thought existing production arrangements far from ideal: in nine-tenths of cases there are principal–agent problems (not his terminology). All said, he suggested, the choice should turn on the most important issue of all: which system 'is consistent with the greatest amount of human liberty and spontaneity'? (1848, Book II, Ch. 1, p. 208).

2. In the very next chapter Mill argued for a distinction between the right of private ownership and the right to bequeath and inherit. On the one hand, the power to bequeath might be inconsistent with the permanent interest of the race; on the other, the essential principle of property – to assure to all what they themselves have produced – cannot apply to the raw materials of the earth. After universally agreed exceptions, Mill observed, where doubt is present the presumption should be against the owner (1848, Book II, Ch. 2).

3. In Book IV, Chapter 4, Mill adumbrated his own non-Smithian tendency for the rate of profits to fall. He accepted the tendency, but argued that it reflects not only the natural (Ricardian) consequences of the extension of cultivation, but also the progress of civilization. As people become more rational they also become more self-controlled, and find lower rates of interest and profits acceptable. Not only are rational people less apt to discount the future; they also save against contingencies even in the absence of any immediate need. In a more civilized world, moreover, risks are lower because the strong social spirit renders capital and wealth generally more secure.

4. Building on the arguments just listed, Mill was also able to contemplate a future with zero growth (the stationary state: Book IV, Ch. 6). Here he reiterated the theme that 'a population might be too crowded' for that solitariness and tranquillity so essential to depth of character. Quite apart from that, zero growth of course does not preclude 'improving the Art of Living'. And in any case, the social ideal cannot be the elbowing, crushing competition all around us. We should be able to get beyond the struggle for (relative) riches, so as to realize a state in which 'while no one is poor, no one desires to be richer, nor has any reason to fear being thrust back' (1848, p. 754).

5. A third chapter in Book IV, 'On the Probably Futurity of the Labouring Classes', expands on all this, but stresses the importance of making people more 'rational' by increasing their independence, this by reversing the hiring–service relationship and replacing it with employer–employee associations (1848, p. 763). As so often, Mill qualified this sweepingly optimistic view with a pragmatic caution: competition need not be dispensed with; after all, cheaper goods come of it and labour must therefore benefit (1848, p. 794).

6. Finally, in Book V, especially Chapter 11, there is an exploration of laissez-faire, the general rule, and the 'large exceptions' to it that Mill also deemed necessary. The positive role of government should extend to education; the care of minors (from which category he was careful to exclude women); and a long list of cases where private initiative would be preferable if only it were not generally lacking for one reason or another. The list reads quite like the one Smith provided, of desirable projects for which no individual or small group can find the necessary financing; only Mill extended it beyond roads, harbours, canals, and so on, to hospitals, schools, colleges and printing presses (1848, pp. 944, 947, 950, 970).

NEIL DE MARCHI

See also **competition; cooperation; property rights.**

Selected works

1823. Malthus's measure of value. In *Collected Works*, vol. 23.
1826. Paper currency and commercial distress. In *Collected Works*, vol. 4.
1836. On the definition of political economy; and on the method of investigation proper to it. In *Collected Works*, vol. 4.
1838. Bentham. In *Collected Works*, vol. 10.
1840. Coleridge. In *Collected Works*, vol. 10.
1843. *A System of Logic, Ratiocinative and Inductive*. In *Collected Works*, vols 7 and 8.
1844. Of the laws of interchange between nations. In *Essays on Some Unsettled Questions of Political Economy*. In *Collected Works*, vol. 4.
1844. On the influence of consumption on production. In *Essays on Some Unsettled Questions of Political Economy*. In *Collected Works*, vol. 4.
1848. *Principles of Political Economy, with Some of Their Applications to Social Philosophy*. In *Collected Works*, vols 2 and 3.
1861. Utilitarianism. In *Collected Works*, vol. 10.
1865. Auguste Comte and positivism. In *Part I, Collected Works*, vol. 10.
1873. Autobiography. In *Collected Works*, vol. 1.
1963–91. *Collected Works of John Stuart Mill*, 33 vols. ed. J.M. Robson. Toronto and London: University of Toronto Press and Routledge & Kegan Paul.

Bibliography

Bentham, J. 1827. *Rationale of Judicial Evidence, Specially Applied to English Practice*, 5 vols. ed. J.S. Mill. London: Hunt & Clarke.
De Marchi, N. 2002. Putting evidence in its place: John Mill's early struggles with 'facts in the concrete'. In *Fact and Fiction in Economics. Models, Realism, and Social Construction*, ed. U. Maki. Cambridge: Cambridge University Press.
Dumont, P.É.L. 1802. *Traité de législation civile et pénale*, vols. 3. Paris: Boussange, Masson, Besson.
Hayek, F.A. 1944. *The Road to Serfdom*. London: Routledge.
Hollander, S. 1985. *The Economics of John Stuart Mill*. Oxford: Basil Blackwell.
Jevons, W.S. 1871. *The Theory of Political Economy*. London: Macmillan.
Lardner, D. 1850. *Railway Economy*. New York: A.M. Kelley, 1968.
Maas, H. 2005. *William Stanley Jevons and the Making of Modern Economics*. Cambridge: Cambridge University Press.
Malthus, T.R. 1823. *The Measure of Value Stated and Illustrated*. London: John Murray.
Malthus, T.R. 1827. *Definitions in Political Economy*. London: John Murray.
Marshall, A. 1879. *The Pure Theory of Foreign Trade. The Pure Theory of Domestic Values*. Circulated privately; repr. London: London School of Economics and Political Science, 1930.
Marshall, A. 1890. *The Principles of Economics*, 9th (variorum) edn. vol. 2, ed. C. Guillebaud. London: Macmillan for the Royal Economic Society, 1961.
Mill, J. 1821. *The Elements of Political Economy*. London: Baldwin, Cradock & Joy.
Ricardo, D. 1817. *The Principles of Political Economy and Taxation*. London: John Murray.
Robson, J.M. 1968. *The Improvement of Mankind*. London: Routledge & Kegan Paul.
Smith, A. 1759. In *The Theory of Moral Sentiments*, ed. A.L. Macfie and D.D. Raphael. Oxford: Oxford University Press, 1976.
Smith, A. 1776. *An Inquiry into the Nature and Causes of the Wealth of Nations*, vol. 2, ed. R.H. Campbell and A.S. Skinner. Oxford: Oxford University Press, 1976.
Tooke, T. 1826. *Considerations on the State of the Currency*. London: John Murray.
Tozer, J.E. 1838. *Mathematical Investigation of the effect of Machinery on the Wealth of a Community in which it is Employed and on the Fund for the Payment of Wages*. Cambridge: Cambridge Philosophical Society, Transaction 6.

Miller, Merton (1923–2000)

From the late 1950s to the early 1970s the field of finance changed fundamentally. A reader of the *Journal of Finance* in the early 1950s would find a field that was mostly descriptive. After the early 1970s the field had become a science. Merton Miller was at the centre of that transformation. His work started it in 1958. For the rest of his life he was at the heart of modern finance. (Grundy, 2001, provides a complete list of Merton Miller's publications.)

After obtaining a Ph.D. in economics from Johns Hopkins University in 1952 and a brief stay at the London School of Economics, he joined the Graduate School of Industrial Administration at what was then known as Carnegie Tech. As an assistant and associate professor there, he made the contributions to the theory of corporate finance with Franco Modigliani, another faculty member, that made him famous. He joined the University of Chicago in 1961. From Chicago he exerted a huge influence on finance which lasted until he died in 2000. Merton Miller's research had a prodigious impact – he made major contributions in monetary economics, operations research, derivatives pricing, and asset pricing, as well as his seminal contributions in corporate finance – but his influence went far beyond the contributions of his papers. He mentored countless Chicago graduate students and faculty members from Chicago and throughout the profession. At times he played the role of the nurturing patriarch, while at other times he used his wit and intellect to keep people on the straight and narrow path of solid economic thinking. From 'his' seat on the left of the speaker in the Rosenwald seminar room, often in a worn-out sweater, he changed the course of numerous papers. Sometimes his intervention went further – for example, he was instrumental in persuading the *Journal of Political Economy* to publish the paper by Black and Scholes that is the foundation of option pricing theory. When he ventured outside of the University of Chicago, he often did so to be 'an activist supporter of free-market solutions to economic problems', as he stated in a brief Nobel autobiography (1991a). He knew how to make his case – he was not the son of an attorney, a Harvard graduate also, for nothing – and had a well-deserved reputation for unparalleled eloquence in the finance profession.

The irrelevance propositions and the role of arbitrage

Merton Miller earned a Nobel Prize in economics in 1990 for his 'fundamental contributions to the theory of corporate finance' (Franco Modigliani already had a Nobel Prize by then for his life cycle theory of saving). Just about every MBA in the world has learned the famous MM irrelevance propositions he developed with Franco Modigliani. (One paper had Modigliani's name first and the other had Miller's name first, so I will proceed using the moniker MM to represent the team.) The two key MM irrelevance propositions are developed in a world with perfect markets, so that there are no frictions. In particular, there are no transactions costs or taxes, and no costs are incurred to induce managers to maximize the value of the firm.

The first irrelevance proposition, Proposition I in the paper titled 'The Cost of Capital, Corporation Finance and the Theory of Investment' published in the *American Economic Review* (1958, p. 268) states that 'the market value of any firm is independent of its capital structure and is given by capitalizing its expected return at the rate. ... appropriate to its class'. The second irrelevance proposition concludes that 'given a firm's investment policy, the dividend payout it chooses to follow will affect neither the current price of its shares nor the total return to its shareholders' (1961, p. 414). In other words, in perfect markets neither capital structure choices nor dividend policy decisions matter. Since then, corporate finance has refined these results and built theories based on the existence of market imperfections.

If we had to remember one thing about Merton Miller's contributions to finance, what should it be? It would not be the irrelevance propositions themselves. Rather, it would be the way the irrelevance propositions were proved (for a more complete analysis, see Stulz, 2000). The approach used to prove these propositions is central to the thinking of practitioners of modern finance. It has spawned many seminal contributions to the field. The method used to prove Proposition I is the method of arbitrage. MM did not invent arbitrage, but made it the foundation of modern finance. MM assume that financial markets are perfect and then show that

> if Proposition I did not hold, an investor could buy and sell stocks and bonds in such a way as to exchange one income stream for another stream, identical in all relevant respects but selling at a lower price. The exchange would therefore be advantageous to the investor quite independently of his attitudes toward risk. As investors exploit these arbitrage opportunities, the value of the overpriced shares will fall and that of the underpriced shares will rise, thereby tending to eliminate the discrepancy between the market values of the firms. (1958, p. 269)

The arbitrage mechanism is how Merton Miller thought about finance phenomena. Results that would lead to arbitrage opportunities could not possibly be important because market forces would step in to make prices right. However, in his thinking arbitrage was never limited to existing financial instruments and institutions. For him, arbitrage opportunities that exist in the real world will eventually disappear because, when needed, financial innovations will occur that will prevent these opportunities from persisting.

Though arbitrage arguments are now pervasive throughout finance and, more generally, economics, the more immediate and direct impact of the arbitrage proof of Proposition I was to provide the foundation for modern corporate finance because it specifies sufficient conditions for leverage not to matter. Because of the proof, we know that, if financial markets are perfect, the value of a firm does not depend on its leverage. As a result, practitioners and academics alike know that, if leverage affects value, it must be that one or more of the assumptions required by the arbitrage proof do not hold.

In their papers MM eliminated once and for all the argument that leverage is costly simply because it increases the interest rate the corporation pays for its debt. As leverage increases in a world of perfect markets, the coupon paid on debt increases, but that is because bondholders bear more risk and must be compensated for this additional risk. This will happen even though the firm's cash flows are unaffected by the additional leverage. Hence, as Merton Miller pointed out in his Nobel lecture (Miller, 1991c), the increase in the risk of debt has no social costs because the firm's total risk is unaffected by the change in leverage.

Beyond the irrelevance propositions

With corporate income taxes, the cost of debt for the firm is the cost after taxes since interest paid on debt is tax deductible at the corporate level. If the only departure from the assumptions leading to Proposition I were a tax subsidy to corporate debt, one would expect firms to maximize the value of that subsidy and therefore have extremely high leverage. Empirically, however, leverage is not extreme. To make sense of the limited levels of leverage in the presence of what appeared to be a large tax subsidy for debt, finance had either to relax other assumptions leading to Proposition I or to conclude that the subsidy was illusory. Initially, the route chosen by finance was to take into account bankruptcy costs. Bankruptcy costs occur because contracting is costly – firms that default on their debt contracts cannot be cost-lessly reorganized. In the presence of bankruptcy costs and tax subsidy to debt, each firm has an optimal debt level such that the increase in the present value of expected bankruptcy costs resulting from an additional dollar of debt equals the present value of the expected tax subsidy from that additional dollar of debt.

Merton Miller always doubted that expected bank-ruptcy costs could be large enough to explain why firms did not take greater advantage of the tax subsidy of debt. His assessment of the evidence on bankruptcy and finan-cial distress costs was that 'neither empirical research nor simple common sense could convincingly sustain these presumed costs of bankruptcy as a sufficient, or even as a major, reason for the failure of so many large, well-managed US corporations to pick up what seemed to be billions upon billions of dollars of potential tax subsidies' (1991b, p. 274). This assessment led him to one of his most memorable statements, namely, that 'the supposed trade-off between tax gains and bankruptcy costs looks suspiciously like the recipe for the fabled horse-and-rabbit stew – one horse and one rabbit' (1976, p. 264).

Since direct bankruptcy costs could not explain why firms were not taking advantage of the apparent tax subsidy of debt, the field of finance turned to other explanations for low leverage based on contracting costs. Jensen and Meckling (1976) showed that, as leverage increases, shareholders have incentives to take advantage of bondholders by undertaking highly risky projects with high payoffs to shareholders in some states even though such projects have a negative net present value. The bondholder–shareholder conflict identified by Jensen and Meckling makes debt more costly because firms either behave inefficiently as a result of leverage or spend real resources to convince bondholders that they will not take advantage of them. A large literature emphasizing contracting costs has developed over time.

Merton Miller always had doubts that the bondholder–shareholder conflict could explain why firms did not take greater advantage of the tax shield of debt. Not surpris-ingly, his scepticism stemmed from the role of arbitrage in his thinking. If the tax shield of debt was so large, why was it that investment bankers would not devise solutions that would enable firms to take advantage of this tax shield and overcome the agency costs of debt through clever con-tracting? As always, he viewed no finance problem as solved unless he could find a solution that would not provide clever arbitrageurs with profit opportunities.

In 1976, in his address as President of the American Finance Association, Merton Miller revisited the issue of the impact of corporate taxation on the MM irrelevance propositions in a classic paper titled 'Debt and Taxes'. This paper shows perhaps better than any of his other papers how he could use arbitrage arguments to change the way finance academics and practitioners understood how the world works. In that paper he pointed out that the tax advantage of corporate debt might be mostly if not completely illusory. Because interest on corporate debt is taxed as income to the bondholder, the interest paid must be sufficiently high to ensure that the after-tax income from holding corporate bonds is attractive relative to the income from equity which, when it accrues as capital gains, is taxed at a lower effective rate. While corporate interest payments generate tax deductions, personal taxes on interest income are higher than on capital gains, and so the before-tax cost of capital on debt must be higher than on equity to induce investors to hold debt. In his paper Merton Miller showed that under specific condi-tions the only feasible equilibrium is the one in which the after-tax cost of debt equals the after-tax cost of equity. When this equilibrium obtains, Proposition I holds in the presence of taxes, and no firm has a financial incentive to alter its mix of debt and equity even though interest payments on debt are tax deductible. 'Debt and Taxes' demonstrated that the perfect-markets assumptions are sufficient, but not necessary, conditions for leverage to be irrelevant. Showing that the assumptions required for Proposition I do not hold is not enough to conclude that leverage matters; rather it must also be the case that clever arbitrageurs cannot profit from the situation.

The legacy

With the contributions to the field of finance that I have described, Merton Miller provided a way to think about financial phenomena that remains at the core of all major theoretical developments in the field. Throughout his life, Merton Miller used arbitrage reasoning to organ-ize his thoughts about important phenomena. His first publication appeared in the 1948 *American Economic Review*. In 1990, he published a paper in the *Journal of Finance* (co-authored with David Hsieh) that analysed the impact on stock prices of changes in margin require-ments. That paper was awarded a Smith–Breeden prize for best paper in the *Journal of Finance*. At the time, Merton Miller was thrilled because he had pub-lished refereed papers in top journals in five different decades. He never stopped wanting to write papers that merited publication in top journals. Three days before his death he was preparing a paper for submission. Throughout his life he was first, last, and foremost a scholar.

RENÉ M. STULZ

See also **arbitrage; Modigliani, Franco; Modigliani–Miller theorem.**

I am grateful for comments from Harry DeAngelo, Linda DeAngelo, Steven Durlauf and Andrew Karolyi.

Selected works

1948. (With R. Musgrave.) Built-in flexibility. *American Economic Review* 38, 122–8.

1958. (With F. Modigliani.) The cost of capital, corporation finance and the theory of investment. *American Economic Review* 48, 261–97.

1961. (With F. Modigliani.) Dividend policy, growth, and the valuation of shares. *Journal of Business* 34, 411–33.

1976. Debt and taxes. *Journal of Finance* 32, 261–75.

1990. (With D. Hsieh.) Margin regulation and stock market volatility. *Journal of Finance* 45, 3–29.

1991a. Autobiography. In *Les Prix Nobel. The Nobel Prizes 1990*, ed. Tore Frängsmyr. Stockholm: Nobel Foundation. Online. Available at http://nobelprize.org/nobel_prizes/economics/laureates/1990/miller-autobio.html, accessed 28 June 2006.

1991b. *Financial Innovations and Market Volatility*. Cambridge, MA and Oxford, UK: Blackwell.

1991c. Leverage. *Journal of Finance* 46, 479–88.

Bibliography

Grundy, B. 2001. M. H. Miller: his contributions to financial economics. *Journal of Finance* 56, 1183–206.

Jensen, M. and Meckling, W. 1976. Theory of the firm: managerial behavior, agency costs and ownership structure. *Journal of Financial Economics* 3, 305–60.

Stulz, R. 2000. Merton Miller and modern finance. *Financial Management* 29, 119–31.

Minard, Charles Joseph (1781–1870)

A French engineer and economist, Charles Joseph Minard was widely recognized as the creator of graphical statistics, a means of figuratively portraying railway traffic routes on illustrated maps. Minard served as professor at the École Nationale des Ponts et Chaussées (ENPC) in the 1830s, where he taught the course on interior navigation, which included roads, rivers, canals and railways. In 1831 Minard wrote a lengthy monograph designed to establish a course in economics that he proposed for ENPC students. Although Minard viewed this work as a manual for practising engineers, J.B. Say immediately recognized the manuscript as a systematic treatise on the economics of public works, and urged Minard to publish it for the benefit of economists as well as engineers. For reasons that are not entirely clear, Minard shelved his manuscript instead – probably owing to the delay by ENPC in establishing an economics chair until 1847. In 1850, a year before his retirement from public service, Minard published his 'Notions élémentaires d'économie politique appliqué aux travaux publics' in the *Annales des Ponts et Chaussées*.

In this monograph Minard explored such fundamental notions as utility, demand, opportunity costs, the value of time and services, the effects of taxes on income distribution, and the use of compound interest in calculating the value of capital expenditures – a treatment lauded by W.S. Jevons in his *Theory of Political Economy* (1871). Despite its unfortunate delay in publication, the ideas in Minard's monograph were clearly part of the oral tradition in economics at ENPC in the first half of the 19th century. Thus, Minard served as an important link between Navier and Dupuit in the development of demand theory and cost–benefit analysis. This claim is based on four major aspects of his work: he introduced subjective elements, such as the value of time, into the operational measure of utility; he insisted that the magnitude of social utility depends on the distribution of income; he recognized that price increases cause substitution effects among existing consumers and that price decreases draw new consumers into the market; and he developed subjective notions of cost associated with public works.

R. F. HÉBERT

See also **cost–benefit analysis; demand theory; Dupuit, Arsene-Jules-Emile Juvenal; Jevons, William Stanley; Navier, Claude Louis Marie Henri; public works; Say, Jean-Baptiste.**

Selected works

1850. Notions élémentaires d'économie politique appliqué aux travaux publics. *Annales des Ponts et Chaussées: Mémoires et Documents*, 2d ser. 19(1), 1–125.

1851. Motifs pour préférer dans les travaux publics des ouvrages moins coûteux, quoique moins durables. *Journal des Economistes* 21, 65–7.

Bibliography

Coronio, G. 1997. *250 ans de L'École des Ponts en cent portraits*. Paris: Presses de l'école des Ponts et Chaussées, 84–5.

Ekelund, R., Jr. and Hébert, R. 1978. French engineers, welfare economics, and public finance in the nineteenth century. *History of Political Economy* 10, 636–68.

Ekelund, R., Jr. and Hébert, R. 1999. *Secret Origins of Modern Microeconomics: Dupuit and the Engineers*. Chicago: University of Chicago Press.

Etner, F. 1987. *Histoire du calcul économique en France*. Paris: Economica.

Hébert, R. 1994. Fondements et développements de l'économie publique. *Revue Du Dix-Huitième Siècle* 26, 37–49.

Jevons, W.S. 1871. *The Theory of Political Economy*. London: Macmillan.

Mincer, Jacob (1922–2006)

Born in Poland, Jacob Mincer was a college freshman in Czechoslovakia when the Germans invaded in early 1939. He spent most of the Second World War in prisons and concentration camps, but survived to enter Emory University in 1948 on an Hillel Foundation scholarship.

After completing his first degree in two years, Mincer began his graduate studies in economics at the University of Chicago. He then transferred to Columbia University, having followed the lady who would be his wife from Chicago to New York for her residency in radiation oncology. Later, Flora Kaplan Mincer, MD, took six years from her practice to bring up their three children. That interruption in her career would be the basis for Mincer's subsequent paper, with his student Solomon Polachek (1974), which was the first to empirically tackle the complications of women's careers in earnings determination.

Jacob Mincer received his Ph.D. from Columbia in 1957, taught for two years at the City College of New York, and then returned to Columbia, where he remained until his 1991 retirement. In the interim, there were visiting appointments at the University of Chicago, the Stockholm School of Economics and the Hebrew University of Jerusalem.

Mincer was one of the very best 20th-century economists. He is one of the four or five who led the way into modern labour economics. The ideas of investing in man per se that were circulating in the early to mid-1950s had become environmental at Chicago and Columbia by the end of the decade. Given publication lags, it is impossible to know who came first, but the three papers that introduced the economics world to human capital were Theodore W. Schultz's 'Capital Formation by Education' (1960), Jacob Mincer's 'Investment in Human Capital and Personal Income Distribution' (1958) and Gary S. Becker's 'Underinvestment in College Education?' (1960).

Schultz argued simply that skills are malleable, that they are durable and acquired at a cost. As such they fit the capital formation rubric nicely. He also demonstrated that the opportunity costs of students who forgo work to remain in school in the aggregate are roughly equal to the costs of all purchased resources of schools and colleges. Soon afterwards he suggested that an extraordinarily large part of US per capita income growth in the first half of the 20th century was due to growth in education of the citizenry (1961). Mincer's 1958 *Journal of Political Economy* (*JPE*) paper was an extension of his thesis, which relied on the 1940, and 1950 decennial censuses. In this paper he challenged the traditional literature regarding income distributions that had focused only on the aggregate shape, with differences among individuals presumably owing only to luck and ability. After presenting a simple theory showing that with the discounted value of lifetime incomes constant, there would nonetheless be differences in income attributable to the time spent in both formal training and informal on-the-job training. The empirical support followed. In addition to laying the groundwork for what would become possibly *the* major area of empirical study in all of economics, he made the fundamental argument that the distribution of lifetime incomes is more, much more, equal than the point in time distributions. Becker simply showed that as a pure and simple investment for subsequent income alone, rates of return to a college education compare favourably to investments in physical capital. The traditional assumptions regarding the consumption and external benefits of education – for example, the ability to enjoy the arts, and so on, improved choices regarding health and life style and the externality of an informed citizenry – were not to be ignored: education is undoubtedly consumption in part, but there is also real productive value.

The introduction of the ideas of human capital to economics cumulated in T.W. Schultz's 1960 Presidential Address to the American Economics Association, 'Investment in Human Capital' (1961), followed by the collection of articles in the October 1962 *JPE* supplement headlined with Becker's, 'Investment in Human Capital: A Theoretical Analysis' and Mincer's, 'On the Job Training: Costs, Returns, and Some Implications'. The ideas presented in these and a few of the others in the supplement, for example, Stigler's article on search, triggered an intellectual excitement and enthusiasm that coloured almost all of labour economics for the two succeeding decades. During that period, labour economics became one of the foremost applied fields of economics.

Although Mincer matched his contemporaries in insight and imagination, his work is distinguished by his insistence on empirical applicability. An elegant case in point is the piece in the 1962 *JPE* supplement. Noting that age–wage profiles have a consistent tendency to rise rapidly early in a career, less rapidly thereafter, and then stabilize or decline slightly, he characterized the shape of the profile as the result of investment in learning on the job. He began by assuming that the individual has as an option a relatively flat profile equal in discounted value to the value of the observed profile. It follows that immediately after leaving school the difference between the flat profile and the lower actual one is an investment in higher subsequent higher wages. As such, the second period opportunity wage exceeds the flat alternative by the return on the first period's investment, and so on. Assuming, further, that investment declines linearly during the early career, Mincer observed that if the rate of return on the investment in training is approximately equal to the rate used for calculating the flat alternative, then the two will intersect a number of years after leaving school, that is, approximately equal to the inverse of the rate of return. This is his famous 'overtaking point'. Some invest heavily and have a steeply inclined wage profile, while others invest less and have a profile that increases less rapidly. Even so, if the rates of return are independent of the intensity of investment, the alternative paths will intersect at the overtaking point. These are simple descriptives that are easy for graduate students to follow. Maybe that is part of the reason Mincer is so revered. The ultimate pedagogic piece came in his 1974 book *Schooling, Experience and Earnings*.

In that most influential work, Mincer specified the details of 'the' human capital earnings equation. In it the left-hand variable is the logarithm of a rate of wages or earnings. The right-hand side has years of schooling (linearly) and a quadratic is years of work experience approximated by the number of years since leaving school. In the mid-1980s Kevin Murphy and I prepared a paper on empirical age earnings profiles. By way of introduction, we wanted an approximate count of the number of articles in economics journals that had used the Mincer specification. Once we saw it was well over 1,000, we gave up and simply noted that fact.

Mincer's early work on human capital and earnings was interspersed with work on the labour force participation of married women (1960a; 1960b; 1962a). As for his work on wages and experience, it set the stage for a voluminous literature to follow. As noted, he introduced work on earnings profiles of women that included interrupted work careers (1974a; 1974b; 1978a; 1979; 1980). Although he subsequently added excellent work on wage growth and job mobility, the nemesis of economists – the minimum wage, and economic growth – I believe that the most outstanding is the 1978 *JPE* paper, 'Family Migration Decisions', where he made the *ex post* obvious point regarding tried husband–wife movers, namely, in two-career families it is more difficult to find superior alternatives than it is for individuals or for one-career families. Moreover, the difficulty of finding superior alternatives increases as the specialization of the careers increases. As is true of most of his work, whether he pioneered or joined an existing literature, he greatly influenced what was to follow.

Mincer thought about and worked on important problems. He was original. You expected to learn any time you read a Mincer paper. Further, he always looked for applications: the theory had an empirical counterpart. Equally important, he was simply very good at what he did. He was an excellent colleague, teacher, and mentor to his doctoral students. He was also a great man. I am honoured to have known him.

Jacob Mincer retired from Columbia University in 1991. In 2002, the Institute for the Study of Labor (IZA) in Bonn awarded him the inaugural IZA Prize in Labor Economics. The prize was announced at his 80th birthday celebration hosted by Columbia University. In 2003 Mincer and Gary Becker were the inaugural recipients of the Society of Labor Economists (SOLE) Career Achievement Award. That award was then renamed the Jacob Mincer Award, in honour of the great man.

FINIS WELCH

See also **returns to schooling; women's work and wages.**

Selected works

1958. Investment in human capital and personal income distribution. *Journal of Political Economy* 66, 281–302.

1960a. Employment and consumption. *Review of Economics and Statistics* 42, 20–6.

1960b. Labor supply, family income and consumption. *Papers and Proceedings of the American Economic Association* 50, 574–83.

1962a. Labor force participation of married women. In *Aspects of Labor Economics*, ed. H.G. Lewis. Princeton: Princeton University Press.

1962b. On the job training: costs, returns, and some implications. In *Investment in Human Beings*, 2, U-NB Conference, printed in *Journal of Political Economy* 70(Suppl), 50–79.

1974a. Family investment in human capital: earnings of women, with S. Polacheck. *Journal of Political Economy* 82, 76–108.

1974b. *Schooling, Experience and Earnings*. New York: NBER.

1978. Family migration decisions. *Journal of Political Economy* 86, 749–73.

1978. (With S. Polachek.) Women's earnings reexamined. *Journal of Human Resources* 13, 118–34.

1979. (With H. Ofek.) Lifetime distribution of labor supply of married women. *Journal of Political Economy* 87, 197–202.

1980. Research in earnings and labor supply of women. In *Conference on Women in the Labor Market*, ed. C. Lloyd, E. Andrews and C. Gilroy. New York: Columbia University Press.

Bibliography

Becker, G.S. 1960. Underinvestment in college education? *American Economic Review* 50, 346–54. Repr. in *Problems of Economic Growth* ed. E. Phelps. New York: Norton, 1962.

Becker, G.S. 1962. Investment in human capital: a theoretical analysis. *Journal of Political Economy* 5, 9–49.

Schultz, T.W. 1960. Capital formation by education. *Journal of Political Economy* 6, 571–83.

Schultz, T.W. 1961. Education and economic growth. In *Social Forces Influencing American Education*, ed. N.B. Henry. Chicago: University of Chicago Press.

Schultz, T.W. 1961. Investment in human capital. *American Economic Review* 51, 1–17.

minimum wages

The term minimum wages refers to various legal restrictions on the lowest wage rate payable by employers to workers. Until relatively recently, wage floors usually had a very specific focus; in Great Britain and the United States, for example, minimum wages were initially limited to women and children. Only following the Great Depression were such laws extended systematically to the general work force in many industrial and industrializing economies. The minimum wage restrictions were often industry specific, in France for example, extensions of trade union legislation (Rosa, 1981). In the United States, industry-specific wage restrictions were held to be unconstitutional; in 1938 a uniform national minimum wage rate was established for non-farm, non-supervisory personnel under the Fair Labor Standards Act. Subsequently, coverage was extended to the bulk of the labour force.

The social appeal of minimum wage legislation appears to be strong, its intuitive base rooted in concern about the equity of market processes. Dissatisfaction with the share of production allocated to the least able members of the work force is prevalent even among individuals impressed with the enormous capacity of the market system to organize productive activity. An obvious solution to this problem, and one that can be implemented with a modest government budget commitment for statute enforcement, is to redefine the wage structure politically to achieve a socially preferable distribution of income. Although the political interests that have formed the most prominent support for minimum wage legislation may have had less socially oriented goals, for example, Colberg (1960) and Silberman and Durden (1978), broad public support for such legislation is, I believe, based on this equity issue and it is usually against the social criterion of poverty reduction that minimum wage legislation has been judged.

Stigler (1946) provides the classic discussion of the potential deficiencies of minimum wage legislation as an antipoverty device; employment may fall more than in proportion to the wage increase from the minimum, thereby reducing earnings: wage rates in uncovered sectors may decrease more than those in the covered sector rise as the uncovered sector is forced to absorb the workers released by the covered sector: the impact of the legislation on family income distribution may be perverse unless the fewer but better jobs are allocated to members of needy families rather than to low-wage workers, most obviously teenagers, from wealthier families. A crucial insight by economists is that minimum wage legislation alters the opportunity set of the least able but does not unambiguously expand it. The legal restriction that employers cannot pay less than a specified wage is equivalent to the legal stipulation that workers cannot work at all in the protected sector unless they find employers willing to hire them at that wage. Much of the progress in the analysis of minimum wage effects in the last several decades has focused on the theoretical and empirical modelling needed to assess the welfare implications of this altered opportunity set.

As the theoretical modelling of the low-wage labour market has become more complete, theoretical predictions of minimum wage law effects have, unfortunately, become qualitatively ambiguous. Most models have been designed to capture the major features of minimum wage legislation in the United States, a uniform wage minimum covering a portion of a competitive economy. The principal implication of such models is that employment in the covered sector will fall with the establishment of an effective minimum wage. If labour supply is inelastic, these disemployed workers will seek and presumably find employment in the uncovered sector. The wages and well-being of workers in the uncovered sector might be expected to fall as that sector is forced to absorb additional workers (Stigler, 1946; Welch, 1974; 1978). Johnson (1969) demonstrates, however, that in a general equilibrium framework with two factors (labour and capital) the well-being of uncovered workers could in fact rise. If the covered sector is sufficiently capital intense and faces a sufficiently high demand elasticity, the quantity of capital released as the covered sector contracts could potentially increase the well-being of workers in the uncovered sector. The introduction of an elastic labour supply function (and implicitly or explicitly some valuable non-market activity) suggests additional parameters that must be estimated before theoretical considerations can be brought to bear on the assessment of the minimum wage (Welch, 1974).

The modelling of minimum wage effects on unemployment and labour force participation is more complex than on employment, requiring careful specification of the search process (Mincer, 1976). The effect of a minimum wage on unemployment, for instance, depends critically on the queuing method required to secure high paying jobs and on the optimal search strategy induced by this hiring regime. If, for example, workers must wait in a union hall to secure jobs in the covered sector, the extent of unemployment will be quite different than if they can maintain their places in the queue for covered employment while in an uncovered sector job or while out of the labour force entirely.

Before turning to the empirical evidence on minimum wage effects, a brief comment on compliance is warranted. Legal compliance with the minimum wage laws in the United States appears to be surprisingly high (Ashenfelter and Smith, 1979). Effective evasion of small minimum wage restrictions, however, is probably quite high since wages are only a portion of the employment compensation package (Wessels, 1980). Non-wage benefits such as paid vacations are almost completely fungible. Indeed, the envelope theorem would suggest that modest adjustments among components in the total compensation package could be made without affecting employer costs or, equally important, worker welfare. Larger minimum wage restrictions would presumably raise covered worker welfare and employer costs, but not at the rate suggested by the wage-only compensation models.

Among other adjustments employers could make to an increase in the wage minimum would be an increase in effort demands or a reduction in the convenience (or number) of scheduled work hours. Perhaps of greater concern to economists is the potential for a reduction in the provision of on-the-job training to the young. The adverse training effects of legal minimum wages appear to be significant (Leighton and Mincer, 1981; Hashimoto, 1982), although perhaps partly offset by increased schooling in a broader picture (Mattila, 1981).

Clearly the effect of minimum wage laws on the wages and well-being of the labour force must be resolved empirically, either by estimation of the parameters in the theoretical models or by direct estimation of labour market effects. The latter approach has been the most common. Unfortunately, the evidence for the United States labour market (for which such estimation is most prevalent) is not as useful as one might hope. The political equilibrium in the United States has apparently kept the legal wage minimum relatively low. Only in a few circumstances has the minimum been so large as to induce major industrial contractions, for example in the South in the early years of the legislation (Colberg, 1960), and in Puerto Rico, most dramatically in that same period (Reynolds and Gregory, 1965). For most of the more recent period, the wage minimum has been primarily limited in impact to teenagers of both sexes and to adult females (Kneisner, 1981), both of which groups have significant non-market alternatives subject to their own exogenous forces.

The empirical literature on employment effects of the legal minimum wage in the United States suggests that the economywide employment effects of wage minimums at recent levels are negative but not large (Eccles and Freeman, 1982; Brown, Gilroy and Kohen, 1982). Most estimates are bounded by employment elasticities of minus 1 (a reduction in employment equiproportional to the increase in the wage minimum) and zero. Brown, Gilroy and Kohen argue for an estimate towards the zero portion of that range. The effects may, however, not be constant over a wider range of minimum wage restrictions; as the potential for substitution within the total compensation package is reduced, the employment effects will almost surely increase. Certainly minimum wage restrictions that are 'large' relative to customary wages appear to have very large effects, whether considered regionally (again Colberg, 1960; Reynolds and Gregory, 1965), or by economic sector (Fleisher, 1981).

Highly visible work by Card and Krueger (1994; 1995) has focused on 'natural experiments' generated by changes in the minimum wage. In 1992 the minimum wage was increased in New Jersey. Card and Krueger estimated the effect of the minimum wage on employment in fast-food restaurants in New Jersey compared with neighbouring Pennsylvania, where there was no increase in the minimum wage, and found that employment increased in New Jersey relative to Pennsylvania. Kennan (1995) discussed this work and potential explanations and subsequent research by Neumark and Wascher (2000) questioned their results.

For most individuals not directly involved in buying or selling low skilled labour, the critical empirical question is not the magnitude of the employment effects of minimum wages but rather the effect on income poverty.

Obviously large negative employment effects would suggest that the antipoverty effects of the minimum wage are small or possibly even perverse. Direct empirical studies of antipoverty effects (Gramlich, 1976; Parsons, 1980) indicate, however, that the antipoverty effects in the United States would be quite modest even if employment effects were zero. The great majority of low-wage workers do not come from families in poverty. Moreover, the groups primarily affected, teenagers and low-skilled adult females, are predominantly part-time workers and any wage-rate effect on earnings and income is strictly proportional to hours worked. Even a fully effective wage minimum with no offsetting employment adjustment would provide little relief to poverty-level families (Parsons, 1980). Negative employment effects simply enhance other fundamental limitations of minimum wage legislation as a poverty programme.

Wage rate restrictions alone appear to be an unsatisfactory solution to social concerns about labour market outcomes. Politically manipulating the price system seems like a direct and inexpensive method of assisting the disadvantaged. Almost surely it is not. Employment opportunities and the factors that limit labour market participation must be considered as well as wage rates if market outcomes are to be supplanted in a socially satisfactory way for low-skilled workers.

ORIGINAL BY DONALD O. PARSONS; REVISED BY BRUCE WEINBERG

See also **labour economics.**

Bibliography

Ashenfelter, O. and Smith, R.S. 1979. Compliance with the minimum wage law. *Journal of Political Economy* 87, 333–50.

Brown, C., Gilroy, C. and Kohen, A. 1982. The effect of the minimum wage on employment and unemployment. *Journal of Economic Literature* 20, 487–528.

Card, D. and Krueger, A.B. 1994. Minimum wages and employment: a case study of the fast-food industry in New Jersey and Pennsylvania. *American Economic Review* 84, 772–93.

Card, D. and Krueger, A.B. 1995. *Myth and Measurement: The New Economics of the Minimum Wage.* Princeton, NJ: Princeton University Press.

Colberg, M.R. 1960. Minimum wage effects on Florida's economic development. *Journal of Law and Economics* 3, 106–17.

Eccles, M. and Freeman, R.B. 1982. What! Another minimum wage study? *American Economic Review* 94, 226–32.

Fleisher, B.M. 1981. *Minimum Wage Regulation in Retail Trade.* Washington, DC: American Enterprise Institute.

Gramlich, E.M. 1976. Impact of minimum wages on other wages, employment, and family incomes. *Brookings Papers on Economic Activity* 1976(2), 409–51.

Hashimoto, M. 1982. Minimum wage effects on training on the job. *American Economic Review* 72, 1070–87.

Johnson, H.J. 1969. Minimum wage laws: a general equilibrium analysis. *Canadian Journal of Economics* 2, 599–604.

Kennan, J. 1995. The elusive effects of minimum wages. *Journal of Economic Literature* 33, 1950–65.

Kneisner, T.J. 1981. The low-wage workers: who are they? In Rottenberg (1981).

Leighton, L. and Mincer, J. 1981. The effects of minimum wages on human capital formation. In Rottenberg (1981).

Mattila, J. 1981. The impact of minimum wages on teenage schooling and part-time full-time employment of youths. In Rottenberg (1981).

Mincer, J. 1976. Unemployment effects of minimum wages. *Journal of Political Economy* 84, S87–S104.

Neumark, D. and Wascher, W. 2000. Minimum wages and employment: a case study of the fast-food industry in New Jersey and Pennsylvania: comment. *American Economic Review* 90, 1362–96.

Parsons, D.O. 1980. *Poverty and the Minimum Wage*. Washington, DC: American Enterprise Institute.

Reynolds, L.G. and Gregory, P. 1965. *Wages, Productivity, and Industrialization in Puerto Rico*. Homewood, IL: Richard D. Irwin.

Rosa, J.J. 1981. The effects of minimum wage regulation in France. In Rottenberg (1981).

Rottenberg, S., ed. 1981. *The Economics of Legal Minimum Wages*. Washington, DC: American Enterprise Institute.

Silberman, J. and Durden, G.C. 1978. Determining legislative preferences on the minimum wage: an economic approach. *Journal of Political Economy* 84, 317–29.

Stigler, G.J. 1946. The economics of minimum wage legislation. *American Economic Review* 36, 358–65.

Welch, F. 1974. Minimum wage legislation in the United States. *Economic Inquiry* 12, 285–318.

Welch, F. 1978. *Minimum Wages: Issues and Evidence*. Washington, DC: American Enterprise Institute.

Wessels, W.J. 1980. The effect of minimum wages on fringe benefits: an expanded model. *Economic Inquiry* 18, 293–13.

Mirrlees, James (born 1936)

Professor Sir James Mirrlees was born in Scotland in 1936 and educated at Edinburgh University and Trinity College, Cambridge. He held academic posts at Trinity College and at Nuffield College, Oxford, and was awarded the Nobel Prize in economics in 1996 for his work on optimal income taxation and its extension to information and incentive problems in general. Mirrlees also made important contributions to growth theory, development economics and public economics.

Growth and development

The initial work of Mirrlees focused upon technical progress in models of economic growth. Kaldor and Mirrlees (1962) assumed technical progress was embodied in new investment with the growth rate of productivity per worker operating on new machines an increasing concave function of the growth rate of investment per worker. The incorporation of externalities between different firms' investment decisions made this paper a precursor of the literature on endogenous growth theory. The problem of optimal growth in an economy subject to deterministic technical change was discussed in Mirrlees (1967). An extension to stochastic diffusion in continuous time showing that increased uncertainty would often lead to more saving rather than less was given in Mirrlees's Ph.D. dissertation and circulated in unpublished work (Mirrlees, 1965). These themes were also addressed in Mirrlees (1974a).

Mirrlees contributed to development economics via the influential Little and Mirrlees (1968; 1974) handbook of project appraisal ('the manual'). The manual was a practical guide to the use of cost–benefit analysis designed to contribute to improvements in the economic conditions of developing countries. It took as its starting point the use of shadow prices to value all inputs and outputs, regardless of whether they were marketable or non-marketable, and showed how shadow prices should be determined. In particular, it emphasized the use of border prices to value inputs and outputs when the project was located in a small country. When goods were not traded, it provided methods for valuing them based on the prices of traded goods. The manual emphasized that investment finance was scarce because of the government's budget constraint, so social profits should be discounted at the internal rate of return for the marginal investment project. The manual also studied constraints upon policy choices and how these affected shadow prices.

The recommendations of the manual provided a simple but powerful methodology. Since its publication they have been subjected to much theoretical scrutiny that has generally confirmed their validity. The practical impact of the Little–Mirrlees approach can be judged from the number of donor agencies that adopted it to guide their decisions. Foremost among these was the World Bank, where cost–benefit analysis was the dominant decision-making method throughout the 1970s. Its use has steadily declined since, which is attributed by Little and Mirrlees (1994) to the changing nature of lending and the internal institutional structure of the World Bank.

Income taxation

In a seminal paper Mirrlees (1971, p. 175) studied 'what principles should govern an optimum income tax; what such a tax schedule would look like; and what degree of inequality would remain once it was established'.

Addressing this question required a model that included a motive for the redistribution of income because of endogenously generated inequality, incentive effects in labour supply and a justification for using an income tax rather than lump-sum taxation. The success of Mirlees's model was that it managed to capture all this but remained tractable and allowed the optimum tax to be characterized. No better model of income taxation has yet been proposed, although new results are still being discovered within the original framework and its specializations – see, for example, Diamond (1998), Saez (2001) and Hashimzade and Myles (2007).

The paper demonstrated that an optimum income tax leads to an allocation in which pre-tax income is increasing with ability, and that the marginal tax rate is between zero and one. Furthermore, unemployment is possible at the optimum and, when it occurs, is of the lowest-ability workers. The numerical analysis provides some of the most surprising findings. The optimal marginal rate of tax is low, at least compared with the rates applied in many countries at the time the paper was written. Furthermore, the marginal tax rate is fairly constant, so the tax function is close to being linear. These results motivated Mirlees's observation (1971, p. 207) that 'I had expected the rigorous analysis of income-taxation in the utilitarian manner to provide an argument for high tax rates. It has not done so.'

The analysis of the model required Mirrlees to formulate and solve a series of novel theoretical problems. In doing so he developed a series of techniques that have since become standard tools of economic analysis. In the income tax problem the government must offer the workers a budget constraint along which each chooses an optimal location through utility maximization. Since the budget constraint can be nonlinear it is possible for there to be multiple optimal choices for a worker, so choice cannot be represented by a demand function. The fundamental contribution of the paper was to show how this problem could be circumvented by viewing the government as selecting an allocation (an income–consumption pair) for each worker. If every worker prefers his allocation to that of any other, then each will willingly select the allocation intended for him. This is the notion of incentive compatibility: a worker of ability level s must find that the allocation designed for someone of this ability gives at least as much utility as the allocation designed for any other ability s'. The government then conducts its optimization over the set of incentive-compatible allocations. The imposition of incentive compatibility reduces the set of feasible allocations and is responsible for the second-best nature of the optimum tax.

The paper also showed that the problem can be reduced further if workers' preferences over allocations are consistently related to ability. The restriction upon preferences introduced in Mirrlees (1971) has since become known as the single-crossing condition and

implies that at every point in income–consumption space the indifference curve of a high-ability worker is flatter than that of a low-ability worker. Under single crossing, incentive compatibility requires high-ability workers to earn higher incomes and enjoy higher levels of consumption. The single-crossing condition has since found countless applications in problems involving the design of contracts for populations with agents of differing characteristics. With a continuum of consumers, it is not practical to state the incentive compatibility constraints directly. Mirlees (1971) surmounted this problem in a simple but ingenious way by showing that incentive compatibility is equivalent to utility being maximized at a worker's true skill level. The first-order condition for this optimization generates a differential equation that determines the evolution of utility as a function of ability. The differential equation can be used as a constraint on the optimization. This technique has since become known as the first-order approach to 'maximization subject to maximization'. The first-order condition is necessary but not sufficient, so there exists the possibility that the tax function arising from the optimization analysis may violate the monotonicity requirement. A direct solution to this problem is to incorporate the second-order condition into the optimization (see Ebert, 1992). The 1971 income tax paper appreciated this issue, and the limitations of the first-order approach remained an issue that was addressed further in Mirlees's later work on the principal–agent problem.

That the optimum involved monotonicity implied an important observation: those with higher skills earn and consume more, so, although the government cannot directly observe skill, in equilibrium it can infer skill from income. Hence, given the optimum tax function, the announcement by a consumer of an income level is just a proxy for the direct announcement of a level of skill. This observation was later formalized in the revelation principle (Dasgupta, Hammond and Maskin, 1979; Myerson, 1979) that shows it is possible to replace the income tax with an equivalent direct mechanism in which each consumer announces a skill level and, furthermore, announcing the true skill level is a dominant strategy. The revelation principle is now applied routinely in the analysis of incentive problems.

Commodity taxation

Diamond and Mirrlees (1971a; 1971b) revolutionized the theory of commodity taxation. The papers clarify the separation between consumer and producer prices and show that the choice of untaxed commodity is just a normalization that plays no role in determining the optimum allocation. They were among the first to employ the emerging duality methods and used the indirect utility function to phrase the problem in terms of the after-tax consumer prices that were the natural choice variables. As well as these innovations, the commodity taxation papers contain two fundamental results. The first is the simple rule of thumb that the imposition of an optimum commodity tax system requires an equal proportionate reduction in compensated demand for all commodities. This conclusion emphasizes that the real effect of a tax system is on consumers' demands and that the effect on prices is of secondary importance. The second result, now known as the production efficiency lemma, is more surprising and of significant practical value for policy.

The production efficiency lemma states that the optimum commodity tax system results in an equilibrium that is on the frontier of the production set. There are some limitations to this result, most notably nonconstant returns to scale, which imply that achieving efficiency may require some firms to be shut down, thus adversely affecting their owners' incomes. Such restrictions are clarified in Mirrlees (1972). The policy value of the lemma follows from observing that efficiency is only possible if there are no distortions in the input prices faced by producers. Input taxes should not therefore be a feature of the optimum set of commodity taxes, implying that intermediate goods should not be taxed. This observation justifies the use of value-added taxation with tax rebates available for producers who purchase intermediate goods. It also suggests that capital held by firms should not be subject to taxation, though dividends paid to consumers can and probably should be, along with their realized capital gains.

Theoretically, the production efficiency lemma is especially surprising when contrasted with the conclusions of Lipsey and Lancaster's (1956) second-best theory. The central message of Lipsey and Lancaster was that a distortion in any sector of the economy should generally be offset by introducing distortions in all other sectors. This finding had achieved great prominence at the time the Diamond–Mirrlees article was published. In contrast, the lemma states that, even when distortionary taxes and subsidies are being introduced into consumer decisions in order to redistribute real income or to finance public goods, there is no reason to distort producer decisions. This special case runs counter to the general message of Lipsey–Lancaster.

Principal–agent

The third area to which Mirrlees made a fundamental contribution is the principal–agent problem that arises when one party wishes another to undertake an act on his or her behalf. If the act undertaken cannot be observed directly and its consequences observed only with some random error, then moral hazard can occur: the agent can attempt to hide behind the randomness to take an action which is less costly to the agent but which yields a lower expected return to the principal. Such a problem can arise in any economic relationship based on contingent contracts, for example between the owner and

the manager of a firm. Mirrlees (1974b; 1975) analysed the problem facing the principal in designing a contract that provides an incentive to the agent to take the action that yields the highest expected payoff to the principal. There are considerable analytical similarities between the design of this contract and the choice of an optimum income tax. These similarities arise because the principal is choosing the contract to maximize expected payoff subject to the agent choosing an action to maximize his or her payoff. This leads again to a situation of maximization subject to maximization and its analysis via incentive compatibility.

When the agent must choose from a finite set of actions the incentive compatibility constraints can be employed directly. This is impractical for the continuous case where there would be an uncountable infinity of constraints. Consequently, it again becomes necessary to use the first-order conditions for the agent's choice problem as a constraint on the optimization of the principal. Although this had been used prior to Mirrlees's analysis of the principal–agent problem (Zeckhauser, 1970), it had not been noticed that the approach might fail to generate the optimum. This possibility was made very clear in Mirrlees (1975), which provided an example where the first-order approach failed to generate the optimum and proceeded to discuss how the problem could be overcome. The method proposed identified the possible maxima and incorporated them as constraints into the optimization. This method works but has proved unwieldy in practice, so most analyses rely on the first-order approach despite its known weaknesses. These issues were explored even further in Mirrlees (1986) and in Mirrlees and Roberts (1980).

A further issue that arises in principal–agent relationships is the conditions that guarantee the reward from the contract is monotonic: that is, the payment to the agent increases as observed output increases. If there are only two possible output levels, monotonicity arises naturally. With three possible output levels, monotonicity can easily fail (Grossman and Hart, 1983). Mirrlees (1976) introduced the monotone likelihood ratio condition that is sufficient for monotonicity. This condition requires that actions that are more costly for the agent to undertake make more profitable outcomes relatively more likely. Although weaker conditions are available (Jewitt, 1988), the monotone likelihood ratio condition has become another essential component of the economic theorist's toolkit. It is, of course, closely related to the single-crossing property that plays such an important role in the income tax paper.

The work of Mirrlees has contributed to the understanding of economic policy via the manual and the papers on tax policy. His work also laid the foundation for the analysis of incentive problems in the presence of asymmetric information. Taken together, incentive compatibility, the extension of the first-order approach, the single-crossing property and the monotone likelihood ratio condition provide the basic tools that no economic theorist can be without. There has not been a single area of economics in which they have not been used to great advantage.

GARETH D. MYLES

See also **incentive compatibility; income taxation and optimal policies; neoclassical growth theory; principal and agent (i); principal and agent (ii); revelation principle.**

Selected works

1962. (With N. Kaldor.) A new model of economic growth. *Review of Economic Studies* 29, 174–90.

1965. Optimal capital accumulation under uncertainty. Unpublished manuscript.

1967. Optimum growth when technology is changing. *Review of Economic Studies* 34, 95–124.

1968. (With I. Little.) *Manual of Industrial Project Analysis in Developing Countries, Vol. II: Social Cost–Benefit Analysis.* Paris: OECD.

1971. An exploration in the theory of optimum income taxation. *Review of Economic Studies* 38, 175–208.

1971a. (With P. Diamond.) Optimal taxation and public production I: Production efficiency. *American Economic Review* 61, 8–27.

1971b. (With P. Diamond.) Optimal taxation and public production II: Tax rules. *American Economic Review* 61, 261–78.

1972. On producer taxation. *Review of Economic Studies* 39, 105–11.

1974a. Optimal allocation under uncertainty. In *Allocation Under Uncertainty*, ed. J. Drèze. London: Macmillan.

1974b. Notes on welfare economics, information and uncertainty. In *Essays in Equilibrium Behavior under Uncertainty*, ed. M. Balch, D. McFadden and S. Wu. Amsterdam: North-Holland.

1974. (With I. Little.) *Project Appraisal and Planning for Developing Countries.* London: Heinemann.

1975. The theory of moral hazard and unobservable behaviour, Part I. Mimeo. Oxford: Nuffield College. Published in *Review of Economic Studies* 66 (1999), 3–21.

1976. The optimal structure of incentives and authority within an organization. *Bell Journal of Economics* 7, 105–31.

1980. (With K. Roberts.) Functions with multiple maxima. Mimeo. Oxford: Nuffield College.

1986. The theory of optimal taxation. In *Handbook of Mathematical Economics*, vol. 3, ed. K. Arrow and M. Intriligator. Amsterdam: North-Holland.

1994. (With I. Little.) The costs and benefits of analysis: project appraisal and planning twenty years on. In *Cost–Benefit Analysis*, ed. R. Layard and S. Glaister. Cambridge: Cambridge University Press.

Bibliography

Dasgupta, P., Hammond, P. and Maskin, E. 1979. The implementation of social choice rules: some general results in incentive compatibility. *Review of Economic Studies* 46, 185–216.

Diamond, P. 1998. Optimal income taxation: an example with a U-shaped pattern of optimal marginal tax rates. *American Economic Review* 88, 83–95.

Ebert, U. 1992. A reexamination of the optimal nonlinear income tax. *Journal of Public Economics* 49, 47–73.

Grossman, S. and Hart, O. 1983. An analysis of the principal–agent problem. *Econometrica* 51, 7–45.

Hashimzade, N. and Myles, G. 2007. The structure of the optimal income tax in the quasi-linear model. *International Journal of Economic Theory* 3, 5–33.

Jewitt, I. 1988. Justifying the first-order approach to principal–agent problems. *Econometrica* 56, 1177–90.

Lipsey, R. and Lancaster, K. 1956. The general theory of second best. *Review of Economic Studies* 24, 11–32.

Myerson, R. 1979. Incentive compatibility and the bargaining problem. *Econometrica* 47, 61–73.

Saez, E. 2001. Using elasticities to derive optimal income tax rules. *Review of Economic Studies* 68, 205–29.

Zeckhauser, R. 1970. Medical insurance: a case study of the tradeoff between risk spreading and appropriate incentives. *Journal of Economic Theory*

Mises, Ludwig Edler von (1881–1973)

Mises was born in Lemberg, Austria-Hungary, on 29 September 1881 and died in New York City on 18 October 1973. The son of a Viennese construction engineer for the Austrian railroads, Mises enrolled in the University of Vienna in 1900. He earned his doctorate in law and economics in 1906, after which he became a leading member of Böhm-Bawerk's famous seminar at the university. From 1913 to 1934, Mises taught as an unpaid *Privatdozent* at the University of Vienna, conducting a seminar on economic theory. From 1909 to 1934, he was an economist for the Vienna Chamber of Commerce, serving as the principal economic adviser to the Austrian government.

Disturbed at encroaching Nazi influence in Austria, Mises accepted a professorship at the Graduate Institute of International Studies in Geneva, where he taught from 1934 to 1940, after which he emigrated to New York City. Mises became a visiting professor at New York University in 1948, where he continued to teach a seminar on economic theory until he retired in 1969, spry and energetic at the age of 87.

Mises' multifaceted achievements in economic theory built upon the insights and methodology of the Menger–Böhm-Bawerk Austrian School of economics. In contrast to the Jevons and Walras branches of marginal utility theory, the Austrians engaged in a logical analysis of the action of individuals, their major focus on a step-by-step process analysis rather than on the necessarily unreal world of static general equilibrium. Furthermore, 'cause', for the Austrians, was a unilinear 'causal-genetic' flow from individual utilities and actions to price, rather than the familiar neoclassical mutual determination of mathematical functions.

Mises' first pioneering accomplishment was to extend Austrian analysis to money. In his *Theory of Money and Credit* (1912) he succeeded in integrating money into micro-theory, demonstrating how the marginal utility of money interacts with utilities of other goods and with the supply of money to determine money prices. In doing so, Mises solved 'the problem of the Austrian circle', a formidable obstacle for any causal-genetic theorist. Since money, unlike other goods, is demanded not for its own sake but to purchase other goods in exchange, a demand to purchase and hold money must assume a pre-existing purchasing power in terms of other goods. How, then, can one explain the existence of that purchasing power; that is, of money prices? In his 'regression theorem', Mises, building on Menger's insights into the origin of money, demonstrated that the demand for money can be pushed back logically to the 'day' before the money-commodity became money, when it had purchasing power only as a commodity valuable in barter. Hence, every money must originate on the market as a valuable non-monetary commodity and cannot begin by being imposed by the state, or in an ad hoc social contract.

There were many other notable contributions in *Money and Credit*. Though superficially similar to the quantity theory of money, Mises' process analysis demonstrated the inevitable non-neutral impact of money on relative prices and incomes. Indeed, he levelled a devastating critique of such neutral-money concepts as Fisher's equation of exchange and the idea of stabilizing 'the price level'. Moreover, Mises developed a cash-balance analysis, independently of the Cambridge School and on an individualistic rather than an aggregative and holistic basis. And before Gustav Cassel, Mises set forth a purchasing-power parity theory of exchange rates under fiat money, based on a Ricardian array of goods rather than on Cassel's price-level approach (Wu, 1939, pp. 115–16, 126–7, 232–5).

Money and Credit also revived the Ricardian–Currency School insight that no quantity of the money supply can be more optimal than any other. Since money's sole function is to exchange, an increase in its quantity can only dilute the purchasing power of each money unit and can confer no social benefit. Mises concluded that fractional reserve banking, or 'circulation credit', is inflationary and distorts prices and production. He showed the ideal banking system to be 100 per cent reserves of bank notes and demand deposits to standard gold or silver. On the other hand, eight years before C.A. Phillips (Phillips, 1920), Mises showed that any individual bank is necessarily severely restricted in expanding credit, so that the abolition of central banking would go far to eliminate the problem of inflationary banking.

Finally, in analysing marginal utility, Mises incorporated the insights of the Czech Franz Cuhel (1907), a fellow member of Böhm-Bawerk's seminar, to demonstrate that marginal utility can in no sense be a measurable, mathematical quantity. Instead, it can only be a strictly ordinal subjective preference ranking; hence there can be no 'total utility' as an integral of marginal utilities. There can only be varying marginal utilities depending on the size of the 'margin', the actual unit of human choice.

Although two semesters of Böhm-Bawerk's seminar were devoted to discussing *Money and Credit*, the older Austrians resisted this new development (Mises, 1978, pp. 59–60). Mises proceeded to found his own 'neo-Austrian' school, centred in his renowned biweekly private seminar at the Chamber of Commerce. Leading participants and followers included F.A. Hayek, Fritz Machlup, Gottfried von Haberler, Oskar Morgenstern, Wilhelm Ropke, Richard von Strigl, Alfred Schutz, Felix Kaufmann, Erich Voegelin, Georg Halm, Paul Rosenstein-Rodan and Lionel Robbins.

During the 1920s Mises developed (from its beginnings in *Money and Credit*) his notable theory of the business cycle, one of the few to be integrated with general micro-theory (Mises, 1923–31). Formed out of the Currency School, Böhm-Bawerk's theory of capital and Wicksell's distinction between natural and loan rates of interest, Mises' 'monetary malinvestment' theory sees the boom–bust cycle as the inevitable product of inflationary credit expansion. This expansion artificially lowers interest rates and induces unsound overinvestments in higher-order capital goods, as well as underinvestment in consumer goods. Any cessation of credit expansion reveals the malinvestments and the lack of sufficient savings, and the ensuing recession liquidates the distortions of the boom and restores a healthy economy.

Mises founded the Austrian Institute for Business Cycle Research in 1926, and his cycle theory later won attention as an explanation of the Great Depression. His most important student and follower, F.A. Hayek, who had elaborated on the theory, emigrated to the London School of Economics in 1931 and strongly influenced a rising generation of English economists. Unfortunately, most of this influence was swept away in the flush of enthusiasm for the Keynesian Revolution.

When socialism emerged after the First World War, Mises wrote a classic article (Mises, 1920; 1922), demonstrating that a socialist government could not calculate economically and therefore could not organize a complex industrial economy. For two decades, socialists in Europe tried to rebut Mises' contentions, but not only had he anticipated their objections, he explicitly refuted them in the late 1940s (Mises, 1949; Hoff, 1949). If socialism could not calculate, and state interventionism only creates problems in the name of solving them (Mises, 1929), then the only viable and truly prosperous economy is laissez-faire. In a century marked by accelerating statism and collectivism, Mises stood out among scholars as an uncompromising stalwart of laissez-faire (Mises, 1927).

Austrian economists had virtually begun with defence of economic theory against the German Historical School (Menger, 1883). Amidst a rising tide of logical positivism, Mises now set forth and elaborated 'praxeology', the methodology of Nassau Senior and of the Austrians (Bowley, 1937). In contrast to the physical sciences, economic laws are discovered by logical deduction from self-evident axioms, such as that human beings exist and pursue goals. Praxeology develops the logical implications of the fact of individual human action (Mises, 1933; 1949). Historical events are the complex resultants of many causal factors; they are not simple, homogeneous events that can, as in the positivist schema, be used to 'test' theory. Instead, prior theory must be used to explain and understand history (Mises, 1957; Robbins, 1932; Kirzner, 1960).

In the culmination of his life-work, Mises put his methodological precepts into practice by constructing a systematic edifice of economic theory, completing the neo-Austrian integration of micro- and macroeconomics. First published in German in 1940, this monumental treatise was refined and expanded in his English-language *Human Action* (Mises, 1949). Some notable features were a resurrection of Fetter's pure time-preference theory of interest; a theory of subjective costs; and a dynamic emphasis on profit-and-loss as the motive power of the economy, and on profit as a reward for successful entrepreneurial forecasting.

Even though an exile late in life, the trend of the world and of academia against him, and remaining only a visiting professor, Mises maintained his good cheer and productivity and gradually built up a new group of followers in the United States. Since his death there has been a veritable renaissance of interest in his thought and works, including the establishment of an institute in his name at Auburn University (Moss, 1976; Andrews, 1981; Kirzner, 1982; Rothbard, 1973).

MURRAY N. ROTHBARD

Selected works

1912. *The Theory of Money and Credit*, 3rd English edn. Indianapolis: Liberty Classics, 1981.
1920. Economic calculation in the socialist commonwealth. In *Collectivist Economic Planning: Critical Studies on the Possibilities of Socialism*, ed. F. von Hayek. London: Routledge & Sons, 1935.
1922. *Socialism: An Economic and Sociological Analysis*, 3rd English edn. Indianapolis: Liberty Classics, 1981.
1923–31. *On the Manipulation of Money and Credit*. Ed. P.E. Greaves, Dobbs Ferry, NY: Free Market Books, 1978.
1927. *Liberalism*, 3rd English edn. Irvington-on-Hudson, NY: Foundation for Economic Education, 1985.
1929. *A Critique of Interventionism*. New Rochelle, NY: Arlington House, 1977.
1933. *Epistemological Problems of Economics*. New York: New York University Press, 1981.

1940. *Nationalökonomie: Theorie des Handelns und Wirtschaftens*. Geneva: Editions Union.
1944a. *Bureaucracy*. New Haven: Yale University Press.
1944b. *Omnipotent Government: The Rise of the Total State and Total War*. Springs Mill, PA: Libertarian Press, 1985.
1949. *Human Action: A Treatise on Economics*, 3rd edn. Chicago: Regnery, 1966.
1957. *Theory and History: An Interpretation of Social and Economic Evolution*, 2nd edn. Auburn, AL: Ludwig von Mises Institute, 1985.
1978. *Notes and Recollections*. South Holland, IL: Libertarian Press.

Bibliography

Andrews, J.K., ed. 1981. *Homage to Mises: The First Hundred Years*. Hillsdale, MO: Hillsdale College Press.
Bien, B., ed. 1969. *The Works of Ludwig von Mises*. Irvington-on-Hudson, NY: Foundation for Economic Education.
Bowley, M. 1937. *Nassau Senior and Classical Economics*. New York: Kelley, 1949.
Cuhel, F. 1907. *Zur Lehre von den Bedürfrissen. Theoretische Untersuchungen über das Grenzgebiet der Ökonomik und Psychologie*. Innsbruck: Wagner.
Hoff, T.J.B. 1949. *Economic Calculation in the Socialist Society*. London: William Hodge.
Kirzner, I.M. 1960. *The Economic Point of View: An Essay in the History of Economic Thought*. Princeton, NJ: Van Nostrand.
Kirzner, I.M., ed. 1982. *Method, Process, and Austrian Economics: Essays in Honor of Ludwig von Mises*. Lexington, MA: Lexington Books.
Menger, C. 1883. *Problems of Economics and Sociology*. Ed. L. Schneider, Urbana, IL: University of Illinois Press, 1963.
Mises, M. von. 1976. *My Years with Ludwig von Mises*, 2nd enlarged edn. Cedar Falls, IA: Center for Futures Education, 1984.
Moss, L., ed. 1976. *The Economics of Ludwig von Mises: Toward a Critical Reappraisal*. Kansas City: Sheed & Ward.
Phillips, C.A. 1920. *Bank Credit*. New York: Macmillan.
Robbins, L. 1932. *An Essay on the Nature and Significance of Economic Science*. London: Macmillan.
Rothbard, M. 1973. *The Essential von Mises*, 3rd edn. Washington, DC: Ludwig von Mises Institute, 1983.
Wu, C.-Y. 1939. *An Outline of International Trade Theories*. London: Routledge.

Misselden, Edward (*fl.* 1608–1654)

Edward Misselden, merchant-economist, held a number of appointments, including that of Deputy Governor of the Merchant Adventurers' Company at Delft, 1623–33, and representative of the Merchant Adventurers and the

East India Company in various trade negotiations. His economic writings stem from his testimony before the Standing Commission on Trade appointed in 1622. His *Free Trade, or the means to make trade flourish* (1622) attributes the 'decay of trade' to the 'undervaluation of His Majesty's coin', 'the want of money', 'the excess of … consuming the commodities of foreign countries', particularly luxury goods (against which he proposed sumptuary laws), the export of bullion by the East India Company, and the decay and inadequate enforcement of regulation of the cloth trades. His proposal to remedy the shortage of money by increasing the denomination of the coin would, he acknowledged, raise general commodity prices, but this would be offset by the 'quickening of trade in every man's hand' that would result from the 'plenty of money'. Landlords and creditors could be protected by requiring that 'contracts made before the raising of monies shall be paid at the value the money went at when the contracts were made'.

Misselden's *Circle of Commerce, or the Balance of Trade* (1623), a long rejoinder to Malynes's attack on his earlier work, effectively sorts out the relation between commodity trade and the international exchange rate. 'It is not the rate of exchange, whether it be higher or lower, that maketh the price of commodities dear or cheap … but it is the plenty or scarcity of commodities, their use or non-use, that maketh them rise or fall in price.' He recognized that actual market prices may deviate from what might be thought to be intrinsic or par values.

Misselden's impressive work on the definition and computation of the balance of trade (explicitly including the earnings from re-exports, profits on fisheries, and freight income) contained an estimate for the year 1621–22, made by multiplying the five per cent customs revenue by 20 to obtain trade volume data. He pointed to the idea of the self-balancing international mechanism in his claim that 'there is a fluxus and refluxus, a flood and ebbe of the monies of Christendom traded within itself: for sometimes there is more in one part … less in another, as one country wanteth and another aboundeth'.

While Misselden advocated a high degree of governmental intervention in the economy, particularly in the granting of exclusive international trading privileges and the regulation of quality standards in domestic trade, he generally opposed the encouragement of monopolies. The free market analogy, which reappears frequently in his arguments, pointed also to the theory of the rate of interest: 'As it is the scarcity of money that maketh the high rates of interest, so the plenty of money will make interest low better than any statute for that purpose.' Misselden's various proposals to correct the 'decay of trade' shared the widespread concern for the state of the 'idle poor'. What was given away as charity, he proposed, should be 'orderly collected and prudently ordered for the employment of the poor'.

DOUGLAS VICKERS

See also **mercantilism.**

Selected works

1622. *Free Trade, or the means to make trade flourish.* London.
1623. *The Circle of Commerce, or the Balance of Trade.* London.

Bibliography

Letiche, J.M. 1959. *Balance of Payments and Economic Growth.* New York: Harper.
Viner, J. 1937. *Studies in the Theory of International Trade.* New York: Harper.

Mitchell, Wesley Clair (1874–1948)

Wesley C. Mitchell was born in Rushville, Illinois, on 5 August 1874 and died on 29 October 1948. Most of his professional life was spent at Columbia University (1913–19, 1922–44) and as Director of Research at the National Bureau of Economic Research in New York (1920–45).

Mitchell's principal contribution to economic theory was indirect – through the emphasis he placed throughout his working life upon the need for close interaction between the development of hypotheses and testing their conformity to fact. This emphasis was explicit both in his own work on business cycles and in the research that he promoted and guided in many fields at the National Bureau. In his final report as Director (1945) he said:

> We like to think of ourselves as helping to lay the foundations of an economics that will consist of statements warranted by evidence a competent reader may judge for himself…. Speculative systems can be quickly excogitated precisely because they do not require the economist to collect and analyze masses of data, to test hypotheses for conformity to fact, to discard those which do not fit, to invent new ones and test them until, at long last, he has established a factually valid theory.

One of the hypotheses that Mitchell formulated has generated one of the longest continued and most widely applied scientific experiments in the field of economics. The hypothesis is that in free enterprise economies business cycles are generated by the continuous interaction of economic activities which lead or lag one another by varying intervals and which differ in amplitude of fluctuation by varying amounts. The processes have been identified and their leads and amplitudes measured on an *ex ante* as well as *ex post* basis. Historical records covering a century or more have been used to test the hypothesis. Private research institutes, governmental and international agencies in more than 30 countries have set up the statistical apparatus required to test the hypothesis, keep the information up-to-date, and derive economic forecasts from it. The information is generally summarized in the form of leading, coincident and lagging indexes.

The types of economic processes that Mitchell considered crucial to his hypothesis were largely identified in his first major work on the subject, *Business Cycles* (1913). The variables included costs, prices and profits; investment decisions and investment expenditures; employment, income and consumption expenditures; interest rates, the volume of money, credit, and bank reserves; inventories and sales. In the original and subsequent treatises he observed how economic agents reacted to changes in economic conditions and how these reactions in turn affected others. To measure leads and lags he defined business cycles in such a way that their peaks and troughs could be dated. Measures of timing, amplitude and rates of change in successive cycles were devised, and summarized across cycles to find out what patterns were typical. Patterns of change within the cycle enabled Mitchell to test whether what happened during one phase had a bearing on what happened in the next, and whether the repetitive sequences corresponded with his expectations based upon economic practices and institutions.

Among the economic processes in business cycles that Mitchell stressed was the imbalance that develops between costs and prices. As an expansion in business activity proceeds, costs of production begin to rise faster than prices. This reduces profit margins and dims the outlook for future profits. This in turn prompts cutbacks in decisions to invest, and leads to reductions in sales, output, and employment. As a recession develops, costs as well as prices increase less rapidly or are reduced, but cost reduction soon begins to exceed price reduction, enhancing prospects for profits and incentives to invest. This in turn helps to bring the recession to an end and get recovery started. Mitchell and others have looked into such questions as what kinds of costs and prices behave in this manner, why they do so, and whether or not the phenomenon is widespread. Comprehensive data bearing on the matter have only become available in recent years, but they show that the pattern has continued to emerge in market-oriented economies some 70 years after Mitchell gave it a central position in his hypothesis about the self-generating character of business cycles.

One of Mitchell's great objectives was to construct a general theory of business cycles consistent with the facts of cyclical experience that he took such pains to observe and record. His respect for the value of economic theory was demonstrated not only by this objective, but also by his long concern with the history of economic thought. For many years he taught a famous course at Columbia University called Types of Economic Theory, and lecture notes taken stenographically by students were subsequently published under that title (1949). The lectures traced the historical origins of economic theories and related their development to particular legal, political, social, and economic institutions and events. Such was his interest in theory that in 1941 Mitchell allowed the theoretical portion (Part III) of his 1913 volume, *Business Cycles*, to be re-published under the title *Business Cycles and Their Causes* (1941). This early effort to construct a dynamic theory, indeed, serves well as an interpretation of Mitchell's last work, *What Happens During Business Cycles* (1951). But the self-generating theory of business cycles, which was the hallmark of Mitchell's ideas on the subject, remained and still remains to be written.

GEOFFREY H. MOORE

Selected works

1903. *A History of the Greenbacks, with Special Reference to the Economic Consequences of their Issue: 1862–65.* Chicago: University of Chicago Press.

1913. *Business Cycles.* Berkeley: University of California Press.

1915. The making and using of index numbers. *Bulletin of the US Bureau of Labor Statistics* No. 173(July), 5–114.

1923. (With others) *Business Cycles and Unemployment.* New York: McGraw-Hill.

1927. *Business Cycles: The Problem and its Setting.* New York: National Bureau of Economic Research.

1937. *The Backward Art of Spending Money, and Other Essays.* New York: McGraw-Hill.

1938. (With A.F. Burns.) *Statistical Indicators of Cyclical Revivals.* Bulletin No. 69. New York: NBER.

1941. *Business Cycles and Their Causes.* Berkeley: University of California Press.

1945. *The National Bureau's First Quarter-Century.* 25th Annual Report of the National Bureau of Economic Research. New York: NBER.

1946. (With A.F. Burns.) *Measuring Business Cycles.* New York: NBER.

1949. *Lecture Notes on Types of Economic Theory.* New York: Kelley.

1951. *What Happens during Business Cycles: A Progress Report.* New York: NBER.

Bibliography

Burns, A.F., ed. 1952. *Wesley Clair Mitchell: The Economic Scientist.* New York: NBER.

Mitchell, L.S. 1953. *Two Lives: The Story of Wesley Clair Mitchell and Myself.* New York: Simon & Schuster.

mixed strategy equilibrium

In many strategic situations a player's success depends upon his actions being unpredictable. Competitive sports are replete with examples. One of the simplest occurs repeatedly in soccer (football): if a kicker knows which side of the goal the goalkeeper has chosen to defend, he will kick to the opposite side; and if the goalkeeper knows to which side the kicker will direct his kick, he will choose that side to defend. In the language of game theory, this is a simple 2×2 game which has no pure strategy equilibrium.

John von Neumann's (1928) theoretical formulation and analysis of such strategic situations is generally regarded as the birth of game theory. Von Neumann introduced the concept of a *mixed strategy*: each player in our soccer example should choose his Left or Right action randomly, but according to some particular binomial process. Every *zero sum* two-person game in which each player's set of available strategies is finite must have a *value* (or *security level*) for each player, and each player must have at least one *minimax* strategy – a strategy that assures him that, no matter how his opponent plays, he will achieve at least his security level for the game, in expected value terms. In many such games the minimax strategies are pure strategies, requiring no mixing; in others, they are mixed strategies.

John Nash (1950) introduced the powerful notion of *equilibrium* in games (including non-zero-sum games and games with an arbitrary number of players): an equilibrium is a combination of strategies (one for each player) in which each player's strategy is a *best* strategy for him against the strategies all the other players are using. An equilibrium is thus a sustainable combination of strategies, in the sense that no player has an incentive to change unilaterally to a different strategy. A *mixed-strategy equilibrium* (MSE) is one in which each player is using a mixed strategy; if a game's only equilibria are mixed, we say it is an MSE game. In two-person zero-sum games there is an equivalence between minimax and equilibrium: it is an equilibrium for each player to use a minimax strategy, and an equilibrium can consist only of minimax strategies.

An example or two will be helpful. First consider the game tic-tac-toe. There are three possible outcomes: Player A wins, Player B wins, or the game ends in a draw. Fully defining the players' possible strategies is somewhat complex, but anyone who has played the game more than a few times knows that each player has a strategy that guarantees him no worse than a draw. These are the players' respective minimax strategies and they constitute an equilibrium. Since they are *pure strategies* (requiring no mixing), tic-tac-toe is not an MSE game.

A second example is the game called 'matching pennies'. Each player places a penny either heads up or tails up; the players reveal their choices to one another simultaneously; if their choices match, Player A gives his penny to Player B, otherwise Player B gives his penny to Player A. This game has only two possible outcomes and it is obviously zero-sum. Neither of a player's pure strategies (heads or tails) ensures that he won't lose. But by choosing heads or tails randomly, each with probability one-half (for example, by 'flipping' the coin), he ensures that in expected value his payoff will be zero *no matter how his opponent plays*. This 50–50 mixture of heads and

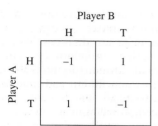

Figure 1

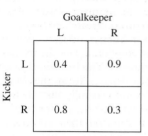

Figure 2

tails is thus a minimax strategy for each player, and it is an MSE of the game for each player to choose his minimax strategy.

Figure 1 provides a matrix representation of matching pennies. Player A, when choosing heads or tails, is effectively choosing one of the matrix's two rows; Player B chooses one of the columns; the cell at the resulting row-and-column intersection indicates Player A's *payoff*. Player B's payoff need not be shown, since it is the negative of Player A's (as always in a zero-sum game). Matching pennies is an example of a 2×2 game: each player has two pure strategies, and the game's matrix is therefore 2×2.

Figure 2 depicts our soccer example, another 2×2 MSE game. The kicker and the goalie simultaneously choose either Left or Right; the number in the resulting cell (at the row-and-column intersection) is the probability a goal will be scored, given the players' choices. The probabilities capture the fact that for each combination of choices by kicker and goalie the outcome is still random – a goal is less likely (but not impossible) when their choices match and is more likely (while not certain) when they don't. The specific probabilities will depend upon the abilities of the specific kicker and goalie: the probabilities in Figure 2 might represent, for example, a situation in which the kicker is more effective kicking to the left half of the goal than to the right half. For the specific game in Figure 2 it can be shown that the kicker's minimax strategy is a 50–50 mix between Left and Right and the goalie's minimax strategy is to defend Left 3/5 of the time and Right 2/5. The reader can easily see that the value of the game is therefore 3/5, that is, in the MSE the kicker will succeed in scoring a goal 60 per cent of the time.

Non-zero-sum games and games with more than two players often have mixed strategy equilibria as well. Important examples are decisions whether to enter a competition (such as an industry, a tournament, or an auction), 'wars of attrition' (decisions about whether and when to exit a competition), and models of price dispersion (which explain how the same good may sell at different prices), as well as many others.

How do people actually behave in strategic situations that have mixed strategy equilibria? Does the MSE provide an accurate description of people's behaviour? Virtually from the moment Nash's 1950 paper was distributed in preprint, researchers began to devise experiments in which human subjects play games that have mixed strategy equilibria. The theory has not fared well in these experiments. The behaviour observed in experiments typically departs from the MSE in two ways: participants do not generally play their strategies in the proportions dictated by the game's particular MSE probability distribution; and their choices typically exhibit negative serial correlation – a player's mixed strategy in an MSE requires that his choices be independent across multiple plays, but experimental subjects tend instead to switch from one action to another more often than chance would dictate. Experimental psychologists have reported similar 'switching too often' in many experiments designed to determine people's ability to intentionally behave randomly. The evidence suggests that humans are not very good at behaving randomly.

The results from experiments were so consistently at variance with the theory that empirical analysis of the concept of MSE became all but moribund for nearly two decades, until interest was revived by Barry O'Neill's (1987) seminal paper. O'Neill pointed out that there were features of previous experiments that subtly invalidated them as tests of the theory of mixed strategy equilibrium, and he devised a clever but simple experiment that avoided these flaws. Although James Brown and Robert Rosenthal (1990) subsequently demonstrated that the behaviour of O'Neill's subjects was still inconsistent with the theory, the correspondence between theory and observation was nevertheless closer in his experiment than in prior experiments.

Mark Walker and John Wooders (2001) were the first to use field data instead of experiments to evaluate the theory of mixed strategy equilibrium. They contended that, while the rules and mechanics of a simple MSE game may be easy to learn quickly, as required in a laboratory experiment, substantial experience is nevertheless required in order to develop an understanding of the strategic subtleties of playing even simple MSE games. In short, an MSE game may be easy to play but not easy to play *well*. This fact alone may account for much of the theory's failure in laboratory experiments.

Instead of using experiments, Walker and Wooders applied the MSE theory to data from professional tennis matches. The 'serve' in tennis can be described as a 2×2

MSE game exactly like the soccer example in Figure 2: the server chooses which direction to serve, the receiver chooses which direction to defend, and the resulting payoff is the probability the server wins the point. Walker and Wooders obtained data from matches between the best players in the world, players who have devoted their lives to the sport and should therefore be expert in the strategic subtleties of this MSE game. Play by these world-class tennis players was found to correspond quite closely to the MSE predictions. Subsequent research by others, with data from professional tennis and soccer matches, has shown a similar correspondence between theory and observed behaviour.

Thus, the empirical evidence to date indicates that MSE is effective for explaining and predicting behaviour in strategic situations at which the competitors are experts and that it is less effective when the competitors are novices, as experimental subjects typically are. This leaves several obvious open questions. In view of the enormous disparity in expertise between world-class athletes and novice experimental subjects, how can we determine, for specific players, whether the MSE yields an appropriate prediction or explanation of their play? And when MSE is not appropriate, what *is* a good theory of play? We clearly need a generalization of current theory, one that includes MSE, that tells us in addition when MSE is 'correct', and that explains behavior when MSE is not correct. Moreover, the need for such a theory extends beyond MSE games to the theory of games more generally.

A more general theory will likely comprise either an alternative, more general notion of equilibrium or a theory of out-of-equilibrium behaviour in which some players may, with enough experience, come to play as the equilibrium theory predicts. Recent years have seen research along both lines. Among the most promising developments are the notion of quantal response equilibrium introduced by Richard McKelvey and Thomas Palfrey (1995), the theory of level-*n* thinking introduced by Dale Stahl and Paul Wilson (1994), and the idea of reinforcement learning developed by Ido Erev and Alvin Roth (1998).

MARK WALKER AND JOHN WOODERS

See also **game theory; game theory in economics, origins of; Nash, John Forbes; purification; quantal response equilibria; von Neumann, John.**

Bibliography

Brown, J. and Rosenthal, R. 1990. Testing the minimax hypothesis: a re-examination of O'Neill's game experiment. *Econometrica* 58, 1065–81.
Erev, I. and Roth, A.E. 1998. Predicting how people play games: reinforcement learning in experimental games with unique, mixed strategy equilibria. *American Economic Review* 88, 848–81.

McKelvey, R. and Palfrey, T. 1995. Quantal response equilibria for normal-form games. *Games and Economic Behavior* 10, 6–38.

Nash, J.F. 1950. Equilibrium points in N person games. *Proceedings of the National Academy of Sciences* 36, 48–9.

O'Neill, B. 1987. Nonmetric test of the minimax theory of two-person zerosum games. *Proceedings of the National Academy of Sciences* 84, 2106–9.

Stahl, D. and Wilson, P. 1994. Experimental evidence on players' models of other players. *Journal of Economic Behavior & Organization* 25, 309–27.

von Neumann, J. 1928. Zur Theorie der Gesellschaftsspiele. *Mathematische Annalen* 100, 295–320.

Walker, M. and Wooders, J. 2001. Minimax play at Wimbledon. *American Economic Review* 91, 1521–38.

mixture models

Suppose that $\mathscr{F} = \{F_\theta : \theta \in S\}$ is a parametric family of distributions on a sample space X, and let Q denote a probability distribution defined on the parameter space S. The distribution

$$F_Q = \int F_\theta \, dQ(\theta)$$

is a mixture distribution. An observation X drawn from F_Q can be thought of as being obtained in a two-step procedure: first, a random Θ is drawn from the distribution Q and then, conditional on $\Theta = \theta$, X is drawn from the distribution F_θ. Suppose we have a random sample $X_1, \ldots, X_n$ from F_Q. We can view this as a missing data problem in that the 'full data' consists of pairs $(X_1, \Theta_1), \ldots, (X_n, \Theta_n)$, with $\Theta_i \sim Q$ and $X_i | \Theta_i = \theta \sim F_\theta$, but then only the first member X_i of each pair is observed; the labels Θ_i are hidden.

If the distribution Q is discrete with a finite number k of mass points $\theta_1, \ldots, \theta_k$ then we can write

$$F_Q = \sum_{j=1}^{k} q_j F_{\theta_j},$$

where $q_j = Q\{\theta_j\}$. The distribution F_Q is called a finite mixture distribution, the distributions F_θ are the component distributions and the q_j are the component weights.

There are several reasons why mixture distributions, and in particular finite mixture distributions, are of interest. First, there are many applications where the mechanism generating the data is truly of a mixture form; we sample from a population which we know or suspect is made up of several relatively homogeneous sub-populations in each of which the data of interest have the component distributions. We may wish to draw inferences, based on such a sample, relating to certain characteristics of the component sub-populations (parameters θ_j) or the relative proportions (parameters q_j) of the population in each sub-population, or both. Even the precise number of sub-populations may be unknown to us. An example is a population of fish, where the sub-populations are the yearly spawnings. Interest may focus on the relative abundances of each spawning, an unusually low proportion possibly corresponding to unfavourable conditions one year.

Second, even when there is no a priori reason to anticipate a mixture distribution, families of mixture distributions, in particular finite mixtures, provide us with particularly flexible families of probability distributions and densities which can be used to fit to unusually (skewed, long-tailed, multimodal) shaped data which would otherwise be difficult to describe with a more conventional parametric family of densities. Also, such a fit is often comparable in flexibility to a fully non-parametric estimate but structurally simpler, and often requires less subjective input, for example in terms of choosing smoothing parameters. For example, it has been shown that the very skewed log-normal density can often by well approximated by a two- or three-component mixture of normals, each with possibly different means and variances.

Third, many problems can be recast as mixture problems. An example is the problem of estimating a decreasing density function on the positive half-line. Such a density can be expressed as a mixture of uniform distributions, and, in the nonparametric maximum likelihood estimation of mixing distributions discussed below, we see that the solution to this density estimation problem follows from the solution to the general mixture problem.

Formal interest in finite mixtures dates back to at least Karl Pearson's laborious method-of-moments fitting of a two-component normal mixture to data on physical dimensions of crabs in the late 19th century. The mathematical difficulties inherent in fitting mixtures in that time have been greatly eased with the advent of the expectation-minimization (EM) algorithm in the 1970s. This algorithm yields an iterative method for computing maximum likelihood estimates (or very accurate approximations thereof) in a general missing-data situation. As mentioned above, mixtures have a natural missing-data interpretation and so the EM algorithm, together with improved computing technology, has made the task of fitting mixtures models to data much easier, leading to a renewal of interest in them.

Fitting finite mixtures using maximum likelihood

The EM-algorithm generates a sequence of parameter estimates each of which is guaranteed to give a larger likelihood than its predecessor. It can be used whenever the original log-likelihood $\log f_X(x; \theta)$ is difficult to maximize over θ for given x, but $f_X(x; \theta)$ can be expressed as the marginal distribution of X in a pair (X, J) whose corresponding log-likelihood $\log f_{XJ}(x, j; \theta)$ is easier to maximize over θ for given x and j. Given a 'current estimate' θ_0, the next in the sequence θ_1 is defined as the maximizer of the EM-log-likelihood $\ell_{EM}(\theta; x)$ which is defined as the conditional expectation of $\log f_{XJ}(x, J; \theta)$ over the 'missing data' J given $X = x$ computed under θ_0, that is

$$\ell_{EM}(\theta; x) = E \log f(x, J; \theta) \text{ where } J \text{ has density}$$
$$f_{J|X}(j|x; \theta_0) = f_{XJ}(x, j; \theta_0)/f_X(x; \theta_0).$$

It is guaranteed that $\log f_X(x; \theta_1) \geq \log f_X(x; \theta_0)$.

If we wish to fit a finite mixture

$$f(x; Q) = \sum_{j=1}^{k} q_j f(x; \theta_j)$$

where the number of components k is known, the EM-algorithm works in almost the same way for either one or both of the q_j's or θ_j's unknown. We regard the x_i's as the observed first members of random pairs $(X_1, J_1), \ldots, (X_n, J_n)$, but the J_i's are unobserved. We can write the full data log-likelihood as

$$\sum_{i=1}^{n} \sum_{j=1}^{k} 1\{J_i = j\}\{\log q_j + \log f(x_i; \theta_j)\}$$

(here $q_j = P\{J_i = j\}$). We now outline how to go from an initial set of estimates $q_{01}, \ldots, q_{0k}, \theta_{01}, \ldots, \theta_{0k}$ to the next in the EM-sequence $q_{11}, \ldots, q_{1k}, \theta_{11}, \ldots, \theta_{1k}$. If some of these values are known, then they of course remain unchanged. The first step is to compute the posterior probabilities

$$\pi_{j|i} = P\{J_i = j|X_i = x_i\} \text{ computed under the } q_{0j}s$$
$$\text{and } \theta_{0j}s$$
$$= \frac{q_{0j}f(x_i; \theta_{0j})}{\sum_{j=1}^{k} q_{0j}f(x_i; \theta_{0j})}.$$

The EM-log-likelihood is then obtained by replacing the $1\{J_i = j\}$'s in the full data log-likelihood with the $\pi_{j|i}$'s; note that the EM-log-likelihood thus obtained separates into a term involving the q_j's only and one involving the θ_j's only.

If the q_j's are unknown, we maximize

$$\sum_{j=1}^{k} \log q_j \left\{ \sum_{i=1}^{n} \pi_{j|i} \right\}$$

with respect to the q_j's; this is maximized at

$$q_{1j} = n^{-1} \sum_{i=1}^{n} \pi_{j|i},$$

simply the averages of the posterior probabilities over the data:

If the θ_j's are unknown, we maximize

$$\sum_{j=1}^{k} \sum_{i=1}^{n} \pi_{j|i} \log f(x_i; \theta_j)$$

with respect to the θ_j's. Differentiating with respect to each θ_j and setting to zero yields k weighted score equations:

$$\sum_{i=1}^{n} \pi_{j|i} \frac{\partial \log f(x_i; \theta_j)}{\partial \theta_j} = 0.$$

In many common models these are easily solved. For example, in one-parameter exponential families of the form $f(x; \theta) = e^{\theta x - K(\theta)}f_0(x)$, (for example, normal with known variance, Poisson, and so on) let $\hat{\theta}(t)$ be that value of θ that solves $K'(\theta) = t$. Then for each j one can explicitly find the EM update as

$$\theta_{j1} = \hat{\theta}\left(\frac{\sum_{i=1}^{n} \pi_{j|i} x_i}{\sum_{i=1}^{n} \pi_{j|i}} \right),$$

a known function of a $\pi_{j|i}$-weighted average of the x_is.

Further inferences

Once the model has been fitted, further inferences may consist of confidence intervals for, or hypothesis tests concerning, the component parameters θ_j and/or the mixing proportions q_j's. When the model is correctly specified (that is, there really are k components and all the q_j's are positive), the parameter estimates behave more or less in a standard fashion: they are asymptotically normal with an estimable covariance matrix, subject to the component densities $f(x; \theta_j)$ being suitably regular. Hence confidence regions can be computed in a standard fashion, bearing in mind the restrictions on the q_j's: they are non-negative and add to 1. In addition, one should be aware that, when the weights q_j are small or the parameters θ_j for two or more groups are similar, there is a sharp loss of estimating efficiency as well as good reason to be doubtful of the accuracy of asymptotic approximations. This occurs because of the near loss of identifiability of the parameters near the boundaries of the parameter space.

Hypothesis tests are perhaps not so standard, at least not for tests concerning the q_js. If one wishes to test whether an estimate $\hat{q}_j$ is significantly different from zero, the non-negativity constraints have a significant impact, at least when it comes to using large-sample χ^2 approximations to the p-values. Since such a hypothesis constrains a parameter to be on the boundary of the parameter space, the asymptotic distribution of twice the log-likelihood ratio will be a mixture of χ^2 distributions rather than a pure χ^2, on the assumption that the model is otherwise suitably regular. In such a case, a parametric bootstrap approach can be used to obtain an approximate *p*-value.

An unknown number of components, or completely unknown *Q*

If the number of components of a putatively finite mixture is unknown, we are essentially on the same footing as knowing absolutely nothing about *Q*, for reasons we now explain.

For any given data-set $x_1, \ldots, x_n$ with $d \leq n$ distinct x_i's and any pre-specified *Q*, no matter it be discrete or continuous, so long as the likelihoods $f(x_i; \theta)$ are bounded in θ we can find a discrete $\tilde{Q}$ with $m \leq d$ support points such that *Q* and $\tilde{Q}$ provide exactly the same density values at the observed data. That is, for any mixing distribution *Q* there is a possibly different $\tilde{Q}$ yielding a finite mixture such that *Q* and $\tilde{Q}$ cannot be distinguished, at least in terms of the data $x_1, \ldots, x_n$. So it suffices to restrict attention to such $\tilde{Q}$s.

An implication of this, when the likelihoods are bounded in θ, is that the maximum likelihood estimate of *Q* over all distributions, which we denote by $\hat{Q}$, exists and is finite with at most *d* (the number of distinct x_is) support points. So we never need leave the realm of finite mixtures in this setting.

This is not to say, however, that an estimate of an unknown *k* is readily available. The number of components in $\hat{Q}$ may be an overestimate in that some support points (respectively mixing proportions) may be so close together (small) that combining them into a single point (removing them) hardly decreases the likelihood. This and other issues related to trying to infer something about the number of components in a mixture, like hypothesis tests concerning *k*, are difficult problems. Some problems are still open, others have solutions that are possibly too complex to be useful.

The nonparametric estimate of *Q*

When the estimate $\hat{Q}$ discussed above exists, it is discrete with at most *d* support points. Hence a strategy for computing it is to try to and fit a finite mixture with *d* components using the EM-algorithm. In many situations this yields a sensible result. More sophisticated algorithms exist however which are related to the following gradient function characterization.

The gradient function

$$D_Q(\theta) = \sum_{i=1}^{n} \left[\frac{f(x_i; \theta)}{f(x_i; Q)} - 1 \right]$$

measures the rate of increase in the log-likelihood if we remove a small amount of weight from the mixing distribution *Q* and put it at the point θ. Hence, for a candidate estimate *Q*, if for some θ we have $D_Q(\theta) > 0$, we know that we can increase the log-likelihood by putting some weight at θ.

In light of this the following result is not surprising: if the nonparametric maximum likelihood estimate $\hat{Q}$ exists, then $D_{\hat{Q}}(\theta) \leq 0$ for all θ, and the support points of $\hat{Q}$ are included in the set of values θ where $D_{\hat{Q}}(\theta) = 0$. The fact that $D_{\hat{Q}}(\theta) > 0$ for no θ makes sense; moving mass around from $\hat{Q}$ to any other θ cannot increase the likelihood.

The nonparametric version of the mixture model falls into the class of convex models, a subject with its own independent literature. Often convex models can be written as mixture models. For example, a distribution function that is concave on the positive half-line can also be written as a nonparametric mixture of the form $\int f(x; \theta) \, dQ(\theta)$ with component density $f(x; \theta) = 1\{0 < x < \theta\}/\theta$. One can deduce that the nonparametric likelihood estimator is the least concave majorant of the empirical distribution function using the above gradient characterization. See McLachlan and Peel (2000), Titterington, Smith and Makov (1985) or Lindsay (1995) for further examples and other references.

Mixtures and nonlinear time series

Methods related to mixtures of distributions have in recent times enjoyed a surge in popularity in finance and econometrics, in particular in the area of time series analysis. Traditional (linear) time series models, while intuitive and tractable, are well-known to be unable to capture certain features of much financial or econometric data, including variability that changes over time and marginal distributions that can be multimodal or long-tailed.

Traditional linear time series models with Gaussian innovations have marginal and conditional distributions which are Gaussian. However, in many applications both marginal and conditional distributions can be multimodal, skewed, and fat-tailed, and exhibit other non-Gaussian features. Also, series can exhibit bursts of volatility, where the variability changes in strange ways, sometimes with some dependence on past and current values of the observable series or an unobserved underlying process of 'shocks'. In several different settings, ideas of mixtures have led to new types of models that have been quite successful at capturing many of these problematic features.

One example is the mixture of autoregressive (AR) models idea. The standard autoregressive model, where the observation at time *t*, Y_t, has a conditional distribution, given the past $Y_{t-1}, Y_{t-2}, \ldots$ of the form

$$Y_t = \theta_0 + \sum_{\ell=1}^{L} \theta_\ell Y_{t-\ell} + sZ_t,$$

where the θ_ℓ's are fixed constants and the Z_t's are independent (often standard Gaussian) random variables. Assuming $\theta_k \neq 0$ here, the model is said to be autoregressive of order L (we abbreviate this to AR(L)). The mixture version can be represented by replacing the parameter vector $\theta = (\theta_0, \theta_1, \ldots, \theta_L, s)^T$ above at each time point t with a random version $\Theta_t = (\Theta_{0t}, \Theta_{1t}, \ldots, \Theta_{Lt}, S_t)^T$, yielding

$$Y_t = \Theta_{0t} + \sum_{\ell=1}^{L} \Theta_{\ell t} Y_{t-\ell} + S_t Z_t$$

where $P\left(\Theta_t = \theta^{(j)}\right) = q_j$, each $q_j \geq 0$ and $\sum_{j=1}^{k} q_j = 1$. For each j, we have a different AR *regime* with corresponding parameter vector $\theta^{(j)} = (\theta_0^{(j)}, \ldots, \theta_L^{(j)}, s_j)^T$ which is chosen randomly at each time point according to the probability distribution given by the q_j's, independently of Z_t and past values of the series. All regimes need not be of the same order; an AR(L') regime with $L' < L$ can be obtained by just setting $\theta_{L'+1}^{(j)} = \cdots = \theta_L^{(j)} = 0$.

This so-called mixture autoregressive (MAR) model has several appealing features. Its mathematical form means that it is relatively straightforward to derive its autocorrelation function, and indeed its stationarity properties are similarly easy to derive. An interesting point here is that it is possible to have some of the component regimes non-stationary, but, so long as their mixing proportions q_j are small enough, the overall series can still have a second-order stationarity property (see TIME SERIES ANALYSIS for more details). In looser terms, we can have occasional explosive behaviour but still have a series that is well-behaved in the long run. For example, when the stock market becomes volatile we can have short bursts of heightened activity which eventually settle down. Such features cannot be captured by a single AR model.

Another feature of the MAR model is that the marginal as well as conditional distributions can change with time and be multimodal. Again, during a period of stock market volatility we might expect some sharp increases and/or decreases during these periods which may result in bi- or multimodal conditional distributions. Consider the following example (simplified version of fit to IBM data from Wong and Li, 2000):

$$Y_t = \begin{cases} 0.7Y_{t-1} + 0.3Y_{t-2} + 5Z_t + & \text{with prob. } 0.55; \\ 1.7Y_{t-1} - 0.7Y_{t-2} + 5Z_t + & \text{with prob. } 0.4; \\ Y_{t-1} + 20Z_t & \text{with prob. } 0.5. \end{cases}$$

If the series has been quite volatile and Y_{t-1} and Y_{t-2} are very different, say $Y_{t-1} = 200$ and $Y_{t-2} = 300$, then the conditional distribution of Y_t would be a mixture

of the form

$$Y_t \sim \begin{cases} N(230, 25) & \text{with prob. } 0.55; \\ N(130, 25) & \text{with prob. } 0.4; \\ N(200, 400) & \text{with prob. } 0.05. \end{cases}$$

However, if the series had been quite stable, say with $Y_{t-1} = 200$ and $Y_{t-2} = 201$ say, then the conditional distribution would be

$$Y_t \sim \begin{cases} N(200.3, 25) & \text{with prob. } 0.55; \\ N(199.3, 25) & \text{with prob. } 0.4; \\ N(200, 400) & \text{with prob. } 0.05. \end{cases}$$

So we still have a component for increases, a component for decreases and the same component for outliers. However, the first two components are so similar that the mixture density is markedly unimodal. This example illustrates that the MAR can capture volatility as well as a changing, possibly multimodal conditional distribution.

Estimation

The mixture structure also enables maximum-likelihood estimation of unknown parameters via the EM algorithm. We briefly outline how this would work when fitting a mixture of k AR(L) regimes, although the basic steps are the same in cases where the order of each regime can differ from component to component. As in the i.i.d. case though, the question of choosing k, the number of components of the mixture, is a difficult open problem.

We can represent the mixture in terms of an unobserved label J_t at each time point which indicates which regime applies; it is equal to j with probability q_j, $j = 1, \ldots, k$. If these were known, then the full log-likelihood of observed $(y_{L+1}, \ldots, y_n)^T$ (conditional on $y_1, \ldots, y_L$) would be

$$\ell_{\text{full}}\left(\boldsymbol{q}, \boldsymbol{\theta}^{(1)}, \ldots, \boldsymbol{\theta}^{(k)}\right)$$

$$= \sum_{t=L+1}^{n} \left\{ \sum_{j=1}^{k} 1\{J_t = j\}[\log q_j + \log f \right.$$

$$\left. \times (y_t, \ldots, y_{t-L}; \boldsymbol{\theta}^{(j)})] \right\},$$

where $f(\cdot; \boldsymbol{\theta})$ is the conditional density of Y_t given $Y_{t-1}, \ldots, Y_{t-L}$ under a single AR(L) regime. We now show how a current set of estimates $\tilde{\boldsymbol{q}}, \tilde{\boldsymbol{\theta}}^{(1)}, \ldots, \tilde{\boldsymbol{\theta}}^{(k)}$ would be updated. There are two steps, an E-step and an M-step. At the E-step the missing data is set equal to its conditional expectation, given current parameter estimates and data, which here reduce to the posterior probabilities:

$$\pi_{j|t} = P\{J_t = j | Y_t = y_t, \ldots, Y_{t-L} = y_{t-L}\}$$

$$\text{computed under current estimates}$$

$$= \frac{\tilde{q}_j f\left(y_t, \ldots, y_{t-L}; \tilde{\boldsymbol{\theta}}^{(j)}\right)}{\sum_{t=L+1}^{n} \tilde{q}_j f\left(y_t, \ldots, y_{t-L}; \tilde{\boldsymbol{\theta}}^{(j)}\right)}$$

The M-step consists of firstly defining the EM-log-likelihood $\ell_{EM}\left(\boldsymbol{q}, \boldsymbol{\theta}^{(1)}, \ldots, \boldsymbol{\theta}^{(k)}\right)$ obtained by replacing $1\{J_j = t\}$ with $\pi_{j|t}$, and then maximizing over the remaining parameters. As in the i.i.d. case, the EM-log-likelihood separates into two pieces, one involving just the q_j's, which is maximized at

$$\hat{q}_j = \frac{\sum_{t=L+1}^{n} \pi_{j|t}}{n - L}$$

and another involving the other parameters of the form

$$\sum_{j=1}^{k} \sum_{t=L+1}^{n} \pi_{j|t} \log f\left(y_t, \ldots, y_{t-L}; \boldsymbol{\theta}^{(j)}\right)$$

which when differentiated partially with respect to each $\boldsymbol{\theta}^{(j)}$ yields a separate set of *weighted likelihood* equations just as in the i.i.d. case, for example,

$$\frac{\partial}{\partial \theta_0^{(j)}} \ell_{EM}\left(\boldsymbol{q}, \boldsymbol{\theta}^{(1)}, \ldots, \boldsymbol{\theta}^{(k)}\right)$$

$$= \sum_{t=L+1}^{n} \pi_{j|t} \frac{\partial}{\partial \theta_0} \log f\left(y_t, \ldots, y_{t-L}; \boldsymbol{\theta}\right)\bigg|_{\boldsymbol{\theta} = \boldsymbol{\theta}^{(j)}}.$$

Thus, if one has a computational method to obtain the maximum likelihood estimate for a straight AR(L) model, it is possible to use the same computations on this weighted form in the M-step for the more general mixture case. Note that this method is not restricted to the Gaussian-Z_t case or a linear autoregression function.

As mentioned earlier, the autocorrelation structure of the MAR model is quite straightforward to analyse; in fact, it inherits much of the simplicity of the standard AR model. One thing that one cannot obtain using an AR or MAR model is a first-order stationary series whose square exhibits some autocorrelation, which is a key feature of certain time series models designed to capture time-varying volatility. The main breakthrough in this area was the introduction of the autoregressive conditional heteroscedastic (ARCH) model for time series errors in the early 1980s by Engle, where S_t^2, the variance of the error at time t, is allowed to depend on squares of earlier errors: if Z_t's are i.i.d. mean-zero-unit-variance

errors then the series $\{\varepsilon_t\}$ given by

$$\varepsilon_t = S_t Z_t;$$

$$S_t = \left(\beta_0 + \sum_{\ell=1}^{M} \beta_\ell \varepsilon_{t-\ell}^2\right)$$

is an ARCH(M)-series. One can incorporate this into a mixture setting by using the same specification for the conditional mean as in the MAR case, but allowing the errors to be generated *within each regime* by a different ARCH mechanism. Hence the full specification is

$$Y_t = \Theta_{0t} + \sum_{\ell=1}^{L} \Theta_{\ell t} Y_{t-\ell} + \varepsilon_t,$$

$$\varepsilon_t = S_t Z_t;$$

$$S_t = \left(B_0 + \sum_{\ell=1}^{M} B_\ell \varepsilon_{t-\ell}^2\right),$$

where now (Θ_t, B_t) takes the value $(\theta^{(j)}, \beta^{(j)})$ with probability q_j.

The resulting MAR–ARCH model combines the extra flexibility of the MAR model with the superior modelling of volatility enjoyed by ARCH series. In addition, the ability to fit several different AR–ARCH regimes provides an aid to interpretation; as in the MAR case, we can have a different regime for each of several possible reactions at each time point, and furthermore the choices (that is, conditional distributions) can change with time. The EM-algorithm can be employed in essentially the same way as the MAR model, so long as weighted maximum likelihood estimation can be performed in the M-step for each AR-ARCH regime (allowing the possibility of non-normal errors).

Connection to threshold models

There is some connection between MAR and MAR-ARCH models and another class of non-linear time series known as (self-exciting) threshold autoregressive (SETAR) models. An elementary version is

$$Y_t = \begin{cases} \theta_0^{(1)} + \theta_1^{(1)} Y_{t-1} + s_1 Z_t & \text{if } Y_{t-1} < c, \\ \theta_0^{(2)} + \theta_1^{(2)} Y_{t-1} + s_2 Z_t & \text{if } Y_{t-1} \geq c, \end{cases}$$

That is, follows one of two possible AR(1) regimes, the choice depending on whether the previous value Y_{t-1} exceeds a threshold c, in contrast to the MAR model where the choice is made independently of the earlier values of the series.

It can be shown that if the Z_t's are Gaussian then the marginal distribution of the zeroth order (where $\theta_1^{(j)} \equiv 0$) is a mixture of Gaussians, permitting multimodality.

A class of models intermediate between the SETAR models and MAR involves having several AR regimes, but the choice at each time point is partly influenced by earlier values of the series, but not in a completely deterministic way. A simple version involves replacing the thresholding rule $Y_{t-1} < c$ with $Y_{t-1} + \eta_t < c$ for an independent random variable η_t. In this case, we have a mixture of AR regimes where the mixing proportions $q_j = q_j(Y_{t-1}, c)$ depend on earlier values of the series and the threshold.

These models (MAR, MAR-ARCH, SETAR and intermediate versions) are still being fully developed, however an excellent introduction is provided in Tong (1990).

Summary

Mixture distributions, particularly finite mixtures, in general permit a great increase in flexibility of modelling without an overwhelming increase in computation difficulty, while also helping in interpretation by modelling heterogeneity in a natural way. In particular, if distributions within a certain model can be fitted by maximum likelihood, then finite mixtures of distributions from the same model can in general also by fitted by maximum likelihood using the EM-algorithm. Such finite mixtures can capture heterogeneity or other complex behaviour that single components (that is, when there is no mixture) cannot capture.

BRUCE G. LINDSAY AND MICHAEL STEWART

See also **statistical inference; testing; time series analysis.**

Bibliography

Lindsay, B.G. 1995. *Mixture Models: Theory, Geometry and Applications*, NSF-CBMS Regional Conference Series in Probability and Statistics, 5. Hayward, CA: Institute of Mathematical Statistics and American Statistical Association.

McLachlan, G. and Peel, D. 2000. *Finite Mixture Models*. New York: Wiley-Interscience.

Titterington, D.M., Smith, A.F.M. and Makov, U.E. 1985. *Statistical Analysis of Finite Mixture Distributions*. Chichester: John Wiley.

Tong, H. 1990. *Nonlinear Time Series: A Dynamical System Approach*. Oxford: Clarendon Press.

Wong, C.S. and Li, W.K. 2000. On a mixture autoregressive model. *Journal of the Royal Statistical Society*, Series B 62, 95–115.

model averaging

Model averaging allows the estimation of the distribution of unknown parameters and related quantities of interest across different models. The basic principle of model averaging is to treat models and associated parameters as unobservable and estimate their distributions based on observable data. Model averaging can be employed for inference, prediction and policy analysis in the face of model uncertainty. Many areas of economics give rise to

model uncertainty, including uncertainty about theory, specification and data issues. A naive approach that ignores model uncertainty generally results in biased parameter estimates, overconfident (too narrow) standard errors and misleading inference and predictions (see Draper, 1995). Taking model uncertainty seriously implies a departure from conditioning on a particular model and calculating quantities of interest by averaging across different models instead.

Model averaging is conceptually straightforward. The sample information contained in the likelihood function for a particular model is combined with relative model weights or posterior model probabilities to estimate the distribution of unknown parameters across models. Three main approaches – Bayesian, empirical Bayes, and frequentist – have been developed, and they differ in their underlying statistical foundations and practical implementation.

Bayesian model averaging (BMA) was developed first to systematically deal with model uncertainty. The idea of combining evidence from different models is readily integrated into a Bayesian framework. Jeffreys (1961) laid the foundation for BMA, further developed by Leamer (1978). Hoeting et al. (1999), Wasserman (2000) and Koop (2003) give excellent introductions to BMA. A drawback of the Bayesian approach is that it requires assumptions about prior information about distribution of unknown parameters. In response, *empirical Bayes* (EB) approaches have been developed to estimate elements of the prior using observable data. Chipman, George and McCulloch (2001) argue for a pragmatic approach that introduces objective or frequentist considerations into model averaging. In contrast to Bayesian approaches, *frequentist model averaging* (FMA) methods were developed only relatively recently. Recent contributions include Yang (2001), Hjort and Claeskens (2003) and Hansen (2007).

Model averaging was not widely used until advances in statistical techniques and computing power facilitated its practical use (see Chib, 2001; Geweke and Whiteman, 2006). Economic applications of model averaging include economic growth (Fernandez, Ley and Steel, 2001a; Sala-i-Martin, Doppelhofer and Miller, 2004), finance (Avramov, 2002), policy evaluation (Brock, Durlauf and West, 2003; Levin and Williams, 2003), macroeconomic forecasting (Garratt et al., 2003).

This article is organized as follows. The statistical model averaging framework is introduced in the next section. Different model averaging approaches are illustrated with applications to linear regressions. Finally, implementation issues, including model priors, numerical methods, and software are discussed.

Statistical framework

Suppose a decision maker observes data Y and wishes to learn about quantities of interest related to an unknown parameter (vector) θ, such as the effect of an economic variable (say $\theta > 0$ or $\theta \leq 0$) or predictions of future observations Y^f. The utility (or loss) function of the decision maker describes the relation between parameter of interest θ and action a. For example, the decision maker could maximize expected utility

$$\max_{a} E[u(a, \theta|Y)] = \int u(a, \theta|Y) p(\theta|Y) d\theta. \tag{1}$$

In general, the preferred action depends on the preferences of the decision-maker and the unconditional distribution of parameters. Alternative preference structure can have important consequences for optimal estimators and implied policy conclusions. Bernardo and Smith (1994) give an accessible introduction to statistical decision theory. In the context of economic policy, Brock, Durlauf and West (2003) present an interesting discussion of alternative preferences and implied policies.

A key ingredient in decision making is the *posterior* distribution of the parameter θ, which can be calculated using Bayes's rule:

$$p(\theta|Y) = \frac{L(Y|\theta) p(\theta)}{p(Y)} \propto L(Y|\theta) p(\theta). \tag{2}$$

The posterior distribution is therefore proportional to the *likelihood* function $L(Y|\theta)$, which summarizes all information about θ contained in the observed data, and the *prior* distribution $p(\theta)$. In contrast, the classical approach assumes that the parameter θ is fixed (non-random) and does not have a meaningful distribution. The estimator $\hat{\theta}$ on the other hand is viewed as a random variable.

In many economic and more generally non-experimental applications, a decision maker might face considerable model uncertainty given potentially overlapping, economic theories. Brock and Durlauf (2001) refer to this as 'open-endedness' of economic theories. Also, there might be alternative empirical specifications of these theoretical channels. In sum, the number of observations may be smaller than the number of suggested explanations, and the problem may be compounded by data problems, such as missing data or outliers.

Formally, there may be many candidate models $M_1, \ldots, M_K$ to explain the observed data. A model M_j can be described by a probability distribution $p(Y|\theta_j, M_j)$ with model-specific parameter (vector) θ_j. In a situation of model uncertainty, the decision-maker evaluates the utility function (1) using the posterior distribution of θ. The posterior distribution is unconditional with respect to the set of models and is calculated by averaging conditional or model-specific distributions across all models

$$p(\theta|Y) = \sum_{j=1}^{K} w_j \cdot p(\theta_j|M_j, Y), \tag{3}$$

where the model weights w_j are proportional to the fit in explaining the observable data. In a Bayesian context, the weights are the *posterior model probabilities*, $w_j = p(M_j|Y)$. Using Bayes's rule,

$$p(M_j|Y) = \frac{L(Y|M_j) p(M_j)}{\sum_{j=1}^{K} L(Y|M_j) p(M_j)} \propto L(Y|M_j) p(M_j). \tag{4}$$

The posterior model weights are proportional to the product of prior model probability $p(M_j)$ and model-specific marginal likelihood $L(Y|M_j)$. The marginal likelihood is obtained by integrating a model-specific version of equation (2) with respect to θ_j

$$L(Y|M_j) = \int_{\theta} L(Y|\theta_j, M_j) p(\theta_j|M_j) d\theta_j \tag{5}$$

using the fact that $\int p(\theta_j|M_j, Y) d\theta_j = 1$.

When comparing two models, M_i and M_j say, the posterior model probabilities or *posterior odds ratio* equals the ratio of integrated likelihoods times the prior odds

$$\frac{p(M_i|Y)}{p(M_j|Y)} = \frac{L(Y|M_i)}{L(Y|M_j)} \frac{p(M_i)}{p(M_j)}. \tag{6}$$

Similarly, the weight for model M_i relative to K models under consideration is given by (4), where the normalizing factor $\sum_{j=1}^{K} L(Y|M_j) p(M_j)$ ensures consistency of model weights.

The decision maker may be interested in particular aspects of the unconditional distribution (3), such as posterior mean or variance. Leamer (1978) derives the following expressions for unconditional mean or variance of the parameter θ

$$E(\theta|Y) = \sum_{j=1}^{K} p(M_j|Y) E(\theta_j|Y, M_j). \tag{7}$$

$$\begin{aligned}
Var(\theta|Y) &= E(\theta^2|Y) - [E(\theta|Y)]^2 \\
&= \sum_{j=1}^{K} p(M_j|Y) \{ Var(\theta_j|Y, M_j) \\
&\quad + [E(\theta_j|Y, M_j)]^2 \} - [E(\theta|Y)]^2 \\
&= \sum_{j=1}^{K} p(M_j|Y) Var(\theta_j|Y, M_j) \\
&\quad + \sum_{j=1}^{K} p(M_j|Y) [E(\theta_j|Y, M_j) - E(\theta|Y)]^2.
\end{aligned} \tag{8}$$

The expression for the unconditional mean of θ in (7) is simply the model-weighted sum of conditional means. Notice that the unconditional variance of θ in (8) exceeds the sum of model-weighted conditional variances by an additional term, reflecting the distance between the estimated conditional mean in each model $E(\theta_j|Y, M_j)$ and the unconditional mean $E(\theta|Y)$. Ignoring this last term overestimates the precision of estimated effects and underestimates parameter uncertainty (see Draper, 1995).

The advantage of the Bayesian approach to model averaging is its generality and the explicit treatment of model uncertainty and decision theory. The decision maker simply combines prior information about the distribution of parameters and models with sample information to calculate the unconditional posterior distribution of θ in eq. (3).

However, there are several problems that can make implementation of BMA difficult in practice (see Hoeting et al., 1999; Chipman, George and McCulloch, 2001):

1. The specification of prior distribution of parameters θ requires assumptions about functional forms and unknown hyper-parameters which will in general affect the marginal likelihood (5) and hence posterior model weights (4).
2. The specification of prior probabilities over the model space $p(M_j)$ might have important effects on posterior model weights (4).
3. The number of models K in eq. (3) can be too large for a complete summation across models, implying the use simulation techniques to approximate the unconditional distribution $p(\theta|Y)$ in equation (3).
4. Choices of utility function (1) and class of models are other important issues.

These issues are discussed in turn, contrasting the fully Bayesian, empirical Bayes and frequentist approaches.

Linear regression example

Many of the implementation problems of model averaging and approaches suggested in the literature can be illustrated using the linear regression example (see Koop, 2003). Raftery, Madigan and Hoeting (1997) and Fernandez, Ley and Steel (2001b) discuss BMA for linear regression models.

Consider linear regression models of the form

$$y = x_1\beta_1 + \cdots + x_k\beta_k + \varepsilon = X\beta + \varepsilon, \quad (9)$$

where y is the vector of N observations of the dependent variable and $X = [x_1, \ldots, x_k]$ is a set of k regressors (including a constant) with associated coefficient vector β. Each model M_j is characterized by a subset of explanatory variables X_j with coefficient vector β_j. With k regressors, the set of linear models equals $K = 2^k$. The residuals are drawn from a multivariate normal distribution and are assumed to be conditionally homoskedastic,

$\varepsilon_j \sim N(0, \sigma^2 I)$. Notice that this implies that the residuals are also conditionally exchangeable (see Bernardo and Smith, 1994; Brock and Durlauf, 2001).

Suppose the decision maker is interested in the effect of different explanatory variables, represented by slope parameters β with posterior distribution of $p(\beta|Y)$. As shown in eq. (3), the posterior distribution is estimated by weighting conditional distributions of parameters by posterior model probabilities. The relative posterior model weights in eqs (6) and (4) are proportional to the marginal likelihood and prior model weights.

For the normal regression model, the likelihood function can be written as

$$L(y|\beta_j, \sigma^2)$$
$$= \frac{1}{(2\pi\sigma^2)^{N/2}}$$
$$\times \left\{ \exp\left[-\frac{1}{2\sigma^2}(y - X\beta_j)'(y - X\beta_j) \right] \right\}$$
$$\propto \left\{ \exp\left[-\frac{1}{2\sigma^2}(\beta_j - \hat{\beta}_j)'X_j'X_j(\beta_j - \hat{\beta}_j) \right] \right\}$$
$$\times \left\{ \sigma^{-(v_j+1)}\exp\left[-\frac{v_j s_j^2}{2\sigma^2} \right] \right\}.$$
$$(10)$$

The second line of the likelihood substitutes the ordinary least squares (OLS) estimates for the slope and variance

$$\hat{\beta}_j = (X_j'X_j)^{-1}X_j'y, \quad (11)$$

$$s_j^2 = \frac{(y - X_j\hat{\beta}_j)'(y_j - X_j\hat{\beta}_j)}{v_j}, \quad (12)$$

with degrees of freedom $v_j = N - k_j - 1$. The implementation of model averaging – Bayesian, empirical Bayes, or frequentist – requires the specification of prior distributions $p(\theta_j)$ for the model parameters $\theta_j = (\beta_j, \sigma^2)$.

Bayesian conjugate priors

A standard way to specify priors in Bayesian estimation is to assume a prior structure that is analytically and computationally convenient. A *conjugate prior* distribution leads to a posterior distribution of the same class of distributions when combined with the likelihood. The likelihood (10) is part of the Normal-Gamma family of distributions, proportional to the product of a normal distribution for the slope β_j, conditional on the variance σ^2, and an inverse-Gamma distribution for the variance σ^2. The conjugate prior therefore takes the form

$$p(\beta_j|\sigma^2, M_j) \sim N\left(\beta_{0j}, \sigma^2 V_{0j}\right)$$
$$p(\sigma^2|M_j) = p(\sigma^2) \sim IG(s_0^2, v_0) \quad (13)$$

where the prior hyper-parameters for slope and variance are denoted by subscript 0. Notice that the error variance is assumed to be drawn from the same distribution across all regression models, reflecting the assumption of conditional homoskedasticity and exchangeability of the residuals.

A drawback of the Bayesian approach is that marginal likelihood and posterior model weights depend on unknown hyper-parameters (β_0, V_0, s_0, v_0). Different subjective priors therefore affect the posterior model weights and distribution of parameters, and hence also the decision maker's action. The standard Bayesian approach to check for robustness with respect to the choice of prior parameters is sensitivity analysis. An alternative strategy is to limit the use of subjective prior information and use objective methods based on observed data.

Empirical Bayes priors

Empirical Bayes (EB) approaches make use of sample information to specify prior parameters. Different versions of empirical Bayes methods have been proposed in the literature (see Hoeting et al., 1999; George and Foster, 2000; Chipman, George and McCulloch, 2001). To limit the importance of prior information, EB methods often use non-informative or diffuse priors that are dominated by the sample information (see Leamer, 1978). Jeffreys (1961) proposes non-informative priors to represent lack of prior knowledge and derives a formal relationship to the expected information in the sample.

A drawback of non-informative priors is that they are usually not proper distributions, which can lead to undesirable properties when comparing models with different parameters. In this case, relative model weights can depend on arbitrary constants. However, this problem is not present when comparing models with common parameters, since normalizing constants drop out from *relative* model weights (see Kass and Raftery, 1995). Koop (2003) argues that informative or proper priors should be used for all other (non-common) parameters.

Fernandez, Ley and Steel (2001b) propose *benchmark priors* for BMA that limit the subjective prior information to a minimum while maintaining the Bayesian natural conjugate framework. They suggest the following non-informative priors for the error variance, assumed to be the same in all k models:

$$p(\sigma^2) \propto \frac{1}{\sigma^2}. \qquad (14)$$

The slope parameter β_j is drawn from a normal prior distribution as in eq. (13) with prior mean $\beta_{0j} = 0$ and prior covariance matrix V_{oj} equal to the so-called g-prior suggested by Zellner (1986):

$$V_{oj} = \left(g_0 X_j' X_j\right)^{-1}. \qquad (15)$$

Intuitively, the prior covariance matrix is assumed to be proportional to the sample covariance with a factor of proportionality g_0. The g-prior simplifies the specification of prior covariances to choosing a single parameter g_0. For example, $g_0 = 0$ corresponds to completely non-informative priors, and $g_0 = 1$ implies a very informative prior receiving equal weight to the sample information. Based on extensive simulations, Fernandez, Ley and Steel (2001b) recommend the following benchmark values:

$$g_0 = \begin{cases} 1/k^2, & \text{if } N \leq k^2 \\ 1/N, & \text{if } N > k^2 \end{cases}. \qquad (16)$$

Note that the ratio of prior to sample variance g_0 decreases with the sample size or with the square of estimated parameters. If the number of parameters is relatively large $k^2 \geq N$, the variance is assumed to be relatively more diffuse.

Using this prior structure, the posterior weights for model M_j can be written as

$$p(M_j|Y) \propto p(M_j) \cdot \left(\frac{1+g_0}{g_0}\right)^{-k_j/2} \cdot SSE_j^{-(N-1)/2}. \qquad (17)$$

The weight for model $p(M_j|Y)$ depends on three terms: (i) the prior model weight $p(M_j)$, (ii) a penalty term for the number of regressors $((1+g_0)/g_0)^{-k_j/2}$ implying a preference for parsimonious models, and (iii) a term involving the sum of squared errors of the regression $SSE_j \equiv (y - X_j\beta_j)'(y - X_j\beta_j)$, corresponding to the kernel of the normal likelihood.

Frequentist sample dominated priors

A potential problem of using non-informative g-priors for the error covariance matrix is that the limit of posterior weights may be very sensitive to specification of the prior (see Leamer, 1978). Alternatively, Leamer (1978) assumes that a proper, conjugate Normal-Gamma prior (13) is 'dominated' by the sample information as the number of observations N grows. For stationary regressors with $\lim_{N \to \infty} (X_j'X_j)/N$ converging to a constant, the implied model weight is approximately equal to the (exponentiated) Schwarz (1978) model selection criterion (BIC)

$$p(M_j|Y) \propto p(M_j) \cdot N^{-k_j/2} \cdot SSE_j^{-N/2}. \qquad (18)$$

On closer inspection, the relative model weights using non-informative g-priors (17) or sample-dominated prior (18) are essentially the same, using $g_0 = 1/N$ in eq. (16). This is very reassuring for a decision maker, since the relative model weights are very similar under an empirical Bayesian or frequentist interpretation.

The BIC weights can also be derived from a unit information prior, where the information introduced by the prior corresponds to *one* datapoint from the sample (see Kass and Wasserman, 1995; Raftery, 1995). Klein and Brown (1984) give an alternative derivation of the BIC model weights (18) by minimizing the so-called Shannon information in the prior distribution; this approach also lends support for using the BIC model weights in small samples.

The underlying model space and its interpretation are important issues in the model uncertainty literature. Bernardo and Smith (1994) distinguish between *M*-closed and *M*-open environments, where the former includes the true model and the latter does not necessarily. A set of Akaike (AIC) model weights can be derived in the *M*-open environment as the best approximation to the true distribution (see Burnham and Anderson, 2002). The AIC weights have the disadvantage that they will not be consistent in *M*-closed environments.

Prior over model space

An important ingredient to model averaging is the choice of prior model probability. A popular choice is to impose a uniform prior over the space of models

$$p(M_j) = 1/K. \tag{19}$$

This prior might represent diffuse information about the set of models, but does have important implications for the size of models.

There are different approaches to modelling the inclusion of explanatory variables in the linear regression models (9). Mitchell and Beauchamp (1988) assign a discrete prior probability mass $p(\beta_i = 0|M_j)$ to excluding regressors x_i from the regression model M_j, that is a 'spike' at zero. A more Bayesian approach assigns a mixture of a relatively informative prior at zero (corresponding to a spike at zero) and a more diffuse prior if the variable is included (see George and McCulloch, 1993).

An alternative to specifying prior model probabilities is to think about prior model size and the implied probability of including individual variables. Sala-i-Martin, Doppelhofer and Miller (2004) argue that in the context of economic growth regressions a prior model size $\bar{k}$ smaller than the one implied by uniform priors $k/2$ might be preferable. Notice that this translates into a prior probability $\pi = p(\beta_i \neq 0|M_j) = \bar{k}/k$ of including a regressor x_i in model M_j. The implied model probability can then be written as

$$p(M_j) = \pi^{k_j} \cdot (1 - \pi)^{k - k_j}. \tag{20}$$

Notice that the prior inclusion probabilities π_i and implied prior model weights can also differ across variables, which is used in the 'stratified' sampler of the

BACE approach by Sala-i-Martin, Doppelhofer and Miller (2004) to speed up numerical convergence.

George (1999) observes that, when allowing for a large number of explanatory variables which could be correlated with each other, posterior model probabilities can be spread across models with 'similar' regressors. To address this problem, George (1999) proposes *dilution priors*, which reduce the prior weight on models that include explanatory variables measuring similar underlying theories. Alternatively, one can impose a hierarchical structure on the set of models and variables and partition the model space accordingly (see Chipman, George and McCulloch, 2001; Brock, Durlauf and West, 2003). Doppelhofer and Weeks (2007) propose to estimate the degree of dependence or jointness among regressors over the model space. If we are only interested in prediction, the orthogonalization of regressors greatly reduces the computational burden of model averaging (see Clyde, Desimone and Parmigiani, 1996). The costs are the loss of interpretation of associated coefficient estimates and the need to recalculate orthogonal factors with changing sample information.

Numerical simulation techniques

A major challenge for the practical implementation of model averaging is the computational burden of calculating posterior quantities of interest when the model space is potentially very large. In the linear regressions example, an exhaustive integration over all 2^k models becomes impractical for a relatively moderate number of 30 regressors.

Recent advances in computing power and development of statistical methods have made numerical approximations of posterior distributions feasible. Chib (2001) gives an overview of computationally intensive methods. Such methods include Markov chain Monte Carlo techniques (Madigan and York, 1995), stochastic search variable selection (George and McCulloch, 1993), the Metropolis–Hastings algorithm (Chib and Greenberg, 1995), and the Gibbs sampler (Casella and George, 1992). Chipman, George and McCulloch (2001) contrast different approaches in the context of Bayesian model selection.

The main idea of Monte Carlo simulation techniques is to estimate the empirical distribution of the parameter θ or related functions of interest $g(\theta)$ by sampling from the posterior distribution

$$E[g(\theta)|Y] = \int g(\theta)p(\theta|Y)d\theta, \tag{21}$$

where $g(\theta)$ could be any function, such as variance of θ or predicted values of the dependent variable y. Consider the sample counterpart

$$\widehat{g}_S = \frac{1}{S}\sum_{s=1}^{S} g\left(\theta^{(s)}\right), \tag{22}$$

where $\theta^{(s)}$ is a random *i.i.d.* sample drawn from $p(\theta|Y)$ and S is the number of draws. Provided that $E[g(\theta)|Y] < 0$ exists, a weak law of large numbers implies

$$\widehat{g}_S \xrightarrow{p} E[g(\theta)|Y]. \qquad (23)$$

A central limit theorem implies that

$$\sqrt{S}\{\widehat{g}_S - E[g(\theta)|Y]\} \xrightarrow{d} N(0, \Sigma_g) \qquad (24)$$

where Σ_g is the estimated covariance matrix of $g(\theta)|Y$.

Markov chain Monte Carlo (MCMC) techniques strengthen these results by constructing a Markov chain moving through the model space $\{M(s), s = 1, \ldots, S\}$ that simulates from a transition kernel $p(\theta^{(s)}|\theta^{(s-1)})$, starting from an initial value $\theta^{(0)}$. There are various approaches to constructing a Markov chain that converges to the posterior distribution $p(\theta|Y)$. This limiting distribution can be estimated from simulated values of $\theta^{(s)}$.

Simulation methods differ with respect to the choice of sampling procedure and transition kernels. A sampling algorithm that uses the underlying structure of the model can greatly improve the efficiency of the simulation. For example, the Gibbs sampler uses the structure of the statistical model to partition parameters and their distribution into blocks, which breaks up the simulation into smaller steps. In the linear regression example, the Gibbs sampler can draw from the conditional distributions for slope and variance parameters (13) separately. A disadvantage of numerical methods can be the technical challenges in their implementation (for an excellent introduction, see Gilks, Richardson and Spiegelhalter, 1996). Links to software packages and codes that facilitate implementation, such as BACC, BACE, BUGS and the BMA project website, are listed at the end of this article.

An alternative approach is to limit the set of models and rule out dominated models by Occam's razor, see Hoeting et al. (1999). This can speed up computation of posterior distributions and can be useful tool for model selection. Evidence by Raftery, Madigan and Volinsky (1996) suggests that model averaging leads to important improvements in predictive performance over any single model, and gives a small predictive advantage relative to the restricted set of models. The relative performance of different model averaging techniques and associated model weights depends on sample size and stability of estimated model (see Yuan and Yang, 2005; Hansen, 2007).

GERNOT DOPPELHOFER

See also **Bayesian econometrics; Bayesian methods in macroeconometrics; Bayesian statistics; decision theory in econometrics; econometrics; extreme bounds analysis; hierarchical Bayes models; model uncertainty; shrinkage-biased estimation in econometrics; testing.**

Bibliography

Avramov, D. 2002. Stock return predictability and model uncertainty. *Journal of Financial Economics* 64, 423–58.

Bernardo, J.M. and Smith, A.F.M. 1994. *Bayesian Theory.* New York: Wiley.

Brock, W.A. and Durlauf, S.N. 2001. Growth empirics and reality. *World Bank Economic Review* 15, 229–72.

Brock, W.A., Durlauf, S.N. and West, K. 2003. Policy evaluation in uncertain economic environments. *Brookings Papers on Economic Activity* 2003(1), 235–322.

Burnham, K.P. and Anderson, D.R. 2002. *Model Selection and Multimodel Inference: A Practical Information-Theoretic Approach,* 2nd edn. New York: Springer.

Carlin, B.P. and Louis, T.A. 2000. *Bayes and Empirical Bayes Methods for Data Analysis,* 2nd edn. New York: Chapman & Hall.

Casella, G. and George, E.I. 1992. Explaining the Gibbs sampler. *The American Statistician* 46, 167–74.

Chib, S. 2001. Markov chain Monte Carlo methods: computation and inference. In *Handbook of Econometrics,* vol. 5, ed. J. Heckman and E. Leamer. Amsterdam: North- Holland.

Chib, S. and Greenberg, E. 1995. Understanding the Metropolis–Hastings algorithm. *The American Statistician* 49, 327–35.

Chipman, H., George, E.I. and McCulloch, R.E. 2001. The practical implementation of Bayesian model selection. In *Model Selection. IMS Lecture Notes: Monograph Series,* ed. P. Lahiri. Beachwood, OH: Institute of Mathematical Statistics.

Clyde, M., Desimone, H. and Parmigiani, G. 1996. Prediction via orthogonalized model mixing. *Journal of the American Statistical Association* 91, 1197–208.

Doppelhofer, G. and Weeks, M. 2007. Jointness of growth determinants. *Journal of Applied Econometrics.*

Draper, D. 1995. Assessment and propagation of model uncertainty (with discussion). *Journal of the Royal Statistical Society B* 57, 45–97.

Fernandez, C., Ley, E. and Steel, M.F.J. 2001a. Model uncertainty in cross-country growth regressions. *Journal of Applied Econometrics* 16, 563–76.

Fernandez, C., Ley, E. and Steel, M.F.J. 2001b. Benchmark priors for Bayesian model averaging. *Journal of Econometrics* 100, 381–427.

Garratt, A., Lee, K., Pesaran, M.H. and Shin, Y. 2003. Forecast uncertainties in macroeconomic modelling: an application to the U.K. economy. *Journal of the American Statistical Association* 98, 829–38.

George, E.I. 1999. Discussion of Bayesian model averaging and model search strategies by M.A. Clyde. *Bayesian Statistics* 6, 175–77.

George, E.I. and Foster, D.P. 2000. Calibration and empirical Bayes variable selection. *Biometrika* 87, 731–47.

George, E. and McCulloch, R.E. 1993. Variable selection via Gibbs sampling. *Journal of the American Statistical Association* 88, 881–9.

Geweke, J. 1989. Bayesian inference in econometric models using Monte Carlo integration. *Econometrica* 57, 1317–39.

Geweke, J. and Whiteman, C. 2006. Bayesian forecasting. In *Handbook of Economic Forecasting*, vol. 1, ed. G. Elliott, C.W.J. Granger and A. Timmermann. Amsterdam: North-Holland.

Gilks, W., Richardson, S. and Spiegelhalter, D. 1996. *Markov Chain Monte Carlo in Practice*. New York: Chapman & Hall.

Hansen, B.E. 2007. Least squares model averaging. *Econometrica* 75, 1175–89.

Hjort, N.L. and Claeskens, G. 2003. Frequentist model averaging. *Journal of the American Statistical Association* 98, 879–99.

Hoeting, J.A., Madigan, D., Raftery, A.E. and Volinsky, C.T. 1999. Bayesian model averaging: a tutorial. *Statistical Science* 14, 382–417.

Jeffreys, H. 1961. *Theory of Probability*, 3rd edn. Oxford: Clarendon Press.

Kass, R.E. and Raftery, A.E. 1995. Bayes factors. *Journal of the American Statistical Association* 90, 773–95.

Kass, R.E. and Wasserman, L. 1995. A reference Bayesian test for nested hypotheses and its relationship to the Schwarz criterion. *Journal of the American Statistical Association* 90, 928–34.

Klein, R.W. and Brown, S.J. 1984. Model selection when there is 'minimal' prior information. *Econometrica* 52, 1291–312.

Koop, G. 2003. *Bayesian Econometrics*. Chichester: Wiley.

Leamer, E. 1978. *Specification Searches*. New York: Wiley.

Levin, A.T. and Williams, J.C. 2003. Robust monetary policy with competing reference models. *Journal of Monetary Economics* 50, 945–75.

Madigan, D. and York, J. 1995. Bayesian graphical models for discrete data. *International Statistical Review* 63, 215–32.

Mitchell, T.J. and Beauchamp, J.J. 1988. Bayesian variable selection in linear regression. *Journal of the American Statistical Association* 83, 1023–32.

Raftery, A.E. 1995. Bayesian model selection in social research. *Sociological Methodology* 25, 111–63.

Raftery, A.E., Madigan, D. and Hoeting, J.A. 1997. Bayesian model averaging for linear regression models. *Journal of the American Statistical Association* 92, 179–91.

Raftery, A.E., Madigan, D. and Volinsky, C.T. 1996. Accounting for model uncertainty in survival analysis improves predictive performance. *Bayesian Statistics* 5, 323–49.

Sala-i-Martin, X., Doppelhofer, G. and Miller, R.M. 2004. Determinants of economic growth: a Bayesian averaging of classical estimates (BACE) approach. *American Economic Review* 94, 813–35.

Schwarz, G. 1978. Estimating the dimension of a model, *Annals of Statistics* 6, 461–4.

Wasserman, L. 2000. Bayesian model selection and model averaging. *Journal of Mathematical Psychology* 44, 92–107.

Yang, Y. 2001. Adaptive regression by mixing. *Journal of the American Statistical Association* 96, 574–88.

Yuan, Z. and Yang, Y. 2005. Combining linear regression models: when and how? *Journal of the American Statistical Association* 100, 1202–14.

Zellner, A. 1986. On assessing prior distributions and Bayesian regression analysis with *g*-prior distributions. In *Bayesian Inference and Decision Techniques: Essays in Honor of Bruno de Finetti*, ed. P.K. Goel and A. Zellner. Amsterdam: North-Holland.

Model averaging software and codes

BACC package: http://www2.cirano.qc.ca/~bacc

BACE website: http://www.nhh.no/sam/bace

BMA homepage: http://www.research.att.com/~volinsky/bma.html

BUGS project: http://www.mrc-bsu.cam.ac.uk/bugs

LeSage's Econometrics Toolbox: http://www.spatial-econometrics.com

model selection

The purpose of econometric analysis is to develop mathematical representations of observable phenomena, which we call *models* or *hypotheses* (models subject to restrictions). Such models are then used to perform parameter estimation, test hypotheses, build confidence sets, make forecasts, conduct simulations, analyse policies, and so on. A central feature of modelling activity is the fact that models are usually interpreted as stylized (or simplified) representations that can perform certain tasks – such as prediction – but (eventually) not others, and they are treated *as if they were true* for certain purposes. Indeed, summarizing and stylizing observed phenomena can be viewed as essential components of modelling activity, which make it useful. This feature is not specific to economics and is shared by other sciences (see Cartwright, 1983).

Models can be classified as either *deterministic* or *stochastic*. *Deterministic models*, which often claim to make arbitrarily precise predictions, can be useful in theoretical activity. However, such models are rarely viewed as appropriate representations of observed data; for example, unless they are highly complex or indeterminate, they are typically logically inconsistent with data. For this reason, models used for econometric analysis are usually *stochastic* (or *statistical*).

Formally, a statistical model is a family of probability distributions (or measures) which are proposed to represent observed data. *Model selection*, in this context, is the task of selecting a family of proposed probability distributions, which will then be used to analyse data and perform other statistical inference operations (such as parameter estimation, hypothesis testing, and so on).

A basic feature of probability models is that they are typically *unverifiable*: as for any theory that makes an indefinite number of predictions, we can never be sure that the model will not be at odds with new data. Moreover, they are *logically unfalsifiable*: in contrast with deterministic models, a probabilistic model is usually logically compatible with all the possible observation sets. Consequently, model selection can depend on a wide array of elements, such as the objectives of the model, (economic) theory, the data themselves, and various conventions.

Features which are often viewed as desirable include: (*a*) simplicity or *parsimony* (Zellner, Keuzenkamp and McAleer, 2001); (*b*) the ability to deduce testable (or falsifiable) hypotheses (Popper, 1968); (*c*) the possibility of interpreting model parameters in terms of economic theory, if not consistency with economic theory; (*d*) the ability to satisfactorily perform the tasks for which the model is built (prediction, for example); (*e*) consistency with observed data. It is important to note that these characteristics depend (at least, partially) on conventional elements, such as the objectives of the model, criteria upon which a model will be deemed 'satisfactory', and so on. For further discussions of these general issues, the reader may consult Poirier (1994), Morgan and Morrison (1999), Keuzenkamp (2000), Zellner, Keuzenkamp and McAleer (2001) and Dufour (2003).

In this article, we focus on statistical methods for selecting a model on the basis of the available data. Methods for that purpose can be classified in four broad (not mutually exclusive) categories:

1. hypothesis testing procedures, including specification and diagnostic tests;
2. penalized goodness-of-fit methods, such as information criteria;
3. Bayesian approaches;
4. forecast evaluation methods.

The three first approaches are meant to be applicable 'in-sample', while the last approach *stricto sensu* requires observations that are not available when the model is selected, but may lead to model revision. (For general reviews of the topic of statistical model selection in econometrics and statistics, see Hocking, 1976; Leamer, 1978; 1983; Draper and Smith, 1981; Judge et al., 1985, chs 7 and 21; Sakamoto, Ishiguro and Kitagawa, 1985; Grasa, 1989; Choi, 1992; Gouriéroux and Monfort, 1995, ch. 22; Charemza and Deadman, 1997; McQuarrie and Tsai, 1998; Burnham and Anderson, 2002; Clements and Hendry, 2002; Miller, 2002; Bhatti, Al-Shanfari and Hossain, 2006). It is also interesting to note that classification techniques in statistics contain results that may be relevant to model selection. This topic, however, goes beyond the scope of the present article (for further discussion, see Krishnaiah and Kanal, 1982).

Model selection and specification errors
Most model selection methods deal in different ways with a trade-off between model *realism* – which usually suggests considering relatively general, hence complex models – and *parsimony*. From the viewpoint of estimation, for example, a model which is too simple (or parsimonious) involves *specification errors* and *biases* in parameter estimation, while too complex a model leads to parameter estimates with large variances. If the objective is forecasting, it is usually unclear which effect dominates.

For example, let us consider a linear regression model of the form

$$y_t = x_{t1}\beta_1 + x_{t2}\beta_2 + \cdots + x_{tk}\beta_k + u_t,$$
$$t = 1, \ldots, T,$$

$$(1)$$

where y_t is a dependent variable and $x_{t1}, \ldots, x_{tk}$ are explanatory variables, and u_t is a random disturbance which is typically assumed to be independent of (or uncorrelated with) the explanatory variables. In the classical linear model, it is assumed that the regressors can taken as fixed and that the disturbances $u_1, \ldots, u_T$ are independent and identically distributed (i.i.d.) according to a $N(0, \sigma^2)$ distribution. In this context, model selection typically involves selecting the regressors to be included as well as various distributional assumptions to be made upon the disturbances.

An especially important version of (1) is the autoregressive model:

$$y_t = \beta_0 + \beta_1 y_{t-1} + \cdots + \beta_p y_{t-p} + u_t,$$
$$t = 1, \ldots, T.$$

$$(2)$$

Then a central model selection issue consists in setting the order p of the process. In such models, there is typically little theoretical guidance on the order, so data-based order selection rules can be quite useful. A related set-up where model selection is usually based on statistical methods is the class of autoregressive-moving-average (ARMA) models

$$y_t = \beta_0 + \varphi y_{t-1} + \cdots + \varphi_p y_{t-p} + u_t - \theta_1 u_{t-1} + \cdots + \theta_1 u_{t-q},$$

$$(3)$$

where the orders p and q must be specified.

By considering the simple linear regression model, it is easy to see that excluding irrelevant variables can lead to biases in parameter estimates (Theil, 1957). On the other hand, including irrelevant regressors raises the variances of the estimators. The overall effect on the mean square error (MSE) of the estimator and, more generally, how closely it will tend to approach the parameter value may be ambiguous. It is well known that a biased estimator may have lower MSE than an unbiased estimator. This may be particularly important in forecasting, where a simple 'false' model may easily provide better forecasts than a complicated 'true' model, because the latter may be affected by imprecise parameter estimates (Allen, 1971).

Hypothesis testing approaches

Since hypothesis tests are based on a wide body of statistical theory (see Lehmann, 1986; Gouriéroux and Monfort, 1995), such procedures are widely used for assessing, comparing and selecting models. Furthermore, econometric models are also based on economic theory which suggests basic elements that can be used for specifying models. This entails a form of asymmetry, in which restrictions suggested by economic theory will be abandoned only if 'sufficient evidence' becomes available. Although significance tests are meant to decide whether a given hypothesis (which usually takes the form of a restricted model) is compatible with the data, such procedures can also be used for model selection. It is interesting to note that the methodology originally proposed by Box and Jenkins (1976) for specifying ARMA models was almost exclusively based on significance tests (essentially, autocorrelation tests).

There are two basic ways of using hypothesis tests for that purpose. The first one is *forward* or *specific-to-general* approach, in which one starts from a relatively simple model and then checks whether the model can be deemed 'satisfactory'. This typically involves various specification tests, such as:

1. residual-based tests, including tests for heteroskedasticity, autocorrelation, outliers, distributional assumptions (for example, normality), and so on;
2. tests for unit roots and/or stationarity, to decide whether corrections for integrated variables may be needed;
3. tests for the presence of structural change;
4. exogeneity tests, to decide whether corrections for endogeneity – such as instrumental variable (IV) methods – are required;
5. tests for the addition of explanatory variables;
6. tests of the functional form used (for example, linearity vs. nonlinearity).

There is a considerable literature on specification tests in econometrics (see Godfrey, 1988; MacKinnon, 1992; Davidson and MacKinnon, 1993). Systematic procedures for adding variables are also know in statistics as *forward selection* or *stepwise regression* procedures (Draper and Smith, 1981).

The second way is the *backward* or *general-to-specific* approach, in which one starts from a relatively comprehensive model which includes all the relevant variables. This model is then simplified by checking which variables are significant. *Backward selection* procedures in statistics (Draper and Smith, 1981) and the general-to-specific approach in econometrics (Davidson et al., 1978;

Charemza and Deadman, 1997) can be viewed as illustrations of this approach.

In practical work, the backward and forward approaches are typically combined. Both involve a search for a model which is both parsimonious and consistent with the data. However, the results may differ. Specifying a model through significance tests involves many judgements and depends on idiosyncratic decisions. Further, standard hypothesis tests involve the use of typically conventional levels (such as the commonly used five per cent level). The powers of the tests can also have a strong influence on the results.

Penalized goodness-of-fit criteria

As pointed out by Akaike (1974), it is not clear that hypothesis testing is a good basis for model selection. Instead, the problem of model selection may be better interpreted as an estimation problem involving a well-defined loss function. This leads to the topic of goodness-of-fit criteria.

A common way of assessing the performance of a regression model, such as (1), consists in computing the coefficient of determination, that is, the proportion of the dependent variable variance which is 'explained' by the model:

$$R^2 = 1 - \frac{\hat{V}(u)}{\hat{V}(y)} \tag{4}$$

where $\hat{V}(u) = \sum_{t=1}^{T} \hat{u}_t^2/T$, $\hat{V}(y) = \sum_{t=1}^{T}(y_t - \bar{y})^2/T$, $\bar{y} = \sum_{t=1}^{T} y_t/T$ and $\hat{u}_1, \ldots, \hat{u}_T$ are least squares residuals. This measure, however, has the inconvenient feature that it always increases when a variable is added to the model, even if it is completely irrelevant, and it can be made equal to its maximal value of one by including a sufficient number of regressors (for example, using any set of T linearly independent regressors).

An early way of avoiding this problem was proposed by Theil (1961, p. 213) who suggested that $\hat{V}(u)$ and $\hat{V}(y)$ be replaced by the corresponding unbiased estimators $s^2 = \sum_{t=1}^{T} \hat{u}_t^2/(T-k)$ and $s_y^2 = \sum_{t=1}^{T}(y_t - \bar{y})^2/(T-1)$. This yields the adjusted coefficient of determination:

$$\bar{R}^2 = 1 - \frac{s^2}{s_y^2} = 1 - \frac{T-1}{T-k}(1-R^2)$$

$$= R^2 - \frac{k-1}{T-k}(1-R^2).$$

It is easy to see that $\bar{R}^2$ may increase when the number of regressors increases. Note that maximizing $\bar{R}^2$ is equivalent to minimizing the 'unbiased estimator' s^2 of the disturbance variance. Further, if two regression models (which satisfy the assumptions of the classical linear model) are compared, and if one of these is the 'true' model, then the value of s^2 associated with the true model is smaller on average than the one of the other model (see Theil, 1961, p. 543). On the other hand, in large samples, the rule which consists in maximizing $\bar{R}^2$ does not select the true model with a probability converging to one: that is, it is not consistent (see Gouriéroux and Monfort, 1995, section 2.3).

Another approach consists in evaluating the 'distance' between the selected model and the true (unknown) model. Let $f(y)$ the density associated with the postulated model and $f_o(y)$ the density of the true model, where $Y=(y_1,\dots,y_T)'$. One such distance is the *Kullback distance*:

$$I(f,f_o) = \int \log\left[f_o(y)/f(y)\right]f_o(y)\ dy$$
$$= \underset{f_o}{E}\{\log[f_o(Y)/f(Y)]\}$$
$$= \underset{f_o}{E}\{\log[f_o(Y)]\} - \underset{f_o}{E}\{\log[f(Y)]\}.$$

Minimizing $I(f, f_o)$ with respect to f is equivalent to minimizing $-E\{\log[f(Y)]\}$. We obtain an information criterion by selecting an 'estimator' of $E\{\log[f(Y)]\}$.

For the case where the model f is estimated by maximizing a likelihood function $L_T(\theta)$ over a $K \times 1$ parameter vector θ, Akaike (1973) suggests that $L(\hat{\theta})$ can be viewed as a natural estimator of $E\{\log[f(Y)]\}$. However, the fact that θ has been estimated introduces a bias. This bias is (partially) corrected – using an expansion argument – by subtracting the number K from $L(\hat{\theta})$. This suggests the following information criterion:

$$AIC_L(\hat{\theta}_T) = -2L_T(\hat{\theta}_T) + 2K \tag{5}$$

where K is the dimension of θ (the number of estimated parameters) and multiplication by 2 is introduced to simplify the algebra. Among a given set of models, the one with the lowest AIC is selected.

The above criterion has also been generalized by various authors leading the following general class of criteria:

$$IC_L(\hat{\theta}_T) = -2L_T(\hat{\theta}_T) + c(T,K)K \tag{6}$$

where $c(T, K)$ is a function of T and K. In the case of Gaussian models, such as (1) or (2) with i.i.d. $N(0,\sigma^2)$ disturbances, we have $L_T(\hat{\theta}_T) = -(T/2)\ln(\hat{\sigma}_T^2) + d_T$, where d_T is a constant which only depends on T, so that minimizing $IC_L(\hat{\theta}_T)$ is equivalent to minimizing

$$IC(\hat{\theta}_T) = \ln(\hat{\sigma}_T^2) + c(T,K)\frac{K}{T}. \tag{7}$$

Alternative values of $c(T, K)$ which have been proposed include:

1. $c(T, K)=2$ (Akaike, 1969), which yields what is usually called the AIC criterion;
2. $c(T, K)=\ln(T)$ (Schwarz, 1978);
3. $c(T, K)=2\delta_T \ln(\ln T)$ where $\underset{T\to\infty}{\lim\sup}\,\delta_T > 1$ (Hannan and Quinn, 1979);

4. $c(T,K) = 2 + \frac{2K(K+1)}{T-K-1}$ (Hurvitch and Tsai, 1989), which leads to the AIC_c criterion.

An especially convenient feature of such information criteria is the fact that they can be applied to both regression models (through (7)) as well as to various nonlinear models (using (6)).

Other related rules include: (*a*) criteria based on an estimate of the *final prediction error*, which try to estimate the mean square prediction error taking into account estimation uncertainty (Akaike, 1969; 1970; Mallows, 1973; Amemiya, 1980); (*b*) the *criterion autoregressive transfer* (CAT) function proposed by Parzen (1977) for selecting the order of an autoregressive process; (*c*) Sawa's (1978) Bayesian information criterion (BIC).

By far, the information criteria are the most widely used in practice. Some theoretical (non-)optimality properties have been established. In particular, when one of the models compared is the 'true' one, it was observed by Shibata (1976) that Akaike's criterion is not consistent, in the sense that it does not select the most parsimonious true model with probability converging to one (as the sample size goes to infinity). Instead, even in large samples it has a high probability of picking a model with 'too many parameters'. By contrast, the criterion proposed by Hannan and Quinn (1979) is consistent under fairly general conditions, which also entails that Schwarz's (1978) criterion also leads to consistent model selection. On the other hand, the AIC criterion has a different optimality property, in the sense that it tends to minimize the one-step expected quadratic forecast error (Shibata, 1980).

On consistency, it is also interesting to observe that consistent model selection rules can be obtained provided each model is tested through a consistent test procedure (against all the other models considered) and the level of the test declines with the sample size at an appropriate rate (which depends on the asymptotic behaviour of the test statistic) (see Pötscher, 1983).

Model selection criteria of the information have the advantage of being fairly mechanical. On the other hand, they can be become quite costly to apply in practice when the number of models considered is large.

Bayesian model selection

Bayesian model selection involves comparing models through their 'posterior probabilities' giving observed data. Suppose we have two models M_1 and M_2 each of which postulates that the observation vector **y** follows a probability density which depends on a parameter vector: $p_y(y|\theta_1,M_1)$ under M_1, and $p_y(y|\theta_2,M_2)$ under M_2, where θ_1 and θ_2 are unknown parameter vectors (which may have different dimensions). Further, each one of the parameter vectors is assigned a 'prior distribution' ($p(\theta_1|M_1)$ and $p(\theta_2|M_2)$), and each model a 'prior probability' ($p(M_1)$ and $p(M_2)$). Then one may compute the 'posterior probability' of each model given the data

$$p(M_i|y) = p(M_i) \int p_y(y|\theta_i, M_1)p(\theta_1|M_i) \ d\theta_i,$$

$$i = 1, 2.$$

(8)

This posterior probability of each model provides a direct measure of the 'plausibility' of each model. In such contexts, the ratio

$$K_{12} = \frac{p(M_1|y)}{p(M_2|y)}$$

(9)

is called the 'posterior odds ratio' of M_1 relative to M_2.

A rational decision rule for selecting between M_1 and M_2 then emerges if we can specify a loss function such as

$$L(i, j) = \text{cost of choosing } M_j \text{ when } M_i \text{ is true.}$$

(10)

If $L(i, i)=0$ for $i=1, 2$, expected loss is minimized by choosing M_1 when

$$K_{12} \geq \frac{L(2, 1)}{L(1, 2)},$$

(11)

and M_2 when otherwise. In particular, if $L(1, 2)=L(2, 1)$, expected loss is minimized by choosing the model with the highest posterior probability. Such rules can be extended to problems where more than two models are compared.

The Bayesian approach automatically introduces a penalty for non-parsimony and easily allows the use of decision-theoretic considerations. The main difficulty consists in assigning prior distributions on model parameters and prior probabilities to competing models. For further discussion, see Zellner (1971, ch. 10), Leamer (1978; 1983), Gelman et al. (2003) and Lancaster (2004).

Forecast evaluation

In view of the fact that forecasting is one of the most common objectives for building econometric models, alternative models are often assessed by studying *post-sample* forecasts. Three types of assessments are typically considered in such contexts: (*a*) tests of predictive failure; (*b*) descriptive measures of forecast performance, which can be compared across models; (*c*) tests of predictive ability.

A test of predictive failure involves testing whether the prediction errors associated with a model are consistent with the model. This suggests testing whether forecasts are 'unbiased' or 'too large' to be consistent with the model. The well-known predictive test for structural change proposed by Chow (1960) is an early example of such an approach. (For further discussion and extensions, see Box and Tiao, 1976; Dufour, 1980; Pesaran, Smith and Yeo, 1985; Dufour, Ghysels and Hall, 1994; Dufour and Ghysels, 1996; Clements and Hendry, 1998.)

Common measures of forecast performance involve mean errors, mean square errors, mean absolute errors, and so on (see Theil, 1961; Diebold, 2004). Although commonly used, such measures are mainly descriptive. They can usefully be complemented by tests of predictive ability. Such procedures test whether the difference between expected measures of forecast performance is zero (or less than zero) against an alternative where it is different from zero (or larger than zero). Tests of this type were proposed, among others, by Meese and Rogoff (1988), Diebold and Mariano (1995), Harvey, Leybourne and Newbold (1997), West (1996), West and McCracken (1998) and White (2000) (for reviews, see also Mariano, 2002; McCracken and West, 2002).

It is important to note that predictive performance and predictive accuracy depend on two features: first, whether the theoretical model used is close to the unknown data distribution and, second, the ability to estimate accurately model parameters (hence on sample size available for estimating these). For a given sample size, a false but parsimonious model may well have better predictive ability than the 'true' model.

Post-model selection inference

An important issue often raised in relation with model selection is its effect on the validity of inference – such as estimation, tests and confidence sets – obtained after a process of model selection (or pretesting). This issue is subtle and complex. Not surprisingly, both positive and negative assessments can be found.

On the positive side, it has been observed that pretesting (or model selection) does allow one to produce so-called 'super-efficient' (or Hodges) estimators, whose asymptotic variance can be at least as low as the Cramér–Rao efficiency bound and lower at certain points (see Le Cam, 1953). This may be viewed as a motivation for using consistent pretesting.

Furthermore, consistent model selection does not affect the asymptotic distributions of various estimators and test statistics, so the asymptotic validity of inferences based on a model selected according to such a rule is maintained (see Pötscher, 1991; Dufour, Ghysels and Hall, 1994).

On the negative side, it is important to note that these are only asymptotic results. In particular, these are point-wise convergence results, not uniform convergence results, so they may be quite misleading concerning what happens in finite samples (for some examples, see Dufour, 1997; Pötscher, 2002). For estimation, there is a considerable literature on the finite-sample distribution of pretest estimators, which can be quite different of their limit distributions (Judge and Bock, 1978; Danilov and Magnus, 2004). For a critical discussion of the effect of model selection on tests and confidence sets, see Leeb and Pötscher (2005).

Conclusion

The problem of model selection is one of the most basic and challenging problems of statistical analysis in econometrics. Much progress has been done in recent years in developing better model selection procedures and for understanding the consequences of model selection.

But model building remains largely an art in which subjective judgements play a central role. Developing procedures applicable to complex models, which may involve a large number of candidate variables, and allowing for valid statistical inference in the presence of model selection remain difficult issues to which much further research should be devoted.

JEAN-MARIE DUFOUR

See also **Bayesian statistics; econometrics; endogeneity and exogeneity; forecasting; heteroskedasticity and autocorrelation corrections; linear models; models; serial correlation and serial dependence; specification problems in econometrics; statistical decision theory; statistical inference; structural change; testing; time series analysis.**

Bibliography

Akaike, H. 1969. Fitting autoregressive models for prediction. *Annals of the Institute of Statistical Mathematics* 21, 243–7.

Akaike, H. 1970. Statistical predictor identification. *Annals of the Institute of Statistical Mathematics* 22, 203–17.

Akaike, H. 1973. Information theory and an extension of the maximum likelihood principle. In *Second International Symposium on Information Theory*, ed. B.N. Petrov and F. Csaki. Budapest: Akademiai Kiado.

Akaike, H. 1974. A new look at the statistical model identification. *IEEE Transactions on Automatic Control* AC-19, 716–23.

Allen, D.M. 1971. Mean square error prediction as a criterion for selecting variables. *Technometrics* 13, 469–75.

Amemiya, T. 1980. Selection of regressors. *International Economic Review* 21, 331–54.

Bhatti, M.I., Al-Shanfari, H. and Hossain, M.Z. 2006. *Econometric Analysis of Model Selection and Model Testing*. Aldershot: Ashgate.

Box, G.E.P. and Jenkins, G.M. 1976. *Time Series Analysis: Forecasting and Control*, 2nd edn. San Francisco: Holden-Day.

Box, G.E.P. and Tiao, G.C. 1976. Comparison of forecast and actuality. *Applied Statistics* 64, 195–200.

Burnham, K.P. and Anderson, D.R. 2002. *Model Selection and Multi-model Inference: A Practical Information Theoretic Approach*. New York: Springer.

Cartwright, N. 1983. *How the Laws of Physics Lie*. Oxford: Oxford University Press.

Charemza, W.W. and Deadman, D.F. 1997. *New Directions in Econometric Practice: General to Specific Modelling, Cointegration and Vector Autoregression*, 2nd edn. Aldershot: Edward Elgar.

Choi, B. 1992. *ARMA Model Identification*. New York: Springer.

Chow, G.C. 1960. Tests of equality between sets of coefficients in two linear regressions. *Econometrica* 28, 591–605.

Clements, M.P. and Hendry, D.F. 1998. *Forecasting Economic Time Series*. Cambridge: Cambridge University Press.

Clements, M.P. and Hendry, D.F., eds. 2002. *A Companion to Economic Forecasting*. Oxford: Blackwell.

Danilov, D. and Magnus, J.R. 2004. On the harm that ignoring pretesting can cause. *Journal of Econometrics* 122, 27–46.

Davidson, J.E.H., Hendry, D.F., Srba, F. and Yeo, S. 1978. Econometric modelling of the aggregate time-series relationship between consumers' expenditure and income in the United Kingdom. *Economic Journal* 88, 661–92.

Davidson, R. and MacKinnon, J.G. 1993. *Estimation and Inference in Econometrics*. New York: Oxford University Press.

Diebold, F.X. 2004. *Elements of Forecasting*, 3rd edn. Mason, OH: Thomson South-Western.

Diebold, F.X. and Mariano, R.S. 1995. Comparing predictive accuracy. *Journal of Business and Economic Statistics* 13, 253–63.

Draper, N.R. and Smith, H., eds. 1981. *Applied Regression Analysis*, rev. edn. New York: Wiley.

Dufour, J.-M. 1980. Dummy variables and predictive tests for structural change. *Economics Letters* 6, 241–7.

Dufour, J.-M. 1997. Some impossibility theorems in econometrics, with applications to structural and dynamic models. *Econometrica* 65, 1365–89.

Dufour, J.-M. 2003. Identification, weak instruments and statistical inference in econometrics. *Canadian Journal of Economics* 36, 767–808.

Dufour, J.-M. and Ghysels, E. 1996. Recent developments in the econometrics of structural change. *Journal of Econometrics* 70(1).

Dufour, J.-M., Ghysels, E. and Hall, A. 1994. Generalized predictive tests and structural change analysis in econometrics. *International Economic Review* 35, 199–229.

Gelman, A., Carlin, J.B., Stern, H.S. and Rubin, D.B. 2003. *Bayesian Data Analysis*, 2nd edn. London: Chapman and Hall/CRC.

Godfrey, L.G. 1988. *Misspecification Tests in Econometrics: The Lagrange Multiplier Principle and Other Approaches*. Cambridge: Cambridge University Press.

Gouriéroux, C. and Monfort, A. 1995. *Statistics and Econometric Models*, vols. 1 and 2. Cambridge: Cambridge University Press.

Grasa, A.A. 1989. *Econometric Model Selection: A New Approach*. Dordrecht: Kluwer.

Hannan, E.J. and Quinn, B. 1979. The determination of the order of an autoregression. *Journal of the Royal Statistical Society B* 41, 190–1.

Harvey, D.I., Leybourne, S.J. and Newbold, P. 1997. Testing the equality of prediction mean squared errors. *International Journal of Forecasting* 13, 281–91.

Hocking, R.R. 1976. The analysis and selection of variables in linear regression. *Biometrika* 32, 1–49.

Hurvitch, C.M. and Tsai, C.-L. 1989. Regression and time series model selection in small samples. *Biometrika* 76, 297–307.

Judge, G.G. and Bock, M.E. 1978. *The Statistical Implications of Pre-Test and Stein-Rule Estimators in Econometrics*. Amsterdam: North-Holland.

Judge, G.G., Griffiths, W.E., Carter Hill, R., Lütkepohl, H. and Lee, T.-C. 1985. *The Theory and Practice of Econometrics*, 2nd edn. New York: Wiley.

Keuzenkamp, H.A. 2000. *Probability, Econometrics and Truth: The Methodology of Econometrics*. Cambridge: Cambridge University Press.

Krishnaiah, P.R. and Kanal, L.N. 1982. *Handbook of Statistics 2: Classification, Pattern Recognition and Reduction of Dimensionality*. Amsterdam: North-Holland.

Lancaster, T. 2004. *An Introduction to Modern Bayesian Econometrics*. Oxford: Blackwell.

Le Cam, L. 1953. On some asymptotic properties of maximum likelihood estimates and related Bayes estimates. *University of California Publications in Statistics* 1, 277–330.

Leamer, E. 1978. *Specification Searches: Ad Hoc Inferences with Nonexperimental Data*. New York: Wiley.

Leamer, E.E. 1983. Model choice. In *Handbook of Econometrics*, vol. 1, ed. Z. Griliches and M.D. Intriligator. Amsterdam: North-Holland.

Leeb, H. and Pötscher, B. 2005. Model selection and inference: facts and fiction. *Econometric Theory* 21, 29–59.

Lehmann, E.L. 1986. *Testing Statistical Hypotheses*, 2nd edn. New York: Wiley.

MacKinnon, J.G. 1992. Model specification tests and artificial regressions. *Journal of Economic Literature* 30, 102–46.

Mallows, C.L. 1973. Some comments on *Cp. Technometrics* 15, 661–75.

Mariano, R.S. 2002. Testing forecast accuracy. In Clements and Hendry (2002).

McCracken, M.W. and West, K.D. 2002. Inference about predictive ability. In Clements and Hendry (2002).

McQuarrie, A.D.R. and Tsai, C.-L. 1998. *Regression and Time Series Model Selection*. Singapore: World Scientific.

Meese, R.A. and Rogoff, K. 1988. Was it real? The exchange rate-interest differential relation over the modern floating-rate period. *Journal of Finance* 43, 933–48.

Miller, A. 2002. *Subset Selection in Regression*, 2nd edn. Boca Raton, FL: Chapman & Hall/CRC.

Morgan, M.S. and Morrison, M. 1999. *Models as Mediators: Perspectives on Natural and Social Science*. Cambridge: Cambridge University Press.

Parzen, E. 1977. Multiple time series: determining the order of approximating autoregressive schemes. In *Multivariate Analysis IV: Proceedings of the Fourth International Symposium on Multivariate Analysis*, ed. P.R. Krishnaiah. Amsterdam: North-Holland/Elsevier.

Pesaran, M.H., Smith, R.P. and Yeo, J.S. 1985. Testing for structural stability and predictive failure: a review. *Manchester School* 3, 280–95.

Poirier, D.J. 1994. *The Methodology of Econometrics*, 2 vols. Aldershot: Edward Elgar.

Popper, K. 1968. *The Logic of Scientific Discovery*, rev. edn. New York: Harper Torchbooks.

Pötscher, B.M. 1983. Order estimation in ARMA-models by Lagrange multiplier tests. *Annals of Statistics* 11, 872–85.

Pötscher, B. 1991. Effects of model selection on inference. *Econometric Theory* 7, 163–85.

Pötscher, B. 2002. Lower risk bounds and properties of confidence sets for ill-posed estimation problems with applications to spectral density and persistence estimation, unit roots and estimation of long memory parameters. *Econometrica* 70, 1035–65.

Sakamoto, Y., Ishiguro, M. and Kitagawa, G. 1985. *Akaike Information Criterion Statistics*. Dordrecht: Reidel.

Sawa, T. 1978. Information criteria for discriminating among alternative regression models. *Econometrica* 46, 1273–91.

Schwarz, G. 1978. Estimating the dimension of a model. *Annals of Statistics* 6, 461–4.

Shibata, R. 1976. Selection of the order of an autoregressive model by Akaike's information criterion. *Biometrika* 71, 117–26.

Shibata, R. 1980. Asymptotically efficient selection of the order of the model for estimating parameters of a linear process. *Annals of Statistics* 8, 147–64.

Theil, H. 1957. Specification errors and the estimation of economic relationships. *Review of the International Statistical Institute* 25, 41–51.

Theil, H. 1961. *Economic Forecasts and Policy*, 2nd edn. Amsterdam: North-Holland.

West, K.D. 1996. Asymptotic inference about predictive ability. *Econometrica* 64, 1067–84.

West, K.D. and McCracken, M.D. 1998. Regression-based tests of predictive ability. *International Economic Review* 39, 817–40.

White, H. 2000. A reality check for data snooping. *Econometrica* 68, 1097–126.

Zellner, A. 1971. *An Introduction to Bayesian Inference in Econometrics*. New York: Wiley.

Zellner, A., Keuzenkamp, H.A. and McAleer, M. 2001. *Simplicity, Inference and Modelling: Keeping It Sophisticatedly Simple*. Cambridge: Cambridge University Press.

model uncertainty

Model uncertainty is a condition of analysis when the specification of the model of analysed process is open to doubt. One of the fundamental sources of model uncertainty is the tradition of critical reasoning that, in words of Karl Popper (1962, pp. 151–3), 'admits a plurality of doctrines which all try to approach the truth by means of critical discussion'. Popper traces the critical tradition back to ancient Greek philosophy. He cites Xenophanes, 570–480 BC, who wrote (see Diels, 1951, vol. 1, pp. 133 and 137):

> The gods did not reveal, from the beginning,
> All things to us; but in the course of time,
> Through seeking, men find that which is the better ...
>
> But as for certain truth, no man has known it,
> Nor will he know it; neither of the gods,
> Nor yet of all the things of which I speak.
> And even if by chance he were to utter
> The final truth, he would himself not know it:
> For all is but a woven web of guesses.

Another fundamental source of model uncertainty is the necessity for models to be simple enough to provide an efficient link between theory and reality (see Morgan and Morrison, 1999, for a book-length discussion of the nature of models). Complicated models may be less useful than simple ones even though the accuracy of the simple models' description of the modelled process may be more doubtful.

The understanding of what constitutes a model and how to model model uncertainty itself depends on the research context. For example, for engineers a prototypical model is represented by a system of differential equations:

$$\dot{x}(t) = Ax(t) + Bu(t),$$
$$y(t) = Cx(t) + Du(t),$$

where $x(t)$, $u(t)$, and $y(t)$ are square-integrable functions of $t \in [0, \infty)$, interpreted, respectively, as internal states, inputs and outputs of the modelled mechanism. By means of the Laplace transform, we get an alternative representation of the above model (with zero initial states):

$$\hat{y}(s) = M(s)\hat{u}(s),$$
$$M(s) = D + C(sI - A)^{-1}B,$$

where $\hat{u}(s)$ and $\hat{y}(s)$ are the Laplace transforms of $u(t)$ and $y(t)$ (see Kwakernaak and Sivan, 1972, p. 33).

For engineers, the interest often lies in checking whether particular inputs into the modelled mechanism are such that the corresponding internal states and outputs satisfy an admissibility criterion. Since the model is only an approximation of the mechanism, the check of the admissibility criterion should take into account possible deviations of the model from the truth. These possible deviations constitute model uncertainty, which can be represented by a set of models built around the above reference model.

A model of the uncertainty set which is very flexible and well suited for the purpose of the admissibility checks is the so-called linear fractional model (see Zhou, Doyle and Glover, 1996, chs 10 and 11). It replaces the reference model represented by $M(s)$, by a set of models:

$$M(\Delta) = M(s) + L(s)\Delta(I - \Delta G(s))^{-1}R(s),$$
$$\Delta \in \Lambda,$$

where Λ is a set of block-diagonal matrices with the largest singular value bounded by unity. The number and the structure of the blocks, and the form of matrix functions $L(s)$, $R(s)$, and $G(s)$ must be chosen so that the resulting model uncertainty set accurately represents the engineer's understanding of possible deviations of the reference model from the modelled mechanism.

To take another example, for researchers in statistics a model is often defined as a family of the joint probability distributions of the data. Draper (1995, pp. 45–6) notes that statistical models can be expressed in two parts, the first representing structural assumptions, such as distributional choices for residuals, or a particular functional form of the regression function and so on, and the second representing parameters, whose meaning is specific to the assumed structure. He points out that 'even in controlled experiments and randomized sample surveys key aspects of ... [the structure] will usually be uncertain, and this is even more true with observational studies'. Statistical model uncertainty can be interpreted as the structural uncertainty that Draper is concerned about in the above citation.

A failure to account for statistical model uncertainty often leads to overconfidence in the results of a statistical study. For example, the forecast intervals, which are computed ignoring possible model uncertainty, may be too narrow, p-values of a test of significance of coefficients in a linear regression too small, and so forth.

Typically, statistical models analyse reality, which is much more complicated than man-made mechanisms. Therefore, building a crisp set of models that represent model uncertainty is more problematic in statistics than in engineering. Most of the statistical approaches to modelling model uncertainty are Bayesian. They represent model uncertainty by a prior distribution defined in the model space and propagate this uncertainty to the statistical decisions by integrating models out from the posterior distribution. Such a technique of model uncertainty propagation is called Bayesian model averaging (see Hoeting et al., 1999 for a tutorial).

There are no standardized ways of specifying a prior that would represent model uncertainty. One approach is to expand a given model to a more general class and to formulate a subjective prior over this class. An early example of this approach can be found in Box and Tiao (1962), who re-examine Darwin's paired data on the heights of self- and cross-fertilized plants earlier analysed by Fisher (1935). To take into account a possible mis-specification of Fisher's model for differences in the heights of the i-th pair of plants, y_i:

$$y_i = \theta + \sigma e_i, \quad e_i \propto i.i.d.N(0,1),$$

Box and Tiao expand it to a more general model:

$$y_i = \theta + \sigma e_i, \quad e_i \text{ are i.i.d. with density}$$
$$\text{proportional to } \exp\left(-\tfrac{1}{2}|e|^{2/(1+\beta)}\right),$$

and formulate a beta-type prior distribution for the 'extra' parameter β.

As emphasized by Draper et al. (1987, p. 12), for the model expansion approach to be successful it is important to 'stake out the corners in model space', that is, to find 'the plausible variations on the model... that strongly influence what actions would be taken'. Of course, such an exercise would necessarily be subjective and context specific.

An interesting frequentist alternative to specifying a prior in the model space is to bootstrap the modelling process. Efron and Gong (1983) consider a databased process of explanatory variable selection for a logistic model of the probability of death from a certain disease. They apply the selection process to bootstrap replications of the data, obtaining, thus, a distribution of logistic models, which represents uncertainty about the model whose explanatory variables were chosen on the basis of the original data-set.

If we turn to a discussion of model uncertainty in economics, we first note that the economic model uncertainty is much broader in scope than engineering or statistical model uncertainty. The economic reality is so complex that it may be impossible in principle to approximate it by any model. Different research communities may disagree on what should be understood by economic reality in the first place. For example, Frankel and Rockett (1988, p. 318), in their study of potential gains from cooperation of different countries' monetary authorities, write: 'The assumption that policy makers agree on the true model has little, if any, empirical basis. Different governments subscribe to different economic philosophies.'

The idea of incommensurability of different views of economic reality is a focus of Dow's (2004) methodological study of model uncertainty. Dow puts the incommensurability idea in the context of uncertainty research originating in Keynes's (1921) *Treatise on Probability*, and discusses the role of judgement in a situation when it is impossible in principle to compare models on the basis of their closeness to 'the truth'.

Further, in views of Keynes (1921) and Knight (1921), economic uncertainty may be conceptually different from the uncertainty modelled by randomness. So even if the incommensurability issue does not arise, an economic decision-maker may be hesitant in assigning probabilities to different economic models and comparing them on the basis of these probabilities. Such a view is supported by a range of experimental studies initiated by the Ellsberg paradox.

The Ellsberg paradox shows that people prefer to bet on 50–50 lotteries rather than on lotteries with completely unknown odds. Such behaviour is a variant of a more general phenomenon called ambiguity aversion. It reveals that people fail to assign prior probabilities to events that happen in incomplete information environments.

As Gilboa and Schmeidler (1989) show, failing to assign prior probabilities to events is perfectly rational because it is consistent with axioms of choice as reasonable as those used by Savage (1954). Gilboa and Schmeidler's axioms imply that a rational decision-maker acts as if he or she contemplates a set of probability distributions over the possible events. The decision is then made so as to minimize the expected loss under the worst possible distribution from the set.

Much of modern research on economic model uncertainty concerns monetary policy formulation and evaluation when policymakers do not have a single reliable model of the economy. In the rest of this article we will therefore focus on the model uncertainty arising in monetary policy research.

Global model uncertainty

Different approaches to macroeconomic model uncertainty can roughly be separated in two broad categories, which Brock, Durlauf and West (2003) call global and local approaches. The global approach assumes that a set of possible models consists of the substantially different economic theories. An early example of the global approach is posited by McCallum (1988), who uses a real business cycle model, a monetary misperception model and a Keynesian model to represent model uncertainty confronted by a monetary policymaker. In contrast, the local approach builds the model uncertainty set by continuously expanding a single reference model.

Brock, Durlauf and West (2003) distinguish three different components of model uncertainty in the global approach. The first component is 'theory uncertainty', which represents economists' 'disagreement over fundamental aspects of the economy'. The second component is 'specification uncertainty', which includes uncertainty about lag length specification, functional form, and the choice of proxy variables representing particular theoretical concepts. The last component is 'heterogeneity uncertainty' which 'concerns the extent to which different observations are assumed to obey a common model'.

A model for the global model uncertainty itself is based on a set of models which represent different theories, have different specifications given a particular theory, and may include dummy variables or other devices that capture possible data heterogeneity. Brock, Durlauf and West (2003) propose to complete the model of model uncertainty by specifying a prior distribution over the models in the set. They propose three principles that should guide the formulation of the prior. First, it 'should assign relatively high probability to those areas of the likelihood that are relatively large' (see, however, Chris Sims's critique of this principle in the discussion published with Brock, Durlauf and West, 2003). Second, 'a prior should be robust in the sense that a small change in the prior should not induce a large change in the posterior'. Finally, 'priors should be flexible enough to allow for their use across similar studies'.

To accommodate the possibility of the ambiguity aversion on behalf of policymakers, Brock, Durlauf and West (2003) suggest that the chosen prior, π, be extended to a class of ε-contaminated priors $\{(1 - \varepsilon)\pi + \varepsilon P, P \in P(M)\}$, where $0 \leq \varepsilon \leq 1$ and $P(M)$ is the set of all possible probability measures on the model uncertainty set. The policy which takes into account the model uncertainty can then be chosen by minimizing the expected posterior loss under the worst possible prior from the ε-contaminated class.

Classes of ε-contaminated priors are often used in robust Bayesian analysis to model uncertainty in the prior distribution (see Berger and Berliner, 1986). Such classes are easy to work with, and it is not difficult to show that the policy described above differs from the policy which minimizes expected posterior loss under the original prior by putting an extra weight on the worst possible model from the model uncertainty set. The higher the ε, the larger the extra weight.

In the extreme case when $\varepsilon = 1$, specifying prior probabilities of the models from the model uncertainty set is not necessary. The very set completely describes model uncertainty. The policy is then formulated as if the worst possible model were true. The policy choice under the extreme model uncertainty is often visualized as a zero-sum game between a policymaker and malevolent 'nature' who chooses adversary models from the model uncertainty set. Early advocates of this useful visualization were Brunner and Meltzer (1969) and von zur Muehlen (2001).

Describing model uncertainty by an un-weighted set of models was advocated by John Tukey. He says in his comment on Draper (1995) (see Draper, 1995, p. 78):

> The most acceptable pattern, as far as I am concerned, for the development of a bouquet of models begins with a predata choice of a collection of models likely to be relevant in the field in question, followed by an examination of the reasonability of the data in the light

of each model. For those models for which the data seem unreasonable, we have a choice:

(a) drop them from consideration or

(b) move them sufficiently close to a smoothed version of the data to make the data reasonable.

Here reasonability is a yes-no decision, not a probability reduction, and the models are thought as challenges, trying to mark the boundaries of reasonability, not to represent likely outcomes. Taking the worst of what remains is a conservative but, in my judgment, reasonable step.

Local model uncertainty

An unweighted set description of model uncertainty is also preferred by Lars Hansen and Thomas Sargent, who initiated a broad research programme addressing model uncertainty in macroeconomics (see Hansen and Sargent, 2006, for a book-length development of their research plan). In contrast to Tukey, their choice of the unweighted representation is primarily motivated by the difficulty of formulating a sensible prior over a large set of models.

Hansen and Sargent's approach to model uncertainty is an example of the local approach. They assume that by an unspecified search process a policymaker comes to a single approximating model of the economy. Then, the model uncertainty set is built around this model. The set includes all models that are statistically difficult to distinguish from the original approximating model.

More formally, Hansen and Sargent (2006, p. 8) consider a policymaker whose approximating model can be formalized as a Markov process characterized by transition density $f(y_t|y_{t-1})$, where y_t is a state vector at time t. The policymaker's model uncertainty set consists of the Markov processes with transition densities $g(y_t|y_{t-1})$, which are difficult to statistically distinguish from the approximating model in the sense that the expected discounted sum of conditional relative entropies of models g with respect to model f is reasonably small:

$$E_g \sum_{t=0}^{\infty} \beta^t \int \log\left(\frac{g(z|y_t)}{f(z|y_t)}\right) g(z|y_t) dz \leq \eta.$$

The conditional relative entropy measures the mean information for discrimination between g and f on the basis of a new observation of the state vector, which comes from g (see Kullback and Leibler, 1951). What 'reasonably small' means depends on how uncertain the policymaker is about her approximating model. When η is large, the amount of uncertainty may be very large. Hence, the classification of the Hansen–Sargent approach as 'local' does not mean that the uncertainty they address is insignificant. Anderson, Hansen and Sargent (2003) relate η to a more transparent concept of detection error probability, which can be used to calibrate η.

Using the relative entropy concept for the formulation of the model uncertainty set is very convenient for design of macroeconomic policy that works well across all models from the set. In an engineering context, Petersen, James and Dupuis (2000) show how to construct a risk-sensitive control problem which has the same solution as the problem of finding a controller that maximizes the worst possible performance over the set of models subject to the relative entropy constraint. The risk-sensitive control problem is extensively studied in Whittle (1990). It has a very simple solution, which is a modification of a standard solution of the linear quadratic Gaussian problem. Hansen and Sargent (2006) substantially modify and extend the control methods so that they are applicable to economic problems.

A very important economic setting that calls for an extensive modification of the engineering ideas is that with multiple decision-makers. The rational expectations literature assumes that the economic agents living inside the model and the policymaker who uses the model to formulate her policy agree on the model. The possibility that the agents and the policymaker have doubts about the model calls for a revision of the rational expectations paradigm. Giannoni (2002) is an early example of a study that assumes model uncertainty on behalf of the policymaker but requires the modelled economic agents to know the true model. Hansen and Sargent (2003) consider a situation when the policymaker and the economic agents are uncertain about a common approximating model.

Another example of the local approach to model uncertainty is provided by Schorfheide and Del Negro (2005). In contrast to Hansen and Sargent, they represent model uncertainty about an approximating model by a prior distribution in the model space, centred at the approximating model. To cope with the difficulty of specifying sensible and manageable priors over a vast set of models, they restrict attention to the alternative models that have form of identified vector autoregressions (VARs). The prior density over the alternative models is taken to be proportional to the relative entropy distance between the alternative and the approximating model, which is chosen to be a state-of-the-art dynamic stochastic general equilibrium model.

Using identified VARs for construction of the model uncertainty set potentially raises an extra model uncertainty issue: which identification scheme to use to identify structural shocks in VARs? Different identification schemes cannot be evaluated on the basis of data because the implied identified VARs are observationally equivalent. To take into account uncertainty about the identification schemes, Faust (1998) proposes forming a set of identified VARs so that the corresponding impulse responses look reasonable in the sense that they are consistent with some particularly strong prior beliefs about the effects of structural shocks.

Evolving model uncertainty

Schorfheide and Del Negro's (2005) analysis of policy choice under model uncertainty is one of few studies that allows for changes in the model uncertainty depending on the prospective policy choice. Such flexibility comes from their obtaining the joint posterior distribution for the set of possible models and policy parameters. As long as policy parameters are set in the historically observed region, the policymaker can take as his or her model of model uncertainty the posterior distribution over the set of models conditional on the particular parameter values.

Policymakers' perceptions of model uncertainty may depend on many factors beyond particular policy choices. As new data emerge, policymakers learn and adjust their model uncertainty sets. Even more importantly, unforeseen events may substantially change the set of possible models. This fact is at the heart of Keynes's (1939, p. 567) critique of Tinbergen's econometric method: '[The] main prima facie objection to the application of the method of multiple correlation to complex economic problems lies in the apparent lack of any adequate degree of uniformity in the environment.'

An interesting theory of learning under the condition of model uncertainty in a non-stationary environment is Epstein and Schneider (2006). These authors consider a decision-maker who receives a sequence of signals generated by an uncertain model. Some features of the model are constant over time. Those features are represented by a parameter θ, which the decision-maker hopes to learn about, although it is ambiguous initially. Other features may 'vary over time in a way … [the decision-maker] does not understand well enough even to theorize about and therefore she does not try to learn about them' (see Epstein and Schneider, 2006, p. 3). These features are captured by an assumption that the decision-maker considers a non-singleton set of data distributions, which are all parameterized by θ but have different structure. Which structure is used to deliver observations may erratically change over time.

Epstein and Schneider show how the set of priors for θ changes over time, and prove that, under certain regulatory conditions, it converges to a distribution assigning probability 1 to a single vector θ^* so that the ambiguity about θ is asymptotically resolved. On the contrary, by assumption, the uncertainty associated with the multiplicity of the structures representing the poorly understood factors influencing the dynamics is never resolved or learned about.

Can we form any idea about the nature and the strength of the poorly understood factors? After all, we have to somehow specify a set of distributions representing these factors to analyse model uncertainty. Tetlow (2006) may be a first step in answering this question. He studies the real-time evolution of the principal macroeconomic model of the Federal Reserve Board in the 1996–2003 period. He finds a surprisingly large amount of variation in the model over the period, and shows how the changes in the model were driven by the data and 'the economic issues of the day'.

The literature on model uncertainty is large and rapidly growing. In engineering, the entire field of automatic control is motivated to a large extent by issues of robustness to model uncertainty. Although above we have given an example of engineers' approach to model uncertainty, we have not even scratched upon the surface of the literature. Similarly, many important approaches to model uncertainty in statistics and economics have been left aside. We hope, however, that the reader has gained a general idea about the topic and will find a further discussion in the references provided below.

ALEXEI ONATSKI

See also **ambiguity and ambiguity aversion; model averaging; models; robust control; specification problems in econometrics; uncertainty.**

Bibliography

Anderson, E., Hansen, L.P. and Sargent, T.J. 2003. A quartet of semigroups for model specification, robustness, prices of risk, and model detection. *Journal of the European Economic Association* 1, 68–123.

Berger, J. and Berliner, L.M. 1986. Robust Bayes and empirical Bayes analysis with ε-contaminated priors. *Annals of Statistics* 14, 461–86.

Box, G.E.P. and Tiao, G.C. 1962. A further look at robustness via Bayes's theorem. *Biometrika* 49, 419–32.

Brock, W.A., Durlauf, S.N. and West, K.D. 2003. Policy evaluation in uncertain economic environments. *Brookings Papers on Economic Activity* 2003(1), 235–322.

Brunner, K. and Meltzer, A. 1969. The nature of policy problem. In *Targets and Indicators of Monetary Policy*, ed. K. Brunner and A. Meltzer. San Francisco: Chandler Publishing Company.

Diels, H. 1951. *Die Fragmente der Vorsokratiker*. Berlin: Weidmannsche Verlagsbuchhandlung.

Dow, S.C. 2004. Uncertainty and monetary policy. *Oxford Economic Papers* 56, 539–61.

Draper, D. 1995. Assessment and propagation of model uncertainty. *Journal of the Royal Statistical Society* B 57, 45–97.

Draper, D., Hodges, J.S., Leamer, E.E., Morris, C.N. and Rubin, D.B. 1987. A research agenda for assessment and propagation of model uncertainty. Report No. 2683-RC. Santa Monica: Rand Corporation.

Efron, B. and Gong, G. 1983. A leisurely look at the bootstrap, the jackknife, and cross-validation. *American Statistican* 37, 36–49.

Epstein, L.G. and Schneider, M. 2006. Learning under ambiguity. Working Paper No. 527, Rochester Center for Economic Research.

Faust, J. 1998. The robustness of identified VAR conclusions about money. *Carnegie-Rochester Conference Series on Public Policy* 49, 207–44.

Fisher, R.A. 1935. *The Design of Experiments*. Edinburgh: Oliver & Boyd.

Frankel, J.A. and Rockett, K.E. 1988. International macroeconomic policy coordination when policymakers do not agree on the true model. *American Economic Review* 78, 318–40.

Giannoni, M. 2002. Does model uncertainty justify caution? Robust optimal monetary policy in a forward-looking model. *Macroeconomic Dynamics* 6, 111–44.

Gilboa, I. and Schmeidler, D. 1989. Maximin expected utility with non-unique priors. *Journal of Mathematical Economics* 18, 141–53.

Hansen, L.P. and Sargent, T.J. 2003. Robust control of forward-looking models. *Journal of Monetary Economics* 50, 581–604.

Hansen, L.P. and Sargent, T.J. 2006. Robustness. Working paper, New York University.

Hoeting, J.A., Madigan, D., Raftery, A.E. and Volinsky, C.T. 1999. Bayesian model averaging: a tutorial. *Statistical Science* 14, 382–417.

Keynes, J.M. 1921. *A Treatise on Probability*. London: Macmillan. Repr. for the Royal Economic Society as *Collected Writings*, vol. 8, 1973.

Keynes, J.M. 1939. Professor Tinbergen's method. *Economic Journal* 49, 558–68.

Knight, F.H. 1921. *Risk, Uncertainty and Profit*. New York: Houghton Mifflin.

Kullback, S. and Leibler, R.A. 1951. On information and sufficiency. *Annals of Mathematical Statistics* 22, 79–86.

Kwakernaak, H. and Sivan, R. 1972. *Linear Optimal Control Systems*. New York: John Wiley & Sons.

McCallum, B.T. 1988. Robustness properties of a rule for monetary policy. *Carnegie-Rochester Conference Series on Public Policy* 29, 173–203.

Morgan, M.S. and Morrison, M. 1999. *Models as Mediators*. Cambridge: United Kingdom: Cambridge University Press.

Petersen, I.R., James, M.R. and Dupuis, P. 2000. Minimax optimal control of stochastic uncertain systems with relative entropy constraints. *IEEE Transactions on Automatic Control* 45, 398–412.

Popper, K.R. 1962. *Conjectures and Refutations*. New York, London: Basic Books.

Savage, L.G. 1954. *The Foundations of Statistics*. New York: Dover Publications.

Schorfheide, F. and Del Negro, M. 2005. Monetary policy analysis with potentially misspecified models. Mimeo, University of Pennsylvania.

Tetlow, R.J. 2006. Real-time model uncertainty in the United States: 'robust' policies put to the test. Manuscript, Division of Research and Statistics, Federal Reserve Board.

von zur Muehlen, P. 2001. Activist vs. non-activist monetary policy: optimal rules under extreme uncertainty. Finance and Economics Discussion Series Working Paper No. 2, Federal Reserve Board.

Whittle, P. 1990. *Risk-Sensitive Optimal Control.* New York: Wiley.

Zhou, K., Doyle, J.C. and Glover, K. 1996. *Robust and Optimal Control.* Upper Saddle River, NJ: Prentice Hall.

models

Modelling became the dominant methodology of economics during the 20th century.

Yet, despite its ubiquitous usage in modern economics, the term 'model' was introduced relatively recently. In the late 19th century, 'models' were not even a recognized category in discussions about methodology (as for example in Palgrave's *Dictionary of Political Economy* of the 1890s), although a few existed as practical working objects. The effective usage of the term 'model' in economics is associated with the econometrics movement of the interwar period, a movement whose aim was both to develop and to meld together mathematical and statistical approaches to economics. From this original broad notion, in the 1950s grew separate fields of mathematical economists and econometricians, and both maintained modelling as a central tool of their scientific practice. It became conventional then to think of models in modern economics as either mathematical objects used in economic theory or as econometric objects (involving both statistical and mathematical properties) in empirical work. Historical accounts of models in modern economics may conveniently begin then with this division.

Philosophical commentaries, too, have mostly tended to follow this division, treating the models of economic theory as different kinds of creatures, with different roles, from those which are applied to data. The latter role of models, that of 'fitting theories to the world', is exemplified in the empirical modelling, econometric work and methodological statements of Jan Tinbergen in the 1930s. By contrast, the mathematical models of modern economics are primarily viewed as a way in which economic theory building goes on. This 'modelling as theorizing' view is exemplified in the programmatic pronouncements of Tjalling Koopmans in 1957. A third methodological framework presents 'models as investigative instruments': tools to learn about economic theory or the economic world, a position typified in the late 19th century and early 20th century work of Irving Fisher, who might be seen as another of the founders of modelling in economics.

This article covers the historical emergence and roles of models in economics according to these three different methodological accounts, and discusses how these approaches fit into the modern science of economics.

Modelling as fitting theories to the world

Although a vibrant econometrics community developed in the two decades up to the 1920s, its products (regressions of demand, statistical accounts of business cycles and so forth) were presented as direct descriptions of the underlying economic relations, rather than as models put forward tentatively to represent them (see Morgan, 1990). The difference is a subtle one, but illuminated by Philippe Le Gall's (2007) use of the term 'natural econometrician' for those 19th century economists who believed, in parallel to the natural sciences, that the laws that governed the economy were written in mathematics, and clever manipulation of statistical data (without, it must be said, much in the way of analytical techniques) would reveal these laws.

Into this descriptive statistical framework, Jan Tinbergen not only introduced the term 'model' in 1935 (see Boumans, 1993) but he was also responsible – along with Ragnar Frisch – for the development of such joint mathematical–statistical objects in the econometrics of the 1930s. (Prior to this, the rare use of the term 'model' typically referred to physical object models as Boltzmann defined them in 1911. Paul Ehrenfest is the probable source of a broadening in scope of the term to include mathematical models, and Tinbergen was his assistant during the mid-1920s; see Boumans, 2005, ch. 2.) Frisch in 1933 had developed – in the context of business cycle research – the notion of a 'macro-dynamic scheme': a three-equation model with random errors. He even simulated it to show that it could reproduce the generic characteristics of time-series data of his time. But it was Tinbergen who developed Frisch's design into an econometric model – a model that could be fitted to real data from the economy. As is well known, he built the first generation of macroeconometric models (see Tinbergen, 1937; 1939; and Bodkin, Klein and Marwah, 1991), and in doing so he made explicit the notion of a model as a vehicle for bridging the gap between theories of the business cycle and specific (time and place) statistical data of the cycle, as Morgan (1990, ch. 4) argues. To appreciate the task, it needs to be remembered that most existing theories of the cycle were expressed verbally, and the nascent mathematical theories of the cycle were too small and simplified to represent the characteristics of real cycles, so even building up a system of equations from these theories was a considerable task. The data played a role, too, in deciding the time sequence of the relations and which variables should be included or omitted, for both these elements were determined in the statistical work. In other words, Tinbergen created a set of usable mathematical–statistical relations which both incorporated theoretical ideas about how the economy worked and represented empirically the different parts of the economy. Having fitted theories and data together in the format of the econometric model, he then used the model to test the viability of various theories of the cycle, to explain events in the economy, and to run the model forward with different policy options relevant for the Great Depression years – all this in the pre-computer age using hand calculators! This 'new practice' of models, as Boumans (2005) terms it, involved a creative building of mathematical economic theory in relation to the statistical data of the economic world and of craft skill in using those models. For both Frisch and Tinbergen, modelling was a project to explain how the economic world worked.

The next stage in the history may be marked by Trygve Haavelmo's famous blueprint for econometrics of 1944 which brought another subtle change of focus to the task of econometric modelling. He suggested that econometrics ought to be concerned, not with a process of matching theory and data in an iterative process, but with finding the correct model for the observed data using probability reasoning (see Morgan, 1990, ch. 8). He effectively introduced into econometrics not only the notion of the theoretical model (the mathematical model derived from a priori theory) but also that of the 'true' (but unknown) model: 'the 'true' mechanism under which the data considered are being produced' (Haavelmo, 1944, p. 49). Yet he was by no means a 'natural econometrician' (in Le Gall's sense for the 19th century), arguing of models of economic behaviour that 'whatever be the 'explanations' [of economic phenomena] we prefer, it is not to be forgotten that they are all our own artificial inventions in a search for an understanding of real life; they are not hidden truths to be "discovered"' (Haavelmo, 1944, p. 3). Though he urged that a well-fitting econometric model (a theory which fits the data well) might not be the 'true' model, nevertheless, his blueprint probability approach was destined to alter the accepted task of econometrics. The Cowles Commission approach that followed (whose contributions are analysed by Qin, 1993, and Epstein, 1987) stressed the use of the correct methods of identifying and estimating the theoretically derived complete structural model as the means to discover that true model. The 'strong apriorism' of their approach to econometrics, in which theory proposes the model and the data dispose (or not) of these hypotheses, sparked the famous 'measurement without theory' debate with the more empiricist branch of the field over how to do econometrics in the late 1940s.

It is tempting to see Haavelmo's provision of a philosophical basis for econometrics as paving the way for a post-1950 division of labour in the use of models – namely, the economists provide mathematical models from economic theory, and the job of the econometrician is to use statistics for model estimation and theory testing. To some extent this division of labour is borne out, for it is in this period that a much clearer distinction emerges between theoretical and applied economics (as seen in Backhouse, 1998). However, despite the rhetoric of post-1950 econometrics which talks of 'confronting theory with data', or 'applying theory to data', from the point of view of econometric modelling the practical division is not nearly so clear-cut. There are several reasons. First, it remains a prosaic but generally valid comment that theory rarely provides all the resources needed

to make models that can be immediately applied to the data from the world. This is precisely why econometric models have featured as a necessary intermediary, a matching device, between them. Second, this matching process of fitting theories to the world is done with many different purposes – to test theories, to measure relations, to explain events, and so on – each needing different resources from theory and with different criteria. Third, there are no general scientific rules for modelling. There have been fierce arguments within the econometrics community in recent decades over various scientific principles for modelling (and associated criteria): whether models should be theory driven or data driven; whether the modelling process should be simple to general or general to specific; and so forth (see Heckman, 2000). Regardless of which principles are followed, the creative element is still very much evident wherever applied econometric modelling occurs, whether such modelling is at the pattern-seeking end of the spectrum or theory-led modelling, and whether the field is macro- or micro-econometrics.

A more recent shift in focus, particularly in the macro-econometric field and associated with Robert Lucas, entails giving up on the aim of using theory to make models that represent the true general structure as a way to uncover that structure. As he wrote:

> A 'theory' is not a collection of assertions about the behavior of the actual economy but rather an explicit set of instructions for building a parallel or analogue system – a mechanical, imitation economy. A 'good' model, from this point of view, will not be exactly more 'real' than a poor one, but will provide better imitations. (Lucas, 1980, p. 697)

This move changes the relation between models and theory, for now the task of theory is to produce models as analogues of the world, rather than to use them to explain the behaviour of the world (see Boumans, 1997). At the same time, it shifts the focus of 'fitting': the aim is no longer to fit theory to the world but to fit the model to the world in the particular sense of being able to imitate certain sorts of data characteristics.

Another recent account, developed this time in micro-econometrics by John Sutton (2000), validates itself in relation to the earlier econometric agenda held by Frisch and Tinbergen, for, like those early pioneers, he thinks of models not as devices for the discovery of the true general model as in the Cowles Commission interpretation of Haavelmo's project, nor as mathematical machines that imitate the world as in Lucas's account, but as investigative devices for finding out about the world. In Sutton's view, the economic world produces reasonably stable regularities or variability only within a class of cases, not across all cases; thus, looking for a general model is too ambitious. The aim of modelling is to describe the economic mechanisms that produce the data characteristics that are shared within a subset of all cases and so explain the regularities observed within that subclass. Sutton describes this as a 'class of models' approach. Once again, models appear as an intermediary device between theory and data, but this time function to sort out like cases in the world and so offer explanations for their characteristic behaviour.

Models apparently play a critical epistemological role in econometrics – but there are different ways of characterising this. Econometrics can be seen as fulfilling the function of laboratory experiments in some other sciences – a claim that lies implicit in Haavelmo's discussion of the data of economics as being the result of passive observation of nature's experiments and explicit in his discussion of econometric modelling as designing experiments (see Haavelmo, 1944, chs. 1 and 2). His conceptualization of econometrics appeals to the importance of probability and statistical reasoning as the bases for both model design and statistical inference: models have to be designed to match data that could be observed, and be framed in probability terms. The 'design of experiments' notion requires the econometrician to think about the fitting problem, while the probability set-up gives rules for inferences from the model experiment, ones that are in fact much better specified than those for laboratory experiments in most sciences. Thus Haavelmo's blueprint explicitly buys into a tradition of statistical thinking as a valid mode of scientific reasoning, but reinterprets it as a form of experimental work.

A more recent characterisation of the epistemological function of models in econometrics is to understand them as instruments of observation and measurement that enable economists to identify stable phenomena in the world of economic activity. Kevin Hoover's account of 'econometrics as observation' describes 'econometric calculations' as 'the economist's telescope' (1994, p. 74) where rules for focusing the telescope come from statistical theory and where economic theory, and the purpose engaged in, guide the observation process. Marcel Boumans (2005) understands models as the primary instrument in this process, without which the economists could not 'model the world to number'. Rather than a means of observation, he portrays models as complex scientific instruments that generate the numbers for those economic objects, concepts and relations that cannot be observed directly and that are not yet measured. Like Haavelmo, Boumans's account of model work invokes a careful design of experiments, but he provides a more concrete discussion of how econometric modelling provides measurement structures to deal with *ceteris paribus* clauses; how statistical and other criteria provide ways of assessing the reliability of model instruments (via calibration, filtering and so forth); and how precision and rigour are obtained in the measurement process.

Neither Boumans nor Hoover is instrumentalist about models in the sense that has come to be associated with Milton Friedman's 1953 argument that models need be efficient only for prediction, not for explanation.

(Friedman's essay has been much argued over, and interpretations of this particular point vary; see particularly Hirsch and De Marchi, 1990; INSTRUMENTALISM AND OPERATIONALISM; and Mäki, 2007.) Nor are they operationists in the Bridgmanian sense (that informed, for example, Paul Samuelson's early work in economics; see Bridgeman, 1927), namely, that a concept is defined by its measuring process (such as an econometric model). Both Hoover and Boumans might be termed 'sophisticated instrumentalists' for they regard econometric calculations or models as cleverly designed instruments for observing and measuring the relations of economics, and so understanding and explaining, the world.

Modelling as theorizing

The term 'model' had rarely been used in economics before the 1930s, even though things we would now label 'models' had been developed and used for theorizing before then. We can certainly recognize some earlier examples of modelling in the late 19th century; for example, we can happily denote the Edgeworth–Bowley box diagram, and Alfred Marshall's trade diagrams and supply–demand scissor diagrams as models. These examples signal that modelling was an unrecognized element in the mathematizing process of that earlier period (see Morgan, 2008). Yet it was only after the 1950s that modelling became a widely recognized way of using mathematics in economics and became one of the dominant forms of economic theorizing. Whereas the establishment of the statistical–econometric notion is associated with Tinbergen, the mathematical–theorizing one may be associated with another Dutch econometrician, Tjalling Koopmans, whose account, given in a set of three essays in 1957, is widely understood as a paradigmatic statement of the modelling approach of modern mathematical economics. Koopmans had developed Tinbergen's earlier ideas about modelling to fit with contemporary discussions of the role of mathematics in economics in the 1940s and 1950s and with the formal mathematical idea of a model at that time. As such, his statement fits into a broader history of mathematics and economics treated particularly in Weintraub (2002) and Ingrao and Israel (1987).

Koopmans defined an economic theory as a set of postulates with which we reason in order to work out and make explicit the otherwise implicit effects of the set of postulates taken together: a reasoning practice that apparently involves models. For Koopmans, this reasoning was an important part of theorizing since these implications are not self-evident, nor is any particular set of postulates necessarily fruitful. His portrayal of 'Economic Theory as a Sequence of Models' (to quote his 1957, p. 142, section title) is presented as his answer to the ongoing argument of his day about the status of the assumptions and the predictions of economics in which he explicitly defined the role of models almost as an aside:

> neither are the postulates of economic theory entirely self-evident [as Robbins had argued in 1932], nor are the implications of various sets of postulates readily tested by observation [as Friedman had argued in 1953]. In this situation, it is desirable that we arrange and record our logical deductions in such a manner that any particular conclusion or observationally refutable implication can be traced to the postulates on which it rests ... Considerations of this order suggest that we look upon economic theory as a sequence of conceptional *models* that seek to express in simplified form different aspects of an always more complicated reality. At first these aspects are formalized as much as feasible in isolation, then in combinations of increasing realism. (Koopmans, 1957, p. 142)

Koopmans suggests, then, that models are an essential element in theorizing, and that their role comes in their sequenced ability to express different and combined aspects of a simplified reality. But his projection that such a sequence of models would represent 'combinations of increasing realism' seems not to have been borne out. While tractability suggests that increasing realisticness in some aspects will have to be traded off against simplification in others, the history of modelling suggests that model sequences are more often driven by changes in problems, in questions, and in the mathematical tools available. This last was a possibility that Koopmans himself discusses in the context of the move from arithmetical to diagrammatic to algebraic forms of theorizing. And, as just noted with Lucas, some modern modelling no longer aims to represent the world as it is, but to develop artificial systems that mimic outputs from the world.

There are various ways of characterizing the use of mathematical models in economic theory. For Daniel Hausman, the connection of models with concept formation is both more explicit and more important than Koopmans suggests, for economic modelling is where theory development goes on:

> A theory must identify regularities in the world. But science does not proceed primarily by spotting correlations among various known properties of things. An absolutely crucial step is constructing new concepts – new ways of classifying and describing phenomena. Much of scientific theorizing consists of developing and thinking about such new concepts, relating them to other concepts and exploring their implications.

This kind of endeavor is particularly prominent in economics, where theorists devote a great deal of effort to exploring the implications of perfect rationality, perfect information, and perfect competition. These explorations, which are separate from questions of application and assessment, are, I believe, what

economists (but *not* econometricians) call 'models'. (Hausman, 1984, p. 13)

Nowadays, the explorations would be into bounded rationality, imperfect information and imperfect competition: the agenda has moved on, but the mode of theorizing via modelling remains the same. Hausman's attention to the role of models in conceptual innovation is given credence and depth in his own analysis of Samuelson's 'overlapping generations' model, a story about creative exploration in the theoretical realm. The Edgeworth Box history (see Humphrey, 1996, and Morgan, 2004a) provides another good example of the way modelling is associated with new concepts and descriptions – it is after all where indifference curves, contract curves and so forth were first introduced.

The development of the supply and demand diagram we find in Marshall's *Principles* (1890) exemplifies Hausman's claims. It is not just that Marshall's diagrams describe in new ways some older ideas about the phenomena of supply and demand that go way back in the purely verbal literatures of economics, but that in his hands these curves are fashioned to represent various kinds of markets and relations, resulting in new concepts and classification of types of supply or demand at a level that sits between any general theory and one-off cases (see Morgan, 2002). It is this function of modelling as a classification device that Sutton (2000) reprises in a different form in his 'class of models' work on industrial competition (discussed above). And, historically between these two economists, we can situate, as just one example, the work by Martin Shubik (1959) who used game theoretic models to classify kinds of competition and industry structure according to the kind of game that most matches the economic situation involved.

Hausman is keen to make his account of the methodology of economics not only fit to the practice of modern economics, but philosophically sensible, so he separates the activity of modelling from the more general assertions and truth claims of theories. At first sight this strict separation may look curious to economists who often talk of 'testing models' rather than theories, and do not bother to pull apart the categories of theories and models in their everyday scientific work. This conflation may occur because, as Hausman suggests, 'Models are not themselves empirical applications, but they have the same structure' (Hausman, 1992, p. 80). Having the same structure might enable empirical application by econometricians, though this is not how economists mostly use mathematical models in arguing about the world: rather, they are more often linked to the world in a much more casual fashion.

Indeed, 'casual application' is exactly the term used by Alan Gibbard and Hal Varian to describe how mathematical models are applied 'to explain aspects of the world that can be noticed or conjectured without explicit techniques of measurement' (1978, p. 672). In their view, mathematical models are designed only to *approximate* the world, and, unlike econometric models which go through a serious process of fitting to the world, they are casually connected to the world by 'stories' which interpret the terms in the model to elements in the world. But they stress that such applications of models do not pertain to particular situations or things in the world. In contrast, Hausman (1990) argues that economists do often use their models in this way to discuss particular real world events, and they use narratives to fill in the descriptions given in the model in order to provide explanations of those events in the world. Morgan (2001; 2007) takes a stronger position with regard to these stories, suggesting that they form an integral part of the application of models to the world – both in general and for particular cases – and equally form an essential part of the identity of the model. Steven Rappaport (1998), like Hausman, finds mathematical models to be quite stretchable in function: in conceptual work, in normative work (for example in discussions of policy), and in heuristic explanatory work. However, in other respects Rappaport's account of models and their function contrast with Hausman's and with Morgan's, for he portrays models as 'mini-theories' within a research programme that function in counterfactual format: that is, their function is to provide accounts of what might happen if the model were a true description of the world.

These accounts of how mathematical models connect to the world all suggest a dependence on cognitive, intuitive or informal elements of economists' theorizing with respect to the world, in strong contrast to the statistical and economic criteria that attend the way econometricians use models to fit theories to the world. On the other hand, mathematical models appear to fulfil a wider variety of functions ranging from devices for new concept formation and classificatory work in theorizing to inference devices that purport to give explanations of general or particular events. Policy usage often involves mathematical models for analysis of policy interventions and for mechanism design purposes – as, for example, in the design of auctions. So far there is little historical or reflective philosophical literature on this side of model work (though see Guala, 2001). By contrast, there is a considerable reflective literature on the policy activities associated with empirical or econometric models (see examples and references in Den Butter and Morgan, 2000).

Models as investigative instruments

We have already seen various ways in which models are understood as investigative devices. In the commentaries on econometrics, we found models portrayed as tools or instruments of observation and measurement, and in the early econometric work models were also understood as tools to help explain the world. The idea of models as instruments is also present in the mathematical

modelling literature, but is associated with a more active sense of investigation. Irving Fisher, for his thesis, physically built a three good, three consumer, hydraulic analogue general equilibrium model:

> The mechanism just described is the physical analogue of the ideal economic market. The elements which contribute to the determination of prices are represented each with its appropriate role and open to the scrutiny of the eye. We are thus enabled not only to obtain a clear and analytical *picture* of the interdependence of the many elements in the causation of prices, but also to employ the mechanism as an instrument of investigation and by it, study some complicated variations which could scarcely be successfully followed without its aid. (Fisher, 1892, p. 44)

This chimes well with the commentary from Scott Gordon, who, from his historical and philosophical analysis of economics, claims that 'the purpose of any model is to serve as a tool or instrument of scientific investigation' (1991, p. 108).

The notion of tools in economics has not been well-developed. Arthur Pigou (1929) introduced the distinction between 'tool makers' and 'tool users', labelling Francis Edgeworth as a maker of tools, and Marshall as both a maker and user. For Pigou, the term 'tools' referred not to processes of induction as opposed to deduction, or even to the mathematical as opposed to the literary method, but to something he referred to as a 'wider' analytical movement involving specific statistical and mathematical techniques or 'machinery' (such as the method of analysis of demand and supply). It was in following him that Joan Robinson (1933), in oft-quoted comments, wrote about the 'tool-box of economics' which she presented as consisting of 'assumptions' (theory) and 'geometry' (methods) though we might more naturally think of these combining to form models. Koopmans (1957), too, wrote about tools, referring not only to numerical examples and diagrammatic representations, but also to formal mathematics, computing techniques, input–output analysis and so forth, thus (for our time) mixing up methods or modes of analysis (ones we associate now with modelling) and kinds of models. Yet there is a striking similarity between the way Fisher referred to and used his physical hydraulic model and the way modern economists use their equivalent mathematical models of modern economics as tools of investigation. Both seem to be well covered by the notions of tool using that Pigou introduced.

Indeed, attention to the functions of models has emphasized that much of the classifying and conceptual development work of theorizing discussed in the previous section occurs not so much in building mathematical models as in using them. For example, the models developed by Hicks, Samuelson, Meade and others in the late 1930s based on Keynes's *General Theory* were used to explore, develop and understand that theory in ways that involved substantive conceptual and classifying work of their own (see Darity and Young, 1995). In deriving solutions to theoretical problems, or in exploring the limits of behaviour implied by the theoretical relations represented in the models, and in applying their models to think about problems of the economic world represented in the model, those economists used their models as instruments of investigation. These investigations appear as glorified thought experiments, too complicated to do in the mind and so requiring a representation of the case or system in the form of the model and associated mathematical modes of reasoning about it. In Fisher's case, he had a material object to experiment with. Mathematical models in economics also typically provide such internal resources for experimental manipulation. Morgan (2002) argues the case for regarding mathematical modelling activity as experimental work on mathematical models in parallel with statistical experiments practised on econometric models. But whereas we have well-grounded statistical rules for making inferences from econometric experiments, the application of mathematical models to the world (or inferences from such model experiments) is more casual or approximate, as we have already seen.

This notion that mathematical modelling work is a form of experimental activity is most evident in the founding literature on simulation in economics around 1960 (surveyed at the time by Shubik, 1960a; 1960b). In some other fields of science, simulation has been introduced primarily as a method of numerical, rather than analytical, solution. But in economics, simulation has been more usually presented and used as a process of experiment on models, a process that effectively investigates in a systematic manner the full range of behaviours of the system or the actors portrayed in the model. There were isolated examples of simulation earlier in the history of economics – most particularly Tinbergen's 1936 simulation of his macroeconometric model, Paul Samuelson's (1939) simulation of a little Keynesian mathematical system and Eugen Slutsky's (1927) famous random shock models that mimicked business cycles. The possibilities of simulation were then explored more effectively during 1950s and 1960s Cold War activities that brought the social sciences and mathematics together.

The birth of simulation in economics has usually been attributed to Herbert Simon, but equally important were concurrent developments connected with other pioneers, particularly Frank and Irma Adelman, Martin Shubik and Guy Orcutt (see Morgan, 2004b). Simon's simulation projects in economics involved, for example, programming computers to imitate decisions and choices in the same way that investment bankers made those decisions and choices, that is, on the same information and by the same processes of comparison and assessment (see Clarkson and Simon, 1960). The Adelmans's work was particularly important in the development of simulation

methods in econometrics following the lead of Tinbergen's earlier work (see also Duesenberry, Eckstein and Fromm, 1960), while in economics at that time simulations involved both 'game playing', meaning experiments in which people role-played making economic decisions where the model simulated the environment and all the interest was in the behaviour of the people (for example, managers making decisions), and mathematical model simulations in which the behaviour was taken as given (for example, rational economic behaviour) and the environment varied to see how that altered the outcomes projected by the model. (This broad category of simulations around 1960 thus included some things we would now label experiments.) Shubik was involved in many of these different types of simulations ranging from game-playing experiments, to business games, to model experiments. Orcutt (1960) meanwhile pioneered the method of microsimulation, in which he constructed a representative virtual sample of the population, endowed the sample individuals with characteristics of the real population, and then simulated their behaviour through time to explore the characteristics of the aggregate system as well as the individual parts. This is complicated model-experimental work that was possible only with the new-found computing power of that day. All these economists significantly extended the ways in which models worked as instruments of investigation via different forms of experimental activity in which each 'run' of the model provided a slightly different experiment with the model. Simulation, since its introduction into economics, has been characterized as a form of experiment with models that aims at mimicking a variety of different economic behaviours, at different levels and in different ways.

Model construction

Model making (as opposed to formal or informal definitions of models) has been a fertile ground for philosophical commentators on economics who have presented it as a process of 'idealization', a term that covers a range of things including abstraction, simplification and isolation (see Hamminga and De Marchi, 1994). This general idea goes back to the 'ideal type' concept defined by Max Weber (1904; 1913) for the social sciences. His discussion included notions of the ideal type of individual economic behaviour and the ideal type notion of a market. Certainly it is easy to see the late 19th century portrait of economic man as ideal type, divorced from all but his pure economic motivations without any deeper psychology. The term 'idealization' suggests that models are arrived at by processes of *abstracting* to the level of ideas or concepts; of *simplifying* the case or system treated by omitting irrelevant or negligible influences; of *isolating* the elements that are really thought to be important by *ceteris paribus* clauses; and so forth (see Morgan, 2006). These processes can be understood as working on theories (for example, moving from a full equilibrium account down to a single particular market) or as starting with the complicated world and isolating a small part of it for model representation. Leszek Nowak (for example, 1994) presents a rather general analysis in which 'idealization' takes one from the world to theory and 'concretization' from theory to the world in two rather seamless parallel processes. This account known as the 'Poznań approach' (named after the University that hosted its development: see Hamminga, 1998), was formulated for Marxian economics, but might well be applied more generally. Two other commentators particularly associated with questions of idealization in economic modelling are Nancy Cartwright and Uskali Mäki. Cartwright (1989) is interested in what has been called 'causal' idealization, that is, in isolating the causal capacities that actually work in the world. She associates this aim both with how econometric modelling works and with Millian tendencies (the account of tendency laws in economics provided by John Stuart Mill in the mid-19th century). Mäki (1992) is more interested in 'construct' idealization, that is, in how economic theorizing goes on by constructing versions of theory with more or less scope along different dimensions of isolation. (The distinction between construct and causal idealization used here is due to McMullin, 1985.) We can find both these kinds of process going on in the history of model making. Von Thünen's (1826) construction of his diagrammatic model of an 'isolated state' provides a clear example of model-making by isolating the factors that determine farm profitability. His isolations can be interpreted as creating a theoretical model (that is, he constructed an idealized model) but he was also interested in getting at real causes for he fitted this model to his own farm's statistical data (that is, he isolated the causes, using informal econometric procedures).

Idealization itself may involve not just simplifications or isolations but the addition of false elements. Max Weber (1904) discusses how ideal types present certain features in an exaggerated form, not just by accentuating those features left by the omission of others but as a strategy to present the most ideal form of the type. This notion of exaggeration comes up again in Gibbard and Varian's (1978) notion of caricature modelling in economics, where the exaggeration is designed to enable the economist to investigate the robustness of the model (the virtue that Friedman had, of course, earlier associated with the use of unrealistic assumptions). But if we interpret this caricaturing process to involve not just an extreme degree of exaggeration but the addition of features, then we have an idealization of a qualitatively different kind from those that come from methods of isolation or simplification. For example, Frank Knight's (1921) assumption of perfect information involves adding a feature to the portrait of economic man; the assumption can be specified in different ways, each creates a different model. Caricature models are not to be

confused with the artificial constructions of Lucas's models, which are not derived by idealization from either theory or the world. Idealizations, even in caricaturing form, are still understood as representations of the system or man's behaviour (however unrealistic or positively false these might be) whereas the artificial world models do not seek to represent the system or agent's behaviour – rather, the aim is to mimic the output of such systems or behaviour. In imitating the system outputs, one might of course argue that representational power is sought at a different point.

In economics itself, as opposed to in the analyses of commentators, these processes of model making may all be going on together at the same time. That is, models may be constructed to represent the idealized versions of grander theories, be abstracted from the particularities of economic life, and provide simplifications of the more complicated world. These features are all at play in François Quesnay's famous 18th century *Tableau économique*, a construction that may be regarded as the general ancestor of models in economics. But that model makes a telling example, for as a construction it is only in part a derivation or isolation from a general set of ideas or theory, only in part a simplification of the relations in the world or abstraction into a more conceptual framework. It does not seem to be derived entirely from theory, nor does it appear as a description of his contemporary data. Yet while it does embody elements of all these things, it is also a construction of its own (see Charles, 2004). Quesnay moulded these elements together to create a wonderful table-cum-picture that represents the French economy of his day, one that few later economists can understand easily (at least without translating it into a different form, which of course changes its meaning and working).

This interpretation of Quesnay's modelling assumes that models are neither just derived from theory nor solely built up from data, for they typically involve bits of both and oftentimes other things as well, such as metaphors, imported mathematical forms, and so on. The notion that econometric models are constructed from both theoretical relations and statistical elements is probably not that contentious. The mixture of elements is also obvious in a case like the Phillips–Newlyn model, a real hydraulic machine in which red water, representing the various aggregate stocks and flows of the economy, circulated around the machine and sometime spilt into the lecture room (see Leeson, 2000; Boumans and Morgan, 2004). But these mixtures are equally characteristic in mathematical models, according to the case work account of model building by Boumans (1999), who argues that we should think of model making as like cooking new recipes, in which mathematics provides the means of integrating such several, sometimes disparate, elements into new models. This account of model construction goes against much traditional philosophizing, even by economists, about model making.

Yet more recently economists have begun to write about their modelling work as a much more ad hoc activity in which past practices, new intuitions and even speculations guide their model making (see, for example, Krugman, 1993; Sugden, 2000).

Understanding model making according to Boumans's recipe-making account suggests that models – by construction – are partially independent of both theory and the world (or its data), and this accounts for their apparently autonomous existence as working objects in modern economics. This construction account is part of the 'models as mediators' view of the role of models, which analyses their use as investigative instruments (see Morrison and Morgan, 1999). According to this account, models can function in this autonomous in-between way because of their construction. However, the possibility of learning from using models depends on another element in their construction, namely, that models are devices made to represent in some way or form something in our economic theories or in the economic world or both at once. It is this representing quality, built in at the construction stage, which makes it possible to use a model not just as an instrument of prediction but as an investigative instrument to learn something about the world or the theory which it represents. This account can apply even to the artificial world models proposed by Lucas which are constructed not to represent the workings of the system but the outputs of the system, though here the modellers' ambitions to learn from the modelling in order to understand the economic system and explain the outcome phenomena that they mimic seems somewhat reduced.

This recent recipe account of model-making stands in marked contrast to accounts of how model making goes on according to those mid-20th century commentators discussed earlier. Recall that Koopmans had labelled mathematical models as 'defined by a set of postulates' where the full set of postulates form the theory – a definition consistent with the then current axiomatic approach to theories. In econometrics, the Cowles Commission presented econometric models as being derived – directly given in some sense – from a priori theory. Indeed, it was the basis of their position in the 'measurement without theory' debate that econometrics needed models that were clearly versions of theories to get anywhere at all, against the data-derived models of the National Bureau of Economic Research (NBER) that they decried as unscientific. Another description that fits the philosophical inclinations of the mid-20th century, but is more model-oriented, was given by Friedman, who defined a theory as consisting of two parts: 'a conceptual world or abstract model simpler than the "real world" and containing only the forces that the hypothesis [theory] asserts to be important' and a second part defining the 'class of phenomena for which the "model" can be taken to be an adequate representation of the "real world"' along with the correspondence rules linking the model terms and the phenomena (Friedman, 1953, p. 24). Friedman here neatly depicts the model as both a version of theory and at the same time a representation of the real world, yet the correspondence rules are by no means unproblematic. While one could argue that the main work of econometrics has been to develop both the theory and practices of such correspondence rules for models, for mathematical models, in contrast, methodological accounts have often foundered on how such correspondence criteria might be formulated. Despite the long shadow of these rather formal mid-20th century definitions, it is in keeping with our observations about how models are used in modern economic science that they may now be understood as autonomous working objects, rather than as either proto-theories or versions of data.

Conclusion

There is more that might be said, and that remains to be researched, about the philosophy of modelling, for example about the nature of reasoning with mathematical models; about the role of mathematical models within the design of classroom/laboratory experiments in economics; about the use of models in policy advice and intervention; and about the absence of formal criteria for working with mathematical models that are equivalent to the statistical criteria associated with econometric model work. There is also much to be done in filling in the skeletal history of modelling offered here: in separating the history of modelling from both the history of mathematical economics and the history of econometrics; in demarcating the historical range of scope of modelling; and in discerning why and how the method took hold. Nevertheless, the basic trajectory of the history is clear: modelling becoming defined as a mode of reasoning and working for economics in the 1930s, it was developed and used in various ways in the 1940s and 1950s, setting the scene for modelling to become a dominant methodology in the latter part of the century. And once defined, we can look back and recognize earlier prototypes for such a method going back to Quesnay in the 18th century. When we so look back, and consider the scientific world view that we have lost in economics by adopting modelling as one of our favoured methods of doing economics, what stands out is that the science is a radically different one. No longer do economists believe and enquire into a few grand governing laws, nor even propose wide-ranging general theories – rather, economics has become a science of many different and particular models.

MARY S. MORGAN

See also **econometrics; Edgeworth, Francis Ysidro; Fisher, Irving; instrumentalism and operationalism; Koopmans, Tjalling Charles; mathematics and economics; methodology of economics; Tinbergen, Jan.**

Bibliography

Adelman, I. and Adelman, F.L. 1959. The dynamic properties of the Klein–Goldberger model. *Econometrica* 27, 596–625.

Backhouse, R.E. 1998. The transformation of U.S. economics, 1920–1960. In *From Interwar Pluralism to Postwar Neoclassicism*, ed. M.S. Morgan and M. Rutherford. Annual Supplement to *History of Political Economy*, vol. 30, Durham, NC: Duke University Press.

Bodkin, R.G., Klein, L.R. and Marwah, K. 1991. *A History of Macroeconometric Model-Building*. Aldershot: Elgar.

Boltzmann, L. 1911. Models. In *Encyclopaedia Britannica*, 11th edn. Cambridge: Cambridge University Press.

Boumans, M. 1993. Paul Ehrenfest and Jan Tinbergen: a case of limited physics transfer. In *Non-natural Social Science: Reflecting on the Enterprise of More Heat Than Light*, ed. N. De Marchi. Durham: Duke University Press.

Boumans, M. 1997. Lucas and artificial worlds. In *New Economics and its History*, ed. J.B. Davis. Durham: Duke University Press.

Boumans, M. 1999. Built-in justification. In *Models as Mediators*, ed. M.S. Morgan and M. Morrison. Cambridge: Cambridge University Press.

Boumans, M. 2005. *How Economists Model the World to Numbers*. London: Routledge.

Boumans, M. and Morgan, M.S. 2001. *Ceteris paribus* conditions: materiality and the application of economic theories. *Journal of Economic Methodology* 8, 11–26.

Boumans, M. and Morgan, M.S. 2004. Secrets hidden by two-dimensionality: the economy as a hydraulic machine. In *Models: The Third Dimension of Science*, ed. S. de Chadarevian and N. Hopwood. Stanford: Stanford University Press.

Bridgeman, P. 1927. *The Logic of Modern Physics*. New York: Macmillan.

Cartwright, N. 1989. *Nature's Capacities and their Measurement*. Oxford: Clarendon Press.

Charles, L. 2004. The Tableau économique as rational recreation. *History of Political Economy* 36, 445–74.

Clarkson, G.P.E. and Simon, H.A. 1960. Simulation of individual and group behaviour. *American Economic Review* 50, 920–32.

Darity, W. and Young, W. 1995. IS–LM: an inquest. *History of Political Economy* 27, 1–41.

Den Butter, F. and Morgan, M.S. 2000. *Empirical Models and Policy Making: Interaction and Institutions*. London: Routledge.

Duesenberry, J.S., Eckstein, O. and Fromm, G. 1960. A simulation of the United States economy in recession. *Econometrica* 28, 749–809.

Epstein, R.J. 1987. *A History of Econometrics*. Amsterdam: North-Holland.

Fisher, I. 1892. *Mathematical Investigations in the Theory of Value and Prices*. Yale University thesis, repr. New Haven: Yale University Press, 1925.

Friedman, M. 1953. *Essays in Positive Economics*. Chicago: University of Chicago Press.

Frisch, R. 1933. Propagation and impulse problems in dynamic economics. In *Economic Essays in Honour of Gustav Cassel*. London: Allen & Unwin.

Gibbard, A. and Varian, H.R. 1978. Economic models. *Journal of Philosophy* 75, 664–77.

Gordon, S. 1991. *The History and Philosophy of Social Science*. New York: Routledge.

Guala, F. 2001. Building economic machines: the FCC auctions. *Studies in History and Philosophy of Science* 32, 453–77.

Haavelmo, T. 1944. The probability approach in econometrics. *Econometrica* 12(Supplement), iii–iv, 1–115.

Hamminga, B. 1998. Poznań approach. In *Handbook of Economic Methodology*, ed. J.B. Davis, D. Wade Hands and U. Mäki. Cheltenham: Edward Elgar.

Hamminga, B. and De Marchi, N., eds. 1994. *Idealization in Economics*. Amsterdam: Rodopi.

Hausman, D.M., ed. 1984. *The Philosophy of Economics: An Anthology*. Cambridge: Cambridge University Press.

Hausman, D.M. 1990. Supply and demand explanations and their *ceteris paribus* clauses. *Review of Political Economy* 2, 168–87.

Hausman, D.M. 1992. *The Inexact and Separate Science of Economics*. Cambridge: Cambridge University Press.

Heckman, J. 2000. Causal parameters and policy analysis in economics: a twentieth century retrospective. *Quarterly Journal of Economics* 115, 45–97.

Hirsch, A. and De Marchi, N. 1990. *Milton Friedman: Economics in Theory and Practice*. New York: Harvester Wheatsheaf.

Hoover, K.D. 1994. Econometrics as observation: the Lucas critique and the nature of econometric inference. *Journal of Economic Methodology* 1, 65–80.

Humphrey, T.M. 1996. The early history of the box diagram. *Federal Reserve Board of Richmond Economic Review* 82(1), 37–75.

Ingrao, B. and Israel, G. 1987. *The Invisible Hand: Economic Equilibrium in the History of Science*. Trans. I. McGilvray, Cambridge, MA: MIT Press, 1990.

Knight, F.H. 1921. *Risk, Uncertainty and Profit*. Boston: Houghton Mifflin.

Koopmans, T. 1957. *Three Essays on the State of Economic Science*. New York: McGraw Hill.

Krugman, P. 1993. How I work. *American Economist* 37(2), 25–31.

Le Gall, P. 2007. *A History of Econometrics in France: From Nature to Models*. Routledge: London.

Leeson, R. 2000. *A.W.H. Phillips: Collected Works in Contemporary Perspective*. Cambridge: Cambridge University Press.

Lucas, R.E. 1980. Methods and problems in business cycle theory. *Journal of Money, Credit and Banking* 12, 696–715.

Mäki, U. 1992. On the method of isolation ineconomics. In *Idealization IV: Intelligibility in Science*, ed. C. Dilworth. Amsterdam: Rodopi.

Mäki, U., ed. 2002. *Fact and Fiction in Economics.* Cambridge: Cambridge University Press.

Mäki, M., ed. 2007. *The Methodology of Positive Economics: Milton Friedman's Essay Fifty Years Later.* Cambridge: Cambridge University Press.

Marshall, A.W. 1890. *Principles of Economics.* 8th edn, London: Macmillan, 1930.

McMullin, E. 1985. Galilean idealization. *Studies in History and Philosophy of Science* 16, 247–73.

Morgan, M.S. 1990. *The History of Econometric Ideas.* Cambridge: Cambridge University Press.

Morgan, M.S. 2001. Models, stories and the economic world. *Journal of Economic Methodology* 8, 361–84 Repr. in Mäki (2002).

Morgan, M.S. 2002. Model experiments and models in experiments. In *Model-Based Reasoning: Science, Technology, Values*, ed. L. Magnani and N. Nersessian. New York: Kluwer Academic/Plenum Press.

Morgan, M.S. 2004a. Imagination and imaging in economic model-building. *Philosophy of Science* 71, 753–66.

Morgan, M.S. 2004b. Simulation: the birth of a technology to create 'evidence' in economics. *Revue d'Histoire des Sciences* 57, 341–77.

Morgan, M.S. 2006. Economic man as model man: ideal types, idealization and caricatures. *Journal of the History of Economic Thought* 28, 1–27.

Morgan, M.S. 2007. The curious case of the Prisoner's Dilemma: model situation? Exemplary narrative? In *Science Without Laws: Model Systems, Cases, and Exemplary Narratives*, ed. A. Creager, E. Lunbeck and N. Wise. Durham, NC: Duke University Press.

Morgan, M.S. 2008. *The World in the Model.*

Morgan, M.S. and Morrison, M. 1999. *Models as Mediators: Perspectives on Natural and Social Science.* Cambridge: Cambridge University Press.

Morrison, M. and Morgan, M.S. 1999. Models as mediating instruments. In Morgan and Morrison (1999).

Nowak, L. 1994. The idealization methodology and econometrics. In Hamminga and De Marchi (1994).

Orcutt, G.H. 1960. Simulation of economic systems. *American Economic Review* 50, 893–907.

Pigou, A.C. 1929. The function of economic analysis. The Sidney Ball Lecture, University of Oxford, May. In *Economic Essays and Addresses* with D.H. Robertson. London: P.S. King, 1931.

Qin, D. 1993. *The Formation of Econometrics.* Oxford: Clarendon Press.

Rappaport, S. 1998. *Models and Reality in Economics.* Cheltenham: Edward Elgar.

Robbins, L. 1932. *An Essay on the Nature and Significance of Economic Science.* London: Macmillan.

Robinson, J. 1933. *The Economics of Imperfect Competition.* London: Macmillan.

Samuelson, P.A. 1939. Interactions between the multiplier analysis and the principle of acceleration. *Review of Economics and Statistics* 21, 75–8.

Shubik, M. 1959. *Strategy and Market Structure.* New York: Wiley.

Shubik, M. 1960a. Bibliography on simulation, gaming, artificial intelligence and allied topics. *Journal of the American Statistical Association* 55, 736–51.

Shubik, M. 1960b. Simulation of the industry and the firm. *American Economic Review* 50, 908–19.

Slutsky, E.E. 1927. The summation of random causes as the source of cycle processes. *Econometrica* 5 (1937), 105–46.

Sugden, R. 2000. Credible worlds: the status of theoretical models in economics. *Journal of Economic Methodology* 7, 1–31.

Sutton, J. 2000. *Marshall's Tendencies: What Can Economists Know?* Cambridge, MA: MIT Press.

Tinbergen, J. 1937. *An Econometric Approach to Business Cycle Problems.* Paris: Hermann.

Tinbergen, J. 1939. *Statistical Testing of Business Cycle Theories.* Geneva: League of Nations.

Von Thünen, J.H. 1826. *Der Isolierte Staat.* Hamburg: Perthes. Trans. C. Wartenberg as *Von Thünen's Isolated State*, Oxford: Pergamon, 1966.

Weber, M. 1904. 'Objectivity' in social science and social policy. In *The Methodology of the Social Sciences*, trans. and ed. E.A. Shils and H.A. Finch. New York: Free Press, 1949.

Weber, M. 1913. *The Theory of Social and Economic Organisations*, trans. A.M. Henderson and T. Parsons as Part I of *Wirtschaft und Gesellschaft*. New York: Free Press, 1947.

Weintraub, E.R. 2002. *How Economics Became a Mathematical Science.* Durham, NC: Duke University Press.

Modigliani, Franco (1918–2003)

Franco Modigliani was awarded the Sveriges Riksbank (Bank of Sweden) Prize in Economic Sciences in Memory of Alfred Nobel in 1985 for 'pioneering studies of saving and of financial markets'. A life-long Keynesian, his contributions to macroeconomics and finance transformed both fields. The life-cycle approach to consumption and saving pioneered a microfoundations approach to macroeconomic theory and remains the standard model of consumption in macroeconomics. The Modigliani–Miller theorems on the cost of capital had a profound influence on subsequent research in finance. He was also a pioneer in modelling expectations in macroeconomic models. Modigliani was an influential and critical voice on macroeconomic policy in the United States, in his native country of Italy, and in the European community.

Biography and intellectual development

Modigliani was born in Rome, Italy on 10 June 1918. His father, who died when Modigliani was only 14, was a pediatrician. He entered the University of Rome to study law at 17. In his second year he won a national competition in economics with an essay on the price controls imposed in Italy during the annexation of Abyssinia (now Ethiopia). He records in his autobiography (2001) that, following the receipt of this award, he began a self-study of economics reading the classics, an approach he deemed more satisfactory then taking courses during the fascist regime.

At about the same time he became a committed anti-fascist. After the Italian government promulgated anti-Semitic laws in 1938, he and his fiancée, Serena Calabi, fled to Paris, where they were married in 1939. He and Serena applied for an immigration visa to the United States and arrived in New York in August 1939, a few days before the beginning of the Second World War. Modigliani was immediately taken on as a postgraduate scholar by the New School for Social Research, which had been newly created as a haven for social scientists fleeing Europe. He was mentored there in economic theory and econometrics by Jacob Marschak. Modigliani always took care to acknowledge the powerful influence that Marschak had on his development as an economist. During 1941–3 Modigliani taught as an instructor at the New Jersey College for Women (now Douglass College and at the time part of Rutgers University) and at Bard College of Columbia University (now independent). During these years he continued to work on his doctoral dissertation in social sciences for the New School, and received a Ph.D. in 1944. This work was reported in the same year in his first published article, 'Liquidity Preference and the Theory of Interest and Money'. He then returned to the New School as a lecturer.

Modigliani taught briefly at the University of Illinois (1949–52), where he was promoted from associate professor to full professor in 1950 at the age of 32. There he found a friend and collaborator, Richard Brumberg, a graduate student. Together they developed the life-cycle theory of saving, which became Modigliani's most important contribution and one of the two cited by the Nobel judges. He next taught at the Carnegie Institute of Technology (now Carnegie–Mellon) as a Professor of Economics and Industrial Administration (1952–60). Most of the other projects now associated with his name were begun there including his collaboration with Merton Miller on the founding theorems of corporate finance. These theorems were the second contribution cited in 1985 by the Nobel committee.

Modigliani visited Harvard University (1957–8) and the Massachusetts Institute of Technology (1960–1). He was appointed to the faculty at Northwestern University (1960–2) and taught there one year before returning to MIT in 1962 as a Professor of Economics and Finance. He remained at MIT for the balance of his career. By the mid-1960s MIT was regarded as the premier graduate school in the world for the study of economics.

Modigliani's scientific output is impressive for its breadth of coverage, the depth to which each topic was pursued, and the sheer volume of brilliant, highly original papers. In six volumes of collected papers (1980–2005), Modigliani assembled 87 published papers from a corpus of nearly 200 (and a famous previously unpublished paper with Richard Brumberg, 1980). Modigliani also wrote or coauthored ten books and edited several more. This huge output is all the more remarkable when one considers that throughout his academic career Modigliani always subjected his economic theory to rigorous empirical verification, often employing sophisticated statistical technique with ingeniously (and laboriously) derived data.

In 1970 Modigliani was named an Institute Professor, an honorific title that MIT reserves for scholars of great distinction. He was elected President of the American Economic Association (1975–6). He also served as President of the Econometric Society and the American Finance Association. He became Professor Emeritus in 1988.

Franco Modigliani died on 25 September 2003 at the age of 85 in Cambridge, Massachusetts. MIT Institute Professor Paul Samuelson, a colleague and friend, said, 'Franco Modigliani could have been a multiple Nobel winner. When he died he was the greatest living macroeconomist. He revised Keynesian economics from its Model-T, Neanderthal, Great Depression model to its modern-day form' (MIT, 2003).

The Keynesian revolution and the debate over stabilization policy

When he arrived in New York in 1939, Modigliani began several years of study of macroeconomics (and mathematics and statistics as well) under the tutelage of Jacob Marschak, Abba Lerner, Oskar Lange and Tjalling Koopmans. The hot topic, of course, was *The General Theory of Employment, Interest, and Money* by John Maynard Keynes. Published in 1936, Keynes's analysis was truly revolutionary. Keynes pioneered modern macroeconomics by proposing a novel and compelling explanation of the gyrations of the economic system. Those fluctuations had had a devastating impact on the US economy during the Great Depression of the 1930s, a catastrophe whose lingering effects were still evident in 1939. The Keynesian model also suggested a set of active policy prescriptions that might be used, first, to lift an economy out of depression and, second, to prevent recessions and depressions from occurring in the first place. Furthermore, Keynes suggested that if the curative policies were not applied, the economy might languish with mass unemployment for a long time.

Neither the theoretical formulation nor the policy prescriptions of *The General Theory* were easy to accept in the early 1940s. Keynes's argument was complicated and subtle, the book's prose was at points cumbersome and inelegant, and the concepts that Keynes introduced were unfamiliar to economists and sometimes counter-intuitive. The policy implications seemed almost impossibly unorthodox. Government spending should not be based on the need for public services. Taxes should not be based on the need for revenue to pay for the government services. Instead government spending and taxation should be directed to restoring and then maintaining full employment which might lead to levels of spending far in excess of the perceived need for public services and to a level of taxation that might produce substantial deficits.

Working in 1942 and 1943, Modigliani sought to reduce the confusion generated by the debate over what Keynes was saying and to articulate the common sense of the Keynesian policy message. In the process he made an important clarification of the Keynesian argument. The result was his now famous *Econometrica* paper of 1944, 'Liquidity Preference and the Theory of Interest and Money'. The paper did three things. First, Modigliani reduced the 384 pages of Keynes's complex argument to a mathematical system of nine simultaneous equations. The virtue of a mathematical representation is that it served to insure that the variables considered important by Keynes were consistently and precisely defined and that the relationships among them were made rigorously explicit. Modigliani was not the first to attempt a mathematical reduction to clarify the logical structure of *The General Theory*. One of his mentors, Oskar Lange, the noted Polish economist, had preceded him. But Modigliani's version became the standard, taught to graduate students for decades (who generally left *The General Theory* unread), until it was replaced by a revised (and more complex) presentation produced by Modigliani in 1963, 'The Monetary Mechanism and its Interaction with Real Phenomena.' Second, Modigliani clarified the role played in the model by Keynes's assumption that money wages were inflexible. We return to this point below. Third, Modigliani argued that fiscal policy was not the only weapon available for fighting recessions. Monetary policy could be effective in many, if not all cases. In this third effort, Modigliani was taking issue with another of his mentors, Abba Lerner, who was suggesting at that time that fiscal policy, and only fiscal policy, would work.

The mathematical formulation of the determinants of macroeconomic equilibrium did much to make Keynes acceptable to economists, though it must be said that the mathematics required was most easily mastered by young economists still in graduate school or only recently accepted into the professorship. Many of the 'old guard' seemed unable or unwilling to shed their pre-Keynesian conceptions. By salvaging and later defending a role for monetary policy, Modigliani had a major influence on the conduct of anti-recession policy, particularly in the 1950s and 1960s. But it was the clarification of the role of 'sticky wages' that helped to transform Keynesian economics into its modern form.

Modigliani established that both the classics and Keynes shared a conception of the macroeconomic demand for money derived from basic microeconomic principles. Any such model would necessarily connect money to real variables such as output and employment only when money entered the formulation as a ratio to the price level. This ratio is known as *real* money and was defined by Keynes and Modigliani in terms of 'wage units'. The 'classical' quantity theory of money, for example, made real money proportional to real output. If changes in the nominal money supply are to influence real output, there must be some reason why those changes are not immediately followed by an equiproportionate change in wages. In the pre-Keynesian, 'classical' model wages would adjust rapidly, unemployment would thus be briefly transitory, and monetary policy would be both ineffective and unnecessary to increase output and employment.

Modigliani's equations revealed that idle resources and price flexibility could simultaneously exist only in the extreme case when the demand for money became infinite. Modigliani considered this an unlikely situation which he called the 'Keynesian case'. It later became better known as the 'liquidity trap'. In the *General Theory* Keynes had been critical of the flexible wage assumption and introduced what Modigliani considered the more realistic assumption that, in the short run at least, money wages would not adjust in the downward direction. With this specification added to the system of equations, underemployment equilibrium was possible even when liquidity trap conditions were not present. Modigliani argued on this basis that the hypothesis of wage rigidity was a necessary part of the Keynesian system if monetary policy was to play a role in influencing real variables.

As a corollary of the argument, Modigliani pointed out that the economy could not be 'dichotomized' into real and monetary sectors that operated independently of each other. In his demonstration Modigliani was following John Hicks who made the same point with the IS–LM apparatus made famous by introductory textbooks. In Hicks's (1937) diagram the interest rate and the level of output are jointly determined by the intersection of an LM curve reflecting an equilibrium of the demands and supplies that characterize the monetary sector (L for 'liquidity preference' and M for the money supply) with the IS curve reflecting the equilibrium of real forces (I for the demand for investment and S for the supply of saving). It might be noted, however, that Hicks expressed the IS–LM relationship in terms of the rate of interest and *money* income. It was Modigliani who gave it the appropriate interpretation in terms of the interest rate and *real* income.

Modigliani considered the 1944 paper one of his most significant contributions. It set the stage for the 'neo-classical synthesis' of the Keynesian and the classical traditions. This synthesis came to dominate the economics profession for the next three or four decades. That approach accepted that labour and capital would be underutilized over the course of the business cycle, that unemployment was not a transitory problem but a variable that helped clear the money market, and that activist monetary and fiscal policies can be welfare improving. Indeed, avoiding unemployment would take close management of the money supply and interest rates. In the United States these views became most influential during the 1960s when the administration of John F. Kennedy put them into practice in a serious way. But these academic and political developments pulled Modigliani into an extended debate with the 'monetarists'. Led by Milton Friedman, the monetarists held that the quantity of money is the key factor in determining economic change and that the fiscal variables advocated by Modigliani and other Keynesians are not important. Modigliani was particularly disturbed by Friedman's proposal that neither discretionary fiscal nor monetary policy should be employed; rather, the money supply should be strictly regulated to grow at a constant rate (say three per cent per year). Modigliani ridiculed this prescription as a 'blind rule' and consistently argued that wise discretionary control of the money supply was essential.

In a pair of empirical papers, one with Albert Ando, his student at Carnegie, Modigliani, went on the attack (1964; 1965). In his presidential address to the American Economic Association, Modigliani rejected the idea that Keynesians did not think that money mattered, and he cited his 1944 and 1963 papers as proof (1977). After winning the rhetorical and empirical debate with Friedman, he sought to 'make peace' with the monetarists by declaring 'We are all monetarists'. And yet he went on to defend the case for policy discretion in a fashion he later described as 'a full, passionate, and polemical'. In an interview conducted in 1999, he declared victory. 'There is not a country in the world today that uses a mechanical rule' (2000, p. 236). He might have added that the highly praised success of Alan Greenspan as the Chairman of the U.S. Federal Reserve Board was based on the careful discretionary management of money and interest rates. In a series of lectures, later published as *The Debate over Stabilization Policy* (1986c), Modigliani traced the history of these disputes.

The monetarist debates of the 1960s, and the empirical success of the work testing Keynesian propositions, led to another important direction for Modigliani's research. He was asked to construct an econometric model of the US economy by the Federal Reserve. The model would be an empirically estimated system of simultaneous equations that would be used by the Federal Reserve to make and guide policy and forecast future developments. He asked Albert Ando to join him on the project and they created what was first known as the 'MIT model' and, after Ando moved to the University of Pennsylvania, as the 'Federal Reserve-MIT-University of Pennsylvania

Model' (FMP) (1975a). The result embodied many of Modigliani's ideas about the structure of the economy, the consumption function, the structure of interest rates, and the workings of other financial markets. Emblematic of Modigliani's willingness to learn from the data were the many modifications he made to his early formulations in the process of constructing the FMP model. In particular he explicitly extended the theories to include the causes and consequences of inflation which had only begun to become a noticeable problem for the American economy in the 1970s (for his major contributions on inflation see Part III of *Collected Papers*, vol. 5). The model proved sufficiently valuable that the Federal Reserve continued to use it into the 1980s.

The life-cycle model of saving and consumption

In his 1944 paper on the Keynesian model, Modigliani presented an equation for the national flow of saving that described saving as a positive function of aggregate income in a manner consistent with the 'consumption function' famously introduced by John Maynard Keynes in the *General Theory*. Keynes had postulated a 'fundamental psychological law' whereby an individual's consumption would increase as his or her income increased but not as much as the increase in income. Thus saving, defined as income less consumption, should increase when income grows and the aggregate saving rate, defined as the national saving–income ratio, should increase with aggregate income. According to this part of the *General Theory*, rich people saved, poor people did not; rich countries saved, poor countries did not. Despite his acceptance of this simple Keynesian formulation in 1944, Modigliani reports that he was not convinced that the saving–income ratio should rise with aggregate income, and began to systematically reconsider the Keynesian law in 1946. He was particularly unhappy with the notion that saving should be regarded as a luxury good that would be 'purchased' in greater quantities by the rich than poor in order to 'bequeath a fortune'. 'This explanation satisfied me not a jot' (2001, p. 52).

In the late 1940s Modigliani's alternative suggestion was that the saving–income ratio should fluctuate around a constant (or slowly moving) trend and that these fluctuations would be driven by the relationship of actual income to the normal income that the household could expect. In other words, the household's saving rate was explained not by its absolute level of income (as Keynes would have it) but by its income *relative* to the aggregate mean income in the economy. Modigliani formulated his hypothesis in an elegant linear model in which the saving–income ratio was related negatively to the ratio of income at its previous peak to the current level of income (1949). When the economy was in recession (and current income was below its previous peak), saving and the saving–income ratio would both fall. This movement reflected the cyclical movement of consumption emphasized by Keynes. But, when the economy was growing and incomes were pushed above their previous peak, saving would rise and the saving–income ratio would return to its previous level. Thus the aggregate consumption function would shift upward in a ratcheting movement as aggregate income set new records.

Modigliani tested this formulation and estimated the parameters of the model using aggregate data for 1921 to 1940. James Duesenberry independently hit upon a very similar formulation. Duesenberry's 'relative income hypothesis' reconciled the time series and cross-sectional data by suggesting that the higher consumption of the poor was an attempt to keep up with those better situated economically. Both contributions were published in 1949. The differences in their theoretical justifications were generally glossed over by subsequent commentators and the empirical model became known as the Duesenberry–Modigliani hypothesis.

The success of the Duesenberry-Modigliani empirical work (and the growing sophistication of econometric technique) produced a flurry of follow-up empirical studies. Modigliani and his collaborator Richard Brumberg described the state of affairs, in a passage that reflects Modigliani's scientific philosophy (2001, p. 129). Empirical work should test theory; theory should be inspired by empirical observation; and progress would be made only through the constant interplay between the two:

> It may be said that, at the date of this writing (1952), the analysis of the consumption function has degenerated into a morass of seemingly contradictory, or at least disconnected, results, with each new empirical finding adding less to our understanding than to the existing confusion. Further empirical analysis is not likely to advance us very far until the economic theorist has been able to provide a conceptual framework to give coherence to past findings and guidance for the collection of more 'facts.'

Shortly after arriving at the University of Illinois, Modigliani began working with Brumberg to provide the missing conceptual foundation for the macroeconomic theory of consumption based on microeconomic marginal utility analysis. They produced two papers in 1952. The first, 'Utility Analysis and the Consumption Function,' was published in 1954. The other, 'Utility Analysis and Aggregate Consumption Functions,' was unpublished at the time of Blumberg's sudden and tragic death from a cerebral embolism in 1955. Modigliani was devastated by his friend's death and 'lost all interest in revising the manuscript' for publication (2001, p. 66). It remained unpublished for a quarter of century. It finally appeared in Modigliani's Collected Papers (1980) exactly as it had been left at the time of Blumberg's death. Together the two papers describe the life-cycle hypothesis (LCH).

The microeconomic model of consumption and saving proposed by Modigliani and Brumberg took the perspective of a forward-looking individual (or a couple) with a finite lifespan and no desire to bequeath a fortune to heirs (Keynes's proposed motive for aggregate saving was thus explicitly rejected). The model recognized that income will vary over the lifetime, rising at first as the individual's career advances and he or she gains experience and skill, but income will ultimately fall with age and may even disappear during retirement. With this view saving behaviour would vary over a person's lifetime. When young, the individual would save very little (when income is low relative to what can be expected in middle age). During the period of peak earnings in middle age, the individual's saving will be high as assets are accumulated to finance late life consumption and to afford retirement. When retired, the individual dissaves (saving is negative) as the accumulated assets are sold to support a planned retirement lifestyle.

The most familiar (and most simplified) exposition of the microeconomic model is that published by Modigliani in Social Research in 1966. That version pictured the expected income profile as flat and constant until retirement when it fell to zero and the desired consumption profile as flat throughout life. Over the lifespan the total of consumption would exactly exhaust the total income earned, but, since consumption must be maintained during the retirement years, consumption is less than income during the earning years. The 1966 article first introduced the diagram of the 'Modigliani pyramid', made famous by macroeconomic textbooks, that was reproduced in Modigliani's Nobel lecture, and which he came to view as his 'trademark' (2001, p. 60). In this diagram, the lifetime profile of wealth rises linearly with age until it reaches a maximum on the day of retirement and then declines linearly with age until death, thus tracing out the pyramid shape. In the more general case, the wealth profile would be hump-shaped.

In the elementary formulation of the model it was assumed for convenience (and also to make a sharp contrast to the common view) that individuals had no desire to make a net bequest to heirs; that is, they had no reason to make net accumulations in order to bequeath a greater inheritance then they had received. Modigliani had always argued, however, that a bequest motive could be added to the LCH without disturbing its implications. Yet he maintained that empirically a bequest motive would be 'relevant for the very rich (and especially for the *nouveaux riches*)'. At the same time Modigliani argued that in the absence of bequest motives there would still be substantial bequests left at death. If individuals knew the date of their death in advance, as assumed in the simplified exposition, then each individual over his lifetime would consume one hundred per cent of his or her lifetime income. The 'life-time propensity to consume' would be 1. Since people do not generally foresee the timing of their death, they must plan their saving to be sufficient to support them to a very old age. Since, alas, many die at a younger age then this, inheritance bequests are commonplace, but are for the most part unintended.

The importance of Modigliani–Brumberg *micro*economic model of saving lies in the *macro*economic implications of life-cycle behaviour. Aggregate saving in the LCH does not depend upon current income but on life-cycle income. Thus the age structure of the population matters. In a population that is growing rapidly because of natural increase or immigration, there will be more young and middle-aged savers than older retired dissavers. Aggregate saving will be higher. Likewise, in an economy that is experiencing rapid economic growth, perhaps produced by new technologies and strong investment in new capital, the young and middle-aged savers will look forward to higher lifetime earnings while the older dissavers are consuming at a level commensurate with their assets accumulated over a lifetime when productivity was lower. Thus growth is good for saving. Moreover, the higher aggregate rates of saving generated by either population growth or by economic growth can help sustain the forward progress by financing investment at continuing high levels. Saving is good for growth.

Another important long-run implication of the life-cycle hypothesis is that sustained government deficits will be a drag on economic growth. Modigliani called attention to the burden of the national debt in a famous paper published in the *Economic Journal* (1961). The government finances its deficit spending by issuing government bonds which are a form of net worth for those who purchase them. When members of the public hold some of their wealth in the form of bonds, the bonds substitute for the physical capital (machines, structures, and other productive capital) that would otherwise be created to satisfy the demand for life-cycle assets. The burden of the national debt is the reduced rate of growth attributable to the reduced rate of capital formation. This burden can be said to fall on future generations by reducing their income below what it would be otherwise.

Modigliani's analysis of the burden of the national debt was criticized by Robert Barro (1974). Barro's approach to the issue is also known as the 'Ricardian equivalence theorem' because it echoed a suggestion of David Ricardo. Barro rejected Modigliani's view that an individual's planning horizon is constrained to his expected lifetime and took the extreme opposite position that the planning horizon is infinite. Government deficits today, Barro argued, should lead to an increase in saving as taxpayers reasoned that taxes would have to be raised in some indefinite future to pay off the debt. To have the assets needed to meet this forecast tax increase, taxpayers would temporarily increase saving to set the required sum aside. Modigliani viewed Barro's assumption of an infinite horizon as 'incredible' and the equivalence theorem 'untenable' (2000, p. 235). In characteristic fashion, however, he responded with carefully designed empirical tests rather than theoretical

debate. In his presentation of the data, the LCH and the burden of the debt were supported and Ricardian equivalence rejected (1983a; 1986b).

The simple version of the LCH made no allowance for the Social Security pension system as an alternative to private saving. Modigliani argued that incorporating a mandatory government retirement plan into the model was straightforward and, more importantly, that treating Social Security consistently would clear up several important misunderstandings. As he would model it, Social Security's payroll taxes should be considered a form of forced or 'compulsory' saving that builds up 'Social Security wealth'. The benefits received in old age should then be seen as drawing down those assets. When Social Security is included as a form of wealth, the empirical wealth profile has the hump shape predicted by the LCH (1983 with Arlie Sterling; 1987 and 2005 with Tullio Jappelli). This answered those critics who failed to find much dissaving in old age when using a conventional definition of saving. The critics had simply defined wealth too narrowly.

The introduction of Social Security into an economy that previously relied exclusively on private saving, according to Modigliani, would have two effects on the private saving rate. One is the replacement effect. Because the Social Security tax is a form of forced saving, individuals who count on the promised benefits can save less and on this account the society's wealth–income ratio will be reduced. On the other hand, there might be an offsetting 'retirement effect'. A Social Security system will encourage earlier retirement both directly and through a social emulation effect. Longer retirement periods require greater wealth accumulation and thus increased saving rates. Empirical work reported by Modigliani and his coauthor Arlie Sterling suggests that the two effects roughly cancel each other out (1983).

The long-run implications of the LCH that saving is increased by economic growth, that the national debt produces a burden, and that there is little reason to think that the introduction of Social Security significantly reduced the saving rate challenged conventional views at the time. Not surprisingly, there were many critics. Modigliani's persistent defence of the logic of the theory and his continuous production (with the help of many coauthors) of ingeniously designed and carefully executed empirical verifications and rejoinders kept the model in the forefront of academic analysis and policy debate. It remains the accepted view.

Yet it was the short-run or cyclical implications – not the long-run consequences – that received the more immediate attention. In a pair of papers coauthored with Albert Ando, Modigliani directed attention to the short-run considerations and the implications for the aggregate time-series consumption function (1963; 1965). The underlying theory had been formulated in the still unpublished second paper with Richard Brumberg but the work with Ando brought the cyclical implications to the attention of the profession. The short-term consumption function proposed by Ando and Modigliani made consumption a linear function of aggregate disposable *labour* income (that is, income excluding the return to asset holdings and less the amount of personal taxes) and aggregate net worth. The coefficients of the two variables could be taken as empirically constant in the short run determined by the length of life, the length of retirement, and the rate of growth. It was not until estimates of the aggregate stock of net worth became available that the model could be verified empirically. When Raymond Goldsmith published his wealth estimates (1962), the life-cycle consumption function passed the battery of tests designed by Ando and Modigliani with the highest marks (Ando and Modigliani, 1963; Modigliani, 1966).

The cyclical properties of the LCH equation were not in themselves particularly novel. The LCH behaved in the short run not unlike the Duesenberry–Modigliani model or the roughly contemporaneous theory of consumption put forward by Milton Friedman, the permanent income hypothesis (1957). The saving–income ratio would fall during recessions and rise during upturns, but would fluctuate about a fairly stable long-run average. And, like the simpler Keynesian model, the Ando–Modigliani formulation implied that tax cuts could stimulate consumption and thus help counteract recessionary tendencies. There were, however two novel implications of the cyclical formulation of the LCH with important policy implications. The short-run life-cycle consumption function postulates that consumption would be responsive to the value of assets; thus a stock market crash, like that of 1929, would tend to reduce consumption as individuals sought to restore their lost wealth. This was not an implication of the alternative models. As another contrast, Friedman suggested that consumption each period should depend upon the current rate of interest since consumers would be willing to save more (and consume less) when the reward to asset holding is high. Modigliani conjectured that the saving rate would be 'largely independent' of the interest rate. While accepting Friedman's point that an increase in the reward for saving (higher interest rates) would induce an increase in saving, Modigliani pointed out another consequence of high rates. High interest rates would allow the stock of assets to accumulate more rapidly, thus requiring less saving to reach the target level of assets needed for retirement. Modigliani suggested the two effects would largely cancel out. If Modigliani is correct, short-term policy strategies to increase saving by manipulating the rate of interest would be ruled out.

Expectations and fluctuations

One of Keynes's foremost contributions, according to his own view, was his emphasis on the importance of expectations. The central conclusion of his *General Theory*, announced in the Preface, was that a 'monetary economy … is essentially one in which changing views about the future are capable of influencing the quantity of employment and not merely its direction' (1936). It is somewhat ironic, then, that Modigliani's 1944 reformulation of the *General Theory* took expectations as given. We are told that this was a simplification for 'convenience' since the paper was concerned with 'the determinants of equilibrium, and not with the explanation of business cycles' (1944, p. 46). Most of the equations of his equilibrium model, to be sure, contain variables that represent the expectations of economic agents. But, to take account of any relevant *change* of views about the future, the analyst would have to shift one or more of the relationships expressed in the system of equations.

A few years after formulating the equilibrium model with static expectations, Modigliani began a far-ranging investigation of the role of anticipations and uncertainty in the explanation of business cycles. In 1949 Modigliani began work on a project he called 'Economic Expectations and Fluctuations'. It would occupy him for more than ten years. Modigliani moved the project to Carnegie Tech in 1952. There he collaborated with Herbert Simon, Charles Holt, and John Muth (1960) and Kalman Cohen (1961) on two books concerned with anticipations, forecasting, and the use of inventories to smooth production. While the work on the life cycle and production smoothing explicitly recognized the importance of expectations in microeconomic models, a breakthrough came when Modigliani turned his attention to modelling the formation of expectations in a macroeconomic context. Modigliani collaborated with Emile Grunberg, a colleague at Carnegie, on the 'Predictability of Social Events' (1954), a famous paper that is widely recognized as introducing the concept of 'rational expectations' into economic theory. The concept itself is simple. Rational expectations are forecasts of the future that are consistent with the way the economy is believed to work. To adopt any other expectation would be to ignore whatever knowledge one had about the workings of the economy. The macroeconomic implications of rational expectations, however, proved to be profound. In the hands of others, rational expectation formation was used to question the effectiveness of Keynesian monetary and fiscal stabilization policy, and thus Modigliani's 'invention' reappeared later as a challenge to the legitimacy of Keynesian economics.

The problem that Grunberg and Modigliani set out to explore was whether a widely believed public prediction of a future event might change individuals' behaviour in such a way as to invalidate the prediction. Their answer was that a correct private prediction would be a wrong public prediction. Nevertheless, accurate public prediction was possible because the reaction of the public to the announcement can be taken into account by the social scientist. Accurate public predictions are predictions that are 'internally consistent' in the sense that they recognize and incorporate any change in public expectations induced by the prediction itself that would influence the course of events.

It was left to Modigliani's student at Carnegie, John Muth, to extend the concept of internally consistent expectations to become 'rational expectations', an exercise Muth (1961) carried out in a microeconomic context. Ten years later Robert Lucas (1972) returned the concept to a macroeconomic setting (in the context of a market-clearing model) and suggested that stabilization policies could not change real output in a predictable way if those policies were fully anticipated. The macroeconomic rational expectations model became the foundation of the 'new classical macroeconomics', so called because money had no real effects in this model. These developments took place in the 1970s and were led by others; meanwhile, Modigliani's thinking about expectations had been developing in another direction during the 1950s and 1960s. In his paper with Brumberg, Modigliani argued that, while anticipations about the future life course would be relevant to the individual's decision about current consumption, it was not necessary to take explicit account of uncertainty about the future. Uncertainty would simply give rise to an additional precautionary motive for saving, but the assets accumulated to satisfy the life-cycle motive would do double duty as a buffer stock to insure against emergencies. In making this argument Modigliani was echoing arguments that he had advanced in the books on business planning. In this work Modigliani observed firm behaviour and offered a description of how businesses form expectations about the future and how they make use of those anticipations in current decision making. The upshot was that, while knowledge about the future would be important, firms need not (and therefore did not) attempt to acquire all possible information. Much information about the future would be beyond the relevant planning horizon and therefore irrelevant, other information would not need to be precise, and some information might not be worth the effort to acquire. Businesses in the real world attempt to make the best possible forecasts of the variables deemed important, but sometimes best practice would be a rule of thumb or a simple extrapolation of the past. Any uncertainty that remained would be adequately hedged since inventory could do double duty and serve as a buffer stock against inadequately foreseen contingencies as well as smooth production.

This is a clearly pragmatic approach to expectations. Modigliani suggested that a pragmatic formulation was realistic. The 'expectation function will, at best, appear in the form of broad statistical generalizations' since expectations about the future range in practice 'from the elaborate scientific forecast of the large business enterprise to primitive guesses and dark hunches' (Grunberg and Modigliani, 1954, p. 471). It was this realistic approach to expectations that Modigliani later carried over to macroeconomic models. It is important to note, however, that

Modigliani was not opposed to the idea of rational expectations in principle. He declared the concept 'a good starting point' for analysis and thought the assumption would be 'sensible' in some circumstances, for example, in financial markets (1983b, pp. 123–4). He considered Muth's contribution 'fundamental' and an improvement over 'naïve or *ad hoc* assumptions' regarding the formation of expectations (1986b, p. 25). But when rational expectations were used to support the new classical economics and its startling proposition that stabilization policy would be ineffective, he thought that this was 'pushing the idea of rationality well beyond the range where it is useful' (1983b, p. 123). 'It is a 'wonderful theory … [but] it is *not* a description of the world' (2000, p. 235).

Characteristically, Modigliani was not content to simply debate the logical merits of a model or the realism of its assumptions. The new classical macroeconomics could be rejected because its conclusions were inconsistent with the empirical evidence. The model implied that fluctuations in unemployment should be mild, short-lived, and random, contrary to all experience. The new classical model was also inconsistent with the existence of long-term contracts. If such contracts are rational, then wages are rigid, contrary to a postulate of the new classical view. If they are not rational, then they 'should have long ago disappeared'.

Modigliani's pragmatic approach to modelling expectations was put to work in a series of papers on the term structure of interest rates (Modigliani and Sutch, 1966; 1967; Modigliani and Shiller, 1973). The 'term structure' refers to the relationship between interest rates on assets with different terms to maturity. In his collaboration with Sutch the long-term rate of interest was linked to the short-term rate through financial arbitrage. Since the investor could obtain a return over the long term by investing either in a long-term bond or alternatively in a sequence of short-term bills, the choice between the two would be influenced by the investor's expectations about the future course of short-term interest rates. Because the expectations would be subject to uncertainty, each investor would have a natural preference for assets with a maturity that matched their needs. But they could be tempted out of this 'preferred maturity habitat' if the advantage with shorter or longer maturities were forecast to be large enough.

An empirical characterization of expectation formation was required to complete the model of the relationship between short- and long-term rates. Here again Modigliani looked to how investors actually behaved. Modigliani and Sutch suggested that future expected rates were formulated by extrapolating past movements. They proposed that the recent trend in the rate would be anticipated to continue for a while, but that the best guess for the long run was that rates would return to their long historical average (as Keynes had suggested). Modigliani and Sutch considered this formulation a 'plausible' representation of how investors actually thought about the problem. Modigliani and Shiller went on to demonstrate that the Modigliani–Sutch model of expectations was also rational in the sense that it represented the best forecast possible on the basis of all information available.

Corporate finance

A key component of the Keynesian macroeconomic structure is the investment function, which held that the aggregate volume of investment would be responsive to the cost of capital. In the 1950s Modigliani turned his attention to this topic as well. The result was spectacular. In citing Franco Modigliani for the Nobel Prize in 1986, the Nobel Foundation's judges singled out both the life-cycle hypothesis and the path-breaking Modigliani–Miller theorems on corporate dividends, leverage, and the cost of capital (Modigliani and Miller, 1958; 1963; Miller and Modigliani, 1961; Modigliani. 1982). The two MM theorems, as they are called, not only overturned the existing thinking about the cost of capital but launched modern finance theory. Indeed, this line of research was deemed so important that Merton Miller later received his own Nobel Prize in 1990 for his contribution to the joint work. In 1956 Merton Miller was an assistant professor auditing Modigliani's course at the Carnegie Institute of Technology. He became excited when Modigliani introduced the topic in class and agreed to join him in working out the proof.

The first Modigliani–Miller theorem establishes, when a firm's investment policy is fixed, that the market evaluation of a firm would be unaffected by its volume of debt in a simplified world with well-functioning financial markets, rational investors, and neutral taxes (1958). The second theorem, an extension of the first, states under the same assumptions that the value of the firm is independent of its dividend policy (1961). Taken together they suggest that 'financial policy does not matter!' (1982, p. 255).

The contribution to the scientific analysis of finance was profound. First, the MM papers introduced the application of microeconomic theory – and in particular the notion of arbitrage – to problems in corporate finance. Rigorous mathematical modelling has been the hallmark of the field ever since. Second, the two theorems taken together allow the separation for analytical and management purposes of investment decisions from financial decisions. The implication for the structuring of corporate management has led over time to the division of managerial responsibilities between the CEO and the CFO. Third, the MM theorems were established in the context of a highly stylized model, so a good deal of subsequent theoretical and empirical work has been devoted to understanding the impact of relaxing the simplifying assumptions and extending the application of the model. This research agenda has enriched the field

immeasurably. The MM theorems, for example, have led directly to subsequent developments in the evaluations of options.

At the time the first MM theorem was published it was held to be self-evident that borrowing and taking on debt would lower the cost of capital to the firm because the rate of interest on the loans was below the cost of raising capital through the sale of equity. Modigliani and Miller elegantly demonstrated that the old theory was seriously flawed. As is typical of Modigliani's work, the result rests on the clear application of a microeconomic principle, in this case, the role of arbitrage. The intuition behind the two theorems is simple. No matter what the debt–equity structure of the firm (or its dividend–retained earnings policy) the investor can always undo the impact on his or her own stock portfolio by adding or subtracting other equities or forms of debt to the mix. The resulting arbitrage will mean that the market value of the firm will depend only on the income stream generated by its assets.

Despite the enormous literature that the MM theorems generated and despite the transformation of the field of corporate finance as a consequence, Modigliani was fond of trivializing the idea behind MM as 'obvious' and said that the theorems were written with 'tongue-in-cheek' as a way of chastising the 'old school' of finance for its reliance on anecdotes and rules of thumb relayed through case studies and the reminiscences of managers and accountants (2000, pp. 233–4). Yet the papers from 1958 and 1963 are among the top three most-cited papers by Modigliani and also among those he listed as his 'personal favorites' (Merton, 1987).

Other topics

In 1997 Modigliani published with Leah Modigliani, his granddaughter and a financial analyst, a paper entitled 'Risk-Adjusted Performance: How to Measure It and Why'. Together they proposed a measure of the rate of return on an investment portfolio that was adjusted for risk so that the performance of different fund portfolios could be compared with the same measuring rod. Their technique of risk adjustment is now widely used on Wall Street and has become known as M^2 – 'M-squared' – for the two Modiglianis. It applies the same concept of arbitrage introduced by Modigliani and Miller to neutralize the risk. If the historical volatility of a portfolio has been high relative to a benchmark (say the S&P 500), its risk could hypothetically be reduced to match that of the benchmark by adding treasury bills in sufficient quantity to the mix. If the investment portfolio under study has a volatility below that of the benchmark, it could hypothetically be levered up to match the risk standard by borrowing on margin and investing additional sums in the fund. The rates of return can then be calculated and compared for these blended portfolios.

A longer review of Modigliani's work would have to find space to discuss his writings on the Italian economy with La Malfa (1967), Tarantelli (1975), Padoa-Schioppa and Rossi (1986), and Jappelli (1987) and on the European economy and international finance (Part III of *Collected Papers*, vol. 3), to mention just a few of the papers that were published in English. For Modigliani's recounting of this work, much of which is in Italian, see chapters 2 and 3 of his autobiography, *Adventures of an Economist* (2001). A review of those contributions will suggest that there are serious omissions from the present survey.

Retrospect

Modigliani was a brilliant economist who took the real problems of the real world seriously and then developed powerful theories to explain what he saw. Yet he was uncomfortable with his theories until he had rigorously tested them against the data and against alternative explanations. These econometric explorations invariably stimulated him to re-examine his thinking. For him, it was a process without end. Modigliani rarely let a topic go, he worked continuously to refine, improve, and, when necessary, to defend each of his signature contributions. He was driven by a strong faith in the power of an economic theory so derived to inform policy, to solve problems, and to right social wrongs. He acted on his beliefs by becoming an advisor to – or, when they would not listen, a public opponent of – those who made economic policy. He changed his mind when logic or facts dictated it, yet he remained steadfast in his belief that economics was a science with the potential to make the world a better place. This combination of dedication, intellectual honesty, and liberal values made him one of the most influential macroeconomists of the 20th century.

His personal characteristics were an important ingredient of his success. He was warm and caring, intense and excitable, enthusiastic and full of an infectious joy for life. He was a charismatic teacher, a tenacious debater, and a seminal thinker with the rare ability to stimulate others to think and imagine beyond their usual capacity.

RICHARD SUTCH

See also **expectations; Keynesian revolution; Miller, Merton; Modigliani–Miller theorem; rational expectations; term structure of interest rates.**

Partial support for this research was provided by the National Science Foundation and the Center for Social and Economic Policy at the University of California, Riverside.

Selected works

The most important scientific contributions of Modigliani have been collected and reprinted in *The Collected Papers of Franco Modigliani*, 6 vols., ed. A. Abel,

S. Johnson and F. Franco (1980–2005), Cambridge, MA: MIT Press.

1944. Liquidity preference and the theory of interest and money. *Econometrica* 12, 45–88.

1949. Fluctuations in the saving–income ratio: a problem in economic forecasting. In *Studies in Income and Wealth*, vol. 11. New York: NBER.

1954. (With R. Brumberg.) Utility analysis and the consumption function: an interpretation of cross-section Data. In *Post-Keynesian Economics*, ed. K. Kurihara. New Brunswick, NJ: Rutgers University Press.

1954. (With E. Grunberg.) The predictability of social events. *Journal of Political Economy* 62, 465–78.

1958. (With M. Miller.) The cost of capital, corporation finance, and the theory of investment. *American Economic Review* 48, 261–97.

1960. (With C. Holt, J. Muth and H Simon.) *Planning Production, Inventories, and Work Force.* Englewood Cliffs, NJ: Prentice-Hall.

1961. Long-run implications of alternative fiscal policies and the burden of the national debt. *Economic Journal* 71, 730–55.

1961. (With K. J. Cohen.) *The Role of Anticipations and Plans in Economic Behavior and their Use in Economic Analysis and Forecasting.* Urbana: University of Illinois.

1961. (With M. Miller.) Dividend policy, growth, and the valuation of shares. *Journal of Business* 34, 411–33.

1963. The monetary mechanism and its interaction with real phenomena. *Review of Economics and Statistics* 45(1) Part 2, Supplement, 79–107.

1963. (With A. Ando.) The 'life-cycle' hypothesis of saving: aggregate implications and tests. *American Economic Review* 53, 55–84.

1963. (With M. Miller.) Corporate income tax and the cost of capital: a correction. *American Economic Review* 53, 433–43.

1964. Some empirical tests of monetary management and of rules versus discretion. *Journal of Political Economy* 72, 211–45.

1965. (With A. Ando.) The relative stability of monetary velocity and the investment multiplier. *American Economic Review* 55, 693–728.

1966. The life-cycle hypothesis of saving: the demand for wealth and the supply of capital. *Social Research* 33, 160–217.

1966. (With R. Sutch.) Innovations in interest rate policy. *American Economic Review* 56, 178–97.

1967. (With G. La Malfa.) Inflation, balance of payments deficit, and their cure through monetary policy: the Italian example. *Banca Nazionale del Lavoro Quarterly Review* 80, 3–47.

1967. (With R. Sutch.) Debt management and the term structure of interest rates: an empirical analysis. *Journal of Political Economy* 75, 569–89.

1969. (With A. Ando.) Econometric analysis of stabilization policies. *American Economic Review* 59, 296–314.

1973. (With R. Shiller.) Inflation, rational expectations and the term structure of interest rates. *Economica* 40, 12–43.

1975a. Channels of monetary policy in the Federal Reserve-MIT-University of Pennsylvania Econometric Model of the United States. In *Modelling the Economy*, ed. G. Renton. London: Heinemann Educational Books.

1975b. The life-cycle hypothesis of saving twenty years later. In *Contemporary Issues in Economics*, ed. M. Parkin and A. Nobay. Manchester: Manchester University Press.

1975. (With E. Tarantelli.) The consumption function in a developing economy and the Italian experience. *American Economic Review* 65, 825–42.

1977. The monetarist controversy or, Should we forsake stabilization policies? Presidential address delivered at the American Economic Association. *American Economic Review* 67, 1–19.

1980. (With R. Brumberg.) Utility analysis and aggregate consumption functions: an attempt at integration. In *The Collected Papers of Franco Modigliani*, vol. 2, ed. A. Abel. Cambridge, MA: MIT Press.

1982. Debt, dividend policy, taxes, inflation, and market valuation. Presidential address delivered at the American Finance Association. *Journal of Finance* 37, 255–73.

1983a. Government deficits, inflation, and future generations. In *Deficits: How Big and How Bad?*, ed. D. Conklin and T. Courchene. Ontario: Ontario Economic Council.

1983b. Interview with Franco Modigliani. In *Conversations with Economists: New Classical Economists and Their Opponents Speak Out on the Current Controversy in Macroeconomics*, ed. A. Klamer. Totowa, NJ: Rowman and Littlefield.

1983. (With A. Sterling.) Determinants of private saving with special reference to the role of Social Security – cross-country tests. In *The Determinants of National Saving and Wealth*, ed. F. Modigliani and R. Hemming. London: Macmillan.

1986a. Autobiography. *Les Prix Nobel. The Nobel Prizes 1985*, ed. W. Odelberg. Stockholm: Nobel Foundation. Online. Available at http://nobelprize.org/nobel_prizes/economics/laureates/1985/modigliani-autobio.html, accessed 9 September 2006.

1986b. Life cycle, individual thrift, and the wealth of nations. Nobel Prize Lecture, 1985. Reprinted in *American Economic Review* 76, 297–313.

1986c. *The Debate over Stabilization Policy*. Cambridge: Cambridge University Press.

1986. (With F. Padoa-Schioppa and N. Rossi.) Aggregate unemployment in Italy, 1960–1983. *Economica* 53, S245–S273, S347–S352.

1986. (With A. Sterling.) Government debt, government spending, and private sector behavior: comment. *American Economic Review* 76, 1168–79.

1987. (With T. Jappelli.) Fiscal policy and saving in Italy since 1860. In *Private Saving and Public Debt*, ed. M. Boskin, J. Flemming and S. Gorini. Oxford: Basil Blackwell.

1988a. The role of intergenerational transfers and life cycle saving in the accumulation of wealth. *Journal of Economic Perspectives* 2(2), 15–40.

1988b. MM – past, present, future. *Journal of Economic Perspectives* 2(4), 149–58.

1997. (With L. Modigliani.) Risk-adjusted performance: how to measure it and why. *Journal of Portfolio Management* 23(2), 45–54.

2000. An interview with Franco Modigliani. Interviewed by W. Barnett and R. Solow, 5–6 November 1999. *Macroeconomic Dynamics* 4, 222–56.

2001. *Adventures of an Economist*. New York: Texere.

2005. (With T. Jappelli.) The age–saving profile and the life–cycle hypothesis. In *The Collected Papers of Franco Modigliani*, vol. 6, ed. F. Franco. Cambridge, MA: MIT Press.

Bibliography

Barro, R. 1974. Are government bonds net worth? *Journal of Political Economy* 82, 1095–117.

Duesenberry, J. 1949. *Income, Saving, and the Theory of Consumer Behavior*. Cambridge, MA: Harvard University Press.

Friedman, M. 1957. *A Theory of the Consumption Function*. Princeton, NJ: Princeton University Press.

Goldsmith, R. 1962. *The National Wealth of the United States in the Postwar Period*. Princeton: Princeton University Press.

Hicks, J. 1937. Mr Keynes and the 'Classics'. *Econometrica* 5, 147–59.

Keynes, J.M. 1936. *The General Theory of Employment, Interest, and Money*. New York: Harcourt, Brace.

Lucas, R., Jr. 1972. Expectations and the neutrality of money. *Journal of Economic Theory* 4, 103–24.

Merton, R. 1987. In honor of Nobel Laureate, Franco Modigliani. *Journal of Economic Perspectives* 1(2), 145–55.

MIT (Massachusetts Institute of Technology). 2003. 'Nobel laureate Franco Modigliani dies at 85'. News Office, MIT. Online. Available at http://web.mit.edu/newsoffice/2003/modigliani.html, accessed 11 November 2003.

Muth, J.F. 1961. Rational expectations and the theory of price movements. *Econometrica* 29, 315–35.

Modigliani–Miller theorem

The Modigliani–Miller theorem is a cornerstone of modern corporate finance. At its heart, the theorem is an irrelevance proposition: it provides conditions under which a firm's financial decisions do not affect its value. Modigliani explains the theorem as follows:

> … with well-functioning markets (and neutral taxes) and rational investors, who can 'undo' the corporate financial structure by holding positive or negative amounts of debt, the market value of the firm – debt

plus equity – depends *only* on the income stream generated by its assets. It follows, in particular, that the value of the firm should not be affected by the share of debt in its financial structure or by what will be done with the returns – paid out as dividends or reinvested (profitably). (Modigliani, 1980, p. xiii)

In fact, what is currently understood as the Modigliani–Miller theorem comprises four distinct results from a series of papers (1958; 1961; 1963). The first proposition establishes that under certain conditions, a firm's debt–equity ratio does not affect its market value. The second proposition establishes that a firm's leverage has no effect on its weighted average cost of capital (that is, the cost of equity capital is a linear function of the debt–equity ratio). The third proposition establishes that firm market value is independent of its dividend policy. The fourth proposition establishes that equity-holders are indifferent about the firm's financial policy.

Miller (1991, p. 5) explains the intuition for the theorem with a simple analogy. 'Think of the firm as a gigantic tub of whole milk. The farmer can sell the whole milk as it is. Or he can separate out the cream, and sell it at a considerably higher price than the whole milk would bring.' He continues: 'The Modigliani–Miller proposition says that if there were no costs of separation (and, of course, no government dairy support programme), the cream plus the skimmed milk would bring the same price as the whole milk.' The essence of the argument is that increasing the amount of debt (cream) lowers the value of outstanding equity (skimmed milk) – selling off safe cash flows to debt-holders leaves the firm with more lower-valued equity, keeping the total value of the firm unchanged. Put differently, any gain from using more of what might seem to be cheaper debt is offset by the higher cost of now riskier equity. Hence, given a fixed amount of total capital, the allocation of capital between debt and equity is irrelevant because the weighted average of the two costs of capital to the firm is the same for all possible combinations of the two.

The theorem makes two fundamental contributions. In the context of the modern theory of finance, it represents one of the first formal uses of a no arbitrage argument (though the 'law of one price' is long-standing). More fundamentally, it structured the debate on why irrelevance fails around the theorem's assumptions: (i) neutral taxes; (ii) no capital market frictions (that is, no transaction costs, asset trade restrictions or bankruptcy costs); (iii) symmetric access to credit markets (that is, firms and investors can borrow or lend at the same rate); and (iv) firm financial policy reveals no information. Modigliani and Miller (1958) also assumed that each firm belonged to a 'risk class', a set of firms with common earnings across states of the world, but Stiglitz (1969) showed that this assumption is not essential. The relevant assumptions are important because they set conditions for effective arbitrage: When a financial

market is not distorted by taxes, transaction or bankruptcy costs, imperfect information or any other friction which limits access to credit, then investors can costlessly replicate a firm's financial actions. This gives investors the ability to 'undo' firm decisions, if they so desire. Attempts to overturn the theorem's controversial irrelevance result were a fortiori arguments about which of the assumptions to reject or amend. The systematic analysis of these assumptions led to an expansion of the frontiers of economics and finance.

The importance of taxes for the irrelevance of debt versus equity in the firm's capital structure was considered in Modigliani and Miller's original paper (1958). Modigliani and Miller (1963) and Miller (1977) addressed the issue more specifically, showing that under some conditions, the optimal capital structure can be complete debt finance due to the preferential treatment of debt relative to equity in a tax code. For example, in the United States, interest payments on debt are excluded from corporate taxes. As a consequence, substituting debt for equity generates a surplus by reducing firm tax payments to the government. Firms can then pass this surplus on to investors in the form of higher returns. This raised the further provocative question – were firms that issued equity leaving stockholder money on the table in the form of unnecessary corporate income tax payments? Miller (1977) resolved this problem by showing that a firm could generate higher after-tax income by increasing the debt–equity ratio, and this additional income would result in a higher payout to stockholders and bondholders, but the value of the firm need not increase. The crux of the argument is that as debt is substituted for equity, the proportion of firm payouts in the form of interest on debt rises relative to payouts in the form of dividends and capital gains on equity. Taxes that are higher on interest payments than on equity returns reduce or eliminate the advantage of debt finance to the firm.

The remaining Modigliani–Miller assumptions deal with various types of capital market frictions (for example, transaction costs or imperfect information) that are at the heart of arbitrage. The driving force in a perfect market for a homogeneous good is the 'law of one price'. If debt and equity are merely different packages of an underlying homogeneous good – capital – and there are no market imperfections, then it follows immediately that the law of one price holds due to arbitrage. Investors simply engage in arbitrage until any deviation in the price of the two forms of capital is eliminated. Thus, the remaining discussion is organized around the implications of the theorem for firm capital structure, dividend policy, and the method of capital finance (lease versus buy).

With regard to firm capital structure, the theorem opened a literature on the fundamental nature of debt versus equity. Are debt and equity distinct forms of capital? Why and in what specific ways? In order to answer these questions about the nature of capital, the optimal contract literature examines debt and equity as financial contracts that arise optimally in response to particular market frictions, when contracting possibilities are complete or incomplete. Complete contracts can be written on all states if this is optimal; incomplete contacts cannot depend on some states of nature.

In one of the earliest contributions, Townsend (1979) combines elements of imperfect information and bankruptcy costs to examine the nature of debt in a complete contracting environment. In his costly state verification model, debt is an optimal response to costly monitoring and differential information: all agents know *ex ante* the distribution of firm returns, but only the firm privately and costlessly observes the return *ex post*. The lender can acquire this information, but must irrevocably commit to pay a deadweight verification cost. Townsend shows that debt is optimal because it minimizes this cost. When the firm makes the required fixed debt repayment, no cost is incurred. Only when the firm is insolvent, and hence cannot repay its debt fully, does verification occur. Townsend interprets this as costly bankruptcy (liquidation): the firm is shut down; firm assets are seized by a 'court', which verifies their magnitude and transfers the residual to the lender, net of the verification cost. Lacker and Weinberg (1989) extend the approach by specifying conditions under which equity is optimal in an analogue of the model, costly state falsification. Neither debt nor equity is *ex post* efficient in this class of models because no agent wishes to request costly intervention and incur the deadweight cost, *ex post*. Agents know that bankruptcy occurs only when the firm is truly unable to repay due to a low realization, but they are implicitly assumed to be committed to the decisions they made *ex ante*. Otherwise, debt is no longer optimal.

Krasa and Villamil (2000) show that a firm–lender investment problem with multiple stages, costly enforcement, limited commitment and an explicit enforcement decision, can illuminate debt's distinct properties. The analysis also solves the *ex post* inefficiency problem in the costly state verification model. Agents write a contract in the initial period, knowing only the distribution of project returns. The contract specifies payments and when enforcement will occur, and can be altered if agents receive new information. In the next period, the borrower privately observes the return and can make the unenforceable payment specified in the original contract or propose an alternative payment (that is, renegotiate). In the final stage the investor can seek costly enforcement of the contractually specified payment or renegotiate enforcement. The opportunity to renegotiate is important because it introduces a new source of information: any positive renegotiation payment by the firm would reveal information to the investor about the firm's state. Debt is optimal because it minimizes information revelation. Renegotiation, which imposes a constraint on the contract problem, is only relevant when an agent acquires new information and can use the information to alter the

initial contract. Debt weakens agents' incentive to renegotiate by minimizing information revelation (a fixed face value reveals no information about the firm). The contract is *ex post* efficient because all decisions are chosen optimally as part of a perfect Bayesian Nash equilibrium. This minimal information revelation of debt stands in sharp contrast to the active information revelation in signalling models of equity. For example, in Leland and Pyle (1977) retained equity by a firm signals a profit increase sufficient to offset the owner's forgone diversification. In Myers and Majluf (1984), issuing equity signals bad news – owners with inside information sell shares when markets overvalue them. These signalling models leave open why a firm would use financial decisions to reveal information, a problem that does not arise in Krasa and Villamil.

In incomplete contracting models, control rights are an alternative justification for debt and equity contracts. Aghion and Bolton (1992) view debt as a particular assignment of control rights with important incentive properties. They show that when contracting possibilities are exogenously incomplete and control rights are assigned entirely to the investor or the firm, the first-best contract cannot be implemented. If the investor has sole control, the investor may force the firm to expand to a suboptimal level. Alternatively, if the firm has sole control it may not liquidate optimally. Aghion and Bolton show that, under some conditions, debt is the optimal contract because it assigns control to the firm in good states but to the investor in bad states. This ensures that optimal decisions are made in solvency and default states. Zender (1991) extends the model to include both debt and equity contracts. Grossman and Hart (1988) and Harris and Raviv (1988) examine control in the context of voting rights. They focus on the 'one vote per share' property of equity and majority voting, showing circumstances under which equity is optimal and when other 'extreme securities' are optimal.

Instead of focusing on the properties of debt and equity per se, Allen and Gale (1988; 1991) examine the properties of optimal securities more broadly, especially financial innovation. They study the problem of a firm that can issue securities in a market where the transaction cost of issuing securities makes the market incomplete. Market structure is endogenous in the sense that firms choose the securities they issue, which determines the transaction costs they incur. Allen and Gale (1988) prohibit short sales and show that neither debt nor equity is optimal. In contrast, Allen and Gale (1991) permit unlimited short sales, and show by example that debt and equity can be optimal. They note that the example is a special case; in general their model predicts that optimal securities are much more complex than those typically observed. The debt–equity puzzle unleashed by Modigliani and Miller continues to be an active area of research. The common theme of both the complete and incomplete contracting literatures is that debt, equity, and hybrid securities arise endogenously to overcome frictions in capital markets. Debt and equity have unique properties that resolve these frictions.

The Miller and Modigliani (1961) and Miller (1977) result that firm value is independent of dividend policy has also been examined extensively. Bhattacharya (1979) and others show that firm dividend policy can be a costly device to signal a firm's state, and hence relevant, in a class of models with: (i) asymmetric information about stochastic firm earnings; (ii) shareholder liquidity (a need to sell makes firm valuation relevant); and (iii) deadweight costs (to pay dividends, refinance cash flow shocks or cover underinvestment). In a separating equilibrium, only firms with high anticipated earnings pay high dividends, thus signalling their prospects to the stock market. As in other costly signalling models, the question as to why a firm would use financial decisions to reveal information, rather than direct disclosure, must be addressed. As noted previously, taxes are another important friction that effect dividend policy (for example, see Allen, Bernardo and Welch, 2000).

Finally, Miller and Upton (1976) show that firms are indifferent between leasing and buying capital, except when they face different tax rates. Myers, Dill and Bautista (1976) develop a formula to evaluate the lease versus buy decision, where different tax rates across firms create different discount rates. They show it is optimal for low tax rate, and hence high discount rate firms, to lease. Alchian and Demsetz (1972) show that leasing involves agency costs due to the separation of ownership and control of capital; a lessee may not have the same incentive as an owner to properly use or maintain the capital. Coase (1972) and Bulow (1986) argue that a durable goods monopolist may lease in order to avoid time inconsistency, and Hendel and Lizzari (1999; 2002) show that it may lease to reduce competition or adverse selection in secondary (used goods) markets. Eisfeldt and Rampini (2007) show that leasing has a repossession advantage relative to buying via secured lending. The trade-off involves the benefit of the enforcement advantage for leased capital, relative to the cost of the ownership, versus a standard control agency problem which arises because ownership and control are separated.

In addition to these specific advances in financial structure, an essential part of Modigliani and Miller's innovation was to put agents on an equal footing. They, and others, then asked what types of friction would cause agents to have different market opportunities, information sets or commitment friction? This perspective, which was novel at the time, has been used productively to analyse problems in monetary economics, public finance, international economics, and a number of other applications. In summary, the most profound and lasting impacts of the Modigliani–Miller theorem have been this notion of 'even footedness' and the systematic investigation of the theorem's assumptions. The approach has motivated decades of research in economics and finance in a search for what *is* relevant in a host of economic problems (between borrowers and lenders, governments and citizens, and countries). As Miller (1988, p. 100) said: 'Showing what doesn't matter can also show, by implication, what does.'

ANNE P. VILLAMIL

See also **arbitrage; finance; Miller, Merton; Modigliani, Franco.**

Bibliography

Aghion, P. and Bolton, P. 1992. An incomplete contracts approach to financial contracting. *Review of Economic Studies* 59, 473–94.

Alchian, A. and Demsetz, H. 1972. Production, information costs and economic organization. *American Economic Review* 62, 777–95.

Allen, F., Bernardo, A. and Welch, I. 2000. A theory of dividends based on tax clienteles. *Journal of Finance* 55, 2499–536.

Allen, F. and Gale, D. 1988. Optimal security design. *Review of Financial Studies* 1, 229–63.

Allen, F. and Gale, D. 1991. Arbitrage, short sales and financial innovation. *Econometrica* 59, 1041–68.

Bhattacharya, S. 1979. Imperfect information, dividend policy, and the 'bird in the hand' fallacy. *Bell Journal of Economics* 10, 259–70.

Bulow, J. 1986. An economic theory of planned obsolescence. *Quarterly Journal of Economics* 101, 729–49.

Coase, R. 1972. Durability and monopoly. *Journal of Law and Economics* 15, 142–9.

Eisfeldt, A. and Rampini, A. 2007. Leasing, ability to repossess and debt capacity. *Review of Financial Studies*, forthcoming.

Grossman, S. and Hart, O. 1988. One share one vote and the market for corporate control. *Journal of Financial Economics* 20, 175–202.

Harris, M. and Raviv, A. 1988. Corporate governance: voting rights and majority rule. *Journal of Financial Economics* 20, 203–35.

Hendel, I. and Lizzari, A. 1999. Interfering with secondary markets. *RAND Journal of Economics* 30, 1–21.

Hendel, I. and Lizzari, A. 2002. The role of leasing under adverse selection. *Journal of Political Economy* 110, 113–43.

Krasa, S. and Villamil, A.P. 2000. Optimal contracts when enforcement is a decision variable. *Econometrica* 68, 119–34.

Lacker, J. and Weinberg, J. 1989. Optimal contracts under costly state falsification. *Journal of Political Economy* 97, 1345–63.

Leland, H. and Pyle, D. 1977. Informational asymmetries, financial structure and financial intermediation. *Journal of Finance* 32, 371–87.

Miller, M.H. 1977. Debt and taxes. *Journal of Finance* 32, 261–75.

Miller, M.H. 1988. The Modigliani-Miller proposition after thirty years. *Journal of Economic Perspectives* 2(4), 99–120.

Miller, M.H. 1991. *Financial Innovations and Market Volatility*. Cambridge, MA: Blackwell.

Miller, M.H. and Modigliani, F. 1961. Dividend policy, growth and the valuation of shares. *Journal of Business* 34, 411–33.

Miller, M.H. and Upton, C. 1976. Leasing, buying and the cost of capital services. *Journal of Finance* 31, 761–86.

Modigliani, F. 1980. Introduction. In *The Collected Papers of Franco Modigliani*, vol. 3, ed. A. Abel. Cambridge, MA: MIT Press.

Modigliani, F. and Miller, M.H. 1958. The cost of capital, corporate finance and the theory of investment. *American Economic Review* 48, 261–97.

Modigliani, F. and Miller, M.H. 1963. Corporate income taxes and the cost of capital: a correction. *American Economic Review* 53, 433–43.

Myers, S., Dill, D. and Bautista, A. 1976. Valuation of financial lease contracts. *Journal of Finance* 31, 799–819.

Myers, S. and Majluf, N. 1984. Corporate financing and investment when firms have information that investors do not have. *Journal of Financial Economics* 11, 187–221.

Stiglitz, J. 1969. A re-examination of the Modigliani–Miller theorem. *American Economic Review* 59, 784–93.

Townsend, R. 1979. Optimal contracts and competitive markets with costly state verification. *Journal of Economic Theory* 22, 265–93.

Zender, J. 1991. Optimal financial instruments. *Journal of Finance* 46, 1645–63.

monetarism

Monetarism is the view that the quantity of money has a major influence on economic activity and the price level and that the objectives of monetary policy are best achieved by targeting the rate of growth of the money supply.

Background and initial development

Monetarism is most closely associated with the writings of Milton Friedman who advocated control of the money supply as superior to Keynesian fiscal measures for stabilizing aggregate demand. Friedman (1948) had proposed that the government finance budget deficits by issuing new money and use budget surpluses to retire money. The resulting countercyclical variations in the money stock would stabilize the economy, provided that the government set its expenditures and tax rates to balance the budget at full employment. In his *A Program for Monetary Stability* (1960), however, Friedman proposed that constant growth of the money stock, divorced from the government budget, would be simpler and equally effective for stabilizing the economy.

In their emphasis on the importance of money, these proposals followed a tradition of the Chicago School of economics. Preceding Friedman at the University of Chicago, Henry Simons (1936) had advocated control of the money stock to achieve a stable price level, and Lloyd Mints (1950) laid out a specific monetary programme for stabilizing an index of the price level. These writers rejected reliance on the gold standard because it had failed in practice to stabilize the price level or economic activity. Such views were not confined to the University of Chicago. In the 1930s James Angell of Columbia University (1933) advocated constant monetary growth, and in the post-Second World War period Karl Brunner and Allan Meltzer were influential proponents of monetarism. The term 'monetarism' was first used by Brunner (1968). He and Meltzer founded the 'Shadow Open Market Committee' in the 1970s to publicize monetarist views on how the Federal Reserve should conduct monetary policy. Monetarism gradually gained adherents not only in the United States but also in Britain (Laidler, 1978) and other Western European countries, and subsequently around the world. The growing prominence of monetarism led to intense controversy among economists over the desirability of a policy of targeting monetary growth.

The roots of monetarism lie in the quantity theory of money which formed the basis of classical monetary economics from at least the 18th century. The quantity theory explains changes in nominal aggregate expenditures – reflecting changes in both the physical volume of output and the price level – in terms of changes in the money stock and in the velocity of circulation of money (the ratio of aggregate expenditures to the money stock). Over the long run changes in velocity are usually smaller than those in the money stock and in part are a result of prior changes in the money stock, so that aggregate expenditures are determined largely by the latter. Moreover, over the long run growth in the physical volume of output is determined mainly by real (that is, non-monetary) factors, so that monetary changes mainly influence the price level. The observed long-run association between money and prices confirms that inflation results from monetary overexpansion and can be prevented by proper control of the money supply. This is the basis for Friedman's oft-repeated statement that inflation is always and everywhere a monetary phenomenon.

The importance of monetary effects on price movements had been supported in empirical studies by classical and neoclassical economists such as Cairnes, Jevons and Cassel. But these studies suffered from limited data, and the widespread misinterpretation of monetary influences in the Great Depression of the 1930s fostered doubts about their importance in business cycles. As Keynesian theory revolutionized thinking in the late 1930s and 1940s, it offered an influential alternative to monetary interpretations of business cycles.

The first solid empirical support for a monetary interpretation of business cycles came in a series of studies of the United States by Clark Warburton (for example, 1946). Subsequently Friedman and Anna J. Schwartz compiled new data at the National Bureau of Economic Research in an extension of Warburton's work. In 1962 they demonstrated that fluctuations in monetary growth preceded peaks and troughs of all US business cycles since the Civil War. Their dates for significant steps to higher or lower rates of monetary growth showed a lead over corresponding business cycle turns on the average by about a half year at peaks and by about a quarter year at troughs, but the lags varied considerably. Other studies have found that monetary changes take one to two years or more to affect the price level.

In *A Monetary History of the United States, 1867–1960* (1963b) Friedman and Schwartz detailed the role of money in business cycles and argued in particular that severe business contractions like that of 1929–33 were directly attributable to unusually large monetary contractions. Their monetary studies were continued in *Monetary Statistics of the United States* (1970) and *Monetary Trends in the United States and the United Kingdom* (1982). A companion National Bureau study *Determinants and Effects of Changes in the Stock of Money* (1965) by Phillip Cagan presented evidence that the reverse effect of economic activity and prices on money did not account for the major part of their observed correlation, which therefore pointed to an important causal role of money.

The monetarist proposition that monetary changes are responsible for business cycles was widely contested, but by the end of the 1960s the view that monetary policy had important effects on aggregate activity was generally accepted. The obvious importance of monetary growth in the inflation of the 1970s restored money to the centre of macroeconomics.

Monetarism versus Keynesianism

Monetarism and Keynesianism differ sharply in their research strategies and theories of aggregate expenditures. The Keynesian theory focuses on the determinants of the components of aggregate expenditures and assigns a minor role to money holdings. In monetarist theory money demand and supply are paramount in explaining aggregate expenditures.

To contrast the Keynesian and monetarist theories, Friedman and David Meiselman (1963) focused on the basic hypothesis about economic behaviour underlying each theory: for the Keynesian theory the consumption multiplier posits a stable relationship between consumption and income, and for the monetarist theory the velocity of circulation of money posits a stable demand function for money. Friedman and Meiselman tested the two theories empirically using US data for various periods by relating consumption expenditures in one

regression to investment expenditures, assuming a constant consumption multiplier, and in a second regression to the money stock, assuming a constant velocity. They reported that the monetarist regression generally fitted the data much better. These dramatic results were not accepted by Keynesians, who argued that the Keynesian theory was not adequately represented by a one-equation regression and that econometric models of the entire economy, based on Keynesian theory, were superior to small-scale models based solely on monetary changes.

The alleged superiority of Keynesian models was contested by economists at the Federal Reserve Bank of St Louis (see Andersen and Jordan, 1968). They tested a 'St Louis equation' in which changes in nominal GNP depended on current and lagged changes in the money stock, current and lagged changes in government expenditures, and a constant term reflecting the trend in monetary velocity. When fitted to historical US data, the equation showed a strong permanent effect of money on GNP and a weak transitory (and in later work, non-existent) effect of the fiscal variables, contradicting the Keynesian claim of the greater importance of fiscal than monetary policies. Although the St Louis equation was widely criticized on econometric issues, it was fairly accurate when first used in the late 1960s to forecast GNP, which influenced academic opinion and helped bring monetarism to the attention of the business world.

Although budget deficits and surpluses change interest rates and thus can affect the demand for money, monetarists believe that fiscal effects on aggregate demand are small because of the low interest elasticity of money demand. Government borrowing crowds out private borrowing and associated spending, and so deficits have little net effect on aggregate demand. The empirical results of the St Louis equation are taken as confirmation of weak transitory effects. The debate over the effectiveness of fiscal policy as a stabilization tool has produced a large literature.

In their analysis of the transmission of monetary changes through the economy, Brunner and Meltzer (1976) compare the effects of government issues of money and bonds. If the government finances increased expenditures in a way that raises the money supply, aggregate expenditures increase and nominal income rises. Moreover, the increased supply of money adds to the public's wealth, and greater wealth increases the demand for goods and services. This too raises nominal income. The rise in nominal income is at first mainly a rise in real income and later a rise in prices. They compare this result with one in which the government finances its increased expenditures by issuing bonds rather than money. Again wealth increases, and this raises aggregate expenditures. As long as the government issues either money or bonds to finance a deficit, nominal income must rise due to the increase in wealth. Brunner and Meltzer therefore agree with Keynesians that in principle a deficit financed by bonds as well as by new money is expansionary. However, they show that the empirical magnitudes of the economy are such that national income rises more from issuing a dollar of money than a dollar of bonds.

Policy implications of monetarism

Because monetary effects have variable lags of one to several quarters or more, countercyclical monetary policy actions are difficult to time properly. Friedman as well as Brunner and Meltzer argued that an active monetary policy, in the absence of an impossibly ideal foresight, tends to exacerbate, rather than smooth, economic fluctuations. In their view a stable monetary growth rate would avoid monetary sources of economic disturbances, and could be set to produce an approximately constant price level over the long run. Remaining instabilities in economic activity would be minor and, in any event, were beyond the capabilities of policy to prevent. A commitment by the monetary authorities to stable monetary growth would also help deflect constant political pressures for short-run monetary stimulus and would remove the uncertainty for investors of the unexpected effects of discretionary monetary policies.

A constant monetary growth policy can be contrasted with central bank practices that impart pro-cyclical variations to the money supply. It is common for central banks to lend freely to banks at times of rising credit demand in order to avoid increases in interest rates. Although such interest-rate targeting helps to stabilize financial markets, the targeting often fails to allow rates to change sufficiently to counter fluctuations in credit demands. By preventing interest rates from rising when credit demands increase, for example, the policy leads to monetary expansion that generates higher expenditures and inflationary pressures. Such mistakes of interest-rate targeting were clearly demonstrated in the 1970s, when for some time increases in nominal interest rates did not match increases in the inflation rate, and the resulting low rates of interest in real terms (that is, adjusted for inflation) overstimulated investment and aggregate demand.

The same accommodation of market demands for bank credit results from the common practice of targeting the volume of borrowing from the central bank. Attempts to keep this volume at some designated level require the central bank to supply reserves through open market operations as an alternative to borrowing by banks when rising market credit demands tighten bank reserve positions, and to withdraw reserves in the opposite situation. The resulting procyclical behaviour of the money supply could be avoided by operations designed to maintain a constant growth rate of money.

Brunner and Meltzer (1964a) developed an analytic framework describing how monetary policy should aim at certain intermediate targets as a way of influencing aggregate expenditures. The intermediate targets are such variables as the money supply or interest rates. (Since the Federal Reserve does not control long-term interest rates or the money stock directly, it operates through instrumental variables, such as bank reserves or the federal funds rate, which it can affect directly.) The question of the appropriate intermediate targets of monetary policy soon became the most widely discussed issue in monetary policy.

In recognition of the deficiencies of interest-rate targeting, some countries turned during the 1970s to a modified monetary targeting in which annual growth ranges were announced and adhered to, though with frequent exceptions to allow for departures deemed appropriate because of disturbances from foreign trade and other sources. Major countries adopting some form of monetary targeting included the Federal Republic of Germany, Japan, and Switzerland, all of which kept inflation rates low and thus advertised by example the anti-inflationary virtues of monetarism. In the United States the Federal Reserve also began to set monetary target ranges during the 1970s but generally did not meet them and continued to target interest rates. In October 1979, when inflation was escalating sharply, the Federal Reserve announced a more stringent targeting procedure for reducing monetary growth. Although the average growth rate was reduced, the large short-run fluctuations in monetary growth were criticized by monetarists. In late 1982 the Federal Reserve relaxed its pursuit of monetary targets.

By the mid-1980s the US and numerous other countries were following a partial form of monetary targeting, in which relatively broad bands of annual growth rates are pursued but still subject to major departures when deemed appropriate. These policies are monetarist only in the sense that one or more monetary aggregates are an important indicator of policy objectives; they fall short of a firm commitment to a steady, let alone a non-inflationary, monetary growth rate.

Monetarist theory

Monetarist theory of aggregate expenditures is based on a demand function for monetary assets that is claimed to be stable in the sense that successive residual errors are generally offsetting and do not accumulate. Given the present inconvertible-money systems, the stock of money is treated as under the control of the government. Although a distinction is made in theory between the determinants of household and business holdings of money, money demand is usually formulated for households and applied to the total. In these formulations the demand for money depends on the volume of transactions, the fractions of income and of wealth the public wishes to hold in the form of money balances, and the opportunity costs of holding money rather than other income-producing assets (that is, the difference between yields on money and on alternative assets). The alternative assets are viewed broadly to include not only financial instruments but also such physical assets as durable consumer goods, real property, and business plant and equipment. The public is presumed to respond to changes in the amount of money supplied by undertaking transactions to bring actual holdings of both money and other assets into equilibrium with desired holdings. As a result of substitutions between money and assets, starting with close substitutes, yields change on a broad range of assets, including consumer durables and capital goods, in widening ripples that affect borrowing, investment, consumption, and production throughout the economy.

The end result is reflected in *aggregate* expenditures and the average level of prices. Independently of this monetary influence on aggregate expenditures and the price level, developments specific to particular sectors determine the distribution of expenditures among goods and services and relative prices. Thus monetarist theory rejects the common technique for forecasting aggregate output by adding up the forecasts for individual industries or the common practice of explaining changes in the price level in terms of price changes for particular goods and services.

Monetarists were early critics of the once influential Keynesian theory of a highly elastic demand for money with respect to short-run changes in the interest rate on liquid short-term assets, which in extreme form became a 'liquidity trap'. Empirical studies have found instead that interest rates on savings deposits and on short-term market securities have elasticities smaller even than the $-\frac{1}{2}$ implied by the simple Baumol–Tobin cash balance theory (Baumol, 1952; Tobin, 1956).

In empirical work a common form of the demand function for money includes one or two interest rates and real GNP as a proxy for real income. A gradual adjustment of actual to desired money balances is allowed for, implying that a full adjustment to a change in the stock is spread over several quarters. The lagged adjustment is subject to an alternative interpretation in which money demand reflects 'permanent' instead of current levels of income and interest rates. This interpretation de-emphasizes the volume of transactions as the major determinant of money demand in favour of the monetarist view of money as a capital asset yielding a stream of particular services and dependent on 'permanent' values of wealth, income, and interest rates (in most studies captured empirically by a lagged adjustment). Treatment of the demand for money as similar to demands for other assets stocks is now standard practice.

The monetarist view of money as a capital asset suggests that the demand for it depends on a variety of characteristics, and not uniquely on its transactions services. The definition of money for policy purposes depends on two considerations: the ability of the monetary authorities to control its quantity, and the empirical stability of a function describing the demand for it. In their study of the United States Friedman and Schwartz used an early version of M2, which included time and savings deposits at commercial banks, but they argued that minor changes in coverage would not greatly affect their findings. Subsequently the quantity of transaction balances M1 has become the most widely used definition of money for most countries, though many central banks claim to pay attention also to broader aggregates in conducting monetary policy.

In view of the wide range of assets into which the public may shift any excess money balances, the transmission of monetary changes through the economy to affect aggregate expenditures and other variables can follow a variety of paths. Monetarists doubt that these effects can be adequately captured by a detailed econometric model which prescribes a fixed transmission path. Instead they prefer models that dispense with detailed transmission paths and focus on a stable overall relationship between changes in money and in aggregate expenditures.

In both the monetarist model and large-scale econometric models, changes in the money stock are usually treated as exogenous (that is, as determined outside the model). It is clear that money approaches a strict exogeneity only in the long run. The US studies by Friedman and Schwartz and by Cagan established that the money supply not only influences economic activity but also is influenced by it in turn. This creates difficulties in testing empirically for the monetary effects on activity because allowance must be made for the feedback effect of economic activity on the money supply. Econometric models of the money supply can allow for feedback through the banking system (Brunner and Meltzer, 1964b). Under modern systems of inconvertible money, however, the feedback is dominated by monetary policies of the central banks, and attempts to model central bank behaviour have been less than satisfactory. Statistical tests of the exogeneity of the money supply using the Granger–Sims methodology have given mixed results. Although the concurrent mutual interaction between money and economic activity remains difficult to disentangle, the longer the lag in monetary effects the less likely that the feedback from activity to money can account for the observed association. In the St Louis equation, for example, while the correlation between changes in GNP and in money concurrently could largely reflect feedback from GNP to money, the correlation between changes in GNP and lagged changes in money are less likely to be dominated by such feedback.

Opposition to monetary targeting

While monetarism has refocused attention on money and monetary policy, there is widespread doubt that velocity is sufficiently stable to make targeting of monetary growth desirable. Movements in velocity when monetary growth is held constant produce expansionary and contractionary effects on the economy. In the United States the trend of velocity was fairly stable and predictable from the early 1950s to the mid-1970s, but money demand equations based on that period showed large overpredictions after the mid-1970s (Judd and Scadding, 1982). Financial innovations providing new ways of making payments and close substitutes for holding money were changing the appropriate definition of money and the parameters of the demand function. In the United States the gradual removal of ceilings on interest rates banks could pay on deposits played a major role in these developments by increasing competition in banking. In Great Britain the removal of domestic controls over international financial transactions led to unusual movements in money holdings in 1979–80. Germany and Switzerland also found growing international capital inflows at certain times a disruptive influence on their monetary policies.

The 'monetary theory of the balance of payments' (Frenkel and Johnson, 1976) is an extension of monetarism to open economies where money supply and demand are interrelated among countries through international payments. A debated issue is whether individual countries, even under flexible exchange rates, can pursue largely independent monetary policies. The growing internationalization of capital markets is often cited as an argument against the monetarist presumption that velocity and the domestic money supply under flexible foreign exchange rates are largely independent of foreign influences.

Uncertainties over the proper definition of money and instability in the velocity of money as variously defined led to monetarist proposals to target the monetary liabilities of the central bank, that is, the 'monetary base' consisting of currency outstanding and bank reserves. The monetary base has the advantage of not being directly affected by market innovations and so of not needing redefinitions when innovations occur. Monetarists have proposed maintaining a constant growth rate of the base also because it would simplify – indirectly virtually eliminate – the monetary policy function of central banks and governments. Some of the European central banks have found targeting the monetary base preferable to targeting the money supply, though not without important discretionary departures from the target.

Yet financial market developments can also produce instabilities in the relationship between the monetary base and aggregate expenditures. Economists opposed to monetarism propose instead that stable growth of aggregate expenditures be the target of monetary policy and that it be pursued by making discretionary changes as deemed appropriate in growth of the base. This contrasts sharply with the monetarist opposition to discretion in the conduct of policy.

The Phillips curve trade-off

The inflationary outcome of discretionary monetary policy since the Second World War can be explained in terms of the Phillips curve trade-off between inflation and unemployment. Along the Phillips curve lower and lower unemployment levels are associated with higher and higher inflation rates. Such a relationship, first found in historical British data, was shown to fit US data for the 1950s and 1960s and earlier. The trade-off depends on sticky wages and prices. As aggregate demand increases, the rise in wages and prices trails behind, inducing an expansion of output to absorb part of the increase in demand. US experience initially suggested that any desired position on the Phillips curve could be maintained by the management of aggregate demand. Thus a lower rate of unemployment could be achieved and maintained by tolerating an associated higher rate of inflation. Given this presumed trade-off, policymakers tended to favour lower unemployment at the cost of higher inflation.

In the 1970s, however, the Phillips curve shifted towards higher rates of inflation for given levels of unemployment. Friedman (1968) argued that the economy gravitates toward a 'natural rate of unemployment' which in the long run is largely independent of the inflation rate and cannot be changed by monetary policy. Wages and prices adjust sluggishly to unanticipated changes in aggregate demand but adjust more rapidly to maintained increases in demand and prices that are anticipated. Consequently, the only way to hold unemployment below the natural rate is to keep aggregate demand rising faster than the anticipated rate of inflation. Since the anticipated rate tends to follow the actual rate upward, this leads to faster and faster inflation. This 'acceleration principle' implies that there is no permanent trade-off between inflation and unemployment. The existence of a natural rate of unemployment also implies that price stability does not lead to higher unemployment in the long run.

Monetarist thought puts primary emphasis on the long-run consequences of policy actions and procedures. It rejects attempts to reduce short-run fluctuations in interest rates and economic activity as usually beyond the capabilities of monetary policy and as generally inimical to the otherwise achievable goals of long-run price stability and maximum economic growth. Monetarists believe that economic activity, apart from monetary disturbances, is inherently stable. Much of their disagreement with Keynesians can be traced to this issue.

Rational expectations

One version of the rational expectations theory goes beyond monetarism by contending that there is little or no Phillips curve trade-off between inflation and unemployment even in the short run, since markets are allegedly able to anticipate any systematic countercyclical policy pursued to stabilize the economy. Only unanticipated departures from such stabilization policies affect output; all anticipated monetary changes are fully absorbed by price changes. Since unsystematic policies would have little countercyclical effectiveness or purpose, the best policy is to minimize uncertainty with a predictable monetary growth.

This theory shares the monetarist view that unpredictable fluctuations in monetary growth are an undesirable source of uncertainty with little benefit. But the two views disagree on the speed of price adjustments to predictable monetary measures and on the associated effects on economic activity. Monetarists do not claim that countercyclical policies have no real effects, but they are sceptical of our ability to use them effectively. It is the ill-timing of countercyclical policies as a result of variable lags in monetary effects that underlies the monetarist preference for constant monetary growth to avoid uncertainty and inflation bias.

Interest in private money supplies

Monetarism is the fountainhead of a renewed interest in a subject neglected during the Keynesian revolution: the design of monetary systems that maintain price-level stability. Scepticism that price-level stability can be achieved even by a constant growth rate of money however defined or of the monetary base has led to proposals for a strict gold standard or for a monetary system in which money is supplied by the private sector under competitive pressures to maintain a stable value. While monetarists are sympathetic to proposals to eliminate discretionary monetary policies, they view such alternative systems as impractical and believe that a nondiscretionary government policy of constant monetary growth is the best policy.

Associated views of the Monetarist School

Monetarism is associated with various related attitudes towards government (see Mayer, 1978). Monetarism shares with laissez-faire a belief in the long-run benefits of a competitive economic system and of limited government intervention in the economy. It opposes constraints on the free flow of credit and on movements of interest rates, such as the US ceilings on deposit interest rates (removed by the mid-1980s except on demand deposits). The disruptive potential of such ceilings became evident in the 1970s when financial innovations, partly undertaken to circumvent the ceilings, produced the transitional shifts in the traditional money-demand functions that created difficulties for the conduct of monetary policy. Government control over the quantity of money is viewed as a justifiable exception to laissez-faire, however, in order to ensure the stability of the value of money.

PHILLIP CAGAN

See also **Friedman, Milton; Keynesianism; monetary policy, history of; new classical macroeconomics; quantity theory of money; rational expectations.**

Bibliography

Andersen, L.C. and Jordan, J.L. 1968. Monetary and fiscal actions: a test of their relative importance in economic stabilization. *Federal Reserve Bank of St Louis Review* 50(November), 11–24.

Angell, J. 1933. Monetary control and general business stabilization. In *Economic Essays in Honour of Gustav Cassel*. London: Allen and Unwin.

Baumol, W.J. 1952. The transactions demand for cash: an inventory theoretic approach. *Quarterly Journal of Economics* 66, 545–56.

Brunner, K. 1968. The role of money and monetary policy. *Federal Reserve Bank of St Louis Review* 50(July), 8–24.

Brunner, K. and Meltzer, A. 1964a. The Federal Reserve's attachment to the free reserve concept. U.S. Congress House Committee on Banking and Currency, Subcommittee on Domestic Finance, April.

Brunner, K. and Meltzer, A. 1964b. Some further investigations of demand and supply functions for money. *Journal of Finance* 19, 240–83.

Brunner, K. and Meltzer, A. 1976. An aggregative theory for a closed economy. In *Studies in Monetarism*, ed. J. Stein. Amsterdam: North-Holland.

Cagan, P. 1965. *Determinants and Effects of Changes in the Stock of Money 1875–1960*. New York: Columbia University Press for the NBER.

Frenkel, J.A. and Johnson, H.G., eds. 1976. *The Monetary Approach to the Balance of Payments*. Toronto: University of Toronto Press.

Friedman, M. 1948. A monetary and fiscal framework for economic stability. *American Economic Review* 38, 256–64.

Friedman, M. 1960. *A Program for Monetary Stability*. New York: Fordham University Press.

Friedman, M. 1968. The role of monetary policy. *American Economic Review* 58, 1–17.

Friedman, M. and Meiselman, D. 1963. The relative stability of monetary velocity and the investment multiplier in the United States, 1897–1958. In Commission on Money and Credit, *Stabilization Policies*. Englewood Cliffs, NJ: Prentice–Hall.

Friedman, M. and Schwartz, A.J. 1963a. Money and business cycles. *Review of Economics and Statistics* 45(1), Part II, Supplement, 32–64.

Friedman, M. and Schwartz, A. 1963b. *A Monetary History of the United States 1867–1960*. Princeton: Princeton University Press for the NBER.

Friedman, M. and Schwartz, A. 1970. *Monetary Statistics of the United States Estimates, Sources, Methods*. New York: NBER.

Friedman, M. and Schwartz, A. 1982. *Monetary Trends in the United States and the United Kingdom Their Relation to*

Income, Prices and Interest Rates, 1867–1975. Chicago: University of Chicago Press.

Judd, J.P. and Scadding, J.L. 1982. The search for a stable money demand function: a survey of the post-1973 literature. *Journal of Economic Literature* 20, 993–1023.

Laidler, D. 1978. Mayer on monetarism: comments from a British point of view. In *The Structure of Monetarism*, ed. T. Mayer. New York: Norton.

Mayer, T., ed. 1978. *The Structure of Monetarism.* New York: Norton.

Mints, L.W. 1950. *Monetary Policy for a Competitive Society.* New York: McGraw-Hill.

Simons, H. 1936. Rules versus authorities in monetary policy. *Journal of Political Economy* 44(February), 1–30.

Tobin, J. 1956. The interest elasticity of transactions demand for cash. *Review of Economics and Statistics* 38(August), 241–7.

Warburton, C. 1946. The misplaced emphasis in contemporary business-fluctuation theory. *Journal of Business* 19, 199–220.

monetary aggregation

Aggregation theory and index-number theory have been used to generate official governmental data since the 1920s. One exception still exists. The monetary quantity aggregates and interest rate aggregates supplied by many central banks are not based on index-number or aggregation theory, but rather are the simple unweighted sums of the component quantities and quantity-weighted or arithmetic averages of interest rates. The predictable consequence has been induced instability of money demand and supply functions, and a series of 'puzzles' in the resulting applied literature. In contrast, the Divisia monetary aggregates, originated by Barnett (1980), are derived directly from economic index-number theory. Financial aggregation and index number theory was first rigorously connected with the literature on micro-economic aggregation and index number theory by Barnett (1980; 1987). A collection of many of his contributions to that field is available in Barnett and Serletis (2000).

Data construction and measurement procedures imply the theory that can rationalize the procedure. The assumptions implicit in the data construction procedures must be consistent with the assumptions made in producing the models within which the data are to be used. Unless the theory is internally consistent, the data and its applications are incoherent. Without that coherence between aggregator function structure and the econometric models within which aggregates are embedded, stable structure can appear to be unstable. This phenomenon has been called the 'Barnett critique' by Chrystal and MacDonald (1994).

Aggregation theory versus index number theory

The exact aggregates of microeconomic aggregation theory depend on unknown aggregator functions, which typically are utility, production, cost, or distance functions. Such functions must first be econometrically estimated. Hence the resulting exact quantity and price indexes become estimator- and specification-dependent. This dependency is troublesome to governmental agencies, which therefore view aggregation theory as a research tool rather than a data construction procedure.

Statistical index-number theory, on the other hand, provides indexes which are computable directly from quantity and price data, without estimation of unknown parameters. Such index numbers depend jointly on prices and quantities, but not on unknown parameters. In a sense, index number theory trades joint dependency on prices and quantities for dependence on unknown parameters. Examples of such statistical index numbers are the Laspeyres, Paasche, Divisia, Fisher ideal, and Törnqvist indexes.

The loose link between index number theory and aggregation theory was tightened, when Diewert (1976) defined the class of second-order 'superlative' index numbers. Statistical index number theory became part of microeconomic theory, as economic aggregation theory had been for decades, with statistical index numbers judged by their nonparametric tracking ability to the aggregator functions of aggregation theory.

For decades, the link between statistical index number theory and microeconomic aggregation theory was weaker for aggregating over monetary quantities than for aggregating over other goods and asset quantities. Once monetary assets began yielding interest, monetary assets became imperfect substitutes for each other, and the 'price' of monetary-asset services was no longer clearly defined. That problem was solved by Barnett (1978; 1980), who derived the formula for the user cost of demanded monetary services. Subsequently Barnett (1987) derived the formula for the user cost of supplied monetary services. A regulatory wedge can exist between the demand and supply-side user costs if non-payment of interest on required reserves imposes an implicit tax on banks.

Barnett's results on the user cost of the services of monetary assets set the stage for introducing index number theory into monetary economics.

The economic decision

Consider a decision problem over monetary assets that illustrates the capability of monetary aggregation theory. The decision problem will be defined so that the relevant literature on economic aggregation over goods is immediately applicable. Initially we shall assume perfect certainty.

Let $\mathbf{m}'_t = (m_{1t}, m_{2t}, \ldots m_{nt})$ be the vector of real balances of monetary assets during period t, let r_t be the vector of nominal holding-period yields for monetary assets during period t, and let R_t be the one-period holding yield on the benchmark asset during period t. The benchmark asset is defined to be a pure investment that provides no services other than its yield, R_t, so that the asset is held solely to accumulate wealth. Thus, R_t is the maximum holding period yield in the economy in period t.

Let y_t be the real value of total budgeted expenditure on monetary services during period t. Under simplifying assumptions for data within one country, the conversion between nominal and real expenditure on the monetary services of one or more assets is accomplished using the true cost of living index on consumer goods. But for multi-country data or data aggregated across heterogeneous regions, the correct deflator can be found in Barnett (2003; 2007. The optimal portfolio allocation decision is:

$$\text{maximize } u(\mathbf{m}_t) \qquad (1)$$

$$\text{subject to } \boldsymbol{\pi}_t' \, \mathbf{m}_t = y_t,$$

where $\boldsymbol{\pi}_t' = (\pi_{1t}, \ldots, \pi_{nt})$ is the vector of monetary-asset real user costs, with

$$\pi_{it} = \frac{R_t - r_{it}}{1 + R_t}. \qquad (2)$$

This function u is the decision maker's utility function, assumed to be monotonically increasing and strictly concave. The user cost formula (2), derived by Barnett (1978; 1980), measures the forgone interest or opportunity cost of holding monetary asset i, when the higher yielding benchmark asset could have been held.

To be an admissible quantity aggregator function, the function u must be weakly separable within the consumer's complete utility function over all goods and services. Producing a reliable test for weak separability is the subject of much intensive research by an international group of econometricians (see, for example, Jones, Dutkowsky and Elger, 2005; Fleissig and Whitney, 2003; De Peretti, 2005). Two approaches exist. One approach uses stochastic extensions of nonparametric revealed preference tests, while the other uses parametric econometric models.

Let $\mathbf{m}_t^*$ be derived by solving decision (1). Under the assumption of linearly homogeneous utility, the exact monetary aggregate of economic theory is the utility level associated with holding the portfolio, and hence is the optimized value of the decision's objective function:

$$M_t = u(\mathbf{m}_t^*). \qquad (3)$$

The Divisia index

Although equation (3) is exactly correct, it depends upon the unknown function, u. Nevertheless, statistical index-number theory enables us to track M_t exactly without estimating the unknown function, u. In continuous time, the exact monetary aggregate, $M_t = u(\mathbf{m}_t^*)$, can be tracked exactly by the Divisia index, which solves the differential equation

$$\frac{d \log M_t}{dt} = \sum_i s_{it} \frac{d \log m_{it}^*}{dt} \qquad (4)$$

for M_t, where

$$s_{it} = \frac{\pi_{it} m_{it}^*}{y_t}$$

is the i'th asset's share in expenditure on the total portfolio's service flow. In equation (4), it is understood that the result is in continuous time, so the time subscripts are a shorthand for functions of time. We use t to be the time period in discrete time, but the instant of time in continuous time. The dual user cost price aggregate $\Pi_t = \Pi(\boldsymbol{\pi}_t)$, can be tracked exactly by the Divisia price index, which solves the differential equation

$$\frac{d \log \Pi_t}{dt} = \sum_i s_{it} \frac{d \log \pi_{it}}{dt}. \qquad (5)$$

The user cost dual satisfies Fisher's factor reversal in continuous time:

$$\Pi_t M_t = \boldsymbol{\pi}_t' \, \mathbf{m}_t. \qquad (6)$$

As a formula for aggregating over quantities of perishable consumer goods, that index was first proposed by François Divisia (1925) with market prices of those goods inserted in place of the user costs in equation (4). In continuous time, the Divisia index, under conventional neoclassical assumptions, is exact. In discrete time, the Törnqvist approximation is:

$$\log M_t - \log M_{t-1} = \sum_i \bar{s}_{it} (\log m_{it}^* - \log m_{i,t-1}^*), \qquad (7)$$

where

$$\bar{s}_{it} = \tfrac{1}{2}(s_{it} + s_{i,t-1}).$$

In discrete time, we often call equation (7) simply the Divisia quantity index. After the quantity index is computed from (7), the user cost aggregate most commonly is computed directly from equation (6).

Diewert (1976) defines a 'superlative index number' to be one that is exactly correct for a quadratic approximation to the aggregator function. The discretization (7) to the Divisia index is in the superlative class, since it is exact for the quadratic translog specification to an aggregator function. With weekly or monthly monetary data, Barnett (1980) has shown that the Divisia index growth rates, (7), are accurate to within three decimal places. In addition, the difference between the Fisher ideal index and the discrete Divisia index growth rates are third order and comparably small. That third-order differential error typically is smaller than the round-off error in the component data.

Prior applications

Divisia monetary aggregates were first constructed for the United States by Barnett (1980), when he was on the staff of the Special Studies Section of the Board of Governors of the Federal Reserve System, and are now maintained by the Federal Reserve Bank of Saint Louis in its data base, called FRED (see Anderson, Jones and Nesmith, 1997, who produced the Divisia data for FRED). A Divisia monetary-aggregates data base also has been produced for the United Kingdom by the Bank of England. An overview of Divisia data maintained by many central banks throughout the world can be found in Belongia and Binner (2000; 2005) and in Barnett, Fisher and Serletis (1992), along with a survey of empirical results with that data. The most extensive collection of relevant applied and theoretical research in that area is in Barnett and Serletis (2000) and Barnett and Binner (2004).

The state of the art

The European Central Bank is implementing a multi-lateral extension of the Divisia monetary aggregates for monetary quantity and interest rate aggregation within the euro area. This aggregation is multilateral in the recursive sense that it permits aggregation of monetary service flows first within countries, then over countries. The resulting aggregation will be in a strictly nested, internally consistent manner. The multilateral extension of the theory was produced by Barnett (2003; 2007). This extension was produced under three increasingly strong sets of assumptions: (a) with the weakest being produced from heterogeneous agents theory, (b) followed by the somewhat stronger assumption of existence of a multi-lateral representative agent, and (c) finally with the strongest being the assumption of the existence of a unilateral representative agent. The intent is to move from the weakest towards the strongest assumptions, as progress is made within the European Monetary Union towards its harmonization and economic convergence goals. Since Barnett's three assumption structures are nested, construction of the data under the most general heterogeneous countries approach would continue to be valid, as the stronger assumptions become more reasonable and are attained within the euro area.

Extension of index number theory to the case of risk was introduced by Barnett, Liu and Jensen (2000), who derived the extended theory from Euler equations rather than from the perfect-certainty first-order conditions used in the earlier index number-theory literature. Since

that extension is based upon the consumption capital-asset-pricing model (CCAPM), the extension is subject to the 'equity premium puzzle' of smaller than necessary adjustment for risk. We believe that the under-correction produced by CCAPM results from its assumption of intertemporal blockwise strong separability of goods and services within preferences. Barnett and Wu (2005) have extended Barnett, Liu, and Jensen's result to the case of risk aversion with intertemporally non-separable tastes.

The extension to risk is likely to be especially important to countries whose residents hold significant deposits in foreign denominated assets, since exchange-rate risk can cause rates of return on monetary assets to be subject to non-negligible risk. With the recent trend towards financial integration in many parts of the world, exchange-rate risk is likely to grow in importance in monetary aggregation. In many countries, the largest holder of foreign-denominated deposits is the central bank itself. Within the United States, the extension to risk is highly relevant to the so called 'missing M2' episode of the early 1990s, when substitutability among small time deposits, stock funds, and bond funds produced 'puzzles'.

User cost aggregates are duals to monetary quantity aggregates. Either implies the other uniquely. In addition, user-cost aggregates imply the corresponding interest-rate aggregates uniquely. The interest-rate aggregate r_t implied by the user-cost aggregate Π_t is the solution for r_t to the equation:

$$\frac{R_t - r_t}{1 + R_t} = \Pi_t.$$

Accordingly, any monetary policy that operates through the opportunity cost of money (that is, interest rates) has a dual policy operating through the monetary quantity aggregate, and vice versa. Aggregation theory implies no preference for either of the two dual policy procedures or for any other approach to policy, so long as the policy does not violate principles of aggregation theory.

Conclusion

Aggregation theory is about measurement, and has little, if anything, to say about the choice of policy instrument, such as the funds rate or the base. But accurate measurement, through proper application of aggregation theory, has much to say about the transmission of policy, modelling of structure, and the measurement of intermediate targets (if any) and final targets.

Policies that violate aggregation theoretic principles include the following oversimplified approaches: (a) inflation targeting that targets one arbitrary consumer-good price as a final target, while ignoring all other consumer goods prices, rather than targeting the true cost-of-living index over all consumer goods prices; (b) interest rate targeting that analogously targets one arbitrary interest rate as an intermediate target while ignoring all other interest rates, rather than targeting the aggregation-theoretic interest-rate or user-cost aggregate over a weakly separable collection of monetary assets; (c) monetary quantity targeting that targets a simple-sum monetary aggregate as an intermediate target rather than the aggregator function over a weakly separable collection of monetary assets; and (d) policy simulations using money-demand or money-supply functions containing simple-sum monetary aggregates or quantity-weighted interest-rate aggregates. The measurement defects in the above four cases are unrelated to the choice of the funds rate or monetary base as an instrument of policy. Unlike intermediate targets, final targets, and variables in models, the chosen instruments of policy tend to be highly controllable, disaggregated variables, presenting few serious measurement problems.

The objective of the Divisia monetary aggregates is measurement of the economy's monetary service flow and its dual opportunity cost (user cost) and implied interest rate aggregate, not advocacy of any particular policy use of the correctly measured variables. But all uses of data are adversely affected by improper measurement, and a long series of 'puzzles' in monetary economics have been shown to have been produced by improper measurement (see, for example, Barnett and Serletis, 2000, ch. 24).

WILLIAM A. BARNETT

See also **European Central Bank; Federal Reserve System; foreign direct investment; inflation targeting; measurement; monetary and fiscal policy overview; monetary economics, history of; statistics and economics.**

Bibliography

Anderson, R., Jones, B. and Nesmith, T. 1997. Building new monetary services indexes: concepts, data and methods. *Federal Reserve Bank of St Louis Review* 79, 53–82.

Barnett, W. 1978. The user cost of money. *Economics Letters* 1, 145–49. Repinted in Barnett and Serletis (2000, ch. 1).

Barnett, W. 1980. Economic monetary aggregates: an application of aggregation and index number theory. *Journal of Econometrics* 14, 11–48. Reprinted in Barnett and Serletis (2000, ch. 2).

Barnett, W. 1987. The microeconomic theory of monetary aggregation. In *New Approaches in Monetary Economics*, ed. W. Barnett and K. Singleton. Cambridge: Cambridge University Press. Reprinted in Barnett and Serletis (2000, ch. 3).

Barnett, W. 2003. Aggregation-theoretic monetary aggregation over the euro area, when countries are heterogeneous. Working Paper No. 260. Frankfurt: European Central Bank.

Barnett, W. 2007. Multilateral aggregation-theoretic monetary aggregation over heterogeneous countries. *Journal of Econometrics* 136, 457–82.

Barnett, W. and Binner, J. 2004. *Functional Structure and Approximation in Econometrics*. Amsterdam: North-Holland.

Barnett, W., Fisher, D. and Serletis, A. 1992. Consumer theory and the demand for money. *Journal of Economic Literature* 30, 2086–119. Reprinted in Barnett and Serletis (2000, ch. 18).

Barnett, W., Liu, Y. and Jensen, M. 2000. CAPM risk adjustment for exact aggregation over financial assets. *Macroeconomic Dynamics* 1, 485–512.

Barnett, W. and Serletis, A., eds. 2000. *The Theory of Monetary Aggregation*. Amsterdam: North-Holland.

Barnett, W. and Wu, S. 2005. On user costs of risky monetary assets. *Annals of Finance* 1, 35–50.

Belongia, M. and Binner, J. 2000. *Divisia Monetary Aggregates: Theory and Practice*. Basingstoke: Palgrave.

Belongia, M. and Binner, J. 2005. *Money, Measurement, and Computation*. Basingstoke: Palgrave.

Chrystal, A. and MacDonald, R. 1994. Empirical evidence on the recent behaviour and usefulness of simple-sum and weighted measures of the money stock. *Federal Reserve Bank of St. Louis Review* 76, 73–109.

De Peretti, P. 2005. Testing the significance of the departures from utility maximization. *Macroeconomic Dynamics* 9(3), 373–97.

Diewert, W. 1976. Exact and superlative index numbers. *Journal of Econometrics* 4, 115–45.

Divisia, F. 1925. L'Indice monétaire et la théorie de la monnaie. *Revue d'Economie Politique* 39, 980–1008.

Fleissig, A. and Whitney, G. 2003. A new PC-based test for Varian's weak separability conditions. *Journal of Business and Economic Statistics* 21, 133–44.

Jones, B., Dutkowsky, D. and Elger, T. 2005. Sweep programs and optimal monetary aggregation. *Journal of Banking and Finance* 29, 483–508.

monetary approach to the balance of payments

The monetary approach to the balance of payments is an analytical formulation which emphasizes the interaction between the supply and the demand for money in determining the country's overall balance of payments position. It could be seen as an extension, to the case of an open economy, of traditional closed-economy monetary theory, which stresses the stability of the money demand function and considers the various channels through which changes in the money supply affect the economy. If changes in the money supply are not matched by equivalent changes in demand, then a stock disequilibrium arises. In responding to the stock disequilibrium, individuals alter their spending patterns. These adjustments are subject to the budget constraints which link the excess flow supply of money to the corresponding excess flow demand for goods and services. In a closed economy nominal income rises and interest rates may change so as to eliminate the disequilibrium in the money market; the increase in prices, and possibly output, in conjunction with the change in interest rates, raises the nominal demand for money to a level equivalent to the rise in the nominal money stock.

In contrast to the closed economy, the open economy has additional channels through which monetary imbalances are resolved. In the open economy changes in the money stock can arise from domestic credit creation as well as from the foreign exchange operations of the monetary authorities. As a result, the monetary approach to the balance of payments stresses that money market disequilibria are reflected not only in changes in nominal income but also in the country's overall balance of payments, as represented by changes in foreign exchange reserves. Thus the monetary approach to the balance of payments focuses on the relation among prices, output, interest rates, *and* the balance of payments.

In developing the simplest version of the monetary approach to the balance of payments, it is assumed that the country is small, fully employed, that it has a fixed exchange rate, and that there is perfect international mobility of goods and financial assets. These assumptions mean that domestic prices and interest rates equal their respective (exogenously given) world values, and that output is determined exogenously. Under such circumstances, any disequilibrium emerging from the money market is fully reflected in the balance of payments. For example, an excess supply of money arising from domestic credit expansion results in a loss of international reserves. This loss reduces the outstanding money stock to its equilibrium level consistent with the given demand. By concentrating on the direct connection between the money market and the balance of payments, rather than working through the implied changes in the goods or financial assets markets, the monetary approach distinguishes itself from other analytical approaches to balance of payments theory.

The development of the approach
The monetary approach to the balance of payments has a long intellectual history originating with the 18th-century writings of David Hume. The continuity of its development, however, was reversed for upwards of a quarter of a century by the events of the 1930s. This included the international monetary collapse of 1931 and after, and the 'Keynesian revolution'.

The modern revival of the monetary approach originated with the writings of James Meade in the early 1950s followed by Harry G. Johnson and Robert A. Mundell in the 1960s. At the same time, important contributions to the formal development of the approach were carried out, under the leadership of Jacques J. Polak at the International Monetary Fund, thereby yielding analytical foundations to the Fund's operational practices.

By the late 1960s a long series of articles, subsequently collected in Mundell (1968, 1971), Frenkel and Johnson (1976) and International Monetary Fund (1977), gave an increasing stimulus to the rapid development of theoretical and empirical work on the monetary approach. Many of the contributions are surveyed in Kreinin and Officer (1978) and in Frenkel and Mussa (1985).

Theoretical underpinnings
In order to assess the major implications of the monetary approach to the balance of payments, it is useful to present a simplified model which embodies the central characteristics of the analytical approach. The stripdown basic model considers a small, fully employed country operating under a fixed exchange rate system and assumes full integration of domestic and foreign goods and capital markets. Perfect arbitrage determines the prices of domestic commodities and of financial assets.

Because of its concentration on the money market, the monetary approach to the balance of payments involves the explicit specification of the money supply process and of a demand for money function. The supply of money (M^s) is the product of the stock of high-powered money (H) and the money supply multiplier (m) where the latter reflects the behaviour of asset-holders and the banking system:

$$M^s = mH. \tag{1}$$

By definition, the stock of high-powered money (the liabilities of the monetary authorities) is equal to the domestic currency value of the stock of international reserves, eR (where e is the exchange rate, defined as the domestic-currency price of foreign exchange, and R is the foreign currency value of international reserves), and the domestic asset (net of liabilities) holdings of monetary authorities (D):

$$H = eR + D. \tag{2}$$

The demand for real money balances is specified as a positive function of real income and a negative function of the opportunity cost of holding money. This opportunity cost is measured by the yield on alternative financial assets, usually represented by the rate of interest. The demand for money in nominal terms (M^d) can be written as:

$$M^d = Pf(Y, i) \tag{3}$$

where P denotes the domestic price level, Y is the level of domestic real income, and i stands for the domestic nominal interest rate.

Money market equilibrium implies that $M^s = M^d$. Under the assumptions of the simplified model, the mechanism responsible for maintaining equilibrium operates through changes in international reserves. Accordingly, using equations (1), (2), and (3) the (endogenously determined) stock of international reserves can be specified as:

$$R = g(P, Y, i, m, D). \qquad (4)$$

Equation (4) represents the key relationship implied by the monetary approach to the balance of payments under a fixed exchange rate system. The assumed specifications of M^s and M^d imply that an increase in real income and in (world) prices raises the stock of international reserves while an increase in the rate of interest, in the money multiplier, and in the net domestic assets of the central bank reduces the stock of international reserves. These changes in the stock of international reserves are reflected in balance of payments surpluses or deficits. The size of the income and interest rate effects depends on the elasticities of the money demand function. In this simple model a rise in the money supply brought about by an open-market purchase (an increase in D) is completely offset by a corresponding fall in R.

An important implication of the analysis is that under a fixed exchange rate regime the nominal money supply is no longer within the direct control of the monetary authorities and becomes an endogenous variable of the system. The monetary authorities, however, do retain control over the volume of domestic credit, which is one of the sources of money creation. The distinction between high-powered money and its domestic credit component becomes crucial: the central bank controls the latter but not the former. Given a rate of growth in the demand for money, an equivalent growth in the supply can be obtained by an appropriate increase in domestic credit. However, if the rate of domestic credit expansion differs from the growth in demand, then the difference between the two is made up by changes in net foreign assets, brought about through a balance of payments surplus or deficit.

Extensions and analytical applications

The simplified model presented in the previous section may be seen as a prototype of the monetary approach to the balance of payments and can also be regarded as a representation of its long-run equilibrium characteristics, when all adjustments have taken place. In these circumstances, monetary imbalances tend to affect primarily the balance of payments. However, if the degree of international capital mobility is not high and if the share of non-tradeable goods in GNP is relatively high, then the speed of adjustment to monetary disturbances is reduced. In the short run, therefore, monetary imbalances also affect prices, output, and interest rates, and the relative importance of these effects depends on various factors such as the nature of exchange rate management, the degree of openness of the economy in both the goods and the capital markets, the proportion of tradeable and non-tradeable goods, the degree of resource utilization, the degree of nominal and real wage rigidities, and so forth. Many of those elements have been specifically modelled

within the framework of the monetary approach, and the effects of considering different sets of alternative assumptions have been carefully analysed. A central feature of most of the short-term extensions of the basic model is that the excess demand in the commodity market, caused by excess supply in the money market, results in a combination of price increases (which reduce the real value of the outstanding nominal money stock) and balance of payments deficits (which, by depleting the level of international reserves, reduce the level of the nominal money stock). These changes take place in addition to income changes, which in the short run depend on the degree of resource utilization and on the degree to which the public has anticipated the monetary expansion. The effects of monetary disequilibrium fall more heavily on the domestic price level and on the domestic interest rate, and less on the balance of payments, the lower the degree to which the economy is integrated into the world markets for goods and capital. Therefore, the effects of monetary imbalances on the domestic price level and interest rate are stronger the larger are the relative shares of nontraded goods and financial assets, and the more prohibitive are import tariffs, quantitative restrictions and exchange controls.

Further extensions of the basic framework have considered the effects of exchange rate changes on prices and on the balance of payments. In contrast with other approaches to balance of payments analysis (notably the elasticities approach), the monetary approach stresses that the effects of a once-and-for-all exchange rate adjustment in a small economy are transitory. A devaluation (a rise in e) raises the price of internationally tradeable goods. This increase in price reduces the real value of the nominal money stock and, in order to restore money market equilibrium, a balance of payments surplus is generated as foreign exchange reserves flow into the country. As monetary equilibrium is restored, the flow of reserves stops.

The negative relationship between the rate of expansion of domestic credit and the rate of change of foreign exchange reserves implied by the monetary approach does not necessarily imply a unidirectional causality. In fact, it is possible that central banks manipulate their domestic assests in order to sterilize the impact of exogenous changes in foreign reserves on the domestic supply of money. Assume, for example, a reserve-gaining country which desires to avoid an increase in its money supply. The central bank will tend to counteract the inflow of reserves by reducing its credit to commercial banks or its lending to the government. The required volume and the effects of these sterilization operations could easily be analysed within the framework of the monetary approach, if the parameters underlying the money demand function and the money supply process were known.

The effects of income growth and of external shocks can also be examined within the same set-up. As shown by equation (4), changes in the level of income have a direct impact on the balance of payments through their effect on the demand for money. Therefore, an acceleration in a country's rate of growth, by increasing the demand for liquidity, tends to improve the balance of payments provided that domestic credit policy does not expand accordingly. Similarly, external shocks, such as terms of trade changes, which affect domestic activity, also affect the balance of payments through the same mechanism. In particular, a negative external shock which reduces real income results in a once-and-for-all reduction in the demand for money and (in the absence of domestic credit policy) results in foreign exchange reserves.

The basic model can also be used to determine the effects of commercial policies such as an import tariff. A tariff affects the balance of payments by raising the domestic price level and thereby, by lowering the real value of the outstanding money stock. These changes are likely to induce an excess demand for money which, other things being equal, results in an inflow of international reserves. Similar principles can be used to analyse the effects of other forms of taxation and commercial policies.

Finally, the model could be generalized to the 'large-country' case. When the country is not small relative to the rest of the world, one needs to take account of the impacts of its policy and economic behaviour on the world price of tradeable goods and on the world rate of interest. While the monetary mechanism of balance of payments adjustment is more complicated for the large-country case, the basic elements of this mechanism are essentially the same. Starting from a situation in which the domestic nominal money supply is below its long-run equilibrium level and, correspondingly, the foreign money supply is above its long-run equilibrium level, reserve flows associated with trade imbalances gradually move the economic system to long-run equilibrium by raising the domestic money supply and reducing the foreign money supply to their respective long-run equilibrium levels. As in the case of the small country, the essential ingredient underlying this adjustment process is the relationship through which a deficiency in a country's money supply relative to its long-run equilibrium level leads to an excess of domestic income over domestic expenditure which implies a trade surplus which brings an inflow of foreign exchange reserves and a gradual restoration of money balances to their long-run equilibrium level.

In the two-country world, it remains true that a given initial divergence of a country's money supply will ultimately lead to a cumulative payments surplus and change in reserves just equal to this initial divergence, assuming there is no change in the non-reserve assets of central banks.

Overview

In general, a proper analysis of the balance of payments emphasizes the budget constraint imposed on the country's international spending and views the various accounts of the balance of payments as the 'windows' to the outside world, through which the excesses of domestic flow demands over domestic flow supplies, and of excess domestic flow supplies over domestic flow demands, are cleared. Accordingly, surpluses in the trade account and the capital account, respectively, represent excess flow supplies of goods and securities, and a surplus in the money account reflects an excess domestic flow demand for money. Consequently, in analysing the money account, or more familiarly the rate of increase or decrease in the country's international reserves, the monetary approach focuses on the determinants of the excess domestic flow demand for or supply of money.

Although it concentrates on the money account of the balance of payments, the monetary approach should, in principle, give an answer not different from that provided by a correct analysis in terms of the other balance of payments accounts. The surplus or deficit in the goods account (more generally the current account) measures the extent to which the economy's income is greater than consumption ('absorption') and the economy is therefore accumulating claims on future income (assets) from abroad or vice versa. By virtue of the budget constraint, the sum of the deficit on the capital account (net purchase of foreign securities) and the surplus on the money account equally represents the accumulation of foreign assets (decumulation if negative). The so-called 'absorption approach' to the balance of payments, associated with Sidney Alexander (1952), emphasizes the rate of accumulation or decumulation of foreign assets (securities plus money). In so doing, it differs from the 'elasticity approach', which emphasizes relative-price mechanisms.

The monetary approach selects for emphasis a subset of the spectrum of foreign assets whose accumulation or decumulation is emphasized by the absorption approach. The main reasons for this are, firstly, that the accumulation of foreign assets does not necessarily imply the accumulation of money through the balance of payments – it may mean the opposite, as for example when a monetary policy of lowering interest rates leads domestic asset-holders to move their funds from domestic to foreign securities. Secondly, the monetary authorities, in their role as stabilizers of the exchange rate in a fixed rate system, are concerned with what causes the stock of international reserves to change and how to prevent such changes. Thirdly, the monetary authorities, as the ultimate source of domestic money, control the rate of change of the domestic credit component of the monetary base – the other component being international reserves. The assumption that the residents of the country have a demand for money which depends on variables at least in part different from those that determine the quantity of domestic credit extended by the banking system, or alternatively, that the rate of change of money demanded (the rate of hoarding) is independent of the rate of change of the domestic credit source component of the monetary base, implies that the money account of the balance of payments is influenced directly by monetary policy.

MARIO I. BLEJER AND JACOB A. FRENKEL

See also **absorption approach to the balance of payments; elasticities approach to the balance of payments; international finance; purchasing power parity; specie-flow mechanism.**

Bibliography

Alexander, S.S. 1952. Effects of a devaluation on a trade balance. *IMF Staff Papers* 2, June, 263–78.

Frenkel, J.A. and Johnson, H.G., eds. 1976. *The Monetary Approach to the Balance of Payments*. London: Allen & Unwin; Toronto: University of Toronto Press.

Frenkel, J.A. and Mussa, M.L. 1985. Asset markets, exchange rates and the balance of payments. In *Handbook of International Economics*, Vol. II, ed. R.W. Jones and P.B. Kenen. New York: Elsevier.

International Monetary Fund. 1977. *The Monetary Approach to the Balance of Payments*. Washington, DC: International Monetary Fund.

Kreinin, M. and Officer, L. 1978. *The Monetary Approach to the Balance of Payments: A Survey*. Princeton Studies in International Finance No. 43, Princeton: Princeton University Press.

Meade, J.E. 1951. *The Theory of International Economic Policy*, Vol. I: The Balance of Payments, Oxford: Oxford University Press.

Mundell, R.A. 1968. *International Economics*. New York: Macmillan.

Mundell, R.A. 1971. *Monetary Theory*. Pacific Palisades, Cal.: Goodyear Publishing Company.

monetary business cycle models (sticky prices and wages)

Since the earliest analysis of the monetary transmission mechanism by pre-eminent classical economists of the 18th and early 19th century, sticky prices and wages have been identified as playing a central role (Humphrey, 2004). The classical economists believed that prices adjusted gradually to a change in the nominal money stock, so that monetary changes could exert substantial short-run effects on output. Nominal wages were regarded as particularly slow to change, and thus helped account for gradual price adjustment by mitigating short-run pressures on factor costs.

The classical economists and their successors used this framework both to guide recommendations about policy and to evaluate alternative monetary regimes. For example, the belief that prices would respond slowly to a monetary contraction led Thornton and Ricardo to recommend a gradualist approach to deflation.

Early Keynesian models, and some critiques

A major contribution of Keynes (1936) and prominent successors such as Hicks to understanding the monetary transmission mechanism consisted in developing an explicit theoretical framework expressed in terms of equilibrium conditions in goods and asset markets. This IS–LM framework was of great value in illuminating the channels through which monetary shocks affected interest rates and output. However, the assumption of fixed prices and wages was a major shortcoming. It was eventually supplanted by the famous 'Phillips curve' relation linking nominal wage inflation to the unemployment rate, or variants relating price inflation to the output gap:

$$p(t) - p(t-1) = b * (y(t) - y(t)^*) \quad b > 0 \tag{1}$$

where $p(t)$ is (the log of) the price level, $y(t)$ output, $y(t)^*$ potential output, and b is a parameter. The Phillips curve filled a missing link in earlier 'fixed price' IS–LM analysis by making it feasible to trace the dynamic effects of a monetary shock on prices and output. Thus, an initial rise in output following a monetary expansion boosts prices via (1), which in turn causes real balances and output to revert gradually to pre-shock levels. However, the Phillips curve had weak theoretical underpinnings, so that there was little economic rationale for what determined the sensitivity of prices to the output gap (that is, 'b' in (1)), for the activity variable(s) driving price dynamics, and for how inflation might be influenced by expectations.

A series of remarkable critiques beginning with the analysis of Friedman (1968) and Phelps (1968) provided impetus for developing more theoretically coherent models of price and wage dynamics. These authors argued that the Phillips curve should be augmented so that actual inflation depended directly on inflation expectations in addition to real activity. In this framework, output could be pushed above potential only through surprising private agents by keeping inflation above the level that they had forecast in previous periods. Since such surprises could not continue indefinitely, there could be no long-run trade-off between inflation and output: expansionary monetary policy would eventually raise expected inflation, resulting in higher inflation with no output stimulus.

Shortly thereafter, Lucas (1972) derived an 'expectations-augmented' Phillips curve in a clearly specified rational expectations model. Lucas adopted a signal extraction framework in which agents partly misinterpreted aggregate nominal shocks as shocks to the relative price of their own output good (due to limited information), and responded by adjusting their supply. Consistent with Friedman and Phelps, Lucas's model implied that aggregate output varied positively with the unanticipated component of inflation (with anticipated inflation exerting no real effects). But because unanticipated inflation was linked explicitly to a 'rational expectations' forecast error in Lucas's model – which would be expected to die away quickly as agents learned about the nature of underlying shocks – monetary shocks could exert only transient effects on output. This posed a serious challenge to traditional Keynesian models by suggesting that their ability to derive persistent effects in response to a monetary injection relied on ad hoc assumptions about price dynamics or expectations formation. Moreover, because only unanticipated changes in inflation affected output, Lucas's supply relation implied that any predictable policy was as good as any other (the 'policy ineffectiveness' proposition). This point, emphasized by Sargent and Wallace (1975), contrasted sharply with the activist policy stance that emerged from typical Keynesian models.

Monetary transmission in optimization-based MBC models

Since the mid-1990s a new generation of optimization-based MBC models has emerged that can generate 'traditional' Keynesian implications, but in a framework consistent with rational expectations and rigorous microfoundations. Roughly speaking, these new MBC models graft features that can induce sluggish price and/or wage adjustment onto an underlying real business cycle (RBC) model. (Blanchard, 2000, and Taylor, 1999, provide comprehensive surveys of the foundations of modern optimization-based MBC models, which were laid in a series of important contributions spanning several decades.)

To highlight salient features of the modern approach, it is helpful to examine a specific characterization of price-setting that has been utilized extensively in the literature. This relation, often called the 'New Keynesian Phillips curve (NKPC)', takes the form

$$p(t) - p(t-1) = B * E(t) \left[p(t+1) - p(t) \right] + b * (y(t) - y(t)^*) \quad (2)$$

where $E(t)$ is the conditional expectation operator, and B is the discount factor.

Following Calvo (1983) and Yun (1996), the NKPC can be derived in a framework consistent with intertemporal optimization. Firms are assumed to behave as monopolistic competitors in the output market, and face downward-sloping demand curves for their distinctive products. Firms face a dynamic decision problem, because they are constrained to set a price that remains fixed in nominal terms over some random duration of time (referred to as the 'contract period', since firms are assumed to meet all demand at this fixed price until allowed to adjust). When a firm receives a signal enabling it to adjust its price, the firm resets it based on estimates of current and future marginal costs expected to prevail over the contract period. Because not all firms can change their price in a given period, price-setting is

staggered – similar to the decentralized price-setting in actual economies. (See STICKY WAGES AND STAGGERED WAGE SETTING for a discussion of the staggered contracts model.)

From a qualitative perspective, an MBC model in which prices are determined by the NKPC provides a conventional Keynesian account of the monetary transmission mechanism. Thus, a monetary shock increases nominal spending and, since the price level adjusts gradually, real output exhibits a persistent increase (in contrast to the transient real effects in Lucas's model). But as time passes, a larger proportion of firms receive a signal that allows them to raise their price in response to higher projected marginal costs. At an aggregate level, these relative price adjustments translate into a higher price level, which eventually restores real balances and output to pre-shock levels.

A major virtue of the microfounded approach is that it illuminates how the monetary policy rule and various structural features of the economy affect the transmission of nominal (and real) shocks. First, given that price adjustment is influenced directly by inflation expectations (as in (2)), monetary surprises have smaller effects on current inflation to the extent that the policy rule is expected to keep future inflation near target (that is, 'anchors' inflation expectations). Second, while the sensitivity of price inflation to the output gap ('b') clearly plays a key role in determining how quickly prices and output adjust to a monetary injection, this parameter is itself determined by features of the microeconomic environment. Quite intuitively, the parameter 'b' varies inversely with the mean duration of price contracts, so that longer contracts imply slower price adjustment and more persistent effects on output. But 'b' also depends on the responsiveness of firm-level marginal costs to the aggregate output gap, which in turn hinges on features of the specific microeconomic environment, including assumptions about factor mobility, capital utilization, and preferences. While some assumptions constrain 'b' to be large, a considerable literature has emerged showing how various 'real rigidities' such as firm-specific capital and labour can account for a low 'b' (even with fairly short-lived contracts); an insightful overview is provided in Woodford (2003). Such real rigidities appear important in allowing macro models to account for persistent output effects, while remaining consistent with disaggregate price data suggesting that firms change prices frequently (Bils and Klenow, 2004).

The NKPC in (2), in which the output gap enters as the activity variable, is derived under the assumption that wages are fully flexible. But, as noted above, there is a long precedent in macroeconomics suggesting that sticky wages play an important role in the transmission process. As shown by Erceg, Henderson and Levin (2000), wage rigidity may be modelled in a framework isomorphic to that rationalizing price rigidity, with households acting as monopolistic suppliers of differentiated labour services.

Christiano, Eichenbaum and Evans (2005) have shown that a model that incorporates both wage and price rigidity can account remarkably well for the estimated dynamic effects of a monetary shock on output, prices, and interest rates. The presence of wage rigidity damps the rise in marginal cost due to a positive monetary injection, helping account for estimated persistence in the response of output. Moreover, a model including both types of rigidities can help account for the observed acyclicality of the real wage. By contrast, sticky prices alone imply too much procyclicality in the real wage, while sticky wages alone (in the spirit of the classical economists and Keynes) imply too much counter-cyclicality.

Real shocks and alternative policies in MBC models

Given that monetary policy is widely perceived to have been much more stable since the mid-1980s, the literature has focused greater attention on how policy should respond to real shocks. Modern optimization-based MBC models are useful in this regard, because they provide a coherent framework for examining the transmission of real shocks in the presence of sticky wages and prices, and for assessing the role of monetary policy in affecting the economy's responses.

The presence of nominal rigidities can markedly affect the economy's responses to real shocks. Following Gali (1999), this can be illustrated by contrasting the effects of a persistent rise in technology in an RBC model (in which prices and wages are flexible) with the effects in an MBC model in which prices adjust according to eq. (2). For simplicity, it is assumed that money demand takes the interest-inelastic form $M = P*Y$, and that the monetary authority holds the nominal money stock constant. In either model, money market equilibrium implies that output can expand only if prices fall proportionally. But as prices can drop instantaneously in the RBC model, the money supply rule is irrelevant in determining the real effects of the shock. Thus, the technology shock immediately boosts employment (as the substitution effect dominates the income effect), and the (percentage) jump in output exceeds the magnitude of the shock. By contrast, prices fall gradually in the MBC model, so that output is constrained to rise slowly given the fixed money stock. With prices determined by the NKPC, negative output gaps are required to induce prices to fall, consistent with employment remaining persistently below its pre-shock level.

As in the case of nominal shocks, the effects of real shocks may be highly sensitive to underlying features of the microeconomic framework, including those that determine the speed of price or wage adjustment. Thus, features that affect 'b' in the NKPC can markedly change how real shocks impact the economy. In the case of the technology shock, additional price sluggishness would translate into a smaller short-run expansion in output and greater employment contraction. Similarly, the inclusion of wage stickiness can markedly affect the responses to technology shocks. For example, while the NKPC derived under the assumption of flexible wages (eq. (2)) implies that price inflation stabilization also keeps output at potential, the same policy could generate large output gap fluctuations if wages were sticky as well as prices.

Modern MBC models have also been applied fruitfully to normative issues. Optimal policy is derived by maximizing an objective function subject to the model's behavioural equations. Importantly, the objective function used in ranking alternative policies is typically derived from the utility functions of the economy's households (Woodford provides an extensive treatment).

A compelling message of this normative literature is that a well-designed policy must take account of its ability to influence inflation through an expectations channel. Thus, a policymaker acting 'under discretion' in an environment where inflation was determined by (2) would act as if the only margin on which to trade in devising a policy involved current inflation and output. However, such a 'discretionary' policy is suboptimal, because it fails to take account of its influence on the expected inflation term in (2). The analysis of Clarida, Gali and Gertler (1999) and Woodford shows that rules that are devised to take account of their influence on future expected inflation can perform much better in maximizing social welfare than discretionary policies that take future inflation as outside the central bank's control. For example, these authors show that well-designed policies can reduce substantially the impact of an adverse cost-push shock on current inflation (relative to the effects under discretion) by creating the perception that future policy will bring inflation back quickly to baseline.

Woodford emphasizes that the optimal monetary policy rule in an environment with forward-looking price-setting exhibits history dependence, so that current monetary policy actions depend on past inflation and activity. This inertial character reflects that the optimal policy rule is derived in a framework in which future policy is expected to take full account of its influence on inflation expectations at earlier dates, much as optimal tax rules recognize their impact on previous investment decisions. Consistent with this history dependence, Woodford shows that it is generally optimal for monetary policy to reverse spikes in inflation above its target value, rather than follow the conventional wisdom of allowing 'bygones to be bygones'. Interestingly, this analysis provides strong support for some form of price level targeting – as recommended by Fisher and Keynes nearly a century ago – with the twist that the modern justification highlights the role it can play in optimally anchoring inflation expectations.

CHRISTOPHER J. ERCEG

See also **IS–LM in modern macro; monetary transmission mechanism; Phillips curve (new views); real rigidities; sticky wages and staggered wage setting.**

Bibliography

Bils, M. and Klenow, P. 2004. Some evidence on the importance of sticky prices. *Journal of Political Economy* 112, 947–85.

Blanchard, O. 2000. What do we know about macroeconomics that Fisher and Wicksell did not? *Quarterly Journal of Economics* 115, 1375–409.

Calvo, G. 1983. Staggered prices in a utility-maximizing framework. *Journal of Monetary Economics* 12, 383–98.

Christiano, L., Eichenbaum, M. and Evans, C. 2005. Nominal rigidities and the dynamic effects of shocks to monetary policy. *Journal of Political Economy* 113, 1–45.

Clarida, R., Gali, J. and Gertler, M. 1999. The science of monetary policy: a new Keynesian perspective. *Journal of Economic Literature* 37, 1661–707.

Erceg, C., Henderson, D. and Levin, A. 2000. Optimal monetary policy with staggered wage and price contracts. *Journal of Monetary Economics* 46, 281–313.

Fisher, I. 1920. *Stabilizing the Dollar.* Norwood, MA: Norwood Press.

Friedman, M. 1968. The role of monetary policy. *American Economic Review* 58(1), 1–17.

Gali, J. 1999. Technology, employment, and the business cycle: do technology shocks explain aggregate fluctuations? *American Economic Review* 89, 249–71.

Humphrey, T. 2004. Classical deflation theory. *Federal Bank of Richmond Economic Quarterly* 90, 11–32.

Keynes, J. 1936. *The General Theory of Interest, Employment, and Money.* London: Macmillan.

Lucas, R. 1972. Expectations and the neutrality of money. *Journal of Economic Theory* 4, 103–24.

Phelps, E. 1968. Money–wage dynamics and labor market equilibrium. *Journal of Political Economy* 76, 678–711.

Sargent, T. and Wallace, N. 1975. Rational expectations, the optimal monetary instrument, and the optimal money supply rule. *Journal of Political Economy* 83, 169–83.

Taylor, J. 1999. Staggered wage and price setting in macroeconomics. In *Handbook of Macroeconomics*, ed. J.B. Taylor and M. Woodford. Amsterdam: North-Holland.

Woodford, M. 2003. *Interest and Prices.* Princeton: Princeton University Press.

Yun, T. 1996. Nominal price rigidity, money supply endogeneity, and business cycles. *Journal of Monetary Economics* 37, 345–70.

monetary business cycles (imperfect information)

Business cycle theories based on incomplete information start from the premise that key economic decisions on pricing, investment or production are often made on the basis of incomplete knowledge of constantly changing aggregate economic conditions. As a result, decisions tend to respond slowly to changes in economic fundamentals, and small or temporary economic shocks may have large and long-lasting effects on macroeconomic aggregates.

Incomplete information theories have been popular in particular for explaining sluggish price or wage adjustment in response to monetary shocks. At the heart of this theory lies the assumption that firms or households only pay attention to a relatively small number of indicators regarding conditions in markets relevant to their own activities, but they may not acquire information more broadly about aggregate economic activity. With imprecise information about these aggregate conditions, it takes the firms some time to sort out temporary from permanent changes, or nominal from real disturbances. Prices then respond with a delay to changes in nominal spending, and monetary shocks may have significant effects on real economic activity in the intervening periods – despite the fact that firms have the opportunity to constantly readjust their decisions.

This basic idea was proposed first by Phelps (1970) and formalized by Lucas (1972). In Lucas (1972), economic agents produce in localized markets, in which they observe the market-clearing price at which they can sell their output. This price is affected both by aggregate spending shocks and by market-specific supply shocks. Under perfect information, quantities adjust in response to local supply shocks, but not prices, and prices respond to aggregate spending shocks, but not quantities. With imperfect information, agents are unable to filter out the magnitudes of the aggregate and market-specific shocks from the observed prices in the short run. Output then responds positively to price changes and spending shocks in the short run, but not in the long run, once agents have been able to sort out the spending shocks from the market-specific supply shocks.

Lucas (1972) formulated this idea in a rational expectations market equilibrium model, in which agents' expectations are fully Bayesian, and the resulting output responses are optimal. His model also includes stark assumptions about the nature of local versus aggregate market interactions, as well as the nature of shocks (monetary versus real, demand versus supply, aggregate versus market-specific) and the information to which firms have access.

Importantly, the model lacks a natural internal amplification mechanism: the extent of incomplete nominal adjustment depends almost entirely on the degree of informational incompleteness. Subsequent work has tried to address these issues, for example by introducing richer information structures. Townsend (1983) considers an investment model in which firms get to observe how much some of the other firms invest. Therefore, they need to form forecasts about each others' beliefs – forecasting the forecasts of others. This leads to a complicated infinite regress problem, whereby a firm's current investment level depends on its observation of other firms' past investment, which in turn depended on observations about past investment… Townsend showed that this type of problem does not admit a simple finite-dimensional recursive structure. As a result, firms must draw inference about all past realizations of shocks simultaneously, leading to an infinite-dimensional filtering and fixed point problem, with no easily characterized solution.

These and other important technical and computational hurdles effectively imposed limitations on the complexity and economic realism of the early incomplete information models. Moreover, the model is open to the criticism that if incomplete information is a major source of business cycle fluctuations, then there seems to be an important societal benefit to making the relevant information publicly available to everyone. In part because of these difficulties, economists have, from the mid-1980s, turned their attention to New Keynesian sticky price theories that emphasize the role of adjustment and coordination frictions in price-setting. (Among others, see Calvo, 1983; Blanchard and Kiyotaki, 1987.)

Recently, the incomplete information theories have made a comeback, which can be traced to two factors. First, technological progress has made models such as Townsend (1983) computationally tractable. Second, new game-theoretic results regarding equilibrium analysis with a lack of common knowledge and heterogeneity in beliefs, as well as insights borrowed from the sticky price literature regarding the role of real rigidities and pricing complementarities (Ball and Romer, 1990) have enabled us to paint a much richer picture of the adjustment dynamics resulting from incomplete information models. The empirical performance of these new incomplete information models, however, still remains to be seen.

In the remainder of this article I provide a unified exposition of the main ideas behind the incomplete information theories, from the original contributions to the more recent renewal. I also attempt to chart out some of the challenges that lie ahead. This is a lively and active area of research, with many open questions and few definite answers.

A canonical framework

Consider the following model, which is based on the New Keynesian models of monopolistic competition. There is a large number of firms, indexed by $i \in [0,1]$. In each period, each firm sets its (log-)price $p_t(i)$ equal to its expectation of a target price p_t^*, $p_t(i) = E(p_t^* | \mathscr{I}_t^i)$, where $\mathscr{I}_t^i$ denotes the information set of firm i at date t, that is all signals on which it can condition its pricing decision. p_t^* is characterized as

$$p_t^* = k y_t + p_t, \qquad (1)$$

where $p_t = \int p_t(i)\, di$ denotes the average of the firms' pricing decisions, y_t denotes the aggregate real output in period t, relative to its trend level that would prevail with complete information, and $k > 0$ measures the response of optimal pricing decisions to real output. A firm's ideal relative price $p_t^* - p_t$ is determined by real output deviations from trend.

We augment this pricing rule by a quantity equation, $y_t + p_t = m_t$, where m_t denotes nominal spending. Combining the two, we find

$$p_t^* = k m_t + (1 - k) p_t. \qquad (2)$$

Nominal spending m_t is driven by exogenous shocks; for simplicity, assume that $m_t = m_{t-1} + \varepsilon_t$, where $\{\varepsilon_t\}$ is i.i.d. white noise.

Each firm's target price is therefore a linear combination of the exogenous shocks and the prices set by the other firms. If $k \in (0,1)$, prices are complementary, that is, an increase in the average price level implies that each firm has an incentive to raise its own price. The parameter value of k depends on the substitution elasticity between the firms' products, the firms' returns to scale parameter in the technology, and the Frisch elasticity of labour supply.

To complete the model description, we need to specify each firm's information set $\mathscr{I}_t^i$ – this is where different incomplete information theories vary. An equilibrium of this model requires that prices satisfy the optimality condition $p_t(i) = E(p_t^* | \mathscr{I}_t^i)$, taking into account that p_t^* itself depends on the aggregate price level.

Common information

Suppose first that all firms have identical information sets, $\mathscr{I}_t^i = \mathscr{I}_t$. Then, they will set identical prices, equal to $p_t(i) = p_t = E(m_t | \mathscr{I}_t)$. This reflects the implications of the original Lucas model that prices adjust to the common expectation of the underlying shocks. When information is incomplete, firms will only learn gradually about m_t, prices adjust slowly, and monetary surprises have real effects: y_t is determined directly by the discrepancy between the realized and the expected value of m_t. However, if the available information on which these expectations are based is sufficiently precise, then $E(m_t | \mathscr{I}_t)$ cannot be far from the true value of m_t. As discussed above, the real effects of monetary shocks are bounded by the degree of informational incompleteness – as firms have better information, their prices track m_t more closely, and monetary shocks have smaller real effects.

Heterogeneous beliefs, but independent strategies

A similar conclusion emerges when firms have different information sets, but their target prices do not respond to the other firms' decisions ($k = 1$). Each firm's price is set equal to its expectation of the spending shock

$p_t(i) = E(m_t|\mathscr{I}_t^i)$, and the average price adjusts according to the average expectation $p_t = \bar{E}(m_t) = \int E(m_t|\mathscr{I}_t^i)\,di$ of the spending shock. Once again, if firms are sufficiently well informed, their pricing decisions will on average not be far from the nominal spending shock, which implies little delay in price adjustment and only small real output effects.

Heterogeneous beliefs and complementary strategies

Suppose now that instead $k \in (0,1)$, so that there are complementarities in pricing decisions. Averaging the pricing equation, and substituting forward, firm i's equilibrium price is given by

$$p_t(i) = k \sum_{s=0}^{\infty} (1-k)^s E\left[\bar{E}^{(s)}(m_t)|\mathscr{I}_t^i\right] \quad (3)$$

where $\bar{E}^{(s)}(m_t)$ denotes the s-order average expectation of m_t, or the average expectation of the average expectation of … (repeat s times) … of m_t. A firm's optimal price is therefore given as a geometrically weighted average of higher-order expectations – a firm needs to forecast not only the realized shock but also the other firms' expectations of the shock, the other firms' expectations of the other firms' expectations of the shock, and so on.

If the firms all had identical information, the law of iterated expectations would simply collapse the right-hand side above into the common first-order expectation of m_t. The model thus derives its interest from the fact that with heterogeneous information, higher-order expectations respond differently to new information than first-order expectations about m_t.

The following example illustrates this point and serves also to derive the main results of this model. Suppose that all firms observe m_{t-1} exactly, but only a fraction λ (the *informed*) gets to observe m_t. Then, $\bar{E}(m_t) = \lambda m_t + (1-\lambda)m_{t-1}$, but the second order average expectation is $\bar{E}^{(2)}(m_t) = \lambda[\lambda m_t + (1-\lambda)m_{t-1}] + (1-\lambda)m_{t-1} = \lambda^2 m_t + (1-\lambda^2)m_{t-1}$. By iteration, the s-order average expectation of m_t is $\bar{E}^{(s)}(m_t) = \lambda^s m_t + (1-\lambda^s)m_{t-1}$. The average price is

$$p_t = k \sum_{s=0}^{\infty} (1-k)^s \bar{E}^{(s+1)}(m_t)$$

$$= m_{t-1} + \frac{k\lambda}{1-(1-k)\lambda}(m_t - m_{t-1}). \quad (4)$$

Two important conclusions emerge. First, note that $\frac{k\lambda}{1-(1-k)\lambda} < \lambda$. The informed firms whose prices may react to m_t take into account that the uninformed firms won't respond, which in turn reduces their incentives to adjust prices. Therefore, while incomplete information serves

as the initial source of sluggish price adjustment, the complementarity and the heterogeneity in beliefs dampen the response of prices far beyond what the initial degree of informational incompleteness would suggest. To illustrate the strength of this amplification effect, consider the following numerical example: suppose that $k = 0.15$ (as in standard parametrizations of New Keynesian sticky price models), and that half the firms are informed. Then, the contemporaneous response of average prices is $\frac{k\lambda}{1-(1-k)\lambda} \approx 0.13$, that is a one per cent increase in nominal spending leads to only a 0.13 per cent increase in prices, and a 0.87 per cent increase in real output – despite the fact that half of the firms actually observe the increase in nominal spending and are hence able to respond to it!

Second, this amplification can be large, even if the degree of informational incompleteness is small. If λ is close to 1, almost all firms exactly observe the current realization m_t. Nevertheless, if k is close to 0, that is if there is a strong pricing complementarity, they still won't respond to the monetary shock. The presence of only a few uninformed firms is therefore enough to radically overturn the conclusions of the complete information model.

These two observations apply quite generally, once firms have heterogeneous beliefs. They form the central insight of the new incomplete information theories. In Mankiw and Reis (2002), heterogeneous beliefs result because, in any given period, only a fraction of firms observe new information. This generalizes the above example to allow for richer adjustment dynamics. In Woodford (2002), all firms observe a conditionally independent idiosyncratic signal x_t^i of the current realization of m_t in each period. The resulting inference problem is more complicated but can be solved numerically. Again, the response of prices to monetary shocks is significantly dampened by the fact that firms do not share in common information, yet their pricing decisions are complementary.

The role of public information

Hellwig (2002) provides a simplified version of Woodford (2002), providing closed-form solutions to a general class of information structures. This simplified model also accommodates the presence of additional public sources of information such as central bank announcements. Besides dampening the response to idiosyncratic private signals, the complementarity in prices generates overreaction to public news. Public announcements thus speed up price adjustment and reduce the real effects of monetary shocks, but the noise in public news creates an additional source of volatility, which in some cases may increase rather than decrease real output fluctuations. (Similar results are derived by Amato and Shin, 2003, for Woodford's model, and by Ui, 2003, in the original Lucas island model.)

Looking ahead

These new contributions have provided promising insights into the amplification and propagation mechanisms of incomplete information models. But they also abstract from important modelling issues that need to be addressed before a comprehensive quantitative evaluation becomes possible.

So far, much of the analysis is based on a stylized price-setting model that captures the essence of pricing complementarities as described above, without deriving them within a fully specified dynamic general equilibrium model. This short-cut is not without problems. First, the lack of a proper context of markets makes it difficult to interpret these propagation results. Presumably in a market firms obtain some information about price and quantity variables – so far, this is not formally modelled.

Second, the assumption that firms are heterogeneously informed implies that other frictions must be present – in particular, the extent to which information about fundamental shocks can be inferred from publicly observable prices must be limited, implying that the asset market must be incomplete. But then, one faces the problem of isolating the effects of informational heterogeneity from the effects of other market imperfections. In Lorenzoni, (2006) for instance, a precautionary savings motive generates a multiplier effect in household spending, which is further amplified by the presence of heterogeneous information.

Third, there is an issue of interpretation. At this point, there exist several different interpretations regarding the source of the differences in beliefs across firms, and they may lead to radically different model conclusions. In Mankiw and Reis (2002), firms update their information only infrequently, and in the intervening periods set prices on the basis of outdated information; Reis (2006) further develops this idea on the basis of menu costs in updating decisions. Woodford (2002) instead bases his model on the notion of 'rational inattention', developed by Sims (2003; 2006a). Sims argues that decision makers only have a finite capacity to process new information, which constrains the quality of the signals they observe in any given period. Heterogeneity in beliefs then arises naturally through the idiosyncratic noise in each individual's information processing channel (see Sims, 2006b, for further discussion of the resulting conceptual and modelling issues). A third interpretation suggests that individuals are Bayesian, but access to information is limited – for example, firms observe the demand for their own products, but not the demand for competitors' products. If each firm is subject to idiosyncratic, as well as common shocks, then an information structure much like the above with idiosyncratic private signals emerges. On the other hand, firms also observe market prices, which generates a source of common information.

Finally, all these models treat the information structure as an exogenous primitive. In reality, firms and households have access to overwhelming amounts of information, and information processing becomes a matter of choice, given the existing constraints and trade-offs. By and large, the effects of information costs and choices and the strategic interaction that results from these choices remains unexplored. Preliminary developments in this direction include Mackowiak and Wiederholt (2005) and Hellwig and Veldkamp (2005). In Mackowiak and Wiederholt, firms need to allocate a fixed information processing capacity between firm-specific and aggregate variables. Hellwig and Veldkamp explore how the pricing complementarities that are relevant for business cycle implications also shape incentives for information acquisition.

In summary, the most important issue that remains to be resolved is the grounding of new incomplete information theories within a fully specified model of goods and asset markets, with special emphasis on the origins of the informational frictions. Beyond that, the new incomplete information theories raise many intriguing questions, which merit further attention, or have already been addressed to some extent: for example, Ball, Mankiw and Reis (2005) reconsider the role of monetary policy, and Morris and Shin (2002), Hellwig (2005) and Angeletos and Pavan (2004; 2007) discuss the welfare effects of information disclosures. Finally, the combination of new evidence on the cross-sectional and business cycle properties of expectations (Mankiw, Reis and Wolfers, 2004) and new micro-level data on price adjustments (Bils and Klenow, 2004) promises to provide an interesting avenue for evaluating the empirical performance of the model's cross-sectional and business cycle implications.

CHRISTIAN HELLWIG

See also **information aggregation and prices; Lucas, Robert; monetary business cycle models (sticky prices and wages); monetary transmission mechanism; Phelps, Edmund.**

Bibliography

Amato, J. and Shin, H.S. 2003. Public and private information in monetary policy models. Working Paper No. 138, Bank of International Settlements.

Angeletos, G.-M. and Pavan, A. 2004. Transparency of information and coordination in economies with investment complementarities. *American Economic Review* 94, 91–8.

Angeletos, G.-M. and Pavan, A. 2007. Efficient use of information and social value of information. *Econometrica* 75, 1103–42.

Ball, L., Mankiw, G. and Reis, R. 2005. Monetary policy for inattentive economies. *Journal of Monetary Economics* 52, 703–25.

Ball, L. and Romer, D. 1990. Real rigidities and the non-neutrality of money. *Review of Economic Studies* 57, 183–203.

Bils, M. and Klenow, P. 2004. Some evidence on the importance of sticky prices. *Journal of Political Economy* 112, 947–85.

Blanchard, O. and Kiyotaki, N. 1987. Monopolistic competition and the effects of aggregate demand. *American Economic Review* 77, 647–66.

Calvo, G. 1983. Staggered prices in a utility maximizing framework. *Journal of Monetary Economics* 12, 383–98.

Hellwig, C. 2002. Public announcements, adjustment delays and the business cycle. Discussion paper, University of California, Los Angeles.

Hellwig, C. 2005. Heterogeneous information and the welfare effects of public information disclosures. Discussion paper, University of California, Los Angeles.

Hellwig, C. and Veldkamp, L. 2005. Knowing what others know: coordination motives in information acquisition. Discussion paper, University of California, Los Angeles and New York University.

Lorenzoni, G. 2006. A theory of demand shocks. Discussion paper, Massachusetts Institute of Technology.

Lucas, R. 1972. Expectations and the neutrality of money. *Journal of Economic Theory* 4, 103–24.

Mackowiak, B. and Wiederholt, M. 2005. Optimal sticky prices under rational inattention. Discussion paper, Humboldt University Berlin.

Mankiw, G. and Reis, R. 2002. Sticky information versus sticky prices: a proposal to replace the new Kaynesian Phillips curve. *Quarterly Journal of Economics* 117, 1295–328.

Mankiw, G., Reis, R. and Wolfers, J. 2004. Disagreement about inflation expectations. In *NBER Macroeconomics Annual 2003*. Cambridge, MA: MIT Press.

Morris, S. and Shin, H.S. 2002. The social value of public information. *American Economic Review* 92, 1521–34.

Phelps, E. 1970. Introduction: the new microeconomics in employment and inflation theory. In *Microeconomic Foundations of Employment and Inflation Theory*. New York: Norton.

Reis, R. 2006. Inattentive producers. *Review of Economic Studies* 73, 1–29.

Sims, C. 2003. Implications of rational inattention. *Journal of Monetary Economics* 50, 665–90.

Sims, C. 2006a. Rational inattention: beyond the linear-quadratic case. *American Economic Review* 96, 158–63.

Sims, C. 2006b. Rational inattention: a research agenda. Discussion paper, Princeton University.

Townsend, R. 1983. Forecasting the forecasts of others. *Journal of Political Economy* 91, 546–88.

Ui, T. 2003. A note on the Lucas model: iterated expectations and the non-neutrality of money. Discussion paper, Yokohama National University.

Woodford, M. 2002. Imperfect common knowledge and the effects of monetary policy. In *Knowledge, Information and Expectations in Modern Macroeconomics*, ed. P. Aghion et al. Princeton: Princeton University Press.

monetary cranks

The history of ideas tends to concentrate on the successful ideas – ideas which appear to have been precursors of the orthodoxy of the day. As a result, ideas which had large followings but which are later considered 'cranky' tend to be ignored. This is especially true of the ideas of those who we can loosely call the monetary cranks.

These persons have placed money at the centre of their economic analysis, have usually placed major blame for society's evils on alleged financial conspiracies and bankers' ramps – on the 'Money Power' – and have advocated a variety of monetary experiments. Over the past century particularly, such concerns can be found in all Western countries, on both the Left and the Right of politics. This article can only provide the broadest of overviews of the voluminous literature in this field.

Opposition to financial oligarchies has a long history. The Medicis of 15th-century Florence aroused suspicion and hostility. In *Lombard Street* (1873), Walter Bagehot described the streets around the Bank of England in London as 'by far the greatest combination of power and economic oligarchy that the world has ever seen'. But it was the fiery late-19th-century American populist, William Jennings Bryan, who popularized the term 'Money Power' (cited in Douglas, 1924, Preface):

> The Money Power preys upon the nation in times of peace and conspires against it in times of adversity. It is more despotic than monarchy, more insolent than autocracy, more bureaucratic than bureaucracy. It denounces, as public enemies, all who question its methods, or throw light upon its crimes. It can only be overthrown by the awakened conscience of the nation.

Monetary parables have a long history, ranging from David Hume's 1752 hope that 'by miracle, every man in Great Britain should have five pounds slipped into his pocket in one night', through to Milton Friedman's 1969 postulated helicopter miracle, whereby dollars would be dropped from the heavens. (These are discussed in Clayton, Gilbert and Sedgwick, 1971, p. 6.) Over the past three centuries, however, actual monetary experiments have taken two main forms: attempts to overcome economic fluctuations by means of adjusting note issue; and attempts to achieve a more stable price level through the formulation and adoption of a new or different monetary standard.

Such experiments were first undertaken in the North American colonies. The first paper money issued by any government in Europe or the Americas was printed by Massachusetts to pay the wages of its soldiers engaged in conflict with the French in Canada at the end of the 17th century. Other New England colonies followed suit and a competitive depreciation of the individual currencies followed. The French Canadians even used playing cards as a form of money.

In 1721, a Mr Wise of Chebacco, Massachusetts, concerned at the depreciation of the notes admonished his fellow colonists (cited in Lester, 1939):

> Gentleman! You must do by your Bills, as all Wise Men do by their Wives; Make the Best of them... Wise Men Love their Wives; and what ill-conveniences they find in them they bury; and what Vertues they are inrich't with they Admire and Magnifie. And thus you must do by your Bills for there is not doing without them; if you Divorce or Disseize yourselves of them you are undone.

Hence the American colonies developed the practice of adjusting note issue to stimulate business or countervail a recession. They believed that there is a very close relationship between money, prices and business conditions and that the appropriate note issue would greatly stimulate business. Their efforts were made easier by the fact that there was no bank-issued money.

In England, after the Napoleonic Wars, the first great debate about monetary reform occurred, with persons such as Joseph Lowe, John Rooke and Poulett Scrope, proposing a 'managed currency', the volume of which was to be controlled according to changing prices in such a way as to keep the price level steady. Similarly, Henry Thornton's *Paper Credit* (1802) argued that contraction or expansion of the money supply had real effects on the level of economic activity. In the 1840s, Thomas Attwood claimed that if Britain's coinage 'were accommodated to man and man to our coinage then world would be capable of multiplying its production to an unlimited extent'. However, David Ricardo's and John Stuart Mill's failure to appreciate that credit expansion might stimulate the level of economic activity, rather than just increase prices, dominated economic thinking for the rest of the 19th century (see Viner, 1937).

This opened the door for the monetary cranks, who argued that money did matter. Their main inspiration came from the underconsumptionist tradition. A number of authorities have emphasized that underconsumptionist literature is difficult to categorize (for example, Schumpeter, 1954, p. 740; Haberler, 1937, ch. 5; Bleaney, 1976, ch. 1). Still, the argument that there is a permanent deficiency of purchasing power produced all kinds of suggestions as to how such a deficiency could be remedied.

In the interwar period, underconsumptionist ideas fell on particularly receptive ears. Many persons, particularly those concerned with high unemployment, were prepared to believe that the schemes of the monetary cranks would increase demand and hence create jobs. The quantity of pamphlet literature on monetary reform over this era is thus enormous. A common argument was that because the First World War was financed by printing money, the same method could be used to eliminate unemployment. Opposition to the gold standard usually accompanied this argument.

Academic discussion of monetary matters was disparate and disputatious (see, for example the famous debate between F.A. von Hayek and P. Sraffa in the *Economic Journal*, March–June 1932) and this was seized upon by the monetary reformers, who sought to penetrate what they claimed were the obfuscations of the academics. They also pointed to the fact that discussion of money and banking tended to be confined to tendentious tomes written for bank employees, while economic theory textbooks devoted little space to arguments against Say's Law.

Major C.H. Douglas was probably the best-known reformer in English-speaking countries in this era (see Douglas, 1924) but there were many, many others who wrote on monetary reform. These included: A.H. Abbati, who attracted the interest of John Maynard Keynes and D.H. Robertson; Sir Normal Angel, whose set of cards *The Money Game* was widely used in high schools in Britain and the US; W.T. Foster and W. Catchings, who were probably the best known US reformers; and Frederick Soddy of Oxford University, who, after being awarded the Nobel Prize for chemistry, set out to solve the money problem inspired by John Ruskin's *Unto this Last* (1862) and an Australian invention. Soddy argued that the gold standard could be replaced with a machine based on the automatic totalizator at Sydney's Randwick Racecourse (Soddy, 1931). Cole (1933) discusses some of this literature.

Strangely, Schumpeter (1954) contains no reference to Douglas but he does mention (pp. 1090–91) G.F. Knapp's *The State Theory of Money* (1924), which promoted similar ideas and had considerable impact in interwar Germany. For example, in the dying days of the Weimar Republic, at the suggestion of H.J. Rustow and W. Lavtenbach of the Ministry of Economics, interest-bearing tax certificates were issued in lieu of treasury bills and exchequer bonds. Employers were given these certificates if they employed additional employees and reduced the wages of existing employees (see Rustow, 1978).

With the Keynesian revolution and the increased emphasis given to monetary theory by academic economists in recent decades, the monetary cranks have largely disappeared from public debate, although underconsumptionist ideas will probably have supporters while ever there is unemployment.

Any explanation of the appeal of these ideas over generations would have to invoke sociology and psychology. Such ideas found strong support because they enabled persons to impress their peers with their apparent understanding of economics, even though they had no formal training in the discipline. They offered the false hope that there were simple solutions to the complexities of modern economic life. They also transcended party political allegiances – similar passages about 'credit slavery' and 'Shylocks' can be found in Hitler's *Mein Kampf* and left-wing pamphlets of the same era. A very wide range of individuals can be opposed to private banks and the 'Money Power' without their opposition leading to more sophisticated political analysis. In fact, as the history of populism shows, 'Funny Money' beliefs provided a kind of ideological release valve.

The history of ideas contains numerous examples of the power of the phrase-monger. The simpler the panacea, the greater the chance the agitator will have of attracting a following. As the Chartist agitator Ernest Jones once advised (cited in Martin and Rubinstein, 1979, p. 43): 'We say to the great minds of the day, come among the people, write for the people and your fame will live forever.'

DAVID CLARK

Bibliography

Angell, N. 1936. *The Money Mystery: An Explanation for Beginners*. London: Dent. (*The Money Game*, a set of cards for teaching purposes, was sold in conjunction with this book.)

Bleaney, M. 1976. *Underconsumption Theories: A History and Critical Analysis*. London: Lawrence & Wishart.

Clayton, G., Gilbert, J.C. and Sedgwick, R., eds. 1971. *Monetary Theory and Policy in the 1970s*. London: Oxford University Press.

Cole, G.D.H. 1933. *What Everybody Wants to Know about Money: A Planned Outline of Monetary Problems*. London: Victor Gollancz.

Douglas, C.H. 1924. *Social Credit*. London: Eyre & Spottiswoode.

Durbin, E.F.M. 1934. *Purchasing Power and Trade Depression*. London: Chapman & Hall.

Haberler, G. 1937. *Prosperity and Depression*. Cambridge, MA: Harvard University Press.

Lester, R.A. 1939. *Monetary Experiments: Early American and Recent Scandinavian*. Princeton: Princeton University Press.

Martin, D. and Rubinstein, D., eds. 1979. *Ideology and the Labour Movement*. London: Croom Helm.

Rustow, H.J. 1978. The economic crisis of the Weimar Republic and how it was overcome. *Cambridge Journal of Economics* 2, 409–21.

Schumpeter, J.A. 1954. *A History of Economic Analysis*. London: George Allen & Unwin.

Soddy, F. 1931. *Money versus Man*. London: Elkin Mathews & Marrot.

Viner, J. 1937. *Studies in the Theory of International Trade*. London: George Allen & Unwin.

monetary economics, history of

Origins of monetary economics

As with so much else in the Western tradition, theorizing about the role of money can be traced back to Plato and Aristotle in the fourth century BCE, although they may have drawn on pre-Socratic philosophers whose works survive, if at all, only in fragments. In his *Republic* (1974), Plato remarked that money was a symbol devised to make exchange easier. He disapproved of gold and silver as money, preferring a currency that would have value only internally, not in external commerce. The analysis in Aristotle's *Nicomachean Ethics* (1996) and *Politics* (1984) of what constitutes just exchange led Aristotle to a more systematic discussion of a medium of exchange. His account of the functions of money, and of the properties that suit a commodity such as gold or silver to be the medium of exchange, as well as his use of the myth of Midas to distinguish between gold and wealth, influenced comparable presentations by Nicolas Oresme in about 1360 (Oresme, de Sassoferrato and Buridan, 1989), Adam Smith (1776), and, through Smith, any number of 19th-century textbooks (see Menger, 1892; Monroe, 1923). Barter might be the most basic form of exchange, but it involves accepting goods one does not wish to consume in order to make a further exchange for what is desired. Aristotle noted the convenience of a generally accepted medium of exchange in reducing the number of transactions required. He saw the convenience of stating prices in terms of the medium of exchange, and that, if a commodity is to serve as a medium of exchange, it must also be a store of value, retaining purchasing power between being received and being spent (but he did not mention the function of money as a standard of deferred payment). Precious metals provided a suitable medium of exchange because of being homogenous, divisible, portable, and sufficiently scarce to a have a high value relative to their weight, although that value could change. Unlike Plato, Aristotle viewed the weight and purity of the precious metals as the source of the purchasing power of money, with coinage just saving the inconvenience of having to weigh and assay the metals at every transaction.

The quantity theory of money, described by David Laidler (1991b) as 'always and everywhere controversial' and by Mark Blaug as 'the oldest surviving theory in economics' (Blaug et al., 1995), holds that the price level (the inverse of the purchasing power of money) depends on how large the stock of money is compared with the demand for real money balances, with the direction of causation running from money to prices (Hegeland, 1951). The quantity theory originated in the 16th century, when Martin de Azpilcueta Navarro in Salamanca in 1556 and Jean Bodin in France in 1568 identified the inflow of silver from the Spanish colonies of Mexico and Upper Peru as the cause of the rise in prices and depreciation of silver throughout Europe, a phenomenon now known as the 'price revolution' (Grice-Hutchinson, 1952; O'Brien, 2000). In contrast to the recognition by Navarro and Bodin of the inverse relationship between the quantity of the precious metals and their purchasing power, contemporaries such as the Seigneur de Malestroit had attributed rising prices of commodities to the debasement of various national coinages. The astronomer

Copernicus had remarked earlier that money usually depreciates when it is too abundant (Grice-Hutchinson, 1952, p. 34), but Navarro and Bodin went beyond such passing insights to formulate a theory they could use to explain the observed trend of commodity prices. Later research has shown that the 16th century quadrupling of prices was also due in part to the growing output of central European silver mines and to an increase in the velocity of circulation of money as systems of payment and communication evolved, notably the use of bills of exchange.

Mercantilists also took note of the inflow of precious metals from Spain's conquest in the New World, viewing this gold and silver as the 'sinews of war' with which Spain could pay armies in Europe. Although both alchemy and seizure of the Spanish treasure fleet were attempted (the physicist Isaac Newton was both Master of the Royal Mint and an avid alchemist), mercantilists such as Thomas Mun advocated interventionist government policies to achieve a surplus of exports over imports as the way to bring gold and silver into a country that lacked its own mines. Mercantilists held that increased circulation of gold and silver in a country would both increase national power and stimulate real economic activity (Viner, 1937; Vickers, 1959). Isaac Gervaise (1720), Richard Cantillon (2001, written c. 1730 and published posthumously in 1755), and, most fully and forcefully, David Hume (1752) used the quantity theory of money to develop the specie-flow mechanism of international payments adjustment that rendered such mercantilist schemes futile. An increase in gold and silver circulating in a country, whether due to colonial conquests, discovery of new mines, or a trade surplus engineered by tariffs on imports and bounties on exports, would increase spending. Although Hume recognized that one immediate, temporary effect of such increased spending would be to stimulate production (see Humphrey, 1993) in due course prices and wages would rise, making domestic goods more expensive in relation to foreign goods. This would reduce exports and increase imports, eliminating the trade surplus, so that the only lasting result would be the misallocation of resources caused by tariffs, bounties and quotas. For Adam Smith (1776), a small open economy such as that of Scotland took prices under the gold standard as given by the world market, so the balance of payments adjustment would take place without any change in the relative price of foreign and domestic goods. An excess supply of money in a country would directly cause more imports and more exportable goods to be purchased domestically (and the contrary in a country with an excess demand for money) unless the world's supply of monetary metal was distributed across countries in proportion to their demand for money. Humphrey (1993) and Laidler (2003, ch. 1) show that Smith's analysis bore a closer resemblance than that of Hume to the modern monetary approach to the balance of payments.

From Aristotle and the Bible onwards, payment of interest on loans had been condemned as usury on the grounds that it was unnatural for gold ('barren metal') to breed and that interest violated justice (exchange of equal values), as the amount of money repaid exceeded the initial loan. Cantillon, Hume, A.R.J. Turgot, and Jeremy Bentham argued for the legitimacy of an interest rate set by market forces of supply and demand, with Turgot invoking time preference to point out that the amount of money lent and the larger amount of money repaid represented the same present value. Contrary to his general stand against government intervention, Adam Smith (1776) endorsed legal limits on interest to prevent high-risk lending for speculation and reckless consumption, and was rebuked for inconsistency by the young Bentham (West, 1997).

Monetary controversies in classical economics

Monetary theory was advanced by two British debates, the Bullionist Controversy, which surrounded the suspension of the convertibility of Bank of England notes into gold from 1797 to 1821, and the clash between the Banking School and the Currency School in the 1840s leading up to and following the Bank Act revision that separated and regulated the Bank of England's Issue Department (whose liabilities were bank notes, with gold held in reserve) and Banking Department (whose liabilities were deposits, with Bank of England notes held in reserve). During the suspension of convertibility during the Napoleonic Wars, Henry Thornton (1802) and, from 1809 onwards, David Ricardo (1810) argued the high price of bullion and foreign exchange showed that the Bank of England had engaged in over-issue of bank notes, raising commodity prices and depreciating the pound sterling (Fetter, 1965; Marcuzzo and Rosselli, 1991). Christiernin (1761) had made a similar argument in Sweden, but appears not to have been known in Britain. Thornton was the leading figure on a House of Commons Select Committee on the High Price of Gold Bullion in 1810 that adopted this view in the Bullion Report, but the directors of the Bank of England persuaded the full House not to act on the committee's report. The directors, invoking the authority of Adam Smith, held that they could not have been guilty of any inflationary overissue of notes beyond what the needs of trade required as long as they issued notes only by discounting bills of exchange created by genuine commercial transactions, rather than financial speculation. This version of the real bills doctrine ignored Smith's assumption that bank notes were convertible into gold upon demand, so that any increase in the quantity of notes sufficient to depress their value below their gold par would cause the excess notes to be redeemed. Without convertibility as a constraint on overissue, the demand for bills would be unbounded as long as the discount rate was less than the prevailing rate of profit. The distinction between real and fictitious bills also failed to recognize that the length of time a bill was discounted need not correspond to the length of time goods were in process (Mints, 1945; Laidler, 2003; Davis, 2005).

The depression that accompanied the end of the Napoleonic Wars and Britain's subsequent return to the gold standard stimulated a debate over the possibility of a general glut of commodities. Thomas Robert Malthus and J.C.L. Simonde de Sismondi attributed the depression to an insufficiency of effective demand. Malthus's argument was acclaimed by John Maynard Keynes a century later, although, unlike Keynes, Malthus did not distinguish between a decision to save and a decision to invest (see Keynes's 1933 essay on Malthus). Ricardo and Jean-Baptiste Say upheld Say's (or James Mill's) Law of Markets, denying the possibility of a general glut of commodities or an insufficiency of aggregate effective demand, since a commodity was offered for sale only with the intention of acquiring the means to purchase some other commodity, not with intent to hoard money, which is only a medium of exchange (Say was not quite as unambiguous as James Mill). Ricardo and Say recognized that unemployment would occur during the adjustment to a major change in the mix of commodities demanded, as the end of the Napoleonic Wars curtailed military and naval spending and as the purchasing power of money changed: Ricardo was prepared to accept restoration of gold convertibility at the depreciated parity, to avoid the price deflation associated with going back to the pre-war parity, and Say endorsed public works to employ those who would otherwise be jobless during the transition period. But, according to Ricardo, Say and James Mill, such distress resulted from a temporary mismatch between the mix of commodities produced and those demanded, with excess supply in some markets and excess demand in others, not from generalized excess supply.

Throughout the 19th century, classical economists such as John Stuart Mill struggled to formulate an acceptable version of the law of markets that would be stronger than what Oskar Lange later labelled Say's Equality but weaker than what Lange called Say's Identity (Corry, 1962; Sowell, 1972; Baumol, 1977; 1999; Davis, 2005). Say's equality, which held that at equilibrium prices the value of excess demand sums to zero across all markets except that for money, is a trivial implication of the market-clearing equilibrium condition that at market-clearing prices supply equals demand in each market. Say's identity, which held that at any prices the value of excess demand always sums to zero across all markets except money, implies (when combined with the summation of individual budget constraints) that money demand always equals the money supply at any prices, which leaves the absolute price level (the inverse of the purchasing power of money) indeterminate. In the 1870s, Leon Walras reformulated Say's Law as what Lange termed Walras's Law: the value of aggregate excess demand summed over all markets (including money) is identically zero, from the summation of individual budget constraints (the net value of each individual's transactions is at most zero, since people must pay for their purchases) plus local non-satiation (so that no one is willing to throw away purchasing power). Robert Clower (1984), seeking to understand Keynes's rejection of Say's Law of Markets, argued that Walras's Law only applies to notional demands, not to quantity-constrained effective demands when markets do not clear (in Keynes's case, the labour market): if workers cannot sell all the labour they wish at the prevailing wage rate, then the quantity of labour they cannot sell multiplied by the wage rate that they would have received should not be included in their budget constraint for demanding goods.

Currency School adherents (for example, J.R. McCulloch, G.W. Norman and Lord Overstone), whose ideas shaped Sir Robert Peel's Bank Act of 1844, urged that, beyond maintaining convertibility, the Bank of England should conduct its operations so that a mixed metallic and paper currency would fluctuate in the same way that a purely metallic currency would. Building on Ricardo's presentation of the quantity theory of money and the price specie-flow mechanism, the Currency School wished the central bank to follow a stabilizing policy that would prevent gold outflows, rather than waiting for such international cash drains to bring about adjustment. The Currency School attributed the banking crises of 1825, 1832 and 1836–37 to monetary mismanagement by the Bank of England, which could have regulated the volume of coin and notes in circulation so as to stabilize prices. In contrast, Banking School writers such as Thomas Tooke and John Fullarton, drawing on Thornton, emphasized the endogeneity of the total volume of credit (financial instruments convertible into gold), of which bank notes were only a small part (Fullarton, 1836; 1845; Fetter, 1965; Arnon, 1991; Cassidy, 1998; Skaggs, 1999). Karl Marx also held that the volume of money adjusted to satisfy the equation of exchange (de Brunhoff, 1976). Elements of both Currency School and Banking School positions appeared in the writings of John Stuart Mill. The Banking School thought that the volume of credit was as likely to respond to changes in prices as to cause them, and so did not share the Currency School view of the banking system as the initiator of credit cycles. The Banking School prescription was for the Bank of England to hold a bullion reserve large enough to ride out temporary disturbances in credit and international payments. While the Currency and Banking Schools differed on the appropriate policy for a central bank, another group of writers, including Henry Dunning Macleod (1855), James Wilson of The Economist and Jean-Gustave Courcelle-Seneuil, opposed having a central bank with a legally protected dominant position and special privileges. Instead, they advocated a system of free banking, with the market valuing the notes of competing banks, a proposal revived by Vera Smith (1936) and later by

Friedrich Hayek (1976), who had been her dissertation adviser. Walter Bagehot's *Lombard Street* (1873) established the monetary orthodoxy, emerging from the Currency School–Banking School debates, on how the central bank should manage the discount rate to maintain convertibility and its role as a lender of last resort to preserve the liquidity of the banking system, rather than simply acting in the interests of its shareholders.

The golden age of the quantity theory

In studies collected posthumously in Jevons (1884), William Stanley Jevons used index numbers, with equal weights on different commodities, to show the rise in prices following the gold rushes in California in 1849 and Australia in 1851, as did John Elliot Cairnes. Commodity prices tended downwards from 1873 to 1896 as the world's demand for real money balances grew faster than its money supply, a decline halted by the introduction of the cyanide process for extracting gold from low-grade ores and by gold discoveries in South Africa and the Klondike. Together with the return of the United States to gold convertibility of the dollar in 1873 after the issue of inconvertible greenbacks during the Civil War, this deflation contributed to bimetallist agitation that reached its peak in William Jennings Bryan's presidential campaign in 1896, in which Bryan spoke against 'crucifying mankind on a cross of gold'. The bimetallists argued that monetizing silver as well as gold would raise the price by increasing the quantity of money, and this would have lasting real benefits. This led hard-money, classical economists such as J. Laurence Laughlin of the University of Chicago to associate the quantity theory of money with claims of long-run non-neutrality (Skaggs, 1995). In place of the quantity theory, Laughlin (1903) derived the value of money from the convertibility into gold, whose value depended on its cost of production, a view which David Glasner (1985; 2000) shows had figured alongside the quantity theory in classical political economy. The quantity theorists David Kinley (1904), Edwin Kemmerer (1907) and Irving Fisher (with Harry G. Brown, *The Purchasing Power of Money*, 1911, in Fisher, 1997, vol. 4) responded by seeking to show, contrary to Laughlin and his Chicago associates, that exogenous changes in the quantity of money explained the behaviour of prices (given the trend in money demand), and, contrary to the bimetallists, that money is neutral in the long run. These quantity theorists extended earlier statements of the equation of exchange by Simon Newcomb (to whom Fisher dedicated his 1911 book) and Sir John Lubbock. Fisher allowed currency (M) and bank deposits (M′) to have different velocities of circulation, restating the equation of exchange as MV+M′V′ = PT, where T is an index of the volume of transactions and P is the price level. To use the equation of exchange to make the case that the changing money supply explained the observed movements of US prices (rather than just having the

equation as a tautology defining the velocity of circulation) required independent measures of the velocity of circulation. To estimate V, Fisher persuaded 116 people at Yale (including 113 male undergraduates) to keep daily records of their spending and cash balances. For V′, the velocity of circulation of bank deposits, Fisher used linear interpolation between the estimates from two empirical studies by David Kinley counting all bank clearings in the United States for a day in 1896 (for the Comptroller of the Currency) and a day in 1910 (for the National Monetary Commission). From an Austrian perspective, Ludwig von Mises (1935) objected to the aggregative reasoning of the quantity theorists, arguing that an index number of the price level gives a distorted picture of how agents respond to prices.

Systematically developing earlier remarks by John Stuart Mill and Alfred Marshall and an article by Jacob de Haas, Irving Fisher argued in *Appreciation and Interest* (1896, in Fisher, 1997, vol. 1) that that nominal interest is the sum of real interest and the expected rate of inflation, so that only unanticipated changes in the purchasing power of money change the real interest rate and redistribute wealth. Contrary to bimetallist claims, expected inflation or deflation would have no real effects. Fisher's 1896 analysis included uncovered interest arbitrage parity (the difference between nominal interest rates in two currencies is the expected rate of change of the exchange rate) and the expectations theory of the term structure of interest rates (variations in nominal interest on loans of different duration reflects expectations of the time-path of prices). But from *The Purchasing Power of Money* onwards, while continuing to insist on the long-run neutrality of money, Fisher argued that money was not neutral during transition periods (of up to ten years), as nominal interest adjusted only slowly to monetary shocks, and that the 'so-called "business cycle"' was really a 'dance of the dollar'. While Ralph Hawtrey (1919) and Fisher advanced monetary theories of economic fluctuations, many economists in the late 19th and early 20th centuries, from Jevons on sunspot cycles to Joseph Schumpeter on clusters of innovations, emphasized real shocks and truly periodic cycles of varying lengths such as Juglar, Kondratiev and Kitchin cycles. Fisher's article, 'A Statistical Relationship between Unemployment and Price Level Changes' (1926) correlated unemployment with a distributed lag of past price level changes and was reprinted in the *Journal of Political Economy* in 1973 as 'Lost and Found: I Discovered the Phillips Curve'. Fisher correlated nominal interest with a distributed lag of price changes (a version of adaptive expectations) to show the slow adjustment of nominal interest and inflation expectations (*The Theory of Interest*, 1930), resulting from what he termed *The Money Illusion* (the title of his 1928 book), the widespread tendency to think in nominal rather than real terms.

Bimetallism foundered on its insistence on fixing the relative price of gold and silver, at 15 or 16 ounces of silver per ounce of gold. As the relative market valuation changed, due to changing marginal costs of production or shifts in non-monetary demand for precious metals, one of the two metals would disappear from circulation and its coins be melted down. Alfred Marshall's (1887) suggestion of symmetallism, a unit of value consisting of a quantity of gold plus a quantity of silver (reprinted in Pigou, 1925), was more practical, but did not seem so to bimetallists or the general public. Marshall's tentative proposal to peg the monetary value of a basket of two commodities instead of just one (gold) marked a step towards a monetary policy of targeting the price level (or its rate of change) rather than the exchange rate with gold. Like Jevons (1884), Marshall suggested voluntary indexation, with contracts made in terms of a 'standard unit of purchasing power', which Marshall argued would reduce cyclical fluctuations (Laidler, 1991a, pp. 172–8). Irving Fisher and Senator Robert Owen attempted unsuccessfully to get such a price level target into the Federal Reserve Act of 1913. The Federal Reserve Act, influenced by J.L. Laughlin and his student H. Parker Willis, instead adopted a fixed price of gold and, inconsistent with that goal, a version of the real bills doctrine that the volume of currency and bank credit should vary pro-cyclically with the needs of trade. As Knut Wicksell (1915) and others objected, Fisher compromised his compensated dollar plan by disguising it as a version of the gold standard, with the gold weight of the dollar changed periodically to peg the dollar price of a basket of commodities, a system vulnerable to speculative attacks. By 1935, when Fisher endorsed open market operations under a floating exchange rate to achieve a price-level target, he had lost his audience.

While Fisher distinguished nominal and real interest rates, Knut Wicksell (1898; 1915) stressed the distinction between the market rate of interest, set by the banking system, and the natural rate of interest that would equilibrate desired investment and saving (Laidler, 1991a; Humphrey, 1993). As long as the market rate is less than the natural rate, entrepreneurs can profit by borrowing and investing, causing total spending to increase and prices to rise. Such a cumulative inflation would continue until the growth of loans and deposits and a drain of cash out of the banking system reduced the ratio of reserves to bank deposits, forcing banks to raise the market rate to restore their liquidity. Wicksell pointed out that in a cashless economy, with only bank money used for transactions and no reserves held by banks, there would be no such force to automatically halt a cumulative inflation or deflation, and stability would depend on deliberate action by the monetary authority to match the market rate to the changing natural rate. To explain observed price movements, Wicksell emphasized real shocks that changed the natural rate as initiating fluctuations. Wicksell's two-rate model greatly influenced the Stockholm School (Karin Kock, Erik Lindahl, Erik Lundberg, Gunnar Myrdal, Bertil Ohlin) and John

Maynard Keynes's *Treatise on Money* (1930). Recent financial innovations, diminishing the role of money as a means of payment and as an asset, have renewed attention to Wicksell's analysis of a cashless economy in which the monetary authority pursues stabilization by setting the interest rate rather than the quantity of money. The title of Michael Woodford's (2003) *Interest and Prices* deliberately echoes the title of Wicksell's (1898) *Interest and Prices* and a change of emphasis from Don Patinkin's (1965) *Money, Interest and Prices*. The 'Taylor rule', the influential monetary policy rule proposed by John Taylor, amounts to an attempt to set the market rate of interest equal to a Wicksellian natural rate that changes over time and is not directly observable.

Cambridge monetary theory and the Keynesian revolution

In his lectures at Cambridge, evidence to official inquiries (collected by Keynes after Marshall's death as Marshall, 1926), and manuscripts from the 1870s that half a century later formed the basis of Marshall (1923), Alfred Marshall expounded the quantity theory of money in a version that emphasized that desired cash balances are proportional to nominal income, $M = kPY$ (see Robertson, 1922; Marget, 1938–42; Eshag, 1963; Bridel, 1987; Laidler, 1999 on Cambridge monetary economics). The Cambridge coefficient k is the reciprocal of V, the income velocity of circulation of money in the equation of exchange, so that the two versions of the quantity theory are formally equivalent, although Marshall's disciples A.C. Pigou and J.M. Keynes claimed that Cambridge discussions of the determinants of k were more choice-theoretic and less mechanical than Fisher's discussion of the determinants of velocity. Related contributions emerged from both traditions: Fisher was the first to correctly state the marginal opportunity cost of holding real money balances (1930), Keynes the first to explicitly write money demand as a function of income and nominal interest (*General Theory*, 1936). Writing in a time of floating exchange rates and Continental European hyperinflations after the First World War, the young Keynes, in *A Tract on Monetary Reform* (1923), extended Marshall's monetary economics to analyse inflation as a tax on holding money and government bonds, the social costs of inflation (both distortions from incorrectly anticipated inflation and higher transactions costs as expected inflation reduces the demand for real money balances), and covered interest arbitrage parity (the spread between spot and forward exchange rates is the difference between nominal interest in two currencies). Keynes opposed Britain's return to the gold standard at the pre-war parity in 1925 as entailing domestic deflation and, until wages declined, unemployment. Keynes's position recalled Ricardo's preference for restoring convertibility as a depreciated parity after the Napoleonic Wars. D.H. Robertson (1926), deeply Marshallian although a student of Keynes and Pigou rather than directly of Marshall, examined the effect of price level changes on saving and investment, notably how an increase in the price level causes forced saving ('induced lacking') to restore real money balances (Laidler, 1999).

Reflecting on Britain's stagnation after the return to gold and on the worldwide Great Depression of the 1930s, Keynes's *General Theory of Employment, Interest and Money* (1936) denied the automatic restoration of full employment in a monetary economy after a negative demand shock. Keynes lumped together economists from Ricardo to Marshall and Pigou as 'classical' economists who accepted Say's Law (summarized by Keynes as 'supply creates its own demand'). Keynes subsequently clarified that he did not regard Fisher, Hawtrey, Robertson or Wicksell's Swedish followers as classical (but he did think that Wicksell himself was trying to be classical), and, as Ellis (1934) showed, German monetary theorists such as Joseph Schumpeter and L. Albert Hahn were far from classical about the real effects of an expansion of the banking system. In contrast to von Mises (1935) and Hayek (1931), who viewed depressions as necessary corrections of earlier overinvestment, Keynes held that depressions were calamities that the government and monetary authority could overcome by increasing aggregate demand, rather than relying on wage and price deflation to restore full employment. Keynes considered it crucial that wage bargains are made in money terms, so that workers concerned about relative wages might accept a price level increase to clear the labour market while quite rationally opposing money wage cuts as staggered contracts came up for renegotiation (1936, ch. 2). Wage cuts, and the associated deflation of prices, would increase demand for real money balances, exerting a contractionary effect on aggregate demand (1936, ch. 19). Keynes identified volatile private investment, resulting from fundamental uncertainty about future profitability, as the source of economic fluctuations, and, like the generations of Keynesian, New Keynesian and Post Keynesian economists after him, saw a need for management of aggregate demand to stabilize the economy.

The revival of the quantity theory of money

While Keynes was arguing the case for stabilization policy, Henry Simons of the University of Chicago made the case for rules rather than discretion in monetary policy (Simons, 1936). Keynes saw a role for government to counteract the instability resulting from volatile private spending, but Chicago quantity theorists (later called monetarists) such as Simons (1936) and Milton Friedman and his students (Friedman, 1956) blamed volatile, unpredictable monetary policy for economic instability. Keynesians invoked the Great Depression of the 1930s as demonstrating the need for government stabilization of an unstable private sector in a monetary

economy, but Friedman and Anna J. Schwartz (1963) blamed the depression on a misguided Federal Reserve system that permitted a 'great contraction' of the money supply. Misled by the real bills doctrine, the Federal Reserve Board had not paid sufficient attention to the quantity of money. Where Keynes had emphasized the fundamental uncertainty underlying long-period expectations of profitability, Friedman (like Fisher) stressed the endogeneity of expectations of inflation: people cannot be fooled indefinitely by inflation into working more for a lower real wage that they think they are getting, because they will learn from experience (see Friedman and his critics in Gordon, 1974). Keynes worried about involuntary unemployment – an excess supply of labour because the labour market did not clear – while Friedman held that at any correctly anticipated inflation rate unemployment would be at its natural rate, reflecting voluntary investment in search and consumption of leisure. Friedman claimed in 1956 to be following a Chicago oral tradition of monetary theory taught by Frank Knight, Jacob Viner, Henry Simons and Lloyd Mints that had replaced J. Laurence Laughlin's opposition to the quantity theory. Don Patinkin (1981) and David Laidler (2003), who both held Chicago Ph.D.s, argued that Friedman overstated the purely Chicago sources of his monetarism: Friedman's teachers had taught the works of non-Chicago quantity theorists such as Fisher as well as Keynes's earlier Marshallian *Tract on Monetary Reform* (1923) and his Wicksell-influenced *Treatise on Money* (1930). Friedman took a course in which the main textbook was Keynes's *Treatise*, which Keynes's detailed and extensive contribution to monetary analysis. Fisher had advocated a monetary policy rule (a price level target, rather than the constant of money growth proposed by Friedman), while Keynes's *Tract* was as attentive as any Chicago monetarist to the social costs of inflation. A key element of Friedman's monetarism, money demand as a function of a small list of variables, had first appeared in Keynes's *General Theory*. There were also parallel, independent revivals of the quantity theory of money far from Chicago, such as that associated with Marius Holtrop, longtime president of the Netherlands central bank (De Jong, 1973).

Integrating the theory of money into general economic theory

Rationalizing the use of money has been a problem in the development of general equilibrium theory: if markets are complete, or all debts will be repaid with certainty, there is no need for a particular asset to be singled out as a generally accepted means of payment. Irving Fisher's 1892 dissertation introduced general equilibrium analysis in North America, but he did not integrate his later monetary economics into a general equilibrium framework. Leon Walras, the founder of general equilibrium theory, wrote on the theory of money (for example,

Walras, 1886), starting with the equation of exchange and later discussing desired cash balances, *encaisse désirée*, but simply assumed that monetary exchange is superior to barter, rather than demonstrating that the use of money reduces transactions costs: 'In Walras's economy, agents hold money not out of choice but of a technological necessity' (Bridel, 1997, p. 119; see also Patinkin, 1965, pp. 531–72). In Walras's analysis, prices were stated in terms of a particular commodity, the *numéraire*, but it was not clear why transactions should use that commodity. The idea that money is only a veil over the real side of the economy long predates the introduction of the term 'veil of money' in English by Dennis Robertson (1922) and of 'neutrality of money' by Hayek (1931): (see Pigou, 1949; Patinkin and Steiger, 1989). Don Patinkin (1965) argued that a long list of classical and neoclassical economists postulated, at least implicitly, an invalid dichotomy between the real and nominal sides of the economy, in which an equi-proportional change in all money prices (so that no relative prices changed) would not affect the excess demands for commodities. Such a dichotomy would exclude the real balance effect that would bring the general price level to equilibrium. The valid dichotomy would hold that an equi-proportional change in all money prices, the quantity of money, and any exogenous nominal variables (such as quantities of government bonds) would have no real effects.

John Hicks (1935) set the agenda for much later work integrating the theory of money into the more general theory of value, seeking choice-theoretic explanations of why fiat money, not backed by convertibility into a commodity such as gold or silver, has a positive purchasing power, and why people choose to hold part of their wealth in money (either non-interest-bearing high-powered money or highly liquid close substitutes paying low rates of interest) rather than in alternative assets that pay a higher rate of return. Following Hicks's argument for treating the decision to hold money as part of the allocation of wealth across a portfolio of assets, James Tobin (1958) introduced money as a riskless asset (at least in nominal terms) into Harry Markowitz's theory of portfolio choice. Risk-averse individuals would divide their wealth between money (zero return, zero risk) and a portfolio of risky assets with positive expected return. Each investor would combine risky assets in the same proportions, differing from other investors only in the fraction of wealth held in the riskless asset. If returns were normally distributed or investors had quadratic loss functions, this portfolio choice could be conveniently captured by a two-dimensional diagram (the mean and standard distribution of portfolio returns), and if investors had constant relative risk aversion, the share of wealth held in each asset (including money) would be independent of the level of wealth (see Tobin, 1958; 1969; Tobin and Golub, 1998). However, money is a risky asset in real terms, as its purchasing power may be eroded by inflation, and is dominated in rate of return by such

short-term, highly liquid assets as Treasury bills, which, like money, have no default risk. While Treasury bills have some nominal risk, since a rise in nominal interest would lower their market price, this risk is limited by the short maturity of the bills. Tobin (1969) extended his portfolio approach to a 'general equilibrium approach to monetary theory' that treated money as one of a range of imperfectly substitutable assets whose rates of return are determined simultaneously, with an adding-up constraint that asset demands sum to total wealth, but without assuming continuous clearing of non-financial markets (Tobin, 1971; Tobin and Golub, 1998).

Another approach to a choice-theoretic explanation of demand for fiat money assumes that money must be used as a means of payment and that it is costly to trade between money and interest-bearing assets, so that individuals trade off the interest forgone by holding money against the transaction costs (including the value of one's time spent going to the bank) incurred by having to liquidate interest-bearing assets when having to make payments. Maurice Allais in 1947, William Baumol in 1952, and James Tobin in 1956 independently derived the square-root rule for this inventory approach to the transactions demand for money by minimizing the total cost of cash management, forgone interest plus transactions costs (see Allais, 1947, pp. 238–41; Tobin and Golub, 1998), unaware that Francis Ysidro Edgeworth (1888), followed by Wicksell (1898, pp. 57–8), had derived a similar square-root rule for the demand for reserves by banks given randomness in withdrawals of deposits.

Another explanation for a positive value of fiat money is provided by overlapping generations (OLG) models, pioneered independently by Allais (1947) and Paul Samuelson (1958). In OLG models, agents live for two periods, but produce consumption goods only when young. The young trade goods to the old in return for money in anticipation of being able to exchange that money for goods in the next period when they themselves are old. Such models explain the existence of positive-valued fiat money on the assumption that no other assets exist. Other efforts to provide micro-economic foundations for fiat money emphasize monitoring costs and default risks, so that liabilities of a single, more easily monitored monetary authority are less risky than private promissory notes and therefore more acceptable as means of payments.

The long history of monetary economics reveals several recurring issues: why fiat money has value, how the real and monetary sides of the economy are related, whether a central bank should follow a rule (and if so which rule) or have discretion (or whether a central bank should even exist), is the lender of last resort function consistent with a policy rule, whether money has a special role or is just one of many assets and forms of credit, how should monetary exchange be incorporated in the general theory of value. Monetary analysis has also been focused and stimulated by external events and current policy issues: the 'price revolution' of the 16th century, the high price of bullion while the convertibility of Bank of England notes was suspended during the Napoleonic Wars, the Bank of England's charter coming up for renewal in 1844 after several banking crises, the decline in the purchasing power of gold following the California and Australian gold rushes and its appreciation from 1873 to 1896, the Continental European hyperinflations after the First World War, Britain's return to the gold exchange standard at the pre-war parity in 1925, and the Great Depression.

ROBERT W. DIMAND

See also **Banking School, Currency School, Free Banking School; bullionist controversies (empirical evidence); equation of exchange; natural rate and market rate of interest; quantity theory of money; real bills doctrine versus the quantity theory.**

Bibliography

Allais, M. 1947. *Économie et intérêt*. Paris: Librairie des Publications Officieles.

Aristotle. 1984. *The Politics*, tr. Carnes Lord. Chicago: University of Chicago Press.

Aristotle. 1996. *The Nicomachean Ethics*, tr. Harris Rackham Ware, Herts., UK: Wordsworth Editions.

Arnon, A. 1991. *Thomas Tooke, Pioneer of Monetary Theory.* Aldershot, UK, and Brookfield, VT: Edward Elgar.

Bagehot, W. 1873. *Lombard Street*. In Bagehot (1974–86).

Bagehot, W. 1974–86. *The Collected Works of Walter Bagehot.* London: The Economist.

Baumol, W.J. 1977. Say's (at least) eight laws, or what Say and James Mill may really have meant. *Economica* NS 44, 145–62.

Baumol, W.J. 1999. Retrospectives: Say's law. *Journal of Economic Perspectives* 13, 195–204.

Blaug, M., Eltis, W., O'Brien, D., Patinkin, D., Skidelsky, R. and Wood, G.E. 1995. *The Quantity Theory of Money from Locke to Keynes and Friedman*. Aldershot, UK, and Brookfield, VT: Edward Elgar.

Boyer, J.de. 2003. *La pensée monétaire: Histoire et analyse.* Paris: Éditions Les Solos.

Bridel, P. 1987. *Cambridge Monetary Thought: The Development of Saving-Investment Analysis*. Basingstoke: Macmillan.

Bridel, P. 1997. *Money and General Equilibrium Theory: From Walras to Pareto (1870–1923)*. Cheltenham: Edward Elgar.

Brunhoff, S. de 1976. *Marx on Money*, tr. M. Goldbloom. New York: Urizen.

Cantillon, R. 2001. *Essay on the Nature of Commerce in General*, tr. H. Higgs. New Brunswick, NJ: Transaction.

Cassidy, M. 1998. The development of John Fullarton's monetary thought. *European Journal of the History of Economic Thought* 5, 509–36.

Christiernin, P.N. 1761. *Lectures on the High Price of Foreign Exchange in Sweden*, tr. in R.V. Eagly, ed., *The Swedish Bullionist Controversy*. Philadelphia: American Philosophical Society, 1967.

Clower, R.W. 1984. *Money and Markets: Essays by Robert W. Clower*, ed. Donald A. Walker. Cambridge: Cambridge University Press.

Corry, B. 1962. *Money, Saving and Investment in English Economics 1800–1850*. London: Macmillan.

Davis, T. 2005. *Ricardo's Macroeconomics: Money, Trade Cycles and Growth*. Cambridge: Cambridge University Press.

De Jong, F.J. 1973. *Developments of Monetary Theory in the Netherlands*. Rotterdam: Rotterdam University Press.

Edgeworth, F.Y. 1888. Mathematical theory of banking. *Journal of the Royal Statistical Society* 51, 113–27.

Ellis, H.S. 1934. *German Monetary Theory 1905–1933*. Cambridge, MA: Harvard University Press.

Eshag, E. 1963. *From Marshall to Keynes: An Essay on the Monetary Theory of the Cambridge School*. Oxford: Basil Blackwell.

Fetter, F.W. 1965. *The Development of British Monetary Orthodoxy 1797–1875*. Cambridge, MA: Harvard University Press.

Fisher, I. 1892. *Mathematical Investigations in the Theory and Value of Prices*. New York: Macmillan In Fisher (1997), vol. 1.

Fisher, I. 1896. *Appreciation and Interest*. In Fisher (1997), vol. 1.

Fisher, I. and Brown, H. 1911. *The Purchasing Power of Money*. In Fisher (1997), vol. 4.

Fisher, I. 1926. 'A statistical relationship between unemployment and price level changes'. In *International Labour Review* 13, 785–92. Repr. 1973 as 'Lost and found: I discovered the Phillips curve', *Journal of Political Economy* 81, 496–502. Also in Fisher (1997), vol. 8.

Fisher, I. 1928. *The Money Illusion*. In Fisher (1997), vol. 8.

Fisher, I. 1930. *The Theory of Interest*. In Fisher (1997), vol. 9.

Fisher, I. 1997. *The Works of Irving Fisher*, 14 vols. ed. W.J. Barber, assisted R.W. Dimand and K. Foster. London: Pickering & Chatto.

Friedman, M. 1956. *Studies in the Quantity Theory of Money*. Chicago: University of Chicago Press.

Friedman, M. and Schwartz, A.J. 1963. *A Monetary History of the United States 1867–1960*. Princeton, NJ: Princeton University Press for the NBER.

Fullarton, J. 1836. Response to a proposal for a bank of India. Repr. 1998 in *European Journal of the History of Economic Thought* 5, 480–508.

Fullarton, J. 1845. *Regulation of Currencies of the Bank of England*. New York: Augustus M. Kelley, 1969.

Gervaise, I. 1720. *The System or Theory of Trade of the World*. London: J. Roberts; repr. Baltimore: Johns Hopkins Press, 1954.

Glasner, D. 1985. A reinterpretation of classical monetary theory. *Southern Economic Journal* 52, 46–68.

Glasner, D. 2000. Classical monetary theory and the quantity theory. *History of Political Economy* 32, 39–59.

Gonnard, R. 1936. *Histoire des doctrines monétaires, dans ses rapports avec l'histoire des monnaies*, 2 vols. Paris: Sirey.

Gordon, R.J. 1974. *Milton Friedman's Monetary Framework: A Debate with his Critics*. Chicago: University of Chicago Press.

Grice-Hutchinson, M. 1952. *The Salamanca School: Readings in Spanish Monetary Theory 1544–1605*. Oxford: Clarendon Press.

Guggenheim, T. 1989. *Preclassical Monetary Theories*. London and New York: Pinter.

Hawtrey, R.G. 1919. *Currency and Credit*. London: Longmans, Green, 3rd edn. 1934.

Hayek, F.A. 1931. *Prices and Production*. London: Routledge.

Hayek, F.A. 1976. *The Denationalisation of Money*. London: Institute of Economic Affairs.

Hegeland, H. 1951. *The Quantity Theory of Money*. Göteborg: Elanders Boktryckeri; New York: Augustus M. Kelley, 1969.

Hicks, J.R. 1935. A suggestion for simplifying the theory of money. *Economica* NS 2, 1–19.

Hume, D. 1752. *Writings on Economics*, ed. E. Rotwein. Madison: University of Wisconsin Press, 1955.

Humphrey, T.M. 1993. *Money, Banking, and Inflation: Essays in the History of Economic Thought*. Aldershot, UK, and Brookfield, VT: Edward Elgar.

Jevons, W.S. 1875. *Money and the Mechanism of Exchange*. New York: D. Appleton, 1897.

Jevons, W.S. 1884. *Investigations in Credit and Prices*, ed. H.S. Foxwell. London: Macmillan.

Kemmerer, E.W. 1907. *Money and Credit Instruments in their Relation to General Prices*. New York: Henry Holt.

Keynes, J.M. 1923. *A Tract on Monetary Reform*. In Keynes (1971–89), vol. 4.

Keynes, J.M. 1930. *Treatise on Money*. In Keynes (1971–89), vols 5 and 6.

Keynes, J.M. 1933. Robert Malthus: the first of the Cambridge economists. In J.M. Keynes, *Essays in Biography*, London: Macmillan. Repr. in Keynes (1971–89), vol. 9.

Keynes, J.M. 1936. *General Theory of Employment, Interest and Money*. In Keynes (1971–89), vol. 7.

Keynes, J.M. 1971–89. *Collected Writings of John Maynard Keynes*, 30 vols. ed. D.E. Moggridge and E.A.G. Robinson. London: Macmillan, and New York: Cambridge University Press, for the Royal Economic Society.

Kinley, D. 1904. *Money, a Study of the Theory of the Medium of Exchange*. New York: Macmillan.

Laidler, D. 1991a. *The Golden Age of the Quantity Theory*. Princeton, NJ: Princeton University Press.

Laidler, D. 1991b. The quantity is always and everywhere controversial – why? *Economic Record* 67, 289–306.

Laidler, D. 1999. *Fabricating the Keynesian Revolution*. Cambridge: Cambridge University Press.

Laidler, D. 2003. *Macroeconomics in Retrospect: Selected Essays*. Cheltenham: Edward Elgar.

Laughlin, J.L. 1903. *The Principles of Money*. New York: Scribner.

Lowry, S. Todd. 1987. *The Archaeology of Economic Ideas: The Classical Greek Tradition*. Durham, NC: Duke University Press.

Macleod, H.D. 1855. *The Theory and Practice of Banking*, 5th edn. London: Longmans, Green, 1893.

Marcuzzo, M.C. and Rosselli, A. 1991. *Ricardo and the Gold Standard: The Foundations of the International Monetary Order*. London: Macmillan.

Marget, A.W. 1938–42. *The Theory of Prices: A Re-examination of the Central Problems of a Monetary Theory*, 2 vols. New York: Augustus M. Kelley, 1966.

Marshall, A. 1887. Remedies for fluctuations in general prices. *Contemporary Review*, reprinted in *Memorials of Alfred Marshall*, ed. A.C. Pigou. London: Macmillan, 1925.

Marshall, A. 1923. *Money, Credit and Commerce*. London: Macmillan.

Marshall, A. 1926. *Official Papers*, ed. J.M. Keynes. London: Macmillan.

Menger, C. 1892. On the origin of money. *Economic Journal* 2, 239–55.

Mints, L. 1945. *A History of Banking Theory in Great Britain and the United States*, 5th edn. Chicago: University of Chicago Press, 1970.

Mises, L. Von. 1935. *The Theory of Money and Credit*, tr. H. Batson. London: Cape.

Monroe, A.E. 1923. *Monetary Theory before Adam Smith*. New York: Augustus M. Kelley, 1969.

O'Brien, D.P. 2000. Bodin's analysis of inflation. *History of Political Economy* 32, 267–92.

Oresme, N., de Sassoferrato, B. and Buridan, J. 1989. *Traité des monnaies et autres écrits monétaires du XIVe siècle*, ed. C. Dupuy, tr. F. Chartrain. Lyon: La Manufacture.

Patinkin, D. 1965. *Money, Interest and Prices*, 2nd edn. New York: Harper & Row.

Patinkin, D. 1981. *Essays on and in the Chicago Tradition*. Durham, NC: Duke University Press.

Patinkin, D. and Steiger, O. 1989. In search of the 'Veil of Money' and the 'Neutrality of Money': a note on the origin of terms. *Scandinavian Journal of Economics* 91, 131–46.

Pigou, A.C. 1925. *Memorials of Alfred Marshall*. London: Macmillan.

Pigou, A.C. 1949. *The Veil of Money*. London: Macmillan.

Plato. 1974. *The Republic*, tr. G.M.A. Grube. Indianapolis: Hackett Publishing.

Ricardo, D. 1810. *The High Price of Bullion, a Proof of the Depreciation of Bank Notes*. London: John Murray, 4th edn 1811. Repr. in Ricardo (1951–73), vol. 3.

Ricardo, D. 1951–73. *Works and Correspondence of David Ricardo*, Cambridge: Cambridge University Press 11 vols, ed. P. Sraffa and M.H. Dobb.

Rist, C. 1938. *Histoire des doctrines relative au crédit et à la monnaie depuis John Law jusqu'à nos jours*. Paris: Sirey. Tr. as *History of Monetary and Credit Theory from John Law to the Present Day*, New York: Augustus M. Kelley, 1966.

Robertson, D.H. 1922. *Money*. Cambridge: Cambridge Economic Handbooks.

Robertson, D.H. 1926. *Banking Policy and the Price Level*. London: P.S. King.

Samuelson, P.A. 1958. An exact consumption-loan model of interest with or without the social contrivance of money. *Journal of Political Economy* 66, 467–82.

Simons, H.C. 1936. Rules versus authorities in monetary policy. *Journal of Political Economy* 44, 1–30.

Skaggs, N.T. 1995. The methodological roots of J. Laurence Laughlin's anti-quantity theory of money and prices. *Journal of the History of Economic Thought* 17, 1–20.

Skaggs, N.T. 1999. Changing views: twentieth-century opinion on the banking school-currency school controversy. *History of Political Economy* 31, 361–91.

Smith, A. 1776. *An Inquiry into the Nature and Causes of the Wealth of Nations*, ed. E. Cannan. New York: Random House, 1937.

Smith, V.C. 1936. *The Rationale of Central Banking*. London: P.S. King.

Sowell, T. 1972. *Say's Law: An Historical Analysis*. Princeton, NJ: Princeton University Press.

Thornton, H. 1802. *An Enquiry into the Nature and Effects of the Paper Credit of Great Britain*, with an introduction by F.A. Hayek. London: George Allen & Unwin, 1939. New York: Augustus M. Kelley, 1965.

Tobin, J. 1958. Liquidity preference as behavior towards risk. *Review of Economic Studies* 25, 65–86.

Tobin, J. 1969. A general equilibrium approach to monetary theory. *Journal of Money, Credit and Banking* 1, 15–29.

Tobin, J. 1971. *Essays in Economics*, vol. 1, *Macroeconomics*. Chicago: Markham.

Tobin, J. and Golub, S. 1998. *Money, Credit, and Capital*. New York: McGraw-Hill.

Vickers, D. 1959. *Studies in the Theory of Money 1690–1776*. New York: Chilton.

Viner, J. 1937. *Studies in the Theory of International Trade*. London: George Allen & Unwin.

Walker, D.A. 1984. *Money and Markets: Selected Essays of Robert Clower*. Cambridge: Cambridge University Press.

Walras, L. 1886. *Théorie de la monnaie*. Paris: Èditions Larose et Forcel.

West, E.G. 1997. Adam Smith's support for money and banking regulation: a case of inconsistency. *Journal of Money, Credit and Banking* 29, 127–35.

Wicksell, K.G. 1898. *Interest and Prices*, tr. R.F. Kahn. London: Macmillan, 1936.

Wicksell, K.G. 1915. *Lectures on Political Economy*, vol. 2, *Money*, tr. E. Claasen. London: Routledge, 1935.

Woodford, M. 2003. *Interest and Prices: Foundations of a Theory of Monetary Policy*. Princeton, NJ: Princeton University Press.

monetary and fiscal policy overview

In this article I provide an overview of economic thinking about monetary and fiscal policy. There are three terms that need to be defined in this sentence: policy, monetary, and fiscal. I begin by defining each in turn.

A government's *policy* is akin to a strategy in game theory. It specifies a function at each date that maps the government's information at that date into the government's actions. This information typically takes two forms. First, it includes *endogenous* variables such as past prices, past quantities or past actions of the government. For example, under the famous Taylor rule, a government's choice of current short-term interest rates is based on past observations of the consumer price index and gross domestic product. Second, the government's information includes *exogenous* variables, like the realizations of shocks to productivity or to money demand.

These sources of information may be public or they may be known only to the government. Thus, in the United States the Federal Reserve collects information about the state of the economy that it uses for making decisions but is kept confidential from households in the economy. Note, too, that the government's actions themselves may be private information to the government; for example, until recently, the Federal Open Market Committee publicly announced its decisions only with a lag.

In the popular press, the term 'policy' is commonly used in a different way, to refer only to the *current* choice of the government. However, as long as *some* economic actors (firms, households or the government itself) are forward-looking, such a specification of policy is intrinsically incomplete. Forward-looking decision-makers need to know not just the government's choice of policy today but also how the government will respond to new information in the future. (This is true even if these forward-looking actors have expectations that are far from rational.) Thus, if the government raises taxes today, my response to that increase depends crucially on whether I believe it will persist for a long time. To make that judgement, I need to know not just the government's choices today but also how its choices in the future depend on new information that the government receives.

Whether a policy is monetary or fiscal or neither depends on the nature of the actions specified by that policy. A policy is said to be *monetary* if the relevant actions are those generally undertaken by a central bank. These may include the size of monetary injections, reserve requirements, the discount rate, or the scale of interventions in bond or foreign exchange markets. A policy is said to be *fiscal* if the relevant actions are tax rates and/or expenditures on various commodities. Of course, many government policies (should Iran be invaded or not?) are neither fiscal nor monetary.

In the body of this article, I discuss several lessons from the study of monetary and fiscal policy. Before doing so, though, it is useful to understand the methodology that was used to learn those lessons (see Lucas, 1980, and Prescott, 2005, for a fuller discussion of this methodology). Any analysis of policy starts with the following question: on the assumption that no other exogenous variables change, how does the economy respond to a change in policy? This kind of question is really asking about the outcome of a controlled *experiment*. It would be best answered by constructing giant national or super-national laboratories in order to conduct these experiments. But it is clearly impossible to perform controlled experiments of this kind. How then do macroeconomists proceed?

The approach taken by macroeconomists is closely related to the methods used by other non-experimental sciences. Consider for example the issue of global warming. There have been no prior episodes in world history in which man has been able to generate such a large amount of CO_2 in such a short period of time. Hence, there is no way to use prior data to understand the impact of this build-up on climatic variables like temperature. Instead, climatologists rely on computer simulations of abstract models to understand the impact of greenhouse gases on the world's climate.

Similarly, macroeconomists build abstract computational models to answer questions about the impact of monetary and fiscal policy. It is well-understood from many years of computational experimentation that useful models must have certain elements to provide reliable answers to policy questions. The models need to be both dynamic and stochastic in nature. The models need to be explicit about aggregate resource constraints: the amount of goods consumed by governments and households cannot exceed the amount of goods produced. The models should feature households with well-defined objectives and budget constraints. The households and firms in the models should be forward-looking (although they may or may not be fully informed about the state of the economy).

To provide a quantitative answer about the impact of a particular policy, macroeconomists need to be specific about many other elements of the computational model (preferences of households, shocks hitting the economy, and so on). Again, it is useful to refer to the natural sciences as a way to understand how macroeconomists proceed. Consider a biologist that wants to understand the impact of a new drug on human beings. At least initially, she experiments on animals. For some kinds of drugs, she may use mice. For others, she may use more expensive animals like monkeys or dogs. Her decision about which proxy to use is a complex one, grounded in theory, collective prior experience about other drugs and these animals, and individual judgement.

In the same fashion, macroeconomists do not use the same model for all policy questions. Instead, they choose the model based on the question at hand. Thus, for questions concerning the short-run impact of monetary policies, they may include adjustment costs in physical capital and/or prices. For other questions concerning the long-run impact of monetary policy, they may neglect these elements. Like the biologist, their decisions are based on theory, collective prior experience and judgement.

One aspect of this decision-making that receives particular attention in macroeconomics is how to quantify the various elements of the model. How risk-averse are the households in the model economy? What is the elasticity of substitution between capital and labour in the model economy? Fortunately, for many of these parameter choices, there is a profession-wide consensus, informed by many years of experience and discussion. For other parameters, new choices have to be made. Generally, macroeconomists use a mix of information from both microeconomic and macroeconomic sources to make these choices. There may well be a range of plausible choices for a given parameter, and then the answer to the policy question under consideration is really a set, not a single point.

In the remainder of this article, I discuss some of the conclusions about monetary and fiscal policy that macroeconomists have reached from using this methodology. I focus on results that are highly robust, in the sense that they occur across a wide class of models. I begin by looking at lessons from the *positive* approach to policy, which studies the response of the private sector to different specifications of policy. I then look at lessons from the *normative* approach, which looks at properties of *ex ante* optimal policies. Finally, I discuss some difficulties associated with modelling policy choices as being an endogenous response to economic conditions.

The positive approach to policy

There is a large amount of macroeconomic research that treats monetary and fiscal policy as wholly exogenous to the economy. It asks questions of the sort: how does some aspect of private sector economic behaviour respond to a given specification of monetary and fiscal policy? Macroeconomists have described the outcomes to many specific experiments of this kind. There is no useful way to summarize this knowledge. However, there are several general lessons that one can draw from this research. In what follows, I discuss three of these.

Lesson 1: fiscal vs. monetary policy

I have drawn a distinction between fiscal and monetary policy. However, this distinction is more than a little artificial for two reasons. First, in macroeconomic models households face budget constraints and aggregate resource constraints are satisfied. Together, these imply that the government itself must satisfy a budget constraint in equilibrium: the present value of the government's revenues must equal the present value of its expenditures. (There are overlapping-generations model economies in which this restriction need not be satisfied. However, these models are typically not thought to be empirically relevant; Abel et al., 1989.) This constraint implies a sharp linkage between fiscal and monetary policy. Changes in monetary policies affect the government's revenue from money creation. Hence, the two types of policies are inextricably linked, because they cannot be changed separately. (This fundamental linkage between fiscal and monetary policy was made especially clear by Sargent and Wallace, 1981.)

The second reason is that, in terms of its impact on the economy, monetary policy is merely fiscal policy by another name. People and firms who hold money are forgoing the interest that they could receive by holding bonds instead. They hold that money because it helps them buy goods and services that are difficult to purchase using bonds. Higher interest rates makes money more costly to hold, and makes those goods and services more costly to buy. The interest rate acts like a sales tax on those goods and services.

Monetary policy has still other distorting effects on the economy when some prices are more flexible than others. For example, suppose nominal wages do not respond rapidly to changes in inflation, but gas prices do. Then, the relative price of labour and gasoline may vary in response to variations in monetary instruments. Again, though, a particular kind of fiscal policy – variations in the gasoline tax – can affect the economy in exactly the same way. (This equivalence between fiscal and monetary policy is stressed by Correia, Nicolini and Teles, 2004.)

Lesson 2: Ricardian equivalence

I pointed out above that the present value of government expenditures must equal the present value of government revenues. This simple fact has surprising consequences. Consider two policies with the same government purchases. Suppose one policy generates lower tax revenue in the next ten years than the other policy. Obviously, under the first policy, the government must borrow more. This extra demand in loans puts upward pressure on interest rates.

However, the government's intertemporal budget constraint also implies that the first policy must necessarily generate *higher* tax revenue in the future. Forward-looking households anticipate this increase in their future tax burden. They respond by saving more to meet this tax burden. In a classic paper, Barro (1974) shows that, if households are sufficiently forward-looking, and markets are frictionless, then the households' extra demand for savings under the first policy is exactly equal to the government's extra demand for loans. Hence, even though the government is borrowing more, there is no extra pressure on interest rates; they should be the same under the two policies. This result is generally termed *Ricardian equivalence* (because of some antecedents in the work of David Ricardo).

The exact Ricardian equivalence result is not robust to adding plausible frictions like borrowing constraints on households. Nonetheless, there is a qualitative lesson that holds much more generally and is often forgotten in policy discussions: economics does not predict a stable relationship between current government debt or deficits and interest rates.

Lesson 3: Expectations matter

I have emphasized above that households' expectations about future government actions matter for current outcomes. However, in many macroeconomic models a given household's behaviour depends also on its expectations of other households' current and future actions. This feedback generates the possibility of multiple equilibrium outcomes for a given government policy.

Here's a simple example of this phenomenon. Suppose both government investment and household labour are necessary inputs into production – that is, either zero government investment or zero labour input leads to zero output. Suppose as well that the government collects resources to fund its investment by taxing output. In such a world, regardless of the government's policy, there is always an equilibrium in which households do not work at all. In this equilibrium, because other households are not working, a given household realizes that the government cannot fund any investment. Hence, it is individually optimal for that household not to provide any labour input.

This kind of multiplicity leads to the possibility of what are called *sunspot* fluctuations in macroeconomic variables. The idea here is that households use some arbitrary random variable to coordinate their behavior. Thus, if they all see rain in Peoria, they decide not to work. If they see sun in Peoria, they decide to work. Whether it is sunny or not in Peoria, of course, is irrelevant for economic fundamentals – but in this economy, this variable can still affect equilibrium outcomes. (For early expositions of the concept of sunspot equilibria, see Azariadis, 1981, and Cass and Shell, 1983.)

Note that this example is only an illustration of a much more general phenomenon. It is especially prevalent in monetary economies. In these settings, a household's decision about how many real balances to hold today depends crucially on the household's expectations about future inflation rates. Obstfeld and Rogoff (1983) demonstrate how this intertemporal feedback can generate a continuum of welfare-indexed possible inflation paths as equilibria, even if the money supply is fixed. Sargent and Wallace (1975) demonstrate how this intertemporal feedback can generate a continuum of welfare-indexed possible inflation paths as equilibria even if interest rates are fixed. (Pareto-ranked equilibria do not occur in all economies. In many economies – especially non-monetary ones – it may be possible to prove that any equilibrium allocation solves a maximization problem in which the objective is a weighted average of households' utilities. In such settings, equilibrium allocations are necessarily Pareto non-comparable. Without such a proof in hand, though, one has to be aware that there is the potential for sunspot fluctuations between Pareto-ranked outcomes. Many macroeconomists restrict attention to so-called recursive equilibria or Markov-perfect equilibria. Under these notions of equilibrium, outcomes have the property that they depend on the past only through a small number of state variables. This restriction is undoubtedly useful for simplifying computational or econometric work. However, the restriction may inadvertently rule out important sources of potential multiplicity. See, for example, Woodford's, 1994, analysis of Lucas and Stokey's, 1987, model economy.)

The normative approach to policy

I now turn to the second approach to studying macroeconomic policy. This approach posits a government that chooses a policy at the beginning of time; its objective is to maximize some weighted average of household utilities. Crucially, the government is able to commit to never change the policy. This kind of commitment power is clearly artificial; the goal of the second approach is to tell us what kinds of policies maximize *ex ante* social welfare, not what policies are actually adopted by governments. By construction, there is no requirement that the optimal policies be realistic: normative analyses tell us what the government should do, not what they actually do. Thus, economists use normative analyses to argue strongly in favour of free trade, which is a policy that has never been followed by any country at any time.

Everything in this approach hinges on what is assumed about the set of instruments available to the government. It is well-known that *lump-sum* taxes are a highly desirable taxation instrument. A lump-sum tax is a tax on a household or firm which is independent of their actions. Such a tax is desirable because it does not distort the choices of the household or the firm.

But lump-sum taxes are typically not used by governments. Once one notices this fact, there are at least two ways to proceed in thinking about optimal taxes. One can assume that the governments can only use a limited set of tax instruments that does not include lump-sum taxes. This approach is generally called the *Ramsey* approach. Alternatively, one can build model economies in which governments have access to all possible tax instruments, but *choose*, because of a particular private information friction, not to use lump-sum taxes. This approach is generally called the Mirrlees approach.

The Ramsey approach and its lessons

Suppose the government can impose a linear tax on capital income, a linear tax on labour income, and can print money. It must optimally choose these instruments so as to finance an optimally chosen process for government purchases. What are the properties of the optimal taxes? An enormous amount of work has been done on this question; see Chari and Kehoe (1999) for a survey. I first briefly describe the mathematical approach, and then turn to the properties of the optimal taxes.

One way to proceed here would be to solve for the households' and firms' response to all possible tax policies. Then, given this response function, we could solve

the government's optimization problem. This problem turns out to be difficult in most circumstances.

Fortunately, there is a way to substitute out the tax schedules; we can instead think of the government directly choosing quantities subject to two types of restrictions. The first is the usual physical feasibility constraints. The other is a set of constraints called *implementability* constraints. These look like household budget constraints, except that we substitute the household marginal rates of substitution in for all prices; the constraints then contain only physical quantities. Somewhat remarkably, these simple implementability constraints turn out to capture exactly the seemingly complicated restriction that the government can use only linear taxes.

Of course, because it is couched only in terms of quantities, the solution to this problem does not contain direct information about optimal taxes. Once one solves the optimization problem, one sees that there are differences (commonly termed *wedges*) between marginal rates of substitution and marginal rates of transformation in the solution. The optimal taxes in equilibrium are equal to these wedges from the solution of the optimization problem. Note these wedges exist only because of the implementability constraints; without them, all wedges would be zero, and it would be optimal to set all taxes to zero.

What then are the properties of optimal taxes when we apply this kind of analysis? In general, the quantitative properties of the optimal taxes depend on many precise details of the specification of the environment. However, there are (at least) two remarkably robust properties of the optimal taxes. The first is that if the government can accumulate assets, the long-run optimal capital income tax rate is zero. (This result was originally derived by Chamley, 1986, and Judd, 1985.) Intuitively, suppose the long-run capital income tax is positive. This tax rate affects the rate of return in every period, and its impact cumulates as the horizon of the investment grows. Hence, the tax rate on accumulating capital between period t and period $t+s$ gets arbitrarily large as t, s get large. This arbitrarily large tax rate creates too much social waste, given that it is raising only a finite amount of revenue. The second property of optimal taxes is that, under very general conditions, the optimal nominal interest rate is zero (in all periods, not just in the long run) (see Chari, Christiano and Kehoe, 1996; Correia and Teles, 1999; Correia, Nicolini and Teles, 2004).

Here, the basic intuition is that any positive nominal interest rate is a tax on money holdings (as discussed above). But money is not a final good; it is only an intermediate input into production and consumption. A tax on intermediate inputs creates two distortions: people are deterred both from using the intermediate input and from consuming any final goods that use the intermediate input. It is generally optimal to eliminate this double distortion by simply taxing final goods and not taxing any intermediate inputs, including money.

Even though the nominal interest rate is zero, the real interest rate can still be positive as long as the price index is falling over time. If prices are fully flexible, then this consistent deflation has no real effects. However, if prices are sticky, this steady deflation may create inefficiencies in a world with sticky prices. In particular, if some prices are adjusted downward more frequently than others, then any consistent deflation creates distortions in relative prices.

Correia, Nicolini and Teles (2004) demonstrate that this kind of systematic distortion can be fixed by using *sales* taxes. Their key observation is that the nominal interest rate can be zero and the real interest rate can be positive as long as the *after-tax* price level is falling over time. Hence, if the government sets the sales tax to fall at the correct rate, firms will find it optimal to never change their prices even though the nominal interest rate is zero.

The Mirrlees approach and its lessons
The Ramsey approach simply assumes that governments cannot use lump-sum taxes. But why do governments not use lump-sum taxes? One problem is that, if the government imposes a tax of, say, $10,000 per head, then some people will have the ability to generate this income and others will not. This is not a difficulty if the government can tell who is in which group – it can just exempt those who cannot pay.

Unfortunately, people can *pretend* to be unable to generate this level of income by pretending to have back pain, mental illness or other sources of disability. The government cannot figure out whom to exempt from the head tax.

This observation suggests that governments are deterred from using lump-sum taxes because people are privately informed about their abilities or skills. The Mirrlees approach starts with this informational restriction. The government is allowed to use any form of taxes that it wishes (linear, nonlinear, and so on) on any private sector choice. Because it is not restricted to linear taxes, the implementability constraint discussed above vanishes. Instead, the government faces an *incentive-compatibility constraint* that reflects the ability of people to pretend to be less able than they truly are.

Given this difference in constraints, one can proceed much as in the Ramsey approach. The first step is to set up a maximization problem in which the government maximizes *ex ante* welfare subject to feasibility constraints and incentive-compatibility constraints. This type of maximization problem is roughly equivalent to the kind of dynamic contracting problems originally considered by Green (1987). One considerable complication is that abilities may change over time due to health shocks. Dynamic contracting models with persistent shocks are highly challenging to solve even with a computer (see Fernandes and Phelan, 2000).

The next step is to design a tax system such that the optimal allocations emerge as equilibrium outcomes.

These tax systems are complicated objects when abilities evolve over time. Nonetheless, we can draw remarkably strong conclusions about the structure of optimal capital income taxes. If preferences are additively separable between consumption and leisure, then one can show that there exists an optimal tax system which is *linear* in capital income. (Remember that the government is free to use an arbitrarily nonlinear system.) The optimal tax system *subsidizes* the capital income of surprisingly highly skilled people and *taxes* the capital income of surprisingly low-skilled people. While seemingly regressive, this tax system actually provides better social insurance. Intuitively, the tax system provides better incentives because it deters people from accumulating lots of wealth and then pretending to be low-skilled. These better incentives expand the scope for social insurance.

The heterogeneity in tax rates across people means that the Mirrlees prescription for optimal capital taxes differs from the Ramsey prescription for optimal capital tax rates. However, the two approaches do coincide in their recommendations for total and average capital income taxes. The Mirrlees approach recommends subsidies on some people and taxes on others. However, one can prove that, in the optimal tax system, both the average tax rate (across people) and the total tax revenue from capital income taxes are zero at every date. (See Kocherlakota, 2006, for a survey article on the Mirrlees approach.)

Making government endogenous
In both the positive approach and the normative approach, the government is a pre-programmed robot during the life of the economy. It would be useful to develop models in which the government is another economic actor (or, even more realistically, a collection of economic actors) that makes choices at intervals based on its information. Such models would allow us to understand what forces lead to the kinds of policy choices that we see in reality. (See Persson and Tabellini, 2000, for a much more complete discussion of these issues.)

These models need to capture at least two types of conflict. One source of conflict is heterogeneity. Households differ in their attributes and so in their preferences over policies. Old people have shorter horizons and typically prefer to set public investment to lower levels than young people. People with lots of capital prefer lower capital tax rates than do people with little capital. People with lots of nominal debt would like to raise nominal interest rates; their lenders prefer the opposite.

There is a great deal of research studying these kinds of conflicts. Unfortunately, it has been hard to generate the kind of robust answers that macroeconomists have obtained from the positive and normative approaches. There is no real consensus about how to model the games that get played by the different groups. Some researchers use voting games, while others use bargaining games.

Some researchers treat conflicts in isolation, while others model conflicts as being resolved in bundles. These different modelling choices generate substantially different predictions about policy formation.

In a classic article, Kydland and Prescott (1977) set forth a second source of conflict. Suppose the world lasts two periods, and a government wants to raise taxes to finance purchases using capital income taxes and labour income taxes. Assume that all households are identical – so that the first type of conflict is removed – and that the government cares only about maximizing household welfare. It would seem that all sources of conflict have been removed in this situation.

But this is not true. The period 1 government's preferences over period 2 capital taxes are fundamentally different from the period 2 government's preferences. In period 2, the amount of capital in the economy is fixed – there is no way to get any more. The period 2 government would like to set a high tax rate on this fixed tax base to raise as much revenue as possible.

In period 1, though, the amount of capital in period 2 has yet to be determined. The period 1 government has to consider how the tax rate in period 2 affects the size of the period 2 tax base. Its preferred period 2 tax rate is much smaller than the tax rate that the period 1 government likes.

Thus, even if governments at different dates are all benevolent, there is a dynamic conflict between them. How this conflict gets resolved is, again, a non-trivial matter. The dynamic game does have a unique equilibrium in a finite horizon. Unfortunately, this unique equilibrium is unrealistic in most countries: capital tax rates are set very high in every period. On the other hand, if the game has an infinite horizon, then there are an infinite number of equilibrium outcomes, including ones with high capital tax rates, low capital tax rates, and paths that vary between the two (see Chari and Kehoe, 1990). The predictive power of the model is then quite limited.

Conclusions

There is an old joke to the effect that if you ask 10 macroeconomists about a policy question, you'll get 11 different answers. This joke provided a disturbingly accurate picture of the state of the field in the 1970s and 1980s. To a remarkable extent, it was no longer applicable as of 2005. There is a profession-wide consensus on methods that simply did not exist in the early 1980s. This consensus has led to a set of results about monetary and fiscal policy that are sharp, robust and surprising.

NARAYANA R. KOCHERLAKOTA

See also **optimal taxation; 'political economy'; Ricardian equivalence theorem; social insurance.**

I thank Barbara McCutcheon for her comments. The opinions expressed herein are mine and not necessarily those of the Federal Reserve Bank of Minneapolis or the Federal Reserve System.

Bibliography

Abel, A., Mankiw, N.G., Summers, L. and Zeckhauser, R. 1989. Assessing dynamic efficiency: theory and evidence. *Review of Economic Studies* 56, 1–19.

Azariadis, C. 1981. Self-fulfilling prophecies. *Journal of Economic Theory* 25, 380–96.

Barro, R. 1974. Are government bonds net wealth? *Journal of Political Economy* 82, 1095–117.

Cass, D. and Shell, K. 1983. Do sunspots matter? *Journal of Political Economy* 91, 193–227.

Chamley, C. 1986. Optimal taxation of capital income in general equilibrium with infinite lives. *Econometrica* 54, 607–22.

Chari, V.V., Christiano, L. and Kehoe, P. 1996. Optimality of the Friedman rule in economies with distorting taxes. *Journal of Monetary Economics* 37, 203–23.

Chari, V.V. and Kehoe, P. 1990. Sustainable plans. *Journal of Political Economy* 98, 783–802.

Chari, V.V. and Kehoe, P. 1999. Optimal fiscal and monetary policy. In *Handbook of Macroeconomics*, vol. 1C, ed. J.B. Taylor and M. Woodford. Amsterdam: North-Holland.

Correia, I. and Teles, P. 1999. The optimal inflation tax. *Review of Economic Dynamics* 2, 325–46.

Correia, I., Nicolini, J.-P. and Teles, P. 2004. Optimal fiscal and monetary policy: equivalence results. Working paper, Centre for Economic Performance, London School of Economic.

Fernandes, A. and Phelan, C. 2000. A recursive formulation for repeated agency with history dependence. *Journal of Economic Theory* 91, 223–47.

Green, E. 1987. Lending and smoothing of uninsurable income. In *Contractual Agreements for Intertemporal Trade*, ed. E. Prescott and N. Wallace. Minneapolis: University of Minnesota Press.

Judd, K. 1985. Redistributive taxation in a perfect foresight model. *Journal of Public Economics* 28, 59–84.

Kocherlakota, N. 2006. Advances in dynamic optimal taxation. *Advances in Economics and Econometrics: Theory and Applications: Ninth World Congress of the Econometric Society*, vol. 1, ed. R. Blundell, W. K. Newey and T. Persson. Cambridge: Cambridge University Press.

Kydland, F. and Prescott, E. 1977. Rules rather than discretion: the inconsistency of optimal plans. *Journal of Political Economy* 85, 473–91.

Lucas, R.E., Jr. 1980. Methods and problems in business cycle theory. *Journal of Money, Credit, and Banking* 12, 696–715.

Lucas, R.E., Jr. and Stokey, N. 1987. Money and interest in a cash-in-advance economy. *Econometrica* 55, 491–513.

Obstfeld, M. and Rogoff, K. 1983. Speculative hyperinflations in maximizing models: can we rule them out? *Journal of Political Economy* 91, 675–87.

Persson, T. and Tabellini, G. 2000. *Political Economics, Explaining Economic Policy.* Cambridge, MA: MIT Press.

Prescott, E. 2005. The transformation of macroeconomic policy and research. In *Les Prix Nobel. The Nobel Prizes 2004*, ed. T. Frängsmyr. Stockholm: Nobel Foundation.

Online. Available at http://nobelprize.org/nobel_prizes/economics/laureates/2004/prescott-lecture.pdf, accessed 18 October 2006.

Sargent, T. and Wallace, N. 1975. Rational expectations, the optimal monetary instrument and the optimal money supply rule. *Journal of Political Economy* 83, 241–54.

Sargent, T. and Wallace, N. 1981. Some unpleasant monetarist arithmetic. *Federal Reserve Bank of Minneapolis Quarterly Review* 5(3), 1–18.

Woodford, M. 1994. Monetary policy and price level determinacy in a cash-in-advance economy. *Economic Theory* 4, 345–80.

monetary overhang

In functioning market economies, an excess of nominal money supply over nominal money demand is resolved through a combination of price, interest rate and real income changes. If these adjustment mechanisms are effectively blocked, a *monetary overhang* may emerge. Periods of pervasive monetary overhangs occurred in 1940s Europe (Gurley, 1953; Ames, 1954; Dornbusch and Wolf, 2001) and in the final period of some centrally planned economies, though for the latter episodes the magnitude of monetary overhangs – and thus the degree to which they contributed to rapid inflation in the aftermath of liberalization – has been debated (Nuti, 1989; Cochrane and Ickes, 1991; Chawluk and Cross, 1997).

A pure monetary overhang requires three conditions. Individuals (*a*) face a binding upper limit on nominal expenditures on goods and services (typically reflecting rationing of goods at controlled prices), (*b*) face binding limits on the purchase of (non-monetary) assets, and (*c*) are holding monetary balances that exceed the levels they would choose to hold in the absence of restrictions on goods and asset purchases. In practice, for a number of reasons discussed below, these constraints are unlikely to bind absolutely for all individuals; the term monetary overhang is hence also used more loosely to describe situations of extensive constraints on monetary spending.

First, access to unofficial markets may allow consumers a choice between converting monetary balances into goods at the higher unofficial price (hidden inflation) and holding cash balances (possibly in expectation of greater availability of rationed products at the lower official price in the future). As access to black markets is often limited and subject to penalties, the aggregate situation may still be described as a monetary overhang. Second, individuals may be able to convert cash into savings accounts. If interest rates are controlled, a situation may arise in which individuals prefer buying more goods at controlled prices to holding either cash or deposits, but, unable to buy goods, prefer the interest-bearing asset to cash. In this setting, the overhang situation persists, but now becomes a broader financial asset overhang (forced savings).

A monetary overhang – which might be alternatively characterized as a situation of excess nominal money supply, of below equilibrium prices (repressed inflation) and of below equilibrium velocity – can be eliminated by a combination of (*a*) a cut in the nominal money supply, (*b*) an increase in prices, (*c*) a decrease in equilibrium velocity, and (*d*) an increase in output.

In practice, the degree of disequilibrium is typically such that an increase in money demand through the third and fourth channel does not provide more than a partial solution. In episodes of often substantial uncertainty, higher nominal interest rates on demand deposits are unlikely to elicit pronounced increases in desired holdings and may, moreover, adversely affect stability in financial sectors often characterized by significant non-performing loans accrued during the period of price and interest rate controls. Rapid output growth following a return to free prices has at times acted as an anti-inflation force in a post-monetary-reform period, but rarely suffices to raise money demand sufficiently.

Severe monetary overhangs consequently tend to be cured by a reduction in the real money supply, either through an increase in the price level measured from the controlled price baseline (some black market prices may well fall after price liberalization) or through a cut in the nominal money supply (typically accompanied by the removal of price controls).

A cut in money supply (often embedded in a more comprehensive reform package) may be voluntary, for instance through the issue of bonds (with fiscal implications), or involuntary, either through a straight cancellation of part of the outstanding monetary balances or a forced conversion into public assets (again with associated fiscal implications). In principle, the cut in the nominal money supply can be set so that the post-reform equilibrium price level coincides with the pre-reform controlled price level. Determining the necessary cut requires estimates of the reform-induced change in velocity and output levels. The combination of extensive economic distortions in the pre-reform period, possible responses to anticipated monetary reform and the endogeneity of the post-reform developments to the success of the reform renders this estimation highly challenging. In economies with a recent market experience, historical velocity provides a useful baseline. Alternatively, velocity estimates can be based on comparable market economies. On the implementation side, the difficulty can be overcome by a two-stage approach combining an outright cancellation of part of the nominal money supply with a freeze on a further part, with an option to either cancel or release the frozen balances at a future point depending on the post-reform evolution of output and velocity.

Price liberalization relies on market forces to restore monetary equilibrium and avoids the need to estimate the extent of the overhang. If price controls kept prices for all goods below their equilibrium by the same proportion, the monetary overhang can in principle be resolved with a one-time proportionate jump in all prices. In practice, the disequilibrium price level typically combines with a disequilibrium relative price structure. Price liberalization may then lead to a period of inflation depending on the wage and price setting structures, possibly reinforced by an adverse fiscal impact of inflation.

HOLGER C. WOLF

See also **command economy; forced saving; inflation; inflation dynamics; rationing.**

Bibliography

Ames, E. 1954. Soviet bloc currency conversions. *American Economic Review* 44, 339–53.

Chawluk, A. and Cross, R. 1997. Measures of shortage and monetary overhang in the Polish economy. *Review of Economics and Statistics* 79, 105–15.

Cochrane, J. and Ickes, B. 1991. Inflation stabilization in reforming socialist economies. *Comparative Economic Studies* 33, 97–122.

Dornbusch, R. and Wolf, H. 2001. Curing a monetary overhang. In *Money, Capital Mobility, and Trade: Essays in Honor of Robert A. Mundell*, ed. G.A. Calvo, M. Obstfeld and R. Dornbusch. Cambridge, MA: MIT Press.

Gurley, J. 1953. Excess liquidity and European monetary reforms. *American Economic Review* 43, 76–100.

Nuti, D. 1989. Hidden and repressed inflation in soviet type economies. *Contributions to Political Economy* 5, 37–82.

monetary policy. *See* **inflation targeting; international monetary institutions; monetary transmission mechanism; money supply; optimum quantity of money; real bills doctrine versus the quantity theory; Taylor rules.**

monetary policy, history of

Today monetary policy is the principle way in which governments influence the macroeconomy. To implement monetary policy the monetary authority uses its policy instruments (short-term interest rates or the monetary base) to achieve its desired goals of low inflation and real output close to potential. Monetary policy has evolved over the centuries, along with the development of the money economy.

The origins

Debate swirls between historians, economists, anthropologists and numismatists over the origins of money. In the West it is commonly believed that coins first appeared in ancient Lydia in the eighth century BC. Some date the origins to ancient China.

Money evolved as a medium of exchange, a store of value and unit of account. According to one authority – Hicks (1969), following Menger (1892) – its rise was associated with the growth of commerce. Traders would hold stocks of another good, in addition to the goods they traded in, which was easily stored, widely recognized, and divisible, with precious metals evolving as the best example. This good would serve as the unit of account and then as a medium of exchange. According to this story money first emerged from market activity.

Governments became involved when the monarch realized that it was easier to pay his soldiers in terms of generalized purchasing power than with particular goods. This led to the origin of seigniorage or the government's prerogative in the coining of money. Seigniorage originally represented the fee that the royal mint collected from the public to convert their holdings of bullion into coin. Governments generally since ancient times had a monopoly over the issue of coins (either licensing their production or producing them themselves).

The earliest predecessors to monetary policy seem to be those of debasement, where the government would call in the coins, melt them down and mix them with cheaper metals. They would alter either the weight or the quality of the coins (fineness). An alternative method used was to alter the unit of account (see Redish, 2000; Sussman, 1993; Sargent and Velde, 2002). The practice of debasement was widespread in the later years of the Roman Empire (Schwartz, 1973), but reached its perfection in western Europe in the late Middle Ages. Sussman (1993) describes how the French monarchs of the 15th century, unable to collect more normal forms of taxes, used debasement as a form of inflation tax to finance the ongoing Hundred Years War with the English. Debasement was really a form of fiscal rather than monetary policy, but it set the stage for the later development of monetary policy using fiduciary money.

Fiduciary or paper money evolved from the operations of early commercial banks in Italy (Cipolla, 1967) to economize on the precious metals used in coins (although there is evidence that paper money was issued by imperial decree in China centuries earlier: see Chown, 1994). This development has its origins in the practice of goldsmiths who would issue warehouse receipts as evidence of their storing gold coins and bullion for their clients. Eventually these certificates circulated as media of exchange. Once the goldsmiths learned that not all the claims were redeemed at the same time, they were able to circulate claims of value greater than their specie reserves. Thus was borne fiduciary money (money not fully backed by specie) and fractional reserve banking. The goldsmiths and early commercial bankers learned by experience to hold a precautionary reserve sufficient to meet the demands for redemption in the normal course of business.

Governments began issuing paper money in Europe only in the 18th century. An early example was Sweden's note issue, initiated to finance its participation in the Seven Years War (Eagly, 1969). Fiat money reached its maturity during the American Revolutionary Wars when the Congress issued continentals to finance military expenditures. These were promissory notes to be convertible into specie; but the promise was not kept. They were issued in massive quantities. However, the rate of issue and the average inflation rate of 65 per cent per annum (Rockoff, 1984) was not far removed from the revenue-maximizing rate of issue by a monopoly fiat money issuing central bank of the 20th century (Bailey, 1956). During the French Revolution the overissue of paper money, the *assignats*, which were based initially on the value of seized Church lands, led to hyperinflation (White, 1995).

An early predecessor of monetary policy was John Law's system. In 1719 Law persuaded the Regent of France to convert the French national debt into stock in his Compagnie des Indes. He then used the stock as backing for the issue of notes in his Banque Royale. Note issue could then support and finance the issue of further shares. Law then conducted a proto typical form of monetary policy in 1720 to save his system when he attempted both to peg the exchange rate of notes in terms of specie and provide a support price to stem the collapse in the price of shares (Bordo, 1987; Velde, 2007).

Central banks

Monetary policy is conducted by the monetary authority. It is the issuer of national currency and the source of the monetary base. Usually we think of central banks as fulfilling these functions, but in many countries, until well into the 20th century, in the absence of a central bank, these were performed by the Treasury or in some cases (Australia, Canada, New Zealand) by a large commercial bank entrusted with the government's tax revenues (Goodhart, 1989). The earliest central banks were established in the 17th century (the Swedish Riksbank founded in 1664, the Bank of England founded in 1694, the Banque de France, founded in 1800, and the Netherlands Bank in 1814) to aid the fisc of the newly emerging nation states.

In the case of the Bank of England a group of private investors was granted a royal charter to set up a bank to purchase and help market government debt. The establishment of the bank helped ensure the creation of a deep and liquid government debt market which served as the base of growing financial system (Dickson, 1969; Rousseau and Sylla, 2003. The bank eventually evolved into a bankers' bank by taking deposits from other nascent commercial banks. Its large gold reserves and monopoly privilege eventually allowed it to become a lender of last resort, that is, to provide liquidity to its correspondents in the face of a banking panic – a scramble by the public for liquidity.

Monetary policy as we know it today began by the bank discounting the paper of other financial institutions, both government debt and commercial paper. The interest rate at which the bank would lend, based on this collateral became known as bank rate (in other countries as the discount rate). By altering this rate the bank could influence credit conditions in the British economy. It could also influence credit conditions in the rest of the world by attracting or repelling short-term funds (Sayers, 1957).

A second wave of central banks was initiated at the end of the 19th century. This was not based explicitly on the fiscal revenue motive as had been the case with the first wave, but on following the rules of the gold standard and ironing out swings in interest rates induced by seasonal forces and by the business cycle. Included in this group are the Swiss National Bank founded in 1907 (Bordo and James, 2007) and the Federal Reserve founded in 1913 (Meltzer, 2003). Subsequent waves of new central banks followed in the interwar period as countries in the British Empire, the new states of central Europe and Latin America attempted to emulate the experiences of the advanced countries (Capie et al., 1994).

Central bank independence

Although the early central banks had public charters, they were privately owned and they had policy independence. A problem that plagued the Bank of England in its early years was that it placed primary weight on its commercial activities and on several occasions of financial distress was criticized for neglecting the public good. Walter Bagehot formulated the responsibility doctrine in 1873 according to which the bank was to place primary importance on its public role as lender of last resort (Bagehot, 1873).

From the First World War onwards central banks focused entirely on public objectives, and many fell under public control. Their objectives also changed from emphasis on maintaining specie convertibility towards shielding the domestic economy from external shocks and stabilizing real output and prices. This trend continued in the 1930s and after the Second World War. Moreover, the Great Depression led to a major reaction against central banks, which were accused of creating and exacerbating the depression. In virtually every country monetary policy was placed under the control of the Treasury and fiscal policy became dominant. In every country central banks followed a low interest peg to both stimulate the economy and aid the Treasury in marketing its debt.

Monetary policy was restored to the central banks in the 1950s (for example, in the United States, after the Treasury–Federal Reserve Accord of 1951), and there followed a brief period of price stability until the mid-1960s. This was followed by a significant run up in inflation worldwide. The inflation was broken in the early 1980s by concerted tight monetary policies in the United States, the United Kingdom and other countries and a new emphasis placed on the importance of low inflation based on credible monetary policies. Central banks in many countries were granted goal independence and were given a mandate to keep inflation low.

Classical monetary policy

The true origin of modern monetary policy occurred under the classical gold standard, which prevailed from 1880 to 1914. The gold standard evolved from the earlier bimetallic regime. Under the gold standard all countries would define their currencies in terms of a fixed weight of gold and then all fiduciary money would be convertible into gold. The key role of central banks was to maintain gold convertibility. Central banks were also supposed to use their discount rates to speed up the adjustment to external shocks to the balance of payments, that is, they were supposed to follow the 'rules of the game' (Keynes, 1930). In the case of a balance of payments deficit, gold would tend to flow abroad and reduce a central bank's gold reserves. According to the rules, the central bank would raise its discount rate. This would serve to depress aggregate demand and offset the deficit. At the same time the rise in rates would stimulate a capital inflow. The opposite set of policies was to be followed in the case of a surplus.

There is considerable debate on whether the rules were actually followed (Bordo and MacDonald, 2005). There is evidence that central banks sterilized gold flows and prevented the adjustment mechanism from working (Bloomfield, 1959). Others paid attention to the domestic objectives of price stability or stable interest rates or stabilizing output (Goodfriend, 1988). There is also evidence that because the major central banks were credibly committed to maintaining gold convertibility they had some policy independence to let their interest rates depart from interest rate parity and to pursue domestic objectives (Bordo and MacDonald, 2005).

After the First World War the gold standard was restored, but in the face of a changing political economy – the extension of suffrage and organized labour (Eichengreen, 1992) – greater emphasis was placed by central banks on the domestic objectives of price stability and stable output and employment than on external convertibility. Thus for example the newly created Federal Reserve sterilized gold flows and followed countercyclical policies to offset two recessions in the 1920s (Meltzer, 2003).

The depression beginning in 1929 was probably caused by inappropriate monetary policy. The Federal Reserve followed the flawed real bills doctrine, which exacerbated the downturn, and the gold sterilization policies followed by the Fed and the Banque de France greatly weakened the adjustment mechanism of the gold standard. As mentioned above, the central banks were blamed for the depression and monetary policy was downgraded until the mid-1950s.

The goals of monetary policy

The goals of monetary policy have changed across monetary regimes. Until 1914, the dominant monetary regime was the gold standard. Since then the world has gradually shifted to a fiat money regime. Under the classical gold standard the key goal was gold convertibility with limited focus on the domestic economy. By the interwar period gold convertibility was being overshadowed by emphasis on domestic price level and output stability, and the regime shifted towards fiat money. This continued after the Second World War. Under the 1944 Bretton Woods Articles of Agreement, member countries were to maintain pegged exchange rates and central banks were to intervene in the foreign exchange market to do this, but the goal of domestic full employment was also given predominance. The Bretton Woods system evolved into a dollar gold exchange standard in which member currencies were convertible on a current account basis into dollars and the dollar was convertible into gold (Bordo, 1993). A continued conflict between the dictates of internal and external balance was a dominant theme from 1959 to 1971 as was the concern over global imbalance because the United States, as centre country of the system, would provide through its balance of payments deficits and its role as a financial intermediary more dollars than could be safely backed by its gold reserves (Triffin, 1960).

The collapse of Bretton Woods between 1971 and 1973 was brought about largely because the United States followed an inflationary policy to finance both the Vietnam War and expanded social welfare programmes like Medicare under President Johnson's Great Society, thus ending any connection of the monetary regime to gold and propelling the world to a pure fiat regime. In this new environment the balance was largely tipped in favour of domestic stability and was coupled with the now dominant belief by central bankers in the Phillips curve trade-off between unemployment and inflation (Phillips, 1958): this led to a focus on maintaining full employment at the expense of inflation.

The resulting 'great inflation' of the 1970s finally came to an end in the early 1980s by central banks following tight monetary policies. Since then the pendulum has again swung towards the goal of low inflation and the belief that central banks should eschew control of real variables (Friedman, 1968; Phelps, 1968).

The instruments of monetary policy

The original policy instrument was the use of the discount rate and rediscounting. Open market operations (the buying and selling of government securities) was first developed in the 1870s and 1880s by the Bank of England in order to make bank rate effective, that is to force financial institutions to borrow (Sayers, 1957). Other countries with less developed money markets than those of Britain used credit rationing (France) and gold policy operations to alter the gold points and impede the normal flow of gold (Sayers, 1936).

In the interwar period the newly established Federal Reserve initially used the discount rate as its principal tool, but after heavy criticism for its use in rolling back the post-First World War inflation and thereby creating one of the worst recessions of the 20th century in 1920–1 (Meltzer, 2003), the Fed shifted to open market policy, its principal tool ever since. In the 1930s it also began changing reserve requirements. Its policy of doubling reserve requirements in 1936 was later blamed as the cause for the recession of 1937–8 (Friedman and Schwartz, 1963). In the 1930s and 1940s, along with the downgrading of monetary policy, came an increased use of various types of controls and regulations such as margin requirements on stock purchases, selective credit controls on consumer durables and interest rate ceilings. Similar policies were adopted elsewhere. The return to traditional monetary policy in the 1950s restored open market operations to the position of predominance.

Intermediate targets

Traditionally, central banks altered interest rates as the mechanism to influence aggregate spending, prices and output. In the 1950s, the monetarists revived the quantity theory of money and posited the case for using money supply as the intermediate target (Friedman, 1956; Brunner and Meltzer, 1993). The case for money was based on evidence of a stable relationship between the growth of money supply, on the one hand, and nominal income and the price level, on the other hand, and the evidence that, by focusing on interest rates, the Fed and other central banks aggravated the business cycle, and then – in part because of their inability to distinguish between real and nominal rates – generated the great inflation of the 1970s (Brunner and Meltzer, 1993).

By the 1970s most central banks had monetary aggregate targets. However, the rise in inflation in the 1970s (which was followed by disinflation) as well as continuous financial innovation (which was in turn exacerbated by inflation uncertainty) made the demand for money function less predictable (Laidler, 1980; Judd and Scadding, 1982). This meant that central banks had difficulty in meeting their money growth targets. In addition, the issue was raised as to which monetary aggregate to target (Goodhart, 1984). By the late 1980s most countries had abandoned monetary aggregates and returned to interest rates. But since the early 1990s monetary policy in many countries has been based on pursuing an inflation target (implicit or explicit) with the policy rate set to allow inflation to hit the target, a policy which seems to be successful.

Theories of monetary policy

The development of the practice of monetary policy described above was embedded in major advances in monetary theory that began in the first quarter of the

19th century. A major controversy in England, the Currency Banking School debate, has shaped subsequent thinking on monetary policy ever since. That debate evolved out of the Bullionist debate during the Napoleonic wars over whether inflation in Britain was caused by monetary or real forces (Viner, 1937). In a later debate, Currency School advocates emphasized the importance for the Bank of England to change its monetary liabilities in accordance with changes in its gold reserves – that is, according to the currency principle, which advocated a rule tying money supply to the balance of payments. The opposing Banking School emphasized the importance of disturbances in the domestic economy and the domestic financial system as the key variables the Bank of England should react to. They advocated that the bank directors should use their discretion rather than being constrained by a rigid rule. The controversy still rages.

Later in the 19th century, the two principles became embedded in central banking lore (Meltzer, 2003, ch. 2). The Federal Reserve and other central banks (including the Swiss National Bank) were founded on two pillars that evolved from this debate – the gold standard and the real bills doctrine.

The latter evolved from 19th-century practice and the Banking School theory. The basic premise of real bills is that as long as commercial banks lend on the basis of self-liquidating short-term real bills they will be sound. Moreover, as long as central banks discount only eligible real bills the economy will always have the correct amount of money and credit. Adherence to real bills sometimes clashed with the first pillar, gold adherence, for example when the economy was expanding and real bills dictated ease while the balance of payments was deteriorating, which dictated tightening. This conflict erupted in the United States on a number of occasions in the 1920s (Friedman and Schwartz, 1963).

Adherence to the two pillars led to disaster in the 1930s. The Fed made a serious policy error by following real bills. A corollary of that theory urged the Fed to defuse the stock market boom because it was believed that speculation would lead to inflation, which would ultimately lead to deflation (Meltzer, 2003). According to Friedman and Schwartz, Meltzer and others, the Fed's tight policy triggered a recession in 1929 and its inability to stem the banking panics that followed in the early 1930s led to the Great Depression. The depression was spread globally by the fixed exchange rate gold standard. In addition, the gold standard served as 'golden fetters' for most countries because, lacking the credibility they had before 1914, they could not use monetary policy to allay banking panics or stimulate the economy lest it trigger a speculative attack (Eichengreen, 1992).

The Great Depression gave rise to the Keynesian view that monetary policy was impotent. This led to the dominance of fiscal policy over monetary policy for the next two decades. The return to traditional monetary policy in the 1950s was influenced by Keynesian monetary theory. According to this approach monetary policy should influence short-term rates and then by a substitution process across the financial portfolio would affect the real rate of return on capital. This money market approach dominated policy until the 1960s.

The monetarists criticized the Fed for failing to stabilize the business cycle, for still adhering to vestiges of real bills (for example, free reserves: Calomiris and Wheelock, 1998), and for its belief in a stable Phillips curve – that unemployment could be permanently reduced at the expense of inflation. This, they argued, led to an acceleration of inflation as market agents' expectations adjusted to the higher inflation rate, which produced the great inflation of the 1970s. As mentioned above, the subsequent adoption of monetary aggregate targeting was short lived because of unpredictable shifts in velocity.

The approach to monetary policy followed since the early 1990s has learned the basic lesson from the monetarists of the primacy of price stability. It also learned about the distinction between nominal and real interest rates (Fisher, 1922). Moreover, it has adopted a principle from the earlier gold standard literature, Wicksell's (1898) distinction between the natural rate of interest and the bank rate (Woodford, 2003). In Wicksell's theory, central banks should gear their lending rate to the natural rate (the real rate of return on capital). If it keeps bank rate too low, inflation will ensue, which under the gold standard will lead to gold outflows and upward market pressure on the bank rate. Today's central banks, dedicated to low inflation, can be viewed as following the Taylor rule, according to which they set the nominal policy interest rate relative to the natural interest rate as a function of the deviation of inflation forecasts from their targets and real output from its potential (Taylor, 1999).

Rules versus discretion

A key theme in the monetary policy debate is the issue of rules versus discretion. The question that followed the Currency Banking School debate was whether monetary policy should be entrusted to well meaning authorities with limited knowledge or to a rule that cannot be designed to deal with unknown shocks (Simons, 1936; Friedman, 1960).

A more recent approach focuses on the role of time inconsistency. According to this approach a rule is a credible commitment mechanism that ties the hands of policymakers and prevents them from following time-inconsistent policies – policies that take past policy commitments as given and react to the present circumstances by changing policy (Kydland and Prescott, 1977; Barro and Gordon, 1983). In this vein, today's central bankers place great emphasis on accountability and transparency to support the credibility of their commitments to

maintain interest rates geared towards low inflation (Svensson, 1999).

Conclusion

Monetary policy has evolved since the early 19th century. It played a relatively minor role before 1914, although it was then that many of its tools and principles were developed. The role of monetary policy in stabilizing prices and output came to fruition in the 1920s, but for the Federal Reserve, which used a flawed model – the real bills doctrine – and adhered to a less than credible gold standard, the policy was a recipe for disaster and led to the great contraction of 1929–33. When monetary policy was restored in the 1950s in the United States, it still was influenced by real bills (Calomiris and Wheelock, 1998), which may have led to the policy mistakes that created the great inflation. The rest of the world was tied to the United States by the pegged exchange rates of Bretton Woods. Since the early 1990s monetary policy in many countries has returned back to a key principle of the gold standard era – price stability based on a credible nominal anchor (Bordo and Schwartz, 1999) and to Wicksell's distinction between real and nominal interest rates. Yet it is based on a fiat regime and the commitment of central banks to follow credible and predictable policies.

MICHAEL D. BORDO

See also **Bank of England; central bank independence; fiat money; gold standard; inflation targeting; monetary and fiscal policy overview.**

Bibliography

Barro, R.I. and Gordon, D.B. 1983. Rules, discretion and reputation in a model of monetary policy. *Journal of Monetary Economics* 12, 101–21.

Bloomfield, A.I. 1959. *Monetary Policy under the International Gold Standard*. New York: Federal Reserve Bank of New York.

Bagehot, W. 1873. *Lombard Street: A Description of the Money Market*. Reprint edn. London: John Murray, 1917.

Bailey, M.J. 1956. The welfare costs of inflationary finance. *Journal of Political Economy* 64, 93–110.

Bordo, M.D. 1987. John Law. In *The New Palgrave: A Dictionary of Economic Theory and Doctrine*, ed. J. Eatwell and M. Milgate. London: Macmillan.

Bordo, M.D. 1993. The Bretton Woods international monetary system: a historical overview. In *A Retrospective on the Bretton Woods System: Lessons for International Monetary Reform*, ed. M.D. Bordo and B. Eichengreen. Chicago: University of Chicago Press.

Bordo, M.D. and James, H. 2007. The SNB 1907–1946: a happy childhood or a troubled adolescence? In Swiss National Bank. Centenary Conference volume, Zurich.

Bordo, M.D. and MacDonald, R. 2005. Interest rate interactions in the classical gold standard: 1880–1914: was there monetary independence? *Journal of Monetary Economics* 52, 307–27.

Bordo, M.D. and Schwartz, A.J. 1999. Monetary policy regimes and economic performance: the historical record. In *Handbook of Macroeconomics*, ed. J.B. Taylor and M. Woolford. New York: North-Holland.

Brunner, K. and Meltzer, A.H. 1993. *Money and the Economy: Issues in Monetary Analysis*. Cambridge: Cambridge University Press.

Calomiris, C.W. and Wheelock, D.C. 1998. Was the great depression a watershed for American monetary policy? In *The Defining Moment: The Great Depression and the American Economy in the Twentieth Century*, ed. M.D. Bordo, C. Goldin and E.N. White. Chicago: University of Chicago Press.

Capie, F., Goodhart, C., Fischer, S. and Schnadt, N. 1994. *The Future of Central Banking*. Cambridge: Cambridge University Press.

Chown, J.F. 1994. *The History of Money from AD 800*. London: Routledge.

Cipolla, C.M. 1967. *Money, Prices, and Civilization in the Mediterranean World, Fifth to Seventeenth Century*. New York: Gordian Press.

Dickson, P.M. 1969. *The Financial Revolution in England: A Study in the Development of Public Credit, 1688–1756*. London: Macmillan.

Eagly, R.U. 1969. Monetary policy and politics in mid-eighteenth century Sweden. *Journal of Economic History* 29, 739–57.

Eichengreen, B. 1992. *Golden Fetters*. New York: Oxford University Press.

Fisher, I. 1922. *The Purchasing Power of Money*. New York: Augustus M. Kelley, 1965.

Friedman, M. 1956. Quantity theory of money: a restatement. In *Studies in the Quality Theory of Money*, ed. M. Friedman. Chicago: University of Chicago Press.

Friedman, M. 1960. *A Program for Monetary Stability*. New York: Fordham University Press.

Friedman, M. 1968. The role of monetary policy. *American Economic Review* 58, 1–17.

Friedman, M. and Schwartz, A.J. 1963. *A Monetary History of the United States, 1867–1960*. Princeton: Princeton University Press.

Goodfriend, M. 1988. Central banking under the gold standard. *Carnegie Rochester Conference Series on Public Policy* 19, 85–124.

Goodhart, C.A.E. 1984. Chapter 3 problems of monetary management. In *Monetary Theory and Practice. The UK Experience*. London: Macmillan.

Goodhart, C. 1989. *The Evolution of Central Banks*. Cambridge, MA: MIT Press.

Hicks, J.R. 1969. *A Theory of Economic History*. Oxford: Clarendon Press.

Judd, J.P. and Scadding, J.L. 1982. The search for a stable money demand function: a survey of the post-1973 literature. *Journal of Economic Literature* 20, 993–1023.

Keynes, J.M. 1930. *A Treatise on Money*, vol. 2: *The Applied Theory of Money*. Repr. in *The Collected Writings of John Maynard Keynes*. 30 vols, ed. A. Robinson and D. Moggridge, vol. 6. London: Macmillan for the Royal Economic Society, 1971.

Kydland, F.E. and Prescott, E.C. 1977. Rules rather than discretion: the inconsistency of optimal plans. *Journal of Political Economy* 85, 473–92.

Laidler, D. 1980. The demand for money in the United States – yet again. In *The State of Macro-Economics, Carnegie-Rochester Conference Series on Public Policy*, vol. 12, ed. K. Brunner and A.H. Meltzer. New York: North-Holland.

Meltzer, A.H. 2003. *A History of the Federal Reserve*, vol. 1. Chicago: University of Chicago Press.

Menger, K. 1892. On the origins of money. *Economic Journal* 2, 238–58.

Phillips, A.W. 1958. The relation between unemployment and the rate of change of money wage rates in the United Kingdom 1861–1957. *Economica* 25, 283–99.

Phelps, E.S. 1968. Money-wage dynamics and labor market equilibrium. *Journal of Political Economy* 76, 678–711.

Redish, A. 2000. *Bimetallism: An Economic and Historical Analysis*. Cambridge: Cambridge University Press.

Ricardo, D. 1811. High price of bullion: a proof of the depreciation of bank notes. In *The Works and Correspondence of David Ricardo*, ed. P. Sraffa. Cambridge: Cambridge University Press.

Rockoff, H. 1984. *Drastic Measures: A History of Wage and Price Controls in the United States*. New York: Cambridge University Press.

Rousseau, P. and Sylla, R. 2003. Financial systems ,economic growth and globalization. In *Globalization in Historical Perspective*, ed. M.D. Bordo, A. Taylor and J. Williamson. Chicago: University of Chicago Press.

Sargent, T. and Velde, F. 2002. *The Big Problem of Small Change*. Princeton: Princeton University Press.

Sayers, R.S. 1936. *Bank of England Operations, 1890–1914*. London: P.S. King & Son.

Sayers, R.S. 1957. *Central Banking after Bagehot*. Oxford: Oxford University Press.

Schwartz, A.J. 1973. Secular price change in historical perspective. *Journal of Money, Credit and Banking* 5, 243–69.

Simons, H.C. 1936. Rule versus authorities in monetary policy. *Journal of Political Economy* 44, 1–30.

Sussman, N. 1993. Debasement, royal reviews and inflation in France during the second stage of the Hundred Years War. *Journal of Economic History* 56, 789–808.

Svensson, L.E.O. 1999. Inflation targeting as a monetary policy rule. *Journal of Monetary Economics* 43, 607–54.

Taylor, J.B. 1999. A historical analysis of monetary policy rules. In *Monetary Policy Rule*, ed. J.B. Taylor. Chicago: University of Chicago Press.

Thornton, H. 1802. *An Inquiry into the National Effects of the Paper Credit of Great Britain*. Fairfield, NJ: Augustus M. Kelley, 1978.

Triffin, R. 1960. *Gold and the Dollar Crisis*. New Haven: Yale University Press.

Velde, F. forthcoming. *Government Equity and Money: John Laws System in 1720 France*. Princeton: Princeton University Press.

Viner, J. 1937. *Studies in the Theory of International Trade*. New York: Augustus M. Kelley, 1975.

Woodford, M. 2003. *Interest and Prices: Foundations of a Theory of Monetary Policy*. Princeton: Princeton University Press.

Wicksell, K. 1898. *Interest and Prices*. New York: Augustus M. Kelley, 1965.

White, E.N. 1995. The French Revolution and the politics of government finance, 1770–1815. *Journal of Economic History* 55, 227–55.

monetary policy rules. *See* **inflation targeting; money supply; Taylor rules.**

monetary transmission mechanism

The monetary transmission mechanism describes how policy-induced changes in the nominal money stock or the short-term nominal interest rate impact on real variables such as aggregate output and employment.

Key assumptions

Central bank liabilities include both components of the monetary base: currency and bank reserves. Hence, the central bank controls the monetary base. Indeed, monetary policy actions typically begin when the central bank changes the monetary base through an open market operation, purchasing other securities – most frequently, government bonds – to increase the monetary base or selling securities to decrease the monetary base.

If these policy-induced movements in the monetary base are to have any impact beyond their immediate effects on the central bank's balance sheet, other agents must lack the ability to offset them exactly by changing the quantity or composition of their own liabilities. Thus, any theory or model of the monetary transmission mechanism must assume that there exist no privately issued securities that substitute perfectly for the components of the monetary base. This assumption holds if, for instance, legal restrictions prevent private agents from issuing liabilities having one or more characteristics of currency and bank reserves.

Both currency and bank reserves are nominally denominated, their quantities measured in terms of the economy's unit of account. Hence, if policy-induced movements in the nominal monetary base are to have real effects, nominal prices must not be able to respond immediately to those movements in a way that leaves the real value of the monetary base unchanged. Thus, any theory or model of the monetary transmission mechanism must also assume that some friction in the economy works to prevent nominal prices from adjusting immediately and proportionally to at least some changes in the monetary base.

The monetary base and the short-term nominal interest rate

If, as in the US economy today, neither component of the monetary base pays interest or if, more generally, the components of the monetary base pay interest at a rate that is below the market rate on other highly liquid assets such as short-term government bonds, then private agents' demand for real base money M/P can be described as a decreasing function of the short-term nominal interest rate i: $M/P = L(i)$. This function L summarizes how, as the nominal interest rate rises, other highly liquid assets become more attractive as short-term stores of value, providing stronger incentives for households and firms to economize on their holdings of currency and banks to economize on their holdings of reserves. Thus, when the price level P cannot adjust fully in the short run, the central bank's monopolistic control over the nominal quantity of base money M also allows it to influence the short-term nominal interest rate i, with a policy-induced increase in M leading to whatever decline in i is necessary to make private agents willing to hold the additional volume of real base money and, conversely, a policy-induced decrease in M leading to a rise in i. In the simplest model where changes in M represent the only source of uncertainty, the deterministic relationship that links M and i implies that monetary policy actions can be described equivalently in terms of their effects on either the monetary base or the short-term nominal interest rate.

Poole's (1970) analysis shows, however, that the economy's response to random shocks of other kinds can depend importantly on whether the central bank operates by setting the nominal quantity of base money and then allowing the market to determine the short-term nominal interest rate or by setting the short-term nominal interest rate and then supplying whatever quantity of nominal base money is demanded at that interest rate. More specifically, Poole's analysis reveals that central bank policy insulates output and prices from the effects of large and unpredictable disturbances to the money demand relationship by setting a target for i rather than M. Perhaps reflecting the widespread belief that money demand shocks are large and unpredictable, most central banks around the world today – including the Federal Reserve in the United States – choose to conduct monetary policy with reference to a target for the short-term nominal interest rate as opposed to any measure of the money supply. Hence, in practice, monetary policy actions are almost always described in terms of their impact on a short-term nominal interest rate – such as the federal funds rate in the United States – even though, strictly speaking, those actions still begin with open market operations that change the monetary base.

The channels of monetary transmission

Mishkin (1995) usefully describes the various channels through which monetary policy actions, as summarized by changes in either the nominal money stock or the short-term nominal interest rate, impact on real variables such as aggregate output and employment.

According to the traditional Keynesian *interest rate channel*, a policy-induced increase in the short-term nominal interest rate leads first to an increase in longer-term nominal interest rates, as investors act to arbitrage away differences in risk-adjusted expected returns on debt instruments of various maturities as described by the expectations hypothesis of the term structure. When nominal prices are slow to adjust, these movements in nominal interest rates translate into movements in real interest rates as well. Firms, finding that their real cost of borrowing over all horizons has increased, cut back on their investment expenditures. Likewise, households facing higher real borrowing costs scale back on their purchases of homes, automobiles and other durable goods. Aggregate output and employment fall. This interest rate channel lies at the heart of the traditional Keynesian textbook IS–LM model, due originally to Hicks (1937), and also appears in the more recent New Keynesian models described below.

In open economies, additional real effects of a policy-induced increase in the short-term interest rate come about through the *exchange rate channel*. When the domestic nominal interest rate rises above its foreign counterpart, equilibrium in the foreign exchange market requires that the domestic currency gradually depreciate at a rate that, again, serves to equate the risk-adjusted returns on various debt instruments, in this case debt instruments denominated in each of the two currencies – this is the condition of uncovered interest parity. Both in traditional Keynesian models that build on Fleming (1962), Mundell (1963), and Dornbusch (1976) and in the New Keynesian models described below, this expected future depreciation requires an initial appreciation of the domestic currency that, when prices are slow to adjust, makes domestically produced goods more expensive than foreign-produced goods. Net exports fall; domestic output and employment fall as well.

Additional *asset price channels* are highlighted by Tobin's (1969) *q*-theory of investment and Ando and Modigliani's (1963) life-cycle theory of consumption. Tobin's *q* measures the ratio of the stock market value of a firm to the replacement cost of the physical capital that is owned by that firm. All else equal, a policy-induced increase in the short-term nominal interest rate makes debt instruments more attractive than equities in the eyes of investors; hence, following a monetary tightening, equilibrium across securities markets must be re-established in part through a fall in equity prices. Facing a lower value of *q*, each firm must issue more new shares of stock in order to finance any new investment project; in this sense, investment becomes more costly for the firm. In the aggregate across all firms, therefore, investment projects that were only marginally profitable before the monetary tightening go unfunded after the fall in *q*, leading output and employment to decline as well. Meanwhile, Ando and Modigliani's life-cycle theory of consumption assigns a role to wealth as well as income as key determinants of consumer spending. Hence, this theory also identifies a channel of monetary transmission: if stock prices fall after a monetary tightening, household financial wealth declines, leading to a fall in consumption, output and employment.

According to Meltzer (1995), asset price movements beyond those reflected in interest rates alone also play a central role in *monetarist* descriptions of the transmission mechanism. Indeed, monetarist critiques of the traditional Keynesian model often start by questioning the view that the full thrust of monetary policy actions is completely summarized by movements in the short-term nominal interest rate. Monetarists argue instead that monetary policy actions impact on prices simultaneously across a wide variety of markets for financial assets and durable goods, but especially in the markets for equities and real estate, and that those asset price movements are all capable of generating important wealth effects that impact, through spending, on output and employment.

Two distinct *credit channels*, the *bank lending channel* and the *balance sheet channel*, also allow the effects of monetary policy actions to propagate through the real economy. Kashyap and Stein (1994) trace the origins of thought on the bank lending channel back to Roosa (1951) and also highlight Blinder and Stiglitz's (1983) resurrection of the loanable funds theory and Bernanke and Blinder's (1988) extension of the IS–LM model as two approaches that account for this additional source of monetary non-neutrality. According to this lending view, banks play a special role in the economy not just by issuing liabilities – bank deposits – that contribute to the broad monetary aggregates but also by holding assets – bank loans – for which few close substitutes exist. More specifically, theories and models of the bank lending channel emphasize that for many banks, particularly small banks, deposits represent the principal source of funds for lending and that for many firms, particularly small firms, bank loans represent the principal source of funds for investment. Hence, an open market operation that leads first to a contraction in the supply of bank reserves and then to a contraction in bank deposits requires banks that are especially dependent on deposits to cut back on their lending, and firms that are especially dependent on bank loans to cut back on their investment spending. Financial market imperfections confronting individual banks and firms thereby contribute, in the aggregate, to the decline in output and employment that follows a monetary tightening.

Bernanke and Gertler (1995) describe a broader credit channel, the balance sheet channel, where financial market imperfections also play a key role. Bernanke and Gertler emphasize that, in the presence of financial market imperfections, a firm's cost of credit, whether from banks or any other external source, rises when the strength of its balance sheet deteriorates. A direct effect of monetary policy on the firm's balance sheet comes about when an increase in interest rates works to increase the payments that the firm must make to service its floating rate debt. An indirect effect arises, too, when the same increase in interest rates works to reduce the capitalized value of the firm's long-lived assets. Hence, a policy-induced increase in the short-term interest rate not only acts immediately to depress spending through the traditional interest rate channel, it also acts, possibly with a lag, to raise each firm's cost of capital through the balance sheet channel, deepening and extending the initial decline in output and employment.

Recent developments

Recent theoretical work on the monetary transmission mechanism seeks to understand how the traditional Keynesian interest rate channel operates within the context of dynamic, stochastic, general equilibrium models. This recent work builds on early attempts by Fischer (1977) and Phelps and Taylor (1977) to combine the key assumption of nominal price or wage rigidity with the assumption that all agents have rational expectations so as to overturn the policy ineffectiveness result that McCallum (1979) associates with Lucas (1972) and Sargent and Wallace (1975). This recent work builds on those earlier studies by deriving the key behavioural equations of the New Keynesian model from more detailed descriptions of the objectives and constraints faced by optimizing households and firms.

More specifically, the basic New Keynesian model consists of three equations involving three variables: output y_t, inflation π_t, and the short-term nominal interest rate i_t. The first equation, which Kerr and King (1996) and McCallum and Nelson (1999) dub the expectational IS curve, links output today to its expected future value and to the *ex ante* real interest rate, computed in the usual way by subtracting the expected rate of inflation from the nominal interest rate:

$$y_t = E_t y_{t+1} - \sigma(i_t - E_t \pi_{t+1}),$$

where σ, like all of the other parameters to be introduced below, is strictly positive. This equation corresponds to a log-linearized version of the Euler equation linking an optimizing household's intertemporal marginal rate of substitution to the inflation-adjusted return on bonds, that is, to the real interest rate. The second equation, the New Keynesian Phillips curve, takes the form

$$\pi_t = \beta E_t \pi_{t+1} + \gamma y_t$$

and corresponds to a log-linearized version of the first-order condition describing the optimal behavior of monopolistically competitive firms that either face explicit costs of nominal price adjustment, as suggested by Rotemberg (1982), or set their nominal prices in randomly staggered fashion, as suggested by Calvo (1983). The third and final equation is an interest rate rule for monetary policy of the type proposed by Taylor (1993),

$$i_t = \alpha \pi_t + \psi y_t,$$

according to which the central bank systematically adjusts the short-term nominal interest in response to movements in inflation and output. This description of monetary policy in terms of interest rates reflects the observation, noted above, that most central banks today conduct monetary policy using targets for the interest rate as opposed to any of the monetary aggregates. A money demand equation could be appended to this three-equation model, but that additional equation would serve only to determine the amount of money that the central bank and the banking system would need to supply to clear markets, given the setting for the central bank's interest rate target (see Ireland, 2004, for a detailed discussion of this last point).

In this benchmark New Keynesian model, monetary policy operates through the traditional Keynesian interest rate channel. A monetary tightening in the form of a shock to the Taylor rule that increases the short-term nominal interest rate translates into an increase in the real interest rate as well when nominal prices move sluggishly due to costly or staggered price setting. This rise in the real interest rate then causes households to cut back on their spending, as summarized by the IS curve. Finally, through the Phillips curve, the decline in output puts downward pressure on inflation, which adjusts only gradually after the shock.

Importantly, however, the expectational terms that enter into the IS and Phillips curves displayed above imply that policy actions will differ in their quantitative effects depending on whether these actions are anticipated or unanticipated; hence, this New Keynesian model follows the earlier rational expectations models of Lucas and Sargent and Wallace by stressing the role of expectations in the monetary transmission mechanism. And, as emphasized by Kimball (1995), by deriving these expectational forms for the IS and Phillips curves from completely spelled-out descriptions of the optimizing behaviour of households and firms, the New Keynesian model takes advantage of the powerful microeconomic foundations introduced into macroeconomics through Kydland and Prescott's (1982) real business cycle model while also drawing on insights from earlier work in New Keynesian economics as exemplified, for instance, by the articles collected in Mankiw and Romer's (1991) two-volume set.

Clarida, Gali and Gertler (1999) and Woodford (2003) trace out the New Keynesian model's policy implications in much greater detail. Obstfeld and Rogoff (1995) develop an open-economy extension in which the exchange rate channel operates together with the interest rate channel of monetary transmission. Andres, Lopez-Salido and Nelson (2004) enrich the New Keynesian specification to open up a broader range of asset price channels and, similarly, Bernanke, Gertler and Gilchrist (1999) extend the basic model to account for the balance sheet channel of monetary transmission. Hence, all of these papers contribute to a large and still growing body of literature that examines the workings of various channels of monetary transmission within dynamic, stochastic, general equilibrium models.

Other recent research on the monetary transmission mechanism focuses on the problem of the zero lower bound on nominal interest rates – a problem that appears most starkly in the basic New Keynesian model sketched out above, in which monetary policy affects the economy exclusively through the Keynesian interest rate channel. Private agents always have the option of using currency as a store of value; hence, equilibrium in the bond market requires a non-negative nominal interest rate. In a low-inflation environment where nominal interest rates are also low on average, the central bank may bump up against this zero lower bound and find itself unable to provide further monetary stimulus after the economy is hit by a series of adverse shocks. Interest in the zero lower bound grew during the late 1990s and early 2000s when, in fact, nominal interest rates approached zero in Japan, the United States and a number of other countries. Among recent studies, Summers (1991) and Fuhrer and Madigan (1997) rank among the first to call for renewed attention to the problem of the zero lower bound; Krugman (1998) draws parallels between the zero lower bound and the traditional Keynesian liquidity trap; and Eggertsson and Woodford (2003), Svensson (2003), and Bernanke, Reinhart and Sack (2004) propose and evaluate alternative monetary policy strategies for coping with the zero lower bound.

Finally, on the empirical front, quite a bit of recent work looks for evidence of quantitatively important credit channels of monetary transmission. Kashyap and Stein (1994) and Bernanke, Gertler and Gilchrist (1996) survey this branch of the literature. Also, the striking rise in equity and real estate prices that began in the mid-1990s in the United States, the United Kingdom, and elsewhere has sparked renewed interest in quantifying the importance of the asset price channels described above. Noteworthy contributions along these lines include Lettau and Ludvigson (2004) and Case, Quigley and Shiller (2005).

PETER N. IRELAND

See also **inflation dynamics; liquidity trap; monetary business cycles (imperfect information); monetary business cycle models (sticky prices and wages); money supply; Phillips curve (new views); Taylor rules.**

I would like to thank Steven Durlauf and Jeffrey Fuhrer for extremely helpful comments and suggestions.

Bibliography

Ando, A. and Modigliani, F. 1963. The 'life cycle' hypothesis of saving: aggregate implications and tests. *American Economic Review* 53, 55–84.
Andres, J., Lopez-Salido, J. and Nelson, E. 2004. Tobin's imperfect asset substitution in optimizing general equilibrium. *Journal of Money, Credit, and Banking* 36, 665–90.
Bernanke, B. and Blinder, A. 1988. Credit, money, and aggregate demand. *American Economic Review* 78, 435–39.
Bernanke, B. and Gertler, M. 1995. Inside the black box: the credit channel of monetary policy transmission. *Journal of Economic Perspectives* 9(4), 27–48.
Bernanke, B., Gertler, M. and Gilchrist, S. 1996. The financial accelerator and the flight to quality. *Review of Economics and Statistics* 78, 1–15.
Bernanke, B., Gertler, M. and Gilchrist, S. 1999. The financial accelerator in a quantitative business cycle framework. In *Handbook of Macroeconomics*, ed. J. Taylor and M. Woodford. Amsterdam: North-Holland.
Bernanke, B., Reinhart, V. and Sack, B. 2004. Monetary policy alternatives at the zero bound: an empirical assessment. *Brookings Papers on Economic Activity* 2004(2), 1–78.
Blinder, A. and Stiglitz, J. 1983. Money, credit constraints, and economic activity. *American Economic Review* 73, 297–302.
Calvo, G. 1983. Staggered prices in a utility-maximizing framework. *Journal of Monetary Economics* 12, 383–98.
Case, K., Quigley, J. and Shiller, R. 2005. Comparing wealth effects: the stock market versus the housing market. *Advances in Macroeconomics* 5 . http://www.bepress.com/bejm/advances/vol5/iss1/art1/.
Clarida, R., Gali, J. and Gertler, M. 1999. The science of monetary policy: a New Keynesian perspective. *Journal of Economic Literature* 37, 1661–707.
Dornbusch, R. 1976. Expectations and exchange rate dynamics. *Journal of Political Economy* 84, 1161–76.
Eggertsson, G. and Woodford, M. 2003. The zero bound on interest rates and optimal monetary policy. *Brookings Papers on Economic Activity* 2003(1), 139–211.
Fischer, S. 1977. Long-term contracts, rational expectations, and the optimal money supply rule. *Journal of Political Economy* 85, 191–205.
Fleming, J. 1962. Domestic financial polices under fixed and under floating exchange rates. *International Monetary Fund Staff Papers* 9, 369–79.

Fuhrer, J. and Madigan, B. 1997. Monetary policy when interest rates are bounded at zero. *Review of Economics and Statistics* 79, 573–85.

Hicks, J. 1937. Mr. Keynes and the 'Classics': a suggested interpretation. *Econometrica* 5, 147–59.

Ireland, P. 2004. Money's role in the monetary business cycle. *Journal of Money, Credit, and Banking* 36, 969–83.

Kashyap, A. and Stein, J. 1994. Monetary policy and bank lending. In *Monetary Policy*, ed. N. Mankiw. Chicago: University of Chicago Press.

Kerr, W. and King, R. 1996. Limits on interest rate rules in the IS model. *Federal Reserve Bank of Richmond Economic Quarterly* 82, 47–75.

Kimball, M. 1995. The quantitative analytics of the basic neomonetarist model. *Journal of Money, Credit, and Banking* 27, 1241–77.

Krugman, P. 1998. It's baaack: Japan's slump and the return of the liquidity trap. *Brookings Papers on Economic Activity* 1998(2), 137–87.

Kydland, F. and Prescott, E. 1982. Time to build and aggregate fluctuations. *Econometrica* 50, 1345–70.

Lettau, M. and Ludvigson, S. 2004. Understanding trend and cycle in asset values: reevaluating the wealth effect on consumption. *American Economic Review* 94, 276–99.

Lucas Jr., R. 1972. Expectations and the neutrality of money. *Journal of Economic Theory* 4, 103–24.

Mankiw, N. and Romer, D. 1991. *New Keynesian Economics. Volume 1: Imperfect Competition and Sticky Prices. Volume 2: Coordination Failures and Real Rigidities.* Cambridge, MA: MIT Press.

McCallum, B. 1979. The current state of the policy-ineffectiveness debate. *American Economic Review* 69, 240–5.

McCallum, B. and Nelson, E. 1999. An optimizing IS–LM specification for monetary policy and business cycle analysis. *Journal of Money, Credit, and Banking* 31, 296–316.

Meltzer, A. 1995. Monetary, credit and (other) transmission processes: a monetarist perspective. *Journal of Economic Perspectives* 9, 49–72.

Mishkin, F. 1995. Symposium on the monetary transmission mechanism. *Journal of Economic Perspectives* 9(4), 3–10.

Mundell, R. 1963. Capital mobility and stabilization policy under fixed and flexible exchange rates. *Canadian Journal of Economics and Political Science* 29, 475–85.

Obstfeld, M. and Rogoff, K. 1995. Exchange rate dynamics redux. *Journal of Political Economy* 103, 624–60.

Phelps, E. and Taylor, J. 1977. Stabilizing powers of monetary policy under rational expectations. *Journal of Political Economy* 85, 163–90.

Poole, W. 1970. Optimal choice of monetary policy instruments in a simple stochastic macro model. *Quarterly Journal of Economics* 84, 197–216.

Roosa, R. 1951. Interest rates and the central bank. In *Money, Trade, and Economic Growth: Essays in Honor of John Henry Williams.* New York: Macmillan.

Rotemberg, J. 1982. Sticky prices in the United States. *Journal of Political Economy* 90, 1187–211.

Sargent, T. and Wallace, N. 1975. 'Rational' expectations, the optimal monetary instrument, and the optimal money supply rule. *Journal of Political Economy* 83, 241–54.

Summers, L. 1991. How should long-term monetary policy be determined? *Journal of Money, Credit, and Banking* 23, 625–31.

Svensson, L. 2003. Escaping from a liquidity trap and deflation: the foolproof way and others. *Journal of Economic Perspectives* 17(4), 145–66.

Taylor, J. 1993. Discretion versus policy rules in practice. *Carnegie-Rochester Conference Series on Public Policy* 39, 195–214.

Tobin, J. 1969. A general equilibrium approach to monetary theory. *Journal of Money, Credit, and Banking* 1, 15–29.

Woodford, M. 2003. *Interest and Prices: Foundations of a Theory of Monetary Policy.* Princeton: Princeton University Press.

money

Money as a social institution and public good

Among the conventions of almost every human society of historical record has been the use of *money*, that is, particular commodities or tokens as measures of value and media of exchange in economic transactions. Somehow the members of a society agree on what will be acceptable tender in making payments and settling debts among themselves. General agreement to the convention, not the particular media agreed upon, is the source of money's immense value to the society. In this respect money is similar to language, standard time, or the convention designating the side of the road for passing.

The reason for the universality of money as a social institution is that it facilitates trade. Trade among individuals enables them to achieve much higher standards of living than if each person or family were restricted to autarchic subsistence. Because of economies of scale, division of labour among specialists yields enormous gains. Of course, trades have always taken place by barter, and even in modern economies many exchanges occur without money. Barter is usually bilateral, thus in Jevons's famous phrase it requires 'a double coincidence [of wants], which will rarely happen' (1875: 3). Multilateral trade is much more efficient, permitting each trader bilateral imbalances provided her trade in aggregate is balanced. Imagine, for example, that for lack of double coincidences no bilateral trades are possible among A, B and C because A wants C's goods, B wants A's and C wants B's. Obviously three-way exchange would benefit everyone.

Multilateral barter is conceivable. It could be arranged by putting participants in simultaneous communication with each other – in person as at a village market or a commodity or stock exchange, or by modern telecommunications. But any multi-participant multi-commodity market would need a clearing mechanism. A trader would not have to be balanced with every other trader. But in the absence of a money each trader would have to be balanced in every commodity. This would be awkward and inefficient. Participants would need to come to market with inventories of many goods. A natural conclusion of any one market session would be intertemporal deals, commodities acquired today in exchange for promised future deliveries of the same or other commodities. Without money, this too would be awkward: a typical trader would end up with debts to or claims on other traders in many specific commodities.

One could imagine using intrinsically valueless tokens during a market session to lubricate barter – like poker chips for scorekeeping in a stakeless poker game. The tokens would make it possible to price each commodity in a common *numéraire* rather than in each of numerous other commodities. But if the tokens became worthless at the end of the session, each participant would have to be required to return as many tokens as he or she started with. Otherwise no one would sell useful goods for tokens, for fear of leaving the market with them rather than with commodities of value. If instead the tokens will be acceptable tenders in this and other markets in future – well, then they are money (on these issues see Hawtrey, 1927, ch. 1; Starr, 1972; Shubik, 1984; Kareken and Wallace, 1980).

The social convention makes a society's money generally acceptable within it, and the practice of general acceptability reinforces the convention. Y accepts money from X in exchange for goods and services and other things of value because Y is confident that Z, A, B,…, and indeed X will in turn accept that same money. Moreover, money is accepted from the bearer immediately and impersonally – without delay, without identification. Since an economic agent's purchases and sales, outlays and receipts, are not perfectly synchronous, each agent's inventory of money fluctuates in size as money circulates throughout the economy. These fluctuations in individual money holdings enable essential intertemporal exchanges to take place. Workers are paid for their labour today, and next week they buy the food and clothing that are the truly desired proceeds of their work. The farmer and the tailor accumulate money from those sales; on payday they pay it out to their hired hands.

The moneys chosen by societies have varied tremendously over human history. So have their languages. In each case, what is universal and important is that something is chosen, not what is chosen. The variety of choice defies generalizations about the intrinsic properties of moneys. Livestock, salt, glass beads and seashells have served as money. Major grain crops were natural media for payments of wages and rents, and therefore in other transactions and accounts. Cigarettes were money in

prisoner-of-war camps. On the island of Yap debts were settled by changing the ownership of large immovable stone wheels. The practice continued after the sea flooded their site and the stones were invisible at the bottom of a lagoon. (Similarly when gold was international money in the twentieth-century title to it often changed while the gold itself, safe in underground vaults, never moved.)

Some moneys have been commodities valued independently of their monetary role, intrinsically useful in production or consumption. Others have been tokens of no intrinsic utility and negligible cost of production, coins or pieces of paper. Commodity moneys derive their value partly, and token moneys wholly, from the social convention that designates them as money.

In modern nation-states the sovereign government can generally determine the society's money. For example, the United States constitution assigns to the federal government (thus, not to the states) the power 'to coin money, regulate the value thereof, and of foreign coin'. The central government defines the monetary unit, decides in what media taxes and other debts to the government itself may be paid, and defines what media are legal tender in the settlement of other debts and contracts (Starr, 1974).

Precious metals as money

Gold and silver have histories going back many centuries as the moneys of choice of many societies and as international media of exchange. Copper coinage antedates them, but copper became too abundant and was relegated to subsidiary coins. The precious metals are durable. They are divisible into convenient denominations. They can be made into ingots, bars and coins of standard weights. When used as moneys, they have been sufficiently scarce – relative to the non-monetary demands for them – as to pack considerable value into convenient portable forms. They glitter. They have long been prized for ornament and display. Gold and silver, one or the other or both, were the basic moneys of Europe and of European dominions and settlements throughout the world from the 17th century, or before, until recently. In modern times gold, in particular, acquired awesome mystique (Keynes, 1930).

Sovereigns minted these precious metals on demand into coins of their own realms, with their own names. In addition to minting *full-bodied* coins for public circulation, sovereigns commonly provided *token* coins made of metals, convenient for retail transactions, negligible in intrinsic value but convertible into the basic money of the realm. Many full-bodied coins circulated across national boundaries with values equivalent to their weight. For example, the original monetary unit of the United States was the silver dollar of Spanish America.

Until the late nineteenth century silver was more prevalent than gold as a monetary commodity. From medieval times silver was the English money of account; the pound sterling was initially a weight of silver. England and many other countries coined both silver and gold, but there were frequent periods when bimetallism degenerated *de facto* into one standard or the other. This happened when their prices at the mint diverged enough from their relative values in other countries or in commerce to offset the costs of arbitrage. Then 'Gresham's law' would take over, and the metal undervalued at the mint, the 'good money', would disappear from monetary circulation, 'driven out' by the 'bad money' overpriced at the mint (Hawtrey, 1927: 202–4, 283).

In England in 1717 Isaac Newton, Master of the Mint, unintentionally overvalued gold, pushing silver out of circulation and in effect putting England on a gold standard. The switch was formalized in 1816. During the nineteenth century other European countries and the United States likewise gravitated from bimetallism to gold. Alexander Hamilton, America's first Secretary of the Treasury, complemented the silver dollar with gold coins. But it was not until the late nineteenth century that gold overtook silver as the basic money of the United States. The values of sterling and dollars in gold set by Newton and Hamilton, implying an exchange rate of $4.86 per pound, lasted until 1931, with several wartime interruptions.

The heyday of the international gold standard was 1880–1914, when all major national currencies were convertible into gold at fixed rates. Silver, like copper before it, was eventually demoted to token coin status (Hawtrey, 1927, chs 16–20).

Functions of money

A triad long familiar to students of introductory economics lists the functions of money: (1) unit of account, or *numéraire*, (2) means of payment, or medium of exchange, and (3) store of value.

The US dollar, for example, is the unit of account in the United States. Prices of everything are quoted in dollars, and accounts are kept in dollars. The various media that change hands in transactions – coins, paper currency, deposits – are denominated in dollars. That does not prevent anyone who cares to do so from quoting prices in a foreign currency or in bushels of wheat, or from finding sellers who will accept them in payment for other things. It just would not be very efficient as a general practice.

To be sure, some societies have used, and kept accounts in, more than one money – in both gold and silver or, for example, in Japan two centuries ago, both in coins and in standard weights of rice. Today some national currencies may be acceptable means of payment in other jurisdictions – dollars in Russia, srael and Canada, yen in Hawaii, Deutschemarks in Eastern Europe. The reason may be the frequency of cross-border tourism and trade. Or it may be that as a consequence of hyperinflation people turn to a 'hard' foreign currency as unit of account. For still a different reason, a new European currency, the ecu, may become a *numéraire* parallel to national currencies like pounds, francs and Deutschemarks during the period of transition to a common currency.

A society's money is necessarily a store of value. Otherwise it could not be an acceptable means of payment. (New York subway tokens cannot be generally acceptable money; they can become valueless any day, even for use as subway fare. US food stamps, intended to be in-kind welfare benefits, are exchanged with cash at par, while grocery brands' discount coupons are disqualified by their expiration dates.)

Money is the principal means of payment of a society, but it is only one of many stores of value – and quantitatively a minor one at that. Through most of human history land has been the major form of wealth, increasingly augmented by livestock and reproducible capital – buildings, tools, machines and durable goods of all kinds. Claims to much of this wealth today take the form of bonds and shares and other securities. In the United States, basic money is only 6 per cent of total privately owned wealth.

Even though a particular commodity or token is established as the generally acceptable medium for discharging debts denominated in the unit of account, it need not be and generally is not the sole means of payment in use. *Derivative* media, often termed *representative* money, arise and circulate as media of exchange. They are promises to pay the *basic*, sometimes called *definitive*, money on demand. In the commercial city states of northern Italy, merchants left gold with goldsmiths for safekeeping. They then found it convenient to circulate the 'warehouse' receipts in place of the gold. Those payable to bearers were precursors of paper currency and banknotes. Those payable to named persons, and on their order to third parties, were precursors of cheques. Indeed, once the goldsmiths realized that they need not keep 100 percent gold reserves against the outstanding claims upon them, and that they could lend their certificates to merchants promising to deliver gold later, they became banks.

Besides providing token coins, states issued paper currency redeemable in gold or silver, or delegated the privilege to a private bank chartered to serve the state, like the Bank of England, founded in 1694. In addition, ordinary private banks issued their own notes, backed only by their own promises to pay basic money, gold or silver. In the nineteenth and twentieth centuries, governments and their central banks came to monopolize the issue of paper currency. This was not a catastrophe for banks. In modern economies, demand deposits in banks, transferable to third parties by cheque or wire or other order, have become the most important derivative media of exchange.

Whether derivative moneys were officially or privately issued, the ability of the issuers to carry out their promises to redeem them in basic money, gold or silver, was a recurrent problem. In wars and other emergencies governments often suspended these promises and issued irredeemable paper money. The trend in the twentieth century was to dispense with commodity money and to replace it with fiat money of no intrinsic value. Within each nation, the official derivative money, government currency, became the basic money. In 1933 United States paper dollars became inconvertible into gold except by foreign governments or central banks.

Internationally, gold was dethroned in 1971 as the medium for settlement of imbalances of payments between countries. Governments are no longer prepared to buy or sell gold at prices fixed in their own currencies. Gold is traded freely in private markets all over the world. Its price fluctuates as people speculate about its future. In the United States there is still an official weight of gold that theoretically corresponds to the dollar – 0.0231 oz, that is a gold price of $43.22, about one eighth of the free market price. But the US government is not prepared to sell any gold for dollars at the official price – or at the free market price, for that matter.

The US monetary base (M0) is the amount of fiat currency the government, mainly its central bank, the Federal Reserve System, has issued. It is a 'debt' to the public on which the government pays no interest and against which the government holds virtually no assets (other than its remaining gold stock, $11 billion at the official price, and its drawing rights at the International Monetary Fund, $19 billion). Derivative promises to pay dollars are now, directly or indirectly, commitments to pay this fiat money. Those promises include bank deposits and all other debts, private and public, denominated in dollars and payable at specified future times, tomorrow or 30 years hence.

In the United States in the fourth quarter of 1991 the stock of *transactions money* (M1) held by economic agents other than the federal government and banks averaged $890 billion, $265 of currency (paper and coin) and $617 of chequable deposits available on demand. The banks held reserves of $53 billion in currency in their vaults or on deposit in the 12 Federal Reserve Banks, collectively the American central bank. The sum of the currency in public circulation and the currency or equivalent held as bank reserves is the *monetary base* (M0), $318 billion. It is often called *high-powered* money: every dollar of M0 was supporting $2.80 of Ml, and GNP transactions of $18.20 a year.

Sovereigns have long profited from their money monopolies. Their mints charged 'seigniorage' fees – and sometimes they cheated. Likewise, issue of currency bearing zero interest is a way for a government to pay its bills, easier than taxation and cheaper than interest-bearing debt. By regularly issuing base money to keep up with economic growth and inflation, the sovereign collects seigniorage year after year. In the United States today seigniorage is a minor source of revenue. Since base money is only 6 per cent of GNP, growth of dollar GNP at 7 per cent a year means new issue of base money of only 0.42 per cent of GNP, 1.68 per cent of the federal budget. But for many less developed countries printing money is a major way of financing public expenditures; seigniorage is a major source of revenue, because implicit taxation by inflation is politically easier than explicit taxation.

Commodity money vs fiat money

The age of fiat money, first in one nation after another and finally internationally as well, has been more inflationary than the century of silver and gold standards between the Napoleonic wars and the First World War. During and following the 1914–18 war the gold standard broke down, and attempts to re-establish it during the Great Depression did not succeed. The Bretton Woods regime established in 1945 linked the world's currencies to gold via their fixed parities with the US dollar, because foreign governments could convert dollars into gold at a fixed price. But this system differed radically from the pre-1914 gold standard in that currency exchange rates could be and were frequently changed. The discipline imposed on a government and economy by an exchange parity fixed for a long time was diluted. In 1971, when this discipline became too much for the US itself, the gold–dollar parity gave way, and the international monetary system was wholly a regime of fiat money.

Discontent with inflation since the Second World War, and with the volatility of currency exchange rates since 1971, has led to agitation for return to the gold standard or some other commodity money. A commodity standard, if adhered to, provides a real anchor for nominal prices; its discipline prevents hyperinflation.

However, although the long-run trend of prices during the gold standard period was flat, there were violent inflationary and deflationary fluctuations around it. More important, real economic activity was highly volatile, to a degree that would be politically unacceptable nowadays (Cooper, 1982, 1991).

Irving Fisher, writing during the gold standard era, was greatly concerned by the instability of prices. He was complaining, in effect, about the volatility of the relative price of gold. Ideally, he would define the dollar in terms of a representative package of goods and services, the bundle priced in a comprehensive index number. Thus he revived the idea of a 'tabular standard', proposed by several early-nineteenth-century writers, and described with approval by Jevons (1875, ch. 25). But exchange between paper currency and such bundles is impractical. Fisher proposed instead to make periodic adjustments of the gold content of the dollar, raising or lowering it in proportion to the rise or fall in the price index since the previous adjustment. In effect, the Treasury would be selling gold for dollars to fight inflation and buying gold for dollars to fight deflation (Fisher, 1920).

A recent proposal by Robert Hall (1982) would tie the dollar to a composite commodity 'ANCAP' of ammonium nitrate, copper, aluminium and plywood. Because ANCAP's prices have historically mirrored general indices, it is meant to be a feasible proxy for the economy's aggregate market basket (other proposals for commodity standards are described in Cooper, 1991).

The Fisher strategy could be followed, even imposed as a nondiscretionary rule on the central bank, in a regime of fiat money. The market operations to implement it would be carried out in securities rather than in gold. The fundamental issue is not the monetary standard but whether stabilizing a price index should be the exclusive objective of monetary policy, to the exclusion of stabilization of real output growth and employment.

Free market money?

Would it be possible to privatize money? Certainly it is possible to privatíze derivative issues of money, promises to pay fixed amounts of base money on demand. But United States experience suggests that the supply of money, even derivative 'low-powered' money, cannot safely be left to free market competition.

Before the establishment of the national banking system in 1864, private banknotes were the only paper currency of the United States. The several states freely chartered banks, and those banks freely issued their own banknotes. These were promises to pay silver dollars, but so-called 'wildcat' banks contrived to make it tough for noteholders to find them. There was no central bank to control the aggregate issue of banknotes. The notes circulated at varying discounts from par and often became worthless, stranding innocent holders.

As a result, Congress established a system of nationally chartered banks in 1864, and taxed state banknotes out of existence. Only nationally chartered banks could issue notes, and these had to be fully backed by US Treasury debt securities. In effect, they were Treasury currency, supplementing various direct issues of Treasury currency (including the inconvertible 'greenbacks' the union government issued during the 1861–5 Civil War, which were made convertible into specie in 1879). Central banking did not begin in the United States until the Federal Reserve Act of 1914, which confined the issue of banknotes to Federal Reserve Banks.

Although private banks, state and national, were out of the business of issuing demand notes, they were still in the business of accepting demand deposits, the increasingly prevalent form of derivative money. Banks' balance sheets were regulated, but depositors were at risk. Their banks might not be able to pay in gold or equivalent on demand. After the epidemic bank failures of the 1920s and 1930s, Congress initiated a system of federal deposit insurance. Deposits in banks and other financial institutions became governmentally guaranteed, like banknotes after 1864. In the 1980s, these deposit guarantees became an expensive burden on federal taxpayers.

Could government get out of the money business altogether? It seems barely possible with commodity money and not possible with fiat money. If the government defined the *dollar* as a certain weight of gold or ANCAP or some other commodity or bundle, then private entrepreneurs could issue 'dollars', either chequable deposits or paper notes. They would be promises to pay the bearer the equivalent in the chosen commodities. The commodities themselves would not necessarily circulate on their own; indeed ANCAP and other composites could not.

The money entrepreneurs would have to keep inventories of the commodity as reserves. If one hundred per cent reserves were required, the currency would be like goldsmiths' warehouse receipts, and the private issuers would earn just a small fee for 'minting' the commodity into paper. Left to themselves, they would become banks, acquiring risky and illiquid assets while incurring demand liabilities. *Caveat emptor* would reign. The rates various banks would have to pay to attract funds would reflect depositors' appraisals of the risks. Notes and cheques of risky banks would not be honoured at par. In short, the very problems that resulted in consensus that issue of money cannot safely be left to unregulated free markets would recur.

Could the government's role be confined to defining the unit of account, the commodity equivalent of a dollar, in the same way that the government – through the Bureau of Standards in the United States – defines weights and measures? Could the system operate without any government-owned or government-issued base money? In its absence, clearings among private banks would require awkward transfers of ownership of the commodities kept as reserves against their liabilities. Very probably some one bank or consortium would arise as an unofficial central bank, and its liabilities would play the role of base money, the medium in which clearing imbalances among other banks are settled. The central bank, official or unofficial, would have to hold inventories of the standard commodity, gold or ANCAP or whatever, and be prepared to convert currency into the commodity and vice versa. That institution, history also suggests, would eventually be nationalized.

A fortiori, if there is neither an official definition of the 'dollar' nor any issue of dollars by the government or a quasi-governmental institution, there would be no standard commodity for private banks to compete in supplying to the public. Barter trading would be the rule, and the public-good advantages of social agreement on money would be lost. Since the institution of money is a public good, it is not surprising that its advantages cannot be realized by private market competition unassisted and uncontrolled.

How can money have positive value in exchange?

Economists have long regarded the theory of value as the central question of their discipline. What determines the prices at which goods and services are traded for each other? The prices in question include the wages of labour in terms of consumer goods, the rent of land in terms of its produce, and many other relative prices. They encompass interest rates and asset prices, thus the terms of trade of commodities to be delivered in future for commodities available today. They cover interregional and international trade, where the prices of concern are the terms on which imports can be obtained by exports.

Money, however, is an embarrassment to value theory. According to standard theory, something can have positive value only if it generates positive marginal utility in individuals' consumption or positive marginal productivity in the making of goods and services that do generate marginal utility. The embarrassing puzzle is sharpest for fiat money. All of its value comes from the fiat that makes it money. Fiat money has no intrinsic non-monetary source of value. It cannot be eaten or worn or be used in any other way that generates utility for consumers, except a few numismatists. Nor can it contribute to the production of things that consumers do value. It can be produced at zero social cost. Yet it is a scarce commodity for any individual agent. Why is it worth anything at all? That the institution of money is of value to the society as a whole as a public good does not automatically give it value to individuals in market exchanges.

The uphill struggle of modern economic theorists to cope with these challenges is exhibited in the proceedings of a recent conference (Kareken and Wallace, 1980). Their solutions relied principally on the overlapping generations model, which unrealistically assigns to money the function of being the sole or the principal store of value that links one generation to the next. The most careful, thoughtful and perceptive formal models of the roles of credit and money in transactions and strategies, in partial equilibrium and general equilibrium systems, are those of the game theorist Martin Shubik (1984).

It was argued at the beginning that a condition for fiat money to be held and valued today is that it will be acceptable in exchange for intrinsically useful commodities tomorrow. But this bootstrap story may not work. Suppose the world itself is known to be finite; its end will come at a definite future time. In the last period, one minute before midnight so to speak, you may need money to buy whatever consumer goods might generate utility, at least solace. Otherwise you will be confined to your own resources. But who will sell you anything, knowing that the money will be worthless while the goods might be a source of some utility? Thus money is worthless one minute before midnight, and by iterations of the same argument, it is worthless today. Even if the institution of money had public-good value between now and the end of the

world, the money itself would have no market value to individuals.

The escape from this logical impasse is that we do not all and will not all expect with certainty the end of the world at any definite time. We always do, always will, assign some probability to its continuation. Since there are many other paradoxes involved in thinking about human behaviour in a world with no chance of a future beyond a definite time, it is best not to take that prospect seriously in economic modelling.

Formal general equilibrium theory, which describes the imaginary world of frictionless barter, does of course express the prices of goods and services in a *numéraire*. It is tempting to identify *numéraire* prices as money prices. But the *numéraire* is just a mathematical normalization convenient for handling the fact that the supply equals-demand equations for N commodities determine only the $N - 1$ relative prices. Those relative prices are, by construction, independent of the scalar arbitrarily attached to the *numéraire*.

Standard value theory does, of course, have something to say about the value of commodity money in terms of other goods and services. In a gold standard regime, the relative prices of gold in other commodities have to be the same at the mint and in the market; they cannot depend on whether the gold is circulating in coins or being used in jewellery, dentistry or rocketry. That is simply a condition of the absence of arbitrage profits. It definitely does not say that under the gold standard the relative price of gold is the same as it would be if gold were not money. As argued above, gold's role as money must increase the demand for it, and that must affect its price unless it is supplied perfectly elastically. The same will be true of any other commodity or bundle of commodities chosen as the monetary standard. A substantial part of the value of any commodity used as money arises from the convention or the fiat that makes it money. The distinction between commodity money and fiat money is not absolute.

The neutrality of money

Although business managers, financiers, politicians and workers worry a great deal about monetary institutions and policies and their consequences for economic activity and well-being, pure economic theory minimizes these consequences. Theory puts the burden of proof on anyone who contends that money and monetary inflations or deflations do much good or much ill.

Classical economists liked to insist that money is a veil, obscuring but not altering the real economic scenario (Robertson, [1922] 1959:7). Their modern descendants expound 'real business cycle theory', premised on the view that economic developments that matter to societies and individuals are independent of monetary events and policies (Prescott, 1986). It is true that economic fluctuations and trends are frequently misinterpreted by stressing superficial monetary phenomena to the neglect of resources, technologies and tastes. But money does matter, really.

Does an economy arrive at the same *real* outcomes (in variables like volumes of production, consumption and employment, and in relative prices such as the purchasing power of wages and the price of oil relative to that of bread) as it would without the institution of money? Clearly not. Without money, confined to barter, the economy would produce a different menu of products, less of most things. People would spend more time searching for trades and less in actual production, consumption and leisure.

That is not the comparison the classical economists, old and new, intend by the 'veil' metaphor. Their fantasy is a frictionless, costless system of multilateral barter, in which relative prices and the allocations of labour and capital among various productive activities are determined in competitive markets. Their proposition is that the outcomes of an economy with money are the same as those that would arise from their ideal barter model. The corollary is that real economic outcomes are independent of the particular nature of the monetary institutions (Dillard, 1988).

These propositions cannot be true of commodity money. Real economic outcomes with commodity money will differ from those with fiat money, and will also depend on what commodity is selected as money. Inventories of the chosen commodity have to be held for exchange purposes and for governmental and bank reserves, beyond the stocks held in connection with the commodity's non-monetary uses in production and consumption. In growing economies demands for monetary inventories will be steadily increasing. The relative demands for monetary and non-monetary inventories are bound to change with economic and technological developments that alter the incentives to produce the commodity and change its prices in terms of other goods and services. Examples are discoveries or exhaustions of gold and silver deposits and innovations in mining and processing technologies. Since the monetary commodity's price is fixed in money, its output will decline when there is general inflation and rise when there is deflation. Intertemporal choices involving the monetary commodity, as well as contemporaneous choices, will be significantly affected by its monetary use.

The availability of moneys, whether commodity or fiat, whether basic or derivative, as stores of value necessarily brings about significant deviations in real outcomes from the hypothetical regime of frictionless barter. This is true even though that regime is postulated to include markets in state-contingent commodity futures, 'Arrow–Debreu' contracts (Arrow and Debreu, 1954). Holding monetary assets gives agents more flexibility: they can convert them into consumption of any kind at any time in any 'state of nature', though not at predictable prices. The flexibility is a convenience to individual agents. But, as Keynes saw, it opens the door to 'coordination failures' which are the essence of macroeconomics – demand for goods and services may at times diverge seriously from supplies (Keynes, 1936, chs 16, 17).

The classical dichotomy

It is possible to recognize that an economy with monetary institutions is different in real outcomes from a barter economy, even from an ideal frictionless barter economy, and still to argue that its real outcomes are independent of the purely nominal parameters of those institutions. It would be terribly convenient if the determination of the absolute price level, the reciprocal of the value of the monetary unit in a representative bundle of consumer goods, could be split off from the determination of relative prices and the associated real quantities.

Don Patinkin (1956) called this separation the *classical dichotomy*. Only monetary shocks would affect the general price level, and those shocks would raise or lower the nominal prices of all commodities in the same proportions. Only real shocks – to tastes, technologies and resource supplies – would affect relative prices and real quantities. This proposition would not exclude the fact that the monetary institutions themselves matter. The choice between commodity money and fiat money, the choice among possible commodity standards, and the arrangements for derivative moneys might well affect the social efficiency of markets and trade.

What are the nominal parameters whose settings, according to the classical dichotomy, would make no real difference? For a commodity money, such a parameter is the definition of the monetary unit in terms of the standard commodity, for example the weight in gold of a dollar. For fiat money, the key nominal parameter is the quantity of money – base money, all transactions money, or some even more inclusive aggregate.

Why should cutting the gold content of the dollar from 0.0484 ounces to 0.0286 ounces, raising the dollar price of gold from $20.67 to $35.00 (as Franklin Roosevelt did in 1933), make any real difference? The dollar values of existing public and private stocks of gold, and of monetary claims to gold would rise in the same proportion. Will not all other commodity prices do likewise? Then all relative prices and real quantities, including those of gold, will be the same as before.

For fiat money systems, and for commodity standards where issues of derivative moneys have become essentially independent of the commodity, the *quantity theory of money* achieved similar dichotomization. According to the theory, which might more accurately be called the quantity-of-money theory of prices, an increase in the nominal quantity of money would raise all nominal commodity prices in the same proportion, leaving relative prices and real quantities unchanged. Quantity theorists argue that an increase in the quantity of money is equivalent to a change in the monetary unit.

A hundred-fold increase in the stock of French francs would be – would it not? – the same as De Gaulle's decree changing the unit of account to a new franc equivalent to 100 old francs. Since the units change could make no real difference, the other way of multiplying the money stock could not either.

These analogies fail, for several related reasons. In most economies money is by no means the only asset denominated in the monetary unit. There are many promises to pay base money on demand or at specified dates. If there is a thorough units change, like De Gaulle's, all these assets are automatically converted to the new unit of account. Roosevelt's devaluation of the dollar relative to gold was not a pure units change. He did not scale up the dollar values of outstanding currency or even of Treasury bonds with provisions for such revaluation. Naturally private assets and debts expressed in dollars were not scaled up either. Likewise, when the quantity of money is changed by normal operations of governments or central banks or by other events, the outstanding amounts of other nominally denominated assets are not scaled up or down in the same proportion. They may remain constant, as when money is printed to finance government expenditures. They may move in the opposite direction, as when central banks engage in open-market operations, which typically increase the amount of base money outstanding by buying bills or bonds, thus reducing the quantities of them in the hands of the public.

The quantity theory

The quantity theory goes back to David Hume, probably farther, but its major and most effective protagonists have been Irving Fisher (1911) and Milton Friedman (1956).

In its crudest form, the quantity theory is a mechanistic proposition strangely alien to the assumptions of rational maximizing behaviour on which classical and neoclassical economic theories generally rely, as J.R. Hicks eloquently pointed out in a famous article (1935). Specifically, it ignores the effects of the returns to holding money on the amounts economic agents choose to hold. The technology of monetary circulation fixes the annual turnover of a unit of money. Suppose that every dollar 'sitting' supports just V dollars per year 'on the wing', to use D.H. Robertson's famous terms ([1922] 1959: 30). Suppose, further, that the economy is assumed to be in real equilibrium and the supply of money is doubled. The public will not wish to hold the additional money until the dollar value of transactions is doubled, and this requires prices to double.

Surely the demand for money to hold is not so mechanical. The velocity of money can be speeded up if people put up with more inconvenience and risk more illiquidity in managing their transactions. Money holdings depend, therefore, on the opportunity costs, the expected changes in the value of money and the real

yields of other assets into which the same funds could be placed. Fisher and Friedman would agree.

The quantity theory can still be rationalized, as a proposition in comparative statics. Compare, for example, two stationary situations of a given economy, in each of which the money supply and price level are constant over time. Let the money supply in the second situation be twice that in the first. Then an equilibrium in the second situation will be the equilibrium of the first with a nominal price level twice as high. This will be true even if the demand for money is modelled as behavioural, not mechanical, and is allowed to depend on interest rates, expected inflation and other variables.

However, it is not sufficient to double solely the quantity of money, narrowly defined. All exogenous nominal quantities, including outstanding stocks of debts and assets, must also be doubled. Or the second equilibrium must be interpreted as a stationary state that will be reached only when all these other nominal stocks have had time to adjust endogenously to the new quantity of money. This quantity theory does not apply to short-run changes in monetary quantities engineered by central banks, for the same reasons that render the 'units change' metaphor inapplicable.

In its interpretation as a proposition in long-run comparative statics, the quantity theory supports 'neutrality' as asserted in the classical dichotomy. Neutrality has come to have two meanings in monetary economics. Simple *neutrality* means that real economic outcomes are independent of the levels of nominal prices. *Superneutrality* means that those outcomes are also independent of the rates of change of nominal prices.

The case for superneutrality appeals to, and depends upon, the 'Fisher equation'. Early on, Fisher (1896) saw the importance of distinguishing between nominal and real rates of interest on assets and debts denominated in monetary units. *Ex post*, the algebraic difference between them is by definition the rate of inflation or deflation. This is a tautology. But Fisher (1911) is also credited with a meaningful proposition: anticipation of inflation (deflation) raises (lowers) nominal rates of interest but does not alter real rates of interest. The corollary is that whatever is the time path of money stocks that determines the path of prices, the paths of real economic variables are the same. Fisher himself was enough of a classical economist to believe this as a long-run theoretical truth, but enough of a pragmatic empiricist to find that nominal rates were very slow to incorporate adjustments for ongoing inflations and deflations.

The price of money

A 1975 conference on monetarism at Brown University is remembered for a pithy observation by Milton Friedman, offered only half in jest:

> For the monetarist/non-monetarist dichotomy, I suspect that the simplest litmus test would be the

conditioned reflex to the question, 'What is the price of money?' The monetarist will answer, 'The inverse of the price level'; the non-monetarist (Keynesian or central banker) will answer, 'the interest rate'. The key difference is whether the stress is on money viewed as an asset with special characteristics, or on credit and credit markets, which leads to the analysis of monetary policy and monetary change operating through organized 'money', i.e. 'credit', markets, rather than through actual and desired cash balances. Though not so obvious, the answer given also affects attitudes toward prices: whether their adjustment is regarded as an integral part of the economic process analyzed, or as an institutional datum to which the rest of the system will adjust (Stein, 1976: 316).

'What am I', asked the chairman of the session, George Borts, 'if I answer "one"?'

Any durable good has at least two 'prices', the price at which it can be bought or sold, and the price of the services it renders per unit time. The price of the good itself is the present value of the expected, though uncertain, values of the services it will render in future. For money, the first price is its purchasing power. Its services come in two forms: as a store of value, the capital gain or loss from changes in its purchasing power, and, as a medium of exchange, the benefits it yields in convenience, effort-saving and risk reduction. Without cash on hand, an economic agent may find it costly to make desirable transactions, or to forgo them. The marginal productivity of holding money is the value of an additional dollar in reducing those costs.

What is the marginal opportunity cost to which agents will equate the marginal productivity of holding money? It depends on what alternatives are available. If money proper were the only store of value in the economy, the opportunity cost of holding money would be the marginal utility of immediate consumption relative to future consumption. Although this set-up is all too common in the literature, it confuses theories of money and of saving. Acknowledging the availability of other stores of value makes the cost of holding money the difference between the real capital gain or loss on money and the real rate of return on the non-money assets in which a marginal dollar could be invested.

If money proper were the only store of value in the monetary unit of account, though not the only one in the economy at large, the relevant opportunity cost would be the return on real capital, that is storable or durable commodities. In modern economies, however, the immediate substitutes for money are promises to pay money in future. Since money and these substitutes are affected equally by price level changes, the opportunity cost is simply the nominal interest rate on those non-money substitutes. (This assumes zero nominal interest on money itself.)

Friedman's Keynesian is careless if he calls any of these opportunity cost concepts the price of money. These are prices of the services of money. Friedman's monetarist is right, therefore, to say that the price of money is the reciprocal of the commodity price level – the real price, that is, for Borts was right about money's nominal price. Of course, there are as many relative prices as there are non-monetary commodities, and any average value of money requires using an arbitrary commodity price index.

To implement Friedman's asset valuation approach to the price of money, suppose that the nominal supply of money per capita, real per capita output and the real interest rate all follow arbitrary variable paths, anticipated in advance. Assume, at least for illustrative purposes, the Allais–Baumol–Tobin model of the demand for money (Baumol and Tobin, 1989). The marginal productivity of nominal cash holdings for a representative agent is the reduction in the frequency and cost of exchanges back and forth between money and dollar-denominated interest-bearing substitutes. It is, by the usual approximation equal to $a(t)y(t)/(2m(t)^2v(t))$, where a is the real cost of one of those exchanges, y is the agent's real income per period, m is the agent's average nominal cash holding, and v is the value of money, the reciprocal of the price level. Of these, a, y and m are arbitrary exogenous functions of time, while the valuation v is a function of time to be determined. Let $r(t)$ be the exogenous path of the real interest rate. The value of money at any time T is the discounted value of its future marginal productivities:

$$v(T) = a(T) \int_T^\infty \exp\left(-\int_T^t r(s)\mathrm{d}s\right)y(t)/$$
$$(2m(t)^2v(t))\mathrm{d}t, \tag{1}$$

$$v'(T) = r(T)v(T) - a(T)y(T)/(2m(T)^2v(T)), \tag{2}$$

$$r(T) - v'(T)/v(T) = a(t)y(T)/(2m(T)^2v(T)^2). \tag{3}$$

Equation (3), with the nominal interest rate on the left, is the familiar equation for optimal *real* cash holdings. It involves the stronger Fisher equation, because the real rate has been taken as exogenous.

Interpreted as the price dynamics of the economy, these equations describe the time path of the 'price of money'. The level of prices at each time converts the autonomous nominal money supply into the real quantity on which its marginal productivity depends. The price path itself generates the rates of price change which, added to the autonomous real interest rates, give the nominal rates. The marginal productivity of money at each point in time is equated to the nominal interest rate. Future as well as current values of money supplies, as well as other variables, affect current prices. An expected increase in future money supply raises prices today, and so does an expected future increase in real rates of interest. The Fisher equation is essential to maintain the assumed dichotomy between the paths of real and nominal variables (for a calculation in this same spirit, see Sargent and Wallace 1981).

Money and macroeconomics

In the above scenario, a key institutional fact is that the nominal interest rate on money proper is fixed, at zero. Expected inflation makes money's real interest rate negative and reduces the attraction of holding money compared to assets bearing the economy's real interest rate. For the same reason, an increase in that real interest rate is a disincentive to hold money.

However, the same institution – the fixed nominal interest rate on money – threatens the classical dichotomy. It calls into question the Fisher equation, which is central to the independence from monetary influence of the real rate of interest and related real variables. It calls it into question in principle, in long runs and short, in equilibrium and in disequilibrium. If expected inflation diminishes demand for money, it by the same token increases demands for other assets, both interest-bearing promises to pay money and real capital. These substitutions will reduce the real interest rates on those assets; their nominal interest rates will rise less than the full inflation premium. This effect – associated in the literature with the names of Mundell (1963) and Tobin (1965, 1969) – refutes superneutrality, which is essential to neutrality in any general dynamic meaning. That is to say, it is not possible to determine the real interest rate and related real variables independently of the money equation, or to determine the value of money from the demand=supply equation for money by itself.

This is true whether the economy is assumed to be classical, with full employment assured by flexibility of nominal interest rates and prices, or Keynesian, with aggregate demand short of full employment. However, the real effects of expected price inflation and deflation are a reason for doubting the efficacy of price flexibility in sustaining or restoring full employment equilibrium in the face of aggregate demand shocks (Fisher, 1933; Keynes, 1936, ch. 19; Tobin, 1975).

Irving Fisher, Alfred Marshall and other monetary economists of the early twentieth century regarded neutrality in any sense as properties of long-run static equilibrium, not of the dynamic transitions that dominate empirical observations of monetary and real variables. According to them, people are slow in translating experience of inflation into their expectations of the future. This is how Fisher interpreted the strong positive

correlations he found between inflation rates and real output (Fisher, 1911). However, the Mundell–Tobin effect suggests a still stronger conclusion, since it calls into question the Fisher equation even when inflation expectations are correct and people are not victims of 'money illusion'.

In Friedman's litmus test there is much more at stake than meets the eye. The issue is how the price level, whose reciprocal is the 'price of money', is determined. The monetarist's trained instinct is to think of it as determined by the demand = supply equation for money 'as an asset with special characteristics'. With the absolute price level thus determined, the function of markets for goods and services is to generate real, relative prices, just as in Walrasian general equilibrium theory. Those real variables, in turn, are exogenous to the path of the 'price of money'.

The Keynesian's trained instinct, on the other hand, is to think of the price level as an index of nominal prices of goods and services. As Keynes (1936, Book I) emphasized – for labour markets especially – markets in our monetary economies determine in the first instance nominal prices, not real prices. The pricel 'level' is a synthetic aggregate of multitudes of individual prices determined in diverse imperfect markets, often decided by administrative decisions or by negotiations. For price determination the most relevant equations of a macroeconomic model are price and wage equations, often members of the Phillips curve family. These specify inertia of varying degrees in nominal prices and relate their changes to measures of real excess demand or supply. As a result, price indices move smoothly and sluggishly over time, not 'jumping' like the price of a financial asset sensitive to market views of the future.

With the price level determined in goods markets, the function of the money demand = supply equation is to generate interest rates. That explains the Keynesian's instinctive response to the test question. Of course, the Keynesian recognizes that the endogenous variables of a simultaneous equations system are determined jointly, not equation by equation. That real variables are among those endogenous variables can be attributed to the fact that there is usually a non-zero discrepancy between the price path determined by the full system and the path that would be generated by the monetarist's asset price of money. The non-monetarist view does not take prices 'as an institutional datum to which the rest of the system will adjust', but it does rely on variables besides prices to equate 'actual and desired cash balances'.

The equation of money demand and supply is just one of many relations in a theoretical or econometric macroeconomic model. The small tail cannot wag the big dog. That was too much to expect. The price level is a factor common to the valuation of many assets denominated in the monetary unit, many of them close substitutes for transactions money. Their quantities now and in future must make a difference. Of course monetary policies and supplies, current and prospective, are important determinants of the price level, and so are credit markets. But the channels of these influences run through demands and supplies in markets for goods and services. Understanding the process belongs to the messy subject of macroeconomics. Finance theory, however elegant, cannot provide a shortcut.

Monetary events and policies are not a sideshow to the main performance. The real variables of a monetary economy are hopelessly entangled with monetary phenomena. They do not behave as if an economy enjoying the societal advantages of money were a frictionless multilateral barter economy seen through a veil. That barter economy would never have business cycles characterized by economy-wide excess demands and supplies of labour and other goods and services. The public-good advantages of the institution of money do not come so cheap. Among their costs are fluctuations in business activity and in the value of money itself. Pragmatic monetary economics is a central part of macroeconomics in general.

JAMES TOBIN

See also **fiat money; financial intermediation; gold standard; international finance; monetarism; new classical macroeconomics; quantity theory of money; rational expectations.**

Bibliography

Arrow, K.J. and Debreu, G. 1954. Existence of equilibrium for a competitive economy. *Econometrica* 22, 265–90.

Baumol, W.J. and Tobin, J. 1989. The optimal cash balance proposition: Maurice Allais's priority. *Journal of Economic Literature* 27 , 1160–62.

Cooper, R.N. 1982. The gold standard: historical facts and future prospects. *Brookings Papers on Economic Activity* 1982(1), 1–45.

Cooper, R.N. 1991. Toward an international commodity standard? In *Money, Macroeconomics, and Economic Policy*. ed. W.C. Brainard, W.D. Nordhaus and H.W. Watts. Cambridge, MA: MIT Press.

Dillard, D. 1988. The barter illusion in classical and neoclassical economics. *Eastern Economic Journal* 14 , 299–318.

Fisher, I. 1896. *Appreciation and Interest*. Publications of the American Economic Association, 3rd series 11(4); reprinted, Fairfield, NJ: A.M. Kelley, 1991.

Fisher, I. 1906. *The Nature of Capital and Income*. New York: Macmillan.

Fisher, I. 1911. *The Purchasing Power of Money*. New York: Macmillan.

Fisher, I. 1920. *Stabilizing the Dollar*. New York: Macmillan.

Fisher, I. 1933. The debt-deflation theory of great depressions. *Econometrica* 1, 337–57.

Friedman, M. 1956. *Studies in the Quantity Theory of Money*. Chicago: University of Chicago Press.

Hall, R.E. 1982. Explorations in the gold standard and related policies for stabilizing the dollar. In *Inflation: Causes and Effects*, ed. R.E. Hall. Chicago: University of Chicago Press.

Hawtrey, R.G. 1927. *Currency and Credit*. 3rd edn. London: Longmans, Green & Co.

Hicks, J.R. 1935. A suggestion for simplifying the theory of money. *Economica*, NS 2(1), 1–19.

Jevons, W.S. 1875. *Money and the Mechanism of Exchange*. London: King.

Kareken, J.H. and Wallace, N., eds. 1980. *Models of Monetary Economics*. Minneapolis, MN: Federal Reserve Bank.

Keynes, J.M. 1930. Auri sacra fames. In *Essays in Persuasion*, reprinted in *The Collected Writings of John Maynard Keynes*, vol. 9, London: Macmillan, 1972; New York: Harcourt Brace.

Keynes, J.M. 1936. *The General Theory of Employment, Interest, and Money*. Reprinted in *The Collected Writings of John Maynard Keynes*, vol. 7.London: Macmillan, 1973; New York: Harcourt Brace.

Mundell, R.A. 1963. Inflation and real interest. *Journal of Political Economy* 71, 280–83.

Patinkin, D. 1956. *Money, Interest, and Prices*. New York: Harper and Row; 2nd edn, 1965.

Prescott, E. 1986. Theory ahead of business cycle measurement. *Federal Reserve Bank of Minneapolis Quarterly Review* 10(4), 9–22.

Robertson, D.H. 1922. *Money*. Cambridge Economic Handbook, 4th edn, Chicago: University of Chicago Press, 1959.

Sargent, T.J. and Wallace, N. 1981. Some unpleasant monetarist arithmetic. *Federal Reserve Bank of Minneapolis Quarterly Review* 5(3), 1–17.

Shubik, M. 1984. *A Game-Theoretic Approach to Political Economy*. Cambridge, MA: MIT Press.

Starr, R.M. 1972. The structure of exchange in barter and monetary economies. *Quarterly Journal of Economics* 86, 290–302.

Starr, R.M. 1974. The price of money in a pure exchange economy with taxation. *Econometrica* 42, 45–54.

Stein, J.L., ed. 1976. *Monetarism*. Amsterdam: North-Holland.

Tobin, J. 1965. Money and economic growth. *Econometrica* 33, 671–84.

Tobin, J. 1969. A general equilibrium approach to monetary theory. *Journal of Money, Credit, and Banking* 1(1), 15–29.

Tobin, J. 1975. Keynesian models of recession and depression. *American Economic Review* 65, 195–202.

money, classical theory of

The classical theory of money is an integral part of the classical theory of value and distribution; and its conceptual categories have real counterparts in historical experience. These categories begin with metallic money and progress to the more complex forms of fiduciary money and credit.

Classical framework

The equation of exchange forms a common point of reference for all approaches to monetary theory, since the relationships it expresses simply constitute a truism and do not in themselves imply causality: $MV = PT$, where M denotes the money supply, V the velocity of circulation, P an index of prices and T the number of commodity transactions. This equation may also be written: $MV = PY$, where Y denotes total output, the index P is correspondingly adjusted and V no longer reflects the circulation of a stock of commodities but the rate of expenditure of a flow of income (corresponding to the flow of output). We use this alternative formulation to specify the classical approach to monetary theory. The only difference of substance is the replacement of the sum of commodity transactions with a measure of net output over a given period, hence excluding non-produced assets (such as land) from the exchange process.

The classical theory of money was developed largely as a response to the practical issue of the relationship between changes in the money supply and the price level. This issue was central to three historical episodes which form the background to our discussion: the Price Revolution of the 16th and 17th centuries, the Napoleonic war inflation and the industrial crises of the mid-19th century. It was not the existence of an empirical correlation that was in dispute, but the direction of causation. A solution would therefore require a *theoretical* approach as well as knowledge of the facts.

The basic structure of the solution arose from discussion of the Price Revolution. Instead of augmenting wealth in the manner suggested by mercantilist doctrine, the influx of gold and silver from the newly discovered American mines seemed only to devalue the unit of account. An immediate interpretation was offered by the quantity theory of money, which attributed the increase in the price level throughout Europe entirely to monetary expansion. According to David Hume, money had no intrinsic value and was simply a means of circulation, in which capacity it served simultaneously as money of account (1752, p. 33). This approach 'essentially amounted to treating money not as a commodity but as a voucher for buying goods' (Schumpeter, 1954, p. 313). Once in circulation, money acquired merely a 'fictitious value', whose magnitude was established by demand and supply (Hume, 1752, p. 48; also Montesquieu, 1748, pp. 50–1; Vanderlint, 1734, pp. 2–3; Locke, 1691, p. 233).

Classical economists, by contrast, treated money as a *real commodity*, whose value was determined like other commodities by the labour time socially necessary for its production (Petty, 1963, vol. 1, pp. 43–4; Smith, 1776, p. 24; Ricardo, 1821, pp. 85–6). They traced the cause of the Price Revolution not to monetary phenomena but to

lowered production costs at the mines (Nef, 1941; Outhwaite, 1969, esp. p. 29; Vilar, 1976, esp. p. 343). It followed that, in the long run, when economic activity is regulated by permanent forces, the magnitude of P in the equation of exchange is determined on the basis of value theory and both Y and V are fixed due to Say's Law and institutional factors respectively. Hence P is the independent variable in the equation and M the dependent variable. Any movement in P as a result of changes in the production costs of commodities (or money) has a commensurate effect on M. This determination of aggregate monetary requirements in the 'real' sector of the economy became known as the 'classical dichotomy' and constitutes the basic classical law of circulation (Petty, 1963, vol. 1, p. 36; Smith, 1776, pp. 332–3; Ricardo, 1923, p. 158; Marx, 1867, pp. 123–4). In other words, causation runs from prices to money in classical economics and not the reverse as we find in both traditional quantity theory and neoclassical monetarism (Eatwell, 1983; Green, 1982). All things being equal, 'The quantity of money that can be employed in a country must depend on its value' (Ricardo, 1821, p. 352). The type of money employed in the circulation process has no bearing on this conclusion, since V will be determinate whatever *its* numerical value.

Had the scope of classical economics extended no further than the study of permanent economic forces, the question of whether it possessed a 'quantity theory of money' would not have arisen. But the limitations of a long-run approach in explaining concrete developments and formulating relevant policies convinced most classical writers to take into account the role of temporary factors. In particular, the effect of exogenous changes in the money supply needed to be explained. Now the problem became complicated by the definition of money and the nature of financial organization. If Say's Law kept Y constant, only two possibilities remained open: a price adjustment, that is, a change in P, or a quantity adjustment, that is, a change in V (by hoarding or dishoarding). This was the essence of the division among the classical economists. One group was led by Ricardo and included the bullionists (that is, supporters of the 1810 Bullion Report), and later, the Currency School. The other group comprised the anti-bullionists and the Banking School and was given qualified approval by Marx.

The dominant Ricardian group held consistently that both Y and V were always fixed. The quantity 'theory' of money was therefore no theory at all in this view, but simply a logical outcome of assuming Say's Law. The inflationary process was seen as the transitional mechanism by which monetary deviations were corrected: 'That commodities would rise or fall in price, in proportion to the increase of diminution of money, *I assume as a fact which is incontrovertible*' (Ricardo, 1923, p. 93 fn., emphasis added).

The opponents of quantity theory, on the other hand, were prepared to sacrifice logical consistency in an attempt to interpret the real events with which they were confronted. Their often pioneering expositions generally placed the weight of adjustment on V, although the extent was seen as contingent upon the composition of M – whether the money supply was metallic, fiduciary or credit. The flaw in their approach was their failure to overthrow Say's Law and develop an analysis of the saving–investment process, that is, a theory of output. Had they done so, their challenge to the incorporation of quantity theory into classical economics may have been more successful.

Currency and credit

By the time the Bank of England suspended cash payments in 1797, a body of principles on the role and behaviour of paper money had already been formed. The collapse of Law's system led to considerable discussion which culminated in Smith's authoritative exposition of banking in the *Wealth of Nations*. There Cantillon's view was accepted – as against Law and Steuart – that banking could not increase the quantity of capital but only its turnover (Smith, 1776, p. 246). This accorded with the given output assumption of Say's Law. It was also established that paper money would not depreciate provided its total amount did not exceed the value of gold and silver that would otherwise have circulated at any given level of economic activity (1776, p. 227).

More contentiously, Smith argued that the economic convertibility of paper and metallic money could be maintained not only by enforcing legal convertibility but also by having banks adopt the practice of discounting 'real bills', that is, securities backed by real assets (1776, p. 239 and *passim*). This became known as the 'real bills doctrine'. It was repudiated first by Thornton and then by Ricardo and the Currency School, but rehabilitated as the 'law of reflux' by the Banking School.

The Bank Restriction period was marked by high inflation accompanied by a rise in the market price of bullion over its mint price. This indicated a depreciation of paper currency in terms of the monetary standard, a phenomenon which could not have existed when convertibility was enforced by law. The central problem was to explain the appearance of this premium on bullion, and to find a principle whose practical implementation would restore and maintain economic convertibility, thus ensuring that the bank notes conformed to the behaviour of metallic currency. The explanation which gained widest acceptance was based upon the quantity theory of money. It was presented officially in the Bullion Report and then developed by Ricardo. The remedy for inflation implied by this approach was control over the money supply by the authorities.

Ricardo began his analysis by recognizing the need to replace gold and silver in the sphere of circulation by paper – provided only that it was issued in the same amount, that is, the amount prescribed by the value of

the metal which served as the monetary standard: 'A currency is in its most perfect state when it consists wholly of paper money, but of paper money with an equal value with the gold which it professes to represent' (Ricardo, 1821, p. 355). Ricardo's discussion of legally convertible bank notes followed Smith, with some of Thornton's modifications. Since their equivalence with gold was guaranteed, they could not be issued in a greater quantity than the value of the coin which would otherwise have circulated. Any attempt to exceed this sum would precipitate a return of notes for specie, a depreciation of both paper and metallic currency, and the subsequent export of superfluous bullion (Ricardo, 1923, pp. 7–13). Overextension of inconvertible notes in a 'mixed currency' of notes and coins had the same effect so long as the degree of excess was no greater than the amount of coin in circulation (1923, p. 13, n., pp. 108–12).

In 1809, however, when Ricardo entered the bullion controversy, the currency was composed almost entirely of inconvertible paper. He therefore ascribed the rise in commodity prices, in so far as it corresponded with the premium on bullion, wholly to monetary overissue. Such an overissue would have no other effect than to 'raise the *money* price of bullion without lowering its *value*, in the same manner, and in the same proportion, as it will raise the prices of other commodities'. In other words, although paper money was depreciated, the 'bullion price' of commodities was unaltered. Hence the deterioration of the foreign exchanges 'will only be a *nominal*, not a *real* fall, and will not occasion the exportation of bullion' (1923, p. 13 n. and p. 109).

Ricardo was criticized for ignoring the real reasons for the inflation, which had more to do with harvest failures, war subsidies and the Napoleonic blockade (Morgan, 1965, pp. 46–7). Moreover, he left himself open to the charge of superimposing a theory of *fiduciary* money on a *credit* system. Had bank notes been issued at will by the state, Ricardo would have been correct in his characterization of their relationship to the price level. Fiduciary money only *represents* gold in the circulation process, and is depreciated to the extent of its overissue. The depreciation persists until the quantity is reduced, for there are no self-correcting tendencies as in the case of convertible paper. However, the fact that the notes of the Bank Restriction period were not forced currency but credit responding to the demand of the non-bank public was excluded from Ricardo's consideration by Say's Law. He treated the notes as though they were fiduciary because output and velocity were independently given. The possibility of disintermediation when the authorities tried to contract the note issue was also excluded. The fixed velocity assumption implied that the rest of the spectrum of credit would shrink commensurately with the notes. In fact, as the Banking School was to demonstrate, credit instruments simply expanded in their place.

The resumption of specie payments in 1819 on the advice of Ricardo and the bullionist spokesmen did nothing to eliminate price instability from Britain's developing industrial economy. In 1825 and 1836, phases of vigorous expansion ended with an adverse balance of payments, a gold drain from the Bank of England and an inflationary collapse into recession. The Currency School – a new orthodoxy which Morgan describes as the 'heirs of the Bullion Report' – attributed the recurrent dislocation to excessive monetary growth. The convertibility of bank notes was no longer seen as a sufficient safeguard against overissue and consequent depreciation. The Currency School argued that rules would have to be devised to make the paper currency fluctuate as though it were metallic, in other words to replicate the 'automatic' operation of Ricardo's international specie-flow mechanism. This implied regulation of the note issue by the monetary authorities in strict conformity with the foreign exchanges; the export and import of bullion was treated as an index of monetary excess or deficiency, and thus of the value of the notes.

The currency principle was given practical effect by the Bank Charter Act of 1844, which set the pattern of the UK financial system for almost a century. It was challenged by the Banking School, which Morgan calls 'the heirs to the opposition to the Bullion Report, but the opposition as it might have been rather than as it was'.

The long-run determination of aggregate monetary requirements by nominal output – the 'supply side' of the equation of exchange – was common ground in the debate. The real point at issue was again the *short-run* behaviour of the variables. Whereas the Currency School adopted Ricardian quantity theory and applied it to a credit system made up of convertible bank notes, the Banking School took the alternative view of metallic circulation and tried to develop a theory specific to credit. Both sides recognized the importance of theorizing the laws of metallic circulation as a precondition for the analysis of paper currency. The entire Currency School case for monetary control rested upon the assertion that the note issue would not by itself emulate the behaviour of a metallic system. Despite legal convertibility, it might depart at least temporarily from the amount and value of the metallic money which would otherwise have circulated. In practice, therefore, economic convertibility could be ensured only by quantitative intervention on the part of the authorities (Torrens to Lord Melbourne, *cit.* Tooke, 1844, p. 7).

Banking School criticism took three main lines. First, starting from the assumption that legal convertibility necessarily implied economic convertibility, they pointed out that any discrepancy between the note issue and a purely metallic system arose from the Currency School's erroneous theory of metallic circulation rather than from the supposed autonomy of the notes. Second, any effect of prices attributed to bank notes could not be denied to a range of financial assets excluded by the Currency School from their definition of money. Third, bank notes were in any case not money but credit, and therefore never could be overissued, through the credit structure as a whole might be extended beyond the limits of real accumulation by 'speculation and overtrading'.

The Banking School emphasized that the volume of notes in circulation could not be increased at will by the authorities, but only in response to the demand of the non-bank public. This crucial difference between fiduciary money and bank notes was explained by Tooke as consisting, 'not only in the limit prescribed by their convertibility to the amount of them, but in the *mode of issue*' (Tooke, 1844, pp. 70–1, emphasis added; see also Fullarton, 1845, ch. 3, and Wilson, 1859, pp. 48, 51–2, 57–8). The currency principle, by contrast, 'completely identifies *monetary turnover* with *credit*, which is economically wrong' (Marx, 1973, p. 123). An advance of bank notes did not *add* to the money supply, but merely changed its *composition*, allowing the substitution of one financial asset for another in the hands of the public. Excess notes returned automatically to the bank 'in the shape of deposits or of a demand for bullion' (Tooke, 1844, p. 60; see also Wilson, 1859, p. 58; Marx, 1867, III, pt. 5). This was the basis of the law of reflux, which Fullarton called 'the great regulating principle of the internal currency'. It held that economic convertibility could be ensured not only by a legal right to exchange notes for specie but also by maintaining a balance between the notes advanced on loan and those returned to the bank at maturity. Provided lending took place on commercial paper which represented a real or (within a given timescale) potential sum of values, 'the reflux and the issue will, in the long run, always balance each other' (1845, pp. 64–7; also p. 207; Marx, 1973, p. 131).

The Banking School did not imagine that the economic cycle could be eliminated by monetary measures. Instead, they evolved a new set of criteria by which the authorities could operate on the 'state of credit' through interest rate and reserve management (Tooke, 1844, p. 124; Fullarton, 1845, p. 164; Marx, 1867, III, p. 447). In practice, all that lay between the Currency and Banking Schools was ultimately a matter of timing, but this reflected profound theoretical differences. Within the framework of classical analysis, it was the Banking School which came closer to constructing a modern philosophy of monetary regulation.

ROY GREEN

See also **Banking School, Currency School, Free Banking School; bullionist controversies (empirical evidence); Hume, David; quantity theory of money; Ricardo, David; Thornton, Henry.**

Bibliography

Cantillon, R. 1775. *Essai sur la nature du commerce en général.* London: Macmillan, 1931.

Eatwell, J. 1983. The analytical foundations of monetarism. In *Keynes's Economics and the Theory of Value and Distribution*, ed. J. Eatwell and M. Milgate. London: Duckworth.

Fullarton, J. 1845. *On the Regulation of the Currency*. London: John Murray.

Green, R. 1982. Money, output and inflation in classical economics. *Contributions to Political Economy* 1, 59–85.

Hume, D. 1752. *Writings on Economics*. Oxford: Oxford University Press, 1955.

Law, J. 1705. *Money and Trade Considered*. Edinburgh: Anderson.

Locke, J. 1691. Consequences of the lowering of interest and raising the value of money. In *Principles of Political Economy*, ed. J.R. McCulloch. London: Ward, Lock & Co., 1825.

Marx, K. 1867. *Capital*. Moscow: Progress Publishers, 1971.

Marx, K. 1973. *Grundrisse*. Harmondsworth: Penguin.

Montesquieu, C. 1748. *The Spirit of Laws*. London: George Bell & Sons, 1900.

Morgan, E.V. 1965. *The Theory and Practice of Central Banking, 1797–1913*. London: Frank Cass.

Nef, J.U. 1941. Silver production in central Europe: 1450–1618. *Journal of Political Economy* 49, 575–91.

Outhwaite, R.B. 1969. *Inflation in Tudor and Early Stuart England*. London: Macmillan.

Petty, W. 1963. *The Economic Writings of Sir William Petty*. New York: Kelley.

Ricardo, D. 1821. *Principles of Political Economy and Taxation*. Ed. P. Sraffa, Cambridge: Cambridge University Press, 1951.

Ricardo, D. 1923. *Economic Essays*. London: Frank Cass.

Schumpeter, J. 1954. *A History of Economic Analysis*. London: Allen & Unwin.

Smith, A. 1776. *An Inquiry into the Nature and Causes of the Wealth of Nations*. London: Routledge, 1890.

Steuart, J. 1767. *An Inquiry into the Principles of Political Economy*. Edinburgh: Oliver and Boyd, 1966.

Thornton, H. 1802. *An Enquiry into the Nature and Effects of the Paper Credit of Great Britain*. London: LSE reprint series, 1939.

Tooke, T. 1844. *An Inquiry into the Currency Principle*. London: LSE reprint series, 1959.

Vanderlint, J. 1734. *Money Answers All Things*. London: T. Cox.

Vilar, P. 1976. *A History of Gold and Money: 1450–1920*. London: New Left Books.

Viner, J. 1937. *Studies in the Theory of International Trade*. London: Allen & Unwin.

Wilson, J. 1859. *Capital, Currency and Banking*. 2nd edn, London: The Economist.

money and general equilibrium

The general equilibrium theory of value, as developed by Walras (1874–77) and his followers, determines the relative prices of goods in terms of non-monetary factors such as technology, preferences, and endowments. Monetary factors are used to determine the nominal price level once relative prices have been determined. Relative prices are determined by the market-clearing conditions for goods whereas the general price level is determined by the market-clearing condition for money. Given a vector of nominal prices $p = (p_1, \ldots, p_\ell)$, the market excess demand functions can be denoted by $f(p) = (f_1(p), \ldots, f_\ell(p))$, where p_h denotes the nominal price of good h and $f_h(p)$ denotes the market excess demand for good h. The functions $f(p)$ are assumed to be homogeneous of degree zero in nominal prices:

$$f(p) = f(tp),$$

for any positive scalar $t > 0$. The market-clearing conditions for goods require that the excess demand for each good vanishes at the equilibrium price vector p^*, that is $f(p^*)=0$. These conditions can at most determine relative prices, because if p^* is an equilibrium price vector, then so is tp^*, for any positive scalar $t > 0$.

To determine the nominal price level, a demand function for money is introduced. The aggregate demand for money is assumed to be a function of prices $M(p)$. Money demand is homogeneous of degree one in prices:

$$M(tp) = tM(p),$$

for any price vector p and any scalar $t > 0$. For any vector of nominal prices p^* satisfying the goods market-clearing condition $f(p^*)=0$, there is a unique value of $t > 0$ such that

$$M(tp^*) = \overline{M},$$

where $\overline{M} > 0$ is the exogenous money supply. Thus, once relative prices have been determined by the real factors, the level of nominal prices is determined by monetary factors. This doctrine, which became known as the classical dichotomy, characterized the classical (pre-Keynesian) thinking about monetary economics (see Fisher, 1963, for example).

The integration of monetary theory and the theory of value was stimulated by the appearance of Keynes's General Theory (Keynes, 1936). Pigou (1943) argued that the demand for goods could not be homogeneous of degree zero in prices, because a general fall in prices would increase the real value of money and the wealth effect would in turn increase demand for goods. The Pigou effect (the effect of a general fall in prices on the aggregate demand for goods) is a special case of the real balance effect: that is, the effect of any change in real balances on the aggregate demand for goods. In an attempt to make sense of Keynes's short period analysis, Hicks (1946) introduced the concept of temporary equilibrium, in which prices adjust to clear markets in a particular time period, taking as given expectations about prices in future periods. Building on the work of Hicks and Pigou, Patinkin (1965) argued that the real balance effect is essential for the existence and stability of equilibrium. The classical writers assumed that the market excess demand functions satisfy Say's Law, that is, the value of excess demands for goods sum to zero or

$$p \cdot f(p) = 0,$$

for any price vector p. However, Patinkin pointed out that Walras's Law should also be satisfied: that is, the value of the excess demands for goods and money should sum to zero, or

$$p \cdot f(p) + M(p) - \overline{M} = 0,$$

for any price vector p. Say's Law and Walras's Law together imply that

$$M(p) = \overline{M},$$

for any price vector p. Then homogeneity of the excess demand function $f(p)$ once again implies that, if p^* is a market-clearing price vector, so is tp^* for any $t > 0$ and the price level is once again undetermined. To avoid this indeterminacy, Patinkin argued that there must be a real balance effect: a change in the general price level implies a change in real balances, and hence a change in wealth which must change the demand for commodities. Thus, in a monetary economy the excess demand for goods $f(p, \overline{M})$ is a (homogeneous of degree zero) function of nominal prices and the money supply.

Hahn (1965) pointed out another problem in the theory of monetary equilibrium, viewed from the Walrasian perspective. The problem was the lack of a proof that money has positive value in equilibrium. Hahn observed that the uses of money that might be expected to give rise to a positive demand for money all require money to have positive value in exchange. If the value of money were zero, the economy would be identical to a barter economy. Under the usual assumptions on the excess demand functions, such a non-monetary economy would possess an equilibrium, but it would not be a monetary equilibrium, because money would have no role in exchange.

Grandmont (1983) provided an elegant solution to the problem posed by Hahn (1965). He showed that, while the real balance effect might be necessary, it was not sufficient for the existence of an equilibrium in which the value of money is positive. A strong intertemporal substitution effect is needed as well. Consider an economy in which there are two periods (the present and the future). In the first period, agents buy and sell goods for immediate consumption. They also demand money as a store of value, which they hold until the following period. The value of money is given by an indirect utility function $v(m, p')$, where $m > 0$ is the amount of money held until the future and p' is the vector of future nominal prices. An agent's expectations are represented by a probability measure μ on the space of price vectors. Expectations of future prices depend on current prices p via the expectation function $\mu = \psi(p)$. Then the expected utility associated with the cash balance m is simply the expected value of $\tilde{v}(m, p')$, conditional on the current price vector p:

$$v(m, p) = \int \tilde{v}(m, p') \mathrm{d}\psi(p).$$

Let $u(x)$ denote the utility associated with the consumption of a vector of current goods x. Then the agent seeks to maximize

$$u(x) + v(m, p)$$

subject to the budget constraint

$$p \cdot x + m \leq p \cdot e + \bar{m},$$

where e is the agent's endowment of goods and $\bar{m}$ his endowment of money. The crucial assumption (sufficient condition) for the existence of an equilibrium in which money has a positive value is that the expectation function $\psi(p)$ satisfies the uniform tightness property: for any number $\varepsilon > 0$ and for every current price vector p, there is a compact set K in the space of positive prices such that $\psi(p)$ assigns probability at least $1 - \varepsilon$ to the event that the future price vector p' belongs to K.

While the classical dichotomy cannot hold in the short run, Archibald and Lipsey (1958) argued that it would hold in the long run because the allocation of money balances is endogenous in the long run. This gave rise to the study of stationary states (see Grandmont, 1983).

The cash-in-advance constraint

Introduced by Clower (1967), the cash-in-advance constraint provides a simple motivation for the use of money as a medium of exchange. Lucas (1980) derives the cash-in-advance constraint as follows. Every household is assumed to consist of two agents, one of whom is responsible for selling the household's endowment of goods (for example, supplying labour) and the other is responsible for purchasing goods. At the beginning of each day, the seller sets off for the market with a bundle of goods to sell, while the buyer sets of for a different set of markets to buy the goods they need. Following Clower's dictum that 'money buys goods and goods buy money but goods do not buy goods', the buyer needs to have a stock of money at the beginning of the day. The money earned by the seller is not available until the end of the day, so the buyer's purchases are constrained by the amount of money she has at the beginning of the day. The money brought home by the seller must be held until the next day. If $\bar{m}$ is the amount of money held initially and m is the amount carried forward to the next day, the budget constraint can be written as

$$p \cdot x + m \leq p \cdot e + \bar{m}$$

and the cash-in-advance constraint can be written as

$$p \cdot (x - e)^+ \leq \bar{m},$$

where ξ^+ denotes the vector consisting of the non-negative part of the vector ξ.

Grandmont and Younes (1973) used a cash-in-advance constraint to study the efficiency of monetary equilibrium. They considered stationary equilibria of an infinite-horizon, pure-exchange economy in which a finite number of individuals $i = 1, \ldots, I$ maximize the discounted sum of utilities $\sum_{s=t}^{\infty} \delta^{s-t} u_i(x_i(s))$ subject to a sequence of budget constraints and a cash-in-advance constraint in the form

$$p(t) \cdot (x_i(t) - e_i)^+ + kp \cdot (x_i(t) - e)^- \leq m(t-1),$$

where $0 \leq k \leq 1$. For $k = 0$ this constraint reduces to the Clower–Lucas version. Grandmont and Younes established Friedman's optimum quantity of money result: any laissez-faire, stationary equilibrium of this economy is Pareto inefficient but, if the rate of price deflation equals the subjective rate as time preference, this is sufficient to guarantee that equilibrium is efficient. Grandmont and Laroque (1975) also showed that the payment of interest on money has no effect on efficiency. More precisely, it is the gap between the inflation rate and the interest rate which has an effect, and this is attributable to the lump-sum taxes rather than the interest payments.

The cash-in-advance constraint has played an important role in macroeconomics, particularly in the study of the effect of fiscal and monetary policy (see, for example, Lucas and Stokey, 1983; 1987; Sargent, 1987).

Financial securities

The classical model of general competitive equilibrium assumes that markets are complete. Hart (1975) showed that, with incomplete markets, the existence of equilibrium is no longer guaranteed and the fundamental theorems of welfare economics no longer hold. In Hart's model, incomplete markets are represented by trade in real securities, which are promises to deliver bundles of commodities at some future date and event. Cass (2006) and Werner (1985) introduced financial securities, whose payoffs are denominated in units of money, and showed that this resolved the existence problem. However, as Balasko and Cass (1989) and Geanakoplos and Mas-Colell (1989) showed, financial securities also introduced indeterminacy of equilibrium. The problem is that a change in the price level in some state changes the real purchasing power of money and hence changes the real payoffs of the financial securities. Magill and Quinzii (1992) pointed out that the indeterminacy arises from

the fact that 'money' serves only as a unit of account in the Cass–Werner model. Money has no role in exchange or savings and investment, and hence there is no well defined demand for money.

To address this problem, Magill and Quinzii introduce a cash-in-advance constraint in the spirit of Clower (1967). There are two dates, $t = 0, 1$, and S states of nature, $s = 1, \ldots, S$. The state is unknown at date 0; the true state is revealed at date 1. It is convenient to treat the situation at date 0 as another state, denoted $s = 0$. Then each period s is divided into three sub-periods, denoted s_1, s_2, and s_3. In sub-period s_1, agents sell their entire endowment of money to a central exchange and receive money instead. In sub-period s_2, they invest in financial securities (at date 0) and receive dividends (at date 1). In sub-period s_3, they use money to purchase goods from the central exchange. The separation of the sale and purchase of goods between sub-periods s_1 and s_3 forces agents to hold money in equilibrium. Money can also be used to store wealth between periods 0 and 1, but agents will do this only if they anticipate deflation. The supply of money is determined exogenously by the government.

Three main results were established by Magill and Quinzii. First, they showed that, *generically in endowments and money supply, an economy has a finite number of locally unique monetary equilibria*. This means that equilibrium is locally determinate: the well-defined demand for money has eliminated the indeterminacy of the price level. Second, *if money is used as a medium of exchange only, local changes in the money supply have no real effects if the asset markets are complete* – changes in the money supply will change the price level but this will have no effect on the real allocation as long as markets are complete – *whereas, if markets are incomplete, local changes in money supply translate into an $S - 1$ dimensional submanifold of real allocations*. When markets are incomplete, any change in the price level implies a change in the real payoffs of the securities, and this translates into a real change in the allocation. Finally, *if money is used as a store of value, local changes in the money supply translate into an S-dimensional submanifold of real allocations in the case of both complete and incomplete markets*. This follows because the use of money as a store of value to transfer wealth between periods implies that the real allocation is directly impacted by changes in the real payoffs from holding money.

A related study by Geanakoplos and Dubey (1992) addresses a similar set of questions, but does so in the context of a model with a banking system.

Market games

To provide microeconomic foundations for monetary equilibrium, Shubik (1972) introduced a game that integrates the use of money as a medium of exchange with a generalized Nash–Cournot model of markets. The generalization by Shapley and Shubik (1977) can be summarized as follows. There is an exchange economy with ℓ commodities, indexed by $h = 1, \ldots, \ell$, and I traders, indexed by $I = 1, \ldots, I$. Each trader is characterized by a consumption set $\mathbf{R}_+^\ell$, an endowment $e_i \in \mathbf{R}_+^\ell$, and a utility function $u_i : \mathbf{R}_+^\ell \to \mathbf{R}$. The utility functions are assumed to be C^1, non-decreasing and concave. We assume that each commodity has a positive aggregate endowment $e_h > 0$ and that each individual has a non-zero endowment $e_i > 0$.

For simplicity, we assume that traders offer their entire endowment of assets for sale and then bid for the assets they want to hold using fiat money as a means of payment. Each trader i has an endowment of fiat money $m_i > 0$. The amount of money he bids for asset h is denoted by $b_{ih} \geq 0$ and the vector consisting of his bids is denoted by $b_i \in \mathbf{R}_+^\ell$.

A trader cannot bid more money than he holds, so the bid vector chosen by trader i must satisfy the cash-in-advance constraint

$$\sum_{h=1}^{\ell} b_{ih} \leq m_i.$$

The set of bid vectors satisfying the cash-in-advance constraint for trader i is denoted by B_i, where it is understood that the initial balance m_i is exogenously given.

For any strategy profile $b = (b_1, \ldots, b_I)$, define an attainable allocation of commodities as follows. Let the price of commodity h be denoted by $p_h(b)$ and defined by

$$p_h(b) = \frac{b_h}{e_h},$$

where $b_h \equiv \sum_{i=1}^I b_{ih}$ and $e_h = \sum_{i=1}^I e_{ih}$. Then let the quantity of commodity h received by trader i be denoted by $\xi_{ih}(b)$ and defined by

$$\xi_{ih}(b) = \begin{cases} b_{ih}/p_h & \text{if } p_h > 0, \\ 0 & \text{if } p_h = 0. \end{cases}$$

Then the commodity bundle achieved by i for any strategy profile b is denoted by $\xi_i(b)$. It is easy to see that the I-tuple $\{\xi_i(b)\}$ is an attainable allocation for any $b \in B$.

The traders must return their initial balances of fiat money to the government at the end of the game. This means that trader i must end the trading period with at least m_i units of money. We assume that any choice of b_i resulting in end-of-period money balances that are lower than m_i will yield a payoff of $-\infty$. The terminal balance for trader i equals his initial balance m_i minus the sum of his bids $\sum_{h=1}^\ell b_{ih}$ plus the revenue from the sale of his initial portfolio $p(b) \cdot e_i$. It is easy to show that the terminal balance satisfies

$$m_i - \sum_{h=1}^{\ell} b_{ih} + p(b) \cdot e_i = m_i - p(b) \cdot (\xi_i(b) - e_i),$$

so the terminal constraint is satisfied if and only if $p(b) \cdot (\xi_i(b) - e_i) \leq 0$. For any strategy profile b, let trader i's payoff be denoted by $\pi_i(b)$ and defined by

$$\pi_i(b) = \begin{cases} u_i(\xi_i(b)) & \text{if } p(b) \cdot (\xi_i(b) - e_i) \leq 0, \\ -\infty & \text{if } p(b) \cdot (\xi_i(b) - e_i) > 0. \end{cases}$$

Shapley and Shubik (1977) demonstrate the existence of a Nash equilibrium for this game under the additional assumption that for each commodity h there are at least two individuals whose utility is increasing in that commodity. They also provide conditions under which the equilibrium allocation converges to a competitive equilibrium as the number of traders increases without bound.

Concluding remarks

As Joseph Ostroy wrote in the first edition of *The New Palgrave* (1987, p. 515),

> We shall argue that the incorporation of monetary exchange tests the limits of general equilibrium theory, exposing its implicitly centralized conception of trade and calling for more decentralized models of exchange.

That comment is just as true today as it was then, and remains the great challenge for economists who want to develop more satisfactory models of the process of monetary exchange at the level of the economy as a whole.

DOUGLAS GALE

See also **monetary approach to the balance of payments; monetary cranks; monetary policy, history of; money illusion; money supply.**

Bibliography

Archibald, G. and Lipsey, R. 1958. Monetary and value theory: a critique of Patinkin and Lange. *Review of Economic Studies* 26, 1–22.
Balasko, Y. and Cass, D. 1989. The structure of financial equilibrium: I. exogenous yields and unrestricted participation. *Econometrica* 57, 135–62.
Cass, D. 2006. Competitive equilibrium with incomplete financial markets. *Journal of Mathematical Economics* 42, 384–405.
Clower, R. 1967. A reconsideration of the microfoundations of monetary theory. *Economic Inquiry* 6, 1–8.
Fisher, I. 1963. *The Purchasing Power of Money*, rev. edn. New York: Kelley.
Geanakoplos, J. and Mas-Colell, A. 1989. Real indeterminacy with financial assets. *Journal of Economic Theory* 47, 22–38.
Geanakoplos, J. and Dubey, P. 1992. The value of money in a finite-horizon economy: a role for banks. In *Economic Analysis of Markets and Games*, ed. P. Dasgupta et al. Cambridge, MA: MIT Press.

Grandmont, J.-M. 1983. *Money and Value: A Reconsideration of Classical and Neoclassical Monetary Theories.* Cambridge: Cambridge University Press; Paris: Maison des Sciences de l'Homme.

Grandmont, J.-M. and Laroque, G. 1975. On money and banking. *Review of Economic Studies* 42, 207–36.

Grandmont, J.-M. and Younes, Y. 1973. On the efficiency of monetary equilibrium. *Review of Economic Studies* 40, 149–65.

Hahn, F. 1965. On some problems of proving the existence of an equilibrium in a monetary economy. In *The Theory of Interest Rates*, ed. F. Hahn and F. Brechling. London: Macmillan.

Hart, O. 1975. On the optimality of equilibrium when the market structure is incomplete. *Journal of Economic Theory* 11, 418–43.

Hicks, J. 1946. *Value and Capital: An Inquiry into Some Fundamental Principles of Economic Theory*, 2nd edn. Oxford: Clarendon.

Keynes, J. 1936. *The General Theory of Employment, Interest and Money.* London: Macmillan.

Lucas, R. 1980. Equilibrium in a pure currency economy. *Economic Enquiry* 18, 203–20.

Lucas, R. and Stokey, N. 1983. Optimal fiscal and monetary policy in an economy without capital. *Journal of Monetary Economics* 12, 55–93.

Lucas, R. and Stokey, N. 1987. Money and interest in a cash-in-advance economy. *Econometrica* 55, 491–513.

Magill, M. and Quinzii, M. 1992. Real effects of money in general equilibrium. *Journal of Mathematical Economics* 21, 301–42.

Ostroy, J.M. 1987. Money and general equilibrium. In *The New Palgrave: A Dictionary of Economics*, vol. 3, ed. J. Eatwell, M. Milgate and P. Newman. London: Macmillan.

Patinkin, D. 1965. *Money, Interest, and Prices: An Integration of Monetary and Value Theory*, 2nd edn. New York: Harper and Row.

Pigou, A.C. 1943. The classical stationary state. *Economic Journal* 53, 343–51.

Sargent, T. 1987. *Dynamic Macroeconomic Theory.* Cambridge, MA: Harvard University Press.

Shapley, L. and Shubik, M. 1977. Trade using one commodity as a means of payment. *Journal of Political Economy* 85, 937–68.

Shubik, M. 1972. Commodity money, oligopoly, credit and bankruptcy in a general equilibrium model. *Western Economic Journal* 10, 24–38.

Werner, J. 1985. Equilibrium in economies with incomplete financial markets. *Journal of Economic Theory* 36, 110–19.

money illusion

The term money illusion is commonly used to describe any failure to distinguish monetary from real magnitudes. It seems to have been coined by Irving Fisher, who defined it as 'failure to perceive that the dollar, or any other unit of money, expands or shrinks in value' (1928, p. 4). To Fisher, money illusion was an important factor in business-cycle fluctuations. Rising prices during the upswing would stimulate investment demand and induce business firms to increase their borrowing, thus causing a rise in the nominal rate of interest. Lenders would accommodate them by increasing their savings in response to the rise in the nominal rate, not taking into account that, because of the rise in inflation, the real rate of interest had not risen but had actually fallen (Fisher, 1922, esp. ch. 4).

Beginning with Haberler (1941, p. 460, fn. 1) other writers have used the term money illusion as synonymous with a violation of what Leontief (1936) called the 'homogeneity postulate', the postulate that demand and supply functions be homogeneous of degree zero in all nominal prices; that is, that they depend upon relative prices but not upon the absolute price level. This usage differs from Fisher's in two senses. It refers to people's reactions to a change in the level of prices rather than to a change in the rate of change of prices, and it is cast in operational terms, as a property of potentially observable supply and demand functions rather than as a property of people's perceptions or lack thereof.

Patinkin (1949) objected to the latter use of the term money illusion on the grounds that it failed to take into account the real balance effect. A doubling of all money prices should affect household demand functions even if people are perfectly rational and suffer from no illusions, because it reduces at least one component of the real wealth that constrains their demands – the real value of their initial money holdings. Accordingly he defined the absence of money illusion as the zero-degree homogeneity of net demand functions in all money prices and the money values of initial holdings of assets.

In a fiat money economy in Hicksian temporary equilibrium, under the assumption of static expectations, the absence of money illusion in Patinkin's sense is operationally equivalent to the assumption of rational behaviour, in the following sense. Let each agent's demand functions $\hat{x}_i(p_1,\ldots,p_n,W)$ for goods $i=1,\ldots,n$, together with his demand-for-money function $M(p_1,\ldots,p_n,W)$ be defined as the maximizers of the utility function $U(x_1,\ldots,x_n; M,p_1,\ldots,p_n)$ subject to the budget constraint: $p_1x_1+\ldots+p_nx_n+M=W$, where W is initial nominal wealth. The utility function includes M and the money prices p_i because M is assumed to yield unspecified services whose value depends upon the vector of prices expected to prevail next period, and those expected prices are proportional to today's prices.

A rational agent would realize that a proportional change in M and all prices would leave unaffected the purchasing power of M, and thus also the services rendered by M. Accordingly U is said to be illusion-free if it is homogeneous of degree zero in $(M, p_1, \ldots, p_n)$. This homogeneity property was first assumed explicitly in the context of demand theory by Samuelson (1947, p. 118) although it was implicit in the earlier analysis of Leser (1943), who used the equivalent formulation: $U(x_1, \ldots, x_n; M/p_1, \ldots, M/P_n)$. It is easily verified that the $\hat{x}$'s are illusion-free in Patinkin's sense if and only if they can be derived from an illusion-free U (see Howitt and Patinkin, 1980).

The assumption of static expectations is crucial to this equivalence. If expected future prices were not proportional to current prices then a proportional change in $p_1, \ldots, p_n, W$ would alter intertemporal relative prices and it would not be irrational for the agent to respond by changing his demands. Patinkin's original definition can be generalized to take this possibility into account and to allow for the presence of productive non-money assets by requiring demand functions for real goods to be unaffected by a proportional change in W, all current prices, and all expected future prices, holding constant the rates of return on all non-money assets. If future prices p_i' were uncertain then current demands would depend upon the probability distribution $F(p_i', \ldots, p_n')$, and the proportional change in future expected prices in the above statement would have to be replaced by a change from $F(p_i', \ldots, p_n')$ to $F_\lambda(p_i', \ldots, p_n') \equiv F(p_l'/\lambda, \ldots, p_n'/\lambda)$ where λ is the factor of proportionality.

The absence of money illusion is the main assumption underlying the long-run neutrality proposition of the quantity theory of money. But the presence of money illusion has also frequently been invoked to account for the short-run non-neutrality of money, sometimes by quantity theorists themselves, as in the case of Fisher. On the other hand, many monetary economists have reacted adversely to explanations based on such illusions, partly because illusions contradict the maximizing paradigm of microeconomic theory and partly because invoking money illusion is often too simplistic an explanation of phenomena that do not fit well into the standard equilibrium mould of economics. Behaviour that seems irrational in a general equilibrium framework may actually be a rational response to systemic coordination problems that are assumed away in that framework.

Thus, for example, Leontief (1936) attributed Keynes's denial of the quantity theory to an assumption of money illusion. He interpreted Keynes as saying that the supply of labour depended upon the nominal wage rate whereas the demand depended upon the real wage. A rise in the price level would thus raise the equilibrium quantity of employment. Leijonhufvud (1968, ch. 2) questioned this interpretation and argued that Keynes was dealing with information problems that don't exist in Leontief's general equilibrium analysis. Specifically, Leijonhufvud argued that workers might continue supplying the same amount of labour services in the event of a rise in the general price level, not because they irrationally identified nominal with real wages but because in a world of less than perfect information it would take time for them to learn of the changed value of money.

Likewise, Friedman (1968) objected to the then standard formulation of the Phillips-relation between unemployment and the rate of wage-inflation. Friedman argued that the rate at which firms raised their wage offers and households raised their reservations wages, given any existing amount of unemployment, should depend upon these agents' expectations of the future value of money. To assume otherwise would be to assume money illusion. Friedman's argument implied that an expected-inflation term should be added to the usual specification of the Phillips curve. His analysis of the expectations-augmented Phillips curve was similar to Leijonhufvud's imperfect-information argument.

More recently, Barro (1977) has argued against the assumption of nominal wage stickiness in the work of Fischer (1977) and others, on the grounds that microeconomic theories of wage contracts imply that these contracts should be signed in real, not nominal terms, unless people suffer from money illusion.

Although monetary economists have thus been reluctant to attribute money illusion to private agents they have not hesitated to attribute it to governments. Indeed, as Patinkin (1961) demonstrated, money illusion on the part of the monetary authority is necessary for an economy to possess a determinate equilibrium price level. More recently, several writers have attributed real effects of inflation to money-illusion in tax laws (e.g., Feldstein, 1983). Specifically, in many countries interest income and expenses are taxed at the same rate regardless of the rate of inflation, and historical money costs rather than current replacement costs are used for evaluating inventories and calculating depreciation allowances. Because of these effects inflation can distort the after-tax cost of capital.

In short, the attitude of economists to the assumption of money illusion can best be described as equivocal. The assumption is frequently invoked and frequently resisted. The persistence of a concept so alien to economists' pervasive belief in rationality indicates a deeper failure to understand the importance of money and of nominal magnitudes in economic life. This failure is evident, for example, in the lack of any convincing explanation for why people persist in signing non-indexed debt contracts, or why the objective of reducing the rate of inflation, even at the cost of a major recession, should have such wide popular support in times of high inflation.

PETER HOWITT

See also **neutrality of money; real balances.**

Bibliography

Barro, R.J. 1977. Long-term contracting, sticky prices, and monetary policy. *Journal of Monetary Economics* 3(3), July, 305–16.

Feldstein, M. 1983. *Inflation, Tax Rules, and Capital Formation.* Chicago: University of Chicago Press.

Fischer, S. 1977. Long-term contracts, rational expectations, and the optimal money supply rule. *Journal of Political Economy* 85(1), February,191–205.

Fisher, I. 1922. *The Purchasing Power of Money*. 2nd edn, New York: Macmillan.

Fisher, I. 1928. *The Money Illusion*. New York: Adelphi.

Friedman, M. 1968. The role of monetary policy. *American Economic Review* 58(1), March, 1–17.

Haberler, G. 1941. *Prosperity and Depression*. 3rd edn, Geneva: League of Nations.

Howitt, P. and Patinkin, D. 1980. Utility function transformations and money illusion: comment. *American Economic Review* 70(3), September, 819–22.

Leijonhufvud, A. 1968. *On Keynesian Economics and the Economics of Keynes*. New York: Oxford University Press.

Leontief, W. 1936. The fundamental assumptions of Mr Keynes' monetary theory of unemployment. *Quarterly Journal of Economics* 5(November), 192–7.

Leser, C.E.V. 1943. The consumer's demand for money. *Econometrica* 11(2), April, 123–40.

Patinkin, D. 1949. The indeterminacy of absolute prices in classical economic theory. *Econometrica* 17(1), January, 1–27.

Patinkin, D. 1961. Financial intermediaries and the logical structure of monetary theory. *American Economic Review* 51(1), March, 95–116.

Samuelson, P.A. 1947. *Foundations of Economic Analysis*. Cambridge, Mass.: Harvard University Press.

money supply

Supplying money for use in everyday transactions, so as to obviate the need for cumbersome barter, has been a function of governments for more than 2,000 years. Not surprisingly, government-issued money, once in existence, rapidly became a store of value as well. As an aspect of the history of human society and institutions, the process by which governments supply money has naturally attracted substantial attention. But the primary interest in money supply within the discipline of economics has stemmed from the proposition that movements in money are an important – according to some views, the most important – determinant of movements in prices, in output and employment, and in other economic phenomena of well-established interest on their own account.

Two analytical frameworks that rose to prominence in the latter half of the 20th century – indeed, that dominated macroeconomic thinking during much of that period – attached just this importance to money: quantity-theory monetarism, and IS–LM Keynesianism. Both these frameworks, however, took for granted that governments conduct their affairs (specifically in this context, that central banks conduct monetary policy) in such a way as to create independent movements in the supply of money, as opposed to merely passive movements in response to changes in money demand that therefore could not plausibly be the cause of movements in either prices or real economic activity. As of the outset of the 21st century, however, the number of central banks that in fact carry out their responsibilities in such a way is small and shrinking. Instead, most central banks implement monetary policy by setting some designated short-term interest rate.

As a result, interest in how money is supplied has sharply diminished among economists, and the details of the money supply process are now often omitted from the standard economics curriculum. (Examples at the graduate level are the instructional text by David Romer, 2006, and the theoretical treatise by Michael Woodford, 2003.) In the absence of some substantive knowledge of how money is supplied, however, just how a central bank can set 'the interest rate' would remain mysterious. Even if the number of central banks that actively seek to influence money supply as an element of the conduct of monetary policy shrinks to zero, therefore, money supply is unlikely to disappear from the purview of economics altogether.

The analytical basics

The first recognized monies supplied by governments for ordinary economic use mostly consisted of precious metals. The authorities' role was to provide standardized units, together with what amounted to stamped certification that the amount of metal in the coin or other object conformed. Apart from the certification, therefore, anyone who had an adequate quantity of the chosen metal could supply money along with the government.

In the more modern conception of money supply, relevant only since the 19th century, money is a form of debt. Most government-issued money consists of currency, which represents the liability of a partly or wholly government-owned central bank. Currency is typically not interest-bearing, and so the motives for holding it do not stem from its role as an earning asset. And although it is the government's (the central bank's) liability, in modern times it usually does not represent an obligation on the government's part to pay the bearer in some other form. Instead, both private citizens and businesses hold these government liabilities for their convenient use in everyday transactions, normally enforced by their statutory status as legal tender.

The fact that government-issued money is supplied as the liability of the central bank, and the presumption that the central bank has control over its balance sheet, together create the conceptual foundation for viewing the supply of money as a tool of economic policy. Indeed, much of the initial interest in this subject in the modern era arose from the experience of countries where the central bank had lost control of its balance sheet for some period of time, often in the aftermath of war or under other circumstances that prevented the government from raising ordinary revenues to cover its ongoing expenditures. The observation that such episodes often led to spiralling hyperinflation, with rising prices requiring the government to issue more money (in the absence of other revenues) and the larger supply of money leading to further increases in prices, immediately suggested a connection between money supply and prices, if not real economic activity as well.

Apart from situations of runaway money supply and hyperinflation, however, the issuance of currency is usually not the focus of economists' interest in how the supply of money relates to economic activity. While the great majority of government-issued money in the economically advanced countries now consists of currency held by the public (as of 2006, 69 per cent in the United Kingdom, and 95 per cent in the United States), currency is nonetheless only a small part of the money that individuals and firms use for savings and to execute everyday economic transactions. The money that individuals and firms use mostly consists of deposits issued by banks and other financial institutions. In the United Kingdom, deposit money outweighs currency by more than 30 to 1. Even in the United States, where the country's currency is also commonly used in both legal and illegal transactions around the world, the ratio is more than 8 to 1. Moreover, although in principle a central bank could seek to influence the economy by manipulating how much currency it supplies, in practice most central banks supply currency passively to accommodate whatever demands the public may have. (The role of currency issuance as a source of government finance – the heart of most examples of hyperinflation – is likewise limited in most economically advanced countries. Even in the United States, with demand for the currency enlarged by the use of US dollars in other countries, issuance of currency in a typical year amounts to only one to two per cent of the federal government's spending.) The simple construct of an economy in which the public depends entirely on government-issued currency to execute economic transactions, and the central bank exerts its economic influence by expanding or contracting the supply of that currency, is a textbook instructional device with limited relevance to most actual economies.

From the perspective of any active connection to either nonfinancial economic activity or the pricing of assets in the financial markets, therefore, what matters is the larger money supply issued by banks and other depository institutions (hereafter simply 'banks' for short). And in most modern banking systems, what gives the central bank the ability to influence the volume of deposits that banks in the aggregate create is its control over the amount of its own liabilities that it supplies for banks to hold. While most of the central bank's liabilities consist of currency held by the public, the remainder (31 per cent in the United Kingdom, and only five per cent in the United States, as of 2006) are held as assets – normally called 'reserves' – by the banks. The link between the banks' creation of deposits for the public to hold and their own holdings of reserves at the central bank constitutes the heart of the money supply process for purposes of a connection to most matters of concern to monetary policy.

Banks hold central bank reserves – and, importantly, hold more reserves as they have more deposits outstanding (all other things equal) – for several reasons. First, in traditional 'fractional reserve' banking systems, banks are required by law to hold such reserves in amounts equal to at least some fixed percentage of their outstanding deposits. Hence a larger supply of reserves makes it possible for the banks to do more lending (or buy more securities) and therefore create more money. Conversely, contracting the supply of reserves requires banks to shrink the amount of deposits they have outstanding, normally by not extending new loans to replace existing credits that mature or are otherwise repaid, or by selling securities.

Second, banks need a supply of currency to satisfy customers who draw on their accounts or present checks or other negotiable instruments for payment. In some banking systems, currency held by banks (as opposed to currency held by the public) is counted as part of banks' reserves. When a customer cashes a check, therefore, bank reserves fall and there is a corresponding increase in currency held by the public. (Because the central bank is not a party to the transaction, the total amount of central bank liabilities remains unchanged.) But banks cannot satisfy such demands unless they are holding an adequate amount of currency to begin with. And the greater the bank's volume of business, including in particular the amount of deposits it has outstanding against which its customers may want to draw, the more currency – hence the more reserves, if bank-held currency counts as reserves – the bank will ordinarily hold.

Third, banks also need to settle transactions with one another. If a customer of one bank deposits a check written against an account at another bank, the two banks must transfer some asset from one to the other. The same is true if one bank sells a security to another. Although banks in most countries have various mechanisms, like private clearing houses, for effecting such transfers without involving the central bank, some inter-bank transactions do normally settle by transferring reserves at the central bank from the paying bank to the receiving bank. In order to participate in that process, banks therefore need to hold at least some amount of reserves; and the more deposits the bank has outstanding, the more inter-bank transactions it may have to settle on a given day, and so the more reserves it will ordinarily hold. Moreover, in some banking systems the central bank reinforces the demand for its reserves by requiring banks to settle certain classes of inter-bank transactions in this way. Especially in systems where there are no reserve requirements in the traditional form of a stated minimum percentage of outstanding deposits, requiring the banks to settle inter-bank transactions in this way reinforces the banks' need to hold central bank reserves.

Banks' demand for reserves, therefore, is in many ways analogous to the public's demand for money. Reserves provide banks with an ability to do business, just as the money that individuals and nonfinancial firms hold enables them carry out their everyday economic affairs. That ability has value, but not infinite value. Hence the more expensive it is for banks to hold reserves, in terms of interest forgone by holding reserves instead of some other asset, the more banks will seek to economize on their reserve holdings in relation to their outstanding volume of deposits. For a given amount of deposits, therefore, banks' demand for reserves is negatively elastic with respect to the interest rate on alternative assets (typically loans or securities), just as the public's demand for money is negatively interest elastic for a given amount of income being earned or transacting being done. If reserves at the central bank bear an interest rate that varies in close step with what banks can get from holding other earning assets, this negative interest elasticity is likely to be small, or even trivial. But if the interest rate that the central bank pays on reserves is fixed (in the United States, for example, it is fixed at zero), or even if it varies together with market returns but only imperfectly, the negative interest elasticity in banks' reserve demand is likely to be significant. (The classic paper making this point is Dewald, 1963.)

The analytical mirror image of banks' negatively elastic demand for reserves, for a given volume of deposits outstanding, is their positively elastic willingness to create deposits for a given amount of reserves that they hold. The higher are market interest rates on earning assets, compared to whatever rate the central bank pays on reserves, the greater is the incentive for banks to stretch their reserves further by making more loans and buying more securities – and in the process creating more deposits – rather than leaving an increasingly expensive cushion of reserves that may provide benefits (less risk of having to take abrupt action in the event of a shortfall, for example) but are costly nonetheless.

The result is a positively interest-elastic supply of money, representing the behaviour of banks, to go along with the usual negatively interest-elastic demand for money representing the behaviour of the households and firms that hold bank deposits, together with currency, as the money that they use for economic purposes. In the absence of some pathology, the intersection of this positively interest-elastic money supply and negatively interest-elastic money demand determines the equilibrium quantity of money created and held, for a given supply of reserves and a given level of income, together with the interest rate at which the market clears. (And, because the positively interest-elastic supply of money is simply the mirror image of the negatively interest-elastic demand for reserves – both represent the same aspect of banks' behaviour – the market for reserves is likewise

in equilibrium, with demand equal to whatever quantity of reserves the central bank is supplying, at the same interest rate.) Integrating this partial equilibrium of the money market (and the reserves market) with the demand for goods and services then completes a simple representation of the economy's aggregate demand. Further integrating that aggregate demand representation with aggregate supply, importantly including the labour market, in turn completes the economy's short-run general equilibrium (short-run in that such dynamic elements as the stocks of capital, technology, and other relevant factors are still unaccounted for).

In some treatments of money supply within the economics literature, this explicit supply–demand equilibrium in the markets for money and reserves is, instead, implicitly represented by a simple 'money multiplier' stating the relationship between the total liabilities supplied by the central bank – often called the 'monetary base' – and the resulting amount of money, including bank deposits as well as currency. Purely as a matter of arithmetic, specifying the ratio of reserves to deposits that the banks choose to hold (influenced in part by whatever reserve requirements and other institutional strictures banks face), and the ratio of currency to deposits that the public chooses within its holdings of money, is sufficient to determine the quantity of money that goes along with any given monetary base set by the central bank. But the banks' reserve-to-deposit ratio depends in part on interest rates as well, and the public's demand for currency often varies with a host of factors (confidence in the banking system, use of currency abroad or for purposes of illegal transactions, and so on), so that the 'money multiplier' representation is really just a short-hand simplification that works well or badly depending on the strength of the relevant interest elasticities and the extent of variation in interest rates and the many other factors involved. (See, for example, Cagan, 1965. A brief statement of the central ideas appeared in Friedman and Schwartz, 1963, ch. 2, sec. 4.) Underneath, the supply–demand equilibrium established by the central bank's supply of reserves, banks' behaviour in demanding reserves and supplying deposits, and the public's behaviour in demanding both deposits and currency, is what establishes an economy's money supply. (For a fully articulated treatment, see Modigliani, Rasche, and Cooper, 1970.)

The link to monetary policy

The logical starting point in this process is the central bank's supply of its own liabilities, and it is the central bank's control over the liabilities it issues that gives the supply of money its place in economic policy. Until fairly recently – well into the 19th century – governments issued either coins or paper currency mostly as a means of payment for goods and services they purchased. Such actions were, in effect, a combination of what have come to be known as fiscal and monetary policies. In the modern era, however, especially with the advent of central banks as distinct and often quasi-independent governmental institutions, economists have thought of fiscal and monetary policies as likewise distinct.

In the absence of a securities market, or some similar set of financial institutions, it is difficult to conceive of how monetary policy would operate independently of fiscal policy: how could the government, in such a setting, increase the amount of money outstanding without simultaneously making either a purchase or at least a transfer payment? One metaphor sometimes used in the theoretical economics literature to represent such an action – and which only serves to indicate how far-fetched such a situation is – is to picture the government dropping money from a helicopter. While monetary and fiscal policies are distinguishable in most modern economies, central banks, of course, do not drop money from helicopters. The reason is that the economies in which they operate in fact have securities markets.

The primary means by which central banks in most modern economies change the amount of their liabilities outstanding is to purchase, or sell, securities – actions typically called 'open market operations'. When the central bank buys a security, it makes payment by increasing the amount of reserves credited to the seller's bank. (In systems in which bank-held currency is counted as part of reserves, the consequence is the same even if the central bank makes payment by delivering currency to the seller's bank.) When the central bank sells a security, it correspondingly receives payment by reducing the amount of reserves credited to the buyer's bank. In either case, the central bank's assets, consisting mostly of the securities it holds, and its liabilities, consisting partly of the reserves credited to banks, rise or fall in lockstep. But because of the ways in which banks' ability to create deposits depends on their holdings of reserves, the change is not economically irrelevant. Changes in the supply of reserves, effected via open market operations, shift a key underpinning of the equilibrium in the reserves market and the money market, thereby changing not only the resulting quantity of money but the yields and prices of non-money assets and ultimately the equilibrium of the nonfinancial economy as well.

Not all open market operations carried out by central banks change the quantity of reserves. Most importantly, the central bank also needs to accommodate the public's changing demand for currency. In a growing economy with rising prices, the demand for currency is usually increasing. When individuals and businesses go to their banks to get more currency, their doing so increases the amount of currency in public circulation but reduces the amount of the banks' reserves (as long as bank-held currency is counted as reserves). As a part of their normal ongoing procedures, therefore, most central banks routinely purchase securities – that is, carry out open market operations – in order to offset such reductions in

reserves due to increasing public demand for currency. Central banks also regularly carry out open market purchases or sales in order to prevent short-run fluctuation in other technical factors, such as international transactions and variations in the amount of checks currently in the clearing process, from affecting the supply of reserves.

Central banks can also create reserves by lending to banks, rather than buying earning assets from them, and in some countries' systems the lending of reserves is more important for purposes of carrying out monetary policy than open market operations. Whether banks distinguish between reserves that they have borrowed from the central bank and reserves that they simply own outright (often called 'nonborrowed reserves' to distinguish the two) depends on the specifics of the individual system's institutions. Most obviously, borrowed reserves are a liability of the bank, on which it presumably has to pay interest, while its nonborrowed reserves are an asset on which it may or may not earn interest. In addition, in some systems (the United States, for example), borrowing reserves from the central bank exposes a bank to regulatory oversight with implicit costs well beyond what the interest rate paid would suggest.

Whether reserves are borrowed or nonborrowed, however, the essence of monetary policy is the central bank's provision of reserves to the banking system. The recognition of the way in which that role played by the central bank potentially affects an economy's money supply, interest rates, asset prices, nonfinancial activity, and prices and wages, in turn sets the stage for both normative and positive consideration of monetary policy. The ensuing economics literature has become vast. In most countries the corresponding public discussion is likewise active and intense.

The modern economist most identified with emphasizing the role of money supply in the conduct of monetary policy – as opposed to focusing on interest rates, or measures of reserves in the banking system, or other relevant indicators of what a central bank is doing in this respect – is Milton Friedman. At the most fundamental normative level, Friedman advocated a long-run policy of shrinking the supply of money (by which he meant government-issued money) at a rate adequate to render nominal interest rates on assets closely substitutable for money equal to zero on average over time. The basic logic was that, since the government could create such money at essentially no cost, it should be costless for the public to hold; the public's effort to economize on holdings of money balances, when market interest rates on money substitutes are positive, represents a deadweight loss to the economy (see Friedman, 1969). Given the demonstrated dangers of deflation, however – with a positive real rate of interest, negative inflation would be necessary to achieve a zero average nominal interest rate – this recommendation had little impact on actual monetary policy.

At a more practical level, however, over short- and medium-run horizons Friedman advocated keeping the supply of money (by which he meant the deposits and currency held by the public) growing at a constant rate. Here the argument was that the influence of monetary policy on both prices and real economic activity operates with lengthy delays, subject to unpredictable variation, and that active attempts by the central bank to use monetary policy to offset nonmonetary influences on the economy were likely to be destabilizing (see Friedman, 1953; 1956). Many other economists, more optimistic about the prospects for using active variation in monetary policy to blunt the influence on the economy of factors that the central bank could either foresee or at least recognize quickly once they had occurred, followed Friedman in advocating the use of growth in the money supply as the way to gauge whether the central bank was exerting a stimulative or a contractionary force on economic activity. Beginning in the 1960s, but more so in the 1970s, many central banks around the world implemented these recommendations by adopting one or another form of explicit target for the growth of its money supply.

The role of empirical evidence

The crucial empirical underpinning of such policy frameworks, whether they involved constant money growth or attempts at active stabilization nonetheless benchmarked by money growth, was the observation that movements in money bore a reliable relationship to movements in income and prices. Early in the post-Second World War period, Philip Cagan documented such a relationship between money growth and price inflation in several well-known episodes of hyperinflation in Europe that had followed each of the two world wars (Cagan, 1956). But hyperinflation in the context of post-war chaos (especially for the war's losers) bore only limited implications for the conduct of monetary policy under more normal circumstances. In a massive historical study, Milton Friedman and Anna J. Schwartz documented the relationships between money and prices, and also money and income, for the United States during the period 1867–1960 – including the Great Depression of the 1930s but also many more ordinary business fluctuations as well – and following their work many other empirical researchers attempted similar (though mostly smaller-scale) studies for other countries and other time periods (Friedman and Schwartz, 1963).

At the conceptual level, the central idea linking this empirical research to the implied role of money supply in conducting monetary policy was that, if fluctuations in money growth and fluctuations in income and/or prices are systematically related, and if the observed fluctuations in money growth within those relationships represent independent movements of money supply, then the central bank can exploit those relationships by purposefully steering the money supply along an optimally chosen course (which may or may not be a simply constant-growth path). Following the work of Friedman and Schwartz, and the many other researchers who applied ever more sophisticated empirical methodologies to the same line of enquiry, questions about each of these two underlying issues – how strong the observed relationships are, and whether they result from independent movements of money supply – generated a similarly large literature.

One immediate difficulty, recognized early on, is that, since money supply necessarily equals money demand, inferences about the money–income or money–price relationship on the basis of observed movements in money are subject to the usual problem of statistical identification. (An early paper making this point was Teigen, 1964. Another, addressed more explicitly to the work of Friedman and Schwartz, was Tobin, 1970.) Hence what may look like a relationship between movements of prices and income induced by movements in money supply may in reality be movements in money demand induced by movements in prices and income. Further, unless the central bank takes its decisions affecting money supply with no regard for the behaviour of prices and income, the observed relationships may also represent the reactive behaviour of the central bank itself. Indeed, under some plausible accounts of how central banks make monetary policy, relationships of the kind observed in the data would spuriously emerge. (An early paper making this point was Goldfeld and Blinder, 1972.) Still more fundamentally, even if the relationships observed between money and either income or prices actually did represent exactly the kind of causal influence of money supply that was claimed, the attempt by the central bank to exploit such a relationship for policy purposes, once widely recognized, could cause the relationship to change or even break down altogether. (The classic statement of this proposition in a general context is Lucas, 1976. For a formulation in the specific context of monetary policy, see Goodhart, 1984; the original formulation of 'Goodhart's Law' dates to 1975 when this paper was first presented.)

Starting in the mid-1970s, however, and then increasingly so over the next two decades, these questions became moot. Fluctuations in money growth no longer appeared to bear much observed relation to fluctuations in either income or prices over time horizons that were useful for conducting monetary policy, especially after controlling for other obvious information like past movements of income and prices themselves. In parallel, the evidence indicated that money demand was unstable. The presumption of a stable functional relationship between money demand and income or prices had always been central to the claim that money supply was a useful tool for purposes of monetary policy. But now evidence for a stable money demand gave way, in one country after another, to evidence of instability.

The reasons for the disappearance of stable money demand were many, and, at a qualitative level, straightforward to understand. (The empirical money demand literature is a separate subject; for a survey, see Goldfeld and Sichel, 1990. For an earlier survey, written before the instability became so widespread or so evident, see Laidler, 1977, ch. 7.) One reason was changing regulation (in the United States, for example, the removal of the prohibition against banks' paying interest on checkable deposits, and also of the ceilings limiting the interest that banks could pay on interest-bearing savings deposits). Another, in part prompted by regulatory changes, was innovation in the kinds of deposits and deposit-like instruments that banks and other financial institutions offered their customers (for example, money market mutual funds). A third was the electronic revolution, which made various forms of financial transactions ever easier and less costly (for example, shifting funds between checkable and noncheckable accounts). A fourth was rapid globalization, which made businesses in particular, but many individuals as well, increasingly willing to hold assets, and to borrow, in multiple currencies, and to substitute readily among them. But regardless of the precise reasons, which presumably varied from one country to another, money demand no longer appeared to be stable. Nor, in parallel, did the relationships of a simpler form between money and either income or prices that had spurred policy interest in money supply in the first place.

The decline of money supply as a tool of monetary policy

In the absence of empirical evidence of stable money demand, the rationale for the role of money supply as a tool of monetary policy collapsed as well. If money demand is unstable, then even perfectly stable money supply introduces into income and prices the influence of whatever disturbances to the public's money-holding behaviour occur. Under those circumstances, the central bank can do a better job of stabilizing either prices or income, over the short or medium run, by fixing some interest rate and thereby allowing fluctuations in money supply to accommodate fluctuations in money demand that occur for reasons unrelated to movements of income and prices. (The classic paper making this point is Poole, 1970; for a survey of the optimal monetary policy literature along these lines, including the role of money supply behaviour along with money demand, see Friedman, 1990. In the long run, however, there must be at least some absolute nominal element in the policy mechanism to anchor the price level; the interest rate is a relative price, not an absolute price.) Following the increasing evidence of money demand instability, and the collapse of money–price and money–income relationships, that is precisely what an increasing number of central banks have done.

The experience in the Unites States is illustrative. The Federal Reserve System, the US central bank, first began to take explicit note of money supply movements in formulating its monetary policy in 1970. In 1975 the US Congress adopted a resolution requiring the Federal Reserve to announce, in advance, quantitative targets for the growth of key money (and credit) aggregates and, after the fact, to report to the relevant Congressional oversight committees on its success or failure in meeting these targets. In 1979 the Federal Reserve publicly declared an intensified dedication to controlling money growth, with the main focus on the narrow M1 aggregate (consisting primarily of currency and checkable deposits), and adopted new day-to-day operating procedures, centred on the supply of nonborrowed reserves, designed to enhance its ability to achieve control of M1.

The movement towards ever greater emphasis on money supply in US monetary policy took less than a decade; unwinding it took only a little longer. In 1982, the Federal Reserve recognized the increasing instability of demand for M1 and shifted its focus to the broader M2 (including not only currency and demand deposits but also most forms of time and savings deposits). Soon thereafter, it abandoned its operating system based on nonborrowed reserves, in favour of simply setting the federal funds rate (the overnight interest rate on bank reserves) at the level most likely to achieve the desired M2 growth. After 1986 the Federal Reserve stopped setting a target for M1 growth, but continued to do so for M2 and M3 (a still broader aggregate). In the late 1980s evidence based on how the Federal Reserve changed the federal funds rate in response to observed movements of money suggested that the M2 growth target still bore significant influence on US monetary policy. (See, for example, Friedman, 1997; but the empirical literature on this issue is voluminous.)

That influence had mostly dissipated by 1990, and in 1993 the Federal Reserve publicly 'downgraded' the role of its M2 target. Thereafter it continued to set 'ranges' for M2 and M3 growth, but it made clear that these were not actual money growth targets; they were merely 'intended to communicate its expectation as to the growth of these monetary aggregates that would result' under specified assumed conditions. In 1998 the Federal Reserve further confirmed that these ranges were not 'guides to policy'. In 2001 it stopped setting such ranges altogether.

The pattern in most other countries was roughly parallel. By 1980 the use of money supply targets for monetary policy was an idea whose time had come. Most of the major central banks had put such targets at the core of their policymaking process. By 1990 money growth targets were already largely a thing of the past. By the mid-1990s most central banks had either de-emphasized such targets or dropped them altogether. By 2000 it had become standard that central banks carry out monetary policy by setting some short-term interest rate. Money supply mostly disappeared from public discussion, and the professional economics literature largely dispensed with the now-unnecessary apparatus of money demand, money supply, and likewise demand and supply in the market for reserves. (See, for example, Clarida, Gali and Gertler, 1999.)

Implicitly, however, that conceptual apparatus nonetheless stands behind the ability of central banks to set the designated interest rate in the first place. In principle, a central bank – or anyone else with large enough resources, for that matter – could fix the price or yield on any asset simply by buying or selling that asset in sufficient volume to shift the entire market equilibrium, ultimately including the real returns established by the fundamental economic forces of thrift and productivity. (Given the lags with which monetary policy influences price inflation, in the short run the interest rate the central bank is setting is a real interest rate.) But in fact most central banks normally move the interest rate they use for monetary policy purposes by executing only very small transactions, and in an increasing number of cases they do so without executing any transactions at all; often the mere announcement of what the central bank would like the designated rate to be is sufficient.

What gives a central bank the ability to do so is, presumably, market participants' knowledge that the interest rate being set is closely tied to that on the central bank's own liabilities (in systems like that in the United States, it is exactly that rate), and that the central bank can make the supply of those liabilities whatever it chooses. But market equilibrium requires that the demand for those liabilities equal the supply, and the demand for central bank liabilities in turn is an aspect of the same behavioural process that determines the supply of money. Hence money supply remains a part of the story, even if now mostly a hidden one.

BENJAMIN M. FRIEDMAN

See also **Friedman, Milton; inside and outside money; monetary and fiscal policy overview; monetary policy, history of; monetary transmission mechanism; money.**

Bibliography

Cagan, P. 1956. The monetary dynamics of hyperinflation. In *Studies in the Quantity Theory of Money*, ed. M. Friedman. Chicago: University of Chicago Press.

Cagan, P. 1965. *Determinants and Effects of Changes in the Stock of Money, 1875–1960*. New York: NBER.

Clarida, R., Gali, J. and Gertler, M. 1999. The science of monetary policy: a new Keynesian perspective. *Journal of Economic Literature* 37, 1661–1707.

Dewald, W.G. 1963. Free reserves, total reserves and monetary control. *Journal of Political Economy* 71, 141–53.

Friedman, B.M. 1990. Targets and instruments of monetary policy. In *Handbook of Monetary Economics*, vol. 2, ed. B.M. Friedman and F. Hahn. Amsterdam: North-Holland.

Friedman, B.M. 1997. The rise and fall of money growth targets as guidelines for U.S. monetary policy. In *Towards More Effective Monetary Policy*, ed. I. Kuroda. London: Macmillan.

Friedman, M. 1953. The effects of a full-employment policy on economic stability: a formal analysis. In *Essays in Positive Economics*. Chicago: University of Chicago Press.

Friedman, M. 1956. The quantity theory of money: a restatement. In *Studies in the Quantity Theory of Money*. Chicago: University of Chicago Press.

Friedman, M. 1969. The optimum quantity of money. In *The Optimum Quantity of Money and Other Essays*. Chicago: Aldine.

Friedman, M. and Schwartz, A.J. 1963. *A Monetary History of the United States, 1867–1960*. Princeton: Princeton University Press.

Goldfeld, S.M. and Blinder, A.S. 1972. Some implications of endogenous stabilization policy. *Brookings Papers on Economic Activity* 1972(3), 585–644.

Goldfeld, S.M. and Sichel, D.E. 1990. The demand for money. In *Handbook of Monetary Economics*, vol. 2, ed. B.M. Friedman and F. Hahn. Amsterdam: North-Holland.

Goodhart, C. 1984. Problems of monetary management: the U.K. experience. In *Monetary Theory and Practice: The U.K. Experience*. London: Macmillan.

Laidler, D.E. 1977. *The Demand for Money: Theories and Evidence*, 2nd edn. New York: Harper & Row.

Lucas, R.E., Jr. 1976. Econometric policy evaluation: a critique. In *The Phillips Curve and Labor Markets*, ed. K. Brunner and A.H. Meltzer. Amsterdam: North-Holland.

Modigliani, F., Rasche, R. and Cooper, J.P. 1970. Central bank policy, the money supply and the short-term rate of interest. *Journal of Money, Credit and Banking* 2, 166–218.

Poole, W. 1970. Optimal choice of monetary policy instruments in a simple stochastic macro model. *Quarterly Journal of Economics* 84, 197–216.

Romer, D. 2006. *Advanced Macroeconomics*, 3rd edn. Boston: McGraw-Hill/Irwin.

Teigen, R.L. 1964. Demand and supply functions for money in the Unites States: some structural estimates. *Econometrica* 32, 467–509.

Tobin, J. 1970. Money and income: post hoc ergo propter hoc? *Quarterly Journal of Economics* 84, 301–17.

Woodford, M. 2003. *Interest and Prices: Foundations of a Theory of Monetary Policy*. Princeton: Princeton University Press.

moneylenders in developing countries

Moneylenders are a principal source of credit in developing countries, especially in rural areas, but are notoriously difficult to classify. They may be shopkeepers, millers, traders, landlords, or professional financiers. Moneylenders operate within a broad spectrum of lending 'formality' bounded above by the activities of commercial or agricultural banks and below by credit from friends, relatives, and fellow clan members. Banks normally take deposits, ask lenders for collateral, have formal procedures for loan applications with written contracts, and operate within the legal system; moneylenders may do none of the above. Friends, relatives and clan-members, on the other hand, do not require their loans to be secured, make verbal agreements, generally do not charge interest, and often allow state-contingent repayment (Udry, 1994). Reciprocity and social pressure, rather than legal sanctions, enforce such kin- or clan-based credit (La Ferrara, 2003). Moneylenders, by contrast, are less flexible about the terms of repayment, more likely to charge interest, and less able to mobilize social opprobrium to punish default.

Formal sector lending is limited by the value of collateral, which in agricultural areas is usually in the form of land. Land is useful as collateral only to the extent that it can be legally repossessed upon default of the loan. This, in turn, requires that land be titled, or that ownership be otherwise documented, and that foreclosure be enforceable in court. Moneylenders thrive in settings where collateral is scarce or legal enforcement of debt contracts is weak or non-existent. But such conditions are not sufficient for the presence of moneylenders, who ultimately face the same problem as do banks; earning profit in the face of potential default. One way to do so is by setting a low interest rate and rationing credit, as in Stiglitz and Weiss (1981). This presumes, however, that moneylenders have no particular informational advantage over banks.

What, then, is the comparative advantage of the moneylender? There are three, not mutually exclusive, answers to this question, all related to the fact that the moneylender either resides in the same village or locality as his clientele, and is thus likely to have much more personal knowledge of and contact with them than would a bank, or is simultaneously dealing with his borrowers in another market. By virtue of proximity, a moneylender may, first of all, have a better idea as to whether a borrower can successfully implement a given project and thus repay the loan. In other words, it is mainly the bank, not the moneylender, that faces asymmetric information about the creditworthiness of the borrower.

A second advantage the moneylender may have over a bank is in enforcing repayment. Traders or millers often advance credit against the forthcoming harvest. By acquiring the right to market his debtor's harvest as a condition of the loan, and to deduct principal and interest at the time of sale, the trader–lender effectively guarantees debt seniority. Indeed, the trade–credit linkage may serve the dual purpose of enforcement and screening. The frequent exclusivity of such marketing agreements insures that the lender can observe the *entire* output of his borrowers, so as to monitor their ability to repay, as well as that of his prospective borrowers, so as to assess their future creditworthiness; at the same time, no other lender can have access to this information and thereby compete away borrowers (Siamwalla et al., 1990; Aleem, 1990). Moneylenders may also have more effective means of preventing their clients from absconding with the loan principal or diverting it to non-productive uses (Giné, 2005). While banks cannot legally prevent such strategic default beyond confiscating what collateral they hold, moneylenders may be able to exert various kinds of physical and psychological pressures to ensure repayment.

Lastly, moneylenders may more readily exchange information about borrowers' repayment histories than banks in developing countries. An informal borrower with a reputation for default will not only be unable to obtain future loans from the same moneylender but may lose access to all local creditors. Kletzer and Wright (2000) show that, when credit histories are public information, punishing default by a debt moratorium until such time as the lender is repaid is a credible strategy. If any competing moneylender fails to respect this punishment by subsequently lending to the delinquent borrower, the other moneylenders can induce the borrower to default on this loan by offering him a better deal, thus 'cheating the cheater'. When there is a high enough probability that credit histories are 'forgotten' or hidden, however, this type of equilibrium breaks down (Hoff and Stiglitz, 1997). Reputation equilibria are thus sensitive to the extent of village information networks, about which little is known.

These arguments aside, collecting on a past debt may not be an unalloyed benefit to the moneylender. When the borrower's output or investment depends importantly on his unverifiable effort, debt creates an incentive problem. The higher the debt burden, the more the borrower is working merely to pay off the loan, the less willing he is to work, the lower his output, and, consequently, the more likely he is to default. Given 'debt overhang', the moneylender has to trade off higher debt collection against higher probability of default and collecting nothing. The resolution may involve forgiving debt. Evidence on the extent of debt forgiveness in informal credit markets is lacking (Fafchamps and Gubert, 2004, is a notable exception), but there are at least two reasons to believe that it is not widespread. First, in a long-term credit relationship, the moneylender has the option of rescheduling debt in the hopes that the borrower's fortunes will improve, a less drastic step than forgiveness. Second, the impact of forgiveness on incentives is diluted when the borrower and lender are not in an exclusive credit relationship. Since other creditors can free ride on the lowering of total debt, there may be too little forgiveness in equilibrium.

Landlord–moneylenders have motivated a considerable literature on 'interlinked' tenancy-credit contracts.

Because the landlord must always verify the harvest of a share-tenant, he is in a better position to enforce debt repayment than an outside moneylender. Perhaps more importantly, however, the landlord has a stronger incentive to provide credit to his share-tenant than any other moneylender. This is because the landlord, in general, captures a larger share of incremental surplus due to an increase in the tenant's working capital than does an otherwise equivalent outside moneylender (see, for example, Basu, Bell and Bose, 2000). Even if the landlord himself faces relatively high credit costs, given his enforcement advantage, he may still prefer to on-lend funds to his tenant from a moneylender under a so-called 'credit-layering' arrangement (Mansuri, 2007).

The boundaries of moneylending are further obscured by the multifarious nature of credit. Traders, for example, often advance inputs in kind rather than cash, with interest collected through a markup on the price. Burkhart and Ellingsen (2004) rationalize this form of trade credit on the grounds that inputs are less easily diverted to non-productive uses than cash; in-kind loans thus alleviate a monitoring problem. Another form of in-kind lending occurs when landlords defer rental payments until after the harvest. Besides the possible monitoring advantage, such debt contracts have better incentive properties than share-contracts when the tenant's liability is limited (Innes, 1990) or when tenant risk aversion and yield variability are not too high (Arimoto, 2005). Since land is far and away the most important factor of agricultural production, the value of deferred rent may dwarf that of other seasonal borrowing.

Interest in moneylenders has centred around their role in modulating the impact of government policies, such as interest rate subsidies or controls, that can be effectively implemented only in the formal sector. The effects of such policies depend critically on the relationship between moneylenders and banks. The literature has taken two approaches to the formal–informal sector interaction. The first assumes a vertical structure whereby moneylenders act as middlemen, borrowing from the formal sector and on-lending to uncollateralized peasants (Hoff and Stiglitz, 1997; Floro and Ray, 1998). In the second approach, moneylenders and bankers compete with one another, with the residual demand for credit in the formal sector spilling over into the informal sector. Bell, Srinivasan and Udry (1997) and Kochar (1997) have moneylenders coexisting with banks by virtue of exogenous ceilings on formal sector credit, whereas Giné (2005) and Jain (1999) explicitly model moneylenders' informational advantage over banks to obtain coexistence in equilibrium without imposing formal sector credit rationing.

HANAN G. JACOBY

See also **adverse selection; agricultural finance; micro-credit; sharecropping.**

Bibliography

Aleem, I. 1990. Imperfect information, screening and the costs of informal lending: a study of rural credit markets in Pakistan. *World Bank Economic Review* 4, 329–49.

Arimoto, Y. 2005. State-contingent rent reduction and tenancy contract choice. *Journal of Development Economics* 76, 355–75.

Basu, K., Bell, C. and Bose, P. 2000. Interlinkage, limited liability and strategic interaction. *Journal of Economic Behavior and Organization* 42, 445–62.

Bell, C., Srinivasan, T. and Udry, C. 1997. Rationing, spillover and interlinking in credit markets: the case of rural Punjab. *Oxford Economic Papers* 49, 557–87.

Burkhart, M. and Ellingsen, T. 2004. In-kind finance: a theory of trade credit. *American Economic Review* 94, 569–90.

Fafchamps, M. and Gubert, F. 2004. Contingent loan repayment in the Philippines. Discussion Paper No. 215. Department of Economics, Oxford University. Online.

Floro, M. and Ray, D. 1998. Vertical links between formal and informal financial institutions. *Review of Development Economics* 1, 34–56.

Giné, X. 2005. Access to capital in rural Thailand: an estimated model of formal vs. informal credit. Policy Research Working Paper No. 3502. Washington, DC: World Bank.

Hoff, K. and Stiglitz, J. 1997. Moneylenders and bankers, price–increasing subsidies in a monopolistically competitive market. *Journal of Development Economics* 52, 429–62.

Innes, R. 1990. Limited liability and incentive contracting with ex-ante action choices. *Journal of Economic Theory* 52, 45–67.

Jain, S. 1999. Symbiosis vs. crowding-out, the interaction of formal vs. informal credit markets in developing countries. *Journal of Development Economics* 59, 419–44.

Kletzer, K. and Wright, B. 2000. Sovereign debt as inter-temporal barter. *American Economic Review* 90, 621–39.

Kochar, A. 1997. An empirical investigation of rationing constraints in rural credit markets in India. *Journal of Development Economics* 53, 339–71.

La Ferrara, E. 2003. Kin groups and reciprocity: a model of credit transactions in Ghana. *American Economic Review* 93, 1730–50.

Mansuri, G. 2007. Credit Layering in informal financial markets. *Journal of Development Economics* 84, 715–30.

Siamwalla, A., Pithong, C., Poapongsakorn, N., Satsanguan, P., Nettayarak, P., Mingmaneenakin, W. and Tubpun, Y. 1990. The Thai Rural credit system: public subsidies, private information, and segmented markets. *World Bank Economic Review* 4, 271–96.

Stiglitz, J. and Weiss, A. 1981. Credit rationing in markets with imperfect information. *American Economic Review* 71, 383–410.

Udry, C. 1994. Risk and insurance in a rural credit market: an empirical investigation in Northern Nigeria. *Review of Economic Studies* 61, 495–526.

monocentric versus polycentric models in urban economics

The formal modelling of urban spatial structure originated in the monocentric city model by Alonso (1964). The model was extended to include production, transportation and housing by Mills (1967; 1972) and Muth (1969), and was eventually integrated into a unified framework by Fujita (1989). In these traditional models, the city is a priori assumed to be monocentric, that is, all production activities within a city are supposed to take place in a point representing the *central business district* (CBD), and all workers living in the surrounding area are supposed to commute to the CBD. The success of this model is primarily due to its compatibility with the competitive paradigm, since the existence of the CBD is a priori assumed. In order to explain the urban morphology, however, it is essential to endogenize the CBD formation. For this purpose, Fujita (1986) provided a very useful insight based on the spatial impossibility theorem of Starrett (1978): in order to have endogenous formation of economic agglomeration, the model must have at least one of the following three elements: (*a*) heterogeneous space, (*b*) non-market externalities in production and/or consumption, and (*c*) imperfectly competitive markets.

The approach based on (*a*) explains the formation of the CBD by *comparative advantage* among locations, while otherwise retaining the competitive paradigm. One of the earliest such attempts was made by Schweizer, Varaiya and Hartwick (1976).

Most models of type (*b*) are based on *externalities from non-market interactions*. The earliest attempt was made by Solow and Vickrey (1971). In the one-dimensional location space, they considered the optimal allocation of urban land between business areas and roads when each unit of business area is assumed to generate a given number of trips to every other unit. But the first model of residential land use of this type is by Beckmann (1976), where the utility of each individual directly depends on the average distance to all other individuals and the amount of her land consumption. This preference leads to a *bell-shaped spatial population distribution as well as land rent curves*, where the CBD is represented by a densely inhabited area around the central location.

While Beckmann, Solow and Vickrey considered only a single type of agents (firms or consumers), Ogawa and Fujita (1980) and Imai (1982) developed two-sector monocentric models of a one-dimensional city. The dispersion force in this case is generated through land and labour markets. That is, the agglomeration of firms increases the commuting distance for their workers on average, which in turn pushes up the wage rate and land rent around the agglomeration, and this higher cost of labour and land discourages further agglomeration of firms. The most recent contribution along this line is by Lucas and Rossi-Hansberg (2002), who formally demonstrate the existence of an equilibrium and the endogenous formation of the CBD.

In the endogenous monocentric models discussed so far, the optimal distribution of firms requires greater concentration near the centre than does the equilibrium distribution. The reason is the locational externality generated by individuals: while the location of each individual directly affects the travelling cost for others to make contact with this individual, it is not taken into account when each individual makes a location decision.

Building on Ogawa and Fujita (1980), the first model of a *polycentric city* was developed by Fujita and Ogawa (1982). Their key assumption is that the benefit from interactions between two firms is a negative exponential function of the distance between them, unlike the linear dependence in previous models. When commuting costs are relatively high, this assumption leads to the formation of *multiple business districts* and the possibility of *multiple equilibria*.

The first urban economic model based on (*c*) is by Fujita (1988). His model demonstrated that pure market interactions alone can explain the agglomeration of economic activities with the use of the Chamberlinian monopolistic competition model. The agglomeration force is generated from the interaction among preference for product variety, transport costs, and increasing returns at the level of individual producers. In this model, the city may be monocentric or polycentric. Also it is possible that business and residential districts are mixed. These works were critical for the emergence of *the new economic geography* (NEG) in the 1990s (Krugman, 1991a; 1991b; Fujita, 1993).

In the application of the NEG to urban economics initiated by Fujita and Krugman (1995), there are two key features. The first is the *general equilibrium modelling of an entire spatial economy* unlike all the models presented so far. The second is its focus on *the spatial distribution of cities*, while abstracting from the intra-city spatial structure. In particular, it is assumed that mobile firms and workers do not occupy land, so that an agglomeration of firms and population, that is, a city, forms at a point on the continuous location space. The second feature dramatically increases the tractability of the model. The agglomeration force in this model is essentially the same as in Fujita (1988), while the dispersion force is generated from the presence of immobile resources through transport costs between cities and non-city locations. The key to this approach is the recognition that the profitability of any given location for a firm can be represented by an *index of market potential*. The market potential at a given location reflects the trade-off among the proximity to consumers, the degree of competition, and the production cost at that location. In particular, the market potential of a given industry sharply decreases when it moves away from a city in which this industry is agglomerated, and then starts increasing again after a certain distance, exhibiting the presence of an *agglomeration shadow*. Differences in the degree of product differentiation and/or transport costs among industries lead to differences in the size of the agglomeration shadow, which in turn result in variations in the (roughly constant) spacing of agglomerations among industries (Fujita and Mori, 1997). In the presence of multiple industries, the *inter-industry demand externalities* lead to a formation of *hierarchical city systems* (Fujita, Krugman and Mori, 1999). This is reminiscent of Christaller (1933): the set of industries found in a smaller city is a subset of those found in a larger city. Furthermore, the relative decrease in transport costs for urban sectors may eventually lead to the formation of a *megalopolis* consisting of large core cities that are connected by an *industrial belt*, that is, *a continuum of small cities* (Mori, 1997). NEG remains the only general location-equilibrium framework which can investigate the spatial distribution of cities and their industrial structure in a unified manner.

There is also a large literature of spatial oligopoly (hence, type *c*) aiming to explain the spatial concentration of stores through *statistical economies of scale*. These models assume that consumers have imperfect information regarding the types (and the prices) of commodities sold by stores before they visit them. The greater the agglomeration of stores, the more likely it is that consumers will find their favourite commodities. The concentration of stores is explained by the market-size effect due to taste uncertainty and/or lower price expectation (see, for example, Konishi, 2005).

Finally, in all the models introduced thus far, all agents are assumed to be atomistic. Hence, land and labour markets are perfectly competitive. In contrast, Henderson and Mitra (1996) offer a model of *suburbanization* in which new *edge cities* are formed by *large land-developers* in the suburbs of the old CBD, formalizing Garreau's observation (1991) on the recent development of edge cities within large US metro areas. Given an existing CBD, the developer of a new edge city chooses the location and capacity of its business district strategically to maximize profits. The developer exercises monopsony power in the labour market in the edge city though her control over aggregate employment there. The proximity to the old CBD increases production efficiency through easier communication of firms between the CBD and the edge city, while it also increases residential land rents and wages of workers in the edge city. This model thus incorporates elements (*b*) and (*c*).

TOMOYA MORI

See also **location theory; spatial economics; urban agglomeration; urban economics; urban growth; urban production externalities; urbanization.**

Bibliography

Alonso, W. 1964. *Location and Land Use*. Cambridge, MA: Harvard University Press.

Beckmann, M. 1976. Spatial equilibrium in the dispersed city. In *Mathematical Land Use Theory*, ed. Y. Papageorgiou. Lexington MA: Lexington Books.

Christaller, W. 1933. *Central Places in Southern Germany*, trans. C. Baskin. London: Prentice Hall, 1966.

Fujita, M. 1986. Urban land use theory. In *Location Theory*, ed. R. Arnott. London: Harwood Academic Publishers.

Fujita, M. 1988. A monopolistic competition model of spatial agglomeration: a differentiated product approach. *Regional Science and Urban Economics* 18, 87–124.

Fujita, M. 1989. *Urban Economic Theory: Land Use and City Size*. Cambridge: Cambridge University Press.

Fujita, M. 1993. Monopolistic competition and urban systems. *European Economic Review* 37, 308–15.

Fujita, M. and Krugman, P. 1995. When is the economy monocentric?: von Thünen and Chamberlin unified. *Regional Science and Urban Economics* 25, 505–28.

Fujita, M., Krugman, P. and Mori, T. 1999. On the evolution of hierarchical urban systems. *European Economic Review* 43, 209–51.

Fujita, M. and Mori, T. 1997. Structural stability and evolution of urban systems. *Regional Science and Urban Economics* 27, 399–442.

Fujita, M. and Ogawa, H. 1982. Multiple equilibria and structural transition of non-monocentric urban configurations. *Regional Science and Urban Economics* 12, 161–96.

Fujita, M. and Thisse, J.-F. 2002. *Economics of Agglomeration: Cities, Industrial Location, and Regional Growth*. Cambridge: Cambridge University Press.

Garreau, J. 1991. *Edge City: Life on the New Frontier*. New York: Doubleday.

Henderson, J. and Mitra, A. 1996. The new urban landscape: developers and edge cities. *Regional Science and Urban Economics* 26, 613–43.

Imai, H. 1982. CBD hypothesis and economies of agglomeration. *Journal of Economic Theory* 28, 275–99.

Krugman, P. 1991a. Increasing returns and economic geography. *Journal of Political Economy* 99, 483–99.

Krugman, P. 1991b. *Geography and Trade*. Cambridge, MA: MIT Press.

Konishi, H. 2005. Concentration of competing retail stores. *Journal of Urban Economics* 58, 488–512.

Lucas, R. and Rossi-Hansberg, E. 2002. On the internal structure of cities. *Econometrica* 70, 1445–76.

Mills, E. 1967. An aggregative model of resource allocation in a metropolitan area. *American Economic Review* 57, 197–210.

Mills, E. 1972. *Studies in the Structure of the Urban Economy*. Baltimore, MD: Johns Hopkins University Press.

Mori, T. 1997. A modeling of megalopolis formation: the maturing of city systems. *Journal of Urban Economics* 42, 133–57.

Muth, R. 1969. *Cities and Housing*. Chicago: University of Chicago Press.

Ogawa, H. and Fujita, M. 1980. Equilibrium land use patterns in a non-monocentric city. *Journal of Regional Science* 20, 455–75.

Schweizer, U., Varaiya, P. and Hartwick, J. 1976. General equilibrium and location theory. *Journal of Urban Economics* 3, 285–303.

Solow, R. and Vickrey, W. 1971. Land use in a long narrow city. *Journal of Economic Theory* 3, 1468–88.

Starrett, D. 1978. Market allocations of location choice in a model with free mobility. *Journal of Economic Theory* 9, 418–48.

monopolistic competition

There is at least an oral tradition that the origin of theories of monopolistic competition is Sraffa's (1926). In the case of Joan Robinson (1933) this may well be true. In the case of Edward Chamberlin (1933) it cannot be: the book was developed from a Ph.D. thesis supervised by Allyn A. Young submitted on 1 April 1927. Indeed, Chamberlin (1933, p. 5 n.) refers to Sraffa's paper as appearing 'since the above was written'.

It is, none the less, convenient to take Sraffa's implicit criticism of Marshall (1890) as a starting point. The increasing-marginal-cost condition, necessary for a competitive equilibrium, was, he asserted, not satisfied in many firms that could not possibly be described as 'Marshallian monopolies'. Thus there existed no appropriate model for an apparently common class of firms (or markets – Sraffa was quite aware of the problems of product heterogeneity). The works of Chamberlin and Mrs Robinson, however diversely prompted, may be seen as attempts to fill what became known as the gap between Marshall's polar cases of monopoly and perfect competition. The gap they had in mind was not filled by oligopoly models, which were already well known. Chamberlin certainly had a 'more competitive' model in mind (free entry). Mrs Robinson was so vague about the construction of the demand curve that it is hard to be sure where 'imperfect competition' leaves off and oligopoly begins, but I read her as in the same spirit as Chamberlin. Whether we can in fact reasonably construct a model of imperfect or monopolistic competition which is not an oligopoly model is still an open question.

The work of Edward Chamberlin and Joan Robinson

It would not, I think, be a wise use of space to review here the old dispute between Chamberlin (persistent and vociferous) and Mrs Robinson (reluctant and *dégagée*) about whether or not their models were 'the same'. Nor do I wish to dismiss the question as merely 'braces versus suspenders'. Instead, I shall note briefly what it seems to me they had in common and what not. I start with what they had in common.

Both had downward-sloping demand curves (although their construction differed somewhat; see below), but tried to distinguish their models from that of simple or Marshallian monopoly.

This they were able to do because they assumed that the competitive mechanism worked not only through prices but, most importantly, through entry of firms (products). Thus both made an important generalization and extension of Marshall's proposition that competition would ensure that pure profits were only quasi-rents. Indeed, both thought that free entry is a sufficient condition for the elimination of all pure profit in full equilibrium, and thus both exhibited the famous tangency solution.

Thanks to the downward-sloping demand curve, both were able to exhibit profit-maximizing equilibria consistent with non-convexities in the technology, that is to answer Sraffa. (One consequent result, the familiar excess-capacity theorem, is discussed below.)

Both should, in my judgement, be credited with a major extension of the marginal productivity theory of distribution.

There are, none the less, some differences, and they may explain why, in spite of the many elegant features of Mrs Robinson's analysis, Chamberlin's 'monopolistic competition' seems to have been the more enduring model (or, at least, title).

First, there are the famous Chamberlinian 'groups' or industries, groups of similar but not identical products, ill-defined as they may have been. The lack of identity justified the downward slope of the individual demand curve; the assumptions of large numbers and symmetry were carefully stated to justify the assumption of Cournot–Nash behaviour instead of the recognition of oligopolistic interdependence. (The famous construction of the 'perceived' demand curve, *DD'* and the 'share-of-the-market' demand curve, *dd'* was designed to explain disequilibrium adjustment behaviour. It has little to do with the properties of full equilibrium which, as in Mrs Robinson's version, is characterized by the elimination of super-normal profit.)

By contrast, Mrs Robinson's treatment of the demand curve seems cavalier. She simply asserted (1933, p. 21) that it shows what the firm will sell at each price when all other adjustments are completed. Whether she had in mind the Cournot–Nash assumption of Chamberlin, or intended to encompass in her model some types of oligopolistic behaviour, is obscure. No adjustment mechanism was suggested. The existence of a full-adjustment demand curve, on which the firm's profit-maximizing decisions are based, was simply postulated as a primitive of the model.

Chamberlin was much more ambitious than Mrs Robinson: he attempted to include product-choice and advertising in the model. I say 'attempted' because it was here that his technique let him down most seriously. Two-dimensional geometry only allowed him to illustrate equilibrium conditions pairwise, and he was never able to exhibit the full set of simultaneous equilibrium conditions, to consider second-order conditions, or to carry out any comparative static analysis. Mrs Robinson confined her attention to what her two-dimensional geometry could handle, omitting advertising and quality from the model, and gave us her elegant analysis of discriminating monopoly and monopsony (with its arresting application to the theory of labour market discrimination).

Criticisms

It would be impossible to review the whole debate over monopolistic competition in limited space. I shall concentrate on those criticisms which seem to be still with us, and lead us to recent advances.

There is no doubt that 'groups' were ill-defined. A common definition, still employed, is that we have a group if we can isolate a set of products such that (i) cross-elasticities of demand between them are 'large' and (ii) cross-elasticities of demand between all members of the set and its complement are 'small'. Triffin (1940) pointed out that there is no analytical cut-off between small and large, and concluded that there was no valid analytical construct between the individual firm and the whole economy. We may take this a little further. We may say that a satisfactory taxonomy induces the discrete metric. A continuous function, such as a cross-elasticity, cannot induce the discrete metric and, accordingly, cannot generate a satisfactory taxonomy. I shall argue below that there now exists an analytically satisfactory way of defining groups, that is, one that induces the discrete metric.

Kaldor (1934; 1935) suggested very early in the discussion that chains of overlapping oligopolies might be empirically more likely than competitive groups operating in virtual isolation from other groups. This raises sharply a question which is still with us: what are the necessary and sufficient conditions for competition to be general, or 'diffuse', that is for the assumption of Cournot–Nash behaviour to be plausible, as opposed to localized or oligopolistic so that the possibility of strategic behaviour has to be admitted.

Several writers on spatial competition have shown recently that free entry cannot be relied upon as a sufficient condition to eliminate super-normal profit, that is to generate the tangency solution (see, for example, Eaton, 1976; Eaton and Lipsey, 1978). This follows basically from the idea that capital is product- (location-) specific, and long-lasting, and has accordingly to be *committed*. Hotelling (1929) and Chamberlin (1957) thought that monopolistic and spatial competition were, in some sense, the 'same' subject. Given the spatial results, the 'sameness' of the subjects, or models, becomes an urgent question.

Application of Samuelson's (1947) programme, the 'qualitative calculus', to Chamberlin's model, even when 'making the best of it' (to make the criticism more effective) by, for example ignoring the fact that groups were ill-defined, unfortunately showed it to be qualitatively

almost empty in the sense of generating few qualitative comparative-static predictions (Archibald, 1961). For the individual firm, the reason is the now familiar one: in the multivariate case, the assumption that sufficient extremum conditions are satisfied is not enough to sign the cofactors of off-diagonal elements in the matrix of second-order coefficients. For the group, the reason is essentially the non-convexity of the technology. If, for example demand falls (due, say, to an excise tax), firms exit. When full equilibrium is restored, surviving firms may be producing more or less, that is incurring lower or higher average costs. It also turned out that even the excess capacity theorem did not survive the explicit introduction of advertising in the model (excess capacity remains a possibility but not an entailment). Demsetz (1964) made the interesting suggestion that, by the processes of spin-off, merger, and subcontracting, firms would become so structured that the quantity that minimized average production costs would also minimize average selling costs, in which case equilibrium could not entail excess capacity. It unfortunately turned out that, analytically, this model was inadequately specified (Archibald, 1967), but the idea might still be worth pursuing.

Some reactions to the welfare implications of Chamberlin's model were strange. The reaction of several writers to the excess capacity theorem seems to have been 'It can't be true, but, if it is, it is wicked'. Chamberlin replied (1957), quite reasonably, that optimality conditions for an economy with homogeneous product-groups would not necessarily serve as benchmarks for an economy with some increasingness in returns and differentiated product-groups. Little was in fact known about the welfare economics of an economy with non-convexities in its technology.

Some recent advances and unsolved problems

After some years in which the theory of monopolistic competition was relatively neglected, or at least not much advanced, there has been a recent revival of interest, and a new approach to the subject has emerged. The standard approach, which I shall call the 'goods approach', is in the traditional Walrasian (or Hicksian) style: see the papers by Dixit and Stiglitz (1977), Hart (1979) and Spence (1976). The new, or 'characteristics approach', follows the work of Lancaster: see his (1966), (1971), (1975) and (1979), also Gorman (1980). This approach to monopolistic competition was advocated in Archibald, Eaton and Lipsey (1986). I note briefly the main features of these two quite distinct approaches.

The goods approach is familiar and traditional, but some features deserve emphasis in the present context. Goods themselves are, of course, the primitives of analysis. There is a fixed vector of possible goods, usually either finite or countably infinite. The utility function is defined on the goods, and there is usually a 'representative consumer' (in some sense that requires definition) who consumes some of each of the goods actually produced. If groups are to be identified, the cross-elasticity taxonomy is employed. If individual firm behaviour is considered, the Cournot–Nash assumption is commonly employed. Full equilibrium is characterized by normal profit.

There are some points to notice here. In some models, the assumption of a fixed vector of goods implies that the technology is not continuous: a firm may choose to produce a good (or quality) x_0 or x_1, say, but cannot produce a good arbitrarily close to either of them (in some space of attributes). Now, if these attributes (characteristics) of goods are continuous (for example, the fuel consumption of automobiles, the alcohol content of beer), this is a restrictive, and somewhat strange, assumption. Furthermore, it induces an immediate, and perhaps unwelcome, answer to the question, 'are models of monopolistic and spatial competition in some sense the same?', as Hotelling and Chamberlin thought. The space in most spatial models is a continuum, whether in one dimension or two, whence any analogy between the models breaks down at the first step in their construction.

The assumption of a representative consumer who, necessarily, consumes some of each good produced prevents us from taking into account that diversity of tastes which is an obvious feature of the real world. In a characteristics model, the consumer buys no more goods than there are characteristics that he wishes to consume, and if the number of goods produced exceeds the number of 'relevant' characteristics, he buys none of many (perhaps most) goods. This seems to capture an important feature of reality; but it must immediately be admitted that tractable methods of modelling the diversity of preferences have yet to be developed.

The characteristics model is doubtless now familiar too, and only a few points need to be made. The characteristics of goods, rather than the goods themselves, are the primitives of analysis. The technology is assumed to be continuous, in the sense that, if y_1 and y_2 are two goods embodying different mixes of two characteristics, z_1 and z_2 say, then it is possible to produce any good y_i embodying a convex combination of the quantities of z_1 and z_2 embodied in y_1 and y_2. It is thus always possible to produce a good $\in$-close to any other good in the characteristics space. As in spatial models, possible locations form a continuum. Some increasingness of returns is necessarily assumed: with everywhere constant returns, we might expect a 'production point' at every 'consumption point', whether in physical or characteristics space. Thus out of the continuum of possibilities, only a finite number of goods is produced at any time. None the less, it is assumed that, at least in developed economies, the number of goods produced exceeds the number of characteristics desired by consumers. This can only be the consequence of diversity of tastes: if all consumers wanted the same characteristics mix, the number of goods produced would be *less* than the number of characteristics.

An immediate advantage of the characteristics approach is that it allows us to give an analytic definition of a 'group' or industry. It is assumed that the consumption technology is linear, that is, characteristics are 'produced' by goods according to $z = Ay$ where z is the $1 \times m$ vector of characteristics, A is $m \times n$, and y is the $n \times 1$ vector of produced goods. Suppose now that we can partition z, and correspondingly y, so that the corresponding arrangement of the elements of A is block diagonal. Consider one such block, and the corresponding subsets of z and y. We may call this a group: the elements of the subset of y produce only elements of the corresponding subset of z, and no elements of the complement of this subset in y produce any elements of this subset in z.

This taxonomy induces the discrete metric: two goods either do or do not unambiguously belong to the same group. Whether or not there exist, empirically, any groups corresponding to this definition is yet to be discovered.

To complete this sketch of the characteristics approach, let us consider a group of possible goods embodying only two characteristics, z_1 and z_2, say. Then any produced good, y_i say, can be described by θ_i where $\tan \theta_i = z_2/z_1$. The good is completely described by the pair of numbers (p_i, θ_i) where p_i is the price (reciprocal of the length of the vector θ_i to the z_1, z_2 point that can be bought for some fixed amount). The firm's problem is to choose θ_i as well as p_i. The economist's first problem is to characterize the equilibrium vector of θ's as well as p's. His second problem is to characterize the optimal vector of θ's as well as p's. For the first problem, he needs, of course, to know whether competition is oligopolistic or diffuse. (The prior problem of existence has, of course, been thoroughly investigated for the competitive general equilibrium model, and for some partial equilibrium spatial and small-group models. Little seems to have been done on existence in a Chamberlinian model, at least in the characteristics approach.)

The problem of the socially optimal product choice is of great practical as well as theoretical interest. There is evidence, mostly anecdotal, that the planned economies frequently produce the 'wrong' goods. In the planning literature a fixed vector of homogeneous goods is commonly assumed, and the problem of product choice is not addressed. We similarly lack welfare criteria to tell us if a capitalist economy makes a good job of product selection.

The problem is in fact most difficult. Lancaster (1979) showed that, given some increasingness in returns, considerations of efficiency cannot be successfully divorced from distributional considerations. The problem appears even more starkly in a series of papers by Brown and Heal (1979), (1980), (1981), since they stay with the conventional goods approach. Consider an 'economy' as described by an endowment of resources, a given but non-convex technology, and tastes. They show that, for an arbitrary distribution of ownership, there may exist no efficient allocation of resources. They are also able to show that, for the given 'economy', there always exists a share-ownership distribution (in particular, the equal distribution) such that an efficient allocation does exist.

If this is true for an economy with a fixed product vector, we might conjecture that it is true for an economy in which the product vector is yet to be chosen. We can at least see why efficiency and distribution are entangled in a spatial model (whether the space be geographical or of characteristics). Let there be a given distribution of consumers, whether by location or preferred characteristics mix, and a distribution of stores or products. Assume that the capital specific to one product or location (store) wears out, and is due for replacement. Assume further that some of the mass of demand has shifted (arbitrarily, to the left in the appropriate space). 'Common sense' suggests that the new capital be installed to the left of the old. But this is not a Pareto-efficient move: those consumers remaining to the right will unambiguously lose.

Spence (1976) investigates optimality in monopolistic competition. He adopts the conventional goods model, assuming away income effects, and takes the sum of consumer and producer surplus as his welfare criterion. He is able to show (i) that if sellers can price-discriminate, their profit function will coincide with the welfare maximand, and the optimal product vector (from the possible set) will be produced; and (ii) if not, not: there may be too many or too few products marketed. The reason, roughly speaking, is that, with some increasingness of returns, and products to be chosen, price is not a sufficient signal: we have a species of market failure. Thus there is no market in which you and I and the producers may arrange side-payments such that, by agreeing on the same good(s), we all benefit from the increasingness of returns.

I conjecture that Spence has given us all the pure efficiency results that are to be had. If we follow Lancaster, and Brown and Heal, and do not ignore distributional considerations, it is not obvious what results we may hope for.

We urgently need to know the necessary and sufficient conditions for competition to be diffuse (Chamberlinian) as opposed to local or oligopolistic. The next question follows: on what conditions does the small-group model become asymptotically competitive? So far, we have only a scattering of results.

Consider the set of products in a space of two characteristics, or of stores along a line. It is obvious that no product, or store, can have more than two neighbours: we appear to have Kaldor's chain of overlapping oligopolies. What happens if we increase the number of consumers and products, or stores, without limit is less obvious. While each outlet still has no more than two neighbours, its scope for price setting is evidently diminished. We might conjecture that the asymptotic results in

this case will be approximately competitive. Now let the dimensions of the tangency solution space increase. It has been shown, by Archibald and Rosenbluth (1975), that when the number of tangency solution is four, the number of neighbours (immediate competitors) each product may have approaches half the number of products in the space. This is a necessary condition for competition among diverse products to be Chamberlinian. Sufficient conditions have not been established. These authors, and others, also considered the possibility of 'pre-emptive entry': an incumbent firm in a growing market occupies a point (in physical or characteristics space) before it is normally profitable to do so in order to deter new competition.

Hart (1979) gets asymptotically competitive results in a goods model. He assumes, however that the output of each firm is bounded from above so that the output of each firm can be made as small as we like relative to the whole economy. Further, replication involves increasing the number of consumers each of whom has one of a finite set of preferences, that is, cloning them. What is not yet known is what happens asymptotically in an economy in which (i) the output of the individual firm is not bounded, (ii) the 'address' of products, in the sense of Archibald, Eaton and Lipsey matters, and (iii) as the number of consumers increases, so does the diversity of preferences.

G.C. ARCHIBALD

See also **advertising; Chamberlin, Edward Hastings; competition; market structure; oligopoly; product differentiation; Robinson, Joan Violet.**

Bibliography

Archibald, G.C. 1961. Chamberlin versus Chicago. *Review of Economic Studies* 24, 9–28.

Archibald, G.C. 1967. Monopolistic competition and returns to scale. *Economic Journal* 77, 405–12.

Archibald, G.C. and Rosenbluth, G. 1975. The 'new' theory of consumer demand and monopolistic competition. *Quarterly Journal of Economics* 80, 569–90.

Archibald, G.C., Eaton, B.C. and Lipsey, R.G. 1986. Address models of value theory. In *New Developments in the Analysis of Market Structure*, ed. J.E. Stiglitz. Cambridge, MA: MIT Press.

Brown, D.J. and Heal, G. 1979. Equity, efficiency and increasing returns. *Review of Economic Studies* 57, 571–85.

Brown, D.J. and Heal, G.M. 1980. Two-part tariffs, marginal cost pricing and increasing returns in a general equilibrium model. *Journal of Public Economics* 13, 25–49.

Brown, D.J. and Heal, G. 1981. Welfare theorems for economies with increasing returns. Essex Economic Papers No. 179.

Chamberlin, E.H. 1933. *The Theory of Monopolistic Competition*. Cambridge, MA: Harvard University Press; London: Oxford University Press.

Chamberlin, E.H. 1957. *Towards a More General Theory of Value*. New York: Oxford University Press.

Demsetz, H. 1964. The welfare and empirical implications of monopolistic competition. *Economic Journal* 74, 623–41.

Dixit, A.K. and Stiglitz, J.E. 1977. Monopolistic competition and optimum product diversity. *American Economic Review* 67, 297–308.

Eaton, B.C. 1976. Free entry in one dimensional models. *Journal of Regional Science* 16, 21–33.

Eaton, B.C. and Lipsey, R.G. 1978. Freedom of entry and the existence of pure profit. *Economic Journal* 88, 455–69.

Gorman, W.M. 1980. A possible procedure for analysing quality differentials in the egg market. *Review of Economic Studies* 47, 843–57.

Hart, O. 1979. Monopolistic competition in a large economy with differentiated commodities. *Review of Economic Studies* 46, 1–30.

Hotelling, H. 1929. Stability in competition. *Economic Journal* 39, 41–57.

Kaldor, N. 1934. Mrs. Robinson's 'Economics of imperfect competition'. *Economica* NS 1, 335–41.

Kaldor, N. 1935. Market imperfections and excess capacity. *Economica* NS 2, 33–50.

Lancaster, K.J. 1966. A new approach to consumer theory. *Journal of Political Economy* 74, 132–57.

Lancaster, K. 1971. *Consumer Demand: A New Approach*. New York: Columbia University Press.

Lancaster, K. 1975. Socially optimal product differentiation. *American Economic Review* 65, 567–85.

Lancaster, K.J. 1979. *Variety, Equity, and Efficiency*. New York: Columbia University Press.

Marshall, A. 1890. *Principles of Economics*. London: Macmillan.

Robinson, J. 1933. *The Economics of Imperfect Competition*. London: Macmillan.

Samuelson, P.A. 1947. *Foundations of Economic Analysis*. Cambridge, MA: Harvard University Press.

Spence, A.M. 1976. Product selection, fixed costs, and monopolistic competition. *Review of Economic Studies* 43, 217–35.

Sraffa, P. 1926. The laws of returns under competitive conditions. *Economic Journal* 36, 535–50.

Triffin, R. 1940. *Monopolistic Competition and General Equilibrium Theory*. Cambridge, MA: Harvard University Press.

monopoly

Irving Fisher (1923), once defined monopoly simply as an 'absence of competition'. From this point of view various attitudes to, or criticisms of, monopoly are connected with the particular vision of competition that each writer has in mind. To the neoclassical economist monopoly is the polar opposite to the now familiar 'perfect competition' of the textbooks. Modern writers in the classical tradition, on the other hand, complain that perfect competition neglects the *process* of competitive activity, overlooks the importance of time to competitive processes and assumes away transaction or information costs.

In effect, 'perfect competition' to the neoclassical implies perfect decentralization wherein exchange costs happen to be zero. But the modern critics insist that exchange is not costless. And for this reason competition can be consistent with a wide variety of institutions that are employed to accommodate time, uncertainty and the costs of transacting (Demsetz, 1982). Such arrangements include, for example, tie-in sales, vertical integration and manufacturer-sponsored resale price maintenance. Such price-making behaviour means that in the real world decentralization is imperfect. And it is imperfect decentralization that is embodied in the classical paradigm of laissez-faire. Consequently many phenomena that are automatically treated by the neoclassical as the absence of perfect competition or the presence of behaviour that *looks* monopolistic, are often viewed approvingly by those in the classical tradition.

It is widely believed that, historically, Adam Smith's *Wealth of Nations* provided the most sustained and devastating attack on monopoly. It is true that he speaks of 'monopoly' quite frequently, but typically he uses the term in a wide 18th-century sense to include all kinds of political restrictions. Monopoly under the modern meaning of a single uncontested firm was not Smith's usual target. He employed the term most often to refer to multi-firm industries enjoying statutory protection. Thus, 'the law gave a monopoly to our boot-makers and shoe-makers, not only against our graziers, but against our tanners' (Smith [1776], 1960, vol. 2, p. 153). Again, the whole system of mercantilism was condemned as monopolistic: 'Monopoly of one kind or another, indeed, seems to be the sole engine of the mercantile system' (ibid., p. 129).

The Ricardians too were more concerned with general restrictions, and especially with the fixed supply of land. Ricardo's *Principles of Political Economy and Taxation* in fact has only five pages out of 292 that discuss monopoly, while John Stuart Mill's *Principles of Political Economy* has only two out of 1,004. Following the Ricardians, the development of Darwinian philosophy in the mid-19th century only served to reinforce the classical emphasis on the necessity, if not inevitability, of competition. It is true that the 'modern' and more rigorous theory of monopoly, showing equilibrium to be determined by the equality of marginal revenue with marginal cost, was introduced by Cournot in 1838. But it received very little attention until much later.

In America the classical laissez-faire view of competition and imperfect decentralization prevailed at least to the end of the 19th century. When the Sherman Antitrust Act was passed in 1890, economists were almost unanimously opposed to it. Thus, despite his general disposition for widespread government intervention, the founder of the

American Economic Association, Richard T. Ely (1900), firmly rejected the politically popular policy of 'trust busting'. In the late 1880s John Bates Clark similarly feared that antitrust laws would involve a loss of the efficiency advantages of combinations or trusts. Combination itself was often necessary to generate adequate capital and to insure against adversity during the depressing period of the business cycle. Other contemporary economists, including Simon N. Patten, David A. Wells and George Gunton, had similar views. The last argued that the concentration of capital does not drive small producers out of business, 'but simply integrates them into a larger and more complex system of production, in which they are enabled to produce wealth more cheaply for the community and obtain a larger income for themselves'. Instead of the concentration of capital tending to destroy competition, the reverse was true: 'By the use of large capital, improved machinery and better facilities, the trust can and does undersell the corporation' (Gunton, 1888, p. 385).

Consider now, and in contrast, the subsequent neoclassical approach which eventually involved the comparison of monopoly with what is said to be its polar opposite market structure of perfect competition. The method was gradually developed from the last part of the 19th century and ultimately, in the 1950s, reached the stage of empirical measurement of what was described as the social cost of monopoly. The most influential study has been that of Harberger (1954), whose basic argument can be summarized in terms of Figure 1.

Assume that long-run average costs are constant for both firm and industry and are represented by the line $M_c = A_c$. The perfectly competitive output would be at Q_c where M_c intersects the demand curve DD. If a monopolist were substituted, he could maximize profits by producing Q_m at price P. His monopoly profit, π, would be represented by the rectangle $ABCP$. The loss of

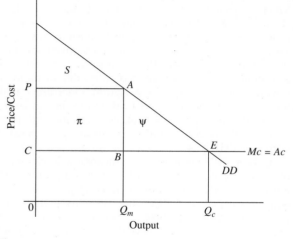

Figure 1

consumers' surplus is measured by the trapezoid $AECP$. The part of this area represented by $ABCP$, however, is not destroyed welfare but simply a transfer of wealth from consumers to the monopolist. The net loss to society as a whole from the monopoly is given by the 'welfare triangle' ABE, denoted in Figure 1 by ω. After making some heroic assumptions, in particular that marginal cost (M_c) was constant for all industries and that the price elasticity of demand was unity everywhere, Harberger estimated an annual welfare loss of $59 million for the US manufacturing sector in the 1920s. This figure was surprisingly small since it represented only one-tenth of 1 per cent of the US national income for that period.

Subsequent writers have argued that Harberger's measure was a serious underestimate for statistical and other reasons. George Stigler (1956) objected that (1) monopolists normally produce in the range where elasticity is greater than unity; (2) some monopoly advantages become embodied in the accounted costs of assets, so leading to an underestimate in reported profits. Subsequent studies that allowed for Stigler's objections reported social costs of monopoly much higher than Harberger's. Thus D.R. Kamerschen (1966) reported an annual welfare loss due to monopoly in the 1956–61 period amounting to around 6 per cent of national income. D.A. Worcester, Jr. (1973), on the other hand, using *firm* rather than *industry* data, and assuming an elasticity of (minus) 2, reported a maximum estimate of welfare loss in the range of 0.5 per cent of national income for the period 1965–9. Focusing on the complaint that Harberger assumed the normal competitive profit rate to be represented by the actual average profit rate earned, whereas the latter itself contains a monopoly profit element, Cowling and Mueller (1978), reported that 734 large firms in the US generated welfare losses totalling $15 billion annually over the period 1963–6, and this amounted to 13 per cent of Gross Corporate Product. All such criticisms have obviously been of a technical nature and implicitly accept Harberger's basic methodology.

Consider next another type of qualification that also accepts the same central methodology. In the frictionless world of the neoclassical model, where all exchange costs are zero, it would be profitable for the monopolist to produce more than Q_m in Figure 1. This would be the case, for example, with the institution of a two-part tariff where a second price is charged for all purchases in excess of Q_m. If this price were located exactly halfway between P and C, it could be shown that the triangle of welfare loss would shrink to one-quarter of the existing size of ω. An extension of such multi-part pricing, of course, would reduce the welfare triangle of loss still further. With the presence of zero exchange costs, which pertains to the neoclassical world, perfect price discrimination is possible. In this case the whole of the trapezoid $CPAE$ would consist of transferred wealth from consumers to producers. Deadweight welfare loss from monopoly would be zero.

If the neoclassical analyst objects that perfect price discrimination does not exist in the real world, he has to offer reasons. It is difficult, meanwhile, to conceive of any practical explanation that could be couched in terms of anything else but significant costs of exchange, such as positive information costs and risk. But such explanation undermines the 'purity' of the neoclassical model and points us back in the direction of the classical world of imperfect decentralization featuring real-world limitations on knowledge, and the existence of dynamic change under uncertainty.

It will be helpful now to describe classical analysis in terms of Figure 1. But first recall that, instead of the notion of perfect competition as a static long-term equilibrium, we start with the view of competition, espoused by Adam Smith and his successors, as a process of rivalry within a time dimension. In Schumpeter, for instance, competition is seen as 'a perennial gale of creative destruction'. It is the possibility of profit, of course, that drives the innovating entrepreneur. Without it the laissez-faire model of decentralization would collapse. But once profits are obtained by a successful pioneer his operation is immediately copied by others, so that there is a constant tendency for entrepreneurial profit to be competed away. It is this focus on a continual series of short runs that distinguishes the analysis from that of 'perfect competition', which is always expressed in terms of the very long run.

Assume then the discovery of a new product, product X, by an entrepreneur who proceeds to offer Q_m of it at price P (see Figure 1). It is only academically true that he is restricting output compared with what potential rivals would produce if they possessed his knowledge and business acumen. But since, in reality, they do not, the only alternative to Q_m supply of product X is some positive quantity of conventional products that the factors were previously producing (the supply of X being zero). The result of his activity in producing X, therefore, is pure social gain, and this is measured in Figure 1 by the profit plus the consumer surplus S. The welfare triangle of social loss (ω) does not exist. It can be expected that the entrepreneur's action will lead to the eventual entry of rivals. At this stage competition will lead to a lowering of price towards cost. This process will then involve a transfer of wealth from the original entrepreneur to consumers. But the latter's original and temporary profit is necessary to induce him to introduce the product at an earlier time than otherwise. It is this earlier introduction indeed that produces the social gains. So while such temporary profit may be described as proceeding from the market structure of 'imperfect competition', nevertheless, according to the Smithian/Schumpeterian analysis, the monopolies so described are necessary institutions, since economic growth would be much weaker without them. Indeed, society recognizes such logic

when it grants temporary legal monopolies in the form of patents.

It is necessary now to examine the special place that is usually accorded to the phenomenon of what is called 'natural monopoly'. This is said to exist when it is technically more efficient to have a single producer or enterprise. The ultimate survival of such a single firm is usually the natural outcome of initial rivalry between several competitors. J.S. Mill ([1848], 1965, p. 962) appears to have been the first to use the adjective 'natural' and to use it interchangeably with 'practical'. Examples quoted by Mill included gas supply, water supply, roads, canals and railways.

In his *Social Economics* (1914) Friedrich von Wieser was probably the first to distinguish the modern from the classical doctrine of monopoly. The classical (Marxian?) attribution to monopoly of the 'favoured' market position of capital over labour was incorrect. So was Ricardo's reference to the 'monopoly' of agricultural soil. The price of urban rents was a competitive price. A typical real monopoly for von Wieser consisted of what he called the 'single-unit enterprise', that was identical to the organization that Mill had previously identified as a 'natural monopoly'. The postal service was an excellent illustration:

> In the face of [such] single-unit administration, the principle of competition becomes utterly abortive. The parallel network of another postal organization, beside the one already functioning, would be economically absurd; enormous amounts of money for plant and management would have to be expended for no purpose whatever. [von Wieser [1914], 1967, pp. 216–17]

The conclusion was that some kind of government control such as price regulation was required.

One must conjecture that von Wieser would have been astonished by the application (in the 1980s) to natural monopolies of the new theory of 'the contestable market'. According to its promulgators, this is a situation in which 'entry is absolutely free, and exit is absolutely costless' (Baumol, 1982). To such economists, even von Wieser's postal service is, at least conceptually, open to such market contestability (although the main example quoted by the new analysts has been that of airlines). The essence of a contestable market is that it is vulnerable to hit-and-run entry: 'Even a very transient profit opportunity need not be neglected by a potential entrant, for he can go in, and before prices change, collect his gains and then depart without cost, should the climate grow hostile' (Baumol, 1982, p. 4).

In effect, such new analysis is a theoretical development of the neoclassical concern with perfect competition and especially with its condition of free entry. Indeed, one writer prefers the term 'ultra-free entry' to 'perfect contestability' (Shepherd, 1984). What is involved is not only the possibility of a new firm gaining a foothold (which is conventional 'free entry') but the ability to duplicate immediately and entirely replace the existing monopolist. The entrant can, moreover, establish itself before the existing firm makes any price response (the Bertrand–Nash assumption). Finally, exit is perfectly free and without cost. Sunk cost, in other words, is zero. Given these conditions, even the threat of entry (potential competition) may hold price down to cost. A government scheme of regulated prices might therefore be socially detrimental.

Although such theoretical innovation is challenging, it has given rise to considerable controversy concerning both the internal consistency of the theory and empirical support for it. The assumption of zero sunk costs has been the one that has come under most attack. It has been observed for instance that in most markets sunk costs are more obvious in the short run than in the long run; and this is by definition. With *any* element of sunk cost the existing firm has a proportionate potential pricing advantage over an entrant. But it is in the very short period that the pure contestability theory stipulates a zero-price response from the incumbent. Meanwhile, with respect to the question of the empirical basis for the theory, Baumol et al. concede that very little is available so far.

Doubts about the efficiency of government price regulation of natural monopolies have also been raised by Demsetz (1968). He has proposed that formal regulation is unnecessary where governments can allow 'rivalrous competitors' to bid for the exclusive rights to supply a good or service over a given 'contract period'. The appearance of a single firm may not imply monopoly pricing, because competition could have previously asserted itself at the franchise bidding stage. Monopoly *structure* therefore does not inevitably predict monopoly *behaviour*, although some element of the latter could appear if conditions, say of production, change during the period of the contract.

An ostensibly similar line of argument to that of Demsetz was offered by Bentham and Chadwick. Chadwick's investigation into water supply in London in the 1850s revealed circumstances of natural monopoly. But he argued that inefficiency was prevalent because the field was divided among 'seven separate companies and establishments of which six were originally competing within the field of supply, with two and three sets of pipes down many of the same streets' (quoted in Crain and Ekelund, 1976). Following Chadwick's recommendation, rivalry was channelled into what he called competition *for* the field and away from (costly) competition '*within* the field'. The same reasoning applied to the railways. Public ownership was advocated while management (operation) of the services was to be contracted out via a competitive franchise bidding process from among potential private enterprises.

It must next be recognized that very many monopolies, if not most, are *unnatural;* that is, they arise not from inexorable economic conditions but from man-made arrangements, usually through the exercise of political power. In these cases the monopoly is typically awarded by government but not usually with the intention of encouraging the introduction of a new product (as with patents). Instead, one supplier is granted the sole right of trading an existing product or service to the exclusion of all other suppliers. A natural state of competition is thus converted by fiat into one of (statutory) monopoly. In this case the classical analyst might see more potential relevance in Harberger's model of welfare loss from monopoly.

Where the monopoly right is granted by the government, and assuming that price discrimination is prohibitively costly, it would seem, again at first sight, that the monopoly rent or 'prize' to the successful producer could indeed be represented by a rectangle such as *ABCP* in Figure 1. But since the seminal writing of Tullock (1967), economists have come to recognize that the pursuit of such monopoly rents is itself a competitive activity, and one that consumes resources. Since Krueger (1974) this process has become known as 'rent seeking' and it frequently takes the form of lobbying, offering campaign contributions, bribery, and other ways of influencing the authorities to grant exclusive rights to production, rights that are then policed by the coercive powers of government.

Recent work has modified the conclusion that the value of resources used in pursuit of the rents would exactly equal the value of the rents. Some writers have urged that lobbying by consumers might to some extent offset that of potential monopolists such that a regulated price at a magnitude lower than *P* (but higher than *C*) in Figure 1 would result. In this case, of course, the expected rectangle of monopoly rent would be reduced and the producers collectively would not spend more than this in rent seeking.

Jadlow (1985) has reduced still further the expected magnitude of such monopoly rent rectangles by introducing a multi-period model wherein other rent seekers continue to compete for the valued monopoly prize while consumers, regulators and antitrusters continue their endeavours to eliminate the rents over a protracted period into the future. Since, therefore, instead of a one-time prize, the monopoly rent is viewed as the expected present value of a stream of rents over a series of future time periods in which uncertainty is present, there is likely to be a significant reduction of resources invested in rent-seeking activities.

It is usually implied by economists that the task of public policy with regard to monopoly is to eliminate monopoly profit by one means or another. The above analysis reveals, however, that the conventional measures of social losses via the welfare triangles, plus the rectangles of potential transfers that are partially 'eaten up' by resources devoted to rent-seeking, are predominantly applicable to monopolies that are politically bestowed. We are thus left with the conclusion that appropriate public policy (according to usual economic reasoning) involves government 'correcting for' something it has created itself. The direct way of solving such a problem, at least to the innocent, would be for the government simply to abstain from granting statutory monopoly privileges in the first place. The newer 'economics of politics', however, has produced reasons why the legislative activity of monopoly rent creation is inherent in the very structure of majority voting democracies. Indeed, some writers (Brennan and Buchanan, 1980) argue that the very institution of government is usually a monopoly. In so far as this is true, we face the paradoxical situation that the public policy prescribed in economics textbooks is one whereby monopoly in general is policed or controlled by an institution that is itself a monopoly.

The problem of government sponsored monopolies is currently receiving considerable attention. Indeed, it constitutes one of the most profound issues of the day. For hopeful developments we must look again, presumably, to still further research in the modern economics of politics.

EDWIN G. WEST

See also **competition; contestable markets; market structure; monopoly.**

Bibliography

Baumol, W.J. 1982. Contestable markets: an uprising in the theory of industry structure. *American Economic Review* 72(1), March, 1–15.

Brennan, G. and Buchanan, J. 1980. *The Power to Tax: Analytical Foundations of the Fiscal Constitution.* Cambridge: Cambridge University Press.

Cowling, K. and Mueller, D.C. 1978. The social costs of monopoly power. *Economic Journal* 88, December, 727–48.

Crain, W.M. and Ekelund, R.E., Jr. 1976. Chadwick and Demsetz on competition and regulation. *Journal of Law and Economics* 19(1), April, 149–62.

Demsetz, H. 1968. Why regulate utilities? *Journal of Law and Economics* 11, April, 55–65.

Demsetz, H. 1982. *Economic, Legal, and Political Dimensions of Competition, Professor Dr. F. de Vries Lectures in Economics.* Vol. 4, Amsterdam: North-Holland.

Ely, R.T. 1900. *Monopolies and Trusts.* New York: Macmillan.

Fisher, I. 1923. *Elementary Principles of Economics.* New York: Macmillan.

Gunton, G. 1888. The economic and social aspects of trusts. *Political Science Quarterly* 3(3), September, 385–408.

Harberger, A.C. 1954. Monopoly and resource allocation. *American Economic Association, Papers and Proceedings* 44, May, 77–87.

Jadlow, J.M. 1985. Monopoly rent-seeking under conditions of uncertainty. *Public Choice* 45(1), 73–87.

Kamerschen, D.R. 1966. An estimation of the 'welfare losses' from monopoly in the American economy. *Western Economic Journal* 4, Summer, 221–36.

Krueger, A.O. 1974. The political economy of the rent-seeking society. *American Economic Review* 64, June, 291–303.

Mill, J.S. 1848. *Principles of Political Economy.* Ed. W.J. Ashley. Reprinted, New York: A.M. Kelley, 1965.

Shepherd, W.G. 1984. 'Contestability' vs. competition. *American Economic Review* 74(2), September, 572–87.

Smith, A. 1776. *An Inquiry into the Nature and Causes of the Wealth of Nations.* 2 vols, ed. E. Cannan, London: Methuen, 1960.

Stigler, G. 1956. The statistics of monopoly and merger. *Journal of Political Economy* 64, February, 33–40.

Tullock, G. 1967. The welfare costs of tariffs, monopolies, and theft. *Western Economic Journal* 5, June, 224–32.

von Wieser, F. 1914. *Social Economics.* Trans. A. Ford Hinrichs, New York: A.M. Kelley, 1967.

Worcester, D.A., Jr. 1973. New estimates of the welfare loss to monopoly, United States: 1956–69. *Southern Economic Journal* 40(2), October, 234–45.

monopoly capitalism

Among Marxian economists 'monopoly capitalism' is the term widely used to denote the stage of capitalism which dates from approximately the last quarter of the 19th century and reaches full maturity in the period after World War II. Marx's *Capital*, like classical political economy from Adam Smith to John Stuart Mill, was based on the assumption that all commodities are produced by industries consisting of many firms, or capitals in Marx's terminology, each accounting for a negligible fraction of total output and all responding to the price and profit signals generated by impersonal market forces. Unlike the classical economists, however, Marx recognized that such an economy was inherently unstable and impermanent. The way to succeed in a competitive market is to cut costs and expand production, a process which requires incessant accumulation of capital in ever new technological and organizational forms. In Marx's words: 'The battle of competition is fought by cheapening of commodities. The cheapness of commodities depends, *ceteris paribus*, on the productiveness of labour, and this again on the scale of production. Therefore the larger capitals beat the smaller.' Further, the credit system which 'begins as a modest helper of accumulation' soon 'becomes a new and formidable weapon in the competitive struggle, and finally it transforms itself into an immense social mechanism for the centralization of capitals' (Marx, 1867, ch. 25, sect. 2). Marx, and even more clearly Engels when preparing the second and third volumes of *Capital* for the printer two decades later, concluded, in the latter's words, that 'the long cherished freedom of competition has reached the end of its tether and is compelled to announce its own palpable bankruptcy' (Marx, 1894, ch. 27).

There is thus no doubt that Marx and Engels believed capitalism had reached a turning point. In their view, however, the end of the competitive era marked not the beginning of a new stage of capitalism but rather the beginning of a transition to the new mode of production that would take the place of capitalism. It was only somewhat later, when it became clear that capitalism was far from on its last legs that Marx's followers, recognizing that a new stage had actually arrived, undertook to analyse its main features and what might be implied for capitalism's 'laws of motion'.

The pioneer in this endeavour was the Austrian Marxist Rudolf Hilferding whose magnum opus *Das Finanzkapital* appeared in 1910. A forerunner was the American economist Thorstein Veblen, whose book *The Theory of Business Enterprise* (1904) dealt with many of the same problems as Hilferding's: corporation finance, the role of banks in the concentration of capital, etc. Veblen's work, however, was apparently unknown to Hilderding, and neither author had a significant impact on mainstream economic thought in the English-speaking world, where the emergence of corporations and related new forms of business activity and organization, though the subject of a vast descriptive literature, was almost entirely ignored in the dominant neoclassical orthodoxy.

In Marxist circles, however, Hilferding's work was hailed as a breakthrough, and its pre-eminent place in the Marxist tradition was assured when Lenin strongly endorsed it at the beginning of his Imperialism, the Highest Stage of Capitalism. 'In 1910,' Lenin wrote, 'there appeared in Vienna the work of the Austrian Marxist, Rudolf Hilferding, Finance Capital … . This work gives a very valuable theoretical analysis of "the latest phase of capitalist development", the subtitle of the book.'

As far as economic theory in the narrow sense is concerned, Lenin added little to Finance Capital, and in retrospect it is evident that Hilferding himself was not successful in integrating the new phenomena of capitalist development into the core of Marx's theoretical structure (value, surplus value, and above all the process of capital accumulation). In chapter 15 of his book ('Price Determination in the Capitalist Monopoly. Historical Tendency of Finance Capital') Hilferding, in seeking to deal with some of these problems, came up with a very striking conclusion which has been associated with his name ever since. Prices under conditions of monopoly, he thought, are indeterminate and hence unstable. Wherever concentration enables capitalists to achieve higher than average profits, suppliers and customers are put under pressure to create counter combinations which will enable them to appropriate part of the extra profits for themselves. Thus monopoly spreads in all directions from every point of origin. The question then arises as to the limits of 'cartellization' (the term is used synonymously with monopolization). Hilferding answers:

The answer to this question must be that there is no absolute limit to cartellization. What exists rather is a tendency to the continuous spread of cartellization. Independent industries, as we have seen, fall more and more under the sway of the cartellized ones, ending up finally by being annexed by the cartellized ones. The result of this process is then a *general cartel*. The entire capitalist production is consciously controlled from one center which determines the amount of production in all its spheres … . It is the consciously controlled society in antagonistic form.

There is more about this vision of a future totally monopolized society, but it need not detain us. Three quarters of a century of monopoly capitalist history has shown that while the tendency to concentration is strong and persistent, it is by no means as ubiquitous and overwhelming as Hilferding imagined. There are powerful counter-tendencies – the breakup of existing firms and the founding of new ones – which have been strong enough to prevent the formation of anything even remotely approaching Hilferding's general cartel.

The first signs of important new departures in Marxist economic thinking began to appear toward the end of the interwar years, i.e., the 1920s and 1930s; but on the whole this was a period in which Lenin's *Imperialism* was accepted as the last word on monopoly capitalism, and the rigid orthodoxy of Stalinism discouraged attempts to explore changing developments in the structure and functioning of contemporary capitalist economies. Meanwhile, academic economists in the West finally got around to analysing monopolistic and imperfectly competitive markets (especially Edward Chamberlin and Joan Robinson), but for a long time these efforts were confined to the level of individual firms and industries. The so-called Keynesian revolution which transformed macroeconomic theory in the 1930s was largely untouched by these advances in the theory of markets, continuing to rely on the time-honoured assumption of atomistic competition.

The 1940s and 1950s witnessed the emergence of new trends of thought within the general framework of Marxian economics. These had their roots on the one hand in Marx's theory of concentration and centralization which, as we have seen, was further developed by Hilferding and Lenin; and on the other hand in Marx's famous Reproduction Schemes presented and analysed in Volume II of *Capital*, which were the focal point of a prolonged debate on the nature of capitalist crises involving many of the leading Marxist theorists of the period between Engels' death (1895) and World War I. Credit for the first attempt to knot these two strands of thought into an elaborated version of Marxian accumulation theory goes to Michal Kalecki, whose published works in Polish in the early 1930s articulated, according to Joan Robinson and others, the main tenets of the contemporaneous Keynesian 'revolution' in the West. Kalecki had been introduced to economics through the works of Marx and the great Polish Marxist Rosa Luxemburg, and he was consequently free of the inhibitions and preconceptions that went with a training in neoclassical economics. He moved to England in the mid-1930s, entering into the intense discussions and debates of the period and making his own distinctive contributions along the lines of his previous work and that of Keynes and his followers in Cambridge, Oxford and the London School of Economics. In April 1938 Kalecki published an article in *Econometrica* ('The Distribution of the National Income') which highlighted differences between his approach and that of Keynes, especially with respect to two crucially important and closely related subjects, namely, the class distribution of income and the role of monopoly. With respect to monopoly, Kalecki stated at the end of the article a position which had deep roots in his thinking and would henceforth be central to his theoretical work:

> The results arrived at in this essay have a more general aspect. A world in which the degree of monopoly determines the distribution of the national income is a world far removed from the pattern of free competition. Monopoly appears to be deeply rooted in the nature of the capitalist system: free competition, as an assumption, may be useful in the first stage of certain investigations, but as a description of the normal state of capitalist economy it is merely a myth.

A further step in the direction of integrating the two strands of Marx's thought – concentration and centralization on the one hand and crisis theory on the other – was marked by the publication in 1942 of *The Theory of Capitalist Development* by Paul M. Sweezy, which contained a fairly comprehensive review of the pre-war history of Marxist economics and at the same time made explanatory use of concepts introduced into mainstream monopoly and oligopoly theory during the preceding decade. This book, soon translated into several foreign languages, had a significant effect in systematizing the study and interpretation of Marxian economic theories.

It should not be supposed, however, that these new departures were altogether a matter of theoretical speculation. Of equal if not greater importance were the changes in the structure and functioning of capitalism which had emerged during the 1920s and 1930s. On the one hand the decline in competition which began in the late 19th century proceeded at an accelerated pace – as chronicled in the classic study by Arthur R. Burns, *The Decline of Competition: A Study of the Evolution of American Industry* (1936) – and on the other hand the unprecedented severity of the depression of the 1930s provided dramatic proof of the inadequacy of conventional business cycle theories. The Keynesian revolution was a partial answer to this challenge, but the renewed upsurge of the advanced capitalist economies during and after the war cut short further development of critical analysis among mainstream economists, and it was left to

the Marxists to carry on along the lines that had been pioneered by Kalecki before the war.

Kalecki spent the war years at the Oxford Institute of Statistics whose Director, A.L. Bowley, had brought together a distinguished group of scholars, most of them emigrés from occupied Europe. Among the latter was Josef Steindl, a young Austrian economist who came under the influence of Kalecki and followed in his footsteps. Later on, Steindl recounted the following:

> On one occasion I talked with Kalecki about the crisis of capitalism. We both, as well as most socialists, took it for granted that capitalism was threatened by a crisis of existence, and we regarded the stagnation of the 1930s as a symptom of such a major crisis. But Kalecki found the reasons, given by Marx, why such a crisis should develop, unconvincing; at the same time he did not have an explanation of his own. I still do not know, he said, why there should be a crisis of capitalism, and he added: Could it have anything to do with monopoly? He subsequently suggested to me and to the Institute, before he left England, that I should work on this problem. It was a very Marxian problem, but my methods of dealing with it were Kaleckian (Steindl, 1985).

Steindl's work on this subject was completed in 1949 and published in 1952 under the title *Maturity and Stagnation in American Capitalism*. While little noticed by the economics profession at the time of its publication, this book nevertheless provided a crucial link between the experiences, empirical as well as theoretical, of the 1930s, and the development of a relatively rounded theory of monopoly capitalism in the 1950s and 1960s, a process which received renewed impetus from the return of stagnation to American (and global) capitalism during the 1970s and 1980s.

The next major work in the direct line from Marx through Kalecki and Steindl was Paul Baran's book, *The Political Economy of Growth*, which presented a theory of the dynamics of monopoly capitalism and opened up a new perspective on the nature of the interaction between developed and underdeveloped capitalist societies. This was followed by the joint work of Baran and Sweezy, *Monopoly Capital: An Essay on the American Economic and Social Order*, incorporating ideas from both of their earlier works and attempting to elucidate, in the words of their Introduction, the 'mechanism linking the foundation of society (under monopoly capitalism) with what Marxists call its political, cultural, and ideological superstructure'. Their effort, however, still fell short of a comprehensive theory of monopoly capitalism since it neglected 'a subject which occupies a central place in Marx's study of capitalism', that is, a systematic inquiry into 'the consequences which the particular kinds of technological change characteristic of the monopoly capitalist period have had for the nature of work, the composition (and differentiation) of the working class, the psychology of workers, the forms of working-class organization and struggle, and so on.' A pioneering effort to fill this gap in the theory of monopoly capitalism was taken by Harry Braverman a few years later (Braverman, 1974) which in turn did much to stimulate renewed research into changing trends in work processes and labour relations in the late 20th century.

Marx wrote in the Preface to the first edition of Volume 1 of *Capital* that 'it is the ultimate aim of this work to lay bare the economic law of motion of modern society'. What emerged, running like a red thread through the whole work, could perhaps better be called a theory of the accumulation of capital. In what respect, if at all, can it be said that latter-day theories of monopoly capitalism modify or add to Marx's analysis of the accumulation process?

As far as form is concerned, the theory remains basically unchanged, and modifications in content are in the direction of putting even greater emphasis on certain tendencies already demonstrated by Marx to be inherent in the accumulation process. This is true of concentration and centralization, and even more spectacularly so of the role of what Marx called the credit system, now grown to monstrous proportions compared to the small beginnings of his day. In addition, and perhaps most important, the new theories seek to demonstrate that monopoly capitalism is more prone than its competitive predecessor to generating unsustainable rates of accumulation, leading to crises, depressions, and prolonged periods of stagnation.

The reasoning here follows a line of thought which recurs in Marx's writings, especially in the unfinished later volumes of *Capital* (including *Theories of Surplus Value*): individual capitalists always strive to increase their accumulation to the maximum extent possible and without regard for the ultimate overall effect on the demand for the increasing output of the economy's expanding capacity to produce. Marx summed this up in the well-known formula that 'the real barrier of capitalist production is capital itself'. The upshot of the new theories is that the widespread introduction of monopoly raises this barrier still higher. It does this in three ways.

(1) Monopolistic organization gives capital an advantage in its struggle with labour, hence tends to raise the rate of surplus value and to make possible a higher rate of accumulation.

(2) With monopoly (or oligopoly) prices replacing competitive prices, a uniform rate of profit gives way to a hierarchy of profit rates – highest in the most concentrated industries, lowest in the most competitive. This means that the distribution of surplus value is skewed in favour of the larger units of capital which characteristically accumulate a greater proportion of their profits than smaller units of capital, once again making possible a higher rate of accumulation.

(3) On the demand side of the accumulation equation, monopolistic industries adopt a policy of slowing down and carefully regulating the expansion of productive capacity in order to maintain their higher rates of profit.

Translated into the language of Keynesian macro theory, these consequences of monopoly mean that the savings potential of the system is increased, while the opportunities for profitable investment are reduced. Other things being equal, therefore, the level of income and employment under monopoly capitalism is lower than it would be in a more competitive environment.

To convert this insight into a dynamic theory, it is necessary to see monopolization (the concentration and centralization of capital) as an ongoing historical process. At the beginning of the transition from the competitive to the monopolistic stage, the accumulation process is only minimally affected. But with the passage of time the impact grows and tends sooner or later to become a crucial factor in the functioning of the system. This, according to monopoly capitalist theory, accounts for the prolonged stagnation of the 1930s as well as for the return of stagnation in the 1970s and 1980s following the exhaustion of the long boom caused by World War II and its multifaceted aftermath effects.

Neither mainstream economics nor traditional Marxian theory had been able to offer a satisfactory explanation of the stagnation phenomenon which has loomed increasingly large in the history of the capitalist world during the 20th century. It is thus the distinctive contribution of monopoly capitalist theory to have tackled this problem head on and in the process to have generated a rich body of literature which draws on and adds to the work of the great economic thinkers of the last 150 years. A representative sampling of this literature, together with editorial introductions and interpretations, is contained in Foster and Szlajfer (1984).

PAUL M. SWEEZY

See also **Baran, Paul Alexander; capitalism; finance; foreign direct investment; Marx, Karl Heinrich.**

Bibliography

Baran, P.A. 1957. *The Political Economy of Growth.* New York: Monthly Review Press.

Baran, P.A. and Sweezy, P.M. 1966. *Monopoly Capital: An Essay on the American Economic and Social Order.* New York: Monthly Review Press.

Braverman, H. 1974. *Labor and Monopoly Capital: The Degradation of Work in the Twentieth Century.* New York: Monthly Review Press.

Burns, A.R. 1936. *The Decline of Competition: A Study of the Evolution of American Industry.* New York: McGraw-Hill.

Foster, J.B. and Szlajfer, H., eds. 1984. *The Faltering Economy: The Problem of Accumulation Under Monopoly Capitalism.* New York: Monthly Review Press.

Hilferding, R. 1910. *Das Finanzkapital.* Trans. M. Watnick and S. Gordon as *Finance Capital*, ed. T. Bottomore, London: Routledge & Kegan Paul, 1981.

Kalecki, M. 1938. The distribution of the national income. *Econometrica*, April.

Lenin, V.I. 1917. *Imperialism, The Highest Stage of Capitalism.*

Marx, K. 1867. *Capital*, Vol. 1. Moscow: Progress Publishers.

Marx, K. 1885. *Capital*, Vol. 2. Moscow: Progress Publishers.

Marx, K. 1894. *Capital*, Vol. 3. Moscow: Progress Publishers.

Steindl, J. 1952. *Maturity and Stagnation in American Capitalism.* Oxford: Blackwell.

Steindl, J. 1985. The present state of economics. *Monthly Review*, February.

Sweezy, P.M. 1942. *The Theory of Capitalist Development.* New York: Monthly Review Press.

Sweezy, P.M. 1966. See Baran and Sweezy (1966).

Veblen, T. 1904. *The Theory of Business Enterprise.* New York: Charles Scribner's Sons.

monopsony

The definition of a monopsony in the *Oxford English Dictionary* (OED) is 'a market situation in which there is only one buyer'. Joan Robinson (1933) is credited with inventing the term (but see Thornton, 2004, for a discussion of the origins of the term) as a counterpart to the more commonly used and understood term 'monopoly'.

Taken literally, it is very likely that a pure monopsony has never existed in any market, but the term is more generally used to denote a situation in which the supply curve to an individual firm has an input price elasticity that is finite, that is, is increasing in the input price, and this article follows that usage. If one is pedantic, one might think that 'oligopsony' is a more accurate term to use (defined by the OED as 'a state of the market in which only a small number of buyers exists for a product'), or 'oligopsonistic competition' if one believes that free entry of firms will bid away any monopsony rents.

The market for any type of good or service could, in principle, be monopsonistic. To give some examples from the economic literature, Schroeter (1988) considers the meat-packing industry as an oligopsonistic buyer of cattle, Just and Chern (1980) consider the tomato-canning industry as an oligopsonistic buyer of tomatoes, and Murray (1995) considers saw-mills as oligopsonistic buyers of logs. But the idea of monopsony is most commonly applied to the labour market, and this article focuses on that application. Employers are often felt to have monopsony power only in a few specific labour markets – those for professional athletes in the United States, nurses and teachers (for whom outside cities there may only be one potential employer), and miners and mill workers in company towns in the early days of the Industrial Revolution are some of the more common examples. But,

in recent years, some labour economists have argued that monopsony is pervasive in all labour markets.

The plan of this article is the following. We first review the simple partial equilibrium of monopsony, discussing the differences from and similarities to the more conventional perfectly competitive model. We then discuss why it is plausible to believe that employers have some monopsony power over their workers, after which we discuss how the monopsony perspective can help us to a better understanding of the workings of labour markets. The monopsonistic approach is more in line with the way that workers and employers experience the labour market, and can explain a wide range of what are puzzles and anomalies from the perspective of labour markets as perfectly competitive. Many of these puzzles and anomalies have other potential explanations but monopsony offers a simple unified account of their existence.

The simple textbook model of monopsony

In a perfectly competitive labour market, an employer can hire as many workers of a particular type as it wants at the market wage for that type of workers (and none at all if it tries to pay below the market wage). But, if an employer has some Monopsony power, the labour supply to an individual employer depends positively on the wage paid. The wage elasticity of the labour supply curve facing the firm is therefore finite not infinite. Figure 1 represents such a labour supply curve.

How does this affect the decisions of employers? Denote the supply of labour to the firm if it pays w by $N(w)$ and the inverse of this relationship by $w(N)$. Total labour costs are given by $w(N)N$. Assume that the firm has a revenue function $Y(N)$ and is a simple monopsonist who has to pay a single wage to all its workers. It wants to choose N to maximize profits which are given by:

$$\pi = Y(N) - w(N)N. \qquad (1)$$

This leads to the first-order condition:

$$Y'(N) = w(N) + w'(N)N. \qquad (2)$$

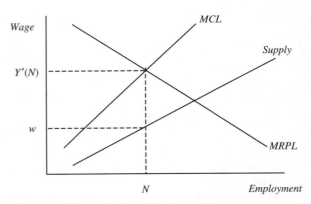

Figure 1   The textbook model of monopsony

The left-hand side of (2) is the marginal revenue product of labour. The right-hand side is the marginal cost of labour, the increase in total labour costs when an extra worker is hired. The marginal cost of labour (MCL) has two parts: the wage, w, that must be paid to the new worker hired and the increase in wages that must be paid to all existing workers. The MCL is always above the labour supply curve to the firm and is also drawn on Figure 1. The profit maximizing employer will choose the level of employment where MRPL = MCL and the wage necessary to supply this amount of labour – the solution is represented graphically in Figure 1.

In equilibrium, the wage paid to workers is less than their marginal revenue product. Although the employer is making positive profit on the marginal worker they have no incentive to increase employment because doing so would require increasing the wage (to attract the extra worker) and this higher wage must be paid not just to the new worker but also to all the existing workers. One particularly useful way of representing the choice of the firm is that marginal cost of labour is a mark-up on the wage, the mark-up being given by the elasticity of the labour supply curve facing the firm. Write the elasticity of the labour supply curve facing the firm as $\varepsilon_{Nw} = \frac{wN'(w)}{N(w)}$ and let ε be the inverse of this elasticity. Then (2) can be written as:

$$\frac{Y' - w}{w} = \frac{1}{\varepsilon_{Nw}} = \varepsilon \qquad (3)$$

so that the proportional gap between the wage and the marginal revenue product is a function of the elasticity of the labour supply curve facing the firm. Perfect competition can be thought of as a special case of this model where $\varepsilon_{Nw} = \infty$ and $\varepsilon = 0$, in which case (3) says that the wage will be equal to the marginal revenue product.

Some of the comparative statics of the monopsony model are the same as the perfectly competitive model and some are different. For example, consider an increase in the marginal revenue product of labour for a single firm – this will lead to an increase in employment and a rise in wages in a monopsony model. The former would occur in a competitive model but the latter would not, as a competitive firm would simply continue to pay the market wage (which would not change if the change in the MRPL affected only a single firm). The impact of shifts in the labour supply curve to the firm is more complicated as the impact depends on how the change affects the marginal cost of labour and not just the average cost of labour. An increase in the supply of labour to the firm that keeps the elasticity the same will result in a rise in employment and a fall in wages, just as in the competitive model. But matters are more complicated if the elasticity of the labour supply curve can also change as the average and marginal cost of labour can move in opposite directions, the most familiar example of which is the impact of a minimum wage. The minimum wage raises the average cost of labour but (if it is binding) reduces $w'(N)$ so its effect on the marginal cost of labour (see (2)) is ambiguous. In fact, one can show that a minimum wage that just binds must raise employment (a demonstration of this can be found in most labour economics textbooks).

Although the model described here captures the fundamentals of a monopsonistic labour market, there are a number of ways in which it is too simplistic, and it is important to be aware of its limitations. First, we have assumed that the employer is a simple monopsonist who must pay the same wage to all workers – that is, wage discrimination is not allowed by assumption.

Second, the simple model assumes that the only way an employer can raise employment is by raising the wage paid, something that is quite implausible. Manning (2006) considers the case where employers can also increase their employment by spending resources on recruitment activities. He shows that monopsony can be thought of as the case where the marginal cost of recruiting an extra worker is increasing in the number of workers recruited.

Third, the simple model is a model of partial equilibrium – it ignores the interactions with other employers that are very important in reality. One would expect the actions of other employers to affect the labour supply curve facing an individual firm; for example, if other firms pay higher wages we would expect the labour supply to this firm to fall for a given wage. Taking account of these interactions is particularly important when considering the impact of policies like the minimum wage that will affect all employers in a market. Manning (2003a, ch. 12) shows that, while in the simple monopsony model a just-binding minimum wage always raises employment, this is not necessarily the case in general equilibrium models of oligopsony, where there is more than one employer.

The sources of monopsony power

Labour economists have often doubted whether many employers have significant monopsony power over their employees (though this scepticism has diminished in recent years – see Boal and Ransom, 1997, for a generally sympathetic survey). So it is important to think about why employers are likely to have monopsony power over their workers.

Traditionally, employers are thought to have monopsony power only in labour markets in which there is a small number of employers. A typical example would be a mill town or mine village in the early days of industrialization, where the employer dominated the local labour market. Most economists are rightly sceptical of the view that the number of employers in many labour markets is small. Classical monopsony could also occur when there are many employers but they collude in wage-setting so that there are only a few effective employers in the labour market. But most economists do not think employer collusion is important in labour markets. (Yet Adam Smith, 1776, p. 169, strongly believed that employer collusion was a frequent outcome in labour markets:

> ... we rarely hear, it has been said, of the combinations of masters, though frequently of those of workmen. But, whoever imagines, upon this account, that masters rarely combine, is as ignorant of the world as of the subject. Masters are always and everywhere in a sort of tacit, but constant and uniform combination, not to raise the wages of labour above their actual rate. To violate this combination is everywhere a most unpopular action, and a sort of reproach to a master among his neighbours and equals. We seldom, indeed hear of this combination, because it is the usual, and one may say, the natural state of things.)

However, modern theories of monopsony do not generally argue that employer market power over their workers derives from there being a small number of employers. They tend to emphasize the role of frictions in the labour market. The perfectly competitive model implies that an employer who cuts wages by one cent will find all their existing workers quit immediately. While it is likely that cutting wages will increase the quit rate and make it harder to recruit replacements, these effects are not as strong as the perfectly competitive model would have us believe.

To illustrate how this can lead to a model from the perspective of firms that looks something like Figure 1, suppose that the quit rate of workers is a negative function of the wage, $q(w)$ and the flow of recruits to the firm is a positive function of the wage, $R(w)$. Then, in steady state employment in the firm is:

$$N = \frac{R(w)}{q(w)} \qquad (4)$$

which will be a positive function of the wage – that is, the employer will face an upward-sloping labour supply curve as represented in Figure 1.

What are the sources of these frictions in labour markets? In *The Economics of Imperfect Competition* (1933, p. 296), Joan Robinson argued that ignorance (about what all employers are offering), heterogeneous preferences and mobility costs are the most plausible sources of frictions in the labour market. The formal models of recent years are built on these ideas. Models based on worker ignorance are typically search models (the canonical versions of which are probably Albrecht and Axell, 1984, and Burdett and Mortensen, 1998) in which it takes time and/or money for workers to change jobs. One the other hand, there are the models that assume workers have full information and no mobility costs but that jobs are differentiated in some way (a canonical model of this sort is Bhaskar and To, 1999, though all such models have

roots in the model of product differentiation by Salop, 1979). In these models, jobs might be differentiated by physical location or skill or any other plausible characteristic. This product differentiation gives employers some monopsony power over their workers because employers are not perfect substitutes from the perspective of workers, so a cut in the wage does not cause all workers to leave for other firms.

These theories of 'modern monopsony' might appear to be very different to classical models of monopsony, but Manning (2003b) argues that they are more similar than one might have thought as they all use different mechanisms to argue that the choice of employers of a particular worker is limited at a particular moment in time.

It is plausible to think that labour markets have frictions; but is this any more than a complication? The next three sections argues that it does matter, emphasizing how our analysis of labour markets from the perspective of workers, employers and public policy is affected in important ways by the recognition that employers have monopsony power over their workers.

Monopsony from an employer perspective

Here the key idea of the monopsony model is that the labour supply curve facing an individual employer is not perfectly elastic. It is helpful to think about the decisions employers must make about pay, the structure of pay and non-wage aspects of jobs.

First, monopsonistic employers who want, for whatever reason, to be large will have to pay higher wages as they need to be further up their labour supply curve. Hence monopsony offers a simple explanation for the very robust empirical correlation between employer size and wages (see Brown and Medoff, 1989). It can also explain why wages seem to be positively correlated with measures of how 'good' an employer is like productivity and profitability (for example, Blanchflower, Oswald and Sanfey, 1996). As noted in the previous section, 'good' firms that have a higher MRPL curve will choose to pay higher wages, something that should not happen in a perfectly competitive labour market.

We also have robust evidence that low-wage employers find it harder to recruit and retain workers, as predicted by monopsony. Low-wage employers have higher vacancy rates, take longer to fill vacancies and have higher quit rates among their workers.

As already mentioned, employers have an incentive to wage discriminate, to pay different wages to workers who might have the same level of productivity. In particular, we would expect them to pay wages that rise with seniority, since pushing the rewards of employment into the future helps to deter quits as workers get the high wages only if they remain with the firm (see Stevens, 2004). This is consistent with the empirical evidence (admittedly a bit patchy) that pay varies more strongly than productivity with seniority, though there are also incentive theories that make similar predictions.

Monopsony also offers a simple explanation of why employers often seem to pay for general training of their workers. In a perfectly competitive market this is something of a puzzle; since workers should receive all the returns to general training, employers should not be prepared to pay for it. But in a monopsonistic labour market, where wages are below marginal products, some of the returns to general training are likely to accrue to employers, giving them an incentive to provide training.

Monopsony from a worker perspective

From the perspective of workers, a monopsonistic labour market will appear to be one in which there is heterogeneity in the jobs available (definitely in the wage but quite likely in other dimensions as well) and jobs are hard to find, so getting and losing jobs are occasions for joy and sadness. If one wants a formal model to capture these ideas, a search model is the right conceptual framework to use. Of course, one can use search models to think about workers' choices whenever they face a distribution of wages even if the origin of that distribution is not the monopsony power of employers, so this area of research is not distinctive to monopsony.

First, it can explain the existence of wage dispersion even in very tightly defined labour markets. This violation of the 'law of one wage' was first documented by the so-called neo-realist labour economists (see Kaufman, 1988) in the United States in the 1940s, but most subsequent studies have confirmed it (for example, Groshen, 1991). This wage dispersion is exactly what we would expect to see in a monopsonistic labour market in which different employers will choose different wages even if faced with the same labour supply curve. This can then help to explain why high-wage workers are, other things equal, less likely to quit and less likely to be looking for another job as these workers have been lucky enough to find themselves in one of the good jobs in their segment of the labour market.

Second, monopsony can explain part of the rapid growth in earnings over the early stages of the life cycle (as first identified by Mincer, 1974). The human capital explanation of this is that workers are accumulating skills but monopsony/search suggests that workers are working themselves into the best jobs in the market (what might be called the accumulation of search capital, the knowledge of which employers pay higher wages). Consistent with this, Topel and Ward (1992) find that one-third of the wage growth of young men in the US labour market is the result of job mobility.

Third, monopsony can explain the earnings losses suffered by displaced workers. It is well-documented that workers who lose their jobs through no fault of their own (for example, through plant closure) tend to suffer losses in earnings (see Kletzer, 1998, for a review) and the losses

do not completely fit the pattern suggested by human capital theory – in particular, older workers suffer greater losses, even when we control for job tenure.

Monopsony can also explain systematic wage differentials between workers, even if they do not differ in their productivity. For example, if women are less attached to market employment or their decisions on which jobs to take are less motivated by money (Manning, 2003a, provides evidence on both these points), then women will earn less than men even if the wage offer distribution they face is the same. The reason is that women will find it harder to accumulate search capital. There may also be incentives for employers to then pay lower wages to women, giving a further twist to their earnings disadvantage. Ransom and Oaxaca (2005) provides some evidence that the quit rate for women is less sensitive to the wage than is the quit rate for men.

Monopsony also has implications for the incentives to acquire human capital. Because the wage is below the marginal product, it is quite likely that some of the returns to investments in human capital accrue to future employers of the worker, though the interests of these employers are not internalized in the education decision. Hence, the social return to education is likely to exceed the private return, leading, in a free market, to underinvestment.

Monopsony from a public policy perspective

Thinking of labour markets as pervasively monopsonistic rather than perfectly competitive has implications for how one thinks about the likely effects of interventions in the labour market. In a perfectly competitive labour market one tends to think of the free market outcome as efficient, of any intervention as causing some inefficiency and justifiable only on equity grounds, especially if the equity effect is large and/or the efficiency cost is small. In contrast, if the labour market is monopsonistic, then there is no presumption that the free market is efficient and interventions might be justifiable on efficiency grounds alone. Based on the simple textbook model of a monopsonist presented earlier, one might be tempted to go further and argue that, because wages are below marginal products, interventions to raise wages must, over some range, improve efficiency. However, in more sophisticated models of monopsony or models of oligopsonistic competition, such a simple conclusion is not necessarily valid. So the monopsonistic approach does suggest approaching the analysis of the impact of interventions with a more open mind than a true believer in perfect competition might be inclined to do.

A good example is the employment impact of the minimum wage. If the labour market is perfectly competitive, one can prove with nothing more than pencil and paper that the minimum wage must reduce employment, and the only purpose of empirical analysis is to decide on how large the reduction is. However, a monopsony approach suggests going to the data with a less certain view about the 'right' answer. The intuition is that, while a rise in the minimum wage reduces the profitability of employing workers for firms, it increases the incentives for workers to work, and the net effect on employment depends on whether the 'demand' or 'supply' effect is dominant. Hence monopsony can explain why the empirical literature often fails to find evidence that it reduces employment (Card and Krueger, 1995; Dickens, Machin and Manning, 1999).

Another good example of apparently 'perverse' employment effects can be found in the impact of equal pay legislation. In the UK, this legislation led to a big increase in the pay of women relative to that of men but did not, as the perfectly competitive model would predict, lead to big falls in the relative employment of women (Manning, 1996).

Conclusions

There are good reasons to believe that employers have some monopsony power over their workers. Assuming labour markets are monopsonistic also brings the thinking of labour economists in line with the way in which agents perceive the workings of labour markets. Workers do not perceive labour markets as frictionless and changing; getting and losing jobs are routinely reported as major life events. And employers perceive they have discretion over the wages paid, as a reading of any human resource management textbook can confirm. And, as demonstrated in this article, a whole range of puzzles and anomalies melt away once one adopts the monopsony perspective. However, the impact of regulations is more ambiguous than in perfectly competitive markets, and the theoretical perspective should go hand-in-hand with an open-minded empirical approach.

There is much work yet to be done. For example, the size of the wage elasticity of the labour supply curve to an individual firm is very much unknown. The literature on the subject is small and not entirely convincing. The best estimates we do have (probably from Staiger, Spetz and Phibbs, 1999; Falch, 2001; Clotfelter et al., 2006) suggest quite a low wage elasticity, with the implication that employers do have significant monopsony power.

ALAN MANNING

See also **labour market search; minimum wages; Robinson, Joan Violet; wage inequality, changes in.**

Bibliography

Albrecht, J. and Axell, B. 1984. An equilibrium model of search unemployment. *Journal of Political Economy* 92, 824–40.

Bhaskar, V. and To, T. 1999. Minimum wages for Ronald McDonald monopsonies: a theory of monopsonistic competition. *Economic Journal* 109, 190–203.

Blanchflower, D., Oswald, A. and Sanfey, P. 1996. Wages, profits, and rent-sharing. *Quarterly Journal of Economics* 111, 227–51.

Boal, W. and Ransom, M. 1997. Monopsony in the labor market. *Journal of Economic Literature* 35, 86–112.

Brown, C. and Medoff, J. 1989. The employer size–wage effect. *Journal of Political Economy* 97, 1027–59.

Burdett, K. and Mortensen, D. 1998. Wage differentials, employer size, and unemployment. *International Economic Review* 39, 257–73.

Card, D. and Krueger, A. 1995. *Myth and Measurement: The New Economics of the Minimum Wage*. Princeton: Princeton University Press.

Clotfelter, C., Glennie, E., Ladd, H. and Vigdor, J. 2006. Would higher salaries keep teachers in high-poverty schools? Evidence from a policy intervention in North Carolina. Working Paper No. 12285. Cambridge, MA: NBER.

Dickens, R., Machin, S. and Manning, A. 1999. The effects of minimum wages on employment: theory and evidence from Britain. *Journal of Labor Economics* 17, 1–22.

Falch, T. 2001. Estimating the elasticity of labor supply utilizing a quasi–natural experiment. Working Paper, Norwegian University of Science and Technology, Trondheim.

Groshen, E. 1991. Sources of intra-industry wage dispersion: how much do employers matter? *Quarterly Journal of Economics* 106, 869–84.

Just, R. and Chern, W. 1980. Tomatoes, technology, and oligopsony. *Bell Journal of Economics* 11, 584–602.

Kaufman, B. 1988. *How Labor Markets Work*. Lexington, MA: Lexington Books.

Kletzer, L. 1998. Job displacement. *Journal of Economic Perspectives* 12(1), 115–36.

Manning, A. 1996. The Equal Pay Act as an experiment to test theories of the labour market. *Economica* 63, 191–212.

Manning, A. 2003a. *Monopsony in Motion: Imperfect Competition in Labor Markets*. Princeton: Princeton University Press.

Manning, A. 2003b. The real thin theory: monopsony in modern labour markets. *Labour Economics* 10(2), 105–31.

Manning, A. 2006. A generalised model of monopsony. *Economic Journal* 116, 84–100.

Mincer, J. 1974. *Schooling, Experience and Earnings*. New York: NBER.

Murray, B. 1995. Measuring oligopsony power with shadow Prices: U.S. markets for pulpwood and sawlogs. *Review of Economics and Statistics* 77, 486–98.

Ransom, M. and Oaxaca, R. 2005. Sex Differences in Pay in a 'New Monopsony' Model of the Labor Market. Discussion Paper No. 1870. Bonn: IZA.

Robinson, J. 1933. *The Economics of Imperfect Competition*. London: Macmillan.

Salop, S. 1979. A model of the natural rate of unemployment. *American Economic Review* 69, 117–25.

Schroeter, J. 1988. Estimating the degree of market power in the beef packing industry. *Review of Economics and Statistics* 70, 158–62.

Smith, A. 1776. *The Wealth of Nations*. London: Penguin, 1986.

Staiger, D., Spetz, J. and Phibbs, C. 1999. Is there monopsony in the labor market? Evidence from a natural experiment. Working Paper No. 7258. Cambridge, MA: NBER.

Stevens, M. 2004. Wage-tenure contracts in a frictional labour market: strategies for recruitment and retention. *Review of Economic Studies* 71, 535–51.

Thornton, R. 2004. Retrospectives: how Joan Robinson and B. L. Hallward named Monopsony. *Journal of Economic Perspectives* 18(2), 257–61.

Topel, R. and Ward, M. 1992. Job mobility and the careers of young men. *Quarterly Journal of Economics* 107, 439–79.

Moore, Henry Ludwell (1869–1958)

An outstanding pioneer econometrician, Moore was a retiring, highly sensitive, intensely dedicated man, who devoted his whole life to the construction of 'a statistical complement to economics', as he termed it. He was born at Moore's Rest, Maryland, on 21 November 1869. After graduating from Randolph Macon College in 1892, he studied under Carl Menger in Vienna, and Simon Newcomb and John Bates Clark at Johns Hopkins, where in 1896 he completed his Ph.D. dissertation on von Thünen's theory of the natural wage. Following a year's instructorship at Hopkins, and five years at Smith College, Moore taught at Columbia, mainly mathematical economics and statistics, from 1902 to 1929. Essentially a researcher rather than a pedagogue, he attended Karl Pearson's courses on mathematical statistics and correlation in London, in 1909 and 1913, and for several years took a voluntary salary reduction in order to avoid undergraduate teaching. Ill health forced his early retirement.

In a series of powerful and highly original volumes Moore endeavoured, among other things, to verify the marginal productivity of wages, render the Walrasian system statistically operational, and reveal the fundamental law and cause of cycles – wherein he concluded that 'the law of the cycles of rainfall is the law of the cycles of the crops and the law of Economic Cycles' (1914, p. 135). Needless to say, this immensely ambitious undertaking was often severely attacked by contemporaries and subsequent commentators who exposed the data deficiencies, lax hypotheses, unavoidably heroic oversimplifications, and other shortcomings (cf. Stigler, 1965; 1968). Nevertheless, the strength and purity of Moore's scientific vision, and the careful and sophisticated statistical methods he employed, commanded respect and admiration.

Not surprisingly, Moore founded no school. Yet his principal disciple, Henry Schultz, was only one among the many economists who produced the 20th-century 'avalanche of statistical demand curves' (Schumpeter, 1954, p. 213) inspired by Moore, whose researches exerted a major impact on agricultural economics. Thus Moore may be credited in part with the high scientific standing American agricultural economics now enjoys (Leontief, 1971). However, despite his seminal efforts to develop empirical estimates of theoretical economic relationships, Moore's achievements have been insufficiently acknowledged, partly, no doubt, because he was unwilling to propagandize his methods among his fellow professionals.

A.W. COATS

Selected works

1908. The statistical complement of pure economics. *Quarterly Journal of Economics* 23, November, 1–33.

1911. *Laws of Wages: An Essay in Statistical Economics*: New York: Macmillan Co.

1914. *Economic Cycles: Their Law and Cause.* New York: Macmillan. (Japanese translation, Tokyo, 1926).

1917. *Forecasting the Yield and Price of Cotton.* New York: Macmillan.

1923. *Generating Economic Cycles.* New York: Macmillan.

1929. *Synthetic Economics.* New York: Macmillan.

Bibliography

Leontief, W. 1971. Theoretical assumptions and non-observed facts. *American Economic Review* 61, 1–7.

Schumpeter, J.A. 1954. *History of Economic Analysis.* New York: Oxford University Press.

Stigler, G.J. 1965. Henry L. Moore and statistical analysis. In *Essays in the History of Economics*, ed. G.J. Stigler. Chicago: University of Chicago Press.

Stigler, G.J. 1968. Moore, H.L. In *International Encyclopedia of the Social Sciences*, vol. 10, ed. David, L. Sills. New York: Macmillan and Free Press.

moral hazard

The problem of moral hazard is pervasive in economic activities. Economists have been well aware of its existence as the following quote from the *Wealth of Nations* will testify:

> The directors of such companies, however, being the managers rather of other peoples' money than of their own, it cannot well be expected, that they should watch over it with the same anxious vigilance with which the partners in a private copartnery frequently watch over their own ... Negligence and profusion, therefore, must always prevail, more or less, in the management of the affairs of such a company. (Smith, 1776, p. 700)

However, theoretical developments and their application to specific problems have only proceeded since the 1960s and are still the subject of vigorous research. While we have a considerable understanding of the problem, we do not as yet understand fully market and social responses to it. In the following I shall attempt to explain the nature of the problem and selectively illustrate the flavour of current theoretical developments.

Moral hazard may be defined as actions of economic agents in maximizing their own utility to the detriment of others, in situations where they do not bear the full consequences or, equivalently, do not enjoy the full benefits of their actions *due to uncertainty and incomplete information or restricted contracts* which prevent the assignment of *full* damages (benefits) to the agent responsible. It is immediately apparent that this definition includes a wide variety of externalities, and thus may lead to nonexistence of equilibria or to inefficiencies of equilibria when they exist.

It is a special form of incompleteness of contracts which creates the conflict between the agent's utility and that of others. Such incompleteness may arise due to several reasons: the coexistence of unequal information and risk aversion or joint production, costs and legal barriers to contracting and costs of contract enforcement. We shall analyse each in turn.

Unequal information

Agents may possess exclusive information. Arrow (1985) classifies such informational advantages as 'hidden action' and 'hidden information'. The first involves actions which cannot be accurately observed or inferred by others. It is therefore impossible to condition contracts on these actions. The second involves states of nature about which the agent has some, possibly incomplete information, information which determines the appropriateness of the agent's actions, but which are imperfectly observable by others. Thus, even if agents' actions are costlessly observable by others, they do not know with certainty whether the actions were in their interest.

Commonly analysed examples of hidden actions are: workers' effort, which cannot be costlessly monitored by employers, precautions taken by insured to reduce the probability of accidents or damages due to them, which cannot be costlessly monitored by insurers. Criminal activity clearly belongs in this category as well.

Examples of hidden information are expert services – such as physicians, lawyers, repairmen, managers and politicians.

Where consequences of specific agents' actions can be separated from those of others, even though the consequences may be affected by random, unobservable states of nature, the problem may be easily solved if agents are risk neutral, by simply assigning the full consequences to the agent, in exchange for a fixed fee. This is in effect a complete contract. The problem of contract incompleteness arises when agents are risk averse or where assignment of responsibility to one agent cannot be made.

When agents are risk averse, assigning full damages (benefits) to them assigns them all risk due to random states of nature. Risk-averse agents would like to purchase insurance against such risks. However, it is impossible for others to separate the consequences of agents' actions from random elements which cannot be controlled by the agent. Insurance against the latter will inevitably insulate agents from the consequences of their own actions. The agent may, of course, offer to supply information about the unobserved actions or states – but such information cannot be credible.

Optimal contracts generally involve some degree of insurance and hence lead to a conflict between incentives and risk sharing. Most of the literature on moral hazard has concentrated on this case. We shall come back to it.

When precise assignment of responsibility to individual agents is impossible, full assignment of consequences to individual agents cannot be achieved. By definition, this is the case for crime, where the identity of the perpetrator is generally not known with certainty. The design of punishments and the interaction with enforcement activities to apprehend and convict criminals is treated extensively in the literature (see for example Becker, 1968).

Group production is another area where assignment may be impossible. Some forms of collective punishment on the group as a whole when output falls short of a specified quota, with some allocation rule when output meets or exceeds the quota may serve to elicit the desired output (Holmstrom, 1982). However, the conditions under which this is possible are quite restricted.

Similar problems arise where quality of products is difficult to ascertain because they must be used jointly with another service or product, because their performance is affected by conditions and nature of use. For example drugs must be used in conjunction with physicians' services. Failure of the drug may result from its poor quality, from misdiagnosis by the physician (who may prescribe the wrong drug) or from failure to follow instructions by the patient. In the absence of these complications, it would be optimal for the manufacturer, who knows the quality of his product, to supply a guarantee of performance, in order to remove the incentive to supply lower quality. As well, the guarantee serves at least partly to insure risk averse consumers against random variations in the performance of the drug. Even if the manufacturer is risk-averse, his risk is mitigated by the 'law of large numbers', so it is optimal for him to act as insurer.

However, under the circumstances above such insurance creates a moral hazard problem for the physician and the patient, who may use insufficient care in diagnosis and use. Any risk sharing among the relevant parties therefore induces a moral hazard problem which cannot be avoided in the presence of private information, even if all parties are risk neutral.

Barriers to contracting

Incomplete contracts may also arise in the absence of private information due to costs of writing detailed contingent contracts. This problem is particularly severe in contracts involving complex transactions and long periods. When uncertainty about the future is great, the number and nature of eventualities to be considered is clearly very large. The cost of anticipating them and writing a contract which specifies or elicits desired actions may be very large. The cost of reaching agreement on the proper actions in each eventuality may well be prohibitive. If the probability of any event is small, and the cost of agreement high, it may pay to leave the contract vague and wait for the resolution of uncertainty before reaching agreement. Of course, this is precisely the case in spot market transactions. However, frequently decisions must be made prior to the resolution of uncertainty. For example, specialized investments in physical or human capital must be made by the parties before production and trading begin (Becker, 1964). The nature of the investment may well depend on the transaction price, which may in turn depend on information revealed after the investment is made. A limited agreement on investment and trading may be optimal, leaving transaction price to future negotiation. This, however, may lead to a moral hazard problem. Opportunistic behaviour in subsequent periods by one of the parties may lead to termination of trading or unfavourable contract terms, for the party which invested in specialized capital. Knowing that this may occur, the incentive to invest is reduced. The resulting inefficiency may well fall short of the costs of complete contracts. Williamson (1985) argues that such problems may give rise to vertical integration.

Contracts are too costly to write when transactions are infrequent and small. Most spot market transactions between retailers and consumers falls in this category. Blanket contracts offered by sellers in the form of 'money back guarantees' or exchange privileges may be substituted for explicit contingent contracts – but they are subject to moral hazard on the consumers' side. Alternatively the state legislates fair trading laws which serve as generalized contracts.

Contracts are lacking altogether when transactions are random or involuntary. Accidental damages inflicted on one party by another as in a traffic accident are good examples. Here again, the law must form a generalized contract. It is obvious that such a law cannot possibly allow for all contingencies, so that it constitutes an incomplete contract, giving rise to moral hazard problems. The question of the design of liability rules has been extensively analysed in the law and economics literature (Posner, 1977).

Finally, contracts may be restricted by law or by limited financial resources of agents. For example, even if managers are risk neutral, their financial resources may be insufficient to become sole proprietors, without relying on outside capital. Shareholders and bondholders must then share in the risk – raising a moral hazard problem due to the informational advantages of managers. For an extensive analysis of these problems, see Jensen and Meckling (1976).

Similarly, when punishments are limited by law, moral hazard may not be resolved even where actions can be costlessly observed *ex post*. Thus, for example, bankruptcy and limited liability provisions insure borrowers against extremely unfavourable states of nature without limiting the gains from extremely favourable ones. This creates a moral hazard problem, inducing borrowers to undertake riskier projects. Stiglitz and Weiss (1981) show that lenders will sometimes require collateral and ration loans in attempting to overcome these difficulties.

Problems of enforcement

A related barrier to complete contracting arises from costs and other limitation on enforcement. When enforcement is costly, it may be more efficient to live with the inefficiencies generated by the moral hazard, than to try to enforce the optimal contingent contract. A common way to overcome such difficulties is by way of posting a bond, which is forfeit in the event of non-performance. However, restricted financial resources generally prevent bonding.

Under conditions where enforcement is not economical, contracts must be *self-enforcing*. It is unimportant whether contracts are explicit or implicit, as they frequently are in labour markets. To be viable contracts must make subsequent actions by contracting parties consistent with their self-interest, that is, they must allow for the potential exercise of moral hazard. This problem is at the heart of non-cooperative game theory, which defines moral hazard as opportunistic behaviour.

So far we have surveyed the conditions under which a moral hazard problem cannot be trivially resolved. This raises three questions which theorists have begun tackling in the past two decades: (*a*) the nature of optimal contracts in the presence of moral hazard; (*b*) market and institutional/legal response to mitigate these problems; and (*c*) welfare consequences.

Optimal contracts

The problem has mainly been tackled by agency theory. Following seminal work by Wilson (1969) and Ross (1973) the optimal (typically second best) reward structure for an agent is derived on the basis of observed variables, usually under 'hidden action' assumptions. Some of the main results for risk-averse agents are: (*a*) Optimal contracts require risk sharing between principal and agent which creates a moral hazard problem in the form of insufficient incentives. (*b*) Efficient contracts should utilize all the information available, that is they should be constructed on the basis of statistical inference from the information available on the hidden action of the agent (Holmstrom, 1979). Thus monitoring, which reduces inference errors, is productive. (c) The nature of the reward schedule is sensitive to the nature of the information available, the residual uncertainty and the degree of risk aversion of the agent and principal. This observation is troubling because incentive contracts observed in reality are generally simple and uniform across a variety of agents and information sets. Long-term contracts, explicit or implicit (client relations), tend to mitigate moral hazard problems, by introducing a reward for not exploiting short-term informational advantages, and because cumulative information reduces uncertainty. Hence, for example, experience rating in insurance contracts.

Market and institutional responses

Market responses may invalidate or reinforce the special features of contracts to mitigate the moral hazard problem. These responses depend on the nature of competition. Free entry and the existence of unobserved differences among agents create the additional problem of adverse selection. We shall therefore reflect only on market responses which are mainly a consequence of moral hazard.

As indicated above, contracts typically require some risk sharing (coinsurance) between the parties when agents are risk averse. Therefore, agents generally bear more risk than they desire. If they are able to purchase additional insurance from third parties, the moral hazard problem is aggravated, making the original contract inefficient. This requires exclusivity in contracting. Thus for example, insurance companies do not allow insurance claims for damage due to fire, health or accident insurance from more than one company. It is obvious that any restriction on coinsurance can be circumvented if such claims are allowed. At the extreme, agents might have more than full coverage, inducing intentional damages, such as arson.

This tendency for exclusivity is reinforced by the advantages of long-term contracting. In the presence of risk aversion or limits on agents' capital which prevent effective bonding, it may be necessary to promise future rewards to mitigate short term opportunistic behaviour. Termination of the agreement will deny these rewards and thus operates as a threat. This requires that contracts yield some rents to agents, so that their removal may constitute a punishment. Thus for example, the utility of being employed must exceed the utility of being unemployed (Shapiro and Stiglitz, 1984).

This requires rationing, which is not undone by competition. If being fired by one's employer leads to immediate employment elsewhere at the same wage, rather than to a significant period of unemployment, the threat of firing is ineffective. An equilibrium must be supported by transaction costs of finding new employment or by a collective use of the information contained in the firing. Such information is indeed relevant for hiring decisions by other

firms. Its use depends on the costs of obtaining such information. Markets develop to supply such information, thereby increasing the effectiveness of such agreements. Credit information bureaus and employment agencies are some examples. Fama (1980) argues that such 'reputation' mechanisms eliminate moral hazard problems in executive markets. However, as the information is subject to noise, it is clear that moral hazard problems cannot be entirely resolved.

Non-market institutions may develop to mitigate some of these problems. Professional licensing and certification limit the number of physicians, lawyers and many other professionals. Aside from issues of assurance of minimum quality and monopoly, these arrangements insure rents to the professions involved and, hence, make license removal a significant penalty (Arrow, 1963).

The consequences of moral hazard in political processes have largely been neglected by economists. Exceptions are Stigler (1971) and Peltzman (1976), who analysed the motivations of regulators, and Buchanan and Tullock (1962). The theoretical tools of agency, contract and game theory have yet to be fruitfully employed in this area. Given the expanding role of government and the evidence of widespread abuses in the political process, such application promises to yield significant dividends.

General equilibrium and welfare effects

There has been little research on the welfare implications of moral hazard. An exception is Stiglitz (see for example Arnott and Stiglitz, 1985), who noted that the existence of moral hazard creates second best contracts. In an economy characterized by such contracts, changes in contracts between any two parties have significant first order effects on social welfare, in contrast to the Arrow–Debreu economy, where first order effects of individual actions are zero at an optimum. As we have seen, moral hazard may lead to rationing and queues, suboptimal expenditure of hidden actions and imperfections in capital markets.

This is not surprising because moral hazard is basically a form of externality. It is well known that uninternalized externalities lead to non-concavities, possible non-existence of equilibria and inefficiencies. The existence of such inefficiencies signals a possible role for government. However, government intervention may well cause more problems than it solves. For example, attempts to supplement deficient insurance markets in the form of universal income (social security, income taxation) insurance have run into serious moral hazard problems of work incentives, tax avoidance and evasion, and so on. It is at least partly because of these moral hazard problems that such markets failed to develop. It is therefore unclear whether government supply of these services enhances welfare.

In contrast, government policies which enhance complete contracts and improve their enforcement, can be welfare enhancing. Examples are contract law, liability rules and trade regulations.

Y. KOTOWITZ

See also **adverse selection; health economics; incomplete contracts; principal and agent (i); principal and agent (ii).**

Bibliography

Arnott, R. and Stiglitz, J. 1985. Labor turnover, wage structures, and moral hazard: the inefficiency of competitive markets. *Journal of Labor Economics* 3, 434–62.

Arrow, K. 1963. Uncertainty and the welfare economics of medical care. *American Economic Review* 53, 541–67.

Arrow, K. 1985. The economics of agency. In *Principals and Agents: The Structure of Business*, ed. J. Pratt and R. Zeckhauser. Boston: Harvard Business School Press.

Becker, G. 1964. *Human Capital*. New York: Columbia University Press.

Becker, G. 1968. Crime and punishment – an economic approach. *Journal of Political Economy* 76, 169–217.

Becker, G. and Stigler, G. 1974. Law enforcement, malfeasance and compensation of enforcers. *Journal of Legal Studies* 3, 1–18.

Buchanan, J.M. and Tullock, G. 1962. *The Calculus of Consent*. Ann Arbor: University of Michigan Press.

Fama, E. 1980. Agency problems and theory of the firm. *Journal of Political Economy* 88, 288–307.

Green, J. 1985. Differential information, the market and incentive compatibility. In *Frontiers of Economics*, ed. K.J. Arrow and S. Honkapohja. Oxford: Basil Blackwell.

Harris, M. and Raviv, A. 1979. Optimal incentive contracts with imperfect information. *Journal of Economic Theory* 20, 231–59.

Holmstrom B. 1979. Moral hazard and observability. *Bell Journal of Economics* 10, 74–91.

Holmstrom, B. 1982. Moral hazard in teams. *Bell Journal of Economics* 13, 314–40.

Jensen, M. and Meckling, W. 1976. Theory of the firm: managerial behavior, agency costs, and capital structure. *Journal of Financial Economics* 3, 305–60.

Peltzman, S. 1976. Towards a more general theory of regulation. *Journal of Law and Economics* 19, 211–40.

Posner, R. 1977. *The Economic Analysis of Law*. 2nd edn. Boston: Little, Brown.

Ross, S. 1973. The economic theory of agency: the principal's problem. *American Economic Review* 63, 134–9.

Shapiro, C. and Stiglitz, J. 1984. Equilibrium unemployment as a worker incentive device. *American Economic Review* 74, 433–44.

Shavell, S. 1979. Risk sharing and incentives in the principal and agent relationship. *Bell Journal of Economics* 10, 55–73.

Smith, A. 1776. *An Inquiry into the Nature and the Causes of the Wealth of Nations*. Ed. E. Cannan, New York: Modern Library, 1937.

Stigler, G. 1971. The theory of economic regulation. *Bell Journal of Economics and Management Science* 2, 3–21.

Stiglitz, J. and Weiss, A. 1981. Credit rationing in markets with imperfect information. *American Economic Review* 71, 393–410.

Williamson, O. 1985. *The Economic Institutions of Capitalism*. New York: Free Press.

Wilson, R. 1969. The structure of incentives for decentralisation under uncertainty. In *La Décision*. Paris: Editions du CNRS.

Morgenstern, Oskar (1902–1977)

Morgenstern was born in Goerlitz, Silesia, on 24 January 1902. He died on 26 July 1977 at his home in Princeton, New Jersey. The two main intellectual centres of his life were Vienna and Princeton. In each case the source of his intellectual stimulation was not primarily the university but institutions such as the Wienerkreis of Moritz Schlick in Vienna, where he counted among his friends Karl Popper, Kurt Gödel and Karl Schlesinger, and the Institute for Advanced Study at Princeton. He obtained his doctorate in 1925 from the University of Vienna, where he was greatly influenced by Karl Menger and the writings of Eugen Böhm-Bawerk.

Morgenstern's first major work, *Wirtschaftsprognose* (1928), which was published in Vienna, served as his Habilitation thesis leading to his appointment as a *privatdozent* at the University of Vienna in 1929. In this book he began to consider the difficulties and paradoxes inherent in economic prediction, being particularly concerned with prediction where the action of a few powerful individuals could influence the outcome. He illustrated some of these difficulties with the example of Sherlock Holmes's pursuit of Professor Moriarty (an example repeated in the *Theory of Games*, 1944).

He became a professor at the University of Vienna in 1935, and in the same year published in the *Zeitschrift für Nationalökonomie* (of which he was managing editor) an article on fundamental difficulties with the assumption of perfect foresight in the study of economic equilibrium. It was then that the mathematician Edward Čech noted that the problems raised by Morgenstern were related to those treated by von Neumann in his article 'Zur Theorie der Gesellschaftsspiele', published in 1928.

Morgenstern did not have the opportunity to meet von Neumann until somewhat later. They both recalled meeting at the Nassau Inn in Princeton on 1 February 1939, although each believed that they had met once before. They became close friends and remained so until von Neumann's death on 8 February 1957.

In Vienna, Morgenstern was also director of the Austrian Institute for Business Cycle Research (1931–8) where he employed Abraham Wald, whom he later helped go to the United States. In 1938, due to his opposition to the Nazis, Morgenstern was dismissed from the University of Vienna as 'politically unbearable' and he accepted an offer from Princeton, to some extent because of the presence of von Neumann at the Institute for Advanced Study. Their close collaboration resulted in the publication in 1944 of their book, *The Theory of Games and Economic Behavior*. This major work contained a radical reconceptualization of the basic problems of competition and collaboration as a game of strategy among several agents, as well as an important novel approach to utility theory (presented in detail in the second edition, 1947).

Both Morgenstern and von Neumann were well aware of the limitations of their great work. They stressed that they were beginning by offering a sound basis for a static theory of conscious individually rational economic behaviour and that the history of science indicated that a dynamic theory might be considerably different. They warned against premature generalization.

In his years at Princeton from 1938 until his retirement in 1970, Morgenstern encouraged the work of a distinguished roster of younger scholars in game theory and combinatoric methods. This was feasible primarily through the strength of the Mathematics Department and its connections with the Institute. There was little interest in the subject in the Department of Economics at the time. The ideas of the *Theory of Games* were so radical that they have taken many years to permeate the social sciences. Even at the time of his death many in the economics profession were sceptical of or indifferent to its contributions.

Although his work on the theory of games was undoubtedly Morgenstern's greatest contribution and collaboration, his interests were wide-ranging. His two books, *On the Accuracy of Economic Observations* (1950), and *Predictability of Stock Market Prices* (1970), written jointly with Clive W. Granger, indicate these interests. He was also concerned with matters of national defence and in 1959 published *The Question of National Defense*.

In 1959 he was one of the founders of Mathematica, a highly successful and sophisticated consulting firm, and served as Chairman of the Board. After retiring from Princeton he was Distinguished Professor at New York University until his death.

MARTIN SHUBIK

Selected works

1928. *Wirtschaftsprognose: Eine Untersuchung ihrer Voraussetzungen und Möglichkeiten*. Vienna: Julius Springer.

1935. Vollkommene Voraussicht und wirtschaftliches Gleichgewicht. *Zeitschrift für Nationalökonomie* 6(3), 337–57.

1944. (With J. von Neumann.) *Theory of Games and Economic Behavior*. Princeton: Princeton University Press. 2nd edn, 1947.

1950. *On the Accuracy of Economic Observations*. Princeton: Princeton University Press.

1959. *The Question of National Defense*. New York: Random House.

1970. (With C.W.J. Granger.) *Predictability of Stock Market Prices*. Lexington, MA: Heath Lexington Books.

Morishima, Michio (1923–2004)

Michio Morishima was one of the most distinguished economic theorists of his generation. He taught in Japan at Kyoto and Osaka Universities, and in the UK he was the Keynes Visiting Professor at the University of Essex 1969–70 and Professor of Economics, later the John Hicks Professor of Economics, at the London School of Economics 1970–84 and Emeritus Professor for the rest of his life. He was awarded the Order of Culture [Bunka Kunsho] of Japan by the Emperor in 1976, a Fellowship of the British Academy in 1981 and an Honorary Fellowship of the LSE upon his retirement. Morishima became the first Japanese to be the President of the Econometric Society in 1965. He died aged 80 on 13 July 2004, leaving behind his wife Yoko and two sons and a daughter.

Morishima's work encompasses general equilibrium theory with heterogeneous capital, growth and money, as part of a coherent attempt to tackle one of the most intractable problems in economic theory, namely, the construction of an adequate theory of a dynamic growing economy with heterogeneous capital and money as well as credit or, to put it another way, a theory of how the capitalist system works.

Morishima's Ph.D. thesis at Kyoto University (published in Japanese in 1950 and in English in 1996 under the title *Dynamic Economic Theory*) dealt with stability of equilibrium. The standard (Hicksian) theory says that if the market starts out at a price away from the equilibrium given by the intersection of the demand and supply curves, then the price must change until the equilibrium point is reached. But how? Walrasians posit an auctioneer who would call out prices and register demands and supplies at each price. No trades are made until the auctioneer is satisfied that demands and supplies balance, that is, no false trading. The corollary of a no false trading equilibrium is that there can be never be involuntary unemployment, raising the issue of the consistency of micro and macro theories with each other.

Morishima prefers the case in which trading takes place at each price, but the price changes if, at that price, after transactions are closed, there is excess supply or demand. This would be a non-tâtonnement process, where some traders may buy (sell) at a price higher (lower) than the equilibrium price. He does not, however, develop this any further in the thesis but asks: are we exploring the path of convergence of the 'groping' prices, that is, virtual prices at which no trades are carried out and hence within 'the market day', or are we talking of the path of equilibrium prices arrived at, at the end of the tâtonnement in each market day from one day to the next?

Within the Hicksian week, the groping process traces out a path of virtual prices which converge to equilibrium under certain well-known conditions. But what of the sequence over several weeks of the equilibrium price? What are the dynamics of the path itself? It is this question that Morishima poses in *Dynamic Economic Theory* and pursues over his entire career. It is obviously connected to the stability of a growth path, since the path of income is analogous to the path of equilibrium prices. Morishima's discussion of growth paths was therefore always concerned not only with the quantity variables such as income and the stock of capital but also prices and interest rates.

Morishima's first book in English, *Equilibrium, Stability and Growth* (1964), tried to integrate Walras into the growth story, which had not hitherto been attempted, and also gave prominence to Marx's work on accumulation at the same time. Morishima constructed Walras–Leontieff and Marx–von Neumann models, which are pioneer efforts. *Equilibrium, Stability and Growth* is growth-oriented with an emphasis on linear technology and balanced maximal growth paths with fixed coefficients. But there is also a chapter on a spectrum of techniques. This is Morishima's response to the then ongoing capital controversy between Cambridge England and Cambridge Massachusetts.

Very soon after *Equilibrium, Stability and Growth* was published, Morishima came out with his most ambitious work to date, *Theory of Economic Growth* (1969). Here Morishima sets out a rigorous multisectoral framework – the von Neumann model – and integrates Walras as well as Hicks into this framework. Prices are solved out along with quantities throughout. Turnpikes are discussed under various assumptions. But Morishima also deals with the issue of the optimality of the maximal growth paths.

Morishima was not happy with *Theory of Economic Growth*. Thus started his long detour via Marx, Walras and Ricardo, until he could come back to his major concern. Morishima's book *Marx's Economics* (1973) deals with the statics and dynamics of Marx's growth and exploitation theory and tackled joint production with innovative insights. It shows that labour values can be used to tackle the aggregation problem for heterogeneous capital.

The crucial next step is provided by Walras. Most economists think that Walras provided consistent microfoundations for a full employment–all markets clearing theory of the macroeconomy. Morishima had a different Walras in his 1977 book with the intriguing title *Walras' Economics: A Pure Theory of Capital and Money*. Morishima's purpose in the book is to see whether he can exploit Walras's work to provide the microfoundations of

Keynesian macroeconomics. He focuses on the contrast between nominal demands (neoclassical) and effective demands (Keynesian) as well as the alternative hypotheses that investments adjust to savings (neoclassical) and that investments are prior and saving adjust (Keynesian). Walras's entrepreneurs have no income; they work on altruistic principles. Morishima adjusts Walras's investment function as well as giving entrepreneurs an income (profits) which makes the model closer to real capitalism. But he also shows why one needs a theory of accumulation and growth, that is, a story with time and future in it, in order to have a rationale for holding money in a Walrasian world. In a static general equilibrium, money can, and does, play no role.

The heart of Morishima's book *Ricardo's Economics* (1989) is in the final section entitled 'Three Paradigms Compared'. Say's Law is at issue. Ricardo established Say's Law as a dominant mode of theorizing. Usual departures from Say's Law involve a non-trivial role for money and/ or a growth process via an active investment function. Ricardo had neither and so could subscribe to Say's Law. Marx had both but his investment function was very restrictive and made no use of money or credit. Walras had money towards the end of *Elements* but his growth theory lacked an investment function which led the way for savings to adjust to investment. Keynes of course had money and investment functions, but he did not spell out the microfoundations. Growth is not sufficient to justify a violation of Say's Laws; money or an investment function which has a role for entrepreneurs to respond to uncertainty is required.

In *Ricardo's Economics* a model is set up in which excess demand and supply for labour and capital are modelled in a simple diagram (1989, fig. 6, p. 218). Here, around an equilibrium point, zones of excess supply and demand for the two factors are mapped out. Morishima's axes are the real wage and the output capital ratio. Within the same general model all the three paradigms are embedded. Again, the investment function turns out to be the crucial relationship for the Anti-Say's Law result that Keynes established.

Capital and Credit: A New Formulation of General Equilibrium Theory (1992) brings together all the major themes of money, heterogeneous capital, underemployment equilibria and growth. The major innovation in *Capital and Credit* is that banks play a crucial role in financing production. This is Schumpeter rather than Keynes. While in Keynes's scheme entrepreneurs may underinvest because of expectations or a low marginal efficiency of capital relative to the rate of interest, Schumpeter allows for overshooting of credit creation by bankers. Thus, inflation as well as underemployment is possible.

Capital and Credit is therefore concerned with innovations and their financing and monetary disequilibrium. The economy is split into Say's Law and Anti-Say's Law activities. There is a scope for Anti-Say's Law if production is financed by credit, and this of course requires that it is not instantaneous but has an input–output lag. With instantaneous production and investment adjusting to savings, Say's Law is confirmed. But in any realistic capitalist economy it breaks down due to the presence of credit. The amount of credit determines activity in the Anti-Say's Law sector (manufacturing industry, in other words), and this, via the multiplier, determines the overall levels of activity and employment. This need not be full employment.

The separation of the economy as between relative prices determined by demand/supply and absolute prices as determined by money –'the classical dichotomy' is no longer valid. It is only by omitting banks and the financial requirements for production that the dichotomy is sustained.

In the last chapter, on 'Monetary Disequilibrium', Wicksell's cumulative process is examined from the point of view of von Neumann. The real system establishes the rate of profits (= rate of growth), but it leaves the price level indeterminate. Credit creation by bankers determines the nominal level of interest with the natural rate given by the real system. Then the monetary side determines the price level by the intersection of the money demand function and the real growth rate. But it is not a stable equilibrium. It is a kind of IS–LM model, but with its axes as interest rate and price level rather than income.

So we now enter a new development in monetary and growth theory. If the economy is growing and/or if the natural rate is a variable, then we need to extend Wicksell's analysis, which assumed a constant natural interest rate. But the natural rate may be above or below the von Neumann rate, and if the natural rate is also variable then the gap between the natural and the money rate is variable over the cycle. Thus, if the natural rate is above the money rate and the von Neumann rate, then inflation follows, but that may reduce the natural rate. If it then crosses over to being below the money rate, deflation follows and the natural rate may approach the von Neumann rate from above. Prices keep falling, and the economy may converge to the von Neumann rate.

In the converse case, the economy starts off with the natural rate below the money rate and below the von Neumann rate, and then deflation comes first as the natural rate approaches the von Neumann rate from below. Once it crosses over the constant money rate, then inflation follows and the economy approaches the von Neumann rate in an explosive inflationary situation.

This is the most sophisticated discussion of money and growth in the classical Wicksell framework. A variable natural rate is seldom modelled, and the deflation–inflation cycles enrich the Wicksell model greatly. But we are still in the world of Say's Law. What happens if we break away from it? The shortage of credit will restrict the economy below full employment, as Keynes envisaged, and abundance of credit will start off an inflationary growth process, as Schumpeter said. This

then is the climax of the entire edifice of Morishima's work. He can now combine Anti-Say's Law with credit and disequilibrium. Credit creation determines the natural rate via the Anti-Say's Law sector, which is often the most innovative and dynamic. Morishima can then tackle the classical dichotomy.

This is the homogeneity postulate whereby nominal variables cannot have real effects and so money must be a veil. But the homogeneity postulate requires that a monetary shock be evenly spread across all agents. It also requires that the elasticity of demand with respect to money balances be identical across all agents. Morishima shows in the final pages of *Capital and Credit* that neither of these assumptions is likely to be fulfilled in a monetary economy. Agents including households and firms and the Anti-Say's Law firms are much more credit-sensitive than other firms, for one thing. And if the homogeneity postulate falls, so does the quantity theory.

The challenge of integrating money and growth with general equilibrium but without Say's Law has been accomplished. There is much more to be gained from a careful study of these writings and one can only hope that future scholars will mine the rich source of theoretical insights in the decades to come.

MEGHNAD DESAI

See also **capitalism; dynamic models with non-clearing markets; growth models, multisector; Say's Law.**

Selected works

1950. *Degaakuteki Keizai Riron*. Tokyo: Kobundo.
1964. *Equilibrium, Stability and Growth*. Oxford: Clarendon Press.
1969. *Theory of Economic Growth*. Oxford: Clarendon Press.
1973. *Marx's Economics: A Dual Theory of Value and Growth*. Cambridge: Cambridge University Press.
1973. (ed.) *Theory of Demand: Real and Monetary*. New York: McGraw Hill.
1976. *Economic Theory of Modern Society*. Cambridge: Cambridge University Press.
1976. *Walras' Economics: A Pure Theory of Capital and Money*. Cambridge: Cambridge University Press.
1978. (With G. Catephores.) *Value, Exploitation and Growth*. London: McGraw Hill.
1986. *The Economics of Industrial Society*. Cambridge: Cambridge University Press.
1989. *Ricardo's Economics: A General Equilibrium Theory of Distribution and Growth*. Cambridge: Cambridge University Press.
1992. *Capital and Credit: A New Formulation of General Equilibrium Theory*. Cambridge: Cambridge University Press.
1996. *Dynamic Economic Theory* [an English translation of *Degaakuteki Keizai Riron*, 1950, with additional articles]. Cambridge: Cambridge University Press.

mortality

Mortality is one of the three demographic components that shape the size, structure, and dynamics of populations; the other two are fertility and migration. Death rates have declined remarkably in modern times. The populations of the more developed countries have been aging for more than 100 years and the process of rising life expectancy also has begun in most of the less developed countries. Survival is increasing as a result of progress in economic development, social improvements, and advances in medicine. Mortality has been falling steadily especially in wealthier, economically advanced countries and has continued to do so during the second half of the 20th century and after, particularly at higher ages. We are getting older and the number of the elderly is increasing in most countries.

While the reduction in human mortality can be considered one of the greatest achievements of modern civilization, rising longevity and the increasing number of elderly will pose major challenges to health care and social security systems. Declines in birth rates and increases in adult life-expectancy result in aging societies. These demographic changes will impact the life-course decisions of individuals, social interaction, economic development, and policy reforms in the countries involved.

Rising life expectancy has globally been a widespread phenomenon, but mortality differentials remain. Death rates vary significantly in different parts of the world and are particularly high in sub-Saharan Africa by global standards. Mortality conditions have changed throughout history and vary among and within populations. Death rates differ according to the country of origin, place of residence, sex, socio-economic status, level of education and marital status.

Mortality and life expectancy

Various indicators exist to measure mortality. Two of the indicators most often used and cited are the central death rate and life expectancy. The former, which is age-specific and time-specific, is defined as the number of deaths occurring at a given age during a given year, divided by the mean population of that age and year.

Life expectancy is an estimate of average age at death under current death rates. It is calculated by imposing the age-specific death rates of the respective year on a hypothetical cohort of newborns. In 2004, Japan reached the highest female life expectancy (85.59 years) ever obtained by a country. Lowest life expectancy is generally recorded in sub-Saharan Africa. An example is Zimbabwe, a country that in 2004 suffered the world's lowest life expectancy, 34 years for men and 37 years for women, according to WHO (2006). The United Nations estimated worldwide life expectancy for 2000–5 at 67.7 and 63.2 for women and men, respectively (United Nations, 2005).

Remaining life expectancy at age x is usually denoted as e_x and e^o_x. A value of $x = 0$ leads to the most often published indicator, 'life expectancy at birth'. Note that 'life expectancy' for a given year is based on a hypothetical cohort. Only if death rates are not changing can the average newborn be expected to live the number of years indicated by life expectancy. If age-specific mortality continues to decrease – as was the case in many developed countries during recent decades – then the actual average age at death of a birth cohort would be higher than the one estimated for the hypothetical cohort.

Age trajectories of human mortality and the Gompertz law of mortality

As individuals age, they tend to suffer an increasing loss of physical function and greater susceptibility to disease and injury. Benjamin Gompertz, a British actuary, described in 1825 the gradual increase in mortality rates with age, using an exponential curve, today known as the 'Gompertz law of mortality'. The model implies that there is a constant rate of increase in the age-specific mortality of adult populations; for many populations this rate of increase is about ten per cent per year. The Gompertz model fits human mortality rates well for adults aged 30 to 85 in most modern populations with high life expectancies.

The overall age trajectory of human mortality is roughly U-shaped. Mortality is high immediately after birth. During infancy it decreases rapidly with age to reach a minimum between the ages of 10 and 15. Thereafter, the risk of dying rises more or less exponentially according to the Gompertz law of mortality, with some excess mortality among young adults. A rise in mortality during early adulthood is often referred to as 'accident hump', as it is mainly caused by accidents in many modern populations (Heligman and Pollard, 1980). Especially in industrialized countries, this hump is more pronounced for men than for women. The hazards associated with being a woman of childbearing age have been greatly reduced in developed countries, but those connected with the transition to manhood are still substantial. Maternal mortality, in contrast, is confined almost exclusively to developing countries. Among women worldwide, those in sub-Saharan Africa are at highest risk of dying during pregnancy and at childbirth: The lifetime risk was estimated by WHO at 1 in 16 in 2002; this compares to a risk of 1 in 2,500 in the United States (WHO, 2004).

Most deaths in developed countries today are concentrated at older ages. Death rates at older ages have, however, declined markedly during the second half of the 20th century. Furthermore, after age 80 death rates rise more slowly than predicted by the Gompertz exponential formula, and may roughly level off around age 110, albeit at the high level of about 50 per cent mortality per year (Thatcher, Kannisto and Vaupel, 1998; Robine and Vaupel, 2002).

Rising life expectancy in industrialized countries

The rise in life expectancy is one of the great achievements of modern times. In the countries with the highest levels, female life expectancy has been rising for 160 years at a steady pace of almost three months per year (Oeppen and Vaupel, 2002). The four-decade increase in best-practice life expectancy is so extraordinarily linear that it may be the most remarkable regularity of mass endeavour observed. On average, women live longer than men, but record life expectancy has also risen linearly for men since 1840, albeit a little more slowly than for women. The improvements in survival leading to the linear climb in record life expectancy result from the intricate interplay of advances in income, salubrity, nutrition, education, sanitation and, in recent decades, medicine (Riley, 2001).

When we look at individual countries, gains in life expectancy have not progressed as linearly. The gap between the record level and the national level can be regarded as a measure of how much better a country might do. Neither the trend in record life expectancy nor the life expectancy trajectories in different countries suggest that a limit to life expectancy is in sight. Although rapid progress in catch-up periods is typically followed by slower increases, none of the curves appear to be approaching a maximum value (Oeppen and Vaupel, 2002).

The rising numbers of centenarians in developed countries is another striking piece of evidence for the continuing increase in longevity. Lifespans exceeding 100 years, which seemed almost impossible to achieve in the past, despite spectacular reports, are increasingly becoming part of our reality today.

It is unlikely that any person living in Sweden before 1800 attained the age of 100 (Jeune, 1995) and throughout the world centenarians must have been very rare (Wilmoth, 1995). Data on the pre-18th century period have to be interpreted with caution. Few reliable statistics are available on mortality levels among the very old living under conditions of low life expectancy. The lower life expectancy is, the greater is the tendency to exaggerate age at older ages (Kannisto, 1994). Today, the number of centenarians in developed countries is increasing at an exceptionally rapid rate of six to nine per cent per year in many countries. While 265 centenarians were counted in England and Wales in 1950, there were 5,895 of them 50 years later, that is, more than 20 times the 1950 figure (Kannisto–Thatcher Database). In developed countries, the number of people celebrating their 100th birthday doubled each decade between 1950 and 1980; by the end of the 20th century it was multiplying by a factor of 2.4 per decade.

The history of mortality decline

How can the transition from high to low mortality be explained? Over most of the course of human existence, life expectancy hovered between 20 and 30 years. Infant mortality was high, people fell victim to infectious and parasitic diseases or simply to the harshness of everyday living conditions. Even in western Europe life expectancy did not reach age 40 until after 1800, and it stayed below age 50 until after 1900 (Vaupel and Jeune, 1995). Over the course of the 20th century, life expectancy rose dramatically by more than 30 years in many industrialized countries. Rising life expectancy in industrialized countries since the 19th century is related to a fundamental epidemiological transition. There was a shift from the predominance of high mortality from infectious disease to conditions in which non-communicable and degenerative diseases among the elderly became more important. By the beginning of the 19th century in European areas of the world epidemics had been reduced, food supply became more stable, and fluctuations in mortality decreased. Over the course of the 19th century, the standard of living and hygiene improved and some public health services were established in a number of countries (Bongaarts and Bulatao, 2000). Infectious disease was the greatest scourge of mankind until the first half of the 20th century, that is, until vaccination, antibiotics, and other medical advances finally began to combat successfully many of the life-threatening diseases in industrialized countries. By the same token, they lowered the rates of infant and child mortality and limited the devastating effects of the largest epidemics, although some outbreaks of influenza and the HIV/AIDS epidemic are exceptions. Parallel to these changes, there was a shift from high to low fertility. Mortality associated with pregnancy and birth decreased considerably.

The second half of the 20th century saw a dramatic reduction in death rates at advanced ages (Vaupel and Jeune, 1995; Kannisto, 1994; Kannisto et al., 1994; Vaupel, 1997). The time around 1950 marks a distinct change in mortality conditions among the 'oldest old' (85 or more years of age) in developed countries: While improvements in survival were slow in the years preceding 1950, progress made after 1950 and especially after 1970 has been impressive. Data from England, Wales, France, Iceland, Japan, and the United States show clearly that old-age survival has been increasing since 1950 (Vaupel, 1997; Vaupel et al., 1998). The population of centenarians and even super-centenarians (persons older than 110 years) is growing rapidly. The increase in the number of births about a century ago coupled with a sharp decline in mortality from childhood to age 80 contributed to the rising numbers. Demographic analyses, however, demonstrate that the most important factor behind the explosion of the centenarian population has been the decline in the mortality rate after age 80, a factor that has been two to three times more important than the other factors combined (Vaupel and Jeune, 1995). The ongoing increase in life expectancy is largely attributable to continuous improvements in survival at advanced ages (Vaupel and Jeune, 1995; Vaupel, 1997).

In developed countries, the decline in mortality caused by infectious diseases and the postponement of degenerative diseases has delayed deaths to increasingly older ages. Today, cardiovascular disease and cancer are the major causes of death in industrialized countries. In 2002, heart disease and stroke accounted for more than half of all deaths, and cancers were responsible for around 20 per cent of all deaths in Europe (WHO, 2004).

The human survival curve, which depicts the proportion of an initial (hypothetical) cohort still alive, has changed its shape as a consequence. The survival curve is becoming more rectangular due to the concentration of deaths at higher ages. To provide an example, the 2002 life table for Japanese women shows that more than 95 per cent of the initial hypothetical cohort would be still alive under current mortality rates at age 60. Mortality decline is neither a regular process in industrialized countries nor is it a process confined to these nations. Life expectancy has risen in most developing countries, too, especially in many Asian states and in Latin America. The mortality transition is driven by the same factors as in the developed countries – combating infectious disease plays a major role here. However, the transition proceeds much faster than it did in industrialized nations and there are considerable differences in the degree of progress (Bongaarts and Bulatao, 2000).

The plateau in late-life mortality

Human death rates increase slowly after age 80. Data analyses of very large cohorts reveal that death rates reach a plateau at advanced ages and may level off around age 110 (Thatcher, Kannisto and Vaupel, 1998; Robine and Vaupel, 2002). This observation is not unique to humans, however. Late-life mortality deceleration has been noticed in and confirmed for a number of model organisms as diverse as yeast, nematodes, or fruit flies. For all species for which large cohorts have been followed to extinction, age-specific mortality decelerates and, for the largest populations studied, even declines at older ages (Vaupel et al., 1998).

Some concepts contributing to an understanding of the astonishing improvement in survival at late ages come from biodemography, a subject that has emerged at the confluence of demography and biology. One biodemographic explanation builds on heterogeneity in frailty. All populations are heterogeneous, and even genetically identical populations display phenotypic differences. Frailer individuals have a lower probability of survival to late ages; robust individuals have a higher one. The frail tend to suffer high mortality, leaving a select subset of robust survivors. This results in compositional change in the surviving, aging population and in slower increases in age-specific death rates (Vaupel, Manton and Stallard, 1979; Curtsinger et al., 1992; Vaupel and Carey, 1993; Yashin, Vaupel and Iachine, 1994). Another biodemographic explanation refers to

changes in survival capacities at the individual level. Generally, the longevity of individual organisms is influenced by the living conditions to which they are exposed. Studies with different species have shown that several environmental factors of non-lethal stress, for example dietary restriction or heat shock, can induce increases in both resistance and longevity (Lithgow et al., 1995; Murakami and Johnson, 1996; Masoro, 2000). Hormesis, a biologically favourable response to low exposure to stress or toxins, is a well-known physiological phenomenon. Caloric restriction has proven to be an effective way to extend life span in a wide range of species, from yeast to mammals (Masoro, 2000). It is not clear, however, whether fasting is a way of prolonging life in humans.

The influence of current conditions on age-specific death rates

Studies involving model organisms have provided valuable insights into the biological processes of aging. An example can be drawn from a study on the Drosophila fruit fly. When flies fed a restricted diet were switched to a full diet, mortality soared to the level suffered by flies that had been fully fed all their lives. Conversely, when the diet of fully fed Drosophila was restricted, mortality plunged within 48 hours to the level enjoyed by flies that had experienced a lifelong restricted diet (Mair et al., 2003). The results support the repeated finding that age-specific death rates for humans (and other species) are strongly influenced by current conditions and behaviour (Kannisto, 1994; Vaupel et al., 1998).

Placed in a broader context, the conclusion drawn from the fruit fly study also applies to humans. This can be illustrated neatly by an unplanned 'natural experiment' in Germany's recent history. Before reunification, both East and West Germany saw a radical decline in old-age mortality, as is characteristic for most developed countries. In the former GDR, however, mortality was considerably higher than in West Germany. Following unification (1989–1990), old-age mortality in East Germany declined to reach the levels prevailing in the West (Gjonca, Brockmann and Maier, 2000), a development largely attributed to improved health care for the elderly after unification. Thus, interventions even late in life can switch death rates to a lower, healthier trajectory. It's never too late to start prolonging your life (Vaupel, Carey and Christensen, 2003).

Longevity in humans has a relatively low heritability. Studies of twins indicate that a modest 25 per cent of the variation in life spans is attributable to genetic differences among people (McGue et al., 1993; Herskind et al., 1996; Finch and Tanzi, 1997). The discoveries of genetic and environmental factors that contribute to extensions of the lifespan do not fully explain the malleability of aging. Nevertheless, the findings show that there are means and ways of delaying aging.

The plasticity of aging

The rise in life expectancy has provoked discussion of the question whether we are approaching a limit to life expectancy, a biologically determined maximum lifespan that inevitably halts further improvements of old-age survival.

A common assumption still widely held is that lifespan cannot be extended beyond a biologically determined limit. The notion of an inevitable maximum lifespan also influences scientific studies of longevity (Fries, 1980; Olshansky, Carnes and Cassel, 1990). Ever since research into longevity began, attempts have been made to determine the maximum life expectancy that humans could reach. The ceilings proposed by various authors differ but all have been exceeded, apart from those proposed most recently (Oeppen and Vaupel, 2002). The assumption of a finite, biological limit to life can be traced back to Aristotle (350 BC). In his treatise 'On Youth and Old Age, On Life and Death', Aristotle contrasted two types of death: premature death caused by disease or accident, and senescent death due to old age. He believed that nothing could be done about old age and thus about the end to life. More than 2,300 years later, James Fries quantified Aristotle's distinction in a widely cited article published in the *New England Journal of Medicine*. If life is not cut short by accident or illness, then the lifespan of man will inevitably approach a potential maximum limit that is fixed for every human but differs from individual to individual (Fries, 1980). According to Fries, the fixed value of the maximum lifespan is normally distributed with a mean of 85 years and a standard deviation of seven years. Fries emphasizes that nothing can be done to alter a person's maximum lifespan as the latter is beyond the influence of environmental, behavioural, or medical intervention currently conceivable. Accordingly, death rates at older ages are intractable. The notion of unavoidable senescent death has been reinforced by evolutionary biologists who hypothesize that mortality must rise with age as the force of selection against deleterious, late-acting mutations declines (Hamilton, 1966).

The notion of an upper biological limit to lifespan may be commonly accepted, yet there is no empirical evidence of a proximate limit to human longevity. The steady rise in human life expectancy shows no signs of levelling off. Experts repeatedly asserting that life expectancy is approaching a ceiling have repeatedly been proven wrong. If life expectancy were approaching an unavoidable biological maximum, then the increase in life expectancy should be slowing, especially in countries such as Japan or France, both of which enjoy exceptionally low death rates. This, however, is not the case (Oeppen and Vaupel, 2002; Vaupel, 1997). Mortality is plastic even at advanced ages.

The prevailing causes of rising life expectancy have undergone changes and are complex. Combined, they have nonetheless led to a stable and linear increase in life expectancy since 1840. This will probably also apply to the future. Just as medical breakthroughs – for example, the discovery of antibiotics or advances in organ transplantation – were not foreseen, we do not know what major technological innovations the future will bring to promote long and healthy lives. There is no reason, however, to assume that progress in technological knowledge and its exploitation will come to a halt. It would not make sense to take the standards of today to estimate the conditions influencing life expectancy tomorrow. Future advances in life expectancy will be made as we progress in the prevention, diagnosis, and treatment of deadly age-related diseases (Barbi and Vaupel, 2005).

Future prospects of longevity

Because best-practice life expectancy has been increasing by 2.5 years per decade for the past 160 years, one reasonable scenario is that this trend will continue in the coming decades. To date, there is no indication that a change in the trend is in sight. If the trend continues, there may be a country in about six decades' time with life expectancy beyond the threshold of 100 years (Oeppen and Vaupel, 2002).

An application of this extrapolation in conjunction with methods from time-series analysis to project the gap between best-practice and national life expectancy results in national forecasts that are considerably higher than many official projections. From the use of this method, female life expectancy for Germany, for example, is expected to rise significantly above 90 years by 2050. Official projections, however, do not exceed 87 years (medium scenario). In many countries, official projections assume a deceleration in reductions of death rates. Such projections made in the past have resulted in underestimates of actual increases in life expectancy. These errors distort planning for future pensions, health care, and other social needs as well as the decision-making of individuals drawing up saving plans or planning for retirement. Increases in life expectancy of a few years can produce large changes in the numbers of old and oldest old who will need support and care. In developed countries, centenarians may well become commonplace during the lifetime of people alive today.

Mortality divergences

Although health trends have been generally positive throughout the world and remarkable improvements in survival have been achieved in developed and many developing countries (Tuljapurkar, Li and Boe, 2000; Vallin and Meslé, 2005), death rates still vary among countries and even within countries. In the 1970s and early 1980s, many demographers expected a convergence in life expectancies worldwide by assuming gains would be higher for the countries with lower life expectancies (McMichael et al., 2004). A quarter of a century later, however, it is clear that this assumption did not hold.

On the one hand, increases in life expectancy of some of the best-performing countries, such as Japan or France, did not show any levelling off at all and life expectancy climbed higher than expected. On the other hand, there have been exceptions to the widespread phenomenon of general mortality decline in the second half of the 20th century. Mortality reversals were observed in the 1980s and 1990s in as many as 42 countries (McMichael et al., 2004; Caselli, Meslé and Vallin, 2002; Vallin and Meslé, 2005) as life expectancy fell. Most of these countries are situated in sub-Saharan Africa or in eastern Europe. Life expectancy in several sub-Saharan countries was more than ten years lower in 2004 than predicted by the UN Population Division about 20 years earlier (United Nations, 1981). Other countries that experienced reversals in life expectancy at the end of the 20th century are North Korea, Haiti, Fiji, the Bahamas, and Iraq. Setbacks apart from those caused by war and famine were not taken into account by early demographers, with the result that future setbacks in national mortality were considered unlikely (McMichael et al., 2004).

In sub-Saharan Africa, HIV/AIDS and other infectious diseases, such as tuberculosis and malaria, caused death rates to rise, and many of the countries involved were additionally faced with economic hardships, political conflicts, and violence between groups or individuals. Russia, like other countries of the former USSR or of eastern Europe, experienced increased mortality among working-age adults, especially among men aged between 20 and 65 (Shkolnikov et al., 1998; Meslé et al., 2003). Adults are normally less vulnerable to mortality increase than are children or the elderly. The drastic political and socio-economic transition increased unemployment rates and income inequalities, and led to weakened safety nets and to psycho-social stress among those most affected, particularly the less educated population groups (Shapiro, 1995; Shkolnikov et al., 1998; Bobak et al., 2000). Adverse male behaviours, such as alcohol abuse, crime, and violence, contributed to male excess adult mortality. In addition, rates of cardiovascular disease and cancer mortality are high in Russia.

Some industrialized countries perform less well than others. Since the mid-1980s in the United States, for example, death rates have declined more slowly than in most other developed countries. Until about 1980, the United States enjoyed relatively low death rates for both women and men after aged 65. Since then, however, death rates at older ages have fallen less rapidly than in Japan, France and other countries. The reasons for the slow increase in life expectancy in the United States are not yet well understood.

Mortality differentials
The U-shape of the mortality risk trajectory applies to all humans. Nevertheless, remarkable differentials exist by geographical region and along other dimensions. The best-known differential is between females and males. In most developed countries, the difference between female and male life expectancy is between four and seven years. The gap between women and men is typically smaller in less developed countries. It is not clear how much of the gap is biological as opposed to social, in part because biological factors interact with social ones. While men take more health risks (such as smoking), women are more careful about their health (for example, visits to the doctor).

Socio-economic status (SES) and mortality have an inverse relationship: individuals with higher SES usually enjoy lower mortality, regardless of how SES is measured (Goldman, 2001). Although measures of SES are correlated with each other, they address different dimensions: education is related to health behaviour and knowledge of healthy lifestyle, occupation to health hazards of the job, and income to access to health care as well as to the ability to provide a healthy living environment (such as housing conditions).

Marital status is another important mortality determinant. Married individuals usually have lower death rates than do never-married women and men, the widowed, or the divorced. Two different hypotheses have been discussed in the literature to explain this differential. On the one hand, marriage is expected to have a protective effect via pooled financial resources, higher social support, the adoption of healthier lifestyles, and other factors. On the other hand, it is argued that there is a selection effect into marriage: healthy women and men have higher chances of finding a spouse than less healthy individuals (Goldman, 1993).

JAMES W. VAUPEL, KRISTÍN G. VON KISTOWSKI AND ROLAND RAU

See also **fertility in developing countries; fertility in developed countries; retirement.**

Bibliography

Aristotle. 350 BC. On youth and old age, on life and death, on breathing. Trans. G. Ross. Online. Available at http://classics.mit.edu/Aristotle/youth_old.html, accessed 20 August 2006.

Barbi, E. and Vaupel, J. 2005. Comment on 'Inflammatory exposure and historical change in human life-spans'. *Science* 308, 1743.

Bobak, M., Pikhart, H., Hertzman, C., Rose, R. and Marmot, M. 2000. Socioeconomic factors, material inequalities, and perceived control in self-rate health: cross-sectional data from seven post-communist countries. *Social Science and Medicine* 51, 1343–50.

Bongaarts, J. and Bulatao, R., eds. 2000. *Beyond the Billion: Forecasting the World's Population*. Washington, DC: National Academy Press.

Caselli, G., Meslé, F. and Vallin, J. 2002. Epidemiologic transition theory exceptions. *Genus* 58(1), 9–51.

Curtsinger, J., Fukui, H., Townsend, D. and Vaupel, J. 1992. Demography of genotypes: failure of the limited life-span paradigm in *Drosophila melanogaster*. *Science* 258, 461–63.

Finch, C. and Tanzi, R. 1997. Genetics of aging. *Science* 278, 407–11.

Fries, J. 1980. Aging, natural death, and the compression of morbidity. *New England Journal of Medicine* 303, 130–5.

Gjonca, A., Brockmann, H. and Maier, H. 2000. Old-age mortality in Germany prior to and after reunification. *Demographic Research* 3(1). Online. Available at http://www.demographic-research.org/volumes/vol3/1/3-1.pdf, accessed 20 August 2006.

Goldman, N. 1993. Marriage selection and mortality patterns: inferences and fallacies. *Demography* 30, 189–208.

Goldman, N. 2001. Mortality differentials: selection and causation. In *International Encyclopedia of the Social and Behavioral Sciences*, ed. N. Smelser and P. Baltes. Oxford: Elsevier Science.

Gompertz, B. 1825. On the nature of the function expressive of the law of human mortality, and on a new mode of determining the value of life contingencies. *Philosophical Transactions of the Royal Society of London* 11, 513–83.

Hamilton, W. 1966. The moulding of senescence by natural selection. *Journal of Theoretical Biology* 12, 12–45.

Heligman, M. and Pollard, J. 1980. The age pattern of mortality. *Journal of the Institute of Actuaries* 107, 49–80.

Herskind, A., McGue, M., Soerensen, T. and Vaupel, J. 1996. The heritability of human longevity: a population-based study of 2872 Danish twin pairs born 1870–1900. *Human Genetics* 97, 319–23.

Jeune, B. 1995. In search for the first centenarians. In *Exceptional Longevity: From Prehistory to the Present*, ed. B. Jeune and J. Vaupel. Odense: Odense University Press.

Kannisto, V. 1994. *Development of the Oldest-Old mortality, 1950– 1990*. Odense: Odense University Press.

Kannisto, V., Lauritsen, J., Thatcher, A. and Vaupel, J. 1994. Reductions in mortality at advanced ages: several decades of evidence from 27 countries. *Population and Development Review* 20, 793–30.

Kannisto Thatcher Database on old age mortality. Online: available at http://www.demogr.mpg.de/databases/ktdb/, accessed 20 August 2006.

Lithgow, G., White, T., Melov, S. and Johnson, T. 1995. Thermotolerance and extended life-span conferred by single-gene mutations and induced by thermal stress. *Proceedings of the National Academy of Sciences USA* 92, 7540–4.

Mair, W., Goymer, P., Pletcher, S. and Partridge, L. 2003. Demography of dietary restriction and death in *Drosophila*. *Science* 301, 1731–3.

Masoro, E.J. 2000. Caloric restriction and aging: an update. *Experimental Gerontology* 35, 299–305.

McGue, M., Vaupel, J., Holm, N. and Harvald, B. 1993. Longevity is moderately heritable in a sample of Danish twins born 1870–1880. *Journals of Gerontology: Series A, Biological Sciences and Medical Sciences* 48, B237–B244.

McMichael, A., McKee, M., Shkolnikov, V. and Valkonen, T. 2004. Mortality trends and setbacks: global convergence or divergence? *The Lancet* 262, 1155–9.

Meslé, F., Vallin, J., Hertrich, V., Andreev, E. and Shkolnikov, V. 2003. Causes of death in Russia: assessing trends since the 1950s. In *Population of Central and Eastern Europe. Challenges and Opportunities*, ed. I. Kotowska and J. Joswiak. Warsaw: Statistical Publishing Establishment.

Murakami, S. and Johnson, T. 1996. A genetic pathway conferring life extension and resistance to UV stress in *Caenorhabditis elegans*. *Genetics* 143, 1207–18.

Oeppen, J. and Vaupel, J. 2002. Broken limits to life expectancy. *Science* 296, 1029–31.

Olshansky, S., Carnes, B. and Cassel, C. 1990. In search of Methuselah: estimating the upper limits of human longevity. *Science* 250, 634–40.

Riley, J. 2001. *Rising Life Expectancy: A Global History*. Cambridge: Cambridge University Press.

Robine, J. and Vaupel, J. 2002. Emergence of supercentenarians in low mortality countries. *North American Actuarial Journal* 6, 54–63.

Shapiro, J. 1995. The Russian mortality crisis and its causes. In *Russian Economic Reform at Risk*, ed. A. Aslund. London: Pinter.

Shkolnikov, V., Cornia, G., Leon, D. and Meslé, F. 1998. Causes of the Russian mortality crisis: evidence and interpretations. *World Development* 26, 1995–2011.

Thatcher, A., Kannisto, V. and Vaupel, J. 1998. *The Trajectory of Mortality from Age 80 to 120*. Odense: Odense University Press.

Tuljapurkar, S., Li, N. and Boe, C. 2000. A universal pattern of mortality decline in the G7 countries. *Nature* 405, 789–92.

United Nations. 1981. *World Population Prospects As Assessed in 1980*. New York, United Nations.

United Nations. 2005. *World Population Prospects, The 2004 Revision, Highlights*. New York: Department of Economic and Social Affairs, United Nations.

Vallin, J. and Meslé, F. 2005. Convergences and divergences: an analytical framework of national and sub-national trends in life expectancy. *Genus* 61(1), 83–123.

Vaupel, J. 1997. The remarkable improvements in survival at old ages. *Philosophical Transactions of the Royal Society of London, Series B* 352, 1799–804.

Vaupel, J. and Carey, J. 1993. Compositional interpretations of medfly mortality. *Science* 260, 1666–7.

Vaupel, J.W., Carey, J. and Christensen, K. 2003. It's never too late. *Science* 301, 1679–81.

Vaupel, J., Carey, J., Christensen, K., Johnson, T., Yashin, A., Holm, N., Iachine, I., Kannisto, V., Khazaeli, A., Liedo, P., Longo, V., Zeng, Y., Manton, K. and Curtsinger, J. 1998. Biodemographic trajectories of longevity. *Science* 280, 855–60.

Vaupel, J. and Jeune, B. 1995. The emergence and proliferation of centenarians. In *Exceptional Longevity:*

From Prehistory to the Present, ed. B. Jeune and J. Vaupel. Odense: Odense University Press.

Vaupel, J.W., Manton, K.G. and Stallard, E. 1979. The impact of heterogeneity in individual frailty on the dynamics of mortality. *Demography* 16, 439–54.

WHO (World Health Organization). 2004. *Maternal Mortality in 2000: Estimates Developed by WHO, UNICEF, and UNFPA*. Geneva: WHO.

WHO 2006. *World Health Report 2006: Working Together for Health*. Geneva: WHO.

Wilmoth, J. 1995. The earliest centenarians: a statistical analysis. In *Exceptional Longevity: From Prehistory to the Present*, ed. B. Jeune and J. Vaupel. Odense: Odense University Press.

Yashin, A., Vaupel, J. and Iachine, I. 1994. A duality in aging: the equivalence of mortality models based on radically different concepts. *Mechanisms of Ageing and Development* 74, 1–14.

Free internet sources on mortality data

The Human Mortality Database contains calculations of the death rates and life tables of almost 30 countries. Access to the data requires registration, which is free at http://www.mortality.org, accessed 20 August 2006.

The Kannisto–Thatcher Database on Old Age Mortality is tailored to analyse mortality at ages 80 and over. It has death and population counts by sex, age, birth year, and calendar year for more than 30 countries for ages 80 and above. Available at http://www.demogr.mpg.de/databases/ktdb., accessed 20 August 2006.

The Human Life-Table Database is a collection of life tables for more than 30 countries. Available at http://www.lifetable.de, accessed 20 August 2006.

motion pictures, economics of

The business of motion pictures is a fascinating laboratory for applied researchers in the social sciences. The glamorous subject matter makes the industry inherently interesting, but more important for empirical research is the availability of project-level data on investment and financial returns. Most studies of investment decisions are conducted at the industry or firm level, so that the researcher observes the return only on a portfolio of projects. In the movie business, the unit of observation is the individual project, and data are collected and reported in fine detail by many industry sources.

Early research on the movie business applied micro-economic theory to the industry and made little use of its detailed data and rich institutions. This early literature is important in providing the historical context in which many of the movie industry's business practices emerged. Kindem (1982) has collected in his volume many papers that provide organizational and institutional analyses of the motion-picture industry from its origins through the modern era. More recent papers in this line of applied research provide revisionist analyses of the industry's history and development (Chisholm, 1993; 1997; De Vany and Eckert, 1991; De Vany and McMillan, 2004; Sedgwick, 2000).

The market for motion pictures is difficult to understand quantitatively, though the intuition is transparent. Film-goers discover the films they like by consuming them, and through the exchange of information the demand for motion pictures evolves over time. Supply adjusts as the available screens respond to demand through flexible state-contingent exhibition contracts. The present article provides an overview of the economics of motion pictures. The focus is on the how the demand process affects the distribution of outcomes, how the distribution of outcomes can be quantified, and how this relates to the industry's organization and business practices.

Movie-goer choices and outcome uncertainty

Understanding demand is essential if one is to make sense of the movie industry's contracts and business practices. Early viewers of a movie affect the choices of potential viewers – behaviour that goes under the names of herding, contagion, network effects, bandwagons, path-dependence, momentum, and information cascades. The particular models differ in their details, but they are dynamic in that demand depends on revealed demand, or more generally on how group behaviour arises from the interaction of individual decision-makers (Epstein and Axtell, 1996). Initial advantages in movie attendance can lead to extreme differences in outcomes when demand has recursive feedback. De Vany and Walls (1996) showed that box-office revenues have a contagion-like property where the week-to-week change in demand is stochastically dependent on previous demand. A big opening of a bad movie can kill it but a big opening of a good movie can lead to an avalanche of attendance and large revenues. Let's examine the demand for movies more closely to see the origins of extreme success and failure.

Assume for simplicity initially that there was only one movie that could be viewed by one consumer at any one time. Consumers choose in random sequence whether or not to go to the movie. If we further assume that the consumers have a common prior belief about the film's quality, then there is a common probability p that a randomly chosen person will choose to see the film. If we let X be the number attending the film, then X is a binomial random variable; it follows that when consumers share a common prior the film's revenues would follow a binomial distribution. When quality is unknown and priors over quality differ among viewers, p is a random variable. By conditioning on p and integrating over the binomial distribution, we see that each of the $n + 1$ possible outcomes is equally likely; adding uncertainty to the priors transforms the distribution of revenue from the binomial to the uniform distribution.

Now consider information sharing, as has been modelled by Jovanovic (1987), where potential consumers can use information revealed during a film's run to refine their prior on its quality; this sort of information includes the opinions of other viewers, such as expert reviewers, advertising, and information from box office reports and queuing at cinemas. De Vany and Walls (1996) let the distribution of customers over screens be multinomial uniform, so the movie search problem – a search for quality with an unknown distribution – is similar to the search for price with an unknown distribution. Viewers who do not know the distribution begin with a uniform prior and adapt from there. The result of this process is the Bose–Einstein distribution which has the property that all of the possible outcome vectors are equally likely! This means the vector in which the attendance at every theatre is equal to zero is as likely as one in which all n trials go to only one theatre and every other vector is equally likely (Feller, 1957). The Bose–Einstein distribution has uniform mass over a space of $s + 1$-vectors; the s-vectors correspond to the revenues of the s theatres and one bin collects those who go to no film.

What is important about the evolution of choice probabilities under the Bose–Einstein choice logic is the way past successes are leveraged into future successes: as soon as individual differences emerge among the films, they are compounded by information feedback into very large differences over the course of a film's theatrical lifetime. A broad opening at many theatres can produce large and rapidly growing audiences, but it also can lead to early failure if the large crowd relays negative information. Movie customers sequentially select movies, and the probability that a given customer selects a particular movie is proportional to the fraction of previous customers who selected that movie. This result obtains because the probabilities are not known and sampling reveals information that causes previous selections to attract new ones.

Quantifying the distribution of movie outcomes

Box-office revenue is asymptotically power law or Pareto distributed (De Vany and Walls, 1999; 2002). One of the attractions of the power law distributions in explaining the movie business is that they allow for the heavy tails and skewness that are characteristic of box-office outcomes. Power laws emerge in many other systems with feedback of the type discussed above (Brock, 1999).

The stable Paretian model

Mandelbrot (1963) proposed the stable Paretian distribution as a general model for natural and social systems; it is applied in economics, finance, biology, geology, physiology, and other sciences (McCulloch, 1996; Uchaikin and Zolotarev, 1999; Mantegna and Stanley, 1995; Levy and Soloman, 1997). The stable distribution is the limiting distribution of all stable processes so that it contains the other well-known stable distributions (Cauchy, Lévy, Gaussian) as special cases. Motion picture profit is well fit by a stable distribution with infinite variance and positive skew (Walls, 2000; De Vany and Walls, 2004). The stable distribution's ability to capture the empirical regularities found in motion picture data and the distribution's statistical foundation on the most general form of central limit theorem make it a natural model of motion picture outcomes. The theoretical reason for thinking that a stable distribution might apply to motion pictures is that Mandelbrot (1963) showed that a dynamic process that is stable under choice, mixture, and aggregation converges in distribution to the stable distribution. If motion picture revenues and costs are discrete time processes with stable increments, then profit will converge to a stable distribution.

Conditional stable distribution

In empirical studies it is possible to model the stable Paretian distribution of movie outcomes conditional on a vector of explanatory variables with the use of McCulloch's (1998) stable regression model in which the index of stability α and the regression coefficients are estimated jointly. The stable regression model has the familiar form of a linear regression $y_i = \beta_0 + \sum_{j=1}^{k} \beta_{ij} x_i + \varepsilon_i$ where the β's are the coefficients to be estimated and the x's are the regressors, but the random disturbance term is assumed to follow a stable distribution with median zero. Estimation of the stable regression model results in an estimate of the regression coefficient β's as well as an estimate of the characteristic exponent α. The regression coefficients in this model represent what is known about the correlates of film success while at the same time permitting the variance of film success at the box office to be infinite. Estimates of this model show that the distribution of returns conditional on a movie's attributes has infinite variance and that returns to production budgets are substantially larger and returns to stars substantially lower than one would estimate using an improperly specified least-squares model (Walls, 2005b).

Stretched exponentials

Concavity in log-log plots of size against rank, also known as a parabolic power law, are interpreted as evidence of increasing returns to information in the demand for motion pictures (De Vany and Walls, 1996; Walls, 1997; Hand, 2001). Frisch and Sornette (1997) propose a multiplicative stochastic process that can explain the deviation of the data relative to a power law distribution, and Sornette (1998) provides rigorous technical details on multiplicative processes leading to power laws and stretched exponentials. Walls (2005a) finds that the stretched exponential distribution fits motion-picture revenue data remarkably well. The stretched exponential distribution does not truncate the upper tail in its estimates of the probability of a movie earning a larger amount than previous movies. The distribution also accounts for the deviation from the strict Pareto power law in a way that does not place artificial restrictions on the possibility that a movie can earn far more than our experience suggests.

Understanding the movie business

We now discuss how the behavioural and statistical models help us to understand the way the motion-picture industry operates and how contracts and business practices adjust the supply of theatrical engagements to capture the increasing returns inherent in the demand process.

The opening

Stars, large production budgets and national advertising campaigns can place a film on many exhibitor screens when it opens. This can generate high initial revenues and, if viewers like the film and spread the word, it will earn high revenues in the following weeks. But a wide release is vulnerable to negative feedback – if viewers do not like the film, the large opening audience transmits a large flow of negative information, and revenue may decline at a rapid rate. A wide release lowers the gross revenue per theatre, and this may cause exhibitors to drop the film sooner than they would otherwise. The willingness of exhibitors and downstream sources of revenue like cable television, videocassette distributors, pay per view and network television as well as foreign distributors to pay advance guarantees for motion pictures before their theatrical run is a major inducement for distributors to produce big budget films and promote them heavily. The theatrical market can be less important than other sources of revenues (Rusco and Walls, 2004).

Decentralization

Each film's run through the market is sequential in order to exploit information dynamics. The run is self-organized because it decentralizes the decision to extend the run to each theatre and uses only local information to extend or close the run at each location. The initial release is modified over time through this process, and new engagements can be added subject to prior contractual obligations. These contractual features interact to adaptively capture revenue and generate strongly increasing returns from highly successful films. When demand has positive feedback, supply responds flexibly to allow some films to become blockbusters.

Admission pricing

Fixed admission prices (across films but within a given customer class or time of day) are a common industry practice. As a result, demand is accommodated by lengthening a film's run. A relatively stationary admission price combined with a count of admissions gives a reliable signal of demand, and this signal is transmitted throughout the industry by real time reporting of box office revenues. This reporting is required in the exhibition contract and encouraged by other means as well. If the admission price were increased to ration excess demand, the number of people who would see the film in the opening weeks would fall and this would reduce the flow of information from this source to potential viewers. This lower rate of information transfer would lead to a shorter run and a lower total level of demand. The ability to extend the run makes an almost perfectly elastic supply response possible, so there is no need for price to rise to ration excess demand. Fixed admission prices lead to a pure quantity signal and an adaptive supply response to accommodate demand discovery.

Contracting

Optimal contract theory does not fit the environment of motion pictures where expected values are dominated by the rare and unpredictable events that are so large. The incentive clauses of optimal contract theory are designed to alter the probabilities of favourable outcomes and raise expected values, but the asymmetric information often emphasized by optimal contract theory is not a factor because both principal and agent are in a state of symmetric ignorance about the prospects of a movie owing to the 'nobody knows' property (Caves, 2000).

A difficult problem to solve contractually is how to keep a film on screens long enough for it to build an audience. If an exhibitor takes such a film, it is with the risk that it may build so slowly during his or her run that only exhibitors who show it later will benefit from information feedback. Because the Paramount decrees bar long-term, exclusive showings, it is difficult to guarantee that the exhibitor who takes the risk of introducing the film will benefit if the film later becomes a success (De Vany and Eckert, 1991). When the audience grows recursively, the Paramount contracting restrictions may prevent risk-taking exhibitors from capturing the demand externality which they create.

Extreme events drive the business, so contracts condition pay on rare events with compensation related to the outcome of the movie. Many Hollywood superstar movie contracts contain some form of profit participation (Weinstein, 1998). Many contracts are contingent on theatrical box office revenues, which are readily monitored. In this case, the share of gross revenue paid often is nonlinear, with the share rising at higher outcomes, to reflect the nonlinear dependence of profit on revenue. In a complex contract, there may be several breakpoints where the star's percentage share increases, this nonlinearity reflecting the nonlinearity of profit in revenue.

Film rentals

The exhibition contracts are rich in contingencies that make them highly adaptive: they rely on locally generated information; they set the rental fee in a precise and nonlinear way in response to demand; they share risk between exhibitors and distributors; and they create incentives for exhibitors to show films by granting a measure of exclusivity. The rental price adapts to the state of demand and the rental schedule is nonlinear. Events in the tail are the high-revenue weeks during a movie's theatrical run, and these weeks can occur at any time during the run. During these high-revenue weeks, the rental clause allows the exhibitor to retain his or her (negotiated) cost per week of operation plus ten per cent while allocating the remaining 90 per cent to the distributor (De Vany and Eckert, 1991).

Star power

Movies with superstars have a different distribution of profit from other movies (De Vany and Walls, 2004). The profit distribution for superstar movies is an asymmetric stable distribution with infinite variance. Stars place much more mass in the upper tail of the profit distribution. The probability of extreme catastrophes – losses in excess of $95 million, say – is higher for movies *without* stars than for movies with stars. This is not at all obvious and may not be observed in a given sample. Putting a star in a movie places more mass on the upper tail and less on the lower tail. Expected profit is positive for star movies and negative for non-star movies. These values are consistent with the fact that probability is skewed to the positive tail in superstar movies and to the negative tail for others. Superstar movies are more profitable and less risky than other movies.

Success breeds success

An interesting property of the stable Paretian distribution discussed above is that conditional expectation does not converge. The tails of stable distributions are Paretian and the conditional probability that $x \geq x_0$ is $P[x > x_0] = (x_0/x)^\alpha$. The conditional mean, given that $x > x_0$ equals $\bar{x}_{x_0} = x_0\alpha/(\alpha - 1)$. Since α is a constant, the conditional expected value of profit depends linearly on x_0. Conditional on having earned a profit, the expected profit continues to rise with current profit, and this does not end as the movie earns more profit. This is not paradoxical because movies that make it into the upper tail of the profit distribution have been selected from among their competitors. The heavy tails of the stable distribution imply that probability does not decline rapidly enough for the conditional expectation to converge. For the Gaussian or log Gaussian distributions, the conditional expectation converges to a constant as the conditioning event increases. The linear conditional expectation of the Paretian distribution means that blockbuster movies that have already attained high profit have an expectation of even higher profit, and this prospect does not diminish as profit grows. This captures the idea of demand momentum.

Conclusion

When movie audiences see a movie they like, they make a discovery and they tell their friends about it. This and other information is transmitted to other consumers, and demand develops dynamically as the audience sequentially discovers which movies it likes. Supply adapts to revealed demand through flexible exhibition contracts and other business practices that permit the increasing returns in film demand to be realized.

W. DAVID WALLS

See also **information cascades; Pareto distribution; path dependence; power laws; superstars, economics of.**

Bibliography

Brock, W. 1999. Scaling in economics: a reader's guide. *Industrial and Corporate Change* 8, 403–46.

Caves, R. 2000. *Creative Industries: Contracts between Art and Commerce*. Cambridge, MA: Harvard University Press.

Chisholm, D. 1993. Asset specificity and long-term contracts: the case of the motion-pictures industry. *Eastern Economic Journal* 19, 143–55.

Chisholm, D. 1997. Profit-sharing versus fixed-payment contracts: evidence from the motion pictures industry. *Journal of Law, Economics, and Organization* 13, 169–201.

De Vany, A. and Eckert, R. 1991. Motion picture antitrust: the Paramount cases revisited. *Research in Law and Economics* 14, 51–112.

De Vany, A. and McMillan, H. 2004. Was the antitrust action that broke up the movie studios good for the movies? Evidence from the stock market. *American Law and Economics Review* 6, 135–53.

De Vany, A. and Walls, W.D. 1996. Bose–Einstein dynamics and adaptive contracting in the motion picture industry. *Economic Journal* 106, 1493–514.

De Vany, A. and Walls, W.D. 1999. Uncertainty in the movie industry: does star power reduce the terror of the box office? *Journal of Cultural Economics* 23, 285–318.

De Vany, A. and Walls, W.D. 2002. Does Hollywood make too many R-rated movies?: Risk, stochastic dominance, and the illusion of expectation. *Journal of Business* 75, 425–51.

De Vany, A. and Walls, W.D. 2004. Motion picture profit, the stable Paretian hypothesis, and the curse of the superstar. *Journal of Economic Dynamics and Control* 28, 1035–57.

Epstein, J. and Axtell, R. 1996. *Growing Artificial Societies: Social Science from the Bottom Up*. Cambridge, MA: Brookings Institution and MIT Press.

Feller, W. 1957. *An Introduction to Probability Theory and Its Applications*. New York: Wiley.

Frisch, U. and Sornette, D. 1997. Extreme deviations and applications. *Journal de Physique* 1, 1155–71.

Hand, C. 2001. Increasing returns to information: further evidence from the UK film market. *Applied Economics Letters* 8, 419–21.

Jovanovic, B. 1987. Micro shocks and aggregate risk. *Quarterly Journal of Economics* 17, 395–409.

Kindem, G., ed. 1982. *The American Movie Industry: The Business of Motion Pictures*. Carbondale: Southern Illinois University Press.

Levy, M. and Soloman, S. 1997. New evidence for the power law distribution of wealth. *Physica A* 242, 90–4.

Mandelbrot, B. 1963. New methods in statistical economics. *Journal of Political Economy* 71, 421–40.

Mantegna, R. and Stanley, H. 1995. Scaling in financial markets. *Nature* 376, 46–9.

McCulloch, J. 1996. Financial applications of stable distributions. In *Statistical Methods in Finance*, vol. 14 of *Handbook of Statistics*, ed. G. Maddala and C. Rao. New York: North-Holland.

McCulloch, J. 1998. Numerical approximation of the symmetric stable distribution and density. In *A Practical Guide to Heavy Tails: Statistical Techniques and Applications*, ed. R. Adler, R. Feldman and M. Taqqu. Berlin: Birkhäuser.

Rusco, F. and Walls, W.D. 2004. Independent film finance, pre-sale agreements, and the distribution of film earnings. In *The Economics of Art and Culture*. Contributions to Economic Analysis No. 260, ed. V. Ginsburgh. Amsterdam: Elsevier.

Sedgwick, J. 2000. *Popular Filmgoing in 1930s Britain: A Choice of Pleasures*. Exeter: University of Exeter Press.

Sornette, D. 1998. Multiplicative processes and power laws. *Physical Review E* 57, 4811–13.

Uchaikin, V. and Zolotarev, V. 1999. *Chance and Stability: Stable Distributions and their Applications*. Utrecht: VSP.

Walls, W.D. 1997. Increasing returns to information: evidence from the Hong Kong movie market. *Applied Economics Letters* 4, 187–90.

Walls, W.D. 2000. Measuring and managing uncertainty with an application to the Hong Kong movie business. *International Journal of Management* 17, 118–27.

Walls, W.D. 2005a. Demand stochastics, supply adaptation, and the distribution of film earnings. *Applied Economics Letters* 12, 619–23.

Walls, W.D. 2005b. Modeling movie success when 'nobody knows anything': conditional stable-distribution analysis of film returns. *Journal of Cultural Economics* 29(3), 177–90.

Weinstein, M. 1998. Profit-sharing contracts in Hollywood: evolution and analysis. *Journal of Legal Studies* 27, 67–112.

multilingualism

Multilingualism or linguistic diversity is an important societal phenomenon that can generate gains or losses resulting from the economic interactions between individuals, regions or countries. The effects of multilingualism have recently come to the forefront of public policy debates. Linguistic issues and, in particular, the treatment of minority languages are almost unparalleled in terms of their explosiveness and emotional appeal, much more so than any other question of resource allocation or responsibility sharing within a polity. As noted by Bretton (1976, p. 447), 'language may be the most explosive issue universally and over time. This mainly because language alone, unlike all other concerns associated with nationalism and ethnocentrism is so closely tied to the individual self. Fear of being deprived of communicating skills seems to raise political passion to fever pitch.'

Language policies in multilingual societies are beset by the trade-off between standardization and disenfranchisement. Linguistic *standardization* comprises any set of policies that promote the dominant use of a unique or several languages while limiting the usage of languages spoken by other population groups. Indeed, linguistic standardization may deliver important benefits in terms of greater ease of communication, reducing costs of translation, increased trade, improved economic performance and administrative efficiency. However, excessive standardization may exacerbate the alienation of large minorities and widen the existing chasm between linguistic communities (Laponce, 2003). A restriction of basic linguistic rights may create *disenfranchisement* of groups of individuals and cause citizens to lose their ability to communicate in the language of their choice. Standardization, which is often represented by a selection of official languages and allocation of linguistic rights, may alienate those groups of individuals whose cultural, societal and historical values and sensibilities are not represented by the official languages (Laitin, 1989). As Pool (1991) points out, nonofficial languages may suffer from their 'minority status' and limit employment and advancement possibilities of their native speakers.

Since in many cases it is not feasible to include all the languages in the set of official ones, a multilingual society must design some language standardization policies (for example, the 'three-language formula' in India; Baldridge, 1996) and the implementation of certain standardization measures (De Swaan, 2001; Grin, 2004). However, the explosive and uncompromising nature of linguistic conflicts, the reluctance of linguistic majorities to concede rights to minorities, makes the choice of official languages a challenging and daunting task. Thus, the choice of the set of official languages has to take into account the sensitivity of a society towards possible disenfranchisement of large groups of its citizens (Ginsburgh, Ortuño-Ortín and Weber, 2005) and has to rely on a delicate resolution of the interplay between administrative and cost efficiency, on the one hand, and the rights and desires of various linguistic groups, on the other (Van Parijs, 2005).

To illustrate the individual and aggregate cost and benefits of standardization and disenfranchisement, we consider a society M and the set of languages L spoken in this society. We assume that every citizen i is endowed with a unique native language $n(i) \in L$ and a set of languages $L(i) \subset L$ that, to simplify, she commands with identical ease. A linguistic profile of each individual i is the pair $(n(i), L(i))$, and society's linguistic profile is given by $P = (n(i), L(i))_{i \in M}$. A linguistic policy is represented by a set of official languages $K \subset L$ that is chosen for administrative, educational, and official communication functions in the society (Pool, 1991; 1996, and the extensive list of references therein; Ginsburgh, Ortuño-Ortín and Weber, 2005.) The choice of the set K represents a linguistic *standardization policy*. If the set of official languages K is non-empty and smaller than L, those members of the society whose native language is not included in K will be *disenfranchised* and some of their linguistic rights will be denied.

In order to evaluate the costs of disenfranchisement, we assume that every citizen i has utility function u_i defined over all subsets of L. We will denote $u_i(K)$ for $i \in M$ and $K \subset L$, where citizens with the same linguistic profiles have identical utility functions. It is important to stress that the functions u_i are defined over the set of languages as a whole, rather than being dissected into preferences over single languages. Though citizens may have preferences over single languages, their evaluation of the set of official languages could be crucially affected by inclusion or exclusion of their native language. The aggregate utility (welfare) function for the entire society is given by $W(u, P, K)$, where u is the vector of u_i's.

Our description indicates the special role played by the native languages of citizens in M, which can be viewed as the union of linguistic clusters M_l, where, for each $l \in L$, M_l consists of citizens whose native language is l. Assuming additivity of the aggregate utility, we have $W(u, P, K) = \sum_{l \in L} \sum_{i \in M_l} u_i(K)$. As a simple example, consider the *dichotomous* function based on the citizens' native languages (Ginsburgh and Weber, 2005), for which the value of $u_i(K)$ is 1 if i's native language, $n(i)$, is included in K, and zero if it is not. The latter group contains individuals who are *disenfranchised* by the imposed standardized measures. The value taken by the function W is the number of citizens whose native language belongs to the set K, $W^1(u, P, K) = \sum_{\{i \in N | n(i) \in K\}} 1$. One generalization of the dichotomous approach is to take into account the entire language profile of every citizen rather than her native language only. Then, the value of her utility function is 1 if at least one of the languages spoken by her is included in K and zero otherwise. Here, the notion of disenfranchisement is limited to those who speak no official language: $W^2(u, P, K) = \sum_{\{i \in N | L(i) \cap K \neq \emptyset\}} 1$.

In evaluating citizens' preferences over subsets of languages one may take into account the similarity or the proximity between languages (see, for example, Dyen, Kruskal and Black, 1992, for a matrix of distances between 95 Indo-European languages). Let $\delta(l, l')$ be the linguistic distance between two languages l and l'. Denote the linguistic distance between any two subsets T, T' of L as the minimal distance between a language from T and a

language from T': $\delta(T, T') = \min_{l \in T, l' \in T'} \delta(l, l')$. Then, the 'linguistic welfare' of the society is function of the distances between citizens' native languages and the set of official languages $K : W^3(u, P, K) = w(\delta(n(1), K), \delta(n(2), K), \ldots, \delta(n(M), K))$, where $w : \mathfrak{R}_+^M \to \mathfrak{R}$ is decreasing in each of its M arguments. Again, a modified utility function could be defined over the distances between the sets $L(i)$ and K instead: $W^4(u, P, K) = w(\delta(L(1), K), \delta(L(2), K), \ldots, \delta(L(M), K))$.

Note that enlarging the set of official language is welfare improving in all four specifications above. Thus, if the only goal of the society is to maximize aggregate utility, it should set $K = L$. However, there are also other considerations to take into account. Difficulties of communication, costs incurred by translation and interpretation, possible errors causing delays and sometimes paralysing multilateral discussions and negotiations impose a non-negligible burden on societies with a large number of official languages (in 2007, the European Union had to manage 23 official languages at a cost over \$1.5 billion). Denote then by $C(K)$ the cost of maintaining the set K of official languages. Obviously, C is increasing, but its specific form depends on the intensity of the linguistic regime. There could be various requirements, including a 'full' regime that every official document needs to exist in all official languages.

There is thus a trade-off between language standardization (and disenfranchisement of some citizens) and the translation, interpretation and communication costs generated by every additional official language. Formally, the society's objective is to find a set of languages K that maximizes the difference between aggregate utility and costs: $\max_{K \subset L} W(u, P, K) - C(K)$. A solution to this problem is discussed by Grin (2004, p. 201), who argues that there must be an optimum, since 'it is reasonable to assume that the benefits of diversity increase at a decreasing rate, while its costs increase at an increasing rate', and is addressed in Ginsburgh, Ortuño-Ortín and Weber (2005).

Language profiles considered so far are assumed given. In fact, they can be remarkably dynamic and change over time as individuals may decide to learn other languages. The reasons that induce citizens to do so can be analysed by examining the benefits and the costs that such learning generates. Benefits are often linked with the increased earning potential, especially in the case of immigrants who acquire the native language of the country in which they live (see, for example, MacManus, Gould and Welsch, 1978; Grenier, 1985; Lang, 1986; Chiswick, 1998; and references in Grin and Vaillancourt, 1997). We consider the Selten and Pool (1991, p. 66) 'communicative benefits' approach that frees itself from the restriction that 'earnings [are] a mechanism and firms a milieu of the incentive to learn languages'. For every language l consider the set M_l of its native speakers, whose number is denoted by m_l. Assume for simplicity that $L = j, k$ and that all citizens speak only their native language, so that the linguistic profile $L(i)$ consists of $n(i)$ for every $i \in M$. Citizens may learn the other language. Denote by $m_{j,k}(m_{j,k})$ the number of citizens in $M_j(M_k)$ who do so. A citizen $i \in M_j$ who learns language k incurs a cost $C(\delta(j, k))$, where C is an increasing function of linguistic distance. Let $u_j(m_j, \cdot)$ be the utility of $i \in M_j$, where the second argument indicates the number of individuals i can communicate with. We assume that the utility functions are increasing and, moreover, identical for all individuals with the same native language. If i learns k, it costs her $C_{j,k}$ but she will be able to communicate with all citizens in M_k. Her gross benefit will be given by $u_j(m_j, m_k)$. If i does not learn k, she will be able to communicate with those in M_k who learn language j, and her gross (and net) benefit will be $u_j(m_j, m_k)$. This formulation leads to the following equilibrium condition that makes individuals in M_k indifferent between learning the other language and deciding not to do so: $u_j(m_j, m_k) - C_{j,k} = u_j(m_j, m_{k,j})$. This equation allows us to determine the number of citizens in group M_k who learn j, and in a similar manner the number of those in group M_j who learn k (see Selten and Pool, 1991; Church and King, 1993; Shy, 2001; Gabszewicz, Ginsburgh and Weber, 2005; Ginsburgh, Ortuño-Ortín and Weber, 2007). By imposing some additional conditions, such as continuity, concavity and super-modularity of the utility functions one can derive some comparative statics results. In particular, one can show that the number of learners of the foreign language j in country k is positively correlated with the number of j-speakers in other countries and negatively correlated with the population size of their own country k (Lazear, 1999; Ginsburgh, Ortuño-Ortín and Weber, 2007). These results also show that public policies may be useful in stimulating learning (for a cost–benefit analysis of linguistic policies in Quebec, see, for example, Breton and Mieskowski, 1975, Vaillancourt, 1987; see also Fidrmuc and Ginsburgh, 2007, for policy suggestions in the EU).

In short, the questions raised by multilingualism offer serious challenges and the main reason is that linguistic policies are concerned not only with difficult trade-offs and resource allocation issues, but enter also the area of public policies that touch so closely personal values, beliefs and traditions.

VICTOR GINSBURGH AND SHLOMO WEBER

See also **culture and economics; social welfare function.**

We should like to thank Yuval Weber for his help in preparing this manuscript.

Bibliography

Baldridge, J. 1996. Reconciling linguistic diversity: the history and future of linguistic policies in India. Discussion paper, University of Pennsylvania.

Breton, A. and Mieskowski, P. 1975. The returns to investment in language: The economics of bilingualism.

Working Paper No. 7512, Toronto Institute for the Quantitative Analysis of Social and Economic Policy, University of Toronto.

Bretton, H. 1976. Political science, language, and politics. In *Language and Politics*, ed. W.M. O'Barr and J.F. O'Barr. The Hague: Mouton.

Chiswick, B. 1998. Hebrew language usage: determinants and effects on earnings among immigrants in Israel. *Journal of Population Economics* 15, 253–71.

Church, J. and King, I. 1993. Bilingualism and network externalities. *Canadian Journal of Economics* 26, 337–45.

De Swaan, A. 2001. *Words of the World*. Cambridge: Polity Press.

Dyen, I., Kruskal, J.B. and Black, P. 1992. An Indo-European classification: a lexicostatistical experiment. *Transactions of the American Philosophical Society* 82(5).

Fidrmuc, J. and Ginsburgh, V. 2007. Languages in the European Union: the quest for equality and its cost. *European Economic Review* 51, 1351–69.

Gabszewicz, J., Ginsburgh, V. and Weber, S. 2005. Bilingualism and communicative benefits. Discussion paper, CORE, Catholic University of Louvain.

Ginsburgh, V., Ortuño-Ortín, I. and Weber, S. 2005. Language disenfranchisement in linguistically diverse societies: the case of European Union. *Journal of the European Economic Association* 3, 946–65.

Ginsburgh, V., Ortuño-Ortín, I. and Weber, S. 2007. Learning foreign languages: theoretical and empirical implications of the Selten and Pool model. *Journal of Economic Behavior and Organization* 64, 337–47.

Ginsburgh, V. and Weber, S. 2005. Language disenfranchisement in the European Union. *Journal of Common Market Studies* 43, 273–86.

Grenier, G. 1985. Bilinguisme, transferts linguistiques et revenus du travail au Québec, quelques éléments d'interaction. In *Economie et Langue*, ed. F. Vaillancourt. Québec: Editeur officiel.

Grin, F. 2004. On the costs of cultural diversity. In *Cultural Diversity versus Economic Solidarity*, ed. F. Van Parijs. Brussels: De Boeck Université.

Grin, F. and Vaillancourt, F. 1997. The economics of multilingualism: overview of the literature and analytical framework. In *Multilingualism and Multilingual communities*, ed. W. Grabbe. Cambridge, MA: Cambridge University Press.

Laitin, D. 1989. Language policy and political strategy in India. *Policy Sciences* 21, 415–36.

Lang, K. 1986. A language theory of discrimination. *Quarterly Journal of Economics* 100, 363–81.

Laponce, J.A. 2003. Minority languages and globalization. *Nationalism and Ethnic Policies* 10, 15–24.

Lazear, E. 1999. Culture and language. *Journal of Political Economy* 107, 95–126.

MacManus, W., Gould, W. and Welsch, F. 1978. Earnings of Hispanic men: the role of English language proficiency. *Journal of Labor Economics* 1, 101–30.

Pool, J. 1991. The official language problem. *American Political Science Review* 85, 495–514.

Pool, J. 1996. Optimal language regimes for the European Union. *International Journal of Sociology of Language* 121, 159–79.

Selten, R. and Pool, J. 1991. The distribution of foreign language skills as a game equilibrium. In *Game Equilibrium Models*, vol. 4, ed. R. Selten. Berlin: Springer-Verlag.

Shy, O. 2001. *The Economics of Network Industries*. Cambridge: Cambridge University Press.

Van Parijs, P. 2005. Europe's three language problems. In *The Challenge of Multilingualism in Law and Politics*, ed. D. Castiglione and C. Longman. Oxford: Hart Publishing.

Vaillancourt, F. 1987. The benefits and costs of language policies in Quebec, 1974–1984: some partial estimates. In *The Economics of Language Use*, ed. H. Tonkin and K. Johnson-Weiner. New York: Center for Research and Documentation on World Language Problems.

multinational firms. *See* **foreign direct investment.**

multiple equilibria in macroeconomics

The multiple equilibrium literature seeks explanations for excessive economic volatility, persistent poverty, market fads and fashions, and related macroeconomic phenomena that appear to be anomalies in standard models of rational economic behaviour. Terms like *animal spirits, sunspots, irrational exuberance, indeterminacy*, and *bubbles* describe situations of multiple equilibrium. All of these ideas assert that future values of macroeconomic states cannot be predicted accurately from current values of these states or from knowledge of economic fundamentals, even if households and firms behave with complete rationality.

Most of the economics research community has been sceptical of multiple equilibrium (cf. McCallum, 1990), believing that it undermines the comparative statics and comparative dynamics exercises that are essential for policy evaluation and econometric prediction. Is it unreasonable, ask the sceptics, to know how the economy selects one equilibrium when many are possible, and how the expectations of economic actors settle on that particular outcome?

Economists have to weigh these legitimate reservations against direct evidence from laboratory experiments that beliefs do matter (Duffy and Fisher, 2005) as well as against the continuing difficulties of unique equilibrium models to come to grips with an expanding array of empirical anomalies in many sub-fields of macroeconomics, from excessively volatile asset prices and exchange rates to persistent underdevelopment. This article describes briefly four types of multiple equilibria common in macroeconomics, discusses what causes them, and reviews briefly what they teach us about economic policy.

Typology and examples

Multiple equilibria occur in dynamic economies whenever the laws of motion that describe macroeconomic states over time admit more than one solution sequence or, more broadly, several asymptotic states. The simplest mathematical example is a set valued, piecewise linear, deterministic law of motion for a scalar state variable $x(t)$, expressed in terms of a vector $v = (A, B, m, a, b)$ of fundamental parameters:

$$x(t + 1) = f(x(t), v) = mx(t) + a \ \text{if} \ 0 < x(t) < A$$
$$= g(x(t), v) = mx(t) + b \ \text{if} \ B < x(t)$$

$$(1)$$

for all $t = 0, 1, \ldots,$ *with* $0 < m < 1, 0 < A, 0 < B, 0 < a < b$, *and possibly some initial condition* $x(0) > 0$ *fixed by history.*

For different values of the parameter vector v, eq. (1) illustrates explicitly three major types of multiple equilibria: *indeterminacy from missing initial conditions*, *indeterminacy from multiple laws of motion*, and *multiple attractors*. A fourth type, *non-fundamental state variables* or *sunspots*, occurs when we randomly combine the two laws of motion f and g. All four types are associated with excessively volatile behaviour, that is, with macroeconomic states exhibiting abnormal sensitivity to small changes in fundamentals.

Missing initial conditions is the simplest and best-known type of indeterminacy. Suppose, for example, that there is a unique law of motion f, that is, the parameters A and B are infinitely large. If $x(0)$ is an initial price or, more generally, a *jump variable* that is not predetermined by history but emerges instead from forward-looking markets, then there is a one-dimensional continuum of solutions $x(t,a)$ to eq. (1) indexed on the indeterminate initial condition $x(0)$:

$$log(x(t, a) - a/(1 - m))$$
$$= t \ log \ m + log(x(0) - a/(1 - m))$$

$$(2)$$

More generally, an indeterminacy with $S - I$ degrees of freedom appears in any dynamic economy when: (*a*) history predetermines I initial conditions; (*b*) the law of motion has S stable eigenvalues; and (*c*) $I < S$. Equation (2) illustrates the case $(S, I) = (1, 0)$. A major set of economic examples for this kind of multiplicity comes from overlapping generations models. Fiat money in a dynamically inefficient exchange economy (Wallace, 1980) has an indeterminate steady state with worthless money at which $(S, I) = (1, 0)$ because history does not fix the initial price of money. Public debt in a dynamically inefficient production economy (Diamond, 1965) leads to an indeterminate steady state, with worthless public debt and $(S, I) = (2, 1)$ because the price of debt is also a jump variable. Finally, two-sector growth environments (Galor, 1992), in which the distribution of capital between sectors is again a jump variable, exhibit indeterminacy with $(S, I) = (2, 1)$ whenever the consumption good is more capital-intensive than the investment good.

Multiple laws of motion describe a less understood but more pernicious kind of indeterminacy that arises even if there are no jump variables. Examples of this phenomenon are growth models with private information or limited enforcement (Azariadis and Smith, 1998; Azariadis and Kaas, 2008) as well as Markov switching models in time-series econometrics and empirical finance (Hamilton, 1994). To illustrate, let us choose the parameter vector v in eq. (1) so that

$$(1 - m)B < a < b < (1 - m)A \qquad (3)$$

Then the two laws of motion, f and g, overlap in the interval (B, A); each of them has a steady state, $a/(1 - m)$ and $b/(1 - m)$ respectively, which is a suitable initial condition for the *other* law. If $x(t, a)$ and $x(t, b)$ are dynamic equilibria for the two laws in eq. (2), then for any initial condition $x(0)$ in the interval (B, A), we can write down a deterministic general solution $z(t)$ that combines regimes f and g in *any arbitrary time sequence*, that is,

$$z(t) = x(t, a) \quad \text{for some } t$$
$$= x(t, b) \quad \text{for all other } t \qquad (4)$$

For each $x(0)$, we may freely select either regime in each time period. In particular, choosing the same regime every period leads to the steady state of that regime; switching regimes periodically leads to deterministic periodic cycles, as in Grandmont (1985), and so on.

Sunspot equilibria are mixtures of multiple deterministic equilibria – static ones as in Cass and Shell (1983) or dynamic ones as in Azariadis (1981) – connected by a *non-fundamental* or *extraneous* random variable. Market sentiment, investor beliefs, and consensus forecasts are three examples of extraneous random variables which often take on more colourful names like 'animal spirits', 'sunspots' or 'self-fulfilling prophecies'. A simple illustration of a non-fundamental state variable is a lottery $s(t)$ played each period over the intercept, a or b, of the two laws of motion in eq. (1). For instance, if $s(t)$ is a two-state Markov process, then $s(t) = s(t - 1)$, with probability $p(a)$ if $s(t - 1) = a$, and with probability $p(b)$ if $s(t - 1) = b$. The general stochastic solution $Z(t, s(t))$ to eq. (1) shows how outcomes depend on the non-fundamental macroeconomic state $s(t)$. Specifically,

$$\textit{If } s(t - 1) = a, \textit{then } z(t, s(t)) = x(t, a) \;\; w.p.p(a)$$
$$= x(t, b) \;\; w.p.1 - p(a)$$
$$\textit{If } s(t - 1) = b, \textit{then } z(t, s(t)) = x(t, a) \;\; w.p.1 - p(b)$$
$$= x(t, b) \;\; w.p.p(b)$$
$$(5)$$

The last type of non-uniqueness, *multiple attractors*, describes environments with several asymptotic states. Here long-run values of macroeconomic states depend on the corresponding initial values, as in Murphy, Shleifer and Vishny (1989), Azariadis and Drazen (1990), and Matsuyama (1991). We call these environments 'non-ergodic' or ones in which 'history matters'. For example, suppose we pick the parameter vector v in eq. (1) to eliminate the overlap between regimes f and g, and obtain one piecewise linear law of motion. Specifically, we replace (3) by

$$a < (1 - m)A < (1 - m)B < b \qquad (6)$$

Then, for each initial $x(0)$, the general deterministic solution $z(t)$ to eq. (1) is a unique step function, which traces the law f up to $x = A$, and jumps to the other law g at that point. Mathematically,

$$z(t) = x(t, a) \;\; \textit{if } z(t - 1) < A$$
$$= x(t, b) \;\; \textit{if } z(t - 1) > A \qquad (7)$$

Equilibrium here is completely determinate and utterly predictable if history fixes $x(0)$, but the asymptotic state is $a/(1 - m)$ if $x(0) < A$, and $b/(1 - m)$ if $x(0) > A$. History *matters* in this situation because small or temporary shocks to the macroeconomic state $z(t)$ can have substantial and long-lasting consequences if that state is anywhere near the critical value A.

Causes

Dynamic inefficiency and dynamic complementarities are the two most common proximate causes of multiple equilibrium in macroeconomic models. Dynamic inefficiency is a property of economies with very patient consumers who are energetic savers at low interest rates. For example, holders of short-term US Treasury bills in the last 50 years seem content with an average real pre-tax annual yield of about one per cent. Very patient savers are willing to invest in *bubbles*, paying top dollar for assets with low dividends. Bubbles themselves (Tirole, 1985; Shiller, 1989) are notoriously indeterminate objects in their initial conditions and laws of motion; they may deflate now, later or not at all, depending on investor sentiment.

Economies with externalities, increasing returns and, most notably, imperfect asset markets often exhibit complementarities in production or consumption which cause excess demands for consumption goods and productive factors to bend backward instead of sloping downward. The typical outcome is several steady states and several laws of motion or *stable manifolds*, each one leading to a distinct asymptotic state. In particular, multiple equilibria occur when externalities or increasing returns link the payoffs of each agent with the actions of others, both in strategic environments (Cooper and John, 1988) and in competitive ones (Benhabib and Farmer, 1994). Producers, for example, find it advantageous to raise, hold steady, or lower output in tandem with their industry or the whole national economy.

Imperfect asset markets, especially restrictions on debt and short sales (Bewley, 1986; Kehoe and Levine, 1993; Kiyotaki and Moore, 1997) are an intellectually bountiful and empirically compelling source of complementarities in consumption. This literature motivates restrictions on short sales by the collateral requirements of creditors and, more generally, as a deterrent to debtor default. Short-sales constraints depend on the excess payoff of solvency (which guarantees unfettered participation in future asset markets) over default (which restricts trading in future asset markets). Constraints on short sales are tighter the smaller this excess payoff is because smaller excess payoffs strengthen the temptation to default.

Debt constraints cause two dynamic complementarities in consumption, one through prices and the other through quantities (Azariadis and Kaas, 2007). Either one may be sufficient to overcome the intertemporal substitution effect embedded in the consumer's utility function. Specifically, price changes create a dynamic complementarity when the ordinary income effect is amplified by a relaxation of binding short-sale restrictions. The same outcome is achieved by quantity changes when an anticipated relaxation of future constraints increases the current payoff to solvency, and to continued market participation, thus slackening today's constraints.

Lessons for policy

What is the function of economic policy in a deterministic world of many steady states like the one described in eq. (7)? What should policy do in the stochastic world of eq. (5) where non-fundamental variables like beliefs, forecasts, consumer sentiment, 'sunspots', or 'animal spirits' could be every bit as important as fundamentals? Dynamic economies with several asymptotic states have two special properties: long-run performance depends on the starting state $x(0)$; and temporary shocks may have permanent consequences. Any economy that is headed towards an inferior or undesirable steady state may be shocked temporarily until it finds a path leading to a more desirable state. In growth models with many asymptotic states, these shocks are easy to achieve in principle via short-lasting gifts of physical or human capital, by forgiving international debt, and so on. The

US-supported Marshall Plan for Europe did exactly that in the 1940s and 1950s. Africa seems in need of a similar plan now but the internal situation in that continent is more problematic than Europe's was at the end of the Second World War.

A bigger conceptual, as distinct from political, challenge is to formulate policies appropriate for environments swayed by non-fundamental variables and vulnerable to spurious volatility. If equilibria were well described by the stochastic process of eq. (5), could we find an economic policy to eliminate the unnecessary randomness, and bolster among consumers the belief that the economy is headed toward the more desirable of the two steady states, say, $b/(1 - m)$? Viewing economic policy as *equilibrium selection* is fairly widespread in the monetary policy literature (Woodford, 2003), and broadly consistent with monetary neutrality. On this view, credible monetary policy may be unable to influence the set of possible long-run equilibria, but it does bear on which one the economy selects. In eq. (5), for example, reactive policy rules may be unable to change the laws of motion f and g but they can still deliver the long-run state $b/(1 - m)$ if they influence the public's beliefs about the long-run likelihood of each state. All it takes to achieve the high state is nudging the two mixing probabilities, $p(a)$ towards zero and $p(b)$ towards 1.

COSTAS AZARIADIS

See also **animal spirits; bubbles.**

Bibliography

Azariadis, C. 1981. Self-fulfilling prophecies. *Journal of Economic Theory* 25, 380–96.

Azariadis, C. and Drazen, A. 1990. Threshold externalities in economic development. *Quarterly Journal of Economics* 105, 501–26.

Azariadis, C. and Kaas, L. 2008. Credit and growth under limited commitment. *Macroeconomic Dynamics* 12 (Supp. 1).

Azariadis, C. and Smith, B. 1998. Financial intermediation and regime switching in business cycles. *American Economic Review* 88, 516–36.

Benhabib, J. and Farmer, R. 1994. Indeterminacy and increasing returns. *Journal of Economic Theory* 63, 19–41.

Bewley, T. 1986. Dynamic implications of the form of the budget constraint. In *Models of Economic Dynamics*, ed. H. Sonnenschein. New York: Springer Verlag.

Cass, D. and Shell, K. 1983. Do sunspots matter? *Journal of Political Economy* 91, 193–227.

Cooper, R. and John, A. 1988. Coordinating coordination failures in Keynesian models. *Quarterly Journal of Economics* 103, 441–64.

Diamond, P. 1965. National debt in a neoclassical growth model. *American Economic Review* 55, 1126–50.

Duffy, J. and Fisher, E. 2005. Sunspots in the laboratory. *American Economic Review* 95, 510–29.

Galor, O. 1992. A two-sector overlapping generations model. *Econometrica* 60, 351–86.

Grandmont, J.-M. 1985. On endogenous competitive business cycles. *Econometrica* 53, 995–1045.

Hamilton, J. 1994. *Time Series Analysis*. Princeton: Princeton University Press.

Kehoe, T. and Levine, D. 1993. Debt-constrained asset markets. *Review of Economic Studies* 60, 865–88.

Kiyotaki, N. and Moore, J. 1997. Credit cycles. *Journal of Political Economy* 105, 221–48.

Matsuyama, K. 1991. Increasing returns, industrialization, and indeterminacy of equilibrium. *Quarterly Journal of Economics* 106, 617–50.

McCallum, B. 1990. New classical macroeconomics: a sympathetic account. In *The State of Macroeconomics*, ed. S. Honkapohja. Oxford: Basil Blackwell.

Murphy, K., Shleifer, A. and Vishny, R. 1989. Industrialization and the big push. *Journal of Political Economy* 97, 1003–26.

Shiller, R. 1989. *Market Volatility*. Cambridge, MA: MIT Press.

Tirole, J. 1985. Asset bubbles and overlapping generations. *Econometrica* 53, 1499–528.

Wallace, N. 1980. The overlapping generations model of fiat money. In *Models of Monetary Economies*, ed. J. Kareken and N. Wallace. Minneapolis: Federal Reserve Bank of Minneapolis.

Woodford, M. 2003. *Interest and Prices*. Princeton: Princeton University Press.

multiplier–accelerator interaction

The phrase 'multiplier–accelerator' refers to a combination of a theory of income as determined by investment and a theory of investment as determined by the rate of change of income.

The concept of multiplier is usually attributed to Richard Kahn (1931), from whom it was adopted by Keynes and used as a building block for his General Theory. The idea was probably shared by a number of European economists in the Thirties and was certainly known to Michael Kalecki, independently of Keynesian influence.

The theory of multiplier in its pure (and static) form can be described thus. In a capitalist economy, investment can always be realized in real terms. The necessary saving will be made available by means of corresponding variations of the level of income, given the propensity to save. With generally underutilized capacity and labour and fixed prices – the most common hypothesis – *real* income will take whatever value generates a flow of saving equal to planned investment. Alternatively, in the presence of supply constraints, the level of prices will adjust and deflate consumption expenditure so as to make available the real resources required for investment.

The former, 'fixprice' version of this simple relation can be stated in the form of algebraic equations, as follows

$$Y = C + I, \tag{1}$$

$$C = cY, \quad c = 1 - s \tag{2}$$

$$I = \bar{I} \tag{3}$$

where Y, C, I indicate, respectively, actual income, consumption and investment; $\bar{I}$ is desired investment; c and s are the propensities to consume and to save, respectively.

Elementary manipulation yields:

$$Y = (1/s)\bar{I} \tag{4}$$

where $(1/s)$ measures the multiplier and the causal relation runs from right to left.

The concept of accelerator appeared in the economic literature much earlier than the *General Theory* and was perhaps first developed by Aftalion (1909) and J.M. Clark (1917). It is based on the idea that the relation between productive capacity (somewhat measured by a scalar quantity, the capital stock) and production can vary only within narrow limits and, in a first approximation, may be taken as a constant.

The constancy of the capital–output ratio may be defended on the basis of two main arguments:

(i) Technical coefficients are fixed (or change little) even though the interest rate may vary: in economists' parlance, the isoquants are L-shaped. Whatever the plausibility of this hypothesis may be from an engineering point of view, it is difficult to accept it on economic grounds. Indeed, when 'capital' is a vectorial quantity (i.e. a list of different capital goods), the capital–output ratio depends both on technical coefficients and on relative prices and the rate of interest.

(ii) Technical coefficients vary, within a certain technology, as functions of the rate of interest. If the latter is constant so are the former.

The assumption on (ii) may be accepted or rejected for lack of realism but is formally correct. On the other hand, it is also consistent with the fix-price approach to income determination. In its starkest form, the accelerator (Harrod called it 'the Relation') can be described by the equation

$$K = vY, \tag{5}$$

(where K indicates the capital stock and v the desired capital–output ratio) or, in its incremental form

$$I = v\dot{Y} \tag{6}$$

where an overdot indicates the derivative with respect to time.

The idea came naturally to combine multiplier and accelerator and derive a model 'complete' in the sense that, given initial conditions, it determines the time evolution of capital stock and income. This was first attempted in the late 1930s by Harrod (1936, 1939) and, in a more mathematical manner, by Samuelson (1939). In the subsequent years, a substantial part of the literature on cycle and growth was also based on the interaction between multiplier and accelerator.

In order to discuss this idea formally, let us couple equations (4) and (6). We shall obtain

$$sY = v\dot{Y} \tag{7}$$

and

$$(\dot{Y}/Y) = (s/v) \tag{8}$$

Equation (8) represents the proportional rate of growth of income as a function of the propensity to save and the acceleration coefficient and was first investigated by Harrod and Domar, after whom it has been named ever since.

The model described by equations (1)–(8) implicitly assumes that equality always holds between demand (=consumption+investment) and supply (=income), as well as between actual and desired consumptions, the results may become drastically different. This line of research was pursued early by Samuelson, Hicks and, in an apparently very different context, Kalecki, and provided the basis for a theory of the trade cycle which prevailed in the economic profession in the early post-World War II years (the best reference is perhaps Phillips, 1954).

Suppose that, while desired and actual consumption are still equal, discrepancies are permitted to exist between demand and supply and between actual and desired investment. We therefore need to replace the relevant equilibrium conditions

$$\dot{Y} = C + I \qquad (\text{or equivalently, } sY = I)$$

and

$$I = v\dot{Y}$$

by adjustment mechanisms which reflect economic agents' reactions to undesired situations.

The most commonly used such adjustments are those of a tâtonnement type, according to which the relevant variables change at a rate proportional to the differences between their desired and actual values. In terms of our model, we have

$$\dot{Y} = \tau_y[(C + I) - Y] = \tau_y[I - sY], \tag{9}$$

$$\dot{I} = \tau_y[v\dot{Y} - I], \tag{10}$$

where τ_y and τ_i are the (positive) speeds of adjustment of income and investment. The equation (9) can be interpreted as a (typically Keynesian) situation in which,

prices being fixed and potential supply unlimited, producers are constrained only by demand and adjust their production in relation to (positive or negative) excess demand.

The system (9)–(10) can be easily transformed into a single second-order differential equation in Y. By choosing the arbitrary unit of measure of time such that $\tau_i = 1$ we have

$$\ddot{Y} + [1 + \tau_y s = \tau_y v]\dot{Y} + \tau_y sY = 0 \tag{11}$$

System (11) has a unique position of stationary equilibrium at $Y = 0$. ('Zero' must be taken here to indicate a level of income determined by factors not considered in the present discussion, such as government expenditure.) Its dynamic behaviour depends on the structural coefficients and may induce decline or growth, in either case with or without fluctuations.

Generally speaking, we may say that the accelerator is an explosive factor in so far as, for given s and τ_y the greater v the more likely it is for the system to grow in time. Moreover, the relative size of the accelerator affects the oscillatory behaviour of the system: if the motion is damped, a large v tends to make the system fluctuate; vice versa, if the motion is explosive, a strong acceleration leads to sustained growth without fluctuations. In agreement with intuitive considerations, large speeds of adjustment tend to produce explosive behaviour, whereas the saving ratio acts as a damper. The effect of these factors on oscillations is more complicated and cannot be ascertained in any obvious way.

A very special and unlikely case arises when we have

$$1 + \tau_y(s - v) = 0 \tag{12}$$

and the time path followed by the system is a pure sinusoid describing a persistent and perfectly regular cycle, neither damped nor explosive. This of course is a watershed situation which would be destroyed by any small perturbation of the model and is therefore not a suitable idealization of economic cycles.

The multiplier–accelerator model constitutes a rough but effective idealization of certain basic mechanisms deemed to determine or influence cycles and growth in a capitalist economy under certain specific circumstances.

Two major extensions of the model, which have made it theoretically more robust (and complicated), should be mentioned in concluding this entry.

First of all, the assumption that the structural coefficients are constant may be dropped and they may instead be treated as functions of the level (or the rate of change) of income, thus making the model nonlinear. Formal investigation of nonlinear multiplier–accelerator models was initiated in the 1950s by Richard Goodwin (1951a and 1951b) and is still a very active area of research. Nonlinear models have two distinct advantages over the linear ones. For one thing, they better correspond to empirical observation of economic facts. Secondly, and most importantly, they can reproduce a far richer (and economically more interesting) diversity of dynamic behaviours. In particular, only they can represent sustained fluctuations of income, i.e. cycles that neither expire nor explode, without requiring very special configurations of parameters for which no economic justification could be found.

A second important extension of the model has been the generalization of some basic results to the multidimensional case. In an economy with an indefinitely large number of sectors the Harrod–Domar equation (7) can be rewritten as

$$[I - A]x = B\dot{x}, \tag{13}$$

where $A \in R^{nxn}$ is the flow input–output matrix, i.e. the generalized propensity to consume; $B \in R^{nxn}$ is the stock input–output matrix, i.e. the generalized accelerator; $x \in R''$ is the vector of production levels; I is of course the identity matrix.

In analogy to the one-dimensional case we can introduce error-adjustment mechanisms for production and investment, obtaining the system of differential equations

$$\ddot{x} + \left\{ T_i + T_y[I - A] - T_i T_y B \right\} \dot{x} + T_i T_y [I - A]x = 0 \tag{14}$$

where T_y and T_i are diagonal matrices whose (positive) elements are the speeds of adjustment of production and investment, respectively, in the various sectors.

The analysis of system (13) is obviously more complex than that of (11), even in the linear case, as now the coefficients are of order n^2. However, it is possible to define multidimensional equivalents of the main explosive and damping factors, and to indicate the conditions for oscillatory behaviour. It is also possible to show that – in perfect analogy to the one-dimensional case – the loss of stability which takes place when the explosive forces (the accelerators) become too strong vis-à-vis the damping forces (saving and lags), leads to cyclical behaviour of the system.

A. MEDIO

See also **acceleration principle; aggregate demand theory; growth and cycles; multiplier analysis; trade cycle.**

Bibliography

Aftalion, A. 1909. La réalité des surproductions générales. *Revue d'économie politique* 23(March), 81–117, 201–29 and 241–59.
Clark, J.M. 1917. Business acceleration and the law of demand: a technical factor in economic cycles. *Journal of Political Economy* 25(March), 217–35.
Domar, E.D. 1946. Capital expansion, rate of growth and employment. *Econometrica* 14(2), April, 137–47.
Goodwin, R. 1951a. The nonlinear accelerator and the persistence of business cycles. *Econometrica* 19(1), January, 1–17.
Goodwin, R. 1951b. Econometrics in business cycle analysis. In *Business Cycles and National Income*, ed. A.H. Hansen, New York: W.W. Norton.
Harrod, R.F. 1936. *The Trade Cycle.* Oxford: Clarendon Press.
Harrod, R.F. 1939. An essay in dynamic theory, *Economic Journal* 49(March), 14–33.
Hicks, J.R. 1950. *A Contribution to the Theory of the Trade Cycle.* Oxford: Clarendon Press.
Kahn, R.F. 1931. The relation of home investment to employment. *Economic Journal* 41(June), 173–98.
Kalecki, M. 1971. *Selected Essays on the Dynamics of the Capitalist Economy 1933–1970.* Cambridge: Cambridge University Press.
Phillips, A.W. 1954. Stabilization policy in a closed economy. *Economic Journal* 64(June), 290–323.
Samuelson, P.A. 1939. Interactions between the multiplier analysis and the principle of acceleration. *Review of Economics and Statistics* 21(2), May, 75–8.

multiplier analysis

What is the effect of a change in the level of investment? Wicksell (1935) was the first economist to pose this question explicitly in the context of his 'pure credit economy'. Voluntary or anticipated saving is not a requirement if the banking system is willing to supply the necessary credit to finance an increase of investment demand. The effect of this increase of investment demand is an increase in the level of prices (if the level of output is fixed or given), or output if there is idle capacity and unemployed labour.

In his *Treatise on Money* (1930) Keynes analyses the same question. Just as in Wicksell's model, in the *Treatise*, investment is independent of current saving. The effects of a change of investment are studied through the *Treatise*'s 'Fundamental Equations' according to which a difference between current (or voluntary) saving and investment will give rise to a change in the price level. It is a pure excess demand effect. Changes in the price level will lead to unforeseen (or windfall) profits or losses which, in turn, will affect producers' next period decision to produce and employ. Windfall profits will have the effect of inducing producers to increase the level of output; losses will have the opposite effect. The effect may not be as mechanical as described here if new informations (concerning, for example, changes in economic policies) come into the picture.

Book IV of the *Treatise* studies the 'credit cycle', that is, the effects of changes in monetary or banking policies on the rate of interest which may have an effect on the decisions to save and invest, and therefore, on the price and output levels. Changes in both the price and output levels are seen as deviations from their long-period or equilibrium counterparts; they are short-period or disequilibrium levels of price and output which, so to speak, oscillate around the equilibrium as defined by the equality between voluntary saving and investment. However, just as in Wicksell's analysis, once the system deviates from the equilibrium position, very little is said in terms of the path towards a new equilibrium; indeed, the latter is not really determined.

Multiplier analysis is very much related to the adjustment process described above. The real *differentia* is that it focuses predominantly on the notions of stability and equilibrium of the process. The most important contributors for the development of the multiplier analysis were Kahn (1931), Keynes (1936) and Kalecki (1971).

The multiplier as an exercise in comparative statics

Let us consider the effects of a change in the level of investment which is known to all the relevant agents of the economy. Also let us temporarily assume that producers of consumption goods fully anticipate the effects of this change in investment on the demand for their products. An increase in the level of investment demand implies a greater level of production of capital goods. The degrees of capacity utilization and employment in the capital goods sector increase, thus leading to higher profits and a greater wage bill. Part of the extra profits and wages earned will be spent in consumption goods; the rest will be saved. The share of profits and wages spent in consumption goods are determined respectively by the propensities to consume out of profits and wages. These, according to Keynes (1936, chs 8 and 9), depend on objective factors (other than income) such as the money wage rate and agents' rates of time-discounting, and subjective factors such as precaution and avarice.

Thus the main effect of an increase in investment is that it induces an increase in consumption, saving, and income. The final effect on the level of income will depend essentially on the propensity to consume of the economy. The greater the propensity to consume, the greater will be the increase in the demand for consumption goods resulting from an initial increase in the income generated in the capital goods sector. The immediate effect on the demand for consumption goods will be given by $C = cI$ where C and I are respectively the levels of consumption and investment, and c is the weighted average of the propensities to consume out of profits and wages. The immediate effect on the level of income will be given by $\Delta Y = \Delta I + c\Delta I$. Note that a second round of the multiplier process will lead to an increase in the level of income given by $\Delta Y = \Delta I + c\Delta I + c^2\Delta I$. In the limit the effect will be given by $\Delta Y = \Delta I + c\Delta I + c^2\Delta I + \ldots = [1/(1 - c)]\Delta I$. The term $1/(1-c)$ is called the investment multiplier. According to Keynes, the multiplier 'tells us that, when

there is an increment of aggregate investment, income will increase by an amount which is $[1/(1-c)]$ times the increment in investment' (Keynes, 1936, p. 115).

Note that the change in the level of saving (ΔS) is given by the propensity to save ($s=1-c$) times the level of income, that is, $\Delta S = s\Delta Y$, which, according to the above analysis, is also equal to the initial change in the level of investment. Thus, through the multiplier mechanism, a change in the level of investment gives rise to an equal level of saving. The multiplier is essentially an equilibrating mechanism. It refers to the adjustment of the economy given an exogenous change, and it determines the equilibrium levels of income and saving associated with different levels of investment demand. It describes the changes in the level of consumption which eventually makes the latter compatible to each level of investment given the propensity to consume of the economy.

The essential difference between the multiplier mechanism and the description of credit cycles found in Keynes's *Treatise on Money* as well as in the analyses of Wicksell and the Swedish economists (Ohlin and Lindhal for example), is that it emphasizes the notion of equilibrium. It determines the new equilibrium configuration associated with any change in the level of investment demand rather than only its immediate effects. Because it is an equilibrating mechanism it must also take into account the stability conditions of the process. In terms of the simple static version discussed above, the only stability condition is that the propensity to consume must be smaller than one. If it were greater than one the system would always explode either to a situation of full employment or zero-employment of the labour force and capacity utilization. As noted by Keynes, 'if the [community] seek to consume the whole of any increment in income, there will be no point of stability and prices with rise without limit' (Keynes, 1936, p. 117). However, since the propensity to consume is always positive, the multiplier is always greater than one which implies that fluctuations in investment will lead to fluctuations of income of greater magnitude. Thus, the workings of the multiplier mechanism itself may be regarded as a source of instability.

The multiplier as an exercise in dynamics

What makes the analysis of the above section static is the fact that it emphasizes the equilibrium configuration associated with a given (and known) level of investment, and a given propensity to consume. The decision to consumer is rather passive and taking it into account does not really make the analysis dynamic. What is most important, however, is that the decisions to produce are not considered. Production takes time, and therefore decisions to produce involve expectations over a period of time. A dynamic approach to the analysis of the multiplier should emphasize the role of time and expectations associated with the decisions to produce.

What is the appropriate time unit for the analysis of the multiplier process if decisions to produce are to be considered explicitly? Following Keynes we shall take the short period as the appropriate time unit. The short period is associated with 'daily' decisions, and daily here stands 'for the shortest interval of time after which the firm is free to revise its decisions as to how much employment to offer' (Keynes, 1936, p. 47). Producers make their decisions as to how much to produce based on their short-period expectations.

On the demand side the object of such expectations are either the expected sale-proceeds or the expected price, that is, the price which the producer expects to get for his product at the end of the period of production. Let us take the expected price as the relevant variable, and assume that the producer knows the remuneration rates of the variable inputs and the shape of his cost curve. Given this information we may assume that the producer goes through the following optimization exercise in order to determine the levels of output and employment: max $E[p]X - wN$ st. $X = F(N, K)$ where $E[p]$ is the expected price, X and N are the levels of output and employment respectively, w is the money-wage rate, K is the stock of capital (assumed to be given), and F is a production function. The level of employment associated with the expected price must satisfy the following condition: $w/E[p] = F'(N^*)$. The level of output is obviously $X^* = F(N^*)$.

Let us assume that the level of investment has been stable for a rather long period of time. Producers of consumption goods know not only the level of investment but also the demand for their products associated with this level. Therefore they are able to form correct expectations concerning the demand for their products, and their price. In short, in each and every period the expected price corresponds to the market price, that is, $E[p] = p$. We now let the level of investment increase but assume that the producers of consumption goods either do not know that the change has taken place or the effect of the change on the demand for their products. If the latter is the case, assume that they underestimate the effect on demand. In either case the actual price will be greater than the expected price associated with the pre-determined level of output (X^*), that is, $p > E[p]$ where p is the market price. In this example producers will experience a windfall profit given by $Q = (p - E[p])X^*$. The same exercise could be carried on taking stocks rather than the price as the adjustment variable (see Hicks, 1974, ch. 1).

The process initiated with a change in investment demand could go on for a long period. Producers would continue to get their expectations wrong, profits or losses would appear, new decisions would be taken and so on. Will producers ever get their prices (and production decisions) right? If we assume that the level of investment will not be affected by changes in short-period expectations, and depending on the way producers form their expectations, they will eventually converge to an equilibrium position. If, for example, producers form their short-period expectations in an adaptive fashion, for certain values of the parameters of the expectation function, the system will converge to a position of rest. For other values of the parameters the system will not converge. This only implies that the way producers form their expectations may affect the stability of the multiplier process and the trajectory of the relevant variables.

Does the way producers form their expectations affect the equilibrium configuration? The answer here is no. If the level of investment is assumed to be given and the process is assumed to be stable (which, again, depends on the parameters of the expectation function), the equilibrium configuration will be exactly the same as the one associated with a process in which producers form their expectations in a rational fashion. By 'rational' here we mean that expectations are recurrently correct. Keynes was aware of this result: in his lecture notes written in 1937 he argued that his principle of effective demand is substantially the same independently of the way expectations are formed (see Keynes, 1973, pp. 180–1).

The multiplier and the notion of 'shifting equilibrium'

So far we have examined the multiplier mechanism assuming that either the level or the expected level of investment is given. In both the static and dynamic analyses the multiplier tells us the levels of income and saving compatible with a given level or expected level of investment. The advantage of these approaches to the multiplier is that they emphasize the notion of equilibrium, that is, they provide a definite result to the effect of a change in investment.

However, once the notion of equilibrium has become clear, we should turn our attention to the interactive relation between the level of investment and the workings of the multiplier. The level of investment is quite a volatile variable. Long-period expectations (which play a central role in the determination of the level of investment) change for various reasons. They change due to changes in the political or international environments; due to changes in economic policies; or due to objective problems of individual industries which tend to affect the expected performance of other industries of the economy. To different states of long-period expectations there corresponds different levels of investment and, therefore, different 'levels of long-period employment' (Keynes, 1936, p. 48). The extent to which short-period expectations are fulfilled may also affect the level of investment. If the actual demand is persistently greater than the expected demand, producers will tend to revise their long-period expectations and investment decisions.

We may associate the notion of 'shifting equilibrium' with the evolution of the economic system as determined by different states of long-period expectations, and therefore, characterized by a sequence of equilibrium configurations of income and saving. By shifting equilibrium Keynes meant 'the theory of a system in which changing views about the future are capable of influencing the present situation' (1936, p. 293).

Distribution and the multiplier

The relationship between the distribution of income (or the real wage) and the multiplier depends on assumptions about the exogeneity or endogeneity of the real wage. In the *General Theory* Keynes assumed perfect competition *cum* profit maximization and decreasing marginal returns which, for a given money-wage rate, implies that the real wage is endogenously determined. It also implies that the greater the levels of employment and output, the smaller the real wage. This result has an important implication for the workings of the Keynesian multiplier. If we assume – as Keynes and Kalecki usually do – that the propensity to consume out of wages is greater than the propensity to consume out of other types of incomes (profits, interests, and so on), as the level of income increases and the real wage falls, the value of the multiplier decreases. Keynes pointed out to this result in the *General Theory*:

> the increase of employment will tend, owing to the effect of diminishing returns, … to increase the proportion of aggregate income which accrues to the entrepreneurs, whose … propensity to consume is probably less than the average for the community as a whole. (1936, p. 121)

Kalecki (1971) assumed constant marginal returns and gave up profit maximization. Instead he assumed that firms determine their prices through a markup over variable costs which, in a closed economy, also determines the real wage. Therefore, according to Kalecki, the real wage is exogenously determined, and does not change as the levels of output and employment change. This means that the multiplier does not change either as the level of output changes; it depends on the propensity to consume out of wages and profits and the level of the markup, both assumed to be constant over the cycle.

EDWARD J. AMADEO

See also **multiplier–accelerator interaction.**

Bibliography

Hicks, J.R. 1974. *The Crisis in Keynesian Economics.* Oxford: Blackwell.
Kahn, R. 1931. The relation of home investment to unemployment. *Economic Journal* 41(June), 173–98. Reprinted in R. Kahn, *Selected Essays on Employment and Growth.* Cambridge: Cambridge University Press, 1972.
Kalecki, M. 1971. *Selected Essays on the Dynamics of the Capitalist Economy.* Cambridge: Cambridge University Press.
Keynes, J.M. 1930. *A Treatise on Money. Vol. 1: The Pure Theory of Money.* London: Macmillan.
Keynes, J.M. 1936. *The General Theory of Employment, Interest and Money.* London: Macmillan.
Keynes, J.M. 1973. *The Collected Writings of John Maynard Keynes,* vol. 14, ed. D.E. Moggridge and E. Johnson. London: Macmillan for the Royal Economic Society.
Wicksell, K. 1935. *Lectures in Political Economy,* vol. 2. London: Routledge & Kegan Paul.

Mun, Thomas (1571–1641)

Thomas Mun, the distinguished mercantilist, was born in London in June 1571 and died in July 1641. He was the third son of John Mun, a mercer, whose father, also John Mun, held the office of provost of the moneyers in the Royal Mint and received a grant of arms in 1562.

Thomas Mun became an extremely wealthy merchant, and a Director (Member of the Committee) of the East India Company in 1615. In 1624 he had the opportunity to serve as Deputy Governor which he declined, but he remained a director until he died.

The East India Company was much criticized because its trade involved exports of bullion (in order to purchase spices). In 1621 Mun was author of a pamphlet, *A Discourse of Trade, from England unto the East-Indies,* in which he set out the benefits that England derived from this trade. His argument was that the same spices (and he details the amounts) would otherwise have been imported from Turkey at three times the sterling cost, and that the purchase of spices in the Indies thus produced satisfactory results for British consumers, while merchants also benefited, and so ultimately did the balance of trade. On Mun's figures the East India Company exported £100,000 of silver yearly to import silk and spices which sold in England for £500,000 (out of which customs duties took a substantial fraction). But only £120,000 of these goods were actually consumed in England, and the remaining £380,000 were re-exported with the consequence that England gained back considerably more bullion than the original outflow of £100,000.

In 1622 he was the leading member of a committee of merchants which submitted evidence to a Commission set up by James I to investigate the causes of the fall in the exchange rate and the loss of specie from which Britain was suffering. Mun was principal author of their first memorandum in 1622, and sole author of later memoranda submitted in 1623. He strongly opposed Malynes' view that the fall in the exchange rate was attributable to conspiratorial behaviour by foreign merchants, and argued that the balance of *trade* was the principal determinant of specie flows and the exchange rate. His memoranda resurfaced in 1664, as chapters in his posthumously published magnum opus, *England's Treasure by Forraign Trade, or the Ballance of our Forraign Trade is* the *Rule of our Treasure*, which Schumpeter has referred to as 'the classic of English mercantilism'. This was published by his son, John Mun, with the imprimatur and personal approval of Charles II's Secretary of State, Sir Henry Bennet.

England's Treasure demolished the previous mercantilist literature which advocated detailed interventionist policies to sustain the English money supply and the exchange rate, such as banning gold exports, currency appreciation, lowering the metallic content of the currency, and encouraging the domestic circulation of foreign coin. Mun reiterated the fundamental balance of payments equation that specie flows must be determined primarily by the excess of exports over imports, and therefore insisted that there could not be a sustained loss of gold and silver while there was a trade surplus, while none of the above expedients could prevent a monetary outflow in the face of a sustained deficit.

His book hammered home the significance of the balance of payments equation, with numerous examples to demonstrate the impotence of detailed interventionist policies to hold or attract bullion while trade was in deficit. At the same time, he developed examples like those in his earlier *Discourse of Trade*, to show how it was ultimately the domestic consumption of imports and not imports as such that needed to be compared with exports to determine the net balance of trade. Imports by English merchants which were not destined for consumption in England were bound to result in equivalent exports, plus of course merchants' profits and duties for the King.

Mun went on to explain the relationship between the balance of trade and the excess of home production over consumption, and to distinguish carefully between the financial interests and impact on the trade balance of Merchants, the Commonwealth (the whole population) and the King. Merchants were solely concerned with profit. The Commonwealth determined the trade balance via the relationship between the aggregate expenditures and incomes of the whole population, while the Sovereign's interest in trade depended considerably upon customs and excise, 'the King by his Customs and Imposts may get notoriously, even when the Merchant notwithstanding shall lose grievously' (p. 147).

Mun may well have been the first to state the celebrated proposition (which Lord Kaldor made much of in the 1970s) that the current account trade surplus must correspond to the sum of the financial surpluses of the public and private sectors. He set out an example where a King enjoys revenues of £900,000, spends £400,000 and accumulates the resulting budget surplus of £500,000. Then if the trade surplus is merely £200,000, the King will

lay up £300,000 more in his Coffers than the whole Kingdom gains from strangers by forraign trade: who sees not then that all the money in such a State, would suddenly be drawn into the Princes treasure, whereby the life of lands and arts must fail and fall to the ruin

both of the publick and private wealth? So that a King who desires to lay up much money must endeavour by all good means to maintain and encrease his forraign trade. (pp. 188–9)

Mun believed that the achievement of a trade surplus on which monetary inflows depended would be best achieved where the population moderated consumption, and merchants enjoyed maximum freedom to exploit opportunities for trade. He has been much praised in the secondary literature for his perception that it was the trade balance that determined specie flows. This has been universally judged vastly superior to the previous literature which recommended piecemeal interventionism in financial markets. According to McCulloch's 1847 *Edinburgh Review* article 'Mun's book was received as the gospel of finance and commercial policy; and his principles ruled for above a century the policy of England, and much longer that of the rest of Europe' (p. 450).

Mun's analysis was superseded in 18th-century England because he failed to go a vital stage further and appreciate the potentially self-correcting nature of the balance of payments. This led Hume and his followers to cease to regard the trade balance as a primary policy objective in comparison with the achievement of a growing capital stock, and increasing levels of output and employment, about which Mun was also deeply concerned.

But those who have been satisfied that the trade balance is self-correcting have sometimes failed to appreciate that a continuing deficit is inevitable where consumption (modern writers would say, domestic absorption) exceeds production. They also lost Mun's perception that in a protectionist world, winning trade away from other countries may permit increases in domestic capital and employment with would not otherwise occur.

WALTER ELTIS

Selected works

1621. *A Discourse of Trade, from England unto the East-Indies*. London.
1664. *England's Treasure by Forraign Trade. Or, The Ballance of our Forraign Trade is the Rule of our Treasure*. London. Repr. in the Economic History Society Reprints of Economic Classics, Oxford, 1928. These works by Mun are both reprinted in J.R. McCulloch, ed., *Early English Tracts on Commerce*, Cambridge: Cambridge University Press, 1952, which is itself a reprint of the London *Political Economy Club's* 1856 publication, and page references are to this edition.

Bibliography

Appleby, J.O. 1978. *Economic Thought and Ideology in Seventeenth-Century England*. Princeton: Princeton University Press.
Heckscher, E.F. 1955. *Mercantilism*, 2 vols. London: Allen & Unwin.

McCulloch, J.R. 1847. Primitive political economy of England. *Edinburgh Review* 172, 426–52.

Schumpeter, J.A. 1954. *History of Economic Analysis*. New York: Oxford University Press.

Supple, B.E. 1970. *Commercial Crisis and Change in England 1600–42*. Cambridge: Cambridge University Press.

Wilson, C. 1957. *Profit and Power: A Study of England and the Dutch Wars*. London: Longmans.

Mundell, Robert (born 1932)

Robert Mundell is one of the key figures in the development of thought in international monetary economics. His work on the IS–LM model in open economies, equilibrium in a world of perfect capital mobility, monetary dynamics in open economies, and optimal currency areas constitutes the core of the research for which Mundell is best known. His work continues to this day to be influential in the analysis of policy decisions in open economies, but an equally important legacy of Mundell's is the role his work played in determining the direction of research in open-economy macroeconomics in the 1960s, 1970s and through to the present. Mundell's work had such a great impact in part because it combined theoretical rigor with elegant presentation. Mundell was awarded the Nobel Prize in 1999 for 'his analysis of monetary and fiscal policy under different exchange rate regimes and his analysis of optimum currency areas'.

Mundell was born in Kingston, Ontario, in 1932. His undergraduate education was undertaken at the University of British Columbia and the University of Washington. He engaged in postgraduate studies at the London School of Economics and received his Ph.D. from MIT in 1956. He taught at Stanford University and the Bologna Center of the School of Advanced International Studies of the Johns Hopkins University, and joined the staff of the International Monetary Fund in 1961. He was a Professor of Economics at the University of Chicago from 1966 to 1971. In 1974 he joined the faculty at Columbia University, where he has spent the remainder of his career.

Mundell is perhaps best known for his work creating an open-economy version of the IS–LM model. Mundell's (1960; 1961; 1962; 1963a) model is still the workhorse model of most undergraduate texts in international macroeconomics. Mundell, like Meade, Metzler, and a few others whose work preceded Mundell's, recognized that the analysis of exchange rates and balance of payments flows must proceed in a monetary general equilibrium framework. Under Mundell's initial formulation, the equilibrium conditions in money markets and goods markets were augmented by an external balance condition. Mundell's concept of external balance was a balance of payments equilibrium, in which the net flow demand for foreign exchange is zero. Demand for foreign exchange comes from importers of goods and from importers of foreign assets. In his initial work, Mundell modelled the demand for foreign assets as a flow that depended on the difference between home and foreign interest rates. As long as there was a positive spread between home and foreign interest rates, capital inflows would persist at a steady rate.

Mundell's special interest was in the analysis of monetary and fiscal policy. He emphasized the importance of the speed of adjustment in capital markets and the role of fixed versus flexible exchange rates in determining the impact of policy changes and the determination of a desirable monetary–fiscal policy mix. His framework was extended and used to consider policy issues by academics and central bankers for many years.

One basic insight of these models concerns the difference in the impact of fiscal and monetary policy under fixed and floating exchange rates. Consider a monetary expansion. Under a floating exchange rate, external balance requires a depreciation of the domestic currency. The monetary expansion lowers interest rates, leading to a capital outflow and a decline in demand for the domestic currency. With sticky nominal goods prices (the hallmark of the Keynesian IS–LM analysis), the depreciation makes imported goods more expensive, so expenditure switches to home goods. This expenditure switching effect would not be present if exchange rates were fixed. Indeed, Mundell (1961) makes the point that in the absence of sterilization (see below) the monetary expansion would be reversed over time. That is, under fixed exchange rates, the monetary expansion leads to a balance of payments deficit. Under a balance of payments deficit, as the central bank's foreign reserves decline, the money supply falls.

In contrast, an expansionary fiscal policy might have greater impact under fixed exchange rates, when capital mobility is high. In the IS–LM framework, an increase in aggregate demand raises interest rates. This should lead to an inflow of capital and an appreciation of the home currency under flexible exchange rates. But the appreciation switches demand away from home goods, thereby dampening the effect of the fiscal expansion. Under fixed exchange rates, the expenditure switching does not occur. Moreover, in the absence of sterilization operations the balance of payments surplus that ensues from the fiscal expansion will lead to a domestic monetary expansion as the central bank acquires foreign reserves.

Note how the analysis of the effects of fiscal expansions depends on the assumption that capital flows respond significantly to changes in the interest rate. If capital flows were not significant, the analysis would be reversed. A fiscal expansion leads to an increase in domestic income. Some of that increased income is spent on imports. There may be increased capital inflows because the interest rate has risen domestically, but if these flows are slight then the decline in the trade balance dominates, so the country's balance of payments deteriorates. Under floating exchange rates, then, there will be a currency depreciation that further boosts aggregate demand. That effect is not present under fixed exchange rates, and indeed there could be a contractionary effect of the balance of payments deficit in the absence of sterilization.

Of special note is Mundell's (1963a) version of his model under the assumption of perfect capital mobility, so that the rates of return on home and foreign nominal bonds are equalized. At one level this paper is a simple extension of his earlier work to consider the extreme case in which capital flows infinitely quickly to equalize rates of return. But at another level the model is fundamentally different. In essence this case turns the external balance condition from a flow equilibrium (analogous to the IS curve) into an asset-market equilibrium condition (analogous to the LM curve.) In this model, for asset markets to be in equilibrium households must be satisfied not only with their holdings of money relative to interest-earning assets (LM) but also with their holdings of domestic bonds relative to foreign bonds. This model laid the foundation for virtually all later work in the field that understands the market for foreign exchange to be an asset market.

The key distinction analytically is that the flow of assets plays no role per se in determining equilibrium in this formulation. For example, the trade balance plays no direct role in establishing the equilibrium in the foreign exchange market. In contrast to many models of the 1950s in which the exchange rate adjusted to set the trade balance to zero, here the trade balance plays a role only in its contribution to the net demand for domestic output. The balance of payments simply reflects the central bank's net accumulation of foreign assets. As Obstfeld (2001) points out, the balance of payments is no longer a relevant indicator of external balance in this setting. By modelling the external balance condition as an asset-market equilibrium, Mundell opened the door for subsequent models that considered the role of expectations in determining exchange rates and laid the foundation for models of balance of payments crises under fixed exchange rates in which speculative attacks play a key role.

Subsequent developments in the field have replaced Mundell's ad hoc formulations of behaviour with optimizing models, and have explicitly modelled expectations formation. But Mundell's work was a cornerstone of the development of more sophisticated models, and open-economy macroeconomic models are still often evaluated by comparing their implications with those of the models of Mundell.

Dynamics was a key concern of Mundell's. Even within the IS–LM framework, Mundell examined the evolution of output, interest rates, exchange rates and prices. Mundell paid special attention to the dynamic effects of balance of payments 'disequilibrium' under fixed exchange rates. When the net private flow demand for foreign exchange is not zero (that is, the sum of the current account and the private component of the capital account is not zero), then, in Mundell's terms, there is balance of payments disequilibrium. Mundell made explicit the distinction between balance of payments flows that were sterilized – so that the monetary base did not change – and policies that allowed the money supply to change automatically when there was balance of payments disequilibrium. Mundell (1961) especially was a precursor of the literature that became known as the 'monetary approach to the balance of payments'. That literature emphasized the automatic adjustment mechanism when there is no sterilization. Most of that analysis was undertaken in classical-style models in which nominal goods prices were assumed to be flexible. Indeed, Mundell (1967) was a contributor in that tradition. But what Mundell's (1961) piece makes clear is that it is the assumption of non-sterilization that is key to understanding the dynamics of adjustment. Even in a world of sticky nominal prices, automatic adjustment to balance of payments disequilibrium can occur through adjustment in the money supply.

Dynamics were central in Mundell's development of what became known as 'the assignment problem'. The question was whether the central bank should be responsible for external balance and fiscal authorities for internal balance, or vice versa. Mundell's answer was that each policy tool should be assigned to the market in which it has the greater effect, which depends on the speed of adjustment of goods markets relative to capital markets. Mundell modelled policymaking in a realistic world in which policymakers have an imperfect understanding of the state of the economy, and in which macroeconomic adjustment to policy changes is slow. These concerns have all but disappeared from more recent research in macroeconomic policymaking, but Mundell's focus still seems relevant. Moreover, Mundell's work recognizes that policymaking at the national level is not in the hands of a single policymaker, but instead involves the interaction of decisions by central banks and fiscal authorities whose actions and goals may not be perfectly coordinated.

Mundell's (1961) paper on optimum currency areas also is still very influential. This paper determines some conditions under which it is optimal for countries to share a common currency. Mundell's view was that there may be some advantage to sharing currencies in terms of reduced transactions costs. But the adoption of a common currency means, of course, that each country is not free to pursue its own independent monetary policy. That loss may not be so large when factors of production can flow freely between the countries in a currency area. If there is a downturn in one country, adjustment can occur through factor flows towards the country with the stronger economy. But if factor mobility is weak, then there is a case for each country to have its own independent money. In general, in Mundell's framework the optimum currency area is determined by a trade-off between these considerations about factor mobility and considerations involving the transactions costs of having many separate currencies. Mundell's work in this area spawned a large literature that considered other factors that determine whether a set of countries were good candidates for adoption of a single currency.

Mundell is also known for his short paper (1963b) that develops what became known as the 'Mundell–Tobin effect'. Mundell argued that inflation reduced the demand for real money balances. That led to a portfolio shift that could induce greater investment in real capital.

Mundell (1957) also made a lasting contribution in pure trade theory. This paper examined the effects of factor mobility in the Heckscher–Ohlin–Samuelson model. Factor mobility could be a substitute for goods trade, just as goods trade could substitute for factor mobility (as in the well-known factor-price equalization theorem.)

The Nobel Prize citation notes that 'Mundell chose his problems with uncommon – almost prophetic – accuracy in terms of predicting the future development of international monetary arrangements and capital markets.' When Mundell wrote much of his influential work in the early 1960s, much of the world was on a fixed-exchange rate system – although his native Canada had a freely floating exchange rate. Moreover, there were still significant barriers to international flows of capital that had been erected in the 1930s and 1940s, even among advanced industrialized countries. Nonetheless, Mundell focused in much of his work on the contrast between the fixed and floating exchange rate systems, with an emphasis on the role of capital mobility. Only in the early 1970s did most of the advanced world move to floating exchange rates, and obstacles to capital flows were gradually eliminated in the decades following Mundell's early writings. His work on optimum currency areas was frequently cited in the economic analysis that preceded the introduction of the euro.

Many of Mundell's contributions are collected in *International Economics* (1968). Excellent brief surveys of Mundell's work can be found in Royal Swedish Academy of Sciences (1999) and Obstfeld (2001). Mundell (2001) provides an interesting history of the development of some of Mundell's work.

CHARLES ENGEL

See also **international capital flows; international financial institutions (IFIs); international monetary institutions.**

Selected works

1957. International trade and factor mobility. *American Economic Review* 47, 321–55.
1960. The monetary dynamics of international adjustment under fixed and flexible exchange rates. *Quarterly Journal of Economics* 74, 227–57.
1961. A theory of optimum currency areas. *American Economic Review* 51, 657–65.
1962. The appropriate use of monetary and fiscal policy for internal and external stability. *IMF Staff Papers* 9, 70–9.

1963a. Capital mobility and stabilization policy under fixed and flexible exchange rates. *Canadian Journal of Economics* 29, 475–85.
1963b. Inflation and real interest. *Journal of Political Economy* 71, 280–3.
1967. Barter theory and the monetary mechanism of adjustment. In *Capital Movements and Economic Development*, ed. J. Adler. London: Macmillan.
1968. *International Economics*. New York: Macmillan.
2001. On the history of the Mundell–Fleming model. Keynote speech. *IMF Staff Papers* 47(special issue), 215–27.

Bibliography

Obstfeld, M. 2001. International macroeconomics: beyond the Mundell–Fleming model. *IMF Staff Papers* 47(special issue) 1–39.
Royal Swedish Academy of Sciences. 1999. *Bank of Sweden Prize in Economic Sciences in Memory of Alfred A. Nobel, 1999*. Online. Available at http://nobelprize.org/economics/laureates/1999/ecoback99.pdf, accessed 9 August 2005.

municipal bonds

Municipal bonds differ from most other securities because of their special tax status. Interest payments on bonds issued by state and local governments in the United States are exempt from federal income tax. Most states with income taxes also exempt their own interest payments from tax. The federal income tax exemption for municipal bond interest is usually justified on the grounds that it reduces borrowing costs for states and localities, thereby facilitating their investment in public infrastructure.

When the federal income tax was enacted in 1913, there was some question as to the constitutionality of such a federal tax on interest paid by states and localities. In 1988, the Supreme Court affirmed the federal prerogative to tax such interest in the case of *South Carolina v. Baker*. The tax exemption for municipal bond interest should therefore be viewed in the same way as any other tax expenditure, namely as a political decision about the structure of income taxation.

There are three types of municipal bonds: *general obligation bonds*, which are backed by the 'full faith and credit' of the borrowing jurisdiction; *revenue bonds*, which are backed by the stream of income from a particular project such as a highway or publicly operated power plant; and *private purpose bonds*, which are tax-exempt bonds issued by private borrowers with the authorization of a state or local government. Only general obligation or 'GO' bonds have a potential claim on the tax revenues of a state and local government. The interest payments on revenue bonds are dependent on the revenues associated with the project that issued the bonds. Private purpose bonds are typically used to finance private sector projects that are deemed beneficial to the state or local economy or community; in practice these bonds finance a wide range of activities. The market value of outstanding tax-exempt bonds in 2006 was 2.3 trillion dollars according to estimates from the Federal Reserve Board Flow of Funds Accounts. GO bonds account for roughly 40 per cent of outstanding tax-exempt debt.

While municipal bond interest is generally exempt from federal income taxation, the relevant tax rules are complicated in some situations. For example, retirees who receive Social Security benefits must include tax-exempt bond interest in the income concept that is used to determine how much of their Social Security income is included in taxable income. In addition, the interest paid on many private purpose bonds is taxable under the federal alternative minimum tax (AMT). While the AMT affected only 3.5 million taxpayers in 2006, projections suggest that provided there are no changes in the basic structure of the tax, it will apply to more than 20 million taxpayers by 2010. Bonds that are not exempt from the AMT typically offer investors a higher yield than bonds that pay interest that is completely tax exempt.

In part as a result of changes in the tax law, there have been changes over time in the ownership patterns for municipal bonds. Prior to 1986, commercial banks were the primary holders of short-term municipal bonds while households and insurance companies were the primary holders of long-term municipals. The Tax Reform Act of 1986 sharply limited the incentives for banks to hold tax-exempt bonds, and since then the ownership mix has shifted towards households. According to Flow of Funds data for the third quarter of 2006, households were the direct owners of 37 per cent of outstanding municipal bonds. Mutual funds, which are largely owned by households, accounted for another 33 per cent. Commercial banks hold seven per cent, while property and casualty insurance companies hold 14 per cent.

Investors who hold municipal bonds avoid paying income taxes on their interest income, but they pay an 'implicit tax' when the pre-tax interest rate on municipal bonds is lower than that on an equally risky taxable bond. The yield spread between taxable and municipal bonds is often summarized by the *implicit tax rate*. This is the value of θ for which $(1 - \theta)R_T = R_M$ where R_T is the yield on newly issued Treasury bonds and R_M is the yield on prime grade municipal bonds of comparable maturity. This relationship is only satisfied by newly issued taxable and municipal bonds under the assumption that investors plan to hold these bonds to maturity. Poterba (1986) shows that with forward-looking investors, the implicit tax rate measured from current bond yields reflects not just current marginal tax rates on taxable interest but future marginal tax rates as well. For seasoned bonds, the tax treatment of differences between the

purchase price of the bond and the par value complicates the calculation of the implicit tax rate. More generally, when investors sell their bonds before maturity, changes in bond prices may result in taxable capital gains or losses. The definition of the implicit tax rate also assumes that Treasury bonds and prime grade municipals are equally risky, an assumption that some might question.

The implicit tax rate on municipal bonds varies across bond maturities at a given point in time, and it varies over time in part as a result of changes in tax rates and tax rules. During the first week of 2007, the interest rate on 30-year GO bonds with an AAA rating was 4.14 per cent, while the yield on a 30-year Treasury bond was 4.59 per cent. The implicit tax rate based on these values is 9.8 per cent, well below the top statutory marginal tax rate on individual investors, 35 per cent. The yield spread between AAA-rated municipal bonds and AAA-rated corporate bonds is larger, but this comparison raises the challenge of risk adjustment. For the same week, the yield on one-year AAA-rated municipals was 3.53 per cent, while that on one-year Treasury bonds was 4.92 per cent. The implicit tax rate at the one year maturity was therefore 28.3 per cent.

One of the challenges in analysing the municipal bond market is explaining why implicit tax rates are substantially below top statutory rates. Chalmers (1998) discusses various potential explanations and rejects the possibility that differential default risk explains this long-standing pattern. The yield curve puzzle has motivated research on the relative pricing of taxable and tax-exempt bonds. Green (1993) argues for moving beyond yield-to-maturity analysis, such as that underlying the foregoing implicit tax rate computations, and developing a more subtle analysis of the tax-exempt bond market.

The key insight in Green (1993) and several subsequent studies is that fully taxable individual investors are unlikely to regard newly issued tax-exempt bonds and newly issued taxable bonds as competitive investment alternatives. If such investors chose to hold taxable bonds, they should do so by holding bonds that generate income in a way that generates less tax liability than a newly issued bond. The opportunities to earn bond returns that face a lighter tax burden are greater at longer than at shorter maturities, because divergences between the purchase price of a bond and its par value are potentially greater at long maturities. This role of tax-wise investing appears to receive empirical support in yield curve comparisons at different maturities. It may help to explain why implied tax rates in the municipal bond market are often lower for longer-maturity than for shorter-maturity bonds.

Whether the policy of exempting interest on state and local government bonds from federal taxation is an efficient method of encouraging capital formation by states and localities is a long-standing subject of debate. The answer turns on the difference between the implicit marginal tax rate on municipal bonds, which determines the interest saving of state and local government borrowers, and the weighted-average marginal tax rate of municipal bond investors, with weights equal to the tax-exempt interest receipts of each investor. The latter determines the federal government's revenue cost from exempting interest on state and local government obligations from tax. If the revenue cost exceeds the interest saving, it would cost less for the federal government to provide cash transfers to state and local governments equal to the amount of their current interest saving, while taxing interest on their bonds, than to pursue the current policy of tax exemption. In 2002, the weighted-average marginal tax rate for individual investors who received tax-exempt interest was 30.2 per cent. Feenberg and Poterba (1991) describe the calculation of such marginal tax rates. Since the implicit tax rate on 20-year municipal bonds and Treasuries varied between ten and 20 per cent during calendar 2002, the revenue cost of the exemption for households appears to exceed the interest saving for state and local government borrowers.

The progressivity of the federal income tax schedule is a key determinant of the efficiency of policies that exempt interest from taxation. When the yield spread between taxable and municipal bonds is determined by the marginal tax rate of the *lowest* tax rate investor who holds those bonds, but the revenue cost is determined by the weighted average marginal tax rate of the investors who hold municipal bonds, then the efficiency cost of the tax exemption will be greater when the top marginal tax rates affect many but not all municipal bond investors, and when the top rates are substantially higher than the rates on lower-income households.

When investors have access to taxable and tax-exempt bonds of equal risk, market equilibrium should involve investor clienteles in which investors segment themselves according to their tax rates. High tax rate investors should hold tax-exempt bonds, while low tax rate investors should hold taxable bonds. In practice, this separation does not occur. Poterba and Samwick (2003) show that among households that hold tax-exempt bonds, 55 per cent also hold taxable bonds. In contrast, only 15 per cent of the households that hold taxable bonds also hold tax-exempt bonds. There are risks inherent to holding municipal bonds, such as the risk of tax change, that are difficult to hedge and may incline investors to diversify their portfolios. This may explain why most investors who hold municipal bonds also hold taxable bonds.

There are many innovative products in the municipal bond market, including variable rate municipals, insured municipal bonds, and zero coupon tax-exempt bonds. The bonds issued by several large issuers, particularly large states and revenue authorities, trade in active aftermarkets, but the markets for many smaller municipal bond issues are not very liquid.

JAMES M. POTERBA

See also **bonds; fiscal federalism; local public finance; tax expenditures; taxation of income.**

Bibliography

Chalmers, J.M.R. 1998. Default risk cannot explain the muni puzzle: evidence from municipal bonds that are secured by U.S. Treasury obligations. *Review of Financial Studies* 11, 281–308.

Feenberg, D.R. and Poterba, J.M. 1991. Which households own municipal bonds? Evidence from tax returns. *National Tax Journal* 44, 93–104.

Green, R.C. 1993. A simple model of the taxable and tax-exempt yield curves. *Review of Financial Studies* 6, 233–64.

Poterba, J.M. 1986. Explaining the yield spread between taxable and tax-exempt bonds. In *Studies in State and Local Public Finance*, ed. H. Rosen. Chicago: University of Chicago Press.

Poterba, J.M. and Samwick, A. 2003. Taxation and household portfolio composition: U.S. evidence from the 1980s and 1990s. *Journal of Public Economics* 87, 5–38.

Musgrave, Richard Abel (1910–2007)

Born in Koenigstein, Germany, Musgrave was educated at Heidelberg (where he obtained a Diplom Volkswirt in 1933) and at Harvard University (where he obtained his Ph.D. in 1937). After serving at the Federal Reserve System in Washington, he held appointments at a number of leading North American universities and ended his formal teaching career at Harvard, where he was Professor Emeritus. He was an economic adviser to a number of governments, headed foreign tax commissions, and served as editor of the *Quarterly Journal of Economics*.

Richard Musgrave is best known for his outstanding treatise *The Theory of Public Finance*, published in 1959 at a time when social expenditures were growing rapidly throughout the industrial world, and when poverty and social justice had become primary policy concerns. This book, which is comprehensive, has served as a fundamental source for scholars and as a teaching reference. In it Musgrave summarizes and extends his original contributions to expenditure theory and the theory of taxation, provides an extensive review of the classical literature in public finance, and includes a thorough discussion of fiscal and monetary policy developed from a Keynesian perspective. One of the great strengths of the book is Musgrave's broad knowledge of the early European masters of public finance, notably Wicksell and Lindahl. By reviewing the classical writers and relating his theory of the public household to their work, Musgrave built an essential bridge between earlier ideas and the development of modern public goods theory.

Musgrave made significant contributions to virtually all areas of public finance. He wrote on the theory of fiscal federalism and revenue sharing, international aspects of taxation, alternative measures of income tax progressivity, land value taxation, the theory of fiscal sociology, and the effects of tax policy on private capital formation, as well as on various aspects of debt and monetary policy. His most original and lasting contributions can be grouped into two categories: taxation theory, which includes three major contributions, and public goods theory, in particular his theory of the public household.

One of Musgrave's most distinguished contributions to taxation theory is his joint paper with E.D. Domar on the effects of taxes on risk taking (1944). The authors show that taxes on capital income will not necessarily decrease investment in relatively risky ventures once the loss offset provisions of the tax and its income effects are accounted for. In fact, it is quite likely that risk taking will be encouraged by an interest income tax. This article ranks with the half-dozen most influential articles on taxation written since the mid-1950s, and it represents the first application of the theory of choice under uncertainty to taxation. Its conclusions have proved to be quite robust to more general formulations of the theory of risk taking.

Musgrave's second contribution to taxation theory is his theoretical and empirical work on tax incidence. He has developed most of the general concepts currently used in incidence analysis, and, in one of the first general equilibrium analyses, established the fundamental equivalences between direct and indirect taxes and between general and specific factor taxes. These contributions clarify a much confused issue: whether general excise taxes are shifted forwards to purchasers of taxed commodities or backwards to providers of factor services. They also established the importance of both uses and sources aspects of incidence theory.

Musgrave's work on the allocation of tax burden (1951) to different income groups is a basic contribution to applied analysis and has been the starting point for all subsequent studies on tax burdens by income classes. More recently (1974) he refined this earlier work and covered the distributive aspects of expenditures as well as taxes. In another important study, *The Shifting of the Corporation Tax* (1963), with M. Krzyzaniak, Musgrave developed the first econometric estimates of incidence and concluded that the corporate profits tax is shifted forwards, a finding which gave rise to a large literature.

Musgrave extended and refined the normative theory of equitable taxation and its implications for income taxation and the concept of horizontal equity (1959, ch. 8). Later, in 1976, he broke new ground by introducing the concept of equal options as the basis for horizontal equity. Within this framework, two persons are considered to be in equal positions and should be treated equally if they face the same options. Thus, two persons with the same present value of lifetime earnings would be considered equal. One of the important insights of this concept is that under

certain assumptions a consumption-based tax system is more equitable than an income tax system: the first treats equals equally while the second discriminates against persons who save relatively more.

The theory of the public household, Musgrave's unifying perspective on public goods, has provided the basis for many of his insights into that fundamental topic. This theory distinguishes between three branches of government – the allocative branch, which provides for social goods and deals with related questions of efficiency, the distribution branch, which modifies the distribution of income as determined by market forces and inheritance, and the stabilization branch, which is concerned with unemployment and overall economic stability.

He stresses that the failure to distinguish between the three different objectives of budget policy will involve unnecessary conflict and inefficient policy design. For instance, different voters may agree on the objective of fiscal stabilization but may fail to enact a proportional cut in taxes in recession if the proposals to combat recession will increase expenditures or change the distribution of income. Hence, one of the practical principles to emerge from the three-budget classification is that expenditure levels and the distribution of income, or tax shares of individual groups, should be determined independently of stabilization objectives. Similarly, the distinction between allocation and distribution leads to the principle that redistribution should be implemented primarily through a tax-transfer process. This will avoid inefficient increases of public expenditures in the name of progressive objectives.

The distinction between allocation and distribution has acquired increased practical significance as much of the expansion of the public sector has consisted of increased transfer payments: Social Security and publicly financed medical care. Also, in a wide variety of policy areas, from the regulation of the prices of energy resources to efficient congestion-pricing of urban highways, the conflict between allocation and distribution has led to poor policy design, as he predicted. Compensation systems are needed to offset the redistributive effects of efficient allocation policies.

The value of the distinction between allocation and distribution has been enhanced by the work of Robert Nozick and John Rawls on social justice. Nozick has restated and extended John Locke's doctrine that one is fully entitled to the fruit of one's labour. Rawls developed a very different theory based on a communal claim to the output of high-ability persons. However, the claim structure is voluntarily agreed upon through a social compact, as risk-averse individuals, not knowing their future position, agree behind a veil of ignorance to share their income. This contractual approach to distribution is fully consistent with Musgrave's separation between the allocation and distribution branches.

Musgrave distinguishes between primary and secondary redistribution. Primary redistribution is determined by the social rights that entitle the individual to some share of the social product based on membership in the community, rather than on property ownership or labour supplied. Secondary redistribution is voluntary giving that occurs either through private charities or collective provision. Secondary redistribution is Pareto optimal in that the donor derives more satisfaction from providing the gift to the poor than from additional personal consumption.

The mix between primary and secondary redistribution will vary across societies, according to differences in social values. Also, some social rights, or primary redistribution, may be provided in part in the form of goods and services, such as education, training programmes and medical care. This possibility blurs the separation of allocation and distribution functions.

The primary shortcoming of the distinction between allocation and distribution, however, is not the existence of transfers in kind and the subsidization of certain goods, which Musgrave has classified as merit goods (1957; 1959). As stressed by Samuelson, the fundamental issue is that numerous allocations between social and private goods are Pareto efficient, and the choice of an efficient allocation, a task for the distribution branch, has allocative consequences. In a planning solution, then, allocation and distribution are decided simultaneously, not separately.

Musgrave agrees to the formal correctness of this argument but he argues that this approach implicitly assumes that the planner knows individual preferences, and that the question of distribution is dealt with *de novo*. If, however, the distribution of income is determined primarily by market forces and preferences are not known, a pricing rule or voting rule that induces preference revelation must be designed. The determination of the pricing rule is the allocative function of government. The determination of money income, in conjunction with the pricing rule, is the distributive function.

When considered from a broader perspective the separation of budgetary functions into allocation and distribution branches has been invaluable, both as a normative theory and as a description of the way public agencies operate. Experience shows that it is very important to develop coordination between branches of government. Also, Musgrave's three-branch theory clarifies many positive issues, such as the causes of large foreign trade deficits and the demise of central cities in metropolitan areas, as well as the design of policies to deal with these trends.

The establishment of a framework for the systematic solution of fiscal problems is Musgrave's most significant contribution. His work combined theory, institutional and historical information, a deep understanding of prior work and empirical testing. Like a number of other outstanding economists educated during the turbulent 1930s, he emphasized the practical and concrete applications of academic research in the belief that 'intelligent conduct of government is at the heart of democracy', and until the end of his life was an active commentator on policy issues. A lovely delineation of his views, along with a contrasting perspective, is found in Buchanan and Musgrave (1999); see also his review of the evolution of ideas on fiscal policy (1987).

ORIGINAL BY PETER MIESZKOWSKI, UPDATED BY THE EDITORS

See also **horizontal and vertical equity; merit goods; public finance.**

Selected works

1939. The voluntary exchange theory of public economy. *Quarterly Journal of Economics* 53, 213–37.

1944. (With E.D. Domar.) Proportional income taxation and risk taking. *Quarterly Journal of Economics* 58, 388–422.

1948. (With T. Thin.) Income tax progression. *Journal of Political Economy* 56, 498–514.

1951. (With J.J. Carrol, L.D. Cook and L. Frane.) Distribution of tax payments by income groups: a case study for 1948. *National Tax Journal* 4, 1–53.

1953. On incidence. *Journal of Political Economy* 61, 306–23.

1957. A multiple theory of budget determination. *Finanz Archiv* NS 17, 333–43.

1959. *The Theory of Public Finance: A Study in Public Economy.* New York: McGraw-Hill.

1963. (With M. Krzyzaniak.) *The Shifting of the Corporation Tax.* Baltimore: Johns Hopkins University Press.

1974. (With K.E. Case and H. Leonard.) The distribution of fiscal burdens and benefits. *Public Finance Quarterly* 2, 259–31.

1976. ET, OT, and SBT. *Journal of Public Economics* 6, 3–16.

1987. A brief history of fiscal doctrine. In *Handbook of Public Economics*, ed. A. Auerbach and M. Feldstein. Amsterdam: North-Holland.

1999. (With J. Buchanan) *Public Finance and Public Choice: Two Contrasting Visions of the State.* Cambridge, MA: MIT Press.

music markets, economics of

On 15 January 1787, Wolfgang Amadeus Mozart wrote from Prague to a friend in Vienna that 'here [in Prague] nothing is talked about but *Figaro*; nothing is played, tootled, sung or whistled but [Mozart's *Marriage of*] *Figaro*.' Music was ubiquitous, and Mozart was at the time Prague's favorite composer. More than two centuries later, music is played and listened to incessantly, usually through some electronic medium, in homes, shops, automobiles, trains, and on the streets. But the diversity of composers and forms is much greater. And in the means by which music is created and reaches the ears of its countless appreciators, the market institutions have changed radically.

Early history

The history of musical performance is as old as the history of humanity. A seven-hole Chinese flute has been carbon-dated to the year 7,000 BC. Prehistoric tribes celebrated military events and other special occasions with music from drums, horns, flutes, and a variety of stringed instruments. By the Middle Ages in Europe, the professional performance of music was concentrated in the churches, following traditions inherited from the Judaic temple music of King David, and in the residences of the wealthy, especially the nobility. The Roman Schola Cantorum was founded in the seventh century AD to perform what came to be called Gregorian chant. The first Holy Roman Emperor, Charlemagne (d. 814), imported from Rome a delegation of 12 specialists to propagate the correct use of Gregorian chant in northern Europe. Chapels established in residences of the nobility maintained their own cadre of instrumentalists and singers. Competition between Protestant and Roman Catholic denominations during the 16th century led to innovations in the richness of church music, ranging from the eminently singable hymns of Martin Luther to the polyphonic masses of Giovanni da Palestrina. The musicians employed in noble chapels also provided entertainment at dinners and celebrations, and during the Renaissance period wealthier nobles initiated further specialization, maintaining one group of musicians for chapel and another for secular entertainment. During the second half of the 17th century, a kind of 'cultural arms race' emerged among the hundreds of noble courts in Germany, Bohemia, and Austria. Each court competed for prestige through the quality of the musicians and composers it employed to entertain visitors (see Elias, 1969; Baumol and Baumol, 1994).

As a golden age of classical music dawned in the 17th century, much of Europe was organized along feudal lines. There was an active market for the hiring of promising musicians, who travelled far and wide in search of the best employment opportunities. But once a musician was retained by a feudal lord, at least throughout much of the European continent, he (seldom she) was often bound to continued servitude at the noble's whim and on the noble's terms. Claudio Monteverdi was able to leave his badly paid, demoralizing position with Duke Vincenzo I of Mantua only after his employer's death in 1612. Johann Sebastian Bach was imprisoned for nearly a month in 1717 when he sought to leave the service of the Duke of Weimar. His contemporary Georg Friedrich Händel was advised by friends to reject an employment offer from the King of Prussia (Scherer, 2004, p. 94):

> For they well knew, that if he once engag'd in the King's service, he must remain in it, whether he liked it, or not; that if he continued to please, it would be reason for not parting with him; and that if he happened to displease, his ruin would be the certain consequence.

When he was discharged in an economy move during 1769, Niccolò Jommelli was denied permission to take with him copies of the music he had written for the Duke of Württemberg.

Gradually, however, a new set of opportunities materialized for musicians to earn a living as freelance artists. Opera was the forerunner of this new tradition (see Bianconi and Pestelli, 1998). Having pioneered the first modern opera *Orpheo* under ducal auspices at Mantua, Monteverdi migrated to the free city of Venice, where operas were financed by a consortium of wealthy patricians, organized by a hired impresario, and written and performed under contracts individually negotiated with composers, librettists, and soloists. The paradigm spread to other parts of Italy, then to England and parts of Germany, and eventually to other European nations and the United States. Opportunities for the performance of instrumental music at private locales also began to emerge. One predecessor appeared in mercantile London, where King Charles II, embarrassed over his perennial money problems and his inability to pay his court musicians adequately, allowed Henry Purcell and others to perform their music privately in local theaters, taverns, and music halls. In 1697 Thomas Hickford opened a 'Great Dancing Room' in London, perfecting the emerging model for private music halls. In 1735 Vauxhall Gardens, south-east across the Thames from today's Victoria Station, began offering open-air summer concerts at admission prices sufficiently modest to draw Londoners of nearly all economic classes (see McVeigh, 1993). These innovations spread to other locations in London and then to many parts of the European continent. By the third decade of the 19th century, private ballrooms had proliferated in Vienna to the point at which they could accommodate some 50,000 music lovers simultaneously, with entertainment provided, inter alia, by 300 musicians under contract to Johann Strauss, sen., and deployed by Strauss in groups of 25. His son Johann was paid $100,000 to conduct his own and others' compositions at the Boston, Massachusetts, Peace Festival in 1872, performed in a huge wooden shed by an orchestra of 2,000 and chorus of 20,000 before audiences of approximately 100,000 persons.

The transition from church and court employment to freelance music composition is depicted in Figure 1. (Scherer, 2004, pp. 69–71). It summarizes by 50-year birth cohort intervals the principal occupational choices of 646 musical composers of enduring fame born between 1650 and 1849. Strong downward trends are evident for court and church employment along with an upward trend for freelance activity. With double-counting allowed to reflect multiple career phases, we see that the fraction employed in noble courts or regularly subsidized by them fell from 62.4 per cent for composers born between 1650 and 1699 to 19.0 per cent for those born in the first half of the 19th century, by which time the Napoleonic wars had undermined much of the feudal

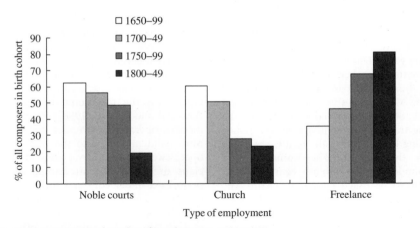

Figure 1   Trends in composers' principal modes of employment, 1650–1849

system. For church employment the sharpest decline occurs for composers born in the second half of the 18th century. The fraction earning a significant component of their living through freelance composition and performance activities increased from 35.5 per cent for composers born in 1650–99 to 81 per cent for those born in 1800–49.

Music market organization

Markets for music are both vertically and horizontally complex. Final demand exists for hearing music performed or for performing it oneself. From that demand are derived a host of other demands: for new musical compositions, for the sheet music through which compositions are disseminated to performers, for training (for example, at conservatories and local schools) in performance, for the concerts and other venues at which music is performed, for the instruments with which it is performed, and for recorded means by which performed music is propagated more widely. The composition, instrument-making, and dissemination stages have for many centuries experienced particularly vigorous innovation. In some subsets, however, such as organ building and violin-making, the technology attained a remarkable degree of perfection as early as the 17th century.

Although data permitting a direct statistical test have not been available, the growth of concert-going during the 18th and 19th centuries in tandem with the commercial and industrial revolutions in Europe implies a substantial income elasticity of demand for music consumption. Indirect evidence is presented in Figure 2 (from Scherer, 2004, p. 35), showing trends in the production of pianos in the United States between 1850 and 1939. Values for years other than those on which specific data were available (points) are interpolated. The implied income elasticity of demand is in the range of 2.4 to 4.3, depending upon what other variables are included in multiple regressions. There is a sharp and lasting break in

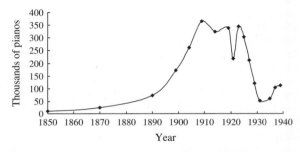

Figure 2   Trends in US piano production, 1850–1939

the series during the mid-1920s, when an economic boom was in full swing. The 1909 and 1923 production peaks were not surpassed over the next 60 years, after which imports began to outweigh domestic production. Two coincident events are responsible for the mid-1920s slump: the introduction of electrical phonographs (with fidelity superior to acoustic phonographs marketed successfully in the 1890s) and the advent of radio broadcasting, including the transmission of classical and popular music. Up to that time, the principal alternative to expensive concert-going (or free summer concerts in urban parks) was the active performance of music within one's home. After the mid-1920s, music could be enjoyed passively at home by listening to radios and phonographs. An era of participatory family musicales began to fade, and a new era dawned.

The marriage of electronics with music wrought further radical changes in markets for music. Through records, radio, television, and still later, the internet, audiences for musical performance were no longer limited to those who could be assembled to hear a specific concert. The whole world was a stage, with four noteworthy consequences. First, for the world as a whole, musical record sales in 1998 (if we count only those sold legally, consistent with applicable copyrights) amounted to more than four billion units. Second, through amplification live performances could be heard by unprecedented numbers of concert-goers. The Woodstock Festival of August 1969 attracted an estimated 300,000 to 500,000 participants. Third, the expansion of potential audiences enhanced incentives for product differentiation. New musical styles proliferated during the second half of the 20th century at an accelerating pace. Fourth, the prerequisite for success as a vocal performer was no longer a beautiful voice that could carry through the expanse of an opera house. Electronics made popular acclaim attainable for faint voices, and even for performers whose histrionics, dancing ability, costuming, and sex appeal outweighed their vocal talent.

The expansion of markets also intensified a phenomenon already in evidence at the start of the 18th century: superstardom. The received theory (see, for example, Rosen, 1981) asserts that the broader the market for talent is, the higher the income differential tends to be between performers with the greatest ability to please and performers of inferior talent. In 1998, for example, the Three Tenors (Luciano Pavarotti, Placedo Domingo, and Jose Carreras) along with their agent received an advance of $18 million for a single performance accompanying the World Cup football finals in Paris, including broadcast and recording rights. Michael Jackson's *Thriller* album, introduced in 1992, achieved an all-time world high of 46 million unit sales, and in 2002, before he plunged into legal and financial difficulties, Jackson's net financial worth was estimated to be in the order of $300 million. But superstardom was not entirely new. In the early 18th century, the leading opera singers made arduous journeys throughout Europe in quest of the most remunerative engagements. The most famous of them all, the castrato Farinelli (Carlo Broschi), is said to have earned £5,000 during the 1735–36 opera season in London at a time when an English building craftsman averaged £30 a year.

For live musical performances that are neither amplified nor broadcast, another economic law operates, known as 'Baumol's cost disease' (Baumol and Bowen, 1965). Many musical works require a more or less fixed complement of musicians expending a nearly fixed amount of rehearsal and performance time. Thus, labour productivity hardly grows from one century to the next. Meanwhile, most other goods and services experience appreciable rates of productivity growth, permitting those who supply them to earn increasing real incomes over time. For musical performers to stay abreast economically with alternative high productivity growth vocational opportunities, musicians' hourly pay levels must rise apace commensurately, which means that the costs of live musical performances increase relative to the prices of all other goods and services, threatening possibly severe adverse substitution effects. To maintain a thriving supply of live musical performances, subsidization becomes increasingly necessary – not by noble patrons, as in the 18th century, but by governments

(preponderantly in Europe and Asia) or affluent concert-goers and private philanthropists (the United States pattern).

For 42 leading US symphony orchestras, all unionized, admissions receipts during the 2002–03 season defrayed on average only 43 per cent of annual budgets. Balancing budgets (which was often not achieved) required voluntary contributions and drawing upon endowments (the latter varying from virtually nothing to $248 million, with a mean of $48 million and median of $19 million). A regression analysis spanning 1980 to 2002 revealed that those orchestras' budgets were higher, if local population is also taken into account, the greater the concentration of manufacturing, mining, and service corporation headquarters assets was in the relevant metropolitan area. A local corporate headquarters presence subsidized symphony orchestra performance both directly through endowment contributions and through the annual donations of well-paid company officials (Scherer, 2005).

Music publication and copyright

For at least three centuries the composers and publishers of new music have complained about the unauthorized use, or 'piracy', of their works. The copyright system – having governments confer upon composers and publishers (including record producers) exclusive rights to their productions, which can then be licensed to others upon payment of royalties and/or performance fees – has been the standard means of compromising the maintenance of economic incentives for creative contributions against widespread public dissemination. The first formal copyright law was enacted in England in 1709, but it was interpreted initially not to cover musical works. Extension to musical works came first in 1777 through a lawsuit brought in England by Johann Christian Bach, the son of Johann Sebastian Bach. Musical works were then included under copyright laws passed in the United States, France, various German states, and then, thanks to an initiative led by Johann Nepomuk Hummel and Ludwig van Beethoven culminating in 1837, the German, Austrian, Italian, Czech, and Hungarian territories that previously comprised the Holy Roman Empire.

Prior to the enactment of copyright laws, some protection against unauthorized use was provided by 'privileges' – ad hoc grants of exclusivity conferred upon composers or publishers by royal sovereigns. Securing such grants required access to the relevant sovereign and, in the politically fragmented territories of the old Holy Roman Empire, the grants were mostly localized and prone to being undermined by competitors producing and selling from another territory. Composers protected their works by contracting with publishers having a reputation for respecting their contracts and keeping manuscripts secret for as long as possible before published versions reached the market. Hand-copying posed a particular threat, for in the early days of the music publishing industry's rapid growth – for example, around 1800 – a copyist could turn out copies by hand at a unit cost lower than the average front-end set-up costs plus variable costs incurred with mechanical printing for production runs of fewer than 25–40 copies (Scherer, 2004, p. 162). Like his contemporaries, Mozart attempted to prevent hand copyists from pirating his works by keeping the copyists he hired under constant supervision and dividing work on any given manuscript among multiple copyists. Publishers combatted piracy through secrecy, announcing fixed prices lower than copyists' minimum costs for publications expected to secure a considerable volume (which would now be called 'limit pricing'), keeping composers' honoraria low for works of limited or uncertain appeal, and entering into collusive anti-piracy agreements with fellow publishers.

Giuseppe Verdi and his publisher Giovanni Ricordi were the first to make aggressive use of the copyright laws enacted in German-speaking and Austrian-controlled regions (for example, northern Italy). Previously, local opera houses had purchased or leased manuscripts at cut-rate prices from copyists. With copyright and a network of local enforcement employees, Verdi and Ricordi were able to extract fees from each house, graduating them in a discriminatory fashion to extract more revenue from those serving large, affluent audiences than those located in small provincial towns. They were also particularly energetic in publishing 'reductions' of each separate overture, aria, and chorus, along with bundles covering a full opera, for a diversity of instruments – for example, voice, piano, violin, flute, clarinet, and various ensembles – played by middle-class citizens in their homes. In this way they were able to create a mass market for their works, and as a result Ricordi could pay unprecedentedly large sums for the rights to publish Verdi's works. Verdi became quite rich, accumulating an estate equivalent to nearly £40,000 at the time of his death in 1901 (when English building craftsmen's annual income averaged £100) and beginning semi-retirement at his Busetto villa in the fifth decade of his nearly nine-decade life.

Verdi's extensive written correspondence leaves little doubt that, as his fortune grew, he consciously reduced his work effort along a backward-bending supply curve. Few 18th and 19th century composers achieved as much prosperity as Verdi did; the terminal wealth distribution is highly skew. (Gioachino Rossini became even wealthier and, after reaching the age of 37, spent the remaining four decades of his life in retirement.) It is unlikely that the majority of composers found themselves on the backward-bending portion of a labour supply curve. It is not unreasonable to suppose that the spectacular financial successes achieved by a relatively few composers under the copyright laws inspired many others to try their luck at musical composition. An attempt to test this hypothesis quantitatively (Scherer, 2004) was inconclusive, largely because of the difficulty of holding

other relevant variables constant. What can be said, however, is that the lack of copyright laws did not prevent classical music from experiencing its golden age of creativity before copyright protection was available in the most musically productive parts of Europe, that is, before the death of Beethoven in 1827 and Schubert in 1828. Despite this limping recommendation, advocates for copyright have been successful in extending greatly both the length of time for which creative individuals and publishers can be protected and, given a continuing stream of new technological challenges, in the range of media over which copyright applies (see Lessig, 2004).

FREDERIC M. SCHERER

See also **art, economics of; intellectual property; superstars, economics of.**

Bibliography

Baumol, W. and Bowen, W. 1965. On the performing arts: the anatomy of their economic problems. *American Economic Review* 55, 495–502.

Baumol, W. and Baumol, H. 1994. On the economics of musical composition in Mozart's Vienna. *Journal of Cultural Economics* 18, 171–98.

Bianconi, L. and Pestelli, G., eds. 1998. *Opera Production and Its Resources*. Chicago: University of Chicago Press.

Elias, N. 1969. *Die höfische Gesellschaft* [The Courtly Society]. Frankfurt: Suhrkamp Verlag.

Lessig, L. 2004. *Free Culture*. New York: Penguin.

McVeigh, S. 1993. *Concert Life in London from Mozart to Haydn*. Cambridge: Cambridge University Press.

Raynor, H. 1972. *A Social History of Music from the Middle Ages to Beethoven*. New York: Schocken.

Rosen, S. 1981. The economics of superstars. *Journal of Political Economy* 71, 845–57.

Scherer, F. 2004. *Quarter Notes and Bank Notes: The Economics of Music Composition in the 18th and 19th Centuries*. Princeton, NJ: Princeton University Press.

Scherer, F. 2005. Corporate structure and the financial support of U.S. symphony orchestras. Working paper.

Muth, John F. (1930–2005)

John F. (Jack) Muth was a brilliant individual, though somewhat awkward socially, and little understood by most people. He was born in Chicago, where his father worked as an accountant at a national accounting firm. Eventually, Jack moved with his parents and two brothers to St. Louis, Missouri. He was very weak as a youngster, suffering from severe asthma and allergies. An avid reader, Jack loved playing the cello and studying mathematics. Jack's cello-playing days continued through the 1980s, and he was a member of the Bloomington symphony orchestra for many years. He studied industrial engineering at Washington University in St. Louis, and continued with graduate work in mathematical economics at Carnegie Tech in Pittsburgh, Pennsylvania. His thesis advisor was Franco Modigliani, with Herb Simon and Merton Miller serving on his committee. All three individuals would later become Nobel laureates in economics.

While a doctoral student, Muth was the first recipient of the Alexander Henderson Award in 1954 (for his work in economics). While finishing his doctorate, he spent the 1957–8 academic year as visiting lecturer at the University of Chicago, returned to Carnegie Tech as an assistant professor during 1959 to 1961, spent the 1961–2 academic year at the Cowles Foundation at Yale University, and finally returned to Carnegie Tech as an associate professor without tenure from 1962 to 1964. It is said that it took him very long to graduate because he did not see the need to take a foreign language examination which would have completed requirements for the Ph.D. degree. Eventually, a colleague whose wife was a French instructor joined the faculty. She tutored Muth in French, and he was finally allowed to graduate. He went on to Michigan State as a professor in 1964, and moved to Indiana University in 1969. He stayed at Indiana University until he retired in 1994.

Throughout his entire academic career John Muth loved to challenge conventional thought. He would explore alternative explanations mathematically, his most famous work being three papers that develop the rational expectations hypothesis (1960; 1961; 1981). Later work by Robert Lucas, the economist, popularized the idea of rational expectations, and Lucas received the Nobel Prize for his efforts. Esther-Mirjam Sent has written a comprehensive paper that describes Muth's work on rational expectations from a historical perspective (Sent, 2002).

Many have asked why Muth did not himself further develop his ideas. If you knew him, this is easy to explain. He knew that there were alternative ways to explain the macroeconomic relationships that were the hot topic of the day. All he wanted to do was show an alternative; in essence, to create an academic debate that challenged conventional wisdom. His colleagues at Carnegie Tech were heavily involved in related research, and he wanted to have some fun and add his thoughts at the same time. Whenever he saw an opening to challenge an idea, he enjoyed developing his elegant ideas, often running concise computer simulations to accompany his mathematical models, subsequently writing up his results. He started doing this very early in his academic career.

A true intellectual, Muth had little interest in promoting his ideas through workshops, presentations or other academic portals. He felt his papers would be interpreted and stand the test of time. Being a good friend, I remember on many occasions Jack talking about invitations to speak at international conferences and at schools. These invitations were usually declined, I am sure not because he was uninterested but rather because he felt these activities would take a significant amount of time, he would probably have trouble with his allergies, and he was more interested in working on his current ideas. He always had something that he was actively working on and would talk about these ideas often over a few beers in the late afternoon at Nick's in Bloomington, Indiana, with his friends.

The late 1960s and early 1970s were spent developing industrial scheduling theory in the field of operations management. He wrote about the importance of the 'aggregate planning' problem and established it in the literature in 1960 with his colleagues at Carnegie Tech (Holt, Modigliani, Muth and Simon, 1960). It was Muth who established the proof of the linear decision rule in aggregate planning. This effort developed into a series of books published with Gerry Thompson and Gene Groff (Muth and Thompson, 1963; Groff and Muth, 1969; 1972).

He spent the late 1970s through the early 1980s studying artificial intelligence. His main interests were in inference engines and inductive and deductive logic. To my knowledge he published only one paper on the topic (Jacobs, Hancock, Mathieson and Muth, 1991). I often heard him refer to his work on artificial intelligence as his 'ten-year sink hole'.

Later in the 1980s he began studying innovation cycles. He would often muse on the fact that many of the most innovative ideas were developed by individuals working at home, and how corporations that spent gigantic sums to develop new ideas so often produced only minor incremental innovations. He wrote simple simulation programs that simulated a random progress function, and matched these results with what was documented in the literature, often musing on the fit. He published an important paper in this area in 1989.

During the late 1980s until his retirement in 1994, Muth spend his time teaching undergraduate courses in process design and scheduling. As one might imagine, he was an awkward teacher and often had difficulty coming down to the level of doctoral students, much less undergraduate students. When he realized during this time that he was going to have to teach undergraduate students to see out his career, it was interesting to observe how he worked to improve. He worked with the teaching resource group at the university, who videotaped his lectures and helped him develop a better teaching style. His colleges in the department were amazed when he was listed as a recommended instructor in the student newspaper in the early 1990s, an event that gave him great personal satisfaction.

He loved sailing in the Florida Keys and had a 30-foot Auburn sailboat that was docked in Marathon until he moved it to Cudjoe Key around 1989. The boat was well suited for sailing around the Florida Keys having a shallow keel. He retired in 1994 and initially split his time between Bloomington and the Keys. For a time, he worked as a consultant to the business school to develop the integrative cases used in the undergraduate core curriculum, taking Indiana's integrative core to yet another level, as he had done in economics and in almost any area in which he became involved. From around 2000, he remained permanently in the Keys.

This article has possibly not emphasized enough the impact of Muth's work. He was truly a brilliant intellectual and influenced numerous doctoral students throughout his career at Michigan State and Indiana University. As an aside, he was also an amazing Trivial Pursuits player. You always wanted Muth on your team since he seldom missed a question! Muth also had a private side as an aggressively loyal and caring person to his close friends. He was always willing to spend time to talk through important career decisions, and always willing to comment quickly and brilliantly on a manuscript (although it might cost you a beer).

Finally, a funny story, I can still remember being in the Keys with my wife and children, and visiting Jack when he first bought the Cudjoe Key house. Late one afternoon we were all driving up from Key West with Jack. We stopped at a store to pick up some food for dinner, my wife and I leaving the kids with Jack in the car. When we returned to the car, there we saw Jack teaching our two young daughters how to make 'unusual noises' by putting their hands over their armpits and pumping their arms up and down. We all still laugh when we think about that time and the other wonderful times we enjoyed with that nervous little genius who was such a great friend.

F. ROBERT JACOBS

Selected works

1960. Optimal properties of exponentially weighted forecasts. *Journal of the American Statistical Association* 55, 299–306.

1960. (With C.C. Holt, F. Modigliani and H.A. Simon.) *Planning Production, Inventories, and Work Force.* Englewood Cliffs, NJ: Prentice-Hall.

1961. Rational expectations and the theory of price movements. *Econometrica* 29, 315–35.

1963. (With G.L. Thompson.) *Industrial Scheduling.* New York: Prentice-Hall.

1969. (With G.K. Groff.) *Operations Management: Selected Readings.* Homewood, IL: Irwin.

1972. (With G.K. Groff.) *Operations Management: Analysis for Decisions.* Homewood, IL: Irwin.

1981. Estimation of economic relationships containing latent expectations variables. In *Rational Expectations and Econometric Practice*, ed. R.E. Lucas and T.J. Sargent. Minneapolis: University of Minnesota Press.

1986. Search theory and the manufacturing progress function. *Management Science* 32, 948–62.

1989. A stochastic theory of the generalized Cobb–Douglas production function. In *Cost Analysis Applications of Economics and Operations Research*, ed. T.R. Gulledge, Jr. and L.A. Litteral. New York: Springer-Verlag.

1991. (With F.R. Jacobs, T. Hancock and K. Mathieson.) A rule–based system to generate NC programs from CAD exchange files. *Computers & Industrial Engineering* 20, 167–76.

Bibliography

Sent, E.-M. 2002. How (not) to influence people: the contrary tale of John F. Muth. *History of Political Economy* 34, 291–319.

Myrdal, Gunnar (1898–1987)

Gunnar Myrdal was born in the province of Dalarná in Sweden. He attributed his faith in Puritan ethics and his egalitarianism to his sturdy farming background.

He was a student of the giant figures Knut Wicksell, David Davidson, Eli Heckscher, Gösta Bagge and above all Gustav Cassel. His personal friendship was warmest with Cassel, to whose chair in Political Economy at Stockholm University he succeeded (1933–9).

At first a pure theorist, Myrdal's year in the United States as a Rockefeller Fellow, following the crash of 1929, turned his interests to political issues. On his return to Sweden from America he, with his wife Alva, became active in politics. In 1935 he became a Member of Parliament. Together, they pioneered modern population policy. His involvements in Swedish politics between 1931 and 1938 turned him from a theoretical economist into a political economist and what he himself describes as an institutionalist. In 1938 the Carnegie Corporation selected him for a major investigation of the Negro problem in America, a project which resulted in *An American Dilemma* (1944a).

He returned to Sweden in 1942 and for five years was again involved in political activities. He headed the committee that drafted the social democratic post-war programme. He returned to Parliament and became a member of the board of directors of the Swedish Bank, chairman of the Swedish Planning Commission, and Minister for Trade and Commerce (1945–7). As Minister he arranged for a highly controversial treaty with the Soviet Union and was also involved in controversy over the dismantling of wartime controls. In 1947 he became Executive Secretary of the United Nations Economic Commission for Europe, to which he recruited an outstandingly able team. After ten years with the Commission in Geneva he embarked on a ten-year study of development in Asia, the result of which was the monumental *Asian Drama* (1968). In 1973 he was awarded the Nobel Prize in economics jointly with Friedrich von Hayek.

Methodological questions occupied Myrdal's thought throughout his life. They were already present in the young Myrdal's *Political Element in the Development of Economic Theory* (1930, English edition 1953). It was under the influence of the remarkable Uppsala University philosopher Axel Hägerström that he had begun to question the wisdom of the economic establishment.

Myrdal's doctoral dissertation on price formation and economic change (1927) introduced expectations systematically into the analysis of prices, profits and changes in capital values. The microeconomic analysis focused on planning by the firm. Many of these ideas were used in his later macroeconomic work, including *Monetary Equilibrium* (1931, English expanded translation 1939).

Much confusion had been caused by the lack of distinction between anticipations and results. The concepts *ex ante* and *ex post* that Myrdal developed greatly clarified the discussion of savings, investment and income, and their effects on prices. In anticipation, intention and planning, savings can diverge from investment; after the event they must be identical, because the community can save only by accumulating real assets. It is the process by which anticipations *ex ante* are adjusted so as to bring about the bookkeeping identity *ex post* that explains unexpected gains and losses as well as fluctuations in prices. Only in equilibrium are *ex ante* savings equal to *ex ante* investment, so that there is no tendency for prices to change. By introducing expectations into the analysis of economic processes he made a major contribution to liberalizing economics from static theory, in which the future is like the past, and to paving the way for dynamics, in which time, uncertainty and expectations enter in an essential way.

What is common to his three important later books, *The Political Element* (1930), *American Dilemma* (1944a) and *Asian Drama* (1968) is the emphasis on realistic and relevant research, whether on economic problems, race relations, or world poverty, and with it the effort to purge economic thinking of systematic biases.

Starting on the study of Blacks in the United States, he soon discovered that he had to study 'American civilization in its entirety, though viewed in its implications for the most disadvantaged population group' (Introduction to *An American Dilemma*, Section 4). The way to reach objectivity was to state explicitly the value premisses of the study. These premisses were not chosen arbitrarily, but were what Myrdal called the 'American Creed' of justice, liberty and equality of opportunity. But while these value premisses were chosen for their relevance to American society, they corresponded to Myrdal's own valuations. The major contribution of the book, which Myrdal regarded as his war service, is the analysis of six decades after Reconstruction as a 'temporary interregnum' not a 'stable equilibrium', and of the incipient changes, on which the prediction of the Black revolt in the South was based.

Apart from his work on expectations and on racial problems, Myrdal is best known for his critique of conventional economic theory applied to underdeveloped countries.

Through his whole work run five lines of criticism of mainstream economic and social theory. First, his appeal for realism is not a critique of abstraction. His criticism is that irrelevant features are selected and relevant ones ignored ('opportunistic ignorance'). A second line of criticism has been the narrow or abstract definitions of development, economic growth, or welfare. The actual needs and valuations of people, not the abstractions of statisticians or the empty concepts of metaphysicians, should be the basis for formulating aims. His third line of criticism is directed at the narrow definitions and the limits of disciplines. The essence of the institutional approach, advocated by Myrdal, is to bring to bear all relevant knowledge and techniques on the analysis of a problem. In an interdependent social system there are no economic, political or social problems, there are only problems. His fourth line of criticism is directed at spurious objectivity which, under the pretence of scientific analysis, conceals political valuations and interests. Myrdal argues that this pseudoscience should be replaced by explicit valuations. He is, of course, aware of the complex nexus between valuations and facts but, ever since his youthful *Political Element*, has constantly fought the inheritance of natural law and utilitarianism, according to which we can derive recommendations from pure analysis. A fifth line of criticism is directed against biases and twisted terminology. He lays bare the opportunistic interests and the 'diplomacy' underlying the use of such concepts as 'United Nations', 'international', 'values', 'welfare', 'developing countries', 'unemployment', 'the free world'. The features against which these lines of criticism are advanced are combined in the technocrat. He isolates economic (or other technical) relations from their social context; he neglects social and political variables and thereby ministers to the vested interests that might otherwise be hurt; he pretends to scientific objectivity and is socially and culturally insensitive. Since the majority of experts, academics and planners are of this type, he has ruffled many feathers.

The question may be asked whether the narrow technocrat cannot be replaced by an approach that introduces social variables openly into the formal model? Myrdal's answer would be, yes and no. In certain areas, a widening or redefinition of concepts can be successful. The productive effects of better nutrition can be studied and the line between investment and consumption be redrawn. The influence of climate, of attitudes, and of institutions can be introduced as constraints or as variables. An agricultural production function can be constructed in which health, education, distance from town, and so on figure as 'inputs'. 'Capital' can be redefined so as to cover anything on which expenditure of resources now raises the flow of output later.

But there are limits to such revisionism. These limits apply both to the analysis of facts and to recommendations of policies. On the factual side, the reformulation runs into difficulties if the connection between expenditure now and 'yield' later is only tenuous, as in the initiation of a birth control programme or a land reform.

In the analysis of values, the construction of a social welfare function is not, in Myrdal's view, a logical task. The unity of a social programme of a party is unlike that of a computer program or a logically consistent system, and more like the unity of a personality. It is discovered not only by deductive reasoning but by empathy, imagination, and even artistic and intuitive understanding. Means and ends, targets and instruments, are misleading ways of grasping the valuations of a class, an interest group or a whole society, for their unity is not logical but psychological.

In *Asian Drama* the explicitly formulated valuations are the 'Modernization Ideals'. A list would include rationality, planning for the future, raising productivity, raising levels of living, social and economic equalization, improved institutions and attitudes, national consolidation, national independence, political democracy, social discipline.

An important idea in Myrdal's arsenal of ideas is that of circular or cumulative causation (or the vicious – or virtuous – circle), first fully developed in *An American Dilemma*. It postulates increasing returns through specialization and economies of scale and shows how small advantages are magnified.

The principle goes back to Wicksell who, in *Interest and Prices* (1898), had analysed divergences between the natural and the market rates of interest in terms of upward or downward cumulative processes, until the divergence was eliminated. Wicksell pointed out that, if banks keep their loan rate of interest below the real rate of return on capital, they will encourage expansion of production and investment in plant and equipment. As a result, prices will rise and will continue to rise cumulatively as long as the lending rate is kept below the real rate.

The principle of cumulative causation can be used to show movements away from an equilibrium position as a result of the interaction of several variables. Myrdal has not always been entirely clear in the formulation of this important principle, and there has been the suggestion that any form of circular or mutual causation or interaction is cumulative and hence disequilibrating. This would be false, for a series of mutually caused events can, after a disturbance, rapidly converge either on the initial or on some other point of stable equilibrium. In order to get instability, a cumulative movement away from the initial situation, the numerical values of the coefficients of interdependence have to be above a critical minimum size. For example, an increase in consumption will raise incomes which in turn will raise consumption, and so on, ad infinitum. But as long as the marginal propensity to consume is less than unity, the infinite series will converge on a finite value.

The notion of cumulative causation was applied by Myrdal most illuminatingly to price expectations (*Monetary Equilibrium*) and to the relations between regions (*Economic Theory and Underdeveloped Regions*, 1957; American title: *Rich Lands and Poor*). He showed how the advantages of growth poles can become cumulative, while the backward region may be relatively or even absolutely impoverished.

Myrdal applied the notion of sociological variables, such as the prejudices against Negroes and their level of performance (low skills, crime, disease, and so on); to economic variables; and, above all, to the interaction of so-called 'economic' and 'non-economic' variables. Thus, the relation between better nutrition, better health and better education, higher productivity and hence ability further to improve health, education and nutrition shows that the inclusion of non-economic variables in the analysis opens up the possibility of numerous cumulative processes to which conventional economic analysis is blind. It also guards against uni-causal explanations and panaceas.

The revolutionary character of the concept of cumulative causation is brought out by the fact that interaction takes place not only within a social system in which the various elements interact, but also in time, so that memory and expectations are of crucial importance. The responses to any given variable, say a price, are different according to what the history of this variable has been. It is this dynamic feature of analysis and its implications for policy that distinguishes Myrdal's approach from that of economists who think in terms of general equilibrium.

In *Economic Theory and Underdeveloped Regions* (1957), and later in *Asian Drama* (1968), he used the concepts 'backwash' and 'spread' effects to analyse the movement of regions or whole countries at different stages of development and the effects of unification. It is a highly suggestive, realistic and fruitful alternative explanation to that of stable equilibrium analysis, usually based on competitive conditions and diminishing returns, and concluding that gains are widely and evenly distributed.

Like the Marxists, Myrdal emphasizes the unequal distribution of power and property as an obstacle not only to equity but also to efficiency and growth. But his conclusion is not Marxist. He regards a direct planning of institutions and shaping of attitudes (what Marx regarded as part of the superstructure) as necessary, though very difficult, partly because he believes that attitudes and institutions are inert, and partly because the policies which aim at reforming attitudes and institutions are themselves part of the social system, part of the power and property structure. There are clearly also logical difficulties in operating on variables that are thought to be fully determined within the system.

In *Asian Drama* Myrdal criticizes the kind of government he calls the 'soft state'. This critique has sometimes been misunderstood. It is plain that 'softness' in Myrdal's sense is quite compatible with a high degree of coercion, violence and cruelty. The Tamils in Sri Lanka, the Indians in Burma, the Chinese in Indonesia, the

Hindus in Pakistan, the Moslems in India, the Biharis in Bangladesh – to take six states he calls 'soft' – could not claim excessively soft treatment. 'Soft states' also go in for military violence, both internal and external. Their 'softness' lies in their unwillingness to coerce in order to implement declared policy goals. It is not the result of gentleness or weakness but reflects the power structure and a gap between real intentions and professions.

Myrdal applied his method to the analysis of inflation combined with widespread unemployment in the developed countries of the West in the 1970s, and either coined or was one of the first to use the term 'stagflation'. He attributes the situation to the organization of producers as pressure groups, and the dispersion and comparative weakness of consumers, to the tax system which encourages speculative expenditures, to the structure of markets and to the methods of oligopoly administrative pricing, and he condemns inflation as a socially highly divisive force.

The approach favoured by Myrdal is one of neither Soviet authority and force nor of capitalist laissez-faire but of a third way: that of using prices for planning purposes and of attacking attitudes and institutions directly to make them the instruments of reform. His approach has more affinity with those socialists who were dismissed by Marx as utopian. The difficulty is that any instrument, even if used with the intention to reform, within a given power structure may serve the powerful and re-establish the old equilibrium. Even well-intentioned allocations, rationing, licensing and controls may reinforce monopoly and big business. How does one break out of this lock? Myrdal does not draw revolutionary conclusions but relies on the, admittedly difficult, possibility of self-reform that arises, in both the American Creed and in the Modernization Ideals, from the tensions between preferred and proclaimed beliefs and actions.

Both *An American Dilemma* and *Asian Drama* are books about the interaction and the conflict between ideals and reality, and about how, when the two conflict, one of them must give way. Much of conventional economic theory is a rationalization whose purpose it is to conceal that conflict. But it is bound to reassert itself sooner or later. When this happens, either the ideals will be scaled down to conform to the reality or the reality will be shaped by the ideals.

PAUL STREETEN

See also **ex ante and ex post; institutional economics.**

Selected works

1927. *Prisbildningsproblemet och föränderligheten.* Uppsala and Stockholm: Almqvist & Wiksell.

1930. *Vetenskap och politik i nationalokonomien.* Stockholm: P.A. Norstedt.

1931. Om penningteoretisk jämvikt. *Ekonomisk Tidskrift* 33, 191–302.

1932. *Das Politische Element in der nationalökonomischen Doktrinbildung.* Berlin: Junker and Dünnhaupt.

1933a. *The Cost of Living in Sweden 1830–1930.* London: P.S. King & Son.

1933b. Der Gleichgewichtsbegriff als Instrument der geldtheoretischen Analyse. In *Beiträge zur Geldtheorie*, ed. P. Friedrich von Hayek. Vienna: Springer-Verlag (expanded version of Myrdal, 1931).

1933c. Konjunktur och offentlig hushållning. Bihang til riksdagens protokoll, 1st collection, Appendix III.

1933d. Das Zweck-Mittel-Denken in der Nationalökonomie. *Zeitschrift für Nationalökonomie* 4, 305–29.

1934a. *Finanspolitikens e konomiska verkningar.* Stockholm: P.A. Norstedt.

1934b. (With A. Myrdal.) *Kris i befolkningsfrågan.* Stockholm: A. Bonnier.

1939. *Monetary Equilibrium.* London: Hodge.

1940. *Population: A Problem for Democracy.* Cambridge, MA: Harvard University Press.

1944a. *An American Dilemma: The Negro Problem and Modern Democracy.* New York: Harper. Paperback edn, New York: McGraw-Hill, 1964.

1944b. *Varning för fredsoptimism.* Stockholm: Bonniers.

1945. *Warnung gegen Friedensoptimismus.* Zurich: Europa Verlag.

1953. *The Political Element in the Development of Economic Theory.* Trans. P. Streeten London: Routledge & Kegan Paul; Cambridge, MA: Harvard University Press. (Originally published in German.)

1955. *Realities and Illusions in Regard to Intergovernmental Organisations.* Oxford: Oxford University Press.

1956a. *Development and Underdevelopment: A Note on the Mechanism of National and International Inequality.* Cairo: National Bank of Egypt.

1956b. *An International Economy: Problems and Prospects.* London: Routledge & Kegan Paul.

1957. *Economic Theory and Underdeveloped Regions.* London: Duckworth; New York: Harper.

1958. *Value in Social Theory: A Selection of Essays on Methodology*, ed. P. Streeten. London: Routledge & Kegan Paul.

1960. *Beyond the Welfare State.* New Haven: Yale University Press.

1961. Value-loaded concepts. In *Money, Growth and Methodology and Other Essays in Honor of Johan Åkerman*, ed. H. Hegeland. Lund: Gleerup.

1963. *Challenge to Affluence.* New York: Pantheon.

1968. *Asian Drama: An Inquiry Into the Poverty of Nations.* New York: Twentieth Century Fund.

1969. *Objectivity in Social Research.* New York: Pantheon.

1970a. *The Challenge of World Poverty: A World Anti-poverty Program in Outline.* New York: Pantheon.

1970b. The 'soft state' in underdeveloped countries. In *Unfashionable Economics*, ed. P. Streeten. London: Weidenfeld & Nicolson.

1972. *Against the Stream: Critical Essays on Economics.* New York: Pantheon.

Bibliographic addendum

Myrdal's intellectual development is described in J. Angresano, *The Political Economy of Gunnar Myrdal*, Cheltenham: Edward Elgar, 1997. The influence of *An American Dilemma* on public policy has been sufficiently great to generate scholarly studies on its genesis and impact, including W. Jackson, *Gunnar Myrdal and America's Conscience: Social Engineering and Racial Liberalism, 1938–1987*, Durham: University of North Carolina Press, 1990, and D. Southern, *Gunnar Myrdal and Black–White Relations: The Use and Abuse of an American Dilemma, 1944–1969*, Baton Rouge: Louisiana State University Press, 1987.

N

Nash, John Forbes (born 1928)

The context of for Nash's work: von Neumann and Morgenstern

Nash's contributions to the theory of games were fundamental to the development of the discipline and its interface with applied fields of study. This section provides is a short account of the state of affairs before Nash's work. For a more detailed account, see the suggestions for further reading at the end of this article.

The first significant step in mathematical modelling of strategic situations was Augustin Cournot's (1838) book on oligopoly, where Cournot presented models of firm interaction that were analysed using what we now call Nash equilibrium. But Cournot did not attempt, or perhaps even recognize, how the analysis might generalize. Further, in the ensuing years confusion persisted regarding whether it would be appropriate for a firm to incorporate a response by its rivals when considering whether to change its own action. The concept of *strategic independence* – that the players' strategies can be considered to be chosen simultaneously and independently – began to be clarified by Emile Borel's (1921) description of a *method of play*.

Game theory became a discipline with the work of John von Neumann (1928), which was incorporated into the path-breaking book by von Neumann and Oscar Morgenstern (1944; 1947). In the book, von Neumann and Morgenstern formally defined both the extensive form (tree-based) and normal form (strategy-based) representations of games, related by the notion of a strategy; they studied for the first time a general class of games, defining solutions and proving existence using fixed-point methods; they introduced the idea of analysing how coalitions of players can take advantage of binding agreements; and they provided a theory of utility and decision-making under risk (the expected utility criterion). With one book, game theory was created and put on solid footing.

Von Neumann and Morgenstern were interested in developing a positive theory of behaviour in games – for any given game, a 'solution'. In a nutshell, their analysis progresses as follows:

1. Formulate a solution concept for two-player *zero-sum games*, which have the defining property that, for each *strategy profile* (one strategy for each player), the players' payoffs sum to zero. Such a game is special because the only economic concern is distributional; in other words, the game models a situation of pure conflict between the players, where one player's winnings come at the other's expense.

2. Analyse n-player zero-sum games by assuming that coalitions of players could bind together and play as a team against the other players. This requires assuming that coalitions can communicate before the game and make binding agreements on how to play. The value of forming a coalition is calculated in reference to the implied zero-sum game that the coalitions play against one another, which ultimately is a two-player game to which the solution from Part 1 above is applied.

3. To evaluate a non-zero-sum, n-player game, imagine the existence of a fictitious player $n+1$ whose payoff is defined as negative of the sum of the other players' payoffs. This creates a zero-sum game to which the preceding applies.

For an illustration of von Neumann and Morgenstern's analysis of two-player zero-sum games (Part 1 above), consider a simple example. Suppose that players 1 and 2 interact in the normal form game depicted in the following table.

1\2	X	Y	Z
A	4, −4	0, 0	−2, 2
B	3, −3	1, −1	1, −1
C	2, −2	1, −1	1, −1

Player 1 selects between strategies A, B, and C. Simultaneously, player 2 chooses between X, Y, and Z. The players' payoffs, which might as well be in monetary terms, are shown in the cells of the table, with player 1's payoff written first. Note that this is a zero-sum game in that, in each cell of the table, the players' payoffs sum to zero.

Von Neumann and Morgenstern motivated their solution concept by considering sequential variations of games in which one player would move first and then the other player, having seen what the first selected, would respond. Their key concept is what is generally known as a 'maximin strategy', also called a 'security strategy'. A security strategy for a given player is a strategy that gives the highest guaranteed payoff level; that is, it maximizes the minimum that the player could get, where the minimum is calculated over all of the strategies of the other player.

In the example, B and C are both security strategies for player 1 because, regardless of what player 2 does, player 1 gets a payoff of at least 1 when using either of these strategies, whereas it is feasible for player 1 to obtain a lower payoff (0 or −2, in particular) by selecting strategy A. For player 2, Y and Z are security strategies and they guarantee a payoff of at least −1.

Von Neumann and Morgenstern's general analysis focuses on mixed strategies (probability distributions over pure strategies) in finite two-player games, to which the maximin definition extends. They prove that the players' security levels (the amounts that the security strategies guarantee) sum to zero. Thus, when each player selects his security strategy, each player obtains exactly his security level payoff. Further, when one player selects his security strategy, the other player can do no better than select her own security strategy; that is, the two players' security strategies are optimal responses to each other. Security strategies also describe optimal play in zero-sum games that are played sequentially. For example, if player 1 had the privilege of selecting among A, B, and C *after* observing player 2's choice, both players would still select security strategies. Finally, security strategies are interchangeable in that the preceding conclusions hold equally well for any combination of security strategies, for instance (B, Y) as well as (B, Z).

Although von Neumann and Morgenstern had developed a theory that applied to all finite games, their theory is essentially empty for non-zero-sum games. For example, in converting a two-player game into a three-player game by adding the fictitious player 3, von Neumann and Morgenstern basically change the rules of the game for the original two players, who now can make binding agreements. The resulting prediction is that the two players will bind themselves to a strategy profile that maximizes the sum of their payoffs, with each player getting at least his security level. Von Neumann and Morgenstern's theory is therefore incomplete and unsatisfying on two fronts. First, for non-zero-sum games, it offers no treatment of rationality in the absence of binding commitments. Second, it offers no way of predicting the outcome of a two-player bargaining problem beyond Francis Ysidro Edgeworth's (1881) contract curve and it relies on transferable utility. Nearly all interesting economic examples involve efficiency concerns and hence are not zero-sum in nature, so economics had little to benefit from game theory until another significant step could be made in the modelling of rational behaviour.

Nash's contributions

Nash's contributions to the emerging discipline of game theory were equally as bold as were von Neumann and Morgenstern's and, in terms of applicability, even more significant. Nash's main contributions were made in a series of four papers published between 1950 and 1953 and summarized in this section.

In his articles in the *Proceedings of the National Academy of Sciences* in 1950 and the *Annals of Mathematics* in 1951, which reported his dissertation research, Nash (*a*) introduced and made clear the distinction between cooperative and non-cooperative games – the latter being games in which players act independently (that is,

without the assumption about coalitions that von Neumann and Morgenstern adopted) – and (*b*) defined a solution concept for non-cooperative games. The first four paragraphs from Nash's *Annals of Mathematics* article describe the context and the contribution succinctly:

> Von Neumann and Morgenstern have developed a very fruitful theory of two-person zero-sum games in their book *Theory of Games and Economic Behavior*. This book also contains a theory of *n*-person games of a type which we would call cooperative. This theory is based on an analysis of the interrelationships of the various coalitions which can be formed by the players of the game.
>
> Our Theory, in contradistinction, is based on the *absence* of coalitions in that it is assumed that each participant acts independently, without collaboration or communication with any of the others.
>
> The notion of an *equilibrium point* is the basic ingredient in our theory. This notion yields a generalization of the concept of the solution of a two-person zero-sum game. It turns out that the set of equilibrium points of a two-person zero-sum game is the set of all pairs of opposing 'good strategies.'
>
> In the immediately following sections we shall define equilibrium points and prove that a finite non-cooperative game always has at least one equilibrium point. We shall also introduce the notions of solvability and strong solvability of a non-cooperative game and prove a theorem on the geometrical structure of the set of equilibrium points of a solvable game. (1951, p. 286)

Nash's equilibrium concept became known as 'Nash equilibrium'. It and the cooperative/non-cooperative distinction were cited by the Royal Swedish Academy of Sciences in awarding Nash the Nobel Prize.

In more mathematical and modern language, here are the definitions of *best response* (in Nash's words, a 'good strategy') and Nash equilibrium. Consider any game defined by a number n of players; a strategy set S_i for each player $i = 1, 2, \ldots, n$; and, for each player i, a payoff function $u_i : S \to \mathbf{R}$, where S is the set of strategy profiles. The strategy sets may be defined as mixed strategies for some underlying set of pure strategies, in which case the payoff functions, as expectations, are linear in the mixed strategies. For a player i, we write '$-i$' to refer to the other players. Given a strategy vector s_{-i} for the other players, player i's strategy s_i is called a best response if player i can do no better than to select s_i; that is, we have $u_i(s_i, s_{-i}) \geq u_i(s_i', s_{-i})$ for every strategy s_i' of player i. Then strategy profile $s^* = (s_1^*, s_2^*, \ldots, s_n^*)$ is called a Nash equilibrium if every player is best responding to the others—that is, if for each player i, it is the case that s_i^* is a best response to s_{-i}^*.

For an illustration of Nash equilibrium and its relation to security strategies, consider the game depicted in the following table.

1\2	X	Y	Z
A	2,3	1,2	6,5
B	1,0	0,2	4,0
C	3,4	2,2	2,0

Observe that, in this game, C and Y are the players' security strategies, so a naive application of von Neumann and Morgenstern's maximin theory (absent binding agreements) would predict that strategy profile (C, Y) be played. However, this strategy profile is plainly inconsistent with the idea that players are rational in responding to each other. In particular, if player 1 is expected to select C then player 2 behaves quite irrationally by choosing Y. In fact, strategy Y is *not even rationalizable* for player 2; it does not survive iterated removal of dominated strategies (see below). Thus, the notion of a security strategy is not a good theory of behaviour for non-zero-sum games, demonstrating the limits of von Neumann and Morgenstern's analysis.

Next, observe that the game has two Nash equilibria in pure strategies, (C, X) and (A, Z). Both of these are reasonable predictions in the sense that, in both cases, the players are best responding to one another. For example, if player 1 is sure that player 2 will select X, then it is best for player 1 to select C; likewise, if player 2 is convinced that player 1 will select C, then it is optimal for player 2 to choose X. There is also a mixed-strategy Nash equilibrium in which player 1 randomizes between A and C, and player 2 randomizes between X and Z. That the game has multiple Nash equilibria demonstrates the general economic problem of coordination, in particular the possibility that the players will coordinate on the less efficient Nash equilibrium. Other games, such as the *Prisoner's Dilemma*, have only inefficient equilibria and thus reveal a fundamental tension between individual and joint incentives.

Nash's intuitive concept of equilibrium facilitated the analysis of *all* non-cooperative games, opening the door to widespread application of game theory. Indeed, Nash equilibrium has become the dominant solution concept for the analysis of games. Through an ingenious fixed-point argument, Nash also proved the existence of an equilibrium point in every finite game. Further, in his dissertation (1950) Nash offered two interpretations of the concept, one based on rational reasoning by individual players and the other describing stability of the distribution of strategies chosen by a population of individuals who interact over time. The latter is a precursor to the methodology of the literature on learning in games and to the modern

theories of *evolutionary stability* in biology (John Maynard Smith, 1984). Nash's 1951 *Annals of Mathematics* article also contains a section that defines 'dominance' (meaning one strategy yields a strictly higher payoff than another, regardless of what the other players do) and explains how an iterated dominance procedure can be used to rule out strategies that are not equilibria. Thus, Nash also made observations that would resurface in the concept of 'rationalizable strategic behaviour' (B. Douglas Bernheim, 1984; David Pearce, 1984), the main non-equilibrium notion of rationality. Nash even was among the first to perform game experiments, as his co-authored article in the volume *Decision Processes* (Kalisch et al., 1954) attests.

In his 1950 *Econometrica* article, Nash tackled the two-person bargaining problem with the objective of determining a unique solution (a precise 'value' that eluded von Neumann and Morgenstern) from the underlying set of alternatives and the players' preferences. Nash took a cooperate-theory approach by positing a system of four axioms that reasonably characterize properties one might expect the outcome of a bargaining process to exhibit: (*a*) a notion of equal bargaining power, (*b*) invariance to inessential utility transformations, (*c*) efficiency, and (*d*) independence of the solution to the removal of so-called irrelevant alternatives. Nash proved that a particular function of parameters (which maximizes the product of surpluses) is exactly characterized by the axioms. The analysis showed that it is possible to reasonably identify a precise outcome of a bargaining problem. It also initiated the axiomatic method for the analysis of bargaining (where theorists explore how different axioms characterize various functional solutions), starting a literature that thrived for several decades. The *Nash bargaining solution* is still the dominant solution in applied economic models.

Nash's second paper on bargaining (the 1953 *Econometrica* article) took another major step by connecting the non-cooperative and cooperative approaches to strategic analysis. At the heart of this theoretical exercise is an underlying non-cooperative game, which gives a set of feasible payoffs, and a technology for the players to make binding commitments about the mixed strategies that they will play in the underlying game. In the model, players first simultaneously make threats, which are mixed strategies they are bound to play if they do not reach an agreement. Then the players interact in a non-cooperative bargaining game in which they simultaneously make payoff demands – this stage is now called the 'Nash demand game'. If their payoff demands are feasible in the underlying game, then the players obtain their demanded payoffs; otherwise, the players get what their threats imply.

Nash observed that the demand game has generally an infinite number of equilibria, revealing a coordination aspect to the bargaining problem. But Nash went further in developing a brilliant method to 'escape from this troublesome non-uniqueness' by looking at the limit of 'smooth' approximations of the demand game.

Amazingly, Nash showed that the limit is unique and coincides with the prediction of his axiomatic model; that is, the limit is the Nash bargaining solution. Nash's limit argument was the forerunner to the enormous literature on *equilibrium refinements*, an area of research that thrived decades later and was the primary subject of Nash's Nobel co-recipients. More significantly, Nash argued that the relation between the cooperative solution concept and the equilibrium in the non-cooperative model justifies wide use of the cooperative solution as a reasonable shorthand for the actual non-cooperative setting. Nash's argument, and fascinating theoretical result, established the profession's understanding of the connection between cooperative and non-cooperative models and initiated the literature on what is now called the 'Nash program'.

After completing the work in game theory just described, Nash made fundamental contributions in pure mathematics – contributions that, in terms of mathematical depth and originality, were of an even higher order of sophistication and importance. According to leading mathematician John Milnor, Nash's

> subsequent mathematical work is far more rich and important [in this mathematical sense]. During the following years he proved that every smooth compact manifold can be realized as a sheet of a real algebraic variety, proved the highly anti-intuitive C1-isometric embedding theorem, introduced powerful and radically new tools to prove the far more difficult C1-isometric embedding theorem in high dimensions, and made a strong start on fundamental existence, uniqueness, and continuity theorems for partial differential equations. (Milnor, 1998, p. 1330)

It is not appropriate to provide here details on Nash's pure mathematics work (nor is it possible, due to the limitations of the author's fields of expertise).

Nash's personal life

Nash's character became legendary with the publication of a biography by Sylvia Nasar (1998) and a 2001 feature film produced by Brian Grazer and Ron Howard. Nash's remarkable personal journey began in Bluefield, West Virginia, where he was born and raised. He explored mathematics and conducted science experiments as a child, and attended Carnegie Institute of Technology, where the mathematics department discovered in him a budding genius. Nash's ideas on bargaining that were published as 'The Bargaining Problem' (1950) were developed while he was an undergraduate student at Carnegie, during the only economics course he took, on international trade.

Nash studied mathematics in the graduate program at Princeton University, where, as his biography describes, he was boorish, cocky, and a renowned adversary in strategic contests. At Princeton, Nash added to his prodigious achievements, finishing his dissertation – the work on non-cooperative games and equilibrium that would bring him the Nobel Prize – in his second year. (Nash also invented the board game *Hex*, a game independently created by Danish mathematician Piet Hein.) Nash taught at Princeton for one year and then took a position at Massachusetts Institute of Technology, where he was on the faculty until 1959. There he conducted the research that won him great acclaim in the mathematics community.

Nash's genius in advancing game theory and mathematics was paired with deep personal challenges. In 1959 Nash began experiencing the severe mental disturbances of paranoid schizophrenia. He resigned from MIT and began a phase of life marked by delusional thinking, an escape to Europe, repeated hospitalizations, unsuccessful medical treatments, and then a long, disengaged presence at Princeton. In the mid-1980s Nash miraculously began to emerge from the delusional haze in what he describes as a gradual rejection of psychotic thinking on intellectual grounds (Nash, 1995). After a quarter century of detachment, Nash's life regained a measure of normality.

Nash's legacy in game theory and economics

There is no simple way of quantifying the enormous reach of Nash's ideas. The notions of Nash equilibrium, the Nash bargaining solution, the Nash demand game, and the Nash program have found such widespread acceptance and application that it has become customary, and perhaps even appropriate, for researchers to forgo formally citing Nash's articles when utilizing these concepts. Nash ideas helped to propel game theory from a mathematical sub-field into a full discipline, with major use and application in not only economics, where it is the main and worthy alternative to the competitive-market framework, but also in theoretical biology, political science, international relations and law.

Beyond its theoretical content, Nash's work also made a stylistic departure from that of von Neumann and Morgenstern, whose book methodically records definitions, examples, and analysis for numerous special cases in the process of developing general theory. Nash, in contrast, used the terse style of the mathematician, presenting his ideas with minimal obscuring features. His 1950 *Proceedings of the National Academy of Sciences* entry, for instance, is generously allotted two pages and could have been typeset on one. The benefit of focusing on the basic mathematical concepts is that it allows for a broad range of interpretations and extensions. For example, there are several motivations for Nash equilibrium, including as a condition for self-enforcement of a contract (which is an important topic in the current literature). A hallmark of excellent theoretical modelling is precise and straightforward expression of assumptions and conclusions, with their relation shown in the most simple and elegant way possible.

Mathematician Milnor, after offering the assessment of Nash's work in pure mathematics that is quoted above, continues with by saying: 'However, when mathematics is applied to other branches of human knowledge, we must really ask a quite different question: To what extent does the new work increase our understanding of the real world? On this basis, Nash's thesis was nothing short of revolutionary' (1998, p. 1330). Two leading game theorists of today say 'Nash's theory of non-cooperative games should now be recognized as one of the outstanding intellectual advances of the twentieth century' (Myerson, 1999, p. 1067) and 'His work lay the foundation of non-cooperative game theory, now the predominant mode of analysis of strategic interactions in economics, political science, and biology' (Crawford, 2002, p. 380).

When viewed from the perspective of five short decades, game theory has caused a revolution in economics and other fields of study. It was with the work of John Nash that the flame so exquisitely ignited by von Neumann and Morgenstern became the torch that would eventually set the social sciences ablaze.

JOEL WATSON

See also **bargaining; game theory; Morgenstern, Oskar; Nash program; non-cooperative games (equilibrium existence); von Neumann, John.**

The author thanks Vincent Crawford, Joel Sobel and Martin Dufwenberg for comments on a preliminary draft.

Bibliography

Items indicated with an asterisk provide good further background reading on John F. Nash, Jr. Also, the *Scandinavian Journal of Economics*, vol. 97, issue 1 (1995), contains articles on John Nash and his co-Nobel Prize recipients, John C. Harsanyi and Reinhard Selten. For a complete list of Nash's publications, including his papers in pure mathematics, see Milnor (1998).

Bernheim, B.D. 1984. Rationalizable strategic behavior. *Econometrica* 52, 1007–28.

Borel, E. 1921. La théorie du jeu et les équations intégrales à noyau symétrique gauche. *Comptes Rendus de l'Académie des Sciences* 173, 1304–08. English translation by L.J. Savage, *Econometrica* 21 (1953), 97–100.

Cournot, A. 1838. *Recherches sur les Principes Mathématiques de la Théorie des Richesses*. Paris: Hatchette. English translation by N.T. Bacon, Researches into the Mathematical Principles of the Theory of Wealth. New York: Macmillan, 1927.

Crawford, V.P. 2002. John Nash and the analysis of strategic behavior. *Economics Letters* 75, 377–82.

Edgeworth, F.Y. 1881. *Mathematical Psychics*. London: Kegan Paul.

Hammerstein, P. et al. 1996. The work of John Nash in game theory: Nobel seminar, December 8, 1994. *Journal of Economic Theory* 69, 153–85.

Kalisch, C., Milnor, J., Nash, J. and Nering, E. 1954. Some experimental n-person games. *Decision Processes*, ed. R.M. Thrall, C.H. Coombs and R.L. Davis. New York: Wiley.

Mayberry, J.P., Nash, J.F. and Shubik, M. 1953. A comparison of treatments of a duopoly situation. *Econometrica* 21, 141–54.

Maynard Smith, J. 1984. *Evolution and the Theory of Games*. New York: Cambridge University Press.

*Milnor, J. 1995. A Nobel Prize for John Nash. *The Mathematical Intelligencer* 17, 11–7.

*Milnor, J. 1998. John Nash and 'A Beautiful Mind'. *Notices of the American Mathematical Society* 45, 1329–32.

Myerson, R.B. 1999. 'Nash equilibrium and the history of economic theory. *Journal of Economic Literature* 37, 1067–82.

*Nasar, S. 1998. *A Beautiful Mind*. New York: Simon and Schuster.

Nash, J.F., Jr. 1950. Equilibrium points in n-person games. *Proceedings of the National Academy of Sciences, USA* 36, 48–9.

Nash, J.F., Jr. 1950. Non-cooperative games. Doctoral dissertation, Princeton University.

Nash, J.F., Jr. 1950. The bargaining problem. *Econometrica* 18, 155–62.

Nash, J.F., Jr. 1951. Non-cooperative games. *Annals of Mathematics* 54, 286–95.

Nash, J.F., Jr. 1953. Two-person cooperative games. *Econometrica* 21, 128–40.

*Nash, J.F., Jr. 1995. Autobiography. *Les Prix Nobel. The Nobel Prizes 1994*, ed. T. Frängsmyr. Stockholm: Nobel Foundation. Online. Available at http://nobelprize.org/nobel_prizes/economics/laureates/1994/nash-autobio.html, accessed 29 November 2006.

Pearce, D. 1984. Rationalizable strategic behavior and the problem of perfection. *Econometrica* 52, 1029–50.

von Neumann, J. 1928. Zur theories der gesellschaftsspiele. *Mathematische Annalen* 100, 295–320. English translation by S. Bergmann in *Contributions to the Theory of Games IV*, ed. R.D. Luce and A.W. Tucker. Princeton: Princeton University Press, 1959.

von Neumann, J. and Morgenstern, O. 1944. *Theory of Games and Economic Behavior*. Princeton: Princeton University Press (2nd edn 1947).

Nash equilibrium, refinements of

Game theory studies decisions by several persons in situations with significant interactions. Two features distinguish it from other theories of multi-person decisions. One is explicit consideration of each person's available strategies and the outcomes resulting from combinations of their choices; that is, a complete and detailed specification of the 'game'. Here a person's strategy is a complete plan specifying his action in each contingency that might arise. In non-cooperative contexts, the other is a focus on optimal choices by each person separately. John Nash

(1950; 1951) proposed that a combination of mutually optimal strategies can be characterized mathematically as an *equilibrium*. According to Nash's definition, a combination is an equilibrium if each person's choice is an optimal response to others' choices. His definition assumes that a choice is optimal if it maximizes the person's expected utility of outcomes, conditional on knowing or correctly anticipating the choices of others. In some applications, knowledge of others' choices might stem from prior agreement or communication, or accurate prediction of others' choices might derive from 'common knowledge' of strategies and outcomes and of optimizing behaviour. Because many games have multiple equilibria, the predictions obtained are incomplete. However, equilibrium is a weak criterion in some respects, and therefore one can refine the criterion to obtain sharper predictions (Harsanyi and Selten, 1988; Hillas and Kohlberg, 2002; Kohlberg, 1990; Kreps, 1990).

Here we describe the main refinements of Nash equilibrium used in the social sciences. Refinements were developed incrementally, often relying on ad hoc criteria, which makes it difficult for a non-specialist to appreciate what has been accomplished. Many refinements have been proposed but we describe only the most prominent ones. First we describe briefly those refinements that select equilibria with simple features, and then we focus mainly on those that invoke basic principles adapted from single-person decision theory.

Equilibria with simple features

Nash's construction allows each person to choose randomly among his strategies. But randomization is not always plausible, so in practice there is a natural focus on equilibria in 'pure' strategies, those that do not use randomization. There is a similar focus on strict equilibria, those for which each person has a unique optimal strategy in response to others' strategies. In games with some symmetries among the players, the symmetric equilibria are those that reflect these symmetries. In applications to dynamic interactions the most useful equilibria are those that, at each stage, depend only on that portion of prior history that is relevant for outcomes in the future. In particular, when the dynamics of the game are stationary one selects equilibria that are stationary or that are Markovian in that they depend only on state variables that summarize the history relevant for the future. Applications to computer science select equilibria or, more often, approximate equilibria, using strategies that can be implemented by simple algorithms. Particularly useful are equilibria that rely only on limited recall of past events and actions and thus economize on memory or computation.

Refinements that require strategies to be admissible

One strategy is strictly dominated by another if it yields strictly inferior outcomes for that person regardless of others' choices. Because an equilibrium never uses a strictly dominated strategy, the same equilibria persist when strictly dominated strategies are deleted, but after deletion it can be that some remaining strategies become strictly dominated. A refinement that exploits this feature deletes strictly dominated strategies until none remain, and then selects those equilibria that remain in the reduced game. If a single equilibrium survives then the game is called 'dominance solvable'. An equilibrium can, however, use a strategy that is weakly dominated in that it would be strictly dominated were it not for ties – in decision theory such a strategy is said to be inadmissible. A prominent criterion selects equilibria that use only admissible strategies, and sometimes this is strengthened by iterative deletion of strictly dominated strategies after deleting the inadmissible strategies. A stronger refinement uses *iterative deletion of* (both strictly and weakly) *dominated strategies* until none remain; however, this procedure is ambiguous because the end result can depend on the order in which weakly dominated strategies are deleted.

A particular order is used for dynamic games that decompose into a succession of subgames as time progresses. In this case, those strategies that are weakly dominated because they are strictly dominated in final subgames are deleted first, then those in penultimate subgames, and so on. In games with 'perfect information' as defined below this procedure implements the criterion called 'backward induction' and the equilibria that survive are among those that are 'subgame-perfect' (Selten, 1965). In general a subgame-perfect equilibrium is one that induces an equilibrium in each subgame. Figure 1 depicts an example in which there are two Nash equilibria, one in which A moves down because she anticipates that B will move down, and a second that is subgame-perfect because in the subgame after A moves across, B also moves across, which yields him a higher payoff than down.

The informal criterion of 'forward induction' has several formulations. Kohlberg and Mertens (1986) require that a refined set of equilibria contains a subset that survives deletion of strategies that are not optimal responses at any equilibrium in the set. Van Damme (1989; 1991) requires that if player A rejects a choice X in favour of Y or Z then another player who knows only that Y or Z was

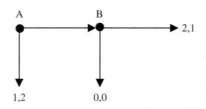

Figure 1   Player A moves down or across, in which case player B moves down or across. Payoffs for A and B are shown at the end of each sequence of moves

chosen should consider Z unlikely if it is chosen only in equilibria that yield player A outcomes worse than choosing X, whereas Y is chosen in an equilibrium whose outcome is better. A typical application mimics backward induction but in reverse – if a person previously rejected a choice with an outcome that would have been superior to the outcomes from all but one equilibrium of the ensuing subgame, then presumably the person is anticipating that favourable equilibrium and intends to use his strategy in that equilibrium of the subgame. In Figure 2, if A rejects the payoff 5 from Down then B can infer that A intends to play Top in the ensuing subgame, yielding payoff 6 for both players.

Dynamic games

Before proceeding further we describe briefly some relevant features of dynamic games, that is, games in which a player acts repeatedly, and can draw inferences about others' strategies, preferences, or private information as the game progresses. A dynamic game is said to have 'perfect information' if each person knows initially all the data of the game, and the prior history of his and others' actions whenever he acts, and they do not act simultaneously. In such a game each action initiates a subgame; hence backward induction yields a unique subgame-perfect equilibrium if there are no ties. But in many dynamic games there are no subgames. This is so whenever some person acts without knowing all data of the game relevant for the future. In Figure 3 player C acts without knowing whether player A or B chose down.

The source of this deficiency is typically that some participant has private information – for example, about his own preferences or about outcomes – or because his actions are observed imperfectly by some others. Among parlour games, chess is a game with perfect information (if players remember whether each king has been castled). Bridge and poker are games with imperfect information because the cards in one player's hand are not known to others when they bet. In practical settings, auctions and negotiations resemble poker because each party acts (bids, offers, and so on) without knowing others' valuations of the transaction. Analyses of practical economic games

usually assume (as we do here) 'perfect recall' in the sense that each player always remembers what he knew and did previously. If bridge is treated as a two-player game between teams, then it has imperfect recall because each team alternately remembers and forgets the cards in one member's hand as the bidding goes round the table, but bridge has perfect recall if it is treated as a four-player game. In card games like bridge and poker each player can derive the probability distribution of others' cards from the assumption that the deck of cards was thoroughly shuffled. Models of economic games impose analogous assumptions; for example, a model of an auction assumes that each bidder initially assesses a probability distribution of others' valuations of the item for sale, and then updates this assessment as he observes their bids. More realism is obtained from more complicated scenarios; for example, it could be that player A is uncertain about player B's assessment of player A's valuation. In principle the model could allow a hierarchy of beliefs – A's probability assessment of B's assessment of A's assessment of ... . To adopt a proposal by John Harsanyi (1967–1968) developed by Mertens and Zamir (1985), such situations are modelled by assuming that each player is one of several types. The initial joint distribution of types is commonly known among the players, but each player knows his own type, which includes a specification of his available strategies, his preferences over outcomes, and, most importantly, his assessment of the conditional probabilities of others' types given his own type. In poker, for instance, a player's type includes the hand of cards he is dealt, and his hand affects his beliefs about others' hands.

Refinements of Nash equilibrium are especially useful in dynamic games. Nash equilibria do not distinguish between the case in which each player commits initially and irrevocably to his strategy throughout the game, and

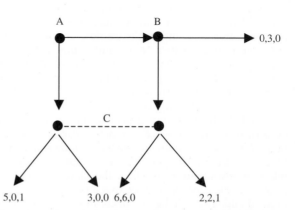

Figure 3   Player A moves down or across, in which case player B moves down or across. Player C does not observe whether it was A or B who moved down when she chooses to move left or right

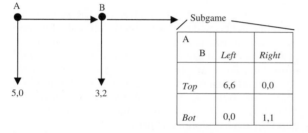

Figure 2   First A and then B can avoid playing the subgame in which simultaneously each chooses between two options

the case in which a player continually re-optimizes as the game progresses. The distinction is lost because the definition of Nash equilibrium presumes that players will surely adhere to their strategies chosen initially. Most refinements of Nash equilibrium are intended to resurrect this important distinction. Ideally one would like each Nash equilibrium to bear a label telling whether it assumes implicit commitment or relies on incredible threats or promises. Such features are usually evident in the equilibria of trivially simple games, but in more complicated games they must be identified by augmenting the definition of Nash equilibrium with additional criteria.

In the sequel we describe two classes of refinements in detail, but first we summarize their main features, identify the main selection criteria they use, and mention the names of some specific refinements. Both classes are generalizations of backward induction and subgame perfection, and they obtain similar results, but their motivation and implementation differ.

1. The criterion of sequential rationality

The presumption that commitment is irrevocable is flawed if other participants in the game do not view commitment to a strategy as credible. Commitment can be advantageous, of course, but if commitment is possible (for example, via enforceable contractual arrangements) then it should properly be treated as a distinct strategy. Absent commitment, some Nash equilibria are suspect because they rely implicitly on promises or threats that are not credible. For example, one Nash equilibrium might enable an incumbent firm to deter another firm from entering its market by threatening a price war. If such a threat succeeds in deterring entry then it is costless to the incumbent because it is never challenged; indeed, it can be that this equilibrium is sustained only by the presumption that the incumbent will never need to carry out the threat. But this threat is not credible if, after entry occurs, the incumbent would recognize that accommodation is more profitable than a price war. In such contexts, the purpose of a refinement is to select an alternative Nash equilibrium that anticipates correctly that entry will be followed by accommodation. For instance, the subgame-perfect equilibrium in Figure 1 satisfies this criterion.

Refinements in the first class exclude strategies that are not credible by requiring explicitly that a strategy is optimal in each contingency, even if it comes as a surprise. (We use the term 'contingency' rather than the technical term 'information set' used in game theory – it refers to any situation in which the player chooses an action.) These generally require that a player's strategy is optimal initially (as in the case of commitment), *and* that in each subsequent contingency in which the player might act his strategy remains optimal for the remainder of the game, even if the equilibrium predicts that the contingency should not occur. This criterion is called 'sequential rationality'. As described later, three such refinements are *perfect Bayes*, *sequential*, and *lexicographic* equilibria, each of which can be strengthened further by imposing additional criteria such as *invariance*, the *intuitive criterion* and *divinity*.

2. The criterion of perfection or stability

The presumption that commitment is irrevocable is also flawed if there is some chance of deviations. If a player might 'tremble' or err in carrying out his intended strategy, or his valuation of outcomes might be slightly different from others anticipated, then other players can be surprised to find themselves in unexpected situations. Refinements that exploit this feature are implemented in two stages. In the first stage one identifies the Nash equilibria of a perturbation of the original game, usually obtained by restricting each player to randomized strategies that assign positive probabilities to all his original pure strategies. In the second stage one identifies those equilibria of the original game that are limits of equilibria of the perturbed game as this restriction is relaxed to allow inferior strategies to have zero probabilities.

Refinements in the second class also exclude strategies that are not credible, but refinements in this class implement sequential rationality indirectly. The general criterion that is invoked is called 'perfection' or 'stability', depending on the context. In each case a refinement is obtained from analyses of perturbed games. This second class of refinements is typically more restrictive than the first class due to the stronger effects of perturbations. As described later, two such refinements are *perfect* and *proper* equilibria. These are equilibria that are perturbed slightly by *some* perturbation of the players' strategies. A more stringent refinement selects a subset of equilibria that is *truly perfect* or *stable* in the sense that it is perturbed only slightly by *every* perturbation of players' strategies. This refinement selects a subset of equilibria rather than a single equilibrium because there need not exist a single equilibrium that is *essential* in that it is perturbed slightly by every perturbation of strategies. A stringent refinement selects a subset that is *hyperstable* in that it is stable against perturbations of both players' strategies and their valuations of outcomes, or against perturbations of their optimal responses; and further, it is *invariant* in that it is unaffected by addition or deletion of redundant strategies.

The crucial role of perturbations in the second class of refinements makes them more difficult for non-specialists to understand and appreciate, but they have a prominent role in game theory because of their desirable properties. For example, in a two-player game a perfect equilibrium is equivalent to an equilibrium that uses only admissible strategies. In general, refinements in the second class have the advantage that they satisfy several selection criteria simultaneously.

After this overview, we now turn to detailed descriptions of the various refinements.

Refinements that require sequential rationality

In dynamic games with perfect information, the implementation of backward induction is unambiguous because in each contingency the player taking an action there knows exactly the subgame that follows. In chess, for example, the current positions of the pieces determine how the game can evolve subsequently. Moreover, if he anticipates his opponent's strategy then he can predict how the opponent will respond to each possible continuation of his own strategy. Using this prediction he can choose an optimal strategy for the remainder of the game by applying the *principle of optimality* – his optimal strategy in the current subgame consists of his initial action that, when followed by his optimal strategies in subsequent subgames, yields his best outcome. Thus, in principle (although not in practice, since chess is too complicated) his optimal strategy can be found by working backward from final positions through all possible positions in the game.

In contrast, in a game with imperfect information a player's current information may be insufficient to identify the prior history that led to this situation, and therefore insufficient to identify how others will respond in the future, even if he anticipates their strategies. In poker, for example, knowledge of his own cards and anticipation of others' strategies are insufficient to predict how they will respond to his bets. Their strategies specify how they will respond conditional on their cards but, since he does not know their cards, he remains uncertain what bets they will make in response to his bets. In this case, it is his assessment of the probability distribution of their cards that enables construction of his optimal strategy. That is, this probability distribution can be combined with their strategies to provide him with a probabilistic prediction of how they will bet in response to each bet he might make. Using this prediction he can again apply the principle of optimality to construct an optimal strategy by working backward from the various possible conclusions of the game.

Those refinements that select equilibria satisfying sequential rationality use an analogous procedure. The analogue of the probability distribution of others' cards is a system of 'beliefs', one for each contingency in which the player might find himself. Each belief is a conditional probability distribution on the prior history of the game given the contingency at which he has arrived. Thus, to whatever extent he is currently uncertain about others' preferences over final outcomes or their prior actions, his current belief provides him with a probability distribution over the various possibilities. As in poker, this probability distribution can be combined with his anticipation of their strategies to provide him with a probabilistic prediction of how they will act in response to each action he might take – and again, using this prediction he can apply the principle of optimality to construct an optimal strategy by working backward from the various possible conclusions of the game.

There is an important proviso, however. These refinements require that, whenever one contingency follows another with positive probability, the belief at the later one must be obtained from the belief at the earlier one by Bayes' rule. This ensures consistency with the rules of conditional probability. But, importantly, it does not restrict a player's belief at a contingency that was unexpected, that is, had zero probability according to his previous belief and the other players' strategies.

In Figure 3, in one Nash equilibrium A chooses down, B chooses across, and C chooses left. This is evidently not sequential because if A were to deviate then B could gain by choosing down. In a sequential equilibrium B chooses down and each of A and C randomizes equally between his two strategies. The strategies of A and B imply that C places equal probabilities on which of A and B chose down.

The weakest refinement selects a *perfect-Bayes* equilibrium (Fudenberg and Tirole, 1991). This requires that each player's strategy is consistent with some system of beliefs such that (*a*) his strategy is optimal given his beliefs and others' strategies, and (*b*) his beliefs satisfy Bayes' rule (wherever it applies) given others' strategies. A stronger refinement selects *sequential* equilibria (Kreps and Wilson, 1982). A sequential equilibrium requires that each player's system of beliefs is consistent with the structure of the game. Consistency is defined formally as the requirement that each player's system of beliefs is the limit of the conditional probabilities induced by players' strategies in some perturbed game, as described previously. A further refinement selects *quasi-perfect* equilibria (van Damme, 1984), which requires admissibility of a player's strategy in continuation from each contingency, excluding any chance that he himself might deviate from his intended strategy. And even stronger are *proper* equilibria (Myerson, 1978), described later. This sequence of progressively stronger refinements is typical. Because proper implies quasi-perfect implies sequential implies perfect-Bayes, one might think that it is sufficient to always use properness as the refinement. However, the prevailing practice in the social sciences is to invoke the weakest refinement that suffices for the game being studied. This reflects a conservative attitude about using unnecessarily restrictive refinements. If, say, there is a unique sequential equilibrium that uses only admissible strategies, then one refrains from imposing stronger criteria.

Additional criteria can be invoked to select among sequential equilibria. In Figure 4 there is a sequential equilibrium in which both types of A move left and B randomizes equally between middle and bottom, and another in which both types of A move right and B chooses middle. An alternative justification for the second, due to Hillas (1998), is shown in Figure 5, where the game is restructured so that A either commits initially to left or they play the subgame with simultaneous choices of strategies. The criterion of subgame perfection selects

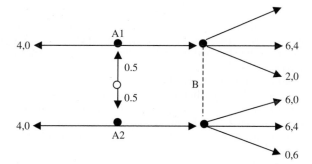

Figure 4   Nature chooses whether player A's type is A1 or A2 with equal probabilities. Then A chooses Left or Right, in which case player B, without knowing A's type, chooses one of three options

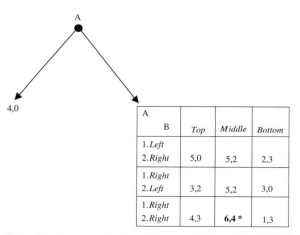

Figure 5   The game in Figure 4 restructured so that either A commits to Left regardless of his type, or plays a subgame with simultaneous moves in which he chooses one of his other three type-contingent strategies. The payoffs 6,4 to A and B from the unique Nash equilibrium of the subgame are shown with an asterisk

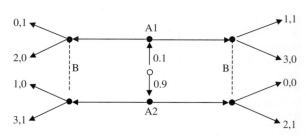

Figure 6   A signalling game in which Nature chooses A's type A1 or A2, then A chooses left or right, and then B, without knowing A's type, chooses up or down

for B to recognize the signal. In effect, these criteria reject equilibria that commit a player to unrealistic beliefs. Another interpretation is that these criteria reject equilibria in which A is 'threatened by B's beliefs' because B stubbornly retains these beliefs in spite of plausible evidence to the contrary.

The simplest version requires that B's belief assigns zero probability to those types of A that cannot possibly gain by deviating, regardless of how B responds. The *intuitive* criterion (Cho and Kreps, 1987) requires that there cannot be some type of A that surely gains from deviating in every continuation for which B responds with a strategy that is optimal based on a belief that assigns zero probability to those types of A that cannot gain from the deviation. That is, an equilibrium fails the intuitive criterion if B's belief fails to recognize that A's deviation is a credible signal about his type. They apply this criterion to the game in Figure 6, which has two sequential equilibria. In one both types of A choose left and B chooses down or up contingent on left or right. In another both types choose right and B chooses up or down contingent on left or right. In both equilibria B's belief in the unexpected event (right or left respectively) assigns probability greater than 0.5 to A's type A1. The intuitive criterion rejects the second equilibrium because if A2 were to deviate by choosing left, and then B recognizes that this deviation credibly signals A's type A2 (because type A1 cannot gain by deviating regardless of B's response) and therefore B chooses down, then type A2 obtains payoff 3 rather than his equilibrium payoff 2.

Cho and Kreps also define an alternative version, called the 'equilibrium domination' criterion. This criterion requires that, for each continuation in which B responds with a strategy that is optimal based on a belief that assigns zero probability to those types of A that cannot gain from deviating, there cannot be some type of A that gains from deviating. More restrictive is the criterion **D1** (Banks and Sobel, 1987), also called 'divinity' when it is applied iteratively, which requires that, if the set of B's responses for which one type of A gains from deviating is larger than the set for which a second type gains, then B's beliefs must assign zero probability to the second type. The criterion **D2** is similar except that some

the second equilibrium in Figure 4 because in Figure 5 the subgame has a unique equilibrium with payoff 6 for A that is superior to his payoff 4 from committing to left.

These refinements can be supplemented with additional criteria that restrict a player's beliefs in unexpected contingencies. The most widely used criteria apply to contexts in which one player B could interpret the action of another player A as revealing private information; that is, A's action might signal something about A's type. These criteria restrict B's belief (after B observes A deviating from the equilibrium) to one that assigns positive probability only to A's types that might possibly gain from the deviation, provided it were interpreted by B as a credible signal about A's type. The purpose of these criteria is to exclude beliefs that are blind to A's attempts to signal what his type is when it would be to A's advantage (rather than just one) types of A gain. All these criteria are weaker than the *never weak best reply* criterion that requires an equilibrium to survive deletion of a player's strategy that is not an optimal reply to any equilibrium with the same outcome. In Figure 6 this criterion is applied by observing that the second equilibrium does not survive deletion of those strategies of A in which type A2 chooses left.

A *lexicographic* equilibrium (Blume, Brandenburger and Dekel, 1991a; 1991b) uses a different construction. Each player is supposed to rely on a sequence of 'theories' about others' strategies. He starts the game by assuming that his first theory of others' strategies is true, and uses his optimal strategy according to that theory. He continues doing so until he finds himself in a situation that cannot be explained by his first theory. In this case, he abandons the first theory and assumes instead that the second theory is true – or if it too cannot explain what has happened then he proceeds to the next theory in the sequence. This provides a refinement of Nash equilibrium because each player anticipates that deviation from his optimal strategy for any theory will provoke others to abandon their current theories and strategies and thus respond with their optimal strategies for their next theories consistent with his deviant action. Lexicographic equilibria can be used to represent nearly any refinement. The hierarchy of a player's theories serves basically the same role as his system of beliefs, but the focus is on predictions of other players' strategies in the future rather than probabilities of what they know or have done in the past. The lexicographic specification has the same effect as considering small perturbations of strategies; for example, the sequence of strategies approximating a perfect or proper equilibrium can be used to construct the hierarchy of theories.

Refinements derived from perturbed games

The other major class of refinements relies on perturbations to select among the Nash equilibria. The motive for this approach stems from a basic principle of decision theory –the *equivalence* of alternative methods of deriving optimal strategies. This principle posits that constructing a player's optimal strategy in a dynamic game by invoking auxiliary systems of beliefs and the iterative application of the principle of optimality (as in perfect-Bayes and sequential equilibria) is a useful computational procedure, but the same result should be obtainable from an initial choice of a strategy, that is, an optimal plan for the entire game of actions taken in each contingency. Indeed, the definition of Nash equilibrium embodies this principle. Proponents therefore argue that whatever improvements come from dynamic analysis can and should be replicated by static analysis of initial choices among strategies, supplemented by additional criteria. (We use the terms 'static' and 'dynamic' analysis rather than the technical terms 'normal-form' and 'extensive-form'

analysis used in game theory.) The validity of this argument is evident in the case of subgame-perfect equilibria of games with perfect information, which can be derived either from the principle of optimality using backward induction, or by iterative elimination of weakly dominated strategies in a prescribed order. The argument is reinforced by major deficiencies of dynamic analysis; for example, we mentioned above that a sequential equilibrium can use inadmissible strategies. Another deficiency is failure to satisfy the criterion of *invariance*, namely, the set of sequential equilibria can depend on which of many equivalent descriptions of the dynamics of the game is used (in particular, on the addition or deletion of redundant strategies).

On this view one should address directly the basic motive for refinement, which is to exclude equilibria that assume implicitly that each player commits initially to his strategy – since Nash equilibria do not distinguish between cases with and without commitment. Thus one considers explicitly that during the game any player might deviate from his equilibrium strategy for some exogenous reason that was not represented in the initial description of the game. Recognition of the possibility of deviations, however improbable they might be, then ensures that a player's strategy includes a specification of his optimal response to others' deviations from the equilibrium. The objective is therefore to characterize those equilibria that are affected only slightly by small probabilities of deviant behaviours or variations in preferences. This programme is implemented by considering perturbations of the game. These can be perturbations of strategies or payoffs, but actually the net effect of a perturbation of others' strategies is to perturb a player's payoffs.

In the following we focus on the perturbations of the static (that is, the normal form) of the game but similar perturbations can also be applied to the dynamic version (that is, the extensive form) by applying them to each contingency separately. This is done by invoking the principle that a dynamic game can also be analysed in a static framework by treating the player acting in each contingency as a new player (interpreted as the player's agent who acts solely in that contingency) in the 'agent-normal-form' of the game, where the new player's payoffs agree with those of the original player.

The construction of a *perfect* equilibrium (Selten, 1975) illustrates the basic method, which uses two steps.

1. For each small positive number ε one finds an ε-*perfect* equilibrium, defined by the requirement that each player's strategy has the following property: every one of his pure strategies is used with positive probability, but any pure strategy that is an inferior response to the others' strategies has probability no more than ε. Thus an ε-perfect equilibrium supposes that every strategy, and therefore every action during the game, might occur, even if it is suboptimal.

2. One then obtains a perfect equilibrium as the limit of a convergent subsequence of ε-perfect equilibria.

One method of constructing an ε-perfect equilibrium starts by specifying for each player i a small probability $\delta_i < \varepsilon$ and a randomized strategy σ_i that uses every pure strategy with positive probability – that is, the strategy combination σ is 'completely mixed'. One then finds an ordinary Nash equilibrium of the perturbed game in which each player's payoffs are as follows: his payoff from each combination of all players' pure strategies is replaced by his expected payoff when each player i's pure strategy is implemented only with probability $1 - \delta_i$ and with probability δ_i that player uses his randomized strategy σ_i instead. In this context one says that the game is perturbed by less than ε toward σ – we use this phrase again later when we describe stable sets of equilibria. An equilibrium of this perturbed game induces an ε-perfect equilibrium of the original game.

An alternative definition of perfect equilibrium requires that each player's strategy is an optimal response to a convergent sequence of others' strategies for which all their pure strategies have positive probability – this reveals explicitly that optimality against small probabilities of deviations is achieved, and that a perfect equilibrium uses only admissible strategies. In fact, a perfect equilibrium of the agent-normal-form induces a sequential equilibrium of the dynamic version of the game. Moreover, if the payoffs of the dynamic game are generic (that is, not related to each other by polynomial equations) then every sequential equilibrium is also perfect.

A stronger refinement selects *proper* equilibria (Myerson, 1978). This refinement supposes that the more inferior the expected payoff from a strategy is, the less likely it is to be used. The construction differs only in step 1: if one pure strategy S is inferior to another T in response to the others' strategies then S has probability no more than ε times the probability of T. A proper equilibrium induces a sequential equilibrium in every one of the equivalent descriptions of the dynamic game.

A perfect or proper equilibrium depends on the particular perturbation used to construct an ε-perfect or ε-proper equilibrium. Sometimes a game has an equilibrium that is *essential* or *truly perfect* in that any σ can be used when perturbing the game by less than ε toward σ, as above. This is usual for a static game with generic payoffs because in this case its equilibria are isolated and vary continuously with perturbations. However, such equilibria rarely exist in the important case that the static game represents a dynamic game, since in this case some strategies have the same equilibrium payoffs. This occurs because there is usually considerable freedom about how a player acts in contingencies off the predicted path of the equilibrium; in effect, the same outcome results whether the player 'punishes' others only barely enough to deter deviations, or more than enough. Indeed, for a dynamic game with generic payoffs, all the equilibria in a connected set yield the same equilibrium outcome because they differ only off the predicted path of equilibrium play. One must therefore consider sets of equilibria when invoking stringent refinements like truly perfect. One applies a somewhat different test to sets of equilibria. When considering a set of equilibria one requires that every sufficiently small perturbation (within a specified class) of the game has an equilibrium near some equilibrium in the set. Some refinements insist on a minimal closed set of equilibria with this property, but here we ignore minimality.

The chief refinement of this kind uses strategy perturbations to generate perturbed games. Kohlberg and Mertens (1986) say that a set of equilibria is *stable* if for each neighbourhood of the set there exists a positive probability ε such that, for every completely mixed strategy combination σ, each perturbation of the game by less than ε toward σ has an equilibrium within the neighbourhood. Stability can be interpreted as truly perfect applied to sets of equilibria and using the class of payoff perturbations generated by strategy perturbations. Besides the fact that a stable set always exists, it satisfies several criteria: it uses only *admissible* strategies, it contains a stable set of the reduced game after deleting a strategy that is weakly dominated or an inferior response to all equilibria in the set (these assure *iterative elimination of weakly dominated strategies* and a version of *forward induction*), and it is *invariant* to addition or deletion of redundant strategies. However, examples are known in which a stable set of a static game does not include a sequential equilibrium of the dynamic game it represents. This failure to satisfy the backward induction criterion can be remedied in various ways that we describe next.

One approach considers the larger class of all payoff perturbations. In this case, invariance to redundant strategies is not assured so it is imposed explicitly. For this, say that two games are equivalent if deletion of all redundant strategies results in the same reduced game. Similarly, randomized strategies in these two games are equivalent if they yield the same randomization over pure strategies of the reduced game. Informally, a set of equilibria is hyperstable if, for every payoff perturbation of every equivalent game, there is an equilibrium equivalent to one near the set. Two formal versions are the following. Kohlberg and Mertens (1986) say that a set S of equilibria is *hyperstable* if, for each neighbourhood N of those strategies in an equivalent game that are equivalent to ones in S, there is a sufficiently small neighbourhood P of payoff perturbations for the equivalent game such that every game in P has an equilibrium in N. A somewhat stronger version is the following. A set S of equilibria of a game G is *uniformly hyperstable* if, for each neighbourhood N of S, there is a $\delta > 0$ such that every game in the δ-neighbourhood of any game equivalent to G has an equilibrium equivalent to one in N. This version emphasizes that uniform hyperstability is closely akin to a kind of continuity with respect to payoff perturbations of equivalent games. Unfortunately, both of these definitions are complex, but the second actually allows a succinct statement in the case that the set S is a 'component' of equilibria, namely, a maximal connected set of the Nash equilibria. In this case the component is uniformly hyperstable if and only if its topological index is non-zero, and thus *essential* in the sense used in algebraic topology to characterize a set of fixed points of a function that is slightly affected by every perturbation of the function. This provides a simply computed test of whether a component is uniformly hyperstable.

Hyperstable sets tend to be larger than stable sets of equilibria because they must be robust against a larger class of perturbations, but for this same reason the criterion is actually stronger. Within a hyperstable component there is always a stable set satisfying the criteria listed previously. There is also a proper equilibrium that induces a sequential equilibrium in every dynamic game with the same static representation – thus, the criterion of *backward induction* is also satisfied. Selecting a stable subset or a proper equilibrium inside a hyperstable component may be necessary because there can be other equilibria within a hyperstable component that use inadmissible strategies. Nevertheless, for a dynamic game with generic payoffs, all the equilibria within a single component yield the same outcome, since they differ only off the path of equilibrium play, so for the purpose of predicting the outcome rather than players' strategies it is immaterial which equilibrium is considered. However, examples are known in which an inessential hyperstable component contains two stable sets with opposite indices with respect to perturbations of strategies.

The most restrictive refinement is the revised definition of stability proposed by Mertens (1989). Although this definition is highly technical, it can be summarized briefly as follows for the mathematically expert reader. Roughly, a closed set of equilibria is (Mertens-) *stable* if the projection map (from its neighbourhood in the graph of the Nash equilibria into the space of games with perturbed strategies) is essential. Such a set satisfies all the criteria listed previously, and several more. For instance, it satisfies the *small-worlds* criterion (Mertens, 1992), which requires that adding other players whose strategies have no effect on the payoffs for the original players has no effect on the selected strategies of the original players. The persistent mystery in the study of refinements is why such sophisticated constructions seem to be necessary if a single definition is to satisfy all the criteria simultaneously. The clue seems to be that, because Nash equilibria are the solutions of a fixed-point problem, a fully adequate refinement must ensure that fixed points exist for every perturbation of this problem.

The state of the art of refinements

The development of increasingly stronger refinements by imposing ad hoc criteria incrementally was a preliminary to more systematic development. Eventually, one wants to identify decision-theoretic criteria that suffice as axioms to characterize refinements. The two groups of refinements described above approach this problem differently. Those that consider perturbations seek to verify whether there exist refinements that satisfy many or (in the case of Mertens-stability) most criteria. From its beginning in the work of Selten (1975), Myerson (1978), and Kohlberg and Mertens (1986), this has been a productive exercise, showing that refinements can enforce more stringent criteria than Nash (1950; 1951) requires. However, the results obtained depend ultimately on the class of perturbations considered, since Fudenberg, Kreps and Levine (1988) show that each Nash equilibrium of a game is the limit of strict equilibria of perturbed games in a very general class. Perturbations are mathematical artefacts used to identify refinements with desirable properties, but they are not intrinsic to a fundamental theory of rational decision making in multi-person situations. Those in the other group directly impose decision-theoretic criteria – admissibility, iterative elimination of dominated or inferior strategies, backward induction, invariance, small worlds, and so on. Their ultimate aim is to characterize refinements axiomatically. But so far none has obtained an ideal refinement of the Nash equilibria.

SRIHARI GOVINDAN AND ROBERT WILSON

See also **behavioural game theory; epistemic game theory: incomplete information; game theory; Harsanyi, John C.; Markov equilibria in macroeconomics; Nash, John Forbes; Nash program; Selten, Reinhard; signalling and screening.**

Bibliography

Banks, J. and Sobel, J. 1987. Equilibrium selection in signaling games. *Econometrica* 55, 647–61.

Blume, L., Brandenburger, A. and Dekel, E. 1991a. Lexicographic probabilities and choice under uncertainty. *Econometrica* 59, 61–79.

Blume, L., Brandenburger, A. and Dekel, E. 1991b. Lexicographic probabilities and equilibrium refinements. *Econometrica* 59, 81–98.

Cho, I. and Kreps, D. 1987. Signaling games and stable equilibria. *Quarterly Journal of Economics* 102, 179–221.

Fudenberg, D., Kreps, D. and Levine, D. 1988. On the robustness of equilibrium refinements. *Journal of Economic Theory* 44, 351–80.

Fudenberg, D. and Tirole, J. 1991. Perfect Bayesian equilibrium and sequential equilibrium. *Journal of Economic Theory* 53, 236–60.

Harsanyi, J. 1967–1968. Games with incomplete information played by 'Bayesian' players, I–III. *Management Science* 14, 159–82, 320–34, 486–502.

Harsanyi, J. and Selten, R. 1988. *A General Theory of Equilibrium Selection in Games*. Cambridge, MA: MIT Press.

Hillas, J. 1998. How much of 'forward induction' is implied by 'backward induction' and 'ordinality'? Mimeo. Department of Economics, University of Auckland.

Hillas, J. and Kohlberg, E. 2002. The foundations of strategic equilibrium. In *Handbook of Game Theory*, vol. 3, ed. R. Aumann and S. Hart. Amsterdam: North-Holland/ Elsevier Science Publishers.

Kohlberg, E. 1990. Refinement of Nash equilibrium: the main ideas. In *Game Theory and Applications*, ed. T. Ichiishi, A. Neyman and Y. Tauman. San Diego: Academic Press.

Kohlberg, E. and Mertens, J.-F. 1986. On the strategic stability of equilibria. *Econometrica* 54, 1003–38.

Kreps, D. 1990. *Game Theory and Economic Modeling*. New York: Oxford University Press.

Kreps, D. and Wilson, R. 1982. Sequential equilibria. *Econometrica* 50, 863–94.

Mertens, J.-F. 1989. Stable equilibria – a reformulation, Part I: definition and basic properties. *Mathematics of Operations Research* 14, 575–624.

Mertens, J.-F. 1992. The small worlds axiom for stable equilibria. *Games and Economic Behavior* 4, 553–64.

Mertens, J.-F. and Zamir, S. 1985. Formulation of Bayesian analysis for games with incomplete information. *International Journal of Game Theory* 14, 1–29.

Myerson, R. 1978. Refinement of the Nash equilibrium concept. *International Journal of Game Theory* 7, 73–80.

Nash, J. 1950. Equilibrium points in n-person games. *Proceedings of the National Academy of Sciences USA* 36, 48–9.

Nash, J. 1951. Non-cooperative games. *Annals of Mathematics* 54, 286–95.

Selten, R. 1965. Spieltheoretische Behandlung eines Oligopolmodells mit Nachfragetragheit. *Zeitschrift fur die gesamte Staatswissenschaft* 121, 301–24, 667–89.

Selten, R. 1975. Reexamination of the perfectness concept for equilibrium points in extensive games. *International Journal of Game Theory* 4, 25–55.

van Damme, E. 1984. A relation between perfect equilibria in extensive form games and proper equilibria in normal form games. *International Journal of Game Theory* 13, 1–13.

van Damme, E. 1989. Stable equilibria and forward induction. *Journal of Economic Theory* 48, 476–96.

van Damme, E. 1991. *Stability and Perfection of Nash Equilibria*. Berlin: Springer-Verlag.

Nash program

In game theory, 'Nash program' is the name given to a research agenda, initiated in Nash (1953), intended to bridge the gap between the cooperative and non-cooperative approaches to the discipline.

Many authors have contributed to the program since its beginnings (see Serrano, 2005, for a comprehensive survey). The current article concentrates on a few salient contributions. One should begin by introducing some preliminaries and providing definitions of some basic concepts.

Preliminaries

The non-cooperative approach to game theory provides a rich language and develops useful tools to analyse strategic situations. One clear advantage of the approach is that it is able to model how specific details of the interaction may affect the final outcome. One limitation, however, is that its predictions may be highly sensitive to those details. For this reason it is worth also analysing more abstract approaches that attempt to obtain conclusions that are independent of such details. The cooperative approach is one such attempt.

Here are the primitives of the basic model in cooperative game theory. Let $N = \{1, \ldots, n\}$ be a finite set of players. For each S, a non-empty subset of N, we shall specify a set $V(S)$ containing $|S|$-dimensional payoff vectors that are feasible for coalition S. Thus, a reduced form approach is taken because one does not explain what strategic choices are behind each of the payoff vectors in $V(S)$. In addition, in this formulation, referred to as the characteristic function, it is implicitly assumed that the actions taken by the complement coalition (those players not in S) cannot prevent S from achieving each of the payoff vectors in $V(S)$. There are more general models in which these sorts of externalities are considered, but for the most part the contributions to the Nash program have been confined to the characteristic function model. Given a collection of sets $V(S)$, one for each S, the theory formulates its predictions on the basis of solution concepts.

A solution is a mapping that assigns a set of payoff vectors in $V(N)$ to each characteristic function $(V(S))_{S \subseteq N}$. Thus, a solution in general prescribes a set, although it can be single-valued (when it assigns a unique payoff vector as a function of the fundamentals of the problem). The leading set-valued cooperative solution concept is the core, while the most used single-valued ones are the Nash bargaining solution and the Shapley value.

There are several criteria to evaluate the reasonableness or appeal of a cooperative solution. One could start by defending it on the basis of its definition alone. In the case of the core, this will be especially relevant: in a context in which players can freely get together in groups, the prediction should be payoff vectors that cannot be improved upon by any coalition. Alternatively, one can propose axioms, abstract principles, that one would like the solution to have, and the next step is to pursue their logical consequences. Historically, this was the first argument to justify the Nash solution and the Shapley value. However, some may think that the definition may be somewhat arbitrary, or one may object that the axiomatic approach is 'too abstract'. By proposing non-cooperative games that specify the details of negotiation, the Nash program may help to counter these criticisms. First, the procedure will tell a story about how coalitions form and what sort of interaction among players is happening. In that process, because the tools of non-cooperative game theory are used for the analysis, the cooperative solution will be understood as the outcome of a series of strategic problems facing individual players. Second, novel connections and differences among solutions may now be uncovered from the distinct negotiation procedures that lead to each of them. Therefore, a result in the Nash program, referred to as a 'non-cooperative foundation' or 'non-cooperative implementation' of a cooperative solution, enhances its significance, being looked at now from a new perspective. Focusing on the features of the rules of negotiation that lead to different cooperative solutions takes one a long way in opening the 'black box' of how a coalition came about, and contributes to a deeper understanding of the circumstances under which one solution versus another may be more appropriate to use.

The Nash bargaining solution

A particular case of a characteristic function is a two-player bargaining problem. In it, $N = \{1, 2\}$ is the set of players. The set $V(\{1, 2\})$, a compact and convex subset of $\mathbb{R}$, is the set of feasible payoffs if the two players reach an agreement. Compactness may follow from the existence of a bounded physical pie that the parties are dividing, and convexity is a consequence of expected utility and the potential use of lotteries. The sets $(V(\{i\}))_{i \in N}$ are subsets of $\mathbb{R}$, and let $d_i = \max V(\{i\})$ be the disagreement payoff for player i, that is, the payoff that i will receive if the parties fail to reach an agreement. It is assumed that $V(\{1, 2\})$ contains payoff vectors that Pareto dominate the disagreement payoffs. A solution assigns a feasible payoff pair to each bargaining problem.

This is the framework introduced in Nash (1950), where he proposes four axioms that a solution to bargaining problems should have. First, expected utility implies that, if payoff functions are rescaled via positive affine transformations, so must be the solution (scale invariance). Second, the solution must prescribe a Pareto efficient payoff pair (efficiency). Third, if the set $V(\{1, 2\})$ is symmetric with respect to the 45 degree line and $d_1 = d_2$, the solution must lie on that line (symmetry). Fourth, the solution must be independent of 'irrelevant' alternatives, that is, it must pick the same point if it is still feasible after one eliminates other points from the feasible set (IIA). Because of scale invariance, there is no loss of generality in normalizing the disagreement payoff to 0. We call the resulting problem a normalized problem.

Nash (1950) shows that there exists a unique solution satisfying scale invariance, efficiency, symmetry and IIA, and it is the one that assigns to each normalized

bargaining problem the point (u_1, u_2) that maximizes the product $v_1 v_2$ over all $(v_1, v_2) \in V(\{1, 2\})$. Today we refer to this as the 'Nash solution'. The use of the Nash solution is pervasive in applications and, following the axioms in Nash (1950), it is usually viewed as a normatively appealing resolution to bargaining problems.

In the first paper of the Nash program, Nash (1953) provides a non-cooperative approach to his axiomatically derived solution. This is done by means of a simple demand game. The two players are asked to demand simultaneously a payoff: player 1 demands v_1 and player 2 demands v_2. If the pair (v_1, v_2) is feasible, so that $(v_1, v_2) \in V(\{1, 2\})$, the corresponding agreement and split of the pie takes place to implement these payoffs. Otherwise, there is disagreement and payoffs are 0. To fix ideas, let us think of the existence of a physical pie of size 1 that is created if agreement is reached, while no pie is produced otherwise. Thus, player i's demand v_i corresponds to demanding a share x_i of the pie, $0 \leq x_i \leq 1$, such that player i's utility or payoff from receiving x_i is v_i.

The Nash demand game admits a continuum of Nash equilibria. Indeed, every point on the Pareto frontier of $V(\{1, 2\})$ is a Nash equilibrium outcome, as is the disagreement payoff point if each player demands the payoff corresponding to having the entire pie. However, Nash (1953) introduces uncertainty concerning the exact size of the pie. Now players, when formulating their demands, must have to take into account the fact that with some probability the pair of demands may lead to disagreement, even if they add up to less than 1. Then, it can be shown that the optimal choice of demands at a Nash equilibrium of the demand game with uncertain pie converges to the Nash solution payoffs as uncertainty becomes negligible. Hence, the Nash solution arises as the rule that equates marginal gain (through the increase in one's demanded share) and marginal loss (via the increase in the probability of disagreement) for each player when the problem is subject to a small degree of noise and demands/commitments are made simultaneously.

Rubinstein (1982) proposes a different non-cooperative procedure. In it, time preferences – impatience – and credibility of threats are the main forces that drive the equilibrium. The game is a potentially infinite sequence of alternating offers. In period 0, player 1 begins by making the first proposal. If player 2 accepts it, the game ends; otherwise, one period elapses and the rejector will make a counter-proposal in period 1, and so on. Let $\delta \in [0, 1)$ be the common per period discount factor, and let $v_i(\cdot)$ be player i's utility function over shares of the pie, assumed to be concave and strictly monotone. Thus, if player i receives a share x_i in an agreement reached in period t, his payoff is $\delta^{t-1} v_i(x_i)$. Perpetual disagreement has a payoff of 0.

Using subgame perfect equilibrium as the solution concept (the standard tool to rule out non-credible threats in dynamic games of complete information), Rubinstein (1982) shows that there exists a unique prediction in his game. Specifically, the unique subgame perfect equilibrium prescribes an immediate agreement on the splits $(x, 1-x)$ – offered by player 1 – and $(y, 1-y)$ – by player 2 – which are described by the following equations:

$$v_1(y) = \delta v_1(x)$$
$$v_2(1-x) = \delta v_2(1-y).$$

That is, at the unique equilibrium, the player acting as a responder in a period is offered a share that makes him exactly indifferent between accepting and rejecting it to play the continuation: the bulk of the proof is to show that any other behaviour relies on non-credible threats.

As demonstrated in Binmore, Rubinstein and Wolinsky (1986), the unique equilibrium payoffs of the Rubinstein game, regardless of who is the first proposer, converge to the Nash solution payoffs as $\delta \to 1$. First, note that the above equations imply that, for any value of δ, the product of payoffs $v_1(x)v_2(1-x)$ is the same as the product $v_1(y)v_2(1-y)$. Thus, both points, $(v_1(x), v_2(1-x))$ and $(v_1(y), v_2(1-y))$, lie on the same hyperbola of equation $v_1v_2 = K$ and, in addition, since they correspond to efficient agreements, both points also lie on the Pareto frontier of $V(\{1, 2\})$. Finally, as $\delta \to 1$, one has that $x \to y$ so that the two proposals (the one made by player 1 and the other by player 2) converge to one and the same, the one that yields the Nash solution payoffs. Thus, credible threats in dynamic negotiations in which both players are equally and almost completely patient also lead to the Nash solution.

The Shapley value

Now consider an n-player coalitional game where payoffs are transferable in a one-to-one rate among different players (for instance, because utility is money for all of them). This means that $V(S)$, the feasible set for coalition S, is the set of payoffs $(x_i)_{i \in S}$ satisfying the inequality $\sum_{i \in S} x_i \leq v(S)$ for some real number $v(S)$. This is called a transferable utility or TU game in characteristic function form. The number $v(S)$ is referred to as the 'worth of S', and it expresses S's initial position (for example, the maximum total utility that the group S of agents can achieve in an exchange economy by redistributing their endowments when utility is quasi-linear).

Therefore, without loss of generality, we can describe a TU game as a collection of real numbers $(v(S))_{S \subseteq N}$. A solution is then a mapping that assigns to each TU game a set of payoffs in the set $V(N)$, that is, vectors $(x_1, \ldots, x_n)$ such that $\sum_{i \in N} x_i \leq v(N)$. In this section, as in the previous one, we shall require that the solution be single-valued. Shapley (1953) is interested in solving in a fair way the problem of distribution of surplus among the players, when taking into account the worth of each coalition. To do this, he resorts to the axiomatic method. First, the payoffs must add up to $v(N)$, which means that the entire surplus is allocated (efficiency). Second, if two players are substitutes because they contribute the same

to each coalition, the solution should treat them equally (symmetry). Third, the solution to the sum of two TU games must be the sum of what it awards to each of the two games (additivity). Fourth, if a player contributes nothing to every coalition, the solution should pay him nothing (dummy).

The result in Shapley (1953) is that there is a unique single-valued solution to TU games satisfying efficiency, symmetry, additivity and dummy. It is what today we call the Shapley value, the function that assigns to each player i the payoff

$$\text{Sh}_i(N, v) = \sum_{S, i \in S} \frac{(|S| - 1)!(|N| - |S|)!}{|N|!}$$
$$\times [v(S) - v(S \setminus \{i\})].$$

That is, the Shapley value awards to each player the average of his marginal contributions to each coalition. In taking this average, all orders of the players are considered to be equally likely. Let us assume, also without loss of generality, that $v(\{i\}) = 0$ for each player i.

Hart and Mas-Colell (1996) propose the following non-cooperative procedure. With equal probability, each player $i \in N$ is chosen to publicly make a feasible proposal to the others: $(x_1, \ldots, x_n)$ is such that the sum of its components cannot exceed $v(N)$. The other players get to respond to it in sequence, following a pre-specified order. If all accept, the proposal is implemented; otherwise, a random device is triggered. With probability $0 \leq \delta < 1$, the same game continues being played among the same n players (thus, a new proposer will be chosen again at random among them), but with probability $1-\delta$ the proposer leaves the game. He is paid 0 and his resources are removed so that, in the next period, proposals to the remaining $n-1$ players cannot add up to more than $v(N \setminus \{i\})$. A new proposer is chosen at random among the set $N \setminus \{i\}$, and so on.

As shown in Hart and Mas-Colell (1996), there exists a unique stationary subgame perfect equilibrium payoff profile of this procedure, and it actually coincides with the Shapley value payoffs for any value of δ. (Stationarity means that strategies cannot be history dependent.) As $\delta \to 1$, the Shapley value payoffs are also obtained not only in expectation but independently of who the proposer is. One way to understand this result, as done in Hart and Mas-Colell (1996), is to check that the rules of the procedure and stationary behaviour in it are in agreement with Shapley's axioms. That is, the equilibrium relies on immediate acceptances of proposals, stationary strategies treat substitute players similarly, the equations describing the equilibrium have an additive structure, and dummy players will have to receive 0 because no resources are destroyed if they are asked to leave. It is also worth stressing the important role in the procedure of players' marginal contributions to coalitions: following a rejection, a proposer incurs the risk of being thrown out and the others of losing his resources, which seem to suggest a 'price' for them.

The core

The idea of agreements that are immune to coalitional deviations was first introduced to economic theory in Edgeworth (1881), who defined the set of coalitionally stable allocations of an economy under the name 'final settlements'. Edgeworth envisioned this concept as an alternative to Walrasian equilibrium (Walras, 1874), and was also the first to investigate the connections between the two concepts. Edgeworth's notion, which today we refer to as 'the core', was rediscovered and introduced to game theory in Gillies (1959). Therefore, the origins of the core were not axiomatic. Rather, its simple definition appropriately describes stable outcomes in a context of unfettered coalitional interaction. (The axiomatizations of the core came much later: see, for example, Peleg, 1985; 1986; Serrano and Volij, 1998).

For simplicity, let us continue to assume that we are studying a TU game. In this context, the core is the set of payoff vectors $x = (x_1, \ldots, x_n)$ that are feasible, that is, $\sum_{i \in N} x_i \leq v(N)$, and such that there does not exist any coalition $S \subseteq N$ for which $\sum_{i \in S} x_i < v(S)$. If such a coalition S exists, we shall say that S can improve upon or block x, and x is deemed unstable. The core usually prescribes a set of payoffs instead of a single one, and it can also prescribe the empty set in some games.

To obtain a non-cooperative implementation of the core, the procedure must embody some feature of anonymity, since the core is usually a large set and it contains payoffs where different players are treated very differently. Perry and Reny (1994) build in this anonymity by assuming that negotiations take place in continuous time, so that anyone can speak at the beginning of the game instead of having a fixed order. The player that gets to speak first makes a proposal consisting of naming a coalition that contains him and a feasible payoff for that coalition. Next, the players in that coalition get to respond. If they all accept the proposal, the coalition leaves and the game continues among the other players. Otherwise, a new proposal may come from any player in N. It is shown that, if the TU game has a non-empty core (as well as any of its subgames), the stationary subgame perfect equilibrium outcomes of this procedure coincide with the core. If a core payoff is proposed to the grand coalition, there are no incentives for individual players to reject it. Conversely, a non-core payoff cannot be sustained because any player in a blocking coalition has an incentive to make a proposal to that coalition, who will accept it (knowing that the alternative, given stationarity, would be to go back to the non-core status quo). Moldovanu and Winter (1995) offer a discrete-time version of the mechanism: in their work, the anonymity required is imposed on the solution concept by looking at order-independent equilibria.

Serrano (1995) sets up a market to implement the core. The anonymity of the procedure stems from the random choice of broker. The broker announces a vector $(x_1, \ldots, x_n)$, where the components add up to $v(N)$. One can interpret x_i as the price for the productive asset held by player i. Following an arbitrary order, the remaining players either accept or reject these prices. If player i accepts, he sells his asset to the broker for the price x_i and leaves the game. Those who reject get to buy from the broker, at the called out prices, the portfolio of assets of their choice if the broker still has them. If a player rejects but does not get to buy the portfolio of assets he would like because someone else took them before, he can always leave the market with his own asset. The broker's payoff is the worth of the final portfolio of assets that he holds, plus the net monetary transfers that he has received. Serrano (1995) shows that the prices announced by the broker will always be his top-ranked vectors in the core. If the TU game is such that gains from cooperation increase with the size of coalitions, the set of all subgame perfect equilibrium payoffs of this procedure will coincide with the core. Core payoffs are here understood as those price vectors where all arbitrage opportunities in the market have been wiped out. Finally, yet another way to build anonymity in the procedure is by allowing the proposal to be made by brokers outside of the set N, as done in Pérez-Castrillo (1994).

ROBERTO SERRANO

See also **bargaining; non-cooperative games (equilibrium existence); Shapley value.**

Bibliography

Binmore, K., Rubinstein, A. and Wolinsky, A. 1986. The Nash bargaining solution in economic modelling. *RAND Journal of Economics* 17, 176–88.
Edgeworth, F. 1881. Mathematical psychics. In *F. Y. Edgeworth's Mathematical Psychics and Further Papers on Political Economy*, ed. P. Newman. Oxford: Oxford University Press, 2003.
Gillies, D. 1959. Solutions to general non-zero-sum games. In *Contributions to the Theory of Games IV*, ed. A. Tucker and R. Luce. Princeton, NJ: Princeton University Press.
Hart, S. and Mas-Colell, A. 1996. Bargaining and value. *Econometrica* 64, 357–80.
Moldovanu, B. and Winter, E. 1995. Order independent equilibria. *Games and Economic Behavior* 9, 21–34.
Nash, J. 1950. The bargaining problem. *Econometrica* 18, 155–62.
Nash, J. 1953. Two person cooperative games. *Econometrica* 21, 128–40.
Peleg, B. 1985. An axiomatizationof the core of cooperative games without side payments. *Journal of Mathematical Economics* 14, 203–14.

Peleg, B. 1986. On the reduced game property and its converse. *International Journal of Game Theory* 15, 187–200.

Pérez-Castrillo, D. 1994. Cooperative outcomes through non-cooperative games. *Games and Economic Behavior* 7, 428–40.

Perry, M. and Reny, P. 1994. A non-cooperative view of coalition formation and the core. *Econometrica* 62, 795–817.

Rubinstein, A. 1982. Perfect equilibrium in a bargaining model. *Econometrica* 50, 97–109.

Serrano, R. 1995. A market to implement the core. *Journal of Economic Theory* 67, 285–94.

Serrano, R. 2005. Fifty years of the Nash program, 1953–2003. *Investigaciones Económicas* 29, 219–58.

Serrano, R. and Volij, O. 1998. Axiomatizations of neoclassical concepts for economies. *Journal of Mathematical Economics* 30, 87–108.

Shapley, L. 1953. A value for *n*-person games. In *Contributions to the Theory of Games II*, ed. A. Tucker and R. Luce. Princeton, NJ: Princeton University Press.

Walras, L. 1874. *Elements of Pure Economics, or the Theory of Social Wealth*, trans. W. Jaffé. Philadelphia: Orion Editions, 1984.

national accounting, history of

National accounting is a product of the 20th century, more precisely of the Great Depression, the Second World War and the subsequent period of recovery and economic growth. However, two and a half centuries earlier, estimates of national income had started with William Petty and Gregory King in England, and Vauban and Boisguilbert in France. This innovation in England, by the end of the 17th century, has been attributed to 'the spirit of the age' (Phyllis Deane, 1955), 'an age of great intellectual vigour, scientific curiosity and inventiveness' (Richard Stone, 1986). This early work had two main purposes: on the one hand, taxation and fiscal reforms, and on the other the assessment of the nations' comparative economic strength in an age when England, France and the Netherlands were frequently at war. Exceptionally, King, an outstanding pioneer, made consistent estimates of various economic magnitudes (income, expenses, increase or decrease in wealth, and so on) for a series of years. However, as a rule, national income was estimated as an isolated magnitude using various methods. Estimates were intermittent and extended slowly (according to Studenski, 1958, national income had been estimated at least once for only eight countries by the end of the 19th century, and for some 20 by 1929. From 1850, earlier in England, evaluations of fortune or wealth, more numerous, were disconnected from national income estimates.

From national income estimate to national accounting

The influence of the First World War was limited, with some exceptions (for example, an NBER 1909–19 series in current and constant dollars published by Wesley Mitchell et al. in 1921–22). The 1929 crisis was a turning point. Official demand appeared (US Senate, 1932; Carson, 1975, p. 156) leading to a 1934 report prepared by Simon Kuznets and his assistants (*National Income 1929–1932*, in current prices, by type of economic activity and distributed income). Estimates were then extended to expenditures (final consumption and capital formation) by Clark Warburton. In a number of countries – the Netherlands (Jan Tinbergen), Sweden, Denmark (Viggo Kampmann) – large programs were developed, such as the one resulting in *National Income in Sweden 1861–1930* published in 1937 by Erik Lindahl, Einar Dahlgren and Karin Koch. Working on his own, Colin Clark in the United Kingdom extended his previous 1932 estimates to a quite comprehensive coverage (*National Income and Outlay*, 1937).

The 1930s were a period of maturation in economics, apart from the conceptual and methodological deepening directly involved in this stream of quantitative estimates. The stimulus to quantitative macroeconomics given by Keynes's *General Theory* (1936) provided the theoretical basis for the estimation of interdependent economic aggregates, for the relationships between income and expenditure and between saving and investment were central to his argument. Such interrelationships had not previously been absent from economic theories (think of Quesnay's *Tableau économique*, Marx's reproduction schemes or Walras's general equilibrium analysis). However, after the Great Depression, such concepts and their statistical representations became central to macroeconomic concerns and policies. Keynes's works were focused on macroeconomic relations, but others sought representations of the economic system as a whole in different ways. Ferdinand Grüning in Germany (1933) analysed the economic circuit at a level later called 'mesoeconomic', half-way between the macro and micro levels. Wassily Leontief's research (1941) introduced input–output analysis at the level of homogeneous industrial groups, with a much broader view, in terms of general equilibrium, than the descriptive detailed balances of relations between branches (industries) prepared by P.I. Popov (1926) in the Soviet Union. The idea of an accounting approach for the economy as a whole, similar to the business accounting approach, was introduced either as a tool for improving national income estimates (as by Morris A. Copeland, following an intuition of Irving Fisher) or as part of a new proposed economic organization (André Vincent in France, Ed Van Cleeff in the Netherlands). The idea of micro/macro relationships was present in much of this work. Coming from a very different perspective, Ragnar Frisch developed an axiomatic, bottom-up representation of economic circulation.

The Second World War was the second, decisive, turning point. National accounting, often called at the beginning social accounting, crystallized in a direct response to the problem of war finance in the UK, as explicitly stated in the April 1941 White Paper (UK Treasury, *An Analysis of the Sources of War Finance and Estimate of the National Income and Expenditure in 1938 and 1940*). This was backed up by a technical paper by James Meade and Richard Stone in 1941. A more elaborated 'social accounting' system was soon proposed by Stone in an appendix to *Measurement of National Income and The Construction of Social Accounts* (published by the United Nations in 1947). Inspired by business accounting, it included sector accounts grouping accounting entities and their transactions organized according to a sequence of sub-accounts, with a set of detailed definitions and the discussion of many unsettled issues. Although it covered neither balance sheets nor a detailed analysis of the productive system, this accounting system was well ahead of its time. Actually, before and during the war, the United States was in advance in both national income and related aggregates estimates and their use, as for instance in the 1942 feasibility study of the Victory Program led by Kuznets or the analysis of the inflationary gap (Carson, 1975, p. 174–7). However, the National Income Division of the Commerce Department, with Milton Gilbert, evolved towards a simple accounting framework rather than a developed accounting system.

Though they encountered many difficulties and though it was a very uneven development, mostly due to deficiencies in statistical information and staffing, national accounting experienced a kind of golden age in the three decades following the war. Economic reconstruction and growth policies, the large increase in the economic role of government and the welfare state, the extension of international cooperation (for example, the Marshall Plan and, later, the Common Market in Europe), with the consequent emphasis on measuring of the rate of growth, led to a great demand for national accounts. This comprised the requirements of Keynesian macroeconomic demand management for short-term economic budget forecasts and longer-term projections needed for various types of indicative planning (the latter being particularly important in France). The development of econometric techniques and national accounts estimates reinforced each other. This trend towards greater use of national accounting data was general, even though the economies involved ranged from basically liberal economies such as the United States to more controlled economies such as France, the Netherlands and Norway.

International harmonization and extensions

Country experiences interacted with the process of international harmonization very early. Discussion between Canada, the UK and the USA took place in September 1944. There was a meeting of a League of Nations Committee, for which Stone prepares a memorandum, in December 1945. Stone played a prominent role in the first generation of standardized systems (OEEC, 1950; 1952; United Nations, 1952). This first attempt at standardization across the Western world as a whole, however, was too limited in scope, and was very far from the ambitions of the 1945 accounting scheme. Conceived as a simplified model for countries that were only beginning to develop their national accounts, it could not meet the needs of countries that were already more advanced, such as Scandinavian countries (Odd Aukrust in Norway, Ingvar Ohlsson in Sweden) or even a country like France. Under the impulse of Claude Gruson, France was, in the 1950s, in order to implement far-reaching economic policies, beginning the process of building a comprehensive and ambitious system of its own, integrating accounts for economic agents, input–output tables and financial transactions in a way that was more integrated than the Copeland's money-flows accounts in the United States.

Until the end of the 1960s the Western stage was characterized by the existence of a variety of national systems that were difficult to reconcile, even among those countries that adopted, in principle, the same comprehensive concept of production, including non-market government services. The new French system adopted a narrower concept of production, limited to market goods and services. The Soviet Union and its satellites used the even more restricted concept of material production, limited to goods and the so-called material services (mostly the transport of goods), following the old tradition of Smith and Marx. However, during the 1960s intense international discussions took place, on the basis of the wide range of national experiences in Europe and North America and the demands of international organizations. The result was the adoption of a second generation of standardized systems, the 1968 System of National Accounts (SNA) and the new European System of Accounts (ESA 1970), prepared on the basis of a report by Stone for the UN (the OECD deleting its system) and a French expert for the European Community. The European Community, thinking the 1952 system was too narrow and unsuited to harmonizing the accounts of its original six members and to meeting the needs of Community policies, had decided in 1964 to establish its own system.

The new system (they can be described as a single system, for SNA and ESA were very close) was closer to Stone's 1945 inspiration and to the French, Scandinavian and British systems than to the 1952 standardized system, in terms of coverage (in particular of input–output tables and financial accounts), integration and institutional orientation. The main weakness remained the absence of balance sheets, despite the pioneering work of Raymond Goldsmith in the United States at the beginning of the 1960s. Fixed capital formation was limited to tangible assets and the relation between income and changes in wealth was not fully shown.

The System of Balances of the National Economy, built around the material product concept, was also standardized, though little innovation was involved, through the framework of the Council of Mutual Economic Assistance, and then published by the United Nations (1971). Careful comparisons between the SNA and the Material Product System (MPS) were carried out in the UN European Economic Commission in Geneva.

France decided to leave its own peculiar system and join, via ESA 1970, the international system, this being achieved by 1976. The USA was not actively involved in the elaboration of the 1968 SNA, keeping its National Income and Product Accounts, whose accounting and conceptual framework had evolved little since 1947.

A quarter of a century later, a third generation of normalized systems has taken the trend towards a universal system a step further. The 1993 SNA/ESA 1995 closed the accounting framework by including balance sheets and completing the accumulation accounts with the introduction of a revaluation account (holding gains and losses) and an account for other types of capital gains and losses. Intangible capital formation was partly accounted for. In the current accounts, the analysis of income distribution was deepened (primary income distribution, secondary distribution, and redistribution in kind), actual final consumption was differentiated from final consumption expenditures, via the re-routing of social transfers in kind from government to households. This clarification of the accounting relation between income and changes in wealth (net worth) has deep implications (see below).

Nearly full integration was achieved between the SNA and the International Monetary Fund manuals (Balance of Payments, Government Finance Statistics, Monetary and Financial Statistics). The MPS disappeared at the beginning of the 1990s with the collapse of the Soviet Union and the fast transition of China towards a market economy. Paradoxically, the USA followed a slower path towards adopting the SNA framework.

During this long process of extension and harmonization of the accounting framework, the substance of the accounts changed dramatically in comparison with what was involved when the focus was on estimating national income. The product aggregate soon became the most important one, on a par with the expenditure aggregate. The income aggregate not only lost its position of being the single aggregate, but was often given a secondary position. From that, a series of consequences resulted.

The factor cost method of valuation, when still in use, was reduced to a lower rank than the market price valuation (in spite of the recurrent objection of 'double counting'). The latter was much more convenient for the valuation of expenditure and the analysis of consumer behaviour. In an integrated framework, the market price valuation was then applied also to the product aggregate (domestic product takes progressively the first place) and much later on to the income aggregate. In the 1993 SNA,

full recognition was given to the concept of national income at market prices, which is in fact the new name given to the earlier concept of national product (which was not actually a product but an income concept).

Partly for similar reasons, gross concepts have generally come to be preferred in practice, even though net concepts, that is, after deduction of consumption of fixed capital (depreciation in the usual business terminology), were considered closer to what was generally understood by the idea of national income. Both gross and net concepts of product, income and expenditure are finally considered part of the SNA/ESA.

The analysis and measurement of production and flows of products (goods and services), both in current value and in volume, have been given an increasing importance in relation to the integration of supply and use or input–output tables (a characteristic feature of the 1968 SNA/ESA 1970). This is increasingly done using the framework of annual tables. The integration with income estimates is less clear in practice, though the concept of value added, a significant improvement, and not only in words, on the old expression 'net output' or 'net product', provides the necessary link.

In this context, thanks to Stone's contribution, significant improvements in valuation concepts were made in the 1968 SNA. This widens and differentiates the usual notion of market prices. Basic prices, excluding net taxes on products, were introduced on the output side, resulting in the measurement of value added at basic prices. All taxes, minus subsidies, on products are then introduced. On the use side, acquisition prices are defined as purchasers' prices including only non-deductible taxes.

Measures in constant prices (described as volume measures), combining quantity and quality changes, also changed significantly. The trend was from globally deflating national income using a single price index in the 1930s, to deflating each of the main items in the balance of products (output, final consumption, and so on) using specific indices, and finally to an integrated system of price and volume measures, at a detailed level, using an input–output framework when annual tables were available (with Denmark, France, the Netherlands and Norway leading here). Double deflation, of output and inputs respectively, was used for value added in this context. International manuals by Stone (1956; 1968 SNA, ch. 4) and Peter Hill (1972; United Nations, 1979) recommended such an approach. Later on the 1993 SNA/ESA 1995 recommended replacing the traditional fixed base indices with chain indices, preferably Fisher volume and price indices or acceptable alternatives.

Much more complex, both conceptually and practically, international comparisons of volume levels of aggregates were the object of an International Comparison Project (ICP), launched in 1968, after the pioneering research of Colin Clark (1940) and Gilbert and Irving Kravis (1954) at the OEEC. Purchasing power parities, more significant than exchange rates, were calculated.

The results of the ICP, however, were not as widely implemented or as widely accepted as national volume measures, something that is unfortunate in a globalized world.

Beyond the progressive completion of its integrated framework, attempts were made to broaden the scope of national accounting by developing semi-integrated additional constructs, such as the satellite accounts whose idea was introduced (by Vanoli) by the end of the 1960 (for example, accounts for social protection, health, education, and environmental protection). In such an approach, the fully integrated system itself becomes the central framework (the expression often used, 'core accounts', is ambiguous).

Social accounting matrices (SAMs) were designed by Stone and Alan Brown in 1962, in order to achieve more flexibility than was possible using the usual account presentation. Though the word 'social' here means only 'for the whole economy', it gave rise to a certain ambiguity. SAMs are sometimes presented as a kind of alternative framework.

In the late 1980s, the Dutch proposed an ambitious 'system of economy-related statistics' as a way of organizing a vast array of statistics. A 'core system', narrower than the SNA central framework, was linked with 'system modules', such as social and environmental modules. This proposal had some similarity with the unsuccessful attempt by Stone, in the first half of the 1970s, to design for the United Nations a system of social and demographic statistics. It echoes the growing importance given to the micro–macro linkages (for example, Richard and Nancy Ruggles, 1986), in parallel with the increased availability of micro-databases.

Concern for statistical coordination had, of course, been present in national accounting from the very beginning.

New challenges since the mid-1970s

The achievements of national accounting, in the face of an enormous development of statistics, have been impressive. However, many countries are still far from fully implementing the international system (for example, few countries prepare integrated balance sheets), and economic and social conditions have changed drastically, especially since the mid-1970s. As a result national accounting, often questioned, sometimes radically, has had to face new challenges.

Since around 1980, after the supply shocks of the 1970s and the decreasing role played by macroeconometric models, national accounting has no longer been supported by the Keynesian paradigm. Some people even think it is obsolete. However, the demand for national accounts continues to grow, even if it also changes. Predominantly short-term concerns have led to a pressing demand for quarterly accounts, and even sometimes for a monthly GDP, resulting in conflicts between timeliness

(early estimates are required) and accuracy. Though more accurate, through successive revisions, annual accounts seem less used and their results are less commented upon.

In the opposite direction, computable general equilibrium models have multiplied since the mid-1970s as a means of studying policies aimed at structural change. Without any concern for the setting up of time series, they are based on the accounts of a single year supplemented, as required, by other data dictated by the models' specificities and purposes. Although they use the somewhat misleading SAM terminology, they actually need national accounts bases.

It remains true, however, that for the study of structural and social policies economists and social researchers, since the last two decades of the 20th century, have generally preferred to make use of micro-simulation models. The role of national accounts data is relatively reduced in this context.

In contrast, a considerable extension of the institutional and political role of national accounting took place during the 1990s, mostly in Europe. Certain aggregates (GDP or GNP) had been used fairly early for administrative purposes such as country contributions to international organizations, eligibility thresholds to preferential World Bank loans, regional allocation of European structural funds, and the 'Fourth own budgetary resource' of the Community budget. However, the debate over accession criteria to the European Economic and Monetary Union (the creation of the euro) marked a qualitative jump in the consideration of national accounting by policymakers and public opinion. Most Maastricht criteria were defined in reference to the ESA (ratios of public deficit and public debt to GDP). The ESA became compulsory for member states of the European Union. This marked the culmination of the European statistical strategy adopted in the 1960s. Closely related to the international statistical systems, like the SNA, European statistical tools are in effect very often legally based.

The policy uses of the ESA necessitate effective harmonization of the content of the accounts. A procedure of verification and evaluation of the comparability and representativeness of GDP is established. Full harmonization is, however, difficult. Because conceptual and statistical issues and political considerations intervene, especially in the procedure for identifying excessive deficits, specific cases have to be studied, sometimes through a rather difficult process. Here, and in issues such as the ratio between compulsory levies and GDP, national accounts appear at the forefront of sensitive political concerns. While it clearly shows their importance, this situation may also have less positive aspects for the national accounts. There is the possibility of political pressures, though this is rare; there may be lack of flexibility; official obligations and procedures can be very time-consuming and, as a result of limited human resources, European national accountants may become insufficiently involved in research work.

No similar policy-led process is taking place at the world level. However the need for regulation on a global scale is increasingly felt. Monitoring and intervention aimed at remedying local and regional crises and at preventing systemic crises falls to the International Monetary Fund, in agreement with the principal economic powers. Hence the growing role of the IMF in the supply, by member states, of timely and well-documented harmonized information. In the last decade of the 20th century, the Fund set up a system of standards to guide countries in data dissemination, including meta-information concerning various characteristics of the data. The structuring role of national accounts has been particularly highlighted. The Fund has conducted assessment missions in order to evaluate the quality of countries' national accounts and data systems.

The impressive increase in the demand for and use of national accounts statistics has taken place against the background of economies which have become much more complex, and hence more difficult to describe and measure, than was the case in the three decades following the Second World War. The number and sophistication of available products have grown; changes in product quality have become more rapid; the share of services, generally more difficult to measure, especially in volume, has increased. The effects of technical change, opening the global economy, the transformation of enterprises and groups, refinements of price policies and consumer behaviour, continuing financial innovations, frequent extension of informal activities, and so on have caused a tendency for economic information systems to maladjust. Hence many controversies arise, notably on price and volume measurements of capital goods – quality change based on performances (Robert Gordon) or on resource cost (the traditional solution championed by Edward Denison) – or measurement of consumption goods and services, where the Boskin Report in the United States (Boskin, Dulberger and Griliches, 1996) argued that the price increase was overestimated.

Significant methodological progress has been in areas such as the measurement of quality change of durable goods based on the change in their performance, the US having taken the lead. However the field is huge, and research is mostly concentrated on information and communication technology products. The measurement of financial and insurance services is in progress. Intangible assets are increasingly investigated. For non-market services, the necessary focusing on direct output–volume measurement instead of the traditional input–volume approach opens, at the start of the 21st century, another wide field of research. It soon appears that the relationship between the concepts of output and outcome must be clarified. On the other hand, some very important issues, like interest and inflation, the treatment of R&D expenditures and the extraction of subsoil resources, have remained outstanding for a long time, defying consensus, though relevant solutions do exist.

After a long emphasis on the relationship between production, income and expenditure, national accounting concerns have in recent decades been extended to the full set of relations between production, income, accumulation and wealth. This raises complex issues concerning the analysis and measurement of capital, particularly intangible assets, and consequently income. By the end of the 20th century business accountants faced similar difficulties with the emerging international accounting standards, moving from historical cost, which national accounting always rejected, to fair value valuation of assets.

Thus, national accounting is fighting for a better coverage of its traditional object at the same time that, at least since the early 1970s, new social concerns have given rise to requests for aggregate monetary indicators synthesizing broader sets of phenomena. There remain things that national accountants cannot do. One is the provision of a welfare indicator, a function that Kuznets assigned to national income, and which gave rise, in the 1940s, to an intense debate involving John Hicks and Paul Samuelson that reached negative conclusions. (William Nordhaus and James Tobin, 1973, later tried to provide such a measure with their 'measure of economic welfare'.) Another is the measurement of an environmentally adjusted domestic product. The suggestions in this direction included in the 1993 United Nations Handbook, *Integrated Environmental and Economic Accounting*, do not reach a consensus and are not implemented. There was then a move towards wanting a sustainable product or income measure, but this does not make any answer easier, though Hicks's concept of income (the maximum amount that can be consumed in a period while expecting total wealth to be unchanged at the end of it) has increasingly been advocated in recent decades.

Most difficulties relate to the observation and measurement of non-market non-monetary flows and stocks. Economists propose at least partial measurement solutions, within the framework of standard economic theory, using, for instance, contingent valuation methods (which raises problems of combination with actual exchange values, transfer of results and aggregation), or theoretical constructs with idealized conditions, seeking to justify a possible interpretation of net domestic product in terms of both welfare and sustainability. Other approaches, however, lean towards synthetic indicators combining both monetary and non-monetary variables.

Tensions between social concerns, theoretical issues and observation constraints of actual economies are increasingly at stake.

ANDRÉ VANOLI

See also **green national accounting; Kuznets, Simon; national accounting, history of; national income; Stone, John Richard Nicholas; Tableau économique.**

Bibliography

Aukrust, O. 1994. The Scandinavian contribution to national accounting. In *The Accounts of Nations*, ed. Z. Kenessey. Amsterdam: IOS Press.

Boskin, M.J., Dulberger, E.R. and Griliches, Z. 1996. *Toward a More Accurate Measure of the Cost of Living*. Final Report to the Senate Finance Committee from the Advisory Commission to Study the Consumer Price Index. Washington, DC: Government Printing Office.

Carson, C.S. 1975. The history of the United States National Income and Product Accounts: the development of an analytical tool. *Review of Income and Wealth* 21, 153–81.

Clark, C. 1937. *National Income and Outlay*. London: Macmillan.

Clark, C. 1940. *The Conditions of Economic Progress*. London: Macmillan.

Commission of the European Communities, International Monetary Fund, Organisation for Economic Co-operation and Development, United Nations, World Bank. 1993. *System of National Accounts 1993*. Brussels/Luxembourg, New York, Paris, Washington, DC.

Deane, P. 1955. The implications of early national income estimates for the measurement of long term economic growth in the United Kingdom. *Economic Development and Cultural Change* 4, 3–38.

Eurostat. 1996. *European System of Accounts ESA 1995*. Luxembourg: Eurostat.

Gilbert, M. and Kravis, I.B. 1954. *An International Comparison of National Products and the Purchasing Power of Currencies*. Paris: OEEC.

Grüning, F. 1933. *Der Wirtschaftskreislauf*. München: Beck.

Hill, T.P. 1972. *A System of Integrated Price and Volume Measures (Indices)*. Luxembourg: Statistical Office of the European Communities.

Kenessey, Z., ed. 1994. *The Accounts of Nations*. Amsterdam: IOS Press.

Kuznets, S. 1934. *National Income 1929–1932*. US Senate Document No. 124, 73rd Congress, 2nd session. Washington, DC: Government Printing Office.

Kuznets, S. 1942. U.S. War Production Board, Planning Committee Document No. 151. A memorandum to the Planning Committee from Simon Kuznets on 'Analysis of the Production program', dated 12 August.

Leontief, W. 1941. *The Structure of the American Economy 1919–1929: An Empirical Application of Equilibrium Analysis*. Cambridge, MA: Harvard University Press.

Lindahl, E., Dahlgren, E. and Koch, K. 1937. *National Income in Sweden 1861–1930*. London: P.S. King.

Meade, J. and Stone, R. 1941. The construction of tables of national income, expenditure, savings and investment. *Economic Journal* 51, 216–233.

Mitchell, W.C., King, W.I., Macaulay, F.R. and Knauth, O.W. 1921; 1922. *Income in the United States: Its Amount and Distribution, 1909–1919*, Parts I and II. New York: NBER.

Nordhaus, W. and Tobin, J. 1973. Is growth obsolete? In *The Measurement of Economic and Social Performance*, ed. M. Moss. New-York: Columbia University Press for NBER.

OEEC (Organisation for European Economic Co-operation). 1950. *A Simplified System of National Accounts*. Paris: OEEC.

OEEC. 1952. *A Standardised System of National Accounts*. Paris: OEEC.

Popov, P.I., ed. 1926. *Balans narodnogo khoziaistva Soyuza SSSR 1923-1924 goda*. Moskva: Trudi Tsentralnogo Statisticheskogo Upravlenia, Tom XXIX.

Ruggles, R. and Ruggles, N.D. 1986. The integration of macro and micro data for the household sector. *Review of Income and Wealth* 32, 245–76.

Statistical Office of the European Communities. 1970. *European System of Integrated Economic Accounts (ESA)*. Luxembourg: OSCE.

Stone, R. 1947. Definition and measurement of the national income and related totals. Appendix to *Measurement of National Income and the Construction of Social Accounts*. Geneva: United Nations.

Stone, R. 1956. *Quantity and Price Indexes in National Accounts*. Paris: OEEC.

Stone, R. 1986. Nobel Memorial Lecture 1984: the accounts of society. *Journal of Applied Econometrics* 1, 5–28.

Studenski, P. 1958. *The Income of Nations*. New York: New York University Press.

UK Treasury. 1941. *An Analysis of the Sources of War Finance and an Estimate of the National Income and Expenditure in 1938 and 1940*. Cmd. 6261. London: HMSO.

United Nations. 1952. *A System of National Accounts and Supporting Tables*. New York: United Nations.

United Nations. 1968. *A System of National Accounts*. Studies in Methods Serie F n° 2 Rev. 3. New-York: United Nations.

United Nations. 1971. *Basic Principles of the System of Balances of the National Economy*. New York: United Nations.

United Nations. 1979. *Manual on National Accounts at Constant Prices*. New York: United Nations.

United Nations. 1993. *Integrated Environmental and Economic Accounting*. Interim version. New York: United Nations.

US Senate. 1932. S. Res. 220, 72nd Cong., 1st sess., *Congressional Record* 75, 12285.

Vanoli, A. 2005. *A History of National Accounting*. Amsterdam: IOS Press.

National Bureau of Economic Research

The National Bureau of Economic Research (NBER) was founded in January 1920, and from the moment of its founding was seen as one of the leading independent research organizations in economics in the world (Fabricant, 1984).

The NBER was established as an independent, non-partisan, research organization focused on empirical investigation. The original research orientation was towards 'basic' knowledge of the economy, but was, nevertheless, clearly intended to inform and improve the policymaking process. More recently the research focus has shifted to become more explicitly applied and policy orientated, but empirical work is still central to the bureau's mission. From the first, its Board included a large number of directors from various universities, scientific associations and other organizations. This and the system of manuscript review were designed to ensure the scientific impartiality of its work. These aspects of bureau organization still exist today.

The idea for an independent research bureau in economics sprang from discussions between Malcolm Rorty and N.I. Stone in 1916. Rorty was a statistician with AT&T, Stone an economist working as an arbitrator and economic advisor. Their policy views clashed but they could agree on the need for more reliable information. They involved Wesley Mitchell (Columbia), Edwin Gay (Harvard), and John R. Commons (Wisconsin, and then President of the American Economic Association). The First World War interrupted progress, but the experience of the war made the lack of quantitative information concerning the economy even more apparent, and by the AEA meeting of December 1919 all the necessary elements were in place.

The NBER began with a research agenda directed at the measurement of the size and distribution of national income, and the problem of business cycles. Wesley Mitchell was the first director of research, Edwin Gay the first president, while Rorty and Stone were members of the Board of Directors. Funding was obtained for a small research staff, originally consisting of Mitchell, Willford King, Frederick Macaulay and Oswald Knauth. The major financial contributors were the Commonwealth Fund, followed by the Carnegie Corporation, and, after 1923, the Laura Spelman Rockefeller Memorial Foundation (and its successor organization, the Social Science Division of the Rockefeller Foundation). The NBER also sold subscriptions and engaged in research commissioned by the President's Conference on Unemployment. In 1921 and 1922 the NBER published its first national income estimates: *Income in the United States: Its Amount and Distribution*. This was followed in 1923 by *Business Cycles and Unemployment*, produced by a special staff of the NBER for the President's Conference on Unemployment.

The NBER grew and prospered during the 1920s and early 1930s. The senior research staff were paid a modest stipend by the bureau, but generally held university appointments in the New York area. The bureau also employed research assistants and received funding for research fellowships and for statistical laboratory and library facilities. The research staff came to include Leo Wolman, F.C. Mills, Simon Kuznets, Arthur Burns and

Solomon Fabricant. The bureau's research expanded to include Wolman's work on trade union membership, a substantial project on the topic of labour migration (undertaken by Harry Jerome, who was 'borrowed' from Wisconsin), F.C. Mills's extensive series of price studies, as well as further work on national income and business cycles. Mitchell produced the first of his projected volumes on business cycles, *Business Cycles: The Problem and its Setting*, in 1927. The bureau also continued its association with the President's Conference on Unemployment by contributing the research for *Recent Economic Changes in the United States* (1929). Kuznets took over the work on national income from King in 1931, and from 1933 he was 'loaned' to the Department of Commerce to work on the construction of official national income estimates. The first result of Kuznets's efforts was his report *National Income, 1929–32*, published in 1934.

A financial crisis in 1932 resulted in significant retrenchment at the bureau, which had suffered loss of income due to the Depression and faced uncertainty over the future of Carnegie support. The crisis was overcome thanks to the flexibility shown by Edmund Day of the Social Science Division of the Rockefeller Foundation, but Day expressed concerns with the bureau – its dependence on Rockefeller funding, its domination by a staff drawn heavily from Columbia University, and its lack of interaction with the broader academic community (Rutherford, 2005).

Rockefeller continued to fund the NBER core programmes on national income, business cycles, price and price relationships, the labour market, and savings and capital formation. The bureau also took on a programme of financial research funded by the Association of Reserve City Bankers and headed by Ralph Young. Mitchell and Burns developed what became known as the 'NBER method' of specific and reference cycles to deal with the variations they found between cycles, but the project became ever larger. By the late 1930s the bureau's financial position had recovered and staff numbers again grew substantially, with Milton Friedman joining as an assistant to Kuznets in 1937 (he took over Kuznets's work on *Incomes from Independent Professional Practice*), Moses Abramovitz and Julius Shiskin arriving in 1938, and Geoffery Moore, among numerous others, in 1939.

Day's concerns were not without results. A Universities National Bureau Committee was established in 1935 to examine the potential of NBER–university cooperation. Out of this came the Conference on Income and Wealth (headed by Kuznets) and the Conference on Prices (headed by Mills). The first of these was particularly successful, producing the series Studies in Income and Wealth from 1938 onwards. In addition, Joseph Willits joined the bureau in 1936 as executive director, to deal with administration and fund raising. In 1939, Willits was appointed as Director of the Division of Social Science of the Rockefeller Foundation, and the NBER enjoyed strong support from Rockefeller until Willits left that position in 1954 Rutherford 2005.

Mitchell retired as Director of Research and was succeeded by Arthur Burns in 1945. Kuznets and Burns disagreed over the future direction of the bureau. Kuznets wished to shift the research emphasis to long-run growth, while Burns wished to maintain the focus on business cycles. Kuznets was to pursue his interests through the Conference on Income and Wealth with the financial support of the Social Science Research Council. Burns stayed as Director of Research until appointed to the Council of Economic Advisers in 1953. He was succeeded by Solomon Fabricant. Burns, however, returned to the bureau as President in 1957 and regained much of his previous authority within the organization.

In 1946, Burns and Mitchell published *Measuring Business Cycles*, the result of almost 20 years of effort on the business-cycle project, and the much delayed second volume of the three that were planned. The final, theoretical, volume was never completed. *Measuring Business Cycles* drew sharp criticism from Tjalling Koopmans of the Cowles Commission for its failure to utilize a formal model. Although Koopman's 1947 characterization of the work as 'measurement without theory' is a misrepresentation of the Mitchell–Burns programme, there can be no doubt that Burns and others at the bureau were sceptical of what might be achieved by the econometric methods being pioneered at Cowles. Also at this time Burns was engaged in a criticism of Keynesian economics as represented by Alvin Hansen. For Burns, Keynesian theorizing was too speculative and not sufficiently well grounded empirically (Burns, 1946).

The period from the late 1940s through to the mid-1960s was a mixed time for the bureau. Some excellent projects were undertaken. Milton Friedman and Anna Schwartz began their work on US monetary history in 1948, a project that took until 1963 to publish. Friedman did other important work, particularly on consumption theory. Abramovitz worked on inventories and business cycles. George Stigler, who had joined the bureau staff in1943, worked on output and employment trends. Geoffrey Moore refined the system of leading indicators for business cycles, and Morris Copeland developed the analysis of money flows, later to become flow of funds accounts. All the same, the focus of the bureau's efforts had become less sharp; it was conducting much work of lesser value, and running into considerable financial difficulty. Once Willits left Rockefeller, those at Rockefeller were not so sympathetic to the bureau's plight. With the exception of a programme on international economic relations, Rockefeller declined to continue funding the NBER, and in 1958 the bureau turned to the Ford Foundation. Ford established a review committee of Gardiner Ackley, Richard Ruggles, and George Stocking. They criticized the bureau, but recommended that Ford provide funding, which they did. This allowed the bureau to continue, with relatively few changes until 1965. The research conducted over this period covered a wide range of projects that were loosely grouped into the categories of economic fluctuations, economic growth, wages and other incomes, the economic impact of government and international economic relations.

In 1965, Solomon Fabricant retired as Director of Research and was replaced by Geoffrey Moore, which was seen by many as a decision by the bureau to stay pretty much on its existing track. At the same time, Ford embarked on a major review of the bureau, again with a committee, but this time consisting of Emile Despres, R.A. Gordon, Lawrence Klein, Lloyd Reynolds, Theodore Schultz, George Shultz and James Tobin. This committee was sharply critical of the bureau, its leadership, project selection and research methods. Burns resigned as President and was replaced by John Meyer of Harvard. Meyer took over many of the functions previously held by the Director of Research, created two Vice Presidents of Research, and reorganized the bureau's efforts into specific programmes under their own Directors. Meyer also shifted the focus of the bureau's research into a number of new areas of social policy importance such as urban economics, health, human resources, education, environmental standards, the economics of the family, and crime and punishment. A number of important NBER studies were published during Meyer's term on subjects such as these by Theodore Schultz, Gary Becker, William Landes, Jacob Mincer and Victor Fuchs. Work on cycles was carried on, but no longer using the older NBER methods (Rutherford, 2005).

Meyer left the bureau in 1977 and was replaced as President by Martin Feldstein, also of Harvard. Feldstein has remained as President except for a few years when he was with the Council of Economic Advisors (1982–4), and Eli Shapiro took over. Feldstein brought about further changes at the bureau, doing away with the senior research staff employed directly by the bureau, and changing the bureau into an organization designed to promote and coordinate research being conducted by university-based 'research associates' funded largely by National Science Foundation and other research grants. This rearrangement vastly increased the bureau's involvement with the larger academic community.

The focus has remained on empirical and policy-related research. Feldstein added programmes on issues such as aging, and asset pricing, and reinvigorated the NBER programmes on macroeconomics and on taxation. As of 2007, the NBER lists 17 major research programmes each involving 20 or more NBER research associates and each with its own director(s). These include aging, asset pricing, children, corporate finance, education, economic fluctuations and growth, health, industrial organization, international finance, labour, law and economics, monetary economics, productivity and public economics. In addition are smaller working groups working on another 16 topics from behavioural finance to the Chinese economy. The Conference on

Income and Wealth also continues. Details of these programmes, those involved, and their publications can be found on the NBER website. The NBER's Research Associates now number about 600, and the NBER working paper series is a major research outlet. Links to the original NBER emphasis on measurement and business cycles are still to be found, however, notably in the NBER's data collection and in the Business Cycle Dating Committee.

MALCOLM RUTHERFORD

See also **Burns, Arthur Frank; business cycle measurement; Kuznets, Simon; Mitchell, Wesley Clair; national accounting, history of.**

Bibliography

Committee of the President's Conference on Unemployment. 1923. *Business Cycles and Unemployment.* New York: McGraw Hill.

Committee on Recent Economic Changes of the President's Conference on Unemployment. 1929. *Recent Economic Changes in the United States.* New York: McGraw Hill.

Burns, A.F. 1946. Economic research and the Keynesian thinking of our times. *Twenty Sixth Annual Report of the National Bureau of Economic Research.* New York: NBER.

Burns, A.F. and Mitchell, W.C. 1946. *Measuring Business Cycles.* New York: NBER.

Fabricant, S. 1984. Toward a firmer basis of economic policy: the founding of the National Bureau of Economic Research. www.nber.org/nberhistory/sfabricantrev.pdf.

Friedman, M. and Schwartz, A.J. 1963. *A Monetary History of the United States, 1867–1960.* Princeton, NJ: Princeton University Press.

Koopmans, T.C. 1947. Measurement without theory. *Review of Economic Statistics* 29, 161–72.

Kuznets, S. 1934. *National Income, 1929–1932.* New York: NBER.

Kuznets, S. and Friedman, M. 1939. *Incomes from Independent Professional Practice, 1919–1936.* New York: NBER.

Mitchell, W.C. 1927. *Business Cycles: The Problem and its Setting.* New York: NBER.

Mitchell, W.C., King, W.I., Macaulay, F.R. and Knauth, O.W. 1921. *Income in the United States: Its Amount and Distribution, 1909–1919, Part 1, Summary.* New York: NBER.

Mitchell, W.C., King, W.I., Macaulay, F.R. and Knauth, O.W. 1922. *Income in the United States: Its Amount and Distribution, 1909–1919, Part 2, Detailed Report.* New York: NBER.

National Bureau of Economic Research.Online. Available at http://www.nber.org, accessed 4 May 2007.

Rutherford, M. 2005. 'Who's afraid of Arthur Burns?' The NBER and the foundations. *Journal of the History of Economic Thought* 27, 109–39.

national income

Comprehensive systems of national accounts consist today of traditional national income, expenditure and product accounts, input output or production accounts, financial transactions and revaluation accounts (Rymes, 1992) and national balance sheets. While many parts of this modern system are expressed in current and constant prices, national income, its factor and individual income distributions are meaningfully expressed only in current prices. Constant price, or 'quantity', indexes are used to measure 'real' expenditures over time and across nations, in productivity studies both partial and for all factors again over time and across industries and countries (see Erwin W. Diewert's contributions in ILO, 2004, and IMF, 2004). Indeed, much of modern economic history can now be written in terms of the nominal and real economic accounts over time.

Yet, to date, no one has put together a comprehensive examination of the whole accounting system seen from a particular set or sets of economic theory. Theorists, such as J.R. Hicks, Richard Stone, Wassily Leontief and James Meade, and quantitative economic historians such as Simon Kuznets have made notable contributions to national accounting and have been so recognized with Nobel Prizes. The general lack of emphasis on the connection with economic theory, however, causes the poor student of economics to find the structure of the official accounts a bewildering maze of 'uses and resources', which seem more the product of much worthwhile international compromise than the development of the accounts from basic principles of economic theory. Anyone who has tried to teach economics students with the assistance of the 1993 System of National Accounts (SNA 1993, Washington, DC.; Commission of the European Communities; International Monetary Fund; OECD; United Nations; and the World Bank (*sic*)) will not find in all the bureaucratic compromises of admittedly needed reconciliation and international comparisons those flashes of illumination which economic theories can give. A recent OEDC publication (Blades and Lequiller, 2006) further illustrates dangers of the lack of economic theory. It never adequately explains the economic meaning behind consumers 'real' expenditures and producers 'real' outputs making up GDP, though such knowledge must be held if the reader is to understand the very useful warnings about 'real shares' and additivity problems associated with index numbers. Thus it is sad to read one of the best practitioners of national accounting today asserting '… the conceptual foundations of the present model of the national accounts are being progressively undermined by the shifting quicksand of economic theory…' (Ward, 2006, p. 327). Of course, Ward describes other eroding forces, but to give economic theory priority of place in conceptually undermining the accounts seems to me an error resulting from a despairing denigration of economic theory.

I concentrate here on how economic theory contributed to and conditioned national income accounting developments and to some extent how problems in constructing national accounts condition good economic theory. The central theme of this article, then, is the interplay between economic theory and national income accounting. Modern readers, especially students, once they see the interconnection between the accounts and economic theory, should find the national accounts as fascinating and exciting as I do and will each become, I hope, a '... passionate accountant' (Lathen, 1974, p. 183).

Classical and neoclassical national income theories

David Ricardo argued the principal problem of political economy was the determination of the laws governing the distribution of national income among the classes of society (Ricardo, 1971, vol. 1, p. 5). His question was a major concern of classical economic theorists and it has returned to some pre-eminence among economists today (Milanovic, 2005). Consider the following set of extremely simple national income and expenditure accounts set out for a market economy to examine classical economic theory.

Incomes		Expenditures
WL		$P_C C$
$RP_K K$		$P_{K\Delta} K$
$RP_N N$		
$D_N P_N N$		
$D_K P_K K$		
Y	$\equiv$	E

where National Income (Y) is shown as identically equal to National Final Expenditures (E) or Product.

Examining the accounts for one country among many, one must distinguish between National Income and Domestic Product whereas, of course, World Income (WI) and World Expenditure or Product (WP) will be the same. Some economists regard the Domestic Product concept as more useful since it extracts from effects of the international redistribution of returns to capital. (For a contrary opinion, see Beckerman, 1987.) More technical but telling objections can be raised against the Domestic Product concept when it is expressed in constant price terms in a world experiencing technical change in which international trade takes place in intermediate inputs of production.

Why however, does Y identically equal E? If we imagine the accounts were for an even simpler world where there was no capital, then the equality among the circular flows would be clear. Owners of labour would sell their time to producers and the value of their expenditures

for the goods produced would cover the cost of the producers. For an extensive discussion of circular flows and the crucial capital-theoretic problems in national accounting, see Hulten (2006).

The notation involves the income of workers (WL), with W the set of money wage rates and L the corresponding set of the working times (hours, days, and so on) offered and demanded by the suppliers and demanders of labour; $RP_N N$ is the net rents earned by the natural agents of production, which, for illustrative purposes, we shall take mainly to be the inalienable and inexhaustible powers of the soil, where R is net rates of return, P_N is prices of the stocks of land so that RP_N is the net rents on the stocks of land (N); and RP_K is rentals earned by the stocks (K) of reproducible capital goods like machines, inventories and buildings. Inanimate things like land and capital goods earn nothing by themselves, and clearly what the classical economists had in mind when then they wrote of the factoral distribution of income was that the net rents on land were garnered by landowners for their husbandry, and the net rents being earned by capital were the net flow of income being earned by the owners of the capital goods, capitalists playing their rentier roles as savers and holders of the stock of capital in the economy. By the 'factoral distribution of income' classical economists meant the distribution of income among people, aggregated as the classes of society: labourers, landlords and capitalists. When it is borne in mind that the classical economists also saw labour, land and capital as factors of production, it can be clearly seen that classical theoretical economics was an immensely great scientific undertaking, one which still echoes throughout economics today.

The notation $D_N P_N N$ and $D_K P_K K$ refers to the rates of depletion or exhaustion of natural agents of production, such as the using up of pools of oil, which do not apply to our simple theoretical case of N being Ricardian land. Nor is there any discussion here of the rate of degradation of the environment capital (see Rymes, 1991). Very importantly, $D_K P_K K$ refers to the rates of depreciation or using up of capital in production.

On the Expenditure side of the accounts, $P_C C$ is the values of the final consumption of the society, which, to many economists, is the be all and end all of economics. $P_{K\Delta} K$ represents the values of the gross capital formation taking place in the society. It is gross in that no allowance is taken of the fact that the new capital goods being produced may or may not be sufficient to replace the wear and tear on existing capital goods. Y and E refer then to Gross National Income and Expenditure respectively.

One of the major theoretical problems in contemporary theory and classical and contemporary national income accounting is the meaning of capital and the conception and measurement of 'maintaining capital intact'. Even today, despite advances in accounting and economic theory, it is difficult if not almost impossible empirically to measure well the 'wear and tear' on capital in modern economic systems. Where depreciation arises from obsolescence, so severe are the problems of measurement that almost all economists today use Gross Domestic Income (Product) or Expenditure as the principal aggregate for economic analysis. National income analysis, then, is greatly hampered by the fact that good estimates of capital consumption and the depletion of natural agents of production, again to say nothing of the degradation of the environment, are generally not available.

If we did have such estimates, the National Accounts just set out could be revised further to appear as

Incomes		Expenditures
WL		PcC
$RP_K K$		$P_K(G - D)K = P_K nK$
$RP_N N$		
Y*N	$\equiv$	E*N

where $P_K (G - D)K = P_K nK$ is net capital formation, with n being the rate of growth so that one would be able to see how important net returns were to capital in net national income, which also in this case is said to measure 'sustainable' consumption.

The importance of the capital problem extends to the measurement of labour income as well. Today, wages are paid not so much for the application of pure labour time but for the services of the human capital accumulated by the individuals through expenditures on education, health and even the raising of families. On such capital expenditures, though there is a direct link between the forgoing of present consumption and the accumulation of capital by the individuals, the difficulties of measuring the depreciation on intangible human capital in the so-called knowledge economies are as bad as, if not worse than, those for physical capital. Yet the problem of measuring the returns to human capital gripped the classical economists as well.

One could argue that the consumption of the workers was not final at all, but was perhaps just sufficient to maintain the labour force either at a particular level or at a certain growth rate. Suppose we could extend all of the capital measurement thinking previously outlined to the classical and modern neoclassical treatment of labour. We could write off the consumption of the workers as required inputs into the maintenance of the labour force. Much of PC would vanish along with WL. The above accounts could be then even further dramatically

reduced to

Incomes		Expenditures
$RP_K K$		PcC^*
$RP_N N$		$P_K(G - D)K = P_K nK$
Y**N	$\equiv$	E**N

where PcC^* is the consumption of the capitalists (and landholders). The extreme classical Ricardian stationary state comes into focus, where the economy is said to have converged to a position where savings and accumulation have been pushed to the point where R, the net rates of return, *are* positive but so low that net savings and the rate of growth of net capital stock and national income, n, would be zero.

Though classical economists were aware that capital accumulation was unlikely to occur in given states of technology, the modern treatment of technical progress is to assume that it serendipitously occurs or, more interestingly, is an endogenous function of the rate of capital accumulation. If, however, technical progress were steadily occurring, then the long-period equilibrium of modern classical analysis and *theory* comes into view. If we ignore land and landholders, and if the consumption of the capitalists were some function of their income and the rate of return so that $PC^* = c((R), RPK)$, then national income for steady growth, the modern variant of the Ricardian stationary state, becomes

	Incomes		Expenditures
	$RPK - c((R)RPK)$	$\equiv$	$Pn'K$
or	$(1 - c((R)RPK))$	$\equiv$	$Pn'K$
	$s(R)R$	$\equiv$	n'

that is, the economy may be said to have converged to an equilibrium where rates of return to capital exceeds the rate of growth of the income of the economy arising from technical progress, n', if the fraction of returns to capital saved, s, is less than 1. If one assumes that the rate of technical progress is a function of R, then the whole structure of the classical and neoclassical national income accounts can be boiled down to reflect basic theories

$$S(R)R = n'(R(R^*(R))$$

where the net rates of return to capital, the intertemporal prices in modern economies, are seen by the simplest accounts to be a function of the rates of saving, or intertemporal choice, and rates of technical change, itself the product of investing and expected rates of return, R^*, themselves seen as some function of R. Thus, we see that, when asking questions about the distribution of national income, the national accounts can be set out to illuminate the forces of growth which play vital roles in determining national income. It can also be seen that Ricardo's question about the determinants of the factoral distribution of national income lies at the very heart of modern economic analysis, of both the neoclassical and neo-Ricardian growth varieties (see Barro and Sala-i-Martin, 1995, in particular the chapter on growth accounting; and Pasinetti, 1995). While economic theories may be said to generate the accounts designed to illuminate them, we have seen that they also illuminate the great theoretical difficulties and aggregation problems associated with Professor Hulten's questions about capital theory.

Readers should please note that I am largely by-passing the *severe* capital-theoretic difficulties alluded to by him. One of Hulten's observations that '... all aspects of capital ultimately are derived from the decision to defer current consumption in order to enhance or maintain expected future consumption' (2006, p. 195) means that capital is not a factor of production independently of the 'willingness to wait' and that multifactor productivity advance should be conceived as the improvement in the efficiency of working and waiting, n', rather than an improvement in the efficiency of labour and capital. The deep theoretical questions involved in measuring capital, the growth of nations and the aggregation questions may be resolved to some extent by the application of Leontief's disaggregated production and capital accumulation accounts (see Cas and Rymes, 1991; Rymes, 1997).

Keynesian theory

The Keynesian revolution clashed with classical and neoclassical theories and led to some of the modern 'advances' in national income accounting. Indeed, some national accountants argue that, partly as a result of Keynes and other theorists such as Jan Tinbergern, modern national accounting started in the 1930s (Bos, 2003; 2006). At the same time economic theory started paying increased attention to institutional forms such as corporations and governments. Under these influences, our simplified national accounts now appear as

Incomes		Expenditures
WL		$P_C C$
Ω		$P_{K\Delta} K$
Y	$\equiv$	E

where the net returns to capital and net rents on natural agents of production are largely replaced by corporate profits, Ω, which generally have measures of depreciation of limited economic meaning, and may or may not well reflect the distribution of interest to bondholders and dividends to shareholders with almost certainly no

account being taken of capital gains and losses, and where the switch away from national income to gross national product reflects concern with unemployment rather than the level and the distribution of national income. When the revaluation accounts are added to the standard income accounts, theory again comes to the forefront.

Suppose that modern corporations distribute none of the profits or returns to capital they earn as dividends to their shareholders, ignoring for simplicity the payment of interest to bondholders, but reinvest their profits in the acquisition of capital goods for their firms. The value of the shares held by shareholders (and bought and sold among them) rise along with increases in the corporate stock of capital. It would appear from the national accounts as if the corporations did the saving whereas they may be used to test theories which have the corporations as mere intermediaries, whose investment decisions reflect the wishes of their shareholders.

The neo-Ricardian and Keynesian theories can be put together for the determination of not just the level but also the distribution of national income. If good estimates of the wear and tear on capital are available, one can revert from gross to net income and develop arguments addressed to the question of whether corporate firms and governments can affect the level and the distribution of national income. Here the national accounts can contribute to our knowledge of the extent to which individual households can be said to 'see through' corporate firms and governments in such matters as the Ricardian equivalence theorem (see Gillespie, 1980; 1991). To do this, the accounts must be prepared with the various theories of institutional forms in mind; otherwise they may be dismissed with some derision by contemporary theorists (Prescott, 2006).

When the personal distribution of national income is considered, national income accounts must be supplemented by longitudinal surveys of the distribution of income and wealth among individuals and families, the latter of which can be taken as representing constellations of individuals through time. Here again the theory of why certain families have such time preferences as to permit them to form dynasties requires much work if national income is to be so disaggregated so that those forces playing upon it may be extended to portray and explain individual and dynastic distributions of income and wealth.

Controversies among modern monetary theories and national accounting

Recent developments in monetary theory present great challenges to national accounting. Some monetary theories, those based fundamentally on the quantity theory of money, assert that once-over changes in 'costless' fiat money cannot have effects on such real phenomenon as national income, whereas continuous changes in such monies, affecting continuous changes in price indexes, may have rather dramatic effects. Yet, as national balance sheets and wealth accounts show, outside fiat monies are becoming increasingly marginal. How is national income affected by these matters?

National income reflects differences in the underlying classical, neoclassical and Keynesian theories. Keynesian models of unemployment rest upon the empirical and theoretical unimportance of outside or fiat money. Friedman argues, against the Keynesian position, that with real capital gains (losses) accruing to holders of money because of Keynesian disequilibria, real national income will tend to equilibrate at classical economic levels. Thus, if money wage rates and prices are falling because of unemployment, then, according to Friedman, the real income of people, holding given amounts of outside fiat money, will be positive, and will rise faster and faster and become bigger and bigger the more quickly prices fall, thus causing the unemployment to vanish even if there were some adverse effects on expenditures while the deflations were going on (Friedman, 1976, pp. 319–21). As monetary economies are characterized by less and less outside or fiat money, the less and less important is the Friedman counter to Keynes. The question which must be asked is this: is it meaningful to introduce capital gains and losses associated with deflations and inflations and the holding of fiat money into the revaluation accounts associated with national income estimates when, under modern monetary and central banking theory, such holdings, at least in the form of reserves with central banks, are vanishing?

The basic problem with the current national accounts is that we do not have meaningful measures of the output of private banks nor, even more importantly, of the output of central banks. If we applied the current method of imputation for the output of banks to modern central banks, their output would be seen to be zero (Rymes, 2004). Since the banks are the principal producers of transactions services and affect monetary production technologies, it follows that the inability of the national accounts to arrive at satisfactory measures of the output of banks in general means that they cannot measure satisfactorily production in monetary economies (see Fixler and Reinsdorf, 2006). Thus, though one of the central questions dividing Keynesian and neoclassical analyses and the effects of monetary developments on the concepts and measures of national income cannot be currently understood using the current national income accounts, even deeper questions emerge. Does the growth of banks and central bank policies affect capital accumulation, technical progress and national income? We simply do not know now!

Conclusion

The national income accounts have played central roles in the development of economic theory and analysis. Concepts and measures must be improved and developed to reflect better the fact that we live in monetary economies where we do not understand and do not accordingly measure well the outputs of banks and central banks, capital inputs, accumulation and technical progress, all which affect the distribution of national income. Ricardo's question still needs answers. Our current theories and measures of national income need work. Readers and students should therefore realize that there is much exciting and profitable theoretical and empirical study remaining to be done in national income accounting.

Acknowledgements

I am indebted to Dr Harry Postner, with whom I collaborated in preparing a paper given at a session we organized on 'National accounts and the teaching of economics' at the 1998 meetings of the International Association for Research in Income and Wealth (IARIW), for his continued criticisms of my work. The most dispiriting finding of that session was how few departments around the world maintained courses in national accounting as part of their curricula. I think the reason is that official national accounting places too little emphasis on connecting with modern economic theories and accordingly lose too much academic contact. I alone am responsible for this basic theme in this article. I also record with much gratitude the extremely critical and penetrating comments on the initial draft made by Professor Duncan McDowall of the history department at Carleton. Professor McDowall took valuable time away from writing a history of the Canadian national accounts to comment on my manuscript. I am also much obliged to Professor Mark Bils whose suggestion for tightening the monetary part of the argument was useful indeed. Finally, I thank Michael James for making my article far more readable than I could.

THOMAS K. RYMES

See also **national accounting, history of.**

Bibliography

Barro, R. and Sala-i-Martin, X. 1995. *Economic Growth.* Toronto: McGraw Hill.
Beckerman, W. 1987. National income. In *The New Palgrave: A Dictionary of Economics*, vol. 3, ed. J. Eatwell, M. Milgate and P. Newman. Toronto: Macmillan.
Blades, D. and Lequiller, F. 2006. *Understanding National Accounts.* Paris: OECD.
Bos, F. 2003. The national accounts as a tool for analysis and policy; past, present and future. Ph.D. thesis, Twente University.
Bos, F. 2006. The development of the Dutch national accounts as a tool for analysis and policy. *Statistica Neerlandica* 60, 225–58.

Cas, A. and Rymes, T.K. 1991. *On Concepts and Measures of Multifactor Productivity in Canada, 1961–81*. Cambridge: Cambridge University Press, 2006.

Fixler, D. and Reinsdorf, M. 2006. Computing real bank services. A paper prepared for the NBER/CRIW Workshop, 18 July.

Friedman, M. 1976. *Price Theory*. Chicago: Aldine.

Gillespie, I. 1980. *The Redistribution of Income in Canada*. Ottawa: Carleton Library.

Gillespie, I. 1991. *Tax, Borrow and Spend: Financing Federal Spending in Canada 1867–1990*. Ottawa: Carleton University Press.

Hulten, C. 2006. The 'architecture' of capital accounting: basic design principles. In *A New Architecture for the U.S. National Accounts*, ed. D.W. Jorgenson, J.S. Landefeld and W.D. Nordhaus. Chicago: University of Chicago Press.

ILO (International Labour Organization). 2004. *Consumer Price Index Manual: Theory and Practice*. Geneva: ILO.

IMF (International Monetary Fund). 2004. *Producer Price Index Manual: Theory and Practice*. Washington, DC: IMF.

Lathen, E. 1974. *Accounting for Murder*. Richmond Hill, ON: Pocket Books.

Milanovic, B. 2005. *Worlds Apart: Measuring International and Global Inequality*. Princeton: Princeton University Press.

Pasinetti, L. 1995. *Structural Change and Economic Growth*. Cambridge: Cambridge University Press.

Prescott, E.C. 2006. The transformation of macroeconomic policy and research. *Journal of Political Economy* 114, 203–35.

Ricardo, D. 1971. On the principles of political economy and taxation. In *The Works and Correspondence of David Ricardo*, vol. 1, ed. P. Sraffa. Cambridge: Cambridge University Press.

Rymes, T.K. 1991. Some theoretical problems in accounting for sustainable consumption. In *Approaches to Environmental Accounting*, ed. A. Franz and C. Stahmer. Heidelberg: Physica.

Rymes, T.K. 1992. National accounting and financial flows. In *The New Palgrave Dictionary of Money and Finance*, vol. 3, ed. P. Newman, M. Milgate and J. Eatwell. London: Macmillan.

Rymes, T.K. 1997. The productivity of working and waiting. In *Capital Controversy: Post-Keynesian Economics And The History Of Economic Thought*, ed. P. Arestis, G. Palma and M. Sawyer. London: Routledge.

Rymes, T.K. 2004. Modern central banks only have *real* effects. In *Central Banking in the Modern World: Alternative Perspectives*, ed. M. Lavoie and M. Seccareccia. Cheltenham: Edward Elgar.

Ward, M. 2006. An intellectual history of national accounting: a review of André Vanoli. *A History of National Accounting*. *Review of Income and Wealth* 52, 327–40.

national system

The term 'national system of political economy' stems from a filiation of American and German ideas that arose in opposition to the universalist character of classical economics and were designed to promote public policies serving the economic development of the nation. The development was visualized as one that would yield a balance of agriculture and industry and make the most of a country's potential economic strength. The term 'American system' occurs as early as 1787 in No. 11 of *The Federalist*, where Alexander Hamilton launches this appeal to his readers: 'Let the thirteen states, bound together in a strict and indissoluble Union, concur in erecting one great American system, superior to the control of all transatlantic force or influence and able to dictate the terms of the connection between the old and the new world.'

Hamilton's more detailed proposals regarding the ways and means to construct the American system can be found in his great state papers, written when he served as Secretary of the Treasury in President Washington's cabinet, and dealing with manufactures, a national bank, and the public debt. With the help of these three instruments he wished to emancipate the new nation from the rural economy of its forefathers, one that Thomas Jefferson, Hamilton's great antagonist, attempted to preserve. Among Hamilton's specific devices to promote industrial development, bounties, or subsidies, stood out. Later writers emphasized protective tariffs rather than bounties.

These writers included Daniel Raymond, a Baltimore attorney, whose *Thoughts on Political Economy* of 1820, while not elaborating the notion of a national system in so many words, made a substantial contribution to the later interpretation of the term by introducing the concept of 'capacity' to produce goods, identified by him with national wealth. Raymond placed on government the duty of utilizing and enlarging this capacity by a policy of protection. His plea for protective tariffs was supported both by the infant-industry argument and the employment argument, in conjunction with which Raymond wrote explicitly of 'full employment.'

The next step in elaborating the concept of a national system was taken by Frederick List, the German writer and promoter, who in 1827 during his residence in the United States published *Outlines of American Political Economy*. Like Hamilton, List writes of the 'American system', which was to realize its potential with the help of tariff protection. This work was written and distributed at the behest of a Pennsylvania manufacturers association whose members clamoured for tariff protection. Composed ostensibly in the form of letters addressed to a leading protectionist, the work appeared serially in the *National Gazette* of Philadelphia and was reprinted by more than 50 other newspapers. When published in pamphlet form, it was distributed in 'many thousand' copies, as List later reported. It was sent to the members of Congress and was apparently helpful in securing the adoption of the Tariff Act of 1828.

In an abortive attempt to win a prize, List wrote in French in 1837 an essay on *The Natural System of Political Economy*, which remained, however, unpublished until 1927, when it was printed in French and German. An English translation appeared only in 1983. This work anticipates in a number of respects List's principal work, *National System of Political Economy*, in which the national-system doctrine reached its full flowering. This work was published in German in 1841; an English translation, sponsored by protectionist interests in the United States, appeared in 1856, and another one, published in England, in 1885. The work, while substantial enough in itself, was intended to be the first part of a larger project, which, however, was never completed. Of the English translations, the earlier one omits the preface, while the later one contains extracts from the preface but omits the introductory chapter that provides a summary of the work.

In the *National System*, List finds fault with the classics for a variety of reasons. He takes them to task for having constructed a system of thought that is permeated by individualism and cosmopolitanism but neglects the nation. According to List, the community of nations is not a homogenous group but made up of members that find themselves at different stages of their development. List then goes on to construct a stage theory which visualizes progress from the agricultural stage to one in which agriculture is combined with industry, and to still another one in which agriculture, industry, and trade are joined together. List tends to equate agriculture with poverty and low level of culture, whereas industry and urbanization bring wealth and cultural achievement. The classics, with their homogenized picture of the world which neglected national differences, would tend to perpetuate the underdeveloped status of the United States and continental Europe vis-à-vis the highly developed Britain. According to List, each stage, or each nation at its respective stage, requires a different set of economic doctrines, whereas the classics claimed universal validity for their doctrines.

At heart, List wanted to improve on Providence by turning all people into Englishmen. To allow the underdeveloped countries of his time to participate in the march toward higher stages, attention would have to be paid to their productive capacities. The development and utilization of these was a task that List placed squarely on the national governments. In this connection List called for liberal political institutions, for the construction of what is now known as social overhead, especially in the form of transportation facilities, for balanced growth and for tariff protection for infant industries (not for agricultural products). The free-trade orientation of the classics List was willing to endorse as valid for the future, when all nations had utilized their potential and attained the most progressive stage. Then free trade would be combined with universal peace and a world federation.

There are a number of questions that List left unanswered. To begin with the most often heard objection to the infant-industry argument for protection, what tests are there to identify infant industries and to mark their eventual attainment of maturity, when protection presumably is to terminate? Moreover, List did not explain how the type of economic warfare that he envisaged would prepare the ground for universal peace. Nor did he show awareness of the likelihood that, once all nations had progressed to what he called the normal state one nation would again get ahead of the others, perhaps for reasons of technological advances, a matter treated with so much insight by Hume in his analysis of the migration of economic opportunities.

List had been a protectionist of sorts already in his young years in his native Germany. His protectionist leanings came to the fore in the United States, where he encountered an even richer potential for economic development and where changing economic conditions were more rapid and conspicuous. Here List's strictures on the classics fell on fertile ground because so many features of their dismal science did not seem to fit into the American environment, especially Malthus's population doctrine and Ricardo's theories of subsistence wages, diminishing returns, and free trade. Thus List's work coalesced with the works of native American critics of the classics, especially of Henry Carey, who developed theories of increasing rather than diminishing returns and of rising wages and profits and declared that each successive addition to the population brings a consumer and a producer. According to Samuelson, Carey's 'logic was often bad and his prolix style atrocious. But his fundamental empirical inferences seem correct for his time and place' (p. 1,732). Beginning in 1848, Carey became an ardent exponent of protectionism. By this time List was dead and it is uncertain to what extent, if any, Carey was indebted to List's thought. Neither of the two developed his proposal for tariff protection in isolation but as parts of a wider system of thought, of a theory of economic development in the case of List and of a theory of a harmoniously ordered society in the case of Carey.

Among political leaders in the United States Henry Clay is often mentioned as an architect of the American system, in which the industrial east and the agrarian west were allied in a powerful union. He pleaded for such a system in a famous speech in 1824, in which he supported protective tariffs as instruments of industrial development. Later still, in 1870, Francis Bowen, an early teacher of economics at Harvard, would publish *American Political Economy*, in which he supported tariff protection and which caused him to lose his teaching job in economics, the president easing him into the presumably less controversial field of history.

In Germany, List's ideas had a profound and lasting influence. He promoted the customs union, which by 1844 covered almost all of Germany, and agitated for railroad construction and tariff protection. The very name of economics in Germany, Nationalökonomie, conveys associations with List. Some German interpreters of the history of economics have compared List with Marx. Both had utopian visions of a society to come in the fullness of time. Both made much of a fusion of theory and practice and of economics and politics. Both are linked by their reputation as rebels who opposed the established order. It is an interesting trivium that in 1841 List turned down an offer to serve as the editor of a newspaper that was to be published under the name of *Rheinische Zeitung*, a post that Marx filled the following year.

List's thought has an affinity with the historical schools and institutional economists, who had ideas of their own about the possibility of universally valid economic doctrines. The word 'system', cleansed of its protectionist implications, continued to play a key role in the writings of such 20th-century German economists as Walter Eucken and Werner Sombart. An equally faint echo of the Hamiltonian idea can be discerned in the current usage of the word in conjunction with the study of comparative economic *systems*.

HENRY W. SPIEGEL

See also **comparative advantage; Corn Laws, free trade and protectionism; growth and international trade; infant-industry protection.**

Bibliography

Bowen, F. 1870. *American Political Economy*. New York: Scribner.

Carey, H. 1858–59. *Principles of Social Science*. 3 vols, Philadelphia: Lippincott.

Conkin, P.K. 1980. *Prophets of Prosperity: America's First Political Economists*. Bloomington: Indiana University Press.

Dorfman, J. 1946. *The Economic Mind in American Civilization*, Vols 1–2. New York: Viking Press.

Hamilton, A. 1934. *Papers on Public Credit, Commerce and Finance*. Ed. S. McKee, New York: Columbia University Press.

Henderson, W.O. 1983. *Friedrich List: Economist and Visionary 1789–1846*. London: Cass.

Hirst, M.E. 1909. *Life of Friedrich List and Selections from His Writings*. London: Smith, Elder.

List, F. 1827. *Outlines of American Political Economy*. Reprinted in *The Life of Friedrich List and Selection from his Writings*, ed. M.E. Hirst. London: Smith, Elder & Co., 1909.

List, F. 1837. *The Natural System of Political Economy*. Trans. and ed. W.O. Henderson, London: Cass, 1983.

List, F. 1956. *National System of Political Economy*. Philadelphia: Lippincott.

Samuelson, P.A. 1960. American economics. In *Postwar Economic Trends in the United States*, ed. R.E. Freeman, New York: Harper. Reprinted in *P.A. Samuelson, Collected Scientific Papers*, Vol. 2, ed. J.E. Stiglitz, Cambridge, Mass.: MIT Press, 1966, 1732–47.

Spiegel, H.W. 1960. *The Rise of American Economic Thought*. Philadelphia: Chilton.

Spiegel, H.W. 1983. *The Growth of Economic Thought*. Revised and expanded edn, Durham, North Carolina: Duke University Press.

natural and warranted rates of growth

The concepts of the natural and warranted rates of growth of national income, associated with the work of R.F. Harrod and E.D. Domar, were first developed in the 1930s and 1940s as part of the rethinking of the theory of economic fluctuations generated by Keynes's *General Theory*. Somewhat paradoxically, they formed an initial impetus for the theories for long-run steady growth elaborated in the 1950s and 1960s.

In the early 1930s Harrod criticized the static nature of economic analysis, suggesting that it be supplemented by a 'dynamic' theory: static theory determined the levels of variables, dynamic theory should explain the 'rates of change' of the variables taken at a point in time. Harrod's first attempt at dynamic theory, *The Trade Cycle* (1936), appeared almost simultaneously with Keynes's book, which Harrod considered limited to statics, even though it argued that the system could achieve equilibrium at less than full employment, because it dealt with the equilibrium *levels* of output and employment. After a lengthy correspondence with Keynes (cf. Keynes, 1973, pp. 151ff), Harrod published a new version of his theory, 'An Essay on Dynamic Theory', (1939) in which he formulated a 'dynamic equilibrium' for income, Y, defined as the 'warranted rate of growth' $g_w = (\mathrm{d}Y/\mathrm{d}t)/Y$, to complement Keynes's static equilibrium. Due to the outbreak of war the theory did not attract attention until he presented it in a series of popular lectures (Harrod, 1948) after the war.

In Keynes's theory any level of output and employment, including full employment as a special case, was a potential equilibrium; the actual equilibrium was determined by the point of effective demand given the general state of expectations expressed in the propensity to consume, the marginal efficiency of capital and liquidity preference. Harrod was thus led to analyse a 'dynamised version of Keynes' ... effective demand' (Harrod, 1959), defined as the rate of growth produced by the rate of investment chosen by entrepreneurs which is warranted in the sense of maintaining a rate of expansion of effective demand which is consistent with entrepreneurial expectation and with individuals' autonomous decisions to save. The level of income, Y_0, prevailing at any point in time in the actual development of the economy will be determined by the entrepreneurs' expectations of the rate of growth of income $(\mathrm{d}Y/\mathrm{d}t)/Y_0$. On the basis of the expected $\mathrm{d}Y/\mathrm{d}t$ they will decide the investment necessary to satisfy this expected expansion in demand. This decision is made on the basis of the 'capital coefficient' (which Harrod called C, but is now generally written as v), $(I_0 = v(\mathrm{d}Y/\mathrm{d}t))$, defined as the total money expenditure that must be made on new investment projects to create an additional £ of output. The public's decisions to spend and save expressed as $S = sY_0$ will then determine the actual increase in income via the multiplier $(dI/dt)/s = dY/dt$. Entrepreneurs' expectations will only be confirmed if $v(dY/dt) = sY_0$ which when rearranged produces Harrod's famous growth equation $g_w = (dY/dt)/Y_0 = s/v$, with $S/Y_0 = I/Y_0$ which is Keynes's equilibrium. The rate of expansion of income is thus warranted and since entrepreneurs' expectations have been confirmed they are presumed to expect income to continue to expand at that rate. Thus, given Y_0 and s there is a set of expectations which produces a dynamic equilibrium rate which will describe an expansion of income through time of $Y = Y_t \exp(g_w t)$.

For Harrod, the analytical importance of his dynamics was to be found in the proposition that while in static analysis any departure from equilibrium produced centripetal forces driving the variable back to its equilibrium value, in dynamic analysis any movement away from equilibrium (in this case the warranted rate of growth of income) would set up centrifugal forces which would move the system further away from its equilibrium position. For example, if income were growing at the warranted rate and investment rose above the warranted rate, $I_t > I_0 \exp(g_w t)$, income would expand at a higher rate, inventories would be drawn down and additional investment would be required to restore them to normal; the expectations which produced the warranted rate would be revised upwards as investment would appear insufficient relative to the expansion in sales, leading to further increases which would eventually surpass available labour and resources. Thus, instead of returning to the equilibrium rate, g_w, an inflationary boom in which expectations would eventually be disappointed by shortages of supply, leads to a collapse of investment and expectations. Since the dynamic equilibrium is unstable, Harrod thus concludes that the warranted rate of growth is inherently unstable.

Just as in Keynes's theory, there is no reason for the warranted rate to be associated with full employment, nor is there any reason for a disturbance of the system from a dynamic equilibrium to lead to a full employment rate. Disturbances will in general lead to a series of erratic booms and slumps of variable duration with respect to the warranted rate. The full employment rate of growth does however play a role in this cyclical process by setting a limit beyond which it is impossible for the economy permanently to grow, either in equilibrium or disequilibrium. If the rate of growth of potentially employable labour, given by the rate of population growth, is $n = (dN/dt)/N$, the full employment rate of growth representing the maximum sustainable growth rate would be $g = n = s/v$ unless technical progress expanded output per man employed. When available technical progress is used to increase labour QJ;productivity by $\tau = (d(Y/N)dt)/(Y/N)$ the maximum sustainable rate, which Harrod called the 'natural' rate, would be $g = n + \tau$ The natural rate will only be an

equilibrium position, i.e. a warranted rate, if households save the required proportion of income s_r which given the optimal introduction of new production techniques producing v_n, is required to produce $g_n = s_r/v_r = n + \tau$. Since there is no economic mechanism that links s and v to n and τ the natural rate is unstable, but for different reasons than if it happened by chance to be a warranted rate.

Thus, for any actual state of the economy there will be a value for $g_w \leq g_n$ which is given by the values of Y_0, v and s determined by the past history of the economy. There can, of course, be only one value for g_w since there cannot be more than one value of Y_0, s or v for any given point in time. If the economy grows at some other rate, say g_a, then Y will not expand along the warranted path $Y_t = Y_0\exp(g_w t)$, so that the rate which would be required to produce warranted growth from any subsequent point in time, t, would depend on the actual values of Y_t, s and v.

For example, if $g_a = s_a/v > g_w = s/v$, then $s_a > s$ and investment will continue to increase g_a until the upper limit of g_n is surpassed. This may be conceivable, for example in the period after a deep slump, but physical bottlenecks and increases in money wages due to labour market shortages will eventually lead to inflationary boom and a subsequent collapse back into a slump which will cause incomes and investment to fall, causing s_a to fall. At any time in this process it would be possible to calculate on the basis of the level of income, Y_t, and associated s and v, the rate of investment which, if adopted would produce warranted equilibrium growth from that time onwards. Although it is highly unlikely that the economy would adopt this rate, it serves as a benchmark with which to compare the actual behaviour of the economy and thus to predict the direction of its subsequent cyclical movements.

There will thus be a different, but unique, value of g_w for every actual position of the system as it develops through time. Only if g_w is in fact attained will the economy exhibit stable, non-cyclical growth, while departures from the rate will not set up self-correcting movements to instantly restore it.

These two aspects of Harrod's theory have caused much misunderstanding. The fact that there is only one 'unique' or 'knife-edge' equilibrium growth path for any given t and condition of the system has led some economists to consider this as the main cause of instability. Yet Harrod himself considered 'instability' to be an inherent property of the general concept of dynamic equilibrium as represented by the warranted growth rate. Since there would be only one warranted rate for any given condition of the economy it could be used to explain the cyclical behaviour of the economy if g_a diverged from g_w. But in Harrod's theory there would be a new warranted rate for every new combination of Y, s and v thrown up by the actual growth of the economy; g_w was only unique because each point in time was characterized by unique conditions. The role of the instability property of the warranted rate, given the natural rate, was to explain how the system would move when it was not growing at its dynamic equilibrium rate.

Domar (1946, 1947), writing after the publication of the *General Theory*, reacted to a specific problem in Keynes's theory, pointing out that the very investment expenditure that provides the demand for the output of existing productive capacity implies increased productive capacity in future periods. Investment as a means of increasing aggregate demand is thus a 'mixed blessing', for if the investment sufficient to prevent unemployment today creates excess capacity tomorrow then even more investment will be required tomorrow. Long-run unemployment could be avoided only by increasing investment at an increasing rate. To analyse this problem it was inevitable that Domar recast Keynes's analysis in terms of rates of change.

Domar approached the problem by separating the influence of investment on aggregate demand and on productive capacity or supply. Keynes had already provided the analysis of demand in terms of the multiplier ($k = 1/s$) giving the expansion in demand resulting from increasing investment as $dY_d/dt = k(dI/dt)$. On the supply side, however, since all of net investment, and not only the increase, expands productive capacity Domar amends Keynes's approach and considers the fraction of the labour force employed as a function of the ratio of income to *potential* productive capacity rather than as a simple function of income. Defining α as the net value added produced by a £ of net investment, potential productive capacity will then increase by αI where I is the aggregate cost of new investment projects. On the micro level, however, some new capacity will be competing with older capacity, and since some investment projects will be carried out on the basis of expectations which will not be realized, Domar defines σ as the 'potential social average productivity of investment' for the economy. The divergence between α and σ (as well as the assumption that $\alpha < \sigma$) thus represents errors in investment decisions, investment outpacing the growth in the labour force or investments incorporating inappropriate technology. The supply-side effect is thus $dY_s/dt = \sigma I$. The answer to Domar's question of whether there is a constant rate of growth of investment at which the demand will rise sufficiently rapidly to offset the effect of investment on supply is thus found where $dY_d/dt = dY_s/dt$ or where $k(dI/dt) = \sigma I$. This equality can be rewritten as $(dI/dt)/I = \sigma/k$ which Domar calls the 'required' rate of growth of investment.

Domar's assumption that unemployment is determined by the relation of income to potential capacity means that the 'required' rate implies full capacity utilization and thus full employment. The failure of the economy to grow at this rate implies excess capacity. If productive potential arising from net investment σI is defined as P, $\sigma = (dP/dt)/I$, then a coefficient of utilization determined by the relative expansion of demand and capacity can be defined as, $\theta = (dY_d/dt)/(dP/dt)$. Since $dY_d/dt = k(dI/dt)$ and $dP/dt = \sigma I$, θ can be

written as $(dI/dt)/I \cdot k/\sigma$ assuming that $\alpha = \sigma$ If investment is expanding at the required rate $(dI/dt)/I = \sigma/k$, $dY_d/dt = dP/dt$ and $\theta = 100$ per cent capacity utilization. Domar's required rate is thus equivalent to Harrod's natural rate of growth (s_r/v_r) when $\alpha = \sigma$ since $k = 1/s$ and $\sigma = (dY/dt)/I = 1/v_r$, $\sigma/k = s/v_r$.

Domar's analysis of divergence of the actual growth rate from the 'required' rate also produces an analysis of instability, for when $(dI/dt)/I$ is below k/σ the required rate, dY_d/dt is less than dP/dt, so part $(1 - \theta)$ of new productive potential is unused. This excess capacity thus implies the existence of unemployment. A higher rate of growth of investment would be required to eliminate the excess capacity and unemployment, but since current productive capacity is already excess to needs, entrepreneurs are more likely to try to reduce than to increase their desired capacity by lowering $(dI/dt)/I$, which will increase rather than decrease both unemployment and excess capacity, producing a slump. Thus, in difference from Harrod's analysis, the natural rate is a unique equilibrium or 'knife edge' rate as well as being unstable. For Domar instability is not linked to the conceptual definition of dynamic equilibrium by means of a warranted rate, but rather to the 'paradox' that is the dynamic equivalent to the Keynesian paradox of saving: given s, the elimination of excess capacity, whether it is caused by the effects of investment on the expansion of demand or productive capacity, requires more capital to be built, while a shortage of productive capacity requires a reduction in the rate of growth of investment. This result is parallel to Harrod's statement to the effect that a general glut of commodities is due to entrepreneurs producing too little rather than too much.

While both Harrod and Domar sought to use the concepts of warranted and natural or required rates as an aid to understanding the cyclical implications of Keynes's analysis, and despite the differences in their approach, their work served to form the basis of what came to be known as the 'Harrod–Domar' theory of steady growth. By interpreting the variables s and v as being given exogenously the theory produced what Kaldor (1951) called 'Harrod's problem', or as Joan Robinson (1965, p. 52) put it:

> Given s,... and v,... g is determined. There is only one value of g which (provided it does not exceed n) is not impossible. The uniqueness of g, not any question about the stability of the corresponding growth path, created the problem of the 'knife edge'.

This 'problem' was 'resolved' by introducing differential savings propensities from wages and profits to make s a variable determined by the distribution of income, which would allow multiple long-period unemployment growth equilibria, as in the post-Keynesian theories of growth and distribution. Alternatively (cf. e.g. Solow, 1970, ch. 2), if movements in relative prices of capital and labour services are allowed to produce substitution of capital for labour, as in an aggregate production function, then v would become variable over time and lead to the full employment of both factors, despite Domar's (1952, pp. 23–6) explicit warning that the introduction of a Cobb–Douglas production function to solve this problem would lead directly to this traditional pre-Keynesian result.

These two conflicting interpretations of the applicability of Keynes's unemployment equilibrium in the long period, soon enlarged to include the wider question of capital theory, created a debate in which steady state theories overwhelmed the interests of both Harrod and Domar in the implications of Keynes's theory for the problem of economic fluctuations and dynamics.

J.A. KREGEL

See also **aggregate demand theory.**

Bibliography

Domar, E.D. 1946. Capital expansion, rate of growth, and employment. *Econometrica* 14(April), 137–47. Reprinted in Domar (1957), 70–82.
Domar, E.D. 1947. Expansion and employment. *American Economic Review* 37(March), 34–55. Reprinted in Domar (1957).
Domar, E.D. 1952. Economic growth: an econometric approach. *American Economic Review, Papers and Proceedings* 42(May), 479–95. Reprinted as 'A theoretical analysis of economic growth', in Domar (1957).
Domar, E.D. 1957. *Essays in the Theory of Economic Growth*. New York and Oxford: Oxford University Press.
Harrod, R.F. 1936. *The Trade Cycle*. Oxford: Clarendon Press.
Harrod, R.F. 1939. An essay in dynamic theory. *Economic Journal* 49(March), 14–33.
Harrod, R.F. 1948. *Towards a Dynamic Economics*. London: Macmillan.
Harrod, R.F. 1959. Domar and dynamic economics. *Economic Journal* 69(September), 451–64.
Kaldor, N. 1951. Mr Hicks on the trade cycle. *Economic Journal* 61(December), 833–47.
Keynes, J.M. 1973. *The Collected Writings of J.M. Keynes*, Vol. 14: *The General Theory and After* – Part II, *Defence and Development*. Ed. D. Moggridge, London: Macmillan.
Robinson, J. 1965. Harrod's knife edge. In J. Robinson, *Collected Economic Papers*, Vol. 3, Oxford: Basil Blackwell.
Solow, R.M. 1970. *Growth Theory: an Exposition*. Oxford: Clarendon Press.

natural experiments and quasi-natural experiments

The term 'natural experiment' has been used in many, often, contradictory, ways. It is not unfair to say that the term is frequently employed to describe situations that are neither 'natural' nor 'experiments' or situations which are 'natural, but not experiments' or vice versa.

It will serve the interests of clarity to initially direct most of our attention to the second term – experiment. A useful, albeit philosophically charged definition of an experiment 'is a set of actions and observations, performed in the context of solving a particular problem or question, to support or falsify a hypothesis or research concerning phenomena' (Wikipedia, 2006).

With such a broad definition in hand, it may not be surprising to observe a wide range of views among economists about whether or not they perform experiments. Vernon Smith, for example, in EXPERIMENTAL METHODS IN ECONOMICS, begins with the premise that 'historically, the method and subject matter of economics have *presupposed* that it was a *non–experimental … science more like astronomy or meteorology than physics or chemistry*' (emphasis added). As he makes clear, his observation implies that *today*, economics is an experimental science. Bastable's article on the same subject in the first edition of *The New Palgrave* overlaps only superficially with Smith's and divides experiments along the lines suggested by Bacon: *experimenta lucifera*, in which 'theoretical' concerns dominate, and *experimenta fructifera*, which concern themselves with 'practical' matters. In sharp contrast to Smith, Bastable concludes that *experimenta lucifera* are 'a very slight resource' (1987, p. 240) in economics.

These two views of experiment, however, do not seem helpful in understanding the controversy regarding natural experiments. 'Experiment' in our context is merely the notion of putting one's view to the most 'severe' test possible. A good summary of the the spirit of experiment (natural or otherwise) comes from the American philosopher Charles Sanders Peirce (and see Mayo, 1996 for a nice exposition of this and related points):

> [After posing a question or theory], the next business in order is to commence deducing from it whatever experimental predictions are extremest and most unlikely … in order to subject them to the *test of experiment*.
>
> The process of testing it will consist, not in examining the facts, in order to see how well they accord with the hypothesis, but on the contrary in examining such of the probable consequences of the hypothesis as would be capable of direct verification, especially those consequences which would be very unlikely or surprising in case the hypothesis were not true.
>
> When the hypothesis has sustained a testing as severe as the present state of our knowledge … renders imperative, it will be admitted provisionally … subject of course to reconsideration. (Peirce, 1958, 7.182 (emphasis added) and 7.231 as cited in Mayo, 1996)

The philosophy of experimentation in natural science

In the emergence of modern natural science during the 16th century, experiments represented an important break with a long historical tradition in which observation of phenomenon was used *in* theories as a way to justify or support a priori reasoning. In Drake's (1981) view: 'The Aristotelian principle of appealing to experience had degenerated among philosophers into dependence on reasoning supported by casual examples among philosophers and the refutation of opponents by pointing to apparent exceptions not carefully examined.' In the useful historical account provided by Shadish, Cook, and Campbell (2002) it is suggested that this 'break' was twofold: first, experiments were frequently employed to correct or refute theories. This naturally led to conflict with political and religious authorities: Galileo Galilei's conflict with the Church and his fate at the hands of the Inquisition is among the best-known examples of this conflict. Second, experiments increasingly involved 'manipulation' to learn about 'causes'. Passive observation was not sufficient. As Hacking (1983, p. 149) says of early experimenter Sir Francis Bacon: 'He taught that not only must we observe nature in the raw, but that we must also "twist the lion's tale", that is, manipulate our world in order to learn its secrets.'

Indeed, at some level in the natural sciences there has been comparatively little debate about the centrality of experiment – ironically, it has typically been only philosophers of science who have downplayed the importance of experiment. Hacking (1983) makes a strong case that philosophers typically have exhibited a remarkably high degree of bias in minimizing their importance in favour of 'theory'. Until the 19th century, the term experiment was typically reserved for studies in the natural sciences.

In the low sciences such as economics and medicine, the role of experiment is been the subject of extensive debate, much tied up with the debate on whether all the types of experiments possible in real science are possible in economics as well as with debates about the many meanings of the word 'cause'.

A key distinction between much real science and economics involves the centrality of 'randomization'. No randomization is required, for example, to study whether certain actions will produce nuclear fission, since 'control' is possible: if a set of procedures applied to a piece of plutonium – under certain pre-specified experimental conditions – regularly produces nuclear fission, as long as agreement exists on the pre-specified conditions and on what constitutes plutonium, and so on, it is possible to put the implied propositions to the type of severe test that would gain widespread assent – all without randomization. Put in a different way, randomization is required only when it is difficult to put a proposition to a severe test without it.

A related issue is whether a study of 'causes' requires some notion of 'manipulation'. Most definitions of 'cause' in social science involve some notion of 'manipulation' (Heckman, 2005) – Bacon's 'twisting of the tail', so to speak. In physics, by way of contrast, some important 'causes' do not involve manipulation per se. One might argue that Newton's law of gravitation was an example of a mere empirical regularity that became a 'cause'. Indeed, when proposed by Newton, Leibnitz objected to this new 'law': in the prevailing intellectual and scientific climate where the world was understood in terms of 'mechanical pushes and pulls', this new law seemed to require the invocation of 'occult powers' (Hacking, 1983). (There is an element of irony in Leibnitz's objection. Leibnitz is believed by some to be the object of Voltaire's satire as the character Dr Pangloss in *Candide* of whom it is said that he 'proved admirably that there is no effect without a cause … in this the best of all possible worlds' – a very different notion of causation! Voltaire, 1759, ch. 1.)

In this article, we take the view that, even if manipulation were not necessary to *define* causality, manipulation is central to whether it is possible to discuss the idea intelligibly in social sciences and whether some kind of 'severe test' is possible (DiNardo, 2007). Some philosophers have sought to *define* science around issues related to 'control', arguing that the phenomena economists try to investigate are impossible to study scientifically at all. Philosophers have articulated numerous reasons for the difference between social and natural science. A few examples may be helpful: Nelson (1990, pp. 102–6) argues, for example, that the objects of enquiry by the economist do not constitute 'a natural kind'. Put very crudely, the issue is the extent to which all the phenomena that we lump into the category 'commodity', for example, can be refined to some essence that is sufficiently 'similar' so that a scientific theory about commodities is possible in the same way as a 'body' is in Newtonian mechanics. This is often discussed as the issue of whether the relevant taxonomy results in 'carving nature at the joints'. Hacking (2000) introduces the notions of 'indifferent kinds' – the objects in the physical science – atoms, quarks, and so on with 'interactive' kinds – the objects of study in medicine or the social sciences. We might interact with plutonium or bacteria, but neither the plutonium nor the bacteria are aware of how we are classifying them or what we are doing to them. This can be contrasted with 'interactive kinds' that are aware and for which 'looping' is possible. For example, mental retardation might lead to segregation of those so designated. This segregation might lead to new behaviours which then might not fall under the old label, and so on. Consequently, investigation of such phenomena might be likened to 'trying to hit a moving target'. Searle (1995) on the other hand, notes that the objects of interest in social science while epistemologically objective, are ontologically subjective. While the loss of 100 dollars may be very 'real' to someone, the notion of money requires groups of individual to accept money as a medium of exchange. Again the existence of atoms does not require us to recognize their existence.

Randomization: an attempt to evade the problems of imperfect 'control'

If one accepts the centrality of manipulation (or something like it), it will not be surprising that the application of principles of experimentation to humans who have free will, make choices, and so on entails a host of issues that, inter alia, sharply constrain what might be reasonable to expect of experiments, natural, or otherwise.

If it is not possible, desirable, or ethical to 'control' humans or their 'environment' as it sometimes is in the natural sciences, is it possible to learn anything at all from experiment broadly construed? *Randomization* in experiments developed in part to try to evade the usual problems of isolating the role of the single phenomenon in situations. In the 19th century, it was discovered that by the use of 'artificial randomizers' (such as a coin toss) it was possible, in principle, to create two groups of individuals which were the same 'on average' apart from a single 'treatment' (cause) which was under (at least partial) control of the experimenter. Hacking (1988, p. 427) has observed that their use began primarily in contexts 'marked by complete ignorance': the economist F. Y. Edgeworth was early to apply the mathematical logic of both Bayesian and 'classical' statistics to a randomized trial of the existence of 'telepathy'.

Although economists played an important role in the development of randomization, economists as a whole were quite slow to embrace the new tools. In an echo of debates that faced natural sciences in the 1600s, this was due in part 'because the theory [of economics] was not in doubt, applied workers sought neither to verify nor to disprove' (Morgan, 1987, pp. 171–2).

Over time, the term 'experiment' evolved to include both experiments of the 'hard sciences' where a measure of control was possible as well as situations in which artificial randomizers were used to assign individuals (or plots of land, and so on) to different 'treatments'. A key role was played by R. A. Fisher (1935) and his seminal *Design of Experiments* as well subsequent publications which discussed the theory and practice of using artificial randomizers to learn about causes.

There are at least two key limitations of randomized experiments relative to experiments where 'scientific' control is possible:

- Without real control, one only has a weak understanding of the 'cause' in question. For instance, one can do a randomized controlled trial of the effect of aspirin on heart failure while understanding nothing of the mechanism by which aspirin affects the outcome. Moreover, it is clear that the experiment is 'context specific'. One's generalization about atoms in a laboratory often extends to atoms in other contexts in a way not possible in social science.
- Any single experiment – even under the ideal situation – does not always reveal the true answer. In the logic of randomized design, the usual inference procedure is merely one that *would* give the right answer on average *if* the experiment were repeated. At best, the true answer is just a 'long-run tendency' in repeated identical experiments.

Social experiments: why not do a 'real' randomized trial?

Even without these limitations, there is a long list of reasons why economists frequently have little interest in randomized trials. The most important reason is that many of the real randomized experiments (often called 'Social experiments') of which one could conceive (or have been implemented), are immoral or unethical. At a most basic level, the decision as to who 'performs an experiment' and who 'decides' or is recruited to be experimented upon often reflects deep-seated social injustice. Even Brandeisian (see below) experiments can take on a sinister cast – state governments surely do not consider the interests of all their citizens equally.

Indeed, historically the conduct of experiments on persons has told us as much or more about the structure of society than anything else: one well-known example is the series of 'experiments' conducted by the US Public Health Service from 1932 to 1972 on about 400 poor black men who had advanced syphilis. One aim of the experiment was to determine the effect of untreated syphilis. To this end, the medical doctors misrepresented themselves to the subjects (the sons and grandsons of slaves), claiming to provide free medical care. For example, when penicillin became the standard of care, the subjects were deliberately not provided with the medication: rather, the doctors were content to observe the horrific progress of the disease as some went blind or insane.

Another set of reasons is practical – experiments are costly to administer. Another reason is attrition: often people drop out of such experiments (often in non-random ways), greatly complicating the problem of inference. A distinct, although sometimes related, reason is that the results of social experiments involving randomization are sometimes difficult to interpret. One often cited reason is that those recruited to participate in such experiments may be different from those for whom the policy is ultimately intended. In even the simplest experiments, 'compliance' is imperfect. Not everyone assigned to a treatment takes it up – indeed, it is often the case that analysis is made on an 'intent to treat' basis. That is, those 'assigned' to treatment are compared to those assigned to the control whether or not those assigned to treatment actually 'took' the treatment. Another often cited reason is that what is likely when a social experiment is conducted with a small number of persons might be very different when applied to much larger numbers of persons. Persons, unlike atomic particles, enjoy free will. In the world of persons, the 'experiment' does not necessarily stop after the experimenters have made their observations. For example, even in the context of a true randomized experiment, those denied treatment often have the opportunity to find it elsewhere (see Heckman and Smith, 1995, with references, for one discussion of the merits of randomized trials in the social science).

Types of natural experiments
Thus far we have seen that the word 'experiment' can be used in two very different senses: one to denote situations where real 'control' is possible and second involving artificial randomizers. As a consequence, the term 'natural experiment' has been used in very different senses. I now turn to the origins of the term and the different ways the term has been used, although we focus on natural experiments most frequently arising in economics.

Natural experiments in natural science
An early use of the term 'natural experiment' in English describes an investigation into the functioning of 'nature'. The term comes from a translation *Saggi di naturali esperienze fatte nell'Accademia del Cimento* published in Italian in 1667 which appeared in an English translation by Richard Waller in 1684 as *Essayes of natural experiments made in the Academie del Cimento* (Waller, 1684). The short-lived Accademia del Cimento was founded in Florence in 1657 by the Medici brothers, Prince Leopold and Grand Duke Ferdinand II, and the *Saggi* record a small subset of the large number of experiments by the Cimento that involved such issues as 'smells do not traverse Glass', and 'the failure to confirm Existence of Atoms of cold' (1684, p. xx). Although the experiments of the Academy included trials involving humans, they did not involve randomization. Indeed, the legacy of these investigations into humans is more relevant to the study of 16th-century culture and authority relations than 16th-century science. (Tribby, 1994, for example, discusses an investigation into a 'gentler' laxative that could 'satisfy' the needs of Grand Duke Ferdinand II as well as those of the many 'delicate persons' who visited or had dealings with the court that involved experimentation on individuals described variously as 'a mercenary', 'a vagrant', 'the Little Moor', and so on.)

Over time, in the hard sciences, the term natural experiment has also come to describe both cases where 'nature' provides an experiment that resembles the controlled situation that scientists would like observe but are unable to create themselves. An unsuccessful experiment may help make the point clear: in a famous quote by Albert Einstein to Erwin Findlay Freundlich (who was attempting to assess the whether path of a ray of light was affected by gravity), Einstein wrote: 'If only we had a considerably larger planet than Jupiter! But nature has not made it a priority to make it easy for us to discover its laws.' ('Wenn wir nur einen ordentlich grösseren Planeten als Jupiter hätten! Aber die Natur hat es sich nicht angelegen sein lassen, uns die Auffindung ihrer

Gesetze bequem zu machen', (as cited in Ashtekar et al., 2003; translation from the *New York Times*, 24 March 1992).

Natural experiments as serendipitous randomized trials
In contrast to the natural experiment of the hard sciences, the term natural experiment is often used by economists to denote a situation where real randomization was employed, without the intent of providing a randomized experiment. For example, between 1970 and 1972 men from specific birth cohorts were conscripted into the US military by way of a draft lottery. Each day of the year was randomly assigned a number which (in part) determined whether or not one was at risk of being inducted into the military service to fight in the US war on Indochina. As a consequence, men of specific birth cohorts born only a day apart, for example, had very different risks of serving in the military. In Hearst, Newman and Hulley (1986), the authors asked whether the war continued to kill after the warrior returned home. The authors compared, among other things, the suicide rates among individuals who on average were *ex ante* similar, but who had very different probabilities of having completed military service.

The example is sufficiently simple to make a number of points about the limitations of natural experiments. *If* one can assume that the mere fact of having such a birth date put one at high risk of military duty, and that having a birth date raised (or did not lower) any person's risk of serving in the military, then it is possible to use something akin to two stage least squares (2SLS) to estimate an 'average' effect of military service for those who were induced to serve in the military by the draft lottery. However, Hearst, Newman and Hulley (1986) are quick to observe that *whether or not* one actually served in the military, the mere fact of having been put at risk of the lottery might have had an effect on delayed mortality. In econometric terms, this would be a violation of the 'exclusion restriction' of 2SLS. If such is the case, it is apparent that a comparison of men with high-risk birthdays to those with low-risk birthdays will be an admixture of the effect of the military service on later mortality *and* any direct effect of the lottery itself. An additional problem is the possibility of non-random selection induced by men dying while at war. This was judged to be small due since the fraction of US soldiers who died while serving in action was a small fraction of the total.

Returning to how one might go from an estimate generated in this way to more general inference, one has a number of other obstacles. For example, the delayed mortality effects of military service on those *induced* to serve by an unlucky birth date might be different from the effect on those who *volunteered* to fight in the war. If the effects are very different, it would obviously be incorrect to use estimates generated by those induced to serve to extrapolate to the broader population of interest.

More generally, our ability to generalize the valid results of an experiment is much more limited when we can only manipulate the cause indirectly (as in the example above) than when we can manipulate the cause directly: there is often the possibility of important differences between persons who take up the treatment as a result of having been encouraged to participate and those who were similarly encouraged but did not take up the treatment.

The regression discontinuity design as a natural experiment

One research design that involves the 'serendipitous' randomization of individuals into a treatment is called the regression discontinuity design. Since it is a relatively 'clean' example of something that approaches a truly randomized experiment without involving explicit randomization, it provides a good illustration of the strengths and weaknesses of natural experiments. (For an analysis of the relationship between the regression discontinuity design and randomized controlled trials see Lee, 2007.) For illustration, let us consider DiNardo and Lee's (2004) analysis of the causal effect of 'unionization' on firms in the United States. The naive approach would be to compare unionized firms to non-unionized firms.

The basis of the regression discontinuity design is the existence of a 'score' or a 'vote' which assigns persons to one treatment or another. In the US context, workers at a firm can win the right to form a labour union by means of a secret ballot election. If 50 per cent plus one of the workers votes in favour of the union, the workers win the right to be represented by a union; less than that, and they are denied such rights.

To understand how this works, consider elections at two different sets of work sites that employ large numbers of workers. In one set, $0.5 + \Delta$ of the workers vote in favour of the union and win the right to bargain collectively where Δ is some small number. In another set, slightly less than 50 per cent vote in favour of the union, and are denied the right to bargain collectively. The vote share in these sites is $0.5 - \Delta$. Suppose we have large amounts of data on such elections and can accurately estimate the average outcome (say the fraction of firms that continue to exist 15 years after the vote).

Using almost exactly the same set-up as before, we compare those places where the union wins with those where the union loses:

$$E[\bar{y}_{\text{Union}} - \bar{y}_{\text{No Union}}] = E[y|\text{vote} = 0.5 + \Delta]$$
$$- E[y|\text{vote} = 0.5 - \Delta]$$

If firm survival is described by the same 'model' as in å above, where now $T = 1$ denotes winning the right to

bargain collectively, we get:

$$E[\bar{y}_{\text{Union}} - \bar{y}_{\text{No Union}}]$$

$$= \beta + \left(\underbrace{E[f(X)|\text{vote} = 0.5 + \Delta] - E[f(X)|\text{vote} = 0.5 - \Delta]}_{\text{Observable Differences}} \right)$$

$$+ \left(\underbrace{E[\varepsilon|\text{vote} = 0.5 + \Delta] - E[\varepsilon|\text{vote} = 0.5 - \Delta]}_{\text{Unobservable Differences}} \right)$$

The 'trick' is that if we choose Δ to be small enough (that is, close to zero), then

$$E[f(X)|\text{vote} = 0.5 + \Delta] \approx E[f(X)|\text{vote} = 0.5 - \Delta]$$
$$\text{and}$$
$$E[\varepsilon|\text{vote} = 0.5 + \Delta] \approx E[\varepsilon|\text{vote} = 0.5 - \Delta]$$

and we get a 'good' estimate of the 'effect of unions' in the same sense that we get a good estimate of the effect of a treatment in a randomized controlled trial. That is, if we focus our attention on the difference in outcomes between 'near winners' and 'near losers' such a contrast is formally equivalent to a randomized controlled trial if there is at least some 'random' component to the vote share. For example, sometimes people take ill on the day of the vote – if that happens randomly in some sites, two sites that would have had the same final vote tally had everyone shown up are now different. When such differences are the difference between recognition or not, one has the practical equivalent of a randomized controlled trial. The mere existence of a 'score' that discontinuously exposes one to a treatment is not enough. This design would not be appropriate, for example, to analyse the causal effects of US Congressional votes on various issues. Substantial 'manipulation' – that is, through negotiation, and so on – of the final vote tally is common and suggests that individuals near but on opposite sides of the threshold are not otherwise similar (see REGRESSION-DISCONTINUITY ANALYSIS).

A few moments' reflection will make clear both the appeal of such experiments and their limits. Advocates of a natural experiment approach point to the fact that the implicit randomization involved in this design means that we can be more confident with such a comparison than a naive comparison that merely compares unionized to non-unionized firms. This would almost certainly confound the true 'effect' with pre-existing differences in unionized and non-unionized firms with 'unionization'. Advocates will also point to the fact that the experiment is relevant to a potential policy – say lowering the threshold required to win representation rights by a small amount.

Detractors will observe many limitations. Is the effect of a union that is set into a place by a 51 per cent vote the same as the effect of a union where the workers vote unanimously? Possibly not. Stipulating the validity of the estimate, is it reasonable to suggest that the effect of unionization would be the same if all workplaces were allowed to vote on a union? Probably not. Is it possible that a union at one work site affects other work sites? What about the effect on the firm's competitors? Indeed, it is even possible to question the premise that a union is a 'treatment' at all. Does it make sense to talk of a single effect of a labour union when there is such heterogeneity in what the notion 'labour union' represents? While the anarcho-syndicalist Industrial Workers of the World (IWW) of Joe Hill (a famous militant IWW member and subject of a well-known folksong) and the American Federation of Labor and Congress of Industrial Organizations (AFL–CIO) of George Meany (a conservative 'anti-communist' who was its president for many years) were both labour unions, they had virtually contrary aims and wildly different political structures.

More generally, 'causes', 'treatments', and so on are much more fragile objects for the types of things usually interesting to economists than the types of things interesting to natural science. The concepts of natural science are often capable of quite substantial refinement in a way that concepts in the human sciences rarely are.

'Natural natural experiments'?

As I have already mentioned, the term 'natural experiment' has been used in several different ways inconsistent with our definition. It seems pointless, however, to claim that our definition is the 'true' or correct one. We shall therefore consider some cases that use the term which do not obviously involve randomization of a treatment or something that approximates such randomization.

Rosenzweig and Wolpin (2000) for instance, have coined the expression 'natural natural experiments' to denote a wide range of studies involving the use of twins. The emphasis on the word 'natural' is intended to highlight the role of nature in providing the variation. Twins have been of inordinate interest to the social scientists since they seem to offer the possibility of 'controlling' for 'genetics'. Consider one case of interest to economists, 'returns to schooling'. Does acquiring an additional year of school result in higher wages in the labour market? How much higher? To fix ideas consider a simple model of the sort:

$$y_{ij} = \beta S_{ij} + a_j + \varepsilon_{ij}.$$

We are interested in some outcome, say hourly wages, and the causal effect of years of schooling S. It will greatly simplify the discussion if we assume that all persons 'treated' with 'schooling' experience the same increase in their wages – that is, the treatment effect is a constant across individuals. We have gathered a random sample of $j = 1, \ldots, J$ 'identical' (monozygotic) twins ($i = 1, 2$). The term a_j is not directly observable but includes everything that the twins have in common – genetics, environment, and so on. The error term ε_{ij} includes everything that the twins do not have in common and cannot be observed as

well as the effects of misspecification, and so on. Though this simple set-up can be greatly elaborated (see Ashenfelter and Krueger, 1994, for a clear exposition) the essential idea is that the *difference* between the twins purges the outcome of the a_j term so that an ordinary least squares regression of the difference in wages Δy_{ij} on ΔS_{ij} yields a good estimate of

$$\hat{\beta} \text{ is a good estimate of } \beta + \frac{\text{Var}(\Delta \varepsilon, \Delta S)}{\text{Var}(\Delta S)}.$$

The first term is the goal of such studies. The second term points to the possibility that there are other influences which might be correlated both with schooling and that affect the outcome. The second term can be interpreted as the slope coefficient from the following hypothetical ordinary least squares (OLS) regression, where δ is the slope of the 'best-fitting' line in this expression:

$$\varepsilon = \text{constant} + S\delta + \text{error}.$$

When will $\hat{\beta}$ to be a good estimate of the returns to schooling β? The conditions are essentially the same as for the randomized controlled trial: if we can treat the assignment of schooling to the two twins as if it were determined by a random coin toss then differences in the level of schooling between the two twins – ΔS_{ij} – will be independent of differences between the two twins in unobserved influences on wages – $\Delta \varepsilon_{ij}$. Detractors of this approach doubt that such an assumption is plausible. In simple language, if the twins are so 'identical' why do they have different levels of schooling? Perhaps the parents noticed that one twin was more interested or had more 'aptitude' for schoolwork than another. If that were the case, estimates of the returns to schooling would be confounded with differences in the aptitude for schooling despite the fact that we had 'controlled' for a large number of other factors. The key difference between this case and what I have identified as a natural experiment is the lack of an obvious approximation to randomization. Bound and Solon (1999) discuss, inter alia, a host of difficulties in treating twin differences as experimental variation. I do not discuss twins studies that utilize twins as a 'surprise' to family size which have some element of randomization.

Other research designs: quasi-experiments

Finally, I should make note of the fact that some authors use the term natural experiment more broadly than I have construed it here. Meyer (1995, p. 151) for instance, considers natural experiments the broad class of research designs 'patterned after randomized experiments' but not (generally) involving actual randomization. One term often used for such situations is 'quasi-experiment'. The relationship between these quasi-experiments and the natural experiments I have been describing is quite varied and ranges from those whose difference from the standard of randomized assignment is merely a matter of 'degree' to those in which assignment to treatment differs so much from the standard of randomization that it is really a difference in 'kind'.

Most of these quasi-experiments are variants of a 'before and after' where an observation is made before and after a treatment. Often a before–after comparison for one set of observations (the treatment – T) is compared to another set (the control – C). A typical set-up might compute a treatment effect by taking the difference in two differences:

$$\text{Treatment Effect} = \left\{ \bar{y}_{T,\text{after}} - \bar{y}_{T,\text{before}} \right\} - \left\{ \bar{y}_{C,\text{after}} - \bar{y}_{C,\text{before}} \right\}.$$

For this reason, such quasi-experiments are described as using 'difference-in-differences' approach to identifying a causal relationship.

In the United States, the fact that the state (or city) governments have some liberty to enact laws independently of the federal government, for example, has led to a great deal of research using 'Brandeisian' experiments. The term comes by way of US Supreme Court Justice Louis Brandeis, in the case *New State Ice* v. *Liebmann*:

> There must be power in the States and the Nation to remould, through experimentation, our economic practices and institutions to meet changing social and economic needs. ... It is one of the happy incidents of the federal system that a single courageous State may, if its citizens choose, serve as a laboratory; and try novel social and economic experiments without risk to the rest of the country. (U.S. Supreme Court *New State Ice Co.* v. *Liebmann*, 285 U.S. 262 (1932))

To give one such example, consider DiNardo and Lemieux's (2001) evaluation of the effect of changing the age at which it is legal to purchase alcohol or the consumption of marijuana. At the beginning of the 1980s states generally enforced two types of legal regimes. In one set, alcohol could not be legally sold to those under the age of 21. In another, the legal minimum drinking age (LMDA) was 18. In the mid-1980s, the federal government put a great deal of pressure on those states with LMDA of 18 to raise them to 21 and by the end of the 1980s, in all states drinking age was 21.

The assignment of drinking age statutes to the states at the beginning of the 1980s could not be considered 'approximately' random. Utah, for example, which is home to a large number of adherents to the Mormon religion – which proscribes alcohol use – had a 21-year drinking age at the beginning of the 1980s. However, due to a federal policy implemented in the mid-1980s of eventually denying federal highway funds to states with legal minimums less than 21 years old, something perhaps approximating an 'experiment' can be arrived at by comparing *changes* in alcohol or marijuana consumption during the 1980s in those states which were forced to

change (and changed early) with those who were forced to but raised their drinking age later.

Let Δy_t denote the change in the fraction of 18–21 year olds who reported smoking marijuana in the previous 30 days from 1980 to 1990 in states that had 18-year-old drinking ages that were increased, and Δy_c denote the similar change in states whose drinking age was always 21. Then an estimate of the effect of the drinking age might be:

$$\Delta y_t - \Delta y_c = \text{Effect of LMDA}.$$

Although randomization is not employed per se, the credibility of these exercises can be at least partially evaluated. For instance, if the outcome of interest has been approximately constant in both the treatment and control groups for a long time preceding the change in legal regime, the estimate is generally more credible. Less credible is the case in which the outcomes in the control group and the treatment group are quite variable over time, the control group and the treatment group do not follow similar patterns *before* the proposed experiment, or when both are true.

Controversies: concluding remarks

Natural experiments and their like have been at the heart of much work in economics. Nonetheless, they are the subject of considerable debate. One of the most cited limitations of natural experiments – by both supporters and detractors – is that such experiments are context specific. Indeed, one frequently encountered 'strength' of natural experiments is that it often concerns the evaluation of an actual policy. There are limitations, however. If we assume that the experiment is 'internally valid' we still have to ask: how do we generalize from one experiment to the broader questions of policy? The foregoing has suggested that it is difficult. There are at least three broad classes of reasons:

1. While a natural experiment might provide a credible estimate of some particular serendipitous 'intervention', this may have only a weak relation to the type of interventions being contemplated as policies. Many of the potential reasons for a weak relationship are similar to those encountered in social experiments (among other things, for example, the effect of a treatment in a demonstration programme might be quite different from the outcome that would obtain if the treatment were applied more broadly or to different persons).

2. Some interesting questions are unanswerable with such an approach because serendipitous randomized experiments are few and far between. The extent to which this criticism is warranted, of course, depends on the availability of alternative ways of putting our views to a severe test.

3. More generally, without a 'theory', estimates from natural experiments are uninterpretable.

I am sympathetic with all three criticisms although (3) deserves some qualification. While it has been argued that even in the natural sciences it is impossible to have 'pre-theoretical' observations or experiments, Hacking (1983) makes a strong case that experimentation has a life of its own, sometimes suggesting ideas in advance of theory, other times the consequence of theory, and sometimes testing theories. Much of this debate in the natural sciences revolves around the notion of what constitutes a 'theory'. Whatever the validity of the view that one cannot experiment in advance of 'theory' in the natural sciences, in the social sciences, it is clear that no theory has the same standing as, say, general relativity in physics. This is the sense in which Noam Chomsky observes that 'as soon as questions of will or decision or reason or choice of action arise, human science is pretty much at a loss' (Magee, 2001, p. 184). Indeed, the standing of randomized experiments – in some fields of enquiry regarded as 'the gold standard' of evidence – is a great deal lower than the best experiments of natural science; they are most often useful in situations otherwise marked by 'complete ignorance' (Hacking, 1988). In short, while the human sciences might have the same ambition as natural science, the status of what we know will almost surely be quite limited.

Nonetheless, one does not need a 'correct' theory to hand, nor an understanding as rich as that found in some of the natural sciences to find an experiment useful. At the risk of over-using such metaphors, the fact that the Michelson–Morley experiments were in part about testing for the existence of 'ether' did not make them uninteresting. Experiments are just ways to use things we (think we) understand to learn about something we do not. And while the sorts of 'natural' experiments 'serendipitously' provided by society may be very limited and are often the product of unhappy social realities, they can sometimes perhaps serve a small role in enhancing our understanding.

Any assessment of the usefulness of natural experiments depends on how one judges the power of other methods of enquiry. Such a discussion is well beyond the scope of this article. Nonetheless, not discounting their many limitations, one benefit of natural experiments I have tried to highlight is that for some they might open up the possibility of revising their beliefs in light of evidence or suggest new ways to think about old problems, however limited. A key aspect of experiments (natural or otherwise) is the willingness to put one's ideas 'to the test'. Often, careful study of a natural experiment, however limited, may also make one aware of how complicated and difficult are the problems we call 'economics'. Even if the success we might have in generalizing natural experiments more broadly may be quite limited, if they bring nothing but humility to the claims social scientists make about much we actually understand, that alone would justify an interest in natural experiments.

J. DINARDO

See also **difference-in-difference estimators; experimental economics; experimental economics, history of; experimental labour economics; experimental methods in economics; experiments and econometrics; Fisher, Ronald Aylmer; regression-discontinuity analysis.**

Bibliography

Ashenfelter, O. and Krueger, A.B. 1994. Estimates of the economic returns to schooling from a new sample of identical twins. *American Economic Review* 84, 1157–73.

Ashtekar, A., Cohen, R.S., Howard, D. Renn, J. Sarkear, S. and Shimony, A. 2003. *Revisiting the Foundations of Relativistic Physics: Festschrift in Honor of John Stachel.* Boston Studies in the Philosophy of Science, vol. 234. Dordrecht: Kluwer Academic.

Bastable, C.F. 1987. Experimental methods in economics (i). In *The New Palgrave: A Dictionary of Economics*, vol. 2, ed. J. Eatwell, M. Milgate and P. Newman. London: Macmillan.

Bound, J. and Solon, G. 1999. Double trouble: on the value of twins-based estimation of the return to schooling. *Economics of Education Review* 18, 169–82.

DiNardo, J. 2007. Interesting questions in freakonomics. *Journal of Economic Literature.*

DiNardo, J. and Lee, D.S. 2002. The impact of unionization on establishment closure: a regression discontinuity analysis of representation elections. Working Paper No. 8993. Cambridge, MA: NBER.

DiNardo, J. and Lee, D.S. 2004. Economic impacts of new unionization on private sector employers: 1984–2001. *Quarterly Journal of Economics* 119, 1383–441.

DiNardo, J. and Lemieux, T. 2001. Alcohol, marijuana, and American youth: the unintended consequences of government regulation. *Journal of Health Economics* 20, 991–1010.

Drake, S. 1981. *Cause, Experiment, and Science: A Galilean Dialogue, Incorporating a New English Translation of Galileo's Bodies that Stay atop Water, or Move in It.* Chicago: University of Chicago Press.

Fisher, R.A. 1935. *Design of Experiments.* Edinburgh, London: Oliver & Boyd.

Hacking, I. 1983. *Representing and Intervening: Introductory Topics in the Philosophy of Natural Science.* Cambridge: Cambridge University Press.

Hacking, I. 1988. Telepathy: origins of randomization in experimental design. *Isis* 79, 427–51.

Hacking, I. 2000. *The Social Construction of What?* Cambridge, MA: Harvard University Press.

Hearst, N., Newman, T.B. and Hulley, S.B. 1986. Delayed effects of the military draft on mortality: a randomized natural experiment. *New England Journal of Medicine* 314, 620–4.

Heckman, J.J. 2005. The scientific model of causality. *Sociological Methodology* 35, 1–97.

Heckman, J.J. and Smith, J.A. 1995. Assessing the case for social experiments. *Journal of Economic Perspectives* 9(2), 85–110.

Lee, D.S. 2008. Randomized experiments from non-random selection in U.S. house elections. *Journal of Econometrics.*

Magee, B. 2001. *Talking Philosophy: Dialogues with Fifteen Leading Philosphers.* Oxford: Oxford University Press.

Mayo, D.G. 1996. *Error and the Growth of Experimental Knowledge Science and Its Conceptual Foundations.* Chicago: University of Chicago Press.

Meyer, B. 1995. Natural and quasi-experiments in economics. *Journal of Business and Economic Statistics* 13, 151–61.

Morgan, M.S. 1987. Statistics without probability and Haavelmo's revolution in econometrics. In *The Probabilistic Revolution: Ideas in the Sciences*, vol. 2, ed. L. Krüger, G. Gigerenzer and M.S. Morgan. Cambridge, MA: MIT Press.

Nelson, A. 1990. Are economic kinds natural? In *Scientific Theories of Minnesota Studies in the Philosophy of Science*, vol. 14, ed. C. Wade Savage. Minneapolis: University of Minnesota Press.

Peirce, C.S. 1958. In *Collected Papers*, vols. 7–8, ed. A. Burks. Cambridge, MA: Harvard University Press.

Rosenzweig, M.R. and Wolpin, K.I. 2000. Natural 'natural experiments' in economics. *Journal of Economic Literature* 38, 827–74.

Searle, J. 1995. *The Construction of Social Reality.* New York: Free Press.

Shadish, W.R., Cook, T.D. and Campbell, D.T. 2002. *Experimental and Quasi–Experimental Designs for Generalized Causal Inference.* Boston: Houghton Mifflin.

Tribby, J. 1994. Club Medici: natural experiment and the imagineering of 'Tuscany'. *Configurations* 2, 215–35.

Voltaire. 1759. *The History of Candide; or All for the Best*, ed. C. Cooke. London, 1796.

Waller, R. 1684. *Essayes of natural experiments made in the academie del cimento, under the protection of the most serene Prince Leopold of Tuscany.* Facsimile edn, ed. R. Hall, trans. R. Waller. New York and London, 1964.

Wikipedia. 2006. Experiment. http://en.wikipedia.org, accessed 28 September 2006.

natural price

In the *Wealth of Nations* Smith says that

> when the price of any commodity is neither more nor less than what is sufficient to pay the rent of the land, the wages of labour, and the profits of the stock employed in the raising, preparing and bringing it to market, according to their natural rates, the commodity is then sold for what may be called its natural price. (Smith, 1776, p. 72)

In the same chapter he explains that in economic theory this particular price level is important because it is a sort of benchmark for the actual price of the commodity, its market price (p. 73). The market price is different from the natural price but tends to move towards it all the time because of competition between producers. 'The natural price, therefore, is, as it were, the central price, to which the prices of all commodities are continuously gravitating' (p. 73). Smith's concept of natural price and his description of the competitive mechanism which guarantees that the market prices tend to move towards it became an important element in classical political economy. Smith's analysis was entirely subscribed to by Ricardo (Ricardo, 1821, pp. 88–91), and was a central point in the classical theory of value and in the price theories of some neoclassical economists.

Smith's notion of natural price is part of a more general analysis of the normal and regular causes which determine the value of commodities. Smith's theory can be divided into three main aspects. First of all, there is the definition of natural price, which is made up of three component parts, wages, profits, and rent. In Chapter 6 of the *Wealth of Nations*, Smith explains that the price of all commodities resolves itself into wages, profits and rent, as soon as we abandon the 'early and rude state of society which precedes both the accumulation of stock and the appropriation of land' (Smith, 1776, p. 65). The price must also repay the raw materials and the capital equipment consumed in production, but the prices of these commodities are also made up of the wages, profits and rent required in their own production (p. 68). Thus ultimately the price of each product is entirely made up of those three parts, which include the incomes of workers, landlords and capitalists who take part in the final production of the good and also the incomes of all those who have indirectly contributed to produce it in previous years. The techniques of production of a commodity have an important influence on its natural price, because they determine the relative shares of profits, rent, and wages. But the natural price also depends on the distribution of income, that is to say, on the level of the natural rates at which wages, rent and profits must be paid.

According to Smith, each rate is determined on a different market and this depends on several circumstances. Therefore the natural price of each commodity is determined by the methods of production and by the exogenously given values of the rates which remunerate the three classes which take part in production. It is worth noticing that for Smith, society is made up of different classes, labourers, landlords and capitalist entrepreneurs, whose economic functions are clearly separated. When all the commodities that make up the output of society are assessed according to their natural prices, the part of this value given by wages is the capital stock of society (p. 110), while rent and profits make up the net product, or surplus.

The second feature of Smith's price theory is the description of the reasons why the natural price is the price level which prevails in the long run, and around which market prices gravitate. This price mechanism is an important element in the notion of natural price because it guarantees that the permanent causes of value are those which influence the natural price, while market price deviations are due to temporary circumstances. The market price fluctuates and may differ from the natural price, but there are forces which compel it towards the natural price.

The factors affecting natural prices must be regarded as the permanent and fundamental forces that determine the value of produced commodities, quite independently from the day-to-day changes in their market prices. This second part of Smith's analysis of natural prices contains several concepts. First, there is the notion of effectual demand which is used to explain the differences between natural and market prices. Effectual demand is the 'demand of those who are willing to pay the natural price of a commodity' (p. 73). Of course a change in this price affects the effectual demand. The quantity produced and brought to the market may be lower (or higher) than the effectual demand, in which case the market price of the commodity will be higher (or lower) than the natural one. This mechanism explains why there are differences between natural and market prices.

The second step in Smith's analysis of the gravitation of market prices around natural prices consists in the competitive mechanism itself. Here, too, several logical stages may be distinguished. (a) For Smith the fact that the market price is higher than the natural one implies that at least one of the three parts which make up the price of a product is higher than it would have been if its contribution to production was remunerated according to its natural rate; it seems reasonable to assume that profits are the share which takes advantage of the favourable market conditions (but the process works in the same way if wages and rent are higher than their natural rates). (b) Entrepreneurs are aware of the existence of these different rates of profit in the different sectors of the economy. (c) There are no barriers to the free circulation of capital, thus entrepreneurs move towards the most remunerative sectors; this is the crucial aspect of Smith's analysis of competition (see Sylos-Labini, 1976). (d) These capital movements lead to an increase in the output of the products which yield the highest rates of profit. (e) Since the quantity produced and brought to the market of these products increases while the effectual demand in unchanged, the market price falls. This does not mean that there is a downward-sloping demand schedule. In Smith's price theory there is no continuous differentiable inverse relationship between quantities and prices, as is found in neoclassical economics (Garegnani, 1983).

Free competition tends to bring about a uniform rate of profit throughout the economy. Hence the concept of natural price is related to the existence of a single rate of profit on the capital invested in all sectors, and is regarded by Smith as 'a centre of repose and continuance' for the actual market price (Smith, 1776, p. 75).

The view that it is possible and useful to separate the day-to-day fluctuations in market prices from the stable and permanent causes of the value of commodities can be traced back to the 16th century. It was part of Scholastic tradition to believe that there was a logical distinction between the actual price of a product and its *true* value. The former price can vary quite a lot according to the state of trade, while the value is always the same. Von Pufendorf believed that the value, or just price, of a commodity depended mostly on the difficulty of acquiring and producing it (Pufendorf, 1688, pp. 684–9). Theoreticians of the just price regarded it as the level to which actual prices ought to conform. They gave no indication of any spontaneous mechanism which should guarantee that market values would adapt to these just levels.

As a student, Adam Smith read the works of von Pufendorf, and his teacher, Francis Hutcheson, wrote a book entitled *A System of Moral Philosophy* in which the distinction between value and price was restated along very similar lines (Hutcheson, 1754–5, pp. 53–5). At the end of the 17th century, Dudley North and John Locke maintained that regulations and government interventions could not affect the price of commodities, which depended on market conditions (North, 1691, Preface; Locke, 1691, pp. 4, 11, 13).

Some years before the publication of the works of Locke and North, Sir William Petty regarded the cost of production of commodities as the main cause determining their true value. Ultimately all commodities are produced by two common denominators, land and labour, and their exchange values are in proportion to the quantities of these non-produced goods which have been employed in their production (Petty, 1662, p. 44). The value of goods is regulated by the physical cost of production, which is regarded as the true measure of the difficulty of acquiring them. For Petty, the natural price depends upon the amount of labour required to produce a commodity with the best available technique (pp. 50–1).

Richard Cantillon developed Petty's analysis of land and labour as the original components of the value of each commodity. He transformed the amount of labour employed in production into an equivalent quantity of land. Thus, the value of each commodity is given by the quantity of land which has been directly and indirectly used in its production (Cantillon, 1755, p. 29). This is the intrinsic value of the products, and their market price fluctuates around it (pp. 28–30). Moreover, Cantillon presented the well-known theory of the 'three rents'; the farmer receives two thirds of the products of land, one third is required to pay workers' wages and other expenses, the second third is the profit from his enterprise; the final third accrues to landlords as rent (p. 43).

Quesnay and the Physiocrats also distinguish the permanent value of commodities from their market price. For Quesnay, the fundamental price is the lowest level of the selling price for the producer. This value is the minimum level of the market price: it is the sum of all the expenses incurred by the cultivator in the production of a commodity, and there is a loss when the market price is lower than this value (Quesnay, 1757, p. 555). The fundamental value of commodities is stable and varies quite slowly, on the other hand market prices change rapidly. Quesnay concentrated his attention on the fundamental price of primary commodities, which included the technical costs of production plus the annual rent paid to the landlords (1757, p. 555; Quesnay, 1756, p. 443). Quesnay believed that two elements contribute to determining the fundamental value of agricultural products: farming techniques, which determine the physical cost of production, and the rule which fixes the distribution of income, at least in the form of rent. The inclusion of an element, rent (which is part of the country's surplus), in the fundamental value of a commodity is an important step towards Smith's concept of natural price. Now the permanent value of commodities is not only the result of technical conditions but also of the social rules and customs which determine the distribution of the net product.

Quesnay used the term 'natural price' to indicate the state of prices when free and unobstructed competition in all the markets regulates the exchanges between buyers and sellers (Quesnay, 1766, pp. 829–30). In this case the actual exchange value of the products of land is a *bon prix*, it exceeds the fundamental price and leaves the farmer with a profit (Quesnay, 1757, p. 529). Quesnay provided a good explanation of the reasons why the market price cannot be lower than the fundamental one, but there is no indication of the existence of market forces which lead the actual price towards the *bon prix*. In Quesnay's value theory the notion of fundamental price is only a sort of threshold which fixes the lowest market price, but profits are still not part of the fundamental price.

In 1767 Sir James Steuart published *An Inquiry into the Principles of Political Oeconomy* in which he made at least two important contributions to the classical theory of value. The first was the notion of the real, or intrinsic, value of the goods. He says that two things make up the price of a product, 'the real value of a commodity and the profit upon alienation' (Steuart, 1767, p. 159). The real value is the cost of production, which depends upon the average techniques which have been adopted and which establishes the amount of time needed to produce a commodity. The 'profit upon alienation' is the positive difference between the actual price and the real value (1767, p. 159). Thus profits are not part of the value of commodities, but according to Steuart 'such profits subsisting for a long time, they insensibly become *consolidated*, or as it were, transformed into the intrinsic

value of the goods' (1767, p. 193, Steuart's italics). Thus, in the normal condition of the market, the value of commodities must also include entrepreneurs' profits, which are a permanent feature of the exchange value of goods. Steuart's second contribution to price theory is the concept of effectual demand; this notion indicates the demand of consumers who can actually pay for a product and is clearly distinguished from wants and desires (1767, pp. 151–3). Steuart's analysis does not provide a theory of profit capable of explaining the level which becomes consolidated in the intrinsic value of commodities. The normal value is not yet defined in a way which explains the existence of a regular element of profit in the exchange value of commodities.

In the *Obsérvations sur le mémoire de Saint Péravy*, Turgot distinguished the fundamental and market price of commodities. The first concept is defined as the cost of production, which includes wages, raw materials and interests on the capital advanced. The fundamental value is fairly stable, while the exchange value is ruled by supply and demand and 'it has a tendency to approach it (the fundamental price) continually, and can never move away from it permanently' (Turgot, 1767, p. 120, n. 16). There is an important difference between Quesnay's and Turgot's use of the term 'fundamental price'. Turgot's notion does not simply indicate the lowest level of the market price, but is the value to which this price must tend. Turgot included a regular profit among the necessary expenses of production (Meek, 1973, p. 17). Turgot's interest on the capital advanced is not only a depreciation allowance but includes profit for the entrepreneur. In *Réflexions sur la formation et la distribution des richesses* (1766) Turgot clearly says that the return to the capitalist entrepreneur must be divided into three main categories: 'depreciation of the capital', 'wages of superintendence and direction as well as the risk premium' and 'pure return on his capital which he could have earned if he had not employed it in industry' (Groenewegen, 1971, p. 333; see Turgot, 1766, pp. 152, 154). Now profits are an essential part of the permanent value of commodities, but above all Turgot's notion of profit is different from those of Steuart and Quesnay. Profit is defined as a rate on the capital invested. This definition of profits is quite different from that of profit upon alienation, according to which profits are influenced by market conditions where the products are sold. For Turgot, on the contrary, the rate of profit depends mainly on competition between capitalist producers who act with a view to obtaining the highest possible rate of profit. This mechanism explains the existence of a continuous tendency towards the equalization of rates of return in all of the capital.

In the *Lectures on Jurisprudence* which Adam Smith gave at Glasgow in the academic year 1762–3, we already find the distinction between natural and market price, together with the description of the mechanism by which the latter price gravitates around the natural value

(Smith, 1762–3, pp. 353 ff.). Smith's analysis of competition among producers explains that natural prices are bound with the existence of a uniform rate of profit in all the sectors of the economy. The existence of this uniform rate has been traditionally adopted to describe the prices which prevail in the long run, when it is possible to abstract from all the accidental causes which influence market prices. In Smith's economics, technology and income distribution are the permanent forces which determine the value of natural prices.

In classical economics, the notion of natural price is necessary to build up an abstract analysis of the main features of the economy. This notion helps to single out the main characteristics of the capitalistic process of development and their relationships to changes in the distribution of income. Thus the concept of natural price is part of the study of the long-term changes in economic systems, which derive from capital accumulation. Natural price is an essential element of the classical method of analysis, which investigates the features of the long-term positions of the economy, when demand does not affect prices and income distribution (Garegnani, 1976, section 1).

In Chapter 4 of *On the Principles of Political Economy and Taxation*, Ricardo subscribes to Smith's theory of natural prices (1821, pp. 88–92). He was interested in the analysis of the permanent changes in income distribution, and was not interested in the temporary deviation of market prices from their natural value.

However, there is a major difference between Smith's and Ricardo's theories of profit. Smith says that profits and wages are determined on separate markets and that the natural price is the sum of these shares plus rent, while Ricardo says that the rate of profit and the real wage are inversely related.

Marx's notion of prices of production shares many of the features of Smith's natural price; both concepts are associated with the existence of a uniform rate of profit in all sectors of the economy (see Marx, 1894, pp. 153–8). Moreover, Marx accepted Ricardo's analysis of the reasons why market prices fluctuate around natural ones (1894, p. 179). Like Ricardo, he believed that real wages and the rate of profit vary in opposite directions. In his 1951 Introduction to *The Works and Correspondence of David Ricardo*, Sraffa clearly singled out the implications of Ricardo's theory of profit determining commodities natural value. Sraffa explicitly mentioned the concepts of natural price and prices of production in presenting his theory of price determination and retained the notion of a uniform rate of profit throughout the economy (Sraffa, 1960, pp. 9, 6).

In the *Principles of Economics* (1920), Alfred Marshall referred to Smith's natural price, for which he substituted the notion of normal price (Marshall, 1920, p. 289). In his discussion of the causes which influence the value of commodities he said that in general, market values are deeply affected by demand, while normal prices depend on the cost of production of commodities. The former price prevails in the short run, but 'the longer the period, the more important becomes the influence of cost of production on value' (1920, p. 291). Normal prices are determined by the persistent causes of value, and are not influenced by fitful and irregular events (1920, pp. 304–5). It should be pointed out that Marshall's notion of cost of production is not the same as the notion put forward by Ricardo and Marx. Moreover, he was sceptical about the existence of a tendency towards the equalization of the rates of profit in all economic activities (1920, pp. 506–7, 512). Nevertheless inside each branch of trade there can be a fair rate of profit which must be reckoned as a component element of the normal price (1920, pp. 513–14).

G. VAGGI

See also **British classical economics; market price.**

Bibliography

Cantillon, R. 1755. *Essai sur la nature du commerce en général*. Ed. H. Higgs, London: Cass, 1959.
Garegnani, P. 1976. On a change in the notion of equilibrium in recent work on value and distribution. In *Essays in Modern Capital Theory*, ed. M. Brown, K. Sato and P. Zarembka. Amsterdam: North-Holland.
Garegnani, P. 1983. The classical theory of wages and the role of demand schedules in the determination of relative prices. *American Economic Review* 73, 309–13.
Groenewegen, P.D. 1971. A reinterpretation of Turgot's theory of capital and interest. *Economic Journal* 81, 327–40.
Hutcheson, F. 1754–5. *A System of Moral Philosophy*. Glasgow: Robert and Andrew Foulis.
Locke, J. 1691. Some considerations of the consequences of the lowering of interest and raising the value of money. In *The Works of John Locke*, vol. 5. London, 1823.
Marshall, A. 1920. *Principles of Economics*, 8th edn. Reprinted, London: Macmillan, 1972.
Marx, K. 1894. *Capital*, vol. 3. London: Lawrence & Wishart, 1977.
Meek, R.L. 1962. *The Economics of Physiocracy*. London: George Allen & Unwin.
Meek, R.L., ed. 1973. *Turgot on Progress, Sociology and Economics*. Cambridge: Cambridge University Press.
North, D. 1691. Discourses upon trade. In *Early English Tracts on Commerce*, London: The Political Economy Club. Reprinted, ed. J.R. McCulloch, Cambridge: Cambridge University Press, 1954.
Petty, W. 1662. A treatise of taxes and contributions. In *The Economic Writings of Sir William Petty*, ed. C.H. Hull. Cambridge: Cambridge University Press, 1899.
Pufendorf, S. von. 1688. *De jure naturae et gentium – libri octo*. Oxford: Clarendon Press, 1934.
Quesnay, F. 1756. Fermiers. In *François Quesnay et la Physiocratie*, Paris: INED, 1958.
Quesnay, F. 1757. Hommes. In *François Quesnay et la Physiocratie*, Paris: INED, 1958.

Quesnay, F. 1766. Du commerce. In *François Quesnay et la Physiocratie*, Paris: INED, 1958.

Ricardo, D. 1821. On the principles of political economy and taxation. In *The Works and Correspondence of David Ricardo*, ed. P. Sraffa with the collaboration of M.H. Dobb. Cambridge: Cambridge University Press, 1951.

Smith, A. 1762–3. *Lectures on Jurisprudence*. Ed. R.L. Meek, D.D. Raphael and P.G. Stein, Oxford: Oxford University Press, 1978.

Smith, A. 1776. *An Inquiry into the Nature and Causes of the Wealth of Nations*. Oxford: Oxford University Press, 1976.

Sraffa, P. 1951. *Introduction to The Works and Correspondence of David Ricardo*, vol. 1. Cambridge: Cambridge University Press.

Sraffa, P. 1960. *Production of Commodities by Means of Commodities*. Cambridge: Cambridge University Press.

Steuart, J. 1767. *An Inquiry into the Principles of Political Oeconomy*. Ed. A. Skinner, Edinburgh and London: Oliver & Boyd, 1966.

Sylos-Labini, P. 1976. Competition: the product market. In *The Market and the State*, ed. T. Wilson and A. Skinner. Oxford: Clarendon Press.

Turgot, A.R.J. 1766. Réflexions sur la formation et la distribution des richesses. In Meek (1973).

Turgot, A.R.J. 1767. Observations sur le mémoire de Saint-Péravy. In *The Economics of A.R.J. Turgot*, ed. P.D. Groenewegen. The Hague: Martinus Nijhoff, 1977.

natural rate and market rate of interest

The main analytical elements of Knut Wicksell's *Interest and Prices* can be found in the works of earlier writers. Wicksell was familiar with Ricardo's distinction between the direct and indirect transmission of monetary impulses. Although unknown to Wicksell in 1898, Henry Thornton had provided a clear account of the cumulative process in 1802, as had Thomas Joplin of the saving–investment analysis somewhat later (cf. Humphrey, 1986).

Yet Wicksell did not just coin the terms 'natural rate' and 'market rate of interest'. His development (1898; 1906) of these ideas made the nexus between money creation, intertemporal resource allocation disequilibrium and movements in money income the dominant theme in macroeconomics for three decades until it was submerged in Keynesian economics. His starting point was the quantity theory, understood as the proposition that in the long run the price level will tend to be proportional to the money stock. His objective was to explain how both money and prices come to move from one equilibrium level to another. This inter-equilibrium movement became his famous 'cumulative process'. The maladjustment of the interest rate was the key hypothesis in Wicksell's explanation.

The 'market rate' denotes the actual value of the real rate of interest while the 'natural rate' refers to an equilibrium value of the same variable. The latter term by itself divulges Wicksell's engagement in the ancient quest for a 'neutral' monetary system, that is, a system neutral in the original sense that all relative prices develop as they would in a hypothetical world without paper money. Wicksell asserted three equilibrium conditions that the interest rate should satisfy; the first of these was that the market rate should equal the rate that would prevail if capital goods were lent and borrowed in kind (*in natura*). This criterion was later shown by Myrdal, Sraffa and others not to have an unambiguous meaning outside the single input–single output world of Wicksell's example. The further development of Wicksellian theory, therefore, centred around the two remaining criteria: saving–investment coordination and price level stability.

The interest rate has two jobs to do. It should coordinate household saving decisions with entrepreneurial investment decisions and it should balance the supply and demand for credit. If the supply of credit were always to equal saving and the demand for credit investment, the two conditions could always be met simultaneously. But there is no such necessary relationship between saving and investment on the one hand and credit supply and demand on the other. In Wicksell's system the banks make the market for credit; they may, for instance, go beyond the mere intermediation of saving and finance additional investment by creating money; the injection of money drives a wedge between saving and investment; this could only be so if the banks set the market rate below the 'natural' value required for the intertemporal coordination of real activities. The resulting inflation and endogenous growth of the money supply would continue as long as the banking system maintained the market rate below the natural rate. Wicksell analysed the case of a 'pure credit' economy in which the cumulative process could go on indefinitely, but he also pointed out that, in a gold standard world, the banks would eventually be checked by the need to maintain precautionary balances of reserve media in some proportion to their demand obligations.

Wicksell used the model to explain long-term trends in the price level and was critical of those who, like Gustav Cassel, used it to explain the business cycle. Nonetheless, subsequent developments of his ideas went altogether in the direction of shorter-run macroeconomic theory. In Sweden, Erik Lindahl (1939) and Gunnar Myrdal (1939) refined the conceptual apparatus, in particular by introducing the distinction between *ex ante* plans and *ex post* realizations and thereby clarifying the relationship between Wicksellian theory and national income analysis. The attempts by the Stockholm School to improve on Wicksell's treatment of expectations were less successful, however, producing a brand of generalized process-analysis in which almost 'everything could happen'.

In Austria, Ludwig von Mises and Friedrich von Hayek focused on the allocational consequences of the Wicksellian inflation story. The Austrian overinvestment theory of the business cycle became known to English-speaking economists primarily through Hayek's *Prices and Production* (1931). In expanding the money supply, the banks hold market rate below natural rate. At this disequilibrium interest rate, the business sector will plan to accumulate capital at a rate higher than the planned saving of the household sector. If the banks lend only to business, the entrepreneurs are able to realize their investment plans whereas households will be unable to realize their consumption plans ('forced saving'). The too rapid accumulation of capital (which also has the wrong temporal structure) cannot be sustained indefinitely. The eventual collapse of the boom may then be exacerbated by a credit crisis as some entrepreneurs are unable to repay their bank loans.

The Austrian 'monetary' theory of the cycle has been overshadowed first by Keynesian 'real' macrotheory and later by monetarist theory. One problem with it is the firm association of inflation with overinvestment. The US stagflation in the 1970s, for example, will not fit. The reasons lie largely in the changes that the monetary system has undergone. Most obviously, commercial banks now lend to all sectors and not only to business. More importantly, however, inflation in a pure fiat regime does not tend to distort intertemporal values in any particular direction (although it may destroy the system's capacity for coordinating activities over time): it simply blows up the nominal scale of real magnitudes at a more or less steady or predictable rate. In contrast, the Austrian situation that preoccupied Mises and Hayek in the late 1920s was one of credit expansion by a small open economy on the gold standard. Given the inelastic nominal expectations appropriate to this regime, the growth of inside money would be associated with the distortion of relative prices and misallocation effects predicted by the Austrian theory.

In England, Dennis Robertson and J. Maynard Keynes both worked along Wicksellian lines in the 1920s. The novel and complicated terminology of Robertson's *Banking Policy and the Price Level* (1926) may have made the work less influential than it deserved. Keynes's *Treatise on Money* (1930), although also remembered as a flawed work, nonetheless remains important as a link in the development of macroeconomics from Wicksell to the *General Theory*.

In the *Treatise*, Keynes, like Wicksell, assumes that the process starts with a real impulse, that is, a change in investment expectations. Unlike Wicksell, he focuses on deflation rather than inflation. For Keynes with his City experience, *the* interest rate was determined on the Exchange rather than set by the banks. Consequently, a deflationary situation with the market rate exceeding the natural rate can only arise when bearish speculation keeps the rate from declining. When saving exceeds investment, therefore, money leaks out of the circular spending flow into the idle balances of bear-speculators. Thus the analysis stresses declining velocity rather than endogenously declining money stock. At this stage of the development of Keynesian economics, the banks are already edging out of the theoretical field of vision and the original connection of natural rate theorizing with criteria for neutral money is by and large severed.

The model of the *Treatise* still assumes that, when market rate exceeds the natural rate, the resulting excess supply of present goods will cause falling spot prices but not unemployment of present resources. Although the focus is on a disequilibrium process, at a deeper level the theory is still comfortably classical. As long as the economy remains at full employment, the bear-speculators who are maintaining the disequilibrium are forced, period after period, to sell income-earning securities and accumulate cash at a rate corresponding to the difference between household saving and business sector investment. Automatic market forces, therefore, are seen to put those responsible for the undervaluation of physical capital under inexorably mounting pressure to allow correction of the market rate. And the longer those agents acting on incorrect expectations persist in obstructing the intertemporal coordination of activities, the larger the losses that they will eventually suffer.

In the *General Theory*, Keynes starts the story in the same way: investment expectations take a turn for the worse – 'the marginal efficiency of capital declines'; the speculative demand for money prevents the interest rate from falling sufficiently to equate *ex ante* saving with investment. But at this point the *General Theory* takes a different tack: the excess supply of present resources, which is the immediate result of the failure of intertemporal price adjustments to bring intertemporal coordination, is eliminated through falling output and employment. Real income falls until saving has been reduced to the new lower investment level.

This change in the lag-structure of Keynes's theory ('quantities reacting before prices') is not necessarily revolutionary by itself. But Keynes combines it with the assumption that the subsequent price adjustments will be governed, in Clower's terminology, not by 'notional' but by 'effective' excess demands. For the economy to reach a new general equilibrium, on a lower growth path, interest rates should fall but money wages stay what they are. Following the real income response, however, saving no longer exceeds investment so there is no accumulating pressure on the interest rate from this quarter; at the same time, unemployment does put effective pressure on wage rates. Interest rates, which should fall, do not; wages, which should not, do. From this point, Keynes went on to argue that nominal wage reductions would not eliminate unemployment unless, in the process, they happened to produce a correction of relative prices (an eventuality that he considered unlikely). This argument was the basis for his 'revolutionary' claim that a failure of saving–investment coordination could end with the economy in 'unemployment equilibrium'.

Prior to the *General Theory*, writers in the Wicksellian tradition had generally treated 'saving exceeds investment' and 'market rate exceeds natural rate' as interchangeable characterizations of the same intertemporal disequilibrium. The basic proposition could be couched equally well in terms of quantities as in terms of prices. In the *General Theory*, Keynes moved away from this language. Constructing a model with output and employment variable in the short run was a novel task and Keynes, as the pioneer, was unsure in his handling of expected, intended and realized magnitudes. Thus his preoccupation with the 'necessary equality' of saving and investment (*ex post*) was to produce endless confusion over interest theory. If saving and investment are always equal, the interest rate cannot be governed by the difference between them; nor can the interest rate mechanism possibly coordinate saving and investment decisions. To Keynes, two things seemed to follow. One was the substitution of the liquidity preference theory of the interest rate for the loanable funds theory; the other was the abandonment of the concept of a 'natural' rate of interest (Leijonhufvud, 1981, pp. 169 ff.)

These were not innocent terminological adjustments. The brand of Keynesian economics that developed on the basis of the IS–LM model had only a shaky grasp at the best of times of the intertemporal coordination problem originally at the heart of Keynes's theory. The Keynesian position shifted already at an early stage back to the pre-Keynesian hypothesis of money wage 'rigidity' as the cause of unemployment. This switched the focus of analytical attention away from the role of intertemporal relative prices (the market rate) in the coordination of saving and investment to the relationship between aggregate money expenditures and money wages. This brand of 'Keynesian' theory which excludes the saving–investment problem (that is, excludes the market-natural rate problem) could hardly be distinguished from Monetarism in any theoretically significant way.

Monetarism gained enormously in influence during the inflationary 1970s. But its period of dominance was brief. This was so in part because, in its New Classical form, it was both theoretically implausible and empirically weak. In part, however, it was swept aside by a wave of innovations in payments technology and in forms of short-term credit that undermined the stability of the relationship between the money stock and income which had been the very linchpin of monetarist doctrine.

Most recently, this has led to a return to a basically Wicksellian doctrine of what monetary policy should aim to accomplish and how it should be conducted. Leading central banks are now committed to targeting the inflation rate (rather than the price level) and use the interest rate as their primary instrument for pursuing that goal. This policy doctrine has been elaborated in the book by Woodford (2003) which borrows its title from Wicksell.

AXEL LEIJONHUFVUD

See also **Stockholm School; Wicksell, Johan Gustav Knut.**

Bibliography

Cassel, G. 1928. The rate of interest, the bank rate, and the stabilization of prices. *Quarterly Journal of Economics* 42(August), 511–29.

Hayek, F.A. 1931. *Prices and Production*. London: Routledge & Kegan Paul.

Humphrey, T.M. 1986. Cumulative process models from Thornton to Wicksell. *Federal Reserve Bank of Richmond Economic Review*, May–June, 18–25.

Keynes, J.M. 1930. *A Treatise on Money*, 2 vols. London: Macmillan.

Keynes, J.M. 1936. *The General Theory of Employment, Interest and Money*. London: Macmillan.

Leijonhufvud, A. 1981. The Wicksell connection. In A. Leijonhufvud, *Information and Coordination*. New York: Oxford University Press.

Lindahl, E. 1939. *Studies in the Theory of Money and Capital*. New York: Holt, Rinehart & Winston.

Myrdal, G. 1939. *Monetary Equilibrium*. Edinburgh: William Hodge.

Palander, T. 1941. On the concepts and methods of the Stockholm School. *International Economic Papers* No. 3, London: Macmillan, 1953.

Robertson, D.H. 1926. *Banking Policy and the Price Level*. New York: Augustus M. Kelley, 1949.

Taylor, J.B., ed. 1999. *Monetary Policy Rules*. Chicago: University of Chicago Press.

Wicksell, K. 1898. *Interest and Prices*. New York: Augustus M. Kelley, 1962.

Wicksell, K. 1906. *Lectures on Political Economy*, vol. 2. London: Routledge & Kegan Paul, 1934.

Woodford, M. 2003. *Interest and Prices: Foundations of a Theory of Monetary Policy*. Princeton: Princeton University Press.

natural rate of unemployment

In his 1968 presidential address to the American Economics Association, Milton Friedman famously defined the natural rate of unemployment as

> ... the level that would be ground out by the Walrasian system of general equilibrium equations, provided there is imbedded in them the actual structural characteristics of the labor and commodity markets, including market imperfections, stochastic variability in demands and supplies, the cost of gathering information about job vacancies and labor availabilies, the costs of mobility, and so on. (1968, p. 8)

This definition is incomplete, however, because it conspicuously lacks any mention of inflation. A more complete definition emerges from the remainder of Friedman's presidential address, in which he extensively examined the relationship between the unemployment rate and inflation. He argued that, whereas the natural rate of unemployment is determined by the real factors described in the passage quoted above, deviations from the natural rate are monetary phenomena: 'I use the term "natural" for the same reason Wicksell did – to try to separate real forces from monetary forces' (Friedman, 1968, p. 9).

The unemployment–inflation trade-off

Friedman's 'natural rate hypothesis' maintained that '... there is a 'natural rate of unemployment' which is consistent with the real forces and with accurate perceptions; unemployment can be kept below that level only by an accelerating inflation; or above it only by accelerating deflation' (Friedman, 1976, p. 458). This view of the relationship between the unemployment rate and inflation grew out of the experiences of the previous decades. In 1958, Phillips had observed a negative empirical relationship between the unemployment rate and the growth rate of wages (Phillips, 1958). Understanding that high wage growth would ultimately translate into inflation, policymakers believed that there was a stable trade-off between unemployment and inflation that they could exploit. In other words, monetary and fiscal policy could be used to drive down unemployment at the cost of a certain degree of inflation. Experience showed, however, that the relationship was not stable. As individuals started to anticipate the inflation that resulted from attempts to exploit the trade-off, stimulative policy ceased to lower unemployment. Consequently, the Phillips curve appeared to have shifted outward, with higher inflation accompanying higher unemployment.

Friedman provided an explanation for this apparent shift. Over the long run, there is an unemployment rate determined by real factors that cannot be affected by monetary policy: the natural rate. In the short run, unanticipated inflation can temporarily push the unemployment rate below its natural rate. If workers do not perceive the higher inflation, then they will respond to higher nominal wages by increasing labour supply; similarly, employers who do not immediately perceive the higher inflation will respond to a higher price for their product by demanding more labour. This temporarily lowers unemployment, but the unemployment rate returns to its natural level when workers and employers begin to perceive the inflation. As emphasized in the literature on rational expectations (for example, Lucas, 1973) that followed Friedman, inflation has no impact on real variables like the unemployment rate once individuals have already built the level of inflation into their expectations. In other words, as expectations about inflation change, the Phillips curve shifts.

Although the absence of any long-run trade-off between inflation and unemployment has gained wide acceptance, the possibility of a short-run trade-off has kept the natural rate of unemployment at the centre of policymaking. In particular, policy rules such as the Taylor rule (see Taylor, 1999) maintain that central banks can stabilize the inflation rate by assessing where the economy stands relative to economic benchmarks such as the natural rate of unemployment, 'potential output', or the 'natural rate of interest'. When unemployment is high relative to the natural rate, and when output is below potential output, the policy rules call for stimulative monetary policy.

However, several important questions arise when one contemplates the usefulness of the natural rate of unemployment as a policy benchmark. First, although the natural rate clearly cannot be observed directly, can it be estimated with enough accuracy to be useful for policy? Or do movements in the natural rate itself make it too difficult to distinguish the natural rate and deviations from the natural rate in a sufficiently timely manner to be useful for policymakers? Second, rather than focusing so much on deviations from the natural rate, should policymakers also focus on policies that would alter the natural rate, either at low frequencies or perhaps even at business cycle frequencies? What would those policies be?

Identifying the natural rate

Although the natural rate is often simplistically described as the long-run average unemployment rate, economists widely recognize that this rate varies over time. Friedman (1968, p. 9) was clear on this point:

> To avoid misunderstanding, let me emphasize that by using the term 'natural' rate of unemployment, I do not mean to suggest that it is immutable and unchangeable. On the contrary, many of the market characteristics that determine its level are man-made and policy-made.... Improvements in employment exchanges, in availability of information about job vacancies and labor supply, and so on, would tend to lower the natural rate of unemployment.

Friedman (1968, p. 10) further argued that the mutability of the natural rate of unemployment significantly reduces its policy usefulness:

> What if the monetary authority chose the 'natural' rate – either of interest or unemployment – as its target? One problem is that it cannot know what the 'natural' rate is. Unfortunately, we have as yet devised no method to estimate accurately and readily the natural rate of either interest or unemployment. And the 'natural' rate will itself change from time to time.

Since Friedman's work, however, economists have achieved additional understanding of some of the factors that contribute to low-frequency fluctuations in the natural rate of unemployment. It is now generally under-stood that demographic changes can have a significant impact on the natural rate of unemployment (see Shimer, 1998). For instance, young workers experience substan-tially more job turnover than more experienced workers, with the spells between jobs often spent in unemploy-ment. Accordingly, when younger workers make up a larger fraction of the workforce (as they did in the 1970s when the baby boom generation entered the workforce in significant numbers), unemployment will be higher on average. Nevertheless, it is not clear whether this greater understanding of the factors that affect the natural rate can be translated into an estimate of the natural rate that is accurate enough to be useful for policy. Often changes in the natural rate can only be detected with a significant lag, after which time a policy response may actually increase volatility by causing the economy to overshoot its target.

Further complicating the question of the natural rate's usefulness as a policy benchmark is the question of whether even higher-frequency (that is, business cycle) fluctuations in the unemployment rate could in fact rep-resent movements in the natural rate. For example, modern search theory views unemployment fluctuations at business cycle frequencies as movements in the natural rate, in the sense that they result from real rather than monetary forces. Evidence from data on job flows shows that jobs are constantly being reallocated across firms, industries, geographical regions, and so on (see Davis, Haltiwanger and Schuh, 1996). Moreover, periods of above-average unemployment rates tend to coincide with an increased level of this reallocative activity. In this sense, unemployment rate fluctuations at business cycle frequencies can be viewed as the outcome of real phenomena of the type described in Friedman's famous quote – that is, as cyclical movements in the natural rate.

This emphasis on the real determinants of movements in the unemployment rate is part of the broader view that a significant portion of economic fluctuations reflects real factors as opposed to monetary phenomena. The vast real business cycle literature has explored this prop-osition since the seminal paper by Kydland and Prescott (1982). Hall (2005b) argues that real fluctuations, and the difficulty of distinguishing them from monetary phenomena, render useless the various benchmark con-cepts such as the natural rate of unemployment, potential output, and the equilibrium real interest rate.

Optimality of the natural rate and policies to alter it
If real sources of unemployment fluctuations are in fact as important as monetary sources, then the proper response by monetary policymakers to the fluctuations is much less clear. However, even if unemployment fluctu-ations are primarily driven by real factors, it would be incorrect to conclude that either the level or fluctuations

of the natural rate are optimal. Accordingly, there may be a role for policy to improve welfare by affecting the nat-ural rate (either at low frequencies or perhaps even at high frequencies). This suggests that research on the optimality of the natural rate, and on policies that can affect it, is as important as research aimed at detecting and proposing policies to counteract deviations from it.

The idea that the natural rate can be either too high or too low has been a primary focus of modern search and matching models of the labour market. In those models, the process whereby workers and firms meet may be subject to various externalities. When a worker chooses to search for a job, it has a positive externality on the probability that employers will find a suitable worker and a negative externality on the probability that other workers will find a job. Employers' search decisions cause similar externalities.

Hosios (1990) analyses the conditions under which, in a broad class of search and matching models, the various externalities result in an unemployment rate that is either too high or too low. He finds that in general there is no economic force that draws the unemployment rate towards its optimal level. One suspects that the wage might play that role. When employers decide whether to open job vacancies (the number of which ultimately determines the unemployment rate), they anticipate the wages that they will have to pay and the profits that they will earn when they form an employment relationship. However, the level of those wages and the resulting profits are determined after the fact by bargaining between workers and firms who have been matched, and who are not contemplating the impact that their bargain has on firms posting new vacancies. If the wages that result from bargaining are too low (high), firms anticipate this and create many (few) vacancies, and the unemployment rate is inefficiently low (high).

As a complement to this more theoretical examination of the optimal level of the natural rate, there is a more applied literature that tries to understand cross-country differences (particularly between continental Europe and the United States) in the average unemployment rate and how those differences relate to various policies. For example, Hopenhayn and Rogerson (1992) examine the impact of firing costs on unemployment and on pro-ductivity. They find that, in addition to increasing aver-age unemployment, firing costs reduce productivity by impeding the reallocation of workers towards more pro-ductive employers. Ljungqvist and Sargent (1998) argue that the interaction between generous unemployment insurance in many western European countries and an increased turbulence in labour markets can explain the secular rise in European unemployment rates relative to the US rate over the last several decades.

In addition to this work on the determinants of average unemployment rates in the long run, recent work has also focused on trying to better understand the sources of non-monetary movements in the unemployment rate over the business cycle, and whether they are efficient. What real factors contribute to spikes in unemployment, and why is the subsequent recovery so slow? Pries (2004) argues that the slow recovery occurs because workers who lose their job in the initial spike may pass through several short-lived jobs, and several intervening unemployment spells, before ultimately settling into more stable employment. In this environment, policies that try to accelerate a recovery may be counterproductive if they encourage worker–firm pairs to hang on to low-quality matches.

Shimer (2005), on the other hand, argues that the slow recovery of the unemployment rate during economic downturns results from a significant reduction in posted vacancies and, consequently, a decline in workers' job-finding rates. More research is needed to understand the causes of the decline in posted vacancies. The canonical Mortensen–Pissarides (1994) matching model, in which wages are flexibly renegotiated as part of a Nash bargaining solution, struggles to produce a sizeable decline in vacancies during recessions. In the model, wages fall considerably during economic downturns, and the lower wages mean that firms still find it quite profitable to post vacancies. This model's failure to deliver the observed cyclicality in vacancies leads Hall (2005a) to suggest that in fact wages are much less flexible than assumed in Mortensen–Pissarides (1994). If so, then should the fluctuations be seen as monetary in nature, and is stimulative monetary policy the correct policy response? Or are tax incentives for investment, which may spur the creation of new jobs, a better policy response? As with countercyclical monetary policy, tax incentives may take effect with a lag and exacerbate fluctuations.

Milton Friedman's assertion in 1968 that there is a natural rate of unemployment that is determined by real economic forces and is impervious to monetary policy has become relatively uncontroversial. Nevertheless, important unresolved questions about the natural rate remain. What is the optimal natural rate? To what extent do unemployment rate fluctuations reflect movements in the natural rate as opposed to deviations from it? What policies, if any, are appropriate for counteracting movements in the natural rate or deviations from it?

MICHAEL J. PRIES

See also **Friedman, Milton; Phillips curve; real business cycles; search models of unemployment; Taylor rules.**

Bibliography

Davis, S., Haltiwanger, J. and Schuh, S. 1996. *Job Creation and Destruction.* Cambridge, MA: MIT Press.

Friedman, M. 1968. The role of monetary policy. *American Economic Review* 58, 1–17.

Friedman, M. 1976. Nobel lecture: Inflation and unemployment. *Journal of Political Economy* 85, 451–72.

Hall, R. 2005a. Employment fluctuations with equilibrium wage stickiness. *American Economic Review* 95, 50–65.

Hall, R. 2005b. Separating the business cycle from other economic fluctuations. In *The Greenspan Era: Lessons for the Future* Proceedings of the Federal Reserve Bank of Kansas City Symposium, August.

Hopenhayn, H. and Rogerson, R. 1992. Job turnover and policy evaluation: a general equilibrium analysis. *Journal of Political Economy* 101, 915–38.

Hosios, A. 1990. On the efficiency of matching and related models of search and unemployment. *Review of Economic Studies* 57, 279–98.

Kydland, F. and Prescott, E. 1982. Time to build and aggregate fluctuations. *Econometrica* 50, 1345–71.

Ljungqvist, L. and Sargent, T. 1998. The European unemployment dilemma. *Journal of Political Economy* 106, 514–50.

Lucas, R. 1973. Some international evidence on output-inflation tradeoffs. *American Economic Review* 63, 326–34.

Mortensen, D. and Pissarides, C. 1994. Job creation and job destruction in the theory of unemployment. *Review of Economic Studies* 61, 397–415.

Phillips, A. 1958. The relationship between unemployment and the rate of change of money wage rates in the United Kingdom, 1861–1957. *Economica* 58, 283–99.

Pries, M. 2004. Persistence of employment fluctuations: a model of recurring job loss. *Review of Economic Studies* 71, 193–215.

Shimer, R. 1998. Why is the U.S. unemployment rate so much lower? In *NBER Macroeconomics Annual*, vol. 13, ed. B. Bernanke and J. Rotemberg. Cambridge, MA: MIT Press.

Shimer, R. 2005. The cyclical behavior of equilibrium unemployment and vacancies. *American Economic Review* 95, 25–49.

Taylor, J. 1999. *Monetary Policy Rules.* NBER Conference Report series. Chicago and London: University of Chicago Press.

Navier, Louis Marie Henri (1785–1836)

A French engineer and economist, Louis Marie Henri Navier was a pioneer in the construction of suspension bridges, and is also known as the creator of that branch of mechanics known as structural analysis. In his economic inquiries, he sought a practical measure of public utility that provided the springboard for Dupuit's pioneer contributions to demand theory. Orphaned at the age of nine, Navier was adopted by his great-uncle, the celebrated architect–engineer, Émiland-Marie Gauthey (1732–1806), who likely inspired his adopted son to follow in his illustrious footsteps. Navier died prematurely at the age of 51, thus cutting short a distinguished career of public service.

Navier was one of the earliest formulators of a cost–benefit rule to guide the construction of public works. His rule advocates expenditures on public works if the total benefit derived – in the form of before–after cost savings – exceeds the total recurring costs of the new construction. In choosing recurring costs over total costs as the element to be covered by tolls, Navier was showing a greater appreciation of consumption externalities than Pigou (1947, p. 3n.), who wrote more than a century later. In fact, Navier's rule is a somewhat less sophisticated version of Stephen Marglin's (1967, pp. 22–4) 'myopic rule' of public investment.

Navier's rule was the proximate cause of Dupuit's innovative attempt to establish demand based on subjective utility. Dupuit (1844) objected to Navier's attempt to measure utility on two grounds: (*a*) in competitive markets the proper measure of utility of the quantity of goods and services consumed is not the reduction of transport costs but rather the reduction of production costs; (*b*) increases in the quantity taken at lower prices do not all have the same utility, but rather take on smaller values as more is consumed. Thus, Dupuit's rule overcame the limitations of Navier's rule, and, in addition, launched the neoclassical theory of demand. Kölm (1968) argues that, in the context of public finance, Dupuit's rule moves us closer to Samuelson's (1954, pp. 387–9) decision rule regarding public goods. However, a valid comparison of Dupuit's performance with Samuelson's must recognize that Samuelson employed a highly restrictive definition of a public good and the assumption of true consumption jointness – aspects missing from Dupuit's analysis or from Navier's.

R. F. HÉBERT

See also **consumption externalities; cost–benefit analysis; Dupuit, Arsene-Jules-Emile-Juvenal; Pigou, Arthur Cecil; public goods; public works.**

selected works

1832. De l'exécution des travaux publics, et particulièrement des concessions. *Annales des Ponts et Chaussées: Mémoires et Documents*, 1 ser. 3, 1–31.
1835. Note sur la comparaison des avantages respectifs de diverse lignes de chemins de fer, et sur l'emploi des machines locomotives. *Annales des Ponts et Chaussées: Mémoires et Documents*, 1 ser. 9, 129–79.

Bibliography

Coronio, G. 1997. *250 ans de L'École des Ponts en cent portraits*. Paris: Presses de l'école des Ponts et Chaussées, 86–7.
Dupuit, J. 1844. On the measurement of the utility of public works. *Annales des ponts et chaussées*, 2d ser. 8, 332–75. Trans. R. Barback, *International Economic Papers* 2 (1952), 83–110.
Ekelund, R., Jr. and Hébert, R. 1978. French engineers, welfare economics, and public finance in the nineteenth century. *History of Political Economy* 10, 636–68.
Ekelund, R., Jr. and Hébert, R. 1999. *Secret Origins of Modern Microeconomics: Dupuit and the Engineers*. Chicago: University of Chicago Press.
Etner, F. 1987. *Histoire du calcul économique en France*. Paris: Economica.
Hébert, R. 1994. Fondements et développements de l'économie publique. *Revue Du Dix-Huitième Siècle* 26, 37–49.
Kölm, S.-C. 1968. Léon Walras' correspondence and related papers: the birth of mathematical economics. *American Economic Review* 58, 1330–41.
Marglin, S. 1967. *Public Investment Criteria: Studies in the Economic Development of India*. Cambridge, MA: MIT Press.
Pigou, A. 1947. *A Study in Public Finance*, 3rd edn. London: Macmillan.
Samuelson, P. 1954. The pure theory of public expenditures. *Review of Economics and Statistics* 36, 387–9.

neighbours and neighbourhoods

The concept of neighbourhood has long been a topic of popular discourse and a subject of academic interest. Despite this attention, there is little agreement on what the term 'neighbourhood' means. The *American Heritage Dictionary* (Pickett, 2000) simply defines a neighbourhood as 'a district or an area with distinctive characteristics'.

'A district or an area' is not very specific, and social scientists (outside of economics) have struggled for decades to define more precisely the geographic boundaries of neighbourhoods (Keller, 1968). Beyond the fact that neighbourhoods are sub-jurisdictional units, characterized by some degree of social cohesion, there is no accepted standard. The report prepared by the National Commission on Neighborhoods (1979, p. 7) stated that 'each neighborhood is what the inhabitants think it is'. Yet the evidence suggests that such subjective perceptions vary greatly (Keller, 1968).

For economists, who generally focus on externalities when considering neighbourhoods, an individual's neighbourhood should theoretically extend as far as the individuals or facilities that affect her satisfaction with the community (Segal, 1979; Galster, 1986). In practice, economists and other social scientists studying neighbourhoods in the United States typically use census tracts to proxy for neighbourhoods. Including between 2,500 and 8,000 people on average, census tracts are close in size to what most envision as a neighbourhood and have the practical advantage of supplying demographic and economic data from the decennial census. In Australia and Europe, census data are typically available at sub-jurisdictional levels, defined by electoral wards or postcodes, and in some cases, smaller enumeration or collection districts (Overman, 2002; Bolster et al., 2004; Drever, 2004). Increasingly, researchers in the United States and Europe are able to link individual census data and other national household surveys to geographic identifiers, and they are experimenting with smaller and more flexible neighbourhood definitions (Bolster et al., 2004; Ioannides, 2004; Bayer, Ross and Topa, 2005).

As for the term 'distinctive characteristics', economists identify several types of goods or services delivered by neighbourhoods. First, neighbourhoods offer distinct physical amenities, ranging from the style and condition of local housing to the number and quality of local parks. Second, neighbourhoods embody a particular set of 'neighbours', who have a distribution of income, human capital, and racial characteristics. Third, neighbourhoods often approximate local public service delivery areas such as attendance zones for public elementary schools, which often vary significantly in performance, even within the same jurisdictions. Fourth, neighbourhoods provide accessibility to shopping and employment opportunities. Finally, economists increasingly view neighbourhoods as possessing a stock of social capital, or norms and networks that facilitate interaction and can help residents work together to address problems like crime (Glaeser, 2000).

Social scientists have been preoccupied with the evolution and nature of neighbourhoods for decades. Modern academic discourse on neighbourhoods has its roots in the Chicago School of the 1920s. These University of Chicago sociologists hypothesized that cities naturally grow outward in a series of concentric rings. Through this growth, a neighbourhood life cycle emerges, from richer residents to poorer, as more affluent residents opt for newer, less dense and quieter areas (Park, Burgess and McKenzie, 1925).

Economists came later to the study of neighbourhoods, also initially drawn by an interest in the transition of neighbourhoods from high to low income and from predominantly white to predominantly minority residents. Muth (1972) and Sweeney (1974) propose variations of the filtering model, which, similar to the Chicago School theory, posits that neighbourhoods decline because, as their housing ages and deteriorates, higher-income residents exit, opting for newer neighbourhoods with newer housing. Other economists focused instead on the role of racial or class preferences in driving neighbourhood change (Bailey, 1959). In his simple, elegant model, Schelling (1971) shows that, if households care about the composition of their neighbours, then small changes in demographic make-up can lead to the rapid tipping of a neighbourhood from one group to another.

Another strand of economic literature examines the relationship between various neighbourhood attributes and housing prices, typically using hedonic regression analysis (Kain and Quigley, 1970; Bartik and Smith, 1987). Mills and Hamilton (1994) argue that economists have historically failed to identify the external effects of housing quality and neighbourhood conditions. But more recent research finds strong evidence that housing prices are lower in areas with higher crime, lower-quality schools, dilapidated housing and vacant lots, and fewer homeowners (Grieson and White, 1989; Black, 1999; Coulson, Hwang and Imai, 2003; Schwartz, Susin and Voicu, 2003; Schwartz et al., 2005). As for the impacts of racial composition, more recent papers find that a neighbourhood's housing prices are negatively correlated with the percentage of black residents (Yinger, 1976; Kiel and Zabel, 1996; Myers, 2004).

Finally, following Wilson (1987), economists have more recently turned to the study of how neighbourhoods and social interactions in them influence resident behaviour and outcomes.

INGRID GOULD ELLEN

See also **ghettoes; residential segregation; spatial mismatch hypothesis; urban housing demand.**

Bibliography

Bailey, M. 1959. Note on the economics of residential zoning and urban renewal. *Land Economics* 35, 288–92.

Bartik, T. and Smith, K. 1987. Urban amenities and public policy. In *Handbook of Regional and Urban Economics*, vol. 2, ed. E. Mills. Amsterdam: North-Holland.

Bayer, P., Ross, S. and Topa, G. 2005. Place of work and place of residence: informal hiring networks and labor market outcomes. Working Paper 11019. Cambridge, MA: NBER.

Black, S. 1999. Do better schools matter? Parental valuation of elementary education. *Quarterly Journal of Economics* 114, 579–99.

Bolster, A., Burgess, S., Johnston, R., Jones, K., Propper, C. and Sarker, R. 2004. Neighbourhoods, households, and income dynamics: a semi-parametric investigation of neighbourhood effects. Research Discussion Paper 4611. London: Centre for Economic Policy.

Coulson, N., Hwang, S.-J. and Imai, S. 2003. The value of owner-occupation in neighborhoods. *Journal of Housing Research* 13(2), 153–74.

Drever, A. 2004. Separate spaced, separate outcomes? Neighbourhood impacts on minorities in Germany. *Urban Studies* 41, 1423–39.

Galster, G. 1986. What is a neighborhood? *International Journal of Urban and Regional Research* 10, 243–63.

Glaeser, E. 2000. The future of urban research: non-market interactions. *Brookings-Wharton Papers on Urban Affairs* 2000, 101–38.

Grieson, R. and White, J. 1989. The existence and capitalization of neighborhood externalities: a reassessment. *Journal of Urban Economics* 25, 68–76.

Ioannides, Y. 2004. Neighborhood income distributions. *Journal of Urban Economics* 56, 435–57.

Kain, J. 1968. Housing segregation, negro unemployment, and metropolitan decentralization. *Quarterly Journal of Economics* 82, 175–97.

Kain, J. and Quigley, J. 1970. Measuring the value of housing quality. *Journal of the American Statistical Association* 5, 532–48.

Katz, L., Kling, J. and Liebman, J. 2001. Moving to opportunity in Boston: early results of a randomized mobility experiment. *Quarterly Journal of Economics* 116, 607–54.

Keller, S. 1968. *The Urban Neighborhood: A Sociological Perspective*. New York: Random House.

Kiel, K. and Zabel, J. 1996. House price differentials in U.S. cities: household and neighborhood racial effects. *Journal of Housing Economics* 5, 143–65.

Mills, E. and Hamilton, B. 1994. *Urban Economics*. 5th edn. New York: HarperCollins College Publishers.

Muth, R. 1972. A vintage model of the housing stock. *Regional Science Association Papers Proceedings* 30(2), 141–56.

Myers, C. 2004. Discrimination and neighborhood effects: understanding racial differences in U.S. house prices. *Journal of Urban Economics* 56, 279–302.

National Commission on Neighborhoods. 1979. *People, Building Neighborhoods*. Final Report to the President and the Congress of the United States. Washington, DC: Government Printing Office.

Overman, H. 2002. Neighbourhood effects in large and smallneighbourhoods. *Urban Studies* 39, 117–30.

Park, R. Burgess, E. and McKenzie, R., eds. 1925. *The City*. Chicago: University of Chicago Press.

Pickett, J., ed. 2000. *The American Heritage® Dictionary of the English Language*. 4th edn. Boston: Houghton Mifflin Company.

Schelling, T. 1971. Dynamic models of segregation. *Journal of Mathematical Sociology* 1, 143–86.

Schwartz, A., Ellen, I., Voicu, I. and Schill, M. 2005. The external effects of place-based, subsidized housing. Working paper. New York: Furman Center for Real Estate and Urban Policy, New York University.

Schwartz, A., Susin, S. and Voicu, I. 2003. Has falling crime driven New York City's real estate boom? *Journal of Housing Research* 14, 101–36.

Segal, D. 1979. Introduction. In *The Economics of Neighborhood*, ed. D. Segal. New York: Academic Press.

Sweeney, J. 1974. A commodity hierarchy model of the rental housing market. *Journal of Urban Economics* 1, 288–323.

Wilson, W. 1987. *The Truly Disadvantaged: The Inner-City, the Underclass and Public Policy*. Chicago: University of Chicago Press.

Yinger, J. 1976. Racial prejudice and racial residential segregation in an urban model. *Journal of Urban Economics* 3, 383–96.

Nemchinov, Vasily Sergeevich (1894–1964)

Born the son of a State Bank messenger in Grabovo, Russia, on 2 January 1894; died in Moscow on 5 November 1964. Nemchinov graduated from the Moscow Commercial Institute between the February and October Revolutions of 1917, but joined the Communist Party only in 1940 on appointment as Director of the K.A. Timiryazev Agricultural Institute, the Statistics Faculty of which he had headed since 1928. He showed courage in prohibiting from his Institute the pseudo-genetics ('Michurinism') of T.D. Lysenko, but when at Stalin's instigation mainstream genetics were condemned in 1948 he was forced from the directorship. The Academy of Sciences (to which he had been elected in 1946) then made him chairman of its Council for the Study of Productive Resources, a post retained (with a chair at the party's Academy of Social Sciences) until his fatal illness. In 1958 he established the first group in the USSR to study mathematical economics (from 1963 the Central Economic Mathematical Institute) and was posthumously awarded a Lenin Prize for elaborating linear programming and economic modelling for the USSR.

The research embodied in Nemchinov (1926; 1928) was distorted to justify Stalin's coercion of the peasantry: his data on rural social stratification gave cover to 'liquidation of the kulaks as a class' (though Nemchinov had avoided the term 'kulak'); his measurement of absolute gross harvest (Nemchinov, 1932) was used to extort deliveries from collective farms. As soon as Stalin died, Nemchinov campaigned for the publication of official statistics and for more sophisticated techniques to utilize them – cybernetics had been damned as a pseudo-science serving capitalist interests. His organization of experimental national and regional input–output tables led him to question the meaningfulness of administered pricing, and his last book (1962) sought, as his widow put it (Nemchinova, 1985, pp. 202–21), 'a broad-based system of social valuations … as a single, internally consistent set of values'.

M.C. KASER

Selected works

1926. O statisticheskom izuchenii klassovogo rassloenniya derevni [On the statistical study of rural class stratification]. *Bulleten' Ural'skogo oblastnogo statisticheskogo upravleniya* [Bulletin of the Urals Regional Statistical Administration] 1. Reprinted in *Selected Works*, vol. 1.

1928. Opyt kalssifikatsii krest'yanskikh khozyaistv [Experience from the classification of peasant households]. *Vestnik statistiki* [Statistical bulletin] 1. Reprinted in *Selected Works*, vol. 1.

1932. Vyborochnye izmereniya urozhainosti [Sampling measurement of yields]. *Narodnoe khozyaistvo SSSR* [National economy of the USSR] 5–6. Reprinted in *Selected Works*, vol. 1.

1962. *Ekonomiko-matematicheskie metody i modeli* [Methods and models of mathematical economics]. Moscow: Sotsegiz. 2nd (posthumous) edn, 1965. Reprinted in *Selected Works*, vol. 3.

1967–9. *Izbrannye proizvedeniya* [Selected Works]. 6 vols. Moscow: Izdatel'stvo Nauka.

Bibliography

Nemchinova, M.B. 1985. The scientific work of Vasily Sergeevich Nemchinov (on the 90th anniversary of his birth). *Matekon. Translations of Russian and East European Mathematical Economics* 21(2) (1984–5), 3–25; translation of an article in *Ekonomika i matematicheskie metody* [Economics and mathematical methods] 20(1) (1984).

'neoclassical'

The term 'neoclassical' was first used by Veblen (1900, pp. 242, 260–2, 265–8), in order to characterize Marshall and Marshallian economics. Veblen did not appeal to any similarity in theoretical structure between the economics of Marshall and classical economics in order to defend this novel designation. Rather, he perceived Marshall's Cambridge School to have a continuity with classical economics on the alleged basis of a common utilitarian approach and the common assumption of a hedonistic psychology. Derivative from Veblen's use, this meaning of the term subsequently gained some currency, particularly in the 1920s and 1930s; for example, in the writings of Wesley Mitchell, J.A. Hobson, Maurice Dobb and Eric Roll. It is evident that the emergence of this notion of Marshallian economics as a 'neoclassical' project also involved, at least in part, an acquiescence to Marshall's portrayal of his own economics as a continuation of the classical tradition, though Marshall's sense of the continuity is not really that perceived by Veblen. Keynes (1936, pp. 177–8) also employed the term, though in an idiosyncratic matter, derivative from his equally idiosyncratic notion of classical economics.

The use of the term with the meaning which became the accepted convention after the Second World War, extending it to embrace marginalist theory in general, can be traced to Hicks (1932, p. 84) and Stigler (1941, pp. 8, 13, 297). From what source they derived the term is not certain. It is highly unlikely that either of them coined it independently. Perhaps the likeliest source of Hicks's use is Dobb's article, published as it was in the London School of Economics' 'house journal', *Economica*. Following Hamilton (1923), Dobb (1924, p. 68) writes that 'neo-classical' is not an entirely inappropriate term to describe Marshallian economics, 'for what the Cambridge School has done is to divest Classical Political Economy of its more obvious crudities, to sever its connection with the philosophy of natural law, and to restate it in terms of the differential calculus. The line of descent is fairly direct from Smith, Malthus, and Ricardo'. Hicks's article, or Veblen, is the most likely source of Stigler's use. He refers to both of them. Hicks and Stigler were certainly more correct than Veblen in perceiving the unifying core of the marginalist theories to be, on the one hand, methodological individualism and on the other, the marginal productivity theory of distribution developed in connection with the subjective theory of value. However, neither of them offered any significant defence for their (then) implicit view that the writings of the classical economists also can be characterized in terms of this theoretical approach. Subsequently this characterization – and the nomenclature for marginalism associated with it – has given way to a recognition of the sharp theoretical disjuncture between classical and marginalist economics. Stigler's use, albeit hesitant, was probably as influential as his book. The term first gained wide currency in the debates on capital and growth in the 1950s and 1960s. It was no doubt also popularized by the extensive use made of it in Samuelson's textbook. From the third edition, Samuelson (1955, p. vi) presents the book as setting forth a 'grand neoclassical synthesis'. (For a fuller account, see Aspromourgos, 1986.)

The question may be raised whether the depiction of 'neoclassical economics' in the mid-20th century, understood as a characterization of the mainstream of the discipline, continues to represent an accurate picture of dominant beliefs within economics. Colander (2000), for example, has questioned this. But, even though the term was never sensible, the majority of the profession remains committed to the fundamental convictions which were at issue in those earlier capital and growth debates – in particular, the notion that competition brings about a tendency to full employment of resources (especially labour) and the marginal productivity theory of functional income distribution.

TONY ASPROMOURGOS

See also **Robinson Crusoe; supply and demand.**

Bibliography

Aspromourgos, T. 1986. On the origins of the term 'neoclassical'. *Cambridge Journal of Economics* 10, 265–70.

Colander, D. 2000. The death of neoclassical economics. *Journal of the History of Economic Thought* 22, 127–43.

Dobb, M. 1924. The entrepreneur myth. *Economica* 4, 66–81.

Hamilton, W.H. 1923. Vestigial economics. *New Republic*, 4 April.

Hicks, J.R. 1932. Marginal productivity and the principle of variation. *Economica* 12, 79–88.

Keynes, J.M. 1936. *The General Theory of Employment, Interest and Money*. London: Macmillan.

Samuelson, P.A. 1955. *Economics: An Introductory Analysis.*
3rd edn, New York: McGraw-Hill.

Stigler, G.J. 1941. *Production and Distribution Theories.* New
York: Macmillan.

Veblen, T.B. 1900. The preconceptions of economic science
III. *Quarterly Journal of Economics* 14, 240–69.

neoclassical growth theory

Neoclassical growth theory is not a theory of history. In a
sense it is not even a theory of growth. Its aim is to
supply an element in an eventual understanding of certain important elements in growth and to provide a
way of organizing one's thoughts on these matters. For
instance, the question of whether technical progress is
bound to be associated with unemployment cannot be
decisively answered by the theory but it goes a long way
in pinpointing those considerations on which an answer
depends.

Most of the theory is that of the equilibrium of a
competitive economy through time. In particular, attention is paid to the accumulation of capital goods, growth
in population and technical progress. Two kinds of
equilibria are distinguished. One is the short period or
momentary equilibrium of the economy when the stock
of capital goods, the working population and technical
know how can be taken as fixed. The other is the *long-run*
equilibrium when none of these three elements are taken
as given. It is important to understand that while long-
run equilibrium implies momentary equilibrium for all
dates it is not the case that a sequence of momentary
equilibria constitutes a long-run equilibrium. For the
latter has the property that the actions of agents taken at
a given date in the light of their expectations of events at
subsequent dates are not regretted when these dates
arrive. In other words, it is what we would now call a
rational expectations equilibrium. Harrod (1939) called a
path of an economy with this property the *warranted
path.*

In principle a warranted path (say of output or output
per man) could be quite irregular. Indeed it could be
cyclical (Lucas, 1975). But except in very simple models
such generality is intractable and most of the attention
has been devoted to long-run equilibria which are *steady-
state* or *quasi-stationary.* (If a variable $x(t)$ obeys the
dynamic equation $x(t) = e^{gt}x(0)$ then $\hat{x}(t) = x(t)e^{-gt} =
x(0)$ is a constant, that is x is stationary.) This is one of
the reasons why the theory is not really a theory of
growth. It is also unwise to identify the steady state – say,
the steady state rate or growth in output per head – with
historical trends in the variable. That would require a
good deal more argument than the theories provide. A
steady state equilibrium is simply an extension of stationary equilibrium (an equilibrium in which the stock of
capital goods, the population and technical knowledge

are all constant). But it allows this now to include
accumulation and technical change.

It is of interest to ask whether a steady state equilibrium is possible and if it is, whether a sequence of short
period equilibria guides the economy to it. There is also
another question: do all warranted paths eventually
become steady states? That is can long-run equilibrium
be said 'eventually' to be independent of an economy's
starting point? (See Hahn, 1987.) However the literature
on these matters is sometimes confused and confusing.
Short period equilibrium plainly depends on agents'
expectations and so if they are not postulated to be
always correct there are many possible evolutions of such
equilibria. In fact except for Harrod's (1939) pioneering
discussion of *actual* growth paths and one or two others,
little attention has been paid to the expectational problem. Instead the path of the economy has been studied on
the hypothesis that what is saved is also invested without
explicit attention to what this implies for expectations
concerning prices and interest rates. When that is made
explicit it turns out that only warranted paths have
been examined and not a sequence of short period
equilibria. This procedure has been also adopted by the
'new macroeconomics' (e.g. Lucas, 1975).

Connected with this is the treatment of investment
and savings. The latter are usually taken to be either
proportional to income or to come only from profits.
Savings are not explained by the optimizing choices of
households. This, however, is against the spirit of neoclassical economics. In order to improve on conventional
savings theory one either takes a world which one can
study 'as if' agents were infinitely long lived or one considers an economy of *overlapping generations* first studied
by Samuelson (1958). Neither of these moves is discussed
in what follows. But I re-emphasize that until savings
behaviour has been explained the theories are not fully
neoclassical.

Investment behaviour is a more difficult matter. Since
the bulk of the theory is one of the warranted path, the
marginal return to any investor is always equal to the
marginal cost of investment. Thus investment is never
regretted and is simply explained by it not being profitable to undertake more or less investment than is thus
warranted. But difficulties arise if the warranted path and
particularly the steady state is not unique, and also if
investment is in some sense the carrier of technical
progress. 'Animal spirits', as Keynes called entrepreneurial
investment propensities, may be determinants of the rate
of growth which the economy is capable of. Equally
important is the circumstance that investment behaviour
will be of prime importance in the evolution of a
sequence of short run equilibria. neoclassical theory has
little to offer on these matters and is open to criticism on
these grounds.

This brings me back to the beginning. As will be seen
from what follows neoclassical theory states quite precisely what kind of economy in what kind of state is being

considered. This economy and this state may be considered to be of low descriptive power. That, however, needs empirical argument and neither proponents nor opponents have produced any clinching ones. But an equally interesting question is whether the theory provides a good base camp for sallies into the study of particular economies. For instance, does it allow us to find just that feature of such an economy which is at variance with the postulates of the theory and thence to a modification of the latter, step by step? To this question at the moment the answer must be yes.

There is one last matter. The theories here discussed have provided the arena for much controversy concerning the *logical* coherence of neoclassical theory in general (Robinson, 1965; Harcourt, 1969). This controversy is not here discussed. For what it is worth it is this writer's view that neoclassical theory has survived this controversy unscathed. But the emphasis here is on 'logical'. There is little to be said for those economists who have taken the question of the descriptive merit of the theory as having been decisively settled in its favour.

1. The simple model

1.1. The single good economy: no technical progress

Consider an economy in which a single good is produced by means of itself and labour. The good can also be consumed. The stock of it devoted to production is denoted by K and called capital. The stock does not depreciate either through use or the passage of time. Further notation is as follows: Y is output, L is the amount of labour used in production, L^0 is the labour force, $y = Y/L$, $k = K/L$, $e = L/L^0$.

Assumption 1.1 The production possibilities of the economy can be represented by a C^2 production function.

$$Y = F(K, L)$$

with the following properties:

(a) For all $h > 0 : hY = F(hK, hL)$. (Constant Returns to Scale)
(b) $f'(k) > 0$, $f''(k) < 0$ for $k \in [0, \infty]$. Also $f'(0) = \infty$, $f'(\infty) = 0$

(The 'Inada Conditions'; see Inada, 1963).

From these assumptions it follows that we may represent the production possibilities by

$$y = f(k). \tag{1.1}$$

Assumption 1.2 The working population L^0 grows at a constant geometric rate λ [i.e. $\dot{L}^0(t) = L^0(0)e^{\lambda t}$].

Assumption 1.3 A constant fraction s of output is not consumed.

It will thus be a condition of equilibrium that output which is not consumed is invested:

$$sf[k(t)] = sy(t) = \frac{\dot{K}(t)}{L(t)} = \dot{k}(t) + k(t)\frac{\dot{L}(t)}{L(t)}. \tag{1.2}$$

Definition 1.1 The economy is said to be in steady state equilibrium if $k(t)$ and $e(t)$ are constants, profits are maximized and (1.2) holds.

If $e(t)$ is constant then

$$\frac{\dot{L}(t)}{L(t)} = \frac{\dot{L}^0(t)}{L^0(t)} = \lambda.$$

Using this and the condition $\dot{k}(t) = 0$ in (1.2) yields

$$\lambda = \frac{sf(k)}{k} \tag{1.3}$$

as a condition for steady state equilibrium. Harrod (1939) called $sf(k)/k$ the *warranted rate of growth* and we shall abbreviate by writing

$$\frac{sf(k)}{k} \equiv w(k).$$

Clearly $w(k)$ gives us the rate of growth of output required to keep investment and savings equal to each other in steady state. On the other hand, λ is the rate of growth of employment which is needed to keep the proportion employed (possibly = unity) constant. Harrod called it the *natural rate of growth* of output for it tells us the rate at which output grows at a constant e.

Now by A.1.1.(b) one has $w(0) > \lambda$ and $w(\infty) < \lambda$ so there exists k^* satisfying (1.3). Since $w'(k) < 0$ everywhere, k^* is the only value of the capital labour ratio satisfying 1.3. But then for profit maximization, the real wage w^* and the real interest rate, ρ in steady state equilibrium are:

$$w^* = f(k^*) - k^*f'(k^*) \quad \text{and} \quad \rho^* = f'(k^*). \tag{1.4}$$

So the steady state equilibrium exists and is uniquely characterized by (1.4) and

$$\lambda = w(k^*) \tag{1.5'}$$

Now return to (1.2) and consider the path $k(t)$ out of steady state but with $e(t)$ constant at e. In our new notation we find

$$\frac{\dot{k}}{k} = [w(k) - \lambda] \tag{1.5}$$

by dividing (1.2) by k and rearranging. Now let

$$V(k) = \frac{1}{2}[w(k) - \lambda]^2$$

so that $V(k)$ is a measure of the deviation of the warranted from the natural rate of growth. One has:

$$V(k) \geq 0 \quad \text{all } k \text{ and } V(k^*) = 0. \quad (1.6)$$

Also using (1.5):

$$\begin{aligned}\dot{V}(k) &= [w(k) - \lambda]w'(k)\dot{k} \\ &= [w(k) - \lambda]^2 kw'(k) < 0 \quad \text{all } k > \\ & \quad 0 \text{ and } k^* \neq k. \end{aligned} \quad (1.7)$$

These two results together with the Inada conditions suffice for the conclusion:

$$\text{For all } k(0) \geq 0, \quad \lim_{t \to \infty} k(t) = k^*.$$

We sum up:

Proposition P.1.1 An economy satisfying A.1.1 – A.1.3 has the following properties:

(a) There exists a unique steady state equilibrium
(b) The path of the economy along which savings are always equal to investment and the proportion of the workforce employed is constant (e is constant) approaches the steady state equilibrium as $t \to \infty$.

1.2. Discussion of the model
There are many lacunae in the theory just presented and we shall be able to fill in some of these below. But first I discuss what can be learned from it.

Harrod (1939) writing in a Keynesian spirit held the view that a steady state equilibrium might not exist. He was particularly interested in the possibility that the warranted growth rate was always above the natural rate. In that case output would have to grow faster than is physically possible in order for investment to take up the savings generated and that is not possible. There would be a permanent tendency to depression. For many commentators this view of Harrod's rested implicitly on an assumed production function of the form:

$$Y = \min[aK, bL] \quad (1.8)$$

that is on fixed coefficients of production (see e.g. Solow, 1956). However, a careful reading of Harrod suggests that he rather based his argument on the Keynesian liquidity trap. That is he thought that monetary forces set a positive lower bound on the rate of interest which thus on neoclassical theory set an upper bound on k and so, given s, a lower bound on $w(k)$.

This argument, however, is suspect. It is the real and not the nominal interest rate which governs (together with the real wage) the choice of k. Liquidity preference may set a lower bound on the nominal interest rate (the cost of holding money) but not on the real rate. Thus suppose r is the nominal interest rate. Then

$$\rho = r - \frac{\dot{p}}{p}$$

where p is the price of the good. Then if r is at its minimum level $\underline{r}$ we have from (1.4)

$$\left(\frac{\dot{p}}{p}\right)^* = \underline{r} - f'(k^*) \quad (1.9)$$

as a condition of steady state equilibrium. By assumption $f'(k^*) < \underline{r}$ so for such an equilibrium one requires a constant inflation rate:

$$\left(\frac{\dot{p}}{p}\right)^* > 0.$$

So provided we can graft a monetary sector onto the simple model it would seem that the liquidity trap is not an obstacle to the existence of steady state equilibrium.

But this argument reveals a central weakness in the reasoning which supports P.1.1(b). For suppose at a historically given k one has $w(k) > \lambda$. If we *impose* the condition that savings are equal to investment, then indeed there would be pressure on resources and one could tell a story to explain the generation of the required inflation rate of (1.8). But we have no good reason for imposing that condition. By doing so we are not really asking: what actually happens?, that is, what is the actual growth rate?, but rather we are implicitly postulating that the inflation rate is always such that excess savings for k constant are taken up by capital deepening ($\dot{k} > 0$). But why should this be so? If, for instance, the economy grew at λ then there would be excess supply of the good and normal arguments would lead us to suspect falling prices. But these would raise the real rate of interest and raise $w(k)$ above λ even further. The steady state equilibrium even if it exists is an unstable 'knife-edge' (Harrod, 1939).

(b) Solow's celebrated paper (1956) established P.1.1. But Solow was mistaken in his belief that it disposed of Harrod's knife-edge. The latter does not deal with paths on which the condition: savings = investment at a constant e has been imposed. That is Harrod did not postulate that the actual path was an equilibrium path. In this he was right since there is no good explanation of the Solow condition.

(c) An alternative procedure leading to P.1.1(a) even if 1.8 is the form of the production function is to drop A.1.3 (Hahn, 1951; Kaldor, 1955; Robinson, 1965). This is done by supposing that the saving ratio out of profits is higher than that out of wages. Now if there are fixed coefficients of production (1.8) the equilibrium conditions (1.4) have no meaning since marginal products are not defined. This leaves it open to determine the real wage and interest rate by the requirement that they should generate that distribution of income between wages and profits which makes the warranted growth rate equal to the natural rate. From (1.8) one finds

$$\frac{Y}{K} = a, \quad \frac{Y}{L} = b \text{ and } k = \frac{b}{a} \equiv \beta \text{ say.}$$

Let s_0 be the saving propensity out of wages and s_1 the saving propensity out of profits, with $s_0 < s_1$. Then the aggregate saving propensity, s, of the economy is given by

$$\frac{s_1 \rho}{a} + s_0 \frac{w}{b} = s.$$

Imposing the condition $sa = \lambda$ (the warranted rate = natural rate) yields

$$s_1 \rho + s_0 \frac{w}{\beta} = \lambda. \tag{1.10}$$

But also

$$\frac{\rho}{a} + \frac{w}{\beta} = 1 \tag{1.11}$$

so that we have two equations to determine what w^* and ρ^* must be in steady state equilibrium. A special case arises when $s_0 = 0$ (no saving out of wages) and $s_1 = 1$ (no consumption out of profits). Then

$$\rho^* = \lambda \tag{1.12}$$

is the condition of equilibrium. The reader should avoid interpreting (1.12) as saying that λ 'determines' the rate of profit. Equation (1.12) tells us what ρ must be if there is to be steady state equilibrium.

Once again a version of P.1.1(a) survives. Also stability fares slightly better than in (a). For if the actual growth rate is less than the warranted rate (because w and ρ have the 'wrong' values), and the latter is greater than λ then investment will be less than savings and competition between firms may lead to lower prices, higher real wages and so a fall in s. This will lower the warranted rate and bring it closer to λ as well as reducing the investment-savings gap. This *may* be so but what has just been said is not a proof. Indeed, as for instance Meade (1966) has shown, falling profitability may reduce the willingness to invest and so lead the system away from steady state equilibrium.

(d) Of course, (1.8) is not a plausible production function. Suppose we combine the savings assumption of (c) with a neoclassical production function satisfying A.1.1. Then certainly (1.4) must hold in equilibrium.

But (1.3) will now read

$$(s_1 + s_0)f'(k) + s_0 \frac{f(k)}{k} = \lambda \tag{1.13}$$

from which we can find k^*. Since

$$s_1 \rho \frac{K}{Y} + s_0 \frac{wL}{Y} = s.$$

So

$$s_1 \rho + s_0 \frac{w}{k} = s \frac{Y}{K} = \lambda.$$

Then substitute from (1.4) for ρ and w. So while the saving hypothesis will be reflected in the steady state value of k it will leave the equality between marginal productivity and factor rewards as an equilibrium condition. Indeed without this, the steady state values of w and ρ would be unknown. This is so even under the 'classical' savings assumption that $s_0 = 0$. The equation derived from (1.13) is then

$$s_1 f'(k) = \lambda$$

and it tells us what k must be in order to generate a profit rate which, given the savings hypothesis, generates just the right amount of savings required for a growth in the capital stock at the rate λ. Thus the savings hypothesis has no direct bearing on the neoclassical equilibrium condition that the rate of profit must equal the marginal product of k.

(e) If workers save and invest their savings at the current rate of return on capital then the foregoing arithmetic needs to be changed. This was first noticed by Pasinetti (1962) whos paper gave rise to a number of others (Meade and Hahn, 1965; Modigliani and Samuelson, 1966).

Let $\sigma = s_1 - s_0 > 0$ Let μ be the fraction of k owned by capitalists – that is by agents who have no income from work. Then savings per employed worker are given by

$$s_0 f(k) + \sigma f'(k) \mu k.$$

So in steady state equilibrium one requires

$$\frac{s_0 f(k)}{k} + \sigma f'(k) \mu = \lambda. \tag{1.14}$$

From which

$$\frac{\mu f'(k)k}{f(k)} = \frac{1}{\sigma} \left[\frac{\lambda k}{f(k)} - s_0 \right]. \tag{1.15}$$

The left-hand side measures the capitalists' share in income which cannot be negative. But there is nothing which guarantees a solution to (1.15) with $\lambda k \geq s_0 f(k)$. Pasinetti (1962) simply made the latter (with strict inequality) a condition of the model. But God may have made the world otherwise.

In fact there are two possibilities. Suppose (1.15) has an admissible solution. One notes that in steady state one must have

$$1 - \mu = \frac{s_0[f(k) - \mu k f'(k)]}{\lambda k}. \tag{1.16}$$

That is the ratio of workers' capital to total capital must equal the ratio of their savings to total savings which in steady state equilibrium is equal to λk. Solving (1.16) for μ yields.

$$\frac{\lambda k - s_0 f(k)}{k[\lambda - s_0 f'(k)]} = \mu. \tag{1.17}$$

Solving (1.14) for μ yields

$$\left[\frac{\lambda k - s_0 f(k)}{k}\right] \frac{1}{\sigma f'(k)} = \mu. \tag{1.18}$$

Equating (1.17) to (1.18) then yields

$$s_1 f'(k) = \lambda. \tag{1.19}$$

So even though workers save, the long run equilibrium rate of profit bears the same relation to λ as it does under the classical savings hypothesis. Note that $\lambda k > s_0 f(k)$ is here required as before. In particular write (1.18) as

$$\max\left[0, \frac{\lambda k - s_0 f(k)}{k}\right] \frac{1}{\sigma f'(k)} = \mu. \tag{1.18'}$$

Then this always has an admissible solution. If that gives $\mu = 0$ then from (1.14)

$$\frac{s_0 f(k)}{k} = \lambda \tag{1.20}$$

Harrod solution. It should now be emphasized that $\mu = 0$ does *not* mean that capitalists own no capital. All it means is that their share in total capital is zero.

Modigliani and Samuelson (1966) have shown how a warranted growth path may converge to k^* given by (1.12) or to k^{**} given by (1.20) depending on the technology and savings propensities.

(f) It will have been noticed that the whole of the above discussion has been conducted for L/L^0 constant and not $L/L^0 = 1$; that is the steady state is consistent with permanent unemployment. This should cause no surprise since the assumption of constant returns to scale and of constant savings propensities makes all equilibrium conditions independent of scale. if there is unemployment in a steady state equilibrium it can be argued with equal lack of real sense that either the capital stock is too low or that the real wage is too high. The present model is not suited to a discussion of whether falling interest rates and or money wages as long as there is unemployment would lead the economy to a steady state with full employment.

1.3. The single good economy with technical progress

Growth theory without technical progress seems pretty useless. Yet no really satisfactory account exists of the determinants of technical progress, at least no such account based solely on considerations of economic theory exists. (Schumpeter (1934) is probably still the most interesting attempt but it excludes the possibility of steady state equilibrium.) What follows is therefore rather ad hoc and mechanical.

Technical progress shifts the production function through time and so in its most general form when technical progress is *disembodied*, one writes

$$Y(t) = F[K(t), L(t), t] \tag{1.21}$$

and retains the assumption of constant returns to scale for each t. Progress is disembodied if it can be taken full advantage of by the stock of the good (capital) accumulated in the past and by the same kind of labour. Even with this strong assumption we need more structure to build a model and accordingly postulate that all technical progress is *factor-augmenting*, that is (1.21) can be written as

$$Y(t) = F[\alpha(t)K(t), \beta(t)L(t)]$$
$$\text{with } \alpha(t) \geq 0, \quad \beta(t) \geq 0 \text{ all } t.$$

Let

$$\hat{K}(t) = \alpha(t)K(t), \quad \hat{L}(t) = \beta(t)L(t)$$

and

$$\hat{k}(t) = \frac{\hat{K}(t)}{\hat{L}(t)}, \quad \hat{y}(t) = \frac{Y(t)}{\hat{L}(t)}.$$

Then the equilibrium real interest rate is given by $\alpha f'[\hat{k}(t)]$ when $\hat{y}(t) = f[\hat{k}(t)]$.

In steady state equilibrium the real interest rate is constant. Let the operator E applied to a function $g(x)$ denote its elasticity

$$\left[Eg(x) = \frac{g'(x)}{g(x)} x\right].$$

Then for the real interest rate to be constant one requires:

$$\frac{\dot{\alpha}}{\alpha} + \left\{Ef'[\hat{k}(t)]\right\} \left[\frac{\dot{\alpha}}{\alpha} - \frac{\dot{\beta}}{\beta} + \frac{\dot{k}}{k}\right] = 0. \tag{1.22}$$

Suppose first that $\alpha(0) = \beta(0) = 1$ and that $\dot{\alpha}(t) = 0$ all t, $\dot{\beta}(t) = b\beta(t)$ all t. Technical progress is purely labour augmenting (at a constant rate) or *Harrod-Neutral*. Clearly $\beta(t) = e^{bt}$. Hence (1.22) will be satisfied if

$$\frac{\dot{k}(t)}{k(t)} - b = 0 \quad \text{or} \quad \frac{\dot{K}}{K} = b + \lambda. \tag{1.23}$$

Let $n = b + \lambda$ and call it the *natural rate of growth*. If savings are proportional to income, equilibrium requires

$$\frac{\alpha(0)sf[\hat{k}(t)]}{\hat{k}(t)} = n \qquad (1.24)$$

which can be uniquely solved for $\hat{k}^*$ when the production function is concave and satisfies the Inada conditions. By (1.23), $\dot{k}(t) = 0$ and so we conclude that (i) the capital output ratio and the real interest rate are both constant and (ii) the real wage and the capital labour ratio (k) are rising at the rate b. But the wage per efficiency unit of labour and capital per efficiency unit of labour are both constant. Hence we are essentially in the same situation as that discussed for the absence of technical progress.

Next suppose that $\dot{\alpha}(t) = a\alpha(t)$ and $a = b$. Technical progress is said to be *Hicks-neutral*. Then (1.22) becomes

$$a + \{Ef'[k(t)]\}\frac{\dot{k}}{k} = 0. \qquad (1.22')$$

Suppose that the production function is characterized by an elasticity of substitution equal to minus one. Then since with Hicks-neutrality one can write: $Y = e^{bt}F[K(t), L(t)]$ one has that KF_k/F is constant when K is changed but F is constant (if one is moving along an isoquant). This implies

$$Ef'[\hat{k}(t)] = -1$$

and so once again (using (1.22')) one obtains (1.23). A constant rate of profit and a constant share of profits then implies a constant capital output ratio. In other words, Harrod-neutrality is equivalent to Hicks-neutrality with a unit elasticity of substitution (Robinson, 1938). Uzawa (1961) has shown that only a Cobb–Douglas production function will give this equivalence.

If $a \neq b$ technical progress is 'biased' in favour of the higher of a and b. However, there is no fundamental reason why technical progress should be of the factor-augmenting type nor, if it is, why it should proceed at a steady rate. Hence technical progress makes the idea of steady state equilibrium somewhat unconvincing.

However, there have been attempts to formulate a theory which focuses on endogenous economic forces that may cause technical progress to be of a certain kind (Kennedy, 1964; Samuelson, 1965). These attempts are not notably successful or convincing and will only be sketched. Given a factor-augmenting production function which exhibits constant returns to scale, one can write the minimum unit cost function as

$$c = c[q(t)/\alpha(t), \quad w(t)/\beta(t)]$$

where $q(t)$ is the rental of capital of $w(t)$ the wage. Let s_K and s_L respectively be the shares in unit cost of capital and labour. Then from elementary Duality Theory

(e.g. Varian, 1978), if $\dot{w}(t) = \dot{q}(t) = 0$:

$$\frac{\dot{c}}{c} = -[s_K a(t) + s_L b(t)] \qquad (1.25)$$

where $b(t) = \dot{\beta}(t)/\beta(t)$, $a(t) = \dot{\alpha}(t)/\alpha(t)$. The idea now is as follows. Firms can choose to 'produce' $a(t)$ and $b(t)$ according to a 'production possibility' function.

$$T[a(t), b(t)] = g[b(t)] - a(t) \geq 0 \qquad (1.26)$$

and the pairs (a, b) satisfying (1.26) form a convex compact set with a differentiable boundary. Also $g'(b) < 0$. If the firm's objective is to minimize $\dot{c}/c$ subject to (1.26) it will choose $b(t)$ so as to satisfy

$$-g'[b(t)] = \frac{s_L}{s_K}. \qquad (1.27)$$

As Samuelson (1965) has noted, (1.27) is *not* some novel theory of income distribution unrelated to the Neo-classical one. The latter was needed in the definition of c and the derivation of (1.25).

Now s_L/s_K will depend on the relative prices of efficiency units. Since $g(\cdot)$ is monotone (1.27) can be inverted:

$$b(t) = (g')^{-1}(s_L/s_K)$$

and so we write

$$b(t) = h\left[\frac{w(t)}{q(t)}\frac{\alpha(t)}{\beta(t)}\right]. \qquad (1.28)$$

The equations (1.26) and (1.28) are two differential equations in $\alpha(t)$, $\beta(t)$ and relative factor prices. It is easy to show that

$$h'(1 - \sigma) \geq 0$$

where σ is the elasticity of substitution.

If one can take w/q constant then one proceeds as follows.

$$b(t) - a(t) = \frac{d \log[\beta(t)/\alpha(t)]}{dt}$$
$$= b(t) - g[b(t)] = v[b(t)] \text{ say.}$$

Substituting from (1.28) one obtains the differential equation

$$\frac{d \log[\beta(t)/\alpha(t)]}{dt} = v\left\{h\left[\frac{w}{q}\frac{\alpha(t)}{\beta(t)}\right]\right\}. \qquad (1.29)$$

This equation gives the evolution of relative factor augmentation. If for some $[\alpha/\beta]^*$ one has a critical point of v and (1.29) is convergent then there will be a constant relative rate of labour augmentation so $b(t) - a(t) \to 0$. (This does not necessarily imply that $b(t)$ and $a(t)$ become constant.) In that situation innovations are derived to be Hicks-Neutral. Even if the rate of innovation is then constant we know that this will not be consistent with steady state unless the elasticity of substitution is unity. But Samuelson (1965) has shown that the stipulated convergence of (1.29) requires an elasticity of substitution which is less than one in absolute value.

All of this is on the assumption w/q = constant. In fact we know from our earlier discussion that w/q will depend on $\hat{k}(t)$ so we can replace the r.h.s. of (1.29) by:

$$v^* \left[k(t) \frac{\alpha(t)}{\beta(t)} \right].$$

We then need a differential equation for the evolution of $k(t)$ which we can obtain from the appropriate warranted growth path.

Samuelson (1965) has studied the case: $\dot{k}(t) = 0$. The literature can be consulted for further detail. At this level of aggregation the story is hardly persuasive nor can much be said in favour of the objective function which has been stipulated. On the other hand, all of this is a considerable advance on meaningless claims like: 'high wages induce labour-saving innovation' first exposed by Fellner (1961). After all, the marginal return per unit cost of the factor is the same for all factors in equilibrium. None the less one must conclude that the theory of induced innovations and their relations to growth have a long way to go yet.

1.4. The one sector model with embodied technical progress

In this section two related ideas are considered. The first is that capital and labour are substitutable *ex ante* ('putty') before investment has been congealed in concrete machines but it is not substitutable *ex post* ('clay') once the investment has been made. The second is that technical progress does not benefit old machines; it is embodied in the latest machines. These two ideas are related but can be combined in various ways. Thus one can have embodied technical progress with (traditional) putty–putty (Solow, 1970) or with clay–clay (Solow et al., 1967). One can also have disembodied technical progress as in the previous section with putty–clay. The main lessons are perhaps best learned by combining embodied technical progress with putty–clay. The classic reference here is Bliss (1968).

Some of the technicalities of the analysis now called for are somewhat involved and what follows is more in the nature of a summary of the economic implications.

An investment undertaken at date θ gives rise to machines of vintage θ. If at that date the investment is $I(\theta)$ and employment is $L(\theta, \theta)$, output per man is $y(\theta, \theta)$ and given by

$$y(\theta, \theta) = e^{a\theta} f(k(\theta)) \text{ where } k(\theta) = I(\theta)/L(\theta, \theta)e^{a\theta}.$$

Let $f(\cdot)$ satisfy Assumption 1.1. The output per man on vintage θ at date $t \geq \theta$ is written as $y(t, \theta)$. It is assumed that as long as output is produced on vintage θ that

$$y(t, \theta) = y(\theta, \theta) \tag{1.30}$$

This departs somewhat from the 'clay' assumption. It will be noticed that Harrod-neutral technical progress has been assumed. It can be shown (Bliss, 1968) that this is necessary for a steady state equilibrium to exist.

Any firm in this technological environment will make its investment and employment decisions in the light of long term expectations. For once machines have been installed they no longer share in technical progress yet the latter will raise real wages and reduce quasi-rents on old machines. These will be scrapped when quasi-rents have fallen to zero so that the economic life of the machines is endogenous to the economic process. The economic life is relevant to the investment decision and hence expectations of the course of real wages are relevant. In the theory it is assumed that all expectations are always correct. None of these considerations apply to the case of disembodied technical progress with putty-putty.

If $w(t)$ is the real wage at t then if $y(t, \theta) - w(t) > 0$ it will pay the firm to set $L(t, \theta) = L(\theta, \theta)$ because of (1.30). It will set $L(t, \theta) = 0$ when $y(t, \theta) - w(t) = 0$. These conditions determine the economic life of a machine. It is easy to show that if T is the economic life of a machine that it must be constant in steady state equilibrium. The value of T is determined by the condition $w(t) = y(t - T, t - T)$, that is, the wage equals its average product on the last vintage in use. When that is the case the firm is indifferent whether it employs labour on that vintage or not. If it does employ some then if the economy had a little more or less labour it would be employment on the last vintage in use which is varied and so $w(t)$ would measure labour's marginal social product. If no labour is employed of the last vintage then a small reduction in labour would mean reducing employment on the next oldest vintage. If there is a continuum of vintages then the economy would still lose just $y(t - T, t - T)$.

Now let $n = a + \lambda$ as in (1.2). We are looking for a steady state equilibrium as before in which output and investment grow at the rate n because gross savings are proportional to income. As before also the ratio of capital to labour measured in efficiency units of the latest vintage (i.e. $k(\theta)$) should be constant. So if $Y(t)$ is aggregate output at t and $Y(\theta, \theta)$ total output with capital of vintage θ we have

$$Y(t) = \int_{t-T}^{t} y(\theta, \theta) L(\theta, \theta) d\theta = \int_{t-T}^{t} Y(\theta, \theta) d\theta$$
$$= \frac{e^{nt} Y(t - T, t - T)(1 - e^{-nT})}{n}.$$

$$\tag{1.31}$$

If $I(\theta)$ is investment at θ then $I(t) = e^{nt}I(t-T)$ and that must equal $sY(t)$. So using (1.31) and writing $v = Y(t-T)/I(t-T)$ we obtain

$$sv = \frac{n}{1 - e^{-nT}}. \tag{1.32}$$

The left-hand side of (1.32) is again Harrod's warranted growth rate. But the rate at which the economy is capable of expanding indefinitely now depends on T, the economic life of equipment and that is an economic variable and *not* a parameter like n. One must, of course, show that (1.32) has a solution. If as in Solow et al. (1967) the technology is clay–clay then v is given as fixed. Profit maximization together with the condition that the present value of quasi-rents equals the cost of the investment which gives rise to them at the scrapping, fix the equilibrium value of T. It is then possible that Harrod's view that (1.32) has no solution is valid. This is a fortiori true if the solution of (1.32) requires $s > 1$.

One can show that the real interest rate (= profit rate) must be constant in steady state equilibrium (see Bliss, 1968). However, the relation between the latter and the equilibrium value of T is not straightforward and depends on the elasticity of substitution. That is because in steady state the scrapping condition is $t = 1/a \log$ (inverse of share of wages in vintage $(t-T)$) and the share will depend on the elasticity of substitution. One can also show that if a steady state exists that the warranted growth path of the economy will approach the steady state. This is even the case with clay–clay.

All in all the simple neoclassical model survives 'the bolting down' of concrete machines and embodied technical progress rather well. That does not mean that the resulting model is satisfactorily 'realistic'. What it does mean is that the theory is a good deal more robust than critics once thought it to be. This is also illustrated by the following episode in the related theory of technical progress.

Kaldor took the view that it was not possible to distinguish between finding another 'page in the book of blueprints' (Robinson, 1965), i.e. movements along the production function and finding a new page, i.e. innovations. He proposed that all that could be observed was a relation between the rate of growth in labour productivity and investment per man. This relation he called the 'technical progress function' and justified by the view that every act of investment led to learning. He and Mirrlees (1962) constructed a model on this basis. However, except for the assumption that firms required investment 'to pay for itself' in a predetermined period, the results of the model were not notably different from the ones already discussed. (A linear technical progress function can be integrated into a Cobb–Douglas production function. A non-linear one of the right shape has the advantage of making steady state equilibrium investment be at the rate at which the capital output ratio is constant, i.e. Harrod-neutrality is a consequence and not a hypothesis of the model.)

Arrow (1962) kept the production function (he uses clay–clay) but made technical improvement depend on the total investment undertaken over the past. This was again justified by learning. The steady state again is one of Harrod-neutral progress which is explained endogenously. There are now obvious external benefits from investment but otherwise the 'learning by doing' steady state equilibrium is of the kind we have already discussed.

2. Two sector growth models
One considers an economy with a consumption good and an investment good sector. This was first proposed by Uzawa (1961) and then gave rise to a very large literature (e.g. Solow, 1962; Inada, 1963; Takayama, 1963). We shall discuss only the case where both sectors have 'well behaved' constant returns to scale production functions, capital does not depreciate and there is no technical progress. For the latter see Diamond (1965).

2.1. Steady state
It is well known (e.g. Samuelson, 1957; Mirrlees, 1969) that given these assumptions, the equilibrium relative prices of the two goods are determined once ρ (the real interest rate) is determined. So with a classical saving hypothesis we know that steady state requires:

$$\rho = \lambda$$

and so q the price of the investment good in terms of the consumption good can be written as $q(\lambda)$. If w is the wage in terms of consumption good, y_c is output per man employed in the consumption good sector and $\mu = L_c/L$ is the proportion of the labour force employed in that sector, the classical savings assumption yields the equilibrium condition

$$w = y_c\mu \quad \text{or} \quad \mu = w/y_c. \tag{2.1}$$

(Demand for consumption good equals supply.) But w/y_c is a unique function of ρ. For by profit maximization the marginal product of capital in the consumption sector must equal $\rho q = \lambda q(\lambda)$. So λ determines a unique capital/labour ratio and so a unique share of wages in the consumption sector. Hence we can write $\mu = \mu(\lambda)$. If k is the overall capital labour ratio, k_c and k_I the capital/labour ratios in the consumption and investment sectors respectively then $k = \mu k_c + (1-\mu)k_I$ It is plain that k is uniquely determined by λ.

Matters are somewhat more complicated with a proportional saving function and we shall not derive all the results in full. Let v be the capital output ratio *in value terms*. In steady state, as usual, we require $s = v\lambda$. The question now is whether putting $v = s/\lambda$ uniquely determines k, k_c k_I and hence the rate of profit and real wage. The answer is: no.

Let ψ be the wage rental ratio. A rise in that ratio will lower q if the consumption goods sector is more labour intensive than the investment goods sector. Hence k_c and k_I will be raised and v will be lowered. But the value of investment output is a constant fraction s of the value of output and q is lower so that output of investment good must rise relatively to that of consumption good and so μ must be lower ($1 - \mu$ is higher). Hence k will be higher (since $k_I > k_c$) and this will tend to increase v. It follows that v can have the same value at different k's and ψ's. This is really the story of what Professor Robinson (1965) called the Wicksell effect. To get uniqueness one needs the not very persuasive assumption: $k_c > k_I$ always, or some assumption on the elasticities of substitution (Takayama, 1963).

2.2. Stability

The question may be asked whether a sequence of short period equilibria of the economy starting with an arbitrary $k(0)$ at time $t = 0$ lead the economy to steady state equilibrium.

At any moment of time k is given from the past. A short period equilibrium is a division of the capital stock and of the labour between the two sectors such that at the resulting prices all markets clear and profits are maximised. The resulting investment good output will augment the capital stock. At the next moment there will also be more labour so we know the new value of k. So given $k(0)$ it looks as if we could deduce $k(t)$ for all $t > 0$ and so study the convergence to steady state.

But this is only true if momentary equilibrium is unique. If it is not then there will be a variety of paths the system can follow and we do not know which it will be. More seriously in this case we may have, say, there equilibria for some k and only one for another k'. In that case at the point at which we 'lose' equilibria there is a 'catastrophe' (in the technical sense). For this see Inada (1963).

Now consider the proportional savings assumption. It says that consumption and investment are proportional to *aggregate income*, that is, the distribution of income has no effect on the demand for either good. But this is just the case for which non-intersecting community indifference maps exist (see Gorman, 1953) and in that case momentary equilibrium must be unique: it is given by the tangency of the transformation curve between investment and consumption good and the indifference curve. So in this case momentary equilibrium is unique.

But this is not true for the classical saving function where it is clear that demand does depend on the distribution of income so that in general no community indifference maps exist and there may be multiple momentary equilibria. Once again more detailed assumptions concerning elasticities of substitution or

$k_c > k_I$ can rescue the situation. They really amount to the postulate of a certain kind of gross-substitutability (Hahn, 1965).

Once uniqueness of momentary equilibrium is assured it is not hard to show that the sequence of momentary equilibria approach the steady state (see Hahn and Matthews, 1964, for an intuitive account). For instance, for a classical saving postulate, $k(0)$ must be inversely related to $\psi(k(0))$, the wage rental ratio. So if k^* is the steady state capital labour ratio, $\rho(k(0)) < \rho(k^*)$ whenever $k(0) > k^*$. But $\rho[k(0)] = K/K$ while $\rho(k^*) = \lambda$ hence

$$\frac{\dot{k}}{k} = \rho[k(0)] - \rho(k^*) < 0$$

and $k(0)$ in declining at $t = 0$. In fact the reader can check that $[k(t) - k^*]^2$ is always declining with t as long as $k(t) \neq k^*$ which suffices here to establish convergence to the steady state value k^*.

On the other hand, it should be noted that this argument is very much at risk when there is a variety of capital goods (see Hagemann, 1987).

2.3. Technical progress

With two sectors the nature of technological change in the economy as a whole will clearly depend on what kind of progress occurs in each of the sectors and on the composition of output. For instance, if by Harrod neutrality we mean that the capital/output ratio in value terms is constant when the rate of profit is constant we need to know how the capital/output ratio in each of the sectors is changing as well as what is happening to the relative outputs of the two sectors.

The case of disembodied technical progress is fully analysed in Diamond (1965) while there seems to be no literature on two-sector embodied technical progress.

As an example consider steady state with a proportional savings function. The value share of investment in output must remain constant. Technical progress in the investment sector will have to be Harrod-neutral because the rate of profit equality with the marginal product of capital is there independent of relative prices (input and output are the same). So in steady state the marginal product of capital should remain constant. If the capital labour ratio in both sectors remains constant then technical progress in the consumption goods sector must also be Harrod-neutral. Differences in the rate of technical progress in the two sectors will be reflected in a changing price of consumption good in terms of investment good. However, there could be steady state equilibrium with the labour allocation between the two sectors changing. In that case in general technical progress in the consumption good sector will not be Harrod-neutral.

It is not profitable to go into greater detail.

3. Many sectors

As long as one is only concerned with steady state equilibrium there is no difficulty for neoclassical theory when there are many sectors. Although it was somewhat special the foundations for the study of this case were laid by von Neumann (1945). (He assumed labour to be in infinitely elastic supply (in fact producible) at a given vector input of consumption goods. He also considered a 'spectrum' of techniques.) More recent formulations are best studied in Morishima (1964). For a survey see Hahn and Matthews (1964).

The essentials of this case can be illustrated for a classical savings function with only intermediate goods used in production (i.e. no long lived inputs) and no joint production.

Suppose there are N produced goods and one non-produced good (e.g. labour). Production takes time. Let q be the price vector of the N produced goods in terms of the non-produced good. Let all inputs be paid for when purchased and let $c(q)$ be the minimum unit cost function in terms of labour. That is $c(q)$ is the unit cost of production when inputs have been chosen to minimise costs. We can write it in this way because constant returns prevail everywhere. If that were not so there would be no hope of finding a steady state equilibrium.

In such an equilibrium if all goods are produced and relative prices are constant it must be that

$$q = (1 + \rho)c(q). \tag{3.1}$$

If the economy is productive and indecomposable and every good needs labour in its production then one can solve (3.1) uniquely for $q(p) \gg 0$ provided ρ lies in some bounded interval. The function $q(\rho)$ is the *factor-price frontier*.

It is easy to prove that

$$\frac{\partial q_j}{\partial \rho} > 0. \tag{3.2}$$

Provided that the ratio in which wage earners consume goods depends only on q and not on their level of income one can now complete the story. The solution $q(\rho)$ is plainly independent of the scale or composition of output. So one can always make demand equal to supply in each sector provided there is enough labour in the economy. Suppose that labour is inelastically supplied. Then the scale of output can be anything. But if the ratio of employed to unemployed is to remain constant then output must grow at the rate λ hence so must investment and we get $\rho = \lambda$ as a further equilibrium condition. Relative prices will then be given by $q(\lambda)$. In equilibrium the present value of an input's marginal product will equal its price. Moreover ρ can be shown to measure the increase, at constant prices, in consumption made possible tomorrow if there is a little less consumption today and resources saved thereby are allocated efficiently.

An alternative scenario is to suppose that labour can always be had at a constant real wage w^* where the real wage is written as some function of q, say, $w(q)$. Then $w^* = w(q)$ together with (3.1) determine both q^* and ρ^* for steady state equilibrium. Given that there are classical savings the economy will grow at the rate ρ^* which will in fact be the highest (balanced) rate of growth the economy is capable of.

Perhaps a more general insight into these models can be gained as follows. Let Y and X be two n-vectors where the latter is the input of goods at one date and Y the output resulting at the subsequent date. Let L be the labour input. Then

$$T(Y, X, L) \geq 0 \tag{3.3}$$

is the economy's transformation locus which is homogeneous of degree one in its argument. Now a perfectly competitive economy is production efficient. So if all goods are produced in the steady state $(Y^*/L^*, X^*/L^*)$ there must be prices q^* and profit rate p^* such that

$$q^*Y^* - (1 + \rho^*)[q^*X^* + L^*] = 0 \tag{3.4}$$

is a supporting hyperplane of the set of (Y, X, L) satisfying (3.3) at (λ^*, X^*, L^*) Net output is $q^*(Y^* - X^*)$. If there are proportional savings at the rate s then one requires

$$sq^*(Y^* - X^*) = \lambda(q^*X^*) \tag{3.5}$$

if employment is to grow at the rate λ and Y/L and X/L are constant. But that is just the Harrod equation.

Now

$$q^*Y^* - (1 + \rho^*)[q^*X^* + L^*]$$
$$\geq q^*Y - (1 + \rho^*)[q^*X + L] \tag{3.6}$$

for all (Y, X, L) satisfying (3.3). Hence (3.4) is the maximum value of the r.h.s. of (3.6) subject to (3.3). Hence if T is differentiable:

$$q_i^* = \frac{T_{X_i}}{T_L} = -(1 + \rho^*)\frac{T_{Y_i}}{T_L} \tag{3.7}$$

as can be verified by carrying out the maximization. Write (3.3) as

$$T(Y, kX, L) \geq 0 \tag{3.8}$$

take $k = 1$ and differentiate with respect to k at (Y^*, X^*, L^*) to get

$$\left[\sum T_{Y_i}\frac{dY_i}{dk} + \sum T_{X_i}X_i\right]dk = 0. \tag{3.9}$$

Substitute from (3.7) into (3.9) writing

$$\Delta y_i = \frac{dY_i}{dk}dk, \quad \Delta x_i = X_i dk,$$

to obtain

$$\sum q_i^* \Delta y_i = (1 + \rho^*) \sum q_i^* \Delta x_i$$

or

$$\frac{\sum q_i^* \Delta y_i - \sum q_i^* \Delta x_i}{\sum q_i^* \Delta x_i} = \rho^* \qquad (3.10)$$

Hence the equilibrium rate of profit measures the increase in the value of net output at equilibrium prices as a fraction of the increase in the value of inputs at equilibrium prices. Or the rate of substitution between present and future consumption bundles of constant composition, evaluated at q^*. Of course, there is no sense to the claim that (3.10) 'determines' ρ^*.

The literature on growth theory is vast and this essay can usefully be supplemented by other accounts such as Meade (1962), Hahn and Matthews (1964) and Solow (1970).

F.H. HAHN

See also **classical growth model; neoclassical growth theory (new perspective); Ramsey model; two-sector models; von Neumann, John.**

Bibliography

Arrow, K.J. 1962. The economic implications of learning by doing. *Review of Economic Studies* 28(3), 155–73.

Bliss, C.J. 1968. On putty-clay. *Review of Economic Studies* 35(2), 105–32.

Diamond, P. 1965. Disembodied technical change in a two-sector model. *Review of Economic Studies* 32(2), 161–8.

Fellner, W. 1961. Two propositions in the theory of induced innovations. *Economic Journal* 71, 305–8.

Gorman, W.M. 1953. Community preference fields. *Econometrica* 21(1), 63–80.

Hagemann, H. 1987. Capital goods. In *The New Palgrave: A Dictionary of Economics*, vol. 1, ed. J. Eatwell, M. Milgate and P. Newman. London: Macmillan.

Hahn, F.H. 1951. The share of wages in national income. *Oxford Economic Papers* 3(2), 149–57.

Hahn, F.H. 1965. On two sector growth models. *Review of Economic Studies* 32(4), 339–46.

Hahn, F.H. 1987. 'Hahn problem'. In The *New Palgrave: A Dictionary of Economics*, vol. 2, ed. J. Eatwell, M. Milgate and P. Newman. London: Macmillan.

Hahn, F.H. and Matthews, R.C.O. 1964. The theory of economic growth: a survey. *Economic Journal* 74, 779–902. Reprinted in *Surveys of Economic Theory*, vol. 2. London: Macmillan 1965.

Harcourt, G.C. 1969. Some Cambridge controversies in the theory of capital. *Journal of Economic Literature* 7(2), 369–405.

Harrod, R.F. 1939. An essay in dynamic theory. *Economic Journal* 49, 14–33.

Inada, K. 1963. On a two-sector model of economic growth: comments and a generalisation. *Review of Economic Studies* 30, 119–27.

Inada, K. 1964. On the stability of growth equilibrium in two-sector models. *Review of Economic Studies* 31(2), 127–42.

Kaldor, N. 1955. Alternative theories of distribution. *Economic Journal* 23(2), 83–100.

Kaldor, N. and Mirrlees, J. 1962. A new model of economic growth. *Review of Economic Studies* 29(3), 174–92.

Kennedy, C. 1964. Induced bias in innovation and the theory of distribution. *Economic Journal* 74, 841–7.

Lucas, R. 1975. An equilibrium model of the trade cycle. *Journal of Political Economy* 83, 1113–44.

Meade, J.E. 1962. *A Neoclassical Theory of Economic Growth*. London: Allen & Unwin.

Meade, J.E. 1966. The outcome of the Pasinetti process: a note. *Economic Journal* 76, 161–5.

Meade, J.E. and Hahn, F.H. 1965. The rate of profit in a growing economy. *Economic Journal* 75, 445–48.

Mirrlees, J.A. 1969. The dynamic non-substitution theorem. *Review of Economic Studies* 36(1), 67–76.

Modigliani, F. and Samuelson, P.A. 1966. The Pasinetti Paradox in neo-classical and more general models. *Review of Economic Studies* 33, 269–301.

Morishima, M. 1964. *Equilibrium, Stability and Growth*. Oxford: Clarendon Press.

Neumann, J. von. 1945. A model of general economic equilibrium. *Review of Economic Studies* 13, 1–9.

Pasinetti, L.L. 1962. Rate of profit and income distribution in relation to the rate of economic growth. *Review of Economic Studies* 29(4), 267–79.

Robinson, J.V. 1938. The classification of inventions. *Review of Economic Studies* 5(2), 139–42.

Robinson, J.V. 1965. *The Accumulation of Capital*. 2nd edn. London: Macmillan.

Samuelson, P.A. 1957. Wages and interest: a modern dissection of Marxian economic models. *American Economic Review* 47, 884–912.

Samuelson, P.A. 1958. An exact consumption-loan model of interest with or without the social contrivance of money. *Journal of Political Economy* 66, 467–82.

Samuelson, P.A. 1965. A theory of induced innovations along Kennedy–Weizsacker lines. *Review of Economics and Statistics* 47, 343–56.

Schumpeter, J.A. 1934. *The Theory of Economic Development*. Cambridge, MA: Harvard University Press.

Solow, R.M. 1956. A contribution to the theory of economic growth. *Quarterly Journal of Economics* 70(1), 65–94.

Solow, R.M. 1962. Comment (on Uzawa 1961). *Review of Economic Studies* 29(3), 255–7.

Solow, R.M. 1970. *Growth Theory: An Exposition*. Oxford: Clarendon Press.

Solow, R.M., Tobin, J., Weizsacker, C.C. von. and Yaari, M. 1967. Neo-classical growth with fixed proportions. *Review of Economic Studies* 33(2), 79–115.

Takayama, A. 1963. On a two-sector model of economic growth: a comparative statics analysis. *Review of Economic Studies* 36, 95–104.

Uzawa, H. 1961. On a two-sector model of economic growth. *Review of Economic Studies* 29(1), 40–47.

Varian, H. 1978. *Micro-economic Analysis*. New York: W.W. Norton.

neoclassical growth theory (new perspectives)

This article complements NEOCLASSICAL GROWTH THEORY. It discusses some developments of the neoclassical growth theory that endogenize the saving rates.

Infinite horizons

The planning problem

The standard neoclassical growth model assumes that the planning horizon is infinite. One justification is that forward-looking parents act 'as if' they were to live forever. To see this, assume that each individual lives for one period and has exactly one descendant. The utility of a member of generation 0 is given by

$$U_0 = u(c_0) + \beta U_1, \qquad (1)$$

where u is an increasing, continuous and concave function of consumption at time t, c_t. Iterating on this expression yields

$$U_0 = \sum_{t=0}^{\infty} \beta^t u(c_t), \qquad \beta = \frac{1}{1+\rho}, \rho > 0, \qquad (2)$$

which shows that altruism implies that the effective planning horizon for each individual is infinite.

In the simplest one-sector version of the model, the technology is summarized by

$$c_t + x_t \le zf(k_t), \qquad t = 0, 1, \ldots \qquad (3a)$$

$$k_{t+1} \le (1 - \delta_k)k_t + x_t, \qquad t = 0, 1, \ldots \qquad (3b)$$

$$k_0 > 0, \qquad given, \qquad (3c)$$

where k_t is the stock of capital per person available at the beginning of period t, x_t is gross investment, z is a measure of productivity, and δ_k is the depreciation rate of capital. The function f is assumed to be increasing, continuous and strictly concave.

The planning problem corresponds to the maximization of the utility criterion (2), subject to the feasibility constraints (3). The analysis of this problem was initially carried out by Ramsey (1928), Cass (1965) and Koopmans (1965). A thorough analysis of the model can be found in Stokey and Lucas (1989).

The model has sharp predictions for the properties of an optimal development path. The relevant first-order conditions (in the interior case) require that the marginal rate of substitution between consumption at time t and $t+1$ equal the marginal rate of transformation,

$$\frac{u(c_t)}{\beta u(c_{t+1})} = 1 - \delta_k + zf'(k_{t+1}), \qquad t = 0, 1, \ldots, \qquad (4)$$

and a transversality condition which is naturally interpreted as requiring that the value, at time 0, of the stock of capital at time $T+1$ converge to 0 as $T \to \infty$. Formally, the condition is

$$\lim_{T \to \infty} \beta^T u'(c_T)k_{T+1} = 0.$$

Some properties of the solution are as follows:

1. There exists a unique steady state; that is, there are constant sequences of consumption, investment and capital that satisfy (3) (except at time 0) and (4). From (4) it follows that, in the steady state, the marginal product of capital equals the sum of the discount rate, ρ, and the depreciation factor, δ_k,

$$\rho + \delta_k = zf'(k^*), \qquad (5)$$

which determines capital per worker. The steady state level of consumption is given by

$$c^* = zf(k^*) - \delta_k k^*. \qquad (6)$$

2. For any $k_0 > 0$, the solution to the problem converges to the steady state. Convergence is monotone.

3. In general, the savings rate – defined as $1 - c_t/zf(k_t)$ – is not constant, or even monotone. This distinguishes the optimal neoclassical growth model from the Solow–Swan version that assumes exogenous (and generally constant) saving rates.

The steady state is the model's prediction about the long-run levels of capital, consumption and investment. From the point of view of a theory of growth there are some interesting results:

1. The steady state level of output per worker is independent of the form of the utility function.

2. If a fixed level of government consumption, g, is introduced in the model, the steady state condition (5) remains unchanged. The new steady state level of consumption is $c^* = zf(k^*) - \delta_k k^* - g$. Thus the model predicts that, in the long run, permanent increases in government spending have no impact on output per worker, and they crowd out private consumption one for one, with no effect on investment.

The basic model has been extended in many dimensions. In the case of multiple sectors, existence of optimal paths has been established very generally. Burmeister (1980) provides conditions for the existence and uniqueness of steady states with many capital goods.

The properties of optimal paths depend on the specification of the economic environment. In the case of a discounted twice differentiable utility and dominance diagonal of a matrix of first-order conditions, it is possible to show that the turnpike property holds (see the excellent survey in McKenzie, 1986). Formally, McKenzie shows that if $\{k_t\}$ is an optimal path starting from k_0, then, for every capital stock k_0' near k_0 the associated unique optimal path converges exponentially to $\{k_t\}$.

The monotonicity properties of optimal paths do not extend to the multicapital or multisector case. In general, optimal paths can display cycles (see Burmeister, 1980) and even more complex behaviour.

To illustrate this let the feasible technology set be described as

$$c_t \leq T(k_t, k_{t+1}),$$

and let the (indirect) utility function over capital stocks be

$$v(k_t, k_{t+1}) \equiv u(T(k_t, k_{t+1})).$$

With this notation, the planning problem reduces to

$$\max_{\{k_{t+1}\}} \sum_{t=0}^{\infty} \beta^t v(k_t, k_{t+1}).$$

Let's denote a candidate solution by a function g where

$$k_{t+1} = g(k_t).$$

Boldrin and Montrucchio (1986) showed that – under standard conditions – given any twice differentiable function g, there exists a pair (v, β) so that the associated planner's problem has g as its optimal policy function. Since g can exhibit arbitrary complex dynamics, the result shows that in order to endow the theory with predictive power it is necessary to 'force' the chosen specification to quantitatively match moments of the (actual) economy under study. Most recent research using the neoclassical growth model disciplines the choices of functional forms and parameters by requiring that they predict behaviour consistent with the empirical evidence.

Equilibrium growth
Even though the analysis of the growth model was motivated by normative considerations, under the stated assumptions the planner's solution of the growth model coincides with the competitive equilibrium of the economy. The argument – using the traditional definition of a competitive equilibrium – follows from Debreu (1954). In macro applications – the field in which the model has proved to be most useful – it is more natural to define a competitive equilibrium using the notion of recursive equilibrium first introduced by Prescott and Mehra (1980).

In order to account for wages, let the production function be given by

$$y \leq zF(k, n),$$

where F is concave and homogeneous of degree one, and it satisfies

$$f(k) \equiv F(k, 1).$$

Even though there are many alternative ways of defining an equilibrium, it is easiest to consider the case in which there are rental spot markets for capital and labour, and the households trade consumption, labour and capital services and one-period bonds. The problem solved by the representative household is

$$\max \sum_{t=0}^{\infty} \beta^t u(c_t)$$

subject to

$$b_{t+1} + c_t + x_t \leq w_t n_t + q_t k_t + (1 + r_t)b_t, t = 0, 1, \ldots$$
$$k_{t+1} \leq (1 - \delta_k)k_t + x_t, t = 0, 1, \ldots$$
$$0 \leq n_t \leq 1, t = 0, 1, \ldots$$

and the initial conditions, $[(1+r_0)b_0, k_0]$, given. As stated, this problem has no solution since the budget set is unbounded. Different alternative assumptions on how to deal with debt at infinity have been used to guarantee that the problem is well defined. The most general specification is to rule out Ponzi games by imposing that the present value of debt be nonnegative. Formally, any solution must satisfy

$$\lim_{T \to \infty} \prod_{j=0}^{T} \frac{1}{1 + r_j} b_{T+1} \geq 0.$$

which is the analogue – in the market setting – of the transversality condition in the planning problem.

Firms solve a static problem

$$\max_{k_t, n_t} zF(k_t, n_t) - q_t k_t - w_t n_t.$$

A competitive equilibrium is an allocation $[\{c_t\}, \{n_t\}, \{x_t\}, \{k_{t+1}\}]_{t=0}^{\infty}$, a price system $[\{q_t\}\{w_t\}, \{r_{t+1}\}]_{t=0}^{\infty}$ and a sequence of bond holdings $\{b_{t+1}\}_{t=0}^{\infty}$, such that:

1. Given the price system, the allocation solves the maximization problems of households and firms.
2. Markets clear.

Given that Debreu (1954) shows that the solution to the planner's problem can be decentralized as a competitive equilibrium, the first-order conditions (on the assumption of interiority and differentiability) corresponding to the maximization of utility and profits imply that equilibrium prices (as a function of the planner's allocation) are given by

$$q_t = zf'(k_t), \tag{7a}$$

$$w_t = zf(k_t) - k_t zf'(k_t), \tag{7b}$$

$$r_{t+1} = q_{t+1} - \delta_k. \tag{7c}$$

It is possible to state the implications of the neoclassical growth model more intuitively using equilibrium prices. The consumer's optimal choice between consumption and saving requires that

$$\frac{u(c_t)}{\beta u(c_{t+1})} = 1 + r_{t+1},$$

that is, that the marginal rate of substitution between present and future consumption equal to (gross) interest rate. Optimality on the part of firms requires that the marginal product of labour be equal to the wage rate and that the marginal product of capital equal the cost of capital, $r_t + \delta_k$.

The basic neoclassical growth model (and some of the extensions mentioned) has had a significant impact on how economists view the process of development and the role of markets supporting optimal development paths. It is clear that there is nothing special about dynamic problems that make it more (or less) likely for competitive markets to fail to deliver optimal allocations. In the basic model of this note, Theorems I and II of welfare economics apply.

Applications

Some of the most notable extensions are as follows.

Technology shocks

Brock and Mirman (1972) studied a version of the neoclassical growth model in which the representative agent maximizes the expected value of the discounted flow of utility, and the technology is as in the deterministic growth model except that the technology level, z, is replaced by a stochastic process $\{z_t\}$. Brock and Mirman assumed that the process $\{z_t\}$ is i.i.d. They established the existence of a solution and they showed that, under standard concavity assumptions, the resulting stochastic process of the capital stock has a unique invariant measure, which is the stochastic analogue of the steady state in the deterministic version of the problem. They also showed that the optimal policy function which determines k_{t+1} as a function of k_t and z_t is monotone. The results were extended to the case of serially correlated shocks by Donaldson and Mehra (1983).

This research has provided the theoretical foundations for a large literature that analyses the impact of economic fluctuations on savings and growth. When the model is extended to include an elastic labour supply, this is a natural setting in which to study cyclical movements of employment. For an introduction to this literature see Cooley (1995).

Human capital and development

The neoclassical growth model, extended to allow for human capital accumulation, is a natural candidate to understand the role that technological differences play in accounting for differences in output per worker. In the standard specification – using a Cobb–Douglas specification for f – it follows that output per worker is given by

$$y = z^{1/(1-\alpha)} \bar{y}_0$$

where α corresponds to capital share, and $\bar{y}_0$ (and all the $\bar{y}_j$ in this section) is a constant. This version of the theory implies that the elasticity of output per worker with respect to z is $1/(1-\alpha)$. Since accepted estimates of α cluster around 0.33 – which, approximately, correspond to the share of national income that accrues to capital – the elasticity is estimated to be approximately 1.5. If this model is to explain the differences in output per worker between the richest and poorest countries (which are of the order of 15–20 to 1), it must assume fairly large differences in productivity that exceed the best available estimates.

Klenow and Rodríguez-Claire (1997) (see also, Bils and Klenow, 2000) consider a production function of the form

$$y = zk^\alpha (h^e)^{1-\alpha},$$

and they use the specification $h^e = e^{\psi s}$, where s corresponds to years of schooling to estimate the role of human capital. In this case, the equilibrium level of output per worker is given by

$$y = z^{1/(1-\alpha)} e^{\psi s} \bar{y}_1$$

Klenow and Rodríguez-Claire use data to determine s and ψ. To highlight the role of productivity differences, let $e^{\psi s} = z^v$. Output per worker is

$$y = z^{1/(1-\alpha)+v} \bar{y}_1.$$

Klenow and Rodríguez-Claire find that the implied v is not large. They conclude that productivity differences account for much of the differences in output.

Manuelli and Seshadri (2007a) endogenize the human capital decision. They adopt Ben Porath's (1967) specification. In discrete time, their model assumes that human capital evolves according to

$$h_{t+1} = z_h (n_t h_t)^{\gamma_1} x_{ht}^{\gamma_2} + (1 - \delta_h) h_t,$$

where $n_t h_t$ is the fraction of the available time allocated to producing human capital, and x_{ht} denotes market goods used in the production of human capital. In this setting, $h^e = (1-n)h$. It is possible to show that, in the steady state, output per worker is given by

$$y = z^{\gamma_2/[(1-\alpha)(1-\gamma_1-\gamma_2)]}\bar{y}_2.$$

This version of the model implies that the elasticity of output with respect to the productivity parameter z is $\gamma_2/[(1-\alpha)(1-\gamma_1-\gamma_2)]$. Manuelli and Seshadri use life age–earnings profile evidence to estimate that $\gamma_1 = 0.63$ and $\gamma_2 = 0.30$. This results in an elasticity of output per worker with respect to productivity of 6.5. This high elasticity implies that productivity differences have a large impact on (endogenously chosen) human capital. As a result, even small productivity differences are consistent with large variations in output per worker. The relative importance of human capital and productivity is an active area of research. More work is needed before the roles of technology and education in accounting for differences in output can be accurately estimated.

The role of taxation

The neoclassical growth model has been widely used to analyse the effect of specific tax policies and to derive properties of optimal tax systems.

Consider a version of the model in which labour is elastically supplied. Let the period utility function be given by $u(c, \ell)$, where ℓ is interpreted as leisure. In an economy in which consumption, capital income and labour income are taxed (at constant rates) it follows that the steady state is characterized by

$$\rho = (1 - \tau^k)(F_k(k, n) - \delta_k) \tag{8a}$$

$$u_\ell(c, 1 - n) = u_c(c, 1 - n)F_n(k, n)\frac{1 - \tau^n}{1 + \tau^c} \tag{8b}$$

$$F(k, n) = c + \delta_k k \tag{8c}$$

$$\rho = (1 - \tau^b)r^b. \tag{8d}$$

From a formal point of view the system of eqs (8) contains four equations in four unknowns. Let $\Phi(c, \ell) = u_\ell(c, 1 - n)/u_c(c, 1 - n)$, and assume that $\Phi(c, \ell)$ is increasing in c and decreasing in ℓ. In this case, it is possible to show that:

1. An increase in the tax rate of capital income, τ^k, decreases the amount of capital, but has ambiguous effects on employment.
2. An increase in tax rate on labour income (consumption) decreases both k and n.

The effect of taxes on employment and growth is a subject that continues to receive substantial attention.

In the mid-1980s Chamley (1986) and Judd (1985) asked the following question: If a government has to finance a given (say, constant) stream of consumption, and if the only available taxes are distortionary taxes (for example, in the previous example, set $\tau^c = 0$ and add

government spending to (8c)), how should those taxes be chosen? Chamley and Judd showed that the optimal tax system is such that, in the steady state, capital income taxes are zero while labour income taxes are positive.

This result is delicate in the sense that it does not hold if some of the assumptions are slightly modified. For example, if the function F is strictly concave, and pure profits cannot be taxed away, then the optimal long-run tax rate on capital income need not be zero. Similarly, if there are different types of labour (for example, high and low skill) and it is possible for the planner to distinguish between them, then the zero taxation result is overturned. For other examples see Correia (1996) and Jones, Manuelli and Rossi (1997).

Money and growth

Since the neoclassical growth model satisfies the assumptions of the convex economy studied by Debreu (1959), it is impossible to find an equilibrium in which a non-interest earning asset (for example, money) has positive value in equilibrium. In order to introduce money, the neoclassical growth model has been modified in a variety of ways. One of the first attempts corresponds to Sidrauski's (1967) analysis of a monetary model. Sidrauski studied the case in which money enters the utility function, as a reduced form that captures the services provided by money balances.

In Sidrauski's formulation (adapted to discrete time), the consumer problem is

$$\max \sum_{t=0}^{\infty} \beta^t u(c_t, m_{t+1}/p_t)$$

subject to

$$c_t + \frac{m_{t+1}}{p_t} + x_t + \frac{B_{t+1}}{p_t} \leq w_t + q_t k_t$$
$$+ \frac{m_t}{p_t} + \frac{(1 + i_t)B_t}{p_t} + \frac{M_{t+1} - M_t}{p},$$

where m_t is nominal money balances chosen by the household, M_t is the economy-wide per capita money supply (that the individual takes as given), p_t is the price level, B_t is the nominal value of one period bonds purchased at time $t-1$, and $(1+i_t)$ is the gross nominal interest rate. The specification of the budget constraint reflects the assumption that the government exogenously increases the stock of money through lump-sum transfers.

The first order conditions for this problem are (imposing the standard equilibrium conditions)

$$u_1(c_t, m_{t+1}/p_t) = \lambda_t, \tag{9a}$$

$$u_2(c_t, m_{t+1}/p_t) = \lambda_t \frac{i_{t+1}}{1 + i_{t+1}}, \tag{9b}$$

$$\lambda_t = \beta\lambda_t[1 - \delta_k + zf'(k_{t+1})], \tag{9c}$$

and feasibility. In this version of the model, money is superneutral in the steady state. In the steady state eq. (9c) reduces to eq. (5a) and, hence, the rate of money growth has no impact on the long-run level of output. This result is not robust. If labour is supplied elastically, inflation has (in general) real effects through its impact on the marginal rate of substitution between real money balances and leisure. The one case in which money is still neutral is when the utility function is separable in real money balances (see Fischer, 1979).

In an economy in which nominal money balances grow at the (gross) rate $1+\pi$, the nominal interest rate is given by

$$1 + i = (1 + \rho)(1 + \pi),$$

and satisfies the Fisher equation. Friedman (1969) argued that since money is costless to produce, its optimal level should be such that individuals are satiated. This corresponds to $u_2(c_t, m_{t+1}/p_t) = 0$. Inspection of eq. (9b) shows that the optimal quantity of money requires that the nominal interest rate be 0. This can be implemented by engineering a deflation (that is, setting $1 + \pi = (1+\rho)^{-1}$) or by keeping the price level constant and paying interest on money holdings.

In general, in the non-separable case, the Friedman rule needs to be modified (see Turnovsky and Brock, 1980).

Fertility and growth

The neoclassical growth model can be easily extended to the case of exogenous population growth and exogenous technical change. It has also been used to understand the interplay between economic forces and fertility decisions (see Barro and Becker, 1989; Becker and Barro, 1988).

To illustrate the relationship between growth and fertility, assume that individuals live for just one period and that each agent gives birth to η offspring. The utility function of a member of generation t is given by

$$U_t = u(c_t) + \beta \eta_t^{(1-\phi)} U_{t+1}, \qquad 0 \le \phi \le 1,$$

where η_t is the number of children. When $\phi > 0$, these preferences display imperfect altruism as increases in the number of children result in lower marginal contribution of the last child to utility.

It is assumed that each child costs v units of labour, and the per capita labour endowment is normalized to 1. The planner's problem for this economy can be expressed as

$$\max \sum_{t=0}^{\infty} \beta^t N_t u(c_t),$$

subject to

$$c_t + \eta_t(a + k_{t+1}) \le zF(k_t, 1 - \eta_t v) + (1 - \delta_k)k_t,$$
$$k_0 > 0, \qquad N_{t+1} \le N_t \eta_t^{(1-\phi)}, \qquad N_0 = 1$$

Thus, from a formal point of view, endogenous fertility plays the role of another good, N_t, which is 'produced' with a linear technology with current fertility as its only input. This is a special case of a two-sector model. Barro and Becker showed that if the utility function is of the form $u(c) = c^\sigma$ – a standard specification – the model can have multiple steady states, with some stable and some unstable.

The model has been used to study the effect of changes in child mortality on fertility (see Doepke, 2005), the impact of introducing social security (see Boldrin and Jones, 2005), and the relationship between fertility, growth and human capital (see Manuelli and Seshadri, 2007b). In general, the ability of the model to match the evidence depends on the specific parameterization used, and finding the appropriate specification is an active area of research.

Finite lifetimes

What are the properties of the neoclassical growth model if economic agents have short – relative to the economy – horizons? The simplest case is study an economy in which individuals live for two periods, and have preferences defined over first- and second-period consumption. This model was originally analysed by Diamond (1965), and an excellent textbook treatment can be found in Azariadis (1993).

Each agent inelastically offers one unit of labour in his first period, and $e \le 1$ units in his second period. The representative agent problem is

$$\max U(c_t^t, c_{t+1}^t)$$

subject to

$$c_t^t + (1 + r_{t+1})^{-1} c_{t+1}^t \le w_t + (1 + r_{t+1})^{-1} w_{t+1} e,$$

where c_t^j denotes consumption at time t of an individual born in period j, and w_t is the wage rate. Feasible allocations satisfy

$$c_t^t + c_t^{t-1} + x_t \le zF(k_t, 1 + e),$$
$$k_{t+1} \le (1 - \delta_k)k_t + x_t, \quad t = 0, 1, \dots.$$

where, as before, we assume that F is homogeneous of degree 1.

Since the solution to an individual optimization problem is completely summarized (in the two period setting) by its saving function, let

$$s_t = s(w_t, w_{t+1}, r_{t+1}) \qquad (10)$$

denote saving by a member of generation t. Firms, as in the case of infinite horizons, are assumed to solve static problems. Equilibrium input prices, satisfy the appropriate version of (7).

An equilibrium in this economy consists of sequences of capital stocks and prices such that individuals and firms optimize and markets clear. A simple (and intuitive) condition that characterizes all the equilibria is the requirement that saving by the young at time t equal the capital stock at the beginning of period $t+1$. Formally, this corresponds to

$$k_{t+1} = s(\bar{w}(k_t), \bar{w}(k_{t+1}), \bar{r}(k_{t+1})), \qquad (11)$$

where,

$$\bar{w}(k) \equiv zF_2(k, 1+e),$$
$$\bar{r}(k) = zF_1(k, 1+e) - \delta_k.$$

For a given k_0, any sequence that satisfies (11) and that does not violate other feasibility conditions (for example, $k_t \geq 0$) is an equilibrium sequence of capital stocks. The other components of an equilibrium (for example, consumption and prices) can be readily obtained from the household and firm optimization problems.

Even though this set-up (with only one type of consumer) appears very close to the infinite horizon model, its implications are quite different. An (incomplete) list of the most interesting properties includes the following:

1. Even if $e = 0$ (young individuals are net savers), and if both consumption goods are normal, the equilibrium need not be unique. A sufficient condition for uniqueness is that the two goods be gross substitutes. This corresponds to the saving function being an increasing function of the interest rate.
2. If $e = 0$ and saving is increasing in the interest rate, eq. (11) can be solved for k_{t+1}. Let the solution be denoted $k_{t+1} = G(k_t)$. Then, if $G'(0) > 1$, then this map can have and odd number $(2j + 1)$ of nontrivial steady states, of which $j + 1$ are asymptotically stable and j are unstable. If $G'(0) < 1$ there may be an even number of nontrivial steady states.
3. If $e = 0$ and saving is not increasing in the interest rate, eq. (11) can be solved for k_{t+1} only locally. The major impact of this is that stable steady states need not be separated by unstable steady states.
4. Equilibrium paths of capital may display cycles and, depending on the specification, chaotic dynamics.
5. Equilibria – even stationary equilibria – need not be optimal.

This last result shows that when the individual horizon differs from the economy's horizon, then optimal saving at the individual level need not imply optimality in the aggregate, even in the absence of the standard arguments (for example, externalities) for market failure.

To illustrate what can go wrong, consider an economy in which U is strictly quasi-concave and that, in a stationary equilibrium, the stock of capital is such that $\bar{r}(\bar{k}) = zF_1(\bar{k}, 1) - \delta_k < 0$. Let the levels of consumption in young and old age be denoted $(\bar{c}_1, \bar{c}_2)$. The key condition is that the gross interest rate be less that the gross rate of population growth, which is assumed to be 1 in this example. Consider next the problem of maximizing the utility of a given generation subject to the constraint

that allocations be constant and the stock of capital also remains constant. Let k^* be the solution to

$$\max U(c_1, c_2)$$

subject to

$$c_1 + c_2 \leq zF(k, 1) - \delta_k k.$$

Let the solution of this problem be (c_1^*, c_2^*, k^*). Given that k^* is such that $zF_1(k^*, 1) - \delta_k = 0$, it follows that $k^* < \bar{k}$. Since $(\bar{c}_1, \bar{c}_2, \bar{k})$ is feasible, it must be the case that $U(c_1^*, c_2^*) > U(\bar{c}_1, \bar{c}_2)$. Thus all generations, starting with generation 1, are better off under this alternative allocation. What about the initial old? Since they only care about consumption they are also better off as fewer resources are allocated to investment.

To summarize, when individual horizons are shorter than the economy's horizon, even the simplest specification of the neoclassical growth model can result in very complicated equilibrium paths.

Concluding comments

For many years, the neoclassical growth model has been the workhorse of researchers interested in fluctuations and growth. The model is not without weaknesses. Perhaps the most important is its inability to explain long-run growth: in the steady state the growth rate is exogenous. Endogenous growth models – versions of which are very close to the neoclassical growth model – can be used to understand the effects of policies and shocks on long-run growth. Currently, there are isolated attempts to integrate both views. This has been done for versions of the models that assume convex technologies. For example, endogenous growth models have been used to eliminate the need for arbitrary detrending in the study of business fluctuations (see, for example, Jones, Manuelli and Siu, 2005). The versions of the models that have been studied so far are, of necessity, the simplest ones. It is too early to tell whether the integration of the two strands will succeed.

A large literature on endogenous growth departs from the assumption of convex technologies and no external effects. This body of research views innovation as a form of public good, and emphasizes the role of institutions (for example, how property rights are protected) in determining growth. Since these assumptions amount to departures from the convexity assumptions of the neoclassical model, competitive equilibria are no longer optimal, and this alternative view suggests that a variety of interventions are needed to attain optimality. Thus, the major difference relies on the presence (or absence) of departures from the assumption that technologies form a convex cone.

If the neoclassical growth model is narrowly interpreted (as in this article) as assuming that government policies are exogenous (and markets are competitive), then it follows that the fundamental cause of cross-country differences in output are differences in policies. More recently, the analysis of the determinants of development has emphasized the role of (endogenous) institutions and geography. Endogenizing the institutional structure seems like a natural next step in the development of the theory. However, serious theoretical limitations of our understanding of social choice theory in dynamic settings has limited progress so far. The direct role of geography is easily incorporated into the framework. However, to the extent that the geographic dimension is viewed as influencing (or determining) institutions and or policies, the same limitations apply.

In summary, the neoclassical growth model is still the basic framework to study questions that require understanding differences across countries, regions or individuals, in the *level* of some economic variable. The main challenge for future research is to develop a theory of social choices (policy choices) that is consistent with the dynamic framework.

RODOLFO E. MANUELLI

See also **neoclassical growth theory.**

Bibliography

Azariadis, C. 1993. *Intertemporal Macroeconomics.* Cambridge: Blackwell Publishers.

Barro, R.J. and Becker, G.S. 1989. Fertility choice in a model of economic growth. *Econometrica* 57, 481–501.

Becker, G.S. and Barro, R.J. 1988. A reformulation of the economic theory of fertility. *Quarterly Journal of Economics* 103, 1–25.

Ben Porath, Y. 1967. The production of human capital and the life cycle of earnings. *Journal of Political Economy* 75, 352–65.

Bils, M. and Klenow, P. 2000. Does schooling cause growth? *American Economic Review* 90, 1160–83.

Boldrin, M. and Jones, L.E. 2005. Fertility and social security. Staff Report No. 359, Federal Reserve Bank of Minneapolis.

Boldrin, M. and Montrucchio, L. 1986. On the indeterminacy of capital accumulation paths. *Journal of Economic Theory* 40, 26–39.

Brock, W.A. and Mirman, L.J. 1972. Optimal economic growth and uncertainty. *Journal of Economic Theory* 4, 479–513.

Burmeister, E. 1980. *Capital Theory and Dynamics.* Cambridge: Cambridge University Press.

Cass, D. 1965. Optimum growth in an aggregative model of capital accumulation. *Review of Economic Studies* 32, 233–40.

Chamley, C. 1986. Optimal taxation of capital income in general equilibrium with infinite lifetimes. *Econometrica* 54, 607–22.

Cooley, T.F. 1995. *Frontiers of Business Cycle Research.* Princeton: Princeton University Press.

Correia, I. 1996. Should capital be taxed in the steady state? *Journal of Public Economics* 60, 147–51.

Debreu, G. 1954. Valuation equilibrium and Pareto optimum. *Proceedings of the National Academy of Sciences* 40, 588–92.

Debreu, G. 1959. *The Theory of Value.* New Haven and London: Yale University Press.

Diamond, P.A. 1965. National debt in a neoclassical growth model. *American Economic Review* 55, 1126–50.

Doepke, M. 2005. Child mortality and fertility decline: does the Barro–Becker model fit the facts? *Journal of Population Economics* 18, 337–66.

Donaldson, J.B. and Mehra, R. 1983. Stochastic growth with correlated production shocks. *Journal of Economic Theory* 29, 282–312.

Fischer, S. 1979. Capital accumulation on the transition path in a monetary optimizing model. *Econometrica* 47, 1433–39.

Friedman, M. 1969. The optimum supply of money. In *The Optimum Supply of Money and Other Essays*, ed. M. Friedman. Chicago: Aldine.

Jones, L.E., Manuelli, R.E. and Rossi, P.E. 1997. On the optimal taxation of capital income. *Journal of Economic Theory* 73, 93–117.

Jones, L.E., Manuelli, R.E. and Siu, H. 2005. Fluctuations in convex models of endogenous growth II: business cycle properties. *Review of Economic Dynamics* 8, 805–28.

Judd, K.J. 1985. Redistributive taxation in a perfect foresight model. *Journal of Public Economics* 28, 59–84.

Klenow, P. and Rodríguez-Clare, A. 1997. The neoclassical revival in growth economics: has it gone too far? In *Macroeconomics Annual 1997*, ed. B. Bernanke and J. Rotenberg. Cambridge, MA: MIT Press.

Koopmans, T.J. 1965. On the concept of optimal economic growth. In *The Econometric Approach to Development Planning*, Chicago: Rand McNally.

Manuelli, R.E. and Seshadri, A. 2007a. Human capital and the wealth of nations. Working paper, University of Wisconsin.

Manuelli, R.E. and Seshadri, A. 2007b. Explaining international fertility differences. Working paper, University of Wisconsin.

McKenzie, L.W. 1986. Optimal economic growth, Turnpike theorems and comparative dynamics. In *Handbook of Mathematical Economics*, vol. 3, ed. K.J. Arrow and M.D. Intriligator. Amsterdam: North-Holland.

Prescott, E.J. and Mehra, R. 1980. Recursive competitive equilibrium: the case of homogeneous households. *Econometrica* 48, 1365–79.

Ramsey, F.P. 1928. A mathematical theory of saving. *Economic Journal* 28, 543–59.

Sidrauski, M. 1967. Inflation and economic growth. *Journal of Political Economy* 75, 796–810.

Stokey, N.L. and Lucas, R.E. (with E.C. Prescott). 1989. *Recursive Methods in Economic Dynamics*. Cambridge, MA: Harvard University Press.

Turnovsky, S.J. and Brock, W.A. 1980. Time consistency and optimal government policies in perfect Foresight equilibrium. *Journal of Public Economics* 13, 183–212.

neoclassical synthesis

The term 'neoclassical synthesis' appears to have been coined by Paul Samuelson to denote the consensus view of macroeconomics which emerged in the mid-1950s in the United States. In the third edition of *Economics* (1955, p. 212), he wrote:

> In recent years 90 per cent of American Economists have stopped being 'Keynesian economists' or 'anti-Keynesian economists'. Instead they have worked toward a synthesis of whatever is valuable in older economics and in modern theories of income determination. The result might be called neo-classical economics and is accepted in its broad outlines by all but about 5 per cent of extreme left wing and right wing writers.

Unlike the old neoclassical economics, the new synthesis did not expect full employment to occur under laissez-faire; it believed, however, that, by proper use of monetary and fiscal policy, the old classical truths would come back into relevance.

This synthesis was to remain the dominant paradigm for another 20 years, in which most of the important contributions, by Hicks, Modigliani, Solow, Tobin and others, were to fit quite naturally. Its apotheosis was probably the large econometric models, in particular the MPS model developed by Modigliani and his collaborators, which incorporated most of these contributions in an empirically based and mathematically coherent model of the US economy. The synthesis had, however, suffered from the start from schizophrenia in its relation to microeconomics. This schizophrenia was eventually to lead to a serious crisis from which it is only now re-emerging. I describe in turn the initial synthesis, the mature synthesis, the crisis and the new emerging synthesis.

The initial synthesis

The post-war consensus was a consensus about two main beliefs. The first was that the decisions of firms and of individuals were largely rational, and as such amenable to study using standard methods from microeconomics. Modigliani, in the introduction to his collected papers, stated it strongly:

> [One of the] basic themes that has dominated my scientific concern [has been to integrate] the main building blocks of the General Theory with the more established methodology of economics, which rests on the basic postulate of rational maximizing behavior on the part of economic agents...' (1980, p. xi)

The faith in rationality was far from blind: animal spirits were perceived as the main source of movements in aggregate demand through investment. For example, the possibility that corporate saving was too high and not offset by personal saving was considered a serious issue, and discussed on empirical rather than theoretical grounds.

This faith in rationality did not, however, extend to a belief in the efficient functioning of markets. The second main belief was indeed that prices and wages did not adjust very quickly to clear markets. There was broad agreement that markets could not be seen as competitive. But, somewhat surprisingly given the popularity of imperfect competition theories at the time, there was no attempt to think in terms of theories of price and wage setting, with explicit agents setting prices and wages. Instead, the prevailing mode of thinking was in terms of tâtonnement, with prices adjusting to excess supply or demand, along the lines of the dynamic processes of adjustment studied by Samuelson in his *Foundations of Economic Analysis* (1947). The Phillips curve, imported to the United States by Samuelson and Solow in 1960, was in that context both a blessing and a curse. It gave strong empirical support to a tâtonnement-like relation between the rate of change of nominal wages and the level of unemployment, but it also made less urgent the need for better microeconomic underpinnings of market adjustment. Given the existence of a reliable empirical relation and the perceived difficulty of the theoretical task, it made good sense to work on other and more urgent topics, where the marginal return was higher.

These twin beliefs had strong implications for the research agenda as well as for policy. Because prices and wages eventually adjusted to clear markets, and because policy could avoid prolonged disequilibrium anyway, macroeconomic research could progress along two separate lines. One could study long-run movements in output, employment and capital, ignoring business cycle fluctuations as epiphenomena along the path and using the standard tools of equilibrium analysis: 'Solving the vital problems of monetary and fiscal policy by the tools of income analysis will validate and bring back into relevance the classical verities' (Samuelson, 1955, p. 360). Or one could instead study short-run fluctuations around that trend, ignoring the trend itself. This is indeed where most of the breakthroughs had been made by the mid-1950s. Work by Hicks (1937) and Hansen (1949), attempting to formalize the major elements of Keynes's informal model, had led to the IS–LM model. Modigliani (1944) had made clear the role played by nominal wage rigidity in the Keynesian model. Metzler (1951) had shown the importance of wealth effects, and the role of government debt. Patinkin (1956) had clarified the structure of the macroeconomic model, and the relation between the demands for goods, money and bonds, in the case of flexible prices and wages. There was general agreement that, except in unlikely and exotic cases, the IS curve was downward sloping and the LM curve upward sloping. Post-war interest rates were high enough – compared with pre-war rates – to make the liquidity trap less of an issue. There was still, however, considerable uncertainty about the effect of interest rates on investment, and thus about the slope of the IS relation. The assumption of fixed nominal wages made by Keynes and early Keynesian models had been relaxed in favour of slow adjustment of prices and wages to market conditions. This was not seen, however, as modifying substantially earlier conclusions. The 'Pigou effect' (so dubbed by Patinkin in 1948), according to which low enough prices would increase real money and wealth, was not considered to be of much practical significance. Only activist policy could avoid large fluctuations in economic activity.

Refinements of the model were not taken as implying that the case for policy activism was any less strong than Keynes had suggested. Because prices and wages did not adjust fast enough, active countercyclical policy was needed to keep the economy close to full employment. Because prices and wages, or policies themselves, eventually got the economy to remain not far from its growth path, standard microeconomic principles of fiscal policy should be used to choose the exact mix of fiscal measures at any point in time. The potential conflict between their relative efficacy in terms of demand management, and their effect on the efficiency of economic allocation, were considered an issue but not a major problem. Nor was the fact that the market failure which led to short-run fluctuations in the first place was not fully understood or even identified.

The ground rules for cyclical fiscal policy were laid in particular by Samuelson in a series of contributions (1951, for example). Countercyclical fiscal policy was to use both taxes and spending; in a depression, the best way to increase demand was to increase both public investment and private investment through tax breaks, so as to equalize social marginal rates of return on both. Where the synthesis stood on monetary policy is less clear. While the potential of monetary policy to smooth fluctuations was generally acknowledged, one feels that fiscal policy was still the instrument of predilection, that policy was thought of as fiscal policy in the lead with accommodating monetary policy in tow.

The mature synthesis

For the next 20 years the initial synthesis was to supply a framework in which most macroeconomists felt at home and in which contributions fitted naturally. As Lucas remarks in his critique of the synthesis, 'those

economists, like Milton Friedman, who made no use of the framework, were treated with some impatience by its proponents' (1980, p. 702). The research programme was largely implied by the initial synthesis, the emphasis on the behavioural components of IS–LM and its agnostic approach to price and wage adjustment; to quote Modigliani, 'the Keynesian system rests on four basic blocks: the consumption function, the investment function, the demand and the supply of money, and the mechanisms determining prices and wages' (1980, p. xii). Progress on many of these fronts was extraordinary; I summarize it briefly as these developments are reviewed in more depth elsewhere in this dictionary.

The failure of the widely predicted post-war over-saving to materialize had led to a reassessment of consumption theory. The theory of intertemporal utility maximization progressively emerged as the main contender. It was developed independently by Friedman (1957) as the 'permanent income hypothesis' and Modigliani and collaborators (1954 in particular) as the 'life cycle hypothesis'. The life-cycle formulation, modified to allow for imperfect financial markets and liquidity constraints, was, however, to dominate most of empirical research. Part of the reason was that it emphasized more explicitly the role of wealth in consumption, and, through wealth, the role of interest rates. Neither wealth effects nor interest rate effects on consumption had figured prominently in the initial synthesis.

Research on the investment function was less successful. Part of the difficulty arose from the complexity of the empirical task, the heterogeneity of capital, and the possibility of substituting factors *ex ante* but not *ex post*. Many of the conceptual issues were clarified by work on growth, but empirical implementation was harder. Part of the difficulty, however, came from the ambiguity of neoclassical theory about price behaviour, about whether firms could be thought of as setting prices or whether the slow adjustment of prices implied that firms were in fact output constrained. The 'neoclassical theory of investment' developed by Jorgenson and collaborators (for example, Hall and Jorgenson, 1967) was ambiguous in this respect, assuming implicitly that price is equal to marginal cost, but estimating empirical functions with output rather than real wages.

Research on the demand for and supply of money was extended to include all assets. Solid foundations for the demand for money were given by Tobin (1956) and Baumol (1952), and the theory of finance provided a theory of the demand for all assets (Tobin, 1958). The expectations hypothesis, which alleviated the need to estimate full demand and supply models of financial markets, was thoroughly tested and widely accepted as an approximation to reality.

In keeping with the initial synthesis, work on prices and wages was much less grounded in theory than work on the other components of the Keynesian model. While research on the microeconomic foundations of wage and price behaviour was proceeding (Phelps, 1972 in particular), it was poorly integrated in empirical wage and price equations. To a large extent, this block of the Keynesian synthesis remained throughout the period the ad hoc but empirically successful Phillips curve, respecified through time to allow for a progressively larger effect of past inflation on current wage inflation.

All these blocks, together with work on growth theory, were largely developed in relation with and then combined in macroeconometric models, starting with the models estimated by Klein (for example, Goldberger and Klein, 1955). The most important model was probably the MPS–FMP model developed by Modigliani and collaborators. This model, while maintaining the initial IS–LM Phillips curve structure of its ancestors, showed the richness of the channels through which shocks and policy could affect the economy. It could be used to derive optimal policy, show the effects of structural changes in financial markets, and so on. By the early 1970s the synthesis appeared to have been highly successful and the research programme laid down after the war to have been mostly completed. Only a few years later, however, the synthesis was in crisis and fighting for survival.

The crisis and the reconstruction
The initial trigger for the crisis was the failure of the synthesis to explain events. The scientific success of the synthesis had been largely due to its empirical success, especially during the Kennedy and the first phase of the Johnson administrations in the United States. As inflation increased in the late 1960s, the empirical success and, in turn, the theoretical foundations of the synthesis were more and more widely questioned. The more serious blow was, however, the stagflation of the mid-1970s in response to the increases in the price of oil: it was clear that policy was not able to maintain steady growth and low inflation. In a clarion call against the neoclassical synthesis, Lucas and Sargent (1978) judged its predictions to have been an 'econometric failure on a grand scale'.

One cannot, however, condemn a theory for failing to anticipate the shape and the effects of shocks which have not been observed before; few theories would pass such a test and, as long as the events can be explained after the fact, there is no particular cause for concern. In fact, soon thereafter models were expanded to allow for supply shocks such as changes in the price of oil. It became clear, however, that while the models could indeed be adjusted *ex post*, there was a more serious problem behind the failure to predict the events of the 1970s. To quote again from the polemical article by Lucas and Sargent, 'That the doctrine on which [these predictions] were made is fundamentally flawed is simply a matter of fact' (1978, p. 49). The 'fundamental flaw' was the asymmetric treatment of agents as being highly rational and of markets as

being inefficient in adjusting wages and prices to their appropriate levels. The tension between the treatment of rational agents and that of myopic impersonal markets had been made more obvious by the developments of the 1960s, and the representation of consumers and firms as highly rational intertemporal decision makers. It was further highlighted by the research on fixed price equilibria, which went to the extreme of taking prices as unexplained and solving for macroeconomic equilibrium under non-market clearing. That research made clear, in a negative way, that progress could be made only if one understood why markets did not clear, why prices and wages did not adjust.

The solution proposed by Lucas and others in the 'new classical synthesis' was thoroughly unappealing to economists trained in the neoclassical synthesis. It was to formalize the economy as if markets were competitive and clearing instantaneously. The 'as if' assumption seemed objectionable on a priori grounds, in that direct evidence on labour and goods markets suggested important departure from competition; it also appeared to many to be an unpromising approach if the goal was to explain economic fluctuations and unemployment. Soon papers by Fischer (1977) and Taylor (1980) showed that one could replace the Phillips curve by a model of explicit nominal price and wage setting and still retain most of the traditional results of the neoclassical synthesis. These papers led the way to a major overhaul and reconstruction, and by the mid-1990s a new synthesis had emerged, a synthesis now dubbed the 'new neoclassical synthesis' (Goodfriend and King, 1997) or the 'new Keynesian synthesis' (for example, Clarida, Gali and Gertler, 1999).

This new synthesis is described in more detail elsewhere in this dictionary, and I shall limit myself to a few remarks and comparisons between the old and the new. Like the old synthesis, the new synthesis has two major features: on the one hand, optimizing behaviour by firms, consumers and workers; on the other, the presence of distortions, most importantly nominal rigidities. In contrast to the old synthesis, however, the distortions are introduced explicitly, and price and wage behaviour is derived from optimizing behaviour by price and wage setters. These distortions imply that, as in the old synthesis, monetary policy and fiscal policy have a major role to play.

Like the old synthesis, the new synthesis is derived from microfoundations, utility maximization by consumers, and profit maximization by firms. But, while models in the old synthesis used theory as a loose guide to empirical specifications and allowed the data to determine the ultimate specification, models in the new synthesis remain much closer to their microfoundations. Dynamics are derived from the model itself, and the implied behavioural equations, rather than being estimated, are typically derived from assumptions about underlying technological and utility parameters.

These more explicit microfoundations allow for a more careful welfare analysis of the implications of policy than was possible with the old models.

The models in the new synthesis are referred to as 'dynamic stochastic general equilibrium', or DSGE, models. Because they are typically difficult to solve, even the larger models are smaller than the models of the old synthesis, and their formalization of markets such as those for goods and labour remains primitive compared with the spirit of the formalizations in the old models. Improvements both in the formalization of these markets and in numerical techniques are, however, allowing for steadily richer and larger models.

To parallel the quotation from Samuelson given at the beginning, it is fair to say that the new neoclassical synthesis is attracting wide support, although less so than the old one. Some researchers, particularly those in the 'real business cycle' tradition, are sceptical about the importance of nominal rigidities in fluctuations. Others find the rationality assumptions embodied in the new synthesis to be too strong, and the methodology too constraining to capture the complexity present in the data.

Nevertheless, DSGE models are increasingly used to guide policy. Many challenges remain, for example in capturing the relevant distortions in goods, labour, financial, and credit markets, or in using econometrics to assess the fit of both the specific components and the overall model to reality. Progress is rapid, however. When I wrote the first version of this contribution in 1991, the emergence of a new synthesis appeared uncertain, and at best far in the future. In updating this contribution, I am struck by the progress that has taken place since then, and by the speed at which progress continues to be made today.

OLIVIER BLANCHARD

See also **Friedman, Milton; Hicks, John Richard; Klein, Lawrence R.; Lucas, Robert; microfoundations; Modigliani, Franco; Patinkin, Don; Phillips curve (new views); Samuelson, Paul Anthony; Tobin, James.**

Bibliography

Baumol, W. 1952. The transactions demand for cash. *Quarterly Journal of Economics* 66, 545–6.
Clarida, R., Gali, J. and Gertler, M. 1999. The science of monetary policy: a New Keynesian perspective. *Journal of Economic Literature* 37, 1661–707.
Fischer, S. 1977. Long-term contracts, rational expectations, and the optimal money supply rule. *Journal of Political Economy* 85, 191–205.
Friedman, M. 1957. *A Theory of the Consumption Function*. New York: NBER.
Goldberger, A. and Klein, L. 1955. *An Econometric Model of the United States, 1929–1952*. Amsterdam: North-Holland.
Goodfriend, M. and King, R. 1997. The new neoclassical synthesis and the role of monetary policy. In *NBER Macroeconomics Annual 1997*, ed. B. Bernanke and J. Rotemberg. Cambridge: MIT Press.
Hall, R. and Jorgenson, D. 1967. Tax policy and investment behavior. *American Economic Review* 57, 391–414.
Hansen, A. 1949. *Monetary Theory and Fiscal Policy*. New York: McGraw-Hill.
Hicks, J. 1937. Mr Keynes and the 'classics': a suggested interpretation. *Econometrica* 5, 147–59.
Lucas, R. 1980. Methods and problems in business cycle theory. *Journal of Money, Credit and Banking* 12, 696–715.
Lucas, R. and Sargent, T. 1978. After Keynesian macroeconomics. In *After the Phillips Curve: Persistence of High Inflation and High Unemployment*. Boston: Federal Reserve of Boston.
Metzler, L. 1951. Wealth, saving and the rate of interest. *Journal of Political Economy* 59, 93–116.
Modigliani, F. 1944. Liquidity preference and the theory of interest and money. *Econometrica* 12, 45–88.
Modigliani, F. 1980. *Collected Papers. Vol. 1: Essays in Macroeconomics*. Cambridge, MA: MIT Press.
Modigliani, F. and Brumberg, R. 1954. Utility analysis and the consumption function: an interpretation of cross section data. In *Post-Keynesian Economics*, ed. K. Kurihara. New Brunswick, NJ: Rutgers University Press.
Patinkin, D. 1948. Price flexibility and full employment. *American Economic Review* 38, 543–64.
Patinkin, D. 1956. *Money, Interest and Prices*. New York: Harper and Row.
Phelps, E. 1972. *Inflation Policy and Unemployment Theory*. London: Macmillan.
Samuelson, P.A. 1947. *Foundations of Economic Analysis*. Cambridge, MA: Harvard University Press.
Samuelson, P. 1951. Principles and rules in modern fiscal policy: a neoclassical reformulation. In *Money, Trade and Economic Growth: Essays in Honor of John Henry Williams*, ed. H. Waitzman. New York: Macmillan.
Samuelson, P. 1955. *Economics*, 3rd edn. New York: McGraw-Hill.
Taylor, J. 1980. Aggregate dynamics and staggered contracts. *Journal of Political Economy* 88, 1–23.
Tobin, J. 1956. The interest-elasticity of transactions demand for cash. *Review of Economics and Statistics* 38, 241–7.
Tobin, J. 1958. Liquidity preference as behavior towards risk. *Review of Economic Studies* 25, 65–86.

neo-Ricardian economics

The term 'neo-Ricardian economics', as it is understood today, can mean several things. It was coined in the aftermath of the publication of *The Works and Correspondence of David Ricardo*, edited by Piero Sraffa with the collaboration of Maurice H. Dobb (Ricardo, 1951–73), and the publication of Sraffa's *Production of Commodities by Means of Commodities* (Sraffa, 1960).

One meaning of the term simply refers to these facts and interprets Sraffa's work in the way Sraffa himself saw it: as a return to the 'standpoint of the old classical economists from Adam Smith to Ricardo, [which] has been submerged and forgotten since the advent of the "marginal" method' (Sraffa, 1960, p. v; see Smith, 1776, and Ricardo, 1951–73). However, the term was first used by Marxist economists to distinguish Sraffa's approach to the theory of value and distribution, which explained relative prices and income distribution strictly in material terms (that is, quantities of commodities and labour), from the Marxist one, which starts from labour values (see Rowthorn, 1974). In some contributions Sraffa's analysis is described in a derogatory manner as a 'peanut theory of profits' and rejected together with marginalist (or 'neoclassical') theory as a variant of 'vulgar economics', dealing with 'appearances' only, whereas Marxist theory is taken to investigate 'the real relations of production in bourgeois society' (Marx, 1867, p. 85n). Neoclassical economists in turn occasionally (see, for example, Hahn, 1982) applied the term to the analysis of those critics who, in the so-called Cambridge controversies on the theory of capital, had attacked marginalism, especially its long-period version, showing it to be logically flawed (see Kurz and Salvadori, 1995, ch. 14). Because of the nationalities of the critics – especially Joan Robinson, Nicholas Kaldor, Piero Sraffa, Pierangelo Garegnani and Luigi Pasinetti – they also spoke of an 'Anglo-Italian school'.

Such an unfortunate diversity of meanings may reflect a misunderstanding both of Sraffa's achievement and of the relation of his analysis to that of Marxist and marginalist economics respectively. What Sraffa in fact provides is a reformulation of the *classical* approach to the problem of value and distribution that sheds the weaknesses of its earlier formulations and builds upon their strengths. Put briefly, profits and all property incomes (such as interest and land rents) are explained in terms of the *social surplus* left over after the necessary means of production and the wages in the support of workers have been deducted from the gross outputs produced during a year. As Ricardo had stressed: 'Profits come out of the surplus produce' (*Works*, vol. 2, pp. 130–1; cf. vol. 1, p. 95). Therefore, instead of 'neo-Ricardian economics' it would be more appropriate to speak of that part of classical economics that deals with value and distribution. As is well known, this part was designed to constitute the foundation of all other economic analysis, including the investigation of capital accumulation and technical progress, of development and growth, of social transformation and structural change, and of taxation and public debt. The pivotal role of the theory of value and distribution in the classical authors can be inferred from the fact that it is typically developed at the beginning of their major works. By rectifying this part, Sraffa revived interest in classical economics. In addition to this constructive task Sraffa also pursued a critical task: the propositions of

his book were explicitly 'designed to serve as the basis for a critique of [the marginal theory of value and distribution]' (1960, p. vi).

In the following we first summarize the achievements of Sraffa and his followers with respect to the constructive task. We then turn to the criticism of marginalist theory. In conclusion, we point out some of the problems that are currently being tackled by scholars working in the classical tradition.

Reformulating the classical theory of value and distribution

The concern of the classical economists, especially Smith and Ricardo, was the laws governing the emerging capitalist economy, characterized by the stratification of society into three classes: workers, landowners, and the rising class of capitalists; wage labour as the dominant form of the appropriation of other people's capacity to work; an increasingly sophisticated division of labour within and between firms; the coordination of economic activity through a system of interdependent markets in which transactions were mediated through money; and significant technical, organizational and institutional change. In short, they were concerned with an economic system incessantly in motion. How to analyse such a system? The ingenious device of the classical authors to see through the complexities of the modern economy consisted in distinguishing between the 'actual' values of the relevant variables – the distributive rates and prices – and their 'normal' values. The former were taken to reflect all kinds of influences, many of an accidental or temporary nature, about which no general propositions were possible, whereas the latter were conceived of as expressing the persistent, non-accidental and non-temporary factors governing the economic system, which could be systematically studied.

The method of analysis adopted by the classical economists is known as the method of 'long-period positions' of the economy. Any such position is the situation towards which the system is taken to gravitate as the result of the self-seeking actions of agents, thereby putting into sharp relief the fundamental forces at work. In conditions of free competition the resulting long-period position is characterized by a *uniform rate of profits* (subject perhaps to persistent inter-industry differentials reflecting different levels of risk and of agreeableness of the business; see Kurz and Salvadori, 1995, ch. 11) and uniform rates of remuneration for each particular kind of primary input. Competitive conditions were taken to engender *cost-minimizing behaviour* of profit-seeking producers.

Alfred Marshall (1920) had interpreted the classical economists as essentially early and somewhat crude demand and supply theorists, with the demand side in its infancy. It was this interpretation and the underlying continuity thesis in economics that Sraffa challenged. As he showed, the classical economists' approach to the theory of value and distribution was fundamentally different from the later marginalist one, and explained profits in terms of basically two data: (*a*) the system of production in use and (*b*) a given real wage rate (or, alternatively, a given share of wages). Profits (and rents) were thus conceived of as a *residual* income. Whereas in marginalist theory wages and profits are treated symmetrically, in classical theory they are treated *asymmetrically*. On a still deeper methodological level the divide between the classical and the later marginalist authors could hardly be more pronounced. While the classical authors took the economic system to exist independently of the single agent and actually exert a considerable influence upon the latter depending upon the role ascribed to him as worker, capitalist or landowner, the marginalist authors advocated one version or another of 'methodological individualism', which takes a set of assumedly optimizing agents who exist independently of the system as a whole and who shape the system rather than the other way round.

Let us now examine more closely the scope, content and analytical structure of classical theory. The classical economists proceeded essentially in two steps. In the first step they isolated the kinds of factors that were seen to determine income distribution and the prices supporting that distribution in specified conditions, that is, *in a given place and time*. The theory of value and distribution was designed to identify *in abstracto* the dominant factors at work and to analyse their interaction. In the second step they turned to an investigation of the causes which *over time* affected systematically the factors at work from within the economic system. This was the realm of the classical analysis of capital accumulation, technical change, economic growth and socio-economic development.

It is another characteristic feature of the classical approach to profits, rents and relative prices that these are explained essentially in terms of magnitudes that can, in principle, be observed, measured or calculated. The *objectivist* orientation of classical economics has received its perhaps strongest expression in a famous proclamation by William Petty, who was arguably its founding father. Keen to assume what he called the '"physician's" outlook', Petty in his *Political Arithmetick*, published in 1690, stressed that he was to express himself exclusively 'in Terms of *Number, Weight* or *Measure*' (Petty, 1986, p. 244). And James Mill noted significantly that '*The agents of production are the commodities themselves* …. They are the food of the labourer, the tools and the machinery with which he works, and the raw materials which he works upon' (Mill, 1826, p. 165, emphasis added). According to Sraffa the classical authors advocated essentially a concept of *physical real cost*. Man cannot create matter, man can only change its form and move it. Production involves destruction, and the real cost of a commodity consists in the commodities destroyed in the course of its production. This concept differs markedly from the later marginalist concepts, with their emphasis on 'psychic cost', reflected in such notions as 'utility' and 'disutility'.

In line with what may be called their 'thermodynamic' view, the classical authors saw production as a *circular flow*. This idea can be traced back to William Petty and Richard Cantillon, and was most effectively expressed by François Quesnay (1759) in the *Tableau économique*: commodities are produced by means of commodities. This is in stark contrast with the view of production as a one-way avenue leading from the services of original factors of production via some intermediate products to consumption goods, as was entertained by the 'Austrian' economists.

Why then did the classical economists fail to elaborate a consistent theory of value and distribution on the basis of the twin concepts of (*a*) physical real costs and (*b*) a circular flow of production? According to Sraffa (see Kurz and Salvadori, 2005) a main, if not *the* main, reason consisted in a mismatch between highly sophisticated analytical concepts on the one hand and inadequate tools available to the classical authors to deal with them on the other. More specifically, the tool needed in order to bring to fruition an analysis based on these twin concepts was simultaneous equations: knowledge of how to solve them and how to discover what their properties are. This indispensable tool (alas!) was not at their disposal. They therefore tried to solve the problems they encountered in a roundabout way, typically by first identifying an 'ultimate standard of value' by means of which *heterogeneous* commodities could be rendered *homogeneous*. Several authors, including Smith, Ricardo and Marx, had then reached the conclusion that 'labour' was the standard they sought and had therefore arrived in one way or another at some version of the labour theory of value. This preserved the objectivist character of the theory by taking as data, or known quantities, only measurable things, such as amounts of commodities actually produced and amounts actually used up, including the means of subsistence in the support of workers. This was understandable in view of the unresolved tension between concepts and tools. However, with production as a circular flow, even labour values cannot be known independently of solving a system of simultaneous equations. Hence the route via labour values was not really a way out of the impasse in which the classical authors found themselves: it rather landed them right in that impasse again. Commodities were produced by means of commodities and there was no way to circumnavigate the simultaneous equations approach.

What made it so difficult, if not impossible, for the classical authors to see that the theory of value and distribution could be firmly grounded in the concept of physical real cost? Given their primitive tools of analysis, they did not see that the information about the system of production in use and the quantities of the means of subsistence in support of workers was all that was needed in order to determine *directly* the system of necessary prices and the rate of profits. Sraffa understood this as early as November 1927, as we can see from his hitherto unpublished papers kept at Trinity College Library,

Cambridge (UK), with respect to what he called his 'first' (without a surplus) and 'second' (with a surplus) 'equations'.

We may start with James Mill's aforementioned case with three kinds of commodities, tools (t), raw materials (m), and the food of the labourer (f). Production in the three industries may then be depicted by the following system of quantities

$$T_t \oplus M_t \oplus F_t \rightarrow T$$
$$T_m \oplus M_m \oplus F_m \rightarrow M \qquad (1)$$
$$T_f \oplus M_f \oplus F_f \rightarrow F$$

where T_i, M_i and F_i designate the inputs of the three commodities (employed as means of production *and* means of subsistence) in industry i ($i = t, m, f$), and T, M and F total outputs in the three industries; the symbol $\oplus$ indicates that all inputs on the LHS of $\rightarrow$, representing production are required to generate the output on its RHS. Invoking classical concepts, Sraffa called these relations 'the methods of production and productive consumption' (1960, p. 3). In the hypothetical case in which the economy is just viable, that is, able to reproduce itself without any surplus (or deficiency), we have $T = \Sigma_i T_i$, $M = \Sigma_i M_i$, and $F = \Sigma_i F_i$.

From this schema of reproduction and reproductive consumption we may directly derive the corresponding system of 'absolute' or 'natural' values, which expresses the idea of physical real cost-based values in an unadulterated way. Denoting the value of one unit of commodity i by p_i ($i = t, m, f$), we have

$$T_t p_t + M_t p_m + F_t p_f = T p_t$$
$$T_m p_t + M_m p_m + F_m p_f = M p_m \qquad (2)$$
$$T_f p_t + M_f p_m + F_f p_f = F p_f$$

These linear equations are homogeneous and therefore only relative prices can be determined. Further, only two of the three equations are independent of one another. This is enough to determine the two relative prices. Alternatively, it is possible to fix a standard of value whose price is *ex definitione* equal to unity. This provides an additional (non-homogeneous) equation without adding a further unknown, and allows one to solve for the remaining dependent variables.

A numerical example illustrates the important finding that the given socio-technical relations rigidly fix relative values:

Values

$$2p_t + 15p_m + 20p_f = 17p_t \qquad p_t = 3p_m$$
$$5p_t + 7p_m + 4p_f = 28p_m \qquad p_m = \tfrac{2}{3}p_f$$
$$10p_t + 6p_m + 11p_f = 35p_f \qquad p_f = \tfrac{1}{2}p_t$$

These values depend exclusively on necessities of production. They are the only ones that allow the initial distribution of resources to be restored. Apparently, the value of one commodity may be 'reduced' to a certain amount of another commodity needed directly or indirectly in the production of the former. For example, one might reduce one unit of commodity t to an amount needed of commodity m. Hence one might say that each of the three commodities could serve as a 'common measure' and that, for example, commodities t and f exchange for one another in the proportion 1:2 because commodity t 'contains' or 'embodies' twice as much of commodity m as commodity f.

There is no need even to talk about labour values at this stage of the argument. The same applies to the next stage, which refers to a system with a surplus and given commodity (or real) wages advanced at the beginning of the production period. In conditions of free competition the surplus will be distributed in terms of a *uniform* rate of profits on the 'capitals' advanced in the different industries.

We start again from the system of quantities consumed productively and produced (1), but now we assume that $T \geq \Sigma_i T_i$, $M \geq \Sigma_i M_i$, and $F \geq \Sigma_i F_i$, where at least with regard to one commodity the strict inequality sign holds. In conditions of free competition 'normal' prices, or 'prices of production', have to satisfy the following system of price equations:

$$(T_t p_t + M_t p_m + F_t p_f)(1 + r) = T p_t$$
$$(T_m p_t + M_m p_m + F_m p_f)(1 + r) = M p_m$$
$$(T_f p_t + M_f p_m + F_f p_f)(1 + r) = F p_f$$

$$(3)$$

The case of a uniform rate of physical surplus across all commodities contemplated by David Ricardo and Robert Torrens

$$\frac{T - \Sigma_i T_i}{\Sigma_i T_i} = \frac{M - \Sigma_i M_i}{\Sigma_i M_i} = \frac{F - \Sigma_i F_i}{\Sigma_i F_i} = r$$

$$(4)$$

denotes a very special constellation: in it the general rate of profits, r, equals the uniform material rate of produce. *Here we see the rate of profits in the commodities themselves, as having nothing to do with their values.* In this case only two of the eqs. (3) are linearly independent so that eq. (4) determines the rate of profits, and eqs. (3), following the same procedure used for eqs. (2), determine relative prices. In general, the rates of physical surplus will be different for different commodities. Unequal rates of commodity surplus do not, however, by themselves imply unequal rates of profit across industries.

In this case there are three numbers, each of which substituted for r in eqs. (3) makes them linearly dependent on one another with respect to prices. It is possible to show that, when the highest real number among such numbers is substituted for r, the corresponding relative prices are positive, whereas when any of the other numbers is substituted for r some relative prices are negative. Since a negative relative price has no economic meaning in the present context, we can assert that there is a single solution which is relevant from an economic point of view. Fixing a standard of value provides a fourth equation and no extra unknown, so that the system of equations can be solved.

The important point to note here is the following. With the real wage rate given and paid at the beginning of the periodical production cycle, the problem of the determination of the rate of profits consists in distributing the surplus product in proportion to the capital advanced in each industry. Obviously,

> such a proportion between two aggregates of heterogeneous goods (in other words, the rate of profits) cannot be determined before we know the prices of the goods. On the other hand, we cannot defer the allotment of the surplus till after the prices are known, for … the prices cannot be determined before knowing the rate of profits. *The result is that the distribution of the surplus must be determined through the same mechanism and at the same time as are the prices of commodities.* (Sraffa, 1960, p. 6; emphasis added)

This passage shows that the idea which underlies Marx's so-called 'transformation' of labour values into prices of production (see Marx, 1894, part 2) cannot generally be sustained. Marx had proceeded in two steps; Ladislaus von Bortkiewicz (1906–7, essay 2, p. 38) aptly dubbed his approach 'successivist' (as opposed to 'simultaneous'). In a first step Marx had assumed that the general rate of profits is determined independently of, and prior to, the determination of prices as the ratio between the labour value of the social surplus and that of social capital, consisting of 'constant capital' (means of production) and 'variable capital' (wages or means of subsistence). In a second step he had then used this rate to calculate prices.

So far we have assumed that real wages are given in kind at some level of subsistence. The classical economists, however, saw clearly that wages may rise above mere sustenance of labourers, which makes necessary a new wage concept. This case had made Ricardo adopt a *share* concept of wages and establish the inverse relationship between the share of wages in the product and the rate of profits: 'The greater the *portion of the result of labour* that is given to the labourer, the smaller must be the *rate* of profits, and vice versa' (*Works*, vol. 8, p. 194; emphasis added). The concept of 'proportional wages', as Sraffa called it, was then adopted by Marx in terms of a given rate of surplus value. Sraffa also adopted the concept, albeit with two important changes. First, when workers participate in the sharing out of the surplus product, the original classical idea of wages being entirely paid out of social capital can no longer be sustained. After some deliberation Sraffa decided to treat wages as a whole as paid out of the product. Second, he did not express the share of wages in terms of labour but as the ratio of total wages to the net product expressed in terms of normal prices, w. These changes necessitated reformulating the price equations by taking explicitly into account the amounts of labour expended in the different industries, L_i $(i = t, m, f)$, because wages are taken to be paid in proportion to these amounts, and by defining these amounts as fractions of the total annual labour of society, that is, $L_t + L_m + L_f = 1$. In addition, it is assumed, following the classical economists, that differences in the quality of labour have been previously reduced to equivalent differences in quantity, so that each unit of labour receives the same wage rate (see Kurz and Salvadori, 1995, ch. 11). We may now formulate the corresponding system of production equations again for the case of the three kinds of commodities mentioned by Mill, where now the quantities represented by T_i, M_i and F_i refer exclusively to the inputs of the three commodities employed as means of production. We get (on the assumption that wages are paid *post factum*)

$$(T_t p_t + M_t p_m + F_t p_f)(1 + r) + L_t w = T p_t$$
$$(T_m p_t + M_m p_m + F_m p_f)(1 + r) + L_m w = M p_m$$
$$(T_f p_t + M_f p_m + F_f p_f)(1 + r) + L_f w = F p_f$$

$$(5.1)$$

With the net product taken as standard of value, we have in addition that

$$(T - \Sigma_i T_i)p_t + (M - \Sigma_i M_i)p_m + (F - \Sigma_i F_i)p_f = 1.$$

Taking one of the distributive variables, the share of wages w (or the rate of profits r) as given, allows one to determine the remaining variables: r (or w) and the prices of commodities.

Using this approach, Sraffa was able to show that, whereas the wage rate as a function of the rate of profits is necessarily decreasing (but does not need to be so if commodities are produced jointly), any relative price as a function of the rate of profits typically does not follow a simple rule: the function can alternately be increasing or decreasing, and can pass through unity a number of times (but such a number is constrained by the overall number of commodities involved). This fact is important also because the problem of the choice of technique from among several alternatives can be studied by following substantially the same argument. Suppose, for instance, that commodity t can be produced also with process

$$T'_t \oplus M'_t \oplus F'_t \oplus L'_t \rightarrow T'$$

Then we can add to system (5.1) the equation

$$(T'_t p_t + M'_t p_m + F'_t p_f)(1 + r) + L'_t w = T' p'_t$$

$$(5.2)$$

with the further unknown p'_t. The study of the ratio p'_t/p_t allows one to say when it is profitable to use the old process and when the new one: if p'_t/p_t is smaller than 1, the new process will be chosen by cost-minimizing producers; if it is larger than 1, the old process will be retained, whereas the two processes can coexist in case $p'_t/p_t = 1$. Obviously, if the new process is chosen and has replaced the old one, and if it is assumed that the rate of profits is unchanged, then eqs. (5.1) give way to the following equations, serving as the new system

$$(T'_t p'_t + M'_t p'_m + F'_t p'_f)(1 + r) + L'_t w' = T' p'_t$$
$$(T_m p'_t + M_m p'_m + F_m p'_f)(1 + r) + L_m w' = M p'_m$$
$$(T_f p'_t + M_f p'_m + F_f p'_f)(1 + r) + L_f w' = F p'_f$$

$$(6.1)$$

In this new system prices and the wage are different ($p'_j \neq p_j$ and $w' \neq w$), but they are not so when $p'_j/p_j = 1$ in system (5). If we now evaluate the old process in terms of the prices and wage of the new system by combining system (6.1) and the equation

$$(T_t p'_t + M_t p'_m + F_t p'_f)(1 + r) + L_t w' = T p_t$$

$$(6.2)$$

we can calculate again the ratio p'_t/p_t, and the property that prices and the wage in the two systems coincide when $p'_t/p_t = 1$ is enough to prove that p'_t/p_t is larger (lower) than 1 for a given r in system (6) if and only if it is so in system (5). Hence the comparison between the new process and the old one can be indifferently done at the prices of either the old system or the new system.

In the following a system involving a number of processes equal to the number of commodities involved, each producing a different commodity, is called a *technique*, and a technique which is chosen at a given income distribution is called a *cost-minimizing technique* at that income distribution. The fact that a relative price can pass through unity at several income distributions implies that a technique can be cost-minimizing at different values of the rate of profits, with other techniques being cost minimizing in the interval in between. This fact has been called *reswitching*; it played an important role in the criticism of neoclassical theory.

In the above it has for simplicity been assumed that there is only single production, that is, only circulating capital. While the circulating part of the capital goods advanced in production contributes entirely and exclusively to the output generated, that is, 'disappears' from the scene, so to speak, the fixed part of it contributes to a sequence of outputs over time, that is, after a single round of production its items are still there – older but still useful. For a discussion of joint production, fixed capital and scarce natural resources, see Kurz and Salvadori (1995).

Critique of marginalist theory

The passage quoted above from Sraffa (1960, p. 6) contains the key to his critique of the long-period marginalist concept of capital. This concept hinges crucially on the possibility of defining the 'quantity of capital', whose relative scarcity and thus marginal productivity was taken to determine the rate of profits, independently of the rate of profits. However, according to the logic of Sraffa's above argument the rate of profits and the quantity (that is, value) of social capital ($\Sigma_i T_i p_t + \Sigma_i M_i p_m + \Sigma_i F_i p_f$) can only be determined simultaneously.

We may approach the issues under consideration by first discussing what are known as 'Wicksell effects'. The term was introduced by Joan Robinson (1953, p. 95) during a debate in the theory of capital (see Kurz and Salvadori, 1995, ch. 14). We distinguish between *price Wicksell effects* and *real Wicksell effects* (henceforth PWE and RWE). A PWE relates to a change in relative prices corresponding to a change in income distribution, given the system of production in use. A RWE relates to a change in technique, with the fact taken into account that at the income distribution at which two techniques are both cost-minimizing (one being so at higher, the other at lower levels of the rate of profits) both techniques have the same prices. The 'changes' under consideration refer to comparisons of long-period equilibria.

Marginalist theory contends that both effects are invariably positive. A *positive* PWE means that with a rise (fall) in the rate of interest prices of consumption goods will tend to rise (fall) relative to those of capital goods. The reason given is that consumption goods are said to be produced more capital intensively than capital goods: consumption goods emerge at the end of the production process, whereas capital goods are intermediate products that gradually 'mature' towards the final product. The higher (lower) is the rate of interest the less (more) expensive are the intermediate products in terms of a standard consisting of a (basket of) consumption good(s). At the macro level of a stationary economy (in which the net product contains only consumption goods) this implies that with a rise in the rate of interest the value of the net social product rises relatively to the value of the aggregate of capital goods employed. Clearly, seen from the marginalist perspective, a positive PWE with regard to the relative price of the two aggregates under consideration involves a negative relationship between the aggregate capital-to-net output ratio on the one hand and the interest rate on the other. Let $K/Y = \mathbf{x}\mathbf{p}(r)/\mathbf{y}\mathbf{p}(r)$ ($\mathbf{x}$ is the row vector of capital goods, $\mathbf{y}$ the row vector of net outputs, and $\mathbf{p}(r)$ the column vector of prices (in terms of the consumption vector) which depends on r) designate the capital-output ratio, then the marginalist message is:

$$\frac{\partial(K/Y)}{\partial r} \leq 0$$

Since for a given system of production the amount of labour is constant irrespective of the level of the rate of interest, also the ratio of the value of the capital goods and the amount of labour employed, or capital–labour ratio, K/L, would tend to fall (rise) with a rise (fall) in the rate of interest,

$$\frac{\partial(K/L)}{\partial r} \leq 0 \qquad (7)$$

This is the first claim marginalist authors put forward. The second is that RWEs are also positive. A *positive* RWE means that with a rise (fall) in the rate of interest cost-minimizing producers switch to methods of production that generally exhibit higher (lower) labour intensities, 'substituting' for the 'factor of production' that has become more expensive – 'capital' (labour) – the one that has become less expensive – labour ('capital'). Hence (7) is said to apply also in this case. The assumed positivity of the RWE underlies the marginalist concept of a demand function for labour (capital) that is inversely related to the real wage rate (rate of interest).

Careful scrutiny of the marginalist argument has shown that it cannot generally be sustained: there is no presumption that PWEs and RWEs are invariably positive. In fact there is no presumption that techniques can be ordered monotonically with the rate of interest (Sraffa, 1960). Reswitching implies that, even if PWEs happen to be positive, RWEs cannot always be positive. As Mas-Colell (1989) stressed, the relationship between K/L and r can have almost any shape whatsoever. In the intervals in which K/L is an increasing function of r we say that there is *capital reversal*. It implies that, if the neoclassical approach to value and distribution is followed, the 'demand for capital' is not decreasing, and therefore the resulting equilibrium, provided there is one, is not stable. Hence the finding that PWEs and RWEs need not be positive challenges the received doctrine of the working of the economic system, as it is portrayed by conventional economic theory with its reference to the 'forces' of demand and supply (see Pasinetti, 1966; Garegnani, 1970; see also Harcourt, 1972; Kurz and Salvadori, 1995, ch. 14; 1998c).

Current work in the classical tradition

In more recent times authors working in the classical tradition, as it was revived by Sraffa, have focused attention on a large number of problems. First, there has been a lively interest in generalizing the results provided by Sraffa on joint production, fixed capital, and land. Then the approach was extended to cover renewable and exhaustible resources and to allow for the more realistic case of costly disposal, which leads to the concept of negative prices of products that have to be disposed of. There is also a renewed interest in the problem of economic growth and development. Freed from the straightjacket of Say's Law, which can be said to be an implication of the finding that conventional equilibrium analysis cannot be sustained, there is no presumption that the economy will consistently follow a full-capacity path of economic expansion. Hence the problem of different degrees and modes of utilization of productive capacity and the role of effectual demand (Adam Smith) have to be analysed. This avenue has opened up avenues for cross-fertilization between classical economics on the one hand, and Keynesian economics, based on the principle of effective demand, and evolutionary economics, concerned with complex dynamics, on the other (see Coase, 1976; Nelson, 2005). This fact is also highlighted in comparisons with the so-called new growth theory, and allows one to better understand the latter's merits and demerits (see Kurz and Salvadori, 1998a, ch. 4; 1999).

In the 1960s and 1970s the long-period versions of marginalist theory revolving around the concept of a uniform rate of return on capital were called into question on logical grounds. While many marginalist authors accepted this criticism, some of them contended that intertemporal equilibrium theory, the 'highbrow version' of neoclassicism, was not affected by it (see especially Bliss, 1975; Hahn, 1982). This claim has more recently been subjected to close scrutiny (see Garegnani, 2000, Schefold, 2000, and the special issue of *Metroeconomica*, vol. 56(4), 2006). While the criticism of the long-period versions of marginalist theory is irrefutable, as authors from Paul Samuelson to Andreu Mas-Colell have admitted, surprisingly this has not prevented the economics profession at large from still using this theory. This is perhaps so because in more recent years the way of theorizing in large parts of mainstream economics has fundamentally changed. Whether this change is a response to the criticism need not concern us here. It suffices to draw the reader's attention to a statement by Paul Romer in one of his papers on endogenous growth in which he self-critically pointed out a slip in his earlier argument. The error he had committed, he wrote, 'may seem a trifling matter in an area of theory that depends on so many other short cuts. After all, if one is going to do violence to the complexity of economic activity by assuming that there is an aggregate production function, how much more harm can it do to be sloppy about the difference between rival and nonrival goods?' (Romer, 1994, pp. 15–16) Once economic theory has taken the road indicated, criticism becomes a barren instrument. Indeed, why should someone who seeks to provide 'microfoundations' in terms of a representative agent with an infinite time horizon find fault with the counter-factual but attractive assumption that there is only a single (capital) good?

HEINZ D. KURZ AND NERI SALVADORI

See also **capital theory; capital theory (paradoxes); classical distribution theories; classical growth model; classical production theories; reswitching of technique; Ricardo, David; Smith, Adam; Sraffa, Piero; Sraffian economics; Sraffian economics (new developments).**

Bibliography

Bliss, C. 1975. *Capital Theory and the Distribution of Income.* Amsterdam: North-Holland.
Bortkiewicz, L. von. 1906–7. Wertrechnung und Preisrechnung im Marxschen System. *Archiv für Sozialwissenschaft und Sozialpolitik* 23 (1906), 1–50 (essay 1), 25 (1907), 10–51 (essay 2) and 445–88 (essay 3).
Coase, R. 1976. Adam Smith's view of man. *Journal of Law and Economics* 19, 529–46.
Garegnani, P. 1970. Heterogeneous capital, the production function and the theory of distribution. *Review of Economic Studies* 37, 407–36.
Garegnani, P. 1987. Surplus approach to value and distribution. In *The New Palgrave: A Dictionary of Economics*, vol. 4, ed. J. Eatwell, M. Milgate and P. Newman. London: Macmillan.
Garegnani, P. 2000. Savings, investment and the quantity of capital in general intertemporal equilibrium. In Kurz (2000).
Hahn, F. 1982. The neo-Ricardians. *Cambridge Journal of Economics* 6, 353–74.
Harcourt, G. 1972. *Some Cambridge Controversies in the Theory of Capital.* Cambridge: Cambridge University Press.
Kurz, H., ed. 2000. *Critical Essays on Piero Sraffa's Legacy in Economics.* Cambridge: Cambridge University Press.
Kurz, H. and Salvadori, N. 1995. *Theory of Productio: A Long-period Analysis.* Cambridge: Cambridge University Press.
Kurz, H. and Salvadori, N. 1998a. *Understanding 'Classical' Economics: Studies in Long-Period Theory.* London: Routledge.
Kurz, H. and Salvadori, N., eds. 1998b. *The Elgar Companion to Classical Economics*, 2 vols. Cheltenham and Northhampton, MA: Edward Elgar.
Kurz, H. and Salvadori, N. 1998c. Reverse capital deepening and the numeraire: a note. *Review of Political Economy* 10, 415–26.
Kurz, H. and Salvadori, N. 1999. Theories of 'endogenous' growth in historical perspective. In *Contemporary Economic Issues. Proceedings of the Eleventh World Congress of the International Economic Association, volume 4: Economic Behaviour and Design*, ed. M. Sertel. London: Macmillan.
Kurz, H. and Salvadori, N. 2005. Representing the production and circulation of commodities in material terms: on Sraffa's objectivism. *Review of Political Economy* 17, 414–41.
Marshall, A. 1920. *Principles of Economics*, 8th edn. London: Macmillan.
Marx, K. 1867. *Capital*, vol. 1. Moscow: Progress Publishers, 1954.
Marx, K. 1894. 1959. *Capital*, vol. 3. Moscow: Progress Publishers, 1959.
Mas-Colell, A. 1989. Capital theory paradoxes: anything goes. In *Joan Robinson and Modern Economic Theory*, ed. R. Feiwel. London: Macmillan.
Mill, J. 1826. *Elements of Political Economy*, 3rd edn, reprinted 1844. London: Baldwin, Cradock, and Joy.
Nelson, R. 2005. *Technology, Institutions, and Economic Growth.* Cambridge, MA, and London: Harvard University Press.
Petty, W. 1986. *The Economic Writings of Sir William Petty.* New York: Kelley.
Quesnay, F. 1759. *Quesnay's Tableau Economique*, ed. M. Kuczynski and R. Meek. London: Macmillan, 1972.
Pasinetti, L. 1966. Changes in the rate of profit and switches of techniques. *Quarterly Journal of Economics* 80, 503–17.
Ricardo, D. 1951–73. *The Works and Correspondence of David Ricardo*, 11 vols, ed. P. Sraffa with the collaboration of M. Dobb. Cambridge: Cambridge University Press. (In the text referred to as *Works*, volume number.)
Robinson, J. 1953. The production function and the theory of capital. *Review of Economic Studies* 21, 81–106.
Romer, P. 1994. The origins of endogenous growth. *Journal of Economic Perspectives* 8(1), 3–22.
Rowthorn, R. 1974. Neo-classicism, neo-Ricardianism and Marxism. *New Left Review* 86, 63–87.
Schefold, B. 2000. Paradoxes of capital and counter-intuitive changes of distribution in an intertemporal equilibrium model. In Kurz (2000).
Smith, A. 1776. *An Inquiry into the Nature and Causes of the Wealth of Nations.* Oxford: Oxford University Press, 1976.
Sraffa, P. 1960. *Production of Commodities by Means of Commodities: Prelude to a Critique of Economic Theory.* Cambridge: Cambridge University Press.

network formation

A growing literature in economics examines the formation of networks and complements a rich literature in sociology and recently emerging literatures in computer science and statistical physics. Research on network formation is generally motivated by the observation that social structure is important in a wide range of interactions, including the buying and selling of many goods and services, the transmission of job information, decisions on whether to undertake criminal activity, and informal insurance networks.

Networks are often modelled using tools and terminology from graph theory. Most models of networks view a network as either a non-directed or a directed graph; which type of graph is more appropriate depends on the context. For instance, if a network is a social network of people and links represent friendships or acquaintances, then it would tend to be non-directed. Here the people would be modelled as the nodes of the network and the relationships would be the links. (In terms of a graph, the people would be vertices and the relationships would be edges.) If, instead, the network represents citations from one article to another, then each article would be a node and the links would be directed, as one article could cite another. While many social and economic relationships are reciprocal or require the consent of both parties, there are also enough applications that take a directed form, so that both non-directed and directed graphs are useful as modelling tools.

Models of how networks form can be roughly divided into two classes. One derives from random graph theory, and views an economic or social relationship as a random variable. The other views the people (or firms or other actors involved) as exercising discretion in forming their relationships, and uses game theoretic tools to model formation. Each of these techniques is discussed in turn.

Models of random networks

Bernoulli random graphs

Some of the earliest formal models used to understand the formation of networks are random graphs: the canonical example is that of a pure Bernoulli process of link formation (for example, see the seminal study of Erdös and Rényi, 1960). For instance, consider a network where the (non-directed) link between any two nodes is formed with some probability p (where $1 > p > 0$), and this process occurs independently across pairs of nodes. While such a random method of forming links allows any network to potentially emerge, some networks are much more likely to do so than others. Moreover, as the number of nodes becomes large, there is much that can be deduced about the structure the network is likely to take, as a function of p. For instance, one can examine the probability that the resulting network will be connected in the sense that one can find a path (sequence of links) leading from any given node to any other node. We can also ask what the average

distance will be in terms of path length between different nodes, among other things. As Erdös and Rényi showed, such a random graph exhibits a number of 'phase' transitions as the probability of forming links, p, is varied in relation to the number of nodes, n; that is, resulting networks exhibit different characteristics depending on the relative sizes of p and n.

Whether or not such a uniformly random graph model is a good fit as a model of network formation, it is of interest because it indicates that networks with different densities of links might tend to have very different structures and also provides some comparisons for network formation processes more generally. Some of the basic properties that such a random graph exhibits can be summarized as follows. When p is small in relation to n, so that $p < 1/n$ (that is, the average number of links per node is less than one), then with a probability approaching 1 as n grows the resulting graph consists of a number of disjointed and relatively small components, each of which has a tree-like structure. (A component of a network is a subgraph, so that each node in the subgraph can be reached from any other node in the subgraph via a path that lies entirely in the subgraph, and there are no links between any nodes in the subgraph and any nodes outside the subgraph.) Once p is large enough in relation to n, so that $p > 1/n$, then a single 'giant component' emerges; that is, with a probability approaching 1 the graph consists of one large component, which contains a nontrivial fraction of the nodes, and all other components are vanishingly small in comparison. Why there is just one giant component and all other components are of a much smaller order is fairly intuitive. In order to have two 'large' components each having a nontrivial fraction of n nodes, there would have to be no links between any node in one of the components and any node in the other. For large n, it becomes increasingly unlikely to have two large components with absolutely no links between them. Thus, nontrivial components mesh into a giant component, and any other components must be of a much smaller order. As p is increased further, there is another phase transition when p is proportional to $log(n)/n$. This is the threshold at which the network becomes 'connected' so that all nodes are path-connected to each other and the network consists of a single component. Once we hit the threshold at which the network becomes connected, we also see further changes in the diameter of the network as we continue to increase p relative to n. (The diameter is the maximal distance between two nodes, where distance is the minimal number of links that are needed to pass from one node to another.) Below the threshold, the diameter of a giant component is of the order of $log(n)$, then at the threshold of connectedness it hits $log(n)/loglog(n)$, and it continues to shrink as p increases.

Similar properties and phase transitions have been studied in the context of other models of random graphs.

For example, Molloy and Reed (1995), among others (see Newman, 2003), have studied component size and connectedness in a 'configuration model'. There, a set of nodes is given together with the number of links that each node should have, and then links are randomly formed to leave each node with the pre-specified number of links.

Clustering and Markov graphs

Although the random graphs of Erdös and Rényi are a useful starting point for modelling network formation, they lack many characteristics observed in most social and economic networks. This has led to a series of richer random graph-based models of networks. The most basic property that is absent from such random networks is that the presence of links tends to be correlated. For instance, social networks tend to exhibit significant clustering. Clustering refers to the following property of a network. If we examine triples of nodes so that two of them are each connected to the third, what is the frequency with which those two nodes are linked to each other? This tends to be much larger in real social networks than one would see in a Bernoulli random graph. On an intuitive level, models of network formation where links are formed independently tend to look too much like 'trees', while observed social and economic networks tend to exhibit substantial clustering, with many more cycles than would be generated at random (see Watts, 1999, for discussion and evidence).

Frank and Strauss (1986) identified a class of random graphs that generalize Bernoulli random graphs, which they called 'Markov graphs' (also referred to as p^* networks). Their idea was to allow the chance that a given link forms to be dependent on whether or not neighbouring links are formed. Specific interdependencies require special structures, because, for instance, making one link dependent on a second, and the second on the third, can imply some interdependencies between the first and third. These sorts of dependencies are difficult to analyse in a tractable manner, but nevertheless some special versions of such models have been useful in statistical estimation of networks.

Small worlds

Another variation on a Bernoulli network was explored by Watts and Strogatz (1998) in order to generate networks that exhibit both relatively low distances (in terms of minimum path length) between nodes and relatively high clustering – two features that are present in many observed networks but not in the Bernoulli random graphs unless the number of links per node (p(n−1)) is extremely high. They started with a very structured network that exhibits a high degree of clustering. Then, by randomly rewiring enough (but not too many) links, one ends up with a network that has a small average distance between links but still has substantial clustering. While such a rewiring process results in networks that exhibit some of the features of social networks, it leads to networks that miss out on other basic characteristics that are present in many social networks. For example, the nodes of such a network tend to be too similar in terms of the number of links that they each have.

Degree distributions

One fundamental characteristic of a social network is a network's degree distribution. The degree of a node is the number of links it has, and the degree distribution keeps track of how varied the degree is across the nodes of the network. That is, the degree distribution is simply the frequency distribution of degrees across nodes. For instance, in a friendship network some individuals might have only a few friends while other individuals might have many, and then the degree distribution quantifies this information.

Price (1965) examined a network of citations (between scientific articles), and found that the degree distribution exhibited 'fat tails' compared with what one would observe in a Bernoulli random graph; that is, there was a higher frequency of articles that had many citations and a higher frequency of articles that had no citations than should be observed if citations were generated independently. In fact, many social networks exhibit such fat tails, and some have even been thought to exhibit what is known as a 'scale-free' degree distribution or said to 'follow a power law'. A scale-free distribution is one where the frequency of degrees can be written in the form $f(d) = ad^{-b}$, for some parameters a and b, where d is the degree and $f(d)$ is the relative frequency of nodes with degree d. Such distributions date to Pareto (1896), and have been observed in a variety of other contexts ranging from the distribution of wealth in a society to the relative use of words in a language. Price (1976) adapted ideas from Simon (1955) to develop a random link formation process that produces networks with such degree distributions. A similar model was later studied by Barabási and Albert (2001), who called the process of link formation 'preferential attachment'. The idea is that nodes gain new links with probabilities that are proportional to the number of links they already have (which is closely related to a lognormal growth process). In a system where new nodes are born over time, this process generates scale-free degree distributions.

A simple preferential attachment model also has its limitations. One is that most social networks do not in fact have degree distributions that are scale-free. Observed degree distributions tend to lie somewhere between the extremes of a scale-free distribution and that corresponding to an independent Bernoulli random graph (sometimes known as a Poisson random graph for its approximate degree distribution). Second, the preferential attachment model fails to produce the type of clustering observed in many social networks, just as

Bernoulli random graphs do. This has led to the construction of hybrid models that allow for richer sets of degree distributions, as well as clustering and correlation in degrees, and allows for the structural fitting of random graph based network formation models to data (for example, see Jackson and Rogers, 2007, and the discussion there).

Strategic models of network formation

Strategic models of network formation have emerged from the economics literature, and offer a very different perspective from that seen in random graph models, and a complementary set of insights (see Jackson, 2006, for comparison and discussion). The starting point for a game theoretic approach is to assume that the nodes are active discretionary agents or players who get payoffs that depend on the social network that emerges. For example, if nodes are countries and links are political alliances, or nodes are firms and links are trading or collaboration agreements, then the relationships are entered into with some care and thought. Even in modelling something like a friendship network, while individuals might not be directly calculating costs and benefits from the relationship, they do react to how enjoyable or worthwhile the relationship is and might tend to spend more effort or time in relationships that are more beneficial and avoid ones that are less so. Different social networks lead to different outcomes for the involved agents (for example, different trades, different access to information or favours, and so on). Links are then formed at the discretion of the agents, and various equilibrium notions are used to predict which networks will form. This differs from the random models not only in that links result as a function of decisions rather than at random, but also in that there are natural costs and benefits associated with networks which then allow a welfare analysis.

Some of the first models to bring explicit utilities and choice to the formation of social links were in the context of modelling the trade-offs between 'strong' and 'weak' ties (links) in labour contact networks. Such models by Boorman (1975) and Montgomery (1991) explored a theory, due to Granovetter (1973), about different strengths of social relationships and their role in finding employment. Granovetter observed that when individuals obtained jobs through their social contacts, while they sometimes did so through strong ties (people whom they knew well and interacted with on a frequent basis), they also quite often obtained jobs through weak ties (acquaintances whom they knew less well and/or interacted with relatively infrequently). This led Granovetter to coin the phrase 'the strength of weak ties'. Boorman's article and Montgomery's articles provided explicit models where costs and benefits could be assigned to strong and weak ties, and trade-offs between them could be explored.

In a very different setting, another use of utility functions involving networks emerged in the work of Myerson (1977). Myerson analysed a class of cooperative games that were augmented with a graph structure. In these games the only coalitions that could produce value are those that are pathwise connected by the graph, and so such graphs indicate the possible cooperation or communication structures. This approach led Myerson to characterize a variation on the Shapley value, now called the Myerson value, which was a cooperative game solution concept for the class of cooperative games where constraints on coalitions were imposed by a graph structure. Although the graphs in Myerson's analysis are tools to define a special class of cooperative games, they allow the graph structure to influence the allocation of societal value among a set of players. Aumann and Myerson (1988), recognizing that different graph structures led to different allocations of value, used this to study a game where the graph structure was endogenous. They studied an extensive form game where links are considered one by one according to some exogenous order, and formed if both agents involved agree. While that game turns out to be hard to analyse even in three-person examples, it was an important precursor to the more recent economic literature on network formation.

In contrast to the cooperative game setting, Jackson and Wolinsky (1996) explicitly considered networks, rather than coalitions, as the primitive. Thus, rather than deducing utilities indirectly through a cooperative game on a graph, they posited that networks were the primitive structure and agents derived utilities based on the network structure in place. So, once a social network structure is in place, one can then deduce what the agent's payoffs will be. Using such a formulation where players' payoffs are determined as a function of the social network in place, it is easy to model network formation using game theoretic techniques.

Pairwise stability

In modelling network formation from a game theoretic perspective, one needs to have some notion of equilibrium or stable networks. Since it is natural to require mutual consent in many applications, standard Nash equilibrium based ideas are not very useful. For instance, consider a game where each agent simultaneously announces which other agents he or she is willing to link to. It is always a Nash equilibrium for each agent to say that he or she does not want to form any links, anticipating that the others will do the same. Generally, this allows for a multiplicity of equilibria, many of which make little sense from a social network perspective. Even equilibrium refinements (such as undominated Nash or perfect equilibrium) do not avoid this problem. Given that it is natural in a network setting for the agents prospectively forming a link to be able to communicate with each other, they should also be able to coordinate with each other on the forming of a link. An approach taken by Jackson and Wolinsky (1996) is to define a stability notion that directly incorporates the mutual consent needed to form links. Jackson and Wolinsky (1996) defined the following notion of 'pairwise stability': a network is pairwise stable if (i) no player would be better off if he or she severed one of his or her links, and (ii) no pair of players would both benefit (with at least one of the pair seeing a strict benefit) from adding a link that is not in the network. The requirement that no player wishes to delete a link that he or she is involved in implies that a player has the discretion to unilaterally terminate relationships that he or she is involved in. The second part of the definition captures the idea that if we are at a network where the creation of a new link would benefit both players involved, then the network g is not stable, as it will be in the players' interests to add the link.

Pairwise stability is a fairly permissive stability concept – for instance, it does not consider deviations where players delete some links and add others at the same time. While pairwise stability is easy to work with and often makes fairly pointed predictions, the consideration of further refinements can make a difference. A variety of refinements and alternative notions have been introduced, including allowing agents to form and sever links at the same time, allowing coalitions of agents to add and sever links in a coordinated fashion, or behaviour where agents anticipate how the formation of one link might influence others to form further links (see Jackson, 2004, for discussion and references). There are also dynamic models (for example, Watts, 2001) in which the possibility of forming links arises (repeatedly) over time, and agents might 'tremble' when they form links (see Jackson, 2004, for references). These various equilibrium/stability concepts have different properties and are appropriate in different contexts.

With pairwise stability, or some other solution in hand, one can address a series of questions. One fundamental question is whether, from society's point of view, efficient or optimal networks will be stable when agents form links with their selfish interests in mind. Given that transfers are being considered here, one natural definition of an 'efficient' or 'optimal' network is one that maximizes the total value or the sum of utilities of all agents in the society. Another basic question is to ask whether in situations where no efficient network is pairwise stable, is it possible for some sort of intervention (for example, in the form of taxing or subsidizing links), to lead efficient networks to form.

A connections model of social networks

One stylized example from Jackson and Wolinsky (1996) gives some feeling for the issues involved in the above questions and is useful for illustrating the relationship between efficient and pairwise stable networks. Jackson

and Wolinsky called this example the 'symmetric connections model', in which the links represent social relationships between players such as friendships. These relationships offer benefits in terms of favours, information, and so on, and also involve some costs. Moreover, players benefit from having indirect relationships. A 'friend of a friend' produces benefits or utility for a player, although of a lesser value than the direct benefits that come from a 'friend'. The same is true of 'friends of a friend of a friend', and so forth. Benefit deteriorates in the 'distance' of the relationship, as represented by a factor δ between 0 and 1, which indicates the benefit from a direct relationship between two agents and is raised to higher powers for more distant relationships. For instance, in the network where player 1 is linked to 2, 2 is linked to 3, and 3 is linked to 4; player 1 gets a benefit of δ from the direct connection with player 2, an indirect benefit of δ^2 from the indirect connection with player 3, and an indirect benefit of δ^3 from the indirect connection with player 4. For $\delta < 1$ this leads to a lower benefit from an indirect connection than a direct one. Players also pay some cost c for maintaining each of their direct relationships (but not for indirect ones). Once the benefit parameter, δ, and the cost parameter, $c > 0$ are specified, it is possible to determine each agent's payoff from every possible network, allowing a characterization of the pairwise stable networks as well as the efficient networks. The efficient network structures are the complete network if $c < \delta - \delta^2$, a 'star' (a network where one agent is connected to each other agent and there are no other connections) encompassing all nodes if $\delta - \delta^2 < c < \delta + \frac{(n-2)}{2}\delta^2$, and the empty network if $\delta + \frac{(n-2)}{2}\delta^2 < c$. The idea is that if costs are very low it will be efficient to include all links in the network, because shortening any path leads to higher payoffs. When the link cost is at an intermediate level, then the unique efficient network structure is to have all players arranged in a star network, since such a structure has the minimal number of links $(n-1)$ needed to connect all individuals, and yet still has all nodes within at most two links from one another. Once links become so costly that a star results in more cost than benefit, then the empty network is efficient. One can also examine a directed version of such a model, as in Bala and Goyal (2000), who find related results, but with some differences that depend on whether both agents or just one of the agents enjoys the benefits from a directed link.

Inefficiency of stable networks

The set of pairwise stable networks does not always coincide with the efficient ones, and sometimes do not even intersect with the set of efficient networks. For instance, if the cost of a link is greater than the direct benefit $(c > \delta)$, then relationships are only valuable to a given agent if they generate indirect benefits as well as direct ones. In such a situation a star is not pairwise stable since the centre player gets benefit of the direct value from each of his or her links, which is less than the cost of each of those links. This model of social networks makes it obvious that there will be situations where individual incentives are not aligned with overall societal benefits.

As it will generally be the case that in economic and social networks there are some sort of externalities present, since two agents' decisions of whether or not to form a relationship can affect the well-being of other agents, one should expect that there will be situations where the networks formed through the selfish decisions of the agents do not coincide with those that are efficient from society's perspective. In such situations, it is natural to ask whether intervention in the form of transfers among agents might help align individual and overall societal incentives to form the right network. For instance, in the connections model, it would make sense to have the peripheral agents in a star pay the centre of the star in order to maintain their links. The peripheral agents benefit much more from the relationship with the centre agent than vice versa, as the centre agent provides access to many indirect agents. Although a simple set of transfers can align individual and overall incentives in the connections model, it is impossible to always correct this tension between individual incentives and overall efficiency by taxing and subsidizing agents for the links they form (even in a complete information setting). The fact that there are very simple, natural network settings where no 'reasonable' set of transfers can help rectify the disparity stability and efficiency was shown in Jackson and Wolinsky (1996). Without providing details, the impossibility of reconciling stability and efficiency stems from the following considerations: from any given network, there are many other networks that can be reached. In fact, if there are n nodes, then there are $n(n-1)/2$ possible links that can be added to or deleted from any given network. In order to ensure that a given efficient network is pairwise stable, payoffs to all neighbouring networks have to be configured so that no agent finds it in his or her interest to delete a link and no two agents find it in their interests to add a link. It is impossible to assign all the necessary taxes and subsidies in such a way that (i) the transfers are feasible (and are not given to unattached agents), (ii) identical agents are treated identically, and (iii) it is always the case that at least one efficient network is pairwise stable.

Much more has been learned about the relationship between stable and efficient networks and possible transfers to ensure that efficient networks form. For instance, one can characterize some classes of settings where the efficient networks and the stable ones coincide (see Jackson and Wolinsky, 1996). One can also design transfers that ensure that some efficient network

is stable by treating agents unequally (for example, taxing or subsidizing them differently even though the agents are identical in the problem as shown by Dutta and Mutuswami, 1997). Another important point was made by Currarini and Morelli (2000), who showed that if agents bargain over the division of payoffs generated by network relationships at the time when they form link, then in a nontrivial class of settings equilibrium networks are efficient. While the conclusions hinge on the structure of the link-formation-bargaining game, and in particular on an asymmetry in bargaining power across the agents, such a result tells us that it can be important to model the formation of the links of a network together with any potential bargaining over payoffs or transfers. Further study in this area shows how the types of transfers needed to reach efficient networks relate to the types of network externalities that are present in the setting.

Small worlds and strategic network formation
Beyond understanding the relationship between stable and efficient networks, strategic models of network formation have also shed light on some empirical regularities and helped predict which networks will arise in settings of particular interest. For instance, strategic models of network formation provide substantial insight into the 'small-worlds' properties of social networks: the simultaneous presence of high clustering (a high density of links on a local level) and short average path length between nodes (see Jackson, 2006, for references). The reasoning is based on a premise that different nodes have different distances from each other, either geographically or according to some other characteristic, such as profession, tastes, and so on. The low cost of forming links to other nodes that are nearby then naturally explains high clustering. High benefits from forming links that bridge disparate parts of the network, due to the access and indirect connections that they bring, naturally explain low average path length.

Networks and markets
There is a rich set of studies of markets and networks from an economics perspective, including models that explicitly examine whether or not buyers and sellers have incentives to form an efficient network of relationships (for example, Kranton and Minehart, 2001). The incentives to form efficient networks depend on the setting and which agents bear the cost of forming relationships. In some settings competitive forces lead to the right configuration of links, and in others buyers and sellers over-connect in order to improve their relative bargaining positions. Other studies focus on the context of specific markets, such as labour markets, where people benefit from connections with neighbours who provide information about job opportunities (see

Ioannides and Loury, 2004, for an overview and references).

In addition to studies of networks of relationships between buyers and sellers, firms also form relationships amongst themselves that affect their costs and the sets of products they offer. Such oligopoly settings where network formation is important (see Bloch, 2004, for a recent survey), again provide a rich set of results regarding the structure of networks that emerge, and contrasts between settings where efficient networks naturally emerge and others where only inefficient networks are formed.

Network formation has also been studied in the context of many other applications, including risk-sharing in developing countries, social mobility, criminal activity, international trade and banking deposits.

Finally, there have been a number of experiments on network formation, using human subjects. These examine a variety of questions, ranging from how forward-looking agents are when they form social ties, to whether or not agents overcome coordination problems when forming links, to whether there are pronounced differences between network formation when links can be formed unilaterally as opposed to when they require mutual consent, to whether efficient networks will tend to result and how that depends on symmetries or asymmetries in the efficient network structure (see Falk and Kosfeld, 2003, for some discussion and references).

MATTHEW O. JACKSON

See also **business networks; learning and information aggregation in networks; mathematics of networks; power laws; psychology of social networks; social networks in labour markets.**

Bibliography

Aumann, R. and Myerson, R. 1988. Endogenous formation of links between players and coalitions: an application of the Shapley value. In *The Shapley Value*, ed. A. Roth. Cambridge: Cambridge University Press.

Bala, V. and Goyal, S. 2000. A non-cooperative model of network formation. *Econometrica* 68, 1181–230.

Barabási, A. and Albert, R. 1999. Emergence of scaling in random networks. *Science* 286, 509–12.

Bloch, F. 2004. Group and network formation in industrial organization: a survey. In *Group Formation in Economics; Networks, Clubs and Coalitions*, ed. G. Demange and M. Wooders. Cambridge: Cambridge University Press.

Bollobás, B. 2001. *Random Graphs*, 2nd edn. Cambridge: Cambridge University Press.

Boorman, S. 1975. A combinatorial optimization model for transmission of job information through contact networks. *Bell Journal of Economics* 6, 216–49.

Currarini, S. and Morelli, M. 2000. Network formation with sequential demands. *Review of Economic Design* 5, 229–50.

Dutta, B. and Mutuswami, S. 1997. Stable networks. *Journal of Economic Theory* 76, 322–44.

Erdös, P. and Rényi, A. 1960. On the evolution of random graphs. *Publication of the Mathematical Institute of the Hungarian Academy of Sciences* 5, 17–61.

Falk, A. and Kosfeld, M. 2003. It's all about connections: evidence on network formation. Mimeo, University of Zurich.

Frank, O. and Strauss, D. 1986. Markov graphs. *Journal of the American Statistical Association* 81, 832–42.

Granovetter, M. 1973. The strength of weak ties. *American Journal of Sociology* 78, 1360–80.

Ioannides, Y.M. and Loury, L.D. 2004. Job information networks, neighborhood effects and inequality. *Journal of Economic Literature* 42, 1056–93.

Jackson, M.O. 2004. A survey of models of network formation: stability and efficiency. In *Group Formation in Economics: Networks, Clubs and Coalitions*, ed. G. Demange and M. Wooders. Cambridge: Cambridge University Press.

Jackson, M.O. 2006. The economics of social networks. In *Chapter 1, Volume 1 in Advances in Economics and Econometrics, Theory and Applications: Ninth World Congress of the Econometric Society*, ed. R. Blundell, W. Newey and T. Persson. Cambridge: Cambridge University Press.

Jackson, M.O. and Rogers, B.W. 2007. Meeting strangers and friends of friends: how random are socially generated networks? *American Economic Review* 97, 890–915.

Jackson, M.O. and Wolinsky, A. 1996. A strategic model of social and economic networks. *Journal of Economic Theory* 71, 44–74.

Kranton, R. and Minehart, D. 2001. A theory of buyer–seller networks. *American Economic Review* 91, 485–508.

Molloy, M. and Reed, B. 1995. A critical point for random graphs with a given degree sequence. *Random Structures and Algorithms* 6, 161–79.

Montgomery, J. 1991. Social networks and labor market outcomes. *American Economic Review* 81, 1408–18.

Myerson, R. 1977. Graphs and cooperation in games. *Math. Operations Research* 2, 225–9.

Newman, M. 2003. The structure and function of complex networks. *SIAM Review* 45, 167–256.

Page, F., Wooders, M. and Kamat, S. 2005. Networks and farsighted stability. *Journal of Economic Theory* 120, 257–69.

Price, D.J.S. 1965. Networks of scientific papers. *Science* 149, 510–5.

Price, D.J.S. 1976. A general theory of bibliometric and other cumulative advantage processes. *Journal of* the *American Society for Information Science* 27, 292–306.

Simon, H. 1955. On a class of skew distribution functions. *Biometrika* 42, 425–40.

Watts, A. 2001. A dynamic model of network formation. *Games and Economic Behavior* 34, 331–41.

Watts, D.J. 1999. *Small Worlds: The Dynamics of Networks between Order and Randomness*. Princeton: Princeton University Press.

Watts, D.J. and Strogatz, S. 1998. Collective dynamics of 'small-world' networks. *Nature* 393, 440–2.

network goods (empirical studies)

A network effect exists if the consumption benefits of a good or service increase with the total number of consumers who purchase compatible products. The literature distinguishes between direct and indirect network effects.

In the case of a direct (or physical) network effect, an increase in the number of consumers on the same network raises the consumption benefits for everyone on the network. Communication networks such as telephone and e-mail networks are examples of goods with direct network effects.

A network effect can also arise in a setting with a 'hardware/software' system. Here, the benefits of the hardware good increase when the variety of compatible software increases. An indirect (or virtual) network effect arises endogenously in this case because an increase in the number of users of compatible hardware increases the demand for compatible software. Since software goods are typically characterized by economies of scale, the increase in demand leads to increases in the supply of software varieties. Examples of settings where virtual network effects arise include consumer electronics such as CD players and compact discs, computer operating systems and applications programs, and television sets and programming.

Given the dramatic growth of the internet and information technology industries, and the importance of interconnection in these networks, it is not surprising that there is a large theoretical literature on competition in industries with network goods. Important questions in this literature include

- the examination of the private and social incentives to attain compatibility;
- the trade-off between standardization and variety;
- modelling the dynamics of competition between competing networks; and
- how the private and social choice among competing incompatible networks differs when there are both early and late adopters.

See Farrell and Klemperer (2007) for further discussion.

Although relatively small, a growing empirical literature has developed to examine technological adoption of products with network effects. In this short article, I briefly discuss this literature. The empirical work can be organized by the issues addressed and the methodology employed. The primary issue addressed by the early literature is whether network effects are indeed significant; this work typically employed reduced form models. The article first surveys early work in this genre, then examines papers that employed structural methodology. The main advantage of this methodology is that it can address aspects of firm strategy, such as incentives to provide compatible products. The article closes by examining key issues in empirical work on network industries.

Early work: indirect evidence of network effects

Greenstein (1993), Gandal (1994; 1995), and Saloner and Shepard (1995) provide early evidence that the value of the 'hardware' good depends on the variety of compatible complementary software. (Shy, 2001, surveys many of the empirical papers discussed in this article in greater detail than space permits here.)

Software for the IBM 1400 mainframe could not run on succeeding generations of IBM mainframes while software for the IBM 360 could run on succeeding models. Greenstein (1993) finds that, other things being equal, a firm with an IBM 1400 was no more likely than any other firm to purchase an IBM mainframe when making a future purchase. On the other hand, a firm with an IBM 360 was more likely to purchase an IBM mainframe than a firm that did not own an IBM 360. This result can be interpreted as a demand for compatible software.

Gandal (1994) estimates hedonic (quality-adjusted) price equations for spreadsheets to examine whether spreadsheet programs that were compatible with Lotus – the de facto standard – command a premium. The results – that consumers place a positive value on compatibility – suggest (*a*) direct network effects because people want to share files and (*b*) indirect network effects because compatible software enables the transfer of data among a variety of software programs. Gandal (1995) extends the analysis to database management software (DMS) and multiple standards and finds that only the Lotus file compatibility standard is significant in explaining price variations, suggesting that indirect network effects are important in the DMS market.

Saloner and Shepard (1995) test for network effects in the automated teller machine (ATM) industry. In particular, they test whether banks with a larger expected number of ATM locations will adopt the ATM technology sooner. Since expected network size is not an observable variable, they use the number of branches as a proxy. The results suggest that banks with more branches will adopt earlier, which is consistent with virtual network effects.

Structural models: explicitly modelling the complementary goods market

Because hedonic price equations are a reduced form, rather than a structural model, parameter estimates associated with compatibility in Gandal (1994; 1995) may be capturing demand effects or supply effects or some combination of both. In other words, are consumers really willing to pay a premium for compatibility or is the marginal cost of compatibility relatively high? In the case of software, fixed costs of providing characteristics are quite significant, while marginal production costs associated with the characteristics are typically very small; they primarily include duplication of digital material. Hence, in these papers the estimated hedonic price coefficients on compatibility indeed measure consumer willingness to pay for compatibility.

Nevertheless, reduced form models are not suitable for examining business strategies or conducting counterfactuals. Gandal, Kende and Rob (2000) develop a dynamic structural model of consumer adoption and software entry, and use the model to estimate the feedback from hardware to software and vice versa in the CD industry. The advantage of the structural methodology is that it enables researchers to assess business strategies as well as examine conduct counterfactuals. In the case of business strategies, Gandal, Kende and Rob (2000) show that a five per cent reduction in price would have had the same effect as a ten per cent increase in CD variety in terms of increasing sales of CD players. They also show that, if it had been possible to make CD players compatible with LPs, compatibility could have accelerated the adoption process by more than a year. This is just a 'thought experiment' for CD players, but it has policy relevance for other systems like HDTV.

Rysman (2004) develops a structural model to examine the importance of network effects in the market for Yellow Pages. The model includes a consumer adoption equation, advertiser demand for space, and a firm's profit maximizing behaviour. He finds that consumers value advertising and advertisers value consumer adoption, suggesting virtual network effects.

In several recent papers, advances in the estimation of discrete choice models of product differentiation – see Berry (1994) and Berry, Levinsohn and Pakes (1995) – have also been employed when testing for indirect network effects in differentiated product markets. Ohashi and Clements (2005), for example, use a logit model to test for indirect network effects in the US video game market.

Key issues in empirical work

As in most fields, empirical work is typically limited by the available data. A key problem exists when one tries to estimate network effects in homogeneous product industries using time series data. For many network industries, technological progress drives down prices and costs. Hence an increase in the number of users on a network might be due

to a network effect or to falling prices (see Gowrisankaran and Stavins, 2004, for further discussion). In order to estimate these effects, one must have additional data.

Gandal, Kende and Rob (2000), for example, have data on the number of available compact disc titles at each point in time. Hence, in their model the two main effects that lead to greater adoption of CD players – lower prices of the hardware good and network effects due to increases in the number of titles – are measured separately. Nevertheless, that is only a start, since both of these variables are typically endogenous. Identification in Gandal, Kende, and Rob (2000) was possible only because there were data on the fixed costs of entering the CD production industry over time. These data were used as an instrument for CD (title) availability. Additionally, case studies indicated that the CD player industry was quite competitive, leading the authors to assume that the price of CD players was exogenous. Without both of these assumptions, it would not have been possible to identify the model.

Additionally, there is the thorny issue of pricing in dynamic models of competition in network industries. Since hardware firms may want to subsidize early adopters in order to build up a network advantage and then (perhaps) charge a higher price when the installed base grows, pricing issues are dynamic; firms will take into account (current and expected future) network size when choosing their prices. Park (2004) develops a dynamic structural model of competition in an oligopolistic market with network effects that addresses the dynamic pricing issues; he then estimates the model for VCRs. To the best of my knowledge, this is the only empirical paper that deals explicitly with dynamic pricing issues.

A similar issue arises in dynamic models of competition in network industries when firms make investment in quality over time. Markovich (2001) examines the trade-off between standardization and variety in a dynamic setting using numerical methods. With suitable data one might be able to use her framework to empirically examine investment incentives and pricing decisions in a dynamic setting with network effects.

Finally, there is a budding empirical literature on standardization via committees. Papers include Simcoe (2006), who examines the standardization process in various committees of the Internet Engineering Task Force, and Gandal, Gantman and Genesove (2006), who examine firms' incentives to participate in Telecommunication Industry Association standardization meetings.

NEIL GANDAL

See also **hedonic prices; network goods (theory).**

Bibliography

Berry, S. 1994. Estimating discrete-choice models of product differentiation. *RAND Journal of Economics* 25, 334–47.

Berry, S., Levinsohn, J. and Pakes, A. 1995. Automobile prices in market equilibrium. *Econometrica* 63, 841–90.

Farrell, J. and Klemperer, P. 2007. Coordination and lock-in: effects competition with switching costs and network effects. In *Handbook of Industrial Organization*, vol. 3, ed. M. Armstrong and R. Porter. Amsterdam: North-Holland.

Gandal, N. 1994. Hedonic price indexes for spreadsheets and an empirical test for network externalities. *RAND Journal of Economics* 25, 160–70.

Gandal, N. 1995. A Selective survey of the literature on indirect network externalities. *Research in Law and Economics* 17, 23–31.

Gandal, N., Gantman, N. and Genesove, D. 2006. Intellectual property and standardization committee participation in the U.S. modem industry. In *Standards and Public Policy*, ed. S. Greenstein and V. Stango. Cambridge: Cambridge University Press.

Gandal, N., Kende, M. and Rob, R. 2000. The dynamics of technological adoption in hardware/software systems: the case of compact disc players. *RAND Journal of Economics* 31, 43–61.

Gowrisankaran, G. and Stavins, J. 2004. Network externalities and technology adoption: lessons from electronic payments. *RAND Journal of Economics* 35, 260–76.

Greenstein, S. 1993. Did installed base give an incumbent any (measurable) advantages in federal computer procurement? *RAND Journal of Economics* 24, 19–39.

Markovich, S. 2001. Snowball: the evolution of dynamic markets with network externalities. Mimeo. Tel Aviv University.

Ohashi, H. and Clements, M. 2005. Indirect network effects and the product cycle: video games in the U.S., 1994–2002. *Journal of Industrial Economics* 53.

Park, S. 2004. Quantitative analysis of network externalities in competing technologies: the VCR case. *Review of Economics and Statistics* 86, 937–45.

Rysman, M. 2004. competition between networks: a study of the market for Yellow Pages. *Review of Economic Studies* 71, 483–512.

Saloner, G. and Shepard, A. 1995. Adoption of technologies with network externalities: an empirical examination of the adoption of automated teller machines. *RAND Journal of Economics* 26, 479–501.

Shy, O. 2001. *The Economics of Network Industries*. Cambridge: Cambridge University Press.

Simcoe, T. 2006. Committees and the creation of technical standards. In *Standards and Public Policy*, ed. S. Greenstein and V. Stango. Cambridge: Cambridge University Press.

network goods (theory)

Direct network effects arise if each user's payoff from the adoption of a good, and his incentive to adopt it, increase as more others adopt it; that is, if adoption by users is complementary. For example, telecommunications users gain directly from more widespread adoption, and telecommunications networks with more are also more attractive to non-users contemplating adoption.

Indirect network effects arise if adoption is complementary because of its effect on a related market. For example, users of hardware may gain when other users join them, not because of any direct benefit, but because it encourages the provision of more and better software.

Extensive case studies and more formal econometric evidence document significant network effects in many areas including, for example, telecommunications, radio and television, computer hardware and software, applications software and operating systems (including Microsoft's), securities markets and exchanges (including Ebay), and credit cards (see, for example, Gabel, 1991; Rohlfs, 2001; Shy, 2001; and the article on NETWORK GOODS (EMPIRICAL STUDIES) in this dictionary).

Usually adoption prices do not fully internalize the network effects, so there is a positive externality from adoption. A single network product therefore tends to be under-adopted at the margin – this issue was the main focus of the early literature (see, for example, Leibenstein, 1950; Rohlfs, 1974). However, if two networks compete, then adopting one network means not adopting the other, which dilutes or reverses the externality.

More interestingly – and what is the starting point for the more recent literature – network effects create incentives to 'herd' with others. In a static (simultaneous-adoption) game there are often multiple equilibria, so expectations are crucial, and self-fulfilling. Likewise, a dynamic (sequential-adoption) game exhibits positive feedback or 'tipping' – a network that looks like succeeding will *as a result* do so (see, for example, David, 1985; Arthur, 1989; Arthur and Rusczcynski, 1992).

How well competition among incompatible networks works depends dramatically on how adopters form expectations and coordinate their choices. If adopters smoothly coordinate on the best deals, vendors face strong pressure to offer them. Competition may then be unusually fierce because all-or-nothing competition neutralizes horizontal differentiation – since adopters focus not on matching a product to their own tastes but on joining the expected winner.

However, coordination is not easy. With simultaneous adoption, adopters may fail to coordinate at all and 'splinter' among different networks, or may coordinate on a different equilibrium from the one that is best for them – for example, each adopter may expect others to choose a low-quality product because it is produced by a firm that was successful in the past. Furthermore, consensus standard-setting (informally or through standards organizations) can be painfully slow when different adopters prefer different coordinated outcomes (see

different
munica-
...ption,
...sers
...ing

915

...99). Coordination through ... in theory (see, for exam- ... Segal, 1999), but seems

...ual, we see *early instability* ... example, Arthur, 1989) – this ... multiple equilibria that arise with ...option. Because early adoptions influ- ...ones, long-term behaviour is determined ...y early events, whether accidental or strategic. ...heory, at least, fully sequential adoption achieves the ...fficient outcome if it is best for all adopters, but more generally early adopters' preferences count for more than later adopters': this is 'excess early power'. Note that 'excess early power' does not depend on 'excess inertia', that is, on incompatible transitions being too hard *given ex post* incompatibility. (Both 'excess inertia', and its opposite, 'excess momentum', are theoretically possible; see Farrell and Saloner, 1985.)

Firms promoting incompatible networks compete to win the pivotal early adopters, and so achieve *ex post* dominance and monopoly rents. Strategies such as pen- etration pricing and pre-announcements (see, for exam- ple, Farrell and Saloner, 1986) are common. History, and especially market share, matter because an installed base both directly means a firm offers more network benefits and boosts expectations about its future sales. Such 'Schumpeterian' competition 'for the market' can neu- tralize (or even overturn) excess early power if promoters of networks that will be more efficient later on set low penetration prices in anticipation of this (see Katz and Shapiro, 1986a). More commonly, though, late develop- ers struggle while networks that are preferred by early pivotal customers thrive.

So early preferences and early information are likely to be excessively important in determining long-term outcomes. For example, whether or not the Dvorak typewriter keyboard is really much better than QWERTY (as David, 1985, contends), there clearly was a chance in the 1800s that a keyboard superior to QWERTY would later be developed, and it is not clear what could have persuaded early generations of typists to wait, or to adopt diverse keyboards, *if* that was socially desirable. So it seems unlikely that the market gave a very good test of whether or not waiting was efficient. (Liebowitz and Margolis, 1990, and Liebowitz, 2002, contest both the details of the QWERTY example and the claim that network effects are significant more generally, but at least the second view is probably a minority one.)

Despite the possibility of competition for the market passing *ex post* rents through to earlier buyers, incom- patibility often reduces efficiency and harms consumers in several ways.

Incompatibility means that consumers are faced with either a segmented market with low network benefits, or – if the market does 'tip' all the way to one network – with reduced product variety and without the option value from the possibility that a currently inferior technology might later become superior. Product variety is more sustainable if niche products are compatible with the mainstream, and so don't force users to sacrifice network effects.

These direct costs of poor coordination by adopters may be exacerbated by weaker incentives for vendors to offer good deals. For example, if a firm like Microsoft is widely believed to have the ability to offer the highest quality, it may never bother to do so: the fact that every- one expects Microsoft to recapture the market if it ever lost any one cohort of customers (or lost any one cohort of providers of complementary products) means every- one rationally chooses Microsoft even if it never actually produces high quality or offers a low price (see Katz and Shapiro, 1992).

Ex post rents are often not fully dissipated by *ex ante* competition, especially if expectations fail to track relative surplus. Worse, the rent dissipation that does occur may be wasteful, such as socially inefficient marketing. At best, *ex ante* competition induces 'bargain- then-rip-off' pricing (low to attract business, high to extract surplus) but this distorts buyers' quantity choices and gives them artificial incentives to be or appear pivotal.

Furthermore, outcomes are biased in favour of a pro- prietary technology (for example, Microsoft's) whose single owner has the incentive to market it strategically over 'open' unsponsored alternatives (for example, Linux) – see, for example, Katz and Shapiro (1986b). As discussed above, outcomes are also often biased in favour of networks that are more efficient early on, and are generally biased in favour of established firms on whom expectations focus. The last bias implies entry with proprietary network effects is often nearly impos- sible (and frequently much too hard from the social viewpoint even *given* incompatibility). And this in turn makes it easier to recoup profits after predatory behav- iour that eliminates a rival, and so encourages such predation.

So while incompatibility does not necessarily damage competition, it often does, and firms may therefore also dissipate further resources creating and defending incompatibility.

If firms offer compatible products, then consumers don't need to buy from the same firm to enjoy full net- work benefits, and (differentiated) products will be better matched with customers. Consumers will be willing to pay more for these benefits, and this may encourage firms to choose compatibility. But compatibility often inten- sifies competition and nullifies the competitive advantage of a large installed base, whereas proprietary networks tend to make competition all-or-nothing, with the advantage going to large firms, and may completely shut out weaker firms. So large firms and those who are good at steering adopters' expectations may prefer their products to be incompatible with rivals' (see, for example, Katz and Shapiro, 1985; Bresnahan, 2001), and may be able to use their intellectual property to enforce this.

Competition with incompatible network effects is closely related to other forms of competition when market share is important, especially competition when consumers have switching costs (see, for example, Klemperer, 1995; Farrell and Klemperer, 2007; and the companion-piece to this article, SWITCHING COSTS), and has similar broader implications (for example, for international trade, see Froot and Klemperer, 1989).

Because competition 'for the market' differs greatly from conventional competition 'in the market', and especially because capturing consumers' and complementors' expectations can be so profitable, competition policy needs to be vigilant against predatory or exclusionary tactics by advantaged firms, including deliberately creating incompatibility by misusing intellectual property protection. Thus, for example, the network effect by which more popular operating systems attract more applications software took centre stage in both the US and European Microsoft cases (see, for example, Bresnahan, 2001). And because coordination is often important and difficult, institutions such as standards organizations matter, and government procurement policy takes on more significance than usual.

In summary, network effects *can* involve efficient competition for larger units of business – 'competition for the market' – but very often make competition, especially entry, less effective. So I, and others, recommend that public policymakers should have a cautious presumption in favour of compatibility, and should look particularly carefully at markets where incompatibility is strategically chosen rather than inevitable.

Farrell and Klemperer (2007) contains a recent and comprehensive survey of network effects.

PAUL KLEMPERER

See also **network goods (empirical studies); switching costs.**

The views expressed here are personal and should not be attributed to the UK Competition Commission or to any of its individual Members other than myself. Furthermore, although some observers thought some of the behaviour discussed warranted regulatory investigation, I do not intend to suggest that any of it violates any applicable rules or laws.

Bibliography

Arthur, W.B. 1989. Competing technologies, increasing returns, and lock-in by historical events. *Economic Journal* 99, 116–31.

Arthur, W.B. and Rusczcynski, A. 1992. Dynamic equilibria in markets with a conformity effect. *Archives of Control Sciences* 37, 7–31.

Bresnahan, T. 2001. Network effects in the Microsoft case. Discussion Paper No. 00-51, Stanford Institute for Economic Policy Research, Stanford University.

Bulow, J. and Klemperer, P.D. 1999. The generalized war of attrition. *American Economic Review* 89, 175–89.

David, P. 1985. Clio and the economics of QWERTY. *American Economic Review* 75, 332–7.

Dybvig, P.H. and Spatt, C.S. 1983. Adoption externalities as public goods. *Journal of Public Economics* 20, 231–47.

Farrell, J. and Klemperer, P.D. 2007. Coordination and lock-in: competition with switching costs and network effects. In *Handbook of Industrial Organization*, vol. 3, ed. M. Armstrong and R. Porter. Amsterdam: North-Holland.

Farrell, J. and Saloner, G. 1985. Standardization, compatibility and innovation. *RAND Journal of Economics* 16, 70–83.

Farrell, J. and Saloner, G. 1986. Installed base and compatibility: innovation, product preannouncements, and predation. *American Economic Review* 76, 940–55.

Froot, K.A. and Klemperer, P.D. 1989. Exchange rate pass-through when market share matters. *American Economic Review* 79, 637–54.

Gabel, H.L. 1991. *Competitive Strategies for Product Standards*. New York: McGraw-Hill.

Katz, M.L. and Shapiro, C. 1985. Network externalities, competition and compatibility. *American Economic Review* 75, 424–40.

Katz, M.L. and Shapiro, C. 1986a. Product compatibility choice in a market with technological progress. *Oxford Economic Papers* 38, 146–65.

Katz, M.L. and Shapiro, C. 1986b. Technology adoption in the presence of network externalities. *Journal of Political Economy* 94, 822–41.

Katz, M.L. and Shapiro, C. 1992. Product introduction with network externalities. *Journal of Industrial Economics* 40, 55–83.

Klemperer, P.D. 1995. Competition when consumers have switching costs. *Review of Economic Studies* 62, 515–39.

Leibenstein, H. 1950. Bandwagon, Snob and Veblen effects in the theory of consumers' demand. *Quarterly Journal of Economics* 64, 183–207.

Liebowitz, S. 2002. *Re-Thinking the Network Economy: The True Forces that Drive the Digital Marketplace*. New York: American Management Association.

Liebowitz, S.J. and Margolis, S.E. 1990. The fable of the keys. *Journal of Law and Economics* 33, 1–25.

Rohlfs, J. 1974. A theory of interdependent demand for a communications service. *Bell Journal of Economics* 5, 16–37.

Rohlfs, J. 2001. *Bandwagon Effects in High Technology Industries*. Cambridge, MA: MIT Press.

Segal, I. 1999. Contracting with externalities. *Quarterly Journal of Economics* 114, 337–88.

Shy, O. 2001. *The Economics of Network Industries*. Cambridge: Cambridge University Press.